THE AMERICAN
SHORT STORY
AND ITS WRITER

THE AMERICAN SHORT STORY AND ITS WRITER

An Anthology

ANN CHARTERS

University of Connecticut

BEDFORD/ST. MARTIN'S

Boston • New York

FOR BEDFORD/ST. MARTIN'S

Developmental Editor: Maura Shea
Production Editor: Karen S. Baart
Production Supervisor: Cheryl Mamaril
Marketing Manager: Karen Melton
Editorial Assistants: Nicole R. Simonsen, Jeannine Thibodeau
Production Assistants: Arthur B. Johnson, Coleen O'Hanley
Copyeditor: Nancy Bell Scott
Text Design: Anna George
Cover Design: Donna Lee Dennison
Cover Photographs: Top row (details): Nathaniel Hawthorne, CORBIS/Hulton-Deutsch Collection; Edgar Allan Poe, CORBIS/Bettmann; Sarah Orne Jewett, CORBIS/Bettmann; Mark Twain (Samuel Langhorne Clemens), CORBIS/Bettmann; Zitkala-Sä (Gertrude Simmons Bonnin), CORBIS/Bettmann-UPI; Willa Cather, CORBIS/Bettmann. Bottom row (details): Ernest Hemingway, CORBIS/Bettmann; Zora Neale Hurston, CORBIS; William Faulkner, CORBIS/Bettmann; James Baldwin, CORBIS/Bettmann; Joyce Carol Oates, CORBIS/Oscar White; Bharati Mukherjee, New York, 1988, © Arvind Garg.
Composition: Stratford Publishing Services, Inc.
Printing and Binding: R. R. Donnelley & Sons Company

President: Charles H. Christensen
Editorial Director: Joan E. Feinberg
Director of Editing, Design, and Production: Marcia Cohen
Managing Editor: Elizabeth M. Schaaf

Library of Congress Catalog Card Number: 99–61995

For information, write: Bedford/St. Martin's, 75 Arlington Street, Boston, MA 02116   (617-426-7440)

ISBN: 0–312–19176–6

ACKNOWLEDGMENTS

Sherman Alexie. "The Only Traffic Signal on the Reservation Doesn't Flash Red Anymore" from *The Lone Ranger and Tonto Fistfight in Heaven.* Copyright © 1993 by Sherman Alexie. Reprinted with the permission of Grove/Atlantic, Inc.

Paula Gunn Allen. "Whirlwind Man Steals Yellow Woman" from *The Woman Who Owned the Shadows.* Copyright © 1983 by Paula Gunn Allen. Reprinted with the permission of Aunt Lute Books.

Acknowledgments and copyrights are continued at the back of the book on pages 1492–95, which constitute an extension of the copyright page. It is a violation of the law to reproduce these selections by any means whatsoever without the written permission of the copyright holder.

PREFACE

I have wanted to compile this anthology of American short stories for a long time. For the past fifteen years, the process of editing five editions of *The Story and Its Writer* has given me ample opportunity to research the development of the genre. More than three years ago I decided that the time was right to create an anthology that would represent the rich history of the American short story and reflect the exciting new directions of literary scholarship. I also wanted a book that was large enough in its scope to attempt a consolidation of this material into a more inclusive paradigm. In *The American Short Story and Its Writer* I have aimed to provide — through chapter introductions, headnotes, commentaries by the writers themselves, an annotated bibliography, and an appendix — literary, historical, and cultural contexts that suggest the extraordinary range and vitality of the American story and its writer.

In this endeavor I have assembled 106 works of short fiction from every historical period, along with 50 commentaries about the genre and about specific stories by authors and critics. In order to present a diverse selection of authors, I have included just one story by each writer. I have attempted to strike a balance between canonical works — by major authors such as Edgar Allan Poe, Nathaniel Hawthorne, Sherwood Anderson, Ernest Hemingway, Flannery O'Connor, and Joyce Carol Oates — and significant works by authors such as Frances E. W. Harper, Charles W. Chesnutt, Zitkala-Sä, and Mary McCarthy who have until recent years been excluded from the canon. I have also selected several important but less frequently anthologized stories by major authors in order to offer a fresh perspective on these writers. Regretfully, this collection does not include the work of J. D. Salinger, because Salinger does not allow his short fiction to be anthologized. The 50 commentaries, more than half of them by authors whose work is in this book, give the storytellers space to express their authority about their craft, the genre, and the works of their predecessors and contemporaries. Also included are important statements by critics that have shaped the way we read and write about the American short story.

ORGANIZATION

The American story originated in oral form long before Washington Irving's publication of the first successful short story in 1819. Accordingly, this anthology begins with an introduction that includes three precursors of the American story representing the oral myths of Native American storytellers, whose artistry nourished and preserved their culture on this continent for thousands of years. Also included are examples of foundation myths of early European settlers, an African American folktale, a tall tale of the Western frontier, and a European folktale that contributed to the cultural background available to later authors of the American short story.

The next five chapters contain 106 short stories, organized in five chronological groupings, from the early nineteenth century to the late twentieth century. Each chapter begins with a discussion of the historical and literary background of a particular period, mapping the genre's development in the United States. The chapter introduction is then followed by a group of stories presented in order of the date of their first publication, with an accompanying headnote for each author providing biographical and historical information. At the end of many of the headnotes are cross-references that connect specific authors and stories to their related commentaries. The final section offers a selection of fifty important commentaries and major critical statements on the literary genre and on specific stories arranged alphabetically by author. The selected annotated bibliography lists the sources mentioned in each chapter introduction and suggests books and articles for further study of the short story. The appendix of stories with their original date and place of publication reveals the important role of periodicals in shaping and publishing short fiction; it also provides readers with material for additional research.

ONLINE RESOURCES

For those readers who are interested in conducting literary research online, Bedford/St. Martin's has created LitLinks, a collection of concise annotations that guide readers to over 250 professionally maintained Web sites built around major writers, texts, and literary periods. These can be accessed at <http://www.bedfordstmartins.com>.

ACKNOWLEDGMENTS

Many people helped me through the long process of my research and preparation for this volume. In particular, two were steadfast supporters of the project: My husband, Samuel Charters, offered invaluable comments that helped me to clarify my ideas about the American short story in the chapter introductions; and my editor Maura Shea at Bedford/St. Martin's was an unfailing source of historical insight, short story materials, and organizational support at every stage of the book. Production editor Karen Baart expertly navigated the book's course through design and production. Thanks are due to Anna George for her elegant text design and to Nancy Bell Scott for her careful copyediting. Arthur Johnson, Coleen O'Hanley, Frederick Courtright, Jeannine Thibodeau, Jessica Foz, and Nicole Simonsen provided valuable production, permissions, and editorial assistance. Stephen Scipione, Elizabeth Schaaf, John Amburg, Charles Christensen, and Joan Feinberg of Bedford/St. Martin's were also good sources of advice and counsel.

My colleagues Veronica Makowsky, Robert S. Tilton, J. D. O'Hara, Margaret Higonnet, and Wally Lamb of the University of Connecticut, Susan Lohafer of the University of Iowa, Charles E. May of California State University at Long Beach, Pat Meanor of the State University of New York at Oneonta, and Rolf Lunden of the English Institute at Uppsala University listened patiently to my enthusiastic but not always coherent ideas about this anthology as it progressed. William R. Hatcher of Burlington County College kindly furnished information for an essential footnote to Irving's "Rip Van Winkle." The writers Ann Beattie, John Edgar Wideman, and Joyce Johnson helped shape my view of the American story by their knowledge of the genre and their estimation of the achievement of various authors. This book benefited from the insightful reviews of Carl Bredahl, University of Florida; Susan Koppelman; Don Kunz, University of Rhode Island; Wendy Martin, Claremont Graduate University; Patrick O'Donnell, Michigan State University; David Richter, Queens College of the City University of New York; and Margaret Whitt, University of Denver. Mary Rohrberger and the two International Conferences on the Short Story in English that I attended provided invaluable contacts with scholars and authors and increased my knowledge considerably. My friends Mel and Bob Chatain, Jenny Hartig, and Jenny Schuesler, and my daughters Mallay and Nora Charters, generously shared their favorite books and told me in no uncertain terms what new short stories I had to read. The staff of the Research Division of the Homer Babbidge Library at the University of Connecticut, the New York Public Library, the Pierpont Morgan Library, the Mashantucket Pequot Museum and Research Center, the Boston Public Library, the Nobel Library in Stockholm, and the Humanities Center Library at Uppsala University assisted in various ways. Suzanne Staubach and Anne Goshdigian at the University of Connecticut Co-Op Bookstore gave courteous, knowledgeable, and unflagging service when what I wanted was not to be found at the library. To all these friends and associates, I am grateful. This book would not exist without them.

CONTENTS

Stories

4. MID–TWENTIETH CENTURY: 1941–1965 789

5. LATE TWENTIETH CENTURY: 1966–PRESENT   *1030*

Commentaries

THE AMERICAN
SHORT STORY
AND ITS WRITER

INTRODUCTION

SOME PRECURSORS
OF THE AMERICAN
SHORT STORY

What is an American story? Most literary critics define it as a short fictional prose narrative written by someone born or living in the United States. The adjective *American* necessarily suggests the many diverse geographical and ethnic segments of the continental United States, Alaska, and Hawaii, and could also include other countries on the North and South American continents whose historical and cultural traditions are very different from those of the United States.

Note that not only the word *American* but also nearly every other word in this definition can be modified or questioned. For example, how short is *short*? Can a piece be as short as a single paragraph or as long as a hundred printed pages and still qualify as a story? And *fictional*—must a story be totally imagined by the author, or can parts or even the whole of it be based on a true-life experience? Although such definitions are easily challenged, in actuality most readers instinctively recognize that protean entity we define as a modern short story. Perhaps a more useful question to ask, since storytelling is one of the universal behaviors of our human species, is how do American stories differ from stories originating in other parts of the world?

The answer is that most modern short stories do not differ in their basic structure as short fictional prose narratives because authors in every country employ the same elements of fiction: plot, characterization, setting, point of view, style, and theme. But the content of stories in different countries reflects the cultural traditions and social conditions experienced by each writer. Each American short story, like each Colombian or French or Turkish or Korean or Australian short story, has been shaped by its author's unique cultural heritage and can be read as a manifestation of some segment of its country's history.

What particularly distinguishes the American story is that its authors played a significant role in the earliest years of the short story's development as a distinct literary form. Novels had been written in Europe for over a century before American authors began to write them, but the

1

short story was a genre that Americans consciously sought to shape as it emerged in books and periodicals during the early nineteenth century.

Certainly storytelling existed centuries before the emergence of modern short stories. Compared with older European and Asian civilizations, where myths and legends can be traced back for thousands of years, North Americans have a relatively brief record of written storytelling. However, native people, who have lived here for more than ten thousand years, told stories about the origin of the cosmos and their tribal nations. Each generation passed its stories orally to the next generation; many of these were thought to be sacred texts. Because the power of the words was in the telling, Native Americans often feared that their stories would be misunderstood when written down and taken into a different cultural context after contact with Europeans—especially since Europeans believed in their own cultural superiority, which enabled them to justify claiming native land and imposing their social, economic, and religious values on native people.

Our legacy of stories told in the Native American oral tradition, as well as the stories of early European settlers and African slaves that have been transcribed by historians and folklorists, goes back only a few hundred years in our written records. However, some of them can be considered precursors of the modern short story because they suggest important themes and techniques developed later by American authors working in this literary genre.

One of the most significant themes is the conflict between Native Americans and the Europeans exploring what they regarded as "the new land" in the seventeenth century. The legend of Captain John Smith's rescue by Pocahontas after his capture by Native Americans is questionable as history, but it survived as a story after being included in a section of Smith's 1624 account of *The Generall Historie of Virginia, New England and the Summer Isles*.

The Smith-Pocahontas Legend

*A*t last they brought him to *Meronocomoco*, where was *Powhatan* their Emperor.[1] Here more than two hundred of those grim Courtiers stood wondering at him, as he had beene a monster; till *Powhatan* and his trayne had put themselves in their greatest braveries. Before a fire upon a seat like a bedsted, he sat covered with a great robe, made of *Rarowcun*[2] skinnes, and all the tayles hanging by. On either hand did sit a young wench of 16

---

[1]To conform to modern usage, Smith's use of the letters *u* and *v* has been altered throughout this selection.
[2]Raccoon.

or 18 yeares, and along on each side of the house, two rowes of men, and behind them as many women, with all their heads and shoulders painted red: many of their heads bedecked with the white downe of Birds; but every one with something: and a great chayne of white beads about their necks.

At his entrance before the King, all the people gave a great shout. The Queene of *Appamatuck* was appointed to bring him water to wash his hands, and another brought him a bunch of feathers, in stead of a Towell to dry them: having feasted him after their best barbarous manner they could, a long consultation was held, but the conclusion was, two great stones were brought before *Powhatan:* then as many as could layd hands on him, dragged him to them, and thereon laid his head, and being ready with their clubs, to beate out his braines, *Pocahontas* the Kings dearest daughter, when no intreaty could prevaile, got his head in her armes, and laid her owne upon his to save him from death: whereat the Emperour was contented he should live to make him hatchets, and her bells, beads, and copper; for they thought him as well of all occupations as themselves. For the King himselfe will make his owne robes, shooes, bowes, arrowes, pots; plant, hunt, or doe any thing so well as the rest.

> They say he bore a pleasant shew,
> But sure his heart was sad.
> For who can pleasant be, and rest,
> That lives in feare and dread:
> And having life suspected, doth
> It still suspected lead.

Two days after, *Powhatan* having disguised himselfe in the most fearefullest manner he could, caused Captain *Smith* to be brought forth to a great house in the woods, and there upon a mat by the fire to be left alone. Not long after from behinde a mat that divided the house, was made the most dolefullest noyse he ever heard; then *Powhatan* more like a devill then a man, with some two hundred more as blacke as himselfe, came unto him and told him now they were friends, and presently he should goe to *Iames* towne, to send him two great gunnes, and a gryndstone, for which he would give him the Country of *Capahowosick,* and for ever esteeme him as his sonne *Nantaquoud.*

So to *Iames* towne with 12 guides *Powhatan* sent him. That night they quarterd in the woods, he still expecting (as he had done all this long time of his imprisonment) every houre to be put to one death or other: for all their feasting. But almightie God (by his divine providence) had mollified the hearts of those sterne *Barbarians* with compassion. The next morning betimes they came to the Fort, where *Smith* having used the Salvages for what kindnesse he could, he shewed *Rawhunt, Powhatans* trusty servant, two demi-Culverings and a millstone to carry *Powhatan:* they found them somewhat too heavie; but when they did see him discharge them, being loaded with stones, among the boughs of a great tree loaded with Isickles, the yce and branches came so tumbling downe, that the poore Salvages ran away halfe dead with feare. But at last we regained some conference with them, and gave them such toyes; and sent to *Powhatan,* his women, and children such presents, as gave them in generall full content.

———

What is important to our understanding of this legend is not whether it is true or false that Pocahontas rescued Captain John Smith in the way he described, but that the story of the rescue entered our mythology or stock of tales about the founding of America. The Jamestown colony actually survived because the Powhatans supplied the starving English colonists with food. When Pocahontas became an American heroine, it was not only because of her action as the brave young daughter of a "barbarian" chieftain but also because of her story, the demonstration of her spirit as the compassionate savior of John Smith and his Jamestown colony. Her intervention for him was interpreted as an act that validated the mission of all Europeans to carry on the work of developing their settlements in the North American wilderness.

The only other story that shared the appeal of the story of Pocahontas as an early American foundation myth was the famous account of George Washington and the cherry tree. According to legend, George Washington's father gave him a hatchet for a birthday present when he was a child, and he used it to cut down a cherry tree. When his father asked if he knew who had destroyed the tree, young George replied, "I cannot tell a lie," and confessed that he had cut it down.

Americans loved these two stories for good reasons. The critic Robert S. Tilton observed in *Pocahontas: The Evolution of an American Narrative* (1994) that "each is a story of bravery in a moment of crisis. And, most importantly, at the heart of each is a defiance of patriarchal power, a fearlessness of the consequences of such defiance, and an appeal to a form of honesty." John Smith's story of his abduction by the Indians was also an archetypal captivity narrative, a form of story that appealed to the imagination of many historically minded nineteenth-century American authors, such as James Hall, Nathaniel Hawthorne, and Harriet Prescott Spofford, who wrote early short prose tales.

Before the European explorers and settlers described their experiences in the new land, Native Americans created richly detailed accounts of their tribal origins. Their oral tradition was the earliest repository of American narratives. In 1735 Governor James Oglethorpe of Georgia, who established trading relations with the Creek Indians, encouraged Chekilli, the head chief of the upper and lower Creeks in Savannah, Georgia, to narrate "The Origin of the Creek Confederacy." Chekilli spoke in his native language, an interpreter translated the narrative into English, and a scribe wrote it on a buffalo skin. When Governor Oglethorpe took a party of Native

Americans from the Yamacraw village near Savannah back to England to meet King George II, the Archbishop of Canterbury, and various Trustees of the Colony of Georgia, this is the American story Chekilli told them:

The Origin of the Creek Confederacy

At a certain time the Earth opened in the West, where its mouth is. The Earth opened and the Kasihtas came out of its mouth, and settled nearby. But the Earth became angry and ate up their children; therefore they moved farther West. A part of them, however, turned back, and came again to the same place where they had been, and settled there. The greater number remained behind, because they thought it best to do so. Their children, nevertheless, were eaten by the Earth, so that, full of dissatisfaction, they journeyed toward the sunrise.

They came to a thick, muddy, slimy river — came there, camped there, rested there, and stayed overnight there. The next day they continued their journey and came, in one day, to a red, bloody river. They lived by this river, and ate of its fishes for two years; but there were low springs there; and it did not please them to remain. They went toward the end of this bloody river, and heard a noise as of thunder. They approached to see whence the noise came. At first they perceived a red smoke, and then a mountain which thundered; and on the mountain was a sound as of singing. They sent to see what this was; and it was a great fire which blazed upward, and made this singing noise. This mountain they named the King of Mountains. It thunders to this day; and men are very much afraid of it.

They here met a people of three different Nations. They had taken and saved some of the fire from the mountain; and, at this place, they also obtained a knowledge of herbs and of other things.

From the East, a white fire came to them; which, however, they would not use. From the South came a fire which was [blue?]; neither did they use it. From the West, came a fire which was black; nor would they use it. At last, came a fire from the North, which was red and yellow. This they mingled with the fire they had taken from the mountain; and this is the fire they use today; and this, too, sometimes sings. On the mountain was a pole which was very restless and made a noise, nor could any one say how it could be quieted. At length they took a motherless child, and struck it against the pole; and thus killed the child. They then took the pole, and carry it with them when they go to war. It was like a wooden tomahawk, such as they now use, and of the same wood.

Here they also found four herbs or roots, which sang and disclosed their virtues: first, Pasaw, the rattlesnake root; second Micoweanochaw, red-root; third Sowatchko, which grows like wild fennel; and fourth, Eschalapootchke, little tobacco. These herbs, especially the first and third, they use as the best medicine to purify themselves at their Busk. At this Busk, which is held yearly, they fast, and make offerings of the first fruits. Since they have learned the virtues of these herbs, their women, at certain times, have a separate fire, and remain apart from the men five, six, and seven days, for the sake of purification. If they neglected this, the power of the herbs would depart; and the women would not be healthy.

About this time a dispute arose, as to which was the oldest, and which should rule; and they agreed, as they were four Nations, they would set up four poles, and make them red with clay which is yellow at first, but becomes red by burning. They would go to war; and whichever Nation should first cover its pole, from top to bottom, with the scalps of their enemies, should be oldest.

They all tried, but the Kasihtas covered their pole first, and so thickly that it was hidden from sight. Therefore, they were looked upon, by the whole Nation, as the oldest. The Chickasaws covered their pole next; then the Alabamas; but the Abihkas did not cover their pole higher than to the knee.

At that time there was a bird of large size, blue in color, with a long tail, and swifter than an eagle, which came every day and killed and ate their people. They made an image in the shape of a woman, and placed it in the way of this bird. The bird carried it off, and kept it a long time, and then brought it back. They left it alone, hoping it would bring something forth. After a long time, a red rat came forth from it, and they believed the bird was the father of the rat. They took council with the rat how to destroy its father. Now the bird had a bow and arrows; and the rat gnawed the bowstring, so that the bird could not defend itself, and the people killed it. They called this bird the King of Birds. They think the eagle is a great King; and they carry its feathers when they go to War or make Peace; the red mean War; the white, Peace. If an enemy approaches with white feathers and a white mouth, and cries like an eagle, they dare not kill him.

After this they left that place, and came to a white footpath. The grass and everything around were white; and they plainly perceived that people had been there. They crossed the path, and slept near there. Afterward they turned back to see what sort of path that was, and who the people were who had been there, in the belief that it might be better for them to follow that path. They went along it to a creek called Coloose-hutche, that is, Coloose-creek, because it was rocky there and smoked.

They crossed it, going toward the sunrise, and came to a people and a town named Coosa. Here they remained four years. The Coosas complained that they were preyed upon by a wild beast, which they called man-eater or lion, which lived in a rock.

The Kasihtas said they would try to kill the beast. They dug a pit and stretched over it a net made of hickory-bark. They then laid a number of branches, crosswise, so that the lion could not follow them, and, going to the place where he lay, they threw a rattle into his den. The lion rushed forth in great anger, and pursued them through the branches. Then they thought it better that one should die rather than all; so they took a motherless child, and threw it before the lion as he came near the pit. The lion rushed at it, and fell in the pit, over which they threw the net, and killed him with blazing pine-wood. His bones, however, they keep to this day; on one side, they are red, on the other blue.

The lion used to come every seventh day to kill the people; therefore, they remained there seven days after they had killed him. In remembrance of him, when they prepare for War, they fast six days and start on the seventh. If they take his bones with them, they have good fortune.

After four years they left the Coosas, and came to a river which they called Nowphawpe, now Callasi-hutche. There they tarried two years; and, as they had no corn, they lived on roots and fishes, and made bows, pointing the arrows with beaver teeth and flint-stones, and for knives they used split canes.

They left this place, and came to a creek, called Wattoola-hawka-hutche, Whooping-creek, so called from the whooping of cranes, a great many being there; they slept there one night. They next came to a river, in which there was a waterfall; this they named the Owatunka-river. The next day they reached another river, which they called the Aphoosa pheeskaw.

The following day they crossed it, and came to a high mountain, where were people who, they believed, were the same who made the white path. They, therefore, made white arrows and shot at them, to see if they were good people. But the people took their white arrows, painted them red, and shot them back. When they showed these to their chief, he said that it was not a good sign; if the arrows returned had been white, they could have gone there and brought food for their children, but as they were red they must not go. Nevertheless, some of them went to see what sort of people they were; and found their houses deserted. They also saw a trail which led into the river; and, as they could not see the trail on the opposite bank, they believed that the people had gone into the river, and would not again come forth.

At that place is a mountain, called Moterelo, which makes a noise like beating on a drum; and they think this people live there. They hear this noise on all sides when they go to war.

They went along the river, till they came to a waterfall, where they saw great rocks, and on the rocks were bows lying; and they believed the people who made the white path had been there.

They always have, on their journeys, two scouts who go before the main body. These scouts ascended a high mountain and saw a town. They shot white arrows into the town; but the people of the town shot back red arrows. Then the Kasihtas became angry, and determined to attack the town, and each one have a house when it was captured.

They threw stones into the river until they could cross it, and took the town (the people had flattened heads) and killed all but two persons. In pursuing these they found a white dog, which they slew. They followed the two who escaped, until they came again to the white path, and saw the smoke of a town, and thought that this must be the people they had so long been seeking. This is the place where now the tribe of Apalachicolas live, from whom Tomochichi is descended.

The Kasihtas continued bloody-minded; but the Apalachicolas gave them black drink, as a sign of friendship, and said to them: "Our hearts are white, and yours must be white, and you must lay down the bloody tomahawk, and show your bodies as a proof that they shall be white." Nevertheless, they were for the tomahawk; but the Apalachicolas got it by persuasion, and buried it under their beds. The Apalachicolas likewise gave them white feathers, and asked to have a chief in common. Since then they have always lived together.

Some settled on one side of the river, some on the other. Those on one side are called Kasihtas, those on the other, Cowetas; yet they are one people, and the principal towns of the Upper and Lower Creeks. Nevertheless, as the Kasihtas first saw the red smoke and the red fire, and make bloody towns, they cannot yet leave their red hearts, which, though white on one side, are red on the other. They now know that the white path was the best for them: for, although Tomochichi was a stranger, they see he has done them good; because he went to see the great King with Esquire Oglethorpe, and hear his talk, and had related it to them, and they had listened to it, and believed it.

Native Americans also created an imaginative oral tradition of mythological stories describing an age of supernatural beings before the arrival of human beings. These myths and legends sometimes had animals as the main characters, like the stories of the trickster Coyote's exploits told by members of the Shasta tribe on the Oregon coast. Creation myths such as the Shasta account of "The Theft of Fire" attempting to explain how important things came into existence are also found in the mythologies of most other cultures throughout the world. This American story, with its memorable detail of fire being originally owned by the Pain people, and the motif of the relay race of the various birds as Coyote's accomplices, probably originated well before the nineteenth century. It was first published in Roland Dixon's account of "Shasta Myths" in the *Journal of American Folklore*, 23 (1911).

The Theft of Fire

Long ago, in the beginning, people had only stones for fire. In the beginning every one had only that sort of fire-stone. "Do you hear? There is fire over there. Where Pain lives there is fire." So Coyote went, and came to the house where Pain lived. The children were at home; but all the old people were away, driving game with fire. They had told their children, "If anyone comes, it will be Coyote." So they went to drive game by setting fires.

Coyote went into the house. "Oh, you poor children! Are you all alone here?" said he. "Yes, we are all alone. They told us they were all going hunting. If anyone comes, it will be Coyote. I think you are Coyote," they said. "I am not Coyote," he said. "Look! Way back there, far off in the mountains, is Coyote's country. There are none near here." Coyote stretched his feet out toward the fire, with his long blanket in which he had run away. "No, you smell like Coyote," said the children. "No, there are none about here," he said.

Now, his blanket began to burn, he was ready to run. He called to Chicken-Hawk, "You stand there! I will run there with the fire. I will give it to you, and then you run on. Eagle, do you stand there! Grouse, do you stand there! Quail, do you stand there!" Turtle alone did not know about it. He was walking along by the river.

Now, Coyote ran out of the house; he stole Pain's fire. He seized it, and ran with it. Pain's children ran after him. Coyote gave the fire to Chicken-Hawk, and he ran on. Now Chicken-Hawk gave it to Eagle, and he ran on. Eagle gave it to Grouse, and he ran on. He gave it to Quail, and he ran far away with it. Turtle was there walking about. The Pains were following, crying, "Coyote has stolen fire!" Now, Turtle was walking about; he knew nothing, he was singing. "I'll give you the fire," said Quail. "Here! Take it!" Just then the Pains got there. Turtle put the fire under his armpit, and jumped into the water. Pain shot at him, shot him in the rear. "Oh, oh, oh! That is going to be a tail," said Turtle, and dove deep down into the river.

All the Pains stood together. By and by they gave it up, and went away. Coyote came up, and asked, "Where is the fire?"

"Turtle dove with it," they said. "Curse it! Why did you dive with it?" Coyote said. He was very angry. After a while Turtle crawled out of the water on the other side. Coyote saw him. "Where is the fire?" he called out. Turtle did not answer. "I say to you, where did you put the fire?" said Coyote. "Curse it! Why did you jump into the water?" After a while Turtle threw the fire all about. "You keep quiet! I will throw the fire about," said Turtle. "O children, poor children!" said Coyote; he said all kinds of things, he was glad. Now, everybody came and got fire. Now we have got fire. Coyote was the first to get it, at Pain's that way. That is all. That is one story.

In addition to stories in the oral tradition relating their tribal origins and myths, Native Americans told stories based on the heroic exploits of their ancestors. These were usually included within a larger narrative framework. For example, around the fifteenth century, five Iroquoian tribes unified under the moral leadership of Tekanawita, who with the aid of the reformer Hiawatha persuaded the Mohawk, Oneida, Onondaga, Cayuga, and Seneca tribes to become a peaceful nation. Here is a story about Tekanawita included in *Concerning the League,* a narrative account of the Iroquois tradition as dictated in Onondaga by John Arthur Gibson. This translation of the ancient story about how Tekanawita attempted to end the practice of cannibalism in the tribes was published in the *Algonquian and Iroquois Linguistics Memoir* in 1992.

From *Concerning the League*[1]

After Tekanawita had departed in that direction he came to a house belonging to a cannibal who had his house there. Then Tekanawita went close to the house. Then, when he saw the man coming out, departing, sliding down the hill to the river, and dipping water, thereupon Tekanawita hurriedly climbed onto the house to the place where there was a chimney for the smoke to escape; he lay down on his stomach and looking into the house he saw that the task of breaking up meat and piling it had been completed. Then the man returned, and he was carrying a drum with water in it. Thereupon he poured it into a vessel, put meat into the liquid, and hung the vessel up over the fire until it boiled. Moreover, the man watched it, and when it was done, he took down the vessel, placing it near the embers. Thereupon he said, "Now indeed it is done. Moreover, now I will eat." Thereupon he set up a seat, a bench, thinking that he will put it there when he eats. Thereupon he went to where the vessel sat, intending to take the meat out of the liquid, when he saw, from inside the vessel, a man looking out. Thereupon he moved away without removing the meat, and sat down again on the long bench, for it was a surprise to him, seeing the man in the vessel. Thereupon he thought, "Let me look again." Thereupon he, Tekanawita, looked again from above where the smoke hole was, again causing a reflection in the vessel, and then the man, standing up again, went to where the vessel sat, looked into the vessel again, saw the man looking out, and he was handsome, he having a nice face. Thereupon the man moved away again, and he sat down again on the long bench, and then he bowed his head, pondering and thinking: "I am exceedingly handsome and I have a nice face; it is probably not right, my habit of eating humans. So I will now stop, from now on I ought not to

---

[1]Edited and translated by Hanni Woodbury in collaboration with Reg Henry and Harry Webster.

kill humans anymore." Thereupon he stood up again, went to where the vessel sat, picked up the vessel with the meat in it, and then he went out, sliding straight down the slope beside the river and near an uprooted tree he poured out the vessel full of meat.

The traditional Native American storytellers' oral presentations of tales such as "The Theft of Fire" and stirring accounts of the adventures of tribal leaders like Tekanawita continued for centuries before the stories were written down by anthropologists for a print-dominated culture. As the scholar Karl Kroeber understood in *Artistry in Native American Myths* (1998), "We read traditional American Indian myths in distorting translations, not merely of the original language but also of transient oral events transposed into enduring printed objects. . . . [The traditional myths were] constructed to encourage variability of interpretation, not finality of meaning." It was not until the beginning of the twentieth century that Native American storytellers began to write their own accounts of their tribal legends as carefully crafted short stories.

One hundred fifty years earlier, European settlers had told fanciful tales about how Native Americans viewed the arrival of the colonists in the new land. John Heckewelder, for example, wrote his account of "The Arrival of the Dutch" in New York Harbor as he imagined it had been experienced by members of the Monhegan tribe. Heckewelder's story was collected in 1765 and published by the New York Historical Society.

The Arrival of the Dutch

A long time ago, when there was no such thing known to the Indians as people with a *white skin,* (their expression,) some Indians who had been out a-fishing, and where the sea widens, espied at a great distance something remarkably large swimming, or floating on the water, and such as they had never seen before. They immediately returning to the shore apprised their countrymen of what they had seen, and pressed them to go out with them and discover what it might be. These together hurried out, and saw to their great surprise the phenomenon, but could not agree what it might be; some concluding it either to be an uncommon large fish, or other animal, while others were of opinion it must be some very large house. It was at length agreed among those who were spectators, that as this phenomenon moved towards the land, whether or not it was an animal, or anything that had life in it, it would be well to inform all the Indians on the inhabited islands of what they had seen, and put them on their guard. Accordingly, they sent runners and watermen off to carry the news to their scattered chiefs, that these might send off in every direction for the warriors to come in. These arriving in numbers, and themselves viewing the strange appearance, and that it was actually moving towards them, (the entrance of the river or bay,) concluded it to be a large canoe or house, in which the great Mannitto (great or Supreme Being) *himself* was, and that he probably was coming to visit them. By this time the chiefs of the different tribes were assembled on York Island, and were counselling (or deliberating) on the manner they should receive their Mannitto on his arrival. Every step had been taken to be well provided with a plenty of meat for a sacrifice; the women were required to prepare the best of victuals; idols or images were examined and put in order; and a grand dance was supposed not only to be an agreeable entertainment for the Mannitto, but might, with the addition of a sacrifice, contribute towards appeasing him, in case he was angry with them. The conjurors were also set to work, to determine what the meaning of this phenomenon was, and what the result would be. Both to these, and to the chiefs and wise men of the nation, men, women, and children were looking up for advice and protection. Between hope and fear, and in confusion, a dance commenced. While in this situation fresh runners arrive declaring it a house of various colours, and crowded with living creatures. It now appears to be certain that it is the great Mannitto bringing them some kind of game, such as they had not before; but other runners soon after arriving, declare it a large house of various colours, full of people, yet of quite a different colour than they (the Indians) are of; that they were also dressed in a different manner from them, and that one in particular appeared altogether red, which must be the *Mannitto* himself. They are soon hailed from the vessel, though in a language they do not understand; yet they shout (or yell) in their way. Many are for running off to the woods, but are pressed by others to stay, in order not to give offence to their visitors, who could find them out, and might destroy them. The house (or large canoe, as some will have it,) stops, and a smaller canoe comes ashore with the red man and some others in it; some stay by this canoe to guard it. The chiefs and wise men (or councillors) had composed a large circle, unto which the red-clothed man with two others approach. He salutes them with friendly countenance, and they return the salute after their manner. They are lost in admiration, both as to the colour of the skin (of these whites) as also to their manner of dress, yet most as to the habit of him who wore the red clothes, which shone with something they could not account for. He *must* be the great Mannitto (Supreme Being,) they think, but why should he have a *white skin*? A large hockhack [Their word for gourd, bottle, decanter] is brought forward by one of the (supposed) Mannitto's servants, and from this a substance is poured out into a small cup (or glass) and handed to the Mannitto. The (expected) Mannitto drinks; has the glass filled again, and hands it to the chief next to him to drink. The chief receives the glass, but only smelleth at it, and passes it on to the next chief, who does the same. The glass thus passes through the circle without the contents being tasted by any one; and is upon the point of being returned again to the red-clothed man, when one of their number, a spirited man and great warrior jumps up — harangues the assembly on the impropriety of returning the glass with the contents in it; that the same was handed them by the Mannitto in order that they should drink it, as he himself had done before them; that this would please him; but to return what he had given to them might provoke him, and be the cause of their being destroyed by him. And that, since he believed it for the good of the nation that the contents offered them *should* be drank, and as no one was willing to drink it *he would*, let the consequence be what it would; and that it was better for one man to die, than a whole nation to be destroyed. He then took the glass and bidding the assembly a farewell, *drank it off.* Every eye was fixed on their resolute companion to see what an effect this would have upon him, and he soon beginning to stagger about, and at last dropping to the ground, they bemoan him. He falls into a sleep, and they view him as expiring. He awakes again, jumps up, and declares that he never felt himself before so happy as after he had drank the cup. Wishes for more. His wish is granted; and the whole assembly soon join him, and become intoxicated. [The Delawares call this place (New-York Island) *Mannahattanink* or *Mannahachtanink* to this day. They have frequently told me that it derived its name from this general *intoxication,* and that the word comprehended the same as to say, *the island or place of general intoxication.* The Mahicanni, (otherwise called Mohiggans by the English, and Mahicanders by the Low Dutch,) call this place by the same name as the Delawares do; yet think it is owing or given in consequence of a kind of wood which grew there, and of which the Indians used to make their bows and arrows. This wood the latter (Mohiccani) call *"gawaak."* The universal name the Monseys have for New-York, is *Laaphawachking,* which is interpreted, *the place of stringing beads (wampum).* They say this name was given in consequence of beads being here distributed among them by the Europeans; and that after the European vessel had returned, wherever one looked, one would see the Indians employed in stringing the beads or wampum the whites had given them.]

After this general intoxication had ceased, (during which time the whites had confined themselves to their vessel,) the man with the red clothes returned again to them, and distributed presents among them, to wit, beads, axes, hoes, stockings, &c. They say that they had become familiar to each other, and were made to understand by signs; that they now would return home, but would visit them next year again, when they would bring them more presents, and stay with them awhile; but that, as they could not live without eating, they should then want a little land of them to sow some seeds in order to raise herbs to put in their broth. That the vessel arrived the season following, and they were much rejoiced at seeing each other; but that the whites laughed at them (the Indians,) seeing they knew not the use of the axes, hoes, &c., they had given them, they having had these hanging to their breasts as ornaments; and the stockings they had made use of as tobacco pouches. The whites now put handles (or helves) in the former, and cut trees down before their eyes, and dug the ground, and showed them the use of the stockings. Here (say they) a general laughter ensued among them (the Indians), that they had remained for so long a time ignorant of the use of so valuable implements; and had borne with the weight of such heavy metal hanging to their necks for such a length of time. They took every white man they saw for a Mannitto, yet inferior and attendant to the *supreme Mannitto,* to wit, to the one which wore the red and laced clothes. Familiarity daily increasing between them and the whites, the latter now proposed to stay with them, asking them only for so much land as the hide of a bullock would cover (or encompass,) which hide was brought forward and spread on the ground before them. That they readily granted this request; whereupon the whites took a knife, and beginning at one place on this hide, cut it up into a rope not thicker than the finger of a little child, so that by the time this hide was cut up there was a great heap. That this rope was drawn out to a great distance, and then brought round again, so that both ends might meet. That they carefully avoided its breaking, and that upon the whole it encompassed a large piece of ground. That they (the Indians) were surprised at the superior wit of the whites, but did not wish to contend with them about a little land, as they had enough. That they and the whites lived for a long time content-edly together, although these asked from time to time more land of them; and proceeding higher up the Mahicanittuk (Hudson river), they believed they would soon want all their country, and which at this time was already the case.

A different type of early imaginative American story is the African American folktale. Africans who were seized in their own land and brought to America as slaves arrived with a storehouse of tribal myths and legends that were intended for oral delivery like the Native American nar-ratives. Many African American tales—such as "All God's Chillen Had Wings," told by Caesar Grant, a laborer from Johns Island, South Car-olina—were collected and written down in the late nineteenth and early twentieth centuries. Grant's poignant story was published in John Ben-net's *Doctor to the Dead* (1943, 1946) and in Langston Hughes and Arna Bontemps's *Book of Negro Folklore* (1958). Later African American writers such as Ralph Ellison were influenced by this story's imagery.

All God's Chillen Had Wings

Once all Africans could fly like birds; but owing to their many transgressions, their wings were taken away. There remained, here and there, in the sea islands and out-of-the-way places in the low country, some who had been overlooked, and had retained the power of flight, though they looked like other men.

There was a cruel master on one of the sea islands who worked his people till they died. When they died he bought others to take their places. These also he killed with overwork in the burning summer sun, through the middle hours of the day, although this was against the law.

One day, when all the worn-out Negroes were dead of overwork, he bought, of a broker in the town, a company of native Africans just brought into the country, and put them at once to work in the cottonfield.

He drove them hard. They went to work at sunrise and did not stop until dark. They were driven with unsparing harshness all day long, men, women and children. There was no pause for rest during the unendurable heat of the midsummer noon, though trees were plenty and near. But through the hardest hours, when fair plantations gave their Negroes rest, this man's driver pushed the work along without a moment's stop for breath, until all grew weak with heat and thirst.

There was among them one young woman who had lately borne a child. It was her first; she had not fully recovered from bearing, and should not have been sent to the field until her strength had come back. She had her child with her, as the other women had, astraddle on her hip, or piggyback.

The baby cried. She spoke to quiet it. The driver could not understand her words. She took her breast with her hand and threw it over her shoulder that the child might suck and be content. Then she went back to chopping knot-grass; but being very weak, and sick with the great heat, she stumbled, slipped and fell.

The driver struck her with his lash until she rose and staggered on.

She spoke to an old man near her, the oldest man of them all, tall and strong, with a forked beard. He replied; but the driver could not understand what they said; their talk was strange to him.

She returned to work; but in a little while she fell again. Again the driver lashed her until she got to her feet. Again she spoke to the old man. But he said: "Not yet, daughter; not yet." So she went on working, though she was very ill.

Soon she stumbled and fell again. But when the driver came running with his lash to drive her on with her work, she turned to the old man and asked: "Is it time yet, daddy?" He answered: "Yes, daughter; the time has come. Go; and peace be with you!" . . . and stretched out his arms toward her . . . so.

15

With that she leaped straight up into the air and was gone like a bird, flying over field and wood.

The driver and overseer ran after her as far as the edge of the field; but she was gone, high over their heads, over the fence, and over the top of the woods, gone, with her baby astraddle of her hip, sucking at her breast.

Then the driver hurried the rest to make up for her loss; and the sun was very hot indeed. So hot that soon a man fell down. The overseer himself lashed him to his feet. As he got up from where he had fallen the old man called to him in an unknown tongue. My grandfather told me the words that he said; but it was a long time ago, and I have forgotten them. But when he had spoken, the man turned and laughed at the overseer, and leaped up into the air, and was gone, like a gull, flying over field and wood.

Soon another man fell. The driver lashed him. He turned to the old man. The old man cried out to him, and stretched out his arms as he had done for the other two; and he, like them, leaped up, and was gone through the air, flying like a bird over field and wood.

Then the overseer cried to the driver, and the master cried to them both: "Beat the old devil! He is the doer!"

The overseer and the driver ran at the old man with lashes ready; and the master ran too, with a picket pulled from the fence, to beat the life out of the old man who had made those Negroes fly.

But the old man laughed in their faces, and said something loudly to all the Negroes in the field, the new Negroes and the old Negroes.

And as he spoke to them they all remembered what they had forgotten, and recalled the power which once had been theirs. Then all the Negroes, old and new, stood up together; the old man raised his hands; and they all leaped up into the air with a great shout; and in a moment were gone, flying, like a flock of crows, over the field, over the fence, and over the top of the wood; and behind them flew the old man.

The men went clapping their hands; and the women went singing; and those who had children gave them their breasts; and the children laughed and sucked as their mothers flew, and were not afraid.

The master, the overseer, and the driver looked after them as they flew, beyond the wood, beyond the river, miles on miles, until they passed beyond the last rim of the world and disappeared in the sky like a handful of leaves. They were never seen again.

Where they went I do not know; I never was told. Nor what it was that the old man said . . . that I have forgotten. But as he went over the last fence he made a sign in the master's face, and cried "Kuli-ba! Kuli-ba!" I don't know what that means.

But if I could only find the old wood sawyer, he could tell you more; for he was there at the time, and saw the Africans fly away with their women and children. He is an old, old man, over ninety years of age, and remembers a great many strange things.

Another important precursor of the American short story was the "brag" or tall tale created by settlers in the western territory in the early years of the nineteenth century. These imaginative stories influenced early storytellers such as Thomas Bangs Thorpe and later journalists, such as Bret Harte and Mark Twain, whose careers began after the Civil War. "Sunrise in My Pocket," from the *Davy Crockett Almanacs* of 1835–56, exemplifies the concise and humorous hyperbole of these early narratives as well as their strong flavor of local dialect. The pages of the yearly almanacs were filled with humorous anecdotes and sketches along with informative planting instructions and weather predictions for the unsophisticated farm families who bought the crudely printed pamphlets and were eager to be entertained. "Sunrise in My Pocket" expresses the vigorous spirit and lusty vernacular speech of the pioneers engaged in the herculean task of domesticating the new continent.

Sunrise in My Pocket

*O*ne January morning it was so all screwen cold that the forest trees were stiff and they couldn't shake, and the very daybreak froze fast as it was trying to dawn. The tinder box in my cabin would no more ketch fire than a sunk raft at the bottom of the sea. Well, seein' daylight war so far behind time I thought creation war in a fair way for freezen fast: so, thinks I, I must strike a little fire from my fingers, light my pipe, an' travel out a few leagues, and see about it. Then I brought my knuckles together like two thunderclouds, but the sparks froze up afore I could begin to collect 'em, so out I walked, whistlin' "Fire in the mountains!" as I went along in three double quick time. Well, arter I had walked about twenty miles up the Peak O'Day and Daybreak Hill I soon discovered what war the matter. The airth had actually friz fast on her axes, and couldn't turn round; the sun had got jammed between two cakes o' ice under the wheels, an' thar he had been shinin' an' workin' to get loose till he friz fast in his cold sweat. C-r-e-a-t-i-o-n! thought I, this ar the toughest sort of suspension, an' it mustn't be endured. Somethin' must be done, or human creation is done for. It war then so anteluvian an' premature cold that my upper and lower teeth an' tongue war all collapsed together as tight as a friz oyster; but I took a fresh twenty-pound bear off my back that I'd picked up on my road, and beat the animal agin the ice till the hot ile began to walk out on him at all sides. I then took an' held him over the airth's axes an' squeezed him till I'd thawed 'em loose, poured about a ton on't over the sun's face, give the airth's cog-wheel one kick backward till I got the sun loose — whistled "Push along, keep movin'!" an' in about fifteen seconds the airth gave a grunt, an' began movin'. The sun walked up beautiful, salutin' me with sich a wind o' gratitude that it made me sneeze. I lit my pipe by the blaze o' his top-knot, shouldered my bear, an' walked home, introducin' people to the fresh daylight with a piece of sunrise in my pocket.

═══════════

By the beginning of the nineteenth century, American authors had a legacy of several different narrative traditions from within the new nation. Many of them could also draw upon their heritage of European literature as well. The direct ancestor of Washington Irving's "Rip Van Winkle," generally considered the first successful American short story, was a transcription of a German folktale from the oral tradition titled "Peter Klaus the Goatherd," collected and transcribed by J. C. C. Nachtigal. Nachtigal was a German folklorist who published under the pseudonym "Otmar" when *Folkssagen, Nacherzhaht von Otmar* (*Folktales, Transcribed by Otmar*), his collection of folk narratives, appeared in Bremen in 1800. Here is a translation of "Peter Klaus the Goatherd," by Irving's English contemporary Thomas Roscoe:

Peter Klaus the Goatherd

*I*n the village of Littendorf at the foot of a mountain lived Peter Klaus, a goatherd, who was in the habit of pasturing his flock upon the Kyffhausen hills. Towards evening he generally let them browse upon a green plot not far off, surrounded with an old ruined wall from which he could take a muster of his whole flock.

For some days past he had observed that one of his prettiest goats, soon after its arrival at this spot, usually disappeared, nor joined the fold again until late in the evening. He watched her again and again, and at last found that she slipped through a gap in the old wall, whither he followed her. It led into a passage which widened as he went into a cavern; and here he saw the goat employed in picking up the oats that fell through some crevices in the place above. He looked up, shook his ears at this odd shower of oats, but could discover nothing. Where the deuce could it come from? At length he heard over his head the neighing and stamping of horses; he listened, and concluded that the oats must have fallen through the manger when they were fed. The poor goatherd was sadly puzzled what to think of these horses in this uninhabited part of the mountain, but so it was, for a groom making his appearance, without saying a word beckoned him to follow him. Peter obeyed, and followed him up some steps which brought him into an open court-yard surrounded by old walls. At the side of this was a still more spacious cavern, surrounded by rocky heights which only admitted a kind of twilight, through the overhanging trees and shrubs. He went on, and came to a smooth shaven green, where he saw twelve ancient knights none of whom spoke a word, engaged in playing at nine pins. His guide now beckoned to Peter in silence, to pick up the nine pins and went his way. Trembling in every joint Peter did not venture to disobey, and at times he cast a stolen glance at the players, whose long beards and slashed doublets were not at all in the present fashion. By degrees his looks grew bolder; he took particular notice of every thing around him; among other things observing a tankard near him filled with wine, whose odour was excellent, he took a good draught. It seemed to inspire him with life; and whenever he began to feel tired of running, he applied with fresh ardour to the tankard, which always renewed his strength. But finally it quite overpowered him, and he fell asleep.

When he next opened his eyes, he found himself on the grass-plot again, in the old spot where he was in the habit of feeding his goats. He rubbed his eyes, he looked round, but could see neither dog nor flock; he was surprised at the long rank grass that grew around him, and at trees and bushes which he had never before seen. He shook his head and walked a little farther, looking for the old sheep path and the hillocks and roads where he used daily to drive his flock; but he could find no traces of them left. Yet he saw the village just before him; it was the same Littendorf, and scratching his head he hastened at a quick pace down the hill to enquire after his flock.

All the people whom he met going into the place were strangers to him, were differently dressed, and even spoke in a different style to his old neighbors. When he asked about his goats, they only stared at him, and fixed their eyes upon his chin. He put his hand unconsciously to his mouth, and to his great surprise found that he had got a beard, at least a foot long. He now began to think that both he and all the world about him were in a dream; and yet he knew the mountain for that of the Kyffhausen (for he had just come down it) well enough. And there were the cottages, with their gardens and grass-plots, much as he had left them. Besides the lads who had all collected round him, answered to the enquiry of a passenger, what place it was: "Littendorf, sir."

Still shaking his head, he went farther into the village to look for his own house. He found it, but greatly altered for the worse; a strange goatherd in an old tattered frock lay before the door, and near him his old dog, which growled and showed its teeth at Peter when he called him. He went through the entrance which had once a door, but all within was empty and deserted; Peter staggered like a drunken man out of the house, and called for his wife and children by their names. But no one heard him, and no one gave him any answer.

Soon, however, a crowd of women and children got round the inquisitive stranger, with the long hoary beard; and asked him what it was he wanted. Now Peter thought it was such a strange kind of thing to stand before his own house, enquiring for his own wife and children, as well as about himself, that evading these inquiries he pronounced the first name that came into his head: "Kurt Steffen, the blacksmith?" Most of the spectators were silent, and only looked at him wistfully, till an old woman at last said, "Why, for these twelve years he has been at Sachsenburg, whence I suppose you are not come today." "Where is Valentine Meier, the tailor?" "The Lord rest his soul," cried another woman leaning on her crutch, "he has been lying more than fifteen years in a house he will never leave."

Peter recognized in the speakers, two of his young neighbours who seemed to have grown old very suddenly, but he had no inclination to enquire any farther. At this moment there appeared making her way through the crowd of spectators, a sprightly young woman with a year old baby in her arms, and a girl about four taking hold of her hand, all three as like his wife he was seeking for as possible. "What are your names?" he enquired in a tone of great surprise. "Mine is Maria." "And your father's?" continued Peter. "God rest his soul! Peter Klaus for sure. It's now twenty years ago since we were all looking for him day and night upon the Kyffhausen; for his flock came home without him, and I was then," continued the woman, "only seven years old."

The goatherd could no longer bear this. "I am Peter Klaus," he said. "Peter and no other," and he took his daughter's child and kissed it. The spectators appeared struck dumb with astonishment, until first one and then another began to say, "Yes, indeed, this is Peter Klaus! Welcome, good neighbour, after twenty years' absence, welcome home."

———————————

The earliest published American short prose tales evolved at the end of the eighteenth century and in the first decades of the nineteenth century out of the background of myths, legends, folktales, sentimental anecdotes, comic parodies, travel and character sketches, and the short fictional narratives that were popular at the time. The spirit of the age that nurtured the development of the short story was romanticism, when originality and imagination were valued over the emphasis on tradition and reason that had shaped the attitude of earlier eighteenth-century neoclassical writers.

For the first time, educated Europeans interested themselves in the oral narratives that had been passed down for centuries by uneducated, rural storytellers. In Germany, J. C. C. Nachtigal and Jakob and Wilhelm Grimm, among others, believed in these stories' cultural value as repositories of the folk imagination. Eager to sympathize with the emotions of what they considered exotic, primitive humanity, the early collectors began to write down the oral tales and publish them in books that were ultimately read all over the world. As the historian Roger Paulin has stated in *The Brief Compass: The Nineteenth-Century German Novelle* (1985), for the first time the subject matter of narrative fiction expanded "to take in more moral and social awareness, satire, and the realm of the fancy and romantic imagination."

In the first decades of the nineteenth century, American writers began to develop a new and highly original form of storytelling. This coincided with the modification of the existing forms of periodical literature, as the content of newspapers and magazines expanded beyond a brief report of current events "to occupy the field of literature rather than of journalism, and to serve as a *Museum, Depository,* or *Magazine* of the polite arts and sciences," according to the anonymous author of an article on "American Magazine-Literature of the Last Century" in an early issue of *The Atlantic Monthly.* Discovering the appeal of imaginative stories for readers in a rapidly expanding age of print, American writers created entertaining short prose tales that enabled them to explore a new subject matter: their own emerging national consciousness. Often the stories dramatized the themes of social injustice or cultural conflicts between Native Americans and Europeans, or reflected the effects of the rapid changes brought about by the exploration and settlement of the new land. These early prose tales caught the spirit of the young country and ushered in the first flourishing period of the American short story.

STORIES

1

EARLY NINETEENTH CENTURY

1819–1860

*W*ashington Irving was the first author to create what most readers recognize as an American short story. In 1818, while living in London, he set himself the task of learning German by translating J. C. C. Nachtigal's collection of *Folkssagen* into English. Before going to Europe, Irving had published a humorous history of New York City that had been very popular. Bored with his translations of the German folktales, he turned his hand during one particularly inspired day to creating an Americanized version of one of them. The result was what is generally considered to be the first successful American short story, "Rip Van Winkle."

On March 3, 1819, Washington Irving sent the manuscript of "Rip Van Winkle" and five other chapters making up the first part of *The Sketch Book of Geoffrey Crayon, Gent.* from London to his brother Ebenezer in New York City, who was to see the book through the press. Along with the manuscript, Irving included a letter expressing his hope that his "literary experiment" would find favor among American readers:

> I consider myself at present as making a literary experiment, in the course of which I only care to be kept in bread and cheese. Should it not succeed—should my writings not acquire critical applause, I am content to throw up the pen and take to any commonplace employment. But if they should succeed, it would repay me for a world of care and privation to be placed among the established authors of my country, and to win the affections of my countrymen.

Irving understood that he was attempting something entirely new in *The Sketch Book*. Earlier prose tales published in American periodicals usually had been either rambling, discursive narratives in the form of political allegories that justified the Revolutionary War or fictional accounts lacking the sufficiently developed settings, characters, or plots that would qualify them as specifically American short stories. In rewriting "Peter Klaus the Goatherd" as an entertaining American story, Irving experimented with using elements of the eighteenth-century character sketch and descriptive travel essay to develop the brief German folktale. He chose the Hudson River valley as his setting to add color and interest to the plot for his American and British readers.

Knowledgeable about the early Dutch settlements in New York, Irving also drew upon the historical background of Henry Hudson's exploration of the region to enrich the story, humorously inventing bogus documents to suggest its authenticity. Letting his imagination play with memories of a distant American homeland while seated at his writing desk in London, Irving cast the warm glow of nostalgia on his descriptions of the majestic Catskill Mountains and their picturesque rural inhabitants.

Despite its humorous tone, "Rip Van Winkle" portrayed life in the Hudson River valley at the time of the Revolutionary War with historical fidelity. During these first decades of the new republic, Irving and his contemporaries were writing in a time of literary nationalism, in which authorship was conceived as public service contributing to the development of an authentic American culture. As Ralph Waldo Emerson wrote in "The American Scholar" in 1837, "We have listened too long to the courtly muses of Europe."

Eighteen years before, "Rip Van Winkle" and its companion story, "The Legend of Sleepy Hollow," which was based on another German legend, had been the earliest imaginative prose works by an American author to impress European readers as authentic portraits of life in the new land. Irving's stories succeeded because of his consummate artistry and his belief that the skill with which he shaped his materials into a tale was more important than its plot or subject matter.

Irving paid a New York printer to produce two thousand copies of *The Sketch Book,* which his brother placed with a bookshop for distribution. Irving wanted to safeguard his earnings from subsequent editions of the work, under an American copyright law guaranteeing financial remuneration for authors whose work was published in this country. Because magazines and newspapers were just beginning to find a precarious financial foothold in the United States, they were usually filled with excerpts from English literature, reprinted without payment to the writers in the absence of an international copyright law.

In both England and America original work was slighted in favor of extracts from previously published English books. The novelist Jane Austen tartly commented in *Northanger Abbey* (1818) on the common practice of filling the pages of books and periodicals with excerpts from the writing of well-known authors:

> And while the abilities . . . of the man who collects and publishes in a volume some dozen lines of Milton, Pope, or Prior, with a paper from the *Spectator* and a chapter from Sterne, are eulogized by a thousand pens—there seems almost a general wish of decrying and undervaluing the labour of the novelist, and of slighting the performances which have only genius, wit, and taste to recommend them.

The first edition of Irving's *Sketch Book* rapidly sold out and was an inspiration to authors in both America and England. They began creating original short prose tales in the manner of *The Sketch Book,* featuring enchanted settings and characters and often basing them on picturesque legends and adventures. One of these early stories, William Austin's "Peter Rugg, the Missing Man" (1824), was serialized in the *New England Galaxy.* Twenty years later the influence of "Rip Van Winkle" was still evident when William Gilmore Simms used Irving's model of a bewitched hunter and a shrewish wife who drove her husband away from home in his tale "The Arm-Chair of Tustenuggee" (1845). Irving's family had the means to finance the publication of his work in New York City, and Augustus Baldwin Longstreet owned the print shop in Augusta that published his book of sketches, *Georgia Scenes,* in 1835. Most American writers of short prose tales, however, depended on periodicals to publish their stories. From the beginning, American short stories developed along with the earliest newspapers, magazines, and books that featured them.

The evolution of this literary form accelerated during the second quarter of the nineteenth century when mechanized printing machinery became available in Europe and America. Before this time, every stage of book and magazine production was done by hand on presses similar to those used by Gutenberg three centuries earlier. The new mechanized techniques revolutionized the production of printed materials and contributed to the proliferation of periodicals, which established a marketplace for the short story.

Original works of short fiction became so popular that less than a decade after *The Sketch Book* they had supplanted the vogue for reprinted articles and stories that had whetted earlier readers' appetites for entertaining short prose narratives. In addition, publishers began to market annual collections of original sketches, tales, and poetry in fancy, tooled-leather bindings as gift books at Christmas and New Year's in the United States. Primarily directed toward women readers, these annuals were popular for almost twenty years. The fad began in 1826 with *The Atlantic Souvenir,* which featured the short fiction of the best-selling novelist Catharine Maria Sedgwick. Other gift books included *The Token* (1827), *The Talisman* (1828), *The Western Souvenir* (1830), *The Literary Souvenir* (1840), and *The Gift* (1842).

The prose tales in these annuals relied heavily on romantic stories of adventure, love, and travel, but they also included material that suggested the darker side of American life in the early nineteenth century. When Catharine Maria Sedgwick introduced "Mary Dyre" in *The Token* of 1831, she wrote that "the subject of the following sketch, a Quaker Martyr, may appear to the fair holiday readers of souvenirs, a very unfit personage to be introduced into the romantic and glorious company of lords, and ladye loves; of doomed brides; and all-achieving heroines; chivalric soldiers; suffering outlaws; and Ossianic sons of the forest." The anonymous sketch

"The Young Backwoodsman," which told of a New England family who relocated to the South, revealed that the northerners had barely survived their first year as farmers without owning slaves to clear their fields and cultivate their crops in the unbearably hot, humid weather. (The story was reprinted in *Lights and Shadows of American Life*, 1832.)

"The Almshouse," by the popular writer Lydia Sigourney, was a tale about "the homeless poor of one of the thriving villages in New England" (*The Token and Atlantic Souvenir*, 1839). William E. Burton's "The Iroquois Slave" (*The Literary Souvenir*, 1840) began with an eight-line quotation from Shakespeare and an informative opening paragraph:

> Among the numerous advantages which the early voyagers to America expected to reap from the discovery of the New World, were the profits to be derived from extensive seizures of the aborigines, who were to be sold to foreign slavery. The sons of Spain, England, and France successively practised the unhallowed scheme, with various degrees of success; but while the English government discountenanced the kidnapping propensities of its officers, and, in some instances, insisted upon ample restitution being made, the courts of Ferdinand and Louis not only allowed the stealing of the red men of the forest, but positively insisted upon its execution in various decrees and proclamations.

Most authors of early prose tales—including James Hall and Nathaniel Hawthorne—depended on gift books and periodicals to publish their work when they embarked on their literary careers, but they overestimated the incomes they could earn. As a young writer, Hawthorne published nearly thirty tales in *The Token*, all anonymously. Authors such as Edgar Allan Poe who created short fiction for the magazines were paid poorly for their original tales and had to supplement their income by turning out reviews and editing periodicals if they wanted to support themselves with their writing. Poe, for example, worked for *The Southern Literary Messenger* in Richmond, *Gentleman's Magazine* and *Graham's Magazine* in Philadelphia, and *The Evening Mirror* and *The Broadway Journal* in New York City, over the course of a decade. Only gradually was it possible to think of authorship as a profession in America. Very few writers, among them Irving and the novelist James Fenimore Cooper, had been able to earn their living by their pens.

As the country became more settled and prosperous, literacy increased. Improved printing techniques and more efficient marketing and distribution of texts meant that authors were no longer dependent on the patronage of their families or wealthy benefactors who had supported their literary efforts in previous centuries. Now sufficient members of a literate American middle class were eager to read books, newspapers, and magazines filled with original works of short fiction. As Susan Coultrap-McQuin wrote in *Doing Literary Business* (1990), "Between 1820 and 1850 the publishing industry expanded tenfold in response to increasing national levels of literacy, people's growing interest in reading as cheap entertainment, and an expanding railroad system making national distribution of books possible."

The first American works of short fiction, such as Irving's "Rip Van Winkle" (1819) and Austin's "Peter Rugg, the Missing Man" (1824), often reflected earlier themes, dramatizing the colonist's sense of dislocation and the rapidity of social change. These two stories also relied on European sources in their retelling of a German folktale and the Faustian myth of eternal damnation. Earlier captivity myths also continued to fascinate American storytellers, as in James Hall's "The Indian Hater" (1830) and Harriet Prescott Spofford's "Circumstance" (1860). Southern writers exhibited a particular talent for humorous, dialect stories influenced by the oral tradition, such as Augustus Baldwin Longstreet's "The Dance" (1833) and Thomas Bangs Thorpe's "The Big Bear of Arkansas" (1841), as well as skillful renditions of tales based on Native American legends, such as William Gilmore Simms's "The Arm-Chair of Tustenuggee: A Tradition of the Catawba" (1845).

After the success of "Rip Van Winkle" and "The Legend of Sleepy Hollow," Irving continued to produce works of short fiction while he lived and traveled in Europe, but none of them had the appeal of the two early stories. In the 1830s and 1840s, Hawthorne and Poe created the most imaginative American tales, which were praised for their originality. In allegorical stories such as "The Minister's Black Veil" (1836), Hawthorne dramatized the theme of moral guilt, which Herman Melville understood in his review article "Hawthorne and His Mosses" to be quintessentially American, as it "derives its force from its appeals to that Calvinistic sense of Innate Depravity and Original Sin, from whose visitations, in some shape or other, no deeply thinking mind is always and wholly free."

The contents of the gift books and annuals were particularly directed to the large audience of leisured young women who were expected to remain at home until marriage. These women had been educated to read and write, and in an age when nearly every family employed servants, their domestic duties were light. Although the early sketches and tales were usually published anonymously, we now know that before long many women readers had become the women writers of the periodical sketches. They participated alongside men as authors of the earliest stories and tales and comprised about a third of the number of writers who published fiction in America before 1830.

The fact that American and English authors shared a common language was of crucial importance to the early development of our short fiction. At this stage in the evolution of the short story, literary influence went back and forth across the Atlantic. As a young man, Irving had modeled his prose style on the essays in the *Spectator* and *Tatler* by the English authors Joseph Addison and Richard Steele. In 1821, encouraged by Irving's success, the English playwright Mary Russell Mitford began to produce prose sketches of country manners, scenery, and characters that appeared in British magazines. They were collected in five volumes as *Our Village* and published in London between 1824 and 1832. Mitford's approach to her material was so congenial to American women writers in the 1820s that they began to imitate her descriptive sketches and tales about domestic life rather than try to produce work like Irving's travel sketches and exotic tales or Sir Walter Scott's and James Fenimore Cooper's historical romances.

By 1830 American tales were so popular that Mitford was asked to make a selection of short fiction from the American gift annuals. The London publishers Colburn and Bentley sold her anthology as *Stories of American Life by American Writers*. In Mitford's introduction to the book, she wrote that she had compiled the tales in "the attempt to make American manners better known in England" in order to "promote kindly feelings between two nations," since they were both "descended from a common ancestry, possessing the same rich and noble language, and alike distinguished by a love of public freedom and domestic virtue." Mitford announced that she had collected her tales from "a great mass of Annuals, Magazines, and other periodicals" in America with the intent of keeping the stories "as national and characteristic as possible." Her concern was to show "local manners" and "local scenery." She admitted that "many a graceful tale has been thrown aside for no graver fault, than that, with an assortment of new names, it might have belonged to France, or Switzerland, or Italy, or any land in Christendom, where love is spoken and tears are shed."

Including stories by well-known authors such as Catharine Maria Sedgwick, Lydia Maria Child, Caroline Kirkland, and James Hall, Mitford's first anthology of stories found so receptive an audience that she gathered another, *Collection of Native American Sketches,* in London in 1832. Later that year she produced a third collection, *Lights and Shadows of American Life,* announcing in her preface that

> the customs and scenery of a foreign country can never be more truly
> and vividly portrayed than in the familiar fictions of its inhabitants,
> who, writing entirely for domestic circulation, must necessarily make
> it a first object to present an unvarnished picture of the scenes and
> manners amongst which they and their readers mutually reside.

Short prose tales were still such a novelty that literature of this kind carried little prestige. In the 1840s, for example, Hawthorne's stories appeared on the front pages of New England small-town newspapers like the *Lowell Morning Courier* alongside advertisements for ornamental fruit trees, lamp oil, groceries, and ladies' bonnets. In 1850 Hawthorne humorously suggested in the introduction to his novel *The Scarlet Letter,* " 'What is he?' murmurs one grey shadow of my forefathers to the other. 'A writer of story-books? . . . Why, the degenerate fellow might as well have been a fiddler!' "

By the middle of the nineteenth century, women authors had come to dominate the periodical market, and they wrote about half of the best-selling novels. Their presence so irritated Hawthorne that he referred to them in an 1855 letter to his editor as the "damned mob of scribbling women." Most of their short fiction tended toward a pale and hasty imitation of English romances. Mrs. Sarah Josepha Hale, for forty years the editor of *Godey's Lady's Book,* the first monthly magazine modeled on the gift books in 1830, defended with her characteristic enthusiasm the prevailing sentimentality of the so-called feminine fiction. "When woman," she wrote in 1837 in *Godey's Lady's Book,* "enjoys the advantages of education in a manner appropriate to her character and duties, proportionally with man, she will no longer deserve or incur from him the epithet of 'romantic animal.'" By this time *Godey's Lady's Book* had the largest circulation of any American monthly, which it kept for nearly fifty years.

As early as 1830, Catharine Maria Sedgwick humorously dramatized the situation of the "scribbling women" in her story "Cacoethes Scribendi," which described the excitement generated in an isolated New England village by the fad of writing short fiction for the new magazines and gift annuals. Later women writers such as "Fanny Fern" (the pen name for Sarah Payson Parton) championed the resourcefulness of female authors in an 1853 sketch titled "A Practical Blue-Stocking," in which a proud husband revealed how his wife supported him, after he became an invalid, with the money she earned when she "made application as a writer to several papers and magazines. She soon became very popular" and not long after placed in his hands "the sum of three hundred dollars, the product of her labor."

All that was needed for anyone to succeed as a writer of stories, according to Fanny Fern, was "a little light-stand" or table "in the corner, with pen, ink, and papers scattered over it." Harriet Beecher Stowe, the most celebrated writer of her time, was more realistic about the unlikely chances of success. In the early 1860s she wrote a sketch, "What Will You Do With Her? Or, the Woman Question," in which she dramatized the plight of magazine editors faced with the task of turning down unsolicited manuscripts by amateur women contributors:

> For instance, you get a letter in a delicate hand, setting forth the old distress — she is poor, and she has looking to her for support those that are poorer and more helpless than herself; she has tried sewing, but can make little at it; tried teaching, but cannot now get a school; — all places being filled, and more than filled; at last has tried literature, and written some little things, of which she sends you a modest specimen, and wants your opinion whether she can gain her living by writing. . . . [You] perceive at a glance that there is no hope or use of her trying to do anything at literature; and then you ask yourself mentally, "What is to be done with her? What can she do?"

The flood of women's stories seemed to many readers as ephemeral as the gift annuals and magazines that published them. In Rufus Wilmot Griswold's pioneering anthology *The Prose Writers of America* (1846), he novels. Their presence so irritated Hawthorne that he referred to them in an 1855 letter to his editor as the "damned mob of scribbling women." Most of their short fiction tended toward a pale and hasty imitation of English romances. Mrs. Sarah Josepha Hale, for forty years the editor of *Godey's Lady's Book,* the first monthly magazine modeled on the gift books in 1830, defended with her characteristic enthusiasm the prevailing sentimentality of the so-called feminine fiction. "When woman," she wrote in 1837 in *Godey's Lady's Book,* "enjoys the advantages of education in a manner appropriate to her character and duties, proportionally with man, she will no longer deserve or incur from him the epithet of 'romantic animal.'" By this time *Godey's Lady's Book* had the largest circulation of any American monthly, which it kept for nearly fifty years.

As early as 1830, Catharine Maria Sedgwick humorously dramatized the situation of the "scribbling women" in her story "Cacoethes Scribendi," which described the excitement generated in an isolated New England village by the fad of writing short fiction for the new magazines and gift annuals. Later women writers such as "Fanny Fern" (the pen name for Sarah Payson Parton) championed the resourcefulness of female authors in an 1853 sketch titled "A Practical Blue-Stocking," in which a proud husband revealed how his wife supported him, after he became an invalid, with the money she earned when she "made application as a writer to several papers and magazines. She soon became very popular" and not long after placed in his hands "the sum of three hundred dollars, the product of her labor."

All that was needed for anyone to succeed as a writer of stories, according to Fanny Fern, was "a little light-stand" or table "in the corner, with pen, ink, and papers scattered over it." Harriet Beecher Stowe, the most celebrated writer of her time, was more realistic about the unlikely chances of success. In the early 1860s she wrote a sketch, "What Will You Do With Her? Or, the Woman Question," in which she dramatized the plight of magazine editors faced with the task of turning down unsolicited manuscripts by amateur women contributors:

> For instance, you get a letter in a delicate hand, setting forth the old distress—she is poor, and she has looking to her for support those that are poorer and more helpless than herself; she has tried sewing, but can make little at it; tried teaching, but cannot now get a school;—all places being filled, and more than filled; at last has tried literature, and written some little things, of which she sends you a modest specimen, and wants your opinion whether she can gain her living by writing. . . . [You] perceive at a glance that there is no hope or use of her trying to do anything at literature; and then you ask yourself mentally, "What is to be done with her? What can she do?"

The flood of women's stories seemed to many readers as ephemeral as the gift annuals and magazines that published them. In Rufus Wilmot Griswold's pioneering anthology *The Prose Writers of America* (1846), he singled out the work of male authors of short fiction for special praise, elaborating on the achievements of Irving, Hawthorne, and Poe, while only listing the work of notable women writers such as Lydia Maria Child and Caroline Kirkland as "possessing various and peculiar merits."

Griswold was writing before the publication of Hawthorne and Melville's greatest novels; he asserted that American prose writers had done their best work in the genre of the short prose tale. Griswold felt that Hawthorne's tales and sketches in *Twice-Told Tales* and *Mosses from an Old Manse* were "the perfection of pensive, graceful, humorous writing, quite equal to the finest things of Diedrich Knickerbocker or Geoffrey Crayon [Washington Irving's pseudonyms in *The Sketch Book*], and superior to all else of a similar description in the English Language."

Griswold also found Poe's tales "peculiar and impressive," noting that "his mind is in the highest degree analytical" and describing at considerable length his skillful deployment of "imagination and fancy" in tales written in the gothic mode. These were short fictions, such as "The Fall of the House of Usher," that dramatized sensational plots to achieve a heightened emotional effect, evoking mystery, terror, and suggestions of the supernatural. Griswold noted with approval that

> the reader of Mr. Poe's tales is compelled almost at the outset to surrender his mind to his author's control. Unlike that of the greater number of suggestive authors his narrative is most minute, and unlike most who attend so carefully to detail he has nothing superfluous — nothing which does not tend to the production of the desired result. . . . No one ever delighted more or was more successful in oppressing the brain with anxiety or startling it with images of horror.

Singled out as the most gifted writer of prose tales of his time, Poe was praised by Griswold for his artistic control, the characteristic that Poe claimed essential for producing "the single effect" on the reader in his groundbreaking analytical reviews of Hawthorne's tales in *Graham's Magazine* (1842) and *Godey's Lady's Book* (1847). In these articles Poe argued that the prose tale was an ideal genre second only to poetry in its appeal to genius. Poe understood that "the whole tendency of the age is Magazine-ward. . . . We need the curt, the condensed, the painted, the readily diffused, in place of the verbose, the detailed, the voluminous, the inaccessible."

Poe became one of the first American authors to be read by Europeans after several of his tales were translated into French and published with an introduction by the symbolist poet Charles Baudelaire in 1856. Even after Poe's death, his tales continued to be the standard by which others were measured. When Melville published "Bartleby, the Scrivener" in 1853, his story was praised by a reviewer as "a Poeish tale with an infusion of natural sentiment."

During this early period, the popularity of the short prose tale resulted in several distinguished collections of work in the new genre. Notable among them were Irving's *The Sketch Book* (1819), Longstreet's *Georgia Scenes* (1835), Hawthorne's *Twice-Told Tales* (1837, enlarged 1842) and *Mosses from an Old Manse* (1846), Poe's *Tales of the Grotesque and Arabesque* (1840) and *Tales* (1845), Kirkland's *Western Clearings* (1845), Simms's *The Wigwam and the Cabin* (1845), and Melville's *Piazza Tales* (1856). Irving's American tales were so popular that in 1849 he collected them in *Book of the Hudson,* introducing them with the heartfelt statement, "I thank God that I was born on the banks of the Hudson."

While the leading male writers of the period, such as Irving, Austin, Hall, Hawthorne, Melville, Poe, Thorpe, and Simms, chose to write romances or fantasy fiction — romantic, allegorical, gothic, and tall tales — most of the accomplished women writers preferred to create domestic tales about their own times. Exceptions did exist, such as Harriet Prescott Spofford's "Circumstance," a brilliant fantasy based on a captivity narrative involving a member of her family that had occurred years before. But for the most part the gifted women authors of short prose tales dramatized contemporary social conflicts and argued the need for social reform.

Lydia Maria Child described the widespread suffering that resulted from "the peculiar institution" of slavery in the Southern states in "Slavery's Pleasant Homes" (1843). In "The Two Altars" (1851), Harriet Beecher Stowe dramatized the tragic curtailment of human rights resulting from the enforcement of the Fugitive Slave Law in the Northern states. Caroline Kirkland revealed the greed and opportunism rampant among the settlers of the western territory in "The Land-Fever" (1845). Elizabeth Stuart Phelps's "The Angel over the Right Shoulder" (1852) and Frances E. W. Harper's "The Two Offers" (1859), the latter being the first published short story by an African American, expressed the grievances of women chafing against the dominant patriarchal tradition that fostered feminine passivity and set strict limits on their education and employment outside marriage.

The issues of slavery and women's rights were often entwined in antebellum America. For example, Harper wrote antislavery articles for *The Liberator,* a newspaper published weekly in Boston by William Lloyd Garrison, the noted abolitionist, advocating immediate freedom for the slaves. In 1840 Garrison joined in the protest of the women delegates to a world convention of antislavery forces in London when they were not allowed seats in the hall. After this rejection, the women were determined to have their own convention in America, agreeing with Garrison's statement in *The Liberator* of August 28, 1840, that it was wrong to exclude a woman delegate like Lucretia Mott from the London meeting "on account of her sex. I have the same credentials. If hers were dishonored, so were mine."

In the summer of 1848, the first meeting in the New World devoted to women's rights took place in Seneca Falls, New York. The participants drafted their own Declaration of Independence, paraphrasing Jefferson in their assertion, "We hold these truths to be self-evident: that all men and women are created equal." The then revolutionary ideas of women's rights and the abolition of slavery were made accessible to Americans in widely circulated short prose tales before Harriet Beecher Stowe's provocative best-seller *Uncle Tom's Cabin* (1852), which itself was first published as a magazine serial. Using the new form of the short story, the "scribbling women" could communicate their sense of injustice to both male and female readers alike as the young nation faced its first crucial test over the issues of slavery and secession at the beginning of the 1860s — the Civil War.

RELATED COMMENTARIES: *Mary Russell Mitford, "Stories of American Life," page 1416; Edgar Allan Poe, "Review of Hawthorne's* Twice-Told Tales," *page 1438.*

WASHINGTON IRVING

Washington Irving (1783–1859), named after George Washington, was the youngest of eleven children born in New York City to a mother of English descent and a Scottish father who was a prosperous merchant. After studying law with Judge Josiah Hoffman, Irving went on a Grand Tour of Europe for two years. Returning to New York City, he published the Salmagundi Papers *(1807–08) and a comic* History of New York *(1809), in which he invented the figure of a talkative elderly narrator named Diedrich Knickerbocker who told anecdotes about the early history of the Dutch colony. Irving's writing was so successful that his comical gentleman "Knickerbocker" came to personify New York City, and the name survives today in the professional basketball team the New York Knicks.*

Anguished by the death of his fiancée, Judge Hoffman's daughter, Irving left New York in 1815 to join his brother Peter in the European branch of the family's business in Liverpool. When the venture failed, Irving moved to London and began to meet British authors, including Sir Walter Scott, one of the most successful playwrights and novelists of his time. They shared an enthusiasm for German literature, which Irving read in translation. He began an intensive study of German, making his own translation of the folktale "Peter Klaus the Goatherd" and other stories. Then Irving started "scribbling" original short prose tales based on his translations.

In "Rip Van Winkle" Irving went to ingenious lengths to disguise his borrowing. First he invented the tongue-in-cheek character "Geoffrey Crayon" as the author of The Sketch Book *(1819), attempting to hide that he was an American writer trying to interest English readers in his work. Then Irving created a frame for "Rip Van Winkle," with Crayon telling the reader that he found the tale "among the papers of the late Diedrich Knickerbocker." Irving's use of pseudonyms and mock documentation in the opening and closing paragraphs of "Rip Van Winkle" underscores the humorous tone of his tale, which gave the story an enduring new life as an American legend. Irving wrote two other books of sketches,* Bracebridge Hall *(1822) and* Tales of a Traveller *(1824), but they didn't equal his success with* The Sketch Book*. It was so popular that Scott followed Irving's lead and published his first short story, "The Two Drovers," in 1827. After years abroad Irving returned to New York in 1832 and settled in Tarrytown on the Hudson. He involved himself in politics and continued to publish books, most notably the travel sketches* A Tour on the Prairies *(1835) and the multivolume* Life of Washington *(1859).*

RELATED STORY: *J. C. C. Nachtigal, "Peter Klaus the Goatherd," page 18.*
RELATED COMMENTARY: *Washington Irving, "Letter to Henry Brevoort, December 11, 1824," page 1373.*

Rip Van Winkle

A Posthumous Writing of Diedrich Knickerbocker

> By Woden, God of Saxons,
> From whence comes Wensday, that is Wodensday,
> Truth is a thing that ever I will keep
> Unto thylke day in which I creep into
> My sepulchre —
>
> — CARTWRIGHT[1]

[The following Tale was found among the papers of the late Diedrich Knickerbocker, an old gentleman of New York, who was very curious in the Dutch history of the province, and the manners of the descendants from its primitive settlers. His historical researches, however, did not lie so much among books as among men; for the former are lamentably scanty on his favorite topics; whereas he found the old burghers, and still more their wives, rich in that legendary lore so invaluable to true history. Whenever, therefore, he happened upon a genuine Dutch family, snugly shut up in its low-roofed farmhouse, under a spreading sycamore, he looked upon it as a little clasped volume of black-letter, and studied it with the zeal of a book-worm.

The result of all these researches was a history of the province during the reign of the Dutch governors, which he published some years since. There have been various opinions as to the literary character of his work, and, to tell the truth, it is not a whit better than it should be. Its chief merit is its scrupulous accuracy, which indeed was a little questioned on its first appearance, but has since been completely established; and it is now admitted into all historical collections as a book of unquestionable authority.

The old gentleman died shortly after the publication of his work; and now that he is dead and gone, it cannot do much harm to his memory to say that his time might have been much better employed in weightier labors. He, however, was apt to ride his hobby his own way; and though it did now and then kick up the dust a little in the eyes of his neighbors, and grieve the spirit of some friends, for whom he felt the truest deference and affection, yet his errors and follies are remembered "more in sorrow than in anger," and it begins to be suspected that he never intended to offend. But however his memory may be appreciated by critics, it is still held dear by many folk whose good opinion is well worth having; particularly by certain biscuit-makers, who have gone so far as to imprint his likeness on their New-Year cakes; and have thus given him a chance for immortality, almost equal to being stamped on a Waterloo Medal, or a Queen Anne's Farthing.]

---

[1]William Cartwright (1611–1643) was an English playwright. The lines are from his play *The Ordinary* (3.1.1050–54).

36

Whoever has made a voyage up the Hudson must remember the Kaat-skill mountains. They are a dismembered branch of the great Appalachian family, and are seen away to the west of the river, swelling up to a noble height, and lording it over the surrounding country. Every change of season, every change of weather, indeed, every hour of the day, produces some change in the magical hues and shapes of these mountains, and they are regarded by all the good wives, far and near, as perfect barometers. When the weather is fair and settled, they are clothed in blue and purple, and print their bold outlines on the clear evening sky; but sometimes, when the rest of the landscape is cloudless, they will gather a hood of gray vapors about their summits, which, in the last rays of the setting sun, will glow and light up like a crown of glory.

At the foot of these fairy mountains, the voyager may have descried the light smoke curling up from a village, whose shingle-roofs gleam among the trees, just where the blue tints of the upland melt away into the fresh green of the nearer landscape. It is a little village, of great antiquity, having been founded by some of the Dutch colonists in the early times of the province, just about the beginning of the government of the good Peter Stuyvesant, (may he rest in peace!) and there were some of the houses of the original settlers standing within a few years, built of small yellow bricks brought from Holland, having latticed windows and gable fronts, surmounted with weathercocks.

In that same village, and in one of these very houses (which, to tell the precise truth, was sadly time-worn and weather-beaten), there lived, many years since, while the country was yet a province of Great Britain, a simple, good-natured fellow, of the name of Rip Van Winkle. He was a descendant of the Van Winkles who figured so gallantly in the chivalrous days of Peter Stuyvesant, and accompanied him to the siege of Fort Christina. He inherited, however, but little of the martial character of his ancestors. I have observed that he was a simple, good-natured man; he was, moreover, a kind neighbor, and an obedient, hen-pecked husband. Indeed, to the latter circumstance might be owing that meekness of spirit which gained him such universal popularity; for those men are most apt to be obsequious and conciliating abroad, who are under the discipline of shrews at home. Their tempers, doubtless, are rendered pliant and malleable in the fiery furnace of domestic tribulation; and a curtain-lecture is worth all the sermons in the world for teaching the virtues of patience and long-suffering. A termagant wife may, therefore, in some respects, be considered a tolerable blessing; and if so, Rip Van Winkle was thrice blessed.

Certain it is, that he was a great favorite among all the good wives of the village, who, as usual with the amiable sex, took his part in all family squabbles; and never failed, whenever they talked those matters over in their evening gossipings, to lay all the blame on Dame Van Winkle. The children of the village, too, would shout with joy whenever he approached. He assisted at their sports, made their playthings, taught them to fly kites and shoot marbles, and told them long stories of ghosts, witches, and Indians. Whenever he went dodging about the village, he was surrounded by a troop of them, hanging on his skirts, clambering on his back, and playing a thousand tricks on him with impunity; and not a dog would bark at him throughout the neighborhood.

The great error in Rip's composition was an insuperable aversion to all kinds of profitable labor. It could not be from the want of assiduity or per-severance; for he would sit on a wet rock, with a rod as long and heavy as a Tartar's lance, and fish all day without a murmur, even though he should not be encouraged by a single nibble. He would carry a fowling-piece on his shoulder for hours together, trudging through woods and swamps, and up hill and down dale, to shoot a few squirrels or wild pigeons. He would never refuse to assist a neighbor even in the roughest toil, and was a foremost man at all country frolics for husking Indian corn, or building stone fences; the women of the village, too, used to employ him to run their errands, and to do such little odd jobs as their less obliging husbands would not do for them. In a word, Rip was ready to attend to anybody's business but his own; but as to doing family duty, and keeping his farm in order, he found it impossible.

In fact, he declared it was of no use to work on his farm; it was the most pestilent little piece of ground in the whole country; everything about it went wrong, and would go wrong, in spite of him. His fences were continually falling to pieces; his cow would either go astray, or get among the cabbages; weeds were sure to grow quicker in his fields than anywhere else; the rain always made a point of setting in just as he had some out-door work to do; so that though his patrimonial estate had dwindled away under his management, acre by acre, until there was little more left than a mere patch of Indian corn and potatoes, yet it was the worst conditioned farm in the neighborhood.

His children, too, were as ragged and wild as if they belonged to nobody. His son Rip, an urchin begotten in his own likeness, promised to inherit the habits, with the old clothes, of his father. He was generally seen trooping like a colt at his mother's heels, equipped in a pair of his father's cast-off galligaskins, which he had much ado to hold up with one hand, as a fine lady does her train in bad weather.

Rip Van Winkle, however, was one of those happy mortals, of foolish, well-oiled dispositions, who take the world easy, eat white bread or brown, whichever can be got with least thought or trouble, and would rather starve on a penny than work for a pound. If left to himself, he would have whistled life away in perfect contentment; but his wife kept continually dinning in his ears about his idleness, his carelessness, and the ruin he was bringing on his family. Morning, noon and night, her tongue was inces-santly going, and everything he said or did was sure to produce a torrent of household eloquence. Rip had but one way of replying to all lectures of the kind, and that, by frequent use, had grown into a habit. He shrugged his shoulders, shook his head, cast up his eyes, but said nothing. This, however, always provoked a fresh volley from his wife; so that he was fain to draw off his forces, and take to the outside of the house — the only side which, in truth, belongs to a hen-pecked husband.

Rip's sole domestic adherent was his dog Wolf, who was as much hen-pecked as his master; for Dame Van Winkle regarded them as companions in idleness, and even looked upon Wolf with an evil eye, as the cause of his master's going so often astray. True it is, in all points of spirit befitting an honorable dog, he was as courageous an animal as ever scoured the woods; but what courage can withstand the ever-enduring and all-besetting terrors of a woman's tongue? The moment Wolf entered the house his crest fell, his tail drooped to the ground, or curled between his legs, he sneaked about with a gallows air, casting many a sidelong glance at Dame Van Winkle, and at the least flourish of a broomstick or ladle he would fly to the door with yelping precipitation.

Times grew worse and worse with Rip Van Winkle as years of matrimony rolled on; a tart temper never mellows with age, and a sharp tongue is the only edged tool that grows keener with constant use. For a long while he used to console himself, when driven from home, by frequenting a kind of perpetual club of the sages, philosophers, and other idle personages of the village, which held its sessions on a bench before a small inn, designated by a rubicund portrait of His Majesty George the Third. Here they used to sit in the shade through a long, lazy summer's day, talking listlessly over village gossip, or telling endless sleepy stories about nothing. But it would have been worth any statesman's money to have heard the profound discussions that sometimes took place, when by chance an old newspaper fell into their hands from some passing traveller. How solemnly they would listen to the contents, as drawled out by Derrick Van Bummel, the schoolmaster, a dapper learned little man, who was not to be daunted by the most gigantic word in the dictionary; and how sagely they would deliberate upon public events some months after they had taken place.

The opinions of this junto[2] were completely controlled by Nicholas Vedder, patriarch of the village, and landlord of the inn, at the door of which he took his seat from morning till night, just moving sufficiently to avoid the sun and keep in the shade of a large tree; so that the neighbors could tell the hour by his movements as accurately as by a sun-dial. It is true he was rarely heard to speak, but smoked his pipe incessantly. His adherents, however (for every great man has his adherents), perfectly understood him, and knew how to gather his opinions. When anything that was read or related displeased him, he was observed to smoke his pipe

---

[2]A group brought together by a common purpose.

vehemently, and to send forth short, frequent, and angry puffs; but when pleased, he would inhale the smoke slowly and tranquilly, and emit it in light and placid clouds; and sometimes, taking the pipe from his mouth, and letting the fragrant vapor curl about his nose, would gravely nod his head in token of perfect approbation.

From even this stronghold the unlucky Rip was at length routed by his termagant wife, who would suddenly break in upon the tranquillity of the assemblage and call the members all to naught; nor was that august personage, Nicholas Vedder himself, sacred from the daring tongue of this terrible virago, who charged him outright with encouraging her husband in habits of idleness.

Poor Rip was at last reduced almost to despair; and his only alternative, to escape from the labor of the farm and clamor of his wife, was to take gun in hand and stroll away into the woods. Here he would sometimes seat himself at the foot of a tree, and share the contents of his wallet with Wolf, with whom he sympathized as a fellow-sufferer in persecution. "Poor Wolf," he would say, "thy mistress leads thee a dog's life of it, but never mind, my lad, whilst I live thou shalt never want a friend to stand by thee!" Wolf would wag his tail, look wistfully in his master's face, and if dogs can feel pity, I verily believe he reciprocated the sentiment with all his heart.

In a long ramble of the kind on a fine autumnal day, Rip had unconsciously scrambled to one of the highest parts of the Kaatskill mountains. He was after his favorite sport of squirrel-shooting, and the still solitudes had echoed and re-echoed with the reports of his gun. Panting and fatigued, he threw himself, late in the afternoon, on a green knoll, covered with mountain herbage, that crowned the brow of a precipice. From an opening between the trees he could overlook all the lower country for many a mile of rich woodland. He saw at a distance the lordly Hudson, far, far below him, moving on its silent but majestic course, with the reflection of a purple cloud, or the sail of a lagging bark, here and there sleeping on its glassy bosom, and at last losing itself in the blue highlands.

On the other side he looked down into a deep mountain glen, wild, lonely, and shagged, the bottom filled with fragments from the impending cliffs, and scarcely lighted by the reflected rays of the setting sun. For some time Rip lay musing on this scene; evening was gradually advancing; the mountains began to throw their long blue shadows over the valleys; he saw that it would be dark long before he could reach the village, and he heaved a heavy sigh when he thought of encountering the terrors of Dame Van Winkle.

As he was about to descend, he heard a voice from a distance, hallooing, "Rip Van Winkle, Rip Van Winkle!" He looked around, but could see nothing but a crow winging its solitary flight across the mountain. He thought his fancy must have deceived him, and turned again to descend, when he heard the same cry ring through the still evening air: "Rip Van

Winkle! Rip Van Winkle!"—at the same time Wolf bristled up his back, and giving a low growl, skulked to his master's side, looking fearfully down into the glen. Rip now felt a vague apprehension stealing over him; he looked anxiously in the same direction, and perceived a strange figure slowly toiling up the rocks, and bending under the weight of something he carried on his back. He was surprised to see any human being in this lonely and unfrequented place; but supposing it to be some one of the neighborhood in need of his assistance, he hastened down to yield it.

On nearer approach he was still more surprised at the singularity of the stranger's appearance. He was a short, square-built old fellow, with thick bushy hair, and a grizzled beard. His dress was of the antique Dutch fashion,—a cloth jerkin strapped around the waist—several pair of breeches, the outer one of ample volume, decorated with rows of buttons down the sides, and bunches at the knees. He bore on his shoulders a stout keg, that seemed full of liquor, and made signs for Rip to approach and assist him with the load. Though rather shy and distrustful of this new acquaintance, Rip complied with his usual alacrity; and mutually relieving one another, they clambered up a narrow gully, apparently the dry bed of a mountain torrent. As they ascended, Rip every now and then heard long, rolling peals, like distant thunder, that seemed to issue out of a deep ravine, or rather cleft, between lofty rocks, toward which their rugged path conducted. He paused for an instant, but supposing it to be the muttering of one of those transient thunder-showers which often take place in mountain heights, he proceeded. Passing through the ravine, they came to a hollow, like a small amphitheatre, surrounded by perpendicular precipices, over the brinks of which impending trees shot their branches, so that you only caught glimpses of the azure sky and the bright evening cloud. During the whole time Rip and his companion had labored on in silence; for though the former marvelled greatly what could be the object of carrying a keg of liquor up this wild mountain, yet there was something strange and incomprehensible about the unknown, that inspired awe and checked familiarity.

On entering the amphitheatre, new objects of wonder presented themselves. On a level spot in the centre was a company of odd-looking personages playing at ninepins. They were dressed in a quaint, outlandish fashion; some wore short doublets, others jerkins, with long knives in their belts, and most of them had enormous breeches, of similar style with that of the guide's. Their visages, too, were peculiar: one had a large beard, broad face, and small piggish eyes; the face of another seemed to consist entirely of nose, and was surmounted by a white sugar-loaf hat, set off with a little red cock's tail. They all had beards, of various shapes and colors. There was one who seemed to be the commander. He was a stout old gentleman, with a weather-beaten countenance; he wore a laced doublet, broad belt and hanger, high crowned hat and feather, red stockings, and high-heeled shoes, with roses in them. The whole group reminded Rip of the figures in an old Flemish painting, in the parlor of Dominie Van Shaick, the village parson, and which had been brought over from Holland at the time of the settlement.

What seemed particularly odd to Rip was, that, though these folks were evidently amusing themselves, yet they maintained the gravest faces, the most mysterious silence, and were, withal, the most melancholy party of pleasure he had ever witnessed. Nothing interrupted the stillness of the scene but the noise of the balls, which, whenever they rolled, echoed along the mountains like rumbling peals of thunder.

As Rip and his companion approached them, they suddenly desisted from their play, and stared at him with such fixed, statue-like gaze, and such strange, uncouth, lack-lustre countenances, that his heart turned within him, and his knees smote together. His companion now emptied the contents of the keg into large flagons, and made signs to him to wait upon the company. He obeyed with fear and trembling; they quaffed the liquor in profound silence, and then returned to their game.

By degrees Rip's awe and apprehension subsided. He even ventured, when no eye was fixed upon him, to taste the beverage, which he found had much of the flavor of excellent Hollands. He was naturally a thirsty soul, and was soon tempted to repeat the draught. One taste provoked another; and he reiterated his visits to the flagon so often that at length his senses were overpowered, his eyes swam in his head, his head gradually declined, and he fell into a deep sleep.

On waking, he found himself on the green knoll whence he had first seen the old man of the glen. He rubbed his eyes—it was a bright sunny morning. The birds were hopping and twittering among the bushes, and the eagle was wheeling aloft, and breasting the pure mountain breeze. "Surely," thought Rip, "I have not slept here all night." He recalled the occurrences before he fell asleep. The strange man with a keg of liquor—the mountain ravine—the wild retreat among the rocks—the woe-begone party at ninepins—the flagon—"Oh! that flagon! that wicked flagon!" thought Rip, "what excuse shall I make to Dame Van Winkle?"

He looked round for his gun, but in place of the clean, well-oiled fowling-piece, he found an old firelock lying by him, the barrel encrusted with rust, the lock falling off, and the stock worm-eaten. He now suspected that the grave roisters of the mountains had put a trick upon him, and, having dosed him with liquor, had robbed him of his gun. Wolf, too, had disappeared, but he might have strayed away after a squirrel or partridge. He whistled after him, and shouted his name, but all in vain; the echoes repeated his whistle and shout, but no dog was to be seen.

He determined to revisit the scene of the last evening's gambol, and if he met with any of the party, to demand his dog and gun. As he rose to walk, he found himself stiff in the joints, and wanting in his usual activity.

"These mountain beds do not agree with me," thought Rip, "and if this frolic should lay me up with a fit of the rheumatism, I shall have a blessed time with Dame Van Winkle." With some difficulty he got down into the glen: he found the gully up which he and his companion had ascended the preceding evening; but to his astonishment a mountain stream was now foaming down it, leaping from rock to rock, and filling the glen with babbling murmurs. He, however, made shift to scramble up its sides, working his toilsome way through thickets of birch, sassafras, and witch-hazel, and sometimes tripped up or entangled by the wild grape-vines that twisted their coils or tendrils from tree to tree, and spread a kind of network in his path.

At length he reached to where the ravine had opened through the cliffs to the amphitheatre; but no traces of such opening remained. The rocks presented a high, impenetrable wall, over which the torrent came tumbling in a sheet of feathery foam, and fell into a broad deep basin, black from the shadows of the surrounding forest. Here, then, poor Rip was brought to a stand. He again called and whistled after his dog; he was only answered by the cawing of a flock of idle crows, sporting high in air about a dry tree that overhung a sunny precipice; and who, secure in their elevation, seemed to look down and scoff at the poor man's perplexities. What was to be done? the morning was passing away, and Rip felt famished for want of his breakfast. He grieved to give up his dog and gun; he dreaded to meet his wife; but it would not do to starve among the mountains. He shook his head, shouldered the rusty firelock, and, with a heart full of trouble and anxiety, turned his footsteps homeward.

As he approached the village he met a number of people, but none whom he knew, which somewhat surprised him, for he had thought himself acquainted with every one in the country round. Their dress, too, was of a different fashion from that to which he was accustomed. They all stared at him with equal marks of surprise, and whenever they cast their eyes upon him, invariably stroked their chins. The constant recurrence of this gesture induced Rip, involuntarily, to do the same, when, to his astonishment, he found his beard had grown a foot long!

He had now entered the skirts of the village. A troop of strange children ran at his heels, hooting after him, and pointing at his gray beard. The dogs, too, not one of which he recognized for an old acquaintance, barked at him as he passed. The very village was altered; it was larger and more populous. There were rows of houses which he had never seen before, and those which had been his familiar haunts had disappeared. Strange names were over the doors—strange faces at the windows—everything was strange. His mind now misgave him; he began to doubt whether both he and the world around him were not bewitched. Surely this was his native village, which he had left but the day before. There stood the Kaatskill mountains—there ran the silver Hudson at a distance—there was every hill and dale precisely as it had always been. Rip was sorely perplexed. "That flagon last night," thought he, "has addled my poor head sadly!"

It was with some difficulty that he found the way to his own house, which he approached with silent awe, expecting every moment to hear the shrill voice of Dame Van Winkle. He found the house gone to decay—the roof fallen in, the windows shattered, and the doors off the hinges. A half-starved dog that looked like Wolf was skulking about it. Rip called him by name, but the cur snarled, showed his teeth, and passed on. This was an unkind cut indeed. "My very dog," sighed poor Rip, "has forgotten me!"

He entered the house, which to tell the truth, Dame Van Winkle had always kept in neat order. It was empty, forlorn, and apparently abandoned. This desolateness overcame all his connubial fears—he called loudly for his wife and children—the lonely chambers rang for a moment with his voice, and then all again was silence.

He now hurried forth, and hastened to his old resort, the village inn, but it too was gone. A large rickety wooden building stood in its place, with great gaping windows, some of them broken and mended with old hats and petticoats, and over the door was painted, "The Union Hotel, by Jonathan Doolittle." Instead of the great tree that used to shelter the quiet little Dutch inn of yore, there now was reared a tall naked pole, with something on top that looked like a red night-cap, and from it was fluttering a flag, on which was a singular assemblage of stars and stripes—all this was strange and incomprehensible. He recognized on the sign, however, the ruby face of King George, under which he had smoked so many a peaceful pipe; but even this was singularly metamorphosed. The red coat was changed for one of blue and buff, a sword was held in the hand instead of a sceptre, the head was decorated with a cocked hat, and underneath was painted in large characters, GENERAL WASHINGTON.

There was, as usual, a crowd of folk about the door, but none that Rip recollected. The very character of the people seemed changed. There was a busy, bustling, disputatious tone about it, instead of the accustomed phlegm and drowsy tranquillity. He looked in vain for the sage Nicholas Vedder, with his broad face, double chin, and fair long pipe, uttering clouds of tobacco-smoke instead of idle speeches; or Van Bummel, the schoolmaster, doling forth the contents of an ancient newspaper. In place of these, a lean, bilious-looking fellow, with his pockets full of handbills, was haranguing vehemently about rights of citizens—elections—members of congress—liberty—Bunker's Hill—heroes of seventy-six—and other words, which were a perfect Babylonish jargon to the bewildered Van Winkle.

The appearance of Rip, with his long, grizzled beard, his rusty fowling-piece, his uncouth dress, and an army of women and children at his heels, soon attracted the attention of the tavern-politicians. They crowded round him, eyeing him from head to foot with great curiosity. The orator bustled up to him, and, drawing him partly aside, inquired "On which side he voted?" Rip stared in vacant stupidity. Another short but busy little fellow pulled him by the arm, and, rising on tiptoe, inquired in his ear, "Whether he was Federal or Democrat?" Rip was equally at a loss to comprehend the question; when a knowing, self-important old gentleman, in a sharp cocked hat, made his way through the crowd, putting them to the right and left with his elbows as he passed, and planting himself before Van Winkle, with one arm akimbo, the other resting on his cane, his keen eyes and sharp hat penetrating, as it were, into his very soul, demanded in an austere tone, "What brought him to the election with a gun on his shoulder, and a mob at his heels; and whether he meant to breed a riot in the village?" — "Alas! gentlemen," cried Rip, somewhat dismayed, "I am a poor quiet man, a native of the place, and a loyal subject of the King, God bless him!"

Here a general shout burst from the by-standers — "A tory! a tory! a spy! a refugee! hustle him! away with him!" It was with great difficulty that the self-important man in the cocked hat restored order; and, having assumed a tenfold austerity of brow, demanded again of the unknown culprit, what he came there for, and whom he was seeking? The poor man humbly assured him that he meant no harm, but merely came there in search of some of his neighbors, who used to keep about the tavern.

"Well — who are they? — name them."

Rip bethought himself a moment, and inquired, "Where's Nicholas Vedder?"

There was a silence for a little while, when an old man replied, in a thin piping voice, "Nicholas Vedder! why, he is dead and gone these eighteen years! There was a wooden tombstone in that churchyard that used to tell all about him, but that's rotten and gone too."

"Where's Brom Dutcher?"

"Oh, he went off to the army in the beginning of the war; some say he was killed at the storming of Stony Point — others say he was drowned in a squall at the foot of Antony's Nose. I don't know — he never came back again."

"Where's Van Bummel, the schoolmaster?"

"He went off to the wars too, was a great militia general, and is now in congress."

Rip's heart died away at hearing of these sad changes in his home and friends, and finding himself thus alone in the world. Every answer puzzled him too, by treating of such enormous lapses of time, and of matters which he could not understand: war — congress — Stony Point — he had no courage to ask after any more friends, but cried out in despair, "Does nobody here know Rip Van Winkle?"

"Oh, Rip Van Winkle!" exclaimed two or three. "Oh, to be sure! that's Rip Van Winkle yonder, leaning against the tree."

Rip looked, and he beheld a precise counterpart of himself, as he went up the mountain; apparently as lazy, and certainly as ragged. The poor fellow was now completely confounded. He doubted his own identity, and whether he was himself or another man. In the midst of his bewilderment, the man in the cocked hat demanded who he was, and what was his name.

"God knows," exclaimed he, at his wit's end; "I'm not myself—I'm somebody else—that's me yonder—no—that's somebody else got into my shoes—I was myself last night, but I fell asleep on the mountain, and they've changed my gun, and everything's changed, and I'm changed, and I can't tell what's my name, or who I am!"

The by-standers began now to look at each other, nod, wink significantly, and tap their fingers against their foreheads. There was a whisper, also, about securing the gun, and keeping the old fellow from doing mischief, at the very suggestion of which the self-important man in the cocked hat retired with some precipitation. At this critical moment a fresh, comely woman pressed through the throng to get a peep at the gray-bearded man. She had a chubby child in her arms, which, frightened at his looks, began to cry. "Hush, Rip," cried she, "hush, you little fool; the old man won't hurt you." The name of the child, the air of the mother, the tone of her voice, all awakened a train of recollections in his mind. "What is your name, my good woman?" asked he.

"Judith Gardenier."

"And your father's name?"

"Ah, poor man, Rip Van Winkle was his name, but it's twenty years since he went away from home with his gun, and never has been heard of since—his dog came home without him; but whether he shot himself, or was carried away by the Indians, nobody can tell. I was then but a little girl."

Rip had but one question more to ask; but he put it with a faltering voice:

"Where's your mother?"

"Oh, she too died but a short time since; she broke a blood vessel in a fit of passion at a New England peddler."

There was a drop of comfort, at least, in this intelligence. The honest man could contain himself no longer. He caught his daughter and her child in his arms. "I am your father!" cried he—"Young Rip Van Winkle once—old Rip Van Winkle now!—Does nobody know poor Rip Van Winkle?"

All stood amazed, until an old woman, tottering out from among the crowd, put her hand to her brow, and peering under it in his face for a moment, exclaimed, "Sure enough! it is Rip Van Winkle—it is himself! Welcome home again, old neighbor. Why, where have you been these twenty long years?"

Rip's story was soon told, for the whole twenty years had been to him but as one night. The neighbors stared when they heard it; some were seen to wink at each other, and put their tongues in their cheeks: and the self-important man in the cocked hat, who, when the alarm was over, had returned to the field, screwed down the corners of his mouth, and shook his head—upon which there was a general shaking of the head throughout the assemblage.

It was determined, however, to take the opinion of old Peter Vanderdonk, who was seen slowly advancing up the road. He was a descendant of the historian of that name, who wrote one of the earliest accounts of the province. Peter was the most ancient inhabitant of the village, and well versed in all the wonderful events and traditions of the neighborhood. He recollected Rip at once, and corroborated his story in the most satisfactory manner. He assured the company that it was a fact, handed down from his ancestor the historian, that the Kaatskill mountains had always been haunted by strange beings. That it was affirmed that the great Hendrick Hudson, the first discoverer of the river and country, kept a kind of vigil there every twenty years, with his crew of the *Half-moon;* being permitted in this way to revisit the scenes of his enterprise, and keep a guardian eye upon the river and the great city called by his name. That his father had once seen them in their old Dutch dresses playing at ninepins in a hollow of the mountain; and that he himself had heard, one summer afternoon, the sound of their balls, like distant peals of thunder.

To make a long story short, the company broke up and returned to the more important concerns of the election. Rip's daughter took him home to live with her; she had a snug, well-furnished house, and a stout, cheery farmer for a husband, whom Rip recollected for one of the urchins that used to climb upon his back. As to Rip's son and heir, who was the ditto of himself, seen leaning against the tree, he was employed to work on the farm; but evinced an hereditary disposition to attend to anything else but his business.

Rip now resumed his old walks and habits; he soon found many of his former cronies, though all rather the worse for the wear and tear of time; and preferred making friends among the rising generation, with whom he soon grew into great favor.

Having nothing to do at home, and being arrived at that happy age when a man can be idle with impunity, he took his place once more on the bench at the inn-door, and was reverenced as one of the patriarchs of the village, and a chronicle of the old times "before the war." It was some time before he could get into the regular track of gossip, or could be made to comprehend the strange events that had taken place during his torpor. How that there had been a revolutionary war—that the country had thrown off the yoke of old England—and that, instead of being a subject of his Majesty George the Third, he was now a free citizen of the United States. Rip, in fact, was no politician; the changes of states and empires made but little impression to him; but there was one species of despotism under which he long groaned, and that was—petticoat government. Happily that was at an end; he had got his neck out of the yoke of matrimony, and could go in and out whenever he pleased, without dreading the tyranny of Dame

Van Winkle. Whenever her name was mentioned, however, he shook his head, shrugged his shoulders, and cast up his eyes; which might pass either for an expression of resignation to his fate, or joy at his deliverance.

He used to tell his story to every stranger that arrived at Mr. Doolittle's hotel. He was observed, at first, to vary on some points every time he told it, which was, doubtless, owing to his having so recently awaked. It at last settled down precisely to the tale I have related, and not a man, woman, or child in the neighborhood but knew it by heart. Some always pretended to doubt the reality of it, and insisted that Rip had been out of his head, and that this was one point on which he always remained flighty. The old Dutch inhabitants, however, almost universally gave it full credit. Even to this day they never hear a thunderstorm of a summer afternoon about the Kaatskill, but they say Hendrick Hudson and his crew are at their game of ninepins; and it is a common wish of all hen-pecked husbands in the neighborhood, when life hangs heavy on their hands, that they might have a quieting draught out of Rip Van Winkle's flagon.

NOTE

The foregoing Tale, one would suspect, had been suggested to Mr. Knickerbocker by a little German superstition about the Emperor Frederick *der Rothbart,* and the Kypphäuser mountain: the subjoined note, however, which he had appended to the tale, shows that it is an absolute fact, narrated with his usual fidelity.

"The story of Rip Van Winkle may seem incredible to many, but nevertheless I give it my full belief, for I know the vicinity of our old Dutch settlements to have been very subject to marvellous events and appearances. Indeed, I have heard many stranger stories than this, in the villages along the Hudson; all of which were too well authenticated to admit of a doubt. I have even talked with Rip Van Winkle myself, who, when last I saw him, was a very venerable old man, and so perfectly rational and consistent on every other point, that I think no conscientious person could refuse to take this into the bargain; nay, I have seen a certificate on the subject taken before a country justice and signed with a cross, in the justice's own handwriting. The story, therefore, is beyond the possibility of doubt." — "D.K."   [1819]

WILLIAM AUSTIN

William Austin (1778–1841) was born in Lunenburg, Massachusetts, the son of Nathaniel and Margaret Rand Austin, whose families had emigrated from England to Massachusetts in 1651. Austin attended Haverhill preparatory school and enrolled as a student at Harvard College at the age of sixteen. Graduating with an A.B. at the age of twenty, he castigated the college as "the death-bed of genius" because students had no legal rights. Austin went on to study law in London from 1802 to 1803. The following year he returned to Charlestown, Massachusetts, to establish his law practice. For nearly forty years, he also served in local politics as a state senator and a representative in the General Court of Massachusetts, as well as a justice of the peace for the County of Middlesex.

At Harvard in 1798, Austin published his first work—his highly critical Strictures on Harvard University. *He followed it with various essays on religion and politics before his story "Peter Rugg, the Missing Man" appeared in three installments in the* New England Galaxy *(September 10, 1824; September 1, 1826; and January 19, 1827). In this fantastic tale, Austin presents Rugg as a phantom figure suffering the consequences of an oath he uttered in anger around the time of the Boston Massacre in 1770. Because he profanely defied the elements in an uncontrollable burst of temper, Rugg was not permitted to return home to Boston from Concord with his young daughter Jenny. As a consequence of his oath, Rugg and his daughter have been banished to a limbo outside of time: "Cut off from the last age," they "can never be fitted to the present." Spectators who catch sight of him are never sure of what they have seen, for as Austin remarks, their "fancy was doubtless at fault. It is a very common thing for the imagination to paint for the senses, both the visible and invisible world."*

Austin published only five stories, most of them didactic moral fables advocating virtues such as patience, honesty, and temperance. In his best work, he dramatized extreme psychological states, as in the story "The Man with the Cloaks: A Vermont Legend" (American Monthly Magazine, *January 1836). There Austin's narrator remarks that "the body is often the plaything of the mind. The imagination can produce a fever; and why may it not turn the heart to an icicle?" As the critic Dean G. Hall has stated,*

> *William Austin's place in American literary history is minor but revealing, for, earlier than others, he explained traditional supernatural events as possible imaginative products of the human mind. As Hawthorne does, Austin blurs the edges of his fictional reality so that facts are never certain, and the ambiance is mystical, a place where psychological causes are as plausible as any.*

Peter Rugg, the Missing Man

FROM JONATHAN DUNWELL[1] OF NEW YORK
TO MR. HERMAN KRAUFF

SIR,—Agreeably to my promise, I now relate to you all the particulars of the lost man and child which I have been able to collect. It is entirely owing to the humane interest you seemed to take in the report, that I have pursued the inquiry to the following result.

You may remember that business called me to Boston in the summer of 1820. I sailed in the packet to Providence, and when I arrived there I learned that every seat in the stage was engaged. I was thus obliged either to wait a few hours or accept a seat with the driver, who civilly offered me that accommodation. Accordingly, I took my seat by his side, and soon found him intelligent and communicative. When we had travelled about ten miles, the horses suddenly threw their ears on their neck, as flat as a hare's. Said the driver, "Have you a surtout with you?"

"No," said I; "why do you ask?"

"You will want one soon," said he. "Do you observe the ears of all the horses?"

"Yes; and was just about to ask the reason."

"They see the storm-breeder, and we shall see him soon."

At this moment there was not a cloud visible in the firmament. Soon after, a small speck appeared in the road.

"There," said my companion, "comes the storm-breeder. He always leaves a Scotch mist behind him. By many a wet jacket do I remember him. I suppose the poor fellow suffers much himself,—much more than is known to the world."

Presently a man with a child beside him, with a large black horse, and a weather-beaten chair, once built for a chaise-body, passed in great haste, apparently at the rate of twelve miles an hour. He seemed to grasp the reins of his horse with firmness, and appeared to anticipate his speed. He seemed dejected, and looked anxiously at the passengers, particularly at the stage-driver and myself. In a moment after he passed us, the horse's ears were up, and bent themselves forward so that they nearly met.

"Who is that man?" said I; "he seems in great trouble."

"Nobody knows who he is, but his person and the child are familiar to me. I have met him more than a hundred times, and have been so often asked the way to Boston by that man, even when he was travelling directly from that town, that of late I have refused any communication with him; and that is the reason he gave me such a fixed look."

"But does he never stop anywhere?"

---

[1]Austin's pseudonym.

"I have never known him to stop anywhere longer than to inquire the way to Boston; and let him be where he may, he will tell you he cannot stay a moment, for he must reach Boston that night."

We were now ascending a high hill in Walpole; and as we had a fair view of the heavens, I was rather disposed to jeer the driver for thinking of his surtout, as not a cloud as big as a marble could be discerned.

"Do you look," said he, "in the direction whence the man came; that is the place to look. The storm never meets him; it follows him."

We presently approached another hill; and when at the height, the driver pointed out in an eastern direction a little black speck about as big as a hat. "There," said he, "is the seed-storm. We may possibly reach Polley's before it reaches us, but the wanderer and his child will go to Providence through rain, thunder, and lightning."

And now the horses, as though taught by instinct, hastened with increased speed. The little black cloud came on rolling over the turnpike, and doubled and trebled itself in all directions. The appearance of this cloud attracted the notice of all the passengers, for after it had spread itself to a great bulk it suddenly became more limited in circumference, grew more compact, dark, and consolidated. And now the successive flashes of chain lightning caused the whole cloud to appear like a sort of irregular net-work, and displayed a thousand fantastic images. The driver bespoke my attention to a remarkable configuration in the cloud. He said every flash of lightning near its centre discovered to him, distinctly, the form of a man sitting in an open carriage drawn by a black horse. But in truth I saw no such thing; the man's fancy was doubtless at fault. It is a very common thing for the imagination to paint for the senses, both in the visible and invisible world.

In the mean time the distant thunder gave notice of a shower at hand; and just as we reached Polley's tavern the rain poured down in torrents. It was soon over, the cloud passing in the direction of the turnpike toward Providence. In a few moments after, a respectable-looking man in a chaise stopped at the door. The man and child in the chair having excited some little sympathy among the passengers, the gentleman was asked if he had observed them. He said he had met them; that the man seemed bewildered, and inquired the way to Boston; that he was driving at great speed, as though he expected to outstrip the tempest; that the moment he had passed him, a thunder-clap broke directly over the man's head, and seemed to envelop both man and child, horse and carriage. "I stopped," said the gentleman, "supposing the lightning had struck him, but the horse only seemed to loom up and increase his speed; and as well as I could judge, he travelled just as fast as the thunder-cloud."

While this man was speaking, a pedler with a cart of tin merchandise came up, all dripping; and on being questioned, he said he had met that man and carriage, within a fortnight, in four different States; that at each time he had inquired the way to Boston; and that a thunder-shower like the present had each time deluged his wagon and his wares, setting his tin pots, etc. afloat, so that he had determined to get a marine insurance for the future. But that which excited his surprise most was the strange conduct of his horse, for long before he could distinguish the man in the chair, his own horse stood still in the road, and flung back his ears. "In short," said the pedler, "I wish never to see that man and horse again; they do not look to me as though they belonged to this world."

This was all I could learn at that time; and the occurrence soon after would have become with me, "like one of those things which had never happened," had I not, as I stood recently on the door-step of Bennett's hotel in Hartford, heard a man say, "There goes Peter Rugg and his child! he looks wet and weary, and farther from Boston than ever." I was satisfied it was the same man I had seen more than three years before; for whoever has once seen Peter Rugg can never after be deceived as to his identity.

"Peter Rugg!" said I; "and who is Peter Rugg?"

"That," said the stranger, "is more than any one can tell exactly. He is a famous traveller, held in light esteem by all innholders, for he never stops to eat, drink, or sleep. I wonder why the government does not employ him to carry the mail."

"Ay," said a by-stander, "that is a thought bright only on one side; how long would it take in that case to send a letter to Boston, for Peter has already, to my knowledge, been more than twenty years travelling to that place."

"But," said I, "does the man never stop anywhere; does he never converse with any one? I saw the same man more than three years since, near Providence, and I heard a strange story about him. Pray, sir, give me some account of this man."

"Sir," said the stranger, "those who know the most respecting that man, say the least. I have heard it asserted that Heaven sometimes sets a mark on a man, either for judgment or a trial. Under which Peter Rugg now labors, I cannot say; therefore I am rather inclined to pity than to judge."

"You speak like a humane man," said I; "and if you have known him so long, I pray you will give me some account of him. Has his appearance much altered in that time?"

"Why, yes. He looks as though he never ate, drank, or slept; and his child looks older than himself, and he looks like time broken off from eternity, and anxious to gain a resting-place."

"And how does his horse look?" said I.

"As for his horse, he looks fatter and gayer, and shows more animation and courage than he did twenty years ago. The last time Rugg spoke to me he inquired how far it was to Boston. I told him just one hundred miles."

" 'Why,' said he, 'how can you deceive me so? It is cruel to mislead a traveller. I have lost my way; pray direct me the nearest way to Boston.'

"I repeated, it was one hundred miles.

" 'How can you say so?' said he; 'I was told last evening it was but fifty, and I have travelled all night.'

" 'But,' said I, 'you are now travelling from Boston. You must turn back.'

" 'Alas,' said he, 'it is all turn back! Boston shifts with the wind, and plays all around the compass. One man tells me it is to the east, another to the west; and the guide-posts too, they all point the wrong way.'

" 'But will you not stop and rest?' said I; 'you seem wet and weary.'

" 'Yes,' said he, 'it has been foul weather since I left home.'

" 'Stop, then, and refresh yourself.'

" 'I must not stop; I must reach home to-night, if possible: though I think you must be mistaken in the distance to Boston.'

"He then gave the reins to his horse, which he restrained with difficulty, and disappeared in a moment. A few days afterward I met the man a little this side of Claremont,[2] winding around the hills in Unity, at the rate, I believe, of twelve miles an hour."

"Is Peter Rugg his real name, or has he accidentally gained that name?"

"I know not, but presume he will not deny his name; you can ask him, — for see, he has turned his horse, and is passing this way."

In a moment a dark-colored, high-spirited horse approached, and would have passed without stopping, but I had resolved to speak to Peter Rugg, or whoever the man might be. Accordingly I stepped into the street; and as the horse approached, I made a feint of stopping him. The man immediately reined in his horse. "Sir," said I, "may I be so bold as to inquire if you are not Mr. Rugg? for I think I have seen you before."

"My name is Peter Rugg," said he. "I have unfortunately lost my way; I am wet and weary, and will take it kindly of you to direct me to Boston."

"You live in Boston, do you; and in what street?"

"In Middle Street."

"When did you leave Boston?"

"I cannot tell precisely; it seems a considerable time."

"But how did you and your child become so wet? It has not rained here to-day."

"It has just rained a heavy shower up the river. But I shall not reach Boston to-night if I tarry. Would you advise me to take the old road or the turnpike?"

"Why, the old road is one hundred and seventeen miles, and the turnpike is ninety-seven."

"How can you say so? You impose on me; it is wrong to trifle with a traveller; you know it is but forty miles from Newburyport to Boston."

---

[2]In New Hampshire.

"But this is not Newburyport; this is Hartford."

"Do not deceive me, sir. Is not this town Newburyport, and the river that I have been following the Merrimack?"

"No, sir; this is Hartford, and the river the Connecticut."

He wrung his hands and looked incredulous. "Have the rivers, too, changed their courses, as the cities have changed places? But see! the clouds are gathering in the south, and we shall have a rainy night. Ah, that fatal oath!"

He would tarry no longer; his impatient horse leaped off, his hind flanks rising like wings: he seemed to devour all before him, and to scorn all behind.

I had now, as I thought, discovered a clew to the history of Peter Rugg; and I determined, the next time my business called me to Boston, to make a further inquiry. Soon after, I was enabled to collect the following particulars from Mrs. Croft, an aged lady in Middle Street, who has resided in Boston during the last twenty years. Her narration is this:

Just at twilight last summer a person stopped at the door of the late Mrs. Rugg. Mrs. Croft on coming to the door perceived a stranger, with a child by his side, in an old weather-beaten carriage, with a black horse. The stranger asked for Mrs. Rugg, and was informed that Mrs. Rugg had died at a good old age, more than twenty years before that time.

The stranger replied, "How can you deceive me so? Do ask Mrs. Rugg to step to the door."

"Sir, I assure you Mrs. Rugg has not lived here these twenty years; no one lives here but myself, and my name is Betsy Croft."

The stranger paused, looked up and down the street, and said, "Though the paint is rather faded, this looks like my house."

"Yes," said the child, "that is the stone before the door that I used to sit on to eat my bread and milk."

"But," said the stranger, "it seems to be on the wrong side of the street. Indeed, everything here seems to be misplaced. The streets are all changed, the people are all changed, the town seems changed, and what is strangest of all, Catherine Rugg has deserted her husband and child. Pray," continued the stranger, "has John Foy come home from sea? He went a long voyage; he is my kinsman. If I could see him, he could give me some account of Mrs. Rugg."

"Sit," said Mrs. Croft, "I never heard of John Foy. Where did he live?"

"Just above here, in Orange-tree Lane."

"There is no such place in this neighborhood."

"What do you tell me! Are the streets gone? Orange-tree Lane is at the head of Hanover Street, near Pemberton's Hill."

"There is no such lane now."

"Madam, you cannot be serious! But you doubtless know my brother, William Rugg. He lives in Royal Exchange Lane, near King Street."

"I know of no such lane; and I am sure there is no such street as King Street in this town."

"No such street as King Street! Why, woman, you mock me! You may as well tell me there is no King George. However, madam, you see I am wet and weary, I must find a resting-place. I will go to Hart's tavern, near the market."

"Which market, sir? for you seem perplexed; we have several markets."

"You know there is but one market near the town dock."

"Oh, the old market; but no such person has kept there these twenty years."

Here the stranger seemed disconcerted, and uttered to himself quite audibly: "Strange mistake; how much this looks like the town of Boston! It certainly has a great resemblance to it; but I perceive my mistake now. Some other Mrs. Rugg, some other Middle Street.—Then," said he, "madam, can you direct me to Boston?"

"Why, this is Boston, the city of Boston; I know of no other Boston."

"City of Boston it may be; but it is not the Boston where I live. I recollect now, I came over a bridge instead of a ferry. Pray, what bridge is that I just came over?"

"It is Charles River bridge."

"I perceive my mistake: there is a ferry between Boston and Charlestown; there is no bridge. Ah, I perceive my mistake. If I were in Boston my horse would carry me directly to my own door. But my horse shows by his impatience that he is in a strange place. Absurd, that I should have mistaken this place for the old town of Boston! It is a much finer city than the town of Boston. It has been built long since Boston. I fancy Boston must lie at a distance from this city, as the good woman seems ignorant of it."

At these words his horse began to chafe, and strike the pavement with his forefeet. The stranger seemed a little bewildered, and said, "No home to-night;" and giving the reins to his horse, passed up the street, and I saw no more of him.

It was evident that the generation to which Peter Rugg belonged has passed away.

This was all the account of Peter Rugg I could obtain from Mrs. Croft; but she directed me to an elderly man, Mr. James Felt, who lived near her, and who had kept a record of the principal occurrences for the last fifty years. At my request she sent for him; and after I had related to him the object of my inquiry, Mr. Felt told me he had known Rugg in his youth, and that his disappearance had caused some surprise; but as it sometimes happens that men run away,—sometimes to be rid of others, and sometimes to be rid of themselves,—and Rugg took his child with him, and his own horse and chair, and as it did not appear that any creditors made a stir, the occurrence soon mingled itself in the stream of oblivion; and Rugg and his child, horse, and chair were soon forgotten.

"It is true," said Mr. Felt, "sundry stories grew out of Rugg's affair, whether true or false I cannot tell; but stranger things have happened in my day, without even a newspaper notice."

"Sir," said I, "Peter Rugg is now living. I have lately seen Peter Rugg and his child, horse, and chair; therefore I pray you to relate to me all you know or ever heard of him."

"Why, my friend," said James Felt, "that Peter Rugg is now a living man, I will not deny; but that you have seen Peter Rugg and his child, is impossible, if you mean a small child; for Jenny Rugg, if living, must be at least—let me see—Boston massacre, 1770—Jenny Rugg was about ten years old. Why, sir, Jenny Rugg, if living, must be more than sixty years of age. That Peter Rugg is living, is highly probable, as he was only ten years older than myself, and I was only eighty last March; and I am as likely to live twenty years longer as any man."

Here I perceived that Mr. Felt was in his dotage, and I despaired of gaining any intelligence from him on which I could depend.

I took my leave of Mrs. Croft, and proceeded to my lodgings at the Marlborough Hotel.

"If Peter Rugg," thought I, "has been travelling since the Boston massacre, there is no reason why he should not travel to the end of time. If the present generation know little of him, the next will know less, and Peter and his child will have no hold on this world."

In the course of the evening, I related my adventure in Middle Street.

"Ha!" said one of the company, smiling, "do you really think you have seen Peter Rugg? I have heard my grandfather speak of him, as though he seriously believed his own story."

"Sir," said I, "pray let us compare your grandfather's story of Mr. Rugg with my own."

"Peter Rugg, sir,—if my grandfather was worthy of credit,—once lived in Middle Street, in this city. He was a man in comfortable circumstances, had a wife and one daughter, and was generally esteemed for his sober life and manners. But unhappily, his temper, at times, was altogether ungovernable, and then his language was terrible. In these fits of passion, if a door stood in his way, he would never do less than kick a panel through. He would sometimes throw his heels over his head, and come down on his feet, uttering oaths in a circle; and thus in a rage, he was the first who performed a somerset, and did what others have since learned to do for merriment and money. Once Rugg was seen to bite a tenpenny nail in halves. In those days everybody, both men and boys, wore wigs; and Peter, at these moments of violent passion, would become so profane that his wig would rise up from his head. Some said it was on account of his terrible language; others accounted for it in a more philosophical way, and said it was caused by the expansion of his scalp, as violent passion, we know, will swell the veins and expand the head. While these fits were on him, Rugg had no respect for heaven or earth. Except this infirmity, all agreed that Rugg was a good sort of man; for when his fits were over, nobody was so ready to commend a placid temper as Peter.

"One morning, late in autumn, Rugg, in his own chair, with a fine large bay horse, took his daughter and proceeded to Concord. On his return a violent storm overtook him. At dark he stopped in Menotomy, now West Cambridge, at the door of a Mr. Cutter, a friend of his, who urged him to tarry the night. On Rugg's declining to stop, Mr. Cutter urged him vehemently. 'Why, Mr. Rugg,' said Cutter, 'the storm is over-whelming you. The night is exceedingly dark. Your little daughter will per-ish. You are in an open chair, and the tempest is increasing.' *'Let the storm increase,'* said Rugg, with a fearful oath, *'I will see home to-night, in spite of the last tempest, or may I never see home!"* At these words he gave his whip to his high-spirited horse and disappeared in a moment. But Peter Rugg did not reach home that night, nor the next; nor, when he became a miss-ing man, could he ever be traced beyond Mr. Cutter's, in Menotomy.

"For a long time after, on every dark and stormy night the wife of Peter Rugg would fancy she heard the crack of a whip, and the fleet tread of a horse, and the rattling of a carriage passing her door. The neighbors, too, heard the same noises, and some said they knew it was Rugg's horse; the tread on the pavement was perfectly familiar to them. This occurred so repeatedly that at length the neighbors watched with lanterns, and saw the real Peter Rugg, with his own horse and chair and the child sitting beside him, pass directly before his own door, his head turned toward his house, and himself making every effort to stop his horse, but in vain.

"The next day the friends of Mrs. Rugg exerted themselves to find her husband and child. They inquired at every public house and stable in town; but it did not appear that Rugg made any stay in Boston. No one, after Rugg had passed his own door, could give any account of him, though it was asserted by some that the clatter of Rugg's horse and car-riage over the pavements shook the houses on both sides of the streets. And this is credible, if indeed Rugg's horse and carriage did pass on that night; for at this day, in many of the streets, a loaded truck or team in pass-ing will shake the houses like an earthquake. However, Rugg's neighbors never afterward watched. Some of them treated it all as a delusion, and thought no more of it. Others of a different opinion shook their heads and said nothing.

"Thus Rugg and his child, horse, and chair were soon forgotten; and probably many in the neighborhood never heard a word on the subject.

"There was indeed a rumor that Rugg was seen afterward in Con-necticut, between Suffield and Hartford, passing through the country at headlong speed. This gave occasion to Rugg's friends to make further inquiry; but the more they inquired, the more they were baffled. If they heard of Rugg one day in Connecticut, the next they heard of him wind-ing round the hills in New Hampshire; and soon after a man in a chair, with a small child, exactly answering the description of Peter Rugg, would be seen in Rhode Island inquiring the way to Boston.

"But that which chiefly gave a color of mystery to the story of Peter Rugg was the affair at Charlestown bridge. The toll-gatherer asserted that sometimes, on the darkest and most stormy nights, when no object could be discerned, about the time Rugg was missing, a horse and wheel-carriage, with a noise equal to a troop, would at midnight, in utter contempt of the rates of toll, pass over the bridge. This occurred so frequently that the toll-gatherer resolved to attempt a discovery. Soon after, at the usual time, apparently the same horse and carriage approached the bridge from Charlestown square. The toll-gatherer, prepared, took his stand as near the middle of the bridge as he dared, with a large three-legged stool in his hand; as the appearance passed, he threw the stool at the horse, but heard nothing except the noise of the stool skipping across the bridge. The toll-gatherer on the next day asserted that the stool went directly through the body of the horse, and he persisted in that belief ever after. Whether Rugg, or whoever the person was, ever passed the bridge again, the toll-gatherer would never tell; and when questioned, seemed anxious to waive the subject. And thus Peter Rugg and his child, horse, and carriage, remain a mystery to this day."

This, sir is all that I could learn of Peter Rugg in Boston.

FURTHER ACCOUNT OF PETER RUGG
BY JONATHAN DUNWELL

In the autumn of 1825 I attended the races at Richmond in Virginia. As two new horses of great promise were run, the race-ground was never better attended, nor was expectation ever more deeply excited. The partisans of Dart and Lightning, the two race-horses, were equally anxious and equally dubious of the result. To an indifferent spectator, it was impossible to perceive any difference. They were equally beautiful to behold, alike in color and height, and as they stood side by side they measured from heel to forefeet within half an inch of each other. The eyes of each were full, prominent, and resolute; and when at times they regarded each other, they assumed a lofty demeanor, seemed to shorten their necks, project their eyes, and rest their bodies equally on their four hoofs. They certainly showed signs of intelligence, and displayed a courtesy to each other unusual even with statesmen.

It was now nearly twelve o'clock, the hour of expectation, doubt, and anxiety. The riders mounted their horses; and so trim, light, and airy they sat on the animals as to seem a part of them. The spectators, many deep in a solid column, had taken their places, and as many thousand breathing statues were there as spectators. All eyes were turned to Dart and Lightning and their two fairy riders. There was nothing to disturb this calm except a busy woodpecker on a neighboring tree. The signal was given, and Dart and Lightning answered it with ready intelligence. At first they proceed at a slow trot, then they quicken to a canter, and then a gallop; presently they sweep the plain. Both horses lay themselves flat on the ground, their riders bending forward and resting their chins between their horses' ears. Had not the ground been perfectly level, had there been any undulation, the least rise and fall, the spectator would now and then have lost sight of both horses and riders.

While these horses, side by side, thus appeared, flying without wings, flat as a hare, and neither gaining on the other, all eyes were diverted to a new spectacle. Directly in the rear of Dart and Lightning, a majestic black horse of unusual size, drawing an old weather-beaten chair, strode over the plain; and although he appeared to make no effort, for he maintained a steady trot, before Dart and Lightning approached the goal the black horse and chair had overtaken the racers, who, on perceiving this new competitor pass them, threw back their ears, and suddenly stopped in their course. Thus neither Dart nor Lightning carried away the purse.

The spectators now were exceedingly curious to learn whence came the black horse and chair. With many it was the opinion that nobody was in the vehicle. Indeed, this began to be the prevalent opinion; for those at a short distance, so fleet was the black horse, could not easily discern who, if anybody, was in the carriage. But both the riders, very near to whom the black horse passed, agreed in this particular,—that a sad-looking man and a little girl were in the chair. When they stated this I was satisfied that the man was Peter Rugg. But what caused no little surprise, John Spring, one of the riders (he who rode Lightning) asserted that no earthly horse without breaking his trot could, in a carriage, outstrip his race-horse; and he persisted, with some passion, that it was not a horse,—or, he was sure it was not a horse, but a large black ox. "What a great black ox can do," said John, "I cannot pretend to say; but no race-horse, not even flying Childers, could out-trot Lightning in a fair race."

This opinion of John Spring excited no little merriment, for it was obvious to every one that it was a powerful black horse that interrupted the race; but John Spring, jealous of Lightning's reputation as a horse, would rather have it thought that any other beast, even an ox, had been the victor. However, the "horse-laugh" at John Spring's expense was soon suppressed; for as soon as Dart and Lightning began to breathe more freely, it was observed that both of them walked deliberately to the track of the race-ground, and putting their heads to the earth, suddenly raised them again and began to snort. They repeated this till John Spring said,— "These horses have discovered something strange; they suspect foul play. Let me go and talk with Lightning."

He went up to Lightning and took hold of his mane; and Lightning put his nose toward the ground and smelt of the earth without touching it, then reared his head very high, and snorted so loudly that the sound echoed from the next hill. Dart did the same. John Spring stooped down to examine the spot where Lightning had smelled. In a moment he raised himself up, and the countenance of the man was changed. His strength failed him, and he sidled against Lightning.

At length John Spring recovered from his stupor and exclaimed, "It was an ox! I told you it was an ox. No real horse ever yet beat Lightning."

And now, on a close inspection of the black horse's tracks in the path, it was evident to every one that the forefeet of the black horse were cloven. Notwithstanding these appearances, to me it was evident that the strange horse was in reality a horse. Yet when the people left the race-ground, I presume one half of all those present would have testified that a large black ox had distanced two of the fleetest coursers that ever trod the Virginia turf. So uncertain are all things called historical facts.

While I was proceeding to my lodgings, pondering on the events of the day, a stranger rode up to me, and accosted me thus, — "I think your name is Dunwell, sir."

"Yes, sir," I replied.

"Did I not see you a year or two since in Boston, at the Marlborough Hotel?"

"Very likely, sir, for I was there."

"And you heard a story about one Peter Rugg."

"I recollect it all," said I.

"The account you heard in Boston must be true, for here he was to-day. The man has found his way to Virginia, and for aught that appears, has been to Cape Horn. I have seen him before to-day, but never saw him travel with such fearful velocity. Pray, sir, where does Peter Rugg spend his winters, for I have seen him only in summer, and always in foul weather, except this time?"

I replied, "No one knows where Peter Rugg spends his winters; where or when he eats, drinks, sleeps, or lodges. He seems to have an indistinct idea of day and night, time and space, storm and sunshine. His only object is Boston. It appears to me that Rugg's horse has some control of the chair; and that Rugg himself is, in some sort, under the control of his horse."

I then inquired of the stranger where he first saw the man and horse.

"Why, sir," said he, "in the summer of 1824, I travelled to the North for my health; and soon after I saw you at the Marlborough Hotel I returned homeward to Virginia, and, if my memory's correct, I saw this man and horse in every State between here and Massachusetts. Sometimes he would meet me, but oftener overtake me. He never spoke but once, and that once was in Delaware. On his approach he checked his horse with some difficulty. A more beautiful horse I never saw; his hide was as fair and rotund and glossy as the skin of a Congo beauty. When Rugg's horse approached mine he reined in his neck, bent his ears forward until they met, and looked my horse full in the face. My horse immediately withered into half a horse, his hide curling up like a piece of burnt leather; spell-bound, he was fixed to the earth as though a nail had been driven through each hoof.

"'Sir,' said Rugg, 'perhaps you are travelling to Boston; and if so, I should be happy to accompany you, for I have lost my way, and I must reach home to-night. See how sleepy this little girl looks; poor thing, she is a picture of patience.'

" 'Sir,' said I, 'it is impossible for you to reach home to-night, for you are in Concord, in the county of Sussex, in the State of Delaware.'

" 'What do you mean,' said he, 'by State of Delaware? If I were in Concord, that is only twenty miles from Boston, and my horse Lightfoot could carry me to Charlestown ferry in less than two hours. You mistake, sir; you are a stranger here; this town is nothing like Concord. I am well acquainted with Concord. I went to Concord when I left Boston.'

" 'But,' said I, 'you are in Concord, in the State of Delaware.'

" 'What do you mean by State?' said Rugg.

" 'Why, one of the United States.'

" 'States!' said he, in a low voice; 'the man is a wag, and would persuade me I am in Holland.' Then, raising his voice, he said, 'You seem, sir, to be a gentleman, and I entreat you to mislead me not: tell me, quickly, for pity's sake, the right road to Boston, for you see my horse will swallow his bits, he has eaten nothing since I left Concord.'

" 'Sir,' said I, 'this town is Concord, — Concord in Delaware, not Concord in Massachusetts; and you are now five hundred miles from Boston.'

"Rugg looked at me for a moment, more in sorrow than resentment, and then repeated, 'Five hundred miles! Unhappy man, who would have thought him deranged; but nothing in this world is so deceitful as appearances. Five hundred miles! This beats Connecticut River.'

"What he meant by Connecticut River, I know not; his horse broke away, and Rugg disappeared in a moment."

I explained to the stranger the meaning of Rugg's expression, "Connecticut River," and the incident respecting him that occurred at Hartford, as I stood on the door-stone of Mr. Bennett's excellent hotel. We both agreed that the man we had seen that day was the true Peter Rugg.

Soon after, I saw Rugg again, at the toll-gate on the turnpike between Alexandria and Middleburgh. While I was paying the toll, I observed to the toll-gatherer that the drought was more severe in his vicinity than farther south.

"Yes," said he, "the drought is excessive; but if I had not heard yesterday, by a traveller, that the man with the black horse was seen in Kentucky a day or two since, I should be sure of a shower in a few minutes."

I looked all around the horizon, and could not discern a cloud that could hold a pint of water.

"Look, sir," said the toll-gatherer, "you perceive to the eastward, just above that hill, a small black cloud not bigger than a blackberry, and while I am speaking it is doubling and trebling itself, and rolling up the turnpike steadily, as if its sole design was to deluge some object."

"True," said I, "I do perceive it; but what connection is there between a thunder-cloud and a man and horse?"

"More than you imagine, or I can tell you; but stop a moment, sir, I may need your assistance. I know that cloud; I have seen it several times before, and can testify to its identity. You will soon see a man and black horse under it."

While he was speaking, true enough, we began to hear the distant thunder, and soon the chain-lightning performed all the figures of a country-dance. About a mile distant we saw the man and black horse under the cloud; but before he arrived at the toll-gate, the thunder-cloud had spent itself, and not even a sprinkle fell near us.

As the man, whom I instantly knew to be Rugg, attempted to pass, the toll-gatherer swung the gate across the road, seized Rugg's horse by the reins, and demanded two dollars.

Feeling some little regard for Rugg, I interfered, and began to question the toll-gatherer, and requested him not to be wroth with the man. The toll-gatherer replied that he had just cause, for the man had run his toll ten times, and moreover that the horse had discharged a cannon-ball at him, to the great danger of his life; that the man had always before approached so rapidly that he was too quick for the rusty hinges of the toll-gate; "but now I will have full satisfaction."

Rugg looked wistfully at me, and said, "I entreat you, sir, to delay me not; I have found at length the direct road to Boston, and shall not reach home before night if you detain me. You see I am dripping wet, and ought to change my clothes."

The toll-gatherer then demanded why he had run his toll so many times.

"Toll! Why," said Rugg, "do you demand toll? There is no toll to pay on the king's highway."

"King's highway! Do you not perceive this is a turnpike?"

"Turnpike! there are no turnpikes in Massachusetts."

"That may be, but we have several in Virginia."

"Virginia! Do you pretend I am in Virginia?"

Rugg, then, appealing to me, asked how far it was to Boston.

Said I, "Mr. Rugg, I perceive you are bewildered, and am sorry to see you so far from home; you are, indeed, in Virginia."

"You know me, then, sir, it seems; and you say I am in Virginia. Give me leave to tell you, sir, you are the most impudent man alive; for I was never forty miles from Boston, and I never saw a Virginian in my life. This beats Delaware!"

"Your toll, sir, your toll!"

"I will not pay you a penny," said Rugg; "you are both of you highway robbers. There are no turnpikes in this country. Take toll on the king's highway! Robbers take toll on the king's highway!" Then in a low tone, he said, "Here is evidently a conspiracy against me; alas, I shall never see Boston! The highways refuse me a passage, the rivers change their courses, and there is no faith in the compass."

But Rugg's horse had no idea of stopping more than one minute; for in the midst of this altercation, the horse, whose nose was resting on the upper bar of the turnpike-gate, seized it between his teeth, lifted it gently off its staples, and trotted off with it. The toll-gatherer, confounded, strained his eyes after his gate.

"Let him go," said I, "the horse will soon drop your gate, and you will get it again."

I then questioned the toll-gatherer respecting his knowledge of this man; and he related the following particulars: —

"The first time," said he, "that man ever passed this toll-gate was in the year 1806, at the moment of the great eclipse. I thought the horse was frightened at the sudden darkness, and concluded he had run away with the man. But within a few days after, the same man and horse repassed with equal speed, without the least respect to the toll-gate or to me, except by a vacant stare. Some few years afterward, during the late war, I saw the same man approaching again, and I resolved to check his career. Accordingly I stepped into the middle of the road, and stretched wide both my arms, and cried, 'Stop, sir, on your peril!' At this the man said, 'Now, Lightfoot, confound the robber!' at the same time he gave the whip liberally to the flank of his horse, which bounded off with such force that it appeared to me two such horses, give them a place to stand, would overcome any check man could devise. An ammunition wagon which had just passed on to Baltimore had dropped an eighteen pounder in the road; this unlucky ball lay in the way of the horse's heels, and the beast, with the sagacity of a demon, clinched it with one of his heels and hurled it behind him. I feel dizzy in relating the fact, but so nearly did the ball pass my head, that the wind thereof blew off my hat; and the ball embedded itself in that gate-post, as you may see if you will cast your eye on the post. I have permitted it to remain there in memory of the occurrence,—as the people of Boston, I am told, preserve the eighteen-pounder which is now to be seen half imbedded in Brattle Street church."

I then took leave of the toll-gatherer, and promised him if I saw or heard of his gate I would send him notice.

A strong inclination had possessed me to arrest Rugg and search his pockets, thinking great discoveries might be made in the examination; but what I saw and heard that day convinced me that no human force could detain Peter Rugg against his consent. I therefore determined if I ever saw Rugg again to treat him in the gentlest manner.

In pursuing my way to New York, I entered on the turnpike in Trenton; and when I arrived at New Brunswick, I perceived the road was newly macadamized. The small stones had just been laid thereon. As I passed this piece of road, I observed that, at regular distances of about eight feet, the stones were entirely displaced from spots as large as the circumference of a half-bushel measure. This singular appearance induced me to inquire the cause of it at the turnpike-gate.

"Sir," said the toll-gatherer, "I wonder not at the question, but I am unable to give you a satisfactory answer. Indeed, sir, I believe I am bewitched, and that the turnpike is under a spell of enchantment; for what appeared to me last night cannot be a real transaction, otherwise a turnpike-gate is a useless thing."

"I do not believe in witchcraft or enchantment," said I; "and if you will relate circumstantially what happened last night, I will endeavor to account for it by natural means."

"You may recollect the night was uncommonly dark. Well, sir, just after I had closed the gate for the night, down the turnpike, as far as my eye could reach, I beheld what at first appeared to be two armies engaged. The report of the musketry, and the flashes of their firelocks, were incessant and continuous. As this strange spectacle approached me with the fury of a tornado, the noise increased; and the appearance rolled on in one compact body over the surface of the ground. The most splendid fireworks arose out of the earth and encircled this moving spectacle. The divers tints of the rainbow, the most brilliant dyes that the sun lays in the lap of spring, added to the whole family of gems, could not display a more beautiful, radiant, and dazzling spectacle than accompanied the black horse. You would have thought all the stars of heaven had met in merriment on the turnpike. In the midst of this luminous configuration sat a man, distinctly to be seen, in a miserable-looking chair, drawn by a black horse. The turnpike-gate ought, by the laws of Nature and the laws of the State, to have made a wreck of the whole, and have dissolved the enchantment; but no, the horse without an effort passed over the gate, and drew the man and chair horizontally after him without touching the bar. This was what I call enchantment. What think you, sir?"

"My friend," said I, "you have grossly magnified a natural occurrence. The man was Peter Rugg, on his way to Boston. It is true, his horse travelled with unequalled speed, but as he reared high his forefeet, he could not help displacing the thousand small stones on which he trod, which flying in all directions struck one another, and resounded and scintillated. The top bar of your gate is not more than two feet from the ground, and Rugg's horse at every vault could easily lift the carriage over that gate."

This satisfied Mr. McDoubt, and I was pleased at that occurrence; for otherwise Mr. McDoubt, who is a worthy man, late from the Highlands, might have added to his calendar of superstitions. Having thus disenchanted the macadamized road and the turnpike-gate, and also Mr. McDoubt, I pursued my journey homeward to New York.

Little did I expect to see or hear anything further of Mr. Rugg, for he was now more than twelve hours in advance of me. I could hear nothing of him on my way to Elizabethtown, and therefore concluded that during the past night he had turned off from the turnpike and pursued a westerly direction; but just before I arrived at Powles's Hook, I observed a considerable collection of passengers in the ferry-boat, all standing motionless, and steadily looking at the same object. One of the ferry-men, Mr. Hardy, who knew me well, observing my approach delayed a minute, in order to afford me a passage, and coming up, said, "Mr. Dunwell, we have a curiosity on board that would puzzle Dr. Mitchell."

"Some strange fish, I suppose, has found its way into the Hudson."

"No," said he, "it is a man who looks as if he had lain hidden in the ark, and had just now ventured out. He has a little girl with him, the counterpart of himself, and the finest horse you ever saw, harnessed to the queerest-looking carriage that ever was made."

"Ah, Mr. Hardy," said I, "you have, indeed, hooked a prize; no one before you could ever detain Peter Rugg long enough to examine him."

"Do you know the man?" said Mr. Hardy.

"No, nobody knows him, but everybody has seen him. Detain him as long as possible; delay the boat under any pretence, cut the gear of the horse, do anything to detain him."

As I entered the ferry-boat, I was struck at the spectacle before me. There, indeed, sat Peter Rugg and Jenny Rugg in the chair, and there stood the black horse, all as quiet as lambs, surrounded by more than fifty men and women, who seemed to have lost all their senses but one. Not a motion, not a breath, not a rustle. They were all eye. Rugg appeared to them to be a man not of this world; and they appeared to Rugg a strange generation of men. Rugg spoke not, and they spoke not; nor was I disposed to disturb the calm, satisfied to reconnoitre Rugg in a state of rest. Presently, Rugg observed in a low voice, addressed to nobody, "A new contrivance, horses instead of oars; Boston folks are full of notions."

It was plain that Rugg was of Dutch extraction. He had on three pairs of small clothes, called in former days of simplicity breeches, not much the worse for wear; but time had proved the fabric, and shrunk one more than another, so that they showed at the knees their different qualities and colors. His several waistcoats, the flaps of which rested on his knees, made him appear rather corpulent. His capacious drab coat would supply the stuff for half a dozen modern ones; the sleeves were like meal bags, in the cuffs of which you might nurse a child to sleep. His hat, probably once black, now of a tan color, was neither round nor crooked, but in shape much like the one President Monroe wore on his late tour. This dress gave the rotund face of Rugg an antiquated dignity. The man, though deeply sunburned, did not appear to be more than thirty years of age. He had lost his sad and anxious look, was quite composed, and seemed happy. The chair in which Rugg sat was very capacious, evidently made for service, and calculated to last for ages; the timber would supply material for three modern carriages. This chair, like a Nantucket coach, would answer for everything that ever went on wheels. The horse, too, was an object of curiosity; his majestic height, his natural mane and tail, gave him a commanding appearance, and his large open nostrils indicated inexhaustible wind. It was apparent that the hoofs of his forefeet had been split, probably on some newly macadamized road, and were now growing together again; so that John Spring was not altogether in the wrong.

How long this dumb scene would otherwise have continued I cannot tell. Rugg discovered no sign of impatience. But Rugg's horse having been quiet more than five minutes, had no idea of standing idle; he began to whinny, and in a moment after, with his right forefoot he started a plank. Said Rugg, "My horse is impatient, he sees the North End. You must be quick, or he will be ungovernable."

At these words, the horse raised his left forefoot; and when he laid it down every inch of the ferry-boat trembled. Two men immediately seized Rugg's horse by the nostrils. The horse nodded, and both of them were in the Hudson. While we were fishing up the men, the horse was perfectly quiet.

"Fret not the horse," said Rugg, "and he will do no harm. He is only anxious, like myself, to arrive at yonder beautiful shore; he sees the North Church, and smells his own stable."

"Sir," said I to Rugg, practising a little deception, "pray tell me, for I am a stranger here, what river is this, and what city is that opposite, for you seem to be an inhabitant of it?"

"This river, sir, is called Mystic River, and this is Winnisimmet ferry,— we have retained the Indian names,—and that town is Boston. You must, indeed, be a stranger in these parts, not to know that yonder is Boston, the capital of the New England provinces."

"Pray, sir, how long have you been absent from Boston?"

"Why, that I cannot exactly tell. I lately went with this little girl of mine to Concord, to see my friends; and I am ashamed to tell you, in returning lost the way, and have been travelling ever since. No one would direct me right. It is cruel to mislead a traveller. My horse, Lightfoot, has boxed the compass; and it seems to me he has boxed it back again. But, sir, you perceive my horse is uneasy; Lightfoot, as yet, has only given a hint and a nod. I cannot be answerable for his heels."

At these words Lightfoot reared his long tail, and snapped it as you would a whiplash. The Hudson reverberated with the sound. Instantly the six horses began to move the boat. The Hudson was a sea of glass, smooth as oil, not a ripple. The horses, from a smart trot, soon pressed into a gallop; water now ran over the gunwale; the ferry-boat was soon buried in an ocean of foam, and the noise of the spray was like the roaring of many waters. When we arrived at New York, you might see the beautiful white wake of the ferry-boat across the Hudson.

Though Rugg refused to pay toll at turnpikes, when Mr. Hardy reached his hand for the ferriage, Rugg readily put his hand into one of his many pockets, took out a piece of silver, and handed it to Mr. Hardy.

"What is this?" said Mr. Hardy.

"It is thirty shillings," said Rugg.

"It might once have been thirty shillings, old tenor," said Mr. Hardy, "but it is not at present."

"The money is good English coin," said Rugg; "my grandfather brought a bag of them from England, and had them hot from the mint."

Hearing this, I approached near to Rugg, and asked permission to see the coin. It was a half-crown, coined by the English Parliament, dated in the year 1649. On one side, "The Commonwealth of England," and St. George's cross encircled with a wreath of laurel. On the other, "God with us," and a harp and St. George's cross united. I winked at Mr. Hardy, and pronounced it good current money; and said loudly, "I will not permit the gentleman to be imposed on, for I will exchange the money myself."

On this, Rugg spoke, — "Please to give me your name, sir."

"My name is Dunwell, sir," I replied.

"Mr. Dunwell," said Rugg, "you are the only honest man I have seen since I left Boston. As you are a stranger here, my house is your home; Dame Rugg will be happy to see her husband's friend. Step into my chair, sir, there is room enough; move a little, Jenny, for the gentleman, and we will be in Middle Street in a minute."

Accordingly I took a seat by Peter Rugg.

"Were you never in Boston before?" said Rugg.

"No," said I.

"Well, you will now see the queen of New England, a town second only to Philadelphia, in all North America."

"You forget New York," said I.

"Poh, New York is nothing; though I never was there. I am told you might put all New York in our mill-pond. No, sir, New York, I assure you, is but a sorry affair; no more to be compared with Boston than a wigwam with a palace."

As Rugg's horse turned into Pearl Street, I looked Rugg as fully in the face as good manners would allow, and said, "Sir, if this is Boston, I acknowledge New York is not worthy to be one of its suburbs."

Before we had proceeded far in Pearl Street, Rugg's countenance changed: his nerves began to twitch; his eyes trembled in their sockets; he was evidently bewildered. "What is the matter, Mr. Rugg; you seem disturbed."

"This surpasses all human comprehension; if you know, sir, where we are, I beseech you to tell me."

"If this place," I replied, "is not Boston, it must be New York."

"No, sir, it is not Boston; nor can it be New York. How could I be in New York, which is nearly two hundred miles from Boston?"

By this time we had passed into Broadway, and then Rugg, in truth, discovered a chaotic mind. "There is no such place as this in North America. This is all the effect of enchantment; this is a grand delusion, nothing real. Here is seemingly a great city, magnificent houses, shops and goods, men and women innumerable, and as busy as in real life, all sprung up in one night from the wilderness; or what is more probable, some tremendous convulsion of Nature has thrown London or Amsterdam on the shores of New England. Or, possibly, I may be dreaming, though the night seems rather long; but before now I have sailed in one night to Amsterdam, bought goods of Vandogger, and returned to Boston before morning."

At this moment a hue-and-cry was heard, "Stop the madmen, they will endanger the lives of thousands!" In vain hundreds attempted to stop Rugg's horse. Lightfoot interfered with nothing; his course was straight as a shooting-star. But on my part, fearful that before night I should find myself behind the Alleghanies, I addressed Mr. Rugg in a tone of entreaty, and requested him to restrain the horse and permit me to alight.

"My friend," said he, "we shall be in Boston before dark, and Dame Rugg will be most exceeding glad to see us."

"Mr. Rugg," said I, "you must excuse me. Pray look to the west; see that thunder-cloud swelling with rage, as if in pursuit of us."

"Ah!" said Rugg, "it is in vain to attempt to escape. I know that cloud; it is collecting new wrath to spend on my head." Then checking his horse, he permitted me to descend, saying, "Farewell, Mr. Dunwell, I shall be happy to see you in Boston; I live in Middle Street."

It is uncertain in what direction Mr. Rugg pursued his course, after he disappeared in Broadway; but one thing is sufficiently known to every-body, — that in the course of two months after he was seen in New York, he found his way most opportunely to Boston.

It seems the estate of Peter Rugg had recently fallen to the Common-wealth of Massachusetts for want of heirs; and the Legislature had ordered the solicitor-general to advertise and sell it at public auction. Happening to be in Boston at the time, and observing his advertisement, which described a considerable extent of land, I felt a kindly curiosity to see the spot where Rugg once lived. Taking the advertisement in my hand, I wan-dered a little way down Middle Street, and without asking a question of any one, when I came to a certain spot I said to myself, "This is Rugg's estate; I will proceed no farther. This must be the spot; it is a counterpart of Peter Rugg." The premises, indeed, looked as if they had fulfilled a sad prophecy. Fronting on Middle Street, they extended in the rear to Ann Street, and embraced about half an acre of land. It was not uncommon in former times to have half an acre for a house-lot; for an acre of land then, in many parts of Boston, was not more valuable than a foot in some places at present. The old mansion-house had become a powder-post, and been blown away. One other building, uninhabited, stood ominous, courting dilapidation. The street had been so much raised that the bed-chamber had descended to the kitchen and was level with the street. The house seemed conscious of its fate; and as though tired of standing there, the front was fast retreating from the rear, and waiting the next south wind to project itself into the street. If the most wary animals had sought a place of refuge, here they would have rendezvoused. Here, under the ridge-pole, the crow would have perched in security; and in the recesses below, you might have caught the fox and the weasel asleep. "The hand of destiny," said I, "has pressed heavy on this spot; still heavier on the former owners. Strange that so large a lot of land as this should want an heir! Yet Peter Rugg, at this day, might pass by his own door-stone, and ask, 'Who once lived here?'"

The auctioneer, appointed by the solicitor to sell this estate, was a man of eloquence, as many of the auctioneers of Boston are. The occasion seemed to warrant, and his duty urged, him to make a display. He addressed his audience as follows, —

"The estate, gentlemen, which we offer you this day, was once the property of a family now extinct. For that reason it has escheated to the Commonwealth. Lest any one of you should be deterred from bidding on so large an estate as this for fear of a disputed title, I am authorized by the solicitor-general to proclaim that the purchaser shall have the best of all titles, — a warranty-deed from the Commonwealth. I state this, gentlemen, because I know there is an idle rumor in this vicinity, that one Peter Rugg, the original owner of this estate, is still living. This rumor, gentlemen, has no foundation, and can have no foundation in the nature of things. It originated about two years since, from the incredible story of one Jonathan Dunwell, of New York. Mrs. Croft, indeed, whose husband I see present, and whose mouth waters for this estate, has countenanced this fiction. But, gentlemen, was it ever known that any estate, especially an estate of this value, lay unclaimed for nearly half a century, if any heir, ever so remote, were existing? For, gentlemen, all agree that old Peter Rugg, if living, would be at least one hundred years of age. It is said that he and his daughter, with a horse and chaise, were missed more than half a century ago; and because they never returned home, forsooth, they must be now living, and will some day come and claim this great estate. Such logic, gentlemen, never led to a good investment. Let not this idle story cross the noble purpose of consigning these ruins to the genius of architecture. If such a contingency could check the spirit of enterprise, farewell to all mercantile excitement. Your surplus money, instead of refreshing your sleep with the golden dreams of new sources of speculation, would turn to the nightmare. A man's money, if not employed, serves only to disturb his rest. Look, then, to the prospect before you. Here is half an acre of land, — more than twenty thousand square feet, — a corner lot, with wonderful capabilities; none of your contracted lots of forty feet by fifty, where in dog-days, you can breathe only through your scuttles. On the contrary, an architect cannot contemplate this lot of land without rapture, for here is room enough for his genius to shame the temple of Solomon. Then the prospect — how commanding! To the east, so near to the Atlantic that Neptune, freighted with the select treasures of the whole earth, can knock at your door with his trident. From the west, the produce of the river of Paradise — the Connecticut — will soon, by the blessings of steam, railways, and canals pass under your windows; and thus, on this spot, Neptune shall marry Ceres, and Pomona from Roxbury, and Flora from Cambridge, shall dance at the wedding.

"Gentlemen of science, men of taste, ye of the literary emporium, — for I perceive many of you present — to you this is holy ground. If the spot on which in times past a hero left only the print of a footstep is now sacred, of what price is the birthplace of one who all the world knows was born in Middle Street, directly opposite to this lot; and who, if his birthplace were not well known, would now be claimed by more than seven cities. To you, then, the value of these premises must be inestimable. For ere long there will arise in full view of the edifice to be erected here, a monument, the wonder and veneration of the world. A column shall spring to the clouds; and on that column will be engraven one word which will convey all that is wise in intellect, useful in science, good in morals, prudent in counsel, and benevolent in principle, — a name of one who, when living, was the patron of the poor, the delight of the cottage, and the admiration of kings; now dead, worth the whole seven wise men of Greece. Need I tell you his name? He fixed the thunder and guided the lightning.

"Men of the North End! Need I appeal to your patriotism, in order to enhance the value of this lot? The earth affords no such scenery as this; there, around that corner, lived James Otis; here, Samuel Adams; there, Joseph Warren; and around that other corner, Josiah Quincy. Here was the birthplace of Freedom; here Liberty was born, and nursed, and grew to manhood. Here man was newly created. Here is the nursery of American Independence — I am too modest — here began the emancipation of the world; a thousand generations hence millions of men will cross the Atlantic just to look at the north end of Boston. Your fathers — what do I say — yourselves, — yes, this moment, I behold several attending this auction who lent a hand to rock the cradle of Independence.

"Men of speculation, — ye who are deaf to everything except the sound of money, — you, I know, will give me both of your ears when I tell you the city of Boston must have a piece of this estate in order to widen Ann Street. Do you hear me, — do you all hear me? I say the city must have a large piece of this land in order to widen Ann Street. What a chance! The city scorns to take a man's land for nothing. If it seizes your property, it is generous beyond the dreams of avarice. The only oppression is, you are in danger of being smothered under a load of wealth. Witness the old lady who lately died of a broken heart when the mayor paid her for a piece of her kitchen-garden. All the faculty agreed that the sight of the treasure, which the mayor incautiously paid her in dazzling dollars, warm from the mint, sped joyfully all the blood of her body into her heart, and rent it with raptures. Therefore, let him who purchases this estate fear his good fortune, and not Peter Rugg. Bid, then, liberally, and do not let the name of Rugg damp your ardor. How much will you give per foot for this estate?"

Thus spoke the auctioneer, and gracefully waved his ivory hammer. From fifty to seventy-five cents per foot were offered in a few moments. The bidding labored from seventy-five to ninety. At length one dollar was offered. The auctioneer seemed satisfied; and looking at his watch, said he would knock off the estate in five minutes, if no one offered more.

There was a deep silence during this short period. While the hammer was suspended, a strange rumbling noise was heard, which arrested the attention of every one. Presently, it was like the sound of many shipwrights driving home the bolts of a seventy-four. As the sound approached nearer, some exclaimed, "The buildings in the new market are falling in promiscuous ruins." Others said, "No, it is an earthquake; we perceive the earth tremble." Others said, "Not so; the sound proceeds from Hanover Street, and approaches nearer;" and this proved true, for presently Peter Rugg was in the midst of us.

"Alas, Jenny," said Peter, "I am ruined; our house has been burned, and here are all our neighbors around the ruins. Heaven grant your mother, Dame Rugg, is safe."

"They don't look like our neighbors," said Jenny; "but sure enough our house is burned, and nothing left but the door-stone and an old cedar post. Do ask where mother is."

In the mean time more than a thousand men had surrounded Rugg and his horse and chair. Yet neither Rugg personally, nor his horse and carriage, attracted more attention than the auctioneer. The confident look and searching eyes of Rugg carried more conviction to every one present that the estate was his, than could any parchment or paper with signature and seal. The impression which the auctioneer had just made on the company was effaced in a moment; and although the latter words of the auctioneer were, "Fear not Peter Rugg," the moment the auctioneer met the eye of Rugg his occupation was gone; his arm fell down to his hips, his late lively hammer hung heavy in his hand, and the auction was forgotten. The black horse, too, gave his evidence. He knew his journey was ended; for he stretched himself into a horse and a half, rested his head over the cedar post, and whinnied thrice, causing his harness to tremble from headstall to crupper.

Rugg then stood upright in his chair, and asked with some authority, "Who has demolished my house in my absence, for I see no signs of conflagration? I demand by what accident this has happened, and wherefore this collection of strange people has assembled before my doorstep. I thought I knew every man in Boston, but you appear to me a new generation of men. Yet I am familiar with many of the countenances here present, and I can call some of you by name; but in truth I do not recollect that before this moment I ever saw any one of you. There, I am certain, is a Winslow, and here a Sargent; there stands a Sewall, and next to him a Dudley. Will none of you speak to me,—or is this all a delusion? I see, indeed, many forms of men, and no want of eyes, but of motion, speech, and hearing, you seem to be destitute. Strange! Will no one inform me who has demolished my house?"

Then spake a voice from the crowd, but whence it came I could not discern: "There is nothing strange here but yourself, Mr. Rugg. Time, which destroys and renews all things, has dilapidated your house, and placed us here. You have suffered many years under an illusion. The tempest which you profanely defied at Menotomy has at length subsided; but you will never see home, for your house and wife and neighbors have all disappeared. Your estate, indeed, remains, but no home. You were cut off from the last age, and you can never be fitted to the present. Your home is gone, and you can never have another home in this world."   [1824–27]

JAMES HALL

James Hall (1793–1868) was born in Philadelphia, where his father was employed as the secretary of the Pennsylvania land office and as a U.S. marshal. Hall was educated at home by his mother, an academic's daughter. At eighteen he studied law in an uncle's law office and then served in the Washington Guards as a soldier in the War of 1812. Hall began to publish essays in various periodicals in 1816, before he bought a half-interest in a newspaper while practicing law in Illinois and Ohio. In 1828 he launched what he hoped would be a series of annual gift books featuring western subjects, titled The Western Souvenir, A Christmas and New Year's Gift for 1829. *At the time Hall's idea seemed a promising novelty, but he had so few contributors that he wrote five tales and nineteen poems in the volume himself, almost half of its 324 pages, and gave up his plan to publish many future issues. Included in* The Western Souvenir (1830) *was his story "The Indian Hater."*

Hall continued to practice law while he wrote tales, as he said, "to develop the character and resources of Illinois" as a fitting subject for American literature. He also composed articles for popular periodicals on Illinois wildlife and wrote biographical sketches of leading citizens such as Daniel Boone and others. In 1832 Hall collected twenty-five tales in Legends of the West, *published by his brother Harrison Hall. Three years later he was ready with another volume of stories,* Tales of the Border (1835), *which featured "The Pioneer," his sequel to "The Indian Hater." In the later tale, the Anglo-American Indian Hater finds that his sister, abducted by the Indians as a child, has grown up to become a contented member of the tribe as a wife and mother. Profoundly moved by his reunion with her, the Indian Hater relinquishes his vendetta: "For the first time in my life, I began to think it possible, that mutual aggression had placed both parties in the wrong, and that either might justly complain of the aggressions of the other." Turning "the other cheek" as a true Christian and devoting himself to a religious life, the Indian Hater wisely concludes:*

> *It is one of the strongest arguments against the principle of revenge, that it is directed by no rule, and bounded by no limit. The aggrieved party is the judge of his own wrong, and the executioner of his own sentence; and the measure of recompense is seldom in proportion to the degree of offence.*

The critic Fred Lewis Pattee labeled Hall "the real pioneer of Western fiction," while noting his undeniable deficiencies as a storyteller with an inflated and clichéd literary style. Yet by publishing a large number of sketches and tales between 1820 and 1832, Hall became a significant early American short story writer. He published his last volume of short fiction, The Wilderness and the War Path, *in 1846. In his later years, his most important work was his coauthorship of* The History of the Indian Tribes of North America, *published in twenty parts from 1836 to 1844 and illustrated with paintings by Charles King and George Catlin.*

The Indian Hater

In the course of a journey, which I lately took through Illinois, I stopped one day at a village for a few hours, and stepped into a store to purchase some trifling article of which I stood in need. Finding a number of persons there, and being not unwilling to while away a few minutes in conversation, I leaned my back against the counter, and addressed myself to a well dressed farmer, who answered my inquiries respecting the country with intelligence and civility.

While thus engaged, my attention was drawn to a person who stood near. He was a man who might have been about fifty years of age. His height did not exceed the ordinary stature, and his person was rather slender than otherwise; but there was something in his air and features, which distinguished him from common men. The expression of his countenance was keen and daring. His forehead was elevated, his cheek-bones high, his lips small and compressed—while long exposure to the climate had tanned his complexion to a deep olive. The same cause seemed to have hardened his skin and muscles, so as to give him the appearance of a living petrefaction. There was over all a settled gloom—a kind of forced composure, which indicated resignation, but not content. In his eye, there was something peculiar, yet it was difficult to tell in what that peculiarity consisted. It was a small grey orb, whose calm, bold, direct glance seemed to vouch, that it had not cowered with shame, or quailed in danger. There was blended in that eye a searching keenness, with a quiet vigilance—a watchful, sagacious, self-possession—so often observable in the physiognomy of those who are in the habit of expecting, meeting, and overcoming peril. His heavy eyebrows had once been black; but time had touched them with his pencil.—He was dressed in a coarse, grey hunting shirt, girded round the waist with a broad, leathern belt, tightly drawn, in which rested a long knife, a weapon common to the western hunter. Upon the whole, there was about this man an expression of grim and gloomy sternness, fixedness of purpose, and intense, but smothered passion, which stamped him as of no common mould: yet there were indications of openness and honesty, which forbade distrust. His was not the unblushing front of hardy guilt, nor the lurking glance of underhanded villainy. A stranger would not have hesitated to confide in his faith or courage, but would have trembled at the idea of provoking his hostility.

I had barely time to make these observations, when several Indians, who had strolled into the village, entered the store. The effect of their presence upon the backwoodsman, whom I have described, was instantaneous and violent. His eyes rolled wildly, as if he had been suddenly stung to madness, gleaming with a strange fierceness; a supernatural lustre, like that which flashes from the eye-balls of the panther, when crouched in a dark covert, and ready to dart upon his prey. His hollow cheek was flushed—the muscles, that but a moment before seemed so rigid, became flexible, and moved convulsively. His hand, sliding quietly to the hilt of his large knife, as if by instinct, grasped it firmly; and it was easy to perceive, that a single breath would be sufficient to blow up the smothered fire. — But, except these indications, he remained motionless as a statue, gazing with a look of intense ferocity at the intruders. The Indians halted when their eyes met his, and exchanged glances of intelligence with each other. Whether it was from instinct, or that they knew the man, or whether that sagacity, which is natural to their race, led them to read danger in his scowling visage, they seemed willing to avoid him, and retired. — The backwoodsman made a motion as if to follow; but several of the persons present, who had watched this silent scene with interest, gently withheld him, and after conversing with him a few moments in an earnest, but under tone, led him off in one direction, while the Indians rode away in another.

Having understood from the farmer, with whom I had been talking, that he was about to return home, and that my route led through his neighbourhood, I cheerfully accepted the offer of his company, and we set out together. Our discourse very naturally fell upon the scene we had witnessed, and I expressed a curiosity to learn something of the history and character of the man, whose image had impressed itself so forcibly upon my mind.

"He is a strange, mysterious looking being," said I, "and I should think he must be better, or worse, than other men."

"Samuel Monson is a very good neighbour," — replied the farmer, cautiously.

"You say that in a tone," rejoined I, "which seems to imply, that in some other respects he may not be so good?"

"Well, as to that — I cannot say, of my own knowledge, that I know any harm of the man."

"And what do other people say of him?"

The farmer hesitated, and then with a caution very common among people of this description, replied —

"People often say more than they can prove. It's not good to be talking of one's neighbours. And Monson, as I said before, is a good neighbour."

"But a bad man, as I understand you?"

"No — far from it: the man's well enough — except —" and here he lowered his tone, and looked cautiously around. "The folks do say he is rather too keen with his rifle."

"How so; — does he shoot his neighbour's cattle?"

"No, sir — Samuel Monson is as much above a mean action, as any other man."

"What, then; — is he quarrelsome?"

"Oh, bless you, no! — There's not a peaceabler man in the settlement; — but he used to be a great Indian fighter in the last war, and he got sort o' haunt to the woods! — and folks do say, he is still rather too keen on the track of a moccasin."

"I do not exactly comprehend you, my dear sir.—The Indians are, I believe, now quiet, and at peace with us."

"Why, yes, they are very peaceable. They never come near us, except now and then a little party comes in to trade."

"They are civil, are they not?"

"Yes, Sir, quite agreeable—bating the killing of a hog once in a while—and that we don't vally—seeing that it is but just natural to the poor savage to shoot any thing that runs in the woods."

"In what way, then, does this Monson interfere with them?"

"I did not say, stranger, that Monson done it. No, no; I wouldn't hurt no man's character; but the fact and truth are about this. Now and then an Indian is missing; and sometimes one is found dead in the range; and folks will have their notions, and their talk, and their suspicions about it—and some talk hard of Monson."

"But why charge it upon him?"

"Why, if you must have it out, stranger, in this country we all know the bore of every man's rifle.—Monson's gun carries just eighty to the pound.—Now the bullet-holes in all these Indians that have been shot, are the same, and we know whose rifle they suit. Besides this, horse tracks have been seen on the trail of the moccasin. They were very particular tracks, and just suited the hoof of a certain horse. Then a certain man was known to be lying out about that same time; and when all these things are put together, it don't take a Philadelphia lawyer to tell who done the deed. Then he sometimes goes off, and is gone for weeks, and people guess that he goes to their own hunting grounds to lie in wait for them. They do say, he can scent a red skin like a hound, and never lets a chance slip."

"But is it possible, that in a civilized country, within the reach of our laws, a wretch is permitted to hunt down his fellow creatures like wild beasts? To murder a defenceless Indian, who comes into our territory in good faith, believing us a Christian people?"

"Why it is not exactly permitted; we don't know for certain who does it, nor is it any particular man's business to inquire more than another. Many of the settlers have had their kin murdered by the savages in early times; and all who have been raised in the back woods, have been taught to fear and dislike them. Then Monson is an honest fellow, works hard, pays his debts, and is always willing to do a good turn, and it seems hard to break neighbourhood with him, for the matter of an Indian or so."

"But the wickedness—the shame—the breach of law and hospitality!"

"Well, so it is.—It is a sin; and sorry would I be to have it on my conscience. But then some think an Indian or two, now and then, will never be missed; others again hate to create an interruption in the settlement; others, who pretend to know the law, say that the general government has the care of the Indians; and that our state laws won't kiver the case; and withal Monson keeps his own counsel, and so among hands he escapes. After all, to come to the plain downright truth, Monson has good cause to hate them; and many a man, that would not dip his own hand in the blood of an Indian, would as soon die as betray Monson; for few of us could lay our hands on our hearts, and say that we would not do the same in his situation."

At this point of the conversation, we were joined by several horsemen, who were pursuing the same road with ourselves; and my companion seeming unwilling to pursue the subject in their hearing, I was unable to learn from him what injury the Indian-hater had received, to provoke his sanguinary career of vengeance. Nor did another opportunity occur; for we soon came to a point where the road diverged; and although my friendly companion, with the usual hospitality of the country, invited me to his house, I was obliged to decline the invitation, and we parted.

I continued my journey into the Northwestern part of Illinois, which was then just beginning to attract the attention of land purchasers, and contained a few scattered settlements. Delighted with this beautiful country, and wishing to explore the lands lying between this tract and the Wabash, I determined, on my return, to strike directly across, through an uninhabited wilderness of about a hundred and fifty miles in extent. I hired an Indian guide, who was highly recommended to me, and set out under his protection.

It is not easy to describe the sensations of a traveller, unaccustomed to such scenery, on first beholding the vast prairies which I was about to explore. Those which I had heretofore seen, were comparatively small. The points of woodland which break into them like so many capes or promontories, and the groves which are interspersed like islands, are, in these lesser prairies, always sufficiently near to be clearly defined to the eye, and to give the scene an interesting variety. We see a plain of several miles in extent, not perfectly level, but gently rolling or undulating, like the swelling of the ocean when nearly calm. The graceful curve of the surface is seldom broken, except when here and there the eye rests upon one of those huge mounds, which are so pleasing to the poet, and so perplexing to the antiquarian. The whole is overspread with grass and flowers, constituting a rich and varied carpet, in which a ground of lively green is ornamented with a profusion of the gaudiest hues. Deep recesses in the edge of the timber, resemble the bays and inlets of a lake; while occasionally a long vista, opening far back into the forest, suffers the eye to roam off, and refresh itself with the calm beauty of a distant perspective.

The traveller, as he rides along these smaller prairies, finds his eye continually attracted to the edges of the forest, and his imagination employed in tracing the beautiful outline, and in finding out resemblances between these wild scenes, and the most highly embellished productions of art. The fairest pleasure grounds, the noblest parks of European princes, where millions have been expended to captivate the fancy with Elysian scenes, are but mimic representations of the beauties which are here spread by nature; for here are clumps, and lawns, and avenues, and groves—the tangled

thicket, and the solitary tree—and all the varieties of scenic attraction—
but on a scale so extensive, as to offer an endless succession of changes to
the eye. There is an air of civilization here, that wins the heart—even here,
where no human residence is seen, where no foot intrudes, and where not
an axe has ever trespassed on the beautiful domain. So different is this feeling from any thing inspired by mountain, or woodland scenery, that the
instant the traveller emerges from the forest into the prairie, he no longer
feels solitary. The consciousness that he is travelling alone, and in a wilderness, escapes him; and he indulges the same pleasing sensations which are
enjoyed by one who, having been lost among the labyrinths of a savage
mountain, suddenly descends into rich and highly cultivated fields. The
gay landscape charms him. He is surrounded by the refreshing sweetness,
and graceful beauty of the rural scene; and recognises at every step some
well remembered spot, enlarged and beautified, and, as it were, retouched
by nature's hand. The clusters of trees so fancifully arranged, seemed to
have been disposed by the hand of taste, and so complete is the delusion,
that it is difficult to dispel the belief, that each avenue leads to a village,
and each grove conceals a splendid mansion.

Widely different was the prospect exhibited in the more northern
prairies. Vast in extent, the distant forest was barely discoverable in the
shapeless outline of blue, faintly impressed on the horizon. Here and there
a solitary tree, torn by the wind, stood alone like a dismantled mast in the
ocean. As I followed my guide through this desolate region, my sensations
were similar to those of the voyager, when his barque is launched into the
ocean. Alone, in a wide waste, with my faithful pilot only, I was dependent
on him for support, guidance, and protection. With little to diversify the
path, and less to please the eye, a sense of dreariness crept over me—a desolation and withering of the spirit, as when the heart, left painfully alone,
finds nothing to love, nothing to admire, nothing from which to reap
instruction or amusement. But these are feelings, which, like the sea sickness of the young mariner, are soon dispelled. I began to find a pleasure in
gazing over this immense, unbroken waste; in watching the horizon in the
vague hope of meeting a traveller, and in following the deer with my eyes,
as they galloped off—their forms growing smaller and smaller, as they
receded, until they faded gradually from the sight.—Sometimes I descried
a dark spot at an immense distance, and pointed it out to my companion
with a joy, like that of the seaman who discovers a distant sail in the speck
which floats on the ocean. When such an object happened to be in the direction of our path, I watched it as it rose and enlarged upon the vision—supposing it one moment to be a man—and at another a buffalo; until, after
it had seemed to approach for hours, I found it to be a tree.

Nor was I entirely destitute of company; for my Pottowattomie guide
proved to be both intelligent and good humoured, and although his stock
of English was but slender, his conversational powers were by no means
contemptible. His topographical knowledge was extensive and accurate,
so that he was able not only to choose the best route, but to point out to

me all the localities. When we halted, he kindled a fire, spread my pallet, and formed a shelter to protect me from the weather. When we came to a stream which was too deep to ford, he framed a raft to cross me over with my baggage, while he mounted my horse and plunged into the water. Throughout the journey, his assiduities were as kind and unremitting, as all his arrangements were sagacious and considerate. A higher motive, than the mere pecuniary reward which he expected for his services, governed his actions; a genuine integrity of purpose, a native politeness and dignity of heart, raised him above the ordinary savage, and rendered him not only a respectable, but an interesting man.

After travelling nearly five days without beholding a human habitation, we arrived at the verge of a settlement on the Wabash. We passed along a rich bottom, covered with large trees, whose thick shade afforded a strong contrast to the scenes we had left behind us, and then ascending a gentle rise, stood on a high bluff bank of the Wabash. A more secluded and beautiful spot has seldom been seen. A small river, with a clear stream, rippling over a rocky bed, meandered round the point on which we stood, and then turning abruptly to the left, was lost among the trees. The opposite shore was low, thickly wooded, and beautifully rich in the variety of mellow hues painted by the autumn sun. The spot we occupied was a slip of table land, a little higher than the surrounding country. It had once been cleared for cultivation, but was now overgrown with hazle-bushes, vines, and briars, while a few tall, leafless trunks, once the proudest oaks of the forest, still adhered tenaciously to the soil. A heap of rubbish, intermingled with logs, half burnt and nearly rotten, showed the remains of what had once been a chimney — but all else had been destroyed by time or fire. One spot only, which had been beaten hard, was covered with a smooth, green sward, unmixed with brush; and here we stood gazing at this desolate spot, and that beautiful stream. It was but a moment, and neither of us had broken silence, when the report of a rifle was heard, and my guide, uttering a dismal yell, fell prostrate. Recovering his senses for an instant, he grasped his gun, partly raised his body, and cast upon me a look of reproach, which I shall never forget; and then, as if satisfied by the concern and alarm of my countenance, and my prompt movement to assist him, he gave me one hand, and pointing with the other towards the woods, exclaimed — "Bad — bad, white man! — Take care!" — and expired.

I was so much surprised and shocked at this catastrophe, that I stood immovable, thoughtless of my own safety, mourning over the brave Indian, who lay weltering in his gore, when I was startled by a slight rustling in the bushes close behind me, and raising my eyes, I beheld Monson! Advancing without the least appearance of shame or fear, until he came to the corpse, and paying not the slightest attention to me, he stood and gazed sternly at the fallen warrior.

"There's another of the cursed crew," said he, at length, "gone to his last account! — He is not the first, nor shall he be the last. — It's an old debt, but it shall be paid to the last drop."

As he spoke, he gnashed his teeth, and his eyes gleamed with the malignity of gratified revenge. Then turning to me, and observing the deep abhorrence with which I shrunk back, he said: —

"May be, stranger, you don't like this sort of business?"

"Wretch—miscreant—murderer! begone! Approach me not," I exclaimed, drawing a large pistol from my belt; but, before I was aware, the backwoodsman, with a sudden spring, caught my arm, and wrested the weapon from me; and then remaining perfectly calm, while I was ready to burst with rage, he said: —

"This is a poor shooting-iron for a man to have about him—it might do for young men to 'tote' in a settlement, but it is of no use in the woods—no more than a shot-gun."

"Scoundrel!" said I, "you shall repent your violence——"

"Young man!" interrupted he, very coolly, "I am no scoundrel;—you mistake—you do not know me."

"Murderer!" repeated I, "for such I know you to be.—Think not this bloody deed shall go unpunished. My life is in your power, but I dread not your vengeance!"

While I was thus exhausting myself in the expression of my rage and horror, the more politic Monson, having possessed himself of the Indian's gun, dropped it, together with my unlucky pistol, on the ground, and placing one foot on them, he proceeded deliberately to reload his rifle.

"Don't be alarmed, young man," said he, in reply to my last remark, "I shall not hurt a hair of your head.—You cannot provoke me to it.—I never harmed a Christian man to my knowledge."

"See here!" he continued, as he finished loading his piece.—Then pointing to the ruins of the cabin, he proceeded in a hurried tone: —

"This was my home.—Here I built a house with my own labour.— With the sweat of my brow I opened this clearing.—Here I lived with my wife, my children, and my mother.—We worked hard—lived well—and were happy. One night—it was in the fall—I had gathered my corn, the labour of the year was done, and I was sitting by the fire among the family, with the prospect of plenty and comfort around me,—when I heard a yell! I never was a coward, but I knew that sound too well; and when I looked round upon the women and the helpless babes that depended on me for protection, a cold chill ran over me, and my heart seemed to die. I ran to the door, and beheld my stacks in a blaze. I caught up my gun—but in a moment, a gang of yelling savages came pouring in at my door like so many howling wolves. I fired, and one of them fell.—I caught up an axe, and rushed at them with such fury that I cleared the cabin. The monsters then set fire to the roof, and we saw the flames spreading around us. What could I do? Here was my poor old mother, and my wife, and my little children, unable to fight or fly.—I burst the door, and rushed madly out; but they pushed me back. The blazing timbers came falling among us—my wife hung on my neck, and called on me to save her children—our pious mother prayed—while the savage wretches roared, and laughed, and mocked us. I grasped my axe, and rushed out again. I killed several of them;—but they overpowered me, bound me, and led me to witness the ruin of all that was dear to me. All—all perished here in the flames before my eyes.—They perished in lingering torments. I saw their agonies—I heard their cries—they called on my name.—Oh, heaven! can I ever forget it?"

Here he stopped, overcome with his emotions, and looked wildly around.—Tears came to his relief, but the man of sorrows brushed them away, and continued:—

"They carried me off a prisoner. I was badly wounded, and so heart broken, that for three days I was helpless as a child. Then a desire of revenge grew up in my heart, and I got strong. I gnawed the ropes they had bound me with, and escaped from them in the night. In the Indian war that followed, I joined every expedition—I was foremost in every fight;—but I could not quench my thirst for the blood of those monsters. I swore never to forgive them; and when peace came, I continued to make war. I made it a rule to kill every red skin that came in my way; and so long as my limbs have strength, I shall continue to slay the savage.

"Go!" he continued, "pursue your own way, and leave me to mine. If you have a parent that prays for you, a wife and children that love you, they will receive you with joy, and you will be happy. I am alone;—there is none to mourn with me, no one to rejoice at my coming. When all that you cherish is torn from you in one moment, condemn me, if you can: but not till then. Go!—That path will lead you to a house;—there you will get a guide."   [1830]

CATHARINE MARIA SEDGWICK

Catharine Maria Sedgwick (1789–1867), once one of America's most popular authors along with her contemporaries Washington Irving and James Fenimore Cooper, was born in Stockbridge, Massachusetts, where she lived most of her life. Her mother was descended from a prosperous family in the Connecticut River valley. Her father graduated from Yale College, studied law, was a member of the Continental Congress, Speaker of the House of Representatives, and eventually chief justice of the Massachusetts Supreme Court. Because their mother was an invalid, Sedgwick and her six brothers and sisters were raised by an African American nurse, Elizabeth Freeman. Both parents died when Sedgwick was young, and an older brother encouraged her to attempt a career as a writer. Sedgwick's conversion from Calvinism to Unitarianism in 1821 led her to write a pamphlet against religious intolerance, which developed into her first novel, A New-England Tale; or, Sketches of New-England Character and Manners, *published anonymously in 1822. In her preface Sedgwick explained that she had made a "humble effort to add something to the scanty stock of native American literature." This book became a best-seller, and she followed it in 1824 with her second novel,* Redwood, *another popular success.* Hope Leslie *(1827), her third, dramatized a conflict between English colonists and Native Americans. Very widely read, it made her the most famous woman writer in America.*

Sedgwick continued to produce a series of best-selling books for nearly a quarter century, including Married or Single? *(1857), a novel arguing that women should refuse to marry if they believed they would lose their self-respect. The eminent English novelist Maria Edgeworth credited her with creating fictional characters that "were to America what [Sir Walter] Scott's characters are to Scotland, valuable as original pictures." Sedgwick's fame as a novelist guaranteed her access to periodicals as a story writer, and she published short fiction voluminously from the 1820s to the 1850s, including a sketch in the first volume of the first American gift book,* The Atlantic Souvenir and New Year's Offering for 1826. *Her story collections include* Tales and Sketches *(1835),* Stories for Young Persons *(1841), and* Tales of City Life *(1850). In "The Literati of New York City" (Godey's Lady's Book, 1840), Edgar Allan Poe acknowledged her reputation, saying that she "has marked talent but no genius."*

The critic Judith Fetterly has characterized Sedgwick's authorial voice as "strong, clear, confident, unconflicted," understanding that early praise for Sedgwick's writing established "the right of women to the territory of American fiction." Yet in "Cacoethes Scribendi," Sedgwick humorously suggests her own ambivalence about the hordes of "scribbling women" who swelled the tide of sketches and articles flooding the literary marketplace in the 1820s and 1830s. Her title can be translated as "writer's itch," a term found in the classic Roman author Juvenal's seventh Satire. *Sedgwick's tale was first published in*

The Atlantic Souvenir *for 1830 and collected in* Tales and Sketches. *When it was included in* Stories of American Life, *the editor, Mary Russell Mitford, commented, "This story is a curious illustration of the universality of the fashion of the day. Many editors of our splendid English Annuals could, I suspect, bear testimony to a similar passion for literary fame on this side of the water."*

Cacoethes Scribendi

> Glory and gain the industrious tribe provoke.
> – POPE

The little secluded and quiet village of H. lies at no great distance from our "literary emporium."[1] It was never remarked or remarkable for any thing, save one mournful pre-eminence, to those who sojourned within its borders — it was duller, even, than common villages. The young men of the better class all emigrated. The most daring spirits adventured on the sea. Some went to Boston; some to the south; and some to the west; and left a community of women who lived like nuns, with the advantage of more liberty and fresh air, but without the consolation and excitement of a religious vow. Literally, there was not a single young gentleman in the village — nothing in manly shape to which these desperate circumstances could give the form and quality, and use of a beau. Some dashing city blades, who once strayed accidentally to this sequestered spot, averred that the girls stared at them as if, like Miranda, they would have exclaimed —

> What is't? a spirit?
> Lord, how it looks about! Believe me, sir,
> It carries a brave form: — But 'tis a spirit.[2]

A peculiar fatality hung over this devoted place. If death seized on either head of a family, he was sure to take the husband; every woman in H. was a widow or maiden: and it is a sad fact, that when the holiest office of the church was celebrated, they were compelled to borrow deacons from an adjacent village. But, incredible as it may seem, there was no great diminution of happiness in consequence of the absence of the nobler sex. Mothers were occupied with their children and housewifery, and the young ladies read their books with as much interest as if they had lovers to discuss them with, and worked their frills and capes as diligently, and wore them as complacently, as if they were to be seen by manly eyes. Never were there pleasanter gatherings or parties (for that was the word even in their

---

[1]Boston. Sedgwick is describing a fictitious Berkshire village.
[2]From William Shakespeare's *The Tempest* (1.2.410–12); Miranda speaks these lines when she first encounters the spirit Ariel.

nomenclature) than those of the young girls of H. There was no mincing—
no affectation—no hope of passing for what they were not—no envy of the
pretty and fortunate—no insolent triumph over the plain, and demure,
and neglected—but all was good-will and good-humour. They were a
pretty circle of girls—a garland of bright fresh flowers. Never were there
more sparkling glances—never sweeter smiles—nor more of them. Their
present was all health and cheerfulness; and their future, not the gloomy
perspective of dreary singleness, for somewhere in the passage of life they
were sure to be mated. Most of the young men who had abandoned their
native soil, as soon as they found themselves *getting along,* loyally returned
to lay their fortunes at the feet of the companions of their childhood.

The girls made occasional visits to Boston, and occasional journeys to
various parts of the country, for they were all enterprising and independent; and had the characteristic New England avidity for seizing a "privilege"; and in these various ways, to borrow a phrase of their good
grandames, "a door was opened for them," and in due time they fulfilled
the destiny of women.

We spoke strictly, and à la lettre, when we said that in the village of H.
there was not a single *beau*. But on the outskirts of the town, at a pleasant
farm, embracing hill and valley, upland and meadow land—in a neat house,
looking to the south, with true economy of sunshine and comfort, and over-
looking the prettiest winding stream that ever sent up its sparkling beauty
to the eye; and flanked on the north by a rich maple grove, beautiful in
spring and summer, and glorious in autumn, and the kindest defence in
winter;—on this farm, and in this house dwelt a youth, to fame unknown;
but known and loved by every inhabitant of H., old and young, grave and
gay, lively and severe. Ralph Hepburn was one of nature's favourites. He
had a figure that would have adorned courts and cities; and a face that
adorned human nature, for it was full of good humour, kind-heartedness,
spirit and intelligence; and, driving the plough, or wielding the scythe, his
cheek flushed with manly and profitable exercise, he looked as if he had
been moulded in a poet's fancy—as farmers look in Georgics[3] and Pas-
torals. His gifts were by no means all external. He wrote verses in every
album in the village, and very pretty album verses they were, and numerous too—for the number of albums was equivalent to the whole female
population. He was admirable at pencil sketches; and once, with a little
paint, the refuse of a house-painting, he achieved an admirable portrait of
his grandmother and her cat. There was, to be sure, a striking likeness
between the two figures; but he was limited to the same colours for both;
and besides, it was not out of nature, for the old lady and her cat had
purred together in the chimney corner, till their physiognomies bore an
obvious resemblance to each other. Ralph had a talent for music too. His

---

[3]A poem on the subject of rural life and agriculture; *Georgics* also refers to a
poem of this type by Virgil.

voice was the sweetest of all the Sunday choir; and one would have fancied, from the bright eyes that were turned on him, from the long line and double lines of treble and counter singers, that Ralph Hepburn was a notebook; or that the girls listened with their eyes as well as their ears. Ralph did not restrict himself to psalmody. He had an ear so exquisitely susceptible to the "touches of sweet harmony," that he discovered, by the stroke of his axe, the musical capacities of certain species of wood, and he made himself a violin of chesnut, and drew strains from it, that if they could not create a soul under the ribs of death, could make the prettiest feet and the lightest heart dance; an achievement far more to Ralph's taste than the aforesaid miracle. In short, it seemed as if nature, in her love of compensation, had showered on Ralph all the gifts that are usually diffused through a community of beaux. Yet Ralph was no prodigy; none of his talents were in excess, but all in moderate degree. No genius was ever so good humoured, so useful, so practical; and though, in his small and modest way, a Crichton,[4] he was not, like most universal geniuses, good for nothing for any particular office in life. His farm was not a pattern farm — a prize farm, for an agricultural society; but in wonderful order, considering his miscellaneous pursuits. He was the delight of his grandfather, for his sagacity in hunting bees — the old man's favourite — in truth his only pursuit. He was so skilled in woodcraft, that the report of his gun was as certain a signal of death, as the tolling of a church bell. The fish always caught at his bait. He manufactured half his farming utensils; improved upon old inventions, and struck out some new ones; tamed partridges — the most untameable of all the feathered tribe; domesticated squirrels; rivalled Scheherazade herself in telling stories, strange and long — the latter quality being essential at a country fireside; and, in short, Ralph made a perpetual holiday of a life of labour.

Every girl in the village-street knew when Ralph's waggon or sleigh traversed it; indeed, there was scarcely a house to which the horses did not, as if by instinct, turn up, while their master greeted its fair tenants. This state of affairs had continued for two winters and two summers, since Ralph came to his majority, and by the death of his father, to the sole proprietorship of the "Hepburn farm," — the name his patrimonial acres had obtained from the singular circumstance, (in our *moving* country,) of their having remained in the same family for four generations. Never was the matrimonial destiny of a young lord, or heir just come to his estate, more thoroughly canvassed than young Hepburn's, by mothers, aunts, daughters, and nieces. But Ralph, perhaps from sheer good nature, seemed reluctant to give to one the heart, that diffused rays of sunshine through the whole village.

With all decent people, he eschewed the doctrines of a certain erratic female lecturer, on the odious monopoly of marriage; yet Ralph, like a

---

[4]A reference to James Crichton (1560–1582), a Scottish scholar, linguist, and adventurer, who was perceived to be a model of the cultured Scottish gentleman.

tender-hearted judge, hesitated to place on a single brow the crown matrimonial, which so many deserved, and which, though Ralph was far enough from a coxcomb, he could not but see so many coveted.

Whether our hero perceived that his mind was becoming elated or distracted with this general favour, or that he observed a dawning of rivalry among the fair competitors, or whatever was the cause, the fact was, that he by degrees circumscribed his visits, and finally concentrated them in the family of his aunt Courland.

Mrs. Courland was a widow, and Ralph was the kindest of nephews to her, and the kindest of cousins to her children. To their mother, he seemed their guardian angel. That the five lawless, darling little urchins did not drown themselves when they were swimming, nor shoot themselves when they were shooting, was, in her eyes, Ralph's merit; and then, "he was so attentive to Alice, her only daughter—a brother could not be kinder." But who would not be kind to Alice?—She was a sweet girl of seventeen, not beautiful—not handsome, perhaps—but pretty enough—with soft hazel eyes; a profusion of light brown hair, always in the neatest trim; and a mouth, that could not but be lovely and loveable, for all kind and tender affections were playing about it. Though Alice was the only daughter of a doting mother, the only sister of five loving boys, the only niece of three single, fond aunts; and last and greatest, the only cousin of our only beau, Ralph Hepburn—no girl of seventeen was ever more disinterested, unassuming, unostentatious, and unspoiled. Ralph and Alice had always lived on terms of cousinly affection; an affection of a neutral tint, that they never thought of being shaded into the deep dye of a more tender passion. Ralph rendered her all cousinly offices. If he had twenty damsels to escort, not an uncommon case, he never forgot Alice. When he returned from any little excursion, he always brought some graceful offering to Alice.

He had lately paid a visit to Boston. It was at the season of the periodical inundation of annuals. He brought two of the prettiest to Alice. Ah! little did she think, they were to prove Pandora's box to her. Poor simple girl! she sat down to read them, as if an annual were meant to be read; and she was honestly interested and charmed. Her mother observed her delight. "What have you there, Alice?" she asked. "Oh, the prettiest story, mamma!—two such tried, faithful lovers, and married at last! It ends beautifully: I hate love stories that don't end in marriage!"

"And so do I, Alice," exclaimed Ralph, who entered at the moment; and, for the first time, Alice felt her cheeks tingle at his approach. He had brought a basket, containing a choice plant he had obtained for her; and she laid down the annual, and went with him to the garden, to see it set by his own hand.

Mrs. Courland seized upon the annual with avidity. She had imbibed a literary taste at Boston; where the best and happiest years of her life were passed. She had some literary ambition too. She read the North American Review from beginning to end; and she fancied no conversation could be sensible or improving, that was not about books. But she had been effectually prevented, by the necessities of a narrow income, and by the unceasing wants of five teasing boys, from indulging her literary inclinations; for Mrs. Courland, like all New England women, had been taught to consider domestic duties as the first temporal duties of her sex. She had recently seen some of the native productions with which the press is daily teeming; and which certainly have a tendency to dispel our early illusions about the craft of authorship. She had even felt some obscure intimations, within her secret soul, that she might herself become an author. The annual was destined to fix her fate. She opened it — the publisher had written the names of the authors of the anonymous pieces against their productions. Among them she found some of the familiar friends of her childhood and youth.

If, by a sudden gift of second sight, she had seen them enthroned as kings and queens, she would not have been more astonished. She turned to their pieces, and read them, as perchance no one else did, from beginning to end — faithfully. Not a sentence — a sentence! not a word was skipped. She paused to consider commas, colons, and dashes. All the art and magic of authorship were made level to her comprehension, and when she closed the book, she *felt a call* to become an author, and before she retired to bed she obeyed the call, as if it had been, in truth, a divinity stirring within her. In the morning she presented an article to *her* public, consisting of her own family and a few select friends. All applauded, and every voice, save one, was unanimous for publication — that one was Alice. She was a modest, prudent girl; she feared failure, and feared notoriety still more. Her mother laughed at her childish scruples. The piece was sent off, and in due time graced the pages of an annual. Mrs. Courland's fate was now decided. She had, to use her own phrase, started in the career of letters, and she was no Atalanta to be seduced from her straight onward way. She was a social, sympathetic, good-hearted creature too, and she could not bear to go forth in the golden field to reap alone.

She was, besides, a prudent woman, as most of her countrywomen are, and the little pecuniary equivalent for this delightful exercise of talent was not overlooked. Mrs. Courland, as we have somewhere said, had three single sisters — worthy women they were — but nobody ever dreamed of their taking to authorship. She, however, held them all in sisterly estimation. Their talents were magnified as the talents of persons who live in a circumscribed sphere are apt to be, particularly if seen through the dilating medium of affection.

Miss Anne, the eldest, was fond of flowers, a successful cultivator, and a diligent student of the science of botany. All this taste and knowledge, Mrs. Courland thought, might be turned to excellent account; and she persuaded Miss Anne to write a little book entitled "Familiar Dialogues on Botany." The second sister, Miss Ruth, had a turn for education, ("bachelor's wives and maid's children are always well taught,") and Miss Ruth undertook a popular treatise on that subject. Miss Sally, the youngest, was the saint of the family, and she doubted about the propriety of a literary occupation, till her scruples were overcome by the fortunate suggestion that her coup d'essai should be a Saturday night book, entitled "Solemn Hours,"—and solemn hours they were to their unhappy readers. Mrs. Courland next besieged her old mother. "You know, mamma," she said, "you have such a precious fund of anecdotes of the revolution and the French war, and you talk just like the 'Annals of the Parish,' and I am certain you can write a book fully as good."

"My child, you are distracted! I write a dreadfully poor hand, and I never learned to spell—no girls did in my time."

"Spell! that is not of the least consequence—the printers correct the spelling."

But the honest old lady would not be tempted on the crusade, and her daughter consoled herself with the reflection, that if she would not write, she was an admirable subject to be written about, and her diligent fingers worked off three distinct stories in which the old lady figured.

Mrs. Courland's ambition, of course, embraced within its widening circle her favourite nephew, Ralph. She had always thought him a genius, and genius in her estimation was the philosopher's stone. In his youth she had laboured to persuade his father to send him to Cambridge, but the old man uniformly replied that Ralph "was a smart lad on the farm, and steady, and by that he knew he was no genius." As Ralph's character was developed, and talent after talent broke forth, his aunt renewed her lamentations over his ignoble destiny. That Ralph was useful, good, and happy—the most difficult and rare results achieved in life—was nothing, so long as he was but a farmer in H. Once she did half persuade him to turn painter, but his good sense and filial duty triumphed over her eloquence, and suppressed the hankerings after distinction that are innate in every human breast, from the little ragged chimneysweep that hopes to be a *boss*, to the political aspirant, whose bright goal is the presidential chair.

Now Mrs. Courland fancied Ralph might climb the steep of fame without quitting his farm; occasional authorship was compatible with his vocation. But, alas! she could not persuade Ralph to pluck the laurels that she saw ready grown to his hand. She was not offended, for she was the best-natured woman in the world, but she heartily pitied him, and seldom mentioned his name without repeating that stanza of Gray's, inspired for the consolation of hopeless obscurity:

"Full many a gem of purest ray serene," &c.

Poor Alice's sorrows we have reserved to the last, for they were the heaviest. "Alice," her mother said, "was gifted; she was well educated, well informed; she was every thing necessary to be an author." But Alice resisted; and, though the gentlest and most complying of all good daughters, she would have resisted to the death—she would as soon have stood in a pillory as have appeared in print. Her mother, Mrs. Courland, was not an obstinate woman, and gave up in despair. But still our poor heroine was destined to be the victim of this *cacoethes scribendi;* for Mrs. Courland divided the world into two classes, or rather parts—authors and subjects for authors; the one active, and the other passive. At first blush one would have thought the village of H. rather a barren field for such a reaper as Mrs. Courland, but her zeal and indefatigableness worked wonders. She converted the stern scholastic divine of H. into as much of a La Roche[5] as she could describe; a tall wrinkled bony old woman, who reminded her of Meg Merrilies,[6] sat for a witch; the schoolmaster for an Ichabod Crane;[7] a poor half-witted boy was made to utter as much pathos, and sentiment, and wit, as she could put into his lips; and a crazy vagrant was a God-send to her. Then every "wide spreading elm," "blasted pine," or "gnarled oak," flourished on her pages. The village church and school-house stood there according to their actual dimensions. One old *pilgrim* house was as prolific as haunted tower or ruined abbey. It was surveyed outside, ransacked inside, and again made habitable for the reimbodied spirits of its founders.

The most kind-hearted of women, Mrs. Courland's interests came to be so at variance with the prosperity of the little community of H., that a sudden calamity, a death, a funeral, were fortunate events to her. To do her justice she felt them in a twofold capacity. She wept as a woman, and exulted as an author. The days of the calamities of authors have passed by. We have all wept over Otway,[8] and shivered at the thought of Tasso.[9] But times are changed. The lean sheaf is devouring the full one. A new class of sufferers has arisen, and there is nothing more touching in all the memoirs Mr. D'Israeli[10] has collected, than the trials of poor Alice, tragi-comic though they were. Mrs. Courland's new passion ran most naturally in the worn channel of maternal affection. Her boys were too purely boys for her art—but Alice, her sweet Alice, was pre-eminently lovely in the new light in which she now placed every object. Not an incident in her life but was inscribed on her mother's memory, and thence transferred to her pages, by way of precept, or example, or pathetic or ludicrous circumstance. She regretted now, for the first time, that Alice had no lover whom she might introduce among her dramatis personæ. Once her thoughts did glance on Ralph, but she had not quite merged the woman in the author; she knew instinctively that Alice would be particularly offended at being thus paired

---

[5]Sophie von La Roche (1731–1807), a German author who introduced passion and a "confessional" aspect to the German novel.

[6]A gypsy character in Sir Walter Scott's novel *Guy Mannering* (1815), and the title character of a poem (1838) by John Keats.

[7]The homely schoolmaster who is the protagonist of Washington Irving's story "The Legend of Sleepy Hollow."

[8]Thomas Otway (1652–1685), an English dramatist.

[9]Torquato Tasso (1544–1595), an Italian poet.

[10]Benjamin Disraeli (1804–1881), a British politician and novelist who was prime minister in 1868 and from 1874 to 1880.

with Ralph. But Alice's *public life* was not limited to her mother's productions. She was the darling niece of her three aunts. She had studied botany with the eldest, and Miss Anne had recorded in her private diary all her favourite's clever remarks during their progress in the science. This diary was now a mine of gold to her, and faithfully worked up for a circulating medium. But, most trying of all to poor Alice, was the attitude in which she appeared in her aunt Sally's "solemn hours." Every aspiration of piety to which her young lips had given utterance was there *printed*. She felt as if she were condemned to say her prayers in the market place. Every act of kindness, every deed of charity, she had ever performed, were produced to the public. Alice would have been consoled if she had known how small that public was; but, as it was, she felt like a modest country girl when she first enters an apartment hung on every side with mirrors, when, shrinking from observation, she sees in every direction her image multiplied and often distorted; for, notwithstanding Alice's dutiful respect for her good aunts, and her consciousness of their affectionate intentions, she could not but perceive that they were unskilled painters. She grew afraid to speak or to act, and from being the most artless, frank, and, at home, social little creature in the world, she became as silent and as stiff as a statue. And, in the circle of her young associates, her natural gaiety was constantly checked by their winks and smiles, and broader allusions to her multiplied portraits; for they had instantly recognized them through the thin veil of feigned names of persons and places. They called her a blue stocking too; for they had the vulgar notion that every body must be tinged that lived under the same roof with an author. Our poor victim was afraid to speak of a book—worse than that, she was afraid to touch one, and the last Waverley novel[11] actually lay in the house a month before she opened it. She avoided wearing even a blue ribbon, as fearfully as a forsaken damsel shuns the colour of green.

It was during the height of this literary fever in the Courland family, that Ralph Hepburn, as has been mentioned, concentrated all his visiting there. He was of a compassionate disposition, and he knew Alice was, unless relieved by him, in solitary possession of their once social parlour, whilst her mother and aunts were driving their quills in their several apartments.

Oh! what a changed place was that parlour! Not the tower of Babel, after the builders had forsaken it, exhibited a sadder reverse; not a Lancasterian school,[12] when the boys have left it, a more striking contrast. Mrs. Courland and her sisters were all "talking women," and too generous to encroach

---

[11]One in a series of more than two dozen historical novels by Sir Walter Scott written between 1814 and 1832. Including titles such as *Rob Roy* and *Ivanhoe*, the novels were published together in a series called *Waverley* (1829–33).

[12]A school using the Lancasterian or "monitorial" method of teaching, formulated by English educator Joseph Lancaster, in which advanced students teach the weaker ones. This system was implemented throughout much of Europe in the nineteenth century.

on one another's rights and happiness. They had acquired the power to hear and speak simultaneously. Their parlour was the general gathering place, a sort of village exchange, where all the innocent gossips, old and young, met together. "There are tongues in trees," and surely there seemed to be tongues in the very walls of that vocal parlour. Every thing there had a social aspect. There was something agreeable and conversable in the litter of netting and knitting work, of sewing implements, and all the signs and shows of happy female occupation.

Now, all was as orderly as a town drawing-room in company hours. Not a sound was heard there save Ralph's and Alice's voices, mingling in soft and suppressed murmurs, as if afraid of breaking the chain of their aunt's ideas, or perchance, of too rudely jarring a tenderer chain. One evening, after tea, Mrs. Courland remained with her daughter, instead of retiring, as usual, to her writing desk. "Alice, my dear," said the good mother, "I have noticed for a few days past that you look out of spirits. You will listen to nothing I say on that subject; but if you would try it, my dear, if you would only try it, you would find there is nothing so tranquillizing as the occupation of writing."

"I shall never try it, mamma."

"You are afraid of being called a blue stocking.—Ah! Ralph, how are you?"—Ralph entered at this moment.—"Ralph, tell me honestly, do you not think it a weakness in Alice to be afraid of blue stockings?"

"It would be a pity, aunt, to put blue stockings on such pretty feet as Alice's."

Alice blushed and smiled, and her mother said—"Nonsense, Ralph; you should bear in mind the celebrated saying of the Edinburgh wit—'no matter how blue the stockings are, if the petticoats are long enough to hide them.'"

"Hide Alice's feet! Oh aunt, worse and worse!"

"Better hide her feet, Ralph, than her talents—that is a sin for which both she and you will have to answer. Oh! you and Alice need not exchange such significant glances! You are doing yourselves and the public injustice, and you have no idea how easy writing is."

"Easy writing, but hard reading, aunt."

"That's false modesty, Ralph. If I had but your opportunities to collect materials"—Mrs. Courland did not know that in literature, as in some species of manufacture, the most exquisite productions are wrought from the smallest quantity of raw material—"There's your journey to New York, Ralph," she continued, "you might have made three capital articles out of that. The revolutionary officer would have worked up for the 'Legendary;' the mysterious lady for the 'Token;' and the man in black for the 'Remember Me;'—all founded on fact, all romantic and pathetic."

"But mamma," said Alice, expressing in words what Ralph's arch smile expressed almost as plainly, "you know the officer drank too much; and the mysterious lady turned out to be a runaway milliner; and the man in black—oh! what a theme for a pathetic story!—the man in black was a widower, on his way to Newhaven, where he was to select his third wife from three *recommended* candidates."

"Pshaw! Alice: do you suppose it is necessary to tell things precisely as they are?"

"Alice is wrong, aunt, and you are right; and if she will open her writing desk for me, I will sit down this moment, and write a story—a true story—true from beginning to end; and if it moves you, my dear aunt, if it meets with your approbation, my destiny is decided."

Mrs. Courland was delighted; she had slain the giant, and she saw fame and fortune smiling on her favourite. She arranged the desk for him herself; she prepared a folio sheet of paper, folded the ominous margins, and was so absorbed in her bright visions, that she did not hear a little by-talk between Ralph and Alice, nor see the tell-tale flush on their cheeks, nor notice the perturbation with which Alice walked first to one window and then to another, and, finally, settled herself to that best of all sedatives—hemming a handkerchief. Ralph chewed off the end of his quill, mended his pen twice, though his aunt assured him "printers did not mind the penmanship," and had achieved a single line when Mrs. Courland's vigilant eye was averted by the entrance of her servant girl, who put a packet into her hands. She looked at the direction, cut the string, broke the seals, and took out a periodical fresh from the publisher. She opened at the first article—a strangely-mingled current of maternal pride and literary triumph rushed through her heart and brightened her face. She whispered to the servant a summons to all her sisters to the parlour, and an intimation, sufficiently intelligible to them, of her joyful reason for interrupting them.

Our readers will sympathize with her, and with Alice too, when we disclose to them the secret of her joy. The article in question was a clever composition written by our devoted Alice when she was at school. One of her fond aunts had preserved it; and aunts and mother had combined in the pious fraud of giving it to the public, unknown to Alice. They were perfectly aware of her determination never to be an author. But they fancied it was the mere timidity of an unfledged bird; and that when, by their innocent artifice, she found that her pinions could soar in a literary atmosphere, she would realize the sweet fluttering sensations they had experienced at their first flight. The good souls all hurried to the parlour, eager to witness the coup de théatre. Miss Sally's pen stood emblematically erect in her turban; Miss Ruth, in her haste, had overset her inkstand, and the drops were trickling down her white dressing, or, as she now called it, writing gown; and Miss Anne had a wild flower in her hand, as she hoped, of an undescribed species, which, in her joyful agitation, she most unluckily picked to pieces. All bit their lips to keep impatient congratulation from bursting forth. Ralph was so intent on his writing, and Alice on her hemming, that neither noticed the irruption; and Mrs. Courland was obliged twice to speak to her daughter before she could draw her attention.

"Alice, look here — Alice, my dear."

"What is it, mamma? something new of yours?"

"No; guess again, Alice."

"Of one of my aunts, of course?"

"Neither, dear, neither. Come and look for yourself, and see if you can then tell whose it is."

Alice dutifully laid aside her work, approached and took the book. The moment her eye glanced on the fatal page, all her apathy vanished — deep crimson overspread her cheeks, brow, and neck. She burst into tears of irrepressible vexation, and threw the book into the blazing fire.

The gentle Alice! Never had she been guilty of such an ebullition of temper. Her poor dismayed aunts retreated; her mother looked at her in mute astonishment; and Ralph, struck with her emotion, started from the desk, and would have asked an explanation, but Alice exclaimed — "Don't say any thing about it, mamma — I cannot bear it now."

Mrs. Courland knew instinctively that Ralph would sympathize entirely with Alice, and quite willing to avoid an éclaircissement,[13] she said — "Some other time, Ralph, I'll tell you the whole. Show me now what you have written. How have you begun?"

Ralph handed her the paper with a novice's trembling hand.

"Oh! how very little! and so scratched and interlined! but never mind — 'ce n'est que le premier pas qui coute.' "[14]

While making these general observations, the good mother was getting out and fixing her spectacles, and Alice and Ralph had retreated behind her. Alice rested her head on his shoulder, and Ralph's lips were not far from her ear. Whether he was soothing her ruffled spirit, or what he was doing, is not recorded. Mrs. Courland read and re-read the sentence. She dropped a tear on it. She forgot her literary aspirations for Ralph and Alice — forgot she was herself an author — forgot every thing but the mother; and rising, embraced them both as her dear children, and expressed, in her raised and moistened eye, the consent to their union, which Ralph had dutifully and prettily asked in that short and true story of his love for his sweet cousin Alice.

In due time the village of H. was animated with the celebration of Alice's nuptials: and when her mother and aunts saw her the happy mistress of the Hepburn farm, and the happiest of wives, they relinquished, without a sigh, the hope of ever seeing her an AUTHOR.   [1830]

---

[13]A clarification.

[14]"The first step is the hardest."

AUGUSTUS BALDWIN LONGSTREET

Augustus Baldwin Longstreet (1790–1870), author of the earliest humorous sketches that set the pattern for the realistic local-color stories of the American South, was born in Augusta, Georgia, when it was a boisterous frontier town featuring tobacco and cotton warehouses, stagecoaches, and racetracks. As a young teenager, he disliked formal schooling, boasting that his ambition was to "outrun, outjump, outshoot, throw down any man in the district." After becoming friends with a roomer in his mother's boardinghouse who read aloud from books and newspapers, Longstreet wrote that he found it "first irksome, then tolerable, then delightful. Thus I acquired my first taste for reading." He graduated from Yale College in 1813 and went on to study law in Litchfield, Connecticut, before returning to Georgia, where, in the 1820s, he served as a Superior Court judge. In 1833 he bought a newspaper, which he renamed the States Rights Sentinel, *and began to write and publish nonpolitical local-color stories in it as well as in other Georgia papers. "The Dance," one of his earliest sketches, appeared in the* Milledgeville Southern Recorder *on October 30, 1833. Two years later Longstreet collected eighteen of his stories in the first edition of* Georgia Scenes, *published in Augusta at his own* States Rights Sentinel *office.*

The title page of the book read "Georgia Scenes, Characters, Incidents, &c. in the First Half Century of the Republic by a Native Georgian." Longstreet remarked later that he wrote the stories to fill "a chasm in history which has always been overlooked—the manners, customs, amusements, wit, dialect, as they appear in all grades of society," especially in the "common walks of life . . . their remarks upon the dresses of their characters, the horses, their mode of driving, and their blunders; upon the pugilistic combatants, their appearance, their muscle . . . their own private games, quarrels, and fights." In sketches such as "The Horse-Swap," "The Fight," "The Shooting-Match," and "The Character of a Native Georgian," he used dialect to suggest the social classes of his characters. The speech of upper-class educated southerners was characterized by standard grammar, whereas black speech was dialectical in syntax and spelling, and lower-class whites' speech was somewhere in between.

Despite its liveliness, Longstreet's humor in Georgia Scenes *often escapes modern readers, but in his own time the book went through multiple printings and editions. Reviewing it, Edgar Allan Poe praised the anonymous author for his "penetrating understanding of character in general and of Southern character in particular." Poe admitted that "seldom—perhaps never in our lives—have we laughed so immoderately over any book as over the one now before us." Three years after publishing* Georgia Scenes, *Longstreet discontinued writing humorous short fiction when he became a Methodist minister and began another career as a college president. At the end of his life, he told the Reverend J. T. Wightman that he "intended to redeem the humor" of his famous book by writing another one "of a religious character, but the [Civil] War kept his pen at rest."*

The Dance

Some years ago I was called by business to one of the frontier counties, then but recently settled. It became necessary for me, while there, to enlist the services of Thomas Gibson, Esq., one of the magistrates of the county, who resided about a mile and a half from my lodgings; and to this circumstance was I indebted for my introduction to him. I had made the intended disposition of my business, and was on the eve of my departure for the city of my residence, when I was induced to remain a day longer by an invitation from the squire to attend a dance at his house on the following day. Having learned from my landlord that I would probably "be expected at the frolic" about the hour of 10 in the forenoon, and being desirous of seeing all that passed upon the occasion, I went over about an hour before the time.

The squire's dwelling consisted of but one room, which answered the threefold purpose of dining-room, bedroom, and kitchen. The house was constructed of logs, and the floor was of *puncheons;* a term which, in Georgia, means split logs, with their faces a little smoothed with the axe or hatchet. To gratify his daughters, Polly and Silvy, the old gentleman and his lady had consented to *camp out* for a day, and to surrender the habitation to the girls and their young friends.

When I reached there I found all things in readiness for the promised amusement. The girls, as the old gentleman informed me, had compelled the family to breakfast under the trees, for they had completely stripped the house of its furniture before the sun rose. They were already attired for the dance, in neat but plain habiliments of their own manufacture. "What!" says some weakly, sickly, delicate, useless, affected, "charming creature" of the city, "dressed for a ball at 9 in the morning!" Even so, my delectable Miss Octavia Matilda Juliana Claudia Ipecacuanha: and what have you to say against it? If people must dance is it not much more rational to employ the hour allotted to exercise in that amusement, than the hours sacred to repose and meditation? And which is entitled to the most credit; the young lady who rises with the dawn, and puts herself and whole house in order for a ball four hours before it begins, or the one who requires a fortnight to get herself dressed for it?

The squire and I employed the interval in conversation about the first settlement of the country, in the course of which I picked up some useful and much interesting information. We were at length interrupted, however, by the sound of a violin, which proceeded from a thick wood at my left. The performer soon after made his appearance, and proved to be no other than Billy Porter, a negro fellow of much harmless wit and humour, who was well known throughout the state. Poor Billy! "his harp is now hung upon the willow;" and I would not blush to offer a tear to his memory, for his name is associated with some of the happiest scenes of my life, and he sleeps with many a dear friend, who used to join me in provoking

95

his wit and in laughing at his eccentricities; but I am leading my reader to the grave instead of the dance, which I promised. If, however, his memory reaches twelve years back, he will excuse this short tribute of respect to BILLY PORTER.

Billy, to give his own account of himself, "had been taking a turn with the brethren (the Bar); and, hearing the ladies wanted to see *pretty Billy,* had come to give them a benefit." The squire had not seen him before; and it is no disrespect to his understanding or politeness to say, that he found it impossible to give me his attention for half an hour after Billy arrived. I had nothing to do, therefore, while the young people were assembling, but to improve my knowledge of Billy's character, to the squire's amusement. I had been thus engaged about thirty minutes, when I saw several fine, bouncing, ruddy-cheeked girls descending a hill about the eighth of a mile off. They, too, were attired in manufactures of their own hands. The refinements of the present day in female dress had not even reached our republican *cities* at this time; and, of course, the *country girls* were wholly ignorant of them. They carried no more cloth upon their arms or straw upon their heads than was necessary to cover them. They used no artificial means of spreading their frock tails to an interesting extent from their ankles. They had no boards laced to their breasts, nor any corsets laced to their sides; consequently, they looked, for all the world, like human beings, and could be distinctly recognised as such at the distance of two hundred paces. Their movements were as free and active as nature would permit them to be. Let me not be understood as interposing the least objection to any lady in this land of liberty dressing just as she pleases. If she choose to lay her neck and shoulders bare, what right have I to look at them? much less to find fault with them. If she choose to put three yards of muslin in a frock sleeve, what right have I to ask why a little strip of it was not put in the body? If she like the pattern of a hoisted umbrella for a frock, and the shape of a cheese-cask for her body, what is all that to me? But to return.

The girls were met by Polly and Silvy Gibson at some distance from the house, who welcomed them — "with a kiss, of course" — oh, no; but with something much less equivocal: a hearty shake of the hand and smiling countenances, which had some meaning.

[*Note.* — The custom of kissing, as practised in these days by the *amiables,* is borrowed from the French, and by them from Judas.]

The young ladies had generally collected before any of the young men appeared. It was not long, however, before a large number of both sexes were assembled, and they adjourned to the *ballroom.*

But for the snapping of a fiddle-string, the young people would have been engaged in the amusement of the day in less than three minutes from the time they entered the house. Here were no formal introductions to be given, no drawing for places or partners, no parade of managers, no ceremonies. It was perfectly understood that all were invited *to dance,* and that none were invited who were unworthy to be danced with; consequently, no gentleman hesitated to ask any lady present to dance with him, and no lady refused to dance with a gentleman merely because she had not been made acquainted with him.

In a short time the string was repaired, and off went the party to a good old republican six reel. I had been thrown among *fashionables* so long that I had almost forgotten my native dance. But it revived rapidly as they wheeled through its mazes, and with it returned many long-forgotten, pleasing recollections. Not only did the reel return to me, but the very persons who used to figure in it with me, in the heyday of youth.

Here was my old sweetheart, Polly Jackson, identically personified in Polly Gibson; and here was Jim Johnson's, in Silvy; and Bill Martin's, in Nancy Ware. Polly Gibson had my old flame's very steps as well as her looks. "Ah!" said I, "squire, this puts me in mind of old times. I have not seen a six reel for five-and-twenty years. It recalls to my mind many a happy hour, and many a jovial friend who used to enliven it with me. Your Polly looks so much like my old sweetheart, Polly Jackson, that, were I young again, I certainly should fall in love with her."

"That was the name of her mother," said the squire.

"Where did you marry her?" inquired I.

"In Wilkes," said he; "she was the daughter of old Nathan Jackson, of that county."

"It isn't possible!" returned I. "Then it is the very girl of whom I am speaking. Where is she?"

"She's out," said the squire, "preparing dinner for the young people; but she'll be in towards the close of the day. But come along, and I'll make you acquainted with her at once, if you'll promise not to run away with her, for I tell you what it is, she's the likeliest *gal* in all these parts yet."

"Well," said I, "I'll promise not to run away with her, but you must not let her know who I am. I wish to make myself known to her; and, for fear of the worst, you shall witness the introduction. But don't get jealous, squire, if she seems a little too glad to see me; for, I assure you, we had a strong notion of each other when we were young."

"No danger," replied the squire; "she hadn't seen *me* then, or she never could have loved such a hard favoured man as you are."

In the mean time the dance went on, and I employed myself in selecting from the party the best examples of the dancers of my day and Mrs. Gibson's for her entertainment. In this I had not the least difficulty; for the dancers before me and those of my day were in all respects identical.

Jim Johnson kept up the double shuffle from the beginning to the end of the reel: and here was Jim over again in Sammy Tant. Bill Martin always set to his partner with the same step; and a very curious step it was. He brought his right foot close behind his left, and with it performed precisely the motion of the thumb in cracking that insect which Burns has immortalized; then moved his right back, threw his weight upon it, brought his left behind it, and *cracked* with that as before; and so on alternately. Just so did Bill Kemp, to a nail. Bob Simons danced for all the world like a "Suple Jack" (or, as we commonly call it, a "*Suple* Sawney"), when the string is pulled with varied force, at intervals of seconds: and so did *Jake* Slack. Davy Moore went like a suit of clothes upon a clothing line on a windy day: and here was his antitype in Ned Clark. Rhoda Noble swam through the reel like a cork on wavy waters; always giving two or three pretty little perchbite *diddles* as she rose from a coupee: Nancy Ware was her very self. Becky Lewis made a business of dancing; she disposed of her part as quick as possible, stopped dead short as soon as she got through, and looked as sober as a judge all the time; even so did Chloe Dawson. I used to tell Polly Jackson, that Becky's countenance, when she closed a dance, always seemed to say, "Now, if you want any more dancing, you may do it yourself."

The dance grew merrier as it progressed; the young people became more easy in each other's company, and often enlivened the scene with most humorous remarks. Occasionally some sharp cuts passed between the boys, such as would have produced half a dozen duels at a city ball; but here they were taken as they were meant, in good humour. Jim Johnson being a little tardy in meeting his partner at a turn of the reel, "I *ax* pardon, Miss Chloe," said he, "Jake Slack went to make a crosshop just now, and tied his legs in a hard knot, and I stop'd to help him untie them." A little after, Jake hung his toe in a crack of the floor, and nearly fell; "Ding my buttons," said he, "if I didn't know I should stumble over Jim Johnson's foot at last; Jim, draw your foot up to your own end of the reel." (Jim was at the other end of the reel, and had, in truth, a prodigious foot.)

Towards the middle of the day, many of the neighbouring farmers dropped in, and joined the squire and myself in talking of old times. At length dinner was announced. It consisted of plain *fare,* but there was a profusion of it. Rough planks, supported by stakes driven in the ground, served for a table; at which the old and young of both sexes seated themselves at the same time. I soon recognised Mrs. Gibson from all the matrons present. Thirty years had wrought great changes in her appearance, but they had left some of her features entirely unimpaired. Her eye beamed with all its youthful fire; and, to my astonishment, her mouth was still beautified with a full set of teeth, unblemished by time. The rose on her cheek had rather freshened than faded, and her smile was the very same that first subdued my heart; but her fine form was wholly lost, and, with it, all the grace of her movements. Pleasing but melancholy reflections occupied my mind as I gazed on her dispensing her cheerful hospitalities. I thought of the sad history of many of her companions and mine, who used to carry light hearts through the merry dance. I compared my after life with the cloudless days of my attachment to Polly. Then I was light hearted, gay, contented, and happy. I aspired to nothing but a good name, a good wife, and an easy competence. The first and last were mine already; and Polly had given me too many little tokens of her favour to leave a doubt now that the second was at my command. But I was foolishly told that my talents were of too high an order to be employed in the drudgeries of a farm, and I more foolishly believed it. I forsook the pleasures which I had tried and proved, and went in pursuit of those imaginary joys which seemed to encircle the seat of Fame. From that moment to the present, my life had been little else than one unbroken scene of disaster, disappointment, vexation, and toil. And now, when I was too old to enjoy the pleasures which I had discarded, I found that my aim was absolutely hopeless; and that my pursuits had only served to unfit me for the humbler walks of life, and to exclude me from the higher. The gloom of these reflections was, however, lightened in a measure by the promises of the coming hour, when I was to live over again with Mrs. Gibson some of the happiest moments of my life.

After a hasty repast the young people returned to their amusement, followed by myself, with several of the elders of the company. An hour had scarcely elapsed before Mrs. Gibson entered, accompanied by a goodly number of matrons of her own age. This accession to the company produced its usual effects. It raised the tone of conversation a full octave, and gave it a triple time movement; added new life to the wit and limbs of the young folks, and set the old men to cracking jokes.

At length the time arrived for me to surprise and delight Mrs. Gibson. The young people insisted upon the old folks taking a reel; and this was just what I had been waiting for; for, after many plans for making the discovery, I had finally concluded upon that which I thought would make *her* joy general among the company: and that was, to announce myself, just before leading her to the dance, in a voice audible to most of the assembly. I therefore readily assented to the proposition of the young folks, as did two others of my age, and we made to the ladies for our partners. I, of course, offered my hand to Mrs. Gibson.

"Come," said I, "Mrs. Gibson, let us see if we can't out-dance these young people."

"Dear me, sir," said she, "I haven't danced a step these twenty years."

"Neither have I; but I've resolved to try once more, if you will join me, just for old time's sake."

"I really cannot think of dancing," said she.

"Well," continued I (raising my voice to a pretty high pitch, on purpose to be heard, while my countenance kindled with exultation at the astonishment and delight which I was about to produce), "you surely will dance with an old friend and sweetheart, who used to dance with you when a girl!"

At this disclosure her features assumed a vast variety of expressions; but none of them responded precisely to my expectation: indeed, some of them were of such an equivocal and alarming character, that I deemed it advisable not to prolong her suspense. I therefore proceeded:

"Have you forgot your old sweetheart, Abram Baldwin?"

"What!" said she, looking more astonished and confused than ever. "Abram Baldwin! Abram Baldwin! I don't think I ever heard the name before."

"Do you remember Jim Johnson?" said I.

"Oh, yes," said she, "mighty well," her countenance brightening with a smile.

"And Bill Martin?"

"Yes, perfectly well; why, *who* are you?"

Here we were interrupted by one of the gentlemen, who had led his partner to the floor, with, "Come, stranger, we're getting mighty tired o' standing. It won't do for old people that's going to dance to take up much time in standing; they'll lose all their *spryness*. Don't stand begging Polly Gibson, she never dances; but take my Sal there, next to her; she'll run a reel with you, to old Nick's house and back *agin*."

No alternative was left me, and therefore I offered my hand to Mrs. Sally—I didn't know who.

"Well," thought I, as I moved to my place, "the squire is pretty secure from jealousy; but Polly will soon remember me when she sees my steps in the reel. I will dance precisely as I used to in my youth, if it tire me to death." There was one step that was almost exclusively my own, for few of the dancers of my day could perform it at all, and none with the grace and ease that I did. "She'll remember Abram Baldwin," thought I, "as soon as she sees the *double cross-hop*." It was performed by rising and crossing the legs twice or thrice before lighting, and I used to carry it to the third cross with considerable ease. It was a step solely adapted to setting or balancing, as all will perceive; but I thought the occasion would justify a little perversion of it, and therefore resolved to lead off with it, that Polly might be at once relieved from suspense. Just, however, as I reached my place, Mrs. Gibson's youngest son, a boy about eight years old, ran in and cried out, "Mammy, old Boler's jump'd upon the planks, and dragg'd off a great hunk o' meat as big as your head, and broke a dish and two plates all to darn smashes!" Away went Mrs. Gibson, and off went the music. Still I hoped that matters would be adjusted in time for Polly to return and see the double cross-hop; and I felt the mortification which my delay in getting a partner had occasioned somewhat solaced by the reflection that it had thrown me at the foot of the reel.

The first and second couples had nearly completed their performances, and Polly had not returned. I began to grow uneasy, and to interpose as many delays as I could without attracting notice.

The six reel is closed by the foot couple balancing at the head of the set, then in the middle, then at the foot, again in the middle, meeting at the head, and leading down.

My partner and I had commenced balancing at the head, and Polly had not returned. I balanced until my partner forced me on. I now deemed it advisable to give myself up wholly to the double cross-hop; so that, if Polly should return in time to see any step, it should be this, though I was already nearly exhausted. Accordingly, I made the attempt to introduce it in the turns of the reel; but the first experiment convinced me of three things at once; 1st. That I could not have used the step in this way in my best days; 2nd. That my strength would not more than support it in its proper place for the remainder of the reel; and, 3rd. If I tried it again in this way, I should knock my brains out against the puncheons; for my partner, who seemed determined to confirm her husband's report of her, evinced no disposition to wait upon experiments; but, fetching me a jerk while I was up and my legs crossed, had wellnigh sent me head foremost to Old Nick's house, sure enough.

We met in the middle, my back to the door, and from the silence that prevailed in the yard, I flattered myself that Polly might be even now catching the first glimpse of the favourite step, when I heard her voice at some distance from the house: "Get you gone! G-e-e-t you gone! G-e-e-e-e-t you gone!" Matters out doors were now clearly explained. There had been a struggle to get the meat from Boler; Boler had triumphed, and retreated to the woods with his booty, and Mrs. Gibson was heaping indignities upon him in the last resort.

The three *"Get-you-gones"* met me precisely at the three closing balances; and the last brought my moral energies to a perfect level with my physical.

Mrs. Gibson returned, however, in a few minutes after, in a good humour; for she possessed a lovely disposition, which even marriage could not spoil. As soon as I could collect breath enough for regular conversation (for, to speak in my native dialect, I was *"mortal tired"*), I took a seat by her, resolved not to quit the house without making myself known to her, if possible.

"How much," said I, "your Polly looks and dances like you used to, at her age."

"I've told my old man so a hundred times," said she. "Why, who upon earth are you!"

"Did you ever see two persons dance more alike than Jim Johnson and Sammy Tant?"

"Never. Why, who can you be!"

"You remember Becky Lewis?"

"Yes!"

"Well, look at Chloe Dawson, and you'll see her over again."

"Well, law me! Now I know I must have seen you somewhere; but, to save my life, I can't tell where. Where did your father live?"

"He died when I was small."

"And where did you use to see me?"

"At your father's, and old Mr. Dawson's, and at Mrs. Barnes's, and at Squire Noble's, and many other places."

"Well, goodness me! it's mighty strange I can't call you to mind."

I now began to get petulant, and thought it best to leave her.

The dance wound up with the old merry jig, and the company dispersed.

The next day I set out for my residence. I had been at home rather more than two months, when I received the following letter from Squire Gibson:

"DEAR SIR: I send you the money collected on the notes you left with me. Since you left here, Polly has been thinking about old times, and she says, to save her life, she can't recollect you."   [1833]

NATHANIEL HAWTHORNE

Nathaniel Hawthorne (1804–1864), was born in Salem, Massachusetts, into an eminent family who traced their lineage back to the Puritans. After his graduation from Bowdoin College in 1825, Hawthorne lived at home while he wrote works of short fiction he called "tales" or "articles" that he tried to sell to periodicals. American magazines of the time were mostly interested in publishing ghost stories, Indian legends, and "village tales" based on historical or fanciful anecdotes. Hawthorne (like his contemporary Edgar Allan Poe) created stories that transcended the limitations of conventional romanticism. His imagination was stirred by what he called "an inveterate love of allegory."

After publishing his stories anonymously in gift annuals, Hawthorne collected his first volume of short fiction, Twice-Told Tales, in 1837; a second book of stories, Mosses from an Old Manse, appeared in 1846. That year he stopped writing to earn a better living for his family as surveyor of customs for the port of Salem. This was a political appointment, and after the Whigs won the presidency three years later, Hawthorne—a Democrat—was out of a job. He returned to writing fiction, sketching his "official life" at the Custom House in the introduction to his novel The Scarlet Letter in 1850. During the last half of his career as a writer he published three other novels, several books for children, and another collection of tales, The Snow Image and Other Twice-Told Tales (1851). In "The Custom House," Hawthorne humorously suggested that his profession would not have impressed his Puritan ancestors:

> *"What is he?" murmurs one grey shadow of my forefathers to the other. "A writer of story-books! What kind of business in life, what manner of glorifying God, or being serviceable to mankind in his day and generation, may that be? Why, the degenerate fellow might as well have been a fiddler!" Such are the compliments bandied between my great-grandsires and myself across the gulf of time! And yet, let them scorn me as they will, strong traits of their nature have intertwined themselves with mine.*

Originally Hawthorne intended to publish "The Scarlet Letter" as part of a volume of short stories, but he revised it to novel length on the advice of his publisher James Fields. Hawthorne wrote Fields, "If the book is made up entirely of 'The Scarlet Letter' it will be too somber. . . . It was my purpose to conjoin the one long story with half a dozen shorter ones, so that, failing to kill the public outright with my biggest and heaviest lump of lead, I might have other chances with the smaller bits." Despite Hawthorne's portrait of himself as an unappreciated artist, he was recognized by contemporaries such as Herman Melville and Edgar Allan Poe as a "genius of a very lofty order." Hawthorne wrote about 120 short tales and sketches in addition to his novels. His notebooks are filled with ideas for stories, more often jottings of abstract ideas than detailed observations of "real" individuals, as when he wrote, "In every heart there is a secret sin, and sad mysteries, which we hide from our nearest and dearest, and would feign conceal from our own consciousness." "The Minister's Black Veil," set in the early years of the New Colonies and first published in The Token *in 1836, is one of his most famous moral tales.*

RELATED COMMENTARIES: *Nathaniel Hawthorne, Preface to* Twice-Told Tales, *page 1362; Henry James, From* Hawthorne, *page 1378; Herman Melville, From "Hawthorne and His Mosses," page 1407; Edgar Allan Poe, "Review of Hawthorne's* Twice-Told Tales," *page 1438.*

The Minister's Black Veil
A Parable[1]

The sexton stood in the porch of Milford meeting-house, pulling lustily at the bell-rope. The old people of the village came stooping along the street. Children, with bright faces, tript merrily beside their parents, or mimicked a graver gait, in the conscious dignity of their Sunday clothes. Spruce bachelors looked sidelong at the pretty maidens, and fancied that the Sabbath sunshine made them prettier than on week-days. When the throng had mostly streamed into the porch, the sexton began to toll the bell, keeping his eye on the Reverend Mr. Hooper's door. The first glimpse of the clergyman's figure was the signal for the bell to cease its summons.

"But what has good Parson Hooper got upon his face?" cried the sexton in astonishment.

All within hearing immediately turned about, and beheld the semblance of Mr. Hooper, pacing slowly his meditative way towards the meeting-house. With one accord they started, expressing more wonder than if some strange minister were coming to dust the cushions of Mr. Hooper's pulpit.

"Are you sure it is our parson?" inquired Goodman Gray of the sexton.

"Of a certainty it is good Mr. Hooper," replied the sexton. "He was to have exchanged pulpits with Parson Shute of Westbury; but Parson Shute sent to excuse himself yesterday, being to preach a funeral sermon."

The cause of so much amazement may appear sufficiently slight. Mr. Hooper, a gentlemanly person of about thirty, though still a bachelor, was

---

[1]Another clergyman in New England, Mr. Joseph Moody, of York, Maine, who died about eighty years since, made himself remarkable by the same eccentricity that is here related of the Reverend Mr. Hooper. In his case, however, the symbol had a different import. In early life he had accidentally killed a beloved friend; and from that day till the hour of his own death, he hid his face from men. [Hawthorne's note.]

dressed with due clerical neatness, as if a careful wife had starched his band, and brushed the weekly dust from his Sunday's garb. There was but one thing remarkable in his appearance. Swathed about his forehead, and hanging down over his face, so low as to be shaken by his breath, Mr. Hooper had on a black veil. On a nearer view, it seemed to consist of two folds of crape, which entirely concealed his features, except the mouth and chin, but probably did not intercept his sight, farther than to give a darkened aspect to all living and inanimate things. With this gloomy shade before him, good Mr. Hooper walked onward, at a slow and quiet pace, stooping somewhat and looking on the ground, as is customary with abstracted men, yet nodding kindly to those of his parishioners who still waited on the meeting-house steps. But so wonder-struck were they, that his greeting hardly met with a return.

"I can't really feel as if good Mr. Hooper's face was behind that piece of crape," said the sexton.

"I don't like it," muttered an old woman, as she hobbled into the meeting-house. "He has changed himself into something awful, only by hiding his face."

"Our parson has gone mad!" cried Goodman Gray, following him across the threshold.

A rumor of some unaccountable phenomenon had preceded Mr. Hooper into the meeting-house, and set all the congregation astir. Few could refrain from twisting their heads towards the door; many stood upright, and turned directly about; while several little boys clambered upon the seats, and came down again with a terrible racket. There was a general bustle, a rustling of the women's gowns and shuffling of the men's feet, greatly at variance with that hushed repose which should attend the entrance of the minister. But Mr. Hooper appeared not to notice the perturbation of his people. He entered with an almost noiseless step, bent his head mildly to the pews on each side, and bowed as he passed his oldest parishioner, a white-haired great-grandsire, who occupied an arm-chair in the centre of the aisle. It was strange to observe, how slowly this venerable man became conscious of something singular in the appearance of his pastor. He seemed not fully to partake of the prevailing wonder, till Mr. Hooper had ascended the stairs, and showed himself in the pulpit, face to face with his congregation, except for the black veil. That mysterious emblem was never once withdrawn. It shook with his measured breath as he gave out the psalm; it threw its obscurity between him and the holy page, as he read the Scriptures; and while he prayed, the veil lay heavily on his uplifted countenance. Did he seek to hide it from the dread Being whom he was addressing?

Such was the effect of this simple piece of crape, that more than one woman of delicate nerves was forced to leave the meeting-house. Yet perhaps the pale-faced congregation was almost as fearful a sight to the minister, as his black veil to them.

Mr. Hooper had the reputation of a good preacher, but not an ener-getic one: he strove to win his people heavenward, by mild persuasive influences, rather than to drive them thither, by the thunders of the Word. The sermon which he now delivered was marked by the same characteris-tics of style and manner, as the general series of his pulpit oratory. But there was something, either in the sentiment of the discourse itself, or in the imagination of the auditors, which made it greatly the most powerful effort that they had ever heard from their pastor's lips. It was tinged, rather more darkly than usual, with the gentle gloom of Mr. Hooper's temperament. The subject had reference to secret sin, and those sad mys-teries which we hide from our nearest and dearest, and would fain conceal from our own consciousness, even forgetting that the Omniscient can detect them. A subtle power was breathed into his words. Each member of the congregation, the most innocent girl, and the man of hardened breast, felt as if the preacher had crept upon them, behind his awful veil, and dis-covered their hoarded iniquity of deed or thought. Many spread their clasped hands on their bosoms. There was nothing terrible in what Mr. Hooper said; at least, no violence; and yet, with every tremor of his melan-choly voice, the hearers quaked. An unsought pathos came hand in hand with awe. So sensible were the audience of some unwonted attribute in their minister, that they longed for a breath of wind to blow aside the veil, almost believing that a stranger's visage would be discovered, though the form, gesture, and voice were those of Mr. Hooper.

At the close of the services, the people hurried out with indecorous confusion, eager to communicate their pent-up amazement, and con-scious of lighter spirits, the moment they lost sight of the black veil. Some gathered in little circles, huddled closely together, with their mouths all whispering in the centre; some went homeward alone, wrapt in silent meditation; some talked loudly, and profaned the Sabbath-day with osten-tatious laughter. A few shook their sagacious heads, intimating that they could penetrate the mystery; while one or two affirmed that there was no mystery at all, but only that Mr. Hooper's eyes were so weakened by the midnight lamp, as to require a shade. After a brief interval, forth came good Mr. Hooper also, in the rear of his flock. Turning his veiled face from one group to another, he paid due reverence to the hoary heads, saluted the middle-aged with kind dignity, as their friend and spiritual guide, greeted the young with mingled authority and love, and laid his hands on the little children's heads to bless them. Such was always his custom on the Sabbath-day. Strange and bewildered looks repaid him for his courtesy. None, as on former occasions, aspired to the honor of walking by their pastor's side. Old Squire Saunders, doubtless by an accidental lapse of memory, neglected to invite Mr. Hooper to his table, where the good cler-gyman had been wont to bless the food, almost every Sunday since his settlement. He returned, therefore, to the parsonage, and, at the moment of closing the door, was observed to look back upon the people, all of whom had their eyes fixed upon the minister. A sad smile gleamed faintly from beneath the black veil, and flickered about his mouth, glimmering as he disappeared.

"How strange," said a lady, "that a simple black veil, such as any woman might wear on her bonnet, should become such a terrible thing on Mr. Hooper's face!"

"Something must surely be amiss with Mr. Hooper's intellects," observed her husband, the physician of the village. "But the strangest part of the affair is the effect of this vagary, even on a sober-minded man like myself. The black veil, though it covers only our pastor's face, throws its influence over his whole person, and makes him ghost-like from head to foot. Do you not feel it so?"

"Truly do I," replied the lady; "and I would not be alone with him for the world. I wonder he is not afraid to be alone with himself!"

"Men sometimes are so," said her husband.

The afternoon service was attended with similar circumstances. At its conclusion, the bell tolled for the funeral of a young lady. The relatives and friends were assembled in the house, and the more distant acquaintances stood about the door, speaking of the good qualities of the deceased, when their talk was interrupted by the appearance of Mr. Hooper, still covered with his black veil. It was now an appropriate emblem. The clergy-man stepped into the room where the corpse was laid, and bent over the coffin, to take a last farewell of his deceased parishioner. As he stooped, the veil hung straight down from his forehead, so that, if her eye-lids had not been closed for ever, the dead maiden might have seen his face. Could Mr. Hooper be fearful of her glance, that he so hastily caught back the black veil? A person, who watched the interview between the dead and living, scrupled not to affirm, that, at the instant when the clergyman's features were disclosed, the corpse had slightly shuddered, rustling the shroud and muslin cap, though the countenance retained the composure of death. A superstitious old woman was the only witness of this prodigy. From the coffin, Mr. Hooper passed into the chamber of the mourners, and thence to the head of the staircase, to make the funeral prayer. It was a tender and heart-dissolving prayer, full of sorrow, yet so imbued with celestial hopes, that the music of a heavenly harp, swept by the fingers of the dead, seemed faintly to be heard among the saddest accents of the minister. The people trembled, though they but darkly understood him, when he prayed that they, and himself, and all of mortal race, might be ready, as he trusted this young maiden had been, for the dreadful hour that should snatch the veil from their faces. The bearers went heavily forth, and the mourners fol-lowed, saddening all the street, with the dead before them, and Mr. Hooper in his black veil behind.

"Why do you look back?" said one in the procession to his partner.

"I had a fancy," replied she, "that the minister and the maiden's spirit were walking hand in hand."

"And so had I, at the same moment," said the other.

That night, the handsomest couple in Milford village were to be joined in wedlock. Though reckoned a melancholy man, Mr. Hooper had a placid cheerfulness for such occasions, which often excited a sympathetic smile, where livelier merriment would have been thrown away. There was no quality of his disposition which made him more beloved than this. The company at the wedding awaited his arrival with impatience, trusting that the strange awe, which had gathered over him throughout the day, would now be dispelled. But such was not the result. When Mr. Hooper came, the first thing that their eyes rested on was the same horrible black veil, which had added deeper gloom to the funeral, and could portend nothing but evil to the wedding. Such was its immediate effect on the guests, that a cloud seemed to have rolled duskily from beneath the black crape, and dimmed the light of the candles. The bridal pair stood up before the minister. But the bride's cold fingers quivered in the tremulous hand of the bridegroom, and her death-like paleness caused a whisper, that the maiden who had been buried a few hours before, was come from her grave to be married. If ever another wedding were so dismal, it was that famous one, where they tolled the wedding-knell. After performing the ceremony, Mr. Hooper raised a glass of wine to his lips, wishing happiness to the new-married couple, in a strain of mild pleasantry that ought to have brightened the features of the guests, like a cheerful gleam from the hearth. At that instant, catching a glimpse of his figure in the looking-glass, the black veil involved his own spirit in the horror with which it overwhelmed all others. His frame shuddered—his lips grew white—he spilt the untasted wine upon the carpet—and rushed forth into the darkness. For the Earth, too, had on her Black Veil.

The next day, the whole village of Milford talked of little else than Parson Hooper's black veil. That, and the mystery concealed behind it, supplied a topic for discussion between acquaintances meeting in the street, and good women gossiping at their open windows. It was the first item of news that the tavern-keeper told to his guests. The children babbled of it on their way to school. One imitative little imp covered his face with an old black handkerchief, thereby so affrighting his playmates, that the panic seized himself, and he well nigh lost his wits by his own waggery.

It was remarkable, that, of all the busy-bodies and impertinent people in the parish, not one ventured to put the plain question to Mr. Hooper, wherefore he did this thing. Hitherto, whenever there appeared the slightest call for such interference, he had never lacked advisers, nor shown himself averse to be guided by their judgment. If he erred at all, it was by so painful a degree of self-distrust, that even the mildest censure would lead him to consider an indifferent action as a crime. Yet, though so well acquainted with this amiable weakness, no individual among his parishioners chose to make the black veil a subject of friendly remonstrance. There was a feeling of dread, neither plainly confessed nor carefully concealed, which caused each to shift the responsibility upon another, till at length it was found expedient to send a deputation of the church, in order to deal with Mr. Hooper about the mystery, before it should grow into a scandal. Never did an embassy so ill discharge its duties. The minister received them with friendly courtesy, but became silent, after they were seated, leaving to his visitors the whole burthen of introducing their important business. The topic, it might be supposed, was obvious enough. There was the black veil, swathed round Mr. Hooper's forehead, and concealing every feature above his placid mouth, on which, at times, they could perceive the glimmering of a melancholy smile. But that piece of crape, to their imagination, seemed to hang down before his heart, the symbol of a fearful secret between him and them. Were the veil but cast aside, they might speak freely of it, but not till then. Thus they sat a considerable time, speechless, confused, and shrinking uneasily from Mr. Hooper's eye, which they felt to be fixed upon them with an invisible glance. Finally, the deputies returned abashed to their constituents, pronouncing the matter too weighty to be handled, except by a council of the churches, if, indeed, it might not require a general synod.

But there was one person in the village, unappalled by the awe with which the black veil had impressed all beside herself. When the deputies returned without an explanation, or even venturing to demand one, she, with the calm energy of her character, determined to chase away the strange cloud that appeared to be settling round Mr. Hooper, every moment more darkly than before. As his plighted wife, it should be her privilege to know what the black veil concealed. At the minister's first visit, therefore, she entered upon the subject, with a direct simplicity, which made the task easier both for him and her. After he had seated himself, she fixed her eyes steadfastly upon the veil, but could discern nothing of the dreadful gloom that had so overawed the multitude: it was but a double fold of crape, hanging down from his forehead to his mouth, and slightly stirring with his breath.

"No," said she aloud, and smiling, "there is nothing terrible in this piece of crape, except that it hides a face which I am always glad to look upon. Come, good sir, let the sun shine from behind the cloud. First lay aside your black veil: then tell me why you put it on."

Mr. Hooper's smile glimmered faintly.

"There is an hour to come," said he, "when all of us shall cast aside our veils. Take it not amiss, beloved friend, if I wear this piece of crape till then."

"Your words are a mystery too," returned the young lady. "Take away the veil from them, at least."

"Elizabeth, I will," said he, "so far as my vow may suffer me. Know, then, this veil is a type and a symbol, and I am bound to wear it ever, both in light and darkness, in solitude and before the gaze of multitudes, and as with strangers, so with my familiar friends. No mortal eye will see it withdrawn. This dismal shade must separate me from the world: even you, Elizabeth, can never come behind it!'

"What grievous affliction hath befallen you," she earnestly inquired, "that you should thus darken your eyes for ever?"

"If it be a sign of mourning," replied Mr. Hooper, "I, perhaps, like most other mortals, have sorrows dark enough to be typified by a black veil."

"But what if the world will not believe that it is the type of an innocent sorrow?" urged Elizabeth. "Beloved and respected as you are, there may be whispers, that you hide your face under the consciousness of secret sin. For the sake of your holy office, do away this scandal!"

The color rose into her cheeks, as she intimated the nature of the rumors that were already abroad in the village. But Mr. Hooper's mildness did not forsake him. He even smiled again — that same sad smile, which always appeared like a faint glimmering of light, proceeding from the obscurity beneath the veil.

"If I hide my face for sorrow, there is cause enough," he merely replied; "and if I cover it for secret sin, what mortal might not do the same?"

And with this gentle, but unconquerable obstinacy, did he resist all her entreaties. At length Elizabeth sat silent. For a few moments she appeared lost in thought, considering, probably, what new methods might be tried, to withdraw her lover from so dark a fantasy, which, if it had no other meaning, was perhaps a symptom of mental disease. Though of a firmer character than his own, the tears rolled down her cheeks. But, in an instant, as it were, a new feeling took the place of sorrow: her eyes were fixed insensibly on the black veil, when, like a sudden twilight in the air, its terrors fell around her. She arose, and stood trembling before him.

"And do you feel it then at last?" said he mournfully.

She made no reply, but covered her eyes with her hand, and turned to leave the room. He rushed forward and caught her arm.

"Have patience with me, Elizabeth!" cried he passionately. "Do not desert me, though this veil must be between us here on earth. Be mine, and hereafter there shall be no veil over my face, no darkness between our souls! It is but a mortal veil — it is not for eternity! Oh! you know not how lonely I am, and how frightened to be alone behind my black veil. Do not leave me in this miserable obscurity for ever!"

"Lift the veil but once, and look me in the face," said she.

"Never! It cannot be!" replied Mr. Hooper.

"Then, farewell!" said Elizabeth.

She withdrew her arm from his grasp, and slowly departed, pausing at the door, to give one long, shuddering gaze, that seemed almost to penetrate the mystery of the black veil. But, even amid his grief, Mr. Hooper smiled to think that only a material emblem had separated him from happiness, though the horrors which it shadowed forth, must be drawn darkly between the fondest of lovers.

From that time no attempts were made to remove Mr. Hooper's black veil, or, by a direct appeal, to discover the secret which it was supposed to hide. By persons who claimed a superiority to popular prejudice, it was reckoned merely an eccentric whim, such as often mingles with the sober actions of men otherwise rational, and tinges them all with its own semblance of insanity. But with the multitude, good Mr. Hooper was irreparably a bugbear. He could not walk the streets with any peace of mind, so conscious was he that the gentle and timid would turn aside to avoid him, and that others would make it a point of hardihood to throw themselves in his way. The impertinence of the latter class compelled him to give up his customary walk, at sunset, to the burial ground; for when he leaned pensively over the gate, there would always be faces behind the grave-stones, peeping at his black veil. A fable went the rounds, that the stare of the dead people drove him thence. It grieved him, to the very depth of his kind heart, to observe how the children fled from his approach, breaking up their merriest sports, while his melancholy figure was yet afar off. Their instinctive dread caused him to feel, more strongly than aught else, that a preternatural horror was interwoven with the threads of the black crape. In truth, his own antipathy to the veil was known to be so great, that he never willingly passed before a mirror, nor stooped to drink at a still fountain, lest, in its peaceful bosom, he should be affrighted by himself. This was what gave plausibility to the whispers, that Mr. Hooper's conscience tortured him for some great crime, too horrible to be entirely concealed, or otherwise than so obscurely intimated. Thus, from beneath the black veil, there rolled a cloud into the sunshine, an ambiguity of sin or sorrow, which enveloped the poor minister, so that love or sympathy could never reach him. It was said, that ghost and fiend consorted with him there. With self-shudderings and outward terrors, he walked continually in its shadow, groping darkly within his own soul, or gazing through a medium that saddened the whole world. Even the lawless wind, it was believed, respected his dreadful secret, and never blew aside the veil. But still good Mr. Hooper sadly smiled, at the pale visages of the worldly throng as he passed by.

Among all its bad influences, the black veil had the one desirable effect, of making its wearer a very efficient clergyman. By the aid of his mysterious emblem — for there was no other apparent cause — he became a man of awful power, over souls that were in agony for sin. His converts always regarded him with a dread peculiar to themselves, affirming, though but figuratively, that, before he brought them to celestial light, they had been with him behind the black veil. Its gloom, indeed, enabled him to sympathize with all dark affections. Dying sinners cried aloud for Mr. Hooper, and would not yield their breath till he appeared; though ever, as he stooped to whisper consolation, they shuddered at the veiled face so near their own. Such were the terrors of the black veil, even when Death had bared his visage! Strangers came long distances to attend service at his church, with the mere idle purpose of gazing at his figure, because it was forbidden them to behold his face. But many were made to quake ere they departed! Once, during Governor Belcher's administration, Mr. Hooper was appointed to preach the election sermon. Covered with his black veil, he stood before the chief magistrate, the council, and the representatives, and wrought so deep an impression, that the legislative measures of that year, were characterized by all the gloom and piety of our earliest ancestral sway.

In this manner Mr. Hooper spent a long life, irreproachable in outward act, yet shrouded in dismal suspicions; kind and loving, though unloved, and dimly feared; a man apart from men, shunned in their health and joy, but ever summoned to their aid in mortal anguish. As years wore on, shedding their snows above his sable veil, he acquired a name throughout the New-England churches, and they called him Father Hooper. Nearly all his parishioners, who were of mature age when he was settled, had been borne away by many a funeral: he had one congregation in the church, and a more crowded one in the church-yard; and having wrought so late into the evening, and done his work so well, it was now good Father Hooper's turn to rest.

Several persons were visible by the shaded candlelight, in the death-chamber of the old clergyman. Natural connections he had none. But there was the decorously grave, though unmoved physician, seeking only to mitigate the last pangs of the patient whom he could not save. There were the deacons, and other eminently pious members of his church. There, also, was the Reverend Mr. Clark, of Westbury, a young and zealous divine, who had ridden in haste to pray by the bedside of the expiring minister. There was the nurse, no hired handmaiden of death, but one whose calm affection had endured thus long, in secrecy, in solitude, amid the chill of age, and would not perish, even at the dying hour. Who, but Elizabeth! And there lay the hoary head of good Father Hooper upon the death-pillow, with the black veil still swathed about his brow and reaching down over his face, so that each more difficult gasp of his faint breath caused it to stir. All through life that piece of crape had hung between him and the world: it had separated him from cheerful brotherhood and woman's love, and kept him in that saddest of all prisons, his own heart; and still it lay upon his face, as if to deepen the gloom of his darksome chamber, and shade him from the sunshine of eternity.

For some time previous, his mind had been confused, wavering doubtfully between the past and the present, and hovering forward, as it were, at intervals, into the indistinctness of the world to come. There had been feverish turns, which tossed him from side to side, and wore away what little strength he had. But in his most convulsive struggles, and in the wildest vagaries of his intellect, when no other thought retained its sober influence, he still showed an awful solicitude lest the black veil should slip aside. Even if his bewildered soul could have forgotten, there was a faithful woman at his pillow, who, with averted eyes, would have covered that aged face, which she had last beheld in the comeliness of manhood. At length the death-stricken old man lay quietly in the torpor of mental and bodily exhaustion, with an imperceptible pulse, and breath that grew fainter and fainter, except when a long, deep, and irregular inspiration seemed to prelude the flight of his spirit.

The minister of Westbury approached the bedside.

"Venerable Father Hooper," said he, "the moment of your release is at hand. Are you ready for the lifting of the veil, that shuts in time from eternity?"

Father Hooper at first replied merely by a feeble motion of his head; then, apprehensive, perhaps, that his meaning might be doubtful, he exerted himself to speak.

"Yea," said he, in faint accents, "my soul hath a patient weariness until that veil be lifted."

"And is it fitting," resumed the Reverend Mr. Clark, "that a man so given to prayer, of such a blameless example, holy in deed and thought, so far as mortal judgment may pronounce; is it fitting that a father in the church should leave a shadow on his memory, that may seem to blacken a life so pure? I pray you, my venerable brother, let not this thing be! Suffer us to be gladdened by your triumphant aspect, as you go to your reward. Before the veil of eternity be lifted, let me cast aside this black veil from your face!"

And thus speaking, the Reverend Mr. Clark bent forward to reveal the mystery of so many years. But, exerting a sudden energy, that made all the beholders stand aghast, Father Hooper snatched both his hands from beneath the bedclothes, and pressed them strongly on the black veil, resolute to struggle, if the minister of Westbury would contend with a dying man.

"Never!" cried the veiled clergyman. "On earth, never!"

"Dark old man!" exclaimed the affrighted minister, "with what horrible crime upon your soul are you now passing to the judgment?"

Father Hooper's breath heaved; it rattled in his throat; but, with a mighty effort, grasping forward with his hands, he caught hold of life, and held it back till he should speak. He even raised himself in bed; and there he sat, shivering with the arms of death around him, while the black veil hung down, awful, at that last moment, in the gathered terrors of a lifetime. And yet the faint, sad smile, so often there, now seemed to glimmer from its obscurity, and linger on Father Hooper's lips.

"Why do you tremble at me alone?" cried he, turning his veiled face round the circle of pale spectators. "Tremble also at each other! Have men avoided me, and women shown no pity, and children screamed and fled, only for my black veil? What, but the mystery which it obscurely typifies, has made this piece of crape so awful? When the friend shows his inmost heart to his friend; the lover to his best-beloved; when man does not vainly shrink from the eye of his Creator, loathsomely treasuring up the secret of his sin; then deem me a monster, for the symbol beneath which I have lived, and die! I look around me, and, lo! on every visage a Black Veil!"

While his auditors shrank from one another, in mutual affright, Father Hooper fell back upon his pillow, a veiled corpse, with a faint smile lingering on the lips. Still veiled, they laid him in his coffin, and a veiled corpse they bore him to the grave. The grass of many years has sprung up and withered on that grave, the burial-stone is moss-grown, and good Mr. Hooper's face is dust; but awful is still the thought, that it mouldered beneath the Black Veil!   [1836]

EDGAR ALLAN POE

Edgar Allan Poe (1809–1849), the son of poor traveling actors, was adopted by the merchant John Allan of Richmond, Virginia, after the death of Poe's mother when Poe was three years old. He was educated in England and Virginia, enlisted and served two years in the army, then entered the military academy at West Point, from which he was expelled for absenteeism after a year. When John Allan disinherited him, Poe became a writer to earn his living.

In 1833 Poe's story "A MS. Found in a Bottle" won a fifty-dollar prize for the best story in a popular Baltimore periodical, and soon afterward he assumed editorship of the Southern Literary Messenger. *In 1836 he married his cousin Virginia Clemm, shortly before her fourteenth birthday. Poe's brilliant reviews, poems, and stories attracted wide attention, but in 1837 he quarreled with the owner of the* Messenger *over his salary and the degree of his independence as an editor, and he resigned from the magazine.*

In 1841 he became an editor of Graham's Magazine, *and during his yearlong tenure he quadrupled subscriptions by publishing his own stories and articles. He left* Graham's *to start his own magazine, which failed. His remaining years as a freelance writer were a struggle with poverty, depression, poor health aggravated by addiction to drugs and alcohol, and—after 1847—grief over the death of his wife. The writer Jorge Luis Borges observed that Poe's life "was short and unhappy, if unhappiness can be short."*

Poe's first collection of twenty-five short stories appeared in two volumes in 1840, Tales of the Grotesque and Arabesque. *His second collection of twelve stories,* Tales, *published in 1845, was so successful that it was followed by* The Raven and Other Poems *the same year. Poe was industrious, and his books of short fiction and poetry sold well, but his total income from them in his lifetime was less than three hundred dollars.*

Most of Poe's best stories can be divided into two categories: melodramatic tales of gothic terror, symbolic psychological fiction that became the source of the modern horror story, such as "The Fall of the House of Usher"; and stories of intellect or reason, analytic tales that were precursors of the modern detective story. After critics accused Poe of imitating the extravagant "mysticism" of German romantic writers in his monologues of inspired madness, Poe asserted his originality in the preface to his first story collection: "If in many of my productions terror has been the thesis, I maintain that terror is not of Germany, but of the soul."

Known as a literary critic as well as a poet and writer of short fiction, Poe published more than seventy tales. He is important as one of the earliest writers to attempt to formulate an aesthetic theory about the short story form, or "prose tale" as it was called in his time. Some of his most extensive comments on this subject are found in his reviews of Hawthorne's Twice-Told Tales *for* Graham's Magazine *in 1842 and Godey's Lady's Book in 1847. In these essays he also described his own philosophy of composition. Poe believed that* unity of a "single effect" was the most essential quality of all successful short fiction. He praised Hawthorne for his "invention, creation, imagination, originality"—qualities Poe himself possessed in abundance. In June 1846, Hawthorne returned the compliment by sending Poe a graceful letter with a copy of his second collection, Mosses from an Old Manse, saying that he would never fail to recognize Poe's "force and originality" as a writer of tales even if he sometimes disagreed with Poe's opinions as a critic.

Poe's stories were widely translated, and he became the first American writer of short fiction to be internationally celebrated. Interpretations of his creative work by writers living abroad usually focused on aspects of his genius that supported their views of America. The Russian novelist Fyodor Dostoevsky admired Poe's "strangely material" imagination and recognized that Poe, unlike the German romantic writers, did not give a large role to supernatural agents in his gothic tales. Instead, Dostoevsky felt that the "power of details" in Poe's descriptions was presented "with such stupendous plasticity that you cannot but believe in the reality or possibility of a fact which actually never has occurred."

The French poet Charles Baudelaire, who translated Poe's tales and championed his genius, regarded Poe from a completely different perspective when he identified him as an alienated artist—"le poète maudit"—a writer outside his society who reflected the derangement of a hypocritical country that professed individual freedom yet permitted slavery in the southern states and bigamy among the Mormons in Utah.

Other readers were more critical—for instance, the transcendentalist writer Margaret Fuller, who took Poe to task for what she considered his careless use of language. Perhaps the most sweeping dismissal of Poe's writing originated with Henry James, who—despite his interest in the psychological presentation of fictional characters—declared that "an enthusiasm for Poe is the mark of a decidedly primitive stage of reflection."

"The Fall of the House of Usher" first appeared in Gentleman's Magazine in 1839 and was collected in Tales of the Grotesque and Arabesque the following year.

RELATED COMMENTARIES: James Russell Lowell, "Edgar Allan Poe and 'The Fall of the House of Usher,'" page 1394; Charles E. May, "Edgar Allan Poe—Critical Context," page 1401; Edgar Allan Poe, "Review of Hawthorne's Twice-Told Tales," page 1438.

The Fall of the House of Usher

Son cœur est un luth suspendu;
Sitôt qu'on le touche il résonne.[1]
– DE BÉRANGER

During the whole of a dull, dark, and soundless day in the autumn of the year, when the clouds hung oppressively low in the heavens, I had been passing alone, on horseback, through a singularly dreary tract of country, and at length found myself, as the shades of the evening drew on, within view of the melancholy House of Usher. I know not how it was — but, with the first glimpse of the building, a sense of insufferable gloom pervaded my spirit. I say insufferable; for the feeling was unrelieved by any of that half-pleasurable, because poetic, sentiment, with which the mind usually receives even the sternest natural images of the desolate or terrible. I looked upon the scene before me — upon the mere house, and the simple landscape features of the domain — upon the bleak walls — upon the vacant eye-like windows — upon a few rank sedges — and upon a few white trunks of decayed trees — with an utter depression of soul which I can compare to no earthly sensation more properly than to the after-dream of the reveller upon opium — the bitter lapse into every-day life — the hideous dropping off of the veil. There was an iciness, a sinking, a sickening of the heart — an unredeemed dreariness of thought which no goading of the imagination could torture into aught of the sublime. What was it — I paused to think — what was it that so unnerved me in the contemplation of the House of Usher? It was a mystery all insoluble; nor could I grapple with the shadowy fancies that crowded upon me as I pondered. I was forced to fall back upon the unsatisfactory conclusion, that while, beyond doubt, there *are* combinations of very simple natural objects which have the power of thus affecting us, still the analysis of this power lies among considerations beyond our depth. It was possible, I reflected, that a mere different arrangement of the particulars of the scene, of the details of the picture, would be sufficient to modify, or perhaps to annihilate its capacity for sorrowful impression; and, acting upon this idea, I reined my horse to the precipitous brink of a black and lurid tarn that lay in unruffled lustre by the dwelling, and gazed down — but with a shudder even more thrilling than before — upon the remodelled and inverted images of the gray sedge, and the ghastly tree-stems, and the vacant and eye-like windows.

Nevertheless, in this mansion of gloom I now proposed to myself a sojourn of some weeks. Its proprietor, Roderick Usher, had been one of my boon companions in boyhood; but many years had elapsed since our last meeting. A letter, however, had lately reached me in a distant part of the country — a letter from him — which, in its wildly importunate nature, had

---

[1]His heart is a hanging lute; / Which resonates as soon as touched.

admitted of no other than a personal reply. The MS. gave evidence of nervous agitation. The writer spoke of acute bodily illness—of a mental disorder which oppressed him—and of an earnest desire to see me, as his best, and indeed his only personal friend, with a view of attempting, by the cheerfulness of my society, some alleviation of his malady. It was the manner in which all this, and much more, was said—it was the apparent *heart* that went with his request—which allowed me no room for hesitation; and I accordingly obeyed forthwith what I still considered a very singular summons.

Although, as boys, we had been even intimate associates, yet I really knew little of my friend. His reserve had been always excessive and habitual. I was aware, however, that his very ancient family had been noted, time out of mind, for a peculiar sensibility of temperament, displaying itself, through long ages, in many works of exalted art, and manifested, of late, in repeated deeds of munificent yet unobtrusive charity, as well as in a passionate devotion to the intricacies, perhaps even more than to the orthodox and easily recognizable beauties, of musical science. I had learned, too, the very remarkable fact, that the stem of the Usher race, all time-honoured as it was, had put forth, at no period, any enduring branch; in other words, that the entire family lay in the direct line of descent, and had always, with very trifling and very temporary variation, so lain. It was this deficiency, I considered, while running over in thought the perfect keeping of the character of the premises with the accredited character of the people, and while speculating upon the possible influence which the one, in the long lapse of centuries, might have exercised upon the other—it was this deficiency, perhaps of collateral issue, and the consequent undeviating transmission, from sire to son, of the patrimony with the name, which had, at length, so identified the two as to merge the original title of the estate in the quaint and equivocal apellation of the "House of Usher"—an appellation which seemed to include, in the minds of the peasantry who used it, both the family and the family mansion.

I have said that the sole effect of my somewhat childish experiment— that of looking down within the tarn—had been to deepen the first singular impression. There can be no doubt that the consciousness of the rapid increase of my superstition—for why should I not so term it?—served mainly to accelerate the increase itself. Such, I have long known, is the paradoxical law of all sentiments having terror as a basis. And it might have been for this reason only, that, when I again uplifted my eyes to the house itself, from its image in the pool, there grew in my mind a strange fancy— a fancy so ridiculous, indeed, that I but mention it to show the vivid force of the sensations which oppressed me. I had so worked upon my imagination as really to believe that about the whole mansion and domain there hung an atmosphere peculiar to themselves and their immediate vicinity— an atmosphere which had no affinity with the air of heaven, but which had reeked up from the decayed trees, and the gray wall, and the silent tarn— a pestilent and mystic vapour, dull, sluggish, faintly discernible, and leaden-hued.

Shaking off from my spirit what *must* have been a dream, I scanned more narrowly the real aspect of the building. Its principal feature seemed to be that of an excessive antiquity. The discoloration of ages had been great. Minute fungi overspread the whole exterior, hanging in a fine tangled web-work from the eaves. Yet all this was apart from an extraordinary dilapidation. No portion of the masonry had fallen; and there appeared to be a wild inconsistency between its still perfect adaptation of parts, and the crumbling condition of the individual stones. In this there was much that reminded me of the specious totality of the old woodwork which has rotted for long years in some neglected vault, with no disturbance from the breath of the external air. Beyond this indication of extensive decay, however, the fabric gave little token of instability. Perhaps the eye of a scrutinizing observer might have discovered a barely perceptible fissure, which, extending from the roof of the building in front, made its way down the wall in a zigzag direction, until it became lost in the sullen waters of the tarn.

Noticing these things, I rode over a short causeway to the house. A servant in waiting took my horse, and I entered the Gothic archway of the hall. A valet, of stealthy step, thence conducted me, in silence, through many dark and intricate passages in my progress to the *studio* of his master. Much that I encountered on the way contributed, I know not how, to heighten the vague sentiments of which I have already spoken. While the objects around me — while the carvings of the ceilings, the sombre tapestries of the walls, the ebon blackness of the floors, and the phantasmagoric armorial trophies which rattled as I strode, were but matters to which, or to such as which, I had been accustomed from my infancy — while I hesitated not to acknowledge how familiar was all this — I still wondered to find how unfamiliar were the fancies which ordinary images were stirring up. On one of the staircases, I met the physician of the family. His countenance, I thought, wore a mingled expression of low cunning and perplexity. He accosted me with trepidation and passed on. The valet now threw open a door and ushered me into the presence of his master.

The room in which I found myself was very large and lofty. The windows were long, narrow, and pointed, and at so vast a distance from the black oaken floor as to be altogether inaccessible from within. Feeble gleams of encrimsoned light made their way through the trellised panes, and served to render sufficiently distinct the more prominent objects around; the eye, however, struggled in vain to reach the remoter angles of the chamber, or the recesses of the vaulted and fretted ceiling. Dark draperies hung upon the walls. The general furniture was profuse, comfortless, antique, and tattered. Many books and musical instruments lay scattered about, but failed to give any vitality to the scene. I felt that I breathed an atmosphere of sorrow. An air of stern, deep, and irredeemable gloom hung over and pervaded all.

Upon my entrance, Usher arose from a sofa on which he had been lying at full length, and greeted me with a vivacious warmth which had much in it, I at first thought, of an overdone cordiality—of the constrained effort of the *ennuyé* man of the world. A glance, however, at his countenance convinced me of his perfect sincerity. We sat down; and for some moments, while he spoke not, I gazed upon him with a feeling half of pity, half of awe. Surely, man had never before so terribly altered, in so brief a period, as had Roderick Usher! It was with difficulty that I could bring myself to admit the identity of the wan being before me with the companion of my early boyhood. Yet the character of his face had been at all times remarkable. A cadaverousness of complexion; an eye large, liquid, and luminous beyond comparison; lips somewhat thin and very pallid, but of a surpassingly beautiful curve; a nose of a delicate Hebrew model, but with a breadth of nostril unusual in similar formations; a finely moulded chin, speaking, in its want of prominence, of a want of moral energy; hair of a more than web-like softness and tenuity; these features, with an inordinate expansion above the regions of the temple, made up altogether a countenance not easily to be forgotten. And now in the mere exaggeration of the prevailing character of these features, and of the expression they were wont to convey, lay so much of change that I doubted to whom I spoke. The now ghastly pallor of the skin, and the now miraculous lustre of the eye, above all things startled and even awed me. The silken hair, too, had been suffered to grow all unheeded, and as, in its wild gossamer texture, it floated rather than fell about the face, I could not, even with effort, connect its Arabesque expression with any idea of simple humanity.

In the manner of my friend I was at once struck with an incoherence—an inconsistency; and I soon found this to arise from a series of feeble and futile struggles to overcome an habitual trepidancy—an excessive nervous agitation. For something of this nature I had indeed been prepared, no less by his letter, than by reminiscences of certain boyish traits, and by conclusions deduced from his peculiar physical conformation and temperament. His action was alternately vivacious and sullen. His voice varied rapidly from a tremulous indecision (when the animal spirits seemed utterly in abeyance) to that species of energetic concision—that abrupt, weighty, unhurried, and hollow-sounding enunciation—that leaden, self-balanced, and perfectly modulated guttural utterance, which may be observed in the lost drunkard, or the irreclaimable eater of opium, during the periods of his most intense excitement.

It was thus that he spoke of the object of my visit, of his earnest desire to see me, and of the solace he expected me to afford him. He entered, at some length, into what he conceived to be the nature of his malady. It was, he said, a constitutional and a family evil, and one for which he despaired to find a remedy—a mere nervous affection, he immediately added, which would undoubtedly soon pass off. It displayed itself in a host of unnatural sensations. Some of these, as he detailed them, interested and bewildered me; although, perhaps, the terms and the general manner of their narration had their weight. He suffered much from a morbid acuteness of the senses; the most insipid food was alone endurable; he could wear only garments of certain texture; the odours of all flowers were oppressive; his eyes were tortured by even a faint light; and there were but peculiar sounds, and these from stringed instruments, which did not inspire him with horror.

To an anomalous species of terror I found him a bounden slave. "I shall perish," said he, "I *must* perish in this deplorable folly. Thus, thus, and not otherwise, shall I be lost. I dread the events of the future, not in themselves, but in their results. I shudder at the thought of any, even the most trivial, incident, which may operate upon this intolerable agitation of soul. I have, indeed, no abhorrence of danger, except in its absolute effect—in terror. In this unnerved—in this pitiable condition—I feel that the period will sooner or later arrive when I must abandon life and reason together, in some struggle with the grim phantasm, FEAR."

I learned, moreover, at intervals, and through broken and equivocal hints, another singular feature of his mental condition. He was enchained by certain superstitious impressions in regard to the dwelling which he tenanted, and whence, for many years, he had never ventured forth—in regard to an influence whose supposititious force was conveyed in terms too shadowy here to be re-stated—an influence which some peculiarities in the mere form and substance of his family mansion had, by dint of long sufferance, he said, obtained over his spirit—an effect which the *physique* of the gray wall and turrets, and of the dim tarn into which they all looked down, had, at length, brought about upon the *morale* of his existence.

He admitted, however, although with hesitation, that much of the peculiar gloom which thus afflicted him could be traced to a more natural and far more palpable origin—to the severe and long-continued illness—indeed to the evidently approaching dissolution—of a tenderly beloved sister, his sole companion for long years, his last and only relative on earth. "Her decease," he said, with a bitterness which I can never forget, "would leave him (him the hopeless and the frail) the last of the ancient race of the Ushers." While he spoke, the lady Madeline (for so was she called) passed slowly through a remote portion of the apartment, and, without having noticed my presence, disappeared. I regarded her with an utter astonishment not unmingled with dread—and yet I found it impossible to account for such feelings. A sensation of stupor oppressed me, as my eyes followed her retreating steps. When a door, at length, closed upon her, my glance sought instinctively and eagerly the countenance of the brother—but he had buried his face in his hands, and I could only perceive that a far more than ordinary wanness had overspread the emaciated fingers through which trickled many passionate tears.

The disease of the lady Madeline had long baffled the skill of her physicians. A settled apathy, a gradual wasting away of the person, and frequent although transient affections of a partially cataleptical character were the unusual diagnosis. Hitherto she had steadily borne up against the pressure of her malady, and had not betaken herself finally to bed; but on the closing in of the evening of my arrival at the house, she succumbed (as her brother told me at night with inexpressible agitation) to the prostrating power of the destroyer; and I learned that the glimpse I had obtained of her person would thus probably be the last I should obtain — that the lady, at least while living, would be seen by me no more.

For several days ensuing, her name was unmentioned by either Usher or myself: and during this period I was busied in earnest endeavours to alleviate the melancholy of my friend. We painted and read together, or I listened, as if in a dream, to the wild improvisations of his speaking guitar. And thus, as a closer and still closer intimacy admitted me more unreservedly into the recesses of his spirit, the more bitterly did I perceive the futility of all attempt at cheering a mind from which darkness, as if an inherent positive quality, poured forth upon all objects of the moral and physical universe in one unceasing radiation of gloom.

I shall ever bear about me a memory of the many solemn hours I thus spent alone with the master of the House of Usher. Yet I should fail in any attempt to convey an idea of the exact character of the studies, or of the occupations, in which he involved me, or led me the way. An excited and highly distempered ideality threw a sulphureous lustre over all. His long improvised dirges will ring forever in my ears. Among other things, I hold painfully in mind a certain singular perversion and amplification of the wild air of the last waltz of Von Weber. From the paintings over which his elaborate fancy brooded, and which grew, touch by touch, into vagueness at which I shuddered the more thrillingly, because I shuddered knowing not why; — from these paintings (vivid as their images now are before me) I would in vain endeavour to educe more than a small portion which should lie within the compass of merely written words. By the utter simplicity, by the nakedness of his designs, he arrested and overawed attention. If ever mortal painted an idea, that mortal was Roderick Usher. For me at least — in the circumstances then surrounding me — there arose out of the pure abstractions which the hypochondriac contrived to throw upon his canvas, an intensity of intolerable awe, no shadow of which I felt ever yet in the contemplation of the certainly glowing yet too concrete reveries of Fuseli.

One of the phantasmagoric conceptions of my friend, partaking not so rigidly of the spirit of abstraction, may be shadowed forth, although feebly, in words. A small picture presented the interior of an immensely long and rectangular vault or tunnel, with low walls, smooth, white, and without interruption or device. Certain accessory points of the design served well to convey the idea that this excavation lay at an exceeding depth below the surface of the earth. No outlet was observed in any portion of its vast extent, and no torch or other artificial source of light was discernible; yet a flood of intense rays rolled throughout, and bathed the whole in a ghastly and inappropriate splendour.

I have just spoken of that morbid condition of the auditory nerve which rendered all music intolerable to the sufferer, with the exception of certain effects of stringed instruments. It was, perhaps, the narrow limits to which he thus confined himself upon the guitar, which gave birth, in great measure, to the fantastic character of his performances. But the fervid *facility* of his *impromptus* could not be so accounted for. They must have been, and were, in the notes, as well as in the words of his wild fantasias (for he not unfrequently accompanied himself with rhymed verbal improvisations), the result of that intense mental collectedness and concentration to which I have previously alluded as observable only in particular moments of the highest artificial excitement. The words of one of these rhapsodies I have easily remembered. I was, perhaps, the more forcibly impressed with it, as he gave it, because, in the under or mystic current of its meaning, I fancied that I perceived, and for the first time, a full consciousness on the part of Usher, of the tottering of his lofty reason upon her throne. The verses, which were entitled "The Haunted Palace," ran very nearly, if not accurately, thus:

I
In the greenest of our valleys,
    By good angels tenanted,
Once a fair and stately palace —
    Radiant palace — reared its head.
In the monarch Thought's dominion —
    It stood there!
Never seraph spread a pinion
    Over fabric half so fair.

II
Banners yellow, glorious, golden,
    On its roof did float and flow;
(This — all this — was in the olden
    Time long ago)
And every gentle air that dallied,
    In that sweet day,
Along the ramparts plumed and pallid,
    A winged odour went away.

III
Wanderers in that happy valley
    Through two luminous windows saw
Spirits moving musically
    To a lute's well-tunèd law,
Round about a throne, where sitting
    (Porphyrogene!)
In state his glory well befitting,
    The ruler of the realm was seen.

IV
And all with pearl and ruby glowing
    Was the fair palace door,
Through which came flowing, flowing, flowing
    And sparkling evermore,
A troop of Echoes whose sweet duty
    Was but to sing,

In voices of surpassing beauty,
    The wit and wisdom of their king.

V

But evil things, in robes of sorrow,
    Assailed the monarch's high estate;
(Ah, let us mourn, for never morrow
    Shall dawn upon him, desolate!)
And, round about his home, the glory
    That blushed and bloomed
Is but a dim-remembered story
    Of the old time entombed.

VI

And travellers now within that valley,
    Through the red-litten windows see
Vast forms that move fantastically
    To a discordant melody;
While, like a rapid ghastly river,
    Through the pale door,
A hideous throng rush out forever,
    And laugh — but smile no more.

I well remember that suggestions arising from this ballad led us into a train of thought wherein there became manifest an opinion of Usher's which I mention not so much on account of its novelty (for other men[2] have thought thus,) as on account of the pertinacity with which he maintained it. This opinion, in its general form, was that of the sentience of all vegetable things. But, in his disordered fancy, the idea had assumed a more daring character, and trespassed, under certain conditions, upon the kingdom of inorganization. I lack words to express the full extent, or the earnest *abandon* of his persuasion. The belief, however, was connected (as I have previously hinted) with the gray stones of the home of his forefathers. The conditions of the sentience had been here, he imagined, fulfilled in the method of collocation of these stones — in the order of their arrangement, as well as in that of the many *fungi* which overspread them, and of the decayed trees which stood around — above all, in the long undisturbed endurance of this arrangement, and in its reduplication in the still waters of the tarn. Its evidence — the evidence of the sentience — was to be seen, he said (and I here started as he spoke), in the gradual yet certain condensation of an atmosphere of their own about the waters and the walls. The result was discoverable, he added, in that silent yet importunate and terrible influence which for centuries had moulded the destinies of his family, and which made *him* what I now saw him — what he was. Such opinions need no comment, and I will make none.

---

[2]Watson, Dr. Percival, Spallanzani, and especially the Bishop of Landaff. — See *Chemical Essays,* vol. v. [Poe's note.]

Our books—the books which, for years, had formed no small portion of the mental existence of the invalid—were, as might be supposed, in strict keeping with his character of phantasm. We pored together over such works as the Ververt et Chartreuse of Gresset; the Belphegor of Machiavelli; the Heaven and Hell of Swedenborg; the Subterranean Voyage of Nicholas Klimm of Holberg; the Chiromancy of Robert Flud, of Jean D'Indaginé, and of De la Chambre; the Journey into the Blue Distance of Tieck; and the City of the Sun of Campanella. One favourite volume was a small octavo edition of the *Directorium Inquisitorum,* by the Dominican Eymeric de Gironne; and there were passages in Pomponius Mela, about the old African Satyrs and Ægipans, over which Usher would sit dreaming for hours. His chief delight, however, was found in the perusal of an exceedingly rare and curious book in quarto Gothic—the manual of a forgotten church—the *Vigiliæ Mortuorum secundum Chorum Ecclesiæ Maguntinæ.*

I could not help thinking of the wild ritual of this work, and of its probable influence upon the hypochondriac, when, one evening, having informed me abruptly that the lady Madeline was no more, he stated his intention of preserving her corpse for a fortnight, (previously to its final interment,) in one of the numerous vaults within the main walls of the building. The worldly reason, however, assigned for this singular proceeding, was one which I did not feel at liberty to dispute. The brother had been led to his resolution (so he told me) by consideration of the unusual character of the malady of the deceased, of certain obtrusive and eager inquiries on the part of her medical men, and of the remote and exposed situation of the burial-ground of the family. I will not deny that when I called to mind the sinister countenance of the person whom I met upon the staircase, on the day of my arrival at the house, I had no desire to oppose what I regarded as at best but a harmless, and by no means an unnatural, precaution.

At the request of Usher, I personally aided him in the arrangements for the temporary entombment. The body having been encoffined, we two alone bore it to its rest. The vault in which we placed it (and which had been so long unopened that our torches, half smothered in its oppressive atmosphere, gave us little opportunity for investigation) was small, damp, and entirely without means of admission for light; lying, at great depth, immediately beneath that portion of the building in which was my own sleeping apartment. It had been used, apparently, in remote feudal times, for the worst purposes of a donjon-keep, and, in later days, as a place of deposit for powder, or some other highly combustible substance, as a portion of its floor, and the whole interior of a long archway through which we reached it, were carefully sheathed with copper. The door, of massive iron, had been, also, similarly protected. Its immense weight caused an unusually sharp grating sound, as it moved upon its hinges.

Having deposited our mournful burden upon tressels within this region of horror, we partially turned aside the yet unscrewed lid of the coffin, and looked upon the face of the tenant. A striking similitude between the brother and sister now first arrested my attention; and Usher, divining, perhaps, my thoughts, murmured out some few words from which I learned that the deceased and himself had been twins, and that sympathies of a scarcely intelligible nature had always existed between them. Our glances, however, rested not long upon the dead — for we could not regard her unawed. The disease which had thus entombed the lady in the maturity of youth, had left, as usual in all maladies of a strictly cataleptical character, the mockery of a faint blush upon the bosom and the face, and that suspiciously lingering smile upon the lip which is so terrible in death. We replaced and screwed down the lid, and, having secured the door of iron, made our way, with toil, into the scarcely less gloomy apartments of the upper portion of the house.

And now, some days of bitter grief having elapsed, an observable change came over the features of the mental disorder of my friend. His ordinary manner had vanished. His ordinary occupations were neglected or forgotten. He roamed from chamber to chamber with hurried, unequal, and objectless step. The pallor of his countenance had assumed, if possible, a more ghastly hue — but the luminousness of his eye had utterly gone out. The once occasional huskiness of his tone was heard no more; and a tremulous quaver, as if of extreme terror, habitually characterized his utterance. There were times, indeed, when I thought his unceasingly agitated mind was labouring with some oppressive secret, to divulge which he struggled for the necessary courage. At times, again, I was obliged to resolve all into the mere inexplicable vagaries of madness, for I beheld him gazing upon vacancy for long hours, in an attitude of the profoundest attention, as if listening to some imaginary sound. It was no wonder that his condition terrified — that it infected me. I felt creeping upon me, by slow yet certain degrees, the wild influences of his own fantastic yet impressive superstitions.

It was, especially, upon retiring to bed late in the night of the seventh or eighth day after the placing of the lady Madeline within the donjon, that I experienced the full power of such feelings. Sleep came not near my couch — while the hours waned and waned away. I struggled to reason off the nervousness which had dominion over me. I endeavoured to believe that much, if not all of what I felt, was due to the bewildering influence of the gloomy furniture of the room — of the dark and tattered draperies, which, tortured into motion by the breath of a rising tempest, swayed fitfully to and fro upon the walls, and rustled uneasily about the decorations of the bed. But my efforts were fruitless. An irrepressible tremour gradually pervaded my frame; and, at length, there sat upon my very heart an incubus of utterly causeless alarm. Shaking this off with a gasp and a struggle, I uplifted myself upon the pillows, and, peering earnestly within the intense darkness of the chamber, hearkened — I know not why, except that an instinctive spirit prompted me — to certain low and indefinite sounds which came, through the pauses of the storm, at long intervals, I knew not whence.

Overpowered by an intense sentiment of horror, unaccountable yet unendurable, I threw on my clothes with haste, (for I felt that I should sleep no more during the night,) and endeavoured to arouse myself from the pitiable condition into which I had fallen, by pacing rapidly to and fro through the apartment.

I had taken but few turns in this manner, when a light step on an adjoining staircase arrested my attention. I presently recognised it as that of Usher. In an instant afterward he rapped, with a gentle touch, at my door, and entered, bearing a lamp. His countenance was, as usual, cadaverously wan—but, moreover, there was a species of mad hilarity in his eyes—an evidently restrained *hysteria* in his whole demeanour. His air appalled me—but anything was preferable to the solitude which I had so long endured, and I even welcomed his presence as a relief.

"And you have not seen it?" he said abruptly, after having stared about him for some moments in silence—"you have not then seen it?—but, stay! you shall." Thus speaking, and having carefully shaded his lamp, he hurried to one of the casements, and threw it freely open to the storm.

The impetuous fury of the entering gust nearly lifted us from our feet. It was, indeed, a tempestuous yet sternly beautiful night, and one wildly singular in its terror and its beauty. A whirlwind had apparently collected its force in our vicinity; for there were frequent and violent alterations in the direction of the wind; and the exceeding density of the clouds (which hung so low as to press upon the turrets of the house) did not prevent our perceiving the life-like velocity with which they flew careering from all points against each other, without passing away into the distance. I say that even their exceeding density did not prevent our perceiving this—yet we had no glimpse of the moon or stars—nor was there any flashing forth of the lightning. But the under surfaces of the huge masses of agitated vapour, as well as all terrestrial objects immediately around us, were glowing in the unnatural light of a faintly luminous and distinctly visible gaseous exhalation which hung about and enshrouded the mansion.

"You must not—you shall not behold this!" said I, shudderingly, to Usher, as I led him, with a gentle violence, from the window to a seat. "These appearances, which bewilder you, are merely electrical phenomena not uncommon—or it may be that they have their ghastly origin in the rank miasma of the tarn. Let us close this casement;—the air is chilling and dangerous to your frame. Here is one of your favourite romances. I will read, and you shall listen;—and so we will pass away this terrible night together."

The antique volume which I had taken up was the "Mad Trist" of Sir Launcelot Canning; but I had called it a favourite of Usher's more in sad jest than in earnest; for, in truth, there is little in its uncouth and unimaginative prolixity which could have had interest for the lofty and spiritual ideality of my friend. It was, however, the only book immediately at hand; and I indulged a vague hope that the excitement which now agitated the hypochondriac might find relief (for the history of mental disorder is full of similar anomalies) even in the extremeness of the folly which I could read. Could I have judged, indeed, by the wild overstrained air of vivacity with which he hearkened, or apparently hearkened, to the words of the tale, I might well have congratulated myself upon the success of my design.

I had arrived at that well-known portion of the story where Ethelred, the hero of the Trist, having sought in vain for peaceable admission into the dwelling of the hermit, proceeds to make good an entrance by force. Here, it will be remembered, the words of the narrative run thus:

"And Ethelred, who was by nature of a doughty heart, and who was now mighty withal, on account of the powerfulness of the wine which he had drunken, waited no longer to hold parley with the hermit, who, in sooth, was of an obstinate and maliceful turn, but, feeling the rain upon his shoulders, and fearing the rising of the tempest, uplifted his mace outright, and, with blows, made quickly room in the plankings of the door for his gauntleted hand; and now pulling therewith sturdily, he so cracked, and ripped, and tore all asunder, that the noise of the dry and hollow-sounding wood alarmed and reverberated throughout the forest."

At the termination of this sentence I started and, for a moment, paused; for it appeared to me (although I at once concluded that my excited fancy had deceived me)—it appeared to me that, from some very remote portion of the mansion, there came, indistinctly, to my ears, what might have been, in its exact similarity of character, the echo (but a stifled and dull one certainly) of the very cracking and ripping sound which Sir Launcelot had so particularly described. It was, beyond doubt, the coincidence alone which had arrested my attention; for, amid the rattling of the sashes of the casements, and the ordinary commingled noises of the still increasing storm, the sound, in itself, had nothing, surely, which should have interested or disturbed me. I continued the story:

"But the good champion Ethelred, now entering within the door, was sore enraged and amazed to perceive no signal of the maliceful hermit; but, in the stead thereof, a dragon of a scaly and prodigious demeanour, and of a fiery tongue, which sate in guard before a palace of gold, with a floor of silver; and upon the wall there hung a shield of shining brass with this legend enwritten—

> Who entereth herein, a conqueror hath bin;
> Who slayeth the dragon, the shield he shall win.

And Ethelred uplifted his mace, and struck upon the head of the dragon, which fell before him, and gave up his pesty breath, with a shriek so horrid and harsh, and withal so piercing, that Ethelred had fain to close his ears with his hands against the dreadful noise of it, the like whereof was never before heard."

Here again I paused abruptly, and now with a feeling of wild amazement—for there could be no doubt whatever that, in this instance, I did actually hear (although from what direction it proceeded I found it impossible to say) a low and apparently distant, but harsh, protracted, and most unusual screaming or grating sound—the exact counterpart of what my fancy had already conjured up for the dragon's unnatural shriek as described by the romancer.

Oppressed, as I certainly was, upon the occurrence of the second and most extraordinary coincidence, by a thousand conflicting sensations, in which wonder and extreme terror were predominant, I still retained sufficient presence of mind to avoid exciting, by any observation, the sensitive nervousness of my companion. I was by no means certain that he had noticed the sounds in question; although, assuredly, a strange alteration had, during the last few minutes, taken place in his demeanour. From a position fronting my own, he had gradually brought round his chair, so as to sit with his face to the door of the chamber; and thus I could but partially perceive his features, although I saw that his lips trembled as if he were murmuring inaudibly. His head had dropped upon his breast—yet I knew that he was not asleep, from the wide and rigid opening of the eye as I caught a glance of it in profile. The motion of his body, too, was at variance with this idea—for he rocked from side to side with a gentle yet constant and uniform sway. Having rapidly taken notice of all this, I resumed the narrative of Sir Launcelot, which thus proceeded:

"And now, the champion, having escaped from the terrible fury of the dragon, bethinking himself of the brazen shield, and of the breaking up of the enchantment which was upon it, removed the carcass from out of the way before him, and approached valorously over the silver pavement of the castle to where the shield was upon the wall; which in sooth tarried not for his full coming, but fell down at his feet upon the silver floor, with a mighty great and terrible ringing sound."

No sooner had these syllables passed my lips, than—as if a shield of brass had indeed, at the moment, fallen heavily upon a floor of silver—I became aware of a distinct, hollow, metallic, and clangorous, yet apparently muffled reverberation. Completely unnerved, I leaped to my feet; but the measured rocking movement of Usher was undisturbed. I rushed to the chair in which he sat. His eyes were bent fixedly before him, and throughout his whole countenance there reigned a stony rigidity. But, as I placed my hand upon his shoulder, there came a strong shudder over his whole person; a sickly smile quivered about his lips; and I saw that he spoke in a low, hurried, and gibbering murmur, as if unconscious of my presence. Bending closely over him, I at length drank in the hideous import of his words.

"Not hear it?—yes, I hear it, and *have* heard it. Long—long—long— many minutes, many hours, many days, have I heard it—yet I dared not— oh, pity me, miserable wretch that I am!—I dared not—I *dared* not speak! *We have put her living in the tomb!* Said I not that my senses were acute? I *now* tell you that I heard her first feeble movements in the hollow coffin. I heard them—many, many days ago—yet I dared not—I *dared not speak!* And now—to-night—Ethelred—ha! ha!—the breaking of the hermit's door, and the death-cry of the dragon, and the clangour of the shield!—say, rather, the rending of her coffin, and the grating of the iron hinges of her prison, and her struggles within the coppered archway of the vault! Oh whither shall I fly? Will she not be here anon? Is she not hurrying to upbraid me for my haste? Have I not heard her footsteps on the stair? Do I not distinguish that heavy and horrible beating of her heart? MADMAN!"—here he sprang furiously to his feet, and shrieked out his syllables, as if in the effort he were giving up his soul—"MADMAN! I TELL YOU THAT SHE NOW STANDS WITHOUT THE DOOR!"

As if in the superhuman energy of his utterance there had been found the potency of a spell—the huge antique panels to which the speaker pointed threw slowly back, upon the instant, their ponderous and ebony jaws. It was the work of the rushing gust—but then without those doors there *did* stand the lofty and enshrouded figure of the lady Madeline of Usher. There was blood upon her white robes, and the evidence of some bitter struggle upon every portion of her emaciated frame. For a moment she remained trembling and reeling to and fro upon the threshold, then, with a low moaning cry, fell heavily inward upon the person of her brother, and in her violent and now final death-agonies, bore him to the floor a corpse, and a victim to the terrors he had anticipated.

From that chamber, and from that mansion, I fled aghast. The storm was still abroad in all its wrath as I found myself crossing the old causeway. Suddenly there shot along the path a wild light, and I turned to see whence a gleam so unusual could have issued; for the vast house and its shadows were alone behind me. The radiance was that of the full, setting, and blood-red moon, which now shone vividly through that once barely discernible fissure, of which I have before spoken as extending from the roof of the building, in a zigzag direction, to the base. While I gazed, this fissure rapidly widened—there came a fierce breath of the whirlwind—the entire orb of the satellite burst at once upon my sight—my brain reeled as I saw the mighty walls rushing asunder—there was a long tumultuous shouting sound like the voice of a thousand waters—and the deep and dank tarn at my feet closed sullenly and silently over the fragments of the "HOUSE OF USHER."   [1839]

THOMAS BANGS THORPE

Thomas Bangs Thorpe (1815–1878) was born in Westfield, Massachusetts, the son of a Methodist minister whose ancestors had settled in Connecticut before 1639. Thorpe was educated in New York City, where he began to study figure painting at age fifteen with John Quidor, an artist who made his living painting the panels of fire engines. In 1833 Thorpe exhibited his first portrait in the National Academy of Design. Its subject was one of Washington Irving's fictional characters, in tribute to that author's work. After two years at Wesleyan University, Thorpe moved to Louisiana for health reasons. When he was unable to make a living as a portrait painter, he turned to writing tales and sketches. His work from 1839 to 1843 was published in Knickerbocker Magazine *and* Spirit of the Times, *a New York humor and sporting newspaper edited by William T. Porter.*

"The Big Bear of Arkansas," a comic story in dialect, was published in the Spirit *on March 27, 1841, and helped establish Thorpe as a writer of tall tales about the Southwest. In the 1840s he also edited five Louisiana newspapers to support his wife and children. His stories were included in an 1845 collection edited by Porter,* The Big Bear of Arkansas and Other Sketches. *It became one of the most popular books of southwestern humor of its time.*

After moving back to New York City in 1854, Thorpe wrote articles on southern life for Harper's Magazine. *A collection of twenty-four of his tales was published that year under the title* The Hive of "The Bee-Hunter," A Repository of Sketches, Including Peculiar American Characters, Scenery, and Rural Sports. *He also wrote a reply to Harriet Beecher Stowe's* Uncle Tom's Cabin *in his only novel,* The Master's House: A Tale of Southern Life (1854). *A loyal Unionist during the Civil War, Thorpe served as a colonel in the occupation forces in New Orleans after the city was captured by the Union army. After the war he practiced law in New York City, worked at the Custom House, and wrote articles on American art for various periodicals. Thorpe is best known as the author of "The Big Bear of Arkansas," in which he used the vernacular comic style with consummate artistry. William Faulkner later paid Thorpe the ultimate compliment when he said, "That's a fine story. A writer is afraid of a story like that. He's afraid he'll try to rewrite it. A writer has to learn when to run from a story."*

The Big Bear of Arkansas

A steamboat on the Mississippi, frequently, in making her regular trips, carries between places varying from one to two thousand miles apart; and, as these boats advertise to land passengers and freight at "all intermediate landings," the heterogeneous character of the passengers of one of these up-country boats can scarcely be imagined by one who has never seen it with his own eyes.

Starting from New Orleans in one of these boats, you will find yourself associated with men from every State in the Union, and from every portion of the globe; and a man of observation need not lack for amusement or instruction in such a crowd, if he will take the trouble to read the great book of character so favorably opened before him.

Here may be seen, jostling together, the wealthy Southern planter and the pedler of tin-ware from New England—the Northern merchant and the Southern jockey—a venerable bishop, and a desperate gambler—the land speculator, and the honest farmer—professional men of all creeds and characters—Wolvereens, Suckers, Hoosiers, Buckeyes, and Corn-crackers, beside a "plentiful sprinkling" of the half-horse and half-alligator species of men, who are peculiar to "old Mississippi," and who appear to gain a livelihood by simply going up and down the river. In the pursuit of pleasure or business, I have frequently found myself in such a crowd.

On one occasion, when in New Orleans, I had occasion to take a trip of a few miles up the Mississippi, and I hurried on board the well-known "high-pressure-and-beat-every-thing" steamboat "Invincible," just as the last note of the last bell was sounding; and when the confusion and bustle that is natural to a boat's getting under way had subsided, I discovered that I was associated in as heterogeneous a crowd as was ever got together. As my trip was to be of a few hours' duration only, I made no endeavors to become acquainted with my fellow-passengers, most of whom would be together many days. Instead of this, I took out of my pocket the "latest paper," and more critically than usual examined its contents; my fellow-passengers, at the same time, disposed of themselves in little groups.

While I was thus busily employed in reading, and my companions were more busily still employed, in discussing such subjects as suited their humors best, we were most unexpectedly startled by a loud Indian whoop, uttered in the "social hall," that part of the cabin fitted off for a bar; then was to be heard a loud crowing, which would not have continued to interest us—such sounds being quite common in that *place of spirits*—had not the hero of these windy accomplishments stuck his head into the cabin, and hallooed out, "Hurra for the Big Bear of Arkansaw!"

Then might be heard a confused hum of voices, unintelligible, save in such broken sentences as "horse," "screamer," "lightning is slow," &c.

As might have been expected, this continued interruption attracted the attention of every one in the cabin; all conversation ceased, and in the midst of this surprise, the "Big Bear" walked into the cabin, took a chair, put his feet on the stove, and looking back over his shoulder, passed the general and familiar salute—"Strangers, how are you?"

He then expressed himself as much at home as if he had been at "the Forks of Cypress," and "prehaps a little more so."

Some of the company at this familiarity looked a little angry, and some astonished; but in a moment every face was wreathed in a smile. There was something about the intruder that won the heart on sight. He appeared to be a man enjoying perfect health and contentment; his eyes were as sparkling as diamonds, and good-natured to simplicity. Then his perfect confidence in himself was irresistibly droll.

"Prehaps," said he, "gentlemen," running on without a person interrupting, "prehaps you have been to New Orleans often; I never made *the first visit before,* and I don't intend to make another in a crow's life. I am thrown away in that ar place, and useless, that ar a fact. Some of the gentlemen thar called me *green*—well, prehaps I am, said I, *but I arn't so at home;* and if I ain't off my trail much, the heads of them perlite chaps themselves wern't much the hardest; for according to my notion, they were *real know-nothings,* green as a pumpkin-vine—couldn't, in farming, I'll bet, raise a crop of turnips; and as for shooting, they'd miss a barn if the door was swinging, and that, too, with the best rifle in the country. And then they talked to me 'bout hunting, and laughed at my calling the principal game in Arkansaw poker, and high-low-jack.

"'Prehaps,' said I, 'you prefer checkers and roulette;' at this they laughed harder than ever, and asked me if I lived in the woods, and didn't know what *game* was?

"At this, I rather think *I* laughed.

"'Yes,' I roared, and says I, 'Strangers, if you'd ask me *how we got our meat* in Arkansaw, I'd a told you at once, and given you a list of varmints that would make a caravan, beginning with the bar, and ending off with the cat; that's *meat* though, not game.'

"Game, indeed,—that's what city folks call it; and with them it means chippen-birds and shite-pokes; may be such trash live in my diggins, but I arn't noticed them yet: a bird anyway is too trifling. I never did shoot at but one, and I'd never forgiven myself for that, had it weighed less than forty pounds. I wouldn't draw a rifle on anything less heavy than that; and when I meet with another wild turkey of the same size, I will drap him."

"A wild turkey weighing forty pounds!" exclaimed twenty voices in the cabin at once.

"Yes, strangers, and wasn't it a whopper? You see, the thing was so fat that it couldn't fly far; and when he fell out of the tree, after I shot him, on striking the ground he bust open behind, and the way the pound gobs of tallow rolled out of the opening was perfectly beautiful."

"Where did all that happen?" asked a cynical-looking Hoosier.

"Happen! happened in Arkansaw: where else could it have happened, but in the creation State, the finishing-up country—a State where the *sile* runs down to the centre of the 'arth, and government gives you a title to every inch of it? Then its airs—just breathe them, and they will make you snort like a horse. It's a State without a fault, it is."

"Excepting mosquitoes," cried the Hoosier.

"Well, stranger, except them; for it ar a fact that they are rather *enormous,* and do push themselves in somewhat troublesome. But, stranger, they never stick twice in the same place; and give them a fair chance for a few months, and you will get as much above noticing them as an alligator. They can't hurt my feelings, for they lay under the skin; and I never knew but one case of injury resulting from them, and that was to a Yankee: and they take worse to foreigners, any how, than they do to natives. But the way they used that fellow up! first they punched him until he swelled up and busted; then he sup-per-a-ted, as the doctor called it, until he was as raw as beef; then, owing to the warm weather, he tuck the ager, and finally he tuck a steamboat and left the country. He was the only man that ever tuck mosquitoes at heart that I knowd of.

"But mosquitoes is natur, and I never find fault with her. If they ar large, Arkansaw is large, her varmits ar large, her trees ar large, her rivers ar large, and a small mosquito would be of no more use in Arkansaw than preaching in a cane-brake."

This knock-down argument in favor of big mosquitoes used the Hoosier up, and the logician started on a new track, to explain how numerous bear were in his "diggins," where he represented them to be "about as plenty as blackberries, and a little plentifuller."

Upon the utterance of this assertion, a timid little man near me inquired, if the bear in Arkansaw ever attacked the settlers in numbers.

"No," said our hero, warming with the subject, "no stranger, for you see it ain't the natur of bear to go in droves; but the way they squander about in pairs and single ones is edifying.

"And then the way I hunt them—the old black rascals know the crack of my gun as well as they know a pig's squealing. They grown thin in our parts, it frightens them so, and they do take the noise dreadfully, poor things. That gun of mine is a perfect *epidemic among bear*: if not watched closely, it will go off as quick on a warm scent as my dog Bowieknife will: and then that dog—whew! why the fellow thinks that the world is full of bear, he finds them so easy. It's lucky he don't talk as well as think; for with his natural modesty, if he should suddenly learn how much he is acknowledged to be ahead of all other dogs in the universe, he would be astonished to death in two minutes.

"Strangers, that dog knows a bear's way as well as a horse-jockey knows a woman's: he always barks at the right time, bites at the exact place, and whips without getting a scratch.

"I never could tell whether he was made expressly to hunt bear, or whether bear was made expressly for him to hunt; any way, I believe they were ordained to go together as naturally as Squire Jones says a man and woman is, when he moralizes in marrying a couple. In fact, Jones once said, said he, 'Marriage according to law is a civil contract of divine origin; it's common to all countries as well as Arkansaw, and people take to it as naturally as Jim Doggett's Bowieknife takes to bear.'"

"What season of the year do your hunts take place?" inquired a gentlemanly foreigner, who, from some peculiarities of his baggage, I suspected to be an Englishman, on some hunting expedition, probably at the foot of the Rocky Mountains.

"The season for bear hunting, stranger," said the man of Arkansaw, "is generally all the year round, and the hunts take place about as regular. I read in history that varmints have their fat season, and their lean season. That is not the case in Arkansaw, feeding as they do upon the *spontenacious* productions of the sile, they have one continued fat season the year round; though in winter things in this way is rather more greasy than in summer, I must admit. For that reason bear with us run in warm weather, but in winter they only waddle.

"Fat, fat! it's an enemy to speed; it tames every thing that has plenty of it. I have seen wild turkeys, from its influence, as gentle as chickens. Run a bear in this fat condition, and the way it improves the critter for eating is amazing; it sort of mixes the ile up with the meat, until you can't tell t'other from which. I've done this often.

"I recollect one perty morning in particular, of putting an old he fellow on the stretch, and considering the weight he carried, he run well. But the dogs soon tired him down, and when I came up with him wasn't he in a beautiful sweat—I might say fever; and then to see his tongue sticking out of his mouth a feet, and his sides sinking and opening like a bellows, and his cheeks so fat that he couldn't look cross. In this fix I blazed at him, and pitch me naked into a briar patch, if the steam didn't come out of the bullet-hole ten foot in a straight line. The fellow, I reckon, was made on the high-pressure system, and the lead sort of bust his biler."

"That column of steam was rather curious, or else the bear must have been very *warm*," observed the foreigner, with a laugh.

"Stranger, as you observe, that bear was WARM, and the blowing off of the steam show'd it, and also how hard the varmint had been run. I have no doubt if he had kept on two miles farther his insides would have been stewed; and I expect to meet with a varmint yet of extra bottom, that will run himself into a skinfull of bear's grease: it is possible; much onlikelier things have happened."

"Whereabouts are these bears so abundant?" inquired the foreigner, with increasing interest.

"Why stranger, they inhabit the neighborhood of my settlement, one of the prettiest places on old Mississipp—a perfeet location, and no mistake; a place that had some defects until the river made the cut-off at 'Shirt-tail bend,' and that remedied the evil, as it brought my cabin on the edge of the river—a great advantage in wet weather, I assure you, as you can now roll a barrel of whiskey into my yard in high water from a boat, as easy as falling off a log. It's a great improvement, as toting it by land in a jug, as I used to do, *evaporated* it too fast, and it became expensive.

"Just stop with me, stranger, a month or two, or a year, if you like, and you will appreciate my place. I can give you plenty to eat; for beside hog and hominy, you can have bear-ham, and bear-sausages, and a mattrass of bear-skins to sleep on, and a wildcat-skin, pulled off hull, stuffed with cornshucks, for a pillow. That bed would put you to sleep if you had the rheumatics in every joint in your body. I call that ar bed, a *quietus.*

"Then look at my 'pre-emption'—the government ain't got another like it to dispose of. Such timber, and such bottom land,—why you can't preserve anything natural you plant in it unless you pick it young, things thar will grow out of shape so quick.

"I once planted in those diggins a few potatoes and beets; they took a fine start, and after that, an ox team couldn't have kept them from growing. About that time I went off to old Kaintuck on business, and did not hear from them things in three months, when I accidentally stumbled on a fellow who had drapped in at my place, with an idea of buying me out.

" 'How did you like things?' said I.

" 'Pretty well,' said he; 'the cabin is convenient, and the timber land is good; but that bottom land ain't worth the first red cent.'

" 'Why?' said I.

" 'Cause,' said he.

" 'Cause it's full of cedar stumps and Indian mounds, and *can't be cleared.*'

" 'Lord,' said I, 'them ar "cedar stumps" is beets, and them ar "Indian mounds" tater hills.'

"As I had expected, the crop was overgrown and useless: the sile is too rich, *and planting in Arkansaw is dangerous.*

"I had a good-sized sow killed in that same bottom land. The old thief stole an ear of corn, and took it down to eat where she slept at night. Well, she left a grain or two on the ground, and lay down on them: before morning the corn shot up, and the percussion killed her dead. I don't plant any more: natur intended Arkansaw for a hunting ground, and I go according to natur."

The questioner, who had thus elicited the description of our hero's settlement, seemed to be perfectly satisfied, and said no more; but the "Big Bear of Arkansaw" rambled on from one thing to another with a volubility perfectly astonishing, occasionally disputing with those around him, particularly with a "live Sucker" from Illinois, who had the daring to say that our Arkansaw friend's stories "smelt rather tall."

The evening was nearly spent by the incidents we have detailed; and conscious that my own association with so singular a personage would probably end before morning, I asked him if he would give me a description of some particular bear hunt; adding, that I took great interest in such things, though I was no sportsman. The desire seemed to please him, and he squared himself round towards me, saying, that he could give me an idea of a bear hunt that was never beat in this world, or in any other. His manner was so singular, that half of his story consisted in his excellent way of telling it, the great peculiarity of which was, the happy manner he had of emphasizing the prominent parts of his conversations. As near as I can recollect, I have italicized the words, and given the story in his own way.

"Stranger," said he, "in bear hunts *I am numerous,* and which particular one, as you say, I shall tell, puzzles me.

"There was the old she devil I shot at the Hurricane last fall—then there was the old hog thief I popped over at the Bloody Crossing, and then—Yes, I have it! I will give you an idea of a hunt, in which the greatest bear was killed that ever lived, *none excepted;* about an old fellow that I hunted, more or less, for two or three years; and if that ain't a *particular bear hunt,* I ain't got one to tell.

"But in the first place, stranger, let me say, I am pleased with you, because you ain't ashamed to gain information by asking and listening; and that's what I say to Countess's pups every day when I'm home; and I have got great hopes of them ar pups, because they are continually *nosing* about; and though they stick it sometimes in the wrong place, they gain experience any how, and may learn something useful to boot.

"Well, as I was saying about this big bear, you see when I and some more first settled in our region, we were drivin to hunting naturally; we soon liked it, and after that we found it an easy matter to make the thing our business. One old chap who had pioneered 'afore us, gave us to understand that we had settled in the right place. He dwelt upon its merits until it was affecting, and showed us, to prove his assertions, more scratches on the bark of the sassafras trees, than I ever saw chalk marks on a tavern door 'lection time.

"'Who keeps that ar reckoning?' said I.

"'The bear,' said he.

"'What for?' said I.

"'Can't tell,' said he; 'but so it is: the bear bite the bark and wood too, at the highest point from the ground they can reach, and you can tell, by the marks,' said he, 'the length of the bear to an inch.'

"'Enough,' said I; 'I've learned something here a'ready, and I'll put it in practice.'

"Well, stranger, just one month from that time I killed a bear, and told its exact length before I measured it, by those very marks; and when I did that, I swelled up considerable—I've been a prouder man ever since.

"So I went on, larning something every day, until I was reckoned a buster, and allowed to be decidedly the best bear hunter in my district; and that is a reputation as much harder to earn than to be reckoned first man in Congress, as an iron ramrod is harder than a toadstool.

"Do the varmints grow over-cunning by being fooled with by greenhorn hunters, and by this means get troublesome, they send for me, as a matter of course; and thus I do my own hunting, and most of my neighbors'. I walk into the varmints though, and it has become about as much the same to me as drinking. It is told in two sentences—

"A bear is started, and he is killed.

"The thing is somewhat monotonous now—I know just how much they will run, where they will tire, how much they will growl, and what a thundering time I will have in getting their meat home. I could give you the history of the chase with all the particulars at the commencement, I know the signs so well—*Stranger, I'm certain*. Once I met with a match, though, and I will tell you about it; for a common hunt would not be worth relating.

"On a fine fall day, long time ago, I was trailing about for bear, and what should I see but fresh marks on the sassafras trees, about eight inches above any in the forests that I knew of. Says I, 'Them marks is a hoax, or it indicates the d—t bear that was ever grown.' In fact, stranger, I couldn't believe it was real, and I went on. Again I saw the same marks, at the same height, and *I knew the thing lived*. That conviction came home to my soul like an earthquake.

"Says I, 'Here is something a-purpose for me: that bear is mine, or I give up the hunting business.' The very next morning, what should I see but a number of buzzards hovering over my corn-field. 'The rascal has been there,' said I, 'for that sign is certain'; and, sure enough, on examining, I found the bones of what had been as beautiful a hog the day before, as was ever raised by a Buckeye. Then I tracked the critter out of the field to the woods, and all the marks he left behind, showed me that he was *the bear*.

"Well, stranger, the first fair chase I ever had with that big critter, I saw him no less than three distinct times at a distance; the dogs run him over eighteen miles and broke down, my horse gave out, and I was as nearly used up as a man can be, made on *my* principle, *which is patent*.

"Before this adventure, such things were unknown to me as possible; but, strange as it was, the bear got me used to it before I was done with him; for he got so at last, that he would leave me on a long chase *quite easy*. How he did it, I never could understand.

"That a bear runs at all, is puzzling; but how this one could tire down and bust up a pack of hounds and a horse, that were used to overhauling everything they started after in no time, was past my understanding. Well, stranger, that bear finally got so sassy, that he used to help himself to a hog off my premises whenever he wanted one; the buzzards followed after what he left, and so, between *bear and buzzard,* I rather think I got *out of pork*.

"Well, missing that bear so often took hold of my vitals, and I wasted away. The thing had been carried too far, and it reduced me in flesh faster than an ager. I would see that bear in every thing I did: *he hunted me,* and that, too, like a devil, which I began to think he was.

"While in this shaky fix, I made preparations to give him a last brush, and be done with it. Having completed everything to my satisfaction, I started at sunrise, and to my great joy, I discovered from the way the dogs run, that they were near him. Finding his trail was nothing, for that had become as plain to the pack as a turnpike road.

"On we went, and coming on an open country, what should I see but the bear very leisurely ascending a hill, and the dogs close at his heels, either a match for him this time in speed, or else he did not care to get out of their way—I don't know which. But wasn't he a beauty, though! I loved him like a brother.

"On he went, until he came to a tree, the limbs of which formed a crotch about six feet from the ground. Into this crotch he got and seated himself, the dogs yelling all around it; and there he sat eyeing them as quiet as a pond in low water.

"A greenhorn friend of mine, in company, reached shooting distance before me, and blazed away, hitting the critter in the centre of his forehead. The bear shook his head as the ball struck it, and then walked down from the tree, as gently as a lady would from a carriage.

"'Twas a beautiful sight to see him do that—he was in such a rage, that he seemed to be as little afraid of the dogs as if they had been sucking pigs; and the dogs warn't slow in making a ring around him at a respectful distance, I tell you; even Bowieknife himself, stood off. Then the way his eyes flashed!—why the fire of them would have singed a cat's hair; in fact, that bear was in a *wrath all over.* Only one pup came near him, and he was brushed out so totally with the bear's left paw, that he entirely disappeared; and that made the old dogs more cautious still. In the mean time, I came up, and taking deliberate aim, as a man should do, at his side, just back of his foreleg, *if my gun did not snap,* call me a coward, and I won't take it personal.

"Yes, stranger, *it snapped,* and I could not find a cap about my person. While in this predicament, I turned round to my fool friend—'Bill,' says I, 'you're an ass—you're a fool—you might as well have tried to kill that bear by barking the tree under his belly, as to have done it by hitting him in the head. Your shot made a tiger of him; and blast me, if a dog gets killed or wounded when they come to blows, I will stick a knife into your liver, I will—.' My wrath was up. I had lost my caps, my gun had snapped, the fellow with me had fired at the bear's head, and I expected every moment to see him close in with the dogs and kill a dozen of them at least. In this thing I was mistaken; for the bear leaped over the ring formed by the dogs, and giving a fierce growl, was off—the pack, of course, in full cry after him. The run this time was short, for coming to the edge of a lake, the varmint jumped in, and swam to a little island in the lake, which it reached, just a moment before the dogs.

"'I'll have him now,' said I, for I had found my caps in the *lining of my coat*—so, rolling a log into the lake, I paddled myself across to the island, just as the dogs had cornered the bear in a thicket. I rushed up and fired—at the same time the critter leaped over the dogs and came within three feet of me, running like mad; he jumped into the lake, and tried to mount the log I had just deserted, but every time he got half his body on it, it would roll over and send him under; the dogs, too, got around him, and pulled him about, and finally Bowieknife clenched with him, and they sunk into the lake together.

"Stranger, about this time I was excited, and I stripped off my coat, drew my knife, and intended to have taken a part with Bowieknife myself, when the bear rose to the surface. But the varmint staid under—Bowieknife came up alone, more dead than alive, and with the pack came ashore.

"'Thank God!' said I, 'the old villain has got his deserts at last.'

"Determined to have the body, I cut a grape-vine for a rope, and dove down where I could see the bear in the water, fastened my rope to his leg and fished him, with great difficulty, ashore. Stranger, may I be chawed to death by young alligators, if the thing I looked at wasn't a *she bear, and not the old critter after all.*

"The way matters got mixed on that island was onaccountably curious, and thinking of it made me more than ever convinced that I was hunting the devil himself. I went home that night and took to my bed—the thing was killing me. The entire team of Arkansaw in bear-hunting acknowledged himself used up, and the fact sunk into my feelings as a snagged boat will in the Mississippi. I grew as cross as a bear with two cubs and a sore tail. The thing got out 'mong the neighbors, and I was asked how come on that individ-u-al that never lost a bear when once started? and if that same individ-u-al didn't wear telescopes when he turned a she-bear, of ordinary size, into an old he one, a little larger than a horse?

"Prehaps,' said I, 'friends'—getting wrathy—'prehaps you want to call somebody a liar?'

"'Oh, no,' said they, 'we only heard of such things being *rather common* of late, but we don't believe one word of it; oh, no'—and then they would ride off, and laugh like so many hyenas over a dead nigger.

"It was too much, and I determined to catch that bear, go to Texas, or die,—and I made my preparations accordin'.

"I had the pack shut up and rested. I took my rifle to pieces, and iled it.

"I put caps in every pocket about my person, *for fear of the lining.*

"I then told my neighbors, that on Monday morning—naming the day—I would start THAT BEAR, and bring him home with me, or they might divide my settlement among them, the owner having disappeared.

"Well, stranger, on the morning previous to the great day of my hunting expedition, I went into the woods near my house, taking my gun and Bowieknife along, just *from habit,* and there sitting down, also from habit, what should I see, getting over my fence, but *the bear!* Yes, the old varmint was within a hundred yards of me, and the way he walked *over that fence*—stranger; he loomed up like a *black mist,* he seemed so large, and he walked right towards me.

"I raised myself, took deliberate aim, and fired. Instantly the varmint wheeled, gave a yell, and *walked through the fence,* as easy as a falling tree would through a cobweb.

"I started after, but was tripped up by my inexpressibles, which, either from habit or excitement of the moment, were about my heels, and before I had really gathered myself up, I heard the old varmint groaning, like a thousand sinners, in a thicket near by, and, by the time I reached him, he was a corpse.

"Stranger, it took five niggers and myself to put that carcass on a mule's back, and old long-ears waddled under his load, as if he was foundered in every leg of his body; and with a common whopper of a bear, he would have trotted off, and enjoy himself.

" 'Twould astonish you to know how big he was: I made a *bedspread of his skin*, and the way it used to cover my bear mattress, and leave several feet on each side to tuck up, would have delighted you. It was, in fact, a creation bear, and if it had lived in Samson's time, and had met him in a fair fight, he would have licked him in the twinkling of a dice-box.

"But, stranger, I never liked the way I hunted him, *and missed him.* There is something curious about it, that I never could understand,—and I never was satisfied at his giving in *so easy at last.* Perhaps he had heard of my preparations to hunt him the next day, so he jist guv up, like Captain Scott's coon, to save his wind to grunt with in dying; but that ain't likely. My private opinion is, that that bear was an *unhuntable bear, and died when his time come.*"

When this story was ended, our hero sat some minutes with his auditors, in a grave silence; I saw there was a mystery to him connected with the bear whose death he had just related, that had evidently made a strong impression on his mind. It was also evident that there was some superstitious awe connected with the affair,—a feeling common with all "children of the wood," when they meet with any thing out of their every-day experience.

He was the first one, however, to break the silence, and, jumping up, he asked all present to "liquor" before going to bed,—a thing which he did, with a number of companions, evidently to his heart's content.

Long before day, I was put ashore at my place of destination, and I can only follow with the reader, in imagination, our Arkansas friend, in his adventures at the "Forks of Cypress," on the Mississippi.   [1841]

LYDIA MARIA CHILD

*L*ydia Maria Child (1802–1880), who wrote short fiction as an outspoken champion of Native American rights, African American emancipation, and women's suffrage, was born in Medford, Massachusetts, into a family she later described as "hardworking people, who had had small opportunity for culture." Her father owned a bakery, which was run as a family business. He sent his most promising son, Convers, to Harvard; but he distrusted his twelve-year-old daughter Lydia's "increasing fondness for books," so he insisted that she live with a married sister in the backwoods of Maine. Child became a schoolteacher and moved back to Massachusetts in 1822, the year Convers became a Unitarian minister. At his home she met Ralph Waldo Emerson, Bronson Alcott, Margaret Fuller, and other leading intellectuals of that period, and participated in their discussions about politics and literature.

Child wrote her first novel, Hobomok (1824), as a response to proslavery forces in Georgia who proposed to take over the prosperous farms of the Cherokees. In this novel Child created a fictional heroine who rebelled against her Puritan father by marrying two men he considered unacceptable: the first a Native American and the second an Episcopalian. Child's radical attempts to suggest that intermarriage and assimilation were preferable alternatives to racial and religious bigotry outraged the critics in the North American Review in 1824 and 1825, who thought her book "revolting . . . to every feeling of delicacy in man or woman." Yet her novel sold so well that publishers were eager to print her work. Until 1830 Child continued to teach school for her livelihood, but she also turned out a stream of novels, short fiction, biographies, histories, and domestic science books aimed primarily at the women's market. She also founded and edited the first successful children's magazine in America, Juvenile Miscellany. Her two-volume History of the Condition of Women in Various Ages and Nations (1835) was read by pioneering feminists such as Elizabeth Cady Stanton and Susan B. Anthony. This work as well as Child's remarkable volume An Appeal in Favor of That Class of Americans Called Africans (1833), which advocated immediate emancipation and argued the case for racial equality and integration, lost her the support of a large popular audience.

In Child's prolific outpourings of sketches and stories written for periodicals and annual gift books in the 1820s and 1830s, she tirelessly championed the cause of civil rights. As the critic Carolyn L. Karcher noted, "Child's contribution to the genre of Indian fiction was to sever it from its origins in the Puritan narratives of captivity and Indian war that justified white conquest, and to turn it instead into a medium for dramatizing the wrongs committed against the Indian." An advocate for the abolitionist cause, Child wrote short fiction that broke new ground. In stories such as "Slavery's Pleasant Homes" (The Liberty Bell, 1843), she attempted to make her readers sympathetic to the plight of black women slaves. In 1860 she published a pamphlet of her letters in *defense of John Brown, who was executed after his raid on Harpers Ferry. The pamphlet sold three hundred thousand copies. Until her death, Child played a key role in the most important reform movements of her time, and her writing has inspired generations of American women.*

Slavery's Pleasant Homes
A Faithful Sketch

Thy treasures of gold
Are dim with the blood of the hearts thou hast sold;
Thy home may be lovely, but round it I hear
The crack of the whip, and the footsteps of fear.

When Frederic Dalcho brought his young bride from New-Orleans to her Georgian home, there were great demonstrations of joy among the slaves of the establishment, — dancing, shouting, clapping of hands, and eager invocations of blessing on the heads of "massa and missis"; for well they knew that he who manifested most zeal was likely to get the largest coin, or the brightest handkerchief.

The bride had been nurtured in seclusion, almost as deep as that of the oriental harem. She was a pretty little waxen plaything, as fragile and as delicate as the white Petunia blossom. She brought with her two slaves. Mars, a stalwart mulatto, of good figure, but a cunning and disagreeable expression of countenance. Rosa, a young girl, elegantly formed, and beautiful as a dark velvet carnation. The blush, so easily excited, shone through the transparent brown of her smooth cheek, like claret through a bottle in the sunshine. It was a beautiful contrast to see her beside her mistress, like a glittering star in attendance upon the pale and almost vanishing moonsickle. They had grown up from infancy together; for the mother of Rosa was foster-mother of Marion; and soon as the little white lady could speak, she learned to call Rosa *her* slave. As they grew older, the wealthy planter's daughter took pride in her servant's beauty, and loved to decorate her with jewels. "You shall wear my golden ornaments whenever you ask for them," said she; "they contrast so well with the soft, brown satin of your neck and arms. I will wear pearls and amethysts; but gold needs the dark complexion to show its richness. Besides, you are a handsome creature, Rosa, and gold is none too good for you."

Her coachman, Mars, was of the same opinion: but the little petted coquette tossed her graceful head at him, and paid small heed to his flattering words. Not so with George, the handsome quadroon brother of Frederic Dalcho, and his favorite slave; but the master and mistress were too much absorbed with their own honeymoon, to observe them. Low talks among the rose-bushes, and stolen meetings by moonlight, passed unnoticed, save by the evil eyes of Mars. Thus it passed on for months. The young slaves had uttered the marriage vow to each other, in the silent presence of the stars.

It chanced, one day, that Rosa was summoned to the parlor to attend her mistress, while George stood respectfully, hat in hand, waiting for a note, which his master was writing. She wore about her neck a small heart and cross of gold, which her lover had given her the night before. He smiled archly, as he glanced at it, and the answer from her large, dark eyes was full of joyful tenderness. Unfortunately, the master looked up at that moment, and at once comprehended the significance of that beaming expression. He saw that it spoke whole volumes of mutual, happy love; and it kindled in him an unholy fire. He had never before realized that the girl was so very handsome. He watched her, as she pursued her work, until she felt uneasy beneath his look. From time to time, he glanced at his young wife. She, too, was certainly very lovely; but the rich, mantling beauty of the slave had the charm of novelty. The next day, he gave her a gay dress; and when he met her among the garden shrubbery, he turned her glossy ringlets over his finger, and called her a pretty darling. Poor Rosa hastened away, filled with terror. She wanted to tell her mistress all this, and claim her protection; but she dared not. As for George, he was of a proud and fiery nature, and she dreaded the storm it would raise in his breast. Her sleeping apartment adjoined that of her mistress, and she was now called to bring water to her master at a much later hour than had been usual with him. One night, no answer was given to the summons. Rosa was not in her room. When questioned in the morning, she stammered out an incoherent excuse, and burst into tears. She was ordered, somewhat sternly, to be very careful not to be again absent when called for.

Marion took an early opportunity to plead her favorite's cause. "I have suspected, for some time," said she, "that George and Rosa are courting; and for my part, I should like very well to have them married." Her husband made no reply, but abruptly left the room. His conduct towards George became singularly capricious and severe. Rosa wept much in secret, and became shy as a startled fawn. Her mistress supposed it was because Mr. Dalcho objected to her marriage, and suspected nothing more. She tried to remonstrate with him, and learn the nature of his objections; but he answered sharply, and left her in tears.

One night, Marion was awakened by the closing of the door, and found that Frederic was absent. She heard voices in Rosa's apartment, and the painful truth flashed upon her. Poor young wife, what a bitter hour was that!

In the morning, Rosa came to dress her, as usual, but she avoided looking in her face, and kept her eyes fixed on the ground. As she *knelt* to tie the satin shoe, Marion spoke angrily of her awkwardness, and gave her a blow. It was the first time she had ever struck her; for they really loved each other. The beautiful slave looked up with an expression of surprise, which was answered by a strange, wild stare. Rosa fell at her feet, and sobbed

out, "Oh, mistress, I am not to blame. Indeed, indeed, I am very wretched."
Marion's fierce glance melted into tears. "Poor child," said she, "I ought not
to have struck you; but, oh, Rosa, I am wretched, too." The foster-sisters
embraced each other, and wept long and bitterly; but neither sought any
further to learn the other's secrets.

At breakfast, George was in attendance, but he would not look at
Rosa, though she watched for a glance with anxious love. When she found
an opportunity to see him alone, he was sullen, and rejected her proffered
kiss. "Rosa, where were you last night?" said he, hastily. The poor girl
blushed deeply, and strove to take his hand; but he flung her from him, with
so much force that she reeled against the wall. "Oh, George," said she,
with bitter anguish, "what *can* I do? I am his *slave*." The justice of her plea,
and the pathos of her tones, softened his heart. He placed her head on his
shoulder, and said more kindly, "Keep out of his way, dear Rosa; keep out
of his way."

Rosa made strong efforts to follow this injunction; and dearly did she
rue it. George was sent away from the house, to work on the plantation,
and they were forbidden to see each other, under penalty of severe punishment. His rival, Mars, watched them, and gave information of every attempt
to transgress this cruel edict. But love was more omnipotent than fear of
punishment, and the lovers did sometimes catch a stolen interview. The
recurrence of this disobedience exasperated their master beyond endurance.
He swore he would overcome her obstinacy, or kill her; and one severe
flogging succeeded another, till the tenderly-nurtured slave fainted under
the cruel infliction, which was rendered doubly dangerous by the delicate
state of her health. Maternal pains came on prematurely, and she died a
few hours after.

George wandered into the woods, and avoided the sight of his reckless
master, who, on his part, seemed willing to avoid an interview. Four days
had passed since Rosa's death, and the bereaved one had scarcely tasted
food enough to sustain his wretched life. He stood beside the new-made
grave, which he himself had dug. "Oh, Father in Heaven!" he exclaimed,
"what would I give, if I had not flung her from me! Poor girl, *she* was not
to blame." He leaned his head against a tree, and looked mournfully up to
the moon struggling through clouds. Cypresses reared their black forms
against the sky, and the moss hung from bough to bough, in thick, funereal
festoons. But a few months ago, how beautiful and bright was Nature—and
now, how inexpressibly gloomy. The injustice of the past, and the hopelessness of the future, came before him with dreary distinctness. "He is my
brother," thought he, "we grew up side by side, children of the same father;
but I am his slave. Handsomer, stronger, and more intelligent than he; yet
I am his *slave*. And now he will sell me, because the murdered one will forever come up between us."

He thought of Rosa as he first saw her, so happy, and so beautiful; of
all her gushing tenderness; of her agonized farewell, when they last met; of

her graceful form bleeding under the lash, and now lying cold and dead beneath his feet.

He looked toward his master's house. "Shall I escape now and forever?" said he; "or shall I first"—he paused, threw his arms widely upward, gnashed his teeth, and groaned aloud, "God, pity me! He murdered my poor Rosa."

On that night, Marion's sleep was disturbed and fitful. The memory of her foster-sister mingled darkly with all her dreams. Was that a shriek she heard? It was fearfully shrill in the night-silence! Half sleeping and half waking, she called wildly, "Rosa! Rosa!" But a moment after, she remembered that Rosa's light step would never again come at her call. At last a drowsy slave answered the loud summons of her bell. "I left your master reading in the room below," said she; "go and see if he is ill." The girl came back, pallid and frightened. "Oh, mistress, he is dead!" she exclaimed; "there is a dagger through his heart."

Neighbors were hastily summoned, and the slaves secured. Among them was George, who, with a fierce and haggard look, still lingered around Rosa's grave.

The dagger found in Frederic Dalcho's heart was the one he had himself been accustomed to wear. He lay upon the sofa, with an open book beside him, as if he had fallen asleep reading. A desk in the room was broken open, and a sum of money gone. Near it, was dropped a ragged handkerchief, known to belong to Mars. Suspicion hovered between him and George. Both denied the deed. Mars tried hard to fix the guilt on his hated rival, and swore to many falsehoods. But as some of these falsehoods were detected, and the stolen money was found hidden in his bed, the balance turned against him. After the brief, stern trial awarded to slaves, with slaveholders for judges and jurors, Mars was condemned to be hung. George thought of his relentless persecutions, and for a moment triumphed over the cunning enemy, who had so often dogged poor Rosa's steps; but his soul was too generous to retain this feeling.

The fatal hour came. Planters rode miles to witness the execution, and stood glaring at their trembling victim, with the fierceness of tigers. The slaves from miles around were assembled, to take warning by his awful punishment. The rope was adjusted on the strong bough of a tree. Mars shook like a leaf in the wind. The countenance of George was very pale and haggard, and his breast was heaving with tumultuous thoughts. "He is my enemy," said he to himself; "tis an awful thing to die thus. The *theft* I did not commit; but if I take all the blame, they can do no more than hang me."

They led the shivering wretch towards the tree, and were about to fasten the fatal noose. But George rushed forward with a countenance ghastly pale, and exclaimed, "Mars is innocent. I murdered him—for he killed my wife, and hell was in my bosom."

No voice praised him for the generous confession. They kicked and cursed him; and hung up, like a dog or a wolf, a man of nobler soul than any of them all.

The Georgian papers thus announced the deed: *"Fiend-like Murder.* Frederic Dalcho, one of our most wealthy and respected citizens, was robbed and murdered last week, by one of his slaves. The black demon was caught and hung; and hanging was too good for him."

The Northern papers copied this version; merely adding, "These are the black-hearted monsters, which abolition philanthropy would let loose upon our brethren of the South."

Not one was found to tell how the slave's young wife had been torn from him by his own brother, and murdered with slow tortures. Not one recorded the heroism that would not purchase life by another's death, though the victim was his enemy. His very *name* was left unmentioned; he was only Mr. Dalcho's *slave!*   [1843]

CAROLINE KIRKLAND

Caroline Kirkland (1801–1864) was born in New York City to educated middle-class parents and began to attend her aunt's Quaker school at the age of eight. She taught school until her marriage in 1828 to William Kirkland, whose grandfather had founded Hamilton College. In 1835 the couple and their young daughter moved to Detroit and bought acreage in the Michigan back-country. Settling near the village of Pinckney, Kirkland began to write a series of letters describing frontier life to friends back East, who encouraged her to turn them into a book. A New Home—Who'll Follow? *(1839), her first publica-tion, was such a boldly realistic account of life in the West that it caused what Edgar Allan Poe termed "an undoubted sensation." Kirkland followed with* Forest Life *(1842), a second book of sketches about pioneering in the wilder-ness. Unfortunately, by the time it was published, an unscrupulous land agent had swindled Kirkland and her husband out of their Michigan property, and they were forced to return to New York City to support themselves by teaching and writing for periodicals. She continued to describe the frontier experience in another collection of sketches,* Western Clearings, *published in 1845. Kirkland's later work included* The Helping Hand, Comprising an Account of the Home for Discharged Female Convicts and an Appeal in Behalf of that Institution *(1853) and* Personal Memoirs of George Washington *(1857). She died of a stroke after participating in a fund-raiser for the Sanitary Commis-sion in New York City, an organization that later became the Red Cross.*

Like Mary Russell Mitford, her greatest literary influence, Kirkland wrote as a commonsense moralist. Presenting what she called "actual reality" in her sketches of the frontier, Kirkland refused to idealize her descriptions of life as it was lived in the harsh conditions of the backwoods settlements. In the opening pages of A New Home, *she confessed that she had been sadly disillusioned after arriving in Michigan because she had believed the accounts of earlier writ-ers, which she later understood were "touched by the glowing pencil of fancy." Instead she resolved to produce in her sketches "an unimpeachable transcript of reality." Poverty, boredom, and discomfort predominate in her descriptions of drenching rainstorms, crowded and filthy living conditions in the log cabins, hungry and insubordinate children, and shiftless woodsmen "continually sub-ject to accidents of the most appalling kind."*

*In her sketches of the West, including "The Land-Fever" (*Western Clear-ings, *1845), Kirkland emphasized a woman's perspective. Her descriptions of domestic life evoke an unforgettable sense of the casual and makeshift arrange-ments in the frontier settlements. This realism suggests her understanding of the hardships endured by pioneering women. Feminist critics such as Judith Fetterley also have argued that Kirkland's stories not only run counter to pre-vious romanticism but also are "designed equally to counter that masculine 'realism' that believes the whole story has been told when the man's story has been told."*

The Land-Fever

The years 1835 and 1836 will long be remembered by the Western settler — and perhaps by some few people at the East, too — as the period when the madness of speculation in lands had reached a point to which no historian of the time will ever be able to do justice. A faithful picture of those wild days would subject the most veracious chronicler to the charge of exaggeration; and our great-grand-children can hope to obtain an adequate idea of the infatuation which led away their forefathers, only by the study of such detached facts as may be noted down by those in whose minds the feeling recollection of the delusion is still fresh. Perhaps when our literary existence shall have become sufficiently confirmed to call for the collection of Ana, something more may be gleaned from the correspondence in which were embodied the exultings of the successful, and the lamentations of the disappointed.

"Seeing is believing," certainly, in most cases; but in the days of the land-fever, we, who were in the midst of the infected district, scarcely found it so. The whirl, the fervour, the flutter, the rapidity of step, the sparkling of eyes, the beating of hearts, the striking of hands, the utter *abandon* of the hour, were incredible, inconceivable. The "man of one idea" was every where: no man had two. He who had no money, begged, borrowed, or stole it; he who had, thought he made a generous sacrifice, if he lent it at cent per cent. The tradesman forsook his shop; the farmer his plough; the merchant his counter; the lawyer his office; nay, the minister his desk, to join the general chase. Even the schoolmaster, in his longing to be "abroad" with the rest, laid down his birch, or in the flurry of his hopes, plied it with diminished unction.

> Tramp! tramp! along the land they rode,
> Splash! splash! along the sea!

The man with one leg, or he that had none, could at least get on board a steamer, and make for Chicago or Milwaukie; the strong, the able, but above all, the "enterprising," set out with his pocket-map and his pocket-compass, to thread the dim woods, and see with his own eyes. Who would waste time in planting, in building, in hammering iron, in making shoes, when the path to wealth lay wide and flowery before him?

A ditcher was hired by the job to do a certain piece of work in his line. "Well, John, did you make any thing?"

"Pretty well; I cleared about two dollars a day: but I should have made more by *standing round*," i.e., watching the land-market for bargains.

This favourite occupation of all classes was followed by its legitimate consequences. Farmers were as fond of "standing round" as any body; and when harvest time came, it was discovered that many had quite forgotten that the best land requires sowing; and grain, and of course other articles

149

of general necessity, rose to an unprecedented price. The hordes of travellers flying through the country in all directions were often cited as the cause of the distressing scarcity; but the true source must be sought in the diversion, or rather suspension, of the industry of the entire population. Be this as it may, of the wry faces made at the hard fare, the travellers contributed no inconsiderable portion; for they were generally city gentlemen, or at least gentlemen who had lived long enough in the city to have learned to prefer oysters to salt pork. This checked not their ardour, however; for the golden glare before their eyes had power to neutralize the hue of all present objects. On they pressed, with headlong zeal: the silent and pathless forest, the deep miry marsh, the gloom of night, and the fires of noon, beheld alike the march of the speculator. Such searching of trees for town lines! Such ransacking of the woods for section corners, ranges, and base lines! Such anxious care in identifying spots possessing particular advantages! And then, alas! after all, such precious blunders!

These blunders called into action another class of operators, who became popularly known as "land-lookers." These met you at every turn, ready to furnish "water-power," "pine lots," "choice farming tracts," or any thing else, at a moment's notice. Bar-rooms and street-corners swarmed with these prowling gentry. It was impossible to mention any part of the country which they had not personally surveyed. They would tell you, with the gravity of astrologers, what sort of timber predominated on any given tract, drawing sage deductions as to the capabilities of the soil. Did you incline to city property? Lo! a splendid chart, setting forth the advantages of some unequalled site, and your confidential friend, the land-looker, able to tell you more than all about it, or to accompany you to the happy spot; though that he would not advise; "bad roads," "nothing fit to eat," etc.; and all this from a purely disinterested solicitude for your welfare.

These amiable individuals were, strange to tell, no favourites with the actual settlers. If they disliked the gentleman speculator, they hated with a perfect hatred him who aided by his local knowledge the immense purchases of non-residents. These short-sighted and prejudiced persons forgot the honour and distinction which must result from their insignificant farms being surrounded by the possessions of the magnates of the land. They saw only the solitude which would probably be entailed on them for years; and it was counted actual treason in a settler to give any facilities to the land-looker, of whatever grade. "Let the land-shark do his own hunting," was their frequent reply to applications of this kind; and some thought them quite right. Yet this state of feeling among the Hard-handed, was not without its inconvenient results to city gentlemen, as witness the case of our friend Mr. Willoughby, a very prim and smart bachelor, from ————.

It was when the whirlwind was at its height, that a gentleman wearing the air of a bank-director, at the very least—in other words, that of an uncommonly fat pigeon—drew bridle at the bars in front of one of the roughest log houses in the county of ————. The horse and his rider were loaded with all those unnecessary defences, and cumbrous comforts, which the fashion of the time prescribed in such cases. Blankets, valise, saddle-bags, and holsters nearly covered the steed; a most voluminous enwrap-ment of India-rubber cloth completely enveloped the rider. The gallant sorrel seemed indeed fit for his burden. He looked as if he might have swam any stream in Michigan

> Barded from counter to tail,
> And the rider arm'd complete in mail;

yet he seemed a little jaded, and hung his head languidly, while his master accosted the tall and meagre tenant of the log cabin.

This individual and his dwelling resembled each other in an unusual degree. The house was, as we have said, of the roughest; its ribs scarcely half filled in with clay; its "looped and windowed raggedness" rendered more conspicuous by the tattered cotton sheets which had long done duty as glass, and which now fluttered in every breeze; its roof of oak shingles, warped into every possible curve; and its stick chimney, so like its owner's hat, open at the top, and jammed in at the sides; all shadowed forth the contour and equipments of the exceedingly easy and self-satisfied person who leaned on the fence, and snapped his long cart-whip, while he gave such answers as suited him to the gentleman in the India-rubbers, taking especial care not to invite him to alight.

"Can you tell me, my friend, ——" civilly began Mr. Willoughby.

"Oh! *friend!*" interrupted the settler; "who told you I was your friend? Friends is scuss in these parts."

"You have at least no reason to be otherwise," replied the traveller, who was blessed with a very patient temper, especially where there was no use in getting angry.

"I don't know that," was the reply. "What fetch'd you into these woods?"

"If I should say 'my horse,' the answer would perhaps be as civil as the question."

"Jist as you like," said the other, turning on his heel, and walking off.

"I wished merely to ask you," resumed Mr. Willoughby, talking after the nonchalant son of the forest, "whether this is Mr. Pepper's land."

"How do you know it an't mine?"

"I'm not likely to know, at present, it seems," said the traveller, whose patience was getting a little frayed. And taking out his memorandum-book, he ran over his minutes: "South half of north-west quarter of sec-tion fourteen —— Your name is Leander Pepper, is it not?"

"Where did you get so much news? You a'n't the sheriff, be ye?"

"Pop!" screamed a white-headed urchin from the house, "Mam says supper's ready."

"So ain't I," replied the papa; "I've got all my chores to do yet." And he busied himself at a log pig-stye on the opposite side of the road, half as large as the dwelling-house. Here he was soon surrounded by a squealing multitude, with whom he seemed to hold a regular conversation.

Mr. Willoughby looked at the westering sun, which was not far above the dense wall of trees that shut in the small clearing; then at the heavy clouds which advanced from the north, threatening a stormy night; then at his watch, and then at his note-book; and after all, at his predicament—on the whole, an unpleasant prospect. But at this moment a female face showed itself at the door. Our traveller's memory reverted at once to the testimony of Ledyard and Mungo Park;[1] and he had also some floating and indistinct poetical recollections of woman's being useful when a man was in difficulties, though hard to please at other times. The result of these reminiscences, which occupied a precious second, was, that Mr. Willoughby dismounted, fastened his horse to the fence, and advanced with a brave and determined air, to throw himself upon female kindness and sympathy.

He naturally looked at the lady, as he approached the door, but she did not return the compliment. She looked at the pigs, and talked to the children, and Mr. Willoughby had time to observe that she was the very duplicate of her husband; as tall, as bony, as ragged, and twice as cross-looking.

"Malviny Jane!" she exclaimed, in no dulcet treble, "be done a-paddlin' in that 'ere water! If I come there, I'll——"

"You'd better look at Sophrony, I guess!" was the reply.

"Why, what's she a-doing?"

"Well, I guess if you look, you'll see!" responded Miss Malvina, coolly, as she passed into the house, leaving at every step a full impression of her foot in the same black mud that covered her sister from head to foot.

The latter was saluted with a hearty cuff, as she emerged from the puddle; and it was just at the propitious moment when her shrill howl aroused the echoes, that Mr. Willoughby, having reached the threshold, was obliged to set about making the agreeable to the mamma. And he called up for the occasion all his politeness.

"I believe I must become an intruder on your hospitality for the night, madam," he began. The dame still looked at the pigs. Mr. Willoughby tried again, in less courtly phrase.

"Will it be convenient for you to lodge me to-night, ma'am? I have been disappointed in my search for a hunting-party, whom I had engaged to meet, and the night threatens a storm."

"I don't know nothin' about it; you must ask the old man," said the lady, now for the first time taking a survey of the new comer; "with *my* will, we'll lodge nobody."

This was not very encouraging, but it was a poor night for the woods; so our traveller persevered, and making so bold a push for the door that

---

[1]Explorers who had written books about their travels in Africa.

the lady was obliged to retreat a little, he entered, and said he would await her husband's coming.

And in truth he could scarcely blame the cool reception he had experienced, when he beheld the state of affairs within those muddy precincts. The room was large, but it swarmed with human beings. The huge open fire-place, with its hearth of rough stone, occupied nearly the whole of one end of the apartment; and near it stood a long cradle, containing a pair of twins, who cried—a sort of hopeless cry, as if they knew it would do no good, yet could not help it. The schoolmaster, (it was his week,) sat reading a tattered novel, and rocking the cradle occasionally, when the children cried *too* loud. An old grey-headed Indian was curiously crouched over a large tub, shelling corn on the edge of a hoe; but he ceased his noisy employment when he saw the stranger, for no Indian will ever willingly be seen at work, though he may be sometimes compelled by the fear of starvation or the longing for whiskey, to degrade himself by labour. Near the only window was placed the work-bench and entire paraphernalia of the shoemaker, who in these regions travels from house to house, shoeing the family and mending the harness as he goes, with various interludes of songs and jokes, ever new and acceptable. This one, who was a little, bald, twinkling-eyed fellow, made the smoky rafters ring with the burden of that favourite ditty of the west:

> All kinds of game to hunt, my boys, also the buck and doe,
> All down by the banks of the river O-hi-o;

and children of all sizes, clattering in all keys, completed the picture and the concert.

The supper-table, which maintained its place in the midst of this living and restless mass, might remind one of the square stone lying bedded in the bustling leaves of the acanthus; but the associations would be any but those of Corinthian elegance. The only object which at that moment diversified its dingy surface was an iron hoop, into which the mistress of the feast proceeded to turn a quantity of smoking hot potatoes, adding afterward a bowl of salt, and another of pork fat, by courtesy denominated gravy: plates and knives dropped in afterward, at the discretion of the company.

Another call of "Pop! pop!" brought in the host from the pig-stye; the heavy rain which had now began to fall, having no doubt, expedited the performance of the chores. Mr. Willoughby, who had established himself resolutely, took advantage of a very cloudy assent from the proprietor, to lead his horse to a shed, and to deposit in a corner his cumbrous outer gear; while the company used in turn the iron skillet which served as a wash-basin, dipping the water from a large trough outside, overflowing with the abundant drippings of the eaves. Those who had no pocket-handkerchiefs, contented themselves with a nondescript article which seemed to stand for the family towel; and when this ceremony was concluded, all seriously addressed themselves to the demolition of the potatoes. The grown people were accommodated with chairs and chests; the children prosecuted a series of flying raids upon the good cheer, snatching a potato now and then as they could find an opening under the raised arm of one of the family, and then retreating to the chimney corner, tossing the hot prize from hand to hand, and blowing it stoutly the while. The old Indian had disappeared.

To our citizen, though he felt inconveniently hungry, this primitive meal seemed a little meagre; and he ventured to ask if he could not be accommodated with some tea.

"An't my victuals good enough for you?"

"Oh!—the potatoes are excellent, but I'm very fond of tea."

"So be I, but I can't have every thing I want—can you?"

This produced a laugh from the shoemaker, who seemed to think his patron very witty, while the schoolmaster, not knowing but the stranger might happen to be one of his examiners next year, produced only a faint giggle, and then reducing his countenance instantly to an awful gravity, helped himself to his seventh potato.

The rain which now poured violently, not only outside but through many a crevice in the roof, naturally kept Mr. Willoughby cool; and finding that dry potatoes gave him the hiccups, he withdrew from the table, and seating himself on the shoemaker's bench, took a survey of his quarters.

Two double-beds and the long cradle, seemed all the sleeping apparatus; but there was a ladder which doubtless led to a lodging above. The sides of the room were hung with abundance of decent clothing, and the dresser was well stored with the usual articles, among which a tea-pot and canister shone conspicuous; so that the appearance of inhospitality could not arise from poverty, and Mr. Willoughby concluded to set it down to the account of rustic ignorance.

The eating ceased not until the hoop was empty, and then the company rose and stretched themselves, and began to guess it was about time to go to bed. Mr. Willoughby inquired what was to be done with his horse.

"Well! I s'pose he can stay where he is."

"But what can he have to eat?"

"I reckon you won't get nothing for him, without you turn him out on the mash."

"He would get off, to a certainty!"

"Tie his legs."

The unfortunate traveller argued in vain. Hay was "scuss," and potatoes were "scusser;" and in short the "mash" was the only resource, and these natural meadows afford but poor picking after the first of October. But to the "mash" was the good steed despatched, ingloriously hampered, with the privilege of munching wild grass in the rain, after his day's journey.

Then came the question of lodging for his master. The lady, who had by this time drawn out a trundle-bed, and packed it full of children, said there was no bed for him, unless he could sleep "up chamber" with the boys.

Mr. Willoughby declared that he should make out very well with a blanket by the fire.

"Well! just as you like," said his host; "but Solomon sleeps there, and if you like to sleep by Solomon, it is more than *I* should."

This was the name of the old Indian, and Mr. Willoughby once more cast woful glances toward the ladder.

But now the schoolmaster, who seemed rather disposed to be civil, declared that he could sleep very well in the long cradle, and would relinquish his place beside the shoemaker to the guest, who was obliged to content himself with this arrangement, which was such as was most usual in those times.

The storm continued through the night, and many a crash in the woods attested its power. The sound of a storm in the dense forest is almost precisely similar to that of a heavy surge breaking on a rocky beach; and when our traveller slept, it was only to dream of wreck and disaster at sea, and to wake in horror and affright. The wild rain drove in at every crevice, and wet the poor children in the loft so thoroughly, that they crawled shivering down the ladder, and stretched themselves on the hearth, regardless of Solomon, who had returned after the others were in bed.

But morning came at last; and our friend, who had no desire farther to test the vaunted hospitality of a western settler, was not among the latest astir. The storm had partially subsided; and although the clouds still lowered angrily, and his saddle had enjoyed the benefit of a leak in the roof during the night, Mr. Willoughby resolved to push on as far as the next clearing, at least, hoping for something for breakfast besides potatoes and salt. It took him a weary while to find his horse, and when he had saddled him, and strapped on his various accoutrements, he entered the house, and inquired what he was to pay for his entertainment—laying somewhat of a stress on the last word.

His host, nothing daunted, replied that he guessed he would let him off for a dollar.

Mr. Willoughby took out his purse, and as he placed a silver dollar in the leathern palm outspread to receive it, happening to look toward the hearth, and perceiving the preparations for a very substantial breakfast, the long pent-up vexation burst forth.

"I really must say, Mr. Pepper——" he began: his tone was certainly that of an angry man, but it only made his host laugh.

"If this is your boasted western hospitality, I can tell you——"

"You'd better tell me what the dickens you are peppering me up this fashion for! My name isn't Pepper, no more than yours is! May be that *is* your name; you seem pretty warm."

"Your name not Pepper! Pray what is it, then?"

"Ah! there's the thing now! You land-hunters ought to know such things without asking."

"Land-hunter! I'm no land-hunter!"

"Well! you're a land-shark, then—swallowin' up poor men's farms. The less I see of such cattle, the better I'm pleased."

"Confound you!" said Mr. Willoughby, who waxed warm, "I tell you I've nothing to do with land. I wouldn't take your whole state for a gift."

"What did you tell my woman you was a land-hunter for, then?"

And now the whole matter became clear in a moment; and it was found that Mr. Willoughby's equipment, with the mention of a "hunting party," had completely misled both host and hostess. And to do them justice, never were regret and vexation more heartily expressed.

"You needn't judge our new-country folks by me," said Mr. Handy, for such proved to be his name; "any man in these parts would as soon bite off his own nose, as to snub a civil traveller that wanted a supper and a night's lodging. But somehow or other, your lots o' fixin', and your askin' after that 'ere Pepper—one of the worst land-sharks we've ever had here— made me mad; and I know I treated you worse than an Indian."

"Humph!" said Solomon.

"But," continued the host, "you shall see whether my old woman can't set a good breakfast, when she's a mind to. Come, you shan't stir a step till you've had breakfast; and just take back this plaguey dollar. I wonder it didn't burn my fingers when I took it!"

Mrs. Handy set forth her very best, and a famous breakfast it was, considering the times. And before it was finished, the hunting party made their appearance, having had some difficulty in finding their companion, who had made no very uncommon mistake as to section corners and town-lines.

"I'll tell ye what," said Mr. Handy, confidentially, as the cavalcade with its baggage-ponies, loaded with tents, gun-cases, and hampers of provisions, was getting into order for a march to the prairies, "I'll tell ye what; if you've occasion to stop any where in the Bush, you'd better tell 'em at the first goin' off that you a'n't land-hunters."

But Mr. Willoughby had already had "a caution."   [1845]

WILLIAM GILMORE SIMMS

William Gilmore Simms (1806–1870), whose talent and industry made him the leading antebellum writer in southern literature, was born in Charleston, South Carolina. His Irish father was so devastated by the death of Simms's mother in another childbirth that he left his son, not yet two years old, in Charleston and went to Mississippi to start a plantation on the frontier. Simms was raised by his maternal grandmother, who encouraged his production of patriotic verses and plays as a child. By his late teens he was editing periodicals as a professional writer. He published the first of his six collections of short fiction, The Book of My Lady, *in 1833. Over Simms's lifetime he saw more than eighty books of his own poetry, romances, historical novels, essays, and literary criticism through the press. Despite the grace and polish of his literary style, his popularity declined after the Civil War, primarily because of his racism as a loyal southerner outspoken in his support of slavery and secession.*

With the success of his romance novels in the 1830s, most notably The Yemassee *(1835), Simms considered himself primarily a writer of long fiction. The economic recession in the early 1840s, however, made him return to the production of sketches and short stories. In 1841 he told a correspondent that his book sales "are terribly diminished within the last few years. You will perceive that [Washington] Irving now writes almost wholly for magazines and [James Fenimore] Cooper & myself are almost the only ones whose novels are printed." Forced back into editing periodicals, Simms made an important contact with Evert Duyckinck, an influential editor in New York City, who arranged for the publication of a volume of Simms's stories in a series advertised as a "Library of American Books" by Wiley and Putnam.*

The series—which included Poe's The Raven and Other Poems *(1845), Melville's* Typee *(1846), and Hawthorne's* Mosses from an Old Manse *(1846)—was enriched by the addition of Simms's* The Wigwam and the Cabin, *issued in two volumes in 1845. The series promoted American poetry and fiction based on native materials instead of on the imitation of British authors. Simms created his finest work in tales like "The Arm-Chair of Tustenuggee" in* The Wigwam and the Cabin. *Some of the stories in this collection originally appeared in shorter form in periodicals, but Simms expanded them for book publication, drawing upon his research into folk legends and the oral tradition of storytelling in the South.*

The Arm-Chair of Tustenuggee

A Tradition of the Catawba

-I-

The windy month had set in, the leaves were falling, and the light-footed hunters of Catawba set forth upon the chase. Little groups went off in every direction, and before two weeks had elapsed from the beginning of the campaign, the whole nation was broken up into parties, each under the guidance of an individual warrior. The course of the several hunting bands was taken according to the tastes or habits of these leaders. Some of the Indians were famous for their skill in hunting the otter, could swim as long with head under water as himself, and be not far from his haunches, when he emerged to breathe. These followed the course of shallow waters and swamps, and thick, dense bays, in which it was known that he found his favorite haunts. The bear hunter pushed for the cane brakes and the bee trees; and woe to the black bear whom he encountered with his paws full of honeycomb, which he was unwilling to leave behind him. The active warrior took his way towards the hills, seeking for the brown wolf and the deer; and, if the truth were known, smiled with wholesale contempt at the more timorous who desired less adventurous triumphs. Many set forth in couples only, avoiding with care all the clamorous of the tribe; and some few, the more surly or successful—the inveterate bachelors of the nation—were content to make their forward progress alone. The old men prepared their traps and nets, the boys their blow guns, and followed with the squaws slowly, according to the division made by the hunters among themselves. They carried the blankets and bread stuffs, and camped nightly in noted places, to which, according to previous arrangement, the hunters might repair at evening and bring their game. In this way, some of the tribes followed the course of the Catawba, even to its source. Others darted off towards the Pacolet and Broad rivers, and there were some, the most daring and swift of foot, who made nothing of a journey to the Tiger River, and the rolling mountains of Spartanburg.

There were two warriors who pursued this course. One of them was named Conattee, and a braver man and more fortunate hunter never lived. But he had a wife who was a greater scold than Xantippe.[1] She was the wonder and the terror of the tribe, and quite as ugly as the one-eyed squaw of Tustenuggee, the grey demon of Enoree. Her tongue was the signal for "slinking," among the bold hunters of Turkey-town; and when they heard it, "now," said the young women, who sympathised, as all proper young women will do, with the handsome husband of an ugly wife, "now," said they, "we know that poor Conattee has come home." The

---

[1]The notoriously ill-tempered wife of the Greek philosopher Socrates.

return of the husband, particularly if he brought no game, was sure to be followed by a storm of that "dry thunder," so well known, which never failed to be heard at the farthest end of the village.

The companion of Conattee on the present expedition was named Selonee — one of the handsomest lads in the whole nation. He was tall and straight like a pine tree, had proved his skill and courage in several expeditions against the Chowannee red sticks, and had found no young warriors of the Cherokee, though he had been on the war path against them and had stricken all their posts, who could circumvent him in stratagem or conquer him in actual blows. His renown as a hunter was not less great. He had put to shame the best wolf-takers of the tribe, and the lodge of his venerable father, Chifonti, was never without meat. There was no good reason why Conattee, the married man, should be so intimate with Selonee, the single — there was no particular sympathy between the two; but, thrown together in sundry expeditions, they had formed an intimacy, which, strange to say, was neither denounced nor discouraged by the virago wife of the former. She who approved of but few of her husband's movements, and still fewer of his friends and fellowships, forbore all her reproaches when Selonee was his companion. She was the meekest, gentlest, sweetest tempered of all wives whenever the young hunter came home with her husband; and he, poor man, was consequently, never so well satisfied as when he brought Selonee with him. It was on such occasions, only, that the poor Conattee could persuade himself to regard Macourah as a tolerable personage. How he came to marry such a creature — such a termagant, and so monstrous ugly — was a mystery which none of the damsels of Catawba could elucidate, though the subject was one on which, when mending the young hunter's moccasins, they expended no small quantity of conjecture. Conattee, we may be permitted to say, was still quite popular among them, in spite of his bad taste, and manifest unavailableness; possibly, for the very reason that his wife was universally detested; and it will, perhaps, speak something for their charity, if we pry no deeper into their motives, to say that the wish was universal among them that the Opitchi Manneyto, or Black Devil of their belief, would take the virago to himself, and leave to the poor Conattee some reasonable hope of being made happy by a more indulgent spouse.

–II–

Well, Conattee and Selonee were out of sight of the smoke of "Turkey-town," and, conscious of his freedom as he no longer heard the accents of domestic authority, the henpecked husband gave a loose to his spirits, and made ample amends to himself, by the indulgence of joke and humor, for the sober constraints which fettered him at home. Selonee joined with him in his merriment, and the resolve was mutual that they should give the squaws the slip and not linger in their progress till they had thrown the

Tiger River behind them. To trace their course till they came to the famous hunting ground which bordered upon the Pacolet, will scarcely be necessary, since, as they did not stop to hunt by the way, there were necessarily but few incidents to give interest to their movements. When they had reached the river, however, they made for a cove, well known to them on previous seasons, which lay between the parallel waters of the Pacolet, and a little stream called the Thicketty—a feeder of the Eswawpuddenah, in which they had confident hopes of finding the game which they desired. In former years the spot had been famous as a sheltering place for herds of wolves; and, with something like the impatience of a warrior waiting for his foe, the hunters prepared their strongest shafts and sharpest flints, and set their keen eyes upon the closest places of the thicket, into which they plunged fearlessly. They had not proceeded far, before a single boar-wolf, of amazing size, started up in their path; and, being slightly wounded by the arrow of Selonee, which glanced first upon some twigs beneath which he lay, he darted off with a fearful howl in the direction of Conattee, whose unobstructed shaft, penetrating the side beneath the fore shoulders, inflicted a fearful, if not a fatal wound, upon the now thoroughly enraged beast. He rushed upon Conattee in his desperation, but the savage was too quick for him; leaping behind a tree, he avoided the rashing stroke with which the white tusks threatened him, and by this time was enabled to fit a second arrow to his bow. His aim was true, and the stone blade of the shaft went quivering into the shaggy monster's heart; who, under the pang of the last convulsion, bounded into the muddy waters of the Thicketty Creek, to the edge of which the chase had now brought all the parties. Conattee beheld him plunge furiously forward—twice—thrice—then rest with his nostrils in the water, as the current bore him from sight around a little elbow of the creek. But it was not often that the Indian hunter of those days lost the game which he had stricken. Conattee stripped to it, threw his fringed hunting shirt of buckskin on the bank, with his bow and arrows, his moccasins and leggins beside it, and reserving only his knife, he called to Selonee, who was approaching him, to keep them in sight, and plunged into the water in pursuit of his victim. Selonee gave little heed to the movements of his companion, after the first two or three vigorous strokes which he beheld him make. Such a pursuit, as it promised no peril, called for little consideration from this hardy and fearless race, and Selonee amused himself by striking into a thick copse which they had not yet traversed, in search of other sport. There he startled the she-wolf, and found sufficient employment on his own hands to call for all his attention to himself. When Selonee first came in sight of her, she was lying on a bed of rushes and leaves, which she had prepared under the roots of a gigantic Spanish oak. Her cubs, to the number of five, lay around her, keeping a perfect silence, which she had no doubt enforced upon them after her own fashion, and which was rigidly maintained until they saw him. It was then that the instincts of the fierce beasts could no longer be suppressed, and they joined at once in a short chopping bark, or cry, at the stranger, while their little eyes flashed fire, and their red jaws, thinly sprinkled with the first teeth, were gnashed together with a show of that ferocious hatred of man, which marks their nature, but which, fortunately for Selonee, was too feeble at that time to make his approach to them dangerous. But the dam demanded greater consideration. With one sweep of her forepaw she drew all the young ones behind her, and showing every preparedness for flight, she began to move backward slowly beneath the overhanging limbs of the tree, still keeping her keen, fiery eye fixed upon the hunter. But Selonee was not disposed to suffer her to get off so easily. The success of Conattee had just given him sufficient provocation to make him silently resolve that the she-wolf—who is always more to be dreaded than the male, as, with nearly all his strength, she has twice his swiftness, and, with her young about her, more than twice his ferocity— should testify more completely to his prowess than the victory just obtained by his companion could possibly speak for his. His eye was fixed upon hers, and hers, never for a moment, taken from him. It was his object to divert it, since he well knew, that with his first movement, she would most probably spring upon him. Without lifting his bow, which he nevertheless had in readiness, he whistled shrilly as if to his dog; and answered himself by a correct imitation of the bark of the Indian cur, the known enemy of the wolf, and commonly his victim. The keen eye of the angry beast looked suddenly around as if fearing an assault upon her young ones from behind. In that moment, the arrow of Selonee was driven through her neck, and when she leaped forward to the place where he stood, he was no longer to be seen.

From a tree which he had thrown between them, he watched her movements and prepared a second shaft. Meanwhile she made her way back slowly to her young, and before she could again turn towards him a second arrow had given her another and severer wound. Still, as Selonee well knew the singular tenacity of life possessed by these fierce animals, he prudently changed his position with every shaft, and took especial care to place himself in the rear of some moderately sized tree, sufficiently large to shelter him from her claws, yet small enough to enable him to take free aim around it. Still he did not, at any time, withdraw more than twenty steps from his enemy. Divided in her energies by the necessity of keeping near her young, he was conscious of her inability to pursue him far. Carrying on the war in this manner, he had buried no less than five arrows in her body, and it was not until his sixth had penetrated her eye, that he deemed himself safe in the nearer approach which he now meditated. She had left her cubs, on receiving his last shot, and was writhing and leaping, blinded, no less than maddened, by the wound, in a vain endeavor to approach her assailant. It was now that Selonee determined on a closer conflict. It was the great boast of the Catawba warriors to grapple with the wolf, and while he yet struggled, to tear the quick quivering heart from his bosom.

He placed his bow and arrows behind the tree, and taking in his left hand a chunk or fragment of a bough, while he grasped his unsheathed knife in his right, he leapt in among the cubs, and struck one of them a severe blow upon the head with the chunk. Its scream, and the confusion among the rest, brought back the angry dam, and though she could see only imperfectly, yet, guided by their clamor, she rushed with open jaws upon the hunter. With keen, quick eyes, and steady resolute nerves, he waited for her approach, and when she turned her head aside, to strike him with her sharp teeth, he thrust the pine fragment which he carried in his left hand, into her extended jaws, and pressing fast upon her, bore back her haunches to the earth. All this while the young ones were impotently gnawing at the heels of the warrior, which had been fearlessly planted in the very midst of them. But these he did not heed. The larger and fiercer combatant called for all his attention, and her exertions, quickened by the spasms of her wounds, rendered necessary all his address and strength to preserve the advantage he had gained. The fierce beast had sunk her teeth by this into the wood, and, leaving it in her jaws, he seized her with the hand, now freed, by the throat, and, bearing her upward, so as to yield him a plain and easy stroke at her belly, he drove the deep knife into it, and drew the blade upwards, until resisted by the bone of the breast. It was then, while she lay writhing and rolling upon the ground in the agonies of death, that he tore the heart from the opening he had made, and hurled it down to the cubs, who seized on it with avidity. This done, he patted and caressed them, and while they struggled about him for the meat, he cut a fork in the ears of each, and putting the slips in his pouch, left the young ones without further hurt, for the future sport of the hunter. The dam he scalped, and with this trophy in possession, he pushed back to the place where he had left the accoutrements of Conattee, which he found undisturbed in the place where he had laid them.

– III –

But where was Conattee himself during all this period? Some hours had elapsed since he had taken the river after the tiger that he had slain, and it was something surprising to Selonee that he should have remained absent and without his clothes so long. The weather was cold and unpleasant, and it could scarce be a matter of choice with the hunter, however hardy, to suffer all its biting bleaknesses when his garments were within his reach. This reflection made Selonee apprehensive that some harm had happened to his companion. He shouted to him, but received no answer. Could he have been seized with the cramp while in the stream, and drowned before he could extricate himself? This was a danger to which the very best of swimmers is liable at certain seasons of the year, and in certain conditions of the body. Selonee reproached himself that he had not waited beside the stream until the result of Conattee's experiment was known.

The mind of the young hunter was troubled with many fears and doubts. He went down the bank of the river, and called aloud with all his lungs, until the woods and waters re-echoed, again and again, the name of Conattee. He received no other response. With a mind filled with increasing fears, each more unpleasant than the last, Selonee plunged into the creek, and struck off for the opposite shore, at the very point at which the tiger had been about to turn, under the influence of the current, when Conattee went in after him. He was soon across, and soon found the tracks of the hunter in the gray sands upon its margin. He found, too, to his great delight, the traces made by the carcass of the tiger—the track was distinct enough from the blood which dropped from the reeking skin of the beast, and Selonee rejoiced in the certainty that the traces which he followed would soon lead him to his friend. But not so. He had scarcely gone fifty yards into the woods when his tracks failed him at the foot of a crooked, fallen tree, one of the most gnarled and complicated of all the crooked trees of the forest; here all signs disappeared. Conattee was not only not there, but had left no sort of clue by which to follow him further. This was the strangest thing of all. The footprints were distinct enough till he came to the spot where lay the crooked tree, but there he lost them. He searched the forest around him, in every direction. Not a copse escaped his search— not a bay—not a thicket—not an island—and he came back to the spot where the tiger had been skinned, faint and weary, and more sorrowful than can well be spoken. At one time he fancied his friend was drowned, at another, that he was taken prisoner by the Cherokees. But there were his tracks from the river, and there were no other tracks than his own. Besides, so far as the latter supposition was concerned, it was scarcely possible that so brave and cunning a warrior would suffer himself to be so completely entrapped and carried off by an enemy, without so much as being able to give the alarm; and, even had that been the case, would it be likely that the enemy would have suffered him to pass without notice? "But," here the suggestion naturally arose in the mind of Selonee, "may they not even now be on the track!" With the suggestion the gallant youth bounded to his feet. "It is no fat turkey that they seek!" he exclaimed, drawing out an arrow from the leash that hung upon his shoulders, and fitting it to his bow, while his busy, glancing eye watched every shadow in the wood, and his keen, quick ear noted every sound. But there were no signs of an enemy, and a singular and mournful stillness hung over the woods. Never was creature more miserable than Selonee. He called aloud, until his voice grew hoarse, and his throat sore, upon the name of Conattee. There was no answer, but the gibing echoes of his own hoarse accents. Once more he went back to the river, once more he plunged into its bosom, and with lusty sinews struck out for a thick green island that lay some quarter of a mile below, to which he thought it not improbable that the hunter might have wandered in pursuit of other game. It was a thickly wooded but small island, which he traversed in an hour. Finding nothing, he made his weary way back to the spot from which his friend had started on leaving him. Here he found his clothes where he had hidden them. The neighborhood of this region he traversed in like manner with the opposite — going over ground, and into places, which it was scarcely on the verge of physical possibility that his friend's person could have gone.

The day waned and night came on, and still the persevering hunter gave not up his search. The midnight found him at the foot of the tree, where they had parted, exhausted but sleepless, and suffering bitterly in mind from those apprehensions which every moment of hopeless search had necessarily helped to accumulate and strengthen. Day dawned, and his labor was renewed. The unhappy warrior went resolutely over all the ground which he had traversed the night before. Once more he crossed the river, and followed, step by step, the still legible foot tracks of Conattee. These, he again noted, were all in the opposite direction to the stream, to which it was evident he had not returned. But, after reaching the place where lay the fallen tree, all signs failed. Selonee looked round the crooked tree, crawled under its sprawling and twisted limbs, broke into the hollow which was left by its uptorn roots, and again shouted, until all the echoes gave back his voice, the name of Conattee, imploring him for an answer if he could hear him and reply. But the echoes died away, leaving him in a silence that spoke more loudly to his heart than before, that his quest was hopeless. Yet he gave it not up until the day had again failed him. That night, as before, he slept upon the ground. With the dawn, he again went over it, and with equally bad success. This done, he determined to return to the camp. He no longer had any spirit to pursue the sports for which alone he had set forth. His heart was full of sorrow, his limbs were weary, and he felt none of that vigorous elasticity which had given him such great renown as a brave and a hunter, among his own and the neighboring nations. He tied the clothes of Conattee upon his shoulders, took his bows and arrows, now sacred in his sight, along with him, and turned his eyes homeward. The next day, at noon, he reached the encampment.

–IV–

The hunters were all in the woods, and none but the squaws and the papooses left in the encampment. Selonee came within sight of their back settlements, and seated himself upon a log at the edge of the forest with his back carefully turned towards the smoke of the camp. Nobody ventured to approach him while in this situation; but, at night, when the hunters came dropping in, one by one, Selonee drew nigh to them. He called them apart from the women, and then told them his story.

"This is a strange tale which the wolf-chief tells us," said one of the old men, with a smile of incredulity.

"It is a true tale, father," was the reply.

"Conattee was a brave chief!"

"Very brave, father," said Selonee.

"Had he not eyes to see?"

"The great bird, that rises to the sun, had not better," was the reply.

"What painted jay was it that said Conattee was a fool?"

"The painted bird lied, that said so, my father," was the response of Selonee.

"And comes Selonee, the wolf-chief, to us, with a tale that Conattee was blind, and could not see; a coward that could not strike the she-wolf; a fool that knew not where to set down his foot; and shall we not say Selonee lies upon his brother, even as the painted bird that makes a noise in my ears? Selonee has slain Conattee with his knife. See, it is the blood of Conattee upon the war-shirt of Selonee."

"It is the blood of the she-wolf," cried the young warrior, with a natural indignation.

"Let Selonee go to the woods behind the lodges, till the chiefs say what shall be done to Selonee, because of Conattee, whom he slew."

"Selonee will go, as Emathla, the wise chief, has commanded," replied the young warrior. "He will wait behind the lodges, till the chiefs have said what is good to be done to him, and if they say that he must die because of Conattee, it is well. Selonee laughs at death. But the blood of Conattee is not upon the war-shirt of Selonee. He has said it is the blood of the wolf's mother." With these words the young chief drew forth the skin of the wolf which he had slain, together with the tips of the ears taken from the cubs, and leaving them in the place where he had sat, withdrew, without further speech, from the assembly which was about to sit in judgment upon his life.

– V –

The consultation that followed was close and earnest. There was scarcely any doubt in the minds of the chiefs that Conattee was slain by his companion. He had brought back with him the arms and all the clothes of the hunter. He was covered with his blood, as they thought; and the grief which filled his heart and depressed his countenance, looked, in their eyes, rather like the expression of guilt than suffering. For a long while did they consult together. Selonee had friends who were disposed to save him; but he had enemies also, as merit must have always, and these were glad of the chance afforded them to put out of their reach, a rival of whom they were jealous, and a warrior whom they feared. Unfortunately for Selonee, the laws of the nation but too well helped the malice of his foes. These laws, as peremptory as those of the Medes and Persians, held him liable in his own life for that of the missing hunter; and the only indulgence that could be accorded to Selonee, and which was obtained for him, was, that he might be allowed a single moon in which to find Conattee, and bring him home to his people.

"Will Selonee go seek Conattee—the windy moon is for Selonee— let him bring Conattee home to his people." Thus said the chiefs, when the young warrior was again brought before them.

"Selonee would die to find Conattee," was the reply.

"He will die if he finds him not!" answered the chief, Emathla.

"It is well!" calmly spoke the young warrior. "Is Selonee free to go?"

"The windy moon is for Selonee. Will he return to the lodges if he finds not Conattee?" was the inquiry of Emathla.

"Is Selonee a dog, to fly?" indignantly demanded the warrior. "Let Emathla send a young warrior on the right and on the left of Selonee, if he trusts not what is spoken by Selonee."

"Selonee will go alone, and bring back Conattee."

–VI–

The confidence thus reposed in one generally esteemed a murderer, and actually under sentence as such, is customary among the Indians; nor is it often abused. The loss of caste which would follow their flight from justice, is much more terrible among them than any fear of death—which an Indian may avoid, but not through fear. Their loss of caste among themselves, apart from the outlawry which follows it, is, in fact, a loss of the soul. The heaven of the great Manneyto is denied to one under outlawry of the nation, and such a person is then the known and chosen slave of the demon, Opitchi-Manneyto. It was held an unnecessary insult on the part of Emathla, to ask Selonee if he would return to meet his fate. But Emathla was supposed to favor the enemies of Selonee.

With such a gloomy alternative before him in the event of his proving unsuccessful, the young hunter retraced his steps to the fatal waters where Conattee had disappeared. With a spirit no less warmly devoted to his friend, than anxious to avoid the disgraceful doom to which he was destined, the youth spared no pains, withheld no exertion, overlooked no single spot, and omitted no art known to the hunter, to trace out the mystery which covered the fate of Conattee. But days passed of fruitless labor, and the last faint slender outlines of the moon which had been allotted him for the search, gleamed forth a sorrowful light upon his path, as he wearily traced it onward to the temporary lodges of the tribe.

Once more he resumed his seat before the council and listened to the doom which was in reserve for him. When the sentence was pronounced, he untied his arrows, loosened the belt at his waist, put a fillet around his head made of the green bark of a little sapling which he cut in the neighboring woods, then rising to his feet, he spoke thus, in language, and with a spirit, becoming so great a warrior.

"It is well. The chiefs have spoken, and the wolf-chief does not tremble. He loves the chase, but he does not weep like a woman, because it is forbidden that he go after the deer—he loves to fright the young hares of the Cherokee, but he laments not that ye say ye can conquer the Cherokee without his help. Fathers, I have slain the deer and the wolf—my lodge is full of their ears. I have slain the Cherokee, till the scalps are about my knees when I walk in the cabin. I go not to the dark valley without glory— I have had the victories of grey hairs, but there is no grey hair in my own. I have no more to say—there is a deed for every arrow that is here. Bid the young men get their bows ready, let them put a broad stone upon their arrows that may go soon into the life—I will show my people how to die."

They led him forth as he commanded, to the place of execution—a little space behind the encampment, where a hole had been already dug for his burial. While he went, he recited his victories to the youths who attended him. To each he gave an arrow which he was required to keep, and with this arrow, he related some incident in which he had proved his valor, either in conflict with some other warrior, or with the wild beasts of the woods. These deeds, each of them was required to remember and relate, and show the arrow which was given with the narrative on occasion of this great state solemnity. In this way, their traditions are preserved. When he reached the grave, he took his station before it, the executioners, with their arrows, being already placed in readiness. The whole tribe had assembled to witness the execution, the warriors and boys in the foreground, the squaws behind them. A solemn silence prevailed over the scene, and a few moments only remained to the victim; when the wife of Conattee darted forward from the crowd bearing in her hands a peeled wand, with which, with every appearance of anger, she struck Selonee over the shoulders, exclaiming as she did so:

"Come, thou dog, thou shalt not die—thou shalt lie in the doorway of Conattee, and bring venison for his wife. Shall there be no one to bring meat to my lodge? Thou shalt do this, Selonee—thou shalt not die."

A murmur arose from the crowd at these words.

"She hath claimed Selonee for her husband, in place of Conattee— well, she hath the right."

The enemies of Selonee could not object. The widow had, in fact, exercised a privilege which is recognized by the Indian laws almost universally; and the policy by which she was governed in the present instance, was sufficiently apparent to all the village. It was evident, now that Conattee was gone, that nobody could provide for the woman who had no sons, and no male relations, and who was too execrably ugly, and too notorious as a scold, to leave it possible that she could ever procure another husband so inexperienced or so flexible as the one she had lost. Smartly striking Selonee on his shoulders, she repeated her command that he should rise and follow her.

"Thou wilt take this dog to thy lodge, that he may hunt thee venison?" demanded the old chief, Emathla.

"Have I not said?" shouted the scold—"Hear you not? The dog is mine—I bid him follow me."

"Is there no friendly arrow to seek my heart?" murmured the young warrior, as, rising slowly from the grave into which he had previously descended, he prepared to obey the laws of his nation, in the commands of the woman who claimed him to replace the husband who was supposed to have died by his hands. Even the foes of Selonee looked on him with lessened hostility, and the pity of his friends was greater now than when he stood on the precipice of death. The young women of the tribe wept bitterly as they beheld so monstrous a sacrifice. Meanwhile, the exulting hag, as if conscious of her complete control over the victim, goaded him forward with repeated strokes of her wand. She knew that she was hated by all the young women, and she was delighted to show them a conquest which would have been a subject of pride to any among them. With this view she led the captive through their ranks. As they parted mournfully, on either hand, to suffer the two to pass, Selonee stopped short and motioned one of the young women who stood at the greatest distance behind the rest, looking on with eyes which, if they had no tears, yet gave forth an expression of desolateness more woeful than any tears could have done. With clasped hands, and trembling as she came, the gentle maiden drew nigh.

"Was it a dream," said Selonee sorrowfully, "that told me of the love of a singing bird, and a green cabin by the trickling waters? Did I hear a voice that said to me sweetly, wait but a little, till the green corn breaks the hill, and Medoree will come to thy cabin and lie by thy side? Tell me, is this thing true, Medoree?"

"Thou sayest, Selonee—the thing is true," was the reply of the maiden, uttered in broken accents that denoted a breaking heart.

"But they will make Selonee go to the lodge of another woman— they will put Macourah into the arms of Selonee."

"Alas! Alas!"

"Wilt thou see this thing, Medoree? Can'st thou look upon it, then turn away, and going back to thy own lodge, can'st thou sing a gay song of forgetfulness as thou goest?"

"Forgetfulness!—Ah, Selonee."

"Thou art the beloved of Selonee, Medoree—thou shalt not lose him. It would vex thy heart that another should take him to her lodge!"

The tears of the damsel flowed freely down her cheeks, and she sobbed bitterly, but said nothing.

"Take the knife from my belt, Medoree, and put its sharp tooth into my heart, ere thou sufferest this thing! Wilt thou not?"

The girl shrunk back with an expression of undisguised horror in her face.

"I will bless thee, Medoree," was the continued speech of the warrior. She turned from him, covering her face with her hands.

"I cannot do this thing, Selonee—I cannot strike thy heart with the knife. Go—let the woman have thee. Medoree cannot kill thee—she will herself die."

"It is well," cried the youth, in a voice of mournful self-abandonment, as he resumed his progress towards the lodge of Macourah.

–VII–

It is now time to return to Conattee, and trace his progress from the moment when, plunging into the waters, he left the side of Selonee in pursuit of the wolf, whose dying struggles in the stream he had beheld. We are already acquainted with his success in extricating the animal from the water, and possessing himself of its hide. He had not well done this when he heard a rushing noise in the woods above him, and fancying that there was a prospect of other game at hand, and inflated with the hope of adding to his trophies, though without any weapon but his knife, Conattee hastened to the spot. When he reached it, however, he beheld nothing. A gigantic and singularly deformed pine tree, crooked and most irregular in shape, lay prostrate along the ground, and formed such an intricate covering above it, that Conattee deemed it possible that some beast of prey might have made its den among the recesses of its roots. With this thought, he crawled under the spreading limbs, and searched all their intricacies. Emerging from the search, which had been fruitless, he took a seat upon the trunk of the tree, and spreading out the wolf's hide before him, proceeded to pare away the particles of flesh which, in the haste with which he had performed the task of flaying him, had been suffered to adhere to the skin. But he had scarcely commenced the operation, when two gigantic limbs of the fallen tree upon which he sat, curled over his thighs and bound him to the spot. Other limbs, to his great horror, while he strove to move, clasped his arms and covered his shoulders. He strove to cry aloud, but his jaws were grasped before he could well open them, by other branches; and, with his eyes, which were suffered to peer through little openings in the bark, he could see his legs encrusted by like coverings with his other members. Still seeing, his own person yet escaped his sight. Not a part of it now remained visible to himself. A bed of green velvet-like moss rested on his lap. His knees shot out a thorny excrescence; and his hands, flattened to his thighs, were enveloped in as complete a casing of bark as covered the remainder of the tree around him. Even his knife and wolf skin, to his great surprise, suffered in like manner, the bark having contracted them into one of those huge bulging knobs that so numerously deformed the tree. With all his thoughts and consciousness remaining, Conattee had yet lost every faculty of action. When he tried to scream aloud, his jaws felt the contraction of a pressure upon them, which resisted all their efforts, while an oppressive thorn growing upon a wild vine that hung before his face, was brought by every movement of himself or of the tree into his very mouth. The poor hunter immediately conceived his situation — he was in the power of Tustenuggee, the Grey Demon of Enoree. The tree upon which he sat was one of those magic trees which the tradition of his people entitled the "Arm-chair of Tustenuggee." In these traps for the unwary the wicked demon caught his victim, and exulted in his miseries. Here he sometimes remained until death released him; for it was not often that the power into whose clutches he had fallen, suffered his prey to escape through a sudden feeling of lenity and good humor. The only hope of Conattee was that Selonee might suspect his condition; in which event his rescue was simple and easy enough. It was only to hew off the limbs, or pare away the bark, and the victim was uncovered in his primitive integrity. But how improbable that this discovery should be made! He had no voice to declare his bondage. He had no capacity for movement by which he might reveal the truth to his comrade's eyes; and unless some divine instinct should counsel his friend to an experiment which he would scarcely think upon, of himself, the poor prisoner felt that he must die in the miserable bondage into which he had fallen. While these painful convictions were passing through his mind, he heard the distant shoutings of Selonee. In a little while he beheld the youth anxiously seeking him in every quarter, following his trail at length to the very tree in which he was bound, crawling like himself beneath its branches, but not sitting like himself to be caught upon its trunk. Vainly did the poor fellow strive to utter but a few words, however faintly, apprising the youth of his condition. The effort died away in the most imperfect breathing, sounding in his own ears like the faint sigh of some budding flower. With equal ill success did he aim to struggle with his limbs. He was too tightly grasped, in every part, to stir in the slightest degree a single member. He saw the fond search, meanwhile, which his comrade maintained, and his heart yearned the more in fondness for the youth. But it was with consummate horror that he saw him depart as night came on. Miserable, indeed, were his feelings that night. The voice of the Grey Demon alone kept him company, and he and his one-eyed wife made merry with his condition, goading him the livelong night with speeches of cruel gibe and mischievous reflection, such as the following:

"There is no hope for you, Conattee, till some one takes your place. Some one must sit in your lap, whom you are willing to leave behind you, before you can get out of mine," was the speech of the Grey Demon, who, perched upon Conattee's shoulders, bent his huge knotty head over him, while his red eyes looked into the half-hidden ones of the environed hunter, and glared upon him with the exultation of the tyrant at last secure of his prey. Night passed away at length, and, with the dawn, how was the hopeless heart of Conattee refreshed as he again saw Selonee appear! He then remembered the words of Tustenuggee, which told him that he could not escape until some one sat in his lap whom he was willing to leave behind him. The fancy rose in his mind that Selonee would do this; but could it be that he would consent to leave his friend behind him? Life was sweet, and great was the temptation. At one moment he almost wished that Selonee would draw nigh and seat himself after his fatigue. As if the young hunter knew his wish, he drew nigh at that instant; but the better feelings in Conattee's heart grew strong as he approached, and, striving to twist and writhe in his bondage, and laboring at the same time to call out in warning to his friend, he manifested the noble resolution not to avail himself of his friend's position to relieve his own; and, as if the warning of Conattee had really reached the understanding of Selonee, the youth retraced his steps, and once more hurried away from the place of danger. With his final departure the fond hopes of the prisoner sunk within him; and when hour after hour had gone by without the appearance of any of his people, and without any sort of change in his condition, he gave himself up utterly for lost. The mocks and jeers of the Grey Demon and his one-eyed squaw filled his ears all night, and the morning brought him nothing but flat despair. He resigned himself to his fate with the resolution of one who, however unwilling he might be to perish in such a manner, had yet faced death too frequently not to yield him a ready defiance now.

– VIII –

But hope had not utterly departed from the bosom of Selonee. Perhaps the destiny which had befallen him had made him resolve the more earnestly to seek farther into the mystery of that which hung above the fate of his friend. The day which saw him enter the cabin of Macourah saw him the most miserable man alive. The hateful hag, hateful enough as the wife of his friend, whose ill treatment was notorious, was now doubly hateful to him as his own wife; and now, when, alone together, she threw aside the harsh and termagant features which had before distinguished her deportment, and, assuming others of a more amorous complexion, threw her arms about the neck of the youth and solicited his endearments, a loathing sensation of disgust was coupled with the hate which had previously possessed his mind. Flinging away from her embrace, he rushed out of the lodge with feelings of the most unspeakable bitterness and grief, and bending his way towards the forest, soon lost sight of the encampment of his people. Selonee was resolved on making another effort for the recovery of his friend. His resolve went even farther than this. He was bent never to return to the doom which had been fastened upon him, and to pursue his way into more distant and unknown forests — a self-doomed exile — unless he could restore Conattee to the nation. Steeled against all those ties of love or of country, which at one time had prevailed in his bosom over all, he now surrendered himself to friendship or despair. In Catawba, unless he restored Conattee, he could have no hope; and without Catawba he had neither hope nor love. On either hand he saw nothing but misery; but the worst form of misery lay behind him in the lodge of Macourah. But Macourah was not the person to submit to such a determination. She was too well satisfied with the exchange with which fortune had provided her, to suffer its gift to be lost so easily; and when Selonee darted from the cabin in such fearful haste, she readily conjectured his determination. She hurried after him with all possible speed, little doubting that those thunders — could she overtake him — with which she had so frequently overawed the pliant Conattee, would possess an effect not less influential upon his more youthful successor. Macourah was gaunt as a greyhound, and scarcely less fleet of foot. Besides, she was as tough as a greysquirrel in his thirteenth year. She did not despair of overtaking Selonee, provided she suffered him not to know that she was upon his trail. Her first movements therefore were marked with caution. Having watched his first direction, she divined his aim to return to the hunting grounds where he had lost or slain his companion; and these hunting grounds were almost as well known to herself as to him. With a rapidity of movement, and a tenacity of purpose, which could only be accounted for by a reference to that wild passion which Selonee had unconsciously inspired in her bosom for himself, she followed his departing footsteps; and when, the next day, he heard her shouts behind him, he was absolutely confounded. But it was with a feeling of surprise and not of dissatisfaction that he heard her voice. He — good youth — regarding Conattee as one of the very worthiest of the Catawba warriors, seemed to have been impressed with an idea that such also was the opinion of his wife. He little dreamed that she had any real design upon himself; and believed that, to show her the evidences which were to be seen, which led to the fate of her husband, might serve to convince her that not only he was not the murderer, but that Conattee might not, indeed, be murdered at all. He coolly waited her approach, therefore, and proceeded to renew his statements, accompanying his narrative with the expression of the hope which he entertained of again restoring her husband to herself and the nation. But she answered his speech only with upbraidings and entreaties; and when she failed, she proceeded to thump him lustily with the wand by which she had compelled him to follow her to the lodge the day before. But Selonee was in no humor to obey the laws of the nation now. The feeling of degradation which had followed in his mind, from the moment when he left the spot where he had stood up for death, having neither fear nor shame, was too fresh in his consciousness to suffer him to yield a like acknowledgment to it now; and though sorely tempted to pummel the Jezabel in return for the lusty thwacks which she had already inflicted upon his shoulders, he forbore, in consideration of his friend, and contented himself with simply setting forward on his progress, determined to elude her pursuit by an exercise of all his vigor and elasticity. Selonee was hardy as the grisly bear, and fleeter than the wild turkey; and Macourah, virago as she was, soon discovered the difference in the chase when Selonee put forth his strength and spirit. She followed with all her pertinacity, quickened as it was by an increase of fury at the presumption which had ventured to disobey her commands; but Selonee fled faster than she pursued, and every additional moment served to increase the space between them. The hunter lost her from his heels at length, and deemed himself fortunate that she was no longer in sight and hearing, when he again approached the spot where his friend had so mysteriously disappeared. Here he renewed his search with a painful care and minuteness, which the imprisoned Conattee all the while beheld. Once more Selonee crawled beneath those sprawling limbs and spreading arms that wrapped up in their solid and coarse rinds the person of the warrior. Once more he emerged from the spot disappointed and hopeless. This he had hardly done when, to the great horror of the captive, and the annoyance of Selonee, the shrill shrieks and screams of the too well-known voice of Macourah rang through the forests. Selonee dashed forward as he heard the sounds, and when Macourah reached the spot, which she did unerringly in following his trail, the youth was already out of sight.

"I can go no further," cried the woman — "a curse on him and a curse on Conattee, since in losing one I have lost both. I am too faint to follow. As for Selonee, may the one-eyed witch of Tustenuggee take him for her dog."

With this delicate imprecation, the virago seated herself in a state of exhaustion upon the inviting bed of moss which formed the lap of Conattee. This she had no sooner done, than the branches relaxed their hold upon the limbs of her husband. The moment was too precious for delay, and sliding from under her with an adroitness and strength which were beyond her powers of prevention, and, indeed, quite too sudden for any effort at resistance, she had the consternation to behold her husband starting up in full life before her, and, with the instinct of his former condition, preparing to take flight. She cried to him, but he fled the faster — she strove to follow him, but the branches which had relaxed their hold upon her husband had resumed their contracted grasp upon her limbs. The brown bark was already forming above her on every hand, and her tongue, allotted a brief term of liberty, was alone free to assail him. But she had spoken but few words when the bark encased her jaws, and the ugly thorn of the vine which had so distressed Conattee, had taken its place at their portals.

– IX –

The husband looked back but once, when the voice ceased — then, with a shivering sort of joy that his own doom had undergone a termination, which he now felt to be doubly fortunate — he made a wide circuit that he might avoid the fatal neighborhood, and pushed on in pursuit of his friend, whom his eyes, even when he was surrounded in the tree, had followed in his flight. It was no easy task, however, to overtake Selonee, flying, as he did, from the supposed pursuit of the termagant. Great however was the joy of the young warriors when they did encounter, and long and fervent was their mutual embrace. Conattee described his misfortunes, and related the manner in which he was taken; showed how the bark had encased his limbs, and how the intricate magic had even engrossed his knife and the wolf skin which had been the trophy of his victory. But Conattee said not a word of his wife and her entrapment, and Selonee was left in the conviction that his companion owed his escape from the toils to some hidden change in the tyrannical mood of Tustenuggee, or the one-eyed woman, his wife.

"But the skin and the knife, Conattee, let us not leave them," said Selonee, "let us go back and extricate them from the tree."

Conattee showed some reluctance. He soon said, in the words of Macbeth, which he did not use however as a quotation, "I'll go no more." But Selonee, who ascribed this reluctance to very natural apprehensions of the demon from whose clutches he had just made his escape, declared his readiness to undertake the adventure if Conattee would only point out to his eyes the particular excrescence in which the articles were enclosed. When the husband perceived that his friend was resolute, he made a merit of necessity.

"If the thing is to be done," said he, "why should you have the risk, I myself will do it. It would be a woman-fear were I to shrink from the danger. Let us go."

The process of reasoning by which Conattee came to this determination was a very sudden one, and one, too, that will not be hard to comprehend by every husband in his situation. It was his fear that if Selonee undertook the business, an unlucky or misdirected stroke of his knife might sever a limb, or remove some portions of the bark which did not merit or need removal. Conattee trembled at the very idea of the revelations which might follow such an unhappy result. Strengthening himself, therefore, with all his energies, he went forward with Selonee to the spot, and while the latter looked on and witnessed the operation, he proceeded with a nicety and care which amused and surprised Selonee, to the excision of the swollen scab upon the tree in which he had seen his wolf skin encompassed. While he performed the operation, which he did as cautiously as if it had been the extraction of a mote from the eye of a virgin, the beldam in the tree, conscious of all his movements, and at first flattered with the hope that he was working for her extrication, maintained the most ceaseless efforts of her tongue and limbs, but without avail. Her slight breathing, which Conattee knew where to look for, more like the sighs of an infant zephyr than the efforts of a human bosom, denoted to his ears an overpowering but fortunately suppressed volcano within; and his heart leaped with a new joy, which had been unknown to it for many years before, when he thought that he was now safe, and, he trusted, for ever, from any of the tortures which he had been fain to endure patiently so long. When he had finished the operation by which he had re-obtained his treasures, he ventured upon an impertinence which spoke surprisingly for his sudden acquisition of confidence; and looking up through the little aperture in the bark, from whence he had seen every thing while in the same situation, and from whence he concluded she was also suffered to see, he took a peep—a quick, quizzical and taunting peep, at those eyes which he had not so dared to offend before. He drew back suddenly from the contact—so suddenly, indeed, that Selonee, who saw the proceeding, but had no idea of the truth, thought he had been stung by some insect, and questioned him accordingly.

"Let us be off, Selonee," was the hurried answer, "we have nothing to wait for now."

"Yes," replied Selonee, "and I had forgotten to say to you that your wife, Macourah, is on her way in search of you. I left her but a little ways behind, and thought to find her here. I suppose she is tired, however, and is resting by the way."

"Let her rest," said Conattee, "which is an indulgence much greater than any she ever accorded me. She will find me out soon enough, without making it needful that I should go in search of her. Come."

Selonee kindly suppressed the history of the transactions which had taken place in the village during the time when the hunter was supposed to be dead; but Conattee heard the facts from other quarters, and loved Selonee the better for the sympathy he had shown, not only in coming again to seek for him, but in not loving his wife better than he did himself. They returned to the village, and every body was rejoiced to behold the return of the hunters. As for the termagant Macourah, nobody but Conattee knew her fate; and he, like a wise man, kept his secret until there was no danger of its being made use of to rescue her from her predicament. Years had passed, and Conattee had found among the young squaws one that pleased him much better than the old. He had several children by her, and years and honors had alike fallen numerously upon his head, when, one day, one of his own sons, while hunting in the same woods, knocked off one of the limbs of the Chair of Tustenuggee, and to his great horror discovered the human arm which they enveloped. This led him to search farther, and limb after limb became detached under the unscrupulous action of his hatchet, until the entire but unconnected members of the old squaw became visible. The lad knocked about the fragments with little scruple, never dreaming how near was his relation to the form which he treated with so little veneration. When he came home to the lodge and told his story, Selonee looked at Conattee, but said nothing. The whole truth was at once apparent to his mind. Conattee, though he still kept his secret, was seized with a sudden fit of piety, and taking his sons with him, he proceeded to the spot which he well remembered, and, gathering up the bleached remains, had them carefully buried in the trenches of the tribe.

It may properly end this story, to say that Selonee wedded the sweet girl who, though willing to die herself to prevent him from marrying Macourah, yet positively refused to take his life to defeat the same event. It may be well to state, in addition, that the only reason Conattee ever had for believing that Selonee had not kept his secret from every body, was that Medoree, the young wife of the latter, looked on him with a very decided coolness. "But, we will see," muttered Conattee as he felt this conviction. "Selonee will repent of this confidence, since now it will never be possible for him to persuade her to take a seat in the Arm-chair of Tustenuggee. Had he been a wise man he would have kept his secret, and then there would have been no difficulty in getting rid of a wicked wife."

[1845]

HARRIET BEECHER STOWE

Harriet Beecher Stowe (1811–1896) was born in Litchfield, Connecticut, the seventh child of Congregational minister Lyman Beecher and his wife, Roxana. When Harriet was five, her mother died of tuberculosis and her older sister Catharine became her surrogate mother. Educated at Litchfield Female Academy, Harriet, by the age of twelve, was admired for the easy fluency of her writing. She continued her studies at Hartford Female Seminary, a school run by her sister Catharine, where Harriet also taught rhetoric and composition. The Beecher family moved to Cincinnati in 1832, when Lyman Beecher became president of the Lane Theological Seminary. Homesick for New England, Harriet began publishing stories and reviews in the Western Monthly Magazine, *including "Isabelle and Her Sister Kate" (February 1834), which won first prize in a contest sponsored by the magazine. In 1836 she married Calvin Ellis Stowe, a theology professor at Lane. Within a year, Harriet was the mother of twin girls; she eventually gave birth to five more children. Despite the work of caring for her family, she continued to write for periodicals such as* Godey's Lady's Book *and the* New-York Evangelist.*

In 1843 Stowe published her first book of fiction—fifteen domestic sketches collected in The Mayflower; or, Sketches of Scenes and Characters among the Descendents of the Puritans. *Eight years later* Uncle Tom's Cabin, *her most famous work, was serialized in the* National Era *and became a best-seller. In the South the response to Stowe's novel was virulently hostile. William Gilmore Simms accused her of possessing "a malignity so remarkable that the petticoat lifts of itself, and we see the hoof of the beast under the table." But in 1863, during the Civil War, Stowe was invited to the White House, and legend has it that she was greeted by President Lincoln as "the little lady who started this big war." She followed* Uncle Tom's Cabin *with another antislavery novel,* Dred: A Tale of the Great Dismal Swamp *(1856), as well as a dozen other novels and story collections.*

"The Two Altars; or, Two Pictures in One" consists of two paired stories that appeared in the New-York Evangelist *in June 1851, a week after the first installment of* Uncle Tom's Cabin. *In "The Two Altars" Stowe dramatizes the contrast between the ideals of the American Revolution and the realities of life in America before the abolition of slavery. In regard to both her long and short fiction, Stowe told the editor of the* National Era *that she considered herself "a painter" more than a writer, because "there is no arguing with pictures, and everybody is impressed by them, whether they mean to be or not." Her children recalled a sultry summer night when they were frightened by a thunderstorm and found her awake and alert, watching it from her bed. "I have been writing a description of a storm for my book [Dred]," she said, "and I am watching to see if I need to correct it in any particular." Stowe's pictorial approach to writing fiction was to stand her in good stead in the decade after* Uncle Tom's Cabin *when she developed the realistic local-color genre in stories published in*

The Atlantic Monthly and collected in Oldtown Fireside Stories *(1872) and* Sam Lawson's Oldtown Fireside Stories *(1881). Here her evocation of the New England past and her vivid portraits of the villagers inspired the next generation of women writers, most notably Rose Terry Cooke, Sarah Orne Jewett, and Mary Wilkins Freeman.*

The Two Altars; or, Two Pictures in One

I. THE ALTAR OF LIBERTY, OR 1776

The well-sweep of the old house on the hill was relieved dark and clear, against the reddening sky, as the early winter sun was going down in the west. It was a brisk, clear, metallic evening; the long drifts of snow blushed crimson red on their tops, and lay in shades of purple and lilac in the hollows; and the old wintry wind brushed shrewdly along the plain, tingling people's noses, blowing open their cloaks, puffing in the back of their necks, and showing other unmistakable indications that he was getting up steam for a real roistering night.

"Hurrah! How it blows!" said little Dick Ward, from the top of the mossy wood-pile.

Now Dick had been sent to said wood-pile, in company with his little sister Grace, to pick up chips, which, everybody knows, was in the olden time considered a wholesome and gracious employment, and the peculiar duty of the rising generation. But said Dick, being a boy, had mounted the wood-pile, and erected there a flagstaff, on which he was busily tying a little red pocket-handkerchief, occasionally exhorting Grace "to be sure and pick up fast."

"Oh, yes, I will," said Grace; "but you see the chips have got ice on 'em, and make my hands so cold!"

"Oh, don't stop to suck your thumbs! Who cares for ice? Pick away, I say, while I set up the flag of liberty."

So Grace picked away as fast as she could, nothing doubting but that her cold thumbs were in some mysterious sense an offering on the shrine of liberty; while soon the red handkerchief, duly secured, fluttered and snapped in the brisk evening wind.

"Now you must hurrah, Gracie, and throw up your bonnet," said Dick, as he descended from the pile.

"But won't it lodge down in some place in the wood-pile?" suggested Grace thoughtfully.

"Oh, never fear; give it to me, and just holler now, Gracie, 'Hurrah for liberty!' and we'll throw up your bonnet and my cap; and we'll play, you know, that we are a whole army and I'm General Washington."

So Grace gave up her little red hood, and Dick swung his cap, and up they both went into the air; and the children shouted, and the flag snapped and fluttered, and altogether they had a merry time of it. But then the wind—good-for-nothing, roguish fellow!—made an ungenerous plunge at poor Grace's little hood, and snipped it up in a twinkling, and whisked it off, off, off,—fluttering and bobbing up and down, quite across a wide, waste, snowy field,—and finally lodged it on the top of a tall, strutting rail, that was leaning, very independently, quite another way from all the other rails of the fence.

"Now see, do see!" said Grace; "there goes my bonnet! What will Aunt Hitty say?" and Grace began to cry.

"Don't you cry, Gracie; you offered it up to liberty, you know: it's glorious to give up everything for liberty."

"Oh, but Aunt Hitty won't think so."

"Well, don't cry, Gracie, you foolish girl! Do you think I can't get it? Now, only play that that great rail is a fort, and your bonnet is a prisoner in it, and see how quick I'll take the fort and get it!" and Dick shouldered a stick, and started off.

"What upon *airth* keeps those children so long? I should think they were *making* chips!" said Aunt Mehetabel; "the fire's just a-going out under the tea-kettle."

By this time Grace had lugged her heavy basket to the door, and was stamping the snow off her little feet, which were so numb that she needed to stamp, to be quite sure they were yet there. Aunt Mehetabel's shrewd face was the first that greeted her as the door opened.

"Gracie— What upon *airth!*—wipe your nose, child; your hands are frozen. Where alive is Dick?—and what's kept you out all this time?—and where's your bonnet?"

Poor Grace, stunned by this cataract of questions, neither wiped her nose nor gave any answer, but sidled up into the warm corner where grandmamma was knitting, and began quietly rubbing and blowing her fingers, while the tears silently rolled down her cheeks, as the fire made the former ache intolerably.

"Poor little dear!" said grandmamma, taking her hands in hers; "Hitty sha'n't scold you. Grandma knows you've been a good girl,—the wind blew poor Gracie's bonnet away;" and grandmamma wiped both eyes and nose, and gave her, moreover, a stalk of dried fennel out of her pocket, whereat Grace took heart once more.

"Mother always makes fools of Roxy's children," said Mehetabel, puffing zealously under the tea-kettle. "There's a little maple sugar in that saucer up there, mother, if you will keep giving it to her," she said, still vigorously puffing. "And now, Gracie," she said, when, after a while, the fire seemed in tolerable order, "will you answer my question? Where is Dick?"

"Gone over in the lot to get my bonnet."

"How came your bonnet off?" said Aunt Mehetabel. "I tied it on firm enough."

"Dick wanted me to take it off for him, to throw up for liberty," said Grace.

"Throw up for fiddlestick! Just one of Dick's cut-ups; and you was silly enough to mind him!"

"Why, he put up a flagstaff on the wood-pile, and a flag to liberty, you know, that papa's fighting for," said Grace more confidently, as she saw her quiet, blue-eyed mother, who had silently walked into the room during the conversation.

Grace's mother smiled, and said encouragingly, "And what then?"

"Why, he wanted me to throw up my bonnet and he his cap, and shout for liberty; and then the wind took it and carried it off, and he said I ought not to be sorry if I did lose it, — it was an offering to liberty."

"And so I did," said Dick, who was standing as straight as a poplar behind the group; "and I heard it in one of father's letters to mother that we ought to offer up everything on the altar of liberty and so I made an altar of the wood-pile."

"Good boy!" said his mother; "always remember everything your father writes. He has offered up everything on the altar of liberty, true enough; and I hope you, son, will live to do the same."

"Only, if I have the hoods and caps to make," said Aunt Hitty, "I hope he won't offer them up every week, — that's all!"

"Oh, well, Aunt Hitty, I've got the hood; let me alone for that. It blew clear over into the Daddy Ward pasture lot, and there stuck on the top of the great rail; and I played that the rail was a fort, and besieged it, and took it."

"Oh, yes! you're always up to taking forts, and anything else that nobody wants done. I'll warrant, now, you left Gracie to pick up every blessed one of them chips."

"Picking up chips is girls' work," said Dick; "and taking forts and defending the country is men's work."

"And pray, Mister Pomp, how long have you been a man?" said Aunt Hitty.

"If I ain't a man, I soon shall be; my head is 'most up to my mother's shoulder, and I can fire off a gun, too. I tried, the other day, when I was up to the store. Mother, I wish you'd let me clean and load the old gun, so that, if the British should come" —

"Well, if you are so big and grand, just lift me out that table, sir," said Aunt Hitty; "for it's past supper-time."

Dick sprang, and had the table out in a trice, with an abundant clatter, and put up the leaves with quite an air. His mother, with the silent and gliding motion characteristic of her, quietly took out the table-cloth and spread it, and began to set the cups and saucers in order, and to put on the plates and knives, while Aunt Hitty bustled about the tea.

"I'll be glad when the war's over, for one reason," said she. "I'm pretty much tired of drinking sage tea, for one, I know."

"Well, Aunt Hitty, how you scolded that peddler, last week, that brought along that real tea!"

"To be sure I did. S'pose I'd be taking any of his old tea, bought of the British?—fling every teacup in his face first."

"Well, mother," said Dick, "I never exactly understood what it was about the tea, and why the Boston folks threw it all overboard."

"Because there was an unlawful tax laid upon it, that the government had no right to lay. It wasn't much in itself; but it was a part of a whole system of oppressive meanness, designed to take away our rights, and make us slaves of a foreign power."

"Slaves!" said Dick, straightening himself proudly. "Father a slave!"

"But they would not be slaves! They saw clearly where it would all end, and they would not begin to submit to it in ever so little," said the mother.

"I wouldn't, if I was they," said Dick.

"Besides," said his mother, drawing him towards her, "it wasn't for themselves alone they did it. This is a great country, and it will be greater and greater; and it's very important that it should have free and equal laws, because it will by and by be so great. This country, if it is a free one, will be a light of the world,—a city set on a hill, that cannot be hid; and all the oppressed and distressed from other countries shall come here to enjoy equal rights and freedom. This, dear boy, is why your father and uncles have gone to fight, and why they do stay and fight, though God knows what they suffer and"— And the large blue eyes of the mother were full of tears; yet a strong, bright beam of pride and exultation shone through those tears.

"Well, well, Roxy, you can always talk, everybody knows," said Aunt Hitty, who had been not the least attentive listener of this little patriotic harangue; "but, you see, the tea is getting cold, and yonder I see the sleigh is at the door, and John's come; so let's set up our chairs for supper."

The chairs were soon set up, when John, the eldest son, a lad of about fifteen, entered with a letter. There was one general exclamation, and stretching out of hands towards it. John threw it into his mother's lap; the tea-table was forgotten, and the tea-kettle sang unnoticed by the fire, as all hands crowded about mother's chair to hear the news. It was from Captain Ward, then in the American army at Valley Forge. Mrs. Ward ran it over hastily, and then read it aloud. A few words we may extract.

"There is still," it said, "much suffering. I have given away every pair of stockings you sent me, reserving to myself only one; for I will not be one whit better off than the poorest soldier that fights for his country. Poor fellows! it makes my heart ache sometimes to go round among them, and see them with their worn clothes and torn shoes, and often bleeding feet, yet cheerful and hopeful, and every one willing to do his very best. Often the spirit of discouragement comes over them, particularly at night, when, weary, cold, and hungry, they turn into their comfortless huts, on the snowy ground. Then sometimes there is a thought of home, and warm fires, and some speak of giving up; but next morning out come Washington's general orders,—little short note, but 's wonderful the good it does; and then they all resolve to hold on, come what may. There are commissioners going all through the country to pick up supplies. If they come to you, I need not to tell you what to do. I know all that will be in your hearts."

"There, children, see what your father suffers," said the mother, "and what it costs these poor soldiers to gain our liberty."

"Ephraim Scranton told me that the commissioners had come as far as the Three Mile Tavern, and that he rather 'spected they'd be along here to-night," said John, as he was helping round the baked beans to the silent company at the tea-table.

"To-night?—do tell, now!" said Aunt Hitty. "Then it's time we were awake and stirring. Let's see what can be got."

"I'll send my new overcoat, for one," said John. "That old one isn't cut up yet, is it, Aunt Hitty?"

"No," said Aunt Hitty; "I was laying out to cut it over next Wednesday, when Desire Smith could be here to do the tailoring."

"There's the south room," said Aunt Hitty, musing; "that bed has the two old Aunt Ward blankets on it, and the great blue quilt, and two comforters. Then mother's and my room, two pair—four comforters—two quilts—the best chamber has got"—

"Oh, Aunt Hitty, send all that's in the best chamber! If any company comes, we can make it up off from our beds," said John. "I can send a blanket or two off from my bed, I know,—can't but just turn over in it, so many clothes on, now."

"Aunt Hitty, take a blanket off from our bed," said Grace and Dick at once.

"Well, well, we'll see," said Aunt Hitty, bustling up.

Up rose grandmamma, with great earnestness, now, and going into the next room, and opening a large cedar-wood chest, returned, bearing in her arms two large snow-white blankets, which she deposited flat on the table, just as Aunt Hitty was whisking off the table-cloth.

"Mortal! mother, what are you going to do?" said Aunt Hitty.

"There," she said, "I spun those, every thread of 'em, when my name was Mary Evans. Those were my wedding-blankets, made of real nice wool, and worked with roses in all the corners. I've got *them* to give!" and grandmamma stroked and smoothed the blankets, and patted them down, with great pride and tenderness. It was evident she was giving something that lay very near her heart; but she never faltered.

"La! mother, there's no need of that," said Aunt Hitty. "Use them on your own bed, and send the blankets off from that; they are just as good for the soldiers."

"No, I sha'n't!" said the old lady, waxing warm; "'t isn't a bit too good for 'em. I'll send the very best I've got, before they shall suffer. Send 'em the *best!*" and the old lady gestured oratorically.

They were interrupted by a rap at the door, and two men entered, and announced themselves as commissioned by Congress to search out supplies for the army. Now the plot thickens. Aunt Hitty flew in every direction,—through entry passage, meal-room, milk-room, down cellar, up chamber,—her cap border on end with patriotic zeal; and followed by John, Dick, and Grace, who eagerly bore to the kitchen the supplies that she turned out, while Mrs. Ward busied herself in quietly sorting and arranging, in the best possible traveling order, the various contributions that were precipitately launched on the kitchen floor.

Aunt Hitty soon appeared in the kitchen with an armful of stockings, which, kneeling on the floor, she began counting and laying out.

"There," she said, laying down a large bundle on some blankets, "that leaves just two pair apiece all round."

"La!" said John, "what's the use of saving two pair for me? I can do with one pair, as well as father."

"Sure enough," said his mother; "besides, I can knit you another pair in a day."

"And I can do with one pair," said Dick.

"Yours will be too small, young master, I guess," said one of the commissioners.

"No," said Dick; "I've got a pretty good foot of my own, and Aunt Hitty will always knit my stockings an inch too long, 'cause she says I grow so. See here,—these will do;" and the boy shook his triumphantly.

"And mine, too," said Grace, nothing doubting, having been busy all the time in pulling off her little stockings.

"Here," she said to the man who was packing the things into a wide-mouthed sack; "here's mine," and her large blue eyes looked earnestly through her tears.

Aunt Hitty flew at her. "Good land! the child's crazy. Don't think the men could wear your stockings,—take 'em away!"

Grace looked around with an air of utter desolation, and began to cry. "I wanted to give them something," said she. "I'd rather go barefoot on the snow all day than not send 'em anything."

"Give me the stockings, my child," said the old soldier tenderly. "There, I'll take 'em, and show 'em to the soldiers, and tell them what the little girl said that sent them. And it will do them as much good as if they could wear them. They've got little girls at home, too." Grace fell on her mother's bosom completely happy, and Aunt Hitty only muttered,—

"Everybody does spile that child; and no wonder, neither!"

Soon the old sleigh drove off from the brown house, tightly packed and heavily loaded. And Grace and Dick were creeping up to their little beds.

"There's been something put on the altar of Liberty to-night, hasn't there, Dick?"

"Yes, indeed," said Dick; and, looking up to his mother, he said, "But, mother, what did you give?"

"I?" said the mother musingly.

"Yes, you, mother; what have you given to the country?"

"All that I have, dears," said she, laying her hands gently on their heads,— "my husband and my children!"

II. The Altar of ——, or 1850

The setting sun of chill December lighted up the solitary front window of a small tenement on——Street, in Boston, which we now have occasion to visit. As we push gently aside the open door, we gain sight of a small room, clean as busy hands can make it, where a neat, cheerful young mulatto woman is busy at an ironing-table. A basket full of glossy-bosomed shirts, and faultless collars and wrist-bands, is beside her, into which she is placing the last few items with evident pride and satisfaction. A bright black-eyed boy, just come in from school, with his satchel of books over his shoulder, stands, cap in hand, relating to his mother how he has been at the head of his class, and showing his school tickets, which his mother, with untiring admiration, deposits in the little real china teapot, which, as being their most reliable article of gentility, is made the deposit of all the money and most especial valuables of the family.

"Now, Henry," says the mother, "look out and see if father is coming along the street;" and she begins filling the little black tea-kettle, which is soon set singing on the stove.

From the inner room now daughter Mary, a well-grown girl of thirteen, brings the baby, just roused from a nap, and very impatient to renew his acquaintance with his mamma.

"Bless his bright eyes!—mother will take him," ejaculates the busy little woman, whose hands are by this time in a very floury condition, in the incipient stages of wetting up biscuit,—"in a minute;" and she quickly frees herself from the flour and paste, and, deputing Mary to roll out her biscuit, proceeds to the consolation and succor of young master.

"Now, Henry," says the mother, "you'll have time, before supper, to take that basket of clothes up to Mr. Sheldin's; put in that nice bill that you made out last night. I shall give you a cent for every bill you write out for me. What a comfort it is, now, for one's children to be gettin' learnin' so!"

Henry shouldered the basket and passed out the door, just as a neatly dressed colored man walked up with his pail and whitewash brushes.

"Oh, you've come, father, have you? Mary, are the biscuits in? You may as well set the table now. Well, George, what's the news?"

"Nothing, only a pretty smart day's work. I've brought home five dollars, and shall have as much as I can do, these two weeks;" and the man, having washed his hands, proceeded to count out his change on the ironing-table.

"Well, it takes you to bring in the money," said the delighted wife; "nobody but you could turn off that much in a day."

"Well, they do say—those that's had me once—that they never want any other hand to take hold in their rooms. I s'pose it's a kinder practice I've got, and kinder natural!"

"Tell ye what," said the little woman, taking down the family strong box,—to wit, the china teapot aforenamed,—and pouring the contents on the table, "we're getting mighty rich now! We can afford to get Henry his new Sunday cap, and Mary her mousseline-de-laine dress—Take care, baby, you rogue!" she hastily interposed, as young master made a dive at a dollar bill, for his share in the proceeds.

"He wants something, too, I suppose," said the father; "let him get his hand in while he's young."

The baby gazed, with round, astonished eyes, while mother, with some difficulty, rescued the bill from his grasp; but, before any one could at all anticipate his purpose, he dashed in among the small change with such zeal as to send it flying all over the table.

"Hurrah! Bob's a smasher!" said the father, delighted; "he'll make it fly, he thinks;" and, taking the baby on his knee, he laughed merrily as Mary and her mother pursued the rolling coin all over the room.

"He knows now, as well as can be that he's been doing mischief," said the delighted mother, as the baby kicked and crowed uproariously; "he's such a forward child, now, to be only six months old! Oh, you've no idea, father, how mischievous he grows;" and therewith the little woman began to roll and tumble the little mischief-maker about, uttering divers frightful threats, which appeared to contribute, in no small degree, to the general hilarity.

"Come, come, Mary," said the mother at last, with a sudden burst of recollection; "you mustn't be always on your knees fooling with this child! Look in the oven at them biscuits."

"They're done exactly, mother,—just the brown!" and, with the word, the mother dumped baby on to his father's knee, where he sat contentedly munching a very ancient crust of bread, occasionally improving the flavor thereof by rubbing it on his father's coat-sleeve.

"What have you got in that blue dish there?" said George, when the whole little circle were seated around the table.

"Well, now, what do you suppose?" said the little woman, delighted; "a quart of nice oysters,—just for a treat, you know. I wouldn't tell you till this minute," said she, raising the cover.

"Well," said George, "we both work hard for our money, and we don't owe anybody a cent; and why shouldn't we have our treats, now and then, as well as rich folks?"

And gayly passed the supper hour; the tea-kettle sung, the baby crowed, and all chatted and laughed abundantly.

"I'll tell you," said George, wiping his mouth; "wife, these times are quite another thing from what it used to be down in Georgia. I remember then old mas'r used to hire me out by the year; and one time, I remember,

I came and paid him in two hundred dollars,—every cent I'd taken. He just looked it over, counted it, and put it in his pocket-book, and said, 'You are a good boy, George,'—and he gave me half a dollar!"

"I want to know, now!" said his wife.

"Yes, he did, and that was every cent I ever got of it; and, I tell you, I was mighty bad off for clothes, them times."

"Well, well, the Lord be praised, they're over, and you are in a free country now!" said the wife, as she rose thoughtfully from the table, and brought her husband the great Bible. The little circle were ranged around the stove for evening prayers.

"Henry, my boy, you must read—you are a better reader than your father—thank God, that let you learn early!"

The boy, with a cheerful readiness, read, "The Lord is my Shepherd," and the mother gently stilled the noisy baby to listen to the holy words. Then all kneeled, while the father, with simple earnestness, poured out his soul to God.

They had but just risen—the words of Christian hope and trust scarce died on their lips—when, lo! the door was burst open, and two men entered; and one of them, advancing, laid his hand on the father's shoulder. "This is the fellow," said he.

"You are arrested in the name of the United States!" said the other.

"Gentlemen, what is this?" said the poor man, trembling.

"Are you not the property of Mr. B., of Georgia?" said the officer.

"Gentlemen, I've been a free, hard-working man these ten years."

"Yes; but you are arrested, on suit of Mr. B., as his slave."

Shall we describe the leave-taking,—the sorrowing wife, the dismayed children, the tears, the anguish, that simple, honest, kindly home, in a moment so desolated? Ah, ye who defend this because it is law, think for one hour what if this that happens to your poor brother should happen to you!

It was a crowded court-room, and the man stood there to be tried—for life?—no; but for the life of life—for liberty!

Lawyers hurried to and fro, buzzing, consulting, bringing authorities,—all anxious, zealous, engaged,—for what? To save a fellow man from bondage? No; anxious and zealous lest he might escape; full of zeal to deliver him over to slavery. The poor man's anxious eyes follow vainly the busy course of affairs, from which he dimly learns that he is to be sacrificed—on the altar of the Union; and that his heart-break and anguish, and the tears of his wife, and the desolation of his children are, in the eyes of these well-informed men, only the bleat of a sacrifice, bound to the horns of the glorious American altar!

Again it is a bright day, and business walks brisk in this market. Senator and statesman, the learned and patriotic, are out, this day, to give their countenance to an edifying and impressive and truly American spectacle,—the sale of a man! All the preliminaries of the scene are there: dusky-browed mothers, looking with sad eyes while speculators are turning round their children, looking at their teeth, and feeling of their arms; a poor, old, trembling woman, helpless, half blind, whose last child is to be sold, holds on to her bright boy with trembling hands. Husbands and wives, sisters and friends, all soon to be scattered like the chaff of the threshing-floor, look sadly on each other with poor nature's last tears; and among them walk briskly glib, oily politicians, and thriving men of law, letters, and religion, exceedingly sprightly and in good spirits—for why?—it isn't *they* that are going to be sold; it's only somebody else. And so they are very comfortable, and look on the whole thing as quite a matter-of-course affair, and, as it is to be conducted to-day, a decidedly valuable and judicious exhibition.

And now, after so many hearts and souls have been knocked and thumped this way and that way by the auctioneer's hammer, comes the *instructive* part of the whole; and the husband and father, whom we saw in his simple home, reading and praying with his children, and rejoicing in the joy of his poor ignorant heart that he lived in a free country, is now set up to be admonished of his mistake.

Now there is great excitement, and pressing to see, and exultation and approbation; for it is important and interesting to see a man put down that has tried to be a *free man*.

"That's he, is it? Couldn't come it, could he?" says one.

"No; and he will never come it, that's more," says another triumphantly.

"I don't generally take much interest in scenes of this nature," says a grave representative; "but I came here to-day for the sake of the principle!"

"Gentlemen," says the auctioneer, "we've got a specimen here that some of your Northern abolitionists would give any price for; but they sha'n't have him! no! we've looked out for that. The man that buys him must give bonds never to sell him to go North again!"

"Go it!" shout the crowd; "good! good! hurrah!" "An impressive idea!" says a Senator; "a noble maintaining of principle!" and the man is bid off, and the hammer falls with a last crash on his heart, his hopes, his manhood, and he lies a bleeding wreck on the altar of Liberty!

Such was the altar in 1776; such is the altar in 1850!   [1851]

ELIZABETH STUART PHELPS

Elizabeth Stuart Phelps (1815–1852) was born in Andover, Massachusetts, as the second daughter in a family of five children, each born less than a year apart. Her father was a minister and a professor of Greek and Hebrew literature at Andover Theological Society. Her mother was an invalid whose death in 1855 prompted her friend Harriet Beecher Stowe to write "of life's long sickness healed / A saint has risen, where pain no more may come." Elizabeth grew up with an obsessive desire for her father's approval and a deep fear of becoming an invalid like her mother. After an early education at Abbott Academy, she went to Boston at age sixteen to attend Mount Vernon school, living with the family of the Reverend Jacob Abbott, author of religious books for children. There she published her first stories in a magazine edited by Abbott. Later she recalled that her father's saying "Well done" after reading one of her stories meant more to her than the praise she received from thousands of readers of her novels.

In 1834 Elizabeth returned to her family in Andover, showing symptoms of a nervous breakdown or "cerebral disease," as it was then called. For the next four years she suffered from persistent severe headaches, partial blindness, and temporary paralysis. She wrote that her "suppressed longings, and unsatisfied tastes, and despised capacities, at length took their revenge . . . [but] from the very first half hour in which I broke down the barriers of my old system, and took up my pencil, I said, 'Goodbye to doctors!'" In 1842, after her marriage to Austin Phelps—one of her father's divinity students at Andover—the couple moved to Boston, where he became a minister and she gave birth to their daughter in 1845. Then the young family returned to Andover, where she had a second child. Her daughter recalled her "first distinct vision" of her mother reading aloud children's stories she had written, "never meant to go beyond that little public of two, and illustrated in colored crayons by her own pencil." These stories were published posthumously as Little Mary; or Talks and Tales for Children *(1854).*

Phelps was thirty years old before she embarked on a writing career. Because her early works were formulaic religious stories that appeared anonymously, she had difficulty recognizing them after they were published. Her husband recalled that "she has several times been seen bending over the counter of a bookstore, in perplexity as to the authorship of some little book she held in her hand, seeming to detect some familiar traces of her former self, and yet unable at last to decide whether she were the author or not." Finally Phelps achieved renown by writing a novel based on the life of a friend, The Sunny Side; or, A Country Minister's Wife *(1851). It sold 100,000 copies in its first year. She followed it with a companion novel,* Number Five; or, A Chapter in the Life of a City Pastor *(1852). She also wrote two collections of short fiction, including the story "Angel over the Right Shoulder." It originally appeared as a Christmas pamphlet in 1852, a month after she died of complications from her third childbirth. Today Phelps is primarily remembered as the author of this powerful, disheartening story. Her daughter and namesake grew up to become a successful novelist who summed up her mother's stressful life as "a wife, a mother, a housekeeper, a hostess, in delicate health," who had taken on a "deadly load" with her literary career.*

The Angel over the Right Shoulder

"There! a woman's work is never done," said Mrs James. "I thought, for once, I was through; but just look at that lamp, now! it will not burn, and I must go and spend half an hour over it."

"Don't you wish you had never been married?' said Mr James, with a good-natured laugh.

"Yes"—rose to her lips, but was checked by a glance at the group upon the floor where her husband was stretched out, and two little urchins with sparkling eyes and glowing cheeks were climbing and tumbling over him, as if they found in this play the very essence of fun.

She did say, "I should like the good, without the evil, if I could have it."

"You have no evils to endure," replied her husband.

"That is just all you gentlemen know about it. What would you think, if you could not get an uninterrupted half hour to yourself, from morning till night? I believe you would give up trying to do anything."

"There is no need of that; all you want, is *system*. If you arranged your work systematically, you would find that you could command your time."

"Well," was the reply, "all I wish is, that you could just follow me around for one day, and see what I have to do. If you could reduce it all to system, I think you would show yourself a genius."

When the lamp was trimmed, the conversation was resumed. Mr James had employed the "half hour," in meditating on this subject.

"Wife," said he, as she came in, "I have a plan to propose to you, and I wish you to promise me beforehand, that you will accede to it. It is to be an experiment, I acknowledge, but I wish it to have a fair trial. Now to please me, will you promise?'

Mrs James hesitated. She felt almost sure that his plan would be quite impracticable, for what does a man know of a woman's work? Yet she promised.

"Now I wish you," said he, "to set apart two hours of every day for your own private use. Make a point of going to your room, and locking yourself in; and also make up your mind to let the work which is not done, go undone, if it must. Spend this time on just those things which will be most profitable to yourself. I shall bind you to your promise for one month— then, if it has proved a total failure, we will devise something else."

"When shall I begin?"

"Tomorrow."

The morrow came. Mrs James had chosen the two hours before dinner as being, on the whole, the most convenient and the least liable to interruption. They dined at one o'clock. She wished to finish her morning work, get dressed for the day, and enter her room at eleven.

Hearty as were her efforts to accomplish this, the hour of eleven found her with her work but half done; yet, true to her promise, she left all, retired to her room and locked the door.

With some interest and hope, she immediately marked out a course of reading and study, for these two precious hours: then arranging her table, her books, pen and paper, she commenced a schedule of her work with much enthusiasm. Scarcely had she dipped her pen in ink, when she heard the tramping of little feet along the hall, and then a pounding at her door.

"Mamma! mamma! I cannot find my mittens, and Hannah is going to slide without me."

"Go to Amy, my dear; mamma is busy."

"So Amy busy too; she say she can't leave baby."

The child began to cry, still standing close to the fastened door. Mrs James knew the easiest, and indeed the only way of settling the trouble, was to go herself and hunt up the missing mittens. Then a parley must be held with Frank, to induce him to wait for his sister, and the child's tears must be dried, and little hearts must be all set right before the children went out to play; and so favorable an opportunity must not be suffered to slip, without impressing on young minds the importance of having a "place for everything, and everything in its place." This took time; and when Mrs James returned to her study, her watch told her that *half* her portion had gone. Quietly resuming her work, she was endeavoring to mend her broken train of thought, when heavier steps were heard in the hall, and the fastened door was once more besieged. Now, Mr James must be admitted.

"Mary," said he, "cannot you come and sew a string on for me? I do believe there is not a bosom in my drawer in order, and I am in a great hurry. I ought to have been down town an hour ago."

The schedule was thrown aside, the work-basket taken, and Mrs James followed him. She soon sewed on the tape, but then a button needed fastening; and, at last, a rip in his glove was to be mended. As Mrs James stitched away on the glove, a smile lurked in the corners of her mouth, which her husband observed.

"What are you laughing at?" asked he.

"To think how famously your plan works."

"I declare!" said he, "is this your study hour? I am sorry, but what can a man do? He cannot go down town without a shirt-bosom!"

"Certainly not," said his wife, quietly.

When her liege lord was fairly equipped and off, Mrs James returned to her room. A half an hour yet remained to her, and of this she determined to make the most. But scarcely had she resumed her pen, when there was another disturbance in the entry. Amy had returned from walking out with the baby, and she entered the nursery with him, that she might get him to sleep. Now it happened that the only room in the house which Mrs James could have to herself with a fire, was the one adjoining the nursery. She had become so accustomed to the ordinary noise of the children, that it did not disturb her; but the very extraordinary noise which master Charley sometimes felt called upon to make, when he was fairly on his back in the cradle, did disturb the unity of her thoughts. The words which she was reading rose and fell with the screams and lulls of the child, and she felt obliged to close her book, until the storm was over. When quiet was restored in the cradle, the children came in from sliding, crying with cold fingers; and just as she was going to them, the dinner-bell rang.

"How did your new plan work this morning?" inquired Mr James.

"Famously," was the reply; "I read about seventy pages of German, and as many more in French."

"I am sure *I* did not hinder you long."

"No—yours was only one of a dozen interruptions."

"O, well! you must not get discouraged. Nothing succeeds well the first time. Persist in your arrangement, and by and by the family will learn that if they want anything of you, they must wait until after dinner."

"But what can a man do?" replied his wife; "he cannot go down town without a shirt-bosom."

"I was in a bad case," replied Mr James, "it may not happen again. I am anxious to have you try the month out faithfully, and then we will see what has come of it."

The second day of trial was a stormy one. As the morning was dark, Bridget overslept, and consequently breakfast was too late by an hour. This lost hour Mrs James could not recover. When the clock struck eleven, she seemed but to have commenced her morning's work, so much remained to be done. With mind disturbed and spirits depressed, she left her household matters "in the suds," as they were, and punctually retired to her study. She soon found, however, that she could not fix her attention upon any intellectual pursuit. Neglected duties haunted her, like ghosts around the guilty conscience. Perceiving that she was doing nothing with her books, and not wishing to lose the morning wholly, she commenced writing a letter. Bridget interrupted her before she had proceeded far on the first page.

"What, ma'am, shall we have for dinner? No marketing ha'n't come."

"Have some steaks, then."

"We ha'n't got none, ma'am."

"I will send out for some, directly."

Now there was no one to send but Amy, and Mrs James knew it. With a sigh, she put down her letter and went into the nursery.

"Amy, Mr James has forgotten our marketing. I should like to have you run over to the provision store, and order some beef-steaks; I will stay with the baby."

Amy was not much pleased to be sent out on this errand. She remarked, that she "must change her dress first."

"Be as quick as possible," said Mrs James, "for I am particularly en-gaged at this hour."

Amy neither obeyed, nor disobeyed, but managed to take her own time, without any very deliberate intention to do so. Mrs James, hoping to get along with a sentence or two, took her German book into the nursery. But this arrangement was not to master Charley's mind. A fig did he care for German, but "the kitties" he must have, whether or no—and kitties he would find in that particular book—so he turned its leaves over in great haste. Half of the time on the second day of trial had gone when Amy returned, and Mrs James, with a sigh, left the nursery. Before one o'clock, she was twice called into the kitchen to superintend some important din-ner arrangement, and thus it turned out that she did not finish one page of her letter.

On the third morning the sun shone, and Mrs James rose early, made every provision which she deemed necessary for dinner, and for the com-fort of her family; and then, elated by her success, in good spirits, and with good courage, she entered her study precisely at eleven o'clock, and locked her door. Her books were opened, and the challenge given to a hard German lesson. Scarcely had she made the first onset, when the door-bell was heard to ring, and soon Bridget, coming nearer and nearer,— then, tapping at the door.

"Somebodies wants to see you in the parlor, ma'am."

"Tell them I am engaged, Bridget."

"I told 'em you were to home, ma'am, and they sent up their names, but I ha'n't got 'em, jist."

There was no help for it—Mrs James must go down to receive her callers. She had to smile when she felt little like it—to be sociable when her thoughts were busy with her task. Her friends made a long call—they had nothing else to do with their time, and when they went, others came. In very unsatisfactory chit-chat, her morning slipped away.

On the next day, Mr James invited company to tea, and her morning was devoted to preparing for it; she did not enter her study. On the day following, a sick-head-ache confined her to bed; and on Saturday, the care of the baby devolved upon her, as Amy had extra work to do. Thus passed the first week.

True to her promise, Mrs James patiently persevered for a month, in her efforts to secure for herself this little fragment of her broken time, but with what success, the first week's history can tell. With its close, closed the month of December.

On the last day of the old year, she was so much occupied in her prepa-rations for the morrow's festival, that the last hour of the day was approach-ing, before she made her good night's call in the nursery. She first went to the crib and looked at the baby. There he lay in his innocence and beauty, fast asleep. She softly stroked his golden hair—she kissed gently his rosy cheek—she pressed the little dimpled hand in hers; and then carefully drawing the coverlet over it, tucked it in,—and stealing yet another kiss, she left him to his peaceful dreams,—and sat down on her daughter's bed. She also slept sweetly, with her dolly hugged to her bosom. At this her mother smiled, but soon grave thoughts entered her mind, and these deepened into sad ones. She thought of her disappointment and the failure of her plans. To her, not only the past month but the whole past year, seemed to have been one of fruitless effort—all broken and disjointed— even her hours of religious duty had been encroached upon, and disturbed. She had accomplished nothing, that she could see, but to keep her house and family in order, and even this, to her saddened mind, seemed to have been but indifferently done. She was conscious of yearnings for a more earnest life than this. Unsatisfied longings for something which she had not attained, often clouded what, otherwise, would have been a bright day to her; and yet the causes of these feelings seemed to lie in a dim and misty region, which her eye could not penetrate.

What then did she need? To see some *results* from her life's work? To know that a golden cord bound her life-threads together into *unity* of purpose—notwithstanding they seemed, so often, single and broken?

She was quite sure that she felt no desire to shrink from duty, however humble, but she sighed for some comforting assurance of what *was duty*. Her employments, conflicting as they did with her tastes, seemed to her frivolous and useless. It seemed to her that there was some better way of living, which she, from deficiency in energy of character, or of principle, had failed to discover. As she leaned over her child, her tears fell fast upon its young brow.

Most earnestly did she wish, that she could shield that child from the disappointments and mistakes and self-reproach from which the mother was then suffering; that the little one might take up life where she could give it to her—all mended by her own experience. It would have been a comfort to have felt that, in fighting the battle, she had fought for both; yet she knew that so it could not be—that for ourselves must we all learn what are those things which "make for our peace."

The tears were in her eyes, as she gave the goodnight to her sleeping daughter; then, with soft steps, she entered an adjoining room, and there fairly kissed out the old year on another chubby cheek, which nestled among the pillows. At length she sought her own rest.

Soon she found herself in a singular place. She was traversing a vast plain. No trees were visible, save those which skirted the distant horizon, and on their broad tops rested wreaths of golden clouds. Before her was a female, who was journeying towards that region of light. Little children were about her, now in her arms, now running by her side, and as they travelled, she occupied herself in caring for them. She taught them how to place their little feet; she gave them timely warnings of the pitfalls; she gently lifted them over the stumbling-blocks. When they were weary, she soothed them by singing of that brighter land, which she kept ever in view, and towards which she seemed hastening with her little flock. But what was most remarkable was, that, all unknown to her, she was constantly watched by two angels, who reposed on two golden clouds which floated above her. Before each was a golden book, and a pen of gold. One angel, with mild and loving eyes, peered constantly over her right shoulder; another, kept as strict watch over her left. Not a deed, not a word, not a look, escaped their notice. When a good deed, word, look, went from her, the angel over the right shoulder, with a glad smile, wrote it down in his book; when an evil, however trivial, the angel over the left shoulder recorded it in his book,—then, with sorrowful eyes, followed the pilgrim until he observed penitence for the wrong, upon which he dropped a tear on the record, and blotted it out, and both angels rejoiced.

To the looker-on, it seemed that the traveller did nothing which was worthy of such careful record.

Sometimes, she did but bathe the weary feet of her little children, but the angel over the *right shoulder*—wrote it down. Sometimes, she did but patiently wait to lure back a little truant who had turned his face away from the distant light, but the angel over the *right shoulder*—wrote it down. Sometimes, she did but soothe an angry feeling or raise a drooping eyelid, or kiss away a little grief; but the angel over the right shoulder— *wrote it down.*

Sometimes, her eye was fixed so intently on that golden horizon, and she became so eager to make progress thither, that the little ones, missing her care, did languish or stray. Then it was that the angel over the *left shoulder,* lifted his golden pen, and made the entry, and followed her with sorrowful eyes, until he could blot it out. Sometimes, she seemed to advance rapidly, but in her haste the little ones had fallen back, and it was the sorrowing angel who recorded her progress. Sometimes, so intent was she to gird up her loins, and have her lamp trimmed and burning, that the little children wandered away quite into forbidden paths, and it was the angel over the *left shoulder* who recorded her diligence.

Now the observer as she looked, felt that this was a faithful and true record, and was to be kept to that journey's end. The strong clasps of gold on those golden books, also impressed her with the conviction that, when they were closed, it would only be for a future opening.

Her sympathies were warmly enlisted for the gentle traveller, and with a beating heart she quickened her steps that she might overtake her. She wished to tell her of the angels keeping watch above her—to entreat her to be faithful and patient to the end—for her life's work was all written down—every item of it—and the *results* would be known when those golden books should be unclasped. She wished to beg of her to think no duty trivial which must be done, for over her right shoulder and over her left were recording angels, who would surely take note of all!

Eager to warn the traveller of what she had seen, she touched her. The traveller turned, and she recognized or seemed to recognize *herself.* Startled and alarmed, she awoke in tears. The gray light of morning struggled through the half-open shutter, the door was ajar, and merry faces were peeping in.

"Wish you a happy new year, mamma!"—"Wish you a *Happy New Year!*" — "A happy noo ear!"

She returned the merry greeting most heartily. It seemed to her as if she had entered upon a new existence. She had found her way through the thicket in which she had been entangled, and a light was now about her path. The *Angel over the Right Shoulder* whom she had seen in her dream, would bind up in his golden book her life's work, if it were but well done. He required of her no great deeds, but faithfulness and patience to the end of the race which was set before her. Now she could see, plainly enough, that, though it was right and important for her to cultivate her own mind and heart, it was equally right and equally important, to meet and perform faithfully all those little household cares and duties on which the comfort and virtue of her family depended; for into these things the angels carefully looked—and these duties and cares acquired a dignity from the strokes of that golden pen—they could not be neglected without danger.

Sad thoughts and sadder misgivings—undefined yearnings and ungratified longings seemed to have taken their flight with the Old Year, and it was with fresh resolution and cheerful hope, and a happy heart, she welcomed the *Glad* New Year. The *Angel over the Right Shoulder* would go with her, and if she were found faithful, would strengthen and comfort her to its close.   [1852]

HERMAN MELVILLE

*H*erman Melville (1819–1891) published his first short story in 1853 as "Bartleby, the Scrivener: A Story of Wall Street." Behind him were seven years of writing novels beginning with the burst of creative energy that produced his early books of sea adventure: Typee (1846), Omoo (1847), Mardi (1849), Redburn (1849), and White-Jacket (1850). All of these were based on his experiences onboard ship. Melville had been left in poverty at the age of fifteen when his father went bankrupt, and in 1839 he went to sea as a cabin boy. Two years later he sailed on a whaler bound for the Pacific, but he deserted in the Marquesas Islands and lived for a time with cannibals. Having little formal education, Melville later boasted that "a whale ship was my Yale College and my Harvard." His most ambitious book was Moby-Dick (1851), a work of great allegorical complexity heavily indebted to the influence of Nathaniel Hawthorne, Melville's neighbor in the Berkshires at the time he wrote it. Moby-Dick was not a commercial success, however, and the novel that followed it, Pierre (1852), was dismissed by critics as incomprehensible trash.

It was at this point that Melville turned to the short story. Between 1853 and 1856 he published fifteen sketches and stories and a serialized historical novel, promising the popular magazines that his stories would "contain nothing of any sort to shock the fastidious." But when this work and another novel (The Confidence Man, 1857) failed to restore his reputation, he ceased trying to support his family by his pen. He moved from his farm in the Berkshires to a house in New York City bought for him by his father-in-law, and worked for more than twenty years as an inspector of customs. He published a few books of poems and wrote a short novel, Billy Budd, which critics acclaimed as one of his greatest works when it was published—thirty years after his death.

Melville stood at the crossroads in the early history of American short fiction. When he began to publish in magazines, Hawthorne and Poe had already done their best work in the romantic vein of tales and sketches, and the realistic local-color school of short stories had not yet been established. Melville created something new in "Bartleby, the Scrivener," a fully developed, if discursive, short story set in a contemporary social context. It baffled readers of Putnam's Monthly Magazine in 1853, when it was published in two installments. For the rest of his stories, Melville used the conventional form of old-fashioned tales, but he continued to explore the idea that point of view can serve as theme as well as technique in storytelling. In stories like "Bartleby, the Scrivener" and "Benito Cereno," Melville demonstrated, as the critic Marvin Fisher understood, "where one stands determines his view of the truth and reality, and shapes his values."

RELATED COMMENTARIES: Herman Melville, From "Hawthorne and His Mosses," page 1407; J. Hillis Miller, "A Deconstructive Reading of Melville's 'Bartleby, the Scrivener,'" page 1411.

Bartleby, the Scrivener
A Story of Wall Street

I am a rather elderly man. The nature of my avocations, for the last thirty years, has brought me into more than ordinary contact with what would seem an interesting and somewhat singular set of men, of whom, as yet, nothing, that I know of, has ever been written—I mean, the law-copyists, or scriveners. I have known very many of them, professionally and privately, and, if I pleased, could relate divers histories, at which good-natured gentlemen might smile, and sentimental souls might weep. But I waive the biographies of all other scriveners, for a few passages in the life of Bartleby, who was a scrivener, the strangest I ever saw, or heard of. While, of other law-copyists, I might write the complete life, of Bartleby nothing of that sort can be done. I believe that no materials exist, for a full and satisfactory biography of this man. It is an irreparable loss to literature. Bartleby was one of those beings of whom nothing is ascertainable, except from the original sources, and, in his case, those are very small. What my own astonished eyes saw of Bartleby, *that* is all I know of him, except, indeed, one vague report, which will appear in the sequel.

Ere introducing the scrivener, as he first appeared to me, it is fit I make some mention of myself, my *employés,* my business, my chambers, and general surroundings, because some such description is indispensable to an adequate understanding of the chief character about to be presented. Imprimis:[1] I am a man who, from his youth upwards, has been filled with a profound conviction that the easiest way of life is the best. Hence, though I belong to a profession proverbially energetic and nervous, even to turbulence, at times, yet nothing of that sort have I ever suffered to invade my peace. I am one of those unambitious lawyers who never address a jury, or in any way draw down public applause; but, in the cool tranquillity of a snug retreat, do a snug business among rich men's bonds, and mortgages, and title-deeds. All who know me, consider me an eminently *safe* man. The late John Jacob Astor, a personage little given to poetic enthusiasm, had no hesitation in pronouncing my first grand point to be prudence; my next, method. I do not speak it in vanity, but simply record the fact, that I was not unemployed in my profession by the late John Jacob Astor; a name which, I admit, I love to repeat; for it hath a rounded and orbicular sound to it, and rings like unto bullion. I will freely add, that I was not insensible to the late John Jacob Astor's good opinion.

Some time prior to the period at which this little history begins, my avocations had been largely increased. The good old office, now extinct in the State of New York, of a Master in Chancery, had been conferred upon

---

[1]In the first place.

me. It was not a very arduous office, but very pleasantly remunerative. I seldom lose my temper; much more seldom indulge in dangerous indignation at wrongs and outrages; but I must be permitted to be rash here and declare, that I consider the sudden and violent abrogation of the office of Master in Chancery, by the new Constitution, as a —— premature act; inasmuch as I had counted upon a life-lease of the profits, whereas I only received those of a few short years. But this is by the way.

My chambers were up stairs, at No. — Wall Street. At one end, they looked upon the white wall of the interior of a spacious skylight shaft, penetrating the building from top to bottom.

This view might have been considered rather tame than otherwise, deficient in what landscape painters call "life." But, if so, the view from the other end of my chambers offered, at least, a contrast, if nothing more. In that direction, my windows commanded an unobstructed view of a lofty brick wall, black by age and everlasting shade; which wall required no spyglass to bring out its lurking beauties, but, for the benefit of all nearsighted spectators, was pushed up to within ten feet of my window-panes. Owing to the great height of the surrounding buildings, and my chambers being on the second floor, the interval between this wall and mine not a little resembled a huge square cistern.

At the period just preceding the advent of Bartleby, I had two persons as copyists in my employment, and a promising lad as an office-boy. First, Turkey; second, Nippers; third, Ginger Nut. These may seem names, the like of which are not usually found in the Directory. In truth, they were nicknames, mutually conferred upon each other by my three clerks, and were deemed expressive of their respective persons or characters. Turkey was a short, pursy Englishman, of about my own age — that is, somewhere not far from sixty. In the morning, one might say, his face was of a fine florid hue, but after twelve o'clock, meridian — his dinner hour — it blazed like a grate full of Christmas coals; and continued blazing — but, as it were, with a gradual wane — till six o'clock, P.M., or thereabouts; after which, I saw no more of the proprietor of the face, which, gaining its meridian with the sun, seemed to set with it, to rise, culminate, and decline the following day, with the like regularity and undiminished glory. There are many singular coincidences I have known in the course of my life, not the least among which was the fact, that, exactly when Turkey displayed his fullest beams from his red and radiant countenance, just then, too, at that critical moment, began the daily period when I considered his business capacities as seriously disturbed for the remainder of the twenty-four hours. Not that he was absolutely idle, or averse to business then; far from it. The difficulty was, he was apt to be altogether too energetic. There was a strange, inflamed, flurried, flighty recklessness of activity about him. He would be incautious in dipping his pen into his inkstand. All his blots upon my documents were dropped there after twelve o'clock, meridian. Indeed, not only would he be reckless, and sadly given to making blots in the afternoon, but, some days, he went further, and was rather noisy. At such times, too, his face flamed with augmented blazonry, as if cannel coal had been heaped on anthracite. He made an unpleasant racket with his chair; spilled his sand-box; in mending his pens, impatiently split them all to pieces, and threw them on the floor in a sudden passion; stood up, and leaned over his table, boxing his papers about in a most indecorous manner, very sad to behold in an elderly man like him. Nevertheless, as he was in many ways a most valuable person to me, and all the time before twelve o'clock, meridian, was the quickest, steadiest creature, too, accomplishing a great deal of work in a style not easily to be matched—for these reasons, I was willing to overlook his eccentricities, though, indeed, occasionally, I remonstrated with him. I did this very gently, however, because, though the civilest, nay, the blandest and most reverential of men in the morning, yet, in the after-noon, he was disposed, upon provocation, to be slightly rash with his tongue—in fact, insolent. Now, valuing his morning services as I did, and resolved not to lose them—yet, at the same time, made uncomfortable by his inflamed ways after twelve o'clock—and being a man of peace, unwill-ing by my admonitions to call forth unseemly retorts from him, I took upon me, one Saturday noon (he was always worse on Saturdays) to hint to him, very kindly, that, perhaps, now that he was growing old, it might be well to abridge his labors; in short, he need not come to my chambers after twelve o'clock, but, dinner over, had best go home to his lodgings, and rest himself till tea-time. But no; he insisted upon his afternoon devo-tions. His countenance became intolerably fervid, as he oratorically assured me—gesticulating with a long ruler at the other end of the room—that if his services in the morning were useful, how indispensable, then, in the afternoon?

"With submission, sir," said Turkey, on this occasion, "I consider myself your right-hand man. In the morning I but marshal and deploy my columns; but in the afternoon I put myself at their head, and gallantly charge the foe, thus"—and he made a violent thrust with the ruler.

"But the blots, Turkey," intimated I.

"True; but, with submission, sir, behold these hairs! I am getting old. Surely, sir, a blot or two of a warm afternoon is not to be severely urged against gray hairs. Old age—even if it blot the page—is honorable. With submission, sir, we *both* are getting old."

This appeal to my fellow-feeling was hardly to be resisted. At all events, I saw that go he would not. So, I made up my mind to let him stay, resolving, nevertheless, to see to it that, during the afternoon, he had to do with my less important papers.

Nippers, the second on my list, was a whiskered, sallow, and, upon the whole, rather piratical-looking young man, of about five-and-twenty. I always deemed him the victim of two evil powers—ambition and indiges-tion. The ambition was evinced by a certain impatience of the duties of a mere copyist, an unwarrantable usurpation of strictly professional affairs such as the original drawing up of legal documents. The indigestion seemed betokened in an occasional nervous testiness and grinning irritability, causing the teeth to audibly grind together over mistakes committed in copying; unnecessary maledictions, hissed, rather than spoken, in the heat of business; and especially by a continual discontent with the height of the table where he worked. Though of a very ingenious mechanical turn, Nippers could never get this table to suit him. He put chips under it, blocks of various sorts, bits of pasteboard, and at last went so far as to attempt an exquisite adjustment, by final pieces of folded blotting paper. But no invention would answer. If, for the sake of easing his back, he brought the table-lid at a sharp angle well up towards his chin, and wrote there like a man using the steep roof of a Dutch house for his desk, then he declared that it stopped the circulation in his arms. If now he lowered the table to his waistbands, and stooped over it in writing, then there was a sore aching in his back. In short, the truth of the matter was, Nippers knew not what he wanted. Or, if he wanted anything, it was to be rid of a scrivener's table altogether. Among the manifestations of his diseased ambition was a fondness he had for receiving visits from certain ambiguous-looking fellows in seedy coats, whom he called his clients. Indeed, I was aware that not only was he, at times, considerable of a ward-politician, but he occasionally did a little business at the justices' courts, and was not unknown on the steps of the Tombs.[2] I have good reason to believe, however, that one individual who called upon him at my chambers, and who, with a grand air, he insisted was his client, was no other than a dun, and the alleged title-deed, a bill. But, with all his failings, and the annoyances he caused me, Nippers, like his compatriot Turkey, was a very useful man to me; wrote a neat, swift hand; and, when he chose, was not deficient in a gentlemanly sort of deportment. Added to this, he always dressed in a gentlemanly sort of way; and so, incidentally, reflected credit upon my chambers. Whereas, with respect to Turkey, I had much ado to keep him from being a reproach to me. His clothes were apt to look oily, and smell of eating-houses. He wore his pantaloons very loose and baggy in summer. His coats were execrable, his hat not to be handled. But while the hat was a thing of indifference to me, inasmuch as his natural civility and deference, as a dependent Englishman, always led him to doff it the moment he entered the room, yet his coat was another matter. Concerning his coats, I reasoned with him; but with no effect. The truth was, I suppose, that a man with so small an income could not afford to sport such a lustrous face and a lustrous coat at one and the same time. As Nippers once observed, Turkey's money went chiefly for red ink. One winter day, I presented Turkey with a highly respectable-looking coat of my own—a padded gray coat, of a most comfortable warmth, and which buttoned straight up from the knee to the neck. I thought Turkey would appreciate

---

[2]A prison in New York City.

the favor, and abate his rashness and obstreperousness of afternoons. But no; I verily believe that buttoning himself up in so downy and blanket-like a coat had a pernicious effect upon him upon the same principle that too much oats are bad for horses. In fact, precisely as a rash, restive horse is said to feel his oats, so Turkey felt his coat. It made him insolent. He was a man whom prosperity harmed.

Though, concerning the self-indulgent habits of Turkey, I had my own private surmises, yet, touching Nippers, I was well persuaded that, whatever might be his faults in other respects, he was, at least, a temperate young man. But, indeed, nature herself seemed to have been his vintner, and, at his birth, charged him so thoroughly with an irritable, brandy-like disposition, that all subsequent potations were needless. When I consider how, amid the stillness of my chambers, Nippers would sometimes impatiently rise from his seat, and stooping over his table, spread his arms wide apart, seize the whole desk, and move it, and jerk it, with a grim, grinding motion on the floor, as if the table were a perverse voluntary agent, intent on thwarting and vexing him, I plainly perceive that, for Nippers, brandy-and-water were altogether superfluous.

It was fortunate for me that, owing to its peculiar cause—indigestion—the irritability and consequent nervousness of Nippers were mainly observable in the morning, while in the afternoon he was comparatively mild. So that, Turkey's paroxysms only coming on about twelve o'clock, I never had to do with their eccentricities at one time. Their fits relieved each other, like guards. When Nippers' was on, Turkey's was off; and *vice versa*. This was a good natural arrangement, under the circumstances.

Ginger Nut, the third on my list, was a lad, some twelve years old. His father was a carman, ambitious of seeing his son on the bench instead of a cart, before he died. So he sent him to my office, as student at law, errand-boy, cleaner, and sweeper, at the rate of one dollar a week. He had a little desk to himself, but he did not use it much. Upon inspection, the drawer exhibited a great array of the shells of various sorts of nuts. Indeed, to this quick-witted youth, the whole noble science of the law was contained in a nutshell. Not the least among the employments of Ginger Nut, as well as one which he discharged with the most alacrity, was his duty as cake and apple purveyor for Turkey and Nippers. Copying lawpapers being proverbially a dry, husky sort of business, my two scriveners were fain to moisten their mouths very often with Spitzenbergs, to be had at the numerous stalls nigh the Custom House and Post Office. Also, they sent Ginger Nut very frequently for that peculiar cake—small, flat, round, and very spicy—after which he had been named by them. Of a cold morning, when business was but dull, Turkey would gobble up scores of these cakes, as if they were mere wafers—indeed, they sell them at the rate of six or eight for a penny—the scrape of his pen blending with the crunching of the crisp particles in his mouth. Of all the fiery afternoon blunders and flurried rashness of Turkey, was his once moistening a ginger-cake between his lips, and clapping it on to a mortgage, for a seal. I came within an ace of dismissing him then. But he mollified me by making an oriental bow, and saying —

"With submission, sir, it was generous of me to find you in stationery on my own account."

Now my original business — that of a conveyancer and title hunter, and drawer-up of recondite documents of all sorts — was considerably increased by receiving the Master's office. There was now great work for scriveners. Not only must I push the clerks already with me, but I must have additional help.

In answer to my advertisement, a motionless young man one morning stood upon my office threshold, the door being open, for it was summer. I can see that figure now — pallidly neat, pitiably respectable, incurably forlorn! It was Bartleby.

After a few words touching his qualifications, I engaged him, glad to have among my corps of copyists a man of so singularly sedate an aspect, which I thought might operate beneficially upon the flighty temper of Turkey, and the fiery one of Nippers.

I should have stated before that ground-glass folding-doors divided my premises into two parts, one of which was occupied by my scriveners, the other by myself. According to my humor, I threw open these doors, or closed them. I resolved to assign Bartleby a corner by the folding-doors, but on my side of them, so as to have this quiet man within easy call, in case any trifling thing was to be done. I placed his desk close up to a small side-window in that part of the room, a window which originally had afforded a lateral view of certain grimy brickyards and bricks, but which, owing to subsequent erections, commanded at present no view at all, though it gave some light. Within three feet of the panes was a wall, and the light came down from far above, between two lofty buildings, as from a very small opening in a dome. Still further to a satisfactory arrangement, I procured a high green folding screen, which might entirely isolate Bartleby from my sight, though not remove him from my voice. And thus, in a manner, privacy and society were conjoined.

At first, Bartleby did an extraordinary quantity of writing. As if long famishing for something to copy, he seemed to gorge himself on my documents. There was no pause for digestion. He ran a day and night line, copying by sunlight and by candle-light. I should have been quite delighted with his application, had he been cheerfully industrious. But he wrote on silently, palely, mechanically.

It is, of course, an indispensable part of a scrivener's business to verify the accuracy of his copy, word by word. Where there are two or more scriveners in an office, they assist each other in this examination, one reading from the copy, the other holding the original. It is a very dull, wearisome, and lethargic affair. I can readily imagine that, to some sanguine temperaments, it would be altogether intolerable. For example, I cannot credit that the mettlesome poet, Byron, would have contentedly sat down with Bartleby to examine a law document of, say five hundred pages, closely written in a crimpy hand.

Now and then, in the haste of business, it had been my habit to assist in comparing some brief document myself, calling Turkey or Nippers for this purpose. One object I had, in placing Bartleby so handy to me behind the screen, was, to avail myself of his services on such trivial occasions. It was on the third day, I think, of his being with me, and before any necessity had arisen for having his own writing examined, that, being much hurried to complete a small affair I had in hand, I abruptly called to Bartleby. In my haste and natural expectancy of instant compliance, I sat with my head bent over the original on my desk, and my right hand sideways, and somewhat nervously extended with the copy, so that, immediately upon emerging from his retreat, Bartleby might snatch it and proceed to business without the least delay.

In this very attitude did I sit when I called to him, rapidly stating what it was I wanted him to do—namely, to examine a small paper with me. Imagine my surprise, nay, my consternation, when, without moving from his privacy, Bartleby, in a singularly mild, firm voice, replied, "I would prefer not to."

I sat awhile in perfect silence, rallying my stunned faculties. Immediately it occurred to me that my ears had deceived me, or Bartleby had entirely misunderstood my meaning. I repeated my request in the clearest tone I could assume; but in quite as clear a one came the previous reply, "I would prefer not to."

"Prefer not to," echoed I, rising in high excitement, and crossing the room with a stride. "What do you mean? Are you moonstruck? I want you to help me compare this sheet here—take it," and I thrust it towards him.

"I would prefer not to," said he.

I looked at him steadfastly. His face was leanly composed; his gray eye dimly calm. Not a wrinkle of agitation rippled him. Had there been the least uneasiness, anger, impatience, or impertinence in his manner; in other words, had there been anything ordinarily human about him, doubtless I should have violently dismissed him from the premises. But as it was, I should have as soon thought of turning my pale plaster-of-paris bust of Cicero out of doors. I stood gazing at him awhile, as he went on with his own writing, and then reseated myself at my desk. This is very strange, thought I. What had one best do? But my business hurried me. I concluded to forget the matter for the present, reserving it for my future leisure. So, calling Nippers from the other room, the paper was speedily examined.

A few days after this, Bartleby concluded four lengthy documents, being quadruplicates of a week's testimony taken before me in my High Court of Chancery. It became necessary to examine them. It was an important suit, and great accuracy was imperative. Having all things arranged, I called

Turkey, Nippers, and Ginger Nut, from the next room, meaning to place the four copies in the hands of my four clerks, while I should read from the original. Accordingly, Turkey, Nippers, and Ginger Nut had taken their seats in a row, each with his document in his hand, when I called to Bartleby to join this interesting group.

"Bartleby! quick, I am waiting."

I heard a slow scrape of his chair legs on the uncarpeted floor, and soon he appeared standing at the entrance of his hermitage.

"What is wanted?" said he, mildly.

"The copies, the copies," said I, hurriedly. "We are going to examine them. There"—and I held towards him the fourth quadruplicate.

"I would prefer not to," he said, and gently disappeared behind the screen.

For a few moments I was turned into a pillar of salt, standing at the head of my seated column of clerks. Recovering myself, I advanced towards the screen, and demanded the reason for such extraordinary conduct.

"*Why* do you refuse?"

"I would prefer not to."

With any other man I should have flown outright into a dreadful passion, scorned all further words, and thrust him ignominiously from my presence. But there was something about Bartleby that not only strangely disarmed me, but, in a wonderful manner, touched and disconcerted me. I began to reason with him.

"These are your own copies we are about to examine. It is labor saving to you, because one examination will answer for your four papers. It is common usage. Every copyist is bound to help examine his copy. Is it not so? Will you not speak? Answer!"

"I prefer not to," he replied in a flute-like tone. It seemed to me that, while I had been addressing him, he carefully revolved every statement that I made; fully comprehended the meaning; could not gainsay the irresistible conclusion; but, at the same time, some paramount consideration prevailed with him to reply as he did.

"You are decided, then, not to comply with my request—a request made according to common usage and common sense?"

He briefly gave me to understand, that on that point my judgment was sound. Yes: his decision was irreversible.

It is not seldom the case that, when a man is browbeaten in some unprecedented and violently unreasonable way, he begins to stagger in his own plainest faith. He begins, as it were, vaguely to surmise that, wonderful as it may be, all the justice and all the reason is on the other side. Accordingly, if any disinterested persons are present, he turns to them for some reinforcement for his own faltering mind.

"Turkey," said I, "what do you think of this? Am I not right?"

"With submission, sir," said Turkey, in his blandest tone, "I think that you are."

"Nippers," said I, "what do *you* think of it?"

"I think I should kick him out of the office."

(The reader of nice perceptions will have perceived that, it being morning, Turkey's answer is couched in polite and tranquil terms, but Nippers replies in ill-tempered ones. Or, to repeat a previous sentence, Nippers' ugly mood was on duty, and Turkey's off.)

"Ginger Nut," said I, willing to enlist the smallest suffrage in my behalf, "what do *you* think of it?"

"I think, sir, he's a little *luny*," replied Ginger Nut, with a grin.

"You hear what they say," said I, turning towards the screen, "come forth and do your duty."

But he vouchsafed no reply. I pondered a moment in sore perplexity. But once more business hurried me. I determined again to postpone the consideration of this dilemma to my future leisure. With a little trouble we made out to examine the papers without Bartleby, though at every page or two Turkey deferentially dropped his opinion, that this proceeding was quite out of the common; while Nippers, twitching in his chair with a dyspeptic nervousness, ground out, between his set teeth, occasional hissing maledictions against the stubborn oaf behind the screen. And for his (Nippers') part, this was the first and the last time he would do another man's business without pay.

Meanwhile Bartleby sat in his hermitage, oblivious to everything but his own peculiar business there.

Some days passed, the scrivener being employed upon another lengthy work. His late remarkable conduct led me to regard his ways narrowly. I observed that he never went to dinner; indeed, that he never went anywhere. As yet I had never, of my personal knowledge, known him to be outside of my office. He was a perpetual sentry in the corner. At about eleven o'clock though, in the morning, I noticed that Ginger Nut would advance towards the opening in Bartleby's screen, as if silently beckoned thither by a gesture invisible to me where I sat. The boy would then leave the office, jingling a few pence, and reappear with a handful of ginger-nuts, which he delivered in the hermitage, receiving two of the cakes for his trouble.

He lives, then, on ginger-nuts, thought I; never eats a dinner, properly speaking; he must be a vegetarian, then, but no; he never eats even vegetables, he eats nothing but ginger-nuts. My mind then ran on in reveries concerning the probable effects upon the human constitution of living entirely on ginger-nuts. Ginger-nuts are so called, because they contain ginger as one of their peculiar constituents, and the final flavoring one. Now, what was ginger? A hot, spicy thing. Was Bartleby hot and spicy? Not at all. Ginger, then, had no effect upon Bartleby. Probably he preferred it should have none.

Nothing so aggravates an earnest person as a passive resistance. If the individual so resisted be of a not inhumane temper, and the resisting one perfectly harmless in his passivity, then, in the better moods of the former, he will endeavor charitably to construe to his imagination what proves impossible to be solved by his judgment. Even so, for the most part, I regarded Bartleby and his ways. Poor fellow! thought I, he means no mischief; it is plain he intends no insolence; his aspect sufficiently evinces that his eccentricities are involuntary. He is useful to me. I can get along with him. If I turn him away, the chances are he will fall in with some less indulgent employer, and then he will be rudely treated, and perhaps driven forth miserably to starve. Yes. Here I can cheaply purchase a delicious self-approval. To befriend Bartleby; to humor him in his strange wilfulness, will cost me little or nothing, while I lay up in my soul what will eventually prove a sweet morsel for my conscience. But this mood was not invariable with me. The passiveness of Bartleby sometimes irritated me. I felt strangely goaded on to encounter him in new opposition—to elicit some angry spark from him answerable to my own. But, indeed, I might as well have essayed to strike fire with my knuckles against a bit of Windsor soap. But one afternoon the evil impulse in me mastered me, and the following little scene ensued:

"Bartleby," said I, "when those papers are all copied, I will compare them with you."

"I would prefer not to."

"How? Surely you do not mean to persist in that mulish vagary?"

No answer.

I threw open the folding-doors nearby, and turning upon Turkey and Nippers, exclaimed:

"Bartleby a second time says, he won't examine his papers. What do you think of it, Turkey?"

It was afternoon, be it remembered. Turkey sat glowing like a brass boiler; his bald head steaming; his hands reeling among his blotted papers.

"Think of it?" roared Turkey. "I think I'll just step behind his screen, and black his eyes for him!"

So saying, Turkey rose to his feet and threw his arms into a pugilistic position. He was hurrying away to make good his promise, when I detained him, alarmed at the effect of incautiously rousing Turkey's combativeness after dinner.

"Sit down, Turkey," said I, "and hear what Nippers has to say. What do you think of it, Nippers? Would I not be justified in immediately dismissing Bartleby?"

"Excuse me, that is for you to decide, sir. I think his conduct quite unusual, and, indeed, unjust, as regards Turkey and myself. But it may only be a passing whim."

"Ah," exclaimed I, "you have strangely changed your mind, then—you speak very gently of him now."

"All beer," cried Turkey; "gentleness is effects of beer—Nippers and I dined together to-day. You see how gentle *I* am, sir. Shall I go and black his eyes?"

"You refer to Bartleby, I suppose. No, not to-day, Turkey," I replied; "pray, put up your fists."

I closed the doors, and again advanced towards Bartleby. I felt additional incentives tempting me to my fate. I burned to be rebelled against again. I remembered that Bartleby never left the office.

"Bartleby," said I, "Ginger Nut is away; just step around to the Post Office, won't you?" (it was but a three minutes' walk) "and see if there is anything for me."

"I would prefer not to."

"You *will* not?"

"I *prefer* not."

I staggered to my desk, and sat there in a deep study. My blind inveteracy returned. Was there any other thing in which I could procure myself to be ignominiously repulsed by this lean, penniless wight? my hired clerk? What added thing is there, perfectly reasonable, that he will be sure to refuse to do?

"Bartleby!"

No answer.

"Bartleby," in a louder tone.

No answer.

"Bartleby," I roared.

Like a very ghost, agreeably to the laws of magical invocation, at the third summons, he appeared at the entrance of his hermitage.

"Go to the next room, and tell Nippers to come to me."

"I would prefer not to," he respectfully and slowly said, and mildly disappeared.

"Very good, Bartleby," said I, in a quiet sort of serenely-severe self-possessed tone, intimating the unalterable purpose of some terrible retribution very close at hand. At the moment I half intended something of the kind. But upon the whole, as it was drawing towards my dinner-hour, I thought it best to put on my hat and walk home for the day, suffering much from perplexity and distress of mind.

Shall I acknowledge it? The conclusion of this whole business was, that it soon became a fixed fact of my chambers, that a pale young scrivener, by the name of Bartleby, had a desk there; that he copied for me at the usual rate of four cents a folio (one hundred words); but he was permanently exempt from examining the work done by him, that duty being transferred to Turkey and Nippers, out of compliment, doubtless, to their superior acuteness; moreover, said Bartleby was never, on any account, to be dispatched on the most trivial errand of any sort; and that even if entreated to take upon him such a matter, it was generally understood that he would "prefer not to" — in other words, that he would refuse point blank.

As days passed on, I became considerably reconciled to Bartleby. His steadiness, his freedom from all dissipation, his incessant industry (except when he chose to throw himself into a standing revery behind his screen), his great stillness, his unalterableness of demeanor under all circumstances, made him a valuable acquisition. One prime thing was this—*he was always there*—first in the morning, continually through the day, and the last at night. I had a singular confidence in his honesty. I felt my most precious papers perfectly safe in his hands. Sometimes, to be sure, I could not, for the very soul of me, avoid falling into sudden spasmodic passions with him. For it was exceeding difficult to bear in mind all the time those strange peculiarities, privileges, and unheard-of exemptions, forming the tacit stipulations on Bartleby's part under which he remained in my office. Now and then, in the eagerness of dispatching pressing business, I would inadvertently summon Bartleby, in a short, rapid tone, to put his finger, say, on the incipient tie of a bit of red tape with which I was about compressing some papers. Of course, from behind the screen the usual answer, "I prefer not to," was sure to come; and then, how could a human creature, with the common infirmities of our nature, refrain from bitterly exclaiming upon such perverseness—such unreasonableness? However, every added repulse of this sort which I received only tended to lessen the probability of my repeating the inadvertence.

Here it must be said, that, according to the custom of most legal gentlemen occupying chambers in densely populated law buildings, there were several keys to my door. One was kept by a woman residing in the attic, which person weekly scrubbed and daily swept and dusted my apartments. Another was kept by Turkey for convenience sake. The third I sometimes carried in my own pocket. The fourth I knew not who had.

Now, one Sunday morning I happened to go to Trinity Church, to hear a celebrated preacher, and finding myself rather early on the ground I thought I would walk round to my chambers for a while. Luckily I had my key with me; but upon applying it to the lock, I found it resisted by something inserted from the inside. Quite surprised, I called out; when to my consternation a key was turned from within; and thrusting his lean visage at me, and holding the door ajar, the apparition of Bartleby appeared, in his shirt-sleeves, and otherwise in a strangely tattered *deshabille,* saying quietly that he was sorry, but he was deeply engaged just then, and preferred not admitting me at present. In a brief word or two, he moreover added, that perhaps I had better walk round the block two or three times, and by that time he would probably have concluded his affairs.

Now, the utterly unsurmised appearance of Bartleby, tenanting my law-chambers of a Sunday morning, with his cadaverously gentlemanly *nonchalance,* yet withal firm and self-possessed, had such a strange effect upon me, that incontinently I slunk away from my own door, and did as desired. But not without sundry twinges of impotent rebellion against the mild effrontery of this unaccountable scrivener. Indeed, it was his wonderful mildness chiefly, which not only disarmed me, but unmanned me, as it were. For I consider that one, for the time, is sort of unmanned when he tranquilly permits his hired clerk to dictate to him, and order him away from his own premises. Furthermore, I was full of uneasiness as to what Bartleby could possibly be doing in my office in his shirt-sleeves, and in an otherwise dismantled condition on a Sunday morning. Was anything amiss going on? Nay, that was out of the question. It was not to be thought of for a moment that Bartleby was an immoral person. But what could he be doing there?—copying? Nay again, whatever might be his eccentricities, Bartleby was an eminently decorous person. He would be the last man to sit down to his desk in any state approaching to nudity. Besides, it was Sunday; and there was something about Bartleby that forbade the supposition that he would by any secular occupation violate the proprieties of the day.

Nevertheless, my mind was not pacified; and full of a restless curiosity, at last I returned to the door. Without hindrance I inserted my key, opened it, and entered. Bartleby was not to be seen. I looked round anxiously, peeped behind his screen; but it was very plain that he was gone. Upon more closely examining the place, I surmised that for an indefinite period Bartleby must have ate, dressed, and slept in my office, and that too without plate, mirror, or bed. The cushioned seat of a rickety old sofa in one corner bore the faint impress of a lean, reclining form. Rolled away under his desk, I found a blanket; under the empty grate, a blacking box and brush; on a chair, a tin basin, with soap and a ragged towel; in a newspaper a few crumbs of ginger-nuts and a morsel of cheese. Yes, thought I, it is evident enough that Bartleby has been making his home here, keeping bachelor's hall all by himself. Immediately then the thought came sweeping across me, what miserable friendlessness and loneliness are here revealed! His poverty is great; but his solitude, how horrible! Think of it. Of a Sunday, Wall Street is deserted as Petra;[3] and every night of every day it is an emptiness. This building, too, which of week-days hums with industry and life, at nightfall echoes with sheer vacancy, and all through Sunday is forlorn. And here Bartleby makes his home; sole spectator of a solitude which he has seen all populous—a sort of innocent and transformed Marius[4] brooding among the ruins of Carthage!

For the first time in my life a feeling of overpowering stinging melancholy seized me. Before, I had never experienced aught but a not unpleasing sadness. The bond of a common humanity now drew me irresistibly to gloom. A fraternal melancholy! For both I and Bartleby were sons of Adam. I remembered the bright silks and sparkling faces I had seen that

---

[3]A city in what is now Jordan, once the center of an Arab kingdom. It was deserted for more than ten centuries, until its rediscovery by explorers in 1812.

[4]Gaius Marius (157?–86 B.C.), a Roman general, several times elected consul. Marius's greatest military successes came in the Jugurthine War, in Africa. Later, when his opponents gained power and he was banished, he fled to Africa. Carthage was a city in North Africa.

day, in gala trim, swan-like sailing down the Mississippi of Broadway; and I contrasted them with the pallid copyist, and thought to myself, Ah, happiness courts the light, so we deem the world is gay; but misery hides aloof, so we deem that misery there is none. These sad fancyings—chimeras, doubtless, of a sick and silly brain—led on to other and more special thoughts, concerning the eccentricities of Bartleby. Presentiments of strange discoveries hovered round me. The scrivener's pale form appeared to me laid out, among uncaring strangers, in its shivering winding-sheet.

Suddenly I was attracted by Bartleby's closed desk, the key in open sight left in the lock.

I mean no mischief, seek the gratification of no heartless curiosity, thought I; besides, the desk is mine, and its contents, too, so I will make bold to look within. Everything was methodically arranged, the papers smoothly placed. The pigeon-holes were deep, and removing the files of documents, I groped into their recesses. Presently I felt something there, and dragged it out. It was an old bandanna handkerchief, heavy and knotted. I opened it, and saw it was a saving's bank.

I now recalled all the quiet mysteries which I had noted in the man. I remembered that he never spoke but to answer; that, though at intervals he had considerable time to himself, yet I had never seen him reading—no, not even a newspaper; that for long periods he would stand looking out, at his pale window behind the screen, upon the dead brick wall; I was quite sure he never visited any refectory or eating-house; while his pale face clearly indicated that he never drank beer like Turkey; or tea and coffee even, like other men; that he never went anywhere in particular that I could learn; never went out for a walk, unless, indeed, that was the case at present; that he had declined telling who he was, or whence he came, or whether he had any relatives in the world; that though so thin and pale, he never complained of ill-health. And more than all, I remembered a certain unconscious air of pallid—how shall I call it?—of pallid haughtiness, say, or rather an austere reserve about him, which had positively awed me into my tame compliance with his eccentricities, when I had feared to ask him to do the slightest incidental thing for me, even though I might know, from his long-continued motionlessness, that behind his screen he must be standing in one of those dead-wall reveries of his.

Revolving all these things, and coupling them with the recently discovered fact, that he made my office his constant abiding place and home, and not forgetful of his morbid moodiness; revolving all these things, a prudential feeling began to steal over me. My first emotions had been those of pure melancholy and sincerest pity; but just in proportion as the forlornness of Bartleby grew and grew to my imagination, did that same melancholy merge into fear, that pity into repulsion. So true it is, and so terrible, too, that up to a certain point the thought or sight of misery enlists our best affections; but, in certain special cases, beyond that point it does not. They err who would assert that invariably this is owing to the inherent selfishness of the human heart. It rather proceeds from a certain hopelessness of remedying excessive and organic ill. To a sensitive being, pity is not seldom pain. And when at last it is perceived that such pity cannot lead to effectual succor, common sense bids the soul be rid of it. What I saw that morning persuaded me that the scrivener was the victim of innate and incurable disorder. I might give alms to his body; but his body did not pain him; it was his soul that suffered, and his soul I could not reach.

I did not accomplish the purpose of going to Trinity Church that morning. Somehow, the things I had seen disqualified me for the time from church-going. I walked homeward, thinking what I would do with Bartleby. Finally, I resolved upon this—I would put certain calm questions to him the next morning, touching his history, etc., and if he declined to answer them openly and unreservedly (and I supposed he would prefer not), then to give him a twenty dollar bill over and above whatever I might owe him, and tell him his services were no longer required; but that if in any other way I could assist him, I would be happy to do so, especially if he desired to return to his native place, wherever that might be, I would willingly help to defray the expenses. Moreover, if, after reaching home, he found himself at any time in want of aid, a letter from him would be sure of a reply.

The next morning came.

"Bartleby," said I, gently calling to him behind his screen.

No reply.

"Bartleby," said I, in a still gentler tone, "come here; I am not going to ask you to do anything you would prefer not to do—I simply wish to speak to you."

Upon this he noiselessly slid into view.

"Will you tell me, Bartleby, where you were born?"

"I would prefer not to."

"Will you tell me *anything* about yourself?"

"I would prefer not to."

"But what reasonable objection can you have to speak to me? I feel friendly towards you."

He did not look at me while I spoke, but kept his glance fixed upon my bust of Cicero, which, as I then sat, was directly behind me, some six inches above my head.

"What is your answer, Bartleby?" said I, after waiting a considerable time for a reply, during which his countenance remained immovable, only there was the faintest conceivable tremor of the white attenuated mouth.

"At present I prefer to give no answer," he said, and retired into his hermitage.

It was rather weak in me I confess, but his manner, on this occasion, nettled me. Not only did there seem to lurk in it a certain calm disdain, but his perverseness seemed ungrateful, considering the undeniable good usage and indulgence he had received from me.

Again I sat ruminating what I should do. Mortified as I was at his behavior, and resolved as I had been to dismiss him when I entered my office, nevertheless I strangely felt something superstitious knocking at my heart, and forbidding me to carry out my purpose, and denouncing me for a villain if I dared to breathe one bitter word against this forlornest of mankind. At last, familiarly drawing my chair behind his screen, I sat down and said: "Bartleby, never mind, then, about revealing your history; but let me entreat you, as a friend, to comply as far as may be with the usages of this office. Say now, you will help to examine papers tomorrow or next day: in short, say now, that in a day or two you will begin to be a little reasonable:—say so, Bartleby."

"At present I would prefer not to be a little reasonable," was his mildly cadaverous reply.

Just then the folding-doors opened, and Nippers approached. He seemed suffering from an unusually bad night's rest, induced by severer indigestion than common. He overheard those final words of Bartleby.

"*Prefer not,* eh?" gritted Nippers—"I'd *prefer* him, if I were you, sir," addressing me—"I'd *prefer* him; I'd give him preferences, the stubborn mule! What is it, sir, pray, that he *prefers* not to do now?"

Bartleby moved not a limb.

"Mr. Nippers," said I, "I'd prefer that you would withdraw for the present."

Somehow, of late, I had got into the way of involuntarily using this word "prefer" upon all sorts of not exactly suitable occasions. And I trembled to think that my contact with the scrivener had already and seriously affected me in a mental way. And what further and deeper aberration might it not yet produce? This apprehension had not been without efficacy in determining me to summary measures.

As Nippers, looking very sour and sulky, was departing, Turkey blandly and deferentially approached.

"With submission, sir," said he, "yesterday I was thinking about Bartleby here, and I think that if he would but prefer to take a quart of good ale every day, it would do much towards mending him, and enabling him to assist in examining his papers."

"So you have got the word, too," said I, slightly excited.

"With submission, what word, sir?" asked Turkey, respectfully crowding himself into the contracted space behind the screen, and by so doing, making me jostle the scrivener. "What word, sir?"

"I would prefer to be left alone here," said Bartleby, as if offended at being mobbed in his privacy.

"*That's* the word, Turkey," said I—"*that's* it."

"Oh, *prefer?* oh yes—queer word. I never use it myself. But, sir, as I was saying, if he would but prefer—"

"Turkey," interrupted I, "you will please withdraw."

"Oh certainly, sir, if you prefer that I should."

As he opened the folding-door to retire, Nippers at his desk caught a glimpse of me, and asked whether I would prefer to have a certain paper copied on blue paper or white. He did not in the least roguishly accent the word "prefer." It was plain that it involuntarily rolled from his tongue. I thought to myself, surely I must get rid of a demented man, who already has in some degree turned the tongues, if not the heads of myself and clerks. But I thought it prudent not to break the dismission at once.

The next day I noticed that Bartleby did nothing but stand at his window in his dead-wall revery. Upon asking him why he did not write, he said that he had decided upon doing no more writing.

"Why, how now? what next?" exclaimed I, "do no more writing?"

"No more."

"And what is the reason?"

"Do you not see the reason for yourself?" he indifferently replied.

I looked steadfastly at him, and perceived that his eyes looked dull and glazed. Instantly it occurred to me, that his unexampled diligence in copying by his dim window for the first few weeks of his stay with me might have temporarily impaired his vision.

I was touched. I said something in condolence with him. I hinted that of course he did wisely in abstaining from writing for a while; and urged him to embrace that opportunity of taking wholesome exercise in the open air. This, however, he did not do. A few days after this, my other clerks being absent, and being in a great hurry to dispatch certain letters by the mail, I thought that, having nothing else earthly to do, Bartleby would surely be less inflexible than usual, and carry these letters to the Post Office. But he blankly declined. So, much to my inconvenience, I went myself.

Still added days went by. Whether Bartleby's eyes improved or not, I could not say. To all appearance, I thought they did. But when I asked him if they did he vouchsafed no answer. At all events, he would do no copying. At last, in replying to my urgings, he informed me that he had permanently given up copying.

"What!" exclaimed I; "suppose your eyes should get entirely well — better than ever before — would you not copy then?"

"I have given up copying," he answered, and slid aside.

He remained as ever, a fixture in my chamber. Nay — if that were possible — he became still more of a fixture than before. What was to be done? He would do nothing in the office; why should he stay there? In plain fact, he had now become a millstone to me, not only useless as a necklace, but afflictive to bear. Yet I was sorry for him. I speak less than truth when I say that, on his own account, he occasioned me uneasiness. If he would but have named a single relative or friend, I would instantly have written, and urged their taking the poor fellow away to some convenient retreat. But he seemed alone, absolutely alone in the universe. A bit of wreck in the mid-Atlantic. At length, necessities connected with my business tyrannized over all other considerations. Decently as I could, I told Bartleby that in six days' time he must unconditionally leave the office. I warned him to take measures, in the interval, for procuring some other abode. I offered to assist him in this endeavor, if he himself would but take the first step towards a removal. "And when you finally quit me, Bartleby," added I, "I shall see that you go not away entirely unprovided. Six days from this hour, remember."

At the expiration of that period, I peeped behind the screen, and lo! Bartleby was there.

I buttoned up my coat, balanced myself; advanced slowly towards him, touched his shoulder, and said, "The time has come; you must quit this place; I am sorry for you; here is money; but you must go."

"I would prefer not," he replied, with his back still towards me.

"You *must*."

He remained silent.

Now I had an unbounded confidence in this man's common honesty. He had frequently restored to me sixpences and shillings carelessly dropped upon the floor, for I am apt to be very reckless in such shirt-button affairs. The proceeding, then, which followed will not be deemed extraordinary.

"Bartleby," said I, "I owe you twelve dollars on account; here are thirty-two; the odd twenty are yours—Will you take it?" and I handed the bills towards him.

But he made no motion.

"I will leave them here, then," putting them under a weight on the table. Then taking my hat and cane and going to the door, I tranquilly turned and added—"After you have removed your things from these offices, Bartleby, you will of course lock the door—since every one is now gone for the day but you—and if you please, slip your key underneath the mat, so that I may have it in the morning. I shall not see you again; so good-bye to you. If, hereafter, in your new place of abode, I can be of any service to you, do not fail to advise me by letter. Good-bye, Bartleby, and fare you well."

But he answered not a word; like the last column of some ruined temple, he remained standing mute and solitary in the middle of the otherwise deserted room.

As I walked home in a pensive mood, my vanity got the better of my pity. I could not but highly plume myself on my masterly management in getting rid of Bartleby. Masterly I call it, and such it must appear to any dispassionate thinker. The beauty of my procedure seemed to consist in its perfect quietness. There was no vulgar bullying, no bravado of any sort, no choleric hectoring, and striding to and fro across the apartment, jerking out vehement commands for Bartleby to bundle himself off with his beggarly traps. Nothing of the kind. Without loudly bidding Bartleby depart—as an inferior genius might have done—I *assumed* the ground that depart he must; and upon that assumption built all I had to say. The more I thought over my procedure, the more I was charmed with it. Nevertheless, next morning, upon awakening, I had my doubts—I had somehow slept off the fumes of vanity. One of the coolest and wisest hours a man has, is just after he awakes in the morning. My procedure seemed as sagacious as ever—but only in theory. How it would prove in practice—there was the rub. It was truly a beautiful thought to have assumed Bartleby's departure; but, after all, that assumption was simply my own, and none of Bartleby's. The great point was, not whether I had assumed that he would quit me, but whether he would prefer to do so. He was more a man of preferences than assumptions.

After breakfast, I walked down town, arguing the probabilities *pro* and *con*. One moment I thought it would prove a miserable failure, and Bartleby would be found all alive at my office as usual; the next moment it seemed certain that I should find his chair empty. And so I kept veering about. At the corner of Broadway and Canal Street, I saw quite an excited group of people standing in earnest conversation.

"I'll take odds he doesn't," said a voice as I passed.

"Doesn't go?—done!" said I, "put up your money."

I was instinctively putting my hand in my pocket to produce my own, when I remembered that this was an election day. The words I had overheard bore no reference to Bartleby, but to the success or non-success of some candidate for the mayoralty. In my intent frame of mind, I had, as it were, imagined that all Broadway shared in my excitement, and were debating the same question with me. I passed on, very thankful that the uproar of the street screened my momentary absent-mindedness.

As I had intended, I was earlier than usual at my office door. I stood listening for a moment. All was still. He must be gone. I tried the knob. The door was locked. Yes, my procedure had worked to a charm; he indeed must be vanished. Yet a certain melancholy mixed with this: I was almost sorry for my brilliant success. I was fumbling under the door mat for the key, which Bartleby was to have left there for me, when accidentally my knee knocked against a panel, producing a summoning sound, and in response a voice came to me from within—"Not yet; I am occupied."

It was Bartleby.

I was thunderstruck. For an instant I stood like the man who, pipe in mouth, was killed one cloudless afternoon long ago in Virginia, by summer lightning; at his own warm open window he was killed, and remained leaning out there upon the dreamy afternoon, till someone touched him, when he fell.

"Not gone!" I murmured at last. But again obeying that wondrous ascendancy which the inscrutable scrivener had over me, and from which ascendancy, for all my chafing, I could not completely escape, I slowly went down stairs and out into the street, and while walking round the block, considered what I should next do in this unheard-of perplexity. Turn the man out by an actual thrusting I could not; to drive him away by calling him hard names would not do; calling in the police was an unpleasant idea; and yet, permit him to enjoy his cadaverous triumph over me — this, too, I could not think of. What was to be done? or, if nothing could be done, was there anything further that I could *assume* in the matter? Yes, as before I had prospectively assumed that Bartleby would depart, so now I might retrospectively assume that departed he was. In the legitimate carrying out of this assumption, I might enter my office in a great hurry, and pretending not to see Bartleby at all, walk straight against him as if he were air. Such a proceeding would in a singular degree have the appearance of a home-thrust. It was hardly possible that Bartleby could withstand such an application of the doctrine of assumption. But upon second thoughts the success of the plan seemed rather dubious. I resolved to argue the matter over with him again.

"Bartleby," said I, entering the office, with a quietly severe expression, "I am seriously displeased. I am pained, Bartleby. I had thought better of you. I had imagined you of such a gentlemanly organization, that in any delicate dilemma a slight hint would suffice — in short, an assumption. But it appears I am deceived. Why," I added, unaffectedly starting, "you have not even touched that money yet," pointing to it, just where I had left it the evening previous.

He answered nothing.

"Will you, or will you not, quit me?" I now demanded in a sudden passion, advancing close to him.

"I would prefer *not* to quit you," he replied, gently emphasizing the *not*.

"What earthly right have you to stay here? Do you pay any rent? Do you pay my taxes? Or is this property yours?"

He answered nothing.

"Are you ready to go on and write now? Are your eyes recovered? Could you copy a small paper for me this morning? or help examine a few lines? or step round to the Post Office? In a word, will you do anything at all, to give a coloring to your refusal to depart the premises?"

He silently retired into his hermitage.

I was now in such a state of nervous resentment that I thought it but prudent to check myself at present from further demonstrations. Bartleby and I were alone. I remembered the tragedy of the unfortunate Adams and the still more unfortunate Colt in the solitary office of the latter; and how poor Colt, being dreadfully incensed by Adams, and imprudently permitting himself to get wildly excited, was at unawares hurried into his fatal act — an act which certainly no man could possibly deplore more than the actor himself.[5] Often it had occurred to me in my ponderings upon the

---

[5]John C. Colt murdered Samuel Adams in January 1842. Later that year, after his conviction, Colt committed suicide a half-hour before he was to be hanged. The case received wide and sensationalistic press coverage at the time.

subject that had that altercation taken place in the public street, or at a private residence, it would not have terminated as it did. It was the circumstance of being alone in a solitary office, up stairs, of a building entirely unhallowed by humanizing domestic associations—an uncarpeted office, doubtless, of a dusty, haggard sort of appearance—this it must have been, which greatly helped to enhance the irritable desperation of the hapless Colt.

But when this old Adam of resentment rose in me and tempted me concerning Bartleby, I grappled him and threw him. How? Why, simply by recalling the divine injunction: "A new commandment give I unto you, that ye love one another." Yes, this it was that saved me. Aside from higher considerations, charity often operates as a vastly wise and prudent principle—a great safeguard to its possessor. Men have committed murder for jealousy's sake, and anger's sake, and hatred's sake, and selfishness' sake, and spiritual pride's sake; but no man, that ever I heard of, ever committed a diabolical murder for sweet charity's sake. Mere self-interest, then, if no better motive can be enlisted, should, especially with high-tempered men, prompt all beings to charity and philanthropy. At any rate, upon the occasion in question, I strove to drown my exasperated feelings towards the scrivener by benevolently construing his conduct. Poor fellow, poor fellow! thought I, he don't mean anything; and besides, he has seen hard times, and ought to be indulged.

I endeavored, also, immediately to occupy myself, and at the same time to comfort my despondency. I tried to fancy, that in the course of the morning, at such time as might prove agreeable to him, Bartleby, of his own free accord, would emerge from his hermitage and take up some decided line of march in the direction of the door. But no. Half-past twelve o'clock came; Turkey began to glow in the face, overturn his inkstand, and become generally obstreperous; Nippers abated down into quietude and courtesy; Ginger Nut munched his noon apple; and Bartleby remained standing at his window in one of his profoundest dead-wall reveries. Will it be credited? Ought I to acknowledge it? That afternoon I left the office without saying one further word to him.

Some days now passed, during which, at leisure intervals I looked a little into "Edwards[6] on the Will," and "Priestley[7] on Necessity." Under the circumstances, those books induced a salutary feeling. Gradually I slid into

---

[6]Jonathan Edwards, *Freedom of the Will* (1754). Edwards was an important American theologian, a rigidly orthodox Calvinist who believed in the doctrine of predestination and was a leader of the Great Awakening, the religious revival that swept the North American colonies in the 1740s.

[7]Joseph Priestley (1733–1803), English scientist and clergyman. Priestley began as a Unitarian but developed his own radical ideas on "natural determinism." As a scientist, he did early experiments with electricity and was one of the first to discover the existence of oxygen. As a political philosopher, he championed the French Revolution—a cause so unpopular in England that he had to flee that country and spend the last decade of his life in the United States.

the persuasion that these troubles of mine, touching the scrivener, had been all predestined from eternity, and Bartleby was billeted upon me for some mysterious purpose of an all-wise Providence, which it was not for a mere mortal like me to fathom. Yes, Bartleby, stay there behind your screen, thought I; I shall persecute you no more; you are harmless and noiseless as any of these old chairs; in short, I never feel so private as when I know you are here. At last I see it, I feel it; I penetrate to the predestined purpose of my life. I am content. Others may have loftier parts to enact; but my mission in this world, Bartleby, is to furnish you with office-room for such period as you may see fit to remain.

I believe that this wise and blessed frame of mind would have continued with me, had it not been for the unsolicited and uncharitable remarks obtruded upon me by my professional friends who visited the rooms. But thus it often is, that the constant friction of illiberal minds wears out at last the best resolves of the more generous. Though to be sure, when I reflected upon it, it was not strange that people entering my office should be struck by the peculiar aspect of the unaccountable Bartleby, and so be tempted to throw out some sinister observations concerning him. Sometimes an attorney, having business with me, and calling at my office, and finding no one but the scrivener there, would undertake to obtain some sort of precise information from him touching my whereabouts; but without heeding his idle talk, Bartleby would remain standing immovable in the middle of the room. So after contemplating him in that position for a time, the attorney would depart, no wiser than he came.

Also, when a reference was going on, and the room full of lawyers and witnesses, and business driving fast, some deeply-occupied legal gentleman present, seeing Bartleby wholly unemployed, would request him to run round to his (the legal gentleman's) office and fetch some papers for him. Thereupon, Bartleby would tranquilly decline, and yet remain idle as before. Then the lawyer would give a great stare, and turn to me. And what could I say? At last I was made aware that all through the circle of my professional acquaintance, a whisper of wonder was running round, having reference to the strange creature I kept at my office. This worried me very much. And as the idea came upon me of his possibly turning out a long-lived man, and keeping occupying my chambers, and denying my authority; and perplexing my visitors; and scandalizing my professional reputation; and casting a general gloom over the premises; keeping soul and body together to the last upon his savings (for doubtless he spent but half a dime a day), and in the end perhaps outlive me, and claim possession of my office by right of his perpetual occupancy: as all these dark anticipations crowded upon me more and more, and my friends continually intruded their relentless remarks upon the apparition in my room; a great change was wrought in me. I resolved to gather all my faculties together, and forever rid me of this intolerable incubus.

Ere revolving any complicated project, however, adapted to this end, I first simply suggested to Bartleby the propriety of his permanent departure.

In a calm and serious tone, I commended the idea to his careful and mature consideration. But, having taken three days to meditate upon it, he apprised me, that his original determination remained the same; in short, that he still preferred to abide with me.

What shall I do? I now said to myself, buttoning up my coat to the last button. What shall I do? what ought I to do? what does conscience say I *should* do with this man, or, rather, ghost. Rid myself of him, I must; go, he shall. But how? You will not thrust him, the poor, pale, passive mortal—you will not thrust such a helpless creature out of your door? you will not dishonor yourself by such cruelty? No, I will not, I cannot do that. Rather would I let him live and die here, and then mason up his remains in the wall. What, then, will you do? For all your coaxing, he will not budge. Bribes he leaves under your own paper-weight on your table; in short, it is quite plain that he prefers to cling to you.

Then something severe, something unusual must be done. What! surely you will not have him collared by a constable, and commit his innocent pallor to the common jail? And upon what ground could you procure such a thing to be done?—a vagrant, is he? What! he a vagrant, a wanderer, who refuses to budge? It is because he will not be a vagrant, then, that you seek to count him *as* a vagrant. That is too absurd. No visible means of support: there I have him. Wrong again: for indubitably he *does* support himself, and that is the only unanswerable proof that any man can show of his possessing the means so to do. No more, then. Since he will not quit me, I must quit him. I will change my offices; I will move elsewhere, and give him fair notice, that if I find him on my new premises I will then proceed against him as a common trespasser.

Acting accordingly, next day I thus addressed him: "I find these chambers too far from the City Hall; the air is unwholesome. In a word, I propose to remove my offices next week, and shall no longer require your services. I tell you this now, in order that you may seek another place."

He made no reply, and nothing more was said.

On the appointed day I engaged carts and men, proceeded to my chambers, and, having but little furniture, everything was removed in a few hours. Throughout, the scrivener remained standing behind the screen, which I directed to be removed the last thing. It was withdrawn; and, being folded up like a huge folio, left him the motionless occupant of a naked room. I stood in the entry watching him a moment, while something from within me upbraided me.

I re-entered, with my hand in my pocket—and—and my heart in my mouth.

"Good-bye, Bartleby; I am going—good-bye, and God some way bless you; and take that," slipping something in his hand. But it dropped upon the floor, and then—strange to say—I tore myself from him whom I had so longed to be rid of.

Established in my new quarters, for a day or two I kept the door locked, started at every footfall in the passages. When I returned to my rooms, after any little absence, I would pause at the threshold for an instant, and attentively listen, ere applying my key. But these fears were needless. Bartleby never came nigh me.

I thought all was going well, when a perturbed-looking stranger visited me, inquiring whether I was the person who had recently occupied rooms at No. — Wall Street.

Full of forebodings, I replied that I was.

"Then, sir," said the stranger, who proved a lawyer, "you are responsible for the man you left there. He refuses to do any copying; he refuses to do anything; he says he prefers not to; and he refuses to quit the premises."

"I am very sorry, sir," said I, with assumed tranquillity, but an inward tremor, "but, really, the man you allude to is nothing to me — he is no relation or apprentice of mine, that you should hold me responsible for him."

"In mercy's name, who is he?"

"I certainly cannot inform you. I know nothing about him. Formerly I employed him as a copyist; but he has done nothing for me now for some time past."

"I shall settle him, then — good morning, sir."

Several days passed, and I heard nothing more; and, though I often felt a charitable prompting to call at the place and see poor Bartleby, yet a certain squeamishness, of I know not what, withheld me.

All is over with him, by this time, thought I, at last, when, through another week, no further intelligence reached me. But, coming to my room the day after, I found several persons waiting at my door in a high state of nervous excitement.

"That's the man here — he comes," cried the foremost one, whom I recognized as the lawyer who had previously called upon me alone.

"You must take him away, sir, at once," cried a portly person among them, advancing upon me, and whom I knew to be the landlord of No. — Wall Street. "These gentlemen, my tenants, cannot stand it any longer; Mr. B——" pointing to the lawyer, "has turned him out of his room, and he now persists in haunting the building generally, sitting upon the banisters of the stairs by day, and sleeping in the entry by night. Everybody is concerned; clients are leaving the offices; some fears are entertained of a mob; something you must do, and that without delay."

Aghast at this torrent, I fell back before it, and would fain have locked myself in my new quarters. In vain I persisted that Bartleby was nothing to me — no more than to any one else. In vain — I was the last person known to have anything to do with him, and they held me to the terrible account. Fearful, then, of being exposed in the papers (as one person present obscurely threatened), I considered the matter, and, at length, said, that if the lawyer would give me a confidential interview with the scrivener, in his (the lawyer's) own room, I would, that afternoon, strive my best to rid them of the nuisance they complained of.

Going up stairs to my old haunt, there was Bartleby silently sitting upon the banister at the landing.

"What are you doing here, Bartleby?" said I.

"Sitting upon the banister," he mildly replied.

I motioned him into the lawyer's room, who then left us.

"Bartleby," said I, "are you aware that you are the cause of great tribulation to me, by persisting in occupying the entry after being dismissed from the office?"

No answer.

"Now one of two things must take place. Either you must do something, or something must be done to you. Now what sort of business would you like to engage in? Would you like to re-engage in copying for some one?"

"No; I would prefer not to make any change."

"Would you like a clerkship in a dry-goods store?"

"There is too much confinement about that. No, I would not like a clerkship; but I am not particular."

"Too much confinement," I cried, "why, you keep yourself confined all the time!"

"I would prefer not to take a clerkship," he rejoined, as if to settle that little item at once.

"How would a bar-tender's business suit you? There is no trying of the eye-sight in that."

"I would not like it at all; though, as I said before, I am not particular."

His unwonted wordiness inspirited me. I returned to the charge.

"Well, then, would you like to travel through the country collecting bills for the merchants? That would improve your health."

"No, I would prefer to be doing something else."

"How, then, would going as a companion to Europe, to entertain some young gentleman with your conversation—how would that suit you?"

"Not at all. It does not strike me that there is anything definite about that. I like to be stationary. But I am not particular."

"Stationary you shall be, then," I cried, now losing all patience, and, for the first time in all my exasperating connections with him, fairly flying into a passion. "If you do not go away from these premises before night, I shall feel bound—indeed, I *am* bound—to—to—to quit the premises myself!" I rather absurdly concluded, knowing not with what possible threat to try to frighten his immobility into compliance. Despairing of all further efforts, I was precipitately leaving him, when a final thought occurred to me—one which had not been wholly unindulged before.

"Bartleby," said I, in the kindest tone I could assume under such exciting circumstances, "will you go home with me now not to my office, but my dwelling—and remain there till we can conclude upon some convenient arrangement for you at our leisure? Come, let us start now, right away."

"No: at present I would prefer not to make any change at all."

I answered nothing; but, effectually dodging every one by the suddenness and rapidity of my flight, rushed from the building, ran up Wall

Street towards Broadway, and, jumping into the first omnibus, was soon removed from pursuit. As soon as tranquillity returned, I distinctly perceived that I had now done all that I possibly could, both in respect to the demands of the landlord and his tenants, and with regard to my own desire and sense of duty, to benefit Bartleby, and shield him from rude persecution. I now strove to be entirely care-free and quiescent; and my conscience justified me in the attempt; though, indeed, it was not so successful as I could have wished. So fearful was I of being again hunted out by the incensed landlord and his exasperated tenants, that, surrendering my business to Nippers, for a few days, I drove about the upper part of the town and through the suburbs, in my rockaway; crossed over to Jersey City and Hoboken, and paid fugitive visits to Manhattanville and Astoria. In fact, I almost lived in my rockaway for the time.

When again I entered my office, lo, a note from the landlord lay upon the desk. I opened it with trembling hands. It informed me that the writer had sent to the police, and had Bartleby removed to the Tombs as a vagrant. Moreover, since I knew more about him than any one else, he wished me to appear at that place, and make a suitable statement of the facts. These tidings had a conflicting effect upon me. At first I was indignant; but, at last, almost approved. The landlord's energetic, summary disposition, had led him to adopt a procedure which I do not think I would have decided upon myself; and yet, as a last resort, under such peculiar circumstances, it seemed the only plan.

As I afterwards learned, the poor scrivener, when told that he must be conducted to the Tombs, offered not the slightest obstacle, but, in his pale, unmoving way, silently acquiesced.

Some of the compassionate and curious by-standers joined the party; and headed by one of the constables arm-in-arm with Bartleby, the silent procession filed its way through all the noise, and heat, and joy of the roaring thoroughfares at noon.

The same day I received the note, I went to the Tombs, or, to speak more properly, the Halls of Justice. Seeking the right officer, I stated the purpose of my call, and was informed that the individual I described was, indeed, within. I then assured the functionary that Bartleby was a perfectly honest man, and greatly to be compassionated, however unaccountably eccentric. I narrated all I knew, and closed by suggesting the idea of letting him remain in as indulgent confinement as possible, till something less harsh might be done—though, indeed, I hardly knew what. At all events, if nothing else could be decided upon, the alms-house must receive him. I then begged to have an interview.

Being under no disgraceful charge, and quite serene and harmless in all his ways, they had permitted him freely to wander about the prison, and, especially, in the inclosed grass-platted yards thereof. And so I found him there, standing all alone in the quietest of the yards, his face towards a high wall, while all around, from the narrow slits of the jail windows, I thought I saw peering out upon him the eyes of murderers and thieves.

"Bartleby!"

"I know you," he said, without looking round—"and I want nothing to say to you."

"It was not I that brought you here, Bartleby," said I, keenly pained at his implied suspicion. "And to you, this should not be so vile a place. Nothing reproachful attaches to you by being here. And see, it is not so sad a place as one might think. Look, there is the sky, and here is the grass."

"I know where I am," he replied, but would say nothing more, and so I left him.

As I entered the corridor again, a broad meat-like man, in an apron, accosted me, and, jerking his thumb over my shoulder, said "Is that your friend?"

"Yes."

"Does he want to starve? If he does, let him live on the prison fare, that's all."

"Who are you?" asked I, not knowing what to make of such an unofficially speaking person in such a place.

"I am the grub-man. Such gentlemen as have friends here, hire me to provide them with something good to eat."

"Is this so?" said I, turning to the turnkey.

He said it was.

"Well, then," said I, slipping some silver into the grub-man's hands (for so they called him), "I want you to give particular attention to my friend there; let him have the best dinner you can get. And you must be as polite to him as possible."

"Introduce me, will you?" said the grub-man, looking at me with an expression which seemed to say he was all impatience for an opportunity to give a specimen of his breeding.

Thinking it would prove of benefit to the scrivener, I acquiesced; and, asking the grub-man his name, went up with him to Bartleby.

"Bartleby, this is a friend; you will find him very useful to you."

"Your sarvant, sir, your sarvant," said the grub-man, making a low salutation behind his apron. "Hope you find it pleasant here, sir; nice grounds—cool apartments—hope you'll stay with us some time—try to make it agreeable. What will you have for dinner to-day?"

"I prefer not to dine to-day," said Bartleby, turning away. "It would disagree with me; I am unused to dinners." So saying, he slowly moved to the other side of the inclosure, and took up a position fronting the dead-wall.

"How's this?" said the grub-man, addressing me with a stare of astonishment. "He's odd, ain't he?"

"I think he is a little deranged," said I, sadly.

"Deranged? deranged is it? Well, now, upon my word, I thought that friend of yourn was a gentleman forger; they are always pale and genteel-like, them forgers. I can't help pity 'em—can't help it, sir. Did you know

Monroe Edwards?" he added, touchingly, and paused. Then, laying his hand piteously on my shoulder, sighed, "he died of consumption at Sing-Sing. So you weren't acquainted with Monroe?"

"No, I was never socially acquainted with any forgers. But I cannot stop longer. Look to my friend yonder. You will not lose by it. I will see you again."

Some few days after this, I again obtained admission to the Tombs, and went through the corridors in quest of Bartleby; but without finding him.

"I saw him coming from his cell not long ago," said a turnkey, "may be he's gone to loiter in the yards."

So I went in that direction.

"Are you looking for the silent man?" said another turnkey, passing me. "Yonder he lies — sleeping in the yard there. 'Tis not twenty minutes since I saw him lie down."

The yard was entirely quiet. It was not accessible to the common prisoners. The surrounding walls, of amazing thickness, kept off all sounds behind them. The Egyptian character of the masonry weighed upon me with its gloom. But a soft imprisoned turf grew under foot. The heart of the eternal pyramids, it seemed, wherein, by some strange magic, through the clefts, grass-seed, dropped by birds, had sprung.

Strangely huddled at the base of the wall, his knees drawn up, and lying on his side, his head touching the cold stones, I saw the wasted Bartleby. But nothing stirred. I paused; then went close up to him; stooped over, and saw that his dim eyes were open; otherwise he seemed profoundly sleeping. Something prompted me to touch him. I felt his hand, when a tingling shiver ran up my arm and down my spine to my feet.

The round face of the grub-man peered upon me now. "His dinner is ready. Won't he dine to-day, either? Or does he live without dining?"

"Lives without dining," said I, and closed the eyes.

"Eh! — He's asleep, ain't he?"

"With kings and counselors,"[8] murmured I.

There would seem little need for proceeding further in this history. Imagination will readily supply the meagre recital of poor Bartleby's interment. But, ere parting with the reader, let me say, that if this little narrative has sufficiently interested him, to awaken curiosity as to who Bartleby was, and what manner of life he led prior to the present narrator's making his acquaintance, I can only reply, that in such curiosity I fully share, but am wholly unable to gratify it. Yet here I hardly know whether I should

---

[8]A reference to Job 3:14. Job, who has lost his family and all his property and been stricken by a terrible disease, wishes he had never been born: "Then had I been at rest with kings and counselors of the earth, which built desolate places for themselves."

divulge one little item of rumor, which came to my ear a few months after the scrivener's decease. Upon what basis it rested, I could never ascertain; and hence, how true it is I cannot now tell. But, inasmuch as this vague report has not been without a certain suggestive interest to me, however sad, it may prove the same with some others; and so I will briefly mention it. The report was this: that Bartleby had been a subordinate clerk in the Dead Letter Office at Washington, from which he had been suddenly removed by a change in the administration. When I think over this rumor, hardly can I express the emotions which seize me. Dead letters! does it not sound like dead men? Conceive a man by nature and misfortune prone to a pallid hopelessness, can any business seem more fitted to heighten it than that of continually handling these dead letters, and assorting them for the flames? For by the cart-load they are annually burned. Sometimes from out the folded paper the pale clerk takes a ring—the finger it was meant for, perhaps, moulders in the grave; a bank-note sent in swiftest charity—he whom it would relieve, nor eats nor hungers any more; pardon for those who died despairing; hope for those who died unhoping; good tidings for those who died stifled by unrelieved calamities. On errands of life, these letters speed to death.

Ah, Bartleby! Ah, humanity!   [1853]

FRANCES E. W. HARPER

Frances E. W. Harper (1825–1911), author of the first published short story by an African American, was born to free parents in Baltimore, Maryland. She was orphaned by the age of three and later described her feelings of desolation: "Have I yearned for a mother's love? The grave was my robber. Before three years had scattered their blight around my path, death had won my mother from me. Would a strong arm of a brother have been welcome? I was my mother's only child." Raised by her uncle, who founded the William Watkins Academy for free colored children, she was educated as a teacher but found herself unhappy trying to control a classroom of what she described as "fifty-three untrained little urchins." She quit her job as a teacher and began to support herself as a professional lecturer for the abolitionist cause, hired at first by the Maine Anti-Slavery Society. Greatly moved by Harriet Beecher Stowe's Uncle Tom's Cabin, *she published a volume of* Poems on Miscellaneous Subjects *in 1854 containing several classic antislavery poems such as "The Slave Auction" and "The Fugitive's Wife," which went into twenty printings in her lifetime.*

During Harper's long career at the lecture podium, she published many of her essays written for the New York City Anti-Slavery Society, the Pennsylvania Society for Promoting the Abolition of Slavery, and other temperance, civil rights, and world peace organizations. For more than half a century, she involved herself in radical protest demonstrations against racial discrimination and used her experiences in her writing. For example, in The Liberator *she described an act of civil disobedience when she refused to stand on the crowded platform of a Philadelphia streetcar in 1858, a time when blacks were legally prohibited from riding inside the cars. She insisted on remaining in her seat during the journey, and when the conductor would not accept her fare, she threw the money at his feet.*

Harper produced almost as many volumes of poetry and long fiction as she did essays and lectures, but she published few short stories. The first was "The Two Offers," in the September-October 1859 issue of The Anglo-African Magazine, *which advertised that it was "devoted to Literature, Science, Statistics, and the advancement of the cause of human freedom." In this work of short fiction, Harper argues that marriage is not the only option for intelligent women and that there are worse fates than becoming "an old maid." Ironically, "The Two Offers" appeared a year before she married Fenton Harper, who brought her to what she described as a "humble log house" in rural Ohio, where she lived for five years as a housewife and mother. In 1864, after the untimely death of her husband left her responsible for the support of her children, she resumed writing long fiction and returned to the lecture circuit. Nearly a quarter century later she experienced her greatest popular success as a novelist with* Iola Leroy; or, Shadows Uplifted *(1892).*

The Two Offers

"What is the matter with you, Laura, this morning? I have been watching you this hour, and in that time you have commenced a half dozen letters and torn them all up. What matter of such grave moment is puzzling your dear little head, that you do not know how to decide?"

"Well, it is an important matter: I have two offers for marriage, and I do not know which to choose."

"I should accept neither, or to say the least, not at present."

"Why not?"

"Because I think a woman who is undecided between two offers, has not love enough for either to make a choice; and in that very hesitation, indecision, she has a reason to pause and seriously reflect, lest her marriage, instead of being an affinity of souls or a union of hearts, should only be a mere matter of bargain and sale, or an affair of convenience and selfish interest."

"But I consider them both very good offers, just such as many a girl would gladly receive. But to tell you the truth, I do not think that I regard either as a woman should the man she chooses for her husband. But then if I refuse, there is the risk of being an old maid, and that is not to be thought of."

"Well, suppose there is, is that the most dreadful fate that can befall a woman? Is there not more intense wretchedness in an ill-assorted marriage —more utter loneliness in a loveless home, than in the lot of the old maid who accepts her earthly mission as a gift from God, and strives to walk the path of life with earnest and unfaltering steps?"

"Oh! what a little preacher you are. I really believe that you were cut out for an old maid; that when nature formed you, she put in a double portion of intellect to make up for a deficiency of love; and yet you are kind and affectionate. But I do not think that you know anything of the grand, over-mastering passion, or the deep necessity of woman's heart for loving."

"Do you think so?" resumed the first speaker; and bending over her work she quietly applied herself to the knitting that had lain neglected by her side, during this brief conversation; but as she did so, a shadow flitted over her pale and intellectual brow, a mist gathered in her eyes, and a slight quivering of the lips, revealed a depth of feeling to which her companion was a stranger.

But before I proceed with my story, let me give you a slight history of the speakers. They were cousins, who had met life under different auspices. Laura Lagrange, was the only daughter of rich and indulgent parents, who had spared no pains to make her an accomplished lady. Her cousin, Janette Alston, was the child of parents, rich only in goodness and affection. Her father had been unfortunate in business, and dying before he could retrieve his fortunes, left his business in an embarrassed state. His widow was unacquainted with his business affairs, and when the estate was settled, hungry creditors had brought their claims and the lawyers had received their fees, she found herself homeless and almost penniless, and she who had been sheltered in the warm clasp of loving arms, found them too powerless to shield her from the pitiless pelting storms of adversity. Year after year she struggled with poverty and wrestled with want, till her toil-worn hands became too feeble to hold the shattered chords of existence, and her tear-dimmed eyes grew heavy with the slumber of death. Her daughter had watched over her with untiring devotion, had closed her eyes in death, and gone out into the busy, restless world, missing a precious tone from the voices of earth, a beloved step from the paths of life. Too self reliant to depend on the charity of relations, she endeavored to support herself by her own exertions, and she had succeeded. Her path for a while was marked with struggle and trial, but instead of uselessly repining, she met them bravely, and her life became not a thing of ease and indulgence, but of conquest, victory, and accomplishments. At the time when this conversation took place, the deep trials of her life had passed away. The achievements of her genius had won her a position in the literary world, where she shone as one of its bright particular stars. And with her fame came a competence of worldly means, which gave her leisure for improvement, and the riper development of her rare talents. And she, that pale intellectual woman, whose genius gave life and vivacity to the social circle, and whose presence threw a halo of beauty and grace around the charmed atmosphere in which she moved, had at one period of her life, known the mystic and solemn strength of an all-absorbing love. Years faded into the misty past, had seen the kindling of her eye, the quick flushing of her cheek, and the wild throbbing of her heart, at tones of a voice long since hushed to the stillness of death. Deeply, wildly, passionately, she had loved. Her whole life seemed like the pouring out of rich, warm and gushing affections. This love quickened her talents, inspired her genius, and threw over her life a tender and spiritual earnestness. And then came a fearful shock, a mournful waking from that "dream of beauty and delight." A shadow fell around her path; it came between her and the object of her heart's worship; first a few cold words, estrangement, and then a painful separation; the old story of woman's pride — digging the sepulchre of her happiness, and then a new-made grave, and her path over it to the spirit world; and thus faded out from that young heart her bright, brief and saddened dream of life. Faint and spirit-broken, she turned from the scenes associated with the memory of the loved and lost. She tried to break the chain of sad associations that bound her to the mournful past; and so, pressing back the bitter sobs from her almost breaking heart, like the dying dolphin, whose beauty is born of its death anguish, her genius gathered strength from suffering and wonderous power and brilliancy from the agony she hid within the desolate chambers of her soul. Men hailed her as one of earth's strangely gifted children, and wreathed the garlands of fame for her brow, when it was throbbing with a wild and fearful unrest. They breathed her name with applause, when through the lonely halls of her stricken spirit, was an earnest cry for peace, a deep yearning for sympathy and heart-support.

But life, with its stern realities, met her; its solemn responsibilities confronted her, and turning, with an earnest and shattered spirit, to life's duties and trials, she found a calmness and strength that she had only imagined in her dreams of poetry and song. We will now pass over a period of ten years, and the cousins have met again. In that calm and lovely woman, in whose eyes is a depth of tenderness, tempering the flashes of her genius, whose looks and tones are full of sympathy and love, we recognize the once smitten and stricken Janette Alston. The bloom of her girlhood had given way to a higher type of spiritual beauty, as if some unseen hand had been polishing and refining the temple in which her lovely spirit found its habitation; and this had been the fact. Her inner life had grown beautiful, and it was this that was constantly developing the outer. Never, in the early flush of womanhood, when an absorbing love had lit up her eyes and glowed in her life, had she appeared so interesting as when, with a countenance which seemed overshadowed with a spiritual light, she bent over the death-bed of a young woman, just lingering at the shadowy gates of the unseen land.

"Has he come?" faintly but eagerly exclaimed the dying woman. "Oh! how I have longed for his coming, and even in death he forgets me."

"Oh, do not say so, dear Laura, some accident may have detained him," said Janette to her cousin; for on that bed, from whence she will never rise, lies the once-beautiful and light-hearted Laura Lagrange, the brightness of whose eyes has long since been dimmed with tears, and whose voice had become like a harp whose every chord is tuned to sadness—whose faintest thrill and loudest vibrations are but the variations of agony. A heavy hand was laid upon her once warm and bounding heart, and a voice came whispering through her soul, that she must die. But, to her, the tidings was a message of deliverance—a voice, hushing her wild sorrows to the calmness of resignation and hope. Life had grown so weary upon her head—the future looked so hopeless—she had no wish to tread again the track where thorns had pierced her feet, and clouds overcast her sky; and she hailed the coming of death's angel as the footsteps of a welcome friend. And yet, earth had one object so very dear to her weary heart. It was her absent and recreant husband; for, since that conversation, she had accepted one of her offers, and become a wife. But, before she married, she learned that great lesson of human experience and woman's life, to love the man who bowed at her shrine, a willing worshipper. He had a pleasing address, raven hair, flashing eyes, a voice of thrilling sweetness, and lips of persuasive eloquence; and being well versed in the ways of the world, he won his way to her heart, and she became his bride, and he was proud of his prize. Vain and superficial in his character, he looked upon marriage not as a divine sacrament for the soul's development and human progression, but as the title-deed that gave him possession of the woman he thought he loved. But alas for her, the laxity of his principles had rendered him unworthy of the deep and undying devotion of a pure-hearted woman; but, for awhile, he hid from her his true character, and she blindly loved him, and for a short period was happy in the conscious-ness of being beloved; though sometimes a vague unrest would fill her soul, when, overflowing with a sense of the good, the beautiful, and the true, she would turn to him, but find no response to the deep yearnings of her soul—no appreciation of life's highest realities—its solemn grandeur and significant importance. Their souls never met, and soon she found a void in her bosom, that his earth-born love could not fill. He did not sat-isfy the wants of her mental and moral nature—between him and her there was no affinity of minds, no intercommunion of souls.

Talk as you will of woman's deep capacity for loving, of the strength of her affectional nature. I do not deny it; but will the mere possession of any human love, fully satisfy all the demands of her whole being? You may paint her in poetry or fiction, as a frail vine, clinging to her brother man for support, and dying when deprived of it; and all this may sound well enough to please the imaginations of schoolgirls, or love-lorn maidens. But woman—the true woman—if you would render her happy, it needs more than the mere development of her affectional nature. Her con-science should be enlightened, her faith in the true and right established, and scope given to her Heaven-endowed and God-given faculties. The true aim of female education should be, not a development of one or two, but all the faculties of the human soul, because no perfect womanhood is developed by imperfect culture. Intense love is often akin to intense suf-fering, and to trust the whole wealth of a woman's nature on the frail bark of human love, may often be like trusting a cargo of gold and precious gems, to a bark that has never battled with the storm, or buffetted the waves. Is it any wonder, then, that so many life-barks go down, paving the ocean of time with precious hearts and wasted hopes? that so many float around us, shattered and dismasted wrecks? that so many are stranded on the shoals of existence, mournful beacons and solemn warnings for the thoughtless, to whom marriage is a careless and hasty rushing together of the affections? Alas that an institution so fraught with good for humanity should be so perverted, and that state of life, which should be filled with happiness, become so replete with misery. And this was the fate of Laura Lagrange. For a brief period after her marriage her life seemed like a bright and beautiful dream, full of hope and radiant with joy. And then there came a change—he found other attractions that lay beyond the pale of home influences. The gambling saloon had power to win him from her side, he had lived in an element of unhealthy and unhallowed excitements, and the society of a loving wife, the pleasures of a well-regulated home, were enjoyments too tame for one who had vitiated his tastes by the plea-sures of sin. There were charmed houses of vice, built upon dead men's loves, where, amid a flow of song, laughter, wine, and careless mirth, he would spend hour after hour, forgetting the cheek that was paling through his neglect, heedless of the tear-dimmed eyes, peering anxiously into the darkness, waiting, or watching his return.

The influence of old associations was upon him. In early life, home had been to him a place of ceilings and walls, not a true home, built upon goodness, love and truth. It was a place where velvet carpets hushed his tread, where images of loveliness and beauty invoked into being by painter's art and sculptor's skill, pleased the eye and gratified the taste, where magnificence surrounded his way and costly clothing adorned his person; but it was not the place for the true culture and right development of his soul. His father had been too much engrossed in making money, and his mother in spending it, in striving to maintain a fashionable position in society, and shining in the eyes of the world, to give the proper direction to the character of their wayward and impulsive son. His mother put beautiful robes upon his body, but left ugly scars upon his soul; she pampered his appetite, but starved his spirit. Every mother should be a true artist, who knows how to weave into her child's life images of grace and beauty, the true poet capable of writing on the soul of childhood the harmony of love and truth, and teaching it how to produce the grandest of all poems — the poetry of a true and noble life. But in his home, a love for the good, the true and right, had been sacrificed at the shrine of frivolity and fashion. That parental authority which should have been preserved as a string of precious pearls, unbroken and unscattered, was simply the administration of chance. At one time obedience was enforced by authority, at another time by flattery and promises, and just as often it was not enforced [at] all. His early associations were formed as chance directed, and from his want of home-training, his character received a bias, his life a shade, which ran through every avenue of his existence, and darkened all his future hours. Oh, if we would trace the history of all the crimes that have o'ershadowed this sin-shrouded and sorrow-darkened world of ours, how many might be seen arising from the wrong home influences, or the weakening of the home ties. Home should always be the best school for the affections, the birth-place of high resolves, and the altar upon which lofty aspirations are kindled, from whence the soul may go forth strengthened, to act its part aright in the great drama of life, with conscience enlightened, affections cultivated, and reason and judgment dominant. But alas for the young wife. Her husband had not been blessed with such a home. When he entered the arena of life, the voices from home did not linger around his path as angels of guidance about his steps; they were not like so many messages to invite him to deeds of high and holy worth. The memory of no sainted mother arose between him and deeds of darkness; the earnest prayers of no father arrested him in his downward course: and before a year of his married life had waned, his young wife had learned to wait and mourn his frequent and uncalled-for absence. More than once had she seen him come home from his midnight haunts, the bright intelligence of his eye displaced by the drunkard's stare, and his manly gait changed to the inebriate's stagger; and she was beginning to know the bitter agony that is compressed in the mournful words, a drunkard's wife. And then there came a bright but brief episode in her experience; the angel of life gave to her existence a deeper meaning and loftier significance: she sheltered in the warm clasp of her loving arms, a dear babe, a precious child, whose love filled every chamber of her heart, and felt the fount of maternal love gushing so new within her soul. That child was hers. How overshadowing was the love with which she bent over its helplessness, how much it helped to fill the void and chasms in her soul. How many lonely hours were beguiled by its winsome ways, its answering smiles and fond caresses. How exquisite and solemn was the feeling that thrilled her heart when she clasped the tiny hands together and taught her dear child to call God "Our Father."

What a blessing was that child. The father paused in his headlong career, awed by the strange beauty and precocious intellect of his child; and the mother's life had a better expression through her ministrations of love. And then there came hours of bitter anguish, shading the sunlight of her home and hushing the music of her heart. The angel of death bent over the couch of her child and beaconed it away. Closer and closer the mother strained her child to her wildly heaving breast, and struggled with the heavy hand that lay upon its heart. Love and agony contended with death, and the language of the mother's heart was,

> Oh, Death, away! that innocent is mine;
> I cannot spare him from my arms
> To lay him, Death, in thine.
> I am a mother, Death; I gave that darling birth
> I could not bear his lifeless limbs
> Should moulder in the earth.

But death was stronger than love and mightier than agony and won the child for the land of crystal founts and deathless flowers, and the poor, stricken mother sat down beneath the shadow of her mighty grief, feeling as if a great light had gone out from her soul, and that the sunshine had suddenly faded around her path. She turned in her deep anguish to the father of her child, the loved and cherished dead. For awhile his words were kind and tender, his heart seemed subdued, and his tenderness fell upon her worn and weary heart like rain on perishing flowers, or cooling waters to lips all parched with thirst and scorched with fever; but the change was evanescent, the influence of unhallowed associations and evil habits had vitiated and poisoned the springs of his existence. They had bound him in their meshes, and he lacked the moral strength to break his fetters, and stand erect in all the strength and dignity of a true manhood, making life's highest excellence his ideal, and striving to gain it.

And yet moments of deep contrition would sweep over him, when he would resolve to abandon the wine-cup forever, when he was ready to forswear the handling of another card, and he would try to break away from the associations that he felt were working his ruin; but when the hour of temptation came his strength was weakness, his earnest purposes were cobwebs, his well-meant resolutions ropes of sand, and thus passed year after year of the married life of Laura Lagrange. She tried to hide her agony from the public gaze, to smile when her heart was almost breaking. But year after year her voice grew fainter and sadder, her once light and bounding step grew slower and faltering. Year after year she wrestled with agony, and strove with despair, till the quick eyes of her brother read, in the paling of her cheek and the dimming eye, the secret anguish of her worn and weary spirit. On that wan, sad face, he saw the death-tokens, and he knew the dark wing of the mystic angel swept coldly around her path. "Laura," said her brother to her one day, "you are not well, and I think you need our mother's tender care and nursing. You are daily losing strength, and if you will go I will accompany you." At first, she hesitated, she shrank almost instinctively from presenting that pale sad face to the loved ones at home. That face was such a tell-tale; it told of heart-sickness, of hope deferred, and the mournful story of unrequited love. But then a deep yearning for home sympathy woke within her a passionate longing for love's kind words, for tenderness and heart-support, and she resolved to seek the home of her childhood, and lay her weary head upon her mother's bosom, to be folded again in her loving arms, to lay that poor, bruised and aching heart where it might beat and throb closely to the loved ones at home. A kind welcome awaited her. All that love and tenderness could devise was done to bring the bloom to her cheek and the light to her eye; but it was all in vain; hers was a disease that no medicine could cure, no earthly balm would heal. It was a slow wasting of the vital forces, the sickness of the soul. The unkindness and neglect of her husband, lay like a leaden weight upon her heart, and slowly oozed away its life-drops. And where was he that had won her love, and then cast it aside as a useless thing, who rifled her heart of its wealth and spread bitter ashes upon its broken altars? He was lingering away from her when the death-damps were gathering on her brow, when his name was trembling on her lips! lingering away! when she was watching his coming, though the death films were gathering before her eyes, and earthly things were fading from her vision. "I think I hear him now," said the dying woman, "surely that is his step;" but the sound died away in the distance. Again she started from an uneasy slumber, "that is his voice! I am so glad he has come." Tears gathered in the eyes of the sad watchers by that dying bed, for they knew that she was deceived. He had not returned. For her sake they wished his coming. Slowly the hours waned away, and then came the sad, soul-sickening thought that she was forgotten, forgotten in the last hour of human need, forgotten when the spirit, about to be dissolved, paused for the last time on the threshold of existence, a weary watcher at the gates of death. "He has forgotten me," again she faintly murmured, and the last tears she would ever shed on earth sprung to her mournful eyes, and clasping her hands together in silent anguish, a few broken sentences issued from her

pale and quivering lips. They were prayers for strength and earnest pleading for him who had desolated her young life, by turning its sunshine to
shadows, its smiles to tears. "He has forgotten me," she murmured again,
"but I can bear it, the bitterness of death is passed, and soon I hope to
exchange the shadows of death for the brightness of eternity, the rugged
paths of life for the golden streets of glory, and the care and turmoils of
earth for the peace and rest of heaven." Her voice grew fainter and fainter,
they saw the shadows that never deceive flit over her pale and faded face,
and knew that the death angel waited to soothe their weary one to rest, to
calm the throbbing of her bosom and cool the fever of her brain. And
amid the silent hush of their grief the freed spirit, refined through suffering, and brought into divine harmony through the spirit of the living
Christ, passed over the dark waters of death as on a bridge of light, over
whose radiant arches hovering angels bent. They parted the dark locks
from her marble brow, closed the waxen lids over the once bright and
laughing eye, and left her to the dreamless slumber of the grave. Her
cousin turned from that death-bed a sadder and wiser woman. She
resolved more earnestly than ever to make the world better by her example, gladden by her presence, and to kindle the fires of her genius on
the altars of universal love and truth. She had a higher and better object in
all her writings than the mere acquisition of gold, or acquirement of fame.
She felt that she had a high and holy mission on the battle-field of existence, that life was not given her to be frittered away in nonsense, or
wasted away in trifling pursuits. She would willingly espouse an unpopular
cause but not an unrighteous one. In her the down-trodden slave found an
earnest advocate; the flying fugitive remembered her kindness as he
stepped cautiously through our Republic, to gain his freedom in a monar-
chial land, having broken the chains on which the rust of centuries had
gathered. Little children learned to name her with affection, the poor
called her blessed, as she broke her bread to the pale lips of hunger. Her
life was like a beautiful story, only it was clothed with the dignity of reality
and invested with the sublimity of truth. True, she was an old maid, no
husband brightened her life with his love, or shaded it with his neglect. No
children nestling lovingly in her arms called her mother. No one appended
Mrs. to her name; she was indeed an old maid, not vainly striving to keep
up an appearance of girlishness, when departed was written on her youth.
Not vainly pining at her loneliness and isolation, the world was full of
warm, loving hearts and her own beat in unison with them. Neither was
she always sentimentally sighing for something to love, objects of affection
were all around her, and the world was not so wealthy in love that it had
no use for hers; in blessing others she made a life and benediction, and as
old age descended peacefully and gently upon her, she had learned one of
life's most precious lessons, that true happiness consists not so much in the
fruition of our wishes as in the regulation of desires and the full development and right culture of our whole natures.   [1859]

HARRIET PRESCOTT SPOFFORD

Harriet Prescott Spofford (1835–1921), a prolific author of short stories for The Atlantic Monthly, Harper's Bazaar, *and other periodicals for almost sixty years, began writing short fiction to support her parents and four younger brothers and sisters when she was in her early twenties. Born in Calais, Maine, she had six years of schooling before her father left for Oregon hoping to make his fortune. When he returned a penniless invalid in 1856, he was dependent on his family's efforts to earn money running a boardinghouse in Newburyport, Massachusetts. To supplement their meager income, Spofford began to place her earliest stories anonymously in Boston newspapers.*

Her career officially began when The Atlantic Monthly *published "In a Cellar" in its February 1859 issue. This was a melodramatic story about the recovery of a stolen diamond in Paris, and Spofford's descriptions of Europe were so vivid that James Russell Lowell, chief editor of the magazine, called in the eminent minister Thomas Wentworth Higginson to convince the other editors that "a demure little Yankee girl could have written it." With Higginson's encouragement, Spofford published "The Amber Gods" in the magazine in January and February of 1860. It presents a daring monologue by a woman recounting from beyond the grave the story of how she stole her cousin's fiancé. That same year Spofford also completed her first novel, a gothic romance titled* Sir Rohan's Ghost, *as well as "Circumstance," which appeared in the May 1860 issue of* The Atlantic Monthly. *Spofford based this story on an anecdote told in her family about one of her father's ancestors.*

"Circumstance" was so compelling that the poet Emily Dickinson told her brother's wife, Sue, that "it is the only thing I ever read in my life that I didn't think I could have imagined." In the story, musical images provide an ingenious if improbable narrative structure as the heroine saves her life by singing ballads and hymns throughout the night in order to divert an "Indian devil," a panther who trapped her in the forest close to home. It was included in The Amber Gods and Other Stories *(1863), the first of Spofford's several volumes of short fiction. In her productive lifetime she published more than thirty books of poetry, long fiction, essays, and plays as well as 275 short stories. Henry James praised the "united strength and brilliance of her descriptions" in Spofford's first collection; but the following year, in a review of her novel* Azarian *(1864), he castigated her for producing "a wearisome series of word-pictures linked by a slight thread of narrative" and urged her to learn from the new realist school of writers. Today Spofford is remembered for a few works of short fiction, including "Circumstance" and "Her Story," a forceful account of a woman driven to insanity by her marriage. "Her Story" appeared in* Lippincott's *magazine in 1872 and was a forerunner of Charlotte Perkins Gilman's "The Yellow Wallpaper."*

Circumstance

She had remained, during all that day, with a sick neighbor,—those eastern wilds of Maine in that epoch frequently making neighbors and miles synonymous,—and so busy had she been with care and sympathy that she did not at first observe the approaching night. But finally the level rays, reddening the snow, threw their gleam upon the wall, and, hastily donning cloak and hood, she bade her friends farewell and sallied forth on her return. Home lay some three miles distant, across a copse, a meadow, and a piece of woods,—the woods being a fringe on the skirts of the great forests that stretch far away into the North. That home was one of a dozen log-houses lying a few furlongs apart from each other, with their half-cleared demesnes[1] separating them at the rear from a wilderness untrodden save by stealthy native or deadly panther tribes.

She was in a nowise exalted frame of spirit,—on the contrary, rather depressed by the pain she had witnessed and the fatigue she had endured; but in certain temperaments such a condition throws open the mental pores, so to speak, and renders one receptive of every influence. Through the little copse she walked slowly, with her cloak folded about her, lingering to imbibe the sense of shelter, the sunset filtered in purple through the mist of woven spray and twig, the companionship of growth not sufficiently dense to band against her, the sweet homefeeling of a young and tender wintry wood. It was therefore just on the edge of the evening that she emerged from the place and began to cross the meadowland. At one hand lay the forest to which her path wound; at the other the evening star hung over a tide of failing orange that slowly slipped down the earth's broad side to sadden other hemispheres with sweet regret. Walking rapidly now, and with her eyes wide-open, she distinctly saw in the air before her what was not there a moment ago, a winding-sheet,—cold, white, and ghastly, waved by the likeness of four wan hands,—that rose with a long inflation, and fell in rigid folds, while a voice, shaping itself from the hollowness above, spectral and melancholy, sighed,—"The Lord have mercy on the people! The Lord have mercy on the people!" Three times the sheet with its corpse-covering outline waved beneath the pale hands, and the voice, awful in its solemn and mysterious depth, sighed, "The Lord have mercy on the people!" Then all was gone, the place was clear again, the gray sky was obstructed by no deathly blot; she looked about her, shook her shoulders decidedly, and, pulling on her hood, went forward once more.

She might have been a little frightened by such an apparition, if she had led a life of less reality than frontier settlers are apt to lead; but dealing with hard fact does not engender a flimsy habit of mind, and this woman

---

[1]Acreage surrounding a household.

was too sincere and earnest in her character, and too happy in her situation, to be thrown by antagonism, merely, upon superstitious fancies and chimeras of the second-sight. She did not even believe herself subject to an hallucination, but smiled simply, a little vexed that her thought could have framed such a glamour from the day's occurrences, and not sorry to lift the bough of the warder of the woods and enter and disappear in their sombre path. If she had been imaginative, she would have hesitated at her first step into a region whose dangers were not visionary; but I suppose that the thought of a little child at home would conquer that propensity in the most habituated. So, biting a bit of spicy birch, she went along. Now and then she came to a gap where the trees had been partially felled, and here she found that the lingering twilight was explained by that peculiar and perhaps electric film which sometimes sheathes the sky in diffused light for many hours before a brilliant aurora. Suddenly, a swift shadow, like the fabulous flying-dragon, writhed through the air before her, and she felt herself instantly seized and borne aloft. It was that wild beast — the most savage and serpentine and subtle and fearless of our latitudes — known by hunters as the Indian Devil, and he held her in his clutches on the broad floor of a swinging fir-bough. His long sharp claws were caught in her clothing, he worried them sagaciously a little, then, finding that ineffectual to free them, he commenced licking her bare arm with his rasping tongue and pouring over her the wide streams of his hot, foetid breath. So quick had this flashing action been that the woman had had no time for alarm; moreover, she was not of the screaming kind: but now, as she felt him endeavoring to disentangle his claws, and the horrid sense of her fate smote her, and she saw instinctively the fierce plunge of those weapons, the long strips of living flesh torn from her bones, the agony, the quivering disgust, itself a worse agony, — while by her side, and holding her in his great lithe embrace, the monster crouched, his white tusks whetting and gnashing, his eyes glaring through all the darkness like balls of red fire, — a shriek, that rang in every forest hollow, that startled every winter-housed thing, that stirred and woke the least needle of the tasselled pines, tore through her lips. A moment afterward, the beast left the arm, once white, now crimson, and looked up alertly.

She did not think at this instant to call upon God. She called upon her husband. It seemed to her that she had but one friend in the world; that was he; and again the cry, loud, clear, prolonged, echoed through the woods. It was not the shriek that disturbed the creature at his relish; he was not born in the woods to be scared of an owl, you know; what then? It must have been the echo, most musical, most resonant, repeated and yet repeated, dying with long sighs of sweet sound, vibrated from rock to river and back again from depth to depth of cave and cliff. Her thought flew after it; she knew, that, even if her husband heard it, he yet could not reach her in time; she saw that while the beast listened he would not gnaw, — and this she *felt* directly, when the rough, sharp, and multiplied stings of his tongue retouched her arm. Again her lips opened by instinct, but the sound that issued thence came by reason. She had heard that music charmed wild beasts,—just this point between life and death intensified every faculty,— and when she opened her lips the third time, it was not for shrieking, but for singing.

A little thread of melody stole out, a rill of tremulous motion; it was the cradle-song with which she rocked her baby;—how could she sing that? And then she remembered the baby sleeping rosily on the long settee before the fire,—the father cleaning his gun, with one foot on the green wooden rundle,—the merry light from the chimney dancing out and through the room, on the rafters of the ceiling with their tassels of onions and herbs, on the log walls painted with lichens and festooned with apples, on the king's-arm slung across the shelf with the old pirate's-cutlass, on the snow-pile of the bed, and on the great brass clock,—dancing, too, and lingering on the baby, with his fringed-gentian eyes, his chubby fists clenched on the pillow, and his fine breezy hair fanning with the motion of his father's foot. All this struck her in one, and made a sob of her breath, and she ceased.

Immediately the long red tongue thrust forth again. Before it touched, a song sprang to her lips, a wild sea-song, such as some sailor might be singing far out on trackless blue water that night, the shrouds whistling with frost and the sheets glued in ice,—a song with the wind in its burden and the spray in its chorus. The monster raised his head and flared the fiery eyeballs upon her, then fretted the imprisoned claws a moment and was quiet; only the breath like the vapor from some hell-pit still swathed her. Her voice, at first faint and fearful, gradually lost its quaver, grew under her control and subject to her modulation; it rose on long swells, it fell in subtile cadences, now and then its tones pealed out like bells from distant belfries on fresh sonorous mornings. She sung the song through, and, wondering lest his name of Indian Devil were not his true name, and if he would not detect her, she repeated it. Once or twice now, indeed, the beast stirred uneasily, turned, and made the bough sway at his movement. As she ended, he snapped his jaws together, and tore away the fettered member, curling it under him with a snarl,—when she burst into the gayest reel that ever answered a fiddle-bow. How many a time she had heard her husband play it on the homely fiddle made by himself from birch and cherrywood! how many a time she had seen it danced on the floor of their one room, to the patter of wooden clogs and the rustle of homespun petticoat! how many a time she had danced it herself!—and did she not remember once, as they joined clasps for eight-hands-round, how it had lent its gay, bright measure to her life? And here she was singing it alone, in the forest, at midnight, to a wild beast! As she sent her voice trilling up and down its quick oscillations between joy and pain, the creature who grasped her uncurled his paw and scratched the bark from the bough; she must vary the spell; and her voice spun leaping along the projecting points of tune of a hornpipe. Still singing, she felt herself twisted about with a low growl and a lifting of the red lip from the glittering teeth; she broke the hornpipe's thread, and commenced unravelling a lighter, livelier thing, an Irish jig. Up and down and round about her voice flew, the beast threw back his head so that the diabolical face fronted hers, and the torrent of his breath prepared her for his feast as the anaconda slimes his prey. Franticly she darted from tune to tune; his restless movements followed her. She tired herself with dancing and vivid national airs, growing feverish and singing spasmodically as she felt her horrid tomb yawning wider. Touching in this manner all the slogan and keen clan cries, the beast moved again, but only to lay the disengaged paw across her with heavy satisfaction. She did not dare to pause; through the clear cold air, the frosty starlight, she sang. If there were yet any tremor in the tone, it was not fear,—she had learned the secret of sound at last; nor could it be chill,—far too high a fever throbbed her pulses; it was nothing but the thought of the log-house and of what might be passing within it. She fancied the baby stirring in his sleep and moving his pretty lips,—her husband rising and opening the door, looking out after her, and wondering at her absence. She fancied the light pouring through the chink and then shut in again with all the safety and comfort and joy, her husband taking down the fiddle and playing lightly with his head inclined, playing while she sang, while she sang for her life to an Indian Devil. Then she knew he was fumbling for and finding some shining fragment and scoring it down the yellowing-hair, and unconsciously her voice forsook the wild wartunes and drifted into the half-gay, half-melancholy "Rosin the Bow."

Suddenly she woke pierced with a pang, and the daggered tooth penetrating her flesh;—dreaming of safety, she had ceased singing and lost it. The beast had regained the use of all his limbs, and now, standing and raising his back, bristling and foaming, with sounds that would have been like hisses but for their deep and fearful sonority, he withdrew step by step toward the trunk of the tree, still with his flaming balls upon her. She was all at once free, on one end of the bough, twenty feet from the ground. She did not measure the distance, but rose to drop herself down, careless of any death, so that it were not this. Instantly, as if he scanned her thoughts, the creature bounded forward with a yell and caught her again in his dreadful hold. It might be that he was not greatly famished; for, as she suddenly flung up her voice again, he settled himself composedly on the bough, still clasping her with invincible pressure to his rough, ravenous breast, and listening in a fascination to the sad, strange U-la-lu that now moaned forth in loud, hollow tones above him. He half closed his eyes, and sleepily reopened and shut them again.

What rending pains were close at hand! Death! and what a death! worse than any other that is to be named! Water, be it cold or warm, that which buoys up blue icefields, or which bathes tropical coasts with currents of balmy bliss, is yet a gentle conqueror, kisses as it kills, and draws you down gently through darkening fathoms to its heart. Death at the sword is the festival of trumpet and bugle and banner, with glory ringing out around you and distant hearts thrilling through yours. No gnawing disease can bring such hideous end as this; for that is a fiend bred of your own flesh, and this—is it a fiend, this living lump of appetites? What dread comes with the thought of perishing in flames! but fire, let it leap and hiss never so hotly, is something too remote, too alien, to inspire us with such loathly horror as a wild beast; if it have a life, that life is too utterly beyond our comprehension. Fire is not half ourselves; as it devours, arouses neither hatred nor disgust; is not to be known by the strength of our lower natures let loose; does not drip our blood into our faces with foaming chaps, nor mouth nor slaver above us with vitality. Let us be ended by fire, and we are ashes, for the winds to bear, the leaves to cover; let us be ended by wild beasts, and the base, cursed thing howls with us forever through the forest. All this she felt as she charmed him, and what force it lent to her song God knows. If her voice should fail! If the damp and cold should give her any fatal hoarseness! If all the silent powers of the forest did not conspire to help her! The dark, hollow night rose indifferently over her; the wide, cold air breathed rudely past her, lifted her wet hair and blew it down again; the great boughs swung with a ponderous strength, now and then clashed their iron lengths together and shook off a sparkle of icy spears or some long-lain weight of snow from their heavy shadows. The green depths were utterly cold and silent and stern. These beautiful haunts that all the summer were hers and rejoiced to share with her their bounty, these heavens that had yielded their largess, these stems that had thrust their blossoms into her hands, all these friends of three moons ago forgot her now and knew her no longer.

Feeling her desolation, wild, melancholy, forsaken songs rose thereon from that frightful aerie,—weeping, wailing tunes, that sob among the people from age to age, and overflow with otherwise unexpressed sadness,—all rude, mournful ballads,—old tearful strains, that Shakespeare heard the vagrants sing, and that rise and fall like the wind and tide,—sailor-songs, to be heard only in lone mid-watches beneath the moon and stars,—ghastly rhyming romances, such as that famous one of the Lady Margaret, when

> She slipped on her gown of green
>   A piece below the knee,–
> And 't was all a long cold winter's night
>   A dead corse followed she.[2]

Still the beast lay with closed eyes, yet never relaxing his grasp. Once a half-whine of enjoyment escaped him,—he fawned his fearful head upon her; once he scored her cheek with his tongue—savage caresses that hurt like wounds. How weary she was! and yet how terribly awake! How fuller

---

[2]From "Sweet William's Ghost" (variation "Lady Margaret"), an old ballad collected in *The English and Scottish Popular Ballads* (1882–98) by Francis James Childs.

and fuller of dismay grew the knowledge that she was only prolonging her anguish and playing with death! How appalling the thought that with her voice ceased her existence! Yet she could not sing forever; her throat was dry and hard; her very breath was a pain; her mouth was hotter than any desert-worn pilgrim's;—if she could but drop upon her burning tongue one atom of the ice that glittered about her!—but both of her arms were pinioned in the giant's vice. She remembered the winding-sheet, and for the first time in her life shivered with spiritual fear. Was it hers? She asked herself, as she sang, what sins she had committed, what life she had led, to find her punishment so soon and in these pangs,—and then she sought eagerly for some reason why her husband was not up and abroad to find her. He failed her,—her one sole hope in life; and without being aware of it, her voice forsook the songs of suffering and sorrow for old Covenanting hymns,—hymns with which her mother had lulled her, which the class-leader pitched in the chimney-corners,—grand and sweet Methodist hymns, brimming with melody and with all fantastic involutions of tune to suit that ecstatic worship,—hymns full of the beauty of holiness, steadfast, relying, sanctified by the salvation they had lent to those in worse extremity than hers,—for they had found themselves in the grasp of hell, while she was but in the jaws of death. Out of this strange music, peculiar to one character of faith, and than which there is none more beautiful in its degree nor owning a more potent sway of sound, her voice soared into the glorified chants of churches. What to her was death by cold or famine or wild beasts? "Though He slay me, yet will I trust in him," she sang. High and clear through the frore fair night, the level moonbeams splintering in the wood, the scarce glints of stars in the shadowy roof of branches, these sacred anthems rose,—rose as a hope from despair, as some snowy spray of flower-bells from blackest mould. Was she not in God's hands? Did not the world swing at his will? If this were in his great plan of providence, was it not best, and should she not accept it?

"He is the Lord our God; his judgments are in all the earth."

Oh, sublime faith of our fathers, where utter self-sacrifice alone was true love, the fragrance of whose unrequired subjection was pleasanter than that of golden censers swung in purple-vapored chancels!

Never ceasing in the rhythm of her thoughts, articulated in music as they thronged, the memory of her first communion flashed over her. Again she was in that distant place on that sweet spring morning. Again the congregation rustled out, and the few remained, and she trembled to find herself among them. How well she remembered the devout, quiet faces, too accustomed to the sacred feast to glow with their inner joy! how well the snowy linen at the altar, the silver vessels slowly and silently shifting! and as the cup approached and passed, how the sense of delicious perfume stole in and heightened the transport of her prayer, and she had seemed, looking up through the windows where the sky soared blue in constant freshness, to feel all heaven's balms dripping from the portals, and to scent the lilies of eternal peace! Perhaps another would not have felt so much ecstasy as satisfaction on that occasion; but it is a true, if a later disciple, who has said, "The Lord bestoweth his blessings there, where he findeth the vessels empty."

"And does it need the walls of a church to renew my communion?" she asked. "Does not every moment stand a temple four-square to God? And in that morning, with its buoyant sunlight, was I any dearer to the Heart of the World than now? — 'My beloved is mine, and I am his,'" she sang over and over again, with all varied inflection and profuse tune. How gently all the winter-wrapt things bent toward her then! into what relation with her had they grown! how this common dependence was the spell of their intimacy! how at one with Nature had she become! how all the night and the silence and the forest seemed to hold its breath, and to send its soul up to God in her singing! It was no longer despondency, that singing. It was neither prayer nor petition. She had left imploring, "How long wilt thou forget me, O Lord? Lighten mine eyes, lest I sleep the sleep of death! For in death there is no remembrance of thee," — with countless other such fragments of supplication. She cried rather, "Yea, though I walk through the valley of the shadow of death, I will fear no evil: for thou art with me; thy rod and thy staff, they comfort me," — and lingered, and repeated, and sang again, "I shall be satisfied, when I awake, with thy likeness."

Then she thought of the Great Deliverance, when he drew her up out of many waters, and the flashing old psalm pealed forth triumphantly:

> The Lord descended from above,
>   and bow'd the heavens hie:
> And underneath his feet he cast
>   the darknesse of the skie.
> On cherubs and on cherubins
>   full royally he road:
> And on the wings of all the winds
>   came flying all abroad.

She forgot how recently, and with what a strange pity for her own shapeless form that was to be, she had quaintly sung, —

> O lovely appearance of death!
>   What sight upon earth is so fair?
> Not all the gay pageants that breathe,
>   Can with a dead body compare!

She remembered instead, — "In thy presence is fulness of joy; at thy right hand there are pleasures forevermore. God will redeem my soul from the power of the grave: for he shall receive me. He will swallow up death in victory." Not once now did she say, "Lord, how long wilt thou look on; rescue my soul from their destructions, my darling from the lions," — for she knew that the young lions roar after their prey and seek their meat from God. "O Lord, thou preservest man and beast!" she said.

She had no comfort or consolation in this season, such as sustained the Christian martyrs in the amphitheatre. She was not dying for her faith;

there were no palms in heaven for her to wave; but how many a time had she declared,—"I had rather be a doorkeeper in the house of my God, than to dwell in the tents of wickedness!" And as the broad rays here and there broke through the dense covert of shade and lay in rivers of lustre on crystal sheathing and frozen fretting of trunk and limb and on the great spaces of refraction, they builded up visibly that house, the shining city on the hill, and singing, "Beautiful for situation, the joy of the whole earth, is Mount Zion, on the sides of the North, the city of the Great King," her vision climbed to that higher picture where the angel shows the dazzling thing, the holy Jerusalem descending out of heaven from God, with its splendid battlements and gates of pearls, and its foundations, the eleventh a jacinth, the twelfth an amethyst,—with its great white throne, and the rainbow round about it, in sight like unto an emerald: "And there shall be no night there,—for the Lord God giveth them light," she sang.

What whisper of dawn now rustled through the wilderness? How the night was passing? And still the beast crouched upon the bough, changing only the posture of his head, that again he might command her with those charmed eyes;—half their fire was gone; she could almost have released herself from his custody; yet, had she stirred, no one knows what malevolent instinct might have dominated anew. But of that she did not dream; long ago stripped of any expectation, she was experiencing in her divine rapture how mystically true it is that "he that dwelleth in the secret place of the Most High shall abide under the shadow of the Almighty."

Slow clarion cries now wound from the distance as the cocks caught the intelligence of day and re-echoed it faintly from farm to farm,—sleepy sentinels of night, sounding the foe's invasion, and translating that dim intuition to ringing notes of warning. Still she chanted on. A remote crash of brushwood told of some other beast on his depredations, or some night-belated traveller groping his way through the narrow path. Still she chanted on. The far, faint echoes of the chanticleers died into distance, the crashing of the branches grew nearer. No wild beast that, but a man's step,—a man's form in the moonlight, stalwart and strong,—on one arm slept a little child, in the other hand he held his gun. Still she chanted on.

Perhaps, when her husband last looked forth, he was half ashamed to find what a fear he felt for her. He knew she would never leave the child so long but for some direst need,—and yet he may have laughed at himself, as he lifted and wrapped it with awkward care, and, loading his gun and strapping on his horn, opened the door again and closed it behind him, going out and plunging into the darkness and dangers of the forest. He was more singularly alarmed than he would have been willing to acknowledge; as he had sat with his bow hovering over the strings, he had half believed to hear her voice mingling gayly with the instrument, till he paused and listened if she were not about to lift the latch and enter. As he drew nearer the heart of the forest, that intimation of melody seemed to grow more actual, to take body and breath, to come and go on long swells and ebbs of the night-breeze, to increase with tune and words, till a strange shrill singing grew ever clearer, and, as he stepped into an open space of moonbeams, far up in the branches, rocked by the wind, and singing, "How beautiful upon the mountains are the feet of him that bringeth good tidings, that publisheth peace," he saw his wife,—his wife,—but, great God in heaven! how? Some mad exclamation escaped him, but without diverting her. The child knew the singing voice, though never heard before in that unearthly key, and turned toward it through the veiling dreams. With a celerity almost instantaneous, it lay, in the twinkling of an eye, on the ground at the father's feet, while his gun was raised to his shoulder and levelled at the monster covering his wife with shaggy form and flaming gaze,—his wife so ghastly white, so rigid, so stained with blood, her eyes so fixedly bent above, and her lips, that had indurated into the chiselled pallor of marble, parted only with that flood of solemn song.

I do not know if it were the mother-instinct that for a moment lowered her eyes,—those eyes, so lately riveted on heaven, now suddenly seeing a life-long bliss possible. A thrill of joy pierced and shivered through her like a weapon, her voice trembled in its course, her glance lost its steady strength, fever-flushes chased each other over her face, yet she never once ceased chanting. She was quite aware, that, if her husband shot now, the ball must pierce her body before reaching any vital part of the beast,— and yet better that death, by his hand, than the other. But this her husband also knew, and he remained motionless, just covering the creature with the sight. He dared not fire, lest some wound not mortal should break the spell exercised by her voice, and the beast, enraged with pain, should rend her in atoms; moreover, the light was too uncertain for his aim. So he waited. Now and then he examined his gun to see if the damp were injuring its charge, now and then he wiped the great drops from his forehead. Again the cocks crowed with the passing hour,—the last time they were heard on that night. Cheerful home sound then, how full of safety and all comfort and rest it seemed! what sweet morning incidents of sparkling fire and sunshine, of gay household bustle, shining dresser, and cooing baby, of steaming cattle in the yard, and brimming milk-pails at the door! what pleasant voices! what laughter! what security! and here—

Now, as she sang on in the slow, endless, infinite moments, the fervent vision of God's peace was gone. Just as the grave had lost its sting, she was snatched back again to the arms of earthly hope. In vain she tried to sing, "There remaineth a rest for the people of God,"—her eyes trembled on her husband's, and she could only think of him, and of the child, and of happiness that yet might be, but with what a dreadful gulf of doubt between! She shuddered now in the suspense; all calm forsook her; she was tortured with dissolving heats or frozen with icy blasts; her face contracted, growing small and pinched; her voice was hoarse and sharp,—every tone cut like a knife,—the notes became heavy to lift,—withheld by some hostile pressure,—impossible. One gasp, a convulsive effort, and there was silence,—she had lost her voice.

The beast made a sluggish movement,—stretched and fawned like one awaking,—then, as if he would have yet more of the enchantment, stirred her slightly with his muzzle. As he did so, a sidelong hint of the man standing below with the raised gun smote him; he sprung round furiously, and, seizing his prey, was about to leap into some unknown airy den of the topmost branches now waving to the slow dawn. The late moon had rounded through the sky so that her gleam at last fell full upon the bough with fairy frosting; the wintry morning light did not yet penetrate the gloom. The woman, suspended in mid-air an instant, cast only one agonized glance beneath,—but across and through it, ere the lids could fall, shot a withering sheet of flame,—a rifle-crack, half-heard, was lost in the terrible yell of desperation that bounded after it and filled her ears with savage echoes, and in the wide arc of some eternal descent she was falling;—but the beast fell under her.

I think that the moment following must have been too sacred for us, and perhaps the three have no special interest again till they issue from the shadows of the wilderness upon the white hills that skirt their home. The father carries the child hushed again into slumber, the mother follows with no such feeble step as might be anticipated. It is not time for reaction,—the tension not yet relaxed, the nerves still vibrant, she seems to herself like some one newly made; the night was a dream; the present stamped upon her in deep satisfaction, neither weighed nor compared with the past; if she has the careful tricks of former habit, it is as an automaton; and as they slowly climb the steep under the clear gray vault and the paling morning star, and as she stops to gather a spray of the red-rose berries or a feathery tuft of dead grasses for the chimney-piece of the log-house, or a handful of brown cones for the child's play,—of these quiet, happy folk you would scarcely dream how lately they had stolen from under the banner and encampment of the great King Death. The husband proceeds a step or two in advance; the wife lingers over a singular foot-print in the snow, stoops and examines it, then looks up with a hurried word. Her husband stands alone on the hill, his arms folded across the babe, his gun fallen,—stands defined as a silhouette against the pallid sky. What is there in their home, lying below and yellowing in the light, to fix him with such a stare? She springs to his side. There is no home there. The log-house, the barns, the neighboring farms, the fences, are all blotted out and mingled in one smoking ruin. Desolation and death were indeed there, and beneficence and life in the forest. Tomahawk and scalping-knife, descending during that night, had left behind them only this work of their accomplished hatred and one subtle foot-print in the snow.

For the rest,—the world was all before them, where to choose.[3]

[1860]

------

[3]Allusion to the concluding lines of Milton's *Paradise Lost* describing the exodus of Adam and Eve from the Garden of Eden.

2

LATE
NINETEENTH
CENTURY

1861–1899

*I*n October 1861, *The Atlantic Monthly* featured a story by Rebecca Harding Davis in which she defined the new direction for American short fiction that she had taken six months earlier in her first *Atlantic* story, "Life in the Iron-Mills, or The Korl Woman."

> My own story is very crude and homely,—only a rough sketch of one or two of those people whom you see every day, and call "dregs" sometimes—a dull bit of prose, such as you might pick for yourself out of any of these warehouses or back streets. . . . You want something, in fact, to lift you out of this crowded, tobacco-stained commonplace, to kindle and chafe and glow in you. I want you to dig into this commonplace, this vulgar American life, and see what is in it. Sometimes I think it has a new and awful significance that we do not see.

"Life in the Iron-Mills, or The Korl Woman" had appeared in *The Atlantic* in April 1861, the month the Confederate army fired on Fort Sumter and started the Civil War. In Davis's story the plight of the victims of industrial exploitation laboring in the western Virginia iron mills was described in such harrowing detail that for many readers the workers' tragedy seemed to prefigure the horrors of warfare between the North and South that would continue for four bloody years.

Realism in American short fiction had never approached the ruthless account of human misery that appeared in the pages of "Life in the Iron-Mills." The story was a landmark depiction of "this commonplace, this vulgar American life." It signaled the end of the earlier era of fantastic, romantic tales in the American magazines exemplified by the extravaganzas of Poe and the enigmas of Hawthorne and Melville. In his preface to his 1861 novel *The Marble Faun*, which he set in Italy, Hawthorne acknowledged his difficulty in continuing to produce allegorical fiction about America:

> No author, without a trial, can conceive of the difficulty of writing a romance about a country where there is no shadow, no antiquity, no

mystery, no picturesque and gloomy wrong, nor anything but a commonplace prosperity, in broad and simple daylight, as is happily the
case with my dear native land.

Hawthorne had lived abroad for years and believed that "romance and
poetry, ivy, lichens, and wallflowers, need ruin to make them grow." He was
also writing before the heavy casualties of the Civil War. More than six hundred thousand Americans died in the fight to preserve the Union and end
slavery. The unprecedented toll of human lives lost on the battlefields at
Antietam, at Gettysburg, and in the Virginia campaigns dominated the consciousness of many younger writers of short fiction. They turned from the
romantic to the realistic mode in order to convey a sense of the war's devastating effect. The war was such a traumatic event in American life that
most of the memorable stories about it were written years after it was over.

In "Rodman the Keeper" (1877), Constance Fenimore Woolson
described the grim aftermath of the war, when the hatred between Northerners and Southerners could not be easily assuaged. Ambrose Bierce dramatized the unbearable psychological ordeal of active combat in "One of
the Missing" (1886). Hamlin Garland wrote about the heavy emotional
and economic toll of the war on a midwestern farm family in "The Return
of a Private" (1890). Stephen Crane created perhaps the most brilliant fiction about the conflict in his novel *The Red Badge of Courage* (1895) after
reading illustrated articles about the war in old issues of *Century Magazine*. He went on to imagine memorable war stories and to create short
fiction about many other subjects, including the settling of the western
United States.

In retrospect, young authors such as Bret Harte believed that the
hardships of the Civil War opened up new possibilities for literature. In
"The Rise of the 'Short Story'" (1899), Harte asserted:

> Many cultivated aspirants for literature, as well as many seasoned
> writers for the press, were among the volunteer soldiery. Again, the
> composition of the army was heterogeneous: regiments from the
> West rubbed shoulders with regiments from the East; spruce city
> clerks hobnobbed with backwoodsmen, and the student fresh from
> college shared his rations with the half-educated western farmer. The
> Union, for the first time, recognized its component parts; the natives
> knew each other. . . . Yet it is a mortifying proof of the strength of
> inherited literary traditions, that [a writer] never dared till quite
> recently to make a test of them. It is still more strange that he should
> have waited for the initiative to be taken by a still more crude, wild,
> and more western civilisation — that of California!

Harte also credited the humorous tall tales developed in the oral tradition on the western frontier in the early nineteenth century with having
influenced him and other California short story authors after the Civil War.
These comic anecdotes were "common in the barrooms, the gatherings in

the country store, and finally at public meetings in the mouths of 'stump orators.'" They were so distinctive that they were immediately appreciated as original American stories because of their novelty. As Harte realized, the tall tale as published in newspapers and almanacs voiced

> not only the dialect, but the habits of thought of a people or locality. It gave a new interest to slang. From a paragraph of a dozen lines it grew into a half column, but always retaining its conciseness and felicity of statement. It was a foe to prolixity of any kind, it admitted no fine writing nor affectation of style. It was burdened by no conscientiousness; it was often irreverent; it was devoid of all moral responsibility—but it was original!

In the aftermath of the Civil War, realism became the dominant mode chosen by writers of short fiction. Rebecca Harding Davis's pioneering story had envisioned the brutal exploitation of factory workers as a result of the growing industrialization in the northern cities, but during the late nineteenth century the majority of American stories still reflected a predominantly agrarian society. This was to change after World War I; between 1870 and 1920 a quarter of the population of the United States would leave their farms to live in towns and cities.

The harsh depiction of the misery of Welsh immigrant workers casting rails for the railroads in "Life in the Iron-Mills" reflected the growth of immigration to the United States in the years before the Civil War, which was only to increase by huge numbers at the end of the century. Between 1880 and 1914 more than twenty million immigrants arrived in the United States, mostly from Ireland, Italy, Sweden, Norway, Poland, Russia, and China. The majority flocked to industrialized cities on the eastern seaboard, but many settled in towns and farms in the Midwest.

In 1891 the United States Census Bureau declared that the frontier had ceased to exist. Two years later, when the historian Frederick Jackson Turner postulated that the American character had been formed on the frontier where the European settlers had been changed into "a new product that is American," he had in mind Thomas Jefferson's ideal nation of culturally homogeneous people living on the continent. This, of course, was a fantasy even in Jefferson's day, since a culturally and racially homogeneous America had never existed after the Europeans began to explore the continent. Dutch, Spanish, English, French, German, and African men and women had been interacting with the Native Americans and with each other for hundreds of years.

What was changing in the final decades of the nineteenth century with the swell of immigration from all parts of Europe and China was the unquestioned hegemony of Northern Europeans in America. The new settlers would ultimately challenge the prevailing simple assimilatory ideal that the hordes of immigrants from all over the world would be thrown into the metaphorical "melting pot" that was the challenging experience of living in the United States, and that they somehow would emerge over the course of a few generations as Anglo-Americans, having adopted their linguistic, historical, and cultural heritage from Great Britain. This "melting pot" idea was most memorably expressed by Hector St. John de Crèvecoeur in his *Letters from an American Farmer* (1782) describing life in the British colonies of America: "Here individuals of all nations are melted into a new race of men, whose labours and posterity will one day cause great changes in the world."

The growing industrialization of the nation was another important feature shaping the American character. The transcontinental railroad connecting the Atlantic and Pacific Oceans was completed in 1869, with 200,000 miles of iron track laid by 1890. Stephen Crane's story "The Bride Comes to Yellow Sky"(1898) humorously depicted the domestication of the frontier by the impact of the railroad in Texas, where the outlaw wore a flannel shirt "made, principally, by some [immigrant] Jewish women on the east side of New York."

After the Civil War, radical women's groups, united in their opposition to slavery, splintered on the issue of women's suffrage, which wasn't achieved until 1920. In 1861 Davis had created an impassioned vision of thwarted female creativity in "Life in the Iron-Mills, or The Korl Woman," but by the turn of the century Charlotte Perkins Gilman was the most important social activist for women's rights among short story authors. Gilman, who wrote nearly two hundred short stories, many urging women's financial independence, was best known for her treatise on *Women and Economics* (1896). Her story "The Yellow Wallpaper" (1892), based on her own experience of a mental breakdown during a postpartum depression aggravated by inappropriate medical treatment, was enormously influential. She acknowledged that "the story was meant to be dreadful, and succeeded."

Gilman was writing at the end of the century, when a second generation of women writers of short fiction finally became accepted as literary artists as well as "scribbling women." In 1857 the first generation of women publishing stories and tales had discovered a powerful champion when *The Atlantic Monthly* magazine was founded in Boston. It immediately established itself as the most important magazine in America when the country's most distinguished cultural spokesmen—the poets and essayists Henry Wadsworth Longfellow, Oliver Wendell Holmes, Ralph Waldo Emerson, and John Greenleaf Whittier—all agreed to write for it. *The Atlantic Monthly*'s first editor, the distinguished poet James Russell Lowell, announced that the magazine's policy was to print three short stories in each issue, with emphasis on fiction of quality by American women authors. This was a radical decision because in the absence of an international copyright law, most leading periodicals in the United States were still filled with the reprinted fiction of best-selling English authors. In February 1865, for example, *Harper's Magazine* offered twenty-page installments of Charles Dickens's novel *Our Mutual Friend* and Wilkie Collins's *Armadale*.

Earlier, *Putnam's* and *Knickerbocker's* magazines had attempted a high literary standard, but under the three years of Lowell's leadership *The Atlantic* ushered in a new stage in the development of American short fiction. When James T. Fields succeeded Lowell as editor of the magazine for the next decade, he and his wife, Annie Fields, were even more ardent supporters of women's writing. They championed the work of Rebecca Harding Davis, invited her to Boston, introduced her to prominent literary lions such as Emerson and Hawthorne, and encouraged her work. In 1870 the founding of *Scribner's Monthly* magazine in New York City continued to widen the marketplace for quality short fiction. By 1872 women writers produced nearly 75 percent of the fiction published in the United States.

The last decades of the nineteenth century witnessed the flowering of local-color or regional stories, realistic short fiction about the people and life of a particular geographical section of the United States. These stories followed upon the popularity of Western tales by writers such as Mark Twain and Bret Harte. In the first issue of *The Atlantic,* Harriet Beecher Stowe had published "The Mourning Veil," a tale set in New England that was more sermon than story. She later consciously set out to change her writing style, explaining in the preface to her collection *Oldtown Folks* (1869) that in her stories she "tried to maintain the part simply of a sympathetic spectator. I propose neither to teach nor preach through them, any farther than any spectator of life is preached to by what he sees of the workings of human nature around him."

Stowe wrote a series of stories set in New England, but her short fiction never attained the popularity of her great novel *Uncle Tom's Cabin*. By the 1870s she had refined her narrative approach in her "Sam Lawson" stories, which were dialect tales set in rural New England. Her work influenced many women writers in Connecticut, Massachusetts, and Maine, including Rose Terry Cooke, Mary Wilkins Freeman, and Sarah Orne Jewett. George Washington Cable, Kate Chopin, and Alice Dunbar-Nelson, among others, wrote local-color tales set in Louisiana. Hamlin Garland's *Main-Travelled Roads* presented a realistic depiction of the harsh living conditions in the Midwest. In 1894 Garland wrote an essay, "Local Color in Art," in which he defined local-color fiction as a text that "could not have been written in any other place or by any one else than a native."

Scholars have traced important lines of influence between the women writers of this period which contributed to their increasing sense of achievement as literary artists. Stowe's writing influenced Jewett, who admired the earlier author's novel *The Pearl of Orr's Island* (1862). In a letter to her friend Annie Fields, Jewett called Stowe's work "classical — historical — anything you like to say, if you can give it high praise enough." Jewett also admired the stories of Rose Terry Cooke and became the mentor of the young Willa Cather, who wrote part of her novel *Death Comes for the Archbishop* (1926) in the Santa Fe home of the short story author Mary Austin. According to the editor Per Seyersted, Kate Chopin regarded Mary Wilkins

Freeman as a "great genius" and believed that she knew of "no one better than Miss Jewett to study for technique and nicety of construction."

By the 1890s, women authors were questioning many aspects of their traditional role in the American family, and a new sharpness entered their challenge to the passivity of the so-called feminine ideal. Unlike Charlotte Perkins Gilman, the short story writers Mary Wilkins Freeman, Rose Terry Cooke, and Kate Chopin did not regard themselves as radical feminists; nevertheless, they created realistic stories that mirrored the frustrations of many women in the patriarchal society. Others, such as Sarah Orne Jewett, celebrated the independence of women who lived alone in remote pockets of the country, where their imaginations flowered in their solitude and their affections encouraged them to form supportive if far-flung communities. Often the women writers in the local-color tradition were nostalgic for the agrarian past, before the advent of industrialization, when women had vital duties to perform on the farm instead of being expected to take on the passive role of "the angel in the house."

In the aftermath of the Civil War and the failure of Reconstruction, the difficulties faced by African Americans adjusting to their new role in society, and the lack of understanding and support extended to them by the white majority, were cruelly reflected in their short stories. Charles W. Chesnutt attempted to show white readers the complex response of educated blacks to their slave heritage in "The Wife of His Youth" (1898). Alice Dunbar-Nelson poignantly captured a sense of the helplessness of the underclass who lacked the means to fight social injustice in "Tony's Wife" (1899).

While continuing to thrive during this period in both the United States and Europe, the short prose narrative finally came into its own as a distinct literary genre. In the 1880s the term *short story* (it appeared both hyphenated and unhyphenated at the time in critical terminology) was taken to mean a literary entity in its own right and not just as a story that happened to be short. Previously these original works of prose narrative had been called "tales," "stories," "sketches," or "articles," all terms that could be used to describe other narratives in the oral tradition or in nonfiction.

After the genre had received a name of its own, it slowly began to take on a new dignity. In 1880, *Scribner's Monthly*, in reference to one of Bret Harte's works, stated that "short story though it be, it is an honor to American literature." Four years later, the American critic Brander Matthews defended the genre by writing in the London *Saturday Review* that he believed "the short story, properly and technically so called, is a work of art of a distinct kind, and the writing of short stories is a distinct department of literary art." The international copyright law of 1891 also encouraged the production of short stories, guaranteeing an income for authors writing for the steadily growing number of periodicals.

In Hamlin Garland's autobiography, *A Son of the Middle Border* (1920), he described the importance of getting his first story accepted in

1890 by B. O. Flowers, the editor of *The Arena,* a new Boston magazine that had what he called a "frankly radical" editorial policy. Flowers sent Garland a letter of acceptance with a check for one hundred dollars as payment for using the story in the magazine's next issue. Flowers also advised Garland to restore paragraphs that the young writer had crossed out, saying, "When I ask a man to write for me, I want him to utter his mind with perfect freedom."

Flowers accepted several of Garland's stories for *The Arena;* the editor included a story in each issue of the magazine to enliven the articles on politics and current issues. He apologized to Garland for being unable to "match the prices of magazines like the *Century*" for his contributions, but Garland was delighted to have become a regular contributor to *The Arena,* which made him feel financially secure. A short time later *Century Magazine* also accepted one of his stories, and Garland wrote to his father offering to loan him money to buy "seed wheat" for the family farm. Magazine publication was often the start of a literary career for young American writers. Garland confessed, "Like the miner who, having suddenly uncovered a hidden vein of gold, bends to his pick in a confident belief in his 'find,' so I humped above my desk without doubts, without hesitations. I had found my work in the world." In 1892 stories had become so popular that more collections of short fiction than novels were published in the United States.

By 1895 William Dean Howells, reviewing eight short story collections, concluded that "the artistry of the women seems finer than that of the men." He thought that the local-color stories of this period had "a solidity, an honest observation, in the work of such women, which often leaves little to be desired." Some prominent authors, however, stubbornly disagreed with Howells about the superiority of realism over romanticism in fiction. In 1897 Ambrose Bierce complained in his essay "The Short Story" that for years Howells "conducted a department of criticism with a purpose single to expounding the after-thought theories and principles which are the offspring of his own limitations." Bierce argued that

> fiction has nothing to say to probability; the capable writer gives it not a moment's attention, except to make what is related *seem* probable in the reading—*seem* true. Suppose he relates the impossible; what then? Why, he has passed over the line into the realm of romance, the kingdom of Scott, Defoe, Hawthorne, and the authors of the *Arabian Nights*—the land of the poets, the home of all that is good and lasting in the literature of the imagination. Do these little fellows, the so-called realists, ever think of the goodly company which they deny themselves by confining themselves to their clumsy feet and pursuing their stupid noses through the barren hitherland, while just beyond the Delectable Mountains lies in light the Valley of Dreams, with its tall immortals, poppy-crowned? Why, the society of the historians alone would be a distinction and a glory!

By the end of the century, with the rapid shifts in literary fashion dictated by the magazines, both romance fiction and local-color stories had come to seem old-fashioned to many readers of mainstream periodicals. In the October 1897 issue of *The Atlantic Monthly,* the leading article discussed what critic James Lane Allen called "Two Principles in Recent American Fiction," "the Feminine Principle" and "the Masculine Principle." What Allen meant by "the Feminine Principle" was the fiction of the women authors of the realistic, local-color school (although he did not identify any of the writers by name or use that term in his essay). He identified fiction created on the basis of "the Feminine Principle" by its appearance "some twenty-five or thirty years" before and dissected its "essential characteristics" as literary refinement, delicacy, grace, smallness, rarity, and tact. Writers employing "the Feminine Principle" created a body of American short stories "quite definite, quite new, quite unlike anything we had produced before, and to us of quite inestimable value."

Allen credited the writers developing "the Feminine Principle" over the past quarter century with the improvement of the artistic standard of American short fiction:

> Before it began its work, the literature of our fiction was well-nigh barren of names that stood accepted both at home and abroad as those of masters of style. There was Irving, there was Hawthorne, there was Poe: who, with the assurance that his claim would everywhere pass unchallenged, could add to these a fourth? More significant still, there prevailed no universal either conscious or unconscious recognition of style as an attainment vitally inseparable from the writing of any acceptable American short story. . . . There can be no doubt that this great change, this widespread development among us of the purely artistic appreciation of literature in its form and finish, has been directly and indirectly the work of the Feminine Principle.

Since Allen believed in a "law of constant growth and change" that required literature to strive toward "complete expression," he understood that a "perfectly natural temper of dissatisfaction" had begun to discredit works of the Feminine Principle "for what they had never meant to be, to upbraid them for the lack of what they could not possibly contain." Instead, Allen advocated new fiction exemplifying his idea of "the Masculine Principle." He urged young writers to "try for a while the literary virtues and the literary materials of less self-consciousness, of larger self-abandonment, and thus impart to our fiction the free, the uncaring, the tremendous fling and swing that are the very genius of our time and spirit."

Disregarding the work of notable American authors such as Twain, Crane, James, Garland, and Howells, Allen believed that fiction by the British author Rudyard Kipling (then living in the United States) was the ideal blend of masculine and feminine art. Ironically, *The Atlantic Monthly* that featured Allen's article was a fortieth anniversary issue that concluded with a long summary of the magazine's history. It included a lengthy passage praising the notable contributors to the magazine and ended with the names of twenty-eight women authors of short fiction.

Readers of *The Atlantic Monthly, Scribner's,* and *Harper's* were beginning to favor a new type of brief, highly contrived story, often with a surprise ending. The earliest model for this type of narrative was Frank R. Stockton's "The Lady or the Tiger," the short story sensation of 1884. This was a short prose entertainment in which the setting and the characters were abstractions and the conclusion of the plot unresolved. Like Madelene Yale Wynne's popular story "The Little Room" (1895), it was more anecdote than story, its effectiveness due to its manner of telling.

The transition from romance to realism as the dominant mode during this period can be traced through the decades in several outstanding books of short fiction. George Washington Cable's *Old Creole Days* (1879) was one of the last important collections of romantic short fiction. But the genre as a whole had been eclipsed by the earlier local-color brilliance of Mark Twain's *The Celebrated Jumping Frog of Calaveras County and Other Stories* (1867) and Bret Harte's *The Luck of Roaring Camp and Other Sketches* (1870). Stories about the physical and psychological damage of the Civil War dominated Ambrose Bierce's *Tales of Soldiers and Civilians* (1891) and appeared as well in Constance Fenimore Woolson's *Southern Sketches* (1880), Hamlin Garland's *Main-Travelled Roads* (1891), and Stephen Crane's *The Little Regiment* (1896).

The artistry of women writers of short fiction at the end of the century is evident in several collections. Mary Wilkins Freeman's *A New England Nun and Other Stories* and Rose Terry Cooke's *Huckleberries Gathered from New England Hills* (both published in 1891) preceded Kate Chopin's *Bayou Folk* (1894) and *A Night in Arcadie* (1897). Sarah Orne Jewett's *The Country of the Pointed Firs* (1896), a book of linked stories, is generally considered the masterpiece of the local-color school.

Two other notable collections of short fiction from this period were Stephen Crane's *The Open Boat and Other Stories* (1898) and *The Monster* (1899). Also at the end of the century, Charles W. Chesnutt's *The Conjure Woman* and *The Wife of His Youth* (both published in 1899) appeared along with Alice Dunbar-Nelson's *The Goodness of St. Rocque and Other Stories* (1899). Such books by late-nineteeth-century local-color authors of short fiction seemed to Hamlin Garland to be "varying phases of the same movement, a movement which is to give us at last a really vital and original literature," as he wrote in *New England Magazine* (1890). The regional movement had Americanized our literature. By 1900, with so many talented writers creating American short stories, the future of this newest literary genre was assured.

RELATED COMMENTARIES: *Hamlin Garland, "Local Color in Art," page 1344; Bret Harte, "The Rise of the 'Short Story,'" page 1356; Brander Matthews, From* The Philosophy of the Short-Story, *page 1398.*

REBECCA HARDING DAVIS

Rebecca Harding Davis (1831–1910), chiefly remembered for her story "Life in the Iron-Mills, or The Korl Woman," a pioneering work of social realism, was born in Washington, Pennsylvania, the eldest of five children. Her mother had come from a genteel Pennsylvania family; her father had emigrated from England, becoming a businessman after moving his wife and children to Wheeling, [West] Virginia, a prosperous industrial milltown on the Mason-Dixon line employing thousands of immigrant workers. First educated at home, Davis was then sent to the Washington Female Seminary to study French, English literature, and religion. There she also listened to abolitionist lectures by the utopian socialist Francis LeMoyne, who awakened her social conscience. After graduating as class valedictorian in 1848, she returned to live with her parents in Wheeling. She began to pay close attention to the Irish and Welsh immigrant millworkers, taking long walks through town, observing the squalor and misery in the lives of the workers exploited in the mills. She trained her "dramatic eye" to register a "quick perception of character, and of the way character shows itself in looks, tones, dress." As a developing writer she felt "just in proportion to . . . feeling more deeply and noticing more keenly" would she acquire "the faculty of expressing more delicately and powerfully. Not inspiration, practice." After publishing editorials in the local Wheeling Intelligencer, *she was ready in "Life in the Iron-Mills" to describe what she saw as "a reality of soul-starvation, of living death, that meets you every day under the besotted faces on the street."*

As Tillie Olsen understood, what gave "Life in the Iron-Mills" its power was that it "was not written out of compassion or condescending pity. The thirty-year-old Rebecca Harding who wrote it wrote with absolute identification with their thwarted, wasted lives." Subtitling her story "The Korl Woman" ("korl" is the porous material left over after the iron ore has been fired in the mills), the author also attacked the artificiality of the Cult of the True Woman in the ideal of female passivity prevailing in Victorian America. She had grown up admiring Hawthorne's fanciful short stories, but the industrial smoke that she breathed daily in Wheeling brought home to her the groundswell of political and social issues fermenting in the 1840s and 1850s— including widespread talk of seccession over the issue of slavery; the Seneca Falls meeting of American feminists in 1848 calling for constitutional rights for women; the publication of Charles Dickens's uncompromising industrial novel Hard Times *in 1854; and the popularity of the Know-Nothing Party in America. This party elected more than forty congressmen in 1854 on a platform hostile to immigrants, a desperate reaction to the increasing numbers pouring into the country from Ireland, Germany, England, and Wales; one out of eight Americans in 1860 was foreign-born.*

"Life in the Iron-Mills" was published in The Atlantic Monthly *in April 1861. Readers of the magazine clamored to read more by the unknown*

"genius" from Wheeling, and the author obliged with another story hastily written for the magazine dramatizing the widening gulf between the social classes produced by the new industrial capitalist order. Later that year it was published as her first novel, Margaret Howth: A Story of To-day. *In 1862 she married the journalist L. Clarke Davis and continued writing with dwindling critical reputation—292 stories, 9 novels, and 124 pieces for children. Her eldest son became such a popular writer that her* New York Times *obituary was headlined, "Mother of Richard Harding Davis Dies at Son's Home in Mt. Kisco, aged 79."*

Life in the Iron-Mills, or The Korl Woman

Is this the end?
O Life, as futile, then, as frail!
What hope of answer of redress?

A cloudy day: do you know what that is in a town of iron-works? The sky sank down before dawn, muddy, flat, immovable. The air is thick, clammy with the breath of crowded human beings. It stifles me. I open the window, and, looking out, can scarcely see through the rain the grocer's shop opposite, where a crowd of drunken Irishmen are puffing Lynchburg tobacco in their pipes. I can detect the scent through all the foul smells ranging loose in the air.

The idiosyncrasy of this town is smoke. It rolls sullenly in slow folds from the great chimneys of the iron-foundries, and settles down in black, slimy pools on the muddy streets. Smoke on the wharves, smoke on the dingy boats, on the yellow river,—clinging in a coating of greasy soot to the house-front, the two faded poplars, the faces of the passers-by. The long train of mules, dragging masses of pig-iron through the narrow street, have a foul vapor hanging to their reeking sides. Here, inside, is a little broken figure of an angel pointing upward from the mantel-shelf; but even its wings are covered with smoke, clotted and black. Smoke everywhere! A dirty canary chirps desolately in a cage beside me. Its dream of green fields and sunshine is a very old dream,—almost worn out, I think.

From the back-window I can see a narrow brick-yard sloping down to the river-side, strewed with rain-butts and tubs. The river, dull and tawny-colored, (*la belle rivière!*) drags itself sluggishly along, tired of the heavy weight of boats and coal-barges. What wonder? When I was a child, I used to fancy a look of weary, dumb appeal upon the face of the negro-like river slavishly bearing its burden day after day. Something of the same idle notion comes to me to-day, when from the street-window I look on the slow stream of human life creeping past, night and morning, to the great mills. Masses of men, with dull, besotted faces bent to the ground, sharpened here and there by pain or cunning; skin and muscle and flesh begrimed with smoke and ashes; stooping all night over boiling caldrons of metal, laired by day in dens of drunkenness and infamy; breathing from infancy to death an air saturated with fog and grease and soot, vileness for soul and body. What do you make of a case like that, amateur psychologist? You call it an altogether serious thing to be alive: to these men it is a drunken jest, a joke, — horrible to angels perhaps, to them commonplace enough. My fancy about the river was an idle one: it is no type of such a life. What if it be stagnant and slimy here? It knows that beyond there waits for it odorous sunlight, — quaint old gardens, dusky with soft, green foliage of apple-trees, and flushing crimson with roses, — air, and fields, and mountains. The future of the Welsh puddler passing just now is not so pleasant. To be stowed away, after his grimy work is done, in a hole in the muddy grave-yard, and after that, — *not* air, nor green fields, nor curious roses.

Can you see how foggy the day is? As I stand here, idly tapping the window-pane, and looking out through the rain at the dirty back-yard and the coal-boats below, fragments of an old story float up before me, — a story of this old house into which I happened to come to-day. You may think it a tiresome story enough, as foggy as the day, sharpened by no sudden flashes of pain or pleasure. — I know: only the outline of a dull life, that long since, with thousands of dull lives like its own, was vainly lived and lost: thousands of them, — massed, vile, slimy lives, like those of the torpid lizards in yonder stagnant water-butt. — Lost? There is a curious point for you to settle, my friend, who study psychology in a lazy, *dilettante* way. Stop a moment. I am going to be honest. This is what I want you to do. I want you to hide your disgust, take no heed to your clean clothes, and come right down with me, — here, into the thickest of the fog and mud and foul effluvia. I want you to hear this story. There is a secret down here, in this nightmare fog, that has lain dumb for centuries: I want to make it a real thing to you. You, Egoist, or Pantheist, or Arminian, busy in making straight paths for your feet on the hills, do not see it clearly, — this terrible question which men here have gone mad and died trying to answer. I dare not put this secret into words. I told you it was dumb. These men, going by with drunken faces and brains full of unawakened power, do not ask it of Society or of God. Their lives ask it; their deaths ask it. There is no reply. I will tell you plainly that I have a great hope; and I bring it to you to be tested. It is this: that this terrible dumb question is its own reply; that it is not the sentence of death we think it, but, from the very extremity of its darkness, the most solemn prophecy which the world has known of the Hope to come. I dare make my meaning no clearer, but will only tell my story. It will, perhaps, seem to you as foul and dark as this thick vapor about us, and as pregnant with death; but if your eyes are free as mine are to look deeper, no perfume-tinted dawn will be so fair with promise of the day that shall surely come.

My story is very simple, — only what I remember of the life of one of these men, — a furnace-tender in one of Kirby & John's rolling-mills, — Hugh Wolfe. You know the mills? They took the great order for the Lower Virginia railroads there last winter; run usually with about a thousand men. I cannot tell why I choose the half-forgotten story of this Wolfe more than that of myriads of these furnace-hands. Perhaps because there is a secret underlying sympathy between that story and this day with its impure fog and thwarted sunshine, — or perhaps simply for the reason that this house is the one where the Wolfes lived. There were the father and son, — both hands, as I said, in one of Kirby & John's mills for making railroad-iron, — and Deborah, their cousin, a picker in some of the cotton-mills. The house was rented then to half a dozen families. The Wolfes had two of the cellar-rooms. The old man, like many of the puddlers and feeders of the mills, was Welsh, — had spent half of his life in the Cornish tin-mines. You may pick the Welsh emigrants, Cornish miners, out of the throng passing the windows, any day. They are a trifle more filthy; their muscles are not so brawny; they stoop more. When they are drunk, they neither yell, nor shout, nor stagger, but skulk along like beaten hounds. A pure, unmixed blood, I fancy: shows itself in the slight angular bodies and sharply-cut facial lines. It is nearly thirty years since the Wolfes lived here. Their lives were like those of their class: incessant labor, sleeping in kennel-like rooms, eating rank pork and molasses, drinking — God and the distillers only know what; with an occasional night in jail, to atone for some drunken excess. Is that all of their lives? — of the portion given to them and these their duplicates swarming the streets to-day? — nothing beneath? — all? So many a political reformer will tell you, — and many a private reformer, too, who has gone among them with a heart tender with Christ's charity, and come out outraged, hardened.

One rainy night, about eleven o'clock, a crowd of half-clothed women stopped outside of the cellar-door. They were going home from the cotton-mill.

"Good-night, Deb," said one, a mulatto, steadying herself against the gas-post. She needed the post to steady her. So did more than one of them.

"Dah's a ball to Miss Potts' to-night. Ye'd best come."

"Inteet, Deb, if hur'll come, hur'll hef fun," said a shrill Welsh voice in the crowd.

Two or three dirty hands were thrust out to catch the gown of the woman, who was groping for the latch of the door.

"No."

"No? Where's Kit Small, then?"

"Begorra! on the spools. Alleys behint, though we helped her, we dud. An wid ye! Let Deb alone! It's ondacent frettin' a quite body. Be the powers, an' we'll have a night of it! there'll be lashin's o' drink, — the Var-gent be blessed and praised for 't!"

They went on, the mulatto inclining for a moment to show fight, and drag the woman Wolfe off with them; but, being pacified, she staggered away.

Deborah groped her way into the cellar, and, after considerable stum-bling, kindled a match, and lighted a tallow dip, that sent a yellow glimmer over the room. It was low, damp, — the earthen floor covered with a green, slimy moss,—a fetid air smothering the breath. Old Wolfe lay asleep on a heap of straw, wrapped in a torn horse-blanket. He was a pale, meek little man, with a white face and red rabbit-eyes. The woman Deborah was like him; only her face was even more ghastly, her lips bluer, her eyes more watery. She wore a faded cotton gown and a slouching bonnet. When she walked, one could see that she was deformed, almost a hunchback. She trod softly, so as not to waken him, and went through into the room beyond. There she found by the half-extinguished fire an iron saucepan filled with cold boiled potatoes, which she put upon a broken chair with a pint-cup of ale. Placing the old candlestick beside this dainty repast, she untied her bonnet, which hung limp and wet over her face, and prepared to eat her supper. It was the first food that had touched her lips since morning. There was enough of it, however: there is not always. She was hungry,—one could see that easily enough,—and not drunk, as most of her companions would have been found at this hour. She did not drink, this woman,—her face told that, too,—nothing stronger than ale. Perhaps the weak, flaccid wretch had some stimulant in her pale life to keep her up,—some love or hope, it might be, or urgent need. When that stimulant was gone, she would take to whiskey. Man cannot live by work alone. While she was skinning the potatoes, and munching them, a noise behind her made her stop.

"Janey!" she called, lifting the candle and peering into the darkness. "Janey, are you there?"

A heap of ragged coats was heaved up, and the face of a young girl emerged, staring sleepily at the woman.

"Deborah," she said, at last, "I'm here the night."

"Yes, child. Hur's welcome," she said, quietly eating on.

The girl's face was haggard and sickly; her eyes were heavy with sleep and hunger: real Milesian eyes they were, dark, delicate blue, glooming out from black shadows with a pitiful fright.

"I was alone," she said, timidly.

"Where's the father?" asked Deborah, holding out a potato, which the girl greedily seized.

"He's beyant,—wid Haley,—in the stone house." (Did you ever hear the word *jail* from an Irish mouth?) "I came here. Hugh told me never to stay me-lone."

"Hugh?"

"Yes."

A vexed frown crossed her face. The girl saw it, and added quickly,—

"I have not seen Hugh the day, Deb. The old man says his watch lasts till the mornin'."

The woman sprang up, and hastily began to arrange some bread and flitch[1] in a tin pail, and to pour her own measure of ale into a bottle. Tying on her bonnet, she blew out the candle.

---

[1]"Flitch" is cured meat, especially salt pork or bacon.

"Lay ye down, Janey dear," she said, gently, covering her with the old rags. "Hur can eat the potatoes, if hur's hungry."

"Where are ye goin', Deb? The rain's sharp."

"To the mill, with Hugh's supper."

"Let him bide till th' morn. Sit ye down."

"No, no,"—sharply pushing her off. "The boy'll starve."

She hurried from the cellar, while the child wearily coiled herself up for sleep. The rain was falling heavily, as the woman, pail in hand, emerged from the mouth of the alley, and turned down the narrow street, that stretched out, long and black, miles before her. Here and there a flicker of gas lighted an uncertain space of muddy footwalk and gutter; the long rows of houses, except an occasional lager-bier shop, were closed; now and then she met a band of mill-hands skulking to or from their work.

Not many even of the inhabitants of a manufacturing town know the vast machinery of system by which the bodies of workmen are governed, that goes on unceasingly from year to year. The hands of each mill are divided into watches that relieve each other as regularly as the sentinels of an army. By night and day the work goes on, the unsleeping engines groan and shriek, the fiery pools of metal boil and surge. Only for a day in the week, in half-courtesy to public censure, the fires are partially veiled; but as soon as the clock strikes midnight, the great furnaces break forth with renewed fury, the clamor begins with fresh, breathless vigor, the engines sob and shriek like "gods in pain."

As Deborah hurried down through the heavy rain, the noise of these thousand engines sounded through the sleep and shadow of the city like far-off thunder. The mill to which she was going lay on the river, a mile below the city-limits. It was far, and she was weak, aching from standing twelve hours at the spools. Yet it was her almost nightly walk to take this man his supper, though at every square she sat down to rest, and she knew she should receive small word of thanks.

Perhaps, if she had possessed an artist's eye, the picturesque oddity of the scene might have made her step stagger less, and the path seem shorter; but to her the mills were only "summat deilish to look at by night."

The road leading to the mills had been quarried from the solid rock, which rose abrupt and bare on one side of the cinder-covered road, while the river, sluggish and black, crept past on the other. The mills for rolling iron are simply immense tent-like roofs, covering acres of ground, open on every side. Beneath these roofs Deborah looked in on a city of fires, that burned hot and fiercely in the night. Fire in every horrible form: pits of flame waving in the wind; liquid metal-flames writhing in tortuous streams through the sand; wide caldrons filled with boiling fire, over which bent ghastly wretches stirring the strange brewing; and through all, crowds of half-clad men, looking like revengeful ghosts in the red light, hurried, throwing masses of glittering fire. It was like a street in Hell. Even Deborah muttered, as she crept through, "'T looks like t' Devil's place!" It did,—in more ways than one.

She found the man she was looking for, at last, heaping coal on a furnace. He had not time to eat his supper; so she went behind the furnace, and waited. Only a few men were with him, and they noticed her only by a "Hyur comes t' hunchback, Wolfe."

Deborah was stupid with sleep; her back pained her sharply; and her teeth chattered with cold, with the rain that soaked her clothes and dripped from her at every step. She stood, however, patiently holding the pail, and waiting.

"Hout, woman! ye look like a drowned cat. Come near to the fire," — said one of the men, approaching to scrape away the ashes.

She shook her head. Wolfe had forgotten her. He turned, hearing the man, and came closer.

"I did no' think; gi' me my supper, woman."

She watched him eat with a painful eagerness. With a woman's quick instinct, she saw that he was not hungry, — was eating to please her. Her pale, watery eyes began to gather a strange light.

"Is't good, Hugh? T'ale was a bit sour, I feared."

"No, good enough." He hesitated a moment. "Ye're tired, poor lass! Bide here till I go. Lay down there on that heap of ash, and go to sleep."

He threw her an old coat for a pillow, and turned to his work. The heap was the refuse of the burnt iron, and was not a hard bed; the half-smothered warmth, too, penetrated her limbs, dulling their pain and cold shiver.

Miserable enough she looked, lying there on the ashes like a limp, dirty rag, — yet not an unfitting figure to crown the scene of hopeless discomfort and veiled crime: more fitting, if one looked deeper into the heart of things, — at her thwarted woman's form, her colorless life, her waking stupor that smothered pain and hunger, — even more fit to be a type of her class. Deeper yet if one could look, was there nothing worth reading in this wet, faded thing, half-covered with ashes? no story of a soul filled with groping passionate love, heroic unselfishness, fierce jealousy? of years of weary trying to please the one human being whom she loved, to gain one look of real heart-kindness from him? If anything like this were hidden beneath the pale, bleared eyes, and dull, washed-out-looking face, no one had ever taken the trouble to read its faint signs: not the half-clothed furnace-tender, Wolfe, certainly. Yet he was kind to her: it was his nature to be kind, even to the very rats that swarmed in the cellar; kind to her in just the same way. She knew that. And it might be that very knowledge had given to her face its apathy and vacancy more than her low, torpid life. One sees that dead, vacant look steal sometimes over the rarest, finest of women's faces, — in the very midst, it may be, of their warmest summer's day; and then one can guess at the secret of intolerable solitude that lies hid beneath the delicate laces and brilliant smile. There was no warmth, no brilliancy, no summer for this woman; so the stupor and vacancy had time to gnaw into her face perpetually. She was young, too, though no one guessed it; so the gnawing was the fiercer.

She lay quiet in the dark corner, listening, through the monotonous din and uncertain glare of the works, to the dull plash of the rain in the far distance,—shrinking back whenever the man Wolfe happened to look towards her. She knew, in spite of all his kindness, that there was that in her face and form which made him loathe the sight of her. She felt by instinct, although she could not comprehend it, the finer nature of the man, which made him among his fellow-workmen something unique, set apart. She knew, that, down under all the vileness and coarseness of his life, there was a groping passion for whatever was beautiful and pure,—that his soul sickened with disgust at her deformity, even when his words were kindest. Through this dull consciousness, which never left her, came, like a sting, the recollection of the dark blue eyes and lithe figure of the little Irish girl she had left in the cellar. The recollection struck through even her stupid intellect with a vivid glow of beauty and of grace. Little Janey, timid, helpless, clinging to Hugh as her only friend: that was the sharp thought, the bitter thought, that drove into the glazed eyes a fierce light of pain. You laugh at it? Are pain and jealousy less savage realities down here in this place I am taking you to than in your own house or your own heart,—your heart, which they clutch at sometimes? The note is the same, I fancy, be the octave high or low.

If you could go into this mill where Deborah lay, and drag out from the hearts of these men the terrible tragedy of their lives, taking it as a symptom of the disease of their class, no ghost Horror would terrify you more. A reality of soul-starvation, of living death, that meets you every day under the besotted faces on the street,—I can paint nothing of this, only give you the outside outlines of a night, a crisis in the life of one man: whatever muddy depth of soul-history lies beneath you can read according to the eyes God has given you.

Wolfe, while Deborah watched him as a spaniel its master, bent over the furnace with his iron pole, unconscious of her scrutiny, only stopping to receive orders. Physically, Nature had promised the man but little. He had already lost the strength and instinct vigor of a man, his muscles were thin, his nerves weak, his face (a meek, woman's face) haggard, yellow with consumption. In the mill he was known as one of the girl-men: "Molly Wolfe" was his *sobriquet*. He was never seen in the cockpit, did not own a terrier, drank but seldom; when he did, desperately. He fought sometimes, but was always thrashed, pommelled to a jelly. The man was game enough, when his blood was up: but he was no favorite in the mill; he had the taint of school-learning on him,—not to a dangerous extent, only a quarter or so in the free-school in fact,[2] but enough to ruin him as a good hand in a fight.

For other reasons, too, he was not popular. Not one of themselves, they felt that, though outwardly as filthy and ash-covered; silent, with foreign thoughts and longings breaking out through his quietness in innumerable

---

[2]The majority of mill workers had no formal education and were illiterate.

curious ways: this one, for instance. In the neighboring furnace-buildings lay great heaps of the refuse from the ore after the pig-metal is run. *Korl* we call it here: a light, porous substance, of a delicate, waxen, flesh-colored tinge. Out of the blocks of this korl, Wolfe, in his off-hours from the furnace, had a habit of chipping and moulding figures,—hideous, fantastic enough, but sometimes strangely beautiful: even the mill-men saw that, while they jeered at him. It was a curious fancy in the man, almost a passion. The few hours for rest he spent hewing and hacking with his blunt knife, never speaking, until his watch came again,—working at one figure for months, and, when it was finished, breaking it to pieces perhaps, in a fit of disappointment. A morbid, gloomy man, untaught, unled, left to feed his soul in grossness and crime, and hard, grinding labor.

I want you to come down and look at this Wolfe, standing there among the lowest of his kind, and see him just as he is, that you may judge him justly when you hear the story of this night. I want you to look back, as he does every day, at his birth in vice, his starved infancy; to remember the heavy years he has groped through as boy and man,—the slow, heavy years of constant, hot work. So long ago he began, that he thinks sometimes he has worked there for ages. There is no hope that it will ever end. Think that God put into this man's soul a fierce thirst for beauty,—to know it, to create it; to *be*—something, he knows not what,—other than he is. There are moments when a passing cloud, the sun glinting on the purple thistles, a kindly smile, a child's face, will rouse him to a passion of pain,—when his nature starts up with a mad cry of rage against God, man, whoever it is that has forced this vile, slimy life upon him. With all this groping, this mad desire, a great blind intellect stumbling through wrong, a loving poet's heart, the man was by habit only a coarse, vulgar laborer, familiar with sights and words you would blush to name. Be just: when I tell you about this night, see him as he is. Be just,—not like man's law, which seizes on one isolated fact, but like God's judging angel, whose clear, sad eye saw all the countless cankering days of this man's life, all the countless nights, when, sick with starving, his soul fainted in him, before it judged him for this night, the saddest of all.

I called this night the crisis of his life. If it was, it stole on him unawares. These great turning-days of life cast no shadow before, slip by unconsciously. Only a trifle, a little turn of the rudder, and the ship goes to heaven or hell.

Wolfe, while Deborah watched him, dug into the furnace of melting iron with his pole, dully thinking only how many rails the lump would yield. It was late,—nearly Sunday morning; another hour, and the heavy work would be done,—only the furnaces to replenish and cover for the next day. The workmen were growing more noisy, shouting, as they had to do, to be heard over the deep clamor of the mills. Suddenly they grew less boisterous,—at the far end, entirely silent. Something unusual had happened. After a moment, the silence came nearer; the men stopped their jeers and drunken choruses. Deborah, stupidly lifting up her head, saw the cause of the quiet. A group of five or six men were slowly approaching, stopping to examine each furnace as they came. Visitors often came to see the mills after night: except by growing less noisy, the men took no notice of them. The furnace where Wolfe worked was near the bounds of the works; they halted there hot and tired: a walk over one of these great foundries is no trifling task. The woman, drawing out of sight, turned over to sleep. Wolfe, seeing them stop, suddenly roused from his indifferent stupor, and watched them keenly. He knew some of them: the overseer, Clarke,—a son of Kirby, one of the mill-owners,—and a Doctor May, one of the town-physicians. The other two were strangers. Wolfe came closer. He seized eagerly every chance that brought him into contact with this mysterious class that shone down on him perpetually with the glamour of another order of being. What made the difference between them? That was the mystery of his life. He had a vague notion that perhaps to-night he could find it out. One of the strangers sat down on a pile of bricks, and beckoned young Kirby to his side.

"This *is* hot, with a vengeance. A match, please?"—lighting his cigar. "But the walk is worth the trouble. If it were not that you must have heard it so often, Kirby, I would tell you that your works look like Dante's Inferno."

Kirby laughed.

"Yes. Yonder is Farinata himself in the burning tomb,"—pointing to some figure in the shimmering shadows.

"Judging from some of the faces of your men," said the other, "they bid fair to try the reality of Dante's vision, some day."

Young Kirby looked curiously around, as if seeing the faces of his hands for the first time.

"They're bad enough, that's true. A desperate set, I fancy. Eh, Clarke?"

The overseer did not hear him. He was talking of net profits just then,—giving, in fact, a schedule of the annual business of the firm to a sharp peering little Yankee, who jotted down notes on a paper laid on the crown of his hat: a reporter for one of the city-papers, getting up a series of reviews of the leading manufactories. The other gentlemen had accompanied them merely for amusement. They were silent until the notes were finished, drying their feet at the furnaces, and sheltering their faces from the intolerable heat. At last the overseer concluded with—

"I believe that is a pretty fair estimate, Captain."

"Here, some of you men!" said Kirby, "bring up those boards. We may as well sit down, gentlemen, until the rain is over. It cannot last much longer at this rate."

"Pig-metal,"—mumbled the reporter,—"um!—coal facilities,— um!—hands employed, twelve hundred,—bitumen,—um!—all right, I believe, Mr. Clarke;—sinking-fund,—what did you say was your sinking-fund?"

"Twelve hundred hands?" said the stranger, the young man who had first spoken. "Do you control their votes, Kirby?"

"Control? No." The young man smiled complacently. "But my father brought seven hundred votes to the polls for his candidate last November. No force-work, you understand,—only a speech or two, a hint to form themselves into a society, and a bit of red and blue bunting to make them a flag. The Invincible Roughs,—I believe that is their name. I forget the motto: 'Our country's hope,' I think."

There was a laugh. The young man talking to Kirby sat with an amused light in his cool gray eye, surveying critically the half-clothed figures of the puddlers, and the slow swing of their brawny muscles. He was a stranger in the city,—spending a couple of months in the borders of a Slave State, to study the institutions of the South,—a brother-in-law of Kirby's,—Mitchell. He was an amateur gymnast,—hence his anatomical eye; a patron, in a *blasé* way, of the prize-ring; a man who sucked the essence out of a science or philosophy in an indifferent, gentlemanly way; who took Kant, Novalis, Humboldt, for what they were worth in his own scales; accepting all, despising nothing, in heaven, earth, or hell, but one-idead men; with a temper yielding and brilliant as summer water, until his Self was touched, when it was ice, though brilliant still. Such men are not rare in the States.

As he knocked the ashes from his cigar, Wolfe caught with a quick pleasure the contour of the white hand, the blood-glow of a red ring he wore. His voice, too, and that of Kirby's, touched him like music,—low, even, with chording cadences. About this man Mitchell hung the impalpable atmosphere belonging to the thoroughbred gentleman. Wolfe, scraping away the ashes beside him, was conscious of it, did obeisance to it with his artist sense, unconscious that he did so.

The rain did not cease. Clark and the reporter left the mills; the others, comfortably seated near the furnace, lingered, smoking and talking in a desultory way. Greek would not have been more unintelligible to the furnace-tenders, whose presence they soon forgot entirely. Kirby drew out a newspaper from his pocket and read aloud some article, which they discussed eagerly. At every sentence, Wolfe listened more and more like a dumb, hopeless animal, with a duller, more stolid look creeping over his face, glancing now and then at Mitchell, marking acutely every smallest sign of refinement, then back to himself, seeing as in a mirror his filthy body, his more stained soul.

Never! He had no words for such a thought, but he knew now, in all the sharpness of the bitter certainty, that between them there was a great gulf never to be passed. Never!

The bells of the mills rang for midnight. Sunday morning had dawned. Whatever hidden message lay in the tolling bells floated past these men unknown. Yet it was there. Veiled in the solemn music ushering the risen saviour was a key-note to solve the darkest secrets of a world gone wrong,—even this social riddle which the brain of the grimy puddler grappled with madly to-night.

The men began to withdraw the metal from the caldrons. The mills were deserted on Sundays, except by the hands who fed the fires, and those who had no lodgings and slept usually on the ash-heaps. The three strangers sat still during the next hour, watching the men cover the furnaces, laughing now and then at some jest of Kirby's.

"Do you know," said Mitchell, "I like this view of the works better than when the glare was fiercest? These heavy shadows and the amphitheatre of smothered fires are ghostly, unreal. One could fancy these red smouldering lights to be the half-shut eyes of wild beasts, and the spectral figures their victims in the den."

Kirby laughed. "You are fanciful. Come, let us get out of the den. The spectral figures, as you call them, are a little too real for me to fancy a close proximity in the darkness,—unarmed, too."

The others rose, buttoning their over-coats, and lighting cigars.

"Raining, still," said Doctor May, "and hard. Where did we leave the coach, Mitchell?"

"At the other side of the works.—Kirby, what's that?"

Mitchell started back, half-frightened, as, suddenly turning a corner, the white figure of a woman faced him in the darkness,—a woman, white, of giant proportions, crouching on the ground, her arms flung out in some wild gesture of warning.

"Stop! Make that fire burn there!" cried Kirby, stopping short.

The flame burst out, flashing the gaunt figure into bold relief.

Mitchell drew a long breath.

"I thought it was alive," he said, going up curiously.

The others followed.

"Not marble, eh?" asked Kirby, touching it.

One of the lower overseers stopped.

"Korl, Sir."

"Who did it?"

"Can't say. Some of the hands; chipped it out in off-hours."

"Chipped to some purpose, I should say. What a flesh-tint the stuff has! Do you see, Mitchell?"

"I see."

He had stepped aside where the light fell boldest on the figure, looking at it in silence. There was not one line of beauty or grace in it: a nude woman's form, muscular, grown coarse with labor, the powerful limbs instinct with some one poignant longing. One idea: there it was in the tense, rigid muscles, the clutching hands, the wild, eager face, like that of a starving wolf's. Kirby and Doctor May walked around it, critical, curious. Mitchell stood aloof, silent. The figure touched him strangely.

"Not badly done," said Doctor May. "Where did the fellow learn that sweep of the muscles in the arm and hand? Look at them! They are groping,—do you see?—clutching: the peculiar action of a man dying of thirst."

"They have ample facilities for studying anatomy," sneered Kirby, glancing at the half-naked figures.

"Look," continued the Doctor, "at this bony wrist, and the strained sinews of the instep! A working-woman,—the very type of her class."

"God forbid!" muttered Mitchell.

"Why?" demanded May. "What does the fellow intend by the figure? I cannot catch the meaning."

"Ask him," said the other, dryly. "There he stands,"—pointing to Wolfe, who stood with a group of men, leaning on his ash-rake.

The Doctor beckoned him with the affable smile which kind-hearted men put on, when talking with these people.

"Mr. Mitchell has picked you out as the man who did this,—I'm sure I don't know why. But what did you mean by it?"

"She be hungry."

Wolfe's eyes answered Mitchell, not the Doctor.

"Oh-h! But what a mistake you have made, my fine fellow! You have given no sign of starvation to the body. It is strong,—terribly strong. It has the mad, half-despairing gesture of drowning."

Wolfe stammered, glanced appealingly at Mitchell, who saw the soul of the thing, he knew. But the cool, probing eyes were turned on himself now,—mocking, cruel, relentless.

"Not hungry for meat," the furnace-tender said at last.

"What then? Whiskey?" jeered Kirby, with a coarse laugh.

Wolfe was silent a moment, thinking.

"I dunno," he said, with a bewildered look. "It mebbe. Summat to make her live, I think,—like you. Whiskey ull do it, in a way."

The young man laughed again. Mitchell flashed a look of disgust somewhere,—not at Wolfe.

"May," he broke out impatiently, "are you blind? Look at that woman's face! It asks questions of God, and says, 'I have a right to know.' Good God, how hungry it is!"

They looked a moment; then May turned to the mill-owner:—

"Have you many such hands as this? What are you going to do with them? Keep them at puddling iron?"

Kirby shrugged his shoulders. Mitchell's look had irritated him.

"*Ce n'est pas mon affaire.* I have no fancy for nursing infant geniuses. I suppose there are some stray gleams of mind and soul among these wretches. The Lord will take care of his own; or else they can work out their own salvation. I have heard you call our American system a ladder which any man can scale. Do you doubt it? Or perhaps you want to banish all social ladders, and put us all on a flat table-land,—eh, May?"

The Doctor look vexed, puzzled. Some terrible problem lay hid in this woman's face, and troubled these men. Kirby waited for an answer, and, receiving none, went on, warming with his subject.

"I tell you, there's something wrong that no talk of '*Liberté*' or '*Éga-lité*' will do away. If I had the making of men, these men who do the lowest part of the world's work should be machines,—nothing more,—hands. It would be kindness. God help them! What are taste, reason, to creatures who must live such lives as that?" He pointed to Deborah, sleeping on the ash-heap. "So many nerves to sting them to pain. What if God had put your brain, with all its agony of touch, into your fingers, and bid you work and strike with that?"

"You think you could govern the world better?" laughed the Doctor.

"I do not think at all."

"That is true philosophy. Drift with the stream, because you cannot dive deep enough to find bottom, eh?"

"Exactly," rejoined Kirby. "I do not think. I wash my hands of all social problems,—slavery, caste, white or black. My duty to my operatives has a narrow limit,—the pay-hour on Saturday night. Outside of that, if they cut korl, or cut each other's throats, (the more popular amusement of the two,) I am not responsible."

The Doctor sighed,—a good honest sigh, from the depths of his stomach.

"God help us! Who is responsible?"

"Not I, I tell you," said Kirby, testily. "What has the man who pays them money to do with their souls' concerns, more than the grocer or butcher who takes it?"

"And yet," said Mitchell's cynical voice, "look at her! How hungry she is!"

Kirby tapped his boot with his cane. No one spoke. Only the dumb face of the rough image looking into their faces with the awful question, "What shall we do to be saved?" Only Wolfe's face, with its heavy weight of brain, its weak, uncertain mouth, its desperate eyes, out of which looked the soul of his class,—only Wolfe's face turned towards Kirby's. Mitchell laughed,—a cool, musical laugh.

"Money has spoken!" he said, seating himself lightly on a stone with the air of an amused spectator at a play. "Are you answered?"—turning to Wolfe his clear, magnetic face.

Bright and deep and cold as Arctic air, the soul of the man lay tranquil beneath. He looked at the furnace-tender as he had looked at a rare mosaic in the morning; only the man was the more amusing study of the two.

"Are you answered? Why, May, look at him! *De profundis clamavi.*' Or to quote in English, 'Hungry and thirsty, his soul faints in him.' And so Money sends back its answer into the depths through you, Kirby! Very clear the answer, too!—I think I remember reading the same words some-where:—washing your hands in Eau de Cologne, and saying, 'I am innocent of the blood of this man. See ye to it!'"

Kirby flushed angrily.

"You quote Scripture freely."

"Do I not quote correctly? I think I remember another line, which may amend my meaning: 'Inasmuch as ye did it unto one of the least of these, ye did it unto me.' Deist? Bless you, man, I was raised on the milk of the Word. Now, Doctor, the pocket of the world having uttered its voice, what has the heart to say? You are a philanthropist, in a small way,—*n'est ce pas?* Here, boy, this gentleman can show you how to cut korl better,—or your destiny. Go on, May!"

"I think a mocking devil possesses you to-night," rejoined the Doctor, seriously.

He went to Wolfe and put his hand kindly on his arm. Something of a vague idea possessed the Doctor's brain that much good was to be done here by a friendly word or two: a latent genius to be warmed into life by a waited-for sun-beam. Here it was: he had brought it. So he went on complacently:—

"Do you know, boy, you have it in you to be a great sculptor, a great man?—do you understand?" (talking down to the capacity of his hearer: it is a way people have with children, and men like Wolfe,)—"to live a better, stronger life than I, or Mr. Kirby here? A man may make himself anything he chooses. God has given you stronger powers than many men,—me, for instance."

May stopped, heated, glowing with his own magnanimity. And it was magnanimous. The puddler had drunk in every word, looking through the Doctor's flurry, and generous heat, and self-approval, into his will, with those slow, absorbing eyes of his.

"Make yourself what you will. It is your right."

"I know," quietly. "Will you help me?"

Mitchell laughed again. The Doctor turned now, in a passion,—

"You know, Mitchell, I have not the means. You know, if I had, it is in my heart to take this boy and educate him for"—

"The glory of God, and the glory of John May."

May did not speak for a moment; then, controlled, he said,—

"Why should one be raised, when myriads are left?—I have not the money, boy," to Wolfe, shortly.

"Money?" He said it over slowly, as one repeats the guessed answer to a riddle, doubtfully. "That is it? Money?"

"Yes, money,—that is it," said Mitchell, rising, and drawing his furred coat about him. "You've found the cure for all the world's diseases.—Come, May, find your good-humor, and come home. This damp wind chills my very bones. Come and preach your Saint-Simonian doctrines to-morrow to Kirby's hands. Let them have a clear idea of the rights of the soul, and I'll venture next week they'll strike for higher wages. That will be the end of it."

"Will you send the coach-driver to this side of the mills?" asked Kirby, turning to Wolfe.

He spoke kindly: it was his habit to do so. Deborah, seeing the puddler go, crept after him. The three men waited outside. Doctor May walked up and down, chafed. Suddenly he stopped.

"Go back, Mitchell! You say the pocket and the heart of the world speak without meaning to these people. What has its head to say? Taste, culture, refinement? Go!"

Mitchell was leaning against a brick wall. He turned his head indolently, and looked into the mills. There hung about the place a thick, unclean odor. The slightest motion of his hand marked that he perceived it, and his insufferable disgust. That was all. May said nothing, only quickened his angry tramp.

"Besides," added Mitchell, giving a corollary to his answer, "it would be of no use. I am not one of them."

"You do not mean" — said May, facing him.

"Yes, I mean just that. Reform is born of need, not pity. No vital movement of the people's has worked down, for good or evil; fermented, instead, carried up the heaving, cloggy mass. Think back through history, and you will know it. What will this lowest deep — thieves, Magdalens, negroes — do with the light filtered through ponderous Church creeds, Baconian theories, Goethe schemes? Some day, out of their bitter need will be thrown up their own light-bringer, — their Jean Paul, their Cromwell, their Messiah."

"Bah!" was the Doctor's inward criticism. However, in practice, he adopted the theory; for, when, night and morning, afterwards, he prayed that power might be given these degraded souls to rise, he glowed at heart, recognizing an accomplished duty.

Wolfe and the woman had stood in the shadow of the works as the coach drove off. The Doctor had held out his hand in a frank, generous way, telling him to "take care of himself, and to remember it was his right to rise." Mitchell had simply touched his hat, as to an equal, with a quiet look of thorough recognition. Kirby had thrown Deborah some money, which she found, and clutched eagerly enough. They were gone now, all of them. The man sat down on the cinder-road, looking up into the murky sky.

"'T be late, Hugh. Wunnot hur come?"

He shook his head doggedly, and the woman crouched out of his sight against the wall. Do you remember rare moments when a sudden light flashed over yourself, your world, God? when you stood on a mountain-peak, seeing your life as it might have been, as it is? one quick instant, when custom lost its force and every-day usage? when your friend, wife, brother, stood in a new light? your soul was bared, and the grave, — a foretaste of the nakedness of the Judgment-Day? So it came before him, his life, that night. The slow tides of pain he had borne gathered themselves up and surged against his soul. His squalid daily life, the brutal coarseness eating into his brain, as the ashes into his skin: before, these things had been a dull aching into his consciousness; to-night, they were reality. He gripped the filthy red shirt that clung, stiff with soot, about him, and tore it savagely from his arm. The flesh beneath was muddy with grease and ashes, — and the heart beneath that! And the soul? God knows.

Then flashed before his vivid poetic sense the man who had left him, — the pure face, the delicate, sinewy limbs, in harmony with all he knew of beauty or truth. In his cloudy fancy he had pictured a Something like this. He had found it in this Mitchell, even when he idly scoffed at his pain: a Man all-knowing, all-seeing, crowned by Nature, reigning, — the keen glance of his eye falling like a sceptre on other men. And yet his instinct taught him that he too—He! He looked at himself with sudden loathing, sick, wrung his hands with a cry, and then was silent. With all the phantoms of his heated, ignorant fancy, Wolfe had not been vague in his ambitions. They were practical, slowly built up before him out of his knowledge of what he could do. Through years he had day by day made this hope a real thing to himself,—a clear, projected figure of himself, as he might become.

Able to speak, to know what was best, to raise these men and women working at his side up with him: sometimes he forgot this defined hope in the frantic anguish to escape,—only to escape,—out of the wet, the pain, the ashes, somewhere, anywhere,—only for one moment of free air on a hill-side, to lie down and let his sick soul throb itself out in the sunshine. But to-night he panted for life. The savage strength of his nature was roused; his cry was fierce to God for justice.

"Look at me!" he said to Deborah, with a low, bitter laugh, striking his puny chest savagely. "What am I worth, Deb? Is it my fault that I am no better? My fault? My fault?"

He stopped, stung with a sudden remorse, seeing her hunchback shape writhing with sobs. For Deborah was crying thankless tears, according to the fashion of women.

"God forgi' me, woman! Things go harder wi' you nor me. It's a worse share."

He got up and helped her to rise; and they went doggedly down the muddy street, side by side.

"It's all wrong," he muttered, slowly,—"all wrong! I dunnot understan'. But it'll end some day."

"Come home, Hugh!" she said, coaxingly; for he had stopped, looking around bewildered.

"Home,—and back to the mill!" He went on saying this over to himself, as if he would mutter down every pain in this dull despair.

She followed him through the fog, her blue lips chattering with cold. They reached the cellar at last. Old Wolfe had been drinking since she went out, and had crept nearer the door. The girl Janey slept heavily in the corner. He went up to her, touching softly the worn white arm with his fingers. Some bitterer thought stung him, as he stood there. He wiped the drops from his forehead, and went into the room beyond, livid, trembling. A hope, trifling, perhaps, but very dear, had died just then out of the poor puddler's life, as he looked at the sleeping, innocent girl,—some plan for the future, in which she had borne a part. He gave it up that moment, then and forever. Only a trifle, perhaps, to us: his face grew a shade paler,—that was all. But, somehow, the man's soul, as God and the angels looked down on it, never was the same afterwards.

Deborah followed him into the inner room. She carried a candle, which she placed on the floor, closing the door after her. She had seen the look on his face, as he turned away: her own grew deadly. Yet, as she came up to him her eyes glowed. He was seated on an old chest, quiet, holding his face in his hands.

"Hugh!" she said, softly.

He did not speak.

"Hugh, did hur hear what the man said,—him with the clear voice? Did hur hear? Money, money,—that it wud do all?"

He pushed her away,—gently, but he was worn out; her rasping tone fretted him.

"Hugh!"

The candle flared a pale yellow light over the cobwebbed brick walls, and the woman standing there. He looked at her. She was young, in deadly earnest; her faded eyes, and wet, ragged figure caught from their frantic eagerness a power akin to beauty.

"Hugh, it is true! Money ull do it! Oh, Hugh, boy, listen till me! He said it true! It is money!"

"I know. Go back! I do not want you here."

"Hugh, it is t' last time. I'll never worrit hur again."

There were tears in her voice now, but she choked them back.

"Hear till me only to-night! If one of t' witch people wud come, them we heard of t' home, and gif hur all hur wants, what then? Say, Hugh!"

"What do you mean?"

"I mean money."

Her whisper shrilled through his brain.

"If one of t' witch dwarfs wud come from t' lane moors to-night, and gif hur money, to go out,—*out,* I say,—out, lad, where t' sun shines, and t' heath grows, and t' ladies walk in silken gownds, and God stays all t' time,—where t' man lives that talked to us to-night,—Hugh knows,— Hugh could walk there like a king!"

He thought the woman mad, tried to check her, but she went on, fierce in her eager haste.

"If *I* were t' witch dwarf, if I had t' money, wud hur thank me? Wud hur take me out o' this place wid hur and Janey? I wud not come into the gran' house hur wud build, to vex hur wid t' hunch,—only at night, when t' shadows were dark, stand far off to see hur."

Mad? Yes! Are many of us mad in this way?

"Poor Deb! poor Deb!" he said, soothingly.

"It is here," she said, suddenly jerking into his hand a small roll. "I took it! I did it! Me, me!—not hur! I shall be hanged, I shall be burnt in hell, if anybody knows I took it! Out of his pocket, as he leaned against t' bricks. Hur knows?"

She thrust it into his hand, and then, her errand done, began to gather chips together to make a fire, choking down hysteric sobs.

"Has it come to this?"

That was all he said. The Welsh Wolfe blood was honest. The roll was a small green pocket-book containing one or two gold pieces, and a check for an incredible amount, as it seemed to the poor puddler. He laid it down, hiding his face again in his hands.

"Hugh, don't be angry wud me! It's only poor Deb,—hur knows?"

He took the long skinny fingers kindly in his.

"Angry? God help me, no! Let me sleep. I am tired."

He threw himself heavily down on the wooden bench, stunned with pain and weariness. She brought some old rags to cover him.

It was late on Sunday evening before he awoke. I tell God's truth, when I say he had then no thought of keeping this money. Deborah had hid it in his pocket. He found it there. She watched him eagerly, as he took it out.

"I must gif it to him," he said, reading her face.

"Hur knows," she said with a bitter sigh of disappointment. "But it is hur right to keep it."

His right! The word struck him. Doctor May had used the same. He washed himself, and went out to find this man Mitchell. His right! Why did this chance word cling to him so obstinately? Do you hear the fierce devils whisper in his ear, as he went slowly down the darkening street?

The evening came on, slow and calm. He seated himself at the end of an alley leading into one of the larger streets. His brain was clear to-night, keen, intent, mastering. It would not start back, cowardly, from any hellish temptation, but meet it face to face. Therefore the great temptation of his life came to him veiled by no sophistry, but bold, defiant, owning its own vile name, trusting to one bold blow for victory.

He did not deceive himself. Theft! That was it. At first the word sickened him; then he grappled with it. Sitting there on a broken cart-wheel, the fading day, the noisy groups, the church-bells' tolling passed before him like a panorama, while the sharp struggle went on within. This money! He took it out, and looked at it. If he gave it back, what then? He was going to be cool about it.

People going by to church saw only a sickly mill-boy watching them quietly at the alley's mouth. They did not know that he was mad, or they would not have gone by so quietly: mad with hunger; stretching out his hands to the world, that had given so much to them, for leave to live the life God meant him to live. His soul within him was smothering to death; he wanted so much, thought so much, and *knew*—nothing. There was nothing of which he was certain, except the mill and things there. Of God and heaven he had heard so little, that they were to him what fairy-land is to a child: something real, but not here; very far off. His brain, greedy, dwarfed, full of thwarted energy and unused powers, questioned these men and women going by, coldly, bitterly, that night. Was it not his right to live as they,—a pure life, a good, true-hearted life, full of beauty and kind words? He only wanted to know how to use the strength within him. His heart warmed, as he thought of it. He suffered himself to think of it longer. If he took the money?

Then he saw himself as he might be, strong, helpful, kindly. The night crept on, as this one image slowly evolved itself from the crowd of other thoughts and stood triumphant. He looked at it. As he might be! What wonder, if it blinded him to delirium,—the madness that underlies all revolution, all progress, and all fall?

You laugh at the shallow temptation? You see the error underlying its argument so clearly,—that to him a true life was one of full development rather than self-restraint? that he was deaf to the higher tone in a cry of voluntary suffering for truth's sake than in the fullest flow of spontaneous harmony? I do not plead his cause. I only want to show you the mote in my brother's eye: then you can see clearly to take it out.

The money,—there it lay on his knee, a little blotted slip of paper, nothing in itself; used to raise him out of the pit; something straight from God's hand. A thief! Well, what was it to be a thief? He met the question at last, face to face, wiping the clammy drops of sweat from his forehead. God made this money—the fresh air, too—for his children's use. He never made the difference between poor and rich. The Something who looked down on him that moment through the cool gray sky had a kindly face, he knew,—loved his children alike. Oh, he knew that!

There were times when the soft floods of color in the crimson and purple flames, or the clear depth of amber in the water below the bridge, had somehow given him a glimpse of another world than this,—of an infinite depth of beauty and of quiet somewhere,—somewhere,—a depth of quiet and rest and love. Looking up now, it became strangely real. The sun had sunk quite below the hills, but his last rays struck upward, touching the zenith. The fog had risen, and the town and river were steeped in its thick, gray damp; but overhead, the sun-touched smoke-clouds opened like a cleft ocean,—shifting, rolling seas of crimson mist, waves of billowy silver veined with blood-scarlet, inner depths unfathomable of glancing light. Wolfe's artist-eye grew drunk with color. The gates of that other world! Fading, flashing before him now! What, in that world of Beauty, Content, and Right, were the petty laws, the mine and thine, of mill-owners and mill-hands?

A consciousness of power stirred within him. He stood up. A man,— he thought, stretching out his hands,—free to work, to live, to love! Free! His right! He folded the scrap of paper in his hand. As his nervous fingers took it in, limp and blotted, so his soul took in the mean temptation, lapped it in fancied rights, in dreams of improved existences, drifting and endless as the cloud-seas of color. Clutching it, as if the tightness of his hold would strengthen his sense of possession, he went aimlessly down the street. It was his watch at the mill. He need not go, need never go again, thank God!—shaking off the thought with unspeakable loathing.

Shall I go over the history of the hours of that night? how the man wandered from one to another of his old haunts, with a half-consciousness of bidding them farewell,—lanes and alleys and back-yards where the mill-hands lodged,—noting, with a new eagerness, the filth and drunkenness, the pig-pens, the ash-heaps covered with potato-skins, the bloated, pimpled women at the doors,—with a new disgust, a new sense of sudden triumph, and, under all, a new, vague dread, unknown before, smothered down, kept under, but still there? It left him but once during the night, when, for the second time in his life, he entered a church. It was a sombre Gothic pile, where the stained light lost itself in far-retreating arches; built to meet the requirements and sympathies of a far other class than Wolfe's. Yet it touched, moved him uncontrollably. The distances, the shadows, the still, marble figures, the mass of silent kneeling worshippers, the mysterious music, thrilled, lifted his soul with a wonderful pain. Wolfe forgot himself, forgot the new life he was going to live, the mean terror gnawing underneath. The voice of the speaker strengthened the charm; it was clear, feeling, full, strong. An old man, who had lived much, suffered much; whose brain was keenly alive, dominant; whose heart was summer-warm with charity. He taught it to-night. He held up Humanity in its grand total; showed the great world-cancer to his people. Who could show it better? He was a Christian reformer; he had studied the age thoroughly; his outlook at man had been free, world-wide, over all time. His faith stood sublime upon the Rock of Ages; his fiery zeal guided vast schemes by which the gospel was to be preached to all nations. How did he preach it to-night? In burning, light-laden words he painted the incarnate Life, Love, the universal Man: words that became reality in the lives of these people,—that lived again in beautiful words and actions, trifling, but heroic. Sin, as he defined it, was a real foe to them; their trials, temptations, were his. His words passed far over the furnace-tender's grasp, toned to suit another class of culture; they sounded in his ears a very pleasant song in an unknown tongue. He meant to cure this world-cancer with a steady eye that had never glared with hunger, and a hand that neither poverty nor strychnine-whiskey had taught to shake. In this morbid, distorted heart of the Welsh puddler he had failed.

Wolfe rose at last, and turned from the church down the street. He looked up; the night had come on foggy, damp; the golden mists had vanished, and the sky lay dull and ash-colored. He wandered again aimlessly down the street, idly wondering what had become of the cloud-sea of crimson and scarlet. The trial-day of this man's life was over, and he had lost the victory. What followed was mere drifting circumstance,—a quicker walking over the path,—that was all. Do you want to hear the end of it? You wish me to make a tragic story out of it? Why, in the police-reports of the morning paper you can find a dozen such tragedies: hints of shipwrecks unlike any that ever befell on the high seas; hints that here a power was lost to heaven,—that there a soul went down where no tide can ebb or flow. Commonplace enough the hints are,—jocose sometimes, done up in rhyme.

Doctor May, a month after the night I have told you of, was reading to his wife at breakfast from this fourth column of the morning-paper: an unusual thing,—these police-reports not being, in general, choice reading for ladies; but it was only one item he read.

"Oh, my dear! You remember that man I told you of, that we saw at Kirby's mill?—that was arrested for robbing Mitchell? Here he is; just listen:—'Circuit Court. Judge Day. Hugh Wolfe, operative in Kirby & John's Loudon Mills. Charge, grand larceny. Sentence, nineteen years hard labor in penitentiary.'—Scoundrel! Serves him right! After all our kindness that night! Picking Mitchell's pocket at the very time!"

His wife said something about the ingratitude of that kind of people, and then they began to talk of something else.

Nineteen years! How easy that was to read! What a simple word for Judge Day to utter! Nineteen years! Half a lifetime!

Hugh Wolfe sat on the window-ledge of his cell, looking out. His ankles were ironed. Not usual in such cases; but he had made two desperate efforts to escape. "Well," as Haley, the jailer, said, "small blame to him! Nineteen years' imprisonment was not a pleasant thing to look forward to." Haley was very good-natured about it, though Wolfe had fought him savagely.

"When he was first caught," the jailer said afterwards, in telling the story, "before the trial, the fellow was cut down at once,—laid there on that pallet like a dead man, with his hands over his eyes. Never saw a man so cut down in my life. Time of the trial, too, came the queerest dodge of any customer I ever had. Would choose no lawyer. Judge gave him one, of course. Gibson it was. He tried to prove the fellow crazy; but it wouldn't go. Thing was plain as day-light: money found on him. 'Twas a hard sentence,—all the law allows; but it was for 'xample's sake. These mill-hands are gettin' onbearable. When the sentence was read, he just looked up, and said the money was his by rights, and that all the world had gone wrong. That night, after the trial, a gentleman came to see him here, name of Mitchell,—him as he stole from. Talked to him for an hour. Thought he came for curiosity, like. After he was gone, thought Wolfe was remarkable quiet, and went into his cell. Found him very low; bed all bloody. Doctor said he had been bleeding at the lungs. He was as weak as a cat; yet, if ye'll b'lieve me, he tried to get a-past me and get out. I just carried him like a baby, and threw him on the pallet. Three days after, he tried it again: that time reached the wall. Lord help you! he fought like a tiger,— giv' some terrible blows. Fightin' for life, you see; for he can't live long, shut up in the stone crib down yonder. Got a death-cough now. 'T took two of us to bring him down that day; so I just put the irons on his feet. There he sits, in there. Goin' to-morrow, with a batch more of 'em. That woman, hunchback, tried with him,—you remember?—she's only got three years. 'Complice. But *she's* a woman, you know. He's been quiet ever since I put on irons: giv' up, I suppose. Looks white, sick-lookin'. It acts different on 'em, bein' sentenced. Most of 'em gets reckless, devilish-like. Some prays awful, and sings them vile songs of the mills, all in a breath. That woman, now, she's desper't'. Been beggin' to see Hugh, as she calls him, for three days. I'm a-goin' to let her in. She don't go with him. Here she is in this next cell. I'm a-goin' now to let her in."

He let her in. Wolfe did not see her. She crept into a corner of the cell, and stood watching him. He was scratching the iron bars of the window with a piece of tin which he had picked up, with an idle, uncertain, vacant stare, just as a child or idiot would do.

"Tryin' to get out, old boy?" laughed Haley. "Them irons will need a crow-bar beside your tin, before you can open 'em."

Wolfe laughed, too, in a senseless way.

"I think I'll get out," he said.

"I believe his brain's touched," said Haley, when he came out.

The puddler scraped away with the tin for half an hour. Still Deborah did not speak. At last she ventured nearer, and touched his arm.

"Blood?" she said, looking at some spots on his coat with a shudder.

He looked up at her. "Why, Deb!" he said, smiling,—such a bright, boyish smile, that it went to poor Deborah's heart directly, and she sobbed and cried out loud.

"Oh, Hugh, lad! Hugh! dunnot look at me, when it wur my fault! To think I brought hur to it! And I loved hur so! Oh, lad, I dud!"

The confession, even in this wretch, came with the woman's blush through the sharp cry.

He did not seem to hear her,—scraping away diligently at the bars with the bit of tin.

Was he going mad? She peered closely into his face. Something she saw there made her draw suddenly back,—something which Haley had not seen, that lay beneath the pinched, vacant look it had caught since the trial, or the curious gray shadow that rested on it. That gray shadow,—yes, she knew what that meant. She had often seen it creeping over women's faces for months, who died at last of slow hunger or consumption. That meant death, distant, lingering: but this—Whatever it was the woman saw, or thought she saw, used as she was to crime and misery, seemed to make her sick with a new horror. Forgetting her fear of him, she caught his shoulders, and looked keenly, steadily, into his eyes.

"Hugh!" she cried, in a desperate whisper,—"oh, boy, not that! for God's sake, not *that!*"

The vacant laugh went off his face, and he answered her in a muttered word or two that drove her away. Yet the words were kindly enough. Sitting there on his pallet, she cried silently a hopeless sort of tears, but did not speak again. The man looked up furtively at her now and then. Whatever his own trouble was, her distress vexed him with a momentary sting.

It was market-day. The narrow window of the jail looked down directly on the carts and wagons drawn up in a long line, where they had unloaded. He could see, too, and hear distinctly the clink of money as it changed hands, the busy crowd of whites and blacks shoving, pushing one another, and the chaffering and swearing at the stalls. Somehow, the sound, more than anything else had done, wakened him up,—made the whole real to him. He was done with the world and the business of it. He let the tin fall, and looked out, pressing his face close to the rusty bars. How they crowded and pushed! And he,—he should never walk that pavement again! There came Neff Sanders, one of the feeders at the mill, with a basket on his arm. Sure enough, Neff was married the other week. He whistled, hoping he would look up; but he did not. He wondered if Neff remembered he was there,—if any of the boys thought of him up there, and thought that he never was to go down that old cinder-road again. Never again! He had not quite understood it before; but now he did. Not for days or years, but never!—that was it.

How clear the light fell on that stall in front of the market! and how like a picture it was, the dark-green heaps of corn, and the crimson beets, and golden melons! There was another with game: how the light flickered on that pheasant's breast, with the purplish blood dripping over the brown feathers! He could see the red shining of the drops, it was so near. In one minute he could be down there. It was just a step. So easy, as it seemed, so natural to go! Yet it could never be—not in all the thousands of years to come—that he should put his foot on that street again! He thought of himself with a sorrowful pity, as of some one else. There was a dog down in the market, walking after his master with such a stately, grave look!—only a dog, yet he could go backwards and forwards just as he pleased: he had good luck! Why, the very vilest cur, yelping there in the gutter, had not lived his life, had been free to act out whatever thought God had put into his brain; while he—No, he would not think of that! He tried to put the thought away, and to listen to a dispute between a countryman and a woman about some meat; but it would come back. He, what had he done to bear this?

Then came the sudden picture of what might have been, and now. He knew what it was to be in the penitentiary,—how it went with men there. He knew how in these long years he should slowly die, but not until soul and body had become corrupt and rotten,—how, when he came out, if he lived to come, even the lowest of the mill-hands would jeer him,—how his hands would be weak, and his brain senseless and stupid. He believed he was almost that now. He put his hand to his head, with a puzzled, weary look. It ached, his head, with thinking. He tried to quiet himself. It was only right, perhaps; he had done wrong. But was there right or wrong for such as he? What was right? And who had ever taught him? He thrust the whole matter away. A dark, cold quiet crept through his brain. It was all wrong; but let it be! It was nothing to him more than the others. Let it be!

The door grated, as Haley opened it.

"Come, my woman! Must lock up for t'night. Come, stir yerself!"

She went up and took Hugh's hand.

"Good-night, Deb," he said, carelessly.

She had not hoped he would say more; but the tired pain on her mouth just then was bitterer than death. She took his passive hand and kissed it.

"Hur'll never see Deb again!" she ventured, her lips growing colder and more bloodless.

What did she say that for? Did he not know it? Yet he would not be impatient with poor old Deb. She had trouble of her own, as well as he.

"No, never again," he said, trying to be cheerful.

She stood just a moment, looking at him. Do you laugh at her, standing there, with her hunchback, her rags, her bleared, withered face, and the great despised love tugging at her heart?

"Come, you!" called Haley, impatiently.

She did not move.

"Hugh!" she whispered.

It was to be her last word. What was it?

"Hugh, boy, not *THAT!*"

He did not answer. She wrung her hands, trying to be silent, looking in his face in an agony of entreaty. He smiled again, kindly.

"It is best, Deb. I cannot bear to be hurted any more."

"Hur knows," she said, humbly.

"Tell my father good-bye; and — and kiss little Janey."

She nodded, saying nothing, looked in his face again, and went out of the door. As she went, she staggered.

"Drinkin' to-day?" broke out Haley, pushing her before him. "Where the Devil did you get it? Here, in with ye!" and he shoved her into her cell, next to Wolfe's, and shut the door.

Along the wall of her cell there was a crack low down by the floor, through which she could see the light from Wolfe's. She had discovered it days before. She hurried in now, and, kneeling down by it, listened, hoping to hear some sound. Nothing but the rasping of the tin on the bars. He was at his old amusement again. Something in the noise jarred on her ear, for she shivered as she heard it. Hugh rasped away at the bars. A dull old bit of tin, not fit to cut korl with.

He looked out of the window again. People were leaving the market now. A tall mulatto girl, following her mistress, her basket on her head, crossed the street just below, and looked up. She was laughing; but, when she caught sight of the haggard face peering out through the bars, suddenly grew grave, and hurried by. A free, firm step, a clear-cut olive face, with a scarlet turban tied on one side, dark, shining eyes, and on the head the basket poised, filled with fruit and flowers, under which the scarlet turban and bright eyes looked out half-shadowed. The picture caught his eye.

It was good to see a face like that. He would try to-morrow, and cut one like it. *To-morrow!* He threw down the tin, trembling, and covered his face with his hands. When he looked up again, the daylight was gone.

Deborah, crouching near by on the other side of the wall, heard no noise. He sat on the side of the low pallet, thinking. Whatever was the mystery which the woman had seen on his face, it came out now slowly, in the dark there, and became fixed,—a something never seen on his face before. The evening was darkening fast. The market had been over for an hour; the rumbling of the carts over the pavement grew more infrequent: he listened to each, as it passed, because he thought it was to be for the last time. For the same reason, it was, I suppose, that he strained his eyes to catch a glimpse of each passer-by, wondering who they were, what kind of homes they were going to, if they had children,—listening eagerly to every chance word in the street, as if—(God be merciful to the man! what strange fancy was this?)—as if he never should hear human voices again.

It was quite dark at last. The street was a lonely one. The last passenger, he thought, was gone. No,—there was a quick step: Joe Hill, lighting the lamps. Joe was a good old chap; never passed a fellow without some joke or other. He remembered once seeing the place where he lived with his wife. "Granny Hill" the boys called her. Bedridden she was; but so kind as Joe was to her! kept the room so clean!—and the old woman, when he was there, was laughing at "some of t' lad's foolishness." The step was far down the street; but he could see him place the ladder, run up, and light the gas. A longing seized him to be spoken to once more.

"Joe!" he called, out of the grating. "Good-bye, Joe!"

The old man stopped a moment, listening uncertainly; then hurried on. The prisoner thrust his hand out of the window, and called again, louder; but Joe was too far down the street. It was a little thing; but it hurt him,—this disappointment.

"Good-bye, Joe!" he called, sorrowfully enough.

"Be quiet!" said one of the jailers, passing the door, striking on it with his club.

Oh, that was the last, was it?

There was an inexpressible bitterness on his face, as he lay down on the bed, taking the bit of tin, which he had rasped to a tolerable degree of sharpness, in his hand,—to play with, it may be. He bared his arms, looking intently at their corded veins and sinews. Deborah, listening in the next cell, heard a slight clicking sound, often repeated. She shut her lips tightly, that she might not scream, the cold drops of sweat broke over her, in her dumb agony.

"Hur knows best," she muttered at last, fiercely clutching the boards where she lay.

If she could have seen Wolfe, there was nothing about him to frighten her. He lay quite still, his arms outstretched, looking at the pearly stream of moonlight coming into the window. I think in that one hour that came then he lived back over all the years that had gone before. I think that all the low, vile life, all his wrongs, all his starved hopes, came then, and stung him with a farewell poison that made him sick unto death. He made neither moan nor cry, only turned his worn face now and then to the pure light, that seemed so far off, as one that said, "How long, O Lord? how long?"

The hour was over at last. The moon, passing over her nightly path, slowly came nearer, and threw the light across his bed on his feet. He watched it steadily, as it crept up, inch by inch, slowly. It seemed to him to carry with it a great silence. He had been so hot and tired there always in the mills. The years had been so fierce and cruel! There was coming now quiet and coolness and sleep. His tense limbs relaxed, and settled in a calm languor. The blood ran fainter and slow from his heart. He did not think now with a savage anger of what might be and was not; he was conscious only of deep stillness creeping over him. At first he saw a sea of faces: the mill-men,—women he had known, drunken and bloated,—Janey's timid and pitiful,—poor old Deb's: then they floated together like a mist, and faded away, leaving only the clear, pearly moonlight.

Whether, as the pure light crept up the stretched-out figure, it brought with it calm and peace, who shall say? His dumb soul was alone with God in judgment. A Voice may have spoken for it from far-off Calvary, "Father, forgive them, for they know not what they do!" Who dare say? Fainter and fainter the heart rose and fell, slower and slower the moon floated from behind a cloud, until, when at last its full tide of white splendor swept over the cell, it seemed to wrap and fold into a deeper stillness the dead figure that never should move again. Silence deeper than the Night! Nothing that moved, save the black nauseous stream of blood dripping slowly from the pallet to the floor!

There was outcry and crowd enough in the cell the next day. The coroner and his jury, the local editors, Kirby himself, and boys with their hands thrust knowingly into their pockets and heads on one side, jammed into the corners. Coming and going all day. Only one woman. She came late, and outstayed them all. A Quaker, or Friend, as they call themselves. I think this woman was known by that name in heaven. A homely body, coarsely dressed in gray and white. Deborah (for Haley had let her in) took notice of her. She watched them all—sitting on the end of the pallet, holding his head in her arms—with the ferocity of a watch-dog, if any of them touched the body. There was no meekness, or sorrow, in her face; the stuff out of which murderers are made, instead. All the time Haley and the woman were laying straight the limbs and cleaning the cell, Deborah sat still, keenly watching the Quaker's face. Of all the crowd there that day, this woman alone had not spoken to her,—only once or twice had put some cordial to her lips. After they all were gone, the woman, in the same still, gentle way, brought a vase of wood-leaves and berries, and placed it by the pallet, then opened the narrow window. The fresh air blew in, and swept the woody fragrance over the dead face. Deborah looked up with a quick wonder.

"Did hur know my boy wud like it? Did hur know Hugh?"

"I know Hugh now."

The white fingers passed in a slow, pitiful way over the dead, worn face. There was a heavy shadow in the quiet eyes.

"Did hur know where they'll bury Hugh?" said Deborah in a shrill tone, catching her arm.

This had been the question hanging on her lips all day.

"In t' town-yard? Under t' mud and ash? T' lad'll smother, woman! He wur born on t' lane moor, where t' air is frick and strong. Take hur out, for God's sake, take hur out where t' air blows!"

The Quaker hesitated, but only for a moment. She put her strong arm around Deborah and led her to the window.

"Thee sees the hills, friend, over the river? Thee sees how the light lies warm there, and the winds of God blow all the day? I live there,—where the blue smoke is, by the trees. Look at me." She turned Deborah's face to her own, clear and earnest. "Thee will believe me? I will take Hugh and bury him there to-morrow."

Deborah did not doubt her. As the evening wore on, she leaned against the iron bars, looking at the hills that rose far off, through the thick sodden clouds, like a bright, unattainable calm. As she looked, a shadow of their solemn repose fell on her face: its fierce discontent faded into a pitiful, humble quiet. Slow, solemn tears gathered in her eyes: the poor weak eyes turned so hopelessly to the place where Hugh was to rest, the grave heights looking higher and brighter and more solemn than ever before. The Quaker watched her keenly. She came to her at last, and touched her arm.

"When thee comes back," she said, in a low, sorrowful tone, like one who speaks from a strong heart deeply moved with remorse or pity, "thee shall begin thy life again,—there on the hills. I came too late; but not for thee,—by God's help, it may be."

Not too late. Three years after, the Quaker began her work. I end my story here. At evening-time it was light. There is no need to tire you with the long years of sunshine, and fresh air, and slow, patient Christ-love, needed to make healthy and hopeful this impure body and soul. There is a homely pine house, on one of these hills, whose windows overlook broad, wooded slopes and clover-crimsoned meadows,—niched into the very place where the light is warmest, the air freest. It is the Friends' meeting-house. Once a week they sit there, in their grave, earnest way, waiting for the Spirit of Love to speak, opening their simple hearts to receive His words. There is a woman, old, deformed, who takes a humble place among them: waiting like them: in her gray dress, her worn face, pure and meek, turned now and then to the sky. A woman much loved by these silent, restful people; more silent than they, more humble, more loving. Waiting: with her eyes turned to hills higher and purer than these on which she lives, — dim and far off now, but to be reached some day. There may be in her heart some latent hope to meet there the love denied her here, — that she shall find him whom she lost, and that then she will not be all-unworthy. Who blames her? Something is lost in the passage of every soul from one eternity to the other, — something pure and beautiful, which might have been and was not: a hope, a talent, a love, over which the soul mourns, like Esau deprived of his birthright. What blame to the meek Quaker, if she took her lost hope to make the hills of heaven more fair?

Nothing remains to tell that the poor Welsh puddler once lived, but this figure of the mill-woman cut in korl. I have it here in a corner of my library. I keep it hid behind a curtain, — it is such a rough, ungainly thing. Yet there are about it touches, grand sweeps of outline, that show a master's hand. Sometimes, — to-night, for instance, — the curtain is accidentally drawn back, and I see a bare arm stretched out imploringly in the darkness, and an eager, wolfish face watching mine: a wan, woful face, through which the spirit of the dead korl-cutter looks out, with its thwarted life, its mighty hunger, its unfinished work. Its pale, vague lips seem to tremble with a terrible question. "Is this the End?" they say, — "nothing beyond? — no more?" Why, you tell me you have seen that look in the eyes of dumb brutes, — horses dying under the lash. I know.

The deep of the night is passing while I write. The gas-light wakens from the shadows here and there the objects which lie scattered through the room: only faintly, though; for they belong to the open sunlight. As I glance at them, they each recall some task or pleasure of the coming day. A half-moulded child's head; Aphrodite; a bough of forest-leaves; music; work; homely fragments, in which lie the secrets of all eternal truth and beauty. Prophetic all! Only this dumb, woful face seems to belong to and end with the night. I turn to look at it. Has the power of its desperate need commanded the darkness away? While the room is yet steeped in heavy shadow, a cool, gray light suddenly touches its head like a blessing hand, and its groping arm points through the broken cloud to the far East, where, in the flickering, nebulous crimson, God has set the promise of the Dawn.   [1861]

MARK TWAIN

Mark Twain was the name under which Samuel Langhorne Clemens (1835–1910) published his works. Clemens was born in the village of Florida, Missouri, the son of a lawyer from Virginia. When he was five, the family moved to Hannibal, Missouri, on the west bank of the Mississippi River—"a heavenly place for a boy," he later remembered. His formal schooling ended at age twelve, when his father died and he was apprenticed to his brother Orion, who edited a country newspaper. At this time he saw his first story printed—"The Dandy Frightening the Squatter," a typical piece of frontier humor. For years he worked as a journeyman printer in St. Louis, New York City, Philadelphia, and Cincinnati. Then he became an apprentice steamboat pilot on the Mississippi in 1857, and he remained on the river until the Civil War. In his book Life on the Mississippi (1883), Twain wrote that on the river he became "acquainted with all the different types of human nature that are to be found in fiction, biography or history." After considering enlisting in the Confederate army, he joined his brother Orion in the Nevada Territory, first prospecting for gold and then working for the Virginia City Enterprise. It was in his writing for this newspaper that he first used the pseudonym Mark Twain, a call of the Mississippi pilots signifying a depth of two fathoms (twelve feet), just barely safe water for riverboats.

Twain's early work for newspapers was influenced by the topical humorists of his time. He first achieved recognition as a writer in 1865 with a tall tale, "Jim Smiley and His Jumping Frog," which was published in the New York Saturday Press. Twain later said he didn't think much of the story, but it was published in book form as "The Celebrated Jumping Frog of Calaveras County" with other sketches in 1867. Two years later his career was established with the travel book The Innocents Abroad. He achieved further fame (and fortune) with the popular success of his novels, The Adventures of Tom Sawyer (1876), The Prince and the Pauper (1882), A Connecticut Yankee in King Arthur's Court (1889), and many other books, including his masterpiece, The Adventures of Huckleberry Finn (1884).

Twain had a sensitive ear for the varied riches of American regional dialects, and he was our first author to write great works using a genuinely colloquial and native American speech. He published collections of short stories throughout his life, beginning with his first book, The Celebrated Jumping Frog of Calaveras County and Other Sketches (1867), and including such titles as Mark Twain's Sketches (1875), Merry Tales (1892), and My Debut as a Literary Person, with Other Essays and Stories (1903). The Complete Stories of Mark Twain, sixty in all, was published in 1957.

RELATED COMMENTARY: Mark Twain, "How to Tell a Story," page 1459.

The Celebrated Jumping Frog
of Calaveras County

In compliance with the request of a friend of mine, who wrote me from the East, I called on good-natured, garrulous old Simon Wheeler, and inquired after my friend's friend, *Leonidas W.* Smiley, as requested to do, and I hereunto append the result. I have a lurking suspicion that *Leonidas W.* Smiley is a myth; that my friend never knew such a personage; and that he only conjectured that, if I asked old Wheeler about him, it would remind him of his infamous *Jim* Smiley, and he would go to work and bore me nearly to death with some infernal reminiscence of him as long and tedious as it should be useless to me. If that was the design, it certainly succeeded.

I found Simon Wheeler dozing comfortably by the bar-room stove of the old, dilapidated tavern in the ancient mining camp of Angel's, and I noticed that he was fat and bald-headed, and had an expression of winning gentleness and simplicity upon his tranquil countenance. He roused up and gave me good-day. I told him a friend of mine had commissioned me to make some inquiries about a cherished companion of his boyhood named *Leonidas W.* Smiley— *Rev. Leonidas W.* Smiley—a young minister of the Gospel, who he had heard was at one time a resident of Angel's Camp. I added that, if Mr. Wheeler could tell me anything about this Rev. Leonidas W. Smiley, I would feel under many obligations to him.

Simon Wheeler backed me into a corner and blockaded me there with his chair, and then sat me down and reeled off the monotonous narrative which follows this paragraph. He never smiled, he never frowned, he never changed his voice from the gentle-flowing key to which he tuned the initial sentence, he never betrayed the slightest suspicion of enthusiasm; but all through the interminable narrative there ran a vein of impressive earnestness and sincerity, which showed me plainly that, so far from his imagining that there was anything ridiculous or funny about his story, he regarded it as a really important matter, and admired its two heroes as men of transcendent genius in finesse. To me, the spectacle of a man drifting serenely along through such a queer yarn without ever smiling, was exquisitely absurd. As I said before, I asked him to tell me what he knew of Rev. Leonidas W. Smiley, and he replied as follows. I let him go on in his own way, and never interrupted him once:

There was a feller here once by the name of *Jim* Smiley, in the winter of '49—or maybe it was the spring of '50—I don't recollect exactly, somehow, though what makes me think it was one or the other is because I remember the big flume wasn't finished when he first came to the camp; but anyway, he was the curiousest man about always betting on anything that turned up you ever see, if he could get anybody to bet on the other side; and if he couldn't, he'd change sides. Any way that suited the other man would suit him — any way just so's he got a bet, *he* was satisfied. But still he was lucky, uncommon lucky; he most always come out winner. He was always ready and laying for a chance; there couldn't be no solit'ry thing mentioned but that feller'd offer to bet on it, and take any side you please, as I was just telling you. If there was a horse race, you'd find him flush, or you'd find him busted at the end of it; if there was a dogfight, he'd bet on it; if there was a cat-fight, he'd bet on it; if there was a chicken-fight, he'd bet on it; why, if there was two birds setting on a fence, he would bet you which one would fly first; or if there was a camp meeting, he would be there reg'lar, to bet on Parson Walker, which he judged to be the best exhorter about here, and so he was, too, and a good man. If he even seen a straddlebug start to go anywheres, he would bet you how long it would take him to get wherever he was going to, and if you took him up, he would foller that straddlebug to Mexico but what he would find out where he was bound for and how long he was on the road. Lots of the boys here has seen that Smiley, and can tell you about him. Why, it never made no difference to *him* — he would bet on *any*thing — the dangdest feller. Parson Walker's wife laid very sick once, for a good while, and it seemed as if they warn't going to save her; but one morning he come in, and Smiley asked how she was, and he said she was considerable better — thank the Lord for his inf'nit mercy — and coming on so smart that, with the blessing of Prov'dence, she'd get well yet; and Smiley, before he thought, says, "Well, I'll risk two-and-a-half that she don't, anyway."

Thish-yer Smiley had a mare — the boys called her the fifteen-minute nag, but that was only in fun, you know, because, of course, she was faster than that — and he used to win money on that horse, for all she was so slow and always had the asthma, or the distemper, or the consumption, or something of that kind. They used to give her two or three hundred yards start, and then pass her under way; but always at the fag end of the race she'd get excited and desperate-like, and come cavorting and straddling up, and scattering her legs around limber, sometimes in the air, and sometimes out to one side amongst the fences, and kicking up m-o-r-e dust, and raising m-o-r-e racket with her coughing and sneezing and blowing her nose — and always fetch up at the stand just about a neck ahead, as near as you could cipher it down.

And he had a little small bull pup, that to look at him you'd think he wan't worth a cent, but to set around and look ornery, and lay for a chance to steal something. But as soon as money was up on him, he was a different dog; his underjaw'd begin to stick out like the fo-castle of a steamboat, and his teeth would uncover, and shine savage like the furnaces. And a dog might tackle him, and bully-rag him, and bite him, and throw him over his shoulder two or three times, and Andrew Jackson — which was the name of the pup — Andrew Jackson would never let on but what *he* was satisfied, and hadn't expected nothing else—and the bets being doubled and doubled on the other side all the time, till the money was all up; and then all of a sudden he would grab that other dog jest by the j'int of his hind leg and freeze to it—not chaw, you understand, but only jest grip and hang on till they throwed up the sponge, if it was a year. Smiley always come out winner on that pup, till he harnessed a dog once that didn't have no hind legs, because they'd been sawed off by a circular saw, and when the thing had gone along far enough, and the money was all up, and he come to make a snatch for his pet holt, he saw in a minute how he'd been imposed on, and how the other dog had him in the door, so to speak, and he 'peared surprised, and then he looked sorter discouraged-like, and didn't try no more to win the fight, and so he got shucked out bad. He give Smiley a look, as much as to say his heart was broke, and it was *his* fault for putting up a dog that hadn't no hind legs for him to take holt of, which was his main dependence in a fight, and then he limped off a piece and laid down and died. It was a good pup, was that Andrew Jackson, and would have made a name for hisself if he'd lived, for the stuff was in him, and he had genius—I know it, because he hadn't had no opportunities to speak of, and it don't stand to reason that a dog could make such a fight as he could under them circumstances, if he hadn't no talent. It always makes me feel sorry when I think of that last fight of his'n, and the way it turned out.

Well, thish-yer Smiley had rat-tarriers, and chicken cocks, and tom-cats, and all them kind of things, till you couldn't rest, and you couldn't fetch nothing for him to bet on but he'd match you. He ketched a frog one day, and took him home, and said he cal'klated to educate him; and so he never done nothing for three months but set in his back yard and learn that frog to jump. And you bet you he *did* learn him, too. He'd give him a little punch behind, and the next minute you'd see that frog whirling in the air like a doughnut—see him turn one summerset, or may be a couple, if he got a good start, and come down flatfooted and all right, like a cat. He got him up so in the matter of catching flies, and kept him in practice so constant, that he'd nail a fly every time as far as he could see him. Smiley said all a frog wanted was education, and he could do most anything—and I believe him. Why, I've seen him set Dan'l Webster down here on this floor—Dan'l Webster was the name of the frog—and sing out, "Flies, Dan'l, flies!" and quicker'n you could wink, he'd spring straight up, and snake a fly off'n the counter there, and flop down on the floor again as solid as a gob of mud, and fall to scratching the side of his head with his hind foot as indifferent as if he hadn't no idea he'd been doin' any more'n any frog might do. You never see a frog so modest and straight-for'ard as he was, for all he was so gifted. And when it come to fair and square jumping on a dead level, he could get over more ground at one straddle than any animal of his breed you ever see. Jumping on a dead level was his strong suit, you understand; and when it come to that, Smiley would ante up money on him as long as he had a red.[1] Smiley was monstrous proud of his frog, and well he might be, for fellers that had traveled and been everywheres, all said he laid over any frog that ever *they* see.

Well, Smiley kept the beast in a little lattice box, and he used to fetch him downtown sometimes and lay for a bet. One day a feller—a stranger in the camp, he was—come across him with his box, and says:

"What might it be that you've got in the box?"

And Smiley says, sorter indifferent like, "It might be a parrot, or it might be a canary, maybe, but it an't—it's only just a frog."

And the feller took it, and looked at it careful, and turned it round this way and that, and says, "H'm—so 'tis. Well, what's *he* good for?"

"Well," Smiley says, easy and careless, "he's good enough for *one* thing, I should judge—he can outjump any frog in Calaveras county."

The feller took the box again, and took another long, particular look, and give it back to Smiley, and says, very deliberate, "Well, I don't see no p'ints about that frog that's any better'n any other frog."

"Maybe you don't," Smiley says. "Maybe you understand frogs, and maybe you don't understand 'em; maybe you've had experience, and maybe you an't only a amature, as it were. Anyways, I've got *my* opinion, and I'll risk forty dollars that he can outjump any frog in Calaveras county."

And the feller studied a minute, and then says, kinder sad like, "Well, I'm only a stranger here, and I an't got no frog; but if I had a frog, I'd bet you."

And then Smiley says, "That's all right—that's all right—if you'll hold my box a minute, I'll go and get you a frog." And so the feller took the box, and put up his forty dollars along with Smiley's, and set down to wait.

So he set there a good while thinking and thinking to hisself, and then he got the frog out and prized his mouth open and took a teaspoon and filled him full of quail shot—filled him pretty near up to his chin—and set him on the floor. Smiley he went to the swamp and slopped around in the mud for a long time, and finally he ketched a frog, and fetched him in, and give him to this feller, and says:

"Now, if you're ready, set him alongside of Dan'l, with his fore-paws just even with Dan'l, and I'll give the word." Then he says, "One—two—three—jump!" and him and the feller touched up the frogs from behind, and the new frog hopped off, but Dan'l give a heave, and hysted up his shoulders—so—like a Frenchman, but it wan't no use—he couldn't budge; he was planted as solid as an anvil, and he couldn't no more stir than if he was anchored out. Smiley was a good deal surprised, and he was disgusted too, but he didn't have no idea what the matter was, of course.

The feller took the money and started away; and when he was going out at the door, he sorter jerked his thumb over his shoulders—this

---

[1]A penny.

way—at Dan'l, and says again, very deliberate, "Well, *I* don't see no p'ints about that frog that's any better'n any other frog."

Smiley he stood scratching his head and looking down at Dan'l a long time, and at last he says, "I do wonder what in the nation that frog throw'd off for—I wonder if there an't something the matter with him— he 'pears to look mighty baggy, somehow." And he ketched Dan'l by the nap of the neck, and lifted him up and says, "Why, blame my cats, if he don't weigh five pound!" and turned him upside down, and he belched out a double handful of shot. And then he see how it was, and he was the maddest man—he set the frog down and took out after that feller, but he never ketched him. And—

[Here Simon Wheeler heard his name called from the front yard, and got up to see what was wanted.] And turning to me as he moved away, he said: "Just set where you are, stranger, and rest easy—I an't going to be gone a second."

But, by your leave, I did not think that a continuation of the history of the enterprising vagabond *Jim* Smiley would be likely to afford me much information concerning the Rev. *Leonidas W.* Smiley, and so I started away.

At the door I met the sociable Wheeler returning, and he buttonholed me and recommenced:

"Well, thish-yer Smiley had a yaller one-eyed cow that didn't have no tail, only jest a short stump like a bannanner, and—"

"Oh! hang Smiley and his afflicted cow," I muttered, good-naturedly, and bidding the old gentleman good-day, I departed.   [1865]

BRET HARTE

Bret Harte (1836–1902) was born in Albany, New York, the third of four children. After the death of his father, his formal schooling ended when he was thirteen. In 1853 his mother moved to California and remarried, and the next year Harte followed her, drifting from job to job and writing pretentious poetry. By the time he was twenty he believed he was a failure and confided in his diary, "The conclusion forced upon me by observation and not by vain enthusiasm is that I am fit for nothing else—[this condition] must impel me to seek distinction and future in literature." He began working as a printer for the Northern Californian newspaper in a town north of San Francisco, filling its columns with his own articles and poetry and developing a sense of what his readers expected. At the beginning of 1859 he lost the job after he used the paper to denounce the townspeople who had massacred a tribe of peaceful Native Americans holding a religious festival near Eureka.

A short time afterward Harte began to work in San Francisco as a compositor at the Golden Era, writing a column titled "Town and Table Talk" about theatrical events. In 1864–65 he managed a weekly newspaper, the Californian. Two years later he collected the short pieces he was writing for periodicals into his first two books: Condensed Novels, and Other Papers, parodies of authors such as James Fenimore Cooper and Charles Dickens, and The Last Galleon and Other Tales. The following year he became editor of a new magazine, The Overland Monthly, for which he did his best work. Two of his short stories for this paper are frequently cited as the beginning of Western local-color fiction: "The Luck of Roaring Camp" (August 1868) and "The Outcasts of Poker Flat" (January 1869). As the critic Henry L. Golemba understood,

> In addition to satisfying audience demand for local-color sketches and providing formulas for hundreds of Western books and movies over the next century, these two stories deployed a cunning narrative strategy which insured their success with genteel readers. The tales argue that society's outcasts—whether gamblers, gold-seekers, prostitutes, or unemployed cowboys—all have hearts of gold. Circumstances can prove them to be nobler than the mainstream society which rejects them. Yet an elegant, polished, and highly cultivated narrative voice distances the narrator from the subjects, thereby shielding genteel readers from a potentially disturbing theme.

In 1864 Harte met Mark Twain, who later claimed that Harte taught him how to write. For the next decade Harte enjoyed financial success as The Luck of Roaring Camp, and Other Sketches, published in Boston by Fields and Osgood in 1870, went through several printings. He left San Francisco the following year and never returned to California, living first in New Jersey and then in London. Having created a portrait gallery of stock Western characters—the softhearted gambler, the sentimental prostitute, the rough miner who is touched *by a chance encounter with a baby—Harte later complained to a friend that "I grind out the old tunes on the old organ and gather up the coppers." For the rest of his career he turned out formula fiction along with occasional spirited essays.*

RELATED COMMENTARY: *Bret Harte, "The Rise of the 'Short Story,'" page 1356.*

The Luck of Roaring Camp

There was commotion in Roaring Camp. It could not have been a fight, for in 1850 that was not novel enough to have called together the entire settlement. The ditches and claims were not only deserted, but "Tuttle's grocery" had contributed its gamblers, who, it will be remembered, calmly continued their game the day that French Pete and Kanaka Joe shot each other to death over the bar in the front room. The whole camp was collected before a rude cabin on the outer edge of the clearing. Conversation was carried on in a low tone, but the name of a woman was frequently repeated. It was a name familiar enough in the camp,— "Cherokee Sal."

Perhaps the less said of her the better. She was a coarse, and, it is to be feared, a very sinful woman. But at that time she was the only woman in Roaring Camp, and was just then lying in sore extremity, when she most needed the ministration of her own sex. Dissolute, abandoned, and irreclaimable, she was yet suffering a martyrdom hard enough to bear even when veiled by sympathizing womanhood, but now terrible in her loneliness. The primal curse had come to her in that original isolation which must have made the punishment of the first transgression so dreadful. It was, perhaps, part of the expiation of her sin, that, at a moment when she most lacked her sex's intuitive tenderness and care, she met only the half-contemptuous faces of her masculine associates. Yet a few of the spectators were, I think, touched by her sufferings. Sandy Tipton thought it was "rough on Sal," and, in the contemplation of her condition, for a moment rose superior to the fact that he had an ace and two bowers in his sleeve.

It will be seen, also, that the situation was novel. Deaths were by no means uncommon in Roaring Camp, but a birth was a new thing. People had been dismissed from the camp effectively, finally, and with no possibility of return; but this was the first time that anybody had been introduced *ab initio*. Hence the excitement.

"You go in there, Stumpy," said a prominent citizen known as "Kentuck," addressing one of the loungers. "Go in there, and see what you kin do. You've had experience in them things."

Perhaps there was a fitness in the selection. Stumpy, in other climes, had been the putative head of two families; in fact, it was owing to some legal informality in these proceedings that Roaring Camp—a city of refuge—

was indebted to his company. The crowd approved the choice, and Stumpy was wise enough to bow to the majority. The door closed on the extempore surgeon and midwife, and Roaring Camp sat down outside, smoked its pipe, and awaited the issue.

The assemblage numbered about a hundred men. One or two of these were actual fugitives from justice, some were criminal, and all were reckless. Physically, they exhibited no indication of their past lives and character. The greatest scamp had a Raphael face, with a profusion of blond hair; Oakhurst, a gambler, had the melancholy air and intellectual abstraction of a Hamlet; the coolest and most courageous man was scarcely over five feet in height, with a soft voice and an embarrassed, timid manner. The term "roughs" applied to them was a distinction rather than a definition. Perhaps in the minor details of fingers, toes, ears, etc., the camp may have been deficient, but these slight omissions did not detract from their aggregate force. The strongest man had but three fingers on his right hand; the best shot had but one eye.

Such was the physical aspect of the men that were dispersed around the cabin. The camp lay in a triangular valley, between two hills and a river. The only outlet was a steep trail over the summit of a hill that faced the cabin, now illuminated by the rising moon. The suffering woman might have seen it from the rude bunk whereon she lay, — seen it winding like a silver thread until it was lost in the stars above.

A fire of withered pine-boughs added sociability to the gathering. By degrees the natural levity of Roaring Camp returned. Bets were freely offered and taken regarding the result. Three to five that "Sal would get through with it"; even, that the child would survive; side bets as to the sex and complexion of the coming stranger. In the midst of an excited discussion an exclamation came from those nearest the door, and the camp stopped to listen. Above the swaying and moaning of the pines, the swift rush of the river, and the crackling of the fire, rose a sharp, querulous cry, — a cry unlike anything heard before in the camp. The pines stopped moaning, the river ceased to rush, and the fire to crackle. It seemed as if Nature had stopped to listen too.

The camp rose to its feet as one man! It was proposed to explode a barrel of gunpowder, but, in consideration of the situation of the mother, better counsels prevailed, and only a few revolvers were discharged; for, whether owing to the rude surgery of the camp, or some other reason, Cherokee Sal was sinking fast. Within an hour she had climbed, as it were, that rugged road that led to the stars, and so passed out of Roaring Camp, its sin and shame forever. I do not think that the announcement disturbed them much, except in speculation as to the fate of the child. "Can he live now?" was asked of Stumpy. The answer was doubtful. The only other being of Cherokee Sal's sex and maternal condition in the settlement was an ass. There was some conjecture as to fitness, but the experiment was tried. It was less problematical than the ancient treatment of Romulus and Remus, and apparently as successful.

When these details were completed, which exhausted another hour, the door was opened, and the anxious crowd of men who had already formed themselves into a queue, entered in single file. Beside the low bunk or shelf, on which the figure of the mother was starkly outlined below the blankets, stood a pine table. On this a candle-box was placed, and within it, swathed in staring red flannel, lay the last arrival at Roaring Camp. Beside the candle-box was placed a hat. Its use was soon indicated. "Gentlemen," said Stumpy, with a singular mixture of authority and *ex officio* complacency,— "Gentlemen will please pass in at the front door, round the table, and out at the back door. Them as wishes to contribute anything toward the orphan will find a hat handy." The first man entered with his hat on; he uncovered, however, as he looked about him, and so, unconsciously, set an example to the next. In such communities good and bad actions are catching. As the procession filed in, comments were audible,—criticisms addressed, perhaps, rather to Stumpy, in the character of showman,— "Is that him?" "mighty small specimen"; "hasn't mor'n got the color"; "ain't bigger nor a derringer." The contributions were as characteristic: A silver tobacco-box; a doubloon; a navy revolver, silver mounted; a gold specimen; a very beautifully embroidered lady's handkerchief (from Oakhurst the gambler); a diamond breastpin; a diamond ring (suggested by the pin, with the remark from the giver that he "saw that pin and went two diamonds better"); a slung shot; a Bible (contributor not detected); a golden spur; a silver teaspoon (the initials, I regret to say, were not the giver's); a pair of surgeon's shears; a lancet; a Bank of England note for £5; and about $200 in loose gold and silver coin. During these proceedings Stumpy maintained a silence as impassive as the dead on his left, a gravity as inscrutable as that of the newly born on his right. Only one incident occurred to break the monotony of the curious procession. As Kentuck bent over the candle-box half curiously, the child turned, and, in a spasm of pain, caught at his groping finger, and held it fast for a moment. Kentuck looked foolish and embarrassed. Something like a blush tried to assert itself in his weather-beaten cheek. "The d—d little cuss!" he said, as he extricated his finger, with, perhaps, more tenderness and care than he might have been deemed capable of showing. He held that finger a little apart from its fellows as he went out, and examined it curiously. The examination provoked the same original remark in regard to the child. In fact, he seemed to enjoy repeating it. "He rastled with my finger," he remarked to Tipton, holding up the member, "the d—d little cuss!"

It was four o'clock before the camp sought repose. A light burnt in the cabin where the watchers sat, for Stumpy did not go to bed that night. Nor did Kentuck. He drank quite freely, and related with great gusto his experience, invariably ending with his characteristic condemnation of the new-comer. It seemed to relieve him of any unjust implication of sentiment, and Kentuck had the weaknesses of the nobler sex. When everybody else had gone to bed, he walked down to the river, and whistled reflectingly. Then he walked up the gulch, past the cabin, still whistling with demonstrative unconcern. At a large redwood tree he paused and retraced his steps, and again passed the cabin. Half-way down to the river's bank he again paused, and then returned and knocked at the door. It was opened by Stumpy. "How goes it?" said Kentuck, looking past Stumpy toward the candle-box. "All serene," replied Stumpy. "Anything up?" "Nothing." There was a pause—an embarrassing one—Stumpy still holding the door. Then Kentuck had recourse to his finger, which he held up to Stumpy. "Rastled with it,—the d—d little cuss," he said, and retired.

The next day Cherokee Sal had such rude sepulture as Roaring Camp afforded. After her body had been committed to the hillside, there was a formal meeting of the camp to discuss what should be done with her infant. A resolution to adopt it was unanimous and enthusiastic. But an animated discussion in regard to the manner and feasibility of providing for its wants at once sprung up. It was remarkable that the argument partook of none of those fierce personalities with which discussions were usually conducted at Roaring Camp. Tipton proposed that they should send the child to Red Dog,—a distance of forty miles,—where female attention could be procured. But the unlucky suggestion met with fierce and unanimous opposition. It was evident that no plan which entailed parting from their new acquisition would for a moment be entertained. "Besides," said Tom Ryder, "them fellows at Red Dog would swap it, and ring in somebody else on us." A disbelief in the honesty of other camps prevailed at Roaring Camp as in other places.

The introduction of a female nurse in the camp also met with objection. It was argued that no decent woman could be prevailed to accept Roaring Camp as her home, and the speaker urged that "they didn't want any more of the other kind." This unkind allusion to the defunct mother, harsh as it may seem, was the first spasm of propriety,—the first symptom of the camp's regeneration. Stumpy advanced nothing. Perhaps he felt a certain delicacy in interfering with the selection of a possible successor in office. But when questioned, he averred stoutly that he and "Jinny"—the mammal before alluded to—could manage to rear the child. There was something original, independent, and heroic about the plan that pleased the camp. Stumpy was retained. Certain articles were sent for to Sacramento. "Mind," said the treasurer, as he pressed a bag of gold-dust into the expressman's hand, "the best that can be got,—lace, you know, and filigree-work and frills,—d—n the cost!"

Strange to say, the child thrived. Perhaps the invigorating climate of the mountain camp was compensation for material deficiencies. Nature took the foundling to her broader breast. In that rare atmosphere of the Sierra foot-hills,—that air pungent with balsamic odor, that ethereal cordial at once bracing and exhilarating,—he may have found food and nourishment, or a subtle chemistry that transmuted asses' milk to lime and phosphorus. Stumpy inclined to the belief that it was the latter and good nursing. "Me and that ass," he would say, "has been father and mother to him! Don't you," he would add, apostrophizing the helpless bundle before him, "never go back on us."

By the time he was a month old, the necessity of giving him a name became apparent. He had generally been known as "the Kid," "Stumpy's boy," "the Cayote" (an allusion to his vocal powers), and even by Kentuck's endearing diminutive of "the d—d little cuss." But these were felt to be vague and unsatisfactory, and were at last dismissed under another influence. Gamblers and adventurers are generally superstitious, and Oakhurst one day declared that the baby had brought "the luck" to Roaring Camp. It was certain that of late they had been successful. "Luck" was the name agreed upon, with the prefix of Tommy for greater convenience. No allusion was made to the mother, and the father was unknown. "It's better," said the philosophical Oakhurst, "to take a fresh deal all round. Call him Luck, and start him fair." A day was accordingly set apart for the christening. What was meant by this ceremony the reader may imagine, who has already gathered some idea of the reckless irreverence of Roaring Camp. The master of ceremonies was one "Boston," a noted wag, and the occasion seemed to promise the greatest facetiousness. This ingenious satirist had spent two days in preparing a burlesque of the church service, with pointed local allusions. The choir was properly trained and Sandy Tipton was to stand godfather. But after the procession had marched to the grove with music and banners, and the child had been deposited before a mock altar, Stumpy stepped before the expectant crowd. "It ain't my style to spoil fun, boys," said the little man, stoutly, eying the faces around him, "but it strikes me that this thing ain't exactly on the squar. It's playing it pretty low down on this yer baby to ring in fun on him that he ain't going to understand. And ef there's going to be any godfathers round, I'd like to see who's got any better rights than me." A silence followed Stumpy's speech. To the credit of all humorists be it said, that the first man to acknowledge its justice was the satirist, thus stopped of his fun. "But," said Stumpy, quickly, following up his advantage, "we're here for a christening, and we'll have it. I proclaim you Thomas Luck, according to the laws of the United States and the State of California, so help me God." It was the first time that the name of the Deity had been uttered otherwise than profanely in the camp. The form of christening was perhaps even more ludicrous than the satirist had conceived; but, strangely enough, nobody saw it and nobody laughed. "Tommy" was christened as seriously as he would have been under a Christian roof, and cried and was comforted in as orthodox fashion.

And so the work of regeneration began in Roaring Camp. Almost imperceptibly a change came over the settlement. The cabin assigned to "Tommy Luck"—or "The Luck," as he was more frequently called—first showed signs of improvement. It was kept scrupulously clean and whitewashed. Then it was boarded, clothed, and papered. The rosewood cradle—packed eighty miles by mule—had, in Stumpy's way of putting it, "sorter killed the rest of the furniture." So the rehabilitation of the cabin became a necessity. The men who were in the habit of lounging in at Stumpy's to see "how The Luck got on" seemed to appreciate the change, and, in self-defence, the rival establishment of "Tuttle's grocery" bestirred itself, and imported a carpet and mirrors. The reflections of the latter on the appearance of Roaring Camp tended to produce stricter habits of personal cleanliness. Again, Stumpy imposed a kind of quarantine upon those who aspired to the honor and privilege of holding "The Luck." It was a cruel mortification to Kentuck—who, in the carelessness of a large nature and the habits of frontier life, had begun to regard all garments as a second cuticle, which, like a snake's, only sloughed off through decay—to be debarred this privilege from certain prudential reasons. Yet such was the subtle influence of innovation that he thereafter appeared regularly every afternoon in a clean shirt, and face still shining from his ablutions. Nor were moral and social sanitary laws neglected. "Tommy," who was supposed to spend his whole existence in a persistent attempt to repose, must not be disturbed by noise. The shouting and yelling which had gained the camp its infelicitous title were not permitted within hearing distance of Stumpy's. The men conversed in whispers, or smoked with Indian gravity. Profanity was tacitly given up in these sacred precincts, and throughout the camp a popular form of expletive, known as "D—n the luck!" and "Curse the luck!" was abandoned, as having a new personal bearing. Vocal music was not interdicted, being supposed to have a soothing, tranquillizing quality, and one song, sung by "Man-o'-War Jack," an English sailor, from her Majesty's Australian colonies, was quite popular as a lullaby. It was a lugubrious recital of the exploits of "the Arethusa, Seventy-four," in a muffled minor, ending with a prolonged dying fall at the burden of each verse, "On b-o-o-o-ard of the Arethusa." It was a fine sight to see Jack holding The Luck, rocking from side to side as if with the motion of a ship, and crooning forth this naval ditty. Either through the peculiar rocking of Jack or the length of his song,—it contained ninety stanzas, and was continued with conscientious deliberation to the bitter end,—the lullaby generally had the desired effect. At such times the men would lie at full length under the trees, in the soft summer twilight, smoking their pipes and drinking in the melodious utterances. An indistinct idea that this was pastoral happiness pervaded the camp. "This 'ere kind o' think," said the Cockney Simmons, meditatively reclining on his elbow, "is 'evingly." It reminded him of Greenwich.

On the long summer days The Luck was usually carried to the gulch, from whence the golden store of Roaring Camp was taken. There, on a blanket spread over pine-boughs, he would lie while the men were working in the ditches below. Latterly, there was a rude attempt to decorate this bower with flowers and sweet-smelling shrubs, and generally some one would bring him a cluster of wild honeysuckles, azaleas, or the painted blossoms of Las Mariposas. The men had suddenly awakened to the fact that there were beauty and significance in these trifles, which they had so long trodden carelessly beneath their feet. A flake of glittering mica, a fragment of variegated quartz, a bright pebble from the bed of the creek, became beautiful to eyes thus cleared and strengthened, and were invariably put aside for "The Luck." It was wonderful how many treasures the woods and hillsides yielded that "would do for Tommy." Surrounded by playthings such as never child out of fairyland had before, it is to be hoped that Tommy was content. He appeared to be securely happy albeit there was an infantine gravity about him—a contemplative light in his round gray eyes that sometimes worried Stumpy. He was always tractable and quiet, and it is recorded that once having crept beyond his "corral,"—a hedge of tessellated pine-boughs, which surrounded his bed,—he dropped over the bank on his head in the soft earth, and remained with his mottled legs in the air in that position for at least five minutes with unflinching gravity. He was extricated without a murmur. I hesitate to record the many other instances of his sagacity, which rest, unfortunately, upon the statements of prejudiced friends. Some of them were not without a tinge of superstition. "I crep' up the bank just now," said Kentuck one day, in a breathless state of excitement, "and dern my skin if he wasn't a talking to a jaybird as was a sittin' on his lap. There they was, just as free and sociable as anything you please, a jawin' at each other just like two cherry-bums." Howbeit, whether creeping over the pine-boughs or lying lazily on his back blinking at the leaves above him, to him the birds sang, the squirrels chattered, and the flowers bloomed. Nature was his nurse and playfellow. For him she would let slip between the leaves golden shafts of sunlight that fell just within his grasp; she would send wandering breezes to visit him with the balm of bay and resinous gums; to him the tall redwoods nodded familiarly and sleepily, the bumble-bees buzzed, and the rooks cawed a slumbrous accompaniment.

Such was the golden summer of Roaring Camp. They were "flush times,"—and the Luck was with them. The claims had yielded enormously. The camp was jealous of its privileges and looked suspiciously on strangers. No encouragement was given to immigration, and, to make their seclusion more perfect, the land on either side of the mountain wall that surrounded the camp they duly preempted. This, and a reputation for singular proficiency with the revolver, kept the reserve of Roaring Camp inviolate. The expressman—their only connecting link with the surrounding world— sometimes told wonderful stories of the camp. He would say, "They've a street up there in 'Roaring,' that would lay over any street in Red Dog. They've got vines and flowers round their houses, and they wash themselves twice a day. But they're mighty rough on strangers, and they worship an Ingin baby."

With the prosperity of the camp came a desire for further improvement. It was proposed to build a hotel in the following spring, and to invite one or two decent families to reside there for the sake of "The Luck,"—

who might perhaps profit by female companionship. The sacrifice that this concession to the sex cost these men, who were fiercely sceptical in regard to its general virtue and usefulness, can only be accounted for by their affection for Tommy. A few still held out. But the resolve could not be carried into effect for three months, and the minority meekly yielded in the hope that something might turn up to prevent it. And it did.

The winter of 1851 will long be remembered in the foot-hills. The snow lay deep on the Sierras, and every mountain creek became a river, and every river a lake. Each gorge and gulch was transformed into a tumultuous watercourse that descended the hillsides, tearing down giant trees and scattering its drift and débris along the plain. Red Dog had been twice under water, and Roaring Camp had been forewarned. "Water put the gold into them gulches," said Stumpy. "It's been here once and will be here again!" And that night the North Fork suddenly leaped over its banks, and swept up the triangular valley of Roaring Camp.

In the confusion of rushing water, crushing trees, and crackling timber, and the darkness which seemed to flow with the water and blot out the fair valley, but little could be done to collect the scattered camp. When the morning broke, the cabin of Stumpy nearest the river-bank was gone. Higher up the gulch they found the body of its unlucky owner; but the pride, the hope, the joy, the Luck, of Roaring Camp had disappeared. They were returning with sad hearts, when a shout from the bank recalled them.

It was a relief-boat from down the river. They had picked up, they said, a man and an infant, nearly exhausted, about two miles below. Did anybody know them, and did they belong here?

It needed but a glance to show them Kentuck lying there, cruelly crushed and bruised, but still holding the Luck of Roaring Camp in his arms. As they bent over the strangely assorted pair, they saw that the child was cold and pulseless. "He is dead," said one. Kentuck opened his eyes. "Dead?" he repeated feebly. "Yes, my man, and you are dying too." A smile lit the eyes of the expiring Kentuck. "Dying," he repeated, "he's a taking me with him, — tell the boys I've got the Luck with me now"; and the strong man, clinging to the frail babe as a drowning man is said to cling to a straw, drifted away into the shadowy river that flows forever to the unknown sea.

[1868]

GEORGE WASHINGTON CABLE

George Washington Cable (1844–1925), born in New Orleans, was the fifth child of parents whose different backgrounds typified the diversity of that city's population. His father came from an old Virginia family and his mother was descended from Calvinists who had settled in New England two hundred years earlier. Cable's formal education ended at fifteen, when he was forced to help support his family as a clerk after his father's death. In 1863 he enlisted in the Confederate army and was wounded twice. After the war he returned to New Orleans, where he married in 1869. The following year he began writing as a columnist and reporter for the New Orleans Picayune. *In 1872 Cable was given access to the city archives at the Cabildo and the St. Louis Cathedral in New Orleans so he could research a series of articles for the newspaper about the city's charities and churches. In these archives he found materials he began to turn into short stories, dramatizing the southern city's records of landhold-ings and legal proceedings that documented its complex racial and cultural diversity since 1718. The critic Fred Lewis Pattee understood Cable's response to the city's archives as mirrored in his stories:*

> *It seemed hardly possible that the new world possessed such a Baghdad of wonder: old Spanish aristocracy, French chivalry of a forgotten* ancien régime, *Creoles, Acadians from the Grand Pré dispersion, adventurers from all the picturesque parts of the earth, slavery with its barbaric atmosphere and its shuddery background of dread, and behind it all and around it all like a mighty moat shutting it close in upon itself and rendering all else in the world a mere hearsay and dream, the swamps and lagoons of the great [Mississippi] river.*

In 1873 Cable showed several of his stories to the journalist Edward King, who had been sent to New Orleans by Scribner's Monthly *to write about the South after the Civil War. On King's recommendation, the magazine began to publish Cable's stories the following year. The publication of Cable's* Old Creole Days *in 1879 established the genre of southern local-color fiction and is one of the pioneering collections of American local-color stories in its use of regional dialect, setting, and character.*

"Belles Demoiselles Plantation," included in Old Creole Days, *first appeared in* Scribner's Monthly *in April 1874. Based on an historical event that occurred around 1820, the story dramatizes the polarization between the two lines of an old New Orleans family in the characters Injin Charlie, the poor half-caste, and his proud but impecunious half-brother, the Creole aristocrat De Charleu. Cable followed the seven stories in* Old Creole Days *with a best-selling novel,* The Grandissimes: A Story of Creole Life *(1880). Five years later he had been so severely criticized by southern readers for his essays and speeches advocating full civil rights for African Americans that he and his family left New Orleans and settled in Northampton, Massachusetts. He continued to write novels and short fiction about the South, publishing three more*

collections of short stories: Strange True Stories of Louisiana *(1889),* Strong Hearts *(1899), and* The Flower of the Chapdelaines *(1918).*

Belles Demoiselles Plantation

The original grantee was Count——, assume the name to be De Charleu; the old Creoles never forgive a public mention. He was the French king's commissary. One day, called to France to explain the lucky accident of the commissariat having burned down with his account books inside, he left his wife, a Choctaw Comtesse, behind.

Arrived at court, his excuses were accepted, and that tract granted to him where afterward stood Belles Demoiselles Plantation. A man cannot remember everything! In a fit of forgetfulness he married a French gentlewoman, rich and beautiful, and "brought her out." However, "All's well that ends well"; a famine had been in the colony, and the Choctaw Comtesse had starved, leaving nought but a half-caste orphan family lurking on the edge of the settlement, bearing our French gentlewoman's own new name, and being mentioned in Monsieur's will.

And the new Comtesse—she tarried but a twelvemonth, left Monsieur a lovely son, and departed, led out of this vain world by the swamp fever.

From this son sprang the proud Creole family of De Charleu. It rose straight up, up, up, generation after generation, tall, branchless, slender, palmlike; and finally, in the time of which I am to tell, flowered with all the rare beauty of a century plant, in Artémise, Innocente, Felicité, the twins Marie and Martha, Leontine and little Septima; the seven beautiful daughters for whom their home had been fitly named Belles Demoiselles.

The Count's grant had once been a long Pointe, round which the Mississippi used to whirl, and seethe, and foam, that it was horrid to behold. Big whirlpools would open and wheel about in the savage eddies under the low bank, and close up again, and others open, and spin, and disappear. Great circles of muddy surface would boil up from hundreds of feet below, and gloss over, and seem to float away—sink, come back again under water, and with only a soft hiss surge up again, and again drift off, and vanish. Every few minutes the loamy bank would tip down a great load of earth upon its besieger, and fall back a foot—sometimes a yard—and the writhing river would press after, until at last the Pointe was quite swallowed up, and the great river glided by in a majestic curve, and asked no more; the bank stood fast, the "caving" became a forgotten misfortune, and the diminished grant was a long, sweeping willowy bend, rustling with miles of sugar cane.

Coming up the Mississippi in the sailing craft of those early days, about the time one first could descry the white spires of the old St. Louis

Cathedral, you would be pretty sure to spy, just over to your right under the levee, Belles Demoiselles Mansion, with its broad veranda and red painted cypress roof, peering over the embankment, like a bird in the nest, half hid by the avenue of willows which one of the departed De Charleus—he that married a Marot—had planted on the levee's crown.

The house stood unusually near the river, facing eastward, and standing foursquare, with an immense veranda about its sides, and a flight of steps in front spreading broadly downward, as we open arms to a child. From the veranda nine miles of river were seen; and in their compass, near at hand, the shady garden full of rare and beautiful flowers; farther away broad fields of cane and rice, and the distant quarters of the slaves, and on the horizon everywhere a dark belt of cypress forest.

The master was old Colonel De Charleu—Jean Albert Henri Joseph De Charleu-Marot, and "Colonel" by the grace of the first American governor. Monsieur—he would not speak to anyone who called him "Colonel"—was a hoary-headed patriarch. His step was firm, his form erect, his intellect strong and clear, his countenance classic, serene, dignified, commanding, his manners courtly, his voice musical—fascinating. He had had his vices—all his life; but had borne them, as his race do, with a serenity of conscience and a cleanness of mouth that left no outward blemish on the surface of the gentleman. He had gambled in Royal Street, drunk hard in Orleans Street, run his adversary through in the dueling ground at Slaughter-house Point, and danced and quarreled at the St. Philippe Street Theater quadroon balls. Even now, with all his courtesy and bounty, and a hospitality which seemed to be entertaining angels, he was bitter-proud and penurious, and deep down in his hard-finished heart loved nothing but himself, his name, and his motherless children. But these!—their ravishing beauty was all but excuse enough for the unbounded idolatry of their father. Against these seven goddesses he never rebelled. Had they even required him to defraud old De Carlos——

I can hardly say.

Old De Carlos was his extremely distant relative on the Choctaw side. With this single exception, the narrow threadlike line of descent from the Indian wife, diminished to a mere strand by injudicious alliances, and deaths in the gutters of old New Orleans, was extinct. The name, by Spanish contact, had become De Carlos; but this one surviving bearer of it was known to all, and known only, as Injin Charlie.

One thing I never knew a Creole to do. He will not utterly go back on the ties of blood, no matter what sort of knots those ties may be. For one reason, he is never ashamed of his or his father's sins; and for another—he will tell you—he is "all heart!"

So the different heirs of the De Charleu estate had always strictly regarded the rights and interests of the De Carloses, especially their ownership of a block of dilapidated buildings in a part of the city which had once been very poor property, but was beginning to be valuable. This block had much more than maintained the last De Carlos through a long and lazy lifetime, and, as his household consisted only of himself, and an aged and crippled Negress, the inference was irresistible that he "had money." Old Charlie, though by alias an "Injin," was plainly a dark white man, about as old as Colonel De Charleu, sunk in the bliss of deep ignorance, shrewd, deaf, and, by repute at least, unmerciful.

The Colonel and he always conversed in English. This rare accomplishment, which the former had learned from his Scotch wife—the latter from up-river traders—they found an admirable medium of communication, answering, better than French could, a similar purpose to that of the stick which we fasten to the bit of one horse and breast gear of another, whereby each keeps his distance. Once in a while, too, by way of jest, English found its way among the ladies of Belles Demoiselles, always signifying that their sire was about to have business with old Charlie.

Now a long-standing wish to buy out Charlie troubled the Colonel. He had no desire to oust him unfairly; he was proud of being always fair; yet he did long to engross the whole estate under one title. Out of his luxurious idleness he had conceived this desire, and thought little of so slight an obstacle as being already somewhat in debt to old Charlie for money borrowed, and for which Belles Demoiselles was, of course, good, ten times over. Lots, buildings, rents, all, might as well be his, he thought, to give, keep, or destroy. "Had he but the old man's heritage. Ah! he might bring that into existence which his *belles demoiselles* had been begging for, 'since many years'; a home—and such a home—in the gay city. Here he should tear down this row of cottages, and make his garden wall; there that long rope-walk should give place to vine-covered arbors; the bakery yonder should make way for a costly conservatory; that wine warehouse should come down, and the mansion go up. It should be the finest in the state. Men should never pass it, but they should say—'the palace of the De Charleus; a family of grand descent, a people of elegance and bounty, a line as old as France, a fine old man, and seven daughters as beautiful as happy; whoever dare attempt to marry there must leave his own name behind him!'

"The house should be of stones fitly set, brought down in ships from the land of 'les Yankees,' and it should have an airy belvedere, with a gilded image tiptoeing and shining on its peak, and from it you should see, far across the gleaming folds of the river, the red roof of Belles Demoiselles, the countryseat. At the big stone gate there should be a porter's lodge, and it should be a privilege even to see the ground."

Truly they were a family fine enough, and fancy-free enough to have fine wishes, yet happy enough where they were, to have had no wish but to live there always.

To those, who, by whatever fortune, wandered into the garden of Belles Demoiselles some summer afternoon as the sky was reddening toward evening, it was lovely to see the family gathered out upon the tiled pavement at the foot of the broad front steps, gaily chatting and jesting, with that ripple of laughter that comes so pleasingly from a bevy of girls. The father would be found seated in their midst, the center of attention and compliment, witness, arbiter, umpire, critic, by his beautiful children's unanimous appointment, but the single vassal, too, of seven absolute sovereigns.

Now they would draw their chairs near together in eager discussion of some new step in the dance, or the adjustment of some rich adornment. Now they would start about him with excited comments to see the eldest fix a bunch of violets in his buttonhole. Now the twins would move down a walk after some unusual flower, and be greeted on their return with the high pitched notes of delighted feminine surprise.

As evening came on they would draw more quietly about their paternal center. Often their chairs were forsaken, and they grouped themselves on the lower steps, one above another, and surrendered themselves to the tender influences of the approaching night. At such an hour the passer on the river, already attracted by the dark figures of the broad-roofed mansion, and its woody garden standing against the glowing sunset, would hear the voices of the hidden group rise from the spot in the soft harmonies of an evening song; swelling clearer and clearer as the thrill of music warmed them into feeling, and presently joined by the deeper tones of the father's voice; then, as the daylight passed quite away, all would be still, and he would know that the beautiful home had gathered its nestlings under its wings.

And yet, for mere vagary, it pleased them not to be pleased.

"Arti!" called one sister to another in the broad hall, one morning— mock amazement in her distended eyes—"something is goin' to took place!"

"*Comm-e-n-t?*"—long-drawn perplexity.

"Papa is goin' to town!"

The news passed upstairs.

"Inno!"—one to another meeting in a doorway—"something is goin' to took place!"

"*Qu'est-ce-que c'est!*"—vain attempt at gruffness.

"Papa is goin' to town!"

The unusual tidings were true. It was afternoon of the same day that the Colonel tossed his horse's bridle to his groom, and stepped up to old Charlie, who was sitting on his bench under a China tree, his head, as was his fashion, bound in a Madras handkerchief. The "old man" was plainly under the effect of spirits, and smiled a deferential salutation without trusting himself to his feet.

"Eh, well, Charlie!"—the Colonel raised his voice to suit his kinsman's deafness, "how is those times with my friend Charlie?"

"Eh?" said Charlie, distractedly.

"Is that goin' well with my friend Charlie?"

"In de house—call her"—making a pretense of rising.

"*Non, non!* I don't want"—the speaker paused to breathe—"ow is collection?"

"Oh!" said Charlie, "every day he make me more poorer!"

"What do you hask for it?" asked the planter indifferently, designating the house by a wave of his whip.

"Ask for w'at?" said Injin Charlie.

"De *house!* What you ask for it?"

"I don't believe," said Charlie.

"What you would *take* for it!" cried the planter.

"Wait for w'at?"

"What you would take for the whole block?"

"I don't want to sell him!"

"I'll give you *ten thousand dollah* for it."

"Ten t'ousand dollah for dis house? Oh, no, dat is no price. He is blame good old house—dat old house." (Old Charlie and the Colonel never swore in presence of each other.) "Forty years dat old house didn't had to be paint! I easy can get fifty t'ousand dollah for dat old house."

"Fifty thousand picayunes; yes," said the Colonel.

"She's a good house. Can make plenty money," pursued the deaf man.

"That's what makes you so rich, eh, Charlie?"

"*Non,* I don't make nothing. Too blame clever, me, dat's de troub'. She's a good house—make money fast like a steamboat—make a barrel full in a week! Me, I lose money all de days. Too blame clever."

"Charlie!"

"Eh?"

"Tell me what you'll take."

"Make? I don't make *nothing*. Too blame clever."

"What will you *take*?"

"Oh! I got enough already—half drunk now."

"What will you take for the 'ouse?"

"You want to buy her?"

"I don't know"—(shrug)—"may*be*—if you sell it cheap."

"She's a bully old house."

There was a long silence. By and by old Charlie commenced——

"Old Injin Charlie is a low-down dog."

"*C'est vrai, oui!*" retorted the Colonel in an undertone.

"He's got Injin blood in him."

The Colonel nodded assent.

"But he's got some blame good blood, too, ain't it?"

The Colonel nodded impatiently.

"*Bien!* Old Charlie's Injin blood says, 'sell de house, Charlie, you blame old fool!' *Mais,* old Charlie's good blood says, 'Charlie! if you sell dat old house, Charlie, you low-down old dog, Charlie, what de Comte de Charleu make for you grace-granmuzzer, de dev' can eat you, Charlie, I don't care.'"

"But you'll sell it anyhow, won't you, old man?"

"No!" And the *no* rumbled off in muttered oaths like thunder out on the Gulf. The incensed old Colonel wheeled and started off.

"Curl!" (Colonel) said Charlie, standing up unsteadily.

The planter turned with an inquiring frown.

"I'll trade with you!" said Charlie.

The Colonel was tempted. "'Ow'l you trade?" he asked.

"My house for yours!"

The old Colonel turned pale with anger. He walked very quickly back, and came close up to his kinsman.

"Charlie!" he said.

"Injin Charlie"—with a tipsy nod.

But by this time self-control was returning. "Sell Belles Demoiselles to you?" he said in a high key, and then laughed "Ho, ho, ho!" and rode away.

A cloud, but not a dark one, overshadowed the spirits of Belles Demoiselles plantation. The old master, whose beaming presence had always made him a shining Saturn, spinning and sparkling within the bright circle of his daughters, fell into musing fits, started out of frowning reveries, walked often by himself, and heard business from his overseer fretfully.

No wonder. The daughters knew his closeness in trade, and attributed to it his failure to negotiate for the Old Charlie buildings—so to call them. They began to depreciate Belles Demoiselles. If a north wind blew, it was too cold to ride. If a shower had fallen, it was too muddy to drive. In the morning the garden was wet. In the evening the grasshopper was a burden. *Ennui* was turned into capital; every headache was interpreted a premonition of ague; and when the native exuberance of a flock of ladies without a want or a care burst out in laughter in the father's face, they spread their French eyes, rolled up their little hands, and with rigid wrists and mock vehemence vowed and vowed again that they only laughed at their misery, and should pine to death unless they could move to the sweet city. "Oh! the theater! Oh! Orleans Street! Oh! the masquerade! the Place d'Armes! the ball!" and they would call upon Heaven with French irreverence, and fall into each other's arms, and whirl down the hall singing a waltz, end with a grand collision and fall, and, their eyes streaming merriment, lay the blame on the slippery floor, that would someday be the death of the whole seven.

Three times more the fond father, thus goaded, managed, by accident—business accident—to see old Charlie and increase his offer; but in vain. He finally went to him formally.

"Eh?" said the deaf and distant relative. "For what you want him, eh? Why you don't stay where you halways be 'appy? Dis is a blame old rat hole—good for old Injin Charlie—da's all. Why you don't stay where you be halways 'appy? Why you don't buy somewheres else?"

"That's none of your business," snapped the planter. Truth was, his reasons were unsatisfactory even to himself.

A sullen silence followed. Then Charlie spoke.

"Well, now, look here; I sell you old Charlie's house."

"*Bien!* And the whole block," said the Colonel.

"Hold on," said Charlie. "I sell you de 'ouse and de block. Den I go and git drunk, and go to sleep; de dev' comes along and says, 'Charlie! old Charlie, you blame low-down old dog, wake up! What you doin' here? Where's de 'ouse what Monsieur le Comte give your grace-granmuzzer? Don't you see dat fine gentyman, De Charleu, done gone and tore him down and make him over new, you blame old fool, Charlie, you low-down old Injin dog!'"

"I'll give you forty thousand dollars," said the Colonel.

"For de 'ouse?"

"For all."

The deaf man shook his head.

"Forty-five!" said the Colonel.

"What a lie? For what you tell me 'What a lie?' I don't tell you no lie."

"*Non, non!* I give you *forty-five!*" shouted the Colonel.

Charlie shook his head again.

"Fifty!"

He shook it again.

The figures rose and rose to——

"Seventy-five!"

The answer was an invitation to go away and let the owner alone, as he was, in certain specified respects, the vilest of living creatures, and no company for a fine gentyman.

The "fine gentyman" longed to blaspheme—but before old Charlie—in the name of pride, how could he? He mounted and started away.

"Tell you what I'll make wid you," said Charlie.

The other, guessing aright, turned back without dismounting, smiling.

"How much Belles Demoiselles hoes me now?" asked the deaf one.

"One hundred and eighty thousand dollars," said the Colonel, firmly.

"Yass," said Charlie. "I don't want Belles Demoiselles."

The old Colonel's quiet laugh intimated it made no difference either way.

"But me," continued Charlie, "me—I'm got le Comte de Charleu's blood in me any'ow—a litt' bit, any'ow, ain't it?"

The Colonel nodded that it was.

"*Bien!* If I go out of dis place and don't go to Belles Demoiselles, de peoples will say—dey will say, 'Old Charlie he been all doze time tell a blame *lie!* He ain't no kin to his old grace-granmuzzer, not a blame bit! He don't got nary drop of De Charleu blood to save his blame low-down old Injin soul!' No, sare! What I want wid money, den? No, sare! My place for yours!"

He turned to go into the house, just too soon to see the Colonel make an ugly whisk at him with his riding whip. Then the Colonel, too, moved off.

Two or three times over, as he ambled homeward, laughter broke through his annoyance, as he recalled old Charlie's family pride and the presumption of his offer. Yet each time he could but think better of—not the offer to swap, but the preposterous ancestral loyalty. It was so much better than he could have expected from his "low-down" relative, and not unlike his own whim withal—the proposition which went with it was forgiven.

This last defeat bore so harshly on the master of Belles Demoiselles that the daughters, reading chagrin in his face, began to repent. They loved their father as daughters can, and when they saw their pretended dejection harassing him seriously they restrained their complaints, displayed more than ordinary tenderness, and heroically and ostentatiously concluded there was no place like Belles Demoiselles. But the new mood touched him more than the old, and only refined his discontent. Here was a man, rich without the care of riches, free from any real trouble, happiness as native to his house as perfume to his garden, deliberately, as it were with premeditated malice, taking joy by the shoulder and bidding her be gone to town, whither he might easily have followed, only that the very same ancestral nonsense that kept Injin Charlie from selling the old place for twice its value prevented him from choosing any other spot for a city home.

But by and by the charm of nature and the merry hearts around him prevailed; the fit of exalted sulks passed off, and after a while the year flared up at Christmas, flickered, and went out.

New Year came and passed; the beautiful garden of Belles Demoiselles put on its spring attire; the seven fair sisters moved from rose to rose; the cloud of discontent had warmed into invisible vapor in the rich sunlight of family affection, and on the common memory the only scar of last year's wound was old Charlie's sheer impertinence in crossing the caprice of the De Charleus. The cup of gladness seemed to fill with the filling of the river.

How high that river was! Its tremendous current rolled and tumbled and spun along, hustling the long funeral flotillas of drift—and how near shore it came! Men were out day and night, watching the levee. On windy nights even the old Colonel took part, and grew lighthearted with occupation and excitement, as every minute the river threw a white arm over the levee's top, as though it would vault over. But all held fast, and, as the summer drifted in, the water sunk down into its banks and looked quite incapable of harm.

On a summer afternoon of uncommon mildness, old Colonel Jean Albert Henri Joseph De Charleu-Marot, being in a mood for revery, slipped the custody of his feminine rulers and sought the crown of the levee, where it was his wont to promenade. Presently he sat upon a stone bench—a favorite seat. Before him lay his broad-spread fields; nearby, his lordly mansion; and being still—perhaps by female contact—somewhat sentimental, he fell to musing on his past. It was hardly worthy to be proud of. All its morning was reddened with mad frolic, and far toward the meridian it was marred with elegant rioting. Pride had kept him well-nigh useless, and despised the honors won by valor; gaming had dimmed prosperity; death had taken his heavenly wife; voluptuous ease had mortgaged his lands; and yet his house still stood, his sweet-smelling fields were still fruitful, his name was fame enough; and yonder and yonder, among the trees and flowers, like angels walking in Eden, were the seven goddesses of his only worship.

Just then a slight sound behind him brought him to his feet. He cast his eyes anxiously to the outer edge of the little strip of bank between the levee's base and the river. There was nothing visible. He paused, with his ear toward the water, his face full of frightened expectation. Ha! There came a single plashing sound, like some great beast slipping into the river, and little waves in a wide semicircle came out from under the bank and spread over the water.

"My God!"

He plunged down the levee and bounded through the low weeds to the edge of the bank. It was sheer, and the water about four feet below. He did not stand quite on the edge, but fell upon his knees a couple of yards away, wringing his hands, moaning and weeping, and staring through his watery eyes at a fine, long crevice just discernible under the matted grass, and curving outward on either hand toward the river.

"My God!" he sobbed aloud; "my God!" and even while he called, his God answered: the tough Bermuda grass stretched and snapped, the crevice slowly became a gape, and softly, gradually, with no sound but the closing of the water at last, a ton or more of earth settled into the boiling eddy and disappeared.

At the same instant a pulse of the breeze brought from the garden behind, the joyous, thoughtless laughter of the fair mistresses of Belles Demoiselles.

The old Colonel sprang up and clambered over the levee. Then, forcing himself to a more composed movement, he hastened into the house and ordered his horse.

"Tell my children to make merry while I am gone," he left word. "I shall be back tonight," and the horse's hoofs clattered down a byroad leading to the city.

"Charlie," said the planter, riding up to a window, from which the old man's nightcap was thrust out, "what you say, Charlie—my house for yours, eh, Charlie—what you say?"

"Ello!" said Charlie; "from where you come from dis time of tonight?"

"I come from the Exchange in St. Louis Street." (A small fraction of the truth.)

"What you want?" said matter-of-fact Charlie.

"I come to trade."

The low-down relative drew the worsted off his ears. "Oh! yass," he said with an uncertain air.

"Well, old man Charlie, what you say: my house for yours—like you said—eh, Charlie?"

"I dunno," said Charlie; "it's nearly mine now. Why you don't stay dare youse'f?"

"Because I don't want!" said the Colonel savagely. "Is dat reason enough for you? You better take me in de notion, old man, I tell you—yes!"

Charlie never winced; but how his answer delighted the Colonel! Quoth Charlie:

"I don't care—I take him!—*mais,* possession give right off."

"Not the whole plantation, Charlie; only——"

"I don't care," said Charlie; "we easy can fix dat. *Mais,* what for you don't want to keep him? I don't want him. You better keep him."

"Don't you try to make no fool of me, old man," cried the planter.

"Oh, no!" said the other. "Oh, no! but you make a fool of yourself, ain't it?"

The dumbfounded Colonel stared; Charlie went on:

"Yass! Belles Demoiselles is more wort' dan tree block like dis one. I pass by dare since two weeks. Oh, pritty Belles Demoiselles! De cane was wave in de wind, de garden smell like a bouquet, de whitecap was jump up and down on de river; seven *belles demoiselles* was ridin' on horses. 'Pritty, pritty, pritty!' says old Charlie. Ah! *Monsieur le père,* 'ow 'appy, 'appy, 'appy!

"Yass!" he continued—the Colonel still staring—"le Comte de Charleu have two familie. One was low-down Choctaw, one was high-up *noblesse.* He gave the low-down Choctaw dis old rat hole; he give Belles Demoiselles to you granfozzer; and now you don't be *satisfait.* What I'll do wid Belles Demoiselles? She'll break me in two years, yass. And what you'll do wid old Charlie's house, eh? You'll tear her down and make you'se'f a blame old fool. I rather wouldn't trade!"

The planter caught a big breathful of anger, but Charlie went straight on:

"I rather wouldn't, *mais* I will do it for you;—just the same, like Monsieur le Comte would say, 'Charlie, you old fool, I want to shange houses wid you.'"

So long as the Colonel suspected irony he was angry, but as Charlie seemed, after all, to be certainly in earnest, he began to feel conscience-stricken. He was by no means a tender man, but his lately discovered misfortune had unhinged him, and this strange, undeserved, disinterested family fealty on the part of Charlie touched his heart. And should he still try to lead him into the pitfall he had dug? He hesitated;—no, he would show him the place by broad daylight, and if he chose to overlook the "caving bank," it would be his own fault;—a trade's a trade.

"Come," said the planter, "come at my house tonight; tomorrow we look at the place before breakfast, and finish the trade."

"For what?" said Charlie.

"Oh, because I got to come in town in the morning."

"I don't want," said Charlie. "How I'm goin' to come dere?"

"I git you a horse at the liberty stable."

"Well—anyhow—I don't care—I'll go." And they went.

When they had ridden a long time, and were on the road darkened by hedges of Cherokee rose, the Colonel called behind him to the "low-down" scion:

"Keep the road, old man."

"Eh?"

"Keep the road."

"Oh, yes; all right; I keep my word; we don't goin' to play no tricks, eh?"

But the Colonel seemed not to hear. His ungenerous design was beginning to be hateful to him. Not only old Charlie's unprovoked good-ness was prevailing; the eulogy on Belles Demoiselles had stirred the depths of an intense love for his beautiful home. True, if he held to it, the caving of the bank, at its present fearful speed, would let the house into the river within three months; but were it not better to lose it so, than sell his birthright? Again—coming back to the first thought—to betray his own blood! It was only Injin Charlie; but had not the De Charleu blood just spoken out in him? Unconsciously he groaned.

After a time they struck a path approaching the plantation in the rear, and a little after, passing from behind a clump of live oaks, they came in sight of the villa. It looked so like a gem, shining through its dark grove, so like a great glowworm in the dense foliage, so significant of luxury and gai-ety, that the poor master, from an overflowing heart, groaned again.

"What?" asked Charlie.

The Colonel only drew his rein, and, dismounting mechanically, con-templated the sight before him. The high, arched doors and windows were thrown wide to the summer air; from every opening the bright light of numerous candelabra darted out upon the sparkling foliage of magnolia and bay, and here and there in the spacious verandas a colored lantern swayed in the gentle breeze. A sound of revel fell on the ear, the music of harps; and across one window, brighter than the rest, flitted, once or twice, the shadows of dancers. But oh! the shadows flitting across the heart of the fair mansion's master!

"Old Charlie," said he, gazing fondly at his house, "you and me is both old, eh?"

"Yaas," said the stolid Charlie.

"And we has both been bad enough in our time, eh, Charlie?"

Charlie, surprised at the tender tone, repeated "Yaas."

"And you and me is mighty close?"

"Blame close, yaas."

"But you never know me to cheat, old man!"

"No"—impassively.

"And do you think I would cheat you now?"

"I dunno," said Charlie. "I don't believe."

"Well, old man, old man"—his voice began to quiver—"I sha'n't cheat you now. My God!—old man, I tell you—you better not make the trade!"

"Because for what?" asked Charlie in plain anger; but both looked quickly toward the house! The Colonel tossed his hands wildly in the air, rushed forward a step or two, and, giving one fearful scream of agony and fright, fell forward on his face in the path. Old Charlie stood transfixed with horror. Belles Demoiselles, the realm of maiden beauty, the home of merriment, the house of dancing, all in the tremor and glow of pleasure, suddenly sunk, with one short, wild wail of terror—sunk, sunk, down, down, down, into the merciless, unfathomable flood of the Mississippi.

Twelve long months were midnight to the mind of the childless father; when they were only half gone, he took to his bed; and every day, and every night, old Charlie, the "low-down," the "fool," watched him tenderly, tended him lovingly, for the sake of his name, his misfortunes, and his broken heart. No woman's step crossed the floor of the sick-chamber, whose western dormer windows overpeered the dingy architecture of old Charlie's block; Charlie and a skilled physician, the one all interest, the other all gentleness, hope, and patience—these only entered by the door; but by the window came in a sweet-scented evergreen vine, transplanted from the caving banks of Belles Demoiselles. It caught the rays of sunset in its flowery net and let them softly in upon the sick man's bed; gathered the glancing beams of the moon at midnight, and often wakened the sleeper to look, with his mindless eyes, upon their pretty silver fragments strewn upon the floor.

By and by there seemed—there was—a twinkling dawn of returning reason. Slowly, peacefully, with an increase unseen from day to day, the light of reason came into his eyes, and speech became coherent; but withal there came a failing of the wrecked body, and the doctor said that monsieur was both better and worse.

One evening, as Charlie sat by the vine-clad window with his fireless pipe in his hand, the old Colonel's eyes fell full upon his own, and rested there.

"Charl—" he said with an effort, and his delighted nurse hastened to the bedside and bowed his best ear. There was an unsuccessful effort or two, and then he whispered, smiling with sweet sadness——

"We didn't trade."

The truth, in this case, was a secondary matter to Charlie; the main point was to give a pleasing answer. So he nodded his head decidedly, as who should say—"Oh, yes, we did, it was a bona-fide swap!" but when he saw the smile vanish, he tried the other expedient and shook his head with still more vigor, to signify that they had not so much as approached a bargain; and the smile returned.

Charlie wanted to see the vine recognized. He stepped backward to the window with a broad smile, shook the foliage, nodded and looked smart.

"I know," said the Colonel, with beaming eyes, — "many weeks."

The next day ——

"Charl ——"

The best ear went down.

"Send for a priest."

The priest came, and was alone with him a whole afternoon. When he left, the patient was very haggard and exhausted, but smiled and would not suffer the crucifix to be removed from his breast.

One more morning came. Just before dawn Charlie, lying on a pallet in the room, thought he was called, and came to the bedside.

"Old man," whispered the failing invalid, "is it caving yet?"

Charlie nodded.

"It won't pay you out."

"Oh, dat makes not'ing," said Charlie. Two big tears rolled down his brown face. "Dat makes not'in."

The Colonel whispered once more:

"*Mes belles demoiselles!* in paradise;—in the garden—I shall be with them at sunrise"; and so it was.   [1874]

CONSTANCE FENIMORE WOOLSON

Constance Fenimore Woolson (1840–1894), a descendent of the American novelist James Fenimore Cooper, was born in Claremont, New Hampshire. A few weeks after her birth, three of her sisters died of scarlet fever, and her parents moved with their three surviving children to Cleveland, Ohio. Except for the few years she attended boarding school in New York City, Woolson remained at home in Cleveland. After her father's death in 1869, she and her mother traveled extensively in varous parts of the United States for ten years while she wrote sketches and stories.

In the 1870s Woolson's stories began to appear in the The Atlantic Monthly, Scribner's Monthly, Harper's Magazine, Lippincott's Monthly, *and other leading periodicals. Her short fiction was marked by her rejection of the sentimentality of the earlier women writers who had produced local-color sketches. In 1875 Woolson wrote to a friend, the poet Paul Hamilton Hayne, about her literary style: "I have the idea that women run too much into mere beauty at the expense of power; and the result is, I fear, that I have gone too far the other way: too rude, too abrupt." That year* Castle Nowhere; Lake-Country Sketches, *set in the Great Lakes region, was Woolson's debut collection. In 1877 "Rodman the Keeper" appeared in* The Atlantic Monthly. *The story was set in Andersonville, Georgia, the site of a notorious Confederate prison in which many thousands of Union soldiers died. When Woolson revised the story for book publication in* Rodman the Keeper: Southern Sketches (1880), *she deleted this passage of dialogue between the federal officer John Rodman and the southern girl Bettina Ward:*

> *"Had I fifty millions to spend on the South tomorrow, every cent should go for schools, and for schools alone."*
>
> *"For the negroes, I suppose," said the girl with bitter scorn.*
>
> *"For the negroes, and for the whites also," answered John Rodman gravely. "The lack of general education is painfully apparent everywhere throughout the South; it is from that cause more than any other that your beautiful country now lies desolate."*
>
> *"Desolate—desolate indeed," said Miss Ward.*

Unlike her contemporaries Sarah Orne Jewett and Mary Wilkins Freeman, Woolson was not grounded in any specific regional boundary. She was more interested in the heterogeneous nature of the various communities in the United States in which she lived, particularly the contrast between Northerners and Southerners after the Civil War. In 1880, after the death of her mother, Woolson left the United States to live and travel in Europe for the next fourteen years, where she wrote five novels and two more collections of stories. In Florence she began a long friendship with Henry James, modeling her novels on his style. In James's Partial Portraits (1887), *he praised the stories in* Rod-man the Keeper *as being "full of interesting artistic work," saying, "As the fruit of a remarkable minuteness of observation and tenderness of feeling on the part of one who evidently did not glance and pass, but lingered and analyzed, they have a high value."*

Rodman the Keeper

"Keeper of what? Keeper of the dead. Well, it is easier to keep the dead than the living; and as for the gloom of the thing, the living among whom I have been lately were not a hilarious set."

John Rodman sat in the doorway and looked out over his domain. The little cottage behind him was empty of life save himself alone. In one room the slender appointments provided by government for the keeper, who being still alive must sleep and eat, made the bareness doubly bare; in the other the desk and the great ledgers, the ink and pens, the register, the loud-ticking clock on the wall, and the flag folded on a shelf, were all for the kept, whose names, in hastily written, blotted rolls of manuscript, were waiting to be transcribed in the new red-bound ledgers in the keeper's best handwriting day by day, while the clock was to tell him the hour when the flag must rise over the mounds where reposed the bodies of fourteen thousand United States soldiers—who had languished where once stood the prison pens, on the opposite slopes, now fair and peaceful in the sunset; who had fallen by the way in long marches to and fro under the burning sun; who had fought and died on the many battlefields that reddened the beautiful state, stretching from the peaks of the marble mountains in the smoky west down to the sea islands of the ocean border. The last rim of the sun's red ball had sunk below the horizon line, and the western sky glowed with deep rose-color, which faded away above into pink, into the salmon tint, into shades of that far-away heavenly emerald which the brush of the earthly artist can never reproduce, but which is found sometimes in the iridescent heart of the opal. The small town, a mile distant, stood turning its back on the cemetery; but the keeper could see the pleasant, rambling old mansions, each with its rose garden and neglected outlying fields, the empty Negro quarters falling into ruin, and everything just as it stood when on that April morning the first gun was fired on Sumter; apparently not a nail added, not a brushful of paint applied, not a fallen brick replaced, or latch or lock repaired. The keeper had noted these things as he strolled through the town, but not with surprise; for he had seen the South in its first estate, when, fresh, strong, and fired with enthusiasm, he, too, had marched away from his village home with the colors flying above and the girls waving their handkerchiefs behind, as the regiment, a thousand strong, filed down the dusty road. That regiment, a weak, scarred two hundred, came back a year later with lagging step and colors tattered and scorched, and the girls could not wave their handkerchiefs, wet and sodden with tears. But the keeper, his wound healed, had gone again; and he had seen with his New England eyes the magnificence and the carelessness of the South, her splendor and negligence, her wealth and thriftlessness, as through Virginia and the fair Carolinas, across Georgia and into sunny Florida, he had marched month by month, first a lieutenant, then captain, and finally major and colonel, as death mowed down those above him, and he and his good conduct were left. Everywhere magnificence went hand in hand with neglect, and he had said so as chance now and then threw a conversation in his path.

"We have no such shiftless ways," he would remark, after he had furtively supplied a prisoner with hardtack and coffee.

"And no such grand ones either," Johnny Reb would reply, if he was a man of spirit; and generally he was.

The Yankee, forced to acknowledge the truth of this statement, qualified it by observing that he would rather have more thrift with a little less grandeur; whereupon the other answered that *he* would not; and there the conversation rested. So now ex-Colonel Rodman, keeper of the national cemetery, viewed the little town in its second estate with philosophic eyes. "It is part of a great problem now working itself out; I am not here to tend the living, but the dead," he said.

Whereupon, as he walked among the long mounds, a voice seemed to rise from the still ranks below: "While ye have time, do good to men," it said. "Behold, we are beyond your care." But the keeper did not heed.

This still evening in early February he looked out over the level waste. The little town stood in the lowlands; there were no hills from whence cometh help — calm heights that lift the soul above earth and its cares; no river to lead the aspirations of the children outward toward the great sea. Everything was monotonous, and the only spirit that rose above the waste was a bitterness for the gained and sorrow for the lost cause. The keeper was the only man whose presence personated the former in their sight, and upon him therefore, as representative, the bitterness fell, not in words, but in averted looks, in sudden silences when he approached, in withdrawals and avoidance, until he lived and moved in a vacuum; wherever he went there was presently no one save himself; the very shopkeeper who sold him sugar seemed turned into a man of wood, and took his money reluctantly, although the shilling gained stood perhaps for that day's dinner. So Rodman withdrew himself, and came and went among them no more; the broad acres of his domain gave him as much exercise as his shattered ankle could bear; he ordered his few supplies by the quantity, and began the life of a solitary, his island marked out by the massive granite wall with which the United States Government has carefully surrounded those sad Southern cemeteries of hers; sad, not so much from the number of the mounds representing youth and strength cut off in their bloom, for that is but the fortune of war, as for the complete isolation which marks them. "Strangers in a strange land" is the thought of all who, coming and going to and from Florida, turn aside here and there to stand for a moment among the closely ranged graves which seem already a part of the past, that near past which in our hurrying American life is even now so far away. The government work was completed before the keeper came; the lines of the trenches were defined by low granite copings, and the comparatively few single mounds were headed by trim little white boards bearing generally the word "Unknown," but here and there a name and an age, in most cases a boy from some far-away Northern state; "twenty-one," "twenty-two," said the inscriptions; the dates were those dark years among the sixties, measured now more than by anything else in the number of maidens widowed in heart, and women widowed indeed, who sit still and remember, while the world rushes by. At sunrise the keeper ran up the stars and stripes; and so precise were his ideas of the accessories belonging to the place, that from his own small store of money he had taken enough, by stinting himself, to buy a second flag for stormy weather, so that, rain or not, the colors should float over the dead. This was not patriotism so-called, or rather miscalled, it was not sentimental fancy, it was not zeal or triumph; it was simply a sense of the fitness of things, a conscientiousness which had in it nothing of religion, unless indeed a man's endeavor to live up to his own ideal of his duty be a religion. The same feeling led the keeper to spend hours in copying the rolls. "John Andrew Warren, Company G, Eighth New Hampshire Infantry," he repeated, as he slowly wrote the name, giving "John Andrew" clear, bold capitals and a lettering impossible to mistake; "died August 15, 1863, aged twenty-two years. He came from the prison pen yonder, and lies somewhere in those trenches, I suppose. Now then, John Andrew, don't fancy I am sorrowing for you; no doubt you are better off than I am at this very moment. But nonetheless, John Andrew, shall pen, ink, and hand do their duty to you. For that I am here."

Infinite pains and labor went into these records of the dead; one hair's-breadth error, and the whole page was replaced by a new one. The same spirit kept the grass carefully away from the low coping of the trenches, kept the graveled paths smooth and the mounds green, and the bare little cottage neat as a man-of-war. When the keeper cooked his dinner, the door toward the east, where the dead lay, was scrupulously closed, nor was it opened until everything was in perfect order again. At sunset the flag was lowered, and then it was the keeper's habit to walk slowly up and down the path until the shadows veiled the mounds on each side, and there was nothing save the peaceful green of earth. "So time will efface our little lives and sorrows," he mused, "and we shall be as nothing in the indistinguishable past." Yet nonetheless did he fulfill the duties of every day and hour with exactness. "At least they shall not say that I was lacking," he murmured to himself as he thought vaguely of the future beyond these graves. Who "they" were, it would have troubled him to formulate, since he was one of the many sons whom New England in this generation sends forth with a belief composed entirely of negatives. As the season advanced, he worked all day in the sunshine. "My garden looks well," he said. "I like this cemetery because it is the original resting place of the dead who lie beneath. They were not brought here from distant places, gathered up by contract, numbered, and described like so much merchandise; their first repose has not been broken, their peace has been undisturbed. Hasty burials the prison authorities gave them; the thin bodies were tumbled into the trenches by men almost as thin, for the whole state went hungry in those dark days. There were not many prayers, no tears, as the dead carts went the rounds. But the prayers had been said, and the tears had fallen, while the poor fellows were still alive in the pens yonder; and when at last death came, it was like a release. They suffered long; and I for one believe that therefore shall their rest be long — long and sweet."

After a time began the rain, the soft, persistent, gray rain of the Southern lowlands, and he stayed within and copied another thousand names into the ledger. He would not allow himself the companionship of a dog lest the creature should bark at night and disturb the quiet. There was no one to hear save himself, and it would have been a friendly sound as he lay awake on his narrow iron bed, but it seemed to him against the spirit of the place. He would not smoke, although he had the soldier's fondness for a pipe. Many a dreary evening, beneath a hastily built shelter of boughs, when the rain poured down and everything was comfortless, he had found solace in the curling smoke; but now it seemed to him that it would be incongruous, and at times he almost felt as if it would be selfish too. "*They* cannot smoke, you know, down there under the wet grass," he thought, as standing at the window he looked toward the ranks of the mounds stretching across the eastern end from side to side — "my parade ground," he called it. And then he would smile at his own fancies, draw the curtain, shut out the rain and the night, light his lamp, and go to work on the ledgers again. Some of the names lingered in his memory; he felt as if he had known the men who bore them, as if they had been boys together, and were friends even now although separated for a time. "James Marvin, Company B, Fifth Maine. The Fifth Maine was in the seven days' battle. I say, do you remember that retreat down the Quaker church road, and the way Phil Kearney held the rearguard firm?" And over the whole seven days he wandered with his mute friend, who remembered everything and everybody in the most satisfactory way. One of the little headboards in the parade ground attracted him peculiarly because the name inscribed was his own: "——Rodman, Company A, One Hundred and Sixth New York."

"I remember that regiment; it came from the extreme northern part of the state. Blank Rodman must have melted down here, coming as he did from the half-arctic region along the St. Lawrence. I wonder what he thought of the first hot day, say in South Carolina, along those simmering rice fields?" He grew into the habit of pausing for a moment by the side of this grave every morning and evening. "Blank Rodman. It might easily have been John. And then, where should *I* be?"

But Blank Rodman remained silent, and the keeper, after pulling up a weed or two and trimming the grass over his relative, went off to his duties again. "I am convinced that Blank is a relative," he said to himself, "distant, perhaps, but still a kinsman."

One April day the heat was almost insupportable; but the sun's rays were not those brazen beams that sometimes in Northern cities burn the air and scorch the pavements to a white heat; rather were they soft and still; the moist earth exhaled her richness, not a leaf stirred, and the whole level country seemed sitting in a hot vapor bath. In the early dawn the keeper had performed his outdoor tasks, but all day he remained almost without stirring in his chair between two windows, striving to exist. At high noon out came a little black bringing his supplies from the town, whistling and shuffling along, gay as a lark. The keeper watched him coming slowly down the white road, loitering by the way in the hot blaze, stopping to turn a somersault or two, to dangle over a bridge rail, to execute various impromptu capers all by himself. He reached the gate at last, entered, and, having come all the way up the path in a hornpipe step, he set down his basket at the door to indulge in one long and final double-shuffle before knocking. "Stop that!" said the keeper through the closed blinds. The little darkey darted back; but as nothing further came out of the window—a boot, for instance, or some other stray missile—he took courage, showed his ivories, and drew near again. "Do you suppose I am going to have you stirring up the heat in that way?" demanded the keeper.

The little black grinned, but made no reply, unless smoothing the hot white sand with his black toes could be construed as such; he now removed his rimless hat and made a bow.

"Is it, or is it not warm?" asked the keeper, as a naturalist might inquire of a salamander, not referring to his own so much as to the salamander's ideas on the subject.

"Dunno, mars'," replied the little black.

"How do *you* feel?"

"'Spects I feel all right, mars'."

The keeper gave up the investigation, and presented to the salamander a nickel cent. "I suppose there is no such thing as a cool spring in all this melting country," he said.

But the salamander indicated with his thumb a clump of trees on the green plain north of the cemetery. "Ole Mars' Ward's place—cole spring dah." He then departed, breaking into a run after he had passed the gate, his ample mouth watering at the thought of a certain chunk of taffy at the mercantile establishment kept by Aunt Dinah in a corner of her one-roomed cabin. At sunset the keeper went thirstily out with a tin pail on his arm, in search of the cold spring. "If it could only be like the spring down under the rocks where I used to drink when I was a boy!" he thought. He had never walked in that direction before. Indeed, now that he had abandoned the town, he seldom went beyond the walls of the cemetery. An old road led across to the clump of trees, through fields run to waste, and following it he came to the place, a deserted house with tumble-down fences and overgrown garden, the outbuildings indicating that once upon a time there were many servants and a prosperous master. The house was of wood, large on the ground, with encircling piazzas; across the front door rough bars had been nailed, and the closed blinds were protected in the same manner; from long want of paint the clapboards were gray and mossy, and the floor of the piazza had fallen in here and there from decay. The keeper decided that his cemetery was a much more cheerful place than this, and then he looked around for the spring. Behind the house the ground sloped down; it must be there. He went around and came suddenly upon a man lying on an old rug outside of a back door. "Excuse me. I thought nobody lived here," he said.

"Nobody does," replied the man; "I am not much of a body, am I?"

His left arm was gone, and his face was thin and worn with long illness; he closed his eyes after speaking, as though the few words had exhausted him.

"I came for water from a cold spring you have here, somewhere," pursued the keeper, contemplating the wreck before him with the interest of one who has himself been severely wounded and knows the long, weary pain. The man waved his hand toward the slope without unclosing his eyes, and Rodman went off with his pail and found a little shady hollow, once curbed and paved with white pebbles, but now neglected, like all the place. The water was cold, however, deliciously cold. He filled his pail and thought that perhaps after all he would exert himself to make coffee, now that the sun was down; it would taste better made of this cold water. When he came up the slope, the man's eyes were open.

"Have some water?" asked Rodman.

"Yes; there's a gourd inside."

The keeper entered, and found himself in a large, bare room; in one corner was some straw covered with an old counterpane, in another a table and chair; a kettle hung in the deep fireplace, and a few dishes stood on a shelf; by the door on a nail hung a gourd; he filled it and gave it to the host of this desolate abode. The man drank with eagerness.

"Pomp has gone to town," he said, "and I could not get down to the spring today, I have had so much pain."

"And when will Pomp return?"

"He should be here now; he is very late tonight."

"Can I get you anything?"

"No, thank you; he will soon be here."

The keeper looked out over the waste; there was no one in sight. He was not a man of any especial kindliness — he had himself been too hardly treated in life for that — but he could not find it in his heart to leave this helpless creature all alone with night so near. So he sat down on the doorstep. "I will rest awhile," he said, not asking but announcing it. The man had turned away and closed his eyes again, and they both remained silent, busy with their own thoughts; for each had recognized the ex-soldier, Northern and Southern, in portions of the old uniforms, and in the accent. The war and its memories were still very near to the maimed, poverty-stricken Confederate; and the other knew that they were, and did not obtrude himself.

Twilight fell, and no one came.

"Let me get you something," said Rodman; for the face looked ghastly as the fever abated. The other refused. Darkness came; still, no one.

"Look here," said Rodman, rising, "I have been wounded myself, was in hospital for months; I know how you feel. You must have food — a cup of tea, now, and a slice of toast, brown and thin."

"I have not tasted tea or wheaten bread for weeks," answered the man; his voice died off into a wail, as though feebleness and pain had drawn the cry from him in spite of himself. Rodman lighted a match; there was no candle, only a piece of pitch pine stuck in an iron socket on the wall; he set fire to this primitive torch and looked around.

"There is nothing there," said the man outside, making an effort to speak carelessly; "my servant went to town for supplies. Do not trouble yourself to wait; he will come presently, and — and I want nothing."

But Rodman saw through proud poverty's lie; he knew that irregular quavering of the voice, and that trembling of the hand; the poor fellow had but one to tremble. He continued his search; but the bare room gave back nothing, not a crumb.

"Well, if you are not hungry," he said briskly, "I am, hungry as a bear; and I'll tell you what I am going to do. I live not far from here, and I live all alone too; I haven't a servant as you have. Let me take supper here with you, just for a change; and, if your servant comes, so much the better, he can wait upon us. I'll run over and bring back the things."

He was gone without waiting for reply; the shattered ankle made good time over the waste, and soon returned, limping a little, but bravely hasting, while on a tray came the keeper's best supplies, Irish potatoes, corned beef, wheaten bread, butter, and coffee; for he would not eat the hot biscuits, the corncake, the bacon and hominy of the country, and constantly made little New England meals for himself in his prejudiced little kitchen. The pine torch flared in the doorway; a breeze had come down from the far mountains and cooled the air. Rodman kindled a fire on the cavernous hearth, filled the kettle, found a saucepan, and commenced operations, while the other lay outside and watched every movement in the lighted room.

"All ready; let me help you in. Here we are now; fried potatoes, cold beef, mustard, toast, butter, and tea. Eat, man; and the next time I am laid up you shall come over and cook for me."

Hunger conquered, and the other ate, ate as he had not eaten for months. As he was finishing a second cup of tea, a slow step came around the house; it was the missing Pomp, an old Negro, bent and shriveled, who carried a bag of meal and some bacon in his basket. "That is what they live on," thought the keeper.

He took leave without more words. "I suppose now I can be allowed to go home in peace," he grumbled to conscience. The Negro followed him across what was once the lawn. "Fin' Mars' Ward mighty low," he said apologetically, as he swung open the gate which still hung between its posts, although the fence was down, "but I hurred and hurred as fas' as I could; it's mighty fur to de town. Proud to see you, sah; hope you'll come again. Fine fambly, de Wards, sah, befo' de war."

"How long has he been in this state?" asked the keeper.

"Ever sence one ob de las' battles, sah; but he's worse sence we come yer, 'bout a mont' back."

"Who owns the house? Is there no one to see to him? has he no friends?"

"House b'long to Mars' Ward's uncle; fine place once, befo' de war; he's dead now, and dah's nobuddy but Miss Bettina, an' she's gone off somewhuz. Propah place, sah, fur Mars' Ward—own uncle's house," said the old slave, loyally striving to maintain the family dignity even then.

"Are there no better rooms—no furniture?"

"Sartin; but—but Miss Bettina, she took de keys; she didn't know we was comin'—"

"You had better send for Miss Bettina, I think," said the keeper, starting homeward with his tray, washing his hands, as it were, of any future responsibility in the affair.

The next day he worked in his garden, for clouds veiled the sun and exercise was possible; but, nevertheless, he could not forget the white face on the old rug. "Pshaw!" he said to himself, "haven't I seen tumble-down old houses and battered human beings before this?"

At evening came a violent thunderstorm, and the splendor of the heavens was terrible. "We have chained you, mighty spirit," thought the keeper as he watched the lightning, "and some time we shall learn the laws of the winds and foretell the storms; then, prayers will no more be offered in churches to alter the weather than they would be offered now to alter an eclipse. Yet back of the lightning and the wind lies the power of the great Creator, just the same."

But still into his musings crept, with shadowy persistence, the white face on the rug.

"Nonsense!" he exclaimed; "if white faces are going around as ghosts, how about the fourteen thousand white faces that went under the sod down yonder? If they could arise and walk, the whole state would be filled and no more carpetbaggers needed." So, having balanced the one with the fourteen thousand, he went to bed.

Daylight brought rain—still, soft, gray rain; the next morning showed the same, and the third likewise, the nights keeping up their part with low-down clouds and steady pattering on the roof. "If there was a river here, we should have a flood," thought the keeper, drumming idly on his window-pane. Memory brought back the steep New England hillsides shedding their rain into the brooks, which grew in a night to torrents and filled the rivers so that they overflowed their banks; then, suddenly, an old house in a sunken corner of a waste rose before his eyes, and he seemed to see the rain dropping from a moldy ceiling on the straw where a white face lay.

"Really, I have nothing else to do today, you know," he remarked in an apologetic way to himself, as he and his umbrella went along the old road; and he repeated the remark as he entered the room where the man lay, just as he had fancied, on the damp straw.

"The weather *is* unpleasant," said the man. "Pomp, bring a chair."

Pomp brought one, the only one, and the visitor sat down. A fire smoldered on the hearth and puffed out acrid smoke now and then, as if the rain had clogged the soot in the long-neglected chimney; from the streaked ceiling oozing drops fell with a dull splash into little pools on the decayed floor; the door would not close; the broken panes were stopped with rags, as if the old servant had tried to keep out the damp; in the ashes a corncake was baking.

"I am afraid you have not been so well during these long rainy days," said the keeper, scanning the face on the straw.

"My old enemy, rheumatism," answered the man; "the first sunshine will drive it away."

They talked awhile, or rather the keeper talked, for the other seemed hardly able to speak, as the waves of pain swept over him; then the visitor went outside and called Pomp out. "*Is* there anyone to help him, or not?" he asked impatiently.

"Fine fambly, befo' de war," began Pomp.

"Never mind all that; is there anyone to help him now—yes or no?"

"No," said the old black with a burst of despairing truthfulness. "Miss Bettina, she's as poor as Mars' Ward, an' dere's no one else. He's had noth'n but hard corncake for three days, an' he can't swaller it no more."

The next morning saw Ward De Rosset lying on the white pallet in the keeper's cottage, and old Pomp, marveling at the cleanliness all around him, installed as nurse. A strange asylum for a Confederate soldier, was it not? But he knew nothing of the change, which he would have fought with his last breath if consciousness had remained; returning fever, how-ever, had absorbed his senses, and then it was that the keeper and the slave had borne him slowly across the waste, resting many times, but accom-plishing the journey at last.

That evening John Rodman, strolling to and fro in the dusky twilight, paused alongside of the other Rodman. "I do not want him here, and that is the plain truth," he said, pursuing the current of his thoughts. "He fills the house; he and Pomp together disturb all my ways. He'll be ready to fling a brick at me too, when his senses come back; small thanks shall I have for lying on the floor, giving up all my comforts, and, what is more, riding over the spirit of the place with a vengeance!" He threw himself down on the grass beside the mound and lay looking up toward the stars, which were coming out, one by one, in the deep blue of the Southern night. "With a vengeance, did I say? That is it exactly—the vengeance of kindness. The poor fellow has suffered horribly in body and in estate, and now ironical Fortune throws him in my way, as if saying, 'Let us see how far your selfishness will yield.' This is not a question of magnanimity; there is no magnanimity about it, for the war is over, and you Northerners have gained every point for which you fought. This is merely a question between man and man; it would be the same if the sufferer was a poor Federal, one of the carpetbaggers, whom you despise so, for instance, or a pagan Chinaman. And Fortune is right; don't you think so, Blank Rodman? I put it to you, now, to one who has suffered the extreme rigor of the other side—those prison pens yonder."

Whereupon Blank Rodman answered that he had fought for a great cause, and that he knew it, although a plain man and not given to speech-making; he was not one of those who had sat safely at home all through the war, and now belittled it and made light of its issues. (Here a murmur came up from the long line of the trenches, as though all the dead had cried out.) But now the points for which he had fought being gained, and strife ended, it was the plain duty of every man to encourage peace. For his part he bore no malice; he was glad the poor Confederate was up in the cottage, and he did not think any the less of the keeper for bringing him there. He would like to add that he thought more of him; but he was sorry to say that he was well aware what an effort it was, and how almost grudgingly the charity began.

If Blank Rodman did not say this, at least the keeper imagined that he did. "That is what he would have said," he thought. "I am glad you do not object," he added, pretending to himself that he had not noticed the rest of the remark.

"We do not object to the brave soldier who honestly fought for his cause, even though he fought on the other side," answered Blank Rodman for the whole fourteen thousand. "But never let a coward, a double-face, or a flippant-tongued idler walk over our heads. It would make us rise in our graves!"

And the keeper seemed to see a shadowy pageant sweep by—gaunt soldiers with white faces, arming anew against the subtle product of peace: men who said, "It was nothing! Behold, we saw it with our eyes!"—stay-at-home eyes.

The third day the fever abated, and Ward De Rosset noticed his surroundings. Old Pomp acknowledged that he had been moved, but veiled the locality: "To a frien's house, Mars' Ward."

"But I have no friends now, Pomp," said the weak voice.

Pomp was very much amused at the absurdity of this. "No frien's! Mars' Ward, no frien's!" He was obliged to go out of the room to hide his laughter. The sick man lay feebly thinking that the bed was cool and fresh, and the closed green blinds pleasant; his thin fingers stroked the linen sheet, and his eyes wandered from object to object. The only thing that broke the rule of bare utility in the simple room was a square of white drawing paper on the wall, upon which was inscribed in ornamental text the following verse:

> *Toujours femme varie,*
> *Bien fou qui s'y fie;*
> *Une femme souvent*
> *N'est qu'une plume au vent.*[1]

With the persistency of illness the eyes and mind of Ward De Rosset went over and over this distich; he knew something of French, but was unequal to the effort of translating; the rhymes alone caught his vagrant fancy. "Toujours femme varie," he said to himself over and over again; and when the keeper entered, he said it to him.

"Certainly," answered the keeper; "bien fou qui s'y fie. How do you find yourself this morning?"

"I have not found myself at all, so far. Is this your house?"

"Yes."

"Pomp told me I was in a friend's house," observed the sick man, vaguely.

"Well, it isn't an enemy's. Had any breakfast? No? Better not talk, then."

He went to the detached shed which served for a kitchen, upset all Pomp's clumsy arrangements, and ordered him outside; then he set to work and prepared a delicate breakfast with his best skill. The sick man eagerly eyed the tray as he entered. "Better have your hands and face sponged off, I think," said Rodman; and then he propped him up skillfully, and left him to his repast. The grass needed mowing on the parade ground; he shouldered his scythe and started down the path, viciously kicking the gravel aside as he walked. "Wasn't solitude your principal idea, John Rodman, when you applied for this place?" he demanded of himself. "How much of it are you likely to have with sick men, and sick men's servants, and so forth?"

The "and so forth," thrown in as a rhetorical climax, turned into reality and arrived bodily upon the scene—a climax indeed. One afternoon,

---

[1]Women are fickle,
  Who trusts in them is certainly crazy;
  A woman is often
  A mere feather in the wind.

returning late to the cottage, he found a girl sitting by the pallet—a girl young and dimpled and dewy; one of the creamy roses of the South that, even in the bud, are richer in color and luxuriance than any Northern flower. He saw her through the door, and paused; distressed old Pomp met him and beckoned him cautiously outside. "Miss Bettina," he whispered gutturally; "she's come back from somewhuz, an' she's awful mad 'cause Mars' Ward's here. I tole her all 'bout 'em—de leaks an' de rheumatiz an' de hard corncake, but she done gone scole me; and Mars' Ward, he know now whar he is, an' he mad too."

"Is the girl a fool?" said Rodman. He was just beginning to rally a little. He stalked into the room and confronted her. "I have the honor of addressing—"

"Miss Ward."

"And I am John Rodman, keeper of the national cemetery."

This she ignored entirely; it was as though he had said, "I am John Jones, the coachman." Coachmen were useful in their way; but their names were unimportant.

The keeper sat down and looked at his new visitor. The little creature fairly radiated scorn; her pretty head was thrown back, her eyes, dark brown fringed with long dark lashes, hardly deigned a glance; she spoke to him as though he was something to be paid and dismissed like any other mechanic.

"We are indebted to you for some day's board, I believe, keeper—medicines, I presume, and general attendance. My cousin will be removed today to our own residence; I wish to pay now what he owes."

The keeper saw that her dress was old and faded; the small black shawl had evidently been washed and many times mended; the old-fashioned knitted purse she held in her hand was lank with long famine.

"Very well," he said; "if you choose to treat a kindness in that way, I consider five dollars a day none too much for the annoyance, expense, and trouble I have suffered. Let me see: five days—or is it six? Yes. Thirty dollars, Miss Ward."

He looked at her steadily; she flushed. "The money will be sent to you," she began haughtily; then, hesitatingly, "I must ask a little time—"

"O Betty, Betty, you know you cannot pay it. Why try to disguise—But that does not excuse *you* for bringing me here," said the sick man, turning toward his host with an attempt to speak fiercely, which ended in a faltering quaver.

All this time the old slave stood anxiously outside of the door; in the pauses they could hear his feet shuffling as he waited for the decision of his superiors. The keeper rose and threw open the blinds of the window that looked out on the distant parade ground. "Bringing you here," he repeated—"*here;* that is my offense, is it? There they lie, fourteen thousand brave men and true. Could they come back to earth they would be the first to pity and aid you, now that you are down. So would it be with you if the case were reversed; for a soldier is generous to a soldier. It was not your own heart that spoke then; it was the small venom of a woman, that here, as everywhere through the South, is playing its rancorous part."

The sick man gazed out through the window, seeing for the first time the far-spreading ranks of the dead. He was very weak, and the keeper's words had touched him; his eyes were suffused with tears. But Miss Ward rose with a flashing glance. She turned her back full upon the keeper and ignored his very existence. "I will take you home immediately, Ward — this very evening," she said.

"A nice, comfortable place for a sick man," commented the keeper, scornfully, "I am going out now, De Rosset, to prepare your supper; you had better have one good meal before you go."

He disappeared, but as he went he heard the sick man say, deprecatingly: "It isn't very comfortable over at the old house now, indeed it isn't, Betty; I suffered" — and the girl's passionate outburst in reply. Then he closed his door and set to work.

When he returned, half an hour later, Ward was lying back exhausted on the pillows, and his cousin sat leaning her head upon her hand; she had been weeping, and she looked very desolate, he noticed, sitting there in what was to her an enemy's country. Hunger is a strong master, however, especially when allied to weakness; and the sick man ate with eagerness.

"I must go back," said the girl, rising. "A wagon will be sent out for you, Ward; Pomp will help you."

But Ward had gained a little strength as well as obstinacy with the nourishing food. "Not tonight," he said.

"Yes, tonight."

"But I cannot go tonight; you are unreasonable, Bettina. Tomorrow will do as well, if go I must."

"If go you must! You do not want to go, then — to go to our own home — and with me" — Her voice broke; she turned toward the door.

The keeper stepped forward. "This is all nonsense, Miss Ward," he said, "and you know it. Your cousin is in no state to be moved. Wait a week or two, and he can go in safety. But do not dare to offer me your money again; my kindness was to the soldier, not to the man, and as such he can accept it. Come out and see him as often as you please. I shall not intrude upon you. Pomp, take the lady home."

And the lady went.

Then began a remarkable existence for the four: a Confederate soldier lying ill in the keeper's cottage of a national cemetery; a rampant little rebel coming out daily to a place which was to her anathema-maranatha;[2] a cynical, misanthropic keeper sleeping on the floor and enduring every variety of discomfort for a man he never saw before — a man belonging to an

---

[2]A loathed invocation or calling. *Anathema* is something loathed; *maranatha* refers to "O Lord, come" which is used as an invocation in I Corinthians 16:22.

idle, arrogant class he detested; and an old black freedman allowing himself to be taught the alphabet in order to gain permission to wait on his master—master no longer in law—with all the devotion of his loving old heart. For the keeper had announced to Pomp that he must learn his alphabet or go; after all these years of theory, he, as a New Englander, could not stand by and see precious knowledge shut from the black man. So he opened it, and mighty dull work he found it.

Ward De Rosset did not rally as rapidly as they expected. The white-haired doctor from the town rode out on horseback, pacing slowly up the graveled roadway with a scowl on his brow, casting, as he dismounted, a furtive glance down toward the parade ground. His horse and his coat were alike old and worn, and his broad shoulders were bent with long service in the miserably provided Confederate hospitals, where he had striven to do his duty through every day and every night of those shadowed years. Cursing the incompetency in high places, cursing the mismanagement of the entire medical department of the Confederate army, cursing the recklessness and indifference which left the men suffering for want of proper hospitals and hospital stores, he yet went on resolutely doing his best with the poor means in his control until the last. Then he came home, he and his old horse, and went the rounds again, he prescribing for whooping cough or measles, and Dobbin waiting outside; the only difference was that fees were small and good meals scarce for both, not only for the man but for the beast. The doctor sat down and chatted awhile kindly with De Rosset, whose father and uncle had been dear friends of his in the bright, prosperous days; then he left a few harmless medicines and rose to go, his gaze resting a moment on Miss Ward, then on Pomp, as if he were hesitating. But he said nothing until on the walk outside he met the keeper, and recognized a person to whom he could tell the truth. "There is nothing to be done; he may recover, he may not; it is a question of strength merely. He needs no medicines, only nourishing food, rest, and careful tendance."

"He shall have them," answered the keeper briefly. And then the old gentleman mounted his horse and rode away, his first and last visit to a national cemetery.

"National!" he said to himself—"national!"

All talk of moving De Rosset ceased, but Miss Ward moved into the old house. There was not much to move: herself, her one trunk, and Marí, a black attendant, whose name probably began life as Maria, since the accent still dwelt on the curtailed last syllable. The keeper went there once, and once only, and then it was an errand for the sick man, whose fancies came sometimes at inconvenient hours—when Pomp had gone to town, for instance. On this occasion the keeper entered the mockery of a gate and knocked at the front door, from which the bars had been removed; the piazza still showed its decaying planks, but quick-growing summer vines had been planted, and were now encircling the old pillars and veiling all defects with their greenery. It was a woman's pathetic effort to cover up what cannot be covered—poverty. The blinds on one side were open, and white curtains waved to and fro in the breeze; into this room he was ushered by Marí. Matting lay on the floor, streaked here and there ominously by the dampness from the near ground. The furniture was of dark mahogany, handsome in its day: chairs, a heavy pier table with low-down glass, into which no one by any possibility could look unless he had eyes in his ankles, a sofa with a stiff round pillow of hair cloth under each curved end, and a mirror with a compartment framed off at the top, containing a picture of shepherds and shepherdesses, and lambs with blue ribbons around their necks, all enjoying themselves in the most natural and lifelike manner. Flowers stood on the high mantelpiece, but their fragrance could not overcome the faint odor of the damp straw-matting. On a table were books—a life of General Lee, and three or four shabby little volumes printed at the South during the war, waifs of prose and poetry of that highly wrought, richly colored style which seems indigenous to Southern soil.

"Some way, the whole thing reminds me of a funeral," thought the keeper.

Miss Ward entered, and the room bloomed at once; at least that is what a lover would have said. Rodman, however, merely noticed that she bloomed, and not the room, and he said to himself that she would not bloom long if she continued to live in such a moldy place. Their conversation in these days was excessively polite, shortened to the extreme minimum possible, and conducted without the aid of the eyes, at least on one side. Rodman had discovered that Miss Ward never looked at him, and so he did not look at her—that is, not often; he was human, however, and she was delightfully pretty. On this occasion they exchanged exactly five sentences, and then he departed, but not before his quick eyes had discovered that the rest of the house was in even worse condition than this parlor, which, by the way, Miss Ward considered quite a grand apartment; she had been down near the coast, trying to teach school, and there the desolation was far greater than here, both armies having passed back and forward over the ground, foragers out, and the torch at work more than once.

"Will there ever come a change for the better?" thought the keeper, as he walked homeward. "What an enormous stone has got to be rolled up hill! But at least, John Rodman, *you* need not go to work at it; *you* are not called upon to lend your shoulder."

Nonetheless, however, did he call out Pomp that very afternoon and sternly teach him "E" and "F," using the smooth white sand for a blackboard, and a stick for chalk. Pomp's primer was a government placard hanging on the wall of the office. It read as follows:

IN THIS CEMETERY REPOSE THE REMAINS OF
FOURTEEN THOUSAND THREE HUNDRED AND TWENTY-ONE
UNITED STATES SOLDIERS.

Tell me not in mournful numbers
Life is but an empty dream;

For the soul is dead that slumbers,
    And things are not what they seem.

Life is real! Life is earnest!
    And the grave is not its goal;
Dust thou art, to dust returnest,
    Was not written of the soul![3]

"The only known instance of the government's condescending to poetry," the keeper had thought, when he first read this placard. It was placed there for the instruction and edification of visitors; but, no visitors coming, he took the liberty of using it as a primer for Pomp. The large letters served the purpose admirably, and Pomp learned the entire quotation; what he thought of it has not transpired. Miss Ward came over daily to see her cousin. At first she brought him soups and various concoctions from her own kitchen — the leaky cavern, once the dining room, where the soldier had taken refuge after his last dismissal from hospital; but the keeper's soups were richer, and free from the taint of smoke; his martial laws of neatness even disorderly old Pomp dared not disobey, and the sick man soon learned the difference. He thanked the girl, who came bringing the dishes over carefully in her own dimpled hands, and then, when she was gone, he sent them untasted away. By chance Miss Ward learned this, and wept bitter tears over it; she continued to come, but her poor little soups and jellies she brought no more.

One morning in May the keeper was working near the flag staff, when his eyes fell upon a procession coming down the road which led from the town and turning toward the cemetery. No one ever came that way: what could it mean? It drew near, entered the gate, and showed itself to be Negroes walking two and two — old uncles and aunties, young men and girls, and even little children, all dressed in their best; a very poor best, sometimes gravely ludicrous imitations of "ole mars'" or "ole miss'," sometimes mere rags bravely patched together and adorned with a strip of black calico or rosette of black ribbon; not one was without a badge of mourning. All carried flowers, common blossoms from the little gardens behind the cabins that stretched around the town on the outskirts — the new forlorn cabins with their chimneys of piled stones and ragged patches of corn; each little darkey had his bouquet and marched solemnly along, rolling his eyes around, but without even the beginning of a smile, while the elders moved forward with gravity, the bubbling, irrepressible gayety of the Negro subdued by the newborn dignity of the freedman.

"Memorial Day," thought the keeper; "I had forgotten it."

"Will you do us de hono', sah, to take de head ob de processio', sah?" said the leader, with a ceremonious bow. Now, the keeper had not much sympathy with the strewing of flowers, North or South; he had seen the

---

[3]The first two stanzas from "A Psalm of Life" (1838) by Henry Wadsworth Longfellow.

beautiful ceremony more than once turned into a political demonstration. Here, however, in this small, isolated, interior town, there was nothing of that kind; the whole population of white faces laid their roses and wept true tears on the graves of their lost ones in the village churchyard when the Southern Memorial Day came round, and just as naturally the whole population of black faces went out to the national cemetery with their flowers on the day when, throughout the North, spring blossoms were laid on the graves of the soldiers, from the little Maine village to the stretching ranks of Arlington, from Greenwood to the far Western burial places of San Francisco. The keeper joined the procession and led the way to the parade ground. As they approached the trenches, the leader began singing and all joined. "Swing low, sweet chariot," sang the freedmen, and their hymn rose and fell with strange, sweet harmony—one of those wild, unwritten melodies which the North heard with surprise and marveling when, after the war, bands of singers came to their cities and sang the songs of slavery, in order to gain for their children the coveted education. "Swing low, sweet chariot," sang the freedmen, and two by two they passed along, strewing the graves with flowers till all the green was dotted with color. It was a pathetic sight to see some of the old men and women, ignorant field hands, bent, dull eyed, and past the possibility of education even in its simplest forms, carefully placing their poor flowers to the best advantage. They knew dimly that the men who lay beneath those mounds had done something wonderful for them and for their children; and so they came bringing their blossoms, with little intelligence but with much love.

The ceremony over, they retired. As he turned, the keeper caught a glimpse of Miss Ward's face at the window.

"Hope we's not makin' too free, sah," said the leader, as the procession, with many a bow and scrape, took leave, "but we's kep' de day now two years, sah, befo' you came, sah, an we's teachin' de chil'en to keep it, sah."

The keeper returned to the cottage. "Not a white face," he said.

"Certainly not," replied Miss Ward, crisply.

"I know some graves at the North, Miss Ward, graves of Southern soldiers, and I know some Northern women who do not scorn to lay a few flowers on the lonely mounds as they pass by with their blossoms on our Memorial Day."

"You are fortunate. They must be angels. We have no angels here."

"I am inclined to believe you are right," said the keeper.

That night old Pomp, who had remained invisible in the kitchen during the ceremony, stole away in the twilight and came back with a few flowers. Rodman saw him going down toward the parade ground, and watched. The old man had but a few blossoms; he arranged them hastily on the mounds with many a furtive glance toward the house, and then stole back, satisfied; he had performed his part.

Ward De Rosset lay on his pallet, apparently unchanged; he seemed neither stronger nor weaker. He had grown childishly dependent upon his host, and wearied for him, as the Scotch say; but Rodman withstood his fancies, and gave him only the evenings, when Miss Bettina was not there. One afternoon, however, it rained so violently that he was forced to seek shelter; he set himself to work on the ledgers; he was on the ninth thousand now. But the sick man heard his step in the outer room, and called in his weak voice, "Rodman, Rodman." After a time he went in, and it ended in his staying; for the patient was nervous and irritable, and he pitied the nurse, who seemed able to please him in nothing. De Rosset turned with a sigh of relief toward the strong hands that lifted him readily, toward the composed manner, toward the man's voice that seemed to bring a breeze from outside into the close room; animated, cheered, he talked volubly. The keeper listened, answered once in a while, and quietly took the rest of the afternoon into his own hands. Miss Ward yielded to the silent change, leaned back, and closed her eyes. She looked exhausted and for the first time pallid; the loosened dark hair curled in little rings about her temples, and her lips were parted as though she was too tired to close them; for hers were not the thin, straight lips that shut tight naturally, like the straight line of a closed box. The sick man talked on. "Come, Rodman," he said, after a while, "I have read that lying verse of yours over at least ten thousand and fifty-nine times; please tell me its history; I want to have something definite to think of when I read it for the ten thousand and sixtieth."

> Toujours femme varie,
> Bien fou qui s'y fie;
> Une femme souvent
> N'est qu'une plume au vent,

read the keeper slowly, with his execrable English accent. "Well, I don't know that I have any objection to telling the story. I am not sure but that it will do me good to hear it all over myself in plain language again."

"Then it concerns yourself," said De Rosset; "so much the better. I hope it will be, as the children say, the truth, and long."

"It will be the truth, but not long. When the war broke out I was twenty-eight years old, living with my mother on our farm in New England. My father and two brothers had died and left me the homestead; otherwise I should have broken away and sought fortune farther westward, where the lands are better and life is more free. But mother loved the house, the fields, and every crooked tree. She was alone, and so I stayed with her. In the center of the village green stood the square, white meeting-house, and near by the small cottage where the pastor lived; the minister's daughter, Mary, was my promised wife. Mary was a slender little creature with a profusion of pale flaxen hair, large, serious blue eyes, and small, delicate features; she was timid almost to a fault; her voice was low and gentle. She was not eighteen, and we were to wait a year. The war came, and I volunteered, of course, and marched away; we wrote to each other often; my letters were full of the camp and skirmishes; hers told of the village, how the widow Brown had fallen ill, and how it was feared that Squire Stafford's boys were lapsing into evil ways. Then came the day when my regiment marched to the field of its slaughter, and soon after our shattered remnant went home. Mary cried over me, and came out every day to the farmhouse with her bunches of violets; she read aloud to me from her good little books, and I used to lie and watch her profile bending over the page, with the light falling on her flaxen hair low down against the small, white throat. Then my wound healed, and I went again, this time for three years; and Mary's father blessed me, and said that when peace came he would call me son, but not before, for these were no times for marrying or giving in marriage. He was a good man, a red-hot abolitionist, and a roaring lion as regards temperance; but nature had made him so small in body that no one was much frightened when he roared. I said that I went for three years; but eight years have passed and I have never been back to the village. First, mother died. Then Mary turned false. I sold the farm by letter and lost the money three months afterward in an unfortunate investment; my health failed. Like many another Northern soldier, I remembered the healing climate of the South; its soft airs came back to me when the snow lay deep on the fields and the sharp wind whistled around the poor tavern where the moneyless, half-crippled volunteer sat coughing by the fire. I applied for this place and obtained it. That is all."

"But it is not all," said the sick man, raising himself on his elbow; "you have not told half yet, nor anything at all about the French verse."

"Oh—that? There was a little Frenchman staying at the hotel; he had formerly been a dancing master, and was full of dry, withered conceits, although he looked like a thin and bilious old ape dressed as a man. He taught me, or tried to teach me, various wise sayings, among them this one, which pleased my fancy so much that I gave him twenty-five cents to write it out in large text for me."

"Toujours femme varie," repeated De Rosset; "but you don't really think so, do you, Rodman?"

"I do. But they cannot help it; it is their nature. I beg your pardon, Miss Ward. I was speaking as though you were not here."

Miss Ward's eyelids barely acknowledged his existence; that was all. But some time after she remarked to her cousin that it was only in New England that one found that pale flaxen hair.

June was waning, when suddenly the summons came. Ward De Rosset died. He was unconscious toward the last, and death, in the guise of sleep, bore away his soul. They carried him home to the old house, and from there the funeral started, a few family carriages, dingy and battered, following the hearse, for death revived the old neighborhood feeling; that honor at least they could pay—the sonless mothers and the widows who lived shut up in the old houses with everything falling into ruin around them, brooding over the past. The keeper watched the small procession as it passed his gate on its way to the churchyard in the village. "There he goes, poor fellow, his sufferings over at last," he said; and then he set the cottage in order and began the old solitary life again.

He saw Miss Ward but once.

It was a breathless evening in August, when the moonlight flooded the level country. He had started out to stroll across the waste; but the mood changed, and climbing over the eastern wall he had walked back to the flag staff, and now lay at its foot gazing up into the infinite sky. A step sounded on the gravel walk; he turned his face that way, and recognized Miss Ward. With confident step she passed the dark cottage, and brushed his arm with her robe as he lay unseen in the shadow. She went down toward the parade ground, and his eyes followed her. Softly outlined in the moonlight, she moved to and fro among the mounds, pausing often, and once he thought she knelt. Then slowly she returned, and he raised himself and waited; she saw him, started, then paused.

"I thought you were away," she said; "Pomp told me so."

"You set him to watch me?"

"Yes. I wished to come here once, and I did not wish to meet you."

"Why did you wish to come?"

"Because Ward was here — and because — because — never mind. It is enough that I wished to walk once among those mounds."

"And pray there?"

"Well — and if I did!" said the girl defiantly.

Rodman stood facing her, with his arms folded; his eyes rested on her face; he said nothing.

"I am going away tomorrow," began Miss Ward again assuming with an effort her old, pulseless manner. "I have sold the place, and I shall never return, I think; I am going far away."

"Where?"

"To Tennessee."

"That is not so very far," said the keeper, smiling.

"There I shall begin a new existence," pursued the voice, ignoring the comment.

"You have scarcely begun the old; you are hardly more than a child, now. What are you going to do in Tennessee?"

"Teach."

"Have you relatives there?"

"No."

"A miserable life — a hard, lonely, loveless life," said Rodman. "God help the woman who must be that dreary thing, a teacher from necessity!"

Miss Ward turned swiftly, but the keeper kept by her side. He saw the tears glittering on her eyelashes, and his voice softened. "Do not leave me in anger," he said; "I should not have spoken so, although indeed it was the truth. Walk back with me to the cottage, and take your last look at the room where poor Ward died, and then I will go with you to your home."

"No; Pomp is waiting at the gate," said the girl, almost inarticulately.

"Very well; to the gate, then."

They went toward the cottage in silence; the keeper threw open the door. "Go in," he said. "I will wait outside."

The girl entered and went into the inner room, throwing herself down upon her knees at the bedside. "O Ward, Ward!" she sobbed; "I am all alone in the world now, Ward—all alone!" She buried her face in her hands and gave way to a passion of tears; and the keeper could not help but hear as he waited outside. Then the desolate little creature rose and came forth, putting on, as she did so, her poor armor of pride. The keeper had not moved from the doorstep. Now he turned his face. "Before you go—go away for ever from this place—will you write your name in my register," he said—"the visitors' register? The government had it prepared for the throngs who would visit these graves; but with the exception of the blacks, who cannot write, no one has come, and the register is empty. Will you write your name? Yet do not write it unless you can think gently of the men who lie there under the grass. I believe you do think gently of them, else why have you come of your own accord to stand by the side of their graves?" As he said this, he looked fixedly at her.

Miss Ward did not answer; but neither did she write.

"Very well," said the keeper; "come away. You will not, I see."

"I cannot! Shall I, Bettina Ward, set my name down in black and white as a visitor to this cemetery, where lie fourteen thousand of the soldiers who killed my father, my three brothers, my cousins; who brought desolation upon all our house, and ruin upon all our neighborhood, all our state, and all our country?—for the South *is* our country, and not your North. Shall I forget these things? Never! Sooner let my right hand wither by my side! I was but a child; yet I remember the tears of my mother, and the grief of all around us. There was not a house where there was not one dead."

"It is true," answered the keeper; "at the South, all went."

They walked down to the gate together in silence.

"Good-by," said John, holding out his hand; "you will give me yours or not as you choose, but I will not have it as a favor."

She gave it.

"I hope that life will grow brighter to you as the years pass. May God bless you!"

He dropped her hand; she turned, and passed through the gateway; then he sprang after her.

"Nothing can change you," he said; "I know it, I have known it all along; you are part of your country, part of the time, part of the bitter hour through which she is passing. Nothing can change you; if it could, you would not be what you are, and I should not—But you cannot change. Good-by, Bettina, poor little child—good-by. Follow your path out into the world. Yet do not think, dear, that I have not seen—have not understood."

He bent and kissed her hand; then he was gone, and she went on alone.

A week later the keeper strolled over toward the old house. It was twilight, but the new owner was still at work. He was one of those sandy-haired, energetic Maine men, who, probably on the principle of extremes, were often found through the South, making new homes for themselves in the pleasant land.

"Pulling down the old house, are you?" said the keeper, leaning idly on the gate, which was already flanked by a new fence.

"Yes," replied the Maine man, pausing; "it was only an old shell, just ready to tumble on our heads. You're the keeper over yonder, an't you?" (He already knew everybody within a circle of five miles.)

"Yes. I think I should like those vines if you have no use for them," said Rodman, pointing to the uprooted greenery that once screened the old piazza.

"Wuth about twenty-five cents, I guess," said the Maine man, handing them over.   [1877]

AMBROSE BIERCE

Ambrose Bierce (1842–1914?), the youngest of nine children, was born in a log cabin in Horse Cave Creek, Ohio. His father was a farmer, and Bierce had only one year of formal education at the Kentucky Military Institute when he was seventeen. During the Civil War he enlisted with the Ninth Indiana Infantry as a drummer boy. Wounded in 1864, he left the army and went to live with a brother in San Francisco. There he began his career as a newspaper writer, publishing his first story, "The Haunted Valley," in The Overland Monthly *in 1871. When Bierce married the daughter of a wealthy Nevada miner, his father-in-law gave the young couple a wedding gift of $10,000, enabling them to live in London for five years. Homesick for California, Bierce returned with his wife and wrote for various newspapers, including William Randolph Hearst's* San Francisco Examiner. *In the 1880s he became very influential in his profession, although in literary circles outside California he was not widely known. Then his wife separated from him, his two sons died tragically, and he became embittered. In his seventies Bierce supervised publication of the twelve volumes of his* Collected Works, *revisited the Civil War battlefields of his youth, and then disappeared across the Mexican border. The Mexican writer Carlos Fuentes imagined Bierce's last months in the novel* The Old Gringo *(1985), which was made into a film.*

Bierce is known as the author of the philosophical epigrams in The Devil's Dictionary *(1906), but his two volumes of short stories are his finest achievement as a writer. He is considered a notable forerunner of American realists such as Stephen Crane. Bierce's first story collection,* In the Midst of Life, *was published privately in San Francisco under the title* Tales of Soldiers and Civilians *(1891). His second collection,* Can Such Things Be?, *was published two years later. "One of the Missing," which was first published in the literary magazine* The Wave *in 1886, was included in this collection.*

Bierce preferred the short story to the novel, defining the novel as a "short story padded." He modeled his creation of suspense leading up to a dramatic crisis after the stories of Edgar Allan Poe, but Bierce described more realistic situations in his fiction. Civil War stories like "One of the Missing" provided vivid images but no escape from the violent death that was Bierce's obsession.

One of the Missing

Jerome Searing, a private soldier of General Sherman's army, then confronting the enemy at and about Kenesaw Mountain, Georgia, turned his back upon a small group of officers, with whom he had been talking in low tones, stepped across a light line of earthworks, and disappeared in a forest. None of the men in line behind the works had said a word to him, nor had he so much as nodded to them in passing, but all who saw understood that this brave man had been intrusted with some perilous duty. Jerome Searing, though a private, did not serve in the ranks; he was detailed for service at division headquarters, being borne upon the rolls as an orderly. "Orderly" is a word covering a multitude of duties. An orderly may be a messenger, a clerk, an officer's servant—anything. He may perform services for which no provision is made in orders and army regulations. Their nature may depend upon his aptitude, upon favour, upon accident. Private Searing, an incomparable marksman, young—it is surprising how young we all were in those days—hardy, intelligent, and insensible to fear, was a scout. The general commanding his division was not content to obey orders blindly without knowing what was in his front, even when his command was not on detached service, but formed a fraction of the line of the army; nor was he satisfied to receive his knowledge of his *vis-à-vis* through the customary channels; he wanted to know more than he was apprised of by the corps commander and the collisions of pickets and skirmishers. Hence Jerome Searing—with his extraordinary daring, his woodcraft, his sharp eyes and truthful tongue. On this occasion his instructions were simple: to get as near the enemy's lines as possible and learn all that he could.

In a few moments he had arrived at the picket line, the men on duty there lying in groups of from two to four behind little banks of earth scooped out of the slight depression in which they lay, their rifles protruding from the green boughs with which they had masked their small defences. The forest extended without a break toward the front, so solemn and silent that only by an effort of the imagination could it be conceived as populous with armed men, alert and vigilant—a forest formidable with possibilities of battle. Pausing a moment in one of the rifle pits to apprise the men of his intention, Searing crept stealthily forward on his hands and knees and was soon lost to view in a dense thicket of underbrush.

"That is the last of him," said one of the men; "I wish I had his rifle; those fellows will hurt some of us with it."

Searing crept on, taking advantage of every accident of ground and growth to give himself better cover. His eyes penetrated everywhere, his ears took note of every sound. He stilled his breathing, and at the cracking of a twig beneath his knee stopped his progress and hugged the earth. It was slow work, but not tedious; the danger made it exciting, but by no physical signs was the excitement manifest. His pulse was as regular, his nerves were as steady, as if he were trying to trap a sparrow.

"It seems a long time," he thought, "but I cannot have come very far; I am still alive."

He smiled at his own method of estimating distance, and crept forward. A moment later he suddenly flattened himself upon the earth and lay motionless, minute after minute. Through a narrow opening in the bushes he had caught sight of a small mound of yellow clay—one of the enemy's rifle pits. After some little time he cautiously raised his head, inch by inch, then his body upon his hands, spread out on each side of him, all the while intently regarding the hillock of clay. In another moment he was upon his feet, rifle in hand, striding rapidly forward with little attempt at concealment. He had rightly interpreted the signs, whatever they were; the enemy was gone.

To assure himself beyond a doubt before going back to report upon so important a matter, Searing pushed forward across the line of abandoned pits, running from cover to cover in the more open forest, his eyes vigilant to discover possible stragglers. He came to the edge of a plantation — one of those forlorn, deserted homesteads of the last years of the war, upgrown with brambles, ugly with broken fences, and desolate with vacant buildings having blank apertures in place of doors and windows. After a keen reconnoissance from the safe seclusion of a clump of young pines, Searing ran lightly across a field and through an orchard to a small structure which stood apart from the other farm buildings, on a slight elevation, which he thought would enable him to overlook a large scope of country in the direction that he supposed the enemy to have taken in withdrawing. This building, which had originally consisted of a single room, elevated upon four posts about ten feet high, was now little more than a roof; the floor had fallen away, the joists and planks loosely piled on the ground below or resting on end at various angles, not wholly torn from their fastenings above. The supporting posts were themselves no longer vertical. It looked as if the whole edifice would go down at the touch of a finger. Concealing himself in the débris of joists and flooring, Searing looked across the open ground between his point of view and a spur of Kenesaw Mountain, a half mile away. A road leading up and across this spur was crowded with troops — the rear guard of the retiring enemy, their gun barrels gleaming in the morning sunlight.

Searing had now learned all that he could hope to know. It was his duty to return to his own command with all possible speed and report his discovery. But the grey column of infantry toiling up the mountain road was singularly tempting. His rifle — an ordinary "Springfield," but fitted with a globe sight and hair trigger — would easily send its ounce and a quarter of lead hissing into their midst. That would probably not affect the duration and result of the war, but it is the business of a soldier to kill. It is also his pleasure if he is a good soldier. Searing cocked his rifle and "set" the trigger.

But it was decreed from the beginning of time that Private Searing was not to murder anybody that bright summer morning, nor was the Confederate retreat to be announced by him. For countless ages events had been so matching themselves together in that wondrous mosaic to some parts of which, dimly discernible, we give the name of history, that the acts which he had in will would have marred the harmony of the pattern.

Some twenty-five years previously the Power charged with the execution of the work according to the design had provided against that mischance by causing the birth of a certain male child in a little village at the foot of the Carpathian Mountains, had carefully reared it, supervised its education, directed its desires into a military channel, and in due time made it an officer of artillery. By the concurrence of an infinite number of favouring influences and their preponderance over an infinite number of opposing ones, this officer of artillery had been made to commit a breach of discipline and fly from his native country to avoid punishment. He had been directed to New Orleans (instead of New York), where a recruiting officer awaited him on the wharf. He was enlisted and promoted, and things were so ordered that he now commanded a Confederate battery some three miles along the line from where Jerome Searing, the Federal scout, stood cocking his rifle. Nothing had been neglected — at every step in the progress of both these men's lives, and in the lives of their ancestors and contemporaries, and of the lives of the contemporaries of their ancestors — the right thing had been done to bring about the desired result. Had anything in all this vast concatenation been overlooked, Private Searing might have fired on the retreating Confederates that morning, and would perhaps have missed. As it fell out, a captain of artillery, having nothing better to do while awaiting his turn to pull out and be off, amused himself by sighting a field piece obliquely to his right at what he took to be some Federal officers on the crest of a hill, and discharged it. The shot flew high of its mark.

As Jerome Searing drew back the hammer of his rifle, and, with his eyes upon the distant Confederates, considered where he could plant his shot with the best hope of making a widow or an orphan or a childless mother — perhaps all three, for Private Searing, although he had repeatedly refused promotion, was not without a certain kind of ambition — he heard a rushing sound in the air, like that made by the wings of a great bird swooping down upon its prey. More quickly than he could apprehend the gradation, it increased to a hoarse and horrible roar, as the missile that made it sprang at him out of the sky, striking with a deafening impact one of the posts supporting the confusion of timbers above him, smashing it into matchwood, and bringing down the crazy edifice with a loud clatter, in clouds of blinding dust!

Lieutenant Adrian Searing, in command of the picket guard on that part of the line through which his brother Jerome had passed on his mission, sat with attentive ears in his breastwork behind the line. Not the faintest sound escaped him; the cry of a bird, the barking of a squirrel, the noise of the wind among the pines — all were anxiously noted by his overstrained sense. Suddenly, directly in front of his line, he heard a faint, confused rumble, like the clatter of a falling building translated by distance. At the same moment an officer approached him on foot from the rear and saluted.

"Lieutenant," said the aide, "the colonel directs you to move forward your line and feel the enemy if you find him. If not, continue the advance until directed to halt. There is reason to think that the enemy has retreated."

The lieutenant nodded and said nothing; the other officer retired. In a moment the men, apprised of their duty by the non-commissioned officers in low tones, had deployed from their rifle pits and were moving forward in skirmishing order, with set teeth and beating hearts. The lieutenant mechanically looked at his watch. Six o'clock and eighteen minutes.

When Jerome Searing recovered consciousness, he did not at once understand what had occurred. It was, indeed, some time before he opened his eyes. For a while he believed that he had died and been buried, and he tried to recall some portions of the burial service. He thought that his wife was kneeling upon his grave, adding her weight to that of the earth upon his breast. The two of them, widow and earth, had crushed his coffin. Unless the children should persuade her to go home, he would not much longer be able to breathe. He felt a sense of wrong. "I cannot speak to her," he thought; "the dead have no voice; and if I open my eyes I shall get them full of earth."

He opened his eyes—a great expanse of blue sky, rising from a fringe of the tops of trees. In the foreground, shutting out some of the trees, a high, dun mound, angular in outline and crossed by an intricate, pattern-less system of straight lines; in the centre a bright ring of metal—the whole an immeasurable distance away—a distance so inconceivably great that it fatigued him, and he closed his eyes. The moment that he did so he was conscious of an insufferable light. A sound was in his ears like the low, rhythmic thunder of a distant sea breaking in successive waves upon the beach, and out of this noise, seeming a part of it, or possibly coming from beyond it, and intermingled with its ceaseless undertone, came the articulate words: "Jerome Searing, you are caught like a rat in a trap—in a trap, trap, trap."

Suddenly there fell a great silence, a black darkness, an infinite tranquillity, and Jerome Searing, perfectly conscious of his rathood, and well assured of the trap that he was in, remembered all, and, nowise alarmed, again opened his eyes to reconnoitre, to note the strength of his enemy, to plan his defence.

He was caught in a reclining posture, his back firmly supported by a solid beam. Another lay across his breast, but he had been able to shrink a little way from it so that it no longer oppressed him though it was immovable. A brace joining it at an angle had wedged him against a pile of boards on his left, fastening the arm on that side. His legs, slightly parted and straight along the ground, were covered upward to the knees with a mass of débris which towered above his narrow horizon. His head was as rigidly fixed as in a vice; he could move his eyes, his chin—no more. Only his right arm was partly free. "You must help us out of this," he said to it. But he could not get it from under the heavy timber athwart his chest, nor move it outward more than six inches at the elbow.

Searing was not seriously injured, nor did he suffer pain. A smart rap on the head from a flying fragment of the splintered post, incurred simultaneously with the frightfully sudden shock to the nervous system, had momentarily dazed him. His term of unconsciousness, including the period of recovery, during which he had had the strange fancies, had probably not exceeded a few seconds, for the dust of the wreck had not wholly cleared away as he began an intelligent survey of the situation.

With his partly free right hand he now tried to get hold of the beam which lay across, but not quite against, his breast. In no way could he do so. He was unable to depress the shoulder so as to push the elbow beyond that edge of the timber which was nearest his knees; failing in that, he could not raise the forearm and hand to grasp the beam. The brace that made an angle with it downward and backward prevented him from doing anything in that direction, and between it and his body the space was not half as wide as the length of his forearm. Obviously he could not get his hand under the beam nor over it; he could not, in fact, touch it at all. Having demonstrated his inability, he desisted, and began to think if he could reach any of the débris piled upon his legs.

In surveying the mass with a view to determining that point, his attention was arrested by what seemed to be a ring of shining metal immediately in front of his eyes. It appeared to him at first to surround some perfectly black substance, and it was somewhat more than a half inch in diameter. It suddenly occurred to his mind that the blackness was simply shadow, and that the ring was in fact the muzzle of his rifle protruding from the pile of débris. He was not long in satisfying himself that this was so — if it was a satisfaction. By closing either eye he could look a little way along the barrel — to the point where it was hidden by the rubbish that held it. He could see the one side, with the corresponding eye, at apparently the same angle as the other side with the other eye. Looking with the right eye, the weapon seemed to be directed at a point to the left of his head, and *vice versa*. He was unable to see the upper surface of the barrel, but could see the under surface of the stock at a slight angle. The piece was, in fact, aimed at the exact centre of his forehead.

In the perception of this circumstance, in the recollection that just previously to the mischance of which this uncomfortable situation was the result, he had cocked the gun and set the trigger so that a touch would discharge it, Private Searing was affected with a feeling of uneasiness. But that was as far as possible from fear; he was a brave man, somewhat familiar with the aspect of rifles from that point of view, and of cannon, too; and now he recalled, with something like amusement, an incident of his experience at the storming of Missionary Ridge, where, walking up to one of the enemy's embrasures from which he had seen a heavy gun throw charge after charge of grape among the assailants, he thought for a moment that the piece had been withdrawn; he could see nothing in the opening but a brazen circle. What that was he had understood just in time to step aside as it pitched another peck of iron down that swarming slope. To face firearms is one of the commonest incidents in a soldier's life — firearms, too, with malevolent eyes blazing behind them. That is what a soldier is for. Still, Private Searing did not altogether relish the situation, and turned away his eyes.

After groping, aimless, with his right hand for a time, he made an ineffectual attempt to release his left. Then he tried to disengage his head, the fixity of which was the more annoying from his ignorance of what held it. Next he tried to free his feet, but while exerting the powerful muscles of his legs for that purpose it occurred to him that a disturbance of the rubbish which held them might discharge the rifle; how it could have endured what had already befallen it he could not understand, although memory assisted him with various instances in point. One in particular he recalled, in which, in a moment of mental abstraction, he had clubbed his rifle and beaten out another gentleman's brains, observing afterward that the weapon which he had been diligently swinging by the muzzle was loaded, capped, and at full cock—knowledge of which circumstance would doubtless have cheered his antagonist to longer endurance. He had always smiled in recalling that blunder of his "green and salad days" as a soldier, but now he did not smile. He turned his eyes again to the muzzle of the gun, and for a moment fancied that it had moved; it seemed somewhat nearer.

Again he looked away. The tops of the distant trees beyond the bounds of the plantation interested him; he had not before observed how light and feathery they seemed, nor how darkly blue the sky was, even among their branches, where they somewhat paled it with their green; above him it appeared almost black. "It will be uncomfortably hot here," he thought, "as the day advances. I wonder which way I am looking."

Judging by such shadows as he could see, he decided that his face was due north; he would at least not have the sun in his eyes, and north—well, that was toward his wife and children.

"Bah!" he exclaimed aloud, "what have they to do with it?"

He closed his eyes. "As I can't get out, I may as well go to sleep. The rebels are gone, and some of our fellows are sure to stray out here foraging. They'll find me."

But he did not sleep. Gradually he became sensible of a pain in his forehead—a dull ache, hardly perceptible at first, but growing more and more uncomfortable. He opened his eyes and it was gone—closed them and it returned. "The devil!" he said irrelevantly, and stared again at the sky. He heard the singing of birds, the strange metallic note of the meadow lark, suggesting the clash of vibrant blades. He fell into pleasant memories of his childhood, played again with his brother and sister, raced across the fields, shouting to alarm the sedentary larks, entered the sombre forest beyond, and with timid steps followed the faint path to Ghost Rock, standing at last with audible heart-throbs before the Dead Man's Cave and seeking to penetrate its awful mystery. For the first time he observed that the opening of the haunted cavern was encircled by a ring of metal. Then all else vanished, and left him gazing into the barrel of his rifle as before. But whereas before it had seemed nearer, it now seemed an inconceivable distance away, and all the more sinister for that. He cried out, and, startled by something in his own voice—the note of fear—lied to himself in denial: "If I don't sing out I may stay here till I die."

He now made no further attempt to evade the menacing stare of the gun barrel. If he turned away his eyes an instant it was to look for assistance (although he could not see the ground on either side the ruin), and he permitted them to return, obedient to the imperative fascination. If he closed them, it was from weariness, and instantly the poignant pain in his forehead — the prophecy and menace of the bullet — forced him to reopen them.

The tension of nerve and brain was too severe; nature came to his relief with intervals of unconsciousness. Reviving from one of these, he became sensible of a sharp, smarting pain in his right hand, and when he worked his fingers together, or rubbed his palm with them, he could feel that they were wet and slippery. He could not see the hand, but he knew the sensation; it was running blood. In his delirium he had beaten it against the jagged fragments of the wreck, had clutched it full of splinters. He resolved that he would meet his fate more manly. He was a plain, common soldier, had no religion and not much philosophy; he could not die like a hero, with great and wise last words, even if there were someone to hear them, but he could die "game," and he would. But if he could only know when to expect the shot!

Some rats which had probably inhabited the shed came sneaking and scampering about. One of them mounted the pile of débris that held the rifle; another followed, and another. Searing regarded them at first with indifference, then with friendly interest; then, as the thought flashed into his bewildered mind that they might touch the trigger of his rifle, he screamed at them to go away. "It is no business of yours," he cried.

The creatures left; they would return later, attack his face, gnaw his nose, cut his throat — he knew that, but he hoped by that time to be dead.

Nothing could now unfix his gaze from the little ring of metal with its black interior. The pain in his forehead was fierce and constant. He felt it gradually penetrating the brain more and more deeply, until at last its progress was arrested by the wood at the back of his head. It grew momentarily more insufferable; he began wantonly beating his lacerated hand against the splinters again to counteract that horrible ache. It seemed to throb with a slow, regular recurrence, each pulsation sharper than the preceding, and sometimes he cried out, thinking he felt the fatal bullet. No thoughts of home, of wife and children, of country, of glory. The whole record of memory was effaced. The world had passed away — not a vestige remained. Here, in this confusion of timbers and boards, is the sole universe. Here is immortality in time — each pain an everlasting life. The throbs tick off eternities.

Jerome Searing, the man of courage, the formidable enemy, the strong, resolute warrior, was as pale as a ghost. His jaw was fallen; his eyes protruded; he trembled in every fibre; a cold sweat bathed his entire body; he screamed with fear. He was not insane — he was terrified.

In groping about with his torn and bleeding hand he seized at last a strip of board, and, pulling, felt it give way. It lay parallel with his body, and by bending his elbow as much as the contracted space would permit, he could draw it a few inches at a time. Finally it was altogether loosened from the wreckage covering his legs; he could lift it clear of the ground its whole length. A great hope came into his mind: perhaps he could work it upward, that is to say backward, far enough to lift the end and push aside the rifle; or, if that were too tightly wedged, so hold the strip of board as to deflect the bullet. With this object he passed it backward inch by inch, hardly daring to breathe, lest that act somehow defeat his intent, and more than ever unable to remove his eyes from the rifle, which might perhaps now hasten to improve its waning opportunity. Something at least had been gained; in the occupation of his mind in this attempt at self-defence he was less sensible of the pain in his head and had ceased to scream. But he was still dreadfully frightened, and his teeth rattled like castanets.

The strip of board ceased to move to the suasion of his hand. He tugged at it with all his strength, changed the direction of its length all he could, but it had met some extended obstruction behind him, and the end in front was still too far away to clear the pile of débris and reach the muzzle of the gun. It extended, indeed, nearly as far as the trigger-guard, which, uncovered by the rubbish, he could imperfectly see with his right eye. He tried to break the strip with his hand, but had no leverage. Perceiving his defeat, all his terror returned, augmented tenfold. The black aperture of the rifle appeared to threaten a sharper and more imminent death in punishment of his rebellion. The track of the bullet through his head ached with an intenser anguish. He began to tremble again.

Suddenly he became composed. His tremor subsided. He clinched his teeth and drew down his eyebrows. He had not exhausted his means of defence; a new design had shaped itself in his mind—another plan of battle. Raising the front end of the strip of board, he carefully pushed it forward through the wreckage at the side of the rifle until it pressed against the trigger guard. Then he moved the end slowly outward until he could feel that it had cleared it, then, closing his eyes, thrust it against the trigger with all his strength! There was no explosion; the rifle had been discharged as it dropped from his hand when the building fell. But Jerome Searing was dead.

A line of Federal skirmishers swept across the plantation toward the mountain. They passed on both sides of the wrecked building, observing nothing. At a short distance in their rear came their commander, Lieutenant Adrian Searing. He casts his eyes curiously upon the ruin and sees a dead body half buried in boards and timbers. It is so covered with dust that its clothing is Confederate grey. Its face is yellowish white; the cheeks are fallen in, the temples sunken, too, with sharp ridges about them, making the forehead forbiddingly narrow; the upper lip, slightly lifted, shows the white teeth, rigidly clinched. The hair is heavy with moisture, the face as wet as the dewy grass all about. From his point of view the officer does not observe the rifle; the man was apparently killed by the fall of the building.

"Dead a week," said the officer curtly, moving on, mechanically pulling out his watch as if to verify his estimate of time. Six o'clock and forty minutes. [1891]

HAMLIN GARLAND

*H*amlin Garland (1860–1940) was born in West Salem, Wisconsin, the son
of a New England father lured west by the prospect of cheap land. When Garland was nine, his family moved to a farm on the unfenced prairie of northern
Iowa, where he was educated at the Cedar Valley Seminary. As a boy Garland
loved literature. His biographer B. R. McElderry Jr., has stated that "Ivanhoe,
Scottish Chiefs, The Life of P. T. Barnum, *and Franklin's* Autobiography,
*available at home or borrowed from neighbors, along with numerous dime nov-
els, put before the boy a mixture of impractical romance and shrewd materialism. . . . Later he became acquainted with Hawthorne and with Shakespeare,
whose great speeches the boy recited as he followed the plow."*

In 1881, after numerous crop failures, the family moved again, this time to
South Dakota, where Garland worked as a carpenter and taught school. When
he was twenty-five, he sold his claim in the Dakota Territory and used the
money to live in Boston, where he began a program of self-directed study at the
public library.

In 1885 Garland modeled his first attempt at fiction, the story "Ten Years
Dead," on Nathaniel Hawthorne's style, but he was dissatisfied with it. He
kept writing, publishing reviews and poems. In 1888 his first magazine story
appeared in Harper's Weekly Magazine; *it was based on an incident his
mother had told him about when he returned to South Dakota to visit his family. After three years in Boston, he saw the limitations and hardships of prairie
life with new eyes. Garland had finally found his subject. He said, "The ugliness, the endless drudgery, and the loneliness of the farmer's lot smote me with
stern insistence. I was the militant reformer." Several other realistic stories
about prairie life, including "The Return of a Private," first published in
Arena in 1890, were inspired by his visit home, when he listened to his father
talk about his memories of the Civil War. Garland wrote these stories soon after
he returned to Boston.*

In 1891 a collection of these prairie stories was published under the title
Main-Travelled Roads. *The book caused an uproar. Garland's bitter picture
of farmers caught in the grip of relentless capitalism provoked a storm of
denials, but the author was established as the voice of the rebellious Populists, a
political party urging agricultural reform. The novelist William Dean Howells
defended the book: "The type caught in Mr. Garland's book is not pretty; it is
ugly and often ridiculous; but it is heart-breaking in its despair."*

Main-Travelled Roads *is one of the first important collections of modern
short stories closely related by a common theme and location, like* The Country of the Pointed Firs *(1896), by Sarah Orne Jewett;* Dubliners *(1916), by
James Joyce; and* Winesburg, Ohio *(1919), by Sherwood Anderson. Garland
published four other books of realistic short stories in the 1890s, but he turned*

to other literary forms for the remainder of his long life, including several memoirs and his autobiography, A Son of the Middle Border *(1917).*

RELATED COMMENTARY: *Hamlin Garland, "Local Color in Art," page 1344.*

The Return of a Private

– I –

The nearer the train drew toward La Crosse, the soberer the little group of "vets" became. On the long way from New Orleans they had beguiled tedium with jokes and friendly chaff; or with planning with elaborate detail what they were going to do now, after the war. A long journey, slowly, irregularly, yet persistently pushing northward. When they entered on Wisconsin territory they gave a cheer, and another when they reached Madison, but after that they sank into a dumb expectancy. Comrades dropped off at one or two points beyond, until there were only four or five left who were bound for La Crosse County.

Three of them were gaunt and brown, the fourth was gaunt and pale, with signs of fever and ague upon him. One had a great scar down his temple, one limped, and they all had unnaturally large, bright eyes, showing emaciation. There were no bands greeting them at the station, no banks of gayly dressed ladies waving handkerchiefs and shouting "Bravo!" as they came in on the caboose of a freight train into the towns that had cheered and blared at them on their way to war. As they looked out or stepped upon the platform for a moment, while the train stood at the station, the loafers looked at them indifferently. Their blue coats, dusty and grimy, were too familiar now to excite notice, much less a friendly word. They were the last of the army to return, and the loafers were surfeited with such sights.

The train jogged forward so slowly that it seemed likely to be midnight before they should reach La Crosse. The little squad grumbled and swore, but it was no use; the train would not hurry, and, as a matter of fact, it was nearly two o'clock when the engine whistled "down brakes."

All of the group were farmers, living in districts several miles out of the town, and all were poor.

"Now, boys," said Private Smith, he of the fever and ague, "we are landed in La Crosse in the night. We've got to stay somewhere till mornin'. Now I ain't got no two dollars to waste on a hotel. I've got a wife and children, so I'm goin' to roost on a bench and take the cost of a bed out of my hide."

"Same here," put in one of the other men. "Hide'll grow on again, dollars'll come hard. It's goin' to be mighty hot skirmishin' to find a dollar these days."

"Don't think they'll be a deputation of citizens waitin' to 'scort us to a hotel, eh?" said another. His sarcasm was too obvious to require an answer.

Smith went on, "Then at daybreak we'll start for home — at least, I will."

"Well, I'll be dummed if I'll take two dollars out o' *my* hide," one of the younger men said. "I'm goin' to a hotel, ef I don't never lay up a cent."

"That'll do f'r you," said Smith; "but if you had a wife an' three young uns dependin' on yeh—"

"Which I ain't, thank the Lord! and don't intend havin' while the court knows itself."

The station was deserted, chill, and dark, as they came into it at exactly a quarter to two in the morning. Lit by the oil lamps that flared a dull red light over the dingy benches, the waiting room was not an inviting place. The younger man went off to look up a hotel, while the rest remained and prepared to camp down on the floor and benches. Smith was attended to tenderly by the other men, who spread their blankets on the bench for him, and, by robbing themselves, made quite a comfortable bed, though the narrowness of the bench made his sleeping precarious.

It was chill, though August, and the two men, sitting with bowed heads, grew stiff with cold and weariness, and were forced to rise now and again and walk about to warm their stiffened limbs. It did not occur to them, probably, to contrast their coming home with their going forth, or with the coming home of the generals, colonels, or even captains — but to Private Smith, at any rate, there came a sickness at heart almost deadly as he lay there on his hard bed and went over his situation.

In the deep of the night, lying on a board in the town where he had enlisted three years ago, all elation and enthusiasm gone out of him, he faced the fact that with the joy of home-coming was already mingled the bitter juice of care. He saw himself sick, worn out, taking up the work on his half-cleared farm, the inevitable mortgage standing ready with open jaw to swallow half his earnings. He had given three years of his life for a mere pittance of pay, and now! —

Morning dawned at last, slowly, with a pale yellow dome of light rising silently above the bluffs, which stand like some huge storm-devastated castle, just east of the city. Out to the left the great river swept on its massive yet silent way to the south. Bluejays called across the water from hillside to hillside through the clear, beautiful air, and hawks began to skim the tops of the hills. The older men were astir early, but Private Smith had fallen at last into a sleep, and they went out without waking him. He lay on his knapsack, his gaunt face turned toward the ceiling, his hands clasped on his breast, with a curious pathetic effect of weakness and appeal.

An engine switching near woke him at last, and he slowly sat up and stared about. He looked out of the window and saw that the sun was lightening the hills across the river. He rose and brushed his hair as well as he could, folded his blankets up, and went out to find his companions. They stood gazing silently at the river and at the hills.

"Looks natcher'l, don't it?" they said, as he came out.

"That's what it does," he replied. "An' it looks good. D' yeh see that peak?" He pointed at a beautiful symmetrical peak, rising like a slightly truncated cone, so high that it seemed the very highest of them all. It was touched by the morning sun and it glowed like a beacon, and a light scarf of gray morning fog was rolling up its shadowed side.

"My farm's just beyond that. Now, if I can only ketch a ride, we'll be home by dinner-time."

"I'm talkin' about breakfast," said one of the others.

"I guess it's one more meal o' hardtack f'r me," said Smith.

They foraged around, and finally found a restaurant with a sleepy old German behind the counter, and procured some coffee, which they drank to wash down their hardtack.

"Time'll come," said Smith, holding up a piece by the corner, "when this'll be a curiosity."

"I hope to God it will! I bet I've chawed hardtack enough to shingle every house in the coolly. I've chawed it when my lampers was down, and when they wasn't. I've took it dry, soaked, and mashed. I've had it wormy, musty, sour, and blue-mouldy. I've had it in little bits and big bits; 'fore coffee an' after coffee. I'm ready f'r a change. I'd like t' git holt jest about now o' some of the hot biscuits my wife c'n make when she lays herself out f'r company."

"Well, if you set there gabblin', you'll never *see* yer wife."

"Come on," said Private Smith. "Wait a moment, boys; less take suthin'. It's on me." He led them to the rusty tin dipper which hung on a nail beside the wooden water-pail, and they grinned and drank. Then shouldering their blankets and muskets, which they were "takin' home to the boys," they struck out on their last march.

"They called that coffee Jayvy," grumbled one of them, "but it never went by the road where government Jayvy resides. I reckon I know coffee from peas."

They kept together on the road along the turnpike, and up the winding road by the river, which they followed for some miles. The river was very lovely, curving down along its sandy beds, pausing now and then under broad basswood trees, or running in dark, swift, silent currents under tangles of wild grapevines, and drooping alders, and haw trees. At one of these lovely spots the three vets sat down on the thick green sward to rest, "on Smith's account." The leaves of the trees were as fresh and green as in June, the jays called cheery greetings to them, and kingfishers darted to and fro with swooping, noiseless flight.

"I tell yeh, boys, this knocks the swamps of Loueesiana into kingdom come."

"You bet. All they c'n raise down there is snakes, niggers, and p'rticler hell."

"An' fightin' men," put in the older man.

"An' fightin' men. If I had a good hook an' line I'd sneak a pick'rel out o' that pond. Say, remember that time I shot that alligator—"

"I guess we'd better be crawlin' along," interrupted Smith, rising and shouldering his knapsack, with considerable effort, which he tried to hide.

"Say, Smith, lemme give you a lift on that."

"I guess I c'n manage," said Smith, grimly.

"Course. But, yo' see, I may not have a chance right off to pay yeh back for the times you've carried my gun and hull caboodle. Say, now, gimme that gun, anyway."

"All right, if yeh feel like it, Jim," Smith replied, and they trudged along doggedly in the sun, which was getting higher and hotter each half-mile.

"Ain't it queer there ain't no teams comin' along," said Smith, after a long silence.

"Well, no, seein's it's Sunday."

"By jinks, that's a fact. It *is* Sunday. I'll git home in time f'r dinner, sure!" he exulted. "She don't hev dinner usially till about *one* on Sundays." And he fell into a muse, in which he smiled.

"Well, I'll git home jest about six o'clock, jest about when the boys are milkin' the cows," said old Jim Cranby. "I'll step into the barn, an' then I'll say: 'He*ah!* why ain't this milkin' done before this time o' day?' An' then won't they yell!" he added, slapping his thigh in great glee.

Smith went on. "I'll jest go up the path. Old Rover'll come down the road to meet me. He won't bark; he'll know me, an' he'll come down waggin' his tail an' showin' his teeth. That's his way of laughin'. An' so I'll walk up to the kitchen door, an' I'll say, '*Dinner* f'r a hungry man!' An' then she'll jump up, an'—"

He couldn't go on. His voice choked at the thought of it. Saunders, the third man, hardly uttered a word, but walked silently behind the others. He had lost his wife the first year he was in the army. She died of pneumonia, caught in the autumn rains while working in the fields in his place.

They plodded along till at last they came to a parting of the ways. To the right the road continued up the main valley; to the left it went over the big ridge.

"Well, boys," began Smith, as they grounded their muskets and looked away up the valley, "here's where we shake hands. We've marched together a good many miles, an' now I s'pose we're done."

"Yes, I don't think we'll do any more of it f'r a while. I don't want to, I know."

"I hope I'll see yeh once in a while, boys, to talk over old times."

"Of course," said Saunders, whose voice trembled a little, too. "It ain't *exactly* like dyin'." They all found it hard to look at each other.

"But we'd ought'r go home with you," said Cranby. "You'll never climb that ridge with all them things on yer back."

"Oh, I'm all right! Don't worry about me. Every step takes me nearer home, yeh see. Well, good-by, boys."

They shook hands. "Good-by. Good luck!"

"Same to you. Lemme know how you find things at home."

"Good-by."

"Good-by."

He turned once before they passed out of sight, and waved his cap, and they did the same, and all yelled. Then all marched away with their long, steady, loping, veteran step. The solitary climber in blue walked on for a time, with his mind filled with the kindness of his comrades, and musing upon the many wonderful days they had had together in camp and field.

He thought of his chum, Billy Tripp. Poor Billy! A "minie" ball fell into his breast one day, fell wailing like a cat, and tore a great ragged hole in his heart. He looked forward to a sad scene with Billy's mother and sweetheart. They would want to know all about it. He tried to recall all that Billy had said, and the particulars of it, but there was little to remember, just that wild wailing sound high in the air, a dull slap, a short, quick, expulsive groan, and the boy lay with his face in the dirt in the ploughed field they were marching across.

That was all. But all the scenes he had since been through had not dimmed the horror, the terror of that moment, when his boy comrade fell, with only a breath between a laugh and a death-groan. Poor handsome Billy! Worth millions of dollars was his young life.

These sombre recollections gave way at length to more cheerful feelings as he began to approach his home coolly. The fields and houses grew familiar, and in one or two he was greeted by people seated in the doorways. But he was in no mood to talk, and pushed on steadily, though he stopped and accepted a drink of milk once at the well-side of a neighbor.

The sun was burning hot on that slope, and his step grew slower, in spite of his iron resolution. He sat down several times to rest. Slowly he crawled up the rough, reddish-brown road, which wound along the hillside, under great trees, through dense groves of jack oaks, with treetops far below him on his left hand, and the hills far above him on his right. He crawled along like some minute, wingless variety of fly.

He ate some hardtack, sauced with wild berries, when he reached the summit of the ridge, and sat there for some time, looking down into his home coolly.

Sombre, pathetic figure! His wide, round, gray eyes gazing down into the beautiful valley, seeing and not seeing, the splendid cloud-shadows sweeping over the western hills and across the green and yellow wheat far below. His head drooped forward on his palm, his shoulders took on a tired stoop, his cheek-bones showed painfully. An observer might have said, "He is looking down upon his own grave."

– II –

Sunday comes in a Western wheat harvest with such sweet and sudden relaxation to man and beast that it would be holy for that reason, if for no other, and Sundays are usually fair in harvest-time. As one goes out into the field in the hot morning sunshine, with no sound abroad save the crick-ets and the indescribably pleasant silken rustling of the ripened grain, the reaper and the very sheaves in the stubble seem to be resting, dreaming.

Around the house, in the shade of the trees, the men sit, smoking, doz-ing, or reading the papers, while the women, never resting, move about at the housework. The men eat on Sundays about the same as on other days, and breakfast is no sooner over and out of the way than dinner begins.

But at the Smith farm there were no men dozing or reading. Mrs. Smith was alone with her three children, Mary, nine, Tommy, six, and little Ted, just past four. Her farm, rented to a neighbor, lay at the head of a coolly or narrow gully, made at some far-off post-glacial period by the vast and angry floods of water which gullied these tremendous furrows in the level prairie—furrows so deep that undisturbed portions of the original level rose like hills on either side, rose to quite considerable mountains.

The chickens wakened her as usual that Sabbath morning from dreams of her absent husband, from whom she had not heard for weeks. The shadows drifted over the hills, down the slopes, across the wheat, and up the opposite wall in a leisurely way, as if, being Sunday, they could take it easy also. The fowls clustered about the housewife as she went out into the yard. Fuzzy little chickens swarmed out from the coops, where their clucking and perpetually disgruntled mothers tramped about, petulantly thrusting their heads through the spaces between the slats.

A cow called in a deep, musical bass, and a calf answered from a little pen near by, and a pig scurried guiltily out of the cabbages. Seeing all this, seeing the pig in the cabbages, the tangle of grass in the garden, the bro-ken fence which she had mended again and again—the little woman, hardly more than a girl, sat down and cried. The bright Sabbath morning was only a mockery without him!

A few years ago they had bought this farm, paying part, mortgaging the rest in the usual way. Edward Smith was a man of terrible energy. He worked "nights and Sundays," as the saying goes, to clear the farm of its brush and of its insatiate mortgage! In the midst of his Herculean struggle came the call for volunteers, and with the grim and unselfish devotion to his country which made the Eagle Brigade able to "whip its weight in wild-cats," he threw down his scythe and grub-axe, turned his cattle loose, and became a blue-coated cog in a vast machine for killing men, and not thistles. While the millionaire sent his money to England for safe-keeping, this man, with his girl-wife and three babies, left them on a mortgaged farm, and went away to fight for an idea. It was foolish, but it was sublime for all that.

That was three years before, and the young wife, sitting on the well-curb on this bright Sabbath harvest morning, was righteously rebellious. It seemed to her that she had borne her share of the country's sorrow. Two brothers had been killed, the renter in whose hands her husband had left the farm had proved a villain; one year the farm had been without crops, and now the over-ripe grain was waiting the tardy hand of the neighbor who had rented it, and who was cutting his own grain first.

About six weeks before, she had received a letter saying, "We'll be discharged in a little while." But no other word had come from him. She had seen by the papers that his army was being discharged, and from day to day other soldiers slowly percolated in blue streams back into the State and county, but still *her* hero did not return.

Each week she had told the children that he was coming, and she had watched the road so long that it had become unconscious; and as she stood at the well, or by the kitchen door, her eyes were fixed unthinkingly on the road that wound down the coolly.

Nothing wears on the human soul like waiting. If the stranded mariner, searching the sun-bright seas, could once give up hope of a ship, that horrible grinding on his brain would cease. It was this waiting, hoping, on the edge of despair, that gave Emma Smith no rest.

Neighbors said, with kind intentions: "He's sick, maybe, an' can't start north just yet. He'll come along one o' these days."

"Why don't he write?" was her question, which silenced them all. This Sunday morning it seemed to her as if she could not stand it longer. The house seemed intolerably lonely. So she dressed the little ones in their best calico dresses and home-made jackets, and, closing up the house, set off down the coolly to old Mother Gray's.

"Old Widder Gray" lived at the "mouth of the coolly." She was a widow woman with a large family of stalwart boys and laughing girls. She was the visible incarnation of hospitality and optimistic poverty. With Western open-heartedness she fed every mouth that asked food of her, and worked herself to death as cheerfully as her girls danced in the neighborhood harvest dances.

She waddled down the path to meet Mrs. Smith with a broad smile on her face.

"Oh, you little dears! Come right to your granny. Gimme a kiss! Come right in, Mis' Smith. How are yeh, anyway? Nice mornin', ain't it? Come in an' set down. Everything's in a clutter, but that won't scare you any."

She led the way into the best room, a sunny, square room, carpeted with a faded and patched rag carpet, and papered with white-and-green-striped wall-paper, where a few faded effigies of dead members of the family hung in variously sized oval walnut frames. The house resounded with singing, laughter, whistling, tramping of heavy boots, and riotous scufflings. Half-grown boys came to the door and crooked their fingers at the children, who ran out, and were soon heard in the midst of the fun.

"Don't s'pose you've heard from Ed?" Mrs. Smith shook her head. "He'll turn up some day, when you ain't lookin' for 'm." The good old soul had said that so many times that poor Mrs. Smith derived no comfort from it any longer.

"Liz heard from Al the other day. He's comin' some day this week. Anyhow, they expect him."

"Did he say anything of—"

"No, he didn't," Mrs. Gray admitted. "But then it was only a short letter, anyhow. Al ain't much for writin', anyhow. — But come out and see my new cheese. I tell yeh, I don't believe I ever had better luck in my life. If Ed should come, I want you should take him up a piece of this cheese."

It was beyond human nature to resist the influence of that noisy, hearty, loving household, and in the midst of the singing and laughing the wife forgot her anxiety, for the time at least, and laughed and sang with the rest.

About eleven o'clock a wagon-load more drove up to the door, and Bill Gray, the widow's oldest son, and his whole family, from Sand Lake Coolly, piled out amid a good-natured uproar. Every one talked at once, except Bill, who sat in the wagon with his wrists on his knees, a straw in his mouth, and an amused twinkle in his blue eyes.

"Ain't heard nothin' o' Ed, I s'pose?" he asked in a kind of bellow. Mrs. Smith shook her head. Bill, with a delicacy very striking in such a great giant, rolled his quid in his mouth, and said:

"Didn't know but you had. I hear two or three of the Sand Lake boys are comin'. Left New Orleenes some time this week. Didn't write nothin' about Ed, but no news is good news in such cases, mother always says."

"Well, go put out yer team," said Mrs. Gray, "an' go 'n bring me in some taters, an', Sim, you go see if you c'n find some corn. Sadie, you put on the water to bile. Come now, hustle yer boots, all o' yeh. If I feed this yer crowd, we've got to have some raw materials. If y' think I'm goin' to feed yeh on pie — you're jest mightily mistaken."

The children went off into the fields, the girls put dinner on to boil, and then went to change their dresses and fix their hair. "Somebody might come," they said.

"Land sakes, *I hope* not! I don't know where in time I'd set 'em, 'less they'd eat at the second table," Mrs. Gray laughed, in pretended dismay.

The two older boys, who had served their time in the army, lay out on the grass before the house, and whittled and talked desultorily about the war and the crops, and planned buying a threshing-machine. The older girls and Mrs. Smith helped enlarge the table and put on the dishes, talking all the time in that cheery, incoherent, and meaningful way a group of such women have, — a conversation to be taken for its spirit rather than for its letter, though Mrs. Gray at last got the ear of them all and dissertated at length on girls.

"Girls in love ain't no use in the whole blessed week," she said. "Sundays they're a-lookin' down the road, expectin' he'll *come*. Sunday afternoons they can't think o' nothin' else, 'cause he's *here*. Monday mornin's they're sleepy and kind o' dreamy and slimpsy, and good f'r nothin' on Tuesday and Wednesday. Thursday they git absent-minded, an' begin to look off toward Sunday agin, an' mope aroun' and let the dishwater git cold, right under their noses. Friday they break dishes, an' go off in the best room an' snivel, an' look out o' the winder. Saturdays they have queer spurts o' workin' like all p'ssessed, an' spurts o' frizzin' their hair. An' Sunday they begin it all over agin."

The girls giggled and blushed, all through this tirade from their mother, their broad faces and powerful frames anything but suggestive of lackadaisical sentiment. But Mrs. Smith said:

"Now, Mrs. Gray, I hadn't ought to stay to dinner. You've got—"

"Now you set right down! If any of them girls' beaus comes, they'll have to take what's left, that's all. They ain't s'posed to have much appetite, nohow. No, you're goin' to stay if they starve, an' they ain't no danger o' that."

At one o'clock the long table was piled with boiled potatoes, cords of boiled corn on the cob, squash and pumpkin pies, hot biscuit, sweet pickles, bread and butter, and honey. Then one of the girls took down a conch-shell from a nail, and going to the door, blew a long, fine, free blast, that showed there was no weakness of lungs in her ample chest.

Then the children came out of the forest of corn, out of the creek, out of the loft of the barn, and out of the garden.

"They come to their feed f'r all the world jest like the pigs when y' holler 'poo-ee!' See 'em scoot!" laughed Mrs. Gray, every wrinkle on her face shining with delight.

The men shut up their jack-knives, and surrounded the horse-trough to souse their faces in the cold, hard water, and in a few moments the table was filled with a merry crowd, and a row of wistful-eyed youngsters circled the kitchen wall, where they stood first on one leg and then on the other, in impatient hunger.

"Now pitch in, Mrs. Smith," said Mrs. Gray, presiding over the table. "You know these men critters. They'll eat every grain of it, if yeh give 'em a chance. I swan, they're made o' India-rubber, their stomachs is, I know it."

"Haf to eat to work," said Bill, gnawing a cob with a swift, circular motion that rivalled a corn-sheller in results.

"More like workin' to eat," put in one of the girls, with a giggle. "More eat 'n work with you."

"*You* needn't say anything, Net. Any one that'll eat seven ears—"

"I didn't, no such thing. You piled your cobs on my plate."

"That'll do to tell Ed Varney. It won't go down here where we know yeh."

"Good land! Eat all yeh want! They's plenty more in the fiel's, but I can't afford to give you young uns tea. The tea is for us women-folks, and 'specially f'r Mis' Smith an' Bill's wife. We're a-goin' to tell fortunes by it."

One by one the men filled up and shoved back, and one by one the children slipped into their places, and by two o'clock the women alone remained around the débris-covered table, sipping their tea and telling fortunes.

As they got well down to the grounds in the cup, they shook them with a circular motion in the hand, and then turned them bottom-side-up quickly in the saucer, then twirled them three or four times one way, and three or four times the other, during a breathless pause. Then Mrs. Gray lifted the cup, and, gazing into it with profound gravity, pronounced the impending fate.

It must be admitted that, to a critical observer, she had abundant preparation for hitting close to the mark, as when she told the girls that "somebody was comin'." "It's a man," she went on gravely. "He is cross-eyed—"

"Oh, you hush!" cried Nettie.

"He has red hair, and is death on b'iled corn and hot biscuit."

The others shrieked with delight.

"But he's goin' to get the mitten, that red-headed feller is, for I see another feller comin' up behind him."

"Oh, lemme see, lemme see!" cried Nettie.

"Keep off," said the priestess, with a lofty gesture. "His hair is black. He don't eat so much, and he works more."

The girls exploded in a shriek of laughter, and pounded their sister on the back.

At last came Mrs. Smith's turn, and she was trembling with excitement as Mrs. Gray again composed her jolly face to what she considered a proper solemnity of expression.

"Somebody is comin' to *you*," she said, after a long pause. "He's got a musket on his back. He's a soldier. He's almost here. See?"

She pointed at two little tea-stems, which really formed a faint suggestion of a man with a musket on his back. He had climbed nearly to the edge of the cup. Mrs. Smith grew pale with excitement. She trembled so she could hardly hold the cup in her hand as she gazed into it.

"It's Ed," cried the old woman. "He's on the way home. Heavens an' earth! There he is now!" She turned and waved her hand out toward the road. They rushed to the door to look where she pointed.

A man in a blue coat, with a musket on his back, was toiling slowly up the hill on the sun-bright, dusty road, toiling slowly, with bent head half hidden by a heavy knapsack. So tired it seemed that walking was indeed a process of falling. So eager to get home he would not stop, would not look aside, but plodded on, amid the cries of the locusts, the welcome of the crickets, and the rustle of the yellow wheat. Getting back to God's country, and his wife and babies!

Laughing, crying, trying to call him and the children at the same time, the little wife, almost hysterical, snatched her hat and ran out into the yard. But the soldier had disappeared over the hill into the hollow beyond, and, by the time she had found the children, he was too far away for her voice to reach him. And, besides, she was not sure it was her husband, for he had not turned his head at their shouts. This seemed so strange. Why didn't he stop to rest at his old neighbor's house? Tortured by hope and doubt, she hurried up the coolly as fast as she could push the baby wagon, the blue-coated figure just ahead pushing steadily, silently forward up the coolly.

When the excited, panting little group came in sight of the gate they saw the blue-coated figure standing, leaning upon the rough rail fence, his chin on his palms, gazing at the empty house. His knapsack, canteen, blankets, and musket lay upon the dusty grass at his feet.

He was like a man lost in a dream. His wide, hungry eyes devoured the scene. The rough lawn, the little unpainted house, the field of clear yellow wheat behind it, down across which streamed the sun, now almost ready to touch the high hill to the west, the crickets crying merrily, a cat on the fence near by, dreaming, unmindful of the stranger in blue—

How peaceful it all was. O God! How far removed from all camps, hospitals, battle lines. A little cabin in a Wisconsin coolly, but it was majestic in its peace. How did he ever leave it for those years of tramping, thirsting, killing?

Trembling, weak with emotion, her eyes on the silent figure, Mrs. Smith hurried up to the fence. Her feet made no noise in the dust and grass, and they were close upon him before he knew of them. The oldest boy ran a little ahead. He will never forget that figure, that face. It will always remain as something epic, that return of the private. He fixed his eyes on the pale face covered with a ragged beard.

"Who *are* you, sir?" asked the wife, or, rather, started to ask, for he turned, stood a moment, and then cried:

"Emma!"

"Edward!"

The children stood in a curious row to see their mother kiss this bearded, strange man, the elder girl sobbing sympathetically with her mother. Illness had left the soldier partly deaf, and this added to the strangeness of his manner.

But the youngest child stood away, even after the girl had recognized her father and kissed him. The man turned then to the baby, and said in a curiously unpaternal tone:

"Come here, my little man; don't you know me?" But the baby backed away under the fence and stood peering at him critically.

"My little man!" What meaning in those words! This baby seemed like some other woman's child, and not the infant he had left in his wife's arms. The war had come between him and his baby—he was only a strange man to him, with big eyes; a soldier, with mother hanging to his arm, and talking in a loud voice.

"And this is Tom," the private said, drawing the oldest boy to him. "*He'll* come and see me. *He* knows his poor old pap when he comes home from the war."

The mother heard the pain and reproach in his voice and hastened to apologize.

"You've changed so, Ed. He can't know yeh. This is papa, Teddy; come and kiss him—Tom and Mary do. Come, won't you?" But Teddy still peered through the fence with solemn eyes, well out of reach. He resembled a half-wild kitten that hesitates, studying the tones of one's voice.

"I'll fix him," said the soldier, and sat down to undo his knapsack, out of which he drew three enormous and very red apples. After giving one to each of the older children, he said:

"*Now* I guess he'll come. Eh, my little man? Now come see your pap."

Teddy crept slowly under the fence, assisted by the overzealous Tommy, and a moment later was kicking and squalling in his father's arms. Then they entered the house, into the sitting room, poor, bare, art-forsaken little room, too, with its rag carpet, its square clock, and its two or three chromos and pictures from *Harper's Weekly* pinned about.

"Emma, I'm all tired out," said Private Smith, as he flung himself down on the carpet as he used to do, while his wife brought a pillow to put under his head, and the children stood about munching their apples.

"Tommy, you run and get me a pan of chips, and Mary, you get the tea-kettle on, and I'll go and make some biscuit."

And the soldier talked. Question after question he poured forth about the crops, the cattle, the renter, the neighbors. He slipped his heavy government brogan shoes off his poor, tired, blistered feet, and lay out with utter, sweet relaxation. He was a free man again, no longer a soldier under command. At supper he stopped once, listened and smiled. "That's old Spot. I know her voice. I s'pose that's her calf out there in the pen. I can't milk her to-night, though. I'm too tired. But I tell you, I'd like a drink o' her milk. What's become of old Rove?"

"He died last winter. Poisoned, I guess." There was a moment of sadness for them all. It was some time before the husband spoke again, in a voice that trembled a little.

"Poor old feller! He'd 'a' known me half a mile away. I expected him to come down the hill to meet me. It 'ud 'a' been more like comin' home if I could 'a' seen him comin' down the road an' waggin' his tail, an' laughin' that way he has. I tell yeh, it kind o' took hold o' me to see the blinds down an' the house shut up."

"But, yeh see, we—we expected you'd write again 'fore you started. And then we thought we'd see you if you *did* come," she hastened to explain.

"Well, I ain't worth a cent on writin'. Besides, it's just as well yeh didn't know when I was comin'. I tell you, it sounds good to hear them chickens out there, an' turkeys, an' the crickets. Do you know they don't have just the same kind o' crickets down South? Who's Sam hired t' help cut yer grain?"

"The Ramsey boys."

"Looks like a good crop; but I'm afraid I won't do much gettin' it cut. This cussed fever an' ague has got me down pretty low. I don't know when I'll get rid of it. I'll bet I've took twenty-five pounds of quinine if I've taken a bit. Gimme another biscuit. I tell yeh, they taste good, Emma. I ain't had anything like it—Say, if you'd 'a' hear'd me braggin' to th' boys about your butter 'n' biscuits I'll bet your ears 'ud 'a' burnt."

The private's wife colored with pleasure. "Oh, you're always a-braggin' about your things. Everybody makes good butter."

"Yes; old lady Snyder, for instance."

"Oh, well, she ain't to be mentioned. She's Dutch."

"Or old Mis' Snively. One more cup o' tea, Mary. That's my girl! I'm feeling better already. I just b'lieve the matter with me is, I'm *starved*."

This was a delicious hour, one long to be remembered. They were like lovers again. But their tenderness, like that of a typical American family, found utterance in tones, rather than in words. He was praising her when praising her biscuit, and she knew it. They grew soberer when he showed where he had been struck, one ball burning the back of his hand, one cutting away a lock of hair from his temple, and one passing through the calf of his leg. The wife shuddered to think how near she had come to being a soldier's widow. Her waiting no longer seemed hard. This sweet, glorious hour effaced it all.

Then they rose, and all went out into the garden and down to the barn. He stood beside her while she milked old Spot. They began to plan fields and crops for next year.

His farm was weedy and encumbered, a rascally renter had run away with his machinery (departing between two days), his children needed clothing, the years were coming upon him, he was sick and emaciated, but his heroic soul did not quail. With the same courage with which he had faced his Southern march he entered upon a still more hazardous future.

Oh, that mystic hour! The pale man with big eyes standing there by the well, with his young wife by his side. The vast moon swinging above the eastern peaks, the cattle winding down the pasture slopes with jangling bells, the crickets singing, the stars blooming out sweet and far and serene; the katydids rhythmically calling, the little turkeys crying querulously, as they settled to roost in the poplar tree near the open gate. The voices at the well drop lower, the little ones nestle in their father's arms at last, and Teddy falls asleep there.

The common soldier of the American volunteer army had returned. His war with the South was over, and his fight, his daily running fight with nature and against the injustice of his fellow-men, was begun again.

[1890]

MARY WILKINS FREEMAN

Mary Wilkins Freeman (1852–1930) was born in Randolph, Massachusetts, the daughter of a carpenter. After a year at Mt. Holyoke Female Seminary in 1870, which she said "combined a thorough intellectual training with careful religious culture," she—like the poet Emily Dickinson before her—returned home. She lived with her parents in Vermont and tried writing for periodicals to earn money. In 1881, after years of rejection slips, Freeman sold her first poem to a children's magazine. A year later she sold her first stories, and her career was launched. She felt she had succeeded because she wrote about the things she knew best, a village like the one in which she lived and people like the ones with whom she had grown up. Later Freeman advised a young writer to "follow the safe course of writing only about those subjects she knows thoroughly, and concerning which she trusts her own convictions."

After her parents died, Freeman returned to Randolph, where she continued writing for magazines and publishing books for young readers. In 1887 her first book of adult fiction, A Humble Romance and Other Stories, *appeared. It was followed in 1891 by* A New England Nun and Other Stories, *a collection that included "The Revolt of 'Mother,'" which had first appeared in* Harper's Magazine *the preceding year. As the critic Perry Westbrook has observed, these two collections contain stories that Freeman never surpassed "either in narrative skill or in psychological insight," although she published books of fiction nearly every year until 1918. In 1902 she married Dr. Charles Freeman and moved to Metuchen, New Jersey, where she resided until the end of her life.*

Along with Sarah Orne Jewett, whose stories she read and admired while learning her craft, Freeman is considered an important New England regional writer. She usually focused her depiction of rural people's lives on a dominant personality, as in "The Revolt of 'Mother,'" which she conceived as a comic fantasy. She later asserted that no woman with the courage and imagination of her central character, Sarah Penn, ever existed in real life. Freeman became angry when President Theodore Roosevelt commented in a speech that American women would do well to emulate Sarah Penn's independence. Deeply conservative, Freeman said she never intended "The Revolt of 'Mother'" to be read as a tract on women's rights. Yet her local-color stories abound in strong-minded women, and if the plot of "The Revolt of 'Mother'" is improbable, it is true to the spirit of fierce individuality Freeman depicted in many of her New England characters.

The Revolt of "Mother"

"Father!"

"What is it?"

"What are them men diggin' over there in the field for?"

There was a sudden dropping and enlarging of the lower part of the old man's face, as if some heavy weight had settled therein; he shut his mouth tight, and went on harnessing the great bay mare. He hustled the collar on to her neck with a jerk.

"Father!"

The old man slapped the saddle upon the mare's back.

"Look here, father, I want to know what them men are diggin' over in the field for, an' I'm goin' to know."

"I wish you'd go into the house, mother, an' 'tend to your own affairs," the old man said then. He ran his words together, and his speech was almost as inarticulate as a growl.

But the woman understood; it was her most native tongue. "I ain't goin' into the house till you tell me what them men are doin' over there in the field," said she.

Then she stood waiting. She was a small woman, short and straight-waisted like a child in her brown cotton gown. Her forehead was mild and benevolent between the smooth curves of gray hair; there were meek downward lines about her nose and mouth; but her eyes, fixed upon the old man, looked as if the meekness had been the result of her own will, never of the will of another.

They were in the barn, standing before the wide open doors. The spring air, full of the smell of growing grass and unseen blossoms, came in their faces. The deep yard in front was littered with farm wagons and piles of wood; on the edges, close to the fence and the house, the grass was a vivid green, and there were some dandelions.

The old man glanced doggedly at his wife as he tightened the last buckles on the harness. She looked as immovable to him as one of the rocks in his pasture-land, bound to the earth with generations of black-berry vines. He slapped the reins over the horse, and started forth from the barn.

"*Father!*" said she.

The old man pulled up. "What is it?"

"I want to know what them men are diggin' over there in the field for."

"They're diggin' a cellar, I s'pose, if you've got to know."

"A cellar for what?"

"A barn."

"A barn? You ain't goin' to build a barn over there where we was goin' to have a house, father?"

The old man said not another word. He hurried the horse into the farm wagon, and clattered out of the yard, jouncing as sturdily on his seat as a boy.

The woman stood a moment looking after him, then she went out of the barn across a corner of the yard to the house. The house, standing at right angles with the great barn and a long reach of sheds and out-buildings, was infinitesimal compared with them. It was scarcely as commodious for people as the little boxes under the barn eaves were for doves.

A pretty girl's face, pink and delicate as a flower, was looking out of one of the house windows. She was watching three men who were digging over in the field which bounded the yard near the road line. She turned quietly when the woman entered.

"What are they digging for, mother?" said she. "Did he tell you?"

"They're diggin' for—a cellar for a new barn."

"Oh, mother, he ain't going to build another barn?"

"That's what he says."

A boy stood before the kitchen glass combing his hair. He combed slowly and painstakingly, arranging his brown hair in a smooth hillock over his forehead. He did not seem to pay any attention to the conversation.

"Sammy, did you know father was going to build a new barn?" asked the girl.

The boy combed assiduously.

"Sammy!"

He turned, and showed a face like his father's under his smooth crest of hair. "Yes, I s'pose I did," he said, reluctantly.

"How long have you known it?" asked his mother.

"'Bout three months, I guess."

"Why didn't you tell of it?"

"Didn't think 'twould do no good."

"I don't see what father wants another barn for," said the girl, in her sweet, slow voice. She turned again to the window, and stared out at the digging men in the field. Her tender, sweet face was full of a gentle distress. Her forehead was as bald and innocent as a baby's, with the light hair strained back from it in a row of curl-papers. She was quite large, but her soft curls did not look as if they covered muscles.

Her mother looked sternly at the boy. "Is he goin' to buy more cows?" said she.

The boy did not reply; he was tying his shoes.

"Sammy, I want you to tell me if he's goin' to buy more cows."

"I s'pose he is."

"How many?"

"Four, I guess."

His mother said nothing more. She went into the pantry, and there was a clatter of dishes. The boy got his cap from a nail behind the door, took an old arithmetic from the shelf, and started for school. He was lightly built, but clumsy. He went out of the yard with a curious spring in the hips, that made his loose home-made jacket tilt up in the rear.

The girl went to the sink, and began to wash the dishes that were piled up there. Her mother came promptly out of the pantry, and shoved her aside. "You wipe 'em," said she; "I'll wash. There's a good many this mornin'."

The mother plunged her hands vigorously into the water, the girl wiped the plates slowly and dreamily. "Mother," said she, "don't you think it's too bad father's going to build that new barn, much as we need a decent house to live in?"

Her mother scrubbed a dish fiercely. "You ain't found out yet we're women-folks, Nanny Penn," said she. "You ain't seen enough of men-folks yet to. One of these days you'll find it out, an' then you'll know that we know only what men-folks think we do, so far as any use of it goes, an' how we'd ought to reckon men-folks in with Providence, an' not complain of what they do any more than we do of the weather."

"I don't care; I don't believe George is anything like that, anyhow," said Nanny. Her delicate face flushed pink, her lips pouted softly, as if she were going to cry.

"You wait an' see. I guess George Eastman ain't no better than other men. You hadn't ought to judge father, though. He can't help it, 'cause he don't look at things jest the way we do. An' we've been pretty comfortable here, after all. The roof don't leak — ain't never but once — that's one thing. Father's kept it shingled right up."

"I do wish we had a parlor."

"I guess it won't hurt George Eastman any to come to see you in a nice clean kitchen. I guess a good many girls don't have as good a place as this. Nobody's ever heard me complain."

"I ain't complained either, mother."

"Well, I don't think you'd better, a good father an' a good home as you've got. S'pose your father made you go out an' work for your livin'? Lots of girls have to that ain't no stronger an' better able to than you be."

Sarah Penn washed the frying-pan with a conclusive air. She scrubbed the outside of it as faithfully as the inside. She was a masterly keeper of her box of a house. Her one living-room never seemed to have in it any of the dust which the friction of life with inanimate matter produces. She swept, and there seemed to be no dirt to go before the broom; she cleaned, and one could see no difference. She was like an artist so perfect that he has apparently no art. To-day she got out a mixing bowl and a board, and rolled some pies, and there was no more flour upon her than upon her daughter who was doing finer work. Nanny was to be married in the fall, and she was sewing on some white cambric and embroidery. She sewed industriously while her mother cooked, her soft milk-white hands and wrists showed whiter than her delicate work.

"We must have the stove moved out in the shed before long," said Mrs. Penn. "Talk about not havin' things, it's been a real blessin' to be able to put a stove up in that shed in hot weather. Father did one good thing when he fixed that stove-pipe out there."

Sarah Penn's face as she rolled her pies had that expression of meek vigor which might have characterized one of the New Testament saints. She was making mince-pies. Her husband, Adoniram Penn, liked them better than any other kind. She baked twice a week. Adoniram often liked a piece of pie between meals. She hurried this morning. It had been later than usual when she began, and she wanted to have a pie baked for dinner. However deep a resentment she might be forced to hold against her husband, she would never fail in sedulous attention to his wants.

Nobility of character manifests itself at loop-holes when it is not provided with large doors. Sarah Penn's showed itself to-day in flaky dishes of pastry. So she made the pies faithfully, while across the table she could see, when she glanced up from her work, the sight that rankled in her patient and steadfast soul — the digging of the cellar of the new barn in the place where Adoniram forty years ago had promised her their new house should stand.

The pies were done for dinner. Adoniram and Sammy were home a few minutes after twelve o'clock. The dinner was eaten with serious haste. There was never much conversation at the table in the Penn family. Adoniram asked a blessing, and they ate promptly, then rose up and went about their work.

Sammy went back to school, taking soft sly lopes out of the yard like a rabbit. He wanted a game of marbles before school, and feared his father would give him some chores to do. Adoniram hastened to the door and called after him, but he was out of sight.

"I don't see what you let him go for, mother," said he. "I wanted him to help me unload that wood."

Adoniram went to work out in the yard unloading wood from the wagon. Sarah put away the dinner dishes, while Nanny took down her curl-papers and changed her dress. She was going down to the store to buy some more embroidery and thread.

When Nanny was gone, Mrs. Penn went to the door. "Father!" she called.

"Well, what is it!"

"I want to see you jest a minute."

"I can't leave this wood nohow. I've got to git it unloaded an' go for a load of gravel afore two o'clock. Sammy had ought to helped me. You hadn't ought to let him go to school so early."

"I want to see you jest a minute."

"I tell ye I can't, nohow, mother."

"Father, you come here." Sarah Penn stood in the door like a queen; she held her head as if it bore a crown; there was that patience which makes authority royal in her voice. Adoniram went.

Mrs. Penn led the way into the kitchen, and pointed to a chair. "Sit down, father," said she; "I've got somethin' I want to say to you."

He sat down heavily; his face was quite stolid, but he looked at her with restive eyes. "Well, what is it, mother?"

"I want to know what you're buildin' that new barn for, father?"

"I ain't got nothin' to say about it."

"It can't be you think you need another barn?"

"I tell ye I ain't got nothin' to say about it, mother; an' I ain't goin' to say nothin'."

"Be you goin' to buy more cows?"

Adoniram did not reply; he shut his mouth tight.

"I know you be, as well as I want to. Now, father, look here"—Sarah Penn had not sat down; she stood before her husband in the humble fashion of a Scripture woman—"I'm goin' to talk real plain to you; I never have sence I married you, but I'm goin' to now. I ain't never complained, an' I ain't goin' to complain now, but I'm goin' to talk plain. You see this room here, father; you look at it well. You see there ain't no carpet on the floor, an' you see the paper is all dirty, an' droppin' off the walls. We ain't had no new paper on it for ten year, an' then I put it on myself, an' it didn't cost but ninepence a roll. You see this room, father; it's all the one I've had to work in an' eat in an' sit in sence we was married. There ain't another woman in the whole town whose husband ain't got half the means you have but what's got better. It's all the room Nanny's got to have her company in; an' there ain't one of her mates but what's got better, an' their fathers not so able as hers is. It's all the room she'll have to be married in. What would you have thought, father, if we had had our weddin' in a room no better than this? I was married in my mother's parlor, with a carpet on the floor, an' stuffed furniture, an' a mahogany card-table. An' this is all the room my daughter will have to be married in. Look here, father!"

Sarah Penn went across the room as though it were a tragic stage. She flung open a door and disclosed a tiny bedroom, only large enough for a bed and bureau, with a path between. "There, father," said she—"there's all the room I've had to sleep in forty year. All my children were born there—the two that died, an' the two that's livin'. I was sick with a fever there."

She stepped into another door and opened it. It led into the small, ill-lighted pantry. "Here," said she, "is all the buttery I've got—every place I've got for my dishes, to set away my victuals in, an' to keep my milk-pans in. Father, I've been takin' care of the milk of six cows in this place, an' now you're goin' to build a new barn, an' keep more cows, an' give me more to do in it."

She threw open another door. A narrow crooked flight of stairs wound upward from it. "There, father," said she. "I want you to look at the stairs that go up to them two unfinished chambers that are all the places our son an' daughter have had to sleep in all their lives. There ain't a prettier girl in town nor a more ladylike one than Nanny, an' that's the place she has to sleep in. It ain't so good as your horse's stall; it ain't so warm an' tight."

Sarah Penn went back and stood before her husband. "Now, father," said she, "I want to know if you think you're doin' right an' accordin' to what you profess. Here, when we was married, forty year ago, you promised me faithful that we should have a new house built in that lot over in the field before the year was out. You said you had money enough, an' you wouldn't ask me to live in no such place as this. It is forty year now, an' you've been makin' more money, an' I've been savin' of it for you ever since, an' you ain't built no house yet. You've built sheds an' cow-houses an' one new barn, an' now you're goin' to build another. Father, I want to know if you think it's right. You're lodgin' your dumb beasts better than you are your own flesh an' blood. I want to know if you think it's right."

"I ain't got nothin' to say."

"You can't say nothin' without ownin' it ain't right, father. An' there's another thing — I ain't complained; I've got along forty year, an' I s'pose I should forty more, if it wa'n't for that — if we don't have another house. Nanny she can't live with us after she's married. She'll have to go somewheres else to live away from us, an' it don't seem as if I could have it so, noways, father. She wa'n't ever strong. She's got considerable color, but there wa'n't never any backbone to her. I've always took the heft of everything off her, an' she ain't fit to keep house an' do everything herself. She'll be all worn out inside of a year. Think of her doin' all the washin' an' ironin' an' bakin' with them soft white hands an' arms, an' sweepin'! I can't have it so, noways, father."

Mrs. Penn's face was burning; her mild eyes gleamed. She had pleaded her little cause like a Webster;[1] she had ranged from severity to pathos; but her opponent employed that obstinate silence which makes eloquence futile with mocking echoes. Adoniram arose clumsily.

"Father, ain't you got nothin' to say?" said Mrs. Penn.

"I've got to go off after that load of gravel. I can't stan' here talkin' all day."

"Father, won't you think it over, an' have a house built there instead of a barn?"

"I ain't got nothin' to say."

Adoniram shuffled out. Mrs. Penn went into her bedroom. When she came out, her eyes were red. She had a roll of unbleached cotton cloth. She spread it out on the kitchen table, and began cutting out some shirts for her husband. The men over in the field had a team to help them this afternoon; she could hear their halloos. She had a scanty pattern for the shirts; she had to plan and piece the sleeves.

---

[1]Daniel Webster (1782–1852) was an American orator, lawyer, and statesman.

Nanny came home with her embroidery, and sat down with her needlework. She had taken down her curl-papers, and there was a soft roll of fair hair like an aureole over her forehead; her face was as delicately fine and clear as porcelain. Suddenly she looked up, and the tender red flamed all over her face and neck. "Mother," said she.

"What say?"

"I've been thinking I don't see how we're goin' to have any—wedding in this room. I'd be ashamed to have his folks come if we didn't have anybody else."

"Mebbe we can have some new paper before then; I can put it on. I guess you won't have no call to be ashamed of your belongin's."

"We might have the wedding in the new barn," said Nanny, with gentle pettishness. "Why, mother, what makes you look so?"

Mrs. Penn had started, and was staring at her with a curious expression. She turned again to her work, and spread out a pattern carefully on the cloth. "Nothin'," said she.

Presently Adoniram clattered out of the yard in his two-wheeled dump cart, standing as proudly upright as a Roman charioteer. Mrs. Penn opened the door and stood there a minute looking out; the halloos of the men sounded louder.

It seemed to her all through the spring months that she heard nothing but the halloos and the noises of saws and hammers. The new barn grew fast. It was a fine edifice for this little village. Men came on pleasant Sundays, in their meeting suits and clean shirt bosoms, and stood around it admiringly. Mrs. Penn did not speak of it, and Adoniram did not mention it to her, although sometimes, upon a return from inspecting it, he bore himself with injured dignity.

"It's a strange thing how your mother feels about the new barn," he said, confidentially, to Sammy one day.

Sammy only grunted after an odd fashion for a boy; he had learned it from his father.

The barn was all completed ready for use by the third week in July. Adoniram had planned to move his stock in on Wednesday; on Tuesday he received a letter which changed his plans. He came in with it early in the morning. "Sammy's been to the post-office," said he, "an' I've got a letter from Hiram." Hiram was Mrs. Penn's brother, who lived in Vermont.

"Well," said Mrs. Penn, "what does he say about the folks?"

"I guess they're all right. He says he thinks if I come up country right off there's a chance to buy jest the kind of a horse I want." He stared reflectively out of the window at the new barn.

Mrs. Penn was making pies. She went on clapping the rolling-pin into the crust, although she was very pale, and her heart beat loudly.

"I dun' know but what I'd better go," said Adoniram. "I hate to go off jest now, right in the midst of hayin', but the ten-acre lot's cut, an' I guess Rufus an' the others can git along without me three or four days. I can't get a horse round here to suit me, nohow, an' I've got to have another for all that wood-haulin' in the fall. I told Hiram to watch out, an' if he got wind of a good horse to let me know. I guess I'd better go."

"I'll get your clean shirt an' collar," said Mrs. Penn calmly.

She laid out Adoniram's Sunday suit and his clean clothes on the bed in the little bedroom. She got his shaving-water and razor ready. At last she buttoned on his collar and fastened his black cravat.

Adoniram never wore his collar and cravat except on extra occasions. He held his head high, with a rasped dignity. When he was all ready, with his coat and hat brushed, and a lunch of pie and cheese in a paper bag, he hesitated on the threshold of the door. He looked at his wife, and his manner was defiantly apologetic. "*If* them cows come to-day, Sammy can drive 'em into the new barn," said he; "an' when they bring the hay up, they can pitch it in there."

"Well," replied Mrs. Penn.

Adoniram set his shaven face ahead and started. When he had cleared the door-step, he turned and looked back with a kind of nervous solemnity. "I shall be back by Saturday if nothin' happens," said he.

"Do be careful, father," returned his wife.

She stood at the door with Nanny at her elbow and watched him out of sight. Her eyes had a strange, doubtful expression in them; her peaceful forehead was contracted. She went in, and about her baking again. Nanny sat sewing. Her wedding-day was drawing nearer, and she was getting pale and thin with her steady sewing. Her mother kept glancing at her.

"Have you got that pain in your side this mornin'?" she asked.

"A little."

Mrs. Penn's face, as she worked, changed, her perplexed forehead smoothed, her eyes were steady, her lips firmly set. She formed a maxim for herself, although incoherently with her unlettered thoughts. "Unsolicited opportunities are the guide-posts of the Lord to the new roads of life," she repeated in effect, and she made up her mind to her course of action.

"S'posin' I *had* wrote to Hiram," she muttered once, when she was in the pantry—"s'posin' I had wrote, an' asked him if he knew of any horse? But I didn't, an' father's goin' wa'n't none of my doin'. It looks like a providence." Her voice rang out quite loud at the last.

"What are you talkin' about, mother?" called Nanny.

"Nothin'."

Mrs. Penn hurried her baking; at eleven o'clock it was all done. The load of hay from the west field came slowly down the cart track, and drew up at the new barn. Mrs. Penn ran out. "Stop!" she screamed—"stop!"

The men stopped and looked; Sammy upreared from the top of the load, and stared at his mother.

"Stop!" she cried out again. "Don't you put the hay in that barn; put it in the old one."

"Why, he said to put it in here," returned one of the haymakers, won-deringly. He was a young man, a neighbor's son, whom Adoniram hired by the year to help on the farm.

"Don't you put the hay in the new barn; there's room enough in the old one, aint there?" said Mrs. Penn.

"Room enough," returned the hired man, in his thick, rustic tones. "Didn't need the new barn, nohow, far as room's concerned. Well, I s'pose he changed his mind." He took hold of the horses' bridles.

Mrs. Penn went back to the house. Soon the kitchen windows were darkened, and a fragrance like warm honey came into the room.

Nanny laid down her work. "I thought father wanted them to put the hay into the new barn?" she said, wonderingly.

"It's all right," replied her mother.

Sammy slid down from the load of hay, and came in to see if dinner was ready.

"I ain't goin' to get a regular dinner to-day, as long as father's gone," said his mother. "I've let the fire go out. You can have some bread an' milk an' pie. I thought we could get along." She set out some bowls of milk, some bread, and a pie on the kitchen table. "You'd better eat your dinner now," said she. "You might jest as well get through with it. I want you to help me afterward."

Nanny and Sammy stared at each other. There was something strange in their mother's manner. Mrs. Penn did not eat anything herself. She went into the pantry, and they heard her moving dishes while they ate. Presently she came out with a pile of plates. She got the clothes-basket out of the shed, and packed them in it. Nanny and Sammy watched. She brought out cups and saucers, and put them in with the plates.

"What you goin' to do, mother?" inquired Nanny, in a timid voice. A sense of something unusual made her tremble, as if it were a ghost. Sammy rolled his eyes over his pie.

"You'll see what I'm goin' to do," replied Mrs. Penn. "If you're through, Nanny, I want you to go upstairs an' pack up your things; an' I want you, Sammy, to help me take down the bed in the bedroom."

"Oh, mother, what for?" gasped Nanny.

"You'll see."

During the next few hours a feat was performed by this simple, pious New England mother which was equal in its way to Wolfe's storming of the Heights of Abraham.[2] It took no more genius and audacity of bravery for Wolfe to cheer his wondering soldiers up those steep precipices, under the sleeping eyes of the enemy, than for Sarah Penn, at the head of her children, to move all their little household goods into the new barn while her husband was away.

---

[2]James Wolfe (1727–1759) was a British general whose troops stormed the French army on the Plains of Abraham above Quebec.

Nanny and Sammy followed their mother's instructions without a murmur; indeed, they were overawed. There is a certain uncanny and superhuman quality about all such purely original undertakings as their mother's was to them. Nanny went back and forth with her light loads, and Sammy tugged with sober energy.

At five o'clock in the afternoon the little house in which the Penns had lived for forty years had emptied itself into the new barn.

Every builder builds somewhat for unknown purposes, and is in a measure a prophet. The architect of Adoniram Penn's barn, while he designed it for the comfort of four-footed animals, had planned better than he knew for the comfort of humans. Sarah Penn saw at a glance its possibilities. Those great box-stalls, with quilts hung before them, would make better bedrooms than the one she had occupied for forty years, and there was a tight carriage-room. The harness-room, with its chimney and shelves, would make a kitchen of her dreams. The great middle space would make a parlor, by-and-by, fit for a palace. Upstairs there was as much room as down. With partitions and windows, what a house would there be! Sarah looked at the row of stanchions before the allotted space for cows, and reflected that she would have her front entry there.

At six o'clock the stove was up in the harness-room, the kettle was boiling, and the table set for tea. It looked almost as home-like as the abandoned house across the yard had ever done. The young hired man milked, and Sarah directed him calmly to bring the milk to the new barn. He came gaping, dropping little blots of foam from the brimming pails on the grass. Before the next morning he had spread the story of Adoniram Penn's wife moving into the new barn all over the little village. Men assembled in the store and talked it over, women with shawls over their heads scuttled into each other's houses before their work was done. Any deviation from the ordinary course of life in this quiet town was enough to stop all progress in it. Everybody paused to look at the staid, independent figure on the side track. There was a difference of opinion with regard to her. Some held her to be insane; some, of a lawless and rebellious spirit.

Friday the minister went to see her. It was in the forenoon, and she was at the barn door shelling pease for dinner. She looked up and returned his salutation with dignity, then she went on with her work. She did not invite him in. The saintly expression of her face remained fixed, but there was an angry flush over it.

The minister stood awkwardly before her, and talked. She handled the pease as if they were bullets. At last she looked up, and her eyes showed the spirit that her meek front had covered for a lifetime.

"There ain't no use talkin', Mr. Hersey," she said. "I've thought it all over an' over, an' I believe I'm doin' what's right. I've made it the subject of prayer, an' it's betwixt me an' the Lord an' Adoniram. There ain't no call for anybody else to worry about it."

"Well, of course, if you have brought it to the Lord in prayer, and feel satisfied that you are doing right, Mrs. Penn," said the minister, helplessly. His thin gray-bearded face was pathetic. He was a sickly man; his youthful confidence had cooled; he had to scourge himself up to some of his pastoral duties as relentlessly as a Catholic ascetic, and then he was prostrated by the smart.

"I think it's right jest as much as I think it was right for our forefathers to come over from the old country 'cause they didn't have what belonged to 'em," said Mrs. Penn. She arose. The barn threshold might have been Plymouth Rock from her bearing. "I don't doubt you mean well, Mr. Hersey," said she, "but there are things people hadn't ought to interfere with. I've been a member of the church for over forty year. I've got my own mind an' my own feet, an' I'm goin' to think my own thoughts an' go my own ways, an' nobody but the Lord is goin' to dictate to me unless I've a mind to have him. Won't you come in an' set down? How is Mis' Hersey?"

"She is well, I thank you," replied the minister. He added some more perplexed apologetic remarks; then he retreated.

He could expound the intricacies of every character study in the Scriptures, he was competent to grasp the Pilgrim Fathers and all historical innovators, but Sarah Penn was beyond him. He could deal with primal causes, but parallel ones worsted him. But, after all, although it was aside from his province, he wondered more how Adoniram Penn would deal with his wife than how the Lord would. Everybody shared the wonder. When Adoniram's four new cows arrived, Sarah ordered three to be put in the old barn, the other in the house shed where the cooking-stove had stood. That added to the excitement. It was whispered that all four cows were domiciled in the house.

Towards sunset on Saturday, when Adoniram was expected home, there was a knot of men in the road near the new barn. The hired man had milked, but he still hung around the premises. Sarah Penn had supper all ready. There were brown-bread and baked beans and a custard pie; it was the supper that Adoniram loved on a Saturday night. She had on a clean calico, and she bore herself imperturbably. Nanny and Sammy kept close at her heels. Their eyes were large, and Nanny was full of nervous tremors. Still there was to them more pleasant excitement than anything else. An inborn confidence in their mother over their father asserted itself.

Sammy looked out of the harness-room window. "There he is," he announced, in an awed whisper. He and Nanny peeped around the casing. Mrs. Penn kept on about her work. The children watched Adoniram leave the new horse standing in the drive while he went to the house door. It was fastened. Then he went around to the shed. That door was seldom locked, even when the family was away. The thought how her father would be confronted by the cow flashed upon Nanny. There was a hysterical sob in her throat. Adoniram emerged from the shed and stood looking about in a dazed fashion. His lips moved; he was saying something, but they could not hear what it was. The hired man was peeping around a corner of the old barn, but nobody saw him.

Adoniram took the new horse by the bridle and led him across the yard to the new barn. Nanny and Sammy slunk close to their mother. The barn doors rolled back, and there stood Adoniram, with the long mild face of the great Canadian farm horse looking over his shoulder.

Nanny kept behind her mother, but Sammy stepped suddenly forward, and stood in front of her.

Adoniram stared at the group. "What on airth you all down here for?" said he. "What's the matter over to the house?"

"We've come here to live, father," said Sammy. His shrill voice quavered out bravely.

"What"—Adoniram sniffed—"what is it smells like cooking?" said he. He stepped forward and looked in the open door of the harness-room. Then he turned to his wife. His old bristling face was pale and frightened. "What on airth does this mean, mother?" he gasped.

"You come in here, father," said Sarah. She led the way into the harness-room and shut the door. "Now, father," said she, "you needn't be scared. I ain't crazy. There ain't nothin' to be upset over. But we've come here to live, an' we're goin' to live here. We've got jest as good a right here as new horses an' cows. The house wa'n't fit for us to live in any longer, an' I made up my mind I wa'n't goin' to stay there. I've done my duty by you forty year, an' I'm goin' to do it now; but I'm goin' to live here. You've got to put in some windows and partitions; an' you'll have to buy some furniture."

"Why, mother!" the old man gasped.

"You'd better take your coat off an' get washed—there's the wash-basin—an' then we'll have supper."

"Why, mother!"

Sammy went past the window, leading the new horse to the old barn. The old man saw him, and shook his head speechlessly. He tried to take off his coat, but his arms seemed to lack the power. His wife helped him. She poured some water into the tin basin, and put in a piece of soap. She got the comb and brush, and smoothed his thin gray hair after he had washed. Then she put the beans, hot bread, and tea on the table. Sammy came in, and the family drew up. Adoniram sat looking dazedly at his plate, and they waited.

"Ain't you goin' to ask a blessin', father?" said Sarah.

And the old man bent his head and mumbled.

All through the meal he stopped eating at intervals, and stared furtively at his wife; but he ate well. The home food tasted good to him, and his old frame was too sturdily healthy to be affected by his mind. But after supper he went out, and sat down on the step of the smaller door at the right of the barn, through which he had meant his Jerseys to pass in stately file, but which Sarah designed for her front house door, and he leaned his head on his hands.

After the supper dishes were cleared away and the milk-pans washed, Sarah went out to him. The twilight was deepening. There was a clear green glow in the sky. Before them stretched the smooth level of field; in the distance was a cluster of hay-stacks like the huts of a village; the air was very cool and calm and sweet. The landscape might have been an ideal one of peace.

Sarah bent over and touched her husband on one of his thin, sinewy shoulders. "Father!"

The old man's shoulders heaved: he was weeping.

"Why, don't do so, father," said Sarah.

"I'll—put up the—partitions, an'—everything you want, mother."

Sarah put her apron up to her face; she was overcome by her own triumph.

Adoniram was like a fortress whose walls had no active resistance, and went down the instant the right besieging tools were used. "Why, mother," he said, hoarsely, "I hadn't no idee you was so set on't as all this comes to."

[1890]

ROSE TERRY COOKE

Rose Terry Cooke (1827–1892) was born on a farm near Hartford, Connecticut. Her father was the son of a bank president, and her mother gave her early training in literature by insisting that she study the dictionary and keep a diary. At the age of sixteen she graduated from Catharine Beecher's Hartford Female Seminary, where Harriet Beecher Stowe had studied and taught a decade earlier. Cooke then taught school for a few years until she inherited money from a great-uncle, enabling her to live at home and write poetry and short fiction while she cared for her aging parents and her deceased sister's children. Her first story, "The Mormon's Wife," was published in the June 1855 issue of Putnam's Monthly. *Two years later another of her stories, "Sally Parson's Duty," appeared in the first issue of* The Atlantic Monthly *(November 1857), whose editor, James Russell Lowell, encouraged her to write as realistically as possible. Cooke's stories appeared regularly in* The Atlantic Monthly *in the late 1850s and 1860s, and she became a friend of Annie and James T. Field during Field's editorship of the magazine from 1861 to 1871.*

In 1873 Rose Terry married Rollin H. Cooke, a widower with two daughters. She continued writing to help support her family, publishing a collection of stories Somebody's Neighbors, *in 1881. After her father-in-law's business failure put the family in desperate financial straits, she published eight books of poetry, religious novels, and short fiction, including the short story collections* The Sphinx's Children and Other Peoples *(1886) and* Huckleberries Gathered from New England Hills *(1891). One of the "huckleberries" in this volume was "How Celia Changed Her Mind," a story representative of her best work.*

*Like her Hartford neighbor Harriet Beecher Stowe, who also published local-color stories in the 1870s, Cooke excelled at creating realistic women characters in humble circumstances. In the early story "Miss Lucinda" (*The Atlantic Monthly, *August 1861), she wrote, "So forgive me once more, patient reader, if I offer to you no tragedy in high life, no sentimental history of fashion and wealth, but only a little story about a woman who could not be a heroine." One of her memorable female characters is Polly Mariner, who first appeared in the story "Ann Potter's Lesson" in 1858. In 1870 the story "Polly Mariner, Tailoress" developed this character further as an independent spinster, and she is again seen briefly in "How Celia Changed Her Mind" as an elderly woman with a young apprentice, the orphan Celia Barnes, whose spirited life is the subject of this story.*

How Celia Changed Her Mind

"If there's anything on the face of the earth I *do* hate, it's an old maid!"

Mrs. Stearns looked up from her sewing in astonishment.

"Why, Miss Celia!"

"Oh, yes! I know it. I'm one myself, but all the same, I hate 'em worse
than p'ison. They ain't nothing nor nobody; they're cumberers of the
ground." And Celia Barnes laid down her scissors with a bang, as if she
might be Atropos herself, ready to cut the thread of life for all the despised
class of which she was a notable member.

The minister's wife was genuinely surprised at this outburst; she herself had been well along in life before she married, and though she had
been fairly happy in the uncertain relationship to which she had attained,
she was, on the whole, inclined to agree with St. Paul, that the woman
who did not marry "doeth better." "I don't agree with you, Miss Celia,"
she said gently. "Many, indeed, most of my best friends are maiden ladies,
and I respect and love them just as much as if they were married women."

"Well, I don't. A woman that's married is somebody; she's got a place
in the world; she ain't everybody's tag; folks don't say, 'Oh, it's nobody
but that old maid Celye Varnes;' it's 'Mis' Price,' and 'Mis' Simms,' or
'Thomas Smith's wife,' as though you was somebody. I don't know how 't
is elsewheres, but here in Bassett you might as well be a dog as an old
maid. I allow it might be better if they all had means or eddication:
money's 'a dreadful good thing to have in the house,' as I see in a book
once, and learning is sort of comp'ny to you if you're lonesome; but then
lonesome you be, and you've got to be, if you're an old maid, and it can't
be helped noway."

Mrs. Stearns smiled a little sadly, thinking that even married life had its
own loneliness when your husband was shut up in his study, or gone off on
a long drive to see some sick parishioner or conduct a neighborhood
prayer-meeting, or even when he was the other side of the fireplace
absorbed in a religious paper or a New York daily, or meditating on his
next sermon, while the silent wife sat unnoticed at her mending or knitting. "But married women have more troubles and responsibilities than
the unmarried, Miss Celia," she said. "You have no children to bring up
and be anxious about, no daily dread of not doing your duty by the family
whom you preside over, and no fear of the supplies giving out that are
really needed. Nobody but your own self to look out for."

"That's jest it," snapped Celia, laying down the boy's coat she was
sewing with a vicious jerk of her thread. "There 't is! Nobody to home to
care if you live or die; nobody to peek out of the winder to see if you're
comin', or to make a mess of gruel or a cup of tea for you, or to throw ye a
feelin' word if you're sick nigh unto death. And old maids is just as li'ble to
up and die as them that's married. And as to responsibility, I ain't afraid to
tackle that. Never! I don't hold with them that cringe and crawl and are
skeert at a shadder, and won't do a living thing that they had ought to do
because they're 'afraid to take the responsibility.' Why, there's Mrs. Deacon Trimble, she durst n't so much as set up a prayer-meetin' for missions
or the temp'rance cause, because 't was 'sech a reesponsibility to take the
lead in them matters.' I suppose it's somethin' of a responsible chore to
preach the gospel to the heathen, or grab a drinkin' feller by the scruff of

his neck and haul him out of the horrible pit anyway, but if it's dooty it's got to be done, whether or no; and I ain't afraid of pitchin' into anything the Lord sets me to do!"

"Except being an old maid," said Mrs. Stearns.

Celia darted a sharp glance at her over her silver-rimmed spectacles, and pulled her needle through and through the seams of Willy's jacket with fresh vigor, while a thoughtful shadow came across her fine old face. Celia was a candid woman, for all her prejudices, a combination peculiarly characteristic of New England, for she was a typical Yankee. Presently she said abruptly, "I had n't thought on 't in that light." But then the minister opened the door, and the conversation stopped.

Parson Stearns was tired and hungry and cross, and his wife knew all that as soon as she saw his face. She had learned long ago that ministers, however good they may be, are still men; so to-day she had kept her husband's dinner warm in the under-oven, and had the kettle boiling to make him a cup of tea on the spot to assuage his irritation in the shortest and surest way; but though the odor of a savory stew and the cheerful warmth of the cooking-stove greeted him as he preceded her through the door into the kitchen, he snapped out, sharply enough for Celia to hear him through the half-closed door, "What do you have that old maid here for so often?"

"There!" said Celia to herself, — "there 't is! *He* don't look upon 't as a dispensation, if she doos. Men-folks run the world, and they know it. There ain't one of the hull caboodle but what despises an onmarried woman! Well, 't ain't altogether my fault. I would n't marry them that I could; I could n't — not and be honest; and them that I would hev had did n't ask me. I don't know as I'm to blame, after all, when you look into 't."

And she went on sewing Willy's jacket, contrived with pains and skill out of an old coat of his father's, while Mrs. Stearns poured out her husband's tea in the kitchen, replenished his plate with stew, and cut for him more than one segment of the crisp, fresh apple-pie, and urged upon him the squares of new cheese that legitimately accompany this deleterious viand of the race and country, the sempiternal, insistent, flagrant, and alas! also fragrant pie.

Celia Barnes was the tailoress of the little scattered country town of Bassett. Early left an orphan, without near relatives or money, she had received the scantiest measure of education that our town authorities deal to the pauper children of such organizations. She was ten years old when her mother, a widow for almost all those ten years, left her to the tender mercies of the selectmen of Bassett. The selectmen of our country towns are almost irresponsible governors of their petty spheres, and gratify the instinct of oligarchy peculiar to, and conservative of, the human race. Men must be governed and tyrannized over, — it is an inborn necessity of their nature; and while a republic is a beautiful theory, eminently fitted for a race who are "non Angli, sed Angeli," it has in practice the effect of producing more than Russian tyranny, but on smaller scales and in far and scattered localities. Nowhere are there more despots than among village selectmen in New England. Those who have wrestled with their absolute monarchism in behalf of some charity that might abstract a few of the almighty dollars made out of poverty and distress from their official pockets know how positive and dogmatic is their use of power—*experto crede*. The Bassett "first selectman" promptly bound out little Celia Barnes to a hard, imperious woman, who made a white slave of the child, and only dealt out to her the smallest measure of schooling demanded by law, because the good old minister, Father Perkins, interfered in the child's behalf.

As she was strong and hardy and resolute, Celia lived through her bondage, and at the "free" age of eighteen apprenticed herself to old Miss Polly Mariner, the Bassett tailoress, and being deft with her fingers and quick of brain, soon outran her teacher, and when Polly died, succeeded to her business.

She was a bright girl, not particularly noticeable among others, for she had none of that delicate flower-like New England beauty which is so peculiar, so charming, and so evanescent; her features were tolerably regular, her forehead broad and calm, her gray eyes keen and perceptive, and she had abundant hair of an uncertain brown; but forty other girls in Bassett might have been described in the same way; Celia's face was one to improve with age; its strong sense, capacity for humor, fine outlines of a rugged sort, were always more the style of fifty than fifteen, and what she said of herself was true.

She had been asked to marry an old farmer with five uproarious boys, a man notorious in East Bassett for his stinginess and bad temper, and she had promptly declined the offer. Once more fate had given her a chance. A young fellow of no character, poor, "shiftless," and given to cider as a beverage, had considered it a good idea to marry some one who would make a home for him and earn his living. Looking about him for a proper person to fill this pleasant situation, he pounced on Celia—and she returned the attention!

"Marry *you*? I wonder you've got the sass to ask any decent girl to marry ye, Alfred Hatch! What be you good for, anyway? I don't know what under the canopy the Lord spares you for,—only He doos let the tares grow amongst the wheat, Scripter says, and I'm free to suppose He knows why, but I don't. No, *sir!* Ef you was the last man in the livin' universe I would n't tech ye with the tongs. If you'd got a speck of grit into you, you'd be ashamed to ask a woman to take ye in and support ye, for that's what it comes to. You go 'long! I can make my hands save my head so long as I hev the use of 'em, and I have n't no call to set up a private poor-house!"

So Alfred Hatch sneaked off, much like a cur that has sought to share the kennel of a mastiff, and been shortly and sharply convinced of his presumption.

Here ended Celia's "chances," as she phrased it. Young men were few in Bassett; the West had drawn them away with its subtle attraction of unknown possibilities, just as it does to-day, and Celia grew old in the service of those established matrons who always want clothes cut over for their children, carpet rags sewed, quilts quilted, and comfortables tacked. She was industrious and frugal, and in time laid up some money in the Dartford Savings' Bank; but she did not, like many spinsters, invest her hard-earned dollars in a small house. Often she was urged to do so, but her reasons were good for refusing.

"I should be so independent? Well, I'm as independent now as the law allows. I've got two good rooms to myself, south winders, stairs of my own and outside door, and some privileges. If I had a house there'd be taxes, and insurance, and cleanin' off snow come winter-time, and hoein' paths; and likely enough I should be so fur left to myself that I should set up a garden, and make my succotash cost a dollar a pint a-hirin' of a man to dig it up and hoe it down. Like enough, too, I should be gettin' flower seeds and things; I'm kinder fond of blows in the time of 'em. My old fish-geran'um is a sight of comfort to me as 't is, and there would be a bill of expense again. Then you can't noway build a house with only two rooms in't, it would be all outside; and you might as well try to heat the universe with a cookin'-stove as such a house. Besides, how lonesome I should be! It's forlorn enough to be an old maid anyway, but to have it sort of ground into you, as you may say, by livin' all alone in a hull house, that ain't necessary nor agreeable. Now, if I'm sick or sorry, I can just step downstairs and have aunt Nabby to help or hearten me. Deacon Everts he did set to work one time to persuade me to buy a house; he said 't was a good thing to be able to give somebody shelter 't was poorer'n I was. Says I, 'Deacon, I've worked for my livin' ever sence I remember, and I know there 's no use in anybody bein' poorer than I be. I have n't no call to take any sech in and do for 'em. I give what I can to missions, — home ones, — and I'm willin', cheerfully willin', to do a day's work now and again for somebody that is strivin' with too heavy burdens; but as for keepin' free lodgin' and board, I sha'n't do it.' 'Well, well, well,' says he, kinder as if I was a fractious young one, and a-sawin' his fat hand up and down in the air till I wanted to slap him, 'just as you'd ruther, Celye, — just as you'd ruther. I don't mean to drive ye a mite, only, as Scripter says, "Provoke one another to love and good works."'

"That did rile me! Says I: 'Well, you've provoked me full enough, though I don't know as you've done it in the Scripter sense; and mabbe I should n't have got so fur provoked if I had n't have known that little red house your grandsir' lived and died in was throwed back on your hands just now, and advertised for sellin'. I see the "Mounting County Herald," Deacon Everts.' He shut up, I tell ye. But I sha'n't never buy no house so long as aunt Nabby lets me have her two south chambers, and use the back stairway and the north door continual."

So Miss Celia had kept on her way till now she was fifty, and to-day making over old clothes at the minister's. The minister's wife had, as we have seen, little romance or wild happiness in her life; it is not often the portion of country ministers' wives; and, moreover, she had two step-daughters who were girls of sixteen and twelve when she married their father. Katy was married herself now, this ten years, and doing her hard duty by an annual baby and a struggling parish in Dakota; but Rosabel, whose fine name had been the only legacy her dying mother left the day-old child she had scarce had time to kiss and christen before she went to take her own "new name" above, was now a girl of twenty-two, pretty, headstrong, and rebellious. Nature had endowed her with keen dark eyes, crisp dark curls, a long chin, and a very obstinate mouth, which only her red lips and white even teeth redeemed from ugliness; her bright color and her sense of fun made her attractive to young men wherever she encountered one of that rare species. Just now she was engaged in a serious flirtation with the station-master at Bassett Centre,—an impecunious youth of no special interest to other people and quite unable to maintain a wife. But out of the "strong necessity of loving," as it is called, and the want of young society or settled occupation, Rosa Stearns chose to fall in love with Amos Barker, and her father considered it a "fall" indeed. So, with the natural clumsiness of a man and a father, Parson Stearns set himself to prevent the matter, and began by forbidding Rosabel to see or speak or write to the youth in question, and thereby inspired in her mind a burning desire to do all three. Up to this time she had rather languidly amused herself by mild and gentle flirtations with him, such as looking at him sidewise in church on Sunday, meeting him accidentally on his way to and from the station, for she spent at least half her time at her aunt's in Bassett Centre, and had even taught the small school there during the last six months. She had also sent him her tintype, and his own was secreted in her bureau drawer. He had invited her to go with him to two sleigh-rides and one sugaring-off, and always came home with her from prayer-meeting and singing-school; but like a wise youth he had never yet proposed to marry her in due form, not so much because he was wise as because he was thoughtless and lazy; and while he enjoyed the society of a bright girl, and liked to dangle after the prettiest one in Bassett, and the minister's daughter too, he did not love work well enough to shoulder the responsibility of providing for another those material but necessary supplies that imply labor of an incessant sort.

Rosabel, in her first inconsiderate anger at her father's command, sat down and wrote a note to Amos, eminently calculated to call out his sympathy with her own wrath, and promptly mailed it as soon as it was written. It ran as follows:—

> DEAR FRIEND,—Pa has forbidden me to speak to you any more, or to correspond with you. I suppose I must submit so far; but he did not say I must return your picture [the parson had not an idea that she possessed that precious thing], so I shall keep it to remind me of the pleasant hours we have passed together.
>
> "Fare thee well, and if forever,
> Still forever fare thee well!"
>
> Your true friend,   ROSABEL STEARNS
> P.S.—I think pa is *horrid!*

So did Amos as he read this heart-rending missive, in which the postscript, according to the established sneer at woman's postscripts, carried the whole force of the epistle.

Now Amos had made a friend of Miss Celia by once telegraphing for her trunk, which she had lost on her way home from the only journey of her life, a trip to Boston, whither she had gone, on the strength of the one share of B.&A.R.R. stock she held, to spend the allotted three days granted to stockholders on their annual excursions, presumably to attend the annual meeting. Amos had put himself to the immense trouble of sending two messages for Miss Celia, and asked her nothing for the civility, so that ever after, in the fashion of solitary women, she held herself deeply in his debt. He knew that she was at work for Mrs. Stearns when he received Rosa's epistle, for he had just been over to Bassett on the train—there was but a mile to traverse—to get her to repair his Sunday coat, and not found her at home, but had no time to look her up at the parson's, as he must walk back to his station. Now he resolved to take his answer to Rosa to Miss Celia in the evening, and so be sure that his abused sweetheart received it, for he had read too many dime novels to doubt that her tyrannic father would intercept their letters, and drive them both to madness and despair. That well-meaning but rather dull divine never would have thought of such a thing; he was a puffy, absent-minded, fat little man, with a weak, squeaky voice, and a sudden temper that blazed up like a bunch of dry weeds at a passing spark, and went out at once in flattest ashes. It had been Mrs. Stearns's step-motherly interference that drove him into his harshness to Rosa. She meant well and he meant well, but we all know what good intentions with no further sequel of act are good for, and nobody did more of that "paving" than these two excellent but futile people.

Miss Celia was ready to do anything for Amos Barker, and she considered it little less than a mortal sin to stand in the way of any marriage that was really desired by two parties. That Amos was poor did not daunt her at all; she had the curious faith that possesses some women, that any man can be prosperous if he has the will so to be; and she had a high opinion of this youth, based on his civility to her. It may be said of men, as of elephants, that it is lucky they do not know their own power; for how many more women would become their worshipers and slaves than are so to-day if they knew the abject gratitude the average woman feels for the least attention, the smallest kindness, the faintest expression of affection or good will. We are all, like the Syrophenician woman,[1] glad and ready to eat of the crumbs which fall from the children's table, so great is our faith—in men.

Miss Celia took the note in her big basket over to the minister's the very next day after that on which we introduced her to our readers. She was perhaps more rejoiced to contravene that reverend gentleman's orders

---

[1]Woman from Phoenicia (or "Phenicia"), an ancient country made up of modern day Syria and Lebanon.

than if she had not heard his querulous and contemptuous remark about her through the crack of the door on the previous afternoon; and it was with a sense of joy that, after all, an old maid could do something, that she slipped the envelope into Rosa's hands, and told her to put it quickly into her pocket, the very first moment she found herself alone with that young woman.

Many a hasty word had Parson Stearns spoken in the suddenness of his petulant temper, but never one that bore direr fruit than that when he called Celia Barnes "that old maid."

For of course Amos and Rosabel found in her an ardent friend. They had the instinct of distressed lovers to cajole her with all their confidences, caresses, and eager gratitude, and for once she felt herself dear and of importance. Amos consulted her on his plans for the future, which of course pointed westward, where he had a brother editing and owning a newspaper. This brother had before offered him a place in his office, but Amos had liked better the easy work of a station-master in a tiny village. Now his ambition was aroused, for the time at least. He wanted to make a home for Rosabel, but, alack! he had not one cent to pay their united expenses to Peoria, and a lion stood in the way. Here again Celia stepped in: she had some money laid up; she would lend it to them.

I do not say that at this stage she had no misgivings, but even these were set at rest by a conversation she had with Mrs. Stearns some six weeks after the day on which Celia had so fully expressed her scorn of spinsters. She was there again to tack a comfortable for Rosabel's bed, and bethought herself that it was a good time to feel her way a little concerning Mrs. Stearns's opinion of things.

"They do say," she remarked, stopping to snip off her thread and twist the end of it through her needle's eye, "that your Rosy don't go with Amos Barker no more. Is that so?"

"Yes," said Mrs. Stearns, with a half sigh. "Husband was rather prompt about it; he don't think Amos Barker ever'll amount to much, and he thinks his people are not just what they should be. You know his father never was very much of a man, and his grandfather is a real old reprobate. Husband says he never knew anything but crows come out of a crow's nest, and so he told Rosa to break acquaintance with him."

"Who does he like to hev come to see her?" asked Celia, with a grim set of her lips, stabbing her needle fiercely through the unoffending calico.

Mrs. Stearns laughed rather feebly. "I don't think he has anybody on his mind, Miss Celia. I don't think there are any young men in Bassett. I dare say Rosa will never marry. I wish she would, for she is n't happy here, and I can't do much to help it, with all my cares."

"And you can't feel for her as though she was your own, if you try ever so," confidently asserted Celia.

"No, I suppose not. I try to do my duty by her, and I am sorry for her; but I know all the time an own mother would understand her better and make it easier for her. Mr. Stearns is peculiar, and men don't know just how to manage girls."

It was a cautious admission, but Miss Celia had sharp eyes, and knew very well that Rosabel neither loved nor respected her father, and that they were now on terms of real if unavowed hostility.

"Well," said she, "I don' know but you will have to have one of them onpleasant creturs, an old maid, in your fam'ly. I declare for't, I'd hold a Thanksgiving Day all to myself ef I'd escaped that marcy."

"You may not always think so, Celia."

"I don't know what'll change me. 'T will be something I don't look forrard to now," answered Celia obstinately.

Mrs. Stearns sighed. "I hope Rosa will do nothing worse than to live unmarried," she said; but she could not help wishing silently that some worthy man would carry the perverse and annoying girl out of the parsonage for good.

After this Celia felt a certain freedom to help Rosabel; she encouraged the lovers to meet at her house, helped plan their elopement, sewed for the girl, and at last went with them as far as Brimfield when they stole away one evening, saw them safely married at the Methodist parsonage there, and bidding them good-speed, returned to Bassett Centre on the midnight train, and walked over to her own dwelling in the full moonshine of the October night, quite fearless and entirely exultant.

But she was not to come off unscathed. There was a scene of wild commotion at the parsonage next day, when Rosa's letter, modeled on that of the last novel heroine she had become acquainted with, was found on her bureau, as per novel aforesaid.

With her natural thoughtlessness she assured her parents that she "fled not uncompanioned," that her "kind and all but maternal friend, Miss Celia Barnes, would accompany her to the altar, and give her support and her countenance to the solemn ceremony that should make Rosabel Stearns the blessed wife of Amos Barker!"

It was all the minister could do not to swear as he read this astounding letter. His flabby face grew purple; his fat, sallow hands shook with rage; he dared not speak, he only sputtered, for he knew that profane and unbecoming words would surely leap from his tongue if he set it free; but he must—he really must—do or say something! So he clapped on his old hat, and with coat tails flying in the breeze, and rage in every step, set out to find Celia Barnes; and find her he did.

It would be unpleasant, and it is needless, to depict this encounter; language both unjust and unsavory smote the air and reverberated along the highway, for he met the spinster on her road to an engagement at Deacon Stiles's. Suffice it to say that both freed their minds with great enlargement of opinion, and the parson wound up with,—

"And I never want to see you again inside of my house, you confounded old maid!"

"There! that's it!" retorted Celia. "Ef I was n't an old maid, you would n't no more have darst to 'a' talked to me this way than nothin'. Ef I'd had a man to stand up to ye you'd have been dumber'n Balaam's ass a great sight,—afore it seen the angel, I mean. I swow to man, I b'lieve I'd marry a hitchin'-post if 't was big enough to trounce ye. You great lummox, if I could knock ye over you would n't peep nor mutter agin, if I be a woman!"

And with a burst of furious tears that asserted her womanhood Miss Celia went her way. Her hands were clinched under her blanket-shawl, her eyes red with angry rain, and as she walked on she soliloquized aloud:—

"I declare for 't, I b'lieve I'd marry the Old Boy himself if he'd ask me. I'm sicker'n ever of bein' an old maid!"

"Be ye?" queried a voice at her elbow. "P'r'aps, then, you might hear to me if I was to speak my mind, Celye."

Celia jumped. As she said afterward, "I vum I thought 't was the Enemy, for certain; and to think 't was only Deacon Everts!"

"Mercy me!" she said now; "is 't you, deacon?"

"Yes, it's me; and I think 't is a real providence I come up behind ye just in the nick of time. I've sold my farm only last week, and I've come to live on the street in that old red house of grand-sir's, that you mistrusted once I wanted you to buy. I'm real lonesome sence I lost my partner" (he meant his wife), "and I've been a-hangin' on by the edges the past two year; hired help is worse than nothing onto a farm, and hard to get at that; so I sold out, and I'm a-movin' yet, but the old house looks forlorn enough, and I was intendin' to look about for a second; so if you'll have me, Celye, here I be."

Celia looked at him sharply; he was an apple-faced little man, with shrewd, twinkling eyes, a hard, dull red still lingering on his round cheeks in spite of the deep wrinkles about his pursed-up lips and around his eye-lids; his mouth gave him a consequential and self-important air, to which the short stubbly hair, brushed up "like a blaze" above his forehead, added; and his old blue coat with brass buttons, his homespun trousers, the old-fashioned aspect of his unbleached cotton shirt, all attested his frugality. Indeed, everybody knew that Deacon Everts was "near," and also that he had plenty of money, that is to say, far more than he could spend. He had no children, no near relations; his first wife had died two years since, after long invalidism, and all her relations had moved far west. All this Celia knew and now recalled; her wrath against Parson Stearns was yet fresh and vivid; she remembered that Simeon Everts was senior deacon of the church, and had it in his power to make the minister extremely uncomfortable if he chose. I have never said Celia was a very good woman; her religion was of the dormant type not uncommon nowadays; she kept up its observances properly, and said her prayers every day, bestowed a part of her savings on each church collection, and was rated as a church-member "in good and regular standing;" but the vital transforming power of that Christianity which means to "love the Lord thy God with all thy heart, and mind, and soul, and strength, and thy neighbor as thyself," had no more entered into her soul than it had into Deacon Everts's; and while she would have honestly admitted that revenge was a very wrong sentiment, and entirely improper for any other person to cherish, she felt that she did well to be angry with Parson Stearns, and had a perfect right to "pay him off" in any way she could.

Now here was her opportunity. If she said "Yes" to Deacon Everts, he would no doubt take her part. Her objections to housekeeping were set aside by the fact that the house-owner himself would have to do those heavy labors about the house which she must otherwise have hired a man to do; and the cooking and the indoor work for two people could not be so hard as to sew from house to house for her daily bread. In short, her mind was slowly turning favorably toward this sudden project, but she did not want this wooer to be too sure; so she said: "W-e-ll, 't is a life sentence, as you may say, deacon, and I want to think on't a spell. Let's see,—today's Tuesday; I'll let ye know Thursday night, after prayer-meetin'."

"Well," answered the deacon.

Blessed Yankee monosyllable that means so much and so little; that has such shades of phrase and intention in its myriad inflections; that is "yes," or "no," or "perhaps," just as you accent it; that is at once preface and peroration, evasion and definition! What would all New England speech be without "well"? Even as salt without any savor, or pepper with no pungency.

Now it meant to Miss Celia assent to her proposition; and in accordance the deacon escorted her home from meeting Thursday night, and received for reward a consenting answer. This was no love affair, but a matter of mere business. Deacon Everts needed a housekeeper, and did not want to pay out wages for one; and Miss Celia's position she expressed herself as she put out her tallow candle on that memorable night, and breathed out on the darkness the audible aspiration, "Thank goodness, I sha'n't hev to die an old maid!"

There was no touch of sanctifying love or consoling affection, or even friendly comradeship, in this arrangement; it was as truly a *marriage de convenance* as was ever contracted in Paris itself, and when the wedding day came, a short month afterward, the sourest aspect of November skies threatening a drenching pour, the dead and sodden leaves that strewed the earth, the wailing northeast wind, even the draggled and bony old horse behind which they jogged over to Bassett Centre, seemed fit accompaniments to the degraded ceremony performed by a justice of the peace, who concluded this merely legal compact, for Miss Celia stoutly refused to be married by Parson Stearns; she would not be accessory to putting one dollar in his pocket, even as her own wedding fee. So she went home to the little red house on Bassett Street, and begun her married life by scrubbing the dust and dirt of years from the kitchen table, making biscuit for tea, washing up the dishes, and at last falling asleep during the deacon's long nasal prayer, wherein he wandered to the ends of the earth, and prayed fervently for the heathen, piteously unconscious that he was little better than a heathen himself.

It did not take many weeks to discover to Celia what is meant by "the curse of a granted prayer." She could not at first accept the situation at all; she was accustomed to enough food, if it was plain and simple, when she herself provided it; but now it was hard to get such viands as would satisfy a healthy appetite.

"You've used a sight of pork, Celye," the deacon would remonstrate. "My first never cooked half what you do. We shall come to want certain, if you're so free-handed."

"Well, Mr. Everts, there was n't a mite left to set by. We eat it all, and I did n't have no more'n I wanted, if you did."

"We must mortify the flesh, Celye. It's hull-some to get up from your victuals hungry. Ye know what Scripter says, 'Jeshurun waxed fat an' kicked.'"

"Well, I ain't Jeshurun, but I expect I shall be more likely to kick if I don't have enough to eat, when it's only pork 'n' potatoes."

"My first used to say them was the best, for steady victuals, of anything, and she never used but two codfish and two quarts of m'lasses the year round; and as for butter, she was real sparin'; she'd fry our bread along with the salt pork, and 't was just as good."

"Look here!" snapped Celia. "I don't want to hear no more about your 'first.' I'm ready to say I wish 't she'd ha' been your last too."

"Well, well, well! this is onseemly contention, Celye," sputtered the alarmed deacon. "Le' 's dwell together in unity so fur as we can, Mis' Everts. I have n't no intention to starve ye, none whatever. I only want to be keerful, so as we sha'n't have to fetch up in the poor-us."

"No need to have a poor-house to home," muttered Celia.

But this is only a mild specimen of poor Celia's life as a married woman. She did not find the honor and glory of "Mrs." before her name a compensation for the thousand evils that she "knew not of" when she fled to them as a desirable change from her single blessedness. Deacon Everts entirely refused to enter into any of her devices against Parson Stearns; he did not care a penny about Celia's wrongs; and he knew very well that no other man than dreamy, unpractical Mr. Stearns, who eked out his minute pittance by writing school-books of a primary sort, would put up with four hundred dollars a year from his parish; yet that was all Bassett people would pay. If they must have the gospel, they must have it at the lowest living rates, and everybody would not assent to that.

So Celia found her revenge no more feasible after her marriage than before, and, gradually absorbed in her own wrongs and sufferings, her desire to reward Mr. Stearns in kind for his treatment of her vanished; she thought less of his futile wrath and more of her present distresses every day.

For Celia, like everybody who profanes the sacrament of marriage, was beginning to suffer the consequences of her misstep. As her husband's mean, querulous, loveless character unveiled itself in the terrible intimacy of constant and inevitable companionship, she began to look woefully back to the freedom and peace of her maiden days. She learned that a husband is by no means his wife's defender always, not even against reviling tongues. It did not suit Deacon Everts to quarrel with any one, whatever they said to him, or of him and his; he "did n't want no enemies," and Celia bitterly felt that she must fight her own battles; she had not even an ally in her husband. She became not only defiant, but also depressed; the consciousness of a vital and life-long mistake is not productive of cheer or content; and now, admitted into the free-masonry of married women, she discovered how few among them were more than household drudges, the servants of their families, worked to the verge of exhaustion, and neither thanked nor rewarded for their pains. She saw here a woman whose children were careless of, and ungrateful to her, and her husband coldly indifferent; there was one on whom the man she had married wreaked all his fiendish temper in daily small injuries, little vexatious acts, petty tyrannies, a "street-angel, house-devil" of a man, of all sorts the most hateful. There were many whose lives had no other outlook than hard work until the end should come, who rose up to labor and lay down in sleepless exhaustion, and some whose days were a constant terror to them from the intemperate brutes to whom they had intrusted their happiness, and indeed their whole existence.

It was no worse with Celia than with most of her sex in Bassett; here and there, there were of course exceptions, but so rare as to be shining examples and objects of envy. Then, too, after two years, there came forlorn accounts of poor Rosabel's situation at the west. Amos Barker had done his best at first to make his wife comfortable, but change of place or new motives do not at once, if ever, transform an indolent man into an active and efficient one. He found work in his brother's office, but it was the hard work of collecting bills all about the country; the roads were bad, the weather as fluctuating as weather always is, the climate did not agree with him, and he got woefully tired of driving about from dawn till after dark, to dun unwilling debtors. Rosa had chills and fever and babies with persistent alacrity; she had indeed enough to eat, with no appetite, and a house, with no strength to keep it. She grew untidy, listless, hysterical; and her father, getting worried by her despondent and infrequent letters, actually so far roused himself as to sell his horse, and with this sacrificial money betook himself to Mound Village, where he found Rosabel with two babies in her arms, dust an inch deep on all her possessions, nothing but pork, potatoes, and corn bread in the pantry, and a slatternly negress washing some clothes in a kitchen that made the parson shudder.

The little man's heart was bigger than his soul. He put his arms about Rosa and the dingy babies, and forgave her all; but he had to say, even while he held them closely and fondly to his breast, "Oh, Rosy, I told you what would happen if you married that fellow."

Of course Rosa resented the speech, for, after all, she had loved Amos; perhaps could love him still if the poverty and malaria and babies could have all been eliminated from her daily life.

Fortunately the parson's horse had sold well, for it was strong and young, and the rack of venerable bones with which he replaced it was bought very cheap at a farmer's auction, so he had money enough to carry Rosa and the two children home to Bassett, where two months after she added another feeble, howling cipher to the miserable sum of humanity.

Miss—no, Mrs.—Celia's conscience stung her to the quick when she encountered this ghastly wreck of pretty Rosabel Stearns, now called Mrs. Barker. She remembered with deep regret how she had given aid and comfort to the girl who had defied and disobeyed parental counsel and authority, and so brought on herself all this misery. She fancied that Parson Stearns glared at her with eyes of bitter accusation and reproach, and not improbably he did, for beside his pity and affection for his daughter, it was no slight burden to take into his house a feeble woman with two children helpless as babies, and to look forward to the expense and anxiety of another soon to come. And Mrs. Stearns had never loved Rosa well enough to be complacent at this addition to her family cares. She gave the parson no sympathy. It would have been her way to let Rosabel lie on the bed she had made, and die there if need be. But the poor worn-out creature died at home, after all, and the third baby lay on its mother's breast in her coffin: they had gone together.

Celia felt almost like a murderess when she heard that Rosabel Barker was dead. She did not reflect that in all human probability the girl would have married Amos if she, Celia, had refused to help or encourage her. It began to be an importunate question in our friend's mind whether she herself had not made a mistake too; whether the phrase "single blessedness" was not an expression of a vital truth rather than a scoff. Celia was changing her mind no doubt, surely if slowly.

Meantime Deacon Everts did not find all the satisfaction with his "second" that he had anticipated. Celia had a will of her own, quite undisciplined, and it was too often asserted to suit her lord and master. Secretly he planned devices to circumvent her purposes, and sometimes succeeded. In prayer-meeting and in Sunday-school the idea haunted him; his malice lay down and rose up with him. Even when he propounded to his Bible class the important question, "How fur be the heathen *ree*sponsible for what they dun know?" and asked them "to ponder on 't through the comin' week," he chuckled inwardly at the thought that Celia could not evade *her* responsibility; she knew enough, and would be judged accordingly: the deacon was not a merciful man.

At last he hit upon that great legal engine whereby men do inflict the last deadly kick upon their wives: he would remodel his will. Yes, he would leave those gathered thousands to foreign missions; he would leave behind him the indisputable testimony and taunt that he considered the wife of his bosom less than the savages and heathen afar off. He forgot conveniently that the man "who provideth not for his own household hath denied the faith, and is worse than an infidel." And in his delight of revenge he also forgot that the law of the land provides for a man's wife and children in spite of his wicked will. Nor did he remember that his life-insurance policy for five thousand dollars was made out in his wife's name, simply as his wife, her own name not being specified. He had paid the premium always from his "first's" small annual income, and agreed that it should be written for her benefit, but he supposed that at her death it had reverted to him. He forgot that he still had a wife when he mentioned that policy in his assets recorded in the will, and to save money he drew that evil document up himself, and had it signed down at "the store" by three witnesses.

Celia had borne her self-imposed yoke for four years, when it was suddenly broken. A late crop of grass was to be mowed in mid-July on the meadow which appertained to the old house, and the deacon, now some seventy years old, to save hiring help, determined to do it by himself. The grass was heavy and over-ripe, the day extremely hot and breathless, and the grim Mower of Man trod side by side with Simeon Everts, and laid him too, all along by the rough heads of timothy and the purpled feather-tops of the blue-grass. He did not come home at noon or at night, and when Celia went down to the lot to call him she heard no summons of hers; he had answered a call far more imperative and final.

After the funeral Celia found his will pushed back in the deep drawer of an old secretary, where he kept his one quill pen, a bottle of dried ink, a lump of chalk, some rat-poison, and various other odds and ends.

She was indignant enough at its tenor; but it was easily broken, and she not only had her "thirds," but the life policy reverted to her also, as it was made out to Simeon Everts's wife, and surely she had occupied that position for four wretched years. Then, also, she had a right to her support for one year out of the estate, and the use of the house for that time.

Oh, how sweet was her freedom! With her characteristic honesty she refused to put on mourning, and even went to the funeral in her usual gray Sunday gown and bonnet. "I won't lie, anyhow!" she answered to Mrs. Stiles's remonstrance. "I ain't a mite sorry nor mournful. I could ha' wished he'd had time to repent of his sins, but sence the Lord saw fit to cut him short, I don't feel to rebel ag'inst it. I wish 't I'd never married him, that's all!"

"But, Celye, you got a good livin'."

"I earned it."

"And he's left ye with means too."

"He done his best not to. I don't owe him nothing for that; and I earned that too,—the hull on 't. It's poor pay for what I've lived through; and I'm a'most a mind to call it the wages of sin, for I done wrong, ondeniably wrong, in marryin' of him; but the Lord knows I've repented, and said my lesson, if I did get it by the hardest."

Yet all Bassett opened eyes and mouth both when on the next Thanksgiving Day Celia invited every old maid in town—seven all told—to take dinner with her. Never before had she celebrated this old New England day of solemn revel. A woman living in two small rooms could not "keep the feast," and rarely had she been asked to any family conclave. We Yankees are conservative at Thanksgiving if nowhere else, and like to gather our own people only about the family hearth; so Celia had but once or twice shared the turkeys of her more fortunate neighbors.

Now she called in Nabby Hyde and Sarah Gillett, Ann Smith, Celestia Potter, Delia Hills, Sophronia Ann Jenkins and her sister Adelia Ann, ancient twins, who lived together on next to nothing, and were happy.

Celia bloomed at the head of the board, not with beauty, but with gratification. "Well," she said, as soon as they were seated, "I sent for ye all to come because I wanted to have a good time, for one thing, and because it seems as though I'd ought to take back all the sassy and disagreeable things I used to be forever flingin' at old maids. 'I spoke in my haste,' as Scripter says, and also in my ignorance, I'm free to confess. I feel as though I could keep Thanksgivin' to-day with my hull soul. I'm so thankful to be an old maid ag'in!"

"I thought you was a widder," snapped Sally Gillett.

Celia flung a glance of wrath at her, but scorned to reply.

"And I'm thankful too that I'm spared to help ondo somethin' done in that ignorance. I've got means, and, as I've said before, I earned 'em. I don't feel noway obleeged to him for 'em; he did n't mean it. But now I can I'm goin' to adopt Rosy Barker's two children, and fetch 'em up to be dyed-in-the-wool old maids; and every year, so long as I live, I'm goin' to keep an old maids' Thanksgivin' for a kind of a burnt-offering, sech as the Bible tells about, for I've changed my mind clear down to the bottom, and I go the hull figure with the 'postle Paul when he speaks about the onmarried, 'It is better if she so abide.' Now let's go to work at the victuals."

[1891]

CHARLOTTE PERKINS GILMAN

Charlotte Perkins Gilman (1860–1935) was born in Hartford, Connecticut. Her father deserted the family shortly after she was born and provided her mother with only meager support. As a teenager Gilman attended the Rhode Island School of Design for a brief period and worked as a commercial artist and teacher. Like her great-aunt Harriet Beecher Stowe, she was concerned at an early age with social injustice and wrote poetry about the hardship of women's lives.

In 1884 she married the artist Charles Walter Stetson. Suffering extreme depression after the birth of a daughter, she left her husband and moved to California in 1888. They were divorced, and she later married George Houghton Gilman, with whom she lived for thirty-four years. In the 1890s Gilman estab-lished her reputation as a lecturer and writer of feminist tracts. Her book Women and Economics *(1898) is considered one of the most important works of the early years of the women's movement in the United States. Gilman's later books—* Concerning Children *(1900),* The Home *(1904), and* Human Work *(1904)—argue that women should be educated to become financially independent; then they could contribute more to the amelioration of systems of justice and the improvement of society. From 1909 to 1917 Gilman published her own journal,* The Forerunner, *for which she wrote volumi-nously. At the end of her life, suffering from cancer, she committed suicide with chloroform.*

Today Gilman's best-known work is "The Yellow Wallpaper," published in the New England Magazine *in 1892, after her own nervous breakdown. A landmark story in its frank depiction of mental illness, it is part autobiography and part fantasy ("I never had hallucinations or objections to my mural deco-rations"). The story is an imaginative account of her suffering and treatment by the physician S. Weir Mitchell, who forbade her any activity, especially writing, the thing she most wanted to do. Disregarding his advice after three months, Gilman said she "went to work again—work, the normal life of every human being; work, in which is joy and growth and service, without which one is a pauper and a parasite; ultimately recovering some measure of power."*

In setting "The Yellow Wallpaper," Gilman uses elements of the conven-tional gothic romances that were a staple in women's popular fiction—an iso-lated mansion, a distant but dominating male figure, and a mysterious household—all of which force the heroine into the role of passive victim of cir-cumstances. But Gilman gives her own twist to the form. Using the brief para-graphs and simple sentences of popular fiction, she narrates her story with a clinical precision that avoids the trite language of typical romances.

RELATED COMMENTARIES: *Sandra M. Gilbert and Susan Gubar, "A Femi-nist Reading of Gilman's 'The Yellow Wallpaper,'" page 1352; Charlotte Perkins Gilman, "Undergoing the Cure for Nervous Prostration," page 1354.*

The Yellow Wallpaper[1]

It is very seldom that mere ordinary people like John and myself secure ancestral halls for the summer.

A colonial mansion, a hereditary estate, I would say a haunted house and reach the height of romantic felicity—but that would be asking too much of fate!

Still I will proudly declare that there is something queer about it.

Else, why should it be let so cheaply? And why have stood so long untenanted?

John laughs at me, of course, but one expects that in marriage.

John is practical in the extreme. He has no patience with faith, an intense horror of superstition, and he scoffs openly at any talk of things not to be felt and seen and put down in figures.

John is a physician, and *perhaps*—(I would not say it to a living soul, of course, but this is dead paper and a great relief to my mind)—*perhaps* that is one reason I do not get well faster.

You see, he does not believe I am sick!

And what can one do?

If a physician of high standing, and one's own husband, assures friends and relatives that there is really nothing the matter with one but temporary nervous depression—a slight hysterical tendency—what is one to do?

My brother is also a physician, and also of high standing, and he says the same thing.

So I take phosphates or phosphites—whichever it is, and tonics, and journeys, and air, and exercise, and am absolutely forbidden to "work" until I am well again.

Personally, I disagree with their ideas.

Personally, I believe that congenial work, with excitement and change, would do me good.

But what is one to do?

I did write for a while in spite of them; but it *does* exhaust me a good deal—having to be so sly about it, or else meet with heavy opposition.

I sometimes fancy that in my condition if I had less opposition and more society and stimulus—but John says the very worst thing I can do is to think about my condition, and I confess it always makes me feel bad.

So I will let it alone and talk about the house.

The most beautiful place! It is quite alone, standing well back from the road, quite three miles from the village. It makes me think of English places that you read about, for there are hedges and walls and gates that lock, and lots of separate little houses for the gardeners and people.

---

[1]This story originally appeared as "The Yellow Wall-Paper" in 1892. We have chosen to preserve the inconsistent hyphenation of the word *wallpaper* from the original text but have followed convention in omitting the hyphen from the story's title.

There is a *delicious* garden! I never saw such a garden—large and shady, full of box-bordered paths, and lined with long grape-covered arbors with seats under them.

There were greenhouses, too, but they are all broken now.

There was some legal trouble, I believe, something about the heirs and co-heirs; anyhow, the place has been empty for years.

That spoils my ghostliness, I am afraid, but I don't care—there is something strange about the house—I can feel it.

I even said so to John one moonlight evening, but he said what I felt was a *draught,* and shut the window.

I get unreasonably angry with John sometimes. I'm sure I never used to be so sensitive. I think it is due to this nervous condition.

But John says if I feel so, I shall neglect proper self-control; so I take pains to control myself—before him, at least, and that makes me very tired.

I don't like our room a bit. I wanted one downstairs that opened onto the piazza and had roses all over the window, and such pretty old-fashioned chintz hangings! but John would not hear of it.

He said there was only one window and not room for two beds, and no near room for him if he took another.

He is very careful and loving, and hardly lets me stir without special direction.

I have a schedule prescription for each hour in the day; he takes all care from me, and so I feel basely ungrateful not to value it more.

He said we came here solely on my account, that I was to have perfect rest and all the air I could get. "Your exercise depends on your strength, my dear," said he, "and your food somewhat on your appetite; but air you can absorb all the time." So we took the nursery at the top of the house.

It is a big, airy room, the whole floor nearly, with windows that look all ways, and air and sunshine galore. It was nursery first and then play-room and gymnasium, I should judge; for the windows are barred for little children, and there are rings and things in the walls.

The paint and paper look as if a boys' school had used it. It is stripped off—the paper—in great patches all around the head of my bed, about as far as I can reach, and in a great place on the other side of the room low down. I never saw a worse paper in my life.

One of those sprawling flamboyant patterns committing every artistic sin.

It is dull enough to confuse the eye in following, pronounced enough to constantly irritate and provoke study, and when you follow the lame uncertain curves for a little distance they suddenly commit suicide—plunge off at outrageous angles, destroy themselves in unheard of contradictions.

The color is repellant, almost revolting; a smouldering unclean yellow, strangely faded by the slow-turning sunlight.

It is a dull yet lurid orange in some places, a sickly sulphur tint in others.

No wonder the children hated it! I should hate it myself if I had to live in this room long.

There comes John, and I must put this away,—he hates to have me write a word.

We have been here two weeks, and I haven't felt like writing before, since that first day.

I am sitting by the window now, up in this atrocious nursery, and there is nothing to hinder my writing as much as I please, save lack of strength.

John is away all day, and even some nights when his cases are serious.

I am glad my case is not serious!

But these nervous troubles are dreadfully depressing.

John does not know how much I really suffer. He knows there is no *reason* to suffer, and that satisfies him.

Of course it is only nervousness. It does weigh on me so not to do my duty in any way!

I meant to be such a help to John, such a real rest and comfort, and here I am a comparative burden already!

Nobody would believe what an effort it is to do what little I am able,—to dress and entertain, and order things.

It is fortunate Mary is so good with the baby. Such a dear baby!

And yet I *cannot* be with him, it makes me so nervous.

I suppose John never was nervous in his life. He laughs at me so about this wall-paper!

At first he meant to repaper the room, but afterward he said that I was letting it get the better of me, and that nothing was worse for a nervous patient than to give way to such fancies.

He said that after the wall-paper was changed it would be the heavy bedstead, and then the barred windows, and then that gate at the head of the stairs, and so on.

"You know the place is doing you good," he said, "and really, dear, I don't care to renovate the house just for a three months' rental."

"Then do let us go downstairs," I said, "there are such pretty rooms there."

Then he took me in his arms and called me a blessed little goose, and said he would go down cellar, if I wished, and have it whitewashed into the bargain.

But he is right enough about the beds and windows and things.

It is an airy and comfortable room as anyone need wish, and, of course, I would not be so silly as to make him uncomfortable just for a whim.

I'm really getting quite fond of the big room, all but that horrid paper.

Out of one window I can see the garden, those mysterious deep-shaded arbors, the riotous old-fashioned flowers, and bushes and gnarly trees.

Out of another I get a lovely view of the bay and a little private wharf belonging to the estate. There is a beautiful shaded lane that runs down there from the house. I always fancy I see people walking in these numerous paths and arbors, but John has cautioned me not to give way to fancy in the least. He says that with my imaginative power and habit of story-making, a nervous weakness like mine is sure to lead to all manner of excited fancies, and that I ought to use my will and good sense to check the tendency. So I try.

I think sometimes that if I were only well enough to write a little it would relieve the press of ideas and rest me.

But I find I get pretty tired when I try.

It is so discouraging not to have any advice and companionship about my work. When I get really well, John says we will ask Cousin Henry and Julia down for a long visit; but he says he would as soon put fireworks in my pillow-case as to let me have those stimulating people about now.

I wish I could get well faster.

But I must not think about that. This paper looks to me as if it *knew* what a vicious influence it had!

There is a recurrent spot where the pattern lolls like a broken neck and two bulbous eyes stare at you upside down.

I get positively angry with the impertinence of it and the everlasting-ness. Up and down and sideways they crawl, and those absurd, unblinking eyes are everywhere. There is one place where two breadths didn't match, and the eyes go all up and down the line, one a little higher than the other.

I never saw so much expression in an inanimate thing before, and we all know how much expression they have! I used to lie awake as a child and get more entertainment and terror out of blank walls and plain furniture than most children could find in a toy-store.

I remember what a kindly wink the knobs of our big, old bureau used to have, and there was one chair that always seemed like a strong friend.

I used to feel that if any of the other things looked too fierce I could always hop into that chair and be safe.

The furniture in this room is no worse than inharmonious, however, for we had to bring it all from downstairs. I suppose when this was used as a playroom they had to take the nursery things out, and no wonder! I never saw such ravages as the children have made here.

The wall-paper, as I said before, is torn off in spots, and it sticketh closer than a brother—they must have had perseverance as well as hatred.

Then the floor is scratched and gouged and splintered, the plaster itself is dug out here and there, and this great heavy bed, which is all we found in the room, looks as if it had been through the wars.

But I don't mind it a bit—only the paper.

There comes John's sister. Such a dear girl as she is, and so careful of me! I must not let her find me writing.

She is a perfect and enthusiastic housekeeper, and hopes for no better profession. I verily believe she thinks it is the writing which made me sick!

But I can write when she is out, and see her a long way off from these windows.

There is one that commands the road, a lovely shaded winding road, and one that just looks off over the country. A lovely country, too, full of great elms and velvet meadows.

This wallpaper has a kind of sub-pattern in a different shade, a particularly irritating one, for you can only see it in certain lights, and not clearly then.

But in the places where it isn't faded and where the sun is just so — I can see a strange, provoking, formless sort of figure, that seems to skulk about behind that silly and conspicuous front design.

There's sister on the stairs!

Well, the Fourth of July is over! The people are all gone, and I am tired out. John thought it might do me good to see a little company, so we just had mother and Nellie and the children down for a week.

Of course I didn't do a thing. Jennie sees to everything now.

But it tired me all the same.

John says if I don't pick up faster he shall send me to Weir Mitchell[2] in the fall.

But I don't want to go there at all. I had a friend who was in his hands once, and she says he is just like John and my brother, only more so!

Besides, it is such an undertaking to go so far.

I don't feel as if it was worthwhile to turn my hand over for anything, and I'm getting dreadfully fretful and querulous.

I cry at nothing, and cry most of the time.

Of course I don't when John is here, or anybody else, but when I am alone.

And I am alone a good deal just now. John is kept in town very often by serious cases, and Jennie is good and lets me alone when I want her to.

So I walk a little in the garden or down that lovely lane, sit on the porch under the roses, and lie down up here a good deal.

I'm getting really fond of the room in spite of the wallpaper. Perhaps *because* of the wallpaper.

It dwells in my mind so!

I lie here on this great immovable bed — it is nailed down, I believe — and follow that pattern about by the hour. It is as good as gymnastics, I assure you. I start, we'll say, at the bottom, down in the corner over there

---

[2]Dr. S. Weir Mitchell (1829–1914) was an eminent Philadelphia neurologist who advocated "rest cures" for nervous disorders. He was the author of *Diseases of the Nervous System, Especially of Women* (1881).

where it has not been touched, and I determine for the thousandth time that I *will* follow that pointless pattern to some sort of a conclusion.

I know a little of the principle of design, and I know this thing was not arranged on any laws of radiation, or alternation, or repetition, or symmetry, or anything else that I ever heard of.

It is repeated, of course, by the breadths, but not otherwise.

Looked at in one way each breadth stands alone, the bloated curves and flourishes—a kind of "debased Romanesque" with *delirium tremens*—go waddling up and down in isolated columns of fatuity.

But, on the other hand, they connect diagonally, and the sprawling outlines run off in great slanting waves of optic horror, like a lot of wallowing seaweeds in full chase.

The whole thing goes horizontally, too, at least it seems so, and I exhaust myself in trying to distinguish the order of its going in that direction.

They have used a horizontal breadth for a frieze, and that adds wonderfully to the confusion.

There is one end of the room where it is almost intact, and there, when the crosslights fade and the low sun shines directly upon it, I can almost fancy radiation after all,—the interminable grotesques seem to form around a common centre and rush off in headlong plunges of equal distraction.

It makes me tired to follow it. I will take a nap, I guess.

I don't know why I should write this.

I don't want to.

I don't feel able.

And I know John would think it absurd. But I *must* say what I feel and think in some way—it is such a relief!

But the effort is getting to be greater than the relief.

Half the time now I am awfully lazy, and lie down ever so much.

John says I mustn't lose my strength, and has me take cod liver oil and lots of tonics and things, to say nothing of ale and wine and rare meat.

Dear John! He loves me very dearly, and hates to have me sick. I tried to have a real earnest reasonable talk with him the other day, and tell him how I wish he would let me go and make a visit to Cousin Henry and Julia.

But he said I wasn't able to go, nor able to stand it after I got there; and I did not make out a very good case for myself, for I was crying before I had finished.

It is getting to be a great effort for me to think straight. Just this nervous weakness I suppose.

And dear John gathered me up in his arms, and just carried me upstairs and laid me on the bed, and sat by me and read to me till it tired my head.

He said I was his darling and his comfort and all he had, and that I must take care of myself for his sake, and keep well.

He says no one but myself can help me out of it, that I must use my will and self-control and not let any silly fancies run away with me.

There's one comfort, the baby is well and happy, and does not have to occupy this nursery with the horrid wallpaper.

If we had not used it, that blessed child would have! What a fortunate escape! Why, I wouldn't have a child of mine, an impressionable little thing, live in such a room for worlds.

I never thought of it before, but it is lucky that John kept me here after all, I can stand it so much easier than a baby, you see.

Of course I never mention it to them any more—I am too wise, but I keep watch of it all the same.

There are things in the wallpaper that nobody knows but me, or ever will.

Behind that outside pattern the dim shapes get clearer every day.

It is always the same shape, only very numerous.

And it is like a woman stooping down and creeping about behind that pattern. I don't like it a bit. I wonder—I begin to think—I wish John would take me away from here!

It is so hard to talk with John about my case, because he is so wise, and because he loves me so.

But I tried it last night.

It was moonlight. The moon shines in all around just as the sun does.

I hate to see it sometimes, it creeps so slowly, and always comes in by one window or another.

John was asleep and I hated to waken him, so I kept still and watched the moonlight on that undulating wallpaper till I felt creepy.

The faint figure behind seemed to shake the pattern, just as if she wanted to get out.

I got up softly and went to feel and see if the paper *did* move, and when I came back John was awake.

"What is it, little girl?" he said. "Don't go walking about like that— you'll get cold."

I thought it was a good time to talk, so I told him that I really was not gaining here, and that I wished he would take me away.

"Why, darling!" said he, "our lease will be up in three weeks, and I can't see how to leave before.

"The repairs are not done at home, and I cannot possibly leave town just now. Of course if you were in any danger, I could and would, but you really are better, dear, whether you can see it or not. I am a doctor, dear, and I know. You are gaining flesh and color, your appetite is better, I feel really much easier about you."

"I don't weigh a bit more," said I, "nor as much; and my appetite may be better in the evening when you are here but it is worse in the morning when you are away!"

"Bless her little heart!" said he with a big hug, "she shall be as sick as she pleases! But now let's improve the shining hours by going to sleep, and talk about it in the morning!"

"And you won't go away?" I asked gloomily.

"Why, how can I, dear? It is only three weeks more and then we will take a nice little trip of a few days while Jennie is getting the house ready. Really dear you are better!"

"Better in body perhaps—" I began, and stopped short, for he sat up straight and looked at me with such a stern, reproachful look that I could not say another word.

"My darling," said he, "I beg you, for my sake and for our child's sake, as well as for your own, that you will never for one instant let that idea enter your mind! There is nothing so dangerous, so fascinating, to a temperament like yours. It is a false and foolish fancy. Can you trust me as a physician when I tell you so?"

So of course I said no more on that score, and we went to sleep before long. He thought I was asleep first, but I wasn't, and lay there for hours trying to decide whether that front pattern and the back pattern really did move together or separately.

On a pattern like this, by daylight, there is a lack of sequence, a defiance of law, that is a constant irritant to a normal mind.

The color is hideous enough, and unreliable enough, and infuriating enough, but the pattern is torturing.

You think you have mastered it, but just as you get well underway in following, it turns a back-somersault and there you are. It slaps you in the face, knocks you down, and tramples upon you. It is like a bad dream.

The outside pattern is a florid arabesque, reminding one of a fungus. If you can imagine a toadstool in joints, an interminable string of toadstools, budding and sprouting in endless convolutions—why, that is something like it.

That is, sometimes!

There is one marked peculiarity about this paper, a thing nobody seems to notice but myself, and that is that it changes as the light changes.

When the sun shoots in through the east window—I always watch for that first long, straight ray—it changes so quickly that I never can quite believe it.

That is why I watch it always.

By moonlight—the moon shines in all night when there is a moon—I wouldn't know it was the same paper.

At night in any kind of light, in twilight, candlelight, lamplight, and worst of all by moonlight, it becomes bars! The outside pattern I mean, and the woman behind it is as plain as can be.

I didn't realize for a long time what the thing was that showed behind, that dim sub-pattern, but now I am quite sure it is a woman.

By daylight she is subdued, quiet. I fancy it is the pattern that keeps her so still. It is so puzzling. It keeps me quiet by the hour.

I lie down ever so much now. John says it is good for me, and to sleep all I can.

Indeed he started the habit by making me lie down for an hour after each meal.

It is a very bad habit I am convinced, for you see I don't sleep.

And that cultivates deceit, for I don't tell them I'm awake—O, no!

The fact is I am getting a little afraid of John.

He seems very queer sometimes, and even Jennie has an inexplicable look.

It strikes me occasionally, just as a scientific hypothesis,—that perhaps it is the paper!

I have watched John when he did not know I was looking, and come into the room suddenly on the most innocent excuses, and I've caught him several times *looking at the paper!* And Jennie too. I caught Jennie with her hand on it once.

She didn't know I was in the room, and when I asked her in a quiet, a very quiet voice, with the most restrained manner possible, what she was doing with the paper—she turned around as if she had been caught stealing, and looked quite angry—asked me why I should frighten her so!

Then she said that the paper stained everything it touched, that she had found yellow smooches on all my clothes and John's, and she wished we would be more careful!

Did not that sound innocent? But I know she was studying that pattern, and I am determined that nobody shall find it out but myself!

Life is very much more exciting now than it used to be. You see I have something more to expect, to look forward to, to watch. I really do eat better, and am more quiet than I was.

John is so pleased to see me improve! He laughed a little the other day, and said I seemed to be flourishing in spite of my wall-paper.

I turned it off with a laugh. I had no intention of telling him it was *because* of the wall-paper—he would make fun of me. He might even want to take me away.

I don't want to leave now until I have found it out. There is a week more, and I think that will be enough.

I'm feeling ever so much better! I don't sleep much at night, for it is so interesting to watch developments; but I sleep a good deal in the daytime.

In the daytime it is tiresome and perplexing.

There are always new shoots on the fungus, and new shades of yellow all over it. I cannot keep count of them, though I have tried conscientiously.

It is the strangest yellow, that wall-paper! It makes me think of all the yellow things I ever saw—not beautiful ones like buttercups, but old foul, bad yellow things.

But there is something else about that paper—the smell! I noticed it the moment we came into the room, but with so much air and sun it was not bad. Now we have had a week of fog and rain, and whether the windows are open or not, the smell is here.

It creeps all over the house.

I find it hovering in the dining-room, skulking in the parlor, hiding in the hall, lying in wait for me on the stairs.

It gets into my hair.

Even when I go to ride, if I turn my head suddenly and surprise it—there is that smell!

Such a peculiar odor, too! I have spent hours in trying to analyze it, to find what it smelled like.

It is not bad—at first, and very gentle, but quite the subtlest, most enduring odor I ever met.

In this damp weather it is awful, I wake up in the night and find it hanging over me.

It used to disturb me at first. I thought seriously of burning the house—to reach the smell.

But now I am used to it. The only thing I can think of that it is like is the *color* of the paper! A yellow smell.

There is a very funny mark on this wall, low down, near the mopboard. A streak that runs round the room. It goes behind every piece of furniture, except the bed, a long, straight, even *smooch,* as if it had been rubbed over and over.

I wonder how it was done and who did it, and what they did it for. Round and round and round—round and round and round—it makes me dizzy!

I really have discovered something at last.

Through watching so much at night, when it changes so, I have finally found out.

The front pattern *does* move—and no wonder! The woman behind shakes it!

Sometimes I think there are a great many women behind, and sometimes only one, and she crawls around fast, and her crawling shakes it all over.

Then in the very bright spots she keeps still, and in the very shady spots she just takes hold of the bars and shakes them hard.

And she is all the time trying to climb through. But nobody could climb through that pattern—it strangles so; I think that is why it has so many heads.

They get through, and then the pattern strangles them off and turns them upside down, and makes their eyes white!

If those heads were covered or taken off it would not be half so bad.

I think that woman gets out in the daytime!

And I'll tell you why—privately—I've seen her!

I can see her out of every one of my windows!

It is the same woman, I know, for she is always creeping, and most women do not creep by daylight.

I see her in that long shaded lane, creeping up and down. I see her in those dark grape arbors, creeping all around the garden.

I see her on that long road under the trees, creeping along, and when a carriage comes she hides under the blackberry vines.

I don't blame her a bit. It must be very humiliating to be caught creeping by daylight!

I always lock the door when I creep by daylight. I can't do it at night, for I know John would suspect something at once.

And John is so queer now, that I don't want to irritate him. I wish he would take another room! Besides, I don't want anybody to get that woman out at night but myself.

I often wonder if I could see her out of all the windows at once.

But, turn as fast as I can, I can only see out of one at one time.

And though I always see her, she *may* be able to creep faster than I can turn!

I have watched her sometimes away off in the open country, creeping as fast as a cloud shadow in a high wind.

If only that top pattern could be gotten off from the under one! I mean to try it, little by little.

I have found out another funny thing, but I shan't tell it this time! It does not do to trust people too much.

There are only two more days to get this paper off, and I believe John is beginning to notice. I don't like the look in his eyes.

And I heard him ask Jennie a lot of professional questions, about me. She had a very good report to give.

She said I slept a good deal in the daytime.

John knows I don't sleep very well at night, for all I'm so quiet!

He asked me all sorts of questions too, and pretended to be very loving and kind.

As if I couldn't see through him!

Still, I don't wonder he acts so, sleeping under this paper for three months.

It only interests me, but I feel sure John and Jennie are secretly affected by it.

Hurrah! This is the last day, but it is enough. John to stay in town over night, and won't be out until this evening.

Jennie wanted to sleep with me — the sly thing! But I told her I should undoubtedly rest better for a night all alone.

That was clever, for really I wasn't alone a bit! As soon as it was moonlight and that poor thing began to crawl and shake the pattern, I got up and ran to help her.

I pulled and she shook, I shook and she pulled, and before morning we had peeled off yards of that paper.

A strip about as high as my head and half around the room.

And then when the sun came and that awful pattern began to laugh at me, I declared I would finish it to-day!

We go away to-morrow, and they are moving all my furniture down again to leave things as they were before.

Jennie looked at the wall in amazement, but I told her merrily that I did it out of pure spite at the vicious thing.

She laughed and said she wouldn't mind doing it herself, but I must not get tired.

How she betrayed herself that time!

But I am here, and no person touches this paper but me,—not *alive!*

She tried to get me out of the room—it was too patent! But I said it was so quiet and empty and clean now that I believed I would lie down again and sleep all I could, and not to wake me even for dinner—I would call when I woke.

So now she is gone, and the servants are gone, and the things are gone, and there is nothing left but that great bedstead nailed down, with the canvas mattress we found on it.

We shall sleep downstairs to-night, and take the boat home to-morrow.

I quite enjoy the room, now it is bare again.

How those children did tear about here!

This bedstead is fairly gnawed!

But I must get to work.

I have locked the door and thrown the key down into the front path.

I don't want to go out, and I don't want to have anybody come in, till John comes.

I want to astonish him.

I've got a rope up here that even Jennie did not find. If that woman does get out, and tries to get away, I can tie her!

But I forgot I could not reach far without anything to stand on!

This bed will *not* move!

I tried to lift and push it until I was lame, and then I got so angry I bit off a little piece at one corner—but it hurt my teeth.

Then I peeled off all the paper I could reach standing on the floor. It sticks horribly and the pattern just enjoys it! All those strangled heads and bulbous eyes and waddling fungus growths just shriek with derision!

I am getting angry enough to do something desperate. To jump out of the window would be admirable exercise, but the bars are too strong even to try.

Besides I wouldn't do it. Of course not. I know well enough that a step like that is improper and might be misconstrued.

I don't like to *look* out of the windows even—there are so many of those creeping women, and they creep so fast.

I wonder if they all come out of that wall-paper as I did?

But I am securely fastened now by my well-hidden rope — you don't get *me* out in the road there!

I suppose I shall have to get back behind the pattern when it comes night, and that is hard!

It is so pleasant to be out in this great room and creep around as I please!

I don't want to go outside. I won't, even if Jennie asks me to.

For outside you have to creep on the ground, and everything is green instead of yellow.

But here I can creep smoothly on the floor, and my shoulder just fits in that long smooch around the wall, so I cannot lose my way.

Why, there's John at the door!

It is no use, young man, you can't open it!

How he does call and pound!

Now he's crying for an axe.

It would be a shame to break down that beautiful door!

"John dear!" said I in the gentlest voice, "the key is down by the front steps, under a plantain leaf!"

That silenced him for a few moments.

Then he said — very quietly indeed, "Open the door, my darling!"

"I can't," said I. "The key is down by the front door under a plantain leaf!"

And then I said it again, several times, very gently and slowly, and said it so often that he had to go and see, and he got it of course, and came in. He stopped short by the door.

"What is the matter?" he cried. "For God's sake, what are you doing!"

I kept on creeping just the same, but I looked at him over my shoulder.

"I've got out at last," said I, "in spite of you and Jane.[3] And I've pulled off most of the paper, so you can't put me back!"

Now why should that man have fainted? But he did, and right across my path by the wall, so that I had to creep over him every time!   [1892]

---

[3]The speaker is most likely referring to "Jane" as the proper name for Jennie.

SARAH ORNE JEWETT

Sarah Orne Jewett (1849–1909) was born in South Berwick, Maine. Her father was a country doctor, and she often accompanied him on his horse-and-buggy rounds among sick people on the local farms. She later said that she got her real education from these trips rather than from her classes at Miss Rayne's School and the Berwick Academy. She had a fine ear for local speech and the native idiom, which she used to good effect in her stories. Impressed as a girl by the sympathetic depiction of local color in the fiction of Harriet Beecher Stowe, Jewett began to write stories herself, publishing her earliest one, "Jenny Garrow's Lovers," in a Boston weekly when she was eighteen years old. Shortly after her twentieth birthday, her work was accepted by the prestigious Atlantic Monthly, and her career was launched. Jewett published her first collection of stories, Deephaven, in 1877. She read the work of Gustave Flaubert, Émile Zola, Leo Tolstoy, and Henry James, and her style gradually matured, as is evident in the stories that make up the 1886 volume A White Heron and Other Stories. Jewett took her favorite motto from Flaubert, "One should write of ordinary life as if one were writing history." Her masterpiece, The Country of the Pointed Firs (1896), is a book of scrupulously observed short sketches linked by the narrator's account of her stay in a Maine seacoast village and her growing involvement in the quiet lives of its people.

Many stories were written about New England in Jewett's time, but hers have a unique quality stemming from her deep sympathy for the native characters and her ear for local speech. Once she laughingly told the younger writer Willa Cather that her head was full of dear old houses and dear old women, and when an old house and an old woman came together in her brain with a click, she knew a story was under way, as in "The Queen's Twin," first published in The Atlantic Monthly in 1895.

Although it is true that Jewett's realism heightens the attractive aspects of the rural New England character at the same time that it diminishes the harsher qualities, her literary technique is so candid and true to the larger aspects of human nature that the darker undercurrents of deprivation, both physical and psychological, are evident beneath the surface of her descriptions. Henry James recognized that Jewett was "surpassed only by Hawthorne as producer of the most finished and penetrating of the numerous 'short stories' that have the domestic life of New England for their general and their doubtless somewhat lean subject." In her time she was lauded for possessing an exquisitely simple, natural, and graceful style; now she is regarded as our most distinguished American regionalist writer.

RELATED COMMENTARIES: Willa Cather, "Miss Jewett," page 1330; Sarah Orne Jewett, "Looking Back on Girlhood," page 1382.

The Queen's Twin

– I –

The coast of Maine was in former years brought so near to foreign shores by its busy fleet of ships that among the older men and women one still finds a surprising proportion of travelers. Each seaward-stretching headland with its high-set houses, each island of a single farm, has sent its spies to view many a Land of Eshcol;[1] one may see plain, contented old faces at the windows, whose eyes have looked at far-away ports and known the splendors of the Eastern world. They shame the easy voyager of the North Atlantic and the Mediterranean; they have rounded the Cape of Good Hope and braved the angry seas of Cape Horn in small wooden ships; they have brought up their hardy boys and girls on narrow decks; they were among the last of the Northmen's children to go adventuring to unknown shores. More than this one cannot give to a young State for its enlightenment; the sea captains and the captains' wives of Maine knew something of the wide world, and never mistook their native parishes for the whole instead of a part thereof; they knew not only Thomaston and Castine and Portland, but London and Bristol and Bordeaux, and the strange-mannered harbors of the China Sea.

One September day, when I was nearly at the end of a summer spent in a village called Dunnet Landing, on the Maine coast, my friend Mrs Todd, in whose house I lived, came home from a long, solitary stroll in the wild pastures, with an eager look as if she were just starting on a hopeful quest instead of returning. She brought a little basket with blackberries enough for supper, and held it towards me so that I could see that there were also some late and surprising raspberries sprinkled on top, but she made no comment upon her wayfaring. I could tell plainly that she had something very important to say.

"You haven't brought home a leaf of anything," I ventured to this practiced herb-gatherer. "You were saying yesterday that the witch-hazel might be in bloom."

"I dare say, dear," she answered in a lofty manner; "I ain't goin' to say it wasn't; I ain't much concerned either way 'bout the facts o' witch-hazel. Truth is, I've been off visitin'; there's an old Indian footpath leadin' over towards the Back Shore through the great heron swamp that anybody can't travel over all summer. You have to seize your time some day just now, while the low ground's summer-dried as it is today, and before the fall rains set in. I never thought of it till I was out o' sight o' home, and I says to myself, 'Today's the day, certain!' and stepped along smart as I could. Yes,

---

[1] Moses's men, sent to "spy out" the land of Canaan, returned from the fertile valley of Eshcol, calling it "the land of milk and honey" (Numbers 13: 21–27).

I've been visitin'. I did get into one spot that was wet underfoot before I noticed; you wait till I get me a pair o' dry woolen stockings, in case of cold, and I'll come an' tell ye."

Mrs Todd disappeared. I could see that something had deeply interested her. She might have fallen in with either the sea-serpent or the lost tribes of Israel, such was her air of mystery and satisfaction. She had been away since just before mid-morning, and as I sat waiting by my window I saw the last red glow of autumn sunshine flare along the gray rocks of the shore and leave them cold again, and touch the far sails of some coast-wise schooners so that they stood like golden houses on the sea.

I was left to wonder longer than I liked. Mrs Todd was making an evening fire and putting things in train for supper; presently she returned, still looking warm and cheerful after her long walk.

"There's a beautiful view from a hill over where I've been," she told me; "yes, there's a beautiful prospect of land and sea. You wouldn't discern the hill from any distance, but 'tis the pretty situation of it that counts. I sat there a long spell, and I did wish for you. No, I didn't know a word about goin' when I set out this morning" (as if I had openly reproached her!); "I only felt one o' them travelin' fits comin' on, an' I ketched up my little basket; I didn't know but I might turn and come back time for dinner. I thought it wise to set out your luncheon for you in case I didn't. Hope you had all you wanted; yes, I hope you had enough."

"Oh, yes, indeed," said I. My landlady was always peculiarly bountiful in her supplies when she left me to fare for myself, as if she made a sort of peace-offering or affectionate apology.

"You know that hill with the old house right on top, over beyond the heron swamp? You'll excuse me for explainin'," Mrs Todd began, "but you ain't so apt to strike inland as you be to go right along shore. You know that hill; there's a path leadin' right over to it that you have to look sharp to find nowadays; it belonged to the up-country Indians when they had to make a carry to the landing here to get to the out' islands. I've heard the old folks say that there used to be a place across a ledge where they'd worn a deep track with their moccasin feet, but I never could find it. 'Tis so overgrown in some places that you keep losin' the path in the bushes and findin' it as you can; but it runs pretty straight considerin' the lay o' the land, and I keep my eye on the sun and the moss that grows one side o' the tree trunks. Some brook's been choked up and the swamp's bigger than it used to be. Yes; I did get in deep enough, one place!"

I showed the solicitude that I felt. Mrs Todd was no longer young, and in spite of her strong, great frame and spirited behavior, I knew that certain ills were apt to seize upon her, and would end some day by leaving her lame and ailing.

"Don't you go to worryin' about me," she insisted, "settin' still's the only way the Evil One'll ever get the upper hand o' me. Keep me movin' enough, an' I'm twenty year old summer an' winter both. I don't know why 'tis, but I've never happened to mention the one I've been to see. I don't know why I never happened to speak the name of Abby Martin, for I often give her a thought, but 'tis a dreadful out-o'-the-way place where she lives, and I haven't seen her myself for three or four years. She's a real good interesting woman, and we're well acquainted; she's nigher mother's age than mine, but she's very young feeling. She made me a nice cup o' tea, and I don't know but I should have stopped all night if I could have got word to you not to worry."

Then there was a serious silence before Mrs Todd spoke again to make a formal announcement.

"She is the Queen's Twin," and Mrs Todd looked steadily to see how I might bear the great surprise.

"The Queen's Twin?" I repeated.

"Yes, she's come to feel a real interest in the Queen, and anybody can see how natural 'tis. They were born the very same day, and you would be astonished to see what a number o' things have corresponded. She was speaking o' some o' the facts to me today, an' you'd think she'd never done nothing but read history. I see how earnest she was about it as I never did before. I've often and often heard her allude to the facts, but now she's got to be old and the hurry's over with her work, she's come to live a good deal in her thoughts, as folks often do, and I tell you 'tis a sight o' company for her. If you want to hear about Queen Victoria, why Mis' Abby Martin'll tell you everything. And the prospect from that hill I spoke of is as beautiful as anything in this world; 'tis worth while your goin' over to see her just for that."

"When can you go again?" I demanded eagerly.

"I should say tomorrow," answered Mrs Todd; "yes, I should say tomorrow; but I expect 'twould be better to take one day to rest, in between. I considered that question as I was comin' home, but I hurried so that there wa'n't much time to think. It's a dreadful long way to go with a horse; you have to go 'most as far as the old Bowden place an' turn off to the left, a master long, rough road, and then you have to turn right round as soon as you get there if you mean to get home before nine o'clock at night. But to strike across country from here, there's plenty o' time in the shortest day, and you can have a good hour or two's visit beside; 'tain't but a very few miles, and it's pretty all the way along. There used to be a few good families over there, but they've died and scattered, so now she's far from neighbors. There, she really cried, she was so glad to see anybody comin'. You'll be amused to hear her talk about the Queen, but I thought twice or three times as I set there 'twas about all the company she'd got."

"Could we go day after tomorrow?" I asked eagerly.

" 'Twould suit me exactly," said Mrs Todd.

– II –

One can never be so certain of good New England weather as in the days when a long easterly storm has blown away the warm late-summer mists, and cooled the air so that however bright the sunshine is by day, the nights come nearer and nearer to frostiness. There was a cold freshness in the morning air when Mrs Todd and I locked the house-door behind us; we took the key of the fields into our own hands that day, and put out across country as one puts out to sea. When we reached the top of the ridge behind the town it seemed as if we had anxiously passed the harbor bar and were comfortably in open sea at last.

"There, now!" proclaimed Mrs Todd, taking a long breath, "now I do feel safe. It's just the weather that's liable to bring somebody to spend the day; I've had a feeling of Mis' Elder Caplin from North Point bein' close upon me ever since I waked up this mornin', an' I didn't want to be hampered with our present plans. She's a great hand to visit; she'll be spendin' the day somewhere from now till Thanksgivin', but there's plenty o' places at the Landin' where she goes, an' if I ain't there she'll just select another. I thought mother might be in, too, 'tis so pleasant; but I run up the road to look off this mornin' before you was awake, and there was no sign o' the boat. If they hadn't started by that time they wouldn't start, just as the tide is now; besides, I see a lot o' mackerel-men headin' Green Island way, and they'll detain William. No, we're safe now, an' if mother should be comin' in tomorrow we'll have all this to tell her. She an' Mis' Abby Martin's very old friends."

We were walking down the long pasture slopes towards the dark woods and thickets of the low ground. They stretched away northward like an unbroken wilderness; the early mists still dulled much of the color and made the uplands beyond look like a very far-off country.

"It ain't so far as it looks from here," said my companion reassuringly, "but we've got no time to spare either," and she hurried on, leading the way with a fine sort of spirit in her step; and presently we struck into the old Indian footpath, which could be plainly seen across the long-unploughed turf of the pastures, and followed it among the thick, low-growing spruces. There the ground was smooth and brown under foot, and the thin-stemmed trees held a dark and shadowy roof overhead. We walked a long way without speaking; sometimes we had to push aside the branches, and sometimes we walked in a broad aisle where the trees were larger. It was a solitary wood, birdless and beastless; there was not even a rabbit to be seen, or a crow high in air to break the silence.

"I don't believe the Queen ever saw such a lonesome trail as this," said Mrs Todd, as if she followed the thoughts that were in my mind. Our visit to Mrs Abby Martin seemed in some strange way to concern the high affairs of royalty. I had just been thinking of English landscapes, and of the solemn hills of Scotland with their lonely cottages and stone-walled sheepfolds, and the wandering flocks on high cloudy pastures. I had often been struck by the quick interest and familiar allusion to certain members of the royal house which one found in distant neighborhoods of New England; whether some old instincts of personal loyalty have survived all changes of time and national vicissitudes, or whether it is only that the Queen's own character and disposition have won friends for her so far away, it is impossible to tell. But to hear of a twin sister was the most surprising proof of intimacy of all, and I must confess that there was something remarkably exciting to the imagination in my morning walk. To think of being presented at Court in the usual way was for the moment quite commonplace.

– III –

Mrs Todd was swinging her basket to and fro like a schoolgirl as she walked, and at this moment it slipped from her hand and rolled lightly along the ground as if there were nothing in it. I picked it up and gave it to her, whereupon she lifted the cover and looked in with anxiety.

"'Tis only a few little things, but I don't want to lose 'em," she explained humbly. "'Twas lucky you took the other basket if I was goin' to roll it round. Mis' Abby Martin complained o' lacking some pretty pink silk to finish one o' her little frames, an' I thought I'd carry her some, and I had a bunch o' gold thread that had been in a box o' mine this twenty year. I never was one to do much fancy work, but we're all liable to be swept away by fashion. And then there's a small packet o' very choice herbs that I gave a good deal of attention to; they'll smarten her up and give her the best of appetites, come spring. She was tellin' me that spring weather is very wiltin' an' trying' to her, and she was beginnin' to dread it already. Mother's just the same way; if I could prevail on mother to take some o' these remedies in good season 'twould make a world o' difference, but she gets all down hill before I have a chance to hear of it, and then William comes in to tell me, sighin' and bewailin', how feeble mother is. 'Why can't you remember 'bout them good herbs that I never let her be without?' I say to him—he does provoke me so; and then off he goes, sulky enough, down to his boat. Next thing I know, she comes in to go to meetin', wantin' to speak to everybody and feelin' like a girl. Mis' Martin's case is very much the same; but she'd nobody to watch her. William's kind o' slow-moulded; but there, any William's better than none when you get to be Mis' Martin's age."

"Hadn't she any children?" I asked.

"Quite a number," replied Mrs Todd grandly, "but some are gone and the rest are married and settled. She never was a great hand to go about visitin'. I don't know but Mis' Martin might be called a little peculiar. Even her own folks has to make company of her; she never slips in and lives right along with the rest as if 'twas at home, even in her own children's houses. I heard one o' her sons' wives say once she'd much rather have the Queen to spend the day if she could choose between the two, but I never thought Abby was so difficult as that. I used to love to have her come; she may have been sort o' ceremonious, but very pleasant and sprightly if you had sense enough to treat her her own way. I always think she'd know just how to live with great folks, and feel easier 'long of them an' their ways. Her son's wife's a great driver with farm-work, boards a great tableful o' men in hayin' time, an' feels right in her element. I don't say but she's a good woman an' smart, but sort o' rough. Anybody that's gentle-mannered an' precise like Mis' Martin would be a sort o' restraint.

"There's all sorts o' folks in the country, same's there is in the city," concluded Mrs Todd gravely, and I as gravely agreed. The thick woods were behind us now, and the sun was shining clear overhead, the morning mists were gone, and a faint blue haze softened the distance; as we climbed the hill where we were to see the view, it seemed like a summer day. There was an old house on the height, facing southward, — a mere forsaken shell of an old house, with empty windows that looked like blind eyes. The frost-bitten grass grew close about it like brown fur, and there was a single crooked bough of lilac holding its green leaves close by the door.

"We'll just have a good piece of bread-an'-butter now," said the commander of the expedition, "and then we'll hang up the basket on some peg inside the house out o' the way o' the sheep, and have a han'some entertainment as we're comin' back. She'll be all through her little dinner when we get there, Mis' Martin will; but she'll want to make us some tea, an' we must have our visit an' be startin' back pretty soon after two. I don't want to cross all that low ground again after it's begun to grow chilly. An' it looks to me as if the clouds might begin to gather late in the afternoon."

Before us lay a splendid world of sea and shore. The autumn colors already brightened the landscape; and here and there at the edge of a dark tract of pointed firs stood a row of bright swamp-maples like scarlet flowers. The blue sea and the great tide inlets were untroubled by the lightest winds.

"Poor land, this is!" sighed Mrs Todd as we sat down to rest on the worn doorstep. "I've known three good hard-workin' families that come here full o' hope an' pride and tried to make something o' this farm, but it beat 'em all. There's one small field that's excellent for potatoes if you let half of it rest every year; but the land's always hungry. Now, you see them little peaked-topped spruces an' fir balsams comin' up over the hill all green an' hearty; they've got it all their own way! Seems sometimes as if wild Natur' got jealous over a certain spot, and wanted to do just as she'd a mind to. You'll see here; she'll do her own ploughin' an' harrowin' with frost an' wet, an' plant just what she wants and wait for her own crops. Man can't do nothin' with it, try as he may. I tell you those little trees mean business!"

I looked down the slope, and felt as if we ourselves were likely to be surrounded and overcome if we lingered too long. There was a vigor of growth, a persistence and savagery about the sturdy little trees that put weak human nature at complete defiance. One felt a sudden pity for the men and women who had been worsted after a long fight in that lonely place; one felt a sudden fear of the unconquerable, immediate forces of Nature, as in the irresistible moment of a thunderstorm.

"I can recollect the time when folks were shy o' these woods we just come through," said Mrs Todd seriously. "The men-folks themselves never'd venture into 'em alone; if their cattle got strayed they'd collect whoever they could get, and start off all together. They said a person was liable to get bewildered in there alone, and in old times folks had been lost. I expect there was considerable fear left over from the old Indian times, and the poor days o' witchcraft; anyway, I've seen bold men act kind o' timid. Some women o' the Asa Bowden family went out one afternoon berryin' when I was a girl, and got lost and was out all night; they found 'em middle o' the mornin' next day, not half a mile from home, scared most to death, an' sayin' they'd heard wolves and other beasts sufficient for a caravan. Poor creatur's! they'd strayed at last into a kind of low place amongst some alders, an' one of 'em was so overset she never got over it, an' went off in a sort o' slow decline. 'Twas like them victims that drowns in a foot o' water; but their minds did suffer dreadful. Some folks is born afraid of the woods and all wild places, but I must say they've always been like home to me."

I glanced at the resolute, confident face of my companion. Life was very strong in her, as if some force of Nature were personified in this simple-hearted woman and gave her cousinship to the ancient deities. She might have walked the primeval fields of Sicily; her strong gingham skirts might at that very moment bend the slender stalks of asphodel and be fragrant with trodden thyme, instead of the brown wind-brushed grass of New England and frost-bitten goldenrod. She was a great soul, was Mrs Todd, and I her humble follower, as we went our way to visit the Queen's Twin, leaving the bright view of the sea behind us, and descending to a lower country-side through the dry pastures and fields.

The farms all wore a look of gathering age, though the settlement was, after all, so young. The fences were already fragile, and it seemed as if the first impulse of agriculture had soon spent itself without hope of renewal. The better houses were always those that had some hold upon the riches of the sea; a house that could not harbor a fishing-boat in some neighboring inlet was far from being sure of everyday comforts. The land alone was not enough to live upon in that stony region; it belonged by right to the forest, and to the forest it fast returned. From the top of the hill where we had been sitting we had seen prosperity in the dim distance, where the land was good and the sun shone upon fat barns, and where warm-looking houses with three or four chimneys apiece stood high on their solid ridge above the bay.

As we drew nearer to Mrs Martin's it was sad to see what poor bushy fields, what thin and empty dwelling-places had been left by those who had chosen this disappointing part of the northern country for their home. We crossed the last field and came into a narrow rain-washed road, and Mrs Todd looked eager and expectant and said that we were almost at our journey's end. "I do hope Mis' Martin'll ask you into her best room where she keeps all the Queen's pictures. Yes, I think likely she will ask you; but 'tain't everybody she deems worthy to visit 'em, I can tell you!" said Mrs Todd warningly. "She's been collectin' 'em an' cuttin' 'em out o' newspapers an' magazines time out o' mind, and if she heard of anybody sailin' for an English port she'd contrive to get a little money to 'em and ask to have the last likeness there was. She's most covered her best-room wall now; she keeps that room shut up sacred as a meetin'-house! 'I won't say but I have my favorites amongst 'em,' she told me t'other day, 'but they're all beautiful to me as they can be!' And she's made some kind o' pretty little frames for 'em all — you know there's always a new fashion o' frames comin' round; first 'twas shell-work, and then 'twas pine-cones, and bead-work's had its day, and now she's much concerned with perforated cardboard worked with silk. I tell you that best room's a sight to see! But you mustn't look for anything elegant," continued Mrs Todd, after a moment's reflection. "Mis' Martin's always been in very poor, strugglin' circumstances. She had ambition for her children, though they took right after their father an' had little for themselves; she wa'n't over an' above well married, however kind she may see fit to speak. She's been patient an' hard-workin' all her life, and always high above makin' mean complaints of other folks. I expect all this business about the Queen has buoyed her over many a shoal place in life. Yes, you might say that Abby'd been a slave, but there ain't any slave but has some freedom."

–**IV**–

Presently I saw a low gray house standing on a grassy bank close to the road. The door was at the side, facing us, and a tangle of snowberry bushes and cinnamon roses grew to the level of the window-sills. On the doorstep stood a bent-shouldered, little old woman; there was an air of welcome and of unmistakable dignity about her.

"She sees us coming," exclaimed Mrs Todd in an excited whisper. "There, I told her I might be over this way again if the weather held good, and if I came I'd bring you. She said right off she'd take great pleasure in havin' a visit from you; I was surprised, she's usually so retirin'."

Even this reassurance did not quell a faint apprehension on our part; there was something distinctly formal in the occasion, and one felt that consciousness of inadequacy which is never easy for the humblest pride to bear. On the way I had torn my dress in an unexpected encounter with a little thornbush, and I could now imagine how it felt to be going to Court and forgetting one's feathers or her Court train.

The Queen's Twin was oblivious of such trifles; she stood waiting with a calm look until we came near enough to take her kind hand. She was a beautiful old woman, with clear eyes and a lovely quietness and genuineness of manner; there was not a trace of anything pretentious about her, or high-flown, as Mrs Todd would say comprehensively. Beauty in age is rare enough in women who have spent their lives in the hard work of a farmhouse; but autumn-like and withered as this woman may have looked, her features had kept, or rather gained, a great refinement. She led us into her old kitchen and gave us seats, and took one of the little straight-backed chairs herself and sat a short distance away, as if she were giving audience to an ambassador. It seemed as if we should all be standing; you could not help feeling that the habits of her life were more ceremonious, but that for the moment she assumed the simplicities of the occasion.

Mrs Todd was always Mrs Todd, too great and self-possessed a soul for any occasion to ruffle. I admired her calmness, and presently the slow current of neighborhood talk carried one easily along; we spoke of the weather and the small adventures of the way, and then, as if I were after all not a stranger, our hostess turned almost affectionately to speak to me.

"The weather will be growing dark in London now. I expect that you've been in London, dear?" she said.

"Oh, yes," I answered. "Only last year."

"It is a great many years since I was there, along in the forties," said Mrs Martin. "'Twas the only voyage I ever made; most of my neighbors have been great travelers. My brother was master of a vessel, and his wife usually sailed with him; but that year she had a young child more frail than the others, and she dreaded the care of it at sea. It happened that my brother got a chance for my husband to go as super-cargo, being a good accountant, and came one day to urge him to take it; he was very ill-disposed to the sea, but he had met with losses, and I saw my own opportunity and persuaded them both to let me go too. In those days they didn't object to a woman's being aboard to wash and mend, the voyages were sometimes very long. And that was the way I come to see the Queen."

Mrs Martin was looking straight in my eyes to see if I showed any genuine interest in the most interesting person in the world.

"Oh, I am very glad you saw the Queen," I hastened to say. "Mrs Todd has told me that you and she were born the very same day."

"We were indeed, dear!" said Mrs Martin, and she leaned back comfortably and smiled as she had not smiled before. Mrs Todd gave a satisfied nod and glance, as if to say that things were going on as well as possible in this anxious moment.

"Yes," said Mrs Martin again, drawing her chair a little nearer, "'twas a very remarkable thing; we were born the same day, and at exactly the same hour, after you allowed for all the difference in time. My father figured it out sea-fashion. Her Royal Majesty and I opened our eyes upon this world together; say what you may, 'tis a bond between us."

Mrs Todd assented with an air of triumph, and untied her hat-strings and threw them back over her shoulders with a gallant air.

"And I married a man by the name of Albert, just the same as she did, and all by chance, for I didn't get the news that she had an Albert too till a fortnight afterward; news was slower coming then than it is now. My first baby was a girl, and I called her Victoria after my mate; but the next one was a boy, and my husband wanted the right to name him, and took his own name and his brother Edward's, and pretty soon I saw in the paper that the little Prince o' Wales had been christened just the same. After that I made excuse to wait till I knew what she'd named her children. I didn't want to break the chain, so I had an Alfred, and my darling Alice that I lost long before she lost hers, and there I stopped. If I'd only had a dear daughter to stay at home with me, same's her youngest one, I should have been so thankful! But if only one of us could have a little Beatrice, I'm glad 'twas the Queen; we've both seen trouble, but she's had the most care."

I asked Mrs Martin if she lived alone all the year, and was told that she did except for a visit now and then from one of her grandchildren, "the only one that really likes to come an' stay quiet 'long o' grandma. She always says quick as she's through her schoolin' she's goin' to live with me all the time, but she's very pretty an' has taking ways," said Mrs Martin, looking both proud and wistful, "so I can tell nothing at all about it! Yes, I've been alone most o' the time since my Albert was taken away, and that's a great many years; he had a long time o' failing and sickness first." (Mrs Todd's foot gave an impatient scuff on the floor.) "An' I've always lived right here. I ain't like the Queen's Majesty, for this is the only palace I've got," said the dear old thing, smiling again. "I'm glad of it too, I don't like changing about, an' our stations in life are set very different. I don't require what the Queen does, but sometimes I've thought 'twas left to me to do the plain things she don't have time for. I expect she's a beautiful house-keeper, nobody couldn't have done better in her high place, and she's been as good a mother as she's been a queen."

"I guess she has, Abby," agreed Mrs Todd instantly. "How was it you happened to get such a good look at her? I meant to ask you again when I was here t'other day."

"Our ship was layin' in the Thames, right there above Wapping. We was dischargin' cargo, and under orders to clear as quick as we could for Bordeaux to take on an excellent freight o' French goods," explained Mrs Martin eagerly. "I heard that the Queen was goin' to a great review of her army, and would drive out o' her Buckin'ham Palace about ten o'clock in the mornin', and I run aft to Albert, my husband, and brother Horace where they was standin' together by the hatchway, and told 'em they must one of 'em take me. They laughed, I was in such a hurry, and said they couldn't go; and I found they meant it and got sort of impatient when I began to talk, and I was 'most broken-hearted; 'twas all the reason I had for makin' that hard voyage. Albert couldn't help often reproachin' me, for he did so resent the sea, an' I'd known how 'twould be before we sailed; but I'd minded nothing all the way till then, and I just crep' back to my cabin an' begun to cry. They was disappointed about their ship's cook, an' I'd cooked for fo'c's'le an' cabin myself all the way over; 'twas dreadful hard work, specially in rough weather; we'd had head winds an' a six weeks' voyage. They'd acted sort of ashamed o' me when I pled so to go ashore, an' that hurt my feelin's most of all. But Albert come below pretty soon; I've never given way so in my life, an' he begun to act frightened, and treated me gentle just as he did when we was goin' to be married, an' when I got over sobbin' he went on deck and saw Horace an' talked it over what they could do; they really had their duty to the vessel, and couldn't be spared that day. Horace was real good when he understood everything, and he come an' told me I'd more than worked my passage an' was goin' to do just as I liked now we was in port. He'd engaged a cook, too, that was comin' aboard that mornin', and he was goin' to send the ship's carpenter with me — a nice fellow from up Thomaston way; he'd gone to put on his ashore clothes as quick's he could. So then I got ready, and we started off in the small boat and rowed up river. I was afraid we were too late, but the tide was setting up very strong, and we landed an' left the boat to a keeper, and I run all the way up those great streets and across a park. 'Twas a great day, with sights o' folks everywhere, but 'twas just as if they was nothin' but wax images to me. I kep' askin' my way an' runnin' on, with the carpenter comin' after as best he could, and just as I worked to the front o' the crowd by the palace, the gates was flung open and out she came; all prancin' horses and shinin' gold, and in a beautiful carriage there she sat; 'twas a moment o' heaven to me. I saw her plain, and she looked right at me so pleasant and happy, just as if she knew there was somethin' different between us from other folks."

There was a moment when the Queen's Twin could not go on and neither of her listeners could ask a question.

"Prince Albert was sitting right beside her in the carriage," she continued. "Oh, he was a beautiful man! Yes, dear, I saw 'em both together just as I see you now, and then she was gone out o' sight in another minute, and the common crowd was all spread over the place pushin' an' cheerin'. 'Twas some kind o' holiday, an' the carpenter and I got separated, an' then I found him again after I didn't think I should, an' he was all for makin' a day of it, and goin' to show me all the sights; he'd been in London before, but I didn't want nothin' else, an' we went back through the streets down to the waterside an' took the boat. I remember I mended an old coat o' my Albert's as good as I could, sittin' on the quarter-deck in the sun all that afternoon, and 'twas all as if I was livin' in a lovely dream. I don't know how to explain it, but there hasn't been no friend I've felt so near to me ever since."

One could not say much — only listen. Mrs Todd put in a discerning question now and then, and Mrs Martin's eyes shone brighter and brighter as she talked. What a lovely gift of imagination and true affection was in this fond old heart! I looked about the plain New England kitchen, with its wood-smoked walls and homely braided rugs on the worn floor, and all its simple furnishings. The loud-ticking clock seemed to encourage us to speak; at the other side of the room was an early newspaper portrait of Her Majesty the Queen of Great Britain and Ireland. On a shelf below were some flowers in a little glass dish, as if they were put before a shrine.

"If I could have had more to read, I should have known 'most everything about her," said Mrs Martin wistfully. "I've made the most of what I did have, and thought it over and over till it came clear. I sometimes seem to have her all my own, as if we'd lived right together. I've often walked out into the woods alone and told her what my troubles was, and it always seemed as if she told me 'twas all right, an' we must have patience. I've got her beautiful book about the Highlands; 'twas dear Mis' Todd here that found out about her printing it and got a copy for me, and it's been a treasure to my heart, just as if 'twas written right to me. I always read it Sundays now, for my Sunday treat. Before that I used to have to imagine a good deal, but when I come to read her book, I knew what I expected was all true. We do think alike about so many things," said the Queen's Twin with affectionate certainty. "You see, there is something between us, being born just at the same time; 'tis what they call a birthright. She's had great tasks put upon her, being the Queen, an' mine has been the humble lot; but she's done the best she could, nobody can say to the contrary, and there's something between us; she's been the great lesson I've had to live by. She's been everything to me. An' when she had her Jubilee, oh, how my heart was with her!"

"There, 'twouldn't play the part in her life it has in mine," said Mrs Martin generously, in answer to something one of her listeners had said. "Sometimes I think, now she's older, she might like to know about us. When I think how few old friends anybody has left at our age, I suppose it may be just the same with her as it is with me; perhaps she would like to know how we came into life together. But I've had a great advantage in seeing her, an' I can always fancy her goin' on, while she don't know nothin' yet about me, except she may feel my love stayin' her heart sometimes an' not know just where it comes from. An' I dream about our being together out in some pretty fields, young as ever we was, and holdin' hands as we walk along. I'd like to know if she ever has that dream too. I used to have days when I made believe she did know, an' was comin' to see me," confessed the speaker shyly, with a little flush on her cheeks; "and I'd plan what I could have nice for supper, and I wasn't goin' to let anybody know she was here havin' a good rest, except I'd wish you, Almira Todd, or dear Mis' Blackett would happen in, for you'd know just how to talk with her. You see, she likes to be up in Scotland, right out in the wild country, better than she does anywhere else."

"I'd really love to take her out to see mother at Green Island," said Mrs Todd with a sudden impulse.

"Oh, yes! I should love to have you," exclaimed Mrs Martin, and then she began to speak in a lower tone. "One day I got thinkin' so about my dear Queen," she said, "an' livin' so in my thoughts, that I went to work an' got all ready for her, just as if she was really comin'. I never told this to a livin' soul before, but I feel you'll understand. I put my best fine sheets and blankets I spun an' wove myself on the bed, and I picked some pretty flowers and put 'em all round the house, an' I worked as hard an' happy as I could all day, and had as nice a supper ready as I could get, sort of telling myself a story all the time. She was comin' an' I was goin' to see her again, an' I kep' it up until nightfall; an' when I see the dark an' it come to me I was all alone, the dream left me, an' I sat down on the doorstep an' felt all foolish an' tired. An', if you'll believe it, I heard steps comin', an' an old cousin o' mine come wanderin' along, one I was apt to be shy of. She wasn't all there, as folks used to say, but harmless enough and a kind of poor old talking body. And I went right to meet her when I first heard her call, 'stead o' hidin' as I sometimes did, an' she come in dreadful willin', an' we sat down to supper together; 'twas a supper I should have had no heart to eat alone."

"I don't believe she ever had such a splendid time in her life as she did then. I heard her tell all about it afterwards," exclaimed Mrs Todd compassionately. "There, now I hear all this it seems just as if the Queen might have known and couldn't come herself, so she sent that poor old creatur' that was always in need!"

Mrs Martin looked timidly at Mrs Todd and then at me. "'Twas childish o' me to go an' get supper," she confessed.

"I guess you wa'n't the first one to do that," said Mrs Todd. "No, I guess you wa'n't the first one who's got supper that way, Abby," and then for a moment she could say no more.

Mrs Todd and Mrs Martin had moved their chairs a little so that they faced each other, and I, at one side, could see them both.

"No, you never told me o' that before, Abby," said Mrs Todd gently. "Don't it show that for folks that have any fancy in 'em, such beautiful dreams is the real part o' life? But to most folks the common things that happens outside 'em is all in all."

Mrs Martin did not appear to understand at first, strange to say, when the secret of her heart was put into words; then a glow of pleasure and comprehension shone upon her face. "Why, I believe you're right, Almira!" she said, and turned to me.

"Wouldn't you like to look at my pictures of the Queen?" she asked, and we rose and went into the best room.

–V–

The mid-day visit seemed very short; September hours are brief to match the shortening days. The great subject was dismissed for a while after our visit to the Queen's pictures, and my companions spoke much of lesser persons until we drank the cup of tea which Mrs Todd had foreseen. I happily remembered that the Queen herself is said to like a proper cup of tea, and this at once seemed to make her Majesty kindly join so remote and reverent a company. Mrs Martin's thin cheeks took on a pretty color like a girl's. "Somehow I always have thought of her when I made it extra good," she said. "I've got a real china cup that belonged to my grandmother, and I believe I shall call it hers now."

"Why don't you?" responded Mrs Todd warmly, with a delightful smile.

Later they spoke of a promised visit which was to be made in the Indian summer to the Landing and Green Island, but I observed that Mrs Todd presented the little parcel of dried herbs, with full directions, for a cure-all in the spring, as if there were no real chance of their meeting again first. As we looked back from the turn of the road the Queen's Twin was still standing on the door-step watching us away, and Mrs Todd stopped, and stood still for a moment before she waved her hand again.

"There's one thing certain, dear," she said to me with great discernment; "it ain't as if we left her all alone!"

Then we set out upon our long way home over the hill, where we lingered in the afternoon sunshine, and through the dark woods across the heron-swamp.   [1895]

MADELENE YALE WYNNE

*M*adelene Yale Wynne (1847–1919?) was born in Newport, New York, the *daughter of the inventor of the Yale lock. She lived comfortably on the income from her father's patent, married, and had a son. A talented artist, she said that as the daughter of an inventor, she "had a training in mechanics and access to shop and machinery." Later she studied at the Boston Museum of Fine Arts and in New York City, specializing in hand-wrought metalwork and enamel Arts and Crafts jewelry. As a gifted writer of short stories, she also contributed to many magazines; however, little is known about how she learned her craft as a writer.*

Wynne's stories were collected posthumously in An Ancestral Invasion and Other Stories *(1920) by Annie Cabot Putnam. In the foreword to that volume, Edward Waldo Emerson wrote that Wynne "knew the New England country people of a generation now past, and in her presentation of their old-time ways, had love and respect for them." Four of the twelve stories in that book rely on dialect for local-color effect, and all of them contain deft touches of humor in their plots and characterizations.*

The lack of plot resolution in "The Little Room" so tantalized contemporary readers that Wynne wrote another story, "The Sequel to the Little Room," without solving its mystery. Published in Harper's Magazine *in 1895, "The Little Room" was often compared to Frank Stockton's popular "The Lady, or the Tiger?"—another magazine story with an unresolved conclusion, narrated in an even, matter-of-fact tone that skillfully dramatized gender conflict. Whereas Wynne added a realistic flavor to "The Little Room" by setting it in Vermont, Stockton set his tale vaguely in a "very olden time" in a "semi-barbaric court," where a cruel king brought prisoners into an amphitheater before thousands of spectators to determine their innocence or guilt. In the arena there were two doors, and the prisoner on trial could choose to open either one of them, guided only by chance. Behind one door stood a hungry tiger, who immediately tore the hapless prisoner to pieces in front of the crowd as punishment for his guilt. Behind the other door stood a lady, who was immediately married to the prisoner in a lavish ceremony as proof of his innocence. When the king discovers that his only daughter is passionately in love with a commoner, he seizes the young man and throws him into the arena. Behind one door is the fierce tiger; behind the other is a lovely young woman whom the princess hates because she is a rival for the young man's affections. The king's daughter sits in the audience and motions to her lover to choose the door on the right. Stockton ended his tale, "And so I leave it with all of you: which came out of the opened door,—the lady, or the tiger?"*

Contemporary readers interested in dramatizations of the gender conflict also often compared Wynne's "The Little Room" to Charlotte Perkins Gilman's "The Yellow Wallpaper."

"How would it do for a smoking-room?"

"Just the very place; only, you know, Roger, you must not think of smoking in the house. I am almost afraid having just a plain common man around, let alone a smoking-man, will upset Aunt Hannah. She is New England—Vermont New England boiled down."

"You leave Aunt Hannah to me; I shall find her tender side. I am going to ask her about the old sea-captain and the yellow calico."

"Not yellow calico—blue chintz."

"Well, yellow *shell*, then."

"No, no! don't mix it up so; you won't know yourself what to expect, and that's half the fun."

"Now you tell me again exactly what to expect; to tell the truth, I didn't half hear about it the other day; I was wool-gathering. It was something queer that happened when you were a child, wasn't it?"

"Something that began to happen long before that, and kept happening, and may happen again; but I hope not."

"What was it?"

"I wonder if the other people in the car can hear us?"

"I fancy not; we don't hear them—not consecutively, at least."

"Well, mother was born in Vermont, you know; she was the only child by a second marriage. Aunt Hannah and Aunt Maria are only half-aunts to me, you know."

"I hope they are half as nice as you are."

"Roger, be still; they certainly will hear us."

"Well, don't you want them to know we are married?"

"Yes, but not just married. There's all the difference in the world."

"You are afraid we look too happy!"

"No; only I want my happiness all to myself."

"Well, the little room?"

"My aunts brought mother up; they were nearly twenty years older than she. I might say Hiram and they brought her up. You see, Hiram was bound out to my grandfather when he was a boy, and when grandfather died Hiram said he 's'posed he went with the farm, 'long o' the critters,' and he has been there ever since. He was my mother's only refuge from the decorum of my aunts. They are simply workers. They make me think of the Maine woman who wanted her epitaph to be, 'She was a *hard* working woman.'"

"They must be almost beyond their working-days. How old are they?"

"Seventy, or thereabouts; but they will die standing; or, at least, on a Saturday night, after all the house-work is done up. They were rather strict with mother, and I think she had a lonely childhood. The house is almost a mile away from any neighbors, and off on top of what they call Stony Hill. It is bleak enough up there even in summer.

"When mamma was about ten years old they sent her to cousins in Brooklyn, who had children of their own, and knew more about bringing them up. She staid there till she was married; she didn't go to Vermont in all that time, and of course hadn't seen her sisters, for they never would leave home for a day. They couldn't even be induced to go to Brooklyn to her wedding, so she and father took their wedding trip up there."

"And that's why we are going up there on our own?"

"Don't, Roger; you have no idea how loud you speak."

"You never say so except when I am going to say that one little word."

"Well, don't say it, then, or say it very, very quietly."

"Well, what was the queer thing?"

"When they got to the house, mother wanted to take father right off into the little room; she had been telling him about it, just as I am going to tell you, and she had said that of all the rooms, that one was the only one that seemed pleasant to her. She described the furniture and the books and paper and everything, and said it was on the north side, between the front and back room. Well, when they went to look for it, there was no little room there; there was only a shallow china-closet. She asked her sisters when the house had been altered and a closet made of the room that used to be there. They both said the house was exactly as it had been built—that they had never made any changes, except to tear down the old wood-shed and build a smaller one.

"Father and mother laughed a good deal over it, and when anything was lost they would always say it must be in the little room, and any exaggerated statement was called 'little-roomy.' When I was a child I thought that was a regular English phrase, I heard it so often.

"Well, they talked it over, and finally they concluded that my mother had been a very imaginative sort of a child, and had read in some book about such a little room, or perhaps even dreamed it, and then had 'made believe,' as children do, till she herself had really thought the room was there."

"Why, of course, that might easily happen."

"Yes, but you haven't heard the queer part yet; you wait and see if you can explain the rest as easily.

"They staid at the farm two weeks, and then went to New York to live. When I was eight years old my father was killed in the war, and mother was broken-hearted. She never was quite strong afterwards, and that summer we decided to go up to the farm for three months.

"I was a restless sort of a child, and the journey seemed very long to me; and finally, to pass the time, mamma told me the story of the little room, and how it was all in her own imagination, and how there really was only a china-closet there.

"She told it with all the particulars; and even to me, who knew before-hand that the room wasn't there, it seemed just as real as could be. She said it was on the north side, between the front and back rooms; that it was very small, and they sometimes called it an entry. There was a door also that opened out-of-doors, and that one was painted green, and was cut in the middle like the old Dutch doors, so that it could be used for a window by opening the top part only. Directly opposite the door was a lounge or couch; it was covered with blue chintz — India chintz — some that had been brought over by an old Salem sea-captain as a 'venture.' He had given it to Maria when she was a young girl. She was sent to Salem for two years to school. Grandfather originally came from Salem."

"I thought there wasn't any room or chintz."

"*That is just it.* They had decided that mother had imagined it all, and yet you see how exactly everything was painted in her mind, for she had even remembered that Hiram had told her that Maria could have married the sea-captain if she had wanted to!

"The India cotton was the regular blue stamped chintz, with the pea-cock figure on it. The head and body of the bird were in profile, while the tail was full front view behind it. It had seemed to take mamma's fancy, and she drew it for me on a piece of paper as she talked. Doesn't it seem strange to you that she could have made all that up, or even dreamed it?

"At the foot of the lounge were some hanging shelves with some old books on them. All the books were leather-colored except one; that was bright red, and was called the *Ladies' Album*. It made a bright break between the other thicker books.

"On the lower shelf was a beautiful pink sea-shell, lying on a mat made of balls of red shaded worsted. This shell was greatly coveted by mother, but she was only allowed to play with it when she had been partic-ularly good. Hiram had showed her how to hold it close to her ear and hear the roar of the sea in it.

"I know you will like Hiram, Roger, he is quite a character in his way.

"Mamma said she remembered, or *thought* she remembered, having been sick once, and she had to lie quietly for some days on the lounge; then was the time she had become so familiar with everything in the room, and she had been allowed to have the shell to play with all the time. She had had her toast brought to her in there, with make-believe tea. It was one of her pleasant memories of her childhood; it was the first time she had been of any importance to anybody, even herself.

"Right at the head of the lounge was a light-stand, as they called it, and on it was a very brightly polished brass candlestick and a brass tray, with snuffers. That is all I remember of her describing, except that there was a braided rag rug on the floor, and on the wall was a beautiful flowered paper — roses and morning-glories in a wreath on a light blue ground. The same paper was in the front room."

"And all this never existed except in her imagination?"

"She said that when she and father went up there, there wasn't any little room at all like it anywhere in the house; there was a china-closet where she had believed the room to be."

"And your aunts said there had never been any such room."

"That is what they said."

"Wasn't there any blue chintz in the house with a peacock figure?"

"Not a scrap, and Aunt Hannah said there had never been any that she could remember; and Maria just echoed her—she always does that. You see, Aunt Hannah is an up-and-down New England woman. She looks just like herself; I mean, just like her character. Her joints move up and down or backward and forward in a plain square fashion. I don't believe she ever leaned on anything in her life, or sat in an easy-chair. But Maria is different; she is rounder and softer; she hasn't any ideas of her own; she never had any. I don't believe she would think it right or becoming to have one that differed from Aunt Hannah's, so what would be the use of having any? She is an echo, that's all.

"When mamma and I got there, of course I was all excitement to see the china-closet, and I had a sort of feeling that it would be the little room after all. So I ran ahead and threw open the door, crying, 'Come and see the little room.'

"And, Roger," said Mrs. Grant, laying her hand in his, "there really was a little room there, exactly as mother had remembered it. There was the lounge, the peacock chintz, the green door, the shell, the morning-glory and rose paper, *everything exactly as she had described it to me.*"

"What in the world did the sisters say about it?"

"Wait a minute and I will tell you. My mother was in the front hall still talking with Aunt Hannah. She didn't hear me at first, but I ran out there and dragged her through the front room, saying, 'The room *is* here—it is all right.'

"It seemed for a minute as if my mother would faint. She clung to me in terror. I can remember now how strained her eyes looked and how pale she was.

"I called out to Aunt Hannah and asked her when they had had the closet taken away and the little room built; for in my excitement I thought that that was what had been done.

"'That little room has always been there,' said Aunt Hannah, 'ever since the house was built.'

"'But mamma said there wasn't any little room here, only a china-closet, when she was here with papa,' said I.

"'No, there has never been any china-closet there; it has always been just as it is now,' said Aunt Hannah.

"Then mother spoke; her voice sounded weak and far off. She said, slowly, and with an effort, 'Maria, don't you remember that you told me that there had *never been any little room here?* and Hannah said so too, and then I said I must have dreamed it?'

"'No, I don't remember anything of the kind,' said Maria, without the slightest emotion. 'I don't remember you ever said anything about any china-closet. The house has never been altered; you used to play in this room when you were a child, don't you remember?'

"'I know it,' said mother, in that queer slow voice that made me feel frightened. 'Hannah, don't you remember my finding the china-closet here, with the gilt-edged china on the shelves, and then *you* said that the *china-closet* had always been here?'

"'No,' said Hannah, pleasantly but unemotionally—'no, I don't think you ever asked me about any china-closet, and we haven't any gilt-edged china that I know of.'

"And that was the strangest thing about it. We never could make them remember that there had ever been any question about it. You would think they could remember how surprised mother had been before, unless she had imagined the whole thing. Oh, it was so queer! They were always pleasant about it, but they didn't seem to feel any interest or curiosity. It was always this answer: 'The house is just as it was built; there have never been any changes, so far as we know.'

"And my mother was in an agony of perplexity. How cold their gray eyes looked to me! There was no reading anything in them. It just seemed to break my mother down, this queer thing. Many times that summer, in the middle of the night, I have seen her get up and take a candle and creep softly down stairs. I could hear the steps creak under her weight. Then she would go through the front room and peer into the darkness, holding her thin hand between the candle and her eyes. She seemed to think the little room might vanish. Then she would come back to bed and toss about all night, or lie still and shiver; it used to frighten me.

"She grew pale and thin, and she had a little cough; then she did not like to be left alone. Sometimes she would make errands in order to send me to the little room for something—a book, or her fan, or her handkerchief; but she would never sit there or let me stay in there long, and sometimes she wouldn't let me go in there for days together. Oh, it was pitiful!"

"Well, don't talk any more about it, Margaret, if it makes you feel so," said Mr. Grant.

"Oh yes, I want you to know all about it, and there isn't much more—no more about the room.

"Mother never got well, and she died that autumn. She used often to sigh, and say, with a wan little laugh, 'There is one thing I am glad of, Margaret: your father knows now all about the little room.' I think she was afraid I distrusted her. Of course, in a child's way, I thought there was something queer about it, but I did not brood over it. I was too young then, and took it as a part of her illness. But, Roger, do you know, it really did affect me. I almost hate to go there after talking about it; I somehow feel as if it might, you know, be a china-closet again."

"That's an absurd idea."

"I know it; of course it can't be. I saw the room, and there isn't any china-closet there, and no gilt-edged china in the house, either."

And then she whispered, "But, Roger, you may hold my hand as you do now, if you will, when we go to look for the little room."

"And you won't mind Aunt Hannah's gray eyes?"

"I won't mind *anything.*"

It was dusk when Mr. and Mrs. Grant went into the gate under the two old Lombardy poplars and walked up the narrow path to the door, where they were met by the two aunts.

Hannah gave Mrs. Grant a frigid but not unfriendly kiss; and Maria seemed for a moment to tremble on the verge of an emotion, but she glanced at Hannah, and then gave her greeting in exactly the same repressed and non-committal way.

Supper was waiting for them. On the table was the *gilt-edged china.* Mrs. Grant didn't notice it immediately, till she saw her husband smiling at her over his teacup; then she felt fidgety, and couldn't eat. She was nervous, and kept wondering what was behind her, whether it would be a little room or a closet.

After supper she offered to help about the dishes, but, mercy! she might as well have offered to help bring the seasons round; Maria and Hannah couldn't be helped.

So she and her husband went to find the little room, or closet, or whatever was to be there.

Aunt Maria followed them, carrying the lamp, which she set down, and then went back to the dish-washing.

Margaret looked at her husband. He kissed her, for she seemed troubled; and then, hand in hand, they opened the door. It opened into a *china-closet.* The shelves were neatly draped with scalloped paper; on them was the gilt-edged china, with the dishes missing that had been used at the supper, and which at that moment were being carefully washed and wiped by the two aunts.

Margaret's husband dropped her hand and looked at her. She was trembling a little, and turned to him for help, for some explanation, but in an instant she knew that something was wrong. A cloud had come between them; he was hurt; he was antagonized.

He paused for an appreciable instant, and then said, kindly enough, but in a voice that cut her deeply, "I am glad this ridiculous thing is ended; don't let us speak of it again."

"Ended!" said she. "How ended?" And somehow her voice sounded to her as her mother's voice had when she stood there and questioned her sisters about the little room. She seemed to have to drag her words out. She spoke slowly: "It seems to me to have only just begun in my case. It was just so with mother when she —"

"I really wish, Margaret, you would let it drop. I don't like to hear you speak of your mother in connection with it. It—" He hesitated, for was not this their wedding-day? "It doesn't seem quite the thing, quite deli-cate, you know, to use her name in the matter."

She saw it all now: *he didn't believe her.* She felt a chill sense of wither-ing under his glance.

"Come," he added, "let us go out, or into the dining-room, some-where, anywhere, only drop this nonsense."

He went out; he did not take her hand now—he was vexed, baffled, hurt. Had he not given her his sympathy, his attention, his belief—and his hand?—and she was fooling him. What did it mean?—she so truthful, so free from morbidness—a thing he hated. He walked up and down under the poplars, trying to get into the mood to go and join her in the house.

Margaret heard him go out; then she turned and shook the shelves; she reached her hand behind them and tried to push the boards away; she ran out of the house on to the north side and tried to find in the darkness, with her hands, a door, or some steps leading to one. She tore her dress on the old rose-trees, she fell and rose and stumbled, then she sat down on the ground and tried to think. What could she think—was she dreaming?

She went into the house and out into the kitchen, and begged Aunt Maria to tell her about the little room—what had become of it, when had they built the closet, when had they bought the gilt-edged china?

They went on washing dishes and drying them on the spotless towels with methodical exactness; and as they worked they said that there had never been any little room, so far as they knew; the china-closet had always been there, and the gilt-edged china had belonged to their mother, it had always been in the house.

"No, I don't remember that your mother ever asked about any little room," said Hannah. "She didn't seem very well that summer, but she never asked about any changes in the house; there hadn't ever been any changes."

There it was again: not a sign of interest, curiosity, or annoyance, not a spark of memory.

She went out to Hiram. He was telling Mr. Grant about the farm. She had meant to ask him about the room, but her lips were sealed before her husband.

Months afterwards, when time had lessened the sharpness of their feelings, they learned to speculate reasonably about the phenomenon, which Mr. Grant had accepted as something not to be scoffed away, not to be treated as a poor joke, but to be put aside as something inexplicable on any ordinary theory.

Margaret alone in her heart knew that her mother's words carried a deeper significance than she had dreamed of at the time. "One thing I am glad of, your father knows now," and she wondered if Roger or she would ever know.

Five years later they were going to Europe. The packing was done; the children were lying asleep, with their traveling things ready to be slipped on for an early start.

Roger had a foreign appointment. They were not to be back in America for some years. She had meant to go up to say good-by to her aunts; but a mother of three children intends to do a great many things that never get done. One thing she had done that very day, and as she paused for a moment between the writing of two notes that must be posted before she went to bed, she said:

"Roger, you remember Rita Lash? Well, she and Cousin Nan go up to the Adirondacks every autumn. They are clever girls, and I have intrusted to them something I want done very much."

"They are the girls to do it, then, every inch of them."

"I know it, and they are going to."

"Well?"

"Why, you see, Roger, that little room —"

"Oh —"

"Yes, I was a coward not to go myself, but I didn't find time, because I hadn't the courage."

"Oh! *that* was it, was it?"

"Yes, just that. They are going, and they will write us about it."

"Want to bet?"

"No; I only want to know."

Rita Lash and Cousin Nan planned to go to Vermont on their way to the Adirondacks. They found they would have three hours between trains, which would give them time to drive up to the Keys farm, and they could still get to the camp that night. But, at the last minute, Rita was prevented from going. Nan had to go to meet the Adirondack party, and she promised to telegraph her when she arrived at the camp. Imagine Rita's amusement when she received this message: "Safely arrived; went to the Keys farm; it is a little room."

Rita was amused, because she did not in the least think Nan had been there. She thought it was a hoax; but it put it into her mind to carry the joke further by really stopping herself when she went up, as she meant to do the next week.

She did stop over. She introduced herself to the two maiden ladies, who seemed familiar, as they had been described by Mrs. Grant.

They were, if not cordial, at least not disconcerted at her visit, and willingly showed her over the house. As they did not speak of any other stranger's having been to see them lately, she became confirmed in her belief that Nan had not been there.

In the north room she saw the roses and morning-glory paper on the wall, and also the door that should open into — what?

She asked if she might open it.

"Certainly," said Hannah; and Maria echoed, "Certainly."

She opened it, and found the china-closet. She experienced a certain relief; she at least was not under any spell. Mrs. Grant left it a china-closet; she found it the same. Good.

But she tried to induce the old sisters to remember that there had at various times been certain questions relating to a confusion as to whether the closet had always been a closet. It was no use; their stony eyes gave no sign.

Then she thought of the story of the sea-captain, and said, "Miss Keys, did you ever have a lounge covered with India chintz, with a figure of a peacock on it, given to you in Salem by a sea-captain, who brought it from India?"

"I dun'no' as I ever did," said Hannah. That was all. She thought Maria's cheeks were a little flushed, but her eyes were like a stone wall.

She went on that night to the Adirondacks. When Nan and she were alone in their room she said, "By-the-way, Nan, what did you see at the farm-house? and how did you like Maria and Hannah?"

Nan didn't mistrust that Rita had been there, and she began excitedly to tell her all about her visit. Rita could almost have believed Nan had been there if she hadn't known it was not so. She let her go on for some time, enjoying her enthusiasm, and the impressive way in which she described her opening the door and finding the "little room." Then Rita said: "Now, Nan, that is enough fibbing. I went to the farm myself on my way up yesterday, and there is *no* little room, and there *never* has been any; it is a china-closet, just as Mrs. Grant saw it last."

She was pretending to be busy unpacking her trunk, and did not look up for a moment; but as Nan did not say anything, she glanced at her over her shoulder. Nan was actually pale, and it was hard to say whether she was most angry or frightened. There was something of both in her look. And then Rita began to explain how her telegram had put her in the spirit of going up there alone. She hadn't meant to cut Nan out. She only thought— Then Nan broke in: "It isn't that; I am sure you can't think it is that. But I went myself, and you did not go; you can't have been there, for *it is a little room.*"

Oh, what a night they had! They couldn't sleep. They talked and argued, and then kept still for a while, only to break out again, it was so absurd. They both maintained that they had been there, but both felt sure the other one was either crazy or obstinate beyond reason. They were wretched; it was perfectly ridiculous, two friends at odds over such a thing; but there it was— "little room," "china-closet,"—"china-closet," "little room."

The next morning Nan was tacking up some tarlatan at a window to keep the midges out. Rita offered to help her, as she had done for the past ten years. Nan's "No, thanks," cut her to the heart.

"Nan," said she, "come right down from that stepladder and pack your satchel. The stage leaves in just twenty minutes. We can catch the afternoon express train, and we will go together to the farm. I am either going there or going home. You better go with me."

Nan didn't say a word. She gathered up the hammer and tacks, and was ready to start when the stage came round.

It meant for them thirty miles of staging and six hours of train, besides crossing the lake; but what of that, compared with having a lie lying round loose between them! Europe would have seemed easy to accomplish, if it would settle the question.

At the little junction in Vermont they found a farmer with a wagon full of meal-bags. They asked him if he could not take them up to the old Keys farm and bring them back in time for the return train, due in two hours.

They had planned to call it a sketching trip, so they said, "We have been there before, we are artists, and we might find some views worth taking, and we want also to make a short call upon the Misses Keys."

"Did ye calculate to paint the old *house* in the picture?"

They said it was possible they might do so. They wanted to see it, anyway.

"Waal, I guess you are too late. The *house* burnt down last night, and everything in it."   [1895]

KATE CHOPIN

*K*ate Chopin (1851–1904) was born in St. Louis. Her father died when she was four, and she was raised by her Creole mother's family. In 1870 she married Oscar Chopin, a cotton broker. They lived in Louisiana, first in New Orleans and then on a large plantation among the French-speaking Acadians. When her husband died in 1882, Chopin moved with her six children back to St. Louis. Friends encouraged her to write, and when she was nearly forty years old she published her first novel, At Fault (1890). Her stories began to appear in Century and Harper's Magazine, and two collections followed: Bayou Folk (1894) and A Night in Acadie (1897). Her last major work, the novel The Awakening (1899), is her masterpiece, but its sympathetic treatment of adultery shocked reviewers and readers throughout America. In St. Louis the novel was taken out of the libraries, and Chopin was denied membership in the St. Louis Fine Arts Club. When her third collection of stories was rejected by her publisher at the end of 1899, Chopin felt herself a literary outcast; she wrote very little in the last years of her life.

What affronted the genteel readers of the 1890s was Chopin's attempt to write frankly about women's emotions in their relations with men, children, and their own sexuality. After her mother's death in 1885, she stopped being a practicing Catholic and accepted the Darwinian view of human evolution. Seeking God in nature rather than through the church, Chopin wrote freely on the subjects of sex and love, but she said she learned to her sorrow that for American authors, "the limitations imposed upon their art by their environment hamper a full and spontaneous expression." Magazine editors turned down her work if it challenged conventional social behavior, but her writing was championed by feminist critics more than half a century after her death.

Chopin adopted Guy de Maupassant as a model after translating his stories from the French. She felt, "Here was life, not fiction; for where were the plots, the old fashioned mechanism and stage trappings that in a vague, unthinking way I had fancied were essential to the art of story making?" If her fiction is sometimes marred by stilted language or improbable coincidence, at her best, as in "Athénaïse," Chopin subtly emphasizes character rather than plot in her depiction of a young woman's psychological growth into an acceptance of her marriage. "Athénaïse" first appeared in 1896 in The Atlantic Monthly and was collected the following year in A Night in Acadie (1897).

RELATED COMMENTARY: Kate Chopin, "On Certain Brisk, Bright Days," page 1333.

Athénaïse

– I –

Athénaïse went away in the morning to make a visit to her parents, ten miles back on rigolet de Bon Dieu. She did not return in the evening, and Cazeau, her husband, fretted not a little. He did not worry much about Athénaïse, who, he suspected, was resting only too content in the bosom of her family; his chief solicitude was manifestly for the pony she had ridden. He felt sure those "lazy pigs," her brothers, were capable of neglecting it seriously. This misgiving Cazeau communicated to his servant, old Félicité, who waited upon him at supper.

His voice was low pitched, and even softer than Félicité's. He was tall, sinewy, swarthy, and altogether severe looking. His thick black hair waved, and it gleamed like the breast of a crow. The sweep of his mustache, which was not so black, outlined the broad contour of the mouth. Beneath the under lip grew a small tuft which he was much given to twisting, and which he permitted to grow, apparently for no other purpose. Cazeau's eyes were dark blue, narrow and overshadowed. His hands were coarse and stiff from close acquaintance with farming tools and implements, and he handled his fork and knife clumsily. But he was distinguished looking, and succeeded in commanding a good deal of respect, and even fear sometimes.

He ate his supper alone, by the light of a single coal-oil lamp that but faintly illuminated the big room, with its bare floor and huge rafters, and its heavy pieces of furniture that loomed dimly in the gloom of the apartment. Félicité, ministering to his wants, hovered about the table like a little, bent, restless shadow.

She served him with a dish of sunfish fried crisp and brown. There was nothing else set before him beside the bread and butter and the bottle of red wine which she locked carefully in the buffet after he had poured his second glass. She was occupied with her mistress's absence, and kept reverting to it after he had expressed his solicitude about the pony.

"Dat beat me! on'y marry two mont', an' got de head turn' a'ready to go 'broad. C'est pas Chrétien, tenez!"[1]

Cazeau shrugged his shoulders for answer, after he had drained his glass and pushed aside his plate. Félicité's opinion of the unchristianlike behavior of his wife in leaving him thus alone after two months of marriage weighed little with him. He was used to solitude, and did not mind a day or a night or two of it. He had lived alone ten years, since his first wife died, and Félicité might have known better than to suppose that he cared. He told her she was a fool. It sounded like a compliment in his modulated,

---

[1] "It's not Christian, you know."

431

caressing voice. She grumbled to herself as she set about clearing the table, and Cazeau arose and walked outside on the gallery; his spur, which he had not removed upon entering the house, jangled at every step.

The night was beginning to deepen, and to gather black about the clusters of trees and shrubs that were grouped in the yard. In the beam of light from the open kitchen door a black boy stood feeding a brace of snarling, hungry dogs; further away, on the steps of a cabin, some one was playing the accordion; and in still another direction a little negro baby was crying lustily. Cazeau walked around to the front of the house, which was square, squat and one-story.

A belated wagon was driving in at the gate, and the impatient driver was swearing hoarsely at his jaded oxen. Félicité stepped out on the gallery, glass and polishing towel in hand, to investigate, and to wonder, too, who could be singing out on the river. It was a party of young people paddling around, waiting for the moon to rise, and they were singing Juanita, their voices coming tempered and melodious through the distance and the night.

Cazeau's horse was waiting, saddled, ready to be mounted, for Cazeau had many things to attend to before bed-time; so many things that there was not left to him a moment in which to think of Athénaïse. He felt her absence, though, like a dull, insistent pain.

However, before he slept that night he was visited by the thought of her, and by a vision of her fair young face with its drooping lips and sullen and averted eyes. The marriage had been a blunder; he had only to look into her eyes to feel that, to discover her growing aversion. But it was a thing not by any possibility to be undone. He was quite prepared to make the best of it, and expected no less than a like effort on her part. The less she revisited the rigolet, the better. He would find means to keep her at home hereafter.

These unpleasant reflections kept Cazeau awake far into the night, notwithstanding the craving of his whole body for rest and sleep. The moon was shining, and its pale effulgence reached dimly into the room, and with it a touch of the cool breath of the spring night. There was an unusual stillness abroad; no sound to be heard save the distant, tireless, plaintive notes of the accordion.

– II –

Athénaïse did not return the following day, even though her husband sent her word to do so by her brother, Montéclin, who passed on his way to the village early in the morning.

On the third day Cazeau saddled his horse and went himself in search of her. She had sent no word, no message, explaining her absence, and he felt that he had good cause to be offended. It was rather awkward to have to leave his work, even though late in the afternoon, — Cazeau had always so much to do; but among the many urgent calls upon him, the task of bringing his wife back to a sense of her duty seemed to him for the moment paramount.

The Michés, Athénaïse's parents, lived on the old Gotrain place. It did not belong to them; they were "running" it for a merchant in Alexandria. The house was far too big for their use. One of the lower rooms served for the storing of wood and tools; the person "occupying" the place before Miché having pulled up the flooring in despair of being able to patch it. Upstairs, the rooms were so large, so bare, that they offered a constant temptation to lovers of the dance, whose importunities Madame Miché was accustomed to meet with amiable indulgence. A dance at Miché's and a plate of Madame Miché's gumbo filé at midnight were pleasures not to be neglected or despised, unless by such serious souls as Cazeau.

Long before Cazeau reached the house his approach had been observed, for there was nothing to obstruct the view of the outer road; vegetation was not yet abundantly advanced, and there was but a patchy, straggling stand of cotton and corn in Miché's field.

Madame Miché, who had been seated on the gallery in a rocking-chair, stood up to greet him as he drew near. She was short and fat, and wore a black skirt and loose muslin sack fastened at the throat with a hair brooch. Her own hair, brown and glossy, showed but a few threads of silver. Her round pink face was cheery, and her eyes were bright and good humored. But she was plainly perturbed and ill at ease as Cazeau advanced.

Montéclin, who was there too, was not ill at ease, and made no attempt to disguise the dislike with which his brother-in-law inspired him. He was a slim, wiry fellow of twenty-five, short of stature like his mother, and resembling her in feature. He was in shirt-sleeves, half leaning, half sitting, on the insecure railing of the gallery, and fanning himself with his broad-rimmed felt hat.

"Cochon!" he muttered under his breath as Cazeau mounted the stairs, — "sacré cochon!"[2]

"Cochon" had sufficiently characterized the man who had once on a time declined to lend Montéclin money. But when this same man had had the presumption to propose marriage to his well-beloved sister, Athénaïse, and the honor to be accepted by her, Montéclin felt that a qualifying epithet was needed fully to express his estimate of Cazeau.

Miché and his oldest son were absent. They both esteemed Cazeau highly, and talked much of his qualities of head and heart, and thought much of his excellent standing with city merchants.

Athénaïse had shut herself up in her room. Cazeau had seen her rise and enter the house at perceiving him. He was a good deal mystified, but no one could have guessed it when he shook hands with Madame Miché. He had only nodded to Montéclin, with a muttered "Comment ça va?"[3]

---

[2]"Pig . . . damn pig!"
[3]"How are things?"

"Tiens! something tole me you were coming to-day!" exclaimed Madame Miché, with a little blustering appearance of being cordial and at ease, as she offered Cazeau a chair.

He ventured a short laugh as he seated himself.

"You know, nothing would do," she went on, with much gesture of her small, plump hands, "nothing would do but Athénaïse mus' stay las' night fo' a li'le dance. The boys wouldn' year to their sister leaving."

Cazeau shrugged his shoulders significantly, telling as plainly as words that he knew nothing about it.

"Comment! Montéclin didn' tell you we were going to keep Athénaïse?" Montéclin had evidently told nothing.

"An' how about the night befo'," questioned Cazeau, "an' las' night? It isn't possible you dance every night out yere on the Bon Dieu!"

Madame Miché laughed, with amiable appreciation of the sarcasm; and turning to her son, "Montéclin, my boy, go tell yo' sister that Monsieur Cazeau is yere."

Montéclin did not stir except to shift his position and settle himself more securely on the railing.

"Did you year me, Montéclin?"

"Oh yes, I yeard you plain enough," responded her son, "but you know as well as me it's no use to tell 'Thénaïse anything. You been talkin' to her yo'se'f since Monday; an' pa's preached himse'f hoa'se on the subject; an' you even had uncle Achille down yere yesterday to reason with her. W'en 'Thénaïse said she wasn' goin' to set her foot back in Cazeau's house, she meant it."

This speech, which Montéclin delivered with thorough unconcern, threw his mother into a condition of painful but dumb embarrassment. It brought two fiery red spots to Cazeau's cheeks, and for the space of a moment he looked wicked.

What Montéclin had spoken was quite true, though his taste in the manner and choice of time and place in saying it were not of the best. Athénaïse, upon the first day of her arrival, had announced that she came to stay, having no intention of returning under Cazeau's roof. The announcement had scattered consternation, as she knew it would. She had been implored, scolded, entreated, stormed at, until she felt herself like a dragging sail that all the winds of heaven had beaten upon. Why in the name of God had she married Cazeau? Her father had lashed her with the question a dozen times. Why indeed? It was difficult now for her to understand why, unless because she supposed it was customary for girls to marry when the right opportunity came. Cazeau, she knew, would make life more comfortable for her; and again, she had liked him, and had even been rather flustered when he pressed her hands and kissed them, and kissed her lips and cheeks and eyes, when she accepted him.

Montéclin himself had taken her aside to talk the thing over. The turn of affairs was delighting him.

"Come, now, 'Thénaïse, you mus' explain to me all about it, so we can settle on a good cause, an' secu' a separation fo' you. Has he been mistreating an' abusing you, the sacré cochon?" They were alone together in her room, whither she had taken refuge from the angry domestic elements.

"You please to reserve yo' disgusting expressions, Montéclin. No, he has not abused me in any way that I can think."

"Does he drink? Come 'Thénaïse, think well over it. Does he ever get drunk?"

"Drunk! Oh, mercy no,—Cazeau never gets drunk."

"I see; it's jus' simply you feel like me; you hate him."

"No, I don't hate him," she returned reflectively; adding with a sudden impulse, "It's jus' being married that I detes' an' despise. I hate being Mrs. Cazeau, an' would want to be Athénaïse Miché again. I can't stan' to live with a man; to have him always there; his coats an' pantaloons hanging in my room; his ugly bare feet—washing them in my tub, befo' my very eyes, ugh!" She shuddered with recollections, and resumed, with a sigh that was almost a sob: "Mon Dieu, mon Dieu! Sister Marie Angélique knew w'at she was saying; she knew me better than myse'f w'en she said God had sent me a vocation an' I was turning deaf ears. W'en I think of a blessed life in the convent, at peace! Oh, w'at was I dreaming of!" and then the tears came.

Montéclin felt disconcerted and greatly disappointed at having obtained evidence that would carry no weight with a court of justice. The day had not come when a young woman might ask the court's permission to return to her mamma on the sweeping ground of a constitutional disinclination for marriage. But if there was no way of untying this Gordian knot of marriage, there was surely a way of cutting it.

"Well, 'Thénaïse, I'm mighty durn sorry you got no better groun's 'an w'at you say. But you can count on me to stan' by you w'atever you do. God knows I don' blame you fo' not wantin' to live with Cazeau."

And now there was Cazeau himself, with the red spots flaming in his swarthy cheeks, looking and feeling as if he wanted to thrash Montéclin into some semblance of decency. He arose abruptly, and approaching the room which he had seen his wife enter, thrust open the door after a hasty preliminary knock. Athénaïse, who was standing erect at a far window, turned at his entrance.

She appeared neither angry nor frightened, but thoroughly unhappy, with an appeal in her soft dark eyes and a tremor on her lips that seemed to him expressions of unjust reproach, that wounded and maddened him at once. But whatever he might feel, Cazeau knew only one way to act toward a woman.

"Athénaïse, you are not ready?" he asked in his quiet tones. "It's getting late; we havn' any time to lose."

She knew that Montéclin had spoken out, and she had hoped for a wordy interview, a stormy scene, in which she might have held her own as she had held it for the past three days against her family, with Montéclin's aid. But she had no weapon with which to combat subtlety. Her husband's looks, his tones, his mere presence, brought to her a sudden sense of hopelessness, an instinctive realization of the futility of rebellion against a social and sacred institution.

Cazeau said nothing further, but stood waiting in the doorway. Madame Miché had walked to the far end of the gallery, and pretended to be occupied with having a chicken driven from her parterre.[4] Montéclin stood by, exasperated, fuming, ready to burst out.

Athénaïse went and reached for her riding skirt that hung against the wall. She was rather tall, with a figure which, though not robust, seemed perfect in its fine proportions. "La fille de son père,"[5] she was often called, which was a great compliment to Miché. Her brown hair was brushed all fluffily back from her temples and low forehead, and about her features and expression lurked a softness, a prettiness, a dewiness, that were perhaps too childlike, that savored of immaturity.

She slipped the riding-skirt, which was of black alpaca, over her head, and with impatient fingers hooked it at the waist over her pink linen-lawn. Then she fastened on her white sunbonnet and reached for her gloves on the mantelpiece.

"If you don' wan' to go, you know w'at you got to do, 'Thénaïse," fumed Montéclin. "You don' set yo' feet back on Cane River, by God, unless you want to,—not w'ile I'm alive."

Cazeau looked at him as if he were a monkey whose antics fell short of being amusing.

Athénaïse still made no reply, said not a word. She walked rapidly past her husband, past her brother; bidding good-bye to no one, not even to her mother. She descended the stairs, and without assistance from any one mounted the pony, which Cazeau had ordered to be saddled upon his arrival. In this way she obtained a fair start of her husband, whose departure was far more leisurely, and for the greater part of the way she managed to keep an appreciable gap between them. She rode almost madly at first, with the wind inflating her skirt balloon-like about her knees, and her sunbonnet falling back between her shoulders.

At no time did Cazeau make an effort to overtake her until traversing an old fallow meadow that was level and hard as a table. The sight of a great solitary oak-tree, with its seemingly immutable outlines, that had been a landmark for ages—or was it the odor of elderberry stealing up from the gully to the south? or what was it that brought vividly back to Cazeau, by some association of ideas, a scene of many years ago? He had passed that old live-oak hundreds of times, but it was only now that the memory of one day came back to him. He was a very small boy that day, seated before

----

[4] Flower bed.
[5] "Her father's daughter."

his father on horse-back. They were proceeding slowly, and Black Gabe was moving on before them at a little dog-trot. Black Gabe had run away, and had been discovered back in the Gotrain swamp. They had halted beneath this big oak to enable the negro to take breath; for Cazeau's father was a kind and considerate master, and every one had agreed at the time that Black Gabe was a fool, a great idiot indeed, for wanting to run away from him.

The whole impression was for some reason hideous, and to dispel it Cazeau spurred his horse to a swift gallop. Overtaking his wife, he rode the remainder of the way at her side in silence.

It was late when they reached home. Félicité was standing on the grassy edge of the road, in the moonlight, waiting for them.

Cazeau once more ate his supper alone; for Athénaïse went to her room, and there she was crying again.

– III –

Athénaïse was not one to accept the inevitable with patient resignation, a talent born in the souls of many women; neither was she the one to accept it with philosophical resignation, like her husband. Her sensibilities were alive and keen and responsive. She met the pleasurable things of life with frank, open appreciation, and against distasteful conditions she rebelled. Dissimulation was as foreign to her nature as guile to the breast of a babe, and her rebellious outbreaks, by no means rare, had hitherto been quite open and aboveboard. People often said that Athénaïse would know her own mind some day, which was equivalent to saying that she was at present unacquainted with it. If she ever came to such knowledge, it would be by no intellectual research, by no subtle analyses or tracing the motives of actions to their source. It would come to her as the song to the bird, the perfume and color to the flower.

Her parents had hoped—not without reason and justice—that marriage would bring the poise, the desirable pose, so glaringly lacking in Athénaïse's character. Marriage they knew to be a wonderful and powerful agent in the development and formation of a woman's character; they had seen its effect too often to doubt it.

"And if this marriage does nothing else," exclaimed Miché in an outburst of sudden exasperation, "it will rid us of Athénaïse; for I am at the end of my patience with her! You have never had the firmness to manage her,"—he was speaking to his wife,—"I have not had the time, the leisure, to devote to her training; and what good we might have accomplished, that maudit Montéclin—Well, Cazeau is the one! It takes just such a steady hand to guide a disposition like Athénaïse's, a master hand, a strong will that compels obedience."

And now, when they had hoped for so much, here was Athénaïse, with gathered and fierce vehemence, beside which her former outbursts appeared mild, declaring that she would not, and she would not, and she would not continue to enact the role of wife to Cazeau. If she had had a reason! as Madame Miché lamented; but it could not be discovered that she had any sane one. He had never scolded, or called names, or deprived her of comforts, or been guilty of any of the many reprehensible acts commonly attributed to objectionable husbands. He did not slight nor neglect her. Indeed, Cazeau's chief offense seemed to be that he loved her, and Athénaïse was not the woman to be loved against her will. She called marriage a trap set for the feet of unwary and unsuspecting girls, and in round, unmeasured terms reproached her mother with treachery and deceit.

"I told you Cazeau was the man," chuckled Miché, when his wife had related the scene that had accompanied and influenced Athénaïse's departure.

Athénaïse again hoped, in the morning, that Cazeau would scold or make some sort of a scene, but he apparently did not dream of it. It was exasperating that he should take her acquiescence so for granted. It is true he had been up and over the fields and across the river and back long before she was out of bed, and he may have been thinking of something else, which was no excuse, which was even in some sense an aggravation. But he did say to her at breakfast, "That brother of yo's, that Montéclin, is unbearable."

"Montéclin? Par exemple!"

Athénaïse, seated opposite to her husband, was attired in a white morning wrapper. She wore a somewhat abused, long face, it is true, — an expression of countenance familiar to some husbands, — but the expression was not sufficiently pronounced to mar the charm of her youthful freshness. She had little heart to eat, only playing with the food before her, and she felt a pang of resentment at her husband's healthy appetite.

"Yes, Montéclin," he reasserted. "He's developed into a firs'-class nuisance; an' you better tell him, Athénaïse, — unless you want me to tell him, — to confine his energies after this to matters that concern him. I have no use fo' him or fo' his interference in w'at regards you an' me alone."

This was said with unusual asperity. It was the little breach that Athénaïse had been watching for, and she charged rapidly: "It's strange, if you detes' Montéclin so heartily, that you would desire to marry his sister." She knew it was a silly thing to say, and was not surprised when he told her so. It gave her a little foothold for further attack, however. "I don't see, anyhow, w'at reason you had to marry me, w'en there were so many others," she complained, as if accusing him of persecution and injury. "There was Marianne running after you fo' the las' five years till it was disgraceful; an' any one of the Dortrand girls would have been glad to marry you. But no, nothing would do; you mus' come out on the rigolet fo' me." Her complaint was pathetic, and at the same time so amusing that Cazeau was forced to smile.

"I can't see w'at the Dortrand girls or Marianne have to do with it," he rejoined; adding, with no trace of amusement, "I married you because I loved you; because you were the woman I wanted to marry, an' the only one. I reckon I tole you that befo'. I thought—of co'se I was a fool fo' taking things fo' granted—but I did think that I might make you happy in making things easier an' mo' comfortable fo' you. I expected—I was even that big a fool—I believed that yo' coming yere to me would be like the sun shining out of the clouds, an' that our days would be like w'at the story-books promise after the wedding. I was mistaken. But I can't imagine w'at induced you to marry me. W'atever it was, I reckon you foun' out you made a mistake, too. I don' see anything to do but make the best of a bad bargain, an' shake han's over it." He had arisen from the table, and, approaching, held out his hand to her. What he had said was common-place enough, but it was significant, coming from Cazeau, who was not often so unreserved in expressing himself.

Athénaïse ignored the hand held out to her. She was resting her chin in her palm, and kept her eyes fixed moodily upon the table. He rested his hand, that she would not touch, upon her head for an instant, and walked away out of the room.

She heard him giving orders to workmen who had been waiting for him out on the gallery, and she heard him mount his horse and ride away. A hundred things would distract him and engage his attention during the day. She felt that he had perhaps put her and her grievance from his thoughts when he crossed the threshold; whilst she—

Old Félicité was standing there holding a shining tin pail, asking for flour and lard and eggs from the storeroom, and meal for the chicks.

Athénaïse seized the bunch of keys which hung from her belt and flung them at Félicité's feet.

"Tiens! tu vas les garder comme tu as jadis fait. Je ne veux plus de ce train là, moi!"[6]

The old woman stooped and picked up the keys from the floor. It was really all one to her that her mistress returned them to her keeping, and refused to take further account of the ménage.[7]

–IV–

It seemed now to Athénaïse that Montéclin was the only friend left to her in the world. Her father and mother had turned from her in what appeared to be her hour of need. Her friends laughed at her, and refused to take seriously the hints which she threw out,—feeling her way to dis-cover if marriage were as distasteful to other women as to herself. Monté-clin alone understood her. He alone had always been ready to act for her and with her, to comfort and solace her with his sympathy and his support. Her only hope for rescue from her hateful surroundings lay in Montéclin.

---

[6]"You are going to keep them as you did in the past. I don't want any more of this nonsense."

[7]Housekeeping.

Of herself she felt powerless to plan, to act, even to conceive a way out of this pitfall into which the whole world seemed to have conspired to thrust her.

She had a great desire to see her brother, and wrote asking him to come to her. But it better suited Montéclin's spirit of adventure to appoint a meeting-place at the turn of the lane, where Athénaïse might appear to be walking leisurely for health and recreation, and where he might seem to be riding along, bent on some errand of business or pleasure.

There had been a shower, a sudden downpour, short as it was sudden, that had laid the dust in the road. It had freshened the pointed leaves of the live-oaks, and brightened up the big fields of cotton on either side of the lane till they seemed carpeted with green, glittering gems.

Athénaïse walked along the grassy edge of the road, lifting her crisp skirts with one hand, and with the other twirling a gay sunshade over her bare head. The scent of the fields after the rain was delicious. She inhaled long breaths of their freshness and perfume, that soothed and quieted her for the moment. There were birds splashing and spluttering in the pools, pluming themselves on the fence-rails, and sending out little sharp cries, twitters, and shrill rhapsodies of delight.

She saw Montéclin approaching from a great distance, — almost as far away as the turn of the woods. But she could not feel sure it was he; it appeared too tall for Montéclin, but that was because he was riding a large horse. She waved her parasol to him; she was so glad to see him. She had never been so glad to see Montéclin before; not even the day when he had taken her out of the convent, against her parents' wishes, because she had expressed a desire to remain there no longer. He seemed to her, as he drew near, the embodiment of kindness, of bravery, of chivalry, even of wisdom; for she had never known Montéclin at a loss to extricate himself from a disagreeable situation.

He dismounted, and, leading his horse by the bridle, started to walk beside her, after he had kissed her affectionately and asked her what she was crying about. She protested that she was not crying, for she was laughing, though drying her eyes at the same time on her handkerchief, rolled in a soft mop for the purpose.

She took Montéclin's arm, and they strolled slowly down the lane; they could not seat themselves for a comfortable chat, as they would have liked, with the grass all sparkling and bristling wet.

Yes, she was quite as wretched as ever, she told him. The week which had gone by since she saw him had in no wise lightened the burden of her discontent. There had even been some additional provocations laid upon her, and she told Montéclin all about them, — about the keys, for instance, which in a fit of temper she had returned to Félicité's keeping; and she told how Cazeau had brought them back to her as if they were something she had accidentally lost, and he had recovered; and how he had said, in that aggravating tone of his, that it was not the custom on Cane river for the negro servants to carry the keys, when there was a mistress at the head of the household.

But Athénaïse could not tell Montéclin anything to increase the disrespect which he already entertained for his brother-in-law; and it was then he unfolded to her a plan which he had conceived and worked out for her deliverance from this galling matrimonial yoke.

It was not a plan which met with instant favor, which she was at once ready to accept, for it involved secrecy and dissimulation, hateful alternatives, both of them. But she was filled with admiration for Montéclin's resources and wonderful talent for contrivance. She accepted the plan; not with the immediate determination to act upon it, rather with the intention to sleep and to dream upon it.

Three days later she wrote to Montéclin that she had abandoned herself to his counsel. Displeasing as it might be to her sense of honesty, it would yet be less trying than to live on with a soul full of bitterness and revolt, as she had done for the past two months.

–V–

When Cazeau awoke, one morning at his usual very early hour, it was to find the place at his side vacant. This did not surprise him until he discovered that Athénaïse was not in the adjoining room, where he had often found her sleeping in the morning on the lounge. She had perhaps gone out for an early stroll, he reflected, for her jacket and hat were not on the rack where she had hung them the night before. But there were other things absent,—a gown or two from the armoire; and there was a great gap in the piles of lingerie on the shelf; and her traveling-bag was missing, and so were her bits of jewelry from the toilet tray—and Athénaïse was gone!

But the absurdity of going during the night, as if she had been a prisoner, and he the keeper of a dungeon! So much secrecy and mystery, to go sojourning out on the Bon Dieu! Well, the Michés might keep their daughter after this. For the companionship of no woman on earth would he again undergo the humiliating sensation of baseness that had overtaken him in passing the old oak-tree in the fallow meadow.

But a terrible sense of loss overwhelmed Cazeau. It was not new or sudden; he had felt it for weeks growing upon him, and it seemed to culminate with Athénaïse's flight from home. He knew that he could again compel her return as he had done once before,—compel her to return to the shelter of his roof, compel her cold and unwilling submission to his love and passionate transports; but the loss of self-respect seemed to him too dear a price to pay for a wife.

He could not comprehend why she had seemed to prefer him above others; why she had attracted him with eyes, with voice, with a hundred womanly ways, and finally distracted him with love which she seemed, in her timid, maidenly fashion, to return. The great sense of loss came from the realization of having missed a chance for happiness,—a chance that would come his way again only through a miracle. He could not think of himself loving any other woman, and could not think of Athénaïse ever—even at some remote date—caring for him.

He wrote her a letter, in which he disclaimed any further intention of forcing his commands upon her. He did not desire her presence ever again in his home unless she came of her free will, uninfluenced by family or friends; unless she could be the companion he had hoped for in marrying her, and in some measure return affection and respect for the love which he continued and would always continue to feel for her. This letter he sent out to the rigolet by a messenger early in the day. But she was not out on the rigolet, and had not been there.

The family turned instinctively to Montéclin, and almost literally fell upon him for an explanation; he had been absent from home all night. There was much mystification in his answers, and a plain desire to mislead in his assurances of ignorance and innocence.

But with Cazeau there was no doubt or speculation when he accosted the young fellow. "Montéclin, w'at have you done with Athénaïse?" he questioned bluntly. They had met in the open road on horseback, just as Cazeau ascended the river bank before his house.

"W'at have you done to Athénaïse?" returned Montéclin for answer.

"I don't reckon you've considered yo' conduct by any light of decency an' propriety in encouraging yo' sister to such an action, but let me tell you"—

"Voyons! you can let me alone with yo' decency an' morality an' fiddle-sticks. I know you mus' 'a' done Athénaïse pretty mean that she can't live with you; an' fo' my part, I'm mighty durn glad she had the spirit to quit you."

"I ain't in the humor to take any notice of yo' impertinence, Montéclin; but let me remine you that Athénaïse is nothing but a chile in character; besides that, she's my wife, an' I hole you responsible fo' her safety an' welfare. If any harm of any description happens to her, I'll strangle you, by God, like a rat, and fling you in Cane river, if I have to hang fo' it!" He had not lifted his voice. The only sign of anger was a savage gleam in his eyes.

"I reckon you better keep yo' big talk fo' the women, Cazeau," replied Montéclin, riding away.

But he went doubly armed after that, and intimated that the precaution was not needless, in view of the threats and menaces that were abroad touching his personal safety.

–VI–

Athénaïse reached her destination sound of skin and limb, but a good deal flustered, a little frightened, and altogether excited and interested by her unusual experiences.

Her destination was the house of Sylvie, on Dauphine Street, in New Orleans,—a three-story gray brick, standing directly on the banquette, with three broad stone steps leading to the deep front entrance. From the second-story balcony swung a small sign, conveying to passers-by the intelligence that within were "*chambres garnies.*"[8]

It was one morning in the last week of April that Athénaïse presented herself at the Dauphine Street house. Sylvie was expecting her, and introduced her at once to her apartment, which was in the second story of the back ell, and accessible by an open, outside gallery. There was a yard below, paved with broad stone flagging; many fragrant flowering shrubs and plants grew in a bed along the side of the opposite wall, and others were distributed about in tubs and green boxes.

It was a plain but large enough room into which Athénaïse was ushered, with matting on the floor, green shades and Nottingham-lace curtains at the windows that looked out on the gallery, and furnished with a cheap walnut suit. But everything looked exquisitely clean, and the whole place smelled of cleanliness.

Athénaïse at once fell into the rocking-chair, with the air of exhaustion and intense relief of one who has come to the end of her troubles. Sylvie, entering behind her, laid the big traveling-bag on the floor and deposited the jacket on the bed.

She was a portly quadroon of fifty or there-about, clad in an ample *volante* of the old-fashioned purple calico so much affected by her class. She wore large golden hoop-earrings, and her hair was combed plainly, with every appearance of effort to smooth out the kinks. She had broad, coarse features, with a nose that turned up, exposing the wide nostrils, and that seemed to emphasize the loftiness and command of her bearing,—a dignity that in the presence of white people assumed a character of respectfulness, but never of obsequiousness. Sylvie believed firmly in maintaining the color line, and would not suffer a white person, even a child, to call her "Madame Sylvie,"—a title which she exacted religiously, however, from those of her own race.

"I hope you be please' wid yo' room, madame," she observed amiably. "Dat's de same room w'at yo' brother, M'sieur Miché, all time like w'en he come to New Orlean'. He well, M'sieur Miché? I receive' his letter las' week, an' dat same day a gent'man want I give 'im dat room. I say, 'No, dat room already ingage'.' Ev-body like dat room on 'count it so quite (quiet). M'sieur Gouvernail, dere in nax' room, you can't pay 'im! He been stay t'ree year' in dat room; but all fix' up fine wid his own furn'ture an' books, 'tel you can't see! I say to 'im plenty time', 'M'sieur Gouvernail, w'y you don't take dat t'ree-story front, now, long it's empty?' He tells me, 'Leave me 'lone, Sylvie; I know a good room w'en I fine it, me.'"

---

[8] Furnished rooms.

She had been moving slowly and majestically about the apartment, straightening and smoothing down bed and pillows, peering into ewer and basin, evidently casting an eye around to make sure that everything was as it should be.

"I sen' you some fresh water, madame," she offered upon retiring from the room. "An' w'en you want an't'ing, you jus' go out on de gall'ry an' call Pousette: she year you plain,—she right down dere in de kitchen."

Athénaïse was really not so exhausted as she had every reason to be after that interminable and circuitous way by which Montéclin had seen fit to have her conveyed to the city.

Would she ever forget that dark and truly dangerous midnight ride along the "coast" to the mouth of Cane river! There Montéclin had parted with her, after seeing her aboard the St. Louis and Shreveport packet which he knew would pass there before dawn. She had received instructions to disembark at the mouth of Red river, and there transfer to the first south-bound steamer for New Orleans; all of which instructions she had followed implicitly, even to making her way at once to Sylvie's upon her arrival in the city. Montéclin had enjoined secrecy and much caution; the clandestine nature of the affair gave it a savor of adventure which was highly pleasing to him. Eloping with his sister was only a little less engaging than eloping with some one else's sister.

But Montéclin did not do the *grand seigneur*[9] by halves. He had paid Sylvie a whole month in advance for Athénaïse's board and lodging. Part of the sum he had been forced to borrow, it is true, but he was not niggardly.

Athénaïse was to take her meals in the house, which none of the other lodgers did; the one exception being that Mr. Gouvernail was served with breakfast on Sunday mornings.

Sylvie's clientèle came chiefly from the southern parishes; for the most part, people spending but a few days in the city. She prided herself upon the quality and highly respectable character of her patrons, who came and went unobtrusively.

The large parlor opening upon the front balcony was seldom used. Her guests were permitted to entertain in this sanctuary of elegance,— but they never did. She often rented it for the night to parties of respectable and discreet gentlemen desiring to enjoy a quiet game of cards outside the bosom of their families. The second-story hall also led by a long window out on the balcony. And Sylvie advised Athénaïse, when she grew weary of her back room, to go and sit on the front balcony, which was shady in the afternoon, and where she might find diversion in the sounds and sights of the street below.

Athénaïse refreshed herself with a bath, and was soon unpacking her few belongings, which she ranged neatly away in the bureau drawers and the armoire.

---

[9]Lord of the manor.

She had revolved certain plans in her mind during the past hour or so. Her present intention was to live on indefinitely in this big, cool, clean back room on Dauphine Street. She had thought seriously, for moments, of the convent, with all readiness to embrace the vows of poverty and chastity; but what about obedience? Later, she intended, in some round-about way, to give her parents and her husband the assurance of her safety and welfare; reserving the right to remain unmolested and lost to them. To live on at the expense of Montéclin's generosity was wholly out of the question, and Athénaïse meant to look about for some suitable and agreeable employment.

The imperative thing to be done at present, however, was to go out in search of material for an inexpensive gown or two; for she found herself in the painful predicament of a young woman having almost literally nothing to wear. She decided upon pure white for one, and some sort of a sprigged muslin for the other.

– VII –

On Sunday morning, two days after Athénaïse's arrival in the city, she went in to breakfast somewhat later than usual, to find two covers laid at table instead of the one to which she was accustomed. She had been to mass, and did not remove her hat, but put her fan, parasol, and prayer-book aside. The dining-room was situated just beneath her own apartment, and, like all rooms of the house, was large and airy; the floor was covered with a glistening oil-cloth.

The small, round table, immaculately set, was drawn near the open window. There were some tall plants in boxes on the gallery outside; and Pousette, a little, old, intensely black woman, was splashing and dashing buckets of water on the flagging, and talking loud in her Creole patois to no one in particular.

A dish piled with delicate river-shrimps and crushed ice was on the table; a caraffe of crystal-clear water, a few *hors d'œuvres,* beside a small golden-brown crusty loaf of French bread at each plate. A half-bottle of wine and the morning paper were set at the place opposite Athénaïse.

She had almost completed her breakfast when Gouvernail came in and seated himself at table. He felt annoyed at finding his cherished privacy invaded. Sylvie was removing the remains of a mutton-chop from before Athénaïse, and serving her with a cup of café au lait.

"M'sieur Gouvernail," offered Sylvie in her most insinuating and impressive manner, "you please leave me make you acquaint' wid Madame Cazeau. Dat's M'sieur Miché's sister; you meet 'im two t'ree time', you rec'lec', an' been one day to de race wid 'im. Madame Cazeau, you please leave me make you acquaint' wid M'sieur Gouvernail."

Gouvernail expressed himself greatly pleased to meet the sister of Monsieur Miché, of whom he had not the slightest recollection. He inquired after Monsieur Miché's health, and politely offered Athénaïse a part of his newspaper,—the part which contained the Woman's Page and the social gossip.

Athénaïse faintly remembered that Sylvie had spoken of a Monsieur Gouvernail occupying the room adjoining hers, living amid luxurious surroundings and a multitude of books. She had not thought of him further than to picture him a stout, middle-aged gentleman, with a bushy beard turning gray, wearing large gold-rimmed spectacles, and stooping somewhat from much bending over books and writing material. She had confused him in her mind with the likeness of some literary celebrity that she had run across in the advertising pages of a magazine.

Gouvernail's appearance was, in truth, in no sense striking. He looked older than thirty and younger than forty, was of medium height and weight, with a quiet, unobtrusive manner which seemed to ask that he be let alone. His hair was light brown, brushed carefully and parted in the middle. His mustache was brown, and so were his eyes, which had a mild, penetrating quality. He was neatly dressed in the fashion of the day; and his hands seemed to Athénaïse remarkably white and soft for a man's.

He had been buried in the contents of his newspaper, when he suddenly realized that some further little attention might be due to Miché's sister. He started to offer her a glass of wine, when he was surprised and relieved to find that she had quietly slipped away while he was absorbed in his own editorial on Corrupt Legislation.

Gouvernail finished his paper and smoked his cigar out on the gallery. He lounged about, gathered a rose for his buttonhole, and had his regular Sunday-morning confab with Pousette, to whom he paid a weekly stipend for brushing his shoes and clothing. He made a great pretense of haggling over the transaction, only to enjoy her uneasiness and garrulous excitement.

He worked or read in his room for a few hours, and when he quitted the house, at three in the afternoon, it was to return no more till late at night. It was his almost invariable custom to spend Sunday evenings out in the American quarter, among a congenial set of men and women,—*des esprits forts*,[10] all of them, whose lives were irreproachable, yet whose opinions would startle even the traditional "sapeur,"[11] for whom "nothing is sacred." But for all his "advanced" opinions, Gouvernail was a liberal-minded fellow; a man or woman lost nothing of his respect by being married.

When he left the house in the afternoon, Athénaïse had already ensconced herself on the front balcony. He could see her through the jalousies when he passed on his way to the front entrance. She had not yet grown lonesome or homesick; the newness of her surroundings made them sufficiently entertaining. She found it diverting to sit there on the front balcony watching people pass by, even though there was no one to talk to. And then the comforting, comfortable sense of not being married!

[10]Freethinkers.
[11]Rebel.

She watched Gouvernail walk down the street, and could find no fault with his bearing. He could hear the sound of her rockers for some little distance. He wondered what the "poor little thing" was doing in the city, and meant to ask Sylvie about her when he should happen to think of it.

– VIII –

The following morning, towards noon, when Gouvernail quitted his room, he was confronted by Athénaïse, exhibiting some confusion and trepidation at being forced to request a favor of him at so early a stage of their acquaintance. She stood in her doorway, and had evidently been sewing, as the thimble on her finger testified, as well as a long-threaded needle thrust in the bosom of her gown. She held a stamped but unaddressed letter in her hand.

And would Mr. Gouvernail be so kind as to address the letter to her brother, Mr. Montéclin Miché? She would hate to detain him with explanations this morning,—another time, perhaps,—but now she begged that he would give himself the trouble.

He assured her that it made no difference, that it was no trouble whatever; and he drew a fountain pen from his pocket and addressed the letter at her dictation, resting it on the inverted rim of his straw hat. She wondered a little at a man of his supposed erudition stumbling over the spelling of "Montéclin" and "Miché."

She demurred at overwhelming him with the additional trouble of posting it, but he succeeded in convincing her that so simple a task as the posting of a letter would not add an iota to the burden of the day. Moreover, he promised to carry it in his hand, and thus avoid any possible risk of forgetting it in his pocket.

After that, and after a second repetition of the favor, when she had told him that she had had a letter from Montéclin, and looked as if she wanted to tell him more, he felt that he knew her better. He felt that he knew her well enough to join her out on the balcony, one night, when he found her sitting there alone. He was not one who deliberately sought the society of women, but he was not wholly a bear. A little commiseration for Athénaïse's aloneness, perhaps some curiosity to know further what manner of woman she was, and the natural influence of her feminine charm were equal unconfessed factors in turning his steps towards the balcony when he discovered the shimmer of her white gown through the open hall window.

It was already quite late, but the day had been intensely hot, and neighboring balconies and doorways were occupied by chattering groups of humanity, loath to abandon the grateful freshness of the outer air. The voices about her served to reveal to Athénaïse the feeling of loneliness that was gradually coming over her. Notwithstanding certain dormant impulses, she craved human sympathy and companionship.

She shook hands impulsively with Gouvernail, and told him how glad she was to see him. He was not prepared for such an admission, but it pleased him immensely, detecting as he did that the expression was as sincere as it was outspoken. He drew a chair up within comfortable conversational distance of Athénaïse, though he had no intention of talking more than was barely necessary to encourage Madame—He had actually forgotten her name!

He leaned an elbow on the balcony rail, and would have offered an opening remark about the oppressive heat of the day, but Athénaïse did not give him the opportunity. How glad she was to talk to some one, and how she talked!

An hour later she had gone to her room, and Gouvernail stayed smoking on the balcony. He knew her quite well after that hour's talk. It was not so much what she had said as what her half saying had revealed to his quick intelligence. He knew that she adored Montéclin and he suspected that she adored Cazeau without being herself aware of it. He had gathered that she was self-willed, impulsive, innocent, ignorant, unsatisfied, dissatisfied; for had she not complained that things seemed all wrongly arranged in this world, and no one was permitted to be happy in his own way? And he told her he was sorry she had discovered that primordial fact of existence so early in life.

He commiserated her loneliness, and scanned his bookshelves next morning for something to lend her to read, rejecting everything that offered itself to his view. Philosophy was out of the question, and so was poetry; that is, such poetry as he possessed. He had not sounded her literary tastes, and strongly suspected she had none; that she would have rejected The Duchess as readily as Mrs. Humphry Ward. He compromised on a magazine.

It had entertained her passably, she admitted, upon returning it. A New England story had puzzled her, it was true, and a Creole tale had offended her, but the pictures had pleased her greatly, especially one which had reminded her so strongly of Montéclin after a hard day's ride that she was loath to give it up. It was one of Remington's Cowboys, and Gouvernail insisted upon her keeping it,—keeping the magazine.

He spoke to her daily after that, and was always eager to render her some service or to do something towards her entertainment.

One afternoon he took her out to the lake end. She had been there once, some years before, but in winter, so the trip was comparatively new and strange to her. The large expanse of water studded with pleasure-boats, the sight of children playing merrily along the grassy palisades, the music, all enchanted her. Gouvernail thought her the most beautiful woman he had ever seen. Even her gown—the sprigged muslin—appeared to him the most charming one imaginable. Nor could anything be more becoming than the arrangement of her brown hair under the white sailor hat, all rolled back in a soft puff from her radiant face. And she carried her parasol and lifted her skirts and used her fan in ways that seemed quite unique and peculiar to herself, and which he considered almost worthy of study and imitation.

They did not dine out there at the water's edge, as they might have done, but returned early to the city to avoid the crowd. Athénaïse wanted to go home, for she said Sylvie would have dinner prepared and would be expecting her. But it was not difficult to persuade her to dine instead in the quiet little restaurant that he knew and liked, with its sanded floor, its secluded atmosphere, its delicious menu, and its obsequious waiter wanting to know what he might have the honor of serving to "monsieur et madame." No wonder he made the mistake, with Gouvernail assuming such an air of proprietorship! But Athénaïse was very tired after it all; the sparkle went out of her face, and she hung draggingly on his arm in walking home.

He was reluctant to part from her when she bade him good-night at her door and thanked him for the agreeable evening. He had hoped she would sit outside until it was time for him to regain the newspaper office. He knew that she would undress and get into her peignoir and lie upon her bed; and what he wanted to do, what he would have given much to do, was to go and sit beside her, read to her something restful, soothe her, do her bidding, whatever it might be. Of course there was no use in thinking of that. But he was surprised at his growing desire to be serving her. She gave him an opportunity sooner than he looked for.

"Mr. Gouvernail," she called from her room, "will you be so kine as to call Pousette an' tell her she fo'got to bring my ice-water?"

He was indignant at Pousette's negligence, and called severely to her over the banisters. He was sitting before his own door, smoking. He knew that Athénaïse had gone to bed, for her room was dark, and she had opened the slats of the door and windows. Her bed was near a window.

Pousette came flopping up with the ice-water, and with a hundred excuses: "Mo pa oua vou à tab c'te lanuite, mo cri you pé gagni déja là-bas; parole! Vou pas cri conté ça Madame Sylvie?" She had not seen Athénaïse at table, and thought she was gone. She swore to this, and hoped Madame Sylvie would not be informed of her remissness.

A little later Athénaïse lifted her voice again: "Mr. Gouvernail, did you remark that young man sitting on the opposite side from us, coming in, with a gray coat an' a blue ban' aroun' his hat?"

Of course Gouvernail had not noticed any such individual, but he assured Athénaïse that he had observed the young fellow particularly.

"Don't you think he looked something, — not very much, of co'se, — but don't you think he had a little faux-air of Montéclin?"

"I think he looked strikingly like Montéclin," asserted Gouvernail, with the one idea of prolonging the conversation. "I meant to call your attention to the resemblance, and something drove it out of my head."

"The same with me," returned Athénaïse. "Ah, my dear Montéclin! I wonder w'at he is doing now?"

"Did you receive any news, any letter from him to-day?" asked Gouvernail, determined that if the conversation ceased it should not be through lack of effort on his part to sustain it.

"Not to-day, but yesterday. He tells me that maman was so distracted with uneasiness that finally, to pacify her, he was fo'ced to confess that he knew w'ere I was, but that he was boun' by a vow of secrecy not to reveal it. But Cazeau has not noticed him or spoken to him since he threaten' to throw po' Montéclin in Cane river. You know Cazeau wrote me a letter the morning I lef', thinking I had gone to the rigolet. An' maman opened it, an' said it was full of the mos' noble sentiments, an' she wanted Montéclin to sen' it to me; but Montéclin refuse' poin' blank, so he wrote to me."

Gouvernail preferred to talk of Montéclin. He pictured Cazeau as unbearable, and did not like to think of him.

A little later Athénaïse called out, "Good-night, Mr. Gouvernail."

"Good-night," he returned reluctantly. And when he thought that she was sleeping, he got up and went away to the midnight pandemonium of his newspaper office.

– IX –

Athénaïse could not have held out through the month had it not been for Gouvernail. With the need of caution and secrecy always uppermost in her mind, she made no new acquaintances, and she did not seek out persons already known to her; however, she knew so few, it required little effort to keep out of their way. As for Sylvie, almost every moment of her time was occupied in looking after her house; and, moreover, her deferential attitude towards her lodgers forbade anything like the gossipy chats in which Athénaïse might have condescended sometimes to indulge with her land-lady. The transient lodgers, who came and went, she never had occasion to meet. Hence she was entirely dependent upon Gouvernail for company.

He appreciated the situation fully; and every moment that he could spare from his work he devoted to her entertainment. She liked to be out of doors, and they strolled together in the summer twilight through the mazes of the old French quarter. They went again to the lake end, and stayed for hours on the water; returning so late that the streets through which they passed were silent and deserted. On Sunday morning he arose at an unconscionable hour to take her to the French market, knowing that the sights and sounds there would interest her. And he did not join the intellectual coterie in the afternoon, as he usually did, but placed himself all day at the disposition and service of Athénaïse.

Notwithstanding all, his manner toward her was tactful, and evinced intelligence and a deep knowledge of her character, surprising upon so brief an acquaintance. For the time he was everything to her that she would have him; he replaced home and friends. Sometimes she wondered if he had ever loved a woman. She could not fancy him loving any one passionately, rudely, offensively, as Cazeau loved her. Once she was so naïve as to ask him outright if he had ever been in love, and he assured her promptly that he had not. She thought it an admirable trait in his character, and esteemed him greatly therefor.

He found her crying one night, not openly or violently. She was leaning over the gallery rail, watching the toads that hopped about in the moonlight, down on the damp flagstones of the courtyard. There was an oppressively sweet odor rising from the cape jessamine. Pousette was down there, mumbling and quarreling with some one, and seeming to be having it all her own way,—as well she might, when her companion was only a black cat that had come in from a neighboring yard to keep her company.

Athénaïse did admit feeling heart-sick, body-sick, when he questioned her; she supposed it was nothing but homesick. A letter from Montéclin had stirred her all up. She longed for her mother, for Montéclin; she was sick for a sight of the cotton-fields, the scent of the ploughed earth, for the dim, mysterious charm of the woods, and the old tumble-down home on the Bon Dieu.

As Gouvernail listened to her, a wave of pity and tenderness swept through him. He took her hands and pressed them against him. He wondered what would happen if he were to put his arms around her.

He was hardly prepared for what happened, but he stood it courageously. She twined her arms around his neck and wept outright on his shoulder; the hot tears scalding his cheek and neck, and her whole body shaken in his arms. The impulse was powerful to strain her to him; the temptation was fierce to seek her lips; but he did neither.

He understood a thousand times better than she herself understood it that he was acting as substitute for Montéclin. Bitter as the conviction was, he accepted it. He was patient; he could wait. He hoped some day to hold her with a lover's arms. That she was married made no particle of difference to Gouvernail. He could not conceive or dream of it making a difference. When the time came that she wanted him,—as he hoped and believed it would come,—he felt he would have a right to her. So long as she did not want him, he had no right to her,—no more than her husband had. It was very hard to feel her warm breath and tears upon his cheek, and her struggling bosom pressed against him and her soft arms clinging to him and his whole body and soul aching for her, and yet to make no sign.

He tried to think what Montéclin would have said and done, and to act accordingly. He stroked her hair, and held her in a gentle embrace, until the tears dried and the sobs ended. Before releasing herself she kissed him against the neck; she had to love somebody in her own way! Even that he endured like a stoic. But it was well he left her, to plunge into the thick of rapid, breathless, exacting work till nearly dawn.

Athénaïse was greatly soothed, and slept well. The touch of friendly hands and caressing arms had been very grateful. Henceforward she would not be lonely and unhappy, with Gouvernail there to comfort her.

– X –

The fourth week of Athénaïse's stay in the city was drawing to a close. Keeping in view the intention which she had of finding some suitable and agreeable employment, she had made a few tentatives in that direction. But with the exception of two little girls who had promised to take piano lessons at a price that would be embarrassing to mention, these attempts had been fruitless. Moreover, the homesickness kept coming back, and Gouvernail was not always there to drive it away.

She spent much of her time weeding and pottering among the flowers down in the courtyard. She tried to take an interest in the black cat, and a mockingbird that hung in a cage outside the kitchen door, and a disreputable parrot that belonged to the cook next door, and swore hoarsely all day long in bad French.

Beside, she was not well; she was not herself, as she told Sylvie. The climate of New Orleans did not agree with her. Sylvie was distressed to learn this, as she felt in some measure responsible for the health and well-being of Monsieur Miché's sister; and she made it her duty to inquire closely into the nature and character of Athénaïse's malaise.

Sylvie was very wise, and Athénaïse was very ignorant. The extent of her ignorance and the depth of her subsequent enlightenment were bewildering. She stayed a long, long time quite still, quite stunned, after her interview with Sylvie, except for the short, uneven breathing that ruffled her bosom. Her whole being was steeped in a wave of ecstasy. When she finally arose from the chair in which she had been seated, and looked at herself in the mirror, a face met hers which she seemed to see for the first time, so transfigured was it with wonder and rapture.

One mood quickly followed another, in this new turmoil of her senses, and the need of action became uppermost. Her mother must know at once, and her mother must tell Montéclin. And Cazeau must know. As she thought of him, the first purely sensuous tremor of her life swept over her. She half whispered his name, and the sound of it brought red blotches into her cheeks. She spoke it over and over, as if it were some new, sweet sound born out of darkness and confusion, and reaching her for the first time. She was impatient to be with him. Her whole passionate nature was aroused as if by a miracle.

She seated herself to write to her husband. The letter he would get in the morning, and she would be with him at night. What would he say? How would he act? She knew that he would forgive her, for had he not written a letter? — and a pang of resentment toward Montéclin shot through her. What did he mean by withholding that letter? How dared he not have sent it?

Athénaïse attired herself for the street, and went out to post the letter which she had penned with a single thought, a spontaneous impulse. It would have seemed incoherent to most people, but Cazeau would understand.

She walked along the street as if she had fallen heir to some magnificent inheritance. On her face was a look of pride and satisfaction that passers-by noticed and admired. She wanted to talk to some one, to tell some person; and she stopped at the corner and told the oyster-woman, who was Irish, and who God-blessed her, and wished prosperity to the race of Cazeaus for generations to come. She held the oyster-woman's fat, dirty little baby in her arms and scanned it curiously and observingly, as if a baby were a phenomenon that she encountered for the first time in life. She even kissed it!

Then what a relief it was to Athénaïse to walk the streets without dread of being seen and recognized by some chance acquaintance from Red river! No one could have said now that she did not know her own mind.

She went directly from the oyster-woman's to the office of Harding & Offdean, her husband's merchants; and it was with such an air of partnership, almost proprietorship, that she demanded a sum of money on her husband's account, they gave it to her as unhesitatingly as they would have handed it over to Cazeau himself. When Mr. Harding, who knew her, asked politely after her health, she turned so rosy and looked so conscious, he thought it a great pity for so pretty a woman to be such a little goose.

Athénaïse entered a dry-goods store and bought all manner of things,—little presents for nearly everybody she knew. She bought whole bolts of sheerest, softest, downiest white stuff; and when the clerk, in trying to meet her wishes, asked if she intended it for infant's use, she could have sunk through the floor, and wondered how he might have suspected it.

As it was Montéclin who had taken her away from her husband, she wanted it to be Montéclin who should take her back to him. So she wrote him a very curt note,—in fact it was a postal card,—asking that he meet her at the train on the evening following. She felt convinced that after what had gone before, Cazeau would await her at their own home; and she preferred it so.

Then there was the agreeable excitement of getting ready to leave, of packing up her things. Pousette kept coming and going, coming and going; and each time that she quitted the room it was with something that Athénaïse had given her,—a handkerchief, a petticoat, a pair of stockings with two tiny holes at the toes, some broken prayer-beads, and finally a silver dollar.

Next it was Sylvie who came along bearing a gift of what she called "a set of pattern',"—things of complicated design which never could have been obtained in any new-fangled bazaar or pattern-store, that Sylvie had acquired of a foreign lady of distinction whom she had nursed years before at the St. Charles hotel. Athénaïse accepted and handled them with reverence, fully sensible of the great compliment and favor, and laid them religiously away in the trunk which she had lately acquired.

She was greatly fatigued after the day of unusual exertion, and went early to bed and to sleep. All day long she had not once thought of

Gouvernail, and only did think of him when aroused for a brief instant by the sound of his foot-falls on the gallery, as he passed in going to his room. He had hoped to find her up, waiting for him.

But the next morning he knew. Some one must have told him. There was no subject known to her which Sylvie hesitated to discuss in detail with any man of suitable years and discretion.

Athénaïse found Gouvernail waiting with a carriage to convey her to the railway station. A momentary pang visited her for having forgotten him so completely, when he said to her, "Sylvie tells me you are going away this morning."

He was kind, attentive, and amiable, as usual, but respected to the utmost the new dignity and reserve that her manner had developed since yesterday. She kept looking from the carriage window, silent, and embarrassed as Eve after losing her ignorance. He talked of the muddy streets and the murky morning, and of Montéclin. He hoped she would find everything comfortable and pleasant in the country, and trusted she would inform him whenever she came to visit the city again. He talked as if afraid or mistrustful of silence and himself.

At the station she handed him her purse, and he bought her ticket, secured for her a comfortable section, checked her trunk, and got all the bundles and things safely aboard the train. She felt very grateful. He pressed her hand warmly, lifted his hat, and left her. He was a man of intelligence, and took defeat gracefully; that was all. But as he made his way back to the carriage, he was thinking, "By heaven, it hurts, it hurts!"

– XI –

Athénaïse spent a day of supreme happiness and expectancy. The fair sight of the country unfolding itself before her was balm to her vision and to her soul. She was charmed with the rather unfamiliar, broad, clean sweep of the sugar plantations, with their monster sugar-houses, their rows of neat cabins like little villages of a single street, and their impressive homes standing apart amid clusters of trees. There were sudden glimpses of a bayou curling between sunny, grassy banks, or creeping sluggishly out from a tangled growth of wood, and brush, and fern, and poison-vines, and palmettos. And passing through the long stretches of monotonous woodlands, she would close her eyes and taste in anticipation the moment of her meeting with Cazeau. She could think of nothing but him.

It was night when she reached her station. There was Montéclin, as she had expected, waiting for her with a two-seated buggy, to which he had hitched his own swift-footed, spirited pony. It was good, he felt, to have her back on any terms; and he had no fault to find since she came of her own choice. He more than suspected the cause of her coming; her eyes and her voice and her foolish little manner went far in revealing the secret that was brimming over in her heart. But after he had deposited her at her own gate, and as he continued his way toward the rigolet, he could not help feeling that the affair had taken a very disappointing, an ordinary, a most commonplace turn, after all. He left her in Cazeau's keeping.

Her husband lifted her out of the buggy, and neither said a word until they stood together within the shelter of the gallery. Even then they did not speak at first. But Athénaïse turned to him with an appealing gesture. As he clasped her in his arms, he felt the yielding of her whole body against him. He felt her lips for the first time respond to the passion of his own.

The country night was dark and warm and still, save for the distant notes of an accordion which some one was playing in a cabin away off. A little negro baby was crying somewhere. As Athénaïse withdrew from her husband's embrace, the sound arrested her.

"Listen, Cazeau! How Juliette's baby is crying! Pauvre ti chou,[12] I wonder w'at is the matter with it?"   [1896]

---

[12]"Poor little dear."

CHARLES W. CHESNUTT

*C*harles *W. Chesnutt (1858–1932), author of short stories, novels, and a pio-neering biography of the abolitionist Frederick Douglass, is generally consid-ered, as Joyce Carol Oates has noted, to be "the first black writer to find a white readership in America." Chesnutt was born in Cleveland, Ohio, and moved with his family to Fayetteville, North Carolina, when he was eight years old. Educated at local schools, he became a schoolteacher and then a lawyer before his short stories began to appear regularly in newspapers and magazines. The quality of his fiction was recognized by William Dean Howells, one of the most influential American writers of the time, who compared Chesnutt's stories to the work of Henry James and Guy de Maupassant.*

Two collections of Chesnutt's short fiction, The Conjure Woman *and* The Wife of His Youth and Other Stories of the Color Line, *appeared in 1899. After publishing three novels a few years later, Chesnutt abandoned his career as a writer and spent the remaining years of his life as a businessman. Committed in his fiction to the theme of the dehumanizing effects of racial prej-udice in the United States, he expressed his ideas with characteristic irony when he stated that "the object of my writings would not be so much the eleva-tion of the colored people as the elevation of the whites—for I consider the unjust spirit of caste which is so insidious as to pervade a whole nation . . . as a barrier to the moral progress of the American people."*

The stories in The Conjure Woman *belong to the genre of regional fiction with their dramatization of the exotic folkways and dialect of characters marooned in backwater poverty and superstition. The title story from the col-lection* The Wife of His Youth *is a more mainstream, realistic narrative about the daunting challenges faced by African Americans after the Civil War. This was a period of white supremacy and black suppression in the South extolled in novels such as Thomas Dixon's* The Clansman *(1905), the best-seller later turned into the popular silent film* The Birth of a Nation. *As the critic William L. Howard recognized, a common thread running throughout Ches-nutt's compassionate stories is "the search for identity and the ambivalences a person of mixed blood experiences on such a search." In "The Wife of His Youth," Chesnutt dramatizes the difficulty of bridging the distance between the "talented tenth" (W. E. B. Du Bois's term to describe African Americans who succeeded in becoming middle class by the end of the nineteenth century), and the uneducated folk they have left behind. The story was first published in* The Atlantic Monthly *in 1898.*

RELATED COMMENTARY: *William Dean Howells, "Mr. Charles W. Ches-nutt's Stories," page 1365.*

The Wife of His Youth

– I –

Mr. Ryder was going to give a ball. There were several reasons why this was an opportune time for such an event.

Mr. Ryder might aptly be called the dean of the Blue Veins. The original Blue Veins were a little society of colored persons organized in a certain Northern city shortly after the war. Its purpose was to establish and maintain correct social standards among a people whose social condition presented almost unlimited room for improvement. By accident, combined perhaps with some natural affinity, the society consisted of individuals who were, generally speaking, more white than black. Some envious outsider made the suggestion that no one was eligible for membership who was not white enough to show blue veins. The suggestion was readily adopted by those who were not of the favored few, and since that time the society, though possessing a longer and more pretentious name, had been known far and wide as the "Blue Vein Society," and its members as the "Blue Veins."

The Blue Veins did not allow that any such requirement existed for admission to their circle, but, on the contrary, declared that character and culture were the only things considered; and that if most of their members were light-colored, it was because such persons, as a rule, had had better opportunities to qualify themselves for membership. Opinions differed, too, as to the usefulness of the society. There were those who had been known to assail it violently as a glaring example of the very prejudice from which the colored race had suffered most; and later, when such critics had succeeded in getting on the inside, they had been heard to maintain with zeal and earnestness that the society was a lifeboat, an anchor, a bulwark and a shield, — a pillar of cloud by day and of fire by night, to guide their people through the social wilderness. Another alleged prerequisite for Blue Vein membership was that of free birth; and while there was really no such requirement, it is doubtless true that very few of the members would have been unable to meet it if there had been. If there were one or two of the older members who had come up from the South and from slavery, their history presented enough romantic circumstances to rob their servile origin of its grosser aspects.

While there were no such tests of eligibility, it is true that the Blue Veins had their notions on these subjects, and that not all of them were equally liberal in regard to the things they collectively disclaimed. Mr. Ryder was one of the most conservative. Though he had not been among the founders of the society, but had come in some years later, his genius for social leadership was such that he had speedily become its recognized adviser and head, the custodian of its standards, and the preserver of its traditions. He shaped its social policy, was active in providing for its entertainment, and when the interest fell off, as it sometimes did, he fanned the embers until they burst again into a cheerful flame.

There were still other reasons for his popularity. While he was not as white as some of the Blue Veins, his appearance was such as to confer distinction upon them. His features were of a refined type, his hair was almost straight; he was always neatly dressed; his manners were irreproachable, and his morals above suspicion. He had come to Groveland a young man, and obtaining employment in the office of a railroad company as messenger had in time worked himself up to the position of stationery clerk, having charge of the distribution of the office supplies for the whole company. Although the lack of early training had hindered the orderly development of a naturally fine mind, it had not prevented him from doing a great deal of reading or from forming decidedly literary tastes. Poetry was his passion. He could repeat whole pages of the great English poets; and if his pronunciation was sometimes faulty, his eye, his voice, his gestures, would respond to the changing sentiment with a precision that revealed a poetic soul and disarmed criticism. He was economical, and had saved money; he owned and occupied a very comfortable house on a respectable street. His residence was handsomely furnished, containing among other things a good library, especially rich in poetry, a piano, and some choice engravings. He generally shared his house with some young couple, who looked after his wants and were company for him; for Mr. Ryder was a single man. In the early days of his connection with the Blue Veins he had been regarded as quite a catch, and young ladies and their mothers had manoeuvred with much ingenuity to capture him. Not, however, until Mrs. Molly Dixon visited Groveland had any woman ever made him wish to change his condition to that of a married man.

Mrs. Dixon had come to Groveland from Washington in the spring, and before the summer was over she had won Mr. Ryder's heart. She possessed many attractive qualities. She was much younger than he; in fact, he was old enough to have been her father, though no one knew exactly how old he was. She was whiter than he, and better educated. She had moved in the best colored society of the country, at Washington, and had taught in the schools of that city. Such a superior person had been eagerly welcomed to the Blue Vein Society, and had taken a leading part in its activities. Mr. Ryder had at first been attracted by her charms of person, for she was very good looking and not over twenty-five; then by her refined manners and the vivacity of her wit. Her husband had been a government clerk, and at his death had left a considerable life insurance. She was visiting friends in Groveland, and, finding the town and the people to her liking, had prolonged her stay indefinitely. She had not seemed displeased at Mr. Ryder's attentions, but on the contrary had given him every proper encouragement; indeed, a younger and less cautious man would long since have spoken. But he had made up his mind, and had only to determine the time when he would ask her to be his wife. He decided to give a ball in her honor, and at some time during the evening of the ball to offer her his heart and hand. He had no special fears about the outcome, but, with a little touch of romance, he wanted the surroundings to be in harmony with his own feelings when he should have received the answer he expected.

Mr. Ryder resolved that this ball should mark an epoch in the social history of Groveland. He knew, of course, — no one could know better, — the entertainments that had taken place in past years, and what must be done to surpass them. His ball must be worthy of the lady in whose honor it was to be given, and must, by the quality of its guests, set an example for the future. He had observed of late a growing liberality, almost a laxity, in social matters, even among members of his own set, and had several times been forced to meet in a social way persons whose complexions and callings in life were hardly up to the standard which he considered proper for the society to maintain. He had a theory of his own.

"I have no race prejudice," he would say, "but we people of mixed blood are ground between the upper and the nether millstone. Our fate lies between absorption by the white race and extinction in the black. The one doesn't want us yet, but may take us in time. The other would welcome us, but it would be for us a backward step. 'With malice towards none, with charity for all,' we must do the best we can for ourselves and those who are to follow us. Self-preservation is the first law of nature."

His ball would serve by its exclusiveness to counteract leveling tendencies, and his marriage with Mrs. Dixon would help to further the upward process of absorption he had been wishing and waiting for.

– II –

The ball was to take place on Friday night. The house had been put in order, the carpets covered with canvas, the halls and stairs decorated with palms and potted plants; and in the afternoon Mr. Ryder sat on his front porch, which the shade of a vine running up over a wire netting made a cool and pleasant lounging place. He expected to respond to the toast "The Ladies" at the supper, and from a volume of Tennyson — his favorite poet — was fortifying himself with apt quotations. The volume was open at "A Dream of Fair Women." His eyes fell on these lines, and he read them aloud to judge better of their effect: —

> At length I saw a lady within call,
>> Stiller than chisell'd marble, standing there;
> A daughter of the gods, divinely tall,
>> And most divinely fair.

He marked the verse, and turning the page read the stanza beginning, —

> O sweet pale Margaret,
> O rare pale Margaret.

He weighed the passage a moment, and decided that it would not do. Mrs. Dixon was the palest lady he expected at the ball, and she was of a rather ruddy complexion, and of lively disposition and buxom build. So he ran over the leaves until his eye rested on the description of Queen Guinevere:—

> She seem'd a part of joyous Spring:
> A gown of grass-green silk she wore,
> Buckled with golden clasps before;
> A light-green tuft of plumes she bore
> Closed in a golden ring.
>
> .   .   .   .   .   .
>
> She look'd so lovely, as she sway'd
> The rein with dainty finger-tips,
> A man had given all other bliss,
> And all his worldly worth for this,
> To waste his whole heart in one kiss
> Upon her perfect lips.

As Mr. Ryder murmured these words audibly, with an appreciative thrill, he heard the latch of his gate click, and a light foot-fall sounding on the steps. He turned his head, and saw a woman standing before his door.

She was a little woman, not five feet tall, and proportioned to her height. Although she stood erect, and looked around her with very bright and restless eyes, she seemed quite old; for her face was crossed and recrossed with a hundred wrinkles, and around the edges of her bonnet could be seen protruding here and there a tuft of short gray wool. She wore a blue calico gown of ancient cut, a little red shawl fastened around her shoulders with an old-fashioned brass brooch, and a large bonnet profusely ornamented with faded red and yellow artificial flowers. And she was very black—so black that her toothless gums, revealed when she opened her mouth to speak, were not red, but blue. She looked like a bit of the old plantation life, summoned up from the past by the wave of a magician's wand, as the poet's fancy had called into being the gracious shapes of which Mr. Ryder had just been reading.

He rose from his chair and came over to where she stood.

"Good-afternoon, madam," he said.

"Good-evenin', suh," she answered, ducking suddenly with a quaint curtsy. Her voice was shrill and piping, but softened somewhat by age. "Is dis yere whar Mistuh Ryduh lib, suh?" she asked, looking around her doubtfully, and glancing into the open windows, through which some of the preparations for the evening were visible.

"Yes," he replied, with an air of kindly patronage, unconsciously flattered by her manner, "I am Mr. Ryder. Did you want to see me?"

"Yas, suh, ef I ain't 'sturbin' of you too much."

"Not at all. Have a seat over here behind the vine, where it is cool. What can I do for you?"

"'Scuse me, suh," she continued, when she had sat down on the edge of a chair, "'scuse me, suh, I's lookin' for my husban'. I heerd you wuz a big man an' had libbed heah a long time, an' I 'lowed you would n't min' ef I'd come roun' an' ax you ef you'd ever heerd of a merlatter man by de name er Sam Taylor 'quirin' roun' in de chu'ches ermongs' de people fer his wife 'Liza Jane?"

Mr. Ryder seemed to think for a moment.

"There used to be many such cases right after the war," he said, "but it has been so long that I have forgotten them. There are very few now. But tell me your story, and it may refresh my memory."

She sat back farther in her chair so as to be more comfortable, and folded her withered hands in her lap.

"My name's 'Liza," she began, "'Liza Jane. W'en I wuz young I us'ter b'long ter Marse Bob Smif, down in ole Missoura. I wuz bawn down dere. W'en I wuz a gal I wuz married ter a man named Jim. But Jim died, an' after dat I married a merlatter man named Sam Taylor. Sam wuz free-bawn, but his mammy and daddy died, an' de w'ite folks 'prenticed him ter my marster fer ter work fer 'im 'tel he wuz growed up. Sam worked in de fiel', an' I wuz de cook. One day Ma'y Ann, ole miss's maid, came rushin' out ter de kitchen, an' says she, ''Liza Jane, ole marse gwine sell yo' Sam down de ribber.'

"'Go way f'm yere,' says I; 'my husban' 's free!'

"'Don' make no diff'ence. I heerd ole marse tell ole miss he wuz gwine take yo' Sam 'way wid 'im ter-morrow, fer he needed money, an' he knowed whar he could git a t'ousan' dollars fer Sam an' no questions axed.'

"W'en Sam come home f'm de fiel' dat night, I tole him 'bout ole marse gwine steal 'im, an' Sam run erway. His time wuz mos' up, an' he swo' dat w'en he wuz twenty-one he would come back an' he'p me run erway, er else save up de money ter buy my freedom. An' I know he'd 'a' done it, fer he thought a heap er me, Sam did. But w'en he come back he did n' fin' me, fer I wuz n' dere. Ole marse had heerd dat I warned Sam, so he had me whip' an' sol' down de ribber.

"Den de wah broke out, an' w'en it wuz ober de cullud folks wuz scattered. I went back ter de ole home; but Sam wuz n' dere, an' I could n' l'arn nuffin' 'bout 'im. But I knowed he'd ben dere to look fer me an' had n' foun' me, an' had gone erway ter hunt fer me.

"I's be'n lookin' fer 'im eber sence," she added simply, as though twenty-five years were but a couple of weeks, "an' I knows he's be'n lookin' fer me. Fer he sot a heap er sto' by me, Sam did, an' I know he's be'n huntin' fer me all dese years,—'less'n he's be'n sick er sump'n, so he could n' work, er out'n his head, so he could n' 'member his promise. I went back down de ribber, fer I 'lowed he'd gone down dere lookin' fer me. I's be'n ter Noo Orleens, an' Atlanty, an' Charleston, an' Richmon'; an' w'en I'd be'n all ober de Souf I come ter de Norf. Fer I knows I'll fin' 'im some er dese days," she added softly, "er he'll fin' me, an' den we'll bofe be as happy in freedom as we wuz in de ole days befo' de wah." A smile stole over her withered countenance as she paused a moment, and her bright eyes softened into a far-away look.

This was the substance of the old woman's story. She had wandered a little here and there. Mr. Ryder was looking at her curiously when she finished.

"How have you lived all these years?" he asked.

"Cookin', suh. I's a good cook. Does you know anybody w'at needs a good cook, suh? I's stoppin' wid a cullud fam'ly roun' de corner yonder 'tel I kin git a place."

"Do you really expect to find your husband? He may be dead long ago."

She shook her head emphatically. "Oh no, he ain' dead. De signs an' de tokens tells me. I dremp three nights runnin' on'y dis las' week dat I foun' him."

"He may have married another woman. Your slave marriage would not have prevented him, for you never lived with him after the war, and without that your marriage does n't count."

"Would n' make no diff'ence wid Sam. He would n' marry no yuther 'ooman 'tel he foun' out 'bout me. I knows it," she added. "Sump'n 's be'n tellin' me all dese years dat I's gwine fin' Sam 'fo' I dies."

"Perhaps he's outgrown you, and climbed up in the world where he would n't care to have you find him."

"No, indeed, suh," she replied, "Sam ain' dat kin' er man. He wuz good ter me, Sam wuz, but he wuz n' much good ter nobody e'se, fer he wuz one er de triflin'es' han's on de plantation. I 'spec's ter haf ter suppo't 'im w'en I fin' 'im, fer he nebber would work 'less'n he had ter. But den he wuz free, an' he did n' git no pay fer his work, an' I don' blame 'im much. Mebbe he's done better sence he run erway, but I ain' 'spectin' much."

"You may have passed him on the street a hundred times during the twenty-five years, and not have known him; time works great changes."

She smiled incredulously. "I 'd know 'im 'mongs' a hund'ed men. Fer dey wuz n' no yuther merlatter man like my man Sam, an' I could n' be mistook. I's toted his picture roun' wid me twenty-five years."

"May I see it?" asked Mr. Ryder. "It might help me to remember whether I have seen the original."

As she drew a small parcel from her bosom he saw that it was fastened to a string that went around her neck. Removing several wrappers, she brought to light an old-fashioned daguerreotype in a black case. He looked long and intently at the portrait. It was faded with time, but the features were still distinct, and it was easy to see what manner of man it had represented.

He closed the case, and with a slow movement handed it back to her.

"I don't know of any man in town who goes by that name," he said, "nor have I heard of any one making such inquiries. But if you will leave me your address, I will give the matter some attention, and if I find out anything I will let you know."

She gave him the number of a house in the neighborhood, and went away, after thanking him warmly.

He wrote the address on the fly-leaf of the volume of Tennyson, and, when she had gone, rose to his feet and stood looking after her curiously. As she walked down the street with mincing step, he saw several persons whom she passed turn and look back at her with a smile of kindly amusement. When she had turned the corner, he went upstairs to his bedroom, and stood for a long time before the mirror of his dressing-case, gazing thoughtfully at the reflection of his own face.

– III –

At eight o'clock the ballroom was a blaze of light and the guests had begun to assemble; for there was a literary programme and some routine business of the society to be gone through with before the dancing. A black servant in evening dress waited at the door and directed the guests to the dressing-rooms.

The occasion was long memorable among the colored people of the city; not alone for the dress and display, but for the high average of intelligence and culture that distinguished the gathering as a whole. There were a number of school-teachers, several young doctors, three or four lawyers, some professional singers, an editor, a lieutenant in the United States army spending his furlough in the city, and others in various polite callings; these were colored, though most of them would not have attracted even a casual glance because of any marked difference from white people. Most of the ladies were in evening costume, and dress coats and dancing pumps were the rule among the men. A band of string music, stationed in an alcove behind a row of palms, played popular airs while the guests were gathering.

The dancing began at half past nine. At eleven o'clock supper was served. Mr. Ryder had left the ballroom some little time before the intermission, but reappeared at the supper-table. The spread was worthy of the occasion, and the guests did full justice to it. When the coffee had been served, the toast-master, Mr. Solomon Sadler, rapped for order. He made a brief introductory speech, complimenting host and guests, and then presented in their order the toasts of the evening. They were responded to with a very fair display of after-dinner wit.

"The last toast," said the toast-master, when he reached the end of the list, "is one which must appeal to us all. There is no one of us of the sterner sex who is not at some time dependent upon woman, — in infancy for protection, in manhood for companionship, in old age for care and comforting. Our good host has been trying to live alone, but the fair faces I see around me to-night prove that he too is largely dependent upon the gentler sex for most that makes life worth living,—the society and love of friends,—and rumor is at fault if he does not soon yield entire subjection to one of them. Mr. Ryder will now respond to the toast,—The Ladies."

There was a pensive look in Mr. Ryder's eyes as he took the floor and adjusted his eye-glasses. He began by speaking of woman as the gift of Heaven to man, and after some general observations on the relations of the sexes he said: "But perhaps the quality which most distinguishes woman is her fidelity and devotion to those she loves. History is full of examples, but has recorded none more striking than one which only to-day came under my notice."

He then related, simply but effectively, the story told by his visitor of the afternoon. He gave it in the same soft dialect, which came readily to his lips, while the company listened attentively and sympathetically. For the story had awakened a responsive thrill in many hearts. There were some present who had seen, and others who had heard their fathers and grandfathers tell, the wrongs and sufferings of this past generation, and all of them still felt, in their darker moments, the shadow hanging over them. Mr. Ryder went on:—

"Such devotion and confidence are rare even among women. There are many who would have searched a year, some who would have waited five years, a few who might have hoped ten years; but for twenty-five years this woman has retained her affection for and her faith in a man she has not seen or heard of in all that time.

"She came to me to-day in the hope that I might be able to help her find this long-lost husband. And when she was gone I gave my fancy rein, and imagined a case I will put to you.

"Suppose that this husband, soon after his escape, had learned that his wife had been sold away, and that such inquiries as he could make brought no information of her whereabouts. Suppose that he was young, and she much older than he; that he was light, and she was black; that their marriage was a slave marriage, and legally binding only if they chose to make it so after the war. Suppose, too, that he made his way to the North, as some of us have done, and there, where he had larger opportunities, had improved them, and had in the course of all these years grown to be as different from the ignorant boy who ran away from fear of slavery as the day is from the night. Suppose, even, that he had qualified himself, by industry, by thrift, and by study, to win the friendship and be considered worthy the society of such people as these I see around me to-night, gracing my board and filling my heart with gladness; for I am old enough to remember the day when such a gathering would not have been possible in this land. Suppose, too, that, as the years went by, this man's memory of the past grew more and more indistinct, until at last it was rarely, except in his dreams, that any image of this bygone period rose before his mind. And then suppose that accident should bring to his knowledge the fact that the wife of his youth, the wife he had left behind him,—not one who had walked by his side and kept pace with him in his upward struggle, but one upon whom advancing years and a laborious life had set their mark,—was alive and seeking him, but that he was absolutely safe from recognition or discovery, unless he chose to reveal himself. My friends, what would the man do? I will presume that he was one who loved honor, and tried to deal justly with all men. I will even carry the case further, and suppose that perhaps he had set his heart upon another, whom he had hoped to call his own. What would he do, or rather what ought he to do, in such a crisis of a lifetime?

"It seemed to me that he might hesitate, and I imagined that I was an old friend, a near friend, and that he had come to me for advice; and I argued the case with him. I tried to discuss it impartially. After we had looked upon the matter from every point of view, I said to him, in words that we all know:—

> 'This above all: to thine own self be true,
> And it must follow, as the night the day,
> Thou canst not then be false to any man.'[1]

Then, finally, I put the question to him, 'Shall you acknowledge her?'

"And now, ladies and gentlemen, friends and companions, I ask you, what should he have done?"

There was something in Mr. Ryder's voice that stirred the hearts of those who sat around him. It suggested more than mere sympathy with an imaginary situation; it seemed rather in the nature of a personal appeal. It was observed, too, that his look rested more especially upon Mrs. Dixon, with a mingled expression of renunciation and inquiry.

She had listened, with parted lips and streaming eyes. She was the first to speak: "He should have acknowledged her."

"Yes," they all echoed, "he should have acknowledged her."

"My friends and companions," responded Mr. Ryder, "I thank you, one and all. It is the answer I expected, for I knew your hearts."

He turned and walked toward the closed door of an adjoining room, while every eye followed him in wondering curiosity. He came back in a moment, leading by the hand his visitor of the afternoon, who stood startled and trembling at the sudden plunge into this scene of brilliant gayety. She was neatly dressed in gray, and wore the white cap of an elderly woman.

"Ladies and gentlemen," he said, "this is the woman, and I am the man, whose story I have told you. Permit me to introduce to you the wife of my youth."   [1898]

---

[1]From William Shakespeare's *Hamlet* (1.3.78–80); Polonius shares this advice with his son, Laertes, upon his departure for France.

STEPHEN CRANE

Stephen Crane (1871–1900) wrote some of the most memorable fiction and poetry ever created by an American, publishing fourteen books in his short lifetime. The poet John Berryman, who wrote a biography of Crane, observed the essential truth about him: "Crane was a writer and nothing else: a man alone in a room with the English language, trying to get human feelings right." Crane's style in his short stories is as intensely personal as Edgar Allan Poe's or Nathaniel Hawthorne's, but he did not use the techniques of fantasy and allegory. "His eyes remained wide open on his world. He was almost illusionless, whether about his subjects or himself. Perhaps his sole illusion was the heroic one; and not even this, especially if he was concerned in it himself as a man, escaped his irony."

Crane was born in Newark, New Jersey, the youngest of fourteen children. His father, a Methodist minister, died when Crane was just a boy, and his mother supported the family by writing articles for Methodist papers and reporting for the New York Tribune *and the* Philadelphia Press. *Crane briefly attended Lafayette College and Syracuse University before going to work in New York City as a freelance journalist. He became interested in life in the Bowery, one of the worst slums in New York, and he used this setting for his novel* Maggie: A Girl of the Streets, *a work so grimly naturalistic in its portrayal of slum life and so frank in its treatment of sex that Crane had to publish it at his own expense in 1893. Two years later he sold a long story about the Civil War to a syndicate for less than a hundred dollars. That work,* The Red Badge of Courage, *was such a vivid account of wartime experience—even though Crane had never been in a battle himself—that it established his literary reputation.*

In the last five years of his life, before he died of tuberculosis in Germany, Crane traveled extensively as a reporter, first to the American West, then to Florida. He couldn't keep away from scenes of war or revolution, believing— as did Ernest Hemingway after him—that "the nearer a writer gets to life, the greater he becomes as an artist." Crane was en route to Florida on the steamship Commodore *when the ship was wrecked on New Year's Day, 1897. He based one of his finest adventure stories, "The Open Boat," on what happened to him in a lifeboat with the other survivors. He had first reported the disaster in an article for his newspaper. Several months later, when he had moved to London with his common-law wife, Cora Crane, he wrote the humorous story "The Bride Comes to Yellow Sky." For its publication in* McClure's Magazine *in 1898, Crane received payment of less than three cents a word.*

The Bride Comes to Yellow Sky

–I–

The great Pullman was whirling onward with such dignity of motion that a glance from the window seemed simply to prove that the plains of Texas were pouring eastward. Vast flats of green grass, dull-hued spaces of mesquite and cactus, little groups of frame houses, woods of light and tender trees, all were sweeping into the east, sweeping over the horizon, a precipice.

A newly married pair had boarded this coach at San Antonio. The man's face was reddened from many days in the wind and sun, and a direct result of his new black clothes was that his brick-colored hands were constantly performing in a most conscious fashion. From time to time he looked down respectfully at his attire. He sat with a hand on each knee, like a man waiting in a barber's shop. The glances he devoted to other passengers were furtive and shy.

The bride was not pretty, nor was she very young. She wore a dress of blue cashmere, with small reservations of velvet here and there and with steel buttons abounding. She continually twisted her head to regard her puff sleeves, very stiff, straight, and high. They embarrassed her. It was quite apparent that she had cooked, and that she expected to cook, dutifully. The blushes caused by the careless scrutiny of some passengers as she had entered the car were strange to see upon this plain, under-class countenance, which was drawn in placid, almost emotionless lines.

They were evidently very happy. "Ever been in a parlor-car before?" he asked, smiling with delight.

"No," she answered. "I never was. It's fine, ain't it?"

"Great! And then after a while we'll go forward to the diner and get a big lay-out. Finest meal in the world. Charge a dollar."

"Oh, do they?" cried the bride. "Charge a dollar? Why, that's too much — for us — ain't it, Jack?"

"Not this trip, anyhow," he answered bravely. "We're going to go the whole thing."

Later, he explained to her about the trains. "You see, it's a thousand miles from one end of Texas to the other, and this train runs right across it and never stops but four times." He had the pride of an owner. He pointed out to her the dazzling fittings of the coach, and in truth her eyes opened wider as she contemplated the sea-green figured velvet, the shining brass, silver, and glass, the wood that gleamed as darkly brilliant as the surface of a pool of oil. At one end a bronze figure sturdily held a support for a separated chamber, and at convenient places on the ceiling were frescoes in olive and silver.

To the minds of the pair, their surroundings reflected the glory of their marriage that morning in San Antonio. This was the environment of

467

their new estate, and the man's face in particular beamed with an elation that made him appear ridiculous to the negro porter. This individual at times surveyed them from afar with an amused and superior grin. On other occasions he bullied them with skill in ways that did not make it exactly plain to them that they were being bullied. He subtly used all the manners of the most unconquerable kind of snobbery. He oppressed them, but of this oppression they had small knowledge, and they speedily forgot that infrequently a number of travelers covered them with stares of derisive enjoyment. Historically there was supposed to be something infinitely humorous in their situation.

"We are due in Yellow Sky at 3:42," he said, looking tenderly into her eyes.

"Oh, are we?" she said, as if she had not been aware of it. To evince surprise at her husband's statement was part of her wifely amiability. She took from a pocket a little silver watch, and as she held it before her and stared at it with a frown of attention, the new husband's face shone.

"I bought it in San Anton' from a friend of mine," he told her gleefully.

"It's seventeen minutes past twelve," she said, looking up at him with a kind of shy and clumsy coquetry. A passenger, noting this play, grew excessively sardonic, and winked at himself in one of the numerous mirrors.

At last they went to the dining-car. Two rows of negro waiters, in glowing white suits, surveyed their entrance with the interest and also the equanimity of men who had been forewarned. The pair fell to the lot of a waiter who happened to feel pleasure in steering them through their meal. He viewed them with the manner of a fatherly pilot, his countenance radiant with benevolence. The patronage, entwined with the ordinary deference, was not plain to them. And yet, as they returned to their coach, they showed in their faces a sense of escape.

To the left, miles down a long purple slope, was a little ribbon of mist where moved the keening Rio Grande. The train was approaching it at an angle, and the apex was Yellow Sky. Presently it was apparent that, as the distance from Yellow Sky grew shorter, the husband became commensurately restless. His brick-red hands were more insistent in their prominence. Occasionally he was even rather absent-minded and far-away when the bride leaned forward and addressed him.

As a matter of truth, Jack Potter was beginning to find the shadow of a deed weigh upon him like a leaden slab. He, the town marshal of Yellow Sky, a man known, liked, and feared in his corner, a prominent person, had gone to San Antonio to meet a girl he believed he loved, and there, after the usual prayers, had actually induced her to marry him, without consulting Yellow Sky for any part of the transaction. He was now bringing his bride before an innocent and unsuspecting community.

Of course, people in Yellow Sky married as it pleased them, in accordance with a general custom; but such was Potter's thought of his duty to his friends, or of their idea of his duty, or of an unspoken form which does not control men in these matters, that he felt he was heinous. He had committed an extraordinary crime. Face to face with this girl in San Antonio, and spurred by his sharp impulse, he had gone headlong over all the social hedges. At San Antonio he was like a man hidden in the dark. A knife to sever any friendly duty, any form, was easy to his hand in that remote city. But the hour of Yellow Sky, the hour of daylight, was approaching.

He knew full well that his marriage was an important thing to his town. It could only be exceeded by the burning of the new hotel. His friends could not forgive him. Frequently he had reflected on the advisability of telling them by telegraph, but a new cowardice had been upon him. He feared to do it. And now the train was hurrying him toward a scene of amazement, glee, and reproach. He glanced out of the window at the line of haze swinging slowly in towards the train.

Yellow Sky had a kind of brass band, which played painfully, to the delight of the populace. He laughed without heart as he thought of it. If the citizens could dream of his prospective arrival with his bride, they would parade the band at the station and escort them, amid cheers and laughing congratulations, to his adobe home.

He resolved that he would use all the devices of speed and plains-craft in making the journey from the station to his house. Once within that safe citadel, he could issue some sort of a vocal bulletin, and then not go among the citizens until they had time to wear off a little of their enthusiasm.

The bride looked anxiously at him. "What's worrying you, Jack?"

He laughed again, "I'm not worrying, girl. I'm only thinking of Yellow Sky."

She flushed in comprehension.

A sense of mutual guilt invaded their minds and developed a finer tenderness. They looked at each other with eyes softly aglow. But Potter often laughed the same nervous laugh. The flush upon the bride's face seemed quite permanent.

The traitor to the feelings of Yellow Sky narrowly watched the speeding landscape. "We're nearly there," he said.

Presently the porter came and announced the proximity of Potter's home. He held a brush in his hand and, with all his airy superiority gone, he brushed Potter's new clothes as the latter slowly turned this way and that way. Potter fumbled out a coin and gave it to the porter, as he had seen others do. It was a heavy and muscle-bound business, as that of a man shoeing his first horse.

The porter took their bag, and as the train began to slow they moved forward to the hooded platform of the car. Presently the two engines and their long string of coaches rushed into the station of Yellow Sky.

"They have to take water here," said Potter, from a constricted throat and in mournful cadence, as one announcing death. Before the train stopped, his eye had swept the length of the platform, and he was glad and astonished to see there was none upon it but the station-agent, who, with a slightly hurried and anxious air, was walking toward the water-tanks. When the train had halted, the porter alighted first and placed in position a little temporary step.

"Come on, girl," said Potter hoarsely. As he helped her down they each laughed on a false note. He took the bag from the negro, and bade his wife cling to his arm. As they slunk rapidly away, his hang-dog glance perceived that they were unloading the two trunks, and also that the station-agent far ahead near the baggage-car had turned and was running toward him, making gestures. He laughed, and groaned as he laughed, when he noted the first effect of his marital bliss upon Yellow Sky. He gripped his wife's arm firmly to his side, and they fled. Behind them the porter stood chuckling fatuously.

– II –

The California Express on the Southern Railway was due at Yellow Sky in twenty-one minutes. There were six men at the bar of the "Weary Gentleman" saloon. One was a drummer who talked a great deal and rapidly; three were Texans who did not care to talk at that time; and two were Mexican sheep-herders who did not talk as a general practice in the "Weary Gentleman" saloon. The barkeeper's dog lay on the board walk that crossed in front of the door. His head was on his paws, and he glanced drowsily here and there with the constant vigilance of a dog that is kicked on occasion. Across the sandy street were some vivid green grass plots, so wonderful in appearance amid the sands that burned near them in a blazing sun that they caused a doubt in the mind. They exactly resembled the grass mats used to represent lawns on the stage. At the cooler end of the railway station a man without a coat sat in a tilted chair and smoked his pipe. The fresh-cut bank of the Rio Grande circled near the town, and there could be seen beyond it a great, plum-colored plain of mesquite.

Save for the busy drummer and his companions in the saloon, Yellow Sky was dozing. The new-comer leaned gracefully upon the bar, and recited many tales with the confidence of a bard who has come upon a new field.

"——and at the moment that the old man fell down stairs with the bureau in his arms, the old woman was coming up with two scuttles of coal, and, of course—"

The drummer's tale was interrupted by a young man who suddenly appeared in the open door. He cried: "Scratchy Wilson's drunk, and has turned loose with both hands." The two Mexicans at once set down their glasses and faded out of the rear entrance of the saloon.

The drummer, innocent and jocular, answered: "All right, old man. S'pose he has. Come in and have a drink, anyhow."

But the information had made such an obvious cleft in every skull in the room that the drummer was obliged to see its importance. All had become instantly solemn. "Say," said he, mystified, "what is this?" His three companions made the introductory gesture of eloquent speech, but the young man at the door forestalled them.

"It means, my friend," he answered, as he came into the saloon, "that for the next two hours this town won't be a health resort."

The barkeeper went to the door and locked and barred it. Reaching out of the window, he pulled in heavy wooden shutters and barred them. Immediately a solemn, chapel-like gloom was upon the place. The drummer was looking from one to another.

"But, say," he cried, "what is this, anyhow? You don't mean there is going to be a gun-fight?"

"Don't know whether there'll be a fight or not," answered one man grimly. "But there'll be some shootin'—some good shootin'."

The young man who had warned them waved his hand. "Oh, there'll be a fight fast enough, if anyone wants it. Anybody can get a fight out there in the street. There's a fight just waiting."

The drummer seemed to be swayed between the interest of a foreigner and a perception of personal danger.

"What did you say his name was?" he asked.

"Scratchy Wilson," they answered in chorus.

"And will he kill anybody? What are you going to do? Does this happen often? Does he rampage around like this once a week or so? Can he break in that door?"

"No, he can't break down that door," replied the barkeeper. "He's tried it three times. But when be comes you'd better lay down on the floor, stranger. He's dead sure to shoot at it, and a bullet may come through."

Thereafter the drummer kept a strict eye upon the door. The time had not yet been called for him to hug the floor, but, as a minor precaution, he sidled near to the wall. "Will he kill anybody?" he said again.

The men laughed low and scornfully at the question.

"He's out to shoot, and he's out for trouble. Don't see any good in experimentin' with him."

"But what do you do in a case like this? What do you do?"

A man responded: "Why, he and Jack Potter—"

"But," in chorus, the other men interrupted, "Jack Potter's in San Anton'."

"Well, who is he? What's he got to do with it?"

"Oh, he's the town marshal. He goes out and fights Scratchy when he gets on one of these tears."

"Wow," said the drummer, mopping his brow. "Nice job he's got."

The voices had toned away to mere whisperings. The drummer wished to ask further questions which were born of an increasing anxiety and bewilderment; but when he attempted them, the men merely looked at him in irritation and motioned him to remain silent. A tense waiting hush was upon them. In the deep shadows of the room their eyes shone as they listened for sounds from the street. One man made three gestures at the barkeeper, and the latter, moving like a ghost, handed him a glass and a bottle. The man poured a full glass of whisky, and set down the bottle noiselessly. He gulped the whisky in a swallow, and turned again toward the door in immovable silence. The drummer saw that the barkeeper, without a sound, had taken a Winchester from beneath the bar. Later he saw this individual beckoning to him, so he tiptoed across the room.

"You better come with me back of the bar."

"No, thanks," said the drummer, perspiring. "I'd rather be where I can make a break for the back door."

Whereupon the man of bottles made a kindly but peremptory gesture. The drummer obeyed it, and finding himself seated on a box with his head below the level of the bar, balm was laid upon his soul at sight of various zinc and copper fittings that bore a resemblance to armorplate. The barkeeper took a seat comfortably upon an adjacent box.

"You see," he whispered, "this here Scratchy Wilson is a wonder with a gun—a perfect wonder—and when he goes on the war trail, we hunt our holes—naturally. He's about the last one of the old gang that used to hang out along the river here. He's a terror when he's drunk. When he's sober he's all right—kind of simple—wouldn't hurt a fly—nicest fellow in town. But when he's drunk—whoo!"

There were periods of stillness. "I wish Jack Potter was back from San Anton'," said the barkeeper. "He shot Wilson up once—in the leg—and he would sail in and pull out the kinks in this thing."

Presently they heard from a distance the sound of a shot, followed by three wild yowls. It instantly removed a bond from the men in the darkened saloon. There was a shuffling of feet. They looked at each other. "Here he comes," they said.

– III –

A man in a maroon-colored flannel shirt, which had been purchased for purposes of decoration and made, principally, by some Jewish women on the east side of New York, rounded a corner and walked into the middle of the main street of Yellow Sky. In either hand the man held a long, heavy, blue-black revolver. Often he yelled, and these cries rang through a semblance of a deserted village, shrilly flying over the roofs in a volume that seemed to have no relation to the ordinary vocal strength of a man. It was as if the surrounding stillness formed the arch of a tomb over him. These cries of ferocious challenge rang against walls of silence. And his boots had red tops with gilded imprints, of the kind beloved in winter by little sledding boys on the hillsides of New England.

The man's face flamed in a rage begot of whisky. His eyes, rolling and yet keen for ambush, hunted the still doorways and windows. He walked with the creeping movement of the midnight cat. As it occurred to him, he roared menacing information. The long revolvers in his hands were as easy as straws; they were moved with an electric swiftness. The little fingers of each hand played sometimes in a musician's way. Plain from the low collar of the shirt, the cords of his neck straightened and sank, straightened and sank, as passion moved him. The only sounds were his terrible invitations. The calm adobes preserved their demeanor at the passing of this small thing in the middle of the street.

There was no offer of fight; no offer of fight. The man called to the sky. There were no attractions. He bellowed and fumed and swayed his revolvers here and everywhere.

The dog of the barkeeper of the "Weary Gentleman" saloon had not appreciated the advance of events. He yet lay dozing in front of his master's door. At sight of the dog, the man paused and raised his revolver humorously. At sight of the man, the dog sprang up and walked diagonally away, with a sullen head, and growling. The man yelled, and the dog broke into a gallop. As it was about to enter an alley, there was a loud noise, a whistling, and something spat the ground directly before it. The dog screamed, and, wheeling in terror, galloped headlong in a new direction. Again there was a noise, a whistling, and sand was kicked viciously before it. Fear-stricken, the dog turned and flurried like an animal in a pen. The man stood laughing, his weapons at his hips.

Ultimately the man was attracted by the closed door of the "Weary Gentleman" saloon. He went to it, and hammering with a revolver, demanded drink.

The door remaining imperturbable, he picked up a bit of paper from the walk and nailed it to the framework with a knife. He then turned his back contemptuously upon this popular resort, and walking to the opposite side of the street, and spinning there on his heel quickly and lithely, fired at the bit of paper. He missed it by a half inch. He swore at himself, and went away. Later, he comfortably fusilladed the windows of his most intimate friend. The man was playing with this town. It was a toy for him.

But still there was no offer of fight. The name of Jack Potter, his ancient antagonist, entered his mind, and he concluded that it would be a glad thing if he should go to Potter's house and by bombardment induce him to come out and fight. He moved in the direction of his desire, chanting Apache scalp-music.

When he arrived at it, Potter's house presented the same still front as had the other adobes. Taking up a strategic position, the man howled a challenge. But this house regarded him as might a great stone god. It gave no sign. After a decent wait, the man howled further challenges, mingling with them wonderful epithets.

Presently there came the spectacle of a man churning himself into deepest rage over the immobility of a house. He fumed at it as the winter wind attacks a prairie cabin in the North. To the distance there should have gone the sound of a tumult like the fighting of 200 Mexicans. As necessity bade him, he paused for breath or to reload his revolvers.

– IV –

Potter and his bride walked sheepishly and with speed. Sometimes they laughed together shamefacedly and low.

"Next corner, dear," he said finally.

They put forth the efforts of a pair walking bowed against a strong wind. Potter was about to raise a finger to point the first appearance of the new home when, as they circled the corner, they came face to face with a man in a maroon-colored shirt who was feverishly pushing cartridges into a large revolver. Upon the instant the man dropped his revolver to the ground, and, like lightning, whipped another from its holster. The second weapon was aimed at the bridegroom's chest.

There was a silence. Potter's mouth seemed to be merely a grave for his tongue. He exhibited an instinct to at once loosen his arm from the woman's grip, and he dropped the bag to the sand. As for the bride, her face had gone as yellow as old cloth. She was a slave to hideous rites gazing at the apparitional snake.

The two men faced each other at a distance of three paces. He of the revolver smiled with a new and quiet ferocity.

"Tried to sneak up on me," he said. "Tried to sneak up on me!" His eyes grew more baleful. As Potter made a slight movement, the man thrust his revolver venomously forward. "No, don't you do it, Jack Potter. Don't you move a finger toward a gun just yet. Don't you move an eyelash. The time has come for me to settle with you, and I'm goin' to do it my own way and loaf along with no interferin'. So if you don't want a gun bent on you, just mind what I tell you."

Potter looked at his enemy. "I ain't got a gun on me, Scratchy," he said. "Honest, I ain't." He was stiffening and steadying, but yet somewhere at the back of his mind a vision of the Pullman floated, the sea-green figured velvet, the shining brass, silver, and glass, the wood that gleamed as darkly brilliant as the surface of a pool of oil—all the glory of the marriage, the environment of the new estate. "You know I fight when it comes to fighting, Scratchy Wilson, but I ain't got a gun on me. You'll have to do all the shootin' yourself."

His enemy's face went livid. He stepped forward and lashed his weapon to and fro before Potter's chest. "Don't you tell me you ain't got no gun on you, you whelp. Don't tell me no lie like that. There ain't a man in Texas ever seen you without no gun. Don't take me for no kid." His eyes blazed with light, and his throat worked like a pump.

"I ain't takin' you for no kid," answered Potter. His heels had not moved an inch backward. "I'm takin' you for a——fool. I tell you I ain't got a gun, and I ain't. If you're goin' to shoot me up, you better begin now. You'll never get a chance like this again."

So much enforced reasoning had told on Wilson's rage. He was calmer. "If you ain't got a gun, why ain't you got a gun?" he sneered. "Been to Sunday-school?"

"I ain't got a gun because I've just come from San Anton' with my wife. I'm married," said Potter. "And if I'd thought there was going to be any galoots like you prowling around when I brought my wife home, I'd had a gun, and don't you forget it."

"Married!" said Scratchy, not at all comprehending.

"Yes, married. I'm married," said Potter distinctly.

"Married?" said Scratchy. Seemingly for the first time he saw the drooping drowning woman at the other man's side. "No!" he said. He was like a creature allowed a glimpse of another world. He moved a pace backward, and his arm with the revolver dropped to his side. "Is this the lady?" he asked.

"Yes, this is the lady," answered Potter.

There was another period of silence.

"Well," said Wilson at last, slowly, "I s'pose it's all off now."

"It's all off if you say so, Scratchy. You know I didn't make the trouble." Potter lifted his valise.

"Well, I 'low it's off, Jack," said Wilson. He was looking at the ground. "Married!" He was not a student of chivalry; it was merely that in the presence of this foreign condition he was a simple child of the earlier plains. He picked up his starboard revolver, and placing both weapons in their holsters, he went away. His feet made funnel-shaped tracks in the heavy sand.   [1898]

ALICE DUNBAR-NELSON

Alice Dunbar-Nelson (1875–1935) was born in New Orleans, the daughter of working-class parents of mixed black, white, and Native American ancestry. Possessing a striking physical appearance, she could pass as white but she identified herself as a person of color. In her 1916 essay "People of Color in Louisiana," she explored the different definitions of Creole, stating that white people in Louisiana defined Creoles as whites who claimed French and Spanish ancestry, whereas people of color felt that everyone born in Louisiana was Creole "with the African strain slightly apparent."

After attending public high school in New Orleans, Dunbar-Nelson graduated from a two-year teachers' college and began a long career as a high school teacher to support her writing. She was twenty when she published her first book of poetry and sketches, Violets and Other Tales *(1895). Four years later appeared* The Goodness of St. Rocque, and Other Stories, *the first short story collection published in the United States by an African American. It contained local-color stories featuring poignant portraits of women who experience gender oppression, such as "Tony's Wife," set in New Orleans. By this time Dunbar-Nelson had left New Orleans to live in New York, Washington, D.C., and Wilmington, Delaware. In 1898 she briefly married the eminent African American poet Paul Laurence Dunbar, but they were separated by the time he died in 1906. Ten years later she married the journalist Robert J. Nelson.*

For most of her career Dunbar-Nelson wrote about race and gender conflicts as a journalist, columnist, and reviewer while continuing to teach and publish occasional stories in magazines and newspapers. She also edited Masterpieces of Negro Eloquence *(1914), which was a collection of speeches, and* The Dunbar Speaker and Entertainer *(1920), a magazine she started in an attempt to support herself after losing her twenty-year teaching job at a Delaware high school because of her political activism. In her short fiction she was not an experimenter like her contemporary Jean Toomer, but she used a conventional literary style to express the highly charged emotions of men and women trapped by poverty and circumstances beyond their control. In 1984 Gloria T. Hull edited* Give Us This Day: The Diary of Alice Dunbar-Nelson *from journals kept during the years 1921 and 1926–31.*

Tony's Wife

"Gimme fi' cents worth o'candy, please." It was the little Jew girl who spoke, and Tony's wife roused herself from her knitting to rise and count out the multi-hued candy which should go in exchange for the dingy nickel grasped in warm, damp fingers. Three long sticks, carefully wrapped

476

in crispest brown paper, and a half dozen or more of pink candy fish for lagniappe, and the little Jew girl sped away in blissful contentment. Tony's wife resumed her knitting with a stifled sigh until the next customer should come.

A low growl caused her to look up apprehensively. Tony himself stood beetle-browned and huge in the small doorway.

"Get up from there," he muttered, "and open two dozen oysters right away; the Eliots want 'em." His English was unaccented. It was long since he had seen Italy.

She moved meekly behind the counter, and began work on the thick shells. Tony stretched his long neck up the street.

"Mr. Tony, mama wants some charcoal." The very small voice at his feet must have pleased him, for his black brows relaxed into a smile, and he poked the little one's chin with a hard, dirty finger, as he emptied the ridiculously small bucket of charcoal into the child's bucket, and gave a banana for lagniappe.

The crackling of shells went on behind, and a stifled sob arose as a bit of sharp edge cut into the thin, worn fingers that clasped the knife.

"Hurry up there, will you?" growled the black brows; "the Eliots are sending for the oysters."

She deftly strained and counted them, and, after wiping her fingers, resumed her seat, and took up the endless crochet work, with her usual stifled sigh.

Tony and his wife had always been in this same little queer old shop on Prytania Street, at least to the memory of the oldest inhabitant in the neighbourhood. When or how they came, or how they stayed, no one knew; it was enough that they were there, like a sort of ancestral fixture to the street. The neighbourhood was fine enough to look down upon these two tumble-down shops at the corner, kept by Tony and Mrs. Murphy, the grocer. It was a semi-fashionable locality, far up-town, away from the old-time French quarter. It was the sort of neighbourhood where millionaires live before their fortunes are made and fashionable, high-priced private schools flourish, where the small cottages are occupied by aspiring school-teachers and choir-singers. Such was this locality, and you must admit that it was indeed a condescension to tolerate Tony and Mrs. Murphy.

He was a great, black-bearded, hoarse-voiced, six-foot specimen of Italian humanity, who looked in his little shop and on the prosaic pavement of Prytania Street somewhat as Hercules might seem in a modern drawing-room. You instinctively thought of wild mountain-passes, and the gleaming dirks of bandit contadini in looking at him. What his last name was, no one knew. Someone had maintained once that he had been christened Antonio Malatesta, but that was unauthentic, and as little to be believed as that other wild theory that her name was Mary.

She was meek, pale, little, ugly, and German. Altogether part of his arms and legs would have very decently made another larger than she. Her

hair was pale and drawn in sleek, thin tightness away from a pinched, pitiful face, whose dull cold eyes hurt you, because you knew they were trying
to mirror sorrow, and could not because of their expressionless quality. No
matter what the weather or what her other toilet, she always wore a thin
little shawl of dingy brick-dust hue about her shoulders. No matter what
the occasion or what the day, she always carried her knitting with her, and
seldom ceased the incessant twist, twist of the shining steel among the
white cotton meshes. She might put down the needles and lace into the
spool-box long enough to open oysters, or wrap up fruit and candy, or
count out wood and coal into infinitesimal portions, or do her housework;
but the knitting was snatched with avidity at the first spare moment, and
the worn, white, blue-marked fingers, half enclosed in kid-glove stalls for
protection, would writhe and twist in and out again. Little girls just learning to crochet borrowed their patterns from Tony's wife, and it was considered quite a mark of advancement to have her inspect a bit of lace done
by eager, chubby fingers. The ladies in larger houses, whose husbands
would be millionaires some day, bought her lace, and gave it to their servants for Christmas presents.

As for Tony, when she was slow in opening his oysters or in cooking
his red beans and spaghetti, he roared at her, and prefixed picturesque
adjectives to her lace, which made her hide it under her apron with a fear-
some look in her dull eyes.

He hated her in a lusty, roaring fashion, as a healthy beefy boy hates a
sick cat and torments it to madness. When she displeased him, he beat her,
and knocked her frail form on the floor. The children could tell when this
had happened. Her eyes would be red, and there would be blue marks on
her face and neck. "Poor Mrs. Tony," they would say, and nestle close to
her. Tony did not roar at her for petting them, perhaps, because they spent
money on the multi-hued candy in glass jars on the shelves.

Her mother appeared upon the scene once, and stayed a short time;
but Tony got drunk one day and beat her because she ate too much, and
she disappeared soon after. Whence she came and where she departed, no
one could tell, not even Mrs. Murphy, the Pauline Pry and Gazette of the
block.

Tony had gout, and suffered for many days in roaring helplessness, the
while his foot, bound and swathed in many folds of red flannel, lay on the
chair before him. In proportion as his gout increased and he bawled from
pure physical discomfort, she became light-hearted, and moved about the
shop with real, brisk cheeriness. He could not hit her then without such
pain that after one or two trials he gave up in disgust.

So the dull years had passed, and life had gone on pretty much the
same for Tony and the German wife and the shop. The children came on
Sunday evenings to buy the stick candy, and on week-days for coal and
wood. The servants came to buy oysters for the larger houses, and to gossip over the counter about their employers. The little dry woman knitted,
and the big man moved lazily in and out in his red flannel shirt, exchanged

politics with the tailor next door through the window, or lounged into Mrs. Murphy's bar and drank fiercely. Some of the children grew up and moved away, and other little girls came to buy candy and eat pink lagniappe fishes, and the shop still thrived.

One day Tony was ill, more than the mummied foot of gout, or the wheeze of asthma; he must keep his bed and send for the doctor.

She clutched his arm when he came, and pulled him into the tiny room.

"Is it——is it anything much, doctor?" she gasped.

Æsculapius shook his head as wisely as the occasion would permit. She followed him out of the room into the shop.

"Do you——will he get well, doctor?"

Æsculapius buttoned up his frock coat, smoothed his shining hat, cleared his throat, then replied oracularly,

"Madam, he is completely burned out inside. Empty as a shell, madam, empty as a shell. He cannot live, for he has nothing to live on."

As the cobblestones rattled under the doctor's equipage rolling leisurely up Prytania Street, Tony's wife sat in her chair and laughed,— laughed with a hearty joyousness that lifted the film from the dull eyes and disclosed a sparkle beneath.

The drear days went by, and Tony lay like a veritable Samson shorn of his strength, for his voice was sunken to a hoarse, sibilant whisper, and his black eyes gazed fiercely from the shock of hair and beard about a white face. Life went on pretty much as before in the shop; the children paused to ask how Mr. Tony was, and even hushed the jingles on their bell hoops as they passed the door. Red-headed Jimmie, Mrs. Murphy's nephew, did the hard jobs, such as splitting wood and lifting coal from the bin; and in the intervals between tending the fallen giant and waiting on the customers, Tony's wife sat in her accustomed chair, knitting fiercely, with an inscrutable smile about her purple compressed mouth.

Then John came, introducing himself, serpent-wise, into the Eden of her bosom.

John was Tony's brother, huge and bluff too, but fair and blond, with the beauty of Northern Italy. With the same lack of race pride which Tony had displayed in selecting his German spouse, John had taken unto himself Betty, a daughter of Erin, aggressive, powerful, and cross-eyed. He turned up now, having heard of this illness, and assumed an air of remarkable authority at once.

A hunted look stole into the dull eyes, and after John had departed with blustering directions as to Tony's welfare, she crept to his bedside timidly.

"Tony," she said,—"Tony, you are very sick."

An inarticulate growl was the only response.

"Tony, you ought to see the priest; you mustn't go any longer without taking the sacrament."

The growl deepened into words.

"Don't want any priest; you're always after some snivelling old woman's fuss. You and Mrs. Murphy go on with your church; it won't make *you* any better."

She shivered under this parting shot, and crept back into the shop. Still the priest came the next day.

She followed him in to the bedside and knelt timidly.

"Tony," she whispered, "here's Father Leblanc."

Tony was too languid to curse out loud; he only expressed his hate in a toss of the black beard and shaggy mane.

"Tony," she said nervously, "won't you do it now? It won't take long, and it will be better for you when you go —— Oh, Tony, don't —— don't laugh. Please, Tony, here's the priest."

But the Titan roared aloud: "No; get out. Think I'm a-going to give you a chance to grab my money now? Let me die and go to hell in peace."

Father Leblanc knelt meekly and prayed, and the woman's weak pleadings continued, ——

"Tony, I've been true and good and faithful to you. Don't die and leave me no better than before. Tony, I do want to be a good woman once, a real-for-true married woman. Tony, here's the priest; say yes." And she wrung her ringless hands.

"You want my money," said Tony, slowly, "and you sha'n't have it, not a cent; John shall have it."

Father Leblanc shrank away like a fading spectre. He came next day and next day, only to see re-enacted the same piteous scene,—the woman pleading to be made a wife ere death hushed Tony's blasphemies, the man chuckling in pain-racked glee at the prospect of her bereaved misery. Not all the prayers of Father Leblanc nor the wailings of Mrs. Murphy could alter the determination of the will beneath the shock of hair; he gloated in his physical weakness at the tenacious grasp on his mentality.

"Tony," she wailed on the last day, her voice rising to a shriek in its eagerness, "tell them I'm your wife; it'll be the same. Only say it, Tony, before you die!"

He raised his head, and turned stiff eyes and gibbering mouth on her; then, with one chill finger pointing at John, fell back dully and heavily.

They buried him with many honours by the Society of Italia's Sons. John took possession of the shop when they returned home, and found the money hidden in the chimney corner.

As for Tony's wife, since she was not his wife after all, they sent her forth in the world penniless, her worn fingers clutching her bundle of clothes in nervous agitation, as though they regretted the time lost from knitting.

[1899]

3

EARLY
TWENTIETH
CENTURY

1900–1940

*T*wenty-one years after publishing *Winesburg, Ohio* (1919), Sherwood Anderson wrote a letter to William Shaw, a sympathetic reader who had asked how Anderson's critics had affected him:

> The question you put to me is however a little difficult to answer. You see I have never been what is called a "Popular" writer nor do I believe I have ever aimed at being one. When some of my earlier books were published, a book like *Winesburg, Ohio,* for example, I was, for a time, rather deeply affected by the tone taken by most of the critics. There was a great deal of talk of what they called "sex-obsession." I was called "dirty-minded." In one New England town the book was publicly burned, in the town square, by the town library board. . . .

On January 6, 1940, when Anderson wrote this letter, the United States was in many ways a different country from what it had been when he first published *Winesburg, Ohio*. His early readers had come of age at the turn of the century, when three-fifths of the population still lived in rural environments.

Almost unbelievably, only 144 miles of roads in the United States had been paved by 1900. At that time the newly established electrical industry promised to bring lighting equipment to every household in towns and cities, but the electrification of rural America did not occur until the 1930s. Commercial radio, along with electric refrigerators and washing machines, arrived in the 1920s, when tractors began to replace horses on farms. In 1900 the average age at death was forty-eight. In 1901 the first international telephone call was made from Key West, Florida, to Havana, Cuba. Completed in 1902, the Flatiron Building in New York City, at twenty stories high, was then the city's tallest building. Orville and Wilbur Wright accomplished the first heavier-than-air flight at Kitty Hawk, North Carolina, in 1903, the same year that Edwin Porter directed *The Great Train Robbery*—at twelve minutes the longest film ever shown in the United

States. Henry Ford didn't sell his first Model T automobile until 1908. Sigmund Freud, the Austrian founder of psychoanalysis, visited the United States in 1909; his theories had not yet become popular, although they would later suggest to many Americans the sexual nature of the human libido and the powerful, masked force of the superego.

There was a tremendous difference between the way people lived in the United States at the beginning of the twentieth century and the way they lived in 1940, but scientific progress was only a part of it. If any single event can be said to have brought about a change in social consciousness, it was the Great War in Europe from 1914 to 1918, even if American casualties abroad were relatively light. "Never such innocence again," wrote the historian Paul Fussell in *The Great War and Modern Memory* (1975), quoting from a poem by the English writer Philip Larkin, who describes a photograph of smiling young men lined up outside a British recruiting station at the start of the war. World War I destroyed more than human lives; it also destroyed an essential social optimism in the United States and Europe. The wreckage of war was so widespread that it did not permit the illusion of heroism on the battlefield, and the failure of the League of Nations to prevent World War II compounded the disillusion.

In the early years of the twentieth century, many social changes began to occur in the United States. The women's movement gained momentum when radical women demonstrated for their rights to vote and earn fair wages. They started calling themselves "feminists" around 1912, the year before Margaret Sanger was jailed for thirty days in New York City for opening the first birth control clinic. In 1920 the sale of alcohol was banned by the Eighteenth Amendment. Later that year American women won the right to vote through the Nineteenth Amendment, legislation that passed by a majority of only one vote in the House of Representatives. The decades of Prohibition—the "Roaring Twenties" (for some) and the Great Depression of the beleaguered thirties—emphasized the fragility of the American social contract and its underlying economic system. The country returned to prosperity only by mobilizing for World War II after the Japanese attack on Pearl Harbor in December 1941.

American poets and novelists such as T. S. Eliot and F. Scott Fitzgerald used images of darkness and disillusionment in powerful works like *The Waste Land* (1922) and *The Great Gatsby* (1925) to dramatize their sense of a watershed in European and American culture after World War I, but American authors of short stories (with the notable exception of Ernest Hemingway) were slower to express their sense of apocalypse. Anderson understood their conservatism. He ended his letter to William Shaw by saying, "Granted the commercialism that, under our system, is a part of all publication, the influence of advertising etc., how can you expect anything but caution and the following of certain patterns, always on the safe side."

By the beginning of the twentieth century, commercialism encouraged the production of short stories in the United States as the market for short fiction rapidly expanded. Although Americans such as Edgar Allan Poe had been pioneers in the earliest years of the genre, the French author Guy de Maupassant and the Russian writer Anton Chekhov had become the most influential creators of short fiction by the 1920s. In particular, the work of Maupassant at the end of the previous century impressed many American writers, including Kate Chopin, Henry James, and Edith Wharton. In Wharton's 1925 monograph, *The Writing of Fiction,* she gave an eloquent account of the international, multicultural background that had shaped the development of the short story in its brief history, and explained the genre's contribution to world literature:

> When the great Russians (who owe to French culture much more than is generally conceded) took over that neat thing, the French *nouvelle,* they gave it the additional dimension it most often lacked. In any really good subject one has only to probe deep enough to come to tears; and the Russians almost always dig to that depth. The result has been to give to the short story, as French and Russian art have combined to shape it, great closeness of texture with profundity of form. Instead of a loose web spread over the surface of life they have made it, at its best, a shaft driven straight into the heart of human experience.

Wharton, who settled permanently in France in 1913, published her first collection of short fiction, *The Greater Inclination,* in 1899, and her last book of short stories, *Ghosts,* in 1937. Like her contemporaries Henry James, Willa Cather, and Theodore Dreiser, she wrote stories before she became a novelist, and yet despite achieving great renown as a novelist, she continued to publish stories throughout her career. "The Other Two" (1904), her ironic depiction of the emotional cost of divorce for a fashionable New York couple, illustrated what Wharton called "the newest social problem" for those wealthy enough to afford it.

Henry James published his earliest tale, "The Story of a Year," in *The Atlantic Monthly* in 1864 and went on to produce more than thirty stories in the next decade before turning to the novel. He explained his aim in writing what he called "short lengths" to the English novelist Robert Louis Stevenson in 1888: "I want to leave a multitude of pictures of my time, projecting my small circular frame upon as many different spots as possible and going in for number as well as quality, so that the number may constitute a total having a certain value as observation and testimony."

As a young writer, James took Hawthorne as his model and wrote a perceptive study of this early American writer's career. Later James repudiated Hawthorne's influence by saying, "I hate old New England stories — which are lean and pale and poor and ugly." In 1869 James traveled to Europe and absorbed European literature; six years later he left America to live permanently in England, returning for only brief visits, some of them to his friend Edith Wharton in her luxurious summer house in the Berkshires

of Massachusetts. He continued to publish occasional short stories along
with his novels in the early years of the new century, among them his
brilliantly imagined fictional account of an expatriate's return to New York
City in "The Jolly Corner" (1908).

Despite Wharton's and James's admiration for European writers of
short fiction, the influence of Europeans is less evident on American short
story authors than on American poets and novelists. The critic Philip Stevick
has argued in *The American Short Story, 1900–1945* (1984):

> If an O. Henry story looks, in certain respects, like a story by Mau-
> passant, it is not that O. Henry learned his craft from Maupassant,
> but that his native talents and the pressures of the marketplace
> encouraged the development of a form that happens to look like
> Maupassant at his most facile. . . . If an Anderson story looks, in cer-
> tain respects, like a story by Chekhov (Paul Rosenfeld, in 1922, called
> Anderson a "phallic Chekhov"), it is not that Anderson learned his
> craft from Chekhov but that, reacting against formula and respond-
> ing to the demands of his subject matter, he developed a form that
> happens to look like Chekhov's.
>
> Surely any number of writers, Hemingway, for example, were far
> better read than they ever chose to appear and, covering their tracks,
> absorbed more of what they had read than we will ever know. And
> any writer would at least have known the Europeans as their trans-
> lated stories appeared in the very magazines in which he published.
> Yet . . . American short fiction tends to make, in Hugh Kenner's
> phrase, "a homemade world."

> In short, then, the stories of the period participate in, and draw
> upon, the life of their time but not exactly in the ways that the other
> genres do. Eliot and Pound, the first generation of modernist poets
> in general, sought to "make it new" while simultaneously drawing
> upon the whole of the Western tradition. Writers of short fiction, on
> the contrary, their antennas remarkably attuned to the changes in our
> general sensibility, still sought to make an art form out of basically
> native materials.

The credit for the most ingenious use of "native materials" to meet his
readers' expectations of novelty in the early years of the new century must
be given to O. Henry, the pen name of William Sydney Porter, who
turned out hundreds of stories illustrating contemporary American settings and situations in his brief career as a writer. His sympathy for characters down on their luck pervades his best stories, such as "The Duplicity of
Hargraves" (1902).

The "O. Henry" surprise or "snapper" ending to a short, entertaining
plot was so widely imitated that it quickly became a formula. Porter was
writing during a boom period in American magazines. The production costs
of printed materials had been drastically reduced after the invention of the
halftone in the printing process, which cut the cost of an illustration in a

newspaper or magazine from $300 to $20. As Frederick Mott stated in *A History of American Magazines, 1865–1905* (1938), technical developments raised circulation considerably: In 1885 only 21 magazines sold more than a hundred thousand copies an issue, whereas in 1905 there were 159 magazines that had reached that figure. These included the *Saturday Evening Post* and the *Ladies' Home Journal,* two periodicals that paid handsomely for short stories to attract new readers to their glossy pages filled with advertisements.

This period of mass-market journalism was the first step toward our own age of film, television, and media innovation and saturation. As the New York *Nation* advertised, "Our short stories move rapidly, but it is a form of speed that is confined within the limits of each paragraph. Every sentence must have 'go' in it and stimulate the desire for the next sentence as an object in itself. . . . You must start at the crack of the pistol, not necessarily to tell your story, but to seize the attention."

Magazines publishing quality fiction now included *Harper's Magazine, Scribner's Magazine,* and *Century Magazine* as well as *The Atlantic Monthly.* In the first decades of the new century they solicited work from established authors such as Jack London after the success of his novel *The Call of the Wild* (1903). In the story "All Gold Canyon" (1905), London's approach went beyond local-color fiction and regionalism to naturalism, as he showed how a man's obsessive greed nearly destroyed him and his environment. Informed by the ideas in Charles Darwin's *The Origin of Species by Means of Natural Selection* (1859), London and his naturalist contemporaries such as Frank Norris and Theodore Dreiser believed that human beings lack free will because their actions are determined by their environment, so they are easily capable of regression to a savage state.

With mass-market journalism, the short story quickly became standardized by commercialization. In 1900 Dreiser complained that the majority of stories in American magazines pandered to their audience and showed "the almost complete absence of any reference to the coarse and the vulgar and the cruel and the terrible. . . . Almost invariably one's dreams came true in the magazines." Yet the outpouring of magazine stories also included works such as Dreiser's "The Lost Phœbe" (1916), a dark account of an old man's obsessive love for his dead wife, as well as quality stories by many young authors possessing distinctive voices who were continuing the tradition of regional short fiction, usually by focusing on the deprivations of American life.

For example, Willa Cather based "A Wagner Matinée" (1904) on her awareness of the pleasure offered by the thriving concert life of Boston to a culturally starved relative from Nebraska. Mary Austin fashioned tales and sketches such as "The Walking Woman" (1907) out of her sensitive responses to a woman's choice to live an independent life in the desert wilderness of New Mexico. Susan Glaspell converted her successful one-act play *Trifles* into the story "A Jury of Her Peers" (1917) for *Everyweek,* a large-circulation magazine, to dramatize the solidarity of women in rural Iowa who supported each other against patriarchal oppression.

By the turn of the century, the prosperity of magazines publishing short fiction encouraged editors to become less conservative and more attentive to minority voices as a growing number of immigrants swelled the cities' populations. By 1915 the industrial working class far outnumbered the middle class, and the poor constituted 65 percent of the population. In 1901 Zitkala-Sä (Gertrude Simmons Bonnin), the first Native American to create autobiographical short fiction, placed her story "The Trial Path" in *Harper's Magazine*. Sui Sin Far (Edith Maud Eaton), a Chinese American journalist, produced some of the earliest stories reflecting an ethnic experience outside the American mainstream in work such as "'Its Wavering Image'" (1912). Anzia Yezierska wrote stories such as "My Own People" (1920) about the difficult adjustment to the New World experienced by recent Jewish immigrants from Eastern Europe. New magazines such as *The Crisis* and *Masses* began to publish stories dramatizing the social issues of homophobia and racism. Sherwood Anderson's "Hands," the first story of his collection *Winesburg, Ohio* (1919), was originally published in *Masses* in 1916.

Short fiction became so abundant that in 1915 the editor Edward J. O'Brien began to publish an annual volume of what he considered to be the best short stories of the year, *Best Short Stories,* later titled *Best American Short Stories*. O'Brien's editorial choices were often ethnically diverse as he deliberately sought good fiction by immigrant and minority writers to illustrate his faith in the American melting pot. Three years later, a second annual volume was inaugurated by the New York Society of Arts and Sciences and published by Doubleday as the *O. Henry Memorial Award Prize Stories;* both annuals have survived to the present day.

Near the end of his life, in 1920, the distinguished author William Dean Howells edited *The Great Modern American Short Stories,* which included Charlotte Perkins Gilman's "The Yellow Wallpaper," Madelene Yale Wynne's "The Little Room," and Dreiser's "The Lost Phœbe." Writing about short fiction, Howells questioned the importance of the magazine story in our cultural life: "Is it because American life is scrappy and desultory and instinctively seeks its expression in the sketch, the little tale, the miniature romance; or because the short story seems in all literatures to find its development earlier than [a new author's] full-sized novel? Did our skill in writing short stories create the demand for them in the magazines or did the demand of the magazines foster the skill?"

Howells's questions might have been prompted by the vitality characterizing the work of a new generation of American short story writers who began to publish after World War I. The pace of modern life had accelerated until every decade seemed to bring with it a new social crisis, and every generation seemed to respond with a new group of talented storytellers who reflected their rapidly changing times.

Sherwood Anderson was the first representative of the group of writers who would be termed modernists by later critics. In 1919, *Winesburg, Ohio,* Anderson's book of linked stories, became a landmark volume in the history of American short fiction. As John Updike recognized in his essay "Twisted Apples" (1984), "the wide-eyed eagerness with which Anderson pursued the mystery of the meager lives of Winesburg opened Michigan to Hemingway, and Mississippi to Faulkner; a way had been shown to a new directness and a freedom from contrivance." Modernist short story authors such as Anderson, Hemingway, William Faulkner, Katherine Anne Porter, Jean Toomer, and Zora Neale Hurston, who wrote in the first half of the twentieth century, were determined to break free of tradition and create a new kind of narrative often relying on thematic irony and linguistic innovation.

One of the earliest modernists was Gertrude Stein, an American who began to write after she moved to Paris. Her book *Three Lives* (1909), three long stories about an uneducated African American woman and two German immigrant women, so impressed Anderson that he began to experiment with a new approach to fiction. Few writers took literary experimentation as far as Gertrude Stein, who lived on an inherited income and could attempt to rival James Joyce and Marcel Proust as an innovative stylist. As Ernest Hemingway remarked in a 1928 letter, since Stein "has taken up not making sense some eighteen years ago [she] has never known a moment's unhappiness with her work."

Hemingway suggested a change in American sensibility in his autobiographical story "Soldier's Home," which was included in his first collection of short fiction, *In Our Time* (1925). But it was his manner of writing as much as his subject matter that made him the most representative writer of his time and the most famous American writer of short stories to readers throughout the world. The English author H. E. Bates understood that Hemingway's style caused a revolution because he "was a man with an ax," cutting away the "cavernous gloom of explanations, discussions, social dilemmas, and philosophizings" in earlier fiction to reveal "the scattered bright scraps of pictorial narrative."

Since Washington Irving, writers of short fiction had used metaphors of art and painting to describe what they were doing. One of the earliest names for a short prose tale was the "sketch." Irving stated that he considered a story "merely as a frame on which to stretch" his materials; Edgar Allan Poe suggested that prose tales assumed the spatial form of painting in his 1842 review of Hawthorne's short fiction; Harriet Beecher Stowe wrote in her preface to *Oldtown Folks* (1869) that her "studies for this object have been Pre-Raphaelite," referring to a contemporary group of English painters; and James told Robert Louis Stevenson that he wanted "to leave a multitude of pictures" of his time.

Developing an interest in imagism, the use of clear and concise images that dominated the work of contemporary poets (Amy Lowell, Hilda

Doolittle, Ezra Pound, T. S. Eliot), Hemingway went further. His revolutionary prose style suggested the influence of Pound's advice in essays written in 1913 on the composition of imagist poetry:

1. Direct treatment of the "thing," without evasion or cliché.
2. The use of absolutely no word that does not contribute to the general design.
3. Fidelity to the rhythms of natural speech.
4. The natural object is always the adequate symbol.

Hemingway's pared-down, direct way of storytelling became the dominant narrative prose style of the twentieth century. His stories were so spare and intensely understated that they created the suspicion, as Eudora Welty understood in *Short Stories* (1949), that his "object is quite dark within, for all its clouds of speed, those primary colors of red and green and blue."

F. Scott Fitzgerald championed Hemingway's early stories and convinced him that an American author could earn substantial money writing short fiction in the 1920s. Fitzgerald confided to Hemingway in a 1925 letter that the *Saturday Evening Post,* flush with advertising revenue, was paying him $2,750 for a story. That year Fitzgerald earned more of his income writing magazine stories than he received from his royalties for his new novel, *The Great Gatsby.* As the writer John O'Hara stated, Fitzgerald "was an artist and at the same time enough of an artisan to sell stories to the *Saturday Evening Post* and still say what he wanted to say." In stories such as "Winter Dreams" (1922), Fitzgerald captured the giddiness and glitter of what he called "the Jazz Age" of the 1920s. He also encouraged his friend Ring Lardner to write sardonic stories such as "The Golden Honeymoon" (1922) to counteract what they both regarded as the prevailing sentimentality of most popular fiction.

In 1928 Edward J. O'Brien listed the top twenty-eight periodicals publishing quality stories. These included the *Saturday Evening Post, Cosmopolitan, MacLean's Magazine, Transition, Woman's Home Companion, McCall's,* the *Ladies' Home Journal, Good Housekeeping, Scribner's Magazine, The Atlantic Monthly,* and *American Mercury.* Their generous payments to talented authors often sustained them through lean times: in the 1930s William Faulkner said that he wrote his stories just to earn the money to pay his rent. Faulkner and Katherine Anne Porter, like Hemingway, were so gifted that their formal innovations expanded the technical possibilities of the short story. Porter's "He" (1927) and Faulkner's "Spotted Horses" (1930) exhibit virtuosic use of symbolic compression, manipulation of point of view, and complex arrangement of time.

The 1925 debut of *The New Yorker,* a new magazine featuring satiric sketches such as Dorothy Parker's "You Were Perfectly Fine" (1929)—a humorous account of a young man's night on the town getting around the restrictions of Prohibition—signaled the increasing sophistication of the short story marketplace. John O'Hara and James Thurber also regularly contributed stories to *The New Yorker;* soon the magazine had developed a style of its own, reflecting the tastes of its educated and affluent readers. As in the past century, American short fiction continued to be a sensitive barometer of social conditions.

In New York City, from 1917 to 1930, the cultural and artistic movement known as the Harlem Renaissance also encouraged the emergence of many young writers of short fiction. Jean Toomer, Zora Neale Hurston, Arna Bontemps, and Langston Hughes, among others, were welcomed in the pages of major black journals such as *The Crisis* and *Opportunity*. Their stories were recognized by literary critics as the work of important young authors who were expressing pride in their racial heritage.

Toomer's "Blood-Burning Moon" (1923) from his collection *Cane* was a pioneering story about southern black life that influenced Zora Neale Hurston's later stories set in Florida in *The Eatonville Anthology* (1927). Toomer brought the perspective of an urban outsider to his material, celebrating what he thought was the authentic spirit of a nearly obsolete black peasantry in rural Georgia; Hurston, on the other hand, had grown up in the type of all-black Florida community she described in stories such as "The Gilded Six-Bits" (1933). She wrote about her characters with an insider's knowledge and humorous affection.

The advent of the Great Depression in the 1930s darkened the mood of American storytellers as they chronicled the hard times in the nation. Arna Bontemps sympathetically depicted a poverty-stricken, devoted old black couple's double suicide in "A Summer Tragedy," first published in *Opportunity* in 1932. Langston Hughes, like Hurston, used a Florida setting for "Red-Headed Baby" (1934), but he wrote this story from a white narrator's point of view to emphasize the distance between whites and blacks in the United States. Richard Wright developed this theme even more subtly in "The Man Who Was Almost a Man" (1940). William Saroyan's "Seventy Thousand Assyrians" (1934) gave the theme of racial persecution a new twist, as two survivors of "ethnic cleansing" in the Old Country discover their common ground in a California barbershop. William Carlos Williams and Jack Conroy eloquently dramatized the strength and courage of recent immigrants and members of the working class in stories such as "The Use of Force" (1934) and "He Is Thousands" (1939).

The range of different voices heard in short fiction during the years of the Depression was made possible by the founding of many new magazines that were committed to experimental writing. Some, such as Jack Conroy's *Masses* and *The New Masses,* were engaged in radical politics. Others, such as *Pagany,* were started by writers who announced in their first issue, January–March 1930, that "it is neither entering into connection nor competition with any magazine trying to make a point, to formulate a policy." *Pagany* published innovative short stories by Williams, Gertrude Stein, and Erskine Caldwell, among others.

The 1930s short fiction written by John Steinbeck and Delmore Schwartz went beyond realism to suggest psychological implications that anticipated stories written after World War II. Steinbeck's "The Snake" (1935) portrayed a haunting encounter between a marine biologist, a caged rattlesnake, and a woman in a Monterey laboratory that troubled many readers. Critics offered Freudian and Jungian interpretations to explain the surrealistic imagery in Schwartz's "In Dreams Begin Responsibilities" (1937), which depicted a young man's anxious dream of a confrontation before his conception with the couple who became his parents. Then, as now, the growing complexity of American life was reflected in its stories.

Distinguished collections of short fiction published during the first decades of the twentieth century demonstrated an unprecedented variety of authors and subjects, beginning in 1901 with Zitkala-Sä's *Old Indian Legends,* the first book of authentic Native American stories. O. Henry's debut anthology, *Cabbages and Kings* (1904), announced the arrival of a writer whose popularity remained uncontested for many years. Willa Cather's first collection, *The Troll Gardens* (1905), which included seven stories, reflected her love of English literature and her sense of the difficulty of being a literary artist in the United States early in the century. Cather began her book with an epigraph from the English poet Christina Rossetti's "Goblin Market":

> We must not look at Goblin men,
>   We must not buy their fruits;
> Who knows upon what soil they fed
>   Their hungry thirsty roots?

Opposite the epigraph, on the handsomely printed title page of Cather's book, she included a quatrain by another English writer, Charles Kingsley, to suggest the theme of many of her stories—the work of the artist was to make "always things rare and strange." Four other collections reflecting the wide range of women's writing during this period were Gertrude Stein's *Three Lives* (1909); Mary Austin's *Lost Borders* (1909); Sui Sin Far's *Mrs. Spring Fragrance* (1912), a novel in the form of linked stories; and Anzia Yezierska's *Hungry Hearts* (1920).

In 1919 Anderson's *Winesburg, Ohio* heralded the beginning of what later critics would call modernism in their overviews of the history of the American short story. Other important collections include F. Scott Fitzgerald's *Flappers and Philosophers* (1920) and *Tales of the Jazz Age* (1922), Jean Toomer's *Cane* (1923), Ernest Hemingway's *In Our Time* (1925)—first printed by a small press in Paris two years before as *in our time*—along with Zora Neale Hurston's *The Eatonville Anthology* (1927), Katherine Anne Porter's *Flowering Judas and Other Stories* (1930) and *Pale Horse, Pale Rider* (1939), William Faulkner's *These Thirteen* (1931), Langston Hughes's *The Ways of White Folks* (1934), William Saroyan's *The Daring Young Man on the Flying Trapeze* (1934) and *My Name Is Aram* (1940),

John Steinbeck's *The Long Valley* (1938), William Carlos Williams's *Life along the Passaic River* (1938), and Richard Wright's *Uncle Tom's Children* (1938). This diversity of voices added new dimensions to the American short story as the country faced the challenge of World War II.

RELATED COMMENTARIES: *Sherwood Anderson, "Form, Not Plot, in the Short Story," page 1291; H. E. Bates, "Hemingway's Short Stories," page 1313; Zora Neale Hurston, "What White Publishers Won't Print," page 1368; Ruth Suckow, "The Short Story," page 1455; John Updike, "Twisted Apples: On* Winesburg, Ohio," *page 1464; Edith Wharton, "Every Subject Must Contain within Itself Its Own Dimensions," page 1473.*

ZITKALA-SÄ

Zitkala-Sä (Gertrude Simmons Bonnin) (1876–1938) was born at the Yankton Sioux Agency in South Dakota, the third child of Tate I Yohin Win (Reaches for the Wind), a full-blood Dakota woman, and a white man who deserted the mother before her daughter's birth. Zitkala-Sä was raised in the Dakota Sioux tribe, but in 1884 she was persuaded to follow missionaries back to a Quaker boarding school for Indians in Wabash, Indiana. She later wrote in American Indian Stories *(1921) that on her journey to Indiana she was "as frightened and bewildered as the captured young of a wild creature." After her first day at the school she felt she was "only one of many little animals driven by a herder." Most traumatic was the obligatory school haircut, since in her Sioux culture "short hair was worn by mourners, and shingled hair by cowards." When she heard the scissors "gnaw off" her thick braids, she felt that she had lost her tribal identity—and her spirit.*

After six years at the boarding school, Zitkala-Sä studied at Earlham College in Richmond, Indiana, from 1895 to 1897 and then began to teach at Carlisle Indian Industrial School in Pennsylvania in 1899. There, under the Lakota name Zitkala-Sä (Red Bird), she started to publish autobiographical stories in magazines. In 1900 The Atlantic Monthly *and* Harper's Magazine *were welcoming controversial material after their early conservatism, featuring articles and sketches responsive to the political movements begun in the 1880s to reform the United States' policy toward Native Americans. In this climate of interest, Zitkala-Sä published* Old Indian Legends, Retold by Zitkala-Sä *(1901) for the Boston educational publisher Ginn and Company, who sent her back to Yankton to collect stories from her tribe. She decided to stay on the reservation to live near her mother again. In 1902 she married Raymond Talesfase Bonnin, also a Yankton Sioux. They moved to the Uintah and Ouray Reservation near Fort Duchesne, Utah, where their son was born in 1903.*

In 1914 Zitkala-Sä became a member of the advisory board of the Society for the American Indian (SAI), founded in 1911. She and her husband and son lived in Washington, D.C., where she edited the SAI journal, the American Indian Magazine. *In 1921 she founded the Indian Welfare Committee, and three years later, when United States citizenship was finally granted to Native Americans, she coauthored the book* Oklahoma's Poor Rich Indians. *For the remainder of her life she tirelessly promoted the cause of Native American rights, and after her death she was buried in Arlington National Cemetery. "The Trial Path" was first published in* Harper's Magazine *in 1901 and was included in her second book,* American Indian Stories, *published in Washington, D.C., in 1921. This was a pioneering collection of autobiographical sketches in which Zitkala-Sä told about her tribal background in her own voice, without editorial intervention.*

The Trial Path

It was an autumn night on the plain. The smoke-lapels of the cone-shaped tepee flapped gently in the breeze. From the low night sky, with its myriad fire points, a large bright star peeped in at the smoke-hole of the wigwam between its fluttering lapels, down upon two Dakotas talking in the dark. The mellow stream from the star above, a maid of twenty summers, on a bed of sweetgrass, drank in with her wakeful eyes. On the opposite side of the tepee, beyond the centre fireplace, the grandmother spread her rug. Though once she had lain down, the telling of a story has aroused her to a sitting posture.

Her eyes are tight closed. With a thin palm she strokes her wind-shorn hair.

"Yes, my grandchild, the legend says the large bright stars are wise old warriors, and the small dim ones are handsome young braves," she reiterates, in a high, tremulous voice.

"Then this one peeping in at the smoke-hole yonder is my dear old grandfather," muses the young woman, in long-drawn-out words.

Her soft rich voice floats through the darkness within the tepee, over the cold ashes heaped on the centre fire, and passes into the ear of the toothless old woman, who sits dumb in silent reverie. Thence it flies on swifter wing over many winter snows, till at last it cleaves the warm light atmosphere of her grandfather's youth. From there her grandmother made answer:

"Listen! I am young again. It is the day of your grandfather's death. The elder one, I mean, for there were two of them. They were like twins, though they were not brothers. They were friends, inseparable! All things, good and bad, they shared together, save one, which made them mad. In that heated frenzy the younger man slew his most intimate friend. He killed his elder brother, for long had their affection made them kin."

The voice of the old woman broke. Swaying her stooped shoulders to and fro as she sat upon her feet, she muttered vain exclamations beneath her breath. Her eyes, closed tight against the night, beheld behind them the light of bygone days. They saw again a rolling black cloud spread itself over the land. Her ear heard the deep rumbling of a tempest in the west. She bent low a cowering head, while angry thunderbirds shrieked across the sky. "Heyä! heyä!" (No! no!) groaned the toothless grandmother at the fury she had awakened. But the glorious peace afterward, when yellow sunshine made the people glad, now lured her memory onward through the storm.

"How fast, how loud my heart beats as I listen to the messenger's horrible tale!" she ejaculates. "From the fresh grave of the murdered man he hurried to our wigwam. Deliberately crossing his bare shins, he sat down unbidden beside my father, smoking a long-stemmed pipe. He had scarce caught his breath when, panting, he began:

"'He was an only son, and a much-adored brother.'

"With wild, suspecting eyes he glanced at me as if I were in league with the man-killer, my lover. My father, exhaling sweet-scented smoke, assented—'How.' Then interrupting the 'Eya' on the lips of the round-eyed tale-bearer, he asked, 'My friend, will you smoke?' He took the pipe by its red-stone bowl, and pointed the long slender stem toward the man. 'Yes, yes, my friend,' replied he, and reached out a long brown arm.

"For many heart-throbs he puffed out the blue smoke, which hung like a cloud between us. But even through the smoke-mist I saw his sharp black eyes glittering toward me. I longed to ask what doom awaited the young murderer, but dared not open my lips, lest I burst forth into screams instead. My father plied the question. Returning the pipe, the man replied: 'Oh, the chieftain and his chosen men have had counsel together. They have agreed it is not safe to allow a man-killer loose in our midst. He who kills one of our tribe is an enemy, and must suffer the fate of a foe.'

"My temples throbbed like a pair of hearts!

"While I listened, a crier passed by my father's tepee. Mounted, and swaying with his pony's steps, he proclaimed in a loud voice these words (hark! I hear them now!): 'Ho-po! Give ear, all you people. A terrible deed is done. Two friends—ay, brothers in heart—have quarrelled together. Now one lies buried on the hill, while the other sits, a dreaded man-killer, within his dwelling. Says our chieftain: "He who kills one of our tribe commits the offence of an enemy. As such he must be tried. Let the father of the dead man choose the mode of torture or taking of life. He has suffered livid pain, and he alone can judge how great the punishment must be to avenge his wrong." It is done.

"'Come, every one, to witness the judgment of a father upon him who was once his son's best friend. A wild pony is now lassoed. The man-killer must mount and ride the ranting beast. Stand you all in two parallel lines from the centre tepee of the bereaved family to the wigwam opposite in the great outer ring. Between you, in the wide space, is the given trialway. From the outer circle the rider must mount and guide his pony toward the centre tepee. If, having gone the entire distance, the man-killer gains the centre tepee still sitting on the pony's back, his life is spared and pardon given. But should he fall, then he himself has chosen death.'

"The crier's words now cease. A lull holds the village breathless. Then hurrying feet tear along, swish, swish, through the tall grass. Sobbing women hasten toward the trialway. The muffled groan of the round camp-ground is unbearable. With my face hid in the folds of my blanket, I run with the crowd toward the open place in the outer circle of our village. In a moment the two long files of solemn-faced people mark the path of the public trial. Ah! I see strong men trying to lead the lassoed pony, pitching and rearing, with white foam flying from his mouth. I choke with pain as I recognize my handsome lover desolately alone, striding with set face toward the lassoed pony. 'Do not fall! Choose life and me!' I cry in my breast, but over my lips I hold my thick blanket.

"In an instant he has leaped astride the frightened beast, and the men have let go their hold. Like an arrow sprung from a strong bow, the pony, with extended nostrils, plunges halfway to the centre tepee. With all his might the rider draws the strong reins in. The pony halts with wooden legs. The rider is thrown forward by force, but does not fall. Now the maddened creature pitches, with flying heels. The line of men and women sways outward. Now it is back in place, safe from the kicking, snorting thing.

"The pony is fierce, with its large black eyes bulging out of their sockets. With humped back and nose to the ground, it leaps into the air. I shut my eyes. I cannot see him fall.

"A loud shout goes up from the hoarse throats of men and women. I look. So! The wild horse is conquered. My lover dismounts at the doorway of the centre wigwam. The pony, wet with sweat and shaking with exhaustion, stands like a guilty dog at his master's side. Here at the entranceway of the tepee sit the bereaved father, mother, and sister. The old warrior father rises. Stepping forward two long strides, he grasps the hand of the murderer of his only son. Holding it so the people can see, he cries, with compassionate voice, 'My son!' A murmur of surprise sweeps like a puff of sudden wind along the lines.

"The mother, with swollen eyes, with her hair cut square with her shoulders, now rises. Hurrying to the young man, she takes his right hand. 'My son!' she greets him. But on the second word her voice shook, and she turned away in sobs.

"The young people rivet their eyes upon the young woman. She does not stir. With bowed head, she sits motionless. The old warrior speaks to her. 'Shake hands with the young brave, my little daughter. He was your brother's friend for many years. Now he must be both friend and brother to you.'

"Hereupon the girl rises. Slowly reaching out her slender hand, she cries, with twitching lips, 'My brother!' The trial ends."

"Grandmother!" exploded the girl on the bed of sweet-grass. "Is this true?"

"Tosh!" answered the grandmother, with a warmth in her voice. "It is all true. During the fifteen winters of our wedded life many ponies passed from our hands, but this little winner, Ohiyesa, was a constant member of our family. At length, on that sad day your grandfather died, Ohiyesa was killed at the grave."

Though the various groups of stars which move across the sky, marking the passing of time, told how the night was in its zenith, the old Dakota woman ventured an explanation of the burial ceremony.

"My grandchild, I have scarce ever breathed the sacred knowledge in my heart. To-night I must tell you one of them. Surely you are old enough to understand.

"Our wise medicine-man said I did well to hasten Ohiyesa after his master. Perchance on the journey along the ghost-path your grandfather will weary, and in his heart wish for his pony. The creature, already bound on the spirit-trail, will be drawn by that subtle wish. Together master and beast will enter the next camp-ground."

The woman ceased her talking. But only the deep breathing of the girl broke the quiet, for now the night wind had lulled itself to sleep.

"Hinnu! hinnu! Asleep! I have been talking in the dark, unheard. I did wish the girl would plant in her heart this sacred tale," muttered she, in a querulous voice.

Nestling into her bed of sweet-scented grass, she dozed away into another dream. Still the guardian star in the night sky beamed compassionately down upon the little tepee on the plain.   [1901]

O. HENRY

O. Henry (1862–1910) was born William Sydney Porter in Greensboro, North Carolina. After rudimentary schooling he worked in a drugstore; then at the age of fourteen he moved to Texas, where he took a series of jobs over the next twenty years as a rancher, a bank teller, and the editor of a humorous weekly magazine called the Rolling Stone. *In 1896 he fled to Honduras after being indicted for alleged embezzlement of funds from the bank that had employed him. He protested his innocence, but he was arrested and convicted of the crime when he returned to the United States to be with his dying wife. While serving three years in the federal penitentiary in Columbus, Ohio, Porter began to write short stories under the pseudonym of O. Henry. It is thought that he got the idea for the name from a reference book he used at his job in the prison pharmacy.*

After his release from prison, O. Henry settled in New York City and began to contribute stories to the New York World *on a regular basis, turning out a story a week for thirty months. He took as his first subject adventure and revolution in Latin America when he debuted with a book of tales,* Cabbages and Kings, *in 1904. This collection became a best-seller, and before O. Henry's death from alcoholism six years later he followed it with twelve more volumes of short stories set in the United States, including* The Four Million *(1906),* Heart of the West *(1907),* The Trimmed Lamp *(1907),* The Gentle Grafter *(1908),* The Voice of the City *(1908),* Options *(1909),* Roads of Destiny *(1909),* Whirligigs *(1910), and* Strictly Business *(1910).*

A prolific writer of short stories, O. Henry was called "a Yankee Maupassant" after the French writer, whose tales in English translation were gaining popularity with American readers about the time O. Henry started his career. Like several of Maupassant's works of short fiction, the typical O. Henry story concludes with a surprise twist to the plot, or what he called a "snapper" ending, as in "The Duplicity of Hargraves," published in 1902 in The Junior Munsey. *Contemporary critics often fault the predictability of his stock story formulas and the facetiousness of his garrulous, breezy narrative style, but the literary historian Arthur Voss has pointed out that in O. Henry's stories the author is trying to "make the point that the humble, insignificant little people" are just as "admirable and their lives as worthy of attention and interest" as the wealthiest members of society.*

The Duplicity of Hargraves

When Major Pendleton Talbot, of Mobile, sir, and his daughter, Miss Lydia Talbot, came to Washington to reside, they selected for a boarding place a house that stood fifty yards back from one of the quietest avenues.

It was an old-fashioned brick building, with a portico upheld by tall white pillars. The yard was shaded by stately locusts and elms, and a catalpa tree in season rained its pink and white blossoms upon the grass. Rows of high box bushes lined the fence and walks. It was the Southern style and aspect of the place that pleased the eyes of the Talbots.

In this pleasant private boarding house they engaged rooms, including a study for Major Talbot, who was adding the finishing chapters to his book, *Anecdotes and Reminiscences of the Alabama Army, Bench, and Bar.*

Major Talbot was of the old, old South. The present day had little interest or excellence in his eyes. His mind lived in that period before the Civil War when the Talbots owned thousands of acres of fine cotton land and the slaves to till them; when the family mansion was the scene of princely hospitality, and drew its guests from the aristocracy of the South. Out of that period he had brought all its old pride and scruples of honor, an antiquated and punctilious politeness, and (you would think) its wardrobe.

Such clothes were surely never made within fifty years. The Major was tall, but whenever he made that wonderful, archaic genuflexion he called a bow, the corners of his frock coat swept the floor. That garment was a surprise even to Washington, which has long ago ceased to shy at the frocks and broad-brimmed hats of Southern Congressmen. One of the boarders christened it a "Father Hubbard," and it certainly was high in the waist and full in the skirt.

But the Major, with all his queer clothes, his immense area of plaited, raveling shirt bosom, and the little black string tie with the bow always slipping on one side, both was smiled at and liked in Mrs. Vardeman's select boarding house. Some of the young department clerks would often "string him," as they called it, getting him started upon the subject dearest to him—the traditions and history of his beloved Southland. During his talks he would quote freely from the *Anecdotes and Reminiscences.* But they were very careful not to let him see their designs, for in spite of his sixty-eight years he could make the boldest of them uncomfortable under the steady regard of his piercing gray eyes.

Miss Lydia was a plump, little old maid of thirty-five, with smoothly drawn, tightly twisted hair that made her look still older. Old-fashioned, too, she was; but antebellum glory did not radiate from her as it did from the Major. She possessed a thrifty common sense, and it was she who handled the finances of the family, and met all comers when there were bills to pay. The Major regarded board bills and wash bills as contemptible nuisances. They kept coming in so persistently and so often. Why, the Major wanted to know, could they not be filed and paid in a lump sum at some convenient period—say when the *Anecdotes and Reminiscences* had been published and paid for? Miss Lydia would calmly go on with her sewing and say, "We'll pay as we go as long as the money lasts, and then perhaps they'll have to lump it."

Most of Mrs. Vardeman's boarders were away during the day, being nearly all department clerks and business men; but there was one of them who was about the house a great deal from morning to night. This was a young man named Henry Hopkins Hargraves—every one in the house addressed him by his full name—who was engaged at one of the popular vaudeville theaters. Vaudeville has risen to such a respectable plane in the last few years, and Mr. Hargraves was such a modest and well-mannered person, that Mrs. Vardeman could find no objection to enrolling him upon her list of boarders.

At the theater Hargraves was known as an all-round dialect comedian, having a large repertoire of German, Irish, Swede, and black-face specialties. But Mr. Hargraves was ambitious, and often spoke of his great desire to succeed in legitimate comedy.

This young man appeared to conceive a strong fancy for Major Talbot. Whenever that gentleman would begin his Southern reminiscences, or repeat some of the liveliest of the anecdotes, Hargraves could always be found, the most attentive among his listeners.

For a time the Major showed an inclination to discourage the advances of the "play actor," as he privately termed him; but soon the young man's agreeable manner and indubitable appreciation of the old gentleman's stories completely won him over.

It was not long before the two were like old chums. The Major set apart each afternoon to read to him the manuscript of his book. During the anecdotes Hargraves never failed to laugh at exactly the right point. The Major was moved to declare to Miss Lydia one day that young Hargraves possessed remarkable perception and a gratifying respect for the old régime. And when it came to talking of those old days—if Major Talbot liked to talk, Mr. Hargraves was entranced to listen.

Like almost all old people who talk of the past, the Major loved to linger over details. In describing the splendid, almost royal, days of the old planters, he would hesitate until he had recalled the name of the negro who held his horse, or the exact date of certain minor happenings, or the number of bales of cotton raised in such a year; but Hargraves never grew impatient or lost interest. On the contrary, he would advance questions on a variety of subjects connected with the life of that time, and he never failed to extract ready replies.

The fox hunts, the 'possum suppers, the hoe-downs and jubilees in the negro quarters, the banquets in the plantation-house hall, when invitations went for fifty miles around; the occasional feuds with the neighboring gentry; the Major's duel with Rathbone Culbertson about Kitty Chalmers, who afterward married a Thwaite of South Carolina; and private yacht races for fabulous sums on Mobile Bay; the quaint beliefs, improvident habits, and loyal virtues of the old slaves—all these were subjects that held both the Major and Hargraves absorbed for hours at a time.

Sometimes, at night, when the young man would be coming upstairs to his room after his turn at the theater was over, the Major would appear at the door of his study and beckon archly to him. Going in, Hargraves would find a little table set with a decanter, sugar bowl, fruit, and a big bunch of fresh green mint.

"It occurred to me," the Major would begin — he was always ceremonious — "that perhaps you might have found your duties at the — at your place of occupation — sufficiently arduous to enable you, Mr. Hargraves, to appreciate what the poet might well have had in his mind when he wrote, 'tired Nature's sweet restorer' — one of our Southern juleps."

It was a fascination to Hargraves to watch him make it. He took rank among artists when he began, and he never varied the process. With what delicacy he bruised the mint; with what exquisite nicety he estimated the ingredients; with what solicitous care he capped the compound with the scarlet fruit glowing against the dark green fringe! And then the hospitality and grace with which he offered it, after the selected oat straws had been plunged into its tinkling depths!

After about four months in Washington, Miss Lydia discovered one morning that they were almost without money. The *Anecdotes and Reminiscences* was completed, but publishers had not jumped at the collected gems of Alabama sense and wit. The rental of a small house which they still owned in Mobile was two months in arrears. Their board money for the month would be due in three days. Miss Lydia called her father to a consultation.

"No money?" said he with a surprised look. "It is quite annoying to be called on so frequently for these petty sums. Really, I——"

The Major searched his pockets. He found only a two-dollar bill, which he returned to his vest pocket.

"I must attend to this at once, Lydia," he said. "Kindly get me my umbrella and I will go downtown immediately. The congressman from our district, General Fulghum, assured me some days ago that he would use his influence to get my book published at an early date. I will go to his hotel at once and see what arrangement has been made."

With a sad little smile Miss Lydia watched him button his "Father Hubbard" and depart, pausing at the door, as he always did, to bow profoundly.

That evening, at dark, he returned. It seemed that Congressman Fulghum had seen the publisher who had the Major's manuscript for reading. That person had said that if the anecdotes, etc., were carefully pruned down about one-half, in order to eliminate the sectional and class prejudice with which the book was dyed from end to end, he might consider its publication.

The Major was in a white heat of anger, but regained his equanimity, according to his code of manners, as soon as he was in Miss Lydia's presence.

"We must have money," said Miss Lydia, with a little wrinkle above her nose. "Give me the two dollars, and I will telegraph to Uncle Ralph for some to-night."

The Major drew a small envelope from his upper vest pocket and tossed it on the table.

"Perhaps it was injudicious," he said mildly, "but the sum was so merely nominal that I bought tickets to the theater to-night. It's a new war drama, Lydia. I thought you would be pleased to witness its first production in Washington. I am told that the South has very fair treatment in the play. I confess I should like to see the performance myself."

Miss Lydia threw up her hands in silent despair.

Still, as the tickets were bought, they might as well be used. So that evening, as they sat in the theater listening to the lively overture, even Miss Lydia was minded to relegate their troubles, for the hour, to second place. The Major, in spotless linen, with his extraordinary coat showing only where it was closely buttoned, and his white hair smoothly roached, looked really fine and distinguished. The curtain went up on the first act of *A Magnolia Flower,* revealing a typical Southern plantation scene. Major Talbot betrayed some interest.

"Oh, see!" exclaimed Miss Lydia, nudging his arm, and pointing to her program.

The Major put on his glasses and read the line in the cast of characters that her fingers indicated.

Col. Webster Calhoun. . . . Mr. Hopkins Hargraves.

"It's our Mr. Hargraves," said Miss Lydia. "It must be his first appearance in what he calls 'the legitimate.' I'm so glad for him."

Not until the second act did Col. Webster Calhoun appear upon the stage. When he made his entry Major Talbot gave an audible sniff, glared at him, and seemed to freeze solid. Miss Lydia uttered a little, ambiguous squeak and crumpled her program in her hand. For Colonel Calhoun was made up as nearly resembling Major Talbot as one pea does another. The long, thin white hair, curly at the ends, the aristocratic beak of a nose, the crumpled, wide, raveling shirt front, the string tie, with the bow nearly under one ear, were almost exactly duplicated. And then, to clinch the imitation, he wore the twin to the Major's supposed to be unparalleled coat. High-collared, baggy, empire-waisted, ample-skirted, hanging a foot lower in front than behind, the garment could have been designed from no other pattern. From then on, the Major and Miss Lydia sat bewitched, and saw the counterfeit presentment of a haughty Talbot "dragged," as the Major afterward expressed it, "through the slanderous mire of a corrupt stage."

Mr. Hargraves had used his opportunities well. He had caught the Major's little idiosyncrasies of speech, accent, and intonation and his pompous courtliness to perfection—exaggerating all to the purpose of the stage. When he performed that marvelous bow that the Major fondly imagined to be the pink of all salutations, the audience sent forth a sudden round of hearty applause.

Miss Lydia sat immovable, not daring to glance toward her father. Sometimes her hand next to him would be laid against her cheek, as if to conceal the smile which, in spite of her disapproval, she could not entirely suppress.

The culmination of Hargraves' audacious imitation took place in the third act. The scene is where Colonel Calhoun entertains a few of the neighboring planters in his "den."

Standing at a table in the center of the stage, with his friends grouped about him, he delivers that inimitable, rambling character monologue so famous in *A Magnolia Flower*, at the same time that he deftly makes juleps for the party.

Major Talbot, sitting quietly, but white with indignation, heard his best stories retold, his pet theories and hobbies advanced and expanded, and the dream of the *Anecdotes and Reminiscences* served, exaggerated and garbled. His favorite narrative—that of his duel with Rathbone Culbertson—was not omitted, and it was delivered with more fire, egotism, and gusto than the Major himself put into it.

The monologue concluded with a quaint, delicious, witty little lecture on the art of concocting a julep, illustrated by the act. Here Major Talbot's delicate but showy science was reproduced to a hair's breadth—from his dainty handling of the fragrant weed—"the one-thousandth part of a grain too much pressure, gentlemen, and you extract the bitterness, instead of the aroma, of this heaven-bestowed plant"—to his solicitous selection of the oaten straws.

At the close of the scene the audience raised a tumultuous roar of appreciation. The portrayal of the type was so exact, so sure and thorough, that the leading characters in the play were forgotten. After repeated calls, Hargraves came before the curtain and bowed, his rather boyish face bright and flushed with the knowledge of success.

At last Miss Lydia turned and looked at the Major. His thin nostrils were working like the gills of a fish. He laid both shaking hands upon the arms of his chair to rise.

"We will go, Lydia," he said chokingly. "This is an abominable—desecration."

Before he could rise, she pulled him back into his seat.

"We will stay it out," she declared. "Do you want to advertise the copy by exhibiting the original coat?" So they remained to the end.

Hargraves's success must have kept him up late that night, for neither at the breakfast nor at the dinner table did he appear.

About three in the afternoon he tapped at the door of Major Talbot's study. The Major opened it, and Hargraves walked in with his hands full of the morning papers—too full of his triumph to notice anything unusual in the Major's demeanor.

"I put it all over 'em last night, Major," he began exultantly. "I had my inning, and, I think, scored. Here's what *The Post* says:

> His conception and portrayal of the old-time Southern colonel,
> with his absurd grandiloquence, his eccentric garb, his quaint idioms

and phrases, his motheaten pride of family, and his really kind heart, fastidious sense of honor, and lovable simplicity, is the best delineation of a character rôle on the boards to-day. The coat worn by Colonel Calhoun is itself nothing less than an evolution of genius. Mr. Hargraves has captured his public.

"How does that sound, Major, for a first-nighter?"

"I had the honor"—the Major's voice sounded ominously frigid—"of witnessing your very remarkable performance, sir, last night."

Hargraves looked disconcerted.

"You were there? I didn't know you ever—I didn't know you cared for the theater. Oh, I say, Major Talbot," he exclaimed frankly, "don't you be offended. I admit I did get a lot of pointers from you that helped out wonderfully in the part. But it's a type, you know—not individual. The way the audience caught on shows that. Half the patrons of that theater are Southerners. They recognized it."

"Mr. Hargraves," said the Major, who had remained standing, "you have put upon me an unpardonable insult. You have burlesqued my person, grossly betrayed my confidence, and misused my hospitality. If I thought you possessed the faintest conception of what is the sign manual of a gentleman, or what is due one, I would call you out, sir, old as I am. I will ask you to leave the room, sir."

The actor appeared to be slightly bewildered, and seemed hardly to take in the full meaning of the old gentleman's words.

"I am truly sorry you took offense," he said regretfully. "Up here we don't look at things just as you people do. I know men who would buy out half the house to have their personality put on the stage so the public would recognize it."

"They are not from Alabama, sir," said the Major haughtily.

"Perhaps not. I have a pretty good memory, Major; let me quote a few lines from your book. In response to a toast at a banquet given in—Milledgeville, I believe—you uttered, and intend to have printed, these words:

> The Northern man is utterly without sentiment or warmth except in so far as the feelings may be turned to his own commercial profit. He will suffer without resentment any imputation cast upon the honor of himself or his loved ones that does not bear with it the consequence of pecuniary loss. In his charity, he gives with a liberal hand; but it must be heralded with the trumpet and chronicled in brass.

"Do you think that picture is fairer than the one you saw of Colonel Calhoun last night?"

"The description," said the Major, frowning "is—not without grounds. Some exag—latitude must be allowed in public speaking."

"And in public acting," replied Hargraves.

"That is not the point," persisted the Major, unrelenting. "It was a personal caricature. I positively decline to overlook it, sir."

"Major Talbot," said Hargraves, with a winning smile, "I wish you would understand me. I want you to know that I never dreamed of insulting you. In my profession, all life belongs to me. I take what I want, and what I can, and return it over the footlights. Now, if you will, let's let it go at that. I came in to see you about something else. We've been pretty good friends for some months, and I'm going to take the risk of offending you again. I know you are hard up for money—never mind how I found out, a boarding house is no place to keep such matters secret—and I want you to let me help you out of the pinch. I've been there often enough myself. I've been getting a fair salary all the season, and I've saved some money. You're welcome to a couple hundred—or even more—until you get——"

"Stop!" commanded the Major, with his arm outstretched. "It seems that my book didn't lie, after all. You think your money salve will heal all the hurts of honor. Under no circumstances would I accept a loan from a casual acquaintance; and as to you, sir, I would starve before I would consider your insulting offer of a financial adjustment of the circumstances we have discussed. I beg to repeat my request relative to your quitting the apartment."

Hargraves took his departure without another word. He also left the house the same day, moving, as Mrs. Vardeman explained at the supper table, nearer the vicinity of the downtown theater, where *A Magnolia Flower* was booked for a week's run.

Critical was the situation with Major Talbot and Miss Lydia. There was no one in Washington to whom the Major's scruples allowed him to apply for a loan. Miss Lydia wrote a letter to Uncle Ralph, but it was doubtful whether that relative's constricted affairs would permit him to furnish help. The Major was forced to make an apologetic address to Mrs. Vardeman regarding the delayed payment for board, referring to "delinquent rentals" and "delayed remittances" in a rather confused strain.

Deliverance came from an entirely unexpected source.

Late one afternoon the door maid came up and announced an old colored man who wanted to see Major Talbot. The Major asked that he be sent up to his study. Soon an old darkey appeared in the doorway, with his hat in hand, bowing, and scraping with one clumsy foot. He was quite decently dressed in a baggy suit of black. His big, coarse shoes shone with a metallic luster suggestive of stove polish. His bushy wool was gray—almost white. After middle life, it is difficult to estimate the age of a negro. This one might have seen as many years as had Major Talbot.

"I be bound you don't know me, Mars' Pendleton," were his first words.

The Major rose and came forward at the old, familiar style of address. It was one of the old plantation darkeys without a doubt; but they had been widely scattered, and he could not recall the voice or face.

"I don't believe I do," he said kindly—"unless you will assist my memory."

"Don't you 'member Cindy's Mose, Mars' Pendleton, what 'migrated 'mediately after de war?"

"Wait a moment," said the Major, rubbing his forehead with the tips of his fingers. He loved to recall everything connected with those beloved days. "Cindy's Mose," he reflected. "You worked among the horses—breaking the colts. Yes, I remember now. After the surrender, you took the name of—don't prompt me—Mitchell, and went to the West—to Nebraska."

"Yassir, yassir,"—the old man's face stretched with a delighted grin—"dat's him, dat's it. Newbraska. Dat's me—Mose Mitchell. Old Uncle Mose Mitchell, dey calls me now. Old mars', your pa, gimme a pah of dem mule colts when I lef' fur to staht me goin' with. You 'member dem colts, Mars' Pendleton?"

"I don't seem to recall the colts," said the Major. "You know. I was married the first year of the war and living at the old Follinsbee place. But sit down, sit down, Uncle Mose. I'm glad to see you. I hope you have prospered."

Uncle Mose took a chair and laid his hat carefully on the floor beside it.

"Yessir; of late I done mouty famous. When I first got to Newbraska, dey folks come all roun' me to see dem mule colts. Dey ain't see no mules like dem in Newbraska. I sold dem mules for three hundred dollars. Yessir—three hundred.

"Den I open a blacksmith shop, suh, and made some money and bought some lan'. Me and my old 'oman done raised up seb'm chillun, and all doin' well 'cept two of 'em what died. Fo' year ago a railroad come along and staht a town slam ag'inst my lan', and, suh, Mars' Pendleton, Uncle Mose am worth leb'm thousand dollars in money, property, and lan'."

"I'm glad to hear it," said the Major heartily. "Glad to hear it."

"And dat little baby of yon, Mars' Pendleton—one what you name Miss Lyddy—I be bound dat little tad done growed up tell nobody wouldn't know her."

The Major stepped to the door and called: "Lydie, dear, will you come?"

Miss Lydia, looking quite grown up and a little worried, came in from her room.

"Dar, now! What'd I tell you? I knowed dat baby done be plum growed up. You don't 'member Uncle Mose, child?"

"This is Aunt Cindy's Mose, Lydia," explained the Major. "He left Sunnymead for the West when you were two years old."

"Well," said Miss Lydia, "I can hardly be expected to remember you, Uncle Mose, at that age. And, as you say, I'm 'plum growed up,' and was a blessed long time ago. But I'm glad to see you, even if I can't remember you."

And she was. And so was the Major. Something alive and tangible had come to link them with the happy past. The three sat and talked over the olden times, the Major and Uncle Mose correcting or prompting each other as they reviewed the plantation scenes and days.

The Major inquired what the old man was doing so far from his home.

"Uncle Mose am a delicate," he explained, "to de grand Baptis' convention in dis city. I never preached none, but bein' a residin' elder in de church, and able fur to pay my own expenses, dey sent me along."

"And how did you know we were in Washington?" inquired Miss Lydia.

"Dey's a cullud man works in de hotel whar I stops, what comes from Mobile. He told me he seen Mars' Pendleton comin' outen dish here house one mawnin'.

"What I come fur," continued Uncle Mose, reaching into his pocket—"besides de sight of home folks—was to pay Mars' Pendleton what I owes him.

"Yessir—three hundred dollars." He handed the Major a roll of bills. "When I lef' old mars' says: 'Take dem mule colts, Mose, and, if it be so you gits able, pay fur 'em.' Yessir—dem was his words. De war had done lef' old mars' po' hisself. Old mars' bein' long ago dead, de debt descends to Mars' Pendleton. Three hundred dollars. Uncle Mose is plenty able to pay now. When dat railroad buy my lan' I laid off to pay fur dem mules. Count de money, Mars' Pendleton. Dat's what I sold dem mules fur. Yessir."

Tears were in Major Talbot's eyes. He took Uncle Mose's hand and laid his other upon his shoulder.

"Dear, faithful, old servitor," he said in an unsteady voice, "I don't mind saying to you that 'Mars' Pendleton' spent his last dollar in the world a week ago. We will accept this money, Uncle Mose, since, in a way, it is a sort of payment, as well as a token of the loyalty and devotion of the old régime. Lydia, my dear, take the money. You are better fitted than I to manage its expenditure."

"Take it, honey," said Uncle Mose. "Hit belongs to you. Hit's Talbot money."

After Uncle Mose had gone, Miss Lydia had a good cry—for joy; and the Major turned his face to a corner, and smoked his clay pipe volcanically.

The succeeding days saw the Talbots restored to peace and ease. Miss Lydia's face lost its worried look. The Major appeared in a new frock coat, in which he looked like a wax figure personifying the memory of his golden age. Another publisher who read the manuscript of the *Anecdotes and Reminiscences* thought that, with a little retouching and toning down of the high lights, he could make a really bright and salable volume of it. Altogether, the situation was comfortable, and not without the touch of hope that is often sweeter than arrived blessings.

One day, about a week after their piece of good luck, a maid brought a letter for Miss Lydia to her room. The postmark showed that it was from New York. Not knowing any one there, Miss Lydia, in a mild flutter of wonder, sat down by her table and opened the letter with her scissors. This was what she read:

> Dear Miss Talbot:
>
> I thought you might be glad to learn of my good fortune. I have received and accepted an offer of two hundred dollars per week by a New York stock company to play Colonel Calhoun in *A Magnolia Flower.*
>
> There is something else I wanted you to know. I guess you'd better not tell Major Talbot. I was anxious to make him some amends for the great help he was to me in studying the part, and for the bad humor he was in about it. He refused to let me, so I did it anyhow. I could easily spare the three hundred.
>
> Sincerely yours,
H. Hopkins Hargraves.
>
> P.S. How did I play Uncle Mose?

Major Talbot, pawing through the hall, saw Miss Lydia's door open and stopped.

"Any mail for us this morning, Lydia, dear?" he asked.

Miss Lydia slid the letter beneath a fold of her dress.

"*The Mobile Chronicle* came," she said promptly. "It's on the table in your study." [1902]

WILLA CATHER

*W*illa *Cather (1873–1947) once wrote that "a creative writer can do his best only with what lies within the range and character of his deepest sympathies." She was thirty-nine before she found her true subject. The oldest of seven children, Cather was raised in a loving home, but she hated the frontier prairie village of Red Cloud, Nebraska, where her family finally settled after leaving Virginia. She went to a preparatory school in Lincoln and continued at the University of Nebraska, studying classics. After her graduation in 1895, she moved to Pittsburgh, where she worked as a journalist for seven years before teaching English and Latin in high schools. At this time her stories and poems began to appear in popular magazines. Her first book was a volume of poetry,* April Twilights *(1903), followed in 1905 by* The Troll Gardens, *which included "A Wagner Matinée," first published in* Everybody's *Magazine the preceding year.*

The most important influence on Cather's work was Sarah Orne Jewett, who taught her that beautiful writing is a consequence of steady concentration on a thoroughly understood subject. Cather met Jewett in Boston, and Jewett urged her to develop her talent, advising her to "find your own quiet center of life and write to the human heart, the great consciousness that all humanity goes to make up." It was not until 1912 that Cather found her subject, after a trip home to Red Cloud. When she no longer saw her adolescence on the prairie as deprived and stifling, she was able to feel that her own experience was significant enough to write about. O Pioneers! *(1913), the first of her three novels about immigrant life on the western frontier, was followed in 1915 by* The Song of the Lark *and in 1918 by* My Ántonia, *a portrait of a pioneer woman that is generally regarded as her masterpiece.*

Cather went on to publish a total of twelve novels and four collections of stories, many about artists, but she did not value her forty-four stories as highly as her novels, including only three of them in the definitive "Library Edition" that represents her final judgment of her work. Many critics have commented on the purity of Cather's prose style. Her early study of classical languages and her admiration of Flaubert helped form her attitudes toward rigorous control in her realistic fiction, but she later realized that as a young writer she had been inhibited by her awe of great writers: "Life began for me when I ceased to admire and began to remember." Cather was also a perceptive literary critic. She published a collection of essays, On Writing *(1949), in which she analyzed the subtle magic of the storyteller's art: "Whatever is felt on the page without being specifically named there—that, one might say, is created."*

R*ELATED* C*OMMENTARY:*   *Willa Cather, "Miss Jewett," page 1330.*

508

A Wagner Matinée

I received one morning a letter, written in pale ink on glassy, blue-lined note-paper, and bearing the postmark of a little Nebraska village. This communication, worn and rubbed, looking as if it had been carried for some days in a coat pocket that was none too clean, was from my uncle Howard, and informed me that his wife had been left a small legacy by a bachelor relative, and that it would be necessary for her to go to Boston to attend to the settling of the estate. He requested me to meet her at the station and render her whatever services might be necessary. On examining the date indicated as that of her arrival, I found it to be no later than tomorrow. He had characteristically delayed writing until, had I been away from home for a day, I must have missed my aunt altogether.

The name of my Aunt Georgiana opened before me a gulf of recollection so wide and deep that, as the letter dropped from my hand, I felt suddenly a stranger to all the present conditions of my existence, wholly ill at ease and out of place amid the familiar surroundings of my study. I became, in short, the gangling farmer-boy my aunt had known, scourged with chilblains and bashfulness, my hands cracked and sore from the corn husking. I sat again before her parlour organ, fumbling the scales with my stiff, red fingers, while she, beside me, made canvas mittens for the huskers.

The next morning, after preparing my landlady for a visitor, I set out for the station. When the train arrived I had some difficulty in finding my aunt. She was the last of the passengers to alight, and it was not until I got her into the carriage that she seemed really to recognize me. She had come all the way in a day coach; her linen duster had become black with soot and her black bonnet grey with dust during the journey. When we arrived at my boarding-house the landlady put her to bed at once and I did not see her again until the next morning.

Whatever shock Mrs. Springer experienced at my aunt's appearance, she considerately concealed. As for myself, I saw my aunt's battered figure with that feeling of awe and respect with which we behold explorers who have left their ears and fingers north of Franz-Joseph-Land, or their health somewhere along the Upper Congo. My Aunt Georgiana had been a music teacher at the Boston Conservatory, somewhere back in the latter sixties. One summer, while visiting in the little village among the Green Mountains where her ancestors had dwelt for generations, she had kindled the callow fancy of my uncle, Howard Carpenter, then an idle, shiftless boy of twenty-one. When she returned to her duties in Boston, Howard followed her, and the upshot of this infatuation was that she eloped with him, eluding the reproaches of her family and the criticism of her friends by going with him to the Nebraska frontier. Carpenter, who, of course, had no money, took up a homestead in Red Willow County, fifty miles from the railroad. There they had measured off their land themselves, driving across the prairie in a wagon, to the wheel of which they had tied a red

509

cotton handkerchief, and counting its revolutions. They built a dug-out in the red hillside, one of those cave dwellings whose inmates so often reverted to primitive conditions. Their water they got from the lagoons where the buffalo drank, and their slender stock of provisions was always at the mercy of bands of roving Indians. For thirty years my aunt had not been farther than fifty miles from the homestead.

I owed to this woman most of the good that ever came my way in my boyhood, and had a reverential affection for her. During the years when I was riding herd for my uncle, my aunt, after cooking the three meals—the first of which was ready at six o'clock in the morning—and putting the six children to bed, would often stand until midnight at her ironing-board, with me at the kitchen table beside her, hearing me recite Latin declensions and conjugations, gently shaking me when my drowsy head sank down over a page of irregular verbs. It was to her, at her ironing or mending, that I read my first Shakspere, and her old text-book on mythology was the first that ever came into my empty hands. She taught me my scales and exercises on the little parlour organ which her husband had bought her after fifteen years during which she had not so much as seen a musical instrument. She would sit beside me by the hour, darning and counting, while I struggled with the "Joyous Farmer." She seldom talked to me about music, and I understood why. Once when I had been doggedly beating out some easy passages from an old score of *Euryanthe* I had found among her music books, she came up to me and, putting her hands over my eyes, gently drew my head back upon her shoulder, saying tremulously, "Don't love it so well, Clark, or it may be taken from you."

When my aunt appeared on the morning after her arrival in Boston, she was still in a semi-somnambulant state. She seemed not to realize that she was in the city where she had spent her youth, the place longed for hungrily half a lifetime. She had been so wretchedly train-sick throughout the journey that she had no recollection of anything but her discomfort, and, to all intents and purposes, there were but a few hours of nightmare between the farm in Red Willow County and my study on Newbury Street. I had planned a little pleasure for her that afternoon, to repay her for some of the glorious moments she had given me when we used to milk together in the straw-thatched cowshed and she, because I was more than usually tired, or because her husband had spoken sharply to me, would tell me of the splendid performance of the *Huguenots* she had seen in Paris, in her youth.

At two o'clock the Symphony Orchestra was to give a Wagner program, and I intended to take my aunt; though, as I conversed with her, I grew doubtful about her enjoyment of it. I suggested our visiting the Conservatory and the Common before lunch, but she seemed altogether too timid to wish to venture out. She questioned me absently about various changes in the city, but she was chiefly concerned that she had forgotten to leave instructions about feeding half-skimmed milk to a certain weakling calf, "old Maggie's calf, you know, Clark," she explained, evidently having forgotten how long I had been away. She was further troubled because she had neglected to tell her daughter about the freshly-opened kit of mackerel in the cellar, which would spoil if it were not used directly.

I asked her whether she had ever heard any of the Wagnerian operas, and found that she had not, though she was perfectly familiar with their respective situations, and had once possessed the piano score of *The Flying Dutchman*. I began to think it would be best to get her back to Red Willow County without waking her, and regretted having suggested the concert.

From the time we entered the concert hall, however, she was a trifle less passive and inert, and for the first time seemed to perceive her surroundings. I had felt some trepidation lest she might become aware of her queer, country clothes, or might experience some painful embarrassment at stepping suddenly into the world to which she had been dead for a quarter of a century. But, again, I found how superficially I had judged her. She sat looking about her with eyes as impersonal, almost as stony, as those with which the granite Rameses in a museum watches the froth and fret that ebbs and flows about his pedestal. I have seen this same aloofness in old miners who drift into the Brown hotel at Denver, their pockets full of bullion, their linen soiled, their haggard faces unshaven; standing in the thronged corridors as solitary as though they were still in a frozen camp on the Yukon.

The matinée audience was made up chiefly of women. One lost the contour of faces and figures, indeed any effect of line whatever, and there was only the colour of bodices past counting, the shimmer of fabrics soft and firm, silky and sheer; red, mauve, pink, blue, lilac, purple, écru, rose, yellow, cream, and white, all the colours that an impressionist finds in a sunlit landscape, with here and there the dead shadow of a frock coat. My Aunt Georgiana regarded them as though they had been so many daubs of tube-paint on a palette.

When the musicians came out and took their places, she gave a little stir of anticipation, and looked with quickening interest down over the rail at that invariable grouping, perhaps the first wholly familiar thing that had greeted her eye since she had left old Maggie and her weakling calf. I could feel how all those details sank into her soul, for I had not forgotten how they had sunk into mine when I came fresh from ploughing forever and forever between green aisles of corn, where, as in a treadmill, one might walk from daybreak to dusk without perceiving a shadow of change. The clean profiles of the musicians, the gloss of their linen, the dull black of their coats, the beloved shapes of the instruments, the patches of yellow light on the smooth, varnished bellies of the 'cellos and the bass viols in the rear, the restless, wind-tossed forest of fiddle necks and bows—I recalled how, in the first orchestra I ever heard, those long bow-strokes seemed to draw the heart out of me, as a conjurer's stick reels out yards of paper ribbon from a hat.

The first number was the *Tannhäuser* overture. When the horns drew out the first strain of the Pilgrim's chorus, Aunt Georgiana clutched my coat sleeve. Then it was I first realized that for her this broke a silence of thirty years. With the battle between the two motives, with the frenzy of the Venusberg theme and its ripping of strings, there came to me an overwhelming sense of the waste and wear we are so powerless to combat; and I saw again the tall, naked house on the prairie, black and grim as a wooden fortress; the black pond where I had learned to swim, its margin pitted with sundried cattle tracks; the rain gullied clay banks about the naked house, the four dwarf ash seedlings where the dish-cloths were always hung to dry before the kitchen door. The world there was the flat world of the ancients; to the east, a cornfield that stretched to daybreak; to the west, a corral that reached to sunset; between, the conquests of peace, dearer-bought than those of war.

The overture closed, my aunt released my coat sleeve, but she said nothing. She sat staring dully at the orchestra. What, I wondered, did she get from it? She had been a good pianist in her day, I knew, and her musical education had been broader than that of most music teachers of a quarter of a century ago. She had often told me of Mozart's operas and Meyerbeer's, and I could remember hearing her sing, years ago, certain melodies of Verdi. When I had fallen ill with a fever in her house she used to sit by my cot in the evening—when the cool, night wind blew in through the faded mosquito netting tacked over the window and I lay watching a certain bright star that burned red above the cornfield—and sing "Home to our mountains, O, let us return!" in a way fit to break the heart of a Vermont boy near dead of home-sickness already.

I watched her closely through the prelude to *Tristan and Isolde,* trying vainly to conjecture what that seething turmoil of strings and winds might mean to her, but she sat mutely staring at the violin bows that drove obliquely downward, like the pelting streaks of rain in a summer shower. Had this music any message for her? Had she enough left to at all comprehend this power which had kindled the world since she had left it? I was in a fever of curiosity, but Aunt Georgiana sat silent upon her peak in Darien. She preserved this utter immobility throughout the number from *The Flying Dutchman,* though her fingers worked mechanically upon her black dress, as if, of themselves, they were recalling the piano score they had once played. Poor hands! They had been stretched and twisted into mere tentacles to hold and lift and knead with;—on one of them a thin, worn band that had once been a wedding ring. As I pressed and gently quieted one of those groping hands, I remembered with quivering eyelids their services for me in other days.

Soon after the tenor began the "Prize Song," I heard a quick drawn breath and turned to my aunt. Her eyes were closed, but the tears were glistening on her cheeks, and I think, in a moment more, they were in my eyes as well. It never really died, then—the soul which can suffer so excruciatingly and so interminably; it withers to the outward eye only; like that strange moss which can lie on a dusty shelf half a century and yet, if placed in water, grows green again. She wept so throughout the development and elaboration of the melody.

During the intermission before the second half, I questioned my aunt and found that the "Prize Song" was not new to her. Some years before there had drifted to the farm in Red Willow County a young German, a tramp cow-puncher, who had sung in the chorus at Bayreuth when he was a boy, along with the other peasant boys and girls. Of a Sunday morning he used to sit on his gingham-sheeted bed in the hands' bedroom which opened off the kitchen, cleaning the leather of his boots and saddle, singing the "Prize Song," while my aunt went about her work in the kitchen. She had hovered over him until she had prevailed upon him to join the country church, though his sole fitness for this step, in so far as I could gather, lay in his boyish face and his possession of this divine melody. Shortly afterward, he had gone to town on the Fourth of July, been drunk for several days, lost his money at a faro table, ridden a saddled Texas steer on a bet, and disappeared with a fractured collar-bone. All this my aunt told me huskily, wanderingly, as though she were talking in the weak lapses of illness.

"Well, we have come to better things than the old *Trovatore*[1] at any rate, Aunt Georgie?" I queried, with a well meant effort at jocularity.

Her lip quivered and she hastily put her handkerchief up to her mouth. From behind it she murmured, "And you have been hearing this ever since you left me, Clark?" Her question was the gentlest and saddest of reproaches.

The second half of the program consisted of four numbers from the *Ring*, and closed with Siegfried's funeral march. My aunt wept quietly, but almost continuously, as a shallow vessel overflows in a rain-storm. From time to time her dim eyes looked up at the lights, burning softly under their dull glass globes.

The deluge of sound poured on and on; I never knew what she found in the shining current of it; I never knew how far it bore her, or past what happy islands. From the trembling of her face I could well believe that before the last number she had been carried out where the myriad graves are, into the grey, nameless burying grounds of the sea; or into some world of death vaster yet, where, from the beginning of the world, hope has lain down with hope and dream with dream and, renouncing, slept.

The concert was over; the people filed out of the hall chattering and laughing, glad to relax and find the living level again, but my kinswoman made no effort to rise. The harpist slipped the green felt cover over his

---

[1]The title character from *Il Trovatore* ("The Troubador"), an opera by Italian composer Giuseppe Verdi first performed in Rome in January of 1853.

instrument; the flute-players shook the water from their mouth-pieces; the men of the orchestra went out one by one, leaving the stage to the chairs and music stands, empty as a winter cornfield.

I spoke to my aunt. She burst into tears and sobbed pleadingly. "I don't want to go, Clark, I don't want to go!"

I understood. For her, just outside the concert hall, lay the black pond with the cattle-tracked bluffs; the tall, unpainted house, with weather-curled boards, naked as a tower; the crook-backed ash seedlings where the dish-cloths hung to dry; the gaunt, moulting turkeys picking up refuse about the kitchen door.   [1904]

EDITH WHARTON

Edith Wharton (1862–1937) was born into a wealthy family in New York City. She later wrote, "My little-girl life, safe, guarded, monotonous, was cradled in the only world about which, according to Goethe [the German poet], it is impossible to write poetry. The small society into which I was born was 'good' in the most prosaic sense of the term, and its only interest, for the generality of readers, lies in the fact of its sudden and total extinction." She was raised by governesses and tutors in the family homes in Paris, New York City, and Newport, Rhode Island. At an early age she decided to become a writer, and when she was only thirteen she disregarded Goethe and published, at her family's expense, a collection of verse.

After her marriage in 1885, Wharton began to write stories for popular magazines. Her first collection of stories, The Greater Inclination *(1899), was followed by books of fiction almost every year for more than a quarter of a century, a total of eleven collections of stories and sixteen novels. She lived most of her life in Paris, but her periodic visits to her country estate in the Berkshires, near Lenox, Massachusetts, helped her write with authority about life in America. Her best works include the early novel* The House of Mirth *(1905);* Ethan Frome *(1911), a laconically powerful New England tragedy; and* The Age of Innocence *(1920), a novel about old New York society. As a rule, Wharton's conventional novels of manners develop characterizations; her short stories, more satiric, emphasize plots. In both forms her point of view is always poised, her prose style elegant and tightly controlled.*

One of Wharton's good friends was another expatriate and keen observer of the society they knew so well, Henry James. James, who also visited her in the Berkshires, had a profound influence on her writing, encouraging her to set a high standard. Like James, Wharton enjoyed defining her artistic methods as a storyteller. In 1925 she published The Writing of Fiction. *"The Other Two" is an early story that first appeared in* Collier's Weekly *in 1904 and was collected in* The Descent of Man *the same year.*

RELATED COMMENTARY: *Edith Wharton, "Every Subject Must Contain within Itself Its Own Dimensions," page 1473.*

The Other Two

Waythorn, on the drawing-room hearth, waited for his wife to come down to dinner.

It was their first night under his own roof, and he was surprised at his thrill of boyish agitation. He was not so old, to be sure—his glass gave him little more than the five-and-thirty years to which his wife confessed—but he had fancied himself already in the temperate zone; yet here he was listening for her step with a tender sense of all it symbolized, with some old trail of verse about the garlanded nuptial doorposts floating through his enjoyment of the pleasant room and the good dinner just beyond it.

They had been hastily recalled from their honeymoon by the illness of Lily Haskett, the child of Mrs. Waythorn's first marriage. The little girl, at Waythorn's desire, had been transferred to his house on the day of her mother's wedding, and the doctor, on their arrival, broke the news that she was ill with typhoid, but declared that all the symptoms were favorable. Lily could show twelve years of unblemished health, and the case promised to be a light one. The nurse spoke as reassuringly, and after a moment of alarm Mrs. Waythorn had adjusted herself to the situation. She was very fond of Lily—her affection for the child had perhaps been her decisive charm in Waythorn's eyes—but she had the perfectly balanced nerves which her little girl had inherited, and no woman ever wasted less tissue in unproductive worry. Waythorn was therefore quite prepared to see her come in presently, a little late because of a last look at Lily, but as serene and well-appointed as if her good-night kiss had been laid on the brow of health. Her composure was restful to him; it acted as ballast to his somewhat unstable sensibilities. As he pictured her bending over the child's bed he thought how soothing her presence must be in illness: her very step would prognosticate recovery.

His own life had been a gray one, from temperament rather than circumstance, and he had been drawn to her by the unperturbed gaiety which kept her fresh and elastic at an age when most women's activities are growing either slack or febrile. He knew what was said about her; for, popular as she was, there had always been a faint undercurrent of detraction. When she had appeared in New York, nine or ten years earlier, as the pretty Mrs. Haskett whom Gus Varick had unearthed somewhere—was it in Pittsburg or Utica?—society, while promptly accepting her, had reserved the right to cast a doubt on its own indiscrimination. Inquiry, however, established her undoubted connection with a socially reigning family, and explained her recent divorce as the natural result of a runaway match at seventeen; and as nothing was known of Mr. Haskett it was easy to believe the worst of him.

Alice Haskett's remarriage with Gus Varick was a passport to the set whose recognition she coveted, and for a few years the Varicks were the most popular couple in town. Unfortunately the alliance was brief and stormy, and this time the husband had his champions. Still, even Varick's stanchest supporters admitted that he was not meant for matrimony, and Mrs. Varick's grievances were of a nature to bear the inspection of the New York courts. A New York divorce is in itself a diploma of virtue, and in the semiwidowhood of this second separation Mrs. Varick took on an air of sanctity, and was allowed to confide her wrongs to some of the most scrupulous ears in town. But when it was known that she was to marry

Waythorn there was a momentary reaction. Her best friends would have preferred to see her remain in the role of the injured wife, which was as becoming to her as crepe to a rosy complexion. True, a decent time had elapsed, and it was not even suggested that Waythorn had supplanted his predecessor. People shook their heads over him, however, and one grudging friend, to whom he affirmed that he took the step with his eyes open, replied oracularly: "Yes—and with your ears shut."

Waythorn could afford to smile at these innuendos. In the Wall Street phrase, he had "discounted" them. He knew that society has not yet adapted itself to the consequences of divorce, and that till the adaptation takes place every woman who uses the freedom the law accords her must be her own social justification. Waythorn had an amused confidence in his wife's ability to justify herself. His expectations were fulfilled, and before the wedding took place Alice Varick's group had rallied openly to her support. She took it all imperturbably; she had a way of surmounting obstacles without seeming to be aware of them, and Waythorn looked back with wonder at the trivialities over which he had worn his nerves thin. He had the sense of having found refuge in a richer, warmer nature than his own, and his satisfaction, at the moment, was humorously summed up in the thought that his wife, when she had done all she could for Lily, would not be ashamed to come down and enjoy a good dinner.

The anticipation of such enjoyment was not, however, the sentiment expressed by Mrs. Waythorn's charming face when she presently joined him. Though she had put on her most engaging tea gown she had neglected to assume the smile that went with it, and Waythorn thought he had never seen her look so nearly worried.

"What is it?" he asked. "Is anything wrong with Lily?"

"No; I've just been in and she's still sleeping." Mrs. Waythorn hesitated. "But something tiresome has happened."

He had taken her two hands, and now perceived that he was crushing a paper between them.

"This letter?"

"Yes—Mr. Haskett has written—I mean his lawyer has written."

Waythorn felt himself flush uncomfortably. He dropped his wife's hands.

"What about?"

"About seeing Lily. You know the courts—"

"Yes, yes," he interrupted nervously.

Nothing was known about Haskett in New York. He was vaguely supposed to have remained in the outer darkness from which his wife had been rescued, and Waythorn was one of the few who were aware that he had given up his business in Utica and followed her to New York in order to be near his little girl. In the days of his wooing, Waythorn had often met Lily on the doorstep, rosy and smiling, on her way "to see papa."

"I am so sorry," Mrs. Waythorn murmured.

He roused himself. "What does he want?"

"He wants to see her. You know she goes to him once a week."

"Well—he doesn't expect her to go to him now, does he?"

"No—he has heard of her illness; but he expects to come here."

"Here?"

Mrs. Waythorn reddened under his gaze. They looked away from each other.

"I'm afraid he has the right. . . . You'll see. . . ." She made a proffer of the letter.

Waythorn moved away with a gesture of refusal. He stood staring about the softly-lighted room, which a moment before had seemed so full of bridal intimacy.

"I'm so sorry," she repeated. "If Lily could have been moved—"

"That's out of the question," he returned impatiently.

"I suppose so."

Her lip was beginning to tremble, and he felt himself a brute.

"He must come, of course," he said. "When is—his day?"

"I'm afraid—tomorrow."

"Very well. Send a note in the morning."

The butler entered to announce dinner.

Waythorn turned to his wife. "Come—you must be tired. It's beastly, but try to forget about it," he said, drawing her hand through his arm.

"You're so good, dear. I'll try," she whispered back.

Her face cleared at once, and as she looked at him across the flowers, between the rosy candleshades, he saw her lips waver back into a smile.

"How pretty everything is!" she sighed luxuriously.

He turned to the butler. "The champagne at once, please. Mrs. Waythorn is tired."

In a moment or two their eyes met above the sparkling glasses. Her own were quite clear and untroubled: he saw that she had obeyed his injunction and forgotten.

– II –

Waythorn, the next morning, went downtown earlier than usual. Haskett was not likely to come till the afternoon, but the instinct of flight drove him forth. He meant to stay away all day—he had thoughts of dining at his club. As his door closed behind him he reflected that before he opened it again it would have admitted another man who had as much right to enter it as himself, and the thought filled him with a physical repugnance.

He caught the elevated at the employees' hour, and found himself crushed between two layers of pendulous humanity. At Eighth Street the man facing him wriggled out, and another took his place. Waythorn glanced up and saw that it was Gus Varick. The men were so close together that it was impossible to ignore the smile of recognition on Varick's handsome overblown face. And after all—why not? They had always been on good terms, and Varick had been divorced before Waythorn's intentions to his wife began. The two exchanged a word on the perennial grievance of the congested trains, and when a seat at their side was miraculously left empty the instinct of self-preservation made Waythorn slip into it after Varick.

The latter drew the stout man's breath of relief. "Lord—I was beginning to feel like a pressed flower." He leaned back, looking unconcernedly at Waythorn. "Sorry to hear that Sellers is knocked out again."

"Sellers?" echoed Waythorn, starting at his partner's name.

Varick looked surprised. "You didn't know he was laid up with the gout?"

"No. I've been away—I only got back last night." Waythorn felt himself reddening in anticipation of the other's smile.

"Ah—yes; to be sure. And Sellers' attack came on two days ago. I'm afraid he's pretty bad. Very awkward for me, as it happens, because he was just putting through a rather important thing for me."

"Ah?" Waythorn wondered vaguely since when Varick had been dealing in "important things." Hitherto he had dabbled only in the shallow pools of speculation, with which Waythorn's office did not usually concern itself.

It occurred to him that Varick might be talking at random, to relieve the strain of their propinquity. That strain was becoming momentarily more apparent to Waythorn, and when, at Cortlandt Street, he caught sight of an acquaintance and had a sudden vision of the picture he and Varick must present to an initiated eye, he jumped up with a muttered excuse.

"I hope you'll find Sellers better," said Varick civilly, and he stammered back: "If I can be of any use to you—" and let the departing crowd sweep him to the platform.

At his office he heard that Sellers was in fact ill with the gout, and would probably not be able to leave the house for some weeks.

"I'm sorry it should have happened so, Mr. Waythorn," the senior clerk said with affable significance. "Mr. Sellers was very much upset at the idea of giving you such a lot of extra work just now."

"Oh, that's no matter," said Waythorn hastily. He secretly welcomed the pressure of additional business, and was glad to think, when the day's work was over, he would have to call at his partner's on the way home.

He was late for luncheon, and turned in at the nearest restaurant instead of going back to his club. The place was full, and the waiter hurried him to the back of the room to capture the only vacant table. In the cloud of cigar smoke Waythorn did not at once distinguish his neighbors: but presently, looking about him, he saw Varick seated a few feet off. This time, luckily, they were too far apart for conversation, and Varick, who faced another way, had probably not even seen him; but there was an irony in their renewed nearness.

Varick was said to be fond of good living, and as Waythorn sat dispatching his hurried luncheon he looked across half enviously at the other's leisurely degustation of his meal. When Waythorn first saw him he had been helping himself with critical deliberation to a bit of Camembert at the ideal point of liquefaction, and now, the cheese removed, he was just pouring his *café double* from its little two-storied earthen pot. He poured slowly, his ruddy profile bent over the task, and one beringed white hand steadying the lid of the coffeepot; then he stretched his other hand to the decanter of cognac at his elbow, filled a liqueur glass, took a tentative sip, and poured the brandy into his coffee cup.

Waythorn watched him in a kind of fascination. What was he thinking of—only of the flavor of the coffee and the liqueur? Had the morning's meeting left no more trace in his thoughts than on his face? Had his wife so completely passed out of his life that even this odd encounter with her present husband, within a week after her remarriage, was no more than an incident in his day? And as Waythorn mused, another idea struck him: had Haskett ever met Varick as Varick and he had just met? The recollection of Haskett perturbed him, and he rose and left the restaurant, taking a circuitous way out to escape the placid irony of Varick's nod.

It was after seven when Waythorn reached home. He thought the footman who opened the door looked at him oddly.

"How is Miss Lily?" he asked in haste.

"Doing very well, sir. A gentleman—"

"Tell Barlow to put off dinner for half an hour," Waythorn cut him off, hurrying upstairs.

He went straight to his room and dressed without seeing his wife. When he reached the drawing room she was there, fresh and radiant. Lily's day had been good; the doctor was not coming back that evening.

At dinner Waythorn told her of Sellers' illness and of the resulting complications. She listened sympathetically, adjuring him not to let himself be overworked, and asking vague feminine questions about the routine of the office. Then she gave him the chronicle of Lily's day; quoted the nurse and doctor, and told him who had called to inquire. He had never seen her more serene and unruffled. It struck him, with a curious pang, that she was very happy in being with him, so happy that she found a childish pleasure in rehearsing the trivial incidents of her day.

After dinner they went to the library, and the servant put the coffee and liqueurs on a low table before her and left the room. She looked singularly soft and girlish in her rosy-pale dress, against the dark leather of one of his bachelor armchairs. A day earlier the contrast would have charmed him.

He turned away now, choosing a cigar with affected deliberation.

"Did Haskett come?" he asked, with his back to her.

"Oh, yes—he came."

"You didn't see him, of course?"

She hesitated a moment. "I let the nurse see him."

That was all. There was nothing more to ask. He swung round toward her, applying a match to his cigar. Well, the thing was over for a week, at any rate. He would try not to think of it. She looked up at him, a trifle rosier than usual, with a smile in her eyes.

"Ready for your coffee, dear?"

He leaned against the mantelpiece, watching her as she lifted the coffeepot. The lamplight struck a gleam from her bracelets and tipped her soft hair with brightness. How light and slender she was, and how each gesture flowed into the next! She seemed a creature all compact of harmonies. As the thought of Haskett receded, Waythorn felt himself yielding again to the joy of possessorship. They were his, those white hands with flitting motions, his the light haze of hair, the lips and eyes. . . .

She set down the coffeepot, and reaching for the decanter of cognac, measured off a liqueur glass and poured it into his cup.

Waythorn uttered a sudden exclamation.

"What is the matter?" she said, startled.

"Nothing; only—I don't take cognac in my coffee."

"Oh, how stupid of me," she cried.

Their eyes met, and she blushed a sudden agonized red.

– III –

Ten days later, Mr. Sellers, still housebound, asked Waythorn to call on his way downtown.

The senior partner, with his swaddled foot propped up by the fire, greeted his associate with an air of embarrassment.

"I'm sorry, my dear fellow; I've got to ask you to do an awkward thing for me."

Waythorn waited, and the other went on, after a pause apparently given to the arrangement of his phrases: "The fact is, when I was knocked out I had just gone into a rather complicated piece of business for—Gus Varick."

"Well?" said Waythorn, with an attempt to put him at his ease.

"Well—it's this way: Varick came to me the day before my attack. He had evidently had an inside tip from somebody, and had made about a hundred thousand. He came to me for advice, and I suggested his going in with Vanderlyn."

"Oh, the deuce!" Waythorn exclaimed. He saw in a flash what had happened. The investment was an alluring one, but required negotiation. He listened quietly while Sellers put the case before him, and, the statement ended, he said: "You think I ought to see Varick?"

"I'm afraid I can't as yet. The doctor is obdurate. And this thing can't wait. I hate to ask you, but no one else in the office knows the ins and outs of it."

Waythorn stood silent. He did not care a farthing for the success of Varick's venture, but the honor of the office was to be considered, and he could hardly refuse to oblige his partner.

"Very well," he said, "I'll do it."

That afternoon, apprised by telephone, Varick called at the office. Waythorn, waiting in his private room, wondered what the others thought of it. The newspapers, at the time of Mrs. Waythorn's marriage, had acquainted their readers with every detail of her previous matrimonial ventures, and Waythorn could fancy the clerks smiling behind Varick's back as he was ushered in.

Varick bore himself admirably. He was easy without being undignified, and Waythorn was conscious of cutting a much less impressive figure. Varick had no experience of business, and the talk prolonged itself for nearly an hour while Waythorn set forth with scrupulous precision the details of the proposed transaction.

"I'm awfully obliged to you," Varick said as he rose. "The fact is I'm not used to having much money to look after, and I don't want to make an ass of myself—" He smiled, and Waythorn could not help noticing that there was something pleasant about his smile. "It feels uncommonly queer to have enough cash to pay one's bills. I'd have sold my soul for it a few years ago!"

Waythorn winced at the allusion. He had heard it rumoured that a lack of funds had been one of the determining causes of the Varick separation, but it did not occur to him that Varick's words were intentional. It seemed more likely that the desire to keep clear of embarrassing topics had fatally drawn him into one. Waythorn did not wish to be outdone in civility.

"We'll do the best we can for you," he said. "I think this is a good thing you're in."

"Oh, I'm sure it's immense. It's awfully good of you—" Varick broke off, embarrassed. "I suppose the thing's settled now—but if—"

"If anything happens before Sellers is about, I'll see you again," said Waythorn quietly. He was glad, in the end, to appear the more self-possessed of the two.

The course of Lily's illness ran smooth, and as the days passed Waythorn grew used to the idea of Haskett's weekly visit. The first time the day came round, he stayed out late, and questioned his wife as to the visit on his return. She replied at once that Haskett had merely seen the nurse downstairs, as the doctor did not wish anyone in the child's sickroom till after the crisis.

The following week Waythorn was again conscious of the recurrence of the day, but had forgotten it by the time he came home to dinner. The crisis of the disease came a few days later, with a rapid decline of fever, and the little girl was pronounced out of danger. In the rejoicing which ensued the thought of Haskett passed out of Waythorn's mind, and one afternoon, letting himself into the house with a latchkey, he went straight to his library without noticing a shabby hat and umbrella in the hall.

In the library he found a small effaced-looking man with a thinnish gray beard sitting on the edge of a chair. The stranger might have been a piano tuner, or one of those mysteriously efficient persons who are summoned in emergencies to adjust some detail of the domestic machinery. He blinked at Waythorn through a pair of gold-rimmed spectacles and said mildly: "Mr. Waythorn, I presume? I am Lily's father."

Waythorn flushed. "Oh—" he stammered uncomfortably. He broke off, disliking to appear rude. Inwardly he was trying to adjust the actual Haskett to the image of him projected by his wife's reminiscences. Waythorn had been allowed to infer that Alice's first husband was a brute.

"I am sorry to intrude," said Haskett, with his over-the-counter politeness.

"Don't mention it," returned Waythorn, collecting himself. "I suppose the nurse has been told?"

"I presume so. I can wait," said Haskett. He had a resigned way of speaking, as though life had worn down his natural powers of resistance.

Waythorn stood on the threshold, nervously pulling off his gloves.

"I'm sorry you've been detained. I will send for the nurse," he said, and as he opened the door he added with an effort: "I'm glad we can give you a good report of Lily." He winced as the *we* slipped out, but Haskett seemed not to notice it.

"Thank you, Mr. Waythorn. It's been an anxious time for me."

"Ah, well, that's past. Soon she'll be able to go to you." Waythorn nodded and passed out.

In his own room he flung himself down with a groan. He hated the womanish sensibility which made him suffer so acutely from the grotesque chances of life. He had known when he married that his wife's former husbands were both living, and that amid the multiplied contacts of modern existence there were a thousand chances to one that he would run against one or the other, yet he found himself as much disturbed by his brief encounter with Haskett as though the law had not obligingly removed all difficulties in the way of their meeting.

Waythorn sprang up and began to pace the room nervously. He had not suffered half as much from his two meetings with Varick. It was Haskett's presence in his own house that made the situation so intolerable. He stood still, hearing steps in the passage.

"This way, please," he heard the nurse say. Haskett was being taken upstairs, then: not a corner of the house but was open to him. Waythorn dropped into another chair, staring vaguely ahead of him. On his dressing table stood a photograph of Alice, taken when he had first known her. She was Alice Varick then—how fine and exquisite he had thought her! Those were Varick's pearls about her neck. At Waythorn's insistence they had been returned before her marriage. Had Haskett ever given her any trinkets—and what had become of them, Waythorn wondered? He realized suddenly that he knew very little of Haskett's past or present situation; but from the man's appearance and manner of speech he could reconstruct with curious precision the surroundings of Alice's first marriage. And it startled him to think that she had, in the background of her life, a phase of existence so different from anything with which he had connected her. Varick, whatever his faults, was a gentleman, in the conventional, traditional sense of the term: the sense which at that moment seemed, oddly enough, to have most meaning to Waythorn. He and Varick had the same social habits, spoke the same language, understood the same allusions. But this other man . . . it was grotesquely uppermost in Waythorn's mind that Haskett had worn a made-up tie attached with an elastic. Why should that ridiculous detail symbolize the whole man? Waythorn was exasperated by his own paltriness, but the fact of the tie expanded, forced itself on him, became as it were the key to Alice's past. He could see her, as Mrs. Haskett, sitting in a "front parlor" furnished in plush, with a pianola, and a copy of *Ben Hur* on the center table. He could see her going to the theater with Haskett—or perhaps even to a "Church Sociable"—she in the "picture hat" and Haskett in a black frock coat, a little creased, with the made-up tie on an elastic. On the way home they would stop and look at the illuminated shop windows, lingering over the photographs of New York actresses. On Sunday afternoons Haskett would take her for a walk, pushing Lily ahead of them in a white enameled perambulator, and Waythorn had a vision of the people they would stop and talk to. He could fancy how pretty Alice must have looked, in a dress adroitly constructed from the hints of a New York fashion paper, and how she must have looked down on the other women, chafing at her life, and secretly feeling that she belonged in a bigger place.

For the moment his foremost thought was one of wonder at the way in which she had shed the phase of existence which her marriage with Haskett implied. It was as if her whole aspect, every gesture, every inflection, every allusion, were a studied negation of that period of her life. If she had denied being married to Haskett she could hardly have stood more convicted of duplicity than in this obliteration of the self which had been his wife.

Waythorn started up, checking himself in the analysis of her motives. What right had he to create a fantastic effigy of her and then pass judgment on it? She had spoken vaguely of her first marriage as unhappy, had hinted, with becoming reticence, that Haskett had wrought havoc among her young illusions. . . . It was a pity for Waythorn's peace of mind that Haskett's very inoffensiveness shed a new light on the nature of those illusions. A man would rather think that his wife has been brutalized by her first husband than that the process has been reversed.

– IV –

"Mr. Waythorn, I don't like that French governess of Lily's."

Haskett, subdued and apologetic, stood before Waythorn in the library, revolving his shabby hat in his hand.

Waythorn, surprised in his armchair over the evening paper, stared back perplexedly at his visitor.

"You'll excuse my asking to see you," Haskett continued. "But this is my last visit, and I thought if I could have a word with you it would be a better way than writing to Mrs. Waythorn's lawyer."

Waythorn rose uneasily. He did not like the French governess either; but that was irrelevant.

"I am not so sure of that," he returned stiffly; "but since you wish it I will give your message to—my wife." He always hesitated over the possessive pronoun in addressing Haskett.

The latter sighed. "I don't know as that will help much. She didn't like it when I spoke to her."

Waythorn turned red. "When did you see her?" he asked.

"Not since the first day I came to see Lily—right after she was taken sick. I remarked to her then that I didn't like the governess."

Waythorn made no answer. He remembered distinctly that, after that first visit, he had asked his wife if she had seen Haskett. She had lied to him then, but she had respected his wishes since; and the incident cast a curious light on her character. He was sure she would not have seen Haskett that first day if she had divined that Waythorn would object, and the fact that she did not divine it was almost as disagreeable to the latter as the discovery that she had lied to him.

"I don't like the woman," Haskett was repeating with mild persistency. "She ain't straight, Mr. Waythorn—she'll teach the child to be underhand. I've noticed a change in Lily—she's too anxious to please—and she don't always tell the truth. She used to be the straightest child, Mr. Waythorn—" He broke off, his voice a little thick. "Not but what I want her to have a stylish education," he ended.

Waythorn was touched. "I'm sorry, Mr. Haskett; but frankly, I don't quite see what I can do."

Haskett hesitated. Then he laid his hat on the table, and advanced to the hearthrug, on which Waythorn was standing. There was nothing aggressive in his manner, but he had the solemnity of a timid man resolved on a decisive measure.

"There's just one thing you can do, Mr. Waythorn," he said. "You can remind Mrs. Waythorn that, by the decree of the courts, I am entitled to have a voice in Lily's bringing-up." He paused, and went on more deprecatingly: "I'm not the kind to talk about enforcing my rights, Mr. Waythorn. I don't know as I think a man is entitled to rights he hasn't known how to hold on to; but this business of the child is different. I've never let go there—and I never mean to."

The scene left Waythorn deeply shaken. Shamefacedly, in indirect ways, he had been finding out about Haskett; and all that he had learned was favorable. The little man, in order to be near his daughter, had sold out his share in a profitable business in Utica, and accepted a modest clerkship in a New York manufacturing house. He boarded in a shabby street and had few acquaintances. His passion for Lily filled his life. Waythorn felt that this exploration of Haskett was like groping about with a dark lantern in his wife's past; but he saw now that there were recesses his lantern had not explored. He had never inquired into the exact circumstances of his wife's first matrimonial rupture. On the surface all had been fair. It was she who had obtained the divorce, and the court had given her the child. But Waythorn knew how many ambiguities such a verdict might cover. The mere fact that Haskett retained a right over his daughter implied an unsuspected compromise. Waythorn was an idealist. He always refused to recognize unpleasant contingencies till he found himself confronted with them, and then he saw them followed by a spectral train of consequences. His next days were thus haunted, and he determined to try to lay the ghosts by conjuring them up in his wife's presence.

When he repeated Haskett's request a flame of anger passed over her face; but she subdued it instantly and spoke with a slight quiver of outraged motherhood.

"It is very ungentlemanly of him," she said.

The word grated on Waythorn. "That is neither here nor there. It's a bare question of rights."

She murmured: "It's not as if he could ever be a help to Lily—"

Waythorn flushed. This was even less to his taste. "The question is," he repeated, "what authority has he over her?"

She looked downward, twisting herself a little in her seat. "I am willing to see him—I thought you objected," she faltered.

In a flash he understood that she knew the extent of Haskett's claims. Perhaps it was not the first time she had resisted them.

"My objecting has nothing to do with it," he said coldly; "if Haskett has a right to be consulted you must consult him."

She burst into tears, and he saw that she expected him to regard her as a victim.

Haskett did not abuse his rights. Waythorn had felt miserably sure that he would not. But the governess was dismissed, and from time to time the little man demanded an interview with Alice. After the first outburst she accepted the situation with her usual adaptability. Haskett had once reminded Waythorn of the piano tuner, and Mrs. Waythorn, after a month or two, appeared to class him with that domestic familiar. Waythorn could not but respect the father's tenacity. At first he had tried to cultivate the suspicion that Haskett might be "up to" something, that he had an object in securing a foothold in the house. But in his heart Waythorn was sure of Haskett's single-mindedness; he even guessed in the latter a mild contempt for such advantages as his relation with the Waythorns might offer. Haskett's sincerity of purpose made him invulnerable, and his successor had to accept him as a lien on the property.

Mr. Sellers was sent to Europe to recover from his gout, and Varick's affairs hung on Waythorn's hands. The negotiations were prolonged and complicated; they necessitated frequent conferences between the two men, and the interests of the firm forbade Waythorn's suggesting that his client should transfer his business to another officer.

Varick appeared well in the transaction. In moments of relaxation his coarse streak appeared, and Waythorn dreaded his geniality; but in the office he was concise and clear-headed, with a flattering deference to Waythorn's judgment. Their business relations being so affably established, it would have been absurd for the two men to ignore each other in society. The first time they met in a drawing-room, Varick took up their intercourse in the same easy key, and his hostess' grateful glance obliged Waythorn to respond to it. After that they ran across each other frequently, and one evening at a ball Waythorn, wandering through the remoter rooms, came upon Varick seated beside his wife. She colored a little, and faltered in what she was saying; but Varick nodded to Waythorn without rising, and the latter strolled on.

In the carriage, on the way home, he broke out nervously: "I didn't know you spoke to Varick."

Her voice trembled a little. "It's the first time—he happened to be standing near me; I didn't know what to do. It's so awkward, meeting everywhere—and he said you had been very kind about some business."

"That's different," said Waythorn.

She paused a moment. "I'll do just as you wish," she returned pliantly. "I thought it would be less awkward to speak to him when we meet."

Her pliancy was beginning to sicken him. Had she really no will of her own—no theory about her relation to these men? She had accepted Haskett—did she mean to accept Varick? It was "less awkward," as she had said, and her instinct was to evade difficulties or to circumvent them. With sudden vividness Waythorn saw how the instinct had developed. She was "as easy as an old shoe"—a shoe that too many feet had worn. Her elasticity was the result of tension in too many different directions. Alice Haskett—Alice Varick—Alice Waythorn—she had been each in turn, and had left hanging to each name a little of her privacy, a little of her personality, a little of the inmost self where the unknown god abides.

"Yes—it's better to speak to Varick," said Waythorn wearily.

–V–

The winter wore on, and society took advantage of the Waythorns' acceptance of Varick. Harassed hostesses were grateful to them for bridging over a social difficulty, and Mrs. Waythorn was held up as a miracle of good taste. Some experimental spirits could not resist the diversion of throwing Varick and his former wife together, and there were those who thought he found a zest in the propinquity. But Mrs. Waythorn's conduct remained irreproachable. She neither avoided Varick nor sought him out. Even Waythorn could not but admit that she had discovered the solution of the newest social problem.

He had married her without giving much thought to that problem. He had fancied that a woman can shed her past like a man. But now he saw that Alice was bound to hers both by the circumstances which forced her into continued relation with it, and by the traces it had left on her nature. With grim irony Waythorn compared himself to a member of a syndicate. He held so many shares in his wife's personality and his predecessors were his partners in the business. If there had been any element of passion in the transaction he would have felt less deteriorated by it. The fact that Alice took her change of husbands like a change of weather reduced the situation to mediocrity. He could have forgiven her for blunders, for excesses; for resisting Haskett, for yielding to Varick; for anything but her acquiescence and her tact. She reminded him of a juggler tossing knives; but the knives were blunt and she knew they would never cut her.

And then, gradually, habit formed a protecting surface for his sensibilities. If he paid for each day's comfort with the small change of his illusions, he grew daily to value the comfort more and set less store upon the coin. He had drifted into a dulling propinquity with Haskett and Varick and he took refuge in the cheap revenge of satirizing the situation. He even began to reckon up the advantages which accrued from it, to ask himself if it were not better to own a third of a wife who knew how to make a man happy than a whole one who had lacked opportunity to acquire the art. For it *was* an art, and made up, like all others, of concessions, eliminations, and embellishments; of lights judiciously thrown and shadows skillfully softened. His wife knew exactly how to manage the lights, and he knew exactly to what training she owed her skill. He even tried to trace the source of his obligations, to discriminate between the influences which had combined to produce his domestic happiness: he perceived that Haskett's commonness had made Alice worship good breeding, while Varick's liberal construction of the marriage bond had taught her to value the conjugal virtues; so that he was directly indebted to his predecessors for the devotion which made his life easy if not inspiring.

From this phase he passed into that of complete acceptance. He ceased to satirize himself because time dulled the irony of the situation and the joke lost its humor with its sting. Even the sight of Haskett's hat on the hall table had ceased to touch the springs of epigram. The hat was often seen there now, for it had been decided that it was better for Lily's father to visit her than for the little girl to go to his boardinghouse. Waythorn, having acquiesced in this arrangement, had been surprised to find how little difference it made. Haskett was never obtrusive, and the few visitors who met him on the stairs were unaware of his identity. Waythorn did not know how often he saw Alice, but with himself Haskett was seldom in contact.

One afternoon, however, he learned on entering that Lily's father was waiting to see him. In the library he found Haskett occupying a chair in his usual provisional way. Waythorn always felt grateful to him for not leaning back.

"I hope you'll excuse me, Mr. Waythorn," he said rising. "I wanted to see Mrs. Waythorn about Lily, and your man asked me to wait here till she came in."

"Of course," said Waythorn, remembering that a sudden leak had that morning given over the drawing room to the plumbers.

He opened his cigar case and held it out to his visitor, and Haskett's acceptance seemed to mark a fresh stage in their intercourse. The spring evening was chilly, and Waythorn invited his guest to draw up his chair to the fire. He meant to find an excuse to leave Haskett in a moment; but he was tired and cold, and after all the little man no longer jarred on him.

The two were enclosed in the intimacy of their blended cigar smoke when the door opened and Varick walked into the room. Waythorn rose abruptly. It was the first time that Varick had come to the house, and the surprise of seeing him, combined with the singular inopportuneness of his arrival, gave a new edge to Waythorn's blunted sensibilities. He stared at his visitor without speaking.

Varick seemed too preoccupied to notice his host's embarrassment.

"My dear fellow," he exclaimed in his most expansive tone, "I must apologize for tumbling in on you in this way, but I was too late to catch you downtown, and so I thought—"

He stopped short, catching sight of Haskett, and his sanguine color deepened to a flush which spread vividly under his scant blond hair. But in a moment he recovered himself and nodded slightly. Haskett returned the bow in silence, and Waythorn was still groping for speech when the footman came in carrying a tea table.

The intrusion offered a welcome vent to Waythorn's nerves. "What the deuce are you bringing this here for?" he said sharply.

"I beg your pardon, sir, but the plumbers are still in the drawing room, and Mrs. Waythorn said she would have tea in the library." The footman's perfectly respectful tone implied a reflection on Waythorn's reasonableness.

"Oh, very well," said the latter resignedly, and the footman proceeded to open the folding tea table and set out its complicated appointments. While this interminable process continued the three men stood motionless, watching it with a fascinated stare, till Waythorn, to break the silence, said to Varick, "Won't you have a cigar?"

He held out the case he had just tendered to Haskett, and Varick helped himself with a smile. Waythorn looked about for a match, and finding none, proffered a light from his own cigar. Haskett, in the background, held his ground mildly, examining his cigar tip now and then, and stepping forward at the right moment to knock its ash into the fire.

The footman at last withdrew, and Varick immediately began: "If I could just say half a word to you about this business—"

"Certainly," stammered Waythorn; "in the dining room—"

But as he placed his hand on the door it opened from without, and his wife appeared on the threshold.

She came in fresh and smiling, in her street dress and hat, shedding a fragrance from the boa which she loosened in advancing.

"Shall we have tea in here, dear?" she began; and then she caught sight of Varick. Her smiled deepened, veiling a slight tremor of surprise. "Why, how do you do?" she said with a distinct note of pleasure.

As she shook hands with Varick she saw Haskett standing behind him. Her smile faded for a moment, but she recalled it quickly, with a scarcely perceptible side glance at Waythorn.

"How do you do, Mr. Haskett?" she said, and shook hands with him a shade less cordially.

The three men stood awkwardly before her, till Varick, always the most self-possessed, dashed into an explanatory phrase.

"We — I had to see Waythorn a moment on business," he stammered, brick-red from chin to nape.

Haskett stepped forward with his air of mild obstinacy. "I am sorry to intrude; but you appointed five o'clock —" he directed his resigned glance to the timepiece on the mantel.

She swept aside their embarrassment with a charming gesture of hospitality.

"I'm so sorry — I'm always late; but the afternoon was so lovely." She stood drawing off her gloves, propitiatory and graceful, diffusing about her a sense of ease and familiarity in which the situation lost its grotesqueness. "But before talking business," she added brightly, "I'm sure everyone wants a cup of tea."

She dropped into her low chair by the tea table, and the two visitors, as if drawn by her smile, advanced to receive the cups she held out.

She glanced about for Waythorn, and he took the third cup with a laugh.   [1904]

JACK LONDON

*J*ack London (1876–1916), unlike Bret Harte, Mark Twain, and most of the early American writers who wrote stories about the American West, was born in that region—in San Francisco. He had a hard childhood, forced to earn his own living by manual labor in a canning factory starting at age fifteen. Later he worked in a laundry, and still later he was a sailor. Descriptive writing came naturally to him, and two years before he graduated from Oakland High School he won first prize in a local newspaper's article contest for "Story of a Typhoon off the Coast of Japan." He attended the University of California at Berkeley for one semester, but he regarded himself as self-taught, reading Karl Marx and Friedrich Engels, Herbert Spencer, and Friedrich Nietzsche as a young man. He joined the Socialist Labor Party after he had become convinced that it was impossible for workers to secure better conditions without organizing to take over the means of production. In 1897 he joined the Klondike gold rush and spent the winter in the Yukon. Two years later, after his return from Alaska on a 2,000-mile boat trip down the Yukon River, he published his first professional story, "To the Man on the Trail," in The Overland Monthly, *and began to write for his living.*

London's first collection of fiction, Son of the Wolf, *appeared in 1900. His novel* The Call of the Wild *(1903) was his biggest success, selling 1.5 million copies, and he became the highest-paid author of his time. He regarded his adventure stories as inferior to his political writing, however; they were merely a means of making money to meet his expanding interests in social reform as a Socialist speaker and political candidate. He covered the Russo-Japanese War as a correspondent, and wrote articles on the San Francisco earthquake of 1906 and the Mexican Revolution of 1914. Shortly before his death at the age of forty, he resigned from the Socialist Party "because of its lack of fire and fight, and its loss of emphasis on the class struggle." London's death, possibly by his own hand, strangely echoed the events of his semiautobiographical novel* Martin Eden *(1909), in which a writer achieves success, but after rejecting Socialist aims finds his life meaningless and commits suicide.*

London produced almost fifty volumes of prose, including several collections of short stories such as Son of the Wolf, South Sea Tales *(1911), and* The House of Pride and Other Tales of Hawaii *(1912). He learned to tell stories, he claimed, when he was bumming across the United States and had to decide exactly the right line to pitch between the moment the housewife opened the door and the moment she asked him what he wanted. He felt that poverty had made him hustle, but that only his good luck had prevented it from destroying him. Claiming "no mentor but myself" as a writer, he placed the highest value on original experience; the stamp of self on a writer's work was "a trademark of far greater value than copyright." London's reputation as a storyteller has declined in the United States in recent times, but he remains one of our most translated authors. His literary style is simple, often journalistic, and his stories are known to countless readers around the world for dramatizing this country's rugged pioneer experience, as in "All Gold Canyon," which first appeared in* Century Magazine *in 1905. As Jorge Luis Borges has observed, the vitality that permeated London's life is apparent in his best work.*

All Gold Canyon

It was the green heart of the canyon, where the walls swerved back from the rigid plan and relieved their harshness of line by making a little sheltered nook and filling it to the brim with sweetness and roundness and softness. Here all things rested. Even the narrow stream ceased its turbulent downrush long enough to form a quiet pool. Knee-deep in the water, with drooping head and half-shut eyes, drowsed a red-coated, many-antlered buck.

On one side, beginning at the very lip of the pool, was a tiny meadow, a cool, resilient surface of green that extended to the base of the frowning wall. Beyond the pool a gentle slope of earth ran up and up to meet the opposing wall. Fine grass covered the slope—grass that was spangled with flowers, with here and there patches of color, orange and purple and golden. Below, the canyon was shut in. There was no view. The walls leaned together abruptly and the canyon ended in a chaos of rocks, moss-covered and hidden by a green screen of vines and creepers and boughs of trees. Up the canyon rose far hills and peaks, the big foothills, pine-covered and remote. And far beyond, like clouds upon the border of the sky, towered minarets of white, where the Sierra's eternal snows flashed austerely the blazes of the sun.

There was no dust in the canyon. The leaves and flowers were clean and virginal. The grass was young velvet. Over the pool three cottonwoods sent their snowy fluffs fluttering down the quiet air. On the slope the blossoms of the wine-wooded manzanita filled the air with springtime odors, while the leaves, wise with experience, were already beginning their vertical twist against the coming aridity of summer. In the open spaces on the slope, beyond the farthest shadow-reach of the manzanita, poised the maripose lilies, like so many flights of jeweled moths suddenly arrested and on the verge of trembling into flight again. Here and there that woods harlequin, the madroña, permitting itself to be caught in the act of changing its pea-green trunk to madder red, breathed its fragrance into the air from great clusters of waxen bells. Creamy white were these bells, shaped like lilies of the valley, with the sweetness of perfume that is of the springtime.

There was not a sigh of wind. The air was drowsy with its weight of perfume. It was a sweetness that would have been cloying had the air been heavy and humid. But the air was sharp and thin. It was as starlight transmuted into atmosphere, shot through and warmed by sunshine, and flower-drenched with sweetness.

An occasional butterfly drifted in and out through the patches of light and shade. And from all about rose the low and sleepy hum of mountain bees—feasting sybarites that jostled one another good-naturedly at the board, nor found time for rough discourtesy. So quietly did the little stream drip and ripple its way through the canyon that it spoke only in faint and occasional gurgles. The voice of the stream was as a drowsy whisper, ever interrupted by dozings and silences, ever lifted again in the awakenings.

The motion of all things was a drifting in the heart of the canyon. Sunshine and butterflies drifted in and out among the trees. The hum of the bees and the whisper of the stream were a drifting of sound. And the drifting sound and drifting color seemed to weave together in the making of a delicate and intangible fabric which was the spirit of the place. It was a spirit of peace that was not of death, but of smooth-pulsing life, of quietude that was not silence, of movement that was not action, of repose that was quick with existence without being violent with struggle and travail. The spirit of the place was the spirit of the peace of the living, somnolent with the easement and content of prosperity, and undisturbed by rumors of far wars.

The red-coated, many-antlered buck acknowledged the lordship of the spirit of the place and dozed knee-deep in the cool, shaded pool. There seemed no flies to vex him and he was languid with rest. Sometimes his ears moved when the stream awoke and whispered; but they moved lazily, with foreknowledge that it was merely the stream grown garrulous at discovery that it had slept.

But there came a time when the buck's ears lifted and tensed with swift eagerness for sound. His head was turned down the canyon. His sensitive, quivering nostrils scented the air. His eyes could not pierce the green screen through which the stream rippled away, but to his ears came the voice of a man. It was a steady, monotonous, singsong voice. Once the buck heard the harsh clash of metal upon rock. At the sound he snorted with a sudden start that jerked him through the air from water to meadow, and his feet sank into the young velvet, while he pricked his ears and again to listen, and faded away out of the canyon like a wraith, soft-footed and without sound.

The clash of steel-shod soles against the rocks began to be heard, and the man's voice grew louder. It was raised in a sort of chant and became distinct with nearness, so that the words could be heard:

> Tu'n around an' tu'n yo' face
> Untoe them sweet hills of grace.
> (D' pow'rs of sin yo' am scornin'!)
> Look about an' look aroun',
> Fling yo' sin pack on d' groun'
> (Yo' will meet wid d' Lord in d' mornin'!)

A sound of scrambling accompanied the song, and the spirit of the place fled away on the heels of the red-coated buck. The green screen was burst asunder, and a man peered out at the meadow and the pool and the sloping sidehill. He was a deliberate sort of man. He took in the scene with one embracing glance, then ran his eyes over the details to verify the general impression. Then, and not until then, did he open his mouth in vivid and solemn approval.

"Smoke of life an' snakes of purgatory! Will you just look at that! Wood an' water an' grass an' a sidehill! A pocket hunter's delight an' a cayuse's paradise! Cool green for tired eyes! Pink pills for pale people ain't in it. A secret pasture for prospectors and a resting place for tired burros, by damn!"

He was a sandy-complexioned man in whose face geniality and humor seemed the salient characteristics. It was a mobile face, quick-changing to inward mood and thought. Thinking was in him a visible process. Ideas chased across his face like windflaws across the surface of a lake. His hair, sparse and unkempt of growth, was as indeterminate and colorless as his complexion. It would seem that all the color of his frame had gone into his eyes, for they were startlingly blue. Also they were laughing and merry eyes, within them much of the naïveté and wonder of the child; and yet, in an unassertive way, they contained much of calm self-reliance and strength of purpose founded upon self-experience and experience of the world.

From out the screen of vines and creepers he flung ahead of him a miner's pick and shovel and gold pan. Then he crawled out himself into the open. He was clad in faded overalls and black cotton shirt, with hobnailed brogans on his feet, and on his head a hat whose shapelessness and stains advertised the rough usage of wind and rain and sun and camp smoke. He stood erect, seeing wide-eyed the secrecy of the scene and sensuously inhaling the warm, sweet breath of the canyon garden through nostrils that dilated and quivered with delight. His eyes narrowed to laughing slits of blue, his face wreathed itself in joy, and his mouth curled in a smile as he cried aloud:

"Jumping dandelions and happy hollyhocks, but that smells good to me! Talk about your attar o' roses an' cologne factories! They ain't in it!"

He had the habit of soliloquy. His quick-changing facial expressions might tell every thought and mood, but the tongue, perforce, ran hard after, repeating, like a second Boswell.[1]

The man lay down on the lip of the pool and drank long and deep of its water. "Tastes good to me," he murmured, lifting his head and gazing across the pool at the sidehill, while he wiped his mouth with the back of his hand. The sidehill attracted his attention. Still lying on his stomach, he studied the hill formation long and carefully. It was a practiced eye that traveled up the slope to the crumbling canyon wall and back and down

---

[1]James Boswell (1740–1795), Scottish author and lawyer known as the friend and biographer of Samuel Johnson. The posthumous publication of Boswell's journals revealed that he was also a devoted diarist, recording Johnson's conversations.

again to the edge of the pool. He scrambled to his feet and favored the side-hill with a second survey.

"Looks good to me," he concluded, picking up his pick and shovel and gold pan.

He crossed the stream below the pool, stepping agilely from stone to stone. Where the sidehill touched the water he dug up a shovelful of dirt and put it into the gold pan. He squatted down, holding the pan in his two hands, and partly immersing it in the stream. Then he imparted to the pan a deft circular motion that sent the water sluicing in and out through the dirt and gravel. The larger and the lighter particles worked to the surface, and these, by a skillful dipping movement of the pan, he spilled out and over the edge. Occasionally, to expedite matters, he rested the pan and with his fingers raked out the large pebbles and pieces of rock.

The contents of the pan diminished rapidly until only fine dirt and the smallest bits of gravel remained. At this stage he began to work very deliberately and carefully. It was fine washing, and he washed fine and finer, with a keen scrutiny and delicate and fastidious touch. At last the pan seemed empty of everything but water; but with a quick semicircular flirt that sent the water flying over the shallow rim into the stream he disclosed a layer of black sand on the bottom of the pan. So thin was this layer that it was like a streak of paint. He examined it closely. In the midst of it was a tiny golden speck. He dribbled a little water in over the depressed edge of the pan. With a quick flirt he sent the water sluicing across the bottom, turning the grains of black sand over and over. A second tiny golden speck rewarded his effort.

The washing had now become very fine—fine beyond all need of ordinary placer mining. He worked the black sand, a small portion at a time, up the shallow rim of the pan. Each small portion he examined sharply, so that his eyes saw every grain of it before he allowed it to slide over the edge and away. Jealously, bit by bit, he let the black sand slip away. A golden speck, no larger than a pinpoint, appeared on the rim, and by his manipulation of the water it returned to the bottom of the pan. And in such fashion another speck was disclosed, and another. Great was his care of them. Like a shepherd he herded his flock of golden specks so that not one should be lost. At last, of the pan of dirt nothing remained but his golden herd. He counted it, and then, after all his labor, sent it flying out of the pan with one final swirl of water.

But his blue eyes were shining with desire as he rose to his feet. "Seven," he muttered aloud, asserting the sum of the specks for which he had toiled so hard and which he had so wantonly thrown away. "Seven," he repeated, with the emphasis of one trying to impress a number on his memory.

He stood still a long while, surveying the hillside. In his eyes was a curiosity, new-aroused and burning. There was an exultance about his bearing and a keenness like that of a hunting animal catching the fresh scent of game.

He moved down the stream a few steps and took a second panful of dirt.

Again came the careful washing, the jealous herding of the golden specks, and the wantonness with which he sent them flying into the stream when he had counted their number.

"Five," he muttered, and repeated, "five."

He could not forbear another survey of the hill before filling the pan farther down the stream. His golden herds diminished. "Four, three, two, two, one," were his memory tabulations as he moved down the stream. When but one speck of gold rewarded his washing he stopped and built a fire of dry twigs. Into this he thrust the gold pan and burned it till it was blue-black. He held up the pan and examined it critically. Then he nodded approbation. Against such a color background he could defy the tiniest yellow speck to elude him.

Still moving down the stream, he panned again. A single speck was his reward. A third pan contained no gold at all. Not satisfied with this, he panned three times again, taking his shovels of dirt within a foot of one another. Each pan proved empty of gold, and the fact, instead of discouraging him, seemed to give him satisfaction. His elation increased with each barren washing, until he arose, exclaiming jubilantly:

"If it ain't the real thing, may God knock off my head with sour apples!"

Returning to where he had started operations, he began to pan up the stream. At first his golden herds increased—increased prodigiously. "Fourteen, eighteen, twenty-one, twenty-six," ran his memory tabulations. Just above the pool he struck his richest pan—thirty-five colors.

"Almost enough to save," he remarked regretfully as he allowed the water to sweep them away.

The sun climbed to the top of the sky. The man worked on. Pan by pan he went up the stream, the tally of results steadily decreasing.

"It's just booful, the way it peters out," he exulted when a shovelful of dirt contained no more than a single speck of gold.

And when no specks at all were found in several pans he straightened up and favored the hillside with a confident glance.

"Aha! Mr. Pocket!" he cried out as though to an auditor hidden somewhere above him beneath the surface of the slope. "Aha! Mr. Pocket! I'm a-comin', I'm a-comin', an' I'm shorely gwine to get yer! You heah me, Mr. Pocket? I'm gwine to get yer as shore as punkins ain't cauliflowers!"

He turned and flung a measuring glance at the sun poised above him in the azure of the cloudless sky. Then he went down the canyon, following the line of shovel holes he had made in filling the pans. He crossed the stream below the pool and disappeared through the green screen. There was little opportunity for the spirit of the place to return with its quietude and repose, for the man's voice, raised in ragtime song, still dominated the canyon with possession.

After a time, with a greater clashing of steel-shod feet on rock, he returned. The green screen was tremendously agitated. It surged back and forth in the throes of a struggle. There was a loud grating and clanging of metal. The man's voice leaped to a higher pitch and was sharp with imperativeness. A large body plunged and panted. There was a snapping and ripping and rending, and amid a shower of falling leaves a horse burst through the screen. On its back was a pack, and from this trailed broken vines and torn creepers. The animal gazed with astonished eyes at the scene into which it had been precipitated, then dropped its head to the grass and began contentedly to graze. A second horse scrambled into view, slipping once on the mossy rocks and regaining equilibrium when its hoofs sank into the yielding surface of the meadow. It was riderless, though on its back was a high-horned Mexican saddle, scarred and discolored by long usage.

The man brought up the rear. He threw off pack and saddle, with an eye to camp location, and gave the animals their freedom to graze. He unpacked his food and got out frying pan and coffeepot. He gathered an armful of dry wood, and with a few stones made a place for his fire.

"My," he said, "but I've got an appetite! I could scoff iron filings an' horseshoe nails an' thank you kindly, ma'am, for a second helpin'."

He straightened up, and while he reached for matches in the pocket of his overalls his eyes traveled across the pool to the sidehill. His fingers had clutched the matchbox, but they relaxed their hold and the hand came out empty. The man wavered perceptibly. He looked at his preparations for cooking and he looked at the hill.

"Guess I'll take another whack at her," he concluded, starting to cross the stream.

"They ain't no sense in it, I know," he mumbled apologetically. "But keepin' grub back an hour ain't goin' to hurt none, I reckon."

A few feet back from his first line of test pans he started a second line. The sun dropped down the western sky, the shadows lengthened, but the man worked on. He began a third line of test pans. He was crosscutting the hillside, line by line, as he ascended. The center of each line produced the richest pans, while the ends came where no colors showed in the pan. And as he ascended the hillside the lines grew perceptibly shorter. The regularity with which their length diminished served to indicate that somewhere up the slope the last line would be so short as to have scarcely length at all, and that beyond could come only a point. The design was growing into an inverted V. The converging sides of this V marked the boundaries of the gold-bearing dirt.

The apex of the V was evidently the man's goal. Often he ran his eye along the converging sides and on up the hill, trying to divine the apex, the point where the gold-bearing dirt must cease. Here resided "Mr. Pocket"—for so the man familiarly addressed the imaginary point above him on the slope, crying out:

"Come down out o' that, Mr. Pocket! Be right smart an' agreeable, an' come down!"

"All right," he would add later, in a voice resigned to determination. "All right, Mr. Pocket. It's plain to me I got to come right up an' snatch you out bald-headed. An' I'll do it! I'll do it!" he would threaten still later.

Each pan he carried down to the water to wash, and as he went higher up the hill the pans grew richer, until he began to save the gold in an empty baking powder can which he carried carelessly in his lap pocket. So engrossed was he in his toil that he did not notice the long twilight of oncoming night. It was not until he tried vainly to see the gold colors in the bottom of the pan that he realized the passage of time. He straightened up abruptly. An expression of whimsical wonderment and awe overspread his face as he drawled:

"Gosh darn my buttons, if I didn't plumb forget dinner!"

He stumbled across the stream in the darkness and lighted his long-delayed fire. Flapjacks and bacon and warmed-over beans constituted his supper. Then he smoked a pipe by the smoldering coals, listening to the night noises and watching the moonlight stream through the canyon. After that he unrolled his bed, took off his heavy shoes, and pulled the blankets up to his chin. His face showed white in the moonlight, like the face of a corpse. But it was a corpse that knew its resurrection, for the man rose suddenly on one elbow and gazed across at his hillside.

"Good night, Mr. Pocket," he called sleepily. "Good night."

He slept through the early gray of morning until the direct rays of the sun smote his closed eyelids, when he awoke with a start and looked about him until he had established the continuity of his existence and identified his present self with the days previously lived.

To dress, he had merely to buckle on his shoes. He glanced at his fireplace and at his hillside, wavered, but fought down the temptation and started the fire.

"Keep yer shirt on, Bill; keep yer shirt on," he admonished himself. "What's the good of rushin'? No use in gettin' all het up an' sweaty. Mr. Pocket'll wait for you. He ain't a-runnin' away before you can get yer breakfast. Now what you want, Bill, is something fresh in yer bill o' fare. So it's up to you to go an' get it."

He cut a short pole at the water's edge and drew from one of his pockets a bit of line and a draggled fly that had once been a royal coachman.

"Mebbe they'll bite in the early morning," he muttered as he made his first cast into the pool. And a moment later he was gleefully crying: "What'd I tell you, eh? What'd I tell you?"

He had no reel or any inclination to waste time, and by main strength, and swiftly, he drew out of the water a flashing ten-inch trout. Three more, caught in rapid succession, furnished his breakfast. When he came to the steppingstones on his way to his hillside, he was struck by a sudden thought, and paused.

"I'd just better take a hike downstream a ways," he said. "There's no tellin' what cuss may be snoopin' around."

But he crossed over on the stones, and with a "I really oughter take that hike" the need of the precaution passed out his mind and he fell to work.

At nightfall he straightened up. The small of his back was stiff from stooping toil, and as he put his hand behind him to soothe the protesting muscles he said:

"Now what d'ye think of that, by damn? I clean forgot my dinner again! If I don't watch out I'll sure be degeneratin' into a two-meal-a-day crank."

"Pockets is the damnedest things I ever see for makin' a man absent-minded," he communed that night as he crawled into his blankets. Nor did he forget to call up the hillside, "Good night, Mr. Pocket! Good night!"

Rising with the sun, and snatching a hasty breakfast, he was early at work. A fever seemed to be growing in him, nor did the increasing richness of the test pans allay this fever. There was a flush in his cheek other than that made by the heat of the sun, and he was oblivious to fatigue and the passage of time. When he filled a pan with dirt he ran down the hill to wash it; nor could he forbear running up the hill again, panting and stumbling profanely, to refill the pan.

He was now a hundred yards from the water, and the inverted V was assuming definite proportions. The width of the pay dirt steadily decreased, and the man extended in his mind's eye the sides of the V to their meeting place far up the hill. This was his goal, the apex of the V, and he panned many times to locate it.

"Just about two yards above that manzanita bush an' a yard to the right," he finally concluded.

Then the temptation seized him. "As plain as the nose on your face," he said as he abandoned his laborious crosscutting and climbed to the indicated apex. He filled a pan and carried it down the hill to wash. It contained no trace of gold. He dug deep, and he dug shallow, filling and washing a dozen pans, and was unrewarded even by the tiniest golden specks. He was enraged at having yielded to the temptation, and cursed himself blasphemously and pridelessly. Then he went down the hill and took up the crosscutting.

"Slow an' certain, Bill; slow an' certain," he crooned. "Short cuts to fortune ain't in your line, an' it's about time you know it. Get wise, Bill; get wise. Slow an' certain's the only hand you can play; so go to it, an' keep to it, too."

As the crosscuts decreased, showing that the sides of the V were converging, the depth of the V increased. The gold trace was dipping into the hill. It was only at thirty inches beneath the surface that he could get colors in his pan. The dirt he found at twenty-five inches from the surface, and at thirty-five inches, yielded barren pans. At the base of the V, by the water's edge, he had found the gold colors at the grass roots. The higher he went up the hill, the deeper the gold dipped. To dig a hole three feet deep in order to get one test pan was a task of no mean magnitude; while between the man and the apex intervened an untold number of such holes to be dug. "An' there's no tellin' how much deeper it'll pitch," he sighed in a moment's pause, while his fingers soothed his aching back.

Feverish with desire, with aching back and stiffening muscles, with pick and shovel gouging and mauling the soft brown earth, the man toiled up the hill. Before him was the smooth slope, spangled with flowers and made sweet with their breath. Behind him was devastation. It looked like some terrible eruption breaking out on the smooth skin of the hill. His slow progress was like that of a slug, be-fouling beauty with a monstrous trail.

Though the dipping gold trace increased the man's work, he found consolation in the increasing richness of the pans. Twenty cents, thirty cents, fifty cents, sixty cents, were the values of the gold found in the pans, and at nightfall he washed his banner pan, which gave him a dollar's worth of gold dust from a shovelful of dirt.

"I'll just bet it's my luck to have some inquisitive cuss come buttin' in here on my pasture," he mumbled sleepily that night as he pulled the blankets up to his chin.

Suddenly he sat upright. "Bill!" he called sharply. "Now listen to me, Bill; d'ye hear! It's up to you, tomorrow mornin', to mosey round an' see what you can see. Understand? Tomorrow morning, an' don't you forget it!"

He yawned and glanced across at his sidehill. "Good night, Mr. Pocket," he called.

In the morning he stole a march on the sun, for he had finished breakfast when its first rays caught him, and he was climbing the wall of the canyon where it crumbled away and gave footing. From the outlook at the top he found himself in the midst of loneliness. As far as he could see, chain after chain of mountains heaved themselves into his vision. To the east his eyes, leaping the miles between range and range and between many ranges, brought up at last against the white-peaked Sierras — the main crest, where the backbone of the Western world reared itself against the sky. To the north and south he could see more distinctly the cross systems that broke through the main trend of the sea of mountains. To the west the ranges fell away, one behind the other, diminishing and fading into the gentle foothills that, in turn, descended into the great valley which he could not see.

And in all that mighty sweep of earth he saw no sign of man nor of the handiwork of man — save only the torn bosom of the hillside at his feet. The man looked long and carefully. Once, far down his own canyon, he thought he saw in the air a faint hint of smoke. He looked again and decided that it was the purple haze of the hills made dark by a convolution of the canyon wall at its back.

"Hey, you, Mr. Pocket!" he called down into the canyon. "Stand out from under! I'm a-comin', Mr. Pocket! I'm a-comin'!"

The heavy brogans on the man's feet made him appear clumsy-footed, but he swung down from the giddy height as lightly and airily as a mountain goat. A rock, turning under his foot on the edge of the precipice, did not disconcert him. He seemed to know the precise time required for the turn to culminate in disaster, and in the meantime he utilized the false footing itself for the momentary earth contact necessary to carry him on into safety. Where the earth sloped so steeply that it was impossible to stand for a second upright, the man did not hesitate. His foot pressed the impossible surface for but a fraction of the fatal second and gave him the bound that carried him onward. Again, where even the fraction of a second's footing was out of the question, he would swing his body past by a moment's handgrip on a jutting knob of rock, a crevice, or a precariously rooted shrub. At last, with a wild leap and yell, he exchanged the face of the wall for an earth slide and finished the descent in the midst of several tons of sliding earth and gravel.

His first pan of the morning washed out over two dollars in coarse gold. It was from the center of the V. To either side the diminution in the values of the pans was swift. His lines of crosscutting holes were growing very short. The converging sides of the inverted V were only a few yards apart. Their meeting point was only a few yards above him. But the pay streak was dipping deeper and deeper into the earth. By early afternoon he was sinking the test holes five feet before the pans could show the gold trace.

For that matter the gold trace had become something more than a trace; it was a placer mine in itself, and the man resolved to come back after he had found the pocket and work over the ground. But the increasing richness of the pans began to worry him. By late afternoon the worth of the pans had grown to three and four dollars. The man scratched his head perplexedly and looked a few feet up the hill at the manzanita bush that marked approximately the apex of the V. He nodded his head and said oracularly:

"It's one o' two things, Bill; one o' two things. Either Mr. Pocket's spilled himself all out an' down the hill, or else Mr. Pocket's that damned rich you maybe won't be able to carry him all away with you. And that'd be hell, wouldn't it, now?" He chuckled at contemplation of so pleasant a dilemma.

Nightfall found him by the edge of the stream, his eyes wrestling with the gathering darkness over the washing of a five-dollar pan.

"Wisht I had an electric light to go on working," he said.

He found sleep difficult that night. Many times he composed himself and closed his eyes for slumber to overtake him; but his blood pounded with too strong desire, and as many times his eyes opened and he murmured wearily, "Wisht it was sunup."

Sleep came to him in the end, but his eyes were open with the first paling of the stars, and the gray of dawn caught him with breakfast finished and climbing the hillside in the direction of the secret abiding place of Mr. Pocket.

The first crosscut the man made, there was space for only three holes, so narrow had become the pay streak and so close was he to the fountainhead of the golden stream he had been following for four days.

"Be ca'm, Bill; be ca'm," he admonished himself as he broke ground for the final hole where the sides of the V had at last come together in a point.

"I've got the almighty cinch on you, Mr. Pocket, an' you can't lose me," he said many times as he sank the hole deeper and deeper.

Four feet, five feet, six feet, he dug his way down into the earth. The digging grew harder. His pick grated on broken rock. He examined the rock. "Rotten quartz," was his conclusion as, with the shovel, he cleared the bottom of the hole of loose dirt. He attacked the crumbling quartz with the pick, bursting the disintegrating rock asunder with every stroke.

He thrust his shovel into the loose mass. His eye caught a gleam of yellow. He dropped the shovel and squatted suddenly on his heels. As a farmer rubs the clinging earth from fresh-dug potatoes, so the man, a piece of rotten quartz held in both hands, rubbed the dirt away.

"Sufferin' Sardanopolis!" he cried. "Lumps an' chunks of it! Lumps an' chunks of it!"

It was only half rock he held in his hand. The other half was virgin gold. He dropped it into his pan and examined another piece. Little yellow was to be seen, but with his strong fingers he crumbled the rotten quartz away till both hands were filled with glowing yellow. He rubbed the dirt away from fragment after fragment, tossing them into the gold pan. It was a treasure hole. So much had the quartz rotted away that there was less of it than there was of gold. Now and again he found a piece to which no rock clung—a piece that was all gold. A chunk, where the pick had laid open the heart of the gold, glittered like a handful of yellow jewels, and he cocked his head at it and slowly turned it around and over to observe the rich play of the light upon it.

"Talk about yer Too Much Gold diggin's!" the man snorted contemptuously. "Why, this diggin'd make it look like thirty cents. This diggin' is all gold. An' right here an' now I name this yere canyon 'All Gold Canyon,' b' gosh!"

Still squatting on his heels, he continued examining the fragments and tossing them into the pan. Suddenly there came to him a premonition of danger. It seemed a shadow had fallen upon him. But there was no shadow. His heart had given a great jump up into his throat and was choking him. Then his blood slowly chilled and he felt the sweat of his shirt cold against his flesh.

He did not spring up nor look around. He did not move. He was considering the nature of the premonition he had received, trying to locate the source of the mysterious force that had warned him, striving to sense the imperative presence of the unseen thing that threatened him. There is an aura of things hostile, made manifest by messengers too refined for the senses to know; and this aura he felt, but knew not how he felt it. His was the feeling as when a cloud passes over the sun. It seemed that between him and life had passed something dark and smothering and menacing; a gloom, as it were, that swallowed up life and made for death — his death.

Every force of his being impelled him to spring up and confront the unseen danger, but his soul dominated the panic, and he remained squatting on his heels, in his hands a chunk of gold. He did not dare to look around, but he knew by now that there was something behind him and above him. He made believe to be interested in the gold in his hand. He examined it critically, turned it over and over, and rubbed the dirt from it. And all the time he knew that something behind him was looking at the gold over his shoulder.

Still feigning interest in the chunk of gold in his hand, he listened intently and he heard the breathing of the thing behind him. His eyes searched the ground in front of him for a weapon, but they saw only the uprooted gold, worthless to him now in his extremity. There was his pick, a handy weapon on occasion; but this was not such an occasion. The man realized his predicament. He was in a narrow hole that was seven feet deep. His head did not come to the surface of the ground. He was in a trap.

He remained squatting on his heels. He was quite cool and collected; but his mind, considering every factor, showed him only his helplessness. He continued rubbing the dirt from the quartz fragments and throwing the gold into the pan. There was nothing else for him to do. Yet he knew that he would have to rise up, sooner or later, and face the danger that breathed at his back. The minutes passed, and with the passage of each minute he knew that by so much he was nearer the time when he must stand up or else — and his wet shirt went cold against his flesh again at the thought—or else he might receive death as he stooped there over his treasure.

Still he squatted on his heels, rubbing dirt from gold and debating in just what manner he should rise up. He might rise up with a rush and claw his way out of the hole to meet whatever threatened on the even footing aboveground. Or he might rise up slowly and carelessly, and feign casually to discover the thing that breathed at his back. His instinct and every fighting fiber of his body favored the mad, clawing rush to the surface. His intellect, and the craft thereof, favored the slow and cautious meeting with the thing that menaced and which he could not see. And while he debated, a loud, crashing noise burst on his ear. At the same instant he received a stunning blow on the left side of the back, and from the point of impact felt a rush of flame through his flesh. He sprang up in the air, but halfway to his feet collapsed. His body crumpled in like a leaf withered in sudden heat, and he came down, his chest across his pan of gold, his face in the dirt and rock, his legs tangled and twisted because of the restricted space at the bottom of the hole. His legs twitched convulsively several times. His body was shaken as with a mighty ague. There was a slow expansion of the lungs, accompanied by a deep sigh. Then the air was slowly, very slowly, exhaled, and his body as slowly flattened itself down into inertness.

Above, revolver in hand, a man was peering down over the edge of the hole. He peered for a long time at the prone and motionless body beneath him. After a while the stranger sat down on the edge of the hole so that he could see into it, and rested the revolver on his knee. Reaching his hand into a pocket, he drew out a wisp of brown paper. Into this he dropped a few crumbs of tobacco. The combination became a cigarette, brown and squat, with the ends turned in. Not once did he take his eyes from the body at the bottom of the hole. He lighted the cigarette and drew its smoke into his lungs with a caressing intake of the breath. He smoked slowly. Once the cigarette went out and he relighted it. And all the while he studied the body beneath him.

In the end he tossed the cigarette stub away and rose to his feet. He moved to the edge of the hole. Spanning it, a hand resting on each edge, and with the revolver still in the right hand, he muscled his body down into the hole. While his feet were yet a yard from the bottom he released his hands and dropped down.

At the instant his feet struck bottom he saw the pocket miner's arm leap out, and his own legs knew a swift, jerking grip that overthrew him. In the nature of the jump his revolver hand was above his head. Swiftly as the grip had flashed about his legs, just as swiftly he brought the revolver down. He was still in the air, his fall in process of completion, when he pulled the trigger. The explosion was deafening in the confined space. The smoke filled the hole so that he could see nothing. He struck the bottom on his back, and like a cat's the pocket miner's body was on top of him. Even as the miner's body passed on top, the stranger crooked in his right arm to fire; and even in that instant the miner, with a quick thrust of elbow, struck his wrist. The muzzle was thrown up and the bullet thudded into the dirt of the side of the hole.

The next instant the stranger felt the miner's hand grip his wrist. The struggle was now for the revolver. Each man strove to turn it against the other's body. The smoke in the hole was clearing. The stranger, lying on his back, was beginning to see dimly. But suddenly he was blinded by a handful of dirt deliberately flung into his eyes by his antagonist. In that moment he felt a smashing darkness descend upon his brain, and in the midst of the darkness even the darkness ceased.

But the pocket miner fired again and again, until the revolver was empty. Then he tossed it from him and, breathing heavily, sat down on the dead man's legs.

The miner was sobbing and struggling for breath. "Measly skunk!" he panted; "a-campin' on my trail an' lettin' me do the work, an' then shootin' me in the back!"

He was half crying from anger and exhaustion. He peered at the face of the dead man. It was sprinkled with loose dirt and gravel, and it was difficult to distinguish the features.

"Never laid eyes on him before," the miner concluded his scrutiny. "Just a common an' ordinary thief, damn him! An' he shot me in the back! He shot me in the back!"

He opened his shirt and felt himself, front and back on his left side.

"Went clean through, and no harm done!" he cried jubilantly. "I'll bet he aimed all right, all right; but he drew the gun over when he pulled the trigger—the cuss! But I fixed 'm! Oh, I fixed 'm!"

His fingers were investigating the bullet hole in his side, and a shade of regret passed over his face. "It's goin' to be stiffer'n hell," he said. "An' it's up to me to get mended an' get out o' here."

He crawled out of the hole and went down the hill to his camp. Half an hour later he returned, leading his pack horse. His open shirt disclosed the rude bandages with which he had dressed his wound. He was slow and awkward with his left-hand movements, but that did not prevent his using the arm.

The bight of the pack rope under the dead man's shoulders enabled him to heave the body out of the hole. Then he set to work gathering up his gold. He worked steadily for several hours, pausing often to rest his stiffening shoulder and to exclaim:

"He shot me in the back, the measly skunk! He shot me in the back!"

When his treasure was quite cleaned up and wrapped securely into a number of blanket-covered parcels, he made an estimate of its value.

"Four hundred pounds, or I'm a Hottentot," he concluded. "Say two hundred in quartz an' dirt—that leaves two hundred pounds of gold. Bill! Wake up! Two hundred pounds of gold! Forty thousand dollars! An' it's yourn—all yourn!"

He scratched his head delightedly and his fingers blundered into an unfamiliar groove. They quested along it for several inches. It was a crease through his scalp where the second bullet had plowed.

He walked angrily over to the dead man.

"You would, would you?" he bullied. "You would, eh? Well, I fixed you good an' plenty, an' I'll give you decent burial, too. That's more'n you'd have done for me."

He dragged the body to the edge of the hole and toppled it in. It struck the bottom with a dull crash, on its side, the face twisted up to the light. The miner peered down at it.

"An' you shot me in the back!" he said accusingly.

With pick and shovel he filled the hole. Then he loaded the gold on his horse. It was too great a load for the animal, and when he had gained his camp he transferred part of it to his saddle horse. Even so, he was compelled to abandon a portion of his outfit—pick and shovel and gold pan, extra food and cooking utensils, and divers odds and ends.

The sun was at the zenith when the man forced the horses at the screen of vines and creepers. To climb the huge boulders the animals were compelled to uprear and struggle blindly through the tangled mass of vegetation. Once the saddle horse fell heavily and the man removed the pack to get the animal on its feet. After it started on its way again the man thrust his head out from among the leaves and peered up at the hillside.

"The measly skunk!" he said, and disappeared.

There was a ripping and tearing of vines and boughs. The trees surged back and forth, marking the passage of the animals through the midst of them. There was a clashing of steel-shod hoofs on stone, and now and again an oath or a sharp cry of command. Then the voice of the man was raised in song:

> Tu'n around an' tu'n yo' face
> Untoe them sweet hills of grace.
> (D' pow'rs of sin yo' am scornin'!)
> Look about an' look aroun',
> Fling yo' sin pack on d' groun'.
> (Yo' will meet wid d' Lord in d' mornin'!)

The song grew faint and fainter, and through the silence crept back the spirit of the place. The stream once more drowsed and whispered; the hum of the mountain's bees rose sleepily. Down through the perfume-weighted air fluttered the snowy fluffs of the cottonwoods. The butterflies drifted in and out among the trees, and over all blazed the quiet sunshine. Only remained the hoofmarks in the meadow and the torn hillside to mark the boisterous trail of the life that had broken the peace of the place and passed on.   [1905]

MARY AUSTIN

Mary Austin (1868–1934) was born in Carlinsville, Illinois. After her graduation from Blackburn College, she moved with her family to homestead in California in 1888. In 1891 she married Stafford Wallace Austin and lived in the desert, where she began to write the sketches about nature published in her first book, The Land of Little Rain *(1903). Two years later she divorced her husband and moved east to join artist colonies in New York City's Greenwich Village and in London, but she soon returned to New Mexico to write about her favorite landscape. Austin supported herself by writing sketches and stories for* The Overland Monthly, The Atlantic Monthly, Harper's Magazine, *and* Century Magazine. *In her autobiography* Earth Horizon *(1932), she explained that her goal as an author was to "write imaginatively not only of people, but of the scene, the totality which is called Nature, and . . . I would give myself intransigently to the quality of experience called Folk, and to the frame of behavior known as Mystical."*

Most of Austin's stories can be found in four collections: The Basket Woman: A Book of Fanciful Tales for Children *(1904),* Lost Borders *(1909),* The Trail Book *(1919), and* One-Smoke Stories *(1934). A posthumous collection of her early work—* Mother of Felipe and Other Stories *(1950), edited by Franklin Walker—also was produced.*

"The Walking Woman," first published in The Atlantic Monthly *in August 1907, was collected in* Lost Borders. *Austin often experimented in her writing, as in her story "The Return of Mr. Wills," in which she rewrote the plot of "Rip Van Winkle" from a woman's point of view, making Mrs. Wills discover after her husband's disappearance that "she not only did not need Mr. Wills, but got on better without him." In* One-Smoke Stories, *another literary experiment, Austin conceived each story in the volume as being told in the time it took its teller to smoke a cigarette. She believed that*

> *your true desert dweller travels light. He makes even of his experience a handy package with the finished neatness that distinguishes his artifacts. How else could they be passed intact from tribe to tribe, from generation to generation? Just before the end, like the rattle that warns that the story is about to strike, comes the fang of experience, most often in the shape of a wise saying. Then the speaker resumes the soul-consoling smoke while another takes up the dropped stitch of narrative and weaves it into the pattern of the talk.*

RELATED COMMENTARY: *Mary Austin, "Regionalism in American Fiction," page 1293.*

The Walking Woman

The first time of my hearing of her was at Temblor. We had come all one day between blunt, whitish bluffs rising from mirage water, with a thick, pale wake of dust billowing from the wheels, all the dead wall of the foothills sliding and shimmering with heat, to learn that the Walking Woman had passed us somewhere in the dizzying dimness, going down to the Tulares on her own feet. We heard of her again in the Carrisal, and again at Adobe Station, where she had passed a week before the shearing, and at last I had a glimpse of her at the Eighteen-Mile House as I went hurriedly northward on the Mojave stage; and afterward sheepherders at whose camps she slept, and cowboys at rodeos, told me as much of her way of life as they could understand. Like enough they told her as much of mine. That was very little. She was the Walking Woman, and no one knew her name, but because she was a sort of whom men speak respectfully, they called her to her face Mrs. Walker, and she answered to it if she was so inclined. She came and went about our western world on no discoverable errand, and whether she had some place of refuge where she lay by in the interim, or whether between her seldom, unaccountable appearances in our quarter she went on steadily walking, was never learned. She came and went, oftenest in a kind of muse of travel which the untrammelled space begets, or at rare intervals flooding wondrously with talk, never of herself, but of things she had known and seen. She must have seen some rare happenings, too—by report. She was at Maverick the time of the Big Snow, and at Tres Piños when they brought home the body of Morena; and if anybody could have told whether De Borba killed Mariana for spite or defence, it would have been she, only she could not be found when most wanted. She was at Tunawai at the time of the cloud-burst, and if she had cared for it could have known most desirable things of the ways of trail-making, burrow-habiting small things.

All of which should have made her worth meeting, though it was not, in fact, for such things I was wishful to meet her; and as it turned out, it was not of these things we talked when at last we came together. For one thing, she was a woman, not old, who had gone about alone in a country where the number of women is as one in fifteen. She had eaten and slept at the herder's camps, and laid by for days at one-man stations whose masters had no other touch of human kind than the passing of chance prospectors, or the halting of the tri-weekly stage. She had been set on her way by teamsters who lifted her out of white, hot desertness and put her down at the crossing of unnamed ways, days distant from anywhere. And through all this she passed unarmed and unoffended. I had the best testimony to this, the witness of the men themselves. I think they talked of it because they were so much surprised at it. It was not, on the whole, what they expected of themselves.

Well I understand that nature which wastes its borders with too eager burning, beyond which rim of desolation it flares forever quick and white, and have had some inkling of the isolating calm of a desire too high to stoop to satisfaction. But you could not think of these things pertaining to the Walking Woman; and if there were ever any truth in the exemption from offence residing in a frame of behavior called ladylike, it should have been inoperative here. What this really means is that you get no affront so long as your behavior in the estimate of the particular audience invites none. In the estimate of the immediate audience — conduct which affords protection in Mayfair gets you no consideration in Maverick. And by no canon could it be considered ladylike to go about on your own feet, with a blanket and a black bag and almost no money in your purse, in and about the haunts of rude and solitary men.

There were other things that pointed the wish for a personal encounter with the Walking Woman. One of them was the contradiction of reports of her — as to whether she was comely, for example. Report said yes, and again, plain to the point of deformity. She had a twist to her face, some said; a hitch to one shoulder; they averred she limped as she walked. But by the distance she covered she should have been straight and young. As to sanity, equal incertitude. On the mere evidence of her way of life she was cracked; not quite broken, but unserviceable. Yet in her talk there was both wisdom and information, and the word she brought about trails and water-holes was as reliable as an Indian's.

By her own account she had begun by walking off an illness. There had been an invalid to be taken care of for years, leaving her at last broken in body, and with no recourse but her own feet to carry her out of that predicament. It seemed there had been, besides the death of her invalid, some other worrying affairs, upon which, and the nature of her illness, she was never quite clear, so that it might very well have been an unsoundness of mind which drove her to the open, sobered and healed at last by the large soundness of nature. It must have been about that time that she lost her name. I am convinced that she never told it because she did not know it herself. She was the Walking Woman, and the country people called her Mrs. Walker. At the time I knew her, though she wore short hair and a man's boots, and had a fine down over all her face from exposure to the weather, she was perfectly sweet and sane.

I had met her occasionally at ranch-houses and road-stations, and had got as much acquaintance as the place allowed; but for the things I wished to know there wanted a time of leisure and isolation. And when the occasion came we talked altogether of other things.

It was at Warm Spring in the Little Antelope I came upon her in the heart of a clear forenoon. The spring lies off a mile from the main trail, and has the only trees about it known in that country. First you come upon a pool of waste full of weeds of a poisonous dark green, every reed ringed about with the water-level with a muddy white incrustation. Then the three oaks appear staggering on the slope, and the spring sobs and blubbers below them in ashy-colored mud. All the hills of that country have the down plunge toward the desert and back abruptly toward the Sierra. The grass is thick and brittle and bleached straw-color toward the end of the season. As I rode up the swale of the spring I saw the Walking Woman sitting where the grass was deepest, with her black bag and blanket, which she carried on a stick, beside her. It was one of those days when the genius of talk flows as smoothly as the rivers of mirage through the blue hot desert morning.

You are not to suppose that in my report of a Borderer I give you the words only, but the full meaning of the speech. Very often the words are merely the punctuation of thought; rather, the crests of the long waves of inter-communicative silences. Yet the speech of the Walking Woman was fuller than most.

The best of our talk that day began in some dropped word of hers from which I inferred that she had had a child. I was surprised at that, and then wondered why I should have been surprised, for it is the most natural of all experiences to have children. I said something of that purport, and also that it was one of the perquisites of living I should be least willing to do without. And that led to the Walking Woman saying that there were three things which if you had known you could cut out all the rest, and they were good any way you got them, but best if, as in her case, they were related to and grew each one out of the others. It was while she talked that I decided that she really did have a twist to her face, a sort of natural warp or skew into which it fell when it was worn merely as a countenance, but which disappeared the moment it became the vehicle of thought or feeling.

The first of the experiences the Walking Woman had found most worth while had come to her in a sand-storm on the south slope of Tehachapi in a dateless spring. I judged it should have been about the time she began to find herself, after the period of worry and loss in which her wandering began. She had come, in a day pricked full of intimations of a storm, to the camp of Filon Geraud, whose companion shepherd had gone a three days' *pasear* to Mojave for supplies. Geraud was of great hardihood, red-blooded, of a full laughing eye, and an indubitable spark for women. It was the season of the year when there is a soft bloom on the days, but the nights are cowering cold and the lambs tender, not yet flockwise. At such times a sand-storm works incalculable disaster. The lift of the wind is so great that the whole surface of the ground appears to travel upon it slantwise, thinning out miles high in air. In the intolerable smother the lambs are lost from the ewes; neither dogs nor man make headway against it.

The morning flared through a horizon of yellow smudge, and by mid-forenoon the flock broke.

"There were but the two of us to deal with the trouble," said the Walking Woman. "Until that time I had not known how strong I was, nor how good it is to run when running is worth while. The flock travelled down the wind, the sand bit our faces; we called, and after a time heard the words broken and beaten small by the wind. But after a little we had not to call. All the time of our running in the yellow dusk of day and the black dark of night, I knew where Filon was. A flock-length away, I knew him. Feel? What should I feel? I knew. I ran with the flock and turned it this way and that as Filon would have.

"Such was the force of the wind that when we came together we held by one another and talked a little between pantings. We snatched and ate what we could as we ran. All that day and night until the next afternoon the camp kit was not out of the cayaques. But we held the flock. We herded them under a butte when the wind fell off a little, and the lambs sucked; when the storm rose they broke, but we kept upon their track and brought them together again. At night the wind quieted, and we slept by turns; at least Filon slept. I lay on the ground when my turn was and beat with the storm. I was no more tired than the earth was. The sand filled in the creases of the blanket, and where I turned, dripped back upon the ground. But we saved the sheep. Some ewes there were that would not give down their milk because of the worry of the storm, and the lambs died. But we kept the flock together. And I was not tired."

The Walking Woman stretched out her arms and clasped herself, rocking in them as if she would have hugged the recollection to her breast.

"For you see," said she, "I worked with a man, without excusing, without any burden on me of looking or seeming. Not fiddling or fumbling as women work, and hoping it will all turn out for the best. It was not for Filon to ask, Can you, or Will you. He said, Do, and I did. And my work was good. We held the flock. And that," said the Walking Woman, the twist coming in her face again, "is one of the things that make you able to do without the others."

"Yes," I said; and then, "What others?"

"Oh," she said, as if it pricked her, "the looking and the seeming."

And I had not thought until that time that one who had the courage to be the Walking Woman would have cared! We sat and looked at the pattern of the thick crushed grass on the slope, wavering in the fierce noon like the waterings in the coat of a tranquil beast; the ache of a world-old bitterness sobbed and whispered in the spring. At last—

"It is by the looking and the seeming," said I, "that the opportunity finds you out."

"Filon found out," said the Walking Woman. She smiled; and went on from that to tell me how, when the wind went down about four o'clock and left the afternoon clear and tender, the flock began to feed, and they had out the kit from the cayaques, and cooked a meal. When it was over, and Filon had his pipe between his teeth, he came over from his side of the fire, of his own notion, and stretched himself on the ground beside her. Of his own notion. There was that in the way she said it that made it seem as if nothing of the sort had happened before to the Walking Woman, and for a moment I thought she was about to tell me one of the things I wished to know; but she went on to say what Filon had said to her of her work with the flock. Obvious, kindly things, such as any man in sheer decency would have said, so that there must have something more gone with the words to make them so treasured of the Walking Woman.

"We were very comfortable," said she, "and not so tired as we expected to be. Filon leaned up on his elbow. I had not noticed until then how broad he was in the shoulders, and how strong in the arms. And we had saved the flock together. We felt that. There was something that said together, in the slope of his shoulders toward me. It was around his mouth and on the cheek high up under the shine of his eyes. And under the shine the look—the look that said, 'We are of one sort and one mind'—his eyes that were the color of the flat water in the toulares—do you know the look?"

"I know it."

"The wind was stopped and all the earth smelled of dust, and Filon understood very well that what I had done with him I could not have done so well with another. And the look—the look in the eyes—"

"Ah-ah—!"

I have always said, I will say again, I do not know why at this point the Walking Woman touched me. If it were merely a response to my unconscious throb of sympathy, or the unpremeditated way of her heart to declare that this, after all, was the best of all indispensable experiences; or if in some flash of forward vision, encompassing the unimpassioned years, the stir, the movement of tenderness were for *me*—but no; as often as I have thought of it, I have thought of a different reason, but no conclusive one, why the Walking Woman should have put out her hand and laid it on my arm.

"To work together, to love together," said the Walking Woman, withdrawing her hand again; "there you have two of the things; the other you know."

"The mouth at the breast," said I.

"The lips and the hands," said the Walking Woman. "The little, pushing hands and the small cry." There ensued a pause of fullest understanding, while the land before us swam in the noon, and a dove in the oaks behind the spring began to call. A little red fox came out of the hills and lapped delicately at the pool.

"I stayed with Filon until the fall," said she. "All that summer in the Sierras, until it was time to turn south on the trail. It was a good time, and longer than he could be expected to have loved one like me. And besides, I was no longer able to keep the trail. My baby was born in October."

Whatever more there was to say to this, the Walking Woman's hand said it, straying with remembering gesture to her breast. There are so many ways of loving and working, but only one way of the first-born. She added after an interval, that she did not know if she would have given up her walking to keep at home and tend him, or whether the thought of her son's small feet running beside her in the trails would have driven her to the open again. The baby had not stayed long enough for that. "And whenever the wind blows in the night," said the Walking Woman, "I wake and wonder if he is well covered."

She took up her black bag and her blanket; there was the ranch-house of Dos Palos to be made before night, and she went as outliers do, without a hope expressed of another meeting and no word of good-bye. She was the Walking Woman. That was it. She had walked off all sense of society-made values, and, knowing the best when the best came to her, was able to take it. Work—as I believed; love—as the Walking Woman had proved it; a child—as you subscribe to it. But look you: it was the naked thing the Walking Woman grasped, not dressed and tricked out, for instance, by prejudices in favor of certain occupations; and love, man love, taken as it came, not picked over and rejected if it carried no obligation of permanency; and a child; *any* way you get it, a child is good to have, say nature and the Walking Woman; to have it and not to wait upon a proper concurrence of so many decorations that the event may not come at all.

At least one of us is wrong. To work and to love and to bear children. *That* sounds easy enough. But the way we live establishes so many things of much more importance.

Far down the dim, hot valley I could see the Walking Woman with her blanket and black bag over her shoulder. She had a queer, sidelong gait, as if in fact she had a twist all through her.

Recollecting suddenly that people called her lame, I ran down to the open place below the spring where she had passed. There in the bare, hot sand the track of her two feet bore evenly and white.   [1907]

HENRY JAMES

Henry James (1843–1916) was born in New York City. His father was a philosopher of religion, and his brother William James was a noted physician, philosopher, and psychologist. Educated mostly by tutors in the United States and Europe, James published his first story at the age of twenty-one. In 1875 he chose to live permanently in England. He formed friendships with several European writers, including Gustave Flaubert and Guy de Maupassant. During the first phase of James's long career, he explored personal relationships, most notably in the novel The Portrait of a Lady *(1881). Then he turned to themes of social reform, as in* The Bostonians *(1886). He constantly experimented with ways to refine his writing and commented on his "art of fiction" in many essays, prefaces, letters, and notebooks. The dense, symbolic style of his later work can be seen in his last three novels,* The Wings of the Dove *(1902),* The Ambassadors *(1903), and* The Golden Bowl *(1904).*

James wrote more than seventy stories. He felt that experience assumes meaning only when the proper form for its expression is found. One of his favorite words was awareness, *and he tried to make his own awareness encompass everything he could observe, relate, weigh, and judge. In the essay "The Art of Fiction," he said that the source of fiction is not mere raw experience but "the power to guess the unseen from the seen, to trace the implication of things, to judge the whole piece by the pattern, the condition of feeling life in general so completely that you are well on your way to knowing any particular corner of it."*

James's stories lack the characteristic compression and dramatic action typical of this literary form. Instead, using the device he called a "central intelligence," he revealed the world through the silent thought of one of his characters, proceeding at a stately pace, through constant self-examination and self-analysis, as in his late story "The Jolly Corner," published in the English Review *in 1908.*

Struck by the remarkable construction of Henry James's sentences, the essayist William Gass has commented in On Being Blue:

> *If any of us were as well taken care of as the sentences of Henry James, we'd never long for another, never wander away; where else would we receive such constant attention, our thoughts anticipated, our feelings understood? Who else would robe us so richly, take us to the best places, or guard our virtue as his own and defend our character in every situation? If we were his sentences, we'd sing ourselves though we were dying and about to be extinguished, since the silence which would follow our passing would not be like the pause left behind by a noisy train. It would be a memorial, well-remarked grave, just as the Master has assured us death itself is: the distinguished thing.*

RELATED COMMENTARIES: *Henry James, "From* Hawthorne," *page 1378; Floyd Stovall, "Henry James's 'The Jolly Corner,'" page 1452.*

The Jolly Corner

"Every one asks me what I 'think' of everything," said Spencer Brydon; "and I make answer as I can — begging or dodging the question, putting them off with any nonsense. It wouldn't matter to any of them really," he went on, "for, even were it possible to meet in that stand-and-deliver way so silly a demand on so big a subject, my 'thoughts' would still be almost altogether about something that concerns only myself." He was talking to Miss Staverton, with whom for a couple of months now he had availed himself of every possible occasion to talk; this disposition and this resource, this comfort and support, as the situation in fact presented itself, having promptly enough taken the first place in the considerable array of rather unattenuated surprises attending his so strangely belated return to America. Everything was somehow a surprise; and that might be natural when one had so long and so consistently neglected everything, taken pains to give surprises so much margin for play. He had given them more than thirty years — thirty-three, to be exact; and they now seemed to him to have organised their performance quite on the scale of that licence. He had been twenty-three on leaving New York — he was fifty-six today: unless indeed he were to reckon as he had sometimes, since his repatriation, found himself feeling; in which case he would have lived longer than is often allotted to man. It would have taken a century, he repeatedly said to himself, and said also to Alice Staverton, it would have taken a longer absence and a more averted mind than those even of which he had been guilty, to pile up the differences, the newnesses, the queernesses, above all the bignesses, for the better or the worse, that at present assaulted his vision wherever he looked.

The great fact all the while however had been the incalculability; since he *had* supposed himself, from decade to decade, to be allowing, and in the most liberal and intelligent manner, for brilliancy of change. He actually saw that he had allowed for nothing; he missed what he would have been sure of finding, he found what he would never have imagined. Proportions and values were upside-down; the ugly things he had expected, the ugly things of his far-away youth, when he had too promptly waked up to a sense of the ugly — these uncanny phenomena placed him rather, as it happened, under the charm; whereas the "swagger" things, the modern, the monstrous, the famous things, those he had more particularly, like thousands of ingenuous enquirers every year, come over to see, were exactly his sources of dismay. They were as so many set traps for displeasure, above all for reaction, of which his restless tread was constantly pressing the spring. It was interesting, doubtless, the whole show, but it would have been too disconcerting hadn't a certain finer truth saved the situation. He had distinctly not, in this steadier light, come over *all* for the monstrosities; he had come, not only in the last analysis but quite on the face of the act, under an impulse with which they had nothing to do. He had come—putting the thing pompously—to look at his "property," which he had thus for a third of a century not been within four thousand miles of; or, expressing it less sordidly, he had yielded to the humour of seeing again his house on the jolly corner, as he usually, and quite fondly, described it—the one in which he had first seen the light, in which various members of his family had lived and had died, in which the holidays of his overschooled boyhood had been passed and the few social flowers of his chilled adolescence gathered, and which, alienated then for so long a period, had, through the successive deaths of his two brothers and the ter-mination of old arrangements, come wholly into his hands. He was the owner of another, not quite so "good"—the jolly corner having been, from far back, superlatively extended and consecrated; and the value of the pair represented his main capital, with an income consisting, in these later years, of their respective rents which (thanks precisely to their original excellent type) had never been depressingly low. He could live in "Europe," as he had been in the habit of living, on the product of these flourishing New York leases, and all the better since, that of the second structure, the mere number in its long row, having within a twelvemonth fallen in, renovation at a high advance had proved beautifully possible.

These were items of property indeed, but he had found himself since his arrival distinguishing more than ever between them. The house within the street, two bristling blocks westward, was already in course of recon-struction as a tall mass of flats; he had acceded, some time before, to over-tures for this conversion—in which, now that it was going forward, it had been not the least of his astonishments to find himself able, on the spot, and though without a previous ounce of such experience, to participate with a certain intelligence, almost with a certain authority. He had lived his life with his back so turned to such concerns and his face addressed to those of so different an order that he scarce knew what to make of this lively stir, in a compartment of his mind never yet penetrated, of a capacity for business and a sense for construction. These virtues, so common all round him now, had been dormant in his own organism—where it might be said of them perhaps that they had slept the sleep of the just. At present, in the splendid autumn weather—the autumn at least was a pure boon in the terrible place—he loafed about his "work" undeterred, secretly agi-tated; not in the least "minding" that the whole proposition, as they said, was vulgar and sordid, and ready to climb ladders, to walk the plank, to handle materials and look wise about them, to ask questions, in fine, and challenge explanations and really "go into" figures.

It amused, it verily quite charmed him; and, by the same stroke, it amused, and even more, Alice Staverton, though perhaps charming her perceptibly less. She wasn't however going to be better off for it, as *he* was—and so astonishingly much: nothing was now likely, he knew, ever to make her better off than she found herself, in the afternoon of life, as the delicately frugal professor and tenant of the small house in Irving Place to which she had subtly managed to cling through her almost unbroken New York career. If he knew the way to it now better than to any other address among the dreadful multiplied numberings which seemed to him to reduce the whole place to some vast ledger-page, overgrown, fantastic, of ruled and criss-crossed lines and figures — if he had formed, for his consolation, that habit, it was really not a little because of the charm of his having encountered and recognised, in the vast wilderness of the wholesale, breaking through the mere gross generalisation of wealth and force and success, a small still scene where items and shades, all delicate things, kept the sharpness of the notes of a high voice perfectly trained, and where economy hung about like the scent of a garden. His old friend lived with one maid and herself, dusted her relics and trimmed her lamps and polished her silver; she stood off, in the awful modern crush, when she could, but she sallied forth and did battle when the challenge was really to "spirit," the spirit she after all confessed to, proudly and a little shyly, as to that of the better time, that of *their* common, their quite far-away and antediluvian social period and order. She made use of the street-cars when need be, the terrible things that people scrambled for as the panic-stricken at sea scramble for the boats; she affronted, inscrutably, under stress, all the public concussions and ordeals; and yet, with that slim mystifying grace of her appearance, which defied you to say if she were a fair young woman who looked older through trouble, or a fine smooth older one who looked young through successful indifference; with her precious reference, above all, to memories and histories into which he could enter, she was as exquisite for him as some pale pressed flower (a rarity to begin with), and, failing other sweetnesses, she was a sufficient reward of his effort. They had communities of knowledge, "their" knowledge (this discriminating possessive was always on her lips) of presences of the other age, presences all overlaid, in his case, by the experience of a man and the freedom of a wanderer, overlaid by pleasure, by infidelity, by passages of life that were strange and dim to her, just by "Europe" in short, but still unobscured, still exposed and cherished, under that pious visitation of the spirit from which she had never been diverted.

She had come with him one day to see how his "apartment-house" was rising; he had helped her over gaps and explained to her plans, and while they were there had happened to have, before her, a brief but lively discussion with the man in charge, the representative of the building-firm that had undertaken his work. He had found himself quite "standing-up" to this personage over a failure on the latter's part to observe some detail of one of their noted conditions, and had so lucidly argued his case that, besides ever so prettily flushing, at the time, for sympathy in his triumph, she had afterwards said to him (though to a slightly greater effect of irony) that he had clearly for too many years neglected a real gift. If he had but stayed at home he would have anticipated the inventor of the sky-scraper. If he had but stayed at home he would have discovered his genius in time really to start some new variety of awful architectural hare and run it till it burrowed in a gold-mine. He was to remember these words, while the weeks elapsed, for the small silver ring they had sounded over the queerest and deepest of his own lately most disguised and most muffled vibrations.

It had begun to be present to him after the first fortnight, it had broken out with the oddest abruptness, this particular wanton wonderment: it met him there—and this was the image under which he himself judged the matter, or at least, not a little, thrilled and flushed with it—very much as he might have been met by some strange figure, some unexpected occupant, at a turn of one of the dim passages of an empty house. The quaint analogy quite hauntingly remained with him, when he didn't indeed rather improve it by a still intenser form: that of his opening a door behind which he would have made sure of finding nothing, a door into a room shuttered and void, and yet so coming, with a great suppressed start, on some quite erect confronting presence, something planted in the middle of the place and facing him through the dusk. After that visit to the house in construction he walked with his companion to see the other and always so much the better one, which in the eastward direction formed one of the corners, the "jolly" one precisely, of the street now so generally dishonoured and disfigured in its westward reaches, and of the comparatively conservative Avenue. The Avenue still had pretensions, as Miss Staverton said, to decency; the old people had mostly gone, the old names were unknown, and here and there an old association seemed to stray, all vaguely, like some very aged person, out too late, whom you might meet and feel the impulse to watch or follow, in kindness, for safe restoration to shelter.

They went in together, our friends; he admitted himself with his key, as he kept no one there, he explained, preferring, for his reasons, to leave the place empty, under a simple arrangement with a good woman living in the neighbourhood and who came for a daily hour to open windows and dust and sweep. Spencer Brydon had his reasons and was growingly aware of them; they seemed to him better each time he was there, though he didn't name them all to his companion, any more than he told her as yet how often, how quite absurdly often, he himself came. He only let her see for the present, while they walked through the great blank rooms, that absolute vacancy reigned and that, from top to bottom, there was nothing but Mrs. Muldoon's broomstick, in a corner, to tempt the burglar. Mrs. Muldoon was then on the premises, and she loquaciously attended the visitors, preceding them from room to room and pushing back shutters and throwing up sashes—all to show them, as she remarked, how little there was to see. There was little indeed to see in the great gaunt shell where the main dispositions and the general apportionment of space, the style of an age of ampler allowances, had nevertheless for its master their honest pleading message, affecting him as some good old servant's, some lifelong retainer's appeal for a character, or even for a retiring-pension; yet it was also a remark of Mrs. Muldoon's that, glad as she was to oblige him by her noonday round, there was a request she greatly hoped he would never make of her. If he should wish her for any reason to come in after dark she would just tell him, if he "plased," that he must ask it of somebody else.

The fact that there was nothing to see didn't militate for the worthy woman against what one *might* see, and she put it frankly to Miss Staverton that no lady could be expected to like, could she? "scraping up to thim top storeys in the ayvil hours." The gas and the electric light were off the house, and she fairly evoked a gruesome vision of her march through the great grey rooms—so many of them as there were too!—with her glimmering taper. Miss Staverton met her honest glare with a smile and the profession that she herself certainly would recoil from such an adventure. Spencer Brydon meanwhile held his peace—for the moment; the question of the "evil" hours in his old home had already become too grave for him. He had begun some time since to "crape," and he knew just why a packet of candles addressed to that pursuit had been stowed by his own hand, three weeks before, at the back of a drawer of the fine old sideboard that occupied, as a "fixture," the deep recess in the dining-room. Just now he laughed at his companions—quickly however changing the subject; for the reason that, in the first place, his laugh struck him even at that moment as starting the odd echo, the conscious human resonance (he scarce knew how to qualify it) that sounds made while he was there alone sent back to his ear or his fancy; and that, in the second, he imagined Alice Staverton for the instant on the point of asking him, with a divination, if he ever so prowled. There were divinations he was unprepared for, and he had at all events averted enquiry by the time Mrs. Muldoon had left them, passing on to other parts.

There was happily enough to say, on so consecrated a spot, that could be said freely and fairly; so that a whole train of declarations was precipitated by his friend's having herself broken out, after a yearning look round: "But I hope you don't mean they want you to pull *this* to pieces!" His answer came, promptly, with his re-awakened wrath: it was of course exactly what they wanted, and what they were "at" him for, daily, with the iteration of people who couldn't for their life understand a man's liability to decent feelings. He had found the place, just as it stood and beyond what he could express, an interest and a joy. There were values other than the beastly rent-values, and in short, in short—! But it was thus Miss Staverton took him up. "In short you're to make so good a thing of your sky-scraper that, living in luxury on *those* ill-gotten gains, you can afford for a while to be sentimental here!" Her smile had for him, with the words, the particular mild irony with which he found half her talk suffused; an irony without bitterness and that came, exactly, from her having so much imagination—not, like the cheap sarcasms with which one heard most people, about the world of "society," bid for the reputation of cleverness, from nobody's really having any. It was agreeable to him at this very moment to be sure that when he had answered, after a brief demur, "Well yes: so, precisely, you may put it!" her imagination would still do him justice. He explained that even if never a dollar were to come to him from the other house he would nevertheless cherish this one; and he dwelt, further, while they lingered and wandered, on the fact of the stupefaction he was already exciting, the positive mystification he felt himself create.

He spoke of the value of all he read into it, into the mere sight of the walls, mere shapes of the rooms, mere sound of the floors, mere feel, in his hand, of the old silver-plated knobs of the several mahogany doors, which suggested the pressure of the palms of the dead; the seventy years of the past in fine that these things represented, the annals of nearly three generations, counting his grandfather's, the one that had ended there, and the impalpable ashes of his long-extinct youth, afloat in the very air like microscopic motes. She listened to everything; she was a woman who answered intimately but who utterly didn't chatter. She scattered abroad therefore no cloud of words; she could assent, she could agree, above all, she could encourage, without doing that. Only at the last she went a little further than he had done himself. "And then how do you know? You may still, after all, want to live here." It rather indeed pulled him up, for it wasn't what he had been thinking, at least in her sense of the words. "You mean I may decide to stay on for the sake of it?"

"Well, *with* such a home—!" But, quite beautifully, she had too much tact to dot so monstrous an *i*, and it was precisely an illustration of the way she didn't rattle. How could any one—of any wit—insist on any one else's "wanting" to live in New York?

"Oh," he said, "I *might* have lived here (since I had my opportunity early in life); I might have put in here all these years. Then everything would have been different enough—and, I dare say, 'funny' enough. But that's another matter. And then the beauty of it—I mean of my perversity, of my refusal to agree to a 'deal'—is just in the total absence of a reason. Don't you see that if I had a reason about the matter at all it would *have* to be the other way, and would then be inevitably a reason of dollars? There are no reasons here *but* of dollars. Let us therefore have none whatever—not the ghost of one."

They were back in the hall then for departure, but from where they stood the vista was large, through an open door, into the great square main saloon, with its almost antique felicity of brave spaces between windows. Her eyes came back from that reach and met his own a moment. "Are you very sure the 'ghost' of one doesn't, much rather, serve—?"

He had a positive sense of turning pale. But it was as near as they were then to come. For he made answer, he believed, between a glare and a grin: "Oh ghosts—of course the place must swarm with them! I should be ashamed of it if it didn't. Poor Mrs. Muldoon's right, and it's why I haven't asked her to do more than look in."

Miss Staverton's gaze again lost itself, and things she didn't utter, it was clear, came and went in her mind. She might even for the minute, off there in the fine room, have imagined some element dimly gathering. Simplified like the death-mask of a handsome face, it perhaps produced for her just then an effect akin to the stir of an expression in the "set" commemorative plaster. Yet whatever her impression may have been she produced instead a vague platitude. "Well, if it were only furnished and lived in—!"

She appeared to imply that in case of its being still furnished he might have been a little less opposed to the idea of a return. But she passed straight into the vestibule, as if to leave her words behind her, and the next moment he had opened the house-door and was standing with her on the steps. He closed the door and, while he re-pocketed his key, looking up and down, they took in the comparatively harsh actuality of the Avenue, which reminded him of the assault of the outer light of the Desert on the traveller emerging from an Egyptian tomb. But he risked before they stepped into the street his gathered answer to her speech. "For me it *is* lived in. For me it *is* furnished." At which it was easy for her to sigh "Ah yes—!" all vaguely and discreetly; since his parents and his favourite sister, to say nothing of other kin, in numbers, had run their course and met their end there. That represented, within the walls, ineffaceable life.

It was a few days after this that, during an hour passed with her again, he had expressed his impatience of the too flattering curiosity—among the people he met—about his appreciation of New York. He had arrived at none at all that was socially producible, and as for that matter of his "thinking" (thinking the better or the worse of anything there) he was wholly taken up with one subject of thought. It was mere vain egoism, and it was moreover, if she liked, a morbid obsession. He found all things come back to the question of what he personally might have been, how he might have led his life and "turned out," if he had not so, at the outset, given it up. And confessing for the first time to the intensity within him of this absurd speculation—which but proved also, no doubt, the habit of too selfishly thinking—he affirmed the impotence there of any other source of interest, any other native appeal. "What would it have made of me, what would it have made of me? I keep for ever wondering, all idiotically; as if I could possibly know! I see what it has made of dozens of others, those I meet, and it positively aches within me, to the point of exasperation, that it would have made something of me as well. Only I can't make out *what,* and the worry of it, the small rage of curiosity never to be satisfied, brings back what I remember to have felt, once or twice, after judging best, for reasons, to burn some important letter unopened. I've been sorry, I've hated it—I've never known what was in the letter. You may of course say it's a trifle—!"

"I don't say it's a trifle," Miss Staverton gravely interrupted.

She was seated by her fire, and before her, on his feet and restless, he turned to and fro between this intensity of his idea and a fitful and unseeing inspection, through his single eyeglass, of the dear little old objects on her chimney-piece. Her interruption made him for an instant look at her harder. "I shouldn't care if you did!" he laughed, however; "and it's only a figure, at any rate, for the way I now feel. *Not* to have followed my perverse young course—and almost in the teeth of my father's curse, as I may say; not to have kept it up, so, 'over there,' from that day to this, without a doubt or a pang; not, above all, to have liked it, to have loved it, so much, loved it, no doubt, with such an abysmal conceit of my own preference: some variation from *that,* I say, must have produced some different effect for my life and for my 'form.' I should have stuck here—if it had been possible; and I was too young, at twenty-three, to judge, *pour deux sous,* whether it *were* possible. If I had waited I might have seen it was, and then I might have been, by staying here, something nearer to one of these types who have been hammered so hard and made so keen by their conditions. It isn't that I admire them so much—the question of any charm in them, or of any charm, beyond that of the rank money-passion, exerted by their conditions *for* them, has nothing to do with the matter: it's only a question of what fantastic, yet perfectly possible, development of my own nature I mayn't have missed. It comes over me that I had then a strange *alter ego* deep down somewhere within me, as the full-blown flower is in the small tight bud, and that I just took the course, I just transferred him to the climate, that blighted him for once and for ever."

"And you wonder about the flower," Miss Staverton said. "So do I, if you want to know; and so I've been wondering these several weeks. I believe in the flower," she continued, "I feel it would have been quite splendid, quite huge and monstrous."

"Monstrous above all!" her visitor echoed; "and I imagine, by the same stroke, quite hideous and offensive."

"You don't believe that," she returned; "if you did you wouldn't wonder. You'd know, and that would be enough for you. What you feel—and what I feel *for* you—is that you'd have had power."

"You'd have liked me that way?" he asked.

She barely hung fire. "How should I not have liked you?"

"I see. You'd have liked me, have preferred me, a billionaire!"

"How should I not have liked you?" she simply again asked.

He stood before her still—her question kept him motionless. He took it in, so much there was of it; and indeed his not otherwise meeting it testified to that. "I know at least what I am," he simply went on; "the other side of the medal's clear enough. I've not been edifying—I believe I'm thought in a hundred quarters to have been barely decent. I've followed strange paths and worshipped strange gods; it must have come to you again and again—in fact you've admitted to me as much—that I was leading, at any time these thirty years, a selfish frivolous scandalous life. And you see what it has made of me."

She just waited, smiling at him. "You see what it has made of *me.*"

"Oh you're a person whom nothing can have altered. You were born to be what you are, anywhere, anyway: you've the perfection nothing else could have blighted. And don't you see how, without my exile, I shouldn't have been waiting till now—?" But he pulled up for the strange pang.

"The great thing to see," she presently said, "seems to me to be that it has spoiled nothing. It hasn't spoiled your being here at last. It hasn't spoiled this. It hasn't spoiled your speaking—" She also however faltered.

He wondered at everything her controlled emotion might mean. "Do you believe then—too dreadfully!—that I *am* as good as I might ever have been?"

"Oh no! Far from it!" With which she got up from her chair and was nearer to him. "But I don't care," she smiled.

"You mean I'm good enough?"

She considered a little. "Will you believe it if I say so? I mean will you let that settle your question for you?" And then as if making out in his face that he drew back from this, that he had some idea which, however absurd, he couldn't yet bargain away: "Oh you don't care either—but very differently: you don't care for anything but yourself."

Spencer Brydon recognised it—it was in fact what he had absolutely professed. Yet he importantly qualified. "*He* isn't myself. He's the just so totally other person. But I do want to see him," he added. "And I can. And I shall."

Their eyes met for a minute while he guessed from something in hers that she divined his strange sense. But neither of them otherwise expressed it, and her apparent understanding, with no protesting shock, no easy derision, touched him more deeply than anything yet, constituting for his stifled perversity, on the spot, an element that was like breathable air. What she said however was unexpected. "Well, *I've* seen him."

"You—?"

"I've seen him in a dream."

"Oh a 'dream'—!" It let him down.

"But twice over," she continued. "I saw him as I see you now."

"You've dreamed the same dream—?"

"Twice over," she repeated. "The very same."

This did somehow a little speak to him, as it also gratified him. "You dream about me at that rate?"

"Ah about *him*!" she smiled.

His eyes again sounded her. "Then you know all about him." And as she said nothing more: "What's the wretch like?"

She hesitated, and it was as if he were pressing her so hard that, resisting for reasons of her own, she had to turn away. "I'll tell you some other time!"

–II–

It was after this that there was most of a virtue for him, most of a cultivated charm, most of a preposterous secret thrill, in the particular form of surrender to his obsession and of address to what he more and more believed to be his privilege. It was what in these weeks he was living for—since he really felt life to begin but after Mrs. Muldoon had retired from the scene and, visiting the ample house from attic to cellar, making sure he was alone, he knew himself in safe possession and, as he tacitly expressed it, let himself go. He sometimes came twice in the twenty-four hours; the moments he liked best were those of gathering dusk, of the short autumn twilight; this was the time of which, again and again, he found himself hoping most. Then he could, as seemed to him, most intimately wander and wait, linger and listen, feel his fine attention, never in his life before so fine, on the pulse of the great vague place: he preferred the lampless hour and only wished he might have prolonged each day the deep crepuscular spell. Later—rarely much before midnight, but then for a considerable vigil—he watched with his glimmering light; moving slowly, holding it high, playing it far, rejoicing above all, as much as he might, in open vistas, reaches of communication between rooms and by passages; the long straight chance or show, as he would have called it, for the revelation he pretended to invite. It was a practice he found he could perfectly "work" without exciting remark; no one was in the least the wiser for it; even Alice Staverton, who was moreover a well of discretion, didn't quite fully imagine.

He let himself in and let himself out with the assurance of calm proprietorship; and accident so far favoured him that, if a fat Avenue "officer" had happened on occasion to see him entering at eleven-thirty, he had never yet, to the best of his belief, been noticed as emerging at two. He walked there on the crisp November nights, arrived regularly at the evening's end; it was as easy to do this after dining out as to take his way to a club or to his hotel. When he left his club, if he hadn't been dining out, it was ostensibly to go to his hotel; and when he left his hotel, if he had spent a part of the evening there, it was ostensibly to go to his club. Everything was easy in fine; everything conspired and promoted: there was truly even in the strain of his experience something that glossed over, something that salved and simplified, all the rest of consciousness. He circulated, talked, renewed, loosely and pleasantly, old relations—met indeed, so far as he could, new expectations and seemed to make out on the whole that in spite of the career, of such different contacts, which he had spoken of to Miss Staverton as ministering so little, for those who might have watched it, to edification, he was positively rather liked than not. He was a dim secondary social success—and all with people who had truly not an idea of him. It was all mere surface sound, this murmur of their welcome, this popping of their corks—just as his gestures of response were the extravagant shadows, emphatic in proportion as they meant little, of some game of *ombres chinoises*.[1] He projected himself all day, in thought, straight over the bristling line of hard unconscious heads and into the other, the real, the

---

[1](French) shadow-graph; shadow play.

waiting life; the life that, as soon as he had heard behind him the click of his great house-door, began for him, on the jolly corner, as beguilingly as the slow opening bars of some rich music follows the tap of the conductor's wand.

He always caught the first effect of the steel point of his stick on the old marble of the hall pavement, large black-and-white squares that he remembered as the admiration of his childhood and that had then made in him, as he now saw, for the growth of an early conception of style. This effect was the dim reverberating tinkle as of some far-off bell hung who should say where? — in the depths of the house, of the past, of that mystical other world that might have flourished for him had he not, for weal or woe, abandoned it. On this impression he did ever the same thing; he put his stick noiselessly away in a corner — feeling the place once more in the likeness of some great glass bowl, all precious concave crystal, set delicately humming by the play of a moist finger round its edge. The concave crystal held, as it were, this mystical other world, and the indescribably fine murmur of its rim was the sigh there, the scarce audible pathetic wail to his strained ear, of all the old baffled forsworn possibilities. What he did therefore by this appeal of his hushed presence was to wake them into such measure of ghostly life as they might still enjoy. They were shy, all but unappeasably shy, but they weren't really sinister; at least they weren't as he had hitherto felt them — before they had taken the Form he so yearned to make them take, the Form he at moments saw himself in the light of fairly hunting on tiptoe, the points of his evening-shoes, from room to room and from storey to storey.

That was the essence of his vision — which was all rank folly, if one would, while he was out of the house and otherwise occupied, but which took on the last verisimilitude as soon as he was placed and posted. He knew what he meant and what he wanted; it was as clear as the figure on a cheque presented in demand for cash. His *alter ego* "walked" — that was the note of his image of him, while his image of his motive for his own odd pastime was the desire to waylay him and meet him. He roamed, slowly, warily, but all restlessly, he himself did — Mrs. Muldoon had been right, absolutely, with her figure of their "craping"; and the presence he watched for would roam restlessly too. But it would be as cautious and as shifty; the conviction of its probable, in fact its already quite sensible, quite audible evasion of pursuit grew for him from night to night, laying on him finally a rigour to which nothing in his life had been comparable. It had been the theory of many superficially-judging persons, he knew, that he was wasting that life in a surrender to sensations, but he had tasted of no pleasure so fine as his actual tension, had been introduced to no sport that demanded at once the patience and the nerve of this stalking of a creature more subtle, yet at bay perhaps more formidable, than any beast of the forest. The terms, the comparisons, the very practices of the chase positively came again into play; there were even moments when passages of his occasional experience as a sportsman, stirred memories, from his younger time, of moor and mountain and desert, revived for him—and to the increase of his keenness—by the tremendous force of analogy. He found himself at moments—once he had placed his single light on some mantel-shelf or in some recess—stepping back into shelter or shade, effacing himself behind a door or in an embrasure, as he had sought of old the vantage of rock and tree; he found himself holding his breath and living in the joy of the instant, the supreme suspense created by big game alone.

He wasn't afraid (though putting himself the question as he believed gentlemen on Bengal tiger-shoots or in close quarters with the great bear of the Rockies had been known to confess to having put it); and this indeed—since here at least he might be frank!—because of the impression, so intimate and so strange, that he himself produced as yet a dread, produced certainly a strain, beyond the liveliest he was likely to feel. They fell for him into categories, they fairly became familiar, the signs, for his own perception, of the alarm his presence and his vigilance created; though leaving him always to remark, portentously, on his probably having formed a relation, his probably enjoying a consciousness, unique in the experience of man. People enough, first and last, had been in terror of apparitions, but who had ever before so turned the tables and become himself, in the apparitional world, an incalculable terror? He might have found this sublime had he quite dared to think of it; but he didn't too much insist, truly, on that side of his privilege. With habit and repetition he gained to an extraordinary degree the power to penetrate the dusk of distances and the darkness of corners, to resolve back into their innocence the treacheries of uncertain light, the evil-looking forms taken in the gloom by mere shadows, by accidents of the air, by shifting effects of perspective; putting down his dim luminary he could still wander on without it, pass into other rooms and, only knowing it was there behind him in case of need, see his way about, visually project for his purpose a comparative clearness. It made him feel, this acquired faculty, like some monstrous stealthy cat; he wondered if he would have glared at these moments with large shining yellow eyes, and what it mightn't verily be, for the poor hard-pressed *alter ego,* to be confronted with such a type.

He liked however the open shutters; he opened everywhere those Mrs. Muldoon had closed, closing them as carefully afterwards, so that she shouldn't notice: he liked—oh this he did like, and above all in the upper rooms!—the sense of the hard silver of the autumn stars through the window-panes, and scarcely less the flare of the street-lamps below, the white electric lustre which it would have taken curtains to keep out. This was human actual social; this was of the world he had lived in, and he was more at his ease certainly for the countenance, coldly general and impersonal, that all the while and in spite of his detachment it seemed to give him. He had support of course mostly in the rooms at the wide front and the prolonged side; it failed him considerably in the central shades and the parts at the back. But if he sometimes, on his rounds, was glad of his optical reach, so none the less often the rear of the house affected him as the very jungle of his prey. The place was there more subdivided; a large "extension" in particular, where small rooms for servants had been multiplied, abounded in nooks and corners, in closets and passages, in the ramifications especially of an ample back staircase over which he leaned, many a time, to look far down—not deterred from his gravity even while aware that he might, for a spectator, have figured some solemn simpleton playing at hide-and-seek. Outside in fact he might himself make that ironic *rapprochement;* but within the walls, and in spite of the clear windows, his consistency was proof against the cynical light of New York.

It had belonged to that idea of the exasperated consciousness of his victim to become a real test for him; since he had quite put it to himself from the first that, oh distinctly! he could "cultivate" his whole perception. He had felt it as above all open to cultivation—which indeed was but another name for his manner of spending his time. He was bringing it on, bringing it to perfection, by practice; in consequence of which it had grown so fine that he was now aware of impressions, attestations of his general postulate, that couldn't have broken upon him at once. This was the case more specifically with a phenomenon at last quite frequent for him in the upper rooms, the recognition—absolutely unmistakeable, and by a turn dating from a particular hour, his resumption of his campaign after a diplomatic drop, a calculated absence of three nights—of his being definitely followed, tracked at a distance carefully taken and to the express end that he should the less confidently, less arrogantly, appear to himself merely to pursue. It worried, it finally quite broke him up, for it proved, of all the conceivable impressions, the one least suited to his book. He was kept in sight while remaining himself—as regards the essence of his position—sightless, and his only recourse then was in abrupt turns, rapid recoveries of ground. He wheeled about, retracing his steps, as if he might so catch in his face at least the stirred air of some other quick revolution. It was indeed true that his fully dislocalised thought of these manœuvres recalled to him Pantaloon, at the Christmas farce, buffeted and tricked from behind by ubiquitous Harlequin; but it left intact the influence of the conditions themselves each time he was reexposed to them, so that in fact this association, had he suffered it to become constant, would on a certain side have but ministered to his intenser gravity. He had made, as I have said, to create on the premises the baseless sense of a reprieve, his three absences; and the result of the third was to confirm the after-effect of the second.

On his return, that night—the night succeeding his last intermission—he stood in the hall and looked up the staircase with a certainty more intimate than any he had yet known. "He's *there,* at the top, and waiting—not, as in general, falling back for disappearance. He's holding his ground, and it's the first time—which is a proof, isn't it? that something has happened for him." So Brydon argued with his hand on the banister and his foot on the lowest stair; in which position he felt as never before the air chilled by his logic. He himself turned cold in it, for he seemed of a sudden to know what now was involved. "Harder pressed?—yes, he takes it in, with its thus making clear to him that I've come, as they say, 'to stay.' He finally doesn't like and can't bear it, in the sense, I mean, that his wrath, his menaced interest, now balances with his dread. I've hunted him till he has 'turned': that, up there, is what has happened—he's the fanged or the antlered animal brought at last to bay." There came to him, as I say—but determined by an influence beyond my notation!—the acuteness of this certainty; under which however the next moment he had broken into a sweat that he would as little have consented to attribute to fear as he would have dared immediately to act upon it for enterprise. It marked none the less a prodigious thrill, a thrill that represented sudden dismay, no doubt, but also represented, and with the selfsame throb, the strangest, the most joyous, possibly the next minute almost the proudest, duplication of consciousness.

"He has been dodging, retreating, hiding, but now, worked up to anger, he'll fight!"—this intense impression made a single mouthful, as it were, of terror and applause. But what was wondrous was that the applause, for the felt fact, was so eager, since, if it was his other self he was running to earth, this ineffable identity was thus in the last resort not unworthy of him. It bristled there—somewhere near at hand, however unseen still—as the hunted thing, even as the trodden worm of the adage *must* at last bristle; and Brydon at this instant tasted probably of a sensation more complex than had ever before found itself consistent with sanity. It was as if it would have shamed him that a character so associated with his own should triumphantly succeed in just skulking, should to the end not risk the open, so that the drop of this danger was, on the spot, a great lift of the whole situation. Yet with another rare shift of the same subtlety he was already trying to measure by how much more he himself might now be in peril of fear; so rejoicing that he could, in another form, actively inspire that fear, and simultaneously quaking for the form in which he might passively know it.

The apprehension of knowing it must after a little have grown in him, and the strangest moment of his adventure perhaps, the most memorable or really most interesting, afterwards, of his crisis, was the lapse of certain instants of concentrated conscious *combat,* the sense of a need to hold on to something, even after the manner of a man slipping and slipping on some awful incline; the vivid impulse, above all, to move, to act, to charge, somehow and upon something—to show himself, in a word, that he wasn't afraid. The state of "holding-on" was thus the state to which he was momentarily reduced; if there had been anything, in the great vacancy, to seize, he would presently have been aware of having clutched it as he might under a shock at home have clutched the nearest chair-back. He had been surprised at any rate—of this he *was* aware—into something unprecedented since his original appropriation of the place; he had closed his eyes, held them tight, for a long minute, as with that instinct of dismay and that terror of vision. When he opened them the room, the other contiguous rooms, extraordinarily, seemed lighter—so light, almost, that at first he took the change for day. He stood firm, however that might be, just where he had paused; his resistance had helped him—it was as if there were something he had tided over. He knew after a little what this was—it had been in the imminent danger of flight. He had stiffened his will against going; without this he would have made for the stairs, and it seemed to him that, still with his eyes closed, he would have descended them, would have known how, straight and swiftly, to the bottom.

Well, as he had held out, here he was—still at the top, among the more intricate upper rooms and with the gauntlet of the others, of all the rest of the house, still to run when it should be his time to go. He would go at his time—only at his time: didn't he go every night very much at the same hour? He took out his watch—there was light for that: it was scarcely a quarter past one, and he had never withdrawn so soon. He reached his lodgings for the most part at two—with his walk of a quarter of an hour. He would wait for the last quarter—he wouldn't stir till then; and he kept his watch there with his eyes on it, reflecting while he held it that this deliberate wait, a wait with an effort, which he recognised, would serve perfectly for the attestation he desired to make. It would prove his courage—unless indeed the latter might most be proved by his budging at last from his place. What he mainly felt now was that, since he hadn't original scuttled, he had his dignities—which had never in his life seemed so many—all to preserve and to carry aloft. This was before him in truth as a physical image, an image almost worthy of an age of greater romance. That remark indeed glimmered for him only to glow the next instant with a finer light; since what age of romance, after all, could have matched either the state of his mind or, "objectively," as they said, the wonder of his situation? The only difference would have been that, brandishing his dignities over his head as in a parchment scroll, he might then—that is in the heroic time—have proceeded downstairs with a drawn sword in his other grasp.

At present, really, the light he had set down on the mantel of the next room would have to figure his sword; which utensil, in the course of a minute, he had taken the requisite number of steps to possess himself of. The door between the rooms was open, and from the second another door opened to a third. These rooms, as he remembered, gave all three upon a common corridor as well, but there was a fourth, beyond them, without issue save through the preceding. To have moved, to have heard his step again, was appreciably a help; though even in recognising this he lingered once more a little by the chimney-piece on which his light had rested.

When he next moved, just hesitating where to turn, he found himself considering a circumstance that, after his first and comparatively vague apprehension of it, produced in him the start that often attends some pang of recollection, the violent shock of having ceased happily to forget. He had come into sight of the door in which the brief chain of communication ended and which he now surveyed from the nearer threshold, the one not directly facing it. Placed at some distance to the left of this point, it would have admitted him to the last room of the four, the room without other approach or egress, had it not, to his intimate conviction, been closed *since* his former visitation, the matter probably of a quarter of an hour before. He stared with all his eyes at the wonder of the fact, arrested again where he stood and again holding his breath while he sounded its sense. Surely it had been *subsequently* closed — that is it had been on his previous passage indubitably open!

He took it full in the face that something had happened between — that he couldn't not have noticed before (by which he meant on his original tour of all the rooms that evening) that such a barrier had exceptionally presented itself. He had indeed since that moment undergone an agitation so extraordinary that it might have muddled for him any earlier view; and he tried to convince himself that he might perhaps then have gone into the room and, inadvertently, automatically, on coming out, have drawn the door after him. The difficulty was that this exactly was what he never did; it was against his whole policy, as he might have said, the essence of which was to keep vistas clear. He had them from the first, as he was well aware, quite on the brain: the strange apparition, at the far end of one of them, of his baffled "prey" (which had become by so sharp an irony so little the term now to apply!) was the form of success his imagination had most cherished, projecting into it always a refinement of beauty. He had known fifty times the start of perception that had afterwards dropped; had fifty times gasped to himself "There!" under some fond brief hallucination. The house, as the case stood, admirably lent itself; he might wonder at the taste, the native architecture of the particular time, which could rejoice so in the multiplication of doors — the opposite extreme to the modern, the actual almost complete proscription of them; but it had fairly contributed to provoke this obsession of the presence encountered telescopically, as he might say, focussed and studied in diminishing perspective and as by a rest for the elbow.

It was with these considerations that his present attention was charged — they perfectly availed to make what he saw portentous. He *couldn't*, by any lapse, have blocked that aperture; and if he hadn't, if it was unthinkable, why what else was clear but that there had been another agent? Another agent? — he had been catching, as he felt, a moment back, the very breath of him; but when had he been so close as in this simple, this logical, this completely personal act? It was so logical, that is, that one might have *taken* it for personal; yet for what did Brydon take it, he asked himself, while, softly panting, he felt his eyes almost leave their sockets. Ah this time at last they *were*, the two, the opposed projections of him, in presence; and this time, as much as one would, the question of danger loomed. With it rose, as not before, the question of courage — for what he knew the blank face of the door to say to him was "Show us how much you have!" It stared, it glared back at him with that challenge; it put to him the two alternatives: should he just push it open or not? Oh to have this consciousness was to *think* — and to think, Brydon knew, as he stood there, was, with the lapsing moments, not to have acted! Not to have acted — that was the misery and the pang — was even still not to act; was in fact *all* to feel the thing in another, in a new and terrible way. How long did he pause and how long did he debate? There was presently nothing to measure it; for his vibration had already changed — as just by the effect of its intensity. Shut up there, at bay, defiant, and with the prodigy of the thing palpably proveably *done,* thus giving notice like some stark signboard — under that accession of accent the situation itself had turned; and Brydon at last remarkably made up his mind on what it had turned to.

It had turned altogether to a different admonition; to a supreme hint, for him, of the value of Discretion! This slowly dawned, no doubt — for it could take its time; so perfectly, on his threshold, had he been stayed, so little as yet had he either advanced or retreated. It was the strangest of all things that now when, by his taking ten steps and applying his hand to a latch, or even his shoulder and his knee, if necessary, to a panel, all the hunger of his prime need might have been met, his high curiosity crowned, his unrest assuaged — it was amazing, but it was also exquisite and rare, that insistence should have, at a touch, quite dropped from him. Discretion — he jumped at that; and yet not, verily, at such a pitch, because it saved his nerves or his skin, but because, much more valuably, it saved the situation. When I say he "jumped" at it I feel the consonance of this term with the fact that — at the end indeed of I know not how long — he did move again, he crossed straight to the door. He wouldn't touch it — it seemed now that he might *if* he would: he would only just wait there a little, to show, to prove, that he wouldn't. He had thus another station, close to the thin partition by which revelation was denied him; but with his eyes bent and his hands held off in a mere intensity of stillness. He listened as if there had been something to hear, but this attitude, while it lasted, was his own communication. "If you won't then — good: I spare you and I give up. You affect me as by the appeal positively for pity: you convince me that for reasons rigid and sublime — what do I know? — we both of us should have suffered. I respect them then, and, though moved and privileged as, I believe, it has never been given to man, I retire, I renounce — never, on my honour, to try again. So rest for ever — and let *me!*"

That, for Brydon was the deep sense of this last demonstration — solemn, measured, directed, as he felt it to be. He brought it to a close, he turned away; and now verily he knew how deeply he had been stirred. He retraced his steps, taking up his candle, burnt, he observed, well-nigh to the socket, and marking again, lighten it as he would, the distinctness of his footfall; after which, in a moment, he knew himself at the other side of the house. He did here what he had not yet done at these hours—he opened half a casement, one of those in the front, and let in the air of the night; a thing he would have taken at any time previous for a sharp rupture of his spell. His spell was broken now, and it didn't matter—broken by his concession and his surrender, which made it idle henceforth that he should ever come back. The empty street—its other life so marked even by the great lamplit vacancy—was within call, within touch; he stayed there as to be in it again, high above it though he was still perched; he watched as for some comforting common fact, some vulgar human note, the passage of a scavenger or a thief, some night-bird however base. He would have blessed that sign of life; he would have welcomed positively the slow approach of his friend the policeman, whom he had hitherto only sought to avoid, and was not sure that if the patrol had come into sight he mightn't have felt the impulse to get into relation with it, to hail it, on some pretext, from his fourth floor.

The pretext that wouldn't have been too silly or too compromising, the explanation that would have saved his dignity and kept his name, in such a case, out of the papers, was not definite to him: he was so occupied with the thought of recording his Discretion—as an effect of the vow he had just uttered to his intimate adversary—that the importance of this loomed large and something had overtaken all ironically his sense of proportion. If there had been a ladder applied to the front of the house, even one of the vertiginous perpendiculars employed by painters and roofers and sometimes left standing overnight, he would have managed somehow, astride of the window-sill, to compass by outstretched leg and arm that mode of descent. If there had been some such uncanny thing as he had found in his room at hotels, a workable fire-escape in the form of notched cable or a canvas shoot, he would have availed himself of it as a proof—well, of his present delicacy. He nursed that sentiment, as the question stood, a little in vain, and even—at the end of he scarce knew, once more, how long—found it, as by the action on his mind of the failure of response of the outer world, sinking back to vague anguish. It seemed to him he had waited an age for some stir of the great grim hush; the life of the town was itself under a spell—so unnaturally, up and down the whole prospect of known and rather ugly objects, the blankness and the silence lasted. Had they ever, he asked himself, the hard-faced houses, which had begun to look livid in the dim dawn, had they ever spoken so little to any need of his spirit? Great builded voids, great crowded stillnesses put on, often, in the heart of cities, for the small hours, a sort of sinister mask, and it was of this large collective negation that Brydon presently became conscious—all the more that the break of day was, almost incredibly, now at hand, proving to him what a night he had made of it.

He looked again at his watch, saw what had become of his time-values (he had taken hours for minutes—not, as in other tense situations, minutes for hours) and the strange air of the streets was but the weak, the sullen flush of a dawn in which everything was still locked up. His choked appeal from his own open window had been the sole note of life, and he could but break off at last as for a worse despair. Yet while so deeply demoralised he was capable again of an impulse denoting—at least by his present measure—extraordinary resolution; of retracing his steps to the spot where he had turned cold with the extinction of his last pulse of doubt as to there being in the place another presence than his own. This required an effort strong enough to sicken him; but he had his reason, which overmastered for the moment everything else. There was the whole of the rest of the house to traverse, and how should he screw himself to that if the door he had since closed were at present open? He could hold to the idea that the closing had practically been for him an act of mercy, a chance offered him to descend, depart, get off the ground and never again profane it. This conception held together, it worked; but what it meant for him depended now clearly on the amount of forbearance his recent action, or rather his recent inaction, had engendered. The image of the "presence," whatever it was, waiting there for him to go—this image had not yet been so concrete for his nerves as when he stopped short of the point at which certainty would have come to him. For, with all his resolution, or more exactly with all his dread, he did stop short—he hung back from really seeing. The risk was too great and his fear too definite: it took at this moment an awful specific form.

He knew—yes, as he had never known anything—that, *should* he see the door open, it would all too abjectly be the end of him. It would mean that the agent of his shame—for his shame was the deep abjection—was once more at large and in general possession; and what glared him thus in the face was the act that this would determine for him. It would send him straight about to the window he had left open, and by that window, be long ladder and dangling rope as absent as they would, he saw himself uncontrollably insanely fatally take his way to the street. The hideous chance of this he at least could avert; but he could only avert it by recoiling in time from assurance. He had the whole house to deal with, this fact was still there; only he now knew that uncertainty alone could start him. He stole back from where he had checked himself—merely to do so was suddenly like safety—and, making blindly for the greater staircase, left gaping rooms and sounding passages behind. Here was the top of the stairs, with a fine large dim descent and three spacious landings to mark off. His instinct was all for mildness, but his feet were harsh on the floors, and, strangely, when he had in a couple of minutes become aware of this, it counted somehow for help. He couldn't have spoken, the tone of his voice would have scared him, and the common conceit or resource of "whistling in the dark" (whether literally or figuratively) have appeared basely vulgar;

yet he liked none the less to hear himself go, and when he had reached his first landing—taking it all with no rush, but quite steadily—that stage of success drew from him a gasp of relief.

The house, withal, seemed immense, the scale of space again inordinate; the open rooms, to no one of which his eyes deflected, gloomed in their shuttered state like mouths of caverns, only the high skylight that formed the crown of the deep well created for him a medium in which he could advance, but which might have been, for queerness of colour, some watery under-world. He tried to think of something noble, as that his property was really grand, a splendid possession; but this nobleness took the form too of the clear delight with which he was finally to sacrifice it. They might come in now, the builders, the destroyers—they might come as soon as they would. At the end of two flights he had dropped to another zone, and from the middle of the third, with only one more left, he recognised the influence of the lower windows, of half-drawn blinds, of the occasional gleam of street-lamps, of the glazed spaces of the vestibule. This was the bottom of the sea, which showed an illumination of its own and which he even saw paved—when at a given moment he drew up to sink a long look over the banisters—with the marble squares of his childhood. By that time indubitably he felt, as he might have said in a commoner cause, better; it had allowed him to stop and draw breath, and the ease increased with the sight of the old black-and-white slabs. But what he most felt was that now surely, with the element of impunity pulling him as by hard firm hands, the case was settled for what he might have seen above had he dared that last look. The closed door, blessedly remote now, was still closed—and he had only in short to reach that of the house.

He came down further, he crossed the passage forming the access to the last flight; and if here again he stopped an instant it was almost for the sharpness of the thrill of assured escape. It made him shut his eyes—which opened again to the straight slope of the remainder of the stairs. Here was impunity still, but impunity almost excessive; inasmuch as the side-lights and the high fan-tracery of the entrance were glimmering straight into the hall; an appearance produced, he the next instant saw, by the fact that the vestibule gaped wide, that the hinged halves of the inner door had been thrown far back. Out of that again the *question* sprang at him, making his eyes, as he felt, half-start from his head, as they had done, at the top of the house, before the sign of the other door. If he had left that one open, hadn't he left this one closed, and wasn't he now in *most* immediate presence of some inconceivable occult activity? It was as sharp, the question, as a knife in his side, but the answer hung fire still and seemed to lose itself in the vague darkness to which the thin admitted dawn, glimmering archwise over the whole outer door, made a semicircular margin, a cold silvery nimbus that seemed to play a little as he looked—to shift and expand and contract.

It was as if there had been something within it, protected by indistinctness and corresponding in extent with the opaque surface behind, the painted panels of the last barrier to his escape, of which the key was in his pocket. The indistinctness mocked him even while he stared, affected him as somehow shrouding or challenging certitude, so that after faltering an instant on his step he let himself go with the sense that here *was* at last something to meet, to touch, to take, to know—something all unnatural and dreadful, but to advance upon which was the condition for him either of liberation or of supreme defeat. The penumbra, dense and dark, was the virtual screen of a figure which stood in it as still as some image erect in a niche or as some black-vizored sentinel guarding a treasure. Brydon was to know afterwards, was to recall and make out, the particular thing he had believed during the rest of his descent. He saw, in its great grey glimmering margin, the central vagueness diminish, and he felt it to be taking the very form toward which, for so many days, the passion of his curiosity had yearned. It gloomed, it loomed, it was something, it was somebody, the prodigy of a personal presence.

Rigid and conscious, spectral yet human, a man of his own substance and stature waited there to measure himself with his power to dismay. This only could it be—this only till he recognised, with his advance, that what made the face dim was the pair of raised hands that covered it and in which, so far from being offered in defiance, it was buried as for dark deprecation. So Brydon, before him, took him in; with every fact of him now, in the higher light, hard and acute—his planted stillness, his vivid truth, his grizzled bent head and white masking hands, his queer actuality of evening-dress, of dangling double eye-glass, of gleaming silk lappet and white linen, of pearl button and gold watch-guard and polished shoe. No portrait by a great modern master could have presented him with more intensity, thrust him out of his frame with more art, as if there had been "treatment," of the consummate sort, in his every shade and salience. The revulsion, for our friend, had become, before he knew it, immense—this drop, in the act of apprehension, to the sense of his adversary's inscrutable manœuvre. That meaning at least, while he gaped, it offered him; for he could but gape at his other self in this other anguish, gape as a proof that *he,* standing there for the achieved, the enjoyed, the triumphant life, couldn't be faced in his triumph. Wasn't the proof in the splendid covering hands, strong and completely spread?—so spread and so intentional that, in spite of a special verity that surpassed every other, the fact that one of these hands had lost two fingers, which were reduced to stumps, as if accidentally shot away, the face was effectually guarded and saved.

"Saved," though, *would* it be?—Brydon breathed his wonder till the very impunity of his attitude and the very insistence of his eyes produced, as he felt, a sudden stir which showed the next instant as a deeper portent, while the head raised itself, the betrayal of a braver purpose. The hands, as he looked, began to move, to open; then, as if deciding in a flash, dropped from the face and left it uncovered and presented. Horror, with the sight, had leaped into Brydon's throat, gasping there in a sound he couldn't utter; for the bared identity was too hideous as *his,* and his glare was the passion of his protest. The face, *that* face, Spencer Brydon's? — he searched it still, but looking away from it in dismay and denial, falling straight from his height of sublimity. It was unknown, inconceivable, awful, disconnected from any possibility —! He had been "sold," he inwardly moaned, stalking such game as this: the presence before him was a presence, the horror within him a horror, but the waste of his nights had been only grotesque and the success of his adventure an irony. Such an identity fitted his at *no* point, made its alternative monstrous. A thousand times yes, as it came upon him nearer now — the face was the face of a stranger. It came upon him nearer now, quite as one of those expanding fantastic images projected by the magic lantern of childhood; for the stranger, whoever he might be, evil, odious, blatant, vulgar, had advanced as for aggression, and he knew himself give ground. Then harder pressed still, sick with the force of his shock, and falling back as under the hot breath and the roused passion of a life larger than his own, a rage of personality before which his own collapsed, he felt the whole vision turn to darkness and his very feet give way. His head went round; he was going; he had gone.

– III –

What had next brought him back, clearly — though after how long? — was Mrs. Muldoon's voice, coming to him from quite near, from so near that he seemed presently to see her as kneeling on the ground before him while he lay looking up at her; himself not wholly on the ground, but half-raised and upheld — conscious, yes, of tenderness of support and, more particularly, of a head pillowed in extraordinary softness and faintly refreshing fragrance. He considered, he wondered, his wit but half at his service; then another face intervened, bending more directly over him, and he finally knew that Alice Staverton had made her lap an ample and perfect cushion to him, and that she had to this end seated herself on the lowest degree of the staircase, the rest of his long person remaining stretched on his old black-and-white slabs. They were cold, these marble squares of his youth; but *he* somehow was not, in this rich return of consciousness — the most wonderful hour, little by little, that he had ever known, leaving him, as it did, so gratefully, so abysmally passive, and yet as with a treasure of intelligence waiting all round him for quiet appropriation; dissolved, he might call it, in the air of the place and producing the golden glow of a late autumn afternoon. He had come back, yes — come back from further away than any man but himself had ever travelled; but it was strange how with this sense what he had come back *to* seemed really the great thing, and as if his prodigious journey had been all for the sake of it. Slowly but surely his consciousness grew, his vision of his state thus completing itself: he had been miraculously *carried* back—lifted and carefully borne as from where he had been picked up, the uttermost end of an interminable grey passage. Even with this he was suffered to rest, and what had now brought him to knowledge was the break in the long mild motion.

It had brought him to knowledge, to knowledge—yes, this was the beauty of his state; which came to resemble more and more that of a man who has gone to sleep on some news of a great inheritance, and then, after dreaming it away, after profaning it with matters strange to it, has waked up again to serenity of certitude and has only to lie and watch it grow. This was the drift of his patience—that he had only to let it shine on him. He must moreover, with intermissions, still have been lifted and borne; since why and how else should he have known himself, later on, with the afternoon glow intenser, no longer at the foot of his stairs—situated as these now seemed at that dark other end of his tunnel—but on a deep window-bench of his high saloon, over which had been spread, couch-fashion, a mantle of soft stuff lined with grey fur that was familiar to his eyes and that one of his hands kept fondly feeling as for its pledge of truth. Mrs. Muldoon's face had gone, but the other, the second he had recognised, hung over him in a way that showed how he was still propped and pillowed. He took it all in, and the more he took it the more it seemed to suffice: he was as much at peace as if he had had food and drink. It was the two women who had found him, on Mrs. Muldoon's having plied, at her usual hour, her latch-key—and on her having above all arrived while Miss Staverton still lingered near the house. She had been turning away, all anxiety, from worrying the vain bell-handle—her calculation having been of the hour of the good woman's visit; but the latter, blessedly, had come up while she was still there, and they had entered together. He had then lain, beyond the vestibule, very much as he was lying now—quite, that is, as he appeared to have fallen, but all so wondrously without bruise or gash; only in a depth of stupor. What he most took in, however, at present, with the steadier clearance, was that Alice Staverton had for a long unspeakable moment not doubted he was dead.

"It must have been that I *was*." He made it out as she held him. "Yes—I can only have died. You brought me literally to life. Only," he wondered, his eyes rising to her, "only, in the name of all the benedictions, how?"

It took her but an instant to bend her face and kiss him, and something in the manner of it, and in the way her hands clasped and locked his head while he felt the cool charity and virtue of her lips, something in all this beatitude somehow answered everything. "And now I keep you," she said.

"Oh keep me, keep me!" he pleaded while her face still hung over him: in response to which it dropped again and stayed close, clingingly close. It was the seal of their situation—of which he tasted the impress for a long blissful moment in silence. But he came back. "Yet how did you know—?"

"I was uneasy. You were to have come, you remember—and you had sent no word."

"Yes, I remember—I was to have gone to you at one today." It caught on to their "old" life and relation—which were so near and so far. "I was still out there in my strange darkness—where was it, what was it? I must have stayed there so long." He could but wonder at the depth and the duration of his swoon.

"Since last night?" she asked with a shade of fear for her possible indiscretion.

"Since this morning—it must have been: the cold dim dawn of today. Where have I been," he vaguely wailed, "where have I been?" He felt her hold him close, and it was as if this helped him now to make in all security his mild moan. "What a long dark day!"

All in her tenderness she had waited a moment. "In the cold dim dawn?" she quavered.

But he had already gone on piecing together the parts of the whole prodigy. "As I didn't turn up you came straight—?"

She barely cast about. "I went first to your hotel—where they told me of your absence. You had dined out last evening and hadn't been back since. But they appeared to know you had been at your club."

"So you had the idea of *this*—?"

"Of what?" she asked in a moment.

"Well—of what has happened."

"I believed at least you'd have been here. I've known, all along," she said, "that you've been coming."

"'Known' it—?"

"Well, I've believed it. I said nothing to you after that talk we had a month ago—but I felt sure. I knew you *would*," she declared.

"That I'd persist, you mean?"

"That you'd see him."

"Ah but I didn't!" cried Brydon with his long wail. "There's somebody—an awful beast; whom I brought, too horribly, to bay. But it's not me."

At this she bent over him again, and her eyes were in his eyes. "No—it's not you." And it was as if, while her face hovered, he might have made out in it, hadn't it been so near, some particular meaning blurred by a smile. "No, thank heaven," she repeated—"it's not you! Of course it wasn't to have been."

"Ah but it *was*," he gently insisted. And he stared before him now as he had been staring for so many weeks. "I was to have known myself."

"You couldn't!" she returned consolingly. And then reverting, and as if to account further for what she had herself done, "But it wasn't only *that*, that you hadn't been at home," she went on. "I waited till the hour at which we had found Mrs. Muldoon that day of my going with you; and she arrived, as I've told you, while, failing to bring any one to the door, I lingered in my despair on the steps. After a little, if she hadn't come, by such a mercy, I should have found means to hunt her up. But it wasn't," said Alice Staverton, as if once more with her fine intention — "it wasn't only that."

His eyes, as he lay, turned back to her. "What more then?"

She met it, the wonder she had stirred. "In the cold dim dawn, you say? Well, in the cold dim dawn of this morning I too saw you."

"Saw *me* — ?"

"Saw *him*," said Alice Staverton. "It must have been at the same moment."

He lay an instant taking it in — as if he wished to be quite reasonable. "At the same moment?"

"Yes — in my dream again, the same one I've named to you. He came back to me. Then I knew it for a sign. He had come to you."

At this Brydon raised himself; he had to see her better. She helped him when she understood his movement, and he sat up, steadying himself beside her there on the window-bench and with his right hand grasping her left. "*He* didn't come to me."

"You came to yourself," she beautifully smiled.

"Ah I've come to myself now — thanks to you, dearest. But this brute, with his awful face — this brute's a black stranger. He's none of *me*, even as I *might* have been," Brydon sturdily declared.

But she kept the clearness that was like the breath of infallibility. "Isn't the whole point that you'd have been different?"

He almost scowled for it. "As different as *that* — ?"

Her look again was more beautiful to him than the things of this world. "Haven't you exactly wanted to know *how* different? So this morning," she said, "you appeared to me."

"Like *him*?"

"A black stranger!"

"Then how did you know it was I?"

"Because, as I told you weeks ago, my mind, my imagination, had worked so over what you might, what you mightn't have been — to show you, you see, how I've thought of you. In the midst of that you came to me — that my wonder might be answered. So I knew," she went on; "and believed that, since the question held you too so fast, as you told me that day, you too would see for yourself. And when this morning I again saw I knew it would be because you had — and also then, from the first moment, because you somehow wanted me. *He* seemed to tell me of that. So why," she strangely smiled, "shouldn't I like him?"

It brought Spencer Brydon to his feet. "You 'like' that horror — ?"

"I *could* have liked him. And to me," she said, "he was no horror. I had accepted him."

"'Accepted' — ?" Brydon oddly sounded.

"Before, for the interest of his difference — yes. And as *I* didn't disown him, as *I* knew him — which you at last, confronted with him in his difference, so cruelly didn't, my dear—well, he must have been, you see, less dreadful to me. And it may have pleased him that I pitied him."

She was beside him on her feet, but still holding his hand—still with her arm supporting him. But though it all brought for him thus a dim light, "You 'pitied' him?" he grudgingly, resentfully asked.

"He has been unhappy; he has been ravaged," she said.

"And haven't I been unhappy? Am not I—you've only to look at me!—ravaged?"

"Ah I don't say I like him *better,*" she granted after a thought. "But he's grim, he's worn—and things have happened to him. He doesn't make shift, for sight, with your charming monocle."

"No"—it struck Brydon: "I couldn't have sported mine 'downtown.' They'd have guyed me there."

"His great convex pince-nez—I saw it, I recognised the kind—is for his poor ruined sight. And his poor right hand—!"

"Ah!" Brydon winced—whether for his proved identity or for his lost fingers. Then, "He has a million a year," he lucidly added. "But he hasn't you."

"And he isn't—no, he isn't—*you!*" she murmured as he drew her to his breast.   [1908]

SUI SIN FAR

Sui Sin Far (1865–1914), born Edith Maud Eaton, was the first person of mixed Asian and European ancestry in the United States to publish fiction about her ethnic identity. Eaton was born in Macclesfield, England, as the oldest of sixteen children; she emigrated with her family first to the United States and then to Montreal, Canada, when she was nine years old. Her father was an Englishman who tried to support his large family by painting landscapes. Her mother was Chinese and was adopted by an English missionary couple who gave her an English education. Eaton took care of her younger siblings and later said that she "abhorred the work" of child care in the poverty-stricken household. Left in poor health after an attack of rheumatic fever, she taught herself shorthand and typing so she could work as a journalist for the Montreal Star, *giving her wages to her parents to alleviate their financial distress. In 1888 she published the first of many articles in a Montreal magazine. Eight years later she began to use the pseudonym Sui Sin Far (a transliteration of the Chinese symbol for water lily) for the stories she published in periodicals edited by her brother-in-law.*

In 1898 Eaton's physician advised her to move to San Francisco for her health. After working there for two years as a typist for the Canadian Pacific Railroad, she relocated to Seattle, where she worked as an English teacher at a Baptist mission in Chinatown. There she wrote stories about the Chinese community that she placed in Century, Ladies' Home Journal, Good Housekeeping, *and other magazines. In 1912 thirty of her linked stories, including "'Its Wavering Image,'" were published as a novel,* Mrs. Spring Fragrance. *Eaton's earlier articles and sketches often exploited melodramatic situations and racial stereotypes, as in her story "The Gamblers" (1896), about a murder in an opium den. But as the writer matured, she dedicated herself to battling the racism oppressing the Chinese people in the United States, as in "'Its Wavering Image.'" She also proved capable in* Mrs. Spring Fragrance *of creating a title character who is a thoroughly westernized, affluent, happily married Chinese American woman.*

In 1909 Eaton said people had advised her that "if I wish to succeed in literature in America I should dress in Chinese costume, carry a fan in my hand, wear a pair of scarlet beaded slippers, live in New York City, and come of high birth." She was alluding to her sister Winnifred's success as a best-selling novelist who wrote under the pseudonym Onoto Watanna in the first years of the twentieth century. Winnifred exploited the vogue for things Japanese in the United States, wearing costly Japanese kimonos and claiming that her mother had been born a Japanese aristocrat. The short story writer Sui Sin Far may have had a more modest career than her sister did, but she wrote honestly about what she knew. By embracing her Chinese heritage, she acquired the authenticity that makes her writing still relevant today.

"Its Wavering Image"

Pan was a half white, half Chinese girl. Her mother was dead, and Pan lived with her father who kept an Oriental Bazaar on Dupont Street. All her life had Pan lived in Chinatown, and if she were different in any sense from those around her, she gave little thought to it. It was only after the coming of Mark Carson that the mystery of her nature began to trouble her.

They met at the time of the boycott of the Sam Yups by the See Yups. After the heat and dust and unsavoriness of the highways and byways of Chinatown, the young reporter who had been sent to find a story, had stepped across the threshold of a cool, deep room, fragrant with the odor of dried lilies and sandalwood, and found Pan.

She did not speak to him, nor he to her. His business was with the spectacled merchant, who, with a pointed brush, was making up accounts in brown paper books and rolling balls in an abacus box. As to Pan, she always turned from whites. With her father's people she was natural and at home; but in the presence of her mother's she felt strange and con-strained, shrinking from their curious scrutiny as she would from the sharp edge of a sword.

When Mark Carson returned to the office, he asked some questions concerning the girl who had puzzled him. What was she? Chinese or white? The city editor answered him, adding: "She is an unusually bright girl, and could tell more stories about the Chinese than any other person in this city—if she would."

Mark Carson had a determined chin, clever eyes, and a tone to his voice which easily won for him the confidence of the unwary. In the reporter's room he was spoken of as "a man who would sell his soul for a story."

After Pan's first shyness had worn off, he found her bewilderingly frank and free with him; but he had all the instincts of a gentleman save one, and made no ordinary mistake about her. He was Pan's first white friend. She was born a Bohemian, exempt from the conventional restric-tions imposed upon either the white or Chinese woman; and the Oriental who was her father mingled with his affection for his child so great a respect for and trust in the daughter of the dead white woman, that every-thing she did or said was right to him. And Pan herself! A white woman might pass over an insult; a Chinese woman fail to see one. But Pan! He would be a brave man indeed who offered one to childish little Pan.

All this Mark Carson's clear eyes perceived, and with delicate tact and subtlety he taught the young girl that, all unconscious until his coming, she had lived her life alone. So well did she learn this lesson that it seemed at times as if her white self must entirely dominate and trample under foot her Chinese.

Meanwhile, in full trust and confidence, she led him about China-town, initiating him into the simple mystery and history of many things, for which she, being of her father's race, had a tender regard and pride. For her sake he was received as a brother by the yellow-robed priest in the joss house, the Astrologer of Prospect Place, and other conservative Chinese. The Water Lily Club opened its doors to him when she knocked, and the Sublimely Pure Brothers' organization admitted him as one of its honorary members, thereby enabling him not only to see but to take part in a ceremony in which no American had ever before participated. With her by his side, he was welcomed wherever he went. Even the little Chinese women in the midst of their babies, received him with gentle smiles, and the children solemnly munched his candies and repeated nursery rhymes for his edification.

He enjoyed it all, and so did Pan. They were both young and light-hearted. And when the afternoon was spent, there was always that high room open to the stars, with its China bowls full of flowers and its big colored lanterns, shedding a mellow light.

Sometimes there was music. A Chinese band played three evenings a week in the gilded restaurant beneath them, and the louder the gongs sounded and the fiddlers fiddled, the more delighted was Pan. Just below the restaurant was her father's bazaar. Occasionally Mun You would stroll upstairs and inquire of the young couple if there was anything needed to complete their felicity, and Pan would answer: "Thou only." Pan was very proud of her Chinese father. "I would rather have a Chinese for a father than a white man," she often told Mark Carson. The last time she had said that he had asked whom she would prefer for a husband, a white man or a Chinese. And Pan, for the first time since he had known her, had no answer for him.

– II –

It was a cool, quiet evening, after a hot day. A new moon was in the sky.

"How beautiful above! How unbeautiful below!" exclaimed Mark Carson involuntarily.

He and Pan had been gazing down from their open retreat into the lantern-lighted, motley-thronged street beneath them.

"Perhaps it isn't very beautiful," replied Pan, "but it is here I live. It is my home." Her voice quivered a little.

He leaned towards her suddenly and grasped her hands.

"Pan," he cried, "you do not belong here. You are white — white."

"No! no!" protested Pan.

"You are," he asserted. "You have no right to be here."

"I was born here," she answered, "and the Chinese people look upon me as their own."

"But they do not understand you," he went on. "Your real self is alien to them. What interest have they in the books you read — the thoughts you think?"

"They have an interest in me," answered faithful Pan. "Oh, do not speak in that way any more."

"But I must," the young man persisted. "Pan, don't you see that you have got to decide what you will be — Chinese or white? You cannot be both."

"Hush! Hush!" bade Pan. "I do not love you when you talk to me like that."

A little Chinese boy brought tea and saffron cakes. He was a picturesque little fellow with a quaint manner of speech. Mark Carson jested merrily with him, while Pan holding a tea-bowl between her two small hands laughed and sipped.

When they were alone again, the silver stream and the crescent moon became the objects of their study. It was a very beautiful evening.

After a while Mark Carson, his hand on Pan's shoulder, sang:

> And forever, and forever,
> As long as the river flows,
> As long as the heart has passions,
> As long as life has woes,
> The moon and its broken reflection,
> And its shadows shall appear,
> As the symbol of love in heaven,
> And its wavering image here.

Listening to that irresistible voice singing her heart away, the girl broke down and wept. She was so young and so happy.

"Look up at me," bade Mark Carson. "Oh, Pan! Pan! Those tears prove that you are white."

Pan lifted her wet face.

"Kiss me, Pan," said he. It was the first time.

Next morning Mark Carson began work on the special-feature article which he had been promising his paper for some weeks.

– III –

"Cursed be his ancestors," bayed Man You.

He cast a paper at his daughter's feet and left the room.

Startled by her father's unwonted passion, Pan picked up the paper, and in the clear passionless light of the afternoon read that which forever after was blotted upon her memory.

"Betrayed! Betrayed! Betrayed to be a betrayer!"

It burnt red hot; agony unrelieved by words, unassuaged by tears.

So till evening fell. Then she stumbled up the dark stairs which led to the high room open to the stars and tried to think it out. Someone had hurt her. Who was it? She raised her eyes. There shone: "Its Wavering Image." It helped her to lucidity. He had done it. Was it unconsciously dealt—that cruel blow? Ah, well did he know that the sword which pierced her through others, would carry with it to her own heart, the pain of all those others. None knew better than he that she, whom he had called "a white girl, a white woman," would rather that her own naked body and soul had been exposed, than that things, sacred and secret to those who loved her, should be cruelly unveiled and ruthlessly spread before the ridiculing and uncomprehending foreigner. And knowing all this so well, so well, he had carelessly sung her heart away, and with her kiss upon his lips, had smilingly turned and stabbed her. She, who was of the race that remembers.

– IV –

Mark Carson, back in the city after an absence of two months, thought of Pan. He would see her that very evening. Dear little Pan, pretty Pan, clever Pan, amusing Pan; Pan, who was always so frankly glad to have him come to her; so eager to hear all that he was doing; so appreciative, so inspiring, so loving. She would have forgotten that article by now. Why should a white woman care about such things? Her true self was above it all. Had he not taught her *that* during the weeks in which they had seen so much of one another? True, his last lesson had been a little harsh, and as yet he knew not how she had taken it; but even if its roughness had hurt and irritated, there was a healing balm, a wizard's oil which none knew so well as he how to apply.

But for all these soothing reflections, there was an undercurrent of feeling which caused his steps to falter on his way to Pan. He turned into Portsmouth Square and took a seat on one of the benches facing the fountain erected in memory of Robert Louis Stevenson. Why had Pan failed to answer the note he had written telling her of the assignment which would keep him out of town for a couple of months and giving her his address? Would Robert Louis Stevenson have known why? Yes—and so did Mark Carson. But though Robert Louis Stevenson would have boldly answered himself the question, Mark Carson thrust it aside, arose, and pressed up the hill.

"I knew they would not blame you, Pan!"

"Yes."

"And there was no word of you, dear. I was careful about that, not only for your sake, but for mine."

Silence.

"It is mere superstition anyway. These things have got to be exposed and done away with."

Still silence.

Mark Carson felt strangely chilled. Pan was not herself to-night. She did not even look herself. He had been accustomed to seeing her in American dress. Tonight she wore the Chinese costume. But for her clear-cut features she might have been a Chinese girl. He shivered.

"Pan," he asked, "why do you wear that dress?"

Within her sleeves Pan's small hands struggled together; but her face and voice were calm.

"Because I am a Chinese woman," she answered.

"You are not," cried Mark Carson, fiercely. "You cannot say that now, Pan. You are a white woman—white. Did your kiss not promise me that?"

"A white woman!" echoed Pan her voice rising high and clear to the stars above them. "I would not be a white woman for all the world. *You* are a white man. And *what* is a promise to a white man!"

When she was lying low, the element of Fire having raged so fiercely within her that it had almost shriveled up the childish frame, there came to the house of Man You a little toddler who could scarcely speak. Climbing upon Pan's couch, she pressed her head upon the sick girl's bosom. The feel of that little head brought tears.

"Lo!" said the mother of the toddler. "Thou wilt bear a child thyself some day, and all the bitterness of this will pass away."

And Pan, being a Chinese woman, was comforted.   [1912]

SHERWOOD ANDERSON

S*herwood Anderson (1876–1941) was born the son of a jack-of-all-trades father in Camden, Ohio. He did not publish his first book until he was over forty years old, after working for many years as a newsboy, farm laborer, stable boy, factory hand, and advertising copywriter. Dissatisfied with the commercial spirit of the advertising business, Anderson made friends with writers in Chicago and began to publish his own poetry and fiction. The poet Carl Sandburg encouraged him, but Anderson's literary style was most influenced by* Three Lives *(1909), an experimental book by the expatriate American writer Gertrude Stein, which he felt revolutionized the language of narrative.*

In 1916 Anderson published his first novel, Windy McPherson's Son. *He followed it with another novel and a volume of poetry, but he did not receive wide recognition until 1919, with the book* Winesburg, Ohio. *This was a collection of related stories, including "Hands" (*Masses, *1916), about life in a small town that explored the devastating consequences of the repressive conventions of a provincial society. It was followed by other important collections of stories:* The Triumph of the Egg *(1921),* Horses and Men *(1923), and* Death in the Woods and Other Stories *(1933). In his time Anderson was a strong influence on Ernest Hemingway, William Faulkner, William Saroyan, Richard Wright, and John Steinbeck. The editor Martha Foley wrote in 1941 that*

> *Sherwood Anderson set out on new paths at a time when the American short story seemed doomed to a formula-ridden, conventionalized, mechanized, and commercialized concept. When* Winesburg, Ohio, *appeared in 1919 it was intensely influential on writers who either had lost heart or had not yet found their way. His vision was his own; his characters were people into whose hearts and minds he seemed intuitively to peer; his prose was simple, deceptively simple, sensuous, rich, and evocative.*

As literary critics have observed, the characteristic tone of Anderson's short fiction is melancholy reminiscence. In an understated fashion, he wove carefully selected realistic details into a narrative that moves by apparently formless associations of thought and feeling but is actually a controlled progression of fully dramatized situations. Anderson's importance in our literature is suggested by Richard Wright's acknowledgment that Anderson's stories made him see that through the powers of fiction, "America could be shaped nearer to the hearts of those who lived in it."

RELATED COMMENTARIES: *Sherwood Anderson, "Form, Not Plot, in the Short Story," page 1291; John Updike, "Twisted Apples: On* Winesburg, Ohio," *page 1464.*

Hands

Upon the half decayed veranda of a small frame house that stood near the edge of a ravine near the town of Winesburg, Ohio, a fat little old man walked nervously up and down. Across a long field that had been seeded for clover but that had produced only a dense crop of yellow mustard weeds, he could see the public highway along which went a wagon filled with berry pickers returning from the fields. The berry pickers, youths and maidens, laughed and shouted boisterously. A boy clad in a blue shirt leaped from the wagon and attempted to drag after him one of the maidens who screamed and protested shrilly. The feet of the boy in the road kicked up a cloud of dust that floated across the face of the departing sun. Over the long field came a thin girlish voice. "Oh, you Wing Biddlebaum, comb your hair, it's falling into your eyes," commanded the voice to the man, who was bald and whose nervous little hands fiddled about the bare white forehead as though arranging a mass of tangled locks.

Wing Biddlebaum, forever frightened and beset by a ghostly band of doubts, did not think of himself as in any way a part of the life of the town where he had lived for twenty years. Among all the people of Winesburg but one had come close to him. With George Willard, son of Tom Willard, the proprietor of the new Willard House, he had formed something like a friendship. George Willard was the reporter on the *Winesburg Eagle* and sometimes in the evenings he walked out along the highway to Wing Biddlebaum's house. Now as the old man walked up and down on the veranda, his hands moving nervously about, he was hoping that George Willard would come and spend the evening with him. After the wagon containing the berry pickers had passed, he went across the field through the tall mustard weeds and climbing a rail fence peered anxiously along the road to the town. For a moment he stood thus, rubbing his hands together and looking up and down the road, and then, fear overcoming him, ran back to walk again upon the porch of his own house.

In the presence of George Willard, Wing Biddlebaum, who for twenty years had been the town mystery, lost something of his timidity, and his shadowy personality, submerged in a sea of doubts, came forth to look at the world. With the young reporter at his side, he ventured in the light of day into Main Street or strode up and down on the rickety front porch of his own house, talking excitedly. The voice that had been low and trembling became shrill and loud. The bent figure straightened. With a kind of wriggle, like a fish returned to the brook by the fisherman, Biddlebaum the silent began to talk, striving to put into words the ideas that had been accumulated by his mind during long years of silence.

Wing Biddlebaum talked much with his hands. The slender expressive fingers, forever active, forever striving to conceal themselves in his pockets or behind his back, came forth and became the piston rods of his machinery of expression.

The story of Wing Biddlebaum is a story of hands. Their restless activity, like unto the beating of the wings of an imprisoned bird, had given him his name. Some obscure poet of the town had thought of it. The hands alarmed their owner. He wanted to keep them hidden away and looked with amazement at the quiet inexpressive hands of other men who worked beside him in the fields, or passed, driving sleepy teams on country roads.

When he talked to George Willard, Wing Biddlebaum closed his fists and beat with them upon a table or on the walls of his house. The action made him more comfortable. If the desire to talk came to him when the two were walking in the fields, he sought out a stump or the top board of a fence and with his hands pounding busily talked with renewed ease.

The story of Wing Biddlebaum's hands is worth a book itself. Sympathetically set forth it would tap many strange, beautiful qualities in obscure men. It is a job for a poet. In Winesburg the hands had attracted attention merely because of their activity. With them Wing Biddlebaum had picked as high as a hundred and forty quarts of strawberries in a day. They became his distinguishing feature, the source of his fame. Also they made more grotesque an already grotesque and elusive individuality. Winesburg was proud of the hands of Wing Biddlebaum in the same spirit in which it was proud of Banker White's new stone house and Wesley Moyer's bay stallion, Tony Tip, that had won the two-fifteen trot at the fall races in Cleveland.

As for George Willard, he had many times wanted to ask about the hands. At times an almost overwhelming curiosity had taken hold of him. He felt that there must be a reason for their strange activity and their inclination to keep hidden away and only a growing respect for Wing Biddlebaum kept him from blurting out the questions that were often in his mind.

Once he had been on the point of asking. The two were walking in the fields on a summer afternoon and had stopped to sit upon a grassy bank. All afternoon Wing Biddlebaum had talked as one inspired. By a fence he had stopped and beating like a giant woodpecker upon the top board had shouted at George Willard, condemning his tendency to be too much influenced by the people about him. "You are destroying yourself," he cried.

"You have the inclination to be alone and to dream and you are afraid of dreams. You want to be like others in town here. You hear them talk and you try to imitate them."

On the grassy bank Wing Biddlebaum had tried again to drive his point home. His voice became soft and reminiscent, and with a sigh of contentment he launched into a long rambling talk, speaking as one lost in a dream.

Out of the dream Wing Biddlebaum made a picture for George Willard. In the picture men lived again in a kind of pastoral golden age. Across a green open country came clean-limbed young men, some afoot, some mounted upon horses. In crowds the young men came to gather about the feet of an old man who sat beneath a tree in a tiny garden and who talked to them.

Wing Biddlebaum became wholly inspired. For once he forgot the hands. Slowly they stole forth and lay upon George Willard's shoulders. Something new and bold came into the voice that talked. "You must try to forget all you have learned," said the old man. "You must begin to dream. From this time on you must shut your ears to the roaring of the voices."

Pausing in his speech, Wing Biddlebaum looked long and earnestly at George Willard. His eyes glowed. Again he raised the hands to caress the boy and then a look of horror swept over his face.

With a convulsive movement of his body, Wing Biddlebaum sprang to his feet and thrust his hands deep into his trousers pockets. Tears came to his eyes. "I must be getting along home. I can talk no more with you," he said nervously.

Without looking back, the old man had hurried down the hillside and across a meadow, leaving George Willard perplexed and frightened upon the grassy slope. With a shiver of dread the boy arose and went along the road toward town. "I'll not ask him about his hands," he thought, touched by the memory of the terror he had seen in the man's eyes. "There's something wrong, but I don't want to know what it is. His hands have something to do with his fear of me and of everyone."

And George Willard was right. Let us look briefly into the story of the hands. Perhaps our talking of them will arouse the poet who will tell the hidden wonder story of the influence for which the hands were but fluttering pennants of promise.

In his youth Wing Biddlebaum had been a school teacher in a town in Pennsylvania. He was not then known as Wing Biddlebaum, but went by the less euphonic name of Adolph Myers. As Adolph Myers he was much loved by the boys of his school.

Adolph Myers was meant by nature to be a rare teacher of youth. He was one of those rare, little-understood men who rule by a power so gentle that it passes as a lovable weakness. In their feeling for the boys under their charge such men are not unlike the finer sort of women in their love of men.

And yet that is but crudely stated. It needs the poet there. With the boys of his school, Adolph Myers had walked in the evening or had sat talking until dusk upon the schoolhouse steps lost in a kind of dream. Here and there went his hands, caressing the shoulders of the boys, playing about the tousled heads. As he talked his voice became soft and musical. There was a caress in that also. In a way the voice and the hands, the stroking of the shoulders and the touching of the hair was a part of the schoolmaster's effort to carry a dream into the young minds. By the caress that was in his fingers he expressed himself. He was one of those men in whom the force that creates life is diffused, not centralized. Under the caress of his hands doubt and disbelief went out of the minds of the boys and they began also to dream.

And then the tragedy. A half-witted boy of the school became enamored of the young master. In his bed at night he imagined unspeakable things and in the morning went forth to tell his dreams as facts. Strange, hideous accusations fell from his loose-hung lips. Through the Pennsylvania town went a shiver. Hidden, shadowy doubts that had been in men's minds concerning Adolph Myers were galvanized into beliefs.

The tragedy did not linger. Trembling lads were jerked out of bed and questioned. "He put his arms about me," said one. "His fingers were always playing in my hair," said another.

One afternoon a man of the town, Henry Bradford, who kept a saloon, came to the schoolhouse door. Calling Adolph Myers into the school yard he began to beat him with his fists. As his hard knuckles beat down into the frightened face of the schoolmaster, his wrath became more and more terrible. Screaming with dismay, the children ran here and there like disturbed insects. "I'll teach you to put your hands on my boy, you beast," roared the saloon keeper, who, tired of beating the master, had begun to kick him about the yard.

Adolph Myers was driven from the Pennsylvania town in the night. With lanterns in their hands a dozen men came to the door of the house where he lived alone and commanded that he dress and come forth. It was raining and one of the men had a rope in his hands. They had intended to hang the schoolmaster, but something in his figure, so small, white, and pitiful, touched their hearts and they let him escape. As he ran away into the darkness they repented of their weakness and ran after him, swearing and throwing sticks and great balls of soft mud at the figure that screamed and ran faster and faster into the darkness.

For twenty years Adolph Myers had lived alone in Winesburg. He was but forty but looked sixty-five. The name Biddlebaum he got from a box of goods seen at a freight station as he hurried through an eastern Ohio town. He had an aunt in Winesburg, a black-toothed old woman who raised chickens, and with her he lived until she died. He had been ill for a year after the experience in Pennsylvania, and after his recovery worked as a day laborer in the fields, going timidly about and striving to conceal his hands. Although he did not understand what had happened he felt that the hands must be to blame. Again and again the fathers of the boys had talked of the hands. "Keep your hands to yourself," the saloon keeper had roared, dancing with fury in the schoolhouse yard.

Upon the veranda of his house by the ravine, Wing Biddlebaum continued to walk up and down until the sun had disappeared and the road beyond the field was lost in the grey shadows. Going into his house he cut slices of bread and spread honey upon them. When the rumble of the evening train that took away the express cars loaded with the day's harvest of berries had passed and restored the silence of the summer night, he went again to walk upon the veranda. In the darkness he could not see the hands and they became quiet. Although he still hungered for the presence of the boy, who was the medium through which he expressed his love of man, the hunger became again a part of his loneliness and his waiting. Lighting a lamp, Wing Biddlebaum washed the few dishes soiled by his simple meal and, setting up a folding cot by the screen door that led to the porch, prepared to undress for the night. A few stray white bread crumbs lay on the cleanly washed floor by the table; putting the lamp upon a low stool he began to pick up the crumbs, carrying them to his mouth one by one with unbelievable rapidity. In the dense blotch of light beneath the table, the kneeling figure looked like a priest engaged in some service of his church. The nervous expressive fingers, flashing in and out of the light, might well have been mistaken for the fingers of the devotee going swiftly through decade after decade of his rosary.   [1916]

THEODORE DREISER

Theodore Dreiser (1871–1945), best known for his novels Sister Carrie *(1900) and* An American Tragedy *(1925), was born in Terre Haute, Indiana. His parents were German immigrants whose marriage resulted in thirteen children. Because his father was often ill and unemployed, the family struggled against poverty throughout Dreiser's childhood. In rebellion against his father's obsessive religiosity, Dreiser left home at fifteen for Chicago. There, after three years of menial jobs, he found work as a newspaper reporter. While Dreiser churned out hack work for various periodicals, he was reading the deterministic philosophy of Herbert Spencer and the novels of Honoré de Balzac, who believed in the evolutionary doctrine that life is a struggle in which instinctive human desires are often in conflict with conventional moral-ity. In 1900 Dreiser published his first book,* Sister Carrie, *now regarded as a classic naturalistic novel, challenging the American myth that honesty and hard work inevitably lead to success. Dreiser's compassion toward his desper-ate fictional characters was less important to the early readers of his novel than the alleged immorality of his book. Sales were poor, but he followed the novel with several other works of long fiction before publishing his first collection of stories in 1918,* Free and Other Stories, *which included "The Lost Phœbe."*

Dreiser wrote "The Lost Phœbe" in 1912, after publishing Jenny Ger-hardt *(1911) and* The Financier *(1912). By this time he had won the respect of critics as the leading realistic novelist in the United States and had signed con-tracts for many more books, including a volume of sketches,* A Traveler at Forty *(1913). Having built a solid literary reputation, Dreiser told his literary agent to sell "The Lost Phœbe" for at least $400. Over the next two years edi-tors at the* Saturday Evening Post, Ladies' Home Journal, Redbook, Amer-ican, Metropolitan, Scribner's Magazine, Women's World, Century Magazine, Good Housekeeping, Collier's, *and* The Atlantic Monthly *refused to pay Dreiser's price for the story, even after he lowered it to $200. In August 1914, the editor of* Redbook *took another look at it and unenthusiasti-cally agreed to pay $125. Dreiser considered the bid, but his friend H. L. Mencken at the* Smart Set *had made a standing offer of $100 per story, so Dreiser took the story to him. Mencken first turned it down before grudgingly agreeing to publish it. Dreiser told him to forget about it and sent the story to other magazine editors, collecting new rejection letters from* Semi-Monthly, Everybody's, Woman's Home Companion, McClure's, Pictorial Review, *and* Lippincott's. *After Dreiser's nineteenth rejection, the editor of* Century Magazine *told him, "I am very much charmed with your story," and paid him $200 to publish it in 1916. "The Lost Phœbe" became the most frequently anthologized story Dreiser ever wrote.*

Dreiser published a second story collection, Chains: Lesser Novels and Stories, *in 1927. Many of these stories dramatized the same theme he had explored in "The Lost Phœbe"—love as the most powerful force in life. Two*

years after Dreiser's death from a heart attack, the novelist Howard Fast edited
The Best Short Stories of Theodore Dreiser *(1947).*

The Lost Phœbe

They lived together in a part of the country which was not so prosperous as it had once been, about three miles from one of those small towns that, instead of increasing in population, is steadily decreasing. The territory was not very thickly settled; perhaps a house every other mile or so, with large areas of corn- and wheat-land and fallow fields that at odd seasons had been sown to timothy and clover. Their particular house was part log and part frame, the log portion being the old original home of Henry's grandfather. The new portion, of now rain-beaten, time-worn slabs, through which the wind squeaked in the chinks at times, and which several overshadowing elms and a butternut-tree made picturesque and reminiscently pathetic, but a little damp, was erected by Henry when he was twenty-one and just married.

That was forty-eight years before. The furniture inside, like the house outside, was old and mildewy and reminiscent of an earlier day. You have seen the what-not of cherry wood, perhaps, with spiral legs and fluted top. It was there. The old-fashioned four poster bed, with its ball-like protuberances and deep curving incisions, was there also, a sadly alienated descendant of an early Jacobean ancestor. The bureau of cherry was also high and wide and solidly built, but faded-looking, and with a musty odor. The rag carpet that underlay all these sturdy examples of enduring furniture was a weak, faded, lead-and-pink-colored affair woven by Phœbe Ann's own hands, when she was fifteen years younger than she was when she died. The creaky wooden loom on which it had been done now stood like a dusty, bony skeleton, along with a broken rocking-chair, a worm-eaten clothes-press — Heaven knows how old — a lime-stained bench that had once been used to keep flowers on outside the door, and other decrepit factors of household utility, in an east room that was a lean-to against this so-called main portion. All sorts of other broken-down furniture were about this place; an antiquated clothes-horse, cracked in two of its ribs; a broken mirror in an old cherry frame, which had fallen from a nail and cracked itself three days before their youngest son, Jerry, died; an extension hat-rack, which once had had porcelain knobs on the ends of its pegs; and a sewing-machine, long since outdone in its clumsy mechanism by rivals of a newer generation.

The orchard to the east of the house was full of gnarled old apple-trees, worm-eaten as to trunks and branches, and fully ornamented with green and white lichens, so that it had a sad, greenish-white, silvery effect in moonlight. The low outhouses, which had once housed chickens, a horse or two, a cow, and several pigs, were covered with patches of moss as to their roof, and the sides had been free of paint for so long that they were blackish gray as to color, and a little spongy. The picket-fence in front, with its gate squeaky and askew, and the side fences of the stake-and-rider type were in an equally run-down condition. As a matter of fact, they had aged synchronously with the persons who lived here, old Henry Reifsneider and his wife Phœbe Ann.

They had lived here, these two, ever since their marriage, forty-eight years before, and Henry had lived here before that from his childhood up. His father and mother, well along in years when he was a boy, had invited him to bring his wife here when he had first fallen in love and decided to marry; and he had done so. His father and mother were the companions of himself and his wife for ten years after they were married, when both died; and then Henry and Phœbe were left with their five children growing lustily apace. But all sorts of things had happened since then. Of the seven children, all told, that had been born to them, three had died; one girl had gone to Kansas; one boy had gone to Sioux Falls, never even to be heard of after; another boy had gone to Washington; and the last girl lived five counties away in the same State, but was so burdened with cares of her own that she rarely gave them a thought. Time and a commonplace home life that had never been attractive had weaned them thoroughly, so that, wherever they were, they gave little thought as to how it might be with their father and mother.

Old Henry Reifsneider and his wife Phœbe were a loving couple. You perhaps know how it is with simple natures that fasten themselves like lichens on the stones of circumstance and weather their days to a crumbling conclusion. The great world sounds widely, but it has no call for them. They have no soaring intellect. The orchard, the meadow, the corn-field, the pig-pen, and the chicken-lot measure the range of their human activities. When the wheat is headed it is reaped and threshed; when the corn is browned and frosted it is cut and shocked; when the timothy is in full head it is cut, and the hay-cock erected. After that comes winter, with the hauling of grain to market, the sawing and splitting of wood, the simple chores of fire-building, meal-getting, occasional repairing, and visiting. Beyond these and the changes of weather—the snows, the rains, and the fair days—there are no immediate, significant things. All the rest of life is a far-off, clamorous phantasmagoria, flickering like Northern lights in the night, and sounding as faintly as cow-bells tinkling in the distance.

Old Henry and his wife Phœbe were as fond of each other as it is possible for two old people to be who have nothing else in this life to be fond of. He was a thin old man, seventy when she died, a queer, crotchety person with coarse gray-black hair and beard, quite straggly and unkempt. He looked at you out of dull, fishy, watery eyes that had deep-brown crow's-feet at the sides. His clothes, like the clothes of many farmers, were aged and angular and baggy, standing out at the pockets, not fitting about the neck, protuberant and worn at elbow and knee. Phœbe Ann was thin and shapeless, a very umbrella of a woman, clad in shabby black, and with a black bonnet for her best wear. As time had passed, and they had only themselves to look after, their movements had become slower and slower, their activities fewer and fewer. The annual keep of pigs had been reduced from five to one grunting porker, and the single horse which Henry now retained was a sleepy animal, not over-nourished and not very clean. The chickens, of which formerly there was a large flock, had almost disappeared, owing to ferrets, foxes, and the lack of proper care, which produces disease. The former healthy garden was now a straggling memory of itself, and the vines and flower-beds that formerly ornamented the windows and dooryard had now become choking thickets. A will had been made which divided the small tax-eaten property equally among the remaining four, so that it was really of no interest to any of them. Yet these two lived together in peace and sympathy, only that now and then old Henry would become unduly cranky, complaining almost invariably that something had been neglected or mislaid which was of no importance at all.

"Phœbe, where's my corn-knife? You ain't never minded to let my things alone no more."

"Now you hush, Henry," his wife would caution him in a cracked and squeaky voice. "If you don't, I'll leave yuh. I'll git up and walk out of here some day, and then where would y' be? Y' ain't got anybody but me to look after yuh, so yuh just behave yourself. Your corn-knife's on the mantel where it's allus been unless you've gone an' put it summers else."

Old Henry, who knew his wife would never leave him in any circumstances, used to speculate at times as to what he would do if she were to die. That was the one leaving that he really feared. As he climbed on the chair at night to wind the old, long-pendulumed, double-weighted clock, or went finally to the front and the back door to see that they were safely shut in, it was a comfort to know that Phœbe was there, properly ensconced on her side of the bed, and that if he stirred restlessly in the night, she would be there to ask what he wanted.

"Now, Henry, do lie still! You're as restless as a chicken."

"Well, I can't sleep, Phœbe."

"Well, yuh needn't roll so, anyhow. Yuh kin let me sleep."

This usually reduced him to a state of somnolent ease. If she wanted a pail of water, it was a grumbling pleasure for him to get it; and if she did rise first to build the fires, he saw that the wood was cut and placed within easy reach. They divided this simple world nicely between them.

As the years had gone on, however, fewer and fewer people had called. They were well-known for a distance of as much as ten square miles as old Mr. and Mrs. Reifsneider, honest, moderately Christian, but too old to be really interesting any longer. The writing of letters had become an almost impossible burden too difficult to continue or even negotiate via others, although an occasional letter still did arrive from the daughter in Pemberton County. Now and then some old friend stopped with a pie or cake or a roasted chicken or duck, or merely to see that they were well; but even these kindly minded visits were no longer frequent.

One day in the early spring of her sixty-fourth year Mrs. Reifsneider took sick, and from a low fever passed into some indefinable ailment which, because of her age, was no longer curable. Old Henry drove to Swinnerton, the neighboring town, and procured a doctor. Some friends called, and the immediate care of her was taken off his hands. Then one chill spring night she died, and old Henry, in a fog of sorrow and uncertainty, followed her body to the nearest graveyard, an unattractive space with a few pines growing in it. Although he might have gone to the daughter in Pemberton or sent for her, it was really too much trouble and he was too weary and fixed. It was suggested to him at once by one friend and another that he come to stay with them awhile, but he did not see fit. He was so old and so fixed in his notions and so accustomed to the exact surroundings he had known all his days, that he could not think of leaving. He wanted to remain near where they had put his Phœbe; and the fact that he would have to live alone did not trouble him in the least. The living children were notified and the care of him offered if he would leave, but he would not.

"I kin make a shift for myself," he continually announced to old Dr. Morrow, who had attended his wife in this case. "I kin cook a little, and, besides, it don't take much more'n coffee an' bread in the mornin's to satisfy me. I'll get along now well enough. Yuh just let me be." And after many pleadings and proffers of advice, with supplies of coffee and bacon and baked bread duly offered and accepted, he was left to himself. For a while he sat idly outside his door brooding in the spring sun. He tried to revive his interest in farming, and to keep himself busy and free from thought by looking after the fields, which of late had been much neglected. It was a gloomy thing to come in of an evening, however, or in the afternoon and find no shadow of Phœbe where everything suggested her. By degrees he put a few of her things away. At night he sat beside his lamp and read in the papers that were left him occasionally or in a Bible that he had neglected for years, but he could get little solace from these things. Mostly he held his hand over his mouth and looked at the floor as he sat and thought of what had become of her, and how soon he himself would die. He made a great business of making his coffee in the morning and frying himself a little bacon at night; but his appetite was gone. The shell in which he had been housed so long seemed vacant, and its shadows were suggestive of immedicable griefs. So he lived quite dolefully for five long months, and then a change began.

It was one night, after he had looked after the front and the back door, wound the clock, blown out the light, and gone through all the selfsame motions that he had indulged in for years, that he went to bed not so much to sleep as to think. It was a moonlight night. The green-lichen-covered orchard just outside and to be seen from his bed where he now lay was a silvery affair, sweetly spectral. The moon shone through the east windows, throwing the pattern of the panes on the wooden floor, and making the old furniture, to which he was accustomed, stand out dimly in the room. As usual he had been thinking of Phœbe and the years when they had been young together, and of the children who had gone, and the poor shift he was making of his present days. The house was coming to be in a very bad state indeed. The bed-clothes were in disorder and not clean, for he made a wretched shift of washing. It was a terror to him. The roof leaked, causing things, some of them, to remain damp for weeks at a time, but he was getting into that brooding state where he would accept anything rather than exert himself. He preferred to pace slowly to and fro or to sit and think.

By twelve o'clock of this particular night he was asleep, however, and by two had waked again. The moon by this time had shifted to a position on the western side of the house, and it now shone in through the windows of the living-room and those of the kitchen beyond. A certain combination of furniture—a chair near a table, with his coat on it, the half-open kitchen door casting a shadow, and the position of a lamp near a paper—gave him an exact representation of Phœbe leaning over the table as he had often seen her do in life. It gave him a great start. Could it be she—or her ghost? He had scarcely ever believed in spirits; and still—— He looked at her fixedly in the feeble half-light, his old hair tingling oddly at the roots, and then sat up. The figure did not move. He put his thin legs out of the bed and sat looking at her, wondering if this could really be Phœbe. They had talked of ghosts often in their lifetime, of apparitions and omens; but they had never agreed that such things could be. It had never been a part of his wife's creed that she could have a spirit that could return to walk the earth. Her after-world was quite a different affair, a vague heaven, no less, from which the righteous did not trouble to return. Yet here she was now, bending over the table in her black skirt and gray shawl, her pale profile outlined against the moonlight.

"Phœbe," he called, thrilling from head to toe and putting out one bony hand, "have yuh come back?"

The figure did not stir, and he arose and walked uncertainly to the door, looking at it fixedly the while. As he drew near, however, the apparition resolved itself into its primal content—his old coat over the high-backed chair, the lamp by the paper, the half-open door.

"Well," he said to himself, his mouth open, "I thought shore I saw her." And he ran his hand strangely and vaguely through his hair, the while his nervous tension relaxed. Vanished as it had, it gave him the idea that she might return.

Another night, because of this first illusion, and because his mind was now constantly on her and he was old, he looked out of the window that was nearest his bed and commanded a hen-coop and pig-pen and a part of the wagon-shed, and there, a faint mist exuding from the damp of the ground, he thought he saw her again. It was one of those little wisps of mist, one of those faint exhalations of the earth that rise in a cool night after a warm day, and flicker like small white cypresses of fog before they disappear. In life it had been a custom of hers to cross this lot from her kitchen door to the pig-pen to throw in any scrap that was left from her cooking, and here she was again. He sat up and watched it strangely, doubtfully, because of his previous experience, but inclined, because of the nervous titillation that passed over his body, to believe that spirits really were, and that Phœbe, who would be concerned because of his lonely state, must be thinking about him, and hence returning. What other way would she have? How otherwise could she express herself? It would be within the province of her charity so to do, and like her loving interest in him. He quivered and watched it eagerly; but, a faint breath of air stirring, it wound away toward the fence and disappeared.

A third night, as he was actually dreaming, some ten days later, she came to his bedside and put her hand on his head.

"Poor Henry!" she said. "It's too bad."

He roused out of his sleep, actually to see her, he thought, moving from his bed-room into the one living-room, her figure a shadowy mass of black. The weak straining of his eyes caused little points of light to flicker about the outlines of her form. He arose, greatly astonished, walked the floor in the cool room, convinced that Phœbe was coming back to him. If he only thought sufficiently, if he made it perfectly clear by his feeling that he needed her greatly, she would come back, this kindly wife, and tell him what to do. She would perhaps be with him much of the time, in the night, anyhow; and that would make him less lonely, this state more endurable.

In age and with the feeble it is not such a far cry from the subtleties of illusion to actual hallucination, and in due time this transition was made for Henry. Night after night he waited, expecting her return. Once in his weird mood he thought he saw a pale light moving about the room, and another time he thought he saw her walking in the orchard after dark. It was one morning when the details of his lonely state were virtually unendurable that he woke with the thought that she was not dead. How he had arrived at this conclusion it is hard to say. His mind had gone. In its place was a fixed illusion. He and Phœbe had had a senseless quarrel. He had reproached her for not leaving his pipe where he was accustomed to find it, and she had left. It was an aberrated fulfillment of her old jesting threat that if he did not behave himself she would leave him.

"I guess I could find yuh ag'in," he had always said. But her cackling threat had always been.

"Yuh'll not find me if I ever leave yuh. I guess I kin git some place where yuh can't find me."

This morning when he arose he did not think to build the fire in the customary way or to grind his coffee and cut his bread, as was his wont, but solely to meditate as to where he should search for her and how he should induce her to come back. Recently the one horse had been dispensed with because he found it cumbersome and beyond his needs. He took down his soft crush hat after he had dressed himself, a new glint of interest and determination in his eye, and taking his black crook cane from behind the door, where he had always placed it, started out briskly to look for her among the nearest neighbors. His old shoes clumped soundly in the dust as he walked, and his gray-black locks, now grown rather long, straggled out in a dramatic fringe or halo from under his hat. His short coat stirred busily as he walked, and his hands and face were peaked and pale.

"Why, hello, Henry! Where're yuh goin' this mornin'?" inquired Farmer Dodge, who, hauling a load of wheat to market, encountered him on the public road. He had not seen the aged farmer in months, not since his wife's death, and he wondered now, seeing him looking so spry.

"Yuh ain't seen Phœbe, have yuh?" inquired the old man, looking up quizzically.

"Phœbe who?" inquired Farmer Dodge, not for the moment connecting the name with Henry's dead wife.

"Why, my wife Phœbe, o' course. Who do yuh spose I mean?" He stared up with a pathetic sharpness of glance from under his shaggy, gray eyebrows.

"Wall, I'll swan, Henry, yuh ain't jokin', are yuh?" said the solid Dodge, a pursy man, with a smooth, hard, red face. "It can't be your wife yuh're talkin' about. She's dead."

"Dead! Shucks!" retorted the demented Reifsneider. "She left me early this mornin', while I was sleepin'. She allus got up to build the fire, but she's gone now. We had a little spat last night, an' I guess that's the reason. But I guess I kin find her. She's gone over to Matilda Race's; that's where she's gone."

He started briskly up the road, leaving the amazed Dodge to stare in wonder after him.

"Well, I'll be switched!" he said aloud to himself. "He's clean out'n his head. That poor old feller's been livin' down there till he's gone outen his mind. I'll have to notify the authorities." And he flicked his whip with great enthusiasm. "Geddap!" he said, and was off.

Reifsneider met no one else in this poorly populated region until he reached the whitewashed fence of Matilda Race and her husband three miles away. He had passed several other houses en route, but these not being within the range of his illusion were not considered. His wife, who had known Matilda well, must be here. He opened the picket-gate which guarded the walk, and stamped briskly up to the door.

"Why, Mr. Reifsneider," exclaimed old Matilda herself, a stout woman, looking out of the door in answer to his knock, "what brings yuh here this mornin'?"

"Is Phœbe here?" he demanded eagerly.

"Phœbe who? What Phœbe?" replied Mrs. Race, curious as to this sudden development of energy on his part.

"Why, my Phœbe, o' course. My wife Phœbe. Who do yuh s'pose? Ain't she here now?"

"Lawsy me!" exclaimed Mrs. Race, opening her mouth. "Yuh pore man! So you're clean out'n your mind now. Yuh come right in and sit down. I'll git yuh a cup o' coffee. O' course your wife ain't here; but yuh come in an' sit down. I'll find her fer yuh after a while. I know where she is."

The old farmer's eyes softened, and he entered. He was so thin and pale a specimen, pantalooned and patriarchal, that he aroused Mrs. Race's extremest sympathy as he took off his hat and laid it on his knees quite softly and mildly.

"We had a quarrel last night, an' she left me," he volunteered.

"Laws! laws!" sighed Mrs. Race, there being no one present with whom to share her astonishment as she went to her kitchen. "The pore man! Now somebody's just got to look after him. He can't be allowed to run around the country this way lookin' for his dead wife. It's turrible."

She boiled him a pot of coffee and brought in some of her new-baked bread and fresh butter. She set out some of her best jam and put a couple of eggs to boil, lying whole-heartedly the while.

"Now yuh stay right there, Uncle Henry, till Jake comes in, an' I'll send him to look for Phœbe. I think it's more'n likely she's over to Swinnerton with some o' her friends. Anyhow, we'll find out. Now yuh just drink this coffee an' eat this bread. Yuh must be tired. Yuh've had a long walk this mornin'." Her idea was to take counsel with Jake, "her man," and perhaps have him notify the authorities.

She bustled about, meditating on the uncertainties of life, while old Reifsneider thrummed on the rim of his hat with his pale fingers and later ate abstractedly of what she offered. His mind was on his wife, however, and since she was not here, or did not appear, it wandered vaguely away to a family by the name of Murray, miles away in another direction. He decided after a time that he would not wait for Jake Race to hunt his wife but would seek her for himself. He must be on, and urge her to come back.

"Well, I'll be goin'," he said, getting up and looking strangely about him. "I guess she didn't come here after all. She went over to the Murrays', I guess. I'll not wait any longer, Mis' Race. There's a lot to do over to the house to-day." And out he marched in the face of her protests taking to the dusty road again in the warm spring sun, his cane striking the earth as he went.

It was two hours later that this pale figure of a man appeared in the Murrays' doorway, dusty, perspiring, eager. He had tramped all of five miles, and it was noon. An amazed husband and wife of sixty heard his strange query, and realized also that he was mad. They begged him to stay to dinner, intending to notify the authorities later and see what could be done; but though he stayed to partake of a little something, he did not stay long, and was off again to another distant farmhouse, his idea of many things to do and his need of Phœbe impelling him. So it went for that day and the next and the next, the circle of his inquiry ever widening.

The process by which a character assumes the significance of being peculiar, his antics weird, yet harmless, in such a community is often involute and pathetic. This day, as has been said, saw Reifsneider at other doors, eagerly asking his unnatural question, and leaving a trail of amazement, sympathy, and pity in his wake. Although the authorities were informed — the county sheriff, no less — it was not deemed advisable to take him into custody; for when those who knew old Henry, and had for so long, reflected on the condition of the county insane asylum, a place which, because of the poverty of the district, was of staggering aberration and sickening environment, it was decided to let him remain at large; for, strange to relate, it was found on investigation that at night he returned peaceably enough to his lonesome domicile there to discover whether his wife had returned, and to brood in loneliness until the morning. Who would lock up a thin, eager, seeking old man with iron-gray hair and an attitude of kindly, innocent inquiry, particularly when he was well known for a past of only kindly servitude and reliability? Those who had known him best rather agreed that he should be allowed to roam at large. He could do no harm. There were many who were willing to help him as to food, old clothes, the odds and ends of his daily life — at least at first. His figure after a time became not so much a common-place as an accepted curiosity, and the replies, "Why, no, Henry; I ain't see her," or "No, Henry; she ain't been here to-day," more customary.

For several years thereafter then he was an odd figure in the sun and rain, on dusty roads and muddy ones, encountered occasionally in strange and unexpected places, pursuing his endless search. Undernourishment, after a time, although the neighbors and those who knew his history gladly contributed from their store, affected his body; for he walked much and ate little. The longer he roamed the public highway in this manner, the deeper became his strange hallucination; and finding it harder and harder to return from his more and more distant pilgrimages, he finally began taking a few utensils with him from his home, making a small package of them, in order that he might not be compelled to return. In an old tin coffee-pot of large size he placed a small tin cup, a knife, fork, and spoon, some salt and pepper, and to the outside of it, by a string forced through a pierced hole, he fastened a plate, which could be released, and which was his woodland table. It was no trouble for him to secure the little food that he needed, and with a strange, almost religious dignity, he had no hesitation in asking for that much. By degrees his hair became longer and longer, his once black hat became an earthen brown, and his clothes threadbare and dusty.

For all of three years he walked, and none knew how wide were his perambulations, nor how he survived the storms and cold. They could not see him, with homely rural understanding and forethought, sheltering himself in hay-cocks, or by the sides of cattle, whose warm bodies protected him from the cold, and whose dull understandings were not opposed to his harmless presence. Overhanging rocks and trees kept him at times from the rain, and a friendly hay-loft or corn-crib was not above his humble consideration.

The involute progression of hallucination is strange. From asking at doors and being constantly rebuffed or denied, he finally came to the conclusion that although his Phœbe might not be in any of the houses at the doors of which he inquired, she might nevertheless be within the sound of his voice. And so, from patient inquiry, he began to call sad, occasional cries, that ever and anon waked the quiet landscapes and ragged hill regions, and set to echoing his thin "O-o-o Phœbe! O-o-o Phœbe!" It had a pathetic, albeit insane, ring, and many a farmer or plowboy came to know it even from afar and say, "There goes old Reifsneider."

Another thing that puzzled him greatly after a time and after many hundreds of inquiries was, when he no longer had any particular dooryard in view and no special inquiry to make, which way to go. These cross-roads, which occasionally led in four or even six directions, came after a time to puzzle him. But to solve this knotty problem, which became more and more of a puzzle, there came to his aid another hallucination. Phœbe's spirit or some power of the air or wind or nature would tell him. If he stood at the center of the parting of the ways, closed his eyes, turned thrice about, and called "O-o-o Phœbe!" twice, and then threw his cane straight before him, that would surely indicate which way to go for Phœbe, or one of these mystic powers would surely govern its direction and fall! In whichever direction it went, even though, as was not infrequently the case, it took him back along the path he had already come, or across fields, he was not so far gone in his mind but that he gave himself ample time to search before he called again. Also the hallucination seemed to persist that at some time he would surely find her. There were hours when his feet were sore, and his limbs weary, when he would stop in the heat to wipe his seamed brow, or in the cold to beat his arms. Sometimes, after throwing away his cane, and finding it indicating the direction from which he had just come, he would shake his head wearily and philosophically, as if contemplating the unbelievable or an untoward fate, and then start briskly off. His strange figure came finally to be known in the farthest reaches of three or four counties. Old Reifsneider was a pathetic character. His fame was wide.

Near a little town called Watersville, in Green County, perhaps four miles from that minor center of human activity, there was a place or

precipice locally known as the Red Cliff, a sheer wall of red sandstone, perhaps a hundred feet high, which raised its sharp face for half a mile or more
above the fruitful corn-fields and orchards that lay beneath, and which was
surmounted by a thick grove of trees. The slope that slowly led up to it
from the opposite side was covered by a rank growth of beech, hickory,
and ash, through which threaded a number of wagon-tracks crossing at
various angles. In fair weather it had become old Reifsneider's habit, so
inured was he by now to the open, to make his bed in some such patch of
trees as this to fry his bacon or boil his eggs at the foot of some tree before
laying himself down for the night. Occasionally, so light and inconsequen-
tial was his sleep, he would walk at night. More often, the moonlight or
some sudden wind stirring in the trees or a reconnoitering animal arousing
him, he would sit up and think, or pursue his quest in the moonlight or
the dark, a strange, unnatural, half wild, half savage-looking but utterly
harmless creature, calling at lonely road crossings, staring at dark and shuttered houses, and wondering where, where Phœbe could really be.

That particular lull that comes in the systole-diastole of this earthly
ball at two o'clock in the morning invariably aroused him, and though he
might not go any farther he would sit up and contemplate the darkness or
the stars, wondering. Sometimes in the strange processes of his mind he
would fancy that he saw moving among the trees the figure of his lost wife,
and then he would get up to follow, taking his utensils, always on a string,
and his cane. If she seemed to evade him too easily he would run, or plead,
or, suddenly losing track of the fancied figure, stand awed or disappointed,
grieving for the moment over the almost insurmountable difficulties of his
search.

It was in the seventh year of these hopeless peregrinations, in the dawn
of a similar springtime to that in which his wife had died, that he came at last
one night to the vicinity of this selfsame patch that crowned the rise to the
Red Cliff. His far-flung cane, used as a divining-rod at the last cross-roads,
had brought him hither. He had walked many, many miles. It was after ten
o'clock at night, and he was very weary. Long wandering and little eating
had left him but a shadow of his former self. It was a question now not so
much of physical strength but of spiritual endurance which kept him up.
He had scarcely eaten this day, and now exhausted he set himself down in
the dark to rest and possibly to sleep.

Curiously on this occasion a strange suggestion of the presence of his
wife surrounded him. It would not be long now, he counseled with himself, although the long months had brought him nothing, until he should
see her, talk to her. He fell asleep after a time, his head on his knees. At
midnight the moon began to rise, and at two in the morning, his wakeful
hour, was a large silver disk shining through the trees to the east. He
opened his eyes when the radiance became strong, making a silver pattern
at his feet and lighting the woods with strange lusters and silvery, shadowy
forms. As usual, his old notion that his wife must be near occurred to him

on this occasion, and he looked about him with a speculative, anticipatory eye. What was it that moved in the distant shadows along the path by which he had entered—a pale, flickering will-o'-the-wisp that bobbed gracefully among the trees and riveted his expectant gaze? Moonlight and shadows combined to give it a strange form and a stranger reality, this fluttering of bogfire or dancing of wandering fireflies. Was it truly his lost Phœbe? By a circuitous route it passed about him, and in his fevered state he fancied that he could see the very eyes of her, not as she was when he last saw her in the black dress and shawl but now a strangely younger Phœbe, gayer, sweeter, the one whom he had known years before as a girl. Old Reifsneider got up. He had been expecting and dreaming of this hour all these years, and now as he saw the feeble light dancing lightly before him he peered at it questioningly, one thin hand in his gray hair.

Of a sudden there came to him now for the first time in many years the full charm of her girlish figure as he had known it in boyhood, the pleasing, sympathetic smile, the brown hair, the blue sash she had once worn about her waist at a picnic, her gay, graceful movements. He walked around the base of the tree, straining with his eyes, forgetting for once his cane and utensils, and following eagerly after. On she moved before him, a will-o'-the-wisp of the spring, a little flame above her head, and it seemed as though among the small saplings of ash and beech and the thick trunks of hickory and elm that she signaled with a young, a lightsome hand.

"O Phœbe! Phœbe!" he called. "Have yuh really come? Have yuh really answered me?" And hurrying faster, he fell once, scrambling lamely to his feet, only to see the light in the distance dancing illusively on. On and on he hurried until he was fairly running, brushing his ragged arms against the trees, striking his hands and face against impeding twigs. His hat was gone, his lungs were breathless, his reason quite astray, when coming to the edge of the cliff he saw her below among a silvery bed of apple-trees now blooming in the spring.

"O Phœbe!" he called. "O Phœbe! Oh, no, don't leave me!" And feeling the lure of a world where love was young and Phœbe as this vision presented her, a delightful epitome of their quondam youth, he gave a gay cry of "Oh, wait, Phœbe!" and leaped.

Some farmer-boys, reconnoitering this region of bounty and prospect some few days afterward, found first the tin utensils tied together under the tree where he had left them, and then later at the foot of the cliff, pale, broken, but elate, a molded smile of peace and delight upon his lips, his body. His old hat was discovered lying under some low-growing saplings the twigs of which had held it back. No one of all the simple population knew how eagerly and joyously he had found his lost mate.   [1916]

SUSAN GLASPELL

*S*usan Glaspell (1876–1948) was born in Davenport, Iowa, into a family that had been among the state's first settlers a generation before. After her graduation from high school, she worked as a reporter and society editor for various newspapers before enrolling at Drake University in Des Moines. There she studied literature, philosophy, and history; edited the college newspaper; and began to write short stories. In 1899 she took a job as statehouse reporter for the Des Moines Daily News. Years later she claimed that the discipline of newspaper work helped her to become a creative writer.

At the age of twenty-five, Glaspell returned to Davenport to live with her family, determined, as she said, to "boldly" quit journalism and "give all my time to my own writing. I say 'boldly,' because I had to earn my living." Slowly she began to publish her fiction, mostly sentimental magazine pieces and an undistinguished first novel—work that, as her biographer C. W. E. Bigsby noted, "suggested little of the originality and power which were to mark her work in the theater." In 1909 Glaspell met George Cram Cook, a novelist and utopian socialist from a wealthy family who divorced his second wife and left his two children to marry her. They moved to Greenwich Village and collaborated on a play for the Washington Square Players in 1915, Suppressed Desires. The following year, after the Players had moved to Provincetown on Cape Cod, Cook urged Glaspell to write a new play for the theater company, renamed the Provincetown Players. Her memory of a murder trial in Iowa that she had covered as a newspaper reporter served as the inspiration for the short play Trifles (1916). Glaspell recalled that she "had meant to do it as a short story, but the stage took it for its own."

Trifles was so successful as an experimental play that Glaspell turned it into a short story a year later, retitling it "A Jury of Her Peers" for publication in Everyweek. Her choice of a limited-omniscient, third-person point of view (via the character Martha Hale's perspective) and her description of the harsh realities of the rural setting in "A Jury of Her Peers" suggest the local-color tradition of such earlier writers as Sarah Orne Jewett, although Glaspell's suffragist sympathies were more radical than the views of most of the nineteenth-century women writers. In 1912 Glaspell published her first book of stories, Lifted Masks, and she continued to write fiction as well as plays for most of her life. In her forty-seven-year career, she published fifty short stories, nine novels, and thirteen plays, including the Pulitzer Prize–winning play Alison's House (1931), based on Genevieve Taggart's biography of Emily Dickinson.

A Jury of Her Peers

When Martha Hale opened the storm-door and got a cut of the north wind, she ran back for her big woolen scarf. As she hurriedly wound that round her head her eye made a scandalized sweep of her kitchen. It was no ordinary thing that called her away — it was probably further from ordinary than anything that had ever happened in Dickson County. But what her eye took in was that her kitchen was in no shape for leaving: her bread all ready for mixing, half the flour sifted and half unsifted.

She hated to see things half done; but she had been at that when the team from town stopped to get Mr. Hale, and then the sheriff came running in to say his wife wished Mrs. Hale would come too — adding, with a grin, that he guessed she was getting scary and wanted another woman along. So she had dropped everything right where it was.

"Martha!" now came her husband's impatient voice. "Don't keep folks waiting out here in the cold."

She again opened the storm-door, and this time joined the three men and the one woman waiting for her in the big two-seated buggy.

After she had the robes tucked around her she took another look at the woman who sat beside her on the back seat. She had met Mrs. Peters the year before at the county fair, and the thing she remembered about her was that she didn't seem like a sheriff's wife. She was small and thin and didn't have a strong voice. Mrs. Gorman, sheriff's wife before Gorman went out and Peters came in, had a voice that somehow seemed to be backing up the law with every word. But if Mrs. Peters didn't look like a sheriff's wife, Peters made it up in looking like a sheriff. He was to a dot the kind of man who could get himself elected sheriff — a heavy man with a big voice, who was particularly genial with the law-abiding, as if to make it plain that he knew the difference between criminals and non-criminals. And right there it came into Mrs. Hale's mind, with a stab, that this man who was so pleasant and lively with all of them was going to the Wrights' now as a sheriff.

"The country's not very pleasant this time of year," Mrs. Peters at last ventured, as if she felt they ought to be talking as well as the men.

Mrs. Hale scarcely finished her reply, for they had gone up a little hill and could see the Wright place now, and seeing it did not make her feel like talking. It looked very lonesome this cold March morning. It had always been a lonesome-looking place. It was down in a hollow, and the poplar trees around it were lonesome-looking trees. The men were looking at it and talking about what had happened. The county attorney was bending to one side of the buggy, and kept looking steadily at the place as they drew up to it.

"I'm glad you came with me," Mrs. Peters said nervously, as the two women were about to follow the men in through the kitchen door.

Even after she had her foot on the door-step, her hand on the knob, Martha Hale had a moment of feeling she could not cross that threshold.

And the reason it seemed she couldn't cross it now was simply because she hadn't crossed it before. Time and time again it had been in her mind, "I ought to go over and see Minnie Foster"—she still thought of her as Minnie Foster, though for twenty years she had been Mrs. Wright. And then there was always something to do and Minnie Foster would go from her mind. But *now* she could come.

The men went over to the stove. The women stood close together by the door. Young Henderson, the county attorney, turned around and said, "Come up to the fire, ladies."

Mrs. Peters took a step forward, then stopped. "I'm not—cold," she said.

And so the two women stood by the door, at first not even so much as looking around the kitchen.

The men talked for a minute about what a good thing it was the sheriff had sent his deputy out that morning to make a fire for them, and then Sheriff Peters stepped back from the stove, unbuttoned his outer coat, and leaned his hands on the kitchen table in a way that seemed to mark the beginning of official business. "Now, Mr. Hale," he said in a sort of semi-official voice, "before we move things about, you tell Mr. Henderson just what it was you saw when you came here yesterday morning."

The county attorney was looking around the kitchen.

"By the way," he said, "has anything been moved?" He turned to the sheriff. "Are things just as you left them yesterday?"

Peters looked from cupboard to sink; from that to a small worn rocker a little to one side of the kitchen table.

"It's just the same."

"Somebody should have been left here yesterday," said the county attorney.

"Oh—yesterday," returned the sheriff, with a little gesture as of yesterday having been more than he could bear to think of. "When I had to send Frank to Morris Center for that man who went crazy—let me tell you. I had my hands full *yesterday*. I knew you could get back from Omaha by today, George, and as long as I went over everything here myself—"

"Well, Mr. Hale," said the county attorney, in a way of letting what was past and gone go, "tell just what happened when you came here yesterday morning."

Mrs. Hale, still leaning against the door, had that sinking feeling of the mother whose child is about to speak a piece. Lewis often wandered along and got things mixed up in a story. She hoped he would tell this straight and plain, and not say unnecessary things that would just make things harder for Minnie Foster. He didn't begin at once, and she noticed that he looked queer—as if standing in that kitchen and having to tell what he had seen there yesterday morning made him almost sick.

"Yes, Mr. Hale?" the county attorney reminded.

"Harry and I had started to town with a load of potatoes," Mrs. Hale's husband began.

Harry was Mrs. Hale's oldest boy. He wasn't with them now, for the very good reason that those potatoes never got to town yesterday and he was taking them this morning, so he hadn't been home when the sheriff stopped to say he wanted Mr. Hale to come over to the Wright place and tell the county attorney his story there, where he could point it all out. With all Mrs. Hale's other emotions came the fear now that maybe Harry wasn't dressed warm enough — they hadn't any of them realized how that north wind did bite.

"We come along this road," Hale was going on, with a motion of his hand to the road over which they had just come, "and as we got in sight of the house I says to Harry, 'I'm goin' to see if I can't get John Wright to take a telephone.' You see," he explained to Henderson, "unless I can get somebody to go in with me they won't come out this branch road except for a price *I* can't pay. I'd spoke to Wright about it once before; but he put me off, saying folks talked too much anyway, and all he asked was peace and quiet — guess you know about how much he talked himself. But I thought maybe if I went to the house and talked about it before his wife, and said all the women-folks liked the telephones, and that in this lonesome stretch of road it would be a good thing — well, I said to Harry that that was what I was going to say — though I said at the same time that I didn't know as what his wife wanted made much difference to John —"

Now there he was! — saying things he didn't need to say. Mrs. Hale tried to catch her husband's eye, but fortunately the county attorney interrupted with:

"Let's talk about that a little later, Mr. Hale. I do want to talk about that, but I'm anxious now to get along to just what happened when you got here."

When he began this time, it was very deliberately and carefully:

"I didn't see or hear anything. I knocked at the door. And still it was all quiet inside. I knew they must be up — it was past eight o'clock. So I knocked again, louder, and I thought I heard somebody say, 'Come in.' I wasn't sure — I'm not sure yet. But I opened the door — this door," jerking a hand toward the door by which the two women stood, "and there, in that rocker" — pointing to it — "sat Mrs. Wright."

Everyone in the kitchen looked at the rocker. It came into Mrs. Hale's mind that that rocker didn't look in the least like Minnie Foster — the Minnie Foster of twenty years before. It was a dingy red, with wooden rungs up the back, and the middle rung was gone, and the chair sagged to one side.

"How did she — look?" the county attorney was inquiring.

"Well," said Hale, "she looked — queer."

"How do you mean—queer?"

As he asked it he took out a note-book and pencil. Mrs. Hale did not like the sight of that pencil. She kept her eye fixed on her husband, as if to keep him from saying unnecessary things that would go into that note-book and make trouble.

Hale did speak guardedly, as if the pencil had affected him too.

"Well, as if she didn't know what she was going to do next. And kind of—done up."

"How did she seem to feel about your coming?"

"Why, I don't think she minded—one way or other. She didn't pay much attention. I said, 'Ho' do, Mrs. Wright? It's cold, ain't it?' And she said, 'Is it?'—and went on pleatin' at her apron.

"Well, I was surprised. She didn't ask me to come up to the stove, or to sit down, but just set there, not even lookin' at me. And so I said: 'I want to see John.'

"And then she—laughed. I guess you would call it a laugh.

"I thought of Harry and the team outside, so I said, a little sharp, 'Can I see John?' 'No,' says she—kind of dull like. 'Ain't he home?' says I. Then she looked at me. 'Yes,' says she, 'he's home.' 'Then why can't I see him?' I asked her, out of patience with her now. 'Cause he's dead' says she, just as quiet and dull—and fell to pleatin' her apron. 'Dead?' says I, like you do when you can't take in what you've heard.

"She just nodded her head, not getting a bit excited, but rockin' back and forth.

"'Why—where is he?' says I, not knowing *what* to say.

"She just pointed upstairs—like this"—pointing to the room above.

"I got up, with the idea of going up there myself. By this time I—didn't know what to do. I walked from there to here; then I says: 'Why, what did he die of?'

"'He died of a rope around his neck,' says she; and just went on pleatin' at her apron."

Hale stopped speaking, and stood staring at the rocker, as if he were still seeing the woman who had sat there the morning before. Nobody spoke; it was as if every one were seeing the woman who had sat there the morning before.

"And what did you do then?" the county attorney at last broke the silence.

"I went out and called Harry. I thought I might—need help. I got Harry in, and we went upstairs." His voice fell almost to a whisper. "There he was—lying over the—"

"I think I'd rather have you go into that upstairs," the county attorney interrupted, "where you can point it all out. Just go on now with the rest of the story."

"Well, my first thought was to get that rope off. It looked—"

He stopped, his face twitching.

"But Harry, he went up to him, and he said, 'No, he's dead all right, and we'd better not touch anything.' So we went downstairs.

"She was still sitting that same way. 'Has anybody been notified?' I asked. 'No,' says she, unconcerned.

"'Who did this, Mrs. Wright?' said Harry. He said it businesslike, and she stopped pleatin' at her apron. 'I don't know,' she says. 'You don't *know?*' says Harry. 'Weren't you sleepin' in the bed with him?' 'Yes,' says she, 'but I was on the inside.' 'Somebody slipped a rope round his neck and strangled him, and you didn't wake up?' says Harry. 'I didn't wake up,' she said after him.

"We may have looked as if we didn't see how that could be, for after a minute she said, 'I sleep sound.'

"Harry was going to ask her more questions, but I said maybe that weren't our business; maybe we ought to let her tell her story first to the coroner or the sheriff. So Harry went fast as he could over to High Road—the Rivers' place, where there's a telephone."

"And what did she do when she knew you had gone for the coroner?" The attorney got his pencil in his hand all ready for writing.

"She moved from that chair to this one over here"—Hale pointed to a small chair in the corner—"and just sat there with her hands held together and looking down. I got a feeling that I ought to make some conversation, so I said I had come in to see if John wanted to put in a telephone; and at that she started to laugh, and then she stopped and looked at me—scared."

At the sound of a moving pencil the man who was telling the story looked up.

"I dunno—maybe it wasn't scared," he hastened: "I wouldn't like to say it was. Soon Harry got back, and then Dr. Lloyd came, and you, Mr. Peters, and so I guess that's all I know that you don't."

He said that last with relief, and moved a little, as if relaxing. Everyone moved a little. The county attorney walked toward the stair door.

"I guess we'll go upstairs first—then out to the barn and around there."

He paused and looked around the kitchen.

"You're convinced there was nothing important here?" he asked the sheriff. "Nothing that would—point to any motive?"

The sheriff too looked all around, as if to re-convince himself.

"Nothing here but kitchen things," he said, with a little laugh for the insignificance of kitchen things.

The county attorney was looking at the cupboard—a peculiar, ungainly structure, half closet and half cupboard, the upper part of it being built in the wall, and the lower part just the old-fashioned kitchen cupboard. As if its queerness attracted him, he got a chair and opened the upper part and looked in. After a moment he drew his hand away sticky.

"Here's a nice mess," he said resentfully.

The two women had drawn nearer, and now the sheriff's wife spoke.

"Oh—her fruit," she said, looking to Mrs. Hale for sympathetic understanding. She turned back to the county attorney and explained: "She worried about that when it turned so cold last night. She said the fire would go out and her jars might burst."

Mrs. Peters' husband broke into a laugh.

"Well, can you beat the women! Held for murder, and worrying about her preserves!"

The young attorney set his lips.

"I guess before we're through with her she may have something more serious than preserves to worry about."

"Oh, well," said Mrs. Hale's husband, with good-natured superiority, "women are used to worrying over trifles."

The two women moved a little closer together. Neither of them spoke. The county attorney seemed suddenly to remember his manners—and think of his future.

"And yet," said he, with the gallantry of a young politician, "for all their worries, what would we do without the ladies?"

The women did not speak, did not unbend. He went to the sink and began washing his hands. He turned to wipe them on the roller towel—whirled it for a cleaner place.

"Dirty towels! Not much of a housekeeper, would you say, ladies?"

He kicked his foot against some dirty pans under the sink.

"There's a great deal of work to be done on a farm," said Mrs. Hale stiffly.

"To be sure. And yet"—with a little bow to her—"I know there are some Dickson County farm-houses that do not have such roller towels." He gave it a pull to expose its full length again.

"Those towels get dirty awful quick. Men's hands aren't always as clean as they might be."

"Ah, loyal to your sex, I see," he laughed. He stopped and gave her a keen look. "But you and Mrs. Wright were neighbors. I suppose you were friends, too."

Martha Hale shook her head.

"I've seen little enough of her of late years. I've not been in this house—it's more than a year."

"And why was that? You didn't like her?"

"I liked her well enough," she replied with spirit. "Farmers' wives have their hands full, Mr. Henderson. And then—" She looked around the kitchen.

"Yes?" he encouraged.

"It never seemed a very cheerful place," said she, more to herself than to him.

"No," he agreed; "I don't think anyone would call it cheerful. I shouldn't say she had the home-making instinct."

"Well, I don't know as Wright had, either," she muttered.

"You mean they didn't get on very well?" he was quick to ask.

"No; I don't mean anything," she answered, with decision. As she turned a little away from him, she added: "But I don't think a place would be any the cheerfuller for John Wright's bein' in it."

"I'd like to talk to you about that a little later, Mrs. Hale," he said. "I'm anxious to get the lay of things upstairs now."

He moved toward the stair door, followed by the two men.

"I suppose anything Mrs. Peters does'll be all right?" the sheriff inquired. "She was to take in some clothes for her, you know—and a few little things. We left in such a hurry yesterday."

The county attorney looked at the two women whom they were leaving alone there among the kitchen things.

"Yes—Mrs. Peters," he said, his glance resting on the woman who was not Mrs. Peters, the big farmer woman who stood behind the sheriff's wife. "Of course Mrs. Peters is one of us," he said, in a manner of entrusting responsibility. "And keep your eye out, Mrs. Peters, for anything that might be of use. No telling; you women might come upon a clue to the motive—and that's the thing we need."

Mr. Hale rubbed his face after the fashion of a showman getting ready for a pleasantry.

"But would the women know a clue if they did come upon it?" he said; and, having delivered himself of this, he followed the others through the stair door.

The women stood motionless and silent, listening to the footsteps, first upon the stairs, then in the room above them.

Then, as if releasing herself from something strange, Mrs. Hale began to arrange the dirty pans under the sink, which the county attorney's disdainful push of the foot had deranged.

"I'd hate to have men comin' into my kitchen," she said testily—"snoopin' round and criticizin'."

"Of course it's no more than their duty," said the sheriff's wife, in her manner of timid acquiescence.

"Duty's all right," replied Mrs. Hale bluffly; "but I guess that deputy sheriff that come out to make the fire might have got a little of this on." She gave the roller towel a pull. "Wish I'd thought of that sooner! Seems mean to talk about her for not having things slicked up, when she had to come away in such a hurry."

She looked around the kitchen. Certainly it was not "slicked up." Her eye was held by a bucket of sugar on a low shelf. The cover was off the wooden bucket, and beside it was a paper bag—half full.

Mrs. Hale moved toward it.

"She was putting this in there," she said to herself—slowly.

She thought of the flour in her kitchen at home—half sifted, half not sifted. She had been interrupted, and had left things half done. What had interrupted Minnie Foster? Why had that work been left half done? She made a move as if to finish it,—unfinished things always bothered her,—and then she glanced around and saw that Mrs. Peters was watching her—and she didn't want Mrs. Peters to get that feeling she had got of work begun and then—for some reason—not finished.

"It's a shame about her fruit," she said, and walked toward the cupboard that the county attorney had opened, and got on the chair, murmuring: "I wonder if it's all gone."

It was a sorry enough looking sight, but "Here's one that's all right," she said at last. She held it toward the light. "This is cherries, too." She looked again. "I declare I believe that's the only one."

With a sigh, she got down from the chair, went to the sink, and wiped off the bottle.

"She'll feel awful bad, after all her hard work in the hot weather. I remember the afternoon I put up my cherries last summer."

She set the bottle on the table, and, with another sigh, started to sit down in the rocker. But she did not sit down. Something kept her from sitting down in that chair. She straightened—stepped back, and, half turned away, stood looking at it, seeing the woman who had sat there "pleatin' at her apron."

The thin voice of the sheriff's wife broke in upon her: "I must be getting those things from the front-room closet." She opened the door into the other room, started in, stepped back. "You coming with me, Mrs. Hale?" she asked nervously. "You—you could help me get them."

They were soon back—the stark coldness of that shut-up room was not a thing to linger in.

"My!" said Mrs. Peters, dropping the things on the table and hurrying to the stove.

Mrs. Hale stood examining the clothes the woman who was being detained in town had said she wanted.

"Wright was close!"[1] she exclaimed, holding up a shabby black skirt that bore the marks of much making over. "I think maybe that's why she kept so much to herself. I s'pose she felt she couldn't do her part; and then, you don't enjoy things when you feel shabby. She used to wear pretty clothes and be lively—when she was Minnie Foster, one of the town girls, singing in the choir. But that—oh, that was twenty years ago."

With a carefulness in which there was something tender, she folded the shabby clothes and piled them at one corner of the table. She looked up at Mrs. Peters, and there was something in the other woman's look that irritated her.

"She don't care," she said to herself. "Much difference it makes to her whether Minnie Foster had pretty clothes when she was a girl."

---

[1]Frugal, tightfisted.

Then she looked again, and she wasn't so sure; in fact, she hadn't at any time been perfectly sure about Mrs. Peters. She had that shrinking manner, and yet her eyes looked as if they could see a long way into things.

"This all you was to take in?" asked Mrs. Hale.

"No," said the sheriff's wife; "she said she wanted an apron. Funny thing to want," she ventured in her nervous little way, "for there's not much to get you dirty in jail, goodness knows. But I suppose just to make her feel more natural. If you're used to wearing an apron—. She said they were in the bottom drawer of this cupboard. Yes—here they are. And then her little shawl that always hung on the stair door."

She took the small gray shawl from behind the door leading upstairs, and stood a minute looking at it.

Suddenly Mrs. Hale took a quick step toward the other woman.

"Mrs. Peters!"

"Yes, Mrs. Hale?"

"Do you think she—did it?"

A frightened look blurred the other thing in Mrs. Peters' eyes.

"Oh, I don't know," she said, in a voice that seemed to shrink away from the subject.

"Well, I don't think she did," affirmed Mrs. Hale stoutly. "Asking for an apron, and her little shawl. Worryin' about her fruit."

"Mr. Peters says—." Footsteps were heard in the room above; she stopped, looked up, then went on in a lowered voice: "Mr. Peters says—it looks bad for her. Mr. Henderson is awful sarcastic in a speech, and he's going to make fun of her saying she didn't—wake up."

For a moment Mrs. Hale had no answer. Then, "Well, I guess John Wright didn't wake up—when they was slippin' that rope under his neck," she muttered.

"No, it's *strange*," breathed Mrs. Peters. "They think it was such a—funny way to kill a man."

She began to laugh; at the sound of the laugh, abruptly stopped.

"That's just what Mr. Hale said," said Mrs. Hale, in a resolutely natural voice. "There was a gun in the house. He says that's what he can't understand."

"Mr. Henderson said, coming out, that what was needed for the case was a motive. Something to show anger—or sudden feeling."

"Well, I don't see any signs of anger around here," said Mrs. Hale, "I don't—" She stopped. It was as if her mind tripped on something. Her eye was caught by a dishtowel in the middle of the kitchen table. Slowly she moved toward the table. One half of it was wiped clean, the other half messy. Her eyes made a slow, almost unwilling turn to the bucket of sugar and the half empty bag beside it. Things begun—and not finished.

After a moment she stepped back, and said, in that manner of releasing herself:

"Wonder how they're finding things upstairs? I hope she had it a little

more redd up[2] up there. You know,"—she paused, and feeling gathered,—
"it seems kind of *sneaking:* locking her up in town and coming out here to
get her own house to turn against her!"

"But, Mrs. Hale," said the sheriff's wife, "the law is the law."

"I s'pose 'tis," answered Mrs. Hale shortly.

She turned to the stove, saying something about that fire not being
much to brag of. She worked with it a minute, and when she straightened
up she said aggressively:

"The law is the law—and a bad stove is a bad stove. How'd you like to
cook on this?"—pointing with the poker to the broken lining. She opened
the oven door and started to express her opinion of the oven; but she was
swept into her own thoughts, thinking of what it would mean, year after
year, to have that stove to wrestle with. The thought of Minnie Foster trying to bake in that oven—and the thought of her never going over to see
Minnie Foster—.

She was startled by hearing Mrs. Peters say: "A person gets discouraged—and loses heart."

The sheriff's wife had looked from the stove to the sink—to the pail
of water which had been carried in from outside. The two women stood
there silent, above them the footsteps of the men who were looking for
evidence against the woman who had worked in that kitchen. That look of
seeing into things, of seeing through a thing to something else, was in the
eyes of the sheriff's wife now. When Mrs. Hale next spoke to her, it was
gently:

"Better loosen up your things, Mrs. Peters. We'll not feel them when
we go out."

Mrs. Peters went to the back of the room to hang up the fur tippet she
was wearing. A moment later she exclaimed, "Why, she was piecing a
quilt," and held up a large sewing basket piled high with quilt pieces.

Mrs. Hale spread some of the blocks on the table.

"It's log-cabin pattern," she said, putting several of them together.
"Pretty, isn't it?"

They were so engaged with the quilt that they did not hear the footsteps on the stairs. Just as the stair door opened Mrs. Hale was saying:

"Do you suppose she was going to quilt it or just knot it?"

The sheriff threw up his hands.

"They wonder whether she was going to quilt it or just knot it!"

There was a laugh for the ways of women, a warming of hands over
the stove, and then the county attorney said briskly:

"Well, let's go right out to the barn and get that cleared up."

"I don't see as there's anything so strange," Mrs. Hale said resentfully,
after the outside door had closed on the three men—"our taking up our

---

[2]Neat.

time with little things while we're waiting for them to get the evidence. I don't see as it's anything to laugh about."

"Of course they've got awful important things on their minds," said the sheriff's wife apologetically.

They returned to an inspection of the block for the quilt. Mrs. Hale was looking at the fine, even sewing, and preoccupied with thoughts of the woman who had done that sewing, when she heard the sheriff's wife say, in a queer tone:

"Why, look at this one."

She turned to take the block held out to her.

"The sewing," said Mrs. Peters, in a troubled way. "All the rest of them have been so nice and even—but—this one. Why, it looks as if she didn't know what she was about!"

Their eyes met—something flashed to life, passed between them; then, as if with an effort, they seemed to pull away from each other. A moment Mrs. Hale sat there, her hands folded over that sewing which was so unlike all the rest of the sewing. Then she had pulled a knot and drawn the threads.

"Oh, what are you doing, Mrs. Hale?" asked the sheriff's wife, startled.

"Just pulling out a stitch or two that's not sewed very good," said Mrs. Hale mildly.

"I don't think we ought to touch things," Mrs. Peters said, a little helplessly.

"I'll just finish up this end," answered Mrs. Hale, still in that mild, matter-of-fact fashion.

She threaded a needle and started to replace bad sewing with good. For a little while she sewed in silence. Then, in that thin, timid voice, she heard:

"Mrs. Hale!"

"Yes, Mrs. Peters?"

"What do you suppose she was so—nervous about?"

"Oh, *I* don't know," said Mrs. Hale, as if dismissing a thing not important enough to spend much time on. "I don't know as she was— nervous. I sew awful queer sometimes when I'm just tired."

She cut a thread, and out of the corner of her eye looked up at Mrs. Peters. The small, lean face of the sheriff's wife seemed to have tightened up. Her eyes had that look of peering into something. But next moment she moved, and said in her thin, indecisive way:

"Well, I must get those clothes wrapped. They may be through sooner than we think. I wonder where I could find a piece of paper—and string."

"In that cupboard, maybe," suggested Mrs. Hale, after a glance around.

One piece of the crazy sewing remained unripped. Mrs. Peters' back turned, Martha Hale now scrutinized that piece, compared it with the dainty, accurate sewing of the other blocks. The difference was startling.

Holding this block made her feel queer, as if the distracted thoughts of the woman who had perhaps turned to it to try and quiet herself were communicating themselves to her.

Mrs. Peters' voice roused her.

"Here's a bird-cage," she said. "Did she have a bird, Mrs. Hale?"

"Why, I don't know whether she did or not." She turned to look at the cage Mrs. Peters was holding up. "I've not been here in so long." She sighed. "There was a man round last year selling canaries cheap—but I don't know as she took one. Maybe she did. She used to sing real pretty herself."

Mrs. Peters looked around the kitchen.

"Seems kind of funny to think of a bird here." She half laughed—an attempt to put up a barrier. "But she must have had one—or why would she have a cage? I wonder what happened to it."

"I suppose maybe the cat got it," suggested Mrs. Hale, resuming her sewing.

"No; she didn't have a cat. She's got that feeling some people have about cats—being afraid of them. When they brought her to our house yesterday, my cat got in the room, and she was real upset and asked me to take it out."

"My sister Bessie was like that," laughed Mrs. Hale.

The sheriff's wife did not reply. The silence made Mrs. Hale turn round. Mrs. Peters was examining the bird-cage.

"Look at this door," she said slowly. "It's broke. One hinge has been pulled apart."

Mrs. Hale came nearer.

"Looks as if someone must have been—rough with it."

Again their eyes met—startled, questioning, apprehensive. For a moment neither spoke nor stirred. Then Mrs. Hale, turning away, said brusquely:

"If they're going to find any evidence, I wish they'd be about it. I don't like this place."

"But I'm awful glad you came with me, Mrs. Hale." Mrs. Peters put the bird-cage on the table and sat down. "It would be lonesome for me—sitting here alone."

"Yes, it would, wouldn't it?" agreed Mrs. Hale, a certain determined naturalness in her voice. She had picked up the sewing, but now it dropped in her lap, and she murmured in a different voice: "But I tell you what I *do* wish, Mrs. Peters. I wish I had come over sometimes when she was here. I wish—I had."

"But of course you were awful busy, Mrs. Hale. Your house—and your children."

"I could've come," retorted Mrs. Hale shortly. "I stayed away because it weren't cheerful—and that's why I ought to have come. I"—she looked around—"I've never liked this place. Maybe because it's down in a hollow and you don't see the road. I don't know what it is, but it's a lonesome place, and always was. I wish I had come over to see Minnie Foster some-times. I can see now—" She did not put it into words.

"Well, you mustn't reproach yourself," counseled Mrs. Peters. "Some-how, we just don't see how it is with other folks till—something comes up."

"Not having children makes less work," mused Mrs. Hale, after a silence, "but it makes a quiet house—and Wright out to work all day—and no company when he did come in. Did you know John Wright, Mrs. Peters?"

"Not to know him. I've seen him in town. They say he was a good man."

"Yes—good," conceded John Wright's neighbor grimly. "He didn't drink, and kept his word as well as most, I guess, and paid his debts. But he was a hard man, Mrs. Peters. Just to pass the time of day with him—." She stopped, shivered a little. "Like a raw wind that gets to the bone." Her eye fell upon the cage on the table before her, and she added, almost bitterly: "I should think she would've wanted a bird!"

Suddenly she leaned forward, looking intently at the cage. "But what do you s'pose went wrong with it?"

"I don't know," returned Mrs. Peters; "unless it got sick and died."

But after she said it she reached over and swung the broken door. Both women watched it as if somehow held by it.

"You didn't know—her?" Mrs. Hale asked, a gentler note in her voice.

"Not till they brought her yesterday," said the sheriff's wife.

"She—come to think of it, she was kind of like a bird herself. Real sweet and pretty, but kind of timid and—fluttery. How—she—did—change."

That held her for a long time. Finally, as if struck with a happy thought and relieved to get back to everyday things, she exclaimed:

"Tell you what, Mrs. Peters, why don't you take the quilt in with you? It might take up her mind."

"Why, I think that's a real nice idea, Mrs. Hale," agreed the sheriff's wife, as if she too were glad to come into the atmosphere of a simple kind-ness. "There couldn't possibly be any objection to that, could there? Now, just what will I take? I wonder if her patches are in here—and her things?"

They turned to the sewing basket.

"Here's some red," said Mrs. Hale, bringing out a roll of cloth. Underneath that was a box. "Here, maybe her scissors are in here—and her things." She held it up. "What a pretty box! I'll warrant that was some-thing she had a long time ago—when she was a girl."

She held it in her hand a moment; then, with a little sigh, opened it.

Instantly her hand went to her nose.

"Why—!"

Mrs. Peters drew nearer—then turned away.

"There's something wrapped up in this piece of silk," faltered Mrs. Hale.

"This isn't her scissors," said Mrs. Peters, in a shrinking voice.

Her hand not steady, Mrs. Hale raised the piece of silk. "Oh, Mrs. Peters!" she cried. "It's—"

Mrs. Peters bent closer.

"It's the bird," she whispered.

"But, Mrs. Peters!" cried Mrs. Hale. "*Look* at it! Its *neck*—look at its neck! It's all—other side *to*."

She held the box away from her.

The sheriff's wife again bent closer.

"Somebody wrung its neck," said she, in a voice that was slow and deep.

And then again the eyes of the two women met—this time clung together in a look of dawning comprehension, of growing horror. Mrs. Peters looked from the dead bird to the broken door of the cage. Again their eyes met. And just then there was a sound at the outside door.

Mrs. Hale slipped the box under the quilt pieces in the basket, and sank into the chair before it. Mrs. Peters stood holding to the table. The county attorney and the sheriff came in from outside.

"Well, ladies," said the county attorney, as one turning from serious things to little pleasantries, "have you decided whether she was going to quilt it or knot it?"

"We think," began the sheriff's wife in a flurried voice, "that she was going to—knot it."

He was too preoccupied to notice the change that came in her voice on that last.

"Well, that's very interesting, I'm sure," he said tolerantly. He caught sight of the bird-cage. "Has the bird flown?"

"We think the cat got it," said Mrs. Hale in a voice curiously even.

He was walking up and down, as if thinking something out.

"Is there a cat?" he asked absently.

Mrs. Hale shot a look up at the sheriff's wife.

"Well, not *now*," said Mrs. Peters. "They're superstitious, you know; they leave."

She sank into her chair.

The county attorney did not heed her. "No sign at all of anyone having come in from the outside," he said to Peters, in the manner of continuing an interrupted conversation. "Their own rope. Now let's go upstairs again and go over it, piece by piece. It would have to have been someone who knew just the—"

The stair door closed behind them and their voices were lost.

The two women sat motionless, not looking at each other, but as if peering into something and at the same time holding back. When they spoke now it was as if they were afraid of what they were saying, but as if they could not help saying it.

"She liked the bird," said Martha Hale, low and slowly. "She was going to bury it."

"When I was a girl," said Mrs. Peters, under her breath, "my kitten—there was a boy took a hatchet, and before my eyes—before I could get there—" She covered her face an instant. "If they hadn't held me back I would have"—she caught herself, looked upstairs where footsteps were heard, and finished weakly—"hurt him."

Then they sat without speaking or moving.

"I wonder how it would seem," Mrs. Hale at last began, as if feeling her way over strange ground—"never to have had any children around?" Her eyes made a slow sweep of the kitchen, as if seeing what that kitchen had meant through all the years. "No, Wright wouldn't like the bird," she said after that—"a thing that sang. She used to sing. He killed that too." Her voice tightened.

Mrs. Peters moved uneasily.

"Of course we don't know who killed the bird."

"I knew John Wright," was Mrs. Hale's answer.

"It was an awful thing was done in this house that night, Mrs. Hale," said the sheriff's wife. "Killing a man while he slept—slipping a thing round his neck that choked the life out of him."

Mrs. Hale's hand went out to the bird-cage.

"His neck. Choked the life out of him."

"We don't *know* who killed him," whispered Mrs. Peters wildly. "We don't *know*."

Mrs. Hale had not moved. "If there had been years and years of—nothing, then a bird to sing to you, it would be awful—still—after the bird was still."

It was as if something within her not herself had spoken, and it found in Mrs. Peters something she did not know as herself.

"I know what stillness is," she said, in a queer, monotonous voice. "When we homesteaded in Dakota, and my first baby died—after he was two years old—and me with no other then—"

Mrs. Hale stirred.

"How soon do you suppose they'll be through looking for the evidence?"

"I know what stillness is," repeated Mrs. Peters, in just the same way. Then she too pulled back. "The law has got to punish crime, Mrs. Hale," she said in her tight little way.

"I wish you'd seen Minnie Foster," was the answer, "when she wore a white dress with blue ribbons, and stood up there in the choir and sang."

The picture of that girl, the fact that she had lived neighbor to that girl for twenty years, and had let her die for lack of life, was suddenly more than she could bear.

"Oh, I *wish* I'd come over here once in a while!" she cried. "That was a crime! Who's going to punish that?"

"We mustn't take on," said Mrs. Peters, with a frightened look toward the stairs.

"I might 'a' *known* she needed help! I tell you, it's *queer,* Mrs. Peters. We live close together, and we live far apart. We all go through the same things—it's all just a different kind of the same thing! If it weren't—why do you and I *understand?* Why do we *know*—what we know this minute?"

She dashed her hand across her eyes. Then, seeing the jar of fruit on the table, she reached for it and choked out:

"If I was you I wouldn't *tell* her her fruit was gone! Tell her it *ain't.* Tell her it's all right—all of it. Here—take this in to prove it to her! She—she may never know whether it was broke or not."

She turned away.

Mrs. Peters reached out for the bottle of fruit as if she were glad to take it—as if touching a familiar thing, having something to do, could keep her from something else. She got up, looked about for something to wrap the fruit in, took a petticoat from the pile of clothes she had brought from the front room, and nervously started winding that round the bottle.

"My!" she began, in a high, false voice, "it's a good thing the men couldn't hear us! Getting all stirred up over a little thing like a—dead canary." She hurried over that. "As if that could have anything to do with—with—My, wouldn't they *laugh?*"

Footsteps were heard on the stairs.

"Maybe they would," muttered Mrs. Hale—"maybe they wouldn't."

"No, Peters," said the county attorney incisively; "it's all perfectly clear, except the reason for doing it. But you know juries when it comes to women. If there was some definite thing—something to show. Something to make a story about. A thing that would connect up with this clumsy way of doing it."

In a covert way Mrs. Hale looked at Mrs. Peters. Mrs. Peters was looking at her. Quickly they looked away from each other. The outer door opened and Mr. Hale came in.

"I've got the team round now," he said. "Pretty cold out there."

"I'm going to stay here awhile by myself," the county attorney suddenly announced. "You can send Frank out for me, can't you?" he asked the sheriff. "I want to go over everything. I'm not satisfied we can't do better."

Again, for one brief moment, the two women's eyes found one another.

The sheriff came up to the table.

"Did you want to see what Mrs. Peters was going to take in?"

The county attorney picked up the apron. He laughed.

"Oh, I guess they're not very dangerous things the ladies have picked out."

Mrs. Hale's hand was on the sewing basket in which the box was concealed. She felt that she ought to take her hand off the basket. She did not seem able to. He picked up one of the quilt blocks which she had piled on to cover the box. Her eyes felt like fire. She had a feeling that if he took up the basket she would snatch it from him.

But he did not take it up. With another little laugh, he turned away, saying:

"No; Mrs. Peters doesn't need supervising. For that matter, a sheriff's wife is married to the law. Ever think of it that way, Mrs. Peters?"

Mrs. Peters was standing beside the table. Mrs. Hale shot a look up at her; but she could not see her face. Mrs. Peters had turned away. When she spoke, her voice was muffled.

"Not—just that way," she said.

"Married to the law!" chuckled Mrs. Peters' husband. He moved toward the door into the front room, and said to the county attorney:

"I just want you to come in here a minute, George. We ought to take a look at these windows."

"Oh—windows," said the county attorney scoffingly.

"We'll be right out, Mr. Hale," said the sheriff to the farmer, who was still waiting by the door.

Hale went to look after the horses. The sheriff followed the county attorney into the other room. Again—for one final moment—the two women were alone in that kitchen.

Martha Hale sprang up, her hands tight together, looking at that other woman, with whom it rested. At first she could not see her eyes, for the sheriff's wife had not turned back since she turned away at that suggestion of being married to the law. But now Mrs. Hale made her turn back. Her eyes made her turn back. Slowly, unwillingly, Mrs. Peters turned her head until her eyes met the eyes of the other woman. There was a moment when they held each other in a steady, burning look in which there was no evasion nor flinching. Then Martha Hale's eyes pointed the way to the basket in which was hidden the thing that would make certain the conviction of the other woman—that woman who was not there and yet who had been there with them all through that hour.

For a moment Mrs. Peters did not move. And then she did it. With a rush forward, she threw back the quilt pieces, got the box, tried to put it in her handbag. It was too big. Desperately she opened it, started to take the bird out. But there she broke—she could not touch the bird. She stood there helpless, foolish.

There was the sound of a knob turning in the inner door. Martha Hale snatched the box from the sheriff's wife, and got it in the pocket of her big coat just as the sheriff and the county attorney came back into the kitchen.

"Well, Henry," said the county attorney facetiously, "at least we found out that she was not going to quilt it. She was going to—what is it you call it, ladies?"

Mrs. Hale's hand was against the pocket of her coat.

"We call it—knot it, Mr. Henderson."   [1917]

ANZIA YEZIERSKA

Anzia Yezierska (1885–1970) was born in a mud hut in the village of Plinsk to Jewish parents living in poverty near the border between Russia and Poland. At fifteen she emigrated with her family to New York City, where she worked in a sweatshop while she studied English at night school. After three years she was granted a scholarship at Columbia University to train as a domestic-science teacher. In 1910 she was briefly married to an attorney, and then she married a teacher. Yezierska gave birth to a daughter, but she found life as a wife and mother so oppressive that she gave up her child to her husband's care. For the rest of her life she devoted herself to her career as a writer.

In the early story "My Own People," about a young woman who cut herself off from her past to live in a crowded Lower East Side tenement in the midst of a poor Jewish immigrant neighborhood, Yezierska describes her difficult beginning as a writer. Her first published piece, in a 1915 issue of Forum *magazine, was the story "Free Vacation House," about the humiliation suffered by a Jewish family that receives condescending charity. Yezierska explained that in her short stories she was trying "to build a bridge of understanding between the American-born and myself. Since their life was shut out from such as me, I began to open my life and the lives of my people to them. . . . Writing about the ghetto, I found America."*

In 1919 the influential editor Edward J. O'Brien was so moved by Yezierska's story "The Fat of the Land" that he included it in Best Stories of 1919 *and dedicated the entire volume to her.* Hungry Hearts, *her first collection of short fiction about Jewish immigrants, including "My Own People," was published in 1920. The film producer Samuel Goldwyn brought her to Hollywood soon afterwards to make a silent movie out of her book. Yezierska was called "Queen of the Ghetto" and "The Immigrant Cinderella" by the Goldwyn studio publicists. After a year on the West Coast, Yezierska returned to New York's Lower East Side, where she felt more at home and resumed her writing. In 1923 she published her second collection of stories,* Children of Loneliness, *and her first novel,* Salome of the Tenements. *Yezierska followed this work with three more novels about the Jewish immigrant experience. During the Depression, as her book royalties diminished, she was hired by the Works Progress Administration's Writers' Project in New York to catalogue the trees in Central Park. In the last years of her life she continued to write autobiographical fiction and book reviews.* The Open Cage: An Anzia Yezierska Collection *(1979) contains a representative sampling of her work.*

My Own People

With the suitcase containing all her worldly possessions under her arm, Sophie Sapinsky elbowed her way through the noisy ghetto crowds. Pushcart peddlers and pullers-in shouted and gesticulated. Women with market-baskets pushed and shoved one another, eyes straining with the one thought — how to get the food a penny cheaper. With the same strained intentness, Sophie scanned each tenement, searching for a room cheap enough for her dwindling means.

In a dingy basement window a crooked sign, in straggling, penciled letters, caught Sophie's eye: "Room to let, a bargain, cheap."

The exuberant phrasing was quite in keeping with the extravagant dilapidation of the surroundings. "This is the very place," thought Sophie. "There could n't be nothing cheaper in all New York."

At the foot of the basement steps she knocked.

"Come in!" a voice answered.

As she opened the door she saw an old man bending over a pot of potatoes on a shoemaker's bench. A group of children in all degrees of rags surrounded him, greedily snatching at the potatoes he handed out.

Sophie paused for an instant, but her absorption in her own problem was too great to halt the question: "Is there a room to let?"

"Hanneh Breineh, in the back, has a room." The old man was so pre-occupied filling the hungry hands that he did not even look up.

Sophie groped her way to the rear hall. A gaunt-faced woman answered her inquiry with loquacious enthusiasm. "A grand room for the money. I'll let it down to you only for three dollars a month. In the whole block is no bigger bargain. I should live so."

As she talked, the woman led her through the dark hall into an airshaft room. A narrow window looked out into the bottom of a chimney-like pit, where lay the accumulated refuse from a score of crowded kitchens.

"Oi weh!" gasped Sophie, throwing open the sash. "No air and no light. Outside shines the sun and here it's so dark."

"It ain't so dark. It's only a little shady. Let me only turn up the gas for you and you'll quick see everything like with sunshine."

The claw-fingered flame revealed a rusty iron cot, an inverted potato barrel that served for a table, and two soap-boxes for chairs.

Sophie felt of the cot. It sagged and flopped under her touch. "The bed has only three feet!" she exclaimed in dismay.

"You can't have Rockefeller's palace for three dollars a month," de-fended Hanneh Breineh, as she shoved one of the boxes under the legless corner of the cot. "If the bed ain't so steady, so you got good neighbors. Upstairs lives Shprintzeh Gittle, the herring-woman. You can buy by her the biggest bargains in fish, a few days older. . . . What she got left over from the Sabbath, she sells to the neighbors cheap. . . . In the front lives Shmendrik, the shoemaker. I'll tell you the truth, he ain't no real shoemaker. He never

625

yet made a pair of whole shoes in his life. He's a learner from the old country — a tzadik, a saint; but every time he sees in the street a child with torn feet, he calls them in and patches them up. His own eating, the last bite from his mouth, he divides up with them."

"Three dollars," deliberated Sophie, scarcely hearing Hanneh Breineh's chatter. "I will never find anything cheaper. It has a door to lock and I can shut this woman out . . . I'll take it," she said, handing her the money.

Hanneh Breineh kissed the greasy bills gloatingly. "I'll treat you like a mother! You'll have it good by me like in your own home."

"Thanks — but I got no time to shmoos. I got to be alone to get my work done."

The rebuff could not penetrate Hanneh Breineh's joy over the sudden possession of three dollars.

"Long years on you! May we be to good luck to one another!" was Hanneh Breineh's blessing as she closed the door.

Alone in her room — *her* room, securely hers — yet with the flash of triumph, a stab of bitterness. All that was hers — so wretched and so ugly! Had her eager spirit, eager to give and give, no claim to a bit of beauty — a shred of comfort?

Perhaps her family was right in condemning her rashness. Was it worth while to give up the peace of home, the security of a regular job — suffer hunger, loneliness, and want — for what? For something she knew in her heart was beyond her reach. Would her writing ever amount to enough to vindicate the uprooting of her past? Would she ever become articulate enough to express beautifully what she saw and felt? What had she, after all, but a stifling, sweatshop experience, a meager, night-school education, and this wild, blind hunger to release the dumbness that choked her?

Sophie spread her papers on the cot beside her. Resting her elbows on the potato barrel, she clutched her pencil with tense fingers. In the note-book before her were a hundred beginnings, essays, abstractions, outbursts of chaotic moods. She glanced through the titles: "Believe in Yourself," "The Quest of the Ideal."

Meaningless tracings on the paper, her words seemed to her now — a restless spirit pawing at the air. The intensity of experience, the surge of emotion that had been hers when she wrote — where were they? The words had failed to catch the life-beat — had failed to register the passion she had poured into them.

Perhaps she was not a writer, after all. Had the years and years of night-study been in vain? Choked with discouragement, the cry broke from her, "O — God — God help me! I feel — I see, but it all dies in me — dumb!"

Tedious days passed into weeks. Again Sophie sat staring into her note-book. "There's nothing here that's alive. Not a word yet says what's in me . . .

"But it *is* in me!" With clenched fist she smote her bosom. "It must be in me! I believe in it! I got to get it out—even if it tears my flesh in pieces—even if it kills me! . . .

"But these words—these flat, dead words . . .

"Whether I can write or can't write—I can't stop writing. I can't rest. I can't breathe. There's no peace, no running away for me on earth except in the struggle to give out what's in me. The beat from my heart—the blood from my veins—must flow out into my words."

She returned to her unfinished essay, "Believe in Yourself." Her mind groping—clutching at the misty incoherence that clouded her thoughts— she wrote on.

"These sentences are yet only wood—lead; but I can't help it—I'll push on—on—I'll not eat—I'll not sleep—I'll not move from this spot till I get it to say on the paper what I got in my heart!"

Slowly the dead words seemed to begin to breathe. Her eyes brightened. Her cheeks flushed. Her very pencil trembled with the eager onrush of words.

Then a sharp rap sounded on her door. With a gesture of irritation Sophie put down her pencil and looked into the burning, sunken eyes of her neighbor, Hanneh Breineh.

"I got yourself a glass of tea, good friend. It ain't much I got to give away, but it's warm even if it's nothing."

Sophie scowled. "You must n't bother yourself with me. I'm so busy—thanks."

"Don't thank me yet so quick. I got no sugar." Hanneh Breineh edged herself into the room confidingly. "At home, in Poland, I not only had sugar for tea—but even jelly—a jelly that would lift you up to heaven. I thought in America everything would be so plenty, I could drink the tea out from my sugar-bowl. But ach! Not in Poland did my children starve like in America!"

Hanneh Breineh, in a friendly manner, settled herself on the sound end of the bed, and began her jeremiad.

"Yosef, my man, ain't no bread-giver. Already he got consumption the second year. One week he works and nine weeks he lays sick."

In despair Sophie gathered her papers, wondering how to get the woman out of her room. She glanced through the page she had written, but Hanneh Breineh, unconscious of her indifference, went right on.

"How many times it is tearing the heart out from my body—should I take Yosef's milk to give to the baby, or the baby's milk to give to Yosef? If he was dead the pensions they give to widows would help feed my children. Now I got only the charities to help me. A black year on them! They should only have to feed their own children on what they give me."

Resolved not to listen to the intruder, Sophie debated within herself: "Should I call my essay 'Believe in Yourself,' or would n't it be stronger to say, 'Trust Yourself'? But if I say, 'Trust Yourself,' would n't they think that I got the words from Emerson?"

Hanneh Breineh's voice went on, but it sounded to Sophie like a faint buzzing from afar. "Gotteniu! How much did it cost me my life to go and swear myself that my little Fannie—only skin and bones—that she is already fourteen! How it chokes me the tears every morning when I got to wake her and push her out to the shop when her eyes are yet shutting themselves with sleep!"

Sophie glanced at her wrist-watch as it ticked away the precious minutes. She must get rid of the woman! Had she not left her own sister, sacrificed all comfort, all association, for solitude and its golden possibilities? For the first time in her life she had the chance to be by herself and think. And now, the thoughts which a moment ago had seemed like a flock of fluttering birds had come so close—and this woman with her sordid wailing had scattered them.

"I'm a savage, a beast, but I got to ask her to get out—this very minute," resolved Sophie. But before she could summon the courage to do what she wanted to do, there was a timid knock at the door, and the wizened little Fannie, her face streaked with tears, stumbled in.

"The inspector said it's a lie. I ain't yet fourteen," she whimpered.

Hanneh Breineh paled. "Woe is me! Sent back from the shop? God from the world—is there no end to my troubles? Why did n't you hide yourself when you saw the inspector come?"

"I was running to hide myself under the table, but she caught me and she said she'll take me to the Children's Society and arrest me and my mother for sending me to work too soon."

"Arrest me?" shrieked Hanneh Breineh, beating her breast. "Let them only come and arrest me! I'll show America who I am! Let them only begin themselves with me! . . . Black is for my eyes . . . the groceryman will not give us another bread till we pay him the bill!"

"The inspector said . . ." The child's brow puckered in an effort to recall the words.

"What did the inspector said? Gotteniu!" Hanneh Breineh wrung her hands in passionate entreaty. "Listen only once to my prayer! Send on the inspector only a quick death! I only wish her to have her own house with twenty-four rooms and each of the twenty-four rooms should be twenty-four beds and the chills and the fever should throw her from one bed to another!"

"Hanneh Breineh, still yourself a little," entreated Sophie.

"How can I still myself without Fannie's wages? Bitter is me! Why do I have to live so long?"

"The inspector said . . ."

"What did the inspector said? A thunder should strike the inspector! Ain't I as good a mother as other mothers? Would n't I better send my children to school? But who'll give us to eat? And who'll pay us the rent?"

Hanneh Breineh wiped her red-lidded eyes with the corner of her apron.

"The president from America should only come to my bitter heart. Let him go fighting himself with the pushcarts how to get the eating a penny cheaper. Let him try to feed his children on the money the charities give me and we'd see if he would n't better send his littlest ones to the shop better than to let them starve before his eyes. Woe is me! What for did I come to America? What's my life—nothing but one terrible, never-stopping fight with the grocer and the butcher and the landlord . . ."

Suddenly Sophie's resentment for her lost morning was forgotten. The crying waste of Hanneh Breineh's life lay open before her eyes like pictures in a book. She saw her own life in Hanneh Breineh's life. Her efforts to write were like Hanneh Breineh's efforts to feed her children. Behind her life and Hanneh Breineh's life she saw the massed ghosts of thousands upon thousands beating—beating out their hearts against rock barriers.

"The inspector said . . ." Fannie timidly attempted again to explain.

"The inspector!" shrieked Hanneh Breineh, as she seized hold of Fannie in a rage. "Hellfire should burn the inspector! Tell me again about the inspector and I'll choke the life out from you—"

Sophie sprang forward to protect the child from the mother. "She's only trying to tell you something."

"Why should she yet throw salt on my wounds? If there was enough bread in the house would I need an inspector to tell me to send her to school? If America is so interested in poor people's children, then why don't they give them to eat till they should go to work? What learning can come into a child's head when the stomach is empty?"

A clutter of feet down the creaking cellar steps, a scuffle of broken shoes, and a chorus of shrill voices, as the younger children rushed in from school.

"Mamma—what's to eat?"

"It smells potatoes!"

"Pfui! The pot is empty! It smells over from Cohen's."

"Jake grabbed all the bread!"

"Mamma—he kicked the piece out from my hands!"

"Mamma—it's so empty in my stomach! Ain't there nothing?"

"Gluttons—wolves—thieves!" Hanneh Breineh shrieked. "I should only live to bury you all in one day!"

The children, regardless of Hanneh Breineh's invectives, swarmed around her like hungry bees, tearing at her apron, her skirt. Their voices rose in increased clamor, topped only by their mother's imprecations. "Gotteniu! Tear me away from these leeches on my neck! Send on them only a quick death! . . . Only a minute's peace before I die!"

"Hanneh Breineh—children! What's the matter?" Shmendrik stood at the door. The sweet quiet of the old man stilled the raucous voices as the coming of evening stills the noises of the day.

"There's no end to my troubles! Hear them hollering for bread, and the grocer stopped to give till the bill is paid. Woe is me! Fannie sent home by the inspector and not a crumb in the house!"

"I got something." The old man put his hands over the heads of the children in silent benediction. "All come in by me. I got sent me a box of cake."

"Cake!" The children cried, catching at the kind hands and snuggling about the shabby coat.

"Yes. Cake and nuts and raisins and even a bottle of wine."

The children leaped and danced around him in their wild burst of joy.

"Cake and wine—a box—to you? Have the charities gone crazy?" Hanneh Breineh's eyes sparkled with light and laughter.

"No—no," Shmendrik explained hastily. "Not from the charities—from a friend—for the holidays."

Shmendrik nodded invitingly to Sophie, who was standing in the door of her room. "The roomerkeh will also give a taste with us our party?"

"Sure will she!" Hanneh Breineh took Sophie by the arm. "Who'll say no in this black life to cake and wine?"

Young throats burst into shrill cries: "Cake and wine—wine and cake—raisins and nuts—nuts and raisins!" The words rose in a triumphant chorus. The children leaped and danced in time to their chant, almost carrying the old man bodily into his room in the wildness of their joy.

The contagion of this sudden hilarity erased from Sophie's mind the last thought of work and she found herself seated with the others on the cobbler's bench.

From under his cot the old man drew forth a wooden box. Lifting the cover he held up before wondering eyes a large frosted cake embedded in raisins and nuts.

Amid the shouts of glee Shmendrik now waved aloft a large bottle of grape-juice.

The children could contain themselves no longer and dashed forward.

"Shah—shah! Wait only!" He gently halted their onrush and waved them back to their seats.

"The glasses for the wine!" Hanneh Breineh rushed about hither and thither in happy confusion. From the sink, the shelf, the windowsill, she gathered cracked glasses, cups without handles—anything that would hold even a few drops of the yellow wine.

Sacrificial solemnity filled the basement as the children breathlessly watched Shmendrik cut the precious cake. Mouths—even eyes—watered with the intensity of their emotion.

With almost religious fervor Hanneh Breineh poured the grape-juice into the glasses held in the trembling hands of the children. So overwhelming was the occasion that none dared to taste till the ritual was completed. The suspense was agonizing as one and all waited for Shmendrik's signal.

"Hanneh Breineh—you drink from my Sabbath wine-glass!"

Hanneh Breineh clinked glasses with Schmendrik. "Long years on you—long years on us all!" Then she turned to Sophie, clinked glasses once more. "May you yet marry yourself from our basement to a millionaire!" Then she lifted the glass to her lips.

The spell was broken. With a yell of triumph the children gobbled the cake in huge mouthfuls and sucked the golden liquid. All the traditions of wealth and joy that ever sparkled from the bubbles of champagne smiled at Hanneh Breineh from her glass of California grape-juice.

"Ach!" she sighed. "How good it is to forget your troubles, and only those that's got troubles have the chance to forget them!"

She sipped the grape-juice leisurely, thrilled into ecstasy with each lingering drop. "How it laughs yet in me, the life, the minute I turn my head from my worries!"

With growing wonder in her eyes, Sophie watched Hanneh Breineh. This ragged wreck of a woman—how passionately she clung to every atom of life! Hungrily, she burned through the depths of every experience. How she flared against wrongs—and how every tiny spark of pleasure blazed into joy!

Within a half-hour this woman had touched the whole range of human emotions, from bitterest agony to dancing joy. The terrible despair at the onrush of her starving children when she cried out, "O that I should only bury you all in one day!" And now the leaping light of the words: "How it laughs yet in me, the life, the minute I turn my head from my worries."

"Ach, if I could only write like Hanneh Breineh talks!" thought Sophie. "Her words dance with a thousand colors. Like a rainbow it flows from her lips." Sentences from her own essays marched before her, stiff and wooden. How clumsy, how unreal, were her most labored phrases compared to Hanneh Breineh's spontaneity. Fascinated, she listened to Hanneh Breineh, drinking her words as a thirst-perishing man drinks water. Every bubbling phrase filled her with a drunken rapture to create.

"Up till now I was only trying to write from my head. It wasn't real—it wasn't life, Hanneh Breineh is real. Hanneh Breineh is life."

"Ach! What do the rich people got but dried-up dollars! Pfui on them and their money!" Hanneh Breineh held up her glass to be refilled. "Let me only win a fortune on the lotteree and move myself in my own bought house. Let me only have my first hundred dollars in the bank and I'll lift up my head like a person and tell the charities to eat their own cornmeal. I'll get myself an automobile like the kind rich ladies and ride up to their houses on Fifth Avenue and feed them only once on the eating they like so good for me and my children."

With a smile of benediction Shmendrik refilled the glasses and cut for each of his guests another slice of cake. Then came the handful of nuts and raisins.

As the children were scurrying about for hammers and iron lasts with which to crack their nuts, the basement door creaked. Unannounced, a woman entered—the "friendly visitor" of the charities. Her look of awful amazement swept the group of merry-makers.

"Mr. Shmendrik!—Hanneh Breineh!" Indignation seethed in her voice. "What's this? A feast—a birthday?"

Gasps—bewildered glances—a struggle for utterance!

"I came to make my monthly visit—evidently I'm not needed."

Shmendrik faced the accusing eyes of the "friendly visitor." "Holiday eating . . ."

"Oh—I'm glad you're so prosperous."

Before any one had gained presence of mind enough to explain things, the door had clanked. The "friendly visitor" had vanished.

"Pfui!" Hanneh Breineh snatched up her glass and drained its contents. "What will she do now? Will we get no more dry bread from the charities because once we ate cake?"

"What for did she come?" asked Sophie.

"To see that we don't over-eat ourselves!" returned Hanneh Breineh. "She's a 'friendly visitor'! She learns us how to cook cornmeal. By pictures and lectures she shows us how the poor people should live without meat, without milk, without butter, and without eggs. Always it's on the end of my tongue to ask her, 'You learned us to do without so much, why can't you yet learn us how to eat without eating?'"

The children seized the last crumbs of cake that Shmendrik handed them and rushed for the street.

"What a killing look was on her face," said Sophie. "Couldn't she be a little glad for your gladness?"

"Charity ladies—gladness?" The joy of the grape-wine still rippled in Hanneh Breineh's laughter. "For poor people is only cornmeal. Ten cents a day—to feed my children!"

Still in her rollicking mood Hanneh Breineh picked up the baby and tossed it like a Bacchante. "Could you be happy a lot with ten cents in your stomach? Ten cents—half a can of condensed milk—then fill yourself the rest with water! . . . Maybe yet feed you with all water and save the ten-cent pieces to buy you a carriage like the Fifth Avenue babies! . . ."

The soft sound of a limousine purred through the area grating and two well-fed figures in seal-skin coats, led by the "friendly visitor," appeared at the door.

"Mr. Bernstein, you can see for yourself." The "friendly visitor" pointed to the table.

The merry group shrank back. It was as if a gust of icy wind had swept all the joy and laughter from the basement.

"You are charged with intent to deceive and obtain assistance by dishonest means," said Mr. Bernstein.

"Dishonest?" Shmendrik paled.

Sophie's throat strained with passionate protest, but no words came to her release.

"A friend—a friend"—stammered Shmendrik—"sent me the holiday eating."

The superintendent of the Social Betterment Society faced him accusingly. "You told us that you had no friends when you applied to us for assistance."

"My friend—he knew me in my better time." Shmendrik flushed painfully. "I was once a scholar—respected. I wanted by this one friend to hold myself like I was."

Mr. Bernstein had taken from the bookshelf a number of letters, glanced through them rapidly and handed them one by one to the deferential superintendent.

Shmendrik clutched at his heart in an agony of humiliation. Suddenly his bent body straightened. His eyes dilated. "My letters—my life—you dare?"

"Of course we dare!" The superintendent returned Shmendrik's livid gaze, made bold by the confidence that what he was doing was the only scientific method of administering philanthropy. "These dollars, so generously given, must go to those most worthy. . . . I find in these letters references to gifts of fruit and other luxuries you did not report at our office."

"He never kept nothing for himself!" Hanneh Breineh broke in defensively. "He gave it all for the children."

Ignoring the interruption Mr. Bernstein turned to the "friendly visitor." "I'm glad you brought my attention to this case. It's but one of the many impositions on our charity . . . Come . . ."

"Kossacks! Pogromschiks!" Sophie's rage broke at last. "You call yourselves Americans? You dare call yourselves Jews? You bosses of the poor! This man Shmendrik, whose house you broke into, whom you made to shame like a beggar—he is the one Jew from whom the Jews can be proud! He gives all he is—all he has—as God gives. *He is* charity.

"But you—you are the greed—the shame of the Jews! *All-right-niks*—fat bellies in fur coats! What do you give from yourselves? You may eat and bust eating! Nothing you give till you've stuffed yourselves so full that your hearts are dead!"

The door closed in her face. Her wrath fell on indifferent backs as the visitors mounted the steps to the street.

Shmendrik groped blindly for the Bible. In a low, quavering voice, he began the chant of the oppressed—the wail of the downtrodden. "I am afraid, and a trembling taketh hold of my flesh. Wherefore do the wicked live, become old, yea, mighty in power?"

Hanneh Breineh and the children drew close around the old man. They were weeping—unconscious of their weeping—deep buried memories roused by the music, the age-old music of the Hebrew race.

Through the grating Sophie saw the limousine pass. The chant flowed on: "Their houses are safe from fear; neither is the rod of God upon them."

Silently Sophie stole back to her room. She flung herself on the cot, pressed her fingers to her burning eyeballs. For a long time she lay rigid, clenched—listening to the drumming of her heart like the sea against rock barriers. Presently the barriers burst. Something in her began pouring itself out. She felt for her pencil—paper—and began to write. Whether she reached out to God or man she knew not, but she wrote on and on all through that night.

The gray light entering her grated window told her that beyond was dawn. Sophie looked up: "Ach! At last it writes itself in me!" she whispered triumphantly. "It's not me—it's their cries—my own people—crying in me! Hanneh Breineh, Shmendrik, they will not be stilled in me, till all America stops to listen."   [1920]

F. SCOTT FITZGERALD

F. *Scott Fitzgerald (1896–1940), regarded as the literary spokesman for the "Lost Generation" of the 1920s in America, was born in St. Paul, Minnesota. His family had some social standing but little money, and it was only with help from a maiden aunt that he was able to go to an eastern preparatory school and then on to Princeton, where he said his family hoped that he would attend to his studies and stop "wasting his time scribbling." He left college before graduating to accept a commission as a second lieutenant in the Regular Army during World War I, but he spent most of his time in the service writing his first novel, which he revised several times before it was published in 1920 as* This Side of Paradise. *The novel was such a success that magazines were eager to print Fitzgerald's stories, and his first story collection,* Flappers and Philosophers, *was rushed into print later the same year to take advantage of the novel's popularity. Another story collection,* Tales of the Jazz Age, *followed in 1922. Years later Fitzgerald would say, writing in the third person, that he was grateful to the Jazz Age because "it bore him up, flattered him, and gave him more money than he had dreamed of, simply for telling people that he felt as they did, that something had to be done with all the nervous energy stored up and unexpended in the War."*

In 1925, with the publication of his novel The Great Gatsby, *Fitzgerald reached the peak of his fame as a writer. His reputation declined rapidly in the harsher years of the 1930s. The Great Depression in the United States and throughout the world coincided with his own emotional and physical collapse, as his marriage and career fell apart because of his wife's mental illness and his alcoholism. Gertrude Stein had coined the term "Lost Generation" to describe the young men who had served in World War I and were forced to grow up "to find all Gods dead, all wars fought, all faiths in man shaken." But Fitzgerald's last years were truly lost, as he confronted the "waste and horror" of his dissipated talent, writing Hollywood screenplays and struggling unsuccessfully to finish his novel* The Last Tycoon.

At the time of his death Fitzgerald had written about 160 stories. As one of his editors, Malcolm Cowley, has said, the exact number is hard to set because some of his work was on the borderline between fiction and the essay or "magazine piece." Simple and clear in style, Fitzgerald's stories make up an informal history of his career, dating from before the publication of his first novel to after his final crack-up. First published in Metropolitan Magazine *in 1922, and later collected in* All the Sad Young Men *(1926), "Winter Dreams" was written shortly before Fitzgerald began* The Great Gatsby.

RELATED COMMENTARY: *Charles Scribner III, "On F. Scott Fitzgerald's Stories," page 1449.*

Winter Dreams

Some of the caddies were poor as sin and lived in one-room houses with a neurasthenic cow in the front yard, but Dexter Green's father owned the second best grocery-store in Black Bear—the best one was "The Hub," patronized by the wealthy people from Sherry Island—and Dexter caddied only for pocket-money.

In the fall when the days became crisp and gray, and the long Minnesota winter shut down like the white lid of a box, Dexter's skis moved over the snow that hid the fairways of the golf course. At these times the country gave him a feeling of profound melancholy—it offended him that the links should lie in enforced fallowness, haunted by ragged sparrows for the long season. It was dreary, too, that on the tees where the gay colors fluttered in summer there were now only the desolate sand-boxes knee-deep in crusted ice. When he crossed the hills the wind blew cold as misery, and if the sun was out he tramped with his eyes squinted up against the hard dimensionless glare.

In April the winter ceased abruptly. The snow ran down into Black Bear Lake scarcely tarrying for the early golfers to brave the season with red and black balls. Without elation, without an interval of moist glory, the cold was gone.

Dexter knew that there was something dismal about this Northern spring, just as he knew there was something gorgeous about the fall. Fall made him clinch his hands and tremble and repeat idiotic sentences to himself, and make brisk abrupt gestures of command to imaginary audiences and armies. October filled him with hope which November raised to a sort of ecstatic triumph, and in this mood the fleeting brilliant impressions of the summer at Sherry Island were ready grist to his mill. He became a golf champion and defeated Mr. T. A. Hedrick in a marvellous match played a hundred times over the fairways of his imagination, a match each detail of which he changed about untiringly—sometimes he won with almost laughable ease, sometimes he came up magnificently from behind. Again, stepping from a Pierce-Arrow automobile, like Mr. Mortimer Jones, he strolled frigidly into the lounge of the Sherry Island Golf Club—or perhaps, surrounded by an admiring crowd, he gave an exhibition of fancy diving from the spring-board of the club raft. . . . Among those who watched him in open-mouthed wonder was Mr. Mortimer Jones.

And one day it came to pass that Mr. Jones—himself and not his ghost—came up to Dexter with tears in his eyes and said that Dexter was the——best caddy in the club, and wouldn't he decide not to quit if Mr. Jones made it worth his while, because every other——caddy in the club lost one ball a hole for him—regularly——

"No, sir," said Dexter decisively, "I don't want to caddy any more." Then, after a pause: "I'm too old."

"You're not more than fourteen. Why the devil did you decide just this morning that you wanted to quit? You promised that next week you'd go over to the State tournament with me."

"I decided I was too old."

Dexter handed in his "A Class" badge, collected what money was due him from the caddy master, and walked home to Black Bear Village.

"The best——caddy I ever saw," shouted Mr. Mortimer Jones over a drink that afternoon. "Never lost a ball! Willing! Intelligent! Quiet! Honest! Grateful!"

The little girl who had done this was eleven—beautifully ugly as little girls are apt to be who are destined after a few years to be inexpressibly lovely and bring no end of misery to a great number of men. The spark, however, was perceptible. There was a general ungodliness in the way her lips twisted down at the corners when she smiled, and in the—Heaven help us!—in the almost passionate quality of her eyes. Vitality is born early in such women. It was utterly in evidence now, shining through her thin frame in a sort of glow.

She had come eagerly out on to the course at nine o'clock with a white linen nurse and five small new golf-clubs in a white canvas bag which the nurse was carrying. When Dexter first saw her she was standing by the caddy house, rather ill at ease and trying to conceal the fact by engaging her nurse in an obviously unnatural conversation graced by startling and irrelevant grimaces from herself.

"Well, it's certainly a nice day, Hilda," Dexter heard her say. She drew down the corners of her mouth, smiled, and glanced furtively around, her eyes in transit falling for an instant on Dexter.

Then to the nurse:

"Well, I guess there aren't very many people out here this morning, are there?"

The smile again—radiant, blatantly artificial—convincing.

"I don't know what we're supposed to do now," said the nurse, looking nowhere in particular.

"Oh, that's all right. I'll fix it up."

Dexter stood perfectly still, his mouth slightly ajar. He knew that if he moved forward a step his stare would be in her line of vision—if he moved backward he would lose his full view of her face. For a moment he had not realized how young she was. Now he remembered having seen her several times the year before—in bloomers.

Suddenly, involuntarily, he laughed, a short abrupt laugh—then, startled by himself, he turned and began to walk quickly away.

"Boy!"

Dexter stopped.

"Boy——"

Beyond question he was addressed. Not only that, but he was treated to that absurd smile, that preposterous smile—the memory of which at least a dozen men were to carry into middle age.

"Boy, do you know where the golf teacher is?"

"He's giving a lesson."

"Well, do you know where the caddy-master is?"

"He isn't here yet this morning."

"Oh." For a moment this baffled her. She stood alternately on her right and left foot.

"We'd like to get a caddy," said the nurse. "Mrs. Mortimer Jones sent us out to play golf, and we don't know how without we get a caddy."

Here she was stopped by an ominous glance from Miss Jones, followed immediately by the smile.

"There aren't any caddies here except me," said Dexter to the nurse, "and I got to stay here in charge until the caddy-master gets here."

"Oh."

Miss Jones and her retinue now withdrew, and at a proper distance from Dexter became involved in a heated conversation, which was concluded by Miss Jones taking one of the clubs and hitting it on the ground with violence. For further emphasis she raised it again and was about to bring it down smartly upon the nurse's bosom, when the nurse seized the club and twisted it from her hands.

"You damn little mean old *thing!*" cried Miss Jones wildly.

Another argument ensued. Realizing that the elements of the comedy were implied in the scene, Dexter several times began to laugh, but each time restrained the laugh before it reached audibility. He could not resist the monstrous conviction that the little girl was justified in beating the nurse.

The situation was resolved by the fortuitous appearance of the caddy-master, who was appealed to immediately by the nurse.

"Miss Jones is to have a little caddy, and this one says he can't go."

"Mr. McKenna said I was to wait here till you came," said Dexter quickly.

"Well, he's here now." Miss Jones smiled cheerfully at the caddy-master. Then she dropped her bag and set off at a haughty mince toward the first tee.

"Well?" The caddy-master turned to Dexter. "What you standing there like a dummy for? Go pick up the young lady's clubs."

"I don't think I'll go out to-day," said Dexter.

"You don't——"

"I think I'll quit."

The enormity of his decision frightened him. He was a favorite caddy, and the thirty dollars a month he earned through the summer were not to be made elsewhere around the lake. But he had received a strong emotional shock, and his perturbation required a violent and immediate outlet.

It is not so simple as that, either. As so frequently would be the case in the future, Dexter was unconsciously dictated to by his winter dreams.

– II –

Now, of course, the quality and the seasonability of these winter dreams varied, but the stuff of them remained. They persuaded Dexter several years later to pass up a business course at the State university—his father, prospering now, would have paid his way—for the precarious advantage of attending an older and more famous university in the East, where he was bothered by his scanty funds. But do not get the impression, because his winter dreams happened to be concerned at first with musings on the rich, that there was anything merely snobbish in the boy. He wanted not association with glittering things and glittering people—he wanted the glittering things themselves. Often he reached out for the best without knowing why he wanted it—and sometimes he ran up against the mysterious denials and prohibitions in which life indulges. It is with one of those denials and not with his career as a whole that this story deals.

He made money. It was rather amazing. After college he went to the city from which Black Bear Lake draws its wealthy patrons. When he was only twenty-three and had been there not quite two years, there were already people who liked to say: "Now *there's* a boy—" All about him rich men's sons were peddling bonds precariously, or investing patrimonies precariously, or plodding through the two dozen volumes of the "George Washington Commercial Course," but Dexter borrowed a thousand dollars on his college degree and his confident mouth, and bought a partnership in a laundry.

It was a small laundry when he went into it but Dexter made a specialty of learning how the English washed fine woollen golf-stockings without shrinking them, and within a year he was catering to the trade that wore knickerbockers. Men were insisting that their Shetland hose and sweaters go to his laundry just as they had insisted on a caddy who could find golf-balls. A little later he was doing their wives' lingerie as well—and running five branches in different parts of the city. Before he was twenty-seven he owned the largest string of laundries in his section of the country. It was then that he sold out and went to New York. But the part of his story that concerns us goes back to the days when he was making his first big success.

When he was twenty-three Mr. Hart—one of the gray-haired men who like to say "Now there's a boy"—gave him a guest card to the Sherry Island Golf Club for a week-end. So he signed his name one day on the register, and that afternoon played golf in a foursome with Mr. Hart and Mr. Sandwood and Mr. T. A. Hedrick. He did not consider it necessary to remark that he had once carried Mr. Hart's bag over this same links, and that he knew every trap and gully with his eyes shut—but he found himself glancing at the four caddies who trailed them, trying to catch a gleam or gesture that would remind him of himself, that would lessen the gap which lay between his present and his past.

It was a curious day, slashed abruptly with fleeting, familiar impressions. One minute he had the sense of being a trespasser—in the next he was impressed by the tremendous superiority he felt toward Mr. T. A. Hedrick, who was a bore and not even a good golfer any more.

Then, because of a ball Mr. Hart lost near the fifteenth green, an enormous thing happened. While they were searching the stiff grasses of the rough there was a clear call of "Fore!" from behind a hill in their rear. And as they all turned abruptly from their search a bright new ball sliced abruptly over the hill and caught Mr. T. A. Hedrick in the abdomen.

"By Gad!" cried Mr. T. A. Hedrick, "they ought to put some of these crazy women off the course. It's getting to be outrageous."

A head and a voice came up together over the hill:

"Do you mind if we go through?"

"You hit me in the stomach!" declared Mr. Hedrick wildly.

"Did I?" The girl approached the group of men. "I'm sorry. I yelled 'Fore!'"

Her glance fell casually on each of the men—then scanned the fairway for her ball.

"Did I bounce into the rough?"

It was impossible to determine whether this question was ingenuous or malicious. In a moment, however, she left no doubt, for as her partner came up over the hill she called cheerfully:

"Here I am! I'd have gone on the green except that I hit something."

As she took her stance for a short mashie shot, Dexter looked at her closely. She wore a blue gingham dress, rimmed at throat and shoulders with a white edging that accentuated her tan. The quality of exaggeration, of thinness, which had made her passionate eyes and down-turning mouth absurd at eleven, was gone now. She was arrestingly beautiful. The color in her cheeks was centered like the color in a picture—it was not a "high" color, but a sort of fluctuating and feverish warmth, so shaded that it seemed at any moment it would recede and disappear. This color and the mobility of her mouth gave a continual impression of flux, of intense life, of passionate vitality—balanced only partially by the sad luxury of her eyes.

She swung her mashie impatiently and without interest, pitching the ball into a sand-pit on the other side of the green. With a quick, insincere smile and a careless "Thank you!" she went on after it.

"That Judy Jones!" remarked Mr. Hedrick on the next tee, as they waited—some moments—for her to play on ahead. "All she needs is to be turned up and spanked for six months and then to be married off to an old-fashioned cavalry captain."

"My God, she's good-looking!" said Mr. Sandwood, who was just over thirty.

"Good-looking!" cried Mr. Hedrick contemptuously, "she always looks as if she wanted to be kissed! Turning those big cow-eyes on every calf in town!"

It was doubtful if Mr. Hedrick intended a reference to the maternal instinct.

"She'd play pretty good golf if she'd try," said Mr. Sandwood.

"She has no form," said Mr. Hedrick solemnly.

"She has a nice figure," said Mr. Sandwood.

"Better thank the Lord she doesn't drive a swifter ball," said Mr. Hart, winking at Dexter.

Later in the afternoon the sun went down with a riotous swirl of gold and varying blues and scarlets, and left the dry, rustling night of Western summer. Dexter watched from the veranda of the Golf Club, watched the even overlap of the waters in the little wind, silver molasses under the harvest-moon. Then the moon held a finger to her lips and the lake became a clear pool, pale and quiet. Dexter put on his bathing-suit and swam out to the farthest raft, where he stretched dripping on the wet canvas of the spring-board.

There was a fish jumping and a star shining and the lights around the lake were gleaming. Over on a dark peninsula a piano was playing the songs of last summer and of summers before that—songs from "Chin-Chin" and "The Count of Luxemburg" and "The Chocolate Soldier"—and because the sound of a piano over a stretch of water had always seemed beautiful to Dexter he lay perfectly quiet and listened.

The tune the piano was playing at that moment had been gay and new five years before when Dexter was a sophomore at college. They had played it at a prom once when he could not afford the luxury of proms, and he had stood outside the gymnasium and listened. The sound of the tune precipitated in him a sort of ecstasy and it was with that ecstasy he viewed what happened to him now. It was a mood of intense appreciation, a sense that, for once, he was magnificently attune to life and that everything about him was radiating a brightness and a glamour he might never know again.

A low, pale oblong detached itself suddenly from the darkness of the Island, spitting forth the reverberate sound of a racing motor-boat. Two white streamers of cleft water rolled themselves out behind it and almost immediately the boat was beside him, drowning out the hot tinkle of the piano in the drone of its spray. Dexter raising himself on his arms was aware of a figure standing at the wheel, of two dark eyes regarding him over the lengthening space of water—then the boat had gone by and was sweeping in an immense and purposeless circle of spray round and round in the middle of the lake. With equal eccentricity one of the circles flattened out and headed back toward the raft.

"Who's that?" she called, shutting off her motor. She was so near now that Dexter could see her bathing-suit, which consisted apparently of pink rompers.

The nose of the boat bumped the raft, and as the latter tilted rakishly he was precipitated toward her. With different degrees of interest they recognized each other.

"Aren't you one of those men we played through this afternoon?" she demanded.

He was.

"Well, do you know how to drive a motor-boat? Because if you do I wish you'd drive this one so I can ride on the surf-board behind. My name is Judy Jones"—she favored him with an absurd smirk—rather, what tried to be a smirk, for, twist her mouth as she might, it was not grotesque, it was merely beautiful—"and I live in a house over there on the Island, and in that house there is a man waiting for me. When he drove up at the door I drove out of the dock because he says I'm his ideal."

There was a fish jumping and a star shining and the lights around the lake were gleaming. Dexter sat beside Judy Jones and she explained how her boat was driven. Then she was in the water, swimming to the floating surf-board with a sinuous crawl. Watching her was without effort to the eye, watching a branch waving or a sea-gull flying. Her arms, burned to butternut, moved sinuously among the dull platinum ripples, elbow appearing first, casting the forearm back with a cadence of falling water, then reaching out and down, stabbing a path ahead.

They moved out into the lake; turning, Dexter saw that she was kneeling on the low rear of the now uptilted surf-board.

"Go faster," she called, "fast as it'll go."

Obediently he jammed the lever forward and the white spray mounted at the bow. When he looked around again the girl was standing up on the rushing board, her arms spread wide, her eyes lifted toward the moon.

"It's awful cold," she shouted. "What's your name?"

He told her.

"Well, why don't you come to dinner to-morrow night?"

His heart turned over like the fly-wheel of the boat, and, for the second time, her casual whim gave a new direction to his life.

–III–

Next evening while he waited for her to come down-stairs, Dexter peopled the soft deep summer room and the sun-porch that opened from it with the men who had already loved Judy Jones. He knew the sort of men they were—the men who when he first went to college had entered from the great prep schools with graceful clothes and the deep tan of healthy summers. He had seen that, in one sense, he was better than these men. He was newer and stronger. Yet in acknowledging to himself that he wished his children to be like them he was admitting that he was but the rough, strong stuff from which they eternally sprang.

When the time had come for him to wear good clothes, he had known who were the best tailors in America, and the best tailors in America had made him the suit he wore this evening. He had acquired that particular reserve peculiar to his university, that set it off from other universities. He recognized the value to him of such a mannerism and he had adopted it; he knew that to be careless in dress and manner required more confidence than to be careful. But carelessness was for his children. His mother's name had been Krimslich. She was a Bohemian of the peasant class and she had talked broken English to the end of her days. Her son must keep to the set patterns.

At a little after seven Judy Jones came down-stairs. She wore a blue silk afternoon dress, and he was disappointed at first that she had not put on something more elaborate. This feeling was accentuated when, after a brief greeting, she went to the door of a butler's pantry and pushing it open called: "You can serve dinner, Martha." He had rather expected that a butler would announce dinner, that there would be a cocktail. Then he put these thoughts behind him as they sat down side by side on a lounge and looked at each other.

"Father and mother won't be here," she said thoughtfully.

He remembered the last time he had seen her father, and he was glad the parents were not to be here to-night—they might wonder who he was. He had been born in Keeble, a Minnesota village fifty miles farther north, and he always gave Keeble as his home instead of Black Bear Village. Country towns were well enough to come from if they weren't inconveniently in sight and used as footstools by fashionable lakes.

They talked of his university, which she had visited frequently during the past two years, and of the near-by city which supplied Sherry Island with its patrons, and whither Dexter would return next day to his prospering laundries.

During dinner she slipped into a moody depression which gave Dexter a feeling of uneasiness. Whatever petulance she uttered in her throaty voice worried him. Whatever she smiled at—at him, at a chicken liver, at nothing—it disturbed him that her smile could have no root in mirth, or even in amusement. When the scarlet corners of her lips curved down, it was less a smile than an invitation to a kiss.

Then, after dinner, she led him out on the dark sun-porch and deliberately changed the atmosphere.

"Do you mind if I weep a little?" she said.

"I'm afraid I'm boring you," he responded quickly.

"You're not. I like you. But I've just had a terrible afternoon. There was a man I cared about, and this afternoon he told me out of a clear sky that he was poor as a church-mouse. He'd never even hinted it before. Does this sound horribly mundane?"

"Perhaps he was afraid to tell you."

"Suppose he was," she answered. "He didn't start right. You see, if I'd thought of him as poor—well, I've been mad about loads of poor men, and fully intended to marry them all. But in this case, I hadn't thought of him that way, and my interest in him wasn't strong enough to survive the shock. As if a girl calmly informed her fiancé that she was a widow. He might not object to widows, but——

"Let's start right," she interrupted herself suddenly. "Who are you, anyhow?"

For a moment Dexter hesitated. Then:

"I'm nobody," he announced. "My career is largely a matter of futures."

"Are you poor?"

"No," he said frankly, "I'm probably making more money than any man my age in the Northwest. I know that's an obnoxious remark, but you advised me to start right."

There was a pause. Then she smiled and the corners of her mouth drooped and an almost imperceptible sway brought her closer to him, looking up into his eyes. A lump rose in Dexter's throat, and he waited breathless for the experiment, facing the unpredictable compound that would form mysteriously from the elements of their lips. Then he saw— she communicated her excitement to him, lavishly, deeply, with kisses that were not a promise but a fulfillment. They aroused in him not hunger demanding renewal but surfeit that would demand more surfeit . . . kisses that were like charity, creating want by holding back nothing at all.

It did not take him many hours to decide that he had wanted Judy Jones ever since he was a proud, desirous little boy.

– IV –

It began like that—and continued, with varying shades of intensity, on such a note right up to the dénouement. Dexter surrendered a part of himself to the most direct and unprincipled personality with which he had ever come in contact. Whatever Judy wanted, she went after with the full pressure of her charm. There was no divergence of method, no jockeying for position or premeditation of effects—there was a very little mental side to any of her affairs. She simply made men conscious to the highest degree of her physical loveliness. Dexter had no desire to change her. Her deficiencies were knit up with a passionate energy that transcended and justified them.

When, as Judy's head lay against his shoulder that first night, she whispered, "I don't know what's the matter with me. Last night I thought I was in love with a man and to-night I think I'm in love with you——"—it seemed to him a beautiful and romantic thing to say. It was the exquisite excitability that for the moment he controlled and owned. But a week later he was compelled to view this same quality in a different light. She took him in her roadster to a picnic supper, and after supper she disappeared, likewise in her roadster, with another man. Dexter became enormously upset and was scarcely able to be decently civil to the other people present.

When she assured him that she had not kissed the other man, he knew she was lying—yet he was glad that she had taken the trouble to lie to him.

He was, as he found before the summer ended, one of a varying dozen who circulated about her. Each of them had at one time been favored above all others—about half of them still basked in the solace of occasional sentimental revivals. Whenever one showed signs of dropping out through long neglect, she granted him a brief honeyed hour, which encouraged him to tag along for a year or so longer. Judy made these forays upon the helpless and defeated without malice, indeed half unconscious that there was anything mischievous in what she did.

When a new man came to town every one dropped out—dates were automatically cancelled.

The helpless part of trying to do anything about it was that she did it all herself. She was not a girl who could be "won" in the kinetic sense—she was proof against cleverness, she was proof against charm; if any of these assailed her too strongly she would immediately resolve the affair to a physical basis, and under the magic of her physical splendor the strong as well as the brilliant played her game and not their own. She was entertained only by the gratification of her desires and by the direct exercise of her own charm. Perhaps from so much youthful love, so many youthful lovers, she had come, in self-defense, to nourish herself wholly from within.

Succeeding Dexter's first exhilaration came restlessness and dissatisfaction. The helpless ecstasy of losing himself in her was opiate rather than tonic. It was fortunate for his work during the winter that those moments of ecstasy came infrequently. Early in their acquaintance it had seemed for a while that there was a deep and spontaneous mutual attraction—that first August, for example—three days of long evenings on her dusky veranda, of strange wan kisses through the late afternoon, in shadowy alcoves or behind the protecting trellises of the garden arbors, of mornings when she was fresh as a dream and almost shy at meeting him in the clarity of the rising day. There was all the ecstasy of an engagement about it, sharpened by his realization that there was no engagement. It was during those three days that, for the first time, he had asked her to marry him. She said "maybe some day," she said "kiss me," she said "I'd like to marry you," she said "I love you"—she said—nothing.

The three days were interrupted by the arrival of a New York man who visited at her house for half September. To Dexter's agony, rumor engaged them. The man was the son of the president of a great trust company. But at the end of a month it was reported that Judy was yawning. At a dance one night she sat all evening in a motor-boat with a local beau, while the New Yorker searched the club for her frantically. She told the local beau that she was bored with her visitor, and two days later he left. She was seen with him at the station, and it was reported that he looked very mournful indeed.

On this note the summer ended. Dexter was twenty-four, and he found himself increasingly in a position to do as he wished. He joined two clubs in the city and lived at one of them. Though he was by no means an integral part of the stag-lines at these clubs, he managed to be on hand at dances where Judy Jones was likely to appear. He could have gone out socially as much as he liked—he was an eligible young man, now, and popular with down-town fathers. His confessed devotion to Judy Jones had rather solidified his position. But he had no social aspirations and rather despised the dancing men who were always on tap for the Thursday or Saturday parties and who filled in at dinners with the younger married set. Already he was playing with the idea of going East to New York. He wanted to take Judy Jones with him. No disillusion as to the world in which she had grown up could cure his illusion as to her desirability.

Remember that—for only in the light of it can what he did for her be understood.

Eighteen months after he first met Judy Jones he became engaged to another girl. Her name was Irene Scheerer, and her father was one of the men who had always believed in Dexter. Irene was light-haired and sweet and honorable, and a little stout, and she had two suitors whom she pleasantly relinquished when Dexter formally asked her to marry him.

Summer, fall, winter, spring, another summer, another fall—so much he had given of his active life to the incorrigible lips of Judy Jones. She had treated him with interest, with encouragement, with malice, with indifference, with contempt. She had inflicted on him the innumerable little slights and indignities possible in such a case—as if in revenge for having ever cared for him at all. She had beckoned him and yawned at him and beckoned him again and he had responded often with bitterness and narrowed eyes. She had brought him ecstatic happiness and intolerable agony of spirit. She had caused him untold inconvenience and not a little trouble. She had insulted him, and she had ridden over him, and she had played his interest in her against his interest in his work—for fun. She had done everything to him except to criticise him—this she had not done—it seemed to him only because it might have sullied the utter indifference she manifested and sincerely felt toward him.

When autumn had come and gone again it occurred to him that he could not have Judy Jones. He had to beat this into his mind but he convinced himself at last. He lay awake at night for a while and argued it over. He told himself the trouble and the pain she had caused him, he enumerated her glaring deficiencies as a wife. Then he said to himself that he loved her, and after a while he fell asleep. For a week, lest he imagined her husky voice over the telephone or her eyes opposite him at lunch, he worked hard and late, and at night he went to his office and plotted out his years.

At the end of a week he went to a dance and cut in on her once. For almost the first time since they had met he did not ask her to sit out with him or tell her that she was lovely. It hurt him that she did not miss these things—that was all. He was not jealous when he saw that there was a new man to-night. He had been hardened against jealousy long before.

He stayed late at the dance. He sat for an hour with Irene Scheerer and talked about books and about music. He knew very little about either. But he was beginning to be master of his own time now, and he had a rather priggish notion that he—the young and already fabulously successful Dexter Green—should know more about such things.

That was in October, when he was twenty-five. In January, Dexter and Irene became engaged. It was to be announced in June, and they were to be married three months later.

The Minnesota winter prolonged itself interminably, and it was almost May when the winds came soft and the snow ran down into Black Bear Lake at last. For the first time in over a year Dexter was enjoying a certain tranquility of spirit. Judy Jones had been in Florida, and afterward in Hot Springs, and somewhere she had been engaged, and somewhere she had broken it off. At first, when Dexter had definitely given her up, it had made him sad that people still linked them together and asked for news of her, but when he began to be placed at dinner next to Irene Scheerer people didn't ask him about her any more—they told him about her. He ceased to be an authority on her.

May at last. Dexter walked the streets at night when the darkness was damp as rain, wondering that so soon, with so little done, so much of ecstasy had gone from him. May one year back had been marked by Judy's poignant, unforgivable, yet forgiven turbulence—it had been one of those rare times when he fancied she had grown to care for him. That old penny's worth of happiness he had spent for this bushel of content. He knew that Irene would be no more than a curtain spread behind him, a hand moving among gleaming tea-cups, a voice calling to children . . . fire and loveliness were gone, the magic of nights and the wonder of the varying hours and seasons . . . slender lips, down-turning, dropping to his lips and bearing him up into a heaven of eyes. . . . The thing was deep in him. He was too strong and alive for it to die lightly.

In the middle of May when the weather balanced for a few days on the thin bridge that led to deep summer he turned in one night at Irene's house. Their engagement was to be announced in a week now—no one would be surprised at it. And to-night they would sit together on the lounge at the University Club and look on for an hour at the dancers. It gave him a sense of solidity to go with her—she was so sturdily popular, so intensely "great."

He mounted the steps of the brownstone house and stepped inside.

"Irene," he called.

Mrs. Scheerer came out of the living-room to meet him.

"Dexter," she said, "Irene's gone up-stairs with a splitting headache. She wanted to go with you but I made her go to bed."

"Nothing serious, I——"

"Oh, no. She's going to play golf with you in the morning. You can spare her for just one night, can't you, Dexter?"

Her smile was kind. She and Dexter liked each other. In the living-room he talked for a moment before he said good-night.

Returning to the University Club, where he had rooms, he stood in the doorway for a moment and watched the dancers. He leaned against the door-post, nodded at a man or two—yawned.

"Hello, darling."

The familiar voice at his elbow startled him. Judy Jones had left a man and crossed the room to him—Judy Jones, a slender enamelled doll in cloth of gold: gold in a band at her head, gold in two slipper points at her dress's hem. The fragile glow of her face seemed to blossom as she smiled at him. A breeze of warmth and light blew through the room. His hands in the pockets of his dinner-jacket tightened spasmodically. He was filled with a sudden excitement.

"When did you get back?" he asked casually.

"Come here and I'll tell you about it."

She turned and he followed her. She had been away—he could have wept at the wonder of her return. She had passed through enchanted streets, doing things that were like provocative music. All mysterious happenings, all fresh and quickening hopes, had gone away with her, come back with her now.

She turned in the doorway.

"Have you a car here? If you haven't, I have."

"I have a coupé."

In then, with a rustle of golden cloth. He slammed the door. Into so many cars she had stepped—like this—like that—her back against the leather, so—her elbow resting on the door—waiting. She would have been soiled long since had there been anything to soil her—except herself—but this was her own self outpouring.

With an effort he forced himself to start the car and back into the street. This was nothing, he must remember. She had done this before, and he had put her behind him, as he would have crossed a bad account from his books.

He drove slowly down-town and, affecting abstraction, traversed the deserted streets of the business section, peopled here and there where a movie was giving out its crowd or where consumptive or pugilistic youth lounged in front of pool halls. The clink of glasses and the slap of hands on the bars issued from saloons, cloisters of glazed glass and dirty yellow light.

She was watching him closely and the silence was embarrassing, yet in this crisis he could find no casual word with which to profane the hour. At a convenient turning he began to zigzag back toward the University Club.

"Have you missed me?" she asked suddenly.

"Everybody missed you."

He wondered if she knew of Irene Scheerer. She had been back only a day—her absence had been almost contemporaneous with his engagement.

"What a remark!" Judy laughed sadly—without sadness. She looked at him searchingly. He became absorbed in the dashboard.

"You're handsomer than you used to be," she said thoughtfully. "Dexter, you have the most rememberable eyes."

He could have laughed at this, but he did not laugh. It was the sort of thing that was said to sophomores. Yet it stabbed at him.

"I'm awfully tired of everything, darling." She called every one darling, endowing the endearment with careless, individual comraderie. "I wish you'd marry me."

The directness of this confused him. He should have told her now that he was going to marry another girl, but he could not tell her. He could as easily have sworn that he had never loved her.

"I think we'd get along," she continued, on the same note, "unless probably you've forgotten me and fallen in love with another girl."

Her confidence was obviously enormous. She had said, in effect, that she found such a thing impossible to believe, that if it were true he had merely committed a childish indiscretion—and probably to show off. She would forgive him, because it was not a matter of any moment but rather something to be brushed aside lightly.

"Of course you could never love anybody but me," she continued. "I like the way you love me. Oh, Dexter, have you forgotten last year?"

"No, I haven't forgotten."

"Neither have I!"

Was she sincerely moved—or was she carried along by the wave of her own acting?

"I wish we could be like that again," she said, and he forced himself to answer:

"I don't think we can."

"I suppose not. . . . I hear you're giving Irene Scheerer a violent rush."

There was not the faintest emphasis on the name, yet Dexter was suddenly ashamed.

"Oh, take me home," cried Judy suddenly; "I don't want to go back to that idiotic dance—with those children."

Then, as he turned up the street that led to the residence district, Judy began to cry quietly to herself. He had never seen her cry before.

The dark street lightened, the dwellings of the rich loomed up around them, he stopped his coupé in front of the great white bulk of the Mortimer Joneses house, somnolent, gorgeous, drenched with the splendor of the damp moonlight. Its solidity startled him. The strong walls, the steel of the girders, the breadth and beam and pomp of it were there only to bring out the contrast with the young beauty beside him. It was sturdy to accentuate her slightness—as if to show what a breeze could be generated by a butterfly's wing.

He sat perfectly quiet, his nerves in wild clamor, afraid that if he moved he would find her irresistibly in his arms. Two tears had rolled down her wet face and trembled on her upper lip.

"I'm more beautiful than anybody else," she said brokenly, "why can't I be happy?" Her moist eyes tore at his stability—her mouth turned slowly downward with an exquisite sadness: "I'd like to marry you if you'll have me, Dexter. I suppose you think I'm not worth having, but I'll be so beautiful for you, Dexter."

A million phrases of anger, pride, passion, hatred, tenderness fought on his lips. Then a perfect wave of emotion washed over him, carrying off with it a sediment of wisdom, of convention, of doubt, of honor. This was his girl who was speaking, his own, his beautiful, his pride.

"Won't you come in?" He heard her draw in her breath sharply.

Waiting.

"All right," his voice was trembling, "I'll come in."

– V –

It was strange that neither when it was over nor a long time afterward did he regret that night. Looking at it from the perspective of ten years, the fact that Judy's flare for him endured just one month seemed of little importance. Nor did it matter that by his yielding he subjected himself to a deeper agony in the end and gave serious hurt to Irene Scheerer and to Irene's parents, who had befriended him. There was nothing sufficiently pictorial about Irene's grief to stamp itself on his mind.

Dexter was at bottom hard-minded. The attitude of the city on his action was of no importance to him, not because he was going to leave the city, but because any outside attitude on the situation seemed superficial. He was completely indifferent to popular opinion. Nor, when he had seen that it was no use, that he did not possess in himself the power to move fundamentally or to hold Judy Jones, did he bear any malice toward her. He loved her, and he would love her until the day he was too old for loving—but he could not have her. So he tasted the deep pain that is reserved only for the strong, just as he had tasted for a little while the deep happiness.

Even the ultimate falsity of the grounds upon which Judy terminated the engagement that she did not want to "take him away" from Irene—Judy, who had wanted nothing else—did not revolt him. He was beyond any revulsion or any amusement.

He went East in February with the intention of selling out his laundries and settling in New York—but the war came to America in March and changed his plans. He returned to the West, handed over the management of the business to his partner, and went into the first officers' training-camp in late April. He was one of those young thousands who greeted the war with a certain amount of relief, welcoming the liberation from webs of tangled emotion.

–VI–

This story is not his biography, remember, although things creep into it which have nothing to do with those dreams he had when he was young. We are almost done with them and with him now. There is only one more incident to be related here, and it happens seven years farther on.

It took place in New York, where he had done well — so well that there were no barriers too high for him. He was thirty-two years old, and, except for one flying trip immediately after the war, he had not been West in seven years. A man named Devlin from Detroit came into his office to see him in a business way, and then and there this incident occurred, and closed out, so to speak, this particular side of his life.

"So you're from the Middle West," said the man Devlin with careless curiosity. "That's funny — I thought men like you were probably born and raised on Wall Street. You know — wife of one of my best friends in Detroit came from your city. I was an usher at the wedding."

Dexter waited with no apprehension of what was coming.

"Judy Simms," said Devlin with no particular interest; "Judy Jones she was once."

"Yes, I knew her." A dull impatience spread over him. He had heard, of course, that she was married — perhaps deliberately he had heard no more.

"Awfully nice girl," brooded Devlin meaninglessly, "I'm sort of sorry for her."

"Why?" Something in Dexter was alert, receptive, at once.

"Oh, Lud Simms has gone to pieces in a way. I don't mean he ill-uses her, but he drinks and runs around ——"

"Doesn't she run around?"

"No. Stays at home with her kids."

"Oh."

"She's a little too old for him," said Devlin.

"Too old!" cried Dexter. "Why, man, she's only twenty-seven."

He was possessed with a wild notion of rushing out into the streets and taking a train to Detroit. He rose to his feet spasmodically.

"I guess you're busy," Devlin apologized quickly. "I didn't realize ——"

"No, I'm not busy," said Dexter, steadying his voice. "I'm not busy at all. Not busy at all. Did you say she was — twenty-seven? No, I said she was twenty-seven."

"Yes, you did," agreed Devlin dryly.

"Go on, then. Go on."

"What do you mean?"

"About Judy Jones."

Devlin looked at him helplessly.

"Well, that's—I told you all there is to it. He treats her like the devil. Oh, they're not going to get divorced or anything. When he's particularly outrageous she forgives him. In fact, I'm inclined to think she loves him. She was a pretty girl when she first came to Detroit."

A pretty girl! The phrase struck Dexter as ludicrous.

"Isn't she—a pretty girl, any more?"

"Oh, she's all right."

"Look here," said Dexter, sitting down suddenly, "I don't understand. You say she was a 'pretty girl' and now you say she's 'all right.' I don't understand what you mean—Judy Jones wasn't a pretty girl, at all. She was a great beauty. Why, I knew her, I knew her. She was——"

Devlin laughed pleasantly.

"I'm not trying to start a row," he said. "I think Judy's a nice girl and I like her. I can't understand how a man like Lud Simms could fall madly in love with her, but he did." Then he added: "Most of the women like her."

Dexter looked closely at Devlin, thinking wildly that there must be a reason for this, some insensitivity in the man or some private malice.

"Lots of women fade just like *that*," Devlin snapped his fingers. "You must have seen it happen. Perhaps I've forgotten how pretty she was at her wedding. I've seen her so much since then, you see. She has nice eyes."

A sort of dulness settled down upon Dexter. For the first time in his life he felt like getting very drunk. He knew that he was laughing loudly at something Devlin had said, but he did not know what it was or why it was funny. When, in a few minutes, Devlin went he lay down on his lounge and looked out the window at the New York sky-line into which the sun was sinking in dull lovely shades of pink and gold.

He had thought that having nothing else to lose he was invulnerable at last—but he knew that he had just lost something more, as surely as if he had married Judy Jones and seen her fade away before his eyes.

The dream was gone. Something had been taken from him. In a sort of panic he pushed the palms of his hands into his eyes and tried to bring up a picture of the waters lapping on Sherry Island and the moonlit veranda, and gingham on the golf-links and the dry sun and the gold color of her neck's soft down. And her mouth damp to his kisses and her eyes plaintive with melancholy and her freshness like new fine linen in the morning. Why, these things were no longer in the world! They had existed and they existed no longer.

For the first time in years the tears were streaming down his face. But they were for himself now. He did not care about mouth and eyes and moving hands. He wanted to care, and he could not care. For he had gone away and he could never go back any more. The gates were closed, the sun was gone down, and there was no beauty but the gray beauty of steel that withstands all time. Even the grief he could have borne was left behind in the country of illusion, of youth, of the richness of life, where his winter dreams had flourished.

"Long ago," he said, "long ago, there was something in me, but now that thing is gone. Now that thing is gone, that thing is gone. I cannot cry. I cannot care. That thing will come back no more." [1922]

RING LARDNER

Ring Lardner (1885–1933) was born the youngest of nine children in Niles, Michigan (population 4,000), where he lived for the first twenty-two years of his life. His parents were the wealthiest people in town, living in a spacious house with a staff of Irish servants, surrounded by several acres including a private baseball diamond, a tennis court, and a stable of horses. After graduating from Niles High School, Lardner stayed at home and worked a series of odd jobs until he was offered the position of society reporter and sports editor for the South Bend, Indiana, Times. *He worked there for two years and discovered that he had a talent as a baseball reporter, covering White Sox and Chicago Cubs games. In 1907, he was hired away by the Chicago* Examiner *and, during the next ten years, made his reputation as a sportswriter and columnist in both Chicago and New York City until the publication of his first book of short stories,* You Know Me Al: A Busher's Letters *(1916). In these casual stories about a novice's career on a professional baseball team, Lardner used slang and colloquial humor to good effect. He followed this book with a second collection of satirical stories,* Gullible's Travels *(1917).*

In 1920 Lardner moved to New York City and began to write "Ring Lardner's Weekly Letter" for a sports syndicate that reached eight million readers in various American newspapers. Paid an annual salary of $30,000, he wrote the column for seven years. The solidly prosperous Lardner then built a mansion in Great Neck, Long Island, for his wife and children and became close neighbors with Scott and Zelda Fitzgerald and their young daughter. Lardner's humor was so much admired by his New York acquaintances that Dorothy Parker commented upon the publication of his stories in Round Up *(1929), "It is difficult to review these spare and beautiful stories; it would be difficult to review the Gettysburg address."*

After publishing "The Golden Honeymoon" in Cosmopolitan *in July 1922 for $1,500, Lardner was approached by Fitzgerald's editor, Maxwell Perkins, at Scribner's and was persuaded to sign a contract for a book of ten short stories. Lardner had a journalist's casualness about his writing; Fitzgerald remembered that his friend hadn't saved any copies of his stories: "The material of* How to Write Short Stories *was obtained by photographing old issues of magazines in the public library." The book, which contained Lardner's best work, was published in 1924. His self-mockery in his introduction to the volume puzzled the critic Edmund Wilson, who sensed that Lardner was "timid about coming forward in the role of serious writer." Wilson found the stories "a series of studies of American types almost equal in importance to those of Sherwood Anderson" and praised Lardner "because he is primarily interested in studying a kind of person rather than in drawing up an indictment" about human failings. Wilson also knew that Lardner was living "at a time when, if one be not sold irredeemably into bondage to the* Saturday Evening Post, *it is far easier for a serious writer to get published and find a* *hearing than it was in Mark Twain's day." For the rest of Lardner's short life, before he died of alcoholism at the age of forty-eight, he tried to prove that he was a serious writer by finishing a novel. Instead he wrote more humorous stories, plays, and song lyrics. Most of this material was published in the collections* What of It? *(1925),* Round Up *(1929), and* First and Last *(1934).*

RELATED COMMENTARY: *Ring Lardner, "How to Write Short Stories," page 1385.*

The Golden Honeymoon

Mother says that when I start talking I never know when to stop. But I tell her the only time I get a chance is when she ain't around, so I have to make the most of it. I guess the fact is neither one of us would be welcome in a Quaker meeting, but as I tell Mother, what did God give us tongues for if He didn't want we should use them? Only she says He didn't give them to us to say the same thing over and over again, like I do, and repeat myself. But I say:

"Well, Mother," I say, "when people is like you and I and been married fifty years, do you expect everything I say will be something you ain't heard me say before? But it may be new to others, as they ain't nobody else lived with me as long as you have."

So she says:

"You can bet they ain't, as they couldn't nobody else stand you that long."

"Well," I tell her, "you look pretty healthy."

"Maybe I do," she will say, "but I looked even healthier before I married you."

You can't get ahead of Mother.

Yes, sir, we was married just fifty years ago the seventeenth day of last December and my daughter and son-in-law was over from Trenton to help us celebrate the Golden Wedding. My son-in-law is John H. Kramer, the real estate man. He made $12,000 one year and is pretty well thought of around Trenton; a good, steady, hard worker. The Rotarians was after him a long time to join, but he kept telling them his home was his club. But Edie finally made him join. That's my daughter.

Well, anyway, they come over to help us celebrate the Golden Wedding and it was pretty crimpy weather and the furnace don't seem to heat up no more like it used to and Mother made the remark that she hoped this winter wouldn't be as cold as the last, referring to the winter previous. So Edie said if she was us, and nothing to keep us home, she certainly wouldn't spend no more winters up here and why didn't we just shut off the water and close up the house and go down to Tampa, Florida? You know we was there four winters ago and staid five weeks, but it cost us over three hundred and fifty dollars for hotel bill alone. So Mother said we wasn't going no place to be robbed. So my son-in-law spoke up and said that Tampa wasn't the only place in the South, and besides we didn't have to stop at no high price hotel but could rent us a couple rooms and board out somewheres, and he had heard that St. Petersburg, Florida, was *the* spot and if we said the word he would write down there and make inquiries.

Well, to make a long story short, we decided to do it and Edie said it would be our Golden Honeymoon and for a present my son-in-law paid the difference between a section and a compartment so as we could have a compartment and have more privatecy. In a compartment you have an upper and lower berth just like the regular sleeper, but it is a shut in room by itself and got a wash bowl. The car we went in was all compartments and no regular berths at all. It was all compartments.

We went to Trenton the night before and staid at my daughter and son-in-law and we left Trenton the next afternoon at 3:23 P.M.

This was the twelfth day of January. Mother set facing the front of the train, as it makes her giddy to ride backwards. I set facing her, which does not affect me. We reached North Philadelphia at 4:03 P.M. and we reached West Philadelphia at 4:14, but did not go into Broad Street. We reached Baltimore at 6:30 and Washington, D.C., at 7:25. Our train laid over in Washington two hours till another train come along to pick us up and I got out and strolled up the platform and into the Union Station. When I come back, our car had been switched on to another track, but I remembered the name of it, the La Belle, as I had once visited my aunt out in Oconomowoc, Wisconsin, where there was a lake of that name, so I had no difficulty in getting located. But Mother had nearly fretted herself sick for fear I would be left.

"Well," I said, "I would of followed you on the next train."

"You could of," said Mother, and she pointed out that she had the money.

"Well," I said, "we are in Washington and I could of borrowed from the United States Treasury. I would of pretended I was an Englishman."

Mother caught the point and laughed heartily.

Our train pulled out of Washington at 9:40 P.M. and Mother and I turned in early, I taking the upper. During the night we passed through the green fields of old Virginia, though it was too dark to tell if they was green or what color. When we got up in the morning, we was at Fayetteville, North Carolina. We had breakfast in the dining car and after breakfast I got in conversation with the man in the next compartment to ours. He was from Lebanon, New Hampshire, and a man about eighty years of age. His wife was with him, and two unmarried daughters and I made the remark that I should think the four of them would be crowded in one compartment, but he said they had made the trip every winter for fifteen years and knowed how to keep out of each other's way. He said they was bound for Tarpon Springs.

We reached Charleston, South Carolina, at 12:50 P.M. and arrived at Savannah, Georgia, at 4:20. We reached Jacksonville, Florida, at 8:45 P.M. and had an hour and a quarter to lay over there, but Mother made a fuss about me getting off the train, so we had the darky make up our berths and retired before we left Jacksonville. I didn't sleep good as the train done a lot of hemming and hawing, and Mother never sleeps good on a train as she says she is always worrying that I will fall out. She says she would rather have the upper herself, as then she would not have to worry about me, but I tell her I can't take the risk of having it get out that I allowed my wife to sleep in an upper berth. It would make talk.

We was up in the morning in time to see our friends from New Hampshire get off at Tarpon Springs, which we reached at 6:53 A.M.

Several of our fellow passengers got off at Clearwater and some at Belleair, where the train backs right up to the door of the mammoth hotel. Belleair is the winter headquarters for the golf dudes and everybody that got off there had their bag of sticks, as many as ten and twelve in a bag. Women and all. When I was a young man we called it shinny and only needed one club to play with and about one game of it would of been a-plenty for some of these dudes, the way we played it.

The train pulled into St. Petersburg at 8:20 and when we got off the train you would think they was a riot, what with all the darkies barking for the different hotels.

I said to Mother, I said:

"It is a good thing we have got a place picked out to go to and don't have to choose a hotel, as it would be hard to choose amongst them if everyone of them is the best."

She laughed.

We found a jitney and I give him the address of the room my son-in-law had got for us and soon we was there and introduced ourselves to the lady that owns the house, a young widow about forty-eight years of age. She showed us our room, which was light and airy with a comfortable bed and bureau and washstand. It was twelve dollars a week, but the location was good, only three blocks from Williams Park.

St. Pete is what folks calls the town, though they also call it the Sunshine City, as they claim they's no other place in the country where they's fewer days when Old Sol don't smile down on Mother Earth, and one of the newspapers gives away all their copies free every day when the sun don't shine. They claim to of only give them away some sixty-odd times in the last eleven years. Another nickname they have got for the town is "the Poor Man's Palm Beach," but I guess they's men that comes there that could borrow as much from the bank as some of the Willie boys over to the other Palm Beach.

During our stay we paid a visit to the Lewis Tent City, which is the headquarters for the Tin-Can Tourists. But maybe you ain't heard about them. Well, they are an organization that takes their vacation trips by auto and carries everything with them. That is, they bring along their tents to sleep in and cook in and they don't patronize no hotels or cafeterias, but they have got to be bona fide auto campers or they can't belong to the organization.

They tell me they's over 200,000 members to it and they call themselves the Tin-Canners on account of most of their food being put up in tin cans. One couple we seen in the Tent City was a couple from Brady, Texas, named Mr. and Mrs. Pence, which the old man is over eighty years of age and they had come in their auto all the way from home, a distance of 1,641 miles. They took five weeks for the trip, Mr. Pence driving the entire distance.

The Tin-Canners hails from every State in the Union and in the summer time they visit places like New England and the Great Lakes region, but in the winter the most of them comes to Florida and scatters all over the State. While we was down there, they was a national convention of them at Gainesville, Florida, and they elected a Fredonia, New York, man as their president. His title is Royal Tin-Can Opener of the World. They have got a song wrote up which everybody has got to learn it before they are a member:

> The tin can forever! Hurrah, boys! Hurrah!
>   Up with the tin can! Down with the foe!
> We will rally round the campfire, we'll rally once again,
>   Shouting, "We auto camp forever!"

That is something like it. And the members has also got to have a tin can fastened on to the front of their machine.

I asked Mother how she would like to travel around that way and she said:

"Fine, but not with an old rattle brain like you driving."

"Well," I said, "I am eight years younger than this Mr. Pence who drove here from Texas."

"Yes," she said, "but he is old enough to not be skittish."

You can't get ahead of Mother.

Well, one of the first things we done in St. Petersburg was to go to the Chamber of Commerce and register our names and where we was from as they's great rivalry amongst the different States in regards to the number of their citizens visiting in town and of course our little State don't stand much of a show, but still every little bit helps, as the fella says. All and all, the man told us, they was eleven thousand names registered, Ohio leading with some fifteen hundred-odd and New York State next with twelve hundred. Then come Michigan, Pennsylvania and so on down, with one man each from Cuba and Nevada.

The first night we was there, they was a meeting of the New York-New Jersey Society at the Congregational Church and a man from Ogdensburg, New York State, made the talk. His subject was Rainbow Chasing. He is a Rotarian and a very convicting speaker, though I forget his name.

Our first business, of course, was to find a place to eat and after trying several places we run on to a cafeteria on Central Avenue that suited us up and down. We eat pretty near all our meals there and it averaged about two dollars per day for the two of us, but the food was well cooked and everything nice and clean. A man don't mind paying the price if things is clean and well cooked.

On the third day of February, which is Mother's birthday, we spread ourselves and eat supper at the Poinsettia Hotel and they charged us seventy-five cents for a sirloin steak that wasn't hardly big enough for one.

I said to Mother: "Well," I said, "I guess it's a good thing every day ain't your birthday or we would be in the poorhouse."

"No," says Mother, "because if every day was my birthday, I would be old enough by this time to of been in my grave long ago."

You can't get ahead of Mother.

In the hotel they had a card room where they was several men and ladies playing five hundred and this new fangled whist bridge. We also seen a place where they was dancing, so I asked Mother would she like to trip the light fantastic toe and she said no, she was too old to squirm like you have got to do now days. We watched some of the young folks at it awhile till Mother got disgusted and said we would have to see a good movie to take the taste out of our mouth. Mother is a great movie heroyne and we go twice a week here at home.

But I want to tell you about the Park. The second day we was there we visited the Park, which is a good deal like the one in Tampa, only bigger, and they's more fun goes on here every day than you could shake a stick at. In the middle they's a big bandstand and chairs for the folks to set and listen to the concerts, which they give you music for all tastes, from "Dixie" up to classical pieces like "Hearts and Flowers."

Then all around they's places marked off for different sports and games—chess and checkers and dominoes for folks that enjoys those kind of games, and roque and horse-shoes for the nimbler ones. I used to pitch a pretty fair shoe myself, but ain't done much of it in the last twenty years.

Well, anyway, we bought a membership ticket in the club which costs one dollar for the season, and they tell me that up to a couple years ago it was fifty cents, but they had to raise it to keep out the riffraff.

Well, Mother and I put in a great day watching the pitchers and she wanted I should get in the game, but I told her I was all out of practice and would make a fool of myself, though I seen several men pitching who I guess I could take their measure without no practice. However, they was some good pitchers, too, and one boy from Akron, Ohio, who could certainly throw a pretty shoe. They told me it looked like he would win the championship of the United States in the February tournament. We come away a few days before they held that and I never did hear if he win. I forget his name, but he was a clean cut young fella and he has got a brother in Cleveland that's a Rotarian.

Well, we just stood around and watched the different games for two or three days and finally I set down in a checker game with a man named Weaver from Danville, Illinois. He was a pretty fair checker player, but he wasn't no match for me, and I hope that don't sound like bragging. But I always could hold my own on a checkerboard and the folks around here will tell you the same thing. I played with this Weaver pretty near all morning for two or three mornings and he beat me one game and the only other time it looked like he had a chance, the noon whistle blowed and we had to quit and go to dinner.

While I was playing checkers, Mother would set and listen to the band, as she loves music, classical or no matter what kind, but anyway she was setting there one day and between selections the woman next to her opened up a conversation. She was a woman about Mother's own age, seventy or seventy-one, and finally she asked Mother's name and Mother told her her name and where she was from and Mother asked her the same question, and who do you think the woman was?

Well, sir, it was the wife of Frank M. Hartsell, the man who was engaged to Mother till I stepped in and cut him out, fifty-two years ago!

Yes, sir!

You can imagine Mother's surprise! And Mrs. Hartsell was surprised, too, when Mother told her she had once been friends with her husband, though Mother didn't say how close friends they had been, or that Mother and I was the cause of Hartsell going out West. But that's what we was. Hartsell left his town a month after the engagement was broke off and ain't never been back since. He had went out to Michigan and become a veterinary, and that is where he had settled down, in Hillsdale, Michigan, and finally married his wife.

Well, Mother screwed up her courage to ask if Frank was still living and Mrs. Hartsell took her over to where they was pitching horse-shoes and there was old Frank, waiting his turn. And he knowed Mother as soon as he seen her, though it was over fifty years. He said he knowed her by her eyes.

"Why, it's Lucy Frost!" he says, and he throwed down his shoes and quit the game.

Then they come over and hunted me up and I will confess I wouldn't of knowed him. Him and I is the same age to the month, but he seems to show it more, some way. He is balder for one thing. And his beard is all white, where mine has still got a streak of brown in it. The very first thing I said to him, I said:

"Well, Frank, that beard of yours makes me feel like I was back north. It looks like a regular blizzard."

"Well," he said, "I guess yourn would be just as white if you had it dry cleaned."

But Mother wouldn't stand that.

"Is that so!" she said to Frank. "Well, Charley ain't had no tobacco in his mouth for over ten years!"

And I ain't!

Well, I excused myself from the checker game and it was pretty close to noon, so we decided to all have dinner together and they was nothing for it only we must try their cafeteria on Third Avenue. It was a little more expensive than ours and not near as good, I thought. I and Mother had about the same dinner we had been having every day and our bill was $1.10. Frank's check was $1.20 for he and his wife. The same meal wouldn't of cost them more than a dollar at our place.

After dinner we made them come up to our house and we all set in the parlor, which the young woman had give us the use of to entertain company. We begun talking over old times and Mother said she was a-scared Mrs. Hartsell would find it tiresome listening to we three talk over old times, but as it turned out they wasn't much chance for nobody else to talk with Mrs. Hartsell in the company. I have heard lots of women that could go it, but Hartsell's wife takes the cake of all the women I ever seen. She told us the family history of everybody in the State of Michigan and bragged for a half hour about her son, who she said is in the drug business in Grand Rapids, and a Rotarian.

When I and Hartsell could get a word in edgeways we joked one another back and forth and I chafed him about being a horse doctor.

"Well, Frank," I said, "you look pretty prosperous, so I suppose they's been plenty of glanders around Hillsdale."

"Well," he said, "I've managed to make more than a fair living. But I've worked pretty hard."

"Yes," I said, "and I suppose you get called out all hours of the night to attend births and so on."

Mother made me shut up.

Well, I thought they wouldn't never go home and I and Mother was in misery trying to keep awake, as the both of us generally always takes a nap after dinner. Finally they went, after we had made an engagement to meet them in the Park the next morning, and Mrs. Hartsell also invited us to come to their place the next night and play five hundred. But she had forgot that they was a meeting of the Michigan Society that evening, so it was not till two evenings later that we had our first card game.

Hartsell and his wife lived in a house on Third Avenue North and had a private setting room besides their bedroom. Mrs. Hartsell couldn't quit talking about their private setting room like it was something wonderful. We played cards with them, with Mother and Hartsell partners against his wife and I. Mrs. Hartsell is a miserable card player and we certainly got the worst of it.

After the game she brought out a dish of oranges and we had to pretend it was just what we wanted, though oranges down there is like a young man's whiskers; you enjoy them at first, but they get to be a pesky nuisance.

We played cards again the next night at our place with the same partners and I and Mrs. Hartsell was beat again. Mother and Hartsell was full of compliments for each other on what a good team they made, but the both of them knowed well enough where the secret of their success laid. I guess all and all we must of played ten different evenings and they was only one night when Mrs. Hartsell and I come out ahead. And that one night wasn't no fault of hern.

When we had been down there about two weeks, we spent one evening as their guest in the Congregational Church, at a social give by the Michigan Society. A talk was made by a man named Bitting of Detroit, Michigan, on How I was Cured of Story Telling. He is a big man in the Rotarians and give a witty talk.

A woman named Mrs. Oxford rendered some selections which Mrs. Hartsell said was grand opera music, but whatever they was my daughter Edie could of give her cards and spades and not made such a hullaballoo about it neither.

Then they was a ventriloquist from Grand Rapids and a young woman about forty-five years of age that mimicked different kinds of birds. I whispered to Mother that they all sounded like a chicken, but she nudged me to shut up.

After the show we stopped in a drugstore and I set up the refreshments and it was pretty close to ten o'clock before we finally turned in. Mother and I would of preferred tending the movies, but Mother said we mustn't offend Mrs. Hartsell, though I asked her had we came to Florida to enjoy ourselves or to just not offend an old chatter-box from Michigan.

I felt sorry for Hartsell one morning. The women folks both had an engagement down to the chiropodist's and I run across Hartsell in the Park and he foolishly offered to play me checkers.

It was him that suggested it, not me, and I guess he repented himself before we had played one game. But he was too stubborn to give up and set there while I beat him game after game and the worst part of it was that a crowd of folks had got in the habit of watching me play and there they all was, looking on, and finally they seen what a fool Frank was making of himself, and they began to chafe him and pass remarks. Like one of them said:

"Who ever told you you was a checker player!"

And:

"You might maybe be good for tiddle-de-winks, but not checkers!"

I almost felt like letting him beat me a couple games. But the crowd would of knowed it was a put up job.

Well, the women folks joined us in the Park and I wasn't going to mention our little game, but Hartsell told about it himself and admitted he wasn't no match for me.

"Well," said Mrs. Hartsell, "checkers ain't much of a game anyway, is it?" She said: "It's more of a children's game, ain't it? At least, I know my boy's children used to play it a good deal."

"Yes, ma'am," I said. "It's a children's game the way your husband plays it, too."

Mother wanted to smooth things over, so she said:

"Maybe they's other games where Frank can beat you."

"Yes," said Mrs. Hartsell, "and I bet he could beat you pitching horseshoes."

"Well," I said, "I would give him a chance to try, only I ain't pitched a shoe in over sixteen years."

"Well," said Hartsell, "I ain't played checkers in twenty years."

"You ain't never played it," I said.

"Anyway," says Frank, "Lucy and I is your master at five hundred."

Well, I could of told him why that was, but had decency enough to hold my tongue.

It had got so now that he wanted to play cards every night and when I or Mother wanted to go to a movie, any one of us would have to pretend we had a headache and then trust to goodness that they wouldn't see us sneak into the theater. I don't mind playing cards when my partner keeps their mind on the game, but you take a woman like Hartsell's wife and how can they play cards when they have got to stop every couple seconds and brag about their son in Grand Rapids?

Well, the New York–New Jersey Society announced that they was going to give a social evening too and I said to Mother, I said:

"Well, that is one evening when we will have an excuse not to play five hundred."

"Yes," she said, "but we will have to ask Frank and his wife to go to the social with us as they asked us to go to the Michigan social."

"Well," I said, "I had rather stay home than drag that Chatter-box everywheres we go."

So Mother said:

"You are getting too cranky. Maybe she does talk a little too much but she is good hearted. And Frank is always good company."

So I said:

"I suppose if he is such good company you wished you had of married him."

Mother laughed and said I sounded like I was jealous. Jealous of a cow doctor!

Anyway we had to drag them along to the social and I will say that we give them a much better entertainment than they had given us.

Judge Lane of Paterson made a fine talk on business conditions and a Mrs. Newell of Westfield imitated birds, only you could really tell what they was the way she done it. Two young women from Red Bank sung a choral selection and we clapped them back and they gave us "Home to Our Mountains" and Mother and Mrs. Hartsell both had tears in their eyes. And Hartsell, too.

Well, some way or another the chairman got wind that I was there and asked me to make a talk and I wasn't even going to get up, but Mother made me, so I got up and said:

"Ladies and gentlemen," I said. "I didn't expect to be called on for a speech on an occasion like this or no other occasion as I do not set myself up as a speech maker, so will have to do the best I can, which I often say is the best anybody can do."

Then I told them the story about Pat and the motorcycle, using the brogue, and it seemed to tickle them and I told them one or two other stories but altogether I wasn't on my feet more than twenty or twenty-five minutes and you ought to of heard the clapping and hollering when I set down. Even Mrs. Hartsell admitted that I am quite a speechifier and said if I ever went to Grand Rapids, Michigan, her son would make me talk to the Rotarians.

When it was over, Hartsell wanted we should go to their house and play cards, but his wife reminded him that it was after 9:30 P.M., rather a late hour to start a card game, but he had went crazy on the subject of cards, probably because he didn't have to play partners with his wife. Anyway, we got rid of them and went home to bed.

It was the next morning, when we met over to the Park, that Mrs. Hartsell made the remark that she wasn't getting no exercise so I suggested that why didn't she take part in the roque game.

She said she had not played a game of roque in twenty years, but if Mother would play she would play. Well, at first Mother wouldn't hear of it, but finally consented, more to please Mrs. Hartsell than anything else.

Well, they had a game with a Mrs. Ryan from Eagle, Nebraska, and a young Mrs. Morse from Rutland, Vermont, who Mother had met down to the chiropodist's. Well, Mother couldn't hit a flea and they all laughed at her and I couldn't help from laughing at her myself and finally she quit and said her back was too lame to stoop over. So they got another lady and kept on playing and soon Mrs. Hartsell was the one everybody was laughing at, as she had a long shot to hit the black ball, and as she made the effort her teeth fell out on to the court. I never seen a woman so flustered in my life. And I never heard so much laughing, only Mrs. Hartsell didn't join in and she was madder than a hornet and wouldn't play no more, so the game broke up.

Mrs. Hartsell went home without speaking to nobody, but Hartsell stayed around and finally he said to me, he said:

"Well, I played you checkers the other day and you beat me bad and now what do you say if you and me play a game of horse-shoes?"

I told him I hadn't pitched a shoe in sixteen years, but Mother said:

"Go ahead and play. You used to be good at it and maybe it will come back to you."

Well, to make a long story short, I give in. I oughtn't to of never tried it, as I hadn't pitched a shoe in sixteen years, and I only done it to humor Hartsell.

Before we started, Mother patted me on the back and told me to do my best, so we started in and I seen right off that I was in for it, as I hadn't pitched a shoe in sixteen years and didn't have my distance. And besides, the plating had wore off the shoes so that they was points right where they stuck into my thumb and I hadn't throwed more than two or three times when my thumb was raw and it pretty near killed me to hang on to the shoe, let alone pitch it.

Well, Hartsell throws the awkwardest shoe I ever seen pitched and to see him pitch you wouldn't think he would ever come nowheres near, but he is also the luckiest pitcher I ever seen and he made some pitches where the shoe lit five and six feet short and then schoonered up and was a ringer. They's no use trying to beat that kind of luck.

They was a pretty fair size crowd watching us and four or five other ladies besides Mother, and it seems like, when Hartsell pitches, he has got to chew and it kept the ladies on the anxious seat as he don't seem to care which way he is facing when he leaves go.

You would think a man as old as him would of learnt more manners.

Well, to make a long story short, I was just beginning to get my distance when I had to give up on account of my thumb, which I showed it to Hartsell and he seen I couldn't go on, as it was raw and bleeding. Even if I could of stood it to go on myself, Mother wouldn't of allowed it after she seen my thumb. So anyway I quit and Hartsell said the score was nineteen to six, but I don't know what it was. Or don't care, neither.

Well, Mother and I went home and I said I hoped we was through with the Hartsells as I was sick and tired of them, but it seemed like she had promised we would go over to their house that evening for another game of their everlasting cards.

Well, my thumb was giving me considerable pain and I felt kind of out of sorts and I guess maybe I forgot myself, but anyway, when we was about through playing Hartsell made the remark that he wouldn't never lose a game of cards if he could always have Mother for a partner.

So I said:

"Well, you had a chance fifty years ago to always have her for a partner, but you wasn't man enough to keep her."

I was sorry the minute I had said it and Hartsell didn't know what to say and for once his wife couldn't say nothing. Mother tried to smooth things over by making the remark that I must of had something stronger than tea or I wouldn't talk so silly. But Mrs. Hartsell had froze up like an iceberg and hardly said good night to us and I bet her and Frank put in a pleasant hour after we was gone.

As we was leaving, Mother said to him: "Never mind Charley's nonsense, Frank. He is just mad because you beat him all hollow pitching horseshoes and playing cards."

She said that to make up for my slip, but at the same time she certainly riled me. I tried to keep ahold of myself, but as soon as we was out of the house she had to open up the subject and begun to scold me for the break I had made.

Well, I wasn't in no mood to be scolded. So I said:

"I guess he is such a wonderful pitcher and card player that you wished you had married him."

"Well," she said, "at least he ain't a baby to give up pitching because his thumb has got a few scratches."

"And how about you," I said, "making a fool of yourself on the roque court and then pretending your back is lame and you can't play no more!"

"Yes," she said, "but when you hurt your thumb I didn't laugh at you, and why did you laugh at me when I sprained my back?"

"Who could help from laughing!" I said.

"Well," she said, "Frank Hartsell didn't laugh."

"Well," I said, "why didn't you marry him?"

"Well," said Mother, "I almost wished I had!"

"And I wished so, too!" I said.

"I'll remember that!" said Mother, and that's the last word she said to me for two days.

We seen the Hartsells the next day in the Park and I was willing to apologize, but they just nodded to us. And a couple days later we heard they had left for Orlando, where they have got relatives.

I wished they had went there in the first place.

Mother and I made it up setting on a bench.

"Listen, Charley," she said. "This is our Golden Honeymoon and we don't want the whole thing spoilt with a silly old quarrel."

"Well," I said, "did you mean that about wishing you had married Hartsell?"

"Of course not," she said, "that is, if you didn't mean that you wished I had, too."

So I said:

"I was just tired and all wrought up. I thank God you chose me instead of him as they's no other woman in the world who I could of lived with all these years."

"How about Mrs. Hartsell?" says Mother.

"Good gracious!" I said. "Imagine being married to a woman that plays five hundred like she does and drops her teeth on the roque court!"

"Well," said Mother, "it wouldn't be no worse than being married to a man that expectorates towards ladies and is such a fool in a checker game."

So I put my arm around her shoulder and she stroked my hand and I guess we got kind of spoony.

They was two days left of our stay in St. Petersburg and the next to the last day Mother introduced me to a Mrs. Kendall from Kingston, Rhode Island, who she had met at the chiropodist's.

Mrs. Kendall made us acquainted with her husband, who is in the grocery business. They have got two sons and five grandchildren and one great-grandchild. One of their sons lives in Providence and is way up in the Elks as well as a Rotarian.

We found them very congenial people and we played cards with them the last two nights we was there. They was both experts and I only wished we had met them sooner instead of running into the Hartsells. But the Kendalls will be there again next winter and we will see more of them, that is, if we decide to make the trip again.

We left the Sunshine City on the eleventh day of February, at 11 A.M. This give us a day trip through Florida and we seen all the country we had passed through at night on the way down.

We reached Jacksonville at 7 P.M. and pulled out of there at 8:10 P.M. We reached Fayetteville, North Carolina, at nine o'clock the following morning, and reached Washington, D.C., at 6:30 P.M., laying over there half an hour.

We reached Trenton at 11:01 P.M. and had wired ahead to my daughter and son-in-law and they met us at the train and we went to their house and they put us up for the night. John would of made us stay up all night, telling about our trip, but Edie said we must be tired and made us go to bed. That's my daughter.

The next day we took our train for home and arrived safe and sound, having been gone just one month and a day.

Here comes Mother, so I guess I better shut up.   [1922]

GERTRUDE STEIN

Gertrude Stein (1874–1946) was born in Allegheny, Pennsylvania. When she was a girl she moved with her family to Oakland, California, where her father, a German immigrant, invested so wisely in San Francisco street railways that he was able to leave a comfortable fortune to each of his children when he died in 1891. In 1897 Stein graduated from Radcliffe College, where she had studied psychology under William James and published a paper on her experiments with spontaneous automatic writing. She went on to study medicine at Johns Hopkins Medical School but, tiring of scientific work before she finished her degree, she joined her brother Leo in Paris and settled with him there in 1903, living on their inherited income. The same year she began to write, starting with a short novel based on her own lesbian experience, Q.E.D., *which she then rewrote as the "Melanctha" section of her first published book,* Three Lives *(1909). This work was modeled on Flaubert's stories in* Three Tales.

After posing for a portrait by Pablo Picasso, Stein abandoned realistic narrative to develop her own prose style further, attempting to use words to create the cubist effects of avant-garde painters such as Picasso, Henri Matisse, and Georges Braque, whose canvases she and her companion, Alice B. Toklas, had begun to collect. Tender Buttons *(1914), a collection of sketches departing from traditional syntax and grammar, and* The Making of Americans *(1925), her most ambitious book, running 925 closely printed pages, exhibit her cubist style. Stein produced nearly six hundred works, but most of them remained unpublished until after her death, with the notable exception of her best-selling memoir,* The Autobiography of Alice B. Toklas *(1933).*

Stein was an acknowledged influence on a number of important writers, including Sherwood Anderson, Ernest Hemingway, and Richard Wright. In her opinion, these writers never freed themselves from the influence of conventional narrative, creating fiction that had plots based on consecutive events. Stein wanted her writing, like the story "Miss Furr and Miss Skeene," to depart from the traditional role of fiction as a mirror of the temporal and spatial relations of people, places, and things in the "real world." She felt that literature should have a self-contained existence, where the words cease to convey conventional meaning and become objects to be manipulated by the writer, who could create a syntactical world with its own sense of internal coherence on the page. "Miss Furr and Miss Skeene" was published in Geography and Plays *in 1922.*

Miss Furr and Miss Skeene

Helen Furr had quite a pleasant home. Mrs. Furr was quite a pleasant woman. Mr. Furr was quite a pleasant man. Helen Furr had quite a pleasant voice a voice quite worth cultivating. She did not mind working. She worked to cultivate her voice. She did not find it gay living in the same place where she had always been living. She went to a place where some were cultivating something, voices and other things needing cultivating. She met Georgine Skeene there who was cultivating her voice which some thought was quite a pleasant one. Helen Furr and Georgine Skeene lived together then. Georgine Skeene liked travelling. Helen Furr did not care about travelling, she liked to stay in one place and be gay there. They were together then and travelled to another place and stayed there and were gay there.

They stayed there and were gay there, not very gay there, just gay there. They were both gay there, they were regularly working there both of them cultivating their voices there, they were both gay there. Georgine Skeene was gay there and she was regular, regular in being gay, regular in not being gay, regular in being a gay one who was not being gay longer than was needed to be one being quite a gay one. They were both gay then there and both working there then.

They were in a way both gay there where there were many cultivating something. They were both regular in being gay there. Helen Furr was gay there, she was gayer and gayer there and really she was just gay there, she was gayer and gayer there, that is to say she found ways of being gay there that she was using in being gay there. She was gay there, not gayer and gayer, just gay there, that is to say she was not gayer by using the things she found there that were gay things, she was gay there, always she was gay there.

They were quite regularly gay there, Helen Furr and Georgine Skeene, they were regularly gay there where they were gay. They were very regularly gay.

To be regularly gay was to do every day the gay thing that they did every day. To be regularly gay was to end every day at the same time after they had been regularly gay. They were regularly gay. They were gay every day. They ended every day in the same way, at the same time, and they had been every day regularly gay.

The voice Helen Furr was cultivating was quite a pleasant one. The voice Georgine Skeene was cultivating was, some said, a better one. The voice Helen Furr was cultivating she cultivated and it was quite completely a pleasant enough one then, a cultivated enough one then. The voice Georgine Skeene was cultivating she did not cultivate too much. She cultivated it quite some. She cultivated and she would sometime go on cultivating it and it was not then an unpleasant one, it would not be then an unpleasant one, it would be a quite richly enough cultivated one, it would be quite richly enough to be a pleasant enough one.

They were gay where there were many cultivating something. The two were gay there, were regularly gay there. Georgine Skeene would have liked to do more travelling. They did some travelling, not very much travelling, Georgine Skeene would have liked to do more travelling, Helen Furr did not care about doing travelling, she liked to stay in a place and be gay there.

They stayed in a place and were gay there, both of them stayed there, they stayed together there, they were gay there, they were regularly gay there.

They went quite often, not very often, but they did go back to where Helen Furr had a pleasant enough home and then Georgine Skeene went to a place where her brother had quite some distinction. They both went, every few years, went visiting to where Helen Furr had quite a pleasant home. Certainly Helen Furr would not find it gay to stay, she did not find it gay, she said she would not stay, she said she did not find it gay, she said she would not stay where she did not find it gay, she said she found it gay where she did stay and she did stay there where very many were cultivating something. She did stay there. She always did find it gay there.

She went to see them where she had always been living and where she did not find it gay. She had a pleasant home there, Mrs. Furr was a pleasant enough woman, Mr. Furr was a pleasant enough man, Helen told them and they were not worrying, that she did not find it gay living where she had always been living.

Georgine Skeene and Helen Furr were living where they were both cultivating their voices and they were gay there. They visited where Helen Furr had come from and then they went to where they were living where they were then regularly living.

There were some dark and heavy men there then. There were some who were not so heavy and some who were not so dark. Helen Furr and Georgine Skeene sat regularly with them. They sat regularly with the ones who were dark and heavy. They sat regularly with the ones who were not so dark. They sat regularly with the ones that were not so heavy. They sat with them regularly, sat with some of them. They went with them regularly went with them. They were regular then, they were gay then, they were where they wanted to be then where it was gay to be then, they were regularly gay then. There were men there then who were dark and heavy and they sat with them with Helen Furr and Georgine Skeene and they went with them with Miss Furr and Miss Skeene, and they went with the heavy and dark men Miss Furr and Miss Skeene went with them, and they sat with them, Miss Furr and Miss Skeene sat with them, and there were other men, some were not heavy men and they sat with Miss Furr and Miss Skeene and Miss Furr and Miss Skeene sat with them, and there were other men who were not dark men and they sat with Miss Furr and Miss Skeene and Miss Furr and Miss Skeene sat with them. Miss Furr and Miss Skeene went with them and they went with Miss Furr and Miss Skeene, some who were not heavy men, some who were not dark men. Miss Furr and Miss Skeene sat regularly, then sat with some men. Miss Furr and Miss

Skeene went and there were some men with them. There were men and Miss Furr and Miss Skeene went with them, went somewhere with them, went with some of them.

Helen Furr and Georgine Skeene were regularly living where very many were living and cultivating in themselves something. Helen Furr and Georgine Skeene were living very regularly then, being very regular then in being gay then. They did then learn many ways to be gay and they were then being gay quite regular in being gay, being gay and they were learning little things, little things in ways of being gay, they were very regular then, they were learning very many little things in ways of being gay, they were being gay and using these little things they were learning to have to be gay with regularly gay with then and they were gay the same amount they had been gay. They were quite gay, they were quite regular, they were learning little things, gay little things, they were gay inside them and the same amount they had been gay, they were gay the same length of time they had been gay every day.

They were regular in being gay, they learned little things that are things in being gay, they learned many little things that are things in being gay, they were gay every day, they were regular, they were gay, they were gay the same length of time every day, they were gay, they were quite regularly gay.

Georgine Skeene went away to stay two months with her brother. Helen Furr did not go then to stay with her father and her mother. Helen Furr stayed there where they had been regularly living the two of them and she would then certainly not be lonesome, she would go on being gay. She did go on being gay. She was not any more gay but she was gay longer every day than they had been being gay when they were together being gay. She was gay then quite exactly the same way. She learned a few more little ways of being in being gay. She was quite gay and in the same way, the same way she had been gay and she was gay a little longer in the day, more of each day she was gay. She was gay longer every day than when the two of them had been being gay. She was gay quite in the way they had been gay, quite in the same way.

She was not lonesome then, she was not at all feeling any need of having Georgine Skeene. She was not astonished at this thing. She would have been a little astonished by this thing but she knew she was not astonished at anything and so she was not astonished at this thing not astonished at not feeling any need of having Georgine Skeene.

Helen Furr had quite a completely pleasant voice and it was quite well enough cultivated and she could use it and she did use it but then there was not any way of working at cultivating a completely pleasant voice when it has become a quite completely well enough cultivated one, and there was not much use in using it when one was not wanting it to be helping to make one a gay one. Helen Furr was not needing using her voice to be a gay one. She was gay then and sometimes she used her voice and she was not using it very often. It was quite completely enough cultivated and it was quite completely a pleasant one and she did not use it very often. She was then, she was quite exactly as gay as she had been, she was gay a little longer in the day than she had been.

She was gay exactly the same way. She was never tired of being gay that way. She had learned very many little ways to use in being gay. Very many were telling about using other ways in being gay. She was gay enough, she was always gay exactly the same way, she was always learning little things to use in being gay, she was telling about using other ways in being gay, she was telling about learning other ways in being gay, she was learning other ways in being gay, she would be using other ways in being gay, she would always be gay in the same way, when Georgine Skeene was there not so long each day as when Georgine Skeene was away.

She came to using many ways in being gay, she came to use every way in being gay. She went on living where many were cultivating something and she was gay, she had used every way to be gay.

They did not live together then Helen Furr and Georgine Skeene. Helen Furr lived there the longer where they had been living regularly together. Then neither of them were living there any longer. Helen Furr was living somewhere else then and telling some about being gay and she was gay then and she was living quite regularly then. She was regularly gay then. She was quite regular in being gay then. She remembered all the little ways of being gay. She used all the little ways of being gay. She was quite regularly gay. She told many then the way of being gay, she taught very many then little ways they could use in being gay. She was living very well, she was gay then, she went on living then, she was regular in being gay, she always was living very well and was gay very well and was telling about little ways one could be learning to use in being gay, and later was telling them quite often, telling them again and again.   [1922]

JEAN TOOMER

Jean Toomer (1894–1967), author of Cane, *generally considered the literary masterpiece of the Harlem or "New Negro" Renaissance of the 1920s, was born in Washington, D.C. When his father deserted his mother soon after his birth, Toomer was raised in the household of his maternal grandfather, Pinckney B. S. Pinchbeck, described in the* Dictionary of American Biography *as "the typical Negro politician of the Reconstruction." A crusader for African American rights, Pinchbeck had served as acting governor of Louisiana before Toomer's birth. In 1890 Pinchbeck had moved his family from New Orleans to Washington, D.C., but he was twice denied a seat in the U.S. Senate because of the claim that he had been fraudulently elected. Toomer formed a close attachment to his grandfather. After brief enrollments at several colleges, Toomer took a job in New York City in 1918 and began to write poetry, fiction, essays, and reviews. Two years later he returned to Washington, D.C., to help nurse his ailing grandfather. There he immersed himself in a study of the conditions of life for blacks in America, believing that the United States could serve as a melting pot transforming all races into one race. As Toomer later wrote in the* Liberator *magazine, "From my own point of view I am naturally and inevitably an American. I have strived for a spiritual fusion analogous to the fact of racial inter-mingling."*

Exhausted by the strain of nursing his grandfather, who was finally hospitalized, Toomer accepted an offer in 1922 to work as the head of a school for African Americans in Sparta, Georgia. There he found what he later said was "the starting point" of his book Cane. *In a later autobiographical sketch, Toomer wrote that his three months in Georgia were a revelation to him:*

> *The setting was crude in a way, but strangely rich and beautiful. . . . There was a valley, the valley of* Cane, *with smoke-wreaths during the day and mist at night. A family of back-country Negroes had only recently moved into a shack not too far away [from where he was living]. They sang. And this was the first time I'd ever heard the folk-songs and spirituals. They were very rich and sad and joyous and beautiful. But I learned that the Negroes of the town objected to them. They called them "shouting." They had victrolas and player-pianos. So, I realized with deep regret, that the spirituals, meeting ridicule, would be certain to die out. . . . And this was the feeling I put into* Cane. Cane *was a swan-song. It was a song of the end.*

Toomer began writing the impressionistic sketches—such as "Blood-Burning Moon"—that made up Cane *while riding the train back to Washington, D.C., to stay with his grandfather, who died a few weeks later. Magazines and journals such as the* Liberator, Broom, *and* Prairie, *which first published "Blood-Burning Moon" (1923), began to accept his work, and his book was published in 1923 to great critical praise. He published one other work,* Essentials *(1931), a privately printed book of aphorisms. Toomer spent the rest of his*

*life in a search for self-realization through Eastern religions and psychoanaly-
sis. He stated that "why people have expected me to write a second and a third
and a fourth book like* Cane *is one of the queer misunderstandings of my life."
The stylistic confidence of works like "Blood-Burning Moon" influenced
younger writers such as Zora Neale Hurston and Langston Hughes.*

RELATED COMMENTARY: *Arna Bontemps, "On Jean Toomer and* Cane,"
page 1320.

Blood-Burning Moon

– 1 –

Up from the skeleton stone walls, up from the rotting floor boards
and the solid hand-hewn beams of oak of the pre-war cotton factory, dusk
came up. Up from the dusk the full moon came. Glowing like a fired pine-
knot, it illumined the great door and soft showered the Negro shanties
aligned along the single street of factory town. The full moon in the great
door was an omen. Negro women improvised songs against its spell.

Louisa sang as she came over the crest of the hill from the white folks'
kitchen. Her skin was the color of oak leaves on young trees in fall. Her
breasts, firm and up-pointed like ripe acorns. And her singing had the low
murmur of winds in fig trees. Bob Stone, younger son of the people she
worked for, loved her. By the way the world reckons things, he had won
her. By measure of that warm glow which came into her mind at thought
of him, he had won her. Tom Burwell, whom the whole town called Big
Boy, also loved her. But working in the fields all day, and far away from her,
gave him no chance to show it. Though often enough of evenings he had
tried to. Somehow, he never got along. Strong as he was with hands upon
the ax or plow, he found it difficult to hold her. Or so he thought. But the
fact was that he held her to factory town more firmly than he thought for.
His black balanced, and pulled against, the white of Stone, when she
thought of them. And her mind was vaguely upon them as she came over
the crest of the hill, coming from the white folks' kitchen. As she sang
softly at the evil face of the full moon.

A strange stir was in her. Indolently, she tried to fix upon Bob or Tom
as the cause of it. To meet Bob in the canebrake, as she was going to do an
hour or so later, was nothing new. And Tom's proposal which she felt on
its way to her could be indefinitely put off. Separately, there was no
unusual significance to either one. But for some reason, they jumbled
when her eyes gazed vacantly at the rising moon. And from the jumble
came the stir that was strangely within her. Her lips trembled. The slow
rhythm of her song grew agitant and restless. Rusty black and tan spotted
hounds, lying in the dark corners of porches or prowling around back

yards, put their noses in the air and caught its tremor. They began plaintively to yelp and howl. Chickens woke up and cackled. Intermittently, all over the countryside dogs barked and roosters crowed as if heralding a weird dawn or some ungodly awakening. The women sang lustily. Their songs were cotton-wads to stop their ears. Louisa came down into factory town and sank wearily upon the step before her home. The moon was rising towards a thick cloud-bank which soon would hide it.

> *Red nigger moon. Sinner!*
> *Blood-burning moon. Sinner!*
> *Come out that fact'ry door.*

– 2 –

Up from the deep dusk of a cleared spot on the edge of the forest a mellow glow arose and spread fan-wise into the low-hanging heavens. And all around the air was heavy with scent of boiling cane. A large pile of cane-stalks lay like ribboned shadows upon the ground. A mule, harnessed to a pole, trudged lazily round and round the pivot of the grinder. Beneath a swaying oil lamp, a Negro alternately whipped out at the mule, and fed cane-stalks to the grinder. A fat boy waddled pails of fresh ground juice between the grinder and the boiling stove. Steam came from the copper boiling pan. The scent of cane came from the copper pan and drenched the forest and the hill that sloped to factory town, beneath its fragrance. It drenched the men in circle seated around the stove. Some of them chewed at the white pulp of stalks, but there was no need for them to, if all they wanted was to taste the cane. One tasted it in factory town. And from factory town one could see the soft haze thrown by the glowing stove upon the low-hanging heavens.

Old David Georgia stirred the thickening syrup with a long ladle, and ever so often drew it off. Old David Georgia tended his stove and told tales about the white folks, about moon-shining and cotton picking, and about sweet nigger gals, to the men who sat there about his stove to listen to him. Tom Burwell chewed cane-stalk and laughed with the others till someone mentioned Louisa. Till some one said something about Louisa and Bob Stone, about the silk stockings she must have gotten from him. Blood ran up Tom's neck hotter than the glow that flooded from the stove. He sprang up. Glared at the men and said, "She's my gal." Will Manning laughed. Tom strode over to him. Yanked him up and knocked him to the ground. Several of Manning's friends got up to fight for him. Tom whipped out a long knife and would have cut them to shreds if they hadnt ducked into the woods. Tom had had enough. He nodded to Old David Georgia and swung down the path to factory town. Just then, the dogs started barking and the roosters began to crow. Tom felt funny. Away from the fight, away from the stove, chill got to him. He shivered. He shuddered when he saw the full moon rising towards the cloud-bank. He who didnt give a godam for the fears of old women. He forced his mind to fasten on Louisa. Bob Stone. Better not be. He turned into the street and saw Louisa sitting before her home. He went towards her, ambling, touched the brim of a marvelously shaped, spotted, felt hat, said he wanted to say something to her, and then found that he didnt know what he had to say, or if he did, that he couldnt say it. He shoved his big fists in his overalls, grinned, and started to move off.

"Youall want me, Tom?"

"Thats what us wants, sho, Louisa."

"Well, here I am—"

"An here I is, but that aint ahelpin none, all th same."

"You wanted to say something? . . ."

"I did that, sho. But words is like the spots on dice: no matter how y fumbles em, there's times when they jes wont come. I dunno why. Seems like th love I feels fo yo done stole'm tongue. I got it now. Whee! Louisa, honey, I oughtnt tell y, I feel I oughtnt cause yo is young an goes t church an I has had other gals, but Louisa I sho do love y. Lil gal, Ise watched y from them first days when youall sat right here befo yo door befo th well an sang sometimes in a way that like t broke m heart. Ise carried y with me into th fields, day after day, an after that, an I sho can plow when yo is there, an I can pick cotton. Yassur! Come near beatin Barlo yesterday. I sho did. Yassur! And next year if ole Stone'll trust me, I'll have a farm. My own. My bales will buy yo what y gets from white folks now. Silk stockings an purple dresses—course I dont believe what some folks been whisperin as t how y gets them things now. White folks always did do for niggers what they likes. An they jes cant help alikin yo, Louisa. Bob Stone likes y. Course he does. But not th way folks is awhisperin. Does he, hon?"

"I dont know what you mean, Tom."

"Course y dont. Ise already cut two niggers. Had t hon, t tell em so. Niggers always tryin t make somethin out a nothin. An then besides, white folks aint up t them tricks so much nowadays. Godam better not be. Least-awise not with yo. Cause I wouldnt stand f it. Nassur."

"What would you do, Tom?"

"Cut him just like I cut a nigger."

"No, Tom—"

"I said I would and there aint no mo to it. But that aint th talk f now. Sing, honey Louisa, an while I'm listenin t y I'll be makin love."

Tom took her hand in his. Against the tough thickness of his own, hers felt soft and small. His huge body slipped down to the step beside her. The full moon sank upward into the deep purple of the cloud-bank. An old woman brought a lighted lamp and hung it on the common well whose bulk shadow squatted in the middle of the road, opposite Tom and Louisa. The old woman lifted the well-lid, took hold the chain, and began drawing up the heavy bucket. As she did so, she sang. Figures shifted, restless-like, between lamp and window in the front rooms of the shanties.

Shadows of the figures fought each other on the gray dust of the road. Figures raised the windows and joined the old woman in song. Louisa and Tom, the whole street, singing:

> *Red nigger moon. Sinner!*
> *Blood-burning moon. Sinner!*
> *Come out that fact'ry door.*

– 3 –

Bob Stone sauntered from his veranda out into the gloom of fir trees and magnolias. The clear white of his skin paled, and the flush of his cheeks turned purple. As if to balance this outer change, his mind became consciously a white man's. He passed the house with its huge open hearth which, in the days of slavery, was the plantation cookery. He saw Louisa bent over the hearth. He went in as a master should and took her. Direct, honest, bold. None of this sneaking that he had to go through now. The contrast was repulsive to him. His family had lost ground. Hell no, his family still owned the niggers, practically. Damned if they did, or he wouldnt have to duck around so. What would they think if they knew? His mother? His sister? He shouldnt mention them, shouldnt think of them in this connection. There in the dusk he blushed at doing so. Fellows about town were all right, but how about his friends up North? He could see them incredible, repulsed. They didnt know. The thought first made him laugh. Then, with their eyes still upon him, he began to feel embarrassed. He felt the need of explaining things to them. Explain hell. They wouldnt understand, and moreover, who ever heard of a Southerner getting on his knees to any Yankee, or anyone. No sir. He was going to see Louisa to-night, and love her. She was lovely—in her way. Nigger way. What way was that? Damned if he knew. Must know. He'd known her long enough to know. Was there something about niggers that you couldnt know? Listening to them at church didnt tell you anything. Looking at them didnt tell you anything. Talking to them didnt tell you anything—unless it was gossip, unless they wanted to talk. Of course, about farming, and licker, and craps—but those werent nigger. Nigger was something more. How much more? Something to be afraid of, more? Hell no. Who ever heard of being afraid of a nigger? Tom Burwell. Cartwell had told him that Tom went with Louisa after she reached home. No sir. No nigger had ever been with his girl. He'd like to see one try. Some position for him to be in. Him, Bob Stone, of the old Stone family, in a scrap with a nigger over a nigger girl. In the good old days . . . Ha! Those were the days. His family had lost ground. Not so much, though. Enough for him to have to cut through old Lemon's canefield by way of the woods, that he might meet her. She was worth it. Beautiful nigger gal. Why nigger? Why not, just gal? No, it was because she was nigger that he went to her. Sweet . . . The scent of boiling cane came to him. Then he saw the rich glow of the stove. He heard the voices of the men circled around it. He was about to skirt the clearing when he heard his own name mentioned. He stopped. Quivering. Leaning against a tree, he listened.

"Bad nigger. Yassur, he sho is one bad nigger when he gets started."

"Tom Burwell's been on th gang three times fo cuttin men."

"What y think he's agwine t do t Bob Stone?"

"Dunno yet. He aint found out. When he does — Baby!"

"Aint no tellin."

"Young Stone aint no quitter and I ken tell y that. Blood of th old uns in his veins."

"Thats right. He'll scrap, sho."

"Be gettin too hot f niggers round this away."

"Shut up, nigger. Y dont know what y talkin bout."

Bob Stone's ears burned as though he had been holding them over the stove. Sizzling heat welled up within him. His feet felt as if they rested on red-hot coals. They stung him to quick movement. He circled the fringe of the glowing. Not a twig cracked beneath his feet. He reached the path that led to factory town. Plunged furiously down it. Halfway along, a blindness within him veered him aside. He crashed into the bordering canebrake. Cane leaves cut his face and lips. He tasted blood. He threw himself down and dug his fingers in the ground. The earth was cool. Cane-roots took the fever from his hands. After a long while, or so it seemed to him, the thought came to him that it must be time to see Louisa. He got to his feet and walked calmly to their meeting place. No Louisa. Tom Burwell had her. Veins in his forehead bulged and distended. Saliva moistened the dried blood on his lips. He bit down on his lips. He tasted blood. Not his own blood; Tom Burwell's blood. Bob drove through the cane and out again upon the road. A hound swung down the path before him towards factory town. Bob couldnt see it. The dog loped aside to let him pass. Bob's blind rushing made him stumble over it. He fell with a thud that dazed him. The hound yelped. Answering yelps came from all over the countryside. Chickens cackled. Roosters crowed, heralding the blood-shot eyes of southern awakening. Singers in the town were silenced. They shut their windows down. Palpitant between the rooster crows, a chill hush settled upon the huddled forms of Tom and Louisa. A figure rushed from the shadow and stood before them. Tom popped to his feet.

"Whats y want?"

"I'm Bob Stone."

"Yassur — an I'm Tom Burwell. Whats y want?"

Bob lunged at him. Tom side-stepped, caught him by the shoulder, and flung him to the ground. Straddled him.

"Let me up."

"Yassur — but watch yo doins, Bob Stone."

A few dark figures, drawn by the sound of scuffle, stood about them. Bob sprang to his feet.

"Fight like a man, Tom Burwell, and I'll lick y."

Again he lunged. Tom side-stepped and flung him to the ground. Straddled him.

"Get off me, you godam nigger you."

"Yo sho has started somethin now. Get up."

Tom yanked him up and began hammering at him. Each blow sounded as if it smashed into a precious, irreplaceable soft something. Beneath them, Bob staggered back. He reached in his pocket and whipped out a knife.

"That my game, sho."

Blue flash, a steel blade slashed across Bob Stone's throat. He had a sweetish sick feeling. Blood began to flow. Then he felt a sharp twitch of pain. He let his knife drop. He slapped one hand against his neck. He pressed the other on top of his head as if to hold it down. He groaned. He turned, and staggered towards the crest of the hill in the direction of white town. Negroes who had seen the fight slunk into their homes and blew the lamps out. Louisa, dazed, hysterical, refused to go indoors. She slipped, crumbled, her body loosely propped against the woodwork of the well. Tom Burwell leaned against it. He seemed rooted there.

Bob reached Broad Street. White men rushed up to him. He collapsed in their arms.

"Tom Burwell. . . ."

White men like ants upon a forage rushed about. Except for the taut hum of their moving, all was silent. Shotguns, revolvers, rope, kerosene, torches. Two high-powered cars with glaring search-lights. They came together. The taut hum rose to a low roar. Then nothing could be heard but the flop of their feet in the thick dust of the roar. The moving body of their silence preceded them over the crest of the hill into factory town. It flattened the Negroes beneath it. It rolled to the wall of the factory, where it stopped. Tom knew that they were coming. He couldnt move. And then he saw the search-lights of the two cars glaring down on him. A quick shock went through him. He stiffened. He started to run. A yell went up from the mob. Tom wheeled about and faced them. They poured down on him. They swarmed. A large man with dead-white face and flabby cheeks came to him and almost jabbed a gun-barrel through his guts.

"Hands behind y, nigger."

Tom's wrists were bound. The big man shoved him to the well. Burn him over it, and when the woodwork caved in, his body would drop to the bottom. Two deaths for a godam nigger. Louisa was driven back. The mob pushed in. Its pressure, its momentum was too great. Drag him to the factory. Wood and stakes already there. Tom moved in the direction indicated. But they had to drag him. They reached the great door. Too many to get in there. The mob divided and flowed around the walls to either side. The big man shoved him through the door. The mob pressed in from the sides. Taut humming. No words. A stake was sunk into the ground. Rotting floor boards piled around it. Kerosene poured on the rotting floor boards. Tom bound to the stake. His breast was bare. Nails scratches let little lines of blood trickle down and mat into the hair. His face, his eyes were set and stony. Except for irregular breathing, one would have thought him already dead. Torches were flung onto the pile. A great flare muffled in black smoke shot upward. The mob yelled. The mob was silent. Now Tom could be seen within the flames. Only his head, erect, lean, like a blackened stone. Stench of burning flesh soaked the air. Tom's eyes popped. His head settled downward. The mob yelled. Its yell echoed against the skeleton stone walls and sounded like a hundred yells. Like a hundred mobs yelling. Its yell thudded against the thick front wall and fell back. Ghost of a yell slipped through the flames and out the great door of the factory. It fluttered like a dying thing down the single street of factory town. Louisa, upon the step before her home, did not hear it, but her eyes opened slowly. They saw the full moon glowing in the great door. The full moon, an evil thing, an omen, soft showering the homes of folks she knew. Where were they, these people? She'd sing, and perhaps they'd come out and join her. Perhaps Tom Burwell would come. At any rate, the full moon in the great door was an omen which she must sing to:

> *Red nigger moon. Sinner!*
> *Blood-burning moon. Sinner!*
> *Come out that fact'ry door.*   [1923]

ERNEST HEMINGWAY

*E*rnest Hemingway (1898–1961) was born in Oak Park, Illinois, but he spent most of his boyhood in Michigan, where his father, a doctor, encouraged his enthusiasm for camping and hunting. Active as a reporter for his high school newspaper, Hemingway decided not to go on to college. Instead he worked as a reporter on the Kansas City Star for a few months before volunteering to serve in an American ambulance unit in France during World War I. Then he went to Italy, served at the front, and was severely wounded in action just before his nineteenth birthday. After the war he was too restless to settle down in the United States, so he lived in Paris and supported himself and his wife as a newspaper correspondent. He worked hard at learning how to write fiction; as he later said, "I found the greatest difficulty, aside from knowing what you really felt, rather than what you were supposed to feel, or had been taught to feel, was to put down what really happened in action: what the actual things were which produced the emotion that you experienced."

In America, Hemingway had admired the work of Sherwood Anderson, especially the colloquial, "unliterary" tone of his stories, and in Paris he came under the influence of Gertrude Stein, telling Anderson in a letter of 1922 that "Gertrude Stein and me are just like brothers." "Soldier's Home" first appeared in an anthology, the Contact Collection of Contemporary Writers, published in Paris in 1925. For his first collection of stories, In Our Time (1925), Hemingway juxtaposed a group of fragmented sketches with short stories to suggest the devastation of World War I. In the middle of that book, before the story "Soldier's Home," for example, he placed what he called "Chapter VII," 135 words printed in italics, beginning:

> While the bombardment was knocking the trench to pieces at Fossalta, he lay very flat and sweated and prayed oh jesus christ get me out of here. Dear jesus please get me out. Christ please please please christ. If you'll only keep me from getting killed I'll do anything you say. I believe in you and I'll tell every one in the world that you are the only one that matters. Please please dear jesus. The shelling moved further up the line. . . .

Hemingway's early novels, The Sun Also Rises (1926) and A Farewell to Arms (1929), established him as a master stylist, probably the most influential writer of American prose in the first half of the twentieth century. In 1938 he collected what he considered his best short fiction, forty-nine stories. After publication of The Old Man and the Sea, he was awarded the Nobel Prize for literature in 1954. Seven years later, in poor health and haunted by the memory of the suicide of his father, who had shot himself with a Civil War pistol in 1929, Hemingway killed himself with a shotgun in his Idaho hunting lodge.

Hemingway once explained how he achieved the intense compression of his literary style by comparing his method to the principle of the iceberg: "There is seven-eighths of it under water for every part that shows. Anything *you know you can eliminate and it only strengthens your iceberg. It is the part that doesn't show. If a writer omits something because he does not know it then there is a hole in the story."* The most authoritative collection of Hemingway's stories, The Complete Short Stories of Ernest Hemingway: The Finca-Vigia Edition, *was published in 1991.*

RELATED COMMENTARY: *H. E. Bates, "Hemingway's Short Stories," page 1313.*

Soldier's Home

Krebs went to the war from a Methodist college in Kansas. There is a picture which shows him among his fraternity brothers, all of them wearing exactly the same height and style collar. He enlisted in the Marines in 1917 and did not return to the United States until the second division returned from the Rhine in the summer of 1919.

There is a picture which shows him on the Rhine with two German girls and another corporal. Krebs and the corporal look too big for their uniforms. The German girls are not beautiful. The Rhine does not show in the picture.

By the time Krebs returned to his home town in Oklahoma the greeting of heroes was over. He came back much too late. The men from the town who had been drafted had all been welcomed elaborately on their return. There had been a great deal of hysteria. Now the reaction had set in. People seemed to think it was rather ridiculous for Krebs to be getting back so late, years after the war was over.

At first Krebs, who had been at Belleau Wood, Soissons, the Champagne, St. Mihiel and in the Argonne did not want to talk about the war at all. Later he felt the need to talk but no one wanted to hear about it. His town had heard too many atrocity stories to be thrilled by actualities. Krebs found that to be listened to at all he had to lie, and after he had done this twice he, too, had a reaction against the war and against talking about it. A distaste for everything that had happened to him in the war set in because of the lies he had told. All of the times that had been able to make him feel cool and clear inside himself when he thought of them; the times so long back when he had done the one thing, the only thing for a man to do, easily and naturally, when he might have done something else, now lost their cool, valuable quality and then were lost themselves.

His lies were quite unimportant lies and consisted in attributing to himself things other men had seen, done, or heard of, and stating as facts certain apocryphal incidents familiar to all soldiers. Even his lies were not sensational at the pool room. His acquaintances, who had heard detailed accounts of German women found chained to machine guns in the

Argonne forest and who could not comprehend, or were barred by their patriotism from interest in, any German machine gunners who were not chained, were not thrilled by his stories.

Krebs acquired the nausea in regard to experience that is the result of untruth or exaggeration, and when he occasionally met another man who had really been a soldier and they talked a few minutes in the dressing room at a dance he fell into the easy pose of the old soldier among other soldiers: that he had been badly, sickeningly frightened all the time. In this way he lost everything.

During this time, it was late summer, he was sleeping late in bed, getting up to walk down town to the library to get a book, eating lunch at home, reading on the front porch until he became bored and then walking down through the town to spend the hottest hours of the day in the cool dark of the pool room. He loved to play pool.

In the evening he practised on his clarinet, strolled down town, read and went to bed. He was still a hero to his two young sisters. His mother would have given him breakfast in bed if he had wanted it. She often came in when he was in bed and asked him to tell her about the war, but her attention always wandered. His father was non-committal.

Before Krebs went away to the war he had never been allowed to drive the family motor car. His father was in the real estate business and always wanted the car to be at his command when he required it to take clients out into the country to show them a piece of farm property. The car always stood outside the First National Bank building where his father had an office on the second floor. Now, after the war, it was still the same car.

Nothing was changed in the town except that the young girls had grown up. But they lived in such a complicated world of already defined alliances and shifting feuds that Krebs did not feel the energy or the courage to break into it. He liked to look at them, though. There were so many good-looking young girls. Most of them had their hair cut short. When he went away only little girls wore their hair like that or girls that were fast. They all wore sweaters and shirt waists with round Dutch collars. It was a pattern. He liked to look at them from the front porch as they walked on the other side of the street. He liked to watch them walking under the shade of the trees. He liked the round Dutch collars above their sweaters. He liked their silk stockings and flat shoes. He liked their bobbed hair and the way they walked.

When he was in town their appeal to him was not very strong. He did not like them when he saw them in the Greek's ice cream parlor. He did not want them themselves really. They were too complicated. There was something else. Vaguely he wanted a girl but he did not want to have to work to get her. He would have liked to have a girl but he did not want to have to spend a long time getting her. He did not want to get into the intrigue and the politics. He did not want to have to do any courting. He did not want to tell any more lies. It wasn't worth it.

He did not want any consequences. He did not want any consequences ever again. He wanted to live along without consequences. Besides he did not really need a girl. The army had taught him that. It was all right to pose as though you had to have a girl. Nearly everybody did that. But it wasn't true. You did not need a girl. That was the funny thing. First a fellow boasted how girls mean nothing to him, that he never thought of them, that they could not touch him. Then a fellow boasted that he could not get along without girls, that he had to have them all the time, that he could not go to sleep without them.

That was all a lie. It was all a lie both ways. You did not need a girl unless you thought about them. He learned that in the army. Then sooner or later you always got one. When you were really ripe for a girl you always got one. You did not have to think about it. Sooner or later it would come. He had learned that in the army.

Now he would have liked a girl if she had come to him and not wanted to talk. But here at home it was all too complicated. He knew he could never get through it all again. It was not worth the trouble. That was the thing about French girls and German girls. There was not all this talking. You couldn't talk much and you did not need to talk. It was simple and you were friends. He thought about France and then he began to think about Germany. On the whole he had liked Germany better. He did not want to leave Germany. He did not want to come home. Still, he had come home. He sat on the front porch.

He liked the girls that were walking along the other side of the street. He liked the look of them much better than the French girls or the German girls. But the world they were in was not the world he was in. He would like to have one of them. But it was not worth it. They were such a nice pattern. He liked the pattern. It was exciting. But he would not go through all the talking. He did not want one badly enough. He liked to look at them all, though. It was not worth it. Not now when things were getting good again.

He sat there on the porch reading a book on the war. It was a history and he was reading about all the engagements he had been in. It was the most interesting reading he had ever done. He wished there were more maps. He looked forward with a good feeling to reading all the really good histories when they would come out with good detail maps. Now he was really learning about the war. He had been a good soldier. That made a difference.

One morning after he had been home about a month his mother came into his bedroom and sat on the bed. She smoothed her apron.

"I had a talk with your father last night, Harold," she said, "and he is willing for you to take the car out in the evenings."

"Yeah?" said Krebs, who was not fully awake. "Take the car out? Yeah?"

"Yes. Your father has felt for some time that you should be able to take the car out in the evenings whenever you wished but we only talked it over last night."

"I'll bet you made him," Krebs said.

"No. It was your father's suggestion that we talk the matter over."

"Yeah. I'll bet you made him," Krebs sat up in bed.

"Will you come down to breakfast, Harold?" his mother said.

"As soon as I get my clothes on," Krebs said.

His mother went out of the room and he could hear her frying something downstairs while he washed, shaved and dressed to go down into the dining-room for breakfast. While he was eating breakfast his sister brought in the mail.

"Well, Hare," she said. "You old sleepy-head. What do you ever get up for?"

Krebs looked at her. He liked her. She was his best sister.

"Have you got the paper?" he asked.

She handed him *The Kansas City Star* and he shucked off its brown wrapper and opened it to the sporting page. He folded *The Star* open and propped it against the water pitcher with his cereal dish to steady it, so he could read while he ate.

"Harold," his mother stood in the kitchen doorway, "Harold, please don't muss up the paper. Your father can't read his *Star* if it's been mussed."

"I won't muss it," Krebs said.

His sister sat down at the table and watched him while he read.

"We're playing indoor over at school this afternoon," she said. "I'm going to pitch."

"Good," said Krebs. "How's the old wing?"

"I can pitch better than lots of the boys. I tell them all you taught me. The other girls aren't much good."

"Yeah?" said Krebs.

"I tell them all you're my beau. Aren't you my beau, Hare?"

"You bet."

"Couldn't your brother really be your beau just because he's your brother?"

"I don't know."

"Sure you know. Couldn't you be my beau, Hare, if I was old enough and if you wanted to?"

"Sure. You're my girl now."

"Am I really your girl?"

"Sure."

"Do you love me?"

"Uh, huh."

"Will you love me always?"

"Sure."

"Will you come over and watch me play indoor?"

"Maybe."

"Aw, Hare, you don't love me. If you loved me, you'd want to come over and watch me play indoor."

Krebs's mother came into the dining-room from the kitchen. She carried a plate with two fried eggs and some crisp bacon on it and a plate of buckwheat cakes.

"You run along, Helen," she said. "I want to talk to Harold."

She put the eggs and bacon down in front of him and brought in a jug of maple syrup for the buckwheat cakes. Then she sat down across the table from Krebs.

"I wish you'd put down the paper a minute, Harold," she said.

Krebs took down the paper and folded it.

"Have you decided what you are going to do yet, Harold?" his mother said, taking off her glasses.

"No," said Krebs.

"Don't you think it's about time?" His mother did not say this in a mean way. She seemed worried.

"I hadn't thought about it," Krebs said.

"God has some work for every one to do," his mother said. "There can be no idle hands in His Kingdom."

"I'm not in His Kingdom," Krebs said.

"We are all of us in His Kingdom."

Krebs felt embarrassed and resentful as always.

"I've worried about you so much, Harold," his mother went on. "I know the temptations you must have been exposed to. I know how weak men are. I know what your own dear grandfather, my own father, told us about the Civil War and I have prayed for you. I pray for you all day long, Harold."

Krebs looked at the bacon fat hardening on his plate.

"Your father is worried, too," his mother went on. "He thinks you have lost your ambition, that you haven't got a definite aim in life. Charley Simmons, who is just your age, has a good job and is going to be married. The boys are all settling down; they're all determined to get somewhere; you can see that boys like Charley Simmons are on their way to being really a credit to the community."

Krebs said nothing.

"Don't look that way, Harold," his mother said. "You know we love you and I want to tell you for your own good how matters stand. Your father does not want to hamper your freedom. He thinks you should be allowed to drive the car. If you want to take some of the nice girls out riding with you, we are only too pleased. We want you to enjoy yourself. But you are going to have to settle down to work, Harold. Your father doesn't care what you start in at. All work is honorable as he says. But you've got to make a start at something. He asked me to speak to you this morning and then you can stop in and see him at his office."

"Is that all?" Krebs said.

"Yes. Don't you love your mother, dear boy?"

"No," Krebs said.

His mother looked at him across the table. Her eyes were shiny. She started crying.

"I don't love anybody," Krebs said.

It wasn't any good. He couldn't tell her, he couldn't make her see it. It was silly to have said it. He had only hurt her. He went over and took hold of her arm. She was crying with her head in her hands.

"I didn't mean it," he said. "I was just angry at something. I didn't mean I didn't love you."

His mother went on crying. Krebs put his arm on her shoulder.

"Can't you believe me, mother?"

His mother shook her head.

"Please, please, mother. Please believe me."

"All right," his mother said chokily. She looked up at him. "I believe you, Harold."

Krebs kissed her hair. She put her face up to him.

"I'm your mother," she said. "I held you next to my heart when you were a tiny baby."

Krebs felt sick and vaguely nauseated.

"I know, Mummy," he said. "I'll try and be a good boy for you."

"Would you kneel and pray with me, Harold?" his mother asked.

They knelt down beside the dining-room table and Krebs's mother prayed.

"Now, you pray, Harold," she said.

"I can't," Krebs said.

"Try, Harold."

"I can't."

"Do you want me to pray for you?"

"Yes."

So his mother prayed for him and then they stood up and Krebs kissed his mother and went out of the house. He had tried so to keep his life from being complicated. Still, none of it had touched him. He had felt sorry for his mother and she had made him lie. He would go to Kansas City and get a job and she would feel all right about it. There would be one more scene maybe before he got away. He would not go down to his father's office. He would miss that one. He wanted his life to go smoothly. It had just gotten going that way. Well, that was all over now, anyway. He would go over to the schoolyard and watch Helen play indoor baseball.   [1925]

KATHERINE ANNE PORTER

*K*atherine Anne Porter (1890–1980) was born Callie Russell Porter in Indian Creek, Texas. When she was only two years old her mother died. Educated at boarding schools and an Ursuline convent, Porter worked briefly as a reporter in Chicago and Denver. As a child she had wanted to be a writer, but it took fifteen years of serious writing before she trusted herself enough as a stylist to approach a publisher. Most of her life during this time was a financial struggle; she spent only 10 percent of her energies on writing, and "the other 90 percent went to keeping my head above water." She nearly lost her life in the influenza epidemic that swept the United States at the end of World War I, and when she recovered she went to Mexico to study Aztec and Mayan art.

Porter achieved acclaim in 1930 with her first collection of short stories, Flowering Judas and Other Stories, which included "He," first published in 1927 in New Masses. Her most productive decade as a writer was the 1930s, when she published Noon Wine (1937) and Pale Horse, Pale Rider: Three Short Novels (1939). She supported herself with lecture tours and teaching jobs at various universities while she worked on her novel Ship of Fools (1962), which took over two decades to complete. In 1965 her Collected Stories won both the Pulitzer Prize and the National Book Award.

Porter's style is not so recognizably "southern" as William Faulkner's or Flannery O'Connor's. She was a southerner by tradition and inheritance, but she had thought of herself since childhood as "always restless, always a roving spirit." She was very conscious of her own art as a storyteller, and of the art of fiction in general; she wrote personal essays on Willa Cather, Flannery O'Connor, and Eudora Welty, among others. Particularly indebted in her best stories to the English writer Katherine Mansfield, Porter attempted to dramatize a character's state of mind rather than develop a complicated plot. Her analysis of Mansfield's literary practice in the essay "The Art of Katherine Mansfield" can also be applied to a story such as "He":

> With fine objectivity, she bares a moment of experience, real experience, in the life of some one human being; she states no belief, gives no motives, airs no theories, but simply presents to the reader a situation, a place, and a character, and there it is; and the emotional content is present as implicitly as the germ is in the grain of wheat.

He

Life was very hard for the Whipples. It was hard to feed all the hungry mouths, it was hard to keep the children in flannels during the winter, short as it was: "God knows what would become of us if we lived north," they would say: keeping them decently clean was hard. "It looks like our luck won't never let up on us," said Mr. Whipple, but Mrs. Whipple was all for taking what was sent and calling it good, anyhow when the neighbors were in earshot. "Don't ever let a soul hear us complain," she kept saying to her husband. She couldn't stand to be pitied. "No, not if it comes to it that we have to live in a wagon and pick cotton around the country," she said, "nobody's going to get a chance to look down on us."

Mrs. Whipple loved her second son, the simple-minded one, better than she loved the other two children put together. She was forever saying so, and when she talked with certain of her neighbors, she would even throw in her husband and her mother for good measure.

"You needn't keep on saying it around," said Mr. Whipple, "you'll make people think nobody else has any feelings about Him but you."

"It's natural for a mother," Mrs. Whipple would remind him. "You know yourself it's more natural for a mother to be that way. People don't expect so much of fathers, some way."

This didn't keep the neighbors from talking plainly among themselves. "A Lord's pure mercy if He should die," they said. "It's the sins of the fathers," they agreed among themselves. "There's bad blood and bad doings somewhere, you can bet on that." This behind the Whipples' back. To their faces everybody said, "He's not so bad off. He'll be all right yet. Look how He grows!"

Mrs. Whipple hated to talk about it, she tried to keep her mind off it, but every time anybody set foot in the house, the subject always came up, and she had to talk about Him first, before she could get on to anything else. It seemed to ease her mind. "I wouldn't have anything happen to Him for all the world, but it just looks like I can't keep Him out of mischief. He's so strong and active, He's always into everything; He was like that since He could walk. It's actually funny sometimes, the way He can do anything; it's laughable to see Him up to His tricks. Emly has more accidents; I'm forever tying up her bruises, and Adna can't fall a foot without cracking a bone. But He can do anything and not get a scratch. The preacher said such a nice thing once when he was here. He said, and I'll remember it to my dying day, 'The innocent walk with God—that's why He don't get hurt.'" Whenever Mrs. Whipple repeated these words, she always felt a warm pool spread in her breast, and the tears would fill her eyes, and then she could talk about something else.

He did grow and He never got hurt. A plank blew off the chicken house and struck Him on the head and He never seemed to know it. He had learned a few words, and after this He forgot them. He didn't whine for food as the other children did, but waited until it was given Him; He ate squatting in the corner, smacking and mumbling. Rolls of fat covered Him like an overcoat, and He could carry twice as much wood and water as Adna. Emly had a cold in the head most of the time—"she takes that after me," said Mrs. Whipple—so in bad weather they gave her the extra blanket off His cot. He never seemed to mind the cold.

Just the same, Mrs. Whipple's life was a torment for fear something might happen to Him. He climbed the peach trees much better than Adna and went skittering along the branches like a monkey, just a regular monkey. "Oh, Mrs. Whipple, you hadn't ought to let Him do that. He'll lose His balance sometime. He can't rightly know what He's doing."

Mrs. Whipple almost screamed out at the neighbor. "He *does* know what He's doing! He's as able as any other child! Come down out of there, you!" When He finally reached the ground she could hardly keep her hands off Him for acting like that before people, a grin all over His face and her worried sick about Him all the time.

"It's the neighbors," said Mrs. Whipple to her husband. "Oh, I do mortally wish they would keep out of our business. I can't afford to let Him do anything for fear they'll come nosing around about it. Look at the bees, now. Adna can't handle them, they sting him up so; I haven't got time to do everything, and now I don't dare let Him. But if He gets a sting He don't really mind."

"It's just because He ain't got sense enough to be scared of anything," said Mr. Whipple.

"You ought to be ashamed of yourself," said Mrs. Whipple, "talking that way about your own child. Who's to take up for Him if we don't, I'd like to know? He sees a lot that goes on, He listens to things all the time. And anything I tell Him to do He does it. Don't never let anybody hear you say such things. They'd think you favored the other children over Him."

"Well, now I don't, and you know it, and what's the use of getting all worked up about it? You always think the worst of everything. Just let Him alone, He'll get along somehow. He gets plenty to eat and wear, don't He?" Mr. Whipple suddenly felt tired out. "Anyhow, it can't be helped now."

Mrs. Whipple felt tired too, she complained in a tired voice. "What's done can't never be undone, I know that as good as anybody; but He's my child, and I'm not going to have people say anything. I get sick of people coming around saying things all the time."

In the early fall Mrs. Whipple got a letter from her brother saying he and his wife and two children were coming over for a little visit next Sunday week. "Put the big pot in the little one," he wrote at the end. Mrs. Whipple read this part out loud twice, she was so pleased. Her brother was a great one for saying funny things. "We'll just show him that's no joke," she said, "we'll just butcher one of the suckling pigs."

"It's a waste and I don't hold with waste the way we are now," said Mr. Whipple. "That pig'll be worth money by Christmas."

"It's a shame and a pity we can't have a decent meal's vittles once in a while when my own family comes to see us," said Mrs. Whipple. "I'd hate for his wife to go back and say there wasn't a thing in the house to eat. My

God, it's better than buying up a great chance of meat in town. There's where you'd spend the money!"

"All right, do it yourself then," said Mr. Whipple. "Christamighty, no wonder we can't get ahead!"

The question was how to get the little pig away from his ma, a great fighter, worse than a Jersey cow. Adna wouldn't try it: "That sow'd rip my insides out all over the pen." "All right, old fraidy," said Mrs. Whipple, "*He's* not scared. Watch *Him* do it." And she laughed as though it was all a good joke and gave Him a little push towards the pen. He sneaked up and snatched the pig right away from the teat and galloped back and was over the fence with the sow raging at His heels. The little black squirming thing was screeching like a baby in a tantrum, stiffening its back and stretching its mouth to the ears. Mrs. Whipple took the pig with her face stiff and sliced its throat with one stroke. When He saw the blood He gave a great jolting breath and ran away. "But He'll forget and eat plenty, just the same," thought Mrs. Whipple. Whenever she was thinking, her lips moved making words. "He'd eat it all if I didn't stop Him. He'd eat up every mouthful from the other two if I'd let Him."

She felt badly about it. He was ten years old now and a third again as large as Adna, who was going on fourteen. "It's a shame, a shame," she kept saying under her breath, "and Adna with so much brains!"

She kept on feeling badly about all sorts of things. In the first place it was the man's work to butcher; the sight of the pig scraped pink and naked made her sick. He was too fat and soft and pitiful-looking. It was simply a shame the way things had to happen. By the time she had finished it up, she almost wished her brother would stay at home.

Early Sunday morning Mrs. Whipple dropped everything to get Him all cleaned up. In an hour He was dirty again, with crawling under fences after a possum, and straddling along the rafters of the barn looking for eggs in the hayloft. "My Lord, look at you now after all my trying! And here's Adna and Emly staying so quiet. I get tired trying to keep you decent. Get off that shirt and put on another, people will say I don't half dress you!" And she boxed Him on the ears, hard. He blinked and blinked and rubbed His head, and His face hurt Mrs. Whipple's feelings. Her knees began to tremble, she had to sit down while she buttoned His shirt. "I'm just all gone before the day starts."

The brother came with his plump healthy wife and two great roaring hungry boys. They had a grand dinner, with the pig roasted to a crackling in the middle of the table, full of dressing, a pickled peach in his mouth and plenty of gravy for the sweet potatoes.

"This looks like prosperity all right," said the brother; "you're going to have to roll me home like I was a barrel when I'm done."

Everybody laughed out loud; it was fine to hear them laughing all at once around the table. Mrs. Whipple felt warm and good about it. "Oh, we've got six more of these; I say it's as little as we can do when you come to see us so seldom."

He wouldn't come into the dining room, and Mrs. Whipple passed it off very well. "He's timider than my other two," she said, "He'll just have to get used to you. There isn't everybody He'll make up with, you know how it is with some children, even cousins." Nobody said anything out of the way.

"Just like my Alty here," said the brother's wife. "I sometimes got to lick him to make him shake hands with his own grandmammy."

So that was over, and Mrs. Whipple loaded up a big plate for Him first, before everybody. "I always say He ain't to be slighted, no matter who else goes without," she said, and carried it to Him herself.

"He can chin Himself on the top of the door," said Emly, helping along.

"That's fine. He's getting along fine," said the brother.

They went away after supper. Mrs. Whipple rounded up the dishes, and sent the children to bed and sat down and unlaced her shoes. "You see?" she said to Mr. Whipple. "That's the way my whole family is. Nice and considerate about everything. No out-of-the-way remarks—they *have* got refinement. I get awfully sick of people's remarks. Wasn't that pig good?"

Mr. Whipple said, "Yes, we're out three hundred pounds of pork, that's all. It's easy to be polite when you come to eat. Who knows what they had in their minds all along?"

"Yes, that's like you," said Mrs. Whipple. "I don't expect anything else from you. You'll be telling me next that my own brother will be saying around that we made Him eat in the kitchen! Oh, my God!" She rocked her head in her hands, a hard pain started in the very middle of her forehead. "Now it's all spoiled, and everything was so nice and easy. All right, you don't like them and you never did—all right, they'll not come here again soon, never you mind! But they *can't* say He wasn't dressed every lick as good as Adna—oh, honest, sometimes I wish I was dead!"

"I wish you'd let up," said Mr. Whipple. "It's bad enough as it is."

It was a hard winter. It seemed to Mrs. Whipple that they hadn't ever known anything but hard times, and now to cap it all a winter like this. The crops were about half of what they had a right to expect; after the cotton was in it didn't do much more than cover the grocery bill. They swapped off one of the plow horses, and got cheated, for the new one died of the heaves. Mrs. Whipple kept thinking all the time it was terrible to have a man you couldn't depend on not to get cheated. They cut down on everything, but Mrs. Whipple kept saying there are things you can't cut down on, and they cost money. It took a lot of warm clothes for Adna and Emly, who walked four miles to school during the three-months session. "He sets around the fire a lot, He won't need so much," said Mr. Whipple.

"That's so," said Mrs. Whipple, "and when He does the outdoor chores He can wear your tarpaullion coat. I can't do no better, that's all."

In February He was taken sick, and lay curled up under His blanket looking very blue in the face and acting as if He would choke. Mr. and Mrs. Whipple did everything they could for Him for two days, and then they were scared and sent for the doctor. The doctor told them they must keep Him warm and give Him plenty of milk and eggs. "He isn't as stout as He looks, I'm afraid," said the doctor. "You've got to watch them when they're like that. You must put more cover onto Him, too."

"I just took off His big blanket to wash," said Mrs. Whipple, ashamed. "I can't stand dirt."

"Well, you'd better put it back on the minute it's dry," said the doctor, "or He'll have pneumonia."

Mr. and Mrs. Whipple took a blanket off their own bed and put His cot in by the fire. "They can't say we didn't do everything for Him," she said, "even to sleeping cold ourselves on His account."

When the winter broke He seemed to be well again, but He walked as if His feet hurt Him. He was able to run a cotton planter during the season.

"I got it all fixed up with Jim Ferguson about breeding the cow next time," said Mr. Whipple. "I'll pasture the bull this summer and give Jim some fodder in the fall. That's better than paying out money when you haven't got it."

"I hope you didn't say such a thing before Jim Ferguson," said Mrs. Whipple. "You oughtn't to let him know we're so down as all that."

"Godamighty, that ain't saying we're down. A man is got to look ahead sometimes. He can lead the bull over today. I need Adna on the place."

At first Mrs. Whipple felt easy in her mind about sending Him for the bull. Adna was too jumpy and couldn't be trusted. You've got to be steady around animals. After He was gone she started thinking, and after a while she could hardly bear it any longer. She stood in the lane and watched for Him. It was nearly three miles to go and a hot day, but He oughtn't to be so long about it. She shaded her eyes and stared until colored bubbles floated in her eyeballs. It was just like everything else in life, she must always worry and never know a moment's peace about anything. After a long time she saw Him turn into the side lane, limping. He came on very slowly, leading the big hulk of an animal by a ring in the nose, twirling a little stick in His hand, never looking back or sideways, but coming on like a sleepwalker with His eyes half shut.

Mrs. Whipple was scared sick of bulls; she had heard awful stories about how they followed on quietly enough, and then suddenly pitched on with a bellow and pawed and gored a body to pieces. Any second now that black monster would come down on Him, my God, He'd never have sense enough to run.

She mustn't make a sound nor a move; she mustn't get the bull started. The bull heaved his head aside and horned the air at a fly. Her voice burst out of her in a shriek, and she screamed at Him to come on, for God's sake. He didn't seem to hear her clamor, but kept on twirling His switch and limping on, and the bull lumbered along behind him as gently as a calf. Mrs. Whipple stopped calling and ran towards the house, praying under her breath: "Lord, don't let anything happen to Him. Lord, you *know* people will say we oughtn't to have sent Him. You *know* they'll say we didn't take care of Him. Oh, get Him home, safe home, safe home, and I'll look out for Him better! Amen."

She watched from the window while He led the beast in, and tied him up in the barn. It was no use trying to keep up, Mrs. Whipple couldn't bear another thing. She sat down and rocked and cried with her apron over her head.

From year to year the Whipples were growing poorer and poorer. The place just seemed to run down of itself, no matter how hard they worked. "We're losing our hold," said Mrs. Whipple. "Why can't we do like other people and watch for our best chances? They'll be calling us poor white trash next."

"When I get to be sixteen I'm going to leave," said Adna. "I'm going to get a job in Powell's grocery store. There's money in that. No more farm for me."

"I'm going to be a schoolteacher," said Emly. "But I've got to finish the eighth grade, anyhow. Then I can live in town. I don't see any chances here."

"Emly takes after my family," said Mrs. Whipple. "Ambitious every last one of them, and they don't take second place for anybody."

When fall came Emly got a chance to wait on table in the railroad eating-house in the town near by, and it seemed such a shame not to take it when the wages were good and she could get her food too, that Mrs. Whipple decided to let her take it, and not bother with school until the next session. "You've got plenty of time," she said. "You're young and smart as a whip."

With Adna gone too, Mr. Whipple tried to run the farm with just Him to help. He seemed to get along fine, doing His work and part of Adna's without noticing it. They did well enough until Christmas time, when one morning He slipped on the ice coming up from the barn. Instead of getting up He thrashed round and round, and when Mr. Whipple got to Him, He was having some sort of fit.

They brought Him inside and tried to make Him sit up, but He blubbered and rolled, so they put Him to bed and Mr. Whipple rode to town for the doctor. All the way there and back he worried about where the money was to come from: it sure did look like he had about all the troubles he could carry.

From then on He stayed in bed. His legs swelled up double their size, and the fits kept coming back. After four months, the doctor said, "It's no use, I think you'd better put Him in the County Home for treatment right away. I'll see about it for you. He'll have good care there and be off your hands."

"We don't begrudge Him any care, and I won't let Him out of my sight," said Mrs. Whipple. "I won't have it said I sent my sick child off among strangers."

"I know how you feel," said the doctor. "You can't tell me anything about that, Mrs. Whipple. I've got a boy of my own. But you'd better listen to me. I can't do anything more for Him, that's the truth."

Mr. and Mrs. Whipple talked it over a long time that night after they went to bed. "It's just charity," said Mrs. Whipple, "that's what we've come to, charity! I certainly never looked for this."

"We pay taxes to help support the place just like everybody else," said Mr. Whipple, "and I don't call that taking charity. I think it would be fine to have Him where He'd get the best of everything . . . and besides, I can't keep up with these doctor bills any longer."

"Maybe that's why the doctor wants us to send Him — he's scared he won't get his money," said Mrs. Whipple.

"Don't talk like that," said Mr. Whipple, feeling pretty sick, "or we won't be able to send Him."

"Oh, but we won't keep Him there long," said Mrs. Whipple. "Soon's He's better, we'll bring Him right back home."

"The doctor has told you and told you time and again He can't ever get better, and you might as well stop talking," said Mr. Whipple.

"Doctors don't know everything," said Mrs. Whipple, feeling almost happy. "But anyhow, in the summer Emly can come home for a vacation, and Adna can get down for Sundays: we'll all work together and get on our feet again, and the children will feel they've got a place to come to."

All at once she saw it full summer again, with the garden going fine, and new white roller shades up all over the house, and Adna and Emly home, so full of life, all of them happy together. Oh, it could happen, things would ease up on them.

They didn't talk before Him much, but they never knew just how much He understood. Finally the doctor set the day and a neighbor who owned a double-seated carryall offered to drive them over. The hospital would have sent an ambulance, but Mrs. Whipple couldn't stand to see Him going away looking so sick as all that. They wrapped Him in blankets, and the neighbor and Mr. Whipple lifted Him into the back seat of the carryall beside Mrs. Whipple, who had on her black shirt waist. She couldn't stand to go looking like charity.

"You'll be all right, I guess I'll stay behind," said Mr. Whipple. "It don't look like everybody ought to leave the place at once."

"Besides, it ain't as if He was going to stay forever," said Mrs. Whipple to the neighbor. "This is only for a little while."

They started away, Mrs. Whipple holding to the edges of the blankets to keep Him from sagging sideways. He sat there blinking and blinking. He worked His hands out and began rubbing His nose with His knuckles, and then with the end of the blanket. Mrs. Whipple couldn't believe what she saw; He was scrubbing away big tears that pulled out of the corners of His eyes. He sniveled and made a gulping noise. Mrs. Whipple kept saying, "Oh, honey, you don't feel so bad, do you? You don't feel so bad, do you?" for He seemed to be accusing her of something. Maybe He remembered that time she boxed His ears, maybe He had been scared that day with the bull, maybe He had slept cold and couldn't tell her about it; maybe He knew they were sending Him away for good and all because they were too poor to keep Him. Whatever it was, Mrs. Whipple couldn't bear to think of it. She began to cry, frightfully, and wrapped her arms tight around Him. His head rolled on her shoulder: she had loved Him as much as she possibly could, there were Adna and Emly who had to be thought of too, there was nothing she could do to make up to Him for His life. Oh, what a mortal pity He was ever born.

They came in sight of the hospital, with the neighbor driving very fast, not daring to look behind him.   [1927]

DOROTHY PARKER

*D*orothy Parker (1893–1967), once considered the wittiest woman in America, was born Dorothy Rothschild in West End, New Jersey. She chose the word mongrel *to describe her heritage because her father was a wealthy Jewish clothing merchant and her mother was a Scottish schoolteacher who died when Dorothy was young. While a student at the Blessed Sacrament Convent School in New York City, Dorothy was expelled for insisting that the Immaculate Conception was a form of "spontaneous combustion." She went on to Miss Dana's School in Morristown, New Jersey, where she excelled at translating and imitating Latin poets whose specialty was the epigram. After her graduation in 1911 she lived in a Manhattan boardinghouse and wrote poetry, supporting herself by working in a bookstore and playing the piano at night in a dancing school. Four years later she published her first verse in* Vogue *magazine, which hired her to write captions for their fashion illustrations. In 1913 she became a drama critic at* Vanity Fair *and married her first husband, Edwin Pond Parker II, who was from an old Hartford, Connecticut, family. Later she confessed, "I married him to change my name."*

In the 1920s Parker was the only woman member of the Algonquin Round Table, a group of witty New York journalists that included Harold Ross, who founded The New Yorker *in 1925 and hired her to write book reviews for the magazine. Parker began to publish volumes of poetry and then went on in the 1930s to publish three collections of short stories marked by her characteristically acerbic wit:* Lament for the Living *(1930),* After Such Pleasures *(1933), and* Here Lies *(1939). Her support for radical political causes and her membership in the Communist Party in 1934 as well as her reportage of the Loyalist cause in Spain for* New Masses *in 1937 caused her to be blacklisted in 1949. After her second marriage, to the actor Alan Campbell, she worked on screenplays with her husband in Hollywood and reviewed books for* Esquire. *Widowed in 1963, she returned to New York City where she died four years later of a heart attack, leaving her papers to the National Association for the Advancement of Colored People.*

As the critic Thomas Grant observed, in Parker's short stories she "concentrated upon a few characters whose self-absorption hampers or prevents true communication . . . [and] dwelt upon those casual, brief encounters in which apparent harmonies suddenly unravel into discord." Writing was such hard work for Parker that she once quipped, "I can't write five words but that I change seven." In 1944 she made a selection of her poetry and fiction for The Portable Dorothy Parker. *Thirty years later the publisher, Viking, reported that of all the volumes in the series, "only* Shakespeare, The World Bible, *and* Dorothy Parker *have remained continuously in print and selling steadily through time and change." "You Were Perfectly Fine" first appeared in* The New Yorker *in 1929.*

RELATED COMMENTARY: *Dorothy Parker, "The Short Story, through a Couple of the Ages," page 1435.*

You Were Perfectly Fine

The pale young man eased himself carefully into the low chair, and rolled his head to the side, so that the cool chintz comforted his cheek and temple.

"Oh, dear," he said. "Oh, dear, oh, dear, oh, dear. Oh."

The clear-eyed girl, sitting light and erect on the couch, smiled brightly at him.

"Not feeling so well today?" she said.

"Oh, I'm great," he said. "Corking, I am. Know what time I got up? Four o'clock this afternoon, sharp. I kept trying to make it, and every time I took my head off the pillow, it would roll under the bed. This isn't my head I've got on now. I think this is something that used to belong to Walt Whitman. Oh, dear, oh, dear, oh, dear."

"Do you think maybe a drink would make you feel better?" she said.

"The hair of the mastiff that bit me?" he said. "Oh, no, thank you. Please never speak of anything like that again. I'm through. I'm all, all through. Look at that hand; steady as a humming-bird. Tell me, was I very terrible last night?"

"Oh, goodness," she said, "everybody was feeling pretty high. You were all right."

"Yeah," he said. "I must have been dandy. Is everybody sore at me?"

"Good heavens, no," she said. "Everyone thought you were terribly funny. Of course, Jim Pierson was a little stuffy, there, for a minute at dinner. But people sort of held him back in his chair, and got him calmed down. I don't think anybody at the other tables noticed it at all. Hardly anybody."

"He was going to sock me?" he said. "Oh, Lord. What did I do to him?"

"Why, you didn't do a thing," she said. "You were perfectly fine. But you know how silly Jim gets, when he thinks anybody is making too much fuss over Elinor."

"Was I making a pass at Elinor?" he said. "Did I do that?"

"Of course you didn't," she said. "You were only fooling, that's all. She thought you were awfully amusing. She was having a marvelous time. She only got a little tiny bit annoyed just once, when you poured the clam-juice down her back."

"My God," he said. "Clam-juice down that back. And every vertebra a little Cabot.[1] Dear God. What'll I ever do?"

---

[1]Wealthy Boston family.

"Oh, she'll be all right," she said. "Just send her some flowers, or something. Don't worry about it. It isn't anything."

"No, I won't worry," he said. "I haven't got a care in the world. I'm sitting pretty. Oh, dear, oh, dear. Did I do any other fascinating tricks at dinner?"

"You were fine," she said. "Don't be so foolish about it. Everybody was crazy about you. The maître d'hôtel was a little worried because you wouldn't stop singing, but he really didn't mind. All he said was, he was afraid they'd close the place again, if there was so much noise. But he didn't care a bit, himself. I think he loved seeing you have such a good time. Oh, you were just singing away, there, for about an hour. It wasn't so terribly loud, at all."

"So I sang," he said. "That must have been a treat. I sang."

"Don't you remember?" she said. "You just sang one song after another. Everybody in the place was listening. They loved it. Only you kept insisting that you wanted to sing some song about some kind of fusiliers or other, and everybody kept shushing you, and you'd keep trying to start it again. You were wonderful. We were all trying to make you stop singing for a minute, and eat something, but you wouldn't hear of it. My, you were funny."

"Didn't I eat any dinner?" he said.

"Oh, not a thing," she said. "Every time the waiter would offer you something, you'd give it right back to him, because you said that he was your long-lost brother, changed in the cradle by a gypsy band, and that anything you had was his. You had him simply roaring at you."

"I bet I did," he said. "I bet I was comical. Society's Pet, I must have been. And what happened then, after my overwhelming success with the waiter?"

"Why, nothing much," she said. "You took a sort of dislike to some old man with white hair, sitting across the room, because you didn't like his necktie and you wanted to tell him about it. But we got you out, before he got really mad."

"Oh, we got out," he said. "Did I walk?"

"Walk! Of course you did," she said. "You were absolutely all right. There was that nasty stretch of ice on the sidewalk, and you did sit down awfully hard, you poor dear. But good heavens, that might have happened to anybody."

"Oh, sure," he said. "Louisa Alcott or anybody. So I fell down on the sidewalk. That would explain what's the matter with my—Yes. I see. And then what, if you don't mind?"

"Ah, now, Peter!" she said. "You can't sit there and say you don't remember what happened after that! I did think that maybe you were just a little tight at dinner—oh, you were perfectly all right, and all that, but I did know you were feeling pretty gay. But you were so serious, from the time you fell down—I never knew you to be that way. Don't you know, how you told me I had never seen your real self before? Oh, Peter, I just couldn't bear it, if you didn't remember that lovely long ride we took together in the taxi! Please, you do remember that, don't you? I think it would simply kill me, if you didn't."

"Oh, yes," he said. "Riding in the taxi. Oh, yes, sure. Pretty long ride, hmm?"

"Round and round and round the park," she said. "Oh, and the trees were shining so in the moonlight. And you said you never knew before that you really had a soul."

"Yes," he said. "I said that. That was me."

"You said such lovely, lovely things," she said. "And I'd never known, all this time, how you had been feeling about me, and I'd never dared to let you see how I felt about you. And then last night—oh, Peter dear, I think that taxi ride was the most important thing that ever happened to us in our lives."

"Yes," he said. "I guess it must have been."

"And we're going to be so happy," she said. "Oh, I just want to tell everybody! But I don't know—I think maybe it would be sweeter to keep it all to ourselves."

"I think it would be," he said.

"Isn't it lovely?" she said.

"Yes," he said. "Great."

"Lovely!" she said.

"Look here," he said, "do you mind if I have a drink? I mean, just medicinally, you know. I'm off the stuff for life, so help me. But I think I feel a collapse coming on."

"Oh, I think it would do you good," she said. "You poor boy, it's a shame you feel so awful. I'll go make you a whisky and soda."

"Honestly," he said, "I don't see how you could ever want to speak to me again, after I made such a fool of myself, last night. I think I'd better go join a monastery in Tibet."

"You crazy idiot!" she said. "As if I could ever let you go away now! Stop talking like that. You were perfectly fine."

She jumped up from the couch, kissed him quickly on the forehead, and ran out of the room.

The pale young man looked after her and shook his head long and slowly, then dropped it in his damp and trembling hands.

"Oh, dear," he said. "Oh, dear, oh, dear, oh, dear."   [1929]

WILLIAM FAULKNER

*W*illiam *Faulkner (1897–1962) was born in New Albany, Mississippi, into an old southern family. When he was a child, his parents moved to the isolated town of Oxford, Mississippi, and except for his service in World War I and some time in New Orleans and Hollywood, he spent the rest of his life there. "I discovered my own little postage stamp of native soil was worth writing about, and that I would never live long enough to exhaust it." His literary career began in New Orleans, where he lived for six months and wrote newspaper sketches and stories for the* Times-Picayune. *He met Sherwood Anderson in New Orleans, and Anderson helped him publish his first novel,* Soldier's Pay, *in 1926.*

Faulkner's major work was written in the late 1920s and the 1930s, when he created an imaginary county adjacent to Oxford, calling it Yoknapatawpha County and chronicling its history in a series of experimental novels, including The Sound and the Fury *(1929),* As I Lay Dying *(1930),* Sanctuary *(1931),* Light in August *(1932),* Absalom, Absalom! *(1936), and* The Hamlet *(1940). In these works he showed himself to be a writer of genius, although "a willfully and perversely chaotic one," as Jorge Luis Borges noted, whose "labyrinthine world" required a no less labyrinthine prose technique to describe in epic manner the disintegration of the South through many generations. Faulkner was awarded the Nobel Prize for literature in 1952.*

Faulkner's literary style is more experimental in his novels than in his stories, where he rarely included poetic imagery or stream-of-consciousness narration. His biographer Frederick Karl has noted that he used short fiction "as a means of working through, or toward, larger ideas." He wrote nearly a hundred stories, often revising them later to fit as sections into a novel. For example, "Spotted Horses," first published in Scribner's Magazine *in 1930, was reworked as part of* The Hamlet. *Four books of his stories were published in his lifetime, and Faulkner thought of each as a collection possessing a discernible internal organization. He wrote his editor Malcolm Cowley that "even to a collection of short stories, form, integration, is as important as to a novel—an entity of its own, single, set for one pitch, contrapuntal in integration, toward one end, one finale."*

RELATED COMMENTARY: *Eudora Welty, "The Sense of Place in Faulkner's 'Spotted Horses,'" page 1471.*

Spotted Horses

– I –

Yes, sir. Flem Snopes has filled that whole country full of spotted horses. You can hear folks running them all day and all night, whooping and hollering, and the horses running back and forth across them little wooden bridges ever now and then kind of like thunder. Here I was this morning pretty near half way to town, with the team ambling along and me setting in the buckboard about half asleep, when all of a sudden something come swurging up outen the bushes and jumped the road clean, without touching hoof to it. It flew right over my team, big as a billboard and flying through the air like a hawk. It taken me thirty minutes to stop my team and untangle the harness and the buckboard and hitch them up again.

That Flem Snopes. I be dog if he ain't a case, now. One morning about ten years ago, the boys was just getting settled down on Varner's porch for a little talk and tobacco, when here come Flem out from behind the counter, with his coat off and his hair all parted, like he might have been clerking for Varner for ten years already. Folks all knowed him; it was a big family of them about five miles down the bottom. That year, at least. Share-cropping. They never stayed on any place over a year. Then they would move on to another place, with the chap or maybe the twins of that year's litter. It was a regular nest of them. But Flem. The rest of them stayed tenant farmers, moving ever year, but here come Flem one day, walking out from behind Jody Varner's counter like he owned it. And he wasn't there but a year or two before folks knowed that, if him and Jody was both still in that store in ten years more, it would be Jody clerking for Flem Snopes. Why, that fellow could make a nickel where it wasn't but four cents to begin with. He skun me in two trades, myself, and the fellow that can do that, I just hope he'll get rich before I do; that's all.

All right. So here Flem was, clerking at Varner's, making a nickel here and there and not telling nobody about it. No, sir. Folks never knowed when Flem got the better of somebody lessen the fellow he beat told it. He'd just set there in the store-chair, chewing his tobacco and keeping his own business to hisself, until about a week later we'd find out it was somebody else's business he was keeping to hisself—provided the fellow he trimmed was mad enough to tell it. That's Flem.

We give him ten years to own ever thing Jody Varner had. But he never waited no ten years. I reckon you-all know that gal of Uncle Billy Varner's, the youngest one; Eula. Jody's sister. Ever Sunday ever yellow-wheeled buggy and curried riding horse in that country would be hitched to Bill Varner's fence, and the young bucks setting on the porch, swarming around Eula like bees around a honey pot. One of these here kind of big, soft-looking gals that could giggle richer than plowed new-ground. Wouldn't none of them leave before the others, and so they would set there on the

702

porch until time to go home, with some of them with nine and ten miles to ride and then get up tomorrow and go back to the field. So they would all leave together and they would ride in a clump down to the creek ford and hitch them curried horses and yellow-wheeled buggies and get out and fight one another. Then they would get in the buggies again and go on home.

Well, one day about a year ago, one of them yellow-wheeled buggies and one of them curried saddle-horses quit this country. We heard they was heading for Texas. The next day Uncle Billy and Eula and Flem come in to town in Uncle Bill's surrey, and when they come back, Flem and Eula was married. And on the next day we heard that two more of them yellow-wheeled buggies had left the country. They mought have gone to Texas, too. It's a big place.

Anyway, about a month after the wedding, Flem and Eula went to Texas, too. They was gone pretty near a year. Then one day last month, Eula come back, with a baby. We figgured up, and we decided that it was as well-growed a three-months-old baby as we ever see. It can already pull up on a chair. I reckon Texas makes big men quick, being a big place. Anyway, if it keeps on like it started, it'll be chewing tobacco and voting time it's eight years old.

And so last Friday here come Flem himself. He was on a wagon with another fellow. The other fellow had one of these two-gallon hats and a ivory-handled pistol and a box of gingersnaps sticking out of his hind pocket, and tied to the tail-gate of the wagon was about two dozen of them Texas ponies, hitched to one another with barbed wire. They was colored like parrots and they was quiet as doves, and ere a one of them would kill you quick as a rattlesnake. Nere a one of them had two eyes the same color, and nere a one of them had ever see a bridle, I reckon; and when that Texas man got down offen the wagon and walked up to them to show how gentle they was, one of them cut his vest clean offen him, same as with a razor.

Flem had done already disappeared; he had went on to see his wife, I reckon, and to see if that ere baby had done gone on to the field to help Uncle Billy plow maybe. It was the Texas man that taken the horses on to Mrs. Littlejohn's lot. He had a little trouble at first, when they come to the gate, because they hadn't never see a fence before, and when he finally got them in and taken a pair of wire cutters and unhitched them and got them into the barn and poured some shell corn into the trough, they durn nigh tore down the barn. I reckon they thought that shell corn was bugs, maybe. So he left them in the lot and he announced that the auction would begin at sunup to-morrow.

That night we was setting on Mrs. Littlejohn's porch. You-all mind the moon was nigh full that night, and we could watch them spotted varmints swirling along the fence and back and forth across the lot same as minnows in a pond. And then now and then they would all kind of huddle up against the barn and rest themselves by biting and kicking one another.

We would hear a squeal, and then a set of hoofs would go Bam! against the barn, like a pistol. It sounded just like a fellow with a pistol, in a nest of cattymounts, taking his time.

– II –

It wasn't ere a man knowed yet if Flem owned them things or not. They just knowed one thing: that they wasn't never going to know for sho if Flem did or not, or if maybe he didn't just get on that wagon at the edge of town, for the ride or not. Even Eck Snopes didn't know, Flem's own cousin. But wasn't nobody surprised at that. We knowed that Flem would skin Eck quick as he would ere a one of us.

They was there by sunup next morning, some of them come twelve and sixteen miles, with seed-money tied up in tobacco sacks in their overalls, standing along the fence, when the Texas man come out of Mrs. Littlejohn's after breakfast and clumb onto the gate post with that ere white pistol butt sticking outen his hind pocket. He taken a new box of gingersnaps outen his pocket and bit the end offen it like a cigar and spit out the paper, and said the auction was open. And still they was coming up in wagons and a horse- and mule-back and hitching the teams across the road and coming to the fence. Flem wasn't nowhere in sight.

But he couldn't get them started. He begun to work on Eck, because Eck holp him last night to get them into the barn and feed them that shell corn. Eck got out just in time. He come outen that barn like a chip on the crest of a busted dam of water, and clumb into the wagon just in time.

He was working on Eck when Henry Armstid come up in his wagon. Eck was saying he was skeered to bid on one of them, because he might get it, and the Texas man says, "Them ponies? Them little horses?" He clumb down offen the gate post and went toward the horses. They broke and run, and him following them, kind of chirping to them, with his hand out like he was fixing to catch a fly, until he got three or four of them cornered. Then he jumped into them, and then we couldn't see nothing for a while because of the dust. It was a big cloud of it, and them blare-eyed, spotted things swoaring outen it twenty foot to a jump, in forty directions without counting up. Then the dust settled and there they was, that Texas man and the horse. He had its head twisted clean around like a owl's head. Its legs was braced and it was trembling like a new bride and groaning like a saw mill, and him holding its head wrung clean around on its neck so it was snuffing sky. "Look it over," he says, with his heels dug too and that white pistol sticking outen his pocket and his neck swole up like a spreading adder's until you could just tell what he was saying, cussing the horse and talking to us all at once: "Look him over, the fiddle-headed son of fourteen fathers. Try him, buy him; you will get the best—" Then it was all dust again, and we couldn't see nothing but spotted hide and mane, and that ere Texas man's boot-heels like a couple of walnuts on two strings, and after a while that two-gallon hat come sailing out like a fat old hen crossing a fence.

When the dust settled again, he was just getting outen the far fence corner, brushing himself off. He come and got his hat and brushed it off and come and clumb onto the gate post again. He was breathing hard. He taken the gingersnap box outen his pocket and et one, breathing hard. The hammer-head horse was still running round and round the lot like a merry-go-round at a fair. That was when Henry Armstid come shoving up to the gate in them patched overalls and one of them dangle-armed shirts of hisn. Hadn't nobody noticed him until then. We was all watching the Texas man and the horses. Even Mrs. Littlejohn; she had done come out and built a fire under the wash-pot in her back yard, and she would stand at the fence a while and then go back into the house and come out again with a arm full of wash and stand at the fence again. Well, here come Henry shoving up, and then we see Mrs. Armstid right behind him, in that ere faded wrapper and sunbonnet and them tennis shoes. "Git on back to that wagon," Henry says.

"Henry," she says.

"Here, boys," the Texas man says; "make room for missus to git up and see. Come on, Henry," he says; "here's your chance to buy that saddle-horse missus has been wanting. What about ten dollars, Henry?"

"Henry," Mrs. Armstid says. She put her hand on Henry's arm. Henry knocked her hand down.

"Git on back to that wagon, like I told you," he says.

Mrs. Armstid never moved. She stood behind Henry, with her hands rolled into her dress, not looking at nothing. "He hain't no more despair than to buy one of them things," she says. "And us not five dollars ahead of the pore house, he hain't no more despair." It was the truth, too. They ain't never made more than a bare living offen that place of theirs, and them with four chaps and the very clothes they wears she earns by weaving by the firelight at night while Henry's asleep.

"Shut your mouth and git on back to that wagon," Henry says. "Do you want I taken a wagon stake to you here in the big road?"

Well, that Texas man taken one look at her. Then he begun on Eck again, like Henry wasn't even there. But Eck was skeered. "I can git me a snapping turtle or a water moccasin for nothing. I ain't going to buy none."

So the Texas man said he would give Eck a horse. "To start the auction, and because you holp me last night. If you'll start the bidding on the next horse," he says, "I'll give you that fiddle-head horse."

I wish you could have seen them, standing there with their seed-money in their pockets, watching that Texas man give Eck Snopes a live horse, all fixed to call him a fool if he taken it or not. Finally Eck says he'll take it. "Only I just starts the bidding," he says. "I don't have to buy the next one lessen I ain't overtopped." The Texas man said all right, and Eck bid a dollar on the next one, with Henry Armstid standing there with his mouth already open, watching Eck and the Texas man like a mad-dog or something. "A dollar," Eck says.

The Texas man looked at Eck. His mouth was already open too, like he had started to say something and what he was going to say had up and died on him. "A dollar?" he says. "One dollar? You mean, *one* dollar, Eck?"

"Durn it," Eck says; "two dollars, then."

Well, sir, I wish you could a seen that Texas man. He taken out that gingersnap box and held it up and looked into it, careful, like it might have been a diamond ring in it, or a spider. Then he throwed it away and wiped his face with a bandanna. "Well," he says. "Well. Two dollars. Two dollars. Is your pulse all right, Eck?" he says. "Do you have ager-sweats at night, maybe?" he says. "Well," he says, "I got to take it. But are you boys going to stand there and see Eck get two horses at a dollar a head?"

That done it. I be dog if he wasn't nigh as smart as Flem Snopes. He hadn't no more than got the words outen his mouth before here was Henry Armstid, waving his hand. "Three dollars," Henry says. Mrs. Armstid tried to hold him again. He knocked her hand off, shoving up to the gate post.

"Mister," Mrs. Armstid says, "we got chaps in the house and not corn to feed the stock. We got five dollars I earned my chaps a-weaving after dark, and him snoring in the bed. And he hain't no more despair."

"Henry bids three dollars," the Texas man says. "Raise him a dollar, Eck, and the horse is yours."

"Henry," Mrs. Armstid says.

"Raise him, Eck," the Texas man says.

"Four dollars," Eck says.

"Five dollars," Henry says, shaking his fist. He shoved up right under the gate post. Mrs. Armstid was looking at the Texas man too.

"Mister," she says, "if you take that five dollars I earned my chaps a-weaving for one of them things, it'll be a curse onto you and yourn during all the time of man."

But it wasn't no stopping Henry. He had shoved up, waving his fist at the Texas man. He opened it; the money was in nickels and quarters, and one dollar bill that looked like a cow's cud. "Five dollars," he says. "And the man that raises it'll have to beat my head off, or I'll beat hisn."

"All right," the Texas man says. "Five dollars is bid. But don't you shake your hand at me."

– III –

It taken till nigh sundown before the last one was sold. He got them hotted up once and the bidding got up to seven dollars and a quarter, but most of them went around three or four dollars, him setting on the gate post and picking the horses out one at a time by mouth-word, and Mrs.

Littlejohn pumping up and down at the tub and stopping and coming to the fence for a while and going back to the tub again. She had done got done too, and the wash was hung on the line in the back yard, and we could smell supper cooking. Finally they was all sold; he swapped the last two and the wagon for a buckboard.

We was all kind of tired, but Henry Armstid looked more like a mad-dog than ever. When he bought, Mrs. Armstid had went back to the wagon, setting in it behind them two rabbit-sized, bone-pore mules, and the wagon itself looking like it would fall all to pieces soon as the mules moved. Henry hadn't even waited to pull it outen the road; it was still in the middle of the road and her setting in it, not looking at nothing, ever since this morning.

Henry was right up against the gate. He went up to the Texas man. "I bought a horse and I paid cash," Henry says. "And yet you expect me to stand around here until they are all sold before I can get my horse. I'm going to take my horse outen that lot."

The Texas man looked at Henry. He talked like he might have been asking for a cup of coffee at the table. "Take your horse," he says.

Then Henry quit looking at the Texas man. He begun to swallow, holding onto the gate. "Ain't you going to help me?" he says.

"It ain't my horse," the Texas man says.

Henry never looked at the Texas man again, he never looked at nobody. "Who'll help me catch my horse?" he says. Never nobody said nothing. "Bring the plowline," Henry says. Mrs. Armstid got outen the wagon and brought the plowline. The Texas man got down offen the post. The woman made to pass him, carrying the rope.

"Don't you go in there, missus," the Texas man says.

Henry opened the gate. He didn't look back. "Come on here," he says.

"Don't you go in there, missus," the Texas man says.

Mrs. Armstid wasn't looking at nobody, neither, with her hands across her middle, holding the rope. "I reckon I better," she says. Her and Henry went into the lot. The horses broke and run. Henry and Mrs. Armstid followed.

"Get him into the corner," Henry says. They got Henry's horse cornered finally, and Henry taken the rope, but Mrs. Armstid let the horse get out. They hemmed it up again, but Mrs. Armstid let it get out again, and Henry turned and hit her with the rope. "Why didn't you head him back?" Henry says. He hit her again. "Why didn't you?" It was about that time I looked around and see Flem Snopes standing there.

It was the Texas man that done something. He moved fast for a big man. He caught the rope before Henry could hit the third time, and Henry whirled and made like he would jump at the Texas man. But he never jumped. The Texas man went and taken Henry's arm and led him outen the lot. Mrs. Armstid come behind them and the Texas man taken some money outen his pocket and he give it into Mrs. Armstid's hand. "Get him into the wagon and take him on home," the Texas man says, like he might have been telling them he enjoyed his supper.

Then here come Flem. "What's that for, Buck?" Flem says.

"Thinks he bought one of them ponies," the Texas man says. "Get him on away, missus."

But Henry wouldn't go. "Give him back that money," he says. "I bought that horse and I aim to have him if I have to shoot him."

And there was Flem, standing there with his hands in his pockets, chewing, like he had just happened to be passing.

"You take your money and I take my horse," Henry says. "Give it back to him," he says to Mrs. Armstid.

"You don't own no horse of mine," the Texas man says. "Get him on home, missus."

Then Henry seen Flem. "You got something to do with these horses," he says. "I bought one. Here's the money for it." He taken the bill outen Mrs. Armstid's hand. He offered it to Flem. "I bought one. Ask him. Here. Here's the money," he says, giving the bill to Flem.

When Flem taken the money, the Texas man dropped the rope he had snatched outen Henry's hand. He had done sent Eck Snopes's boy up to the store for another box of gingersnaps, and he taken the box outen his pocket and looked into it. It was empty and he dropped it on the ground. "Mr. Snopes will have your money for you to-morrow," he says to Mrs. Armstid. "You can get it from him to-morrow. He don't own no horse. You get him into the wagon and get him on home." Mrs. Armstid went back to the wagon and got in. "Where's that ere buckboard I bought?" the Texas man says. It was after sundown then. And then Mrs. Littlejohn come out on the porch and rung the supper bell.

–IV–

I come on in and et supper. Mrs. Littlejohn would bring in a pan of bread or something, then she would go out to the porch a minute and come back and tell us. The Texas man had hitched his team to the buck-board he had swapped them last two horses for, and him and Flem had gone, and then she told that the rest of them that never had ropes had went back to the store with I. O. Snopes to get some ropes, and wasn't nobody at the gate but Henry Armstid, and Mrs. Armstid setting in the wagon in the road, and Eck Snopes and that boy of hisn. "I don't care how many of them fool men gets killed by them things," Mrs. Littlejohn says, "but I ain't going to let Eck Snopes take that boy into that lot again." So she went down to the gate, but she come back without the boy or Eck neither.

"It ain't no need to worry about that boy," I says. "He's charmed." He was right behind Eck last night when Eck went to help feed them. The whole drove of them jumped clean over that boy's head and never touched him. It was Eck that touched him. Eck snatched him into the wagon and taken a rope and frailed the tar outen him.

So I had done et and went to my room and was undressing, long as I had a long trip to make next day; I was trying to sell a machine to Mrs. Bundren up past Whiteleaf; when Henry Armstid opened that gate and went in by hisself. They couldn't make him wait for the balance of them to get back with their ropes. Eck Snopes said he tried to make Henry wait, but Henry wouldn't do it. Eck said Henry walked right up to them and that when they broke, they run clean over Henry like a hay-mow breaking down. Eck said he snatched that boy of hisn out of the way just in time and that them things went through that gate like a creek flood and into the wagons and teams hitched side the road, busting wagon tongues and snapping harness like it was fishing-line, with Mrs. Armstid still setting in their wagon in the middle of it like something carved outen wood. Then they scattered, wild horses and tame mules with pieces of harness and single trees dangling offen them, both ways up and down the road.

"There goes ourn, paw!" Eck says his boy said. "There it goes, into Mrs. Littlejohn's house." Eck says it run right up the steps and into the house like a boarder late for supper. I reckon so. Anyway, I was in my room, in my underclothes, with one sock on and one sock in my hand, leaning out the window when the commotion busted out, when I heard something run into the melodeon in the hall; it sounded like a railroad engine. Then the door to my room come sailing in like when you throw a tin bucket top into the wind and I looked over my shoulder and see something that looked like a fourteen-foot pinwheel a-blaring its eyes at me. It had to blare them fast, because I was already done jumped out the window.

I reckon it was anxious, too. I reckon it hadn't never seen barbed wire or shell corn before, but I know it hadn't never seen underclothes before, or maybe it was a sewing-machine agent it hadn't never seen. Anyway, it swirled and turned to run back up the hall and outen the house, when it met Eck Snopes and that boy just coming in, carrying a rope. It swirled again and run down the hall and out the back door just in time to meet Mrs. Littlejohn. She had just gathered up the clothes she had washed, and she was coming onto the back porch with a armful of washing in one hand and a scrubbing-board in the other, when the horse skidded up to her, trying to stop and swirl again. It never taken Mrs. Littlejohn no time a-tall.

"Git outen here, you son," she says. She hit it across the face with the scrubbing-board; that ere scrubbing-board split as neat as ere a axe could have done it, and when the horse swirled to run back up the hall, she hit it again with what was left of the scrubbing-board, not on the head this time. "And stay out," she says.

Eck and that boy was half-way down the hall by this time. I reckon that horse looked like a pinwheel to Eck too. "Git to hell outen here, Ad!"

Eck says. Only there wasn't time. Eck dropped flat on his face, but the boy never moved. The boy was about a yard tall maybe, in overhalls just like Eck's; that horse swoared over his head without touching a hair. I saw that, because I was just coming back up the front steps, still carrying that ere sock and still in my underclothes, when the horse come onto the porch again. It taken one look at me and swirled again and run to the end of the porch and jumped the banisters and the lot fence like a hen-hawk and lit in the lot running and went out the gate again and jumped eight or ten upside-down wagons and went on down the road. It was a full moon then. Mrs. Armstid was still setting in the wagon like she had done been carved outen wood and left there and forgot.

That horse. It ain't never missed a lick. It was going about forty miles an hour when it come to the bridge over the creek. It would have had a clear road, but it so happened that Vernon Tull was already using the bridge when it got there. He was coming back from town; he hadn't heard about the auction; him and his wife and three daughters and Mrs. Tull's aunt, all setting in chairs in the wagon bed, and all asleep, including the mules. They waked up when the horse hit the bridge one time, but Tull said the first he knew was when the mules tried to turn the wagon around in the middle of the bridge and he seen that spotted varmint run right twixt the mules and run up the wagon tongue like a squirrel. He said he just had time to hit it across the face with his whip-stock, because about that time the mules turned the wagon around on that ere one-way bridge and that horse clumb across one of the mules and jumped down onto the bridge again and went on, with Vernon standing up in the wagon and kicking at it.

Tull said the mules turned in the harness and clumb back into the wagon too, with Tull trying to beat them out again, with the reins wrapped around his wrist. After that he says all he seen was overturned chairs and womenfolks' legs and white drawers shining in the moonlight, and his mules and that spotted horse going on up the road like a ghost.

The mules jerked Tull outen the wagon and drug him a spell on the bridge before the reins broke. They thought at first that he was dead, and while they was kneeling around him, picking the bridge splinters outen him, here come Eck and that boy, still carrying the rope. They was running and breathing a little hard. "Where'd he go?" Eck says.

– V –

I went back and got my pants and shirt and shoes on just in time to go and help get Henry Armstid outen the trash in the lot. I be dog if he didn't look like he was dead, with his head hanging back and his teeth showing in the moonlight, and a little rim of white under his eyelids. We could still hear them horses, here and there; hadn't none of them got more than four-five miles away yet, not knowing the country, I reckon. So we could hear them and folks yelling now and then: "Whooey. Head him!"

We toted Henry into Mrs. Littlejohn's. She was in the hall; she hadn't put down the armful of clothes. She taken one look at us, and she laid down the busted scrubbing-board and taken up the lamp and opened a empty door. "Bring him in here," she says.

We toted him in and laid him on the bed. Mrs. Littlejohn set the lamp on the dresser, still carrying the clothes. "I'll declare, you men," she says. Our shadows was way up the wall, tiptoeing too; we could hear ourselves breathing. "Better get his wife," Mrs. Littlejohn says. She went out, carrying the clothes.

"I reckon we had," Quick says. "Go get her, somebody."

"Whyn't you go?" Winterbottom says.

"Let Ernest git her," Durley says. "He lives neighbors with them."

Ernest went to fetch her. I be dog if Henry didn't look like he was dead. Mrs. Littlejohn come back, with a kettle and some towels. She went to work on Henry, and then Mrs. Armstid and Ernest come in. Mrs. Armstid come to the foot of the bed and stood there, with her hands rolled into her apron, watching what Mrs. Littlejohn was doing, I reckon.

"You men git outen the way," Mrs. Littlejohn says. "Git outside," she says. "See if you can't find something else to play with that will kill some more of you."

"Is he dead?" Winterbottom says.

"It ain't your fault if he ain't," Mrs. Littlejohn says. "Go tell Will Varner to come up here. I reckon a man ain't so different from a mule, come long come short. Except maybe a mule's got more sense."

We went to get Uncle Billy. It was a full moon. We could hear them, now and then, four mile away: "Whooey. Head him." The country was full of them, one on ever wooden bridge in the land, running across it like thunder: "Whooey. There he goes. Head him."

We hadn't got far before Henry begun to scream. I reckon Mrs. Littlejohn's water had brung him to; anyway, he wasn't dead. We went on to Uncle Billy's. The house was dark. We called to him, and after a while the window opened and Uncle Billy put his head out, peart as a peckerwood, listening. "Are they still trying to catch them durn rabbits?" he says.

He come down, with his britches on over his night-shirt and his suspenders dangling, carrying his horse-doctoring grip. "Yes, sir," he says, cocking his head like a woodpecker; "they're still a-trying."

We could hear Henry before we reached Mrs. Littlejohn's. He was going Ah-Ah-Ah. We stopped in the yard. Uncle Billy went on in. We could hear Henry. We stood in the yard, hearing them on the bridges, this-a-way and that: "Whooey. Whooey."

"Eck Snopes ought to caught hisn," Ernest says.

"Looks like he ought," Winterbottom said.

Henry was going Ah-Ah-Ah steady in the house; then he begun to scream. "Uncle Billy's started," Quick says. We looked into the hall. We could see the light where the door was. Then Mrs. Littlejohn come out.

"Will needs some help," she says. "You, Ernest. You'll do." Ernest went into the house.

"Hear them?" Quick said. "That one was on Four Mile bridge." We could hear them; it sounded like thunder a long way off; it didn't last long: "Whooey."

We could hear Henry: "Ah-Ah-Ah-Ah-Ah."

"They are both started now," Winterbottom says. "Ernest too."

That was early in the night. Which was a good thing, because it taken a long night for folks to chase them things right and for Henry to lay there and holler, being as Uncle Billy never had none of this here chloryfoam to set Henry's leg with. So it was considerate in Flem to get them started early. And what do you reckon Flem's comment was?

That's right. Nothing. Because he wasn't there. Hadn't nobody see him since that Texas man left.

– VI –

That was Saturday night. I reckon Mrs. Armstid got home about daylight, to see about the chaps. I don't know where they thought her and Henry was. But lucky the oldest one was a gal, about twelve, big enough to take care of the little ones. Which she did for the next two days. Mrs. Armstid would nurse Henry all night and work in the kitchen for hern and Henry's keep, and in the afternoon she would drive home (it was about four miles) to see to the chaps. She would cook up a pot of victuals and leave it on the stove, and the gal would bar the house and keep the little ones quiet. I would hear Mrs. Littlejohn and Mrs. Armstid talking in the kitchen. "How are the chaps making out?" Mrs. Littlejohn says.

"All right," Mrs. Armstid says.

"Don't they git skeered at night?" Mrs. Littlejohn says.

"Ina May bars the door when I leave," Mrs. Armstid says. "She's got the axe in bed with her. I reckon she can make out."

I reckon they did. And I reckon Mrs. Armstid was waiting for Flem to come back to town; hadn't nobody seen him until this morning; to get her money the Texas man said Flem was keeping for her. Sho. I reckon she was.

Anyway, I heard Mrs. Armstid and Mrs. Littlejohn talking in the kitchen this morning while I was eating breakfast. Mrs. Littlejohn had just told Mrs. Armstid that Flem was in town. "You can ask him for that five dollars," Mrs. Littlejohn says.

"You reckon he'll give it to me?" Mrs. Armstid says.

Mrs. Littlejohn was washing dishes, washing them like a man, like they was made out of iron. "No," she says. "But asking him won't do no hurt. It might shame him. I don't reckon it will, but it might."

"If he wouldn't give it back, it ain't no use to ask," Mrs. Armstid says.

"Suit yourself," Mrs. Littlejohn says. "It's your money."

I could hear the dishes.

"Do you reckon he might give it back to me?" Mrs. Armstid says. "That Texas man said he would. He said I could get it from Mr. Snopes later."

"Then go and ask him for it," Mrs. Littlejohn says.

I could hear the dishes.

"He won't give it back to me," Mrs. Armstid says.

"All right," Mrs. Littlejohn says. "Don't ask him for it, then."

I could hear the dishes; Mrs. Armstid was helping. "You don't reckon he would, do you?" she says. Mrs. Littlejohn never said nothing. It sounded like she was throwing the dishes at one another. "Maybe I better go and talk to Henry about it," Mrs. Armstid says.

"I would," Mrs. Littlejohn says. I be dog if it didn't sound like she had two plates in her hands, beating them together. "Then Henry can buy another five-dollar horse with it. Maybe he'll buy one next time that will out and out kill him. If I thought that, I'd give you back the money, myself."

"I reckon I better talk to him first," Mrs. Armstid said. Then it sounded like Mrs. Littlejohn taken up all the dishes and throwed them at the cookstove, and I come away.

That was this morning. I had been up to Bundren's and back, and I thought that things would have kind of settled down. So after breakfast, I went up to the store. And there was Flem, setting in the store-chair and whittling, like he might not have ever moved since he come to clerk for Jody Varner. I.O. was leaning in the door, in his shirt sleeves and with his hair parted too, same as Flem was before he turned the clerking job over to I.O. It's a funny thing about them Snopes: they all looks alike, yet there ain't ere a two of them that claims brothers. They're always just cousins, like Flem and Eck and Flem and I.O. Eck was there too, squatting against the wall, him and that boy, eating cheese and crackers outen a sack; they told me that Eck hadn't been home a-tall. And that Lon Quick hadn't got back to town, even. He followed his horse clean down to Samson's Bridge, with a wagon and a camp outfit. Eck finally caught one of hisn. It run into a blind lane at Freeman's and Eck and the boy taken and tied their rope across the end of the lane, about three foot high. The horse come to the end of the lane and whirled and run back without ever stopping. Eck says it never seen the rope a-tall. He says it looked just like one of these here Christmas pinwheels. "Didn't it try to run again?" I says.

"No," Eck says, eating a bit of cheese offen his knife blade. "Just kicked some."

"Kicked some?" I says.

"It broke its neck," Eck says.

Well, they was squatting there, about six of them, talking, talking at Flem; never nobody knowed yet if Flem had ere a interest in them horses or not. So finally I come right out and asked him. "Flem's done skun all of us so much," I says, "that we're proud of him. Come on, Flem," I says, "how much did you and that Texas man make offen them horses? You can tell us. Ain't nobody here but Eck that bought one of them; the others ain't got back to town yet, and Eck's your own cousin; he'll be proud to hear, too. How much did you-all make?"

They was all whittling, not looking at Flem, making like they was studying. But you could a heard a pin drop. And I.O. He had been rubbing his back up and down on the door, but he stopped now, watching Flem like a pointing dog. Flem finished cutting the sliver offen his stick. He spit across the porch, into the road. "Twarn't none of my horses," he says.

I.O. cackled, like a hen, slapping his legs with both hands. "You boys might just as well quit trying to get ahead of Flem," he said.

Well, about that time I see Mrs. Armstid come outen Mrs. Littlejohn's gate, coming up the road. I never said nothing. I says, "Well, if a man can't take care of himself in a trade, he can't blame the man that trims him."

Flem never said nothing, trimming at the stick. He hadn't seen Mrs. Armstid. "Yes, sir," I says. "A fellow like Henry Armstid ain't got nobody but hisself to blame."

"Course he ain't," I.O. says. He ain't seen her, neither. "Henry Armstid's a born fool. Always is been. If Flem hadn't a got his money, somebody else would."

We looked at Flem. He never moved. Mrs. Armstid come on up the road.

"That's right," I says. "But, come to think of it, Henry never bought no horse." We looked at Flem; you could a heard a match drop. "That Texas man told her to get that five dollars back from Flem next day. I reckon Flem's done already taken that money to Mrs. Littlejohn's and give it to Mrs. Armstid."

We watched Flem. I.O. quit rubbing his back against the door again. After a while Flem raised his head and spit across the porch, into the dust. I.O. cackled, just like a hen. "Ain't he a beating fellow, now?" I.O. says.

Mrs. Armstid was getting closer, so I kept on talking, watching to see if Flem would look up and see her. But he never looked up. I went on talking about Tull, about how he was going to sue Flem, and Flem setting there, whittling his stick, not saying nothing else after he said they wasn't none of his horses.

Then I.O. happened to look around. He seen Mrs. Armstid. "Pssst!" he says. Flem looked up. "Here she comes!" I.O. says. "Go out the back. I'll tell her you done went in to town to-day."

But Flem never moved. He just set there, whittling, and we watched Mrs. Armstid come up onto the porch, in that ere faded sunbonnet and wrapper and them tennis shoes that made a kind of hissing noise on the porch. She come onto the porch and stopped, her hands rolled into her dress in front, not looking at nothing.

"He said Saturday," she says, "that he wouldn't sell Henry no horse. He said I could get the money from you."

Flem looked up. The knife never stopped. It went on trimming off a sliver same as if he was watching it. "He taken that money off with him when he left," Flem says.

Mrs. Armstid never looked at nothing. We never looked at her, neither, except that boy of Eck's. He had a half-et cracker in his hand, watching her, chewing.

"He said Henry hadn't bought no horse," Mrs. Armstid says. "He said for me to get the money from you today."

"I reckon he forgot about it," Flem said. "He taken that money off with him Saturday." He whittled again. I.O. kept on rubbing his back, slow. He licked his lips. After a while the woman looked up the road, where it went on up the hill, toward the graveyard. She looked up that way for a while, with that boy of Eck's watching her and I.O. rubbing his back slow against the door. Then she turned back toward the steps.

"I reckon it's time to get dinner started," she says.

"How's Henry this morning, Mrs. Armstid?" Winterbottom says.

She looked at Winterbottom; she almost stopped. "He's resting, I thank you kindly," she says.

Flem got up, outen the chair, putting his knife away. He spit across the porch. "Wait a minute, Mrs. Armstid," he says. She stopped again. She didn't look at him. Flem went on into the store, with I.O. done quit rubbing his back now, with his head craned after Flem, and Mrs. Armstid standing there with her hands rolled into her dress, not looking at nothing. A wagon come up the road and passed; it was Freeman, on the way to town. Then Flem come out again, with I.O. still watching him. Flem had one of these little striped sacks of Jody Varner's candy; I bet he still owes Jody that nickel, too. He put the sack into Mrs. Armstid's hand, like he would have put it into a hollow stump. He spit again across the porch. "A little sweetening for the chaps," he says.

"You're right kind," Mrs. Armstid says. She held the sack of candy in her hand, not looking at nothing. Eck's boy was watching the sack, the half-et cracker in his hand; he wasn't chewing now. He watched Mrs. Armstid roll the sack into her apron. "I reckon I better get on back and help with dinner," she says. She turned and went back across the porch. Flem set down in the chair again and opened his knife. He spit across the porch again, past Mrs. Armstid where she hadn't went down the steps yet. Then she went on, in that ere sunbonnet and wrapper all the same color, back down the road toward Mrs. Littlejohn's. You couldn't see her dress move, like a natural woman walking. She looked like an old snag still standing up and moving along on a high water. We watched her turn in at Mrs. Littlejohn's and go outen sight. Flem was whittling. I.O. begun to rub his back on the door. Then he begun to cackle, just like a durn hen.

"You boys might just as well quit trying," I.O. says. "You can't git ahead of Flem. You can't touch him. Ain't he a sight, now?"

I be dog if he ain't. If I had brung a herd of wild cattymounts into town and sold them to my neighbors and kinfolks, they would have lynched me. Yes, sir.   [1930]

ARNA BONTEMPS

Arna Bontemps (1902–1973) was born in Alexandria, Louisiana, the son of Creole parents. His father was a skilled brick mason who moved his family to Los Angeles when Arna was three years old. Tension developed between father and son when Arna refused to be apprenticed as a mason. He was sent away to a white boarding school in San Fernando with his father's command not to "go up there acting colored." Unhappy at what he saw as his father's effort to make him forget his racial heritage, Bontemps went on to Pacific Union College in Angwin, California, graduating in 1923. Later he wrote:

> *Had I not gone home summers and hobnobbed with Negroes, I would have finished college without knowing that any Negro other than Paul Laurence Dunbar ever wrote a poem. I would have come out imagining that the story of the Negro could be told in two short paragraphs: a statement about jungle people in Africa and an equally brief account of the slavery issue in American history.*

In 1924 Bontemps began to publish his poetry in magazines such as The Crisis *and* Opportunity, *which encouraged the work of young African American writers. He had hoped to study for a Ph.D. in English, but after his marriage in 1926 and the subsequent birth of six children, he accepted teaching jobs to support his family. In 1926 he moved to New York City to teach at the Harlem Academy for five years, a period in which he was also close to several important figures of the Harlem Renaissance, including Langston Hughes and Jean Toomer. In 1931 he published his first book,* God Sends Sunday, *a novel about a black St. Louis jockey. That year Bontemps moved to Huntsville, Alabama, to teach at Oakwood Junior College. He had no room for his typewriter in his tiny, rented frame cottage, so he wrote outdoors during his summer vacations, in the sweltering heat, armed with a fly swatter and a large bath towel, on an old table placed on the shady side of the house. There Bontemps created the story "A Summer Tragedy," which won the 1932 prize for fiction from* Opportunity *magazine. This story impressed Richard Wright, who began to publish short fiction with a similarly bleak view of black farm life in Mississippi a short time later.*

At Huntsville, Bontemps said that "I began to suspect that it was fruitless for a Negro in the United States to address serious writing to my generation, and I began to consider the alternative of trying to reach young readers not yet hardened or grown insensitive to man's inhumanity to man, as it is called." For the remaining forty years of his life, Bontemps wrote biographies, children's fiction, and black history, and compiled literary anthologies, often in collaboration with his close friends Langston Hughes and Jack Conroy. In 1943, after completing a master's degree in library science, he served until his retirement as head librarian at Fisk University, developing an archive of African American cultural materials that is a major resource for study in this field.

RELATED COMMENTARY: *Arna Bontemps, "On Jean Toomer and* Cane,*"*
page 1320.

A Summer Tragedy

Old Jeff Patton, the black share farmer, fumbled with his bow tie. His fingers trembled and the high stiff collar pinched his throat. A fellow loses his hand for such vanities after thirty or forty years of simple life. Once a year, or maybe twice if there's a wedding among his kinfolks, he may spruce up; but generally fancy clothes do nothing but adorn the wall of the big room and feed the moths. That had been Jeff Patton's experience. He had not worn his stiff-bosomed shirt more than a dozen times in all his married life. His swallow-tailed coat lay on the bed beside him, freshly brushed and pressed, but it was as full of holes as the overalls in which he worked on weekdays. The moths had used it badly. Jeff twisted his mouth into a hideous toothless grimace as he contended with the obstinate bow. He stamped his good foot and decided to give up the struggle.

"Jennie," he called.

"What's that, Jeff?" His wife's shrunken voice came out of the adjoining room like an echo. It was hardly bigger than a whisper.

"I reckon you'll have to he'p me wid this heah bow tie, baby," he said meekly. "Dog if I can hitch it up."

Her answer was not strong enough to reach him, but presently the old woman came to the door, feeling her way with a stick. She had a wasted, dead-leaf appearance. Her body, as scrawny and gnarled as a string bean, seemed less than nothing in the ocean of frayed and faded petticoats that surrounded her. These hung an inch or two above the tops of her heavy unlaced shoes and showed little grotesque piles where the stockings had fallen down from her negligible legs.

"You oughta could do a heap mo' wid a thing like that'n me — beingst as you got yo' good sight."

"Looks like I oughta could," he admitted. "But ma fingers is gone democrat on me. I get all mixed up in the looking glass an' can't tell wicha way to twist the devilish thing."

Jennie sat on the side of the bed and old Jeff Patton got down on one knee while she tied the bow knot. It was a slow and painful ordeal for each of them in this position. Jeff's bones cracked, his knee ached, and it was only after a half dozen attempts that Jennie worked a semblance of a bow into the tie.

"I got to dress maself now," the old woman whispered. "These is ma old shoes an' stockings, and I ain't so much as unwrapped ma dress."

"Well, don't worry 'bout me no mo', baby," Jeff said. "That 'bout finishes me. All I gotta do now is slip on that old coat 'n ves' an' I'll be fixed to leave."

Jennie disappeared again through the dim passage into the shed room. Being blind was no handicap to her in that black hole. Jeff heard the cane placed against the wall beside the door and knew that his wife was on easy ground. He put on his coat, took a battered top hat from the bedpost and hobbled to the front door. He was ready to travel. As soon as Jennie could get on her Sunday shoes and her old black silk dress, they would start.

Outside the tiny log house, the day was warm and mellow with sunshine. A host of wasps were humming with busy excitement in the trunk of a dead sycamore. Gray squirrels were searching through the grass for hickory nuts and blue jays were in the trees, hopping from branch to branch. Pine woods stretched away to the left like a black sea. Among them were scattered scores of log houses like Jeff's, houses of black share farmers. Cows and pigs wandered freely among the trees. There was no danger of loss. Each farmer knew his own stock and knew his neighbor's as well as he knew his neighbor's children.

Down the slope to the right were the cultivated acres on which the colored folks worked. They extended to the river, more than two miles away, and they were today green with the unmade cotton crop. A tiny thread of a road, which passed directly in front of Jeff's place, ran through these green fields like a pencil mark.

Jeff, standing outside the door, with his absurd hat in his left hand, surveyed the wide scene tenderly. He had been forty-five years on these acres. He loved them with the unexplained affection that others have for the countries to which they belong.

The sun was hot on his head, his collar still pinched his throat, and the Sunday clothes were intolerably hot. Jeff transferred the hat to his right hand and began fanning with it. Suddenly the whisper that was Jennie's voice came out of the shed room.

"You can bring the car round front whilst you's waitin'," it said feebly. There was a tired pause; then it added, "I'll soon be fixed to go."

"A'right, baby," Jeff answered. "I'll get it in a minute."

But he didn't move. A thought struck him that made his mouth fall open. The mention of the car brought to his mind, with new intensity, the trip he and Jennie were about to take. Fear came into his eyes; excitement took his breath. Lord, Jesus!

"Jeff . . . O Jeff," the old woman's whisper called.

He awakened with a jolt. "Hunh, baby?"

"What you doin'?"

"Nuthin. Jes studyin'. I jes been turnin' things round'n round in ma mind."

"You could be gettin' the car," she said.

"Oh yes, right away, baby."

He started round to the shed, limping heavily on his bad leg. There were three frizzly chickens in the yard. All his other chickens had been killed or stolen recently. But the frizzly chickens had been saved somehow.

That was fortunate indeed, for these curious creatures had a way of devouring "Poison" from the yard and in that way protecting against conjure and black luck and spells. But even the frizzly chickens seemed now to be in a stupor. Jeff thought they had some ailment; he expected all three of them to die shortly.

The shed in which the old T-model Ford stood was only a grass roof held up by four corner poles. It had been built by tremulous hands at a time when the little rattletrap car had been regarded as a peculiar treasure. And, miraculously, despite wind and downpour it still stood.

Jeff adjusted the crank and put his weight upon it. The engine came to life with a sputter and bang that rattled the old car from radiator to tail-light. Jeff hopped into the seat and put his foot on the accelerator. The sputtering and banging increased. The rattling became more violent. That was good. It was good banging, good sputtering and rattling, and it meant that the aged car was still in running condition. She could be depended on for this trip.

Again Jeff's thought halted as if paralyzed. The suggestion of the trip fell into the machinery of his mind like a wrench. He felt dazed and weak. He swung the car out into the yard, made a half turn and drove around to the front door. When he took his hands off the wheel, he noticed that he was trembling violently. He cut off the motor and climbed to the ground to wait for Jennie.

A few minutes later she was at the window, her voice rattling against the pane like a broken shutter.

"I'm ready, Jeff."

He did not answer, but limped into the house and took her by the arm. He led her slowly through the big room, down the step and across the yard.

"You reckon I'd oughta lock the do'?" he asked softly.

They stopped and Jennie weighed the question. Finally she shook her head.

"Ne' mind the do'," she said. "I don't see no cause to lock up things."

"You right," Jeff agreed. "No cause to lock up."

Jeff opened the door and helped his wife into the car. A quick shudder passed over him. Jesus! Again he trembled.

"How come you shaking so?" Jennie whispered.

"I don't know," he said.

"You mus' be scairt, Jeff."

"No, baby, I ain't scairt."

He slammed the door after her and went around to crank up again. The motor started easily. Jeff wished that it had not been so responsive. He would have liked a few more minutes in which to turn things around in his head. As it was, with Jennie chiding him about being afraid, he had to keep going. He swung the car into the little pencil-mark road and started off toward the river, driving very slowly, very cautiously.

Chugging across the green countryside, the small battered Ford seemed tiny indeed. Jeff felt a familiar excitement, a thrill, as they came down the first slope to the immense levels on which the cotton was growing. He could not help reflecting that the crops were good. He knew what that meant, too; he had made forty-five of them with his own hands. It was true that he had worn out nearly a dozen mules, but that was the fault of old man Stevenson, the owner of the land. Major Stevenson had the odd notion that one mule was all a share farmer needed to work a thirty-acre plot. It was an expensive notion, the way it killed mules from overwork, but the old man held to it. Jeff thought it killed a good many share farmers as well as mules, but he had no sympathy for them. He had always been strong, and he had been taught to have no patience with weakness in men. Women or children might be tolerated if they were puny, but a weak man was a curse. Of course, his own children —

Jeff's thought halted there. He and Jennie never mentioned their dead children any more. And naturally he did not wish to dwell upon them in his mind. Before he knew it, some remark would slip out of his mouth and that would make Jennie feel blue. Perhaps she would cry. A woman like Jennie could not easily throw off the grief that comes from losing five grown children within two years. Even Jeff was still staggered by the blow. His memory had not been much good recently. He frequently talked to himself. And, although he had kept it a secret, he knew that his courage had left him. He was terrified by the least unfamiliar sound at night. He was reluctant to venture far from home in the daytime. And that habit of trembling when he felt fearful was now far beyond his control. Sometimes he became afraid and trembled without knowing what had frightened him. The feeling would just come over him like a chill.

The car rattled slowly over the dusty road. Jennie sat erect and silent, with a little absurd hat pinned to her hair. Her useless eyes seemed very large, very white in their deep sockets. Suddenly Jeff heard her voice, and he inclined his head to catch the words.

"Is we passed Delia Moore's house yet?" she asked.

"Not yet," he said.

"You must be drivin' mighty slow, Jeff."

"We might just as well take our time, baby."

There was a pause. A little puff of steam was coming out of the radiator of the car. Heat wavered above the hood. Delia Moore's house was nearly half a mile away. After a moment Jennie spoke again.

"You ain't really scairt, is you, Jeff?"

"Nah, baby, I ain't scairt."

"You know how we agreed — we gotta keep on goin'."

Jewels of perspiration appeared on Jeff's forehead. His eyes rounded, blinked, became fixed on the road.

"I don't know," he said with a shiver. "I reckon it's the only thing to do."

"Hm."

A flock of guinea fowls, pecking in the road, were scattered by the passing car. Some of them took to their wings; others hid under bushes. A blue jay, swaying on a leafy twig, was annoying a roadside squirrel. Jeff held an even speed till he came near Delia's place. Then he slowed down noticeably.

Delia's house was really no house at all, but an abandoned store building converted into a dwelling. It sat near a crossroads, beneath a single black cedar tree. There Delia, a cattish old creature of Jennie's age, lived alone. She had been there more years than anybody could remember, and long ago had won the disfavor of such women as Jennie. For in her young days Delia had been gayer, yellower and saucier than seemed proper in those parts. Her ways with menfolks had been dark and suspicious. And the fact that she had had as many husbands as children did not help her reputation.

"Yonder's old Delia," Jeff said as they passed.

"What she doin'?"

"Jes sittin' in the do'," he said.

"She see us?"

"Hm," Jeff said. "Musta did."

That relieved Jennie. It strengthened her to know that her old enemy had seen her pass in her best clothes. That would give the old she-devil something to chew her gums and fret about, Jennie thought. Wouldn't she have a fit if she didn't find out? Old evil Delia! This would be just the thing for her. It would pay her back for being so evil. It would also pay her, Jennie thought, for the way she used to grin at Jeff—long ago when her teeth were good.

The road became smooth and red, and Jeff could tell by the smell of the air that they were nearing the river. He could see the rise where the road turned and ran along parallel to the stream. The car chugged on monotonously. After a long silent spell, Jennie leaned against Jeff and spoke.

"How many bale o' cotton you think we got standin'?" she said.

Jeff wrinkled his forehead as he calculated.

" 'Bout twenty-five, I reckon."

"How many you make las' year?"

"Twenty-eight," he said. "How come you ask that?"

"I's jes thinkin'," Jennie said quietly.

"It don't make a speck o' difference though," Jeff reflected. "If we get much or if we get little, we still gonna be in debt to old man Stevenson when he gets through counting up agin us. It's took us a long time to learn that."

Jennie was not listening to these words. She had fallen into a trance-like meditation. Her lips twitched. She chewed her gums and rubbed her gnarled hands nervously. Suddenly she leaned forward, buried her face in the nervous hands and burst into tears. She cried aloud in a dry cracked voice that suggested the rattle of fodder on dead stalks. She cried aloud like a child, for she had never learned to suppress a genuine sob. Her slight old frame shook heavily and seemed hardly able to sustain such violent grief.

"What's the matter, baby?" Jeff asked awkwardly. "Why you cryin' like all that?"

"I's jes thinkin'," she said.

"So you the one what's scairt now, hunh?"

"I ain't scairt, Jeff. I's jes thinkin' 'bout leavin' eve'thing like this— eve'thing we been used to. It's right sad-like."

Jeff did not answer, and presently Jennie buried her face again and cried.

The sun was almost overhead. It beat down furiously on the dusty wagon-path road, on the parched roadside grass and the tiny battered car. Jeff's hands, gripping the wheel, became wet with perspiration; his forehead sparkled. Jeff's lips parted. His mouth shaped a hideous grimace. His face suggested the face of a man being burned. But the torture passed and his expression softened again.

"You mustn't cry, baby," he said to his wife. "We gotta be strong. We can't break down."

Jennie waited a few seconds, then said, "You reckon we oughta do it, Jeff? You reckon we oughta go 'head an' do it, really?"

Jeff's voice choked; his eyes blurred. He was terrified to hear Jennie say the thing that had been in his mind all morning. She had egged him on when he had wanted more than anything in the world to wait, to reconsider, to think things over a little longer. Now she was getting cold feet. Actually there was no need of thinking the question through again. It would only end in making the same painful decision once more. Jeff knew that. There was no need of fooling around longer.

"We jes as well to do like we planned," he said. "They ain't nothin' else for us now—it's the bes' thing."

Jeff thought of the handicaps, the near impossibility, of making another crop with his leg bothering him more and more each week. Then there was always the chance that he would have another stroke, like the one that had made him lame. Another one might kill him. The least it could do would be to leave him helpless. Jeff gasped—Lord, Jesus! He could not bear to think of being helpless, like a baby, on Jennie's hands. Frail, blind Jennie.

The little pounding motor of the car worked harder and harder. The puff of steam from the cracked radiator became larger. Jeff realized that they were climbing a little rise. A moment later the road turned abruptly and he looked down upon the face of the river.

"Jeff."

"Hunh?"

"Is that the water I hear?"

"Hm. Tha's it."

"Well, which way you goin' now?"

"Down this-a way," he said. "The road runs 'long 'side o' the water a lil piece."

She waited a while calmly. Then she said, "Drive faster."

"A'right, baby," Jeff said.

The water roared in the bed of the river. It was fifty or sixty feet below the level of the road. Between the road and the water there was a long smooth slope, sharply inclined. The slope was dry, the clay hardened by prolonged summer heat. The water below, roaring in a narrow channel, was noisy and wild.

"Jeff."

"Hunh?"

"How far you goin'?"

"Jes a lil piece down the road."

"You ain't scairt, is you, Jeff?"

"Nah, baby," he said trembling. "I ain't scairt."

"Remember how we planned it, Jeff. We gotta do it like we said. Brave-like."

"Hm."

Jeff's brain darkened. Things suddenly seemed unreal, like figures in a dream. Thoughts swam in his mind foolishly, hysterically, like little blind fish in a pool within a dense cave. They rushed, crossed one another, jostled, collided, retreated and rushed again. Jeff soon became dizzy. He shuddered violently and turned to his wife.

"Jennie, I can't do it. I can't." His voice broke pitifully.

She did not appear to be listening. All the grief had gone from her face. She sat erect, her unseeing eyes wide open, strained and frightful. Her glossy black skin had become dull. She seemed as thin, as sharp and bony, as a starved bird. Now, having suffered and endured the sadness of tearing herself away from beloved things, she showed no anguish. She was absorbed with her own thoughts, and she didn't even hear Jeff's voice shouting in her ear.

Jeff said nothing more. For an instant there was light in his cavernous brain. The great chamber was, for less than a second, peopled by characters he knew and loved. They were simple, healthy creatures, and they behaved in a manner that he could understand. They had quality. But since he had already taken leave of them long ago, the remembrance did not break his heart again. Young Jeff Patton was among them, the Jeff Patton of fifty years ago who went down to New Orleans with a crowd of country boys to the Mardi Gras doings. The gay young crowd, boys with candy-striped shirts and rouged-brown girls in noisy silks, was like a picture in his head. Yet it did not make him sad. On that very trip Slim Burns had killed Joe Beasley—the crowd had been broken up. Since then Jeff Patton's world had been the Greenbriar Plantation. If there had been other Mardi Gras carnivals, he had not heard of them. Since then there had been no time; the years had fallen on him like waves. Now he was old, worn out. Another paralytic stroke (like the one he had already suffered) would put him on his back for keeps. In that condition, with a frail blind woman to look after him, he would be worse off than if he were dead.

Suddenly Jeff's hands became steady. He actually felt brave. He slowed down the motor of the car and carefully pulled off the road. Below, the water of the stream boomed, a soft thunder in the deep channel. Jeff ran the car onto the clay slope, pointed it directly toward the stream and put his foot heavily on the accelerator. The little car leaped furiously down the steep incline toward the water. The movement was nearly as swift and direct as a fall. The two old black folks, sitting quietly side by side, showed no excitement. In another instant the car hit the water and dropped immediately out of sight.

A little later it lodged in the mud of a shallow place. One wheel of the crushed and upturned little Ford became visible above the rushing water.

[1932]

ZORA NEALE HURSTON

Zora Neale Hurston (1891–1960) was born to a family of sharecroppers in Notasulga, Alabama. When she was very young she moved to Eatonville, Florida, a town founded by African Americans. After her mother died in 1904, her father, a Baptist preacher, couldn't raise their eight children, so Hurston was forced to move from one relative's home to another. She never finished grade school, but when she was old enough to support herself, she attended Howard University in Washington, D.C. In 1921 she published her first story, "John Redding Goes to Sea," in the student literary magazine.

In 1925 Hurston went to New York City and became active in the cultural renaissance in Harlem, collaborating with Langston Hughes on a folk comedy, Mule Bone. Like Hughes, she was deeply interested in the abiding folk spirit inherent in southern life. With several other writers of that time, she tried to express her cultural heritage by writing short stories. The Eatonville Anthology (1927) was the collection that first brought Hurston's work to the attention of a national audience. After Hurston studied with the famous anthropologist Franz Boas at Barnard College, she returned to Florida to record the oral traditions of her native community. As critics have noted, from this time to the end of her life she tried to achieve a balance in her literary work between the folk culture of her racial background and her individuality as a developing artist. Realizing that average white people used stereotypes to keep African Americans, Asian Americans, Hispanic Americans, and Native Americans in their "place," Hurston insisted that it was

> urgent to realize that minorities do think, and think about something other than the race problem. That they are very human and internally, according to natural endowment, are just like everybody else. So long as this is not conceived, there must remain that feeling of unsurmountable difference, and difference to the average man means something bad. If people were made right, they would be just like him.

During the Great Depression of the 1930s, Hurston turned all her energies to writing. "The Gilded Six-Bits" appeared in Story in 1933. She published Mules and Men (1935), based on material from her field trips to Florida, and Their Eyes Were Watching God (1937), a novel about a woman's search for love and personal identity, in addition to several other books, including an autobiography. Although she published more than any other African American woman writer of her time, in the last two decades of her life she earned very little from her writing. Fifteen years after Hurston's death, her work was rediscovered by black authors such as Alice Walker, and she is now regarded as an important American writer.

RELATED COMMENTARIES: Zora Neale Hurston, "What White Publishers Won't Print," page 1368; Alice Walker, "Zora Neale Hurston: A Cautionary Tale and a Partisan View," page 1469.

The Gilded Six-Bits

It was a Negro yard around a Negro house in a Negro settlement that looked to the payroll of the G and G Fertilizer works for its support.

But there was something happy about the place. The front yard was parted in the middle by a sidewalk from gate to doorstep, a sidewalk edged on either side by quart bottles driven neck down to the ground on a slant. A mess of homey flowers planted without a plan but blooming cheerily from their helter-skelter places. The fence and house were whitewashed. The porch and steps scrubbed white.

The front door stood open to the sunshine so that the floor of the front room could finish drying after its weekly scouring. It was Saturday. Everything clean from the front gate to the privy house. Yard raked so that the strokes of the rake would make a pattern. Fresh newspaper cut in fancy-edge on the kitchen shelves.

Missie May was bathing herself in the galvanized washtub in the bedroom. Her dark-brown skin glistened under the soapsuds that skittered down from her wash rag. Her stiff young breasts thrust forward aggressively like broad-based cones with the tips lacquered in black.

She heard men's voices in the distance and glanced at the dollar clock on the dresser.

"Humph! Ah'm way behind time t'day! Joe gointer be heah 'fore Ah git mah clothes on if Ah don't make haste."

She grabbed the clean meal sack at hand and dried herself hurriedly and began to dress. But before she could tie her slippers, there came the ring of singing metal on wood. Nine times.

Missie May grinned with delight. She had not seen the big tall man come stealing in the gate and creep up the walk grinning happily at the joyful mischief he was about to commit. But she knew that it was her husband throwing silver dollars in the door for her to pick up and pile beside her plate at dinner. It was this way every Saturday afternoon. The nine dollars hurled into the open door, he scurried to a hiding place behind the cape jasmine bush and waited.

Missie May promptly appeared at the door in mock alarm.

"Who dat chunkin' money in mah do'way?" she demanded. No answer from the yard. She leaped off the porch and began to search the shrubbery. She peeped under the porch and hung over the gate to look up and down the road. While she did this, the man behind the jasmine darted to the chinaberry tree. She spied him and gave chase.

"Nobody ain't gointer be chunkin' money at me and Ah not do'em nothin'," she shouted in mock anger. He ran around the house with Missie May at his heels. She overtook him at the kitchen door. He ran inside but could not close it after him before she crowded in and locked with him in a rough and tumble. For several minutes the two were a furious mass of male and female energy. Shouting, laughing, twisting, turning, and Joe trying, but not too hard, to get away.

"Missie May, take yo' hand out mah pocket!" Joe shouted out between laughs.

"Ah ain't, Joe, not lessen you gwine gimme whateve' it is good you got in yo' pocket. Turn it go Jo, do Ah'll tear yo' clothes."

"Go on tear 'em. You de one dat pushes de needles round heah. Move yo' hand Missie May."

"Lemme git dat paper sack out yo' pocket. Ah bet its candy kisses."

"Tain't. Move yo' hand. Woman ain't got no business in a man's clothes nowhow. Go 'way."

Missie May gouged way down and gave an upward jerk and triumphed.

"Unhhunh! Ah got it. It 'tis so candy kisses. Ah knowed you had somethin' for me in yo' clothes. Now Ah got to see whut's in every pocket you got."

Joe smiled indulgently and let his wife go through all of his pockets and take out the things that he had hidden there for her to find. She bore off the chewing gum, the cake of sweet soap, the pocket handkerchief as if she had wrested them from him, as if they had not been bought for the sake of this friendly battle.

"Whew! dat play-fight done got me all warmed up," Joe exclaimed. "Got me some water in de kittle?"

"Yo' water is on de fire and yo' clean things is cross de bed. Hurry up and wash yo'self and git changed so we kin eat. Ah'm hongry." As Missie said this, she bore the steaming kettle into the bedroom.

"You ain't hongry, sugar," Joe contradicted her. "Youse jes's little empty. Ah'm de one whut's hongry. Ah could eat up camp meetin,' back off 'ssociation, and drink Jurdan dry. Have it on de table when Ah git out de tub."

"Don't you mess wid mah business, man. You git in yo' clothes. Ah'm a real wife, not no dress and breath. Ah might not look lak one, but if you burn me, you won't git a thing but wife ashes."

Joe splashed in the bedroom and Missie May fanned around in the kitchen. A fresh red and white checked cloth on the table. Big pitcher of buttermilk beaded with pale drops of butter from the churn. Hot fried mullet, crackling bread, ham hocks atop a mound of string beans and new potatoes, and perched on the window-sill a pone of spicy potato pudding.

Very little talk during the meal but that little consisted of banter that pretended to deny affection but in reality flaunted it. Like when Missie May reached for a second helping of the tater pone. Joe snatched it out of her reach. After Missie May had made two or three unsuccessful grabs at the pan, she begged, "Aw, Joe gimme some mo' dat tater pone."

"Nope, sweetenin' is for us men-folks. Y'all pritty li'l frail eels don't need nothin' lak dis. You too sweet already."

"Please, Joe."

"Naw, naw. Ah don't want you to get no sweeter than whut you is already. We goin' down de road al li'l piece t'night so you go put on yo' Sunday-go-to-meetin' things."

Missie May looked at her husband to see if he was playing some prank. "Sho' nuff, Joe?"

"Yeah. We goin' to de ice cream parlor."

"Where de ice cream parlor at, Joe?"

"A new man done come heah from Chicago and he done got a place and took and opened it up for a ice cream parlor, and bein' as it's real swell, Ah wants you to be one de first ladies to walk in dere and have some set down."

"Do Jesus, Ah ain't knowed nothin' 'bout it. Who de man done it?"

"Mister Otis D. Slemmons, of spots and places — Memphis, Chicago, Jacksonville, Philadelphia, and so on."

"Dat heavy-set man wid his mouth full of gold teethes?"

"Yeah. Where did you see 'im at?"

"Ah went down to de sto' tuh git a box of lye and Ah seen 'im standin' on de corner talkin' to some of de mens, and Ah come on back and went to scrubbin' de floor, and he passed and tipped his hat whilst Ah was scourin' de steps. Ah thought never Ah seen *him* befo'."

Joe smiled pleasantly. "Yeah, he's up to date. He got de finest clothes Ah ever seen on a colored man's back."

"Aw, he don't look no better in his clothes than you do in yourn. He got a puzzlegut on 'im and he so chuckle-headed, he got a pone behind his neck."

Joe looked down at his own abdomen and said wistfully, "Wisht Ah had a build on me lak he got. He ain't puzzle-gutted, honey. He jes' got a corperation. Dat make 'm look lak a rich white man. All rich mens is got some belly on 'em."

"Ah seen de pitchers of Henry Ford and he's a spare-built man and Rockefeller look lak he ain't got but one gut. But Ford and Rockefeller and dis Slemmons and all de rest kin be as many-gutted as dey please, ah'm satisfied wid you jes' lak you is, baby. God took pattern after a pine tree and built you noble. Youse a pretty still man, and if Ah knowed any way to make you mo' pretty still Ah'd take and do it."

Joe reached over gently and toyed with Missie May's ear. "You jes' say dat cause you love me, but Ah know Ah can't hold no light to Otis D. Slemmons. Ah ain't never been nowhere and Ah ain't got nothin' but you."

"How you know dat, Joe."

"He tole us so hisself."

"Dat don't make it so. His mouf is cut cross-ways, ain't it? Well, he kin lie jes' lak anybody els."

"Good Lawd, Missie! You womens sho' is hard to sense into things. He's got a five-dollar gold piece for a stick-pin and he got a ten-dollar gold piece on his watch chain and his mouf is jes' crammed full of gold teethes. Sho' wisht it wuz mine. And whut make it so cool, he got money 'cumulated. And womens give it all to 'im."

"Ah don't see whut de womens see on 'im. Ah wouldn't give 'im a wind if de sherff wuz after 'im."

"Well, he tole us how de white womens in Chicago give 'im all dat gold money. So he don't 'low nobody to touch it at all. Not even put dey finger on it. Dey tole 'im not to. You kin make 'miration at it, but don't tetch it."

"Whyn't he stay up dere where dey so crazy 'bout 'im?"

"Ah reckon dey done made 'im vast-rich and he wants to travel some. He say dey wouldn't leave 'im hit a lick of work. He got mo' lady people crazy 'bout him than he kin shake a stick at."

"Joe, Ah hates to see you so dumb. Dat stray nigger jes' tell y'all anything and y'all b'lieve it."

"Go 'head on now, honey and put on yo' clothes. He talkin' 'bout his pritty womens—Ah want 'im to see *mine*."

Missie May went off to dress and Joe spent the time trying to make his stomach punch out like Slemmons' middle. He tried the rolling swagger of the stranger, but found that his tall bone-and-muscle stride fitted ill with it. He just had time to drop back into his seat before Missie May came in dressed to go.

On the way home that night Joe was exultant. "Didn't Ah say ole Otis was swell? Can't he talk Chicago talk? Wuzn't dat funny whut he said when great big fat ole Ida Armstrong come in? He asted me, 'Who is dat broad wid de forty shake?' Dat's a new word. Us always thought forty was a set of figgers but he showed us where it means a whole heap of things. Sometimes he don't say forty, he jes' say thirty-eight and two and dat mean de same thing. Know whut he tole me when Ah was payin' for our ice cream? He say, 'Ah have to hand it to you, Joe. Dat wife of yours is jes' thirty-eight and two. Yessuh, she's forty!' Ain't he killin?"

"He'll do in case of a rush. But he sho' is got uh heap uh gold on 'im. Dat's de first time Ah ever seed gold money. It lookted good on him sho' nuff, but it'd look a whole heap better on you."

"Who, me? Missie May was youse crazy! Where would a po' man lak me git gold money from?"

Missie May was silent for a minute, then she said, "Us might find some goin' long de road some time. Us could."

"Who would be losin' gold money 'round heah? We ain't even seen none dese white folks wearin' no gold money on dey watch chain. You must be figgeren' Mister Packard or Mister Cadillac goin' pass through heah . . ."

"You don't know whut been lost 'round heah. Maybe somebody way back in memorial times lost they gold money and went on off and it ain't never been found. And then if we wuz to find it, you could wear some 'thout havin' no gang of womens lak dat Slemmons say he got."

Joe laughed and hugged her. "Don't be so wishful 'bout me. Ah'm satisfied de way Ah is. So long as Ah be yo' husband, ah don't keer 'bout nothin' else. Ah'd ruther all de other womens in de world to be dead than for you to have de toothache. Less we go to bed and git our night rest."

It was Saturday night once more before Joe could parade his wife in Slemmons' ice cream parlor again. He worked the night shift and Saturday was his only night off. Every other evening around six o'clock he left home, and dying dawn saw him hustling home around the lake where the challenging sun flung a flaming sword from east to west across the trembling water.

That was the best part of life — going home to Missie May. Their white-washed house, the mock battle on Saturday, the dinner and ice cream parlor afterwards, church on Sunday nights when Missie outdressed any woman in town — all, everything was right.

One night around eleven the acid ran out at the G and G. The foreman knocked off the crew and let the steam die down. As Joe rounded the lake on his way home, a lean moon rode the lake in a silver boat. If anybody had asked Joe about the moon on the lake, he would have said he hadn't paid it any attention. But he saw it with his feelings. It made him yearn painfully for Missie. Creation obsessed him. He thought about children. They had been married for more than a year now. They had money put away. They ought to be making little feet for shoes. A little boy child would be about right.

He saw a dim light in the bedroom and decided to come in through the kitchen door. He could wash the fertilizer dust off himself before presenting himself to Missie May. It would be nice for her not to know that he was there until he slipped into his place in bed and hugged her back. She always liked that.

He eased the kitchen door open slowly and silently, but when he went to set his dinner bucket on the table he bumped it into a pile of dishes, and something crashed to the floor. He heard his wife gasp in fright and hurried to reassure her.

"Iss me, honey. Don't get skeered."

There was a quick, large movement in the bedroom. A rustle, a thud, and a stealthy silence. The light went out.

What? Robbers? Murderers? Some varmint attacking his helpless wife, perhaps. He struck a match, threw himself on guard, and stepped over the door-sill into the bedroom.

The great belt on the wheel of Time slipped and eternity stood still.

By the match light he could see the man's legs fighting with his breeches in his frantic desire to get them on. He had both chance and time to kill the intruder in his helpless condition—half-in and half-out of his pants—but he was too weak to take action. The shapeless enemies of humanity that live in the hours of Time had waylaid Joe. He was assaulted in his weakness. Like Samson awakening after his haircut. So he just opened his mouth and laughed.

The match went out and he struck another and lit the lamp. A howling wind raced across his heart, but underneath its fury he heard his wife sobbing and Slemmons pleading for his life. Offering to buy it with all that he had. "Please, suh, don't kill me. Sixty-two dollars at de sto' gold money."

Joe just stood. Slemmons looked at the window, but it was screened. Joe stood out like a rough-backed mountain between him and the door. Barring him from escape, from sunrise, from life.

He considered a surprise attack upon the big clown that stood there laughing like a chessy cat. But before his fist could travel an inch, Joe's own rushed out to crush him like a battering ram. Then Joe stood over him.

"Git into yo' damn rags, Slemmons, and dat quick."

Slemmons scrambled to his feet and into his vest and coat. As he grabbed his hat, Joe's fury overrode his intentions and he grabbed at Slemmons with his left hand and struck at him with his right. The right landed. The left grazed the front of his vest. Slemmons was knocked a somersault into the kitchen and fled through the open door. Joe found himself alone with Missie May, with the golden watch charm clutched in his left fist. A short bit of broken chain dangled between his fingers.

Missie May was sobbing. Wails of weeping without words. Joe stood, and after awhile she found out that he had something in his hand. And then he stood and felt without thinking and without seeing with his natural eyes. Missie May kept on crying and Joe kept on feeling so much and not knowing what to do with all his feelings, he put Slemmons' watch charm in his pants pocket and took a good laugh and went to bed.

"Missie May, whut you crying for?"

"Cause Ah love you so hard and Ah know you don't love *me* no mo'."

Joe sank his face into the pillow for a spell then he said huskily, "You don't know de feelings of dat yet, Missie May."

"Oh Joe, honey, he said he wuz gointer gimme dat gold money and he jes' kept on after me—"

Joe was very still and silent for a long time. Then he said, "Well, don't cry no mo', Missie May. Ah got yo' gold piece for you."

The hours went past on their rusty ankles. Joe still and quiet on one bed-rail and Missie May wrung dry of sobs on the other. Finally the sun's tide crept upon the shore of night and drowned all its hours. Missie May with her face stiff and streaked towards the window saw the dawn come into her yard. It was day. Nothing more. Joe wouldn't be coming home as usual. No need to fling open the front door and sweep off the porch, making it nice for Joe. Never no more breakfast to cook; no more washing and starching of Joe's jumper-jackets and pants. No more nothing. So why get up?

With this strange man in her bed, she felt embarrassed to get up and dress. She decided to wait till he had dressed and gone. Then she would get up, dress quickly, and be gone forever beyond reach of Joe's looks and laughs. But he never moved. Red light turned to yellow, then white.

From beyond the no-man's land between them came a voice. A strange voice that yesterday had been Joe's.

"Missie May, ain't you gonna fix me no breakfus'?"

She sprang out of bed. "Yeah, Joe. Ah didn't reckon you wuz hongry."

No need to die today. Joe needed her for a few more minutes anyhow.

Soon there was a roaring fire in the cook stove. Water bucket full and two chickens killed. Joe loved fried chicken and rice. She didn't deserve a thing and good Joe was letting her cook him some breakfast. She rushed hot biscuits to the table as Joe took his seat.

He ate with his eyes on his plate. No laughter, no banter.

"Missie May, you ain't eatin' yo' breakfus'."

"Ah don't choose none, Ah thank yuh."

His coffee cup was empty. She sprang to refill it. When she turned from the stove and bent to set the cup beside Joe's plate, she saw the yellow coin on the table between them.

She slumped into her seat and wept into her arms.

Presently Joe said calmly, "Missie May, you cry too much. Don't look back lak Lot's wife and turn to salt."

The sun, the hero of every day, the impersonal old man that beams as brightly on death as on birth, came up every morning and raced across the blue dome and dipped into the sea of fire every evening. Water ran down hill and birds nested.

Missie knew why she didn't leave Joe. She couldn't. She loved him too much. But she couldn't understand why Joe didn't leave her. He was polite, even kind at times, but aloof.

There were no more Saturday romps. No ringing silver dollars to stack beside her plate. No pockets to rifle. In fact the yellow coin in his trousers was like a monster hiding in the cave of his pockets to destroy her.

She often wondered if he still had it, but nothing could have induced her to ask nor yet to explore his pockets to see for herself. Its shadow was in the house whether or no.

One night Joe came home around midnight and complained of pains in the back. He asked Missie to rub him down with liniment. It had been three months since Missie had touched his body and it all seemed strange. But she rubbed him. Grateful for the chance. Before morning, youth triumphed and Missie exulted. But the next day, as she joyfully made up their bed, beneath her pillow she found the piece of money with the bit of chain attached.

Alone to herself, she looked at the thing with loathing, but look she must. She took it into her hands with trembling and saw first thing that it was no gold piece. It was a gilded half-dollar. Then she knew why Slemmons had forbidden anyone to touch his gold. He trusted village eyes at a distance not to recognize his stick-pin as a gilded quarter, and his watch charm as a four-bit piece.

She was glad at first that Joe had left it there. Perhaps he was through with her punishment. They were man and wife again. Then another thought came clawing at her. He had come home to buy from her as if she were any woman in the long house. Fifty cents for her love. As if to say that he could pay as well as Slemmons. She slid the coin into his Sunday pants pocket and dressed herself and left his house.

Halfway between her house and the quarters she met her husband's mother, and after a short talk she turned and went back home. If she had not the substance of marriage, she had the outside show. Joe must leave *her*. She let him see she didn't want his old gold four-bits too.

She saw no more of the coin for some time though she knew that Joe could not help finding it in his pocket. But his health kept poor, and he came home at least every ten days to be rubbed.

The sun swept around the horizon, trailing its robes of weeks and days. One morning as Joe came in from work, he found Missie May chopping wood. Without a word he took the ax and chopped a huge pile before he stopped.

"You ain't got no business choppin' wood, and you know it."

"How come? Ah been choppin' it for de last longest."

"Ah ain't blind. You makin' feet for shoes."

"Won't you be glad to have a li'l baby chile, Joe?"

"You know dat 'thout astin' me."

"Iss gointer be a boy chile and de very spit of you."

"You reckon, Missie May?"

"Who else could it look lak?"

Joe said nothing, but he thrust his hand deep into his pocket and fingered something there.

It was almost six months later Missie May took to bed and Joe went and got his mother to come wait on the house.

Missie May delivered a fine boy. Her travail was over when Joe came in from work one morning. His mother and the old women were drinking great bowls of coffee around the fire in the kitchen.

The minute Joe came into the room his mother called him aside.

"How did Missie May make out?" he asked quickly.

"Who, dat gal? She strong as a ox. She gointer have plenty mo'. We done fixed her wid de sugar and lard to sweeten her for de nex' one."

Joe stood silent awhile.

"You ain't ast 'bout de baby, Joe. You oughter be mighty proud cause he sho' is de spittin' image of yuh, son. Dat's yourn all right, if you never git another one, dat un is yourn. And you know Ah'm mighty proud too, son, cause Ah never thought well of you marryin' Missie May cause her ma used tuh fan her foot 'round right smart and Ah been mighty skeered dat Missie May wuz gointer git misput on her road."

Joe said nothing. He fooled around the house till late in the day then just before he went to work, he went and stood at the foot of the bed and asked his wife how she felt. He did this every day during the week.

On Saturday he went to Orlando to make his market. It had been a long time since he had done that.

Meat and lard, meal and flour, soap and starch. Cans of corn and tomatoes. All the staples. He fooled around town for awhile and bought bananas and apples. Way after while he went around to the candy store.

"Hellow, Joe," the clerk greeted him. "Ain't seen you in a long time."

"Nope, Ah ain't been heah. Been 'round spots and places."

"Want some of them molasses kisses you always buy?"

"Yessuh." He threw the gilded half-dollar on the counter. "Will dat spend?"

"Whut is it, Joe? Well, I'll be doggone! A gold-plated four-bit piece. Where'd you git it, Joe?"

"Offen a stray nigger dat come through Eatonville. He had it on his watch chain for a charm — goin' 'round making out iss gold money. Ha ha! He had a quarter on his tie pin and it wuz all golded up too. Tryin' to fool people. Makin' out he so rich and everything. Ha! Ha! Trying' to tole off folkses wives from home."

"How did you git it, Joe? Did he fool you, too?"

"Who, me? Naw suh! He ain't fooled me none. Know whut Ah done? He come 'round me wid his smart talk. Ah hauled off and knocked 'im down and took his old four-bits 'way from 'im. Gointer buy my wife some good ole 'lasses kisses wid it. Gimme fifty cents worth of dem candy kisses."

"Fifty cents buys a mightly lot of candy kisses, Joe. Why don't you split it up and take some chocolate bars, too. They eat good, too."

"Yessuh, de do, but Ah wants all dat in kisses. Ah got a li'l boy chile home now. Tain't a week old yet, but he kin suck a sugar tit and maybe eat one them kisses hisself."

Joe got his candy and left the store. The clerk turned to the next customer. "Wisht I could be like these darkies. Laughin' all the time. Nothin' worries 'em."

Back in Eatonville, Joe reached his own front door. There was the ring of singing metal on wood. Fifteen times. Missie May couldn't run to the door, but she crept there as quickly as she could.

"Joe Banks, Ah hear you chunkin' money in mah do'way. You wait till Ah got mah strength back and Ah'm gointer fix you for dat."   [1933]

LANGSTON HUGHES

Langston Hughes (1902–1967), who was to become one of the first American poets to reach a wide audience with a direct, personal poetic style created from the rhythms and language of everyday black speech, was born in Joplin, Missouri. In his high school classes he read the poetry of Carl Sandburg and Edgar Lee Masters, and he published several poems in the literary magazine. Hughes's father persuaded him to study engineering at Columbia University, but after only one year Hughes abandoned his studies and signed on as a mess boy on a ship that took him to Africa and Europe. He had begun to place his poetry in the NAACP magazine The Crisis, *including what was to become one of his best-known poems, "The Negro Speaks of Rivers" (which he had written as a teenager), and he was determined to be a writer.*

Hughes's career as an African American poet was launched a few years later with his book The Weary Blues *(1926), poems about a Harlem musician. Hughes completed a B.A. from Lincoln University in Pennsylvania and then settled in New York City. During the Harlem Renaissance he became an important member of the literary group including Zora Neale Hurston, Nella Larsen, Jean Toomer, Countee Cullen, and Claude McKay, writers who emphasized Negro topics — their African heritage, the slave era, and modern city life. Exhibiting an impressive versatility and productivity in his career, Hughes wrote plays as well as poetry and prose and edited twenty-eight collections of African American poetry and folklore. As his biographer Arnold Rampersad wrote, the greatest truth about Hughes's life was that his "true satisfaction came only from the love and regard of the black race, which he earned by placing his finest gift, his skill with language, in its service."*

Hughes's interest in fiction developed later than his talent for poetry. As he described it in his autobiography I Wonder As I Wander *(1956), he was traveling in the Soviet Union in the early 1930s when he picked up a paperback copy of a collection of short stories he had never read before by D. H. Lawrence. He was so impressed with them — especially with "The Rocking-Horse Winner" — that a night or two later he sat down at his well-traveled portable typewriter to write stories of his own. Hughes sent his first three stories to his literary agent in New York, and by the time he returned to the United States, all three had been sold to popular magazines. His early fiction, including "Red-Headed Baby," was published as* The Ways of White Folks *in 1934. During World War II Hughes began to write a series of stories in the* Chicago Defender *newspaper about an imaginary character named Jesse B. Semple, a working-class black man living in Harlem, whose conversations blended urban cynicism and genial mother wit on a wide variety of timely topics, such as war, racial prejudice, women's rights, unemployment, and education for blacks. Hughes published three collections of these stories as well as* The Best of Simple *(1961).* The Short Stories of Langston Hughes *was published in 1996.*

Red-Headed Baby

"Dead, dead as hell, these little burgs on the Florida coast. Lot of half-built skeleton houses left over from the boom. Never finished. Never will be finished. Mosquitoes, sand, niggers. Christ, I ought to break away from it. Stuck five years on same boat and still nothin' but a third mate puttin' in at dumps like this on a damned coast-wise tramp. Not even a good time to be had. Norfolk, Savannah, Jacksonville, ain't bad. Ain't bad. But what the hell kind of port's this? What the hell is there to do except get drunk and go out and sleep with niggers? Hell!"

Feet in the sand. Head under palms, magnolias, stars. Lights and the kid-cries of a sleepy town. Mosquitoes to slap at with hairy freckled hands and a dead hot breeze, when there is any breeze.

"What the hell am I walkin' way out here for? She wasn't nothin' to get excited over — last time I saw her. And that must a been a full three years ago. She acted like she was a virgin then. Name was Betsy. Sure ain't a virgin now, I know that. Not after we'd been anchored here damn near a month, the old man mixed up in some kind of law suit over some rich guy's yacht we rammed in a midnight squall off the bar. Damn good thing I wasn't on the bridge then. And this damn yellow gal, said she never had nothing to do with a seaman before. Lyin' I guess. Three years ago. She's probably on the crib-line now. Hell, how far was that house?"

Crossing the railroad track at the edge of town. Green lights. Sand in the road, seeping into oxfords and the cuffs of dungarees. Surf sounds, mosquito sounds, nigger-cries in the night. No street lights out here. There never is where niggers live. Rickety run-down huts, under palm trees. Flowers and vines all over. Always growing, always climbing. Never finished. Never will be finished climbing, growing. Hell of a lot of stars these Florida nights.

"Say, this ought to be the house. No light in it. Well, I remember this half-fallin'-down gate. Still fallin' down. Hell, why don't it go on and fall? Two or three years, and ain't fell yet. Guess *she's* fell a hell of a lot, though. It don't take them yellow janes long to get old and ugly. Said she was seventeen then. A wonder her old woman let me come in the house that night. They acted like it was the first time a white man had ever come in the house. They acted scared. But she was worth the money that time all right. She played like a kid. Said she liked my red hair. Said she'd never had a white man before. . . . Holy Jesus, the yellow wenches I've had, though. . . . Well, it's the same old gate. Be funny if she had another mule in my stall, now wouldn't it? . . . Say, anybody home there?"

"Yes, suh! Yes, suh! Come right in!"

"Hell, I know they can't recognize my voice. . . . It's the old woman, sure as a yard arm's long. . . . Hello! Where's Betsy?"

"Yes, suh, right here, suh. In de kitchen. Wait till I lights de light. Come in. Come in, young gentleman."

"Hell, I can't see to come in."

Little flare of oil light.

"Howdy! Howdy do, suh! Howdy, if 'tain't Mister Clarence, now, 'pon my word! Howdy, Mister Clarence, howdy! Howdy! After sich a long time."

"You must-a knowed my voice."

"No, suh, ain't recollected, suh. No, suh, but I knowed you was some white man comin' up de walk. Yes, indeedy! Set down, set down. Betsy be here directly. Set *right* down. Lemme call her. She's in de kitchen. . . . You Betsy!"

"Same old woman, wrinkled as hell, and still don't care where the money comes from. Still talkin' loud. . . . She knew it was some white man comin' up the walk, heh? There must be plenty of 'em, then, comin' here now. She knew it was some white man, heh! . . . What yuh sayin', Betsy, old gal? Damn if yuh ain't just as plump as ever. Them same damn moles on your cheek! Com'ere, lemme feel 'em."

Young yellow girl in a white house dress. Oiled hair. Skin like an autumn moon. Gold-ripe young yellow girl with a white house dress to her knees. Soft plump bare legs, color of the moon. Bare-footed.

"Say, Betsy, here is Mister Clarence come back."

"Sure is! Claren—Mister Clarence! Ma, give him a drink."

"Keepin' licker in the house, now, heh? Yes? I thought you was church members last time I saw yuh? You always had to send out and get licker then."

"Well, we's expectin' company some of the times these days," smiling teeth like bright-white rays of moon, Betsy, nearly twenty, and still pretty.

"You usin' rouge, too, ain't yuh?"

"Sweet rouge."

"Yal?"

"Yeah, man, sweet and red like your hair."

"Yal?"

No such wise cracking three years ago. Too young and dumb for flirtation then: Betsy. Never like the old woman, talkative, "This here rum come right off de boats from Bermudy. Taste it, Mister Clarence. Strong enough to knock a mule down. Have a glass."

"Here's to you, Mister Clarence."

"Drinkin' licker, too, heh? Hell of a baby, ain't yuh? Yuh wouldn't even do that last time I saw yuh."

"Sure wouldn't, Mister Clarence, but three years a long time."

"Don't Mister Clarence *me* so much. Yuh know I christened yuh. . . . Auntie, yuh right about this bein' good licker."

"Yes, suh, I knowed you'd like it. It's strong."

"Sit on my lap, kid."

"Sure. . . ."

Soft heavy hips. Hot and browner than the moon—good licker. Drinking it down in little nigger house Florida coast palm fronds scratching roof hum mosquitoes night bugs flies ain't loud enough to keep a man named Clarence girl named Betsy old woman named Auntie from talking and drinking in a little nigger house on Florida coast dead warm night with the licker browner and more fiery than the moon. Yeah, man! A blanket of stars in the Florida sky—outside. In oil-lamp house you don't see no stars. Only a white man with red hair—third mate on a lousy tramp, a nigger girl, and Auntie wrinkled as an alligator bringing the fourth bottle of licker and everybody drinking—when the door . . . slowly . . . opens.

"Say, what the hell? Who's openin' that room door, peepin' in here? It can't be openin' itself?"

The white man stares intently, looking across the table, past the lamp, the licker bottles, the glasses and the old woman, way past the girl. Standing in the door from the kitchen—Look! a damn red-headed baby. Standing not saying a damn word, a damn runt of a red-headed baby.

"What the hell?"

"You Clar—. . . Mister Clarence, 'cuse me! . . . You hatian, you, get back to you' bed this minute—fo' I tan you in a inch o' yo' life!"

"Ma, let him stay."

Betsy's red-headed child stands in the door looking like one of those goggly-eyed dolls you hit with a ball at the County Fair. The child's face got no change in it. Never changes. Looks like never will change. Just staring—blue-eyed. Hell! God damn! A red-headed blue-eyed yellow-skinned baby!

"You Clarence! . . . 'Cuse me, Mister Clarence. I ain't talkin' to you suh. . . . You, Clarence, go to bed. . . . That chile near 'bout worries de soul-case out o' me. Betsy spiles him, that's why. De po' little thing can't hear, nohow. Just deaf as a post. And over two years old and can't even say, 'Da!' No, suh, can't say, 'Da!'"

"Anyhow, Ma, my child ain't blind."

"Might just as well be blind fo' all de good his eyesight do him. I show him a switch and he don't pay it no mind—'less'n I hit him."

"He's mighty damn white for a nigger child."

"Yes, suh, Mister Clarence. He really ain't got much colored blood in him, a-tall. Betsy's papa, Mister Clarence, now he were a white man, too. . . . Here, lemme pour you some licker. Drink, Mister Clarence, drink."

Damn little red-headed stupid-faced runt of a child, named Clarence. Bow-legged as hell, too. Three shots for a quarter like a loaded doll in a County Fair. Anybody take a chance. For Christ's sake, stop him from walking across the floor! Will yuh?

"Hey! Take your hands off my legs, you lousy little bastard!"

"He can't hear you, Mister Clarence."

"Tell him to stop crawlin' around then under the table before I knock his block off."

"You varmint. . . ."

"Hey! Take him up from there, will you?"

"Yes, suh, Mister Clarence."

"Hey!"

"You little . . ."

"Hurry! Go on! Get him out then! What's he doin' crawlin' round dumb as hell lookin' at me up at me. I said, *me*. Get him the hell out of here! Hey, Betsy, get him out!"

A red-headed baby. Moonlight-gone baby. No kind of yellow-white bow-legged goggled-eyed County Fair baseball baby. Get him the hell out of here pulling at my legs looking like me at me like me at myself like me red-headed as me.

"Christ!"

"Christ!"

Knocking over glasses by the oil lamp on the table where the night flies flutter Florida where skeleton houses left over from boom sand in the road and no lights in the nigger section across the railroad's knocking over glasses at edge of town where a moon-colored girl's got a red-headed baby deaf as a post like the dolls you wham at three shots for a quarter in the County Fair half full of licker and can't hit nothing.

"Lemme pay for those drinks, will yuh? How much is it?"

"Ain't you gonna stay, Mister Clarence?"

"Lemme pay for my licker, I said."

"Ain't you gonna stay all night?"

"Lemme pay for that licker."

"Why, Mister Clarence? You stayed before."

"How much is the licker?"

"Two dollars, Mister Clarence."

"Here."

"Thank you, Mister Clarence."

"Go'bye!"

"Go'bye."   [1934]

WILLIAM SAROYAN

*W*illiam Saroyan (1908–1981) was born in Fresno, California, three years *after his father, a survivor of the Turkish massacre of the Armenians, had emigrated to America from the Armenian-Kurdish town of Bitlis in eastern Turkey. When Saroyan's father died in 1911, William, his brother, and his two sisters were placed in an orphanage in Oakland. In 1915 they were taken back to Fresno to live with their mother, who was employed as a domestic servant. Saroyan went to public schools but dropped out of high school and moved to San Francisco to work various jobs while he tried to write fiction. At the age of twenty, after publishing his first story in a local magazine, he decided to make his career as a writer.*

Saroyan had begun writing at fourteen when he read the stories of Guy de Maupassant. Later he said that he was less interested in Maupassant's skill as a craftsman than he was in the powerful "sadness" of the stories. That "sadness," Saroyan added, "contained within itself a power and joyousness which I believed to be more important to me than anything else in the world that I might discover, inherit, earn, or steal." When Saroyan also discovered the short fiction of Sherwood Anderson, he took Anderson as his teacher because Anderson showed him that it was possible for a writer to develop a unique voice. Like Anderson, Saroyan believed that what a story was about was never as important as the way it was told.

After writing a story-length version of his early, unpublished stream-of-consciousness novel Trapeze over the Universe, *retitling it "The Daring Young Man on the Flying Trapeze," Saroyan sold it to* Story *magazine in December 1933 for fifteen dollars. Elated by the sale, Saroyan attempted to complete a book of stories in a month.* Story *agreed to publish several of them, including "Seventy Thousand Assyrians" (1934). By the end of January 1934 he had the material for his first published book,* The Daring Young Man on the Flying Trapeze and Other Stories. *He placed "Seventy Thousand Assyrians" second in the collection to make his Armenian background explicit. By 1940 Saroyan had written five hundred stories, as well as essays, poems, and plays. The best of his fiction can be found in his collections* The Daring Young Man on the Flying Trapeze and Other Stories *(1934),* Inhale and Exhale *(1936), and* My Name Is Aram *(1940). In 1939 Saroyan turned down the Pulitzer Prize for his play* The Time of Your Life *because he said he didn't think businessmen were qualified to judge art. He continued writing and publishing more than fifty books until his death from cancer, ending his last book,* Obituaries *(1979), with the words, "I did my best, and let me urge you to do your best, too. Isn't it the least we can do for one another?"*

RELATED COMMENTARY: *William Saroyan, "Writing Stories," page 1447.*

Seventy Thousand Assyrians

I hadn't had a haircut in forty days and forty nights, and I was beginning to look like several violinists out of work. You know the look: genius gone to pot, and ready to join the Communist Party. We barbarians from Asia Minor are hairy people: when we need a haircut, we *need* a haircut. It was so bad, I had outgrown my only hat. (I am writing a very serious story, perhaps one of the most serious I shall ever write. That is why I am being flippant. Readers of Sherwood Anderson will begin to understand what I am saying after a while; they will know that my laughter is rather sad.) I was a young man in need of a haircut, so I went down to Third Street (San Francisco), to the Barber College, for a fifteen-cent haircut.

Third Street, below Howard, is a district; think of the Bowery in New York, Main Street in Los Angeles: think of old men and boys, out of work, hanging around, smoking Bull Durham, talking about the government, waiting for something to turn up, simply waiting. It was a Monday morning in August and a lot of the tramps had come to the shop to brighten up a bit. The Japanese boy who was working over the free chair had a waiting list of eleven; all the other chairs were occupied. I sat down and began to wait. Outside, as Hemingway (*The Sun Also Rises; Farewell to Arms; Death in the Afternoon; Winner Take Nothing*) would say, haircuts were four bits. I had twenty cents and a half-pack of Bull Durham. I rolled a cigarette, handed the pack to one of my contemporaries who looked in need of nicotine, and inhaled the dry smoke, thinking of America, what was going on politically, economically, spiritually. My contemporary was a boy of sixteen. He looked Iowa; splendid potentially, a solid American, but down, greatly down in the mouth. Little sleep, no change of clothes for several days, a little fear, etc. I wanted very much to know his name. A writer is always wanting to get the reality of faces and figures. Iowa said, "I just got in from Salinas. No work in the lettuce fields. Going north now, to Portland; try to ship out." I wanted to tell him how it was with me: rejected story from *Scribner's,* rejected essay from *The Yale Review,* no money for decent cigarettes, worn shoes, old shirts, but I was afraid to make something of my own troubles. A writer's troubles are always boring, a bit unreal. People are apt to feel, *Well, who asked you to write in the first place?* A man must pretend not to be a writer. I said, "Good luck, north." Iowa shook his head. "I know better. Give it a try, anyway. Nothing to lose." Fine boy, hope he isn't dead, hope he hasn't frozen, mighty cold these days (December, 1933), hope he hasn't gone down; he deserved to live. Iowa, I hope you got work in Portland; I hope you are earning money; I hope you have rented a clean room with a warm bed in it; I hope you are sleeping nights, eating regularly, walking along like a human being, being happy. Iowa, my good wishes are with you. I have said a number of prayers for you. (All the same, I think he is dead by this time. It was in him the day I saw him, the low malicious face of the beast, and at the same time all the theatres in America were showing, over and over again, an animated film-cartoon in which there was a song called "Who's Afraid of the Big Bad Wolf?", and that's what it amounts to; people with money laughing at the death that is crawling slyly into boys like young Iowa, pretending that it isn't there, laughing in warm theatres. I have prayed for Iowa, and I consider myself a coward. By this time he must be dead, and I am sitting in a small room, talking about him, only talking.)

I began to watch the Japanese boy who was learning to become a barber. He was shaving an old tramp who had a horrible face, one of those faces that emerge from years and years of evasive living, years of being unsettled, of not belonging anywhere, of owning nothing, and the Japanese boy was holding his nose back (his own nose) so that he would not smell the old tramp. A trivial point in a story, a bit of data with no place in a work of art, nevertheless, I put it down. A young writer is always afraid some significant fact may escape him. He is always wanting to put in everything he sees. I wanted to know the name of the Japanese boy. I am profoundly interested in names. I have found that those that are unknown are the most genuine. Take a big name like Andrew Mellon. I was watching the Japanese boy very closely. I wanted to understand from the way he was keeping his sense of smell away from the mouth and nostrils of the old man what he was thinking, how he was feeling. Years ago, when I was seventeen, I pruned vines in my uncle's vineyard, north of Sanger, in the San Joaquin Valley, and there were several Japanese working with me, Yoshio Enomoto, Hideo Suzuki, Katsumi Sujimoto, and one or two others. These Japanese taught me a few simple phrases, *hello, how are you, fine day, isn't it, good-bye,* and so on. I said in Japanese to the barber student, "How are you?" He said in Japanese, "Very well, thank you." Then, in impeccable English, "Do you speak Japanese? Have you lived in Japan?" I said, "Unfortunately, no. I am able to speak only one or two words. I used to work with Yoshio Enomoto, Hideo Suzuki, Katsumi Sujimoto; do you know them?" He went on with his work, thinking of the names. He seemed to be whispering, "Enomoto, Suzuki, Sujimoto." He said, "Suzuki. Small man?" I said, "Yes." He said, "I know him. He lives in San Jose now. He is married now."

I want you to know that I am deeply interested in what people remember. A young writer goes out to places and talks to people. He tries to find out what they remember. I am not using great material for a short story. Nothing is going to happen in this work. I am not fabricating a fancy plot. I am not creating memorable characters. I am not using a slick style of writing. I am not building up a fine atmosphere. I have no desire to sell this story or any story to *The Saturday Evening Post* or to *Cosmopolitan* or to *Harper's*. I am not trying to compete with the great writers of short stories, men like Sinclair Lewis and Joseph Hergesheimer and Zane Grey, men who really know how to write, how to make up stories that will sell. Rich men, men who understand all the rules about plot and character and style and atmosphere and all that stuff. I have no desire for fame. I am not out to win the Pulitzer Prize or the Nobel Prize or any other prize. I am out here in the far West, in San Francisco, in a small room on Carl Street, writing a letter to common people, telling them in simple language things they already know. I am merely making a record, so if I wander around a little, it is because I am in no hurry and because I do not know the rules. If I have any desire at all, it is to show the brotherhood of man. This is a big statement and it sounds a little precious. Generally a man is ashamed to make such a statement. He is afraid sophisticated people will laugh at him. But I don't mind. I'm asking sophisticated people to laugh. That is what sophistication is for. I do not believe in races. I do not believe in governments. I see life as one life at one time, so many millions simultaneously, all over the earth. Babies who have not yet been taught to speak any language are the only race of the earth, the race of man: all the rest is pretense, what we call civilization, hatred, fear, desire for strength. . . . But a baby is a baby. And the way they cry, there you have the brotherhood of man, babies crying. We grow up and we learn the words of a language and we see the universe through the language we know, we do not see it through all languages or through no language at all, through silence, for example, and we isolate ourselves in the language we know. Over here we isolate ourselves in English, or American as Mencken[1] calls it. All the eternal things, in our words. If I want to do anything, I want to speak a more universal language. The heart of man, the unwritten part of man, that which is eternal and common to all races.

Now I am beginning to feel guilty and incompetent. I have used all this language and I am beginning to feel that I have said nothing. This is what drives a young writer out of his head, this feeling that nothing is being said. Any ordinary journalist would have been able to put the whole business into a three-word caption. Man is man, he would have said. Something clever, with any number of implications. But I want to use language that will create a single implication. I want the meaning to be precise, and perhaps that is why the language is so imprecise. I am walking around my subject, the impression I want to make, and I am trying to see it from all angles, so that I will have a whole picture, a picture of wholeness. It is the heart of man that I am trying to imply in this work.

Let me try again: I hadn't had a haircut in a long time and I was beginning to look seedy, so I went down to the Barber College on Third Street, and I sat in a chair. I said, "Leave it full in the back. I have a narrow head and if you do not leave it full in the back, I will go out of this place looking like a horse. Take as much as you like off the top. No lotion, no water, comb it dry." Reading makes a full man, writing a precise one, as you see. This is what happened. It doesn't make much of a story, and the reason is that I have left out the barber, the young man who gave me the haircut.

---

[1]Henry Louis Mencken (1880–1956), an American literary critic and author of *The American Language* (1919).

He was tall, he had a dark serious face, thick lips, on the verge of smiling but melancholy, thick lashes, sad eyes, a large nose. I saw his name on the card that was pasted on the mirror, Theodore Badal. A good name, genuine, a good young man, genuine. Theodore Badal began to work on my head. A good barber never speaks until he has been spoken to, no matter how full his heart may be.

"That name," I said, "Badal. Are you an Armenian?" I am an Armenian. I have mentioned this before. People look at me and begin to wonder, so I come right out and tell them. "I am an Armenian," I say. Or they read something I have written and begin to wonder, so I let them know. "I am an Armenian," I say. It is a meaningless remark, but they expect me to say it, so I do. I have no idea what it is like to be an Armenian or what it is like to be an Englishman or a Japanese or anything else. I have a faint idea what it is like to be alive. This is the only thing that interests me greatly. This and tennis. I hope some day to write a great philosophical work on tennis, something on the order of *Death in the Afternoon,* but I am aware that I am not yet ready to undertake such a work. I feel that the cultivation of tennis on a large scale among the peoples of the earth will do much to annihilate racial differences, prejudices, hatred, etc. Just as soon as I have perfected my drive and my lob, I hope to begin my outline of this great work. (It may seem to some sophisticated people that I am trying to make fun of Hemingway. I am not. *Death in the Afternoon* is a pretty sound piece of prose. I could never object to it as prose. I cannot even object to it as philosophy. I think it is finer philosophy than that of Will Durant and Walter Pitkin.[2] Even when Hemingway is a fool, he is at least an accurate fool. He tells you what actually takes place and he doesn't allow the speed of an occurrence to make his exposition of it hasty. This is a lot. It is some sort of advancement for literature. To relate leisurely the nature and meaning of that which is very brief in duration.)

"Are you an Armenian?" I asked.

We are a small people and whenever one of us meets another, it is an event. We are always looking around for someone to talk to in our language. Our most ambitious political party estimates that there are nearly two million of us living on the earth, but most of us don't think so. Most of us sit down and take a pencil and a piece of paper and we take one section of the world at a time and imagine how many Armenians at the most are likely to be living in that section and we put the highest number on the paper, and then we go on to another section, India, Russia, Soviet Armenia, Egypt, Italy, Germany, France, America, South America, Australia,

---

[2]William James Durant (1885–1981) was an American historian and the author of *The Story of Philosophy* (1926). American author Walter Boughton Pitkin (1878–1955) wrote *The Psychology of Happiness* (1929) and *Life Begins at Forty* (1932) and was a professor of journalism at Columbia University.

and so on, and after we add up our most hopeful figures the total comes to something a little less than a million. Then we start to think how big our families are, how high our birth-rate and how low our death-rate (except in times of war when massacres increase the death-rate), and we begin to imagine how rapidly we will increase if we are left alone a quarter of a century, and we feel pretty happy. We always leave out earthquakes, wars, massacres, famines, etc., and it is a mistake. I remember the Near East Relief drives in my home town. My uncle used to be our orator and he used to make a whole auditorium full of Armenians weep. He was an attorney and he was a great orator. Well, at first the trouble was war. Our people were being destroyed by the enemy. Those who hadn't been killed were homeless and they were starving, *our own flesh and blood,* my uncle said, and we all wept. And we gathered money and sent it to our people in the old country. Then after the war, when I was a bigger boy, we had another Near East Relief drive and my uncle stood on the stage of the Civic Auditorium of my home town and he said, "Thank God this time it is not the enemy, but an earthquake. God has made us suffer. We have worshipped Him through trial and tribulation, through suffering and disease and torture and horror and (my uncle began to weep, began to sob) through the madness of despair, and now he has done this thing, and still we praise Him, still we worship Him. We do not understand the ways of God." And after the drive I went to my uncle and I said, "Did you mean what you said about God?" And he said, "That was oratory. We've got to raise money. What God? It is nonsense." "And when you cried?" I asked, and my uncle said, "That was real. I could not help it. I had to cry. Why, for God's sake, why must we go through all this God damn hell? What have we done to deserve all this torture? Man won't let us alone. God won't let us alone. Have we done something? Aren't we supposed to be pious people? What is our sin? I am disgusted with God. I am sick of man. The only reason I am willing to get up and talk is that I don't dare keep my mouth shut. I can't bear the thought of more of our people dying. Jesus Christ, have we done something?"

I asked Theodore Badal if he was an Armenian.

He said, "I am an Assyrian."

Well, it was something. They, the Assyrians, came from our part of the world, they had noses like our noses, eyes like our eyes, hearts like our hearts. They had a different language. When they spoke we couldn't understand them, but they were a lot like us. It wasn't quite as pleasing as it would have been if Badal had been an Armenian, but it was something.

"I am an Armenian," I said. "I used to know some Assyrian boys in my home town, Joseph Sargis, Nito Elia, Tony Saleh. Do you know any of them?"

"Joseph Sargis, I know him," said Badal. "The others I do not know. We lived in New York until five years ago, then we came out west to Turlock. Then we moved up to San Francisco."

"Nito Elia," I said, "is a Captain in the Salvation Army." (I don't want anyone to imagine that I am making anything up, or that I am trying to be funny.) "Tony Saleh," I said, "was killed eight years ago. He was riding a horse and he was thrown and the horse began to run. Tony couldn't get himself free, he was caught by a leg, and the horse ran around and around for a half hour and then stopped, and when they went up to Tony he was dead. He was fourteen at the time. I used to go to school with him. Tony was a very clever boy, very good at arithmetic."

We began to talk about the Assyrian language and the Armenian language, about the old world, conditions over there, and so on. I was getting a fifteen-cent haircut and I was doing my best to learn something at the same time, to acquire some new truth, some new appreciation of the wonder of life, the dignity of man. (Man has great dignity, do not imagine that he has not.)

Badal said, "I cannot read Assyrian. I was born in the old country, but I want to get over it."

He sounded tired, not physically but spiritually.

"Why?" I said. "Why do you want to get over it?"

"Well," he laughed, "simply because everything is washed up over there." I am repeating his words precisely, putting in nothing of my own. "We were a great people once," he went on. "But that was yesterday, the day before yesterday. Now we are a topic in ancient history. We had a great civilization. They're still admiring it. Now I am in America learning how to cut hair. We're washed up as a race, we're through, it's all over, why should I learn to read the language? We have no writers, we have no news—well, there is a little news: once in a while the English encourage the Arabs to massacre us, that is all. It's an old story, we know all about it. The news comes over to us through the Associated Press, anyway."

These remarks were very painful to me, an Armenian. I had always felt badly about my own people being destroyed. I had never heard an Assyrian speaking in English about such things. I felt great love for this young fellow. Don't get me wrong. There is a tendency these days to think in terms of pansies whenever a man says that he has affection for man. I think now that I have affection for all people, even for the enemies of Armenia, whom I have so tactfully not named. Everyone knows who they are. I have nothing against any of them because I think of them as one man living one life at a time, and I know, I am positive, that one man at a time is incapable of the monstrosities performed by mobs. My objection is to mobs only.

"Well," I said, "it is much the same with us. We, too, are old. We still have our church. We still have a few writers, Aharonian, Isahakian, a few others, but it is much the same."

"Yes," said the barber, "I know. We went in for the wrong things. We went in for the simple things, peace and quiet and families. We didn't go in for machinery and conquest and militarism. We didn't go in for diplomacy and deceit and the invention of machine-guns and poison gases. Well, there is no use in being disappointed. We had our day, I suppose."

"We are hopeful," I said. "There is no Armenian living who does not still dream of an independent Armenia."

"Dream?" said Badal. "Well, that is something. Assyrians cannot even dream any more. Why, do you know how many of us are left on earth?"

"Two or three million," I suggested.

"Seventy thousand," said Badal. "That is all. Seventy thousand Assyrians in the world, and the Arabs are still killing us. They killed seventy of us in a little uprising last month. There was a small paragraph in the paper. Seventy more of us destroyed. We'll be wiped out before long. My brother is married to an American girl and he has a son. There is no more hope. We are trying to forget Assyria. My father still reads a paper that comes from New York, but he is an old man. He will be dead soon."

Then his voice changed, he ceased speaking as an Assyrian and began to speak as a barber: "Have I taken enough off the top?" he asked.

The rest of the story is pointless. I said *so long* to the young Assyrian and left the shop. I walked across town, four miles, to my room on Carl Street. I thought about the whole business: Assyria and this Assyrian, Theodore Badal, learning to be a barber, the sadness of his voice, the hopelessness of his attitude. This was months ago, in August, but ever since I have been thinking about Assyria, and I have been wanting to say something about Theodore Badal, a son of an ancient race, himself youthful and alert, yet hopeless. Seventy thousand Assyrians, a mere seventy thousand of that great people, and all the others quiet in death and all the greatness crumbled and ignored, and a young man in America learning to be a barber, and a young man lamenting bitterly the course of history.

Why don't I make up plots and write beautiful love stories that can be made into motion pictures? Why don't I let these unimportant and boring matters go hang? Why don't I try to please the American reading public?

Well, I am an Armenian. Michael Arlen[3] is an Armenian, too. He is pleasing the public. I have great admiration for him, and I think he has perfected a very fine style of writing and all that, but I don't want to write about the people he likes to write about. Those people were dead to begin with. You take Iowa and the Japanese boy and Theodore Badal, the Assyrian; well, they may go down physically, like Iowa, to death, or spiritually, like Badal, to death, but they are of the stuff that is eternal in man and it is this stuff that interests me. You don't find them in bright places, making witty remarks about sex and trivial remarks about art. You find them where I found them, and they will be there forever, the race of man, the part of

---

[3]Michael Arlen (1895–1956), born Dikran Kouyoumdjian (the son of an Armenian merchant), a British novelist whose work reflects the cynicism and disillusionment of London society in the years following World War I.

man, of Assyria as much as of England, that cannot be destroyed, the part that massacre does not destroy, the part that earthquake and war and famine and madness and everything else cannot destroy.

This work is in tribute to Iowa, to Japan, to Assyria, to Armenia, to the race of man everywhere, to the dignity of that race, the brotherhood of things alive. I am not expecting Paramount Pictures to film this work. I am thinking of seventy thousand Assyrians, one at a time, alive, a great race. I am thinking of Theodore Badal, himself seventy thousand Assyrians and seventy million Assyrians, himself Assyria, and man, standing in a barber shop, in San Francisco, in 1933, and being, still, himself, the whole race.

[1934]

WILLIAM CARLOS WILLIAMS

William Carlos Williams (1883–1963), the poet, novelist, playwright, and short story writer, was born in Rutherford, New Jersey. After graduating from the University of Pennsylvania Medical School, he returned to Rutherford, where he practiced as a pediatrician for the rest of his life. While still an undergraduate, he began to write poetry, influenced by his friends the poets Ezra Pound and Hilda Doolittle. Williams published his first book, Poems, *in 1909. Initially he devoted himself to poetry, but his experimental writing in the 1920s led him to the novel and the short story. The story became for him a way to emphasize his social and humanitarian concerns, which influenced the gritty, down-to-earth realism of his literary style.*

Williams wrote most of his stories during the Depression, when his patients in Rutherford were the poor people characterized by President Franklin Delano Roosevelt in 1933 as "ill-fed, ill-housed, and ill-clothed." Williams's patients were often down and out, but he saw them as splendidly vital people. When asked how he managed the two careers of medicine and writing, Williams answered, "It's no strain. In fact, the one [medicine] nourishes the other [writing], even if at times I've groaned to the contrary."

Like the doctor-writer Anton Chekhov before him, Williams understood the moral responsibility of his calling, and he was vigilant against his feelings of arrogance and self-importance. "There's nothing like a difficult patient to show us ourselves," he once told a medical student. "I would learn so much on my rounds, or making home visits. At times I felt like a thief because I heard words, lines, saw people and places—and used it all in my writing. I guess I've told people that, and no one's so surprised! There was something deeper going on, though—the force of all those encounters. I was put off guard again and again, and the result was—well, a descent into myself." Williams collected his stories in four volumes: The Knife of the Times *(1932),* Life along the Passaic River *(1938; includes "The Use of Force," which first appeared in* Blast *in 1934),* Make Light of It *(1950), and* The Farmers' Daughters *(1961). Recently Robert Coles compiled* The Doctor Stories *(1984). Williams used vernacular American speech and direct observation in all his writing. His work includes twenty books of poetry, four novels, several books of nonfiction, a collection of plays, and an autobiography.*

RELATED COMMENTARY: *William Carlos Williams, "Notes on 'A Beginning on the Short Story,'" page 1475.*

The Use of Force

They were new patients to me, all I had was the name, Olson. Please come down as soon as you can, my daughter is very sick. When I arrived I was met by the mother, a big startled looking woman, very clean and apologetic who merely said, Is this the doctor? and let me in. In the back, she added. You must excuse us, doctor, we have her in the kitchen where it is warm. It is very damp here sometimes.

The child was fully dressed and sitting on her father's lap near the kitchen table. He tried to get up, but I motioned for him not to bother, took off my overcoat and started to look things over. I could see that they were all very nervous, eyeing me up and down distrustfully. As often, in such cases, they weren't telling me more than they had to, it was up to me to tell them; that's why they were spending three dollars on me.

The child was fairly eating me up with her cold, steady eyes, and no expression to her face whatever. She did not move and seemed, inwardly, quiet; an unusually attractive little thing, and as strong as a heifer in appearance. But her face was flushed, she was breathing rapidly, and I realized that she had a high fever. She had magnificent blonde hair, in profusion. One of those picture children often reproduced in advertising leaflets and the photogravure sections of the Sunday papers.

She's had a fever for three days, began the father and we don't know what it comes from. My wife has given her things, you know, like people do, but it don't do no good. And there's been a lot of sickness around. So we tho't you'd better look her over and tell us what is the matter.

As doctors often do I took a trial shot at it as a point of departure. Has she had a sore throat?

Both parents answered me together, No . . . No, she says her throat don't hurt her.

Does your throat hurt you? added the mother to the child. But the little girl's expression didn't change nor did she move her eyes from my face.

Have you looked?

I tried to, said the mother, but I couldn't see.

As it happens we had been having a number of cases of diphtheria in the school to which this child went during that month and we were all, quite apparently, thinking of that, though no one had as yet spoken of the thing.

Well, I said, suppose we take a look at the throat first. I smiled in my best professional manner and asking for the child's first name I said, come on, Mathilda, open your mouth and let's take a look at your throat.

Nothing doing.

Aw, come on, I coaxed, just open your mouth wide and let me take a look. Look, I said opening both hands wide, I haven't anything in my hands. Just open up and let me see.

Such a nice man, put in the mother. Look how kind he is to you. Come on, do what he tells you to. He won't hurt you.

At that I ground my teeth in disgust. If only they wouldn't use the word "hurt" I might be able to get somewhere. But I did not allow myself to be hurried or disturbed but speaking quietly and slowly I approached the child again.

As I moved my chair a little nearer suddenly with one catlike movement both her hands clawed instinctively for my eyes and she almost reached them too. In fact she knocked my glasses flying and they fell, though unbroken, several feet away from me on the kitchen floor.

Both the mother and father almost turned themselves inside out in embarrassment and apology. You bad girl, said the mother, taking her and shaking her by one arm. Look what you've done. The nice man . . .

For heaven's sake, I broke in. Don't call me a nice man to her. I'm here to look at her throat on the chance that she might have diphtheria and possibly die of it. But that's nothing to her. Look here, I said to the child, we're going to look at your throat. You're old enough to understand what I'm saying. Will you open it now by yourself or shall we have to open it for you?

Not a move. Even her expression hadn't changed. Her breaths however were coming faster and faster. Then the battle began. I had to do it. I had to have a throat culture for her own protection. But first I told the parents that it was entirely up to them. I explained the danger but said that I would not insist on a throat examination so long as they would take the responsibility.

If you don't do what the doctor says you'll have to go to the hospital, the mother admonished her severely.

Oh yeah? I had to smile to myself. After all, I had already fallen in love with the savage brat, the parents were contemptible to me. In the ensuing struggle they grew more and more abject, crushed, exhausted while she surely rose to magnificent heights of insane fury of effort bred of her terror of me.

The father tried his best, and he was a big man but the fact that she was his daughter, his shame at her behavior and his dread of hurting her made him release her just at the critical times when I had almost achieved success, till I wanted to kill him. But his dread also that she might have diphtheria made him tell me to go on, go on though he himself was almost fainting, while the mother moved back and forth behind us raising and lowering her hands in an agony of apprehension.

Put her in front of you on your lap, I ordered, and hold both her wrists.

But as soon as he did the child let out a scream. Don't, you're hurting me. Let go of my hands. Let them go I tell you. Then she shrieked terrifyingly, hysterically. Stop it! Stop it! You're killing me!

Do you think she can stand it, doctor! said the mother.

You get out, said the husband to his wife. Do you want her to die of diphtheria?

Come on now, hold her, I said.

Then I grasped the child's head with my left hand and tried to get the wooden tongue depressor between her teeth. She fought, with clenched teeth, desperately! But now I also had grown furious — at a child. I tried to hold myself down but I couldn't. I know how to expose a throat for inspection. And I did my best. When finally I got the wooden spatula behind the last teeth and just the point of it into the mouth cavity, she opened up for an instant but before I could see anything she came down again and gripped the wooden blade between her molars. She reduced it to splinters before I could get it out again.

Aren't you ashamed, the mother yelled at her. Aren't you ashamed to act like that in front of the doctor?

Get me a smooth-handled spoon of some sort, I told the mother. We're going through with this. The child's mouth was already bleeding. Her tongue was cut and she was screaming in wild hysterical shrieks. Perhaps I should have desisted and come back in an hour or more. No doubt it would have been better. But I have seen at least two children lying dead in bed of neglect in such cases, and feeling that I must get a diagnosis now or never I went at it again. But the worst of it was that I too had got beyond reason. I could have torn the child apart in my own fury and enjoyed it. It was a pleasure to attack her. My face was burning with it.

The damned little brat must be protected against her own idiocy, one says to one's self at such times. Others must be protected against her. It is a social necessity. And all these things are true. But a blind fury, a feeling of adult shame, bred of a longing for muscular release are the operatives. One goes on to the end.

In the final unreasoning assault I overpowered the child's neck and jaws. I forced the heavy silver spoon back of her teeth and down her throat till she gagged. And there it was — both tonsils covered with membrane. She had fought valiantly to keep me from knowing her secret. She had been hiding that sore throat for three days at least and lying to her parents in order to escape just such an outcome as this.

Now truly she was furious. She had been on the defensive before but now she attacked. Tried to get off her father's lap and fly at me while tears of defeat blinded her eyes.   [1934]

JOHN STEINBECK

John Steinbeck (1902–1968) was born in Salinas and raised near Monterey in the fertile farm country of the Salinas Valley in California. His mother was a former schoolteacher; his father was the county treasurer. In high school Steinbeck wrote for the school newspaper and was president of his class. He enjoyed literature from an early age and read novels by Gustave Flaubert, Fyodor Dostoevsky, and Thomas Hardy in the family library. Enrolled at Stanford University as an English major, Steinbeck dropped out before graduating and worked at odd jobs—fruit picker, caretaker, laboratory assistant—while he practiced writing fiction. Several times he took short-term jobs with the Spreckels Sugar Company and gained a perspective on labor problems, which he would later describe in his novels.

In 1929 Steinbeck began his literary career by publishing Cup of Gold, *a fictionalized biography of Henry Morgan, the seventeenth-century Welsh pirate. His next book,* The Pastures of Heaven (1932), *is a collection of short stories about the people in a farm community in California. The critic Brian Barbour has stated that Steinbeck realized early in his career that the short story form was not congenial to his talents. He needed the more expansive form of the novel to give his characters a chance for what he considered real growth. In 1936 Steinbeck wrote* In Dubious Battle, *his first major political novel. He then published four more novels and another book of short fiction before his greatest work,* The Grapes of Wrath (1939). *This book, about a family from the Dust Bowl who emigrate to California and struggle to make a living despite agricultural exploitation, won Steinbeck the Pulitzer Prize. Among his many other successful novels are* East of Eden (1952) *and* The Winter of Our Discontent (1961). *He received the Nobel Prize for literature in 1962.*

One of the most accomplished popular novelists in the United States, Steinbeck excelled—as did Ernest Hemingway—in the creation of exciting conflicts, convincing dialogue, and recognizable characters to dramatize his philosophy of life. First published in the Monterey Beacon *in 1935, "The Snake" was included in Steinbeck's collection of short stories,* The Long Valley (1938). *In his introduction to a later book,* The Log from the Sea of Cortez (1951), *he said, "I wrote the story just as it happened. . . . I don't know what it means." The story was written after Steinbeck had visited the laboratory of a friend, the marine biologist Ed Ricketts in Monterey (named Dr. Phillips in the story). After a woman visitor dropped and hurt a white mouse used in the experiments, someone suggested she feed it to a caged rattlesnake that had been found on a nearby golf course. Everyone watched as the snake swallowed the whole mouse except for its tail, which extended from its mouth like a cigarette. Critics have offered many interpretations of the story that Steinbeck based on the incident, including Charles E. May's suggestion that the woman is a Jungian anima figure who has emerged from the primal world to shock Dr. Phillips out of his scientific detachment. In this reading, the scientist "has rejected the unconscious to such an extent that the instinctual forces [the woman] rise up in opposition."*

The Snake

It was almost dark when young Dr. Phillips swung his sack to his shoulder and left the tide pool. He climbed up over the rocks and squashed along the street in his rubber boots. The street lights were on by the time he arrived at his little commercial laboratory on the cannery street of Monterey. It was a tight little building, standing partly on piers over the bay water and partly on the land. On both sides the big corrugated-iron sardine canneries crowded in on it.

Dr. Phillips climbed the wooden steps and opened the door. The white rats in their cages scampered up and down the wire, and the captive cats in their pens mewed for milk. Dr. Phillips turned on the glaring light over the dissection table and dumped his clammy sack on the floor. He walked to the glass cages by the window where the rattlesnakes lived, leaned over and looked in.

The snakes were bunched and resting in the corners of the cage, but every head was clear; the dusty eyes seemed to look at nothing, but as the young man leaned over the cage the forked tongues, black on the ends and pink behind, twittered out and waved slowly up and down. Then the snakes recognized the man and pulled in their tongues.

Dr. Phillips threw off his leather coat and built a fire in the tin stove; he set a kettle of water on the stove and dropped a can of beans into the water. Then he stood staring down at the sack on the floor. He was a slight young man with the mild, preoccupied eyes of one who looks through a microscope a great deal. He wore a short blond beard.

The draft ran breathily up the chimney and a glow of warmth came from the stove. The little waves washed quietly about the piles under the building. Arranged on shelves about the room were tier above tier of museum jars containing the mounted marine specimens the laboratory dealt in.

Dr. Phillips opened a side door and went into his bedroom, a book-lined cell containing an army cot, a reading light and an uncomfortable wooden chair. He pulled off his rubber boots and put on a pair of sheepskin slippers. When he went back to the other room the water in the kettle was already beginning to hum.

He lifted his sack to the table under the white light and emptied out two dozen common starfish. These he laid out side by side on the table. His preoccupied eyes turned to the busy rats in the wire cages. Taking grain from a paper sack, he poured it into the feeding troughs. Instantly the rats scrambled down from the wire and fell upon the food. A bottle of milk stood on a glass shelf between a small mounted octopus and a jellyfish.

Dr. Phillips lifted down the milk and walked to the cat cage, but before he filled the containers he reached in the cage and gently picked out a big rangy alley tabby. He stroked her for a moment and then dropped her in a small black painted box, closed the lid and bolted it and then turned on a petcock which admitted gas into the killing chamber. While the short soft struggle went on in the black box he filled the saucers with milk. One of the cats arched against his hand and he smiled and petted her neck.

The box was quiet now. He turned off the petcock, for the airtight box would be full of gas.

On the stove the pan of water was bubbling furiously about the can of beans. Dr. Phillips lifted out the can with a big pair of forceps, opened it, and emptied the beans into a glass dish. While he ate he watched the starfish on the table. From between the rays little drops of milky fluid were exuding. He bolted his beans and when they were gone he put the dish in the sink and stepped to the equipment cupboard. From this he took a microscope and a pile of little glass dishes. He filled the dishes one by one with sea water from a tap and arranged them in a line beside the starfish. He took out his watch and laid it on the table under the pouring white light. The waves washed with little sighs against the piles under the floor. He took an eyedropper from a drawer and bent over the starfish.

At that moment there were quick soft steps on the wooden stairs and a strong knocking at the door. A slight grimace of annoyance crossed the young man's face as he went to open. A tall, lean woman stood in the doorway. She was dressed in a severe dark suit—her straight black hair, growing low on a flat forehead, was mussed as though the wind had been blowing it. Her black eyes glittered in the strong light.

She spoke in a soft throaty voice, "May I come in? I want to talk to you."

"I'm very busy just now," he said half-heartedly. "I have to do things at times." But he stood away from the door. The tall woman slipped in.

"I'll be quiet until you can talk to me."

He closed the door and brought the uncomfortable chair from the bedroom. "You see," he apologized, "the process is started and I must get to it." So many people wandered in and asked questions. He had little routines of explanations for the commoner processes. He could say them without thinking. "Sit here. In a few minutes I'll be able to listen to you."

The tall woman leaned over the table. With the eyedropper the young man gathered fluid from between the rays of the starfish and squirted it into a bowl of water, and then he drew some milky fluid and squirted it in the same bowl and stirred the water gently with the eyedropper. He began his little patter of explanation.

"When starfish are sexually mature they release sperm and ova when they are exposed at low tide. By choosing mature specimens and taking them out of the water, I give them a condition of low tide. Now I've mixed the sperm and eggs. Now I put some of the mixture in each one of these ten watch glasses. In ten minutes I will kill those in the first glass with menthol, twenty minutes later I will kill the second group and then a new group every twenty minutes. Then I will have arrested the process in stages, and I will mount the series on microscope slides for biologic study." He paused. "Would you like to look at this first group under the microscope?"

"No, thank you."

He turned quickly to her. People always wanted to look through the glass. She was not looking at the table at all, but at him. Her black eyes were on him, but they did not seem to see him. He realized why — the irises were as dark as the pupils, there was no color line between the two. Dr. Phillips was piqued at her answer. Although answering questions bored him, a lack of interest in what he was doing irritated him. A desire to arouse her grew in him.

"While I'm waiting the first ten minutes I have something to do. Some people don't like to see it. Maybe you'd better step into that room until I finish."

"No," she said in her soft flat tone. "Do what you wish. I will wait until you can talk to me." Her hands rested side by side on her lap. She was completely at rest. Her eyes were bright but the rest of her was almost in a state of suspended animation. He thought, "Low metabolic rate, almost as low as a frog's, from the looks." The desire to shock her out of her inanition possessed him again.

He brought a little wooden cradle to the table, laid out scalpels and scissors and rigged a big hollow needle to a pressure tube. Then from the killing chamber he brought the limp dead cat and laid it in the cradle and tied its legs to hooks in the sides. He glanced sidewise at the woman. She had not moved. She was still at rest.

The cat grinned up into the light, its pink tongue stuck out between its needle teeth. Dr. Phillips deftly snipped open the skin at the throat; with a scalpel he slit through and found an artery. With flawless technique he put the needle in the vessel and tied it in with gut. "Embalming fluid," he explained. "Later I'll inject yellow mass into the veinous system and red mass into the arterial system — for bloodstream dissection — biology classes."

He looked around at her again. Her dark eyes seemed veiled with dust. She looked without expression at the cat's open throat. Not a drop of blood had escaped. The incision was clean. Dr. Phillips looked at his watch. "Time for the first group." He shook a few crystals of menthol into the first watch-glass.

The woman was making him nervous. The rats climbed about on the wire of their cage again and squeaked softly. The waves under the building beat with little shocks on the piles.

The young man shivered. He put a few lumps of coal in the stove and sat down. "Now," he said. "I haven't anything to do for twenty minutes." He noticed how short her chin was between lower lip and point. She seemed to awaken slowly, to come up out of some deep pool of consciousness. Her head raised and her dark dusty eyes moved about the room and then came back to him.

"I was waiting," she said. Her hands remained side by side on her lap. "You have snakes?"

"Why, yes," he said rather loudly. "I have about two dozen rattlesnakes. I milk out the venom and send it to the anti-venom laboratories."

She continued to look at him but her eyes did not center on him, rather they covered him and seemed to see in a big circle all around him. "Have you a male snake, a male rattlesnake?"

"Well, it just happens I know I have. I came in one morning and found a big snake in—in coition with a smaller one. That's very rare in captivity. You see, I do know I have a male snake."

"Where is he?"

"Why, right in the glass cage by the window there."

Her head swung slowly around but her two quiet hands did not move. She turned back toward him. "May I see?"

He got up and walked to the case by the window. On the sand bottom the knot of rattlesnakes lay entwined, but their heads were clear. The tongues came out and flickered a moment and then waved up and down feeling the air for vibrations. Dr. Phillips nervously turned his head. The woman was standing beside him. He had not heard her get up from the chair. He had heard only the splash of water among the piles and the scampering of the rats on the wire screen.

She said softly, "Which is the male you spoke of?"

He pointed to a thick, dusty grey snake lying by itself in one corner of the cage. "That one. He's nearly five feet long. He comes from Texas. Our Pacific coast snakes are usually smaller. He's been taking all the rats, too. When I want the others to eat I have to take him out."

The woman stared down at the blunt dry head. The forked tongue slipped out and hung quivering for a long moment. "And you're sure he's a male."

"Rattlesnakes are funny," he said glibly. "Nearly every generalization proves wrong. I don't like to say anything definite about rattlesnakes, but—yes—I can assure you he's a male."

Her eyes did not move from the flat head. "Will you sell him to me?"

"Sell him?" he cried. "Sell him to you?"

"You do sell specimens, don't you?"

"Oh—yes. Of course I do. Of course I do."

"How much? Five dollars? Ten?"

"Oh! Not more than five. But—do you know anything about rattlesnakes? You might be bitten."

She looked at him for a moment. "I don't intend to take him. I want to leave him here, but—I want him to be mine. I want to come here and look at him and feed him and to know he's mine." She opened a little purse and took out a five-dollar bill. "Here! Now he is mine."

Dr. Phillips began to be afraid. "You could come to look at him without owning him."

"I want him to be mine."

"Oh, Lord!" he cried. "I've forgotten the time." He ran to the table. "Three minutes over. It won't matter much." He shook menthol crystals into the second watch glass. And then he was drawn back to the cage where the woman still stared at the snake.

She asked, "What does he eat?"

"I feed them white rats, rats from the cage over there."

"Will you put him in the other cage? I want to feed him."

"But he doesn't need food. He's had a rat already this week. Sometimes they don't eat for three or four months. I had one that didn't eat for over a year."

In her low monotone she asked, "Will you sell me a rat?"

He shrugged his shoulders. "I see. You want to watch how rattlesnakes eat. All right. I'll show you. The rat will cost twenty-five cents. It's better than a bullfight if you look at it one way, and it's simply a snake eating his dinner if you look at it another." His tone had become acid. He hated people who made sport of natural processes. He was not a sportsman but a biologist. He could kill a thousand animals for knowledge, but not an insect for pleasure. He'd been over this in his mind before.

She turned her head slowly toward him and the beginning of a smile formed on her thin lips. "I want to feed my snake," she said. "I'll put him in the other cage." She had opened the top of the cage and dipped her hand in before he knew what she was doing. He leaped forward and pulled her back. The lid banged shut.

"Haven't you any sense?" he asked fiercely. "Maybe he wouldn't kill you, but he'd make you damned sick in spite of what I could do for you."

"You put him in the other cage then," she said quietly.

Dr. Phillips was shaken. He found that he was avoiding the dark eyes that didn't seem to look at anything. He felt that it was profoundly wrong to put a rat into the cage, deeply sinful; and he didn't know why. Often he had put rats in the cage when someone or other had wanted to see it, but this desire tonight sickened him. He tried to explain himself out of it.

"It's a good thing to see," he said. "It shows you how a snake can work. It makes you have a respect for a rattlesnake. Then, too, lots of people have dreams about the terror of snakes making the kill. I think because it is a subjective rat. The person is the rat. Once you see it the whole matter is objective. The rat is only a rat and the terror is removed."

He took a long stick equipped with a leather noose from the wall. Opening the trap he dropped the noose over the big snake's head and tightened the thong. A piercing dry rattle filled the room. The thick body writhed and slashed about the handle of the stick as he lifted the snake out and dropped it in the feeding cage. It stood ready to strike for a time, but the buzzing gradually ceased. The snake crawled into a corner, made a big figure eight with its body and lay still.

"You see," the young man explained, "these snakes are quite tame. I've had them a long time. I suppose I could handle them if I wanted to, but everyone who does handle rattlesnakes gets bitten sooner or later. I just don't want to take the chance." He glanced at the woman. He hated to put in the rat. She had moved over in front of the new cage; her black eyes were on the stony head of the snake again.

She said, "Put in a rat."

Reluctantly he went to the rat cage. For some reason he was sorry for the rat, and such a feeling had never come to him before. His eyes went over the mass of swarming white bodies climbing up the screen toward him. "Which one?" he thought. "Which one shall it be?" Suddenly he turned angrily to the woman. "Wouldn't you rather I put in a cat? Then you'd see a real fight. The cat might even win, but if it did it might kill the snake. I'll sell you a cat if you like."

She didn't look at him. "Put in a rat," she said. "I want him to eat."

He opened the rat cage and thrust his hand in. His fingers found a tail and he lifted a plump, red-eyed rat out of the cage. It struggled up to try to bite his fingers and, failing, hung spread out and motionless from its tail. He walked quickly across the room, opened the feeding cage and dropped the rat in on the sand floor. "Now, watch it," he cried.

The woman did not answer him. Her eyes were on the snake where it lay still. Its tongue flicking in and out rapidly, tasted the air of the cage.

The rat landed on its feet, turned around and sniffed at its pink naked tail and then unconcernedly trotted across the sand, smelling as it went. The room was silent. Dr. Phillips did not know whether the water sighed among the piles or whether the woman sighed. Out of the corner of his eye he saw her body crouch and stiffen.

The snake moved out smoothly, slowly. The tongue flicked in and out. The motion was so gradual, so smooth that it didn't seem to be motion at all. In the other end of the cage the rat perked up in a sitting position and began to lick down the fine white hair on its chest. The snake moved on, keeping always a deep S curve in its neck.

The silence beat on the young man. He felt the blood drifting up in his body. He said loudly, "See! He keeps the striking curve ready. Rattlesnakes are cautious, almost cowardly animals. The mechanism is so delicate. The snake's dinner is to be got by an operation as deft as a surgeon's job. He takes no chances with his instruments."

The snake had flowed to the middle of the cage by now. The rat looked up, saw the snake and then unconcernedly went back to licking its chest.

"It's the most beautiful thing in the world," the young man said. His veins were throbbing. "It's the most terrible thing in the world."

The snake was close now. Its head lifted a few inches from the sand. The head weaved slowly back and forth, aiming, getting distance, aiming. Dr. Phillips glanced again at the woman. He turned sick. She was weaving too, not much, just a suggestion.

The rat looked up and saw the snake. It dropped to four feet and back up, and then — the stroke. It was impossible to see, simply a flash. The rat jarred as though under an invisible blow. The snake backed hurriedly into the corner from which it had come, and settled down, its tongue working constantly.

"Perfect!" Dr. Phillips cried. "Right between the shoulder blades. The fangs must almost have reached the heart."

The rat stood still, breathing like a little white bellows. Suddenly it leaped in the air and landed on its side. Its legs kicked spasmodically for a second and it was dead.

The woman relaxed, relaxed sleepily.

"Well," the young man demanded, "it was an emotional bath, wasn't it?"

She turned her misty eyes to him. "Will he eat it now?" she asked.

"Of course he'll eat it. He didn't kill it for a thrill. He killed it because he was hungry."

The corners of the woman's mouth turned up a trifle again. She looked back at the snake. "I want to see him eat it."

Now the snake came out of its corner again. There was no striking curve in its neck, but it approached the rat gingerly, ready to jump back in case it attacked. It nudged the body gently with its blunt nose, and drew away. Satisfied that it was dead, the snake touched the body all over with its chin, from head to tail. It seemed to measure the body and to kiss it. Finally it opened its mouth and unhinged its jaws at the corners.

Dr. Phillips put his will against his head to keep it from turning toward the woman. He thought, "If she's opening her mouth, I'll be sick. I'll be afraid." He succeeded in keeping his eyes away.

The snake fitted its jaws over the rat's head and then with a slow peristaltic pulsing, began to engulf the rat. The jaws gripped and the whole throat crawled up, and the jaws gripped again.

Dr. Phillips turned away and went to his work table. "You've made me miss one of the series," he said bitterly. "The set won't be complete." He put one of the watch glasses under a low-power microscope and looked at it, and then angrily he poured the contents of all the dishes into the sink. The waves had fallen so that only a wet whisper came up through the floor. The young man lifted a trapdoor at his feet and dropped the starfish down into the black water. He paused at the cat, crucified in the cradle and grinning comically into the light. Its body was puffed with embalming fluid. He shut off the pressure, withdrew the needle and tied the vein.

"Would you like some coffee?" he asked.

"No, thank you. I shall be going pretty soon."

He walked to her where she stood in front of the snake cage. The rat was swallowed, all except an inch of pink tail that stuck out of the snake's mouth like a sardonic tongue. The throat heaved again and the tail disappeared. The jaws snapped back into their sockets, and the big snake crawled heavily to the corner, made a big eight and dropped its head on the sand.

"He's asleep now," the woman said. "I'm going now. But I'll come back and feed my snake every little while. I'll pay for the rats. I want him to have plenty. And sometime—I'll take him away with me." Her eyes came out of their dusty dream for a moment. "Remember, he's mine. Don't take his poison. I want him to have it. Goodnight." She walked swiftly to the door and went out. He heard her footsteps on the stairs, but he could not hear her walk away on the pavement.

Dr. Phillips turned a chair around and sat down in front of the snake cage. He tried to comb out his thought as he looked at the torpid snake. "I've read so much about psychological sex symbols," he thought. "It doesn't seem to explain. Maybe I'm too much alone. Maybe I should kill the snake. If I knew—no, I can't pray to anything."

For weeks he expected her to return. "I will go out and leave her alone here when she comes," he decided. "I won't see the damned thing again."

She never came again. For months he looked for her when he walked about in the town. Several times he ran after some tall woman thinking it might be she. But he never saw her again—ever.   [1935]

DELMORE SCHWARTZ

*D*elmore Schwartz (1913–1966) was born in Brooklyn, New York, the son of parents who had emigrated to America from Eastern Europe. His parents had a tempestuous marriage, and when Schwartz was ten his father left his mother and moved to Chicago. Schwartz studied philosophy at the University of Wisconsin and New York University, where he graduated in 1935. In July of that year, before he went off to Harvard as a graduate student, he read a volume of Faulkner stories in his Greenwich Village room that inspired him so much he started to write "In Dreams Begin Responsibilities," which he finished in a weekend. He found his title in a phrase used in William Butler Yeats's epigraph to his collection Responsibilities. Schwartz typed a copy of the story for his mother, who penciled her response on the back of one of the pages: "Dear Delmore, If there is another word besides wonderful I don't know I don't remember telling you all these so accurate. Please save this story and bring it home for me. There are moments in my life, that I believe all my struggles are worth while. Mother"

Schwartz left Harvard and returned to New York City in 1937 when he didn't receive a fellowship. His story appeared in 1937 in the first issue of Partisan Review, a radical magazine that featured European writers. The following year Schwartz published his first book, In Dreams Begin Responsibilities, which combined his title story with poems and a play. In 1940 he moved back to Cambridge to teach at Harvard, but after three years he returned to New York City to write the stories published in The World Is a Wedding (1948), which reprinted "In Dreams Begin Responsibilities." In the introduction to Schwartz's last volume of stories, the critic Irving Howe wrote that Schwartz had captured

> the quality of New York life in the 1930's and 1940's with a fine comic intensity—not, of course, the whole of New York life but that interesting point where intellectual children of immigrant Jews are finding their way into the larger world while casting uneasy, rueful glances over their backs. These were stories that helped one reach an emotional truce with the world of our fathers, for the very distance they established from their subject allowed some detachment and thereby, in turn, a little self-criticism and compassion.

In the remaining years of Schwartz's life he was subject to frightening emotional outbursts. He continued to write poetry and short fiction, along with essays on literary topics. In 1953 he was appointed poetry editor of the New Republic. Seven years later he was awarded the Bollingen Prize for Poetry, the youngest American poet to achieve that honor. In 1961 he published his last book, Successful Love and Other Stories. The poet Robert Lowell later wrote a sonnet, "In Dreams Begin Responsibilities," describing Schwartz's agony as his life deteriorated through mental illness to his final heart attack in 1966.

In Dreams Begin Responsibilities

I think it is the year 1909. I feel as if I were in a motion picture theatre, the long arm of light crossing the darkness and spinning, my eyes
fixed on the screen. This is a silent picture as if an old Biograph one, in
which the actors are dressed in ridiculously old-fashioned clothes, and one
flash succeeds another with sudden jumps. The actors too seem to jump
about and walk too fast. The shots themselves are full of dots and rays, as if
it were raining when the picture was photographed. The light is bad.

It is Sunday afternoon, June 12th, 1909, and my father is walking down
the quiet streets of Brooklyn on his way to visit my mother. His clothes are
newly pressed and his tie is too tight in his high collar. He jingles the coins in
his pockets, thinking of the witty things he will say. I feel as if I had by now
relaxed entirely in the soft darkness of the theatre; the organist peals out
the obvious and approximate emotions on which the audience rocks un-
knowingly. I am anonymous, and I have forgotten myself. It is always so
when one goes to the movies, it is, as they say, a drug.

My father walks from street to street of trees, lawns and houses, once
in a while coming to an avenue on which a street-car skates and gnaws,
slowly progressing. The conductor, who has a handle-bar mustache, helps
a young lady wearing a hat like a bowl with feathers on to the car. She lifts
her long skirts slightly as she mounts the steps. He leisurely makes change
and rings his bell. It is obviously Sunday, for everyone is wearing Sunday
clothes, and the street-car's noises emphasize the quiet of the holiday. Is
not Brooklyn the City of Churches? The shops are closed and their shades
drawn, but for an occasional stationery store or drug-store with great
green balls in the window.

My father has chosen to take this long walk because he likes to walk
and think. He thinks about himself in the future and so arrives at the place
he is to visit in a state of mild exaltation. He pays no attention to the
houses he is passing, in which the Sunday dinner is being eaten, nor to the
many trees which patrol each street, now coming to their full leafage and
the time when they will room the whole street in cool shadow. An occasional carriage passes, the horse's hooves falling like stones in the quiet
afternoon, and once in a while an automobile, looking like an enormous
upholstered sofa, puffs and passes.

My father thinks of my mother, of how nice it will be to introduce her
to his family. But he is not yet sure that he wants to marry her, and once in
a while he becomes panicky about the bond already established. He reas-
sures himself by thinking of the big men he admires who are married:
William Randolph Hearst, and William Howard Taft, who has just become
President of the United States.

My father arrives at my mother's house. He has come too early and so
is suddenly embarrassed. My aunt, my mother's sister, answers the loud

bell with her napkin in her hand, for the family is still at dinner. As my father enters, my grandfather rises from the table and shakes hands with him. My mother has run upstairs to tidy herself. My grandmother asks my father if he has had dinner, and tells him that Rose will be downstairs soon. My grandfather opens the conversation by remarking on the mild June weather. My father sits uncomfortably near the table, holding his hat in his hand. My grandmother tells my aunt to take my father's hat. My uncle, twelve years old, runs into the house, his hair tousled. He shouts a greeting to my father, who has often given him a nickel, and then runs upstairs. It is evident that the respect in which my father is held in this household is tempered by a good deal of mirth. He is impressive, yet he is very awkward.

– 2 –

Finally my mother comes downstairs, all dressed up, and my father being engaged in conversation with my grandfather becomes uneasy, not knowing whether to greet my mother or continue the conversation. He gets up from the chair clumsily and says "hello" gruffly. My grandfather watches, examining their congruence, such as it is, with a critical eye, and meanwhile rubbing his bearded cheek roughly, as he always does when he reflects. He is worried; he is afraid that my father will not make a good husband for his oldest daughter. At this point something happens to the film, just as my father is saying something funny to my mother; I am awakened to myself and my unhappiness just as my interest was rising. The audience begins to clap impatiently. Then the trouble is cared for but the film has been returned to a portion just shown, and once more I see my grandfather rubbing his bearded cheek and pondering my father's character. It is difficult to get back into the picture once more and forget myself, but as my mother giggles at my father's words, the darkness drowns me.

My father and mother depart from the house, my father shaking hands with my mother once more, out of some unknown uneasiness. I stir uneasily also, slouched in the hard chair of the theatre. Where is the older uncle, my mother's older brother? He is studying in his bedroom upstairs, studying for his final examination at the College of the City of New York, having been dead of rapid pneumonia for the last twenty-one years. My mother and father walk down the same quiet streets once more. My mother is holding my father's arm and telling him of the novel which she has been reading; and my father utters judgments of the characters as the plot is made clear to him. This is a habit which he very much enjoys, for he feels the utmost superiority and confidence when he approves and condemns the behavior of other people. At times he feels moved to utter a brief "Ugh,"—whenever the story becomes what he would call sugary. This tribute is paid to his manliness. My mother feels satisfied by the interest which she has awakened; she is showing my father how intelligent she is, and how interesting.

They reach the avenue, and the street-car leisurely arrives. They are going to Coney Island this afternoon, although my mother considers that such pleasures are inferior. She has made up her mind to indulge only in a walk on the boardwalk and a pleasant dinner, avoiding the riotous amusements as being beneath the dignity of so dignified a couple.

My father tells my mother how much money he has made in the past week, exaggerating an amount which need not have been exaggerated. But my father has always felt that actualities somehow fall short. Suddenly I begin to weep. The determined old lady who sits next to me in the theatre is annoyed and looks at me with an angry face, and being intimidated, I stop. I drag out my handkerchief and dry my face, licking the drop which has fallen near my lips. Meanwhile I have missed something, for here are my mother and father alighting at the last stop, Coney Island.

– 3 –

They walk toward the boardwalk, and my father commands my mother to inhale the pungent air from the sea. They both breathe in deeply, both of them laughing as they do so. They have in common a great interest in health, although my father is strong and husky, my mother is frail. Their minds are full of theories of what is good to eat and not good to eat, and sometimes they engage in heated discussions of the subject, the whole matter ending in my father's announcement, made with a scornful bluster, that you have to die sooner or later anyway. On the boardwalk's flagpole, the American flag is pulsing in an intermittent wind from the sea.

My father and mother go to the rail of the boardwalk and look down on the beach where a good many bathers are casually walking about. A few are in the surf. A peanut whistle pierces the air with its pleasant and active whine, and my father goes to buy peanuts. My mother remains at the rail and stares at the ocean. The ocean seems merry to her; it pointedly sparkles and again and again the pony waves are released. She notices the children digging in the wet sand, and the bathing costumes of the girls who are her own age. My father returns with the peanuts. Overhead the sun's lightning strikes and strikes, but neither of them are at all aware of it. The boardwalk is full of people dressed in their Sunday clothes and idly strolling. The tide does not reach as far as the boardwalk, and the strollers would feel no danger if it did. My mother and father lean on the rail of the boardwalk and absently stare at the ocean. The ocean is becoming rough; the waves come in slowly, tugging strength from far back. The moment before they somersault, the moment when they arch their backs so beautifully, showing green and white veins amid the black, that moment is intolerable. They finally crack, dashing fiercely upon the sand, actually driving, full force downward, against the sand, bouncing upward and forward, and at last petering out into a small stream which races up the beach and then is recalled. My parents gaze absentmindedly at the ocean, scarcely interested in its harshness. The sun overhead does not disturb them. But I stare at the terrible sun which breaks up sight, and the fatal, merciless, passionate ocean, I forget my parents. I stare fascinated and finally, shocked by the indifference of my father and mother, I burst out weeping once more. The old lady next to me pats me on the shoulder and says "There, there, all of this is only a movie, young man, only a movie," but I look up once more at the terrifying sun and the terrifying ocean, and being unable to control my tears, I get up and go to the men's room, stumbling over the feet of the other people seated in my row.

– 4 –

When I return, feeling as if I had awakened in the morning sick for lack of sleep, several hours have apparently passed and my parents are riding on the merry-go-round. My father is on a black horse, my mother on a white one, and they seem to be making an eternal circuit for the single purpose of snatching the nickel rings which are attached to the arm of one of the posts. A hand-organ is playing; it is one with the ceaseless circling of the merry-go-round.

For a moment it seems that they will never get off the merry-go-round because it will never stop. I feel like one who looks down on the avenue from the 50th story of a building. But at length they do get off; even the music of the hand-organ has ceased for a moment. My father has acquired ten rings, my mother only two, although it was my mother who really wanted them.

They walk on along the boardwalk as the afternoon descends by imperceptible degrees into the incredible violet of dusk. Everything fades into a relaxed glow, even the ceaseless murmuring from the beach, and the revolutions of the merry-go-round. They look for a place to have dinner. My father suggests the best one on the boardwalk and my mother demurs, in accordance with her principles.

However they do go to the best place, asking for a table near the window, so that they can look out on the boardwalk and the mobile ocean. My father feels omnipotent as he places a quarter in the waiter's hand as he asks for a table. The place is crowded and here too there is music, this time from a kind of string trio. My father orders dinner with a fine confidence.

As the dinner is eaten, my father tells of his plans for the future, and my mother shows with expressive face how interested she is, and how impressed. My father becomes exultant. He is lifted up by the waltz that is being played, and his own future begins to intoxicate him. My father tells my mother that he is going to expand his business, for there is a great deal of money to be made. He wants to settle down. After all, he is twenty-nine, he has lived by himself since he was thirteen, he is making more and more money, and he is envious of his married friends when he visits them in the cozy security of their homes, surrounded it seems, by the calm domestic pleasures, and by delightful children, and then, as the waltz reaches the moment when all the dancers swing madly, then, then with awful daring, then he asks my mother to marry him, although awkwardly enough and puzzled, even in his excitement, at how he had arrived at the proposal, and she, to make the whole business worse, begins to cry, and my father looks nervously about, not knowing at all what to do now, and my mother says: "It's all I've wanted from the moment I saw you," sobbing, and he finds all of this very difficult, scarcely to his taste, scarcely as he had thought it would be, on his long walks over Brooklyn Bridge in the revery of a fine cigar, and it was then that I stood up in the theatre and shouted: "Don't do it. It's not too late to change your minds, both of you. Nothing good will come of it, only remorse, hatred, scandal, and two children whose characters are monstrous." The whole audience turned to look at me, annoyed, the usher came hurrying down the aisle flashing his searchlight, and the old lady next to me tugged me down into my seat, saying: "Be quiet. You'll be put out, and you paid thirty-five cents to come in." And so I shut my eyes because I could not bear to see what was happening. I sat there quietly.

– 5 –

But after awhile I begin to take brief glances, and at length I watch again with thirsty interest, like a child who wants to maintain his sulk although offered the bribe of candy. My parents are now having their picture taken in a photographer's booth along the boardwalk. The place is shadowed in the mauve light which is apparently necessary. The camera is set to the side on its tripod and looks like a Martian man. The photographer is instructing my parents in how to pose. My father has his arm over my mother's shoulder, and both of them smile emphatically. The photographer brings my mother a bouquet of flowers to hold in her hand but she holds it at the wrong angle. Then the photographer covers himself with the black cloth which drapes the camera and all that one sees of him is one protruding arm and his hand which clutches the rubber ball which he will squeeze when the picture is finally taken. But he is not satisfied with their appearance. He feels with certainty that somehow there is something wrong in their pose. Again and again he issues from his hidden place with new directions. Each suggestion merely makes matters worse. My father is becoming impatient. They try a seated pose. The photographer explains that he has pride, he is not interested in all of this for the money, he wants to make beautiful pictures. My father says: "Hurry up, will you? We

haven't got all night." But the photographer only scurries about apologetically, and issues new directions. The photographer charms me. I approve
of him with all my heart, for I know just how he feels, and as he criticizes
each revised pose according to some unknown idea of rightness, I become
quite hopeful. But then my father says angrily: "Come on, you've had
enough time, we're not going to wait any longer." And the photographer,
sighing unhappily, goes back under his black covering, holds out his hand,
says: "One, two, three, Now!", and the picture is taken, with my father's
smile turned to a grimace and my mother's bright and false. It takes a few
minutes for the picture to be developed and as my parents sit in the curious light they become quite depressed.

– 6 –

They have passed a fortune-teller's booth and my mother wishes to go
in, but my father does not. They begin to argue about it. My mother
becomes stubborn, my father once more impatient, and then they begin to
quarrel, and what my father would like to do is walk off and leave my
mother there, but he knows that that would never do. My mother refuses
to budge. She is near to tears, but she feels an uncontrollable desire to hear
what the palm-reader will say. My father consents angrily, and they both
go into a booth which is in a way like the photographer's, since it is draped
in black cloth and its light is shadowed. The place is too warm, and my
father keeps saying this is all nonsense, pointing to the crystal ball on the
table. The fortune-teller, a fat, short woman, garbed in what are supposed
to be Oriental robes, comes into the room from the back and greets them,
speaking with an accent. But suddenly my father feels that the whole thing
is intolerable; he tugs at my mother's arm, but my mother refuses to
budge. And then, in terrible anger, my father lets go of my mother's arm
and strides out, leaving my mother stunned. She moves to go after my
father, but the fortune-teller holds her arm tightly and begs her not to do
so, and I in my seat am shocked more than can ever be said, for I feel as if I
were walking a tight-rope a hundred feet over a circus-audience and suddenly the rope is showing signs of breaking, and I get up from my seat and
begin to shout once more the first words I can think of to communicate
my terrible fear and once more the usher comes hurrying down the aisle
flashing his searchlight, and the old lady pleads with me, and the shocked
audience has turned to stare at me and I keep shouting: "What are they
doing? Don't they know what they are doing? Why doesn't my mother go
after my father? If she does not do that, what will she do? Doesn't my
father know what he is doing?"—But the usher has seized my arm and is
dragging me away, and as he does so, he says: "What are *you* doing? Don't
you know that you can't do whatever you want to do? Why should a
young man like you, with your whole life before you, get hysterical like
this? Why don't you *think* of what you're doing? You can't act like this

even if other people aren't around! You will be sorry if you do not do what you should do, you can't carry on like this, it is not right, you will find that out soon enough, everything you do matters too much," and he said that dragging me through the lobby of the theatre into the cold light, and I woke up into the bleak winter morning of my 21st birthday, the windowsill shining with its lip of snow, and the morning already begun.

[1937]

JACK CONROY

Jack Conroy (1899–1990), a leading force in the proletarian literary move-ment of the 1930s, was born and raised in Moberly, Missouri, a hardscrabble mining camp. His mother was a miner's widow and his father was a renegade Catholic priest working for the miners' union who had converted to Method-ism. As a boy Conroy avidly read radical socialist texts in a series of five-cent leaflets published for the miners by the Haldeman-Julius Company in nearby Girard, Kansas. He attended the University of Missouri for one semester, leav-ing because he refused to join the ROTC. Because he had a heart murmur, Con-roy did not serve in World War I but returned to Moberly and did construction work.

In 1929 Conroy joined the Rebel Poets, a group associated with the Indus-trial Workers of the World, and founded a literary magazine, Rebel Poets, *which he edited in 1931–32. He began to publish sketches, stories, and poetry in the magazine, which captured the attention of the influential editor H. L. Mencken at the* American Mercury. *With Mencken's help, Conroy obtained a book contract with a New York publisher for his first novel,* The Disinherited *(1933). This was a picaresque account of the difficult life of his working-class protagonist, Larry Donovan, who labored in a coal mine, a steel mill, a foundry, a tire plant, and a midwestern farm, all the while encountering others like himself exploited by the oppressive economic system. Conroy followed it with a second novel,* A World to Win *(1935). He also founded and edited a new magazine,* The Anvil *(1933–36), the most successful proletarian literary magazine of its time, publishing work by Richard Wright, Langston Hughes, William Carlos Williams, and Erskine Caldwell, among others. In 1939 Con-roy moved to Chicago to edit the* New Anvil, *but the following year the leftist movement redirected its energies from the workers' cause to the fight against international fascism. During World War II Conroy coauthored children's sto-ries with Arna Bontemps as well as a book about African American migration,* They Seek a City *(1945), revised and expanded in 1966 as* Anyplace But Here. *In 1946 he became a senior editor for* The New Standard Encyclope-dia, *a position he held until his retirement in 1966.* The Jack Conroy Reader, *edited by Jack Salzman and David Ray, was published in 1980.*

Interviewed extensively at the end of his life, Conroy was an articulate source of information about the leftist literary movement in the United States in the 1930s. He pointed out that although ideally proletarian literature means "about the working class" and should be "the worker writing about the troubles and the problems of a working class" person, the term also can describe writing about the working class by middle-class authors. "Workers, if they have suffi-cient learning, like to write about things that they don't know anything about, like comfortable living or swashbuckling or fighting wars or things like that." Conroy believed that literature like his story "He Is Thousands" "inspired action and brought about social change," and if social conditions worsen,

772

"writers will let their voices be heard against injustices." "He Is Thousands"
was published in New Masses *in 1939.*

He Is Thousands

"Oh, get that dopey look offa your face," a fellow named Ed Marsh said to his girl. "You look like you'd bit into a quince or been weaned on a pickle. There ain't going to be no trouble: they's got to be an end of trouble sometime. Look out doors! The sun's still on the job, at least, and yesterday I saw a robin as big as life in Circus Park. The air's like spring, and I bet you the leaves will be out soon if it stays like this. They told me out at Premier Motors to come back tomorrow, and besides, the old man hisself has said in the papers that he's gonna risk all he's got to bring back prosperity. Believe me, if he shoots his whole wad, something's got to break loose. I'll just ease out there bright and early, and the job is as good as mine."

"I hear the guards drive the men away from the Premier every morning," Olga insisted. "And sometimes they club them."

"Not unless they start something, they don't. By this time tomorrow, I'll be a workin' man again."

She did not answer: a man must try to work. When Ed said goodbye, the boys were playing marbles on the street corners and the air was heady and balmy. But shabby men were tramping the streets aimlessly, and a blight seemed to be over the city. The haughty limousines rolled along much the same, and the shop windows glittered like harlots lifting their skirts to entice reluctant customers with the lure of a rhinestone garter. At the mission doors, the long queues writhed like wounded snakes. Grim workers haunted the streets as though seeking something they had lost but had little hope of finding. Factory windows were dust-clouded, sad and blank as dead eyes.

Ed had not worked for over a year—since he had been laid off at Premier Motors—but somehow he had lived. Musing over it, he wondered how. The first thing to go had been his watch. He had saved a long time to buy that watch and his pocket missed its weight. Then one thing and another had been sacrificed. But the second-hand men and pawnbrokers were overstocked with the fragments of broken homes and lives and now they refused to buy anything.

In the night the wind shifted maliciously to the North, and cold stabbed through thin walls where men, women and children huddled together for warmth. But there's not much heat in a body when the last layer of fat has been consumed—as a change from food. The poor had been praying that the false spring would remain, for fuel is hard to get without money. Now they bit their blue lips, wishing for morning. Even if the cold did not abate, the sun always *looked* a little warm. Ed shivered under his single blanket and passed the night figuring what he would do with his first pay check. The landlady must have part of it, for she had been pretty good to wait so long, and he knew that the gas company had threatened to take out her meter if she didn't pay the bill next week. He had to have some shoes, too, for as he had often said of late, his soles were so thin he could stand on a dime and tell whether it was heads or tails.

But what seemed most important was the wrist watch he had promised to buy for Olga. He would be able to make the first payment.

Long before dawn, he rose and dressed. It is hard to fumble buttons with cold fingers. He took a hunk of bologna from a bureau drawer. Ravenously, he bit off a few inches, but prudence, prudence . . . Even *if* he got the job (but, of course, he would get it), it would be two weeks before he could draw a pay. The bologna had been pretty long to begin with, and there were two of them, bought at a chain-store special. This was the last, and it was knawed down to three inches. Ed ate skin and all, wiping off a spot of white mold on his shirt sleeve. Queer, how mold could gather in a place that cold.

Premier Motors was five miles from town, and Ed wanted to start early. The city, in the chill morning air, was a city of the dead, and there were mournful ghosts walking its streets. Shabby men, leaning against the gale, stalking down the highway toward Milltown — toward the Premier Plant. There must have been hundreds of them, obscured in the darkness by the gusts of snow. Ed heard the steady shuffle of their feet.

And panic seized him. He knew how men fought for first place in the line; how, frequently, they lay all night on the ground in the forlorn hope of being chosen in the morning. He did not realize at once that he was running past, outdistancing the other men — an endless legion.

"What's your rush, pal?" somebody shouted after him. Ashamed, he slackened to a nervous walk. There were hundreds of them ahead of him, and his heart sank.

Suddenly, outside the limits of Milltown, the marchers jammed: the men ahead must have stopped. Immediately, they began to shuffle their feet and blow on their blue hands in a wind that pierced to the bone. There was ice on the concrete, as Ed's feet could feel through the holes in his shoes. He had put the heels of his socks on top, so the holes would not be on the bottom, but new ones had worn, as holes will in old cloth. But he stood still too long, and when he lifted his foot, he left part of the skin on the pavement.

A man up ahead was speaking — a vague shape in the faint light.

"Listen, men," the speaking figure called. "What we want to do is march up to the gates and send in a couple of fellows to talk to the old man himself, if he's there. He said in the papers that he would spend everything he had to make more work for a bunch of us. Keep together, and don't lose your heads. If nobody else wants to do it, I'll go inside and talk to him—if they let me. Don't give the plant guards any excuse, or they'll probably sap some of us, or give us a bath with the fire hose. That's what they did last year."

Inside the plant, Everet Howard was having a bad half-hour. He could hear restless movements outside, agitated challenges of the guards. The men who had marched were silent. A guard came in to say that two men from the crowd wanted to speak to Howard.

"Oh, I think I better not," he decided nervously. "It would be establishing a bad precedent and there'll be all kinds of importunities. Business really is rotten, and perhaps it would be better for the sales department to stop issuing optimistic reports about the company's flourishing condition. Call me a gloomy gus, say I'm selling America short, but if that gang keeps increasing, they're sure to get nasty one of these times."

"Naw, naw, I know them babies,"—from John Watson, head of Premier's private police. "Guts! They ain't got none! As for their souls, I'll put the fear of God in their souls. Leave it to me to make 'em scatter and howl like a flock of scared pups."

He picked up the tear bombs from a bench, hitching his revolver holster to have it ready. He climbed into his car, and with his stamp on the starter the engine purred.

"A bunch of Communists has egged them bastards on," he snarled, "but I bet I'll make that bunch cry the next time they see a Bolshevik, leave alone associating with one. Gangway! Lemme Out! LaFollette, we are here!"

A guard threw wide the huge doors, the private police outside parting to let the car pass. Watson drove straight at the shivering jobless. Some fell back. Others stood their ground. None believed the car would actually run into them. Watson thrust his head out and beckoned to the guards.

"Come on! Come on! Don't stand there and let the flies blow you! Get busy! Clear 'em off the premises!"

The car struck a man and sent him reeling. Watson threw a tear gas bomb and whipped out his revolver. When the amazed worker who had been struck by the car arose, his hands were torn and bleeding—but they held a rock.

"Oh, you bastard! You dirty, lousy bastard!" he sobbed, the tear gas rasping his lungs. The fury of months broke loose. With all his might he hurled the stone, but he was too weak to throw very hard. It crashed into the windshield and a spider-web of splinters appeared on the shatterproof glass.

The guards were dragging out a fire hose and its cold stream sent the front ranks of the jobless spinning and rolling. The instant the water struck, it froze. Ed lay spluttering on the ground: blood gushed from his nose. The men were finding rocks and cinders and hurling them at the guards. Then a sound like hail pelting a tin roof, or the roll of a drum. He lifted his head— the guards were firing steadily into the masses of men, some of the bullets striking them, others ploughing into the parked cars across the way. Watson's car had stalled against a barricade of fallen bodies, and he leaped out, racing for the protection of the building, holding his head.

"Give 'em hell," he shouted, as he sprang inside.

The pain, when he tried to rise, caught Ed's breath. So it *was* blood, not water, that was trickling down his belly and into his shoes. And the little hole in his coat—he had not noticed it before. Somebody grasped him under the arms and dragged him along. The police had ceased firing, for the men had no more rocks and many of them were lying still in pools of water and blood that had congealed into mush. A frail breath steamed from the blood, cooling.

From a jagged little hole in one man's arm an erratic geyser spurted— a jet that subsided to a thin dribble.

Whoever was dragging Ed dropped him, was standing, panting. And his head, he had almost lost control of it, as it rolled on his neck. So it had been Olga dragging him!

"Oh, honey!" he gasped, "You mustn't stay here. You must get away from here as fast as you can."

"I thought there would be trouble," she said quietly enough, "I came out on the bus."

"I ain't hurt bad," he lied, getting to his knees. "Let's get away from here." But his eyes were a blur and his knees buckled when he tried to stand.

"I can't see you, sweetheart," he admitted, "I can't hear you, either, honey, come closer. Something I wanted to tell you. Just about the watch. The wrist watch we saw in the window on Third Avenue. I aimed to get it for you. I aimed to get it for you for quite a spell, but you know how it is. I ain't had a cent to spare for months and months and months. I swear, I aimed to get it for you, honey, with my first pay."

It horrified her. In his numbing mind only the wrist watch ticked on. The rest was fading into silence as the clots at the corners of his mouth turned purple. The two holes in the soles of his shoes, like the vacant sockets of eyes, oozed a trickle of blood, for his shoes were full. She would not shed those or any other kind of tears.

The patrol wagons gathered up the men who were not nimble enough to escape. Watson was dashing here and there now, shouting, "Don't let any of 'em get away! Some of 'em will burn in the chair for this! They all *ought* to!"

"Please, please, Mr. Watson!" A newspaper man ran after him, pleading. "How many guards wounded? Any killed? I only got an hour to make the final. Please, how many killed, and how many wounded."

"They busted my head," Watson puffed. "But I counted six rioters dead and at least thirty wounded. That's all I got to tell you, son!"

"Get that jane," Watson shouted to a subordinate.

"You knew this guy?" he quizzed Olga, "I take it you're his girl friend. Then we got plenty on you, plenty. You're going to tell us who started this riot."

"He's dead now," she said, "You can't hurt him any more. But you can let him alone since he's dead."

Watson caught her arm and twisted it.

"What does anything matter? He's dead, I tell you, he's dead!" she screamed, beating Watson's chest with her free fist. "Do you hear me? He's dead, and nothing matters any more!"

For suddenly she felt that the dead man was not only Ed Marsh, but many other things. He stood submissively in bread lines, lay row on row in flop houses, he was one, and he was thousands. And he had been a stoical gladiator before Caesar, awaiting the verdict of a capricious thumb: *"Salve atque vale, Caesar, ego moriturus te saluto."*[1] He was a thousand Chinese coolies with heads hacked away. He was ten thousand Egyptian slaves tearing muscles against massive stones to build the Pyramids. He was every bloated corpse that floated down the Yangtse year after year when the spring thaws sent the floods. He was a huge, patient body gnawed by lice that fattened on his flesh and sweat.

"Something does matter," she said so low that Watson could not hear her.

"Take her to the wagon," he ordered. "If she won't talk now, it'll be a pleasure to when we're finished with her."

Could he have read her eyes aright, he would have known that while Olga might talk, she would never say what he expected to hear.   [1939]

---

[1]"Hail and farewell, Caesar, we who are about to die salute you."

RICHARD WRIGHT

Richard Wright (1908–1960) was born on a plantation near Natchez, Mississippi, the son of a farmhand and a country schoolteacher. His home life was disrupted when his father deserted the family, and Wright later said it was only through reading that he managed to keep himself alive. As soon as he could he moved north, to Memphis, Chicago, and then New York City, where he became involved in radical politics. He was a member of the Communist Party from 1932 to 1944. In the 1930s he worked as a reporter for New Masses, a correspondent for the Harlem bureau of the Daily Worker, and an editor for New Challenge, a left-wing magazine that published his "Blueprint for Negro Writing," an effort to bridge the gap between Marxism and black nationalism, in 1938. He was also then writing the stories that appeared in Uncle Tom's Children (1938), which won first prize in a contest for writers in the Federal Writers' Project during the Depression. Wright's early fiction was strongly influenced by Ernest Hemingway's way of writing stories, but Wright also set himself the problem of how to use a modernist style to write about social issues as a radicalized African American:

> Practically all of us, young writers, were influenced by Ernest Hemingway. We liked the simple, direct way in which he wrote, but a great many of us wanted to write about social problems. The question came up: How could we write about social problems and use a simple style? Hemingway's style is so concentrated on naturalistic detail that there is no room for social comment. One boy said that one way was to dig deeper into the character and try to get something that will live. I decided to try it.

The result was the five stories published in Uncle Tom's Children. Next Wright turned to his first novel, Native Son (1940), an American classic dramatizing a brutal story of racial conflict. This was followed by Black Boy (1945), a brilliant autobiography written when he was not yet forty. The next year he left the United States to spend the last fourteen years of his life in Paris, feeling himself alienated from American values. In 1960, the year Wright died, he gathered for publication his second book of short stories, Eight Men, made up of fiction that had appeared over the years in magazines and anthologies, including "The Man Who Was Almost a Man," first published in Harper's Bazaar in 1940.

Telling stories from a realistic view of his own experience, Wright experimented with literary techniques in all his fiction. His short stories dramatize the same themes as his novels and are equally experimental. "The Man Who Was Almost a Man" weaves the black farm boy's speech so skillfully with standard English narration that most readers are unaware of the effect of the deliberate juxtaposition, but this technique brings us closer to the boy's world while making an implicit social comment about his exclusion from the exploitative white society engulfing him.

The Man Who Was Almost a Man

Dave struck out across the fields, looking homeward through paling light. Whut's the use talkin wid em niggers in the field? Anyhow, his mother was putting supper on the table. Them niggers can't understan nothing. One of these days he was going to get a gun and practice shooting, then they couldn't talk to him as though he were a little boy. He slowed, looking at the ground. Shucks, Ah ain scareda them even ef they are biggern me! Aw, Ah know whut Ahma do. Ahm going by ol Joe's sto n git that Sears Roebuck catlog n look at them guns. Mebbe Ma will lemme buy one when she gits mah pay from ol man Hawkins. Ahma beg her t gimme some money. Ahm ol ernough to hava gun. Ahm seventeen. Almost a man. He strode, feeling his long loose-jointed limbs. Shucks, a man oughta hava little gun aftah he done worked hard all day.

He came in sight of Joe's store. A yellow lantern glowed on the front porch. He mounted steps and went through the screen door, hearing it bang behind him. There was a strong smell of coal oil and mackerel fish. He felt very confident until he saw fat Joe walk in through the rear door, then his courage began to ooze.

"Howdy, Dave! Whutcha want?"

"How yuh, Mistah Joe? Aw, Ah don wanna buy nothing. Ah jus wanted t see ef yuhd lemme look at tha catlog erwhile."

"Sure! You wanna see it here?"

"Nawsuh. Ah wants t take it home wid me. Ah'll bring it back termorrow when Ah come in from the fields."

"You plannin on buying something?"

"Yessuh."

"Your ma lettin you have your own money now?"

"Shucks. Mistah Joe, Ahm gittin t be a man like anybody else!"

Joe laughed and wiped his greasy white face with a red bandanna.

"Whut you plannin on buyin?"

Dave looked at the floor, scratched his head, scratched his thigh, and smiled. Then he looked up shyly.

"Ah'll tell yuh, Mistah Joe, ef yuh promise yuh won't tell."

"I promise."

"Waal, Ahma buy a gun."

"A gun? What you want with a gun?"

"Ah wanna keep it."

"You ain't nothing but a boy. You don't need a gun."

"Aw, lemme have the catlog, Mistah Joe. Ah'll bring it back."

Joe walked through the rear door. Dave was elated. He looked around at barrels of sugar and flour. He heard Joe coming back. He craned his neck to see if he were bringing the book. Yeah, he's got it. Gawddog, he's got it!

"Here, but be sure you bring it back. It's the only one I got."

"Sho, Mistah Joe."

"Say, if you wanna buy a gun, why don't you buy one from me? I gotta gun to sell."

"Will it shoot?"

"Sure it'll shoot."

"Whut kind is it?"

"Oh, it's kinda old . . . a left-hand Wheeler. A pistol. A big one."

"Is it got bullets in it?"

"It's loaded."

"Kin Ah see it?"

"Where's your money?"

"What yuh wan fer it?"

"I'll let you have it for two dollars."

"Just two dollahs? Shucks, Ah could buy tha when Ah git mah pay."

"I'll have it here when you want it."

"Awright, suh. Ah be in fer it."

He went through the door, hearing it slam again behind him. Ahma git some money from Ma n buy me a gun! Only two dollahs! He tucked the thick catalogue under his arm and hurried.

"Where yuh been, boy?" His mother held a steaming dish of black-eyed peas.

"Aw, Ma, Ah jus stopped down the road t talk wid the boys."

"Yuh know bettah t keep suppah waitin."

He sat down, resting the catalogue on the edge of the table.

"Yuh git up from there and git to the well n wash yosef! Ah ain feedin no hogs in mah house!"

She grabbed his shoulder and pushed him. He stumbled out of the room, then came back to get the catalogue.

"Whut this?"

"Aw, Ma, it's jusa catlog."

"Who yuh git it from?"

"From Joe, down at the sto."

"Waal, thas good. We kin use it in the outhouse."

"Naw, Ma." He grabbed for it. "Gimme ma catlog, Ma."

She held onto it and glared at him.

"Quit hollerin at me! Whut's wrong wid yuh? Yuh crazy?"

"But Ma, please. It ain mine! It's Joe's! He tol me t bring it back t im termorrow."

She gave up the book. He stumbled down the back steps, hugging the thick book under his arm. When he had splashed water on his face and hands, he groped back to the kitchen and fumbled in a corner for the towel. He bumped into a chair; it clattered to the floor. The catalogue sprawled at his feet. When he had dried his eyes he snatched up the book and held it again under his arm. His mother stood watching him.

"Now, ef yuh gonna act a fool over that ol book, Ah'll take it n burn it up."

"Naw, Ma, please."

"Waal, set down n be still!"

He sat down and drew the oil lamp close. He thumbed page after page, unaware of the food his mother set on the table. His father came in. Then his small brother.

"Whutcha got there, Dave?" his father asked.

"Jusa catlog," he answered, not looking up.

"Yeah, here they is!" His eyes glowed at blue-and-black revolvers. He glanced up, feeling sudden guilt. His father was watching him. He eased the book under the table and rested it on his knees. After the blessing was asked, he ate. He scooped up peas and swallowed fat meat without chewing. Buttermilk helped to wash it down. He did not want to mention money before his father. He would do much better by cornering his mother when she was alone. He looked at his father uneasily out of the edge of his eye.

"Boy, how come yuh don quit foolin wid tha book n eat yo suppah?"

"Yessuh."

"How you n ol man Hawkins gitten erlong?"

"Suh?"

"Can't yuh hear? Why don yuh lissen? Ah ast yu how wuz yuh n ol man Hawkins gittin erlong?"

"Oh, swell, Pa. Ah plows mo lan than anybody over there."

"Waal, yuh oughta keep you mind on whut yuh doin."

"Yessuh."

He poured his plate full of molasses and sopped it up slowly with a chunk of cornbread. When his father and brother had left the kitchen, he still sat and looked again at the guns in the catalogue, longing to muster courage enough to present his case to his mother. Lawd, ef Ah only had tha pretty one! He could almost feel the slickness of the weapon with his fingers. If he had a gun like that he would polish it and keep it shining so it would never rust. N Ah'd keep it loaded, by Gawd!

"Ma?" His voice was hesitant.

"Hunh?"

"Ol man Hawkins give yuh mah money yit?"

"Yeah, but ain no usa yuh thinking bout throwin nona it erway. Ahm keeping tha money sos yuh kin have cloes t go to school this winter."

He rose and went to her side with the open catalogue in his palms. She was washing dishes, her head bent low over a pan. Shyly he raised the book. When he spoke, his voice was husky, faint.

"Ma, Gawd knows Ah wans one of these."

"One of whut?" she asked, not raising her eyes.

"One of these," he said again, not daring even to point. She glanced up at the page, then at him with wide eyes.

"Nigger, is yuh gone plumb crazy?"

"Aw, Ma — "

"Git outta here! Don yuh talk t me bout no gun! Yuh a fool!"

"Ma, Ah kin buy one fer two dollahs."

"Not ef Ah knows it, yuh ain!"

"But yuh promised me one — "

"Ah don care what Ah promised! Yuh ain nothing but a boy yit!"

"Ma, ef yuh lemme buy one Ah'll *never* ast yuh fer nothing no mo."

"Ah tol yuh t git outta here! Yuh ain gonna toucha penny of tha money fer no gun! Thas how come Ah has Mistah Hawkins t pay yo wages t me, cause Ah knows yuh ain got no sense."

"But, Ma, we needa gun. Pa ain got no gun. We needa gun in the house. Yuh kin never tell whut might happen."

"Now don yuh try to maka fool outta me, boy! Ef we did hava gun, yuh wouldn't have it!"

He laid the catalogue down and slipped his arm around her waist.

"Aw, Ma, Ah done worked hard alla summer n ain ast yuh fer nothing, is Ah, now?"

"Thas whut yuh spose t do!"

"But Ma, Ah wans a gun. Yuh kin lemme have two dollahs outta mah money. Please, Ma. I kin give it to Pa. . . . Please, Ma! Ah loves yuh, Ma."

When she spoke her voice came soft and low.

"What yu wan wida gun, Dave? Yuh don need no gun. Yuh'll git in trouble. N ef yo pa jus thought Ah let yuh have money t buy a gun he'd hava fit."

"Ah'll hide it, Ma. It ain but two dollahs."

"Lawd, chil, whut's wrong wid yuh?"

"Ain nothin wrong, Ma. Ahm almos a man now. Ah wans a gun."

"Who gonna sell yuh a gun?"

"Ol Joe at the sto."

"N it don cos but two dollahs?"

"Thas all, Ma. Jus two dollahs. Please, Ma."

She was stacking the plates away; her hands moved slowly, reflectively. Dave kept an anxious silence. Finally, she turned to him.

"Ah'll let yuh git tha gun ef yuh promise me one thing."

"What's tha, Ma?"

"Yuh bring it straight back t me, yuh hear? It be fer Pa."

"Yessum! Lemme go now, Ma."

She stooped, turned slightly to one side, raised the hem of her dress, rolled down the top of her stocking, and came up with a slender wad of bills.

"Here," she said. "Lawd knows yuh don need no gun. But yer pa does. Yuh bring it right back t me, yuh hear? Ahma put it up. Now ef yuh don, Ahma have yuh pa lick yuh so hard yuh won fergit it."

"Yessum."

He took the money, ran down the steps, and across the yard.

"Dave! Yuuuuuh Daaaaave!"

He heard, but he was not going to stop now. "Now, Lawd!"

The first movement he made the following morning was to reach under his pillow for the gun. In the gray light of dawn he held it loosely, feeling a sense of power. Could kill a man with a gun like this. Kill anybody, black or white. And if he were holding his gun in his hand, nobody could run over him; they would have to respect him. It was a big gun, with a long barrel and a heavy handle. He raised and lowered it in his hand, marveling at its weight.

He had not come straight home with it as his mother had asked; instead he had stayed out in the fields, holding the weapon in his hand, aiming it now and then at some imaginary foe. But he had not fired it; he had been afraid that his father might hear. Also he was not sure he knew how to fire it.

To avoid surrendering the pistol he had not come into the house until he knew that they were all asleep. When his mother had tiptoed to his bed-side late that night and demanded the gun, he had first played possum; then he had told her that the gun was hidden outdoors, that he would bring it to her in the morning. Now he lay turning it slowly in his hands. He broke it, took out the cartridges, felt them, and then put them back.

He slid out of bed, got a long strip of old flannel from a trunk, wrapped the gun in it, and tied it to his naked thigh while it was still loaded. He did not go in to breakfast. Even though it was not yet daylight, he started for Jim Hawkins' plantation. Just as the sun was rising he reached the barns where the mules and plows were kept.

"Hey! That you, Dave?"

He turned. Jim Hawkins stood eying him suspiciously.

"What're yuh doing here so early?"

"Ah didn't know Ah wuz gittin up so early, Mistah Hawkins. Ah was fixin t hitch up ol Jenny n take her t the fiels."

"Good. Since you're so early, how about plowing that stretch down by the woods?"

"Suits me, Mistah Hawkins."

"O.K. Go to it!"

He hitched Jenny to a plow and started across the fields. Hot dog! This was just what he wanted. If he could get down by the woods, he could shoot his gun and nobody would hear. He walked behind the plow, hearing the traces creaking, feeling the gun tied tight to his thigh.

When he reached the woods, he plowed two whole rows before he decided to take out the gun. Finally, he stopped, looked in all directions, then untied the gun and held it in his hand. He turned to the mule and smiled.

"Know whut this is, Jenny? Naw, yuh wouldn know! Yuhs jusa ol mule! Anyhow, this is a gun, n it kin shoot, by Gawd!"

He held the gun at arm's length. Whut t hell, Ahma shoot this thing! He looked at Jenny again.

"Lissen here, Jenny! When Ah pull this ol trigger, Ah don wan yuh t run n acka fool now!"

Jenny stood with head down, her short ears pricked straight. Dave walked off about twenty feet, held the gun far out from him at arm's length, and turned his head. Hell, he told himself, Ah ain afraid. The gun felt loose in his fingers; he waved it wildly for a moment. Then he shut his eyes and tightened his forefinger. Bloom! A report half deafened him and he thought his right hand was torn from his arm. He heard Jenny whinnying and galloping over the field, and he found himself on his knees, squeezing his fingers hard between his legs. His hand was numb; he jammed it into his mouth, trying to warm it, trying to stop the pain. The gun lay at his feet. He did not quite know what had happened. He stood up and stared at the gun as though it were a living thing. He gritted his teeth and kicked the gun. Yuh almos broke mah arm! He turned to look for Jenny; she was far over the fields, tossing her head and kicking wildly.

"Hol on there, ol mule!"

When he caught up with her she stood trembling, walling her big white eyes at him. The plow was far away; the traces had broken. Then Dave stopped short, looking, not believing. Jenny was bleeding. Her left side was red and wet with blood. He went closer. Lawd, have mercy! Wondah did Ah shoot this mule? He grabbed for Jenny's mane. She flinched, snorted, whirled, tossing her head.

"Hol on now! Hol on."

Then he saw the hole in Jenny's side, right between the ribs. It was round, wet, red. A crimson stream streaked down the front leg, flowing fast. Good Gawd! Ah wuzn't shootin at tha mule. He felt panic. He knew he had to stop that blood, or Jenny would bleed to death. He had never seen so much blood in all his life. He chased the mule for half a mile, trying to catch her. Finally she stopped, breathing hard, stumpy tail half arched. He caught her mane and led her back to where the plow and gun lay. Then he stopped and grabbed handfuls of damp black earth and tried to plug the bullet hole. Jenny shuddered, whinnied, and broke from him.

"Hol on! Hol on now!"

He tried to plug it again, but blood came anyhow. His fingers were hot and sticky. He rubbed dirt into his palms, trying to dry them. Then again he attempted to plug the bullet hole, but Jenny shied away, kicking her heels high. He stood helpless. He had to do something. He ran at Jenny; she dodged him. He watched a red stream of blood flow down Jenny's leg and form a bright pool at her feet.

"Jenny . . . Jenny," he called weakly.

His lips trembled. She's bleeding t death! He looked in the direction of home, wanting to go back, wanting to get help. But he saw the pistol lying in the damp black clay. He had a queer feeling that if he only did something, this would not be; Jenny would not be there bleeding to death.

When he went to her this time, she did not move. She stood with sleepy, dreamy eyes; and when he touched her she gave a low-pitched whinny and knelt to the ground, her front knees slopping in blood.

"Jenny . . . Jenny . . ." he whispered.

For a long time she held her neck erect; then her head sank, slowly. Her ribs swelled with a mighty heave and she went over.

Dave's stomach felt empty, very empty. He picked up the gun and held it gingerly between his thumb and forefinger. He buried it at the foot of a tree. He took a stick to cover the pool of blood with dirt—but what was the use? There was Jenny lying with her mouth open and her eyes walled and glassy. He could not tell Jim Hawkins he had shot his mule. But he had to tell something. Yeah, Ah'll tell em Jenny started gittin wil n fell on the joint of the plow. . . . But that would hardly happen to a mule. He walked across the field slowly, head down.

It was sunset. Two of Jim Hawkins' men were over near the edge of the woods digging a hole in which to bury Jenny. Dave was surrounded by a knot of people, all of whom were looking down at the dead mule.

"I don't see how in the world it happened," said Jim Hawkins for the tenth time.

The crowd parted and Dave's mother, father, and small brother pushed into the center.

"Where Dave?" his mother called.

"There he is," said Jim Hawkins.

His mother grabbed him.

"Whut happened, Dave? Whut yuh done?"

"Nothin."

"C mon, boy, talk," his father said.

Dave took a deep breath and told the story he knew nobody believed.

"Waal," he drawled. "Ah brung ol Jenny down here sos Ah could do mah plowin. Ah plowed bout two rows, just like yuh see." He stopped and pointed at the long rows of upturned earth. "Then somethin musta been wrong wid ol Jenny. She wouldn ack right a-tall. She started snortin n kickin her heels. Ah tried t hol her, but she pulled erway, rearin n goin in. Then when the point of the plow was stickin up in the air, she swung erroun n twisted herself back on it. . . . She stuck herself n started t bleed. N fo Ah could do anything, she wuz dead."

"Did you ever hear of anything like that in all your life?" asked Jim Hawkins.

There were white and black standing in the crowd. They murmured. Dave's mother came close to him and looked hard into his face. "Tell the truth, Dave," she said.

"Looks like a bullet hole to me," said one man.

"Dave, whut yuh do wid the gun?" his mother asked.

The crowd surged in, looking at him. He jammed his hands into his pockets, shook his head slowly from left to right, and backed away. His eyes were wide and painful.

"Did he hava gun?" asked Jim Hawkins.

"By Gawd, Ah tol yuh tha wuz a gun wound," said a man, slapping his thigh.

His father caught his shoulders and shook him till his teeth rattled.

"Tell whut happened, yuh rascal! Tell whut. . . ."

Dave looked at Jenny's stiff legs and began to cry.

"Whut yuh do wid tha gun?" his mother asked.

"What wuz he doin wida gun?" his father asked.

"Come on and tell the truth," said Hawkins. "Ain't nobody going to hurt you. . . ."

His mother crowded close to him.

"Did yuh shoot tha mule, Dave?"

Dave cried, seeing blurred white and black faces.

"Ahh ddinn gggo tt sshooot hher. . . . Ah ssswear ffo Gawd Ahh ddin. . . . Ah wuz a-tryin t sssee ef the old gggun would sshoot—"

"Where yuh git the gun from?" his father asked.

"Ah got it from Joe, at the sto."

"Where yuh git the money?"

"Ma give it t me."

"He kept worryin me, Bob. Ah had t. Ah tol im t bring the gun right back t me. . . . It was fer yuh, the gun."

"But how yuh happen to shoot that mule?" asked Jim Hawkins.

"Ah wuzn shootin at the mule, Mistah Hawkins. The gun jumped when Ah pulled the trigger. . . . N fo Ah knowed anythin Jenny was there a-bleedin."

Somebody in the crowd laughed. Jim Hawkins walked close to Dave and looked into his face.

"Well, looks like you have bought you a mule, Dave."

"Ah swear fo Gawd, Ah didn go t kill the mule, Mistah Hawkins!"

"But you killed her!"

All the crowd was laughing now. They stood on tiptoe and poked heads over one another's shoulders.

"Well, boy, looks like yuh done bought a dead mule! Hahaha!"

"Ain tha ershame."

"Hohohohoho."

Dave stood, head down, twisting his feet in the dirt.

"Well, you needn't worry about it, Bob," said Jim Hawkins to Dave's father. "Just let the boy keep on working and pay me two dollars a month."

"Whut yuh wan fer yo mule, Mistah Hawkins?"

Jim Hawkins screwed up his eyes.

"Fifty dollars."

"Whut yuh do wid tha gun?" Dave's father demanded.

Dave said nothing.

"Yuh wan me t take a tree n beat yuh till yuh talk!"

"Nawsuh!"

"Whut yuh do wid it?"

"Ah throwed it erway."

"Where?"

"Ah . . . Ah throwed it in the creek."

"Waal, c mon home. N firs thing in the mawnin git to tha creek n fin tha gun."

"Yessuh."

"Whut yuh pay fer it?"

"Two dollahs."

"Take tha gun n git yo money back n carry it to Mistah Hawkins, yuh hear? N don fergit Ahma lam you black bottom good fer this! Now march yosef on home, suh!"

Dave turned and walked slowly. He heard people laughing. Dave glared, his eyes welling with tears. Hot anger bubbled in him. Then he swallowed and stumbled on.

That night Dave did not sleep. He was glad that he had gotten out of killing the mule so easily, but he was hurt. Something hot seemed to turn over inside him each time he remembered how they had laughed. He tossed on his bed, feeling his hard pillow. N Pa says he's gonna beat me. . . . He remembered other beatings, and his back quivered. Naw, naw, Ah sho don wan im t beat me tha way no mo. Dam em all! Nobody ever gave him anything. All he did was work. They treat me like a mule, n then they beat me. He gritted his teeth. N Ma had t tell on me.

Well, if he had to, he would take old man Hawkins that two dollars. But that meant selling the gun. And he wanted to keep that gun. Fifty dollars for a dead mule.

He turned over, thinking how he had fired the gun. He had an itch to fire it again. Ef other men kin shoota gun, by Gawd, Ah kin! He was still, listening. Mebbe they all sleepin now. The house was still. He heard the soft breathing of his brother. Yes, now! He would go down and get that gun and see if he could fire it! He eased out of bed and slipped into overalls.

The moon was bright. He ran almost all the way to the edge of the woods. He stumbled over the ground, looking for the spot where he had buried the gun. Yeah, here it is. Like a hungry dog scratching for a bone, he pawed it up. He puffed his black cheeks and blew dirt from the trigger and barrel. He broke it and found four cartridges unshot. He looked around; the fields were filled with silence and moonlight. He clutched the gun stiff and hard in his fingers. But, as soon as he wanted to pull the trigger, he shut his eyes and turned his head. Naw, Ah can't shoot wid mah eyes closed n mah head turned. With effort he held his eyes open; then he squeezed. *Blooooom!* He was stiff, not breathing. The gun was still in his hands. Dammit, he'd done it! He fired again. *Blooooom!* He smiled. *Bloooom! Blooooom! Click, click.* There! It was empty. If anybody could shoot a gun, he could. He put the gun into his hip pocket and started across the fields.

When he reached the top of a ridge he stood straight and proud in the moonlight, looking at Jim Hawkins' big white house, feeling the gun sagging in his pocket. Lawd, ef Ah had just one mo bullet Ah'd taka shot at tha house. Ah'd like t scare ol man Hawkins jusa little. . . . Jusa enough t let im know Dave Saunders is a man.

To his left the road curved, running to the tracks of the Illinois Central. He jerked his head, listening. From far off came a faint *hoooof-hoooof; hoooof-hoooof.* . . . He stood rigid. Two dollahs a mont. Les see now. . . . Tha means it'll take bout two years. Shucks! Ah'll be dam!

He started down the road, toward the tracks. Yeah, here she comes! He stood beside the track and held himself stiffly. Here she comes, erroun the ben. . . . C mon, yuh slow poke! C mon! He had his hand on his gun; something quivered in his stomach. Then the train thundered past, the gray and brown box cars rumbling and clinking. He gripped the gun tightly; then he jerked his hand out of his pocket. Ah betcha Bill wouldn't do it! Ah betcha. . . . The cars slid past, steel grinding upon steel. Ahm ridin yuh ternight, so hep me Gawd! He was hot all over. He hesitated just a moment; then he grabbed, pulled atop of a car, and lay flat. He felt his pocket; the gun was still there. Ahead the long rails were glinting in the moonlight, stretching away, away to somewhere, somewhere where he could be a man. . . .   [1940]

4

MID–
TWENTIETH
CENTURY

1941–1965

*I*n 1942, shortly after the Japanese air force's surprise attack on American naval bases in Pearl Harbor led to the United States' entry into World War II, Ernest Hemingway edited a best-selling anthology of short fiction, *Men at War,* described on its title page as "The Best War Stories of All Time." More than a thousand pages in length, this volume was dedicated to Hemingway's three sons, the oldest of whom, at eighteen, was eligible for the draft. Hemingway explained in his introduction that his intention was to tell his readers "how all men from the earliest times we know have fought and died. So when you have read it you will know that there are no worse things to be gone through than men have been through before."

Men at War was so popular that it went through three editions and several reprintings, most recently in 1979. The eighty-two selections in the compilation described (among many others) battles from the Old Testament, the Trojan War, Caesar's conquest of Britain, the battle of Waterloo, the Civil War, the Spanish-American War, World War I, the Russian Revolution, the Japanese invasion of China, and the bombing of Pearl Harbor. In Hemingway's introduction he explained why he believed that good stories about war were hard to find:

> Cowardice, as distinguished from panic, is almost always simply a lack of ability to suspend the functioning of the imagination. Learning to suspend your imagination and live completely in the very second of the present minute with no before and no after is the greatest gift a soldier can acquire. It, naturally, is the opposite of all those gifts a writer should have. That is what makes good writing by good soldiers such a rare thing and why it is so prized when we have it.

Hemingway published his last collection of short fiction, *The Fifth Column and the First Forty-Nine Stories,* in 1938. He wrote articles for *Collier's* magazine about the Allies' invasion of France in 1944, but he didn't write short stories about this war, although he had written about World War I in successful short fiction and novels such as *In Our Time* (1925)

789

and *A Farewell to Arms* (1929) and about the Spanish civil war in *For Whom the Bell Tolls* (1940).

Hemingway's renown reflected the prosperity of the nation as the United States assumed the dominant role in the postwar world. After Pearl S. Buck had been awarded the Nobel Prize for literature in 1938, Hemingway, William Faulkner, and John Steinbeck won Nobel Prizes in the 1950s and early 1960s, securing international recognition for the achievement of American authors. Many readers sensed that these writers represented the end of the modernist era; their ranks had been depleted by the deaths of Fitzgerald, Anderson, and Stein in the early 1940s.

The mid-twentieth century was a transitional time for authors of short stories. They inherited the experimentation of the modernist writers and the social realism developed by the writers of the 1930s, but the earlier moral and ideological certainties were severely tested in the aftermath of World War II. Yet in the years immediately following the war, the popularity of short fiction grew with the increasing affluence of Americans, and the range and assurance of our storytelling also began to mirror the nation's new role as the leading world power.

During World War II, paperback books, which were popular in France and England, were published in the United States for the first time in large printings to be distributed to servicemen overseas. After the war, inexpensive paperbacks became a staple item in American publishing. As early as 1943, Avon Books established the *Modern Short Story Monthly*, a series of paperback books sold for a quarter at newsstands along with magazines and newspapers. The publisher advertised the literary merits of its product on the colorful front covers with a quote from the New York *Herald Tribune:* "Where could there be found prose writing more suited to the short story form, more gracefully developed or subtly complete, than between these covers?"

Avon's choice as number twenty-three in the series was Pearl S. Buck's *The First Wife and Other Stories,* published by special arrangement with the John Day Company, which had originally published the book a dozen years before. On the back pages, Avon listed "Some of the More Popular Titles" in its series: volumes of short stories by John O'Hara, William Saroyan, John Steinbeck, Fannie Hurst, Thomas Wolfe, and Sinclair Lewis, among others, as well as the collection *Twelve Selected Modern Stories by Twelve Famous Writers,* edited by the best-selling novelist Edna Ferber. In 1945, for thirty-five cents, the reader was offered *The Avon Annual,* a special anniversary paperback featuring stories by Hemingway, Dashiell Hammett, Mary Roberts Rinehart, Sally Benson, Marjorie Kinnan Rawlings, William Faulkner, Whit Burnett, Erskine Caldwell, James T. Farrell, and Eudora Welty. In 1948 James Michener's first best-seller was a paperback edition of *Tales of the South Pacific,* a collection of wartime love stories.

The magazine *Story,* featuring the work of almost every major author of American short fiction, also prospered in the 1940s. It was first produced on a mimeograph machine in Vienna, Austria, in 1931 by the American journalists Whit Burnett and Martha Foley, who wanted to establish a periodical for noncommercial short stories. During its first ten years, the magazine relocated to New York City and struggled somewhat precariously under various financial backers, but in 1942 it stabilized under the editorship of Hallie Abbett (later Burnett). In 1965, Whit and Hallie Burnett edited the book *Story Jubilee,* a collection of stories from their magazine. In their foreword, they wrote about what publication in *Story* had meant to some of the young authors whose manuscripts they had accepted or rejected:

> *Story* discovered Richard Wright, and its five-hundred-dollar prize took him off the WPA, and the publication of *Uncle Tom's Children, Native Son,* and *Black Boy* (The Story Press–Harper's) launched a new force in Negro writing in America, years before the emergence of James Baldwin and the racial tumult of today. . . . Joseph Heller, who was to write *Catch-22,* was a discovery of a contest *Story* conducted in the armed services in the forties, the money for his prize-winning story having been put up by another loyal young author, who didn't want his name used — J. D. Salinger. Salinger's first stories had appeared in *Story* before he left Burnett's [writing] class at Columbia University. He had joined the army, sold stories to the *Saturday Evening Post,* and just before the Battle of the Bulge, sent back to America a couple of hundred dollars of his fiction earnings to be given to "any author you think can use it."
>
> Not all have been so generous-minded. The trouble with running a magazine is you must reject many more authors than you can accept. One day we received a small, interesting package in the mail. It was, we saw, from an author. It contained, when we opened it, not a box of candy or a bottle of fine old bonded bourbon, but a length of rope. "Dear Sir," the author wrote, "you rejected me. I reject you. Take this rope and hang yourself."

Many American writers participated in World War II, yet very few short stories about this war continue to be read today. Unlike the Civil War, which gave rise to several works of short fiction that have become classics, American authors attempting to describe World War II were more successful as novelists. John Hersey's *Hiroshima* (1946), Norman Mailer's *The Naked and the Dead* (1948), James Jones's *From Here to Eternity* (1951), Joseph Heller's *Catch-22* (1961), and Kurt Vonnegut Jr.'s *Slaughterhouse Five* (1969) were among the best-selling novels about the war. Perhaps the unimaginable extent of the human capacity for destruction, which culminated with the United States' decision to use the atomic bomb on Japanese cities, was beyond description in fiction limited to a relatively few pages.

Peacetime in post–World War II America segued into an unprecedented period of political tension and social tumult as the country found itself embroiled in the cold war against the Soviet Union and China, following the aggressive Communist expansion into Eastern Europe and Cuba.

In 1950, Congress overrode President Truman's veto of an anticommunist bill, preparing the way for Joseph McCarthy's anticommunist hearings in the Senate. At about the same time, United States military forces were sent to fight in South Korea to keep the world "safe for democracy" against the Chinese and North Korean Communist invaders.

During the 1940s, some direct reportage of the experience of war appeared in short fiction. Pearl S. Buck described the prewar invasion of China by Japanese soldiers in her story "His Own Country" (1941). Ralph Ellison referred to early African American myths about the power of flight in "Flying Home" (1944), his story of a black air force pilot's traumatic accident in training maneuvers, which revealed the racial prejudice still endemic in American society despite the advances of the black middle class. In "Winter Night" (1946), Kay Boyle wrote about an immigrant woman who had cared for a child in a Nazi concentration camp and later found a job as a babysitter for the young daughter of a working mother in New York City. Both Ellison and Boyle dramatized the painful irony of the situations implicit in their realistic stories, sensitively reflecting the impact of the war on Americans at home.

There was also a symbolic depiction of the devastating effect of war in the ruined landscape after a holocaust imagined by Walter Van Tilburg Clark in "The Portable Phonograph" (1941). Later writers such as Shirley Jackson in "The Lottery" (1948) and Kurt Vonnegut Jr. in "Harrison Bergeron" (1961) used fantasy to suggest the mounting pressures of conformity in the United States and the growing tide of social unrest during these years.

In this transitional period at midcentury, many writers continued to create traditional stories based on social realism. On the East Coast, writers for *The New Yorker* developed a keenly observant, often ironic eye for the customs and cruelties of their urban and suburban society. James Thurber humorously analyzed the cut-throat strategies of New York City office politics in "The Catbird Seat" (1942), reflecting an underlying uneasiness about women's increasingly visible role in the workforce, especially after they were mobilized for the war effort to take the place of men drafted into active service. John Cheever used fantasy in "The Enormous Radio" (1947) to suggest a darker mood of moral hypocrisy in an affluent married couple's experience living in a large East Side Manhattan apartment house. In "The Sharks," John O'Hara created a sharply etched portrait of homophobia in a wealthy vacation colony on the eastern seaboard.

In the southern states, postwar writers continued to dissect the manners and morals of their society during a period that has been called the southern renaissance (roughly 1925–1960). Carson McCullers's "A Tree. A Rock. A Cloud" (1942) explored the theme of human loneliness, the bleakness of her vision echoing the existential core of darkness at the heart of Hemingway's short fiction in the 1930s. Caroline Gordon's "The Petrified Woman" (1947) used a child's point of view to hint at the unreconcilable hostility between a newly married couple at a southern family reunion—

the hostility stemming from the husband's alcoholism and resentment of his wife's frigidity. Peter Taylor dramatized a father's bewildered sense of alienation from his teenage son in "Promise of Rain" (1959) as the gap between the generations continued to widen in the postwar years.

Even in this flowering of southern writing, readers could sense a transition. In the early 1960s both Eudora Welty and Flannery O'Connor wrote short fiction responding to the social unrest in the South, as American black and white activists challenged the laws enforcing racial segregation that had prevailed since the years of Reconstruction. In "Where Is the Voice Coming From?" (1963), Welty imagined the thoughts of a white supremacist as he murdered a black civil rights activist in a southern city. Welty modeled the events of her story on the assassination of Medgar Evers, who was shot outside his home in Jackson on June 11, 1963, by Byron De La Beckwith after Evers had worked as field secretary for the National Association for the Advancement of Colored People to organize African American voter registration, sit-ins, and shopping boycotts in Mississippi. Beckwith, who was tried for the crime by two juries of Mississippi white men but not convicted, bragged about shooting "that uppity nigger" until he was tried a third time in 1994, found guilty of murder, and sentenced to life in prison.

In "Everything That Rises Must Converge" (1961), Flannery O'Connor reflected the subtle but unmistakable sense of social change in a single white family as well as in their black neighbors after the city buses were integrated in Atlanta, Georgia. The traditional conventions of regional writing culminated in Welty's and O'Connor's stories, as a new generation of more militant writers emerged in the South after the victories of the civil rights movement in the early 1960s.

In 1963 the Irish writer Frank O'Connor published *The Lonely Voice,* his study of the short story. In this work he speculated that the short story was the chosen form of what he called "submerged population groups." O'Connor meant that this literary form has a special affinity for expressing the point of view of "everyman," the powerless, highly vulnerable character on the sidelines. African Americans, women, and Jews traditionally held this position in the United States, yet in the transitional period between 1940 and 1965 their creative voices took on a new strength as they entered the middle class and began to claim their rightful place in American society.

Gwendolyn Brooks, in "We're the only colored people here" (1945), suggested the sense of alienation she felt as a young, married black woman living in a Chicago tenement, attending a movie with her husband in a predominantly white neighborhood. James Baldwin narrated "Sonny's Blues" (1957) from the point of view of a middle-class schoolteacher, struggling to understand his brother's life in the underworld of drug addiction and jazz in Harlem.

The situation of American women depicted in midcentury short fiction was transformed into a new world encouraging sexual freedom and feminist sensibilities. Mary McCarthy offered a sense of the emancipation of a young, college-educated white woman in her graphic description of a sexual adventure aboard a cross-country train en route to California in "The Man in the Brooks Brothers Shirt" (1941). Tillie Olsen also expressed her revolt against moral stereotyping in "I Stand Here Ironing" (1956), a defiant monologue by a poverty-stricken single parent abandoned by her husband who refused to shoulder the burden of caring for their family.

After the disintegration of the political certainties of the 1930s and the emergence of Israel as a new country in 1948, Philip Roth began to mine the middle-class, Jewish American experience in his short fiction. Treating his material with mordant humor, Roth created the iconoclastic "The Conversion of the Jews" (1959), about a young New Jersey boy's stubborn efforts to understand his religious background and challenge the bigotry of the adults around him. Roth's literary tastes had been shaped in part by his reading in *Commentary* magazine, a monthly funded by the American Jewish Committee, and *Partisan Review,* an intellectually stimulating quarterly from which Roth said he learned his "strategies of cultural attack." As he began placing his stories in different American magazines such as *Commentary,* the *Paris Review,* and *The New Yorker,* Roth found himself exhilarated to find that "magazines embodying such divergent cultural perspectives could sanction his subject matter."

With the increasing prosperity, a new kind of magazine proliferated in the United States. In 1943, Charles Allen stated in the *Sewanee Review* that at that time small-circulation literary magazines were publishing about 80 percent of the first stories by important American authors. After the war, with the expansion of the G.I. Bill that financed college education for returning veterans at universities throughout the United States, courses in creative writing and writers' conferences began to thrive along with literary magazines on campuses.

In 1958 the apprentice writer Raymond Carver was fortunate enough to have the novelist John Gardener as his teacher in his first college creative-writing course at Chico State College in California. Later, Carver recalled that Gardener introduced his class to the "little" magazines or literary periodicals "by bringing a box of these magazines to class one day and passing them around" so that students like Carver could acquaint themselves with their names and "see what they looked like and what they felt like to hold in the hand." Soon, Carver would be sending typed pages of his stories to these little magazines, hoping to get published.

While periodicals such as the *Yale Review, Partisan Review,* the *Paris Review,* and the *Southern Review* supported the work of young writers, mainstream magazines with large circulations like *The Atlantic Monthly, Harper's Magazine,* and *The New Yorker* continued to publish the most popular writers of short fiction, including J. D. Salinger, who contributed to the sense of American culture in transition at midcentury. After returning from active combat in France during World War II, Salinger placed his stories exclusively in *The New Yorker,* the ideal place for his exploration of the lives of members of an imaginary Jewish family on the upper West Side of Manhattan.

As issues of *The New Yorker* containing Salinger stories invariably sold out at newsstands, critics such as Mary McCarthy wondered if Salinger wasn't destined to "inherit the mantle of Papa Hemingway." In 1951, Salinger achieved cult status with his novel *The Catcher in the Rye*. Unlike most successful novelists who began by writing short fiction, Salinger continued to publish only books of stories — *Nine Stories* (1953), *Franny and Zooey* (1961), *Raise High the Roof Beam, Carpenters and Seymour: An Introduction* (1963). Salinger's sense of colloquial speech was so exact, and his psychological studies of sensitive young people unable to function in a world controlled by hypocritical adults were so compelling, that he became the stylist to emulate for many young American prose writers, including John Updike and Joyce Carol Oates.

Traditional realism shaped most of the short stories from this period, although by the end of the 1960s a radically new stylistic experimentation would emerge. Collections by Pearl S. Buck and Kay Boyle had reflected the growing internationalism of American writers, beginning with Buck's first collection in 1933, *The First Wife and Other Stories* (reprinted in 1945), and continuing with *Today and Forever* (1941) and *Far and Near: Stories of Japan, China, and America* (1947). Kay Boyle's experience of living abroad as an expatriate for many years contributed to the stories in her first collection, *The White Horses of Vienna and Other Stories* (1936), as well as in her later book *The Smoking Mountain: Stories of Postwar Germany* (1951).

Traditional realist writer John O'Hara also began to publish story collections in the 1930s, starting in 1935 with *The Doctor's Son and Other Stories*. After a decade of writing novels, O'Hara continued his books of short fiction with *Assembly* (1961), *The Cape Cod Lighter* (1962), and several others. John Cheever began to publish his story collections in the 1940s with *The Way Some People Live* (1942), followed by *The Enormous Radio and Other Stories* (1953) and *The Housebreaker of Shady Hill* (1959). A collection of the short fiction and drawings of *The New Yorker* humorist James Thurber, *The Thurber Carnival* (1945), went through several editions.

Southern writers were also well represented, beginning with Eudora Welty's *A Curtain of Green* in 1941, followed two years later by *The Wide Net and Other Stories*. In 1951, Carson McCullers published her novella *The Ballad of the Sad Café* along with a selection of her short stories. The tradition of southern grotesque fiction found its fullest expression at mid-century in two collections of stories by Flannery O'Connor, *A Good Man Is Hard to Find* (1955) and *Everything That Rises Must Converge* (1965). Caroline Gordon's story collections, *The Forest of the South* (1945) and *Old Red and Other Stories* (1963), along with the short fiction of Peter Taylor, presented a more realistic portrait of the South. Taylor debuted with *A Long Fourth and Other Stories* in 1948 and has continued to publish collections of stories for more than fifty years.

Mary McCarthy, Shirley Jackson, and Tillie Olsen probably evoked stronger reactions from readers of short stories than any other American women writers of their time. McCarthy's collection of linked realistic stories, *The Company She Keeps* (1942), broke ground with its uncompromising sexual explicitness. Jackson's *The Lottery; or, The Adventures of James Harris* (1949) displayed her gift for fantasy and implicit moral comment. Tillie Olsen's four stories in *Tell Me a Riddle* (1961) became a rallying point for feminists in the decades to come.

Among African American writers, the poet Gwendolyn Brooks published her collection of linked stories, *Maud Martha,* in 1953. A dozen years later, the novelist and essayist James Baldwin collected his short fiction in *Going to Meet the Man*. Both collections described the difficulties of black life in the crowded ghettos of large northern cities before the explosive uprisings of the 1970s, which resulted from the urbanization of poverty-stricken African Americans, who, seeking employment, had migrated in large numbers to Chicago and New York City from the rural South and the Caribbean islands.

Philip Roth was among a number of Jewish writers who came to prominence during the postwar period; this group included Isaac Bashevis Singer, Saul Bellow, and Bernard Malamud, who also began their careers writing short fiction. Roth was perhaps the most combative figure among them. As the novelist Robert Stone understood, in Jewish writers of his generation "faith in America's promise was coupled with an impulse to test the limits of its sense of justice." Roth's books of fiction anticipated the sweeping cultural changes at the end of the century. Debuting with *Goodbye, Columbus and Five Short Stories* (1959), Roth admitted in his preface that his literary ambitions were formulated "in direct opposition to the triumphant, suffocating American philistinism of that time" that included "*Time, Life,* Hollywood, television, the best-seller list, advertising copy, McCarthyism, Rotary Clubs, racial prejudice, and the American booster mentality."

By 1968, the range of styles in the stories of Kurt Vonnegut Jr.'s *Welcome to the Monkey House* reflected a darkening mood as the optimistic fiction that had predominated in the middle of the century began to shift to a postmodern spirit. From the euphoria of a victorious United States at the end of World War II to the widespread challenges to authority following the anticommunist hysteria of the cold war and the civil rights actions of the 1950s and early 1960s, authors of the American short story had chronicled and participated in the emergence of a new sensibility.

Ten years later, *The Stories of John Cheever* (1978) won the Pulitzer Prize and became the first postwar collection of short fiction to become a best-seller. When Cheever looked back on the relative innocence of the 1940s and 1950s as described in his stories, his work seemed to him "at times to be stories of a long-lost world when the city of New York was still filled with a river light, when you heard the Benny Goodman quartets from a radio in the corner stationery store, and when almost everybody wore a hat." By 1978, this social complacency had been severely tested. The Vietnam War had ushered in another period of social unrest. Afterward, nothing—including short fiction—would ever be the same.

Related Commentaries: *Raymond Carver, "Creative Writing 101," page 1326; Flannery O'Connor, "Some Aspects of the Grotesque in Southern Fiction," page 1417; Frank O'Connor, "From* The Lonely Voice," *page 1424.*

PEARL S. BUCK

Pearl S. Buck (1892–1973), the first American woman to be awarded the Nobel Prize for literature, was born Pearl Sydenstricker in Hillsboro, West Virginia. Her parents were missionaries who took her at the age of three months to live in China in the city of Chinkiang on the Yangtze River. At seventeen she returned to the United States to attend Randolph-Macon Women's College in Virginia, where as a senior she won a literary prize for the best short story. After graduation she returned to China in 1914 to nurse her mother through a serious illness. Three years later she married her first husband, John Buck, employed by the Presbyterian Mission Board to teach agriculture to the Chinese peasants. In 1921 the Bucks moved to Nanking, where their daughter was born. Both began teaching at various universities in Nanking, where innovative ideas from the West were starting to change the country's traditional culture. In 1922 Buck published her first articles in The Atlantic Monthly, Forum, *and* The Nation, *describing her experiences in China. She also resumed writing short fiction and planned a novel that she began in 1925 while journeying by ship to America in search of medical assistance for her daughter, who was mentally disabled.*

A prolific author, Buck published East Wind: West Wind, *the first of more than sixty novels, in 1930, after she had returned to China.* The Good Earth *appeared the following year and won a Pulitzer Prize. Generally considered her best book, the novel chronicled the rise of a simple Chinese farmer from poverty to riches. By this time Communist soldiers had entered Nanking, and Buck described the tumultuous revolution in her first collection of short fiction,* The First Wife and Other Stories *(1933). The following year Buck returned permanently to the United States to settle in Pennsylvania. There she divorced her first husband and married her second, who helped her adopt eight children. Meanwhile Buck continued her career as an author, winning recognition for her work with the William Dean Howells Medal for distinguished fiction in 1935, membership in the National Institute of Arts and Letters in 1936, and the Nobel Prize in 1938 "for rich and generic epic descriptions of Chinese peasant life and masterpieces of biography." (In 1936 Buck had published two biographies of her missionary parents,* The Exile *and* Fighting Angel.)

Buck's second collection of short fiction, Today and Forever *(1941), begins with stories of old China and goes on to describe the changes brought by the country's war with Japan after the Japanese invasion, as in "His Own Country."* Far and Near: Stories of Japan, China, and America *(1947) was followed by* Fourteen Stories *(1961). Occupied throughout her life with humanitarian concerns, Buck helped establish Welcome House, an adoption agency for Asian American children, and the Pearl S. Buck Foundation, which cares for children overseas.*

His Own Country

John Dewey Chang had always known that Mott Street, New York, was not his own country. People said Chinatown, but it was not the same as his own country. He was perfectly familiar with all these noisy, narrowing streets, he knew the shops whose windows were filled with a mixture of things from across the sea and things American, he knew the men and women and the many children whose skin was yellow like his own, and whose eyes were all black. Many of them, like himself, had been born in these crowded lively streets, and had never seen anything else. But still he knew this was not his country.

Not that he was at all strange or that, at least as a child, he had disliked Chinatown. For a long time, indeed, he had not thought about any other country. He had grown from placid babyhood, eternally carried on his mother's arm when he was awake and staring with her into the moving variety of the street outside his father's curio shop. Asleep he was carried into a little dark inner room smelling of dried herbs and ginger and tea, and these two places were his world, and, so far as he knew, his country.

The first time, indeed, that he knew he did not belong here, that none of them belonged here, was when he went to school. His parents, discussing the matter loudly over their rice bowls, had decided against kindergarten, and he had not minded. It was more fun to dart about the streets with many other small boys, more white than yellow, to crouch on the backs of automobiles, and tease the kindly policemen. But the day came when he was six years old and this sort of thing had to cease. It was time his education began. His mother, her old black cotton Chinese coat unfastened at the throat and her hair yet uncombed, early in the morning dressed him immaculately in a blue striped sailor suit, admonishing him in their own language the while as to how small boys behaved their first day at school. She never had learned English, not in all these years. He spoke her own language to her, but when he was in the streets he forgot that he spoke anything except the jargon of the white boys. He listened to her gravely, aware of some decorum settling upon him that was not of New York. "So small Chinese boys behave," his mother said very gravely, and his father said, "Do not forget you are a son of Han, and that you do not belong to these wild white tribes among whom we must live until I can grow rich. Be polite to your teacher, obey what your elders command, and keep your mind on your books."

All during breakfast, his father and his mother paused, holding their chopsticks above their bowls of rice gruel, to give him further excellent advice. After his breakfast his father had given him his school name, John Dewey Chang. To this time he had been called at home Little Dog, and on the street Chink. But his father had written this name down upon a bit of paper, so that he might give it to the teacher, that it might be written correctly in the records, John Dewey Chang. John Dewey, his father explained, was the name of an American who had helped to start good new schools in China. He had read about it in the papers from his home town there.

Almost immediately after his father had taken him to school and introduced him to the teacher, his education began. For it happened that the pupils were told to form in line and march from this small schoolroom into a larger one. Two by two they must march. John Chang took his place with alacrity, his face beaming with interest. Two by two they went ahead of him and behind him, but no one came to stand beside him. Two by two they stood, with himself alone in the middle, until finally there was only a small fat white girl left, a round little girl with tight light braids tied with bits of red ribbon. She stood alone also.

"Mary," said Miss Pinckney, "you may come and stand by John."

But Mary would not come. To his astonishment John saw the little girl shake her head violently. "I won't," she said unpleasantly. "I won't walk beside a Chinaman."

Miss Pinckney stared severely for a moment at her and then took John's hand herself. "Very well," she said, "you may walk alone, and I will walk with John."

There was intense silence along the double row, and John Dewey Chang knew that it was not the silence of sympathy. He grasped Miss Pinckney's hand gingerly, but without pleasure. He would, he knew, much rather have been walking with Mary. This was the beginning of his education.

His education, thus begun, continued through many years. He became accustomed after a while to other things. Quietly he learned to wait until everyone else found partners, and then, if he were lucky enough to be the odd one, he stood alone at the end. If the number were even, particularly if the other were a girl, he learned to stand a little aloof, delicately, waiting. He grew to feel, as though he had antennae, the atmosphere, whether it was welcome or rebuff. He never complained, never told his parents. He withdrew into himself instead and became a silent, studious youth, very quiet and neat and dark. He made it a point to be first in his classes and to carry off prizes. His parents were very proud of him. They talked together of what they would do when he was old enough to take the shop. But though he spent his evenings over his father's ledgers when his lessons were done, he knew he would never take the shop. For by now he knew this was not his country, and he had one deep secret purpose, one aching ambition. He must find his own country.

The curios, the beads, the idols, the misty paintings on the scrolls, the hundreds of odd bits of strange beauty his father had for sale, only made him more eager to go to their source. He unpacked them tenderly from their straw-stuffed boxes, great wooden boxes, stamped with red and black hieroglyphics, wondering, dreaming, of another land where beauty like theirs was shaped — his own country.

Of this country he had, of course, heard from many. He had learned to read not only Shakespeare and American history and Whittier and Longfellow, but he had learned also the long straight lines of the letters of his own language. At night an old man came to tutor him, and to teach him the sing-song rhythms of old poetry. His neighbors, George Liu and Ruth Kin, rebelled bitterly and never learned enough to understand the inner meaning of those curves and squares. Ruth tossed her pretty curled black head, and, chewing her gum quickly, she said loudly, "Gee, what's it all about! Say, I gotta 'nough without that stuff!" She had a dark slanting eye upon Harry Sills, the young grocery man next door. Not that she would marry a white man, of course, but white men were fun. Of course she'd settle down and marry a Chink one of these days, but not one of the old-fashioned kind. She'd marry a smart fella, maybe George Liu, if he turned out smart enough, and they'd have a little flat with an electric range. When anyone asked her if she ever wanted to go home to China, she screamed with laughter and said, "To what? Not for mine! Say, they tell me they ain't even got electric lights in the ole home town in China! And say, they're still keepin' the girls at home over there!" She screamed again with her high light laughter, a little loudly, for Harry Sills was at the door of his store. He grinned at her lazily. "Say, I'll bet they couldn't keep you at home, if you was there!" he called to her.

"That's no bet—that's sure!" she retorted, narrowing her eyes at him. She'd seen Anna May Wong do that in the movies, and she liked it, liked that Oriental lure.

John Dewey Chang watched her gravely. It was just after sunset and he was home from high school. It was his last year. Next year he'd go to college, and after that he'd go to his own country. His country—that word was now beginning to mean something beautiful and secret. He gazed thoughtfully up and down the street. Noise was everywhere, the noise of cars and of children. On the next street a trolley shrieked around the corner. At his feet his last brother picked industriously at John Dewey's shoestrings. He was not quite two, and with his coming the small flat above the shop was crowded to its last limit. But it had not occurred to them to have more room. They slept more thickly in the two bedrooms, but always decorously, his sisters in the other room, his parents' bed curtained and partitioned away with wall board. But he would be glad to be gone. Staring into the noise and confusion of a late spring evening in that crowded street he thought with longing of his own country. There, there were quiet streets and singing country folk and richly tilled fields and courtesy and stillness and certainty. He would be among his own there, his own kind. He had heard his mother tell such tales of the small country town where she grew up, a town in south China where everybody, she said, was happy. All the girls were pretty and good, not like these girls with yellow hair and painted lips and especially not like silly Ruth Kin. He was suddenly very homesick for that which he had never seen.

All during his four years at the state college he held steadfastly to his plan. He grew very Chinese indeed, and he allowed his fellows to think that he had come, not from that crowded rowdy street in New York, but from the sedate and dignified little Chinese town in south China. It was during these years that his country fell into revolution, and he organized a band of patriots among the seven Chinese boys in the college. He denied himself his luncheon each day and saved the money, and he bullied the other members of the club into paying more than they were able, and when after three months the fund amounted to more than ninety dollars, they debated fiercely as to what it should be given for in China. Studying the newspapers and the bulletins from their country, they perceived there were many things for which this sum could be given; it might be given for the starving, for there was a famine again, or it might be given for the air-planes the new government needed, or it might be given for roads. After weeks of indecision, they decided on new roads. So the money was changed into a note, and sent to the government in Nanking, with a long letter explaining the wishes of the donors. After nearly six months a courteous letter came in reply, to which was affixed the seal of the Republic, saying that the money had been received and would be assuredly spent for roads, and then after words of commendation for such patriotism the letter closed, and was signed by the Third Secretary to the President.

It was the first touch with his country. John, holding the letter in his hand, felt his heart thicken with emotion. When he read the letter aloud to the others, he could scarcely keep from weeping. When Art Lok said with cynicism, "Yeah, it's fine talk—my dad says the same chaps used up all the money they sent over last year to buy an airplane, only there wasn't any airplane!" John Chang flew at him, "Will you revile your own country? Will you say your own President's secretary lies?" he cried.

Art twisted his thin handsome mouth and sneered and fell silent. After all, it was no business of his. He began thinking of an engagement he had to keep that night at a certain small café with a very yellow-haired girl. He began to whistle softly.

But there it was. All during college when the others were playing foot-ball or going to movies or making dates, John Chang worked on his plans for his country. Here was the question: Should he delay his return further by taking some sort of special course—say, be an aviator or an architect or a doctor—or should he go straight home as soon as he was through? He argued it with himself, longing to go straightway, waiting for nothing. After all, a college education was something. He could get a job teaching or in the government—there were jobs everywhere these days, in these new and glorious days in his own country. It was not as it was here in the United States, where people were pushing and jostling each other for work. Over there roads were growing, airplanes were flying, new buildings going up, business developing—the whole nation was moving, running ahead—better to join his youth to it now, without waiting. Anyway, bet-ter to go on and see what was wanted and if necessary he would come back. Only he knew he would never come back. He graduated from col-lege and then hurried back to Mott Street, to bid his parents good-by, to buy a third-class ticket to China.

Then he was delayed after all. He was delayed by his own most surprising reluctance to go. When he had endured the noise and the heat of
the flat for two weeks, when he had bought his ticket and had talked with
his parents about everything, when his mother had said to him over and
over again, "Now when you see my honored mother-in-law, you must say
it is my grief I am not there to serve her, and when you see my honored
father-in-law and my brothers and their ladies—" and when his father had
talked with enthusiasm of the new times, "In my youth there was nothing
a lad could do if he were the eighth son on a little land, and so I had to
seize the chance of my father's eldest cousin to come abroad with him in
his business, and here I have remained and they sent your mother to me,
and here you have been born. I return you proudly to my own country—"
when everything was said and everything was ready, suddenly John Chang
found he did not want to go.

At first he could not understand his reluctance. Certainly it was not
this noisy city which held him. He stood looking at the traffic one night in
a melancholy fashion. He did not love these dashing lights, approaching,
glaring for an instant into his face, disappearing again. There was no music
in the roar and the grind of trolley cars to have made him homesick.
Except the faces of his family there were no faces which he cared if he saw
again or not—no faces—and then with fury he realized there was a face, a
little round merry face under frizzy black hair. It was that face which was
making all the trouble. He wanted to see it again and again and again, and
it was Ruth Kin's face!

When he realized this he went quickly into the house and into a dark
corner of the dark little curio shop and there, among the Buddhas and the
pottery Han horses and the hanging mandarin coats, he sat down and held
his head in his hands. He did not at all wish to love Ruth Kin. He did not
want to marry. If he thought about marrying, it was not to someone like
Ruth Kin. His mother had spoken of the women across the sea, their stillness, their gentleness, their mild sweet eyes, their obedience to their lords.
Some day, perhaps, he had thought, some day, in a little house with a court
and a bamboo grove and an oleander tree he might live with a sweet obedient woman. But not with slangy, lively, noisy Ruth Kin! Yet there it was.
He did not want to leave her.

He had seen her, of course, many times—how, he asked himself bitterly, could one avoid seeing her? She still lived next door, and she came
and went loudly and cheerfully to the business school where she was learning stenography so that she might be her father's assistant. Her father, a
tea and oil merchant, had never learned the intricacies of customs and
accounting, and Ruth long ago had made up her mind that she would take
the business in hand as soon as she could. She was always wanting to take
things in hand—to manage things. So year by year she had managed a little
more and a little more of the stout peaceful old man's affairs, until now,
when American retail men came into the wholesale tea shop, it was a smart

young American who greeted them, an American with coal black hair with a strong tendency to straightness, in spite of sedulous care to curling, and black pointed eyes and a rich smooth olive skin. But the voice was American, clear and a little hard, and the words that came from the vivid red lips were pure New York. The men looked at her with laughter and occasionally with longing, longing at least for a little fun. But she never promised them anything, never quite promised them anything. Everyone knew Ruth Kin could take care of herself.

And of course everyone had thought that she would marry George Liu. Even the two families had thought so. Then suddenly, only six months ago, Ruth Kin changed her mind. "No," she told her father firmly. "I don't want to marry George." Everyone knew how she said it, for he told all his friends and they told their wives and so John Chang had heard his mother tell it at the family supper table.

"That Ruth Kin," she said mournfully, "she is like the Americans. All these years she has been as though betrothed to the son of the Lius, the parents have arranged it, and now she will not marry him."

"Why not?" said the father absently. He was not interested in Ruth Kin or in George Liu, but it was a bit of gossip on Mott Street.

"Who knows?" said his mother, sighing. "She says he is not smart enough. She says she will have only a very smart man."

John Chang, sitting in the curio shop alone, thought of this bitterly. "She will not think me smart," he thought. "She has always made fun of me because I want to go home to my own country. I have heard her say often that I am a fool—that I would do better to take my father's business."

Then remembering Ruth Kin's shining black eyes and her little full red mouth he knew it was no good—he loved her hopelessly.

So he put off his trip a little, not much. He had allowed himself a few more days than necessary in order to see the sights on the west coast. He would see no sights. He said a little sullenly to his parents the next day, "I do not feel well. I will wait a day."

He waited a day, thinking furiously and staying away from Ruth Kin. Ever since he had returned he had made it a habit without knowing it to go and stand at the door and watch for her coming home. Now he would not go, not for a whole day. But the second day was a Saturday, and suddenly he was compelled to see her. He felt if he did not see her just once he could not start next day, and he must start or he would miss his boat. He was angry with himself, he threw himself on his bed and muttered and tossed. Then suddenly he leaped up and ran downstairs and into the shop next door. Because it was a Saturday he knew exactly where he would find Ruth. He would find her in the inner room balancing her father's weekly accounts, her red lips a little pursed, her small brown hands nimble with the pencil.

There she was exactly. He did not waste an instant. He stood before her, his hair still rumpled, his shirt without any tie. He began hostilely, because she had delayed him in his dear plan:

"Will you come to China with me or won't you?"

She looked at him, astonished, her eyes open very wide. She never used any lure with John Chang, never at all. They quarreled too often, and there was too much to say to him. They had quarreled, for instance, over this very going back home to China. She thrust her pencil into her curly mop, and there it stood upright like a feather of defiance.

"Why should I go to China?" she answered instantly. "I don't want to go to China! I'm an American—anybody that's born in New York is an American."

"Because your country has use for you!" he shouted at her. She was so very pretty that he was furious with her. Need she have put on a rose-pink linen dress this morning and need her skin look as smooth as golden cream? "You stay here when your country can use you!"

"Thank you," she said coolly, "I'll think about it when there are a few electric lights and a bath tub in the ole home town."

"You think of nothing but comforts," he said. He wanted to shake her, to slap her, to tell her she must come because—because—"You must come!" he said loudly.

Then she stood up. She put her two little hands on her narrow hips and looked at him from the crown of his stiff rumpled black hair to his rather too yellow oxfords. "Will you please tell me who you think you are, Mr. John Dewey Chang?" she demanded. "You can't talk to an American woman like that and get away with it! And why must I come?"

"Because——because I love you!" he said unexpectedly. He had not really meant to say it.

They stared at each other, and Ruth sat down suddenly and drew the pencil out of her hair and began to figure briskly. "Go away, John Dewey Chang," she said coldly. "Don't be funny."

"It is not funny," he said desperately.

"It is only funny to me," she said. "I go back to China? And with you? It's a joke." She pursed her very red lips merrily and looked at him, for a second, this time with her sidewise look. But when he started toward her, she cried out, "No, I mean it. Go away."

"You mean—to China?" asked John Chang in a small voice.

"Yes, to China," said Ruth Kin, with determination, and shut her mouth hard and turned a page of figures.

He watched her for a second, but she did not change, she did not look up, and he turned. Well, then, he would go. But just at the door she called him again, and he glanced back. She was looking at him thoughtfully and now she said in another voice, a coaxing small voice, and she drooped her lashes a little and looked up at him, "Would you," she said, "would you if I said I would—care about you—stay?"

He stared at her aghast. What—give up his own country, after all these years of dreams, his beloved and beautiful country?

"No!" he shouted. He would not give himself time to think.

She shrugged her shoulders, laughed, and said airily, "Then go—go away to your China!"

So he had gone, in haste and hurry to be gone. Before he could stop to think he was on the train whirling across green country, through great roaring cities, through little towns and vast prairies to the sea coast. Before he could stop to think he was on a great ship, crowded among third-class passengers, and outside there was only the roar of the sea, and inside among all these strangers there was infinite time to think—to think and to dream.

But now his dreams would not come right. They would not take the shapes of old, the shapes of his own people, his coming home to his own race, his life, a leader in the revolution, a governor, a diplomat, a great man of some sort in his own country. No, those dreams came stealing into his mind in the shape of a small round willful face, of black eyes, Chinese under a crop of American-curled hair, of a slim yellow Chinese body in a rose pink American dress. He leaped out of his berth again and again and paced the few feet of deck, for he had not ceased to love her and he had not ceased to be angry with her. He told himself many times that she was full of faults—that she was all those things which a Chinese girl should not be—she talked before men and she laughed too loudly and she was disobedient to her parents. Why, she even made fun of her father's lisp when he tried to speak English! It was true that her father had spoiled her and that he laughed at her, but then she was not respectful. How many times had he not heard his own mother say she came home late at night, every time with a different man! He cast up all her faults and tried to see how well off he was to be alone—and groaned because he loved her and wished he were not alone.

He began to look forward to his country with renewed eagerness. For now his country was the only thing which could make him forget Ruth. There among all that new life, working, serving, achieving, he would forget about her. He would even—of course he would find the woman whom he really sought—not Ruth, but another. There he would live and found his home and have his children, their mother not Ruth, but a dreamy-eyed, quiet, obedient woman in his house. But first he must work and he must achieve. And first of all he must find his country.

But where was his country? Upon the sea it had seemed so near, there where the sea ended, there where the river began. This was his country, this first line upon the horizon. He had passed indifferently in the Inland Sea one lovely isle after another; coldly he had gazed at the rocky exquisitely outlined mountains of Japan, waiting for this first dark edge between sea and sky. He rose early to see it, and soon after dawn, staring into a gray and misty sky he saw it, that silent line of dark land. Soon the ship was embraced as though by two arms of that land. There were no hills, no houses, nothing to speak to him—only those two dark arms reached out into the sea to embrace him, to draw him home. He hung over the rail of the deck, staring, his heart beating in his throat.

Then upon the land appeared tiny low houses, isolated, the color of earth, and then the brown of the earth changed to brilliant green. The sun did not shine and the sky was gray. Against the gray the green was deeply vivid. But houses and fields were small and solitary upon the immensity of these ever broadening arms of land. Here, here was his country. He yearned to it, he gazed upon it, he longed to leap across the yellow waters of the river and feel it beneath his feet, old, sure, unchanged, silent, welcoming him in silence.

Then suddenly he lost it all. Suddenly the ship passed between tall buildings, edged ponderously to a dock, and all silence was gone, all peace was lost. A horde of small brown blue-coated men leaped across the rails, chattering, shrieking a language he did not even understand. He used upon them the tongue he had from his mother, but they stared at him wild-eyed, searching. He pointed out his few bags, neatly strapped and ready to be taken ashore, but they passed him by as though he had not spoken. They were looking, he realized suddenly, not for him. It was nothing to them that he was come home at last. They were looking for richer folk than he, for tourists, for white men. He set his teeth a moment, staring after their tumbling, crowding figures, and then one by one he picked up his own bags and staggered across the narrow gangway to the dock.

It was at that moment that he lost his country completely. For standing among the crowd pouring from the ship, pouring from the streets, he might have been in any country again. He might even have been again in New York. He heard no tongue he understood except the English he had left behind him. About him were tall Western buildings; he heard the din of street cars in his ears. Suddenly the rain poured in a drum of noise upon the tin roof of the dock, and he was walled in by it, and he could do no more than wait, walled in with the crowd of alien motley people, not one of whom he knew, and not one of whom were coming to welcome him home. He stood forlornly staring through the rain across the yellow water. A small junk struggled through the mists, its sails lowered, and an oarsman standing at the oar, his brown body naked except for the loin cloth about his hips. From his unfamiliar form John Chang looked at the ship, the ship from which he had longed so desperately to escape. But now somehow it looked like home to him, a home of a sort, whose ways he knew. At least there he had been safe and sheltered.

Then suddenly he shook himself. This would not do. He must be strong. There was no going back now. In his pocket he had the name of a good inn his father had given him and the name of the cousin who was his partner, upon whom he was to call for aid. He must be bold and remember that somewhere his country lay behind this dock, these crowds, these streets. He laid a hand upon a coolie standing near and pointed to his bags.

"Ricksha!" he said with authority, "ricksha!" The man halted, stared, hesitated, took up the bags with a grunt. In a moment John Chang was rolling along, buttoned behind an oil-cloth curtain. He could see nothing, except the brown bare legs of the puller, streaming with the rain, and above his head upon the thin roof of the ricksha the rain beat steadily down.

Where, where was his country? After three days in the small bare room of the inn he sat and stared across a narrow street into a tenement house. Except that the clothes hung upon bamboo poles were shaped differently, it might have been a tenement in New York. In and out of the cheap houses dirty children ran, naked in the stifling midsummer heat. Women shouted after them; slouching men and furtive-eyed young girls came and went. He had seen them all before and they were not his. They were not his, and yet their eyes were black and pointed like his own and their hair black and their skin his skin. But he would not have them for his own.

Already he loathed the inn and determined he must leave it. Yet, when he asked, his cousin shrugged his fat shoulders. "It is good enough, that inn," he said. "A better one would be very dear."

"It is dirty," said John Chang briefly.

"You are like a foreigner," remarked his cousin. "You will become accustomed."

He had been twice to see that cousin, and twice he had come away angry.

It did not seem possible to him that such a man was his cousin. He lived in half-a-dozen different courts, his many children ran about unwashed, and the noise of quarreling women was everywhere. And with all these women, these wives and these servants, there was no one to brush away the flies from the tea bowls upon the table; and when the cousin invited John Chang to eat with him at his house, the flies sat upon the food. Yet the cousin was not a poor man. He had money, since he was the partner in the curio business, and he it was who shipped the Buddhas and the little ivory boxes and the silver trinkets and the embroidered robes and the incense sticks and all those things which John Chang had known all his life in the shop on Mott Street, all things which had set him dreaming of his own country. Now when he saw the fat brown hand of his cousin and saw the grease upon his silken gown and the rolls of fat about his neck and about his belly, when in the heat of the day he put his gown from him and sat with his upper body uncovered, he wondered that he had ever dreamed.

His cousin's daughters, too, came and went, and the cousin snapped his fingers to them when he wanted tea or his pipe or his old shoes to ease his feet. The man boasted of these girls. He said, "As for my girls, I have kept them where they should be kept, in the home. They have fretted now and again to go to some school or other, but I have seen these bold modern girls on the streets, and I know they are nothing but trouble with all their learning and their boldness—trouble for their father who must feed them, and trouble for the men they must marry. I have married ignorant women and they have done me very well." He puffed at his pipe and shouted at his daughter who stood before him to hear any further commands. "Go to your mother and do not hang about to hear men talk!" When the girl was gone he said with complacence, "You see how obedient she is. She will be as obedient as that one day to her husband. It has been my care to prepare my daughters for marriage, for there is nothing else a woman can do."

And, indeed, John Chang, watching, saw the girl go docilely away; as silently as though no one stepped she went in her little satin shoes. But although her face was very pretty and she was well-mannered and said not one word, and was the sort of maid he had dreamed about once, he did not feel his heart move at all when he looked at her. He said to himself, "It is because she is the daughter of my second cousin," but when he went back to his room in the inn and sat down alone he found in surprise that it was not because she was the daughter of his cousin, but because she seemed stupid to him, and her pretty silent face was only like a doll's face; and, thinking further, he was not sure it would be such pleasure to have a doll for a wife, who put up her arm when she was bade and kissed him when she was bade and came when she was bade and went away when she was bade to do it. Suddenly there flew into his mind the thought of Ruth Kin and how no one could make her do what she would not do, and there she was before him, laughing and willful and mischievous. He was glad she was not here.

But after a while, thinking and staring through the rain, he came to the thought that this was not his country, not this dirty city of Shanghai, noisy with vehicles and crowded with every sort of people. Somewhere beyond these flat horizons was more, miles upon miles of his vast country, for him to discover.

So again he went to his cousin and said, "I want to go further away, into the inlands; I want to see and I want to discover."

At this his cousin fanned himself quickly and said, "I hope you are not one of those young revolutionists who have been the pest of our country in these last years! But if you are, do not tell me—I do not want to hear any of it. But if you want to go inland, then I have an errand for your father on which you may go. You are to go to the regions at the end of the great river, into the province of Szechuan. I hear there have been new graves discovered there of ancient princes, and if it is true, you can find curios cheaply and buy what you can and bring them back. But do not buy this and this—" and then the cousin detailed what he should not buy and what was true and what was false, because at such times among the true there are many false things, made by men who think it possible to sell them mingled together.

Thus John Chang went in search of his own country, following the sweep of the great river.

Everywhere he searched for his country and everywhere he found only the same thing. He found cities crowded and noisy and filthy with generations of filth. He grew afraid to drink anything except the hottest tea, although the summer sun scorched his flesh, and he ate only a little rice and cabbage, because there was no ice and nothing to keep from putridness the slabs of pigs hung in the sun and the fish dying in their tubs of stale water and the crabs upon which the flies sat unceasingly. At night the mosquitoes fed upon him, and if he stopped in inns the insects swarmed to him. He could not see the beauty of the distant hills, nor could he see the rich green banks flourishing in rice and the great nets let down to catch the large river fish, because upon the little river steamer with him were two hundred pilgrims going to an ancient temple on a mountain top to worship there, and holy men have the vilest bodies to be found, and these reeked with all their filth and holiness. Yet they were his countrymen. Yes, they were all his countrymen — the blind he met so often on the streets of any town where the steamer stopped; the children running as they would, unclothed; the brawling women washing by the river's edge and beating out their rags upon the rocks, and quarreling as they worked; and the shrewd petty shopkeepers; and the beggars whining everywhere, full of leprosy and holding out their maimed limbs. One day he stopped among them and cried to his own heart, staring at them, "Is this the country I dreamed of all these years, and can any lifetime save them?"

And for a moment he was conscious of an aching in him for some other place, a homesickness. But he was at home. And then it seemed to him he would give all his years to be back in his father's shop again, in that small clean quiet shop. The street in New York seemed the cleanest best street in the world, and he thought with utter longing of the white clean tub in the bathroom above the shop. He turned and walked back swiftly to his cabin and he sat down and wrote a letter. But it was not to his father and his mother. It was to Ruth Kin, and he said, "You were right and I am but a fool. Stay by your home there. You were very right." And grimly he went on day by day up that great river until it wound small and deep and narrow among the gorges, and so at last he came to where he had been sent.

Time and time again he wrote to Ruth Kin, and why he did not know, since she did not care for him. But it seemed to him that now forever his country was lost. It was not what he dreamed, and not being that, it was nothing. He learned to bicker with the dealers to whom his cousin sent him, to suspect falseness in every bit of pottery or bronze they brought him, to know a poor man who pretended to be a farmer bringing in a bit of something he had unearthed from his field might be as great a liar as another. He learned to twist his tongue to speak their languages, to hold to his money, to haggle, and to postpone and do all the paltry business he must do. At night, lying in his bed, he sneered at himself that he had come to this, he who would not work for his father, but must follow dreams for thousands of miles and come to this, this sorry quarreling search. And so he wrote to Ruth, not because he asked anything of her, so he said, but because he must write somewhere and he could not write his father and he would not write his friends and let them know he was so shamed.

"For filth and flies and beggary," he wrote to Ruth Kin, "I have not seen the like of this country. Yes, I suppose this is my country. And here in my country I must watch daily or I am robbed, and here in my country men are kidnaped and nothing is said. And—"

And so he poured out all his bitter disappointment and his shames, and eased himself a little, although he never ate a meal without a fuss about the dust upon the table or flies upon the meats, so that in that whole city he got a name for himself, and the inn dreaded to see him coming, and he was nicknamed the Foreign Devil, since he was so full of fuss about a little dust and dirt or about a fly or two.

Then like a sharp cold wind across the sea one day he had a letter, sent to his cousin and his cousin sent it on, and it was from Ruth Kin. He had come back to his inn at night after a long day of searching in a newly opened ruin, and there upon his table the letter lay. He opened it and found the inner envelope and opened that and read, like Ruth's voice, her laughing pitiless truthful words. "You sap," she wrote, and whereas once he hated such speech, he only laughed now aloud—it seemed so good to have a word come hard and direct against his cheek—oh, how he was weary of the false polite palavering of the dealers! "You sap, what did you expect? For a penny I'd come—not to marry you, you understand, but just to see if it's what you say. And I'd like to sort of clean things up if it is as bad as you say."

Looking out of his window, down the narrow, crowded street, he knew that he did not want Ruth Kin to come. It was evening in August, and the end of a hot day, and the people were quarrelsome. Their voices rose sharply and angrily into his window. Two women were cursing each other, and there was a crowd about them, listening, to hear and to be amused. Suddenly one snatched at the other's hair, and they rolled in the dust, their curses shrieking. But it was a common sight after all, and the people moved and scattered and brought out their bamboo beds and spread their pallets for the night. Men and women and children lay down to sleep, the men stripped near to nakedness, the children naked, and the women in their thin grass-cloth coats. Above them rose the hum of mosquitoes. He stood looking down on them. A child wailed through the dusk and a dog howled. These, these were his people. He did not want Ruth Kin to come.

He went back into the room and lit the small kerosene oil lamp and sat down to answer her letter. The night insects fluttered about him, and twice he got up and stepped upon the body of a centipede and felt its crusty body crack beneath his American leather shoe. He wrote and wrote, and, pausing at last, he added one more line, "Even the kerosene lamp," he wrote, "is American. You had better stay in America." He went to bed exhausted and silent to the heart. There, he thought, having told her everything, there was the end of Ruth Kin.

There was no going back, of course. He was far too proud to go back. After all these years, after he had organized the Chinese boys' patriotic club in his high school and after he had collected money in college to send to the revolutionary government, after everything he had dreamed, there was no going back. He settled himself grimly to his own country. Once he went to the new capital and walked silently and unknown about the streets. He had, he realized, expected to see something like New York, like Washington, like the postcards he had seen of Paris. Instead he saw a few carelessly made wide streets, fringed by new cheap one-story shops. There were two or three large buildings, new and half empty. When he walked up the steps, a guard stopped him sternly, and he turned and went away. Perhaps if he had had influence he might have gone in, but he had no influence at all. He walked a long way outside the city and came to the grave of the hero of the revolution and stood staring at it. The grave was there, enormous, hideous, new, a treeless scar upon the mountain side, and inside it the hero lay dead. He went away again.

Once he begged a holiday from his cousin and went south to the village of his mother's girlhood, traveling by small rat-ridden steamers and at last by wheelbarrow across the flat fertile fields. It was the last stronghold of his dreams. But when he slipped off the vehicle a dog rushed at him savagely, and though he beat the beast off, he had to watch, and so sidling and wary he came to the village. Yet what was it but a village, after all? It was a small cluster of houses made from brick of the field earth, and the people were like all the country people he had seen. They were quite the same, the men suspicious of his foreignness and the women silent and shrinking away. A narrow filthy street, a dirty teashop or two, the smell of human waste upon the fields for fertilizer, the silent staring girls — he did not even wait to search out his kin. If these were his kin, then let him not know it. He turned and shouted to the wheelbarrow pusher, "Let us go away!" he shouted. "I want to go away at once!"

Shaking along over the cobbled country roads, he said to himself he was very glad he had written so to Ruth Kin. He was very glad he had told her she must stay there where she was and marry George Liu and live in a little clean flat and have an electric stove and ice and cleanness — and cleanness — and cleanness — everywhere.

Then how could he have been prepared for Ruth Kin's letter in Shanghai? It came after three months across the thousands of miles. He almost felt its briskness through the envelope. The paper was crisp beneath his fingers, used now to the soft thin paper of his cousin's ledgers. The letter crackled when he opened it, the words leaped out, incredible, lively, determined words. He could see her snapping eyes, hear her laugh, see her slight straight saucy figure, see her tossing hair. "Well, I'm coming, John Dewey Chang," the letter began straightly. "I've changed my mind. You've got me—I guess the old home town needs me—and you do, too—"

This was her letter. A little news, a joke or two—"George Liu has gone and married the girl at the soda fountain—I always knew he wasn't smart! Anyway, my folks have stopped ragging me," and at the end, "I've got my ticket and I'll be along in a week after you get this. My dad's coming on business. You're my business." At the end, in a small squeezed note he read with difficulty, "You can have the ring ready—if you want to—"

He folded the letter in a daze. All these days she had been coming toward him, and he had not known! Straight as wind and ship and day and night could bring her she was coming. And for the moment his first thought was he did not know what to do with her. He had a frantic feeling that he must clean everything up before she came. He was suddenly ashamed of everything, ashamed of dirt and poverty and silent ignorant women and of his fat cousin and of the inn and of this room. He ran to the mirror and looked into it. Yes, he was ashamed of himself, too. He had let his hair grow long and unkempt and he wore a soiled shirt. He looked as he would not have dreamed of letting himself look in New York. It did not seem worth while to be different—until now. But now—now—what could he possibly do in a week?

But after all, he did everything in a week—that is, nearly everything. In this country of his, he determined, there should be one spot, a little single spot, clean and homelike for Ruth Kin and him. He rushed to his cousin and borrowed money of him extravagantly. "An American girl?" said the cousin, suspiciously, breaking into the words pouring out of John Dewey Chang's lips.

"Certainly not," John Chang said. And then suddenly he paused and thought, "A sort of an American girl," and did not say it, knowing his cousin. His cousin would not lend money on an American girl, and so he shook his head. After all, Ruth Kin was not an American.

With the money he rented a little house, not in the Chinese city where the inn was and where his cousin lived and where the shop was, but a little bungalow on the edge of the foreign concession where the Americans lived. He must spare his Ruth what he had had—the sudden death of dreams. There was a little banksia rose growing over the porch and even in this autumn it put forth a few blossoms. In spring it would be a bouquet of fragrance for them. In the court there was even an oleander tree. The little house had been long empty, and he hired a stout serving woman from his cousin to come and scrub and clean, and then among the foreign shops he searched for things for Ruth, a rug, two chairs, a bed, a table, some dishes, curtains at the window, and some pictures. At the last moment he remembered pictures and he ran to a shop on Avenue Edward VII and bought three pictures of mountains and lakes, brightly colored.

Then almost at once he had to hurry, for Ruth's ship would be at the dock in an hour.

It was, he felt, waiting, impossible that Ruth was coming to this dock. He could not imagine it. He felt newly sensitive when he looked about, as though he were responsible for the ragged coolies, for the vendors outside the palings, with their small baskets of dirty sweetmeats. A few well-dressed white people were standing there also, and he hated them for their cleanliness and their smartness. He saw gratefully two pretty Chinese girls with their mother and a maidservant, dressed in long satin robes. At least there were these. Somewhere, perhaps, hidden behind high walls there were many such people. Sometimes one saw them on the street. Among the great mass of noisy hungry common folk they were as though there were none, being so few. But at least today there were these, and Ruth would see them. She would feel strange—of course she would feel strange. He must let her see it all gradually and not be discouraged. He was glad that there was electricity in the little house.

Then almost before he knew it the ship had bumped the dock and the gangway was thrown and there was Ruth! He ran forward and she took his hand and held it and he stared down at her unbelieving.

"Here's Dad," she reminded him, laughing, and he bowed to the stout old figure behind her. "I have letters from your father and mother," she said, but it did not matter to him. He took the letters she held out to him from her hand bag, and stared on at her. She was prettier than ever, but how foreign! In her little trim blue suit she looked wholly American until he saw her face.

She gazed with interest about her. "Queer," she said, "this doesn't seem funny to me—none of it. I've never seen any of it, but it's just as though I had!"

Beyond the customs and the dock he called to a taxicab, but she laid a swift hand on his arm. "Let's ride in those funny little things," she cried, pointing to a ricksha. "Taxis are so common!"

So in a moment they were gliding along the Bund behind panting coolies. She turned and waved her hand at him, smiling in delight, "It's more fun than a picnic," she cried.

Well, there it was. A week later, settled in the small house with the banksia rose, he was more astonished at her than ever. For some change had crept over her, already, some indefinable, softening change. In New York she had been as slangy and sharp as a little gamin. But here in this house on the edge of the Chinese city the sharpness was leaving her. She was more silent, and the slang in which she used to take such pride because it was American was day by day becoming more rare. He was dismayed. To himself he thought, "She's growing to hate it. She's feeling as I did—disappointed. It's all worse than she thought."

"Where's all the dirt and the poor you used to write about?" she asked once.

He was frightened. "I was too particular, I guess," he said, evading her, and hurried on. "Ruth, the oleander's going to bloom."

For once he had said to her that he chose his own country always, whether she were there or not. Now, knowing what it was to have her by him in the day, across the table from him when he ate, and when the deep of night came, knowing her warmly in his arms, he knew that if she did not choose this country it was no longer his own. No country could be his where she was not. Suppose she was wanting to go back to New York, just now when this little house began to seem home to him, just now when he could look about him on the streets and not have his heart full, because at the end of the day there was this home!

For having this center now, this place to which he might come when his work was done, this clean bright spot, changed his whole country. He could come and go in narrow streets whose gutters ran with filth, he could bear blind and maimed beggars, he could bear ignorance and haggling dishonesty, knowing that he had a home. At night he could come back to Ruth and read and talk and listen to the phonograph and maybe go to a picture show, although he liked better just to hear her talk and laugh.

But here she was, growing daily less merry. "I've got to get her out into the foreign concession more," he thought desperately one night. "It's more like New York there." Aloud he said, "Like to go to a cabaret, honey?" They still talked in English together, since her Chinese was so little yet. They made a joke of their Chinese at first, she asking what this was and this. But now she had been picking up words from her servant woman, and then she asked him by the end of the second week to buy a primer—"the kind that the kids use in school," she explained—and then she wanted a tutor and he had to hire an old scholar to come and teach her how to hold the brush for writing. So they had gone to the cabaret and danced a little, but not much. And she had not seemed to enjoy it especially, after all, although it had cost him a great deal of money, nearly five dollars. It was not a thing to be done often.

By the end of the second month she looked at him sidewise one morning at breakfast and asked him, "What would you say if I quit wearing these New York clothes and put on things like the rest of the women here?" He stared at her. He could not imagine her in a narrow smooth-fitting robe. Her face seemed made for these little ruffly dresses she had brought with her. "Well," he began, when she broke in—"Wait—don't say until you've seen me!"

That very night when he came home there she was. She had gone out and bought herself a long green robe of a close-woven silk. The collar was high. She had smoothed down her short hair, and above the straightness of the robe her little round face stood like a grave, pretty flower. She moved gravely, gracefully. Her very smile was changed. It was not saucy and teasing. He could not imagine this demure creature making eyes at a groceryman on the street. He gazed at her entranced. "Like it?" she said, softly.

"Yes," he answered, and could say no more for watching her. Later, after their dinner, he asked with difficulty, fearing her answer. "Does that— dress—feel strange?" She looked up from some sewing she was doing. "No," she said. "The queer thing is I feel as if I'd never had my own clothes on until now."

But still, he told himself, coming and going every day to his cousin's shop, still the house shielded her. Her life was not hard. In the clean little house upon a macadam street, she need not see the other streets. He came and went everyday in the native city, but she could go the other way into the foreign concession and see great shops and motor cars. He talked a little, guardedly, about famines and bandits and wars in the interior, but she was not much interested. Such things were as remote from this place, seemingly, as they had been from Mott Street. She never read English newspapers and could not read the Chinese ones yet, and the little house bounded her life. He breathed the relief that this thought brought to him. He was keeping her safe and happy, secure from the knowledge of the dark native city. Really, he thought, she lived almost as she might have in an American city, as safe from sorrowful truth. He came home to her and rested in that haven, shut away from the real world. When sometimes she spoke of some chance sight—one morning there was a little dead girl baby thrown out even upon the macadam street—he coaxed her thoughts away. So in the end she was only gay when he came home, gay and demurely seductive. It came to him, as a miracle, that somehow Ruth Kin was often like that girl of whom he had dreamed, that sweet obedient woman in his house.

Then the knowledge he would have spared her came flooding down on her, flooding at the very time when he would most have kept it away. For she was going to have a baby, "a son," she said confidently. Now it appeared why she had wanted to wear a robe instead of the tight little American dresses. "As soon as I knew," she said, "I thought I'd like to wear them." Under the pretty, straightly clinging robe her figure rounded softly and with continued grace. And now he knew he must keep her safe in the world he had made for her, this safe, clean little modern world set in the midst of the huge dark old medieval country which was his. He hurried home from his work, hurried through the packing of cases and the shipping of goods to his father in Mott Street. More than ever now he must work to keep that little spot safe and sheltered.

And then, one morning, one spring morning, when their son was seven months known to them and they were planning his birth and he had chosen the very best foreign hospital in the British concession, they heard the crack of cannon. The deep roar burst, reverberated and ceased, roared and reverberated and ceased. He stared at Ruth and she stared back, astonished, questioning. He knew instantly what it was. He had not taken time to read the papers much of late, but the air had been thunderous with it—the Japanese were at the coast. The cannon burst out again and there was the sound of a falling wall, and they leaped from their seats. But he thought of Ruth, only of Ruth. "Never mind," he cried, and forgetting he spoke in his own tongue—it was natural to him now to speak in his own tongue. "You are not be frightened—I will take care of you somehow—" Oh, that he had never brought her here—oh, that they were back in Mott Street, where she might be safe and their child born in peace!

For soon, in a day, in two days, there was nothing left to hide from Ruth. The streets were full of terrified, wretched people, begging for a bit of shelter. Fire leaped everywhere, to the west of them. He had to spend his days and nights moving the stores of curios into the cellars of friendly houses of business in the foreign concessions. For a day and a night he had to work, not knowing what was become of Ruth, except that the little low house was safer, still, he felt, than any other spot. He watched the fire as he came and went. No, those flames were still safely away. He rushed home at dawn dreading to find Ruth terrified, ill, perhaps even in premature birth.

But when he opened the door she was not there. Instead it seemed as though all the folk in the city from whom he had been guarding her had taken the little house. Upon the rugs he had bought sat packed a crew of men and women and children, little precious bundles upon their knees, their faces haggard with bewilderment and fear and weariness. The house reeked with the odor of their unwashedness. They looked up at him mutely, timidly, silent in the din of the unceasing cannon in the west. Three days and three nights the roar had gone on, punctuated by the crash of the falling buildings a half mile away. But the small low house had still stood sturdily, full of these homeless folk, squeezing into every corner, clutching their poor saved possessions. The room was full of them. He rushed to the kitchen to find the maidservant to demand where Ruth was.

And there she was, standing over the little electric range he had bought with such pride, pots on every spot of its surface. She was desperately weary as he could see, her hair uncombed. But her eyes were not tired. They were elated and exalted. Over her robe was a big American apron, and she and the woman stood stirring the pots of food.

"What—?" he began.

"They are all hungry," she said, "they're starved. The poor things have run away because their houses are burned down."

"We can't feed them all," he began.

She stirred vigorously. "We can, too!" she said. "I've got enough here for everybody."

He stood uncertainly. "There's an awful smell in the house," he said suddenly. The smell of the unwashed crowd was coming even here, overcoming the fragrance of the rice. It was so vile he was ashamed for them before Ruth. He had never told her how the reek of the garlic-eating common folk sickened him, and now he must speak of it first.

She turned on him indignantly. "You ought to be ashamed of yourself," she cried, and then in pure New York, "You great big stiff, what does it matter how they smell if they're your own people?" She removed a pot rapidly and began filling bowls set out on the table. "Gee, if I'd known all I've learned since you've been away—" She dipped, competently, carefully, all the languor about her gone. She was electric with vigor. But he only saw her face, weary but perfectly happy.

"I didn't want you to know," he said. "If they do anything to hurt you now when the baby is about to come I shan't forgive them."

She paused in her dipping to stare at him. "Do you mean to tell me, John Dewey Chang," she demanded, "that you've been deliberately hiding things from me? I've wondered why every time we went anywhere you always took me into the foreign concession. That's just like New York— why, I've been bored to death!"

She dipped again, bowl after bowl, filling them to the brim, running to the stove for another pot.

"Bored?" he repeated.

"Yes," she answered. "There's nothing to do— And all the time there were all these people I didn't know about,—"

"Millions of them," he muttered, "millions upon millions upon millions of them!" He could not understand her.

"Well, that settles it," she said contentedly.

"Settles what?" he asked stupidly.

"Settles whether I like it here or in New York."

He stared at her, still stupidly, and she laughed at him, her old shout of loud laughter. He had not heard it just like that since that morning when she was working on her father's ledgers in Mott Street. "Silly!" she said, beginning on the fresh pot, "don't you see? I like to do things, and here's plenty!"

He began to comprehend. She did not mind these people. She was not in the least disappointed in them. They were only hungry people and she wanted to feed them. If they were dirty—

Almost as though she answered his thought she began, "And when they're all fed, I'm going to begin giving the babies baths—and maybe the grown people can take turns—" She turned around to demand, "How long do you think the war will keep up?"

Why, she was a child, nothing but a child, talking about baths! The sound of cannon was thundering steadily across the city. This morning the forts were down, he had heard. What would be the end of it?

"I don't know," he groaned.

"We might get everybody bathed if it only lasts long enough," she planned.

But he interrupted her, "Oh, Ruth, you should—you should go away for the baby's sake—out of the country—there's no telling about this war—"

But at this she turned and put her hands on her hips.

"My baby?" she said, firmly. "My baby is going to be born in his own country where he belongs." Then her voice changed again. "Now," she commanded him, "you take this trayful in and begin to feed them—the kids first. And hurry!" she added, "there's a lot to do around here!"   [1941]

WALTER VAN TILBURG CLARK

Walter Van Tilburg Clark (1909-1971) was born in East Orland, Maine. When Clark was nine years old, his father became president of the University of Nevada in Reno. Clark grew up in that city, attending public high school and the University of Nevada, where he earned an M.A. in English in 1932. That year he published his first book, Ten Women in Gale's House and Shorter Poems. *Then Clark returned to New England to teach at the University of Vermont, where he later said that he discovered he was tied to his western roots: "My feeling is that landscape is character, not background. It's not a stage. It's an active agent. It must be."*

In 1940, while teaching in Cazenovia, New York, Clark published the novel that made his reputation as an important Western writer, The Ox-Bow Incident. *Narrated in the first person by a cowboy, the story has no strong American hero. Instead Clark dramatized an incident during which a crowd is swayed by the passions of mob rule to act as a posse and murder three innocent men suspected of cattle rustling.*

Clark followed this book with two more novels set in Nevada. He also published about twenty short stories, many of them collected in The Watchful Gods and Other Stories *(1950). "The Portable Phonograph," which first appeared in the 1941* Yale Review, *was frequently anthologized in the 1950s. It seemed to describe the aftermath of an atomic holocaust on a global scale, reminiscent of the bombing of Hiroshima and Nagasaki that brought an end to World War II, although the story was written earlier. In 1962 Clark became a writer-in-residence at the University of Nevada in Reno, where he taught until his death from cancer nine years later.*

The Portable Phonograph

The red sunset, with narrow, black cloud strips like threats across it, lay on the curved horizon of the prairie. The air was still and cold, and in it settled the mute darkness and greater cold of night. High in the air there was wind, for through the veil of the dusk the clouds could be seen gliding rapidly south and changing shapes. A sensation of torment, of two-sided, unpredictable nature, arose from the stillness of the earth air beneath the violence of the upper air. Out of the sunset, through the dead, matted grass and isolated weed stalks of the prairie, crept the narrow and deeply rutted remains of a road. In the road, in places, there were crusts of shallow, brittle ice. There were little islands of an old oiled pavement in the road too, but most of it was mud, now frozen rigid. The frozen mud still bore the toothed impress of great tanks, and a wanderer on the neighboring undulations might have stumbled, in this light, into large, partially filled-in and weed-grown cavities, their banks channeled and beginning to spread into bad-lands. These pits were such as might have been made by falling meteors, but they were not. They were the scars of gigantic bombs, their rawness already made a little natural by rain, seed and time. Along the road there were rak-ish remnants of fence. There was also, just visible, one portion of tangled and multiple barbed wire still erect, behind which was a shelving ditch with small caves, now very quiet and empty, at intervals in its back wall. Otherwise there was no structure or remnant of a structure visible over the dome of the darkling earth, but only, in sheltered hollows, the darker shadows of young trees trying again.

Under the wuthering arch of the high wind a V of wild geese fled south. The rush of their pinions sounded briefly, and the faint, plaintive notes of their expeditionary talk. Then they left a still greater vacancy. There was the smell and expectation of snow, as there is likely to be when the wild geese fly south. From the remote distance, toward the red sky, came faintly the protracted howl and quick yap-yap of a prairie wolf.

North of the road, perhaps a hundred yards, lay the parallel and deeply intrenched course of a small creek, lined with leafless alders and wil-lows. The creek was already silent under ice. Into the bank above it was dug a sort of cell, with a single opening, like the mouth of a mine tunnel. Within the cell there was a little red of fire, which showed dully through the opening, like a reflection or a deception of the imagination. The light came from the chary burning of four blocks of poorly aged peat, which gave off a petty warmth and much acrid smoke. But the precious remnants of wood, old fence posts and timbers from the long-deserted dugouts, had to be saved for the real cold, for the time when a man's breath blew white, the moisture in his nostrils stiffened at once when he stepped out, and the expansive blizzards paraded for days over the vast open, swirling and set-tling and thickening, till the dawn of the cleared day when the sky was a thin blue-green and the terrible cold, in which a man could not live for three hours unwarmed, lay over the uniformly drifted swell of the plain.

Around the smoldering peat four men were seated cross-legged. Behind them, traversed by their shadows, was the earth bench, with two old and dirty army blankets, where the owner of the cell slept. In a niche in the opposite wall were a few tin utensils which caught the glint of the coals. The host was rewrapping in a piece of daubed burlap, four fine, leather-bound books. He worked slowly and very carefully, and at last tied the bundle securely with a piece of grass-woven cord. The other three looked intently upon the process, as if a great significance lay in it. As the host tied the cord, he spoke. He was an old man, his long, matted beard and hair gray to nearly white. The shadows made his brows and cheek-bones appear gnarled, his eyes and cheeks deeply sunken. His big hands, rough with frost and swollen by rheumatism, were awkward but gentle at their task. He was like a prehistoric priest performing a fateful ceremonial rite. Also his voice had in it a suitable quality of deep, reverent despair, yet perhaps, at the moment, a sharpness of selfish satisfaction.

"When I perceived what was happening," he said, "I told myself, 'It is the end. I cannot take much; I will take these.'

"Perhaps I was impractical," he continued. "But for myself, I do not regret, and what do we know of those who will come after us? We are the doddering remnant of a race of mechanical fools. I have saved what I love; the soul of what was good in us here; perhaps the new ones will make a strong enough beginning not to fall behind when they become clever."

He rose with slow pain and placed the wrapped volumes in the niche with his utensils. The others watched him with the same ritualistic gaze.

"Shakespeare, the Bible, *Moby Dick, The Divine Comedy,*" one of them said softly. "You might have done worse; much worse."

"You will have a little soul left until you die," said another harshly. "That is more than is true of us. My brain becomes thick, like my hands." He held the big, battered hands, with their black nails, in the glow to be seen.

"I want paper to write on," he said. "And there is none."

The fourth man said nothing. He sat in the shadow farthest from the fire, and sometimes his body jerked in its rags from the cold. Although he was still young, he was sick, and coughed often. Writing implied a greater future than he now felt able to consider.

The old man seated himself laboriously, and reached out, groaning at the movement, to put another block of peat on the fire. With bowed heads and averted eyes, his three guests acknowledged his magnanimity.

"We thank you, Doctor Jenkins, for the reading," said the man who had named the books.

They seemed then to be waiting for something. Doctor Jenkins understood, but was loath to comply. In an ordinary moment he would have said nothing. But the words of *The Tempest,* which he had been reading, and the religious attention of the three, made this an unusual occasion.

"You wish to hear the phonograph," he said grudgingly.

The two middle-aged men stared into the fire, unable to formulate and expose the enormity of their desire.

The young man, however, said anxiously, between suppressed coughs, "Oh, please," like an excited child.

The old man rose again in his difficult way, and went to the back of the cell. He returned and placed tenderly upon the packed floor, where the firelight might fall upon it, an old, portable phonograph in a black case. He smoothed the top with his hand, and then opened it. The lovely green-felt-covered disk became visible.

"I have been using thorns as needles," he said. "But tonight, because we have a musician among us" — he bent his head to the young man, almost invisible in the shadow — "I will use a steel needle. There are only three left."

The two middle-aged men stared at him in speechless adoration. The one with the big hands, who wanted to write, moved his lips, but the whisper was not audible.

"Oh, don't," cried the young man, as if he were hurt. "The thorns will do beautifully."

"No," the old man said. "I have become accustomed to the thorns, but they are not really good. For you, my young friend, we will have good music tonight.

"After all," he added generously, and beginning to wind the phonograph, which creaked, "they can't last forever."

"No, nor we," the man who needed to write said harshly. "The needle, by all means."

"Oh, thanks," said the young man. "Thanks," he said again, in a low, excited voice, and then stifled his coughing with a bowed head.

"The records, though," said the old man when he had finished winding, "are a different matter. Already they are very worn. I do not play them more than once a week. One, once a week, that is what I allow myself.

"More than a week I cannot stand it; not to hear them," he apologized.

"No, how could you?" cried the young man. "And with them here like this."

"A man can stand anything," said the man who wanted to write, in his harsh, antagonistic voice.

"Please, the music," said the young man.

"Only the one," said the old man. "In the long run we will remember more that way."

He had a dozen records with luxuriant gold and red seals. Even in that light the others could see that the threads of the records were becoming worn. Slowly he read out the titles, and the tremendous, dead names of the composers and the artists and the orchestras. The three worked upon the names in their minds, carefully. It was difficult to select from such a wealth what they would at once most like to remember. Finally the man who wanted to write named Gershwin's "New York."

"Oh, no," cried the sick young man, and then could say nothing more because he had to cough. The others understood him, and the harsh man withdrew his selection and waited for the musician to choose.

The musician begged Doctor Jenkins to read the titles again, very slowly, so that he could remember the sounds. While they were read, he lay back against the wall, his eyes closed, his thin, horny hand pulling at his light beard, and listened to the voices and the orchestras and the single instruments in his mind.

When the reading was done he spoke despairingly. "I have forgotten," he complained. "I cannot hear them clearly.

"There are things missing," he explained.

"I know," said Doctor Jenkins. "I thought that I knew all of Shelley by heart. I should have brought Shelley."

"That's more soul than we can use," said the harsh man. "*Moby Dick* is better.

"By God, we can understand that," he emphasized.

The doctor nodded.

"Still," said the man who had admired the books, "we need the absolute if we are to keep a grasp on anything.

"Anything but these sticks and peat clods and rabbit snares," he said bitterly.

"Shelley desired an ultimate absolute," said the harsh man. "It's too much," he said. "It's no good; no earthly good."

The musician selected a Debussy nocturne. The others considered and approved. They rose to their knees to watch the doctor prepare for the playing, so that they appeared to be actually in an attitude of worship. The peat glow showed the thinness of their bearded faces, and the deep lines in them, and revealed the condition of their garments. The other two continued to kneel as the old man carefully lowered the needle onto the spinning disk, but the musician suddenly drew back against the wall again, with his knees up, and buried his face in his hands.

At the first notes of the piano the listeners were startled. They stared at each other. Even the musician lifted his head in amazement, but then quickly bowed it again, strainingly, as if he were suffering from a pain he might not be able to endure. They were all listening deeply, without movement. The wet, blue-green notes tinkled forth from the old machine, and were individual, delectable presences in the cell. The individual, delectable presences swept into a sudden tide of unbearably beautiful dissonance, and then continued fully the swelling and ebbing of that tide, the dissonant inpourings, and the resolutions, and the diminishments, and the little, quiet wavelets of interlude lapping between. Every sound was piercing and singularly sweet. In all the men except the musician, there occurred rapid sequences of tragically heightened recollection. He heard nothing but what was there. At the final, whispering disappearance, but moving quietly, so that the others would not hear him and look at him, he let his head fall back in agony, as if it were drawn there by the hair, and clenched the fingers of one hand over his teeth. He sat that way while the others were silent, and until they began to breathe again normally. His drawn-up legs were trembling violently.

Quickly Doctor Jenkins lifted the needle off, to save it, and not to spoil the recollection with scraping. When he had stopped the whirling of the sacred disk, he courteously left the phonograph open and by the fire, in sight.

The others, however, understood. The musician rose last, but then abruptly, and went quickly out at the door without saying anything. The others stopped at the door and gave their thanks in low voices. The doctor nodded magnificently.

"Come again," he invited, "in a week. We will have the 'New York.'"

When the two had gone together, out toward the rimed road, he stood in the entrance, peering and listening. At first there was only the resonant boom of the wind overhead, and then, far over the dome of the dead, dark plain, the wolf cry lamenting. In the rifts of clouds the doctor saw four stars flying. It impressed the doctor that one of them had just been obscured by the beginning of a flying cloud at the very moment he heard what he had been listening for, a sound of suppressed coughing. It was not near by, however. He believed that down against the pale alders he could see the moving shadow.

With nervous hands he lowered the piece of canvas which served as his door, and pegged it at the bottom. Then quickly and quietly, looking at the piece of canvas frequently, he slipped the records into the case, snapped the lid shut, and carried the phonograph to his couch. There, pausing often to stare at the canvas and listen, he dug earth from the wall and disclosed a piece of board. Behind this there was a deep hole in the wall, into which he put the phonograph. After a moment's consideration, he went over and reached down his bundle of books and inserted it also. Then, guardedly, he once more sealed up the hole with the board and the earth. He also changed his blankets, and the grass-stuffed sack which served as a pillow, so that he could lie facing the entrance. After carefully placing two more blocks of peat on the fire, he stood for a long time watching the stretched canvas, but it seemed to billow naturally with the first gusts of a lowering wind. At last he prayed, and got in under his blankets, and closed his smoke-smarting eyes. On the inside of the bed, next the wall, he could feel with his hand, the comfortable piece of lead pipe.   [1941]

MARY McCARTHY

*M*ary *McCarthy (1912–1989) was born in Seattle, Washington, into a Catholic family. Her parents died in the influenza epidemic of 1918, and she and her three brothers were raised by their great-aunt in Minnesota. Later McCarthy described the emotional and physical deprivation of her early years in* Memoirs of a Catholic Girlhood *(1957). In 1933 she graduated from Vassar College and began to support herself by writing book reviews for* The Nation *and* The New Republic, *joining the community of New York's left-wing writers and intellectuals at the center of the cultural life of the city. After a brief first marriage ended in divorce, she was married to the novelist and literary critic Edmund Wilson for seven years. She later said, "I would never have written fiction if it hadn't been for him." During the summer of 1938 Wilson locked her in a room with a typewriter and demanded a story. She remembered that she typed out her first story, "Cruel and Barbarous Treatment," in one stretch "straight off, without blotting a line." Over the next few years, she wrote six more stories based on the experiences of her autobiographical protagonist. Five were published in the* Southern Review, Harper's Bazaar, *and* Partisan Review, *which included "The Man in the Brooks Brothers Shirt" in its summer 1941 issue. As the critic Elizabeth Hardwick recalled, McCarthy's stories "were indeed a sensation for candor, for the brilliant, lightning flashes of wit, for the bravado, the confidence, and the splendor of the prose style."*

About halfway through writing the stories, McCarthy began to think of them "as a kind of unified story" that subsequently became her first book, The Company She Keeps *(1942). Her husband proudly wrote to a friend, "Mary is well toward the end of a book that is something between a novel and a book of short stories—which I'm very much impressed by. I'm not sure she isn't the woman Stendhal," referring to the nineteenth-century French social realist novelist. After McCarthy published this book,* The New Yorker *editor William Maxwell asked her to contribute to the magazine. In the 1950s her writing was so greatly admired that she signed a "first reading agreement" with* The New Yorker, *a contract that committed the magazine to paying one-quarter more than its usual fee in exchange for getting a first option on any essays or fiction that she wrote.*

During her long and productive career, McCarthy published another collection of stories, The Hounds of Summer and Other Stories *(1981). Her main interest was in writing literary criticism, political commentary, and long fiction. She published seven novels, including the best-selling* The Group *(1963), which was about the lives of eight Vassar graduates of the class of 1933. Her other books include two personal memoirs and eight collections of essays.*

The Man in the
Brooks Brothers Shirt

The new man who came into the club car was coatless. He was dressed in gray trousers and a green shirt of expensive material that had the monogram "W.B." embroidered in darker green on the sleeve. His tie matched the green of the monogram, and his face, which emerged rather sharply from this tasteful symphony in cool colors, was blush pink. The greater part of his head appeared to be pink, also, though actually toward the back there was a good deal of closely cropped pale gray hair that harmonized with his trousers. He looked, she decided, like a middle-aged baby, like a young pig, like something in a seed catalogue. In any case, he was plainly Out of the Question, and the hope that had sprung up, as for some reason it always did, with the sound of a new step soft on the flowered Pullman carpet, died a new death. Already the trip was half over. They were now several hours out of Omaha; nearly all the Chicago passengers had put in an appearance; and still there was no one, no one at all. She must not mind, she told herself; the trip west was of no importance; yet she felt a curious, shamefaced disappointment, as if she had given a party and no guests had come.

She turned again to the lady on her left, her *vis-à-vis* at breakfast, a person with dangling earrings, a cigarette-holder, and a lorgnette, who was somebody in the New Deal and carried about with her a typewritten report of the hearings of some committee which she was anxious to discuss. The man in the green shirt crowded himself into a loveseat directly opposite, next to a young man with glasses and loud socks who was reading Negley Farson's "Way of a Transgressor." Sustaining her end of a well-bred, well-informed, liberal conversation, she had an air of perfect absorption and earnestness, yet she became aware, without ever turning her head, that the man across the way had decided to pick her up. Full of contempt for the man, for his coatlessness, for his color-scheme, for his susceptibility, for his presumption, she nevertheless allowed her voice to rise a little in response to him. The man countered by turning to his neighbor and saying something excessively audible about Negley Farson. The four voices, answering each other, began to give an antiphonal effect. Negley Farson was a fine fellow, she heard him pronounce; he could vouch for it, he knew him *personally*. The bait was crude, she reflected. She would have preferred the artificial fly to the angleworm, but still. . . . After all, he might have done worse; judged by eternal standards, Farson might not be much, but in the cultural atmosphere of the Pullman car, Farson was a titan. Moreover, if one judged the man by his intention, one could not fail to be touched. He was doing his best to *please* her. He had guessed from her conversation that she was an intellectual, and was placing the name of Farson as a humble offering at her feet. And the simple vulgarity of the offering somehow enhanced its value; it was like one of those home-made cakes with Paris-green icing that she used to receive on her birthday from her colored maid.

Her own neighbor must finally have noticed a certain displacement of attention, for she got up announcing that she was going in to lunch, and her tone was stiff with reproof and disappointment so that she seemed, for a moment, this rococo suffragette, like a nun who discovers that her favorite novice lacks the vocation. As she tugged open the door to go out, a blast of hot Nebraska air rushed into the club car, where the air-cooling system had already broken down.

The girl in the seat had an impulse to follow her. It would surely be cooler in the diner, where there was not so much glass. If she stayed and let the man pick her up, it would be a question of eating lunch together, and there would be a little quarrel about the check, and if she let him win she would have him on her hands all the way to Sacramento. And he was certain to be tiresome. That monogram in Gothic script spelled out the self-made man. She could foresee the political pronouncements, the pictures of the wife and children, the hand squeezed under the table. Nothing worse than that, fortunately, for the conductors on these trains were always very strict. Still, the whole thing would be so vulgar; one would expose oneself so to the derision of the other passengers. It was true, she was always wanting something exciting and romantic to happen; but it was not really romantic to be the-girl-who-sits-in-the-club-car-and-picks-up-men. She closed her eyes with a slight shudder: some predatory view of herself had been disclosed for an instant. She heard her aunt's voice saying, "I don't know why you make yourself so cheap," and "It doesn't pay to let men think you're easy." Then she was able to open her eyes again, and smile a little, patronizingly, for of course it hadn't worked out that way. The object of her trip was, precisely, to tell her aunt in Portland that she was going to be married again.

She settled down in her seat to wait and began to read an advance copy of a new novel. When the man would ask her what-that-book-is-you're-so-interested-in (she had heard the question before), she would be able to reply in a tone so simple and friendly that it could not give offense, "Why, you probably haven't heard of it. It's not out yet." (Yet, she thought, she had not brought the book along for purposes of ostentation: it had been given her by a publisher's assistant who saw her off at the train, and now she had nothing else to read. So, really, she could not be accused of insincerity. Unless it could be that her whole way of life had been assumed for purposes of ostentation, and the book, which looked accidental, was actually part of that larger and truly deliberate scheme. If it had not been this book, it would have been something else, which would have served equally well to impress a pink middle-aged stranger.)

The approach, when it came, was more unorthodox than she had expected. The man got up from his seat and said, "Can I talk to you?" Her retort, "What have you got to say?" rang off-key in her own ears. It was as if Broadway had answered Indiana. For a moment the man appeared to be taken aback, but then he laughed. "Why, I don't know; nothing special. We can talk about that book, I guess."

She liked him, and with her right hand made a gesture that meant, "All right, go on." The man examined the cover. "I haven't heard about this. It must be new."

"Yes." Her reply had more simplicity in it than she would have thought she could achieve. "It isn't out yet. This is an advance copy."

"I've read something else by this fellow. He's good."

"You have?" cried the girl in a sharp, suspicious voice. It was incredible that this well-barbered citizen should not only be familiar with but have a taste for the work of an obscure revolutionary novelist. On the other hand, it was incredible that he should be lying. The artless and offhand manner in which he pronounced the novelist's name indicated no desire to shine, indicated in fact that he placed no value on that name, that it was to him a name like Hervey Allen or Arthur Brisbane or Westbrook Pegler or any other.[1] Two alternatives presented themselves: either the man belonged to that extraordinary class of readers who have perfect literary digestions, who can devour anything printed, retaining what suits them, eliminating what does not, and liking all impartially, because, since they take what they want from each, they are always actually reading the same book (she had had a cousin who was like that about the theatre, and she remembered how her aunt used to complain, saying "It's no use asking Cousin Florence whether the show at the stock company is any good this week; Cousin Florence has never seen a bad play")—either that, or else the man had got the name confused and was really thinking of some popular writer all the time.

Still, the assertion, shaky as it was, had given him status with her. It was as if he had spoken a password, and with a greater sense of assurance and propriety, she went on listening to his talk. His voice was rather rich and dark; the accent was middle-western, but underneath the nasalities there was something soft and furry that came from the South. He lived in Cleveland, he told her, but his business kept him on the go a good deal; he spent nearly half his time in New York.

"You do?" she exclaimed, her spirits rising. "What *is* your business?" Her original view of him had already begun to dissolve, and it now seemed to her that the instant he had entered the club car she had sensed that he was no ordinary provincial entrepreneur.

"I'm a traveling salesman," he replied genially.

---

[1]William Hervey Allen Jr. (1884–1949) was an American poet, biographer, and novelist, whose daring novel *Anthony Adverse* (1933), with its candid passage about sex, influenced popular American literature. Arthur Brisbane (1864–1936), influential American journalist, was editor of the *New York Evening Journal* from 1897 to 1921 and the *Chicago Herald and Examiner* from 1918 to his death. American journalist James Westbrook Pegler (1894–1969) wrote for the United Press, the *Chicago Tribune,* the *New York World-Telegram,* and King Features Syndicate.

In a moment she recognized that this was a joke, but not before he had caught her look of absolute dismay and panic. He leaned toward her and laughed. "If it sounds any better to you," he said, "I'm in the steel business."

"It doesn't," she replied, recovering herself, making her words prim with political disapproval. But he *knew;* she had given herself away; he had trapped her features in an expression of utter snobbery.

"You're a pink, I suppose," he said, as if he had noticed nothing. "It'd sound better to you if I said I was a burglar."

"Yes," she acknowledged, with a comic air of frankness, and they both laughed. Much later, he gave her a business card that said he was an executive in Little Steel, but he persisted in describing himself as a traveling salesman, and she saw at last that it was an accident that the joke had turned on her: the joke was a wry, humble, clownish one that he habitually turned on himself.

When he asked if she would join him in a drink before lunch, she accepted readily. "Let's go into the diner, though. It may be cooler."

"I've got a bottle of whiskey in my compartment. I *know* it's cool there."

Her face stiffened. A compartment was something she had not counted on. But she did not know (she never had known) how to refuse. She felt bitterly angry with the man for having exposed her—so early—to this supreme test of femininity, a test she was bound to fail, since she would either go into the compartment, not wanting to (and he would know this and feel contempt for her malleability), or she would stay out of the compartment, wanting to have gone in (and he would know this, too, and feel contempt for her timidity).

The man looked at her face.

"Don't worry," he said in a kind, almost fatherly voice. "It'll be perfectly proper. I promise to leave the door open." He took her arm and gave it a slight, reassuring squeeze, and she laughed out loud, delighted with him for having, as she thought, once again understood and spared her.

In the compartment, which was off the club car, it *was* cooler. The highballs, gold in the glasses, tasted, as her own never did, the way they looked in the White Rock advertisements. There was something about the efficiency with which his luggage, in brown calf, was disposed in that small space, about the white coat of the black waiter who kept coming in with fresh ice and soda, about the chicken sandwiches they finally ordered for lunch, that gave her that sense of ritualistic "rightness" that the Best People are supposed to bask in. The open door contributed to this sense: it was exactly as if they were drinking in a show window, for nobody went by who did not peer in, and she felt that she could discern envy, admiration, and censure in the quick looks that were shot at her. The man sat at ease, unconscious of these attentions, but she kept her back straight, her shoulders high with decorum, and let her bare arms rise and fall now and then in short parabolas of gesture.

But if for the people outside she was playing the great lady, for the man across the table she was the Bohemian Girl. It was plain that she was a revelation to him, that he had never under the sun seen anyone like her. And he was quizzing her about her way of life with the intense, unashamed, wondering curiosity of a provincial seeing for the first time the sights of a great but slightly decadent city. Answering his questions she was able to see herself through his eyes (brown eyes, which were his only good feature, but which somehow matched his voice and thus enhanced the effect, already striking, of his having been put together by a good tailor). What she got from his view of her was a feeling of uniqueness and identity, a feeling she had once had when, at twenty, she had come to New York and had her first article accepted by a liberal weekly, but which had slowly been rubbed away by four years of being on the inside of the world that had looked magic from Portland, Oregon. Gradually, now, she was becoming very happy, for she knew for sure in this compartment that she was beautiful and gay and clever, and worldly and innocent, serious and frivolous, capricious and trustworthy, witty and sad, bad and really good, all mixed up together, all at the same time. She could feel the power running in her, like a medium on a particularly good night.

As these multiple personalities bloomed on the single stalk of her ego, a great glow of charity, like the flush of life, suffused her. This man, too, must be admitted into the mystery; this stranger must be made to open and disclose himself like a Japanese water flower. With a messianic earnestness she began to ask him questions, and though at first his answers displayed a sort of mulish shyness ("I'm just a traveling salesman," "I'm a suburban business man," "I'm an economic royalist"), she knew that sooner or later he would tell her the truth, the rock-bottom truth, and was patient with him. It was not the first time she had "drawn a man out" —— the phrase puckered her mouth, for it had never seemed like that to her. Certain evenings spent in bars with men she had known for half an hour came back to her; she remembered the beautiful frankness with which the cards on each side were laid on the table till love became a wonderful slow game of double solitaire and nothing that happened afterwards counted for anything beside those first few hours of self-revelation. Now as she put question after question she felt once more like a happy burglar twirling the dial of a well-constructed safe, listening for the locks to click and reveal the combination. When she asked him what the monogram on his shirt stood for, unexpectedly the door flew open.

He told her his name, and went on irrelevantly, "I get these shirts at Brooks Brothers. They'll put the monogram on if you order the shirts custom-made. I always order a dozen at a time. I get everything at Brooks Brothers except ties and shoes. Leonie thinks it's stodgy of me."

Leonie was his wife. They had a daughter, little Angela, and they lived in a fourteen-room house in the Gates Mills section of Cleveland. He also had a son by another marriage, little Frank, and Frank and Leonie got on wonderfully, he was glad to say, but then nobody could deny that Leonie had a wonderful disposition. Leonie was a home girl, quite different from Eleanor, who had been his first wife and was now a decorator in New York. Leonie loved her house and children. Of course, she was interested in culture too, particularly the theatre, and there were always a lot of young men from the Cleveland Playhouse hanging around her; but then she was a Bryn Mawr girl, and you had to expect a woman to have different interests from a man.

Leonie was a Book of the Month Club member and she also subscribed to the two liberal weeklies. "She'll certainly be excited," the man said, grinning with pleasure, "when she hears I met somebody from the *Liberal* on this trip. But she'll never be able to understand why you wasted your time talking to poor old Bill."

The girl smiled at him.

"I *like* to talk to you," she said, suppressing the fact that nothing on earth would have induced her to talk to Leonie.

"I read an article in those magazines once in a while," he continued dreamily. "Once in a while they have something good, but on the whole they're too wishy-washy for me. Now that I've had this visit with you, though, I'll read your magazine every week, trying to guess which of those things in the front you wrote."

"I'm *never* wishy-washy," said the girl, laughing. "But is your wife radical?"

"Good Lord, no! She calls herself a liberal, but actually I'm more of a radical than Leonie is."

"How do you mean?"

"Well, you take the election. I'm going to vote for Landon because it's expected of me, and my vote won't put him in."

"But you're really for Roosevelt?"

"No," said the man, a little impatiently. "I don't like Roosevelt either. I don't like a man that's always hedging his bets. Roosevelt's an old woman. Look at the way he's handling these CIO strikes. He doesn't have the guts to stick up for Lewis,[2] and he doesn't have the sense to stay out of the whole business." He leaned across the table and added, almost in a whisper, "You know who I'd like to vote for?"

The girl shook her head.

"Norman Thomas!"[3]

"But you're a steel man!" said the girl.

The man nodded.

---

[2]John Llewellyn Lewis (1880–1969) was an American labor leader who was founder and president, from 1935 to 1940, of the Congress of Industrial Organizations (CIO).

[3]Norman Mattoon Thomas (1884–1968), American politician who helped to found the American Civil Liberties Union; he ran as a Socialist candidate for president of the United States in every election from 1928 to 1948.

"Nobody knows how I feel, not even Leonie." He paused to think. "I was in the last war," he said finally, "and I had a grand time. I was in the cavalry and there weren't any horses. I was the youngest American major in the World War, and after the armistice we were stationed in Cologne, and we got hold of a Renault and every weekend we'd drive all night so we could have a day on the Riviera." He chuckled to himself. "But the way I look at it, there's a new war coming and it isn't going to be like that. God Almighty, we didn't hate the Germans!"

"And now?"

"You wait," he said. "Last time it was supposed to be what you people call an ideological war—for democracy and all that. But it wasn't. That was just advertising. You liberals have all of a sudden found out that it was Mr. Morgan's war.[4] You think that's terrible. But let me tell you that Mr. Morgan's war was a hell of a lot nicer to fight than this new one will be. Because this one will be ideological, and it'll be too damned serious. You'll wish that you had the international bankers and munitions men to stop the fight when things get too rough. I'd like to see this country stay out of it. That's why I'm for Thomas."

"You're a very interesting man," said the girl, tears coming to her eyes, perhaps because of the whiskey. "I've never known anyone like you. You're not the kind of businessman I write editorials against."

"You people are crazy, though," he said genially. "You're never going to get anywhere in America with that proletariat stuff. Every working man wants to live the way I do. He doesn't want me to live the way he does. You people go at it from the wrong end. I remember a Socialist organizer came down fifteen years ago into Southern Illinois. I was in the coal business then, working for my first wife's father. This Socialist was a nice fellow. . . ."

His voice was dreamy again, but there was an undercurrent of excitement in it. It was as if he were reviving some buried love affair, or, rather, some wispy young tendresse that had never come to anything. The Socialist organizer had been a distant connection of his first wife's; the two men had met and had some talks; later the Socialist had been run out of town; the man had stood aloof, neither helping nor hindering.

"I wonder what's become of him," he said finally. "In jail somewhere, I guess."

"Oh no," said the girl. "You don't understand modern life. He's a big bureaucrat in the CIO. Just like a business man, only not so well paid."

The man looked puzzled and vaguely sad. "He had a lot of nerve," he murmured, then added quickly, in a loud, bumptious tone, "But you're all nuts!"

---

[4]John Pierpont Morgan Jr. (1867–1943), American financier and son of J. P. Morgan. During World War I, he acted as agent for the Allied forces in floating large loans in the U.S.

The girl bit her lips. The man's vulgarity was undeniable. For some time now she had been attempting (for her own sake) to whitewash him, but the crude raw material would shine through in spite of her. It had been possible for her to remain so long in the compartment only on the basis of one of two assumptions, both of them literary, (a) that the man was a frustrated socialist, (b) that he was a frustrated man of sensibility, a kind of Sherwood Anderson character. But the man's own personality kept popping up, per- versely, like a Jack-in-the-box, to confound these theories. The most one could say was that the man was frustrated. She had hoped to "give him back to himself," but these fits of self-assertion on his part discouraged her by making her feel that there was nothing very good to give. She had, moreover, a suspicion that his lapses were deliberate, even malicious, that the man knew what she was about and why she was about it, and had made up his mind to thwart her. She felt a Take-me-as-I-am, an I'll-drag-you- down-to-my-level challenge behind his last words. It was like the resis- tance of the patient to the psychoanalyst, of the worker to the Marxist: she was offering to release him from the chains of habit, and he was standing up and clanking those chains comfortably and impudently in her face. On the other hand, she *knew,* just as the analyst knows, just as the Marxist knows, that somewhere in his character there was the need of release and the humility that would accept aid—and there was, furthermore, a kind- ness and a general cooperativeness which would make him pretend to be a little better than he was, if that would help her to think better of herself.

For the thing was, the man and the little adventure of being with him had a kind of human appeal that she kept giving in to against her judg- ment. *She liked him.* Why, it was impossible to say. The attraction was not sexual, for, as the whiskey went down in the bottle, his face took on a more and more porcine look that became so distasteful to her that she could hardly meet his gaze, but continued to talk to him with a large, remote stare, as if he were an audience of several hundred people. Whenever she did happen to catch his eye, to really look at him, she was as disconcerted as an actor who sees a human expression answering him from beyond the footlights. It was not his air of having money, either, that drew her to him, though that, she thought humorously, helped, but it hindered too. It was partly the homespun quality (the use of the word, "visit," for example, as a verb meaning "talk" took her straight back to her childhood and to her father, carpet-slippered, in a brown leather chair), and partly of course his plain delight in her, which had in it more shrewdness than she had thought at first, for, though her character was new and inexplicable to him, in a gross sense he was clearly a connoisseur of women. But beyond all this, she had glimpsed in him a vein of sympathy and understanding that made him available to any human being, just as he was, apparently, available as a reader to any novelist—and this might proceed, not, as she had assumed out in the club car, from stupidity, but from a restless and perenially hopeful curiosity.

Actually, she decided, it was the combination of provincialism and adventurousness that did the trick. This man *was* the frontier, though the American frontier had closed, she knew, forever, somewhere out in Oregon in her father's day. Her father, when that door had shut, had remained on the inside. In his youth, as she had learned to her surprise, from some yellowed newspaper clippings her aunt had forgotten in an old bureau drawer, he had been some kind of wildcat radical, full of workmen's compensation laws and state ownership of utilities; but he had long ago hardened into a corporation lawyer, Eastern style. She remembered how once she had challenged him with those clippings, thinking to shame him with the betrayal of ideals and how calmly he had retorted, "Things were different then." "But you fought the *railroads*," she had insisted. "And now you're their lawyer." "You had to fight the railroads in those days," he had answered innocently, and her aunt had put in, with her ineffable plebeian sententiousness, "Your father always stands for what is right." But she saw now that her father had honestly perceived no contradiction between the two sets of attitudes, which was the real proof that it was not he, so much as the times, that had changed.

Yet this man she was sitting with had somehow survived, like a lonely dinosaur, from that former day. It was not even a true survival, for if he was, as he said, forty-one, that would make him thirty years younger than her father, and he would be barely able to recall the Golden Age of American imperialism, to which, nevertheless, he plainly belonged. Looking at him, she thought of other young empires and recalled the Roman busts in the Metropolitan, marble faces of business men, shockingly rugged and modern and recognizable after the smooth tranquillity of the Greeks. Those early business men had been omnivorous, too, great readers, eaters, travelers, collectors, and, at the beginning, provincial also, small-town men newly admitted into world-citizenship, faintly uneasy but feeling their oats.

In the course of this analysis she had glided all the way from aversion to tenderness. She saw the man now as a man without a country, and felt a desire to reinstate him. But where? The best she could do was communicate to him a sense of his own isolation and grandeur. She could ensconce him in the dignity of sadness.

Meanwhile, the man had grown almost boisterously merry. It was late afternoon; the lunch things had long ago been taken away; and the bottle was nearly empty. Outside the flat yellow farm-land went by, comfortably dotted with haystacks; the drought and the cow-bones strewn over the Dust Bowl seemed remote as a surrealist painting. Other passengers still paused to look in at the open door on their way to the club car, but the girl was no longer fully aware of them: they existed, as it were, only to give the perspective, to deepen that warm third dimension that had been established within the compartment. The man was lit up with memories of the war, droll stories of horse-play and drinking parties, a hero who was drowned while swimming in a French river, trips to Paris, Notre Dame, and target-practice in the Alps. It had been, she could see, an extension of college days, a sort of lower-middle-class Grand Tour, a wonderful male rough-house that had left a man such as this with a permanent homesickness for fraternity and a loneliness that no stag party could quite ease.

"I suppose I'm boring you," said the man, still smiling to himself, "but—it's a funny thing to say—I haven't had such a good time since the war. So that you remind me of it, and I can't stop talking, I don't know why."

"*I* know," she said, full of gentle omniscience. (This was her best side, and she knew it. But did that spoil it, keep it from being good?) "It's because you've made a new friend, and you probably haven't made one for twenty years, not since the war. Nobody does, after they've grown-up."

"Maybe so," said the man. "Getting married, no matter how many times you do it, isn't the same thing. If you even *think* you'd like to marry a girl, you have to start lying to her. It's a law of nature, I guess. You have to protect yourself. I don't mean about cheating—that's small potatoes. . . ."

A meditative look absorbed his face. "Jesus Christ," he said, "I don't even *know* Leonie any more, and vice versa, but that's the way it ought to be. A man doesn't want his wife to understand him. That's not her job. Her job is to have a nice house and nice kids and give good parties he can have his friends to. If Leonie understood me, she wouldn't be able to do that. Probably we'd both go to pot."

Tears came to her eyes again. The man's life and her own life seemed unutterably tragic.

"I was in love with my husband," she said. "We understood each other. He never had a thought he didn't tell me."

"But you got a divorce," said the man. "Somebody must have misunderstood somebody else *somewhere* along the line."

"Well," she admitted, "maybe he *didn't* understand *me* so well. He was awfully surprised. . . ." She giggled like a soubrette. The giggle was quite out of character at the moment, but she had not been able to resist it. Besides (she was sure) it was these quick darts and turns, these flashing inconsistencies that gave her the peculiar, sweet-sour, highly volatile charm that was her *specialité de la maison*.

"Surprised when you picked up with somebody else?" asked the man. She nodded.

"What happened to that?"

"After I got divorced, I didn't want to marry him any more."

"So now you're on your own?"

The question seemed almost idle, but she replied in a distinct, emphatic voice, as if he were deaf and she had an important message for him.

"No," she said. "I'm going to be married in the fall."

"Are you in love with this one?"

"Oh, yes," she said. "He's charming. And he and I are much more alike than Jim and I were. He's a little bit of a bum and I am too. And he's selfish, which is a good thing for me. Jim was so *good*. And so vulnerable.

The back of his neck was just like a little boy's. I always remember the back of his neck."

She spoke earnestly, but she saw that the man did not understand. Nobody had ever understood — and she herself did not quite know — why this image retained such power over her, why all her feelings of guilt and shame had clustered around the picture of a boyish neck (the face had not been boyish, but prematurely lined) bared like an early martyr's for the sword. "How could I have done it?" she whispered to herself again, as she still did nearly every day, and once again she was suffused with horror.

"He was too good for me," she said at last. "I felt like his mother. Nobody would ever have known it, but he needed to be protected."

That was it. That was what was so awful. Nobody would ever have known. But she had crawled into his secret life and nestled there, like the worm in the rose. How warm and succulent it had been! And when she had devoured it all, she had gone away. "Oh God," she muttered under her breath. It was no excuse that she had loved him. The worm indubitably loves the rose.

Hurriedly, to distract herself, she began to talk about her love affairs. First names with thumbnail descriptions rolled out till her whole life sounded to her like a drugstore novel. And she found herself over-anxious to explain to him why in each case the thing had not borne fruit, how natural it was that she should have broken with John, how reasonable that she should never have forgiven Ernest. It was as if she had been a prosecuting attorney drawing up a brief against each of her lovers, and, not liking the position, she was relieved when the man interrupted her.

"Seems to me," he said, "you're still in love with that husband of yours."

"Do you think so really?" she asked, leaning forward. "Why?" Perhaps at last she had found him, the one she kept looking for, the one who could tell her what she was really like. For this she had gone to palmists and graphologists, hoping not for a dark man or a boat trip, but for some quick blaze of gypsy insight that would show her her own lineaments. If she once knew, she had no doubt that she could behave perfectly; it was merely a question of finding out. How, she thought, can you act upon your feelings if you don't know what they are? As a little girl whispering to a young priest in the confessional she had sometimes felt sure. The Church could classify it all for you. If you talked or laughed in church, told lies, had impure thoughts or conversations, you were bad; if you obeyed your parents or guardians, went to confession and communion regularly, said prayers for the dead, you were good. Protestants, like her father, were neutral; they lived in a gray world beyond good and evil. But when as a homely high-school girl, she had rejected the Church's filing system, together with her aunt's illiterate morality, she had given away her sense of herself. For a while she had believed that it was a matter of waiting until you grew older and your character was formed; then you would be able to recognize it as easily as a photograph. But she was now twenty-four, and had heard other people say she had a strong personality; she herself however was still in the dark. This hearty stranger in the green shirt—perhaps he could really tell whether she was in love with her husband. It was like the puzzle about the men with marks on their foreheads: A couldn't know whether his own forehead was marked, but B and C knew, of course, and he could, if he were bright, deduce it from their behavior.

"Well," replied the man, "of all the fellows you've talked about, Jim's the only one I get a picture of. Except your father—but that's different; he's the kind of a man I know about."

The answer disappointed her. It was too plain and folksy to cover the facts. It was true that she had loved her husband *personally*, for himself, and this had never happened to her with any one else. Nobody else's idiosyncrasies had ever warmed her; nobody else had she ever watched asleep. Yet that kind of love had, unfortunately, rendered her impotent to love him in the ordinary way, had, in fact, made it necessary for her to be unfaithful to him, and so, in the course of time, to leave him altogether. Or could it not be put in another way? Could she not say that all that conjugal tenderness had been a brightly packaged substitute for the Real Thing, for the long carnal swoon she had never quite been able to execute in the marriage bed? She had noticed that in those households where domesticity burns brightest and the Little Attentions rain most prodigally, the husband is seldom admitted to his real conjugal rights.

But it was impossible to explain this to the man. Already the conversation had dropped once or twice into ribaldry, but she was determined to preserve the decorum of the occasion. It was dark outside now and the waiter was back again, serving little brook trout on plates that had the Union Pacific's crest on them. Yet even as she warned herself how impossible it was, she heard her voice rushing on in a torrent of explicitness. (This had all happened so many times before, ever since, as a schoolgirl, she had exchanged dirty jokes with the college boys from Eugene and seen them stop the car and lunge at her across the gearshift. While all the time, she commiserated with herself, she had merely been trying to be a good fellow, to show that she was sophisticated and grown-up, and not to let them suspect (oh, never!) that her father did not allow her to go out with boys and that she was a neophyte, a helpless fledgling, with no small talk and no coquetry at all. It had not been *fair* (she could still italicize it, bitterly) for them to tackle her like a football dummy; she remembered the struggles back and forth on the slippery leather seats of sports roadsters, the physical awkwardness of it all being somehow the crowning indignity; she remembered also the rides home afterwards, and how the boy's face would always be sullen and closed—he was thinking that he had been cheated, made a fool of, and resolving never to ask her again, so that she would finally become notorious for being taken out only once. How indecent and anti-human it had been, like the tussle between the drowning man and the lifeguard! And of course she had invited it, just as she was invit-ing it now, but what she was really asking all along was not that the male should assault her, but that he should believe her a woman. This freedom of speech of hers was a kind of masquerade of sexuality, like the rubber breasts that homosexuals put on for drags, but, like the dummy breasts, its brazen-ness betrayed it: it was a poor copy and a hostile travesty all at once. But the men, she thought, did not look into it so deeply; they could only respond by leaping at her—which, after all, she supposed, was their readi-est method of showing her that her impersonation had been convincing. Yet that response, when it came, never failed to disconcert and frighten her: I had not counted on this, she could always whisper to herself, with a certain sad bewilderment. For it was all wrong, it was unnatural: art is to be admired, not acted on, and the public does not belong on the stage, nor the actors in the audience.)

But once more the man across the table spared her. His face was a little heavy with drink, but she could see no lechery in it, and he listened to her as calmly as a priest. The sense of the nightmare lifted; free will was restored to her.

"You know what my favorite quotation is?" she asked suddenly. She must be getting drunk, she knew, or she would not have said this, and a certain cool part of her personality protested. I must not quote poetry, she thought, I must stop it; God help us, if I'm not careful, we'll be singing Yale songs next. But her voice had broken away from her; she could only follow it, satirically, from a great distance. "It's from Chaucer," she went on, when she saw that she had his attention. "Criseyde says it, 'I am myne owne woman, welle at aise.'"

The man had some difficulty in understanding the Middle English, but when at last he had got it straight, he looked at her with bald admiration.

"Golly," he said, "you are, at that!"

The train woke her the next morning as it jerked into Cheyenne. It was still dark. The Pullman shade was drawn, and she imagined at first that she was in her own lower berth. She knew that she had been drunk the night before, but reflected with satisfaction that Nothing Had Happened. It would have been terrible if . . . She moved slightly and touched the man's body.

She did not scream, but only jerked away in a single spasmodic move-ment of rejection. This can't be, she thought angrily, it can't be. She shut her eyes tight. When I open them again, she said, he will be gone. I can't face it, she thought, holding herself rigid; the best thing to do is to go back to sleep. For a few minutes she actually dozed and dreamed she was back in Lower Seven with the sheets feeling extraordinarily crisp and clean and the curtains hanging protectively about her. But in the dream her pil-low shook under her as the porter poked it to call her for breakfast, and she woke again and knew that the man was still beside her and had moved in his sleep. The train was pulling out of the station. If it had not been so early, outside on the platform there would have been tall men in cowboy hats. Maybe, she thought, I passed out and he put me to bed. But the body next to her was naked, and horror rippled over her again as she realized by the coarseness of the sheets touching her that she was naked too. Oh my God, she said, get me out of this and I will do anything you want.

Waves of shame began to run through her, like savage internal blushes, as fragments of the night before presented themselves for inspection. They had sung songs, all right, she remembered, and there had been some question of disturbing the other passengers, and so the door had been shut. After that the man had come around to her side of the table and kissed her rather greedily. She had fought him off for a long time, but at length her will had softened. She had felt tired and kind, and thought, why not? Then there had been something peculiar about the lovemaking itself—but she could not recall what it was. She had tried to keep aloof from it, to be present in body but not in spirit. Somehow that had not worked out and she had been dragged in and humiliated. There was some comfort in this vagueness, but recollection quickly stabbed her again. There were (oh, holy Virgin!) four-letter words that she had been forced to repeat, and, at the climax, a rain of blows on her buttocks that must surely (dear God!) have left bruises. She must be careful not to let her aunt see her without any clothes on, she told herself, and remembered how once she had visualized sins as black marks on the white soul. This sin, at least, no one would see. But all at once she became aware of the significance of the sheets. The bed had been made up. And that meant that the Pullman porter. . . . She closed her eyes, exhausted, unable to finish the thought. The Negley Farson man, the New Deal lady, the waiter, the porter seemed to press in on her, a crowd of jeering material witnesses. If only nobody could know. . . .

But perhaps it was not too late. She had a sudden vision of herself in a black dress, her face scrubbed and powdered, her hair neatly combed, sitting standoffishly in her seat, watching Wyoming and Nevada go by and reading her publisher's copy of a new *avant-garde* novel. It *could* be done. If she could get back before the first call for breakfast, she might be able to carry it off. There would be the porter, of course, but he would not dare gossip to passengers. Softly, she climbed out of the berth and began to look for her clothes. In the darkness, she discovered her slip and dress neatly hung by the wash basin—the man must have put them there, and it was fortunate, at least, that he was such a shipshape character, for the dress would not be rumpled. On the floor she collected her stockings and a pair of white crepe-de-chine pants, many times mended, with a button off and a little brass pin in its place. Feeling herself blush for the pin, she sat down on the floor and pulled her stockings on. One garter was missing. She put on the rest of her clothes, and then began to look for the garter, but though she groped her way over every inch of the compartment, she could not find it. She sank to the floor again with one stocking hanging loosely down, buried her head in her arms and cried. She saw herself locked in an intolerable but ludicrous dilemma: it was impossible to face the rest of the train with one stocking hanging down; but it was also impossible to wait for the man to wake up and enlist him in retrieving the garter; it was impossible to send the porter for it later in the morning, and more impossible to call for it in person. But as the comic nature of the problem grew plain to her, her head cleared. With a final sob she stripped off her stockings and stuffed them into her purse. She stepped barefooted into her shoes, and was fumbling in her purse for a comb when the man turned over and groaned.

He remembers, she thought in terror, as she saw his arm reach out dimly white and plump in the darkness. She stood very still, waiting. Perhaps he would go back to sleep. But there was a click, and the reading light above the berth went on. The man looked at her in bewilderment. She realized that she had forgotten to buckle her belt.

"Dearest," he said, "what in the world are you doing?"

"I'm dressed," she said. "I've got to get out before they wake up. Good-bye."

She bent over with the intention of kissing him on the forehead. Politeness required something, but this was the most she could bring herself to do. The man seized her arms and pulled her down, sitting up himself beside her. He looked very fat and the short hair on his chest was gray.

"You can't go," he said, quite simply and naturally, but as if he had been thinking about it all night long. "I love you. I'm crazy about you. This is the most wonderful thing that's ever happened to me. You come to San Francisco with me and we'll go to Monterey, and I'll fix it up with Leonie to get a divorce."

She stared at him incredulously, but there was no doubt of it: he was serious. His body was trembling. Her heart sank as she saw that there was no longer any question of her leaving; common decency forbade it. Yet she was more frightened than flattered by his declaration of love. It was as if some terrible natural force were loose in the compartment. His seriousness, moreover, was a rebuke; her own squeamishness and sick distaste, which a moment before had seemed virtuous in her, now appeared heartless, even frivolous, in the face of his emotion.

"But I'm engaged," she said, rather thinly.

"You're not in love with him," he said. "You couldn't have done what you did last night if you were." As the memory of lovemaking returned to him, his voice grew embarrassingly hoarse.

"I was tight," she said flatly in a low voice.

"A girl like you doesn't let a man have her just because she's drunk."

She bowed her head. There was no possible answer she could give. "I must go," she repeated. In a way she knew that she would have to stay, and knew, too, that it was only a matter of hours, but, just as a convict whose sentence is nearly up will try a jail break and get shot down by the guards, so the girl, with Sacramento not far ahead, could not restrain herself from begging, like a claustrophobic, for immediate release. She saw that the man was getting hurt and angry, but still she held herself stiffly in his embrace and would not look at him. He turned her head round with his hand. "Kiss me," he said, but she pulled away.

"I have to throw up."

He pointed to the toilet seat, which was covered with green upholstery. (She had forgotten that Pullman compartments had this indecent feature.) She raised the cover and vomited, while the man sat on the bed and watched her. This was the nadir, she thought bitterly; surely nothing worse than this could ever happen to her. She wiped the tears from her eyes and leaned against the wall. The man made a gesture toward her.

"Don't touch me," she said, "or I'll be sick again. It would be better if I went back to my berth."

"Poor little girl," he said tenderly. "You feel bad, don't you?"

He got out of the berth and took a fresh bottle of whiskey from a suitcase.

"I'll have to save the Bourbon for the conductor," he said in a matter-of-fact, friendly voice. "He'll be around later on, looking for his cut."

For the first time that morning the girl laughed. The man poured out two small drinks and handed her one of them. "Take it like medicine," he advised.

She sat down on the berth and crossed her legs. The man put on a dressing-gown and pulled up a chair opposite her. They raised their glasses. The smell of the whiskey gagged her and she knew that it was out of the question, physically, for her to get drunk a second time. Yet she felt her spirits lift a little. There was an air of professional rowdyism about their drinking neat whiskey early in the morning in a dishevelled compartment that took her fancy.

"What about the porter?"

"Oh," said the man genially. "I've squared him. I gave him ten last night and I'll give him another ten when I get off. He thinks you're wonderful. He said to me, 'Mr. Breen, you sure done better than most.'"

"Oh!" said the girl, covering her face with her hands. "Oh! Oh!" For a moment she felt that she could not bear it, but as she heard the man laugh she made her own discomfiture comic and gave an extra groan or two that were purely theatrical. She raised her head and looked at him shamefaced, and then giggled. This vulgarity was more comforting to her than any assurances of love. If the seduction (or whatever it was) could be reduced to its lowest common denominator, could be seen in farcical terms, she could accept and even, wryly, enjoy it. The world of farce was a sort of moral underworld, a cheerful, well-lit hell where a Fall was only a prat-fall after all.

Moreover, this talk had about it the atmosphere of the locker room or the stag-line, an atmosphere more bracing, more astringent than the air of

Bohemia. The ten-dollar tips, the Bourbon for the conductor indicated competence and connoisseurship, which, while not of the highest order, did extend from food and drink and haberdashery all the way up to women. That was what had been missing in the men she had known in New York—the shrewd buyer's eye, the swift, brutal appraisal. That was what you found in the country clubs and beach clubs and yacht clubs—but you never found it in the café of the Brevoort. The men she had known during these last four years had been, when you faced it, too easily pleased: her success had been gratifying but hollow. It was not difficult, after all, to be the prettiest girl at a party for the sharecroppers. At bottom, she was contemptuous of the men who had believed her perfect, for she knew that in a bathing suit at Southampton she would never have passed muster, and though she had never submitted herself to this cruel test, it lived in her mind as a threat to her. A copy of *Vogue* picked up at the beauty parlor, a lunch at a restaurant that was beyond her means, would suffice to remind her of her peril. And if she had felt safe with the different men who had been in love with her it was because—she saw it now—in one way or another they were all of them lame ducks. The handsome ones, like her fiancé, were good-for-nothing, the reliable ones, like her husband, were peculiar-looking, the well-to-do ones were short and wore lifts in their shoes or fat with glasses, the clever ones were alcoholic or slightly homosexual, the serious ones were Jews or foreigners or else wore beards or black shirts or were desperately poor and had no table manners. Somehow each of them was handicapped for American life and therefore humble in love. And was she too disqualified, did she really belong to this fraternity of cripples, or was she not a sound and normal woman who had been spending her life in self-imposed exile, a princess among the trolls?

She did not know. She would have found out soon enough had she stayed on in Portland, but she had not risked it. She had gone away East to college and never come back until now. And very early in her college life she had got engaged to a painter, so that nothing that happened in the way of cutting in at the dances at Yale and Princeton really "counted." She had put herself out of the running and was patently not trying. Her engagement had been a form of insurance, but the trouble was that it not only insured her against failure but also against success. Should she have been more courageous? She could not tell, even now. Perhaps she *was* a princess because her father was a real gentleman who lunched at his club and traveled by drawing room or compartment; but on the other hand, there was her aunt. She could not find out for herself; it would take a prince to tell her. This man now—surely he came from that heavenly world, that divine position at the center of things where choice is unlimited. And he had chosen *her.*

But that was all wrong. She had only to look at him to see that she had cheated again, had tried to get into the game with a deck of phony cards. For this man also was out of the running. He was too old. Sound as he was in every other respect, time had made a lame duck of him. If she had met him ten years before, would he have chosen her then?

He took the glass from her hands and put his arms around her. "My God," he said, "if this had only happened ten years ago!"

She held herself stony in his embrace, and felt indeed like a rock being lapped by some importunate wave. There was a touch of dignity in the simile, she thought, but what takes place in the end?—Erosion. At that the image suddenly turned and presented another facet to her: dear Jesus, she told herself, frightened, I'm really as hard as nails. Then all at once she was hugging the man with an air of warmth that was not quite spurious and not quite sincere (for the distaste could not quite be smothered but only ignored); she pressed her ten fingers into his back and for the first time kissed him carefully on the mouth.

The glow of self-sacrifice illuminated her. This, she thought decidedly, is going to be the only real act of charity I have ever performed in my life; it will be the only time I have ever given anything when it honestly hurt me to do so. That her asceticism should have to be expressed in terms of sensuality deepened, in a curious way, its value, for the sacrifice was both paradoxical and positive; this was no simple abstention like a meatless Friday or a chaste Sunday: it was the mortification of the flesh achieved through the performance of the act of pleasure.

Quickly she helped him take off the black dress, and stretched herself out on the berth like a slab of white lamb on an altar. While she waited with some impatience for the man to exhaust himself, for the indignity to be over, she contemplated with a burning nostalgia the image of herself, fully dressed, with the novel, in her Pullman seat, and knew, with the firmest conviction, that for once she was really and truly good, not hard or heartless at all.

"You need a bath," said the man abruptly, raising himself on one elbow and looking sharply down at her as she lay relaxed on the rumpled sheet. The curtain was halfway up, and outside the Great Salt Lake surrounded them. They had been going over it for hours, that immense, gray-brown blighting Dead Sea, which looked, not like an actual lake, but like a mirage seen in the desert. She had watched it for a long time, while the man beside her murmured of his happiness and his plans for their future; they had slept a little and when they opened their eyes again, it was still there, an interminable reminder of sterility, polygamy, and waste.

"Get up," he went on, "and I'll ring for the porter to fix it for you."

He spoke harshly: this was the drill sergeant, the voice of authority. She sprang to attention, her lips quivering. Her nakedness, her long, loose hair, which a moment before had seemed voluptuous to her, now all at once became bold and disorderly, like an unbuttoned tunic at an army inspection. This was the first wound he had dealt her, but how deep the sword went in, back to the teachers who could smoke cigarettes and gossip with you in the late afternoon and then rebuke you in the morning class, back to the relations who would talk with you as an equal and then tell your aunt you were too young for silk stockings, back through all the betrayers, the friendly enemies, the Janus-faced overseers, back to the mother who could love you and then die.

"I don't want a bath," she asserted stubbornly. "I'm perfectly clean." But she knew, of course, that she had not bathed since she left New York, and, if she had been allowed to go her own way, would not have bathed until she reached Portland—who would think of paying a dollar for a bath on the train? In the ladies' room, where soot and spilt powder made a film over the dressing-tables and the hair-receivers stared up, archaic as cuspidors, one sponged oneself hastily under one's wrapper, and, looking at one's neighbors jockeying for position at the mirror, with their dirty kimonas, their elaborate make-up kits, and their uncombed permanents, one felt that one had been fastidious enough, and hurried away, out of the sweet, musty, unused smell of middle-aged women dressing. "I'm perfectly clean," she repeated. The man merely pressed the bell, and when the porter announced that the bath was ready, shoved her out into the corridor in his Brooks Brothers dressing-gown with a cake of English toilet soap in her hands.

In the ladies' lounge, the colored maid had drawn the bath and stood just behind the half-drawn curtain, waiting to hand her soap and towels. And though, ordinarily, the girl had no particular physical modesty, at this moment it seemed to her insupportable that anyone should watch her bathe. There was something terrible and familiar about the scene—herself in the tub, washing, and a woman standing tall above her—something terrible and familiar indeed about the whole episode of being forced to cleanse herself. Slowly she remembered. The maid was, of course, her aunt, standing over her tub on Saturday nights to see that she washed every bit of herself, standing over her at the medicine cabinet to see that she took the castor oil, standing over her bed in the mornings to see if the sheets were wet. Not since she had been grown-up, had she felt this peculiar weakness and shame. It seemed to her that she did not have the courage to send the maid away, that the maid was somehow the man's representative, his spy, whom it would be impious to resist. Tears of futile, self-pitying rage came into her eyes, and she told herself that she would stay in the bath all day, rather than go back to the compartment. But the bell rang in the dressing-room, and the maid rustled the curtain, saying, "Do you want anything more? I'll leave the towels here," and the door swung behind her, leaving the girl alone.

She lay in the bath a long time, gathering her forces. In the tepid water, she felt for the first time a genuine socialist ardor. For the first time in her life, she truly hated luxury, hated Brooks Brothers and Bergdorf Goodman and Chanel and furs and good food. All the pretty things she had seen in shops and coveted appeared to her suddenly gross, superfatted, fleshly, even, strangely, unclean. By a queer reversal, the very safety pin in her underwear, which she had blushed for earlier in the morning came to look to her now as a kind of symbol of moral fastidiousness, just as the sores of a mendicant saint can, if thought of in the right way, testify to his spiritual health. A proud, bitter smile formed on her lips, as she saw herself as a citadel of socialist virginity, that could be taken and taken again, but never truly subdued. The man's whole assault on her now seemed to have had a political character; it was an incidental atrocity in the long class war. She smiled again, thinking that she had come out of it untouched, while he had been reduced to a jelly.

All morning in the compartment he had been in a state of wild and happy excitement, full of projects for reform and renewal. He was not sure what ought to happen next; he only knew that everything must be different. In one breath, he would have the two of them playing golf together at Del Monte; in the next, he would imagine that he had given her up and was starting in again with Leonie on a new basis. Then he would see himself throwing everything overboard and going to live in sin in a villa in a little French town. But at that moment a wonderful technical innovation for the manufacture of steel would occur to him, and he would be anxious to get back to the office to put it through. He talked of giving his fortune to a pacifist organization in Washington, and five minutes later made up his mind to send little Frank, who showed signs of being a problem child, to a damn good military school. Perhaps he would enlarge his Gates Mills house; perhaps he would sell it and move to New York. He would take her to the theatre and the best restaurants; they would go to museums and ride on bus-tops. He would become a CIO organizer, or else he would give her a job in the personnel department of the steel company, and she could live in Cleveland with him and Leonie. But no, he would not do that, he would marry her, as he had said in the first place, or, if she would not marry him, he would keep her in an apartment in New York. Whatever happened she must not get off the train. He had come to regard her as a sort of rabbit's foot that he must keep by him at any price.

Naturally, she told herself, the idea was absurd. Yet suddenly her heart seemed to contract and the mood of indulgent pity ebbed away from her. She shivered and pulled herself out of the tub. His obstinacy on this point frightened her. If he should bar her way when the time came . . . ? If there should be a struggle . . . ? If she should have to pull the communication cord . . . ? She told herself that such things do not happen, that during the course of the day she would surely be able to convince him that she must go. (She had noticed that the invocation of her father inevitably moved him. "We mustn't do anything to upset your father," he would say. "He must be a very fine man." And tears would actually come to his eyes. She would play that, she thought, for all it was worth.) Yet her uneasiness did not abate. It was as if, carelessly, inadvertently, almost, she had pulled a switch that had set a whole strange factory going, and now, too late, she discovered that she did not know how to turn it off. She could have run away, but some sense of guilt, of social responsibility, of primitive awe, kept her glued to the spot, watching and listening, waiting to be ground to bits. Once, in a beauty parlor, she had been put under a defective dryer that remained on high no matter where she turned the regulator; her neck seemed to be burning up, and she could, at any time, have freed herself by simply getting out of the chair; yet she had stayed there the full half hour, until the operator came to release her. "I think," she had said then, lightly, "there is something wrong with the machine." And when the operator had examined it, all the women had gathered round, clucking, "How did you ever stand it?" She had merely shrugged her shoulders. It had seemed, at the time, better to suffer than to "make a fuss." Perhaps it was something like this that had held her to the man today, the fear of a scene and a kind of morbid competitiveness that would not allow the man to outdistance her in feeling. Yet suddenly she knew that it did not matter what her motives were: she could not, *could not*, get off the train until the man was reconciled to her doing so, until this absurd, ugly love story should somehow be concluded.

If only she could convert him to something, if she could say, "Give up your business, go to Paris, become a Catholic, join the CIO, join the army, join the Socialist Party, go off to the war in Spain." For a moment the notion engaged her. It would be wonderful, she thought, to be able to relate afterwards that she had sent a middle-aged business man to die for the Republicans at the Alcazar. But almost at once she recognized that this was too much to hope for. The man back in the compartment was not equal to it; he was equal to a divorce, to a change of residence, at most to a change of business, but not to a change of heart. She sighed slightly, facing the truth about him. His gray flannel dressing-gown lay on a chair beside her. Very slowly, she wrapped herself in it; the touch of the material made gooseflesh rise. Something about this garment—the color, perhaps, or the unsuitable size—reminded her of the bathing suits one rents at a public swimming pool. She gritted her teeth and pulled open the door. She did not pause to look about but plunged down the corridor with lowered head; though she passed no one, it seemed to her that she was running the gauntlet. The compartment, with its naked man and disordered bed, beckoned her on now, like a home.

When she opened the door, she found the man dressed, the compartment made up, and a white cloth spread on the collapsible table between the seats. In a few minutes the waiter of the night before was back with orange juice in cracked ice and corned beef hash and fish cakes. It was as if the scenery, which had been struck the night before had been set up again for the matinee. The difference was that the door remained shut. Nevertheless, though there were no onlookers, atmospheric conditions in the compartment had changed; the relationship of the pair took on a certain sociable formality. The little breakfast passed off like a ceremonial feast. All primitive peoples, she thought, had known that a cataclysmic experience, whether joyful or sad, had in the end to be liquidated in an orderly meal. The banquets in Homer came to her mind, the refreshments the Irish put out at a wake, the sweetmeats the Arabs nibble after love, the fairy stories that end And-the-king-ordered-a-great-dinner-to-be-served-to-all-his-people. Upheavals of private feeling, like the one she had just been through, were as incalculable and anti-social as death. With a graceful inclination of her head, she accepted a second fish cake from the waiter, and felt herself restored to the human race.

There was to be no more lovemaking, she saw, and from the moment she felt sure of this, she began to be a little bit in love. The long day passed as if in slow motion, in desultory, lingering, tender talk. Dreamy confidences were murmured, and trailed off, casual and unemphatic, like the dialogue in a play by Chekhov. The great desert lake out the window disappeared and was replaced by the sage brush country, which seemed to her a pleasant, melancholy symbol of the contemporary waste land. The man's life lay before her; it was almost as if she could reach out and touch it, poke it, explore it, shine it up, and give it back to him. The people in it grew distinct to her, though they swam in a poetic ambience. She could see his first wife, an executive in her forties, good-looking, well-turned-out, the kind of woman that eats at Longchamps or the Algonquin; and then Leonie, finer-drawn, younger, with a certain Marie Laurencin look that pale, pretty, neutral-colored rich women get; then herself, still younger, still more highly organized—and all the time the man, a ludicrous and touching Ponce de Leon, growing helplessly older and coarser in inverse relation to the women he needed and wanted.

And she could see the Brussels carpet in a Philadelphia whorehouse, where he had first had a woman, the judge's face at the divorce hearing, the squash court at the club, the aquamarine bathtubs in his house, the barbecue pit, the fraternity brothers, the Audubon prints in his study, the vacuum bottle on the night table. Somehow it had become essential to them both that she should know *everything*. They might have been collaborators, drawing up a dossier for a new "Babbitt."[5] This is what I am, he was saying: the wall paper in the larger guest room is a blue and white Colonial design; I go to bed at ten and Leonie sits up and reads; I like kippers for breakfast; we have Heppelwhite chairs in the sitting room; the doctor is worried about my kidneys, and I feel lonely when I first wake up.

There were the details, the realistic "touches," and then there was the great skeleton of the story itself. In 1917 he was a chemistry major, just out of the State university, with a job for the next year teaching at a high

---

[5]1922 novel by Sinclair Lewis (American novelist, 1885–1951) criticizing middle-class American values. The title character, George Babbitt, came to symbolize conformity, materialism, and anti-intellectualism.

school, and plans, after that, for a master's degree, and perhaps a job in the department at Cornell, where he had an uncle in the Agricultural School. The father had been a small business man in a Pennsylvania coal town, the grandfather a farmer, the mother a little lady from Tennessee. But then there came the Officers' Training Camp, and the brilliant war record, and the right connections, so that the high-school job was never taken, and instead he was playing handball at the Athletic Club in the evenings, and working as a metallurgist for the steel company during the day. Soon he was moved into production, but somehow he was too amiable and easy-going for this, and after his first marriage, he went into the coal business. When he came back to the steel company, it was as a purchasing agent, and here his shrewdness and bonhomie were better employed. He became Chief Purchasing Agent and Fourth Vice-President; it was doubtful whether he would ever go further.

For ten years, he confided, he had been visited now and then by a queer sense of having missed the boat, but it was all vague with him: he had no idea of when the boat had sailed or what kind of boat it was or where it went to. Would he have done better to take the teaching job? It hardly seemed so. Plainly, he was no scientist—the steel company had seen this at once—and, had he taken that other road, at best he would have finished as the principal of a high school or the head of the chemistry department in a small-time state university. No, she thought, he was not a scientist manqué, but simply a nice man, and it was a pity that society had offered him no nicer way of being nice than the job of buying materials for a company in Little Steel. The job, she saw, was one of the least compromising jobs he could have held and still made money; by regarding his business life as a nexus of personal friendships he had tried to hold himself aloof from the banks and the blast furnaces. He was full of fraternal feelings, loyalties, even, toward the tin salesmen and iron magnates and copper executives and their wives who wined him and dined him and took him to the latest musical shows over and over again. ("Don't mistake me," he said, "most of those fellows and their women are mighty fine people"). Still—there was always the contract, waiting to be signed the next morning, lying implacably on the desk.

Here he was, affable, a good mixer, self-evidently a sound guy, and yet these qualities were somehow impeached by the commercial use that was made of them, so that he found himself, as he grew older, hunting, more and more anxiously, for new and non-commercial contexts in which to assert his gregariousness. He refused the conventional social life of Cleveland. At the country club dances, he was generally to be found in the bar, shooting dice with the bartender; he played a little stud poker, but no bridge. In New York, he would stay at the Biltmore or the Murray Hill, buy his clothes at Brooks Brothers, and eat—when Leonie was not with him—at Cavanagh's, Luchow's or the Lafayette. But the greater part of his time he spent on trains, talking to his fellow-passengers, getting their life stories. ("Golly," he interjected, "if I were a writer like you!") This was one of his greatest pleasures, he said, and he would never go by plane if he could help it. In the three and a half days that it took a train to cross the continent, you could meet somebody who was a little bit different, and have a good, long visit with them. Sometimes, also, he would stop over and look up old friends, but lately that had been disappointing—so many of them were old or on the wagon, suffering from ulcers or cirrhosis of the liver. . . .

He spread his hands suddenly. There it was, he indicated; he was sharing it all with her, like a basket lunch. And, as she accepted it, nodding from time to time in pleasure and recognition, supplementing it occasionally from her own store, she knew that the actual sharing of his life was no longer so much in question. During this afternoon of confidences, he had undergone a catharsis. He was at rest now, and happy, and she was free. He would never be alone again, she thought; in fact, it was as if he had never been alone at all, for by a tremendous act of perception, she had thrust herself back into his past, and was settled there forever, like the dear companion, the twin, we pray for as children, while our parents, listening, laugh. She had brought it off, and now she was almost reluctant to leave him. A pang of joy went through her as she examined her own sorrow and found it to be real. All day she believed she had been acting a tragic part in something called One Perfect Night, but slowly, without her being aware of it, the counterfeit had passed into the true. She did not understand exactly how it had happened. Perhaps it was because she had come so very, very close—*tout comprendre, c'est tout aimer*—and perhaps it was because she was good at the task he had assigned her: at the sight of his life, waiting to be understood, she had rolled up her sleeves with all the vigor of a first-class cook confronting a brand-new kitchen.

"I love you," she said suddenly. "I didn't before, but now I do."

The man glanced sharply at her.

"Then you won't get off the train . . . ?"

"Oh, yes," she said, for now at last she could be truthful with him. "I'll certainly get off. One reason I love you, I suppose, is because I *am* getting off."

His dark eyes met hers in perfect comprehension.

"And one reason I'm going to let you do it," he said, "is because you love me."

She lowered her eyes, astonished, once more, at his shrewdness.

"Hell," he said, "it's a funny thing, but I'm so happy now that I don't care whether I ever see you again. I probably won't feel that way after you're gone. Right now I think I can live on this one day for the rest of my life."

"I hope you can," she said, her voice trembling with sincerity. "My dear, dear Mr. Breen, I hope you can." Then they both began to laugh wildly because she could not call him by his first name.

Still, he had not quite relinquished the idea of marrying her, and, once, very late in the afternoon, he struck out at her with unexpected, clumsy ferocity.

"You need a man to take care of you," he exclaimed. "I hate to see you go back to that life you've been living in New York. Your father ought to make you stay home in Portland. In a few years, you'll be one of those Bohemian horrors with oily hair and long earrings. It makes me sick to think about it."

She pressed her lips together, and was amazed to find how hurt she was. It was unthinkable that he should speak of her way of life with such contempt; it was as if he had made a point of telling her that her gayest, wickedest, most extravagant hat was ugly and out-of-fashion.

"But you fell in love with me because I *am* Bohemian," she said, forcing herself to smile, to take a suave and reasonable tone.

"No," he said, in a truculently sentimental voice. "It's because underneath all that you're just a sweet girl."

She shook her head impatiently. It was not true, of course, but it was hopeless to argue with him about it. Clearly, he took some cruel satisfaction in telling her that she was different from what she was. That implied that he had not fallen in love with her at all, but with some other person: the whole extraordinary little idyll had been based on a misunderstanding. Poor Marianna, she thought, poor pickings, to be loved under cover of darkness in Isabella's name! She did not speak for a long time.

Night fell again, and the little dinner that was presently served lacked the glamour of the earlier meals. The Union Pacific's menu had been winnowed out; they were reduced to steak and Great Big Baked Potatoes. She wished that they were out in the diner, in full view, eating some unusual dish and drinking a bottle of white wine. Even here in the compartment, she had hoped that he would offer her wine; the waiter suggested it, but the man shook his head without consulting her; his excesses in drink and love were beginning to tell on him; he looked tired and sick.

But by ten o'clock, when they were well out of Reno, she had warmed to him again. He had been begging her to let him send her a present; the notion displeased her at first; she felt a certain arrogant condescension in it; she refused to permit it, refused, even, to give him her address. Then he looked at her suddenly, with all the old humility and square self-knowledge in his brown eyes.

"Look," he said, "you'll be doing me a kindness. You see, that's the only thing a man like me can do for a woman is buy her things and love her a hell of a lot at night. I'm different from your literary boy friends and your artistic boy friends. I can't write you a poem or paint your picture. The only way I can show that I love you is to spend money on you."

"Money's your medium," she said, smiling, happy in this further insight he had given her, happy in her own gift of concise expression.

He nodded and she gave her consent. It must, however, be a very *small* present, and it must not, on any account, be jewelry, she said, not knowing precisely why she imposed this latter condition.

As they moved into the last hour of the trip, the occasion took on an elegiac solemnity. They talked very little; the man held both of her hands tightly. Toward the end, he broke the silence to say, "I want you to know that this has been the happiest day of my life." As she heard these words, a drowsy, sensuous contentment invaded her; it was as if she had been waiting for them all along; this was the climax, the spiritual orgasm. And it was just as she had known from the very first: in the end, he had not let her down. She had not been wrong in him after all.

They stood on the platform as the train came into Sacramento. Her luggage was piled up around them; one suitcase had a missing handle and was tied up with a rope. The man made a noise of disapproval.

"Your father," he said, "is going to feel terrible when he sees *that*."

The girl laughed; the train slowed down; the man kissed her passionately several times, ignoring the porter who waited beside them with a large, Hollywood-darky smile on his face.

"If I were ten years younger," the man said, in a curious, measured tone, as if he were taking an oath, "I'd never let you get off this train." It sounded, she thought, like an apology to God.

In the station the air was hot and thick. She sat down to wait, and immediately she was damp and grubby; her stockings were wrinkled; her black suede shoes had somehow got dusty, and, she noticed for the first time, one of the heels was run over. Her trip home seemed peculiarly pointless, for she had known for the last eight hours that she was never going to marry the young man back in New York.

On the return trip, her train stopped in Cleveland early in the morning. In a new fall suit she sat in the club car, waiting. Mr. Breen hurried into the car. He was wearing a dark-blue business suit and had two packages in his hand. One of them was plainly a florist's box. She took it from him and opened it, disclosing two of the largest and most garish purple orchids she had ever seen. He helped her pin them on her shoulder and did not appear to notice how oddly they harmonized with her burnt sienna jacket. The other box contained a bottle of whiskey; *in memoriam,* he said.

They had the club car to themselves, and for the fifteen minutes the train waited in the station he looked at her and talked. It seemed to her that he had been talking ever since she left him, talking volubly, desperately, incoherently, over the long-distance telephone, via air mail, by Western Union and Postal Telegraph. She had received from him several pieces of glamour-girl underwear and a topaz brooch, and had been disappointed and a little humiliated by the taste displayed. She was glad now that the train stopped at such an outlandish hour, for she felt that he cut a ridiculous figure, with his gifts in his hand, like a superannuated stage-door johnny.

She herself had little to say, and sat passive, letting the torrent of talk and endearment splash over her. Sooner or later, she knew, the law of diminishing returns would begin to operate, and she would cease to reap these overwhelming profits from the small investment of herself she had made. At the moment, he was begging her to marry him, describing a business conference he was about to attend, and asking her approval of a vacation trip he was planning to take with his wife. Of these three elements in his conversation, the first was predominant, but she sensed that already she was changing for him, becoming less of a mistress and more of a confidante. It was significant that he was not (as she had feared) hoping to ride all the way to New York with her: the business conference, he explained, prevented that.

It never failed, she thought, to be a tiny blow to guess that a man is losing interest in you, and she was tempted, as on such occasions she always had been, to make some gesture that would quicken it again. If she let him think she would sleep with him, he would stay on the train, and let the conference go by the board. He had weighed the conference, obviously, against a platonic interlude, and made the sensible decision. But she stifled her vanity, and said to herself that she was glad that he was showing some signs of self-respect; in the queer, business-English letters he had written her, and on the phone for an hour at a time at her father's house, he had been too shockingly abject.

She let him get off the train, still talking happily, pressed his hand warmly but did not kiss him.

It was three weeks before he came to see her in her New York apartment, and then, she could tell, he was convalescent. He had become more critical of her and more self-assured. Her one-and-a-half rooms in Greenwich Village gave him claustrophobia, he declared, and when she pointed out to him that the apartment was charming, he stated flatly that it was not the kind of place he liked, nor the kind of place she ought to be living in. He was more the business man and less the suitor, and though he continued to ask her to marry him, she felt that the request was somewhat formal; it was only when he tried to make love to her that his real, hopeless, humble ardor showed itself once more. She fought him off, though she had an inclination to yield, if only to reestablish her ascendancy over him. They went to the theater two nights, and danced, and drank champagne, and the third morning he phoned her from his hotel that he had a stomach attack and would have to go home to Cleveland with a doctor.

More than a month went by before she saw him again. This time he refused to come to her apartment, but insisted that she meet him at his suite in the Ambassador. They passed a moderate evening: the man contented himself with dining at Longchamps. He bought her a large Brie cheese at the Voisin down the street, and told her an anti–New-Deal joke. Just below the surface of his genial manner, there was an hostility that hurt her. She found that she was extending herself to please him. All her gestures grew over-feminine and demonstrative; the lift of her eyebrows was a shade too arch: like a passée belle, she was overplaying herself. I must let go, she told herself; the train is pulling out; if I hang on, I'll be dragged along at its wheels. She made him take her home early.

A little later she received a duck he had shot in Virginia. She did not know how to cook it and it stayed in her icebox so long that the neighbors complained of the smell.

When she got a letter from him that had been dictated to his stenographer, she knew that his splurge was over. After that, she saw him once — for cocktails. He ordered double martinis and got a little drunk. Then his friendliness revived briefly, and he begged her with tears in his eyes to "forget all this red nonsense and remember that you're just your father's little girl at heart." Walking home alone, trying to decide whether to eat in a tea room or cook herself a chop, she felt flat and sad, but in the end she was glad that she had never told him of her broken engagement.

When her father died, the man must have read the account in the papers, for she got a telegram that read: SINCEREST CONDOLENCES YOU HAVE LOST THE BEST FRIEND YOU WILL EVER HAVE. She did not file it away with the other messages, but tore it up carefully and threw it in the wastebasket. It would have been dreadful if anyone had seen it.   [1941]

CARSON McCULLERS

Carson McCullers (1917–1967) was born Lula Carson Smith in Columbus, Georgia. Her mother was the dominant influence in her early life, encouraging her to become a pianist and a writer. As a teenager McCullers went to New York City intending to study music at Julliard and writing at Columbia, but after she lost the tuition money for Julliard on the subway, she took creative writing classes with the editor Whit Burnett at Columbia and with Sylvia Chatfield Bates at New York University. Supporting herself as a typist and a waitress, she wrote her first published story, "Wunderkind," for Bates and it was accepted by Burnett for Story *magazine in 1936.*

The following year she married Reeves McCullers, a fellow southerner who also wanted to be a writer and was willing to support her. As a wife, McCullers had more time for her writing, and she completed her first published book during the next two years. It was published in 1940 as The Heart Is a Lonely Hunter. *Her marriage began to disintegrate as her husband's career floundered, and the couple separated. McCullers's response to the situation was to write another novel,* Reflections in a Golden Eye *(1941), about alienation and the failure of love. After she suffered the first in a series of strokes that rendered her an invalid for the rest of her life, her husband returned to care for her. McCullers continued writing in this most productive period of her career, when she worked on the story "A Tree. A Rock. A Cloud," the novel* The Member of the Wedding *(1946), and the novella* The Ballad of the Sad Café *(1951). These established her in the company of Katherine Anne Porter, Eudora Welty, and Flannery O'Connor as a writer whose fiction explored the character of the southern grotesque.*

McCullers wrote "A Tree. A Rock. A Cloud" to test her capacity to create works of fiction after she had recovered from her first stroke. Originally published in Harper's Bazaar *in November 1942, it was selected for inclusion in the* O. Henry Memorial Prize Stories *of 1942. Later, in an essay "The Flowering Dream: Notes on Writing" (1959), McCullers wrote,*

> *Spiritual isolation is the basis of most of my themes. My first book was concerned with this, almost entirely, and all my books since, in one way or another. Love, and especially love of a person who is incapable of receiving it, is at the heart of my selection of grotesque figures to write about—people whose physical incapacity is a symbol of their spiritual incapacity to love or receive love—their spiritual isolation.*

A Tree. A Rock. A Cloud

It was raining that morning, and still very dark. When the boy reached the streetcar café he had almost finished his route and he went in for a cup of coffee. The place was an all-night café owned by a bitter and stingy man called Leo. After the raw, empty street, the café seemed friendly and bright: along the counter there were a couple of soldiers, three spinners from the cotton mill, and in a corner a man who sat hunched over with his nose and half his face down in a beer mug. The boy wore a helmet such as aviators wear. When he went into the café he unbuckled the chin strap and raised the right flap up over his pink little ear; often as he drank his coffee some-one would speak to him in a friendly way. But this morning Leo did not look into his face and none of the men were talking. He paid and was leav-ing the café when a voice called out to him:

"Son! Hey Son!"

He turned back and the man in the corner was crooking his finger and nodding to him. He had brought his face out of the beer mug and he seemed suddenly very happy. The man was long and pale, with a big nose and faded orange hair.

"Hey Son!"

The boy went toward him. He was an undersized boy of about twelve, with one shoulder drawn higher than the other because of the weight of the paper sack. His face was shallow, freckled, and his eyes were round child eyes.

"Yeah Mister?"

The man laid one hand on the paper boy's shoulders, then grasped the boy's chin and turned his face slowly from one side to the other. The boy shrank back uneasily.

"Say! What's the big idea?"

The boy's voice was shrill; inside the café it was suddenly very quiet.

The man said slowly, "I love you."

All along the counter the men laughed. The boy, who had scowled and sidled away, did not know what to do. He looked over the counter at Leo, and Leo watched him with a weary, brittle jeer. The boy tried to laugh also. But the man was serious and sad.

"I did not mean to tease you, Son," he said. "Sit down and have a beer with me. There is something I have to explain."

Cautiously, out of the corner of his eye, the paper boy questioned the men along the counter to see what he should do. But they had gone back to their beer or their breakfast and did not notice him. Leo put a cup of coffee on the counter and a little jug of cream.

"He is a minor," Leo said.

The paper boy slid himself up onto the stool. His ear beneath the upturned flap of the helmet was very small and red. The man was nodding at him soberly. "It is important," he said. Then he reached in his hip pocket and brought out something which he held up in the palm of his hand for the boy to see.

"Look very carefully," he said.

The boy stared, but there was nothing to look at very carefully. The man held in his big, grimy palm a photograph. It was the face of a woman, but blurred, so that only the hat and the dress she was wearing stood out clearly.

"See?" the man asked.

The boy nodded and the man placed another picture in his palm. The woman was standing on a beach in a bathing suit. The suit made her stomach very big, and that was the main thing you noticed.

"Got a good look?" He leaned over closer and finally asked: "You ever seen her before?"

The boy sat motionless, staring slantwise at the man. "Not so I know of."

"Very well." The man blew on the photographs and put them back into his pocket. "That was my wife."

"Dead?" the boy asked.

Slowly the man shook his head. He pursed his lips as though about to whistle and answered in a long-drawn way. "Nuuu—" he said. "I will explain."

The beer on the counter before the man was in a large brown mug. He did not pick it up to drink. Instead he bent down and, putting his face over the rim, he rested there for a moment. Then with both hands he tilted the mug and sipped.

"Some night you'll go to sleep with your big nose in a mug and drown," said Leo. "Prominent transient drowns in beer. That would be a cute death."

The paper boy tried to signal to Leo. While the man was not looking he screwed up his face and worked his mouth to question soundlessly: "Drunk?" But Leo only raised his eyebrows and turned away to put some pink strips of bacon on the grill. The man pushed the mug away from him, straightened himself, and folded his loose crooked hands on the counter. His face was sad as he looked at the paper boy. He did not blink, but from time to time the lids closed down with delicate gravity over his pale green eyes. It was nearing dawn and the boy shifted the weight of the paper sack.

"I am talking about love," the man said. "With me it is a science."

The boy half slid down from the stool. But the man raised his forefinger, and there was something about him that held the boy and would not let him go away.

"Twelve years ago I married the woman in the photograph. She was my wife for one year, nine months, three days, and two nights. I loved her.

Yes. . . ." He tightened his blurred, rambling voice and said again: "I loved her. I thought also that she loved me. I was a railroad engineer. She had all home comforts and luxuries. It never crept into my brain that she was not satisfied. But do you know what happened?"

"Mgneeow!" said Leo.

The man did not take his eyes from the boy's face. "She left me. I came in one night and the house was empty and she was gone. She left me."

"With a fellow?" the boy asked.

Gently the man placed his palm down on the counter. "Why naturally, Son. A woman does not run off like that alone."

The café was quiet, the soft rain black and endless in the street outside. Leo pressed down the frying bacon with the prongs of his long fork. "So you have been chasing the floozie for eleven years. You frazzled old rascal!"

For the first time the man glanced at Leo. "Please don't be vulgar. Besides, I was not speaking to you." He turned back to the boy and said in a trusting and secretive undertone. "Let's not pay any attention to him. O.K.?"

The paper boy nodded doubtfully.

"It was like this," the man continued. "I am a person who feels many things. All my life one thing after another has impressed me. Moonlight. The leg of a pretty girl. One thing after another. But the point is that when I had enjoyed anything there was a peculiar sensation as though it was laying around loose in me. Nothing seemed to finish itself up or fit in with the other things. Women? I had my portion of them. The same. Afterwards laying around loose in me. I was a man who had never loved."

Very slowly he closed his eyelids, and the gesture was like a curtain drawn at the end of a scene in a play. When he spoke again his voice was excited and the words came fast—the lobes of his large, loose ears seemed to tremble.

"Then I met this woman. I was fifty-one years old and she always said she was thirty. I met her at a filling station and we were married within three days. And do you know what it was like? I just can't tell you. All I had ever felt was gathered together around this woman. Nothing lay around loose in me any more but was finished up by her."

The man stopped suddenly and stroked his long nose. His voice sank down to a steady and reproachful undertone: "I'm not explaining this right. What happened was this. There were these beautiful feelings and loose little pleasures inside me. And this woman was something like an assembly line for my soul. I run these little pieces of myself through her and I come out complete. Now do you follow me?"

"What was her name?" the boy asked.

"Oh," he said. "I called her Dodo. But that is immaterial."

"Did you try to make her come back?"

The man did not seem to hear. "Under the circumstances you can imagine how I felt when she left me."

Leo took the bacon from the grill and folded two strips of it between a bun. He had a gray face, with slitted eyes, and a pinched nose saddled by faint blue shadows. One of the mill workers signaled for more coffee and Leo poured it. He did not give refills on coffee free. The spinner ate breakfast there every morning, but the better Leo knew his customers the stingier he treated them. He nibbled his bun as though he grudged it to himself.

"And you never got hold of her again?"

The boy did not know what to think of the man, and his child's face was uncertain with mingled curiosity and doubt. He was new on the paper route; it was still strange to him to be out in the town in the black, queer early morning.

"Yes," the man said. "I took a number of steps to get her back. I went around trying to locate her. I went to Tulsa where she had folks. And to Mobile. I went to every town she had ever mentioned to me, and I hunted down every man she had formerly been connected with. Tulsa, Atlanta, Chicago, Cheehaw, Memphis. . . . For the better part of two years I chased around the country trying to lay hold of her."

"But the pair of them had vanished from the face of the earth!" said Leo.

"Don't listen to him," the man said confidentially. "And also just forget those two years. They are not important. What matters is that around the third year a curious thing begun to happen to me."

"What?" the boy asked.

The man leaned down and tilted his mug to take a sip of beer. But as he hovered over the mug his nostrils fluttered slightly; he sniffed the staleness of the beer and did not drink. "Love is a curious thing to begin with. At first I thought only of getting her back. It was a kind of mania. But then as time went on I tried to remember her. But do you know what happened?"

"No," the boy said.

"When I laid myself down on a bed and tried to think about her my mind became a blank. I couldn't see her. I would take out her pictures and look. No good. Nothing doing. A blank. Can you imagine it?"

"Say Mac!" Leo called down the counter. "Can you imagine this bozo's mind a blank!"

Slowly, as though fanning away flies, the man waved his hand. His green eyes were concentrated and fixed on the shallow little face of the paper boy.

"But a sudden piece of glass on a sidewalk. Or a nickel tune in a music box. A shadow on a wall at night. And I would remember. It might happen in a street and I would cry or bang my head against a lamppost. You follow me?"

"A piece of glass . . ." the boy said.

"Anything. I would walk around and I had no power of how and when to remember her. You think you can put up a kind of shield. But remembering don't come to a man face forward—it corners around sideways. I was at the mercy of everything I saw and heard. Suddenly instead of me combing the countryside to find her she begun to chase me around in my very soul. *She* chasing *me*, mind you! And in my soul."

The boy asked finally: "What part of the country were you in then?"

"Ooh," the man groaned. "I was a sick mortal. It was like smallpox. I confess, Son, that I boozed. I fornicated. I committed any sin that suddenly appealed to me. I am loath to confess it but I will do so. When I recall that period it is all curdled in my mind, it was so terrible."

The man leaned his head down and tapped his forehead on the counter. For a few seconds he stayed bowed over in this position, the back of his stringy neck covered with orange furze, his hands with their long warped fingers held palm to palm in an attitude of prayer. Then the man straightened himself; he was smiling and suddenly his face was bright and tremulous and old.

"It was in the fifth year that it happened," he said. "And with it I started my science."

Leo's mouth jerked with a pale, quick grin. "Well none of we boys are getting any younger," he said. Then with sudden anger he balled up a dishcloth he was holding and threw it down hard on the floor. "You draggle-tailed old Romeo!"

"What happened?" the boy asked.

The old man's voice was high and clear: "Peace," he answered.

"Huh?"

"It is hard to explain scientifically, Son," he said. "I guess the logical explanation is that she and I had fleed around from each other for so long that finally we just got tangled up together and lay down and quit. Peace. A queer and beautiful blankness. It was spring in Portland and the rain came every afternoon. All evening I just stayed there on my bed in the dark. And that is how the science come to me."

The windows in the streetcar were pale blue with light. The two soldiers paid for their beers and opened the door—one of the soldiers combed his hair and wiped off his muddy puttees before they went outside. The three mill workers bent silently over their breakfasts. Leo's clock was ticking on the wall.

"It is this. And listen carefully. I meditated on love and reasoned it out. I realized what is wrong with us. Men fall in love for the first time. And what do they fall in love with?"

The boy's soft mouth was partly open and he did not answer.

"A woman," the old man said. "Without science, with nothing to go by, they undertake the most dangerous and sacred experience in God's earth. They fall in love with a woman. Is that correct, Son?"

"Yeah," the boy said faintly.

"They start at the wrong end of love. They begin at the climax. Can you wonder it is so miserable? Do you know how men should love?"

The old man reached over and grasped the boy by the collar of his leather jacket. He gave him a gentle little shake and his green eyes gazed down unblinking and grave.

"Son, do you know how love should be begun?"

The boy sat small and listening and still. Slowly he shook his head. The old man leaned closer and whispered:

"A tree. A rock. A cloud."

It was still raining outside in the street: a mild, gray, endless rain. The mill whistle blew for the six o'clock shift and the three spinners paid and went away. There was no one in the café but Leo, the old man, and the little paper boy.

"The weather was like this in Portland," he said. "At the time my science was begun. I meditated and I started very cautious. I would pick up something from the street and take it home with me. I bought a goldfish and I concentrated on the goldfish and I loved it. I graduated from one thing to another. Day by day I was getting this technique. On the road from Portland to San Diego——"

"Aw shut up!" screamed Leo suddenly. "Shut up! Shut up!"

The old man still held the collar of the boy's jacket; he was trembling and his face was earnest and bright and wild. "For six years now I have gone around by myself and built up my science. And now I am a master. Son. I can love anything. No longer do I have to think about it even. I see a street full of people and a beautiful light comes in me. I watch a bird in the sky. Or I meet a traveler on the road. Everything, Son. And anybody. All stranger and all loved! Do you realize what a science like mine can mean?"

The boy held himself stiffly, his hands curled tight around the counter edge. Finally he asked: "Did you ever really find that lady?"

"What? What say, Son?"

"I mean," the boy asked timidly. "Have you fallen in love with a woman again?"

The old man loosened his grasp on the boy's collar. He turned away and for the first time his green eyes had a vague and scattered look. He lifted the mug from the counter, drank down the yellow beer. His head was shaking slowly from side to side. Then finally he answered: "No, Son. You see that is the last step in my science. I go cautious. And I am not quite ready yet."

"Well!" said Leo. "Well well well!"

The old man stood in the open doorway. "Remember," he said. Framed there in the gray damp light of the early morning he looked shrunken and seedy and frail. But his smile was bright. "Remember I love you," he said with a last nod. And the door closed quietly behind him.

The boy did not speak for a long time. He pulled down the bangs on his forehead and slid his grimy little forefinger around the rim of his empty cup. Then without looking at Leo he finally asked:

"Was he drunk?"

"No," said Leo shortly.

The boy raised his clear voice higher. "Then was he a dope fiend?"

"No."

The boy looked up at Leo, and his flat little face was desperate, his voice urgent and shrill. "Was he crazy? Do you think he was a lunatic?" The paper boy's voice dropped suddenly with doubt. "Leo? Or not?"

But Leo would not answer him. Leo had run a night café for fourteen years, and he held himself to be a critic of craziness. There were the town characters and also the transients who roamed in from the night. He knew the manias of all of them. But he did not want to satisfy the questions of the waiting child. He tightened his pale face and was silent.

So the boy pulled down the right flap of his helmet and as he turned to leave he made the only comment that seemed safe to him, the only remark that could not be laughed down and despised:

"He sure has done a lot of traveling."   [1942]

JAMES THURBER

James Thurber (1894–1961), the humorist, was born in Columbus, Ohio. When he was a boy he lost an eye, which kept him from military service in World War I. After his graduation from Ohio State University, he worked as a news-paper reporter in Columbus and New York and lived in Paris. He came back to New York in 1926 to submit his humorous sketches to a new magazine, The New Yorker. *He also served a short time as its managing editor, and the mag-azine printed his cartoons, fables, stories, and essays for the rest of his life. Among Thurber's many books are* Fables for Our Time *(1940),* My World — And Welcome to It *(1942),* The Thurber Carnival *(1945), and* Thurber Country *(1953).*

Thurber said he began to write as a young man in "a rather curious style . . . tight journalese laced with heavy doses of Henry James." But his con-tact with E. B. White and Harold Ross at The New Yorker *taught him to value clarity above all else. After he matured as a writer he reflected on why James's way of writing no longer worked for him: "James is like—well, I had a bulldog once who used to drag rails around, enormous ones. . . . Once he brought home a chest of drawers—without the drawers in it. Found it on an ash-heap. Well, he'd start to get these things in the garden gate, everything finely balanced, you see, and then crash, he'd come up against the gate posts. He'd get it through finally, but I had that feeling in some of James's novels: that he was trying to get that rail through a gate not wide enough for it."*

In discussing how he wrote stories, Thurber once quoted a definition of the difference between English and American humor: "The English treat the com-monplace as if it were remarkable and the Americans treat the remarkable as if it were commonplace." He felt at home in the short story, never wanting to write a longer work, yet he recognized that there could also be serious elements in his fiction. "In anything funny you write that isn't close to serious you've missed something along the line." To Thurber, humor was "emotional chaos remembered in tranquility," and although the chaos provoked the immediate comic response, the power of ordered remembering gave the incident its deeper meaning. His best fiction and drawings were inspired by his comic view of the perennial battle of the sexes, as in "The Catbird Seat," which appeared in The New Yorker *in 1942.*

RELATED COMMENTARY: *Earl Rovit, "On James Thurber and* The New Yorker," *page 1443.*

The Catbird Seat

Mr. Martin bought the pack of Camels on Monday night in the most crowded cigar store on Broadway. It was theatre time and seven or eight men were buying cigarettes. The clerk didn't even glance at Mr. Martin, who put the pack in his overcoat pocket and went out. If any of the staff at F & S had seen him buy the cigarettes, they would have been astonished, for it was generally known that Mr. Martin did not smoke, and never had. No one saw him.

It was just a week to the day since Mr. Martin had decided to rub out Mrs. Ulgine Barrows. The term "rub out" pleased him because it suggested nothing more than the correction of an error—in this case an error of Mr. Fitweiler. Mr. Martin had spent each night of the past week working out his plan and examining it. As he walked home now he went over it again. For the hundredth time he resented the element of imprecision, the margin of guesswork that entered into the business. The project as he had worked it out was casual and bold, the risks were considerable. Something might go wrong anywhere along the line. And therein lay the cunning of his scheme. No one would ever see in it the cautious, painstaking hand of Erwin Martin, head of the filing department at F & S, of whom Mr. Fitweiler had once said, "Man is fallible but Martin isn't." No one would see his hand, that is, unless it were caught in the act.

Sitting in his apartment, drinking a glass of milk, Mr. Martin reviewed his case against Mrs. Ulgine Barrows, as he had every night for seven nights. He began at the beginning. Her quacking voice and braying laugh had first profaned the halls of F & S on March 7, 1941 (Mr. Martin had a head for dates). Old Roberts, the personnel chief, had introduced her as the newly appointed special adviser to the president of the firm, Mr. Fitweiler. The woman had appalled Mr. Martin instantly, but he hadn't shown it. He had given her his dry hand, a look of studious concentration, and a faint smile. "Well," she had said, looking at the papers on his desk, "are you lifting the oxcart out of the ditch?" As Mr. Martin recalled that moment, over his milk, he squirmed slightly. He must keep his mind on her crimes as a special adviser, not on her peccadillos as a personality. This he found difficult to do, in spite of entering an objection and sustaining it. The faults of the woman as a woman kept chattering on in his mind like an unruly witness. She had, for almost two years now, baited him. In the halls, in the elevator, even in his own office, into which she romped now and then like a circus horse, she was constantly shouting these silly questions at him. "Are you lifting the oxcart out of the ditch? Are you tearing up the pea patch? Are you hollering down the rain barrel? Are you scraping the bottom of the pickle barrel? Are you sitting in the catbird seat?"

It was Joey Hart, one of Mr. Martin's two assistants, who had explained what the gibberish meant. "She must be a Dodger fan," he had said. "Red Barber announces the Dodger games over the radio and he uses those expressions—picked 'em up down South." Joey had gone on to explain one or two. "Tearing up the pea patch" meant going on a rampage; "sitting in the catbird seat" meant sitting pretty, like a batter with three balls and no strikes on him. Mr. Martin dismissed all this with an effort. It had been annoying, it had driven him near to distraction, but he was too solid a man to be moved to murder by anything so childish. It was fortunate, he reflected as he passed on to the important charges against Mrs. Barrows, that he had stood up under it so well. He had maintained always an outward appearance of polite tolerance. "Why, I even believe you like the woman," Miss Paird, his other assistant, had once said to him. He had simply smiled.

A gavel rapped in Mr. Martin's mind and the case proper was resumed. Mrs. Ulgine Barrows stood charged with willful, blatant, and persistent attempts to destroy the efficiency and system of F & S. It was competent, material, and relevant to review her advent and rise to power. Mr. Martin had got the story from Miss Paird, who seemed always able to find things out. According to her, Mrs. Barrows had met Mr. Fitweiler at a party, where she had rescued him from the embraces of a powerfully built drunken man who had mistaken the president of F & S for a famous Middle Western football coach. She had led him to a sofa and somehow worked upon him a monstrous magic. The aging gentleman had jumped to the conclusion there and then that this was a woman of singular attainments, equipped to bring out the best in him and in the firm. A week later he had introduced her into F & S as his special adviser. On that day confusion got its foot in the door. After Miss Tyson, Mr. Brundage, and Mr. Bartlett had been fired and Mr. Munson had taken his hat and stalked out, mailing in his resignation later, old Roberts had been emboldened to speak to Mr. Fitweiler. He mentioned that Mr. Munson's department had been "a little disrupted" and hadn't they perhaps better resume the old system there? Mr. Fitweiler had said certainly not. He had the greatest faith in Mrs. Barrows' ideas. "They require a little seasoning, a little seasoning, is all," he had added. Mr. Roberts had given it up. Mr. Martin reviewed in detail all the changes wrought by Mrs. Barrows. She had begun chipping at the cornices of the firm's edifice and now she was swinging at the foundation stones with a pickaxe.

Mr. Martin came now, in his summing up, to the afternoon of Monday, November 2, 1942—just one week ago. On that day, at 3 P.M., Mrs. Barrows had bounced into his office. "Boo!" she had yelled. "Are you scraping the bottom of the pickle barrel?" Mr. Martin had looked at her from under his green eyeshade, saying nothing. She had begun to wander about the office, taking it in with her great popping eyes. "Do you really need *all* these filing cabinets?" she demanded suddenly. Mr. Martin's heart had jumped. "Each of these files," he had said, keeping his voice even, "plays an indispensable part in the system of F & S." She had brayed at him, "Well, don't tear up the pea patch!" and gone to the door. From there she had bawled, "But you sure have got a lot of fine scrap in here!" Mr. Martin could no longer doubt that the finger was on his beloved department. Her pickaxe was on the upswing, poised for the first blow. It had not come yet; he had received no blue memo from the enchanted Mr. Fitweiler bearing nonsensical instructions deriving from the obscene woman. But there was no doubt in Mr. Martin's mind that one would be forthcoming. He must act quickly. Already a precious week had gone by. Mr. Martin stood up in his living room, still holding his milk glass. Gentlemen of the jury, he said to himself, I demand the death penalty for this horrible person.

The next day Mr. Martin followed his routine, as usual. He polished his glasses more often and once sharpened an already sharp pencil, but not even Miss Paird noticed. Only once did he catch sight of his victim; she swept past him in the hall with a patronizing "Hi!" At five-thirty he walked home, as usual, and had a glass of milk, as usual. He had never drunk anything stronger in his life—unless you could count ginger ale. The late Sam Schlosser, the S of F & S, had praised Mr. Martin at a staff meeting several years before for his temperate habits. "Our most efficient worker neither drinks nor smokes," he had said. "The results speak for themselves." Mr. Fitweiler had sat by, nodding approval.

Mr. Martin was still thinking about that red-letter day as he walked over to the Schrafft's on Fifth Avenue near Forty-Sixth Street. He got there, as he always did, at eight o'clock. He finished his dinner and the financial page of the *Sun* at a quarter to nine, as he always did. It was his custom after dinner to take a walk. This time he walked down Fifth Avenue at a casual pace. His gloved hands felt moist and warm, his forehead cold. He transferred the Camels from his overcoat to a jacket pocket. He wondered, as he did so, if they did not represent an unnecessary note of strain. Mrs. Barrows smoked only Luckies. It was his idea to puff a few puffs on a Camel (after the rubbing-out), stub it out in the ashtray holding her lipstick-stained Luckies, and thus drag a small red herring across the trail. Perhaps it was not a good idea. It would take time. He might even choke, too loudly.

Mr. Martin had never seen the house on West Twelfth Street where Mrs. Barrows lived, but he had a clear enough picture of it. Fortunately, she had bragged to everybody about her ducky first-floor apartment in the perfectly darling three-story red-brick. There could be no doorman or other attendants; just the tenants of the second and third floors. As he walked along, Mr. Martin realized that he would get there before nine-thirty. He had considered walking north on Fifth Avenue from Schrafft's to a point from which it would take him until ten o'clock to reach the house. At that hour people were less likely to be coming in or going out. But the procedure would have an awkward loop in the straight thread of his casualness, and he had abandoned it. It was impossible to figure when people would be entering or leaving the house, anyway. There was a great risk at any hour. If he ran into anybody, he would simply have to place the rubbing-out of Ulgine Barrows in the inactive file forever. The same thing would hold true if there were someone in her apartment. In that case he would just say that he had been passing by, recognized her charming house, and thought to drop in.

It was eighteen minutes after nine when Mr. Martin turned into Twelfth Street. A man passed him, and a man and a woman, talking. There was no one within fifty paces when he came to the house, halfway down the block. He was up the steps and in the small vestibule in no time, pressing the bell under the card that said "Mrs. Ulgine Barrows." When the clicking in the lock started, he jumped forward against the door. He got inside fast, closing the door behind him. A bulb in a lantern hung from the hall ceiling on a chain seemed to give a monstrously bright light. There was nobody on the stair, which went up ahead of him along the left wall. A door opened down the hall in the wall on the right. He went toward it swiftly, on tiptoe.

"Well, for God's sake, look who's here!" bawled Mrs. Barrows, and her braying laugh rang out like the report of a shotgun. He rushed past her like a football tackle, bumping her. "Hey, quit shoving!" she said, closing the door behind them. They were in her living room, which seemed to Mr. Martin to be lighted by a hundred lamps. "What's after you?" she said. "You're as jumpy as a goat." He found he was unable to speak. His heart was wheezing in his throat. "I—yes," he finally brought out. She was jabbering and laughing as she started to help him off with his coat. "No, no," he said. "I'll put it here." He took it off and put it on a chair near the door. "Your hat and gloves, too," she said. "You're in a lady's house." He put his hat on top of the coat. Mrs. Barrows seemed larger than he had thought. He kept his gloves on. "I was passing by," he said. "I recognized—is there anyone here?" She laughed louder than ever. "No," she said, "we're all alone. You're as white as a sheet, you funny man. Whatever *has* come over you? I'll mix you a toddy." She started toward a door across the room. "Scotch-and-soda be all right? But say, you don't drink, do you?" She turned and gave him her amused look. Mr. Martin pulled himself together. "Scotch-and-soda will be all right," he heard himself say. He could hear her laughing in the kitchen.

Mr. Martin looked quickly around the living room for the weapon. He had counted on finding one there. There were andirons and a poker and something in a corner that looked like an Indian club. None of them would do. It couldn't be that way. He began to pace around. He came to a desk. On it lay a metal paper knife with an ornate handle. Would it be sharp enough? He reached for it and knocked over a small brass jar. Stamps spilled out of it and it fell to the floor with a clatter. "Hey," Mrs. Barrows yelled from the kitchen, "are you tearing up the pea patch?" Mr. Martin gave a strange laugh. Picking up the knife, he tried its point against his left wrist. It was blunt. It wouldn't do.

When Mrs. Barrows reappeared, carrying two highballs, Mr. Martin, standing there with his gloves on, became acutely conscious of the fantasy he had wrought. Cigarettes in his pocket, a drink prepared for him—it was all too grossly improbable. It was more than that; it was impossible. Somewhere in the back of his mind a vague idea stirred, sprouted. "For heaven's sake, take off those gloves," said Mrs. Barrows. "I always wear them in the house," said Mr. Martin. The idea began to bloom, strange and wonderful. She put the glasses on a coffee table in front of a sofa and sat on the sofa. "Come over here, you odd little man," she said. Mr. Martin went over and sat beside her. It was difficult getting a cigarette out of the pack of Camels, but he managed it. She held a match for him, laughing. "Well," she said, handing him his drink, "this is perfectly marvelous. You with a drink and a cigarette."

Mr. Martin puffed, not too awkwardly, and took a gulp of the highball. "I drink and smoke all the time," he said. He clinked his glass against hers. "Here's nuts to that old windbag, Fitweiler," he said, and gulped again. The stuff tasted awful, but he made no grimace. "Really, Mr. Martin," she said, her voice and posture changing, "you are insulting our employer." Mrs. Barrows was now all special adviser to the president. "I am preparing a bomb," said Mr. Martin, "which will blow the old goat higher than hell." He had only had a little of the drink, which was not strong. It couldn't be that. "Do you take dope or something?" Mrs. Barrows asked coldly. "Heroin," said Mr. Martin. "I'll be coked to the gills when I bump that old buzzard off." "Mr. Martin!" she shouted, getting to her feet. "That will be all of that. You must go at once." Mr. Martin took another swallow of his drink. He tapped his cigarette out in the ashtray and put the pack of Camels on the coffee table. Then he got up. She stood glaring at him. He walked over and put on his hat and coat. "Not a word about this," he said, and laid an index finger against his lips. All Mrs. Barrows could bring out was "Really!" Mr. Martin put his hand on the doorknob. "I'm sitting in the catbird seat," he said. He stuck his tongue out at her and left. Nobody saw him go.

Mr. Martin got to his apartment, walking, well before eleven. No one saw him go in. He had two glasses of milk after brushing his teeth, and he felt elated. It wasn't tipsiness, because he hadn't been tipsy. Anyway, the walk had worn off all effects of the whiskey. He got in bed and read a magazine for a while. He was asleep before midnight.

Mr. Martin got to the office at eight-thirty the next morning, as usual. At a quarter to nine, Ulgine Barrows, who had never before arrived at work before ten, swept into his office. "I'm reporting to Mr. Fitweiler now!" she shouted. "If he turns you over to the police, it's no more than you deserve!" Mr. Martin gave her a look of shocked surprise. "I beg your pardon?" he said. Mrs. Barrows snorted and bounced out of the room, leaving Miss Paird and Joey Hart staring after her. "What's the matter with that old devil now?" asked Miss Paird. "I have no idea," said Mr. Martin, resuming his work. The other two looked at him and then at each other. Miss Paird got up and went out. She walked slowly past the closed door of Mr. Fitweiler's office. Mrs. Barrows was yelling inside, but she was not braying. Miss Paird could not hear what the woman was saying. She went back to her desk.

Forty-five minutes later, Mrs. Barrows left the president's office and went into her own, shutting the door. It wasn't until half an hour later that Mr. Fitweiler sent for Mr. Martin. The head of the filing department, neat, quiet, attentive, stood in front of the old man's desk. Mr. Fitweiler was pale and nervous. He took his glasses off and twiddled them. He made a small, bruffing sound in his throat. "Martin," he said, "you have been with us more than twenty years." "Twenty-two, sir," said Mr. Martin. "In that time," pursued the president, "your work and your—uh—manner have been exemplary." "I trust so, sir," said Mr. Martin. "I have understood, Martin," said Mr. Fitweiler, "that you have never taken a drink or smoked." "That is correct, sir," said Mr. Martin. "Ah, yes." Mr. Fitweiler polished his glasses. "You may describe what you did after leaving the office yesterday, Martin," he said. Mr. Martin allowed less than a second for his bewildered pause. "Certainly, sir," he said. "I walked home. Then I went to Schrafft's for dinner. Afterward I walked home again. I went to bed early, sir, and read a magazine for a while. I was asleep before eleven." "Ah, yes," said Mr. Fitweiler again. He was silent for a moment, searching for the proper words to say to the head of the filing department. "Mrs. Barrows," he said finally, "Mrs. Barrows has worked hard, Martin, very hard. It grieves me to report that she has suffered a severe breakdown. It has taken the form of a persecution complex accompanied by distressing hallucinations." "I am very sorry, sir," said Mr. Martin. "Mrs. Barrows is under the delusion," continued Mr. Fitweiler, "that you visited her last evening and behaved yourself in an—uh—unseemly manner." He raised his hand to silence Mr. Martin's little pained outcry. "It is the nature of these psychological diseases," Mr. Fitweiler said, "to fix upon the least likely and most innocent party as the—uh—source of persecution. These matters are not for the lay mind to grasp, Martin. I've just had my psychiatrist, Doctor Fitch, on the phone. He would not, of course, commit himself, but he made enough generalizations to substantiate my suspicions. I suggested to Mrs. Barrows, when she had completed her—uh—story to me this morning, that she visit Doctor Fitch, for I suspected a condition at once. She flew, I regret to say, into a rage, and demanded—uh—requested that I call you on the carpet. You may not know, Martin, but Mrs. Barrows had planned a reorganization of your department—subject to my approval, of course, subject to my approval. This brought you, rather than anyone else, to her mind—but again that is a phenomenon for Doctor Fitch and not for us. So, Martin, I am afraid Mrs. Barrows' usefulness here is at an end." "I am dreadfully sorry, sir," said Mr. Martin.

It was at this point that the door to the office blew open with the suddenness of a gas-main explosion and Mrs. Barrows catapulted through it. "Is the little rat denying it?" she screamed. "He can't get away with that!"

Mr. Martin got up and moved discreetly to a point beside Mr. Fitweiler's chair. "You drank and smoked at my apartment," she bawled at Mr. Martin, "and you know it! You called Mr. Fitweiler an old windbag and said you were going to blow him up when you got coked to the gills on your heroin!" She stopped yelling to catch her breath and a new glint came into her popping eyes. "If you weren't such a drab, ordinary little man," she said, "I'd think you'd planned it all. Sticking your tongue out, saying you were sitting in the catbird seat, because you thought no one would believe me when I told it! My God, it's really too perfect!" She brayed loudly and hysterically, and the fury was on her again. She glared at Mr. Fitweiler. "Can't you see how he has tricked us, you old fool? Can't you see his little game?" But Mr. Fitweiler had been surreptitiously pressing all the buttons under the top of his desk and employees of F & S began pouring into the room. "Stockton," said Mr. Fitweiler, "you and Fishbein will take Mrs. Barrows to her home. Mrs. Powell, you will go with them." Stockton, who had played a little football in high school, blocked Mrs. Barrows as she made for Mr. Martin. It took him and Fishbein together to force her out of the door into the hall, crowded with stenographers and office boys. She was still screaming imprecations at Mr. Martin, tangled and contradictory imprecations. The hubbub finally died out down the corridor.

"I regret that this has happened," said Mr. Fitweiler. "I shall ask you to dismiss it from your mind, Martin." "Yes, sir," said Mr. Martin, anticipating his chief's "That will be all" by moving to the door. "I will dismiss it." He went out and shut the door, and his step was light and quick in the hall. When he entered his department he had slowed down to his customary gait, and he walked quietly across the room to the W20 file, wearing a look of studious concentration.   [1942]

RALPH ELLISON

*R*alph Ellison (1914–1994) was born in Oklahoma City, Oklahoma. When he was three his father, a small-time vendor of ice and coal, died, and thereafter his mother worked as a domestic servant to support herself and her son. Ellison later credited his mother, who recruited black votes for the Socialist Party, for turning him into an activist. She also brought home discarded books and phonograph records from the white households where she worked, and as a boy Ellison developed an interest in literature and music. He played trumpet in his high school band at the same time that he began to relate the works of fiction he was reading to real life. "I began to look at my own life through the lives of fictional characters. When I read Stendhal, I would search until I began to find patterns of a Stendhalian novel within the Negro communities in which I grew up. I began, in other words, quite early to connect the worlds projected in literature . . . with the life in which I found myself."

In 1933 Ellison entered Tuskegee Institute in Alabama, where he studied music for three years. Then he went to New York City and met the black writers Langston Hughes and Richard Wright, whose encouragement helped him to become a writer. Wright turned Ellison's attention to writing short stories and reading "those works in which writing was discussed as a craft . . . to Henry James's prefaces, to Conrad," and to other authors. In 1939 Ellison's short stories, essays, and reviews began to appear in periodicals. "Flying Home," which appeared in Cross Section in 1944, is a story from this period. After World War II, he settled down to work on the novel Invisible Man. Published in 1952, it received the National Book Award for fiction, and in 1965, a Book Week poll listed it as the most distinguished American novel of the preceding twenty years. As the critic Richard D. Lyons recognized, the novel was "a chronicle of a young black man's awakening to racial discrimination and his battle against the refusal of Americans to see him apart from his ethnic background, which in turn leads to humiliation and disillusionment."

Insisting that "art by its nature is social," Ellison began Invisible Man with the words "I am an invisible man. No, I am not a spook like those who haunted Edgar Allan Poe; nor am I one of your Hollywood-movie ectoplasms. I am a man of substance, of flesh and bone, fiber and liquids—and I might even be said to possess a mind. I am invisible, understand, simply because people refuse to see me." At the time of his death from cancer, Ellison left an unfinished novel started in the late 1950s. His initial work on the manuscript was destroyed in a fire, and it was difficult for him to complete the book. In addition to Invisible Man, Ellison published two collections of essays, Shadow and Act (1964) and Going to the Territory (1986). He also held a chair as Albert Schweitzer Professor of Contemporary Literature and Culture at New York University. Flying Home and Other Stories was published in 1996.

Flying Home

When Todd came to, he saw two faces suspended above him in a sun so hot and blinding that he could not tell if they were black or white. He stirred, feeling a pain that burned as though his whole body had been laid open to the sun which glared into his eyes. For a moment an old fear of being touched by white hands seized him. Then the very sharpness of the pain began slowly to clear his head. Sounds came to him dimly. He done come to. Who are they? he thought. Naw he ain't, I coulda sworn he was white. Then he heard clearly:

"You hurt bad?"

Something within him uncoiled. It was a Negro sound.

"He's still out," he heard.

"Give 'im time. . . . Say, son, you hurt bad?"

Was he? There was that awful pain. He lay rigid, hearing their breathing and trying to weave a meaning between them and his being stretched painfully upon the ground. He watched them warily, his mind traveling back over a painful distance. Jagged scenes, swiftly unfolding as in a movie trailer, reeled through his mind, and he saw himself piloting a tailspinning plane and landing and landing and falling from the cockpit and trying to stand. Then, as in a great silence, he remembered the sound of crunching bone, and now, looking up into the anxious faces of an old Negro man and a boy from where he lay in the same field, the memory sickened him and he wanted to remember no more.

"How you feel, son?"

Todd hesitated, as though to answer would be to admit an inacceptable weakness. Then, "It's my ankle," he said.

"Which one?"

"The left."

With a sense of remoteness he watched the old man bend and remove his boot, feeling the pressure ease.

"That any better?"

"A lot. Thank you."

He had the sensation of discussing someone else, that his concern was with some far more important thing, which for some reason escaped him.

"You done broke it bad," the old man said. "We have to get you to a doctor."

He felt that he had been thrown into a tailspin. He looked at his watch; how long had he been here? He knew there was but one important thing in the world, to get the plane back to the field before his officers were displeased.

"Help me up," he said. "Into the ship."

"But it's broke too bad. . . ."

"Give me your arm!"

872

"But, son . . ."

Clutching the old man's arm he pulled himself up, keeping his left leg clear, thinking, "I'd never make him understand," as the leather-smooth face came parallel with his own.

"Now, let's see."

He pushed the old man back, hearing a bird's insistent shrill. He swayed giddily. Blackness washed over him, like infinity.

"You best sit down."

"No, I'm O.K."

"But, son. You jus' gonna make it worse. . . ."

It was a fact that everything in him cried out to deny, even against the flaming pain in his ankle. He would have to try again.

"You mess with that ankle they have to cut your foot off," he heard.

Holding his breath, he started up again. It pained so badly that he had to bite his lips to keep from crying out and he allowed them to help him down with a pang of despair.

"It's best you take it easy. We gon' git you a doctor."

Of all the luck, he thought. Of all the rotten luck, now I have done it. The fumes of high-octane gasoline clung in the heat, taunting him.

"We kin ride him into town on old Ned," the boy said.

Ned? He turned, seeing the boy point toward an ox team browsing where the buried blade of a plow marked the end of a furrow. Thoughts of himself riding an ox through the town, past streets full of white faces, down the concrete runways of the airfield made swift images of humiliation in his mind. With a pang he remembered his girl's last letter. "Todd," she had written, "I don't need the papers to tell me you had the intelligence to fly. And I have always known you to be as brave as anyone else. The papers annoy me. Don't you be contented to prove over and over again that you're brave or skillful just because you're black, Todd. I think they keep beating that dead horse because they don't want to say why you boys are not yet fighting. I'm really disappointed, Todd. Anyone with brains can learn to fly, but then what? What about using it, and who will you use it for? I wish, dear, you'd write about this. I sometimes think they're playing a trick on us. It's very humiliating. . . ." He wiped cold sweat from his face, thinking, What does she know of humiliation? She's never been down South. Now the humiliation would come. When you must have them judge you, knowing that they never accept your mistakes as your own, but hold it against your whole race—that was humiliation. Yes, and humiliation was when you could never be simply yourself, when you were always a part of this old black ignorant man. Sure, he's all right. Nice and kind and helpful. But he's not you. Well, there's one humiliation I can spare myself.

"No," he said, "I have orders not to leave the ship. . . ."

"Aw," the old man said. Then turning to the boy, "Teddy, then you better hustle down to Mister Graves and get him to come. . . ."

"No, wait!" he protested before he was fully aware. Graves might be white. "Just have him get word to the field, please. They'll take care of the rest."

He saw the boy leave, running.

"How far does he have to go?"

"Might' nigh a mile."

He rested back, looking at the dusty face of his watch. But now they know something has happened, he thought. In the ship there was a perfectly good radio, but it was useless. The old fellow would never operate it. That buzzard knocked me back a hundred years, he thought. Irony danced within him like the gnats circling the old man's head. With all I've learned I'm dependent upon this "peasant's" sense of time and space. His leg throbbed. In the plane, instead of time being measured by the rhythms of pain and a kid's legs, the instruments would have told him at a glance. Twisting upon his elbows he saw where dust had powdered the plane's fuselage, feeling the lump form in his throat that was always there when he thought of flight. It's crouched there, he thought, like the abandoned shell of a locust. I'm naked without it. Not a machine, a suit of clothes you wear. And with a sudden embarrassment and wonder he whispered, "It's the only dignity I have. . . ."

He saw the old man watching, his torn overalls clinging limply to him in the heat. He felt a sharp need to tell the old man what he felt. But that would be meaningless. If I tried to explain why I need to fly back, he'd think I was simply afraid of white officers. But it's more than fear . . . a sense of anguish clung to him like the veil of sweat that hugged his face. He watched the old man, hearing him humming snatches of a tune as he admired the plane. He felt a furtive sense of resentment. Such old men often came to the field to watch the pilots with childish eyes. At first it had made him proud; they had been a meaningful part of a new experience. But soon he realized they did not understand his accomplishments and they came to shame and embarrass him, like the distasteful praise of an idiot. A part of the meaning of flying had gone then, and he had not been able to regain it. If I were a prizefighter I would be more human, he thought. Not a monkey doing tricks, but a man. They were pleased simply that he was a Negro who could fly, and that was not enough. He felt cut off from them by age, by understanding, by sensibility, by technology and by his need to measure himself against the mirror of other men's appreciation. Somehow he felt betrayed, as he had when as a child he grew to discover that his father was dead. Now for him any real appreciation lay with his white officers; and with them he could never be sure. Between ignorant black men and condescending whites, his course of flight seemed mapped by the nature of things away from all needed and natural landmarks. Under some sealed orders, couched in ever more technical and mysterious terms, his path curved swiftly away from both the shame the old man symbolized and the cloudy terrain of white men's regard. Flying blind, he knew but one point of landing and there he would receive his wings. After that the enemy would appreciate his skill and he would assume his deepest meaning, he thought sadly, neither from those who condescended nor from those who praised without understanding, but from the enemy who would recognize his manhood and skill in terms of hate. . . .

He sighed, seeing the oxen making queer, prehistoric shadows against the dry brown earth.

"You just take it easy, son," the old man soothed. "That boy won't take long. Crazy as he is about airplanes."

"I can wait," he said.

"What kinda airplane you call this here'n?"

"An Advanced Trainer," he said, seeing the old man smile. His fingers were like gnarled dark wood against the metal as he touched the low-slung wing.

" 'Bout how fast can she fly?"

"Over two hundred an hour."

"Lawd! That's so fast I bet it don't seem like you moving!"

Holding himself rigid, Todd opened his flying suit. The shade had gone and he lay in a ball of fire.

"You mind if I take a look inside? I was always curious to see. . . ."

"Help yourself. Just don't touch anything."

He heard him climb upon the metal wing, grunting. Now the questions would start. Well, so you don't have to think to answer. . . .

He saw the old man looking over into the cockpit, his eyes bright as a child's.

"You must have to know a lot to work all these here things."

He was silent, seeing him step down and kneel beside him.

"Son, how come you want to fly way up there in the air?"

Because it's the most meaningful act in the world . . . because it makes me less like you, he thought.

But he said: "Because I like it, I guess. It's as good a way to fight and die as I know."

"Yeah? I guess you right," the old man said. "But how long you think before they gonna let you all fight?"

He tensed. This was the question all Negroes asked, put with the same timid hopefulness and longing that always opened a greater void within him than that he had felt beneath the plane the first time he had flown. He felt light-headed. It came to him suddenly that there was something sinister about the conversation, that he was flying unwillingly into unsafe and uncharted regions. If he could only be insulting and tell this old man who was trying to help him to shut up!

"I bet you one thing . . ."

"Yes?"

"That you was plenty scared coming down."

He did not answer. Like a dog on a trail the old man seemed to smell out his fears and he felt anger bubble within him.

"You sho' scared me. When I seen you coming down in that thing with it a-rollin' and a-jumpin' like a pitchin' hoss, I thought sho' you was a goner. I almost had me a stroke!"

He saw the old man grinning, "Ever'thin's been happening round here this morning, come to think of it."

"Like what?" he asked.

"Well, first thing I know, here come two white fellers looking for Mister Rudolph, that's Mister Graves's cousin. That got me worked up right away. . . ."

"Why?"

"Why? 'Cause he done broke outta the crazy house, that's why. He liable to kill somebody," he said. "They oughta have him by now though. Then here you come. First I think it's one of them white boys. Then doggone if you don't fall outta there. Lawd, I'd done heard about you boys but I haven't never seen one o' you-all. Cain't tell you how it felt to see somebody what look like me in a airplane!"

The old man talked on, the sound streaming around Todd's thoughts like air flowing over the fuselage of a flying plane. You were a fool, he thought, remembering how before the spin the sun had blazed bright against the billboard signs beyond the town, and how a boy's blue kite had bloomed beneath him, tugging gently in the wind like a strange, odd-shaped flower. He had once flown such kites himself and tried to find the boy at the end of the invisible cord. But he had been flying too high and too fast. He had climbed steeply away in exultation. Too steeply, he thought. And one of the first rules you learn is that if the angle of thrust is too steep the plane goes into a spin. And then, instead of pulling out of it and going into a dive you let a buzzard panic you. A lousy buzzard!

"Son, what made all that blood on the glass?"

"A buzzard," he said, remembering how the blood and feathers had sprayed back against the hatch. It had been as though he had flown into a storm of blood and blackness.

"Well, I declare! They's lots of 'em around here. They after dead things. Don't eat nothing what's alive."

"A little bit more and he would have made a meal out of me," Todd said grimly.

"They bad luck all right. Teddy's got a name for 'em, calls 'em jim-crows," the old man laughed.

"It's a damned good name."

"They the damnedest birds. Once I seen a hoss all stretched out like he was sick, you know. So I hollers, 'Gid up from there, suh!' Just to make sho! An' doggone, son, if I don't see two ole jimcrows come flying right up outa that hoss's insides! Yessuh! The sun was shinin' on 'em and they couldn't a been no greasier if they'd been eating barbecue."

Todd thought he would vomit, his stomach quivered.

"You made that up," he said.

"Nawsuh! Saw him just like I see you."

"Well, I'm glad it was you."

"You see lots a funny things down here, son."

"No, I'll let you see them," he said.

"By the way, the white folks round here don't like to see you boys up there in the sky. They ever bother you?"

"No."

"Well, they'd like to."

"Someone always wants to bother someone else," Todd said. "How do you know?"

"I just know."

"Well," he said defensively, "no one has bothered us."

Blood pounded in his ears as he looked away into space. He tensed, seeing a black spot in the sky, and strained to confirm what he could not clearly see.

"What does that look like to you?" he asked excitedly.

"Just another bad luck, son."

Then he saw the movement of wings with disappointment. It was gliding smoothly down, wings outspread, tail feathers gripping the air, down swiftly—gone behind the green screen of trees. It was like a bird he had imagined there, only the sloping branches of the pines remained, sharp against the pale stretch of sky. He lay barely breathing and stared at the point where it had disappeared, caught in a spell of loathing and admiration. Why did they make them so disgusting and yet teach them to fly so well? It's like when I was up in heaven, he heard, starting.

The old man was chuckling, rubbing his stubbled chin.

"What did you say?"

"Sho', I died and went to heaven . . . maybe by time I tell you about it they be done come after you."

"I hope so," he said wearily.

"You boys ever sit around and swap lies?"

"Not often. Is this going to be one?"

"Well, I ain't so sho', on account of it took place when I was dead."

The old man paused, "That wasn't no lie 'bout the buzzards, though."

"All right," he said.

"Sho' you want to hear 'bout heaven?"

"Please," he answered, resting his head upon his arm.

"Well, I went to heaven and right away started to sproutin' me some wings. Six good ones, they was. Just like them the white angels had. I couldn't hardly believe it. I was so glad that I went off on some clouds by myself and tried 'em out. You know, 'cause I didn't want to make a fool outta myself the first thing. . . ."

It's an old tale, Todd thought. Told me years ago. Had forgotten. But at least it will keep him from talking about buzzards.

He closed his eyes, listening.

". . . First thing I done was to git up on a low cloud and jump off. And doggone, boy, if them wings didn't work! First I tried the right; then I tried the left; then I tried 'em both together. Then Lawd, I started to move on out among the folks. I let 'em see me. . . ."

He saw the old man gesturing flight with his arms, his face full of mock pride as he indicated an imaginary crowd, thinking, It'll be in the newspapers, as he heard, ". . . so I went and found me some colored angels—somehow I didn't believe I was an angel till I seen a real black one, ha, yes! Then I was sho'—but they tole me I better come down 'cause us colored folks had to wear a special kin' a harness when we flew. That was how come they wasn't flyin'. Oh yes, an' you had to be extra strong for a black man even, to fly with one of them harnesses. . . ."

This is a new turn, Todd thought, what's he driving at?

"So I said to myself, I ain't gonna be bothered with no harness! Oh naw! 'Cause if God let you sprout wings you oughta have sense enough not to let nobody make you wear something what gits in the way of flyin'. So I starts to flyin'. Heck, son," he chuckled, his eyes twinkling, "you know I had to let eve'ybody know that old Jefferson could fly good as anybody else. And I could too, fly smooth as a bird! I could even loop-the-loop—only I had to make sho' to keep my long white robe down roun' my ankles. . . ."

Todd felt uneasy. He wanted to laugh at the joke, but his body refused, as of an independent will. He felt as he had as a child when after he had chewed a sugar-coated pill which his mother had given him, she had laughed at his efforts to remove the terrible taste.

". . . Well," he heard, "I was doing all right 'til I got to speeding. Found out I could fan up a right strong breeze, I could fly so fast. I could do all kin'sa stunts too. I started flying up to the stars and divin' down and zooming roun' the moon. Man, I like to scare the devil outa some ole white angels. I was raisin' hell. Not that I meant any harm, son. But I was just feeling good. It was so good to know I was free at last. I accidentally knocked the tips offa some stars and they tell me I caused a storm and a coupla lynchings down here in Macon County—though I swear I believe them boys what said that was making up lies on me. . . ."

He's mocking me, Todd thought angrily. He thinks it's a joke. Grinning down at me . . . His throat was dry. He looked at his watch; why the hell didn't they come? Since they had to, why? One day I was flying down one of them heavenly streets. You got yourself into it, Todd thought. Like Jonah in the whale.

"Justa throwin' feathers in everybody's face. An' ole Saint Peter called me in. Said, 'Jefferson, tell me two things, what you doin' flyin' without a harness; an' how come you flyin' so fast?' So I tole him I was flyin' without a harness 'cause it got in my way, but I couldn'ta been flyin' so fast, 'cause I wasn't usin' but one wing. Saint Peter said, 'You wasn't flyin' with but one wing?' 'Yessuh,' I says, scared-like. So he says, 'Well, since you got such a extra fine pair of wings you can leave off yo' harness awhile. But from now on none of that there one-wing flyin', 'cause you gittin' up too damn much speed!' "

And with one mouth full of bad teeth you're making too damned much talk, thought Todd. Why don't I send him after the boy? His body ached from the hard ground and seeking to shift his position he twisted his ankle and hated himself for crying out.

"It gittin' worse?"

"I . . . I twisted it," he groaned.

"Try not to think about it, son. That's what I do."

He bit his lip, fighting pain with counter-pain as the voice resumed its rhythmical droning. Jefferson seemed caught in his own creation.

". . . After all that trouble I just floated roun' heaven in slow motion. But I forgot, like colored folks will do, and got to flyin' with one wing again. This time I was restin' my old broken arm and got to flyin' fast enough to shame the devil. I was comin' so fast, Lawd, I got myself called befo' ole Saint Peter again. He said, 'Jeff, didn't I warn you 'bout that speedin'?' 'Yessuh,' I says, 'but it was an accident!' He looked at me sad-like and shook his head and I knowed I was gone. He said, 'Jeff, you and that speedin' is a danger to the heavenly community. If I was to let you keep on flyin', heaven wouldn't be nothin' but uproar. Jeff, you got to go!' Son, I argued and pleaded with that old white man, but it didn't do a bit of good. They rushed me straight to them pearly gates and gimme a parachute and a map of the state of Alabama . . ."

Todd heard him laughing so that he could hardly speak, making a screen between them upon which his humiliation glowed like fire.

"Maybe you'd better stop awhile," he said, his voice unreal.

"Ain't much more," Jefferson laughed. "When they gimme the parachute ole Saint Peter ask me if I wanted to say a few words before I went. I felt so bad I couldn't hardly look at him, specially with all them white angels standin' around. Then somebody laughed and made me mad. So I tole him, 'Well, you done took my wings. And you puttin' me out. You got charge of things so's I can't do nothin' about it. But you got to admit just this: While I was up here I was the flyinest sonofabitch what ever hit heaven!' "

At the burst of laughter Todd felt such an intense humiliation that only great violence would wash it away. The laughter which shook the old man like a boiling purge set up vibrations of guilt within him which not even the intricate machinery of the plane would have been adequate to transform and he heard himself screaming, "Why do you laugh at me this way?"

He hated himself at that moment, but he had lost control. He saw Jefferson's mouth fall open, "What—?"

"Answer me!"

His blood pounded as though it would surely burst his temples and he tried to reach the old man and fell, screaming, "Can I help it because they won't let us actually fly? Maybe we are a bunch of buzzards feeding on a dead horse, but we can hope to be eagles, can't we? Can't we?"

He fell back, exhausted, his ankle pounding. The saliva was like straw in his mouth. If he had the strength he would strangle this old man. This grinning, gray-headed clown who made him feel as he felt when watched by the white officers at the field. And yet this old man had neither power, prestige, rank nor technique. Nothing that could rid him of this terrible feeling. He watched him, seeing his face struggle to express a turmoil of feeling.

"What you mean, son? What you talking 'bout . . . ?"

"Go away. Go tell your tales to the white folks."

"But I didn't mean nothing like that. . . . I . . . I wasn't tryin' to hurt your feelings. . . ."

"Please. Get the hell away from me!"

"But I didn't, son. I didn't mean all them things a-tall."

Todd shook as with a chill, searching Jefferson's face for a trace of the mockery he had seen there. But now the face was somber and tired and old. He was confused. He could not be sure that there had ever been laughter there, that Jefferson had ever really laughed in his whole life. He saw Jefferson reach out to touch him and shrank away, wondering if anything except the pain, now causing his vision to waver, was real. Perhaps he had imagined it all.

"Don't let it get you down, son," the voice said pensively.

He heard Jefferson sigh wearily, as though he felt more than he could say. His anger ebbed, leaving only the pain.

"I'm sorry," he mumbled.

"You just wore out with pain, was all. . . ."

He saw him through a blur, smiling. And for a second he felt the embarrassed silence of understanding flutter between them.

"What you was doin' flyin' over this section, son? Wasn't you scared they might shoot you for a crow?"

Todd tensed. Was he being laughed at again? But before he could decide, the pain shook him and a part of him was lying calmly behind the screen of pain that had fallen between them, recalling the first time he had ever seen a plane. It was as though an endless series of hangars had been shaken ajar in the air base of his memory and from each, like a young wasp emerging from its cell, arose the memory of a plane.

The first time I ever saw a plane I was very small and planes were new in the world. I was four-and-a-half and the only plane that I had ever seen was a model suspended from the ceiling of the automobile exhibit at the State Fair. But I did not know that it was only a model. I did not know how large a real plane was, nor how expensive. To me it was a fascinating toy, complete in itself, which my mother said could only be owned by rich little white boys. I stood rigid with admiration, my head straining backwards as I watched the gray little plane describing arcs above the gleaming tops of the automobiles. And I vowed that, rich or poor, someday I would own such a toy. My mother had to drag me out of the exhibit and not even the merry-go-round, the Ferris wheel, or the racing horses could hold my attention for the rest of the Fair. I was too busy imitating the tiny drone of the plane with my lips, and imitating with my hands the motion, swift and circling, that it made in flight.

After that I no longer used the pieces of lumber that lay about our back yard to construct wagons and autos . . . now it was used for airplanes. I built biplanes, using pieces of board for wings, a small box for the fuselage, another piece of wood for the rudder. The trip to the Fair had brought something new into my small world. I asked my mother repeatedly when the Fair would come back again. I'd lie in the grass and watch the sky, and each fighting bird became a soaring plane. I would have been good a year just to have seen a plane again. I became a nuisance to everyone with my questions about airplanes. But planes were new to the old folks, too, and there was little that they could tell me. Only my uncle knew some of the answers. And better still, he could carve propellers from pieces of wood that would whirl rapidly in the wind, wobbling noisily upon oiled nails.

I wanted a plane more than I'd wanted anything; more than I wanted the red wagon with rubber tires, more than the train that ran on a track with its train of cars. I asked my mother over and over again:

"Mamma?"

"What do you want, boy?" she'd say.

"Mamma, will you get mad if I ask you?" I'd say.

"What do you want now? I ain't got time to be answering a lot of fool questions. What you want?"

"Mamma, when you gonna get me one . . . ?" I'd ask.

"Get you one what?" she'd say.

"You know, Mamma; what I been asking you. . . ."

"Boy," she'd say, "if you don't want a spanking you better come on an' tell me what you talking about so I can get on with my work."

"Aw, Mamma, you know. . . ."

"What I just tell you?" she'd say.

"I mean when you gonna buy me a airplane."

"Airplane! Boy, is you crazy? How many times I have to tell you to stop that foolishness. I done told you them things cost too much. I bet I'm gon' wham the living daylight out of you if you don't quit worrying me 'bout them things!"

But this did not stop me, and a few days later I'd try all over again.

Then one day a strange thing happened. It was spring and for some reason I had been hot and irritable all morning. It was a beautiful spring. I could feel it as I played barefoot in the backyard. Blossoms hung from the thorny black locust trees like clusters of fragrant white grapes. Butterflies flickered in the sunlight above the short new dew-wet grass. I had gone in the house for bread and butter and coming out I heard a steady unfamiliar drone. It was unlike anything I had ever heard before. I tried to place the sound. It was no use. It was a sensation like that I had when searching for my father's watch, heard ticking unseen in a room. It made me feel as though I had forgotten to perform some task that my mother had ordered . . . then I located it, overhead. In the sky, flying quite low and about a hundred yards off was a plane! It came so slowly that it seemed barely to move. My mouth hung wide; my bread and butter fell into the dirt. I wanted to jump up and down and cheer. And when the idea struck I trembled with excitement: "Some little white boy's plane's done flew away and all I got to do is stretch out my hands and it'll be mine!" It was a little plane like that at the Fair, flying no higher than the eaves of our roof. Seeing it come steadily forward I felt the world grow warm with promise. I opened the screen and climbed over it and clung there, waiting. I would catch the plane as it came over and swing down fast and run into the house before anyone could see me. Then no one could come to claim the plane. It droned nearer. Then when it hung like a silver cross in the blue directly above me I stretched out my hand and grabbed. It was like sticking my finger through a soap bubble. The plane flew on, as though I had simply blown my breath after it. I grabbed again, frantically, trying to catch the tail. My fingers clutched the air and disappointment surged tight and hard in my throat. Giving one last desperate grasp, I strained forward. My fingers ripped from the screen. I was falling. The ground burst hard against me. I drummed the earth with my heels and when my breath returned, I lay there bawling.

My mother rushed through the door.

"What's the matter, chile! What on earth is wrong with you?"

"It's gone! It's gone!"

"What gone?"

"The airplane . . ."

"Airplane?"

"Yessum, jus' like the one at the Fair. . . . I . . . I tried to stop it an' it kep' right on going. . . ."

"When, boy?"

"Just now," I cried, through my tears.

"Where it go, boy, what way?"

"Yonder, there . . ."

She scanned the sky, her arms akimbo and her checkered apron flapping in the wind as I pointed to the fading plane. Finally she looked down at me, slowly shaking her head.

"It's gone! It's gone!" I cried.

"Boy, is you a fool?" she said. "Don't you see that there's a real airplane 'stead of one of them toy ones?"

"Real . . . ?" I forgot to cry. "Real?"

"Yass, real. Don't you know that thing you reaching for is bigger'n a auto? You here trying to reach for it and I bet it's flying 'bout two hundred miles higher'n this roof." She was disgusted with me. "You come on in this house before somebody else sees what a fool you done turned out to be. You must think these here lil ole arms of you'n is mighty long. . . ."

I was carried into the house and undressed for bed and the doctor was called. I cried bitterly, as much from the disappointment of finding the plane so far beyond my reach as from the pain.

When the doctor came I heard my mother telling him about the plane and asking if anything was wrong with my mind. He explained that I had had a fever for several hours. But I was kept in bed for a week and I constantly saw the plane in my sleep, flying just beyond my fingertips, sailing so slowly that it seemed barely to move. And each time I'd reach out to grab it I'd miss and through each dream I'd hear my grandma warning:

> *Young man, young man,*
> *Yo' arms too short*
> *To box with God. . . .*

"Hey, son!"

At first he did not know where he was and looked at the old man pointing, with blurred eyes.

"Ain't that one of you-all's airplanes coming after you?"

As his vision cleared he saw a small black shape above a distant field, soaring through waves of heat. But he could not be sure and with the pain he feared that somehow a horrible recurring fantasy of being split in twain by the whirling blades of a propeller had come true.

"You think he sees us?" he heard.

"See? I hope so."

"He's coming like a bat outa hell!"

Straining, he heard the faint sound of a motor and hoped it would soon be over.

"How you feeling?"

"Like a nightmare," he said.

"Hey, he's done curved back the other way!"

"Maybe he saw us," he said. "Maybe he's gone to send out the ambulance and ground crew." And, he thought with despair, maybe he didn't even see us.

"Where did you send the boy?"

"Down to Mister Graves," Jefferson said. "Man what owns this land."

"Do you think he phoned?"

Jefferson looked at him quickly.

"Aw sho'. Dabney Graves is got a bad name on accounta them killings but he'll call though. . . ."

"What killings?"

"Them five fellers . . . ain't you heard?" he asked with surprise.

"No."

"Everybody knows 'bout Dabney Graves, especially the colored. He done killed enough of us."

Todd had the sensation of being caught in a white neighborhood after dark.

"What did they do?" he asked.

"Thought they was men," Jefferson said. "An' some he owed money, like he do me. . . ."

"But why do you stay here?"

"You black, son."

"I know, but . . ."

"You have to come by the white folks, too."

He turned away from Jefferson's eyes, at once consoled and accused. And I'll have to come by them soon, he thought with despair. Closing his eyes, he heard Jefferson's voice as the sun burned blood-red upon his lips.

"I got nowhere to go," Jefferson said, "an' they'd come after me if I did. But Dabney Graves is a funny fellow. He's all the time making jokes. He can be mean as hell, then he's liable to turn right around and back the colored against the white folks. I seen him do it. But me, I hates him for that more'n anything else. 'Cause just as soon as he gits tired helping a man he don't care what happens to him. He just leaves him stone cold. And then the other white folks is double hard on anybody he done helped. For him it's just a joke. He don't give a hilla beans for nobody — but hisself. . . ."

Todd listened to the thread of detachment in the old man's voice. It was as though he held his words arm's length before him to avoid their destructive meaning.

"He'd just as soon do you a favor and then turn right around and have you strung up. Me, I stays outa his way 'cause down here that's what you gotta do."

If my ankle would only ease for a while, he thought. The closer I spin toward the earth the blacker I become, flashed through his mind. Sweat ran into his eyes and he was sure that he would never see the plane if his head continued whirling. He tried to see Jefferson, what it was that Jefferson held in his hand. It was a little black man, another Jefferson! A little black Jefferson that shook with fits of belly-laughter while the other Jefferson looked on with detachment. Then Jefferson looked up from the thing in his hand and turned to speak, but Todd was far away, searching the sky for a plane in a hot dry land on a day and age he had long forgotten. He was going mysteriously with his mother through empty streets where black faces peered from behind drawn shades and someone was rapping at a window and he was looking back to see a hand and a frightened face frantically beckoning from a cracked door and his mother was looking down the empty perspective of the street and shaking her head and hurrying him along and at first it was only a flash he saw and a motor was droning as through the sun-glare he saw it gleaming silver as it circled and he was seeing a burst like a puff of white smoke and hearing his mother yell, Come along, boy, I got no time for them fool airplanes, I got no time, and he saw it a second time, the plane flying high, and the burst appeared suddenly and fell slowly, billowing out and sparkling like fireworks and he was watching and being hurried along as the air filled with a flurry of white pinwheeling cards that caught in the wind and scattered over the rooftops and into the gutters and a woman was running and snatching a card and reading it and screaming and he darted into the shower, grabbing as in winter he grabbed for snowflakes and bounding away at his mother's, Come on here, boy! Come on, I say! and he was watching as she took the card away, seeing her face grow puzzled and turning taut as her voice quavered, "Niggers Stay From The Polls," and died to a moan of terror as he saw the eyeless sockets of a white hood staring at him from the card and above he saw the plane spiraling gracefully, agleam in the sun like a fiery sword. And seeing it soar he was caught, transfixed between a terrible horror and a horrible fascination.

The sun was not so high now, and Jefferson was calling and gradually he saw three figures moving across the curving roll of the field.

"Look like some doctors, all dressed in white," said Jefferson.

They're coming at last, Todd thought. And he felt such a release of tension within him that he thought he would faint. But no sooner did he close his eyes than he was seized and he was struggling with three white men who were forcing his arms into some kind of coat. It was too much for him, his arms were pinned to his sides and as the pain blazed in his eyes, he realized that it was a straitjacket. What filthy joke was this?

"That oughta hold him, Mister Graves," he heard.

His total energies seemed focused in his eyes as he searched their faces. That was Graves; the other two wore hospital uniforms. He was poised between two poles of fear and hate as he heard the one called Graves saying, "He looks kinda purty in that there suit, boys. I'm glad you dropped by."

"This boy ain't crazy, Mister Graves," one of the others said. "He needs a doctor, not us. Don't see how you led us way out here anyway. It might be a joke to you, but your cousin Rudolph liable to kill somebody. White folks or niggers, don't make no difference. . . ."

Todd saw the man turn red with anger. Graves looked down upon him, chuckling.

"This nigguh belongs in a straitjacket, too, boys. I knowed that the minit Jeff's kid said something 'bout a nigguh flyer. You all know you cain't let the nigguh git up that high without his going crazy. The nigguh brain ain't built right for high altitudes. . . ."

Todd watched the drawling red face, feeling that all the unnamed horror and obscenities that he had ever imagined stood materialized before him.

"Let's git outta here," one of the attendants said.

Todd saw the other reach toward him, realizing for the first time that he lay upon a stretcher as he yelled.

"Don't put your hands on me!"

They drew back, surprised.

"What's that you say, nigguh?" asked Graves.

He did not answer and thought that Graves's foot was aimed at his head. It landed on his chest and he could hardly breathe. He coughed helplessly, seeing Graves's lips stretch taut over his yellow teeth, and tried to shift his head. It was as though a half-dead fly was dragging slowly across his face and a bomb seemed to burst within him. Blasts of hot, hysterical laughter tore from his chest, causing his eyes to pop and he felt that the veins in his neck would surely burst. And then a part of him stood behind it all, watching the surprise in Graves's red face and his own hysteria. He thought he would never stop, he would laugh himself to death. It rang in his ears like Jefferson's laughter and he looked for him, centering his eyes desperately upon his face, as though somehow he had become his sole salvation in an insane world of outrage and humiliation. It brought a certain relief. He was suddenly aware that although his body was still contorted it was an echo that no longer rang in his ears. He heard Jefferson's voice with gratitude.

"Mister Graves, the Army done tole him not to leave his airplane."

"Nigguh, Army or no, you gittin' off my land! That airplane can stay 'cause it was paid for by taxpayers' money. But you gittin' off. An' dead or alive, it don't make no difference to me."

Todd was beyond it now, lost in a world of anguish.

"Jeff," Graves said, "you and Teddy come and grab holt. I want you to take this here black eagle over to that nigguh airfield and leave him."

Jefferson and the boy approached him silently. He looked away, realizing and doubting at once that only they could release him from his overpowering sense of isolation.

They bent for the stretcher. One of the attendants moved toward Teddy.

"Think you can manage it, boy?"

"I think I can, suh," Teddy said.

"Well, you better go behind then, and let yo' pa go ahead so's to keep that leg elevated."

He saw the white men walking ahead as Jefferson and the boy carried him along in silence. Then they were pausing and he felt a hand wiping his face; then he was moving again. And it was as though he had been lifted

out of his isolation, back into the world of men. A new current of communication flowed between the man and boy and himself. They moved him
gently. Far away he heard a mockingbird liquidly calling. He raised his
eyes, seeing a buzzard poised unmoving in space. For a moment the whole
afternoon seemed suspended and he waited for the horror to seize him
again. Then like a song within his head he heard the boy's soft humming
and saw the dark bird glide into the sun and glow like a bird of flaming
gold.   [1944]

GWENDOLYN BROOKS

G̲wendolyn Brooks (b. 1917), one of the most distinguished African American woman poets of the twentieth century, was born in Topeka, Kansas, the granddaughter of a runaway slave who had fought in the Civil War and settled in Oklahoma. Her parents moved to Chicago's South Side soon after her birth. Her father had graduated from high school and hoped to become a doctor, but he worked as a janitor to support his family. Her mother had studied to become a concert pianist and encouraged Brooks's love of poetry after she discovered her daughter writing a page of rhymes at the age of seven. Struck by the originality and clarity of the rhymes, Brooks's mother stated, "You are going to be a poet." Brooks later commented that as a child she "believed every word" her mother said and "just kept on writing." Brooks's childhood was so contented that she wrote in her autobiography, "I had always felt that to be black was good." She first encountered racial prejudice when she entered grammar school, but she found a refuge in her writing, which was first published when she was a teenager. She read the work of Negro poets in Countee Cullen's Caroling Dusk: An Anthology of Verse by Negro Poets *(1927), and she met Langston Hughes and James Weldon Johnson when they gave poetry readings in Chicago. In 1939 she married Henry Lovington Blakely II, and the young married couple moved into a small kitchenette apartment in the Chicago ghetto. The experience brought her in contact for the first time with poverty-stricken, ordinary working-class people. It also furnished the material for her book of linked impressionistic sketches,* Maud Martha *(1953), about a spunky Negro girl growing up in Chicago whose dearest wish is to be cherished.*

Before publishing her only book of fiction, Brooks had won recognition for two volumes of poetry. Her first, A Street in Bronzeville *(1945), won a series of prizes, and she was awarded a Guggenheim Fellowship that allowed her to spend a year devoted entirely to writing. It was at about this time that Brooks first began to think of writing fiction. "We're the only colored people here" is the earliest narrative she wrote, first published as a poem in* Portfolio *in the summer of 1945. In 1949 her second poetry collection,* Annie Allen, *won the Pulitzer Prize, the first time it had been awarded to an African American writer. In 1952, after the birth of her second child, Brooks resumed work on her novel. She regards* Maud Martha *as autobiographical, although her heroine "is a little nicer and a better coordinated creature than I am. . . . The heroine loves dandelions as 'what she chiefly saw . . . and it was comforting to find that what was common was also a flower.'"*

In 1967 Brooks took part in the Second Black Writers' Conference at Fisk University, where she was swept up in the new militancy of the younger generation of black poet activists such as Imamu Amiri Baraka and Don L. Lee (Haki Madhubuti). Her poetry became more specifically political, and finally she turned to alternative publishing so she could have more control over the way her poetry was presented. Throughout her career she taught creative writing at various colleges and universities. She has also established the Illinois Poet Laureate Awards to encourage young writers.

We're the only colored people here

When they went out to the car there were just the very finest bits of white powder coming down, with an almost comical little ethereal hauteur, to add themselves to the really important, piled-up masses of their kind.

And it wasn't cold.

Maud Martha laughed happily to herself. It was pleasant out, and tonight she and Paul were very close to each other.

He held the door open for her — instead of going on round to the driving side, getting in, and leaving her to get in at her side as best she might. When he took this way of calling her "lady" and informing her of his love she felt precious, protected, delicious. She gave him an excited look of gratitude. He smiled indulgently.

"Want it to be the Owl again?"

"Oh, no, no, Paul. Let's not go there tonight. I feel too good inside for that. Let's go downtown?"

She had to suggest that with a question mark at the end, always. He usually had three protests. Too hard to park. Too much money. Too many white folks. And tonight she could almost certainly expect a no, she feared, because he had come out in his blue work shirt. There was a spot of apricot juice on the collar, too. His shoes were not shined.

. . . But he nodded!

"We've never been to the World Playhouse," she said cautiously. "They have a good picture. I'd feel rich in there."

"You really wanta?"

"Please?"

"Sure."

It wasn't like other movie houses. People from the Studebaker Theatre which, as Maud Martha whispered to Paul, was "all-locked-arms" with the World Playhouse, were strolling up and down the lobby, laughing softly, smoking with gentle grace.

"There must be a play going on in there and this is probably an intermission," Maud Martha whispered again.

"I don't know why you feel you got to whisper," whispered Paul. "Nobody else is whispering in here." He looked around, resentfully, wanting to see a few, just a few colored faces. There were only their own.

Maud Martha laughed a nervous defiant little laugh; and spoke loudly. "There certainly isn't any reason to whisper. Silly, huh."

The strolling women were cleverly gowned. Some of them had flowers or flashers in their hair. They looked — cooked. Well cared-for. And as though they had never seen a roach or a rat in their lives. Or gone without heat for a week. And the men had even edges. They were men, Maud Martha thought, who wouldn't stoop to fret over less than a thousand dollars.

"We're the only colored people here," said Paul.

She hated him a little. "Oh, hell. Who in hell cares."

"Well, what I want to know is, where do you pay the damn fares."

"There's the box office. Go on up."

He went on up. It was closed.

"Well," sighed Maud Martha, "I guess the picture has started already. But we can't have missed much. Go on up to that girl at the candy counter and ask her where we should pay our money."

He didn't want to do that. The girl was lovely and blonde and cold-eyed, and her arms were akimbo, and the set of her head was eloquent. No one else was at the counter.

"Well. We'll wait a minute. And see—"

Maud Martha hated him again. Coward. She ought to flounce over to the girl herself—show him up. . . .

The people in the lobby tried to avoid looking curiously at two shy Negroes wanting desperately not to seem shy. The white women looked at the Negro woman in her outfit with which no special fault could be found, but which made them think, somehow, of close rooms, and wee, close lives. They looked at her hair. They were always slightly surprised, but agreeably so, when they did. They supposed it was the hair that had got her that yellowish, good-looking Negro man without a tie.

An usher opened a door of the World Playhouse part and ran quickly down the few steps that led from it to the lobby. Paul opened his mouth.

"Say, fella. Where do we get the tickets for the movie?"

The usher glanced at Paul's feet before answering. Then he said coolly, but not unpleasantly, "I'll take the money."

They were able to go in.

And the picture! Maud Martha was so glad that they had not gone to the Owl! Here was technicolor, and the love story was sweet. And there was classical music that silvered its way into you and made your back cold. And the theater itself! It was no palace, no such Great Shakes as the Tivoli out south, for instance (where many colored people went every night). But you felt good sitting there, yes, good, and as if when you left it you would be going home to a sweet-smelling apartment with flowers on little gleaming tables; and wonderful silver on night-blue velvet, in chests; and crackly sheets; and lace spreads on such beds as you saw at Marshall Field's. Instead of back to your kit'n't apt., with the garbage of your floor's families in a big can just outside your door, and the gray sound of little gray feet scratching away from it as you drag up those flights of narrow complaining stairs.

Paul pressed her hand. Paul said, "We oughta do this more often."

And again. "We'll have to do this more often. And go to plays, too. I mean at that Blackstone, and Studebaker."

She pressed back, smiling beautifully to herself in the darkness. Though she knew that once the spell was over it would be a year, two years, more, before he would return to the World Playhouse. And he might never go to a real play. But she was learning to love moments. To love moments for themselves.

When the picture was over, and the lights revealed them for what they were, the Negroes stood up among the furs and good cloth and faint perfume, looked about them eagerly. They hoped they would meet no cruel eyes. They hoped no one would look intruded upon. They had enjoyed the picture so they were so happy, they wanted to laugh, to say warmly to the other outgoers, "Good, huh? Wasn't it swell?"

This, of course, they could not do. But if only no one would look intruded upon. . . .   [1945]

KAY BOYLE

K*ay Boyle (1902–1992), author of almost forty volumes of fiction, poetry, essays, and translations, was born in St. Paul, Minnesota, and studied as a teenager at the Cincinnati Conservatory of Music. At the age of twenty she fell in love with the French engineer Richard Brault, a veteran of World War I, who graduated from the University of Cincinnati and, as she later wrote in her memoir, shared her hope that "our life together was going to be a confirmation of our impatience with conventions and our commitment to something called freedom in which we believed so passionately."*

After her marriage, Boyle moved to Greenwich Village with her husband, saving money to live in France, a country she revered because she believed it "did not put its socialists in jail, as Eugene Debs was jailed in America, and did not harass its writers." In New York City she worked as a secretary in the office of the experimental literary magazine Broom *for a year before sailing to France, where she published her first short story in an avant-garde literary magazine in 1925. In Paris she became acquainted with such expatriate modernists as Gertrude Stein, James Joyce, Djuna Barnes, Ernest Hemingway, and Robert McAlmon. The memoir Boyle coauthored with McAlmon,* Being Geniuses Together 1920–1930 *(1984)—he wrote an earlier version of the book by himself—is one of our most vivid accounts of the experimental writers' lives in Paris.*

Boyle lived in Europe and published steadily for thirty years, returning to the United States to teach in various colleges. Thrice married, with six children, she was also a political activist deeply committed to pacifist and feminist causes. Reflecting at the end of her long life, she said that "the older I grow, the more I feel that all writers should be more committed to their times and write of their times and of the issues of their times." Boyle's volumes of short stories include The White Horses of Vienna and Other Stories *(1936),* The Smoking Mountain: Stories of Postwar Germany *(1951),* Nothing Ever Breaks Except the Heart *(1966), and* Fifty Stories *(1980). Published in* The New Yorker *in 1946, "Winter Night" is an early story that dramatizes Boyle's concern for social justice and human suffering.*

Winter Night

There is a time of apprehension which begins with the beginning of darkness, and to which only the speech of love can lend security. It is there, in abeyance, at the end of every day, not urgent enough to be given the name of fear but rather of concern for how the hours are to be reprieved from fear, and those who have forgotten how it was when they were children can remember nothing of this. It may begin around five o'clock on a winter afternoon when the light outside is dying in the windows. At that hour the New York apartment in which Felicia lived was filled with shadows, and the little girl would wait alone in the living room, looking out at the winter-stripped trees that stood black in the park against the isolated ovals of unclean snow. Now it was January, and the day had been a cold one; the water of the artificial lake was frozen fast, but because of the cold and the coming darkness, the skaters had ceased to move across its surface. The street that lay between the park and the apartment house was wide, and the two-way streams of cars and busses, some with their headlamps already shining, advanced and halted, halted and poured swiftly on to the tempo of the traffic signals' altering lights. The time of apprehension had set in, and Felicia, who was seven, stood at the window in the evening and waited before she asked the question. When the signals below would change from red to green again, or when the double-decker bus would turn the corner below, she would ask it. The words of it were already there, tentative in her mouth, when the answer came from the far end of the hall.

"Your mother," said the voice among the sound of kitchen things, "she telephoned up before you came in from nursery school. She won't be back in time for supper. I was to tell you a sitter was coming in from the sitting parents' place."

Felicia turned back from the window into the obscurity of the living room, and she looked toward the open door, and into the hall beyond it where the light from the kitchen fell in a clear yellow angle across the wall and onto the strip of carpet. Her hands were cold, and she put them in her jacket pockets as she walked carefully across the living-room rug and stopped at the edge of light.

"Will she be home late?" she said.

For a moment there was the sound of water running in the kitchen, a long way away, and then the sound of the water ceased, and the high, Southern voice went on:

"She'll come home when she gets ready to come home. That's all I have to say. If she wants to spend two dollars and fifty cents and ten cents' carfare on top of that three or four nights out of the week for a sitting parent to come in here and sit, it's her own business. It certainly ain't nothing to do with you or me. She makes her money, just like the rest of us does. She works all day down there in the office, or whatever it is, just like the rest of us works, and she's entitled to spend her money like she wants to spend it. There's no law in the world against buying your own freedom. Your mother and me, we're just buying our own freedom, that's all we're doing. And we're not doing nobody no harm."

"Do you know who she's having supper with?" said Felicia from the edge of dark. There was one more step to take, and then she would be standing in the light that fell on the strip of carpet, but she did not take the step.

"Do I know who she's having supper with?" the voice cried out in what might have been derision, and there was the sound of dishes striking the metal ribs of the drainboard by the sink. "Maybe it's Mr. Van Johnson, or Mr. Frank Sinatra, or maybe it's just the Duke of Wincers for the evening. All I know is you're having soft-boiled egg and spinach and applesauce for supper, and you're going to have it quick now because the time is getting away."

The voice from the kitchen had no name. It was as variable as the faces and figures of the women who came and sat in the evenings. Month by month the voice in the kitchen altered to another voice, and the sitting parents were no more than lonely aunts of an evening or two who sometimes returned and sometimes did not to this apartment in which they had sat before. Nobody stayed anywhere very long any more, Felicia's mother told her. It was part of the time in which you lived, and part of the life of the city, but when the fathers came back, all this would be miraculously changed. Perhaps you would live in a house again, a small one, with fir trees on either side of the short brick walk, and Father would drive up every night from the station just after darkness set in. When Felicia thought of this, she stepped quickly into the clear angle of light, and she left the dark of the living room behind her and ran softly down the hall.

The drop-leaf table stood in the kitchen between the refrigerator and the sink, and Felicia sat down at the place that was set. The voice at the sink was speaking still, and while Felicia ate it did not cease to speak until the bell of the front door rang abruptly. The girl walked around the table and went down the hall, wiping her dark palms in her apron, and, from the drop-leaf table, Felicia watched her step from the angle of light into darkness and open the door.

"You put in an early appearance," the girl said, and the woman who had rung the bell came into the hall. The door closed behind her, and the girl showed her into the living room, and lit the lamp on the bookcase, and the shadows were suddenly bleached away. But when the girl turned, the woman turned from the living room too and followed her, humbly and in silence, to the threshold of the kitchen. "Sometimes they keep me standing around waiting after it's time for me to be getting on home, the sitting parents do," the girl said, and she picked up the last two dishes from the table and put them in the sink. The woman who stood in the doorway was a small woman, and when she undid the white silk scarf from around her head, Felicia saw that her hair was black. She wore it parted in the middle, and it had not been cut, but was drawn back loosely into a knot behind her head. She had very clean white gloves on, and her face was pale, and there was a look of sorrow in her soft black eyes. "Sometimes I have to stand out there in the hall with my hat and coat on, waiting for the sitting parents to turn up," the girl said, and, as she turned on the water in the sink, the contempt she had for them hung on the kitchen air.

"But you're ahead of time," she said, and she held the dishes, first one and then the other, under the flow of steaming water.

The woman in the doorway wore a neat black coat, not a new-looking coat, and it had no fur on it, but it had a smooth velvet collar and velvet lapels. She did not move, or smile, and she gave no sign that she had heard the girl speaking above the sound of water at the sink. She simply stood looking at Felicia, who sat at the table with the milk in her glass not finished yet.

"Are you the child?" she said at last, and her voice was low, and the pronunciation of the words a little strange.

"Yes, this here's Felicia," the girl said, and the dark hands dried the dishes and put them away. "You drink up your milk quick now, Felicia, so's I can rinse your glass."

"I will wash the glass," said the woman. "I would like to wash the glass for her," and Felicia sat looking across the table at the face in the doorway that was filled with such unspoken grief. "I will wash the glass for her and clean off the table," the woman was saying quietly. "When the child is finished, she will show me where her night things are."

"The others, they wouldn't do anything like that," the girl said, and she hung the dishcloth over the rack. "They wouldn't put their hand to housework, the sitting parents. That's where they got the name for them," she said.

Whenever the front door closed behind the girl in the evening, it would usually be that the sitting parent who was there would take up a book of fairy stories and read aloud for a while to Felicia; or else would settle herself in the big chair in the living room and begin to tell the words of a story in drowsiness to her, while Felicia took off her clothes in the bedroom, and folded them, and put her pajamas on, and brushed her teeth, and did her hair. But this time, that was not the way it happened. Instead, the woman sat down on the other chair at the kitchen table, and she began at once to speak, not of good fairies or bad, or of animals endowed with human speech, but to speak quietly, in spite of the eagerness behind her words, of a thing that seemed of singular importance to her.

"It is strange that I should have been sent here tonight," she said, her eyes moving slowly from feature to feature of Felicia's face, "for you look like a child that I knew once, and this is the anniversary of that child."

"Did she have hair like mine?" Felicia asked quickly, and she did not keep her eyes fixed on the unfinished glass of milk in shyness any more.

"Yes, she did. She had hair like yours," said the woman, and her glance paused for a moment on the locks which fell straight and thick on the shoulders of Felicia's dress. It may have been that she thought to stretch out her hand and touch the ends of Felicia's hair, for her fingers stirred as they lay clasped together on the table, and then they relapsed into passivity again. "But it is not the hair alone, it is the delicacy of your face, too, and your eyes the same, filled with the same spring lilac color," the woman said, pronouncing the words carefully. "She had little coats of golden fur on her arms and legs," she said, "and when we were closed up there, the lot of us in the cold, I used to make her laugh when I told her that the fur that was so pretty, like a little fawn's skin on her arms, would always help to keep her warm."

"And did it keep her warm?" asked Felicia, and she gave a little jerk of laughter as she looked down at her own legs hanging under the table, with the bare calves thin and covered with a down of hair.

"It did not keep her warm enough," the woman said, and now the mask of grief had come back upon her face. "So we used to take every-thing we could spare from ourselves, and we would sew them into cloaks and other kinds of garments for her and for the other children. . . ."

"Was it a school?" said Felicia when the woman's voice had ceased to speak.

"No," said the woman softly, "it was not a school, but still there were a lot of children there. It was a camp—that was the name the place had; it was a camp. It was a place where they put people until they could decide what was to be done with them." She sat with her hands clasped, silent a moment, looking at Felicia. "That little dress you have on," she said, not saying the words to anybody, scarcely saying them aloud. "Oh, she would have liked that little dress, the little buttons shaped like hearts, and the white collar—"

"I have four school dresses," Felicia said. "I'll show them to you. How many dresses did she have?"

"Well, there, you see, there in the camp," said the woman, "she did not have any dresses except the little skirt and the pullover. That was all she had. She had brought just a handkerchief of her belongings with her, like everybody else—just enough for three days away from home was what they told us, so she did not have enough to last the winter. But she had her ballet slippers," the woman said, and her clasped fingers did not move. "She had brought them because she thought during her three days away from home she would have the time to practice her ballet."

"I've been to the ballet," Felicia said suddenly, and she said it so eagerly that she stuttered a little as the words came out of her mouth. She slipped quickly down from the chair and went around the table to where the woman sat. Then she took one of the woman's hands away from the other that held it fast, and she pulled her toward the door. "Come into the living room and I'll do a pirouette for you," she said, and then she stopped speaking, her eyes halted on the woman's face. "Did she—did the little girl—could she do a pirouette very well?" she said.

"Yes, she could. At first she could," said the woman, and Felicia felt uneasy now at the sound of sorrow in her words. "But after that she was hungry. She was hungry all winter," she said in a low voice. "We were all hungry, but the children were the hungriest. Even now," she said, and her voice went suddenly savage, "when I see milk like that, clean, fresh milk standing in a glass, I want to cry out loud, I want to beat my hands on the table, because it did not have to be . . ." She had drawn her fingers abruptly away from Felicia now, and Felicia stood before her, cast off, forlorn, alone again in the time of apprehension. "That was three years ago," the woman was saying, and one hand was lifted, as in weariness, to shade her face. "It was somewhere else, it was in another country," she said, and behind her hand her eyes were turned upon the substance of a world in which Felicia had played no part.

"Did — did the little girl cry when she was hungry?" Felicia asked, and the woman shook her head.

"Sometimes she cried," she said, "but not very much. She was very quiet. One night when she heard the other children crying, she said to me, 'You know, they are not crying because they want something to eat. They are crying because their mothers have gone away.'"

"Did the mothers have to go out to supper?" Felicia asked, and she watched the woman's face for the answer.

"No," said the woman. She stood up from her chair, and now that she put her hand on the little girl's shoulder, Felicia was taken into the sphere of love and intimacy again. "Shall we go into the other room, and you will do your pirouette for me?" the woman said, and they went from the kitchen and down the strip of carpet on which the clear light fell. In the front room, they paused hand in hand in the glow of the shaded lamp, and the woman looked about her, at the books, the low tables with the magazines and ash trays on them, the vase of roses on the piano, looking with dark, scarcely seeing eyes at these things that had no reality at all. It was only when she saw the little white clock on the mantelpiece that she gave any sign, and then she said quickly: "What time does your mother put you to bed?"

Felicia waited a moment, and in the interval of waiting the woman lifted one hand and, as if in reverence, touched Felicia's hair.

"What time did the little girl you knew in the other place go to bed?" Felicia asked.

"Ah, God, I do not know, I do not remember," the woman said.

"Was she your little girl?" said Felicia softly, stubbornly.

"No," said the woman. "She was not mine. At least, at first she was not mine. She had a mother, a real mother, but the mother had to go away."

"Did she come back late?" asked Felicia.

"No, ah, no, she could not come back, she never came back," the woman said, and now she turned, her arm around Felicia's shoulders, and she sat down in the low soft chair. "Why am I saying all this to you, why am I doing it?" she cried out in grief, and she held Felicia close against her. "I had thought to speak of the anniversary to you, and that was all, and now I am saying these other things to you. Three years ago today, exactly, the little girl became my little girl because her mother went away. That is all there is to it. There is nothing more."

Felicia waited another moment, held close against the woman, and listening to the swift, strong heartbeats in the woman's breast.

"But the mother," she said then in the small, persistent voice, "did she take a taxi when she went?"

"This is the way it used to happen," said the woman, speaking in hopelessness and bitterness in the softly lighted room. "Every week they used to come into the place where we were and they would read a list of names out. Sometimes it would be the names of children they would read out, and then a little later they would have to go away. And sometimes it would be the grown people's names, the names of the mothers or big sisters, or other women's names. The men were not with us. The fathers were somewhere else, in another place."

"Yes," Felicia said. "I know."

"We had been there only a little while, maybe ten days or maybe not so long," the woman went on, holding Felicia against her still, "when they read the name of the little girl's mother out, and that afternoon they took her away."

"What did the little girl do?" Felicia said.

"She wanted to think up the best way of getting out so that she could go find her mother," said the woman, "but she could not think of anything good enough until the third or fourth day. And then she tied her ballet slippers up in the handkerchief again, and she went up to the guard standing at the door." The woman's voice was gentle, controlled now. "She asked the guard please to open the door so that she could go out. 'This is Thursday,' she said, 'and every Tuesday and Thursday I have my ballet lessons. If I miss a ballet lesson, they do not count the money off, so my mother would be just paying for nothing, and she cannot afford to pay for nothing. I missed my ballet lesson on Tuesday,' she said to the guard, 'and I must not miss it again today.'"

Felicia lifted her head from the woman's shoulder, and she shook her hair back and looked in question and wonder at the woman's face.

"And did the man let her go?" she said.

"No, he did not. He could not do that," said the woman. "He was a soldier and he had to do what he was told. So every evening after her mother went, I used to brush the little girl's hair for her," the woman went on saying. "And while I brushed it, I used to tell her the stories of the ballets. Sometimes I would begin with *Narcissus,*" the woman said, and she parted Felicia's locks with her fingers, "so if you will go and get your brush now, I will tell it while I brush your hair."

"Oh, yes," said Felicia, and she made two whirls as she went quickly to the bedroom. On the way back, she stopped and held on to the piano with the fingers of one hand while she went up on her toes. "Did you see me?

Did you see me standing on my toes?" she called to the woman, and the woman sat smiling in love and contentment at her.

"Yes, wonderful, really wonderful," she said. "I am sure I have never seen anyone do it so well." Felicia came spinning toward her, whirling in pirouette after pirouette, and she flung herself down in the chair close to her, with her thin bones pressed against the woman's soft, wide hip. The woman took the silver-backed, monogrammed brush and the tortoise-shell comb in her hands, and now she began to brush Felicia's hair. "We did not have any soap at all and not very much water to wash in, so I never could fix her as nicely and prettily as I wanted to," she said, and the brush stroked regularly, carefully down, caressing the shape of Felicia's head.

"If there wasn't very much water, then how did she do her teeth?" Felicia said.

"She did not do her teeth," said the woman, and she drew the comb through Felicia's hair. "There were not any toothbrushes or tooth paste, or anything like that."

Felicia waited a moment, constructing the unfamiliar scene of it in silence, and then she asked the tentative question.

"Do I have to do my teeth tonight?" she said.

"No," said the woman, and she was thinking of something else, "you do not have to do your teeth."

"If I am your little girl tonight, can I pretend there isn't enough water to wash?" said Felicia.

"Yes," said the woman, "you can pretend that if you like. You do not have to wash," she said, and the comb passed lightly through Felicia's hair.

"Will you tell me the story of the ballet?" said Felicia, and the rhythm of the brushing was like the soft, slow rocking of sleep.

"Yes," said the woman. "In the first one, the place is a forest glade with little pale birches growing in it, and they have green veils over their faces and green veils drifting from their fingers, because it is the spring-time. There is the music of a flute," said the woman's voice softly, softly, "and creatures of the wood are dancing—"

"But the mother," Felicia said as suddenly as if she had been awakened from sleep. "What did the little girl's mother say when she didn't do her teeth and didn't wash at night?"

"The mother was not there, you remember," said the woman, and the brush moved steadily in her hand. "But she did send one little letter back. Sometimes the people who went away were able to do that. The mother wrote it in a train, standing up in a car that had no seats," she said, and she might have been telling the story of the ballet still, for her voice was gentle and the brush did not falter on Felicia's hair. "There were perhaps a great many other people standing up in the train with her, perhaps all trying to write their little letters on the bits of paper they had managed to hide on them, or that they had found in forgotten corners as they traveled. When they had written their letters, then they must try to slip them out through the boards of the car in which they journeyed, standing up," said the woman, "and these letters fell down on the tracks under the train, or they were blown into the fields or onto the country roads, and if it was a kind person who picked them up, he would seal them in envelopes and send them to where they were addressed to go. So a letter came back like this from the little girl's mother," the woman said, and the brush followed the comb, the comb the brush in steady pursuit through Felicia's hair. "It said good-by to the little girl, and it said please to take care of her. It said: 'Whoever reads this letter in the camp, please take good care of my little girl for me, and please have her tonsils looked at by a doctor if this is possible to do.'"

"And then," said Felicia softly, persistently, "what happened to the little girl?"

"I do not know. I cannot say," the woman said. But now the brush and comb had ceased to move, and in the silence Felicia turned her thin, small body on the chair, and she and the woman suddenly put their arms around each other. "They must all be asleep now, all of them," the woman said, and in the silence that fell on them again, they held each other closer. "They must be quietly asleep somewhere, and not crying all night because they are hungry and because they are cold. For three years I have been saying 'They must all be asleep, and the cold and the hunger and the seasons or night or day or nothing matters to them—'"

It was after midnight when Felicia's mother put her key in the lock of the front door, and pushed it open, and stepped into the hallway. She walked quickly to the living room, and just across the threshold she slipped the three blue foxskins from her shoulders and dropped them, with her little velvet bag, upon the chair. The room was quiet, so quiet that she could hear the sound of breathing in it, and no one spoke to her in greeting as she crossed toward the bedroom door. And then, as startling as a slap across her delicately tinted face, she saw the woman lying sleeping on the divan, and Felicia, in her school dress still, asleep within the woman's arms.

[1946]

JOHN CHEEVER

John Cheever (1912–1982), the leading exponent of the kind of carefully fash-
ioned story of modern suburban manners that The New Yorker *popularized,*
has been called by the reviewer John Leonard "the Chekhov of the suburbs."
Cheever spent most of his life in New York City and in suburban towns similar
to the ones he described in much of his fiction. Born in Quincy, Massachusetts,
he was raised by parents who owned a prosperous business that failed after the
1929 stock market crash. His parents enjoyed reading literature to him, so as a
small child he was acquainted with the fiction of Charles Dickens, Jack London,
and Robert Louis Stevenson. He started his career at an unusually young age.
Expelled from Thayer Academy for being, by his own account, a "quarrelsome,
intractable . . . and lousy student," he moved to New York City, lived in a cell of
a room on a bread-and-buttermilk diet, and wrote stories. When his first one,
"Expelled," was accepted for publication by Malcolm Cowley, then editor of The
New Republic, *Cheever was launched as a teenager into a career as a writer of*
fiction. Earlier Cowley had told him that his stories were too long to get pub-
lished by magazines that paid, so he made Cheever write a story of not more
than a thousand words every day for four days to encourage discipline.

Cheever's first collection of stories, The Way Some People Live, *appeared*
in 1942, while he was completing a four-year stint of army duty. In 1953 he
strengthened his literary reputation with the book The Enormous Radio and
Other Stories, *a collection of fourteen of his* New Yorker *pieces blending real-*
ism and fantasy. The title story was first published in The New Yorker *in*
1947. Six years later appeared another story collection, The Housebreaker of
Shady Hill. *In the 1960s and 1970s he published three more books of short sto-*
ries and two widely acclaimed novels, Bullet Park *(1969) and* Falconer *(1977).*
The Stories of John Cheever, *published in 1978, won both the Pulitzer Prize*
and the National Book Critics Circle Award and became one of the few collec-
tions of short stories ever to make the New York Times *best-seller list. In more*
than fifty years, Cheever published more than two hundred magazine stories;
he figured that he earned "enough money to feed the family and buy a new suit
every other year."

Usually a rapid writer, Cheever said he liked best the stories that he wrote
in less than a week. Late in his life, he wrote an article for Newsweek *(1978),*
in which he explained why he continued to write short stories: "So long as we
are possessed by experience that is distinguished by its intensity and its
episodic nature, we will have the short story in our literature."

The Enormous Radio

Jim and Irene Westcott were the kind of people who seem to strike that satisfactory average of income, endeavor, and respectability that is reached by the statistical reports in college alumni bulletins. They were the parents of two young children, they had been married nine years, they lived on the twelfth floor of an apartment house near Sutton Place, they went to the theatre on an average of 10.3 times a year, and they hoped someday to live in Westchester. Irene Westcott was a pleasant, rather plain girl with soft brown hair and a wide, fine forehead upon which nothing at all had been written, and in the cold weather she wore a coat of fitch skins dyed to resemble mink. You could not say that Jim Westcott looked younger than he was, but you could at least say of him that he seemed to feel younger. He wore his graying hair cut very short, he dressed in the kind of clothes his class had worn at Andover, and his manner was earnest, vehement, and intentionally naive. The Westcotts differed from their friends, their classmates, and their neighbors only in an interest they shared in serious music. They went to a great many concerts—although they seldom mentioned this to anyone—and they spent a good deal of time listening to music on the radio.

Their radio was an old instrument, sensitive, unpredictable, and beyond repair. Neither of them understood the mechanics of radio—or of any of the other appliances that surrounded them—and when the instrument faltered, Jim would strike the side of the cabinet with his hand. This sometimes helped. One Sunday afternoon, in the middle of a Schubert quartet, the music faded away altogether. Jim struck the cabinet repeatedly, but there was no response; the Schubert was lost to them forever. He promised to buy Irene a new radio, and on Monday when he came home from work he told her that he had got one. He refused to describe it, and said it would be a surprise for her when it came.

The radio was delivered at the kitchen door the following afternoon, and with the assistance of her maid and the handyman Irene uncrated it and brought it into the living room. She was struck at once with the physical ugliness of the large gumwood cabinet. Irene was proud of her living room, she had chosen its furnishings and colors as carefully as she chose her clothes, and now it seemed to her that the new radio stood among her intimate possessions like an aggressive intruder. She was confounded by the number of dials and switches on the instrument panel, and she studied them thoroughly before she put the plug into a wall socket and turned the radio on. The dials flooded with a malevolent green light, and in the distance she heard the music of a piano quintet. The quintet was in the distance for only an instant; it bore down upon her with a speed greater than light and filled the apartment with the noise of music amplified so mightily that it knocked a china ornament from a table to the floor. She rushed to the instrument and reduced the volume. The violent forces that were snared in the ugly gumwood cabinet made her uneasy. Her children came home from school then, and she took them to the Park. It was not until later in the afternoon that she was able to return to the radio.

The maid had given the children their suppers and was supervising their baths when Irene turned on the radio, reduced the volume, and sat down to listen to a Mozart quintet that she knew and enjoyed. The music came through clearly. The new instrument had a much purer tone, she thought, than the old one. She decided that tone was most important and that she could conceal the cabinet behind a sofa. But as soon as she had made her peace with the radio, the interference began. A crackling sound like the noise of a burning powder fuse began to accompany the singing of the strings. Beyond the music, there was a rustling that reminded Irene unpleasantly of the sea, and as the quintet progressed, these noises were joined by many others. She tried all the dials and switches but nothing dimmed the interference, and she sat down, disappointed and bewildered, and tried to trace the flight of the melody. The elevator shaft in her building ran beside the living-room wall, and it was the noise of the elevator that gave her a clue to the character of the static. The rattling of the elevator cables and the opening and closing of the elevator doors were reproduced in her loudspeaker, and, realizing that the radio was sensitive to electrical currents of all sorts, she began to discern through the Mozart the ringing of telephone bells, the dialing of phones, and the lamentation of a vacuum cleaner. By listening more carefully, she was able to distinguish doorbells, elevator bells, electric razors, and Waring mixers, whose sounds had been picked up from the apartments that surrounded hers and transmitted through her loudspeaker. The powerful and ugly instrument, with its mistaken sensitivity to discord, was more than she could hope to master, so she turned the thing off and went into the nursery to see her children.

When Jim Westcott came home that night, he went to the radio confidently and worked the controls. He had the same sort of experience Irene had had. A man was speaking on the station Jim had chosen, and his voice swung instantly from the distance into a force so powerful that it shook the apartment. Jim turned the volume control and reduced the voice. Then, a minute or two later, the interference began. The ringing of telephones and doorbells set in, joined by the rasp of the elevator doors and the whir of cooking appliances. The character of the noise had changed since Irene had tried the radio earlier; the last of the electric razors was being unplugged, the vacuum cleaners had all been returned to their closets, and the static reflected that change in pace that overtakes the city after the sun goes down. He fiddled with the knobs but couldn't get rid of the noises, so he turned the radio off and told Irene that in the morning he'd call the people who had sold it to him and give them hell.

The following afternoon, when Irene returned to the apartment from a luncheon date, the maid told her that a man had come and fixed the radio. Irene went into the living room before she took off her hat or her furs and tried the instrument. From the loudspeaker came a recording of the "Missouri Waltz." It reminded her of the thin, scratchy music from an old-fashioned phonograph that she sometimes heard across the lake where she spent her summers. She waited until the waltz had finished, expecting an explanation of the recording, but there was none. The music was followed by silence, and then the plaintive and scratchy record was repeated. She turned the dial and got a satisfactory burst of Caucasian music — the thump of bare feet in the dust and the rattle of coin jewelry — but in the background she could hear the ringing of bells and a confusion of voices. Her children came home from school then, and she turned off the radio and went to the nursery.

When Jim came home that night, he was tired, and he took a bath and changed his clothes. Then he joined Irene in the living room. He had just turned on the radio when the maid announced dinner, so he left it on, and he and Irene went to the table.

Jim was too tired to make even pretense of sociability, and there was nothing about the dinner to hold Irene's interest, so her attention wandered from the food to the deposits of silver polish on the candlesticks and from there to the music in the other room. She listened for a few minutes to a Chopin prelude and then was surprised to hear a man's voice break in. "For Christ's sake, Kathy," he said, "do you always have to play the piano when I get home?" The music stopped abruptly. "It's the only chance I have," a woman said. "I'm at the office all day." "So am I," the man said. He added something obscene about an upright piano, and slammed a door. The passionate and melancholy music began again.

"Did you hear that?" Irene asked.

"What?" Jim was eating his dessert.

"The radio. A man said something while the music was still going on — something dirty."

"It's probably a play."

"I don't think it *is* a play," Irene said.

They left the table and took their coffee into the living room. Irene asked Jim to try another station. He turned the knob. "Have you seen my garters?" a man asked. "Button me up," a woman said. "Have you seen my garters?" the man said again. "Just button me up and I'll find your garters," the woman said. Jim shifted to another station. "I wish you wouldn't leave apple cores in the ashtrays," a man said. "I hate the smell."

"This is strange," Jim said.

"Isn't it?" Irene said.

Jim turned the knob again. " 'On the coast of Coromandel where the early pumpkins blow,' " a woman with a pronounced English accent said, " 'in the middle of the woods lived the Yonghy-Bonghy-Bò. Two old chairs, and half a candle, one old jug without a handle . . .' "

"My God!" Irene cried. "That's the Sweeneys' nurse."

" 'These were all his worldly goods,' " the British voice continued.

"Turn that thing off," Irene said. "Maybe they can hear *us*." Jim switched the radio off. "That was Miss Armstrong, the Sweeney's nurse," Irene said. "She must be reading to the little girl. They live in 17-B. I've talked with Miss Armstrong in the Park. I know her voice very well. We must be getting other people's apartments."

"That's impossible," Jim said.

"Well, that was the Sweeneys' nurse," Irene said hotly. "I know her voice. I know it very well. I'm wondering if they can hear us."

Jim turned the switch. First from a distance and then nearer, nearer, as if borne on the wind, came the pure accents of the Sweeneys' nurse again: " '*Lady Jingly! Lady Jingly!*' " she said, " '*sitting where the pumpkins blow, will you come and be my wife? said the Yonghy-Bonghy-Bò . . .*' "

Jim went over to the radio and said "Hello" loudly into the speaker.

" '*I am tired of living singly,*' " the nurse went on, " '*on this coast so wild and shingly, I'm a-weary of my life; if you'll come and be my wife, quite serene would be my life . . .*' "

"I guess she can't hear us," Irene said. "Try something else."

Jim turned to another station, and the living room was filled with the uproar of a cocktail party that had overshot its mark. Someone was playing the piano and singing the "Whiffenpoof Song,"[1] and the voices that surrounded the piano were vehement and happy. "Eat some more sandwiches," a woman shrieked. There were screams of laughter and a dish of some sort crashed to the floor.

"Those must be the Fullers, in 11-E," Irene said. "I knew they were giving a party this afternoon. I saw her in the liquor store. Isn't this too divine? Try something else. See if you can get those people in 18-C."

The Westcotts overheard that evening a monologue on salmon fishing in Canada, a bridge game, running comments on home movies of what had apparently been a fortnight at Sea Island, and a bitter family quarrel about an overdraft at the bank. They turned off their radio at midnight and went to bed, weak with laughter. Sometime in the night, their son began to call for a glass of water and Irene got one and took it to his room. It was very early. All the lights in the neighborhood were extinguished, and from the boy's window she could see the empty street. She went into the living room and tried the radio. There was some faint coughing, a moan, and then a man spoke. "Are you all right, darling?" he asked. "Yes," a woman said wearily. "Yes, I'm all right, I guess," and then she added with great feeling, "But, you know, Charlie, I don't feel like myself any more. Sometimes there are about fifteen or twenty minutes in the week when I feel like myself. I don't like to go to another doctor, because the

---

[1]One of the most popular of all college glee club songs, it took its name from the Yale singing group that first performed it in 1909. The lyrics are from a Rudyard Kipling poem.

doctor's bills are so awful already, but I just don't feel like myself, Charlie. I just never feel like myself." They were not young, Irene thought. She guessed from the timbre of their voices that they were middle-aged. The restrained melancholy of the dialogue and the draft from the bedroom window made her shiver, and she went back to bed.

The following morning, Irene cooked breakfast for the family—the maid didn't come up from her room in the basement until ten—braided her daughter's hair, and waited at the door until her children and her husband had been carried away in the elevator. Then she went into the living room and tried the radio. "I don't want to go to school," a child screamed. "I hate school. I won't go to school. I hate school." "You will go to school," an enraged woman said. "We paid eight hundred dollars to get you into that school and you'll go if it kills you." The next number on the dial produced the worn record of the "Missouri Waltz." Irene shifted the control and invaded the privacy of several breakfast tables. She overheard demonstrations of indigestion, carnal love, abysmal vanity, faith, and despair. Irene's life was nearly as simple and sheltered as it appeared to be, and the forthright and sometimes brutal language that came from the loudspeaker that morning astonished and troubled her. She continued to listen until her maid came in. Then she turned off the radio quickly, since this insight, she realized, was a furtive one.

Irene had a luncheon date with a friend that day, and she left her apartment a little after twelve. There were a number of women in the elevator when it stopped at her floor. She stared at their handsome and impassive faces, their furs, and the cloth flowers in their hats. Which one of them had been to Sea Island? she wondered. Which one had overdrawn her bank account? The elevator stopped at the tenth floor and a woman with a pair of Skye terriers joined them. Her hair was rigged high on her head and she wore a mink cape. She was humming the "Missouri Waltz."

Irene had two Martinis at lunch, and she looked searchingly at her friend and wondered what her secrets were. They had intended to go shopping after lunch, but Irene excused herself and went home. She told the maid that she was not to be disturbed; then she went into the living room, closed the doors, and switched on the radio. She heard, in the course of the afternoon, the halting conversation of a woman entertaining her aunt, the hysterical conclusion of a luncheon party, and a hostess briefing her maid about some cocktail guests. "Don't give the best Scotch to anyone who hasn't white hair," the hostess said. "See if you can get rid of that liver paste before you pass those hot things, and could you lend me five dollars? I want to tip the elevator man."

As the afternoon waned, the conversations increased in intensity. From where Irene sat, she could see the open sky above the East River. There were hundreds of clouds in the sky, as though the south wind had broken the winter into pieces and were blowing it north, and on her radio she could hear the arrival of cocktail guests and the return of children and businessmen from their schools and offices. "I found a good-sized diamond on the bathroom floor this morning," a woman said. "It must have fallen out of that bracelet Mrs. Dunston was wearing last night." "We'll sell it," a man said. "Take it down to the jeweler on Madison Avenue and sell it. Mrs. Dunston won't know the difference, and we could use a couple of hundred bucks . . ." "'Oranges and lemons, say the bells of St. Clement's,'" the Sweeneys' nurse sang. "'Halfpence and farthings, say the bells of St. Martin's. When will you pay me? say the bells at old Bailey . . .'" "It's not a hat," a woman cried, and at her back roared a cocktail party. "It's not a hat, it's a love affair. That's what Walter Florell said. He said it's not a hat, it's a love affair," and then, in a lower voice, the same woman added, "Talk to somebody, for Christ's sake, honey, talk to somebody. If she catches you standing here not talking to anybody, she'll take us off her invitation list, and I love these parties."

The Westcotts were going out for dinner that night, and when Jim came home, Irene was dressing. She seemed sad and vague, and he brought her a drink. They were dining with friends in the neighborhood, and they walked to where they were going. The sky was broad and filled with light. It was one of those splendid spring evenings that excite memory and desire, and the air that touched their hands and faces felt very soft. A Salvation Army band was on the corner playing "Jesus Is Sweeter." Irene drew on her husband's arm and held him there for a minute, to hear the music. "They're really such nice people, aren't they?" she said. "They have such nice faces. Actually, they're so much nicer than a lot of the people we know." She took a bill from her purse and walked over and dropped it into the tambourine. There was in her face, when she returned to her husband, a look of radiant melancholy that he was not familiar with. And her conduct at the dinner party that night seemed strange to him, too. She interrupted her hostess rudely and stared at the people across the table from her with an intensity for which she would have punished her children.

It was still mild when they walked home from the party, and Irene looked up at the spring stars. "'How far that little candle throws its beams,'" she exclaimed. "'So shines a good deed in a naughty world.'"[2] She waited that night until Jim had fallen asleep, and then went into the living room and turned on the radio.

Jim came home at about six the next night. Emma, the maid, let him in, and he had taken off his hat and was taking off his coat when Irene ran into the hall. Her face was shining with tears and her hair was disordered. "Go up to 16-C, Jim!" she screamed. "Don't take off your coat. Go up to 16-C. Mr. Osborn's beating his wife. They've been quarreling since four o'clock, and now he's hitting her. Go up there and stop him."

---

[2]A line spoken by Portia in William Shakespeare's *Merchant of Venice* (5.1.91).

From the radio in the living room, Jim heard screams, obscenities, and thuds. "You know you don't have to listen to this sort of thing," he said. He strode into the living room and turned the switch. "It's indecent," he said. "It's like looking in windows. You know you don't have to listen to this sort of thing. You can turn it off."

"Oh, it's so horrible, it's so dreadful," Irene was sobbing. "I've been listening all day, and it's so depressing."

"Well, if it's so depressing, why do you listen to it? I bought this damned radio to give you some pleasure," he said. "I paid a great deal of money for it. I thought it might make you happy. I wanted to make you happy."

"Don't, don't, don't, don't quarrel with me," she moaned, and laid her head on his shoulder. "All the others have been quarreling all day. Everybody's been quarreling. They're all worried about money. Mrs. Hutchinson's mother is dying of cancer in Florida and they don't have enough money to send her to the Mayo Clinic. At least, Mr. Hutchinson says they don't have enough money. And some woman in this building is having an affair with the handyman — with that hideous handyman. It's too disgusting. And Mrs. Melville has heart trouble, and Mr. Hendricks is going to lose his job in April and Mrs. Hendricks is horrid about the whole thing and that girl who plays the 'Missouri Waltz' is a whore, a common whore, and the elevator man has tuberculosis and Mr. Osborn has been beating Mrs. Osborn." She wailed, she trembled with grief and checked the stream of tears down her face with the heel of her palm.

"Well, why do you have to listen?" Jim asked again. "Why do you have to listen to this stuff if it makes you so miserable?"

"Oh, don't, don't, don't," she cried. "Life is too terrible, too sordid and awful. But we've never been like that, have we, darling? Have we? I mean, we've always been good and decent and loving to one another, haven't we? And we have two children, two beautiful children. Our lives aren't sordid, are they, darling? Are they?" She flung her arms around his neck and drew his face down to hers. "We're happy, aren't we, darling? We are happy, aren't we?"

"Of course we're happy," he said tiredly. He began to surrender his resentment. "Of course we're happy. I'll have that damned radio fixed or taken away tomorrow." He stroked her soft hair. "My poor girl," he said.

"You love me, don't you?" she asked. "And we're not hypercritical or worried about money or dishonest, are we?"

"No, darling," he said.

A man came in the morning and fixed the radio. Irene turned it on cautiously and was happy to hear a California-wine commercial and a recording of Beethoven's Ninth Symphony, including Schiller's "Ode to Joy." She kept the radio on all day and nothing untoward came from the speaker.

A Spanish suite was being played when Jim came home. "Is everything all right?" he asked. His face was pale, she thought. They had some cocktails and went in to dinner to the "Anvil Chorus" from *Il Trovatore*. This was followed by Debussy's "La Mer."

"I paid the bill for the radio today," Jim said. "It cost four hundred dollars. I hope you'll get some enjoyment out of it."

"Oh, I'm sure I will," Irene said.

"Four hundred dollars is a good deal more than I can afford," he went on. "I wanted to get something that you'd enjoy. It's the last extravagance we'll be able to indulge in this year. I see that you haven't paid your clothing bills yet. I saw them on your dressing table." He looked directly at her. "Why did you tell me you'd paid them? Why did you lie to me?"

"I just didn't want you to worry, Jim," she said. She drank some water. "I'll be able to pay my bills out of this month's allowance. There were the slipcovers last month, and that party."

"You've got to learn to handle the money I give you a little more intelligently, Irene," he said. "You've got to understand that we don't have as much money this year as we had last. I had a very sobering talk with Mitchell today. No one is buying anything. We're spending all our time promoting new issues, and you know how long that takes. I'm not getting any younger, you know. I'm thirty-seven. My hair will be gray next year. I haven't done as well as I'd hoped to do. And I don't suppose things will get any better."

"Yes, dear," she said.

"We've got to start cutting down," Jim said. "We've got to think of the children. To be perfectly frank with you, I worry about money a great deal. I'm not at all sure of the future. No one is. If anything should happen to me, there's the insurance, but that wouldn't go very far today. I've worked awfully hard to give you and the children a comfortable life," he said bitterly. "I don't like to see all my energies, all of my youth, wasted in fur coats and radios and slipcovers and—"

"Please, Jim," she said. "Please. They'll hear us."

"*Who'll hear us?* Emma can't hear us."

"The radio."

"Oh, I'm sick!" he shouted. "I'm sick to death of your apprehensiveness. The radio can't hear us. Nobody can hear us. And what if they can hear us? Who cares?"

Irene got up from the table and went into the living room. Jim went to the door and shouted at her from there. "Why are you so Christly all of a sudden? What's turned you overnight into a convent girl? You stole your mother's jewelry before they probated her will. You never gave your sister a cent of that money that was intended for her—not even when she needed it. You made Grace Howland's life miserable, and where was all your piety and your virtue when you went to that abortionist? I'll never forget how cool you were. You packed your bag and went off to have that child murdered as if you were going to Nassau. If you'd had any reasons, if you'd had any good reasons—"

Irene stood for a minute before the hideous cabinet, disgraced and sickened, but she held her hand on the switch before she extinguished the music and the voices, hoping that the instrument might speak to her kindly, that she might hear the Sweeneys' nurse. Jim continued to shout at her from the door. The voice on the radio was suave and noncommittal. "An early-morning railroad disaster in Tokyo," the loudspeaker said, "killed twenty-nine people. A fire in a Catholic hospital near Buffalo for the care of blind children was extinguished early this morning by nuns. The temperature is forty-seven. The humidity is eighty-nine."   [1947]

CAROLINE GORDON

Caroline Gordon (1895–1981) was born in Trenton County, Kentucky, on one of her mother's family's farms, Merry Mount. She later said that the first seven years of her childhood were completely happy, "so self-contained, yet so fully peopled and so firmly rooted in time and space that today when its name [Merry Mount] is pronounced I feel a stirring of the heart which no other name can evoke." In 1902 Gordon left the farm to move with her family to Clarksville, Tennessee, where her father opened a school and later became a minister. She graduated from Bethany College in 1916 and worked as a journalist at the Chattanooga News. *In 1924 she met the poet and critic Allen Tate, and they were married the following year. Both wanted to be writers, and Gordon took a job as secretary-typist for the novelist Ford Madox Ford, who encouraged her to work hard on her own writing. Gordon told her friend Sally Wood that Ford insisted she write every morning, and "if I complained it was hard work . . . he observed, 'You have no passion for your art. It's unfortunate,' in such a sinister way that I would reel forth sentences in a sort of panic. Never did I see such a passion for the novel as that man had."*

Gordon published her first novel, Penhally, *in 1931, following it with five more novels in the next dozen years. She also wrote short stories, which she often reworked as chapters in her novels. In 1937, after placing her story "The Brilliant Leaves" in* Harper's Bazaar, *she told the writer Robert Penn Warren that "I am quite seriously determined never to try my hand at another. I can face a lifetime of incessant toil writing novels, but each short story takes as much out of you—me, anyhow, as a novel, and then you have to start all over again."*

Today Gordon's reputation rests primarily on her short stories. In 1945 she published The Forest of the South, *her first collection. Five years later she collaborated with Allen Tate on the textbook* The House of Fiction: An Anthology of the Short Story, with Commentary. *This was a pioneering work of what was then called the New Criticism, advocating close reading of literature to discover structure, symbolism, and irony. Gordon's second collection,* Old Red and Other Stories (1963), *included "The Petrified Woman," which had first appeared in* Mademoiselle *magazine in 1947. As Robert Penn Warren wrote in his introduction to* The Collected Stories of Caroline Gordon *in 1981, she possessed "a disciplined style as unpretentious and clear as running water, but shot through with glints of wit, humor, and poetry."*

The Petrified Woman

We were sitting on the porch at the Fork—it is where two creeks meet—after supper, talking about our family reunion. It was to be held at a place called Arthur's Cave that year (it has the largest entrance in the world, though it is not so famous as Mammoth), and there was to be a big picnic dinner, and we expected all our kin and connections to come, some of them from as far off as California.

Hilda and I had been playing in the creek all afternoon and hadn't had time to wash our legs before we came in to supper, so we sat on the bottom step where it was dark. Cousin Eleanor was in the porch swing with Cousin Tom. She had on a long white dress. It brushed the floor a little every time the swing moved. But you had to listen hard to hear it, under the noise the creek made. Wherever you were in that house you could hear the creek running over the rocks. Hilda and I used to play in it all day long. I liked to stay at her house better than at any of my other cousins'. But they never let me stay there long at a time. That was because she didn't have any mother, just her old mammy, Aunt Rachel—till that spring, when her father, Cousin Tom, married a lady from Birmingham named Cousin Eleanor.

A mockingbird started up in the juniper tree. It was the same one sang all night long that summer; we called him Sunny Jim. Cousin Eleanor got up and went to the end of the porch to try to see him.

"Do they always sing when there's a full moon?" she asked.

"They're worse in August," Cousin Tom said. "Got their crops laid by and don't give a damn if they do stay up all night."

"And in August the Fayerlees repair to Arthur's Cave," she said. "Five hundred people repairing en masse to the womb—what a sight it must be."

Cousin Tom went over and put his arm about her waist. "Do they look any worse than other folks, taking them by and large?" he asked.

The mockingbird burst out as if he was the one who would answer, and I heard Cousin Eleanor's dress brushing the floor again as she walked back to the swing. She had on tiny diamond earrings that night and a diamond cross that she said her father had given her. My grandmother said that she didn't like her mouth. I thought that she was the prettiest person ever lived.

"I'd rather not take them by and large," she said. "Do we *have* to go, Tom?"

"Hell!" he said. "I'm contributing three carcasses to the dinner. I'm going, to get my money's worth."

"One thing, I'm not going to let Cousin Edward Barker kiss me tomorrow," Hilda said. "He's got tobacco juice on his mustaches."

Cousin Tom hadn't sat down in the swing when Cousin Eleanor did. He came and stood on the step above us. "I'm going to shave off my mustache," he said, "and then the women won't have any excuse."

"Which one will you start with?"

"Marjorie Wrenn. She's the prettiest girl in Gloversville. No, she isn't. I'm going to start with Sally. She's living in town now. . . . Sally, you ever been kissed?"

"She's going to kiss me good night right this minute," Cousin Eleanor said, and got up from the swing and came over and bent down and put her hand on each of our shoulders and kissed us, French fashion, she said, first on one cheek and then on the other. We said good night and started for the door. Cousin Tom was there. He put his arms about our waists and bumped our heads together and kissed Hilda first, on the mouth, and then he kissed me and he said, "What about Joe Larrabee now?"

After we got in bed Hilda wanted to talk about Joe Larrabee. He was nineteen years old and the best dancer in town. That was the summer we used to take picnic suppers to the cave, and after supper the band would play and the young people would dance. Once, when we were sitting there watching, Joe Larrabee stopped and asked Hilda to dance, and after that she always wanted to sit on that same bench and when he went past, with Marjorie Wrenn or somebody, she would squeeze my hand tight, and I knew that she thought that maybe he would stop and ask her again. But I didn't think he ever would, and anyway I didn't feel like talking about him that night, so I told her I had to go to sleep.

I dreamed a funny dream. I was at the family reunion at the cave. There were a lot of other people there, but when I'd look into their faces it would be somebody I didn't know and I kept thinking that maybe I'd gone to the wrong picnic, when I saw Cousin Tom. He saw me too, and he stood still till I got to where he was and he said, "Sally, this is Tom." He didn't say Cousin Tom, just Tom. I was about to say something but somebody came in between us, and then I was in another place that wasn't like the cave and I was wondering how I'd ever get back when I heard a *knock, knock, knock,* and Hilda said, "Come on, let's get up."

The knocking was still going on. It took me a minute to know what it was: the old biscuit block was on the downstairs back porch right under our room, and Jason, Aunt Rachel's grandson, was pounding the dough for the beaten biscuits that we were going to take on the picnic.

We got to the cave around eleven o'clock. They don't start setting the dinner out till noon, so we went on down into the hollow, where Uncle Jack Dudley and Richard were tending the fires in the barbecue pits. A funny-looking wagon was standing over by the spring, but we didn't know what was in it, then, so we didn't pay any attention, just watched them barbecuing. Thirteen carcasses were roasting over the pits that day. It was the largest family reunion we ever had. There was a cousin named Robert Dale Owen Fayerlee who had gone off to St. Louis and got rich and he hadn't seen any of his kin in a long time and wanted everybody to have a good time, so he had chartered the cave and donated five cases of whiskey. There was plenty of whiskey for the Negroes too. Every now and then Uncle Jack would go off into the bushes and come back with tin cups that he would pass around. I like to be around Negroes, and so does Hilda. We were just sitting there watching them and not doing a thing, when Cousin Tom came up.

There are three or four Cousin Toms. They keep them straight by their middle names, usually, but they call him Wild Tom. He is not awfully old and has curly brown hair. I don't think his eyes would look so light if his face wasn't so red. He is out in the sun a lot.

He didn't see us at first. He went up to Uncle Jack and asked, "Jack, how you fixed?" Uncle Jack said, "Mister Tom, I ain't fooling you. I done already fixed." "I ain't going to fool with you, then," Cousin Tom said, and he was pulling a bottle out of his pocket when he saw us. He is a man that is particular about little girls. He said, "Hilda, what are you doing here?" and when we said we weren't doing a thing he said, "You go right on up the hill."

The first person I saw up there was my father. I hadn't expected to see him because before I left home I heard him say, "All those mediocre people, getting together to congratulate themselves on their mediocrity! I ain't going a step." But I reckon he didn't want to stay home by himself and, besides, he likes to watch them making fools of themselves.

My father is not connected. He is Professor Aleck Maury and he had a boys' school in Gloversville then. There was a girls' school there too, Miss Robinson's, but he said that I wouldn't learn anything if I went there till I was blue in the face, so I had to go to school with the boys. Sometimes I think that that is what makes me so peculiar.

It takes them a long time to set out the dinner. We sat down on a top rail of one of the benches with Susie McIntyre and watched the young people dance. Joe Larrabee was dancing with Marjorie Wrenn. She had on a tan coat-suit, with buttons made out of brown braid. Her hat was brown straw, with a tan ribbon. She held it in her hand, and it flopped up and down when she danced. It wasn't twelve o'clock but Joe Larrabee already had whiskey on his breath. I smelled it when they went past.

Susie said for us to go out there and dance too. She asked me first, and I started to, and then I remembered last year when I got off on the wrong foot and Cousin Edward Barker came along and stepped on me, and I thought it was better not to try than to fail, so I let Hilda go with Susie.

I was still sitting there on top of the bench when Cousin Tom came along. He didn't seem to remember that he was mad at us. He said, "Hello, Bumps." I am not Bumps. Hilda is Bumps, so I said, "I'm just waiting for Hilda . . . want me to get her?"

He waved his hand and I smelled whiskey on his breath. "Well, hello, anyhow," he said, and I thought for a minute that he was going to kiss me. He is a man that you don't so much mind having him kiss you, even when he has whiskey on his breath. But he went on to where Cousin Eleanor was helping Aunt Rachel set out the dinner. On the way he knocked into a lady and when he stepped back he ran into another one, so after he asked them to excuse him he went off on tiptoe. But he lifted his feet too high and put one of them down in a basket of pies. Aunt Rachel hollered out before she thought, "Lord God, he done ruint my pies!"

Cousin Eleanor just stood there and looked at him. When he got almost up to her and she still didn't say anything, he stopped and looked at her a minute and then he said, "All right!" and went off down the hill.

Susie and Hilda came back and they rang a big bell and Cousin Sidney Grassdale (they call them by the names of their places when there are too many of the same name) said a long prayer, and they all went in.

My father got his plate helped first and then he turned around to a man behind him and said, "You stick to me and you can't go wrong. I know the ropes."

The man was short and fat and had on a cream-colored Palm Beach suit and smiled a lot. I knew he was Cousin Robert Dale Owen Fayerlee, the one that gave all the whiskey.

I didn't fool with any of the barbecue, just ate ham and chicken. And then I had some chicken salad, and Susie wanted me to try some potato salad, so I tried that too, and then we had a good many hot rolls and some stuffed eggs and some pickles and some coconut cake and some chocolate cake. I had been saving myself up for Aunt Rachel's chess pies and put three on my plate when I started out, but by the time I got to them I wasn't really hungry and I let Susie eat one of mine.

After we got through, Hilda said she had a pain in her stomach and we sat down on a bench till it went away. My grandmother and Aunt Maria came and sat down too. They had on white shirtwaists and black skirts and they both had their palm-leaf fans.

Cousin Robert D. Owen got up and made a speech. It was mostly about his father. He said that he was one of nature's noblemen. My grandmother and Aunt Maria held their fans up before their faces when he said that, and Aunt Maria said, "Chh! *Jim* Fayerlee!" and my grandmother said that all that branch of the family was boastful.

Cousin Robert D. Owen got through with his father and started on back. He said that the Fayerlees were descended from Edward the Confessor and Philippe le Bel of France and the grandfather of George Washington.

My father was sitting two seats down, with Cousin Edward Barker. "Now ain't that tooting?" he said.

Cousin Edward Barker hit himself on the knee. "I be damn if I don't write to the *Tobacco Leaf* about that," he said. "The Fayerlees have been plain, honest countrymen since 1600. Don't that fool know anything about his own family?"

Susie touched me and Hilda on the shoulder, and we got up and squeezed past my grandmother and Aunt Maria. "Where you going?" my grandmother asked.

"We're just going to take a walk, Cousin Sally," Susie said.

We went out to the gate. The cave is at the foot of a hill. There are some long wooden steps leading up to the top of the hill, and right by the gate that keeps people out if they haven't paid is a refreshment stand. I thought that it would be nice to have some orange pop, but Susie said, "No, let's go to the carnival."

"There isn't any carnival," Hilda said.

"There is, too," Susie said, "but it costs a quarter."

"I haven't got but fifteen cents," Hilda said.

"Here comes Giles Allard," Susie said. "Make out you don't see him."

Cousin Giles Allard is a member of our family connection who is not quite right in the head. He doesn't have any special place to live, just roams around. Sometimes he will come and stay two or three weeks with you and sometimes he will come on the place and not come up to the house, but stay down in the cabin with some darky that he likes. He is a little warped-looking man with pale blue eyes. I reckon that before a family reunion somebody gives him one of their old suits. He had on a nice gray suit that day and looked just about like the rest of them.

He came up to us and said, "You all having a good time?" and we said, "Fine," and thought he would go on, but he stood and looked at us. "My name is Giles Allard," he said.

We couldn't think of anything to say to that. He pointed his finger at me. "You're named for your grandmother," he said, "but your name ain't Fayerlee."

"I'm Sally Maury," I said, "Professor Maury's daughter." My father being no kin to us, they always call me and my brother Sally Maury and Frank Maury, instead of plain Sally and Frank, the way they would if our blood was pure.

"Let's get away from him," Susie whispered, and she said out loud, "We've got to go down to the spring, Cousin Giles," and we hurried on as fast as we could. We didn't realize at first that Cousin Giles was coming with us.

"There comes Papa," Hilda said.

"He looks to me like he's drunk," Susie said.

Cousin Tom stood still till we got up to him, just as he did in my dream. He smiled at us then and put his hand on Hilda's head and said, "How are you, baby?" Hilda said, "I'm all right," and he said, "You are three sweet, pretty little girls. I'm going to give each one of you fifty cents," and he stuck his hand in his pocket and took out two dollar bills, and when Hilda asked how we were going to get the change out, he said, "Keep the change."

"Whoopee!" Susie said. "Now we can go to the carnival. You come, too, Cousin Tom," and we all started out toward the hollow.

The Negroes were gone, but there were still coals in the barbecue pits. That fat man was kneeling over one, cooking something.

"What you cooking for, fellow?" Cousin Tom asked. "Don't you know this is the day everybody eats free?"

The fat man turned around and smiled at us.

"Can we see the carnival?" Susie asked.

The fat man jumped up. "Yes, *ma'am*," he said, "you sure can see the carnival," and he left his cooking and we went over to the wagon.

On the way the fat man kept talking, kind of singsong: "You folks are in luck. . . . Wouldn't be here now but for a broken wheel . . . but one man's loss is another man's gain . . . I've got the greatest attraction in the world . . . yes, sir. Behind them draperies of pure silk lies the world's greatest attraction."

"Well, what is it?" Cousin Tom asked.

The fat man stopped and looked at us and then he began shouting:

Stell-a, Stell-a, the One and Only Stella!
Not flesh, not bone,
But calkypyrate stone,
Sweet Sixteen a Hundred Years Ago
And Sweet Sixteen Today!

A woman sitting on a chair in front of the wagon got up and ducked around behind it. When she came out again she had on a red satin dress, with ostrich feathers on the skirt, and a red satin hat. She walked up to us and smiled and said, "Will the ladies be seated?" and the man got some little stools down, quick, from where they were hooked on to the end of the wagon, and we all sat down, except Cousin Giles Allard, and he squatted in the grass.

The wagon had green curtains draped at each end of it. Gold birds were on the sides. The man bent down and pushed a spring or something, and one side of the wagon folded back, and there, lying on a pink satin couch, was a girl.

She had on a white satin dress. It was cut so low that you could see her bosom. Her head was propped on a satin pillow. Her eyes were shut. The lashes were long and black, with a little gold on them. Her face was dark and shone a little. But her hair was gold. It waved down on each side of her face and out over the green pillow. *The pillow had gold fringe on it! . . . lightly prest . . . in palace chambers . . . far apart. . . . The fragrant tresses are not stirred . . . that lie upon her charmèd heart. . . .*

The woman went around to the other side of the wagon. The man was still shouting:

Stell-a, Stell-a,
The One and Only Stell-a!

Cousin Giles Allard squeaked like a rabbit. The girl's eyes had opened. Her bosom was moving up and down.

Hilda got hold of my hand and held it tight. I could feel myself breathing. . . . But *her* breathing *is not heard . . . in palace chambers, far apart.* Her eyes were no color you could name. There was a veil over them.

The man was still shouting:

You see her now
As she was then,
Sweet Sixteen a Hundred Years Ago,
And Sweet Sixteen Today!

"How come her bubbies move if she's been dead so long?" Cousin Giles Allard asked.

Cousin Tom stood up, quick. "She's a pretty woman," he said, "I don't know when I've seen a prettier woman . . . lies quiet, too. . . . Well, thank you, my friend," and he gave the man two or three dollars and started off across the field.

I could tell that Susie wanted to stay and watch the girl some more, and it did look like we could, after he had paid all that money, but he was walking straight off across the field and we had to go after him. Once, before we caught up with him, he put his hand into his pocket, and I saw the bottle flash in the sun as he tilted it, but he had it back in his pocket by the time we caught up with him.

"You reckon she is sort of mummied, Cousin Tom, or is she just turned to pure rock?" Susie asked.

He didn't answer her. He was frowning. All of a sudden he opened his eyes wide, as if he had just seen something he hadn't expected to see. But there wasn't anybody around or anything to look at, except that purple weed that grows all over the field. He turned around. He hollered, the way he hollers at the hands on the place: "You come on here, Giles Allard!" and Cousin Giles came running. Once he tried to turn back, but Cousin Tom wouldn't let him go till we were halfway up to the cave. He let him slip off into the bushes then.

The sun was in all our eyes. Hilda borrowed Susie's handkerchief and wiped her face. "What made you keep Cousin Giles with us, Papa?" she asked. "I'd just as soon not have him along."

Cousin Tom sat down on a rock. The sun's fiery glare was full on his face. You could see the pulse in his temple beat. A little red vein was spreading over one of his eyeballs. He pulled the bottle out of his pocket. "I don't want him snooping around Stella," he said.

"How could he hurt her, Papa, if she's already dead?" Hilda asked.

Cousin Tom held the bottle up and moved it so that it caught the sun. "Maybe she isn't dead," he said.

Susie laughed out.

Cousin Tom winked his red eye at Susie and shook the bottle. "Maybe she isn't dead," he said again. "Maybe she's just resting."

Hilda stamped her foot on the ground. "*Papa!* I believe you've had too much to drink."

He drank all there was in the bottle and let it fall to the ground. He stood up. He put his hand out, as if he could push the sun away. "And what business is that of yours?" he asked.

"I just wondered if you were going back to the cave, where everybody is," Hilda said.

He was faced toward the cave then, but he shook his head. "No," he said, "I'm not going up to the cave," and he turned around and walked off down the hill.

We stood there a minute and watched him. "Well, anyhow, he isn't going up there where everybody is," Susie said.

"Where Mama is," Hilda said. "It just drives her crazy when he drinks."

"She better get used to it," Susie said. "All the Fayerlee men drink."

The reunion was about over when we got up to the cave. I thought I had to go back to my grandmother's—I was spending the summer there—but Hilda came and said I was to spend the night at the Fork.

"But you got to behave yourselves," Aunt Rachel said. "Big doings tonight."

We rode back in the spring wagon with her and Richard and the ice-cream freezers and what was left of the dinner. Cousin Robert D. Owen and his wife, Cousin Marie, were going to spend the night at the Fork too, and they had gone on ahead in the car with the others.

Hilda and I had long-waisted dimity dresses made just alike that summer. I had a pink sash and she had a blue one. We were so excited while we were dressing for supper that night that we couldn't get our sashes tied right. "Let's get Mama to do it," Hilda said, and we went into Cousin Eleanor's room. She was sitting at her dressing table, putting rouge on her lips. Cousin Marie was in there, too, sitting on the edge of the bed. Cousin Eleanor tied our sashes—she had to do mine twice before she got it right—and then gave me a little spank and said, "Now! You'll be the belles of the ball."

They hadn't told us to go out, so we sat down on the edge of the bed too. "Mama, where is Papa?" Hilda asked.

"I have *no* idea, darling," Cousin Eleanor said. "Tom is a law unto himself." She said that to Cousin Marie. I saw her looking at her in the mirror.

Cousin Marie had bright black eyes. She didn't need to use any rouge, her face was so pink. She had a dimple in one cheek. She said, "It's a *world* unto itself. Bob's been telling me about it ever since we were married, but I didn't believe him, till I came and saw for myself. . . . These little girls, now, how are they related?"

"In about eight different ways," Cousin Eleanor said.

Cousin Marie gave a kind of little yip. "It's just like an English novel," she said.

"They are mostly Scottish people," Cousin Eleanor said, "descended from Edward the Confessor and Philippe le Bel of France . . ."

"And the grandfather of George Washington!" Cousin Marie said, and rolled back on the bed in her good dress and giggled. "Isn't Bob priceless? But it *is* just like a book."

"I never was a great reader," Cousin Eleanor said. "I'm an outdoor girl."

She stood up. I never will forget the dress she had on that night. It was black but thin and it had a rose-colored bow right on the hip. She sort of dusted the bow off, though there wasn't a thing on it, and looked around the room as if she never had been there before. "I was, too," she said. "I was city champion for three years."

"Well, my dear, you could have a golf course here," Cousin Marie said. "Heaven knows there's all the room in creation."

"And draw off to swing, and a mule comes along and eats your golf ball up!" Cousin Eleanor said, "No, thank you, I'm through with all that."

They went down to supper. On the stairs Cousin Marie put her arm around Cousin Eleanor's waist, and I heard her say, "Wine for dinner. We don't need it." But Cousin Eleanor kept her face straight ahead. "There's no use for us to deny ourselves just because Tom can't control himself," she said.

Cousin Tom was already at the table when we got into the dining room. He had on a clean white suit. His eyes were bloodshot, and you could still see that vein beating in his temple. He sat at the head of the table, and Cousin Eleanor and Cousin Marie sat on each side of him. Cousin Sidney Grassdale and his daughter, Molly, were there. Cousin Sidney sat next to Cousin Marie, and Molly sat next to Cousin Eleanor. They had to do it that way on account of the overseer, Mr. Turner. He sat at the foot of the table, and Hilda and I sat on each side of him.

We usually played a game when we were at the table. It was keeping something going through a whole meal, without the grown folks knowing what it was. Nobody knew we did it except Aunt Rachel, and sometimes when she was passing things she would give us a dig in the ribs, to keep us quiet.

That night we were playing Petrified Woman. With everything we said we put in something from the fat man's song; like Hilda would say, "You want some butter?" and I would come back with "No, thank you, calkypyrate bone."

Cousin Marie was asking who the lady with the white hair in the blue flowered dress was.

"That is Cousin Olivia Bradshaw," Cousin Eleanor said.

"She has a pretty daughter," Cousin Robert D. Owen said.

"Mater pulcher, filia pulchrior,"[1] Cousin Sidney Grassdale said.

"And they live at Summer Hill?" Cousin Marie asked.

Cousin Tom laid his fork down. "I never could stand those Summer Hill folks," he said. "Pretentious."

"But the daughter has a great deal of charm," Cousin Marie said.

"Sweet Sixteen a Hundred Years Ago," Hilda said. "Give me the salt."

"And Sweet Sixteen Today," I said. "It'll thin your blood."

Cousin Tom must have heard us. He raised his head. His bloodshot eyes stared around the table. He shut his eyes. I knew that he was trying to remember.

"I saw a woman today that had real charm," he said.

Cousin Eleanor heard his voice and turned around. She looked him straight in the face and smiled, slowly. "In what did her charm consist, Tom?"

"She was petrified," Cousin Tom said.

I looked at her and then I wished I hadn't. She had blue eyes. I always thought that they were like violets. She had a way of opening them wide whenever she looked at you.

---

[1]"The mother is beautiful, the daughter more beautiful."

"Some women are just petrified in spots," Cousin Tom said. "She was petrified all over."

It was like the violets were freezing, there in her eyes. We all saw it. Molly Grassdale said something, and Cousin Eleanor's lips smiled and she half bent toward her and then her head gave a little shake and she straightened up so that she faced him. She was still smiling.

"In that case, how did she exert her charm?"

I thought, "Her eyes, they will freeze him, too." But he seemed to like for her to look at him like that. He was smiling, too.

"She just lay there and looked sweet," he said. "I like a woman to look sweet. . . . Hell, they ain't got anything else to do!"

Cousin Sidney's nose was working up and down, like a squirrel I had once, named Adji-Daumo. He said, "Harry Crenfew seems to be very much in love with Lucy Bradshaw."

"*I'm* in love!" Cousin Tom shouted. "I'm in love with a petrified woman."

She was still looking at him. I never saw anything as cold as her eyes.

"What is her name, Tom?"

"Stell-a!" he shouted. "The One and Only Stell-a!" He pushed his chair back and stood up, still shouting. "I'm going down to Arthur's Cave and take her away from that fellow."

He must have got his foot tangled up in Cousin Marie's dress, for she shrieked and stood up, too, and he went down on the floor, with his wine-glass in his hand. Somebody noticed us after a minute and sent us out of the room. He was still lying there when we left, his arms flung out and blood on his forehead from the broken glass. . . . I never did even see him get up off the floor.

We moved away that year and so we never went to another family reunion. And I never went to the Fork again. It burned down that fall. They said that Cousin Tom set it on fire, roaming around at night, with a lighted lamp in his hand. That was after he and Cousin Eleanor got divorced. I heard that they both got married again but I never knew who it was they married. I hardly ever think of them anymore. If I do, they are still there in that house. The mockingbird has just stopped singing. Cousin Eleanor, in her long white dress, is walking over to the window, where, on moonlight nights, we used to sit, to watch the water glint on the rocks . . . But Cousin Tom is still lying there on the floor. . . .   [1947]

SHIRLEY JACKSON

S*hirley Jackson (1919–1965) was born in San Francisco, California, her mother a housewife and her father an employee of a lithographing company. Most of her early life was spent in Burlingame, California, which she later used as the setting for her first novel,* The Road Through the Wall *(1948). As a child she was interested in writing, she won a poetry prize at age twelve, and in high school she began keeping a diary to record her writing progress. After high school she briefly attended the University of Rochester but left because of an attack of the mental depression that was to recur periodically in her later years. She recovered her health by living quietly at home and writing, conscientiously turning out a thousand words of prose a day. In 1937 she entered Syracuse University, where she published stories in the student literary magazine. There she met Stanley Edgar Hyman, who was to become a noted literary critic. They were married in 1940, the year she received her degree. They had four children while both continued active literary careers, settling to raise their family in a large Victorian house in Vermont, where Hyman taught literature at Bennington College.*

Jackson's first national publication was a humorous story written after a job at a department store during the Christmas rush: "My Life with R. H. Macy" appeared in The New Republic *in 1941. Her first child was born the next year, but she wrote every day on a disciplined schedule, selling her stories to magazines and publishing three novels. She refused to take herself too seriously as a writer: "I can't persuade myself that writing is honest work. It is a very personal reaction, but 50 percent of my life is spent washing and dressing the children, cooking, washing dishes and clothes, and mending. After I get it all to bed, I turn around to my typewriter and try to—well, to create concrete things again. It's great fun, and I love it. But it doesn't tie any shoes."*

Jackson's best-known work, "The Lottery," is often anthologized, dramatized, and televised. It was first published in The New Yorker *in 1948. She regarded it as a tale in the sense that Nathaniel Hawthorne used the term—a moral allegory revealing the hidden evil of the human soul. She wrote later that "explaining just what I had hoped the story to say is very difficult. I supposed, I hoped, by setting a particularly brutal ancient rite in the present and in my own village, to shock the story's readers with a graphic dramatization of the pointless violence and general inhumanity in their own lives."* Just an Ordinary Day: The Uncollected Stories of Shirley Jackson *was published in 1997.*

RELATED COMMENTARY: *Shirley Jackson, "The Morning of June 28, 1948, and 'The Lottery,'" page 1375.*

The Lottery

The morning of June 27th was clear and sunny, with the fresh warmth of a full-summer day; the flowers were blossoming profusely and the grass was richly green. The people of the village began to gather in the square, between the post office and the bank, around ten o'clock; in some towns there were so many people that the lottery took two days and had to be started on June 26th, but in this village, where there were only about three hundred people, the whole lottery took less than two hours, so it could begin at ten o'clock in the morning and still be through in time to allow the villagers to get home for noon dinner.

The children assembled first, of course. School was recently over for the summer, and the feeling of liberty sat uneasily on most of them; they tended to gather together quietly for a while before they broke into boisterous play, and their talk was still of the classroom and teacher, of books and reprimands. Bobby Martin had already stuffed his pockets full of stones, and the other boys soon followed his example, selecting the smoothest and roundest stones; Bobby and Harry Jones and Dickie Delacroix—the villagers pronounced this name "Dellacroy"—eventually made a great pile of stones in one corner of the square and guarded it against the raids of the other boys. The girls stood aside, talking among themselves, looking over their shoulders at the boys, and the very small children rolled in the dust or clung to the hands of their older brothers or sisters.

Soon the men began to gather, surveying their own children, speaking of planting and rain, tractors and taxes. They stood together, away from the pile of stones in the corner, and their jokes were quiet and they smiled rather than laughed. The women, wearing faded house dresses and sweaters, came shortly after their menfolk. They greeted one another and exchanged bits of gossip as they went to join their husbands. Soon the women, standing by their husbands, began to call to their children, and the children came reluctantly, having to be called four or five times. Bobby Martin ducked under his mother's grasping hand and ran, laughing, back to the pile of stones. His father spoke up sharply, and Bobby came quickly and took his place between his father and his oldest brother.

The lottery was conducted—as were the square dances, the teen-age club, the Halloween program—by Mr. Summers, who had time and energy to devote to civic activities. He was a round-faced, jovial man and he ran the coal business, and people were sorry for him, because he had no children and his wife was a scold. When he arrived in the square, carrying the black wooden box, there was a murmur of conversation among the villagers, and he waved and called, "Little late today, folks." The postmaster, Mr. Graves, followed him, carrying a three-legged stool, and the stool was put in the center of the square and Mr. Summers set the black box down on it. The villagers kept their distance, leaving a space between themselves and the stool, and when Mr. Summers said, "Some of you fellows want to give me a hand?" there was a hesitation before two men, Mr. Martin and his oldest son, Baxter, came forward to hold the box steady on the stool while Mr. Summers stirred up the papers inside it.

The original paraphernalia for the lottery had been lost long ago, and the black box now resting on the stool had been put into use even before Old Man Warner, the oldest man in town, was born. Mr. Summers spoke frequently to the villagers about making a new box, but no one liked to upset even as much tradition as was represented by the black box. There was a story that the present box had been made with some pieces of the box that had preceded it, the one that had been constructed when the first people settled down to make a village here. Every year, after the lottery, Mr. Summers began talking again about a new box, but every year the subject was allowed to fade off without anything's being done. The black box grew shabbier each year; by now it was no longer completely black but splintered badly along one side to show the original wood color, and in some places faded or stained.

Mr. Martin and his oldest son, Baxter, held the black box securely on the stool until Mr. Summers had stirred the papers thoroughly with his hand. Because so much of the ritual had been forgotten or discarded, Mr. Summers had been successful in having slips of paper substituted for the chips of wood that had been used for generations. Chips of wood, Mr. Summers had argued, had been all very well when the village was tiny, but now that the population was more than three hundred and likely to keep on growing, it was necessary to use something that would fit more easily into the black box. The night before the lottery, Mr. Summers and Mr. Graves made up the slips of paper and put them in the box, and it was then taken to the safe of Mr. Summers's coal company and locked up until Mr. Summers was ready to take it to the square next morning. The rest of the year, the box was put away, sometimes one place, sometimes another; it had spent one year in Mr. Graves's barn and another year underfoot in the post office, and sometimes it was set on a shelf in the Martin grocery and left there.

There was a great deal of fussing to be done before Mr. Summers declared the lottery open. There were the lists to make up — of heads of families, heads of households in each family, members of each household in each family. There was the proper swearing-in of Mr. Summers by the postmaster, as the official of the lottery; at one time, some people remembered, there had been a recital of some sort, performed by the official of the lottery, a perfunctory, tuneless chant that had been rattled off duly each year; some people believed that the official of the lottery used to stand just so when he said or sang it, others believed that he was supposed to walk among the people, but years and years ago this part of the ritual had been allowed to lapse. There had been, also, a ritual salute, which the official of the lottery had had to use in addressing each person who came up to draw from the box, but this also had changed with time, until now it was felt necessary only for the official to speak to each person approaching.

Mr. Summers was very good at all this; in his clean white shirt and blue jeans, with one hand resting carelessly on the black box, he seemed very proper and important as he talked interminably to Mr. Graves and the Martins.

Just as Mr. Summers finally left off talking and turned to the assembled villagers, Mrs. Hutchinson came hurriedly along the path to the square, her sweater thrown over her shoulders, and slid into place in the back of the crowd. "Clean forgot what day it was," she said to Mrs. Delacroix, who stood next to her, and they both laughed softly. "Thought my old man was out back stacking wood," Mrs. Hutchinson went on, "and then I looked out the window and the kids was gone, and then I remembered it was the twenty-seventh and came a-running." She dried her hands on her apron, and Mrs. Delacroix said, "You're in time, though. They're still talking away up there."

Mrs. Hutchinson craned her neck to see through the crowd and found her husband and children standing near the front. She tapped Mrs. Delacroix on the arm as a farewell and began to make her way through the crowd. The people separated good-humoredly to let her through; two or three people said, in voices just loud enough to be heard across the crowd, "Here comes your Missus, Hutchinson," and "Bill, she made it after all." Mrs. Hutchinson reached her husband, and Mr. Summers, who had been waiting, said cheerfully, "Thought we were going to have to get on without you, Tessie." Mrs. Hutchinson said, grinning, "Wouldn't have me leave m'dishes in the sink, now, would you, Joe?" and soft laughter ran through the crowd as the people stirred back into position after Mrs. Hutchinson's arrival.

"Well, now," Mr. Summers said soberly, "guess we better get started, get this over with, so's we can go back to work. Anybody ain't here?"

"Dunbar," several people said. "Dunbar, Dunbar."

Mr. Summers consulted his list. "Clyde Dunbar," he said. "That's right. He's broke his leg, hasn't he? Who's drawing for him?"

"Me, I guess," a woman said, and Mr. Summers turned to look at her. "Wife draws for her husband," Mr. Summers said. "Don't you have a grown boy to do it for you, Janey?" Although Mr. Summers and everyone else in the village knew the answer perfectly well, it was the business of the official of the lottery to ask such questions formally. Mr. Summers waited with an expression of polite interest while Mrs. Dunbar answered.

"Horace's not but sixteen yet," Mrs. Dunbar said regretfully. "Guess I gotta fill in for the old man this year."

"Right," Mr. Summers said. He made a note on the list he was holding. Then he asked, "Watson boy drawing this year?"

A tall boy in the crowd raised his hand. "Here," he said. "I'm drawing for m'mother and me." He blinked his eyes nervously and ducked his head as several voices in the crowd said things like "Good fellow, Jack," and "Glad to see your mother's got a man to do it."

"Well," Mr. Summers said, "guess that's everyone. Old Man Warner make it?"

"Here," a voice said, and Mr. Summers nodded.

A sudden hush fell on the crowd as Mr. Summers cleared his throat and looked at the list. "All ready?" he called. "Now, I'll read the names— heads of families first—and the men come up and take a paper out of the box. Keep the paper folded in your hand without looking at it until everyone has had a turn. Everything clear?"

The people had done it so many times that they only half listened to the directions; most of them were quiet, wetting their lips, not looking around. Then Mr. Summers raised one hand high and said, "Adams." A man disengaged himself from the crowd and came forward. "Hi, Steve," Mr. Summers said, and Mr. Adams said, "Hi, Joe." They grinned at one another humorlessly and nervously. Then Mr. Adams reached into the black box and took out a folded paper. He held it firmly by one corner as he turned and went hastily back to his place in the crowd, where he stood a little apart from his family, not looking down at his hand.

"Allen," Mr. Summers said, "Anderson. . . . Bentham."

"Seems like there's no time at all between lotteries any more," Mrs. Delacroix said to Mrs. Graves in the back row. "Seems like we got through with the last one only last week."

"Time sure goes fast," Mrs. Graves said.

"Clark. . . . Delacroix."

"There goes my old man," Mrs. Delacroix said. She held her breath while her husband went forward.

"Dunbar," Mr. Summers said, and Mrs. Dunbar went steadily to the box while one of the women said, "Go on, Janey," and another said, "There she goes."

"We're next," Mrs. Graves said. She watched while Mr. Graves came around from the side of the box, greeted Mr. Summers gravely, and selected a slip of paper from the box. By now, all through the crowd there were men holding the small folded papers in their large hands, turning them over and over nervously. Mrs. Dunbar and her two sons stood together, Mrs. Dunbar holding the slip of paper.

"Harburt. . . . Hutchinson."

"Get up there, Bill," Mrs. Hutchinson said, and the people near her laughed.

"Jones."

"They do say," Mr. Adams said to Old Man Warner, who stood next to him, "that over in the north village they're talking of giving up the lottery."

Old Man Warner snorted. "Pack of crazy fools," he said. "Listening to the young folks, nothing's good enough for *them*. Next thing you know, they'll be wanting to go back to living in caves, nobody work any more, live *that* way for a while. Used to be a saying about 'Lottery in June, corn be heavy soon.' First thing you know, we'd all be eating stewed chickweed and acorns. There's *always* been a lottery," he added petulantly. "Bad enough to see young Joe Summers up there joking with everybody."

"Some places have already quit lotteries," Mrs. Adams said.

"Nothing but trouble in *that*," Old Man Warner said stoutly. "Pack of young fools."

"Martin." And Bobby Martin watched his father go forward. "Overdyke. . . . Percy."

"I wish they'd hurry," Mrs. Dunbar said to her older son. "I wish they'd hurry."

"They're almost through," her son said.

"You get ready to run tell Dad," Mrs. Dunbar said.

Mr. Summers called his own name and then stepped forward precisely and selected a slip from the box. Then he called, "Warner."

"Seventy-seventh year I been in the lottery," Old Man Warner said as he went through the crowd. "Seventy-seventh time."

"Watson." The tall boy came awkwardly through the crowd. Someone said. "Don't be nervous, Jack," and Mr. Summers said, "Take your time, son."

"Zanini."

After that, there was a long pause, a breathless pause, until Mr. Summers, holding his slip of paper in the air, said, "All right, fellows." For a minute, no one moved, and then all the slips of paper were opened. Suddenly, all the women began to speak at once, saying, "Who is it?" "Who's got it?" "Is it the Dunbars?" "Is it the Watsons?" Then the voices began to say, "It's Hutchinson. It's Bill," "Bill Hutchinson's got it."

"Go tell your father," Mrs. Dunbar said to her older son.

People began to look around to see the Hutchinsons. Bill Hutchinson was standing quiet, staring down at the paper in his hand. Suddenly, Tessie Hutchinson shouted to Mr. Summers, "You didn't give him time enough to take any paper he wanted. I saw you. It wasn't fair!"

"Be a good sport, Tessie," Mrs. Delacroix called, and Mrs. Graves said, "All of us took the same chance."

"Shut up, Tessie," Bill Hutchinson said.

"Well, everyone," Mr. Summers said, "that was done pretty fast, and now we've got to be hurrying a little more to get done in time." He consulted his next list. "Bill," he said, "you draw for the Hutchinson family. You got any other households in the Hutchinsons?"

"There's Don and Eva," Mrs. Hutchinson yelled. "Make *them* take their chance!"

"Daughters drew with their husbands' families, Tessie," Mr. Summers said gently. "You know that as well as anyone else."

"It wasn't *fair*," Tessie said.

"I guess not, Joe," Bill Hutchinson said regretfully. "My daughter draws with her husband's family, that's only fair. And I've got no other family except the kids."

"Then, as far as drawing for families is concerned, it's you," Mr. Summers said in explanation, "and as far as drawing for households is concerned, that's you, too. Right?"

"Right," Bill Hutchinson said.

"How many kids, Bill?" Mr. Summers asked formally.

"Three," Bill Hutchinson said. "There's Bill, Jr., and Nancy, and little Dave. And Tessie and me."

"All right, then," Mr. Summers said. "Harry, you got their tickets back?"

Mr. Graves nodded and held up the slips of paper. "Put them in the box, then," Mr. Summers directed. "Take Bill's and put it in."

"I think we ought to start over," Mrs. Hutchinson said, as quietly as she could. "I tell you it wasn't *fair*. You didn't give him time enough to choose. *Every*body saw that."

Mr. Graves had selected the five slips and put them in the box, and he dropped all the papers but those onto the ground, where the breeze caught them and lifted them off.

"Listen, everybody," Mrs. Hutchinson was saying to the people around her.

"Ready, Bill?" Mr. Summers asked, and Bill Hutchinson, with one quick glance around at his wife and children, nodded.

"Remember," Mr. Summers said, "take the slips and keep them folded until each person has taken one. Harry, you help little Dave." Mr. Graves took the hand of the little boy, who came willingly with him up to the box. "Take a paper out of the box, Davy," Mr. Summers said. Davy put his hand into the box and laughed. "Take just *one* paper," Mr. Summers said. "Harry, you hold it for him." Mr. Graves took the child's hand and removed the folded paper from the tight fist and held it while little Dave stood next to him and looked up at him wonderingly.

"Nancy next," Mr. Summers said. Nancy was twelve, and her school friends breathed heavily as she went forward, switching her skirt, and took a slip daintily from the box. "Bill, Jr.," Mr. Summers said, and Billy, his face red and his feet overlarge, nearly knocked the box over as he got a paper out. "Tessie," Mr. Summers said. She hesitated for a minute, look-ing around defiantly, and then set her lips and went up to the box. She snatched a paper out and held it behind her.

"Bill," Mr. Summers said, and Bill Hutchinson reached into the box and felt around, bringing his hand out at last with the slip of paper in it.

The crowd was quiet. A girl whispered, "I hope it's not Nancy," and the sound of the whisper reached the edges of the crowd.

"It's not the way it used to be," Old Man Warner said clearly. "People ain't the way they used to be."

"All right," Mr. Summers said. "Open the papers. Harry, you open little Dave's."

Mr. Graves opened the slip of paper and there was a general sigh through the crowd as he held it up and everyone could see that it was blank. Nancy and Bill, Jr., opened theirs at the same time, and both beamed and laughed, turning around to the crowd and holding their slips of paper above their heads.

"Tessie," Mr. Summers said. There was a pause, and then Mr. Summers looked at Bill Hutchinson, and Bill unfolded his paper and showed it. It was blank.

"It's Tessie," Mr. Summers said, and his voice was hushed. "Show us her paper, Bill."

Bill Hutchinson went over to his wife and forced the slip of paper out of her hand. It had a black spot on it, the black spot Mr. Summers had made the night before with the heavy pencil in the coal-company office. Bill Hutchinson held it up and there was a stir in the crowd.

"All right, folks," Mr. Summers said. "Let's finish quickly."

Although the villagers had forgotten the ritual and lost the original black box, they still remembered to use stones. The pile of stones the boys had made earlier was ready; there were stones on the ground with the blowing scraps of paper that had come out of the box. Mrs. Delacroix selected a stone so large she had to pick it up with both hands and turned to Mrs. Dunbar. "Come on," she said. "Hurry up."

Mrs. Dunbar had small stones in both hands, and she said, gasping for breath, "I can't run at all. You'll have to go ahead and I'll catch up with you."

The children had stones already, and someone gave little Davy Hutchinson a few pebbles.

Tessie Hutchinson was in the center of a cleared space by now, and she held her hands out desperately as the villagers moved in on her. "It isn't fair," she said. A stone hit her on the side of the head.

Old Man Warner was saying, "Come on, come on, everyone." Steve Adams was in the front of the crowd of villagers, with Mrs. Graves beside him.

"It isn't fair, it isn't right," Mrs. Hutchinson screamed and then they were upon her.   [1948]

TILLIE OLSEN

Tillie Olsen (b. 1913) was born in Omaha, Nebraska, the daughter of political refugees from the Russian czarist repression after the revolution of 1905. Her father was a farmer, packing-house worker, housepainter, and jack-of-all-trades; her mother was a factory worker. At the age of sixteen Olsen dropped out of high school to help support her family during the Depression. She was a member of the Young Communist League, involved in the Warehouse Union's labor disputes in Kansas City. At age nineteen she began her first novel, Yonnondio. *Four chapters of this book about a poverty-stricken working-class family were completed in the next four years, during which time she married, gave birth to her first child, and was left with the baby by her husband because, as she later wrote in her autobiographical story "I Stand Here Ironing," he "could no longer endure sharing want" with them. In 1934 a section of the first chapter of her novel was published in* Partisan Review, *but she abandoned the unfinished book in 1937. The year before she had married Jack Olsen, with whom she had three more children; raising the children and working for political causes took up all her time. In the 1940s she was a factory worker; in the 1950s, a secretary. Not until 1953, when her youngest daughter started school, could she begin writing again.*

That year Olsen enrolled in a class in fiction writing at San Francisco State College. She was awarded a Stanford University creative writing fellowship for 1955 and 1956. During the 1950s she wrote the four stories collected in Tell Me a Riddle, *which established her reputation when the book was published as a paperback in 1961. "I Stand Here Ironing" first appeared in the* Pacific Spectator *in 1956. Identified as a champion of the reemerging feminist movement, Olsen wrote a biographical introduction to Rebecca Harding Davis's nineteenth-century proletarian story,* Life in the Iron-Mills, *or The Korl Woman (included in Chapter Two of this anthology), reprinted by the Feminist Press in 1972. Two years later, after several grants and creative writing fellowships, she published the still-unfinished* Yonnondio. Silences, *a collection of essays exploring the different circumstances that obstruct or silence literary creation, appeared in 1978.*

As the Canadian author Margaret Atwood has understood about Olsen,

> *Few writers have gained such wide respect on such a small body of published work. . . . Among women writers in the United States, "respect" is too pale a word: "reverence" is more like it. This is presumably because women writers, even more than their male counterparts, recognize what a heroic feat it is to have held down a job, raised four children, and still somehow managed to become and to remain a writer.*

A radical feminist, Olsen has said that she felt no personal guilt as a single parent over her daughter's predicament, as described in her confessional narrative "I Stand Here Ironing," since "guilt is a word used far too sloppily, to cover up harmful situations in society that must be changed." Her four stories have appeared in more than fifty anthologies and have been translated into many languages. In 1994 she was awarded the Rea Award for the Short Story, a literary prize that honors a living American author who has made "a significant contribution to the short story as an art form."

RELATED COMMENTARY: *Robert Coles, "Tillie Olsen: The Iron and the Riddle," page 1335.*

I Stand Here Ironing

I stand here ironing, and what you asked me moves tormented back and forth with the iron.

"I wish you would manage the time to come in and talk with me about your daughter. I'm sure you can help me understand her. She's a youngster who needs help and whom I'm deeply interested in helping."

"Who needs help." . . . Even if I came, what good would it do? You think because I am her mother I have a key, or that in some way you could use me as a key? She has lived for nineteen years. There is all that life that has happened outside of me, beyond me.

And when is there time to remember, to sift, to weigh, to estimate, to total? I will start and there will be an interruption and I will have to gather it all together again. Or I will become engulfed with all I did or did not do, with what should have been and what cannot be helped.

She was a beautiful baby. The first and only one of our five that was beautiful at birth. You do not guess how new and uneasy her tenancy in her now-loveliness. You did not know her all those years she was thought homely, or see her poring over her baby pictures, making me tell her over and over how beautiful she had been—and would be, I would tell her—and was now, to the seeing eye. But the seeing eyes were few or nonexistent. Including mine.

I nursed her. They feel that's important nowadays, I nursed all the children, but with her, with all the fierce rigidity of first motherhood, I did like the books then said. Though her cries battered me to trembling and my breasts ached with swollenness, I waited till the clock decreed.

Why do I put that first? I do not even know if it matters, or if it explains anything.

She was a beautiful baby. She blew shining bubbles of sound. She loved motion, loved light, loved color and music and textures. She would lie on the floor in her blue overalls patting the surface so hard in ecstasy her hands and feet would blur. She was a miracle to me, but when she was eight months old I had to leave her daytimes with the woman downstairs to whom she was no miracle at all, for I worked or looked for work and for

Emily's father, who "could no longer endure" (he wrote in his good-bye note) "sharing want with us."

I was nineteen. It was the pre-relief, pre-WPA world of the depression. I would start running as soon as I got off the streetcar, running up the stairs, the place smelling sour, and awake or asleep to startle awake, when she saw me she would break into a clogged weeping that could not be comforted, a weeping I can hear yet.

After a while I found a job hashing at night so I could be with her days, and it was better. But it came to where I had to bring her to his family and leave her.

It took a long time to raise the money for her fare back. Then she got chicken pox and I had to wait longer. When she finally came, I hardly knew her, walking quick and nervous like her father, looking like her father, thin, and dressed in a shoddy red that yellowed her skin and glared at the pockmarks. All the baby loveliness gone.

She was two. Old enough for nursery school they said, and I did not know then what I know now — the fatigue of the long day, and the lacerations of group life in the kinds of nurseries that are only parking places for children.

Except that it would have made no difference if I had known. It was the only place there was. It was the only way we could be together, the only way I could hold a job.

And even without knowing, I knew. I knew the teacher that was evil because all these years it has curdled into my memory, the little boy hunched in the corner, her rasp, "why aren't you outside, because Alvin hits you? that's no reason, go out, scaredy." I knew Emily hated it even if she did not clutch and implore "don't go Mommy" like the other children, mornings.

She always had a reason why we should stay home. Momma, you look sick. Momma, I feel sick. Momma, the teachers aren't there today, they're sick. Momma, we can't go, there was a fire there last night. Momma, it's a holiday today, no school, they told me.

But never a direct protest, never rebellion. I think of our others in their three-, four-year-oldness — the explosions, the tempers, the denunciations, the demands — and I feel suddenly ill. I put the iron down. What in me demanded that goodness in her? And what was the cost, the cost to her of such goodness?

The old man living in the back once said in his gentle way: "You should smile at Emily more when you look at her." What *was* in my face when I looked at her? I loved her. There were all the acts of love.

It was only with the others I remembered what he said, and it was the face of joy, and not of care or tightness or worry I turned to them — too late for Emily. She does not smile easily, let alone almost always as her brothers and sisters do. Her face is closed and sombre, but when she wants, how fluid. You must have seen it in her pantomimes, you spoke of her rare gift for comedy on the stage that rouses laughter out of the audience so dear they applaud and applaud and do not want to let her go.

Where does it come from, that comedy? There was none of it in her when she came back to me that second time, after I had to send her away again. She had a new daddy now to learn to love, and I think perhaps it was a better time.

Except when we left her alone nights, telling ourselves she was old enough.

"Can't you go some other time, Mommy, like tomorrow?" she would ask. "Will it be just a little while you'll be gone? Do you promise?"

The time we came back, the front door open, the clock on the floor in the hall. She rigid awake. "It wasn't just a little while. I didn't cry. Three times I called you, just three times, and then I ran downstairs to open the door so you could come faster. The clock talked loud. I threw it away, it scared me what it talked."

She said the clock talked loud again that night I went to the hospital to have Susan. She was delirious with the fever that comes before red measles, but she was fully conscious all the week I was gone and the week after we were home when she could not come near the new baby or me.

She did not get well. She stayed skeleton thin, not wanting to eat, and night after night she had nightmares. She would call for me, and I would rouse from exhaustion to sleepily call back: "You're all right, darling, go to sleep, it's just a dream," and if she still called, in a sterner voice, "now go to sleep, Emily, there's nothing to hurt you." Twice, only twice, when I had to get up for Susan anyhow, I went in to sit with her.

Now when it is too late (as if she would let me hold her and comfort her like I do the others) I get up and go to her at once at her moan or restless stirring. "Are you awake, Emily? Can I get you something?" And the answer is always the same: "No, I'm all right, go back to sleep, Mother."

They persuaded me at the clinic to send her away to a convalescent home in the country where "she can have the kind of food and care you can't manage for her, and you'll be free to concentrate on the new baby." They still send children to that place. I see pictures on the society page of sleek young women planning affairs to raise money for it, or dancing at the affairs, or decorating Easter eggs or filling Christmas stockings for the children.

They never have a picture of the children so I do not know if the girls still wear those gigantic red bows and the ravaged looks on the every other Sunday when parents can come to visit "unless otherwise notified" — as we were notified the first six weeks.

Oh it is a handsome place, green lawns and tall trees and fluted flower beds. High up on the balconies of each cottage the children stand, the girls in their red bows and white dresses, the boys in white suits and giant red ties. The parents stand below shrieking up to be heard and the children shriek down to be heard, and between them the invisible wall "Not To Be Contaminated by Parental Germs or Physical Affection."

There was a tiny girl who always stood hand in hand with Emily. Her parents never came. One visit she was gone. "They moved her to Rose Cottage," Emily shouted in explanation. "They don't like you to love anybody here."

She wrote once a week, the labored writing of a seven-year-old. "I am fine. How is the baby. If I write my leter nicly I will have a star. Love." There never was a star. We wrote every other day, letters she could never hold or keep but only hear read—once. "We simply do not have room for children to keep any personal possessions," they patiently explained when we pieced one Sunday's shrieking together to plead how much it would mean to Emily, who loved so to keep things, to be allowed to keep her letters and cards.

Each visit she looked frailer. "She isn't eating," they told us.

(They had runny eggs for breakfast or mush with lumps, Emily said later, I'd hold it in my mouth and not swallow. Nothing ever tasted good, just when they had chicken.)

It took us eight months to get her released home, and only the fact that she gained back so little of her seven lost pounds convinced the social worker.

I used to try to hold and love her after she came back, but her body would stay stiff, and after a while she'd push away. She ate little. Food sickened her, and I think much of life too. Oh she had physical lightness and brightness, twinkling by on skates, bouncing like a ball up and down up and down over the jump rope, skimming over the hill; but these were momentary.

She fretted about her appearance, thin and dark and foreign-looking at a time when every little girl was supposed to look or thought she should look a chubby blonde replica of Shirley Temple. The doorbell sometimes rang for her, but no one seemed to come and play in the house or to be a best friend. Maybe because we moved so much.

There was a boy she loved painfully through two school semesters. Months later she told me how she had taken pennies from my purse to buy him candy. "Licorice was his favorite and I brought him some every day, but he still liked Jennifer better'n me. Why, Mommy?" The kind of question for which there is no answer.

School was a worry for her. She was not glib or quick in a world where glibness and quickness were easily confused with ability to learn. To her overworked and exasperated teachers she was an overconscientious "slow learner" who kept trying to catch up and was absent entirely too often.

I let her be absent, though sometimes the illness was imaginary. How different from my now-strictness about attendance with the others. I wasn't working. We had a new baby. I was home anyhow. Sometimes, after Susan grew old enough, I would keep her home from school, too, to have them all together.

Mostly Emily had asthma, and her breathing, harsh and labored, would fill the house with a curiously tranquil sound. I would bring the two old dresser mirrors and her boxes of collections to her bed. She would select beads and single earrings, bottle tops and shells, dried flowers and pebbles, old postcards and scraps, all sorts of oddments; then she and Susan would play Kingdom, setting up landscapes and furniture, peopling them with action.

Those were the only times of peaceful companionship between her and Susan. I have edged away from it, that poisonous feeling between them, that terrible balancing of hurts and needs I had to do between the two, and did so badly, those earlier years.

Oh there were conflicts between the others too, each one human, needing, demanding, hurting, taking—but only between Emily and Susan, no, Emily toward Susan that corroding resentment. It seems so obvious on the surface, yet it is not obvious; Susan, the second child, Susan, golden- and curly-haired and chubby, quick and articulate and assured, everything in appearance and manner Emily was not; Susan, not able to resist Emily's precious things, losing or sometimes clumsily breaking them; Susan telling jokes and riddles to company for applause while Emily sat silent (to say to me later: that was *my* riddle, Mother, I told it to Susan); Susan, who for all the five years' difference in age was just a year behind Emily in developing physically.

I am glad for that slow physical development that widened the difference between her and her contemporaries, though she suffered over it. She was too vulnerable for that terrible world of youthful competition, of preening and parading, of constant measuring of yourself against every other, of envy, "If I had that copper hair," "If I had that skin. . . ." She tormented herself enough about not looking like the others, there was enough of unsureness, the having to be conscious of words before you speak, the constant caring—what are they thinking of me? without having it all magnified by the merciless physical drives.

Ronnie is calling. He is wet and I change him. It is rare there is such a cry now. That time of motherhood is almost behind me when the ear is not one's own but must always be racked and listening for the child cry, the child call. We sit for a while and I hold him, looking out over the city spread in charcoal with its soft aisles of light. *"Shoogily,"* he breathes and curls closer. I carry him back to bed, asleep. *Shoogily*. A funny word, a family word, inherited from Emily, invented by her to say: *comfort*.

In this and other ways she leaves her seal, I say aloud. And startle at my saying it. What do I mean? What did I start to gather together, to try and make coherent? I was at the terrible, growing years. War years. I do not remember them well. I was working, there were four smaller ones now, there was not time for her. She had to help be a mother, and housekeeper, and shopper. She had to get her seal. Mornings of crisis and near hysteria trying to get lunches packed, hair combed, coats and shoes found, everyone to school or Child Care on time, the baby ready for transportation. And always the paper scribbled on by a smaller one, the book looked at by Susan then mislaid, the homework not done. Running out to that huge school where she was one, she was lost, she was a drop; suffering over the unpreparedness, stammering and unsure in her classes.

There was so little time left at night after the kids were bedded down. She would struggle over books, always eating (it was in those years she developed her enormous appetite that is legendary in our family) and I would be ironing, or preparing food for the next day, or writing V-mail to Bill, or tending the baby. Sometimes, to make me laugh, or out of her despair, she would imitate happenings or types at school.

I think I said once: "Why don't you do something like this in the school amateur show?" One morning she phoned me at work, hardly understandable through the weeping: "Mother, I did it. I won, I won; they gave me first prize; they clapped and clapped and wouldn't let me go."

Now suddenly she was Somebody, and as imprisoned in her difference as she had been in anonymity.

She began to be asked to perform at other high schools, even in colleges, then at city and statewide affairs. The first one we went to, I only recognized her that first moment when thin, shy, she almost drowned herself into the curtains. Then: Was this Emily? The control, the command, the convulsing and deadly clowning, the spell, then the roaring, stamping audience, unwilling to let this rare and precious laughter out of their lives.

Afterwards: You ought to do something about her with a gift like that — but without money or knowing how, what does one do? We have left it all to her, and the gift has so often eddied inside, clogged and clotted, as been used and growing.

She is coming. She runs up the stairs two at a time with her light graceful step, and I know she is happy tonight. Whatever it was that occasioned your call did not happen today.

"Aren't you ever going to finish the ironing, Mother? Whistler painted his mother in a rocker. I'd have to paint mine standing over an ironing board." This is one of her communicative nights and she tells me everything and nothing as she fixes herself a plate of food out of the icebox.

She is so lovely. Why did you want me to come in at all? Why were you concerned? She will find her way.

She starts up the stairs to bed. "Don't get me up with the rest in the morning." "But I thought you were having midterms." "Oh, those," she comes back in, kisses me, and says quite lightly, "in a couple of years when we'll all be atom-dead they won't matter a bit."

She has said it before. She *believes* it. But because I have been dredging the past, and all that compounds a human being is so heavy and meaningful in me, I cannot endure it tonight.

I will never total it all. I will never come in to say: She was a child seldom smiled at. Her father left me before she was a year old. I had to work
her first six years when there was work, or I sent her home and to his relatives. There were years she had care she hated. She was dark and thin and
foreign-looking in a world where the prestige went to blondeness and curly
hair and dimples, she was slow where glibness was prized. She was a child of
anxious, not proud, love. We were poor and could not afford for her the soil
of easy growth. I was a young mother, I was a distracted mother. There
were other children pushing up, demanding. Her younger sister seemed
all that she was not. There were years she did not want me to touch her.
She kept too much in herself, her life was such she had to keep too much
in herself. My wisdom came too late. She has much to her and probably
little will come of it. She is a child of her age, of depression, of war, of fear.

Let her be. So all that is in her will not bloom — but in how many does
it? There is still enough left to live by. Only help her to know — help make
it so there is cause for her to know — that she is more than this dress on
the ironing board, helpless before the iron.   [1956]

JAMES BALDWIN

James Baldwin (1924–1987) was born the son of a clergyman in Harlem, where he attended Public School 24, Frederick Douglass Junior High School, and DeWitt Clinton High School. While still a high school student he preached at the Fireside Pentecostal Assembly, but when he was seventeen he renounced the ministry. Two years later, living in Greenwich Village, he met Richard Wright, who encouraged him to be a writer and helped him win a Eugene Saxton Fellowship. Soon afterward Baldwin moved to France, as Wright had, to escape the stifling racial oppression he found in the United States. Although France was his more or less permanent residence until his death from cancer nearly forty years later, Baldwin regarded himself as a "commuter" rather than an expatriate. He said,

> *Only white Americans can consider themselves to be expatriates. Once I found myself on the other side of the ocean, I could see where I came from very clearly, and I could see that I carried myself, which is my home, with me. You can never escape that. I am the grandson of a slave, and I am a writer. I must deal with both.*

Baldwin began his career by publishing novels and short stories. In 1953 Go Tell It on the Mountain, *his first novel, was highly acclaimed. It was based on his childhood in Harlem and his fear of his tyrannical father. Baldwin's frank depiction of homosexuality in the novels* Giovanni's Room *(1956) and* Another Country *(1962) drew criticism, but during the civil rights movement a few years later, he established himself as a brilliant essayist. In his lifetime Baldwin published several collections of essays, three more novels, and a book of five short stories,* Going to Meet the Man *(1965).*

"Sonny's Blues," from that collection, is one of Baldwin's strongest psychological dramatizations of the frustrations of African American life in our times. It first appeared in Partisan Review *in 1957. Like Wright's autobiographical books, Baldwin's work is an inspiration to young writers struggling to express their experience of racism. The African writer Chinua Achebe has said that "as long as injustice exists . . . the words of James Baldwin will be there to bear witness and to inspire and elevate the struggle for human freedom."*

RELATED COMMENTARY: *James Baldwin, "Autobiographical Notes," page 1298.*

Sonny's Blues

I read about it in the paper, in the subway, on my way to work. I read it, and I couldn't believe it, and I read it again. Then perhaps I just stared at it, at the newsprint spelling out his name, spelling out the story. I stared at it in the swinging lights of the subway car, and in the faces and bodies of the people, and in my own face, trapped in the darkness which roared outside.

It was not to be believed and I kept telling myself that, as I walked from the subway station to the high school. And at the same time I couldn't doubt it. I was scared, scared for Sonny. He became real to me again. A great block of ice got settled in my belly and kept melting there slowly all day long, while I taught my classes algebra. It was a special kind of ice. It kept melting, sending trickles of ice water all up and down my veins, but it never got less. Sometimes it hardened and seemed to expand until I felt my guts were going to come spilling out or that I was going to choke or scream. This would always be at a moment when I was remembering some specific thing Sonny had once said or done.

When he was about as old as the boys in my classes his face had been bright and open, there was a lot of copper in it; and he'd had wonderfully direct brown eyes, and great gentleness and privacy. I wondered what he looked like now. He had been picked up, the evening before, in a raid on an apartment downtown, for peddling and using heroin.

I couldn't believe it: but what I mean by that is that I couldn't find any room for it anywhere inside me. I had kept it outside me for a long time. I hadn't wanted to know. I had had suspicions, but I didn't name them, I kept putting them away. I told myself that Sonny was wild, but he wasn't crazy. And he'd always been a good boy, he hadn't ever turned hard or evil or disrespectful, the way kids can, so quick, so quick, especially in Harlem. I didn't want to believe that I'd ever see my brother going down, coming to nothing, all that light in his face gone out, in the condition I'd already seen so many others. Yet it had happened and here I was, talking about algebra to a lot of boys who might, every one of them for all I knew, be popping off needles every time they went to the head. Maybe it did more for them than algebra could.

I was sure that the first time Sonny had ever had horse, he couldn't have been much older than these boys were now. These boys, now, were living as we'd been living then, they were growing up with a rush and their heads bumped abruptly against the low ceiling of their actual possibilities. They were filled with rage. All they really knew were two darknesses, the darkness of their lives, which was now closing in on them, and the darkness of the movies, which had blinded them to that other darkness, and in which they now, vindictively, dreamed, at once more together than they were at any other time, and more alone.

When the last bell rang, the last class ended, I let out my breath. It seemed I'd been holding it for all that time. My clothes were wet — I may have looked as though I'd been sitting in a steam bath, all dressed up, all afternoon. I sat alone in the classroom a long time. I listened to the boys outside, downstairs, shouting and cursing and laughing. Their laughter struck me for perhaps the first time. It was not the joyous laughter which — God knows why — one associates with children. It was mocking and insular, its intent to denigrate. It was disenchanted, and in this, also, lay the authority of their curses. Perhaps I was listening to them because I was thinking about my brother and in them I heard my brother. And myself.

One boy was whistling a tune, at once very complicated and very simple, it seemed to be pouring out of him as though he were a bird, and it sounded very cool and moving through all that harsh, bright air, only just holding its own through all those other sounds.

I stood up and walked over to the window and looked down into the courtyard. It was the beginning of the spring and the sap was rising in the boys. A teacher passed through them every now and again, quickly, as though he or she couldn't wait to get out of that courtyard, to get those boys out of their sight and off their minds. I started collecting my stuff. I thought I'd better get home and talk to Isabel.

The courtyard was almost deserted by the time I got downstairs. I saw this boy standing in the shadow of a doorway, looking just like Sonny. I almost called his name. Then I saw that it wasn't Sonny, but somebody we used to know, a boy from around our block. He'd been Sonny's friend. He'd never been mine, having been too young for me, and, anyway, I'd never liked him. And now, even though he was a grown-up man, he still hung around that block, still spent hours on the street corners, was always high and raggy. I used to run into him from time to time and he'd often work around to asking me for a quarter or fifty cents. He always had some real good excuse, too, and I always gave it to him, I don't know why.

But now, abruptly, I hated him. I couldn't stand the way he looked at me, partly like a dog, partly like a cunning child. I wanted to ask him what the hell he was doing in the school courtyard.

He sort of shuffled over to me, and he said, "I see you got the papers. So you already know about it."

"You mean about Sonny? Yes, I already know about it. How come they didn't get you?"

He grinned. It made him repulsive and it also brought to mind what he'd looked like as a kid. "I wasn't there. I stay away from them people."

"Good for you." I offered him a cigarette and I watched him through the smoke. "You come all the way down here just to tell me about Sonny?"

"That's right." He was sort of shaking his head and his eyes looked strange, as though they were about to cross. The bright sun deadened his damp dark brown skin and it made his eyes look yellow and showed up the dirt in his kinked hair. He smelled funky. I moved a little away from him and I said, "Well, thanks. But I already know about it and I got to get home."

"I'll walk you a little ways," he said. We started walking. There were a couple of kids still loitering in the courtyard and one of them said good-night to me and looked strangely at the boy beside me.

"What're you going to do?" he asked me. "I mean, about Sonny?"

"Look. I haven't seen Sonny for over a year. I'm not sure I'm going to do anything. Anyway, what the hell *can* I do?"

"That's right," he said quickly, "ain't nothing you can do. Can't much help old Sonny no more, I guess."

It was what I was thinking and so it seemed to me he had no right to say it.

"I'm surprised at Sonny, though," he went on — he had a funny way of talking, he looked straight ahead as though he were talking to himself — "I thought Sonny was a smart boy, I thought he was too smart to get hung."

"I guess he thought so too," I said sharply, "and that's how he got hung. And how about you? You're pretty goddamn smart, I bet."

Then he looked directly at me, just for a minute. "I ain't smart," he said. "If I was smart, I'd have reached for a pistol a long time ago."

"Look. Don't tell *me* your sad story, if it was up to me, I'd give you one." Then I felt guilty — guilty, probably, for never having supposed that the poor bastard *had* a story of his own, much less a sad one, and I asked, quickly, "What's going to happen to him now?"

He didn't answer this. He was off by himself some place. "Funny thing," he said, and from his tone we might have been discussing the quickest way to get to Brooklyn, "when I saw the papers this morning, the first thing I asked myself was if I had anything to do with it. I felt sort of responsible."

I began to listen more carefully. The subway station was on the corner, just before us, and I stopped. He stopped, too. We were in front of a bar and he ducked slightly, peering in, but whoever he was looking for didn't seem to be there. The juke box was blasting away with something black and bouncy and I half watched the barmaid as she danced her way from the juke box to her place behind the bar. And I watched her face as she laughingly responded to something someone said to her, still keeping time to the music. When she smiled one saw the little girl, one sensed the doomed, still-struggling woman beneath the battered face of the semi-whore.

"I never *give* Sonny nothing," the boy said finally, "but a long time ago I come to school high and Sonny asked me how it felt." He paused, I couldn't bear to watch him, I watched the barmaid, and I listened to the music which seemed to be causing the pavement to shake. "I told him it felt great." The music stopped, the barmaid paused and watched the juke box until the music began again. "It did."

All this was carrying me some place I didn't want to go. I certainly didn't want to know how it felt. It filled everything, the people, the houses, the music, the dark, quicksilver barmaid, with menace; and this menace was their reality.

"What's going to happen to him now?" I asked again.

"They'll send him away some place and they'll try to cure him." He shook his head. "Maybe he'll even think he's kicked the habit. Then they'll let him loose" — he gestured, throwing his cigarette into the gutter. "That's all."

"What do you mean, that's *all*?"

But I knew what he meant.

"I *mean,* that's *all.*" He turned his head and looked at me, pulling down the corners of his mouth. "Don't you know what I mean?" he asked, softly.

"How the hell *would* I know what you mean?" I almost whispered it, I don't know why.

"That's right," he said to the air, "how would *he* know what I mean?" He turned toward me again, patient and calm, and yet I somehow felt him shaking, shaking as though he were going to fall apart. I felt that ice in my guts again, the dread I'd felt all afternoon; and again I watched the barmaid, moving about the bar, washing glasses, and singing. "Listen. They'll let him out and then it'll just start all over again. That's what I mean."

"You mean—they'll let him out. And then he'll just start working his way back in again. You mean he'll never kick the habit. Is that what you mean?"

"That's right," he said, cheerfully. "*You* see what I mean."

"Tell me," I said at last, "why does he want to die? He must want to die, he's killing himself, why does he want to die?"

He looked at me in surprise. He licked his lips. "He don't want to die. He wants to live. Don't nobody want to die, ever."

Then I wanted to ask him—too many things. He could not have answered, or if he had, I could not have borne the answers. I started walking. "Well, I guess it's none of my business."

"It's going to be rough on old Sonny," he said. We reached the subway station. "This is your station?" he asked. I nodded. I took one step down. "Damn!" he said, suddenly. I looked up at him. He grinned again. "Damn it if I didn't leave all my money home. You ain't got a dollar on you, have you? Just for a couple of days, is all."

All at once something inside gave and threatened to come pouring out of me. I didn't hate him any more. I felt that in another moment I'd start crying like a child.

"Sure," I said. "Don't sweat." I looked in my wallet and didn't have a dollar, I only had a five. "Here," I said. "That hold you?"

He didn't look at it—he didn't want to look at it. A terrible closed look came over his face, as though he were keeping the number on the bill a secret from him and me. "Thanks," he said, and now he was dying to see me go. "Don't worry about Sonny. Maybe I'll write him or something."

"Sure," I said. "You do that. So long."

"Be seeing you," he said. I went on down the steps.

And I didn't write Sonny or send him anything for a long time. When I finally did, it was just after my little girl died, he wrote me back a letter which made me feel like a bastard.

Here's what he said:

Dear brother,

You don't know how much I needed to hear from you. I wanted to write you many a time but I dug how much I must have hurt you and so I didn't write. But now I feel like a man who's been trying to climb up out of some deep, real deep and funky hole and just saw the sun up there, outside. I got to get outside.

I can't tell you much about how I got here. I mean I don't know how to tell you. I guess I was afraid of something or I was trying to escape from something and you know I have never been very strong in the head (smile). I'm glad Mama and Daddy are dead and can't see what's happened to their son and I swear if I'd known what I was doing I would never have hurt you so, you and a lot of other fine people who were nice to me and who believed in me.

I don't want you to think it had anything to do with me being a musician. It's more than that. Or maybe less than that. I can't get anything straight in my head down here and I try not to think about what's going to happen to me when I get outside again. Sometime I think I'm going to flip and *never* get outside and sometime I think I'll come straight back. I tell you one thing, though, I'd rather blow my brains out than go through this again. But that's what they all say, so they tell me. If I tell you when I'm coming to New York and if you could meet me, I sure would appreciate it. Give my love to Isabel and the kids and I was sure sorry to hear about little Gracie. I wish I could be like Mama and say the Lord's will be done, but I don't know it seems to me that trouble is the one thing that never does get stopped and I don't know what good it does to blame it on the Lord. But maybe it does some good if you believe it.

Your brother,
Sonny

Then I kept in constant touch with him and I sent him whatever I could and I went to meet him when he came back to New York. When I saw him many things I thought I had forgotten came flooding back to me. This was because I had begun, finally, to wonder about Sonny, about the life that Sonny lived inside. This life, whatever it was, had made him older and thinner and it had deepened the distant stillness in which he had always moved. He looked very unlike my baby brother. Yet, when he smiled, when we shook hands, the baby brother I'd never known looked out from the depths of his private life, like an animal waiting to be coaxed into the light.

"How you been keeping?" he asked me.

"All right. And you?"

"Just fine." He was smiling all over his face. "It's good to see you again."

"It's good to see you."

The seven years' difference in our ages lay between us like a chasm: I wondered if these years would ever operate between us as a bridge. I was remembering, and it made it hard to catch my breath, that I had been there when he was born; and I had heard the first words he had ever spoken. When he started to walk, he walked from our mother straight to me. I caught him just before he fell when he took the first steps he ever took in this world.

"How's Isabel?"

"Just fine. She's dying to see you."

"And the boys?"

"They're fine, too. They're anxious to see their uncle."

"Oh, come on. You know they don't remember me."

"Are you kidding? Of course they remember you."

He grinned again. We got into a taxi. We had a lot to say to each other, far too much to know how to begin.

As the taxi began to move, I asked, "You still want to go to India?"

He laughed. "You still remember that. Hell, no. This place is Indian enough for me."

"It used to belong to them," I said.

And he laughed again. "They damn sure knew what they were doing when they got rid of it."

Years ago, when he was around fourteen, he'd been all hipped on the idea of going to India. He read books about people sitting on rocks, naked, in all kinds of weather, but mostly bad, naturally, and walking barefoot through hot coals and arriving at wisdom. I used to say that it sounded to me as though they were getting away from wisdom as fast as they could. I think he sort of looked down on me for that.

"Do you mind," he asked, "if we have the driver drive alongside the park? On the west side—I haven't seen the city in so long."

"Of course not," I said. I was afraid that I might sound as though I were humoring him, but I hoped he wouldn't take it that way.

So we drove along, between the green of the park and the stony, lifeless elegance of hotels and apartment buildings, toward the vivid, killing streets of our childhood. These streets hadn't changed, though housing projects jutted up out of them now like rocks in the middle of a boiling sea. Most of the houses in which we had grown up had vanished, as had the stores from which we had stolen, the basements in which we had first tried sex, the rooftops from which we had hurled tin cans and bricks. But houses exactly like the houses of our past yet dominated the landscape, boys exactly like the boys we once had been found themselves smothering in these houses, came down into the streets for light and air and found themselves encircled by disaster. Some escaped the trap, most didn't. Those who got out always left something of themselves behind, as some animals amputate a leg and leave it in the trap. It might be said, perhaps, that I had escaped, after all, I was a school teacher; or that Sonny had, he hadn't lived in Harlem for years. Yet, as the cab moved uptown through streets which seemed, with a rush, to darken with dark people, and as I covertly studied Sonny's face, it came to me that what we both were seeking through our separate cab windows was that part of ourselves which had been left behind. It's always at the hour of trouble and confrontation that the missing member aches.

We hit 110th Street and started rolling up Lenox Avenue. And I'd known this avenue all my life, but it seemed to me again, as it had seemed on the day I'd first heard about Sonny's trouble, filled with a hidden menace which was its very breath of life.

"We almost there," said Sonny.

"Almost." We were both too nervous to say anything more.

We live in a housing project. It hasn't been up long. A few days after it was up it seemed uninhabitably new, now, of course, it's already rundown. It looks like a parody of the good, clean, faceless life—God knows the people who live in it do their best to make it a parody. The beat-looking grass lying around isn't enough to make their lives green, the hedges will never hold out the streets, and they know it. The big windows fool no one, they aren't big enough to make space out of no space. They don't bother with the windows, they watch the TV screen instead. The playground is most popular with the children who don't play at jacks, or skip rope, or roller skate, or swing, and they can be found in it after dark. We moved in partly because it's not too far from where I teach, and partly for the kids; but it's really just like the houses in which Sonny and I grew up. The same things happen, they'll have the same things to remember. The moment Sonny and I started into the house I had the feeling that I was simply bringing him back into the danger he had almost died trying to escape.

Sonny has never been talkative. So I don't know why I was sure he'd be dying to talk to me when supper was over the first night. Everything went fine, the oldest boy remembered him, and the youngest boy liked him, and Sonny had remembered to bring something for each of them; and Isabel, who is really much nicer than I am, more open and giving, had gone to a lot of trouble about dinner and was genuinely glad to see him. And she's always been able to tease Sonny in a way that I haven't. It was nice to see her face so vivid again and to hear her laugh and watch her make Sonny laugh. She wasn't, or, anyway, she didn't seem to be, at all uneasy or embarrassed. She chatted as though there were no subject which had to be avoided and she got Sonny past his first, faint stiffness. And thank God she was there, for I was filled with that icy dread again. Everything I did seemed awkward to me, and everything I said sounded freighted with hidden meaning. I was trying to remember everything I'd heard about dope addiction and I couldn't help watching Sonny for signs. I wasn't doing it out of malice. I was trying to find out something about my brother. I was dying to hear him tell me he was safe.

"Safe!" my father grunted, whenever Mama suggested trying to move to a neighborhood which might be safer for children. "Safe, hell! Ain't no place safe for kids, nor nobody."

He always went on like this, but he wasn't, ever, really as bad as he sounded, not even on weekends, when he got drunk. As a matter of fact, he was always on the lookout for "something a little better," but he died before he found it. He died suddenly, during a drunken weekend in the middle of the war, when Sonny was fifteen. He and Sonny hadn't ever got on too well. And this was partly because Sonny was the apple of his father's eye. It was because he loved Sonny so much and was frightened for him, that he was always fighting with him. It doesn't do any good to fight with Sonny. Sonny just moves back, inside himself, where he can't be reached. But the principal reason that they never hit it off is that they were so much alike. Daddy was big and rough and loud-talking, just the opposite of Sonny, but they both had—that same privacy.

Mama tried to tell me something about this, just after Daddy died. I was home on leave from the army.

This was the last time I ever saw my mother alive. Just the same, this picture gets all mixed up in my mind with pictures I had of her when she was younger. The way I always see her is the way she used to be on a Sunday afternoon, say, when the old folks were talking after the big Sunday dinner. I always see her wearing pale blue. She'd be sitting on the sofa. And my father would be sitting in the easy chair, not far from her. And the living room would be full of church folks and relatives. There they sit, in chairs all around the living room, and the night is creeping up outside, but nobody knows it yet. You can see the darkness growing against the windowpanes and you hear the street noises every now and again, or maybe the jangling beat of a tambourine from one of the churches close by, but it's real quiet in the room. For a moment nobody's talking, but every face looks darkening, like the sky outside. And my mother rocks a little from the waist, and my father's eyes are closed. Everyone is looking at something a child can't see. For a minute they've forgotten the children. Maybe a kid is lying on the rug, half asleep. Maybe somebody's got a kid in his lap and is absent-mindedly stroking the kid's head. Maybe there's a kid, quiet and big-eyed, curled up in a big chair in the corner. The silence, the darkness coming, and the darkness in the faces frightens the child obscurely. He hopes that the hand which strokes his forehead will never stop—will never die. He hopes that there will never come a time when the old folks won't be sitting around the living room, talking about where they've come from, and what they've seen, and what's happened to them and their kinfolk.

But something deep and watchful in the child knows that this is bound to end, is already ending. In a moment someone will get up and turn on the light. Then the old folks will remember the children and they won't talk any more that day. And when light fills the room, the child is filled with darkness. He knows that every time this happens he's moved just a little closer to that darkness outside. The darkness outside is what the old folks have been talking about. It's what they've come from. It's what they endure. The child knows that they won't talk any more because if he knows too much about what's happened to *them*, he'll know too much too soon, about what's going to happen to *him*.

The last time I talked to my mother, I remember I was restless. I wanted to get out and see Isabel. We weren't married then and we had a lot to straighten out between us.

There Mama sat, in black, by the window. She was humming an old church song, *Lord, you brought me from a long ways off.* Sonny was out somewhere. Mama kept watching the streets.

"I don't know," she said, "if I'll ever see you again, after you go off from here. But I hope you'll remember the things I tried to teach you."

"Don't talk like that," I said, and smiled. "You'll be here a long time yet."

She smiled, too, but she said nothing. She was quiet for a long time. And I said, "Mama, don't you worry about nothing. I'll be writing all the time, and you be getting the checks. . . ."

"I want to talk to you about your brother," she said, suddenly. "If anything happens to me he ain't going to have nobody to look out for him."

"Mama," I said, "ain't nothing going to happen to you *or* Sonny. Sonny's all right. He's a good boy and he's got good sense."

"It ain't a question of his being a good boy," Mama said, "nor of his having good sense. It ain't only the bad ones, nor yet the dumb ones that gets sucked under." She stopped, looking at me. "Your Daddy once had a brother," she said, and she smiled in a way that made me feel she was in pain. "You didn't never know that, did you?"

"No," I said, "I never knew that," and I watched her face.

"Oh, yes," she said, "your Daddy had a brother." She looked out of the window again. "I know you never saw your Daddy cry. But *I* did— many a time, through all these years."

I asked her, "What happened to his brother? How come nobody's ever talked about him?"

This was the first time I ever saw my mother look old.

"His brother got killed," she said, "when he was just a little younger than you are now. I knew him. He was a fine boy. He was maybe a little full of the devil, but he didn't mean nobody no harm."

Then she stopped and the room was silent, exactly as it had sometimes been on those Sunday afternoons. Mama kept looking out into the streets.

"He used to have a job in the mill," she said, "and, like all young folks, he just liked to perform on Saturday nights. Saturday nights, him and your father would drift around to different places, go to dances and things like that, or just sit around with people they knew, and your father's brother would sing, he had a fine voice, and play along with himself on his guitar. Well, this particular Saturday night, him and your father was coming home from some place, and they were both a little drunk and there was a moon that night, it was bright like day. Your father's brother was feeling kind of good, and he was whistling to himself, and he had his guitar slung over his shoulder. They was coming down a hill and beneath them was a road that turned off from the highway. Well, your father's brother, being always kind of frisky, decided to run down this hill, and he did, with that guitar banging and clanging behind him, and he ran across the road, and he was making water behind a tree. And your father was sort of amused at him and he was still coming down the hill, kind of slow. Then he heard a car motor and that same minute his brother stepped from behind the tree, into the road, in the moonlight. And he started to cross the road. And your father started to run down the hill, he says he don't know why. This car was full of white men. They was all drunk, and when they seen your father's brother they let out a great whoop and holler and they aimed the car straight at him. They was having fun, they just wanted to scare him, the way they do sometimes, you know. But they was drunk. And I guess the boy, being drunk, too, and scared, kind of lost his head. By the time he jumped it was too late. Your father says he heard his brother scream when the car rolled over him, and he heard the wood of that guitar when it give, and he heard them strings go flying, and he heard them white men shouting, and the car kept on a-going and it ain't stopped till this day. And, time your father got down the hill, his brother weren't nothing but blood and pulp."

Tears were gleaming on my mother's face. There wasn't anything I could say.

"He never mentioned it," she said, "because I never let him mention it before you children. Your Daddy was like a crazy man that night and for many a night thereafter. He says he never in his life seen anything as dark as that road after the lights of that car had gone away. Weren't nothing, weren't nobody on that road, just your Daddy and his brother and that busted guitar. Oh, yes. Your Daddy never did really get right again. Till the day he died he weren't sure but that every white man he saw was the man that killed his brother."

She stopped and took out her handkerchief and dried her eyes and looked at me.

"I ain't telling you all this," she said, "to make you scared or bitter or to make you hate nobody. I'm telling you this because you got a brother. And the world ain't changed."

I guess I didn't want to believe this. I guess she saw this in my face. She turned away from me, toward the window again, searching those streets.

"But I praise my Redeemer," she said at last, "that He called your Daddy home before me. I ain't saying it to throw no flowers at myself, but, I declare, it keeps me from feeling too cast down to know I helped your father get safely through this world. Your father always acted like he was the roughest, strongest man on earth. And everybody took him to be like that. But if he hadn't had *me* there—to see his tears!"

She was crying again. Still, I couldn't move. I said, "Lord, Lord, Mama, I didn't know it was like that."

"Oh, honey," she said, "there's a lot that you don't know. But you are going to find it out." She stood up from the window and came over to me.

"You got to hold on to your brother," she said, "and don't let him fall, no matter what it looks like is happening to him and no matter how evil you gets with him. You going to be evil with him many a time. But don't you forget what I told you, you hear?"

"I won't forget," I said. "Don't you worry, I won't forget. I won't let nothing happen to Sonny."

My mother smiled as though she were amused at something she saw in my face. Then, "You may not be able to stop nothing from happening. But you got to let him know you's *there*."

Two days later I was married, and then I was gone. And I had a lot of things on my mind and I pretty well forgot my promise to Mama until I got shipped home on a special furlough for her funeral.

And, after the funeral, with just Sonny and me alone in the empty kitchen, I tried to find out something about him.

"What do you want to do?" I asked him.

"I'm going to be a musician," he said.

For he had graduated, in the time I had been away, from dancing to the juke box to finding out who was playing what, and what they were doing with it, and he had bought himself a set of drums.

"You mean, you want to be a drummer?" I somehow had the feeling that being a drummer might be all right for other people but not for my brother Sonny.

"I don't think," he said, looking at me very gravely, "that I'll ever be a good drummer. But I think I can play a piano."

I frowned. I'd never played the role of the older brother quite so seriously before, had scarcely ever, in fact, *asked* Sonny a damn thing. I sensed myself in the presence of something I didn't really know how to handle, didn't understand. So I made my frown a little deeper as I asked: "What kind of musician do you want to be?"

He grinned. "How many kinds do you think there are?"

"Be *serious*," I said.

He laughed, throwing his head back, and then looked at me. "I *am* serious."

"Well, then, for Christ's sake, stop kidding around and answer a serious question. I mean, do you want to be a concert pianist, you want to play classical music and all that, or—or what?" Long before I finished he was laughing again. "For Christ's *sake*, Sonny!"

He sobered, but with difficulty. "I'm sorry. But you sound so—*scared!*" and he was off again.

"Well, you may think it's funny now, baby, but it's not going to be so funny when you have to make your living at it, let me tell you *that*." I was furious because I knew he was laughing at me and I didn't know why.

"No," he said, very sober now, and afraid, perhaps, that he'd hurt me, "I don't want to be a classical pianist. That isn't what interests me. I mean"—he paused, looking hard at me, as though his eyes would help me to understand, and then gestured helplessly, as though perhaps his hand would help—"I mean, I'll have a lot of studying to do, and I'll have to study *everything*, but, I mean, I want to play *with*—jazz musicians." He stopped. "I want to play jazz," he said.

Well, the word had never before sounded as heavy, as real, as it sounded that afternoon in Sonny's mouth. I just looked at him and I was probably frowning a real frown by this time. I simply couldn't see why on earth he'd want to spend his time hanging around nightclubs, clowning around on bandstands, while people pushed each other around a dance floor. It seemed—beneath him, somehow. I had never thought about it before, had never been forced to, but I suppose I had always put jazz musicians in a class with what Daddy called "good-time people."

"Are you *serious*?"

"Hell, *yes,* I'm serious."

He looked more helpless than ever, and annoyed, and deeply hurt.

I suggested, helpfully: "You mean—like Louis Armstrong?"

His face closed as though I'd struck him. "No. I'm not talking about none of that old-time, down home crap."

"Well, look, Sonny, I'm sorry, don't get mad. I just don't altogether get it, that's all. Name somebody—you know, a jazz musician you admire."

"Bird."

"Who?"

"Bird! Charlie Parker! Don't they teach you nothing in the goddamn army?"

I lit a cigarette. I was surprised and then a little amused to discover that I was trembling. "I've been out of touch," I said. "You'll have to be patient with me. Now. Who's this Parker character?"

"He's just one of the greatest jazz musicians alive," said Sonny, sullenly, his hands in his pockets, his back to me. "Maybe *the* greatest," he added, bitterly, "that's probably why *you* never heard of him."

"All right," I said, "I'm ignorant. I'm sorry. I'll go out and buy all the cat's records right away, all right?"

"It don't," said Sonny, with dignity, "make any difference to me. I don't care what you listen to. Don't do me no favors."

I was beginning to realize that I'd never seen him so upset before. With another part of my mind I was thinking that this would probably turn out to be one of those things kids go through and that I shouldn't make it seem important by pushing it too hard. Still, I didn't think it would do any harm to ask: "Doesn't all this take a lot of time? Can you make a living at it?"

He turned back to me and half leaned, half sat, on the kitchen table. "Everything takes time," he said, "and—well, yes, sure, I can make a living at it. But what I don't seem to be able to make you understand is that it's the only thing I want to do."

"Well, Sonny," I said, gently, "you know people can't always do exactly what they *want* to do —"

"*No,* I don't know that," said Sonny, surprising me. "I think people *ought* to do what they want to do, what else are they alive for?"

"You getting to be a big boy," I said desperately, "it's time you started thinking about your future."

"I'm thinking about my future," said Sonny, grimly. "I think about it all the time."

I gave up. I decided, if he didn't change his mind, that we could always talk about it later. "In the meantime," I said, "you got to finish school." We had already decided that he'd have to move in with Isabel and her folks. I knew this wasn't the ideal arrangement because Isabel's folks are inclined to be dicty and they hadn't especially wanted Isabel to marry me. But I didn't know what else to do. "And we have to get you fixed up at Isabel's."

There was a long silence. He moved from the kitchen table to the window. "That's a terrible idea. You know it yourself."

"Do you have a *better* idea?"

He just walked up and down the kitchen for a minute. He was as tall as I was. He had started to shave. I suddenly had the feeling that I didn't know him at all.

He stopped at the kitchen table and picked up my cigarettes. Looking at me with a kind of mocking, amused defiance, he put one between his lips. "You mind?"

"You smoking already?"

He lit the cigarette and nodded, watching me through the smoke. "I just wanted to see if I'd have the courage to smoke in front of you." He grinned and blew a great cloud of smoke to the ceiling. "It was easy." He looked at my face. "Come on, now. I bet you was smoking at my age, tell the truth."

I didn't say anything but the truth was on my face, and he laughed. But now there was something very strained in his laugh. "Sure. And I bet that ain't all you was doing."

He was frightening me a little. "Cut the crap," I said. "We already decided that you was going to go and live at Isabel's. Now what's got into you all of a sudden?"

"*You* decided it," he pointed out. "*I* didn't decide nothing." He stopped in front of me, leaning against the stove, arms loosely folded. "Look, brother. I don't want to stay in Harlem no more, I really don't." He was very earnest. He looked at me, then over toward the kitchen window. There was something in his eyes I'd never seen before, some thoughtfulness, some worry all his own. He rubbed the muscle of one arm. "It's time I was getting out of here."

"Where do you want to *go,* Sonny?"

"I want to join the army. Or the navy, I don't care. If I say I'm old enough, they'll believe me."

Then I got mad. It was because I was so scared. "You must be crazy. You goddamn fool, what the hell do you want to go and join the *army* for?"

"I just told you. To get out of Harlem."

"Sonny, you haven't even finished *school*. And if you really want to be a musician, how do you expect to study if you're in the *army*?"

He looked at me, trapped, and in anguish. "There's ways. I might be able to work out some kind of deal. Anyway, I'll have the G.I. Bill when I come out."

"*If* you come out." We stared at each other. "Sonny, please. Be reasonable. I know the setup is far from perfect. But we got to do the best we can."

"I ain't learning nothing in school," he said. "Even when I go." He turned away from me and opened the window and threw his cigarette out into the narrow alley. I watched his back. "At least, I ain't learning nothing you'd want me to learn." He slammed the window so hard I thought the glass would fly out, and turned back to me. "And I'm sick of the stink of these garbage cans!"

"Sonny," I said, "I know how you feel. But if you don't finish school now, you're going to be sorry later that you didn't." I grabbed him by the shoulders. "And you only got another year. It ain't so bad. And I'll come back and I swear I'll help you do *whatever* you want to do. Just try to put up with it till I come back. Will you please do that? For me?"

He didn't answer and he wouldn't look at me.

"Sonny. You hear me?"

He pulled away. "I hear you. But you never hear anything *I* say."

I didn't know what to say to that. He looked out of the window and then back at me. "OK," he said, and sighed. "I'll try."

Then I said, trying to cheer him up a little, "They got a piano at Isabel's. You can practice on it."

And as a matter of fact, it did cheer him up for a minute. "That's right," he said to himself. "I forgot that." His face relaxed a little. But the worry, the thoughtfulness, played on it still, the way shadows play on a face which is staring into the fire.

But I thought I'd never hear the end of that piano. At first, Isabel would write me, saying how nice it was that Sonny was so serious about his music and how, as soon as he came in from school, or wherever he had been when he was supposed to be at school, he went straight to that piano and stayed there until suppertime. And, after supper, he went back to that piano and stayed there until everybody went to bed. He was at the piano all day Saturday and all day Sunday. Then he bought a record player and started playing records. He'd play one record over and over again, all day long sometimes, and he'd improvise along with it on the piano. Or he'd play one section of the record, one chord, one change, one progression, then he'd do it on the piano. Then back to the record. Then back to the piano.

Well, I really don't know how they stood it. Isabel finally confessed that it wasn't like living with a person at all, it was like living with sound. And the sound didn't make any sense to her, didn't make any sense to any of them — naturally. They began, in a way, to be afflicted by this presence that was living in their home. It was as though Sonny were some sort of god, or monster. He moved in an atmosphere which wasn't like theirs at all. They fed him and he ate, he washed himself, he walked in and out of their door; he certainly wasn't nasty or unpleasant or rude, Sonny isn't any of those things; but it was as though he were all wrapped up in some cloud, some fire, some vision all his own; and there wasn't any way to reach him.

At the same time, he wasn't really a man yet, he was still a child, and they had to watch out for him in all kinds of ways. They certainly couldn't throw him out. Neither did they dare to make a great scene about that piano because even they dimly sensed, as I sensed, from so many thousands of miles away, that Sonny was at that piano playing for his life.

But he hadn't been going to school. One day a letter came from the school board and Isabel's mother got it — there had, apparently, been other letters but Sonny had torn them up. This day, when Sonny came in, Isabel's mother showed him the letter and asked where he'd been spending his time. And she finally got it out of him that he'd been down in Greenwich Village, with musicians and other characters, in a white girl's apartment. And this scared her and she started to scream at him and what came up, once she began — though she denies it to this day — was what sacrifices they were making to give Sonny a decent home and how little he appreciated it.

Sonny didn't play the piano that day. By evening, Isabel's mother had calmed down but then there was the old man to deal with, and Isabel herself. Isabel says she did her best to be calm but she broke down and started crying. She says she just watched Sonny's face. She could tell, by watching him, what was happening with him. And what was happening was that they penetrated his cloud, they had reached him. Even if their fingers had been a thousand times more gentle than human fingers ever are, he could hardly help feeling that they had stripped him naked and were spitting on that nakedness. For he also had to see that his presence, that music, which was life or death to him, had been torture for them and that they had endured it, not at all for his sake, but only for mine. And Sonny couldn't take that. He can take it a little better today than he could then but he's still not very good at it and, frankly, I don't know anybody who is.

The silence of the next few days must have been louder than the sound of all the music ever played since time began. One morning, before she went to work, Isabel was in his room for something and she suddenly realized that all of his records were gone. And she knew for certain that he was gone. And he was. He went as far as the navy would carry him. He finally sent me a postcard from some place in Greece and that was the first I knew that Sonny was still alive. I didn't see him any more until we were both back in New York and the war had long been over.

He was a man by then, of course, but I wasn't willing to see it. He came by the house from time to time, but we fought almost every time we met. I didn't like the way he carried himself, loose and dreamlike all the time, and I didn't like his friends, and his music seemed to be merely an excuse for the life he led. It sounded just that weird and disordered.

Then we had a fight, a pretty awful fight, and I didn't see him for months. By and by I looked him up, where he was living, in a furnished room in the Village, and I tried to make it up. But there were lots of people in the room and Sonny just lay on his bed, and he wouldn't come downstairs with me, and he treated these other people as though they were his family and I weren't. So I got mad and then he got mad, and then I told him that he might just as well be dead as live the way he was living. Then he stood up and he told me not to worry about him any more in life, that he *was* dead as far as I was concerned. Then he pushed me to the door and the other people looked on as though nothing were happening, and he slammed the door behind me. I stood in the hallway, staring at the door. I heard somebody laugh in the room and then the tears came to my eyes. I started down the steps, whistling to keep from crying, I kept whistling to myself, *You going to need me, baby, one of these cold, rainy days.*

I read about Sonny's trouble in the spring. Little Grace died in the fall. She was a beautiful little girl. But she only lived a little over two years. She died of polio and she suffered. She had a slight fever for a couple of days, but it didn't seem like anything and we just kept her in bed. And we would certainly have called the doctor, but the fever dropped, she seemed to be all right. So we thought it had just been a cold. Then, one day, she was up, playing, Isabel was in the kitchen fixing lunch for the two boys when they'd come in from school, and she heard Grace fall down in the living room. When you have a lot of children you don't always start running when one of them falls, unless they start screaming or something. And, this time, Grace was quiet. Yet, Isabel says that when she heard that *thump* and then that silence, something happened in her to make her afraid. And she ran to the living room and there was little Grace on the floor, all twisted up, and the reason she hadn't screamed was that she couldn't get her breath. And when she did scream, it was the worst sound, Isabel says, that she'd ever heard in all her life, and she still hears it sometimes in her dreams. Isabel will sometimes wake me up with a low, moaning, strangled sound and I have to be quick to awaken her and hold her to me and where Isabel is weeping against me seems a mortal wound.

I think I may have written Sonny the very day that little Grace was buried. I was sitting in the living room in the dark, by myself, and I suddenly thought of Sonny. My trouble made his real.

One Saturday afternoon, when Sonny had been living with us, or, anyway, been in our house, for nearly two weeks, I found myself wandering aimlessly about the living room, drinking from a can of beer, and trying to work up the courage to search Sonny's room. He was out, he was usually out whenever I was home, and Isabel had taken the children to see their grandparents. Suddenly I was standing still in front of the living room window, watching Seventh Avenue. The idea of searching Sonny's room made me still. I scarcely dared to admit to myself what I'd be searching for. I didn't know what I'd do if I found it. Or if I didn't.

On the sidewalk across from me, near the entrance to a barbecue joint, some people were holding an old-fashioned revival meeting. The barbecue cook, wearing a dirty white apron, his conked hair reddish and metallic in the pale sun, and a cigarette between his lips, stood in the doorway, watching them. Kids and older people paused in their errands and stood there, along with some older men and a couple of very tough-looking women who watched everything that happened on the avenue, as though they owned it, or were maybe owned by it. Well, they were watching this, too. The revival was being carried on by three sisters in black, and a brother. All they had were their voices and their Bibles and a tambourine. The brother was testifying and while he testified two of the sisters stood together, seeming to say, amen, and the third sister walked around with the tambourine outstretched and a couple of people dropped coins into it. Then the brother's testimony ended and the sister who had been taking up the collection dumped the coins into her palm and transferred them to the pocket of her long black robe. Then she raised both hands, striking the tambourine against the air, and then against one hand, and she started to sing. And the two other sisters and the brother joined in.

It was strange, suddenly, to watch, though I had been seeing these street meetings all my life. So, of course, had everybody else down there. Yet, they paused and watched and listened and I stood still at the window. *"Tis the old ship of Zion,"* they sang, and the sister with the tambourine kept a steady, jangling beat, *"it has rescued many a thousand!"* Not a soul under the sound of their voices was hearing this song for the first time, not one of them had been rescued. Nor had they seen much in the way of rescue work being done around them. Neither did they especially believe in the holiness of the three sisters and the brother, they knew too much about them, knew where they lived, and how. The woman with the tambourine, whose voice dominated the air, whose face was bright with joy, was divided by very little from the woman who stood watching her, a cigarette between her heavy, chapped lips, her hair a cuckoo's nest, her face scarred and swollen from many beatings, and her black eyes glittering like coal. Perhaps they both knew this, which was why, when, as rarely, they addressed each other, they addressed each other as Sister. As the singing filled the air the watching, listening faces underwent a change, the eyes focusing on something within; the music seemed to soothe a poison out of them; and time seemed, nearly, to fall away from the sullen, belligerent, battered faces, as though they were fleeing back to their first condition, while dreaming of their last. The barbecue cook half shook his head and smiled, and dropped his cigarette and disappeared into his joint. A man fumbled in his pockets for change and stood holding it in his hand impatiently, as though he had just remembered a pressing appointment further up the avenue. He looked furious. Then I saw Sonny, standing on the edge of the crowd. He was carrying a wide, flat notebook with a green cover, and it made him look, from where I was standing, almost like a schoolboy. The coppery sun brought out the copper in his skin, he was very faintly smiling, standing very still. Then the singing stopped, the tambourine turned into a collection plate again. The furious man dropped in his coins and vanished, so did a couple of the women, and Sonny dropped some change in the plate, looking directly at the woman with a little smile. He started across the avenue, toward the house. He has a slow, loping walk, something like the way Harlem hipsters walk, only he's imposed on this his own half-beat. I had never really noticed it before.

I stayed at the window, both relieved and apprehensive. As Sonny disappeared from my sight, they began singing again. And they were still singing when his key turned in the lock.

"Hey," he said.

"Hey, yourself. You want some beer?"

"No. Well, maybe." But he came up to the window and stood beside me, looking out. "What a warm voice," he said.

They were singing *If I could only hear my mother pray again!*

"Yes," I said, "and she can sure beat that tambourine."

"But what a terrible song," he said, and laughed. He dropped his notebook on the sofa and disappeared into the kitchen. "Where's Isabel and the kids?"

"I think they went to see their grandparents. You hungry?"

"No." He came back into the living room with his can of beer. "You want to come some place with me tonight?"

I sensed, I don't know how, that I couldn't possibly say no. "Sure. Where?"

He sat down on the sofa and picked up his notebook and started leafing through it. "I'm going to sit in with some fellows in a joint in the Village."

"You mean, you're going to play, tonight?"

"That's right." He took a swallow of his beer and moved back to the window. He gave me a sidelong look. "If you can stand it."

"I'll try," I said.

He smiled to himself and we both watched as the meeting across the way broke up. The three sisters and the brother, heads bowed, were singing

God be with you till we meet again. The faces around them were very quiet. Then the song ended. The small crowd dispersed. We watched the three women and the lone man walk slowly up the avenue.

"When she was singing before," said Sonny, abruptly, "her voice reminded me for a minute of what heroin feels like sometimes—when it's in your veins. It makes you feel sort of warm and cool at the same time. And distant. And—and sure." He sipped his beer, very deliberately not looking at me. I watched his face. "It makes you feel—in control. Sometimes you've got to have that feeling."

"Do you?" I sat down slowly in the easy chair.

"Sometimes." He went to the sofa and picked up his notebook again. "Some people do."

"In order," I asked, "to play?" And my voice was very ugly, full of contempt and anger.

"Well"—he looked at me with great, troubled eyes, as though, in fact, he hoped his eyes would tell me things he could never otherwise say—"they *think* so. And *if* they think so—!"

"And what do *you* think?" I asked.

He sat on the sofa and put his can of beer on the floor. "I don't know," he said, and I couldn't be sure if he were answering my question or pursuing his thoughts. His face didn't tell me. "It's not so much to *play*. It's to *stand* it, to be able to make it at all. On any level." He frowned and smiled: "In order to keep from shaking to pieces."

"But these friends of yours," I said, "they seem to shake themselves to pieces pretty goddamn fast."

"Maybe." He played with the notebook. And something told me that I should curb my tongue, that Sonny was doing his best to talk, that I should listen. "But of course you only know the ones that've gone to pieces. Some don't—or at least they haven't *yet* and that's just about all *any* of us can say." He paused. "And then there are some who just live, really, in hell, and they know it and they see what's happening and they go right on. I don't know." He sighed, dropped the notebook, folded his arms. "Some guys, you can tell from the way they play, they on something *all* the time. And you can see that, well, it makes something real for them. But of course," he picked up his beer from the floor and sipped it and put the can down again, "they *want* to, too, you've got to see that. Even some of them that say they don't—*some*, not all."

"And what about you?" I asked—I couldn't help it. "What about you? Do *you* want to?"

He stood up and walked to the window and remained silent for a long time. Then he sighed. "Me," he said. Then: "While I was downstairs before, on my way here, listening to that woman sing, it struck me all of a sudden how much suffering she must have had to go through—to sing like that. It's *repulsive* to think you have to suffer that much."

I said: "But there's no way not to suffer—is there, Sonny?"

"I believe not," he said and smiled, "but that's never stopped anyone from trying." He looked at me. "Has it?" I realized, with this mocking look, that there stood between us, forever, beyond the power of time or forgiveness, the fact that I had held silence—so long!—when he had needed human speech to help him. He turned back to the window. "No, there's no way not to suffer. But you try all kinds of ways to keep from drowning in it, to keep on top of it, and to make it seem—well, like *you*. Like you did something, all right, and now you're suffering for it. You know?" I said nothing. "Well you know," he said, impatiently, "why *do* people suffer? Maybe it's better to do something to give it a reason, *any* reason."

"But we just agreed," I said, "that there's no way not to suffer. Isn't it better, then, just to—take it?"

"But nobody just takes it," Sonny cried, "that's what I'm telling you! *Everybody* tries not to. You're just hung up on the *way* some people try—it's not *your* way!"

The hair on my face began to itch, my face felt wet. "That's not true," I said, "that's not true. I don't give a damn what other people do, I don't even care how they suffer. I just care how *you* suffer." And he looked at me. "Please believe me," I said, "I don't want to see you—die—trying not to suffer."

"I won't," he said, flatly, "die trying not to suffer. At least, not any faster than anybody else."

"But there's no need," I said, trying to laugh, "is there? in killing yourself."

I wanted to say more, but I couldn't. I wanted to talk about will power and how life could be—well, beautiful. I wanted to say that it was all within; but was it? or, rather, wasn't that exactly the trouble? And I wanted to promise that I would never fail him again. But it would all have sounded—empty words and lies.

So I made the promise to myself and prayed that I would keep it.

"It's terrible sometimes, inside," he said, "that's what's the trouble. You walk these streets, black and funky and cold, and there's not really a living ass to talk to, and there's nothing shaking, and there's no way of getting it out—that storm inside. You can't talk it and you can't make love with it, and when you finally try to get with it and play it, you realize *nobody's* listening. So *you've* got to listen. You got to find a way to listen."

And then he walked away from the window and sat on the sofa again, as though all the wind had suddenly been knocked out of him. "Sometimes you'll do *anything* to play, even cut your mother's throat." He laughed and looked at me. "Or your brother's." Then he sobered. "Or your own." Then: "Don't worry. I'm all right now and I think I'll *be* all right. But I can't forget—where I've been. I don't mean just the physical place I've been, I mean where I've *been*. And *what* I've been."

"What have you been, Sonny?" I asked.

He smiled—but sat sideways on the sofa, his elbow resting on the back, his fingers playing with his mouth and chin, not looking at me. "I've been something I didn't recognize, didn't know I could be. Didn't know anybody could be." He stopped, looking inward, looking helplessly young, looking old. "I'm not talking about it now because I feel *guilty* or anything like that—maybe it would be better if I did, I don't know. Anyway, I can't really talk about it. Not to you, not to anybody," and now he turned and faced me. "Sometimes, you know, and it was actually when I was most *out* of the world, I felt that I was in it, that I was *with* it, really, and I could play or I didn't really have to *play,* it just came out of me, it was there. And I don't know how I played, thinking about it now, but I know I did awful things, those times, sometimes, to people. Or it wasn't that I *did* anything to them—it was that they weren't real." He picked up the beer can; it was empty; he rolled it between his palms: "And other times—well, I needed a fix, I needed to find a place to lean, I needed to clear a space to *listen*—and I couldn't find it, and I—went crazy, I did terrible things to *me,* I was terrible *for* me." He began pressing the beer can between his hands, I watched the metal begin to give. It glittered, as he played with it, like a knife, and I was afraid he would cut himself, but I said nothing. "Oh well. I can never tell you. I was all by myself at the bottom of something, stinking and sweating and crying and shaking, and I smelled it, you know? *my* stink, and I thought I'd die if I couldn't get away from it and yet, all the same, I knew that everything I was doing was just locking me in with it. And I didn't know," he paused, still flattening the beer can, "I didn't know, I still *don't* know, something kept telling me that maybe it was good to smell your own stink, but I didn't think that *that* was what I'd been trying to do—and—who can stand it?" and he abruptly dropped the ruined beer can, looking at me with a small, still smile, and then rose, walking to the window as though it were the lodestone rock. I watched his face, he watched the avenue. "I couldn't tell you when Mama died—but the reason I wanted to leave Harlem so bad was to get away from drugs. And then, when I ran away, that's what I was running from—really. When I came back, nothing had changed, *I* hadn't changed, I was just—older." And he stopped, drumming with his fingers on the windowpane. The sun had vanished, soon darkness would fall. I watched his face. "It can come again," he said, almost as though speaking to himself. Then he turned to me. "It can come again," he repeated. "I just want you to know that."

"All right," I said, at last. "So it can come again, All right."

He smiled, but the smile was sorrowful. "I had to try to tell you," he said.

"Yes," I said. "I understand that."

"You're my brother," he said, looking straight at me, and not smiling at all.

"Yes," I repeated, "yes. I understand that."

He turned back to the window, looking out. "All that hatred down there," he said, "all that hatred and misery and love. It's a wonder it doesn't blow the avenue apart."

We went to the only nightclub on a short, dark street, downtown. We squeezed through the narrow, chattering, jam-packed bar to the entrance of the big room, where the bandstand was. And we stood there for a moment, for the lights were very dim in this room and we couldn't see. Then, "Hello, boy," said a voice and an enormous black man, much older than Sonny or myself, erupted out of all that atmospheric lighting and put an arm around Sonny's shoulder. "I been sitting right here," he said, "waiting for you."

He had a big voice, too, and heads in the darkness turned toward us.

Sonny grinned and pulled a little away, and said, "Creole, this is my brother. I told you about him."

Creole shook my hand. "I'm glad to meet you, son," he said, and it was clear that he was glad to meet me *there*, for Sonny's sake. And he smiled, "You got a real musician in *your* family," and he took his arm from Sonny's shoulder and slapped him, lightly, affectionately, with the back of his hand.

"Well. Now I've heard it all," said a voice behind us. This was another musician, and a friend of Sonny's, a coal-black, cheerful-looking man, built close to the ground. He immediately began confiding to me, at the top of his lungs, the most terrible things about Sonny, his teeth gleaming like a lighthouse and his laugh coming up out of him like the beginning of an earthquake. And it turned out that everyone at the bar knew Sonny, or almost everyone; some were musicians, working there, or nearby, or not working, some were simply hangers-on, and some were there to hear Sonny play. I was introduced to all of them and they were all very polite to me. Yet, it was clear that, for them, I was only Sonny's brother. Here, I was in Sonny's world. Or, rather: his kingdom. Here, it was not even a question that his veins bore royal blood.

They were going to play soon and Creole installed me, by myself, at a table in a dark corner. Then I watched them, Creole, and the little black man, and Sonny, and the others, while they horsed around, standing just below the bandstand. The light from the bandstand spilled just a little short of them and, watching them laughing and gesturing and moving about, I had the feeling that they, nevertheless, were being most careful not to step into that circle of light too suddenly: that if they moved into the light too suddenly, without thinking, they would perish in flame. Then, while I watched, one of them, the small, black man, moved into the light and crossed the bandstand and started fooling around with his drums. Then—being funny and being, also, extremely ceremonious—Creole took Sonny by the arm and led him to the piano. A woman's voice called Sonny's name and a few hands started clapping. And Sonny, also being funny and being ceremonious, and so touched, I think, that he could have cried, but neither hiding it nor showing it, riding it like a man, grinned, and put both hands to his heart and bowed from the waist.

Creole then went to the bass fiddle and a lean, very bright-skinned brown man jumped up on the bandstand and picked up his horn. So there they were, and the atmosphere on the bandstand and in the room began to change and tighten. Someone stepped up to the microphone and announced them. Then there were all kinds of murmurs. Some people at the bar shushed others. The waitress ran around, frantically getting in the last orders, guys and chicks got closer to each other, and the lights on the bandstand, on the quartet, turned to a kind of indigo. Then they all looked different there. Creole looked about him for the last time, as though he were making certain that all his chickens were in the coop, and then he—jumped and struck the fiddle. And there they were.

All I know about music is that not many people ever really hear it. And even then, on the rare occasions when something opens within, and the music enters, what we mainly hear, or hear corroborated, are personal, private, vanishing evocations. But the man who creates the music is hearing something else, is dealing with the roar rising from the void and imposing order on it as it hits the air. What is evoked in him, then, is of another order, more terrible because it has no words, and triumphant, too, for that same reason. And his triumph, when he triumphs, is ours. I just watched Sonny's face. His face was troubled, he was working hard, but he wasn't with it. And I had the feeling that, in a way, everyone on the bandstand was waiting for him, both waiting for him and pushing him along. But as I began to watch Creole, I realized that it was Creole who held them all back. He had them on a short rein. Up there, keeping the beat with his whole body, wailing on the fiddle, with his eyes half closed, he was listening to everything, but he was listening to Sonny. He was having a dialogue with Sonny. He wanted Sonny to leave the shoreline and strike out for the deep water. He was Sonny's witness that deep water and drowning were not the same thing—he had been there, and he knew. And he wanted Sonny to know. He was waiting for Sonny to do the things on the keys which would let Creole know that Sonny was in the water.

And, while Creole listened, Sonny moved, deep within, exactly like someone in torment. I had never before thought of how awful the relationship must be between the musician and his instrument. He has to fill it, this instrument, with the breath of life, his own. He has to make it do what he wants it to do. And a piano is just a piano. It's made out of so much wood and wires and little hammers and big ones, and ivory. While there's only so much you can do with it, the only way to find this out is to try; to try and make it do everything.

And Sonny hadn't been near a piano for over a year. And he wasn't on much better terms with his life, not the life that stretched before him now. He and the piano stammered, started one way, got scared, stopped; started another way, panicked, marked time, started again; then seemed to have found a direction, panicked again, got stuck. And the face I saw on Sonny I'd never seen before. Everything had been burned out of it, and, at the same time, things usually hidden were being burned in, by the fire and fury of the battle which was occurring in him up there.

Yet, watching Creole's face as they neared the end of the first set, I had the feeling that something had happened, something I hadn't heard. Then they finished, there was scattered applause, and then, without an instant's warning, Creole started into something else, it was almost sardonic, it was *Am I Blue*. And, as though he commanded, Sonny began to play. Something began to happen. And Creole let out the reins. The dry, low, black man said something awful on the drums, Creole answered, and the drums talked back. Then the horn insisted, sweet and high, slightly detached perhaps, and Creole listened, commenting now and then, dry, and driving, beautiful and calm and old. Then they all came together again, and Sonny was part of the family again. I could tell this from his face. He seemed to have found, right there beneath his fingers, a damn brand-new piano. It seemed that he couldn't get over it. Then, for awhile, just being happy with Sonny, they seemed to be agreeing with him that brand-new pianos certainly were a gas.

Then Creole stepped forward to remind them that what they were playing was the blues. He hit something in all of them, he hit something in me, myself, and the music tightened and deepened, apprehension began to beat the air. Creole began to tell us what the blues were all about. They were not about anything very new. He and his boys up there were keeping it new, at the risk of ruin, destruction, madness, and death, in order to find new ways to make us listen. For, while the tale of how we suffer, and how we are delighted, and how we may triumph is never new, it always must be heard. There isn't any other tale to tell, it's the only light we've got in all this darkness.

And this tale, according to that face, that body, those strong hands on those strings, has another aspect in every country, and a new depth in every generation. Listen, Creole seemed to be saying, listen. Now these are Sonny's blues. He made the little black man on the drums know it, and the bright, brown man on the horn. Creole wasn't trying any longer to get Sonny in the water. He was wishing him Godspeed. Then he stepped back, very slowly, filling the air with the immense suggestion that Sonny speak for himself.

Then they all gathered around Sonny and Sonny played. Every now and again one of them seemed to say, amen. Sonny's fingers filled the air with life, his life. But that life contained so many others. And Sonny went all the way back, he really began with the spare, flat statement of the opening phrase of the song. Then he began to make it his. It was very beautiful because it wasn't hurried and it was no longer a lament. I seemed to hear with what burning he had made it his, with what burning we had yet to make it ours, how we could cease lamenting. Freedom lurked around us and I understood, at last, that he could help us to be free if we would listen, that he would never be free until we did. Yet, there was no battle in his face now. I heard what he had gone through, and would continue to go through until he came to rest in earth. He had made it his: that long line, of which we knew only Mama and Daddy. And he was giving it back, as everything must be given back, so that, passing through death, it can live forever. I saw my mother's face again, and felt, for the first time, how the stones of the road she had walked on must have bruised her feet. I saw the moonlit road where my father's brother died. And it brought something else back to me, and carried me past it. I saw my little girl again and felt Isabel's tears again, and I felt my own tears begin to rise. And I was yet aware that this was only a moment, that the world waited outside, as hungry as a tiger, and that trouble stretched above us, longer than the sky.

Then it was over. Creole and Sonny let out their breath, both soaking wet, and grinning. There was a lot of applause and some of it was real. In the dark, the girl came by and I asked her to take drinks to the bandstand. There was a long pause, while they talked up there in the indigo light and after awhile I saw the girl put a Scotch and milk on top of the piano for Sonny. He didn't seem to notice it, but just before they started playing again, he sipped from it and looked toward me, and nodded. Then he put it back on top of the piano. For me, then, as they began to play again, it glowed and shook above my brother's head like the very cup of trembling.

[1957]

PHILIP ROTH

Philip Roth (b. 1933) was born in Newark, New Jersey, and grew up in a Jewish neighborhood there. His father was an insurance salesman whose parents had emigrated from Austria-Hungary. Roth worked on the high school newspaper and studied literature at Rutgers and at Bucknell University before earning his M.A. in literature from the University of Chicago, where he later taught English. He launched his career as a writer with a short novel, Goodbye, Columbus *(1959), published together with five short stories, including "The Conversion of the Jews," which appeared earlier the same year in the* Paris Review. *The book was so successful—it won a National Book Award—that Roth decided to give up teaching. Three years later he followed it with his first full-length novel,* Letting Go. *In 1975 a second collection of stories appeared,* Reading Myself and Others.

Over the years Roth's work has ranged from realistic, serious depictions of characters and events to surreal, comic attacks on such favorite American institutions as baseball and the cult of success to bittersweet, introspective examinations of the personal and moral dilemmas of a writer living among the people he writes about. The autobiographical character Nathan Zuckerman is featured in The Ghost Writer *(1979),* Zuckerman Unbound *(1981), and* The Counterlife *(1986).*

One of Roth's major literary influences was the Czech writer Franz Kafka. In Roth's novel The Breast *(1972), a literature professor experiences a Kafkaesque metamorphosis—"a massive hormonal influx"—which transforms him overnight into a spongy, sightless, six-foot-wide female breast. In* The Professor of Desire *(1977), Roth's main character goes to Prague because he is devoted to Kafka, visits the writer's home, and discusses him with a Czech professor. Roth's fantasy story "Looking for Kafka," from his second collection, imagines Kafka's arrival in Newark in 1942 to become a Hebrew teacher preparing boys for their bar mitzvahs. Roth was actually nine years old at the time, attending Hebrew school in Newark. In reality Kafka had died of tuberculosis in 1924, but the fictional account of their imaginary encounter creates a poignant contrast between the self-denying and self-defeating Kafka and Roth's family, Jewish emigrants who fortunately escaped to the United States instead of suffering the tragedy, like one of Kafka's sisters, of disappearing into Hitler's concentration camps.*

The Conversion of the Jews

"You're a real one for opening your mouth in the first place," Itzie said. "What do you open your mouth all the time for?"

"I didn't bring it up, Itz, I didn't," Ozzie said.

964

"What do you care about Jesus Christ for anyway?"

"I didn't bring up Jesus Christ. He did. I didn't even know what he was talking about. Jesus is historical, he kept saying. Jesus is historical." Ozzie mimicked the monumental voice of Rabbi Binder.

"Jesus was a person that lived like you and me," Ozzie continued. "That's what Binder said—"

"Yeah? . . . So what! What do I give two cents whether he lived or not. And what do you gotta open your mouth!" Itzie Lieberman favored closed-mouthedness, especially when it came to Ozzie Freedman's questions. Mrs. Freedman had to see Rabbi Binder twice before about Ozzie's questions and this Wednesday at four-thirty would be the third time. Itzie preferred to keep *his* mother in the kitchen; he settled for behind-the-back subtleties such as gestures, faces, snarls and other less delicate barnyard noises.

"He was a real person, Jesus, but he wasn't like God, and we don't believe he is God." Slowly, Ozzie was explaining Rabbi Binder's position to Itzie, who had been absent from Hebrew School the previous afternoon.

"The Catholics," Itzie said helpfully, "they believe in Jesus Christ, that he's God." Itzie Lieberman used "the Catholics" in its broadest sense—to include the Protestants.

Ozzie received Itzie's remark with a tiny head bob, as though it were a footnote, and went on. "His mother was Mary, and his father probably was Joseph," Ozzie said. "But the New Testament says his real father was God."

"His *real* father?"

"Yeah," Ozzie said, "that's the big thing, his father's supposed to be God."

"Bull."

"That's what Rabbi Binder says, that it's impossible—"

"Sure it's impossible. That stuff's all bull. To have a baby you gotta get laid," Itzie theologized. "Mary hadda get laid."

"That's what Binder says: 'The only way a woman can have a baby is to have intercourse with a man.'"

"He said *that*, Ozz?" For a moment it appeared that Itzie had put the theological question aside. "He said that, intercourse?" A little curled smile shaped itself in the lower half of Itzie's face like a pink mustache. "What you guys do, Ozz, you laugh or something?"

"I raised my hand."

"Yeah? Whatja say?"

"That's when I asked the question."

Itzie's face lit up. "Whatja ask about—intercourse?"

"No, I asked the question about God, how if He could create the heaven and earth in six days, and make all the animals and the fish and the light in six days—the light especially, that's what always gets me, that He could make the light. Making fish and animals, that's pretty good—"

"That's damn good." Itzie's appreciation was honest but unimaginative: it was as though God had just pitched a one-hitter.

"But making light . . . I mean when you think about it, it's really something," Ozzie said. "Anyway, I asked Binder if He could make all that in six days, and He could *pick* the six days he wanted right out of nowhere, why couldn't He let a woman have a baby without having intercourse."

"You said intercourse, Ozz, to Binder?"

"Yeah."

"Right in class?"

"Yeah."

Itzie smacked the side of his head.

"I mean, no kidding around," Ozzie said, "that'd really be nothing. After all that other stuff, that'd practically be nothing."

Itzie considered a moment. "What'd Binder say?"

"He started all over again explaining how Jesus was historical and how he lived like you and me but he wasn't God. So I said I under*stood* that. What I wanted to know was different."

What Ozzie wanted to know was always different. The first time he had wanted to know how Rabbi Binder could call the Jews "The Chosen People" if the Declaration of Independence claimed all men to be created equal. Rabbi Binder tried to distinguish for him between political equality and spiritual legitimacy, but what Ozzie wanted to know, he insisted vehemently, was different. That was the first time his mother had to come.

Then there was the plane crash. Fifty-eight people had been killed in a plane crash at La Guardia. In studying a casualty list in the newspaper his mother had discovered among the list of those dead eight Jewish names (his grandmother had nine but she counted Miller as a Jewish name); because of the eight she said the plane crash was "a tragedy." During free-discussion time on Wednesday Ozzie had brought to Rabbi Binder's attention this matter of "some of his relations" always picking out the Jewish names. Rabbi Binder had begun to explain cultural unity and some other things when Ozzie stood up at his seat and said that what he wanted to know was different. Rabbi Binder insisted that he sit down and it was then that Ozzie shouted that he wished all fifty-eight were Jews. That was the second time his mother came.

"And he kept explaining about Jesus being historical, and so I kept asking him. No kidding, Itz, he was trying to make me look stupid."

"So what he finally do?"

"Finally he starts screaming that I was deliberately simple-minded and a wise guy, and that my mother had to come, and this was the last time. And that I'd never get bar-mitzvahed if he could help it. Then, Itz, then he starts talking in that voice like a statue, real slow and deep, and he says that I better think over what I said about the Lord. He told me to go to his office and think it over." Ozzie leaned his body towards Itzie. "Itz, I thought it over for a solid hour, and now I'm convinced God could do it."

Ozzie had planned to confess his latest transgression to his mother as soon as she came home from work. But it was a Friday night in November and already dark, and when Mrs. Freedman came through the door she tossed off her coat, kissed Ozzie quickly on the face, and went to the kitchen table to light the three yellow candles, two for the Sabbath and one for Ozzie's father.

When his mother lit the candles she would move her two arms slowly towards her, dragging them through the air, as though persuading people whose minds were half made up. And her eyes would get glassy with tears. Even when his father was alive Ozzie remembered that her eyes had gotten glassy, so it didn't have anything to do with his dying. It had something to do with lighting the candles.

As she touched the flaming match to the unlit wick of a Sabbath candle, the phone rang, and Ozzie, standing only a foot from it, plucked it off the receiver and held it muffled to his chest. When his mother lit candles Ozzie felt there should be no noise; even breathing, if you could manage it, should be softened. Ozzie pressed the phone to his breast and watched his mother dragging whatever she was dragging, and he felt his own eyes get glassy. His mother was a round, tired, gray-haired penguin of a woman whose gray skin had begun to feel the tug of gravity and the weight of her own history. Even when she was dressed up she didn't look like a chosen person. But when she lit candles she looked like something better; like a woman who knew momentarily that God could do anything.

After a few mysterious minutes she was finished. Ozzie hung up the phone and walked to the kitchen table where she was beginning to lay the two places for the four-course Sabbath meal. He told her that she would have to see Rabbi Binder next Wednesday at four-thirty, and then he told her why. For the first time in their life together she hit Ozzie across the face with her hand.

All through the chopped liver and chicken soup part of the dinner Ozzie cried; he didn't have any appetite for the rest.

On Wednesday, in the largest of the three basement classrooms of the synagogue, Rabbi Marvin Binder, a tall, handsome, broad-shouldered man of thirty with thick strong-fibered black hair, removed his watch from his pocket and saw that it was four o'clock. At the rear of the room Yakov Blotnik, the seventy-one-year-old custodian, slowly polished the large window, mumbling to himself, unaware that it was four o'clock or six o'clock, Monday or Wednesday. To most of the students Yakov Blotnik's mumbling, along with his brown curly beard, scythe nose, and two heel-trailing black cats, made of him an object of wonder, a foreigner, a relic, towards whom they were alternately fearful and disrespectful. To Ozzie the mumbling had always seemed a monotonous, curious prayer; what made it curious was that old Blotnik had been mumbling so steadily for so many years, Ozzie suspected he had memorized the prayers and forgotten all about God.

"It is now free-discussion time," Rabbi Binder said. "Feel free to talk about any Jewish matter at all—religion, family, politics, sports—"

There was silence. It was a gusty, clouded November afternoon and it did not seem as though there ever was or could be a thing called baseball. So nobody this week said a word about that hero from the past, Hank Greenberg—which limited free discussion considerably.

And the soul-battering Ozzie Freedman had just received from Rabbi Binder had imposed its limitation. When it was Ozzie's turn to read aloud from the Hebrew book the rabbi had asked him petulantly why he didn't read more rapidly. He was showing no progress. Ozzie said he could read faster but that if he did he was sure not to understand what he was reading. Nevertheless, at the rabbi's repeated suggestion Ozzie tried, and showed a great talent, but in the midst of a long passage he stopped short and said he didn't understand a word he was reading, and started in again at a drag-footed pace. Then came the soul-battering.

Consequently, when free-discussion time rolled around none of the students felt too free. The rabbi's invitation was answered only by the mumbling of feeble old Blotnik.

"Isn't there anything at all you would like to discuss?" Rabbi Binder asked again, looking at his watch. "No questions or comments?"

There was a small grumble from the third row. The rabbi requested that Ozzie rise and give the rest of the class the advantage of his thought.

Ozzie rose. "I forget it now," he said, and sat down in his place.

Rabbi Binder advanced a seat towards Ozzie and poised himself on the edge of the desk. It was Itzie's desk and the rabbi's frame only a dagger's-length away from his face snapped him to sitting attention.

"Stand up again, Oscar," Rabbi Binder said calmly, "and try to assemble your thoughts."

Ozzie stood up. All his classmates turned in their seats and watched as he gave an unconvincing scratch to his forehead.

"I can't assemble any," he announced, and plunked himself down.

"Stand up!" Rabbi Binder advanced from Itzie's desk to the one directly in front of Ozzie; when the rabbinical back was turned Itzie gave it five-fingers off the tip of his nose, causing a small titter in the room. Rabbi Binder was too absorbed in squelching Ozzie's nonsense once and for all to bother with titters. "Stand up, Oscar. What's your question about?"

Ozzie pulled a word out of the air. It was the handiest word. "Religion."

"Oh, now you remember?"

"Yes."

"What is it?"

Trapped, Ozzie blurted the first thing that came to him. "Why can't He make anything He wants to make!"

As Rabbi Binder prepared an answer, a final answer, Itzie, ten feet behind him, raised one finger on his left hand, gestured it meaningfully towards the rabbi's back, and brought the house down.

Binder twisted quickly to see what had happened and in the midst of the commotion Ozzie shouted into the rabbi's back what he couldn't have shouted to his face. It was a loud, toneless sound that had the timbre of something stored inside for about six days.

"You don't know! You don't know anything about God!"

The rabbi spun back towards Ozzie. "What?"

"You don't know—you don't—"

"Apologize, Oscar, apologize!" It was a threat.

"You don't—"

Rabbi Binder's hand flicked out at Ozzie's cheek. Perhaps it had only been meant to clamp the boy's mouth shut, but Ozzie ducked and the palm caught him squarely on the nose.

The blood came in a short, red spurt on to Ozzie's shirt front.

The next moment was all confusion. Ozzie screamed, "You bastard, you bastard!" and broke for the classroom door. Rabbi Binder lurched a step backwards, as though his own blood had started flowing violently in the opposite direction, then gave a clumsy lurch forward and bolted out the door after Ozzie. The class followed after the rabbi's huge blue-suited back, and before old Blotnik could turn from his window, the room was empty and everyone was headed full speed up the three flights leading to the roof.

If one should compare the light of day to the life of man: sunrise to birth; sunset—the dropping down over the edge—to death; then as Ozzie Freedman wiggled through the trapdoor of the synagogue roof, his feet kicking backwards bronco-style at Rabbi Binder's outstretched arms—at that moment the day was fifty years old. As a rule, fifty or fifty-five reflects accurately the age of late afternoons in November, for it is in that month, during those hours, that one's awareness of light seems no longer a matter of seeing, but of hearing: light begins clicking away. In fact, as Ozzie locked shut the trapdoor in the rabbi's face, the sharp click of the bolt into the lock might momentarily have been mistaken for the sound of the heavier gray that had just throbbed through the sky.

With all his weight Ozzie kneeled on the locked door; any instant he was certain that Rabbi Binder's shoulder would fling it open, splintering the wood into shrapnel and catapulting his body into the sky. But the door did not move and below him he heard only the rumble of feet, first loud then dim, like thunder rolling away.

A question shot through his brain. "Can this be *me*?" For a thirteen-year-old who had just labeled his religious leader a bastard, twice, it was not an improper question. Louder and louder the question came to him— "Is it me? It is me?"—until he discovered himself no longer kneeling, but racing crazily towards the edge of the roof, his eyes crying, his throat screaming, and his arms flying everywhichway as though not his own.

"Is it me? Is it me ME ME ME! It has to be me—but is it!"

It is the question a thief must ask himself the night he jimmies open his first window, and it is said to be the question with which bridegrooms quiz themselves before the altar.

In the few wild seconds it took Ozzie's body to propel him to the edge of the roof, his self-examination began to grow fuzzy. Gazing down at the street, he became confused as to the problem beneath the question: was it, is-it-me-who-called-Binder-a-bastard? or, is-it-me-prancing-around-on-the-roof? However, the scene below settled all, for there is an instant in any action when whether it is you or somebody else is academic. The thief crams the money in his pockets and scoots out the window. The bridegroom signs the hotel register for two. And the boy on the roof finds a streetful of people gaping at him, necks stretched backwards, faces up, as though he were the ceiling of the Hayden Planetarium. Suddenly you know it's you.

"Oscar! Oscar Freedman!" A voice rose from the center of the crowd, a voice that, could it have been seen, would have looked like the writing on scroll. "Oscar Freedman, get down from there. Immediately!" Rabbi Binder was pointing one arm stiffly up at him; and at the end of that arm, one finger aimed menacingly. It was the attitude of a dictator, but one — the eyes confessed all — whose personal valet had spit neatly in his face.

Ozzie didn't answer. Only for a blink's length did he look towards Rabbi Binder. Instead his eyes began to fit together the world beneath him, to sort out people from places, friends from enemies, participants from spectators. In little jagged starlike clusters his friends stood around Rabbi Binder, who was still pointing. The topmost point on a star compounded not of angels but of five adolescent boys was Itzie. What a world it was, with those stars below, Rabbi Binder below . . . Ozzie, who a moment earlier hadn't been able to control his own body, started to feel the meaning of the word control: he felt Peace and he felt Power.

"Oscar Freedman, I'll give you three to come down."

Few dictators give their subjects three to do anything; but, as always, Rabbi Binder only looked dictatorial.

"Are you ready, Oscar?"

Ozzie nodded his head yes, although he had no intention in the world — the lower one of the celestial one he'd just entered — of coming down even if Rabbi Binder should give him a million.

"All right then," said Rabbi Binder. He ran a hand through his black Samson hair as though it were the gesture prescribed for uttering the first digit. Then, with his other hand cutting a circle out of the small piece of sky around him, he spoke. "One!"

There was no thunder. On the contrary, at that moment, as though "one" was the cue for which he had been waiting, the world's least thunderous person appeared on the synagogue steps. He did not so much come out the synagogue door as lean out, onto the darkening air. He clutched at the doorknob with one hand and looked up at the roof.

"Oy!"

Yakov Blotnik's old mind hobbled slowly, as if on crutches, and though he couldn't decide precisely what the boy was doing on the roof, he knew it wasn't good—that is, it wasn't-good-for-the-Jews. For Yakov Blotnik life had fractionated itself simply: things were either good-for-the-Jews or no-good-for-the-Jews.

He smacked his free hand to his in-sucked cheek, gently. "Oy, Gut!" And then quickly as he was able, he jacked down his head and surveyed the street. There was Rabbi Binder (like a man at an auction with only three dollars in his pocket, he had just delivered a shaky "Two!"); there were the students, and that was all. So far it-wasn't-so-bad-for-the-Jews. But the boy had to come down immediately, before anybody saw. The problem: how to get the boy off the roof?

Anybody who has ever had a cat on the roof knows how to get him down. You call the fire department. Or first you call the operator and you ask her for the fire department. And the next thing there is great jamming of brakes and clanging of bells and shouting of instructions. And then the cat is off the roof. You do the same thing to get a boy off the roof.

That is, you do the same thing if you are Yakov Blotnik and you once had a cat on the roof.

When the engines, all four of them, arrived, Rabbi Binder had four times given Ozzie the count of three. The big hook-and-ladder swung around the corner and one of the firemen leaped from it, plunging head-long towards the yellow fire hydrant in front of the synagogue. With a huge wrench he began to unscrew the top nozzle. Rabbi Binder raced over to him and pulled at his shoulder.

"There's no fire . . ."

The fireman mumbled back over his shoulder and, heatedly, continued working at the nozzle.

"But there's no fire, there's no fire . . ." Binder shouted. When the fireman mumbled again, the rabbi grasped his face with both his hands and pointed it up at the roof.

To Ozzie it looked as though Rabbi Binder was trying to tug the fire-man's head out of his body, like a cork from a bottle. He had to giggle at the picture they made: it was a family portrait—rabbi in black skullcap, fireman in red fire hat, and the little yellow hydrant squatting beside like a kid brother, bareheaded. From the edge of the roof Ozzie waved at the portrait, a one-handed, flapping, mocking wave; in doing it his right foot slipped from under him. Rabbi Binder covered his eyes with his hands.

Firemen work fast. Before Ozzie had even regained his balance, a big, round, yellowed net was being held on the synagogue lawn. The firemen who held it looked up at Ozzie with stern, feelingless faces.

One of the firemen turned his head towards Rabbi Binder. "What, is the kid nuts or something?"

Rabbi Binder unpeeled his hands from his eyes, slowly, painfully, as if they were tape. Then he checked: nothing on the sidewalk, no dents in the net.

"Is he gonna jump, or what?" the fireman shouted.

In a voice not at all like a statue, Rabbi Binder finally answered. "Yes, Yes, I think so . . . He's been threatening to . . ."

Threatening to? Why, the reason he was on the roof, Ozzie remembered, was to get away; he hadn't even thought about jumping. He had just run to get away, and the truth was that he hadn't really headed for the roof as much as he'd been chased there.

"What's his name, the kid?"

"Freedman," Rabbi Binder answered. "Oscar Freedman."

The fireman looked up at Ozzie. "What is it with you, Oscar? You gonna jump, or what?"

Ozzie did not answer. Frankly, the question had just arisen.

"Look, Oscar, if you're gonna jump, jump—and if you're not gonna jump, don't jump. But don't waste our time, willya?"

Ozzie looked at the fireman and then at Rabbi Binder. He wanted to see Rabbi Binder cover his eyes one more time.

"I'm going to jump."

And then he scampered around the edge of the roof to the corner, where there was no net below, and he flapped his arms at his sides, swishing the air and smacking his palms to his trousers on the downbeat. He began screaming like some kind of engine, "Wheeeee . . . wheeeeee," and leaning way out over the edge with the upper half of his body. The firemen whipped around to cover the ground with the net. Rabbi Binder mumbled a few words to Somebody and covered his eyes. Everything happened quickly, jerkily, as in a silent movie. The crowd, which had arrived with the fire engines, gave out a long, Fourth-of-July fireworks oooh-aahhh. In the excitement no one had paid the crowd much heed, except, of course, Yakov Blotnik, who swung from the doorknob counting heads. "Fier und tsvan-tsik . . . finf und tsvantsik . . . Oy, Gut!" It wasn't like this with the cat.

Rabbi Binder peeked through his fingers, checked the sidewalk and net. Empty. But there was Ozzie racing to the other corner. The firemen raced with him but were unable to keep up. Whenever Ozzie wanted to he might jump and splatter himself upon the sidewalk, and by the time the firemen scooted to the spot all they could do with their net would be to cover the mess.

"Wheeeee . . . wheeeee . . ."

"Hey, Oscar," the winded fireman yelled, "What the hell is this, a game or something?"

"Wheeeee . . . wheeeee . . ."

"Hey, Oscar—"

But he was off now to the other corner, flapping his wings fiercely. Rabbi Binder couldn't take it any longer—the fire engines from nowhere, the screaming suicidal boy, the net. He fell to his knees, exhausted, and with his hands curled together in front of his chest like a little dome, he pleaded, "Oscar, stop it, Oscar. Don't jump, Oscar. Please come down . . . Please don't jump."

And further back in the crowd a single voice, a single young voice, shouted a lone word to the boy on the roof.

"Jump!"

It was Itzie. Ozzie momentarily stopped flapping.

"Go ahead, Ozz—jump!" Itzie broke off his point of the star and courageously, with the inspiration not of a wise-guy but of a disciple, stood alone. "Jump, Ozz, jump!"

Still on his knees, his hands still curled, Rabbi Binder twisted his body back. He looked at Itzie, then, agonizingly, back to Ozzie.

"OSCAR, DON'T JUMP! PLEASE, DON'T JUMP . . . please, please . . ."

"Jump!" This time it wasn't Itzie but another point of the star. By the time Mrs. Freedman arrived to keep her four-thirty appointment with Rabbi Binder, the whole little upside down heaven was shouting and pleading for Ozzie to jump, and Rabbi Binder no longer was pleading with him not to jump, but was crying into the dome of his hands.

Understandably Mrs. Freedman couldn't figure out what her son was doing on the roof. So she asked.

"Ozzie, my Ozzie, what are you doing? My Ozzie, what is it?"

Ozzie stopped wheeeeeing and slowed his arms down to a cruising flap, the kind birds use in soft winds, but he did not answer. He stood against the low, clouded, darkening sky—light clicked down swiftly now, as on a small gear—flapping softly and gazing down at the small bundle of a woman who was his mother.

"What are you doing, Ozzie?" She turned towards the kneeling Rabbi Binder and rushed so close that only a paper-thickness of dusk lay between her stomach and his shoulders.

"What is my baby doing?"

Rabbi Binder gaped up at her but he too was mute. All that moved was the dome of his hands; it shook back and forth like a weak pulse.

"Rabbi, get him down! He'll kill himself. Get him down, my only baby . . ."

"I can't," Rabbi Binder said, "I can't . . ." and he turned his handsome head towards the crowd of boys behind him. "It's them. Listen to them."

And for the first time Mrs. Freedman saw the crowd of boys, and she heard what they were yelling.

"He's doing it for them. He won't listen to me. It's them." Rabbi Binder spoke like one in a trance.

"For them?"

"Yes."

"Why for them?"

"They want him to . . . ."

Mrs. Freedman raised her two arms upward as though she were conducting the sky. "For them he's doing it!" And then in a gesture older than pyramids, older than prophets and floods, her arms came slapping down to her sides. "A martyr I have. Look!" She tilted her head to the roof. Ozzie was still flapping softly. "My martyr."

"Oscar, come down, *please*," Rabbi Binder groaned.

In a startlingly even voice Mrs. Freedman called to the boy on the roof. "Ozzie, come down, Ozzie. Don't be a martyr, my baby."

As though it were a litany, Rabbi Binder repeated her words. "Don't be a martyr, my baby. Don't be a martyr."

"Gawhead, Ozz— *be* a Martin!" It was Itzie. "Be a Martin, be a Martin," and all the voices joined in singing for Martindom, whatever *it* was. "Be a Martin, be a Martin . . . ."

Somehow when you're on a roof the darker it gets the less you can hear. All Ozzie knew was that two groups wanted two new things: his friends were spirited and musical about what they wanted; his mother and the rabbi were even-toned, chanting, about what they didn't want. The rabbi's voice was without tears now and so was his mother's.

The big net stared up at Ozzie like a sightless eye. The big, clouded sky pushed down. From beneath it looked like a gray corrugated board. Suddenly, looking up into that unsympathetic sky, Ozzie realized all the strangeness of what these people, his friends, were asking: they wanted him to jump, to kill himself; they were singing about it now—it made them that happy. And there was an even greater strangeness: Rabbi Binder was on his knees, trembling. If there was a question to be asked now it was not "Is it me?" but rather "Is it us? . . . Is it us?"

Being on the roof, it turned out, was a serious thing. If he jumped would the singing become dancing? Would it? What would jumping stop? Yearningly, Ozzie wished he could rip open the sky, plunge his hands through, and pull out the sun; and on the sun, like a coin, would be stamped JUMP or DON'T JUMP.

Ozzie's knees rocked and sagged a little under him as though they were setting him for a dive. His arms tightened, stiffened, froze, from shoulders to fingernails. He felt as if each part of his body were going to vote as to whether he should kill himself or not—and each part as though it were independent of *him*.

The light took an unexpected click down and the new darkness, like a gag, hushed the friends singing for this and the mother and rabbi chanting for that.

Ozzie stopped counting votes, and in a curiously high voice, like one who wasn't prepared for speech, he spoke.

"Mamma?"

"Yes, Oscar."

"Mamma, get down on your knees, like Rabbi Binder."

"Oscar—"

"Get down on your knees," he said, "or I'll jump."

Ozzie heard a whimper, then a quick rustling, and when he looked down where his mother had stood he saw the top of a head and beneath that a circle of dress. She was kneeling beside Rabbi Binder.

He spoke again. "Everybody kneel." There was the sound of everybody kneeling.

Ozzie looked around. With one hand he pointed towards the synagogue entrance. "Make *him* kneel."

There was a noise, not of kneeling, but of body-and-cloth stretching. Ozzie could hear Rabbi Binder saying in a gruff whisper, ". . . or he'll *kill* himself," and when next he looked there was Yakov Blotnik off the doorknob and for the first time in his life upon his knees in the Gentile posture of prayer.

As for the firemen—it is not as difficult as one might imagine to hold a net taut while you are kneeling.

Ozzie looked around again; and then he called to Rabbi Binder.

"Rabbi?"

"Yes, Oscar."

"Rabbi Binder, do you believe in God?"

"Yes."

"Do you believe God can do Anything?" Ozzie leaned his head out into the darkness. "Anything?"

"Oscar, I think—"

"Tell me you believe God can do Anything."

There was a second's hesitation. Then: "God can do Anything."

"Tell me you believe God can make a child without intercourse."

"He can."

"Tell me!"

"God," Rabbi Binder admitted, "can make a child without intercourse."

"Mamma, you tell me."

"God can make a child without intercourse," his mother said.

"Make *him* tell me." There was no doubt who *him* was.

In a few moments Ozzie heard an old comical voice say something to the increasing darkness about God.

Next, Ozzie made everybody say it. And then he made them all say they believed in Jesus Christ—first one at a time, then all together.

When the catechizing was through it was the beginning of evening. From the street it sounded as if the boy on the roof might have sighed.

"Ozzie?" A woman's voice dared to speak. "You'll come down now?"

There was no answer, but the woman waited, and when a voice finally did speak it was thin and crying, and exhausted as that of an old man who has just finished pulling the bells.

"Mamma, don't you see—you shouldn't hit me. He shouldn't hit me. You shouldn't hit me about God, Mamma. You should never hit anybody about God—"

"Ozzie, please come down now."

"Promise me, promise me you'll never hit anybody about God."

He had asked only his mother, but for some reason everyone kneeling in the street promised he would never hit anybody about God.

Once again there was silence.

"I can come down now, Mamma," the boy on the roof finally said. He turned his head both ways as though checking the traffic lights. "Now I can come down . . ."

And he did, right into the center of the yellow net that glowed in the evening's edge like an overgrown halo.   [1959]

PETER TAYLOR

*P*eter Taylor (b. 1917) was born in Trenton, Tennessee. His maternal grandfather, Robert L. Taylor, served as governor of Tennessee for three terms and as a United States senator. Taylor's father was the president of a life insurance company in St. Louis. After Taylor's boyhood in Nashville, St. Louis, and Memphis, he studied at Vanderbilt University and Kenyon College, where his desire to become a writer was encouraged by his professor, John Crowe Ransom. At Kenyon, Taylor also became friends with the poets Randall Jarrell and Robert Lowell, whose concern for language influenced Taylor's attitude toward his prose.

Taylor served in the army from 1941 to 1945. After the war, he began teaching creative writing at various colleges and universities, including the University of North Carolina, the University of Chicago, Kenyon College, Ohio State University, and the University of Virginia. In 1948 one of his previous professors, the novelist Robert Penn Warren, wrote the introduction to Taylor's first book, A Long Fourth and Other Stories, identifying Taylor's main subject as a writer: "the contemporary, urban, middle-class world of the upper South" after World War II. During the next fifteen years Taylor published three more books of fiction: The Widows of Thornton (1954); Happy Families Are All Alike (1959), which included "Promise of Rain"; and Miss Leonora When Last Seen and Fifteen Other Stories (1963). In 1969 he secured his reputation as one of the finest short story writers in America with the publication of The Collected Stories of Peter Taylor. Since then he has published two more collections, In the Miro District (1977) and The Old Forest (1985), which won the PEN/Faulkner Award for the best work of fiction published in 1985. His short fiction continues to appear in magazines like The New Yorker, and his novels include A Woman of Means (1954) and A Summons to Memphis (1986). Taylor once told an interviewer, "It used to infuriate me, the attitude that you wrote stories until you were good enough to write a novel. I much prefer reading stories; I like James's stories better than his novels, and Faulkner's, and I think D. H. Lawrence's stories are much better than his novels. But people always pressure you, and it does seem like a challenge—the scope of it."

Over the years Taylor has refined his prose technique to the point where he says he now writes the first draft of his stories in verse. "I like [verse] because you get more emphasis on the groups of words and the language and the rhythms. I can't sustain it very long, but I try to finish a story in verse, then go back and put it into prose. I began writing that way as an effort to compress; in a story you have very limited space, so every sentence has to do more."

Promise of Rain

Understand, there was never anything *really* wrong with Hugh Robert. He was a well-built boy, strong and quick and bursting with vitality. That, at least, was the impression of himself he managed to give people. I guess he did it just by carrying himself well and never letting down in front of anyone. Actually, he was no better built than my other boys. And how is one really to know about a person's vitality? He had a bright look in his blue eyes, a fresh complexion, and a shock of black curly hair on a head so handsomely shaped that everybody noticed it. It was the shape of his head, I imagine, that made people feel Hugh was so much better-looking than his older brothers. All the girls were crazy about him. And even if I am his father, I have to say that he was a boy who seemed fairly crazy about himself.

When Hugh was sixteen, I kept a pretty close watch on him — closer than I ever had time to keep on the others. I observed how he seldom left for school in the mornings without stopping a moment before the long gilt-framed mirror in the front hall. Sometimes he would seem to be looking at himself with painful curiosity and sometimes with pure admiration. Either way it was unbecoming of him. But still I wasn't too critical of the morning looks he gave himself. I did mind, however, his doing the same thing again when he got home from school in the afternoons. Many a winter's afternoon I would already be home when he came in, and from where I sat in the living room, or in the library across the hall, I could tell by his footsteps that he was stopping to see himself in that great expanse of looking glass.

For Hugh's own good I used, some afternoons, to let him catch me watching him at the mirror. I thought it might break him of the habit. But his eyes would meet mine without the least shame and he would say something he didn't mean, like "I'm not much to look at, am I, Mr. Perkins?" And he continued to stop there and ogle himself in the mirror whenever it suited him to. He would often call me Mr. Perkins like that, and call his mother Mrs. Perkins. We could never be quite sure how it was meant, and I don't think he intended us to be. When he was being outright playful, he was apt to call us Will and Mary.

Hugh kept his schoolbooks in a compartment of the cupboard in the downstairs hall. The cupboard I speak of was a big oak, antique thing, a very expensive piece of furniture, which Hugh's mother had bought in Europe during our 1924 trip — ten years before. Hugh's schoolbooks seldom got farther into the house than the hall cupboard. If I complained about this to Mary, she would refer me to his report card, with its wall of straight A's. If I carried my attack further and mentioned the silly kinds of subjects he was taking, she would sigh and blame it on his having to go to the public school. As though I *wanted* Hugh to go to the public school! And as though I wanted to be home those afternoons when he came in from school! It was just that Hugh Robert grew up during bad times for us, which, as I see it, was no more my fault than it was his. Those were years when it seemed that my business firm might have to close its doors almost anytime. I couldn't *afford* to keep a boy in private school. And as for myself, I just couldn't bear to hang around the office all of those long, dead winter afternoons at the bottom of the Depression.

I can see Hugh now in his corduroy jacket and sheepskin collar stooping down to slip his books always in the same corner of the same compartment of the hall cupboard. He was orderly and systematic about everything like that. His older brothers had never measured up to him in this respect. In an instant he could tell you the whereabouts of any of his possessions. He had things stashed away—ice skates, baseball gloves, and other athletic equipment, as well as sets of carpentry tools, car tools, and radio parts—had them pushed neatly away in nooks and shelves and drawers all over the house. They were all things he had been very much excited about at one time or another. Hugh would plague us to buy him something, and then when we did and he didn't get the satisfaction out of it he had expected, he would brood about it for weeks. Finally, he would put it away somewhere. If it was something expensive and we asked him what became of it, he would say it was just one of his "mistakes" and that we needn't think he had forgotten it. Sometimes when I was looking for something I had misplaced, I would come on one of those nests of "mistakes" and know at once it was Hugh's. I remember its occurring to me once that it wouldn't take Hugh Robert thirty seconds to lay his hands on anything he owned, and that he would be able in ten minutes' time to assemble *everything* he owned and be on his way, if ever that notion struck him. It wasn't a thought that would ever have occurred to me in connection with the other children.

Our daughter and two older boys were married and gone from the house by this time, but when they were home with their spouses on a Sunday they'd say we were still babying Hugh, and say that they knew what would have happened to *them* if they had ever tried calling us by our first names. I suppose you really can't help babying the youngest, in one way or another, and favoring him a little over the others, especially when he comes along as a sort of trailer after the others are already up in school. But to Hugh's mother it was very annoying to have the older children point this out, and she would deny it hotly. If on a Monday morning, after the others had been there on Sunday, Hugh came down to breakfast and began that first-name or Mr.-and-Mrs. business, Mary was likely to try to talk to him as she used to talk to the other children, and tell him that it was not very respectful of him. It never did any good, though, and she would say afterward that I never supported her in these efforts. I don't know. I do know, though, that disrespectful is hardly the word for my son Hugh Robert Perkins—not when he was sixteen, not when he was younger than that, not even nowadays, when he favors us with one of his rare visits and sits around the house for three days talking mostly about himself and about how broke I was when he was growing up. Mary says he's the only person who can remind me, nowadays, of how hard up we were then without making me mad. If that is so, it is because he seems to take such innocent pleasure in remembering it. He talks about it in a way that makes you feel he is saying, "I owe *everything* to that!"

It got to be the fashion in those days for high-school boys to wear the knee bands of their golf knickers unfastened, letting the baggy pants legs hang loose down to their ankles. They went to school that way, and it looked far worse to me than even the shirttail-out fashion that came along after the war. I had never seen Hugh wearing his own plus fours that way, but I remarked to him one day that I regarded it as the ugliest, sloppiest, most ungentlemanly habit of dress I had ever encountered. And I asked him what in the world possessed those boys to make them do it. I think he took this as a nasty slam against his classmates. "I don't know why they do it," he said, with something of a sneer, "but I could find out for you, Mr. Perkins." I told him never mind, that I didn't want to know.

Next day Hugh appeared at breakfast with his knickers hanging down about his ankles. He lunged into the room with his buckles on his knee bands jangling like spurs. Naturally, I was supposed to blow up and tell him to fasten them. But I pretended not even to notice, and I wouldn't let Mary mention it to him. He wore them that way for a couple of days, and then seeing he wasn't going to get a rise out of me, he stopped. He seemed dispirited and rather gloomy for a day or so. Then, finding me at home after school one afternoon, he said out of the clear, "I made a discovery for you, Dad."

"What's that?" I said. I really didn't know what he meant.

"I found out why those fellows wear their plus fours drooping down. I tried wearing my own that way for a couple of days, though you didn't even notice it." And he had the cheek to wink at me in the hall mirror.

"Well?" I said noncommittally. I remembered I had said I didn't want to know why. But I didn't remind him, because I knew he remembered, too.

He had already put his books away, and he was about to take his jacket to the closet behind the stair. He stood running one finger along the ribbing of the corduroy jacket, which he had thrown over his arm, and he had a dejected look on his face. "It makes them feel kind of reckless and devil-may-care and as if they don't give a darn for what anybody thinks of how they look." This he volunteered, mind you. I had only said, "Well?"

I thought he would continue, but when he didn't I asked, "You don't recommend it? You didn't like the feeling?"

"It didn't make *me* feel that way. It only made me understand how it makes *them* feel. I didn't get any kick out of it. I don't blame them too much, though. Those guys don't have much to make them feel important."

I had to bite my tongue to keep from asking the boy what he had to make him feel important. But I let it go at that, because I saw what he was getting at. I realized I was supposed to feel pretty cheap for having criticized the people he went to school with.

Hugh didn't have any duties at home. We weren't people who lived in any do-it-yourself world in those days, no matter how bad business was. I still kept me a yardman in summer and a furnaceman in winter. I can't help saying that in that respect I did as well by Hugh as by his older brothers. When he came home in the afternoon and had stuck his books in the cupboard he was *free*—free as a bird. He might have looked at himself in the mirror all afternoon if he had wanted to. Or he might have been out on the town with a bunch of the high-school roughnecks. But Hugh wasn't a ruffian, and he wasn't an idler, either; not in the worst sense. He was vain and self-centered, but you knew that while he stood before that looking glass unbuckling his corduroy jacket he was trying to make judgments and decisions about himself; he was checking something he had thought about himself during the day.

In the mirror Hugh's blue eyes would seem to study their own blueness for a time, and then, not satisfied, they would begin to explore the hall—the hall, that is, as reflected in the glass, and with himself, of course, always in the foreground. If I had purposely planted myself in the library doorway, that's when his eyes would light on me. He would look at me curiously for a split second—before he let his eyes meet mine—look at me as he did at everything else in view. The first time it happened, I thought the look meant he was curious and resentful about my being home from the office so early. Next time, I saw that this wasn't so and that he was merely fitting me into his picture of himself. I remember very well what he said to me on one of these occasions: "Mr. Perkins, even among mirrors there's a difference! Especially the big ones. They all give you different ideas of how you look." He rambled on, seemingly without any embarrassment. "I saw myself in a big one downtown one day and there was a second when I couldn't place where I'd seen that uncouth, unkempt, uncanny individual before. And at school there's a huge one in the room where we take typing—don't ask me what it's there for. It makes me look like everybody else in the class, with all of us pecking away at typewriters. We all look so much alike I can hardly find myself in it." When Hugh finished that spiel, I found myself blushing—blushing for him. I hated so to think of the boy gaping at himself in mirrors all over town the way he did in that one in my front hall.

During the summer after Hugh turned seventeen I had the misfortune to learn, firsthand, something about his habits away from home—that is, when he did take a notion to use his freedom differently and go out on the town with his cronies from the high school. I am not speaking of nightlife, though there was beginning to be some of that, too, but of the hours that young people have to kill in the daytime. The city of Chatham, which is where we have always lived, is not the biggest city in our state.

Since the Second World War it has grown substantially, and the newspapers claim that there are now half a million people in the "municipal area," by which they mean almost the whole county. But twenty-five years ago people didn't speak of it as being more than half that size. For me to encounter my son Hugh downtown or riding along Division Boulevard couldn't really be thought a great coincidence—especially not since, almost without knowing it, I had developed the habit of keeping an eye out for that head of his.

I would catch a glimpse of him on the street and, with my mind still on some problem we had at the office, wouldn't know right away what it was I had seen. Often I had to turn around and look to be sure. There Hugh would be, his dark head moving along in a group of other youthful heads—frequently a girl's head for every boy's—out under the boiling July sun, in a section of the city that they couldn't possibly have had any reason for being in. There was at least one occasion when I was certain that Hugh saw me, too. I was in the backseat of the car, and when I turned and looked out the rear window, Hugh was waving. But I was crowded in between two hefty fellows—two of my men from the office—and couldn't have returned his wave even if I had tried. On that occasion, we were riding through a section of town that used long ago to be called the Irish Flats. The men with me were both of them strictly Chatham Irish, and as we rode along I commenced teasing them about how tough that section used to be and how when I was a boy a "white man" didn't dare put foot in that end of town.

Perkins Finance Company, which was the name of our firm before we reorganized in 1946, used to make loans on small properties all over Chatham. Since the boys took over—my two older boys and my daughter's husband—they haven't wanted to deal much in that kind of thing. We have bigger irons in the fire now, and the boys have even put a cable address on the company stationery, along with the new name: Perkins, Hodgeson Investments. (The Hodgeson's for my daughter's husband.) But our small loans were what saved us in the Depression. The boys weren't with me in the firm then, of course. When they came back from college up East, just at the time of the Crash, I wouldn't let them come in with me. I got them jobs in two Chatham banks which I *knew* weren't going to fail. They were locked up down there in their cages all day and went home to their young wives at night without ever having any notion of the kind of hide-and-seek games Hugh and I were playing in our idleness. What I would often do—when I didn't go home in the afternoon—was to ride around town with some of my men and look at the property we had an interest in. Aside from any business reason, it did something for me—more than going home did, more than a round of golf, or going to the ball game even. It did something for me to get out and look at the town, to see how it had stopped building and growing. The feeling I got from it was that Time itself had stopped and was actually waiting for me instead of passing me by and leaving me behind just when I was in my prime. At the time, I already had a son-in-law and two daughters-in-law, but I wasn't an old man. I had just turned fifty. In the hot summertime of the Depression I could sometimes look at Chatham and feel about it that it was a big, powerful, stubborn horse that wouldn't go. I was still in the saddle, it seemed—or I had just dismounted and had a tight grip on the reins near the bit and was meaning to remount. Perhaps I even had in mind beating the brute somehow, to make it go; for I was young enough then to be impatient and to feel that I just couldn't wait for the town to begin to move again. I knew I had to have my second chance. Hugh could take whatever pleasure and instruction he would from exploring the city as it was in those days and getting to know different kinds of people. It corresponded to something in his makeup. Or it answered some need of his temperament. Anyway, he seemed to be born for it. But, as for me, I could hardly wait for things to begin to move again and to be the way they had been before.

Yet I was a man old enough to take a certain reasonable satisfaction in everything's suddenly stopping still the way it did in the Depression and giving me the chance to look at the city the way I could then. It has a beauty, a town like Chatham does. Even with things getting mighty shabby, as they were in 1933, Division Boulevard was a magnificent street with handsome stone and tile-faced office buildings and store buildings downtown, with the automobile showrooms taking up beyond the overpass at the Union Station—a cathedral of a building!—and after that a half mile of old mansions from the last century, most of them long since turned into undertaking parlors, all of them so well built that no amount of abuse or remodeling seemed to alter them much; and then almost a mile of small apartment houses, and after that the clinics and the State Medical Center and the two big hospitals.

Beyond the hospitals, Division Boulevard runs right through Lawton Park. On one side you get a glimpse among the trees of the Art Gallery; farther along on that side, there is the bronze monument to the doughboy. On the other side is a mound with Lawton Park spelled out in sweet alyssum and pinks and ground myrtle; and away over on that side you can see among the treetops the glass dome of the birdhouse at the zoo. It's a handsomely kept park—was all the way through the Depression even—and when you come out at the other end, there before your eyes is the beginning of Singleton Heights!

From Singleton Heights on out past the Country Club to the Hunt and Polo Grounds it's all like a fairyland. Great stucco and stone houses, and whitewashed brick, acres upon acres of them. All of them planted round with evergreens and flowering fruit trees, with wide green lawns—the sprinklers playing like fountains all summer long—lawns that are really meadows, stretching off to low stone walls or rustic fences or even a sluggish little creek with willow trees growing along its banks in places.

It's the sort of thing that when you've been off to New York, or maybe to Europe for the summer, and come back to it, the very prettiness of it nearly breaks your heart.

But I ought to say, before speaking of Hugh again, that Singleton Heights and the Country Club area beyond are not the only fine neighborhoods in Chatham and it is not of those sections of Chatham that I think when I'm up at the lake in the summer or away on a business trip. My own house, for instance, is in one of the gated-off streets that were laid out just north of Lawton Park at the turn of the century. The houses there are mostly big three-story houses. There's a green parkway down the center of the street, and we have so many forest trees you would think you were in the middle of Lawton Park itself. But, actually, it's not even the Lawton Park area that's most typical of Chatham, any more than Singleton Heights or the Country Club area. And, in my mind, it is certainly not the new do-it-yourself ranch-house district that means Chatham to me. . . . It is the block after block of modest two-story houses, built thirty to forty years ago now, that seem most typical and give me a really comfortable feeling. It was the people in those houses who managed to keep paying something on their loans in the Depression. Whenever I think of Chatham when Mary and I go away in the summer and think of how pleasant it can be to be there despite the awful heat, I think first of those bungalows built of good wire-cut brick, with red and orange tile roofs and big screened porches, of the little privet hedges that divide their sixty-foot lots, and of the maples and oaks and sycamores whose summer shade their front yards share.

The summer Hugh was seventeen I must have seen him hoofing it along the sidewalk or standing at the curb of every block of Division Boulevard. I could never be certain that the men with me recognized him, and once I asked Joe McNary, "What were those kids doing back there on the curb?"

"They're hitchhiking, Will," he said.

"Hitchhiking?" I had never heard the term before, but I knew at once what it meant. "Where are they going?" I said.

"Nowhere. They're just doing the town. There's no harm in it, I guess."

I guess he was right. Hugh never got into any trouble that I know of, except over a car that he and his buddies made a down payment on, one time. They put down seven dollars on an old Packard touring car and drove it around town till it ran out of gas. They had bought the car in Hugh's name, and so when the police found it parked at the roadside out near the Polo Club, they gave me a ring. I told them just to take it back to the dealer and that I'd pay whatever fine it was. But they were pretty inquisitive, and I had to go down to the police station and answer a lot of questions. It was an embarrassing experience for me, because I had to confess that I hadn't known of Hugh's part in the adventure and didn't know the names of the other boys who went in on it with him. From the police station I had to get Hugh on the telephone at the high school and find out the names of the other boys. He didn't want to tell me. And we had to argue it out right then, which was the bad part, with him talking from the principal's office and with me at the sergeant's desk at the police station. Hugh ended by giving me the boys' names, and we never heard any more about it from the police, though I did have to pay the used-car dealer something to make him forget the whole business.

Hugh Robert was in the dumps for a couple of weeks afterward. Instead of excusing himself from the dinner table, as he had always done when his mother and I sat dawdling over our coffee, he would sit there pretending to listen to what we had to say, or he would just gaze despairingly up into the glass prisms of the chandelier above the table. One night when I felt I couldn't stand his black mood any longer, I gave his mother a sign to leave us alone. At first she frowned and refused to do it. Finally though, when I grew as silent as Hugh, she invented a reason to have to go to the kitchen. As soon as I heard her and the cook's voices out there, I said, "What's the matter, Hugh. What are you thinking about?"

He said, "I was thinking about how sorry I am. I really am, Dad."

"What's this?" I said.

"I'm sorry you had to pay that money on the car."

"Is that all?"

"No. Worse than that was their having you down at the station. I know you hated that worse than paying the money." Right away, you see, he was making me out as some kind of pantywaist.

"I didn't give a hoot in hell about going to the police station," I said. "But it was a damn-fool idea you boys had."

"You don't have to tell me that," he said. "It was the stupidest idea I've ever had. It was an awful mistake."

What could you say to such a boy? I wanted to ask him where they would have gone if they had had more gas, but his mother came bustling back from the kitchen then, followed by Lucy May, the cook, who began pressing Hugh to have a second helping of chocolate pie, which, if I remember correctly, he did.

One other time, when I was out with another group of men, and in another part of town, I asked, "What do you suppose those kids are doing out here?"

"*Out* here?" one of them said, and I could tell from his lack of interest that he hadn't recognized Hugh. But I think the fellow who was driving the car that day must have known that what I meant was: What was a son of mine doing so far from home?

"Oh," he said, "I can guess pretty well what they're doing. They've heard there's a drugstore in this end of town that sells milk shakes for a nickel. It's something like that; you can just count on it." We were in a perfectly decent neighborhood out on the south side, where a lot of the rich Germans used to live. It's a nice section and didn't get too awfully run-down during the Depression. I could hardly have told the difference between it and my own section if I hadn't known Chatham well.

Still another time, we had parked the car and were crossing the street toward a little Italian grocery store and lunchroom, a place just west of Court Square and near the old canal. It was a pretty rough and slummy part of town. (Not long afterward FDR had the whole area demolished and put one of his housing projects there.) But the little joint, which was called Baccalupo's Quick Lunch & Grocery, was getting to be well known for its rye and prosciutto and its three-point-two draft beer. As we headed across the street, I saw Hugh and two other boys running out of the place, with Tony Baccalupo, a swarthy little dwarf of a man, after them. I watched Tony overtake them and snatch some fruit away from them. Then the boys went off laughing together at Tony, who stood shouting something in Italian at the top of his voice. Tony was himself a sort of half-wit, I suppose. He was not the proprietor but the proprietor's younger brother— or older brother. When we got inside, I found the opportunity to ask him about the boys who had gone out just before we came in.

"They jelly beans," he said. "They just-a jelly beans. They think they plenty smart and I see 'em making the fun of me, winking in the mirror over the counter. But they got no money, got no jobs, not even know how to make-a the real trouble. They steal them grapefruit just-a to make-a me hafta run out in the street and get a sweat." He spat in the sawdust on the floor, and began taking our orders.

It got so, instead of watching for Hugh, I tried not to see him. All summer, he was wandering about town, hitchhiking from one point to another, never with any real destination, sometimes driving my old Pierce-Arrow, when his mother didn't need it. He didn't really like to take the car, however; it was an old limousine with a glass between the front and back seats, and used too much gas. He and his friends drifted about town, not ever knowing where they were, really, because to them the different parts of the city didn't mean anything. I would be riding in the backseat of a car or walking on the sidewalk, aware only of how all business and progress had bogged down, wondering if and when we could ever get it going again, searching for the first sign of a comeback. Hugh and his gang were searching for something, too, you might say. Searching for mirrors to admire themselves in. Or that's how it seemed. Every time I saw them, I would think of Tony's word: jelly beans.

One night when I got up from the dinner table, Hugh was just coming in from one of his days of wandering about town. We met in the dining-room doorway. "I hope you're making the most of your freedom, son," I said.

He looked at me for a moment, almost squinting. Then he opened his eyes wide, and turned his blue gaze on the room in general, blinking his eyelids two or three times as though they were camera shutters, his eyes registering everything, including the black cook; Mary had buzzed for her when she heard Hugh shut the front door, and Lucy May was now holding the swinging door a little way open. Finally he squinted at me again — squinted so that you couldn't have told the color of his eyes. And I repeated, "I hope you're making the most of your freedom."

"I wonder if I *am*," he said, smiling, with a tinge of contempt in his smile and in his voice, I thought.

I looked over my shoulder at his mother, and she shook her head, meaning for me not to say anything more.

It was as though Hugh and I were drifting about through two different cities that were laid out on the very same tract of land. I used to feel we were even occupying two different houses built upon one piece of ground — houses of identical dimensions and filling one and the same area of cubic space. It was just a feeling I had. It first came to me one afternoon when I watched Hugh looking at himself in the mirror. I imagined that the interior that Hugh and I saw there wasn't the same as the one I stood in. That's all there was to it. But probably even to mention that feeling of mine is carrying things too far. I don't want to be misleading about this mirror business. I don't think the mirror-gazing itself was any real fetish with Hugh. In the first place, he didn't *always* make for the mirror as soon as he came in. Sometimes he would slip his books into the hall cupboard and go straight to the telephone; he was a great one for the telephone.

And what a lot of common talk we had to listen to on the telephone: "Did he say that? . . . I saw her looking at me and I wondered what she thought. . . . 'What do you mean?' I mean what she thought about *me*. . . ."

Always himself. Often as not, one of his girls would call him.

There was a girl named Ida, who nearly drove us all crazy. In the beginning, Hugh was mightily smitten by her. Of that I am quite certain. She was the belle of the class when Hugh entered the tenth grade at the high school, and throughout most of that year it seemed as though he looked for excuses to mention Ida Thomas's name at the dinner table. We didn't get much notion of her except that she was "a gorgeous redhead" and that she had so many admirers that Hugh "couldn't get near her with a ten-foot pole." Nevertheless, he clearly liked for us to tease him about her, though he would always insist that "she didn't know he existed." But at last — and after considerable effort, I gather — he managed to make Ida aware of his existence. From that day the girl gave him no peace.

She would telephone him two or three times in one evening: She was a brash little thing and would engage Hugh's mother in conversation if she answered the telephone, or even me, if I answered it: "How are *you*, Mr. Perkins? . . . How's Mrs. Perkins? . . . And how's that good-looking son of yours — your pride and joy, so they tell me?" Hugh had a time shaking her, I guess. He got so he wouldn't come to the telephone if Mary or I answered and recognized Ida's voice, and he would never answer it himself. She took to writing him letters at home and finally tended to embarrass the boy with his family. One card said, "Roses are red, violets are blue. Sugar's sweet and so is Hugh." Another said, "Someday I'll ride in your Pierce-Arrow, Hugh Robert Perkins."

One Sunday, I got Hugh to go for a walk with me while his mother was at church, and I asked him outright why he put up with so much nonsense from the girl. "I feel sorry for her," he said. As though that were any kind of an excuse.

"She's not as popular as she used to be?" I asked.

"Certainly she is!" he said.

"Oh," I said. "Then you feel sorry for her because she has all the other fellows but *not* you?"

He laughed aloud. "I never thought of it that way, Mr. Perkins," he said, as if he thought I was only joking.

So I laughed, too, and took the opportunity to ask another question. "Tell me, son," I said, "what turned you against her? Was it the telephone calls?"

"No. Not exactly. You see, it wasn't even *me* she was interested in. She was impressed by your old Pierce-Arrow. And still more by our living in West Vesey Place."

"But you didn't exactly like those telephone calls. And what about those postcards, Hugh?"

"Why, she didn't know any better, Dad!" For a minute he stopped there on the street on Sunday morning and looked at me as though it was I who didn't have good sense about such things. "That's why I had to put up with it. That's why I felt sorry for her."

He was very cagey, and I didn't bother him any further about Ida, since it was all over by then anyway. But judging from the gloom he dwelt in for several months, he must have considered Ida one of his worst mistakes.

Hugh wouldn't study, and he wasn't really too hot an athlete, although certainly for a while he thought he was going to be. He made several of his "mistakes" in the athletic line, and would, of course, fall into a black mood each time he was dropped from a team or was even kept on the sidelines. His mother said he couldn't excel in athletics because he had to compete with the big, tough fellows who went out for sports at Chatham West High. And she said that the schoolwork at the public school was too easy and didn't occupy him. Maybe she was right. I know that when his two brothers had finished at Chatham Academy they had had trigonometry and Latin and even some Greek. Both of them passed the College Board examinations with flying colors and had a summer in Europe before starting college. Hugh wouldn't even *talk* about going to college — not to any local college that I could afford to send him to. Since the war, of course, he has gotten himself some kind of degree at Columbia University on the G.I. Bill. But during high school, when we mentioned college to him, he only laughed at the idea. One Sunday in his senior year, when the other children were at the house and the subject came up, he said, "Why, I've already been to the best college in our part of the country, the College of William and Mary"—meaning his mother and me, of course. "I've been studying diplomacy, and next June I'll be ready for the foreign service."

The others took this as a joke, but it made me realize how soon he might be gone from us to wherever he had in mind going. I was only half through my meal, but involuntarily I began searching my pockets for my pipe and a match. It's hard having your youngest be the one who disappoints you. I sat there searching for my pipe, thinking that I could just imagine how the letter he would leave would look on the library table, or how he would come down to breakfast one morning and say he had written off and gotten himself a job somewhere away from us—away from Chatham! I suppose it was rather simpleminded and old-fashioned of me to think about it the way I did.

In his senior year, Hugh actually began to show an interest in his schoolwork—in a certain part of it, in a part I wouldn't have called work. You would just hardly believe the things they offered in the curriculum of that school. But anyway, the first indication I had of what was stirring was Hugh's coming to me one morning with a very odd sort of request. From some neat, dark, and no doubt carefully protected corner of the house, known only to himself, he had pulled out an old dictation machine—a Dictaphone—which I had given him as a little fellow. It was an old model that I had brought home from the office and let him use as a plaything. I had forgotten about it. It had been seven or eight years since he had asked me to take the wax cylinders downtown and have them scraped so he could use them again. But he came to me after breakfast one morning, when he was all ready to leave for school, carrying the case of cylinders that came with the Dictaphone. He looked a little shamefaced, I must say, like any big boy caught playing with one of his old toys. I was touched to see that he had hung on to something I had given him so long ago. He handed the case to me and as I examined it I remarked silently that it seemed to be in as good condition as on the day I gave it to him. "Where did you resurrect this from, Hugh?" I asked.

"I've had it put by against a rainy day," he said.

"Do you still have the machine itself?" I asked.

"Oh yes, of course," he said.

I held the case of cylinders and then I said, "You intend to sell it, I suppose—the whole outfit?"

"Why no, Mr. Perkins. I want you to have these cylinders scraped for me."

"You know it costs something to have it done?" It occurred to me that as a child he mightn't have realized that.

"Oh, certainly. I'll pay for it. I have some *money* put by, too," he said, giving me one of his quick winks, "against the same rainy day." He was no spendthrift, to be sure. I doubt that there was ever a week when he spent the whole of the small allowance his mother gave him.

I set the case of cylinders on the floor beside me and picked up the paper I had been reading when he came in. "What are you going to use them for?" I said from behind the paper.

"In connection with one of my classes," he said. "A readings course."

I looked at him over my paper. He was still standing before me and was clearly willing for me to pursue the subject. "A reading course?"

"Oral readings," be explained. "A class in oral readings, for additional speech credit." He was in dead earnest. He said they were graded according to some kind of point system and that it had been wonderful help for him to be able to hear himself on the Dictaphone, that he had already made terrific progress.

"You've already been using the Dictaphone, then?" I inquired. "The cylinders were clean when you got them out?"

"Yes," he said. "Don't you remember, I got you to have them scraped before I ever put them away?"

"No, I didn't remember," I said. "It's been a pretty long time, Hugh."

Now I found myself wondering how many nights had he already been up there in his room listening to his own voice on the Dictaphone. I went back to my paper again, because I knew I didn't want to hear any more about this business. Sooner or later, I thought, he will see it as just another of his mistakes.

But for some months to come, Hugh's concern with his voice was all we did hear about. My theory was that the boy had been trying a long while to decide what it was about himself that charmed him most. And at last he thought he knew. All that winter he was as busy as a beaver with his "speech lessons" and "exercises." I would bring home the set of cylinders freshly scraped, and they wouldn't last him much more than a week. Finally, I guess he wore them out because well before spring he quit asking me to take them. But his interest didn't stop there. He continued to engage me now and then in discussions of his current "problems" in speech, as openly and seriously as though he were talking about math or history. And first thing his mother and I knew, he was on the debating team, was trying out for a part in the class play, was even getting special instructions from the teacher in "newscasting."

It occurred to me once during this time that maybe Hugh had fallen in love with his speech teacher, Miss Arrowood. In recent months his mother had complained of a tendency in him to resent any questions about the girls he was having dates with on the weekends. If, under pressure, he mentioned the name of a particular girl, it wasn't a name that his mother knew. I couldn't explain such a business to Mary—there was no use in it—but I think I understood pretty well what Hugh was going through in that respect. And I could remember that a boy, hating himself for his own fallen and degraded state, is apt at such times to begin idealizing some attractive, sympathetic woman who is enough older than himself to seem quite beyond his aspiration—particularly if she is even vaguely the intellectual type. I didn't ask Hugh how old Miss Arrowood was or what she looked like. I just dropped by the school one afternoon in March when I knew there was to be a rehearsal of the class play.

It wasn't even necessary for me to go inside the auditorium to see what I had come to see. Through a glass panel in one of the rear doors I could see the whole stage. The play they were practicing for was one of those moronic things that they give big grown-up boys and girls to act in. (They did it even in the private schools when my older children were coming along.) This one was called *Mr. Hairbrain's Confession: A Comedy*. I read the title in a notice on the bulletin board beside the auditorium door.

After two seconds I spotted Miss Arrowood, who was giving directions from a position at the side of the stage, and I knew that my conjecture had been a false one. I say "after two seconds" because for about two seconds I mistook that lady to be one of the cast and already in costume and makeup. Her bosom was of a size and shape that one of the youngsters might have effected with a bed pillow. Her orange-colored hair may really have been a wig. On the far end of her unbelievable nose rode the inevitable pince-nez. The woman's every gesture had just the exaggeration that you could expect from any member of the cast on the night of the performance.

I realized who she was when she started giving some directions to Hugh, who was now posturing in the center of the stage. No, she wasn't directing him, after all; she was applauding something he had already done or said. Hugh, like his fellow actors, was reading his lines from the book. Every time he opened his mouth or so much as turned his dark head or struck a new position, she either nodded approval or shook with laughter. She hardly took her eyes off him. Hugh no doubt had a comic role, but I knew that nothing in that play was so funny or so interesting as Miss Arrowood's conduct would have led me to believe. I can't say exactly how long I stood watching, lost in my own damned thoughts. When finally I did leave it was because someone in the cast—not Hugh—saw me and called Miss Arrowood's attention to my presence. At once she began motioning to me to go away, waving her book in the air and shooing me with her other hand. She didn't know who I was and didn't care. Miss Arrowood knew only that she wasn't going to have any interruption of the pleasure she took from watching Hugh.

There was no more to it than that. Miss Arrowood was just another old-maid schoolteacher with a crush on one of her pupils. I doubt very much that Hugh's experience with her had any influence on his finally going into the theater the way he has. Quite naturally she must nowadays imagine herself to have been his first great influence and inspiration, but if Miss Arrowood has ever gotten to New York and found her way over to the East Side, to that little cubbyhole of a theater where my son Hugh Robert directs plays, I'll bet she doesn't understand the kind of plays he puts on any better than I do. At any rate, she didn't succeed in turning him into any radio announcer or even into an actor, thank God. I doubt that she hoped to, even; for in my opinion Hugh Robert didn't have any better voice than any of the rest of the family. Physically he is very much like the rest of us. But it is my opinion also that the lady tried to play upon Hugh's vanity for that year, for the sake of keeping him near her. And it must certainly have been she who arranged for a certain phonograph record, which he made on a machine at school, to be put on the local radio. This happened one miserable Sunday afternoon in May. It capped everything else that had happened.

Hugh rose early that Sunday morning in order to plug in the charger to the batteries of the radio. Our set was an old battery-type table model, one that I had paid a lot of money for when it was new. Hugh was fond of giving it a big thump and saying in his best smart-aleck voice, "They don't make 'em like that anymore." But he would have been the first to admit — especially on the Sunday I'm speaking of — that there are times when the electricity goes off just as you want to hear some program. I hung on to my battery set all through the Depression, just the way I did my Pierce-Arrow. And it is true, of course, that we did sometimes find, when a favorite program was due to come on, that we had forgotten to charge the batteries.

But the batteries didn't need charging at all that Sunday in May, and Hugh knew they didn't. He simply wasn't taking any chances. When I came down to breakfast, I saw the ugly little violet light burning in the charger at the end of the living room. I observed Hugh coming in there to check on them off and on all morning. Apparently when the idea of charging the batteries first struck him, he had jumped out of bed and thrown on some clothes without bothering to comb his hair or put on his shoes. He came down wearing his old run-over bedroom slippers, his everyday corduroy pants, and a wrinkled shirt that he must have pulled out of the clothes hamper. He wandered around the house like that all morning. When his mother was leaving for church at ten-thirty, I asked her if she didn't think she ought to remind him to get properly dressed before the other children came for dinner. But either she forgot to, or she decided against it, or she just "hated to" and didn't.

During the two hours his mother was gone, I could hear Hugh moving about all over the house. First he would be in the basement, then at the closet in the back hall, then upstairs somewhere, even on the third floor. Every so often he would come back to the living room to have a look at the batteries. He would sit down and try to get interested in some section of the Sunday paper. But he couldn't stay still except for short intervals. Every time he got up, the first thing he did was to go and look out one of the living-room windows. I suspect that during his wandering through the house he must now and then have stopped and looked out windows in most of the other rooms, too. To him, that day, the weather outside was the most important matter in the world.

And in spite of its being May, the weather outside was quite wintry and nasty. Rain fell during most of the morning, and there was occasional thunder, with streaks of lightning away off across town. We had been having a series of electrical storms, which generally come to us a month earlier than they did that year. This bad weather was what Hugh had pinned his hopes on. The understanding was that if the ball game—the third of the season—was called that Sunday, then Station WCM was going to fill in the first ten minutes or so of the time with a recorded reading Hugh had made of "A Message to Garcia."[1] Though I had been unaware of it before, it seems that the station made a practice of devoting such free periods to activities of the public schools. Hugh managed that Sunday to make us all keenly aware of the fact.

I seldom missed listening to the Chatham Barons' home games. When it was a good season, I even used to go out to Runnymede Park and watch the games. The Barons, however, hadn't had such a season in almost a decade. The last time they had won their league's pennant was in 1925. But, even so, I have never been one to go running off to Cincinnati or St. Louis to see big-league games when we have a team right in Chatham to support and root for. It happened that this year the Barons had won their first two games, and I was hopeful. In particular, I hoped to be listening to the broadcast of a third game in what might turn into a winning streak. I knew why Hugh kept looking out the windows, and soon I was looking out windows, too. The rain came down pretty steady all morning and only began to let up about noon. I found I was pitting my hopes against his. I was, at least, until I saw how awfully worked up the boy was. Then I tried my best to hope with him. But I don't think I ever before had such mixed feelings about so small a thing as whether or not a ball game would be rained out.

Hugh's mother returned from church at twelve-thirty. The other children came for dinner just before one. Hugh was off upstairs when the others arrived, and had to be called to come to the table. I supposed that he had finally gone up to get himself dressed, but he came down in the same state of undress, with his hair still uncombed, and I saw at once that it offended his brothers and his sister. I saw Sister trying to signal her mother, indicating that Hugh ought at least to go and comb his hair. But her mother's eye was not to be caught that day.

Hugh was unusually silent during the meal, and his silence was contagious. From time to time I saw every member of the family taking a glance

---

[1]An essay written by American Elbert Hubbard in 1899 immediately following the Spanish-American War, it upholds the true story of a man's valiant attempt to deliver a message from U.S. President William McKinley to Cuban revolutionary Calixto Garcia y Iñigues as a model of a good work ethic for the business world.

out the window to see how the weather was. After raining all morning, the skies seemed to be clearing. It was mostly bright while we sat there, with only an occasional dark interval. During those dark intervals, Hugh ate feverishly; otherwise he only picked at his food. I'm afraid that with the rest of us the reverse was true.

Once, while Lucy May was passing around a dish, I even saw her turn her black face toward a sunlit window at Hugh's back. Just as she did so, there came from outside the clear chirping of a redbird, which brought a beautiful smile to her face. The others were making a show of keeping up the conversation while a servant was in the room, and so when she offered Hugh the dish she was able to mumble to him without their taking notice, "You hear that redbird, don't you, Hugh! He say, 'To wet! To wet!' That's a promise of rain, honey!" Hugh may or may not have heard the redbird. But he paid no more attention to Lucy May's encouraging words than he had to the encouragement and applause of Miss Arrowood.

The very instant we rose from the table, there was a flash of lightning so close to us that it brightened the windows. And there followed a deafening crack of thunder. Hugh galloped across the hall into the living room and commenced disconnecting the batteries from the charger and hooking them up to the radio. The rest of us followed, just as if there were no other room in the house we could have gone to. By the time I got in there, Hugh was tuning in on WCM. There was a roar of static, and then, as the static receded, the announcer's voice came through saying, "The next voice you hear will be that of Hugh Robert Perkins," and went on to tell who Hugh's parents were, to give his street address, and to say that he was a senior at West High and a member of Miss Arrowood's class in oral readings. Outside, a sheet of rain was falling, and there was more thunder and lightning than there had been all morning.

Through the loudspeaker the voice of Hugh Robert Perkins began with some introductory remarks, telling us how, why, when, and by whom "A Message to Garcia" had been written. It didn't sound especially like Hugh's voice, but even at the outset the static was so bad that I missed about every third word. After the first half minute of the "Message" itself, it seemed hopeless to try to listen. Yet we had to sit there, all of us — and without any assistance from Miss Arrowood or Lucy May — and suffer through the awful business with Hugh. At least, it seemed to us we had to; and we *thought* that's what we were doing.

Hugh never once looked around from the radio. His eyes were glued to the loudspeaker, which was placed on top of the set. He had pulled up a straight chair, and he sat with his legs crossed and his hands clasped over one knee. He held his neck as straight and stiff as a board and didn't move his head to left or right during the entire ten minutes. The storm and static got worse every second, and he didn't even try to improve the reception. He didn't touch the dials. Toward the very end, I saw his mother raise her eyebrows and tighten her mouth the way she does when she's about to cry, and I shook my head vigorously at her, forbidding it. I knew what she was feeling well enough; we were all feeling it: Poor boy had endured his uncertainty, had for days been pinning his hopes on the chance of rain, and now had to hear himself drowned out by the static on our old radio. I thought it might be more than flesh and blood could bear. I thought that at any moment he might spring up and begin kicking that radio set to bits. But I knew, too, that his mother's tears wouldn't help matters.

What a fortunate thing for us all that I stopped her. Because not ten seconds after I did, the reading was finished and Hugh was on his feet and facing us with a broad grin of satisfaction. I saw at once that for him there had been no static. Or, rather, that he had heard the clear, sweet, reassuring tones of his own voice calling to him through and above the static, and that his last doubts about the kind of glory he yearned for had been swept away. He ran his hand through his tangled hair self-consciously. His blue eyes shone. "There!" he said. And after a moment he said it again, "There!" And I felt as strongly then as I feel it now that that was the real moment of Hugh's departure from our midst. He tried to fix his gaze on me for a second, but it was quite beyond his powers to concentrate on any one of us present. "It's a shame . . ." he began rather vaguely, "it's a shame you had to listen to my sorry voice instead of hearing the game. But maybe the game will come on later. . . . Did you hear the place where my voice cracked? That was the worst part of all, wasn't it? I'm glad it's over with." He gave a deep sigh, and then he said, in a voice full of wonder and excitement and confidence, "Gosh!"

At once, he went upstairs and dressed himself in his Sunday clothes and left the house, saying that he had a date, or maybe it was that he was going to meet some of his cronies somewhere. I didn't bother to listen. I knew that he would be back for supper that night and that he wasn't really going to leave us for some time yet. And I knew it wouldn't be a matter of a letter on the breakfast table when he did go, because it couldn't any longer be a matter of a boy running away from home. While the other children were laughing over what had happened and were talking about what a child Hugh still was, I was thinking to myself that Hugh Robert Perkins hadn't many more of his "mistakes" ahead of him. I felt certain that this afternoon he had seen his way ahead clear, and I imagined that I could see it with him.

The other children left the house soon after lunch that Sunday. Mary went upstairs to take a nap, as she often did when we had been through something that there was no use talking about. I wandered through the downstairs rooms, feeling not myself at all. Once, I looked out a window in the library and saw that the weather had cleared, and I didn't go and turn on the radio. And I had a strange experience that afternoon. I was fifty, but suddenly I felt very young again. As I wandered through the house I kept thinking of how everything must look to Hugh, of what his life was going to be like, and of just what he would be like when he got to be my age. It all seemed very clear to me, and I understood how right it was for him. And because it seemed so clear I realized the time had come when I could forgive my son the difference there had always been between our two natures. I was fifty, but I had just discovered what it means to see the world through another man's eyes. It is a discovery you are lucky to make at any age, and one that is no less marvelous whether you make it at fifty or fifteen. Because it is only then that the world, as you have seen it through your own eyes, will begin to tell you things about yourself.

[1959]

FLANNERY O'CONNOR

*F*lannery O'Connor (1925–1964) was born in Savannah, Georgia, the only child of Roman Catholic parents. When she was thirteen her father was found to have disseminated lupus, an incurable disease in which antibodies in the immune system attack the body's own substances. After her father's death in 1941, O'Connor attended Georgia State College for Women in Milledgeville, where she also published stories and edited the literary magazine. On the strength of these stories, she was awarded a fellowship at the Writers Workshop at the University of Iowa and earned her M.F.A. degree there. Late in 1950 she became ill with what was diagnosed as lupus, and she returned to Milledgeville to start a series of treatments that temporarily arrested the disease. Living with her mother on the family's 500-acre dairy farm, O'Connor began to work again, writing from nine to twelve in the morning and spending the rest of the day resting, reading, writing letters, and raising peacocks.

O'Connor's first book, Wise Blood, *a complex comic novel attacking the contemporary secularization of religion, was published in 1952. It was followed in 1955 by a collection of stories,* A Good Man Is Hard to Find. *O'Connor was able to see a second novel,* The Violent Bear It Away, *through to publication in 1960, but she died of lupus in 1964, having completed enough stories for a second collection,* Everything That Rises Must Converge *(1965). Her total output of just thirty-one stories, collected in her* Complete Stories, *won the National Book Award for fiction in 1972.*

Despite her illness, O'Connor was never a recluse; she accepted as many lecture invitations as her health would permit. A volume of her lectures and occasional pieces was published in 1969 as Mystery and Manners. *It is a valuable companion to her stories and novels, because she often reflected on her writing and interpreted her fiction. As a devout Roman Catholic, O'Connor was uncompromising in her religious views: "For I am no disbeliever in spiritual purpose and no vague believer. This means that for me the meaning of life is centered in our Redemption by Christ and what I see in the world I see in relation to that." As Joyce Carol Oates recognized in her essay "The Visionary Art of Flannery O'Connor," O'Connor is one of the great religious writers of modern times, unique "in her celebration of the necessity of succumbing to the divine through violence that is immediate and irreparable. There is no mysticism in her work that is only spiritual; it is physical as well." O'Connor's stories, like "Everything That Rises Must Converge" (New World Writing, 1961), frequently involve family relationships, but they are not meant to be read as realistic fiction, despite her remarkable ear for dialogue. O'Connor said she wrote them as parables.*

RELATED COMMENTARY: *Flannery O'Connor, "Some Aspects of the Grotesque in Southern Fiction," page 1417.*

Everything That Rises Must Converge

Her doctor had told Julian's mother that she must lose twenty pounds on account of her blood pressure, so on Wednesday nights Julian had to take her downtown on the bus for a reducing class at the Y. The reducing class was designed for working girls over fifty, who weighed from 165 to 200 pounds. His mother was one of the slimmer ones, but she said ladies did not tell their age or weight. She would not ride the buses by herself at night since they had been integrated, and because the reducing class was one of her few pleasures, necessary for her health, and *free,* she said Julian could at least put himself out to take her, considering all she did for him. Julian did not like to consider all she did for him, but every Wednesday night he braced himself and took her.

She was almost ready to go, standing before the hall mirror, putting on her hat, while he, his hands behind him, appeared pinned to the door frame, waiting like Saint Sebastian for the arrows to begin piercing him. The hat was new and had cost her seven dollars and a half. She kept saying, "Maybe I shouldn't have paid that for it. No, I shouldn't have. I'll take it off and return it tomorrow. I shouldn't have bought it."

Julian raised his eyes to heaven. "Yes, you should have bought it," he said. "Put it on and let's go." It was a hideous hat. A purple velvet flap came down on one side of it and stood up on the other; the rest of it was green and looked like a cushion with the stuffing out. He decided it was less comical than jaunty and pathetic. Everything that gave her pleasure was small and depressed him.

She lifted the hat one more time and set it down slowly on top of her head. Two wings of gray hair protruded on either side of her florid face, but her eyes, sky-blue, were as innocent and untouched by experience as they must have been when she was ten. Were it not that she was a widow who had struggled fiercely to feed and clothe and put him through school and who was supporting him still, "until he got on his feet," she might have been a little girl that he had to take to town.

"It's all right, it's all right," he said. "Let's go." He opened the door himself and started down the walk to get her going. The sky was a dying violet and the houses stood out darkly against it, bulbous liver-colored monstrosities of a uniform ugliness though no two were alike. Since this had been a fashionable neighborhood forty years ago, his mother persisted in thinking they did well to have an apartment in it. Each house had a narrow collar of dirt around it in which sat, usually, a grubby child. Julian walked with his hands in his pockets, his head down and thrust forward, and his eyes glazed with the determination to make himself completely numb during the time he would be sacrificed to her pleasure.

The door closed and he turned to find the dumpy figure, surmounted by the atrocious hat, coming toward him. "Well," she said, "you only live once and paying a little more for it, I at least won't meet myself coming and going."

"Some day I'll start making money," Julian said gloomily—he knew he never would—"and you can have one of those jokes whenever you take the fit." But first they would move. He visualized a place where the nearest neighbor would be three miles away on either side.

"I think you're doing fine," she said, drawing on her gloves. "You've only been out of school a year. Rome wasn't built in a day."

She was one of the few members of the Y reducing class who arrived in hat and gloves and who had a son who had been to college. "It takes time," she said, "and the world is in such a mess. This hat looked better on me than any of the others, though when she brought it out I said, 'Take that thing back. I wouldn't have it on my head,' and she said, 'Now wait till you see it on,' and when she put it on me, I said, 'We-ull,' and she said, 'If you ask me, that hat does something for you and you do something for the hat, and besides,' she said, 'with that hat, you won't meet yourself coming and going.'"

Julian thought he could have stood his lot better if she had been selfish, if she had been an old hag who drank and screamed at him. He walked along, saturated in depression, as if in the midst of his martyrdom he had lost his faith. Catching sight of his long, hopeless, irritated face, she stopped suddenly with a grief-stricken look, and pulled back on his arm. "Wait on me," she said. "I'm going back to the house and take this thing off and tomorrow I'm going to return it. I was out of my head. I can pay the gas bill with the seven-fifty."

He caught her arm in a vicious grip. "You are not going to take it back," he said. "I like it."

"Well," she said, "I don't think I ought . . ."

"Shut up and enjoy it," he muttered, more depressed than ever.

"With the world in the mess it's in," she said, "it's a wonder we can enjoy anything. I tell you, the bottom rail is on the top."

Julian sighed.

"Of course," she said, "if you know who you are, you can go anywhere." She said this every time he took her to the reducing class. "Most of them in it are not our kind of people," she said, "but I can be gracious to anybody. I know who I am."

"They don't give a damn for your graciousness," Julian said savagely. "Knowing who you are is good for one generation only. You haven't the foggiest idea where you stand now or who you are."

She stopped and allowed her eyes to flash at him. "I most certainly do know who I am," she said, "and if you don't know who you are, I'm ashamed of you."

"Oh hell," Julian said.

"Your great-grandfather was a former governor of this state," she said.

"Your grandfather was a prosperous landowner. Your grandmother was a Godhigh."

"Will you look around you," he said tensely, "and see where you are now?" and he swept his arm jerkily out to indicate the neighborhood, which the growing darkness at least made less dingy.

"You remain what you are," she said. "Your great-grandfather had a plantation and two hundred slaves."

"There are no more slaves," he said irritably.

"They were better off when they were," she said. He groaned to see that she was off on that topic. She rolled onto it every few days like a train on an open track. He knew every stop, every junction, every swamp along the way, and knew the exact point at which her conclusion would roll majestically into the station: "It's ridiculous. It's simply not realistic. They should rise, yes, but on their own side of the fence."

"Let's skip it," Julian said.

"The ones I feel sorry for," she said, "are the ones that are half white. They're tragic."

"Will you skip it?"

"Suppose we were half white. We would certainly have mixed feelings."

"I have mixed feelings now," he groaned.

"Well let's talk about something pleasant," she said. "I remember going to Grandpa's when I was a little girl. Then the house had double stairways that went up to what was really the second floor—all the cooking was done on the first. I used to like to stay down in the kitchen on account of the way the walls smelled. I would sit with my nose pressed against the plaster and take deep breaths. Actually the place belonged to the Godhighs but your grandfather Chestny paid the mortgage and saved it for them. They were in reduced circumstances," she said, "but reduced or not, they never forgot who they were."

"Doubtless that decayed mansion reminded them," Julian muttered. He never spoke of it without contempt or thought of it without longing. He had seen it once when he was a child before it had been sold. The double stairways had rotted and had been torn down. Negroes were living in it. But it remained in his mind as his mother had known it. It appeared in his dreams regularly. He would stand on the wide porch, listening to the rustle of oak leaves, then wander through the high-ceilinged hall into the parlor that opened onto it and gaze at the worn rugs and faded draperies. It occurred to him that it was he, not she, who could have appreciated it. He preferred its threadbare elegance to anything he could name and it was because of it that all the neighborhoods they had lived in had been a torment to him—whereas she had hardly known the difference. She called her insensitivity "being adjustable."

"And I remember the old darky who was my nurse, Caroline. There was no better person in the world. I've always had a great respect for my colored friends," she said. "I'd do anything in the world for them and they'd . . ."

"Will you for God's sake get off that subject?" Julian said. When he got on a bus by himself, he made it a point to sit down beside a Negro, in reparation as it were for his mother's sins.

"You're mighty touchy tonight," she said. "Do you feel all right?"

"Yes I feel all right," he said. "Now lay off."

She pursed her lips. "Well, you certainly are in a vile humor," she observed. "I just won't speak to you at all."

They had reached the bus stop. There was no bus in sight and Julian, his hands still jammed in his pockets and his head thrust forward, scowled down the empty street. The frustration of having to wait on the bus as well as ride on it began to creep up his neck like a hot hand. The presence of his mother was borne in upon him as she gave a pained sigh. He looked at her bleakly. She was holding herself very erect under the preposterous hat, wearing it like a banner of her imaginary dignity. There was in him an evil urge to break her spirit. He suddenly unloosened his tie and pulled it off and put it in his pocket.

She stiffened. "Why must you look like *that* when you take me to town?" she said. "Why must you deliberately embarrass me?"

"If you'll never learn where you are," he said, "you can at least learn where I am."

"You look like a — thug," she said.

"Then I must be one," he murmured.

"I'll just go home," she said. "I will not bother you. If you can't do a little thing like that for me . . ."

Rolling his eyes upward, he put his tie back on. "Restored to my class," he muttered. He thrust his face toward her and hissed, "True culture is in the mind, the *mind*," he said, and tapped his head, "the mind."

"It's in the heart," she said, "and in how you do things and how you do things is because of who you *are*."

"Nobody in the damn bus cares who you are."

"I care who I am," she said icily.

The lighted bus appeared on top of the next hill and as it approached, they moved out into the street to meet it. He put his hand under her elbow and hoisted her up on the creaking step. She entered with a little smile, as if she were going into a drawing room where everyone had been waiting for her. While he put in the tokens, she sat down on one of the broad front seats for three which faced the aisle. A thin woman with protruding teeth and long yellow hair was sitting on the end of it. His mother moved up beside her and left room for Julian beside herself. He sat down and looked at the floor across the aisle where a pair of thin feet in red and white canvas sandals were planted.

His mother immediately began a general conversation meant to attract anyone who felt like talking. "Can it get any hotter?" she said and removed from her purse a folding fan, black with a Japanese scene on it, which she began to flutter before her.

"I reckon it might could," the woman with the protruding teeth said, "but I know for a fact my apartment couldn't get no hotter."

"It must get the afternoon sun," his mother said. She sat forward and looked up and down the bus. It was half filled. Everybody was white. "I see we have the bus to ourselves," she said. Julian cringed.

"For a change," said the woman across the aisle, the owner of the red and white canvas sandals. "I come on one the other day and they were thick as fleas—up front and all through."

"The world is in a mess everywhere," his mother said. "I don't know how we've let it get in this fix."

"What gets my goat is all those boys from good families stealing automobile tires," the woman with the protruding teeth said. "I told my boy, I said you may not be rich but you been raised right and if I ever catch you in any such mess, they can send you on to the reformatory. Be exactly where you belong."

"Training tells," his mother said. "Is your boy in high school?"

"Ninth grade," the woman said.

"My son just finished college last year. He wants to write but he's selling typewriters until he gets started," his mother said.

The woman leaned forward and peered at Julian. He threw her such a malevolent look that she subsided against the seat. On the floor across the aisle there was an abandoned newspaper. He got up and got it and opened it out in front of him. His mother discreetly continued the conversation in a lower tone but the woman across the aisle said in a loud voice, "Well that's nice. Selling typewriters is close to writing. He can go right from one to the other."

"I tell him," his mother said, "that Rome wasn't built in a day."

Behind the newspaper Julian was withdrawing into the inner compartment of his mind where he spent most of his time. This was a kind of mental bubble in which he established himself when he could not bear to be part of what was going on around him. From it he could see out and judge but in it he was safe from any kind of penetration from without. It was the only place where he felt free of the general idiocy of his fellows. His mother had never entered it but from it he could see her with absolute clarity.

The old lady was clever enough and he thought that if she had started from any of the right premises, more might have been expected of her. She lived according to the laws of her own fantasy world, outside of which he had never seen her set foot. The law of it was to sacrifice herself for him after she had first created the necessity to do so by making a mess of things. If he had permitted her sacrifices, it was only because her lack of foresight had made them necessary. All of her life had been a struggle to act like a Chestny without the Chestny goods, and to give him everything she thought a Chestny ought to have; but since, said she, it was fun to struggle, why complain? And when you had won, as she had won, what fun to look back on the hard times! He could not forgive her that she had enjoyed the struggle and that she thought *she* had won.

What she meant when she said she had won was that she had brought him up successfully and had sent him to college and that he had turned out so well—good looking (her teeth had gone unfilled, so that his could be straightened), intelligent (he realized he was too intelligent to be a success), and with a future ahead of him (there was of course no future ahead of him). She excused his gloominess on the grounds that he was still growing up and his radical ideas on his lack of practical experience. She said he didn't yet know a thing about "life," that he hadn't even entered the real world—when already he was as disenchanted with it as a man of fifty.

The further irony of all this was that in spite of her, he had turned out so well. In spite of going to only a third-rate college, he had, on his own initiative, come out with a first-rate education; in spite of growing up dominated by a small mind, he had ended up with a large one; in spite of all her foolish views, he was free of prejudice and unafraid to face facts. Most miraculous of all, instead of being blinded by love for her as she was for him, he had cut himself emotionally free of her and could see her with complete objectivity. He was not dominated by his mother.

The bus stopped with a sudden jerk and shook him from his meditation. A woman from the back lurched forward with little steps and barely escaped falling in his newspaper as she righted herself. She got off and a large Negro got on. Julian kept his paper lowered to watch. It gave him a certain satisfaction to see injustice in daily operation. It confirmed his view that with a few exceptions there was no one worth knowing within a radius of three hundred miles. The Negro was well dressed and carried a briefcase. He looked round and then sat down on the other end of the seat where the woman with the red and white canvas sandals was sitting. He immediately unfolded a newspaper and obscured himself behind it. Julian's mother's elbow at once prodded insistently into his ribs. "Now you see why I won't ride on these buses by myself," she whispered.

The woman with the red and white canvas sandals had risen at the same time the Negro sat down and had gone further back in the bus and taken the seat of the woman who had got off. His mother leaned forward and cast her an approving look.

Julian rose, crossed the aisle, and sat down in the place of the woman with the canvas sandals. From this position, he looked serenely across at his mother. Her face had turned an angry red. He stared at her, making his eyes the eyes of a stranger. He felt his tension suddenly lift as if he had openly declared war on her.

He would have liked to get in conversation with the Negro and to talk with him about art or politics or any subject that would be above the comprehension of those around them, but the man remained entrenched behind his paper. He was either ignoring the change of seating or had never noticed it. There was no way for Julian to convey his sympathy.

His mother kept her eyes fixed reproachfully on his face. The woman with the protruding teeth was looking at him avidly as if he were a type of monster new to her.

"Do you have a light?" he asked the Negro.

Without looking away from his paper, the man reached in his pocket and handed him a packet of matches.

"Thanks," Julian said. For a moment he held the matches foolishly. A NO SMOKING sign looked down upon him from over the door. This alone would not have deterred him; he had no cigarettes. He had quit smoking some months before because he could not afford it. "Sorry," he muttered and handed back the matches. The Negro lowered the paper and gave him an annoyed look. He took the matches and raised the paper again.

His mother continued to gaze at him but she did not take the advantage of his momentary discomfort. Her eyes retained their battered look. Her face seemed to be unnaturally red, as if her blood pressure had risen. Julian allowed no glimmer of sympathy to show on his face. Having got the advantage, he wanted desperately to keep it and carry it through. He would have liked to teach her a lesson that would last her a while, but there seemed no way to continue the point. The Negro refused to come out from behind his paper.

Julian folded his arms and looked stolidly before him, facing her but as if he did not see her, as if he had ceased to recognize her existence. He visualized a scene in which, the bus having reached their stop, he would remain in his seat and when she said, "Aren't you going to get off?" he would look at her as a stranger who had rashly addressed him. The corner they got off on was usually deserted, but it was well lighted and it would not hurt her to walk by herself the four blocks to the Y. He decided to wait until the time came and then decide whether or not he would let her get off by herself. He would have to be at the Y at ten to bring her back, but he could leave her wondering if he was going to show up. There was no reason for her to think she could always depend on him.

He retired again into the high-ceilinged room sparsely settled with large pieces of antique furniture. His soul expanded momentarily but then he became aware of his mother across from him and the vision shriveled. He studied her coldly. Her feet in little pumps dangled like a child's and did not quite reach the floor. She was training on him an exaggerated look of reproach. He felt completely detached from her. At that moment he could with pleasure have slapped her as he would have slapped a particularly obnoxious child in his charge.

He began to imagine various unlikely ways by which he could teach her a lesson. He might make friends with some distinguished Negro professor or lawyer and bring him home to spend the evening. He would be entirely justified but her blood pressure would rise to 300. He could not push her to the extent of making her have a stroke, and moreover, he had never been successful at making any Negro friends. He had tried to strike up an acquaintance on the bus with some of the better types, with ones that looked like professors or ministers or lawyers. One morning he had sat down next to a distinguished-looking dark brown man who had answered his questions with a sonorous solemnity but who had turned out to be an undertaker. Another day he had sat down beside a cigar-smoking Negro with a diamond ring on his finger, but after a few stilted pleasantries, the Negro had rung the buzzer and risen, slipping two lottery tickets into Julian's hand as he climbed over him to leave.

He imagined his mother lying desperately ill and his being able to secure only a Negro doctor for her. He toyed with that idea for a few minutes and then dropped it for a momentary vision of himself participating as a sympathizer in a sit-in demonstration. This was possible but he did not linger with it. Instead, he approached the ultimate horror. He brought home a beautiful suspiciously Negroid woman. Prepare yourself, he said. There is nothing you can do about it. This is the woman I've chosen. She's intelligent, dignified, even good, and she's suffered and she hasn't thought it *fun*. Now persecute us, go ahead and persecute us. Drive her out of here, but remember, you're driving me too. His eyes were narrowed and through the indignation he had generated, he saw his mother across the aisle, purplefaced, shrunken to the dwarf-like proportions of her moral nature, sitting like a mummy beneath the ridiculous banner of her hat.

He was tilted out of his fantasy again as the bus stopped. The door opened with a sucking hiss and out of the dark a large, gaily dressed, sullen-looking colored woman got on with a little boy. The child, who might have been four, had on a short plaid suit and a Tyrolean hat with a blue feather in it. Julian hoped that he would sit down beside him and that the woman would push in beside his mother. He could think of no better arrangement.

As she waited for her tokens, the woman was surveying the seating possibilities—he hoped with the idea of sitting where she was least wanted. There was something familiar-looking about her but Julian could not place what it was. She was a giant of a woman. Her face was set not only to meet opposition but to seek it out. The downward tilt of her large lower lip was like a warning sign: DON'T TAMPER WITH ME. Her bulging figure was encased in a green crepe dress and her feet overflowed in red shoes. She had on a hideous hat. A purple velvet flap came down on one side of it and stood up on the other; the rest of it was green and looked like a cushion with the stuffing out. She carried a mammoth red pocketbook that bulged throughout as if it were stuffed with rocks.

To Julian's disappointment, the little boy climbed up on the empty seat beside his mother. His mother lumped all children, black and white, into the common category, "cute," and she thought little Negroes were on the whole cuter than little white children. She smiled at the little boy as he climbed on the seat.

Meanwhile the woman was bearing down upon the empty seat beside Julian. To his annoyance, she squeezed herself into it. He saw his mother's face change as the woman settled herself next to him and he realized with satisfaction that this was more objectionable to her than it was to him. Her face seemed almost gray and there was a look of dull recognition in her eyes, as if suddenly she had sickened at some awful confrontation. Julian saw that it was because she and the woman had, in a sense, swapped sons. Though his mother would not realize the symbolic significance of this, she would feel it. His amusement showed plainly on his face.

The woman next to him muttered something unintelligible to herself. He was conscious of a kind of bristling next to him, muted growling like that of an angry cat. He could not see anything but the red pocketbook upright on the bulging green thighs. He visualized the woman as she had stood waiting for her tokens—the ponderous figure, rising from the red shoes upward over the solid hips, the mammoth bosom, the haughty face, to the green and purple hat.

His eyes widened.

The vision of the two hats, identical, broke upon him with the radiance of a brilliant sunrise. His face was suddenly lit with joy. He could not believe that Fate had thrust upon his mother such a lesson. He gave a loud chuckle so that she would look at him and see that he saw. She turned her eyes on him slowly. The blue in them seemed to have turned a bruised purple. For a moment he had an uncomfortable sense of her innocence, but it lasted only a second before principle rescued him. Justice entitled him to laugh. His grin hardened until it said to her as plainly as if he were saying aloud: Your punishment exactly fits your pettiness. This should teach you a permanent lesson.

Her eyes shifted to the woman. She seemed unable to bear looking at him and to find the woman preferable. He became conscious again of the bristling presence at his side. The woman was rumbling like a volcano about to become active. His mother's mouth began to twitch slightly at one corner. With a sinking heart, he saw incipient signs of recovery on her face and realized that this was going to strike her suddenly as funny and was going to be no lesson at all. She kept her eyes on the woman and an amused smile came over her face as if the woman were a monkey that had stolen her hat. The little Negro was looking up at her with large fascinated eyes. He had been trying to attract her attention for some time.

"Carver," the woman said suddenly. "Come heah!"

When he saw that the spotlight was on him at last, Carver drew his feet up and turned himself toward Julian's mother and giggled.

"Carver!" the woman said. "You heah me? Come Heah!"

Carver slid down from the seat but remained squatting with his back against the base of it, his head turned slowly around toward Julian's mother, who was smiling at him. The woman reached a hand across the aisle and snatched him to her. He righted himself and hung backwards on her knees, grinning at Julian's mother. "Isn't he cute?" Julian's mother said to the woman with the protruding teeth.

"I reckon he is," the woman said without conviction.

The Negress yanked him upright but he eased out of her grip and shot across the aisle and scrambled, giggling wildly, onto the seat beside his love.

"I think he likes me," Julian's mother said, and smiled at the woman. It was the smile she used when she was being particularly gracious to an inferior. Julian saw everything lost. The lesson had rolled off her like rain on a roof.

The woman stood up and yanked the little boy off the seat as if she were snatching him from contagion. Julian could feel the rage in her at having no weapon like his mother's smile. She gave the child a sharp slap across his leg. He howled once and then thrust his head into her stomach and kicked his feet against her shins. "Behave," she said vehemently.

The bus stopped and the Negro who had been reading the newspaper got off. The woman moved over and set the little boy down with a thump between herself and Julian. She held him firmly by the knee. In a moment he put his hands in front of his face and peeped at Julian's mother through his fingers.

"I see yoooooooo!" she said and put her hand in front of her face and peeped at him.

The woman slapped his hand down. "Quit yo' foolishness," she said, "before I knock the living Jesus out of you!"

Julian was thankful that the next stop was theirs. He reached up and pulled the cord. The woman reached up and pulled it at the same time. Oh my God, he thought. He had the terrible intuition that when they got off the bus together, his mother would open her purse and give the little boy a nickel. The gesture would be as natural to her as breathing. The bus stopped and the woman got up and lunged to the front, dragging the child, who wished to stay on, after her. Julian and his mother got up and followed. As they neared the door, Julian tried to relieve her of her pocketbook.

"No," she murmured, "I want to give the little boy a nickel."

"No!" Julian hissed. "No!"

She smiled down at the child and opened her bag. The bus door opened and the woman picked him up by the arm and descended with him, hanging at her hip. Once in the street she set him down and shook him.

Julian's mother had to close her purse while she got down the bus step but as soon as her feet were on the ground, she opened it again and began to rummage inside. "I can't find but a penny," she whispered, "but it looks like a new one."

"Don't do it!" Julian said fiercely between his teeth. There was a streetlight on the corner and she hurried to get under it so that she could better see into her pocketbook. The woman was heading off rapidly down the street with the child still hanging backward on her hand.

"Oh little boy!" Julian's mother called and took a few quick steps and caught up with them just beyond the lamppost. "Here's a bright new penny for you," and she held out the coin, which shone bronze in the dim light.

The huge woman turned and for a moment stood, her shoulders lifted and her face frozen with frustrated rage, and stared at Julian's mother. Then all at once she seemed to explode like a piece of machinery that had been given one ounce of pressure too much. Julian saw the black fist swing out with the red pocketbook. He shut his eyes and cringed as he heard the woman shout, "He don't take nobody's pennies!" When he opened his eyes, the woman was disappearing down the street with the little boy staring wide-eyed over her shoulder. Julian's mother was sitting on the sidewalk.

"I told you not to do that," Julian said angrily. "I told you not to do that!"

He stood over her for a minute, gritting his teeth. Her legs were stretched out in front of her and her hat was on her lap. He squatted down and looked her in the face. It was totally expressionless. "You got exactly what you deserved," he said. "Now get up."

He picked up her pocketbook and put what had fallen out back in it. He picked the hat up off her lap. The penny caught his eye on the sidewalk and he picked that up and let it drop before her eyes into the purse. Then he stood up and leaned over and held his hands out to pull her up. She remained immobile. He sighed. Rising above them on either side were black apartment buildings, marked with irregular rectangles of light. At the end of the block a man came out of a door and walked off in the opposite direction. "All right," he said, "suppose somebody happens by and wants to know why you're sitting on the sidewalk?"

She took the hand and, breathing hard, pulled heavily up on it and then stood for a moment, swaying slightly as if the spots of light in the darkness were circling around her. Her eyes, shadowed and confused, finally settled on his face. He did not try to conceal his irritation. "I hope this teaches you a lesson," he said. She leaned forward and her eyes raked his face. She seemed trying to determine his identity. Then, as if she found nothing familiar about him, she started off with a headlong movement in the wrong direction.

"Aren't you going to the Y?" he asked.

"Home," she muttered.

"Well, are we walking?"

For answer she kept going. Julian followed along, his hands behind him. He saw no reason to let the lesson she had had go without backing it up with an explanation of its meaning. She might as well be made to understand what had happened to her. "Don't think that was just an uppity Negro woman," he said. "That was the whole colored race which will no longer take your condescending pennies. That was your black double. She can wear the same hat as you, and to be sure," he added gratuitously (because he thought it was funny), "it looked better on her than it did on you. What all this means," he said, "is that the old world is gone. The old manners are obsolete and your graciousness is not worth a damn." He thought bitterly of the house that had been lost for him. "You aren't who you think you are," he said.

She continued to plow ahead, paying no attention to him. Her hair had come undone on one side. She dropped her pocketbook and took no notice. He stopped and picked it up and handed it to her but she did not take it.

"You needn't act as if the world had come to an end," he said, "because it hasn't. From now on you've got to live in a new world and face a few realities for a change. Buck up," he said, "it won't kill you."

She was breathing fast.

"Let's wait on the bus," he said.

"Home," she said thickly.

"I hate to see you behave like this," he said. "Just like a child. I should be able to expect more of you." He decided to stop where he was and make her stop and wait for a bus. "I'm not going any farther," he said, stopping. "We're going on the bus."

She continued to go on as if she had not heard him. He took a few steps and caught her arm and stopped her. He looked into her face and caught his breath. He was looking into a face he had never seen before. "Tell Grandpa to come get me," she said.

He stared, stricken.

"Tell Caroline to come get me," she said.

Stunned, he let her go and she lurched forward again, walking as if one leg were shorter than the other. A tide of darkness seemed to be sweeping her from him. "Mother!" he cried. "Darling, sweetheart, wait!" Crumpling, she fell to the pavement. He dashed forward and fell at her side, crying, "Mamma, Mamma!" He turned her over. Her face was fiercely distorted. One eye, large and staring, moved slightly to the left as if it had become unmoored. The other remained fixed on him, raked his face again, found nothing, and closed.

"Wait here, wait here!" he cried and jumped up and began to run for help toward a cluster of lights he saw in the distance ahead of him. "Help, help!" he shouted, but his voice was thin, scarcely a thread of sound. The lights drifted farther away the faster he ran and his feet moved numbly as if they carried him nowhere. The tide of darkness seemed to sweep him back to her, postponing from moment to moment his entry into the world of guilt and sorrow. [1961]

JOHN O'HARA

John O'Hara (1905–1970) was born in Pottsville, Pennsylvania, the oldest of eight children of a prominent Irish Catholic surgeon and his wife. Rebellious as a boy, O'Hara was dismissed from three preparatory schools and became alienated from his father. In 1925 his father's death left the family's economic circumstances reduced and ended O'Hara's dream of attending Yale. He went to work as a journalist for various magazines and newspapers in New York City and discovered he had an ability to write short stories, which he began to sell to The New Yorker *in 1928. The mostly brief satiric pieces, which relied on O'Hara's talent for recording colloquial speech, were a staple in the magazine until 1949. That year, after* The New Yorker *reviewed one of his novels unfavorably, O'Hara stopped producing short stories to concentrate on his other writing.*

Appointment in Samarra *(1934), O'Hara's first novel, had a modest success, followed by* Butterfield 8 *(1935) and* Pal Joey *(1940), a collection of his stories about a nightclub entertainer. A* Rage to Live *(1949) was O'Hara's first best-seller; his next novels,* Ten North Frederick *(1955) and* From the Terrace *(1958), also sold widely. A prolific author, O'Hara wrote screenplays in Hollywood and the libretto for* Pal Joey *in Richard Rodgers and Lorenz Hart's prize-winning musical adaptation as well as other novels. In 1960 O'Hara ended his feud with* The New Yorker *and agreed to resume publishing his short fiction in the magazine. By the time of his death from a heart attack he had written 402 stories, many of which were collected in a stream of popular volumes, including* The Doctor's Son and Other Stories *(1935),* Files on Parade *(1939),* Hellbox *(1947),* Assembly *(1961),* The Cape Cod Lighter *(1962),* The Hat on the Bed *(1963),* The Horse Knows the Way *(1964),* Waiting for Winter *(1966), and* And Other Stories *(1968).*

Predominantly a realistic writer, O'Hara said that his goal was "to get it all down on paper while I can. . . . I want to record the way people talked and thought and felt, and do it with complete honesty and variety." O'Hara's short fiction ranged from early brief satiric sketches to the later longer novellas in Sermons and Soda Water *(1960), but his mainstay was what the critic Sheldon Grebstein called the "sensibility" story featured in* The New Yorker, *where the author relinquishes a traditional plot to focus on "a character's confrontation with a hitherto hidden (and usually unpleasant) truth about him/herself in relation to the world." As a social chronicler, O'Hara created an uncompromising description of homophobia in his late story "The Sharks," included in* Assembly *(1961).*

The Sharks

Mr. Plastic Rain Cover for His Hat was taking his daily constitutional. "There he goes, Mr. Plastic Rain Cover," said Betty Denning from her position at the window.

"Let him," said her husband.

"But come here and look at him," said Betty Denning.

"I've seen him."

"No, come here. You've only seen him once."

"Oh—" her husband growled, but he got up, took off his reading glasses and went to the window, still holding his newspaper.

"He's looking up here," said Betty Denning.

"Why don't you wave to him?"

"Shall I?" she said. "I wonder what he'd do."

"Well, you can easily find out."

"No, then we'd have him all the time."

"How do you know?"

"He's the type. I wonder which house he has?"

"How do you know he has a house?"

"Because he's on his way back. Yesterday and the day before, he walked toward the west, then fifteen minutes later he walked toward the east and then I didn't see him again. He's going eastward now, which means he's on the way home. That's how I know he has somebody's house. Also, there are no hotels toward the east of us and there are four toward the west."

"Well, you could ask in the village."

"I think I will."

"And then when you have that information safely tucked away? . . . All you have to do is take the field glasses and see where he leaves the beach. We could easily figure out whose house he has."

"I don't want to stand out in the rain just for that," she said. "And that wouldn't tell me his name."

"Why do you want to know his name? I thought you just wanted to know whose house he has."

"I always like to know people's names when they arouse my curiosity."

"I must say I have damn little curiosity about a man that would wear one of those things. God, they're awful. And the worst of it is, people that wear them never wear good hats."

"You're a sartorial snob," said Betty Denning.

"Indeed I am, and that's hardly news."

"But you don't get anything out of it."

"Of course I do. I get a lot out of it. For instance, a man that wears one of those things isn't likely to be in my circle of friends or any of my friends' circle of friends."

"I know," she said. "I know all that. Therefore you've put your finger on it, why I'm curious about Mr. Plastic Rain Cover."

"How? Or why?"

"Should be obvious," she said. "Who among our circle of friends has rented their house to Mr. Plastic? He's been there now at least three days. Whose house is for rent this summer?"

"Nobody's, up in that direction. All the beach houses are occupied."

"Then who is he visiting?" she said.

"I think you'd better get on the horn and ask around. You could start by calling Fred at the police station."

"Oh, I wouldn't want to do that."

"Fred would know."

"No, I'll ask around more casually when I do the marketing."

"You really don't want to have your mystery spoiled."

"Perhaps," she said.

He began to sing. " 'Perhaps—she's putting on her wraps—perhaps—she's putting on her wraps perhaps.' Now may I finish Mr. Joseph Alsop?"

"Do," she said.

The three-day nor'easter came to an end in the middle of the afternoon, and they went for a swim. "God, the beach is positively filthy," he said.

"You could pick up some driftwood," she said.

"And put it all in a neat pile, and then some kids would come along for a beach picnic and steal it all. I'm through breaking my back for the little bastards."

"It's good exercise if you remember to bend your knees. Uh-oh. We're going to have company. Mr. Plastic Cover."

"I forgot to ask you. Did you find out anything about him?"

"Tell you later."

Mr. Plastic Cover, now not wearing a hat, came toward them. He had on bathing trunks and a Madras jacket. He was walking eastward, and now there could be no doubt that he would stop. "Good afternoon," he said.

"Good afternoon," they said.

"I was admiring your house earlier. That's your house, isn't it?"

"Yes it is," said Betty Denning.

"I was wondering, is it on the market?"

"No, not really," said Betty Denning.

"Not at *all*," said Denning. "We rented it last summer, but to friends."

"But you don't want to sell. Well, I don't blame you. Nice to see the sun out again."

"Very nice," said Denning.

"Well—pleasure talking to you," said Mr. Plastic Cover.

He moved on and when he was out of earshot Denning said, "What'd you find out?"

"He has the Warings' house for the rest of the season, but he's not renting it."

"Who is he?"

"He's supposed to be some relation of Mona Waring's. He seems to have plenty of money. He's from out west and he brought a car with a chauffeur and two of his own servants besides, a cook and a maid."

"You wouldn't think to look at him that he had that kind of money. Aren't the Warings coming down?"

"They were, but now they're going abroad instead. A sudden change of plans."

"A sudden deal with Mr. Hat Cover."

"We don't have to call him Mr. Hat Cover any more. His name is Joshua B. Simmons."

"Well, Joshua's going to be in the hospital with second degree burns if he doesn't stay out of the sun. Did you notice his legs, and his nose and forehead? Wow!"

"I don't think that was the sun. I think that's just Mr. Joshua B. Simmons. He put in a big order for liquor. I found that out. And he buys only the most expensive cuts at the meat market. He gets all the New York and Chicago papers and the air mail edition of the London *Times*. He's having five people down this weekend. And he rented one of the large boxes at the post office, the kind that they usually rent to stores."

"You did quite a job on him. Is he married?"

"I had no trouble at all. The natives were more than willing to talk about him. Naturally they all speak well of him. He's spending money. This is his first summer on Long Island. I haven't answered your question about his marital status because I didn't do so well there. Nobody seems to know. The cook does the marketing by telephone. I guess Mona gave her the names of all the clerks."

"Why would he be interested in buying our house?"

"I think that was just to make conversation."

"More than likely. Well, he's exhausted that topic, and now maybe he won't bother us any more."

"Oh, don't be too hopeful. Tomorrow I'm going to the library and look him up in *Who's Who*. I've become fascinated by him."

Betty Denning was not the only one who was fascinated by Joshua B. Simmons. It soon transpired that he was asking owners of all the most desirable summer houses if their places were for sale, invariably getting no for an answer, and always commenting that he did not blame them. "I don't think he wants to buy," said Betty Denning. "I think it's just a conversational gambit he thought up."

The Warings apparently had made some arrangement for Mr. Simmons to be, in Betty Denning's word, whisked into the golf club and the beach club. It had not been difficult; as soon as his name came up some of the governors recognized it; he was on the board of one of the big Chicago banks and of other imposing corporations. "He was graduated from the University of Chicago," Betty Denning told her husband. "I've never known anyone that graduated from the University of Chicago, have you?"

"Walter Eckersall. Eckie. Great football player before my time, but then he used to officiate. He let me stay in a game once when he could have put me out. There was a Princeton guard named Marlow that was holding me on every play, and I finally smacked him one. Eckie saw me do it and he said to me, 'All right, he had it coming to him, but don't do that again.' And I didn't."

"Was that Tubby Marlow?"

"Yes."

"You didn't hit him hard enough. Anyway, Mr. Joshua B. Simmons is sixty-four years old and not married. Do you want to know what he belongs to?"

"Sure."

"Well, a whole list of clubs in Chicago, and Phi Beta Kappa, and something called Sigma Nu. Unfortunately the *Who's Who* in the village library isn't very up-to-date. In fact, 1940. Nothing about the war, and of course he could have got married since 1940, but I doubt it."

"So do I."

"Do you think the same thing I do?"

"Yes. I think he's a fag."

"You mean his walk?" said Betty Denning.

"Everything about him, not only his walk. I think he's an old queen."

"Well, you're right. I told you he was having five guests last weekend. He did. All men."

"Well, I hope that's not any criterion. I've had five men here during the duck-shooting."

"Huh. That's not what I worry about when you have five men here. Quite the opposite."

"I've never had any women here when you weren't here, and so stop your innuendoes. What about Mr. Simmons and his house party?"

"I'll get to it. Three of the men were young, two of them were about the same age as Simmons."

"Well, that's handy. They could square-dance."

"They would have been better off if they had. Saturday night they all got very tight and went for a moonlight dip without any clothes on. Old Mrs. Howard was kept awake all night and she reported them to Fred. You can imagine her, looking out and seeing six naked men and looking around for six naked women. Fred and one of the other policemen went up to investigate, but by that time they'd all got in cars and gone some place else. But Mr. Simmons has been given his first warning."

"Fred tell you all this?"

"He didn't tell me but he told Jim Carter and Peg relayed it to me. Jim is boiling mad at the Warings, especially Mona."

"Maybe she didn't know about her uncle, or whatever he is."

"Uncle is right. Her mother's brother. No, I can't go along with that. Mona's never liked it here much, and I think she and Billy just took off for Europe and let Uncle Joshua run riot. You can't tell me *Billy* doesn't know about Uncle Joshua."

"No, I guess not. But Billy will overlook anything if he can make a buck out of it, and I imagine Uncle Joshua sends a few bucks his way. He's probably Simmons's New York broker, and if there's thirty-five cents in it, Billy wouldn't care what the old guy did."

"He's having another houseful this weekend, Mr. Simmons."

"I wonder why we haven't seen him on the beach?" said Denning.

"Oh, I've seen him, when you were taking your nap. He prances by, always looks up, but he doesn't see me. Maybe he has his eye on you, dear."

"Maybe. I've always been popular with both sexes. Next time he walks by, wave to him."

"I will not. I don't find the situation very funny. I love this old place, and when an old pansy and his pansy friends start coming here, things aren't the same."

"Things aren't the same anyway, old girl, as you well know. No, it isn't a funny situation. I'm glad our boys are grown up and married."

"Well, Jim and Peg wish theirs were. The thing is that this nasty old man has been inquiring about properties, and the first thing you know we'll have a colony of them. That'll be the end of this place."

"You thought Simmons was just making conversation."

"I was wrong. He made a firm offer to the Ludlows. Forty-five thousand, and they may take him up."

"They wouldn't! Well, maybe they would. They're not getting any younger and their children don't come here any more. Good God, that would bring Simmons that much closer to our house."

"Why don't you and Jim Carter buy the Ludlows', as an investment?"

"I'm afraid that isn't the solution. We might be able to beat him to it on the Ludlow property, but Jim and I can't go on buying every property Simmons bids on."

"What is the solution?"

"There is none. With the best of good will in the world, people like the Ludlows can't afford to let sentiment, nostalgia, interfere."

"You mean that pansy's going to win? He's going to take over and ruin this lovely old place, where we've had such good times? I can't bear it."

"I've often said to you, the Lord doesn't care much about money. Look who He allows to have it."

"That's no comfort, I must say."

"I didn't offer it as comfort, Betty. We're not young ourselves, so let's try to enjoy this summer and next. After that? Well. . . ."

"You wouldn't *sell?*"

"I wouldn't *not* sell if the Simmons types get a toehold."

"Oh, no! Can't we *do* something?"

"Suggest something."

"Let's just kill Mr. Simmons."

"In some ways, the only sensible solution." He squeezed her hand. "You wouldn't even kill a shark."

"What good does it do? Kill the shark, and it only attracts a lot of other sharks."

"Well, we've had a lot of good years here. Between us close to eighty."

"The sixty together were the best. I mean thirty."

On the next Sunday night Mr. Joshua B. Simmons, of Chicago, was murdered. He was stabbed in the chest and neck repeatedly by a young man named Charles W. Randolph. It was all on the radio and in the papers, in time, in fact, for the Monday morning papers.

"Do you know who that is?" said Betty Denning. "That's the boy they call Dipstick Charley, he's always so polite when we get gas. Do you know which one I mean?"

"Sure." Denning was reading the newspaper account of the murder, which differed very little from accounts of similar murders in similar circumstances. The millionaire Chicagoan had taken friends to the station to put them on the Sunday evening train to New York. He had then, according to police, gone to a "cocktail lounge" and there encountered Randolph, whom he invited to his fashionable beach residence for a drink. He made overtures to Randolph, who claimed to have repulsed him, and a scuffle occurred, during which Randolph stabbed him, using a dagger-like letter opener. Randolph then fled in the murdered man's Cadillac sedan and was arrested by state police who suspected him of driving a stolen car. Randolph was brought back to the Simmons beach house, reenacted the crime, and signed a full confession. He was being held without bail in the county prison. There were photographs of Randolph in his army uniform and of Simmons in a business suit, of the dagger-like letter opener and of the beach house and Simmons's Cadillac, and of Randolph in custody between Fred and a state policeman.

Even the tabloids could not keep the story built up for more than the fourth day. "Poor old Mrs. Howard's had a heart attack," said Betty Denning. "She's over at the clinic. Reporters and photographers and you have no idea how many morbid people, mistaking her house for the Warings'."

"They've started to come here."

"What on earth for?"

"The sharks. Do you remember what you said about killing a shark—it only attracts other sharks?"

"Oh, don't remind me."

"It was a very astute remark. While you were doing the marketing I had a caller. He wanted to know if this house was for sale. I said no, and he said he'd been given to understand by a certain friend of his that maybe we might sell. I asked him who the friend was, and he said, 'Well if you must know, it was Josh — Josh Simmons, poor boy.' Poor boy."

"What did you say?"

"I said, 'You get your ass out of here before I kick you out.' He said, 'Oh, you wouldn't do that, would you?' So I showed him I would."

"You kicked him?"

"Of course I kicked him. He won't be back, but others like him will be. You were certainly right about the sharks."

"Oh, dear. Oh, dear," she said.   [1961]

KURT VONNEGUT JR.

*K*urt *Vonnegut Jr. (b. 1922) was born on November 11 in Indianapolis, Indiana. The son of an architect and a homemaker, he attended Cornell University and Carnegie Mellon University before the outbreak of World War II, when he interrupted his studies to serve in the U.S. Army. As a prisoner of war in Dresden, Germany, he survived a devastating air raid on February 13, 1945, by staying in a meat locker under a slaughterhouse during the bombing. After World War II, Vonnegut worked in public relations at the General Electric Company in Schenectady, New York, before becoming a freelance writer.* Player Piano, *his first novel, appeared in 1952, followed by a second fantasy novel,* The Sirens of Titan, *in 1959. Two years later he published* Mother Night, *a first-person fictional narrative about World War II. In 1969 Vonnegut published another novel that has become a classic based on his own experience of the Allies' fire-bombing of Dresden. Vonnegut titled it* Slaughterhouse-Five; or, the Children's Crusade: A Duty-Dance with Death, by Kurt Vonnegut Jr., a Fourth-Generation German-American Now Living in Easy Circumstances on Cape Cod (and Smoking Too Much) Who, as an American Infantry Scout Hors de Combat, as a Prisoner of War, Witnessed the Fire-Bombing of Dresden, Germany, the Florence of the Elbe, Long Time Ago, and Survived to Tell the Tale; This Is a Novel Somewhat in the Telegraphic Schizophrenic Manner of Tales of the Planet Tralfamadore, Where the Flying Saucers Come From.

After Slaughterhouse-Five *was made into a film in 1972, Vonnegut's books achieved cult status. The critic Jerome Klinkowitz has observed that there was a "shift in taste" in the late 1960s and early 1970s that brought more serious appreciation to Vonnegut's fiction after a new generation of writers—Donald Barthelme, John Barth, Richard Brautigan, Jerzy Kosinski, Don DeLillo, Thomas Pynchon, and others—began publishing. "Ten years and several books their elder, Vonnegut by his long exile underground was well prepared to be the senior member of the new disruptive group."*

Before Vonnegut's breakthrough as a novelist, he published short stories, like the fantasy tale "Harrison Bergeron," which first appeared in Fantasy and Science Fiction Magazine *in 1961 and was included in* Canary in a Cathouse *(1961) and* Welcome to the Monkey House *(1968). John Updike understood that Vonnegut "began as a published writer with the so-called slick magazines"—the* Saturday Evening Post, Collier's, *and the* Ladies' Home Journal. *In the 1950s, slickness "was a verbal mechanism that raised the spectre of pain and then too easily delivered us from it. Yet the pain in Vonnegut was always real. Through the transpositions of science fiction, he found a way . . . to vaporize it, to scatter it on the plane of the cosmic and the comic."*

Harrison Bergeron

The year was 2081, and everybody was finally equal. They weren't only equal before God and the law. They were equal every which way. Nobody was smarter than anybody else. Nobody was better looking than anybody else. Nobody was stronger or quicker than anybody else. All this equality was due to the 211th, 212th, and 213th Amendments to the Constitution, and to the unceasing vigilance of agents of the United States Handicapper General.

Some things about living still weren't quite right, though. April, for instance, still drove people crazy by not being springtime. And it was in that clammy month that the H-G men took George and Hazel Bergeron's fourteen-year-old son, Harrison, away.

It was tragic, all right, but George and Hazel couldn't think about it very hard. Hazel had a perfectly average intelligence, which meant she couldn't think about anything except in short bursts. And George, while his intelligence was way above normal, had a little mental handicap radio in his ear. He was required by law to wear it at all times. It was tuned to a government transmitter. Every twenty seconds or so, the transmitter would send out some sharp noise to keep people like George from taking unfair advantage of their brains.

George and Hazel were watching television. There were tears on Hazel's cheeks, but she'd forgotten for the moment what they were about.

On the television screen were ballerinas.

A buzzer sounded in George's head. His thoughts fled in panic, like bandits from a burglar alarm.

"That was a real pretty dance, that dance they just did," said Hazel.

"Huh?" said George.

"That dance—it was nice," said Hazel.

"Yup," said George. He tried to think a little about the ballerinas. They weren't really very good—no better than anybody else would have been, anyway. They were burdened with sashweights and bags of birdshot, and their faces were masked, so that no one, seeing a free and graceful gesture or a pretty face, would feel like something the cat drug in. George was toying with the vague notion that maybe dancers shouldn't be handicapped. But he didn't get very far with it before another noise in his ear radio scattered his thoughts.

George winced. So did two out of the eight ballerinas.

Hazel saw him wince. Having no mental handicap herself, she had to ask George what the latest sound had been.

"Sounded like somebody hitting a milk bottle with a ball peen hammer," said George.

"I'd think it would be real interesting, hearing all the different sounds," said Hazel, a little envious. "All the things they think up."

"Um," said George.

"Only, if I was Handicapper General, you know what I would do?" said Hazel. Hazel, as a matter of fact, bore a strong resemblance to the Handicapper General, a woman named Diana Moon Glampers. "If I was Diana Moon Glampers," said Hazel, "I'd have chimes on Sunday—just chimes. Kind of in honor of religion."

"I could think, if it was just chimes," said George.

"Well—maybe make 'em real loud," said Hazel. "I think I'd make a good Handicapper General."

"Good as anybody else," said George.

"Who knows better'n I do what normal is?" said Hazel.

"Right," said George. He began to think glimmeringly about his abnormal son who was now in jail, about Harrison, but a twenty-one-gun salute in his head stopped that.

"Boy!" said Hazel, "that was a doozy, wasn't it?"

It was such a doozy that George was white and trembling, and tears stood on the rims of his red eyes. Two of the eight ballerinas had collapsed to the studio floor, were holding their temples.

"All of a sudden you look so tired," said Hazel. "Why don't you stretch out on the sofa, so's you can rest your handicap bag on the pillows, honey-bunch." She was referring to the forty-seven pounds of birdshot in a canvas bag, which was padlocked around George's neck. "Go on and rest the bag for a little while," she said. "I don't care if you're not equal to me for a while."

George weighed the bag with his hands. "I don't mind it," he said. "I don't notice it any more. It's just a part of me."

"You been so tired lately—kind of wore out," said Hazel. "If there was just some way we could make a little hole in the bottom of the bag, and just take out a few of them lead balls. Just a few."

"Two years in prison and two thousand dollars fine for every ball I took out," said George. "I don't call that a bargain."

"If you could just take a few out when you came home from work," said Hazel. "I mean—you don't compete with anybody around here. You just set around."

"If I tried to get away with it," said George, "then other people'd get away with it—and pretty soon we'd be right back to the dark ages again, with everybody competing against everybody else. You wouldn't like that, would you?"

"I'd hate it," said Hazel.

"There you are," said George. "The minute people start cheating on laws, what do you think happens to society?"

If Hazel hadn't been able to come up with an answer to this question, George couldn't have supplied one. A siren was going off in his head.

"Reckon it'd fall all apart," said Hazel.

"What would?" said George blankly.

"Society," said Hazel uncertainly. "Wasn't that what you just said?"

"Who knows?" said George.

The television program was suddenly interrupted for a news bulletin. It wasn't clear at first as to what the bulletin was about, since the announcer, like all announcers, had a serious speech impediment. For about half a minute, and in a state of high excitement, the announcer tried to say, "Ladies and gentlemen—"

He finally gave up, handed the bulletin to a ballerina to read.

"That's all right—" Hazel said of the announcer, "he tried. That's the big thing. He tried to do the best he could with what God gave him. He should get a nice raise for trying so hard."

"Ladies and gentlemen—" said the ballerina, reading the bulletin. She must have been extraordinarily beautiful, because the mask she wore was hideous. And it was easy to see that she was the strongest and most graceful of all the dancers, for her handicap bags were as big as those worn by two-hundred-pound men.

And she had to apologize at once for her voice, which was a very unfair voice for a woman to use. Her voice was a warm, luminous, timeless melody. "Excuse me—" she said, and she began again, making her voice absolutely uncompetitive.

"Harrison Bergeron, age fourteen," she said in a grackle squawk, "has just escaped from jail, where he was held on suspicion of plotting to overthrow the government. He is a genius and an athlete, is under-handicapped, and should be regarded as extremely dangerous."

A police photograph of Harrison Bergeron was flashed on the screen—upside down, then sideways, upside down again, then right side up. The picture showed the full length of Harrison against a background calibrated in feet and inches. He was exactly seven feet tall.

The rest of Harrison's appearance was Halloween and hardware. Nobody had ever borne heavier handicaps. He had outgrown hindrances faster than the H-G men could think them up. Instead of a little ear radio for a mental handicap, he wore a tremendous pair of earphones, and spectacles with thick wavy lenses. The spectacles were intended to make him not only half blind, but to give him whanging headaches besides.

Scrap metal was hung all over him. Ordinarily, there was a certain symmetry, a military neatness to the handicaps issued to strong people, but Harrison looked like a walking junkyard. In the race of life, Harrison carried three hundred pounds.

And to offset his good looks, the H-G men required that he wear at all times a red rubber ball for a nose, keep his eyebrows shaved off, and cover his even white teeth with black caps at snaggle-tooth random.

"If you see this boy," said the ballerina, "do not—I repeat, do not—try to reason with him."

There was the shriek of a door being torn from its hinges.

Screams and barking cries of consternation came from the television set. The photograph of Harrison Bergeron on the screen jumped again and again, as though dancing to the tune of an earthquake.

George Bergeron correctly identified the earthquake, and well he might have—for many was the time his own home had danced to the same crashing tune. "My God—" said George, "that must be Harrison!"

The realization was blasted from his mind instantly by the sound of an automobile collision in his head.

When George could open his eyes again, the photograph of Harrison was gone. A living, breathing Harrison filled the screen.

Clanking, clownish, and huge, Harrison stood in the center of the studio. The knob of the uprooted studio door was still in his hand. Ballerinas, technicians, musicians, and announcers cowered on their knees before him, expecting to die.

"I am the Emperor!" cried Harrison. "Do you hear? I am the Emperor! Everybody must do what I say at once!" He stamped his foot and the studio shook.

"Even as I stand here—" he bellowed, "crippled, hobbled, sickened—I am a greater ruler than any man who ever lived! Now watch me become what I *can* become!"

Harrison tore the straps of his handicap harness like wet tissue paper, tore straps guaranteed to support five thousand pounds.

Harrison's scrap-iron handicaps crashed to the floor.

Harrison thrust his thumbs under the bar of the padlock that secured his head harness. The bar snapped like celery. Harrison smashed his headphones and spectacles against the wall.

He flung away his rubber-ball nose, revealed a man that would have awed Thor, the god of thunder.

"I shall now select my Empress!" he said, looking down on the cowering people. "Let the first woman who dares rise to her feet claim her mate and her throne!"

A moment passed, and then a ballerina arose, swaying like a willow.

Harrison plucked the mental handicap from her ear, snapped off her physical handicaps with marvelous delicacy. Last of all, he removed her mask.

She was blindingly beautiful.

"Now—" said Harrison, taking her hand, "shall we show the people the meaning of the word dance? Music!" he commanded.

The musicians scrambled back into their chairs, and Harrison stripped them of their handicaps, too. "Play your best," he told them, "and I'll make you barons and dukes and earls."

The music began. It was normal at first—cheap, silly, false. But Harrison snatched two musicians from their chairs, waved them like batons as he sang the music as he wanted it played. He slammed them back into their chairs.

The music began again and was much improved.

Harrison and his Empress merely listened to the music for a while—listened gravely, as though synchronizing their heartbeats with it.

They shifted their weights to their toes.

Harrison placed his big hands on the girl's tiny waist, letting her sense the weightlessness that would soon be hers.

And then, in an explosion of joy and grace, into the air they sprang!

Not only were the laws of the land abandoned, but the law of gravity and the laws of motion as well.

They reeled, whirled, swiveled, flounced, capered, gamboled, and spun.

They leaped like deer on the moon.

The studio ceiling was thirty feet high, but each leap brought the dancers nearer to it.

It became their obvious intention to kiss the ceiling.

They kissed it.

And then, neutralizing gravity with love and pure will, they remained suspended in air inches below the ceiling, and they kissed each other for a long, long time.

It was then that Diana Moon Glampers, the Handicapper General, came into the studio with a double-barreled ten-gauge shotgun. She fired twice, and the Emperor and the Empress were dead before they hit the floor.

Diana Moon Glampers loaded the gun again. She aimed it at the musicians and told them they had ten seconds to get their handicaps back on.

It was then that the Bergerons' television tube burned out.

Hazel turned to comment about the blackout to George. But George had gone out into the kitchen for a can of beer.

George came back in with the beer, paused while a handicap signal shook him up. And then he sat down again. "You been crying?" he said to Hazel.

"Yup," she said.

"What about?" he said.

"I forget," she said. "Something real sad on television."

"What was it?" he said.

"It's all kind of mixed up in my mind," said Hazel.

"Forget sad things," said George.

"I always do," said Hazel.

"That's my girl," said George. He winced. There was the sound of a riveting gun in his head.

"Gee — I could tell that one was a doozy," said Hazel.

"You can say that again," said George.

"Gee —" said Hazel, "I could tell that one was a doozy."   [1961]

EUDORA WELTY

Eudora Welty (b. 1909) was born in Jackson, Mississippi, where she has spent nearly her whole life. She has a predominantly tranquil view of the South, so her stories and novels provide a strong contrast to the turbulent fiction of William Faulkner and Richard Wright, who also wrote about Mississippi. Welty grew up as one of three children in a close-knit family living two blocks from the state capitol. Her father was the president of an insurance company, and her mother was a thrifty housewife who kept a Jersey cow in a little pasture behind the backyard. An insatiable reader as a child, Welty began writing spontaneously and continued, without any particular encouragement or any plan to be a writer, during her years in college. In her midtwenties she started to publish stories in the Southern Review, *but she credits the persistence of her New York literary agent with helping her get a story published in* The Atlantic Monthly *in 1941. This event led directly to the publication of her first book of stories,* A Curtain of Green, *the same year.*

During World War II Welty was a staff member of the New York Times Book Review *while she lived at home with her mother and continued to write short fiction. Another collection was published in 1943 as* The Wide Net and Other Stories. *After leaving her newspaper work, she turned a short story into her first novel,* Delta Wedding *(1946), on the advice of her agent. She has produced several other story collections over the years. Her novel* The Optimist's Daughter *won the Pulitzer Prize in 1972. In 1980* The Collected Stories of Eudora Welty *appeared, forty-one stories in all. Welty is also a fine critic of the short story. Her essays and reviews of the work of writers such as Anton Chekhov, Willa Cather, Katherine Anne Porter, and Virginia Woolf, as well as some comments on her own work, were collected in* The Eye of the Story *(1977). Eight years later the book* Conversations with Eudora Welty *was a best-seller.*

In the preface to her collected stories, Welty states,

> *I have been told, both in approval and in accusation, that I seem to love all my characters. What I do in writing of any character is to try to enter into the mind, heart, and skin of a human being who is not myself. Whether this happens to be a man or a woman, old or young, with skin black or white, the primary challenge lies in making the jump itself. It is the act of a writer's imagination that I set most high.*

In "Where Is the Voice Coming From?" (The New Yorker, 1963), Welty imagines herself in the consciousness of a white supremacist, Byron De La Beckwith, who shot the black activist Medgar Evers outside his home in Jackson, Mississippi, on the night of June 11, 1963. More recently, the e-mail software used by millions of people was named Eudora after Welty and her story "Why I Live at the P.O." According to inventor Steve Dorner, he felt as if he "lived at the post office" while developing e-mail, so he transposed the short story title into his slogan, "Bringing the P.O. to Where You Live." Later Dorner publicly apologized for being "presumptuous" enough to name his program Eudora, after a living person, but Welty's literary agent said the writer had been "pleased and amused" to hear of the tribute.

RELATED COMMENTARY: *Eudora Welty, "The Sense of Place in Faulkner's 'Spotted Horses,'" page 1471.*

Where Is the Voice Coming From?

I says to my wife, "You can reach and turn it off. You don't have to set and look at a black nigger face no longer than you want to, or listen to what you don't want to hear. It's still a free country."

I reckon that's how I give myself the idea.

I says, I could find right exactly where in Thermopylae that nigger's living that's asking for equal time. And without a bit of trouble to me.

And I ain't saying it might not be because that's pretty close to where *I* live. The other hand, there could be reasons you might have yourself for knowing how to get there in the dark. It's where you all go for the thing you want when you want it the most. Ain't that right?

The Branch Bank sign tells you in lights, all night long even, what time it is and how hot. When it was quarter to four, and 92, that was me going by in my brother-in-law's truck. He don't deliver nothing at that hour of the morning.

So you leave Four Corners and head west on Nathan B. Forrest Road, past the Surplus & Salvage, not much beyond the Kum Back Drive-In and Trailer Camp, not as far as where the signs starts saying "Live Bait," "Used Parts," "Fireworks," "Peaches," and "Sister Peebles Reader and Adviser." Turn before you hit the city limits and duck back towards the I.C. tracks. And his street's been paved.

And there was his light on, waiting for me. In his garage, if you please. His car's gone. He's out planning still some other ways to do what we tell 'em they can't. I *thought* I'd beat him home. All I had to do was pick my tree and walk in close behind it.

I didn't come expecting not to wait. But it was so hot, all I did was hope and pray one or the other of us wouldn't melt before it was over.

Now, it wasn't no bargain I'd struck.

I've heard what you've heard about Goat Dykeman, in Mississippi. Sure, everybody knows about Goat Dykeman. Goat he got word to the Governor's Mansion he'd go up yonder and shoot that nigger Meredith clean out of school, if he's let out of the pen to do it. Old Ross turned *that* over in his mind before saying him nay, it stands to reason.

I ain't no Goat Dykeman, I ain't in no pen, and I ain't ask no Governor Barnett to give me one thing. Unless he wants to give me a pat on the back for the trouble I took this morning. But he don't have to if he don't want to. I done what I done for my own pure-D satisfaction.

As soon as I heard wheels, I knowed who was coming. That was him and bound to be him. It was the right nigger heading in a new white car up his driveway towards his garage with the light shining, but stopping before he got there, maybe not to wake 'em. That was him. I knowed it when he cut off the car lights and put his foot out and I knowed him standing dark against the light. I knowed him then like I know me now. I knowed him even by his still, listening back.

Never seen him before, never seen him since, never seen anything of his black face but his picture, never seen his face alive, any time at all, or anywhere, and didn't want to, need to, never hope to see that face and never will. As long as there was no question in my mind.

He had to be the one. He stood right still and waited against the light, his back was fixed, fixed on me like a preacher's eyeballs when he's yelling "Are you saved?" He's the one.

I'd already brought up my rifle, I'd already taken my sights. And I'd already got him, because it was too late then for him or me to turn by one hair.

Something darker than him, like the wings of a bird, spread on his back and pulled him down. He climbed up once, like a man under bad claws, and like just blood could weigh a ton he walked with it on his back to better light. Didn't get no further than his door. And fell to stay.

He was down. He was down, and a ton load of bricks on his back wouldn't have laid any heavier. There on his paved driveway, yes sir.

And it wasn't till the minute before, that the mockingbird had quit singing. He'd been singing up my sassafras tree. Either he was up early, or he hadn't never gone to bed, he was like me. And the mocker he'd stayed right with me, filling the air till come the crack, till I turned loose of my load. I was like him. I was on top of the world myself. For once.

I stepped to the edge of his light there, where he's laying flat. I says, "Roland? There was one way left, for me to be ahead of you and stay ahead of you, by Dad, and I just taken it. Now I'm alive and you ain't. We ain't never now, never going to be equals and you know why? One of us is dead. What about that, Roland?" I said. "Well, you seen to it, didn't you?"

I stood a minute—just to see would somebody inside come out long enough to pick him up. And there she comes, the woman. I doubt she'd been to sleep. Because it seemed to me she'd been in there keeping awake all along.

It was mighty green where I skint over the yard getting back. That nigger wife of his, she wanted nice grass! I bet my wife would hate to pay her water bill. And for burning her electricity. And there's my brother-in-law's truck, still waiting with the door open. "No Riders"—that didn't mean me.

There wasn't a thing I been able to think of since would have made it to go any nicer. Except a chair to my back while I was putting in my waiting. But going home, I seen what little time it takes after all to get a thing done like you really want it. It was 4:34, and while I was looking it moved to 35. And the temperature stuck where it was. All that night I guarantee you it had stood without dropping, a good 92.

My wife says, "What? Didn't the skeeters bite you?" She said, "Well, they been asking that—why somebody didn't trouble to load a rifle and get some of these agitators out of Thermopylae. Didn't the fella keep drumming it in, what a good idea? The one that writes a column ever' day?"

I says to my wife, "Find *some* way I don't get the credit."

"He says do it for Thermopylae," she says. "Don't you ever skim the paper?"

I says, "Thermopylae never done nothing for me. And I don't owe nothing to Thermopylae. Didn't do it for you. Hell, any more'n I'd do something or other for them Kennedys! I done it for my own pure-D satisfaction."

"It's going to get him right back on TV," says my wife. "You watch for the funeral."

I says, "You didn't even leave a light burning when you went to bed. So how was I supposed to even get me home or pull Buddy's truck up safe in our front yard?"

"Well, hear another good joke on you," my wife says next. "Didn't you hear the news? The N. double A.C.P. is fixing to send somebody to Thermopylae. Why couldn't you waited? You might could have got you somebody better. Listen and hear 'em say so."

I ain't but one. I reckon you have to tell *somebody*.

"Where's the gun, then?" my wife says. "What did you do with our protection?"

I says, "It was scorching! It was scorching!" I told her, "It's laying out on the ground in rank weeds, trying to cool off, that's what it's doing now."

"You dropped it," she says. "Back there."

And I told her, "Because I'm so tired of ever'thing in the world being just that hot to the touch! The keys to the truck, the doorknob, the bedsheet, ever'thing, it's all like a stove lid. There just ain't much going that's worth holding on to it no more," I says, "when it's a hundred and two in the shade by day and by night not too much difference. I wish *you'd* laid *your* finger to that gun."

"Trust you to come off and leave it," my wife says.

"Is that how no-'count I am?" she makes me ask. "*You* want to go back and get it?"

"You're the one they'll catch. I say it's so hot that even if you get to sleep you wake up feeling like you cried all night!" says my wife. "Cheer up, here's one more joke before time to get up. Heard what *Caroline* said? Caroline said, 'Daddy, I just can't wait to grow up big, so I can marry *James Meredith*.' I heard that where I work. One rich-bitch to another one, to make her cackle."

"At least I kept some dern teen-ager from North Thermopylae getting there and doing it first," I says. "Driving his own car."

On TV and in the paper, they don't know but half of it. They know who Roland Summers was without knowing who I am. His face was in front of the public before I got rid of him, and after I got rid of him there it is again—the same picture. And none of me. I ain't ever had one made. Not ever! The best that newspaper could do for me was offer a five-hundred-dollar reward for finding out who I am. For as long as they don't know who that is, whoever shot Roland is worth a good deal more right now than Roland is.

But by the time I was moving around uptown, it was hotter still. That pavement in the middle of Main Street was so hot to my feet I might've been walking the barrel of my gun. If the whole world could've just felt Main Street this morning through the soles of my shoes, maybe it would've helped some.

Then the first thing I heard 'em say was the N. double A. C. P. done it themselves, killed Roland Summers, and proved it by saying the shooting was done by a expert (I hope to tell you it was!) and at just the right hour and minute to get the whites in trouble.

You can't win.

"They'll never find him," the old man trying to sell roasted peanuts tells me to my face.

And it's so hot.

It looks like the town's on fire already, whichever ways you turn, ever' street you strike, because there's those trees hanging them pones of bloom like split watermelon. And a thousand cops crowding ever'where you go, half of 'em too young to start shaving, but all streaming sweat alike. I'm getting tired of 'em.

I was already tired of seeing a hundred cops getting us white people nowheres. Back at the beginning, I stood on the corner and I watched them new babyface cops loading nothing but nigger children into the paddy wagon and they come marching out of a little parade and into the paddy wagon singing. And they got in and sat down without providing a speck of trouble, and their hands held little new American flags, and all the cops could do was knock them flagsticks a-loose from their hands, and not let 'em pick 'em up, that was all, and give 'em a free ride. And children can just get 'em more flags.

Everybody: It don't get you nowhere to take nothing from nobody unless you make sure it's for keeps, for good and all, for ever and amen.

I won't be sorry to see them brickbats hail down on us for a change. Pop bottles too, they can come flying whenever they want to. Hundreds, all to smash, like Birmingham. I'm waiting on 'em to bring out them switchblade knives, like Harlem and Chicago. Watch TV long enough and you'll see it all to happen on Deacon Street in Thermopylae. What's holding it back, that's all?—Because it's *in* 'em.

I'm ready myself for that funeral.

Oh, they may find me. May catch me one day in spite of 'emselves. (But I grew up in the country.) May try to railroad me into the electric chair, and what that amounts to is something hotter than yesterday and today put together.

But I advise 'em to go careful. Ain't it about time us taxpayers starts to calling the moves? Starts to telling the teachers *and* the preachers *and* the judges of our so-called courts how far they can go?

Even the President so far, he can't walk in my house without being invited, like he's my daddy, just to say whoa. Not yet!

Once, I run away from my home. And there was a ad for me, come to be printed in our county weekly. My mother paid for it. It was from her. It says: "SON: You are not being hunted for anything but to find you." That time, I come on back home.

But people are dead now.

And it's so hot. Without it even being August yet.

Anyways, I seen him fall. I was evermore the one.

So I reach me down my old guitar off the nail in the wall. 'Cause I've got my guitar, what I've held on to from way back when, and I never dropped that, never lost or forgot it, never hocked it but to get it again, never give it away, and I set in my chair, with nobody home but me, and I start to play, and sing a-Down. And sing a-down, down, down, down. Sing a-down, down, down, down. Down.   [1963]

5

LATE
TWENTIETH
CENTURY

1966–Present

*I*n 1992, Joyce Carol Oates introduced *The Oxford Book of American Short Stories* by describing the genre and its writers and readers. From her viewpoint,

> most short stories (but hardly all) are restricted in time and place; concentrate upon a very small number of characters; and move toward a single ascending dramatic scene or revelation. And all are generated by conflict.
>
> The artist is the focal point of conflict. Lovers of pristine harmony, those who dislike being upset, shocked, made to think and to feel, are not naturally suited to appreciate art, at least not serious art; which, unlike television dramas and situation comedies, for instance, does not evoke conflict merely to solve it within a brief space of time. Rather, conflict is the implicit subject, itself; as conflict, the establishment of disequilibrium, is the impetus for the evolution of life, so is conflict the genesis, the prime mover, the secret heart of all art.
>
> Discord, then, and not harmony, is the subject our writers share in common. Though the quelling of discord and the reestablishment of harmony may well be the point of the art.

Oates was speaking as a writer of her time when she insisted on the presence of "discord, . . . and not harmony," at the center of American short fiction and emphasized the importance of both the writer's and the reader's tolerance of conflict and disequilibrium. The nation's political, social, and cultural turbulence in the second half of the twentieth century had left a legacy of suspicion and unrest. The nuclear threat during the cold war; the United States' attempt to invade Cuba in the Bay of Pigs fiasco; the assassinations of John F. Kennedy, Robert Kennedy, Martin Luther King Jr., and Malcolm X; the widespread resistance to the war in Vietnam; the race riots in major cities and the battles for civil rights; the hippie counterculture; the rise of poetry readings, pop art, street theater, and a celebration of the avant-garde in all the arts; the second wave of feminism; the controversy surrounding the Supreme Court's decision to legalize abortion; the diminishing resources to fund public education and the soaring costs to maintain American prisons; the environmental movement; the canon wars in college English departments; the rise of multiculturalism — these major events and controversies, among many others, contributed to the mandate to "Question Authority" that became a rallying cry in the United States during the late twentieth century. Whether printed in bold letters as a slogan on an automobile bumper sticker, or published in the latest university press book on race/gender/multicultural studies, or dramatized in a short story, this attitude shaped the writing of many important contemporary literary critics and authors of short fiction. Although the conflicts appeared in new guises in many stories, they actually continued to present the major themes that were rooted in American short fiction from its beginning.

As Frank O'Connor realized in *The Lonely Voice,* "America is largely populated by submerged population groups" that make up an increasingly multicultural society in which nearly everyone could claim to be a member of a beleaguered minority group. Our ancestors were strangers in a strange land, and the themes of American short stories have always reflected different cultural traditions and rapidly changing social conditions. As in the past, conflicts involving race and gender predominate. And as social problems arise, one of the ways in which American authors continue to address the complex questions about life and our place in it is by creating works of short fiction.

In the late 1960s and early 1970s, when faced with radical divisions in a society that appeared to be fractured beyond repair during the Vietnam War, many American authors of short stories began using this literary form to explore the effects of fragmentation and disruption instead of relying on conventional realistic narration. To complicate matters further, the emergence of new and sophisticated critical tools early in this historical period also began to affect the way many authors wrote short fiction, especially if they were employed as faculty in university English departments.

Developed in the classroom by Robert Penn Warren and Cleanth Brooks in the 1940s and 1950s, the "New Critical" method of closely reading a literary text had favored poetry and short fiction. In the last decades of the century, this critical approach was supplanted by what was generally called "theory," which entailed linguistically and philosophically more sophisticated feminist, structuralist, poststructuralist, and new historicist approaches, among others. According to many literary critics, we had entered a postmodernist age.

Despite disagreement among critics about the meaning of *postmodernism,* the first use of the term is generally acknowledged to have described a new sensibility in post–World War II literature both in Randall Jarrell's review of the poet Robert Lowell's *Lord Weary's Castle* (1946) and in the poet Charles Olson's essays published in the early 1950s. By the 1970s, the word had also been widely accepted as a sociological term describing a new phase in Western society marked by an expanding use of electronic reproduction and the mass marketing of products in a global economy.

The term *postmodernism* can appear as ubiquitously as the term *realism* to describe short stories, but literary critics such as Marcel Cornis-Pope in *The Reader's Encyclopedia of American Literature* (1991) have suggested a more exact definition of this literary approach: "Reacting against the traditional master narratives that projected an orderly and coherent universe, the postmodern writers have chosen narrative openness over closure, fiction over truth, and fragmentation over unity and coherence." At times postmodern writers offer a critique of traditional narrative practices by using the self-reflexive technique of "metafiction"—creating stories about language and the process of writing itself. At other times, as John Barth understood in "A Few Words about Minimalism," short story writers experimented with the effects of the minimalist style, using

> a stripped-down vocabulary; a stripped-down syntax that avoids periodic sentences, serial predications, and complex subordinating constructions like these; a stripped-down rhetoric that may eschew figurative language altogether; a stripped-down non-emotive tone. And there are minimalisms of material: minimal characters, minimal exposition ("all that David Copperfield kind of crap," says J. D. Salinger's catcher in the rye), minimal mise-en-scènes, minimal action, minimal plot.

Challenging the traditional modes of representational narrative cohesion through various disruptive techniques of both metafiction and minimalism, Barth published stories like "Title" in his collection of experimental pieces *Lost in the Funhouse* (1968). His contemporary Donald Barthelme often presented satiric parodies of extreme solutions to complex social problems such as inner-city crime by using oversimplification and exaggeration in humorous postmodernist works, as in "The Police Band," which appeared in a 1968 issue of *The New Yorker.*

William Gass, Joyce Carol Oates, Richard Brautigan, Grace Paley, Amy Hempel, Ursula K. Le Guin, and Tim O'Brien, among many other authors, have also written in the experimental mode so successfully that their work suggests alternate approaches to narrative. Gass gradually dissolves the protagonist of his story while sketching a surrealistic map of the flat immensity of the American Midwest in the pages of "In the Heart of the Heart of the Country" (1967). Oates imagines the splintered consciousness of a high school girl from an affluent family who went astray in "How I Contemplated the World from the Detroit House of Correction and Began My Life Over Again" (1969).

Humor is foremost in Brautigan's modest sketch that captures the hippie sense of haphazardly perching on the outskirts of mainstream society, while also being inextricably bound to it, in "⅓, ⅓, ⅓" (1971). Paley's condensed story-within-a-story sympathetically contrasts the conventional values of her immigrant father with the idealistic lifestyle of her Greenwich Village bohemian neighbors in "A Conversation with My Father" (1971). Hempel also uses a minimalist technique to hint at the indescribable confusion and fear of a young woman watching a friend die of cancer in her story "In the Cemetery Where Al Jolson Is Buried" (1985). Le Guin creates a supple prose poem in "Texts" (1991), her tribute to verbal and nonverbal communication; Tim O'Brien uses the technique of the list with stunning effect in his Vietnam War story "The Things They Carried" (1986).

The social, political, and cultural ferment in the United States during the 1970s encouraged the development of feminist literary criticism, which led scholars to the rediscovery of many women writers whose work had been slighted by previous generations of male critics and anthologists. Among these newly appreciated American authors, the academic spotlight illuminated earlier short story writers such as Kate Chopin, Charlotte Perkins Gilman, Zora Neale Hurston, and Tillie Olsen. In the last twenty years, feminist scholars have produced editions of the stories of many nineteenth-century women authors whose work had been out of print for decades, thereby making available a treasure-house of "new" short fiction.

Contemporary women writers have continued to reflect the changes in American women's lives as strong role models such as Betty Friedan, Barbara Jordan, Ruth Bader Ginsburg, and Gloria Steinem became prominent after what has been called the second wave of feminism. Friedan's *The Feminine Mystique* (1963) was the most influential book in radicalizing American women readers; it led to the formation of the National Organization for Women (NOW), which Friedan founded. In 1972 Steinem started the magazine *Ms.*, which issued statements such as "If men could menstruate, abortion would be a sacrament." That year Jordan became the first black woman from the South to be elected to the House of Representatives. Ginsburg was appointed to the Supreme Court in 1993 after President Bill Clinton described her as "the Thurgood Marshall of the women's rights movement," in reference to the civil rights lawyer who became the first black Supreme Court justice, serving from 1967 to 1991.

Early in this period, the prolific author John Updike wrote a traditional story about the breakup of a marriage in "Separating" (1975). By the end of the century, however, the changes in families and in relationships between the sexes resulting in part from the feminist movement had become increasingly evident in stories by many writers. Ann Beattie describes a woman's friendship with two gay lovers, one dying of AIDS, in "Second Question" (1991). Mary Gaitskill explores the destructive bond between a father and his lesbian daughter in "Tiny, Smiling Daddy" (1993). Lorrie Moore perceives the humor in her protagonist's close emotional bond with her cat, whom the woman had known longer than her husband and daughter, in "Four Calling Birds, Three French Hens" (1993).

Issues of race have also continued to be explored in short fiction. Alice Walker dramatizes the importance of tradition and caretaking in black families in "Everyday Use" (1973). John Edgar Wideman creates stories like "newborn thrown in trash and dies" (1992) that challenge the very concept of race; he believes that it is not a viable term outside "the concept of racism, which was invented to separate, oppress, and exploit human beings." As more writers began to explore their multicultural backgrounds, short stories about the African American experience have taken their place beside stories about Native Americans, Hispanic Americans, Asian Americans, and others.

Leslie Marmon Silko revitalizes a traditional Native American legend in "Yellow Woman" (1974), and Sherman Alexie ironically describes contemporary life from a Native American perspective in "The Only Traffic Signal on the Reservation Doesn't Flash Red Anymore" (1993). Helena María Viramontes presents a devastating picture of a Mexican American mother and daughter's response to the American Dream in "Miss Clairol" (1988), showing how the poisonous hyperbole of advertising permeates our culture. Bharati Mukherjee dramatizes the perils of academic life for a woman faculty member from India who has recently arrived at a midwestern university in "The Tenant" (1986). Edwidge Danticat offers a sense of the dislocation felt by a member of a Caribbean family encountering the affluence of some Manhattan residents in "New York Day Woman" (1995). Lan Samantha Chang evokes the mood of estrangement in Chinese American children listening to their grandmother's magic tale of the far distant old country in "Water Names" (1998).

Contemporary writers of traditional stories, such as Raymond Carver, Alice Walker, Charles Baxter, Ann Beattie, Bobbie Ann Mason, Gina Berriault, and Annie Proulx, who sometimes have contributed to but often have withstood the enchantment of experimental postmodernist short fiction, apparently agree with John Cheever's explanation in "Why I Write Short Stories" (*Newsweek*, October 1978): "Modern music has been separated from those rhythms and tonalities that are most deeply ingrained in our memories, but literature still possesses the narrative—the story—and one would defend this with one's life." Carver imagines the feelings of a man facing bankruptcy as he waits for his wife to come home after selling their prized convertible in "Are These Actual Miles?" (1972). Mason darkens the contemporary context of nineteenth-century tall tales in "Big Bertha Stories" (1980). Berriault gives voice to the homeless in the wealthy city of San Francisco in "Who Is It Can Tell Me Who I Am?" (1995).

Carver's realistic short fiction influenced a generation of writers who have created memorable stories about ordinary people down on their luck or baffled by the problems of everyday life, such as Charles Baxter's characters in "Saul and Patsy Are in Labor" (1997). Before Carver's stories began to appear in *The New Yorker*, he had published in the "little" magazines he had read in his creative writing course with John Gardner in the late 1950s. Thirty years later, in his last collection (*Where I'm Calling*

From, 1988), he acknowledged periodicals such as *Antaeus, The Antioch Review, The Carolina Quarterly, Colorado State Review, December, Discourse, The Iowa Review, Kansas Quarterly, The Missouri Review, New England Review, Northwest Review, Sou'wester,* and *Western Humanities Review* as having played an important role in his development as a writer.

In the last decades of the twentieth century, the audience for short fiction has become more specialized. Many mass-circulation magazines, such as the *Saturday Evening Post,* which had included short fiction in every issue, have gone out of business, narrowing the market for writers trying to make a living by publishing short stories. Instead, small presses and university presses, whose journals and books appeal to a different kind of reader, have taken over. Now "average" Americans switch on the television to relax instead of picking up a magazine and immersing themselves in a good short story. Or they increasingly entertain themselves with other electronic media by watching a video, surfing the Internet, or playing interactive games on a home computer.

Two annual anthologies of prize-winning stories continue to promote American writers' careers despite the diminishing marketplace for quality short fiction. *Best American Stories* was edited by Martha Foley from 1941 to 1977. It has been coedited by Katrina Kenison for the past ten years. Each year Kenison reads more than two thousand stories and selects one hundred of them to be sent to a guest editor, who makes the final selection. In recent years her coeditors have included Raymond Carver, John Updike, and Joyce Carol Oates. The other prestigious volume is still the annual collection of the O. Henry Memorial Award prize stories.

The change in the status of periodicals publishing short fiction in the United States is evident in a comparison of the lists of magazines consulted for two volumes of the O. Henry Memorial Award prize stories from 1943 and 1997. There were only four pages listing the American magazines read in choosing the *Prize Stories of 1943,* but the magazines were predominantly mass-market periodicals with large circulations that often paid considerable amounts to authors of short fiction. *The Atlantic Monthly, Collier's, Coronet, Cosmopolitan, Esquire, Glamour, Good Housekeeping, Harper's Bazaar, Harper's Magazine, Ladies' Home Journal, Mademoiselle, McCall's, The New Yorker, Redbook, Saturday Evening Post, Woman's Home Companion,* and *Woman's Day* were among the magazines in New York City, Boston, Philadelphia, and Chicago publishing short stories in 1943.

William Abrahams, the editor of the O. Henry story volumes from 1965 to 1996, is credited with keeping the award meaningful despite the financial decline of the marketplace since the end of what the *New York Times* called "the glory days of the *Saturday Evening Post* and other defunct magazines." For over thirty years, Abrahams culled the stories in magazines and literary journals to make inclusion in the annual O. Henry anthologies a significant award for quality writing. The O. Henry Memorial Award *Prize Stories of 1997* boasts sixteen pages listing magazines consulted for the volume. *The Atlantic Monthly, Esquire, Good Housekeeping,*

Harper's Magazine, The New Yorker, and *Redbook* are still listed, but the other mainstream magazines have disappeared.

In their places are periodicals such as *African American Review* ("quarterly with a focus on African American literature and culture"), *Agni* (Boston University Writing Program), *Alabama Literary Review* (published annually), *Alaska Quarterly Review* (University of Alaska), *America West Airlines Magazine* (an inflight magazine with occasional fiction), *American Short Fiction* (University of Texas Press), *Appalachian Heritage* (Berea College), *Accent* (Concordia College), and *Atlanta Review* (biannual), to list only a few titles from the "A" column. The majority of these periodicals are sponsored by university and college creative writing programs, often with a special focus—gay issues, "narratives of Urban Reality," "L.A. stories," "Zionist concerns." Located throughout the country instead of primarily on the East Coast, these "little" magazines facilitate publication for new writers.

In recent years, literature courses in the short story have also proliferated in the English departments of colleges and universities, with their accompanying textbook anthologies of short fiction. Inclusion in anthologies has become a source of substantial revenue to many contemporary writers, as an increasing number of readers encounter the American short story primarily in high school and college classrooms. These recent developments have brought the genre closer to what the critic Andrew Levy, in *The Culture and Commerce of the American Short Story* (1993), has called "the truly democratic" ideal of the short story: "that anyone could write it, anyone could read it, and everyone would judge it." With the democratization of the short story, the best-selling author Amy Tan has expressed concern about the way readers expect her to be a spokesperson for her ethnic background. She wrote an article for *The Threepenny Review* explaining why she felt she was "In the Canon, for All the Wrong Reasons":

> Until recently, I didn't think it was important for writers to express their private intentions in order for their work to be appreciated; I believed that any analysis of my intentions belonged behind the closed doors of literature classes. But I've come to realize that the study of literature does have its effect on how books are being read, and thus on what might be read, published and written in the future. For that reason, I do believe writers today must talk about their intentions—if for no other reason than to serve as an antidote to what others say our intentions should be.
>
> For the record, I don't write to dig a hole and fill it with symbols. I don't write stories as ethnic themes. I don't write to represent life in general. And I certainly don't write because I have answers. If I knew everything there is to know about mothers and daughters, Chinese and Americans, I wouldn't have any stories left to imagine. If I had to write about only positive role models, I wouldn't have enough imagination left to finish the first story. If I knew what to do about immigration, I would be a sociologist or a politician and not a long-winded storyteller.

Despite the paucity of magazines paying well for short fiction, stories have never been more heavily supported in the United States than they are now. Reading the contributors' notes at the back of the O. Henry Memorial Award volume gives us a sense of our society's strong encouragement of storytelling in the number of fellowships, awards, stipends, teaching appointments, and grants available to writers, along with the variety of Web sites offering information about story writing and desktop publishing.

Notable collections of short stories by contemporary authors abound at the end of the century, beginning in 1968 with three representative volumes of experimental fiction: John Barth's *Lost in the Funhouse,* Donald Barthelme's *Unspeakable Practices, Unnatural Acts,* and William Gass's *In the Heart of the Heart of the Country.* The prolific authors Joyce Carol Oates and John Updike continued throughout the decades to alternate volumes of short fiction with their novels and nonfiction books, including Oates's *The Wheels of Love and Other Stories* (1970) and Updike's *Too Far to Go* (1979), his collection of stories about the Maple family and its marital troubles. In 1991, Tim O'Brien's collection of war stories in *The Things They Carried* marked another high point in experimental short fiction.

For many readers, the stories of Raymond Carver represent some of the best writing of this period. Carver's first collection, *Will You Please Be Quiet, Please?* (1976), was a National Book Award nominee. He followed it with *What We Talk About When We Talk About Love* (1981) and *Cathedral* (1984); the latter earned a nomination for the National Book Critics Circle Award and was a runner-up for the Pulitzer Prize. In 1988, Carver was elected to the American Academy and Institute of Arts and Letters, the same year he published his last book of short fiction before his death from cancer, *Where I'm Calling From: New and Selected Stories.*

Many contemporary authors continue the realist tradition of storytelling in the United States, including Charles Baxter in his fourth collection of stories, *Believers* (1997). Baxter has said that he feels part of a literary community, "walking in the steps where others have been before you. In my case, that means walking where Sherwood Anderson has been, Willa Cather has been. . . ." In an interview for the *Sycamore Review,* Baxter also explained how his work creating short stories illustrates the continuing vitality of regionalism in the United States:

> To be in Winesburg, Ohio, around 1910 meant that you were *really* in Winesburg. There was no radio, no television, telegraph service was intermittent. The mail came, but so what? You were still in Winesburg. You were really there, and you were really living the life of that town. Any of us, anywhere now, live lives that are remarkably more homogeneous because of the way information is moved and processed. . . . I'd rather my own characters don't watch a lot of television because I don't want them to get so processed into the culture that I would have to write a different kind of fiction about people who are like that. Don DeLillo writes beautiful fiction about people

who might live anywhere and a great number of the postmodernists write that sort of fiction. I just don't.

Annie Proulx is another regionalist writer who believes in the importance of setting. Recent stories like "The Bunchgrass Edge of the World" (1998) demonstrate her idea that "if you get the landscape right, the characters will step out of it, and they'll be in the right place."

Along with regionalism, the tradition of women's writing has continued in the late twentieth century. Alice Walker's two collections *In Love and Trouble* (1973) and *You Can't Keep a Good Woman Down* (1981) chronicle the progression of black women as they struggle against social injustice. Bobbie Ann Mason's *Shiloh and Other Stories* (1982), described as "shopping mall realism" by some critics, captures the frustrated lives of her Kentucky characters. Amy Hempel and Mary Gaitskill also publish clear-eyed reflections on the societal dislocations in the wake of the feminist movement in Hempel's *Reasons to Live* (1985) and Gaitskill's *Bad Behavior* (1988). In *The Collected Stories of Grace Paley* (1994), Paley consolidates the short fiction in her earlier volumes, as do Gina Berriault in *Women in Their Beds* (1996) and Ann Beattie in *Park City* (1998).

Multicultural writers are also well represented in collections of short fiction, including Leslie Marmon Silko's *Storyteller* (1981), Helena María Viramontes's *The Moths and Other Stories* (1985), Bharati Mukherjee's *The Middleman and Other Stories* (1988), Sherman Alexie's *The Lone Ranger and Tonto Fistfight in Heaven* (1993), Edwidge Danticat's *Krik? Krak!* (1995), and Lan Samantha Chang's *Hunger* (1998).

The late twentieth century has witnessed a blossoming of stories that continue to be "a way of making America intelligible to itself," as the writer Ruth Suckow realized. Certain themes central to what have long been the dominant concerns of American society in its continually evolving diversity—the conflicts between genders and cultures, the destructive consequences of war, and the effect of rapid social changes—are still relevant and continue to inspire our authors of short fiction. It's probably safe to say that if Washington Irving were alive today, he would find that a man of his talents in the United States would likely be guaranteed the modest portion of "bread and cheese" he asked for. But then, good storytellers have always been appreciated in America; just ask the late Diedrich Knickerbocker.

RELATED COMMENTARIES: *John Barth, "It's a Short Story," page 1302; Richard Ford, "Crazy for Stories," page 1340; Susan Lohafer, "From* Short Story Theory at a Crossroads*," page 1388; Ruth Suckow, "The Short Story," page 1455.*

WILLIAM GASS

*W*illiam Gass (b. 1924) was born in Fargo, North Dakota. Soon after his birth
his family moved to Warren, Ohio, where he attended local schools. After service as an ensign in the navy during World War II, he graduated from Kenyon
College and went on to earn a doctorate in philosophy from Cornell University
in 1954. His dissertation, "A Philosophical Investigation of Metaphor," was
based on his training as a philosopher of language. In graduate school Gass
read the work of Gertrude Stein, who influenced his writing experiments.

Earning a living for himself and his family from university teaching, Gass
began to publish stories that were selected for inclusion in The Best American
Stories of 1959, 1961, and 1962. In 1966 his first novel, Omensetter's Luck,
about life in an Ohio small town in the 1890s, appeared. Critics praised his linguistic virtuosity, establishing Gass as an important writer of fiction. In 1968
he published In the Heart of the Heart of the Country, five stories dramatizing the theme of human isolation and the difficulty of love. The title story, originally published in New American Review in 1967, opens with a reference to
Yeats's poem "Sailing to Byzantium," but Gass's verbal arrangement also suggests that he is punning on the words to be.

In 1971 Gass produced Willie Masters' Lonesome Wife, an experimental
novella illustrated with photographs and typographical constructs intended to
help readers free themselves from the linear conventions of narrative. As Gass
explained in his essay "The Medium of Fiction," "It seems a country-headed
thing to say: that literature is language, that stories and the places and the
people in them are merely made of words as chairs are made of smoothed sticks
and sometimes of cloth or metal tubes." On Being Blue (1976), his next book,
is a long essay that the critic Larry McCaffrey reads as an analysis of "blue" at
"various levels as a word, color, state of mind, and Platonic ideal." Gass has
published several collections of essays, including Finding a Form (1996). For
the past twenty years he has been the David May Distinguished Professor in
Humanities at Washington University in St. Louis. Cartesian Sonata and
Other Novellas was published in 1998.

RELATED COMMENTARY: *William Gass, "From Preface to* In the Heart of
the Heart of the Country," *page 1348.*

In the Heart of the Heart
of the Country

A Place

O I have sailed the seas and come . . .

to B . . .

a small town fastened to a field in Indiana. Twice there have been twelve
hundred people here to answer to the census. The town is outstandingly
neat and shady, and always puts its best side to the highway. On one lawn
there's even a wood or plastic iron deer.

You can reach us by crossing a creek. In the spring the lawns are
green, the forsythia is singing, and even the railroad that guts the town has
straight bright rails which hum when the train is coming, and the train
itself has a welcome horning sound.

Down the back streets the asphalt crumbles into gravel. There's Westbrook's, with the geraniums, Horsefall's, Mott's. The sidewalk shatters.
Gravel dust rises like breath behind the wagons. And I am in retirement
from love.

Weather

In the Midwest, around the lower Lakes, the sky in the winter is heavy
and close, and it is a rare day, a day to remark on, when the sky lifts and
allows the heart up. I am keeping count, and as I write this page, it is
eleven days since I have seen the sun.

My House

There's a row of headless maples behind my house, cut to free the passage of electric wires. High stumps, ten feet tall, remain, and I climb these
like a boy to watch the country sail away from me. They are ordinary
fields, a little more uneven than they should be, since in the spring they
puddle. The topsoil's thin, but only moderately stony. Corn is grown one
year, soybeans another. At dusk starlings darken the single tree — a larch —
which stands in the middle. When the sky moves, fields move under it. I
feel, on my perch, that I've lost my years. It's as though I were living at last
in my eyes, as I have always dreamed of doing, and I think then I know
why I've come here: to see, and so to go out against new things — oh god
how easily — like air in a breeze. It's true there are moments — foolish
moments, ecstasy on a tree stump — when I'm all but gone, scattered I like
to think like seed, for I'm the sort now in the fool's position of having love
left over which I'd like to lose; what good is it now to me, candy ungiven
after Halloween?

A PERSON

There are vacant lots on either side of Billy Holsclaw's house. As the weather improves, they fill with hollyhocks. From spring through fall, Billy collects coal and wood and puts the lumps and pieces in piles near his door, for keeping warm is his one work. I see him most often on mild days sitting on his doorsill in the sun. I notice he's squinting a little, which is perhaps the reason he doesn't cackle as I pass. His house is the size of a single garage, and very old. It shed its paint with its youth, and its boards are a warped and weathered gray. So is Billy. He wears a short lumpy faded black coat when it's cold, otherwise he always goes about in the same loose, grease-spotted shirt and trousers. I suspect his galluses were yellow once, when they were new.

WIRES

These wires offend me. Three trees were maimed on their account, and now these wires deface the sky. They cross like a fence in front of me, enclosing the crows with the clouds. I can't reach in, but like a stick, I throw my feelings over. What is it that offends me? I am on my stump, I've built a platform there and the wires prevent my going out. The cut trees, the black wires, all the beyond birds therefore anger me. When I've wormed through a fence to reach a meadow, do I ever feel the same about the field?

THE CHURCH

The church has a steeple like the hat of a witch, and five birds, all doves, perch in its gutters.

MY HOUSE

Leaves move in the windows. I cannot tell you yet how beautiful it is, what it means. But they do move. They move in the glass.

POLITICS

. . . for all those not in love.

I've heard Batista[1] described as a Mason. A farmer who'd seen him in Miami made this claim. He's as nice a fellow as you'd ever want to meet. Of Castro, of course, no one speaks.

---

[1] Fulgencio Batista y Zaldívar (1901–1973), Cuban soldier and dictator who was president of Cuba from 1940 to 1944 and from 1952 to 1959, when his regime was overthrown by Fidel Castro.

For all those not in love there's law: to rule . . . to regulate . . . to rectify. I cannot write the poetry of such proposals, the poetry of politics, though sometimes—often—always now—I am in that uneasy peace of equal powers which makes a State; then I communicate by passing papers, proclamations, orders, through my bowels. Yet I was not a State with you, nor were we both together any Indiana. A squad of Pershing Rifles at the moment, I make myself Right Face! Legislation packs the screw of my intestines. Well, king of the classroom's king of the hill. You used to waddle when you walked because my sperm between your legs was draining to a towel. Teacher, poet, folded lover—like the politician, like those drunkards, ill, or those who faucet-off while pissing heartily to preach upon the force and fullness of that stream, or pause from vomiting to praise the purity and passion of their puke—I chant, I beg, I orate, I command, I sing—

> *Come back to Indiana—not too late!*
> *(Or will you be a ranger to the end?)*
> *Good-bye . . . Good-bye . . . oh, I shall always wait*
> *You, Larry, traveler—*
> > *stranger,*
> > > *son,*
> > > > *—my friend—*

my little girl, my poem by heart, my self, my childhood.

But I've heard Batista described as a Mason. That dries up my pity, melts my hate. Back from the garage where I have overheard it, I slap the mended fender of my car to laugh, and listen to the metal stinging tartly in my hand.

PEOPLE

Their hair in curlers and their heads wrapped in loud scarves, young mothers, fattish in trousers, lounge about in the speedwash, smoking cigarettes, eating candy, drinking pop, thumbing magazines, and screaming at their children above the whir and rumble of the machines.

At the bank a young man freshly pressed is letting himself in with a key. Along the street, delicately teetering, many grandfathers move in a dream. During the murderous heat of summer, they perch on window ledges, their feet dangling just inside the narrow shelf of shade the store has made, staring steadily into the street. Where their consciousness has gone I can't say. It's not in the eyes. Perhaps it's diffuse, all temperature and skin, like an infant's though more mild. Near the corner there are several large overalled men employed in standing. A truck turns to be weighed on the scales at the Feed and Grain. Images drift on the drugstore window. The wind has blown the smell of cattle into town. Our eyes have been driven in like the eyes of the old men. And there's no one to have mercy on us.

VITAL DATA

There are two restaurants here and a tearoom. two bars. one bank, three barbers, one with a green shade with which he blinds his window. two groceries. a dealer in Fords. one drug, one hardware, and one appliance store. several that sell feed, grain, and farm equipment. an antique shop. a poolroom. a laundromat. three doctors. a dentist. a plumber. a vet. a funeral home in elegant repair the color of a buttercup. numerous beauty parlors which open and shut like night-blooming plants. a tiny dime and department store of no width but several floors. a hutch, homemade, where you can order, after lying down or squirming in, furniture that's been fashioned from bent lengths of stainless tubing, glowing plastic, metallic thread, and clear shellac. an American Legion Post and a root beer stand. little agencies for this and that: cosmetics, brushes, insurance, greeting cards and garden produce — anything — sample shoes — which do their business out of hats and satchels, over coffee cups and dissolving sugar. a factory for making paper sacks and pasteboard boxes that's lodged in an old brick building bearing the legend OPERA HOUSE, still faintly golden, on its roof. a library given by Carnegie. a post office. a school. a railroad station. fire station. lumberyard. telephone company. welding shop. garage . . . and spotted through the town from one end to the other in a line along the highway, gas stations to the number five.

EDUCATION

In 1833, Colin Goodykoontz, an itinerant preacher with a name from a fairytale, summed up the situation in one Indiana town this way:

> Ignorance and her squalid brood. A universal dearth of intellect. Total abstinence from literature is very generally practiced . . . There is not a scholar in grammar or geography, or a *teacher capable* of *instructing* in them, to my knowledge . . . Others are supplied a few months of the year with the most antiquated & unreasonable forms of teaching reading, writing & cyphering . . . Need I stop to remind you of the host of loathsome reptiles such a stagnant pool is fitted to breed! Croaking jealousy; bloated bigotry; coiling suspicion; wormish blindness; crocodile malice!

Things have changed since then, but in none of the respects mentioned.

BUSINESS

One side section of street is blocked off with sawhorses. Hard, thin, bitter men in blue jeans, cowboy boots and hats, untruck a dinky carnival. The merchants are promoting themselves. There will be free rides, raucous music, parades and coneys, pop, popcorn, candy, cones, awards and drawings, with all you can endure of pinch, push, bawl, shove, shout, scream, shriek, and bellow. Children pedal past on decorated bicycles, their wheels a blur of color, streaming crinkled paper and excited dogs. A little later there's a pet show for a prize — dogs, cats, birds, sheep, ponies, goats — none of which wins. The whirlabouts whirl about. The Ferris wheel climbs dizzily into the sky as far as a tall man on tiptoe might be persuaded to reach, and the irritated operators measure the height and width of every child with sour eyes to see if they are safe for the machines. An electrical megaphone repeatedly trumpets the names of the generous sponsors. The following day they do not allow the refuse to remain long in the street.

My House, This Place and Body

I have met with some mischance, wings withering, as Plato says obscurely, and across the breadth of Ohio, like heaven on a table, I've fallen as far as the poet, to the sixth sort of body, this house in B, in Indiana, with its blue and gray bewitching windows, holy magical insides. Great thick evergreens protect its entry. And I live *in*.

Lost in the corn rows, I remember feeling just another stalk, and thus this country takes me over in the way I occupy myself when I am well . . . completely — to the edge of both my house and body. No one notices, when they walk by, that I am brimming in the doorways. My house, this place and body, I've come in mourning to be born in. To anybody else it's pretty silly: love. Why should I feel a loss? How am I bereft? She was never mine; she was a fiction, always a golden tomgirl, barefoot, with an adolescent's slouch and a boy's taste for sports and fishing, a figure out of Twain, or worse, in Riley. Age cannot be kind.

There's little hand-in-hand here . . . not in B. No one touches except in rage. Occasionally girls will twine their arms about each other and lurch along, school out, toward home and play. I dreamed my lips would drift down your back, like a skiff on a river. I'd follow a vein with the point of my finger, hold your bare feet in my naked hands.

The Same Person

Billy Holsclaw lives alone — how alone it is impossible to fathom. In the post office he talks greedily to me about the weather. His head bobs on a wild flood of words, and I take this violence to be a measure of his eagerness for speech. He badly needs a shave, coal dust has layered his face, he spits when he speaks, and his fingers pick at his tatters. He wobbles out in the wind when I leave him, a paper sack mashed in the fold of his arm, the leaves blowing past him, and our encounter drives me sadly home to poetry — where there's no answer. Billy closes his door and carries coal or wood to his fire and closes his eyes, and there's simply no way of knowing how lonely and empty he is or whether he's as vacant and barren and love-less as the rest of us are — here in the heart of the country.

WEATHER

For we're always out of luck here. That's just how it is — for instance in the winter. The sides of the buildings, the roofs, the limbs of the trees are gray. Streets, sidewalks, faces, feelings — they are gray. Speech is gray, and the grass when it shows. Every flank and front, each top is gray. Every-thing is gray: hair, eyes, window glass, the hawkers' bills and touters' posters, lips, teeth, poles and metal signs — they're gray, quite gray. Horses, sheep, and cows, cats killed in the road, squirrels in the same way, sparrows, doves, and pigeons, all are gray, everything is gray, and everyone is out of luck who lives here.

A similar haze turns the summer sky milky, and the air muffles your head and shoulders like a sweater you've got caught in. In the summer light, too, the sky darkens a moment when you open your eyes. The heat is pure distraction. Steeped in our fluids, miserable in the folds of our bodies, we can scarcely think of anything but our sticky parts. Hot cyclonic winds and storms of dust crisscross the country. In many places, given an indif-ferent push, the wind will still coast for miles, gathering resource and edge as it goes, cunning and force. According to the season, paper, leaves, field litter, seeds, snow, fill up the fences. Sometimes I think the land is flat because the winds have leveled it, they blow so constantly. In any case, a gale can grow in a field of corn that's as hot as a draft from hell, and to receive it is one of the most dismaying experiences of this life, though the smart of the same wind in winter is more humiliating, and in that sense even worse. But in the spring it rains as well, and the trees fill with ice.

PLACE

Many small Midwestern towns are nothing more than rural slums, and this community could easily become one. Principally during the first decade of the century, though there were many earlier instances, well-to-do farmers moved to town and built fine homes to contain them in their retirement. Others desired a more social life, and so lived in, driving to their fields like storekeepers to their businesses. These houses are now dying like the bereaved who inhabit them; they are slowly losing their senses — deaf-ness, blindness, forgetfulness, mumbling, an insecure gait, an uncontrol-lable trembling has overcome them. Some kind of Northern Snopes[2] will

---

[2]Refers to the Snopes family, recurring characters in William Faulkner's Yok-napatawpha novels and short stories, including "Spotted Horses" (see p. 702).

occupy them next: large-familied, Catholic, Democratic, scrambling, vigorous, poor; and since the parents will work in larger, nearby towns, the children will be loosed upon themselves and upon the hapless neighbors much as the fabulous Khan loosed his legendary horde. These Snopes will undertake makeshift repairs with materials that other people have thrown away; paint halfway round their house, then quit; almost certainly maintain an ugly loud cantankerous dog and underfeed a pair of cats to keep the rodents down. They will collect piles of possibly useful junk in the back yard, park their cars in the front, live largely leaning over engines, give not a hoot for the land, the old community, the hallowed ways, the established clans. Weakening widow ladies have already begun to hire large rude youths from families such as these to rake and mow and tidy the grounds they will inherit.

PEOPLE

In the cinders at the station boys sit smoking steadily in darkened cars, their arms bent out the windows, white shirts glowing behind the glass. Nine o'clock is the best time. They sit in a line facing the highway—two or three or four of them—idling their engines. As you walk by a machine may growl at you or a pair of headlights flare up briefly. In a moment one will pull out, spinning cinders behind it, to stalk impatiently up and down the dark streets or roar half a mile into the country before returning to its place in line and pulling up.

MY HOUSE, MY CAT, MY COMPANY

I must organize myself. I must, as they say, pull myself together, dump this cat from my lap, stir—yes, resolve, move, do. But do what? My will is like the rosy dustlike light in this room: soft, diffuse, and gently comforting. It lets me do . . . anything . . . nothing. My ears hear what they happen to; I eat what's put before me; my eyes see what blunders into them; my thoughts are not thoughts, they are dreams. I'm empty or I'm full . . . depending; and I cannot choose. I sink my claws in Tick's fur and scratch the bones of his back until his rear rises amorously. Mr Tick, I murmur, I must organize myself. I must pull myself together. And Mr Tick rolls over on his belly, all ooze.

I spill Mr Tick when I've rubbed his stomach. Shoo. He steps away slowly, his long tail rhyming with his paws. How beautifully he moves, I think; how beautifully, like you, he commands his loving, how beautifully he accepts. So I rise and wander from room to room, up and down, gazing through most of my forty-one windows. How well this house receives its loving too. Let out like Mr Tick, my eyes sink in the shrubbery. I am not here; I've passed the glass, passed second-story spaces, flown by branches, brilliant berries, to the ground, grass high in seed and leafage every season;

and it is the same as when I passed above you in my aged, ardent body; it's, in short, a kind of love; and I am learning to restore myself, my house, my body, by paying court to gardens, cats, and running water, and with neighbors keeping company.

Mrs Desmond is my right-hand friend; she's eighty-five. A thin white mist of hair, fine and tangled, manifests the climate of her mind. She is habitually suspicious, fretful, nervous. Burglars break in at noon. Children trespass. Even now they are shaking the pear tree, stealing rhubarb, denting lawn. Flies caught in the screens and numbed by frost awake in the heat to buzz and scrape the metal cloth and frighten her, though she is deaf to me, and consequently cannot hear them. Boards creak, the wind whistles across the chimney mouth, drafts cruise like fish through the hollow rooms. It is herself she hears, her own flesh failing, for only death will preserve her from those daily chores she climbs like stairs, and all that anxious waiting. Is it now, she wonders. No? Then: is it now?

We do not converse. She visits me to talk. My task to murmur. She talks about her grandsons, her daughter who lives in Delphi, her sister or her husband — both gone — obscure friends — dead — obscurer aunts and uncles — lost — ancient neighbors, members of her church or of her clubs — passed or passing on; and in this way she brings the ends of her life together with a terrifying rush: she is a girl, a wife, a mother, widow, all at once. All at once — appalling — but I believe it; I wince in expectation of the clap. Her talk's a fence — a shade drawn, window fastened, door that's locked — for no one dies taking tea in a kitchen; and as her years compress and begin to jumble, I really believe in the brevity of life; I sweat in my wonder; death is the dog down the street, the angry gander, bedroom spider, goblin who's come to get her; and it occurs to me that in my listening posture I'm the boy who suffered the winds of my grandfather with an exactly similar politeness, that I am, right now, all my ages, out in elbows, as angular as badly stacked cards. Thus was I, when I loved you, every man I could be, youth and child — far from enough — and you, so strangely ambiguous a being, met me, heart for spade, play after play, the whole run of our suits.

Mr Tick, you do me honor. You not only lie in my lap, but you remain alive there, coiled like a fetus. Through your deep nap, I feel you hum. You are, and are not, a machine. You are alive, alive exactly, and it means nothing to you — much to me. You are a cat — you cannot understand — you are a cat so easily. Your nature is not something you must rise to. You, not I, live in: in house, in skin, in shrubbery. Yes. I think I shall hat my head with a steeple; turn church; devour people. Mr Tick, though, has a tail he can twitch, he need not fly his Fancy. Claws, not metrical schema, poetry his paws; while smoothing . . . smoothing . . . smoothing roughly, his tongue laps its neatness. O Mr Tick, I know you; you are an electrical penis. Go on now, shoo. Mrs Desmond doesn't like you. She thinks you will tangle yourself in her legs and she will fall. You murder her birds, she knows, and walk upon her roof with death in your jaws. I must gather myself together for a bound. What age is it I'm at right now, I wonder. The heart, don't they always say, keeps the true time. Mrs Desmond is knocking. Faintly, you'd think, but she pounds. She's brought me a cucumber. I believe she believes I'm a woman. Come in, Mrs Desmond, thank you, be my company, it looks lovely, and have tea. I'll slice it, crisp, with cream, for luncheon, each slice as thin as me.

POLITICS

O all ye isolate and separate powers, Sing! Sing, and sing in such a way that from a distance it will seem a harmony, a Strindberg play, a friendship ring . . . so happy—happy, happy, happy—as here we go hand in handling, up and down. Our union was a singing, though we were silent in the songs we sang like single notes are silent in a symphony. In no sense sober, we barbershopped together and never heard the discords in our music or saw ourselves as dirty, cheap, or silly. Yet cats have worn out better shoes than those thrown through our love songs at us. Hush. Be patient—prudent—politic. Still, Cleveland killed you, Mr Crane. Were you not politic enough and fond of being beaten? Like a piece of sewage, the city shat you from its stern three hundred miles from history—beyond the loving reach of sailors. Well, I'm not a poet who puts Paris to his temple in his youth to blow himself from Idaho, or—fancy that—Missouri. My god, I said, this is my country, but must my country go so far as Terre Haute or Whiting, go so far as Gary?

When the Russians first announced the launching of their satellite, many people naturally refused to believe them. Later others were outraged that they had sent a dog around the earth. I wouldn't want to take that mutt from out that metal flying thing if he's still living when he lands, our own dog catcher said; anybody knows you shut a dog up by himself to toss around the first thing he'll be setting on to do you let him out is bite somebody.

This Midwest. A dissonance of parts and people, we are a consonance of Towns. Like a man grown fat in everything but heart, we overlabor; our outlook never really urban, never rural either, we enlarge and linger at the same time, as Alice both changed and remained in her story. You are blond. I put my hand upon your belly; feel it tremble from my trembling. We always drive large cars in my section of the country. How could you be a comfort to me now?

MORE VITAL DATA

The town is exactly fifty houses, trailer, stores, and miscellaneous buildings long, but in places no streets deep. It takes on width as you drive south, always adding to the east. Most of the dwellings are fairly spacious farm houses in the customary white, with wide wraparound porches and tall narrow windows, though there are many of the grander kind—fretted, scalloped, turreted, and decorated with clapboards set at angles or on end, with stained-glass windows at the stair landings and lots of wrought iron full of fancy curls—and a few of these look like castles in their rarer brick. Old stables serve as garages now, and the lots are large to contain them and the vegetable and flower gardens which, ultimately, widows plant and weed and then entirely disappear in. The shade is ample, the grass is good, the sky a glorious fall violet; the apple trees are heavy and red, the roads are calm and empty; corn has sifted from the chains of tractored wagons to speckle the streets with gold and with the russet fragments of the cob, and a man would be a fool who wanted, blessed with this, to live anywhere else in the world.

EDUCATION

Buses like great orange animals move through the early light to school. There the children will be taught to read and warned against Communism. By Miss Janet Jakes. That's not her name. Her name is Helen something— Scott or James. A teacher twenty years. She's now worn fine and smooth, and has a face, Wilfred says, like a mail-order ax. Her voice is hoarse, and she has a cough. For she screams abuse. The children stare, their faces blank. This is the thirteenth week. They are used to it. You will all, she shouts, you will all draw pictures of me. No. She is a Mrs—someone's missus. And in silence they set to work while Miss Jakes jabs hairpins in her hair. Wilfred says an ax, but she has those rimless tinted glasses, graying hair, an almost dimpled chin. I must concentrate. I must stop making up things. I must give myself to life; let it mold me: that's what they say in *Wisdom's Monthly Digest* every day. Enough, enough—you've been at it long enough; and the children rise formally a row at a time to present their work to her desk. No, she wears rims; it's her chin that's dimpleless. Well, it will take more than a tablespoon of features to sweeten that face. So she grimly shuffles their sheets, examines her reflection crayoned on them. I would not dare . . . allow a child . . . to put a line around me. Though now and then she smiles like a nick in the blade, in the end these drawings depress her. I could not bear it—how can she ask?—that anyone . . . draw me. Her anger's lit. That's why she does it: flame. There go her eyes; the pink in her glasses brightens, dims. She is a pumpkin, and her rage is breathing like the candle in. No, she shouts, no—the cartoon trembling— no, John Mauck, John Stewart Mauck, this will not do. The picture flut- ters from her fingers. You've made me too muscular.

I work on my poetry. I remember my friends, associates, my students, by their names. Their names are Maypop, Dormouse, Upsydaisy. Their names are Gladiolus, Callow Bladder, Prince and Princess Oleo, Hieronymus, Cardinal Mummum, Mr Fitchew, The Silken Howdah, Spot. Sometimes you're Tom Sawyer, Huckleberry Finn; it is perpetually summer; your buttocks are my pillow; we are adrift on a raft; your back is our river. Sometimes you are Major Barbara, sometimes a goddess who kills men in battle, sometimes you are soft like a shower of water; you are bread in my mouth.

I do not work on my poetry. I forget my friends, associates, my students, and their names: Gramophone, Blowgun, Pickle, Serenade . . . Marge the Barge, Arena, Uberhaupt . . . Doctor Dildoe, The Fog Machine. For I am now in B, in Indiana: out of job and out of patience, out of love and time and money, out of bread and out of body, in a temper, Mrs Desmond, out of tea. So shut your fist up, bitch, you bag of death; go bang another door; go die, my dearie. Die, life-deaf old lady. Spill your breath. Fall over like a frozen board. Gray hair grown from the nose of your mind. You are a skull already—*memento mori*—the foreskin retracts from your teeth. Will your plastic gums last longer than your bones, and color their grinning? And is your twot still hazel-hairy, or are you bald as a ditch? . . . bitch . . . . . . bitch . . . . bitch. I wanted to be famous, but you bring me age—my emptiness. Was it *that* which I thought would balloon me above the rest? Love? where are you? . . . love me. I want to rise so high, I said, that when I shit I won't miss anybody.

BUSINESS

For most people, business is poor. Nearby cities have siphoned off all but a neighborhood trade. Except for feed and grain and farm supplies, you stand a chance to sell only what one runs out to buy. Chevrolet has quit, and Frigidaire. A locker plant has left its afterimage. The lumberyard has been, so far, six months about its going. Gas stations change hands clumsily, a restaurant becomes available, a grocery closes. One day they came and knocked the cornices from the watch repair and pasted campaign posters on the windows. Torn across, by now, by boys, they urge you still to vote for half an orange beblazoned man who as a whole one failed two years ago to win at his election. Everywhere, in this manner, the past speaks, and it mostly speaks of failure. The empty stores, the old signs and dusty fixtures, the debris in alleys, the flaking paint and rusty gutters, the heavy locks and sagging boards: they say the same disagreeable things. What do the sightless windows see, I wonder, when the sun throws a passerby against them? Here a stair unfolds toward the street—dark, rickety, and treacherous—and I always feel, as I pass it, that if I just went carefully up and turned the corner at the landing, I would find myself out of the world. But I've never had the courage.

THAT SAME PERSON

The weeds catch up with Billy. In pursuit of the hollyhocks, they rise in coarse clumps all around the front of his house. Billy has to stamp down a circle by his door like a dog or cat does turning round to nest up, they're so thick. What particularly troubles me is that winter will find the weeds still standing stiff and tindery to take the sparks which Billy's little mortarless chimney spouts. It's true that fires are fun here. The town whistle, which otherwise only blows for noon (and there's no noon on Sunday), signals the direction of the fire by the length and number of its blasts, the volunteer firemen rush past in their cars and trucks, houses empty their owners along the street every time like an illustration in a children's book. There are many bikes, too, and barking dogs, and sometimes—halleluiah—the fire's right here in town—a vacant lot of weeds and stubble flaming up. But I'd rather it weren't Billy or Billy's lot or house. Quite selfishly I want him to remain the way he is—counting his sticks and logs, sitting on his sill in the soft early sun—though I'm not sure what his presence means to me . . . or to anyone. Nevertheless, I keep wondering whether, given time, I might not someday find a figure in our language which would serve him faithfully, and furnish his poverty and loneliness richly out.

WIRES

Where sparrows sit like fists. Doves fly the steeple. In mist the wires change perspective, rise and twist. If they led to you, I would know what they were. Thoughts passing often, like the starlings who flock these fields at evening to sleep in the trees beyond, would form a family of paths like this; they'd foot down the natural height of air to just about a bird's perch. But they do not lead to you.

> *Of whose beauty it was sung*
> *She shall make the old man young.*

They fasten me.

If I walked straight on, in my present mood, I would reach the Wabash. It's not a mood in which I'd choose to conjure you. Similes dangle like baubles from me. This time of year the river is slow and shallow, the clay banks crack in the sun, weeds surprise the sandbars. The air is moist and I am sweating. It's impossible to rhyme in this dust. Everything—sky, the cornfield, stump, wild daisies, my old clothes and pressless feelings—seem fabricated for installment purchase. Yes. Christ. I am suffering a summer Christmas; and I cannot walk under the wires. The sparrows scatter like handfuls of gravel. Really, wires are voices in thin strips. They are words wound in cables. Bars of connection.

WEATHER

I would rather it were the weather that was to blame for what I am and what my friends and neighbors are—we who live here in the heart of the country. Better the weather, the wind, the pale dying snow . . . the snow—why not the snow? There's never much really, not around the lower Lakes anyway, not enough to boast about, not enough to be useful. My father tells how the snow in the Dakotas would sweep to the roofs of the barns in the old days, and he and his friends could sled on the crust that would form because the snow was so fiercely driven. In Bemidji trees have been known to explode. That would be something—if the trees in Davenport or Francisville or Carbondale or Niles were to go blam some winter—blam! blam! blam! all the way down the gray, cindery, snow-sick streets.

A cold fall rain is blackening the trees or the air is like lilac and full of parachuting seeds. Who cares to live in any season but his own? Still I suspect the secret's in this snow, the secret of our sickness, if we could only diagnose it, for we are all dying like the elms in Urbana. This snow—like our skin it covers the country. Later dust will do it. Right now—snow. Mud presently. But it is snow without any laughter in it, a pale gray pudding thinly spread on stiff toast, and if that seems a strange description, it's accurate all the same. Of course soot blackens everything, but apart from that, we are never sufficiently cold here. The flakes as they come, alive and burning, we cannot retain, for if our temperatures fall, they rise promptly again, just as, in the summer, they bob about in the same feckless way. Suppose though . . . suppose they were to rise some August, climb and rise, and then hang in the hundreds like a hawk through December, what a desert we could make of ourselves—from Chicago to Cairo, from Hammond to Columbus—what beautiful Death Valleys.

PLACE

I would rather it were the weather. It drives us in upon ourselves—an unlucky fate. Of course there is enough to stir our wonder anywhere; there's enough to love, anywhere, if one is strong enough, if one is diligent enough, if one is perceptive, patient, kind enough—whatever it takes; and surely it's better to live in the country, to live on a prairie by a drawing of rivers, in Iowa or Illinois or Indiana, say, than in any city, in any stinking fog of human beings, in any blooming orchard of machines. It ought to be. The cities are swollen and poisonous with people. It ought to be better. Man has never been a fit environment for man—for rats, maybe, rats do nicely, or for dogs or cats and the household beetle.

And how long the street is, nowadays. These endless walls are fallen to keep back the tides of earth. Brick could be beautiful but we have covered it gradually with gray industrial vomits. Age does not make concrete genial, and asphalt is always—like America—twenty-one, until it breaks up in crumbs like stale cake. The brick, the asphalt, the concrete, the dancing signs and garish posters, the feed and excrement of the automobile, the litter of its inhabitants: they compose, they decorate, they line our streets, and there is nowhere, nowadays, our streets can't reach.

A man in the city has no natural thing by which to measure himself. His parks are potted plants. Nothing can live and remain free where he resides but the pigeon, starling, sparrow, spider, cockroach, mouse, moth, fly and weed, and he laments the existence of even these and makes his plans to poison them. The zoo? There *is* the zoo. Through its bars the city man stares at the great cats and dully sucks his ice. Living, alas, among men and their marvels, the city man supposes that his happiness depends on establishing, somehow, a special kind of harmonious accord with others. The novelists of the city, of slums and crowds, they call it love — and break their pens.

Wordsworth feared the accumulation of men in cities. He foresaw their "degrading thirst after outrageous stimulation," and some of their hunger for love. Living in a city, among so many, dwelling in the heat and tumult of incessant movement, a man's affairs are touch and go — that's all. It's not surprising that the novelists of the slums, the cities, and the crowds, should find that sex is but a scratch to ease a tickle, that we're most human when we're sitting on the john, and that the justest image of our life is in full passage through the plumbing.

> *That man, immur'd in cities, still retains*
> *His inborn inextinguishable thirst*
> *Of rural scenes, compensating his loss*
> *By supplemental shifts, the best he may.*

Come into the country, then. The air nimbly and sweetly recommends itself unto our gentle senses. Here, growling tractors tear the earth. Dust roils up behind them. Drivers sit jouncing under bright umbrellas. They wear refrigerated hats and steer by looking at the tracks they've cut behind them, their transistors blaring. Close to the land, are they? good companions to the soil? Tell me: do they live in harmony with the alternating seasons?

It's a lie of old poetry. The modern husbandman uses chemicals from cylinders and sacks, spike-ball-and-claw machines, metal sheds, and cost accounting. Nature in the old sense does not matter. It does not exist. Our farmer's only mystical attachment is to parity. And if he does not realize that cows and corn are simply different kinds of chemical engine, he cannot expect to make a go of it.

It isn't necessary to suppose our cows have feelings; our neighbor hasn't as many as he used to have either; but think of it this way a moment, you can correct for the human imputations later: how would it feel to nurse those strange tentacled calves with their rubber, glass, and metal lips, their stainless eyes?

PEOPLE

Aunt Pet's still able to drive her car — a high square Ford — even though she walks with difficulty and a stout stick. She has a watery gaze, a smooth plump face despite her age, and jet black hair in a bun. She has the slowest smile of anyone I ever saw, but she hates dogs, and not very long ago cracked the back of one she cornered in her garden. To prove her vigor she will tell you this, her smile breaking gently while she raises the knob of her stick to the level of your eyes.

HOUSE, MY BREATH AND WINDOW

My window is a grave, and all that lies within it's dead. No snow is falling. There's no haze. It is not still, not silent. Its images are not an animal that waits, for movement is no demonstration. I have seen the sea slack, life bubble through a body without a trace, its spheres impervious as soda's. Downwound, the whore at wagtag clicks and clacks. Leaves wiggle. Grass sways. A bird chirps, pecks the ground. An auto wheel in penning circles keeps its rigid spokes. These images are stones; they are memorials. Beneath this sea lies sea: god rest it . . . rest the world beyond my window, me in front of my reflection, above this page, my shade. Death is not so still, so silent, since silence implies a falling quiet, stillness a stopping, containing, holding in; for death is time in a clock, like Mr Tick, electric . . . like wind through a windup poet. And my blear floats out to visible against the glass, befog its country and bespill myself. The mist lifts slowly from the fields in the morning. No one now would say: the Earth throws back its covers; it is rising from sleep. Why is the feeling foolish? The image is too Greek. I used to gaze at you so wantonly your body blushed. Imagine: wonder: that my eyes could cause such flowering. Ah, my friend, your face is pale, the weather cloudy; a street has been felled through your chin, bare trees do nothing, houses take root in their rectangles, a steeple stands up in your head. You speak of loving; then give me a kiss. The pane is cold. On icy mornings the fog rises to greet me (as you always did); the barns and other buildings, rather than ghostly, seem all the more substantial for looming, as if they grew in themselves while I watched (as you always did). Oh my approach, I suppose, was like breath in a rubber monkey. Nevertheless, on the road along the Wabash in the morning, though the trees are sometimes obscured by fog, their reflection floats serenely on the river, reasoning the banks, the sycamores in French rows. Magically, the world tips. I'm led to think that only those who grow down live (which will scarcely win me twenty-five from *Wisdom's Monthly Digest*), but I find I write that only those who live down grow; and what I write, I hold, whatever I really know. My every word's inverted, or reversed—or I am. I held you, too, that way. You were so utterly provisional, subject to my change. I could inflate your bosom with a kiss, disperse your skin with gentleness, enter your vagina from within, and make my love emerge like a fresh sex. The pane is cold. Honesty is cold, my inside lover. The sun looks, through the mist, like a plum on the tree of heaven, or a bruise on the slope of your belly. Which? The grass crawls with frost. We meet on this window, the world and I, inelegantly, swimmers of the glass; and swung wrong way round to one another, the world seems in. The world—how grand, how monumental, grave and deadly, that word is: the world, my house and poetry. All poets have their inside lovers. Wee penis does not belong to me, or any of this foggery. It is *his* property which he's thrust through what's womanly of me to set down this. These wooden houses in their squares, gray streets and fallen sidewalks, standing trees, your name I've written sentimentally across my breath into the whitening air, pale birds: they exist in me now because of him. I gazed with what intensity . . . A bush in the excitement of its roses could not have bloomed so beautifully as you did then. It was a look I'd like to give this page. For that is poetry: to bring within about, to change.

POLITICS

Sports, politics, and religion are the three passions of the badly educated. They are the Midwest's open sores. Ugly to see, a source of constant discontent, they sap the body's strength. Appalling quantities of money, time, and energy are wasted on them. The rural mind is narrow, passionate, and reckless on these matters. Greed, however shortsighted and direct, will not alone account for it. I have known men, for instance, who for years have voted squarely against their interests. Nor have I ever noticed that their surly Christian views prevented them from urging forward the smithereening, say, of Russia, China, Cuba, or Korea. And they tend to back their country like they back their local team: they have a fanatical desire to win; yelling is their forte; and if things go badly, they are inclined to sack the coach. All in all, then, Birch[3] is a good name. It stands for the bigot's stick, the wild-child-tamer's cane.

Forgetfulness—is that their object?

Oh, I was new, I thought. A fresh start: new cunt, new climate, and new country—there you were, and I was pioneer, and had no history. That language hurts me, too, my dear. You'll never hear it.

FINAL VITAL DATA

The Modern Homemaker's Demonstration Club. The Prairie Home Demonstration Club. The Night-outers' Home Demonstration Club. The IOOF, FFF, VFW, WCTU, WSCS, 4-H, 40 and 8, Psi Iota Chi, and PTA. The Boy and Girl Scouts, Rainbows, Masons, Indians and Rebekah Lodge. Also the Past Noble Grand Club of the Rebekah Lodge. As well as the Moose and the Ladies of the Moose. The Elks, the Eagles, the Jaynettes

---

[3]Refers to the John Birch Society, an anticollectivist and anticommunist organization founded by Robert Welch in 1958 during the cold war. The group opposes unrestrained government power in any form, including communism and socialism. Still in existence, the John Birch Society denies all accusations of racism and anti-Semitism.

and the Eastern Star. The Women's Literary Club, the Hobby Club, the Art Club, the Sunshine Society, the Dorcas Society, the Pythian Sisters, the Pilgrim Youth Fellowship, the American Legion, the American Legion Auxiliary, the American Legion Junior Auxiliary, the Garden Club, the Bridge for Fun Club, the What-can-you-do? Club, the Get Together Club, the Coterie Club, the Worthwhile Club, the Let's Help Our Town Club, the No Name Club, the Forget-me-not Club, the Merry-go-round Club . . .

EDUCATION

Had a quarter disappeared from Paula Frosty's pocket book? Imagine the landscape of that face: no crayon could engender it; soft wax is wrong; thin wire in trifling snips might do the trick. Paula Frosty and Christopher Roger accuse the pale and splotchy Cheryl Pipes. But Miss Jakes, I *saw* her. Miss Jakes is so extremely vexed she snaps her pencil. What else is missing? I appoint you a detective, John: search her desk. Gum, candy, paper, pencils, marble, round eraser—whose? A thief. I can't watch her all the time, I'm here to teach. Poor pale fossetted Cheryl, it's determined, can't return the money because she took it home and spent it. Cindy, Janice, John, and Pete—you four who sit around her—you will be detectives this whole term to watch her. A thief. In all my time. Miss Jakes turns, unfists, and turns again. I'll handle you, she cries. To think. A thief. In all my years. Then she writes on the blackboard the name of Cheryl Pipes and beneath that the figure twenty-five with a large sign for cents. Now Cheryl, she says, this won't be taken off until you bring that money out of home, out of home straight up to here, Miss Jakes says, tapping her desk.

Which is three days.

ANOTHER PERSON

I was raking leaves when Uncle Halley introduced himself to me. He said his name came from the comet, and that his mother had borne him prematurely in her fright of it. I thought of Hobbes,[4] whom fear of the Spanish Armada had hurried into birth, and so I believed Uncle Halley to honor the philosopher, though Uncle Halley is a liar, and neither the one hundred twenty-nine nor the fifty-three he ought to be. That fall the leaves had burned themselves out on the trees, the leaf lobes had curled, and now they flocked noisily down the street and were broken in the wires of my rake. Uncle Halley was himself (like Mrs Desmond and history generally) both deaf and implacable, and he shooed me down his basement stairs to a room set aside there for stacks of newspapers reaching to the ceiling, boxes of leaflets and letters and programs, racks of photo albums, scrapbooks, bundles of rolled-up posters and maps, flags and pennants and slanting piles of dusty magazines devoted mostly to motoring and the

---

[4]Thomas Hobbes (1588–1679), English philosopher.

Christian ethic. I saw a bird cage, a tray of butterflies, a bugle, a stiff straw boater, and all kinds of tassels tied to a coat tree. He still possessed and had on display the steering lever from his first car, a linen duster, driving gloves and goggles, photographs along the wall of himself, his friend, and his various machines, a shell from the first war, a record of 'Ramona' nailed through its hole to a post, walking sticks and fanciful umbrellas, shoes of all sorts (his baby shoes, their counters broken, were held in sorrow beneath my nose — they had not been bronzed, but he might have them done someday before he died, he said), countless boxes of medals, pins, beads, trinkets, toys, and keys (I scarcely saw — they flowed like jewels from his palms), pictures of downtown when it was only a path by the railroad station, a brightly colored globe of the world with a dent in Poland, antique guns, belt buckles, buttons, souvenir plates and cups and saucers (I can't remember all of it — I won't), but I recall how shamefully, how rudely, how abruptly, I fled, a good story in my mouth but death in my nostrils; and how afterward I busily, righteously, burned my leaves as if I were purging the world of its years. I still wonder if this town — its life, and mine now — isn't really a record like the one of 'Ramona' that I used to crank around on my grandmother's mahogany Victrola through lonely rainy days as a kid.

The First Person

Billy's like the coal he's found: spilled, mislaid, discarded. The sky's no comfort. His house and his body are dying together. His windows are boarded. And now he's reduced to his hands. I suspect he has glaucoma. At any rate he can scarcely see, and weeds his yard of rubble on his hands and knees. Perhaps he's a surgeon cleansing a wound or an ardent and tactile lover. I watch, I must say, apprehensively. Like mine-war detectors, his hands graze in circles ahead of him. Your nipples were the color of your eyes. Pebble. Snarl of paper. Length of twine. He leans down closely, picks up something silvery, holds it near his nose. Foil? cap? coin? He has within him — what, I wonder? Does he know more now because he fingers everything and has to sniff to see? It would be romantic cruelty to think so. He bends the down on your arms like a breeze. You wrote me: something is strange when we don't understand. I write in return: I think when I loved you I fell to my death.

Billy, I could read to you from Beddoes; he's your man perhaps; he held with dying, freed his blood of its arteries; and he said that there were many wretched love-ill fools like me lying alongside the last bone of their former selves, as full of spirit and speech, nonetheless, as Mrs Desmond, Uncle Halley and the Ferris wheel, Aunt Pet, Miss Jakes, Ramona or the megaphone; yet I reverse him finally, Billy, on no evidence but braggadocio, and I declare that though my inner organs were devoured long ago, the worm which swallowed down my parts still throbs and glows like a crystal palace.

Yes, you were younger. I was Uncle Halley, the museum man and infrequent meteor. Here is my first piece of ass. They weren't so flat in those days, had more round, more juice. And over here's the sperm I've spilled, nicely jarred and clearly labeled. Look at this tape like lengths of intestine where I've stored my spew, the endless worm of words I've written, a hundred million emissions or more: oh I was quite a man right from the start; even when unconscious in my cradle, from crotch to cranium, I was erectile tissue; though mostly, after the manner approved by Plato, I had intercourse by eye. Never mind, old Holsclaw, you are blind. We pull down darkness when we go to bed; put out like Oedipus the actually offending organ, and train our touch to lies. All cats are gray, says Mr Tick; so under cover of glaucoma you are sack gray too, and cannot be distinguished from a stallion.

I must pull myself together, get a grip, just as they say, but I feel spilled, bewildered, quite mislaid. I did not restore my house to its youth, but to its age. Hunting, you hitch through the hollyhocks. I'm inclined to say you aren't half the cripple I am, for there is nothing left of me but mouth. However, I resist the impulse. It is another lie of poetry. My organs are all there, though it's there where I fail—at the roots of my experience. Poet of the spiritual, Rilke, weren't you? yet that's what you said. Poetry, like love, is—in and out—a physical caress. I can't tolerate any more of my sophistries about spirit, mind, and breath. Body equals being, and if your weight goes down, you are the less.

HOUSEHOLD APPLES

I knew nothing about apples. Why should I? My country came in my childhood, and I dreamed of sitting among the blooms like the bees. I failed to spray the pear tree too. I doubled up under them at first, admiring the sturdy low branches I should have pruned, and later I acclaimed the blossoms. Shortly after the fruit formed there were falls—not many—apples the size of goodish stones which made me wobble on my ankles when I walked about the yard. Sometimes a piece crushed by a heel would cling on the shoe to track the house. I gathered a few and heaved them over the wires. A slingshot would have been splendid. Hard, an unattractive green, the worms had them. Before long I realized the worms had them all. Even as the apples reddened, lit their tree, they were being swallowed. The birds preferred the pears, which were small—sugar pears I think they're called—with thick skins of graying green that ripen on toward violet. So the fruit fell, and once I made some applesauce by quartering and paring hundreds; but mostly I did nothing, left them, until suddenly, overnight it seemed, in that ugly late September heat we often have in Indiana, my problem was upon me.

My childhood came in the country. I remember, now, the flies on our snowy luncheon table. As we cleared away they would settle, fastidiously scrub themselves and stroll to the crumbs to feed where I would kill them in crowds with a swatter. It was quite a game to catch them taking off. I struck heavily since I didn't mind a few stains; they'd wash. The swatter was a square of screen bound down in red cloth. It drove no air ahead of it to give them warning. They might have thought they'd flown headlong into a summered window. The faint pink dot where they had died did not rub out as I'd supposed, and after years of use our luncheon linen would faintly, pinkly, speckle.

The country became my childhood. Flies braided themselves on the flypaper in my grandmother's house. I can smell the bakery and the grocery and the stables and the dairy in that small Dakota town I knew as a kid; knew as I dreamed I'd know your body, as I've known nothing, before or since; knew as the flies knew, in the honest, unchaste sense: the burned house, hose-wet, which drew a mist of insects like the blue smoke of its smolder, and gangs of boys, moist-lipped, destructive as its burning. Flies have always impressed me; they are so persistently alive. Now they were coating the ground beneath my trees. Some were ordinary flies; there were the large blue-green ones; there were swarms of fruit flies too, and the red-spotted scavenger beetle; there were a few wasps, several sorts of bees and butterflies—checkers, sulphurs, monarchs, commas, question marks—and delicate dragonflies . . . but principally houseflies and horseflies and bottleflies, flies and more flies in clusters around the rotting fruit. They loved the pears. Inside, they fed. If you picked up a pear, they flew, and the pear became skin and stem. They were everywhere the fruit was: in the tree still—apples like a hive for them—or where the fruit littered the ground, squashing itself as you stepped . . . there was no help for it. The flies droned, feasting on the sweet juice. No one could go near the trees; I could not climb; so I determined at last to labor like Hercules. There were fruit baskets in the barn. Collecting them and kneeling under the branches, I began to gather remains. Deep in the strong rich smell of the fruit, I began to hum myself. The fruit caved in at the touch. Glistening red apples, my lifting disclosed, had families of beetles, flies, and bugs, devouring their rotten undersides. There were streams of flies; there were lakes and cataracts and rivers of flies, seas and oceans. The hum was heavier, higher, than the hum of the bees when they came to the blooms in the spring, though the bees were there, among the flies, ignoring me—ignoring everyone. As my work went on and juice covered my hands and arms, they would form a sleeve, black and moving, like knotty wool. No caress could have been more indifferently complete. Still I rose fearfully, ramming my head in the branches, apples bumping against me before falling, bursting with bugs. I'd snap my hand sharply but the flies would cling to the sweet. I could toss a whole cluster into a basket from several feet. As the pear or apple lit, they would explosively rise, like monads for a moment, windowless, certainly, with respect to one another, sugar their harmony. I had to admit, though, despite my distaste, that my arm had never been more alive, oftener or more gently kissed. Those hundreds of feet were light. In washing them off, I pretended the hose was a pump. What have I missed? Childhood is a lie of poetry.

THE CHURCH

Friday night. Girls in dark skirts and white blouses sit in ranks and scream in concert. They carry funnels loosely stuffed with orange and black paper which they shake wildly, and small megaphones through which, as drilled, they direct and magnify their shouting. Their leaders, barely pubescent girls, prance and shake and whirl their skirts above their bloomers. The young men, leaping, extend their arms and race through puddles of amber light, their bodies glistening. In a lull, though it rarely occurs, you can hear the squeak of tennis shoes against the floor. Then the yelling begins again, and then continues; fathers, mothers, neighbors joining in to form a single pulsing ululation—a cry of the whole community—for in this gymnasium each body becomes the bodies beside it, pressed as they are together, thigh to thigh, and the same shudder runs through all of them, and runs toward the same release. Only the ball moves serenely through this dazzling din. Obedient to law it scarcely speaks but caroms quietly and lives at peace.

BUSINESS

It is the week of Christmas and the stores, to accommodate the rush they hope for, are remaining open in the evening. You can see snow falling in the cones of the street lamps. The roads are filling—undisturbed. Strings of red and green lights droop over the principal highway, and the water tower wears a star. The windows of the stores have been bedizened. Shamelessly they beckon. But I am alone, leaning against a pole—no . . . there is no one in sight. They're all at home, perhaps by their instruments, tuning in on their evenings, and like Ramona, tirelessly playing and replaying themselves. There's a speaker perched in the tower, and through the boughs of falling snow and over the vacant streets, it drapes the twisted and metallic strains of a tune that can barely be distinguished—yes, I believe it's one of the jolly ones, it's "Joy to the World." There's no one to hear the music but myself, and though I'm listening, I'm no longer certain. Perhaps the record's playing something else.   [1968]

JOHN BARTH

*J*ohn *Barth (b. 1930) was born in Cambridge, Maryland, on the Eastern Shore of the Chesapeake Bay. Music was Barth's first vocation. He was a student of orchestration for a year at the Juilliard School before he enrolled as a journalism major on a scholarship at Johns Hopkins University. His job as a book filer in the university library stacks developed his taste for fiction: "I was permanently impressed with the size of literature and its wild variety; likewise, as I explored the larger geography of the stacks, with the variety of temperaments, histories, and circumstances from which came the literature I came to love." In his undergraduate writing class he began but did not finish a cycle of one hundred stories about Dorchester County, Maryland, his own version of the* Arabian Nights.

Barth's early fiction is conventional in form and language, but The Sot-Weed Factor *(1960) and* Giles Goat-Boy *(1966) are very long, experimental comic novels, indebted to the fiction of Argentine author Jorge Luis Borges and Russian-born Vladimir Nabokov. Reviewers praised both of these novels for their display of erudition and bawdy wit. Barth's talent for parody is evident in all his works. "At heart I'm an arranger still, whose chiefest literary pleasure is to take a received melody—an old narrative poem, a classical myth, a shop-worn literary convention, a shard of my experience . . . and, improvising like a jazzman within its constraints, reorchestrate it to present purpose." Other publications include* The Literature of Exhaustion *(1982), Barth's analysis of postmodernist literary aesthetics, and the novels* Tidewater Tales *(1987) and* Last Voyage of Somebody the Sailor *(1991).*

Barth's first book of short stories, Lost in the Funhouse *(1968), was subtitled* Fiction for Print, Tape, Live Voice. *It was influenced by his friendships with the philosopher Marshall McLuhan and the scholar and critic Leslie Fiedler. Barth's experimental pieces in this collection, like "Title," suggest that he is self-consciously concerned with what happens when a writer writes, and what happens when a reader reads—"the metaphysical plight of imagination engaging with imagination." "Title" was first published in the* Yale Review *in the same year that it was collected in* Lost in the Funhouse. *Barth's second collection,* On with the Story, *was published in 1996.*

RELATED COMMENTARY: *John Barth, "It's a Short Story," page 1302.*

Title

Beginning: in the middle, past the middle, nearer three-quarters done, waiting for the end. Consider how dreadful so far: passionlessness, abstraction, pro, dis. And it will get worse. Can we possibly continue?

Plot and theme: notions vitiated by this hour of the world but as yet not successfully succeeded. Conflict, complication, no climax. The worst is to come. Everything leads to nothing: future tense; past tense; present tense. Perfect. The final question is, Can nothing be made meaningful? Isn't that the final question? If not, the end is at hand. Literally, as it were. Can't stand any more of this.

I think she comes. The story of our life. This is the final test. Try to fill the blank. Only hope is to fill the blank. Efface what can't be faced or else fill the blank. With words or more words, otherwise I'll fill in the blank with this noun here in my prepositional object. Yes, she already said that. And I think. What now. Everything's been said already, over and over; I'm as sick of this as you are; there's nothing to say. Say nothing.

What's new? Nothing.

Conventional startling opener. Sorry if I'm interrupting the Progress of Literature, she said, in a tone that adjective clause suggesting good-humored irony but in fact defensively and imperfectly masking a taunt. The conflict is established though as yet unclear in detail. Standard conflict. Let's skip particulars. What do you want from me? What'll the story be this time? Same old story. Just thought I'd see if you were still around. Before. What? Quit right here. Too late. Can't we start over? What's past is past. On the contrary, what's forever past is eternally present. The future? Blank. All this is just fill in. Hang on.

Still around. In what sense? Among the gerundive. What is that supposed to mean? Did you think I meant to fill in the blank? Why should I? On the other hand, why not? What makes you think I wouldn't fill in the blank instead? Some conversation this is. Do you want to go on, or shall we end it right now? Suspense. I don't care for this either. It'll be over soon enough in any case. But it gets worse and worse. Whatever happens, the ending will be deadly. At least let's have just one real conversation. Dialogue or monologue? What has it been from the first? Don't ask me. What is there to say at this late date? Let me think; I'm trying to think. Same old story. Or. Or? Silence.

This isn't so bad. Silence. There are worse things. Name three. This, that, the other. Some choices. Who said there was a choice?

Let's try again. That's what I've been doing; I've been thinking while you've been blank. Story of Our Life. However, this may be the final complication. The ending may be violent. That's been said before. Who cares? Let the end be blank; anything's better than this.

It didn't used to be so bad. It used to be less difficult. Even enjoyable. For whom? Both of us. To do what? Complicate the conflict. I am weary of this. What, then? To complete this sentence, if I may bring up a sore subject. That never used to be a problem. Now it's impossible; we just can't manage it. You can't fill in the blank; I can't fill in the blank. Or won't. Is this what we're going to talk about, our obscene verbal problem? It'll be our last conversation. Why talk at all? Are you paying attention? I dare you to quit now! Never dare a desperate person. On with it, calmly, one sentence after another, like a recidivist. A what? A common noun. Or another common noun. Hold tight. Or a chronic forger, let's say; committed to the pen for life. Which is to say, death. The point, for pity's sake! Not yet. Forge on.

We're more than halfway through, as I remarked at the outset: youthful vigor, innocent exposition, positive rising action—all that is behind us. How sophisticated we are today. I'll ignore her, he vowed, and went on. In this dehuman, exhausted, ultimate adjective hour, when every humane value has become untenable, and not only love, decency, and beauty but even compassion and intelligibility are no more than one or two subjective complements to complete the sentence. . . .

This is a story? It's a story, he replied equably, or will be if the author can finish it. Without interruption I suppose you mean? she broke in. I can't finish anything; that is my final word. Yet it's these interruptions that make it a story. Escalate the conflict further. Please let me start over.

Once upon a time you were satisfied with incidental felicities and niceties of technique: the unexpected image, the refreshingly accurate word-choice, the memorable simile that yields deeper and subtler significances upon reflection, like a memorable simile. Somebody please stop me. Or arresting dialogue, so to speak. For example?

Why do you suppose it is, she asked, long participial phrase of the breathless variety characteristic of dialogue attributions in nineteenth-century fiction, that literate people such as we talk like characters in a story? Even supplying the dialogue-tags, she added with wry disgust. Don't put words in her mouth. The same old story, an old-fashioned one at that. Even if I should fill in the blank with my idle pen? Nothing new about that, to make a fact out of a figure. At least it's good for something. Every story is penned in red ink, to make a figure out of a fact. This whole idea is insane.

And might therefore be got away with.

No turning back now, we've gone too far. Everything's finished. Name eight. Story, novel, literature, art, humanism, humanity, the self itself. Wait: the story's not finished. And you and I, Howard? whispered Martha, her sarcasm belied by a hesitant alarm in her glance, flickering as it were despite herself to the blank instrument in his hand. Belied indeed; put that thing away! And what does flickering modify? A person who can't verb adverb ought at least to speak correctly.

A tense moment in the evolution of the story. Do you know, declared the narrator, one has no idea, especially nowadays, how close the end may be, nor will one necessarily be aware of it when it occurs. Who can say how near this universe has come to mere cessation? Or take two people, in a story of the sort it once was possible to tell. Love affairs, literary genres, third item in exemplary series, fourth—everything blossoms and decays, does it not, from the primitive and classical through the mannered and baroque to the abstract, stylized, dehumanized, unintelligible, blank. And you and I, Rosemary? Edward. Snapped! Patience. The narrator gathers that his audience no longer cherishes him. And conversely. But little does he know of the common noun concealed for months in her you name it, under her eyelet chemise. This is a slip. The point is the same. And she fetches it out nightly as I dream, I think. That's no slip. And she regards it and sighs, a quantum grimlier each night it may be. Is this supposed to be amusing? The world might end before this sentence, or merely someone's life. And/or someone else's. I speak metaphorically. Is the sentence ended? Very nearly. No telling how long a sentence will be until one reaches the stop. It sounds as if somebody intends to fill in the blank. What *is* all this nonsense about?

It may not be nonsense. Anyhow it will presently be over. As the narrator was saying, things have been kaput for some time, and while we may be pardoned our great reluctance to acknowledge it, the fact is that the bloody century for example is nearing the three-quarter mark, and the characters in this little tale, for example, are similarly past their prime, as is the drama. About played out. Then God damn it let's ring the curtain. Wait wait. We're left with the following three possibilities, at least in theory. Horseshit. Hold onto yourself, it's too soon to fill in the blank. I hope this will be a short story.

Shorter than it seems. It seems endless. Be thankful it's not a novel. The novel is predicate adjective, as is the innocent anecdote of bygone days when life made a degree of sense and subject joined to complement by copula. No longer are these things the case, as you have doubtless remarked. There was I believe some mention of possibilities, three in number. The first is rejuvenation: having become an exhausted parody of itself, perhaps a form—Of what? Of anything—may rise neoprimitively from its own ashes. A tiresome prospect. The second, more appealing I'm sure but scarcely likely at this advanced date, is that moribund what-have-yous will be supplanted by vigorous new: the demise of the novel and short story, he went on to declare, needn't be the end of narrative art, nor need the dissolution of a used-up blank fill in the blank. The end of one road might be the beginning of another. Much good that'll do me. And you may not find the revolution as bloodless as you think, either. Shall we try it? Never dare a person who is fed up to the ears.

The final possibility is a temporary expedient, to be sure, the self-styled narrator of this so-called story went on to admit, ignoring the hostile impatience of his audience, but what is not, and every sentence completed is a step closer to the end. That is to say, every day gained is a day gone. Matter of viewpoint, I suppose. Go on. I am. Whether anyone's paying attention or not. The final possibility is to turn ultimacy, exhaustion, paralyzing self-consciousness and the adjective weight of accumulated history. . . . Go on. Go on. To turn ultimacy against itself to make something new and valid, the essence whereof would be the impossibility of making something new. What a nauseating notion. And pray how does it bear upon the analogy uppermost in everyone's mind? We've gotten this far, haven't we? Look how far we've come together. Can't we keep on to the end? I think not. Even another sentence is too many. Only if one believes the end to be a long way off; actually it might come at any moment; I'm surprised it hasn't before now. Nothing does when it's expected to.

Silence. There's a fourth possibility, I suppose. Silence. General anesthesia. Self-extinction. Silence.

Historicity and self-awareness, he asseverated, while ineluctable and even greatly to be prized, are always fatal to innocence and spontaneity. Perhaps adjective period Whether in a people, an art, a love affair, or a fourth term added not impossibly to make the third less than ultimate. In the name of suffering humanity cease this harangue. It's over. And the story? Is there a plot here? What's all this leading up to?

No climax. There's the story. Finished? Not quite. Story of our lives. The last word in fiction, in fact. I chose the first-person narrative viewpoint in order to reflect interest from the peculiarities of the technique (such as the normally unbearable self-consciousness, the abstraction, and the blank) to the nature and situation of the narrator and his companion, despite the obvious possibility that the narrator and his companion might be mistaken for the narrator and his companion. Occupational hazard. The technique is advanced, as you see, but the situation of the characters is conventionally dramatic. That being the case, may one of them, or one who may be taken for one of them, make a longish speech in the old-fashioned manner, charged with obsolete emotion? Of course.

I begin calmly, though my voice may rise as I go along. Sometimes it seems as if things could instantly be altogether different and more admirable. The times be damned, one still wants a man vigorous, confident, bold, resourceful, adjective, and adjective. One still wants a woman spirited, spacious of heart, loyal, gentle, adjective, adjective. That man and that woman are as possible as the ones in this miserable story, and a good deal realer. It's as if they live in some room of our house that we can't find the door to, though it's so close we can hear echoes of their voices. Experience has made them wise instead of bitter; knowledge has mellowed instead of souring them; in their forties and fifties, even in their sixties, they're gayer and stronger and more authentic than they were in their twenties; for the twenty-year-olds they have only affectionate sympathy. So? Why aren't the couple in this story that man and woman, so easy to imagine? God, but I am surfeited with clever irony! Ill of sickness! Parallel phrase to wrap up series! This last-resort idea, it's dead in the womb, excuse the figure. A false pregnancy, excuse the figure. God damn me though if that's entirely my fault. Acknowledge your complicity. As you see, I'm trying to do something about the present mess; hence this story. Adjective in the noun! Don't lose your composure. You tell me it's self-defeating to talk about it instead of just up and doing it; but to acknowledge what I'm doing while I'm doing it is exactly the point. Self-defeat implies a victor, and who do you suppose it is, if not blank? That's the only victory left. Right? Forward! Eyes open.

No. The only way to get out of a mirror-maze is to close your eyes and hold out your hands. And be carried away by a valiant metaphor, I suppose, like a simile.

There's only one direction to go in. Ugh. We must make something out of nothing. Impossible. Mystics do. Not only turn contradiction into paradox, but *employ* it, to go on living and working. Don't bet on it. I'm betting my cliché on it, yours too. What is that supposed to mean? On with the refutation; every denial is another breath, every word brings us closer to the end.

Very well: to write this allegedly ultimate story is a form of artistic fill in the blank, or an artistic form of same, if you like. I don't. What I mean is, same idea in other terms. The storyteller's alternatives, as far as I can see, are a series of last words, like an aging actress making one farewell appearance after another, or actual blank. And I mean literally fill in the blank. Is this a test? But the former is contemptible in itself, and the latter will certainly become so when the rest of the world shrugs its shoulders and goes on about its business. Just as people would do if adverbial clause of obvious analogical nature. The fact is, the narrator has narrated himself into a corner, a state of affairs more tsk-tsk than boo-hoo, and because his position is absurd he calls the world absurd. That some writers lack lead in their pencils does not make writing obsolete. At this point they were both smiling despite themselves. At this point they were both flashing hatred despite themselves. Every woman has a blade concealed in the neighborhood of her garters. So disarm her, so to speak, don't geld yourself. At this point they were both despite themselves. Have we come to the point at last? Not quite. Where there's life there's hope.

There's no hope. This isn't working. But the alternative is to supply an alternative. That's no alternative. Unless I make it one. Just try; quit talking about it, quit talking, quit! Never dare a desperate man. Or woman. That's the one thing that can drive even the first part of a conventional metaphor to the second part of same. Talk, talk, talk. Yes yes, go on, I believe literature's not likely ever to manage abstraction successfully, like sculpture for example, is that a fact, what a time to bring up that subject, anticlimax, that's the point, do set forth the exquisite reason. Well, because wood and iron have a native appeal and first-order reality, whereas words are artificial to begin with, invented specifically to represent. Go on, please go on. I'm going. Don't you dare. Well, well, weld iron rods into abstract patterns, say, and you've still got real iron, but arrange words into abstract patterns and you've got nonsense. Nonsense is right. For example. On, God damn it; take linear plot, take resolution of conflict, take third direct object, all that business, they may very well be obsolete notions, indeed they are, no doubt untenable at this late date, no doubt at all, but in fact we still lead our lives by clock and calendar, for example, and though the seasons recur our mortal human time does not; we grow old and tired, we think of how things used to be or might have been and how they are now, and in fact, and in fact we get exasperated and desperate and out of expedients and out of words.

Go on. Impossible. I'm going, too late now, one more step and we're done, you and I. Suspense. The fact is, you're driving me to it, the fact is that people still lead lives, mean and bleak and brief as they are, briefer than you think, and people have characters and motives that we divine more or less inaccurately from their appearance, speech, behavior, and the rest, you aren't listening, go on then, what do you think I'm doing, people still fall in love, and out, yes, in and out, and out and in, and they please each other, and hurt each other, isn't that the truth, and they do these things in more or less conventionally dramatic fashion, unfashionable or not, go on, I'm going, and what goes on between them is still not only the most interesting but the most important thing in the bloody murderous world, pardon the adjectives. And that my dear is what writers have got to find ways to write about in this adjective adjective hour of the ditto ditto same noun as above, or their, that is to say our, accursed self-consciousness will lead them, that is to say us, to here it comes, say it straight out, I'm going to, say it in plain English for once, that's what I'm leading up to, me and my bloody anticlimactic noun, we're pushing each other to fill in the blank.

Goodbye. Is it over? Can't you read between the lines? One more step. Goodbye suspense goodbye.

Blank.

Oh God comma I abhor self-consciousness. I despise what we have come to; I loathe our loathsome loathing, our place our time our situation, our loathsome art, this ditto necessary story. The blank of our lives. It's about over. Let the *dénouement* be soon and unexpected, painless if possible, quick at least, above all soon. Now now! How in the world will it ever   [1968]

DONALD BARTHELME

*D*onald Barthelme (1931–1989) was born in Philadelphia and raised in Texas, where his father was a prominent architect. While a high school student he won awards for his stories and poetry, and at the University of Houston he edited the campus newspaper and wrote film criticism for the Houston Post. At age thirty he became director of the Contemporary Arts Museum in Houston. In 1962 he moved to New York City, where he lived when he was not teaching at the University of Houston as Cullen Distinguished Professor of English.

During the twenty years that Barthelme contributed short fiction to The New Yorker, his minimalist style was often imitated. His stories amused some readers as magazine fiction, but they intrigued others who sensed the heavier substance beneath their light narrative surface. Barthelme compared his style of writing short fiction to that of collage, saying that "the principle of collage is the central principle of all art in the twentieth century." Literary critics have noted that Barthelme, like the French poet Stéphane Mallarmé, whom he admired, plays with the meanings of words, relying on poetic intuition to spark new connections of ideas buried in trite expressions and conventional responses.

Readers sometimes criticized Barthelme's stories—along with those of other authors in the group he called "the alleged postmodernists," such as John Barth and William Gass, for being too obscure. Barthelme replied, "Art is not difficult because it wishes to be difficult, rather because it wishes to be art. However much the writer might long to be straight-forward, these virtues are no longer available to him. He discovers that in being simple, honest, straightforward, nothing much happens." First published in The New Yorker in 1968, "The Police Band" was included in his collection Unspeakable Practices, Unnatural Acts (1968). Barthelme published two novels, Snow White (1967) and The Dead Father (1975), and left a third novel, The King, ready for publication in 1992 after his death from cancer. Of his eight volumes of short stories, Sixty Stories (1981), which won the PEN/Faulkner Award for fiction, is the most representative. More recent publications are The Teachings of Donald Barthelme (1992) and Not Knowing (1997), a collection of essays and interviews.

The Police Band

It was kind of the department to think up the Police Band. The original impulse, I believe, was creative and humanitarian. A better way of doing things. Unpleasant, bloody things required by the line of duty. Even if it didn't work out.

The Commissioner (the old Commissioner, not the one they have now) brought us up the river from Detroit. Where our members had been, typically, working the Sho Bar two nights a week. Sometimes the Glass Crutch. Friday and Saturday. And the rest of the time wandering the streets disguised as postal employees. Bitten by dogs and burdened with third-class mail.

What are our duties? we asked at the interview. Your duties are to wail, the Commissioner said. That only. We admired our new dark-blue uniforms as we came up the river in canoes like Indians. We plan to use you in certain situations, certain tense situations, to alleviate tensions, the Commissioner said. I can visualize great success with this new method. And would you play "Entropy." He was pale, with a bad liver.

We are subtle, the Commissioner said, never forget that. Subtlety is what has previously been lacking in our line. Some of the old ones, the Commissioner said, all they know is the club. He took a little pill from a little box and swallowed it with his Scotch.

When we got to town we looked at those Steve Canyon[1] recruiting posters and wondered if we resembled them. Henry Wang, the bass man, looks like a Chinese Steve Canyon, right? The other cops were friendly in a suspicious way. They liked to hear us wail, however.

The Police Band is a very sensitive highly trained and ruggedly anti-Communist unit whose efficacy will be demonstrated in due time, the Commissioner said to the Mayor (the old Mayor). The Mayor took a little pill from a little box and said, We'll see. He could tell we were musicians because we were holding our instruments, right? Emptying spit valves, giving the horn that little shake. Or coming in at letter E with some sly emotion stolen from another life.

The old Commissioner's idea was essentially that if there was a disturbance on the city's streets—some ethnic group cutting up some other ethnic group on a warm August evening—the Police Band would be sent in. The handsome dark-green band bus arriving with sirens singing, red lights whirling. Hard-pressed men on the beat in their white hats raising a grateful cheer. We stream out of the vehicle holding our instruments at high port. A skirmish line fronting the angry crowd. And play "Perdido." The crowd washed with new and true emotion. Startled, they listen. Our emotion stronger than their emotion. A triumph of art over good sense.

That was the idea. The old Commissioner's *musical* ideas were not very interesting, because after all he was a cop, right? But his police ideas were interesting.

We had drills. Poured out of that mother-loving bus onto vacant lots holding our instruments at high port like John Wayne. Felt we were heroes already. Playing "Perdido," "Stumblin'," "Gin Song," "Feebles."

---

[1]Hero of a World War II comic strip created by cartoonist Milton Caniff.

Laving the terrain with emotion stolen from old busted-up loves, broken marriages, the needle, economic deprivation. A few old ladies leaning out of high windows. Our emotion washing rusty Rheingold cans and parts of old doors.

This city is too much! We'd be walking down the street talking about our techniques and we'd see out of our eyes a woman standing in the gutter screaming to herself about what we could not imagine. A drunk trying to strangle a dog somebody'd left leashed to a parking meter. The drunk and the dog screaming at each other. This city is too much!

We had drills and drills. It is true that the best musicians come from Detroit but there is something here that you have to get in your playing and that is simply the scream. We got that. The Commissioner, a sixty-three-year-old hippie with no doubt many graft qualities and unpleasant qualities, nevertheless understood that. When we'd play "ugly," he understood that. He understood the rising expectations of the world's peoples also. That our black members didn't feel like toting junk mail around Detroit forever until the ends of their lives. For some strange reason.

He said one of our functions would be to be sent out to play in places where people were trembling with fear inside their houses, right? To inspirit them in difficult times. This was the plan. We set up in the street. Henry Wang grabs hold of his instrument. He has a four-bar lead-in all by himself. Then the whole group. The iron shutters raised a few inches. Shorty Alanio holding his horn at his characteristic angle (sideways). The reeds dropping lacy little fill-ins behind him. We're cooking. The crowd roars.

The Police Band was an idea of a very romantic kind. The Police Band was an idea that didn't work. When they retired the old Commissioner (our Commissioner), who it turned out had a little drug problem of his own, they didn't let us even drill anymore. We have never been used. His idea was a romantic idea, they said (right?), which was not adequate to the rage currently around in the world. Rage must be met with rage, they said. (Not in so many words.) We sit around the precinct houses, under the filthy lights, talking about our techniques. But I thought it might be good if you knew that the Department still has us. We have a good group. We still have emotion to be used. We're still here.   [1968]

JOYCE CAROL OATES

Joyce Carol Oates (b. 1938) was born in Lockport, New York, one of three children in a Roman Catholic family. She began to put picture stories down on paper even before she could write, and she remembers that her parents "dutifully" supplied her with lined tablets and gave her a typewriter when she was fourteen. In 1956, after Oates graduated from high school, she went on a scholarship to major in English at Syracuse University, but she did not devote most of her time to writing until after she received her M.A. from the University of Wisconsin in 1961. Discovering by chance that one of her stories had been cited in the honor roll of Martha Foley's annual The Best American Short Stories, *Oates assembled the fourteen stories in her first book,* By the North Gate *(1963). Her career was launched, and as John Updike has speculated, she "was perhaps born a hundred years too late; she needs a lustier audience, a race of Victorian word-eaters to be worthy of her astounding productivity, her tireless gift of self-enthrallment."*

One of our most prolific authors, Oates has published almost seventy books, including over a hundred stories. She also writes poetry and literary criticism, including the volume New Heaven, New Earth *(1974), analyzing the "visionary experience in literature" as exemplified in the work of Henry James, Virginia Woolf, Franz Kafka, D. H. Lawrence, Flannery O'Connor, and others. As a writer, critic, and professor at Princeton University, Oates dedicates her life to "promoting and exploring literature. . . . I am not conscious of being in any particular literary tradition, though I share with my contemporaries an intense interest in the formal aspects of writing; each of my books is an experiment of a kind, an investigation of the relationship between a certain consciousness and its formal aesthetic expression."*

"How I Contemplated the World from the Detroit House of Correction and Began My Life Over Again" (TriQuarterly, 1969) was included in Oates's collection The Wheel of Love and Other Stories *(1970). She explained her intent in the story to Jack Hicks, editor of* Cutting Edges: Young American Fiction for the '70s *(1973):*

> *It is an inside-out concentration on why we all leave home or make vain attempts to leave home, or failing all that, yearn to leave home. People ask "Why?" and we reply, "Why not?" Thereafter the world falls into two parts, and we stand on one shore staring over at the people on the other shore, perplexed, shaken at the distance between us. In Detroit, this story isn't really "fiction" but a kind of off-the-street anecdote; but it's a story with an evil ending, because not only must you return home again (lacking the power, I mean the economic and physical power, to stay away), but while you're away, trying to map out another life, new parents or stray adu'ts or simply anyone with an I.Q. one point above yours conquers you. They just walk up to you and take hold. That's that.*

Oates's recent collections include Heat and Other Stories *(1992),* Haunted: Tales of the Grotesque *(1994),* Will You Always Love Me and Other Stories *(1996), and* The Collector of Hearts *(1998).*

How I Contemplated the World from the Detroit House of Correction and Began My Life Over Again

Notes for an Essay for an English Class at
Baldwin Country Day School; Poking around in
Debris; Disgust and Curiosity; a Revelation
of the Meaning of Life; a Happy Ending . . .

I   EVENTS

1. The girl (myself) is walking through Branden's, that excellent store. Suburb of a large famous city that is a symbol for large famous American cities. The event sneaks up on the girl, who believes she is herding it along with a small fixed smile, a girl of fifteen, innocently experienced. She dawdles in a certain style by a counter of costume jewelry. Rings, earrings, necklaces. Prices from $5 to $50, all within reach. All ugly. She eases over to the glove counter, where everything is ugly too. In her close-fitted coat with its black fur collar she contemplates the luxury of Branden's, which she has known for many years: its many mild pale lights, easy on the eye and the soul, its elaborate tinkly decorations, its women shoppers with their excellent shoes and coats and hairdos, all dawdling gracefully, in no hurry.

2. The girl seated at home. A very small library, paneled walls of oak. Someone is talking to me. An earnest, husky, female voice drives itself against my ears, nervous, frightened, groping around my heart, saying, "If you wanted gloves, why didn't you say so? Why didn't you ask for them?" That store, Branden's, is owned by Raymond Forrest who lives on Du Maurier Drive. We live on Sioux Drive. Raymond Forrest. A handsome man? An ugly man? A man of fifty or sixty, with gray hair, or a man of forty with earnest, courteous eyes, a good golf game; who is Raymond Forrest, this man who is my salvation? Father has been talking to him. Father is not his physician; Dr. Berg is his physician. Father and Dr. Berg refer patients to each other. There is a connection. Mother plays bridge with . . . On Mondays and Wednesdays our maid Billie works at . . . The strings draw together in a cat's cradle, making a net to save you when you fall. . . .

3. *Harriet Arnold's.* A small shop, better than Branden's. Mother in her black coat, I in my close-fitted blue coat. Shopping. Now look at this,

isn't this cute, do you want this, why don't you want this, try this on, take this with you to the fitting room, take this also, what's wrong with you, what can I do for you, why are you so strange . . . ? "I wanted to steal but not to buy," I don't tell her. The girl droops along in her coat and gloves and leather boots, her eyes scan the horizon, which is pastel pink and decorated like Branden's, tasteful walls and modern ceilings with graceful glimmering lights.

4. Weeks later, the girl at a bus stop. Two o'clock in the afternoon, a Tuesday; obviously she has walked out of school.

5. The girl stepping down from a bus. Afternoon, weather changing to colder. Detroit. Pavement and closed-up stores; grillwork over the windows of a pawnshop. What is a pawnshop, exactly?

II   Characters

1. The girl stands five feet five inches tall. An ordinary height. Baldwin Country Day School draws them up to that height. She dreams along the corridors and presses her face against the Thermoplex glass. No frost or steam can ever form on that glass. A smudge of grease from her forehead . . . could she be boiled down to grease? She wears her hair loose and long and straight in suburban teen-age style, 1968. Eyes smudged with pencil, dark brown. Brown hair. Vague green eyes. A pretty girl? An ugly girl? She sings to herself under her breath, idling in the corridor, thinking of her many secrets (the thirty dollars she once took from the purse of a friend's mother, just for fun, the basement window she smashed in her own house just for fun) and thinking of her brother who is at Susquehanna Boys' Academy, an excellent preparatory school in Maine, remembering him unclearly . . . he has long manic hair and a squeaking voice and he looks like one of the popular teen-age singers, one of those in a group, *The Certain Forces, The Way Out, The Maniacs Responsible*. The girl in her turn looks like one of those fieldsful of girls who listen to the boys' singing, dreaming and mooning restlessly, breaking into high sullen laughter, innocently experienced.

2. The mother. A Midwestern woman of Detroit and suburbs. Belongs to the Detroit Athletic Club. Also the Detroit Golf Club. Also the Bloomfield Hills Country Club. The Village Women's Club at which lectures are given each winter on Genet and Sartre and James Baldwin, by the Director of the Adult Education Program at Wayne State University. . . . The Bloomfield Art Association. Also the Founders Society of the Detroit Institute of Arts. Also . . . Oh, she is in perpetual motion, this lady, hair like blown-up gold and finer than gold, hair and fingers and body of inestimable grace. Heavy weighs the gold on the back of her hairbrush and hand mirror. Heavy heavy the candlesticks in the dining room. Very heavy is the big car, a Lincoln, long and black, that on one cool autumn day split a squirrel's body in two unequal parts.

3. The father. Dr.⁣   . He belongs to the same clubs as #2. A player of squash and golf; he has a golfer's umbrella of stripes. Candy stripes. In his mouth nothing turns to sugar, however; saliva works no miracles here. His doctoring is of the slightly sick. The sick are sent elsewhere (to Dr. Berg?), the deathly sick are sent back for more tests and their bills are sent to their homes, the unsick are sent to Dr. Coronet (Isabel, a lady), an excellent psychiatrist for unsick people who angrily believe they are sick and want to do something about it. If they demand a male psychiatrist, the unsick are sent by Dr.⁣   (my father) to Dr. Lowenstein, a male psychiatrist, excellent and expensive, with a limited practice.

4. Clarita. She is twenty, twenty-five, she is thirty or more? Pretty, ugly, what? She is a woman lounging by the side of the road, in jeans and a sweater, hitchhiking, or she is slouched on a stool at a counter in some roadside diner. A hard line of jaw. Curious eyes. Amused eyes. Behind her eyes processions move, funeral pageants, cartoons. She says, "I never can figure out why girls like you bum around down here. What are you looking for anyway?" An odor of tobacco about her. Unwashed underclothes, or no underclothes, unwashed skin, gritty toes, hair long and falling into strands, not recently washed.

5. Simon. In this city the weather changes abruptly, so Simon's weather changes abruptly. He sleeps through the afternoon. He sleeps through the morning. Rising, he gropes around for something to get him going, for a cigarette or a pill to drive him out to the street, where the temperature is hovering around 35°. Why doesn't it drop? Why, why doesn't the cold clean air come down from Canada; will he have to go up into Canada to get it? will he have to leave the Country of his Birth and sink into Canada's frosty fields . . . ? Will the F.B.I. (which he dreams about constantly) chase him over the Canadian border on foot, hounded out in a blizzard of broken glass and horns . . . ?

"Once I was Huckleberry Finn," Simon says, "but now I am Roderick Usher."[1] Beset by frenzies and fears, this man who makes my spine go cold, he takes green pills, yellow pills, pills of white and capsules of dark blue and green . . . he takes other things I may not mention, for what if Simon seeks me out and climbs into my girl's bedroom here in Bloomfield Hills and strangles me, what then . . . ? (As I write this I begin to shiver. Why do I shiver? I am now sixteen and sixteen is not an age for shivering.) It comes from Simon, who is always cold.

III   WORLD EVENTS

Nothing.

---

[1] The protagonist of Edgar Allan Poe's "The Fall of the House of Usher" (see p. 117).

IV PEOPLE AND CIRCUMSTANCES CONTRIBUTING TO THIS DELINQUENCY

Nothing.

V SIOUX DRIVE

George, Clyde G. 240 Sioux. A manufacturer's representative; children, a dog, a wife. Georgian with the usual columns. You think of the White House, then of Thomas Jefferson, then your mind goes blank on the white pillars and you think of nothing. Norris, Ralph W. 246 Sioux. Public relations. Colonial. Bay window, brick, stone, concrete, wood, green shutters, sidewalk, lantern, grass, trees, blacktop drive, two children, one of them my classmate Esther (Esther Norris) at Baldwin. Wife, cars. Ramsey, Michael D. 250 Sioux. Colonial. Big living room, thirty by twenty-five, fireplaces in living room, library, recreation room, paneled walls wet bar five bathrooms five bedrooms two lavatories central air conditioning automatic sprinkler automatic garage door three children one wife two cars a breakfast room a patio a large fenced lot fourteen trees a front door with a brass knocker never knocked. Next is our house. Classic contemporary. Traditional modern. Attached garage, attached Florida room, attached patio, attached pool and cabana, attached roof. A front door mail slot through which pour *Time Magazine, Fortune, Life, Business Week*, the *Wall Street Journal*, the *New York Times*, the *New Yorker*, the *Saturday Review, M.D., Modern Medicine, Disease of the Month* . . . and also. . . . And in addition to all this, a quiet sealed letter from Baldwin saying: *Your daughter is not doing work compatible with her performance on the Stanford-Binet.* . . . And your son is not doing well, not well at all, very sad. Where is your son anyway? Once he stole trick-and-treat candy from some six-year-old kids, he himself being a robust ten. The beginning. Now your daughter steals. In the Village Pharmacy she made off with, yes she did, don't deny it, she made off with a copy of *Pageant Magazine* for no reason, she swiped a roll of Life Savers in a green wrapper and was in no need of saving her life or even in need of sucking candy; when she was no more than eight years old she stole, don't blush, she stole a package of Tums only because it was out on the counter and available, and the nice lady behind the counter (now dead) said nothing. . . . Sioux Drive. Maples, oaks, elms. Diseased elms cut down Sioux Drive runs into Roosevelt Drive. Slow, turning lanes, not streets, all drives and lanes and ways and passes. A private police force. Quiet private police, in unmarked cars. Cruising on Saturday evenings with paternal smiles for the residents who are streaming in and out of houses, going to and from parties, a thousand parties, slightly staggering, the women in their furs alighting from automobiles bought of Ford and General Motors and Chrysler, very heavy automobiles. No foreign cars. Detroit. In 275 Sioux, down the block in that magnificent French-Normandy mansion, lives   himself, who has the C   account itself, imagine that! Look at where he lives and look at the enormous trees and chimneys, imagine his many fireplaces, imagine his wife and children, imagine his wife's hair, imagine her fingernails, imagine her bathtub of smooth clean glowing pink, imagine their embraces, his trouser pockets filled with odd coins and keys and dust and peanuts, imagine their ecstasy on Sioux Drive, imagine their income tax returns, imagine their little boy's pride in his experimental car, a scaled-down C   , as he roars around the neighborhood on the sidewalks frightening dogs and Negro maids, oh imagine all these things, imagine everything, let your mind roar out all over Sioux Drive and Du Maurier Drive and Roosevelt Drive and Ticonderoga Pass and Burning Bush Way and Lincolnshire Pass and Lois Lane.

When spring comes, its winds blow nothing to Sioux Drive, no odors of hollyhocks or forsythia, nothing Sioux Drive doesn't already possess, everything is planted and performing. The weather vanes, had they weather vanes, don't have to turn with the wind, don't have to contend with the weather. There is no weather.

VI   DETROIT

There is always weather in Detroit. Detroit's temperature is always 32°. Fast-falling temperatures. Slow-rising temperatures. Wind from the north-northeast four to forty miles an hour, small-craft warnings, partly cloudy today and Wednesday changing to partly sunny through Thursday . . . small warnings of frost, soot warnings, traffic warnings, hazardous lake conditions for small craft and swimmers, restless Negro gangs, restless cloud formations, restless temperatures aching to fall out the very bottom of the thermometer or shoot up over the top and boil everything over in red mercury.

Detroit's temperature is 32°. Fast-falling temperatures. Slow-rising temperatures. Wind from the north-northeast four to forty miles an hour. . . .

VII   EVENTS

1. The girl's heart is pounding. In her pocket is a pair of gloves! In a plastic bag! Airproof breathproof plastic bag, gloves selling for twenty-five dollars on Branden's counter! In her pocket! Shoplifted! . . . In her purse is a blue comb, not very clean. In her purse is a leather billfold (a birthday present from her grandmother in Philadelphia) with snapshots of the family in clean plastic windows, in the billfold are bills, she doesn't know how many bills. . . . In her purse is an ominous note from her friend Tykie *What's this about Joe H. and the kids hanging around at Louise's Sat. night? You heard anything?* . . . passed in French class. In her purse is a lot of dirty yellow Kleenex, her mother's heart would break to see such very dirty

Kleenex, and at the bottom of her purse are brown hairpins and safety pins and a broken pencil and a ballpoint pen (blue) stolen from somewhere forgotten and a purse-size compact of Cover Girl Make-Up, Ivory Rose. . . . Her lipstick is Broken Heart, a corrupt pink; her fingers are trembling like crazy; her teeth are beginning to chatter; her insides are alive; her eyes glow in her head; she is saying to her mother's astonished face *I want to steal but not to buy.*

2. At Clarita's. Day or night? What room is this? A bed, a regular bed, and a mattress on the floor nearby. Wallpaper hanging in strips. Clarita says she tore it like that with her teeth. She was fighting a barbaric tribe that night, high from some pills; she was battling for her life with men wearing helmets of heavy iron and their faces no more than Christian crosses to breathe through, every one of those bastards looking like her lover Simon, who seems to breathe with great difficulty through the slits of mouth and nostrils in his face. Clarita has never heard of Sioux Drive. Raymond Forrest cuts no ice with her, nor does the C   account and its millions; Harvard Business School could be at the corner of Vernor and 12th Street for all she cares, and Vietnam might have sunk by now into the Dead Sea under its tons of debris, for all the amazement she could show . . . her face is overworked, overwrought, at the age of twenty (thirty?) it is already exhausted but fanciful and ready for a laugh. Clarita says mournfully to me *Honey somebody is going to turn you out let me give you warning.* In a movie shown on late television Clarita is not a mess like this but a nurse, with short neat hair and a dedicated look, in love with her doctor and her doctor's patients and their diseases, enamored of needles and sponges and rubbing alcohol. . . . Or no: she is a private secretary. Robert Cummings is her boss. She helps him with fantastic plots, the canned audience laughs, no, the audience doesn't laugh because nothing is funny, instead her boss is Robert Taylor and they are not boss and secretary but husband and wife, she is threatened by a young starlet, she is grim, handsome, wifely, a good companion for a good man. . . . She is Claudette Colbert. Her sister too is Claudette Colbert. They are twins, identical. Her husband Charles Boyer is a very rich handsome man and her sister, Claudette Colbert, is plotting her death in order to take her place as the rich man's wife, no one will know because they are *twins*. . . . All these marvelous lives Clarita might have lived, but she fell out the bottom at the age of thirteen. At the age when I was packing my overnight case for a slumber party at Toni Deshield's she was tearing filthy sheets off a bed and scratching up a rash on her arms. . . . Thirteen is uncommonly young for a white girl in Detroit, Miss Brock of the Detroit House of Correction said in a sad newspaper interview for the *Detroit News;* fifteen and sixteen are more likely. Eleven, twelve, thirteen are not surprising in colored . . . they are more precocious. What can we do? Taxes are rising and the tax base is falling. The temperature rises slowly but falls rapidly. Everything is falling out the bottom, Woodward Avenue is filthy, Livernois Avenue is filthy!

Scraps of paper flutter in the air like pigeons, dirt flies up and hits you right in the eye, oh Detroit is breaking up into dangerous bits of newspaper and dirt, watch out. . . .

Clarita's apartment is over a restaurant. Simon her lover emerges from the cracks at dark. Mrs. Olesko, a neighbor of Clarita's, an aged white wisp of a woman, doesn't complain but sniffs with contentment at Clarita's noisy life and doesn't tell the cops, hating cops, when the cops arrive. I should give more fake names, more blanks, instead of telling all these secrets. I myself am a secret; I am a minor.

3. My father reads a paper at a medical convention in Los Angeles. There he is, on the edge of the North American continent when the unmarked detective put his hand so gently on my arm in the aisle of Branden's and said, "Miss, would you like to step over here for a minute?"

And where was he when Clarita put her hand on my arm, that wintry dark sulphurous aching day in Detroit, in the company of closed-down barber shops, closed-down diners, closed-down movie houses, homes, windows, basements, faces . . . she put her hand on my arm and said, "Honey, are you looking for somebody down here?"

And was he home worrying about me, gone for two weeks solid, when they carried me off . . . ? It took three of them to get me in the police cruiser, so they said, and they put more than their hands on my arm.

4. I work on this lesson. My English teacher is Mr. Forest, who is from Michigan State. Not handsome, Mr. Forest, and his name is plain, unlike Raymond Forrest's, but he is sweet and rodentlike, he has conferred with the principal and my parents, and everything is fixed . . . treat her as if nothing has happened, a new start, begin again, only sixteen years old, what a shame, how did it happen? — nothing happened, nothing could have happened, a slight physiological modification known only to a gynecologist or to Dr. Coronet. I work on my lesson. I sit in my pink room. I look around the room with my sad pink eyes. I sigh, I dawdle, I pause, I eat up time, I am limp and happy to be home, I am sixteen years old suddenly, my head hangs heavy as a pumpkin on my shoulders, and my hair has just been cut by Mr. Faye at the Crystal Salon and is said to be very becoming.

(Simon too put his hand on my arm and said, "Honey, you have got to come with me," and in his six-by-six room we got to know each other. Would I go back to Simon again? Would I lie down with him in all that filth and craziness? Over and over again.

a Clarita is being betrayed as in front of a Cunningham Drug Store she is nervously eying a colored man who may or may not have money, or a nervous white boy of twenty with sideburns and an Appalachian look, who may or may not have a knife hidden in his jacket pocket, or a husky red-faced man of friendly countenance who may or may not be a member of the Vice Squad out for an early twilight walk.)

I work on my lesson for Mr. Forest. I have filled up eleven pages. Words pour out of me and won't stop. I want to tell everything . . . what was the song Simon was always humming, and who was Simon's friend in a very new trench coat with an old high school graduation ring on his finger . . . ? Simon's bearded friend? When I was down too low for him, Simon kicked me out and gave me to him for three days, I think, on Fourteenth Street in Detroit, an airy room of cold cruel drafts with newspapers on the floor. . . . Do I really remember that or am I piecing it together from what they told me? Did they tell the truth? Did they know much of the truth?

VIII CHARACTERS

1. Wednesdays after school, at four; Saturday mornings at ten. Mother drives me to Dr. Coronet. Ferns in the office, plastic or real, they look the same. Dr. Coronet is queenly, an elegant nicotine-stained lady who would have studied with Freud had circumstances not prevented it, a bit of a Catholic, ready to offer you some mystery if your teeth will ache too much without it. Highly recommended by Father! Forty dollars an hour, Father's forty dollars! Progress! Looking up! Looking better! That new haircut is so becoming, says Dr. Coronet herself, showing how normal she is for a woman with an I.Q. of 180 and many advanced degrees.

2. Mother. A lady in a brown suede coat. Boots of shiny black material, black gloves, a black fur hat. She would be humiliated could she know that of all the people in the world it is my ex-lover Simon who walks most like her . . . self-conscious and unreal, listening to distant music, a little bowlegged with craftiness. . . .

3. Father. Tying a necktie. In a hurry. On my first evening home he put his hand on my arm and said, "Honey, we're going to forget all about this."

4. Simon. Outside, a plane is crossing the sky, in here we're in a hurry. Morning. It must be morning. The girl is half out of her mind, whimpering and vague; Simon her dear friend is wretched this morning . . . he is wretched with morning itself . . . he forces her to give him an injection with that needle she knows is filthy, she has a dread of needles and surgical instruments and the odor of things that are to be sent into the blood, thinking somehow of her father. . . . This is a bad morning, Simon says that his mind is being twisted out of shape, and so he submits to the needle that he usually scorns and bites his lip with his yellowish teeth, his face going very pale. *Ah baby!* he says in his soft mocking voice, which with all women is a mockery of love, *do it like this— Slowly—*And the girl, terrified, almost drops the precious needle but manages to turn it up to the light from the window . . . is it an extension of herself then? She can give him this gift then? *I wish you wouldn't do this to me,* she says, wise in her terror, because it seems to her that Simon's danger—in a few minutes he may be dead—is a way of pressing her against him that is more powerful

than any other embrace. She has to work over his arm, the knotted corded veins of his arm, her forehead wet with perspiration as she pushes and releases the needle, staring at that mixture of liquid now stained with Simon's bright blood. . . . When the drug hits him she can feel it herself, she feels that magic that is more than any woman can give him, striking the back of his head and making his face stretch as if with the impact of a terrible sun. . . . She tries to embrace him but he pushes her aside and stumbles to his feet. *Jesus Christ,* he says. . . .

5. Princess, a Negro girl of eighteen. What is her charge? She is closed-mouthed about it, shrewd and silent, you know that no one had to wrestle her to the sidewalk to get her in here; she came with dignity. In the recreation room she sits reading *Nancy Drew and the Jewel Box Mystery,* which inspires in her face tiny wrinkles of alarm and interest: what a face! Light brown skin, heavy shaded eyes, heavy eyelashes, a serious sinister dark brow, graceful fingers, graceful wristbones, graceful legs, lips, tongue, a sugar-sweet voice, a leggy stride more masculine than Simon's and my mother's, decked out in a dirty white blouse and dirty white slacks; vaguely nautical is Princess' style. . . . At breakfast she is in charge of clearing the table and leans over me, saying, *Honey you sure you ate enough?*

6. The girl lies sleepless, wondering. Why here, why not there? Why Bloomfield Hills and not jail? Why jail and not her pink room? Why downtown Detroit and not Sioux Drive? What is the difference? Is Simon all the difference? The girl's head is a parade of wonders. She is nearly sixteen, her breath is marvelous with wonders, not long ago she was coloring with crayons and now she is smearing the landscape with paints that won't come off and won't come off her fingers either. She says to the matron *I am not talking about anything,* not because everyone has warned her not to talk but because, because she will not talk; because she won't say anything about Simon, who is her secret. And she says to the matron, *I won't go home,* up until that night in the lavatory when everything was changed. . . . "No, I won't go home I want to stay here," she says, listening to her own words with amazement, thinking that weeds might climb everywhere over that marvelous $180,000 house and dinosaurs might return to muddy the beige carpeting, but never never will she reconcile four o'clock in the morning in Detroit with eight o'clock breakfasts in Bloomfield Hills. . . . oh, she aches still for Simon's hands and his caressing breath, though he gave her little pleasure, he took everything from her (five-dollar bills, ten-dollar bills, passed into her numb hands by men and taken out of her hands by Simon) until she herself was passed into the hands of other men, police, when Simon evidently got tired of her and her hysteria. . . . *No, I won't go home, I don't want to be bailed out.* The girl thinks as a *Stubborn and Wayward Child* (one of several charges lodged against her), and the matron understands her crazy white-rimmed eyes that are seeking out some new violence that will keep her in jail, should someone threaten to let her out. Such children try to strangle the matrons,

the attendants, or one another . . . they want the locks locked forever, the doors nailed shut . . . and this girl is no different up until that night her mind is changed for her. . . .

IX THAT NIGHT

Princess and Dolly, a little white girl of maybe fifteen, hardy however as a sergeant and in the House of Correction for armed robbery, corner her in the lavatory at the farthest sink and the other girls look away and file to bed, leaving her. God, how she is beaten up! Why is she beaten up? Why do they pound her, why such hatred? Princess vents all the hatred of a thousand silent Detroit winters on her body, this girl whose body belongs to me, fiercely she rides across the Midwestern plains on this girl's tender bruised body . . . revenge on the oppressed minorities of America! revenge on the slaughtered Indians! revenge on the female sex, on the male sex, revenge on Bloomfield Hills, revenge revenge. . . .

X DETROIT

In Detroit, weather weighs heavily upon everyone. The sky looms large. The horizon shimmers in smoke. Downtown the buildings are imprecise in the haze. Perpetual haze. Perpetual motion inside the haze. Across the choppy river is the city of Windsor, in Canada. Part of the continent has bunched up here and is bulging outward, at the tip of Detroit; a cold hard rain is forever falling on the expressways. . . . Shoppers shop grimly, their cars are not parked in safe places, their windshields may be smashed and graceful ebony hands may drag them out through their shatterproof smashed windshields, crying, *Revenge for the Indians!* Ah, they all fear leaving Hudson's and being dragged to the very tip of the city and thrown off the parking roof of Cobo Hall, that expensive tomb, into the river. . . .

XI CHARACTERS WE ARE FOREVER ENTWINED WITH

1. Simon drew me into his tender rotting arms and breathed gravity into me. Then I came to earth, weighed down. He said, *You are such a little girl,* and he weighed me down with his delight. In the palms of his hands were teeth marks from his previous life experiences. He was thirty-five, they said. Imagine Simon in this room, in my pink room; he is about six feet tall and stoops slightly, in a feline cautious way, always thinking, always on guard, with his scuffed light suede shoes and his clothes that are anyone's clothes, slightly rumpled ordinary clothes that ordinary men might wear to not-bad jobs. Simon has fair long hair, curly hair, spent languid curls that are like . . . exactly like the curls of wood shavings to the

touch, I am trying to be exact . . . and he smells of unheated mornings and coffee and too many pills coating his tongue with a faint green-white scum . . . Dear Simon, who would be panicked in this room and in this house (right now Billie is vacuuming next door in my parents' room; a vacuum cleaner's roar is a sign of all good things), Simon who is said to have come from a home not much different from this, years ago, fleeing all the carpeting and the polished banisters . . . Simon has a deathly face, only desperate people fall in love with it. His face is bony and cautious, the bones of his cheeks prominent as if with the rigidity of his ceaseless thinking, plotting, for he has to make money out of girls to whom money means nothing, they're so far gone they can hardly count it, and in a sense money means nothing to him either except as a way of keeping on with his life. *Each Day's Proud Struggle,* the title of a novel we could read at jail. . . . Each day he needs a certain amount of money. He devours it. It wasn't love he uncoiled in me with his hollowed-out eyes and his courteous smile, that remnant of a prosperous past, but a dark terror that needed to press itself against him, or against another man . . . but he was the first, he came over to me and took my arm, a claim. We struggled on the stairs and I said, *Let me loose, you're hurting my neck, my face,* it was such a surprise that my skin hurt where he rubbed it, and afterward we lay face to face and he breathed everything into me. In the end I think he turned me in.

2. Raymond Forrest. I just read this morning that Raymond Forrest's father, the chairman of the board at   , died of a heart attack on a plane bound for London. I would like to write Raymond Forrest a note of sympathy. I would like to thank him for not pressing charges against me one hundred years ago, saving me, being so generous . . . well, men like Raymond Forrest are generous men, not like Simon. I would like to write him a letter telling of my love, or of some other emotion that is positive and healthy. Not like Simon and his poetry, which he scrawled down when he was high and never changed a word . . . but when I try to think of something to say, it is Simon's language that comes back to me, caught in my head like a bad song, it is always Simon's language:

> There is no reality only dreams
> Your neck may get snapped when you wake
> My love is drawn to some violent end
> She keeps wanting to get away
> My love is heading downward
> And I am heading upward
> She is going to crash on the sidewalk
> And I am going to dissolve into the clouds

XII EVENTS

1. Out of the hospital, bruised and saddened and converted, with Princess' grunts still tangled in my hair . . . and Father in his overcoat

looking like a prince himself, come to carry me off. Up the expressway and out north to home. Jesus Christ, but the air is thinner and cleaner here. Monumental houses. Heartbreaking sidewalks, so clean.

2. Weeping in the living room. The ceiling is two stories high and two chandeliers hang from it. Weeping, weeping, though Billie the maid is *probably listening.* I will never leave home again. Never. Never leave home. Never leave this home again, never.

3. Sugar doughnuts for breakfast. The toaster is very shiny and my face is distorted in it. Is that my face?

4. The car is turning in the driveway. Father brings me home. Mother embraces me. Sunlight breaks in movie-land patches on the roof of our traditional-contemporary home, which was designed for the famous automotive stylist whose identity, if I told you the name of the famous car he designed, you would all know, so I can't tell you because my teeth chatter at the thought of being sued . . . or having someone climb into my bedroom window with a rope to strangle me. . . . The car turns up the blacktop drive. The house opens to me like a doll's house, so lovely in the sunlight, the big living room beckons to me with its walls falling away in a delirium of joy at my return, Billie the maid is *no doubt* listening from the kitchen as I burst into tears and the hysteria Simon got so sick of. Convulsed in Father's arms, I say I will never leave again, never, why did I leave, where did I go, what happened, my mind is gone wrong, my body is one big bruise, my backbone was sucked dry, it wasn't the men who hurt me and Simon never hurt me but only those girls . . . my God, how they hurt me . . . I will never leave home again. . . . The car is perpetually turning up the drive and I am perpetually breaking down in the living room and we are perpetually taking the right exit from the expressway (Lahser Road) and the wall of the rest room is perpetually banging against my head and perpetually are Simon's hands moving across my body and adding everything up and so too are Father's hands on my shaking bruised back, far from the surface of my skin on the surface of my good blue cashmere coat (dry-cleaned for my release). . . . I weep for all the money here, for God in gold and beige carpeting, for the beauty of chandeliers and the miracle of a clean polished gleaming toaster and faucets that run both hot and cold water, and I tell them, *I will never leave home, this is my home, I love everything here, I am in love with everything here. . . .*

I am home. [1969]

RICHARD BRAUTIGAN

*R*ichard Brautigan (1935–1984) was born in Tacoma, Washington. His *father was a laborer, his mother a housewife. Although he never went to college, Brautigan was poet-in-residence at the California Institute of Technology in 1967, the year before he received a grant from the National Endowment for the Arts. He had begun to write poems as a teenager and later told an interviewer that he wrote poetry for seven years in an attempt to learn how to write a sentence.*

Brautigan's early books were published by small presses in San Francisco, beginning in 1957 with the poems in The Return of the Rivers *and later including* Please Plant This Book, *a volume of seeds in a handsome envelope printed in 1968 by Graham MacKintosh. In 1965 Grove Press published his first novel,* A Confederate General from Big Sur, *a playful satire on the hippie lifestyle in the manner of a Stephen Crane Civil War book.* Trout Fishing in America *(written in 1961 and published in 1967), a collage-like book of loosely linked stories, was described by the critic Robert Novak as "Brautigan's Hemingway book, a kind of 'Big Two-Hearted River' as seen through the disillusioned eyes of a flower child." This work sold more than two million copies and established his reputation as the voice of a generation. Like William Saroyan, Brautigan often wrote humorous stories about himself writing stories, or stories that refer to writers he admired, such as the sketch "Ernest Hemingway's Typist" in* Revenge of the Lawn: Stories 1962–1970 *(1971). This twenty-two-line story in which Brautigan imagined hearing from a friend who "had Ernest Hemingway's typist do some typing for him," ended:*

> He said that she does everything for you. You just hand her the copy and like
> a miracle you have attractive, correct spelling and punctuation that is so
> beautiful that it brings tears to your eyes and paragraphs that look like Greek
> temples and she even finishes sentences for you.
> She's Ernest Hemingway's
> She's Ernest Hemingway's typist.

Brautigan's story "1/3, 1/3, 1/3" is also from Revenge of the Lawn.

Sometimes satirizing popular fictional genres, Brautigan continued to produce novels in the 1970s, such as The Abortion: An Historical Romance 1966 *(1971),* The Hawkline Monster: A Gothic Western *(1974), and* Dreaming of Babylon: A Private Eye Novel 1942 *(1977). In his last published novel,* So the Wind Won't Blow It All Away *(1982), Brautigan apparently modeled the narrator after himself as a twelve year old, unsettled by the absence of his father and the frequent moves from town to town in the Pacific Northwest with his mother. The book's dark mood suggests the recurrent depression from which he suffered. In 1984 Brautigan committed suicide, like Ernest Hemingway, with a single gunshot wound to his head.*

1/3, 1/3, 1/3

It was all to be done in thirds. I was to get ⅓ for doing the typing, and she was to get ⅓ for doing the editing, and he was to get ⅓ for writing the novel.

We were going to divide the royalties three ways. We all shook hands on the deal, each knowing what we were supposed to do, the path before us, the gate at the end.

I was made a ⅓ partner because I had the typewriter.

I lived in a cardboard-lined shack of my own building across the street from the rundown old house the Welfare rented for her and her nine-year-old son Freddy.

The novelist lived in a trailer a mile away beside a sawmill pond where he was the watchman for the mill.

I was about seventeen and made lonely and strange by that Pacific Northwest of so many years ago, that dark, rainy land of 1952. I'm thirty-one now and I still can't figure out what I meant by living the way I did in those days.

She was one of those eternally fragile women in their late thirties and once very pretty and the object of much attention in the roadhouses and beer parlors, who are now on Welfare and their entire lives rotate around that one day a month when they get their Welfare checks.

The word "check" is the one religious word in their lives, so they always manage to use it at least three or four times in every conversation. It doesn't matter what you are talking about.

The novelist was in his late forties, tall, reddish, and looked as if life had given him an endless stream of two-timing girlfriends, five-day drunks and cars with bad transmissions.

He was writing the novel because he wanted to tell a story that had happened to him years before when he was working in the woods.

He also wanted to make some money: ⅓.

My entrance into the thing came about this way: One day I was standing in front of my shack, eating an apple and staring at a black ragged toothache sky that was about to rain.

What I was doing was like an occupation for me. I was that involved in looking at the sky and eating the apple. You would have thought that I had been hired to do it with a good salary and a pension if I stared at the sky long enough.

"HEY, YOU!" I heard somebody yell.

I looked across the mud puddle and it was the woman. She was wearing a kind of green mackinaw that she wore all the time, except when she had to visit the Welfare people downtown. Then she put on a shapeless duck-gray coat.

We lived in a poor part of town where the streets weren't paved. The street was nothing more than a big mud puddle that you had to walk around. The street was of no use to cars anymore. They traveled on a different frequency where asphalt and gravel were more sympathetic.

She was wearing a pair of white rubber boots that she always had on in the winter, a pair of boots that gave her a kind of childlike appearance. She was so fragile and firmly indebted to the Welfare Department that she often looked like a child twelve years old.

"What do you want?" I said.

"You have a typewriter, don't you?" she said. "I've walked by your shack and heard you typing. You type a lot at night."

"Yeah, I have a typewriter," I said.

"You a good typist?" she said.

"I'm all right."

"We don't have a typewriter. How would you like to go in with us?" she yelled across the mud puddle. She looked a perfect twelve years old, standing there in her white boots, the sweetheart and darling of all mud puddles.

"What's 'go in' mean?"

"Well, he's writing a novel," she said. "He's good. I'm editing it. I've read a lot of pocketbooks and the *Reader's Digest*. We need somebody who has a typewriter to type it up. You'll get ⅓. How does that sound?"

"I'd like to see the novel," I said. I didn't know what was happening. I knew she had three or four boyfriends that were always visiting her.

"Sure!" she yelled. "You have to see it to type it. Come on around. Let's go out to his place right now and you can meet him and have a look at the novel. He's a good guy. It's a wonderful book."

"OK," I said, and walked around the mud puddle to where she was standing in front of her evil dentist house, twelve years old, and approximately two miles from the Welfare office.

"Let's go," she said.

We walked over to the highway and down the highway past mud puddles and sawmill ponds and fields flooded with rain until we came to a road that went across the railroad tracks and turned down past half a dozen small sawmill ponds that were filled with black winter logs.

We talked very little and that was only about her check that was two days late and she had called the Welfare and they said they mailed the check and it should be there tomorrow, but call again tomorrow if it's not there and we'll prepare an emergency money order for you.

"Well, I hope it's there tomorrow," I said.

"So do I or I'll have to go downtown," she said.

Next to the last sawmill pond was a yellow old trailer up on blocks of wood. One look at that trailer showed that it was never going anywhere again, that the highway was in distant heaven, only to be prayed to. It was really sad with a cemeterylike chimney swirling jagged dead smoke in the air above it.

A kind of half-dog, half-cat creature was sitting on a rough plank porch that was in front of the door. The creature half-barked and half-meowed at us, "Arfeow!" and darted under the trailer, looking out at us from behind a block.

"This is it," the woman said.

The door to the trailer opened and a man stepped out onto the porch. There was a pile of firewood stacked on the porch and it was covered with a black tarp.

The man held his hand above his eyes, shielding his eyes from a bright imaginary sun, though everything had turned dark in anticipation of the rain.

"Hello, there," he said.

"Hi," I said.

"Hello, honey," she said.

He shook my hand and welcomed me to his trailer, then he gave her a little kiss on the mouth before we all went inside.

The place was small and muddy and smelled like stale rain and had a large unmade bed that looked as if it had been a partner to some of the saddest lovemaking this side of The Cross.

There was a green bushy half-table with a couple of insectlike chairs and a little sink and a small stove that was used for cooking and heating.

There were some dirty dishes in the little sink. The dishes looked as if they had always been dirty: born dirty to last forever.

I could hear a radio playing western music someplace in the trailer, but I couldn't find it. I looked all over but it was nowhere in sight. It was probably under a shirt or something.

"He's the kid with the typewriter," she said. "He'll get ⅓ for typing it."

"That sounds fair," he said. "We need somebody to type it. I've never done anything like this before."

"Why don't you show it to him?" she said. "He'd like to take a look at it."

"OK. But it isn't too carefully written," he said to me. "I only went to the fourth grade, so she's going to edit it, straighten out the grammar and commas and stuff."

There was a notebook lying on the table, next to an ashtray that probably had 600 cigarette butts in it. The notebook had a color photograph of Hopalong Cassidy on the cover.

Hopalong looked tired, as if he had spent the previous night chasing starlets all over Hollywood and barely had enough strength to get back in the saddle.

There were about twenty-five or thirty pages of writing in the notebook. It was written in a large grammar school sprawl: an unhappy marriage between printing and longhand.

"It's not finished yet," he said.

"You'll type it. I'll edit it. He'll write it," she said.

It was a story about a young logger falling in love with a waitress. The novel began in 1935 in a cafe in North Bend, Oregon.

The young logger was sitting at a table and the waitress was taking his order. She was very pretty with blond hair and rosy cheeks. The young logger was ordering veal cutlets with mashed potatoes and country gravy.

"Yeah, I'll do the editing. You can type it, can't you? It's not too bad, is it?" she said in a twelve-year-old voice with the Welfare peeking over her shoulder.

"No," I said. "It will be easy."

Suddenly the rain started to come down hard outside, without any warning, just suddenly great drops of rain that almost shook the trailer.

You sur lik veel cutlets dont you Maybell said she was ~~holding~~ holding her pensil up her mowth that was preti and red like an apl!

Onli wen you tak my oder Carl said he was a kind of bassful loger but big and strong lik his dead who ownd the starmill!

Ill mak sur you get plenti of gravi!

Just ten the caf door opend and in cam Rins Adams he was hansom and meen, everi bodi in thos parts was afrad of him but not Carl and his ~~dead~~ dad they wasnt afrad of him no sur!

Maybell shifard wen she saw him standing ther in his blac macinaw he smild at her and Carl felt his blod run hot lik scallding cofee and fiting mad!

Howdi ther Rins said Maybell blushed like a ~~flower~~ flouar while we were all sitting there in that rainy trailer, pounding at the gates of American literature.   [1971]

GRACE PALEY

*Grace Paley (b. 1922) was born in New York City. She studied at Hunter Col-
lege and New York University, and in 1942 she married for the first time. She
had two children from that marriage. In the 1950s she turned from writing
poetry to short fiction. Her first book of stories,* The Little Disturbances of
Man *(1959), established her reputation as a writer with a remarkably supple
gift for language. As Susan Sontag later said, "She is that rare kind of writer, a
natural with a voice like no one else's—funny, sad, lean, modest, energetic,
acute." When this book went out of print in 1965, its reputation survived,
strengthened by the infrequent appearances of her new stories in magazines
such as* The Atlantic Monthly, Esquire, *the* Noble Savage, Genesis West,
the New American Review, Ararat, *and* Fiction.

*During the 1960s and 1970s Paley was prominent as a nonviolent activist
protesting the Vietnam War. She served as secretary of the Greenwich Village
Peace Center, spent time in jail for her antiwar activities, and visited Hanoi
and Moscow as a member of peace delegations, defining herself as a "somewhat
combative pacifist and cooperative anarchist." During the World Peace Congress in Moscow in 1973, she condemned the Soviet Union for silencing political dissidents; the congress disassociated itself from her statement. Paley has
long been a feminist and active in the antinuclear movement. In 1974 her second volume of stories,* Enormous Changes at the Last Minute, *was published. It is a quieter, more openly personal collection of seventeen stories,
many of them, such as "A Conversation with My Father" (New American
Review, 1971), autobiographical. Her third book of stories,* Later the Same
Day, *appeared in 1985. In 1988 Paley was designated the first official New
York State Author by an act of the state legislature.*

*Paley refuses to blame her teaching jobs or her involvements as an activist
for her relatively low productivity as a writer. She says she writes "from distress." What she tries to get at in her stories is "a history of everyday life," and
her subject matter and prose style are unmistakable. Dividing her time
between a Vermont farm and a Manhattan apartment close to the Greenwich
Village School (P.S. 41), Little Tony's Unisex Hair Stylists, the Famous Ray's
Pizza, the H & H Fruit and Vegetable Market, and the Jefferson Market
Branch of the New York Public Library, Paley observes her neighbors, friends,
and family with compassion, humor, and hope. Her spare dissection of her
characters is never performed at the expense of sympathy for the human condition. It is likely that, as was true of her Russian counterpart Isaac Babel, her
production of stories will be limited. As she puts it, "There is a long time in me
between knowing and telling." The Collected Stories of Grace Paley *was
published in 1994.*

RELATED COMMENTARY: *Grace Paley, "A Conversation with Ann Charters," page 1430.*

A Conversation with My Father

My father is eighty-six years old and in bed. His heart, that bloody motor, is equally old and will not do certain jobs any more. It still floods his head with brainy light. But it won't let his legs carry the weight of his body around the house. Despite my metaphors, this muscle failure is not due to his old heart, he says, but to a potassium shortage. Sitting on one pillow, leaning on three, he offers last-minute advice and makes a request.

"I would like you to write a simple story just once more," he says, "the kind de Maupassant wrote, or Chekhov, the kind you used to write. Just recognizable people and then write down what happened to them next."

I say, "Yes, why not? That's possible." I want to please him, though I don't remember writing that way. I *would* like to try to tell such a story, if he means the kind that begins: "There was a woman . . ." followed by plot, the absolute line between two points which I've always despised. Not for literary reasons, but because it takes all hope away. Everyone, real or invented, deserves the open destiny of life.

Finally I thought of a story that had been happening for a couple of years right across the street. I wrote it down, then read it aloud. "Pa," I said, "how about this? Do you mean something like this?"

> Once in my time there was a woman and she had a son. They lived nicely, in a small apartment in Manhattan. This boy at about fifteen became a junkie, which is not unusual in our neighborhood. In order to maintain her close friendship with him, she became a junkie too. She said it was part of the youth culture, with which she felt very much at home. After a while, for a number of reasons, the boy gave it all up and left the city and his mother in disgust. Hopeless and alone, she grieved. We all visit her.

"O.K., Pa, that's it," I said, "an unadorned and miserable tale."

"But that's not what I mean," my father said. "You misunderstood me on purpose. You know there's a lot more to it. You know that. You left everything out. Turgenev wouldn't do that. Chekhov wouldn't do that. There are in fact Russian writers you never heard of, you don't have an inkling of, as good as anyone, who can write a plain ordinary story, who would not leave out what you have left out. I object not to facts but to people sitting in trees talking senselessly, voices from who knows where. . . ."

"Forget that one, Pa, what have I left out now? In this one?"

"Her looks, for instance."

"Oh. Quite handsome, I think. Yes."

"Her hair?"

"Dark, with heavy braids, as though she were a girl or a foreigner."

"What were her parents like, her stock? That she became such a person. It's interesting, you know."

"From out of town. Professional people. The first to be divorced in their county. How's that? Enough?" I asked.

"With you, it's all a joke," he said. "What about the boy's father? Why didn't you mention him? Who was he? Or was the boy born out of wedlock?"

"Yes," I said. "He was born out of wedlock."

"For Godsakes, doesn't anyone in your stories get married? Doesn't anyone have the time to run down to City Hall before they jump into bed?"

"No," I said. "In real life, yes. But in my stories, no."

"Why do you answer me like that?"

"Oh, Pa, this is a simple story about a smart woman who came to N.Y.C. full of interest love trust excitement very up to date, and about her son, what a hard time she had in this world. Married or not, it's of small consequence."

"It is of great consequence," he said.

"O.K.," I said.

"O.K. O.K. yourself," he said, "but listen. I believe you that she's good-looking, but I don't think she was so smart."

"That's true," I said. "Actually that's the trouble with stories. People start out fantastic. You think they're extraordinary, but it turns out as the work goes along, they're just average with a good education. Sometimes the other way around, the person's a kind of dumb innocent, but he outwits you and you can't even think of an ending good enough."

"What do you do then?" he asked. He had been a doctor for a couple of decades and then an artist for a couple of decades and he's still interested in details, craft, technique.

"Well, you just have to let the story lie around till some agreement can be reached between you and the stubborn hero."

"Aren't you talking silly now?" he asked. "Start again," he said. "It so happens I'm not going out this evening. Tell the story again. See what you can do this time."

"O.K.," I said. "But it's not a five-minute job." Second attempt:

Once, across the street from us, there was a fine handsome woman, our neighbor. She had a son whom she loved because she'd known him since birth (in helpless chubby infancy, and in the wrestling, hugging ages, seven to ten, as well as earlier and later). This boy, when he fell into the fist of adolescence, became a junkie. He was not a hopeless one. He was in fact hopeful, an ideologue and successful converter. With his busy brilliance, he wrote persuasive articles for his high-school newspaper. Seeking a wider audience, using important connections, he drummed into Lower Manhattan newsstand distribution a periodical called *Oh! Golden Horse!*

In order to keep him from feeling guilty (because guilt is the stony heart of nine tenths of all clinically diagnosed cancers in America today, she said), and because she had always believed in giving bad habits room at home where one could keep an eye on them, she too became a junkie. Her kitchen was famous for a while — a center for intellectual addicts who knew what they were doing. A few felt artistic like Coleridge[1] and others were scientific and revolutionary like Leary.[2] Although she was often high herself, certain good mothering reflexes remained, and she saw to it that there was lots of orange juice around and honey and milk and vitamin pills. However, she never cooked anything but chili, and that no more than once a week. She explained, when we talked to her, seriously, with neighborly concern, that it was her part in the youth culture and she would rather be with the young, it was an honor, than with her own generation.

One week, while nodding through an Antonioni film, this boy was severely jabbed by the elbow of a stern and proselytizing girl, sitting beside him. She offered immediate apricots and nuts for his sugar level, spoke to him sharply, and took him home.

She had heard of him and his work and she herself published, edited, and wrote a competitive journal called *Man Does Live by Bread Alone*. In the organic heat of her continuous presence he could not help but become interested once more in his muscles, his arteries, and nerve connections. In fact he began to love them, treasure them, praise them with funny little songs in *Man Does Live*. . . .

> the fingers of my flesh transcend
> my transcendental soul
> the tightness in my shoulders end
> my teeth have made me whole

To the mouth of his head (that glory of will and determination) he brought hard apples, nuts, wheat germ, and soybean oil. He said to his old friends, From now on, I guess I'll keep my wits about me. I'm going on the natch. He said he was about to begin a spiritual deep-breathing journey. How about you too, Mom? he asked kindly.

His conversion was so radiant, splendid, that neighborhood kids his age began to say that he had never been a real addict at all, only a journalist along for the smell of the story. The mother tried several times to give up what had become without her son and his friends a lonely habit. This effort only brought it to supportable levels. The boy and his girl took their electronic mimeograph and moved to the bushy edge of another borough. They were very strict. They said they would not see her again until she had been off drugs for sixty days.

At home alone in the evening, weeping, the mother read and reread the seven issues of *Oh! Golden Horse!* They seemed to her as truthful as ever. We often crossed the street to visit and console. But if we mentioned any of our children who were at college or in the hos-

---

[1]Samuel Taylor Coleridge (1772–1834), English romantic poet, was an opium addict.
[2]Timothy Leary (1920–1996), sometime Harvard professor of psychology and early advocate of the use of LSD.

pital or dropouts at home, she would cry out, My baby! My baby! and burst into terrible, face-scarring, time-consuming tears. The End.

First my father was silent, then he said, "Number One: You have a nice sense of humor. Number Two: I see you can't tell a plain story. So don't waste time." Then he said sadly, "Number Three: I suppose that means she was alone, she was left like that, his mother. Alone. Probably sick?"

I said, "Yes."

"Poor woman. Poor girl, to be born in a time of fools, to live among fools. The end. The end. You were right to put that down. The end."

I didn't want to argue, but I had to say, "Well, it is not necessarily the end, Pa."

"Yes," he said, "what a tragedy. The end of a person."

"No, Pa," I begged him. "It doesn't have to be. She's only about forty. She could be a hundred different things in this world as time goes on. A teacher or a social worker. An ex-junkie! Sometimes it's better than having a master's in education."

"Jokes," he said. "As a writer that's your main trouble. You don't want to recognize it. Tragedy! Plain tragedy! Historical tragedy! No hope. The end."

"Oh, Pa," I said. "She could change."

"In your own life, too, you have to look it in the face." He took a couple of nitroglycerin. "Turn to five," he said, pointing to the dial on the oxygen tank. He inserted the tubes into his nostrils and breathed deep. He closed his eyes and said, "No."

I had promised the family to always let him have the last word when arguing, but in this case I had a different responsibility. That woman lives across the street. She's my knowledge and my invention. I'm sorry for her. I'm not going to leave her there in that house crying. (Actually neither would Life, which unlike me has no pity.)

Therefore: She did change. Of course her son never came home again. But right now, she's the receptionist in a storefront community clinic in the East Village. Most of the customers are young people, some old friends. The head doctor has said to her, "If we only had three people in this clinic with your experiences. . . ."

"The doctor said that?" My father took the oxygen tubes out of his nostrils and said, "Jokes. Jokes again."

"No, Pa, it could really happen that way, it's a funny world nowadays."

"No," he said. "Truth first. She will slide back. A person must have character. She does not."

"No, Pa," I said. "That's it. She's got a job. Forget it. She's in that storefront working."

"How long will it be?" he asked. "Tragedy! You too. When will you look it in the face?" [1974]

RAYMOND CARVER

*R*aymond Carver (1938–1988) grew up in a logging town in Oregon, where his father worked in a sawmill and his mother held odd jobs. After graduating from high school, Carver married at the age of nineteen and had two children. Working hard to support his wife and family, he managed to enroll briefly in 1958 as a student at Chico State College in California, where he took a creative writing course taught by the then unknown young novelist John Gardner. Carver credited Gardner for giving him a strong sense of direction as a writer: "A writer's values and craft. This is what the man taught and what he stood for, and this is what I've kept by me in the years since that brief but all-important time." In 1963 Carver received his B.A. degree from Humboldt State College in northern California. The following year he studied writing at the University of Iowa. But the 1960s were difficult for him and his wife.

> I learned a long time ago when my kids were little and we had no money, and we were working our hearts out and weren't getting anywhere, even though we were giving it our best, my wife and I, that there were more important things than writing a poem or a story. That was a very hard realization for me to come to. But it came to me, and I had to accept it or die. Getting milk and food on the table, getting the rent paid, if a choice had to be made, then I had to forgo writing.

Carver's desire to be a writer was so strong that he kept on writing long after the "cold facts" of his life told him he ought to quit. His first collection of stories, Will You Please Be Quiet, Please? was nominated for the National Book Award in 1976. Four more collections of stories followed, along with five books of poetry, before his death from lung cancer. Critics have noted the evolution of Carver's style that resulted in part from the rewriting of his editor, Gordon Lish. Their collaboration is evident in the hard-edged, detached minimalist style of Carver's middle period, exemplified by the stories in his collection What We Talk About When We Talk About Love (1981). In his last years, Carver developed his own more expansive style, as in the collection Cathedral (1983) and the stories in his final book of short fiction, Where I'm Calling From: New and Selected Stories (1988). "Are These Actual Miles?"— originally titled "What Is It?" (Esquire, 1972)—appeared in his first collection under that early title, but was revised for his last. The version included here is from the later volume.

The writer Richard Ford described his experience listening to Carver read "Are These Actual Miles?" at a writers' conference in Dallas in 1977, when Ford felt that "a consequence of the story was seemingly to intensify life, even dignify it, and to locate in it shadowed corners and niches that needed revealing so that we readers could practice life better ourselves." Carver showed his audience

> what a story could do in terms of artifice, concision, strong feeling, shapeliness, high and surprising dramatics. The story was definitely about some-

thing, and you could follow it easily—it was about what two people did in adversity which changed their lives. But here was no ponderous naturalism. Nothing extra. There were barely the rudiments of realism. This was highly stylized, artistic writing with life, not art, as its subject. And to be exposed to it was to be bowled over.

RELATED COMMENTARY: *Raymond Carver, "Creative Writing 101," page 1326.*

Are These Actual Miles?

Fact is the car needs to be sold in a hurry, and Leo sends Toni out to do it. Toni is smart and has personality. She used to sell children's encyclopedias door to door. She signed him up, even though he didn't have kids. Afterward, Leo asked her for a date, and the date led to this. This deal has to be cash, and it has to be done tonight. Tomorrow somebody they owe might slap a lien on the car. Monday they'll be in court, home free—but word on them went out yesterday, when their lawyer mailed the letters of intention. The hearing on Monday is nothing to worry about, the lawyer has said. They'll be asked some questions, and they'll sign some papers, and that's it. But sell the convertible, he said—today, *tonight*. They can hold onto the little car, Leo's car, no problem. But they go into court with that big convertible, the court will take it, and that's that.

Toni dresses up. It's four o'clock in the afternoon. Leo worries the lots will close. But Toni takes her time dressing. She puts on a new white blouse, wide lacy cuffs, the new two-piece suit, new heels. She transfers the stuff from her straw purse into the new patent-leather handbag. She studies the lizard makeup pouch and puts that in too. Toni has been two hours on her hair and face. Leo stands in the bedroom doorway and taps his lips with his knuckles, watching.

"You're making me nervous," she says. "I wish you wouldn't just stand," she says. "So tell me how I look."

"You look fine," he says. "You look great. I'd buy a car from you anytime."

"But you don't have money," she says, peering into the mirror. She pats her hair, frowns. "And your credit's lousy. You're nothing," she says. "Teasing," she says and looks at him in the mirror. "Don't be serious," she says. "It has to be done, so I'll do it. You take it out, you'd be lucky to get three, four hundred and we both know it. Honey, you'd be lucky if you didn't have to pay *them*." She gives her hair a final pat, gums her lips, blots the lipstick with a tissue. She turns away from the mirror and picks up her purse. "I'll have to have dinner or something, I told you that already, that's the way they work, I know them. But don't worry, I'll get out of it," she says. "I can handle it."

"Jesus," Leo says, "did you have to say that?"

She looks at him steadily. "Wish me luck," she says.

"Luck," he says. "You have the pink slip?" he says.

She nods. He follows her through the house, a tall woman with a small high bust, broad hips and thighs. He scratches a pimple on his neck. "You're sure?" he says. "Make sure. You have to have the pink slip."

"I have the pink slip," she says.

"Make sure."

She starts to say something, instead looks at herself in the front window and then shakes her head.

"At least call," he says. "Let me know what's going on."

"I'll call," she says. "Kiss, kiss. Here," she says and points to the corner of her mouth. "Careful," she says.

He holds the door for her. "Where are you going to try first?" he says. She moves past him and onto the porch.

Ernest Williams looks from across the street. In his Bermuda shorts, stomach hanging, he looks at Leo and Toni as he directs a spray onto his begonias. Once, last winter, during the holidays, when Toni and the kids were visiting his mother's, Leo brought a woman home. Nine o'clock the next morning, a cold foggy Saturday, Leo walked the woman to the car, surprised Ernest Williams on the sidewalk with a newspaper in his hand. Fog drifted, Ernest Williams stared, then slapped the paper against his leg, hard.

Leo recalls that slap, hunches his shoulders, says, "You have someplace in mind first?"

"I'll just go down the line," she says. "The first lot, then I'll just go down the line."

"Open at nine hundred," he says. "Then come down. Nine hundred is low bluebook, even on a cash deal."

"I know where to start," she says.

Ernest Williams turns the hose in their direction. He stares at them through the spray of water. Leo has an urge to cry out a confession.

"Just making sure," he says.

"Okay, okay," she says. "I'm off."

It's her car, they call it her car, and that makes it all the worse. They bought it new that summer three years ago. She wanted something to do after the kids started school, so she went back selling. He was working six days a week in the fiber-glass plant. For a while they didn't know how to spend the money. Then they put a thousand on the convertible and doubled and tripled the payments until in a year they had it paid. Earlier, while she was dressing, he took the jack and spare from the trunk and emptied the glove compartment of pencils, matchbooks, Blue Chip stamps. Then he washed it and vacuumed inside. The red hood and fenders shine.

"Good luck," he says and touches her elbow.

She nods. He sees she is already gone, already negotiating.

"Things are going to be different!" he calls to her as she reaches the driveway. "We start over Monday. I mean it."

Ernest Williams looks at them and turns his head and spits. She gets into the car and lights a cigarette.

"This time next week!" Leo calls again. "Ancient history!"

He waves as she backs into the street. She changes gear and starts ahead. She accelerates and the tires give a little scream.

In the kitchen Leo pours Scotch and carries the drink to the backyard. The kids are at his mother's. There was a letter three days ago, his name penciled on the outside of the dirty envelope, the only letter all summer not demanding payment in full. We are having fun, the letter said. We like Grandma. We have a new dog called Mr. Six. He is nice. We love him. Good-bye.

He goes for another drink. He adds ice and sees that his hand trembles. He holds the hand over the sink. He looks at the hand for a while, sets down the glass, and holds out the other hand. Then he picks up the glass and goes back outside to sit on the steps. He recalls when he was a kid his dad pointing at a fine house, a tall white house surrounded by apple trees and a high white rail fence. "That's Finch," his dad said admiringly. "He's been in bankruptcy at least twice. Look at that house." But bankruptcy is a company collapsing utterly, executives cutting their wrists and throwing themselves from windows, thousands of men on the street.

Leo and Toni still had furniture. Leo and Toni had furniture and Toni and the kids had clothes. Those things were exempt. What else? Bicycles for the kids, but these he had sent to his mother's for safekeeping. The portable air-conditioner and the appliances, new washer and dryer, trucks came for those things weeks ago. What else did they have? This and that, nothing mainly, stuff that wore out or fell to pieces long ago. But there were some big parties back there, some fine travel. To Reno and Tahoe, at eighty with the top down and the radio playing. Food, that was one of the big items. They gorged on food. He figures thousands on luxury items alone. Toni would go to the grocery and put in everything she saw. "I had to do without when I was a kid," she says. "These kids are not going to do without," as if he'd been insisting they should. She joins all the book clubs. "We never had books around when I was a kid," she says as she tears open the heavy packages. They enroll in the record clubs for something to play on the new stereo. They sign up for it all. Even a pedigreed terrier named Ginger. He paid two hundred and found her run over in the street a week later. They buy what they want. If they can't pay, they charge. They sign up.

His undershirt is wet; he can feel the sweat rolling from his underarms. He sits on the step with the empty glass in his hand and watches the shadows fill up the yard. He stretches, wipes his face. He listens to the traffic on the highway and considers whether he should go to the basement, stand on the utility sink, and hang himself with his belt. He understands he is willing to be dead.

Inside he makes a large drink and he turns the TV on and he fixes something to eat. He sits at the table with chili and crackers and watches something about a blind detective. He clears the table. He washes the pan and the bowl, dries these things and puts them away, then allows himself a look at the clock.

It's after nine. She's been gone nearly five hours.

He pours Scotch, adds water, carries the drink to the living room. He sits on the couch but finds his shoulders so stiff they won't let him lean back. He stares at the screen and sips, and soon he goes for another drink. He sits again. A news program begins—it's ten o'clock—and he says, "God, what in God's name has gone wrong?" and goes to the kitchen to return with more Scotch. He sits, he closes his eyes, and opens them when he hears the telephone ringing.

"I wanted to call," she says.

"Where are you?" he says. He hears piano music, and his heart moves.

"I don't know," she says. "Someplace. We're having a drink, then we're going someplace else for dinner. I'm with the sales manager. He's crude, but he's all right. He bought the car. I have to go now. I was on my way to the ladies and saw the phone."

"Did somebody buy the car?" Leo says. He looks out the kitchen window to the place in the drive where she always parks.

"I told you," she says. "I have to go now."

"Wait, wait a minute, for Christ's sake," he says. "Did somebody buy the car or not?"

"He had his checkbook out when I left," she says. "I have to go now. I have to go to the bathroom."

"Wait!" he yells. The line goes dead. He listens to the dial tone. "Jesus Christ," he says as he stands with the receiver in his hand.

He circles the kitchen and goes back to the living room. He sits. He gets up. In the bathroom he brushes his teeth very carefully. Then he uses dental floss. He washes his face and goes back to the kitchen. He looks at the clock and takes a clean glass from a set that has a hand of playing cards painted on each glass. He fills the glass with ice. He stares for a while at the glass he left in the sink.

He sits against one end of the couch and puts his legs up at the other end. He looks at the screen, realizes he can't make out what the people are saying. He turns the empty glass in his hand and considers biting off the rim. He shivers for a time and thinks of going to bed, though he knows he will dream of a large woman with gray hair. In the dream he is always leaning over tying his shoelaces. When he straightens up, she looks at him, and he bends to tie again. He looks at his hand. It makes a fist as he watches. The telephone is ringing.

"Where are you, honey?" he says slowly, gently.

"We're at this restaurant," she says, her voice strong, bright.

"Honey, which restaurant?" he says. He puts the heel of his hand against his eye and pushes.

"Downtown someplace," she says. "I think it's New Jimmy's. Excuse me," she says to someone off the line, "is this place New Jimmy's? This is New Jimmy's, Leo," she says to him. "Everything is all right, we're almost finished, then he's going to bring me home."

"Honey?" he says. He holds the receiver against his ear and rocks back and forth, eyes closed. "Honey?"

"I have to go," she says. "I wanted to call. Anyway, guess how much?"

"Honey," he says.

"Six and a quarter," she says. "I have it in my purse. He said there's no market for convertibles. I guess we're born lucky," she says and laughs. "I told him everything. I think I had to."

"Honey," Leo says.

"What?" she says.

"Please, honey," Leo says.

"He said he sympathizes," she says. "But he would have said anything." She laughs again. "He said personally he'd rather be classified a robber or a rapist than a bankrupt. He's nice enough, though," she says.

"Come home," Leo says. "Take a cab and come home."

"I can't," she says. "I told you, we're halfway through dinner."

"I'll come for you," he says.

"No," she says. "I said we're just finishing. I told you, it's part of the deal. They're out for all they can get. But don't worry, we're about to leave. I'll be home in a little while." She hangs up.

In a few minutes he calls New Jimmy's. A man answers. "New Jimmy's has closed for the evening," the man says.

"I'd like to talk to my wife," Leo says.

"Does she work here?" the man asks. "Who is she?"

"She's a customer," Leo says. "She's with someone. A business person."

"Would I know her?" the man says. "What is her name?"

"I don't think you know her," Leo says.

"That's all right," Leo says. "That's all right. I see her now."

"Thank you for calling New Jimmy's," the man says.

Leo hurries to the window. A car he doesn't recognize slows in front of the house, then picks up speed. He waits. Two, three hours later, the telephone rings again. There is no one at the other end when he picks up the receiver. There is only a dial tone.

"I'm right here!" Leo screams into the receiver.

Near dawn he hears footsteps on the porch. He gets up from the couch. The set hums, the screen glows. He opens the door. She bumps the wall coming in. She grins. Her face is puffy, as if she's been sleeping under sedation. She works her lips, ducks heavily and sways as he cocks his fist.

"Go ahead," she says thickly. She stands there swaying. Then she makes a noise and lunges, catches his shirt, tears it down the front. "Bankrupt!" she screams. She twists loose, grabs and tears his undershirt at the neck. "You son of a bitch," she says, clawing.

He squeezes her wrists, then lets go, steps back, looking for something heavy. She stumbles as she heads for the bedroom. "Bankrupt," she mutters. He hears her fall on the bed and groan.

He waits awhile, then splashes water on his face and goes to the bedroom. He turns the lights on, looks at her, and begins to take her clothes off. He pulls and pushes her from side to side undressing her. She says something in her sleep and moves her hand. He takes off her underpants, looks at them closely under the light, and throws them into a corner. He turns back the covers and rolls her in, naked. Then he opens her purse. He is reading the check when he hears the car come into the drive.

He looks through the front curtain and sees the convertible in the drive, its motor running smoothly, the headlamps burning, and he closes and opens his eyes. He sees a tall man come around in front of the car and up to the front porch. The man lays something on the porch and starts back to the car. He wears a white linen suit.

Leo turns on the porch light and opens the door cautiously. Her makeup pouch lies on the top step. The man looks at Leo across the front of the car, and then gets back inside and releases the handbrake.

"Wait!" Leo calls and starts down the steps. The man brakes the car as Leo walks in front of the lights. The car creaks against the brake. Leo tries to pull the two pieces of his shirt together, tries to bunch it all into his trousers.

"What is it you want?" the man says. "Look," the man says, "I have to go. No offense. I buy and sell cars, right? The lady left her makeup. She's a fine lady, very refined. What is it?"

Leo leans against the door and looks at the man. The man takes his hands off the wheel and puts them back. He drops the gear into reverse and the car moves backward a little.

"I want to tell you," Leo says and wets his lips.

The light in Ernest Williams' bedroom goes on. The shade rolls up.

Leo shakes his head, tucks in his shirt again. He steps back from the car. "Monday," he says.

"Monday," the man says and watches for sudden movement.

Leo nods slowly.

"Well, goodnight," the man says and coughs. "Take it easy, hear? Monday, that's right. Okay, then." He takes his foot off the brake, puts it on again after he has rolled back two or three feet. "Hey, one question. Between friends, are these actual miles?" The man waits, then clears his throat. "Okay, look, it doesn't matter either way," the man says. "I have to go. Take it easy." He backs into the street, pulls away quickly, and turns the corner without stopping.

Leo tucks at his shirt and goes back in the house. He locks the front door and checks it. Then he goes to the bedroom and locks that door and turns back the covers. He looks at her before he flicks the light. He takes off his clothes, folds them carefully on the floor, and gets in beside her. He lies on his back for a time and pulls the hair on his stomach, considering. He looks at the bedroom door, outlined now in the faint outside light. Presently he reaches out his hand and touches her hip. She does not move. He turns on his side and puts his hand on her hip. He runs his fingers over her hip and feels the stretch marks there. They are like roads, and he traces them in her flesh. He runs his fingers back and forth, first one, then another. They run everywhere in her flesh, dozens, perhaps hundreds of them. He remembers waking up the morning after they bought the car, seeing it, there in the drive, in the sun, gleaming. [1972, 1988]

ALICE WALKER

Alice Walker (b. 1944) was the eighth and youngest child of Willie Lee and Minnie Lou Grant Walker, sharecroppers in Eatonton, Georgia. Walker did well in school, encouraged by her teachers and her mother, whose stories she loved as "a walking history of our community." For two years, Walker attended Spelman College in Atlanta, the oldest college for black women in the United States. Then she studied at Sarah Lawrence College in New York, where she began her writing career by publishing a book of poetry, Once *(1968). Since that time Walker has published several collections of poetry, novels, volumes of short stories, and* Living by the Word *(1988), a book of essays. Her best-known novel,* The Color Purple *(1982), won the American Book Award and the Pulitzer Prize and was made into a motion picture. Later books are* The Temple of My Familiar *(1989),* Possessing the Secret of Joy *(1992), and* Anything We Love Can Be Saved: A Writer's Activism *(1997).*

Walker's works show her commitment to the idea of radical social change. She was active in the civil rights movement in Mississippi, where she met and married a civil rights lawyer from whom she separated after the birth of their daughter. In confronting the painful struggle of black people's history, Walker asserts that the creativity of black women, the extent to which they are permitted to express themselves, is a measure of the health of the entire American society. She calls herself a "womanist," her term for a black feminist. In her definition, "womanism" is preferable to "feminism" because, as she has said,

> part of our tradition as black women is that we are universalists. Black children, yellow children, red children, brown children, that is the black woman's normal, day-to-day relationship. In my family alone, we are about four different colors. When a black woman looks at the world, it is so different . . . when I look at the people in Iran they look like kinfolk. When I look at the people in Cuba, they look like my uncles and nieces.

Walker credits many writers for influencing her prose style in her short fiction. Virginia Woolf, Zora Neale Hurston, and Gabriel García Márquez seem to Walker to be "like musicians; at one with their cultures and their historical subconscious." Her two books of stories show a clear progression of theme. The women of In Love and Trouble *(1973) struggle against injustice almost in spite of themselves, as does the protagonist in "Everyday Use" from that collection; the heroines of* You Can't Keep a Good Woman Down *(1981) consciously challenge conventions. Walker has said, "Writing really helps you heal yourself. I think if you write long enough, you will be a healthy person. That is, if you write what you need to write, as opposed to what will make money, or what will make fame." "Everyday Use" was first published in* Harper's Magazine *in 1973.*

RELATED COMMENTARY: *Alice Walker, "Zora Neale Hurston: A Cautionary Tale and a Partisan View," page 1469.*

Everyday Use

I will wait for her in the yard that Maggie and I made so clean and wavy yesterday afternoon. A yard like this is more comfortable than most people know. It is not just a yard. It is like an extended living room. When the hard clay is swept clean as a floor and the fine sand around the edges lined with tiny, irregular grooves, anyone can come and sit and look up into the elm tree and wait for the breezes that never come inside the house.

Maggie will be nervous until after her sister goes: she will stand hopelessly in corners, homely and ashamed of the burn scars down her arms and legs, eyeing her sister with a mixture of envy and awe. She thinks her sister has held life always in the palm of one hand, that "no" is a word the world never learned to say to her.

You've no doubt seen those TV shows where the child who has "made it" is confronted, as a surprise, by her own mother and father, tottering in weakly from backstage. (A pleasant surprise, of course: What would they do if parent and child came on the show only to curse out and insult each other?) On TV mother and child embrace and smile into each other's faces. Sometimes the mother and father weep, the child wraps them in her arms and leans across the table to tell how she would not have made it without their help. I have seen these programs.

Sometimes I dream a dream in which Dee and I are suddenly brought together on a TV program of this sort. Out of a dark and soft-seated limousine I am ushered into a bright room filled with many people. There I meet a smiling, gray, sporty man like Johnny Carson who shakes my hand and tells me what a fine girl I have. Then we are on the stage and Dee is embracing me with tears in her eyes. She pins on my dress a large orchid, even though she has told me once that she thinks orchids are tacky flowers.

In real life I am a large, big-boned woman with rough, man-working hands. In the winter I wear flannel nightgowns to bed and overalls during the day. I can kill and clean a hog as mercilessly as a man. My fat keeps me hot in zero weather. I can work outside all day, breaking ice to get water for washing; I can eat pork liver cooked over the open fire minutes after it comes steaming from the hog. One winter I knocked a bull calf straight in the brain between the eyes with a sledge hammer and had the meat hung up to chill before nightfall. But of course all this does not show on television. I am the way my daughter would want me to be: a hundred pounds lighter, my skin like an uncooked barley pancake. My hair glistens in the hot bright lights. Johnny Carson has much to do to keep up with my quick and witty tongue.

But that is a mistake. I know even before I wake up. Who ever knew a Johnson with a quick tongue? Who can even imagine me looking a strange white man in the eye? It seems to me I have talked to them always with one foot raised in flight, with my head turned in whichever way is farthest from them. Dee, though. She would always look anyone in the eye. Hesitation was no part of her nature.

"How do I look, Mama?" Maggie says, showing just enough of her thin body enveloped in pink skirt and red blouse for me to know she's there, almost hidden by the door.

"Come out into the yard," I say.

Have you ever seen a lame animal, perhaps a dog run over by some careless person rich enough to own a car, sidle up to someone who is ignorant enough to be kind to him? That is the way my Maggie walks. She has been like this, chin on chest, eyes on ground, feet in shuffle, ever since the fire that burned the other house to the ground.

Dee is lighter than Maggie, with nicer hair and a fuller figure. She's a woman now, though sometimes I forget. How long ago was it that the other house burned? Ten, twelve years? Sometimes I can still hear the flames and feel Maggie's arms sticking to me, her hair smoking and her dress falling off her in little black papery flakes. Her eyes seemed stretched open, blazed open by the flames reflected in them. And Dee. I see her standing off under the sweet gum tree she used to dig gum out of; a look of concentration on her face as she watched the last dingy gray board of the house fall in toward the red-hot brick chimney. Why don't you do a dance around the ashes? I'd wanted to ask her. She had hated the house that much.

I used to think she hated Maggie, too. But that was before we raised the money, the church and me, to send her to Augusta to school. She used to read to us without pity; forcing words, lies, other folks' habits, whole lives upon us two, sitting trapped and ignorant underneath her voice. She washed us in a river of make-believe, burned us with a lot of knowledge we didn't necessarily need to know. Pressed us to her with the serious way she read, to shove us away at just the moment, like dimwits, we seemed about to understand.

Dee wanted nice things. A yellow organdy dress to wear to her graduation from high school; black pumps to match a green suit she'd made from an old suit somebody gave me. She was determined to stare down any disaster in her efforts. Her eyelids would not flicker for minutes at a time. Often I fought off the temptation to shake her. At sixteen she had a style of her own: and knew what style was.

I never had an education myself. After second grade the school was closed down. Don't ask me why: in 1927 colored asked fewer questions than they do now. Sometimes Maggie reads to me. She stumbles along good-naturedly but can't see well. She knows she is not bright. Like good looks and money, quickness passed her by. She will marry John Thomas (who has mossy teeth in an earnest face) and then I'll be free to sit here and I guess just sing church songs to myself. Although I never was a good singer. Never could carry a tune. I was always better at a man's job. I used to love to milk till I was hooked in the side in '49. Cows are soothing and slow and don't bother you, unless you try to milk them the wrong way.

I have deliberately turned my back on the house. It is three rooms, just like the one that burned, except the roof is tin; they don't make shingle roofs any more. There are no real windows, just some holes cut in the sides, like the portholes in a ship, but not round and not square, with rawhide holding the shutters up on the outside. This house is in a pasture, too, like the other one. No doubt when Dee sees it she will want to tear it down. She wrote me once that no matter where we "choose" to live, she will manage to come see us. But she will never bring her friends. Maggie and I thought about this and Maggie asked me, "Mama, when did Dee ever *have* any friends?"

She had a few. Furtive boys in pink shirts hanging about on washday after school. Nervous girls who never laughed. Impressed with her they worshiped the well-turned phrase, the cute shape, the scalding humor that erupted like bubbles in lye. She read to them.

When she was courting Jimmy T she didn't have much time to pay to us, but turned all her faultfinding power on him. He *flew* to marry a cheap city gal from a family of ignorant flashy people. She hardly had time to recompose herself.

When she comes I will meet—but there they are!

Maggie attempts to make a dash for the house, in her shuffling way, but I stay her with my hand. "Come back here," I say. And she stops and tries to dig a well in the sand with her toe.

It is hard to see them clearly through the strong sun. But even the first glimpse of leg out of the car tells me it is Dee. Her feet were always neat-looking, as if God himself had shaped them with a certain style. From the other side of the car comes a short, stocky man. Hair is all over his head a foot long and hanging from his chin like a kinky mule tail. I hear Maggie suck in her breath. "Uhnnnh," is what it sounds like. Like when you see the wriggling end of a snake just in front of your foot on the road. "Uhnnnh."

Dee next. A dress down to the ground, in this hot weather. A dress so loud it hurts my eyes. There are yellows and oranges enough to throw back the light of the sun. I feel my whole face warming from the heat waves it throws out. Earrings gold, too, and hanging down to her shoulders. Bracelets dangling and making noises when she moves her arm up to shake the folds of the dress out of her armpits. The dress is loose and flows, and as she walks closer, I like it. I hear Maggie go "Uhnnnh" again. It is her sister's hair. It stands straight up like the wool on a sheep. It is black as night and around the edges are two long pigtails that rope about like small lizards disappearing behind her ears.

"Wa-su-zo-Tean-o!" she says, coming on in that gliding way the dress makes her move. The short stocky fellow with the hair to his navel is all grinning and he follows up with "Asalamalakim, my mother and sister!" He moves to hug Maggie but she falls back, right up against the back of my chair. I feel her trembling there and when I look up I see the perspiration falling off her chin.

"Don't get up," says Dee. Since I am stout it takes something of a push. You can see me trying to move a second or two before I make it. She turns, showing white heels through her sandals, and goes back to the car. Out she peeks next with a Polaroid. She stoops down quickly and lines up picture after picture of me sitting there in front of the house with Maggie cowering behind me. She never takes a shot without making sure the house is included. When a cow comes nibbling around the edge of the yard she snaps it and me *and* the house. Then she puts the Polaroid in the back seat of the car, and comes up and kisses me on the forehead.

Meanwhile Asalamalakim is going through the motions with Maggie's hand. Maggie's hand is as limp as a fish, and probably as cold, despite the sweat, and she keeps trying to pull it back. It looks like Asalamalakim wants to shake hands but wants to do it fancy. Or maybe he don't know how people shake hands. Anyhow, he soon gives up on Maggie.

"Well," I say. "Dee."

"No, Mama," she says. "Not 'Dee,' Wangero Leewanika Kemanjo!"

"What happened to 'Dee'?" I wanted to know.

"She's dead," Wangero said. "I couldn't bear it any longer being named after the people who oppress me."

"You know as well as me you was named after your aunt Dicie," I said. Dicie is my sister. She named Dee. We called her "Big Dee" after Dee was born.

"But who was *she* named after?" asked Wangero.

"I guess after Grandma Dee," I said.

"And who was she named after?" asked Wangero.

"Her mother," I said, and saw Wangero was getting tired. "That's about as far back as I can trace it," I said. Though, in fact, I probably could have carried it back beyond the Civil War through the branches.

"Well," said Asalamalakim, "there you are."

"Uhnnnh," I heard Maggie say.

"There I was not," I said, "before 'Dicie' cropped up in our family, so why should I try to trace it that far back?"

He just stood there grinning, looking down on me like somebody inspecting a Model A car. Every once in a while he and Wangero sent eye signals over my head.

"How do you pronounce this name?" I asked.

"You don't have to call me by it if you don't want to," said Wangero.

"Why shouldn't I?" I asked. "If that's what you want us to call you, we'll call you."

"I know it might sound awkward at first," said Wangero.

"I'll get used to it," I said. "Ream it out again."

Well, soon we got the name out of the way. Asalamalakim had a name twice as long and three times as hard. After I tripped over it two or three times he told me to just call him Hakim-a-barber. I wanted to ask him was he a barber, but I didn't really think he was, so I didn't ask.

"You must belong to those beef-cattle peoples down the road," I said. They said "Asalamalakim" when they met you, too, but they didn't shake hands. Always too busy: feeding the cattle, fixing the fences, putting up salt-lick shelters, throwing down hay. When the white folks poisoned some of the herd the men stayed up all night with rifles in their hands. I walked a mile and a half just to see the sight.

Hakim-a-barber said, "I accept some of their doctrines, but farming and raising cattle is not my style." (They didn't tell me, and I didn't ask, whether Wangero [Dee] had really gone and married him.)

We sat down to eat and right away he said he didn't eat collards and pork was unclean. Wangero, though, went on through the chitlins and corn bread, the greens and everything else. She talked a blue streak over the sweet potatoes. Everything delighted her. Even the fact that we still used the benches her daddy made for the table when we couldn't afford to buy chairs.

"Oh, Mama!" she cried. Then turned to Hakim-a-barber. "I never knew how lovely these benches are. You can feel the rump prints," she said, running her hands underneath her and along the bench. Then she gave a sigh and her hand closed over Grandma Dee's butter dish. "That's it!" she said. "I knew there was something I wanted to ask you if I could have." She jumped up from the table and went over in the corner where the churn stood, the milk in it clabber by now. She looked at the churn and looked at it.

"This churn top is what I need," she said. "Didn't Uncle Buddy whittle it out of a tree you all used to have?"

"Yes," I said.

"Uh-huh," she said happily. "And I want the dasher, too."

"Uncle Buddy whittle that, too?" asked the barber.

Dee (Wangero) looked up at me.

"Aunt Dee's first husband whittled the dash," said Maggie so low you almost couldn't hear her. "His name was Henry, but they called him Stash."

"Maggie's brain is like an elephant's," Wangero said, laughing. "I can use the churn top as a centerpiece for the alcove table," she said, sliding a plate over the churn, "and I'll think of something artistic to do with the dasher."

When she finished wrapping the dasher the handle stuck out. I took it for a moment in my hands. You didn't even have to look close to see where hands pushing the dasher up and down to make butter had left a kind of sink in the wood. In fact, there were a lot of small sinks; you could see where thumbs and fingers had sunk into the wood. It was beautiful light yellow wood, from a tree that grew in the yard where Big Dee and Stash had lived.

After dinner Dee (Wangero) went to the trunk at the foot of my bed and started rifling through it. Maggie hung back in the kitchen over the dishpan. Out came Wangero with two quilts. They had been pieced by Grandma Dee and then Big Dee and me had hung them on the quilt frames on the front porch and quilted them. One was in the Lone Star pattern. The other was Walk Around the Mountain. In both of them were scraps of dresses Grandma Dee had worn fifty and more years ago. Bits and pieces of Grandpa Jarrell's Paisley shirts. And one teeny faded blue piece, about the size of a penny matchbox, that was from Great Grandpa Ezra's uniform that he wore in the Civil War.

"Mama," Wangero said sweet as a bird. "Can I have these old quilts?"

I heard something fall in the kitchen, and a minute later the kitchen door slammed.

"Why don't you take one or two of the others?" I asked. "These old things was just done by me and Big Dee from some tops your grandma pieced before she died."

"No," said Wangero. "I don't want those. They are stitched around the borders by machine."

"That'll make them last better," I said.

"That's not the point," said Wangero. "These are all pieces of dresses Grandma used to wear. She did all this stitching by hand. Imagine!" She held the quilts securely in her arms, stroking them.

"Some of the pieces, like those lavender ones, come from old clothes her mother handed down to her," I said, moving up to touch the quilts. Dee (Wangero) moved back just enough so that I couldn't reach the quilts. They already belonged to her.

"Imagine!" she breathed again, clutching them closely to her bosom.

"The truth is," I said, "I promised to give them quilts to Maggie, for when she marries John Thomas."

She gasped like a bee had stung her.

"Maggie can't appreciate these quilts!" she said. "She'd probably be backward enough to put them to everyday use."

"I reckon she would," I said. "God knows I been saving 'em for long enough with nobody using 'em. I hope she will!" I didn't want to bring up how I had offered Dee (Wangero) a quilt when she went away to college. Then she had told me they were old-fashioned, out of style.

"But they're *priceless!*" she was saying now, furiously; for she has a temper. "Maggie would put them on the bed and in five years they'd be in rags. Less than that!"

"She can always make some more," I said. "Maggie knows how to quilt."

Dee (Wangero) looked at me with hatred. "You just will not understand. The point is these quilts, *these* quilts!"

"Well," I said, stumped. "What would *you* do with them?"

"Hang them," she said. As if that was the only thing you *could* do with quilts.

Maggie by now was standing in the door. I could almost hear the sound her feet made as they scraped over each other.

"She can have them, Mama," she said, like somebody used to never winning anything, or having anything reserved for her. "I can 'member Grandma Dee without the quilts."

I looked at her hard. She had filled her bottom lip with checkerberry snuff and it gave her face a kind of dopey, hangdog look. It was Grandma Dee and Big Dee who taught her how to quilt herself. She stood there with her scarred hands hidden in the folds of her skirt. She looked at her sister with something like fear but she wasn't mad at her. This was Maggie's portion. This was the way she knew God to work.

When I looked at her like that something hit me in the top of my head and ran down to the soles of my feet. Just like when I'm in church and the spirit of God touches me and I get happy and shout. I did something I never had done before: hugged Maggie to me, then dragged her on into the room, snatched the quilts out of Miss Wangero's hands and dumped them into Maggie's lap. Maggie just sat there on my bed with her mouth open.

"Take one or two of the others," I said to Dee.

But she turned without a word and went out to Hakim-a-barber.

"You just don't understand," she said, as Maggie and I came out to the car.

"What don't I understand?" I wanted to know.

"Your heritage," she said. And then she turned to Maggie, kissed her, and said, "You ought to try to make something of yourself, too, Maggie. It's really a new day for us. But from the way you and Mama still live you'd never know it."

She put on some sunglasses that hid everything above the tip of her nose and her chin.

Maggie smiled; maybe at the sunglasses. But a real smile, not scared. After we watched the car dust settle I asked Maggie to bring me a dip of snuff. And then the two of us sat there just enjoying, until it was time to go in the house and go to bed.   [1973]

LESLIE MARMON SILKO

Leslie Marmon Silko (b. 1948), a Laguna Pueblo Native American, was born and grew up in New Mexico. She was educated at Board of Indian Affairs schools in Laguna, a Catholic school in Albuquerque, and the University of New Mexico, where she received her B.A. in English in 1969. After teaching at various colleges, she became a professor of English at the University of Arizona at Tucson. Silko's first novel, Ceremony *(1977), is regarded as one of the most important books in modern Native American literature. In it she forged a connection between the shared past of the tribe and the individual life of a Native American returning home after World War II. Silko has received a National Endowment for the Arts fellowship, a Pushcart Prize, and a three-year grant from the MacArthur Foundation, which enabled her to take time off from teaching and become "a little less beholden to the everyday world."*

Storyteller (1981), a collection of tribal folktales, family anecdotes, photographs by her grandfather, and her own poems and stories, is Silko's personal anthology of the Laguna Pueblo culture. "Yellow Woman" was first published in the 1974 collection The Man to Send Rain Clouds *and later collected in* Storyteller. *It illustrates Silko's skill in retelling a traditional Native American legend in a realistic contemporary context that confirms its emotional truth and makes it accessible to a larger audience.*

Tales about a "ka'tsina" mountain spirit who seduces the Yellow Woman away from her husband and family were first told to the fictional heroine by her grandfather. The Yellow Woman in the traditional captivity narratives can be interpreted in several ways—as a girl who runs off with men outside the tribe, as a raped and kidnapped married woman, as a spirit, as a fertility archetype. In creating fiction, Silko works with all the implied meanings of the old legends; she has said that she writes "because I like seeing how I can translate [a] sort of feeling or flavor or sense of a story that's told and heard onto the page." Her recent books include The Almanac of the Dead *(1991),* Sacred Water *(1993),* Yellow Woman and a Beauty of the Spirit: Essays on Native American Life *(1996), and* Gardens in the Dunes *(1999).*

RELATED COMMENTARY: *Paula Gunn Allen, "Whirlwind Man Steals Yellow Woman," page 1290.*

Yellow Woman

–I–

My thigh clung to his with dampness, and I watched the sun rising up through the tamaracks and willows. The small brown water birds came to the river and hopped across the mud, leaving brown scratches in the alkali-white crust. They bathed in the river silently. I could hear the water, almost at our feet where the narrow fast channel bubbled and washed green ragged moss and fern leaves. I looked at him beside me, rolled in the red blanket on the white river sand. I cleaned the sand out of the cracks between my toes, squinting because the sun was above the willow trees. I looked at him for the last time, sleeping on the white river sand.

I felt hungry and followed the river south the way we had come the afternoon before, following our footprints that were already blurred by the lizard tracks and bug trails. The horses were still lying down, and the black one whinnied when he saw me but he did not get up — maybe it was because the corral was made out of thick cedar branches and the horses had not yet felt the sun like I had. I tried to look beyond the pale red mesas to the pueblo. I knew it was there, even if I could not see it, on the sand rock hill above the river, the same river that moved past me now and had reflected the moon last night.

The horse felt warm underneath me. He shook his head and pawed the sand. The bay whinnied and leaned against the gate trying to follow, and I remembered him asleep in the red blanket beside the river. I slid off the horse and tied him close to the other horse. I walked north with the river again, and the white sand broke loose in footprints over footprints.

"Wake up."

He moved in the blanket and turned his face to me with his eyes still closed. I knelt down to touch him.

"I'm leaving."

He smiled now, eyes still closed. "You are coming with me, remember?" He sat up now with his bare dark chest and belly in the sun.

"Where?"

"To my place."

"And will I come back?"

He pulled his pants on. I walked away from him, feeling him behind me and smelling the willows.

"Yellow Woman," he said.

I turned to face him. "Who are you?" I asked.

He laughed and knelt on the low, sandy bank, washing his face in the river. "Last night you guessed my name, and you knew why I had come."

I stared past him at the shallow moving water and tried to remember the night, but I could only see the moon in the water and remember his warmth around me.

1111

"But I only said that you were him and that I was Yellow Woman—I'm not really her—I have my own name and I come from the pueblo on the other side of the mesa. Your name is Silva and you are a stranger I met by the river yesterday afternoon."

He laughed softly. "What happened yesterday has nothing to do with what you will do today, Yellow Woman."

"I know—that's what I'm saying—the old stories about the ka'tsina spirit[1] and Yellow Woman can't mean us."

My old grandpa liked to tell those stories best. There is one about Badger and Coyote who went hunting and were gone all day, and when the sun was going down they found a house. There was a girl living there alone, and she had light hair and eyes and she told them that they could sleep with her. Coyote wanted to be with her all night so he sent Badger into a prairie-dog hole, telling him he thought he saw something in it. As soon as Badger crawled in, Coyote blocked up the entrance with rocks and hurried back to Yellow Woman.

"Come here," he said gently.

He touched my neck and I moved close to him to feel his breathing and to hear his heart. I was wondering if Yellow Woman had known who she was—if she knew that she would become part of the stories. Maybe she'd had another name that her husband and relatives called her so that only the ka'tsina from the north and the storytellers would know her as Yellow Woman. But I didn't go on; I felt him all around me, pushing me down into the white river sand.

Yellow Woman went away with the spirit from the north and lived with him and his relatives. She was gone for a long time, but then one day she came back and she brought twin boys.

"Do you know the story?"

"What story?" He smiled and pulled me close to him as he said this. I was afraid lying there on the red blanket. All I could know was the way he felt, warm, damp, his body beside me. This is the way it happens in the stories, I was thinking, with no thought beyond the moment she meets the ka'tsina spirit and they go.

"I don't have to go. What they tell in stories was real only then, back in time immemorial, like they say."

He stood up and pointed at my clothes tangled in the blanket. "Let's go," he said.

I walked beside him, breathing hard because he walked fast, his hand around my wrist. I had stopped trying to pull away from him, because his hand felt cool and the sun was high, drying the river bed into alkali. I will see someone, eventually I will see someone, and then I will be certain that he is only a man—some man from nearby—and I will be sure that I am not Yellow Woman. Because she is from out of time past and I live now

---

[1]A mountain spirit of the Pueblo Indians.

and I've been to school and there are highways and pickup trucks that Yellow Woman never saw.

It was an easy ride north on horseback. I watched the change from the cottonwood trees along the river to the junipers that brushed past us in the foothills, and finally there were only piñons, and when I looked up at the rim of the mountain plateau I could see pine trees growing on the edge. Once I stopped to look down, but the pale sandstone had disappeared and the river was gone and the dark lava hills were all around. He touched my hand, not speaking, but always singing softly a mountain song and looking into my eyes.

I felt hungry and wondered what they were doing at home now — my mother, my grandmother, my husband, and the baby. Cooking breakfast, saying, "Where did she go? — maybe kidnapped," and Al going to the tribal police with the details: "She went walking along the river."

The house was made with black lava rock and red mud. It was high above the spreading miles of arroyos and long mesas. I smelled a mountain smell of pitch and buck brush. I stood there beside the black horse, looking down on the small, dim country we had passed, and I shivered.

"Yellow Woman, come inside where it's warm."

– II –

He lit a fire in the stove. It was an old stove with a round belly and an enamel coffeepot on top. There was only the stove, some faded Navajo blankets, and a bedroll and cardboard box. The floor was made of smooth adobe plaster, and there was one small window facing east. He pointed at the box.

"There's some potatoes and the frying pan." He sat on the floor with his arms around his knees pulling them close to his chest and he watched me fry the potatoes. I didn't mind him watching me because he was always watching me — he had been watching me since I came upon him sitting on the river bank trimming leaves from a willow twig with his knife. We ate from the pan and he wiped the grease from his fingers on his Levis.

"Have you brought women here before?" He smiled and kept chewing, so I said, "Do you always use the same tricks?"

"What tricks?" He looked at me like he didn't understand.

"The story about being a ka'tsina from the mountains. The story about Yellow Woman."

Silva was silent; his face was calm.

"I don't believe it. Those stories couldn't happen now," I said.

He shook his head and said softly, "But someday they will talk about us, and they will say, 'Those two lived long ago when things like that happened.'"

He stood up and went out. I ate the rest of the potatoes and thought about things — about the noise the stove was making and the sound of the mountain wind outside. I remembered yesterday and the day before, and then I went outside.

I walked past the corral to the edge where the narrow trail cut through the black rim rock. I was standing in the sky with nothing around me but the wind that came down from the blue mountain peak behind me. I could see faint mountain images in the distance miles across the vast spread of mesas and valleys and plains. I wondered who was over there to feel the mountain wind on those sheer blue edges—who walks on the pine needles in those blue mountains.

"Can you see the pueblo?" Silva was standing behind me.

I shook my head. "We're too far away."

"From here I can see the world." He stepped out on the edge. "The Navajo reservation begins over there." He pointed to the east. "The Pueblo boundaries are over here." He looked below us to the south, where the narrow trail seemed to come from. "The Texans have their ranches over there, starting with that valley, the Concho Valley. The Mexicans run some cattle over there too."

"Do you ever work for them?"

"I steal from them," Silva answered. The sun was dropping behind us and shadows were filling the land below. I turned away from the edge that dropped forever into the valleys below.

"I'm cold," I said; "I'm going inside." I started wondering about this man who could speak the Pueblo language so well but who lived on a mountain and rustled cattle. I decided that this man Silva must be Navajo, because Pueblo men didn't do things like that.

"You must be a Navajo."

Silva shook his head gently. "Little Yellow Woman," he said, "you never give up, do you? I have told you who I am. The Navajo people know me, too." He knelt down and unrolled the bedroll and spread the extra blankets out on a piece of canvas. The sun was down, and the only light in the house came from outside—the dim orange light from sundown.

I stood there and waited for him to crawl under the blankets.

"What are you waiting for?" he said, and I lay down beside him. He undressed me slowly like the night before beside the river—kissing my face gently and running his hands up and down my belly and legs. He took off my pants and then he laughed.

"Why are you laughing?"

"You are breathing so hard."

I pulled away from him and turned my back to him.

He pulled me around and pinned me down with his arms and chest. "You don't understand, do you, little Yellow Woman? You will do what I want."

And again he was all around me with his skin slippery against mine, and I was afraid because I understood that his strength could hurt me. I lay underneath him and I knew that he could destroy me. But later, while he slept beside me, I touched his face and I had a feeling—the kind of feeling for him that overcame me that morning along the river. I kissed him on the forehead and he reached out for me.

When I woke up in the morning he was gone. It gave me a strange feeling because for a long time I sat there on the blankets and looked around the little house for some object of his—some proof that he had been there or maybe that he was coming back. Only the blankets and the cardboard box remained. The .30–30[2] that had been leaning in the corner was gone, and so was the knife I had used the night before. He was gone, and I had my chance to go now. But first I had to eat, because I knew it would be a long walk home.

I found some dried apricots in the cardboard box, and I sat down on a rock at the edge of the plateau rim. There was no wind and the sun warmed me. I was surrounded by silence. I drowsed with apricots in my mouth, and I didn't believe that there were highways or railroads or cattle to steal.

When I woke up, I stared down at my feet in the black mountain dirt. Little black ants were swarming over the pine needles around my foot. They must have smelled the apricots. I thought about my family far below me. They would be wondering about me, because this had never happened to me before. The tribal police would file a report. But if old Grandpa weren't dead he would tell them what happened—he would laugh and say, "Stolen by a ka'tsina, a mountain spirit. She'll come home—they usually do." There are enough of them to handle things. My mother and grandmother will raise the baby like they raised me. Al will find someone else, and they will go on like before, except that there will be a story about the day I disappeared while I was walking along the river. Silva had come for me; he said he had. I did not decide to go. I just went. Moonflowers blossom in the sand hills before dawn, just as I followed him. That's what I was thinking as I wandered along the trail through the pine trees.

It was noon when I got back. When I saw the stone house I remembered that I had meant to go home. But that didn't seem important any more, maybe because there were little blue flowers growing in the meadow behind the stone house and the gray squirrels were playing in the pines next to the house. The horses were standing in the corral, and there was a beef carcass hanging on the shady side of a big pine in front of the house. Flies buzzed around the clotted blood that hung from the carcass. Silva was washing his hands in a bucket full of water. He must have heard me coming because he spoke to me without turning to face me.

"I've been waiting for you."

"I went walking in the big pine trees."

---

[2]A rifle.

I looked into the bucket full of bloody water with brown-and-white animal hairs floating in it. Silva stood there letting his hand drip, examining me intently.

"Are you coming with me?"

"Where?" I asked him.

"To sell the meat in Marquez."

"If you're sure it's O.K."

"I wouldn't ask you if it wasn't," he answered.

He sloshed the water around in the bucket before he dumped it out and set the bucket upside down near the door. I followed him to the corral and watched him saddle the horses. Even beside the horses he looked tall, and I asked him again if he wasn't Navajo. He didn't say anything; he just shook his head and kept cinching up the saddle.

"But Navajos are tall."

"Get on the horse," he said, "and let's go."

The last thing he did before we started down the steep trail was to grab the .30–30 from the corner. He slid the rifle into the scabbard that hung from his saddle.

"Do they ever try to catch you?" I asked.

"They don't know who I am."

"Then why did you bring the rifle?"

"Because we are going to Marquez where the Mexicans live."

–III–

The trail leveled out on a narrow ridge that was steep on both sides like an animal spine. On one side I could see where the trail went around the rocky gray hills and disappeared into the southeast where the pale sand-rock mesas stood in the distance near my home. On the other side was a trail that went west, and as I looked far into the distance I thought I saw the little town. But Silva said no, that I was looking in the wrong place, that I just thought I saw houses. After that I quit looking off into the distance; it was hot and the wildflowers were closing up their deep-yellow petals. Only the waxy cactus flowers bloomed in the bright sun, and I saw every color that a cactus blossom can be; the white ones and the red ones were still buds, but the purple and the yellow were blossoms, open full and the most beautiful of all.

Silva saw him before I did. The white man was riding a big gray horse, coming up the trail toward us. He was traveling fast and the gray horse's feet sent rocks rolling off the trail into the dry tumbleweeds. Silva motioned for me to stop and we watched the white man. He didn't see us right away, but finally his horse whinnied at our horses and he stopped. He looked at us briefly before he loped the gray horse across the three hundred yards that separated us. He stopped his horse in front of Silva, and his young fat face was shadowed by the brim of his hat. He didn't look mad, but his small, pale eyes moved from the blood-soaked gunny sacks hanging from my saddle to Silva's face and then back to my face.

"Where did you get the fresh meat?" the white man asked.

"I've been hunting," Silva said, and when he shifted his weight in the saddle the leather creaked.

"The hell you have, Indian. You've been rustling cattle. We've been looking for the thief for a long time."

The rancher was fat, and sweat began to soak through his white cowboy shirt and the wet cloth stuck to the thick rolls of belly fat. He almost seemed to be panting from the exertion of talking, and he smelled rancid, maybe because Silva scared him.

Silva turned to me and smiled. "Go back up the mountain, Yellow Woman."

The white man got angry when he heard Silva speak in a language he couldn't understand. "Don't try anything, Indian. Just keep riding to Marquez. We'll call the state police from there."

The rancher must have been unarmed because he was very frightened and if he had a gun he would have pulled it out then. I turned my horse around and the rancher yelled, "Stop!" I looked at Silva for an instant and there was something ancient and dark—something I could feel in my stomach—in his eyes, and when I glanced at his hand I saw his finger on the trigger of the .30–30 that was still in the saddle scabbard. I slapped my horse across the flank and the sacks of raw meat swung against my knees as the horse leaped up the trail. It was hard to keep my balance, and once I thought I felt the saddle slipping backward; it was because of this that I could not look back.

I didn't stop until I reached the ridge where the trail forked. The horse was breathing deep gasps and there was a dark film of sweat on its neck. I looked down in the direction I had come from, but I couldn't see the place. I waited. The wind came up and pushed warm air past me. I looked up at the sky, pale blue and full of thin clouds and fading vapor trails left by jets.

I think four shots were fired—I remember hearing four hollow explosions that reminded me of deer hunting. There could have been more shots after that, but I couldn't have heard them because my horse was running again and the loose rocks were making too much noise as they scattered around his feet.

Horses have a hard time running downhill, but I went that way instead of uphill to the mountain because I thought it was safer. I felt better with the horse running southeast past the round gray hills that were covered with cedar trees and black lava rock. When I got to the plain in the distance I could see the dark green patches of tamaracks that grew along the river; and beyond the river I could see the beginning of the pale sandrock mesas. I stopped the horse and looked back to see if anyone was coming; then I got off the horse and turned the horse around, wondering if it would go back to its corral under the pines on the mountain. It looked back at me for a moment and then plucked a mouthful of green tumbleweeds before it trotted back up the trail with its ears pointed forward, carrying its head daintily to one side to avoid stepping on the dragging reins. When the horse disappeared over the last hill, the gunny sacks full of meat were still swinging and bouncing.

– IV –

I walked toward the river on a wood-hauler's road that I knew would eventually lead to the paved road. I was thinking about waiting beside the road for someone to drive by, but by the time I got to the pavement I had decided it wasn't very far to walk if I followed the river back the way Silva and I had come.

The river water tasted good, and I sat in the shade under a cluster of silvery willows. I thought about Silva, and I felt sad at leaving him; still, there was something strange about him, and I tried to figure it out all the way back home.

I came back to the place on the river bank where he had been sitting the first time I saw him. The green willow leaves that he had trimmed from the branch were still lying there, wilted in the sand. I saw the leaves and I wanted to go back to him—to kiss him and to touch him—but the mountains were too far away now. And I told myself, because I believe it, he will come back sometime and be waiting again by the river.

I followed the path up from the river into the village. The sun was getting low, and I could smell supper cooking when I got to the screen door of my house. I could hear their voices inside—my mother was telling my grandmother how to fix the Jell-O and my husband, Al, was playing with the baby. I decided to tell them that some Navajo had kidnapped me, but I was sorry that old Grandpa wasn't alive to hear my story because it was the Yellow Woman stories he liked to tell best.   [1974]

JOHN UPDIKE

John Updike (b. 1932) was born in Shillington, Pennsylvania, an only child. His father taught algebra in a local high school, and his mother wrote short stories and novels. His mother's consciousness of a special destiny, combined with his family's meager income—they lived with his mother's parents for the first thirteen years of Updike's life—made him "both arrogant and shy" as a teenager. He wrote stories, drew cartoons, and clowned for the approval of his peers. After earning straight A's in high school, he went to Harvard University on a full scholarship, studying English and graduating summa cum laude in 1954. He spent a year at Oxford on a fellowship, then joined the staff of The New Yorker. *In 1959 Updike published both his first book of short fiction,* The Same Door, *and his first novel,* The Poorhouse Fair. *That year he also moved from New York City to a coastal town in Massachusetts, where he has lived most of the time since.*

In the 1960s, 1970s, and early 1980s, Updike continued to alternate novels and collections of stories, adding occasional volumes of verse, collections of essays, and one play. His novels include Rabbit, Run *(1960),* Couples *(1968),* Rabbit Redux *(1971), and* Marry Me *(1976).* Rabbit Is Rich *(1981), continuing the story of Harry "Rabbit" Angstrom, a suburban Pennsylvanian whom Updike has traced through adolescence, marriage, fatherhood, and middle age, won virtually every major American literary award for the year it appeared; Updike concluded the series with* Rabbit at Rest *(1991). Updike's collections of stories include* Pigeon Feathers *(1962),* Museums and Women *(1972), and* Problems and Other Stories *(1981). In 1989 he published his memoirs,* Self-Consciousness. *Other recent books are* The Afterlife and Other Stories *(1994) and* Toward the End of Time *(1997). Author of forty-nine books, he was the 1998 recipient of the National Book Foundation Medal for Distinguished Contribution to American Letters.*

*Updike has said he is indebted to J. D. Salinger's stories for the literary form he adopted to describe the painful experience of adolescence: "I learned a lot from Salinger's short stories; he did remove the short narrative from the wise-guy, slice-of-life stories of the thirties and forties. Like most innovative artists, he made new room for shapelessness, for life as it is lived." Updike writes realistic narrative, believing that "fiction is a tissue of lies that refreshes and informs our sense of actuality. Reality is—chemically, atomically, biologically—a fabric of microscopic accuracies." His fiction, such as the story "Separating" (*The New Yorker, *1975), concentrates on these "microscopic accuracies," tiny details of characterization and setting brilliantly described.*

RELATED COMMENTARY: *John Updike, "Twisted Apples: On* Winesburg, Ohio," *page 1464.*

Separating

The day was fair. Brilliant. All that June the weather had mocked the Maples' internal misery with solid sunlight—golden shafts and cascades of green in which their conversations had wormed unseeing, their sad murmuring selves the only stain in Nature. Usually by this time of the year they had acquired tans; but when they met their elder daughter's plane on her return from a year in England they were almost as pale as she, though Judith was too dazzled by the sunny opulent jumble of her native land to notice. They did not spoil her homecoming by telling her immediately. Wait a few days, let her recover from jet lag, had been one of their formulations, in that string of gray dialogues—over coffee, over cocktails, over Cointreau—that had shaped the strategy of their dissolution, while the earth performed its annual stunt of renewal unnoticed beyond their closed windows. Richard had thought to leave at Easter; Joan had insisted they wait until the four children were at last assembled, with all exams passed and ceremonies attended, and the bauble of summer to console them. So he had drudged away, in love, in dread, repairing screens, getting the mowers sharpened, rolling and patching their new tennis court.

The court, clay, had come through its first winter pitted and windswept bare of redcoat. Years ago the Maples had observed how often, among their friends, divorce followed a dramatic home improvement, as if the marriage were making one last strong effort to live; their own worst crisis had come amid the plaster dust and exposed plumbing of a kitchen renovation. Yet, a summer ago, as canary-yellow bulldozers gaily churned a grassy, daisy-dotted knoll into a muddy plateau, and a crew of pigtailed young men raked and tamped clay into a plane, this transformation did not strike them as ominous, but festive in its impudence; their marriage could rend the earth for fun. The next spring, waking each day at dawn to a sliding sensation as if the bed were being tipped, Richard found the barren tennis court—its net and tapes still rolled in the barn—an environment congruous with his mood of purposeful desolation, and the crumbling of handfuls of clay into cracks and holes (dogs had frolicked on the court in a thaw; rivulets had evolved trenches) an activity suitably elemental and interminable. In his sealed heart he hoped the day would never come.

Now it was here. A Friday. Judith was reacclimated; all four children were assembled, before jobs and camps and visits again scattered them. Joan thought they should be told one by one. Richard was for making an announcement at the table. She said, "I think just making an announcement is a cop-out. They'll start quarreling and playing to each other instead of focusing. They're each individuals, you know, not just some corporate obstacle to your freedom."

"O.K., O.K. I agree." Joan's plan was exact. That evening, they were giving Judith a belated welcome-home dinner, of lobster and champagne. Then, the party over, they, the two of them, who nineteen years before

1120

would push her in a baby carriage along Fifth Avenue to Washington Square, were to walk her out of the house, to the bridge across the salt creek, and tell her, swearing her to secrecy. Then Richard Jr., who was going directly from work to a rock concert in Boston, would be told, either late when he returned on the train or early Saturday morning before he went off to his job; he was seventeen and employed as one of a golf-course maintenance crew. Then the two younger children, John and Margaret, could, as the morning wore on, be informed.

"Mopped up, as it were," Richard said.

"Do you have any better plan? That leaves you the rest of Saturday to answer any questions, pack, and make your wonderful departure."

"No," he said, meaning he had no better plan, and agreed to hers, though to him it showed an edge of false order, a hidden plea for control, like Joan's long chore lists and financial accountings and, in the days when he first knew her, her too-copious lecture notes. Her plan turned one hurdle for him into four—four knife-sharp walls, each with a sheer blind drop on the other side.

All spring he had moved through a world of insides and outsides, of barriers and partitions. He and Joan stood as a thin barrier between the children and the truth. Each moment was a partition, with the past on one side and the future on the other, a future containing this unthinkable *now.* Beyond four knifelike walls a new life for him waited vaguely. His skull cupped a secret, a white face, a face both frightened and soothing, both strange and known, that he wanted to shield from tears, which he felt all about him, solid as the sunlight. So haunted, he had become obsessed with battening down the house against his absence, replacing screens and sash cords, hinges and latches—a Houdini making things snug before his escape.

The lock. He had still to replace a lock on one of the doors of the screened porch. The task, like most such, proved more difficult than he had imagined. The old lock, aluminum frozen by corrosion, had been deliberately rendered obsolete by manufacturers. Three hardware stores had nothing that even approximately matched the mortised hole its removal (surprisingly easy) left. Another hole had to be gouged, with bits too small and saws too big, and the old hole fitted with a block of wood—the chisels dull, the saw rusty, his fingers thick with lack of sleep. The sun poured down, beyond the porch, on a world of neglect. The bushes already needed pruning, the windward side of the house was shedding flakes of paint, rain would get in when he was gone, insects, rot, death. His family, all those he would lose, filtered through the edges of his awareness as he struggled with screw holes, splinters, opaque instructions, minutiae of metal.

Judith sat on the porch, a princess returned from exile. She regaled them with stories of fuel shortages, of bomb scares in the Underground, of Pakistani workmen loudly lusting after her as she walked past on her way to dance school. Joan came and went, in and out of the house, calmer than she should have been, praising his struggles with the lock as if this were one more and not the last of their long chain of shared chores. The younger of his sons, John, now at fifteen suddenly, unwittingly handsome, for a few minutes held the rickety screen door while his father clumsily hammered and chiseled, each blow a kind of sob in Richard's ears. His younger daughter, having been at a slumber party, slept on the porch hammock through all the noise — heavy and pink, trusting and forsaken. Time, like the sunlight, continued relentlessly; the sunlight slowly slanted. Today was one of the longest days. The lock clicked, worked. He was through. He had a drink; he drank it on the porch, listening to his daughter. "It was so sweet," she was saying, "during the worst of it, how all the butchers and bakery shops kept open by candlelight. They're all so plucky and cute. From the papers, things sounded so much worse here — people shooting people in gas lines, and everybody freezing."

Richard asked her, "Do you still want to live in England forever?" *Forever:* the concept, now a reality upon him, pressed and scratched at the back of his throat.

"No," Judith confessed, turning her oval face to him, its eyes still childishly far apart, but the lips set as over something succulent and satisfactory. "I was anxious to come home. I'm an American." She was a woman. They had raised her; he and Joan had endured together to raise her, alone of the four. The others had still some raising left in them. Yet it was the thought of telling Judith — the image of her, their first baby, walking between them arm in arm to the bridge — that broke him. The partition between his face and the tears broke. Richard sat down to the celebratory meal with the back of his throat aching; the champagne, the lobster seemed phases of sunshine; he saw them and tasted them through tears. He blinked, swallowed, croakily joked about hay fever. The tears would not stop leaking through; they came not through a hole that could be plugged but through a permeable spot in a membrane, steadily, purely, endlessly, fruitfully. They became, his tears, a shield for himself against these others — their faces, the fact of their assembly, a last time as innocents, at a table where he sat the last time as head. Tears dropped from his nose as he broke the lobster's back; salt flavored his champagne as he sipped it; the raw clench at the back of his throat was delicious. He could not help himself.

His children tried to ignore his tears. Judith, on his right, lit a cigarette, gazed upward in the direction of her too energetic, too sophisticated exhalation; on her other side, John earnestly bent his face to the extraction of the last morsels — legs, tail segments — from the scarlet corpse. Joan, at the opposite end of the table, glanced at him surprised, her reproach displaced by a quick grimace, of forgiveness, or of salute to his superior gift of strategy. Between them, Margaret, no longer called Bean, thirteen and large for her age, gazed from the other side of his pane of tears as if into a shopwindow at something she coveted—at her father, a crystalline heap of splinters and memories. It was not she, however, but John who, in the kitchen, as they cleared the plates and carapaces away, asked Joan the question: *"Why is Daddy crying?"*

Richard heard the question but not the murmured answer. Then he heard Bean cry, "Oh, no-oh!"—the faintly dramatized exclamation of one who had long expected it.

John returned to the table carrying a bowl of salad. He nodded tersely at his father and his lips shaped the conspiratorial words "She told."

"Told what?" Richard asked aloud, insanely.

The boy sat down as if to rebuke his father's distraction with the example of his own good manners. He said quietly, "The separation."

Joan and Margaret returned; the child, in Richard's twisted vision, seemed diminished in size, and relieved, relieved to have had the bogie-man at last proved real. He called out to her—the distances at the table had grown immense—"You knew, you always knew," but the clenching at the back of his throat prevented him from making sense of it. From afar he heard Joan talking, levelly, sensibly, reciting what they had prepared: it was a separation for the summer, an experiment. She and Daddy both agreed it would be good for them; they needed space and time to think; they liked each other but did not make each other happy enough, somehow.

Judith, imitating her mother's factual tone, but in her youth off-key, too cool, said, "I think it's silly. You should either live together or get divorced."

Richard's crying, like a wave that has crested and crashed, had become tumultuous; but it was overtopped by another tumult, for John, who had been so reserved, now grew larger and larger at the table. Perhaps his younger sister's being credited with knowing set him off. "Why didn't you *tell* us?" he asked, in a large round voice quite unlike his own. "You should have *told* us you weren't getting along."

Richard was startled into attempting to force words through his tears. "We *do* get along, that's the trouble, so it doesn't show even to us—" *That we do not love each other* was the rest of the sentence; he couldn't finish it.

Joan finished for him, in her style. "And we've always, *especially,* loved our children."

John was not mollified. "What do you care about *us?*" he boomed. "We're just little things you *had.*" His sisters' laughing forced a laugh from him, which he turned hard and parodistic: "Ha ha *ha.*" Richard and Joan realized simultaneously that the child was drunk, on Judith's home-coming champagne. Feeling bound to keep the center of the stage, John took a cigarette from Judith's pack, poked it into his mouth, let it hang from his lower lip, and squinted like a gangster.

"You're not little things we had," Richard called to him. "You're the whole point. But you're grown. Or almost."

The boy was lighting matches. Instead of holding them to his cigarette (for they had never seen him smoke; being "good" had been his way of setting himself apart), he held them to his mother's face, closer and closer, for her to blow out. Then he lit the whole folder — a hiss and then a torch, held against his mother's face. Prismed by his tears, the flame filled Richard's vision; he didn't know how it was extinguished. He heard Margaret say, "Oh stop showing off," and saw John, in response, break the cigarette in two and put the halves entirely into his mouth and chew, sticking out his tongue to display the shreds to his sister.

Joan talked to him, reasoning — a fountain of reason, unintelligible. "Talked about it for years . . . our children must help us . . . Daddy and I both want . . ." As the boy listened, he carefully wadded a paper napkin into the leaves of his salad, fashioned a ball of paper and lettuce, and popped it into his mouth, looking around the table for the expected laughter. None came. Judith said, "Be mature," and dismissed a plume of smoke.

Richard got up from this stifling table and led the boy outside. Though the house was in twilight, the outdoors still brimmed with light, the lovely waste light of high summer. Both laughing, he supervised John's spitting out the lettuce and paper and tobacco into the pachysandra. He took him by the hand — a square gritty hand, but for its softness a man's. Yet, it held on. They ran together up into the field, past the tennis court. The raw banking left by the bulldozers was dotted with daisies. Past the court and a flat stretch where they used to play family baseball stood a soft green rise glorious in the sun, each weed and species of grass distinct as illumination on parchment. "I'm sorry, so sorry," Richard cried. "You were the only one who ever tried to help me with all the goddam jobs around this place."

Sobbing, safe within his tears and the champagne, John explained, "It's not just the separation, it's the whole crummy year, I *hate* that school, you can't make any friends, the history teacher's a scud."

They sat on the crest of the rise, shaking and warm from their tears but easier in their voices, and Richard tried to focus on the child's sad year — the weekdays long with homework, the weekends spent in his room with model airplanes, while his parents murmured down below, nursing their separation. How selfish, how blind, Richard thought; his eyes felt scoured. He told his son, "We'll think about getting you transferred. Life's too short to be miserable."

They had said what they could, but did not want the moment to heal, and talked on, about the school, about the tennis court, whether it would ever again be as good as it had been that first summer. They walked to inspect it and pressed a few more tapes more firmly down. A little stiltedly, perhaps trying now to make too much of the moment, Richard led the boy to the spot in the field where the view was best, of the metallic blue river, the emerald marsh, the scattered islands velvety with shadow in the low light, the white bits of beach far away. "See," he said. "It goes on being beautiful. It'll be here tomorrow."

"I know," John answered, impatiently. The moment had closed.

Back in the house, the others had opened some white wine, the champagne being drunk, and still sat at the table, the three females, gossiping. Where Joan sat had become the head. She turned, showing him a tearless face, and asked, "All right?"

"We're fine," he said, resenting it, though relieved, that the party went on without him.

In bed she explained, "I couldn't cry I guess because I cried so much all spring. It really wasn't fair. It's your idea, and you made it look as though I was kicking you out."

"I'm sorry," he said. "I couldn't stop. I wanted to but couldn't."

"You *didn't* want to. You loved it. You were having your way, making a general announcement."

"I love having it over," he admitted. "God, those kids were great. So brave and funny." John, returned to the house, had settled to a model airplane in his room, and kept shouting down to them, "I'm O.K. No sweat." "And the way," Richard went on, cozy in his relief, "they never questioned the reasons we gave. No thought of a third person. Not even Judith."

"That *was* touching," Joan said.

He gave her a hug. "You were great too. Very reassuring to everybody. Thank you." Guiltily, he realized he did not feel separated.

"You still have Dickie to do," she told him. These words set before him a black mountain in the darkness; its cold breath, its near weight affected his chest. Of the four children, his elder son was most like a conscience. Joan did not need to add, "That's one piece of your dirty work I won't do for you."

"I know. I'll do it. You go to sleep."

Within minutes, her breathing slowed, became oblivious and deep. It was quarter to midnight. Dickie's train from the concert would come in at one-fourteen. Richard set the alarm for one. He had slept atrociously for weeks. But whenever he closed his lids some glimpse of the last hours scorched them—Judith exhaling toward the ceiling in a kind of aversion, Bean's mute staring, the sun-struck growth of the field where he and John had rested. The mountain before him moved closer, moved within him; he was huge, momentous. The ache at the back of his throat felt stale. His wife slept as if slain beside him. When, exasperated by his hot lids, his crowded heart, he rose from bed and dressed, she awoke enough to turn over. He told her then, "Joan, if I could undo it all, I would."

"Where would you begin?" she asked. There was no place. Giving him courage, she was always giving him courage. He put on shoes without socks in the dark. The children were breathing in their rooms, the downstairs was hollow. In their confusion they had left lights burning. He turned off all but one, the kitchen overhead. The car started. He had hoped it wouldn't. He met only moonlight on the road; it seemed a diaphanous companion, flickering in the leaves along the roadside, haunting his rearview mirror like a pursuer, melting under his headlights. The center of town, not quite deserted, was eerie at this hour. A young cop in uniform kept company with a gang of T-shirted kids on the steps of the bank. Across from the railroad station, several bars kept open. Customers, mostly young, passed in and out of the warm night, savoring summer's novelty. Voices shouted from cars as they passed; an immense conversation seemed in progress. Richard parked and in his weariness put his head on the passenger seat, out of the commotion and wheeling lights. It was as when, in the movies, an assassin grimly carries his mission through the jostle of a carnival — except the movies cannot show the precipitous, palpable slope you cling to within. You cannot climb back down; you can only fall. The synthetic fabric of the car seat, warmed by his cheek, confided to him an ancient, distant scent of vanilla.

A train whistle caused him to lift his head. It was on time; he had hoped it would be late. The slender drawgates descended. The bell of approach tingled happily. The great metal body, horizontally fluted, rocked to a stop, and sleepy teen-agers disembarked, his son among them. Dickie did not show surprise that his father was meeting him at this terrible hour. He sauntered to the car with two friends, both taller than he. He said "Hi" to his father and took the passenger's seat with an exhausted promptness that expressed gratitude. The friends got into the back, and Richard was grateful; a few more minutes' postponement would be won by driving them home.

He asked, "How was the concert?"

"Groovy," one boy said from the back seat.

"It bit," the other said.

"It was O.K.," Dickie said, moderate by nature, so reasonable that in his childhood the unreason of the world had given him headaches, stomach aches, nausea. When the second friend had been dropped off at his dark house, the boy blurted, "Dad, my eyes are killing me with hay fever! I'm out there cutting that mothering grass all day!"

"Do we still have those drops?"

"They didn't do any good last summer."

"They might this." Richard swung a U-turn on the empty street. The drive home took a few minutes. The mountain was here, in his throat. "Richard," he said, and felt the boy, slumped and rubbing his eyes, go tense at his tone, "I didn't come to meet you just to make your life easier. I came because your mother and I have some news for you, and you're a hard man to get ahold of these days. It's sad news."

"That's O.K." The reassurance came out soft, but quick, as if released from the tip of a spring.

Richard had feared that his tears would return and choke him, but the boy's manliness set an example, and his voice issued forth steady and dry.

"It's sad news, but it needn't be tragic news, at least for you. It should have no practical effect on your life, though it's bound to have an emotional effect. You'll work at your job, and go back to school in September. Your mother and I are really proud of what you're making of your life; we don't want that to change at all."

"Yeah," the boy said lightly, on the intake of his breath, holding himself up. They turned the corner; the church they went to loomed like a gutted fort. The home of the woman Richard hoped to marry stood across the green. Her bedroom light burned.

"Your mother and I," he said, "have decided to separate. For the summer. Nothing legal, no divorce yet. We want to see how it feels. For some years now, we haven't been doing enough for each other, making each other as happy as we should be. Have you sensed that?"

"No," the boy said. It was an honest, unemotional answer: true or false in a quiz.

Glad for the factual basis, Richard pursued, even garrulously, the details. His apartment across town, his utter accessibility, the split vacation arrangements, the advantages to the children, the added mobility and variety of the summer. Dickie listened, absorbing. "Do the others know?"

"Yes."

"How did they take it?"

"The girls pretty calmly. John flipped out; he shouted and ate a cigarette and made a salad out of his napkin and told us how much he hated school."

His brother chuckled. "He did?"

"Yeah. The school issue was more upsetting for him than Mom and me. He seemed to feel better for having exploded."

"He did?" The repetition was the first sign that he was stunned.

"Yes. Dickie, I want to tell you something. This last hour, waiting for your train to get in, has been about the worst of my life. I hate this. *Hate* it. My father would have died before doing it to me." He felt immensely lighter, saying this. He had dumped the mountain on the boy. They were home. Moving swiftly as a shadow, Dickie was out of the car, through the bright kitchen. Richard called after him, "Want a glass of milk or anything?"

"No thanks."

"Want us to call the course tomorrow and say you're too sick to work?"

"No, that's all right." The answer was faint, delivered at the door to his room; Richard listened for the slam that went with a tantrum. The door closed normally, gently. The sound was sickening.

Joan had sunk into that first deep trough of sleep and was slow to awake. Richard had to repeat, "I told him."

"What did he say?"

"Nothing much. Could you go say goodnight to him? Please."

She left their room, without putting on a bathrobe. He sluggishly changed back into his pajamas and walked down the hall. Dickie was already in bed, Joan was sitting beside him, and the boy's bedside clock radio was murmuring music. When she stood, an inexplicable light—the moon?—outlined her body through the nightie. Richard sat on the warm place she had indented on the child's narrow mattress. He asked him, "Do you want the radio on like that?"

"It always is."

"Doesn't it keep you awake? It would me."

"No."

"Are you sleepy?"

"Yeah."

"Good. Sure you want to get up and go to work? You've had a big night."

"I want to."

Away at school this winter he had learned for the first time that you can go short of sleep and live. As an infant he had slept with an immobile, sweating intensity that had alarmed his babysitters. In adolescence he had often been the first of the four children to go to bed. Even now, he would go slack in the middle of a television show, his sprawled legs hairy and brown. "O.K. Good boy. Dickie, listen. I love you so much, I never knew how much until now. No matter how this works out, I'll always be with you. Really."

Richard bent to kiss an averted face but his son, sinewy, turned and with wet cheeks embraced him and gave him a kiss, on the lips, passionate as a woman's. In his father's ear he moaned one word, the crucial, intelligent word: *"Why?"*

Why. It was a whistle of wind in a crack, a knife thrust, a window thrown open on emptiness. The white face was gone, the darkness was featureless. Richard had forgotten why.   [1975]

BOBBIE ANN MASON

*B*obbie Ann Mason (b. 1942) grew up on a farm outside Mayfield, Kentucky. As a child she loved to read, and her parents always made sure she had books, mostly popular fiction about the Bobbsey Twins and the Nancy Drew mysteries. After majoring in journalism at the University of Kentucky, she took several jobs in New York City with movie magazines, writing articles about Annette Funicello, Troy Donahue, Fabian, and other teen stars. Next she went to graduate school at the University of Connecticut, where she received her Ph.D. in literature with a dissertation on Vladimir Nabokov's Ada. This study was later published in paperback as Nabokov's Garden (1974).

After graduate school, Mason wrote The Girl Sleuth: A Feminist Guide to the Bobbsey Twins, Nancy Drew, and Their Sisters (1975), about her favorite childhood reading; then, in her late thirties, she started writing short stories. In 1980 The New Yorker published her first story after an extensive correspondence between Mason and the magazine's fiction editor, Roger Angell. "It took me a long time to discover my material," she says. "It wasn't a matter of developing writing skills, it was a matter of knowing how to see things. And it took me a very long time to grow up. I'd been writing for a long time, but was never able to see what there was to write about. And I always aspired to things away from home, so it took me a long time to look back at home and realize that that's where the center of my thoughts was." Mason writes about the working-class people of western Kentucky, and her stories have contributed to a renaissance of regional fiction in America. She has said that "the sight of a gigantic strip-mining machine nicknamed 'Big Bertha,' visible from a Kentucky parkway, resulted in 'Big Bertha Stories.'"

Mason's first collection, Shiloh and Other Stories, won the 1982 Hemingway Foundation Award. In 1985 reviewers of her novel In Country compared her to Ann Beattie and other "writers of her generation who chronicle aimless lives in prose that tends to be as laconic and stripped down as her characters' emotional range." Mason doesn't regard herself as a feminist writer. She feels that she writes about ordinary people

> who've got a toe-hold in the middle class. They're people who are from the lower class and who've moved up in the world a little. . . . The people I write about—it seems they either want to get away from home, get away from town, see the world, or they want to stay home, and they're afraid to leave, so they accommodate—or it wouldn't occur to them to leave. But I'm interested in that tension between longing to stay and longing to go. And I think that the world sets up a lot of frustrations and there are a lot of limits set for people.

"Big Bertha Stories" (The New Yorker, 1980) is included in Love Life (1989), her second collection of stories, which was followed by Midnight Magic: Selected Stories (1998).

RELATED COMMENTARY: *Bobbie Ann Mason, "On Tim O'Brien's 'The Things They Carried,'" page 1397.*

Big Bertha Stories

Donald is home again, laughing and singing. He comes home from Central City, near the strip mines, only when he feels like it, like an absentee landlord checking on his property. He is always in such a good humor when he returns that Jeannette forgives him. She cooks for him—ugly, pasty things she gets with food stamps. Sometimes he brings steaks and ice cream, occasionally money. Rodney, their child, hides in the closet when he arrives, and Donald goes around the house talking loudly about the little boy named Rodney who used to live there—the one who fell into a septic tank, or the one stolen by gypsies. The stories change. Rodney usually stays in the closet until he has to pee, and then he hugs his father's knees, forgiving him, just as Jeannette does. The way Donald saunters through the door, swinging a six-pack of beer, with a big grin on his face, takes her breath away. He leans against the door facing, looking sexy in his baseball cap and his shaggy red beard and his sunglasses. He wears sunglasses to be like the Blues Brothers, but he in no way resembles either of the Blues Brothers. I should have my head examined, Jeannette thinks.

The last time Donald was home, they went to the shopping center to buy Rodney some shoes advertised on sale. They stayed at the shopping center half the afternoon, just looking around. Donald and Rodney played video games. Jeannette felt they were a normal family. Then, in the parking lot, they stopped to watch a man on a platform demonstrating snakes. Children were petting a twelve-foot python coiled around the man's shoulders. Jeannette felt faint.

"Snakes won't hurt you unless you hurt them," said Donald as Rodney stroked the snake.

"It feels like chocolate," he said.

The snake man took a tarantula from a plastic box and held it lovingly in his palm. He said, "If you drop a tarantula, it will shatter like a Christmas ornament."

"I hate this," said Jeannette.

"Let's get out of here," said Donald.

Jeannette felt her family disintegrating like a spider shattering as Donald hurried them away from the shopping center. Rodney squalled and Donald dragged him along. Jeannette wanted to stop for ice cream. She wanted them all to sit quietly together in a booth, but Donald rushed them to the car, and he drove them home in silence, his face growing grim.

"Did you have bad dreams about the snakes?" Jeannette asked Rodney the next morning at breakfast. They were eating pancakes made with generic pancake mix. Rodney slapped his fork in the pond of syrup on his pancakes. "The black racer is the farmer's friend," he said soberly, repeating a fact learned from the snake man.

"Big Bertha kept black racers," said Donald. "She trained them for the 500." Donald doesn't tell Rodney ordinary children's stories. He tells him a series of strange stories he makes up about Big Bertha. Big Bertha is what he calls the huge strip-mining machine in Muhlenberg County, but he has Rodney believing that Big Bertha is a female version of Paul Bunyan.

"Snakes don't run in the 500," said Rodney.

"This wasn't the Indy 500 or the Daytona 500—none of your well-known 500s," said Donald. "This was the Possum Trot 500, and it was a long time ago. Big Bertha started the original 500, with snakes. Black racers and blue racers mainly. Also some red-and-white-striped racers, but those are rare."

"We always ran for the hoe if we saw a black racer," Jeannette said, remembering her childhood in the country.

In a way, Donald's absences are a fine arrangement, even considerate. He is sparing them his darkest moods, when he can't cope with his memories of Vietnam. Vietnam had never seemed such a meaningful fact until a couple of years ago, when he grew depressed and moody, and then he started going away to Central City. He frightened Jeannette, and she always said the wrong thing in her efforts to soothe him. If the welfare people find out he is spending occasional weekends at home, and even bringing some money, they will cut off her assistance. She applied for welfare because she can't depend on him to send money, but she knows he blames her for losing faith in him. He isn't really working regularly at the strip mines. He is mostly just hanging around there, watching the land being scraped away, trees coming down, bushes flung in the air. Sometimes he operates a steam shovel, and when he comes home his clothes are filled with the clay and it is caked on his shoes. The clay is the color of butterscotch pudding.

At first, he tried to explain to Jeannette. He said, "If we could have had tanks over there as big as Big Bertha, we wouldn't have lost the war. Strip mining is just like what we were doing over there. We were stripping off the top. The topsoil is like the culture and the people, the best part of the land and the country. America was just stripping off the top, the best. We ruined it. Here, at least the coal companies have to plant vetch and loblolly pines and all kinds of trees and bushes. If we'd done that in Vietnam, maybe we'd have left that country in better shape."

"Wasn't Vietnam a long time ago?" Jeannette asked.

She didn't want to hear about Vietnam. She thought it was unhealthy to dwell on it so much. He should live in the present. Her mother is afraid Donald will do something violent, because she once read in the newspaper that a veteran in Louisville held his little girl hostage in their apartment until he had a shootout with the police and was killed. But Jeannette can't imagine Donald doing anything so extreme. When she first met him, several years ago, at her parents' pit-barbecue luncheonette, where she was working then, he had a good job at a lumberyard and he dressed nicely. He took her out to eat at a fancy restaurant. They got plastered and ended up in a motel in Tupelo, Mississippi, on Elvis Presley Boulevard. Back then, he talked nostalgically about his year in Vietnam, about how beautiful it was, how different the people were. He could never seem to explain what he meant. "They're just different," he said.

They went riding around in a yellow 1957 Chevy convertible. He drives too fast now, but he didn't then, maybe because he was so protective of the car. It was a classic. He sold it three years ago and made a good profit. About the time he sold the Chevy, his moods began changing, his even-tempered nature shifting, like driving on a smooth interstate and then switching to a secondary road. He had headaches and bad dreams. But his nightmares seemed trivial. He dreamed of riding a train through the Rocky Mountains, of hijacking a plane to Cuba, of stringing up barbed wire around the house. He dreamed he lost a doll. He got drunk and rammed the car, the Chevy's successor, into a Civil War statue in front of the courthouse. When he got depressed over the meaninglessness of his job, Jeannette felt guilty about spending money on something nice for the house, and she tried to make him feel his job had meaning by reminding him that, after all, they had a child to think of. "I don't like his name," Donald said once. "What a stupid name. Rodney. I never did like it."

Rodney has dreams about Big Bertha, echoes of his father's nightmare, like TV cartoon versions of Donald's memories of the war. But Rodney loves the stories, even though they are confusing, with lots of loose ends. The latest in the Big Bertha series is "Big Bertha and the Neutron Bomb." Last week it was "Big Bertha and the MX Missile." In the new story, Big Bertha takes a trip to California to go surfing with Big Mo, her male counterpart. On the beach, corn dogs and snow cones are free and the surfboards turn into dolphins. Everyone is having fun until the neutron bomb comes. Rodney loves the part where everyone keels over dead. Donald acts it out, collapsing on the rug. All the dolphins and the surfers keel over, everyone except Big Bertha. Big Bertha is so big she is immune to the neutron bomb.

"Those stories aren't true," Jeannette tells Rodney.

Rodney staggers and falls down on the rug, his arms and legs akimbo. He gets the giggles and can't stop. When his spasms finally subside, he says, "I told Scottie Bidwell about Big Bertha and he didn't believe me."

Donald picks Rodney up under the armpits and sets him upright. "You tell Scottie Bidwell if he saw Big Bertha he would pee in his pants on the spot, he would be so impressed."

"Are you scared of Big Bertha?"

"No, I'm not. Big Bertha is just like a wonderful woman, a big fat woman who can sing the blues. Have you ever heard Big Mama Thornton?"

"No."

"Well, Big Bertha's like her, only she's the size of a tall building. She's slow as a turtle and when she crosses the road they have to reroute traffic. She's big enough to straddle a four-lane highway. She's so tall she can see all the way to Tennessee, and when she belches, there's a tornado. She's really something. She can even fly."

"She's too big to fly," Rodney says doubtfully. He makes a face like a wadded-up washrag and Donald wrestles him to the floor again.

Donald has been drinking all evening, but he isn't drunk. The ice cubes melt and he pours the drink out and refills it. He keeps on talking. Jeannette cannot remember him talking so much about the war. He is telling her about an ammunitions dump. Jeannette had the vague idea that an ammo dump is a mound of shotgun shells, heaps of cartridge casings and bomb shells, or whatever is left over, a vast waste pile from the war, but Donald says that is wrong. He has spent an hour describing it in detail, so that she will understand.

He refills the glass with ice, some 7-Up, and a shot of Jim Beam. He slams doors and drawers, looking for a compass. Jeannette can't keep track of the conversation. It doesn't matter that her hair is uncombed and her lipstick eaten away. He isn't seeing her.

"I want to draw the compound for you," he says, sitting down at the table with a sheet of Rodney's tablet paper.

Donald draws the map in red and blue ballpoint, with asterisks and technical labels that mean nothing to her. He draws some circles with the compass and measures some angles. He makes a red dot on an oblique line, a path that leads to the ammo dump.

"That's where I was. Right there," he says. "There was a water buffalo that tripped a land mine and its horn just flew off and stuck in the wall of the barracks like a machete thrown back-handed." He puts a dot where the land mine was, and he doodles awhile with the red ballpoint pen, scribbling something on the edge of the map that looks like feathers. "The dump was here and I was there and over there was where we piled the sandbags. And here were the tanks." He draws tanks, a row of squares with handles — guns sticking out.

"Why are you going to so much trouble to tell me about a buffalo horn that got stuck in a wall?" she wants to know.

But Donald just looks at her as though she has asked something obvious.

"Maybe I *could* understand if you'd let me," she says cautiously.

"You could never understand." He draws another tank.

In bed, it is the same as it has been since he started going away to Central City — the way he claims his side of the bed, turning away from her. Tonight, she reaches for him and he lets her be close to him. She cries for a while and he lies there, waiting for her to finish, as though she were merely putting on makeup.

"Do you want me to tell you a Big Bertha story?" he asks playfully.

"You act like you're in love with Big Bertha."

He laughs, breathing on her. But he won't come closer.

"You don't care what I look like anymore," she says. "What am I supposed to think?"

"There's nobody else. There's not anybody but you."

Loving a giant machine is incomprehensible to Jeannette. There must be another woman, someone that large in his mind. Jeannette has seen the strip-mining machine. The top of the crane is visible beyond a rise along the parkway. The strip mining is kept just out of sight of travelers because it would give them a poor image of Kentucky.

For three weeks, Jeannette has been seeing a psychologist at the free mental health clinic. He's a small man from out of state. His name is Dr. Robinson, but she calls him The Rapist, because the word *therapist* can be divided into two words, *the rapist*. He doesn't think her joke is clever, and he acts as though he has heard it a thousand times before. He has a habit of saying, "Go with that feeling," the same way Bob Newhart did on his old TV show. It's probably the first lesson in the textbook, Jeannette thinks.

She told him about Donald's last days on his job at the lumberyard—how he let the stack of lumber fall deliberately and didn't know why, and about how he went away soon after that, and how the Big Bertha stories started. Dr. Robinson seems to be waiting for her to make something out of it all, but it's maddening that he won't tell her what to do. After three visits, Jeannette has grown angry with him, and now she's holding back things. She won't tell him whether Donald slept with her or not when he came home last. Let him guess, she thinks.

"Talk about yourself," he says.

"What about me?"

"You speak so vaguely about Donald that I get the feeling that you see him as somebody larger than life. I can't quite picture him. That makes me wonder what that says about you." He touches the end of his tie to his nose and sniffs it.

When Jeannette suggests that she bring Donald in, the therapist looks bored and says nothing.

"He had another nightmare when he was home last," Jeannette says. "He dreamed he was crawling through tall grass and people were after him."

"How do *you* feel about that?" The Rapist asks eagerly.

"I didn't have the nightmare," she says coldly. "Donald did. I came to you to get advice about Donald, and you're acting like I'm the one who's crazy. I'm not crazy. But I'm lonely."

Jeannette's mother, behind the counter of the luncheonette, looks lovingly at Rodney pushing buttons on the jukebox in the corner. "It's a shame about that youngun," she says tearfully. "That boy needs a daddy."

"What are you trying to tell me? That I should file for divorce and get Rodney a new daddy?"

Her mother looks hurt. "No, honey," she says. "You need to get Donald to seek the Lord. And you need to pray more. You haven't been going to church lately."

"Have some barbecue," Jeannette's father booms, as he comes in from the back kitchen. "And I want you to take a pound home with you. You've got a growing boy to feed."

"I want to take Rodney to church," Mama says. "I want to show him off, and it might do some good."

"People will think he's an orphan," Dad says.

"I don't care," Mama says. "I just love him to pieces and I want to take him to church. Do you care if I take him to church, Jeannette?"

"No. I don't care if you take him to church." She takes the pound of barbecue from her father. Grease splotches the brown wrapping paper. Dad has given them so much barbecue that Rodney is burned out on it and won't eat it anymore.

Jeannette wonders if she would file for divorce if she could get a job. It is a thought—for the child's sake, she thinks. But there aren't many jobs around. With the cost of a baby-sitter, it doesn't pay her to work. When Donald first went away, her mother kept Rodney and she had a good job, waitressing at a steak house, but the steak house burned down one night—a grease fire in the kitchen. After that, she couldn't find a steady job, and she was reluctant to ask her mother to keep Rodney again because of her bad hip. At the steak house, men gave her tips and left their telephone numbers on the bill when they paid. They tucked dollar bills and notes in the pockets of her apron. One note said, "I want to hold your muffins." They were real-estate developers and businessmen on important missions for the Tennessee Valley Authority. They were boisterous and they drank too much. They said they'd take her for a cruise on the *Delta Queen*, but she didn't believe them. She knew how expensive that was. They talked about their speedboats and invited her for rides on Lake Barkley, or for spins in their private planes. They always used the word *spin*. The idea made her dizzy. Once, Jeannette let an electronics salesman take her for a ride in his Cadillac, and they breezed down the wilderness road through the Land Between the Lakes. His car had automatic windows and a stereo system and lighted computer-screen numbers on the dash that told him how many miles to the gallon he was getting and other statistics. He said the numbers distracted him and he had almost had several wrecks. At the restaurant, he had been flamboyant, admired by his companions. Alone with Jeannette in the Cadillac, on The Trace, he was shy and awkward, and really not very interesting. The most interesting thing about him, Jeannette thought, was all the lighted numbers on his dashboard. The Cadillac had everything but video games. But she'd rather be riding around with Donald, no matter where they ended up.

While the social worker is there, filling out her report, Jeannette listens for Donald's car. When the social worker drove up, the flutter and wheeze of her car sounded like Donald's old Chevy, and for a moment Jeannette's mind lapsed back in time. Now she listens, hoping he won't drive up. The social worker is younger than Jeannette and has been to college. Her name is Miss Bailey, and she's excessively cheerful, as though in her line of work she has seen hardships that make Jeannette's troubles seem like a trip to Hawaii.

"Is your little boy still having those bad dreams?" Miss Bailey asks, looking up from her clipboard.

Jeannette nods and looks at Rodney, who has his finger in his mouth and won't speak.

"Has the cat got your tongue?" Miss Bailey asks.

"Show her your pictures, Rodney." Jeannette explains, "He won't talk about the dreams, but he draws pictures of them."

Rodney brings his tablet of pictures and flips through them silently. Miss Bailey says, "Hmm." They are stark line drawings, remarkably steady lines for his age. "What is this one?" she asks. "Let me guess. Two scoops of ice cream?"

The picture is two huge circles, filling the page, with three tiny stick people in the corner.

"These are Big Bertha's titties," says Rodney.

Miss Bailey chuckles and winks at Jeannette. "What do you like to read, hon?" she asks Rodney.

"Nothing."

"He can read," says Jeannette. "He's smart."

"Do you like to read?" Miss Bailey asks Jeannette. She glances at the pile of paperbacks on the coffee table. She is probably going to ask where Jeannette got the money for them.

"I don't read," says Jeannette. "If I read, I just go crazy."

When she told The Rapist she couldn't concentrate on anything serious, he said she read romance novels in order to escape from reality. "Reality, hell!" she had said. "Reality's my whole problem."

"It's too bad Rodney's not here," Donald is saying. Rodney is in the closet again. "Santa Claus has to take back all these toys. Rodney would love this bicycle! And this Pac-Man game. Santa has to take back so many things he'll have to have a pickup truck!"

"You didn't bring him anything. You never bring him anything," says Jeannette.

He has brought doughnuts and dirty laundry. The clothes he is wearing are caked with clay. His beard is lighter from working out in the sun, and he looks his usual joyful self, the way he always is before his moods take over, like migraine headaches, which some people describe as storms.

Donald coaxes Rodney out of the closet with the doughnuts.

"Were you a good boy this week?"

"I don't know."

"I hear you went to the shopping center and showed out." It is not true that Rodney made a big scene. Jeannette has already explained that Rodney was upset because she wouldn't buy him an Atari. But she didn't blame him for crying. She was tired of being unable to buy him anything.

Rodney eats two doughnuts and Donald tells him a long, confusing story about Big Bertha and a rock-and-roll band. Rodney interrupts him with dozens of questions. In the story, the rock-and-roll band gives a concert in a place that turns out to be a toxic-waste dump and the contamination is spread all over the country. Big Bertha's solution to this problem is not at all clear. Jeannette stays in the kitchen, trying to think of something original to do with instant potatoes and leftover barbecue.

"We can't go on like this," she says that evening in bed. "We're just hurting each other. Something has to change."

He grins like a kid. "Coming home from Muhlenberg County is like R and R—rest and recreation. I explain that in case you think R and R means rock and roll. Or maybe rumps and rears. Or rust and rot." He laughs and draws a circle in the air with his cigarette.

"I'm not that dumb."

"When I leave, I go back to the mines." He sighs, as though the mines were some eternal burden.

Her mind skips ahead to the future: Donald locked away somewhere, coloring in a coloring book and making clay pots, her and Rodney in some other town, with another man—someone dull and not at all sexy. Summoning up her courage, she says, "I haven't been through what you've been through and maybe I don't have a right to say this, but sometimes I think you act superior because you went to Vietnam, like nobody can ever know what you know. Well, maybe not. But you've still got your legs, even if you don't know what to do with what's between them anymore." Bursting into tears of apology, she can't help adding, "You can't go on telling Rodney those awful stories. He has nightmares when you're gone."

Donald rises from bed and grabs Rodney's picture from the dresser, holding it as he might have held a hand grenade. "Kids betray you," he says, turning the picture in his hand.

"If you cared about him, you'd stay here." As he sets the picture down, she asks, "What can I do? How can I understand what's going on in your mind? Why do you go there? Strip mining's bad for the ecology and you don't have any business strip mining."

"My job is serious, Jeannette. I run that steam shovel and put the top-soil back on. I'm reclaiming the land." He keeps talking, in a gentler voice, about strip mining, the same old things she has heard before, comparing Big Bertha to a supertank. If only they had had Big Bertha in Vietnam. He says, "When they strip off the top, I keep looking for those tunnels where the Viet Cong hid. They had so many tunnels it was unbelievable. Imagine Mammoth Cave going all the way across Kentucky."

"Mammoth Cave's one of the natural wonders of the world," says Jeannette brightly. She is saying the wrong thing again.

At the kitchen table at 2 A.M., he's telling about C-5A's. A C-5A is so big it can carry troops and tanks and helicopters, but it's not big enough to hold Big Bertha. Nothing could hold Big Bertha. He rambles on, and when Jeannette shows him Rodney's drawing of the circles, Donald smiles. Dreamily, he begins talking about women's breasts and thighs — the large, round thighs and big round breasts of American women, contrasted with the frail, delicate beauty of the Orientals. It is like comparing oven broilers and banties, he says. Jeannette relaxes. A confession about another lover from long ago is not so hard to take. He seems stuck on the breasts and thighs of American women — insisting that she understand how small and delicate the Orientals are, but then he abruptly returns to tanks and helicopters.

"A Bell Huey Cobra — my God, what a beautiful machine. So efficient!" Donald takes the food processor blade from the drawer where Jeannette keeps it. He says, "A rotor blade from a chopper could just slice anything to bits."

"Don't do that," Jeannette says.

He is trying to spin the blade on the counter, like a top. "Here's what would happen when a chopper blade hits a power line — not many of those over there! — or a tree. Not many trees, either, come to think of it, after all the Agent Orange." He drops the blade and it glances off the open drawer and falls to the floor, spiking the vinyl.

At first, Jeannette thinks the screams are hers, but they are his. She watches him cry. She has never seen anyone cry so hard, like an intense summer thundershower. All she knows to do is shove Kleenex at him. Finally, he is able to say, "You thought I was going to hurt you. That's why I'm crying."

"Go ahead and cry," Jeannette says, holding him close.

"Don't go away."

"I'm right here. I'm not going anywhere."

In the night, she still listens, knowing his monologue is being burned like a tattoo into her brain. She will never forget it. His voice grows soft and he plays with a ballpoint pen, jabbing holes in a paper towel. Bullet holes, she thinks. His beard is like a bird's nest, woven with dark corn silks.

"This is just a story," he says. "Don't mean nothing. Just relax." She is sitting on the hard edge of the kitchen chair, her toes cold on the floor, waiting. His tears have dried up and left a slight catch in his voice.

"We were in a big camp near a village. It was pretty routine and kind of soft there for a while. Now and then we'd go into Da Nang and whoop it up. We had been in the jungle for several months, so the two months at this village was a sort of rest—an R and R almost. Don't shiver. This is just a little story. Don't mean nothing! This is nothing, compared to what I could tell you. Just listen. We lost our fear. At night there would be some incoming and we'd see these tracers in the sky, like shooting stars up close, but it was all pretty minor and we didn't take it seriously, after what we'd been through. In the village I knew this Vietnamese family—a woman and her two daughters. They sold Cokes and beer to GIs. The oldest daughter was named Phan. She could speak a little English. She was really smart. I used to go see them in their hooch in the afternoon—in the siesta time of day. It was so hot there. Phan was beautiful, like the country. The village was ratty, but the country was pretty. And she was beautiful, just like she had grown up out of the jungle, like one of those flowers that bloomed high up in the trees and freaked us out sometimes, thinking it was a sniper. She was so gentle, with these eyes shaped like peach pits, and she was no bigger than a child of maybe thirteen or fourteen. I felt funny about her size at first, but later it didn't matter. It was just some wonderful feature about her, like a woman's hair, or her breasts."

He stops and listens, the way they used to listen for crying sounds when Rodney was a baby. He says, "She'd take those big banana leaves and fan me while I lay there in the heat."

"I didn't know they had bananas over there."

"There's a lot you don't know! Listen! Phan was twenty-three, and her brothers were off fighting. I never even asked which side they were fighting on." He laughs. "She got a kick out of the word *fan*. I told her that *fan* was the same word as her name. She thought I meant her name was banana. In Vietnamese the same word can have a dozen different meanings, depending on your tone of voice. I bet you didn't know that, did you?"

"No. What happened to her?"

"I don't know."

"Is that the end of the story?"

"I don't know." Donald pauses, then goes on talking about the village, the girl, the banana leaves, talking in a monotone that is making Jeannette's flesh crawl. He could be the news radio from the next room.

"You must have really liked that place. Do you wish you could go back there to find out what happened to her?"

"It's not there anymore," he says. "It blew up."

Donald abruptly goes to the bathroom. She hears the water running, the pipes in the basement shaking.

"It was so pretty," he says when he returns. He rubs his elbow absent-mindedly. "That jungle was the most beautiful place in the world. You'd have thought you were in paradise. But we blew it sky-high."

In her arms, he is shaking, like the pipes in the basement, which are still vibrating. Then the pipes let go, after a long shudder, but he continues to tremble.

They are driving to the Veterans Hospital. It was Donald's idea. She didn't have to persuade him. When she made up the bed that morning—with a finality that shocked her, as though she knew they wouldn't be in it again together—he told her it would be like R and R. Rest was what he needed. Neither of them had slept at all during the night. Jeannette felt she had to stay awake, to listen for more.

"Talk about strip mining," she says now. "That's what they'll do to your head. They'll dig out all those ugly memories, I hope. We don't need them around here." She pats his knee.

It is a cloudless day, not the setting for this sober journey. She drives and Donald goes along obediently, with the resignation of an old man being taken to a rest home. They are driving through southern Illinois, known as Little Egypt, for some obscure reason Jeannette has never understood. Donald still talks, but very quietly, without urgency. When he points out the scenery, Jeannette thinks of the early days of their marriage, when they would take a drive like this and laugh hysterically. Now Jeannette points out funny things they see. The Little Egypt Hot Dog World, Pharaoh Cleaners, Pyramid Body Shop. She is scarcely aware that she is driving, and when she sees a sign, LITTLE EGYPT STARLITE CLUB, she is confused for a moment, wondering where she has been transported.

As they part, he asks, "What will you tell Rodney if I don't come back? What if they keep me here indefinitely?"

"You're coming back. I'm telling him you're coming back soon."

"Tell him I went off with Big Bertha. Tell him she's taking me on a sea cruise, to the South Seas."

"No. You can tell him that yourself."

He starts singing "Sea Cruise." He grins at her and pokes her in the ribs.

"You're coming back," she says.

Donald writes from the VA Hospital, saying that he is making progress. They are running tests, and he meets in a therapy group in which all the veterans trade memories. Jeannette is no longer on welfare because she now has a job waitressing at Fred's Family Restaurant. She waits on families, waits for Donald to come home so they can come here and eat together like a family. The fathers look at her with downcast eyes, and the children throw food. While Donald is gone, she rearranges the furniture. She reads some books from the library. She does a lot of thinking. It occurs to her that even though she loved him, she has thought of Donald primarily as a husband, a provider, someone whose name she shared, the father of her child, someone like the fathers who come to the Wednesday night all-you-can-eat fish fry. She hasn't thought of him as himself. She wasn't brought up that way, to examine someone's soul. When it comes to something deep inside, nobody will take it out and examine it, the way they will look at clothing in a store for flaws in the manufacturing. She tries to explain all this to The Rapist, and he says she's looking better, got sparkle in her eyes. "Big deal," says Jeannette. "Is that all you can say?"

She takes Rodney to the shopping center, their favorite thing to do together, even though Rodney always begs to buy something. They go to Penney's perfume counter. There, she usually hits a sample bottle of cologne — Chantilly or Charlie or something strong. Today she hits two or three and comes out of Penney's smelling like a flower garden.

"You stink!" Rodney cries, wrinkling his nose like a rabbit.

"Big Bertha smells like this, only a thousand times worse, she's so big," says Jeannette impulsively. "Didn't Daddy tell you that?"

"Daddy's a messenger from the devil."

This is an idea he must have gotten from church. Her parents have been taking him every Sunday. When Jeannette tries to reassure him about his father, Rodney is skeptical. "He gets that funny look on his face like he can see through me," the child says.

"Something's missing," Jeannette says, with a rush of optimism, a feeling of recognition. "Something happened to him once and took out the part that shows how much he cares about us."

"The way we had the cat fixed?"

"I guess. Something like that." The appropriateness of his remark stuns her, as though, in a way, her child has understood Donald all along. Rodney's pictures have been more peaceful lately, pictures of skinny trees and airplanes flying low. This morning he drew pictures of tall grass, with creatures hiding in it. The grass is tilted at an angle, as though a light breeze is blowing through it.

With her paycheck, Jeannette buys Rodney a present, a miniature trampoline they have seen advertised on television. It is called Mr. Bouncer. Rodney is thrilled about the trampoline, and he jumps on it until his face is red. Jeannette discovers that she enjoys it, too. She puts it out on the grass, and they take turns jumping. She has an image of herself on the trampoline, her sailor collar flapping, at the moment when Donald returns and sees her flying. One day a neighbor driving by slows down and calls out to Jeannette as she is bouncing on the trampoline, "You'll tear your insides loose!" Jeannette starts thinking about that, and the idea is so horrifying she stops jumping so much. That night, she has a nightmare about the trampoline. In her dream, she is jumping on soft moss, and then it turns into a springy pile of dead bodies.

[1980]

AMY HEMPEL

Amy Hempel (b. 1951) was born in Chicago and grew up in California, where she went to four colleges before moving to New York City. She regarded her years in Los Angeles and San Francisco as "lost," yet found herself "making notes on things that happened many years before I started to write, though at the time I did not know why." In 1982 she attended a fiction workshop at Columbia University taught by Gordon Lish, an editor at Knopf, who arranged for the publication of her first collection of stories, Reasons to Live (1985). Hempel has said that in her writing she was influenced by contemporaries such as Raymond Carver, who have "a kind of compression and distillation in their work that gets to the heart of things and gives the reader credit for being able to keep up without having everything explained."

Often Hempel's stories are only a few paragraphs long—fragments of conversation, whimsical anecdotes, and ironic observations about women's lives written in a style as spare and evocative as a Polaroid snapshot. The novelist Sheila Ballantyne has understood Hempel's method:

> Minimalism has its uses, and can achieve surprisingly varied effects: it can allude and expand, as well as leave out and compress. At its most reductive or repetitive, it can induce corresponding states of boredom or trance. . . . At its worst, minimalism is a kind of fraudulent tic that serves to hide a vacuum or defend against feeling. At its best it can, with economy and restraint, amplify perception and force meaning to leap from the page.

"In the Cemetery Where Al Jolson Is Buried" refers to the popular entertainer who starred in The Jazz Singer, the first "talkie" made in Hollywood. Jolson is buried in Forest Lawn Cemetery in Los Angeles. The story, which first appeared in Triquarterly in 1985, is from Hempel's first collection. Since then she has published At the Gate of the Animal Kingdom (1990) and Tumble Home: A Novella and Short Stories (1997), in which one of her narrators suggests Hempel's rationale as a storyteller: "The lighter the line, the easier it is to get your lure down deep." In an interview published in Glimmer Train (1997), Hempel explained that "compression has always been hugely attractive, and rhythm, whether it's in a sentence or a line," when she writes prose narrative.

> I pay readers the compliment, I mean I'm acknowledging that they're smart enough to get it. They don't need everything spelled out. They live downtown, they've seen tall buildings. . . . I think that my concerns are more a poet's concerns and always have been. I don't understand why these things in a story would be criticized, whereas in a poem it's the norm, it's what you expect. But I guess some have certain expectations of what a story is—that a story can be this, but not that. I think it really has come from a more provincial sense, a restricted, limited sense of story, and what it can do.

In the Cemetery Where
Al Jolson Is Buried

"Tell me things I won't mind forgetting," she said. "Make it useless stuff or skip it."

I began. I told her insects fly through rain missing every drop, never getting wet. I told her no one in America owned a tape recorder before Bing Crosby did. I told her the shape of the moon is like a banana — you see it looking full, you're seeing it end-on.

The camera made me self-conscious and I stopped. It was trained on us from a ceiling mount — the kind of camera banks use to photograph robbers. It played us to the nurses down the hall in Intensive Care.

"Go on, girl," she said. "You get used to it."

I had my audience. I went on. Did she know that Tammy Wynette had changed her tune? Really. That now she sings "Stand By Your Friends"? That Paul Anka did it too, I said. Does "You're Having *Our* Baby." That he got sick of all that feminist bitching.

"What else?" she said. "Have you got something else?"

Oh, yes.

For her I would always have something else.

"Did you know that when they taught the first chimp to talk, it lied? That when they asked her who did it on the desk, she signed back Max, the janitor. And that when they pressed her, she said she was sorry, that it was really the project director. But she was a mother, so I guess she had her reasons."

"Oh, that's good," she said. "A parable."

"There's more about the chimp," I said. "But it will break your heart."

"No, thanks," she says, and scratches at her mask.

We look like good-guy outlaws. Good or bad, I am not used to the mask yet. I keep touching the warm spot where my breath, thank God, comes out. She is used to hers. She only ties the strings on top. The other ones — a pro by now — she lets hang loose.

We call this place the Marcus Welby Hospital. It's the white one with the palm trees under the opening credits of all those shows. A Hollywood hospital, though in fact it is several miles west. Off camera, there is a beach across the street.

She introduces me to a nurse as the Best Friend. The impersonal article is more intimate. It tells me that *they* are intimate, the nurse and my friend.

"I was telling her we used to drink Canada Dry ginger ale and pretend we were in Canada."

"That's how dumb *we* were," I say.

"You could be sisters," the nurse says.

So how come, I'll bet they are wondering, it took me so long to get to such a glamorous place? But do they ask?

They do not ask.

Two months, and how long is the drive?

The best I can explain it is this — I have a friend who worked one summer in a mortuary. He used to tell me stories. The one that really got to me was not the grisliest, but it's the one that did. A man wrecked his car on 101 going south. He did not lose consciousness. But his arm was taken down to the wet bone — and when he looked at it — it scared him to death.

I mean, he died.

So I hadn't dared to look any closer. But now I'm doing it — and hoping that I will live through it.

She shakes out a summer-weight blanket, showing a leg you did not want to see. Except for that, you look at her and understand the law that requires two people to be with the body at all times.

"I thought of something," she says. "I thought of it last night. I think there is a real and present need here. You know," she says, "like for someone to do it for you when you can't do it yourself. You call them up whenever you want — like when push comes to shove."

She grabs the bedside phone and loops the cord around her neck.

"Hey," she says, "the end o' the line."

She keeps on, giddy with something. But I don't know with what.

"I can't remember," she says. "What does Kübler-Ross[1] say comes after Denial?"

It seems to me Anger must be next. Then Bargaining, Depression, and so on and so forth. But I keep my guesses to myself.

"The only thing is," she says, "is where's Resurrection? God knows, I want to do it by the book. But she left out Resurrection."

She laughs, and I cling to the sound the way someone dangling above a ravine holds fast to the thrown rope.

"Tell me," she says, "about that chimp with the talking hands. What do they do when the thing ends and the chimp says, 'I don't want to go back to the zoo'?"

When I don't say anything, she says, "Okay — then tell me another animal story. I like animal stories. But not a sick one — I don't want to know about all the seeing-eye dogs going blind."

No, I would not tell her a sick one.

---

[1]Elisabeth Kübler-Ross (b. 1926), author of popular books on death and dying.

"How about the hearing-ear dogs?" I say. "They're not going deaf, but they are getting very judgmental. For instance, there's this golden retriever in New Jersey, he wakes up the deaf mother and drags her into the daughter's room because the kid has got a flashlight and is reading under the covers."

"Oh, you're killing me," she says. "Yes, you're definitely killing me."

"They say the smart dog obeys, but the smarter dog knows when to disobey."

"Yes," she says, "the smarter anything knows when to disobey. Now, for example."

She is flirting with the Good Doctor, who has just appeared. Unlike the Bad Doctor, who checks the I.V. drip before saying good morning, the Good Doctor says things like "God didn't give epileptics a fair shake." The Good Doctor awards himself points for the cripples he could have hit in the parking lot. Because the Good Doctor is a little in love with her, he says maybe a year. He pulls a chair up to her bed and suggests I might like to spend an hour on the beach.

"Bring me something back," she says. "Anything from the beach. Or the gift shop. Taste is no object."

He draws the curtain around her bed.

"Wait!" she cries.

I look in at her.

"Anything," she says, "except a magazine subscription."

The doctor turns away.

I watch her mouth laugh.

What seems dangerous often is not—black snakes, for example, or clear-air turbulence. While things that just lie there, like this beach, are loaded with jeopardy. A yellow dust rising from the ground, the heat that ripens melons overnight—this is earthquake weather. You can sit here braiding the fringe on your towel and the sand will all of a sudden suck down like an hourglass. The air roars. In the cheap apartments on-shore, bathtubs fill themselves and gardens roll up and over like green waves. If nothing happens, the dust will drift and the heat deepen till fear turns to desire. Nerves like that are only bought off by catastrophe.

"It never happens when you're thinking about it," she once observed. "Earthquake, earthquake, earthquake," she said.

"Earthquake, earthquake, earthquake," I said.

Like the aviaphobe who keeps the plane aloft with prayer, we kept it up until an aftershock cracked the ceiling.

That was after the big one in '72. We were in college; our dormitory was five miles from the epicenter. When the ride was over and my jabbering pulse began to slow, she served five parts champagne to one part orange juice, and joked about living in Ocean View, Kansas. I offered to drive her to Hawaii on the new world psychics predicted would surface the next time, or the next.

I could not say that now — next.

Whose next? she could ask.

Was I the only one who noticed that the experts had stopped saying *if* and now spoke of *when?* Of course not; the fearful ran to thousands. We watched the traffic of Japanese beetles for deviation. Deviation might mean more natural violence.

I wanted her to be afraid with me. But she said, "I don't know. I'm just not."

She was afraid of nothing, not even of flying.

I have this dream before a flight where we buckle in and the plane moves down the runway. It takes off at thirty-five miles an hour, and then we're airborne, skimming the tree tops. Still, we arrive in New York on time.

It is so pleasant.

One night I flew to Moscow this way.

She flew with me once. That time she flew with me she ate macadamia nuts while the wings bounced. She knows the wing tips can bend thirty feet up and thirty feet down without coming off. She believes it. She trusts the laws of aerodynamics. My mind stampedes. I can almost accept that a battleship floats when everybody knows steel sinks.

I see fear in her now, and am not going to try to talk her out of it. She is right to be afraid.

After a quake, the six o'clock news airs a film clip of first-graders yelling at the broken playground per their teacher's instructions.

"*Bad* earth!" they shout, because anger is stronger than fear.

But the beach is standing still today. Everyone on it is tranquilized, numb, or asleep. Teenaged girls rub coconut oil on each other's hard-to-reach places. They smell like macaroons. They pry open compacts like clamshells; mirrors catch the sun and throw a spray of white rays across glazed shoulders. The girls arrange their wet hair with silk flowers the way they learned in *Seventeen*. They pose.

A formation of low-riders pulls over to watch with a six-pack. They get vocal when the girls check their tan lines. When the beer is gone, so are they — flexing their cars on up the boulevard.

Above this aggressive health are the twin wrought-iron terraces, painted flamingo pink, of the Palm Royale. Someone dies there every time the sheets are changed. There's an ambulance in the driveway, so the remaining residents line the balconies, rocking and not talking, one-upped.

The ocean they stare at is dangerous, and not just the undertow. You can almost see the slapping tails of sand sharks keeping cruising bodies alive.

If she looked, she could see this, some of it, from her window. She would be the first to say how little it takes to make a thing all wrong.

There was a second bed in the room when I got back to it!

For two beats I didn't get it. Then it hit me like an open coffin.

She wants every minute, I thought. She wants my life.

"You missed Gussie," she said.

Gussie is her parents' three-hundred-pound, narcoleptic maid. Her attacks often come at the ironing board. The pillowcases in that family are all bordered with scorch.

"It's a hard trip for her," I said. "How is she?"

"Well, she didn't fall asleep, if that's what you mean. Gussie's great—you know what she said? She said, 'Darlin, stop this worriation. Just keep prayin, down on your knees'—me, who can't even get out of bed."

She shrugged. "What am I missing?"

"It's earthquake weather," I told her.

"The best thing to do about earthquakes," she said, "is not to live in California."

"That's useful," I said. "You sound like Reverend Ike—'The best thing to do for the poor is not be one of them.'"

We're crazy about Reverend Ike.

I noticed her face was bloated.

"You know," she said, "I feel like hell. I'm about to stop having fun."

"The ancients have a saying," I said. "'There are times when the wolves are silent; there are times when the moon howls.'"

"What's that, Navajo?"

"Palm Royale lobby graffiti," I said. "I bought a paper there. I'll read you something."

"Even though I care about nothing?"

I turned to the page with the trivia column. I said, "Did you know the more shrimp flamingo birds eat, the pinker their feathers get?" I said, "Did you know that Eskimos need refrigerators? Do you know *why* Eskimos need refrigerators? Did you know that Eskimos need refrigerators because how else would they keep their food from freezing?"

I turned to page three, to a UPI filler datelined Mexico City. I read her "Man Robs Bank with Chicken," about a man who bought a barbe-cued chicken at a stand down the block from a bank. Passing the bank, he got the idea. He walked in and approached a teller. He pointed the brown paper bag at her and she handed over the day's receipts. It was the smell of barbecue sauce that eventually led to his capture.

The story had made her hungry, she said—so I took the elevator down six floors to the cafeteria, and brought back all the ice cream she wanted. We lay side by side, adjustable beds cranked up for optimal TV-viewing, littering the sheets with Good Humor wrappers, picking toasted

almonds out of the gauze. We were Lucy and Ethel, Mary and Rhoda in
extremis. The blinds were closed to keep light off the screen.

We watched a movie starring men we used to think we wanted to sleep
with. Hers was a tough cop out to stop mine, a vicious rapist who went
after cocktail waitresses.

"This is a good movie," she said when snipers felled them both.

I missed her already.

A Filipino nurse tiptoed in and gave her an injection. The nurse
removed the pile of popsicle sticks from the nightstand—enough to splint
a small animal.

The injection made us both sleepy. We slept.

I dreamed she was a decorator, come to furnish my house. She worked
in secret, singing to herself. When she finished, she guided me proudly to
the door. "How do you like it?" she asked, easing me inside.

Every beam and sill and shelf and knob was draped in gay bunting,
with streamers of pastel crepe looped around bright mirrors.

"I have to go home," I said when she woke up.

She thought I meant home to her house in the Canyon, and I had to
say No, *home* home. I twisted my hands in the time-honored fashion of
people in pain. I was supposed to offer something. The Best Friend. I
could not even offer to come back.

I felt weak and small and failed.

Also exhilarated.

I had a convertible in the parking lot. Once out of that room, I would
drive it too fast down the Coast highway through the crab-smelling air. A
stop in Malibu for sangria. The music in the place would be sexy and loud.
They'd serve papaya and shrimp and watermelon ice. After dinner I would
shimmer with lust, buzz with heat, vibrate with life, and stay up all night.

Without a word, she yanked off her mask and threw it on the floor. She
kicked at the blankets and moved to the door. She must have hated having
to pause for breath and balance before slamming out of Isolation, and out of
the second room, the one where you scrub and tie on the white masks.

A voice shouted her name in alarm, and people ran down the corridor.
The Good Doctor was paged over the intercom. I opened the door and
the nurses at the station stared hard, as if this flight had been my idea.

"Where is she?" I asked, and they nodded to the supply closet.

I looked in. Two nurses were kneeling beside her on the floor, talking
to her in low voices. One held a mask over her nose and mouth, the other
rubbed her back in slow circles. The nurses glanced up to see if I was the
doctor—and when I wasn't, they went back to what they were doing.

"There, there, honey," they cooed.

On the morning she was moved to the cemetery, the one where Al Jolson is buried, I enrolled in a Fear of Flying class. "What is your worst fear?" the instructor asked, and I answered, "That I will finish this course and still be afraid."

I sleep with a glass of water on the nightstand so I can see by its level if the coastal earth is trembling or if the shaking is still me.

What do I remember?

I remember only the useless things I hear—that Bob Dylan's mother invented Wite-Out, that twenty-three people must be in a room before there is a fifty-fifty chance two will have the same birthdate. Who cares whether or not it's true? In my head there are bath towels swaddling this stuff. Nothing else seeps through.

I review those things that will figure in the re-telling: a kiss through surgical gauze, the pale hand correcting the position of the wig. I noted these gestures as they happened, not in any retrospect—though I do not know why looking back should show us more than looking at.

It is just possible I will say I stayed the night.

And who is there that can say that I did not?

I think of the chimp, the one with the talking hands.

In the course of the experiment, that chimp had a baby. Imagine how her trainers must have thrilled when the mother, without prompting, began to sign to her newborn.

Baby, drink milk.

Baby, play ball.

And when the baby died, the mother stood over the body, her wrinkled hands moving with animal grace, forming again and again the words, Baby, come hug, Baby, come hug, fluent now in the language of grief.   [1985]

BHARATI MUKHERJEE

Bharati Mukherjee (b. 1940) was born in Calcutta, India. As a young girl she lived in London with her parents and sisters, but she returned to India in 1951 and was educated at the universities of Calcutta and Baroda. While studying for her doctorate at the University of Iowa Writers' Workshop, she married the novelist Clark Blaise in 1963. For ten years they lived in Canada, where she published two novels, The Tiger's Daughter *(1972) and* Wife *(1975). Mukherjee and her husband then lived for a year in India, an experience that led to their collaboration on the journal* Days and Nights in Calcutta *(1977). It describes their different impressions of the country—Blaise was fascinated by his introduction to Bengali life and culture, whereas Mukherjee was angered by the oppression of women in India.*

In 1980 Mukherjee came to live in the United States, where she began teaching at the University of Iowa. In Canada she had been conscious of racism: "I was frequently taken for a prostitute or a shoplifter, frequently assumed to be a domestic, praised by astonished auditors that I didn't have a 'singsong' accent. The society itself . . . routinely made crippling assumptions about me, and about my 'kind.'" In the United States, Mukherjee grew more optimistic. She has described the note card pinned above her writing desk to give her inspiration. It quotes the showman Liberace, whom she admired as an "American original": "Too much of a good thing is simply wonderful." She feels that her writing has lost the "mordant and self-protected irony" she had adopted from her previous literary model, V. S. Naipaul. Her outlook is more tolerant in The Middleman and Other Stories *(1988), the book that established her reputation in this country. "The Tenant," first published in the* Literary Review *in 1986, is included in this collection.*

The critic Ann Mandel has understood that in stories such as "The Tenant," Mukherjee is dramatizing the immigrant's "request for recognition— the desire to be 'visible' in honorable ways, to be recognized as a person rather than as an ethnic stereotype." The characters in The Middleman *represent America's recent wave of Third World immigrants—Filipino, Salvadoran, Iraqi, Indian. Mukherjee's recent novels are* Jasmine *(1989),* The Holder of the World *(1993), and* Leave It to Me *(1997).*

The Tenant

Maya Sanyal has been in Cedar Falls, Iowa, less than two weeks. She's come, books and clothes and one armchair rattling in the smallest truck that U-Haul would rent her, from New Jersey. Before that she was in North Carolina. Before that, Calcutta, India. Every place has something to give. She is sitting at the kitchen table with Fran drinking bourbon for the first time in her life. Fran Johnson found her the furnished apartment and helped her settle in. Now she's brought a bottle of bourbon which gives her the right to stay and talk for a bit. She's breaking up with someone named Vern, a pharmacist. Vern's father is also a pharmacist and owns a drugstore. Maya has seen Vern's father on TV twice already. The first time was on the local news when he spoke out against the selling of painkillers like Advil and Nuprin in supermarkets and gas stations. In the matter of painkillers, Maya is a universalist. The other time he was in a barbershop quartet. Vern gets along all right with his father. He likes the pharmacy business, as business goes, but he wants to go back to graduate school and learn to make films. Maya is drinking her first bourbon tonight because Vern left today for San Francisco State.

"I understand totally," Fran says. She teaches Utopian Fiction and a course in Women's Studies and worked hard to get Maya hired. Maya has a Ph.D. in Comparative Literature and will introduce writers like R. K. Narayan and Chinua Achebe to three sections of sophomores at the University of Northern Iowa. "A person has to leave home. Try out his wings."

Fran has to use the bathroom. "I don't feel abandoned." She pushes her chair away from the table. "Anyway, it was a sex thing totally. We were good together. It'd be different if I'd loved him."

Maya tries to remember what's in the refrigerator. They need food. She hasn't been to the supermarket in over a week. She doesn't have a car yet and so she relies on a corner store—a longish walk—for milk, cereal, and frozen dinners. Someday these exigencies will show up as bad skin and collapsed muscle tone. No folly is ever lost. Maya pictures history as a net, the kind of safety net travelling trapeze artists of her childhood fell into when they were inattentive, or clumsy. Going to circuses in Calcutta with her father is what she remembers vividly. It is a banal memory, for her father, the owner of a steel company, is a complicated man.

Fran is out in the kitchen long enough for Maya to worry. They need food. Her mother believed in food. What is love, anger, inner peace, etc., her mother used to say, but the brain's biochemistry. Maya doesn't want to get into that, but she is glad she has enough stuff in the refrigerator to make an omelette. She realizes Indian women are supposed to be inventive with food, whip up exotic delights to tickle an American's palate, and she knows she should be meeting Fran's generosity and candor with some sort of bizarre and effortless countermove. If there's an exotic spice store in Cedar Falls or in neighboring Waterloo, she hasn't found it. She's looked in the phone book for common Indian names, especially Bengali, but hasn't yet struck up culinary intimacies. That will come—it always does. There's a six-pack in the fridge that her landlord, Ted Suminski, had put in because she'd be thirsty after unpacking. She was thirsty, but she doesn't drink beer. She probably should have asked him to come up and drink the beer. Except for Fran she hasn't had anyone over. Fran is more friendly and helpful than anyone Maya has known in the States since she came to

North Carolina ten years ago, at nineteen. Fran is a Swede, and she is tall, with blue eyes. Her hair, however, is a dull, darkish brown.

"I don't think I can handle anything that heavy-duty," Fran says when she comes back to the room. She means the omelette. "I have to go home in any case." She lives with her mother and her aunt, two women in their mid-seventies, in a drafty farmhouse. The farmhouse now has a computer store catty-corner from it. Maya's been to the farm. She's been shown photographs of the way the corner used to be. If land values ever rebound, Fran will be worth millions.

Before Fran leaves she says, "Has Rab Chatterji called you yet?"

"No." She remembers the name, a good, reliable Bengali name, from the first night's study of the phone book. Dr. Rabindra Chatterji teaches Physics.

"He called the English office just before I left." She takes car keys out of her pocketbook. She reknots her scarf. "I bet Indian men are more sensitive than Americans. Rab's a Brahmin, that's what people say."

A Chatterji has to be a Bengali Brahmin—last names give ancestral secrets away—but Brahminness seems to mean more to Fran than it does to Maya. She was born in 1954, six full years after India became independent. Her India was Nehru's India: a charged, progressive place.

"All Indian men are wife beaters," Maya says. She means it and doesn't mean it. "That's why I married an American." Fran knows about the divorce, but nothing else. Fran is on the Hiring, Tenure, and Reappointment Committee.

Maya sees Fran down the stairs and to the car which is parked in the back in the spot reserved for Maya's car, if she had owned one. It will take her several months to save enough to buy one. She always pays cash, never borrows. She tells herself she's still recovering from the U-Haul drive halfway across the country. Ted Suminski is in his kitchen watching the women. Maya waves to him because waving to him, acknowledging him in that way, makes him seem less creepy. He seems to live alone though a sign, THE SUMINSKIS, hangs from a metal horse's head in the front yard. Maya hasn't seen Mrs. Suminski. She hasn't seen any children either. Ted always looks lonely. When she comes back from campus, he's nearly always in the back, throwing darts or shooting baskets.

"What's he like?" Fran gestures with her head as she starts up her car. "You hear these stories."

Maya doesn't want to know the stories. She has signed a year's lease. She doesn't want complications. "He's all right. I keep out of his way."

"You know what I'm thinking? Of all the people in Cedar Falls, you're the one who could understand Vern best. His wanting to try out his wings, run away, stuff like that."

"Not really." Maya is not being modest. Fran is being impulsively democratic, lumping her wayward lover and Indian friend together as head-strong adventurers. For Fran, a utopian and feminist, borders don't count. Maya's taken some big risks, made a break with her parents' ways. She's done things a woman from Ballygunge Park Road doesn't do, even in fantasies. She's not yet shared stories with Fran, apart from the divorce. She's told her nothing of men she picks up, the reputation she'd gained, before Cedar Falls, for "indiscretions." She has a job, equity, three friends she can count on for emergencies. She is an American citizen. But.

Fran's Brahmin calls her two nights later. On the phone he presents himself as Dr. Chatterji, not Rabindra or Rab. An old-fashioned Indian, she assumes. Her father still calls his closest friend, "Colonel." Dr. Chatterji asks her to tea on Sunday. She means to say no but hears herself saying, "Sunday? Fiveish? I'm not doing anything special this Sunday."

Outside, Ted Suminski is throwing darts into his garage door. The door has painted-on rings: orange, purple, pink. The bull's-eye is gray. He has to be fifty at least. He is a big, thick, lonely man about whom people tell stories. Maya pulls the phone cord as far as it'll go so she can look down more directly on her landlord's large, bald head. He has his back to her as he lines up a dart. He's in black running shoes, red shorts, he's naked to the waist. He hunches his right shoulder, he pulls the arm back; a big, lonely man shouldn't have so much grace. The dart is ready to cut through the September evening. But Ted Suminski doesn't let go. He swings on worn rubber soles, catches her eye in the window (she has to have imagined this), takes aim at her shadow. Could she have imagined the noise of the dart's metal tip on her windowpane?

Dr. Chatterji is still on the phone. "You are not having any mode of transportation, is that right?"

Ted Suminski has lost interest in her. Perhaps it isn't interest, at all; perhaps it's aggression. "I don't drive," she lies, knowing it sounds less shameful than not owning a car. She has said this so often she can get in the right degree of apology and Asian upper-class helplessness. "It's an awful nuisance."

"Not to worry, please." Then, "It is a great honor to be meeting Dr. Sanyal's daughter. In Calcutta business circles he is a legend."

On Sunday she is ready by four-thirty. She doesn't know what the afternoon holds; there are surely no places for "high tea"—a colonial tradition—in Cedar Falls, Iowa. If he takes her back to his place, it will mean he has invited other guests. From his voice she can tell Dr. Chatterji likes to do things correctly. She has dressed herself in a peach-colored nylon georgette sari, jade drop-earrings and a necklace. The color is good on dark skin. She is not pretty, but she does her best. Working at it is a part of self-respect. In the mid-seventies, when American women felt rather strongly about such things, Maya had been in trouble with her women's group at Duke. She was too feminine. She had tried to explain the world she came out of. Her grandmother had been married off at the age of five in a village now in Bangladesh. Her great-aunt had been burned to death over a dowry problem. She herself had been trained to speak softly, arrange flowers, sing, be pliant. If she were to seduce Ted Suminski, she thinks as she waits in the front yard for Dr. Chatterji, it would be minor heroism. She has broken with the past. But.

Dr. Chatterji drives up for her at about five ten. He is a hesitant driver. The car stalls, jumps ahead, finally slams to a stop. Maya has to tell him to back off a foot or so; it's hard to leap over two sacks of pruned branches in a sari. Ted Suminski is an obsessive pruner and gardener.

"My sincerest apologies, Mrs. Sanyal," Dr. Chatterji says. He leans across the wide front seat of his noisy, very old, very used car and unlocks the door for her. "I am late. But then, I am sure you're remembering that Indian Standard Time is not at all the same as time in the States." He laughs. He could be nervous—she often had that effect on Indian men. Or he could just be chatty. "These Americans are all the time rushing and rushing but where it gets them?" He moves his head laterally once, twice. It's the gesture made famous by Peter Sellers. When Peter Sellers did it, it had seemed hilarious. Now it suggests that Maya and Dr. Chatterji have three thousand years plus civilization, sophistication, moral virtue, over people born on this continent. Like her, Dr. Chatterji is a naturalized American.

"Call me Maya," she says. She fusses with the seat belt. She does it because she needs time to look him over. He seems quite harmless. She takes in the prominent teeth, the eyebrows that run together. He's in a blue shirt and a beige cardigan with the K-Mart logo that buttons tightly over the waist. It's hard to guess his age because he has dyed his hair and his moustache. Late thirties, early forties. Older than she had expected. "Not Mrs. Sanyal."

This isn't the time to tell about ex-husbands. She doesn't know where John is these days. He should have kept up at least. John had come into her life as a graduate student at Duke, and she, mistaking the brief breathlessness of sex for love, had married him. They had stayed together two years, maybe a little less. The pain that John had inflicted all those years ago by leaving her had subsided into a cozy feeling of loss. This isn't the time, but then she doesn't want to be a legend's daughter all evening. She's not necessarily on Dr. Chatterji's side is what she wants to get across early; she's not against America and Americans. She makes the story—of marriage outside the Brahminic pale, the divorce—quick, dull. Her unsentimentality seems to shock him. His stomach sags inside the cardigan.

"We've each had our several griefs," the physicist says. "We're each required to pay our karmic debts."

"Where are we headed?"

"Mrs. Chatterji has made some Indian snacks. She is waiting to meet you because she is knowing your cousin-sister who studied in Scottish Church College. My home is okay, no?"

Fran would get a kick out of this. Maya has slept with married men, with nameless men, with men little more than boys, but never with an Indian man. Never.

The Chatterjis live in a small blue house on a gravelly street. There are at least five or six other houses on the street; the same size but in different colors and with different front yard treatments. More houses are going up. This is the cutting edge of suburbia.

Mrs. Chatterji stands in the driveway. She is throwing a large plastic ball to a child. The child looks about four, and is Korean or Cambodian. The child is not hers because she tells it, "Chung-Hee, ta-ta, bye-bye. Now I play with guest," as Maya gets out of the car.

Maya hasn't seen this part of town. The early September light softens the construction pits. In that light the houses too close together, the stout woman in a striped cotton sari, the child hugging a pink ball, the two plastic lawn chairs by a tender young tree, the sheets and saris on the clothesline in the back, all seem miraculously incandescent.

"Go home now, Chung-Hee. I am busy." Mrs. Chatterji points the child homeward, then turns to Maya, who has folded her hands in traditional Bengali greeting. "It is an honor. We feel very privileged." She leads Maya indoors to a front room that smells of moisture and paint.

In her new, deliquescent mood, Maya allows herself to be backed into the best armchair—a low-backed, boxy Goodwill item draped over with a Rajasthani bedspread—and asks after the cousin Mrs. Chatterji knows. She doesn't want to let go of Mrs. Chatterji. She doesn't want husband and wife to get into whispered conferences about their guest's misadventures in America, as they make tea in the kitchen.

The coffee table is already laid with platters of mutton croquettes, fish chops, onion pakoras, ghugni with puris, samosas, chutneys. Mrs. Chatterji has gone to too much trouble. Maya counts four kinds of sweetmeats in Corning casseroles on an end table. She looks into a see-through lid; spongy, white dumplings float in rosewater syrup. Planets contained, mysteries made visible.

"What are you waiting for, Santana?" Dr. Chatterji becomes imperious, though not unaffectionate. He pulls a dining chair up close to the coffee table. "Make some tea." He speaks in Bengali to his wife, in English to Maya. To Maya he says, grandly, "We are having real Indian Green Label Lipton. A nephew is bringing it just one month back."

His wife ignores him. "The kettle's already on," she says. She wants to know about the Sanyal family. Is it true her great-grandfather was a member of the Star Chamber in England?

Nothing in Calcutta is ever lost. Just as her story is known to Bengalis all over America, so are the scandals of her family, the grandfather hauled up for tax evasion, the aunt who left her husband to act in films. This woman brings up the Star Chamber, the glories of the Sanyal family, her father's philanthropies, but it's a way of saying, *I know the dirt.*

The bedrooms are upstairs. In one of those bedrooms an unseen, tormented presence—Maya pictures it as a clumsy ghost that strains to shake off the body's shell—drops things on the floor. The things are heavy and they make the front room's chandelier shake. Light bulbs, shaped like tiny candle flames, flicker. The Chatterjis have said nothing about children. There are no tricycles in the hallway, no small sandals behind the doors. Maya is too polite to ask about the noise, and the Chatterjis don't explain. They talk just a little louder. They flip the embroidered cover off the stereo. What would Maya like to hear? Hemanta Kumar? Manna Dey? Oh, that young chap, Manna Dey! What sincerity, what tenderness he can convey!

Upstairs the ghost doesn't hear the music of nostalgia. The ghost throws and thumps. The ghost makes its own vehement music. Maya hears in its voice madness, self-hate.

Finally the water in the kettle comes to a boil. The whistle cuts through all fantasy and pretense. Dr. Chatterji says, "I'll see to it," and rushes out of the room. But he doesn't go to the kitchen. He shouts up the stairwell. "Poltoo, kindly stop this nonsense straightaway! We're having a brilliant and cultured lady-guest and you're creating earthquakes?" The kettle is hysterical.

Mrs. Chatterji wipes her face. The face that had seemed plump and cheery at the start of the evening now is flabby. "My sister's boy," the woman says.

So this is the nephew who has brought with him the cartons of Green Label tea, one of which will be given to Maya.

Mrs. Chatterji speaks to Maya in English as though only the alien language can keep emotions in check. "Such an intelligent boy! His father is government servant. Very highly placed."

Maya is meant to visualize a smart, clean-cut young man from south Calcutta, but all she can see is a crazy, thwarted, lost graduate student. Intelligence, proper family guarantee nothing. Even Brahmins can do self-destructive things, feel unsavory urges. Maya herself had been an excellent student.

"He was First Class First in B. Sc. from Presidency College," the woman says. "Now he's getting Master's in Ag. Science at Iowa State."

The kitchen is silent. Dr. Chatterji comes back into the room with a tray. The teapot is under a tea cozy, a Kashmiri one embroidered with the usual chinar leaves, loops, and chains. "*Her* nephew," he says. The dyed hair and dyed moustache are no longer signs of a man wishing to fight the odds. He is a vain man, anxious to cut losses. "Very unfortunate business."

The nephew's story comes out slowly, over fish chops and mutton croquettes. He is in love with a student from Ghana.

"Everything was A-Okay until the Christmas break. Grades, assistantship for next semester, everything."

"I blame the college. The office for foreign students arranged a Christmas party. And now, *baapre baap!* Our poor Poltoo wants to marry a Negro Muslim."

Maya is known for her nasty, ironic one-liners. It has taken her friends weeks to overlook her malicious, un-American pleasure in others' misfortunes. Maya would like to finish Dr. Chatterji off quickly. He is pompous;

he is reactionary; he wants to live and work in America but give back nothing except taxes. The confused world of the immigrant—the lostness that Maya and Poltoo feel—that's what Dr. Chatterji wants to avoid. She hates him. But.

Dr. Chatterji's horror is real. A good Brahmin boy in Iowa is in love with an African Muslim. It shouldn't be a big deal. But the more she watches the physicist, the, more she realizes that "Brahmin" isn't a caste; it's a metaphor. You break one small rule, and the constellation collapses. She thinks suddenly that John Cheever—she is teaching him as a "world writer" in her classes, cheek-by-jowl with Africans and West Indians—would have understood Dr. Chatterji's dread. Cheever had been on her mind, ever since the late afternoon light slanted over Mrs. Chatterji's drying saris. She remembers now how full of a soft, Cheeverian light Durham had been the summer she had slept with John Hadwen; and how after that, her tidy graduate-student world became monstrous, lawless. All men became John Hadwen; John became all men. Outwardly, she retained her poise, her Brahminical breeding. She treated her crisis as a literary event; she lost her moral sense, her judgment, her power to distinguish. Her parents had behaved magnanimously. They had cabled from Calcutta: WHAT'S DONE IS DONE. WE ARE CONFIDENT YOU WILL HANDLE NEW SITUATIONS WELL. ALL LOVE. But she knows more than do her parents. Love is anarchy.

Poltoo is Mrs. Chatterji's favorite nephew. She looks as though it is her fault that the Sunday has turned unpleasant. She stacks the empty platters methodically. To Maya she says, "It is the goddess who pulls the strings. We are puppets. I know the goddess will fix it. Poltoo will not marry that African woman." Then she goes to the coat closet in the hall and staggers back with a harmonium, the kind sold in music stores in Calcutta, and sets it down on the carpeted floor. "We're nothing but puppets," she says again. She sits at Maya's feet, her pudgy hands on the harmonium's shiny, black bellows. She sings, beautifully, in a virgin's high voice, "Come, goddess, come, muse, come to us hapless peoples' rescue."

Maya is astonished. She has taken singing lessons at Dakshini Academy in Calcutta. She plays the sitar and the tanpur, well enough to please Bengalis, to astonish Americans. But stout Mrs. Chatterji is a devotee, talking to God.

A little after eight, Dr. Chatterji drops her off. It's been an odd evening and they are both subdued.

"I want to say one thing," he says. He stops her from undoing her seat belt. The plastic sacks of pruned branches are still at the corner.

"You don't have to get out," she says.

"Please. Give me one more minute of your time."

"Sure."

"Maya is my favorite name."

She says nothing. She turns away from him without making her embarrassment obvious.

"Truly speaking, it is my favorite. You are sometimes lonely, no? But you are lucky. Divorced women can date, they can go to bars and discos. They can see mens, many mens. But inside marriage there is so much loneliness." A groan, low, horrible, comes out of him.

She turns back toward him, to unlatch the seat belt and run out of the car. She sees that Dr. Chatterji's pants are unzipped. One hand works hard under his Jockey shorts; the other rests, limp, penitential, on the steering wheel.

"Dr. Chatterji—*really!*" she cries.

The next day, Monday, instead of getting a ride home with Fran— Fran says she *likes* to give rides, she needs the chance to talk, and she won't share gas expenses, absolutely not—Maya goes to the periodicals room of the library. There are newspapers from everywhere, even from Madagascar and New Caledonia. She thinks of the periodicals room as an asylum for homesick aliens. There are two aliens already in the room, both Orientals, both absorbed in the politics and gossip of their far off homes.

She goes straight to the newspapers from India. She bunches her raincoat like a bolster to make herself more comfortable. There's so much to catch up on. A village headman, a known Congress-Indira party worker, has been shot at by scooter-riding snipers. An Indian pugilist has won an international medal—in Nepal. A child drawing well water—the reporter calls the child "a neo-Buddhist, a convert from the now-outlawed untouchable caste"—has been stoned. An editorial explains that the story about stoning is not a story about caste but about failed idealism; a story about promises of green fields and clean, potable water broken, a story about bribes paid and wells not dug. But no, thinks Maya, it's about caste.

Out here, in the heartland of the new world, the India of serious newspapers unsettles. Maya longs again to feel what she had felt in the Chatterjis' living room: virtues made physical. It is a familiar feeling, a longing. Had a suitable man presented himself in the reading room at that instant, she would have seduced him. She goes on to the stack of *India Abroad*s, reads through matrimonial columns, and steals an issue to take home.

Indian men want Indian brides. Married Indian men want Indian mistresses. All over America, "handsome, tall, fair" engineers, doctors, data processors—the new pioneers—cry their eerie love calls.

Maya runs a finger down the first column; her fingertip, dark with newsprint, stops at random.

Hello! Hi! Yes, you *are* the one I'm looking for. You are the new emancipated Indo-American woman. You have a zest for life. You are at ease in USA and yet your ethics are rooted in Indian tradition. The man of your dreams has come. Yours truly is handsome, ear-nose-throat specialist, well-settled in Connecticut. Age is 41 but never married, physically fit, sportsmanly, and strong. I adore idealism, poetry, beauty. I abhor smugness, passivity, caste system. Write with recent photo. Better still, call!!!

Maya calls. Hullo, hullo, hullo! She hears immigrant lovers cry in crowded shopping malls. Yes, you who are at ease in both worlds, you are the one. She feels she has a fair chance.

A man answers. "Ashoke Mehta speaking."

She speaks quickly into the bright-red mouthpiece of her telephone. He will be in Chicago, in transit, passing through O'Hare. United counter, Saturday, two P.M. As easy as that.

"Good," Ashoke Mehta says. "For these encounters I, too, prefer a neutral zone."

On Saturday at exactly two o'clock the man of Maya's dreams floats toward her as lovers used to in shampoo commercials. The United counter is a loud, harassed place but passengers and piled-up luggage fall away from him. Full-cheeked and fleshy-lipped, he is handsome. He hasn't lied. He is serene, assured, a Hindu god touching down in Illinois.

She can't move. She feels ugly and unworthy. Her adult life no longer seems miraculously rebellious; it is grim, it is perverse. She has accomplished nothing. She has changed her citizenship but she hasn't broken through into the light, the vigor, the *hustle* of the New World. She is stuck in dead space.

"Hullo, Hullo!" Their fingers touch.

Oh, the excitement! Ashoke Mehta's palm feels so right in the small of her back. Hullo, hullo, hullo. He pushes her out of the reach of anti-Khomeini Iranians, Hare Krishnas, American Fascists, men with fierce wants, and guides her to an empty gate. They have less than an hour.

"What would you like, Maya?"

She knows he can read her mind, she knows her thoughts are open to him. *You,* she's almost giddy with the thought, with simple desire. "From the snack bar," he says, as though to clarify. "I'm afraid I'm starved."

Below them, where the light is strong and hurtful, a Boeing is being serviced. "Nothing," she says.

He leans forward. She can feel the nap of his scarf—she recognizes the Cambridge colors—she can smell the wool of his Icelandic sweater. She runs her hand along the scarf, then against the flesh of his neck. "Only the impulsive ones call," he says.

The immigrant courtship proceeds. It's easy, he's good with facts. He knows how to come across to a stranger who may end up a lover, a spouse. He makes over a hundred thousand. He owns a house in Hartford, and two income properties in Newark. He plays the market but he's cautious. He's good at badminton but plays handball to keep in shape. He watches all the sports on television. Last August he visited Copenhagen, Helsinki and Leningrad. Once upon a time he collected stamps but now he doesn't have hobbies, except for reading. He counts himself an intellectual, he spends too much on books. Ludlum, Forsyth, MacInnes; other names she doesn't catch. She supresses a smile, she's told him only she's a graduate student. He's not without his vices. He's a spender, not a saver. He's a sensualist: good food—all foods, but easy on the Indian—good wine. Some temptations he doesn't try to resist.

And I, she wants to ask, do I tempt?

"Now tell me about yourself, Maya." He makes it easy for her. "Have you ever been in love?"

"No."

"But many have loved you, I can see that." He says it not unkindly. It is the fate of women like her, and men like him. Their karmic duty, to be loved. It is expected, not judged. She feels he can see them all, the sad parade of need and demand. This isn't the time to reveal all.

And so the courtship enters a second phase.

When she gets back to Cedar Falls, Ted Suminski is standing on the front porch. It's late at night, chilly. He is wearing a down vest. She's never seen him on the porch. In fact there's no chair to sit on. He looks chilled through. He's waited around a while.

"Hi." She has her keys ready. This isn't the night to offer the six-pack in the fridge. He looks expectant, ready to pounce.

"Hi." He looks like a man who might have aimed the dart at her. What has he done to his wife, his kids? Why isn't there at least a dog? "Say, I left a note upstairs."

The note is written in Magic Marker and thumb-tacked to her apartment door. DUE TO PERSONAL REASONS, NAMELY REMARRIAGE, I REQUEST THAT YOU VACATE MY PLACE AT THE END OF THE SEMESTER.

Maya takes the note down and retacks it to the kitchen wall. The whole wall is like a bulletin board, made of some new, crumbly building-material. Her kitchen, Ted Suminski had told her, was once a child's bedroom. Suminski in love: the idea stuns her. She has misread her landlord. The dart at her window speaks of no twisted fantasy. The landlord wants the tenant out.

She gets a glass out of the kitchen cabinet, gets out a tray of ice, pours herself a shot of Fran's bourbon. She is happy for Ted Suminski. She is. She wants to tell someone how moved she'd been by Mrs. Chatterji's singing. How she'd felt in O'Hare, even about Dr. Rab Chatterji in the car. But Fran is not the person. No one she's ever met is the person. She can't talk about the dead space she lives in. She wishes Ashoke Mehta would call. Right now.

Weeks pass. Then two months. She finds a new room, signs another lease. Her new landlord calls himself Fred. He has no arms, but he helps her move her things. He drives between Ted Suminski's place and his twice in his station wagon. He uses his toes the way Maya uses her fingers. He likes to do things. He pushes garbage sacks full of Maya's clothes up the stairs.

"It's all right to stare," Fred says. "Hell, I would."

That first afternoon in Fred's rooming house, they share a Chianti. Fred wants to cook her pork chops but he's a little shy about Indians and meat. Is it beef, or pork? Or any meat? She says it's okay, any meat, but not tonight. He has an ex-wife in Des Moines, two kids in Portland, Oregon. The kids are both normal; he's the only freak in the family. But he's self-reliant. He shops in the supermarket like anyone else, he carries out the garbage, shovels the snow off the sidewalk. He needs Maya's help with one thing. Just one thing. The box of Tide is a bit too heavy to manage. Could she get him the giant size every so often and leave it in the basement?

The dead space need not suffocate. Over the months, Fred and she will settle into companionship. She has never slept with a man without arms. Two wounded people, he will joke during their nightly contortions. It will shock her, this assumed equivalence with a man so strikingly deficient. She knows she is strange, and lonely, but being Indian is not the same, she would have thought, as being a freak.

One night in spring, Fred's phone rings. "Ashoke Mehta speaking." None of this "do you remember me?" nonsense. The god has tracked her down. He hasn't forgotten. "Hullo," he says, in their special way. And because she doesn't answer back, "Hullo, hullo, hullo." She is aware of Fred in the back of the room. He is lighting a cigarette with his toes.

"Yes," she says, "I remember."

"I had to take care of a problem," Ashoke Mehta says. "You know that I have my vices. That time at O'Hare I was honest with you."

She is breathless.

"Who is it, May?" asks Fred.

"You also have a problem," says the voice. His laugh echoes. "You will come to Hartford, I know."

When she moves out, she tells herself, it will not be the end of Fred's world. [1986]

TIM O'BRIEN

Tim O'Brien (b. 1946) was born in Austin, Minnesota, and educated at Macalester College and Harvard University. Drafted into the army during the Vietnam War, he attained the rank of sergeant and received the Purple Heart.

O'Brien's first book, If I Die in a Combat Zone, Box Me Up and Ship Me Home *(1973), is an account of his combat experience presented as "auto-fiction," a mixture of autobiography and fiction. His next book,* Northern Lights *(1974), depicts a conflict between two brothers. O'Brien's novel* Going after Cacciato *(1978) won the National Book Award and was judged by many critics to be the best book by an American about the Vietnam War. This was followed by the novels* The Nuclear Age *(1985),* In the Lake of the Woods *(1994), and* Tomcat in Love *(1998).*

"Soldiers are dreamers," a line by the English poet Siegfried Sassoon, who survived a sniper's bullet during World War I, is the epigraph for Going after Cacciato. *Dreams play an important role in all of O'Brien's fiction, yet the note they sound in a story such as "The Things They Carried" is not surrealistic. The dream is always rooted so firmly in reality that it survives, paradoxically, as the most vital element in an O'Brien story. "The Things They Carried" first appeared in* Esquire *magazine in 1986 and was included in* The Best American Short Stories *when Ann Beattie edited the volume in 1987. It is also the title story in O'Brien's collection* The Things They Carried *(1990).*

RELATED COMMENTARY: *Bobbie Ann Mason, "On Tim O'Brien's 'The Things They Carried,'" page 1397.*

The Things They Carried

First Lieutenant Jimmy Cross carried letters from a girl named Martha, a junior at Mount Sebastian College in New Jersey. They were not love letters, but Lieutenant Cross was hoping, so he kept them folded in plastic at the bottom of his rucksack. In the late afternoon, after a day's march, he would dig his foxhole, wash his hands under a canteen, unwrap the letters, hold them with the tips of his fingers, and spend the last hour of light pretending. He would imagine romantic camping trips into the White Mountains in New Hampshire. He would sometimes taste the envelope flaps, knowing her tongue had been there. More than anything, he wanted Martha to love him as he loved her, but the letters were mostly chatty, elusive on the matter of love. She was a virgin, he was almost sure. She was an English major at Mount Sebastian, and she wrote beautifully about her professors and roommates and midterm exams, about her respect for Chaucer and her great affection for Virginia Woolf. She often quoted lines of poetry; she never mentioned the war, except to say, Jimmy, take care of yourself. The letters weighed ten ounces. They were signed "Love, Martha," but Lieutenant Cross understood that "Love" was only a way of signing and did not mean what he sometimes pretended it meant. At dusk, he would carefully return the letters to his rucksack. Slowly, a bit distracted, he would get up and move among his men, checking the perimeter, then at full dark he would return to his hole and watch the night and wonder if Martha was a virgin.

The things they carried were largely determined by necessity. Among the necessities or near necessities were P-38 can openers, pocket knives, heat tabs, wrist watches, dog tags, mosquito repellant, chewing gum, candy, cigarettes, salt tablets, packets of Kool-Aid, lighters, matches, sewing kits, Military Payment Certificates, C rations, and two or three canteens of water. Together, these items weighed between fifteen and twenty pounds, depending upon a man's habits or rate of metabolism. Henry Dobbins, who was a big man, carried extra rations; he was especially fond of canned peaches in heavy syrup over pound cake. Dave Jensen, who practiced field hygiene, carried a toothbrush, dental floss, and several hotel-size bars of soap he'd stolen on R&R in Sydney, Australia. Ted Lavender, who was scared, carried tranquilizers until he was shot in the head outside the village of Than Khe in mid-April. By necessity, and because it was SOP,[1] they all carried steel helmets that weighed five pounds including the liner and camouflage cover. They carried the standard fatigue jackets and trousers. Very few carried underwear. On their feet they carried jungle boots — 2.1 pounds — and Dave Jensen carried three pairs of socks and a can of Dr. Scholl's foot powder as a precaution against trench foot. Until he was shot, Ted Lavender carried six or seven ounces of premium dope, which for him was a necessity. Mitchell Sanders, the RTO,[2] carried condoms. Norman Bowker carried a diary. Rat Kiley carried comic books. Kiowa, a devout Baptist, carried an illustrated New Testament that had been presented to him by his father, who taught Sunday school in Oklahoma City, Oklahoma. As a hedge against bad times, however, Kiowa also carried his grandmother's distrust of the white man, his grandfather's old hunting hatchet. Necessity dictated. Because the land was mined and booby-trapped, it was SOP for each man to carry a steel-centered, nylon-covered flak jacket, which weighed 6.7 pounds, but which on hot days seemed much heavier. Because you could die so quickly, each man carried at least one large compress bandage, usually in the helmet band for easy access. Because the nights were cold, and because the monsoons were wet, each carried a green plastic poncho that could be used as a raincoat or ground sheet or makeshift tent. With its quilted liner, the poncho weighed almost two pounds, but it was worth every ounce. In April, for instance, when

---

[1]Standard operating procedure.
[2]Radiotelephone operator.

Ted Lavender was shot, they used his poncho to wrap him up, then to carry him across the paddy, then to lift him into the chopper that took him away.

They were called legs or grunts.

To carry something was to "hump" it, as when Lieutenant Jimmy Cross humped his love for Martha up the hills and through the swamps. In its intransitive form, "to hump" meant "to walk," or "to march," but it implied burdens far beyond the intransitive.

Almost everyone humped photographs. In his wallet, Lieutenant Cross carried two photographs of Martha. The first was a Kodachrome snapshot signed "Love," though he knew better. She stood against a brick wall. Her eyes were gray and neutral, her lips slightly open as she stared straight-on at the camera. At night, sometimes, Lieutenant Cross wondered who had taken the picture, because he knew she had boyfriends, because he loved her so much, and because he could see the shadow of the picture taker spreading out against the brick wall. The second photograph had been clipped from the 1968 Mount Sebastian yearbook. It was an action shot—women's volleyball—and Martha was bent horizontal to the floor, reaching, the palms of her hands in sharp focus, the tongue taut, the expression frank and competitive. There was no visible sweat. She wore white gym shorts. Her legs, he thought, were almost certainly the legs of a virgin, dry and without hair, the left knee cocked and carrying her entire weight, which was just over one hundred pounds. Lieutenant Cross remembered touching that left knee. A dark theater, he remembered, and the movie was *Bonnie and Clyde,* and Martha wore a tweed skirt, and during the final scene, when he touched her knee, she turned and looked at him in a sad, sober way that made him pull his hand back, but he would always remember the feel of the tweed skirt and the knee beneath it and the sound of the gunfire that killed Bonnie and Clyde, how embarrassing it was, how slow and oppressive. He remembered kissing her good night at the dorm door. Right then, he thought, he should've done something brave. He should've carried her up the stairs to her room and tied her to the bed and touched that left knee all night long. He should've risked it. Whenever he looked at the photographs, he thought of new things he should've done.

What they carried was partly a function of rank, partly of field specialty.

As a first lieutenant and platoon leader, Jimmy Cross carried a compass, maps, code books, binoculars, and a .45-caliber pistol that weighed 2.9 pounds fully loaded. He carried a strobe light and the responsibility for the lives of his men.

As an RTO, Mitchell Sanders carried the PRC-25 radio, a killer, twenty-six pounds with its battery.

As a medic, Rat Kiley carried a canvas satchel filled with morphine and plasma and malaria tablets and surgical tape and comic books and all the things a medic must carry, including M&M's for especially bad wounds, for a total weight of nearly twenty pounds.

As a big man, therefore a machine gunner, Henry Dobbins carried the M-60, which weighed twenty-three pounds unloaded, but which was almost always loaded. In addition, Dobbins carried between ten and fifteen pounds of ammunition draped in belts across his chest and shoulders.

As PFCs or Spec 4s, most of them were common grunts and carried the standard M-16 gas-operated assault rifle. The weapon weighed 7.5 pounds unloaded, 8.2 pounds with its full twenty-round magazine. Depending on numerous factors, such as topography and psychology, the riflemen carried anywhere from twelve to twenty magazines, usually in cloth bandoliers, adding on another 8.4 pounds at minimum, fourteen pounds at maximum. When it was available, they also carried M-16 maintenance gear—rods and steel brushes and swabs and tubes of LSA oil—all of which weighed about a pound. Among the grunts, some carried the M-79 grenade launcher, 5.9 pounds unloaded, a reasonably light weapon except for the ammunition, which was heavy. A single round weighed ten ounces. The typical load was twenty-five rounds. But Ted Lavender, who was scared, carried thirty-four rounds when he was shot and killed outside Than Khe, and he went down under an exceptional burden, more than twenty pounds of ammunition, plus the flak jacket and helmet and rations and water and toilet paper and tranquilizers and all the rest, plus the unweighed fear. He was dead weight. There was no twitching or flopping. Kiowa, who saw it happen, said it was like watching a rock fall, or a big sandbag or something—just boom, then down—not like the movies where the dead guy rolls around and does fancy spins and goes ass over teakettle—not like that, Kiowa said, the poor bastard just flat-fuck fell. Boom. Down. Nothing else. It was a bright morning in mid-April. Lieutenant Cross felt the pain. He blamed himself. They stripped off Lavender's canteens and ammo, all the heavy things, and Rat Kiley said the obvious, the guy's dead, and Mitchell Sanders used his radio to report one U.S. KIA[3] and to request a chopper. Then they wrapped Lavender in his poncho. They carried him out to a dry paddy, established security, and sat smoking the dead man's dope until the chopper came. Lieutenant Cross kept to himself. He pictured Martha's smooth young face, thinking he loved her more than anything, more than his men, and now Ted Lavender was dead because he loved her so much and could not stop thinking about her. When the dust-off arrived, they carried Lavender aboard. Afterward they burned Than Khe. They marched until dusk, then dug their holes, and that night Kiowa kept explaining how you had to be there, how fast it

---

[3]Killed in action.

was, how the poor guy just dropped like so much concrete. Boom-down, he said. Like cement.

In addition to the three standard weapons—the M-60, M-16, and M-79—they carried whatever presented itself, or whatever seemed appropriate as a means of killing or staying alive. They carried catch-as-catch-can. At various times, in various situations, they carried M-14s and CAR-15s and Swedish Ks and grease guns and captured AK-47s and Chi-Coms and RPGs and Simonov carbines and black-market Uzis and .38-caliber Smith & Wesson handguns and 66 mm LAWs and shotguns and silencers and blackjacks and bayonets and C-4 plastic explosives. Lee Strunk carried a slingshot; a weapon of last resort, he called it. Mitchell Sanders carried brass knuckles. Kiowa carried his grandfather's feathered hatchet. Every third or fourth man carried a Claymore antipersonnel mine—3.5 pounds with its firing device. They all carried fragmentation grenades—fourteen ounces each. They all carried at least one M-18 colored smoke grenade—twenty-four ounces. Some carried CS or tear-gas grenades. Some carried white-phosphorus grenades. They carried all they could bear, and then some, including a silent awe for the terrible power of the things they carried.

In the first week of April, before Lavender died, Lieutenant Jimmy Cross received a good-luck charm from Martha. It was a simple pebble, an ounce at most. Smooth to the touch, it was a milky-white color with flecks of orange and violet, oval-shaped, like a miniature egg. In the accompanying letter, Martha wrote that she had found the pebble on the Jersey shoreline, precisely where the land touched water at high tide, where things came together but also separated. It was this separate-but-together quality, she wrote, that had inspired her to pick up the pebble and to carry it in her breast pocket for several days, where it seemed weightless, and then to send it through the mail, by air, as a token of her truest feelings for him. Lieutenant Cross found this romantic. But he wondered what her truest feelings were, exactly, and what she meant by separate-but-together. He wondered how the tides and waves had come into play on that afternoon along the Jersey shoreline when Martha saw the pebble and bent down to rescue it from geology. He imagined bare feet. Martha was a poet, with the poet's sensibilities, and her feet would be brown and bare, the toenails unpainted, the eyes chilly and somber like the ocean in March, and though it was painful, he wondered who had been with her that afternoon. He imagined a pair of shadows moving along the strip of sand where things came together but also separated. It was phantom jealousy, he knew, but he couldn't help himself. He loved her so much. On the march, through the hot days of early April, he carried the pebble in his mouth, turning it with his tongue, tasting sea salts and moisture. His mind wandered. He had difficulty keeping his attention on the war. On occasion he would yell at his men to spread out the column, to keep their eyes open, but then he would slip away into daydreams, just pretending, walking barefoot along the Jersey shore, with Martha, carrying nothing. He would feel himself rising. Sun and waves and gentle winds, all love and lightness.

What they carried varied by mission.

When a mission took them to the mountains, they carried mosquito netting, machetes, canvas tarps, and extra bug juice.

If a mission seemed especially hazardous, or if it involved a place they knew to be bad, they carried everything they could. In certain heavily mined AOs,[4] where the land was dense with Toe Poppers and Bouncing Betties, they took turns humping a twenty-eight-pound mine detector. With its headphones and big sensing plate, the equipment was a stress on the lower back and shoulders, awkward to handle, often useless because of the shrapnel in the earth, but they carried it anyway, partly for safety, partly for the illusion of safety.

On ambush, or other night missions, they carried peculiar little odds and ends. Kiowa always took along his New Testament and a pair of moccasins for silence. Dave Jensen carried night-sight vitamins high in carotin. Lee Strunk carried his slingshot; ammo, he claimed, would never be a problem. Rat Kiley carried brandy and M&M's. Until he was shot, Ted Lavender carried the starlight scope, which weighed 6.3 pounds with its aluminum carrying case. Henry Dobbins carried his girlfriend's pantyhose wrapped around his neck as a comforter. They all carried ghosts. When dark came, they would move out single file across the meadows and paddies to their ambush coordinates, where they would quietly set up the Claymores and lie down and spend the night waiting.

Other missions were more complicated and required special equipment. In mid-April, it was their mission to search out and destroy the elaborate tunnel complexes in the Than Khe area south of Chu Lai. To blow the tunnels, they carried one-pound blocks of pentrite high explosives, four blocks to a man, sixty-eight pounds in all. They carried wiring, detonators, and battery-powered clackers. Dave Jensen carried earplugs. Most often, before blowing the tunnels, they were ordered by higher command to search them, which was considered bad news, but by and large they just shrugged and carried out orders. Because he was a big man, Henry Dobbins was excused from tunnel duty. The others would draw numbers. Before Lavender died there were seventeen men in the platoon, and whoever drew the number seventeen would strip off his gear and crawl in head first with a flashlight and Lieutenant Cross's .45-caliber pistol. The rest of them would fan out as security. They would sit down or kneel, not facing the hole, listening to the ground beneath them, imagining cobwebs and ghosts, whatever was down there — the tunnel walls squeezing in — how the flashlight seemed impossibly heavy in the hand and how it was tunnel vision in the very strictest sense, compression in all ways, even time, and

---

[4]Areas of operations.

how you had to wiggle in—ass and elbows—a swallowed-up feeling—and how you found yourself worrying about odd things—will your flashlight go dead? Do rats carry rabies? If you screamed, how far would the sound carry? Would your buddies hear it? Would they have the courage to drag you out? In some respects, though not many, the waiting was worse than the tunnel itself. Imagination was a killer.

On April 16, when Lee Strunk drew the number seventeen, he laughed and muttered something and went down quickly. The morning was hot and very still. Not good, Kiowa said. He looked at the tunnel opening, then out across a dry paddy toward the village of Than Khe. Nothing moved. No clouds or birds or people. As they waited, the men smoked and drank Kool-Aid, not talking much, feeling sympathy for Lee Strunk but also feeling the luck of the draw. You win some, you lose some, said Mitchell Sanders, and sometimes you settle for a rain check. It was a tired line and no one laughed.

Henry Dobbins ate a tropical chocolate bar. Ted Lavender popped a tranquilizer and went off to pee.

After five minutes, Lieutenant Jimmy Cross moved to the tunnel, leaned down, and examined the darkness. Trouble, he thought—a cave-in maybe. And then suddenly, without willing it, he was thinking about Martha. The stresses and fractures, the quick collapse, the two of them buried alive under all that weight. Dense, crushing love. Kneeling, watching the hole, he tried to concentrate on Lee Strunk and the war, all the dangers, but his love was too much for him, he felt paralyzed, he wanted to sleep inside her lungs and breathe her blood and be smothered. He wanted her to be a virgin and not a virgin, all at once. He wanted to know her. Intimate secrets—why poetry? Why so sad? Why the grayness in her eyes? Why so alone? Not lonely, just alone—riding her bike across campus or sitting off by herself in the cafeteria. Even dancing, she danced alone—and it was the aloneness that filled him with love. He remembered telling her that one evening. How she nodded and looked away. And how, later, when he kissed her, she received the kiss without returning it, her eyes wide open, not afraid, not a virgin's eyes, just flat and uninvolved.

Lieutenant Cross gazed at the tunnel. But he was not there. He was buried with Martha under the white sand at the Jersey shore. They were pressed together, and the pebble in his mouth was her tongue. He was smiling. Vaguely, he was aware of how quiet the day was, the sullen paddies, yet he could not bring himself to worry about matters of security. He was beyond that. He was just a kid at war, in love. He was twenty-two years old. He couldn't help it.

A few moments later Lee Strunk crawled out of the tunnel. He came up grinning, filthy but alive. Lieutenant Cross nodded and closed his eyes while the others clapped Strunk on the back and made jokes about rising from the dead.

Worms, Rat Kiley said. Right out of the grave. Fuckin' zombie.

The men laughed. They all felt great relief.

Spook City, said Mitchell Sanders.

Lee Strunk made a funny ghost sound, a kind of moaning, yet very happy, and right then, when Strunk made that high happy moaning sound, when he went *Ahhooooo*, right then Ted Lavender was shot in the head on his way back from peeing. He lay with his mouth open. The teeth were broken. There was a swollen black bruise under his left eye. The cheekbone was gone. Oh shit, Rat Kiley said, the guy's dead. The guy's dead, he kept saying, which seemed profound — the guy's dead. I mean really.

The things they carried were determined to some extent by superstition. Lieutenant Cross carried his good-luck pebble. Dave Jensen carried a rabbit's foot. Norman Bowker, otherwise a very gentle person, carried a thumb that had been presented to him as a gift by Mitchell Sanders. The thumb was dark brown, rubbery to the touch, and weighed four ounces at most. It had been cut from a VC corpse, a boy of fifteen or sixteen. They'd found him at the bottom of an irrigation ditch, badly burned, flies in his mouth and eyes. The boy wore black shorts and sandals. At the time of his death he had been carrying a pouch of rice, a rifle, and three magazines of ammunition.

You want my opinion, Mitchell Sanders said, there's a definite moral here.

He put his hand on the dead boy's wrist. He was quiet for a time, as if counting a pulse, then he patted the stomach, almost affectionately, and used Kiowa's hunting hatchet to remove the thumb.

Henry Dobbins asked what the moral was.

Moral?

You know. *Moral*.

Sanders wrapped the thumb in toilet paper and handed it across to Norman Bowker. There was no blood. Smiling, he kicked the boy's head, watched the flies scatter, and said, It's like with that old TV show — Paladin. Have gun, will travel.

Henry Dobbins thought about it.

Yeah, well, he finally said. I don't see no moral.

There it *is*, man.

Fuck off.

They carried USO stationery and pencils and pens. They carried Sterno, safety pins, trip flares, signal flares, spools of wire, razor blades, chewing tobacco, liberated joss sticks and statuettes of the smiling Buddha, candles, grease pencils, *The Stars and Stripes,* fingernail clippers, Psy Ops[5] leaflets, bush hats, bolos, and much more. Twice a week, when the resupply choppers came in, they carried hot chow in green Mermite cans and large canvas

---

[5]Psychological operations.

bags filled with iced beer and soda pop. They carried plastic water containers, each with a two-gallon capacity. Mitchell Sanders carried a set of
starched tiger fatigues for special occasions. Henry Dobbins carried Black
Flag insecticide. Dave Jensen carried empty sandbags that could be filled
at night for added protection. Lee Strunk carried tanning lotion. Some
things they carried in common. Taking turns, they carried the big PRC-77
scrambler radio, which weighed thirty pounds with its battery. They
shared the weight of memory. They took up what others could no longer
bear. Often, they carried each other, the wounded or weak. They carried
infections. They carried chess sets, basketballs, Vietnamese-English dictio-
naries, insignia of rank, Bronze Stars and Purple Hearts, plastic cards
imprinted with the Code of Conduct. They carried diseases, among them
malaria and dysentery. They carried lice and ringworm and leeches and
paddy algae and various rots and molds. They carried the land itself—
Vietnam, the place, the soil—a powdery orange-red dust that covered
their boots and fatigues and faces. They carried the sky. The whole atmosphere, they carried it, the humidity, the monsoons, the stink of fungus and
decay, all of it, they carried gravity. They moved like mules. By daylight
they took sniper fire, at night they were mortared, but it was not battle, it
was just the endless march, village to village, without purpose, nothing
won or lost. They marched for the sake of the march. They plodded along
slowly, dumbly, leaning forward against the heat, unthinking, all blood
and bone, simple grunts, soldiering with their legs, toiling up the hills and
down into the paddies and across the rivers and up again and down, just
humping, one step and then the next and then another, but no volition,
no will, because it was automatic, it was anatomy, and the war was entirely
a matter of posture and carriage, the hump was everything, a kind of iner-
tia, a kind of emptiness, a dullness of desire and intellect and conscience
and hope and human sensibility. Their principles were in their feet. Their
calculations were biological. They had no sense of strategy or mission.
They searched the villages without knowing what to look for, not caring,
kicking over jars of rice, frisking children and old men, blowing tunnels,
sometimes setting fires and sometimes not, then forming up and moving
on to the next village, then other villages, where it would always be the
same. They carried their own lives. The pressures were enormous. In the
heat of early afternoon, they would remove their helmets and flak jackets,
walking bare, which was dangerous but which helped ease the strain. They
would often discard things along the route of march. Purely for comfort,
they would throw away rations, blow their Claymores and grenades, no
matter, because by nightfall the resupply choppers would arrive with more
of the same, then a day or two later still more, fresh watermelons and
crates of ammunition and sunglasses and woolen sweaters—the resources
were stunning—sparklers for the Fourth of July, colored eggs for Easter.
It was the great American war chest—the fruits of science, the smoke-
stacks, the canneries, the arsenals at Hartford, the Minnesota forests, the

machine shops, the vast fields of corn and wheat—they carried like freight trains; they carried it on their backs and shoulders—and for all the ambiguities of Vietnam, all the mysteries and unknowns, there was at least the single abiding certainty that they would never be at a loss for things to carry.

After the chopper took Lavender away, Lieutenant Jimmy Cross led his men into the village of Than Khe. They burned everything. They shot chickens and dogs, they trashed the village well, they called in artillery and watched the wreckage, then they marched for several hours through the hot afternoon, and then at dusk, while Kiowa explained how Lavender died, Lieutenant Cross found himself trembling.

He tried not to cry. With his entrenching tool, which weighed five pounds, he began digging a hole in the earth.

He felt shame. He hated himself. He had loved Martha more than his men, and as a consequence Lavender was now dead, and this was something he would have to carry like a stone in his stomach for the rest of the war.

All he could do was dig. He used his entrenching tool like an ax, slashing, feeling both love and hate, and then later, when it was full dark, he sat at the bottom of his foxhole and wept. It went on for a long while. In part, he was grieving for Ted Lavender, but mostly it was for Martha, and for himself, because she belonged to another world, which was not quite real, and because she was a junior at Mount Sebastian College in New Jersey, a poet and a virgin and uninvolved, and because he realized she did not love him and never would.

Like cement, Kiowa whispered in the dark. I swear to God—boom-down. Not a word.

I've heard this, said Norman Bowker.

A pisser, you know? Still zipping himself up. Zapped while zipping.

All right, fine. That's enough.

Yeah, but you had to see it, the guy just—

I *heard,* man. Cement. So why not shut the fuck *up?*

Kiowa shook his head sadly and glanced over at the hole where Lieutenant Jimmy Cross sat watching the night. The air was thick and wet. A warm, dense fog had settled over the paddies and there was the stillness that precedes rain.

After a time Kiowa sighed.

One thing for sure, he said. The Lieutenant's in some deep hurt. I mean that crying jag—the way he was carrying on—it wasn't fake or anything, it was real heavy-duty hurt. The man cares.

Sure, Norman Bowker said.

Say what you want, the man does care.

We all got problems.

Not Lavender.

No, I guess not, Bowker said. Do me a favor, though.

Shut up?

That's a smart Indian. Shut up.

Shrugging, Kiowa pulled off his boots. He wanted to say more, just to lighten up his sleep, but instead he opened his New Testament and arranged it beneath his head as a pillow. The fog made things seem hollow and unattached. He tried not to think about Ted Lavender, but then he was thinking how fast it was, no drama, down and dead, and how it was hard to feel anything except surprise. It seemed un-Christian. He wished he could find some great sadness, or even anger, but the emotion wasn't there and he couldn't make it happen. Mostly he felt pleased to be alive. He liked the smell of the New Testament under his cheek, the leather and ink and paper and glue, whatever the chemicals were. He liked hearing the sounds of night. Even his fatigue, it felt fine, the stiff muscles and the prickly awareness of his own body, a floating feeling. He enjoyed not being dead. Lying there, Kiowa admired Lieutenant Jimmy Cross's capacity for grief. He wanted to share the man's pain, he wanted to care as Jimmy Cross cared. And yet when he closed his eyes, all he could think was Boom-down, and all he could feel was the pleasure of having his boots off and the fog curling in around him and the damp soil and the Bible smells and the plush comfort of night.

After a moment Norman Bowker sat up in the dark.

What the hell, he said. You want to talk, *talk*. Tell it to me.

Forget it.

No, man, go on. One thing I hate, it's a silent Indian.

For the most part they carried themselves with poise, a kind of dignity. Now and then, however, there were times of panic, when they squealed or wanted to squeal but couldn't, when they twitched and made moaning sounds and covered their heads and said Dear Jesus and flopped around on the earth and fired their weapons blindly and cringed and sobbed and begged for the noise to stop and went wild and made stupid promises to themselves and to God and to their mothers and fathers, hoping not to die. In different ways, it happened to all of them. Afterward, when the firing ended, they would blink and peek up. They would touch their bodies, feeling shame, then quickly hiding it. They would force themselves to stand. As if in slow motion, frame by frame, the world would take on the old logic—absolute silence, then the wind, then sunlight, then voices. It was the burden of being alive. Awkwardly, the men would reassemble themselves, first in private, then in groups, becoming soldiers again. They would repair the leaks in their eyes. They would check for casualties, call in dust-offs, light cigarettes, try to smile, clear their throats and spit and begin cleaning their weapons. After a time someone would shake his head and say, No lie, I almost shit my pants, and someone else would laugh, which meant it was bad, yes, but the guy had obviously not shit his pants, it wasn't that bad, and in any case nobody would ever do such a thing and then go ahead and talk about it. They would squint into the dense, oppressive sunlight. For a few moments, perhaps, they would fall silent, lighting a joint and tracking its passage from man to man, inhaling, holding in the humiliation. Scary stuff, one of them might say. But then someone else would grin or flick his eyebrows and say, Roger-dodger, almost cut me a new asshole, *almost*.

There were numerous such poses. Some carried themselves with a sort of wistful resignation, others with pride or stiff soldierly discipline or good humor or macho zeal. They were afraid of dying but they were even more afraid to show it.

They found jokes to tell.

They used a hard vocabulary to contain the terrible softness. *Greased,* they'd say. *Offed, lit up, zapped while zipping.* It wasn't cruelty, just stage presence. They were actors and the war came at them in 3-D. When someone died, it wasn't quite dying, because in a curious way it seemed scripted, and because they had their lines mostly memorized, irony mixed with tragedy, and because they called it by other names, as if to encyst and destroy the reality of death itself. They kicked corpses. They cut off thumbs. They talked grunt lingo. They told stories about Ted Lavender's supply of tranquilizers, how the poor guy didn't feel a thing, how incredibly tranquil he was.

There's a moral here, said Mitchell Sanders.

They were waiting for Lavender's chopper, smoking the dead man's dope.

The moral's pretty obvious, Sanders said, and winked. Stay away from drugs. No joke, they'll ruin your day every time.

Cute, said Henry Dobbins.

Mind-blower, get it? Talk about wiggy — nothing left, just blood and brains.

They made themselves laugh.

There it is, they'd say, over and over, as if the repetition itself were an act of poise, a balance between crazy and almost crazy, knowing without going. There it is, which meant be cool, let it ride, because oh yeah, man, you can't change what can't be changed, there it is, there it absolutely and positively and fucking well *is*.

They were tough.

They carried all the emotional baggage of men who might die. Grief, terror, love, longing — these were intangibles, but the intangibles had their own mass and specific gravity, they had tangible weight. They carried shameful memories. They carried the common secret of cowardice barely restrained, the instinct to run or freeze or hide, and in many respects this was the heaviest burden of all, for it could never be put down, it required perfect balance and perfect posture. They carried their reputations. They carried the soldier's greatest fear, which was the fear of blushing. Men killed, and died, because they were embarrassed not to. It was what had brought them to the war in the first place, nothing positive, no dreams of glory or honor, just to avoid the blush of dishonor. They died so as not to die of embarrassment. They crawled into tunnels and walked point and advanced under fire. Each morning, despite the unknowns, they made their legs move. They endured. They kept humping. They did not submit to the obvious alternative, which was simply to close the eyes and fall. So easy, really. Go limp and tumble to the ground and let the muscles unwind and not speak and not budge until your buddies picked you up and lifted you into the chopper that would roar and dip its nose and carry you off to the world. A mere matter of falling, yet no one ever fell. It was not courage, exactly; the object was not valor. Rather, they were too frightened to be cowards.

By and large they carried these things inside, maintaining the masks of composure. They sneered at sick call. They spoke bitterly about guys who had found release by shooting off their own toes or fingers. Pussies, they'd say. Candyasses. It was fierce, mocking talk, with only a trace of envy or awe, but even so, the image played itself out behind their eyes.

They imagined the muzzle against flesh. They imagined the quick, sweet pain, then the evacuation to Japan, then a hospital with warm beds and cute geisha nurses.

They dreamed of freedom birds.

At night, on guard, staring into the dark, they were carried away by jumbo jets. They felt the rush of takeoff. *Gone!* they yelled. And then velocity, wings and engines, a smiling stewardess—but it was more than a plane, it was a real bird, a big sleek silver bird with feathers and talons and high screeching. They were flying. The weights fell off, there was nothing to bear. They laughed and held on tight, feeling the cold slap of wind and altitude, soaring, thinking *It's over, I'm gone!*—they were naked, they were light and free—it was all lightness, bright and fast and buoyant, light as light, a helium buzz in the brain, a giddy bubbling in the lungs as they were taken up over the clouds and the war, beyond duty, beyond gravity and mortification and global entanglements—*Sin loi!*[6] they yelled, *I'm sorry, motherfuckers, but I'm out of it, I'm goofed, I'm on a space cruise, I'm gone!*—and it was a restful, disencumbered sensation, just riding the light waves, sailing that big silver freedom bird over the mountains and oceans, over America, over the farms and great sleeping cities and cemeteries and highways and the golden arches of McDonald's. It was flight, a kind of fleeing, a kind of falling, falling higher and higher, spinning off the edge of the earth and beyond the sun and through the vast, silent vacuum where there were no burdens and where everything weighed exactly nothing. *Gone!* they screamed, *I'm sorry but I'm gone!* And so at night, not quite

---

[6]"Sorry about that!"

dreaming, they gave themselves over to lightness, they were carried, they were purely borne.

On the morning after Ted Lavender died, First Lieutenant Jimmy Cross crouched at the bottom of his foxhole and burned Martha's letters. Then he burned the two photographs. There was a steady rain falling, which made it difficult, but he used heat tabs and Sterno to build a small fire, screening it with his body, holding the photographs over the tight blue flame with the tips of his fingers.

He realized it was only a gesture. Stupid, he thought. Sentimental, too, but mostly just stupid.

Lavender was dead. You couldn't burn the blame.

Besides, the letters were in his head. And even now, without photographs, Lieutenant Cross could see Martha playing volleyball in her white gym shorts and yellow T-shirt. He could see her moving in the rain.

When the fire died out, Lieutenant Cross pulled his poncho over his shoulders and ate breakfast from a can.

There was no great mystery, he decided.

In those burned letters Martha had never mentioned the war, except to say, Jimmy, take care of yourself. She wasn't involved. She signed the letters "Love," but it wasn't love, and all the fine lines and technicalities did not matter.

The morning came up wet and blurry. Everything seemed part of everything else, the fog and Martha and the deepening rain.

It was a war, after all.

Half smiling, Lieutenant Jimmy Cross took out his maps. He shook his head hard, as if to clear it, then bent forward and began planning the day's march. In ten minutes, or maybe twenty, he would rouse the men and they would pack up and head west, where the maps showed the country to be green and inviting. They would do what they had always done. The rain might add some weight, but otherwise it would be one more day layered upon all the other days.

He was realistic about it. There was that new hardness in his stomach.

No more fantasies, he told himself.

Henceforth, when he thought about Martha, it would be only to think that she belonged elsewhere. He would shut down the daydreams. This was not Mount Sebastian, it was another world, where there were no pretty poems or midterm exams, a place where men died because of carelessness and gross stupidity. Kiowa was right. Boom-down, and you were dead, never partly dead.

Briefly, in the rain, Lieutenant Cross saw Martha's gray eyes gazing back at him.

He understood.

It was very sad, he thought. The things men carried inside. The things men did or felt they had to do.

He almost nodded at her, but didn't.

Instead he went back to his maps. He was now determined to perform his duties firmly and without negligence. It wouldn't help Lavender, he knew that, but from this point on he would comport himself as a soldier. He would dispose of his good-luck pebble. Swallow it, maybe, or use Lee Strunk's slingshot, or just drop it along the trail. On the march he would impose strict field discipline. He would be careful to send out flank security, to prevent straggling or bunching up, to keep his troops moving at the proper pace and at the proper interval. He would insist on clean weapons. He would confiscate the remainder of Lavender's dope. Later in the day, perhaps, he would call the men together and speak to them plainly. He would accept the blame for what had happened to Ted Lavender. He would be a man about it. He would look them in the eyes, keeping his chin level, and he would issue the new SOPs in a calm, impersonal tone of voice, an officer's voice, leaving no room for argument or discussion. Commencing immediately, he'd tell them, they would no longer abandon equipment along the route of march. They would police up their acts. They would get their shit together, and keep it together, and maintain it neatly and in good working order.

He would not tolerate laxity. He would show strength, distancing himself.

Among the men there would be grumbling, of course, and maybe worse, because their days would seem longer and their loads heavier, but Lieutenant Cross reminded himself that his obligation was not to be loved but to lead. He would dispense with love; it was not now a factor. And if anyone quarreled or complained, he would simply tighten his lips and arrange his shoulders in the correct command posture. He might give a curt little nod. Or he might not. He might just shrug and say Carry on, then they would saddle up and form into a column and move out toward the villages of Than Khe.   [1986]

HELENA MARÍA VIRAMONTES

Helena María Viramontes (b. 1954) was born in East Los Angeles, the daughter of a construction worker and a Chicana housewife who raised six daughters and three sons in a community that offered refuge for relatives and friends crossing the border from Mexico into California. As a child Viramontes witnessed "late night kitchen meetings where everyone talked and laughed in low voices" about having reached the United States, el otro lado ("the other side"). After graduation from Garfield High School, Viramontes worked twenty hours a week while earning her B.A. from Immaculate Heart College, one of five Chicanas in her class. She then entered the graduate program at the University of California at Irvine as a creative writing student, but she left in 1981 and completed the requirements for the M.F.A. degree after the publication of her stories.

As the critic Maria Herrera-Sobek has observed, "the 1980s decade witnessed an explosion in the literary output of Chicana authors," when Chicano-oriented publishers began to "risk investing in Mexican American women writers." Viramontes began to place her stories in small magazines such as Maize *and* XhismArte Magazine *as well as the anthology* Cuentos: Stories by Latinas *(1983). Her first book,* The Moths and Other Stories, *was published in 1985 by Arte Publico Press in Houston, Texas. The same year the University of California at Irvine sponsored the first national conference on Mexican American women writers, resulting in the volume* Beyond Stereotypes: A Critical Analysis of Chicana Literature *(1985). Three years later Viramontes helped organize a second Chicana writers conference at Irvine and coedited the anthology* Chicana Creativity and Criticism *(1988), in which "Miss Clairol" was first published. In 1989 Viramontes received a National Endowment for the Arts Fellowship grant; she was also selected by Gabriel García Márquez to participate in a ten-day storytelling workshop sponsored by the Sundance Institute in Utah. After this experience she began adapting one of her short stories into a film script. In 1993 she published her second book of short stories,* Paris Rats in E.L.A. *Her first novel,* Under the Feet of Jesus, *followed in 1995.*

As a woman of color, Viramontes believes that language is her most powerful tool for survival. She explains in "Why I Write" (1993) that "through writing, I have learned to protect the soles of my feet from the broken glass. . . . Writing is the only way I know how to pray."

Miss Clairol

Arlene and Champ walk to K-Mart. The store is full of bins mounted with bargain buys from T-shirts to rubber sandals. They go to aisle 23, Cosmetics. Arlene, wearing bell bottom jeans two sizes too small, can't bend down to the Miss Clairol boxes, asks Champ.

–Which one mamá–asks Champ, chewing her thumb nail.

–Shit, mija, I dunno.–Arlene smacks her gum, contemplating the decision.–Maybe I need a change, tú sabes. What do you think?–She holds up a few blond strands with black roots. Arlene has burned the softness of her hair with peroxide; her hair is stiff, breaks at the ends and she needs plenty of Aqua Net hairspray to tease and tame her ratted hair, then folds it back into a high lump behind her head. For the last few months she has been a platinum "Light Ash" blond, before that a Miss Clairol "Flame" redhead, before that Champ couldn't even identify the color—somewhere between orange and brown, a "Sun Bronze." The only way Champ knows her mother's true hair color is by her roots which, like death, inevitably rise to the truth.

–I hate it, tú sabes, when I can't decide.–Arlene is wearing a pink, strapless tube top. Her stomach spills over the hip hugger jeans. Spits the gum onto the floor.–Fuck it.–And Champ follows her to the rows of nailpolish, next to the Maybelline rack of make-up, across the false eyelashes that look like insects on display in clear, plastic boxes. Arlene pulls out a particular color of nailpolish, looks at the bottom of the bottle for the price, puts it back, gets another. She has a tattoo of purple XXX's on her left finger like a ring. She finally settles for a purple-blackish color, Ripe Plum, that Champ thinks looks like the color of Frankenstein's nails. She looks at her own stubby nails, chewed and gnawed.

Walking over to the eyeshadows, Arlene slowly slinks out another stick of gum from her back pocket, unwraps and crumbles the wrapper into a little ball, lets it drop on the floor. Smacks the gum.

–Grandpa Ham used to make chains with these gum wrappers–she says, toeing the wrapper on the floor with her rubber sandals, her toes dotted with old nailpolish.–He started one, tú sabes, that went from room to room. That was before he went nuts–she says, looking at the price of magenta eyeshadow.–Sabes que? What do you think?–lifting the eye shadow to Champ.

–I dunno know–responds Champ, shrugging her shoulders the way she always does when she is listening to something else, her own heartbeat, what Gregorio said on the phone yesterday, shrugs her shoulders when Miss Smith says OFELIA, answer my question. She is too busy thinking of things people otherwise dismiss like parentheses, but sticks to her like gum, like a hole on a shirt, like a tattoo, and sometimes she wishes she weren't born with such adhesiveness. The chain went from room to room, round and round like a web, she remembers. That was before he went nuts.

–Champ. You listening? Or in lala land again?–Arlene has her arms akimbo on a fold of flesh, pissed.

–I said, I dunno know.–Champ whines back, still looking at the wrapper on the floor.

–Well you better learn, tú sabes, and fast too. Now think, will this color go good with Pancha's blue dress?–Pancha is Arlene's comadre. Since Arlene has a special date tonight, she lent Arlene her royal blue dress that she keeps in a plastic bag at the end of her closet. The dress is made of chiffon, with satin-like material underlining, so that when Arlene first tried it on and strutted about, it crinkled sounds of elegance. The dress fits too tight. Her plump arms squeeze through, her hips breathe in and hold their breath, the seams do all they can to keep the body contained. But Arlene doesn't care as long as it sounds right.

–I think it will–Champ says, and Arlene is very pleased.

–Think so? So do I mija.–

They walk out the double doors and Champ never remembers her mother paying.

It is four in the afternoon, but already Arlene is preparing for the date. She scrubs the tub, Art Labo on the radio, drops crystals of Jean Nate into the running water, lemon scent rises with the steam. The bathroom door ajar, she removes her top and her breasts flop and sag, pushes her jeans down with some difficulty, kicks them off, and steps in the tub.

–Mija. MIJA–she yells.–Mija, give me a few bobby pins.–She is worried about her hair frizzing and so wants to pin it up.

Her mother's voice is faint because Champ is in the closet. There are piles of clothes on the floor, hangers thrown askew and tangled, shoes all piled up or thrown on the top shelf. Champ is looking for her mother's special dress. Pancha says every girl has one at the end of her closet.

–Goddamn it Champ.–

Amidst the dirty laundry, the black hole of the closet, she finds nothing.

–NOW–

–Alright, ALRIGHT. Cheeze amá, stop yelling–says Champ, and goes in the steamy bathroom, checks the drawers, hairbrushes jump out, rollers, strands of hair, rummages through bars of soap, combs, eyeshadows, finds nothing; pulls open another drawer, powder, empty bottles of oil, manicure scissors, kotex, dye instructions crinkled and botched, finally, a few bobby pins.

After Arlene pins up her hair, she asks Champ,–Sabes que? Should I wear my hair up? Do I look good with it up?–Champ is sitting on the toilet.

–Yea, amá, you look real pretty.–

–Thanks mija–says Arlene, Sabes que? When you get older I'll show you how you can look just as pretty–and she puts her head back, relaxes, like the Calgon commercials.

Champ lays on her stomach, T.V. on to some variety show with pogo stick dancers dressed in outfits of stretchy material and glitter. She is wearing one of Gregorio's white T-shirts, the ones he washes and bleaches himself so that the whiteness is impeccable. It drapes over her deflated ten year old body like a dress. She is busy cutting out Miss Breck models from the stacks of old magazines Pancha found in the back of her mother's garage. Champ collects the array of honey colored haired women, puts them in a shoe box with all her other special things.

Arlene is in the bathroom, wrapped in a towel. She has painted her eyebrows so that the two are arched and even, penciled thin and high. The magenta shades her eyelids. The towel slips, reveals one nipple blind from a cigarette burn, a date to forget. She rewraps the towel, likes her reflection, turns to her profile for additional inspection. She feels good, turns up the radio to . . . your love. For your loveeeee, I will do anything, I will do anything, forrr your love. For your kiss . . .

Champ looks on. From the open bathroom door, she can see Arlene, anticipation burning like a cigarette from her lips, sliding her shoulders to the ahhhh ahhhhh, and pouting her lips until the song ends. And Champ likes her mother that way.

Arlene carefully stretches black eyeliner, like a fallen question mark, outlines each eye. The work is delicate, her hand trembles cautiously, stops the process to review the face with each line. Arlene the mirror is not Arlene the face who has worn too many relationships, gotten too little sleep. The last touch is the chalky, beige lipstick.

By the time she is finished, her ashtray is full of cigarette butts, Champ's variety show is over, and Jackie Gleason's dancing girls come on to make kaleidoscope patterns with their long legs and arms. Gregorio is still not home, and Champ goes over to the window, checks the houses, the streets, corners, roams the sky with her eyes.

Arlene sits on the toilet, stretches up her nylons, clips them to her girdle. She feels good thinking about the way he will unsnap her nylons, and she will unroll them slowly, point her toes when she does.

Champ opens a can of Campbell soup, finds a perfect pot in the middle of a stack of dishes, pulls it out to the threatening rumble of the tower. She washes it out, pours the contents of the red can, turns the knob. After it boils, she puts the pot on the sink for it to cool down. She searches for a spoon.

Arlene is romantic. When Champ begins her period, she will tell her things that only women can know. She will tell her about the first time she made love with a boy, her awkwardness and shyness forcing them to go under the house, where the cool, refined soil made a soft mattress. How she closed her eyes and wondered what to expect, or how the penis was the softest skin she had ever felt against her, how it tickled her, searched for a place to connect. She was eleven and his name was Harry.

She will not not tell Champ that her first fuck was a guy named Puppet who ejaculated prematurely, at the sight of her apricot vagina, so plump and fuzzy.–Pendejo–she said–you got it all over me.–She rubbed the gooey substance off her legs, her belly in disgust. Ran home to tell Rat and Pancha, her mouth open with laughter.

Arlene powder puffs under her arms, between her breasts, tilts a bottle of *Love Cries* perfume and dabs behind her ears, neck and breasts for those tight caressing songs which permit them to grind their bodies together until she can feel a bulge in his pants and she knows she's in for the night.

Jackie Gleason is a bartender in a saloon. He wears a black bow tie, a white apron, and is polishing a glass. Champ is watching him, sitting in the radius of the gray light, eating her soup from the pot.

Arlene is a romantic. She will dance until Pancha's dress turns a different color, dance until her hair becomes undone, her hips jiggering and quaking beneath a new pair of hosiery, her mascara shadowing under her eyes from the perspiration of the ritual, dance spinning herself into Miss Clairol, and stopping only when it is time to return to the sewing factory, time to wait out the next date, time to change hair color. Time to remember or to forget.

Champ sees Arlene from the window. She can almost hear Arlene's nylons rubbing against one another, hear the crinkling sound of satin when she gets in the blue and white shark-finned Dodge. Champ yells goodbye. It all sounds so right to Arlene who is too busy cranking up the window to hear her daughter.   [1988]

ANN BEATTIE

*A*nn Beattie (b. 1947) was born in Washington, D.C. She grew up in Chevy Chase, Maryland, the only child of parents who sent her to a suburban school that she called "a civilized concentration camp" because of its strict dress code and stern disciplinary system. She rebelled by bleaching her hair, wearing fishnet stockings, smoking cigarettes, and graduating in the bottom tenth of her class: "That took a little effort on my part." In 1969 she received a B.A. from American University, and the following year she went on to the University of Connecticut as a graduate student in English literature. Her short stories attracted the interest of Professor J. D. O'Hara there.

> He said that he heard that I wrote, and if I was so good at it, why didn't I let him see what I was doing? So I took one of the few stories I had and put it in his mailbox, and it came back with comments all over it—more comments than I'd ever seen, more words than there were in the story. I would put something in his mailbox every few days and he would return it. He taught me a lot . . . about the technical process of writing.

Beattie began to send her stories to magazines, and her first publication, "A Rose for Judy Garland's Casket," appeared in the Western Humanities Review in 1972. The next year another story won an Atlantic Monthly "first" award, and shortly thereafter she began publishing in The New Yorker. Beattie estimates that she sent thirteen stories to that magazine before one was accepted. "You see, I was living in Eastford, Connecticut, at the time and I was bored. You either wrote a story every night or watched television. I wrote a story every night."

Her first book of nineteen stories, Distortions, was published in 1976, the same year as her first novel, Chilly Scenes of Winter, which was later made into a film. In 1978 she published her second collection of stories, Secrets and Surprises, followed by a third collection, The Burning House, in 1982. Her collection What Was Mine appeared in 1991. Critics have compared Beattie's fiction to the work of John Cheever and John Updike for its exploration of American suburban life and its "weird domesticities." Beattie herself sees little resemblance: "I think they're fine writers, but I don't see any comparison in the world between us. . . . Updike's style, that learned elegance, that intrusion of self into the material, and that very careful way he orchestrates everything, and the same thing with Cheever—they're writing traditionally well-made stories." "Second Question" (The New Yorker, 1991) is from Beattie's 1998 collection Park City. She recalls that "at first The New Yorker was going to turn down" the story "because I wouldn't take all the stuff about the girls (and the hands) out and end the story earlier. But somehow, when I wouldn't cave in, they relented. Which pleased me, because so much is true in that story. Not the way I usually judge my successes or failures, but all that stuff was so painful that I felt triumphant that I'd gotten a lot of it in."

RELATED COMMENTARY: *Ann Beattie, "Where Characters Come From," page 1316.*

Second Question

There we were, in the transfusion room at the end of the corridor at Bishopgate Hospital: Friday morning, the patients being dripped with blood or intravenous medicine so they could go home for the weekend. It was February, and the snow outside had turned the gritty gray of dirty plaster. Ned and I stood at the window, flanking a card table filled with desserts: doughnuts, cakes, pies, brownies, cookies. Some plastic forks and knives were piled in stacks, others dropped pick-up-sticks style between the paper plates. Ned surveyed the table and took a doughnut. In his chair, Richard was sleeping, chin dropped, breathing through his mouth. Half an hour into the transfusion, he always fell asleep. He was one of the few who did. A tall, redheaded man, probably in his mid-fifties, was hearing from a nurse about the hair loss he could expect. "Just remember, honey, Tina Turner wears a wig," she said.

Outside, bigger snowflakes fell, like wadded-up tissues heading for the trash. Which was what I had turned away from when I went to the window: the sight of a nurse holding a tissue for a young woman to blow her nose into. The woman was vomiting, with her nose running at the same time, but she refused to relinquish the aluminum bowl clamped under her thumbs. "Into the tissue, honey," the nurse was still saying, not at all distracted by her posturing colleague's excellent imitation of Tina Turner. I'd stopped listening, too, but I'd stuck on the phrase "Gonna break every rule."

Richard was dying of AIDS. Ned, his ex-lover and longtime business associate, found that instead of reading scripts, typing letters, and making phone calls, his new job description was to place organically grown vegetables in yin/yang positions inside a special steamer, below which we boiled Poland Spring water. A few months earlier, in that period before Richard's AZT had to be discontinued so that he could enter an experimental outpatient-treatment program at Bishopgate, Ned had always slept late. He couldn't call the West Coast before two in the afternoon, anyway—or maybe an hour earlier, if he had the unlisted number of an actor or of a director's car phone. All of the people Richard and Ned did business with worked longer hours than nine-to-fivers, and it was a standing joke among us that I was never busy—I had no real job, and when I did work I was paid much more than was reasonable. Ned joked with me a lot, an edge in his voice, because he was a little jealous of the sudden presence of a third person in Richard's apartment. Richard and I had met in New York when we were seated in adjacent chairs at a cheapo haircutter's on Eighth Avenue. He thought I was an actress in an Off Broadway play he'd seen the night before. I was not, but I'd seen the play. As we talked, we discovered that we often ate at the same restaurants in Chelsea. His face was familiar to me, as well. Then began years of our being neighbors—a concept more important to New Yorkers than to people living in a small town. The day we met, Richard took me home with him so I could shower.

That year, my landlord on West Twenty-seventh Street remained unconcerned that hot water rarely made it up to my top-floor apartment. After I met Richard it became a habit with me to put on my sweatsuit and jog to his apartment, three blocks east and one block over. Richard's own landlord, who lived in the other second-floor apartment, could never do enough for him, because Richard had introduced him to some movie stars and invited him to so many screenings. He would sizzle with fury over the abuse I had to endure, working himself up to what Richard (who made *café filtre* for the three of us) swore was a caffeine-induced sexual high, after which he'd race around doing building maintenance. Now, in the too-bright transfusion room, it was hard for me to believe that only a few months ago I'd been sitting in Richard's dining alcove, with the cluster of phones that rested on top of *Variety* landslides and formed the centerpiece of the long tavern table, sipping freshly ground Jamaica Blue Mountain as my white-gloved hands curved around the pleasant heat of a neon-colored coffee mug. The gloves allowed the lotion to sink in as long as possible. I make my living as a hand model. Every night, I rub on a mixture of Dal Raccolta olive oil with a dash of Kiehl's moisturizer and the liquid from two vitamin E capsules. It was Richard who gave me the nickname "Rac," for "Raccoon." My white, pulled-on paws protect me from scratches, broken nails, chapped skin. Forget the M.B.A.: as everyone knows, real money is made in strange ways in New York.

I turned away from the snowstorm. On a TV angled from a wall bracket above us, an orange-faced Phil Donahue glowed. He shifted from belligerence to incredulity as a man who repossessed cars explained his life philosophy. Hattie, the nicest nurse on the floor, stood beside me briefly, considering the array of pastry on our table as if it were a half-played chess game. Finally, she picked up one of the plastic knives, cut a brownie in half, and walked away without raising her eyes to look at the snow.

Taking the shuttle to Boston every weekend had finally convinced me that I was never going to develop any fondness for Beantown. To be fair about it, I didn't have much chance to see Boston as a place where anyone might be happy. Ned and I walked the path between the apartment (rented by the month) and the hospital. Once or twice I took a cab to the natural-food store, and one night, as irresponsible as the babysitters of every mother's nightmare, we had gone to a bar and then to the movies, while Richard slept a drug-induced sleep, with the starfish night-light Hattie had brought him from her honeymoon in Bermuda shining on the bedside table. In the bar, Ned had asked me what I'd do if time could stop: Richard wouldn't get any better and he wouldn't get any worse, and the days we'd gone through—with the crises, the circumlocutions, the gallows humor, the perplexity, the sudden, all-too-clear medical knowledge—would simply persist. Winter, also, would persist: intermittent snow, strong winds, the harsh late-afternoon sun we couldn't stand without the filter of a curtain. I was never a speculative person, but Ned thrived on speculation. In fact, he had studied poetry at Stanford, years ago, where he had written a series of "What If" poems. Richard, visiting California, answering questions onstage after one of the movies he'd produced had been screened, had suddenly found himself challenged by a student whose questions were complex and rhetorical. In the following fifteen years, they had been lovers, enemies, and finally best friends, associated in work. They had gone from Stanford to New York, New York to London, then from Hampstead Heath back to West Twenty-eighth Street, with side trips to gamble in Aruba and to ski in Aspen at Christmas.

"You're breaking the rules," I said. "No what-ifs."

"What if we went outside and flowers were blooming, and there were a car—a convertible—and we drove to Plum Island," he went on. "Moon on the water. Big Dipper in the sky. Think about it. Visualize it and your negative energy will be replaced by helpful, healing energy."

"Is there such a place as Plum Island or did you make it up?"

"It's famous. Banana Beach is there. Bands play at night in the Prune Pavilion."

"There is a Plum Island," the man next to me said. "It's up by Newburyport. It's full of poison ivy in the summer, so you've got to be careful. I once got poison ivy in my lungs from some asshole who was burning the stuff with his leaves. Two weeks in the hospital, and me with a thousand-dollar deductible."

Ned and I looked at the man.

"Buy you a round," he said. "I just saved a bundle. The hotel I'm staying at gives you a rate equal to the temperature when you check in. It's a come-on. I've got a queen-size bed, an honor bar, and one of those showers you can adjust so it feels like needles shooting into you, all for sixteen dollars. I could live there cheaper than heating my house."

"Where you from?" Ned asked.

"Hope Valley, Rhode Island," the man said, his arm shooting in front of me to shake Ned's hand. "Harvey Milgrim," he said, nodding at my face. "Captain, United States Army Reserve."

"Harvey," Ned said, "I don't think you have any use for guys like me. I'm homosexual."

The man looked at me. I was surprised, too; it wasn't like Ned to talk about this with strangers. Circumstance had thrown me together with Ned; fate precipitated our unlikely bonding. Neither of us could think of life without Richard. Richard opened up to very few people, but when he did he made it a point to be indispensable.

"He's kidding," I said. It seemed the easiest thing to say.

"Dangerous joke," Harvey Milgrim said.

"He's depressed because I'm leaving him," I said.

"Well, now, I wouldn't rush into a thing like that," Harvey said. "I'm Bud on draft. What are you two?"

The bartender walked over the minute the conversation shifted to alcohol.

"Stoli straight up," Ned said.

"Vodka tonic," I said.

"Switch me to Jim Beam," Harvey said. He rolled his hand with the quick motion of someone shaking dice. "Couple of rocks on the side."

"Harvey," Ned said, "my world's coming apart. My ex-lover is also my boss, and his white-blood-cell count is sinking too low for him to stay alive. The program he's in at Bishopgate is his last chance. He's a Friday-afternoon vampire. They pump blood into him so he has enough energy to take part in an experimental study and keep his outpatient status, but do you know how helpful that is? Imagine he's driving the Indy. He's in the lead. He screeches in for gas, and what does the pit crew do but blow him a kiss? The other cars are still out there, whipping past. He starts to yell, because they're supposed to fill the car with gas, but the guys are nuts or something. They just blow air kisses."

Harvey looked at Ned's hand, the fingers fanned open, deep Vs of space between them. Then Ned slowly curled them in, kissing his finger-nails as they came to rest on his bottom lip.

The bartender put the drinks down, one-two-three. He scooped a few ice cubes into a glass and put the glass beside Harvey's shot glass of bour-bon. Harvey frowned, looking from glass to glass without saying any-thing. Then he threw down the shot of bourbon and picked up the other glass, lifted one ice cube out, and slowly sucked it. He did not look at us or speak to us again.

The night after Ned and I snuck off to the bar, Richard started to hyperventilate. In a minute his pajamas were soaked, his teeth chattering. It was morning, 4 A.M. He was holding on to the door frame, his feet in close, his body curved away, like someone windsurfing. Ned woke up groggily from his sleeping bag on the floor at the foot of Richard's bed. I was on the foldout sofa in the living room, again awakened by the slightest sound. Before I'd fallen asleep, I'd gone into the kitchen to get a drink of water, and a mouse had run under the refrigerator. It startled me, but then tears sprang to my eyes because if Richard knew there were mice—mice polluting the environment he was trying to purify with air ionizers, and humidifiers that misted the room with mineral water—he'd make us move. The idea of gathering up the piles of holistic-health books, the pam-phlets on meditation, the countless jars of vitamins and chelated minerals and organically grown grains, the eye of God that hung over the stove, the passages he'd made Ned transcribe from Bernie Siegel and tape to the refrigerator—we'd already moved twice, neither time for any good reason. Something couldn't just scurry in and make us pack it all up again, could it? And where was there left to go anymore? He was too sick to be in a hotel, and I knew there was no other apartment anywhere near the hospital. We would have to persuade him that the mouse existed only in his head. We'd tell him he was hallucinating; we'd talk him out of it, in the same way we patiently tried to soothe him by explaining that the terror he was experiencing was only a nightmare. He was not in a plane that had crashed in the jungle; he was tangled in sheets, not weighed down with concrete.

When I got to the bedroom, Ned was trying to pry Richard's fingers off the door frame. He was having no luck, and looked at me with an expression that had become familiar: fear, with an undercurrent of intense fatigue.

Richard's robe dangled from his bony shoulders. He was so wet that I thought at first he might have blundered into the shower. He looked in my direction but didn't register my presence. Then he sagged against Ned, who began to walk him slowly in the direction of the bed.

"It's cold," Richard said. "Why isn't there any heat?"

"We keep the thermostat at eighty," Ned said wearily. "You just need to get under the covers."

"Is that Hattie over there?"

"It's me," I said. "Ned is trying to get you into the bed."

"Rac," Richard said vaguely. He said to Ned, "Is that my bed?"

"That's your bed," Ned said. "You'll be warm if you get into bed, Richard."

I came up beside Richard and patted his back, and walked around and sat on the edge of the bed, trying to coax him forward. Ned was right: it was dizzyingly hot in the apartment. I got up and turned back the covers, smoothing the contour sheet. Ned kept Richard's hand, but turned to face him as he took one step backward, closer to the bed. The two of us pantomimed our pleasure at the bed's desirability. Richard began to walk toward it, licking his lips.

"I'll get you some water," I said.

"Water," Richard said. "I thought we were on a ship. I thought the bathroom was an inside cabin with no window. I can't be where there's no way to see the sky."

Ned was punching depth back into Richard's pillows. Then he made a fist and punched the center of the bed. "All aboard the S.S. *Fucking A*," he said.

It got a fake laugh out of me as I turned into the kitchen, but Richard only began to whisper urgently about the claustrophobia he'd experienced in the bathroom. Finally he did get back in his bed and immediately fell asleep. Half an hour later, still well before dawn, Ned repeated Richard's whisperings to me as if they were his own. Though Ned and I were very different people, our ability to imagine Richard's suffering united us. We were sitting in wooden chairs we'd pulled away from the dining-room table to put by the window so Ned could smoke. His cigarette smoke curled out the window.

"Ever been to Mardi Gras?" he said.

"New Orleans," I said, "but never Mardi Gras."

"They use strings of beads for barter," he said. "People stand up on the balconies in the French Quarter—women as well as men, sometimes—and they holler down for people in the crowd to flash 'em: you give them a thrill, they toss down their beads. The more you show, the more you win. Then you can walk around with all your necklaces and everybody will know you're real foxy. *Real* cool. You do a bump-and-grind, you can get the good ole boys—the men, that is—and the transvestites all whistling together and throwing down the long necklaces. The real long ones are the ones everybody wants. They're like having a five-carat-diamond ring." He opened the window another few inches so he could stub out his cigarette. One-fingered, he flicked it to the ground. Then he lowered the window, not quite pushing it shut. This wasn't one of Ned's wild stories; I was sure what he'd just told me was true. Sometimes I thought Ned told me certain stories to titillate me, or perhaps to put me down in some way: to remind me that I was straight and he was gay.

"You know what I did one time?" I said suddenly, deciding to see if I could shock him for once. "When I was having that affair with Harry? One night we were in his apartment—his wife was off in Israel—and he was cooking dinner, and I was going through her jewelry box. There was a pearl necklace in there. I couldn't figure out how to open the clasp, but finally I realized I could just drop it over my head carefully. When Harry hollered for me, I had all my clothes off and was lying on the rug, in the dark, with my arms at my side. Finally he came after me. He put on the light and saw me, and then he started laughing and sort of dove onto me, and the pearl necklace broke. He raised up and said, 'What have I done?' and I said, 'Harry, it's your wife's necklace.' He didn't even know she had it. She must not have worn it. So he started cursing, crawling around to pick up the pearls, and I thought, No, if he has it restrung at least I'm going to make sure it won't be the same length."

Ned and I turned our heads to see Richard, his robe neatly knotted in front, kneesocks pulled on, his hair slicked back.

"What are you two talking about?" he said.

"Hey, Richard," Ned said, not managing to disguise his surprise.

"I don't smell cigarette smoke, do I?" Richard said.

"It's coming from below," I said, closing the window.

"We weren't talking about you," Ned said. His voice was both kind and wary.

"I didn't say you were," Richard said. He looked at me. "May I be included?"

"I was telling him about Harry," I said. "The story about the pearls." More and more, it seemed, we were relying on stories.

"I never liked him," Richard said. He waved a hand toward Ned. "Open that a crack, will you? It's too hot in here."

"You already know the story," I said to Richard, anxious to include him. "You tell Ned the punch line."

Richard looked at Ned. "She ate them," he said. "When he wasn't looking she ate as many as she could."

"I didn't want them to fit anymore if she tried to put them over her head," I said. "I wanted her to know something had happened."

Richard shook his head, but fondly: a little gesture he gave to indicate that I was interchangeable with some gifted, troublesome child he never had.

"One time, when I was on vacation with Sander, I picked up a trick in Puerto Rico," Ned said. "We were going at it at this big estate where the guy's employer lived, and suddenly the guy, the employer, hears something and starts up the stairs. So I ran into the closet—"

"He played football in college," Richard said.

I smiled, but I had already heard this story. Ned had told it at a party one night long ago, when he was drunk. It was one of the stories he liked best, because he appeared a little wild in it and a little cagey, and because somebody got his comeuppance. His stories were not all that different from those stories boys had often confided in me back in my college days—stories about dates and sexual conquests, told with ellipses to spare my delicate feelings.

"So I grabbed whatever was hanging behind me—just grabbed down a wad of clothes—and as the guy comes into the room, I throw open the door and spring," Ned was saying. "Buck naked, I start out running, and here's my bad luck: I slam right into him and knock him out. Like it's a cartoon or something. I know he's out cold, but I'm too terrified to think straight, so I keep on running. Turns out what I've grabbed is a white pleated shirt and a thing like a—what do you call those jackets the Japanese wear? Comes halfway down my thighs, thank God."

"These are the things he thanks God for," Richard said to me.

Ned got up, growing more animated. "It's *all* like a cartoon. There's a dog in the yard that sets out after me, but the thing is on a *chain*. He reaches the end of the chain and just rises up in the air, baring his teeth, but he can't go anywhere. So I stand right there, inches in front of the dog, and put on the shirt and tie the jacket around me, and then I stroll over to the gate and slip the latch, and about a quarter of a mile later I'm outside some hotel. I go in and go to the men's room to clean up, and that's the first time I realize I've got a broken nose."

Although I had heard the story before, this was the first mention of Ned's broken nose. For a few seconds he seemed to lose steam, as if he himself were tired of the story, but then he started up again, revitalized.

"And here's the rest of my good luck: I come out and the guy on the desk is a fag. I tell him I've run into a problem and will he please call my boyfriend at the hotel where we're staying, because I don't even have a coin to use the pay phone. So he looks up the number of the hotel, and he dials it and hands me the phone. They connect me with Sander, who is sound asleep, but he snaps to right away, screaming, 'Another night on the town with a prettyboy? Suddenly the bars close and Ned realizes his wallet's back at the hotel? And do you think I'm going to come get you, just because you and some pickup don't have money to pay the bill?'"

Eyes wide, Ned turned first to me, then to Richard, playing to a full house. "While he was ranting, I had time to think. I said, 'Wait a minute, Sander. You mean they didn't get anything? You mean I left my wallet at the hotel?'" Ned sank into his chair. "Can you believe it? I'd actually left my fuckin' wallet in our room, so all I had to do was pretend to Sander that I'd gotten mugged—sons of bitches made me strip and ran off with my pants. Then I told him that the guy at the hotel gave me the kimono to put on." He clicked his fingers. "That's what they're called: 'kimonos.'"

"He didn't ask why a kimono?" Richard said wearily. He ran his hand over the stubble of his beard. His feet were tucked beside him on the sofa.

"Sure. And I tell him it's because there's a Japanese restaurant in the hotel, and if you want to wear kimonos and sit on the floor Japanese style, they let you. And the bellboy thought they'd never miss a kimono."

"He believed you?" Richard said.

"Sander? He grew up in L.A. and spent the rest of his life in New York. He knew you had to believe everything. He drives me back to the hotel saying how great it is that the scum that jumped me didn't get any money. The sun's coming up, and we're riding along in the rental car, and he's holding my hand." Ned locked his thumbs together. "Sander and I are like *that* again."

In the silence, the room seemed to shrink around us. Sander died in 1985.

"I'm starting to feel cold," Richard said. "It comes up my body like somebody's rubbing ice up my spine."

I got up and sat beside him, half hugging him, half massaging his back.

"There's that damn baby again," Richard said. "If that's their first baby, I'll bet they never have another one."

Ned and I exchanged looks. The only sound, except for an intermittent hiss of steam from the radiator, was the humming of the refrigerator.

"What happened to your paws, Rac?" Richard said to me.

I looked at my hands, thumbs pressing into the muscles below his shoulders. For the first time in as long as I could remember, I'd forgotten to put on the lotion and the gloves before going to sleep. I was also reflexively doing something I'd trained myself not to do years ago. My insurance contract said I couldn't use my hands that way: no cutting with a knife, no washing dishes, no making the bed, no polishing the furniture. But I kept pressing my thumbs in Richard's back, rubbing them back and forth. Even after Ned dropped the heavy blanket over Richard's trembling shoulders, I kept pressing some resistance to his hopeless dilemma deep into the bony ladder of Richard's spine.

"It's crazy to hate a baby for crying," Richard said, "but I really hate that baby."

Ned spread a blanket over Richard's lap, then tucked it around his legs. He sat on the floor and bent one arm around Richard's blanketed shins. "Richard," he said quietly, "there's no baby. We've gone through the building floor by floor, to humor you. That noise you get in your ears when your blood pressure starts to drop must sound to you like a baby crying."

"Okay," Richard said, shivering harder. "There's no baby. Thank you for telling me. You promised you'd always tell me the truth."

Ned looked up. "Truth? From the guy who just told the Puerto Rico story?"

"Or maybe you're hearing something in the pipes, Richard," I said. "Sometimes the radiators make noise."

Richard nodded hard, in agreement. But he didn't quite hear me. That was what Ned and I had found out about people who were dying: their minds always raced past whatever was being said, and still the pain went faster, leapfrogging ahead.

Two days later, Richard was admitted to the hospital with a high fever, and went into a coma from which he never awoke. His brother flew to Boston that night, to be with him. His godson, Jerry, came, too, getting there in time to go with us in the cab. The experimental treatment hadn't worked. Of course, we still had no way of knowing—we'll never know—whether Richard had been given the polysyllabic medicine we'd come to call "the real stuff," or whether he'd been part of the control group. We didn't know whether the priest from Hartford was getting the real stuff, either, though it was rumored among us that his flushed face was a good sign. And what about the young veterinarian who always had something optimistic to say when we ran into each other in the transfusion room? Like Clark Kent, with his secret "S" beneath his shirt, the vet wore a T-shirt with a photograph reproduced on the front, a snapshot of him hugging his Border collie on the day the dog took a blue ribbon. He told me he wore it every Friday for good luck, as he sat in oncology getting the I.V. drip that sometimes gave him the strength to go to a restaurant with a friend that night.

Ned and I, exhausted from another all-nighter, took the presence of Richard's brother and godson as an excuse to leave the hospital and go get a cup of coffee. I felt light-headed, though, and asked Ned to wait for me in the lobby while I went to the bathroom. I thought some cold water on my face might revive me.

There were two teenage girls in the bathroom. As they talked, it turned out they were sisters and had just visited their mother, who was in the oncology ward down the hall. Their boyfriends were coming to pick them up, and there was a sense of excitement in the air as one sister teased her hair into a sort of plume, and the other took off her torn stockings and threw them away, then rolled her knee-length skirt up to make it a micro-mini. "Come on, Mare," her sister, standing at the mirror, said, though she was taking her time fixing her own hair. Mare reached into her cosmetic bag and took out a little box. She opened it and began to quickly streak a brush over the rectangle of color inside. Then, to my amazement, she began to swirl the brush over both knees, to make them blush. As I washed and dried my face, a fog of hair spray filtered down. The girl at the mirror fanned the air, put the hair spray back in her purse, then picked up a tube of lipstick, opened it, and parted her lips. As Mare straightened up after one last swipe at her knees, she knocked her sister's arm, so that the lipstick shot slightly above her top lip.

"Jesus! You feeb!" the girl said shrilly. "Look what you made me *do*."

"Meet you at the car," her sister said, grabbing the lipstick and tossing it into her makeup bag. She dropped the bag in her purse and almost skipped out, calling back, "Soap and water's good for that!"

"What a bitch," I said, more to myself than to the girl who remained.

"Our mother's dying, and she doesn't care," the girl said. Tears began to well up in her eyes.

"Let me help you get it off," I said, feeling more light-headed than I had when I'd come in. I felt as if I were sleepwalking.

The girl faced me, mascara smudged in half-moons beneath her eyes, her nose bright red, one side of her lip more pointed than the other. From the look in her eyes, I was just a person who happened to be in the room. The way I had happened to be in the room in New York the day Richard came out of the bathroom, one shirtsleeve rolled up, frowning, saying, "What do you think this rash is on my arm?"

"I'm all right," the girl said, wiping her eyes. "It's not your problem."

"I'd say she does care," I said. "People get very anxious in hospitals. I came in to throw some water on my face because I was feeling a little faint."

"Do you feel better now?" she said.

"Yes," I said.

"We're not the ones who are dying," she said.

It was a disembodied voice that came from some faraway, perplexing place, and it disturbed me so deeply that I needed to hold her for a moment—which I did, tapping my forehead lightly against hers and slipping my fingers through hers to give her a squeeze before I walked out the door.

Ned had gone outside and was leaning against a lamppost. He pointed the glowing tip of his cigarette to the right, asking silently if I wanted to go to the coffee shop down the block. I nodded, and we fell into step.

"I don't think this is a walk we're going to be taking too many more times," he said. "The doctor stopped to talk, on his way out. He's run out of anything optimistic to say. He also took a cigarette out of my fingers and crushed it under his heel, told me I shouldn't smoke. I'm not crazy about doctors, but there's still something about that one that I like. Hard to imagine I'd ever warm up to a guy with tassels on his shoes."

It was freezing cold. At the coffee shop, hot air from the electric heater over the door smacked us in the face as we headed for our familiar seats at the counter. Just the fact that it wasn't the hospital made it somehow pleasant, though it was only a block and a half away. Some of the doctors and nurses went there, and of course people like us—patients' friends and relatives. Ned nodded when the waitress asked if we both wanted coffee.

"Winter in Boston," Ned said. "Never knew there was anything worse than winter where I grew up, but I think this is worse."

"Where did you grow up?"

"Kearney, Nebraska. Right down Route Eighty, about halfway between Lincoln and the Wyoming border."

"What was it like, growing up in Nebraska?"

"I screwed boys," he said.

It was either the first thing that popped into his head, or he was trying to make me laugh.

"You know what the first thing fags always ask each other is, don't you?" he said.

I shook my head no, braced for a joke.

"It's gotten so the second thing is 'Have you been tested?' But the first thing is still always 'When did you know?'"

"Okay," I said. "Second question."

"No," he said, looking straight at me. "It can't happen to me."

"Be serious," I said. "That's not a serious answer."

He cupped his hand over mine. "How the hell do you think I got out of Kearney, Nebraska?" he said. "Yeah, I had a football scholarship, but I had to hitchhike to California—never been to another state but Wyoming—hitched with whatever I had in a laundry bag. And if a truck driver put a hand on my knee, you don't think I knew that was a small price to pay for a ride? Because luck was with me. I always knew that. Just the way luck shaped those pretty hands of yours. Luck's always been with me, and luck's with you. It's as good as anything else we have to hang on to."

He lifted his hand from mine, and yes, there it was: the perfect hand, with smooth skin, tapered fingers, and nails curved and shining under the gloss of a French manicure. There was a small, dark smudge across one knuckle. I licked the middle finger of the other hand to see if I could gently rub it away, that smudge of mascara that must have passed from the hand of the girl in the bathroom to my hand when our fingers interwove as we awkwardly embraced. The girl I had been watching, all the time Ned and I sat talking. She was there in the coffee shop with us — I'd seen them come in, the two sisters and their boyfriends — her hair neatly combed, her eyes sparkling, her makeup perfectly stroked on. Though her sister tried to get their attention, both boys hung on her every word.　　　　　　[1991]

URSULA K. LE GUIN

*U*rsula K. Le Guin (b. 1929) is the daughter of Theodora Kroeber, a writer, and Alfred Louis Kroeber, a pioneering anthropologist at the University of California at Berkeley. From her family background Le Guin acquired a double orientation, humanistic and scientific, that shows in all of her writing. She was educated at Radcliffe College and Columbia University, where she completed a master's thesis in medieval romance literature. In 1953 she married the historian Charles Le Guin, with whom she had three children. Although she wrote her first science-fiction story at the age of twelve, she didn't begin publishing until twenty years later. One of her stories, "Semley's Necklace," grew into her first published novel, Rocannon's World *(1966). Another story, "Winter's King," introduced the setting she developed for her first major success, the novel* The Left Hand of Darkness *(1969). These stories and novels, along with* Planet of Exile *(1966),* City of Illusions *(1967),* The Dispossessed *(1974), the novella* The Word for World Is Forest *(1976), and stories in* The Wind's Twelve Quarters *(1976), form the Hainish cycle, a series of independent works sharing an imaginary historic background. Le Guin has also published several other fantasy novels, four more story collections, and the essay collection* Dancing at the Edge of the World: Thoughts on Words, Women, Places *(1990).*

Although Le Guin's earliest work primarily attracted a devoted audience of science-fiction readers, her later work—especially The Left Hand of Darkness*—has wider appeal. In that novel she explored the theme of androgyny on the planet Winter (Gethen), where inhabitants may adopt alternately male and female roles. Le Guin insists on Aristotle's definition of* Homo sapiens *as a social animal, and she shows how difficult it is to think of our fellow humans as people rather than as men and women.*

Le Guin brings to fantasy fiction a wealth of literary scholarship, crediting Leo Tolstoy, Anton Chekhov, and Virginia Woolf (among others) as her primary influences. Most of her stories are about reciprocal relationships, illustrating "the sort of golden rule that whatever you touch, touches you." This maxim has scientific backings in ecology and philosophical echoes in Taoism and Zen. "Texts," which debuted in American Short Fiction *in 1991, is from* Searoad: Chronicles of Klatsand *(1991), a group of linked stories with their setting on the Oregon coast.*

Texts

Messages came, Johanna thought, usually years too late, or years before one could crack their code or had even learned the language they were in. Yet they came increasingly often and were so urgent, so compelling in their demand that she read them, that she do something, as to force her at last to take refuge from them. She rented, for the month of January, a little house with no telephone in a seaside town that had no mail delivery. She had stayed there several times in summer; winter, as she had hoped, was even quieter than summer. A whole day would go by without her hearing or speaking a word. She did not buy the paper or turn on the television, and the one morning she thought she ought to find some news on the radio she got a program in Finnish from Astoria. But the messages still came. Words were everywhere.

Literate clothing was no real problem. She remembered the first print dress she had ever seen, years ago, a genuine *print* dress with typography involved in the design—green on white, suitcases and hibiscus and the names *Riviera* and *Capri* and *Paris* occurring rather blobbily from shoulder-seam to hem, sometimes right side up, sometimes upside down. Then it had been, as the saleswoman said, very unusual. Now it was hard to find a T-shirt that did not urge political action, or quote lengthily from a dead physicist, or at least mention the town it was for sale in. All this she had coped with, she had even worn. But too many things were becoming legible.

She had noticed in earlier years that the lines of foam left by waves on the sand after stormy weather lay sometimes in curves that looked like handwriting, cursive lines broken by spaces, as if in words; but it was not until she had been alone for over a fortnight and had walked many times down to Wreck Point and back that she found she could read the writing. It was a mild day, nearly windless, so that she did not have to march briskly but could mosey along between the foam-lines and the water's edge where the sand reflected the sky. Every now and then a quiet winter breaker driving up and up the beach would drive her and a few gulls ahead of it onto the drier sand; then as the wave receded she and the gulls would follow it back. There was not another soul on the long beach. The sand lay as firm and even as a pad of pale brown paper, and on it a recent wave at its high mark had left a complicated series of curves and bits of foam. The ribbons and loops and lengths of white looked so much like handwriting in chalk that she stopped, the way she would stop, half willingly, to read what people scratched in the sand in summer. Usually it was "Jason + Karen" or paired initials in a heart; once, mysteriously and memorably, three initials and the dates 1973–1984, the only such inscription that spoke of a promise not made but broken. Whatever those eleven years had been, the length of a marriage? a child's life? they were gone, and the letters and numbers also were gone when she came back by where they had been, with the tide rising. She had wondered then if the person who wrote them had written them to be erased. But these foam words lying on the brown sand now had been written by the erasing sea itself. If she could read them they might tell her a wisdom a good deal deeper and bitterer than she could possibly swallow. Do I want to know what the sea writes? she thought, but at the same time she was already reading the foam, which though in vaguely cuneiform blobs rather than letters of any alphabet was perfectly legible as she walked along beside it. "Yes," it read, "esse hes hetu tokye to' ossusess ekyes. Seham hute' u." (When she wrote it down later she used the apostrophe to represent a kind of stop or click like the last sound in "Yep!") As she read it over, backing up some yards to do so, it continued to say the same thing, so she walked up and down it several times and memorised it. Presently, as bubbles burst and the blobs began to shrink, it changed here and there to read, "Yes, e hes etu kye to' ossusess kye. ham te u." She felt that this was not significant change but mere loss, and kept the original text in mind. The water of the foam sank into the sand and the bubbles dried away till the marks and lines lessened into a faint lacework of dots and scraps, half legible. It looked enough like delicate bits of fancywork that she wondered if one could also read lace or crochet.

When she got home she wrote down the foam words so that she would not have to keep repeating them to remember them, and then she looked at the machine-made Quaker lace tablecloth on the little round dining table. It was not hard to read but was, as one might expect, rather dull. She made out the first line inside the border as "pith wot pith wot pith wot" interminably, with a "dub" every thirty stitches where the border pattern interrupted.

But the lace collar she had picked up at a second-hand clothes store in Portland was a different matter entirely. It was handmade, hand written. The script was small and very even. Like the Spencerian hand she had been taught fifty years ago in the first grade, it was ornate but surprisingly easy to read. "My soul must go," was the border, repeated many times, "my soul must go, my soul must go," and the fragile webs leading inward read, "sister, sister, sister, light the light." And she did not know what she was to do, or how she was to do it.   [1991]

JOHN EDGAR WIDEMAN

John Edgar Wideman (b. 1941) was born in Washington, D.C., and grew up in the Homewood section of Pittsburgh, Pennsylvania, an inner-city ghetto he has written about frequently in his fiction. At the University of Pennsylvania, Wideman was both a star athlete and a brilliant scholar: He earned All-Ivy honors in basketball as well as a place in the Philadelphia Big Five Basketball Hall of Fame, and he was one of two African Americans to receive a Rhodes scholarship in 1963, the year he graduated. Wideman spent the next three years at Oxford University studying English literature and followed this experience with a year at the University of Iowa Writers' Workshop as a Kent fellow. After teaching at the University of Wyoming, he is now a professor of English at the University of Massachusetts, Amherst.

Wideman published three novels in the 1960s and 1970s before his first book of stories, Damballah, *appeared in 1981. This was a volume in what he called the Homewood Trilogy, three books describing the Pittsburgh community of Homewood, founded by a runaway slave. The other two books in the trilogy are the novels* Hiding Place *(1981) and* Sent for You Yesterday *(1983), which won a PEN/Faulkner Award. Wideman received this award a second time for his novel* Philadelphia Fire *(1990).* All Stories Are True: The Stories of John Edgar Wideman—*comprising a total of thirty-five stories, including those in* Fever *(1989), his second book of short fiction— appeared in 1992.* Fatheralong: A Meditation on Fathers and Sons, Race and Society *(1994),* The Cattle Killing *(1996), and* Two Cities *(1998) are his recent works.*

"Newborn thrown in trash and dies," which first appeared in All Stories Are True, *is reminiscent of an earlier story in third-person narration about "dead children in garbage cans" titled "Daddy Garbage" in* Damballah. *Later Wideman read a newspaper account of a newborn infant murdered in New York City, and he said that he felt compelled "out of a sense of sadness, frustration, and pain to create the voice of a child who is witness to its own death and never got a chance to speak." Wideman felt that "the challenge of the story was to give dignity to the short life, and to slow down time when the course of its life was so short." As a teacher of aspiring writers, Wideman tells his students to "find the material that you have a stake in, that you care about immensely, that pins you down." In 1998 he was the recipient of the prestigious Rea Award for the Short Story.*

newborn thrown in trash and dies

They say you see your whole life pass in review the instant before you die. How would *they* know. If you die after the instant replay, you aren't around to tell anybody anything. So much for they and what they say. So much for the wish to be a movie star for once in your life because I think that's what people are hoping, what people are pretending when they say you see your life that way at the end. Death doesn't turn your life into a five-star production. The end is the end. And what you know at the end goes down the tube with you. I can speak to you now only because I haven't reached bottom yet. I'm on my way, faster than I want to be traveling and my journey won't take long, but I'm just beginning the countdown to zero. Zero's where I started also so I know a little bit about zero. Know what they say isn't necessarily so. In fact the opposite's true. You begin and right in the eye of that instant storm your life plays itself out for you in advance. That's the theater of your fate, there's where you're granted a preview, the coming attractions of everything that must happen to you. Your life rolled into a ball so dense, so superheavy it would drag the universe down to hell if this tiny, tiny lump of whatever didn't dissipate as quickly as it formed. Quicker. The weight of it is what you recall some infinitesimal fraction of when you stumble and crawl through your worst days on earth.

Knowledge of what's coming gone as quickly as it flashes forth. Quicker. Faster. Gone before it gets here, so to speak. Any other way and nobody would stick around to play out the cards they're dealt. No future in it. You begin forgetting before the zero's entirely wiped off the clock face, before the next digit materializes. What they say is assbackwards, a saying by the way, assbackwards itself. Whether or not you're treated to a summary at the end, you get the whole thing handed to you, neatly packaged as you begin. Then you forget it. Or try to forget. Live your life as if it hasn't happened before, as if the tape has not been prepunched full of holes, the die cast.

I remember because I won't receive much of a life. A measure of justice in the world, after all. I receive a compensatory bonus. Since the time between my wake-up call and curfew is so cruelly brief, the speeded-up preview of what will come to pass, my life, my portion, my destiny, my career, slowed down just enough to let me peek. Not slow enough for me to steal much, but I know some of what it contains, its finality, the groaning, fatal weight of it around my neck.

Call it a trade-off. A standoff. Intensity for duration. I won't get much and this devastating flash isn't much either, but I get it. Zingo.

But the future remains mysterious. Even if we all put our heads together and became one gigantic brain, a brain lots smarter than the sum of each of our smarts, an intelligence as great as the one that guides ants, whales or birds, because they're smarter, they figure things out not one by one, each

1199

individual locked in the cell of its head, its mortality, but collectively, doing what the group needs to do to survive, relate to the planet. If we were smarter even than birds and bees, we'd still have only a clue about what's inside the first flash of being. I know it happened and that I receive help from it. Scattered help. Sometimes I catch on. Sometimes I don't. But stuff from it's being pumped out always. I know things I have no business knowing. Things I haven't been around long enough to learn myself. For instance, many languages. A vast palette of feelings. The names of unseen things. Nostalgia for a darkness I've never experienced, a darkness another sense I can't account for assures me I will enter again. Large matters. Small ones. Naked as I am I'm dressed so to speak for my trip. Down these ten swift flights to oblivion.

Floor Ten. Nothing under the sun, they say, is new. This time they're right. They never stop talking so percentages guarantee they'll be correct sometimes. Especially since they speak out of both sides of their mouths at once: *Birds of a feather flock together. Opposites attract.* Like the billion billion monkeys at typewriters who sooner or later will bang out this story I think is uniquely mine. Somebody else, a Russian, I believe, with a long, strange-sounding name, has already written about his life speeding past as he topples slow-motion from a window high up in a tall apartment building. But it was in another country. And alas, the Russian's dead.

Floor Nine. In this building they shoot craps. One of many forms of gambling proliferating here. Very little new wealth enters this cluster of buildings that are like high-rise covered wagons circled against the urban night, so what's here is cycled and recycled by games of chance, by murder and other violent forms of exchange. Kids do it. Adults. Birds and bees. The law here is the same one ruling the jungle, they say. They say this is a jungle of the urban asphalt concrete variety. Since I've never been to Africa or the Amazon I can't agree or disagree. But you know what I think about what they say.

Seven come eleven. Snake eyes. Boxcars. Fever in the funkhouse searching for a five. Talk to me, baby. Talk. Talk. Please. Please. Please.

They cry and sing and curse and pray all night long over these games. On one knee they chant magic formulas to summon luck. They forget luck is rigged. Some of the men carry a game called Three Card Monte downtown. They cheat tourists who are stupid enough to trust in luck. Showmen with quick hands shuffling cards to a blur, fast feet carrying them away from busy intersections when cops come to break up their scam or hit on them for a cut. Flimflam artists, con men who daily use luck as bait and hook, down on their knees in a circle of other men who also should know better, trying to sweet-talk luck into their beds. Luck is the card you wish for, the card somebody else holds. You learn luck by its absence. Luck is what separates you from what you want. Luck is always turning its back and you lose.

Like other potions and powders they sell and consume here luck creates dependency. In their rooms people sit and wait for a hit. A yearning unto death for more, more, more till the little life they've been allotted dies in a basket on the doorstep where they abandoned it.

The Floor of Facts. Seventeen stories in this building. The address is 2950 West 23rd Street. My mother is nineteen years old. The trash chute down which I was dropped is forty-five feet from the door of the apartment my mother was visiting. I was born and will die Monday, August 12, 1991. The small door in the yellow cinder block wall is maroon. I won't know till the last second why my mother pushes it open. In 1990 nine discarded babies were discovered in New York City's garbage. As of August this year seven have been found. 911 is the number to call if you find a baby in the trash. Ernesto Mendez, forty-four, a Housing Authority caretaker, will notice my head, shoulders and curly hair in a black plastic bag he slashes open near the square entrance of the trash compactor on the ground floor of this brown-brick public housing project called the Gerald J. Carey Gardens. Gardens are green places where seeds are planted, tended, nurtured. The headline above my story reads "Newborn Is Thrown in Trash and Dies." The headline will remind some readers of a similar story with a happy ending that appeared in March. A baby rescued and surviving after she was dropped down a trash chute by her twelve-year-old mother. The reporter, a Mr. George James who recorded many of the above facts, introduced my unhappy story in the Metro Section of the *New York Times* on Wednesday, August 14, with this paragraph: "A young Brooklyn woman gave birth on Monday afternoon in a stairwell in a Coney Island housing project and then dropped the infant down a trash chute into a compactor ten stories below, the police said yesterday." And that's about it. What's fit to print. My tale in a nutshell followed by a relation of facts obtained by interview and reading official documents. Trouble is I could not be reached for comment. No one's fault. Certainly no negligence on the reporter's part. He gave me sufficient notoriety. Many readers must have shaken their heads in dismay or sighed or blurted Jesus Christ, did you see this, handing the Metro Section across the breakfast table or passing it to somebody at work. As grateful as I am to have my story made public you should be able to understand why I feel cheated, why the newspaper account is not enough, why I want my voice to be part of the record. The awful silence is not truly broken until we speak for ourselves. One chance to speak was snatched away. Then I didn't cry out as I plunged through the darkness. I didn't know any better. Too busy thinking to myself, *This is how it is, this is how it is, how it is* . . . accustoming myself to what it seemed life brings, what life is. Spinning, tumbling, a breathless rush, terror, exhilaration and wonder, wondering is this it, am I doing it right. I didn't know any better. The floors, the other lives packed into this building were going on their merry way as I flew past them in the darkness of my tunnel. No one waved. No one warned me. Said hello or good-bye. And of course I was too busy flailing, trying to catch my breath, trying to stop shivering in the sudden, icy air, welcoming almost the thick, pungent draft rushing up at me as if another pair of thighs were opening below to replace the ones from which I'd been ripped.

In the quiet dark of my passage I did not cry out. Now I will not be still.

A Floor of Questions. Why.

A Floor of Opinions. I believe the floor of fact should have been the ground floor, the foundation, the solid start, the place where all else is firmly rooted. I believe there should be room on the floor of fact for what I believe, for this opinion and others I could not venture before arriving here. I believe some facts are unnecessary and that unnecessary borders on untrue. I believe facts sometimes speak for themselves but never speak for us. They are never anyone's voice and voices are what we must learn to listen to if we wish ever to be heard. I believe my mother did not hate me. I believe somewhere I have a father, who if he is reading this and listening carefully will recognize me as his daughter and be ashamed, heartbroken. I must believe these things. What else do I have. Who has made my acquaintance or noticed or cared or forgotten me. How could anyone be aware of what hurtles by faster than light, blackly, in a dark space beyond the walls of the rooms they live in, beyond the doors they lock, shades they draw when they have rooms and the rooms have windows and the windows have shades and the people believe they possess something worth concealing.

In my opinion my death will serve no purpose. The streetlamps will pop on. Someone will be run over by an expensive car in a narrow street and the driver will hear a bump but consider it of no consequence. Junkies will leak out the side doors of this gigantic mound, nodding, buzzing, greeting their kind with hippy-dip vocalizations full of despair and irony and stylized to embrace the very best that's being sung, played and said around them. A young woman will open a dresser drawer and wonder whose baby that is sleeping peaceful on a bed of dishtowels, T-shirts, a man's ribbed sweat socks. She will feel something slither through the mud of her belly and splash into the sluggish river that meanders through her. She hasn't eaten for days, so that isn't it. Was it a deadly disease. Or worse, some new life she must account for. She opens and shuts the baby's drawer, pushes and pulls, opens and shuts.

I believe all floors are not equally interesting. Less reason to notice some than others. Equality would become boring, predictable. Though we may slight some and rattle on about others, that does not change the fact that each floor exists and the life on it is real, whether we pause to notice or not. As I gather speed and weight during my plunge, each floor adds its share. When I hit bottom I will bear witness to the truth of each one.

Floor of Wishes. I will miss Christmas. They say no one likes being born on Christmas. You lose your birthday, they say. A celebration already on December 25 and nice things happen to everyone on that day anyway, you give and receive presents, people greet you smiling and wish you peace and goodwill. The world is decorated. Colored bulbs draped twinkling in windows and trees, doorways hung with wild berries beneath which you may kiss a handsome stranger. Music everywhere. Even wars truced for twenty-four hours and troops served home-cooked meals, almost. Instead of at least two special days a year, if your birthday falls on Christmas, you lose one. Since my portion's less than a day, less than those insects called ephemera receive, born one morning dead the next, and I can't squeeze a complete life cycle as they do into the time allotted, I wish today were Christmas. Once would be enough. If it's as special as they say. And in some matters we yearn to trust them. Need to trust something, someone, so we listen, wish what they say is true. The holiday of Christmas seems to be the best time to be on earth, to be a child and awaken with your eyes full of dreams and expectations and believe for a while at least that all good things are possible—peace, goodwill, love, merriment, the raven-maned rocking horse you want to ride forever. No conflict of interest for me. I wouldn't lose a birthday to Christmas. Rather than this smoggy heat I wish I could see snow. The city, this building snug under a blanket of fresh snow. No footprints of men running, men on their knees, men bleeding. No women forced out into halls and streets, away from their children. I wish this city, this tower were stranded in a gentle snowstorm and Christmas happens day after day and the bright fires in every hearth never go out, and the carols ring true chorus after chorus, and the gifts given and received precipitate endless joys. The world trapped in Christmas for a day dancing on forever. I wish I could transform the ten flights of my falling into those twelve days in the Christmas song. *On the first day of Christmas my true love said to me* . . . angels, a partridge in a pear tree, ten maids a milking, five gold rings, two turtledoves. I wish those would be the sights greeting me instead of darkness, the icy winter heart of this August afternoon I have been pitched without a kiss through a maroon door.

Floor of Power. El Presidente inhabits this floor. Some say he owns the whole building. He believes he owns it, collects rent, treats the building and its occupants with contempt. He is a bold-faced man. Cheeks slotted nose to chin like a puppet's. Chicken lips. This floor is entirely white. A floury, cracked white some say used to gleam. El Presidente is white also. Except for the pink dome of his forehead. Once, long ago, his flesh was pink head to toe. Then he painted himself white to match the white floor of power. Paint ran out just after the brush stroke that permanently sealed his eyes. Since El Presidente is cheap and mean he refused to order more paint. Since El Presidente is vain and arrogant he pretended to look at his unfinished self in the mirror and proclaimed he liked what he saw, the coat of cakey white, the raw, pink dome pulsing like a bruise.

El Presidente often performs on TV. We can watch him jog, golf, fish, travel, lie, preen, mutilate the language. But these activities are not his job; his job is keeping things in the building as they are, squatting on the floor of power like a broken generator or broken furnace or broken heart, occupying the space where one that works should be.

Floor of Regrets. One thing bothers me a lot. I regret not knowing what is on the floors above the one where I began my fall. I hope it's better up there. Real gardens perhaps or even a kind of heaven for the occupants lucky enough to live above the floors I've seen. Would one of you please mount the stairs, climb slowly up from floor ten, examine carefully, one soft, warm night, the topmost floors and sing me a lullaby of what I missed.

Floor of Love. I'm supposed to be sleeping. I could be sleeping. Early morning and my eyes don't want to open and legs don't want to push me out of bed yet. Two rooms away I can hear Mom in the kitchen. She's fixing breakfast. Daddy first, then I will slump into the kitchen Mom has made bright and smelling good already this morning. Her perkiness, the sizzling bacon, water boiling, wheat bread popping up like jack-in-the-box from the shiny toaster, the Rice Krispies crackling, fried eggs hissing, the FM's sophisticated patter and mincing string trios would wake the dead. And it does. Me and Daddy slide into our places. Hi, Mom. Good morning, Dearheart. The day begins. Smells wonderful. I awaken now to his hand under the covers with me, rubbing the baby fat of my tummy where he's shoved my nightgown up past my panties. He says I shouldn't wear them. Says it ain't healthy to sleep in your drawers. Says no wonder you get those rashes. He rubs and pinches. Little nips. Then the flat of his big hand under the elastic waistband wedges my underwear down. I raise my hips a little bit to help. No reason not to. The whole thing be over with sooner. Don't do no good to try and stop him or slow him down. He said my Mama knows. He said go on fool and tell her she'll smack you for talking nasty. He was right. She beat me in the kitchen. Then took me in to their room and he stripped me butt-naked and beat me again while she watched. So I kinda hump up, wiggle, and my underwear's down below my knees, his hand's on its way back up to where I don't even understand how to grow hairs yet.

The Floor That Stands for All the Other Floors Missed or Still to Come. My stepbrother Tommy was playing in the schoolyard and they shot him dead. Bang. Bang. Gang banging and poor Tommy caught a cap in his chest. People been in and out the apartment all day. Sorry. Sorry. Everybody's so sorry. Some brought cakes, pies, macaroni casseroles, lunch meat, liquor. Two Ebony Cobras laid a joint on Tommy's older brother who hadn't risen from the kitchen chair he's straddling, head down, nodding, till his boys bop through the door. They know who hit Tommy. They know tomorrow what they must do. Today one of those everybody-in-the-family-and-friends-in-dark-clothes-funeral days, the mothers, sisters, aunts, grandmothers weepy, the men motherfucking everybody from god on down. You can't see me among the mourners. My time is different from this time. You can't understand my time. Or name it. Or share it. Tommy is beginning to remember me. To join me where I am falling unseen through your veins and arteries down down to where the heart stops, the square opening through which trash passes to the compactor.

[1992]

SHERMAN ALEXIE

Sherman Alexie (b. 1966) was born in Spokane, Washington. A registered member of the Spokane tribe through his mother, he attended grammar school on the Spokane reservation in Wellpinit, Washington. At Washington State University he took a creative writing course with Alex Kuo and began to pub-lish in magazines such as the Beloit Poetry Journal, *the* Journal of Ethnic Studies, New York Quarterly, Ploughshares, *and* Zyzzyva. *In 1991 he was awarded a poetry fellowship from the Washington State Arts Commission; the following year he received a poetry fellowship from the National Endow-ment for the Arts.*

In 1992 Alexie published his first two books, I Would Steal Horses *and* The Business of Fancydancing: Stories and Poems. *Several more titles fol-lowed in rapid order, including* The Lone Ranger and Tonto Fistfight in Heaven *(1993), which received a PEN/Hemingway Award for best first book of fiction. Alexie also won the American Book Award for his novel* Reserva-tion Blues *(1995), in which he imagined what would happen if the legendary bluesman Robert Johnson were resurrected on the Spokane Indian Reservation.* Indian Killer *(1996) is another recent novel.*

Alexie has stated, "I am a Spokane/Coeur d'Alene Indian from Wellpinit, Washington, where I live on the Spokane Indian Reservation. Everything I do now, writing and otherwise, has its origin in that." His short fiction, such as "The Only Traffic Signal on the Reservation Doesn't Flash Red Anymore" (from The Lone Ranger and Tonto Fistfight in Heaven*), reflects his use of the icons of popular culture—radio and television programs, high school sports, Pepsi, Chevys, the Washington Redskins—to facilitate a rapid crossover between storyteller and reader. Alexie also wrote the script for the 1998 film* Smoke Signals, *which is based on* The Lone Ranger and Tonto Fistfight in Heaven.

The Only Traffic Signal
on the Reservation
Doesn't Flash Red Anymore

"Go ahead," Adrian said. "Pull the trigger."

I held a pistol to my temple. I was sober but wished I was drunk enough to pull the trigger.

"Go for it," Adrian said. "You chickenshit."

While I still held that pistol to my temple, I used my other hand to flip Adrian off. Then I made a fist with my third hand to gather a little bit of courage or stupidity, and wiped sweat from my forehead with my fourth hand.

"Here," Adrian said. "Give me the damn thing."

Adrian took the pistol, put the barrel in his mouth, smiled around the metal, and pulled the trigger. Then he cussed wildly, laughed, and spit out the BB.

"Are you dead yet?" I asked.

"Nope," he said. "Not yet. Give me another beer."

"Hey, we don't drink no more, remember? How about a Diet Pepsi?"

"That's right, enit? I forgot. Give me a Pepsi."

Adrian and I sat on the porch and watched the reservation. Nothing happened. From our chairs made rockers by unsteady legs, we could see that the only traffic signal on the reservation had stopped working.

"Hey, Victor," Adrian asked. "Now when did that thing quit flashing?"

"Don't know," I said.

It was summer. Hot. But we kept our shirts on to hide our beer bellies and chicken-pox scars. At least, I wanted to hide my beer belly. I was a former basketball star fallen out of shape. It's always kind of sad when that happens. There's nothing more unattractive than a vain man, and that goes double for an Indian man.

"So," Adrian asked. "What you want to do today?"

"Don't know."

We watched a group of Indian boys walk by. I'd like to think there were ten of them. But there were actually only four or five. They were skinny, darkened by sun, their hair long and wild. None of them looked like they had showered for a week.

Their smell made me jealous.

They were off to cause trouble somewhere, I'm sure. Little warriors looking for honor in some twentieth-century vandalism. Throw a few rocks through windows, kick a dog, slash a tire. Run like hell when the tribal cops drove slowly by the scene of the crime.

"Hey," Adrian asked. "Isn't that the Windmaker boy?"

"Yeah," I said and watched Adrian lean forward to study Julius Windmaker, the best basketball player on the reservation, even though he was only fifteen years old.

"He looks good," Adrian said.

"Yeah, he must not be drinking."

"Yet."

"Yeah, yet."

Julius Windmaker was the latest in a long line of reservation basketball heroes, going all the way back to Aristotle Polatkin, who was shooting jump-shots exactly one year before James Naismith supposedly invented basketball.

I'd only seen Julius play a few times, but he had that gift, that grace, those fingers like a goddamn medicine man. One time, when the tribal school traveled to Spokane to play this white high school team, Julius scored sixty-seven points and the Indians won by forty.

"I didn't know they'd be riding horses," I heard the coach of the white team say when I was leaving.

I mean, Julius was an artist, moody. A couple times he walked right off the court during the middle of a game because there wasn't enough competition. That's how he was. Julius could throw a crazy pass, surprise us all, and send it out of bounds. But nobody called it a turnover because we all knew that one of his teammates should've been there to catch the pass. We loved him.

"Hey, Julius," Adrian yelled from the porch. "You ain't shit."

Julius and his friends laughed, flipped us off, and shook their tail feathers a little as they kept walking down the road. They all knew Julius was the best ballplayer on the reservation these days, maybe the best ever, and they knew Adrian was just confirming that fact.

It was easier for Adrian to tease Julius because he never really played basketball. He was more detached about the whole thing. But I used to be quite a ballplayer. Maybe not as good as some, certainly not as good as Julius, but I still felt that ache in my bones, that need to be better than everyone else. It's that need to be the best, that feeling of immortality, that drives a ballplayer. And when it disappears, for whatever reason, that ballplayer is never the same person, on or off the court.

I know when I lost it, that edge. During my senior year in high school we made it to the state finals. I'd been playing like crazy, hitting everything. It was like throwing rocks into the ocean from a little rowboat. I couldn't miss. Then, right before the championship game, we had our pregame meeting in the first-aid room of the college where the tournament was held every year.

It took a while for our coach to show up so we spent the time looking at these first-aid manuals. These books had all kinds of horrible injuries. Hands and feet smashed flat in printing presses, torn apart by lawnmowers, burned and dismembered. Faces that had gone through windshields, dragged over gravel, split open by garden tools. The stuff was disgusting, but we kept looking, flipping through photograph after photograph, trading books, until we all wanted to throw up.

While I looked at those close-ups of death and destruction, I lost it. I think everybody in that room, everybody on the team, lost that feeling of immortality. We went out and lost the championship game by twenty points. I missed every shot I took. I missed everything.

"So," I asked Adrian. "You think Julius will make it all the way?"

"Maybe, maybe."

There's a definite history of reservation heroes who never finish high school, who never finish basketball seasons. Hell, there's been one or two guys who played just a few minutes of one game, just enough to show what they could have been. And there's the famous case of Silas Sirius, who made one move and scored one basket in his entire basketball career. People still talk about it.

"Hey," I asked Adrian. "Remember Silas Sirius?"

"Hell," Adrian said. "Do I remember? I was there when he grabbed that defensive rebound, took a step, and flew the length of the court, did a full spin in midair, and then dunked that fucking ball. And I don't mean it looked like he flew, or it was so beautiful it was almost like he flew. I mean, he flew, period."

I laughed, slapped my legs, and knew that I believed Adrian's story more as it sounded less true.

"Shit," he continued. "And he didn't grow no wings. He just kicked his legs a little. Held that ball like a baby in his hand. And he was smiling. Really. Smiling when he flew. Smiling when he dunked it, smiling when he walked off the court and never came back. Hell, he was still smiling ten years after that."

I laughed some more, quit for a second, then laughed a little longer because it was the right thing to do.

"Yeah," I said. "Silas was a ballplayer."

"Real ballplayer," Adrian agreed.

In the outside world, a person can be a hero one second and a nobody the next. Think about it. Do white people remember the names of those guys who dove into that icy river to rescue passengers from that plane wreck a few years back? Hell, white people don't even remember the names of the dogs who save entire families from burning up in house fires by barking. And, to be honest, I don't remember none of those names either, but a reservation hero is remembered. A reservation hero is a hero forever. In fact, their status grows over the years as the stories are told and retold.

"Yeah," Adrian said. "It's too bad that damn diabetes got him. Silas was always talking about a comeback."

"Too bad, too bad."

We both leaned further back into our chairs. Silence. We watched the grass grow, the rivers flow, the winds blow.

"Damn," Adrian asked. "When did that fucking traffic signal quit working?"

"Don't know."

"Shit, they better fix it. Might cause an accident."

We both looked at each other, looked at the traffic signal, knew that about only one car an hour passed by, and laughed our asses off. Laughed so hard that when we tried to rearrange ourselves, Adrian ended up with my ass and I ended up with his. That looked so funny that we laughed them off again and it took us most of an hour to get them back right again.

Then we heard glass breaking in the distance.

"Sounds like beer bottles," Adrian said.

"Yeah, Coors Light, I think."

"Bottled 1988."

We started to laugh, but a tribal cop drove by and cruised down the road where Julius and his friends had walked earlier.

"Think they'll catch them?" I asked Adrian.

"Always do."

After a few minutes, the tribal cop drove by again, with Julius in the backseat and his friends running behind.

"Hey," Adrian asked. "What did he do?"

"Threw a brick through a BIA pickup's windshield," one of the Indian boys yelled back.

"Told you it sounded like a pickup window," I said.

"Yeah, yeah, a 1982 Chevy."

"With red paint."

"No, blue."

We laughed for just a second. Then Adrian sighed long and deep. He rubbed his head, ran his fingers through his hair, scratched his scalp hard.

"I think Julius is going to go bad," he said.

"No way," I said. "He's just horsing around."

"Maybe, maybe."

It's hard to be optimistic on the reservation. When a glass sits on a table here, people don't wonder if it's half filled or half empty. They just hope it's good beer. Still, Indians have a way of surviving. But it's almost like Indians can easily survive the big stuff. Mass murder, loss of language and land rights. It's the small things that hurt the most. The white waitress who wouldn't take an order, Tonto, the Washington Redskins.

And, just like everybody else, Indians need heroes to help them learn how to survive. But what happens when our heroes don't even know how to pay their bills?

"Shit, Adrian," I said. "He's just a kid."

"Ain't no children on a reservation."

"Yeah, yeah, I've heard that before. Well," I said. "I guess that Julius is pretty good in school, too."

"And?"

"And he wants to maybe go to college."

"Really?"

"Really," I said and laughed. And I laughed because half of me was happy and half of me wasn't sure what else to do.

A year later, Adrian and I sat on the same porch in the same chairs. We'd done things in between, like ate and slept and read the newspaper. It was another hot summer. Then again, summer is supposed to be hot.

"I'm thirsty," Adrian said. "Give me a beer."

"How many times do I have to tell you? We don't drink anymore."

"Shit," Adrian said. "I keep forgetting. Give me a goddamn Pepsi."

"That's a whole case for you today already."

"Yeah, yeah, fuck these substitute addictions."

We sat there for a few minutes, hours, and then Julius Windmaker staggered down the road.

"Oh, look at that," Adrian said. "Not even two in the afternoon and he's drunk as a skunk."

"Don't he have a game tonight?"

"Yeah, he does."

"Well, I hope he sobers up in time."

"Me, too."

I'd only played one game drunk and it was in an all-Indian basketball tournament after I got out of high school. I'd been drinking the night before and woke up feeling kind of sick, so I got drunk again. Then I went out and played a game. I felt disconnected the whole time. Nothing seemed to fit right. Even my shoes, which had fit perfectly before, felt too big for my feet. I couldn't even see the basketball or basket clearly. They were more like ideas. I mean, I knew where they were generally supposed to be, so I guessed at where I should be. Somehow or another, I scored ten points.

"He's been drinking quite a bit, enit?" Adrian asked.

"Yeah, I hear he's even been drinking Sterno."

"Shit, that'll kill his brain quicker than shit."

Adrian and I left the porch that night and went to the tribal school to watch Julius play. He still looked good in his uniform, although he was a little puffy around the edges. But he just wasn't the ballplayer we all remembered or expected. He missed shots, traveled, threw dumb passes that we all knew were dumb passes. By the fourth quarter, Julius sat at the end of the bench, hanging his head, and the crowd filed out, all talking about which of the younger players looked good. We talked about some kid named Lucy in the third grade who already had a nice move or two.

Everybody told their favorite Julius Windmaker stories, too. Times like that, on a reservation, a basketball game felt like a funeral and wake all rolled up together.

Back at home, on the porch, Adrian and I sat wrapped in shawls because the evening was kind of cold.

"It's too bad, too bad," I said. "I thought Julius might be the one to make it all the way."

"I told you he wouldn't. I told you so."

"Yeah, yeah. Don't rub it in."

We sat there in silence and remembered all of our heroes, ballplayers from seven generations, all the way back. It hurts to lose any of them because Indians kind of see ballplayers as saviors. I mean, if basketball would have been around, I'm sure Jesus Christ would've been the best point guard in Nazareth. Probably the best player in the entire world. And in the beyond. I just can't explain how much losing Julius Windmaker hurt us all.

"Well," Adrian asked. "What do you want to do tomorrow?"

"Don't know."

"Shit, that damn traffic signal is still broken. Look."

Adrian pointed down the road and he was right. But what's the point of fixing it in a place where the STOP signs are just suggestions?

"What time is it?" Adrian asked.

"I don't know. Ten, I think."

"Let's go somewhere."

"Where?"

"I don't know, Spokane, anywhere. Let's just go."

"Okay," I said, and we both walked inside the house, shut the door, and locked it tight. No. We left it open just a little bit in case some crazy Indian needed a place to sleep. And in the morning we found crazy Julius passed out on the living room carpet.

"Hey, you bum," Adrian yelled. "Get off my floor."

"This is my house, Adrian," I said.

"That's right. I forgot. Hey, you bum, get your ass off Victor's floor."

Julius groaned and farted but he didn't wake up. It really didn't bother Adrian that Julius was on the floor, so he threw an old blanket on top of him. Adrian and I grabbed our morning coffee and went back out to sit on the porch. We had both just about finished our cups when a group of Indian kids walked by, all holding basketballs of various shapes and conditions.

"Hey, look," Adrian said. "Ain't that the Lucy girl?"

I saw that it was, a little brown girl with scarred knees, wearing her daddy's shirt.

"Yeah, that's her," I said.

"I heard she's so good that she plays for the sixth grade boys team."

"Really? She's only in third grade herself, isn't she?"

"Yeah, yeah, she's a little warrior."

Adrian and I watched those Indian children walk down the road, walking toward another basketball game.

"God, I hope she makes it all the way," I said.

"Yeah, yeah," Adrian said, stared into the bottom of his cup, and then threw it across the yard. And we both watched it with all of our eyes, while the sun rose straight up above us and settled down behind the house, watched that cup revolve, revolve, until it came down whole to the ground.

[1993]

MARY GAITSKILL

Mary Gaitskill (b. 1954) was born in Lexington, Kentucky, the daughter of a teacher and a social worker. She had what she describes as a difficult adolescence, running away from home at sixteen to become a stripper and spending time in mental institutions. She has said that

> *this background is of limited relevance to my writing except for one thing: my experience of life as essentially unhappy and uncontrollable taught me to examine the way people, including myself, create survival systems and psychological "safe" places for themselves in unorthodox and sometimes apparently self-defeating ways. These inner worlds, although often unworkable and unattractive in social terms, can have a unique beauty and courage.*

In 1981 Gaitskill graduated from the University of Michigan, where she won an award for her collection of short fiction The Woman Who Knew Judo and Other Stories. *Seven years later she published her first book of stories,* Bad Behavior, *with Poseidon Press. The critic Martin Waxman wrote in the Toronto* Globe and Mail *that her self-destructive characters are "outsiders whose behavior is 'bad' in that it is different . . . unexpected."*

In 1991 Gaitskill published her first novel, Two Girls Fat and Thin, *in which she continued to develop what she called her characters' "confusion of violation with closeness." Her fiction often explores the theme of how people seek intimacy but don't know how to achieve it, as in her story "Tiny, Smiling Daddy," originally published in* The Threepenny Review *in 1993, and then collected in* Because They Wanted To *(1997).*

Tiny, Smiling Daddy

The phone rang five times before he got up to answer it. It was his friend Norm. They greeted each other and then Norm, his voice strangely weighted, said, "I saw the issue of *Self* with Kitty in it."

He waited for an explanation. None came so he said, "What? Issue of *Self*? What's *Self*?"

"Good grief, Stew, I thought for sure you'd of seen it. Now I feel awkward."

"So do I. Do you want to tell me what this is about?"

"My daughter's got a subscription to this magazine, *Self*. And they printed an article that Kitty wrote about fathers and daughters talking to each other, and she well, she wrote about you. Laurel showed it to me."

"My God."

"It's ridiculous that I'm the one to tell you. I just thought—"

"It was bad?"

"No. No, she didn't say anything bad. I just didn't understand the whole idea of it. And I wondered what you thought."

He got off the phone and walked back into the living room, shocked. His daughter Kitty was living in South Carolina working in a record store and making pots, vases, and statuettes which she sold on commission. She had never written anything that he knew of, yet she'd apparently published an article in a national magazine about him without telling him. He lifted his arms and put them on the window sill; the air from the open window cooled his underarms. Outside, the Starlings' tiny dog marched officiously up and down the pavement, looking for someone to bark at. Maybe she had written an article about how wonderful he was, and she was too shy to show him right away. This was doubtful. Kitty was quiet but she wasn't shy. She was untactful and she could be aggressive. Uncertainty only made her doubly aggressive.

He turned the edge of one nostril over with his thumb and nervously stroked his nose-hairs with one finger. He knew it was a nasty habit but it soothed him. When Kitty was a little girl he would do it to make her laugh: "Well," he'd say, "do you think it's time we played with the hairs in our nose?" And she would giggle, holding her hands against her face, eyes sparkling over her knuckles.

Then she was fourteen, and as scornful and rejecting as any girl he had ever thrown a spitball at when he was that age. They didn't get along so well any more. Once, they were sitting in the rec room watching TV, he on the couch, she on the footstool. There was a Charlie Chan movie on TV, but he was mostly watching her back and her long, thick brown hair, which she had just washed and was brushing. She dropped her head forward from the neck to let the hair fall between her spread legs, and began slowly stroking it with a pink nylon brush.

"Say, don't you think it's time we played with the hairs in our nose?"

No reaction from bent back and hair.

"Who wants to play with the hairs in their nose?"

Nothing.

"Hairs in the nose, hairs in the nose," he sang.

She bolted violently up from the stool. "You are so gross you disgust me!" She stormed from the room, shoulders in a tailored jacket of indignation.

Sometimes he said it just to see her exasperation, to feel the adorable, futile outrage of her violated girl delicacy.

He wished that his wife would come home with the car so that he could drive to the store and buy a copy of *Self*. His car was being repaired and he could not walk to the little cluster of stores and parking lots that constituted "town" in this heat. It would take a good twenty minutes and he would be completely worn out when he got there. He would find the magazine and stand there in the drugstore and read it and if it was something bad, he might not have the strength to walk back.

He went into the kitchen, opened a beer and brought it into the living room. His wife had been gone for over an hour, and God knows how much longer she would be. She could spend literally all day driving around the county doing nothing but buying a jar of honey or a bag of apples. Of course, he could call Kitty, but he'd probably just get her answering machine, and besides, he didn't want to talk to her before he understood the situation. He felt helplessness move through his body like a swimmer feels a large sea creature pass beneath him. How could she have done this to him? She knew how he dreaded exposure of any kind, she knew the way he guarded himself against strangers, the way he carefully drew all the curtains when twilight approached so that no one could see them walking through the house. She knew how ashamed he had been when, at sixteen, she had announced that she was lesbian.

The Starling dog was now across the street, yapping at the heels of a bow-legged old lady in a blue dress who was trying to walk down the street. "Dammit," he said. He left the window and got the afternoon opera station on the radio. They were in the final act of *La Bohème*.

He did not remember precisely when it had happened, but Kitty, his beautiful, happy little girl, turned into a glum, weird teenager that other kids picked on. She got skinny and ugly. Her blue eyes, which had been so sensitive and bright, turned filmy, as if the real Kitty had retreated so far from the surface that her eyes existed to shield rather than reflect her. It was as if she deliberately held her beauty away from them, only showing glimpses of it during unavoidable lapses, like the time she sat before the TV, daydreaming and lazily brushing her hair. At moments like this, her dormant charm broke his heart. It also annoyed him. What did she have to retreat from? They had both loved her. When she was little, and she couldn't sleep at night, Marsha would sit with her in bed for hours. She praised her stories and her drawings as if she were a genius. When Kitty was seven, she and her mother had special times, during which they went off together and talked about whatever Kitty wanted to talk about.

He tried to compare the sullen, morbid Kitty of sixteen with the slender, self-possessed twenty-eight-year-old lesbian who wrote articles for *Self*. He pictured himself in court, waving a copy of *Self* before a shocked jury. The case would be taken up by the press. He saw the headlines: Dad Sues Mag—Dyke Daughter Reveals . . . reveals what? What had Kitty found to say about him that was of interest to the entire country that she didn't want him to know about?

Anger overrode his helplessness. Kitty could be vicious. He hadn't seen her vicious side in years, but he knew it was there. He remembered the time he'd stood behind the half-open front door when fifteen-year-old Kitty sat hunched on the front steps with one of her few friends, a homely blond who wore white lipstick and a white leather jacket. He had come to the door to view the weather and say something to the girls, but they were muttering so intently that curiosity got the better of him, and he hung back a moment to listen. "Well, at least your mom's smart," said Kitty. "My mom's not only a bitch, she's stupid."

This after the lullabies and special times! It wasn't just an isolated incident either; every time he'd come home from work, his wife had something bad to say about Kitty. She hadn't set the table until she had been asked four times. She'd gone to Lois's house instead of coming straight home like she'd been told to do. She'd worn a dress to school that was short enough to show the tops of her panty hose.

By the time Kitty came to dinner, looking as if she'd been doing slave labor all day, he would be mad at her. He couldn't help it. Here was his wife doing her damnedest to raise a family and cook dinner and here was this awful kid looking ugly, acting mean and not setting the table. It seemed unreasonable that she should turn out so badly after taking up so much time. Her afflicted expression made him angry too. What had anybody ever done to her?

He sat forward and gently gnawed the insides of his mouth as he listened to the dying girl in *La Bohème*. He saw his wife's car pull into the driveway. He walked to the back door, almost wringing his hands, and waited for her to come through the door. When she did, he snatched the grocery bag from her arms and said, "Give me the keys." She stood open-mouthed in the stairwell, looking at him with idiotic consternation. "Give me the keys!"

"What is it, Stew? What's happened?"

"I'll tell you when I get back."

He got in the car and became part of it, this panting, mobile case propelling him through the incredibly complex and fast-moving world of other people, their houses, their children, their dogs, their lives. He wasn't usually so aware of this unpleasant sense of disconnection between him and everyone else, but he had the feeling that it had been there all along, underneath what he thought of most of the time. It was ironic that it should rear up so visibly at a time when there was in fact a mundane yet invasive and horribly real connection between him and everyone else in Wayne County: the hundreds of copies of *Self* magazine sitting in countless drugstores, bookstores, groceries, and libraries. It was as if there was a tentacle plugged into the side of the car, linking him with the random humans who picked up the magazine, possibly his very neighbors. He stopped at a crowded intersection, feeling like an ant in an enemy swarm.

Kitty had projected herself out of the house and into this swarm very early, ostensibly because life with him and Marsha had been so awful. Well, it had been awful, but because of Kitty, not them. As if it wasn't enough to be sullen and dull, she turned into a lesbian. Kids followed her down the street jeering at her. Somebody dropped her books in a toilet. She got into a fistfight. Their neighbors gave them looks. This reaction seemed only to steel Kitty's grip on her new identity; it made her romanticize herself like the kid she was. She wrote poems about heroic women warriors, she brought home strange books and magazines which, among other things, seemed to glorify prostitutes. Marsha looked for them and threw them away. Kitty screamed at her, the tendons leaping out on her slender neck. He hit Kitty, Marsha tried to stop him and he yelled at her. Kitty leapt between them, as if to defend her mother. He grabbed her and shook her but he could not shake the conviction off her face.

Most of the time though, they continued as always, eating dinner together, watching TV, making jokes. That was the worse thing; he would look at Kitty and see his daughter, now familiar in her withdrawn sullenness, and feel comfort and affection. Then he would remember that she was a lesbian and a morass of complication and wrongness would come down between them, making it impossible for him to see her. Then she would be just Kitty again. He hated it.

She ran away at sixteen and the police found her in the apartment of an eighteen-year-old body builder named Dolores who had a naked woman tattooed on her sinister bicep. Marsha made them put her in a mental hospital so psychiatrists could observe her, but he hated the psychiatrists — mean, supercilious sons of bitches who delighted in the trick question — so he took her back out. She finished school and they told her if she wanted to leave it was all right with them. She didn't waste any time getting out of the house.

She moved into an apartment near Detroit with a girl named George and took a job at a home for retarded kids. She would appear for visits with a huge bag of laundry every few weeks. She was thin and neurotically muscular, her body having the look of a fighting dog on a leash. She wore her hair like a boy's and wore black sunglasses, black leather half-gloves and leather belts. The only remnant of her beauty was her erect martial carriage and her efficient movements; she walked through a room like the commander of a guerrilla force. She would sit at the dining room table with Marsha, drinking tea and having a laconic verbal conversation, her body speaking its precise martial language while the washing machine droned from the utility room and he wandered in and out trying to make sense of what she said. Sometimes she would stay into the evening to eat dinner and watch *All in the Family*. Then Marsha would send her home with a jar of homemade tapioca pudding or a bag of apples and oranges.

One day instead of a visit they got a letter postmarked San Francisco. She had left George, she said. She listed strange details about her current environment and was vague about how she was supporting herself. He had nightmares about Kitty, with her brave, proudly muscular little body, lost among big fleshy women who danced naked in go-go bars and took drugs with needles, terrible women who his confused romantic daughter invested with oppressed heroism and intensely female glamour. He got up at night and stumbled into the bathroom for stomach medicine, the familiar darkness of the house heavy with menacing images that pressed about him, images that he saw reflected in his own expression when he turned on the bathroom light over the mirror.

Then one year she came home for Christmas. She came into the house with her luggage and a shopping bag of gifts for them and he saw that she was beautiful again. It was a beauty that both offended and titillated his senses. Her short spiky hair was streaked with purple, her dainty mouth was lipsticked, her nose and ears were pierced with amethyst and dangling silver. Her face had opened in thousands of petals. Her eyes shone with quick perception as she put down her bag and he knew that she had seen him see her beauty. She moved towards him with fluid hips, she embraced him for the first time in years. He felt her live, lithe body against him and his heart pulsed a message of blood and love. "Merry Christmas, Daddy," she said.

Her voice was husky and coarse, it reeked of knowledge and confidence. Her T-shirt said "Chicks With Balls." She was twenty-two years old.

She stayed for a week, discharging her strange jangling beauty into the house and changing the molecules of its air. She talked about the girls she shared an apartment with, her job at a coffee shop, how Californians were different from Michiganders. She talked about her friends: Lorraine, who was so pretty men fell off their bicycles as they twisted their bodies for a better look at her; Judy, a martial arts expert; and Meredith, who was raising a child with her husband, Angela. She talked of poetry readings, ceramics classes, celebrations of spring.

He realized, as he watched her, that she was now doing things that were as bad as or worse than the things that had made him angry at her five years before, yet they didn't quarrel. It seemed that a large white space existed between him and her, and that it was impossible to enter this space or to argue across it. Besides, she might never come back if he yelled at her.

Instead, he watched her, puzzling at the metamorphosis she had undergone. First she had been a beautiful, happy child turned homely, snotty, miserable adolescent. From there she had become a martinet girl with the eyes of a stifled pervert. Now she was a vibrant imp living, it seemed, in a world constructed of topsy-turvy junk pasted with rhinestones. Where had these three different people come from? Not even Marsha, who had spent so much time with her as a child, could trace the genesis of the new Kitty from the old one. Sometimes he bitterly reflected that he and Marsha weren't even real parents anymore, but bereft old people rattling around in a house, connected not to a real child who was going to college, or who at least had some kind of understandable life, but a changeling who was the product of only their most obscure quirks, a being who came from recesses that neither of them suspected they'd had.

There were only a few cars in the parking lot. He wheeled through it with pointless deliberation before parking near the drugstore. He spent irritating seconds searching for *Self* until he realized that its airbrushed cover girl was grinning right at him. He stormed the table of contents, then headed for the back of the magazine. "Speak Easy" was written sideways across the top of the appointed page in round turquoise letters. At the bottom was his daughter's name in a little box. "Kitty Thorne is a ceramic artist living in South Carolina." His hands were trembling.

It was hard for him to rationally ingest the beginning paragraphs which seemed, incredibly, to be about a phone conversation they'd had some time ago about the emptiness and selfishness of people who have sex but don't get married and have children. A few phrases that stood out clearly: ". . . my father may love me but he doesn't love the way I live." ". . . even more complicated because I'm gay." "Because it still hurts me."

For reasons he didn't understand, he felt a nervous smile tremble under his skin. He suppressed it.

"This hurt has its roots deep in our relationship, starting, I think, when I was a teenager."

He had a horrible sensation of being in public so he paid for the thing and took it out to the car with him. He slowly drove to another spot in the lot, as far away from the drugstore as possible, picked up the magazine, and began again. She described "the terrible difficulties" between him and her. She recounted, briefly and with hieroglyphic politeness, the fighting, the running away, the return, the tacit reconciliation.

"There is an emotional distance that we have both accepted and chosen to work around, hoping the occasional contact—love, anger, something—will get through."

He put the magazine down and looked out the window. It was near dusk; most of the stores in the little mall were closed. There were only two other cars in the parking lot, and a big, slow, frowning woman with two grocery bags was getting ready to drive one away. He was parked before a weedy piece of land at the edge of the parking lot. In it were rough, picky weeds spread out like big green tarantulas, young yellow dandelions, frail old dandelions, and bunches of tough blue chickweed. Even in his distress he vaguely appreciated the beauty of the blue weeds against the cool white and grey sky. For a moment the sound of insects comforted him. Images of Kitty passed through his memory with terrible speed: her nine-year-old forehead bent over her dish of ice cream, her tiny nightgowned form ran up the stairs, her ringed hand brushed her face, the keys on her belt jiggled as she walked her slow blue-jeaned walk away from the house. Gone, all gone.

The article went on to describe how Kitty hung up the phone feeling frustrated and then listed all the things she could've said to him to let him know how hurt she was, paving the way for "real communication," all in ghastly talk-show language. He was unable to put these words together with the Kitty he had last seen lounging around the house. She was twenty-eight now and she no longer dyed her hair or wore jewels in her nose. Her demeanor was serious, bookish, almost old-maidish. Once he'd overheard her talking to Marsha and heard her say, "So then this Italian girl gives me the once-over and says to Joanne, 'You 'ang around with too many Wasp.' And I said, 'I'm not a Wasp, I'm white trash.'"

"Speak for yourself," he'd said.

"If the worst occurred and my father was unable to respond to me in kind, I still would have done a good thing. I would have acknowledged my own needs and created the possibility to connect with what therapists call 'the good parent' in myself."

Well, if that was the kind of thing she was going to say to him, he was relieved she hadn't said it. But if she hadn't said it to him, why was she saying it to the rest of the country?

He turned on the radio. It sang: "Try to remember, and if you remember, then follow, follow." He turned it off. He closed his eyes. When he was nine or ten an uncle of his had told him, "Everybody makes his own world. You see what you want to see and hear what you want to hear. You can do it right now. If you blink ten times and then close your eyes real tight, you can see anything you want to see in front of you." He'd tried it rather half-heartedly and hadn't seen anything but the vague suggestion of a yellowish-white ball moving creepily through the dark. At the time, he'd thought it was perhaps because he hadn't tried hard enough.

He had told Kitty to do the same thing, or something like it, when she was eight or nine. They were on the back porch sitting in striped lawn chairs, holding hands and watching the fire-flies turn off and on.

She closed her eyes for a long time. Then very seriously, she said, "I see big balls of color, like shaggy flowers. They're pink and red and turquoise. I see an island with palm trees and pink rocks. There's dolphins and mermaids swimming in the water around it." He'd been almost awed by her belief in this impossible vision. Then he was sad because she would never see what she wanted to see.

His memory floated back to his boyhood; he was walking down the middle of the street at dusk, sweating lightly after a basketball game. There were crickets and the muted barks of dogs and the low, affirming mumble of people on their front porches. He felt securely held by the warm light and its sounds, he felt an exquisite blend of happiness and sorrow that life could contain this perfect moment, and sadness that he would soon arrive home, walk into bright light and be on his way into the next day, with its loud noise and alarming possibility. He resolved to hold this evening walk in his mind forever, to imprint all the sensations that occurred to him as he walked by the Oatlander's house in a permanent place, so that he could always take it out and look at it. He dimly recalled feeling that if he could successfully do that, he could stop time and hold it.

He knew he had to go home soon. He didn't want to talk about the article with Marsha, but the idea of sitting in the house with her and not talking about it was hard to bear. He imagined the conversation grinding into being, a future conversation with Kitty gestating within it. The conversation was a vast, complex machine like those that occasionally appeared in his dreams; if he could only pull the switch everything would be all right, but he felt too stupefied by the weight and complexity of the thing to do so. Besides, in this case, everything might not be all right. He put the magazine under his seat and started the car.

Marsha was in her armchair reading. She looked up and the expression on her face seemed like the result of internal conflict as complicated and strong as his own, but cross-pulled in different directions, uncomprehending of him and what he knew. In his mind he withdrew from her so quickly that for a moment the familiar room was fraught with the inexplicable horror of a banal nightmare. Then the ordinariness of the scene threw the extraordinary event of the day into relief and he felt so angry and bewildered he could've howled.

"Everything all right, Stew?" asked Marsha.

"No, nothing is all right. I'm a tired old man in a shitty world I don't want to be in. I go out there, it's like walking on knives. Everything is an attack, the ugliness, the cheapness, the rudeness, everything." He sensed her withdrawing from him into her own world of disgruntlement, her lips drawn together in that look of exasperated perseverance she'd gotten from her mother. Like Kitty, like everyone, she was leaving him. "I don't have a real daughter and I don't have a real wife who's here with me because she's too busy running around on some—"

"We've been through this before. We agreed I could—"

"That was different! That was when we had two cars!" His voice tore through his throat in a jagged whiplash and came out a cracked half-scream. "I don't have a car, remember? That means I'm stranded, all alone for hours and Norm Pisarro can just call me up and casually tell me that my lesbian daughter has just betrayed me in a national magazine and what do I think about that?" He wanted to punch the wall until his hand was bloody. He wanted Kitty to see the blood. Marsha's expression broke into soft open-mouthed consternation. The helplessness of it made his anger seem huge and terrible, then impotent and helpless itself. He sat down on the couch and instead of anger felt pain.

"What did Kitty do? What happened? What does Norm have—"

"She wrote an article in *Self* magazine about being a lesbian and her problems and something to do with me. I don't know, I could barely read the crap."

Marsha looked down at her nails.

He looked at her and saw the aged beauty of her ivory skin, sagging under the weight of her years and her cock-eyed bifocals, the emotional receptivity of her face, the dark down on her upper lip, the childish pearl buttons of her sweater, only the top button done.

"I'm surprised at Norm, that he would call you like that."

"Oh, who the hell knows what he thought." His heart was soothed and slowed by her words, even if they didn't address its real unhappiness.

"Here," she said, "let me rub your shoulders."

He allowed her to approach him and they sat sideways on the couch, his weight balanced on the edge by his awkwardly planted legs, she sitting primly on one hip with her legs tightly crossed. The discomfort of the position negated the practical value of the massage, but he welcomed her touch. Marsha had strong, intelligent hands that spoke to his muscles of deep safety and love and delight of physical life. In her effort, she leaned close and her sweatered breast touched him, releasing his tension almost against his will. Through half-closed eyes he observed her sneakers on the floor—he could not quite get over this phenomenon of adult women wearing what had been boys' shoes—in the dim light, one toe atop the other as though cuddling, their laces in pretty disorganization.

Poor Kitty. It hadn't really been so bad that she hadn't set the table on time. He couldn't remember why he and Marsha had been so angry over the table. Unless it was Kitty's coldness, her always turning away, her sarcastic voice. But she was a teenager and that's what teenagers did. Well, it was too bad, but it couldn't be helped now.

He thought of his father. That was too bad too, and nobody was writing articles about that. There had been a distance between them too, so great and so absolute that the word "distance" seemed inadequate to describe it. But that was probably because he had only known his father when he was a very young child; if his father had lived longer, perhaps they would've become closer. He could recall his father's face clearly only at the breakfast table, where it appeared silent and still except for lip and jaw motions, comforting in its constancy. His father ate his oatmeal with one hand working the spoon, one elbow on the table, eyes down, sometimes his other hand holding a cold rag to his head, which always hurt with what seemed to be a noble pain, willingly taken on with his duties as a husband and father. He had loved to stare at the big face with its deep lines and long earlobes, its thin lips and loose, loopily chewing jaws. Its almost god-like stillness and expressionlessness filled him with admiration and reassurance, until one day, his father slowly looked up from his cereal, met his eyes and said, "Stop staring at me, you little shit."

In the other memories, his father was a large, heavy body with a vague oblong face. He saw him sleeping in the armchair in the living room, his large, hairy-knuckled hands grazing the floor. He saw him walking up the front walk with the quick, clipped steps that he always used coming home from work, the straight-backed choppy gait that gave the big body an awesome mechanicalness. His shirt was wet under the arms, his head down, the eyes abstracted but alert, as though keeping careful watch on the outside world in case something nasty came at him, while he attended to the more important business inside.

"The good parent in yourself."

What did the well-meaning idiots who thought of these phrases mean by them? When a father dies, he is gone, there is no tiny, smiling daddy who appears, waving happily, in a secret pocket in your chest. Some kinds of loss are absolute. And no amount of self-realization or self-expression will change that.

As if she heard him, Marsha urgently pressed her weight into her hands and applied all her strength to relaxing his muscles. Her sweat and scented deodorant filtered through her sweater, which added its muted wooliness to her smell. "All righty!" She rubbed his shoulders and briskly patted him. He reached back and touched her hand in thanks.

Across from where they sat had once been a red chair, and in it had once sat Kitty, gripping her face in her hand, her expression mottled by tears. "And if you ever try to come back here I'm going to spit in your face. I don't care if I'm on my deathbed, I'll still have the energy to spit in your face," he had said.

Marsha's hands lingered on him for a moment. Then she moved and sat away from him on the couch.   [1993]

LORRIE MOORE

*L*orrie Moore (b. 1957) was born in Glens Falls, New York, daughter of an
insurance executive and a housewife. After completing her studies at St.
Lawrence University and Cornell University, where she earned an M.F.A. in
1982, Moore began teaching at the University of Wisconsin. As an undergraduate she won a **Seventeen** magazine short story contest in 1976, and she has
been publishing her fiction in magazines such as **Cosmopolitan, Ms.,** and
The New Yorker ever since. In 1987 her first novel, **Anagrams,** was published.

Self-Help, Moore's first collection of short stories, appeared in 1985. As
the title of the book suggests, several of the humorous stories, such as "How to
Become a Writer," were narrated in what Moore calls "second person, mock-
imperative" voices as she parodied the self-improvement manuals popular with
American readers. In the book Moore included sketches to cover various situations — "The Kid's Guide to Divorce," "How to Talk to Your Mother," "How
to Be an Other Woman."

Reviewers noted that typically the fictional characters narrating Moore's
stories were intelligent people whose self-knowledge only contributed to their
sense of distress, so they reacted by attempting to distance themselves from
their dilemmas through humor. A character in Moore's second collection, **Like
Life** (1990), is told, "Everything's a joke with you." She replies, "Nothing's a
joke with me. It just all comes out like one." Moore has said that the stories in
Self-Help, written between 1980 and 1983, were stylistic experiments. She
thought,

> Let's see what happens when one eliminates the subject, leaves the verb shiv-
> ering at the start of a clause; what happens when one appropriates the "how-
> to" form for a fiction, for an irony, for a "how-not-to" . . . the self-help
> proffered here, then, is perhaps only that of art itself, which, if you agree with
> Oscar Wilde, is quite useless.

"Four Calling Birds, Three French Hens" is from **Birds of America**
(1998), Moore's third collection of short fiction. It was originally published in
the **New York Times** in 1993.

Four Calling Birds, Three French Hens

When the cat died on Veterans Day, his ashes then packed into a
cheesy pink-posied tin and placed high upon the mantel, the house
seemed lonely and Aileen began to drink. She had lost all her ties to the
animal world. She existed now in a solely man-made place: the couch was
furless, the carpet dry and unmauled, the kitchen corner where the food

dish had been no longer scabby with Mackerel Platter and hazardous for walking.

Oh, Bert!

He had been a beautiful cat.

Her friends interpreted the duration and intensity of her sorrow as a sign of displaced mourning: her grief was for something larger, more appropriate — it was the impending death of her parents; it was the son she and Jack had never had (though wasn't three-year-old Sofie cute as a zipper?); it was this whole Bosnia, Cambodia, Somalia, Dinkins, Giuliani, NAFTA thing.

No, really, it was just Bert, Aileen insisted. It was just her sweet, handsome cat, her buddy of ten years. She had been with him longer than she had with either Jack or Sofie or half her friends, and he was such a smart, funny guy — big and loyal and verbal as a dog.

"What do you mean, *verbal as a dog?*" Jack scowled.

"I swear it," she said.

"Get a grip," said Jack, eyeing her glass of blended malt. Puccini's "Humming Chorus," the Brahms "Alto Rhapsody," and Samuel Barber's Adagio for Strings all murmured in succession from the stereo. He flicked it off. "You've got a daughter. There are holidays ahead. That damn cat wouldn't have shed one tear over you."

"I really don't think that's true," she said a little wildly, perhaps with too much fire and malt in her voice. She now spoke that way sometimes, insisted on things, ventured out on a limb, lived dangerously. She had already — carefully, obediently — stepped through all the stages of bereavement: anger, denial, bargaining, Häagen-Dazs, rage. Anger to rage — who said she wasn't making progress? She made a fist but hid it. She got headaches, mostly prickly ones, but sometimes the zigzag of a migraine made its way into her skull and sat like a cheap, crazy tie in her eye.

"I'm sorry," said Jack. "Maybe he would have. Fund-raisers. Cards and letters. Who can say? You two were close, I know."

She ignored him. "Here," she said, pointing at her drink. "Have a little festive lift!" She sipped at the amber liquor, and it stung her chapped lips.

"Dewar's," said Jack, looking with chagrin at the bottle.

"Well," she said defensively, sitting up straight and buttoning her sweater. "I suppose you're out of sympathy with Dewar's. I suppose you're more of a *Do-ee.*"

"That's right," said Jack disgustedly. "That's right! And tomorrow I'm going to wake up and find I've been edged out by Truman!" He headed angrily up the stairs, while she listened for the final clomp of his steps and the cracking slam of the door.

Poor Jack: perhaps she had put him through too much. Just last spring, there had been her bunion situation — the limping, the crutch, and the big blue shoe. Then in September, there had been Mimi Andersen's dinner party, where Jack, the only nonsmoker, was made to go out on the porch while everyone else stayed inside and lit up. And *then*, there had been Aileen's one-woman performance of "the housework version of *Lysistrata*."[1] "No Sweepie, No Kissie," Jack had called it. But it had worked. Sort of. For about two weeks. There was, finally, only so much one woman on the vast and wicked stage could do.

"I'm worried about you," said Jack in bed. "I'm being earnest here. And not in the Hemingway sense, either." He screwed up his face. "You see how I'm talking? Things are wacko around here." Their bookcase headboard was so stacked with novels and sad memoirs, it now resembled a library carrel more than a conjugal bed.

"You're fine. I'm fine. Everybody's fine," said Aileen. She tried to find his hand under the covers, then just gave up.

"You're someplace else," he said. "Where are you?"

The birds had become emboldened, slowly reclaiming the yard, filling up the branches, cheeping hungrily in the mornings from the sills and eaves. "What is that *shrieking*?" Aileen asked. The leaves had fallen, but now jays, ravens, and house finches darkened the trees—some of them flying south, some of them staying on, pecking the hardening ground for seeds. Squirrels moved in poking through the old apples that had dropped from the flowering crab. A possum made a home for himself under the porch, thumping and chewing. Raccoons had discovered Sofie's little gym set, and one morning Aileen looked out and saw two of them swinging on the swings. She'd wanted animal life? Here was animal life!

"Not this," she said. "None of this would be happening if Bert were still here." Bert had patrolled the place. Bert had kept things in line.

"Are you talking to me?" asked Jack.

"I guess not," she said.

"What?"

"I think we need to douse this place in repellent."

"You mean, like, bug spray?"

"Bug spray, Bugs Bunny," chanted Sofie. "Bug spray, Bugs Bunny."

"I don't know what I mean," said Aileen.

At her feminist film-critique group, they were still discussing *Cat Man,* a movie done entirely in flashback from the moment a man jumps off the ledge of an apartment building. Instead of being divided into acts or chapters, the movie was divided into floor numbers, in descending order. At the end of the movie, the handsome remembering man lands on his feet.

---

[1]Comedy by Greek playwright Aristophanes (c. 450–c. 388 B.C.). In the play, Lysistrata, a Greek housewife, leads the women of Athens in revolt against their husbands, seizing the city and declaring a ban on sexual activity until their spouses agree to end the Peloponnesian War.

Oh, Bert!

One of the women in Aileen's group — Lila Conch — was angry at the movie. "I just hated the way anytime a woman character said anything of substance, she also happened to be half-naked."

Aileen sighed. "Actually, I found those parts the most true to life," she said. "They were the parts I liked best."

The group glared at her. "Aileen," said Lila, recrossing her legs. "Go to the kitchen for us, dear, and set up the brownies and tea."

"Seriously?" asked Aileen.

"Uh — yes," said Lila.

Thanksgiving came and went in a mechanical way. Aileen and Jack, with Sofie, went out to a restaurant and ordered different things, as if the three of them were strangers asserting their ornery tastes. Then they drove home. Only Sofie, who had ordered the child's Stuffed Squash, was somehow pleased, sitting in the car seat in back and singing a Thanksgiving song she'd learned at day care. " 'Oh, a turkey's not a pig, you doink/He doesn't says *oink*/He says *gobble, gobble, gobble.* ' " Their last truly good holiday had been Halloween, when Bert was still alive and they had dressed him up as Jack. They'd then dressed Jack as Bert, Aileen as Sofie, and Sofie as Aileen. "Now, I'm you, Mommy," Sofie had said when Aileen had tied one of her kitchen aprons around her and pressed lipstick onto her mouth. Jack came up and rubbed his Magic Marker whiskers against Aileen, who giggled in her large pink footie pajamas. The only one who wasn't having that much fun was Bert himself, sporting one of Jack's ties, and pawing at it to get it off. When he didn't succeed, he gamely dragged the tie around for a while, trying to ignore it. Then, cross and humiliated, he waddled over to the corner near the piano and lay there, annoyed. Remembering this, a week later — when Bert was dying in an oxygen tent at the vet's, heart failing, fluid around his lungs (though his ears still pricked up when Aileen came to visit him; she wore her usual perfume so he would know her smell, and hand-fed him cat snacks when no one else could get him to eat) — Aileen had felt overwhelmed with sorrow and regret.

"I think you should see someone," said Jack.

"Are we talking a psychiatrist or an affair?"

"An affair, of course." Jack scowled. "An *affair?*"

"I don't know." Aileen shrugged. The whiskey she'd been drinking lately had caused her joints to swell, so that now when she lifted her shoulders, they just kind of stayed like that, stiffly, up around her ears.

Jack rubbed her upper arm, as if he either loved her or was wiping something off on her sleeve. Which could it be? "Life is a long journey across a wide country," he said. "Sometimes the weather's good. Sometimes it's bad. Sometimes it's so bad, your car goes off the road."

"Really."

"Just go talk to someone," he said. "Our health plan will cover part."

"Okay," she said. "Okay. Just—no more metaphors."

She got recommendations, made lists and appointments, conducted interviews.

"I have a death-of-a-pet situation," she said. "How long does it take for you to do those?"

"I beg your pardon?"

"How long will it take you to get me over the death of my cat, and how much do you charge for it?"

Each of the psychiatrists, in turn, with their slightly different outfits, and slightly different potted plants, looked shocked.

"Look," Aileen said. "Forget Prozac. Forget Freud's abandonment of the seduction theory. Forget Jeffrey Masson[2]—or is it *Jackie* Mason? The only thing that's going to revolutionize *this* profession is Bidding the Job!"

"I'm afraid we don't work that way," she was told again and again—until finally, at last, she found someone who did.

"I specialize in Christmas," said the psychotherapist, a man named Sidney Poe, who wore an argyle sweater vest, a crisp bow tie, shiny black oxfords, and no socks. "Christmas specials. You feel better by Christmas, or your last session's free."

"I like the sound of that," said Aileen. It was already December first. "I like the sound of that a lot."

"Good," he said, giving her a smile that, she had to admit, looked crooked and unsound. "Now, what are we dealing with here, a cat or a dog?"

"A cat," she said.

"Whoa-boy." He wrote something down, muttered, looked dismayed.

"Can I ask you a question first?" asked Aileen.

"Certainly," he said.

"Do you offer Christmas specials because of the high suicide rates around Christmas?"

"'The high suicide rates around Christmas,'" he repeated in an amused and condescending way. "It's a myth, the high suicide rates around Christmas. It's the *homicide* rate that's high. Holiday homicide. All that time the family suddenly gets to spend together, and then *bam,* that *egg*nog."

She went to Sidney Poe on Thursdays—"Advent Thursdays," she called them. She sat before him with a box of designer Kleenex on her lap, recalling Bert's finer qualities and golden moments, his great sense of humor and witty high jinks. "He used to try to talk on the phone, when *I*

---

[2]A controversial psychoanalyst who has criticized Freud for abandoning his early seduction theory, which Masson believes to be correct, in favor of the theory of infantile sexuality.

was on the phone. And once, when I was looking for my keys, I said aloud, 'Where're my keys?' and he came running into the room, thinking I'd said, Where's my *kitty*?"

Only once did she actually have to slap Sidney awake—lightly. Mostly, she could just clap her hands once and call his name—*Sid!*—and he would jerk upright in his psychiatrist's chair, staring wide.

"In the intensive care unit at the animal hospital," Aileen continued, "I saw a cat who'd been shot in the spine with a BB. I saw dogs recovering from jaw surgery. I saw a retriever who'd had a hip replacement come out into the lobby dragging a little cart behind him. He was so happy to see his owner. He dragged himself toward her and she knelt down and spread her arms wide to greet him. She sang out to him and cried. It was the animal version of *Porgy and Bess*." She paused for a minute. "It made me wonder what was going on in this country. It made me think we should ask ourselves, What in hell's going on?"

"I'm afraid we're over our time," said Sidney.

The next week, she went to the mall first. She wandered in and out of the stores with their thick tinsel and treacly Muzak Christmas carols. Everywhere she went, there were little cat Christmas books, cat Christmas cards, cat Christmas wrapping paper. She hated these cats. They were boring, dopey, caricatured, interchangeable—not a patch on Bert.

"I had great hopes for Bert," she said later to Sidney. "They gave him all the procedures, all the medications—but the drugs knocked his kidneys out. When the doctor suggested putting him to sleep, I said, 'Isn't there anything else we can do?' and you know what the doctor said? He said, 'Yes. An autopsy.' A thousand dollars later and he says, 'Yes. An autopsy.'"

"Eeeeyew," said Sid.

"A cashectomy," said Aileen. "They gave poor Bert a cashectomy!" And here she began to cry, thinking of the sweet, dire look on Bert's face in the oxygen tent, the bandaged tube in his paw, the wet fog in his eyes. It was not an animal's way to die like that, but she had subjected him to the full medical treatment, signed him up for all that metallic and fluorescent voodoo, not knowing what else to do.

"Tell me about Sofie."

Aileen sighed. Sofie was adorable. Sofie was terrific. "She's fine. She's great." Except Sofie was getting little notes sent home with her from day care. "Today, Sofie gave the teacher the finger—except it was her index finger." Or "Today, Sofie drew a mustache on her face." Or "Today, Sofie demanded to be called Walter."

"Really."

"Our last really good holiday was Halloween. I took her trick-or-treating around the neighborhood, and she was so cute. It was only by the end of the night that she began to catch on to the whole concept of it. Most of the time, she was so excited, she'd ring the bell, and when someone came to the door, she'd thrust out her bag and say, 'Look! I've got treats for you!'"

Aileen had stood waiting, down off the porches, on the sidewalk, in her big pink footie pajamas. She'd let Sofie do the talking. "I'm my mommy and my mommy's me," Sofie explained.

"I see," said the neighbors. And then they'd call and wave from the doorway. "Hello, Aileen! How are you doing?"

"We've got to focus on Christmas here," said Sidney.

"Yes," said Aileen despairingly. "We've only got one more week."

On the Thursday before Christmas, she felt flooded with memories: the field mice, the day trips, the long naps together. "He had limited notes to communicate his needs," she said. "He had his 'food' mew, and I'd follow him to his dish. He had his 'out' mew, and I'd follow him to the door. He had his 'brush' mew, and I'd go with him to the cupboard where his brush was kept. And then he had his existential mew, where I'd follow him vaguely around the house as he wandered in and out of rooms, not knowing exactly what or why."

Sidney's eyes began to well. "I can see why you miss him," he said.

"You can?"

"Of course! But that's all I can leave you with."

"The Christmas special's up?"

"I'm afraid so," he said, standing. He reached to shake her hand. "Call me after the holiday and let me know how you feel."

"All right," she said sadly. "I will."

She went home, poured herself a drink, stood by the mantel. She picked up the pink-posied tin and shook it, afraid she might hear the muffled banging of bones, but she heard nothing. "Are you sure it's even him?" Jack asked. "With animals, they probably do mass incinerations. One scoop for cats, two for dogs."

"Please," she said. At least she had not buried Bert in the local pet cemetery, with its intricate gravestones and maudlin inscriptions — *Beloved Rexie: I'll be joining you soon.* Or, *In memory of Muffin, who taught me to love.*

"I got the very last Christmas tree," said Jack. "It was leaning against the shed wall, with a broken high heel, and a cigarette dangling from its mouth. I thought I'd bring it home and feed it soup."

At least she had sought something more tasteful than the cemetery, sought the appropriate occasion to return him to earth and sky, get him down off the fireplace and out of the house in a meaningful way, though she'd yet to find the right day. She had let him stay on the mantel and had mourned him deeply — it was only proper. You couldn't pretend you had lost nothing. A good cat had died — you had to begin there, not let your blood freeze over. If your heart turned away at this, it would turn away at something greater, then more and more until your heart stayed averted, immobile, your imagination redistributed away from the world and back only toward the bad maps of yourself, the sour pools of your own pulse, your own tiny, mean, and pointless wants. Stop here! Begin here! Begin with Bert!

Here's to Bert!

Early Christmas morning, she woke Sofie and dressed her warmly in her snowsuit. There was a light snow on the ground and a wind blew powdery gusts around the yard. "We're going to say good-bye to Bert," said Aileen.

"Oh, Bert!" said Sofie, and she began to cry.

"No, it'll be happy!" said Aileen, feeling the pink-posied tin in her jacket pocket. "He wants to go out. Do you remember how he used to want to go out? How he would mee-ow at the door and then we would let him go?"

"Mee-ow, mee-ow," said Sofie.

"Right," said Aileen. "So that's what we're going to do now."

"Will he be with Santa Claus?"

"Yes! He'll be with Santa Claus!"

They stepped outside, down off the porch steps. Aileen pried open the tin. Inside, there was a small plastic bag and she tore that open. Inside was Bert: a pebbly ash like the sand and ground shells of a beach. Summer in December! What was Christmas if not a giant mixed metaphor? What was it about if not the mystery of interspecies love — God's for man! Love had sought a chasm to leap across and landed itself right here: the Holy Ghost among the barn animals, the teacher's pet sent to be adored and then to die. Aileen and Sofie each seized a fistful of Bert and ran around the yard, letting wind take the ash and scatter it. Chickadees flew from the trees. Frightened squirrels headed for the yard next door. In freeing Bert, perhaps they would become him a little: banish the interlopers, police the borders, then go back inside and play with the decorations, claw at the gift wrap, eat the big headless bird.

"Merry Christmas to Bert!" Sofie shouted. The tin was now empty.

"Yes, Merry Christmas to Bert!" said Aileen. She shoved the tin back into her pocket. Then she and Sofie raced back into the house, to get warm.

Jack was in the kitchen, standing by the stove, still in his pajamas. He was pouring orange juice and heating buns.

"Daddy, Merry Christmas to Bert!" Sofie popped open the snaps of her snowsuit.

"Yes," said Jack, turning. "Merry Christmas to Bert!" He handed Sofie some juice, then Aileen. But before she drank hers, Aileen waited for him to say something else. He cleared his throat and stepped forward. He raised his glass. His large quizzical smile said, This is a very weird family. But instead, he exclaimed, "Merry Christmas to everyone in the whole wide world!" and let it go at that.   [1993]

GINA BERRIAULT

Gina Berriault (b. 1926) was born in Long Beach, California, the youngest of three children. Her parents were Russian Jewish immigrants, and she did not go on to college after she graduated from high school. Instead she worked as a clerk, waitress, and news reporter before beginning to write fiction. She also married J. V. Berriault, a musician, with whom she had a daughter before they divorced. In 1958 seven of her stories were included by Scribner's in the collection Short Story 1, two years before the publication of her first novel, The Descent, about the numbing political atmosphere in the United States during the cold war. Berriault went on to publish four more novels, but she is primarily known for her three collections of short stories.

The Mistress, and Other Stories (1965) was Berriault's first book of short fiction. Her second collection, The Infinite Passion of Expectation (1982), includes one of her best-known works, "The Stone Boy." This is a dark story about an act of unintended violence and its crippling moral effect on the entire family of a young boy who kills his brother. In 1984 Berriault rewrote the story as a script for a film of the same name starring Glenn Close and Robert Duvall. Her third collection, Women in Their Beds: New and Selected Stories (1996) contains work previously published in Esquire, the Paris Review, and Ploughshares. Stories in this volume—such as "Who Is It Can Tell Me Who I Am?" (Ploughshares, 1995)—were praised for their depiction of ordinary people in crisis. Reviewing the book, critic Gary Amdahl wrote in the Nation that Berriault's stories "could conceivably vindicate the art [of short story writing], and thereby participate in the saving of the Republic. Whether or not certain kinds of novels and stories train readers in the sympathetic imagining of other's lives—from which spring the civic virtues of tolerance and concern for the welfare of all—can be debated . . . [but] what is incontrovertible is that Berriault writes real fiction."

Teaching creative writing at San Francisco State University for most of her career, Berriault almost never gave interviews or publicly explained her ideas about the craft of writing. In a rare comment to World Authors in 1975, she summarized her goal as a writer:

> My work is an investigation of reality which is, simply, so full of ambiguity and of answers that beget further questions that to pursue it is an impossible task and a completely absorbing necessity. It appears to me that all the terrors that human beings inflict upon one another are countered by a perceptible degree by the attempts of some writers to make us known to one another and thus to impart or revive a reverence for life.

In 1997 Berriault was awarded the National Book Critics Circle Award and the PEN/Faulkner Award for Women in Their Beds, as well as the Rea Award for her lifetime achievement as a fiction writer.

Who Is It Can Tell Me Who I Am?

Alberto Perera, librarian, granted no credibility to police profiles of dangerous persons. Writers, down through the centuries, had that look of being up to no good and were often mistaken for assassins, smugglers, fugitives from justice—criminals of all sorts. But the young man invading his sanctum, hands hidden in the pockets of his badly soiled green parka, could possibly be another lunatic out to kill another librarian. Up in Sacramento, two librarians were shot dead while on duty, and, down in Los Angeles, the main library was sent up in flames by an arsonist. Perera loved life and wished to participate in it further.

"You got a minute?"

"I do not."

"Can I read you something?"

"Please don't." Recalling some emergency advice as to how to dissuade a man from a violent deed—*Engage him in conversation*—he said, "Go ahead," regretting his permission even as he gave it. Was he to hear, as the last words he'd ever hear, a denunciation of all librarians for their heinous liberalism, a damnation for all the lies, the deceptions, the swindles, the sins preserved within the thousands of books they so zealously guarded, even with their lives?

With bafflement in his grainy voice, the fellow read from a scrap of paper.

> *Greet the sun, spider. Show no rancor.*
> *Give God your thanks, O toad, that you exist.*
> *The crab has such thorns as the rose.*
> *In the mollusc are reminiscences of women.*
> *Know what you are, enigmas in forms.*
> *Leave the responsibility to the norms,*
> *Which they in turn leave to the Almighty's care.*
> *Chirp on, cricket, to the moonlight. Dance on, bear.*

The fellow granted his listener a moment to think about what he'd just heard. Then, "What do you make of it?"

"What do I make of it?"

"What I make of it," said the intruder, "is you're supposed to feel great if you're an animal. Like if you're talking about a spider or a toad. Am I supposed to do that?"

"Do what?"

"Like thank God because I'm me?"

"That's for you to decide. Take your time with it." Shuffling papers on his desk. "Take your time but not in here."

Watch your step with anybody playing dumb, Perera cautioned himself. They sneak up on you from behind. This fellow knew just what he was doing, pulling out a poem by Rubén Darío, reading it aloud to a librarian so proud of his Spanish ancestry he kept the name his dear mother had called him, Alberto, and there it was, his foreign name in a narrow frame on his desk for all who passed his open door to see. Maybe this fellow had been stabbed in prison by a Chicano with the name Perera, and now Perera, the librarian, a man of goodwill, a humanitarian, was singled out among his fellow librarians.

"What do you figure this guy's saying? Wake up every day feeling great you're you?"

"If that's what you figure he's saying, that's what he's saying. That's the best you can do with a poem."

Out in fistfuls from his parka pockets, more scraps of paper. So many, some fluttered to the floor. Cigarette packets inside out, gum wrappers, scavenged street papers of many colors that are slipped along underfoot by the winds of traffic, scraps become transcendentally unfamiliar by the use they'd been put to: Lines of poetry in a fixatedly careful, cramped hand-writing.

"That spider, you take that spider." Entranced by a spider that only he could see, swinging between himself and Perera. "That spider is in its web where it belongs. Made it himself, swinging away. Sun comes out, strands all shiny, spider feels the warm sun on his back. Okay, glad he's a spider. I can see that. Same with the cricket. Makes chirpity-chirp to the moon. I can accept that. That toad, too. I can see he likes the mud, they're born in mud. It's the bear I can't figure out. Would you know if bears dance in their natural state?"

"Would I know if bears dance?"

"When they're on their own?" A cough, probably incited by some highly pleasurable secret excitement from tormenting a librarian. "What I know about bears," answering himself before his cough was over, "is bears do not dance. It is not in their genetic code. I'll tell you when they dance. They dance when they got a rope around their neck. That poet slipped up there. A bear with a rope around his neck, do you see him waking up happy, hallooing the sun? Same thing."

"Same thing as what?"

No answer, only another cough, probably called up to cover his amusement over an obtuse librarian with a silk tie around his stiff neck.

"You know anything about the guy who wrote it? The bear didn't write it, that I know."

"No, the bear did not write it. Darío wrote it. A modernist, brought Spanish poetry into the modern age. Born in Chile. No, Nicaragua. Myself, I like Lorca. Lorca, you know, was assassinated by Franco's Guardia Civil." Why that note? Because, if it happened to him, Alberto Perera, here and now, his death might possess a similar meaning. An enlightened heart snuffed out.

"When he says like, Spider, greet the sun, where do you figure he was lying?" Slyly, the fellow waited.

"Was he lying?" Always the assumption that poets lie. Why else do they deliberately twist things around?

"What I mean is," grudgingly patient, "where was he lying when the sun came up?"

"The spider, you mean?" asked Perera. "Lying in wait?"

"The poet."

"The spider was in its web. I don't know where the poet was."

"I'll tell you. The poet was lying in his own bed."

"That's a thought."

"That's not a thought. That's the truth."

"A poem can come to you wherever you are," Perera explained. "Whatever you're doing. Sleeping, eating, even looking in the fridge, or when you think you're dying. I imagine that in his case he wakes up one morning after a bad night, takes a look at the sun, and accepts who he is. He accepts the enigma of himself."

"Are you?"

"Am I what? An enigma?"

"Are you glad you wake up who you are?"

"I can say yes to that."

"You give thanks to God?"

"More or less."

"Great. I bet you wake up in your own bed. That's what I'm saying. What's-his-name wouldn't've thought up that poem if he woke up where he was lying on the sidewalk."

"Darío," said Perera, "could very well have waked up on a sidewalk. He pursued that sort of life. Opium, absinthe. Quite possibly he was visited by that poem while lying on the sidewalk."

"Then he went back to his own bed and slept it off."

With trembling fingers the fellow gathered up his scraps from the desk. Trembling with what? With timidity, if this was a confrontation with a guardian of the virtues of every book in the place? As he bent to the floor to pick up his scraps, the crown of his head was revealed, the hair sprinkled with a scintilla of the stuff of the streets and the culture. How old was he, this fellow? Not more than thirty, maybe younger. Young, with no staying power.

By the door a coughing spell took hold of him. With his back to Perera he drew out from yet another pocket in the murky interior of the parka one of those large Palestinian scarves that Arafat wore around his head and were to be seen in the windows of used-clothing stores, and brought up into it whatever he had tried to keep down. Voiceless, he left, his bare ankles slapped by the grimy cuffs of his pants.

Perera imagined him shuffling down the hall, then down the wide white marble stairs, the grandiose interior stairs, centerpiece of this eternal granite edifice. As for Darío's admonition to the spider to show no rancor, that fellow's rancor was showing all over him. Yet his voice was scratchily respectful and his fingers trembled. Anybody who inquires so relentlessly into the meaning of a poem, and presses the words of poets into the ephemerae of the streets, would surely return, borne up the marble stairs by all those uplifting thoughts in his pockets.

Alberto Perera, a librarian if for just a few months more, shortly to be retired, went out into the cold and misty evening. A rarity, in this time when librarians' ranks were shrinking down as his own head had shrunk while bent for so many years over the invaluable minutiae of his responsibilities, including the selection of belles lettres, of poetry, of literary fiction. The cranium shrinks no matter how much knowledge is crammed inside it. A rarity for another reason—a librarian who did not look like one, who wore a Borsalino fedora, his a classic of thirty years, a Bogart raincoat, English boots John Major would covet, a black silk shirt, a vintage tie.

Never as dashing as he wished to appear, however. Slight, short, and for several years now the bronze-color curls gone gray and the romantically drooping eyelids of his youth now faded flags at half-mast. Dashing, though, in the literary realm, numbering among his pen pals, most dead now: Hemingway, a letter to Perera, the youth, on the Spanish Civil War; Samuel Beckett, on critics mired up to their necks in his plays; Neruda, handwritten lines in green ink of two of his poems. What a prize! Also a note from the lovely British actress Vanessa Redgrave, with whom he'd spent an hour in London when he'd delivered to her an obscure little book of letters by Isadora Duncan, whom she'd portrayed in a film. And more, so much more. Everything kept in a bank vault and to be carried away in their black leather attaché case with double locks when he left this city for warmer climes. It was time to donate it all to an auction of literary memorabilia, on condition that the proceeds be used to establish a fund for down-and-out librarians, himself among them soon enough.

Further, he was a rarity for choosing to reside in what he called the broken heart of the city, or the spleen of it, the Tenderloin, and choosing not to move when the scene worsened. Born into a family of refugees from Franco's Spain, Brooklyn their alien soil, he felt a kinship with the dispossessed everywhere in the world, this kinship deepening with the novels he'd read in his youth. Dostoevski's insulted and injured, Dickens' downtrodden. Eighteen years ago he'd found a fourth-floor apartment, the top, in a tentatively respectable building, a walking distance to the main library in the civic center and to the affordable restaurants on Geary Street. Soon after he moved in, the sidewalks and entrances on every block began to fill up with a surge of outcasts of all kinds. The shaven heads, the never-shaven faces, the battle-maimed, the dope-possessed, the jobless, the homeless, the immigrants, and not far from his own corner six-foot-tall transvestite prostitutes and shorter ones, too, all colors. A wave, gathering momentum, swept around him now as he made his way, mornings and evenings, to and from the library. There was no city in the world that was not inundated in its time, or would be in time to come, by refugees from upheavals of all sorts.

On gray days, as this day was, he was reminded of the poor lunatics, madmen, nuisances, all who were herded out of the towns and onto the ships that carried them up and down the rivers of the Rhineland. An idea! The mayor, having deprived the homeless of their carts and their tents, would welcome an idea to rid the city of the homeless themselves. Herd them aboard one of those World War II battleships, rusting away in dry-dock or muck, and send them out to sea. The thousands—whole families, loners, runaway kids, all to be dropped off in Galveston or New Orleans, under cover of a medieval night.

He ate his supper at Lefty O'Doul's, at a long table in company of other men his age and a woman who looked even older. Retired souls, he called them, come in from their residence hotels, their winter smells of naphthalene and menthol hovering over the aroma of his roast turkey with dressing. One should not be ashamed of eating a substantial meal while the hungry roamed the streets. He told himself this as he'd told himself so many times before, lifelong. He knew from saintly experiments of his youth that when he fasted in sympathy, punishing himself for what he thought was plenitude, his conscience began to starve, unable to survive for very long without a body.

A brandy at the long bar, and the bartender slapping down the napkin, asking the usual. "When you going to sell me that Borsalino?" Then, "This man's a librarian," to the bulky young man in a broadly striped sweater on the stool to the left of Perera. "He's read every book in the public library. Ever been in there?"

"Never was."

"You can ask him anything," said the bartender, and the man to Perera's right did. "Do you know right off the number of dead both sides in the Civil War?"

"Whose civil war?"

Taken for a tricky intellectual, he was left alone.

A theater critic, that's what he wished to be mistaken for, passing the theaters at the right time as the ticket holders were drifting in and the lines forming at the box office. Women's skirts and coats swinging out, swishing against him, and a woman turning to apologize, granting a close glimpse of her face to this man who appeared deserving of it. A critic, that's who he was, of the musical up there on the stage and of the audience so delightedly acceptive of the banal, lustily sung.

Past the lofty Hilton at the Tenderloin's edge, whose ultra-plush interior he had strolled through a time or two, finding gold beyond an interior decorator's wildest dreams. Its penthouse window the highest light in the Tenderloin sky, a shining blind eye. Around a corner of the hotel, and, lying up against the cyclone fence, the bundled and the unbundled to whom he gave a wide berth as he would to the dead, in fear and respect. Over the sidewalks, those slips of refuse paper he'd always noticed but not so closely as now. Alert to approaching figures, to whatever plans they had in mind for him, and warily friendly with the fraternal clusters, exchanging with them joking curses on the weather, he made his way. Until at last he stood before the mesh gate to his apartment building. A gate from sidewalk to the entrance's upper reaches, requiring a swift turn of the key before an assault. The gate, the lock, the fear—none of which had been there when he moved in.

The only man in the Western world to wear a nightcap, he drew his on. Cashmere, dove color, knitted twelve years ago by his dear friend and lover, Barbara, a librarian herself, a beautiful one. Syracuse, New York. Every year, off they'd go. Archaeological tours, walking tours. Three winters ago he was at her bedside, close by in her last hours. She, too, had corresponded with writers. Hers were women—poets, memoirists—and these letters, too, were in his care. Into his plaid flannel robe, also a gift from her, the seat and the elbows worn away. He always read in this robe in his ample chair or at the kitchen table or in bed. Three books lay on the floor by his bed, among the last he'd ever consider ordering for any library. One had seduced and deceived him, the second was unbearably vain, and he was put to sleep by the third, already asleep itself, face down on the carpet.

When he lay down the inevitable happened. At once he wondered where the poetry stalker might be, the librarian stalker with the excitable cough. Could Darío have imagined that his earnest little attempt to accept God's ways would wind up in the parka pocket of a sidewalk sleeper, trying to accept the same a hundred years later?

At his desk he was always attuned to the life of this library, as he'd been to every library where he'd spent his years, even the vaster ones with more locked doors, tonnages of archives. This morning his mind's eye was a benign sensor, following the patrons to their chosen areas. He saw them rising in the slow, creaky elevator, he saw the meandering ones and the fast ones climbing the broad marble stairs, those stairs like a solid promise to the climber of an ennobling of the self on the higher levels. The largest concentration of patrons was in the newspaper and periodical section, always and forever a refuge for men from lonely rooms and also now for those without a room, all observing the proper silence, except the man asleep, head down on the table, his glottal breathing quivering the newspaper before his face. In the past, empty chairs were always available; now every chair was occupied. And where was the young man whose pockets were filled with scraps of poetry? In the poetry section, of course, copying down what the world saw fit to honor with the printed page. *Anything in books represents the godlike and anything in myself represents the vile.* Who said that? A writer, born into grim poverty, whose name he'd recall later. If you felt vile in the midst of all these godlike volumes, what restless rage!

"Am I butting in here?"

Same parka, grimier perhaps. But look! His hair rose higher and had a reddish cast, an almost washed look from the rain. His eyes not clearer, not calmer, and in his arms four books, which he let fall onto the desk.

"This is not a checkout desk," said Perera.

"That I know. Never check out anything. No address. If you try to sneak something out you get the guillotine. You get it in the neck."

To touch or not to touch the books. Since there was no real reason not to touch, Perera set the four books upright, his hands as bookends.

"Who've we got here? Ah, Rilke, the *Elegies*. Good choice. And here we've got Whitman. You know how to pick them. Bishop, she's up there. And who's this? Pound? Sublime, all of them. But don't let yourself be intimidated. Nothing sacred in this place, just a lot of people whose thoughts were driving them crazy, euphoria crazy or doom crazy, and they had to get it out, see what *you* think about what they're thinking. That's all there is to it. Librarians in here are just to give it a semblance of order. I'm not a high priest."

"Never thought you were."

"Ah," said Perera, and the books between his hands resumed their frayed existence, their common humanity. One, he saw, had a bit of green mildew at the spine's bottom edge. It must have been left out in a misty rain or someone had read it while in the tub.

"Can I get you some coffee?" inquired the visitor.

"Strange that you should ask," said Perera. "Got my thermos here. A thirst for coffee comes over me at this hour." How closely he'd been watched! And now forced to take the plunge into familiarity, a plunge he would not have taken without further consideration if this man were the sole homeless man around. They were empowered by their numbers.

From the bottom drawer he brought up his thermos and his porcelain cup. The plastic thermos cup held no pleasure and he never used it. He'd use it now and not bother to guess why, and bring up also the paper bag of macaroons.

"Suppose I sit down?"

Perera nodded, and the guest sat down in the only other chair, a hard chair with an unwelcoming look, a chair used until now only by Alexa Okula, head librarian, and Amy Peck, chief guard, who often described for him the assaults she had suffered that day and where in the library they had occurred.

With both hands around the cup, the guest had no trouble holding it. "This is like dessert," he said. "This is great. Got sugar and cream in it." He was shy around the macaroons. Crumbs were tripping down the parka and when they reached the floor he covered them with his beat-up jogging shoes.

At that moment Perera recalled the very recent tragedy at the Sacramento library. When did the shooting occur? Right after a little party celebrating the library's expanded hours. And what did the assassin do then?

Fled to the rooftop, where he was gunned down by the police. It was simple enough to imagine himself dead on the floor, but not so easy to imagine this fellow fleeing anywhere, hampered by the bone-cold ankles, the flappy shoes, the body's tremble at the core.

"You remember that poem?" his guest asked.

"Not verbatim," said Perera. "I did not memorize it."

"You can remember the bear, can't you, and the spider and the toad, anyway? How they're supposed to greet the sun because they are what they are?"

"That I remember," said Perera.

"What I'd like to know is, what am I?"

"You can figure you're a human being," said Perera.

"That's what I thought you'd say. What else you were going to say is, you're a human being by the sweat of your brow. Beavers, that don't take into account beavers. Beavers are dam builders. Then you take those birds who get stuff together to make a nest for the female of their choice. Other birds, too, I've seen them. Can't stop pulling up weeds or whatever stuff is around for a hundred miles, pull this out, pull that out, and off they go and back in a second. Then there's animals who dig a burrow, one hell of a long tunnel in the ground. They can't sweat but they work. It's work, but that don't make them human."

"Work does not get to the essence, I see your point," said Perera. At a moment's notice he could not get to the essence himself and he wished he had not used that word. It could only mean further trouble.

"Okay, take you," said the visitor. "Would you say you were human?"

"I've been led to believe that I am," said Perera.

"What you base that on," said his guest, "is you get to keep guard over this library and you got every book where it's supposed to be and in addition you got it up on a computer, what is its title, what is its number, who wrote it, and maybe you got in your head the reason why the guy wrote it. So in that way you can say you're human and maybe you're glad about it even if you don't look it. Okay, now let's say you're through work for the day and you walk home. Or you go on and have yourself a turkey or whatever they got there, roast beef, chicken and dumplings. Then you go along by that theater, maybe even drop in yourself at fifty bucks a seat in the balcony. After that you go on to your apartment, which is in a bad, I mean *baaad* neighborhood, and you unlock that gate. And then what?"

"I can't imagine."

"You don't have to imagine. You're in your own bed. Got a mattress that's just right for the shape you're in. Maybe you even got an electric blanket. Got pillows with real feathers inside, maybe even that down stuff from the hind end of a couple hundred ducks. Nighty-night."

"So now I'm sure I'm human?"

"So then the sun comes up and what do you say? You say what that spider says. Halloo, old sun up there, had me a good sleep in my own web and now I get to eat some more fat flies. Halloo, says the toad, now I get to spend the day in this hot mud some more. Halloo, says the bear, now I get to dance some more with this rope around my neck. Halloo, says this guy, Alberto Perera, now I get to go to the library again and talk to this guy who can't figure out why he can't halloo the sun with the rest of them."

A flush had spread over the fellow's face, over the pallor and over the pits, over all that was more appallingly obvious today. From his parka he brought out the Arafat headpiece and hid his face in it, coughing up in there something tormentingly intimate.

Alexa Okula, head librarian, passing by and hearing the commotion, paused a moment to look in and Perera held up his hand to calm her fears for his safety. Nothing escaped her, only all the years of her life in the protective custody of tons of books and tons of granite. Soon to be released, just as he was to be, all she'd have was her stringy emeritus professor of a husband and her poodles. Unlike himself, who'd have the world.

The fellow sat staring at the floor, striving to recover from the losing battle with his cough.

"You suppose I could spend the night in here?"

With *unthinkable* on the tip of his tongue, Perera said nothing. Accommodations ought to be available for queries of every sort at any time in your life.

"Looks like it ought to be safer in here."

"Unsafe in here, too," said Perera. "This fortress is in a state of abject deterioration. The last earthquake did some damage, along with the damage done by the budget cuts, along with the damage by vandals. Time's been creeping around in here, too. The whole place could collapse on you while you slept."

"I can handle it," said the supplicant. "Nobody's going to throw lighter fuel on me and set me on fire in here. Nobody's going to knife me in here, at night anyway. Lost my bedroll. I left my stuff with this woman who's my friend, she got room in her cart. I had a change of shirt in there, I had important papers, had a letter from a guy I worked for up the coast. I was good at hauling in those sea urchins they ship over to Japan, tons of them. They love those things over there, then there wasn't any more. Where the sea urchins were, something else is taking over, messing up the water. I'm telling you this because I don't drink, don't do dope, don't smoke, so I sure would not set this place on fire if I was allowed to sleep in here." He was talking fast, outrunning his cough. "The cops took her stuff, took my stuff, dumped it all into the truck. Ordered by the mayor. She lost family pictures, lost the cat she had tied to the cart that sat on top. She was crying. I was in here talking to you."

"It must be damn cold in here at night," Perera said.

"Maybe, maybe not, and if it's raining maybe the roof don't leak."

"Dark, I imagine," said Perera. "I've never thought about it. I suspect they used to leave a few lights on but now it's dark. Saves money. Let's say that once the lights go out you can't see a thing. Your sense of direction is totally lost, you're blind as a bat, and I'm nowhere around to guide you to the lavatory and I wouldn't know where it was myself. You might be pissing on some of the noblest minds that ever put their thoughts on paper."

"I wouldn't do that."

"They do get pissed on, one time and another, but not by you or me. So let's say you're feeling your way around, looking for a comfortable place. Okula has a rug in her office and it's usually warm in there. She exudes a warmth that might stay the night. But how to get there?"

"I know my way around."

"You do seem to," said Perera.

"What you could do when you take off, like your day is done, see? You just leave me in here and close the door. I wouldn't care if you locked it."

"I can lock it," said Perera, "but not with you inside."

"Is there some of that coffee left?"

Perera, pouring, was planning to wash that porcelain cup thoroughly. If it was pneumonia gripping this young man, it would get a more merciless grip on him, twice as old. Or if it was tuberculosis, it would bring on his end with rapacious haste and just as he was about to embark on his most rewarding years.

This time the guest took longer to drink it down, the hot coffee apparently feeling its way past the throat's lacerations.

"Let's say it's like that darkness upon the face of the deep," Perera said. "That same darkness the Creationists are wanting to take us back to. Dark, dark, and you need to find yourself a comfortable place. Now let's say you're at the top of our marble stairs and you don't know it. You take a step and down you go. Come morning, they open up and find you there."

"You think so?"

"You'll be on the front pages in New York, Paris, Tokyo. A homeless man, seeking shelter in San Francisco's main library, fell down in there and died. A library, imagine it, that monument to mankind's exalted IQ. I'll say you dropped by to chat about poetry. I'll say we spent many pleasant hours discussing Darío's *Filosofía*."

Contempt in the eyes meeting Perera's. "What're you telling me? You're telling me to lie down and die?"

"Not at all. All I'm saying is you cannot spend the night in this library."

Scornfully careful, the fellow placed the porcelain cup on the desk and stood up. "You want me to tell you what that poem is saying? Same thing you're saying. If you can't halloo the sun, if you can't go chirpity-chirp to the moon, what're you doing around here anyway?"

"That is not what it is saying," said Perera.

"To hell with you is what I'm saying."

Gone, leaving his curse behind. A curse so popular, so spread around, it carried little weight.

Closing time, the staff and lingering patrons all forced out through one side entrance and into the early dark, into the rain. Perera hoisted his umbrella, one slightly larger than the ordinary, bought in London the day he met the actress, years ago. It will never turn inside out, the clerk promised, not even in Conrad's[1] typhoon. And it hadn't yet. Lives were being turned inside out, but this snob of an umbrella stayed up there. A stance of superiority, that was his problem. A problem he always knew he had and yet that always took him by surprise. And how did he figure he was so smart, this Alberto Perera? Well, he could engage in the jesting the smart ones enjoy when they're in the presence of those they figure are not so smart. He could engage in that jovial thievery, that light-fingered, light-headed trivializing of another person's tragic truth, a practice he abhorred wherever he came upon it.

Onward through this neon-colored rain, this headlight-glittering rain, every light no match for the dark, only a constant contesting. *There is a certainty in degradation.* You can puzzle over lines all your life and never be satisfied with the meanings you get. Until, slushing onward, you've got at last one meaning for sure, because now its time had come, bringing proof by the thousands wherever they were this night in their concrete burrows and dens. There was no certainty in anything else, no matter what you're storing up, say tons of gold, say ten billion library books, and if you think you can elude that certainty it sneaks up on you, it sneaks up the marble stairs and into your sanctum and you're degraded right along with the rest.

For several days at noontime Perera looked for him in the long line at St. Anthony's, men and women moving slowly in for their free meal. After work he climbed the stairs to Hospitality House and looked around at the men in the collection of discarded chairs, each day different men and each man confounded by being among the unwanted many. Here, too, he knew he would not find him. The fellow was a loner, hiding out, probably afraid his cough was reason to arrest him.

A rolled-up wool blanket, a large thermos filled with hot coffee, a dozen packaged handkerchiefs, a thick turtleneck sweater, a package of athletic socks. Perera carried all this into his office, piecemeal, as the days came and went, and these offerings had the same aspect of futility that he saw in the primitive practice of laying out clothing and nourishment for the departed.

He braved the Albatross used-book store not far from the library, trying not to breathe the invisible dust from the high stacks of disintegrating books, and in the dim poetry section came upon some unexpected finds.

---

[1]Joseph Conrad (1857–1924), Polish-born English novelist and short story writer. Inspired by a trip to Java, his novella *Typhoon* (1902) tells of an English sea captain's harrowing experience caught in a typhoon off the China coast.

Ah, hah! Michaux, *My life, you take off without me,* and Trakl, sad, suicidal soul, *Beneath the stars a man alone,* and Anna Akhmatova, *Before this grief the mountains stoop,* and Ah! Machado, *He was seen walking between rifles.* Comments in the margins, someone's own poem on a title page, bus schedules, indecipherable odds and ends of penciled thoughts intermingling with the printed ones. He wanted to keep these thin volumes for himself and instead he did as planned. He bought a green nylon parka in a discount place on Market Street, slid the books into the deep pockets, and folded the parka on top of the pile.

On the morning of the twelfth day, before the hour when the public was admitted, Perera entered by the side door, bringing a pair of black plastic shoes, oxford style, made in China, recommended for their comfort by a street friend wearing a pair. The door guard silently led him to the foot of the marble stairs, where Okula, cops and paramedics and librarians were gathered around a man lying on the lowest step.

Perera had never fainted and was not going to faint now, even though all the strength of his intelligence was leaving the abode of his head to darkness.

"Mr. Perera," Okula was saying but not to him, "was an acquaintance of this man. Wasn't he?"

Nobody was answering, though Perera gave them time.

"Occasionally," he said, "he stepped into my office. My door is usually open." Sweat was rising from his scalp. "Did he fall?"

"More like he lay down and died." The paramedic's voice was inappropriately young. "T.B. Take a look at that rag."

"You say you knew him?" A cop's voice. "Do you know his name? He's got nothing in his pockets."

"No," said Perera.

"Any idea where he concealed himself in here?"

"Hundreds of places." Okula, responding. "We check carefully. However, anyone wishing to stay in can also check carefully."

"What you might be needing is a couple of dogs. German shepherds are good at it. Dobermans, too. A couple of good dogs could cover this whole place in half an hour."

Kneeling by the body, Perera took a closer look at the face, closer than when they sat in the office, discoursing on the animal kingdom. The young man was now no one, as he'd feared he already was when alive. The absolute unwanted, that's who the dead become.

"Did this man bother you?"

It would take many months, he knew, before he'd be able to speak without holding back. Humans speaking were unbearable to hear and abominable to see, himself among the rest. Worse, was all that was written down instead, the never-ending outpouring, given print and given covers, given shelves up and down and everywhere in this warehouse of fathomless darkness.

"He did not bother me," he said.

The door to his office was closed but unlocked, just as he'd left it. Scattered over his desk were what appeared to be the contents of his wastebasket. But unfamiliar, not his. So many kinds of paper scraps, they were the bits and pieces his visitor had brought forth from that green parka. Throwaway ads, envelopes, a discount drugstore's paper bag, business cards tossed away. On each, the cramped handwriting. By copying down all these stirringly strange ideas, had the fellow hoped to impress upon himself his likeness to these other humans? A break-in of a different sort. A young man breaking into a home of his own.

Perera sat down at his desk, slipped his glasses on, and spread the scraps out before him as heedfully as his shaking hands allowed.   [1995]

EDWIDGE DANTICAT

Edwidge Danticat (b. 1969) was born in Port-au-Prince, Haiti. When she was two, her father immigrated to the United States to look for work. Two years later her mother followed him, leaving Danticat and her younger brother in the care of their uncle, who was a minister. Danticat remembers her childhood fascination with the ritual of storytelling conducted by her aunt's grandmother in Haiti. When she told a story, her listeners said "Krik?" and she would answer "Krak!"

> *She told stories when the people would gather—folk tales with her own spin on them, and stories about the family. It was call-and-response—if the audience seemed bored, the story would speed up, and if they were participating, a song would go in. The whole interaction was exciting to me. These cross-generational exchanges didn't happen often, because children were supposed to respect their elders. But when you were telling stories, it was more equal, and fun.*

At the age of twelve, Danticat joined her parents in Brooklyn, where she began to learn English (the family still speaks Creole at home). Within a year she was writing articles for her high school newspaper, New Youth Connections. *She majored in French literature at Barnard College, graduating in 1990, and went on to study in the MFA program in creative writing at Brown University on a full scholarship. While still a graduate student she sold the manuscript of her first book,* Breath, Eyes, Memory, *to Soho, a small press she discovered in* Writer's Digest. *Published in 1994, the novel dramatized a young Haitian woman's coming of age in a troubled mother-daughter relationship and was chosen by Oprah Winfrey for the June 18, 1994, "meeting" of her television book club. With this endorsement,* Breath, Eyes, Memory *became a paperback best-seller.*

The next year Danticat published Krik? Krak!, *a collection of stories that included the autobiographical "New York Day Woman." This book was nominated for a National Book Award, and she was chosen as one of the twenty "Best Young American Novelists" by* Granta *magazine.* The Farming of Bones, *her third book, published by Soho in 1998, describes the 1937 massacre on the Haitian-Dominican border. Danticat now works with the National Coalition for Haitian Rights on a three-year grant from the Lila Acheson Wallace Foundation. As a spokesperson for her community, Danticat insists that she is free to write as she pleases in her fiction: "My characters are not representative of the community as a whole. As a writer, it's the person who is different from everybody else who might be interesting to you."*

New York Day Woman

Today, walking down the street, I see my mother. She is strolling with a happy gait, her body thrust toward the DON'T WALK sign and the yellow taxicabs that make forty-five-degree turns on the corner of Madison and Fifty-seventh Street.

I have never seen her in this kind of neighborhood, peering into Chanel and Tiffany's and gawking at the jewels glowing in the Bulgari windows. My mother never shops outside of Brooklyn. She has never seen the advertising office where I work. She is afraid to take the subway, where you may meet those young black militant street preachers who curse black women for straightening their hair.

Yet, here she is, my mother, who I left at home that morning in her bathrobe, with pieces of newspapers twisted like rollers in her hair. My mother, who accuses me of random offenses as I dash out of the house.

Would you get up and give an old lady like me your subway seat? In this state of mind, I bet you don't even give up your seat to a pregnant lady.

My mother, who is often right about that. Sometimes I get up and give my seat. Other times, I don't. It all depends on how pregnant the woman is and whether or not she is with her boyfriend or husband and whether or not *he* is sitting down.

As my mother stands in front of Carnegie Hall, one taxi driver yells to another, "What do you think this is, a dance floor?"

My mother waits patiently for this dispute to be settled before crossing the street.

In Haiti when you get hit by a car, the owner of the car gets out and kicks you for getting blood on his bumper.

My mother who laughs when she says this and shows a large gap in her mouth where she lost three more molars to the dentist last week. My mother, who at fifty-nine, says dentures are okay.

You can take them out when they bother you. I'll like them. I'll like them fine.

Will it feel empty when Papa kisses you?

Oh no, he doesn't kiss me that way anymore.

My mother, who watches the lottery drawing every night on channel 11 without ever having played the numbers.

1246

A third of that money is all I would need. We would pay the mortgage, and your father could stop driving that taxicab all over Brooklyn.

I follow my mother, mesmerized by the many possibilities of her journey. Even in a flowered dress, she is lost in a sea of pinstripes and gray suits, high heels and elegant short skirts, Reebok sneakers, dashing from building to building.

My mother, who won't go out to dinner with anyone.

If they want to eat with me, let them come to my house, even if I boil water and give it to them.

My mother, who talks to herself when she peels the skin off poultry.

Fat, you know, and cholesterol. Fat and cholesterol killed your aunt Hermine.

My mother, who makes jam with dried grapefruit peel and then puts in cinnamon bark that I always think is cockroaches in the jam. My mother, whom I have always bought household appliances for, on her birthday. A nice rice cooker, a blender.

I trail the red orchids in her dress and the heavy faux leather bag on her shoulders. Realizing the ferocious pace of my pursuit, I stop against a wall to rest. My mother keeps on walking as though she owns the sidewalk under her feet.

As she heads toward the Plaza Hotel, a bicycle messenger swings so close to her that I want to dash forward and rescue her, but she stands dead in her tracks and lets him ride around her and then goes on.

My mother stops at a corner hot-dog stand and asks for something. The vendor hands her a can of soda that she slips into her bag. She stops by another vendor selling sundresses for seven dollars each. I can tell that she is looking at an African print dress, contemplating my size. I think to myself, Please Ma, don't buy it. It would be just another thing that I would bury in the garage or give to Goodwill.

Why should we give to Goodwill when there are so many people back home who need clothes? We save our clothes for the relatives in Haiti.

Twenty years we have been saving all kinds of things for the relatives in Haiti. I need the place in the garage for an exercise bike.

You are pretty enough to be a stewardess. Only dogs like bones.

This mother of mine, she stops at another hot-dog vendor's and buys a frankfurter that she eats on the street. I never knew that she ate frankfurters. With her blood pressure, she shouldn't eat anything with sodium. She has to be careful with her heart, this day woman.

I cannot just swallow salt. Salt is heavier than a hundred bags of shame.

She is slowing her pace, and now I am too close. If she turns around, she might see me. I let her walk into the park before I start to follow again.

My mother walks toward the sandbox in the middle of the park. There a woman is waiting with a child. The woman is wearing a leotard with biker's shorts and has small weights in her hands. The woman kisses the child good-bye and surrenders him to my mother; then she bolts off, running on the cemented stretches in the park.

The child given to my mother has frizzy blond hair. His hand slips into hers easily, like he's known her for a long time. When he raises his face to look at my mother, it is as though he is looking at the sky.

My mother gives this child the soda that she bought from the vendor on the street corner. The child's face lights up as she puts in a straw in the can for him. This seems to be a conspiracy just between the two of them.

My mother and the child sit and watch the other children play in the sandbox. The child pulls out a comic book from a knapsack with Big Bird on the back. My mother peers into his comic book. My mother, who taught herself to read as a little girl in Haiti from the books that her brothers brought home from school.

My mother, who has now lost six of her seven sisters in Ville Rose and has never had the strength to return for their funerals.

Many graves to kiss when I go back. Many graves to kiss.

She throws away the empty soda can when the child is done with it. I wait and watch from a corner until the woman in the leotard and biker's shorts returns, sweaty and breathless, an hour later. My mother gives the woman back her child and strolls farther into the park.

I turn around and start to walk out of the park before my mother can see me. My lunch hour is long since gone. I have to hurry back to work. I walk through a cluster of joggers, then race to a *Sweden Tours* bus. I stand behind the bus and take a peek at my mother in the park. She is standing in a circle, chatting with a group of women who are taking other people's children on an afternoon outing. They look like a Third World Parent-Teacher Association meeting.

I quickly jump into a cab heading back to the office. Would Ma have said hello had she been the one to see me first?

As the cab races away from the park, it occurs to me that perhaps one day I would chase an old woman down a street by mistake and that old woman would be somebody else's mother, who I would have mistaken for mine.

Day women come out when nobody expects them.

Tonight on the subway, I will get up and give my seat to a pregnant woman or a lady about Ma's age.

My mother, who stuffs thimbles in her mouth and then blows up her cheeks like Dizzy Gillespie while sewing yet another Raggedy Ann doll that she names Suzette after me.

I will have all these little Suzettes in case you never have any babies, which looks more and more like it is going to happen.

My mother who had me when she was thirty-three — *l'âge du Christ* — at the age that Christ died on the cross.

That's a blessing, believe you me, even if American doctors say by that time you can make retarded babies.

My mother, who sews lace collars on my company softball T-shirts when she does my laundry.

Why, you can't you look like a lady playing softball?

My mother, who never went to any of my Parent-Teacher Association meetings when I was in school.

You're so good anyway. What are they going to tell me? I don't want to make you ashamed of this day woman. Shame is heavier than a hundred bags of salt.   [1995]

CHARLES BAXTER

*C*harles Baxter (b. 1947) was born in Minneapolis and graduated from Macalester College in St. Paul, Minnesota. He earned his Ph.D. at the State University of New York at Buffalo in 1974 and began to teach English at Wayne State University. Currently he directs the writing program at the University of Michigan.

In 1984 Baxter published his first collection of short stories, **Harmony of the World**, which won the Associated Writing Programs Award for short fiction. The title story was included in the 1982 Pushcart Prize anthology and in Best American Short Stories 1982 (selected by John Gardner). In 1985 Baxter followed with his second collection, **Through the Safety Net**, which contained his often-reprinted story "Gryphon," about an eccentric substitute teacher who baffles her fourth-grade class with her esoteric knowledge of mythology and superstition. That piece subsequently appeared in Best American Short Stories 1986 (chosen by Raymond Carver) and in Best American Short Stories of the Eighties (1990), edited by Shannon Ravenel.

A Relative Stranger (1990), Baxter's third collection, contained stories illustrating what Baxter has described in his essay "Against Epiphanies" as a state of "bewilderment":

> Characters in short stories, unlike the characters in novels, do not, as a rule, make long-term plans. They tend, instead, to be creatures of impulse.
>
> The ending of the short story often does glance uneasily toward the future, but stories frequently try to keep both the past and the future bracketed and separate. The story form has an extraordinary capacity to sense what's been at stake in any action or encounter because it has a heightened feeling for immediate consequences. . . . What if, as Raymond Carver argued, insights don't help and only make things worse? We can still see people acting meaningfully or stewing in their own juices or acting out of the depths of their bewilderment, and we can make of that what we will.

In Baxter's claim that "anti-epiphanic writing is perfectly capable of sneaking its own visionary eloquence through the back door," he suggests his allegiance with a midwestern "community" of writers including Sherwood Anderson, Willa Cather, and Ernest Hemingway. Believers (1997), Baxter's fourth collection of short fiction, contains "Saul and Patsy Are in Labor," which first appeared in American Short Fiction the same year. He has also published three novels and a book of essays about fiction, **Burning Down the House** (1997). The essays explore the nature of the imagination's grip on the commonplace things of daily life "and how one lives in the pressure of that grip" as a creative writer.

Saul and Patsy Are in Labor

The moonlight on the sheets is as heavy as damp cotton, and Patsy, pregnant in her ninth month with a child who does not care to be born, sits up in bed to glare at whatever is still visible. The moonlight falls on the red oak bedroom floor, the carved polar bear on the bedside table, and her husband, Saul, under his electric blanket. Sleeping, Saul is always cold. His dreams, he has reported, are Arctic. Moonlit, he seems a bit blue. But it soothes her, having him there: his quiet groans and his exhaling supply the rhythms of Patsy's waking nights.

She pulls back the covers, walks to the window, and sheds her nightgown.

Brown-haired, athletic, with a runner's body, she is ordinarily a slender woman, but now her breasts and belly are swollen, the skin stretched taut, her fingers and feet thickened with water. She finds herself tilting backward to balance herself against her new frontal weight. She feels like a human rain forest: hot, choked with life, reeking with reproduction.

Out in the yard the full-faced moon shines through two pine trees this side of the garage and on Saul's motorcycle parked in the driveway. Beyond the garage she sees a single deer passing silently through the field.

Patsy leans toward the desk in front of the window and permits the moon to gaze on her nakedness. She soaks up the moonlight, bathes in it. As she turns, she clasps her hands behind her head. She's had it with pregnancy; now she wants the labor, the full-blast finality of it. When she looks at the desk she sees the ampersand key on the upper row of the typewriter keyboard, the & above the 7. It's shaped like herself, distended and full: the big female *and:* &. The baby gives her a sleepy kick.

Hey, she says to the moonlight, *put me in labor. Pull this child into the world. Help me out here.*

Three hours later, just before dawn, her water breaks.

The labor room: Between contractions and the blips of the fetal monitor, she is dimly aware of Saul. He's donned his green hospital scrubs. They wouldn't let him wear his Detroit Tigers baseball cap in here. He's holding her hand and his eyes are anxious with nervous energy. He thinks he's coaching her. But he keeps miscounting the breaths, and she has to correct him.

After two hours of this, she is moved into the huge circular incandescence of the delivery room. She feels as if she's about to expel her entire body outward in a floorflood. With her hair soaked with sweat and sticking to the back of her neck, she can feel the universe sputtering out for an instant into two flattened dimensions. Everything she sees is suddenly painted on a wall. She screams. Then she swears and loosens her hand from Saul's—his touch maddens her—and swears again. The pain blossoms and blossoms, a huge multicolored floral sprouting of it. When the nurses smile, the smiles—full of professionalism and complacency from the other world—make her furious. The seconds split.

"Okay, here's the head. One last push, please."

Patsy backstrokes through the pain. Then the baby girl presents herself in a mess of blood and fleshy wrappings. After the cord is cut, Patsy hears her daughter's cry and a thud to her right: Saul, on the floor, passed out, gone.

"Can someone see to the dad?" the obstetrician asks, rather calmly. "He's fainted." Then, as an afterthought, she says, "No offense, Patsy, but he looked like the fainting type."

After a moment, during which Patsy feels plumbed out and vacant, they give the baby an Apgar test. While they weigh her, a nurse squats down next to Saul and takes his pulse. "Yes, he's coming back," she says. "He'll be fine." His eyes open, and underneath the face mask he smiles sheepishly. The papery cotton over his mouth crinkles upward. It's typical of Saul, Patsy thinks, to have somebody make a fuss over him at the moment of his daughter's birth. He steals scenes.

"Is my husband okay?" she asks. She can't quite find him. Turning back to herself, she can see, blurred, in the salty recession of this birth, the paint of her toenails through her thin white cotton socks. Saul had painted those toenails when she had grown too wide to bend down and do the job herself.

"Here's the baby," the nurse says. The world has recovered itself and accordioned out into three dimensions again. The nurse's smile and her daughter's ancient sleepy expression sunspot near Patsy's heart, and the huge overhead delivery room light goes out, like a sigh.

Someone takes Patsy's hand. Who but Saul, unsteady but upright? Cold sweat drips down his forehead. He kisses Patsy through his face mask, a sterile kiss, and he informs her that they're parents now. Hi, Mom, he says. He apologizes for his cold sweat and the sudden bout of unconsciousness. Patsy raises her hand and caresses Saul's face. Oh, don't worry, the nurse says, apparently referring to Saul's fainting fit. She pats him on the back, as if he were some sort of good dog.

They name their daughter Mary Esther Carlson-Bernstein. While making dinner, one of his improvised stir-fries, Saul says that he's been having second thoughts: Mary Esther is burdened with a lot of name, a lot of Christianity and Judaism mixed in there. Possibly another name would be better. Jayne, maybe, or Liz. Direct, futuristic American monosyllables. As he theorizes and chops carrots and broccoli before dropping the bamboo shoots and water chestnuts into the pan, Patsy can see that he's so tired that he's only half-awake. His socks don't match, his jeans are beltless, and his hair has gone back to its customary anarchy.

Last night, between feedings, Saul claimed that he didn't know if he could manage it, *it* being the long haul of fatherhood. But that was just

Saul-talk. Right now, Mary Esther is sleeping upstairs. Fingering the pages of her magazine, Patsy leans back in the alcove, still in her bathrobe, watching her husband cook. She wonders what she did with the breast pump and when the diaper guy is going to deliver the new batch.

Standing there, Saul sniffs, adds a spot of peanut oil, stirs again, and after a minute he ladles out dinner onto Patsy's plate. Then with that habit he has of reading her thoughts and rewording them, he turns toward her and says, "You left the breast pump upstairs." And then: "Hey, you think I'm sleepwalking. But I'm not. I'm conscious."

They live in a rented house on a dirt road outside of Five Oaks, Michigan, and for the last few months Saul has glimpsed an albino deer, always at a distance, on the fringes of their property. After work or on weekends, he walks across the unfarmed fields up to the next property line, marked by rusting fence posts, or, past the fields, into the neighboring woods of silver maple and scrub oak, hoping to get a sight of the animal. It gives him the shivers. He thinks this is the most godforsaken locale in which he's ever found himself, certainly worse than Baltimore, and that he feels right at home in it, and so does that deer. It is no easy thing to be a Jew in the Midwest, Saul thinks, where all the trees and shrubs are miserly and soul-shriveled, and where fate beats on your heart like a baseball bat, but he has mastered it. He is suited for brush and lowland undergrowth and the antipicturesque. The fungal smell of wood rot in the culverts strengthens him, he believes.

Clouds, mud, wind. Joy and despair live side by side in Saul with very few emotions in between. Even his depressions are thick with lyric intensity. In the spiritual mildew of the Midwest all winter he lives stranded in an ink drawing. He himself is the suggested figure in the lower righthand corner.

He makes his way back to the house, mud clutching fast to his boots. He has a secret he has not told Patsy, though she probably knows it: he does not have any clue to being a parent. He does not love being one, though he loves his daughter with a newfound intensity close to hysteria. To him, fatherhood is one long unrewritable bourgeois script. Love, rage, and tenderness disable him in the chairs in which he sits, miming calm, holding Mary Esther. At night, when Patsy is fast asleep, Saul kneels on the landing and beats his fists on the stairs.

On the morning when Mary Esther was celebrating her birthday — she was four weeks old — they sat at the breakfast table with the sun in a rare appearance blazing in through the east window and reflecting off the butter knife. With one hand Patsy fed herself cornflakes. With the other hand she held Mary Esther, who was nursing. Patsy was also glancing down at the morning paper on the table and was talking to Saul about his upcoming birthday, what color shirt to get him. She chewed her cornflakes thoughtfully and only reacted when Mary Esther sucked too hard. A deep brown, she says. You'd look good in that. It'd show off your eyes.

Listening, Saul watched them both, rattled by the domestic sensuality of their pairing, and his spirit shook with wild bruised jealous love. He felt pointless and redundant, an ambassador from the tiny principality of irony. His heart, that trapped bird, flapped in its cage. Behind Patsy in the kitchen the spice rack displaced its orderly contents. A delivery truck rumbled by on Whitefeather Road. He felt specifically his shallow and approximate condition. In broad daylight, night enfolded him.

He went off to work feeling superfluous and ecstatic and horny, his body glowing with its confusions.

This semester Saul has been taken off teaching American history and has been assigned remedial English for learning-disabled students in the junior high. The school claims it cannot afford a specialist in this area, and because Saul has loudly been an advocate of the rights of the learning-disabled, and because, he suspects, the principal has it in for him, he has been assigned a group of seven kids in remedial writing, and they all meet in a converted storage room at the back of the school at eight-thirty, following the second bell.

Five of them are pleasant and sweet-tempered and bewildered, but two of them hate the class and appear to hate Saul. They sit as far away from him as possible, close to the brooms, whispering to each other and smiling malevolently. Saul has tried everything with them—jokes, praise, discipline—and nothing has seemed to work.

He thinks of the two boys, Gordy Himmelmann and Bob Pawlak, as the Child Cossacks. Gordy apparently has no parents. He lives with siblings and grandparents and perhaps he coalesced out of the mud of the earth. He wears tee-shirts spotted with blood and manure. His boots are scuffed from the objects he has kicked. On his face there are two rashes, one of acne, the other of blankness. His eyes, on those occasions when they meet Saul's, are cold and lunar. If you were dying on the side of the road in a rainstorm, Gordy's eyes would pass over you and continue on to the next interesting sight.

He has no sense of humor. Bob Pawlak does. He brags about killing animals, and his laughter, describing how he has killed them, rises from chuckles to a sort of rhythmic squeal. His smile is the meanest one Saul has ever seen on an ex-child. It is also visible on the face of Bob Pawlak's father. About his boy, this father has said, "Yeah, he is sure a hell-raiser." He shook his dismayed parental head, smiling meanly at Saul in the school's front office, his eyes glittering with what Saul assumed was Jew-hatred.

Saul can hardly stand to look at Gordy and Bob. There are no windows in the room where he teaches them, and no fan, and after half an hour of everyone's mingled breathing, the air in the room is foul enough to kill a canary.

Yesterday Saul gave the kids pictures clipped from magazines. They were supposed to write a one-sentence story to accompany each picture. For these ninth-graders, the task is a challenge. Now, before school starts, his mind still on Patsy and Mary Esther, Saul begins to read yesterday's sentences. Gordy and Bob have as usual not written anything: Gordy tore his picture to bits, and Bob shredded and ate his.

> It is dangerous to dive into a pool of water without the nolige of the depth because if it is salow you could hit your head that might creat unconsheness and drownding.
> Quite serprisingly the boy finds among the presents rapings which are now discarded into trash a model air plan.

Two sentences, each one requiring ten minutes' work. Saul stares at them, feeling himself stumbling in the usual cognitive limp. The sentences are like glimpses into the shattered mind of God.

> Like the hourse a cow is an animal and the human race feasts on its meat and diary which form the bulky hornd animal.
> The cold blooded crecher the bird will lay an egg and in a piriod of time a new bird will brake out of it as a storm of reproduction.

Saul looks up from his desk at the sputtering overhead lights and the grimy acoustic tile. It is in the storm of reproduction — mouths of babes, etc. — that he himself is currently being tossed.

He looks down at the floor again and spots a piece of paper with the words *your a kick* close to the wastebasket. Finally, a nice compliment. He tosses it away.

The neighbors bring food down Whitefeather Road, indented with the patterned tire-tracked mud of spring, to Saul and Patsy's house. They've read Mary Esther's birth announcement in *The Five Oaks Gazette,* but they might know anyway. Small-city snooping keeps everyone informed. With the gray March overcast behind her, Mrs. O'Neill, beaming fixedly with her brand of insane charity, offers them a plate of the cookies for which she has gained local notoriety. They look like molasses blasted in a kiln and crystallized into teeth-shattering candied rock. Anne McPhee gives Patsy a gallon of homemade potato salad preserved in pink translucent Tupperware. Laurie Welch brings molded green Jell-O. Mad Dog Bettermine hauls a case of discount no-name beer into the living room, roaring approval of the baby. In return, Saul gives Mad Dog a cigar, and together the two men retire to the back porch, lighting up and drinking, belching smoke. Back in town, Harold, Saul's barber, gives Saul a free terrible haircut. Charity is everywhere, specific and ungrudging. Saul can make no sense of it.

They all track mud into the nursery. Fond wishes are expressed. Dressed in her sleep suit, Mary Esther lies in the rickety crib that Saul himself assembled, following the confusing and contradictory instructions enclosed in the shipping box. Above the crib hangs a mobile of cardboard stars and planets. Mary Esther sleeps and cries while the mobile slowly turns in the small breezes caused by the visitors as they bend over the baby.

One night, when Mary Esther is eight weeks old and the smell of spring is pouring into the room from the purple lilacs in the driveway, Patsy awakens and finds herself alone in bed. The clock says that it's three-thirty. Saul has to be up for work in three hours. From downstairs she hears very faintly the sound of groans and music. The groans aren't Saul's. She knows his groans. These are different. She puts on her bathrobe.

In the living room, sitting in his usual overstuffed chair and wearing his blue jeans and tee-shirt, Saul is watching a porn film on the VCR. His head is propped against his arm as if he were listening attentively to a lecture. He glances up at Patsy, flashes her a guilty wave with his left hand, then returns his gaze to the movie. On the TV screen, two people, a man and a woman are having showy sex in a curiously grim manner inside a stalled freight elevator, as if they were under orders.

"What's this, Saul?"

"Film I rented."

"Where'd you get it?"

"The store."

Moans have been dubbed onto the soundtrack. The man and the woman do not look at each other. For some reason, a green ceramic poodle sits in the opposite corner of the elevator. "Not very classy, Saul," she says.

"Well," Saul says, "they're just acting." He points at the screen. "She hasn't taken her shoes off. That's pretty strange. They're having sex in the elevator and her shoes are still on. I guess the boys in the audience don't like feet."

Patsy studies the TV screen. Unexpected sadness locates her and settles in, like a headache. She rests her eyes on the Matisse poster above Saul's chair: naked people dancing in a ring. In this room the human body is excessively represented, and for a moment Patsy has the feeling that everything in life is probably too much, there is just too much to face down.

"Come upstairs, Saul."

"In a minute, after this part."

"I don't like to look at them. I don't like you looking at them."

"It's hell, isn't it?"

She touches his shoulder. "This is sort of furtive."

"That's marriage-driven rhetoric you're using there, Patsy."

"Why are you doing this, Saul?"

"Well, I wanted a real movie and I got this instead. I was in the video place and I went past the musicals into the sad private room where the Xs were. There I was, me, full of curiosity."

"About what?"

"Well, we used to have fun. We used to get hot. So this . . . anyway, it's like nostalgia, you know? Nostalgia for something. It's sort of like going into a museum where the exhibits are happy, and you watch the happiness, and it isn't yours, so you watch more of it."

"This isn't like you, Saul. Doesn't it make you feel like shit or something?"

He sits in his chair, thinking. Then he says, "Yup, it does." He clicks off the TV set, rises, and puts his arms around Patsy, and they stand quietly there for what seems to Patsy a long time. Behind Saul on the living room bookshelf are volumes of history and literature—Saul's collections of Dashiell Hammett and Samuel Eliot Morison—and the Scrabble game on the top shelf. "Don't leave me alone back here," Patsy says. "Don't leave me alone, okay?"

"I love you, Patsy," he says. "You know that. Always have."

"That's not what I'm talking about."

"I know."

"You don't get everything now," she says. "You need to diversify."

They stand for a few moments longer, swaying slightly together.

Two nights later, Saul finishes diapering Mary Esther and then walks into the upstairs hallway toward the bathroom. He brushes against Patsy, who is heading downstairs. Under the ceiling light her eyes are shadowed with fatigue. They do not speak, and for ten seconds, she is a stranger to him. He cannot remember why he married her, and he cannot remember his desire for her. He stands there, staring at the floor, angry and frightened, hoarding his injuries.

When Saul enters his classroom the next day, Gordy and Bob greet his arrival with rattled throat noises. On their foreheads they have written MAD IN THE USA, in pencil. "Mad" or "made," misspelled? Saul doesn't ask. Seated in their broken desks and only vaguely attentive, the other students fidget and smile politely, picking at their frayed clothes uniformly one or two sizes too small.

"Today," Saul says, "we're going to pretend that we're young again. We're going to think about what babies would say if they could talk."

He reaches into his jacket pocket for his seven duplicate photographs of Mary Esther, in which she leans against the back of the sofa, her stuffed gnome in her lap.

"This is my daughter," Saul says, passing the photographs out. "Mary Esther." The four girls in the classroom make peculiar cooing sounds. The boys react with nervous laughter, except for Gordy and Bob, who have suddenly turned to stone. "Babies want to say things, right? What would she say if she could talk? Write it out on a sheet of paper. Give her some words."

Saul knows he is testing the Cossacks. He is screwing up their heads with his parental love. At the back of the room, Gordy Himmelman studies the photograph. His face expresses nothing. All his feelings are bricked up; nothing escapes from him.

His is the zombie point of view.

Nevertheless, he now bends down over his desk, pencil in hand.

At the end of the hour, Saul collects the papers, and his students shuffle out into the hallway. Saul has noticed that poor readers do not lift their feet off the floor. You can hear them coming down the hallway from the slide and scrape and squeal of their shoes.

He searches for Gordy Himmelman's paper. Here it is, mad in America, several lines of scrawled writing.

> They thro me up in to the air. Peopl come in when I screem and thro me up in to the air. They stik my face up. They never catch me.

The next lines are heavily erased.

> her   +   try it out   .   You ink

Saul holds up the paper to read the illegible words, and now he sees the word *kick* again, next to the word *lidle*.

His head randomly swimming, Saul holds the photographs of his daughter, the little kike thoughtfully misspelled by Gordy Himmelman, and brings the photos to his chest absentmindedly. From the hallway he hears the sound of lively laughter.

That night, Saul, fortified with Mad Dog's no-brand beer, reads the want ads, deeply interested. The want ads are full of trash and leavings, employment opportunities and the promise of new lives amid the advertised wreckage of the old. He reads the personals like a scholar, checking for verbal nuance. Sitting in his overstuffed chair, he scans the columns when his eye stops.

> BEEHIVES FOR SALE—Must sell. Shells, frames, extractor. Also incl. smoke and protective hat tools and face covering. Good condition. Any offer considered. Eager to deal. $$$ potential. Call after 7 p.m. 890-7236.

Saul takes Mary Esther out of her pendulum chair and holds her as he walks around the house, thick with plans and vision. In the vision, he stands proudly—regally!—in front of Patsy, holding a jar of honey. Sunlight slithers through its glass and transforms the room itself into pure gold. Sweetness is everywhere. Honey will make all the desires right again between them. Gordy Himmelman, meanwhile, will have erased himself from the planet. He will have caused himself to disappear. Patsy accepts Saul's gift. She can't stop smiling at him. She tears off their clothes. She pours the honey over Saul.

Gazing at the newspapers and magazines piling up next to the TV set as he holds Mary Esther, Saul finds himself shaking with a kind of excitement. Irony, his constant companion, is asleep, or on vacation, and in the heady absence of irony Saul begins to imagine himself as a beekeeper.

He does not accuse Gordy of anti-Semitism, or of anything else. He ignores him, as he ignores Bob Pawlak. At the end of the school year they will go away and fall down into the earth and the dirt they came from and become one with the stones and the inanimate all-embracing horizon.

On a fine warm day in April, Saul drives out to the north side of town, where he buys the wooden frames and the other equipment from a laconic man named Gunderson. Gunderson wears overalls and boots. Using the flat of his hand, he rubs the top of his bald head with a farmer's gesture of suspicion as he examines Saul's white shirt, pressed pants, ten-day growth of beard, and brown leather shoes. "Don't wear black clothes around these fellas," Gunderson advises. "They hate black." Saul pays him in cash, and Gunderson counts the money after Saul has handed it over, wetting his thumb to turn the bills.

With Mad Dog's pickup, Saul brings it all back to Whitefeather Road. He stores his purchases behind the garage. He takes out books on beekeeping from the public library and studies their instructions with care. He takes notes in a yellow notebook and makes calculations about placement. The bees need direct sunlight, and water nearby. By long-distance telephone he buys a hive of bees, complete with a queen, from an apiary in South Carolina, using his credit card number. When the bee box arrives in the main post office, he receives an angry call from the assistant postal manager telling him to come down and pick up this damn humming thing.

As it turns out, the bees like Saul. He is calm and slow around them and talks to them when he removes them from the shipping box and introduces them into the shells and frames, following the instructions that he has learned by heart. The hives and frames sit unsteadily on the platform Saul has laid down on bricks near two fence posts on the edge of the property. But the structure is, he thinks, steady enough for bees. He gorges them with sugar syrup, sprinkling it over them, before letting them free, shaking them into the frames. Some of them settle on his gloved hand and are so drowsy that, when he pushes them off, they waterfall into the hive. When the queen and the other bees are enclosed, he replaces the frames inside the shell, being careful to put a feeder with sugar water nearby.

The books have warned him about the loud buzzing sound of angry bees, but for the first few days Saul never hears it. Something about Saul seems to keep the bees occupied and unirritated. He is stung twice, once on the wrist and once on the back of the neck, but the pain is pointed and directed and so focused that he can manage it. It's unfocused pain that he can't stand.

Out at the back of Saul's property, a quarter mile away from the house, the hives and the bees won't bother anyone, Saul thinks. "Just don't bring them in here," Patsy tells him, glancing through one of his apiary books. "Not that they'd come. I just want them and me to have a little distance between us, is all." She smiles. "Bees, Saul? Honey? You're such a literalist."

And then one night, balancing his checkbook at his desk, with Mary Esther half asleep in the crook of his left arm, Saul feels a moment of calm peacefulness, the rarest of his emotions. Under his desk lamp, with his daughter burping up on his Johns Hopkins sweatshirt, he sits forward, waiting. He turns around and sees Patsy, in worn jeans and a tee-shirt, watching him from the doorway. Her arms are folded, and her breasts are outlined perfectly beneath the cloth. She is holding on her face an expression of sly playfulness. He thinks she looks beautiful and tells her so.

She comes into the room, her bare feet whisking against the wood floor, and she puts her arms around him, pressing herself against him.

"Put Mary Esther into her crib," she whispers. She clicks off the desk lamp.

As they make love, Saul thinks of his bees. Those insects, he thinks, are a kind of solution.

Spring moves into summer, and the mud on Whitefeather Road dries into sculpted gravel. Just before school ends, Saul tells his students about the bees and the hives. Pride escapes from his face, radiating it. When he explains how honey is extracted from the frames, he glances at Gordy Himmelman and sees a look of dumb animal rage directed back at him. The boy looks as if he's taking a bath in lye. What's the big deal? Saul wonders before he turns away.

One night in early June, Patsy is headed upstairs, looking for the Snugli, which she thinks she forgot in Mary Esther's room, when she hears Saul's voice coming from behind the door. She stops on the landing, her hand on the banister. At first she thinks he might be singing to Mary Esther, but, no, Saul is not singing. He's sitting in there—well, he's probably sitting, Saul doesn't like to stand when he speaks—talking to his daughter, and Patsy hears him finishing a sentence: ". . . was never very happy."

Patsy moves closer to the door.

"Who explains?" Saul is saying, apparently to his daughter. "No one."

Saul goes on talking to Mary Esther, filling her in on his mother and several other mysterious phenomena. What does he think he's doing, discussing this stuff with an infant? "I should sing you a song," he announces, interrupting himself. "That's what parents do."

To get away from Saul's song, Patsy retreats to the window for a breath of air. Looking out, she sees someone standing on the front lawn, bathed in moonlight, staring in the direction of the house. He's thin and ugly and scruffy, and he looks a bit like a clod, but a dangerous clod.

"Saul," she says. Then, more loudly, "Saul, there's someone out on the lawn."

He joins her at the window. "I can't see him," Saul says. "Oh, yeah, there." He shouts, "Hello? Can I help you?"

The boy turns around. "Sure, fuckwad. Yeah, you bet, shitbird." He gets on a bike and races away down the driveway and onto Whitefeather Road.

Saul does not move. His hands are planted on the windowsill. "It's Gordy Himmelman," he groans. "That little bastard has come on our property. I'm getting on the phone."

"Saul, why'd he come here? What did you do to him?" She holds her arms against her chest. "What does he have against us?"

"I was his teacher. And we're Jewish," Saul says. "And, uh, we're parents. He never had any. I showed those kids the baby pictures. Big mistake. Somebody must've found Gordy somewhere in a barrel of brine. He was not of woman born." He tries to smile. "I'm kidding, sort of."

"Do you think he'll be back?" she asks.

"Oh yes." Saul wipes his forehead. "They always come back, those kind. And I'll be ready."

It has been a spring and summer of violent weather, and Saul has been reading the Old Testament again, looking for clues. On Thursday, at four in the afternoon, Saul has finished mowing the front lawn and is sitting on the porch drinking the last bottle of Mad Dog's beer when he looks to the west and feels a sudden cooling of the air, a shunting of atmospheres. Just above the horizon a mass of clouds begins boiling. Clouds that look like breasts and handtools—he can't help thinking the way he thinks—advance over him. The wind picks up.

"Patsy," he calls. "Hey Patsy."

Something calamitous is happening in the atmosphere. The pressure is dropping so fast that Saul can feel it in his elbows and knees.

"Patsy!" he shouts.

From upstairs he hears her calling back, "What, Saul?"

"Go to the basement," he says. "Close the upstairs window and take Mary Esther down there. Take a flashlight. We're going to get a huge storm."

Through the house Saul rushes, closing windows and switching off lights, and when he returns to the front door to close it, he sees out in the yard the tall and emaciated apparition of Gordy Himmelman, standing fixedly like an emanation from the dirt and stone of the fields. He has returned. Toward Saul he aims his vacant stare. Saul, who cannot stop thinking even in moments of critical emergency, is struck into stillness by Gordy's presence, his authoritative malevolence standing there in the just mown grass. The volatile ambitious sky and the forlorn backwardness of the fields have together given rise to this human disaster, who, even as Saul watches, yells toward the house, "Hey, Mr. Bernstein. Guess what. Just guess what. Go take a look at your bees."

Feeling like a commando, Saul, who is fast when he has to be, catches up to Gordy who is pumping away on his broken and rusted bicycle. Saul tears Gordy off. He throws and kicks the junk Schwinn into the ditch. In the rain that has just started, Saul grabs Gordy by the shoulders and shakes him back and forth. He presses his thumbs hard enough to bruise. Gordy, violently stinking, smells of neglect and seepage, and Saul nearly gags. Saul cannot stop shaking him. He cannot stop shaking himself. With violent rapid horizontal jerking motions the boy's head is whipped.

Saul wants to see his eyes. But the eyes are as empty as mirrors.

"Hey, stop it," Gordy says. "It hurts. You're hurting. You're hurting him."

"Hurt who?" Saul asks. Thunder rolls toward him. He sees himself reflected in Gordy Himmelman's eyes, a tiny figure backed by lightning. *Who, me?*

"Stop it, don't hurt him." Patsy's voice, repeating Gordy's words, snakes into his ear, and he feels her hand on his arm, restraining him. She's here, out in this rain, less frightened of the rain than she is of Saul. The boy has started to sag, seeing the two of them there, his scarecrow arms raised to protect himself, assuming, probably, that he's about to be killed. There he squats, the child of attention deficit, at Saul's feet.

"Stay there," Saul mumbles. "Stay right there." Through the rain he begins walking, then running, toward his bees.

The storm, empty of content, tucks itself toward the east and is being replaced even now by one of those insincere Midwestern blue skies.

Mary Esther begins to cry and wail as Patsy jogs toward Saul. Gordy Himmelman follows along behind her.

When she is within a hundred feet of Saul's beehives, she sees that the frames have been knocked over, scattered, and kicked. Saul lies, face down, where they once stood. He is touching his tongue to the earth momentarily, where the honey is, for a brief taste. When he rises, he sees Patsy. "All the bees swarmed," he says. "They've left. They're gone."

She holds Mary Esther tightly and examines Saul's face. "How come they didn't attack him? Didn't they sting him?"

"Who knows?" Saul spreads his arms. "They just didn't."

Gordy Himmelman watches them from a hundred yards away, and with his empty gaze he makes Patsy think of the albino deer Saul has insisted he has seen: half blind, wandering these fields day after day without direction.

"Look," Saul says, pointing at Mary Esther, who stopped crying when she saw her father. "Her shoe is untied." He wipes his face with his sleeve and shakes off the dirt from his jeans. Approaching Patsy, he gives off a smell of dirt and honey and sweat. In the midst of his distractedness, he ties Mary Esther's shoe.

His hair is soaked with rain. He glances at Patsy, who, with some difficulty, is keeping her mouth shut. She not only loves Saul but at this moment is in love with him, and she has to be careful not to say so just now. It's strange, she thinks, that she loves him, an odd trick of fate: He is fitful and emotional, a man whose sense of theater begins completely with himself. What she loves is the extravagance of feeling that focuses itself into the tiniest actions of human attention, like the tying of this pink shoe. It's better to keep love a secret for a while than to talk about it all the time. It generates more energy that way. He finishes the knot. He kisses them both. Dirt is attached to his lips.

At a distance of a hundred yards, the boy, Gordy, watches all this, and from her vantage point Patsy cannot guess what that expression on his face may mean, those mortuary eyes. Face it: He's a loss. Whatever they have to give away, they can only give him a tiny portion, and it won't be enough, whatever it is. All the same, he will stick around, she's pretty sure of that. They will have to give him something, because now, like it or not, he's following them back, their faithful zombie, made, or mad, in America, and now he's theirs.

Well, maybe we're missionaries, Patsy thinks, as she stumbles and Saul holds her up. We're the missionaries they left behind when they took all the religion away. On the front porch of the house she can see the empty bottle of Saul's no-brand beer still standing on the lip of the ledge, and she can see the porch swing slowly rock back and forth, as if someone were sitting there, waiting for them.   [1997]

LAN SAMANTHA CHANG

Lan Samantha Chang (b. 1965) was born and raised in Appleton, Wisconsin, the daughter of Chinese parents who survived the World War II Japanese occupation of China and later emigrated to the United States, hoping to give their family the security they never experienced. After graduating from the local high school, Chang attended Yale University, first as a premedical student and then as an East Asian studies major. She went on to Harvard University's Kennedy School of Government but dropped out to take courses in writing at a Boston adult education center before earning an M.F.A. at the University of Iowa Writers' Workshop. At Iowa, Chang felt that she became "somewhat proficient in writing short stories." At the age of twenty-eight she published her first story, "The Eve of the Spirit Festival," in The Atlantic Monthly. *The next year "Pipa's Story" was selected for* Best American Short Stories 1994 *(chosen by Tobias Wolff), and Chang received so many letters from editors and agents interested in her work that she felt frightened. "They had ideas about what they thought I should be doing, and I could sense that I wasn't ready to stand up to that yet." Instead she accepted Wallace Stegner and Truman Capote fellowships at Stanford University to study and teach there for five years. "I decided to put my head down, and not pay attention to any of that yet. As a result, I was able to avoid that whole other world for a lot longer than other people can."*

At Stanford, Chang attempted to write in the novella form. The result was Hunger, *included along with five stories in her first book of the same title (*Hunger, *1998). Chang told the interviewer Arthur Salm how she gained the confidence to try an even longer work after finishing the novella.*

> *When I sat down to write a short story, I learned how to do it first. I told myself, why not write a novel the same way? I learn best when I learn very deliberately, when I give myself goals and assignments. Otherwise, what I'm trying to do overwhelms me. Knowing I was writing something that was one hundred pages was the constraint I needed in order to work creatively. Now that I'm trying to write a novel, I have a whole new set of constraints. . . . Once I learned I could write one hundred pages, I thought, OK, there will be five sections [of a novel] and each section is going to be about one hundred pages. I set myself little creative assignments. It's one of the things I learned to do as a teacher, because a lot of students — some of the most talented — will just freeze up, because it's too big a deal.*

Chang felt that her attempt to write long fiction required courage, but she thought, "Since I've become an adult, I haven't really made any decisions because they're practical. Not a single one. So why start now?"

In Chang's fiction, she focuses on the fragility of family relationships and the Chinese American immigrant experience, as in "Water Names," from Hunger. *She has said:*

There's something central to the immigrant experience that happens in many different groups under many different circumstances. One of the things I like to do in my spare time is to go to antique and collectible shows and flea markets in the San Francisco area. I come across tables filled with items, actual objects from America's past—blue glass Mason jars that somebody's grandmother made plum preserves in, or a chrome fitting from a jukebox that people actually listened to in a diner. I'm struck with this sense of envy for people who can look at that Mason jar and say, "Yes, my grandmother had one like this." Because I don't know anything about what my grandmother might have done when she was in China. All those objects have been lost. Immigrants lose their past faster than anyone else, and that loss sharpens and heightens the tension in families that are trying to build a future. It's difficult to build a future only—everybody needs to have a past.

The recipient of a literature grant from the National Endowment for the Arts, Chang lives in northern California.

Water Names

Summertime at dusk we'd gather on the back porch, tired and sticky from another day of fierce encoded quarrels, nursing our mosquito bites and frail dignities, sisters in name only. At first we'd pinch and slap each other, fighting for the best—least ragged—folding chair. Then we'd argue over who would sit next to our grandmother. We were so close together on the tiny porch that we often pulled our own hair by mistake. Forbidden to bite, we planted silent toothmarks on each others' wrists. We ignored the bulk of house behind us, the yard, the fields, the darkening sky. We even forgot about our grandmother. Then suddenly we'd hear her old, dry voice, very close, almost on the backs of our necks.

"*Xiushila!* Shame on you. Fighting like a bunch of chickens."

And Ingrid, the oldest, would freeze with her thumb and forefinger right on the back of Lily's arm. I would slide my hand away from the end of Ingrid's braid. Ashamed, we would shuffle our feet while Waipuo calmly found her chair.

On some nights she sat with us in silence, the tip of her cigarette glowing red like a distant stoplight. But on some nights she told us stories, "just to keep up your Chinese," she said, and the red dot flickered and danced, making ghostly shapes as she moved her hands like a magician in the dark.

"In these prairie crickets I often hear the sound of rippling waters, of the Yangtze River," she said. "Granddaughters, you are descended on both sides from people of the water country, near the mouth of the great Chang Jiang, as it is called, where the river is so grand and broad that even on clear days you can scarcely see the other side.

"The Chang Jiang runs four thousand miles, originating in the Himalaya mountains where it crashes, flecked with gold dust, down steep cliffs so perilous and remote that few humans have ever seen them. In central China, the river squeezes through deep gorges, then widens in its last thousand miles to the sea. Our ancestors have lived near the mouth of this river, the ever-changing delta, near a city called Nanjing, for more than a thousand years."

"A thousand years," murmured Lily, who was only ten. When she was younger she had sometimes burst into nervous crying at the thought of so many years. Her small insistent fingers grabbed my fingers in the dark.

"Through your mother and I you are descended from a line of great men and women. We have survived countless floods and seasons of ill-fortune because we have the spirit of the river in us. Unlike mountains, we cannot be powdered down or broken apart. Instead, we run together, like raindrops. Our strength and spirit wear down mountains into sand. But even our people must respect the water."

She paused, and a bit of ash glowed briefly as it drifted to the floor.

"When I was young, my own grandmother once told me the story of Wen Zhiqing's daughter. Twelve hundred years ago the civilized parts of China still lay to the north, and the Yangtze valley lay unspoiled. In those days lived an ancestor named Wen Zhiqing, a resourceful man, and proud. He had been fishing for many years with trained cormorants, which you girls of course have never seen. Cormorants are sleek, black birds with long, bending necks which the fishermen fitted with metal rings so the fish they caught could not be swallowed. The birds would perch on the side of the old wooden boat and dive into the river." We had only known blue swimming pools, but we tried to imagine the sudden shock of cold and the plunge, deep into water.

"Now, Wen Zhiqing had a favorite daughter who was very beautiful and loved the river. She would beg to go out on the boat with him. This daughter was a restless one, never contented with their catch, and often she insisted they stay out until it was almost dark. Even then, she was not satisfied. She had been spoiled by her father, kept protected from the river, so she could not see its danger. To this young woman, the river was as familiar as the sky. It was a bright, broad road stretching out to curious lands. She did not fully understand the river's depths.

"One clear spring evening, as she watched the last bird dive off into the blackening waters, she said, 'If only this catch would bring back something more than another fish!'

"She leaned over the side of the boat and looked at the water. The stars and moon reflected back at her. And it is said that the spirits living underneath the water looked up at her as well. And the spirit of a young man who had drowned in the river many years before saw her lovely face."

We had heard about the ghosts of the drowned, who wait forever in the water for a living person to pull down instead. A faint breeze moved through the mosquito screens and we shivered.

"The cormorant was gone for a very long time," Waipuo said, "so long that the fisherman grew puzzled. Then, suddenly, the bird emerged from the waters, almost invisible in the night. Wen Zhiqing grasped his catch, a very large fish, and guided the boat back to shore. And when Wen reached home, he gutted the fish and discovered, in its stomach, a valuable pearl ring."

"From the man?" said Lily.

"Sshh, she'll tell you."

Waipuo ignored us. "His daughter was delighted that her wish had been fulfilled. What most excited her was the idea of an entire world like this, a world where such a beautiful ring would be only a bauble! For part of her had always longed to see faraway things and places. The river had put a spell on her heart. In the evenings she began to sit on the bank, looking at her own reflection in the water. Sometimes she said she saw a handsome young man looking back at her. And her yearning for him filled her heart with sorrow and fear, for she knew that she would soon leave her beloved family.

"'It's just the moon,' said Wen Zhiqing, but his daughter shook her head. 'There's a kingdom under the water,' she said. 'The prince is asking me to marry him. He sent the ring as an offering to you.' 'Nonsense,' said her father, and he forbade her to sit by the water again.

"For a year things went as usual, but the next spring there came a terrible flood that swept away almost everything. In the middle of a torrential rain, the family noticed that the daughter was missing. She had taken advantage of the confusion to hurry to the river and visit her beloved. The family searched for days but they never found her."

Her smoky, rattling voice came to a stop.

"What happened to her?" Lily said.

"It's okay, stupid," I told her. "She was so beautiful that she went to join the kingdom of her beloved. Right?"

"Who knows?" Waipuo said. "They say she was seduced by a water ghost. Or perhaps she lost her mind to desiring."

"What do you mean?" asked Ingrid.

"I'm going inside," Waipuo said, and got out of her chair with a creak. A moment later the light went on in her bedroom window. We knew she stood before the mirror, combing out her long, wavy silver-gray hair, and we imagined that in her youth she too had been beautiful.

We sat together without talking, breathing our dreams in the lingering smoke. We had gotten used to Waipuo's abruptness, her habit of creating a question and leaving without answering it, as if she were disappointed in the question itself. We tried to imagine Wen Zhiqing's daughter. What did she look like? How old was she? Why hadn't anyone remembered her name?

While we weren't watching, the stars had emerged. Their brilliant pinpoints mapped the heavens. They glittered over us, over Waipuo in her room, the house, and the small city we lived in, the great waves of grass that ran for miles around us, the ground beneath as dry and hard as bone.

[1998]

ANNIE PROULX

*A*nnie Proulx (b. 1935) was born in Norwich, Connecticut, the oldest of five sisters. Her mother was a painter and amateur naturalist whose family had lived in Connecticut since 1635 as farmers, millworkers, inventors, and artists. Her father was the vice president of a textile company, and Proulx remembers that "we moved frequently when I was a child, North Carolina, Vermont, Maine, Rhode Island, town after town." She credits her mother for encouraging her to observe the environment closely. "From the time I was extremely small, I was told, 'Look at that.' . . . everything—from the wale of corduroy to the broken button to the loose thread to the disheveled mustache to the clouded eye." Proulx attended Colby College, the University of Vermont, and Concordia University, earning a B.A. and an M.A., as well as passing her doctoral oral examinations in history. In 1975, with few teaching jobs available, she abandoned work on her Ph.D. and began a perilous career in freelance journalism. In the 1980s she published six "how-to" books on a variety of subjects, including Plane and Make Your Own Fences and Gates, Walkways, Walls and Drives (1983). During this time she also raised her three sons from her third marriage while living in an isolated cabin in a rural town in Vermont. Later she said that this life made her "very alert and aware of everything, from tree branches and wild mushrooms to animal tracks. It's an excellent training for the eye. Most of us stagger around deaf and dumb."

Supporting herself and her sons on her meager income as a journalist, Proulx began to write stories for fun, creating one or two a year. "It was my pleasure, my indulgence, when I wanted to do something that wasn't fishing or canoeing." Most of these early stories were written for a men's magazine about hunting and fishing, where her first editor told her that she had to publish under a masculine name, "something like Joe or Zack, retrievers' names," she complained. They compromised on using her initials, E. A. Proulx, the E standing for her first name, Edna. In 1983 and 1987, two of her stories were listed among the "Distinguished Short Stories" in Best American Short Stories. In 1988, Proulx published her first book of fiction, the nine stories set in northern Vermont constituting Heart Songs and Other Stories. Reviewers praised her vivid prose style; Kenneth Rosen wrote in the New York Times that her "sometimes enigmatic, often lyrical images seem to complement New England's lavish but barren beauty."

Proulx's contract with her publisher Charles Scribner's Sons for Heart Songs also required her to produce a novel. She felt she "had not a clue about writing a novel, or even the faintest desire. I thought of myself as a short story writer. Period, period, period." Proulx found the inspiration for her first work of long fiction in a group of old postcards, and after her novel Postcards appeared in 1992, she told interviewer Esther Fein, "It was astonishing how easy writing a novel was compared to writing a short story. I was so used to cramping thoughts and sections and cutting, and suddenly I had room to *expand." In 1993 Proulx was the recipient of the PEN/Faulkner Award for* Postcards. *The following year her second novel,* The Shipping News, *won the National Book Award and the Pulitzer Prize. This was followed by the novel* Accordion Crimes *in 1996. Proulx has moved from Vermont to Wyoming, the location of her recent story "The Bunchgrass Edge of the World," published in* The New Yorker *on November 30, 1998.*

The Bunchgrass Edge of the World

The country appeared as empty ground, big sagebrush, rabbitbrush, intricate sky, flocks of small birds like packs of cards thrown up in the air, and a faint track drifting toward the red-walled horizon. Graves were unmarked, fallen house timbers and corrals burned up in old campfires. Nothing much but weather and distance, the distance punctuated once in a while by ranch gates, and to the north the endless murmur and sun-flash of semis rolling along the interstate.

In this vague region the Touheys ranched—old Red, ninety-six years young, his son Aladdin, Aladdin's wife, Wauneta, their boy, Tyler, object of Aladdin's hopes, the daughters, Shan and (the family embarrassment) Ottaline.

Old Red, born in Lusk in 1902, grew up in an orphan home, a cross-grained boy—wrists knobby and prominent, red hair parted in the middle—and walked off when he was fourteen to work in a tie-hack camp. The year the First World War ended he was in Medicine Bow timber. He quit, headed away from the drought burning the West, drilled wells, prodded cattle in railroad stockyards, pasted up handbills, cobbled a life as though hammering two-bys. In 1930 he was in New York, shoveling the Waldorf-Astoria off the side of a barge into the Atlantic Ocean.

One salty morning, homesick for hard, dry landscape, he turned west again. He found a wife along the way and soon enough had a few dirty kids to feed. In Depression Oklahoma he bombed roosting crows and sold them to restaurants. When crows went scarce, they moved to Wyoming, settled a hundred or two miles from where he'd started.

They leased a ranch in the Red Wall country—log house, straggle of corrals that from a distance resembled dropped sticks. The wind isolated them from the world. To step into that reeling torrent of air was to be forced back. The ranch was adrift on the high plain.

There was the idea of running a few sheep, his wife's idea. In five years they built the sheep up into a prime band. The Second World War held wool prices steady. They bought the ranch for back taxes.

In August of 1946 a green-shaded lamp from Sears Roebuck arrived the same day the wife bore their last child. She named the kid Aladdin.

Peace and thermoplastic resin yarns ruined the sheep market and they went to cattle. The wife, as though disgusted with this bovine veer, complained of nausea as they unloaded the first shipment of scrubby calves. She stayed sick three or four years, finally quit. Red was a hard driver and of the six children only Aladdin remained on the dusty ranch, the giant of the litter, stubborn and abusive, bound to have everything on the platter whether bare bones or beefsteak.

Aladdin came back from Vietnam, where he flew C-123 Bs, spraying defoliants. Now he showed a hard disposition, a taste for pressing on to the point of exhaustion, then going dreamy and stuporous for days. He married Wauneta Hipsag on a scorching May morning in Colorado, the bride's home state. A tornado funnel hung from a green cloud miles away. Wauneta's abundant hair was rolled in an old-fashioned French knot. The wedding guests were her parents and eleven brothers, who threw handfuls of wheat, no rice available. During the ceremony, Wauneta's father smoked cigarette after cigarette. That evening at the Touhey ranch a few kernels of wheat shot from Aladdin's pants cuffs when he somersaulted off the porch, exuberant and playful before his new wife. The grains fell to the ground and in the course of time sprouted, grew, headed out, and reseeded. The wheat seized more ground each year until it covered a quarter-acre, the waving grain ardently protected by Wauneta. She said it was her wedding wheat and if ever cut the world would end.

When he was twenty-six Aladdin wrenched the say of how things should go from old Red. Aladdin had been in the mud since blue morning digging out a spring. The old man rode up on his one-eyed mare. The son slung a shovelful of wet dirt.

"You ain't got it dug out yet?" the old man asked. "Not too swift, are you? Not too smart. Shovel ain't even sharp, I bet. How you got a woman a marry you I don't know. You must a got a shotgun on her. Must a hypatized her. Not that she's much, but probably beats doin it with livestock, that right?" The mud-daubed son climbed out of the hole, picked up clods, pelted his father until he galloped off, pursued him to the house, and continued the attack with stones and sticks of firewood snatched up from the woodpile, hurled the side-cutters he always carried in a back pocket, the pencil behind his ear, the round can filled not with tobacco but with the dark green of homegrown.

Red, knot-headed and bleeding, raised one arm in surrender, backed onto the porch. He was seventy-one then and called out his age as a defense. "I made this ranch and I made you." His spotted hand went to his crotch. Aladdin gathered can, pencil, and side-cutters, and put the old man's horse away. He went back to the spring, head down, picked up the shovel, and dug until his hands went nerveless.

Wauneta moved old Red's belongings out of the big upstairs bedroom and into a ground-floor room off the kitchen, once a pantry and still smelling of raisins and stale flour. A strip of adhesive tape held the cracked window glass together.

"You'll be closer to the bathroom," she said in a voice as smooth as gas through a funnel.

Wauneta taught her two girls to carry pie on a white plate to their grandfather, kiss him good night, while Tyler played with plastic cows and stayed up late. One forenoon she came in from hanging clothes and found four-year-old Ottaline gripped astraddle over old Red's lap and squirming to get down. She ripped the child from him, said, "You keep your dirty old prong away from my girls or I'll pour boilin water on it."

"What? I wasn't—" he said. "Not—never did—"

"I know old men," she said.

"Potty!" screamed Ottaline, too late.

Now she warned the daughters from him, spoke of him in a dark tone, fine with her to let him sit alone in the straight-backed chair, let him limp unaided from porch to kitchen to fusty room. The sooner he knocked on the pearly gates the better, she told Aladdin, who groaned and rolled to his side, fretted by the darkness that kept him from work, a quick-sleeping man who would be up at three, filling the kettle, opening the red coffee can, impatient to start.

"Wauneta, what a you want me a do about it?" he said. "Drown him in the stock tank? He will kick off one a these days."

"You been sayin that for five years. He is takin the scenic route."

Time counted out in calving; first grass; branding; rainfall; clouds; roundup; the visit from old Amendinger the cattle buyer; shipping; early snow; late blizzard. The children grew up. Aladdin got an old Piper Cub, swapping it for two bulls, a set of truck tires, a saddle, the rusted frame and cylinder of an 1860 Colt .44 he'd found at the root of a cedar. Wauneta's sandy hair grayed and every few months she went into the bathroom and gave it a maroon color treatment. Only old Red watched the progression of dates on his little feed-store calendar. He was older than kerosene now and strong to make his century.

Shan, the younger daughter, graduated from high school, moved to Las Vegas. She took a job in the package-design department of a manufacturer of religious CDs, quickly grasped the subtleties of images: breaking waves, shafts of sunlight denoted godly favor, while dark clouds with iridescent edges, babies smiling through tears represented troubles that would soon pass with the help of prayer. Nothing was hopeless and the money came in on wheels.

Ottaline was the oldest, distinguished by a physique approaching the size of a propane tank. She finished school a year behind her younger sister, stayed home. She plaited her reddish-pink hair in two braids as thick as whip handles. In conversation a listener would look back and forth between the pillowy, dimpled mouth and crystal-crack blue eyes and think it a pity she was so big. The first year at home she wore gaily colored XXL skirts and helped out around the house. But her legs were always cold and she suffered from what Wauneta called "minstrel problems," a sudden flow that sent her running for the bathroom, leaving a trail of dark, round blood spots behind her varying in size from a dime to a half-dollar. After bare-legged wades through snow, after scaly chilblain, she gave up drafty skirts and housework, changed to ranch chores with Aladdin. Now she wore manure-caked roper boots, big jeans, and T-shirts that hung to her thighs.

"Yes, keep her out a the house," said Wauneta. "What she don't break she loses and what she don't lose she breaks. Her cookin would kill a pig."

"I hate cookin," said Ottaline. "I'll help Dad." It was a fallback position. She wanted to be away, wearing red sandals with cork soles, sitting in the passenger seat of a pearl-colored late-model pickup, drinking from a bottle shaped like a hula girl. When would someone come for her? She was not audacious, not like her younger sister. She knew her appalling self and there was no way to evade it.

Aladdin saw she was easy with the stock, where the boy Tyler whooped and whistled and rode like a messenger reporting a massacre.

"Had my way, ever hand'd be a woman. A woman got a nice disposition with animals." He intended the remark to sting.

"Oh, Daddy," said Tyler in comic falsetto. He was the horseman of the family, had slept out in the dilapidated bunkhouse since he was thirteen, Wauneta's edict.

"My brothers slept in the bunkhouse." There was in that flat remark all of Wauneta's childhood, sequestered, alert, surrounded by menace.

This only son, Tyler, was a huge, kit-handed youth of nineteen stout enough to frighten any father except Aladdin. The kid stamped around in dirty jeans and a brown hat. He was slack-mouthed in reverie, sported a young man's cat-fur mustache, cheeks marred by strings of tiny pimples. He was only one per cent right about anything, alternated between despondency and quick fury. On Aladdin's birthday Tyler presented him with two coyote ears, the result of weeks of cunning stalk. Aladdin unwrapped them, laid them on the tablecloth, and said, "Aw, what am I supposed a do with two coyote ears?"

"By God," screamed Tyler, "set one a them on your dick and say it won a fur hat in the church raffle. You are all against me." He swept the ears to the floor and walked out.

"He will be back," said Wauneta. "He will be back with dirty clothes and his pockets turned inside out. I know boys."

"I was the wanderin boy," old Red mumbled. "He won't be back. Takes after me. I cowboyed. I killed hogs. I made it through. Worked like a man since I was fourteen. Ninety-six years young. Never knowed my father. Carry you all to hell and spit on you." His finger dragged across the tablecloth, the long-ago self making a way. The old man showed a terrible smile, fumbled with his can of snoose.

Aladdin, face like a shield, curly hair springing, tipped his head toward the tablecloth, mumbled, "O bless this food." Heavy beef slices, encircled by a chain of parsnips and boiled potatoes, slumped on the platter. He had discovered two long-dead cows that afternoon, one bogged, the other without a mark of cause. He lifted a small potato and transferred it to his father's plate without looking at him, ignored the rattling of the old man's fork, though Wauneta, pouring coffee into heavy cups, frowned, and said, "Watch it, John Wayne." A pastel envelope lay between her knife and a flat cake with sugar icing so thin it appeared blue.

"Somethin come from Shan."

"She comin back?" Aladdin crushed his potatoes, flooded them with skim milk. Game and Fish would pay for stock killed by grizzlies or lions. He had not seen lion sign for a decade and grizzly, never.

"Didn't open it yet," she said, tearing the end. There was a short and vague letter that she read aloud and, clipped to it, an astonishing photograph. It showed his daughter in a black bikini, greased muscles starkly outlined, exhibiting bulging biceps and calves, spiky crewcut hair whitened with bleach, her rolling, apricot-size eyes frozen wide open. In the letter she had written, "Got into bodybuilding. Alot of girls here do it!"

"Whatever she has done to her hair," said Wauneta, "somebody talked her into it. I know Shan and that would not be her idea." When Shan left she had been an ordinary young woman with thin arms, blondish chew-ended hair. Her glancing unlevel eyes ricked from face to face. When she spoke, her hands revolved, the fingers flung out. The yearbook had named her "most animated."

"Bodybuildin." Aladdin's tone was neutral. He had the rancher's expectation of disaster, never believed in happy endings. He was satisfied that she was alive, not building bombs or winking at drive-by johns.

Ottaline stared at her coffee. Floating on the surface was a spreading-wing moth the shape of a tiny arrowhead. It pointed at her sister's empty chair.

Aladdin wore boots and a big hat but rarely mounted a horse. He missed the Piper Cub, which had seemed to him very like a horse. Someone had stolen it two years earlier, had unbolted the wings and hauled it away on a flatbed while he slept. He suspected Mormons. Now he was welded to the driver's seat of his truck, tearing over the dusty roll of land, and sometimes, drugged and fallen, he spent the night out in a draw, cramped on the front seat. The windshield glass, discolored by high-altitude light, threw down violet radiance. He had made the headache rack from poles cut on the ranch. He kept a bottle of whiskey, a rope behind the seat. The open glove compartment carried kindling, wrenches, bolts and nuts, several hundred loose fence staples, and a handleless hammerhead. Wauneta tossed an old quilt in the cab and told him to wind up the windows when it rained.

"I know you," she said. "You will let the weather get you."

Every ten days or so Ottaline reared up and said she wanted to go to town and look for a job. Aladdin would not take her. Her weight, he said, ruined the springs on the passenger side. Anyway, there were no jobs, she knew that. She had better stay on the ranch where she didn't know how good she had it.

"I don't know why you would want a leave this ranch."

She said he should let her drive in alone.

"I will tell you when I am ready for advice," he said. "I am steerin my own truck for now. If you want a drive a truck then buy one."

"I am about a million dollars short." It was all hopeless.

"What a you want me a do, rob a bank for you?" he said. "Anyway, you're comin a the bull sale. And I'll give you a pointer you don't want a forget. Scrotal circumference is damn important."

What was there for Ottaline when the work slacked off? Stare at indigo slants of hail forty miles east, regard the tumbled clouds like mechanics' rags, count out he loves me, he loves me not, in nervous lightning crooked as branchwood through all quarters of the sky.

That summer the horses were always wet. It rained uncommonly, the southwest monsoon sweeping in. The shining horses stood out on the prairie, withers streaming, manes dripping, and one would suddenly start off, a fan of droplets coming off its shoulders like a cape. Ottaline and Aladdin wore slickers from morning coffee to good-night yawn. Wauneta watched the television weather while she ironed shirts and sheets. Old Red called it drip and dribble, stayed in his room chewing tobacco, reading Zane Grey in large-print editions, his curved fingernail creasing the page under every line. On the Fourth of July they sat together on the porch watching a distant storm, pretending the thick, ruddy legs of lightning and thunder were fireworks.

Ottaline had seen most of what there was to see around her with nothing new in sight. Brilliant events burst open not in the future but in the imagination. The room she had shared with Shan was a room within a room. In the unshaded moonlight her eyes shone oily white. The calfskin rug on the floor seemed to move, to hunch and crawl a fraction of an inch at a time. The dark frame of the mirror sank into the wall, a rectangular trench. From her bed she saw the moon-bleached grain elevator and behind it immeasurable range flecked with cows like small black seeds. She was no one but Ottaline in that peppery, disturbing light that made her want everything there was to want. The raw loneliness then, the silences of the day, the longing flesh led her to press her mouth into the crook of her own hot elbow. She pinched and pummelled her fat flanks, rolled on the bed, twisted, went to the window a dozen times, heels striking the floor until old Red in his pantry below called out, "What is it? You got a sailor up there?"

Her only chance seemed the semiliterate, off-again, on-again hired man, Hal Bloom, tall legs like chopsticks, T-shirt emblazoned "Aggressive by Nature, Cowboy by Choice." He worked for Aladdin in short bursts between rodeo roping, could not often be pried off his horse (for he cherished a vision of himself as an eighteen-seventies cowboy just in from an Oregon cattle drive). Ottaline had gone with him down into the willows a dozen times, to the damp soil and nests of stinging nettles, where he pulled a pale condom over his small, hard penis and crawled silently onto her. His warm neck smelled of soap and horse.

But then, when Ottaline began working on the ranch for hard money, Aladdin told Hal Bloom to go spin his rope.

"Yeah, well, it's too shit-fire long a haul out here anyways," Bloom said, and was gone. That was that.

Ottaline was dissolving. It was too far to anything. Someone had to come for her. There was not even the solace of television, for old Red dominated the controls, always choosing Westerns, calling out to the film horses in his broken voice, "Buck him off, kick his brains out!"

Ottaline went up to her room, listened to cell-phone conversations on the scanner.

"The balance on account number seven three five five nine is minus two hundred and oh four. . . ."

"Yes, I can see that, maybe. Are you drinkin beer already?" "Ha-ha. Yes."

"I guess maybe you didn't notice." "It wasn't all smashed flat like that, all soft. I took it out of the bag and it was—you goin a carve it?" "Not that one. It's nasty."

"Hey, is it rainin there yet?"

"Is it rainin yet?" she repeated. It was raining everywhere and people were alive in it except in the Red Wall country.

Ottaline studied Shan's photograph, said to her mother, "If it kills me I am goin a walk it off."

"Haven't I heard that before?" said Wauneta. "I know you."

Ottaline marched around outside the house for a few days, then widened the loop to take in the corrals, the toolshed, the root cellar, circumambulated the defunct gravel quarry where Aladdin dragged worn-out equipment, a sample of tractors, one a 1928 blue Rumely OilPull tractor on steel with a chokecherry tree growing through the frame, beside it old Red's secondhand 1935 AC with the four-cylinder overhead valve engine, paint sun-scalded white. Half buried at the foot of a caving bank lay the remains of a stripped Fordson Major, grille and radiator shroud smashed in, and next to a ruined stock tank stood the treacherous John Deere 4030.

She was walking through the rain-slicked wrecks when a voice spoke, barely audible. "Sweetheart, lady-girl."

The low sun poured slanting light under the edge of a cloud mass so dark it seemed charred, the prairie, the tractors, her hand beyond the wrist hem of the yellow slicker, all gilded with saffron brilliance. Colors of otherworld intensity blazed in the washed air, the distant Red Wall a bed of coals.

"Sweet," the voice breathed.

She was alone, there were no alien spacecraft in the sky. She stood quite still. She had eaten from a plateful of misery since childhood, suffered avoirdupois, unfeeling parents, the hard circumstances of the place. Looniness was possible, it could happen to anyone. Her mother's brother Mapston Hipsag had contracted a case of lumpy jaw from the stock and the disease took him by stages from depressive rancher to sniggering maniac. The light glided down to a dying hue and the wrecked machines sank into their own coffee-brown shadows. She heard nothing but mosquito whine, small wind that comes with approaching darkness.

That night, listening to the ramble of talk on the scanner, she wondered if hunger had prompted an invisible voice, went to the kitchen, and ate all of the leftover pork roast.

"I'm worried about you. I hope nobody tries to kill you or something." "Don't miss me too much."

"Nothin been hit." "It just rained like a bastard up here." "Rained like shit, here too." "No point stayin here."

Nothing happened for weeks, common enough in that part of the state. On a roaring noon she went again to the gravel pit.

"Hello, sweetheart. Come here, come here." It was the 4030, Aladdin's old green tractor, burly but with forward-raking lines that falsely indicated an eagerness to run. The machine had killed a ranch hand years earlier in a rollover accident at the weed-filled irrigation ditch — Maurice Ramblewood, or what? Rambletree, Bramblefood, Rumbleseat, Tumbleflood? She was a kid but he always flashed her a smile, asked her what was cooking, and on the fatal day tossed her a candy bar, pliable and warm from his shirt pocket, said she could borrow his sunglasses that turned the world orange. In late afternoon he was dead in bristle grass and spiny clotbur. His ghost.

"Maurice? That you?"

"No. No. It ain't him. That boy's a cinder."

"Who is talkin?"

"Two steps closer."

She stretched out her hand to the side grille. Yellow jackets had built a nest in it and were creeping in and out of the grille's interstices, palping the air suspiciously. She stared fixedly at the insects.

"That is good," said the voice inside the tractor. "Get you a little stick and scratch where all that paint is blistered up." But she backed off.

"I'm just scared to pieces," she said, looking at the sky, the rise and fall of crested prairie, the bunchgrass edge of the world that flared like burning threads.

"Naw, now, don't be. This old world is full a wonders, ain't it? Come on, get up in the cab. Plenty a bounce left. The seat's still good. Pretend you're drivin right through L.A." The voice was hoarse and plangent, just above an injured whisper, a movie gangster's voice.

"No," she said. "I don't like this. I already got enough problems, not makin it worse by gettin in a old tractor cab that's ready to collapse."

"Aw, you think you got problems? Look at me, sweetheart, settin out here in the bakin sun, blizzards and lizards, not even a tarpolean over me, brakes wrecked, battery gone, workin parts seized up, no gas, surrounded by deadheads, covered with birdshit and rust. Here you are at last, won't even give me the time a day."

"It's six-twelve," she said and walked off, fingertips pressing her eyebrows. This was hallucination.

The voice called after her, "Sweetheart, lady-girl, don't go."

She craved to know something of the world, but there was only the scanner.

"Broken, threads stripped, had to take it up and get it welded. You know that fucker used a do that shit but he don't hang around here no more."

"—horns off the steers. I stopped by to see her." "Yeah? They told me you left before three." "I was there at three to change my clothes." "You know you're full a bullshit."

"It's fuckin pourin here, man." "I don't know what else. It was like— Whoa! Oh my God that was a big lightnin! Whoa! I got a get off the fuckin phone."

"I want a be with you, but I look at reality and I say to myself this fuckin woman wants a fuck everbody, I can't even get it on the couch, got a go in the fuckin bedroom." "Yeah, it's all my fault, right?"

It made her sick, it made her jealous to hear those quarrelsome but coupled voices.

She went again to the gravel pit. The choking rasp began when she was twenty feet distant.

"Maurice Stumblebum? Just forget him. Wrench your steerin wheel, jam the brakes, rev, rev, rev. Never change oil or filter, never check brake fluid, never got the ballast right, didn't bother a check the front-wheel toe-in, used a ride the clutch unmerciful, run in heavy mud and never think a the front wheel bearins. They're ground a dust. Jump around in the seat until it made me crazy. Aw, don't drum your fingers like that, take me serious."

She looked away to the Red Wall, something best kept at a distance. It was not a place to go. The distant highway flashed, the reflection from a bottle pitched out of a tourist's car.

"But that ain't why I killed him."

"Then why?"

"Over you," said the tractor. "Over you. I saved you from him. He was goin a get you."

"I could a saved myself," she said, "if I'd a wanted to."

At supper Wauneta opened a pink envelope from Shan.

"What I thought," she said. "I knew it. I knew Tyler'd show up." Shan wrote that Tyler had been living with her and her roommate for a month, that he was trying for a job with the BLM rounding up wild horses and, while he waited to hear, holding down a telephone job for a bill collector. He had bought himself a computer and in the daytime seemed to be studying electronics—the table was covered with bits of wire and tape and springs when she came home from the gym. They had become vegetarians, except Tyler, who ate shrimp and crab legs, foods he had never tasted until Las Vegas. He could not get enough of them. He had, wrote Shan, spent sixty-five dollars for a four-pound box of jumbo shrimp, had cooked and eaten them in solitary gluttony. "Ha-ha, not much has changed. He is still a pig," the letter ended.

Aladdin put a parsnip on old Red's plate.

"Shrimps'll make your pecker curl," said the old man. "Sounds like he's buildin a bomb with them wires."

"He's not doin no such thing," said Wauneta.

After supper Ottaline scraped the dishes, began to snivel. Wauneta slung her hip against her, put her arm around the soft shoulders.

"What are you cryin about? That weight not comin off? Make up your mind to it, you are one a them meant to be big. My mother was the same."

"Not that. It seems like somebody is makin fun a me."

"Who? Who is makin fun a you?"

"I don't know. Somebody." She pointed at the ceiling.

"Well, let me tell you, that Somebody makes fun a everbody. Somebody's got a be laughin at the joke. Way I look at it."

"It's lonesome here."

"There's no lonesome, you work hard enough."

Ottaline went upstairs, set the scanner to rove and seek.

"Please enter your billing number now. I'm sorry, you have either misdialled or dialled a billing number we cannot accept. Please dial again."

"Why would it do that?" "Turn it off, turn it off."

"Hey, git doughnuts. And don't be squirtin around with twelve of em. Git a bunch. Don't be squirtin around, git two boxes."

"If that's fuckin all you have to say—then dang!"

Every day the tractor unloaded fresh complaints, the voice rough and urgent.

"Lady-girl, your daddy is a cocklebur. Get up and he don't get down. Stay in the seat sixteen hours. Aw, come here, I want to show you somethin. Look to the left a the cowl there, yeah, down there. What do you see?"

"Patch a rust. Big patch a rust."

"That's right. A big patch a rust. I won't tell you how that got there. I don't like to tell a girl somethin bad about her daddy. But in all the years I

worked for your daddy I only once had a sweet day and that was the day I
come here straight off the dealer's yard, fourth-hand and abused, and you
was ten years old, your birthday. You patted me and said, 'Hello, Mr. Tractor.' Your daddy put you up in the seat, said, 'You can be the first one a sit
there,' and your little hand was sticky with frostin and you wiggled around in
the seat and I thought—I thought it was goin a be like that ever day and it
never happened again, you never touched me again, never come near me, just
that damn bony-assed Maurice couldn't be bothered a use the rockshaft
lever, I got him with hydraulic oil under pressure, he got a infection. And
your dirty dad. Broke my heart until now. But I'll tell you the truth. If your
daddy was a get up here today I would hurt him for what he done a my brake
system. I will tell you sometime about the beer and what he done with it."

"What?"

"I'd tell you, but I think it would disgust you. I won't turn a lady-girl
against her family. I know you'd hold it against me and I don't want that.
Tell you some other time."

"You tell me now. Don't go around talkin blah-blah. I hate that."

"All right. You asked for it. Stumblebum never bothered a check
nothin. Finally brake fluid's gone. I'm out there with your daddy, on the
slope, we was haulin a horse trailer. He's got his old six-pack with him, way
he drinks he's alcoholic. He mashes his foot on the brake and we just keep
rippin. No way he could stop me, not that I wanted a stop. I didn't care.
Slowed only when we come at a rise. He jumped off before the rollback,
kicked a rock under a back wheel. What he done—poured warm beer in
my master-brake-cylinder reservoir, pumped that beer down the brake
lines. Yeah, he got enough pressure. But it ruined me. That's why I'm
here. You hate me for tellin you, don't you?"

"No. I heard a worse crimes. Like killin somebody in a ditch."

"You goin a pout?"

Another day she stormed out to the gravel pit.

"Shut up," she said. "Don't you see I'm fat?"

"What I like."

"Why don't you fix your attentions on another tractor? Leave me
alone."

"Now, think about it, lady-girl. Tractors don't care nothin about tractors. Tractors and people, that's how it is. Ever tractor craves some human
person, usually ends up with some big old farmer."

"Are you like an enchanted thing? A damn story where some girl lets a
warty old toad sleep in her shoe and in the mornin the toad's a good-
lookin dude makin omelettes?"

"Naw. I could tell you they had a guy work at Deere a few years ago
got fired out a the space program for havin picnics with foreigners and
drinkin vodka but they couldn't prove nothin. He was cross-wired about

it. It was around when they started foolin with computers and digital tapes. Remember them cars that told you to shut the door? Like that. Simple. Computers. He worked me up, fifteen languages. I could tell you that. Want a hear me say somethin in Urdu? Skively, skavelly—"

"You could tell me that, but I would not believe it. Some lame story." And it seemed to her that the inbuilt affection for humans the tractor harped on was balanced by vindictive malevolence.

"That's right, I was lyin."

"You got any kind a sense," she said, "you'd know people don't go crazy over tractors."

"Where you're wrong. Famous over in Iowa, Mr. Bob Ladderrung got himself buried with his tractor. Flat-out loved each other, he didn't care who knew it. And I don't just mean Iowa farmers. There's fellas can't keep away from us. There's girls fell in love with tractors all over this country. There is girls married tractors."

"I'm goin in," she said, turning away. "I'm goin in." She looked at the house, her mother's wedding wheat swaying yellow, old Red's face like a hanging skull in the window. "Oh, please," she said to herself, weeping, "not a tractor or nothin like it."

After supper, in her room, she wished for a ray gun to erase the brilliant needles of light from the isolate highway, silence the dull humming like bees in a high maybush. She wanted the cows to lie down and die, hoped for a tornado, the Second Coming, violent men in suits driving a fast car into the yard. There was the scanner.

"You think he's normal until you start to talk to him."

"I should a called the police, as mean and horrible as he is, but I'm not goin a do that. And this is what I'm thinkin. I'm goin a go after him even though we haven't been married that long. He's goin a pay. He's got it! He's makin two thousand a month. Anyway, I got a headache every day a my life over this. But I'm fine. Just a little insane. Don't worry, I'm fine."

Aladdin lifted a wad of turnip greens from the bowl, lowered it onto Ottaline's plate.

"What are you doin out there in the gravel pit with them tractors? I was lookin for you half a hour."

"Thinkin," she said, "of maybe try a fix up that Deere. Like just mess around with it." That day she had climbed up into the cab, sat on the seat, feeling an awful thrill.

"I wouldn't spend a dime on that damn thing. It never run good."

"I'd spend my own money on parts. I don't know, maybe a foolish idea. Thought I might try."

"We had trouble with that machine from day one. Damn Maurice Gargleguts got done, it wouldn't go much. We hauled that thing to Dig Yant, he replaced some a the wirin, cleaned the fuel tank, blew out the gas line, ten other things, rebuilt the carburetor. Then somethin else went wrong. Ever time they fixed it, it'd blow up somewhere else. They give me a hot iron on that one. I went to raisin heck and the dealer finally admitted it was a lemon. Give me a real good deal on the Case. Now, that's a tractor that's held up. You know, that 4030, you will be strippin it down to grit." He ate his meat loaf. He thought, said, "I could—might give you a hand. Haul it in that blue-door shed. Put a stove out there, run a pipe." He saw himself rising in the black wintry morning while his family slept, going out to the shed to stoke the fire, take a little smoke, and in the cozy warmth breaking loose rusty bolts, cleaning mucky fittings, pins, studs, screws, nuts soaking in a tub of kerosene while he waited for daylight and the start of the real day. "We'll get her in there tomorrow."

"Him," said Ottaline.

"You won't fix it," said old Red. "What you are tryin a fix ain't fixable."

"O.K.," she said, walking up to the tractor. "We are goin a move you into the blue-door shed and operate. My dad is goin a help me and you better stay hunderd per cent quiet or it's all over."

"You want a know my problems? Brakes. Belts shot, block cracked, motor seized, everthing rusted hard, sludge, dirt, lifters need replacin, water pump's shot, camshaft bearins shot, seals shot, magneto, alternator fried—you look inside that clutch housin you'll see a nightmare. Clutch plate needs a be relined, got a replace the tie-rod ends, the fuel shut-off line is bust, the steerin-gear assembly wrecked, the front axle bushings, spindle bushings all bananas and gone, you want a talk differential you'll be listin parts for fifteen minutes. The transmission clutch slipped bad before everthing went blank. I don't want your dirty dad a work on me. He already done that and look at me."

"Different now. Anyway, goin a be mostly me. I'm doin this. What gears was that tranny clutch slippin in?"

"You? You don't know nothin about tractor repair. I don't want you workin on me. I want you should take me a Dig Yant—he's a tractor man. It's men that fixes tractors, not no woman. First and third."

"You don't got much choice. Tell you one thing, I didn't take home ec. I took mechanics and I got a B. First and third? Seal on the underdrive brake piston or more likely the disks bad worn." She had brought a can of penetrating oil with her and began to squirt it on studs, bolts, and screws, to rap on the rusted bolts with a heavy wrench.

"You make a wrong move I might hurt you."

"You know what? I was you I'd lay back and enjoy it." Something Hal Bloom had said.

The rain quit in September and the prairie began to yellow out. There were a few heated days; then the weather cooled and an early storm hoop-rolled out of the northwest, slinging a hash of snow, before they got the tractor dismantled to frame, motor, and transmission.

"We got a get a engine hoist in here," said Aladdin, coughing. The first night of the storm he had got wasted and slept out in his pickup, window down, the snow carousing over him. He woke shuddering, drove home, heard they were out of coffee, drank a glass of cold water, told Wauneta he could not eat any breakfast. By noon he was feverish and strangling, took to the bed.

"That coughin drives me into the water and I don't swim," said old Red. "Better off just smother him, be done with it."

"There is somebody else at the top a my smotherin list," said Wauneta. "I knew this was goin a happen. Sleep in a truck." Aspirin, poultices, glasses of water, steam tent, hot tea were her remedies, but nothing changed. Aladdin roasted in his own dry heat.

"What's tomorrow," he said, rolling his aching head on the hot pillow.

"Friday."

"Bring me my calendar." With swimming eyes he studied the scrawled notes, called for Ottaline.

"She's out feedin. It snowed wet, froze hard crust out there, they can't hardly get grass. Supposed a warm up this weekend."

"God damn it," he whispered, "when she comes in send her here." He shivered and retched.

The snow rattled down on Ottaline in the cab of Aladdin's big Case tractor, a huge round bale on the hydraulic-lift spear. It could keep snowing until June the way it was coming down. At noon she drove back to the house, ravenous, hoping for macaroni and cheese. She left the Case idling.

"Dad wants you," said Wauneta. It was beef and biscuits. Ottaline took a pickle from the cut-glass dish.

She sidled into her parents' bedroom. She was one of those who could not bear sick people, who did not know where to look except away from the bloodshot eyes and swollen face.

"Look," he said. "It's first Friday a the month tomorrow. I got Amendinger comin out at eight o'clock. If I ain't better"—he coughed until he retched—"you are goin a deal with him, take him out there, he can look them over, see what we got, make you a offer." Amendinger, the cattle buyer, was a dark-complexioned man with sagging eyes, a black mustache whose ends plunged down to his jawline like twin divers. He wore black shirts and a black hat, gave off an air of implacable decision and control. He had no sense of humor and every rancher cursed him behind his back.

"Dad, I am scared a death a that man. He will get the best a me. He will make us a low offer and I will get rattled and say yes. Why not Ma? Nobody gets on her bad side."

"Because you know the animals and she don't. If Tyler was here—but he ain't. You're my little cowgirl. You don't have to say nothin. Just take him around, hear his offer, and tell him we'll get back to him." He knew that Amendinger did business on the spot; there was no getting back to him. "I get better of this I am goin a buy a plane I been lookin at. It's the only way to work this big of a ranch. A truck ain't no good, windows and all."

"I could bring him in here, Dad."

"Nobody outside a my family sees me layin flat. God damn it." He coughed. "Ain't that how it goes, first your money and then your clothes."

She had the poorest kind of night and in the morning rose groggy and in a mood. The snow had quit and a warm Chinook blew. Already the plain was bare, the shrinking drifts lingering in cuts and folds of land. They were still out of coffee. Upstairs Aladdin wheezed and panted.

"He don't look good," said Wauneta.

By eight the cattle dealer had not arrived. Ottaline ate two oatmeal cookies, another slice of ham, drank a glass of milk. It was past nine when the dealer's black truck pulled in, Amendinger's black hat bent down as he reached for papers. There were three hound dogs in the back. He got out with the clipboard in his hand, already punching figures on a handheld calculator. Ottaline went outside.

It was not the cattle dealer but his son, Flyby Amendinger, big-nostrilled, heavyset, a cleft in his stubbly chin, as quiet as three in the morning.

"Mr. Touhey around?" he asked, looking at his boots.

"I'm showin you the stock," she said. "He got the flu. Or some kind a thing. We thought you would come at eight. We thought you was goin a be your father."

"I missed a couple turns. Dad's over in Hoyt." He fished in his shirt pocket, drew out newspaper clippings, showed her an ad, Amendinger & Son Livestock Dealers. "I been workin with Dad almost nine years, guess I got a idea what I am doin by now."

"I didn't mean you didn't," she said. "I'm glad it's you. Your dad's mustache scares me." She pictured him driving the red roads to the ranch, roads like heavy red marker traced over the map, cutting the circle of horizon.

"Scare the hell out a me, too, when I was a little kid." He looked at the porch, the house, the wedding wheat, the blue-door shed.

"Well," she said. "Here we go."

"That wheat needs cuttin," he said.

She drove and he stared at the far horizon visible beneath the bellies of cows. They bounced over pasture, the dust in the truck cab shaken loose and suspended in a fine sparkling haze as though an emanation from their private thoughts that might coalesce into audible statement. He opened the gates. Ottaline thanked him, pointed out the good qualities of the cattle, the trim, heavily muscled bodies on straight legs, the rib-eye bulge on each side of the backbone, their large size. He murmured at a coarse-fronted cow with a steery look to her, pointed out some small and sickle-hocked steers with flat loins. He counted, made notes and added figures, offered a fair price.

"You are a knowledgeable girl," he said, "and a damn good-lookin one, though upholstered. Care for a beer?"

Ottaline spent the morning tipping back beer bottles with Flyby, who described the lonely life of a cattle dealer's son, illustrating his sad sentences with long, flat gestures of his hand. It was noon when he left.

She gave the figures to Aladdin from the bedroom doorway, hanging back. Dazed and fiery, bursting with tea, he nodded, said all right. It was all right. He did not need a computer to know the margin to a penny. It was all right, and wasn't that a sad relief. He couldn't say as much for himself.

That night old Red woke from his shallow sleep to a stiff, whistling risp he dreaded to hear. His heart beat, he rose and felt his way to the pantry window. The dirty moonlight fizzed through shredded clouds, glanced off a swinging scythe blade, though it was not Death come for him this time but a man in a dark hat cutting the wedding wheat in hissing swathes, stopping at the end of every row to swig from a bottle. He saw his granddaughter Ottaline, mouth cracked wide, her hundred teeth glinting like a mica bed, leaning against the doorframe of the blue-door shed. She hurled a piece of oily metal into the sky, where it twisted and fell, stooped for another, sent it flying.

Old Red watched, summed it up. "I drove teams. I cowboyed. Worked since I was a kid. Run sheep and run cows. Still present, fork end down, ready as a dog with two dicks. I ain't finished my circle yet."

Tyler and Shan were far away hoping for good luck, but here was Ottaline and her haymaker. He wouldn't waste his dear breath laughing.

There was a wedding in September and a tremendous picnic under the Amendinger cattle-sale canopy, red and white stripes that cast a rose flush, trestle tables in the side yard, pork barbecue, a baron of beef pit-roasted, spitted lamb, prairie oysters, sweet corn, giant shrimp in Tyler's ketchup sauce, oven rolls, a keg of sour pickles, melons, ripe Oregon peaches made into deep-dish pies, and a three-tier wedding cake with pale-blue frosting topped by a tiny plastic bull and cow. The day was hot and clear and the Red Wall trembled on the horizon. Out beyond the fence the stripped frame of the 4030 lay where Aladdin had dragged it, on its side in the sagebrush. Wauneta wept, not for her daughter but for the cut wheat. Tyler inspected the ranch, looking it over with a displeased eye. Everything was smaller and shabbier. Why had he wanted this? He had a cell phone and sat on his horse talking to someone far away. Wauneta told Shan she intended to come out to Las Vegas and visit one of these days.

"Not if I got somethin to say about it," said Aladdin.

The guests dragged the folding chairs back and forth, and when Ottaline smoothed the rayon satin of her dress over her knees she felt the grit, saw the glinting dust caught in the weft. A spot of barbecue sauce marked the bosom. At last she changed into the new aquamarine pants suit and drove away with Flyby Amendinger for a four-day honeymoon among the motels of Nebraska.

Where wheat once grew a row of doghouses stood. There were two trucks in the driveway. Old Red in his pantry wished for deafness when the bedsprings sang above. Otherwise all was the same.

Aladdin applied for a bank loan for another plane. "I said if the Lord spared me I'd get it." He was dreaming of a 1948 Aeronca Sedan, a loose, big-cabined thing with feminine curves and a split crankcase to be replaced with an undamaged one from Donald's Cowboy Junkyard.

"She's so roomy, if I had to I could put a couple calves in her, bales a hay, cake, just about anything, even Ottaline, ha-ha."

The bank approved the loan and on a quiet and gray morning, the wind lying low, Aladdin started his truck, got halfway down the drive, backed up, parked, and came into the kitchen. Old Red dunked his toast in black coffee.

"I am goin a fly that plane home," he said. "I will land in the Triangle pasture. Preciate it you was all out there watchin. You, too, bubba," he said to his son-in-law.

"I got a go look at Trev's cows this mornin." Flyby Amendinger did not like living under the thumb of Aladdin Touhey. In the night he complained to Ottaline that Aladdin was worse than his mustachioed father.

"My block don't fit his tackle," he whispered.

"It sure fits mine," she whispered back.

"Call Trev up. Say you'll come a little later. He won't give a shit. I want a see everybody out wavin. Cause for celebration get a plane on this damn place again. Goin a teach Ottaline how to fly it."

It was midmorning when they heard the drone of the engine.

"Ma!" shouted Ottaline into the house. "He's comin!"

Wauneta came outside and stood with Ottaline and Flyby staring at the horizon. Old Red hobbled onto the porch. The wind had come up and was gusty and chill, the distant line of cliff marking a dull red break in the sere plain. Wauneta ran back into the house for her jacket.

The plane flew over and headed toward the Red Wall, turned, and came again in their direction, very much lower. It passed over them twenty feet off the ground. Aladdin's head was barely visible in the smoke from home-grown that clouded the cabin. The plane soared up, shaking in the wind. It rose in a steep climb, levelled out, and sailed away. When it was only a distant speck it turned and came toward the ranch again, curving and sliding, coming low. At a certain angle it resembled a billboard in the sky.

"He is actin up," said Wauneta. She watched the plane roar in low like a crop duster.

"I think he is goin a land," said Flyby, "or take a soil sample. Or stake out a homestead."

"He is actin up. I know him. YOU GET DOWN HERE!" Wauneta shouted at the plane.

As though obeying her, it touched the ground, sending up a puff of dust, bounced back into the air, and made two more prodigious hops before the left wheel caught the iron frame of the abandoned tractor and the plane fell on its face, crumpled into a mash of cloth, metal, and rancher. There was an explosion like a mighty backfire, but no flame. A ball of dust rose.

Flyby dragged Aladdin to safe ground. His father-in-law's head lolled at an unusual angle.

"He is dead, I think. I think he is dead. Yes, he is dead. His neck is broke."

Wauneta shrieked.

"Look what you done," said Ottaline to her. "You killed him."

"Me! That's what cuttin the wheat's done."

"He done it hisself," called old Red from the porch. It was clear to him the way things had to go. They'd plant Aladdin. Ottaline and her scytheman would run the ranch. Wauneta would pack her suitcase and steer for the slot machines. The minute she was out of sight he intended to move out of the pantry and back upstairs. The main thing in life was staying power. That was it: stand around long enough you'd get to sit down.

[1998]

COMMENTARIES

*T*he next part of this book consists of critical comments on the American short story form and on various individual stories. In the preface to his story collection *Twice-Told Tales,* Nathaniel Hawthorne wrote that a writer "would have reason to be ashamed if he could not criticize his own work as fairly as another man's, and—though it is little his business, and perhaps still less his interest—he can hardly resist a temptation to achieve something of the sort. If writers were allowed to do so, and would perform the task with perfect sincerity and unreserve, their opinions of their own productions would often be more valuable and instructive than the works themselves." Although Hawthorne was not entirely serious in this last statement, there is some truth in what he said. Writers' attitudes about creating short fiction can often clarify their work, place their stories in a larger context of literary history, and shed light on the creative process.

Reading literary criticism can also help stimulate your response to the stories. "Criticism is not literature, and the pleasure of criticism is not the pleasure of literature," observed the noted teacher and critic Lionel Trilling. "But experience suggests that the two pleasures go together, and the pleasure of criticism makes literature and its pleasure the more readily accessible."

The commentaries in this section are arranged alphabetically by author. The headnotes to the stories in the anthology refer you to the related commentaries in this part of the book.

PAULA GUNN ALLEN

Paula Gunn Allen is a poet and professor of literature. This story is from her book of Native American traditional tales, Spider Woman's Granddaughters *(1989).*

Whirlwind Man Steals Yellow Woman

Kochinnenako, Yellow Woman, was grinding corn one day with her three sisters. They looked into the water jars and saw that they were empty. They said, "We need some water." Kochinnenako said she would go, and taking the jars made her way across the mesa and went down to the spring. She climbed the rockhewn stairs to the spring that lay in a deep pool of shade. As she knelt to dip the gourd dipper into the cool shadowed water, she heard someone coming down the steps. She looked up and saw Whirlwind Man. He said, "Gutwatzi, Kochinnenako. Are you here?"

"Da'waa'e," she said, dipping water calmly into the four jars beside her. She didn't look at him.

"Put down the dipper," he said. "I want you to come with me."

"I am filling these jars with water as you can see," she said. "My sisters and I are grinding corn, and they are waiting for me."

"No," Whirlwind Man said. "You must come and go with me. If you won't come, well, I'll have to kill you." He showed her his knife.

Kochinnenako put the dipper down carefully. "All right," she said. "I guess I'll go with you." She got up. She went with Whirlwind Man to the other side of the world where he lived with his mother, who greeted her like his wife.

The jars stayed, tall and fat and cool in the deep shade by the shadowed spring.

That was one story. She knew they laughed about Kochinnenako. Brought her up when some woman was missing for awhile. Said she ran off with a Navajo, or maybe with a mountain spirit, "Like Kochinnenako." Maybe the name had become synonymous with "whore" at Guadalupe. Ephanie knew that Yellow was the color of woman, ritual color of faces painted in death, or for some of the dances. But there was a tone of dismissal, or derision there that she couldn't quite pin down, there anyway. No one told how Kochinnenako went with Whirlwind Man because she was forced. Said, "Then Whirlwind Man raped Kochinnenako." Rather, the story was that his mother had greeted Yellow Woman, and made her at home in their way. And that when Kochinnenako wanted to return home, had agreed, asking only that she wait while the old woman prepared gifts for Kochinnenako's sisters.

1290

Ephanie wondered if Yellow Woman so long ago had known what was happening to her. If she could remember it or if she thought maybe she had dreamed it. If they laughed at her, or threw her out when she returned. She wondered if Kochinnenako cried.   [1989]

SHERWOOD ANDERSON

Sherwood Anderson commented on his practice of writing short stories in his autobiography, A Story Teller's Story, *published in 1924. This book was his first attempt to write his memoirs and authenticate his "legend" — an impoverished childhood, a revolt against business life, and an entrance into the avant-garde literary circles of Chicago, New Orleans, and New York. He was more concerned with the meaning than with the facts of his life. In his rejection of the "plot" story (a story emphasizing plot over character, setting, or theme), which he considered contrived fiction, he became a strong influence on many subsequent writers of short stories and revitalized the American short story tradition.*

Form, Not Plot, in the Short Story

For such men as myself you must understand there is always a great difficulty about telling the tale after the scent has been picked up. . . . Having, from a conversation overheard or in some other way, got the tone of a tale, I was like a woman who has just become impregnated. Something was growing inside me. At night when I lay in my bed I could feel the heels of the tale kicking against the walls of my body. Often as I lay thus every word of the tale came to me quite clearly but when I got out of bed to write it down the words would not come.

I had constantly to seek in roads new to me. Other men had felt what I had felt, had seen what I had seen — how had they met the difficulties I faced? My father when he told his tales walked up and down the room before his audience. He pushed out little experimental sentences and watched his audience narrowly. There was a dull-eyed old farmer sitting in a corner of the room. Father had his eyes on the fellow. "I'll get him," he said to himself. He watched the farmer's eyes. When the experimental sentence he had tried did not get anywhere he tried another and kept trying. Besides words he had — to help the telling of his tales — the advantage of being able to act out those parts for which he could find no words. He could frown, shake his fists, smile, let a look of pain or annoyance drift over his face.

These were his advantages that I had to give up if I was to write my tales rather than tell them and how often I had cursed my fate.

How significant words had become to me! At about this time an American woman living in Paris, Miss Gertrude Stein, had published a book called *Tender Buttons* and it had come into my hands. How it had excited me! Here was something purely experimental and dealing in words separated from sense—in the ordinary meaning of the word sense—an approach I was sure the poets must often be compelled to make. Was it an approach that would help me? I decided to try it.

A year or two before the time of which I am now writing an American painter, Mr. Felix Russman, had taken me one day into his workshop to show me his colors. He laid them out on a table before me and then his wife called him out of the room and he stayed for half an hour. It had been one of the most exciting moments of my life. I shifted the little pans of color about, laid one color against another. I walked away and came near. Suddenly there had flashed into my consciousness, for perhaps the first time in my life, the secret inner world of the painters. Before that time I had wondered often enough why certain paintings, done by the old masters, and hung in our Chicago Art Institute, had so strange an effect upon me. Now I thought I knew. The true painter revealed all of himself in every stroke of his brush. Titian made one feel so utterly the splendor of himself; from Fra Angelico and Sandro Botticelli there came such a deep human tenderness that on some days it fairly brought tears to the eyes; in a most dreadful way and in spite of all his skill Bouguereau gave away his own inner nastiness while Leonardo made one feel all of the grandeur of his mind just as Balzac had made his readers feel the universality and wonder of his mind.

Very well then, the words used by the tale-teller were as the colors used by the painter. Form was another matter. It grew out of the materials of the tale and the teller's reaction to them. It was the tale trying to take form that kicked about inside the tale-teller at night when he wanted to sleep.

And words were something else. Words were the surfaces, the clothes of the tale. I thought I had begun to get something a little clearer now. I had smiled to myself a little at the sudden realization of how little native American words had been used by American story-writers. When most American writers wanted to be very American they went in for slang. Surely we American scribblers had paid long and hard for the English blood in our veins. The English had got their books into our schools, their ideas of correct forms of expression were firmly fixed in our minds. Words as commonly used in our writing were in reality an army that marched in a certain array and the generals in command of the army were still English. One saw the words as marching, always just so—in books—and came to think of them so—in books.

But when one told a tale to a group of advertising men sitting in a barroom in Chicago or to a group of laborers by a factory door in Indiana one instinctively disbanded the army. There were moments then for what have always been called by our correct writers "unprintable words." One got now and then a certain effect by a bit of profanity. One dropped instinctively into the vocabulary of the men about, was compelled to do so to get the full effect sought for the tale. Was the tale he was telling not just the tale of a man named Smoky Pete and how he caught his foot in the trap set for himself?—or perhaps one was giving them the Mama Geigans story. The devil. What had the words of such a tale to do with Thackeray or Fielding? Did the men to whom one told the tale not know a dozen Smoky Petes and Mama Geigans? Had one ventured into the classic English models for tale-telling at that moment there would have been a roar. "What the devil! Don't you go high-toning us!"

And it was sure one did not always seek a laugh from his audience. Sometimes one wanted to move the audience, make them squirm with sympathy. Perhaps one wanted to throw an altogether new light on a tale the audience already knew.

Would the common words of our daily speech in shops and offices do the trick? Surely the Americans among whom one sat talking had felt everything the Greeks had felt, everything the English felt? Deaths came to them, the tricks of fate assailed their lives. I was certain none of them lived felt or talked as the average American novel made them live feel and talk and as for the plot short stories of the magazines—those bastard children of de Maupassant, Poe, and O. Henry—it was certain there were no plot short stories ever lived in any life I had known anything about. [1924]

MARY AUSTIN

Mary Austin wrote "Regionalism in American Fiction" in 1932 for the English Journal, *published by the National Council of Teachers of English. Her views were echoed by many American academics and social reformers of the time, who encouraged the work of regional writers during the Depression years through projects supported by the Works Progress Administration. Austin was also directly influenced by the book* The New Regionalism in American Literature *(1930) by her friend Carey McWilliams, who shared her romantic vision of the traditional agrarian ways of life and was attempting to renew and develop the type of local-color fiction dominant in the late nineteenth century.*

Regionalism in American Fiction

"Regionalism in literature," says Dorothy Canfield in a recent review of what she considers an excellent example of it, "is the answer to the problem of getting any literature at all out of so vast and sprawling a country as ours." She might as truthfully have said it of any art and any country which is large enough to cover more than one type of natural environment. Art, considered as the expression of any people as a whole, is the response they make in various mediums to the impact that the totality of their experience makes upon them, and there is no sort of experience that works so constantly and subtly upon man as his regional environment. It orders and determines all the direct, practical ways of his getting up and lying down, of staying in and going out, of housing and clothing and food-getting; it arranges by its progressions of seed times and harvest, its rain and wind and burning suns, the rhythms of his work and amusements. It is the thing always before his eye, always at his ear, always underfoot. Slowly or sharply it forces upon him behavior patterns such as earliest become the habit of his blood, the unconscious factor of adjustment in all his mechanisms. Of all the responses of his psyche, none pass so soon and surely as these into that field of consciousness from which all invention and creative effort of every sort proceed. Musical experts say that they can trace a racial influence in composition many generations back, and what is a race but a pattern of response common to a group of people who have lived together under a given environment long enough to take a recognizable pattern?

Everybody has known this a long time. We have known it about classic Greek and ancient Egypt. We know that the distinctions between Scotch and Irish and British literature have not been erased, have scarcely been touched by their long association of all three under one political identity; we know in fact that at last the pattern of Irish regionalism has prevailed over polity, and it is still a problem of the Irish Free State to withstand the separative influences of regionalism on their own green island. We recognize Moorish and Iberian elements in Spanish art, at the same time that we fully realize something distinctive that comes to this mixed people out of the various regional backgrounds within the Spanish peninsula. Knowing all this, it is rather surprising to find critics in the United States speaking of regionalism as something new and unprecedented in a territory so immensely varied as ours. The really astonishing thing would have been to find the American people as a whole resisting the influences of natural environment in favor of the lesser influences of a shared language and a common political arrangement.

Actually this notion, that the American people should differ from all the rest of the world in refusing to be influenced by the particular region called home, is a late by-product of the Civil War and goes with another ill-defined notion that there is a kind of disloyalty in such a differentiation and an implied criticism in one section of all the others from which it is distinguished. It would be easy to trace out the growth of such an idea, helped as it is and augmented in its turn by the general American inability to realize the source of all art as deeper than political posture, arising, as people truly and rudely say, in our "guts," the seat of life and breath and heartbeats, of loving and hating and rearing. It is not in the nature of mankind to be all of one pattern in these things any more than it is in the nature of the earth to be all plain, all seashore, or all mountains. Regionalism, since it is of the very nature and constitution of the planet, becomes at last part of the nature and constitution of the men who live on it.

Since already a sense of the truth of these things, as applicable to our own country, has worked through to the common consciousness, our real concern is not to argue the case, but to fortify ourselves against the possibility of our missing the way again by failing to discriminate between a genuine regionalism and mistaken presentiments of it. We need to be prompt about it, before somebody discovers that our resistance so far has been largely owed to intellectual laziness which flinches from the task of competently knowing, not one vast, pale figure of America, but several Americas, in many subtle and significant characterizations.

As a matter of fact, our long disappointed expectation of the "great American novel," for which every critic was once obliged to keep an eye out, probably originated in the genuine inability of the various regions to see greatness in novels that dealt with fine and subtle distinctions in respect to some other region. But we have only to transfer the wishful thinking for a single book, or a single author, who would be able to overcome our inextinguishable ignorance of each other, to Europe to become aware of its absurdity. To Europeans our American regional differentiations, all comprised under one language and one government, are very puzzling. That is one reason why they have seized so promptly on *Main Street* and especially on *Babbitt* as just the broad, thin, generalized surface reflection of the American community and American character which the casual observer receives. Babbitt is an American type, the generalized, "footless" type which has arisen out of a rather wide-spread resistance to regional interests and influences, out of a determined fixation on the most widely shared, instead of the deepest rooted, types of American activity. That Babbitt is exactly that sort of person and that he is unhappy in being it, is probably exactly what Mr. Lewis meant to show. But that millions of Americans rise up to reject him as representing "our part of the country" only goes to show that, deep down and probably unconsciously, all the time that one set of influences has been shaping the shallow Babbitt citizen, another set has been at work to produce half a dozen other regionally discriminated types for whom there is, naturally, no common literary instance.

Perhaps the country does not fully realize that in rejecting Babbitt as our family name, it has declared for the regional types such as the best American fictionists have already furnished us. Probably the American reading public never has understood that its insistence on fiction shallow enough to be common to all regions, so that no special knowledge of other environments than one's own is necessary to appreciation of it, has pulled down the whole level of American fiction. It is more than likely that even the critics, who can be discovered surrendering to the idea of strongly marked regional fiction, have no notion of the work they are cutting out for themselves under the necessity of knowing good regional books when they see them. But there it is, the recognition and the demand. People of the South aren't satisfied to go on forever reading novels about New York and Gopher Prairie, people of the Pacific Coast want occasionally to read "something more like us." They are willing to be tolerant and even interested in other regions on consideration that they get an occasional fair showing for themselves. . . .

Until within the last twenty years the literary expectation of the United States could be quite simply allocated to New England; New York City; a "misty midregion" known as the Middlewest, as weird as Weir and not any more explicitly mapped; to which append the fringing Old South and the Far West. At the present, the last two have completely receded into the dimension of time past. The Old South has given rise to the New South; the Far West has split into the Southwest, the Northwest, the California Coast, and the Movie West. Cleavages begin to appear in the Middlewest, outlining *The Great Meadow,* the title of the best book about the section just south of Ohio. Farther north lies the Middle Border and Chicago. Within New York City we are aware of the East Side and Harlem which is the capital of the new Negro world, each producing its own interpreters. Even in the Indian region there is faint indication of splitting off from the children's Indian country of a meagerly explored adult interest.

To the average citizen, notice of these recent annexations to the literary world comes in the form of a new book which everybody is talking about, dealing with life as it is lived there, as it unmistakably couldn't be lived anywhere else. And immediately the average citizen who, however much he wishes to read what everybody else is reading, secretly hankers to be able to discriminate for himself, begins to cast about for a criterion of what acceptable regionalism in literature should be. For to be able to speak of the credibility of reports of the various countries contained within our country requires a nimble wit and a considerable capacity for traveling in one's mind. How, the reader inquires inwardly, without having lived it myself, shall I feel certain that this book does give in human terms the meaning of that country in which the action of the story takes place? One might answer shortly, by the same means that it has become a proverb in the country where I live that "a wool grower knows a wool buyer." Whoever has lived deeply and experientially into his own environment, is by so much the better prepared to recognize the same experience in another. But there are criteria not to be ignored for recognizing regionalism in literature.

The first of the indispensable conditions is that the region must enter constructively into the story, as another character, as the instigator of plot. A natural scene can never be safely assumed to be the region of the story when it is used merely as a backdrop — not that the scenic backdrop cannot be used effectively by way of contrast, or to add a richer harmonization to a story shaped by alien scenes. Henry James is master of this trick, as when in *The Golden Bowl* he uses aristocratic England as a setting for a group of rich Americans and one Italian Prince; or, as in *The Ambassadors,* he unfolds a New England complication against smart Paris. Edith Wharton does it less handsomely in *The Children,* and Sinclair Lewis less importantly in *Dodsworth.* Willa Cather does it most appealingly in *Death Comes for the Archbishop.* I am often asked if this last is not what I mean by a "regional" book of the Southwest. Not in the least. The hero is a missionary arriving here at an age when the major patterns of his life are already set; a Frenchman by birth, a Catholic by conviction and practice, a priest by vocation, there is little that New Mexico can do for him besides providing him an interesting backdrop against which to play out his missionary part. Miss Cather selects her backgrounds with care, draws them with consummate artistry, in this case perverting the scenes from historical accuracy, and omitting—probably, herself, in complete ignorance of it—the tragic implications of its most significant item and so makes it convincing for her audience. I am not saying that this is not a legitimate literary device. That Archbishop Lamy, who was the historic prototype of Miss Cather's leading character, also missed the calamity to Spanish New Mexican culture, of the coming of the French priests, is the one profoundly human touch that so competent a literary artist as Miss Cather should not have overlooked. It makes her story, with all its true seeming, profoundly untrue to the New Mexican event, which removes it from the category of regional literature.

One of the likeliest mistakes the inexperienced reader will make in allocating books to their proper regional source, is to select stories about the region rather than of it. Such a reader would for example class *Uncle Tom's Cabin* as a southern book, when, in fact, its approach, its moral and intellectual outlook is New England from the ground up, and so are its most telling characters. The South never saw itself in Harriet Beecher Stowe's light, never looked on slavery as she displayed it. Southerners would not deny the book's regional character, but they are still protesting after nearly three-quarters of a century that it is not of their region. In the same manner, old Californians, forty years ago, could be heard denying the regional authenticity of *Ramona.* They recognized neither themselves nor their Indians in Helen Hunt Jackson's presentation. The regionally interpretive book must not only be about the country, it must be of it, flower of its stalk and root, in the way that *Huckleberry Finn* is of the great river, taking its movement and rhythm, its structure and intention, or lack of it, from the scene. In the way that Edna Ferber's *Cimarron* isn't of the land but pleasingly and reasonably about it.

With these two indispensable conditions of the environment entering constructively into the story, and the story reflecting in some fashion the essential qualities of the land, it is not easy to put one's finger on representative regional fiction. *Slow Smoke* by Charles Malam is the novel Dorothy Canfield mentions. A book I have in mind as fulfilling all the conditions competently is Frank Applegate's *Indian Stories from the Pueblos.* These are native tales which he tells in the manner in which the natives would tell them. Work of this kind comes on slowly. Time is the essence of the undertaking, time to live into the land and absorb it; still more time to cure the reading public of its preference for something less than the proverbial bird's-eye view of the American scene, what you might call an automobile eye view, something slithering and blurred, nothing so sharply discriminated that it arrests the speed-numbed mind to understand, characters like garish gas stations picked out with electric lights. The one chance of persuading the young reader to make these distinctions for himself would be to whet his appreciation on the best regional literature of our past so that he may not miss the emerging instance of his own times.   [1932]

JAMES BALDWIN

James Baldwin included this account of how he became a writer in his book Notes of a Native Son *(1955). He admitted that "the most difficult (and most rewarding) thing in my life has been the fact that I was born a Negro and was forced, therefore, to effect some kind of truce with this reality." As his biographer Louis H. Pratt has understood, this "truce" forced Baldwin "into an open confrontation with his experience, enabling him to make an honest assessment of his past. . . . Baldwin the artist has been liberated because he has found a way to use his past and to transform those experiences resulting therefrom into art."*

Autobiographical Notes

I was born in Harlem thirty-one years ago. I began plotting novels at about the time I learned to read. The story of my childhood is the usual bleak fantasy, and we can dismiss it with the unrestrained observation that I certainly would not consider living it again. In those days my mother was given to the exasperating and mysterious habit of having babies. As they were born, I took them over with one hand and held a book with the other. The children probably suffered, though they have since been kind enough to deny it, and in this way I read *Uncle Tom's Cabin* and *A Tale of Two Cities* over and over and over again; in this way, in fact, I read just about everything I could get my hands on—except the Bible, probably because it was the only book I was encouraged to read. I must also confess that I wrote—a great deal—and my first professional triumph, in any case, the first effort of mine to be seen in print, occurred at the age of twelve or thereabouts, when a short story I had written about the Spanish revolution won some sort of prize in an extremely short-lived church newspaper. I remember the story was censored by the lady editor, though I don't remember why, and I was outraged.

Also wrote plays, and songs, for one of which I received a letter of congratulations from Mayor La Guardia, and poetry, about which the less said, the better. My mother was delighted by all these goings-on, but my father wasn't; he wanted me to be a preacher. When I was fourteen I became a preacher, and when I was seventeen I stopped. Very shortly thereafter I left home. For God knows how long I struggled with the world of commerce and industry—I guess they would say they struggled with *me*— and when I was about twenty-one I had enough done of a novel to get a Saxton Fellowship. When I was twenty-two the fellowship was over, the novel turned out to be unsalable, and I started waiting on tables in a Village restaurant and writing book reviews—mostly, as it turned out, about the Negro problem, concerning which the color of my skin made me automatically an expert. Did another book, in company with photographer Theodore Pelatowski, about the store-front churches in Harlem. This book met exactly the same fate as my first—fellowship, but no sale. (It was a Rosenwald Fellowship.) By the time I was twenty-four I had decided to stop reviewing books about the Negro problem—which, by this time, was only slightly less horrible in print than it was in life—and I packed my bags and went to France, where I finished, God knows how, *Go Tell It on the Mountain*.

Any writer, I suppose, feels that the world into which he was born is nothing less than a conspiracy against the cultivation of his talent—which attitude certainly has a great deal to support it. On the other hand, it is only because the world looks on his talent with such a frightening indifference that the artist is compelled to make his talent important. So that any writer, looking back over even so short a span of time as I am here forced to assess, finds that the things which hurt him and the things which helped him cannot be divorced from each other; he could be helped in a certain way only because he was hurt in a certain way; and his help is simply to be enabled to move from one conundrum to the next—one is tempted to say that he moves from one disaster to the next. When one begins looking for influences one finds them by the score. I haven't thought much about my own, not enough anyway; I hazard that the King James Bible, the rhetoric of the store-front church, something ironic and violent and perpetually understated in Negro speech—and something of Dickens' love for bravura—have something to do with me today; but I wouldn't stake my life on it. Likewise, innumerable people have helped me in many ways; but finally, I suppose, the most difficult (and most rewarding) thing in my life has been the fact that I was born a Negro and was forced, therefore, to effect some kind of truce with this reality. (Truce, by the way, is the best one can hope for.)

One of the difficulties about being a Negro writer (and this is not special pleading, since I don't mean to suggest that he has it worse than anybody else) is that the Negro problem is written about so widely. The bookshelves groan under the weight of information, and everyone therefore considers himself informed. And this information, furthermore, operates usually (generally, popularly) to reinforce traditional attitudes. Of traditional attitudes there are only two—For or Against—and I, personally, find it difficult to say which attitude has caused me the most pain. I am perfectly aware that the change from ill-will to good-will, however motivated, however imperfect, however expressed, is better than no change at all.

But it is part of the business of the writer—as I see it—to examine attitudes, to go beneath the surface, to tap the source. From this point of view the Negro problem is nearly inaccessible. It is not only written about so widely; it is written about so badly. It is quite possible to say that the price a Negro pays for becoming articulate is to find himself, at length, with nothing to be articulate about. ("You taught me the language," says Caliban to Prospero,[1] "and my profit on't is I know how to curse.") Consider: The tremendous social activity that this problem generates imposes on whites and Negroes alike the necessity of looking forward, of working to bring about a better day. This is fine, it keeps the waters troubled; it is all, indeed, that has made possible the Negro's progress. Nevertheless, social affairs are not generally speaking the writer's prime concern, whether they ought to be or not; it is absolutely necessary that he establish between himself and these affairs a distance that will allow, at least, for clarity, so that before he can look forward in any meaningful sense, he must first be allowed to take a long look back. In the context of the Negro problem neither whites nor blacks, for excellent reasons of their own, have the faintest desire to look back; but I think that the past is all that makes the present coherent, and further, that the past will remain horrible for exactly as long as we refuse to assess it honestly.

I know, in any case, that the most crucial time in my own development came when I was forced to recognize that I was a kind of bastard of the West; when I followed the line of my past I did not find myself in Europe but in Africa. And this meant that in some subtle way, in a really profound way, I brought to Shakespeare, Bach, Rembrandt, to the stones of Paris, to the cathedral at Chartres, and to the Empire State Building, a special attitude. These were not really my creations, they did not contain my history; I might search in them in vain forever for any reflection of myself. I was an interloper; this was not my heritage. At the same time I had no other heritage which I could possibly hope to use—I had certainly been unfitted for the jungle or the tribe. I would have to appropriate these white centuries, I would have to make them mine—I would have to accept my special attitude, my special place in this scheme—otherwise I would have no place in *any* scheme. What was the most difficult was the fact that I was forced to admit something I had always hidden from myself, which the American Negro has had to hide from himself as the price of his public

---

[1] In Shakespeare's *The Tempest,* the monster Caliban is a servant of the magician Prospero.

progress; that I hated and feared white people. This did not mean that I loved black people; on the contrary, I despised them, possibly because they failed to produce Rembrandt. In effect, I hated and feared the world. And this meant, not only that I thus gave the world an altogether murderous power over me, but also that in such a self-destroying limbo I could never hope to write.

One writes out of one thing only—one's own experience. Everything depends on how relentlessly one forces from this experience the last drop, sweet or bitter, it can possibly give. This is the only real concern of the artist, to recreate out of the disorder of life that order which is art. The difficulty then, for me, of being a Negro writer was the fact that I was, in effect, prohibited from examining my own experience too closely by the tremendous demands and the very real dangers of my social situation.

I don't think the dilemma outlined above is uncommon. I do think, since writers work in the disastrously explicit medium of language, that it goes a little way towards explaining why, out of the enormous resources of Negro speech and life, and despite the example of Negro music, prose written by Negroes has been generally speaking so pallid and so harsh. I have not written about being a Negro at such length because I expect that to be my only subject, but only because it was the gate I had to unlock before I could hope to write about anything else. I don't think that the Negro problem in America can be even discussed coherently without bearing in mind its context; its context being the history, traditions, customs, the moral assumptions and preoccupations of the country; in short, the general social fabric. Appearances to the contrary, no one in America escapes its effects and everyone in America bears some responsibility for it. I believe this the more firmly because it is the overwhelming tendency to speak of this problem as though it were a thing apart. But in the work of Faulkner, in the general attitude and certain specific passages in Robert Penn Warren, and, most significantly, in the advent of Ralph Ellison, one sees the beginnings—at least—of a more genuinely penetrating search. Mr. Ellison, by the way, is the first Negro novelist I have ever read to utilize in language, and brilliantly, some of the ambiguity and irony of Negro life.

About my interests: I don't know if I have any, unless the morbid desire to own a sixteen-millimeter camera and make experimental movies can be so classified. Otherwise, I love to eat and drink—it's my melancholy conviction that I've scarcely ever had enough to eat (this is because it's *impossible* to eat enough if you're worried about the next meal)—and I love to argue with people who do not disagree with me too profoundly, and I love to laugh. I do *not* like bohemia, or bohemians, I do not like people whose principal aim is pleasure, and I do not like people who are *earnest* about anything. I don't like people who like me because I'm a Negro; neither do I like people who find in the same accident grounds for contempt. I love America more than any other country in the world, and, exactly for this reason, I insist on the right to criticize her perpetually. I think all theories are suspect, that the finest principles may have to be modified, or may even be pulverized by the demands of life, and that one must find, therefore, one's own moral center and move through the world hoping that this center will guide one aright. I consider that I have many responsibilities, but none greater than this: to last, as Hemingway says, and get my work done.

I want to be an honest man and a good writer. [1955]

JOHN BARTH

John Barth published his lecture "It's a Short Story," analyzing why he decided to write short fiction, in Further Fridays: Essays, Lectures, and Other Nonfiction 1984–94 *(1995). In a prefatory paragraph he described the origin of his talk, written for the Second International Conference on the Short Story in Iowa and first published in the* Mississippi Review *in 1993.*

It's a Short Story

My high regard for the short story—the literary genre codified by Edgar Poe and purified by the likes of Maupassant and Chekhov—is longstanding and ongoing, but our actual love affair was brief. An early-middlescent fling is all it was, really, in the tumultuous 1960s, when the form was a-hundred-and-thirtysomething and pretty well domesticated, but I was thirty-plus and restless. An unprecedented (and unsuccedented) infidelity, it was, to my true love and helpmeet, the novel—whereto my steadfast commitment had produced four robust offspring already by the time I tell of, and has produced another four since, and bids to produce at least one more yet.[1] For a season, however (a maxi-novelist's season: about six years), I strayed. It was a sweet and productive *liaison dangereuse,* the fruits of which were one volume of short stories in 1968 and a trio of novellas in 1972: resonant dates (the first especially) in our nation's political-cultural history, with a special poignancy in my personal scriptorial history.

One notes in what terms I recollect that interlude, no doubt pumping up the recollection a bit in its retelling. That is because I am by temperament monogamous; it was a relief to put that memorable aberration behind me and come back to husbanding the genre of the novel. And I have gone straight ever since—twenty years clean now! Though I still remember . . .

---

[1]This it has duly done, in the interval since delivery of this address. Furthermore, muse willing, *Once Upon a Time* (1994) may not be its author's last novelistic words. [All notes are Barth's.]

Well: It *is* a short story, even though it commences with a digression. I shall retell it discreetly, as such stories should be told. I'll even drop the sexual metaphor: *Auf Wiedersehen,* sexual metaphor.

The story goes, no doubt apocryphally, that in 1872, just after *War and Peace* had been published, Count Leo Tolstoy woke from a nightmare crying "A yacht race! A yacht race!" (in Russian, it goes something like *"Párusnaya regátta!"*), dismayed that he had neglected to include that item in his vast novel: his only omission from the whole panorama of nineteenth-century human activity.[2]

Whatever the truth of the story, it certainly sounds to me like the bad dream of a novelist, not a short-story writer. That the genre of the novel tends toward inclusion, that of the short story toward exclusion, goes without saying, once one has allowed for plenty of exceptional instances on both sides — minimalist novels, maximalist not-so-short stories. Those exceptions granted, we may safely generalize that short-story writers as a class, from Poe to Paley, incline to see how much they can leave out, and novelists as a class, from Petronius to Pynchon, how much they can leave in. Many a fictionist of the last century and this has moved with apparent ease between the modes, not only at some point in her or his career, but right through it: Joyce Carol Oates, John Updike, who have you. Plenty more work the short form abundantly in the earlier part of their careers and then, for one reason or another, practice it seldom or never thereafter: James Joyce, Ernest Hemingway, William Faulkner, Kurt Vonnegut — the list is long. Do we know of any writers, I wonder, who abandoned the novel form in mid or late career and devoted their literary energies exclusively thereafter to the short story?

In any case, more populous than any of those three categories are the categories (*a*) of congenital short-story writers who seldom, perhaps never, publish a novel (Chekhov, Borges, Alice Munro, Raymond Carver) and (*b*) of congenital novelists who never or seldom publish a short story (Ralph Ellison, William Styron, most of the big Victorians, not to mention Richardson, Fielding, Smollett, Jane Austen, and the other pre-Poe novelists — this category is the most populous of all). It seems reasonable to infer that despite numerous exceptions, by and large there is a temperamental, even a metabolical, difference between devout practitioners of the two modes, as between sprinters and marathoners. To such dispositions as Poe's, Maupassant's, Chekhov's, or Donald Barthelme's, the prospect of addressing a single, discrete narrative project for three, four, five years (perhaps seventeen or twenty-two), would be appalling — *atrocious*, I

---

[2]For that reason, I made certain to incorporate in one of my own novels both a yacht race and this Tolstoy anecdote, so that when unfriendly critics charge me with insufficient social realism, I can reply that I have touched bases overlooked even by Tolstoy.

imagine, would have been Borges's adjective—not to mention aesthetically unseemly, perhaps presumptuous, at this advanced hour of the print medium. Such novels as such writers perpetrate, if any—I think of Barthelme's four, of Maupassant's four also, I believe—are slender, economical: They are the hors d'oeuvres or side dishes, paradoxically, to the chef d'oeuvre of their short stories. Knowing that Donald's novels did not come to him as naturally as his short stories, I once very tentatively asked him, in the period of his wrestling with *The Dead Father,* how that project was coming along. "Oh, it's finished," he replied. "Now all I have to do is *write* the damn thing."

Conversely, to many of us the prospect of inventing every few weeks a whole new ground-conceit, situation, cast of characters, plot, perhaps even voice, is as dismaying as would be the prospect of improvising at that same interval a whole new identity. Indeed, for some of us that analogy is so rigorous as to be more an identity itself than an analogy. Like hermit crabs (up to a point), we comfortably *live* in the shell of our project-in-progress, and do not shed it until we must, and feel naked and uncomfortable until we've found another to inhabit. Once every few years is quite often enough for that.

I say "we," because except for the six-year lapse aforecited I am willy-nilly of the camp of the congenital novelists. This circumstance is nowise an aesthetic principle (congenitality doesn't operate by aesthetic principle; it cobbles up a suitable aesthetics ex post facto); it's a metabolical donnée. I didn't plan or presuppose it; congenitality doesn't make such plans and presuppositions. Like everybody else in post–World War II America, I started out writing short stories in an entry-level creative-writing workshop. More particularly, I happened to stumble into virtual charter membership in the second oldest creative-writing program in our republic, although not the second oldest creative-writing *course*. This was 1947; the Johns Hopkins program had been established just the year before, and the only other such operation in existence then (so we at Hopkins believe, anyhow) was Paul Engle's out in Iowa, already by that time of some dozen years' standing. Up at Harvard, Albert Guerard was coaching the likes of John Hawkes and Robert Creeley, but his was an isolated workshop, not a degree-granting program—of which we now have, god help us, above four hundred in the USA.

The poetry workshops at Johns Hopkins in those maiden years were respectably professional, presided over by Elliott Coleman and Karl Shapiro (who had just won a Pulitzer Prize for *V-Letter and Other Poems*), with the distinguished Spanish poet Pedro Salinas standing by in a neighboring department. But the fiction operation was unavoidably makeshift; one would have had to look far to find a career fiction-writer of any stature employed by an American university in the 1940s.[3]

---

[3]Robert Penn Warren is about the only name that comes to mind—and Warren was one-third poet and one-third critic.

I myself had signed up as a journalism major, an even more makeshift curriculum—although it doesn't seem to have damaged Russell Baker, who was one year ahead of me. Our journalistic requirements, interestingly, included the entry-level fiction-writing course, and so it came to pass that my first creative-writing coach was a veteran Marine Corps combat officer and fledgling literary scholar pressed into service by our shorthanded department while he finished his dissertation on Edgar Poe. The departmental reasoning must have been that inasmuch as Poe first defined the modern short story, a Poe scholar could run the workshop.

I have written of this chap elsewhere: a gentle Southerner who encouraged us raw recruits to call him Bob; whose deep-Dixie accent charmed *writing* into *rotting;* who urged upon our attention such exemplary rotters as William Faulkner, Eudora Welty, and R. P. Warren (one discerns Bob's principle of selection); who, because he had no creative-rotting aspirations himself, was oddly respectful, even a touch deferential, to those of us who callowly so presumed. Bob's seminar—we seem not to call them *workshops* at Johns Hopkins—was a whole academic year long and could be repeated for credit, as the department had not many course offerings in those days. His gentle requirement of apprentice aspirants to the craft of rotting fiction was a story every two weeks—and these, mind you, were the bygone days of honest fifteen-week semesters, before the campus riots of the 1960s frightened administrators into shortening the U.S. college semester to thirteen weeks, a whole storysworth of time (*two* storiesworth per academic year; *four* storiesworth over two years). So: Fifteen weeks times two times two divided by two gives thirty stories minimum that I must have written for Bob in my first two years' apprenticeship. Nowadays the number would be a piddling twenty-six, if any workshop in the land still requires a story every fortnight, no excuses or late papers accepted. Bob was gentle; Bob was respectful and soft-spoken; but Bob was a veteran Marine combat officer, whose deadlines one tended not to diddle with.

It is well for me that all this was the case, for I had been ill-educated in general, had next to no familiarity with the vast corpus of literature and no prior experience of or interest in the art of writing fiction. I was a disappointed musician, a Juilliard dropout scrabbling around for some other vocation, and I had squandered my high-school reading budget mainly on the likes of Ellery Queen and Agatha Christie in mass-market paperbacks, which had just been invented. What I turned out for Bob and my fellow novices in those two years was unrelievedly abysmal in every particular except grammar, spelling, and punctuation, at all of which I was reasonably competent. Those manuscripts were letter-graded: Mine scored C's, mainly; the odd D, the occasional B, for two full years, and this from the most considerate of coaches—who, however, had his standards. It was rotten rotting, altogether talentless twaddle, for although I was in that same period taking unto myself a freight of literature—not just the canonical classics plus Bob's Southerners plus the monumental European and expatriate American High Modernists, Pound/Eliot/Joyce/Proust/Mann/

Kafka (whom the literature departments back then wouldn't touch, but our
maverick writing department did), but also, and extracurricularly, the likes of
Rabelais and Boccaccio and Scheherazade and Somadeva—although, as I
say, I was onloading the literary corpus in straight shifts, it was going unsystematically into an all-but-empty cargo hold, and so it took some stevedor-
ing indeed before the vessel ballasted into even rudimentary stability.

But that is not what this present story means to be about. I don't
want, either, to give the impression that *literature* is the main thing one
needs to learn about if one aspires to write it, although I certainly do
believe it to be *one* of the main things. I can't help wondering, though,
how it would have gone with my apprenticeship if semesters in those days
had been of their present abbreviation, for it was not until story number
thirty—more particularly, it was not until the *closing passage* of that final
item of my two-year stretch of random Bobbing on the ocean of story—
that I had what amounted, by my then standards, to a "breakthrough."
Number Thirty itself was little better than its twenty-nine predecessors: a
presumptuous bit of bogus realism about the postwar adjustment problems
of . . . *a Marine combat veteran,* of all imaginable human categories—the
whole thing largely derivative from Hemingway's "Soldier's Home" without Hemingway's authentic knowledge of his material, not to mention
Hemingway's literary skills. But the story's denouement contrived to soar
from wretchedness up to mediocrity with a most un-Hemingwayish purple
stream-of-consciousness passage that, while also bogus, derivative, and
overwritten to boot, was nonetheless not without a certain rhetorical
force. It was duly praised therefor by Bob and my fellow seminarians, and
published in an ephemeral undergraduate lit mag—tautological adjectives, I suppose.

It took no more than that to persuade me of my vocation, although by
no means yet of my talent for that vocation. Still a junior undergraduate,
two years shy of voting age, I immediately married the woman I was living
with and commenced churning out children and fiction with equal facility
and no thought for the morrow. "The Fifties," John Updike somewhere
says with a sigh, "when everybody was pregnant." The babies survived and
thrived; the short stories (for that is what I was writing: stories, stories, stories) suffered a 100 percent infant mortality rate. Their constituent prose
sentences, it may be, slowly improved in grace and efficiency; the case
could scarcely be otherwise, given the number of them that I was generat-
ing and the stacks of good literature—literal library stacks of it—that I
was unsystematically running through. But my plots were gimmicky and
my characterizations inauthentic; my psychological penetration was barely
subcutaneous and my texture of rendered sensory detail unimpressive.
Moreover, like many another American undergraduate writing apprentice,
I had not anything to say nor, had I had, any Weltanschauung to afford me
a handle on it. (Which of those two is logically prior doesn't matter here;
to paraphrase Beckett, having neither chicken nor egg, I had neither egg nor

chicken.) What I did have were an all but reality-proof sense of calling, an unstoppable narrativity, and, I believe, a not-bad ear for English. I have coached many an apprentice since who manifested something like that mix of strengths and shortcomings, and relatively few of the opposite sort: young aspiring writers with a strong sense of who they are and what their material and their handle on it is, but little sense of either story or language. I regard that latter case as by far the less promising, although I would be reluctant to tell the patient so. Experience may confer narrative focus and authority, perhaps even a worldview; but essential imaginativeness and articulateness, not to say eloquence, are surely much more of a gift.

My other problem — as I came to understand in retrospect but could not then, nor could any just routinely knowledgeable coach have told me — was the *form* that we all were working, and that nearly every fiction-workshopper cuts his/her teeth on, with good pedagogical reason: I mean the form of the modern, post-Poe short story. Its aesthetics were simply not my cup of tea, but in those days (and in many more fiction workshops than not to *this* day) it was the only aesthetic on the menu. *Compression,* it turns out, was not my strong suit. *Showing instead of telling* was not my strong suit; neither were implicativeness, singleness of effect, epiphanic peripety, psychological realism, or for that matter realism in general. But those suits were regarded almost unquestioningly as the indispensable, indeed the only ones for a properly modern writer, which I certainly aspired to be. It would have taken an extraordinarily large-viewed coach in the American academic 1940s to have seen that a subtle and inhibitory conflation was operating there, of the terms *modern* and *Modernist.* What a few of us really needed to do (I see now but could scarcely have seen then) was to invent or be invented by Postmodernism, as I understand that term in its best literary-aesthetic application — but that's another story, to which I'll presently return.

Meanwhile, back in the seminar room, there one was, fretting away at that artistically splendid and pedagogically effective but, for some of us, hyperconstrictive, more or less constipative form, the modern short story. Surely it's a truism by now that the admirable efflorescence of the American short story in recent decades is owing to the proliferation of our college creative-writing programs: not simply the raw number of young writers being spawned therein like blue-crab larvae in Chesapeake Bay (and confronting a similar statistical fate), but the prevailing pedagogical assumption, anyhow belief, that the most suitable vehicle for their training is the "classical" modern short story as afore-described.

Understand, please, that I have no serious quarrel with that prevailing belief; indeed, I rather share it. Novels, to name one alternative vehicle, are more cumbersome and time-intensive to deal with in fiction workshops — more cumbersome to write in timely installments, more cumbersome to revise, to reproduce, to read, to critique, to respond to useful criticism of. The academic year runs out before the dramaturgical bills have been paid; or a whole season of apprenticeship gets invested in what at best is likely to be a single narrative conceit, voice, point of view, cast of characters, and plot, and what at worst may prove to have been a large mistake, without coaching-time left to try something else. A conventional short story, on the other hand, we can hold in the mind's eye of the seminar; in the allotted hour or so we can attend with some critical efficiency both to representative details and to overall matters of pace and plot and narrative viewpoint. What's more, as the season wears on we can come to know the author's *characteristic* strengths and weaknesses and idiosyncrasies of imagination, and can assess a new effort in the light of its predecessors, a sort of mini-*oeuvre*. These are undeniable pedagogical assets. The associated aesthetic values, too—compression, implicativeness, rendition as against mere assertion, precise observation, subtlety of effect—are undeniable literary values (though not the only ones); undeniable especially for apprentices, most of whom will not in fact turn out to be working fiction-writers, but a fair fraction of whom will turn out to be teachers, editors, writers of other sorts of documents, and—the chief and worthy product of those four hundred-plus U.S. creative-writing programs—*readers,* more sensitive and knowledgeable in the art of reading literature than they would likely be if they hadn't practiced writing it.

I assert again, however, that those literary values are not the only ones. In the very best workshops (and by definition there can never be a great many of those), the pedagogical virtues of the conventional modern short story will not be conflated with its aesthetic values, and its aesthetic values will not be assumed to hold for all times, places, temperaments, and talents. There is a narrative metabolism, equally honorable and with at least as long a pedigree, that valorizes expansiveness, even extravagance, complication, non-linearity, even telling instead of showing (telling, after all, is one of the things that language can do better than a camera), and perhaps fabulation or some other admixture of irrealism over unadulterated realism. Such a narrative metabolism may find the now-classical short-story form claustrophobic: Rabelais and Laurence Sterne oughtn't to have to walk in Maupassant's moccasins, or Scheherazade in Chekhov's, and vice versa.

When I first set about, at age twenty, to write a novel, I approached the prospect with all due trepidation. It seemed a presumptuous undertaking, as indeed it was, in a number of ways. True, Thomas Mann had been only twenty when he wrote *Buddenbrooks*—but Mann at twenty was forty already, and what's more, he was Thomas Mann. I went ahead and perpetrated my maiden novel, and it was an unpublishable travesty—turgid tidewater ersatz Faulkner, without Faulkner's moral-historical vision and deep acquaintance with his subject—but I felt immediately at home in the form, as if my hands and feet had been unshackled. "The novel, the novel!" I exulted to myself at the time: "Room to swing a cat in!" "The novel, the

novel," I exulted in some novel many novels later,[4] "with its great galumph-
ing grace, amazing as a whale!" I doubted that I would ever go back to the
short story.

And by puristic standards, I never quite did. My very next apprentice
project (the last, in fact, of my apprenticeship) involved short fictions
again, but with at least two differences from my earlier Bob-Bob-Bobbing
that it pleases me to find significant in retrospect. Having imbibed Boccaccio and Scheherazade and company along with the big Modernists, what I
projected was a cycle of one hundred tales about my native tidewater
county—my salt-marsh Yoknapatawpha—at all periods of its history, but
not in chronological order. In other words, the thing was to be a *book,* a
narrative whole like the *Decameron,* larger than the sum of its parts, not
every one of which would need to be free-standing; and those parts, many
of them anyhow, would be in the nature of *tales* or even anecdotes, not
post-Poe short stories. They would *tell,* here and there, instead of showing: *He was a jealous and miserly old oysterman; she was a wanton young
crab-picker*—whatever. They would ramble and digress; they would
deploy narrative effects from the eighteenth and earlier centuries, tongue
half in cheek and one foot always in the here and now.

This project, too, was a failure (I aborted it round about tale fifty), but
it proved a valuable learning experience, as they say, and in the event I was
able to recycle a number of those *Dorchester Tales* into *The Sot-Weed Factor,* three novels later. What I had in place, although I didn't know it yet
(this was the front end of the 1950s), were some of the field-identification
marks that I now associate with Postmodernist art, at least by my definition: notably, the ironized recycling of premodern forms and devices for
modern readers with uppercase Modernism under their belts.

There is, of course, more to the making of fiction than a geographical
predilection and the deployment of forms and devices, ironized or otherwise. There is, e.g., the little matter of what one aspires to narrate by
means of those predilections and forms and devices. Once the material,
the craftsmanly means, and the aesthetic objective have somehow recipro-
cally clarified one another and jiggered themselves into synergy, with luck
a career of "professional" literary production may ensue. In my fortunate
case, once I had discovered by trial, error, and serendipity my narrative
space and pace, I was not of a mind to do other than vigorously continue
exploring it for a couple thousand pagesworth of novels over the next
dozen years: short novels, midsize novels, long novels, but novels all. Now
that I was not committed to and therefore not straitjacketed by the short
story, I was free to admire it uncovetously and its masters unenviously.
This I did, and taught their works with respectful pleasure to my literature
students and the form with profit to my fiction-writing coachees—until

---

[4]*LETTERS,* first published by Putnam in 1979.

the High 1960s, when three or four factors together led me to give short-storyhood another go.

I happened through the latter Sixties to be living and working in Buffalo, New York, and while many young Americans were crossing the Niagara River from that city into Canada for sanctuary from our war in Vietnam (as Americans had done in numerous of our other wars, long before there was a Peace Bridge to facilitate the crossing), there came back across that bridge, from nearby Toronto, the siren song of Marshall McLuhan advising us "print-oriented bastards" that our Gutenberg Galaxy was not only not the whole universe, but a galaxy perhaps petering out in the electronic global village. Self-bound to the medium of the book like Odysseus to the mast of his vessel, I attended this song with the same constrained fascination that I lately bring to Robert Coover's and George P. Landow's serenades to the medium of hypertext:[5] About Hypertexties in the Nineties, as about Death-of-the-Bookies in the Sixties, I think and thought, "Maybe they're right, maybe they're wrong, maybe some of each; but most important, maybe there's something here that a writer can make good use of."

I had, as it happened, just published my fourth novel, and the latter pair of those four were baggy monsters indeed: *The Sot-Weed Factor* and *Giles Goat-Boy*. The notion of re-attempting brevity, perhaps even terseness, was understandably seductive. Moreover, I had discovered and been duly wowed by the *ficciones* of Jorge Luis Borges, who certainly made maximalist novels seem *demasiado* at that hour of the world. Finally and less creditably (as I have acknowledged in the foreword to the current American edition of *Lost in the Funhouse*), I had by the 1960s been teaching long enough to notice that we congenital novelists do not normally find ourselves included, for obvious reasons, in the standard short-story anthologies on which I had cut my own apprentice teeth and which I regularly assigned to the teething apprentices in my charge. (William Styron, for example, wasn't in those anthologies, either; he doesn't teach school, however, and so perhaps was less aware of his exclusion.) But there were Donald Barthelme and Flannery O'Connor and Grace Paley and John Updike and Eudora Welty, not to mention their illustrious predecessors back to Poe and Hawthorne. Along with the more creditable attractions of the short form was admission to that distinguished club, which I unabashedly hankered after. Even today, I confess, when a new anthology comes across my desk, I look first to see how my stock is doing. If I'm included, I check out my new, younger shipmates with benign interest (aha, Graham Swift; aha, Jane Smiley; ahoy there, Julian Barnes); but if the turkeys leave me

---

[5]See for example Landow's *Hypertext: The Convergence of Contemporary Critical Theory and Technology* (Baltimore and London: Johns Hopkins U. Press, 1992) and Coover's pioneering reports, "The End of Books" and "Hyperfiction: Novels for the Computer," in the *New York Times Book Review* of June 21, 1992, and August 29, 1993, respectively.

out, I toss the thing—unless, as has increasingly become the case, former coachees of mine are represented there, supplanting their erstwhile mentor. Pleasant pain.

Anyhow, for all these reasons I embraced at last the sharp-eyed, relaxless muse of the short story, who, unlike good longwinded Homer, *never* dozes off, even for a second. Just as wary Odysseus, when romancing formidable Circe, covered his butt (let's say) with a sprig of moly, so I put an anchor out to windward by writing a short-story *series*—a book, a book, "for print, tape, and live voice"—in order not to get lost in my own funhouse, excuse the hybrid metaphor. I decided to pay my initiation fee by writing the shortest story in the whole corpus of literature, which however would at the same time be literally endless and a paradigm for the book to boot: a ten-word Möbius-strip narrative called "Frame-Tale" (*ONCE UPON A TIME THERE WAS A STORY THAT BEGAN,* etc. ad inf.). Short on characters, short on plot, short on social realism—but short is the name of the game, no?

That done, I spent an invigorating couple of years fabricating tales to be framed by that frame-tale, enjoying most the longest and most intricate of them, for that is who I am, but attempting here and there as bona fide an old-fashioned modern short story as I could contrive for future anthologists, and where possible looking to see what other marks I might set in my private Guinness Book of World Literary Records. Some years of casual homework on frame-tale literature, for example, had revealed to me that the maximum degree of narrative imbeddedness in the corpus of such literature was about the fifth degree—a tale within a tale within a tale within a tale within a tale—and that the relations among such nested tales was generally at best thematic, seldom functionally dramaturgical. Purely *pour le sport,* therefore, I went for seven degrees (in a story called "Menelaiad"), and saw to it moreover that their concentric plots were rigged for sequential climax-triggering from the inmost out. I hasten to add, however, that Menelaus's story is about love, not about plot-mechanics, for I was in love (love, love, love, love, love, love) with the short story.

And after the short story, with the novella—that sweet, that delicious narrative space, so much neglected in our century. I do hope that there'll be an international conference someday on the novella and that I won't be too superannuated to attend, for there's another love story altogether. Meanwhile, two cheers minimum for the exhausting muse of the short story—exhausting anyhow to us congenital novelists, who are likely to leave her embraces in the condition of Peleus after Thetis's, or Anchises after Venus's.[6] I romanced the novella form for three or four years in the

---

[6]One notices, however, that those old studs aren't complaining in their wheelchairs—and that the issue of their life-altering one-nighters was Achilles, was Aeneas.

same sidelong and tracks-covering but truly heartfelt way as I had romanced the short-story form, pretending that my trinity of more or less linked novellas was really a unity—a book, a book, a book—and even allowing my publisher to market that book (*Chimera*) without any indication whatever on jacket or title page that it's not a novel. This was, after all, exactly twenty years ago, just before the wholesale resurgence of the American short story, when the conventional wisdom among New York trade publishers was that volumes of short fiction don't earn their keep. And the original Chimera, we remember, was neither a menagerie nor a congeries nor a colonial organism, but a tripartite, fire-breathing, single-spirited entity, however genetically self-disparate and, well, chimerical.

Then on Yom Kippur 1973, as you may have noticed, the American Sixties ended. Overnight, women's skirts got longer and men's sideburns shorter; the national economy simultaneously recessed and inflated, and in the general reaction against the 1960s, American fiction swung back to its prevailing aesthetic conservatism and for better or worse has pretty much dwelt there to this hour; nor does it show much sign that I can see of venturing therefrom. At this state of affairs, I shrug my shoulders: Traditionalist excellence is no doubt preferable to innovative mediocrity (but there's not much to be said for conservative mediocrity, and there's a great deal to be said for inspired innovation). This particular congenital novelist went contentedly—nay, happily—back to congenital novelizing; I even made a working rapprochement with social/psychological realism, though not enough of one, evidently, to mollify certain critics.

Ah well, *mes amis, je ne regrette rien*, certainly not my invigorating liaisons with those slender, demanding forms, the short story and the novella. Single-shot dalliances, in their way, but each a novelist's single shot, of several years' concentrated, undivided commitment: quality time. I remain profoundly, satisfyingly wedded to the space of the novel, most particularly the longish-haul novel. Every four years or so, however, when a new one slides down the ways to whatever post-launch fate awaits it, I confess to resolving that I will have one more go, this many decades later and this late in the afternoon, at the perennially beautiful possibilities of the short story. At this hour of our cultural history, I ask myself, who needs another large novel—not to say, more particularly, another hefty *Barth-buch*? In no time at all I accumulate project-notes toward that end—notes not for a story, never for a story, but for a *book* of stories, a book, a book. Next thing I know, the frame has subsumed the picture, the book its constituent stories, and what I'm writing is no longer a book of stories but another book-length story. That mode remains as fitted to my spirit as Homer says Penelope was to Odysseus's, and vice versa. To that question aforeproposed—Who needs another et cetera?—I sigh and reply, "*I* do."

Or rather (as bridegroom says to bride), "I *do*."   [1993]

H. E. BATES

H. E. Bates, the great English short story writer and literary critic, included his analysis of how Ernest Hemingway revolutionized American narrative style in The Modern Short Story (1942).

Hemingway's Short Stories

In *Winesburg, Ohio,* Sherwood Anderson saw his characters thoughtfully, with bemused detachment, with a certain melancholy heaviness behind which glowed a constant kindliness of heart. Undetained and unguided by him, these people moved past the office windows of the young reporter, up and down the hard Chicago streets, through lives that led "out of nowhere into nothing." Anderson set down what he saw and felt about them with a kind of tender bewilderment, as if he were really as troubled by their negation and stupidity and colorless frustration as they were, in a style handled with apparent casualness, offhand, so that its charm arose from what seemed to be a studied stylelessness.

Both the rewards and the dangers of this method are obvious. By a public instructed largely in a literature where characters were stereotyped as good or bad, and the physical processes of life, and especially love, were rendered by means of a patent formula, Anderson was of course branded as immoral. This was natural, and is now irrelevant. The real danger of Anderson's method was that it lay wide open to parody, which Anderson himself accomplished to some extent in *Dark Laughter,* unintentionally, of course, and which Hemingway completed in *Torrents of Spring.* This too, I think, does not matter. In Anderson there is a weakness arising from a certain lack of self-censorship. He lacks the austerity that would prevent him from reveling in the luxury of an emotion. But it does not and cannot detract from the inspirational force of Anderson's example to the short story of his day. *Winesburg, Ohio,* is the first directional signpost of the contemporary American short story, directing the writer to turn inward to the job of establishing, out of indigenous American material, a new American tradition.

The ultimate effect of Anderson's pioneering example was a release of energy that was to have, during the next fifteen or twenty years, immense creative results. The immediate effect was its influence on Ernest Hemingway: for if Anderson stopped creating stories by the old facile methods of stereotyping, Hemingway broke up every known type face with which the American short story had ever been set, and cut for it a more austere, revolutionary, and yet more classic design than it had ever known. In doing so

Hemingway brought down a hammer on all writing done to a fancy design; he stripped of its impossible periodic splendor that style of writing which reaches its limits in the intricacies of Henry James; he sheared away the literary woolliness of English as no one had ever done before.

Like Anderson, Hemingway began publishing obscurely, during the private-press vogue of the early twenties, and some of his stories appeared privately in Paris, where it is obvious that he came under the influence of Gertrude Stein. Somewhere between Stein and Anderson, however, there was a middle course, and Hemingway took it. Hemingway had sense enough to see that it might be a million years before there was a public initiated enough to read its fiction in the bony theoretical rhythms offered by Miss Stein. You cannot feed a public on fancy literary theorems, and Hemingway, who had plenty to say, wanted a public. He took the Stein method, which at its most aggravated seemed to have some appeal to mental deficiency, and, as it were, put sanity into it. For every person who read Stein, pretending to understand it whether he did or not, a potential million could read Hemingway.

His first story, "Up in Michigan," was written in Paris in 1921, and as far as I know there is no record that it caused a sensation. It was collected, together with another fifteen stories, into the volume *In Our Time,* and again I know of no record that a revolution was caused. Yet a revolution had been caused, and in these stories, less good and less famous than the contents of *Men Without Women* though they are, the Hemingway method is already in conscious and advanced production.

What is that method? Why did it cause a revolution? In the first place Hemingway was a man with an ax. For generations—it might almost be said for a hundred years or more—written English had been growing steadily more pompous, more prolix, more impossibly parochial; its continuous tendency had been towards discussing and explaining something rather than projecting and painting an object. It carried a vast burden of words which were not doing a job, and it was time, at last, to cut those words away. In the nineties Samuel Butler too had arrived with an ax, but it was an ax less against English writing than against English morality, and Butler had never dramatized the conflict except in a single book. Hemingway, looking back over what still purports to be the great age of the English novel, must have been struck by an interesting fact, of which there are most notable examples in Hardy. He must have been struck by the fact that out of the cavernous gloom of explanations, discussions, social dilemmas, and philosophizings all that emerged of permanent interest and value were the scattered bright scraps of pictorial narrative. In one generation the philosophy had grown moldy, the social dilemmas were forgotten for others, the moral currency had been changed. But the people, the narrative action, the color of scenes, remained, and could, if properly conceived and painted, never fade. So what one remembers out of Hardy, for example, is not the philosophic vaporings or the spiritual anguish, all impossibly unreal today, but the sharp bright scenes that have been painted by a man with his eye on the object—the pigsticking in *Jude,* Tess working in the winter turnip field, Tess praying with the children, the man selling his wife in *The Mayor of Casterbridge*. No changing currency of social and moral action changes these; nothing can come between them and countless generations of readers.

What Hemingway went for was that direct pictorial contact between eye and object, between object and reader. To get it he cut out a whole forest of verbosity. He got back to clean fundamental growth. He trimmed off explanation, discussion, even comment; he hacked off all metaphorical floweriness; he pruned off the dead, sacred clichés; until finally, through the sparse trained words, there was a view.

> The road of the pass was hard and smooth and not yet dusty in the early morning. Below were the hills with oak and chestnut trees, and far away below was the sea. On the other side were snowy mountains.

The picture is complete. And again:

> The hills across the valley of the Ebro were long and white. On this side there was no shade and no trees and the station was between two lines of rails in the sun. Close against the side of the station there was the warm shadow of the building and a curtain, made of strings of bamboo beads, hung across the open door into the bar, to keep out flies.

And here is a portrait, with background, complete:

> An old man with steel-rimmed spectacles and very rusty clothes sat by the side of the road. There was a pontoon bridge across the river and carts, trucks, and men, women and children were crossing it. The mule-drawn carts staggered up the steep bank from the bridge with soldiers helping push against the spokes of the wheels. The trucks ground up and away heading out of it all and the peasants plodded along in the ankle-deep dust. But the old man sat there without moving. He was too tired to go any farther.

The pictures projected are as natural as life. There are no attempts at falsification, no superimposed colors, no rose glasses, no metaphors. Everything that could cloud or date the scene has been ruthlessly rejected. Examine by contrast:

> No sooner did the rays of the rising sun shine on the dew, and fall in little fiery tongues upon their eyelids, than instinct made them strike camp and move away. All day they would journey, until the setting sun made the air to glow like a damp fire, burning the eyes while it chilled the body. The moon, like a disc of copper, hung behind them and the plain seemed dead.[1]

---

[1]A passage from *The Gothick North* by English author Sir Sacheverell Sitwell (1897–1988).

Here the effort to influence the reader is strenuous. Hemingway in effect says: "Here is the picture. That's all. Keep your eye on it"; and is prepared to trust the reader to absorb the proper impression. But Mr. Sitwell cannot trust the reader. The light must be changed, trick-focused, dimmed or raised for a series of effects. Each sentence has its metaphor; each metaphor is supported by some poetic archaism—"upon," "made the air to glow," "than instinct made them." The result is a decorative backcloth, looking real enough until the wind stirs it, and then suddenly ludicrous— what a Hemingway character would rightly call phony.

But Hemingway carried this purge of style beyond mere description. For a century the novel had staggered along under the weight of a colossal convention of fancy mechanics in the matter of dialogue. The novel had managed somehow to survive it; the short story had been in constant danger of collapsing. In this convention the words of a character had their intonation, flavor, emotion, or meaning underlined by the writer. Thus: "he reiterated with a manifest show of anger"; "she ventured to remark with a melancholy intonation in her voice"; "he declared haltingly"; "he stammered out in frightened accents"; "he interposed"; "he interjected with a low laugh," and so on and so on. Wads of this verbal padding bolstered up the conversation of every novel from Dickens down to the fourpenny paperback.

Hemingway swept every letter of that convention away. In its place he put nothing but his own ability to imply, by the choice, association, and order of the words, whether a character was feeling and speaking with anger, regret, desperation, tenderness; quickly or slowly; ironically or bitterly. All intonation and emotion lay somewhere in the apparently abrupt and casual arrangement of the words ("I feel fine," she said. "There's nothing wrong with me. I feel fine."), and Hemingway asked nothing except the cooperation of the reader in the job of capturing these intonations and emotions.

[1942]

ANN BEATTIE

*A*nn Beattie *originally published "Where Characters Come From" in the* Mississippi Review. *It was collected in the anthology* The Best Writing on Writing *in 1994.*

Where Characters Come From

I'm often asked whether I'm annoyed by being asked the same questions over and over. Quite often the question is asked by someone who has invited me to read and to answer questions afterwards, or by an interviewer hoping to provoke me. The short form of my answer is always, "No," but usually some qualifications are thrown in. There are questions, for example, I am asked by the press or by teachers of creative writing that I've never been asked by anyone in an audience or in a classroom. There are times when questions are so particular to the questioner that I'm at a disadvantage if I can't find out quickly (by subtle questioning) why they asked. There are a few—but only a few—truly boring questions. Even then, my reaction usually has to do with when in the interviewing process they are asked. If the first question is, "Where were you born?," I sometimes lie.

But there are other often asked questions that I not only don't mind, but that interest me. For example: "Where do your characters come from?" My usual response to that is that they aren't taken from real life and plopped into a story—and that the stories themselves are never a-day-in-the-life versions of things I've actually experienced—or actually experienced that way. Then, depending on how strange the whole process of writing seems to me on that particular day, I add that I don't mistake my life for art, or I say that certain characters can indeed be versions of real people, but that I haven't necessarily met these real people (say, Princess Diana, or Queen Latifah); their secret desires, eccentricities and speech patterns have registered with me from photographs or from items in the tabloids.

In retrospect, I've realized that I've never begun a story because I wanted to reveal something about a character. It's absolutely necessary that I do this, of course, but when I'm working on the first draft, I file that in the back of my mind and proceed to name some hypothetical being who, in my mind, is immediately seen clearly in one respect, standing in a room, or on the beach, or on a lawn. Because I see instantly the character's context—because I understand the visual world surrounding the character—I'm able to know instinctively whether the story is in past or present tense. I pick up ambient sound before I begin to register dialogue (or awkward silence), I squint to see the character's first tiny movements (Oh hell: he smokes), and by then, if I'm lucky, the room in which I write has in effect disappeared, and I'm in the room in which my cigarette smoking man stands. I become a fly on the wall because I don't want to be noticed. My sensibility will inevitably be noticed, but any direct confrontation between myself—because I know myself too well—and the character (or, by this time, characters) could only be counterproductive. Without me there to enact the usual social shuffle (entering with a smile; commenting on the obvious), the character, who may intuit he is being spied on, may be provoked into saying or doing something uncharacteristic, and in those off-moments, of course, people tend to reveal more with their impulsive gestures or their outbursts than they reveal when they are being assiduously observed. My characters, hopefully, are the animated equivalents of out-takes during a portrait shoot. I think of Richard Avedon's portrait of Marilyn Monroe: her eyes closed; an unmistakable aura of sadness surrounding her as she sits picture pretty in her low-cut evening gown. It isn't a definitive photograph, but it's a picture that makes you realize other images must be factored in if you have any interest in getting to the complex truth of the woman. Hereafter, you'll have to superimpose this Marilyn with the better known Marilyn who's reached down to stop her big swirl of skirt from blowing up entirely. And if you retain those polarities, you'll probably be prepared to believe anything you continue to see: Marilyn in a head scarf, golfing; Marilyn with the Kennedy brothers; the fuzzy photograph that recently appeared in a European tabloid that was said to depict Marilyn, naked, face-down in bed, dead.

Where do my characters come from? As quickly as possible, they come into focus as people I both recognize and do not recognize, by which I do *not* mean that a personal friend appears in the story, suddenly dressed in an odd way. But I have to have the same empathetic reaction to the character I would have toward a friend — or toward someone who was going to be a friend; I know, I have noticed, only so much — so the character is likely to be someone who makes me comfortable enough to animate him or her but one who retains enough mystery to make me excitedly uncomfortable about the outcome of his or her life.

Where my characters come from varies from story to story. I think part of the answer is that they come from the same places the people in my life come from: as a small child, I outright invented them; there was a Mr. Mandell, who was going to capture me and put me on a boat to China, whose presence I protested every time the lights went out (My mother said, "Let's get another thought." Where my dialogue comes from — or at least where the really good dialogue comes from — is another story). They come from stories friends tell me about their friends whom I don't know. Sometimes I eventually meet these friends of friends, who inevitably think I'm psychic. They say, "You won't believe this, but the same thing happened to me." They come from what I understand of life by going to the movies and by walking down the street and by befriending new dogs. But this gets too diffuse, I realize. These are the things people say (gesturing in all directions) when they want to suggest they have mastered a great complexity. I could probably make "Where I get my characters from" sound like a mixture of my great common sense, which paradoxically accompanies my (some would say) unsophisticated, or at least self-deprecating, sense of wonder at the world, and the ways of the people therein. I could lie, as I sometimes do about where I was born, and explain their evolution so that it would sound reasonable — meaning, reproducible — because I'm sure people's desire to proceed the same way a published writer proceeds is often the subtext of the "Where do they come from?" question. I could remember to add that I'm somewhat mystical, and that I think some characters have been a sort of cosmic gift. I should also be forthcoming and say that it's often been disquieting, feeling so vulnerable to a character's vicissitudes; they can cause you the same trouble as real life people. Which leads me to the final thing I have to say on the subject of characters.

They've come into my life in the same strange way so many things have. Years ago, when I lived with a bunch of people in Connecticut, we didn't have a key to lock the door in our rented house, so through the years I went back to that house to find, for example, a dead raccoon in the sink with ice cubes dumped over its head (courtesy of the garbage man, who knew one of the people who lived there loved to make road kill stew). One day I encountered the dog catcher eating a sandwich in the kitchen. I don't believe the dog had run away. Another time, after an entire day home alone, I went for the first time into the kitchen and found a young man meditating silently on top of the washing machine. He had hitched from Vermont to Connecticut and gone to the wrong house. I'm married to a man who moved to Charlottesville, VA, for a semester to teach. One month before he left, he caved in to pressure from an acquaintance in New York and called me, having found the one expired phone book that printed my unlisted number. My friends are—to make quick sense of them—"diverse." Some appear months later than expected, hauling caravans of trucks pulling trailers that contain two dogs, four cats, two birds, and a much nose-and-ear-pierced daughter, and getting to Maine just in time to have the whole road show sink in the field across from our house during a summer hurricane. For the eccentrics, I don't have to look far. But if I'm amused in real life, why bother to recast people in fiction? It's the less excessive friends who more often appear, standing in the room holding the cigarette they don't smoke, though as they come into focus I see not a snapshot from life, but an instant collage of what's there and what isn't: my sofa; certainly not a painting I'd want to own; and please, a joke's a joke, but couldn't that Inca flute music be turned down? As he walks across the floor to adjust the volume, the character metamorphoses into a total stranger. In a horror film, I'd hold my breath, but this has happened so many times in stories that I only perk up slightly. Finally: something I'm not even slightly in control of. By the time he gets to the stereo, Mozart is playing, and he has the good sense not to turn it off, but simply to put his head on top of the machine and close his eyes. The character who next walks into the room is bound to understand it all, instantly. I'll just be transcribing her actions. From there, the story unfolds—one hopes on some real trajectory—until the moment when characters who have defined themselves suddenly change. One speaks, saying something out-of-character. The other reacts. The answer is even more unexpected. My stories don't always follow this pattern, of course, but once it's all there—text and subtext and characters who have a life of their own—I get to step in, become a part of the final shaping, because by then I can intuit what's needed to make it work as a story. . . .

My characters, who surprise, and enlighten, and dismay me so often, come from familiar worlds with unfamiliar subtexts. Similarly, they are "real"—not made-up—until the very early point in any story when they will not be contained, and then they are transformed so they are beyond my comprehension until the moment something clicks, and then I know what I did not know before, or did not articulate to myself. Inventing characters is for me no different from inventing any day. The best days, though, are the ones that contain real inventions. The days when I write stories.   [1994]

ARNA BONTEMPS

*A*rna Bontemps *wrote his discussion of Jean Toomer and* Cane *as part of his essay "The Negro Renaissance: Jean Toomer and the Harlem of the 1920s" in* Anger and Beyond: The Negro Writer in the United States, *edited by Herbert Hill in 1966.*

On Jean Toomer and *Cane*

"In Jean Toomer, the author of *Cane*," [W. S.] Braithwaite wrote in 1925, "we come upon the very first artist of the race, who with all an artist's passion and sympathy for life, its hurts, its sympathies, its desires, its joys, its defeats and strange yearnings, can write about the Negro without the surrender or compromise of the artist's vision. So objective is it, that we feel that it is a mere accident that birth or association has thrown him into contact with the life he has written about. He would write just as well, just as poignantly, just as transmutingly, about the peasants of Russia, or the peasants of Ireland, had experience brought him in touch with their existence. *Cane* is a book of gold and bronze, of dusk and flame, of ecstasy and pain, and Jean Toomer is a bright morning star of a new day of the race in literature."

Cane was published in 1923 after portions of it had first appeared in *Broom, The Crisis, Double Dealer, Liberator, Little Review, Modern Review, Nomad, Prairie and S 4 N.* But *Cane* and Jean Toomer, its gifted author, presented an enigma — an enigma which has, if anything, deepened in the forty-three years since its publication. Given such a problem, perhaps one may be excused for not wishing to separate the man from his work. Indeed, so separated, Toomer's writing could scarcely be understood at all, and its significance would escape us now as it has escaped so many others in the past.

In any case, *Who's Who in Colored America* listed Toomer in 1927 and gave the following vita:

b. Dec. 26, 1894, Washington, D. C.; s. Nathan and Nina (Pinch-back) Toomer; educ. Public Scho., Washington, D. C.; Dunbar,

High Scho.; Univ. of Wisconsin, 1914–15; taught schools, Sparta, Ga., for four months, traveled, worked numerous occupations; auth. *Cane,* pub. Boni and Liveright, 1923; Short Stories and Literary Criticisms in various magazines; address, c/o Civic Club, 439 W. 23rd St., New York, N. Y.

Needless to say, no subsequent listing of Toomer is to be found in this or any other directory of conspicuous Negro Americans. Judging by the above, however, Toomer had always been elusive, and the interest that *Cane* awakened did nothing to change this. Several years later Toomer faded completely into white obscurity leaving behind a literary mystery almost as intriguing as the disappearance of Ambrose Bierce into Mexico in 1913.

Why did he do it? What did it mean?

Concerned with writing, as we are, we automatically turn to Toomer's book for clues. This could be difficult, because copies are scarce. *Cane's* two printings were small, and the few people who went quietly mad about the strange book were evidently unable to do much toward enlarging its audience. But among these few was practically the whole generation of young Negro writers then just beginning to appear, and their reaction to Toomer's *Cane* marked an awakening that soon thereafter began to be called a Negro renaissance.

Cane's influence was not limited to the happy band that included Langston Hughes, Countee Cullen, Eric Walrond, Zora Neale Hurston, Wallace Thurman, Rudolph Fisher, and their contemporaries of the Twenties. Subsequent writing by Negroes in the United States as well as in the West Indies and Africa has continued to reflect its mood and often its method, and, one feels, it also has influenced the writing about Negroes by others. And certainly no earlier volume of poetry or fiction or both had come close to expressing the ethos of the Negro in the Southern setting as *Cane* did.

There are many odd and provocative things about *Cane,* and not the least is its form. Reviewers who read it in 1923 were generally stumped. Poetry and prose were whipped together in a kind of frappé. Realism was mixed with what they called mysticism, and the result seemed to many of them confusing. Still, one of them could conclude that "*Cane* is an interesting, occasionally beautiful and often queer book of exploration into old country and new ways of writing." Another noted, "Toomer has not interviewed the Negro, has not asked opinions about him, has not drawn conclusions about him from his reactions to outside stimuli, but has made the much more searching, and much more self-forgetting effort of seeing life with him, through him."

Such comment was cautious, however, compared to the trumpetings of Waldo Frank in the Foreword he contributed:

A poet has arisen among our American youth who has known how to turn the essence and materials of his Southland into the essences and materials of literature. A poet has arisen in that land who writes, not as a Southerner, not as a rebel against Southerners, not as a Negro, not as apologist or priest or critic: who writes as a *poet*. The fashioning of beauty is ever foremost in his inspiration: not forcedly but simply, and because these ultimate aspects of his world are to him more real than all its specific problems. He has made songs and lovely stories of his land. . . .

The gifted Negro has been too often thwarted from becoming a poet because his world was forever forcing him to recollect that he was a Negro. The artist must lose such lesser identities in the great well of life. . . . The whole will and mind of the creator must go below the surfaces of race. And this has been an almost impossible condition for the American Negro to achieve, forced every moment of his life into a specific and superficial plane of consciousness. . . .

It seems to me, therefore, that this is a first book in more ways than one. It is a harbinger of the South's literary maturity: of its emergence from the obsession put upon its minds by the unending racial crisis. . . . It marks the dawn of direct and unafraid creation. And, as the initial work of a man of twenty-seven, it is the harbinger of a literary force of whose incalculable future I believe no reader of this book will doubt.

It is well to keep in mind the time of these remarks. Of the novels by which T. S. Stribling is remembered, only *Birthright* had been published. Julia Peterkin had not yet published a book. DuBose Heyward's *Porgy* was still two years away. William Faulkner's first novel was three years away. His Mississippi novels were six or more years in the future. Robert Penn Warren, a student at Vanderbilt University, was just beginning his association with the Fugitive poets. His first novel was still more than a decade and a half ahead. Tennessee Williams was just nine years old.

A chronology of Negro writers is equally revealing. James Weldon Johnson had written lyrics for popular songs, some of them minstrel style, and a sort of documentary novel obscurely published under a pseudonym, but *God's Trombones* was a good four years in the offing. Countee Cullen's *Color* was two and Langston Hughes' *The Weary Blues* three years away, though both of these poets had become known to readers of the Negro magazine *Crisis* while still in their teens, and Hughes at twenty-one, the year of *Cane's* publication, could already be called a favorite.

The first fiction of the Negro Renaissance required apologies. It was not first-rate. But it was an anticipation of what was to come later. Even so, it followed *Cane* by a year or two, and Eric Walrond's *Tropic Death* did not come for three. Zora Neale Hurston's first novel was published in 1931,[1] eight years after *Cane*. Richard Wright made his bow with *Uncle*

---

[1]The author is mistaken. Hurston's first novel, *Jonah's Gourd Vine,* was published in 1934.

Tom's Children in 1938, fifteen years later. *Invisible Man* by Ralph Ellison followed Toomer's *Cane* by just thirty years. James Baldwin was not born when Toomer began to publish.

Waldo Frank's use of "harbinger" as the word for *Cane* becomes both significant and ironic when we recognize the debt most of these individuals owe Toomer. Consciously or unconsciously, one after another they picked up his cue and began making the "more searching" effort to see life *with* the Negro, "through him." *Cane* heralded an awakening of artistic expression by Negroes that brought to light in less than a decade a surprising array of talents, and these in turn made way for others. An equally significant change in the writing about Negroes paralleled this awakening. Strangely, however, *Cane* was not at all the harbinger Frank seemed to imagine. Despite his promise—a promise which must impress anyone who puts this first book beside the early writings of either Faulkner or Hemingway, Toomer's contemporaries—Jean Toomer rejected his prospects and turned his back on greatness.

The book by which we remember this writer is as hard to classify as its author. At first glance it appears to consist of assorted sketches, stories, and a novelette interspersed with poems. Some of the prose is poetic, and often Toomer slips from one form into the other almost imperceptibly. The novelette is constructed like a play.

His characters, always evoked with effortless strength, are as recognizable as they are unexpected in the fiction of that period. Fern is a "creamy brown" beauty so complicated men take her "but get no joy from it." Becky is a white outcast beside a Georgia road who bears two Negro children. Layman, a preacher-teacher in the same area, "knows more than would be good for anyone other than a silent man." The name character in the novelette *Kabnis* is a languishing idealist finally redeemed from cynicism and dissipation by the discovery of underlying strength in his people.

It doesn't take long to discover that *Cane* is not without design, however. A world of black peasantry in Georgia appears in the first section. The scene changes to the Negro community of Washington, D.C., in the second. Rural Georgia comes up again in the third. Changes in the concerns of Toomer's folk are noted as the setting moves from the Georgia pike to the bustling Negro section in the nation's capital. The change in the level of awareness that the author discloses is more subtle, but it is clearly discernible when he returns to the Georgia background.

A young poet-observer moves through the book. Drugged by beauty "perfect as dusk when the sun goes down," lifted and swayed by folk song, arrested by eyes that "desired nothing that *you* could give," silenced by "corn leaves swaying, rusty with talk," he recognized that "the Dixie Pike has grown from a goat path in Africa." A native richness is here, he concluded, and the poet embraces it with the passion of love.

This was the sensual power most critics noticed and most readers remembered about *Cane*. It was the basis for Alfred Kreymborg's remark in *Our Singing Strength* that "Jean Toomer is *one* of the finest artists among the dark people, if not *the* finest." The reviewer for the New York *Herald Tribune* had the rich imagery of *Cane* in mind when he said, "Here are the high brown and black and half-caste colored folk of the cane fields, the gin hovel and the brothel realized with a sure touch of artistry." But there remained much in the book that he could not understand or appreciate. Speaking of Toomer's "sometimes rather strident reactions to the Negro," he added that "at moments his outbursts of emotion approach the inarticulately maudlin," though he had to admit that *Cane* represented "a distinct achievement wholly unlike anything of this sort done before."

Others found "obscurity" and "mysticism" in the novelette which comprises the last third of the book. This is not surprising, for in Toomer's expressed creed "A symbol is as useful to the spirit as a tool is to the hand," and his fiction is full of them. Add to puzzling symbols an itch to find "new ways of writing" that led him to bold experimentation and one may begin to see why Toomer baffled as he pleased readers interested in writing by or about Negroes in the early Twenties.

Kreymborg spoke of Toomer as "a philosopher and a psychologist by temperament" and went on to say that "the Washington writer is now fascinated by the larger, rather than the parochial interest of the human race, and should some day compose a book in the grand manner."

Of course, Toomer didn't, or at least he has not published one up to now, and to this extent Kreymborg has failed as a prophet, but his reference to Toomer as philosopher and psychologist was certainly on the mark, and his rather large estimate of this writer's capacities was significant, considering its date. The "new criticism," as we have come to recognize it, had scarcely been heard from then, and apparently it has still not discovered Toomer, but the chances are it may yet find him challenging. He would have comforted them, I am almost sorry to say, incarnating, as he does, some of their favorite attitudes. But at the same time, he could have served as a healthy corrective for others. Whether or not he would prove less complex or less rewarding than Gertrude Stein or James Joyce, for example, remains to be determined.

Saunders Redding gave *Cane* a close reading fifteen years after its publication and saw it as an unfinished experiment, "the conclusion to which we are fearful of never knowing, for since 1923 Toomer has published practically nothing." He meant, one assumes, that Toomer had published little poetry or fiction, or anything else that seemed closely related to *Cane* or to *Cane*'s author. Toomer had published provocative articles here and there as well as a small book of definitions and aphorisms during that time, and since then he has allowed two of his lectures to be published semi-privately. But Redding must be included in the small group who recognized a problem in *Cane* that has yet to be explained.

To him Toomer was a young writer "fresh from the South," who found a paramount importance in establishing "racial kinship" with Negroes in order to treat them artistically. He was impressed by Toomer's "unashamed and unrestrained" love for the race and for the soil and setting that nourished it. He saw a relationship between the writer's "hot, colorful, primitive" moods and the "naïve hysteria of the spirituals," which he held in contrast to "the sophistic savagery of jazz and the blues." *Cane,* he concluded, "was a lesson in emotional release and freedom."

Chapters about Toomer were included in Paul Rosenfeld's *Men Seen* in 1925 and in Gorham B. Munson's *Destinations* in 1928, and elsewhere there are indications that Toomer continued to write and to experiment for at least a decade after the publication of *Cane.* Long stories by him appeared in the second and third volumes of the *American Caravan.* A thoughtful essay on "Race Problems and Modern Society" became part of a volume devoted to *Problems of Civilization* in Baker Brownell's series on "Man and His World." Seven years later, in the *New Caravan* of 1936, Toomer presented similar ideas in the long poem "Blue Meridian." Meanwhile, contributing a chapter to the book *America & Alfred Stieglitz* in 1934, Toomer was explicit about his own writing as well as several other matters.

The rumor that Toomer had crossed the color line began circulating when his name stopped appearing in print. But a reasonable effort to find out what it was Toomer was trying to say to us subsequently makes it hard to accept "passing" as the skeleton key to the Jean Toomer mystery. He seemed too concerned with truth to masquerade. One wants to believe that Toomer's mind came at last to reject the myth of race as it is fostered in our culture. A man of fair complexion, indistinguishable from the majority of white Americans, he had always had a free choice as to where he would take his place in a color-caste scheme. Having wandered extensively and worked at odd jobs in a variety of cities before he began contributing to little magazines, as he has stated, he could scarcely have escaped being taken at face value by strangers who had no way of knowing that the youth, who looked like Hollywood's conception of an Ivy League basketball star, but who spoke so beautifully, whose very presence was such an influence upon them, was not only a product of the Negro community but a grandson of the man whom the *Dictionary of American Biography* describes as "the typical Negro politician of the Reconstruction."

Men of this kind, such as Walter White of the NAACP or Adam Clayton Powell of the U.S. Congress, sometimes called voluntary Negroes when they elect to remain in the fold, so to speak, have in other circumstances been discovered in strange places in our society—in neo-fascist organizations in the United States, among big city bosses, on movie screens, in the student body at "Ole Miss"—but seldom if ever before in an organization working "for understanding between people." Yet Jean Toomer's first publication, following the rumors and the silence, was "An Interpretation of Friends Worship," published by the Committee on Religious Education of Friends General Conference, 1515 Cherry Street, Philadelphia,

1947. It was followed two years later by a pamphlet, "The Flavor of Man." The writing is eloquent with commitment. It reflects unhurried reading and contemplation, as was also true of his piece on "Race Problems and Modern Society." Toomer did not fail to remind his readers that certain racial attitudes could not be condoned. He certainly did not speak as a Negro bent on escaping secretly into white society. Jean Toomer, who, like his high-spirited grandfather, had exuberantly published his pride in his Negro heritage, appears to have reached a point in his thinking at which categories in this kind tend to clutter rather than classify. The stand he appears to have taken at first involved nothing more clandestine than the closing of a book or the changing of a subject.

Yet he is on record as having denied later that he was a Negro. That is a story in itself. Nevertheless, at that point, it seems, Jean Toomer stepped out of American letters. Despite the richness of his thought, his gift of expression, he ceased to be a writer and, as I have suggested, turned his back on greatness. His choice, whatever else may be said about it, reflects the human sacrifices in the field of the arts exacted by the racial myth on which so much writing in the United States is based. While he may have escaped its strictures and inconveniences in his personal life, he did not get away from the racial problem in any real sense. His dilemmas and frustrations as a writer are equally the dilemmas and frustrations of the Negro writers who have since emerged. The fact that most of them have not been provided with his invisible cloak makes little difference. He is their representative man. He stands as their prototype.   [1966]

RAYMOND CARVER

Raymond Carver offers a fine example of how a contemporary author has responded to the work of earlier writers by following a line of thought that links him with his predecessors. In "Creative Writing 101," Carver credits the influence of the novelist John Gardner for giving him the clearest sense of direction when he was a twenty-year-old college student. Carver wrote his essay as the foreword to Gardner's On Becoming a Novelist *(1983).*

Creative Writing 101

A long time ago—it was the summer of 1958—my wife and I and our two baby children moved from Yakima, Washington, to a little town outside of Chico, California. There we found an old house and paid twenty-five dollars a month rent. In order to finance this move, I'd had to borrow a hundred and twenty-five dollars from a druggist I'd delivered prescriptions for, a man named Bill Barton.

This is by way of saying that in those days my wife and I were stone broke. We had to eke out a living, but the plan was that I would take classes at what was then called Chico State College. But for as far back as I can remember, long before we moved to California in search of a different life and our slice of the American pie, I'd wanted to be a writer. I wanted to write, and I wanted to write anything—fiction, of course, but also poetry, plays, scripts, articles for *Sports Afield, True, Argosy,* and *Rogue* (some of the magazines I was then reading), pieces for the local newspaper—anything that involved putting words together to make something coherent and of interest to someone besides myself. But at the time of our move, I felt in my bones I had to get some education in order to go along with being a writer. I put a very high premium on education then—much higher in those days than now, I'm sure, but that's because I'm older and have an education. Understand that nobody in my family had ever gone to college or for that matter had got beyond the mandatory eighth grade in high school. I didn't know *anything,* but I knew I didn't know anything.

So along with this desire to get an education, I had this very strong desire to write; it was a desire so strong that, with the encouragement I was given in college, and the insight acquired, I kept on writing long after "good sense" and the "cold facts"—the "realities" of my life told me, time and again, that I ought to quit, stop the dreaming, quietly go ahead and do something else.

That fall at Chico State I enrolled in classes that most freshman students have to take, but I enrolled as well for something called Creative Writing 101. This course was going to be taught by a new faculty member named John Gardner, who was already surrounded by a bit of mystery and romance. It was said that he'd taught previously at Oberlin College but had left there for some reason that wasn't made clear. One student said Gardner had been fired—students, like everyone else, thrive on rumor and intrigue—and another student said Gardner had simply quit after some kind of flap. Someone else said his teaching load at Oberlin, four or five classes of freshman English each semester, had been too heavy and that he couldn't find time to write. For it was said that Gardner was a real, that is to say a practicing, writer—someone who had written novels and short stories. In any case, he was going to teach CW 101 at Chico State, and I signed up.

I was excited about taking a course from a real writer. I'd never laid eyes on a writer before, and I was in awe. But where were these novels and short stories, I wanted to know. Well, nothing had been published yet. It was said that he couldn't get his work published and that he carried it around with him in boxes. (After I became his student, I was to see those boxes of manuscript. Gardner had become aware of my difficulty in finding a place to work. He knew I had a young family and cramped quarters at home. He offered me the key to his office. I see that gift now as a turning point. It was a gift not made casually, and I took it, I think, as a kind of mandate—for that's what it was. I spent part of every Saturday and Sunday in his office, which is where he kept the boxes of manuscript. The boxes were stacked up on the floor beside the desk. *Nickel Mountain,* grease-pencilled on one of the boxes, is the only title I recall. But it was in his office, within sight of his unpublished books, that I undertook my first serious attempts at writing.) . . .

For short story writers in his class, the requirement was one story, ten to fifteen pages in length. For people who wanted to write a novel—I think there must have been one or two of these souls—a chapter of around twenty pages, along with an outline of the rest. The kicker was that this one short story, or the chapter of the novel, might have to be revised ten times in the course of the semester for Gardner to be satisfied with it. It was a basic tenet of his that a writer found what he wanted to say in the ongoing process of seeing what he'd said. And this seeing, or seeing more clearly, came about through revision. He *believed* in revision, endless revision; it was something very close to his heart and something he felt was vital for writers, at whatever stage of their development. And he never seemed to lose patience rereading a student story, even though he might have seen it in five previous incarnations.

I think his idea of a short story in 1958 was still pretty much his idea of a short story in 1982; it was something that had a recognizable beginning, middle, and an end to it. Once in a while he'd go to the blackboard and draw a diagram to illustrate a point he wanted to make about rising or falling emotion in a story—peaks, valleys, plateaus, resolution, *denouement,* things like that. Try as I might, I couldn't muster a great deal of interest or really understand this side of things, the stuff he put on the blackboard. But what I did understand was the way he would comment on a student story that was undergoing class discussion. Gardner might wonder aloud about the author's reasons for writing a story about a crippled person, say, and leaving out the fact of the character's crippledness until the very end of the story. "So you think it's a good idea not to let the reader know this man is crippled until the last sentence?" His tone of voice conveyed his disapproval, and it didn't take more than an instant for everyone in class, including the author of the story, to see that it wasn't a good strategy to use. Any strategy that kept important and necessary information away from the reader in the hope of overcoming him by surprise at the end of the story was cheating.

In class he was always referring to writers whose names I was not familiar with. Or if I knew their names, I'd never read the work. . . . He talked about James Joyce and Flaubert and Isak Dinesen as if they lived just down the road, in Yuba City. He said, "I'm here to tell you who to read as well as teach you how to write." I'd leave class in a daze and make straight for the library to find books by these writers he was talking about.

Hemingway and Faulkner were the reigning authors in those days. But altogether I'd probably read at the most two or three books by these fellows. Anyway, they were so well-known and so much talked about, they couldn't be all that good, could they? I remember Gardner telling me, "Read all the Faulkner you can get your hands on, and then read all of Hemingway to clean the Faulkner out of your system."

He introduced us to the "little" or literary periodicals by bringing a box of these magazines to class one day and passing them around so that we could acquaint ourselves with their names, see what they looked like and what they felt like to hold in the hand. He told us that this was where most of the best fiction in the country and just about all of the poetry was appearing. Fiction, poetry, literary essays, book reviews of recent books, criticism of *living* authors *by* living authors. I felt wild with discovery in those days.

For the seven or eight of us who were in his class, he ordered heavy black binders and told us we should keep our written work in these. He kept his own work in such binders, he said, and of course that settled it for us. We carried our stories in those binders and felt we were special, exclusive, singled out from others. And so we were.

I don't know how Gardner might have been with other students when it came time to have conferences with them about their work. I suspect he gave everybody a good amount of attention. But it was and still is my impression that during that period he took my stories more seriously, read them closer and more carefully, than I had any right to expect. I was completely unprepared for the kind of criticism I received from him. Before our conference he would have marked up my story, crossing out unacceptable sentences, phrases, individual words, even some of the punctuation; and he gave me to understand that these deletions were not negotiable. In other cases he would bracket sentences, phrases, or individual words, and these were items we'd talk about, these cases were negotiable. And he wouldn't hesitate to add something to what I'd written—a word here and there, or else a few words, maybe a sentence that would make clear what I was trying to say. We'd discuss commas in my story as if nothing else in the world mattered more at that moment—and, indeed, it did not. He was always looking to find something to praise. When there was a sentence, a line of dialogue, or a narrative passage that he liked, something that he thought "worked" and moved the story along in some pleasant or unexpected way, he'd write "Nice" in the margin, or else "Good!" And seeing these comments, my heart would lift.

It was close, line-by-line criticism he was giving me, and the reasons behind the criticism, why something ought to be this way instead of that; and it was invaluable to me in my development as a writer. After this kind of detailed talk about the text, we'd talk about the larger concerns of the story, the "problem" it was trying to throw light on, the conflict it was trying to grapple with, and how the story might or might not fit into the grand scheme of story writing. It was his conviction that if the words in the story were blurred because of the author's insensitivity, carelessness, or sentimentality, then the story suffered from a tremendous handicap. But there was something even worse and something that must be avoided at all costs: if the words and the sentiments were dishonest, the author was faking it, writing about things he didn't care about or believe in, then nobody could ever care anything about it.

A writer's values and craft. This is what the man taught and what he stood for, and this is what I've kept by me in the years since that brief but all-important time. [1983]

WILLA CATHER

Willa Cather wrote the sketch of her friend Sarah Orne Jewett as the introduction to a two-volume collection of Jewett's stories published in 1925. Cather ended her essay with an analogy: "When we find ourselves on shipboard, among hundreds of strangers, we very soon recognize those who are sympathetic to us. We find our own books in the same way. We like a writer much as we like individuals, for what he is, simply, underneath his accomplishments."

Miss Jewett

In reading over a package of letters from Sarah Orne Jewett, I find this observation: *"The thing that teases the mind over and over for years, and at last gets itself put down rightly on paper—whether little or great, it belongs to Literature."* Miss Jewett was very conscious of the fact that when a writer makes anything that belongs to Literature (limiting the term here to imaginative literature, which she of course meant), his material goes through a process very different from that by which he makes merely a good story. No one can define this process exactly; but certainly persistence, survival, recurrence in the writer's mind, are highly characteristic of it. The shapes and scenes that have "teased" the mind for years, when they do at last get themselves rightly put down, make a much higher order of writing, and a much more costly, than the most vivid and vigorous transfer of immediate impressions.

In some of Miss Jewett's earlier books, *Deephaven, Country Byways, Old Friends and New,* one can find first sketches, first impressions, which later crystallized into almost flawless examples of literary art. One can, as it were, watch in process the two kinds of making: the first, which is full of perception and feeling but rather fluid and formless; the second, which is tightly built and significant in design. The design is, indeed, so happy, so right, that it seems inevitable; the design is the story and the story is the design. The "Pointed Fir" sketches are living things caught in the open, with light and freedom and airspaces about them. They melt into the land and the life of the land until they are not stories at all, but life itself.

A great many stories were being written upon New England themes at the same time that Miss Jewett was writing; stories that to many contemporary readers may have seemed more interesting than hers, because they dealt with more definite "situations" and were more heavily accented. But they are not very interesting to reread today; they have not the one thing that survives all arresting situations, all good writing and clever story-making—inherent, individual beauty.

Walter Pater said that every truly great drama must, in the end, linger in the reader's mind as a sort of ballad. One might say that every fine story must leave in the mind of the sensitive reader an intangible residuum of pleasure; a cadence, a quality of voice that is exclusively the writer's own, individual, unique. A quality which one can remember without the volume at hand, can experience over and over again in the mind but can never absolutely define, as one can experience in memory a melody, or the summer perfume of a garden. The magnitude of the subject-matter is not of primary importance, seemingly. An idyll of Theocritus, concerned with sheep and goats and shade and pastures, is today as much alive as the most dramatic passages of the *Iliad*—stirs the reader's feeling quite as much, perhaps.

It is a common fallacy that a writer, if he is talented enough, can achieve this poignant quality by improving upon his subject-matter, by using his "imagination" upon it and twisting it to suit his purpose. The truth is that by such a process (which is not imaginative at all!) he can at best produce only a brilliant sham, which, like a badly built and pretentious house, looks poor and shabby after a few years. If he achieves anything noble, anything enduring, it must be by giving himself absolutely to his material. And this gift of sympathy is his great gift; is the fine thing in him that alone can make his work fine.

The artist spends a lifetime in pursuing the things that haunt him, in having his mind "teased" by them, in trying to get these conceptions down on paper exactly as they are to him and not in conventional poses supposed to reveal their character; trying this method and that, as a painter tries different lightings and different attitudes with his subject to catch the one that presents it more suggestively than any other. And at the end of a lifetime he emerges with much that is more or less happy experimenting, and comparatively little that is the very flower of himself and his genius.

The best of Miss Jewett's work, read by a student fifty years from now, will give him the characteristic flavour, the spirit, the cadence, of an American writer of the first order,—and of a New England which will then be a thing of the past.

Even in the stories which fall short of being Miss Jewett's best, one has the pleasure of her society and companionship—if one likes that sort of companionship. I remember she herself had a fondness for "The Hiltons' Holiday," the slightest of stories: a hard-worked New England farmer takes his two little girls to town, some seventeen miles away (a long drive by wagon), for a treat. That is all, yet the story is a little miracle. It simply *is* *the look*—shy, kind, a little wistful—which shines out at one from good country faces on remote farms; it is the look *itself*. To have got it down upon the printed page is like bringing the tenderest of early spring flowers from the deep wood into the hot light of noon without bruising its petals.

To note an artist's limitations is but to define his talent. A reporter can write equally well about everything that is presented to his view, but a creative writer can do his best only with what lies within the range and character of his deepest sympathies. These stories of Miss Jewett's have much to do with fisher-folk and seaside villages; with juniper pastures and lonely farms, neat grey country houses and delightful, well-seasoned old men and women. That, when one thinks of it in a flash, is New England. I remember hearing an English actor say that until he made a motor trip through the New England country he had supposed that the Americans killed their aged in some merciful fashion, for he saw none in the cities where he played.

There are many kinds of people in the State of Maine, and neighbouring States, who are not found in Miss Jewett's books. There may be Othellos and Iagos and Don Juans; but they are not highly characteristic of the country, they do not come up spontaneously in the juniper pastures as the everlasting does. Miss Jewett wrote of everyday people who grew out of the soil, not about exceptional individuals at war with their environment. This was not a creed with her, but an instinctive preference.

Born within the scent of the sea but not within sight of it, in a beautiful old house full of strange and lovely things brought home from all over the globe by seafaring ancestors, she spent much of her childhood driving about the country with her doctor father on his professional rounds among the farms. She early learned to love her country for what it was. What is quite as important, she saw it as it was. She happened to have the right nature, the right temperament, to see it so—and to understand by intuition the deeper meaning of what she saw.

She had not only the eye, she had the ear. From her early years she must have treasured up those pithy bits of local speech, of native idiom, which enrich and enliven her pages. The language her people speak to each other is a native tongue. No writer can invent it. It is made in the hard school of experience, in communities where language has been undisturbed long enough to take on colour and character from the nature and experiences of the people. The "sayings" of a community, its proverbs, are its characteristic comment upon life; they imply its history, suggest its attitude toward the world and its way of accepting life. Such an idiom makes the finest language any writer can have; and he can never get it with a notebook. He himself must be able to think and feel in that speech — it is a gift from heart to heart.

Much of Miss Jewett's delightful humour comes from her delicate and tactful handling of this native language of the waterside and countryside, never overdone, never pushed a shade too far; from this, and from her own fine attitude toward her subject-matter. This attitude in itself, though unspoken, is everywhere felt, and constitutes one of the most potent elements of grace and charm in her stories. She had with her own stories and her own characters a very charming relation; spirited, gay, tactful, noble in its essence and a little arch in its expression. In this particular relationship many of our most gifted writers are unfortunate. If a writer's attitude toward his characters and his scene is as vulgar as a showman's, as mercenary as an auctioneer's, vulgar and meretricious will his product for ever remain.   [1925]

KATE CHOPIN

Kate Chopin wrote the following fanciful sketch describing her approach to writing short fiction as an answer to her readers' most persistent questions about how she wrote stories. Untitled when it was originally published in the St. Louis Post-Dispatch on November 26, 1899, the essay was given its current title by Per Seyersted, the scholar who has edited a definitive volume of Chopin's work.

On Certain Brisk, Bright Days

On certain brisk, bright days I like to walk from my home, near Thirty-fourth street, down to the shopping district. After a few such experiments I begin to fancy that I have the walking habit. Doubtless I convey the same impression to acquaintances who see me from the car window "hot-footing" it down Olive street or Washington avenue. But in my sub-consciousness, as my friend Mrs. R— would say, I know that I have not the walking habit.

Eight or nine years ago I began to write stories — short stories which appeared in the magazines, and I forthwith began to suspect I had the writing habit. The public shared this impression, and called me an author. Since then, though I have written many short stories and a novel or two, I am forced to admit that I have not the writing habit. But it is hard to make people with the questioning habit believe this.

"How, where, when, why, what do you write?" are some of the questions that I remember. How do I write? On a lapboard with a block of paper, a stub pen, and a bottle of ink bought at the corner grocery, which keeps the best in town.

Where do I write? In a Morris chair beside the window, where I can see a few trees and a patch of sky, more or less blue.

When do I write? I am greatly tempted here to use slang and reply "any old time," but that would lend a tone of levity to this bit of confidence, whose seriousness I want to keep intact if possible. So I shall say I write in the morning, when not too strongly drawn to struggle with the intricacies of a pattern, and in the afternoon, if the temptation to try a new furniture polish on an old table leg is not too powerful to be denied; sometimes at night, though as I grow older I am more and more inclined to believe that night was made for sleep.

"Why do I write?" is a question which I have often asked myself and never very satisfactorily answered. Story-writing—at least with me—is the spontaneous expression of impressions gathered goodness knows where. To seek the source, the impulse of a story is like tearing a flower to pieces for wantonness.

What do I write? Well, not everything that comes into my head, but much of what I have written lies between the covers of my books.

There are stories that seem to write themselves, and others which positively refuse to be written—which no amount of coaxing can bring to anything. I do not believe any writer has ever made a "portrait" in fiction. A trick, a mannerism, a physical trait or mental characteristic go a very short way towards portraying the complete individual in real life who suggests the individual in the writer's imagination. The "material" of a writer is to the last degree uncertain, and I fear not marketable. I have been told stories which were looked upon as veritable gold mines by the generous narrators who placed them at my disposal. I have been taken to spots supposed to be alive with local color. I have been introduced to excruciating characters with frank permission to use them as I liked, but never, in any single instance, has such material been of the slightest service. I am completely at the mercy of unconscious selection. To such an extent is this true, that what is called the polishing up process has always proved disastrous to my work, and I avoid it, preferring the integrity of crudities to artificialities.

How hard it is for one's acquaintances and friends to realize that one's books are to be taken seriously, and that they are subject to the same laws which govern the existence of others' books! I have a son who is growing wroth over the question: "Where can I find your mother's books, or latest book?"

"The very next time any one asks me that question," he exclaimed excitedly, "I am going to tell them to try the stock yards!"

I hope he won't. He might thus offend a possible buyer. Politeness, besides being a virtue, is sometimes an art. I am often met with the same question, and I always try to be polite. "My latest book? Why, you will find it, no doubt, at the bookseller's or the libraries."

"The libraries! Oh, no, they don't keep it." She hadn't thought of the bookseller's. It's real hard to think of everything! Sometimes I feel as if I should like to get a good, remunerative job to do the thinking for some people. This may sound conceited, but it isn't. If I had space (I have plenty of time; time is my own, but space belongs to the *Post-Dispatch*), I should like to demonstrate satisfactorily that it is not conceited.

I trust it will not be giving away professional secrets to say that many readers would be surprised, perhaps shocked, at the questions which some newspaper editors will put to a defenseless woman under the guise of flattery.

For instance: "How many children have you?" This form is subtle and greatly to be commended in dealing with women of shy and retiring propensities. A woman's reluctance to speak of her children has not yet been chronicled. I have a good many, but they'd be simply wild if I dragged them into this. I might say something of those who are at a safe distance — the idol of my soul in Kentucky; the light of my eye off in Colorado; the treasure of his mother's heart in Louisiana — but I mistrust the form of their displeasure, with poisoned candy going through the mails.

"Do you smoke cigarettes?" is a question which I consider impertinent, and I think most women will agree with me. Suppose I do smoke cigarettes. Am I going to tell it out in meeting? Suppose I don't smoke cigarettes. Am I going to admit such a reflection upon my artistic integrity, and thereby bring upon myself the contempt of the guild?

In answering questions in which an editor believes his readers to be interested, the victim cannot take herself too seriously.   [1899]

ROBERT COLES

*R*obert *Coles, distinguished literary critic and professor of medicine specializing in child psychiatry at Harvard University, majored in English as an undergraduate. At the time he was applying to medical schools, he began a life-long friendship with the Paterson, New Jersey, doctor and poet William Carlos Williams, who encouraged him to continue reading novels and writing down his responses to literature. Williams told the young Coles, "Better to pour yourself into a novel, and then come up with some thoughts about it, than letting yourself go to ruin over a few college courses, or anything else." Coles never forgot this advice and titled his collection of literary essays* That Red Wheelbarrow *(1988) after a favorite poem by Williams.*

Tillie Olsen:
The Iron and the Riddle

The prelude to *Middlemarch* is only three paragraphs long, but in them George Eliot makes one of the most powerful and satisfactory statements about the predicament of women: she refers to "blundering lives," to "a life of mistakes," to "a tragic failure which found no sacred poet and sank unwept into oblivion." She had in mind both masses of women and particular women, all of whom have suffered by virtue of what she describes as "meanness of opportunity," both the general kind so many men and women alike faced in the nineteenth century and the special kind women had to endure then, and still now. The novel is a masterful psychological presentation and analysis of rural, middle-class, early-nineteenth-century England but also, for the most part, a chronicle of loss, sadness, disappointment, and failure. Characters endowed with intelligence and ambition, one after the other, fall upon bad times—not poverty but rather the consequences of fate, the sum of the world's accidents, incidents, and circumstances that exert their enormous, tellingly destructive influence. The novel falls just short of tragedy; a village, a county, all of England's rising bourgeoisie had at least another half-century or so to go, yet the story is littered with unfulfilled dreams.

So with Tillie Olsen's *Tell Me a Riddle;* her four short stories lack Eliot's extended, intricate dedication to character portrayal or the workings of historical change but their sensibility, point of view, and mood are spiritually akin to those aspects of *Middlemarch*. The first and briefest, "I Stand Here Ironing," introduces the reader to a woman who has known and suffered from the "meanness of opportunity" George Eliot mentions, a twentieth-century American version of it. The title reveals the scene and tells of all the action to come—a mother reflects upon the hard, curbed, sad life of her nineteen-year-old daughter, born in the Great Depression of the early 1930s. A social worker or guidance counselor or psychologist or psychiatrist (who knows which, and who cares—a substantial number of them all sound drearily alike) has told the mother that the young woman, her oldest child, "needs help." The mother is skeptical and quietly, thoughtfully scornful, but not defensive or guilty, not lacking in a capacity for psychological introspection either—as might be said of her by the person who wants her to come in for one of these self-conscious talks that have become so much a part of so many lives in recent years. She is determined to hold on to her dignity, to her right as an intelligent woman, however hardpressed by life, to comprehend what has happened to herself and her children, and just as important, to resist the interfering, gratuitous, self-serving, or wrong-headed interpretations of others. "Let her be," the mother says to herself—a remark meant also for the one who, with the barely concealed arrogance and condescension of the clinic, had called and said, "I wish you would manage the time to come in and talk with me about your daughter." The story is a mother's effort to understand for herself how her daughter came to be the person she is, and to do so by taking account of the overwhelming social, economic, and cultural reality of a certain kind of life—a reality that generates rather than merely influences currents in the mind's life. Put differently, the story is an interior monologue devoted to the exterior—the insistent, enduring, molding press of the things of this world upon our dreams, nightmares, hesitations, and aspirations.

"She was a miracle to me," the mother remembers. When the baby was eight months old there was a sudden change: "I had to leave her daytimes with the woman downstairs for whom she was no miracle at all, for I worked or looked for work." The father, desperate for lack of a job, humiliated and beaten, said good-bye. The mother was only nineteen, as old as the daughter she is now thinking about as she does her ironing. The story moves on from there—a chronicle, related in one heartbreaking incident after another, of a girl's growing up under the adversity of the depression years. A chronicle, too, of a mother's attempt to keep her own head above water (she remarried, had more children, pursued work to the best of her ability, and tried to do right by her children and new husband). And a chronicle of a particular child's suffering: nurseries where she was ignored at best; schools where the teachers were callous or mean; clinics where arbitrariness and bureaucratic self-importance determined the way she was treated and the recommendations made to her mother; a convalescent home whose horrors were covered by a veneer of sugary sentiment Charles Dickens would have known how to document. And in her family, a fight for herself, for her rights and her terrain, in the face of the children born later to her mother—an especially hard and bitter fight because there were so few victories possible in a family so impoverished and vulnerable.

But the child did not grow to be a mere victim of the kind so many of us these days are rather eager to recognize—a hopeless tangle of psychopathology. The growing child, even in her troubled moments, revealed herself to be persistent, demanding, and observant. In the complaints we make, in the "symptoms" we develop, we reveal our strengths as well as our weaknesses. The hurt child could summon her intelligence, exercise her will, smile and make others smile: "The control, the command, the convulsing and deadly clowning, the spell, then the roaring, stamping audience, unwilling to let this rare and precious laughter out of their lives." At times her mother could observe, "She is so lovely"; and then immediately wonder why they in the clinic were so anxious to talk about the daughter's "problems."

"Let her be," the mother says, not defiantly and not out of escapist ignorance. "So all that is in her will not bloom," she continues, "but in how many does it? There is still enough left to live by." And in case the people at the unnamed clinic already have in response their various "interpretations," their "insights," the mother has a quiet request to make— that the young lady be accorded respect, be allowed her dignity, be regarded as and told she is "more than this dress on the ironing board, helpless before the iron."

That is all; the last words of the story bring the reader back to the first words, but not in a forced or contrived way—not the all too clever and tidy work of a "literary" writer of short stories who has learned in school about rising action and falling action, and structure, and the need for impact or coherence. A working woman is making the best of *her* situation, even as she expects her daughter to do so. A mother shakes her fist at the universe, not excitedly, and with no great expectation of triumph, but out of a determination to assert her worth, her capabilities, however injured or curbed, her ability to see, to comprehend, and to imagine — and to assert too her daughter's — everyone's.

The other stories reveal the same struggle for personal dignity against the same high, almost impossible odds. They are each sad stories, yet leavened with humor and made compelling, even entertaining (despite the subject matter), by the writer's wonderful, eye-opening ability. She makes her fine social awareness, her strongly felt political passions, her abiding interest in and her fighter's anger at the condition of her sex here and in other countries mere instruments in a commitment to the integrity of the private psychological reverie. She uses it to show the idiosyncratic as well as the representative ideas and emotions of the men, women, and children she chooses to portray and wants desperately (the heart of her effort, the basis perhaps of her special appeal) to uphold and make the rest of us also uphold as, thereby, her companions.

The last story, whose title the author has given to the collection as a whole, is the longest and is again all too easily given a summary — an aging couple, once poor and active in radical politics but now reasonably well-off, comes to terms with death. The author allows herself a bit more leeway than she has before; the story has sustained, compelling dialogue, a more relaxed pace of development, and a thread of humor and sarcasm that offset the grief and heartache. The husband and wife, married forty-seven years, have developed their own ways with each other. He is alternately teasing and encouraging. Most of all he wants to forget the past and make the best of everything. She is suspicious, silent, and quite unwilling to gloss over a lifetime's trials and sorrows. There are marvelous exchanges as he coaxes her and, in the course of the story, calls her a succession of bittersweet names that provide the story's continuity: Mrs. Word-Miser, Mrs. Take It Easy, Mrs. Telepathy, Mrs. In a Hurry, Mrs. Excited Over Nothing. She parries his thrusts and lets him plan, involving her in his hopes for a new life. They will move to one of those "havens" for the elderly. But in the clutch she says no; she is tired, and she will not go along with him. She seems to know that she is sick and will soon die. She has a critical detachment with respect to him, their children, and grandchildren (never mind the world at large) that contrasts with the immediacy and warmth of his response to people, places, and things. A husband and wife in America — old, full of memories, scarred by a life that was not easy either materially or psychologically, and now compelled to face their last challenge together. Tell me a riddle, the grandchildren ask; the grandmother cannot, will not. How can she when she has learned, decade after decade, that life itself, hers and maybe everyone's, is a bundle of riddles? The grandmother can only have silent reveries, occasions for the author to turn into a haunting, brooding poet. And the grandfather's bravado soon enough gives way, as he struggles to face death, his wife's and his own — the final riddle that no one, of whatever disposition or station in life, manages to avoid or figure out.

Since the collection *Tell Me a Riddle* was published fifteen years ago, Tillie Olsen has not come out with more short stories. She was forty-seven then and is now in her sixties. Her own life is well worth knowing. She was the Nebraska-born daughter of a Socialist organizer and worked for years in factories. She married a union man, a printer, and fought alongside him in a long series of working-class struggles during the 1930s and 1940s. She also brought up four children, and being poor and a conscientious political activist, she had little or no spare time for the writing she yet craved to do. She has written about herself and much more in two essays, "Silences: When Writers Don't Write," and "Women Who Are Writers in Our Century: One Out of Twelve." She is (and has been for decades) a feminist—unyielding and strong-minded but never hysterical or shrill. Her essays reveal her to be brilliant, forceful and broadly educated, if without degrees to wave around. She also published in 1974 the novel *Yonnondio* about working-class life in the 1930s—its terrible, lacerating reality. And she has written a long biographical interpretation to accompany a reissue by the Feminist Press of Rebecca Harding Davis's *Life in the Iron Mills,* originally issued in 1861.

At times, in a confessional vein not unlike that of "I Stand Here Ironing," she has allowed herself a moment of regret, if not self-pity: if only there had been more time, an easier life, and hence more stories, novels, and essays written. Proud and stoic, though, she pulls back immediately: that is how it goes—and besides, for others, for the overwhelming majority of the world's people, in the past and now too, there has been *no* spare time, no chance for anything like writing or constructing stories and in them giving expression to ideas and ideals. She need not, however, have one moment of regret. Others have produced more, but she has never once faltered. It is as if she had no time for failure either. Everything she has written has become almost immediately a classic—the short stories especially, but also her two essays, her comment on the life and writing of Rebecca Harding Davis, and her novel. She has been spared celebrity, but hers is a singular talent that will not let go of one, a talent that prompts tears. She offers an artist's compassion and forgiveness but makes plain how fierce the various struggles must continue to be.   [1975]

RICHARD FORD

*R*ichard Ford, *author of the novels* The Sportswriter *(1986) and* Wildlife *(1990) and the story collection* Rock Springs *(1987), published an essay about American short fiction in the* New York Times Book Review *on August 9, 1992.*

Crazy for Stories

I have always supposed that Frank O'Connor, the great and beloved Irish story writer, was only taunting us back in 1962 — the year I wrote *my* first short story — when he said that we Americans have handled the short story so wonderfully, one could say that it is our national art form.

Why, I've thought, would as good a story writer as there ever was from a country where the short story was *already* the national art form decide to cut us in unless it was to make fun with fulsome praise?

Over the decades Americans, of course, *have* written short stories wonderfully, even though I'm not ready to claim them as our national art form, and in fact I can't even see in the great variety of American moods, hues, tones, effects, forms and narrative strategies much difference between our short stories and, say, Irish ones, or ours and the Italian, or the French, or even ours and the English. Place names. A few Giuseppes and Nigels where ours turn out to be Lukes and Cindys. But that's all. Nothing especially fundamental; each nationality producing a sufficient rainbow of stories that O'Connor's rather generic and, for him, liberal definition of a short story as being simply a piece of artistic organization made of words seems to suit.

The Lonely Voice, O'Connor's little book of essays on the short story, is certainly the most provocative and attentive there is on the form, and is probably where anyone, including me, who has an overview of the short story — American and European both — got it. Published in the United States in 1962, and containing a dozen affectionate, rather quirky but lucid essays on Turgenev, Lawrence, Hemingway, Isaac Babel, Mary Lavin, and others, *The Lonely Voice* sets forth what have become famous postulates on the "traditional" short story: that stories have no essential or natural forms, but are made-up things that aren't even always short; that they should be plausible, have exposition, development, and drama; that good stories are almost always about "outlawed figures" hoping to escape from "submerged population groups," rather than about "normal" characters who fit into society as a whole — the latter concern O'Connor reserved for novels; that stories are natively romantic, individualistic, and intransigent; and that America is a brutal place full of dislocated people who sometimes fool you and act nice, thereby making the United States a natural place for short stories to flourish.

The Lonely Voice, in fact, came along just as the latest phase of formal experiment and re-visioning in American short-story writing was creating a tumult among writers and readers, and O'Connor can certainly be excused for not being on the cutting edge of another country's newest writing, particularly when that writing seemed so different from what he liked. Many of O'Connor's firmest convictions, though — about plausibility and character, exposition, development — were, at the beginning of the

'60s, being uprooted and turned upside down by Americans writing what came to be called "anti-stories" or "meta-fiction" and, later on in the '70s, "post-modernist fiction" or just plain "fictions."

This was new work with uncertain settings, stories often without characters *at all;* stories without linear developments or events or closures, stories that goaded conventional plausibility, and in which words were imagined not first as windows to meaning or even to the factual world, as had been the case since slightly before Cervantes, but as narrative *objets* with arbitrary, sometimes ironically assigned references, palpable shapes, audible sounds, rhythms — all of whose intricacies and ironies produced *esthetic* as well as ordinary cognitive pleasures. These were often outrageous, loudly funny, declamatory, brainy, biting, self-referring stories, if in fact they were "stories" at all! (Much chin-pulling went on about this.) They defied the mimetic-realistic unities Frank O'Connor loved so much, and many of us who were beginning to be writers in the '60s loved them and were shocked by them, even if we loved O'Connor's unities, too, and couldn't write in the new way.

These new "fictions" implied an ungracious opinion held by many American writers and readers: that prior generations' work was dull and sleepy and worse; it was irrelevant and compromised and complacent about its own forms, as if these previous writers — America's best ones — considered a story's form to be a template rather than what the new writers thought it was, an infinitely mutable and variegated process that had constantly to be kept fluid and lively. "Process" was a word on many lips in the '60s and '70s. Truth was a process of collaborative myth. Education was a process of boundaryless disciplines. Marriage was a process of evolving harmonies. *Life* was certainly a process of many shocking and ill-fitting things, little of which was being truthfully or even interestingly referred to by such ham-handedly normative conceits as plots, settings, characters, sequential narrative time or knowable point of view — the traditional forms of storyness.

A much-thumbed collection of short fiction from the '60s, *The Anti-Story Anthology,* containing work by Jorge Luis Borges and other foreigners as well as by Americans (William Gass, John Barth, Donald Barthelme), complained in its introduction that American fiction of the '50s was "perhaps the most conservative of mid-century, probably the single mode of artistic expression most self-imitative." Unpretty words — "predictable," "bland," even "formless" — were used to unseat the old in favor of what the editor thought was the *now* stuff then.

I remember reading a column by Gordon Lish in a 1971 *Esquire* relishing his new captaincy of the magazine's fiction duties — a change in command I remember as producing considerable, fidgety curiosity among us American short-story writer wannabes, since *Esquire* had published a great deal of the best American fiction since the '30s and we all wished it would publish ours. "Fiction has now become a vehicle for conveying a feeling," Mr. Lish wrote, and "the principal elements in a piece become tone, mood, atmosphere, style, color, form—the esthetic elements—as against the narrative elements on which were established the great stories of the '50s."

That all sounded fine to me, although "esthetic elements" hadn't seemed exactly lacking in the work of earlier generations I knew about, nor in writing going on at the time. Work I liked—by John Updike, Joyce Carol Oates, Leonard Michaels—was neither predictable nor conservative, even if it went on representing people as people and the dialogue made a kind of usual sense. In any case, Eudora Welty knew plenty about mood and atmosphere, color, and style as long ago as 1941, as did Paul Bowles, whom I was then reading. And there were Flannery O'Connor and James Baldwin. They wrote about feeling. And then there was Faulkner, who seemed to do everything all at once and had no equal.

To me, the new work all around was thrilling, but so was the old, and as a reader I didn't see a need to choose, though my tendencies as a writer were toward the traditional. There were extremes of form—I understood that. But if in stories yet to be written these extremes could be made, by writers, to accommodate one another —language's "poetic qualities" re-certified for wider use, for example—then change, even *refinement* would occur. And probably, I thought, they would occur in the context of traditional convictions proving resilient. That, I thought, would be the short story's future.

And it was. Many of these newly surprising and perplexing "fictions" were, in fact, read by Americans drilled in rather traditional narrative expectations. Anti-stories *were* usually written in sentences one could read as well as "experience" like tone poems. They had beginnings and middles, if not always exactly endings. "Images" seemed abundant. Readers often came to terms with such stories by seizing whatever evidence of narrative cohesion was available, postulating "characters" where there were only voices, seeking correspondences and repetitions, noting things linear which might signal that stories referred outward toward a plausible world instead of inward to themselves or to some other, "magical" realm. These readers may ultimately have appreciated this new work as being only ingenious permutations upon an older and already perfectly good method. But it's worth saying as a base principle that no matter how any story is "understood," its artistic intention is considerably rewarded if someone will simply read it. And these were read, even if among writers and readers they didn't supplant the practice of more traditional forms, a fact that may owe as much to comfort and habit as to the absolute excellence of any particular esthetic.

What's important, though, in nearly 50 years in American story writing—since 1944, the year I was born—is that these were and still are provocative issues among people who read and would write literature. The torque between so-called representational and nonrepresentational writing has prolonged a feeling of unsettlement among writers, as well as a preoccupation with invigorating the story's form as a way of creating effects that would transcend form altogether. Maybe this is not altogether so strange in a country widely perceived to have no literary life, howling around in the dark as Stephen Spender once condescendingly said we all seem to be. Like wolves.

I don't know why people write stories. Raymond Carver said he wrote them because he was drunk a lot and his kids were driving him crazy, and a short story was all he had concentration for. Sometimes, he said, he wrote them in a parked car.

Perhaps, on the slightly more majestic other hand, there's a rage for order in certain of us, a fury that nothing but a nice, compact little short-course bundle like a story can satisfy.

Or maybe story writers—more so than novelists—are moralists at heart, and the form lends itself to acceptable expressions of caution. You! You're not paying enough attention to your life, parceled out as it is in increments smaller and yet more significant than you seem aware of. Here's a form that invites more detailed notice—displaying life not as it is, admittedly, but in flashbacks, in hyper-reality, with epiphanies and without, with closures, time foreshortenings, beauties of all sorts to please you and keep you interested.

Certainly short stories are inherited things. As imprecise as they may be in purely technical and formal terms, we write them now largely because other people wrote them before. American writers usually can't sit still until we've expressed our indebtedness to prior all-stars of the form (Chekhov, Turgenev, de Maupassant being some of our favorites), trying to unite our efforts to the grand tradition. Maybe there's simply an urge in us to imitate something excellent, which, when we do it, makes us feel good.

The book critic Anatole Broyard once wrote of the poet Randall Jarrell that "a poet is a man who, having nothing to do, finds something to do." Extended to writing short stories, Broyard's notion of moral languor on a cruise for moral consequence, eventually finding it in a pretty "glancing" form like a short story, satisfies my appreciation of any art's basic gratuitousness, as well as art's being arbitrary and utterly optional for all involved. Broyard's dictum also, incidentally, rings true to my understanding of contemporary mankind's sense of mission upon the planet, as well as to my experience of other writers and to my experience of being one myself.

My own first effort at the short story was an inept little piece of melancholy I called "Saturday" (as yet unpublished). It was written when I was 17 years old, about a boy, surprisingly enough also 17, who kills a Saturday morning dodging chores and brooding over some feeling of Sartrean loss in life—a feeling he has no apparent right to, nor public words for, but to which the privileged language of my story gave logic and expression. What I think about that story and about most of those I've written since then is that I wrote them because lived life somehow wasn't enough, in some way didn't hit the last note convincingly and was too quickly gone. Not at all that the stuff of my story was especially autobiographical. It may or may not have been; though that doesn't interest me since raw material for stories comes from all corners of experience, and in any case I'm talking about why stories get written, not whether my personal glass is half full or half empty.

Yet consequence, or at least that feeling of greater consequence, possibly *final* consequence—the feeling literature can confer upon the lives of both writers and readers—was something I either felt a need for or saw an opportunity to create. And I wrote my story as an attempt to bring it into existence and perhaps to certify something—my own worth, maybe. God only knows what I might have needed to certify. Maybe this is just another one of those famous neuroses of our time.

In two breaths, Flannery O'Connor said about short stories that they were "one of the most natural and fundamental ways of human expression" and later that "the more I write, the more mysterious I find the process." Short stories indeed feel as though they arise out of *some* fierce schism that they by their very existence mean to reconcile. And fascination edging on to mystery does exist in the discrepancy between the ingenious capacity of great stories to penetrate us and our ineludible awareness of their brevity. "They cast a spell," William Trevor said, speaking of the great ones.

They treat us to language. They stir our moral imaginations. They take our minds off our woes and give order to the previously unordered for the purpose of making beauty and clarity anew. They do the best for us that fiction can do.   [1992]

HAMLIN GARLAND

Hamlin Garland wrote the twelve essays on literature, painting, and drama collected in Crumbling Idols *in 1894, three years after the publication of his book of short stories,* Main-Travelled Roads. Crumbling Idols *was Garland's first and only attempt at literary theory.*

Local Color in Art

Local color in fiction is demonstrably the life of fiction. It is the native element, the differentiating element. It corresponds to the endless and vital charm of individual peculiarity. It is the differences which interest us; the similarities do not please, do not forever stimulate and feed as do the differences. Literature would die of dry rot if it chronicled the similarities only, or even largely.

Historically, the local color of a poet or dramatist is of the greatest value. The charm of Horace is the side light he throws on the manners and customs of his time. The vital in Homer lies, after all, in his local color, not in his abstractions. Because the sagas of the North delineate more exactly how men and women lived and wrought in those days, therefore they have always appealed to me with infinitely greater power than Homer.

Similarly, it is the local color of Chaucer that interests us to-day. We yawn over his tales of chivalry which were in the manner of his contemporaries, but the Miller and the Priest interest us. Wherever the man of the past in literature showed us what he really lived and loved, he moves us. We understand him, and we really feel an interest in him.

Historically, local color has gained in beauty and suggestiveness and humanity from Chaucer down to the present day. Each age has embodied more and more of its actual life and social conformation until the differentiating qualities of modern art make the best paintings of Norway as distinct in local color as its fiction is vital and indigenous.

Every great moving literature to-day is full of local color. It is this element which puts the Norwegian and Russian almost at the very summit of modern novel writing, and it is the comparative lack of this distinctive flavor which makes the English and French take a lower place in truth and sincerity.

Everywhere all over the modern European world, men are writing novels and dramas as naturally as the grass or corn or flax grows. The Provençal, the Hun, the Catalonian, the Norwegian, is getting a hearing. This literature is not the literature of scholars; it is the literature of lovers and doers; of men who love the modern and who have not been educated to despise common things.

These men are speaking a new word. They are not hunting themes, they are struggling to express.

Conventional criticism does not hamper or confine them. They are rooted in the soil. They stand among the corn-fields and they dig in the peat-bogs. They concern themselves with modern and very present words and themes, and they have brought a new word which is to divide in half the domain of beauty.

They have made art the re-creation of the beautiful *and the significant*. Mere beauty no longer suffices. Beauty is the old-world aristocrat who has taken for mate this mighty young plebeian Significance. Their child is to be the most human and humane literature ever seen.

It has taken the United States longer to achieve independence of English critics than it took to free itself from old-world political and economic rule. Its political freedom was won, not by its gentlemen and scholars, but by its yeomanry; and in the same way our national literature will come in its fulness when the common American rises spontaneously to the expression of his concept of life.

The fatal blight upon most American art has been, and is to-day, its imitative quality, which has kept it characterless and factitious,—a forced rose-culture rather than the free flowering of native plants.

Our writers despised or feared the home market. They rested their immortality upon the "universal theme," which was a theme of no interest to the public and of small interest to themselves.

During the first century and a half, our literature had very little national color. It was quite like the utterance of corresponding classes in England. But at length Bryant and Cooper felt the influence of our mighty forests and prairies. Whittier uttered something of New England boy-life, and Thoreau prodded about among newly discovered wonders, and the American literature got its first start.

Under the influence of Cooper came the stories of wild life from Texas, from Ohio, and from Illinois. The wild, rough settlements could not produce smooth and cultured poems or stories; they only furnished forth rough-and-ready anecdotes, but in these stories there were hints of something fine and strong and native.

As the settlements increased in size, as the pressure of the forest and the wild beast grew less, expression rose to a higher plane; men softened in speech and manner. All preparations were being made for a local literature raised to the level of art.

The Pacific slope was first in the line. By the exceptional interest which the world took in the life of the gold fields, and by the forward urge which seems always to surprise the pessimist and the scholiast, two young men were plunged into that wild life, led across the plains set in the shadow of Mount Shasta, and local literature received its first great marked, decided impetus.

To-day we have in America, at last, a group of writers who have no suspicion of imitation laid upon them. Whatever faults they may be supposed to have, they are at any rate, themselves. American critics can depend upon a characteristic American literature of fiction and the drama from these people.

The corn has flowered, and the cotton-boll has broken into speech.

Local color—what is it? It means that the writer spontaneously reflects the life which goes on around him. It is natural and unstrained art.

It is, in a sense, unnatural and artificial to find an American writing novels of Russia or Spain or the Holy Land. He cannot hope to do it so well as the native. The best he can look for is that poor word of praise, "He does it very well, considering he is an alien."

If a young writer complain that there are no themes at home, that he is forced to go abroad for prospective and romance, I answer there is something wrong in his education or his perceptive faculty. Often he is more anxious to win a money success than to be patiently one of art's unhurried devotees.

I can sympathize with him, however, for criticism has not helped him to be true. Criticism of the formal kind and spontaneous expression are always at war, like the old man and the youth. They may politely conceal it, but they are mutually destructive.

Old men naturally love the past; the books they read are the master-pieces; the great men are all dying off, they say; the young man should treat lofty and universal themes, as they used to do. These localisms are petty. These truths are disturbing. Youth annoys them. Spontaneousness is formlessness, and the criticism that does not call for the abstract and the ideal and the beautiful is leading to destruction, these critics say.

And yet there is a criticism which helps, which tends to keep a writer at his best; but such criticism recognizes the dynamic force of a literature, and tries to spy out tendencies. This criticism to-day sees that local color means national character, and is aiding the young writer to treat his themes in the best art.

I assert it is the most natural thing in the world for a man to love his native land and his native, intimate surroundings. Born into a web of cir-cumstances, enmeshed in common life, the youthful artist begins to think. All the associations of that childhood and the love-life of youth combine to make that web of common affairs, threads of silver and beads of gold; the near-at-hand things are the dearest and sweetest after all.

As the reader will see, I am using local color to mean something more than a forced study of the picturesque scenery of a State.

Local color in a novel means that it has such quality of texture and back-ground that it could not have been written in any other place or by any one else than a native.

It means a statement of life as indigenous as the plant-growth. It means that the picturesque shall not be seen by the author, — that every tree and bird and mountain shall be dear and companionable and neces-sary, not picturesque; the tourist cannot write the local novel.

From this it follows that local color must not be put in for the sake of local color. It must go in, it *will* go in, because the writer naturally carries it with him half unconsciously, or conscious only of its significance, its interest to him.

He must not stop to think whether it will interest the reader or not. He must be loyal to himself, and put it in because he loves it. If he is an artist, he will make his reader feel it through his own emotion.

What we should stand for is not universality of theme, but beauty and strength of treatment, leaving the writer to choose his theme because he loves it.

Here is the work of the critic. Recognizing that the theme is beyond his control, let him aid the young writer to delineate simply and with unwavering strokes. Even here the critic can do little, if he is possessed of the idea that the young writer of to-day should model upon Addison or Macaulay or Swift.

There are new criterions to-day in writing as in painting, and individ-ual expression is the aim. The critic can do much to aid a young writer to *not* copy an old master or any other master. Good criticism can aid him to be vivid and simple and unhackneyed in his technique, the subject is his own affair.

I agree with him who says, Local art must be raised to the highest levels in its expression; but in aiding this perfection of technique we must be careful not to cut into the artist's spontaneity. To apply ancient dogmas of criticism to our life and literature would be benumbing to [the] artist and fatal to his art.   [1894]

WILLIAM GASS

William Gass ended the preface to In the Heart of the Heart of the Country *(1968), his collection of short fiction, with an account of the way he wrote the title story.*

From Preface to
In the Heart of the
Heart of the Country

When Henry James, bruised by his failure in the theater, returned to the novel with *The Awkward Age,* he wrote in the scenery himself; he created his actors and gave them their speeches and gestures. More than that, he filled the spaces around them with sensibility—other observations—the perfect vessel of appreciation—himself, or rather, his roundabout writing. His method has become a model. Now, on the page, though the stage is full, the theater is dark and empty. Red bulbs burn above the exits. And when the theater is empty, and the actors continue to speak into the wings and walk from cupboard to sofa as if in the midst of emotion, to whom are they speaking but to themselves? Suddenly the action is all there is; the made-up words are real; the actors are the parts they play; questions are no longer cues; replies are real replies; there's no more drama; the conditions of rehearsal have become the conditions of reality, and the light which streams like colored paper from the spots is all there'll ever be of day.

1. Continue work . . .
2. Study the masters . . .
3. Do deliberate exercises . . .
4. Regularly enter notes . . . sharpen that peculiar and forgetful eye . . .
5. Take to sketching . . . details . . . exactitude . . .
6. Become steeped in history . . .
7. . . . the better word . . . the better word . . . the better word . . .
8. Figure it will be five years before any . . .
9. Wait . . .

A former student, who had reached the lower slopes of a national magazine, charitably wrote to ask if I would do a piece on what it was like to live in the Midwest. Without quite knowing whether my answer would be yes or no, I nevertheless began to gather data on that subject, although it became plain soon enough that the magazine was not interested in the logarithmical disorders of my lyricisms. I had always avoided the autobiographical in my work, reasoning that it was one beginner's trap I'd not fall into (more witless wisdom), and by now I had become suspicious of my own detachment. Could I write close to myself, or would the letter B, which my narrator said he'd sailed to, stand for bathos?

I was living in Brookston, Indiana, then, but I called it B because that's how people and places were sometimes represented in the old days. Pamela is always pulling Mr. B's paw out of her bosom. Turgenev's characters occasionally wait on a low small porch which is fastened like a belt around an inn or posting station, rising like a fresh bump on the road — say — to S, though nothing is in sight yet when we encounter them. Like the reader, they are waiting for the book to begin. (On the other hand, Beckett's roads are letterless, and his figures are waiting for the text to terminate.) Not only has the narrator come to B in a pun (a poor place), with the initial I also wanted to invoke the golden boughs and singing birds of Yeats's Byzantium. Furthermore, I knew that when I'd finished, it wouldn't be Brookston, Indiana, anymore, but a place as full of dream and fabrication as that fabled city itself. Inside my cautious sentences, as against Yeats's monumental poetry, B would become an inverted emblem for man's imagination.

I certainly didn't resort to the letter out of shyness or some belated sense of discretion; but as I got my "facts" straight (clubs, crops, products, prospects, townshape, bar- and barn-size), I remembered how eagerly I'd come to the community, how much I'd needed to feel my mind — just once — run free and openly in peace, in wholesome and unworried amplitude, the way my legs before in Larimore, N.D., had carried me through streets scaled perfectly for childhood; and I slowly realized, while I drew up my lists (jobs, shops, climate), marking social strata like a kid counts layers in a cake, that I was taking down the town in notes so far from sounding anything significant that they would not even let me find a cow; yet I figured my estimates anyway (population changes, transportation, education, housing, love), and I took my polls (of churches and their clientele, of diets and diseases); I made my guesses about the townspeople's privacy (fun, games, hankie-pankies, high or low finance: pitch or catch, cadge, swap or auction), just as any geographer would, impressed by the seriousness of habit, too, of simple talk or an idle spit or prolonged squat — a reflective shit in a distant field; and as I started to distribute my data gingerly across my manuscript, a steady dissolution of the real began; because the more precisely one walks down a verbal street; indeed, the more precisely trash heap and vagrant shadow, weed stand and wind-feel and walkcrack are rendered; when, in fact, all that can conceivably enter consciousness — like snowlight and horse harness, grain spill and oil odor, hedge and grass growth, the cool tin taste of well-water in a bent tin cup—enters like the member of an orchestra, armed with an instrument (the bee's hum and the fly's death, for instance); the more completely, in short, we observe rather than merely note, contemplate rather than perceive, imagine rather than simply ponder; then the more fully, too, must the reader and writer realize, as their sentences foot the page, that they are now in the graciously menacing presence of the Angel of Inwardness, that radiant guardian of Ideas of whom Plato and Rilke spoke so ardently, and Mallarmé and Valéry invoked; since a sense of resonant universality arises in literature whenever some mute and otherwise trivial, though unique, superfluity is experienced with an intensely passionate exactness: through a ring of likeness which defines for each object its land of unlikeness, too (though who says so aside from Schopenhauer, who was also wrong about the world?); and consequently the heart of the country became the heart of the heart with a suddenness which left me uncomforted, in B and not Byzantium, not Brookston, far from the self I thought I might expose, nowhere near a childhood, and with thoughts I kept in paragraphs like small animals caged.

Hours of insanity and escape . . . tear paper into thread-thin strips— not easy . . . then to slide lines of words from one side of a page to another, vainly hoping the difference will be agreeable . . . instead of a passionate particularity, to try for a ringing singularity . . . cancel, scratch, XXXXX . . . stop.

The gentle Turgenev (and one of our masters, surely, if we love this arrogantly modest art), writing about *Fathers and Children*—writing about himself—said: "Only the chosen few are able to transmit to posterity not only the content but also the *form* of their thoughts and views, their personality, which, generally speaking, is of no concern to the masses." *The form*. That is what the long search is for; because form, as Aristotle has instructed us, is the soul itself, the life in any thing, and of any immortal thing the whole. It is the B in being. *The chosen few . . .* the happy few . . . that little band of brothers . . . Well, the chosen cannot choose themselves, however they connive at it.

And he asked his fellow Russian writers to guard their language. "Treat this mighty weapon with respect," he begged, "in skilled hands it can work miracles." But miracles cannot be chosen either. And for those of us who have worked none, respect we can still manage. The folly of a hope sustains us: that next time the skill will be there, and the miracle will ensue.

So I am still the obscure man who wrote these words, and if someone were to ask me once again of the circumstances of my birth, I think I should answer finally that I was born somewhere in the middle of my first book; that life, so far, has not been extensive; that my native state is Anger, a place nowhere on the continent but rather somewhere at the bottom of my belly; that I presently dwell in the Sicily of the soul, the Mexico of the mind, the tower at Duino, the garden house in Rye; and that I shall be

happy to rent, sell, or give away these stories, which I would have furnished far more richly if I could have borne the cost, to anyone who might
want to visit them, or — hallelujah — reside. In lieu of that unlikelihood,
however, I am fashioning a reader for these fictions . . . of what kind, you
ask? well, skilled and generous with attention, for one thing, patient with
longeurs,[1] forgiving of every error and the author's self-indulgence, avid
for details . . . ah, and a lover of lists, a twiddler of lines. Shall this reader
be given occasionally to mouthing a word aloud or wanting to read to a
companion in a piercing library whisper? yes; and shall this reader be one
whose heartbeat alters with the tenses of the verbs? that would be nice; and
shall every allusion be caught like a cold? no, eaten like a fish, whole, fins and
skin; and shall there be a wide brow wrinkled with wonder at the rhetoric?
sharp intakes of breath? and the thoughts found profound and the sentiments felt to be of the best kind? yes, and the patterns applauded . . . but
we won't need to put hair or nose upon our reader, or any other opening
or lure . . . not a muscle need be imagined . . . it is a body quite indifferent
to time, to diet . . . it's only eyes . . . what? oh, it will be a kind of slow-
poke on the page, a sipper of sentences, full of reflective pauses, thus a finger for holding its place should be appointed; a mover of lips, then? just
so, yes, large soft moist ones, naturally red, naturally supple, but made
only for shaping syllables, you understand, for singing . . . singing. And
shall this reader, as the book is opened, shadow the page like a palm? yes,
perhaps that would be best (mind the strain on the spirit, though, no
glasses correct that); and shall this reader sink into the paper? become the
print? and blossom on the other side with pleasure and sensation . . . from
the touch of mind, and the love that lasts in language? yes. Let's imagine
such a being, then. And begin. And then begin.   [1968]

---

[1] Long passages.

SANDRA M. GILBERT
AND SUSAN GUBAR

---

*S*andra M. Gilbert and Susan Gubar present a feminist reading of Charlotte
Perkins Gilman's "The Yellow Wallpaper" in The Madwoman in the Attic:
The Woman Writer and the Nineteenth-Century Literary Imagination
(1979). In this book they argue that a recognizable literary tradition existed in
English and American literature in which the female imagination had demonstrated "the anxiety of authorship." According to Gilbert and Gubar, "Images
of enclosure and escape, fantasies in which maddened doubles functioned as

asocial surrogates for docile selves . . . such patterns reoccurred throughout this tradition, along with obsessive depictions of diseases like anorexia, agoraphobia, and claustrophobia." Gilman's story is securely within this tradition of the "literature of confinement," in which a woman writer, trapped by a patriarchal society, tries to struggle free "through strategic redefinitions of self, art, and society."

A Feminist Reading of Gilman's "The Yellow Wallpaper"

As if to comment on the unity of all these points—on, that is, the anxiety-inducing connections between what women writers tend to see as their parallel confinements in texts, houses, and maternal female bodies—Charlotte Perkins Gilman brought them all together in 1890 in a striking story of female confinement and escape, a paradigmatic tale which (like *Jane Eyre*) seems to tell *the* story that all literary women would tell if they could speak their "speechless woe." "The Yellow Wallpaper," which Gilman herself called "a description of a case of nervous breakdown," recounts in the first person the experiences of a woman who is evidently suffering from a severe postpartum psychosis. Her husband, a censorious and paternalistic physician, is treating her according to methods by which S. Weir Mitchell, a famous "nerve specialist," treated Gilman herself for a similar problem. He has confined her to a large garret room in an "ancestral hall" he has rented, and he has forbidden her to touch pen to paper until she is well again, for he feels, says the narrator, "that with my imaginative power and habit of story-making, a nervous weakness like mine is sure to lead to all manner of excited fancies, and that I ought to use my will and good sense to check the tendency."

The cure, of course, is worse than the disease, for the sick woman's mental condition deteriorates rapidly. "I think sometimes that if I were only well enough to write a little it would relieve the press of ideas and rest me," she remarks, but literally confined in a room she thinks is a one-time nursery because it has "rings and things" in the walls, she is literally locked away from creativity. The "rings and things," although reminiscent of children's gymnastic equipment, are really the paraphernalia of confinement, like the gate at the head of the stairs, instruments that definitively indicate her imprisonment. Even more tormenting, however, is the room's wallpaper: a sulphurous yellow paper, torn off in spots, and patterned with "lame uncertain curves" that "plunge off at outrageous angles" and "destroy themselves in unheard of contradictions." Ancient, smoldering, "unclean" as the oppressive structures of the society in which she finds herself, this paper surrounds the narrator like an inexplicable text, censorious and overwhelming as her physician husband, haunting as the "hereditary estate" in which she is trying to survive. Inevitably she studies its suicidal implications—and inevitably, because of her "imaginative power and habit of story-making," she revises it, projecting her own passion for escape into its otherwise incomprehensible hieroglyphics. "This wallpaper," she decides, at a key point in her story,

> has a kind of sub-pattern in a different shade, a particularly irritating one, for you can only see it in certain lights, and not clearly then.
>
> But in the places where it isn't faded and where the sun is just so—I can see a strange, provoking, formless sort of figure, that seems to skulk about behind that silly and conspicuous front design.

As time passes, this figure concealed behind what corresponds (in terms of what we have been discussing) to the facade of the patriarchal text becomes clearer and clearer. By moonlight the pattern of the wallpaper "becomes bars! The outside pattern I mean, and the woman behind it is as plain as can be." And eventually, as the narrator sinks more deeply into what the world calls madness, the terrifying implications of both the paper and the figure imprisoned behind the paper begin to permeate—that is, to *haunt*—the rented ancestral mansion in which she and her husband are immured. The "yellow smell" of the paper "creeps all over the house," drenching every room in its subtle aroma of decay. And the woman creeps too—through the house, in the house, and out of the house, in the garden and "on that long road under the trees." Sometimes, indeed, the narrator confesses, "I think there are a great many women" both behind the paper and creeping in the garden, "and sometimes only one, and she crawls around fast, and her crawling shakes [the paper] all over. . . . And she is all the time trying to climb through. But nobody could climb through that pattern—it strangles so; I think that is why it has so many heads."

Eventually it becomes obvious to both reader and narrator that the figure creeping through and behind the wallpaper is both the narrator and the narrator's double. By the end of the story, moreover, the narrator has enabled this double to escape from her textual/architectural confinement: "I pulled and she shook, I shook and she pulled, and before morning we had peeled off yards of that paper." Is the message of the tale's conclusion mere madness? Certainly the righteous Doctor John—whose name links him to the anti-hero of Charlotte Brontë's *Villette*—has been temporarily defeated, or at least momentarily stunned. "Now why should that man have fainted?" the narrator ironically asks as she creeps around her attic. But John's unmasculine swoon of surprise is the least of the triumphs Gilman imagines for her madwoman. More significant are the madwoman's own imaginings and creations, mirages of health and freedom with which her author endows her like a fairy godmother showering gold on a sleeping heroine. The woman from behind the wallpaper creeps away, for instance, creeps fast and far on the long road, in broad daylight. "I have watched her sometimes away off in the open country," says the narrator, "creeping as fast as a cloud shadow in a high wind."

Indistinct and yet rapid, barely perceptible but inexorable, the progress of that cloud shadow is not unlike the progress of nineteenth-century literary women out of the texts defined by patriarchal poetics into the open spaces of their own authority. That such an escape from the numb world behind the patterned walls of the text was a flight from disease into health was quite clear to Gilman herself. When "The Yellow Wallpaper" was published she sent it to Weir Mitchell whose strictures had kept her from attempting the pen during her own breakdown, thereby aggravating her illness, and she was delighted to learn, years later, that "he had changed his treatment of nervous prostration since reading" her story. "If that is a fact," she declared, "I have not lived in vain." Because she was a rebellious feminist besides being a medical iconoclast, we can be sure that Gilman did not think of this triumph of hers in narrowly therapeutic terms. Because she knew, with Emily Dickinson, that "Infection in the sentence breeds," she knew that the cure for female despair must be spiritual as well as physical, aesthetic as well as social. What "The Yellow Wallpaper" shows she knew, too, is that even when a supposedly "mad" woman has been sentenced to imprisonment in the "infected" house of her own body, she may discover that, as Sylvia Plath[1] was to put it seventy years later, she has "a self to recover, a queen."   [1979]

---

[1] American poet (1932–1963).

CHARLOTTE PERKINS GILMAN

Charlotte Perkins Gilman wrote her autobiography, The Living of Charlotte Perkins Gilman *(1935), in the last years of her life. Her intelligence and strength of character are evident in this work, as is her modesty after a long career as an eminent American feminist. Her straightforward description of her mental breakdown, which had occurred nearly fifty years earlier, is in marked contrast to the obsessive fantasy of her story "The Yellow Wallpaper," written shortly after her illness.*

Undergoing the Cure
for Nervous Prostration

This was a worse horror than before, for now I saw the stark fact — that I was well while away and sick while at home — a heartening prospect! Soon ensued the same utter prostration, the unbearable inner misery, the ceaseless tears. A new tonic had been invented, Essence of Oats, which was given me, and did some good for a time. I pulled up enough to do a little painting that fall, but soon slipped down again and stayed down. An old friend of my mother's, dear Mrs. Diman, was so grieved at this condition that she gave me a hundred dollars and urged me to go away somewhere and get cured.

At that time the greatest nerve specialist in the country was Dr. S. W. Mitchell of Philadelphia. Through the kindness of a friend of Mr. Stetson's living in that city, I went to him and took "the rest cure"; went with the utmost confidence, prefacing the visit with a long letter giving "the history of the case" in a way a modern psychologist would have appreciated. Dr. Mitchell only thought it proved self-conceit. He had a prejudice against the Beechers. "I've had two women of your blood here already," he told me scornfully. This eminent physician was well versed in two kinds of nervous prostration: that of the business man exhausted from too much work, and the society woman exhausted from too much play. The kind I had was evidently behind him. But he did reassure me on one point—there was no dementia, he said, only hysteria.

I was put to bed and kept there. I was fed, bathed, rubbed, and responded with the vigorous body of twenty-six. As far as he could see there was nothing the matter with me, so after a month of this agreeable treatment he sent me home, with this prescription:

> Live as domestic a life as possible. Have your child with you all the time. (Be it remarked that if I did but dress the baby it left me shaking and crying—certainly far from a healthy companionship for her, to say nothing of the effect on me.) Lie down an hour after each meal. Have but two hours' intellectual life a day. And never touch pen, brush, or pencil as long as you live.

I went home, followed those directions rigidly for months, and came perilously near to losing my mind. The mental agony grew so unbearable that I would sit blankly moving my head from side to side—to get out from under the pain. Not physical pain, not the least "headache" even, just mental torment, and so heavy in its nightmare gloom that it seemed real enough to dodge.

I made a rag baby, hung it on a doorknob, and played with it. I would crawl into remote closets and under beds—to hide from the grinding pressure of that profound distress. . . .

Finally, in the fall of '87, in a moment of clear vision, we agreed to separate, to get a divorce. There was no quarrel, no blame for either one, never an unkind word between us, unbroken mutual affection—but it seemed plain that if I went crazy, it would do my husband no good, and be a deadly injury to my child.

What this meant to the young artist, the devoted husband, the loving father, was so bitter a grief and loss that nothing would have justified breaking the marriage save this worse loss which threatened. It was not a choice between going and staying, but between going, sane, and staying, insane. If I had been of the slightest use to him or to the child, I would have "stuck it," as the English say. But this progressive weakening of the mind made a horror unnecessary to face; better for that dear child to have separated parents than a lunatic mother.

We had been married four years and more. This miserable condition of mind, this darkness, feebleness, and gloom, had begun in those difficult years of courtship, had grown rapidly worse after marriage, and was now threatening utter loss; whereas I had repeated proof that the moment I left home I began to recover. It seemed right to give up a mistaken marriage.

Our mistake was mutual. If I had been stronger and wiser I should never have been persuaded into it. Our suffering was mutual too, his unbroken devotion, his manifold cares and labors in tending a sick wife, his adoring pride in the best of babies, all coming to naught, ending in utter failure—we sympathized with each other but faced a bitter necessity. The separation must come as soon as possible, the divorce must wait for conditions.

If this decision could have been reached sooner it would have been much better for me, the lasting mental injury would have been less. Such recovery as I have made in forty years, and the work accomplished, seem to show that the fear of insanity was not fulfilled, but the effects of nerve bankruptcy remain to this day. So much of my many failures, of misplay and misunderstanding and "queerness" is due to this lasting weakness, and kind friends so unfailingly refuse to allow for it, to believe it, that I am now going to some length in stating the case.   [1935]

BRET HARTE

Bret Harte wrote "The Rise of the 'Short Story'" for the Cornhill Magazine *(July, 1899) to reveal the importance of humor—what he considered "the secret of the American short story"—and to promote the opportunity that the literary genre gave authors "to honestly describe the life around them."*

The Rise of the "Short Story"

As it has been the custom of good-natured reviewers to associate the present writer with the origin of the American "short story," he may have a reasonable excuse for offering the following reflections—partly the result of his own observations during the last thirty years, and partly from his experience in the introduction of this form of literature to the pages of the "Western Magazine," of which he was editor at the beginning of that period. But he is far from claiming the invention, or of even attributing its genesis to that particular occasion. The short story was familiar enough in form in America during the early half of the century; perhaps the proverbial haste of American life was some inducement to its brevity. It had been the medium through which some of the most characteristic work of the best American writers had won the approbation of the public. Poe—a master of the art, as yet unsurpassed—had written; Longfellow and Hawthorne had lent it the graces of the English classics. But it was not the American short story of to-day. It was not characteristic of American life, American habits, nor American thought. It was not vital and instinct with the experience and observation of the average American; it made no attempt to follow his reasoning or to understand his peculiar form of expression—which it was apt to consider vulgar; it had no sympathy with those dramatic contrasts and surprises which are the wonders of American civilisation; it took no account of the modifications of environment and of geographical limitations; indeed, it knew little of American geography. Of all that was distinctly American it was evasive—when it was not apologetic. And even when graced by the style of the best masters, it was distinctly provincial.

It would be easier to trace the causes which produced this than to assign any distinct occasion or period for the change. What we called American literature was still limited to English methods and [based] upon English models. The best writers either wandered far afield for their inspiration, or, restricted to home material, were historical or legendary; artistically contemplative of their own country, but seldom observant. Literature abode on a scant fringe of the Atlantic seaboard, gathering the drift from other shores, and hearing the murmur of other lands rather than the voices of its own; it was either expressed in an artificial treatment of life in the cities, or, as with Irving, was frankly satirical of provincial social ambition. There was much "fine" writing; there were American Addisons, Steeles, and Lambs— there were provincial "Spectators" and "Tatlers." The sentiment was English. Even Irving in the pathetic sketch of "The Wife" echoed the style of "Rosamond Grey." There were sketches of American life in the form of the English Essayists, with no attempt to understand the American character. The literary man had little sympathy with the rough and half-civilised masses who were making his country's history; if he used them at all it was as a foil to bring into greater relief his hero of the unmistakable English pattern. In his slavish imitation of the foreigner, he did not, however, succeed in retaining the foreigner's quick appreciation of novelty. It took an Englishman to first develop the humour and picturesqueness of American or "Yankee" dialect, but Judge Haliburton succeeded better in reproducing "Sam Slick's" speech than his character. Dr. Judd's "Margaret"—one of the early American stories—although a vivid picture of New England farm life and strongly marked with local color, was in incident and treatment a mere imitation of English rural tragedy. It would, indeed, seem that while the American people had shaken off the English yoke in government, politics, and national progression, while they had already startled the old world with invention and originality in practical ideas, they had never freed themselves from the trammels of English literary precedent. The old sneer "Who reads an American book?" might have been answered by another: "There are no *American* books."

But while the American literary imagination was still under the influence of English tradition, an unexpected factor was developing to diminish its power. It was *Humour*—of a quality as distinct and original as the country and civilisation in which it was developed. It was at first noticeable in the anecdote or "story," and after the fashion of such beginnings, was orally transmitted. It was common in the barrooms, the gatherings in the "country store," and finally at public meetings in the mouths of "stump orators." Arguments were clenched, and political principles illustrated, by a "funny story." It invaded even the camp meeting and pulpit. It at last received the currency of the public press. But wherever met it was so distinctively original and novel, so individual and characteristic, that it was at once known and appreciated abroad as "an American story." Crude at first, it received a literary polish in the press, but its dominant quality remained. It was concise and condense [*sic*], yet suggestive. It was delightfully extravagant—or a miracle of understatement. It voiced not only the dialect, but the habits of thought of a people or locality. It gave a new interest to slang. From a paragraph of a dozen lines it grew into a half column, but always retaining its conciseness and felicity of statement. It was a foe to prolixity of any kind, it admitted no fine writing nor affectation of style. It went directly to the point. It was burdened by no conscientiousness; it was often irreverent; it was devoid of all moral responsibility—but it was original! By degrees it developed character with its incident, often, in a few lines gave a striking photograph of a community or a section, but always reached its conclusion without an unnecessary word. It became—and still exists—as an essential feature of newspaper literature. It was the parent of the American "short story."

But although these beginnings assumed more of a national character than American serious or polite literature, they were still purely comic, and their only immediate result was the development of a number of humourists in the columns of the daily press—all possessing the dominant national quality with a certain individuality of their own. For a while it seemed as if they were losing the faculty of story-telling in the elaboration of eccentric character—chiefly used as a vehicle for smart sayings, extravagant incident, or political satire. They were eagerly received by the public and, in their day, were immensely popular, and probably were better known at home and abroad than the more academic but less national humourists of New York or Boston. The national note was always struck even in their individual variations, and the admirable portraiture of the shrewd and humourous showman in "Artemus Ward" survived his more mechanical bad spelling. Yet they did not invade the current narrative fiction; the short and long story-tellers went with their old-fashioned methods, their admirable morals, their well-worn sentiments, their colourless heroes and heroines of the first ranks of provincial society. Neither did social and political convulsions bring anything new in the way of Romance. The Mexican war gave us the delightful satires of Hosea Biglow, but no dramatic narrative. The anti-slavery struggle before the War of the Rebellion produced a successful partizan political novel—on the old lines—with only the purely American characters of the negro "Topsy," and the New England "Miss Ophelia." The War itself, prolific as it was of poetry and eloquence—was barren of romance, except for Edward Everett Hale's artistic and sympathetic *The Man Without a Country*. The tragedies enacted, the sacrifices offered, not only on the battle-field but in the division of families and households; the conflict of superb Quixotism and reckless gallantry against Reason and Duty fought out in quiet border farmhouses and plantations; the reincarnation of Puritan and Cavalier in a wild environment of trackless wastes, pestilential swamps and rugged mountains; the patient endurance of both the conqueror and the conquered; all these found no echo in the romance of the period. Out of the battle smoke that covered half a continent drifted into the pages of magazines shadowy but correct figures of blameless virgins of the North—heroines or fashionable belles—habited as hospital nurses, bearing away the deeply wounded but more deeply misunderstood Harvard or Yale graduate lover who had rushed to bury his broken heart in the conflict. It seems almost incredible that, until the last few years, nothing worthy of that tremendous episode has been preserved by the pen of the romancer.

But if the war produced no characteristic American story it brought the literary man nearer his work. It opened to him distinct conditions of life in his own country, of which he had no previous conceptions; it revealed communities governed by customs and morals unlike his own, yet intensely human and American. The lighter side of some of these he had learned from the humourists before alluded to; the grim realities of war and the stress of circumstances had suddenly given them a pathetic or dramatic reality. Whether he had acquired this knowledge of them with a musket or a gilded strap on his shoulder, or whether he was later a peaceful "carpet-bagger" into the desolate homes of the South and South-West, he knew something personally of their romantic and picturesque value in story. Many cultivated aspirants for literature, as well as many seasoned writers for the press, were among the volunteer soldiery. Again, the composition of the army was heterogeneous: regiments from the West rubbed shoulders with regiments from the East; spruce city clerks hobnobbed with backwoodsmen, and the student fresh from college shared his rations with the half-educated western farmer. The Union, for the first time, recognized its component parts; the natives knew each other. The literary man must have seen heroes and heroines where he had never looked for them, situations that he had never dreamed of. Yet it is a mortifying proof of the strength of inherited literary traditions, that he never dared till quite recently to make a test of them. It is still more strange that he should have waited for the initiative to be taken by a still more crude, wild, and more western civilisation—that of California!

The gold discovery had drawn to the Pacific slope of the continent a still more heterogeneous and remarkable population. The immigration of 1849 and 1850 had taken farmers from the plow, merchants from their desks, and students from their books, while every profession was represented in the motley crowd of gold-seekers. Europe and her colonies had contributed to swell these adventurers—for adventurers they were whatever their purpose; the risks were great, the journey long and difficult—the nearest came from a distance of over a thousand miles; that the men were necessarily pre-equipped with courage, faith, and endurance was a foregone conclusion. They were mainly young; a gray-haired man was a curiosity in the mines in the early days, and an object of rude respect and reverence. They were consequently free from the trammels of precedent or tradition in arranging their lives and making their rude homes. There was a singular fraternity in this ideal republic into which all men entered free and equal. Distinction of previous condition or advantages were unknown, even record and reputation for ill or good were of little benefit or embarrassment to the possessor; men were accepted for what they actually were, and what they could do in taking their part in the camp or settlement. The severest economy, the direst poverty, the most menial labour carried no shame or disgrace with it; individual success brought neither envy nor jealousy. What was one man's fortune to-day might be the luck of another to-morrow. Add to this Utopian simplicity of the people, the environment of magnificent scenery, a unique climate, and a vegetation that was marvelous in its proportions and spontaneity of growth; let it be further considered that the strongest relief was given to this picture by its setting among the crumbling ruins of early Spanish possession—whose monuments still existed in Mission and Presidio, and whose legitimate Castilian descendants still lived and moved in picturesque and dignified contrast to their energetic invaders—and it must be admitted that a condition of romantic and dramatic possibilities was created unrivaled in history.

But the earlier literature of the Pacific slope was, like that of the Atlantic seaboard, national and characteristic only in its humour. The local press sparkled with wit and satire, and, as in the East, developed its usual individual humourists. Of these should be mentioned the earliest pioneers of Californian humour—Lieut. Derby, a United States army engineer officer, author of a series of delightful extravagances known as the "Squibob Papers," and the later and universally known "Mark Twain," who contributed "The Jumping Frog of Calaveras" to the columns of the weekly press. "The San Francisco News Letter," whose whilom contributor, Major Bierce, has since written some of the most graphic romances of the Civil War; "The Golden Era," in which the present writer published his earlier sketches, and "The Californian," to which, as editor, in burlesque imitation of the enterprise of his journalistic betters, he contributed "The Condensed Novels," were the foremost literary weeklies. They were all more or less characteristically American, but it was again remarkable that the more literary, romantic, and imaginative romances had no national flavour. The better remembered serious work in the pages of the only literary magazine, "The Pioneer," was a romance of spiritualism, a psychological study, and a poem on the Chandos picture of Shakespeare.

With this singular experience before him, the present writer was called upon to take the editorial control of the "Overland Monthly," a much more ambitious magazine venture than had yet appeared in California. The best writers had been invited to contribute to its pages. But in looking over his materials on preparing the first number, he was discouraged to find the same notable lack of characteristic fiction. There were good literary articles, sketches of foreign travel, and some essays in description of the natural resources of California—excellent from a commercial and advertising viewpoint. But he failed to discover anything of that wild and picturesque life which had impressed him, first as a truant schoolboy, and afterwards as a youthful schoolmaster among the mining population. In this perplexity he determined to attempt to make good the deficiency himself. He wrote "The Luck of Roaring Camp." However far short it fell of his ideal and his purpose, he conscientiously believed that he had painted much that "he saw, and part of which he was," that his subject and characters were distinctly Californian, as was equally his treatment of them. But an unexpected circumstance here intervened. The publication of the story was objected to by both printer and publisher, virtually for not being in the conventional line of subject, treatment, and morals! The introduction of the abandoned outcast mother of the foundling, "Luck," and the language used by the characters, received a serious warning and protest. The writer was obliged to use his right as editor to save his unfortunate contribution from oblivion. When it appeared at last, he saw with consternation that the printer and publisher had really voiced the local opinion; that the press of California was still strongly dominated by the old conservatism and conventionalism of the East, and that when "The Luck of Roaring Camp" was not denounced as "improper" and "corrupting," it was coldly received as being "singular" and "strange." A still more extraordinary instance of the "provincial note" was struck in the criticism of a religious paper that the story was strongly "unfavourable to immigration" and decidedly unprovocative of the "investment of foreign capital." However, its instantaneous and cordial acceptance as a new departure by the critics of the Eastern States and Europe, enabled the writer to follow it with other stories of like character. More than that, he was gratified to find a disposition on the part of his contributors to shake off their conservative trammels, and in an admirable and original sketch of a wandering circus attendant called "Centrepole Bill," he was delighted to recognize and welcome a convert. The term "Imitator," often used by the critics who, as previously stated, had claimed for the present writer the invention of this kind of literature, could not fairly apply to those who had cut loose from conventional methods, and sought to honestly describe the life around them, and he can only claim to have shown them that it could be done. How well it has since been done, what charm of individual flavour and style has been brought to it by such writers as Harris, Cable, Page, Mark Twain in "Huckleberry Finn," the author of "The Great Smoky Mountains," and Miss Wilkins, the average reader need not be told. It would seem evident, therefore, that the secret of the American short story was the treatment of characteristic American life, with absolute knowledge of its peculiarities and sympathy with its methods; with no fastidious ignoring of its habitual expression, or the inchoate poetry that may be found even hidden in its slang; with no moral determination except that which may be the legitimate outcome of the story itself; with no more elimination than may be necessary for the artistic conception, and never from the fear of the "fetish" of conventionalism. Of such is the American short story of to-day—the germ of American Literature to come.   [1899]

NATHANIEL HAWTHORNE

Nathaniel Hawthorne wrote his preface to the second edition of Twice-Told Tales *in 1851. As Henry James later remarked in his biography of Hawthorne, "There is always a charm in Hawthorne's prefaces which makes one grateful for a pretext to quote from them."*

Preface to *Twice-Told Tales*

The author of TWICE-TOLD TALES has a claim to one distinction, which, as none of his literary brethren will care about disputing it with him, he need not be afraid to mention. He was, for a good many years, the obscurest man of letters in America.

These stories were published in Magazines and Annuals, extending over a period of ten or twelve years, and comprising the whole of the writer's young manhood, without making (so far as he has ever been aware) the slightest impression on the Public. One or two among them— THE RILL FROM THE TOWN-PUMP in perhaps a greater degree than any other—had a pretty wide newspaper-circulation; as for the rest, he has no grounds for supposing, that, on their first appearance, they met with the good or evil fortune to be read by anybody. Throughout the time above-specified, he had no incitement to literary effort in a reasonable prospect of reputation or profit; nothing but the pleasure itself of composition—an enjoyment not at all amiss in its way, and perhaps essential to the merit of the work in hand, but which, in the long run, will hardly keep the chill out of a writer's heart, or the numbness out of his fingers. To this total lack of sympathy, at the age when his mind would naturally have been most effervescent, the Public owe it, (and it is certainly an effect not to be regretted, on either part,) that the Author can show nothing for the thought and industry of that portion of his life, save the forty sketches, or thereabouts, included in these volumes.

Much more, indeed, be wrote; and some very small part of it might yet be rummaged out (but it would not be worth the trouble) among the dingy pages of fifteen-or-twenty-year-old periodicals, or within the shabby morocco-covers of faded Souvenirs. The remainder of the works, alluded to, had a very brief existence, but, on the score of brilliancy, enjoyed a fate vastly superior to that of their brotherhood, which succeeded in getting through the press. In a word, the Author burned them without mercy or remorse, (and, moreover, without any subsequent regret,) and had more than one occasion to marvel that such very dull stuff, as he knew his condemned manuscripts to be, should yet have possessed inflammability enough to set the chimney on fire!

After a long while, the first collected volume of the Tales was published. By this time, if the Author had ever been greatly tormented by literary ambition, (which he does not remember or believe to have been the case,) it must have perished, beyond resuscitation, in the dearth of nutriment. This was fortunate; for the success of the volume was not such as would have gratified a craving desire for notoriety. A moderate edition was "got rid of" (to use the Publisher's very significant phrase) within a reasonable time, but apparently without rendering the writer or his productions much more generally known than before. The great bulk of the reading Public probably ignored the book altogether. A few persons read it, and liked it better than it deserved. At an interval of three or four years, the second volume was published, and encountered much the same sort of kindly, but calm, and very limited reception. The circulation of the two volumes was chiefly confined to New England; nor was it until long after this period, if it even yet be the case, that the Author could regard himself as addressing the American Public, or, indeed, any Public at all. He was merely writing to his known or unknown friends.

As he glances over these long-forgotten pages, and considers his way of life, while composing them, the Author can very clearly discern why all this was so. After so many sober years, he would have reason to be ashamed if he could not criticise his own work as fairly as another man's; and—though it is little his business, and perhaps still less his interest—he can hardly resist a temptation to achieve something of the sort. If writers were allowed to do so, and would perform the task with perfect sincerity and unreserve, their opinions of their own productions would often be more valuable and instructive than the works themselves.

At all events, there can be no harm in the Author's remarking, that he rather wonders how the TWICE-TOLD TALES should have gained what vogue they did, than that it was so little and so gradual. They have the pale tint of flowers that blossomed in too retired a shade—the coolness of a meditative habit, which diffuses itself through the feeling and observation of every sketch. Instead of passion, there is sentiment; and, even in what purport to be pictures of actual life, we have allegory, not always so warmly dressed in its habiliments of flesh and blood, as to be taken into the reader's mind without a shiver. Whether from lack of power, or an unconquerable reserve, the Author's touches have often an effect of tameness; the merriest man can hardly contrive to laugh at his broadest humor; the tenderest woman, one would suppose, will hardly shed warm tears at his deepest pathos. The book, if you would see anything in it, requires to be read in the clear, brown, twilight atmosphere in which it was written; if opened in the sunshine, it is apt to look exceedingly like a volume of blank pages.

With the foregoing characteristics, proper to the productions of a person in retirement, (which happened to be the Author's category, at the time,) the book is devoid of others that we should quite as naturally look for. The sketches are not, it is hardly necessary to say, profound; but it is rather more remarkable that they so seldom, if ever, show any design on the writer's part to make them so. They have none of the abstruseness of idea, or obscurity of expression, which mark the written communications of a solitary mind with itself. They never need translation. It is, in fact, the style of a man of society. Every sentence, so far as it embodies thought or sensibility, may be understood and felt by anybody, who will give himself the trouble to read it, and will take up the book in a proper mood.

This statement of apparently opposite peculiarities leads us to a perception of what the sketches truly are. They are not the talk of a secluded man with his own mind and heart, (had it been so, they could hardly have failed to be more deeply and permanently valuable,) but his attempts, and very imperfectly successful ones, to open an intercourse with the world.

The Author would regret to be understood as speaking sourly or querulously of the slight mark, made by his earlier literary efforts, on the Public at large. It is so far the contrary, that he has been moved to write this preface, chiefly as affording him an opportunity to express how much enjoyment he has owed to these volumes, both before and since their publication. They are the memorials of very tranquil and not unhappy years. They failed, it is true—nor could it have been otherwise—in winning an extensive popularity. Occasionally, however, when he deemed them entirely forgotten, a paragraph or an article, from a native or foreign critic, would gratify his instincts of authorship with unexpected praise;—too generous praise, indeed, and too little alloyed with censure, which, therefore, he learned the better to inflict upon himself. And, by-the-by, it is a very suspicious symptom of a deficiency of the popular element in a book, when it calls forth no harsh criticism. This has been particularly the fortune of the

TWICE-TOLD TALES. They made no enemies, and were so little known and talked about, that those who read, and chanced to like them, were apt to conceive the sort of kindness for the book, which a person naturally feels for a discovery of his own.

This kindly feeling, (in some cases, at least,) extended to the Author, who, on the internal evidence of his sketches, came to be regarded as a mild, shy, gentle, melancholic, exceedingly sensitive, and not very forcible man, hiding his blushes under an assumed name, the quaintness of which was supposed, somehow or other, to symbolize his personal and literary traits. He is by no means certain, that some of his subsequent productions have not been influenced and modified by a natural desire to fill up so amiable an outline, and to act in consonance with the character assigned to him; nor, even now, could he forfeit it without a few tears of tender sensibility. To conclude, however;—these volumes have opened the way to most agreeable associations, and to the formation of imperishable friendships; and there are many golden threads, interwoven with his present happiness, which he can follow up more or less directly, until he finds their commencement here; so that his pleasant pathway among realities seems to proceed out of the Dream-Land of his youth, and to be bordered with just enough of its shadowy foliage to shelter him from the heat of the day. He is therefore satisfied with what the TWICE-TOLD TALES have done for him, and feels it to be far better than fame.   [1851]

WILLIAM DEAN HOWELLS

William Dean Howells, editor of The Atlantic Monthly *from 1871 to 1881, wrote his appreciation of Charles W. Chesnutt's stories for the magazine in May 1900, revealing that when "The Wife of His Youth" was originally published in* The Atlantic *two years earlier, it was not known that "the author of this story is of negro blood."*

Mr. Charles W. Chesnutt's Stories

The critical reader of the story called The Wife of his Youth, which appeared in these pages two years ago, must have noticed uncommon traits in what was altogether a remarkable piece of work. The first was the novelty of the material; for the writer dealt not only with people who were not white, but with people who were not black enough to contrast grotesquely with white people,—who in fact were of that near approach to the ordinary American in race and color which leaves, at the last degree, every one but the connoisseur in doubt whether they are Anglo-Saxon or Anglo-African.

Quite as striking as this novelty of the material was the author's thorough mastery of it, and his unerring knowledge of the life he had chosen in its peculiar racial characteristics. But above all, the story was notable for the passionless handling of a phase of our common life which is tense with potential tragedy; for the attitude, almost ironical, in which the artist observes the play of contesting emotions in the drama under his eyes; and for his apparently reluctant, apparently helpless consent to let the spectator know his real feeling in the matter. Any one accustomed to study methods in fiction, to distinguish between good and bad art, to feel the joy which the delicate skill possible only from a love of truth can give, must have known a high pleasure in the quiet self-restraint of the performance; and such a reader would probably have decided that the social situation in the piece was studied wholly from the outside, by an observer with special opportunities for knowing it, who was, as it were, surprised into final sympathy.

Now, however, it is known that the author of this story is of negro blood, — diluted, indeed, in such measure that if he did not admit this descent few would imagine it, but still quite of that middle world which lies next, though wholly outside, our own. Since his first story appeared he has contributed several others to these pages, and he now makes a showing palpable to criticism in a volume called The Wife of his Youth, and Other Stories of the Color Line; a volume of Southern sketches called The Conjure Woman; and a short life of Frederick Douglass, in the Beacon Series of biographies. The last is a simple, solid, straight piece of work, not remarkable above many other biographical studies by people entirely white, and yet important as the work of a man not entirely white treating of a great man of his inalienable race. But the volumes of fiction *are* remarkable above many, above most short stories by people entirely white, and would be worthy of unusual notice if they were not the work of a man not entirely white.

It is not from their racial interest that we could first wish to speak of them, though that must have a very great and very just claim upon the critic. It is much more simply and directly, as works of art, that they make their appeal, and we must allow the force of this quite independently of the other interest. Yet it cannot always be allowed. There are times in each of the stories of the first volume when the simplicity lapses, and the effect is as of a weak and uninstructed touch. There are other times when the attitude, severely impartial and studiously aloof, accuses itself of a little pompousness. There are still other times when the literature is a little too ornate for beauty, and the diction is journalistic, reporteristic. But it is right to add that these are the exceptional times, and that for far the greatest part Mr. Chesnutt seems to know quite as well what he wants to do in a given case as Maupassant, or Tourguénief,[1] or Mr. James, or Miss Jewett, or Miss

---

[1] Ivan Sergeyevich Turgenev (1818–1883), a Russian writer of poems, plays, criticism, stories, and novels, including his masterpiece *Otsy i deti* (*Fathers and Sons*, 1862).

Wilkins, in other given cases, and has done it with an art of kindred quiet and force. He belongs, in other words, to the good school, the only school, all aberrations from nature being so much truancy and anarchy. He sees his people very clearly, very justly, and he shows them as he sees them, leaving the reader to divine the depth of his feeling for them. He touches all the stops, and with equal delicacy in stories of real tragedy and comedy and pathos, so that it would be hard to say which is the finest in such admirably rendered effects as The Web of Circumstance, The Bouquet, and Uncle Wellington's Wives. In some others the comedy degenerates into satire, with a look in the reader's direction which the author's friend must deplore.

As these stories are of our own time and country, and as there is not a swashbuckler of the seventeenth century, or a sentimentalist of this, or a princess of an imaginary kingdom, in any of them, they will possibly not reach half a million readers in six months, but in twelve months possibly more readers will remember them than if they had reached the half million. They are new and fresh and strong, as life always is, and fable never is; and the stories of The Conjure Woman have a wild, indigenous poetry, the creation of sincere and original imagination, which is imparted with a tender humorousness and a very artistic reticence. As far as his race is concerned, or his sixteenth part of a race, it does not greatly matter whether Mr. Chesnutt invented their motives, or found them, as he feigns, among his distant cousins of the Southern cabins. In either case, the wonder of their beauty is the same; and whatever is primitive and sylvan or campestral in the reader's heart is touched by the spells thrown on the simple black lives in these enchanting tales. Character, the most precious thing in fiction, is as faithfully portrayed against the poetic background as in the setting of the Stories of the Color Line.

Yet these stories, after all, are Mr. Chesnutt's most important work, whether we consider them merely as realistic fiction, apart from their author, or as studies of that middle world of which he is naturally and voluntarily a citizen. We had known the nethermost world of the grotesque and comical negro and the terrible and tragic negro through the white observer on the outside, and black character in its lyrical moods we had known from such an inside witness as Mr. Paul Dunbar; but it had remained for Mr. Chesnutt to acquaint us with those regions where the paler shades dwell as hopelessly, with relation to ourselves, as the blackest negro. He has not shown the dwellers there as very different from ourselves. They have within their own circles the same social ambitions and prejudices; they intrigue and truckle and crawl, and are snobs, like ourselves, both of the snobs that snub and the snobs that are snubbed. We may choose to think them droll in their parody of pure white society, but perhaps it would be wiser to recognize that they are like us because they are of our blood by more than a half, or three quarters, or nine tenths. It is not, in such cases, their negro blood that characterizes them; but it is their negro blood that excludes them, and that will imaginably fortify them and exalt them. Bound in that sad solidarity from which there is no hope of entrance into polite white society for them, they may create a civilization of their own, which need not lack the highest quality. They need not be ashamed of the race from which they have sprung, and whose exile they share; for in many of the arts it has already shown, during a single generation of freedom, gifts which slavery apparently only obscured. With Mr. Booker Washington the first American orator of our time, fresh upon the time of Frederick Douglass; with Mr. Dunbar among the truest of our poets; with Mr. Tanner, a black American, among the only three Americans from whom the French government ever bought a picture, Mr. Chesnutt may well be willing to own his color.

But that is his personal affair. Our own more universal interest in him arises from the more than promise he has given in a department of literature where Americans hold the foremost place. In this there is, happily, no color line; and if he has it in him to go forward on the way which he has traced for himself, to be true to life as he has known it, to deny himself the glories of the cheap success which awaits the charlatan in fiction, one of the places at the top is open to him. He has sounded a fresh note, boldly, not blatantly, and he has won the ear of the more intelligent public.[1900]

ZORA NEALE HURSTON

Zora Neale Hurston continued throughout her life to make what the critic Mary Helen Washington called "unorthodox and paradoxical assertions on racial issues." Often conveyed with great wit and style, Hurston's views were always passionately held, as in her essay "What White Publishers Won't Print," first published in Negro Digest *in April 1950.*

What White Publishers Won't Print

I have been amazed by the Anglo-Saxon's lack of curiosity about the internal lives and emotions of the Negroes, and for that matter, any non-Anglo-Saxon peoples within our borders, above the class of unskilled labor.

This lack of interest is much more important than it seems at first glance. It is even more important at this time than it was in the past. The internal affairs of the nation have bearings on the international stress and strain, and this gap in the national literature now has tremendous weight in world affairs. National coherence and solidarity is implicit in a thorough understanding of the various groups within a nation, and this lack of knowledge about the internal emotions and behavior of the minorities cannot fail to bar our understanding. Man, like all the other animals, fears and is repelled by that which he does not understand, and mere difference is apt to connote something malign.

The fact that there is no demand for incisive and full-dress stories about Negroes above the servant class is indicative of something of vast importance to this nation. This blank is NOT filled by the fiction built around upper-class Negroes exploiting the race problem. Rather, it tends to point it up. A college-bred Negro still is not a person like other folks, but an interesting problem, more or less. It calls to mind a story of slavery time. In this story, a master with more intellectual curiosity than usual, set out to see how much he could teach a particularly bright slave of his. When he had gotten him up to higher mathematics and to be a fluent reader of Latin, he called in a neighbor to show off his brilliant slave, and to argue that Negroes had brains just like the slave-owners had, and given the same opportunities, would turn out the same.

The visiting master of slaves looked and listened, tried to trap the literate slave in Algebra and Latin, and failing to do so in both, turned to his neighbor and said:

"Yes, he certainly knows his higher mathematics, and he can read Latin better than many white men I know, but I cannot bring myself to believe that he understands a thing that he is doing. It is all an aping of our culture. All on the outside. You are crazy if you think that it has changed him inside in the least. Turn him loose, and he will revert at once to the jungle. He is still a savage, and no amount of translating Virgil and Ovid is going to change him. In fact, all you have done is to turn a useful savage into a dangerous beast."

That was in slavery time, yes, and we have come a long, long way since then, but the troubling thing is that there are still too many who refuse to believe in the ingestion and digestion of western culture as yet. Hence the lack of literature about the higher emotions and love life of upper-class Negroes and the minorities in general.

Publishers and producers are cool to the idea. Now, do not leap to the conclusion that editors and producers constitute a special class of unbelievers. That is far from true. Publishing houses and theatrical promoters are in business to make money. They will sponsor anything that they believe will sell. They shy away from romantic stories about Negroes and Jews because they feel that they know the public indifference to such works, unless the story or play involves racial tension. It can then be offered as a study in Sociology, with the romantic side subdued. They know the scepticism in general about the complicated emotions in the minorities. The average American just cannot conceive of it, and would be apt to reject the notion, and publishers and producers take the stand that they are not in business to educate, but to make money. Sympathetic as they might be, they cannot afford to be crusaders.

In proof of this, you can note various publishers and producers edging forward a little, and ready to go even further when the trial balloons show that the public is ready for it. This public lack of interest is the nut of the matter.

The question naturally arises as to the why of this indifference, not to say scepticism, to the internal life of educated minorities.

The answer lies in what we may call the AMERICAN MUSEUM OF UNNATURAL HISTORY. This is an intangible built on folk belief. It is assumed that all non-Anglo-Saxons are uncomplicated stereotypes. Everybody knows all about them. They are lay figures mounted in the museum where all may take them in at a glance. They are made of bent wires without insides at all. So how could anybody write a book about the nonexistent?

The American Indian is a contraption of copper wires in an eternal war-bonnet, with no equipment for laughter, expressionless face, and that says "How" when spoken to. His only activity is treachery leading us to massacres. Who is so dumb as not to know all about Indians, even if they have never seen one, nor talked with anyone who ever knew one?

The American Negro exhibit is a group of two. Both of these mechanical toys are built so that their feet eternally shuffle, and their eyes pop and roll. Shuffling feet and those popping, rolling eyes denote the Negro and no characterization is genuine without this monotony. One is seated on a stump picking away on his banjo and singing and laughing. The other is a most amoral character before a share-cropper's shack mumbling about injustice. Doing this makes him out to be a Negro "intellectual." It is as simple as all that.

The whole museum is dedicated to the convenient "typical." In there is the "typical" Oriental, Jew, Yankee, Westerner, Southerner, Latin, and even out-of-favor Nordics like the German. The Englishman "I say old chappie," and the gesticulating Frenchman. The least observant American can know all at a glance. However, the public willingly accepts the untypical in Nordics, but feels cheated if the untypical is portrayed in others. The author of *Scarlet Sister Mary*[1] complained to me that her neighbors objected to her book on the grounds that she had the characters thinking, "and everybody know that Nigras don't think."

But for the national welfare, it is urgent to realize that the minorities do think, and think about something other than the race problem. That they are very human and internally, according to natural endowment, are just like everybody else. So long as this is not conceived, there must remain that feeling of unsurmountable difference, and difference to the average man means something bad. If people were made right, they would be just like him.

The trouble with the purely problem arguments is that they leave too much unknown. Argue all you will or may about injustice, but as long as the majority cannot conceive of a Negro or a Jew feeling and reacting

---

[1]The 1928 novel by Julia Peterkin (1880–1961) set in South Carolina.

inside just as they do, the majority will keep right on believing that people who do not feel like them cannot possibly feel as they do, and conform to the established pattern. It is well known that there must be a body of waived matter, let us say, things accepted and taken for granted by all in a community before there can be that commonality of feeling. The usual phrase is having things in common. Until this is thoroughly established in respect to Negroes in America, as well as of other minorities, it will remain impossible for the majority to conceive of a Negro experiencing a deep and abiding love and not just the passion of sex. That a great mass of Negroes can be stirred by the pageants of Spring and Fall; the extravaganza of summer, and the majesty of winter. That they can and do experience discovery of the numerous subtle faces as a foundation for a great and selfless love, and the diverse nuances that go to destroy that love as with others. As it is now, this capacity, this evidence of high and complicated emotions, is ruled out. Hence the lack of interest in a romance uncomplicated by the race struggle has so little appeal.

This insistence on defeat in a story where upper-class Negroes are portrayed, perhaps says something from the subconscious of the majority. Involved in western culture, the hero or the heroine, or both, must appear frustrated and go down to defeat, somehow. Our literature reeks with it. Is it the same as saying, "You can translate Virgil, and fumble with the differential calculus, but can you really comprehend it? Can you cope with our subtleties?"

That brings us to the folklore of "reversion to type." This curious doctrine has such wide acceptance that it is tragic. One has only to examine the huge literature on it to be convinced. No matter how high we may *seem* to climb, put us under strain and we revert to type, that is, to the bush. Under a superficial layer of western culture, the jungle drums throb in our veins.

This ridiculous notion makes it possible for that majority who accept it to conceive of even a man like the suave and scholarly Dr. Charles S. Johnson[2] to hide a black cat's bone on his person, and indulge in a midnight voodoo ceremony, complete with leopard skin and drums if threatened with the loss of the presidency of Fisk University, or the love of his wife. "Under the skin . . . better to deal with them in business, etc., but otherwise keep them at a safe distance and under control. I tell you, Carl Van Vechten,[3] think as you like, but they are just not like us."

The extent and extravagance of this notion reaches the ultimate in nonsense in the widespread belief that the Chinese have bizarre genitals, because of that eye-fold that makes their eyes seem to slant. In spite of the fact that no biology has ever mentioned any such difference in reproductive organs

---

[2]Johnson (1893–1956) was the first African American president of Fisk University.

[3]Progressive white champion and patron of African American culture (1880–1964).

makes no matter. Millions of people believe it. "Did you know that a Chinese has . . ." Consequently, their quiet contemplative manner is interpreted as a sign of slyness and a treacherous inclination.

But the opening wedge for better understanding has been thrust into the crack. Though many Negroes denounced Carl Van Vechten's *Nigger Heaven* because of the title, and without ever reading it, the book, written in the deepest sincerity, revealed Negroes of wealth and culture to the white public. It created curiosity even when it aroused scepticism. It made folks want to know. Worth Tuttle Hedden's *The Other Room* has definitely widened the opening. Neither of these well-written works takes a romance of upper-class Negro life as the central theme, but the atmosphere and the background is there. These works should be followed up by some incisive and intimate stories from the inside.

The realistic story around a Negro insurance official, dentist, general practitioner, undertaker, and the like would be most revealing. Thinly disguised fiction around the well-known Negro names is not the answer, either. The "exceptional" as well as the Ol' Man Rivers has been exploited all out of context already. Everybody is already resigned to the "exceptional" Negro, and willing to be entertained by the "quaint." To grasp the penetration of western civilization in a minority, it is necessary to know how the average behaves and lives. Books that deal with people like in Sinclair Lewis' *Main Street* is the necessary metier. For various reasons, the average, struggling, non-morbid Negro is the best-kept secret in America. His revelation to the public is the thing needed to do away with that feeling of difference which inspires fear and which ever expresses itself in dislike.

It is inevitable that this knowledge will destroy many illusions and romantic traditions which America probably likes to have around. But then, we have no record of anybody sinking into a lingering death on finding out that there was no Santa Claus. The old world will take it in its stride. The realization that Negroes are no better nor no worse, and at times just as boring as everybody else, will hardly kill off the population of the nation.

Outside of racial attitudes, there is still another reason why this literature should exist. Literature and other arts are supposed to hold up the mirror to nature. With only the fractional "exceptional" and the "quaint" portrayed, a true picture of Negro life in America cannot be. A great principle of national art has been violated.

These are the things that publishers and producers, as the accredited representatives of the American people, have not as yet taken into consideration sufficiently. Let there be light!   [1950]

WASHINGTON IRVING

Washington Irving wrote a letter from Paris to his friend Henry Brevoort on December 11, 1824, describing the way he had composed his sketches and short tales such as "Rip Van Winkle" five years before, and pointing out why the prose tale seemed to him more difficult to write than the novel. The letter was included in the Life and Letters of Washington Irving, *two volumes published by G. P. Putnam's Sons of New York City in 1869.*

Letter to Henry Brevoort, December 11, 1824

PARIS, RUE RICHELIEU, NO. 89 DEC. 11, 1824.

I cannot tell you what pleasure I have received from long chats with Lynch[1] about old times and old associates. His animated and descriptive manner has put all New York before me, and made me long to be once more there. I do not know whether it be the force of early impressions and associations, or whether it be really well-founded, but there is a charm about that little spot of earth; that beautiful city and its environs, that has a perfect spell over my imagination. The bay, the rivers and their wild and woody shores, the haunts of my boyhood, both on land and water, absolutely have a witchery over my mind. I thank God for my having been born in so beautiful a place among such beautiful scenery; I am convinced I owe a vast deal of what is good and pleasant in my nature to the circumstance.

I feel continually indebted to your kindness for the interest you have taken in my affairs, and in the success of my works in America. I begin to feel extremely anxious to secure a little income from my literary property, that shall put me beyond the danger of recurring penury; and shall render me independent of the necessity of laboring for the press. I should like to write occasionally for my amusement, and to have the power of throwing my writings either into my portfolio, or into the fire. I enjoy the first conception and first sketchings down of my ideas, but the correcting and preparing them for the press is irksome, and publishing is detestable.

My last work has a good run in England, and has been extremely well spoken of by some of the worthies of literature, though it has met with some handling from the press. The fact is, I have kept myself so aloof from all clanship in literature that I have no allies among the scribblers for the

---

[1]A reference to Dominick Lynch of New York.

periodical press; and some of them have taken a pique against me for having treated them a little cavalierly in my writings. However, as I do not read criticism, good or bad, I am out of the reach of attack. If my writings are worth anything, they will outlive temporary criticism; if not, they are not worth caring about. Some parts of my last work were written rather hastily; yet I am convinced that a great part of it was written in a free and happier vein than almost any of my former writings. * * * I fancy much of what I value myself upon in writing, escapes the observation of the great mass of my readers, who are intent more upon the story than the way in which it is told. For my part, I consider a story merely as a frame on which to stretch my materials. It is the play of thought, and sentiment, and language; the weaving in of characters, lightly, yet expressively delineated; the familiar and faithful exhibition of scenes in common life; and the half-concealed vein of humor that is often playing through the whole;—these are among what I aim at, and upon which I felicitate myself in proportion as I think I succeed. I have preferred adopting the mode of sketches and short tales rather than long works, because I choose to take a line of writing peculiar to myself, rather than fall into the manner or school of any other writer; and there is a constant activity of thought and a nicety of execution required in writings of the kind, more than the world appears to imagine. It is comparatively easy to swell a story to any size when you have once the scheme and the characters in your mind; the mere interest of the story, too, carries the reader on through pages and pages of careless writing, and the author may often be dull for half a volume at a time, if he has some striking scene at the end of it; but in these shorter writings, every page must have its merit. The author must be continually piquant; woe to him if he makes an awkward sentence or writes a stupid page; the critics are sure to pounce upon it. Yet if he succeed, the very variety and piquancy of his writings—nay, their very brevity, make them frequently recurred to, and when the mere interest of the story is exhausted, he begins to get credit for his touches of pathos or humor; his points of wit or turns of language. I give these as some of the reasons that have induced me to keep on thus far in the way I had opened for myself; because I find by recent letters from E. I. that you are joining in the oft-repeated advice that I should write a novel. I believe the works that I have written will be oftener re read than any novel of the size that I could have written. It is true other writers have crowded into the same branch of literature, and I now begin to find myself elbowed by men who have followed my footsteps; but at any rate I have had the merit of adopting a line for myself, instead of following others.

[1824]

SHIRLEY JACKSON

Shirley Jackson wrote this "biography of a story" in 1960 as a lecture to be delivered before reading "The Lottery" to college audiences. After her death it was included in Come Along with Me *(1968), edited by her husband, Stanley Edgar Hyman. The lecture also contained extensive quotations from letters she had received from readers who took the story literally. These so disgusted Jackson that she promised her listeners at the conclusion of her talk, "I am out of the lottery business for good."*

The Morning of June 28, 1948, and "The Lottery"

On the morning of June 28, 1948, I walked down to the post office in our little Vermont town to pick up the mail. I was quite casual about it, as I recall—I opened the box, took out a couple of bills and a letter or two, talked to the postmaster for a few minutes, and left, never supposing that it was the last time for months that I was to pick up the mail without an active feeling of panic. By the next week I had had to change my mailbox to the largest one in the post office, and casual conversation with the postmaster was out of the question, because he wasn't speaking to me. June 28, 1948, was the day *The New Yorker* came out with a story of mine in it. It was not my first published story, nor my last, but I have been assured over and over that if it had been the only story I ever wrote or published, there would be people who would not forget my name.

I had written the story three weeks before, on a bright June morning when summer seemed to have come at last, with blue skies and warm sun and no heavenly signs to warn me that my morning's work was anything but just another story. The idea had come to me while I was pushing my daughter up the hill in her stroller—it was, as I say, a warm morning, and the hill was steep, and beside my daughter the stroller held the day's groceries—and perhaps the effort of that last fifty yards up the hill put an edge to the story; at any rate, I had the idea fairly clearly in my mind when I put my daughter in her playpen and the frozen vegetables in the refrigerator, and, writing the story, I found that it went quickly and easily, moving from beginning to end without pause. As a matter of fact, when I read it over later I decided that except for one or two minor corrections, it needed no changes, and the story I finally typed up and sent off to my agent the next day was almost word for word the original draft. This, as any writer of stories can tell you, is not a usual thing. All I know is that when I came to read the story over I felt strongly that I didn't want to fuss with it. I didn't think it was perfect, but I didn't want to fuss with it. It was, I thought, a serious, straightforward story, and I was pleased and a little surprised at the ease with which it had been written; I was reasonably proud of it, and hoped that my agent would sell it to some magazine and I would have the gratification of seeing it in print.

My agent did not care for the story, but—as she said in her note at the time—her job was to sell it, not to like it. She sent it at once to *The New Yorker,* and about a week after the story had been written I received a telephone call from the fiction editor of *The New Yorker;* it was quite clear that he did not really care for the story, either, but *The New Yorker* was going to buy it. He asked for one change—that the date mentioned in the story be changed to coincide with the date of the issue of the magazine in which the story would appear, and I said of course. He then asked, hesitantly, if I had any particular interpretation of my own for the story; Mr. Harold Ross, then the editor of *The New Yorker,* was not altogether sure that he understood the story, and wondered if I cared to enlarge upon its meaning. I said no. Mr. Ross, he said, thought that the story might be puzzling to some people, and in case anyone telephoned the magazine, as sometimes happened, or wrote in asking about the story, was there anything in particular I wanted them to say? No, I said, nothing in particular; it was just a story I wrote.

I had no more preparation than that. I went on picking up the mail every morning, pushing my daughter up and down the hill in her stroller, anticipating pleasurably the check from *The New Yorker,* and shopping for groceries. The weather stayed nice and it looked as though it was going to be a good summer. Then, on June 28, *The New Yorker* came out with my story.

Things began mildly enough with a note from a friend at *The New Yorker:* "Your story has kicked up quite a fuss around the office," he wrote. I was flattered; it's nice to think that your friends notice what you write. Later that day there was a call from one of the magazine's editors; they had had a couple of people phone in about my story, he said, and was there anything I particularly wanted him to say if there were any more calls? No, I said, nothing particular; anything he chose to say was perfectly all right with me; it was just a story.

I was further puzzled by a cryptic note from another friend: "Heard a man talking about a story of yours on the bus this morning," she wrote. "Very exciting. I wanted to tell him I knew the author, but after I heard what he was saying I decided I'd better not."

One of the most terrifying aspects of publishing stories and books is the realization that they are going to be read, and read by strangers. I had never fully realized this before, although I had of course in my imagination dwelt lovingly upon the thought of the millions and millions of people who were going to be uplifted and enriched and delighted by the stories I wrote. It had simply never occurred to me that these millions and millions of people might be so far from being uplifted that they would sit down and write me letters I was downright scared to open; of the three-hundred-odd letters that I received that summer I can count only thirteen that spoke kindly to me, and they were mostly from friends. Even my mother scolded me: "Dad and I did not care at all for your story in *The New Yorker*," she wrote sternly, "it does seem, dear, that this gloomy kind of story is what all you young people think about these days. Why don't you write something to cheer people up?"

By mid-July I had begun to perceive that I was very lucky indeed to be safely in Vermont, where no one in our small town had ever heard of *The New Yorker*, much less read my story. Millions of people, and my mother, had taken a pronounced dislike to me.

The magazine kept no track of telephone calls, but all letters addressed to me care of the magazine were forwarded directly to me for answering, and all letters addressed to the magazine—some of them addressed to Harold Ross personally; these were the most vehement—were answered at the magazine and then the letters were sent me in great batches, along with carbons of the answers written at the magazine. I have all the letters still, and if they could be considered to give any accurate cross section of the reading public, or the reading public of *The New Yorker*, or even the reading public of one issue of *The New Yorker*, I would stop writing now.

Judging from these letters, people who read stories are gullible, rude, frequently illiterate, and horribly afraid of being laughed at. Many of the writers were positive that *The New Yorker* was going to ridicule them in print, and the most cautious letters were headed, in capital letters: NOT FOR PUBLICATION or PLEASE DO NOT PRINT THIS LETTER, or, at best, THIS LETTER MAY BE PUBLISHED AT YOUR USUAL RATES OF PAYMENT. Anonymous letters, of which there were a few, were destroyed. *The New Yorker* never published any comment of any kind about the story in the magazine, but did issue one publicity release saying that the story had received more mail than any piece of fiction they had ever published; this was after the newspapers had gotten into the act, in midsummer, with a front-page story in the San Francisco *Chronicle* begging to know what the story meant, and a series of columns in New York and Chicago papers pointing out that *New Yorker* subscriptions were being canceled right and left.

Curiously, there are three main themes which dominate the letters of that first summer—three themes which might be identified as bewilderment, speculation, and plain old-fashioned abuse. In the years since then, during which the story has been anthologized, dramatized, televised, and even—in one completely mystifying transformation—made into a ballet, the tenor of letters I receive has changed. I am addressed more politely, as a rule, and the letters largely confine themselves to questions like what does this story mean? The general tone of the early letters, however, was a kind of wide-eyed, shocked innocence. People at first were not so much concerned with what the story meant; what they wanted to know was where these lotteries were held, and whether they could go there and watch.   [1968]

Henry James wrote his biography of Nathaniel Hawthorne for the English Men of Letters series, published in London in 1879. Aware of the meager opportunities for American writers to make a living in the early years of the century, James took pleasure in describing Hawthorne's brief employment as an underpaid editor in Boston in 1836 before the publication of his Twice-Told Tales.

From *Hawthorne*

It will be necessary, for several reasons, to give this short sketch the form rather of a critical essay than of a biography. The data for a life of Nathaniel Hawthorne are the reverse of copious, and even if they were abundant they would serve but in a limited measure the purpose of the biographer. Hawthorne's career was probably as tranquil and uneventful a one as ever fell to the lot of a man of letters; it was almost strikingly deficient in incident, in what may be called the dramatic quality. Few men of equal genius and of equal eminence can have led on the whole a simpler life. His six volumes of *Note-Books* illustrate this simplicity; they are a sort of monument to an unagitated fortune. Hawthorne's career had few vicissitudes or variations; it was passed for the most part in a small and homogeneous society, in a provincial, rural community; it had few perceptible points of contact with what is called the world, with public events, with the manners of his time, even with the life of his neighbors. Its literary incidents are not numerous. He produced, in quantity, but little. His works consist of four novels and the fragment of another, five volumes of short tales, a collection of sketches, and a couple of storybooks for children. And yet some account of the man and the writer is well worth giving. Whatever may have been Hawthorne's private lot, he has the importance of being the most beautiful and most eminent representative of a literature. The importance of the literature may be questioned, but at any rate, in the field of letters, Hawthorne is the most valuable example of the American genius. That genius has not, as a whole, been literary; but Hawthorne was on his limited scale a master of expression. He is the writer to whom his countrymen most confidently point when they wish to make a claim to have enriched the mother tongue, and, judging from present appearances, he will long occupy this honorable position. If there is something very fortunate for him in the way that he borrows an added relief from the absence of competitors in his own line and from the general flatness of the literary field that surrounds him, there is also, to a spectator, something almost touching in his situation. He was so modest and delicate a genius that we

may fancy him appealing from the lonely honor of a representative attitude — perceiving a painful incongruity between his imponderable literary
baggage and the large conditions of American life. Hawthorne on the one
side is so subtle and slender and unpretending, and the American world on
the other is so vast and various and substantial, that it might seem to the
author of *The Scarlet Letter* and the *Mosses from an Old Manse* that we render him a poor service in contrasting his proportions with those of a great
civilization. But our author must accept the awkward as well as the graceful side of his fame; for he has the advantage of pointing a valuable moral.
This moral is that the flower of art blooms only where the soil is deep, that
it takes a great deal of history to produce a little literature, that it needs a
complex social machinery to set a writer in motion. American civilization
has hitherto had other things to do than to produce flowers, and before
giving birth to writers it has wisely occupied itself with providing something for them to write about. Three or four beautiful talents of trans-
Atlantic growth are the sum of what the world usually recognizes, and in
this modest nosegay the genius of Hawthorne is admitted to have the
rarest and sweetest fragrance.

His very simplicity has been in his favor; it has helped him to appear
complete and homogeneous. To talk of his being national would be to
force the note and make a mistake of proportion; but he is, in spite of the
absence of the realistic quality, intensely and vividly local. Out of the soil of
New England he sprang — in a crevice of that immitigable granite he
sprouted and bloomed. Half of the interest that he possesses for an American reader with any turn for analysis must reside in his latent New England
savor; and I think it no more than just to say that whatever entertainment he
may yield to those who know him at a distance, it is an almost indispensable
condition of properly appreciating him to have received a personal impression of the manners, the morals, indeed of the very climate, of the great
region of which the remarkable city of Boston is the metropolis. The cold,
bright air of New England seems to blow through his pages, and these, in
the opinion of many people, are the medium in which it is most agreeable
to make the acquaintance of that tonic atmosphere. As to whether it is
worth while to seek to know something of New England in order to extract a
more intimate quality from *The House of the Seven Gables* and *The Blithedale
Romance,* I need not pronounce; but it is certain that a considerable observation of the society to which these productions were more directly addressed
is a capital preparation for enjoying them. I have alluded to the absence in
Hawthorne of that quality of realism which is now so much in fashion, an
absence in regard to which there will of course be more to say; and yet I
think I am not fanciful in saying that he testifies to the sentiments of the
society in which he flourished almost as pertinently (proportions observed)
as Balzac and some of his descendants — MM. Flaubert and Zola — testify to
the manners and morals of the French people. He was not a man with a literary theory; he was guiltless of a system, and I am not sure that he had

ever heard of Realism, this remarkable compound having (although it was invented sometime earlier) come into general use only since his death. He had certainly not proposed to himself to give an account of the social idio-syncrasies of his fellow citizens, for his touch on such points is always light and vague, he has none of the apparatus of an historian, and his shadowy style of portraiture never suggests a rigid standard of accuracy. Neverthe-less, he virtually offers the most vivid reflection of New England life that has found its way into literature. His value in this respect is not diminished by the fact that he has not attempted to portray the usual Yankee of comedy, and that he has been almost culpably indifferent to his opportunities for commemorating the variations of colloquial English that may be observed in the New World. His characters do not express themselves in the dialect of the *Biglow Papers*—their language indeed is apt to be too elegant, too delicate. They are not portraits of actual types, and in their phraseology there is nothing imitative. But nonetheless, Hawthorne's work savors thoroughly of the local soil—it is redolent of the social system in which he had his being.

This could hardly fail to be the case, when the man himself was so deeply rooted in the soil. Hawthorne sprang from the primitive New Eng-land stock; he had a very definite and conspicuous pedigree. He was born at Salem, Massachusetts, on the 4th of July, 1804, and his birthday was the great American festival, the anniversary of the Declaration of national Independence. Hawthorne was in his disposition an unqualified and unflinching American; he found occasion to give us the measure of the fact during the seven years that he spent in Europe toward the close of his life; and this was no more than proper on the part of a man who had enjoyed the honor of coming into the world on the day on which of all the days in the year the great Republic enjoys her acutest fit of self-consciousness. Moreover, a person who has been ushered into life by the ringing of bells and the booming of cannon (unless indeed he be frightened straight out of it again by the uproar of his awakening) receives by this very fact an injunction to do something great, something that will justify such striking natal accompaniments. Hawthorne was by race of the clearest Puritan strain. . . .

In 1850, when *The Scarlet Letter* appeared, Hawthorne was forty-six years old, and this may certainly seem a long-delayed popularity. On the other hand, it must be remembered that he had not appealed to the world with any great energy. The *Twice-Told Tales,* charming as they are, do not constitute a very massive literary pedestal. As soon as the author, resorting to severer measures, put forth *The Scarlet Letter,* the public ear was touched and charmed, and after that it was held to the end. "Well it might have been!" the reader will exclaim. "But what a grievous pity that the dulness of this same organ should have operated so long as a deterrent, and by mak-ing Hawthorne wait till he was nearly fifty to publish his first novel, have abbreviated by so much his productive career!" The truth is, he cannot have been in any very high degree ambitious; he was not an abundant producer, and there was manifestly a strain of generous indolence in his composition. There was a lovable want of eagerness about him. Let the encouragement offered have been what it might, he had waited till he was lapsing from middle life to strike his first noticeable blow; and during the last ten years of his career he put forth but two complete works, and the fragment of a third.

It is very true, however, that during this early period he seems to have been very glad to do whatever came to his hand. Certain of his tales found their way into one of the annuals of the time, a publication endowed with the brilliant title of *The Boston Token and Atlantic Souvenir.* The editor of this graceful repository was S. G. Goodrich, a gentleman who, I suppose, may be called one of the pioneers of American periodical literature. He is better known to the world as Mr. Peter Parley, a name under which he produced a multitude of popular school-books, story-books, and other attempts to vulgarize human knowledge and adapt it to the infant mind. This enterprising purveyor of literary wares appears, incongruously enough, to have been Hawthorne's earliest protector, if protection is the proper word for the treatment that the young author received from him. Mr. Goodrich induced him in 1836 to go to Boston to edit a periodical in which he was interested, *The American Magazine of Useful and Entertaining Knowledge.* I have never seen the work in question, but Hawthorne's biographer gives a sorry account of it. It was managed by the so-called Bewick Company, which "took its name from Thomas Bewick, the English restorer of the art of wood engraving, and the magazine was to do his memory honor by his admirable illustrations. But in fact it never did anyone honor, nor brought anyone profit. It was a penny popular affair, containing condensed information about innumerable subjects, no fiction, and little poetry. The woodcuts were of the crudest and most frightful sort. It passed through the hands of several editors and several publishers. Hawthorne was engaged at a salary of five hundred dollars a year; but it appears that he got next to nothing, and did not stay in the position long." Hawthorne wrote from Boston in the winter of 1836: "I came here trusting to Goodrich's positive promise to pay me forty-five dollars as soon as I arrived; and he has kept promising from one day to another, till I do not see that he means to pay at all. I have now broke off all intercourse with him, and never think of going near him. . . . I don't feel at all obliged to him about the editorship, for he is a stockholder and director in the Bewick Company . . . and I defy them to get another to do for a thousand dollars what I do for five hundred." — "I make nothing," he says in another letter, "of writing a history or biography before dinner." Goodrich proposed to him to write a *Universal History* for the use of schools, offering him a hundred dollars for his share in the work. Hawthorne accepted the offer and took a hand — I know not how large a one — in the job. His biographer has been able to identify a single phrase as our author's. He is speaking of George IV: "Even when he was quite a young man this king cared as much about dress as any young coxcomb. He had a great deal of taste in such matters, and it is a pity that he was a king, for he might otherwise have made an excellent tailor." The *Universal History* had a great vogue and passed through hundreds of editions; but it does not appear that Hawthorne ever received more than his hundred dollars. The writer of these pages vividly remembers making its acquaintance at an early stage of his education—a very fat, stumpy-looking book, bound in boards covered with green paper, and having in the text very small woodcuts of the most primitive sort. He associates it to this day with the names of Sesostris and Semiramis whenever he encounters them, there having been, he supposes, some account of the conquests of these potentates that would impress itself upon the imagination of a child. At the end of four months, Hawthorne had received but twenty dollars—four pounds—for his editorship of the *American Magazine*.

There is something pitiful in this episode, and something really touching in the sight of a delicate and superior genius obliged to concern himself with such paltry undertakings. The simple fact was that for a man attempting at that time in America to live by his pen, there were no larger openings; and to live at all Hawthorne had, as the phrase is, to make himself small. This cost him less, moreover, than it would have cost a more copious and strenuous genius, for his modesty was evidently extreme, and I doubt whether he had any very ardent consciousness of rare talent. He went back to Salem, and from this tranquil standpoint, in the spring of 1837, he watched the first volume of his *Twice-Told Tales* come into the world.   [1879]

SARAH ORNE JEWETT

Sarah Orne Jewett wrote "Looking Back on Girlhood" for the Youth's Companion *magazine. It was published in the issue of January 7, 1892, near the end of her long career as a writer (she published at least 146 stories between 1868 and 1904). Jewett's reminiscence of how she became a writer is marked by the same sympathy for others and love of her native landscape that permeates her local-color fiction. As the critic Richard Cary has noted, her lucid and unassuming prose style conveys her "marked regard for the significance of the ordinary."*

Looking Back on Girlhood

In giving this brief account of my childhood, or, to speak exactly, of the surroundings which have affected the course of my work as a writer, my first thought flies back to those who taught me to observe, and to know the deep pleasures of simple things; and to be interested in the lives of people about me.

With its high hills and pine forests, and all its ponds and brooks and distant mountain views, there are few such delightful country towns in New England as the one where I was born. Being one of the oldest colonial settlements, it is full of interesting traditions and relics of the early inhabitants, both Indians and Englishmen. Two large rivers join just below the village at the head of tidewater, and these, with the great inflow from the sea, make a magnificent stream, bordered on its seaward course now by high-wooded banks of dark pines and hemlocks, and again by lovely green fields that slope gently to long lines of willows at the water's edge.

There is never-ending pleasure in making one's self familiar with such a region. One may travel at home in a most literal sense, and be always learning history, geography, botany, or biography—whatever one chooses.

I have had a good deal of journeying in my life, and taken great delight in it, but I have never taken greater delight than in my rides and drives and tramps and voyages within the borders of my native town. There is always something fresh, something to be traced or discovered, something particularly to be remembered. One grows rich in memories and associations.

I believe that we should know our native towns much better than most of us do, and never let ourselves be strangers at home. Particularly when one's native place is so really interesting as my own [Berwick, Maine]! . . .

My grandfather died in my eleventh year, and presently the Civil War began.

From that time the simple village life was at an end. Its provincial character was fading out; shipping was at a disadvantage, and there were no more bronzed sea-captains coming to dine and talk about their voyages, no more bags of filberts or oranges for the children, or great red jars of olives; but in these childish years I had come in contact with many delightful men and women of real individuality and breadth of character, who had fought the battle of life to good advantage, and sometimes against great odds.

In these days I was given to long, childish illnesses, and it must be honestly confessed, to instant drooping if ever I were shut up in school. I had apparently not the slightest desire for learning, but my father was always ready to let me be his companion in long drives about the country.

In my grandfather's business household, my father, unconscious of tonnage and timber measurement, of the markets of the Windward Islands or the Mediterranean ports, had taken to his book, as old people said, and gone to college and begun that devotion to the study of medicine which only ended with his life.

I have tried already to give some idea of my father's character in my story of *The Country Doctor,* but all that is inadequate to the gifts and character of the man himself. He gave me my first and best knowledge of books by his own delight and dependence upon them, and ruled my early attempts at writing by the severity and simplicity of his own good taste.

"Don't try to write *about* people and things, tell them just as they are!"

How often my young ears heard these words without comprehending them! But while I was too young and thoughtless to share in an enthusiasm for Sterne or Fielding, and Smollett or Don Quixote, my mother and grandmother were leading me into the pleasant ways of *Pride and Prejudice,* and *The Scenes of Clerical Life,*[1] and the delightful stories of Mrs. Oliphant.[2]

The old house was well provided with leather-bound books of a deeply serious nature, but in my youthful appetite for knowledge, I could even in the driest find something vital, and in the more entertaining I was completely lost.

My father had inherited from his father an amazing knowledge of human nature, and from his mother's French ancestry, that peculiarly French trait, called *gaieté de cœur.* Through all the heavy responsibilities and anxieties of his busy professional life, this kept him young at heart and cheerful. His visits to his patients were often made perfectly delightful and refreshing to them by his kind heart, and the charm of his personality.

I knew many of the patients whom he used to visit in lonely inland farms, or on the seacoast in York and Wells. I used to follow him about silently, like an undemanding little dog, content to follow at his heels.

I had no consciousness of watching or listening, or indeed of any special interest in the country interiors. In fact, when the time came that my own world of imaginations was more real to me than any other, I was sometimes perplexed at my father's directing my attention to certain points of interest in the character or surroundings of our acquaintances.

I cannot help believing that he recognized, long before I did myself, in what direction the current of purpose in my life was setting. Now, as I write my sketches of country life, I remember again and again the wise things he said, and the sights he made me see. He was only impatient with affectation and insincerity.

I may have inherited something of my father's and grandfather's knowledge of human nature, but my father never lost a chance of trying to teach me to observe. I owe a great deal to his patience with a heedless little girl given far more to dreams than to accuracy, and with perhaps too little natural sympathy for the dreams of others.

The quiet village life, the dull routine of farming or mill life, early became interesting to me. I was taught to find everything that an imaginative child could ask, in the simple scenes close at hand.

I say these things eagerly, because I long to impress upon every boy and girl this truth: that it is not one's surroundings that can help or hinder — it is having a growing purpose in one's life to make the most of whatever is in one's reach.

---

[1]A book of fictional sketches by Victorian novelist George Eliot [Mary Ann Evans]. Eliot (1819–1880) developed the method of psychological analysis widely used in modern fiction.

[2]Margaret Oliphant (1828–1897), a prolific Victorian novelist, historical writer, and biographer known for her sympathetic depictions of rural life.

If you have but a few good books, learn those to the very heart of them. Don't for one moment believe that if you had different surroundings and opportunities you would find the upward path any easier to climb. One condition is like another, if you have not the determination and the power to grow in yourself.

I was still a child when I began to write down the things I was thinking about, but at first I always made rhymes and found prose so difficult that a school composition was a terror to me, and I do not remember ever writing one that was worth anything. But in course of time rhymes themselves became difficult and prose more and more enticing, and I began my work in life, most happy in finding that I was to write of those country characters and rural landscapes to which I myself belonged, and which I had been taught to love with all my heart.

I was between nineteen and twenty when my first sketch was accepted by Mr. Howells for the *Atlantic*. I already counted myself as by no means a new contributor to one or two other magazines — *Young Folks* and *The Riverside* — but I had no literary friends "at court."

I was very shy about speaking of my work at home, and even sent it to the magazine under an assumed name, and then was timid about asking the postmistress for those mysterious and exciting editorial letters which she announced upon the post office list as if I were a stranger in the town.

[1892]

RING LARDNER

Ring Lardner, the American humorist, published several volumes of short stories, most notably How to Write Short Stories *in 1924. As the scholar James D. Hart commented, Lardner's cynical approach to his material meant that the "'average' characters whom he depicts are reduced by the author's implied bitterness to their essential commonplaceness, cruelty, viciousness, dullness, and stupidity." Lardner intended his essay "How to Write Short Stories" to serve as the preface to his collection of ten stories, which included his best-known works, "The Golden Honeymoon" and "Champion."*

How to Write Short Stories

A glimpse at the advertising columns of our leading magazines shows that whatever else this country may be shy of, there is certainly no lack of correspondence schools that learns you the art of short-story writing. The most notorious of these schools makes the boast that one of their pupils cleaned up $5000.00 and no hundreds dollars writing short stories according to the system learnt in their course, though it don't say if that amount was cleaned up in one year or fifty.

However, for some reason or another when you skim through the pages of high class periodicals, you don't very often find them cluttered up with stories that was written by boys or gals who had win their phi beta skeleton keys at this or that story-writing college. In fact, the most of the successful authors of the short fiction of today never went to no kind of a college, or if they did, they studied piano tuning or the barber trade. They could of got just as far in what I call the literary game if they had of stayed home those four years and helped mother carry out the empty bottles.

The answer is that you can't find no school in operation up to date, whether it be a general institution of learning or a school that specializes in story writing, which can make a great author out of a born druggist.

But a little group of our deeper drinkers has suggested that maybe boys and gals who wants to take up writing as their life work would be benefited if some person like I was to give them a few hints in regards to the technic of the short story, how to go about planning it and writing it, when and where to plant the love interest and climax, and finally how to market the finished product without leaving no bad taste in the mouth.

Well, then, it seems to me like the best method to use in giving out these hints is to try and describe my own personal procedure from the time I get inspired till the time the manuscript is loaded on to the trucks.

The first thing I generally always do is try and get hold of a catchy title, like for instance, "Basil Hargrave's Vermifuge," or "Fun at the Incinerating Plant." Then I set down to a desk or flat table of any kind and lay out 3 or 4 sheets of paper with as many different colored pencils and look at them cock-eyed a few moments before making a selection.

How to begin—or, as we professionals would say, "how to commence"—is the next question. It must be admitted that the method of approach ("L'approchement") differs even among first class fictionists. For example, Blasco Ibáñez usually starts his stories with a Spanish word, Jack Dempsey with an "I" and Charley Peterson with a couple of simple declarative sentences about his leading character, such as "Hazel Gooftree had just gone mah jong. She felt faint."

Personally it has been my observation that the reading public prefers short dialogue to any other kind of writing and I always aim to open my tale with two or three lines of conversation between characters—or, as I call them, my puppets—who are to play important rôles. I have often found that something one of these characters says, words I have perhaps unconsciously put into his or her mouth, directs my plot into channels deeper than I had planned and changes, for the better, the entire sense of my story.

To illustrate this, let us pretend that I have laid a plot as follows: Two girls, Dorothy Abbott and Edith Quaver, are spending the heated term at a famous resort. The Prince of Wales visits the resort, but leaves on the next train. A day or two later, a Mexican reaches the place and looks for accommodations, but is unable to find a room without a bath. The two girls meet him at the public filling station and ask him for a contribution to their autograph album. To their amazement, he utters a terrible oath, spits in their general direction and hurries out of town. It is not until years later that the two girls learn he is a notorious forger and realize how lucky they were after all.

Let us pretend that the above is the original plot. Then let us begin the writing with haphazard dialogue and see whither it leads:

"Where was you?" asked Edith Quaver.

"To the taxidermist's," replied Dorothy Abbott.

The two girls were spending the heated term at a famous watering trough. They had just been bathing and were now engaged in sorting dental floss.

"I am getting sick in tired of this place," went on Miss Quaver.

"It is mutual," said Miss Abbott, shying a cucumber at a passing paper-hanger.

There was a rap at their door and the maid's voice announced that company was awaiting them downstairs. The two girls went down and entered the music room. Garnett Whaledriver was at the piano and the girls tiptoed to the lounge.

The big Nordic, oblivious of their presence, allowed his fingers to form weird, fantastic minors before they strayed unconsciously into the first tones of Chopin's 121st Fugue for the Bass Drum.

From this beginning, a skilled writer could go most anywheres, but it would be my tendency to drop these three characters and take up the life of a mule in the Grand Canyon. The mule watches the trains come in from the east, he watches the trains come in from the west, and keeps wondering who is going to ride him. But she never finds out.

The love interest and climax would come when a man and a lady, both strangers, got to talking together on the train going back east.

"Well," said Mrs. Croot, for it was she, "what did you think of the Canyon?"

"Some cave," replied her escort.

"What a funny way to put it!" replied Mrs. Croot. "And now play me something."

Without a word, Warren took his place on the piano bench and at first allowed his fingers to form weird, fantastic chords on the black keys. Suddenly and with no seeming intention, he was in the midst of the second movement of Chopin's Twelfth Sonata for Flute and Cuspidor. Mrs. Croot felt faint.

That will give young writers an idea of how an apparently trivial thing such as a line of dialogue will upset an entire plot and lead an author far from the path he had pointed for himself. It will also serve as a model for beginners to follow in regards to style and technic. I will not insult my readers by going on with the story to its obvious conclusion. That simple task they can do for themselves, and it will be good practice.

So much for the planning and writing. Now for the marketing of the completed work. A good many young writers make the mistake of enclosing a stamped, self-addressed envelope, big enough for the manuscript to come back in. This is too much of a temptation to the editor.

Personally I have found it a good scheme to not even sign my name to the story, and when I have got it sealed up in its envelope and stamped and addressed, I take it to some town where I don't live and mail it from there. The editor has no idea who wrote the story, so how can he send it back? He is in a quandary.

In conclusion let me warn my pupils never to write their stories—or, as we professionals call them, "yarns"—on used paper. And never to write them on a post-card. And never to send them by telegraph (Morse code).

[1924]

SUSAN LOHAFER

Susan Lohafer edited Short Story Theory at a Crossroads *(1989), a volume of critical essays on the theory of the short story, with Jo Ellyn Clarey. Lohafer is also the author of* Coming to Terms with the Short Story *(1983).*

From *Short Story Theory at a Crossroads*

Until not so long ago, the ones who theorized about stories were the ones who wrote them: Poe, Chekhov, Henry James, H. E. Bates, Frank O'Connor, Eudora Welty. Spottily in the sixties, but afterwards more often, study of the short story as a genre attracted "pure" critics, narrative theorists, people whose lifework is the construction of meaning from literary culture. It is their presence—in growing numbers—that lets us say "field" of short story criticism. Stories can now be career investments.

Stories have always been "there"—in the hunters' camp, the ladies' quarterly, the children's bedroom, the freshman classroom. As listeners, readers, teachers, and critics, we have needed, used, revered them—but taken them for granted till forced to do otherwise. And, of course, those who've done the forcing have had something at stake. Think of Poe. In giving us a prescription for the short story—a thing of power and unity—he was doctoring a psyche that was fragile, unstable. And Frank O'Connor. If we quote, still, his tribute to Gogol, to the "lonely voice" in "submerged populations," it may be because he had a nation at heart. Both of these men made famous critical pronouncements; yet they were only saying what had to be true for the sake of their art. Were they biased? Self-serving? Of course, but they were also intuitive. Failing to be objective, they found the essential.

So, however, did Vladimir Propp, a "pure" critic who had a stake in the objective.[1] Studies of oral folktales, and especially Propp's work with recurrent, serially ordered functions in fairy tales, did give the story a far-reaching phylogeny. Indeed, the earlier work of the Formalists (Shklovsky, Tomashevsky, and especially Boris Eikhenbaum) was a striking development in the twenties. They and structuralists like Propp—all of whom had something to say about kernels of narrative—would later become a rich resource for short story critics. But if we look at what was being written in English about the short story in the twenties, we find little academic criticism. We do find Sherwood Anderson and Ring Lardner making light of the "rules." The thirties and forties give us William Saroyan and Elizabeth Bowen, Katherine Anne Porter and H. E. Bates—artists, proponents, and brilliant describers of the short story form as urgent, exquisite, visceral, impressionistic, and sacredly immune to critical dissection.

By the start of the forties, the "new" aesthetic was firmly established. And it was modernism, rather than the short story per se, that "arrived" in academia. Hindsight, helped by people I'll be mentioning soon, points to Joseph Frank as seminal, and A. L. Bader as representative.[2] Writing in 1945, they viewed narrative as an elliptical, spatially designed network of references, and all but prescribed a certain kind of reader for the modern text—or any text that mattered. Moreover, this reader had to be trained, had to be sensitive to the internal resonances, the patterned imagery, the multiple tensions of syntax and diction. These concerns, now so familiar, were, of course, the litany of New Criticism. And they proved to be the charter of professional short story criticism.

It is hard, if not impossible, to overestimate the importance of a school of critics who put their noses to the page. Once again, the short, artful prose narrative became, as it had been for Poe, second only to the lyric poem in its promise of reward for the "sensitive" reader. More accessible than poetry, more manageable than novels, it was just the right size

---

[1]Vladimir Propp, *Morphology of the Folk Tale* (Bloomington, 1958). [All notes are Lohafer's.]

[2]Joseph Frank, "Spatial Form in Modern Literature," *Sewanee Review,* LIII (1945), 221–40, 433–56, 643–53, rpr. in Frank, *The Widening Gyre: Crisis and Mastery in Modern Literature* (New Brunswick, N.J., 1963), 3–63, copyright © 1963 by Rutgers, The State University; A. L. Bader, "The Structure of the Modern Short Story," *College English,* VII (1945), 86–92, rpr. in Charles E. May (ed.), *Short Story Theories* (Athens, Ohio, 1976), 107–15.

for a demonstration. All that was needed was a way of getting the critical mission into the classroom. It happened in many ways, but none is more important than the publication, in 1943, of Brooks and Warren's classic anthology, *Understanding Fiction.*[3]

A veritable bible for the teacher of short fiction, this many-times-revised book has had an enduring influence on the way short fiction has been analyzed, taught, and generally perceived. In "Letter to the Teacher," substantially reprinted in the 1959 edition, Brooks and Warren offer a view of fiction that implicitly foregrounds the short story form. They tell us that students need to be carried past their "threshold interests" (in a particular subject matter, in simply "what happens") into an appreciation based upon "the total structure, upon a set of organic relationships, upon the logic of the whole." The features of compression, economy, irony, and tension—thought to be the very means by which "the more broadly human values implicit in fiction" reveal themselves—just happen to be the definitive characteristics of the literary short story.[4] Although the editors warn against the tyranny of critical viewpoints, and see interpretation as a highly individual activity, nevertheless the passion and coherence of their approach has guided and inspired generations of "close readers."

Understanding Fiction is a seminal book, and it spawned in the marketplace. Hundreds of anthologies are now available. New ones arrive, it seems, every month. Old ones return—updated. Many of these textbooks are valuable, for they refresh the canon, redo the categories. But few, if any, remake our thinking. Few are the vehicles of new concepts or insights we would honor as "theory." Underneath the slick new covers is, all too often, the same old catechism of theme and tone, character and setting. There are, of course, exceptions. Some anthologies invite the reader to place the stories in relation to ideas about stories—even, in the case of Ann Charters's *The Story and Its Writer* (1988), in the context of short story criticism. Still, it may be that the greatest obstacle to the development of short story criticism has been the simple ubiquity, the serviceability, of the short story textbook. For the majority of doctoral students, staffing undergraduate courses, these texts—even the best loved of them—are utilitarian. And it may be that the story, already in the shadow of the novel, is again demeaned. Ph.D. in hand, how many of us project a career in short fiction studies? Where is the excitement, the timely challenge, the gain in prestige? For whom is there a stake here?

To answer that question, we have to look back to the sixties. Let us imagine that decade, so crowded in every other way, as an empty stage for short story criticism. The curtain in the rear is a flickering of faces: Joyce,

---

[3]Cleanth Brooks and Robert Penn Warren, *Understanding Fiction* (New York, 1943).

[4]*Ibid.*, xii–xiii.

Woolf, Hemingway, Faulkner. . . . In the center hangs a life-size portrait of Edgar Allan Poe holding a volume of Hawthorne's stories.

Onto that stage, in 1961, walk three people. The first two, Eugene Current-Garcia and Walton R. Patrick, are the editors of an anthology— but a very different kind from the many before and after its time. Entitled *What Is the Short Story?—Case Studies in the Development of a Literary Genre,* this book is not about understanding fiction but about studying one genre of fiction: the short story.[5] Interestingly enough, the 1959 edition of *Understanding Fiction* had a new section in which four authors wrote about their own stories. Although these essays are in the old tradition of practitioner commentary, their very presence is the beginning of a critical perspective beyond the close-reading exercise. In 1961, Current-Garcia and Patrick go a step further; they devote a full half of their book to things that have been said about the short story form. The editors, themselves, have no "theory." Their effort is one of retrieval, survey, and education. They offer not only famous dicta by famous authors—Poe on Hawthorne, Joyce on epiphanies, Anderson on (or rather, against) plot— but also clippings from the short story's "press." Most of us have heard of Brander Matthews's *Philosophy of the Short-Story,* but how many of us know it was savaged in England? Here we can read that anonymous review from the London *Academy.* In collecting these snippets of historical editorializing, Current-Garcia and Patrick are building a frame for the second half of their volume. There we find sample stories by Poe, Hawthorne, James, and so on. Once again, we have a classroom anthology of stories for discussion. Its editors are heralds on the stage of criticism. The first main character has yet to arrive.

He is Austin M. Wright, and he, too, enters in 1961. Although not yet the author of the novels for which he will later be honored, he seems very much the inheritor of the writer-critic as well as the modernist tradition. His book, *The American Short Story in the Twenties,* is a writer's tribute to his heritage, a loving analysis of the ways in which short fiction changed in that brilliant decade.[6] He is concerned to a great extent with themes and ideas, and how they differ on either side of that great divide—World War I. He knows, and easily, informally cross-references, hundreds of stories. They are his "canon" of representative works, chosen mainly for their familiarity, but also for their power to reveal what is "new" in the twenties. In a section on form, Wright classifies stories loosely according to the genres of tragedy and comedy, and on the relations between kind of action and kind of effect. Aristotle and Poe are surely in the background, and in the foreground are Anderson and Porter. As we will see in Section III,

---

[5]Eugene Current-Garcia and Walton R. Patrick (eds.), *What Is the Short Story?* (Rev. ed.; Glenview, Ill., 1974).

[6]Austin M. Wright, *The American Short Story in the Twenties* (Chicago, 1961).

Wright moves to much more particular and original notions of form in his later work. His achievement in 1961 is a matter of initiative in dealing with the genre in the first place; it is a matter of using stories as the premise and vehicle of literary history.

Let us imagine 1963 as an interlude on our stage, a bountiful moment that is both an interruption of and an impetus to our parade of critics. In that year, Frank O'Connor publishes *The Lonely Voice: A Study of the Short Story*. In many ways, it is a personal commentary, a practitioner's note-book—as was Sean O'Faolain's *The Short Story* in the previous decade. But it is more; it is a think piece on the relation between storytelling and society. The conclusion: stories prosper in times of social upheaval, and in places where individuals are alienated. Stories are the cry of "the lonely voice." They are also the highest form of narrative art. Not since Poe has anyone spoken with such authority and passion in behalf of the "slight" form. Enduringly quotable, this book is, at last, a *genius loci,* a rallying point.

We should not therefore be surprised by the appearance, in 1964, of an academic journal for articles about stories: *Studies in Short Fiction*. All of us owe a debt to its editors for publishing the comments of, for example, Eileen Baldeshwiler—though the journal was never intended to be a forum solely and specifically for genre theory. The short story had another friend in William H. Peden, whose 1964 book, *The American Short Story,* captured the variety and vitality of the national voice in its characteristic medium of literary expression. In the sixties, too, Russian Formalist essays came to us anew in a collection edited by Lee T. Lemon and Marion J. Reis. And even though few took notice at the time, the University of Michigan's Department of Slavic Languages and Literatures published a translation of Eikhen-baum's *O. Henry and the Theory of the Short Story*.[7]

For a new phase of awareness, we must look to 1966. Someone is entering our stage on the left, near the portrait of Poe holding a volume of Hawthorne. It is Mary Rohrberger, author of *Hawthorne and the Modern Short Story*.[8] From any point of view, her position on the stage is commanding. Her book is tied to the great tradition of attention to imagery (Rohrberger's mentor, after all, was Richard H. Fogle). It is also a study of modernist aesthetics linked to Romantic symbolism. Rhetorically and logically it has a dominant aim: to define the short story as distinct from novels and from "simple" short narratives. At the very least, we might say she is underwriting, theoretically, the class of stories that require "close reading." But her scope is more ambitious; she is relating the short story to major topics and concerns of American criticism. Rohrberger is writing for

---

[7]Lee T. Lemon and Marion J. Reis (eds. and trans.), *Russian Formalist Criticism: Four Essays* (Lincoln, Nebr., 1965); B. M. Eikhenbaum, *O. Henry and the Theory of the Short Story,* trans. I. R. Titunik (Ann Arbor, 1968).

[8]Mary Rohrberger, *Hawthorne and the Modern Short Story: A Study in Genre* (The Hague, 1966).

the benefit of those who must classify texts in order to do their job properly. She has an extraordinarily clear notion of service to a specialized field of literary scholarship. By implication, that field must exist. In a sense, she calls it into being by assuming its presence and giving it guidelines. Still, short story theory did not begin, or even flower, in the sixties; what happened was that the conditions for an academic specialty were finally visible and operative. The curtain comes down on a crowded stage.

In many ways, the seventies was a decade of consolidation. It was time to complete the work of Current-Garcia and Patrick, whose anthology *What is the Short Story?* (revised and reissued in 1974) had paired criticism and stories. In 1976, Charles May eliminated the stories. He wanted an anthology of criticism, not of short story texts for the apprentice reader. From the point of view of strategy, he may have made the first, if not the biggest, move toward a forum for theory. He, too, went searching for scattered essays and articles. Naturally he included some of the same ones that appear in *What Is the Short Story?* (Poe, Matthews), but he could also draw heavily on the journal *Studies in Short Fiction.*

One of May's discoveries was a 1958 essay from *Modern Fiction Studies,* called "What Makes a Short Story Short?"[9] This remarkable piece was written by Norman Friedman, and later found its way into his 1975 book, *Form and Meaning in Fiction.* Using a detailed schema derived from Aristotle's "causes," and borrowing from Elder Olson's list of narrative units (speech, episode, and so on), Friedman explains, systematically, the meaning of size in fiction. In its coolness and rigor, this essay is a constant adversary to subjective commentaries, as well as to any form of short story chauvinism—especially the claims for intrinsic differences between short and long narratives. Controversial as its message may be, this essay transcends its own terms. It does something vital for the future of short story criticism. It asks a purely theoretical question about generic form, regardless of period or literary "movement," and answers in truly theoretical terms. By retrieving this essay and others, by drawing them together, May focused their power as genre criticism. He turned his collection into a resource for academic critics, students of narrative theory, specialists in short fiction studies. Had there been no *Short Story Theories,* the present volume would never have appeared.

Another kind of foundation was laid in 1977. The Barnes and Noble Critical Idiom Series (later taken over by Methuen) added a monograph on the short story form. For many readers, Ian Reid's little book of history and definition draws the lines for future study of the genre per se. It even acknowledges some of the relevant work in fields outside traditional literary studies. Chiefly important here is Gerald Prince's *A Grammar of Stories:*

---

[9]Norman Friedman, "What Makes a Short Story Short?" *Modern Fiction Studies,* IV (1958), 103–17, rpr. in Friedman, *Form and Meaning in Fiction* (Athens, Ga., 1975), copyright © 1975 by the University of Georgia Press.

An Introduction, published in 1973.[10] Coming out of linguistics and heading into discourse analysis, this book can lead us into a whole new arena for genre studies.

And so we come to the eighties. In addition to the Twayne critical histories of the short story, under the general editorship of William H. Peden, two collections of essays appeared in 1982: *The Teller and the Tale: Aspects of the Short Story* (proceedings of the Comparative Literature Symposium in Lubbock) and a special issue of *Modern Fiction Studies.*[11] In the next few years, several single-author books of theory arrived. It is now possible to identify a scattered but committed group of people who are known, professionally, as short story theorists. The trends, problems, contributions, and future of their work are discussed from many points of view in the pages that follow. We hope this collection will be both a companion and a sequel to previous efforts to establish a forum for short story theory.

[1989]

---

[10]Ian Reid, *The Short Story* (1977; rpr. New York, 1979); Gerald Prince, *A Grammar of Stories: An Introduction* (The Hague, 1973).

[11]Wendell M. Aycock (ed.), *The Teller and the Tale: Aspects of the Short Story* (Lubbock, Tex., 1982); *Modern Fiction Studies,* XVIII (Spring, 1982).

JAMES RUSSELL LOWELL

James Russell Lowell was an ambivalent critic of Edgar Allan Poe's work, but at Poe's request Lowell wrote what he termed a "notice of Mr. Poe's life and works," which was published in Graham's Magazine, *February 1845. Three years later, in "A Fable for Critics," Lowell produced what is perhaps his most famous evaluation of Poe in the verse "There comes Poe, with his raven, like Barnaby Rudge/Three fifths of him genius and two fifths sheer fudge. . . ."*

Edgar Allan Poe and "The Fall of the House of Usher"

Mr. Poe has two of the prime qualities of genius, a faculty of vigorous yet minute analysis, and a wonderful fecundity of imagination. The first of these faculties is as needful to the artist in words, as a knowledge of anatomy is to the artist in colors or in stone. This enables him to conceive truly, to maintain a proper relation of parts, and to draw a correct outline, while the second groups, fills up, and colors. Both of these Mr. Poe has displayed with singular distinctness in his prose works, the last predominating in his earlier tales, and the first in his later ones. In judging of the merit of an author, and assigning him his niche among our household gods, we have a right to regard him from our own point of view, and to measure him by our own standard. But, in estimating the amount of power displayed in his works, we must be governed by his own design, and, placing them by the side of his own ideal, find how much is wanting. We differ from Mr. Poe in his opinions of the objects of art. He esteems that object to be the creation of Beauty, and perhaps it is only in the definition of that word that we disagree with him. But in what we shall say of his writings, we shall take his own standard as our guide. The temple of the god of song is equally accessible from every side, and there is room enough in it for all who bring offerings, or seek an oracle.

In his tales, Mr. Poe has chosen to exhibit his power chiefly in that dim region which stretches from the very utmost limits of the probable into the weird confines of superstition and unreality. He combines in a very remarkable manner two faculties which are seldom found united; a power of influencing the mind of the reader by the impalpable shadows of mystery, and a minuteness of detail which does not leave a pin or a button unnoticed. Both are, in truth, the natural results of the predominating quality of his mind, to which we have before alluded, analysis. It is this which distinguishes the artist. His mind at once reaches forward to the effect to be produced. Having resolved to bring about certain emotions in the reader, he makes all subordinate parts tend strictly to the common centre. Even his mystery is mathematical to his own mind. To him x is a known quantity all along. In any picture that he paints, he understands the chemical properties of all his colors. However vague some of his figures may seem, however formless the shadows, to him the outline is as clear and distinct as that of a geometrical diagram. For this reason Mr. Poe has no sympathy with *Mysticism*. The Mystic dwells *in* the mystery, is enveloped with it; it colors all his thoughts; it affects his optic nerve especially, and the commonest things get a rainbow edging from it. Mr. Poe, on the other hand, is a spectator *ab extrà*. He analyzes, he dissects, he watches

——with an eye serene,
The very pulse of the machine,

for such it practically is to him, with wheels and cogs and piston-rods, all working to produce a certain end.

This analyzing tendency of his mind balances the poetical, and, by giving him the patience to be minute, enables him to throw a wonderful reality into his most unreal fancies. A monomania he paints with great power. He loves to dissect one of these cancers of the mind, and to trace all the subtle ramifications of its roots. In raising images of horror, also, he has a strange success conveying to us sometimes by a dusky hint some terrible *doubt* which is the secret of all horror. He leaves to imagination the task of finishing the picture, a task to which only she is competent.

> For much imaginary work was there;
> Conceit deceitful, so compact, so kind,
> That for Achilles' image stood his spear
> Grasped in an armed hand; himself behind
> Was left unseen, save to the eye of mind.

Beside the merit of conception, Mr. Poe's writings have also that of form. His style is highly finished, graceful, and truly classical. It would be hard to find a living author who had displayed such varied powers. As an example of his style we would refer to one of his tales, "The House of Usher," in the first volume of his "Tales of the Grotesque and Arabesque." It has a singular charm for us, and we think that no one could read it without being strongly moved by its serene and sombre beauty. Had its author written nothing else, it would alone have been enough to stamp him as a man of genius, and the master of a classic style. In this tale occurs, perhaps, the most beautiful of his poems.

The great masters of imagination have seldom resorted to the vague and the unreal as sources of effect. They have not used dread and horror alone, but only in combination with other qualities, as means of subjugating the fancies of their readers. The loftiest muse has ever a household and fireside charm about her. Mr. Poe's secret lies mainly in the skill with which he has employed the strange fascination of mystery and terror. In this his success is so great and striking as to deserve the name of art, not artifice. We cannot call his materials the noblest or purest, but we must concede to him the highest merit of construction.

As a critic, Mr. Poe was æsthetically deficient. Unerring in his analysis of dictions, metres, and plots, he seemed wanting in the faculty of perceiving the profounder ethics of art. His criticisms are, however, distinguished for scientific precision and coherence of logic. They have the exactness, and at the same time, the coldness of mathematical demonstrations. Yet they stand in strikingly refreshing contrast with the vague generalisms and sharp personalities of the day. If deficient in warmth, they are also without the heat of partizanship. They are especially valuable as illustrating the great truth, too generally overlooked, that analytic power is a subordinate quality of the critic.

On the whole, it may be considered certain that Mr. Poe has attained an individual eminence in our literature, which he will keep. He has given proof of power and originality. He has done that which could only be done once with success or safety, and the imitation or repetition of which would produce weariness.   [1845]

BOBBIE ANN MASON

Bobbie Ann Mason described her response to Tim O'Brien's story "The Things They Carried" in Ron Hansen and Jim Shepard's collection You've Got to Read This *(1994).*

On Tim O'Brien's
"The Things They Carried"

Of all the stories I've read in the last decade, Tim O'Brien's "The Things They Carried" hit me hardest. It knocked me down, just as if a hundred-pound rucksack had been thrown right at me. The weight of the things the American soldiers carried on their interminable journey through the jungle in Vietnam sets the tone for this story. But the power of it is not just the poundage they were humping on their backs. The story's list of "things they carried" extends to the burden of memory and desire and confusion and grief. It's the weight of America's involvement in the war. You can hardly bear to contemplate all that this story evokes with its matter-of-fact yet electrifying details.

The way this story works makes me think of the Vietnam Veterans Memorial in Washington. The memorial is just a list of names, in a simple, dark — yet soaring — design. Its power is in the simplicity of presentation and in what lies behind each of those names.

In the story, there is a central incident, the company's first casualty on its march through the jungle. But the immediate drama is the effort — by the main character, by the narrator, by the writer himself — to contain the emotion, to carry it. When faced with a subject almost too great to manage or confront, the mind wants to organize, to categorize, to simplify. Restraint and matter-of-factness are appropriate deflective techniques for dealing with pain, and they work on several levels in the story. Sometimes it is more affecting to see someone dealing with pain than it is to know about the pain itself. That's what's happening here.

By using the simplicity of a list and trying to categorize the simple items the soldiers carried, O'Brien reveals the real terror of the war itself. And the categories go from the tangible — foot powder, photographs, chewing gum — to the intangible. They carried disease; memory. When it rained, they carried the sky. The weight of what they carried moves expansively, opens out, grows from the stuff in the rucksack to the whole weight of the American war chest, with its litter of ammo and packaging through the landscape of Vietnam. And then it moves back, away from the huge outer world, back into the interior of the self. The story details the way they carried themselves (dignity, laughter, words) as well as what they carried inside (fear, "emotional baggage").

And within the solemn effort to list and categorize, a story unfolds. PFC Ted Lavender, a grunt who carries tranquilizers, is on his way back from relieving himself in the jungle when he is shot by a sniper. The irony and horror of it are unbearable. Almost instantaneously, it seems, the central character, Lieutenant Cross, changes from a romantic youth to a man of action and duty. With his new, hard clarity, he is carried forward by his determination not to be caught unprepared again. And the way he prepares to lead his group is to list his resolves. He has to assert power over the event by detaching himself. It is a life-and-death matter.

So this effort to detach and control becomes both the drama and the technique of the story. For it is our impulse to deal with unspeakable horror and sadness by fashioning some kind of order, a story, to clarify and contain our emotions. As the writer, Tim O'Brien stands back far enough not to be seen but not so far that he isn't in charge.

"They carried all they could bear, and then some, including a silent awe for the terrible power of the things they carried."   [1994]

BRANDER MATTHEWS

Brander Matthews wrote his remarks on the evolution of the short story in 1885. They were reprinted in his book The Philosophy of the Short-Story *(1931), in which he also responded to some of the controversy in the American and English press resulting from his assertion that American stories were superior to those produced by English writers.*

From *The Philosophy of the Short-Story*

With the recollection that it is more than half a century since Hawthorne and Poe wrote their best Short-stories, it is not a little comic to see now and again in American newspapers a rash assertion that "American literature has hitherto been deficient in good Short-stories," or the reckless declaration that "the art of writing Short-stories has not hitherto been cultivated in the United States." Nothing could be more inexact than these statements. Almost as soon as America began to have any literature at all it had good Short-stories. It is quite within ten, or at the most twenty, years that the American novel has come to the front and forced the acknowledgment of its equality with the British novel and the French novel; but for fifty years the American Short-story has had a supremacy which any competent critic could not but acknowledge. Indeed, the present excellence of the American novel is due in great measure to the Short-story; for nearly every one of the American novelists whose works are now read by the whole English-speaking race began as a writer of Short-stories.

Although as a form of fiction the Short-story is not inferior to the Novel, and although it is not easier, all things considered, yet its brevity makes its composition simpler for the 'prentice hand. Though the Short-stories of the beginner may not be good, yet in the writing of Short-stories he shall learn how to tell a story, he shall discover by experience the elements of the art of fiction more readily and, above all, more quickly, than if he had begun on a long and exhausting novel. The physical strain of writing a full-sized novel is far greater than the reader can well imagine. To this strain the beginner in fiction may gradually accustom himself by the composition of Short-stories. . . .

When we read the roll of American novelists, we see that nearly all of them began as writers of Short-stories. Some of them, Mr. Bret Harte, for instance, and Dr. Edward Everett Hale, never got any farther, or, at least, if they wrote novels, their novels did not receive the full artistic appreciation and the ample popular approval bestowed on their Short-stories. Even Mr. Cable's admirable "Grandissimes" has not made his many readers forget his "Posson Jone." . . . Miss Jewett, Mr. Bunner, Mr. Bishop, and Mr. Julian Hawthorne wrote Short-stories before they wrote novels; and Mr. James has never gathered into a book from the back numbers of magazines the half of his earlier efforts.[1]

In these references to the American magazine I believe I have suggested the real reason of the superiority of the American Short-stories over the British. It is not only that the eye of patriotism may detect more fantasy, more humour, a finer feeling for art, in these younger United States, but there is a more emphatic and material reason for the American proficiency. There is in the United States a demand for Short-stories which does not exist in Great Britain, or at any rate not in the same degree. The

---

[1] In the article from which a quotation has already been made, . . . Colonel Higginson called attention to the skill with which the local short-story in the hands of innumerable writers of both sexes in all parts of the United States has been made to yield the very form and colour of every section of our immense country; and he remarks that "the rapid multiplication of the portable kodak has scarcely surpassed the swift growth of local writers, each apparently having the same equipment of directness and vigor. All the varied elements of our society are being rapidly sought out and exhibited. To begin on the soil longest wrought, Miss Wilkins has produced a series of moral pictures, as true and as terse as anything in literature, though she has, unhappily, left rather out of sight the more cultivated and ancestral aspects of New England life, to which, however, Miss Jewett has done ampler justice." [All notes are Matthews's.]

Short-story is of very great importance to the American magazine. But in the British magazine the serial Novel is the one thing of consequence, and all else is termed "padding." In England the writer of three-volume Novels is the best paid of literary labourers.

So it is to be noted that whoever in England has the gift of story-telling is strongly tempted not to essay the difficult art of writing Short-stories, for which he will receive only an inadequate reward; and he is as strongly tempted to write a long story which may serve first as a serial and afterward as a three-volume Novel. The result of this temptation is seen in the fact that there is not a single British novelist whose reputation has been materially assisted by the Short-stories he has written.[2] More than once in the United States a single Short-story has made a man known; but in Great Britain such an event is well-nigh impossible. The disastrous effect on narrative art of the desire to distend every subject to the three-volume limit has been dwelt on unceasingly by British critics.

. . . It is thus the exact artistic opposite of the American Short-story, of which, as we have seen, the chief characteristics are originality, ingenuity, compression, and, not infrequently, a touch of fantasy. I do not say, of course, that the good and genuine Short-story is not written in England now and then.

. . . Certain of the remarks in the present paper I put forth first anonymously in the columns of the *Saturday Review,* of London. To my intense surprise, they were controverted in the *Nation,* of New York.[3] The critic began by assuming that the writer had said that Americans preferred Short-stories to Novels. What had really been said was that there was a steady demand for Short-stories in American magazines, whereas in England the demand was rather for serial Novels.

"In the first place," said the critic, "Americans do not prefer Short-stories, as is shown by the enormous number of British Novels circulated among us; and in the second place, tales of the quiet, domestic kind, which form the staple of periodicals like *All the Year Round* and *Chambers's Journal,* have here thousands of readers where native productions, however clever and original, have only hundreds, since the former are reprinted by the country papers and in the Sunday editions of city papers as rapidly and regularly as they are produced at home." Now, the answer to this is simply that these British Novels and British stories are reprinted widely in the United States, not because the American people prefer them to anything else, but because, owing to the absence of international copyright, they

---

[2]Since this was written the Short-stories of R. L. Stevenson and of Mr. Kipling have proved again how dangerous it is to generalise from special conditions.

[3]The original article will be found in the *Saturday Review* for Sept. 4, 1884; and the adverse criticism appeared in the *Nation* for July 5, 1885.

cost nothing.[4] That the American people prefer to read American stories when they can get them is shown by the enormous circulation of the periodicals which make a speciality of American fiction. [1885]

---

[4]It is pleasant to be able to remark that the copyright act of 1891 removed the premium of cheapness from the British tales, and that the American writer of Short-stories is no longer compelled to produce in competition with stolen goods.

CHARLES E. MAY

Charles E. May discussed the critical context of Poe's literary theories, summarizing the earlier aesthetic theories that influenced his work, in Edgar Allan Poe: A Study of the Short Fiction *(1991).*

Edgar Allan Poe—Critical Context

The single unifying factor in all of Poe's works is the concept of unity itself. Derived primarily from Poe's familiarity with Augustus William Schlegel's *Course of Lectures on Dramatic Art and Literature* and Samuel Taylor Coleridge's *Biographia Literaria,* Poe's theory is relatively simple and straightforward. This theory so dominated his writing that it can not only be observed throughout his fiction and poetry, but its development can be traced from his early journeyman reviews to his last and most ambitious philosophic prose poem, *Eureka.* As Gerhard Hoffmann has pointed out in the most thought-provoking discussion of Poe's debt to German literature and thought, Coleridge and Schlegel combined to convince Poe that the concept of unity is the fundamental principle of existence.[1] R. D. Gooder, in a recent article, is even more emphatic. The heart of Poe's theory about the validity of literature, says Gooder, is neither the accuracy of the description or the justice of an action, but the "skill in the collocation of words and their effect upon the mind of the reader." Poe's preoccupation with style, continues Gooder, "emerges from an almost preternatural self-consciousness which, having lost touch with external reality, has language as its only resource."[2] And the function of language is not to mirror

---

[1]Gerhard Hoffman, "E. A. Poe and German Literature" in *American-German Literary Interrelations in the Nineteenth Century,* ed. Christoph Wecker (Munich: Wilhelm Fink Verlag, 1983), 52–104. [All notes are May's.]

[2]R. D. Gooder, "Edgar Allen Poe: The Meaning of Style," *Cambridge Quarterly* 16 (1987): 110–23.

external reality but to create a self-contained realm of reality that corresponds only to the basic human desire for total unity.

Since Poe's most significant theoretical statements are collected in part 2 of this volume, and since the sources and nature of his theories have been discussed many times in books and articles listed in the bibliography, here I will only offer a brief survey of the main line of Poe's literary theories, focusing particularly on those ideas relevant to his theory of the short story as a genre.[3]

It can be argued that a literary genre does not really exist so long as it is merely practiced. Because a genre concept is just that—a concept—it truly comes into being only when the rules and conventions that constitute it are articulated within the larger conceptual context of literature as a whole. Poe's rigor as a literary critic and genre theorist is thus as important for understanding his contribution to the short story form as is his skill as a short story writer. As early as the 1836 Drake-Halleck review, Poe was insisting that a theoretical understanding of literature was necessary before one might legitimately discuss individual works.[4] The first task he felt necessary was to identify a basic human faculty, a primal human desire instilled in the human mind by God, that the literary work attempted to fulfill. Terming this faculty "Ideality" or, somewhat more narrowly, the "Poetic Sentiment," Poe argued that literary art both arises from and serves to satisfy the Poetic Sentiment. The poet who is highly calculating and logical while patterning language, the poet with the greatest control of technique and literary conventions, is more likely to create a poem that will fulfill the Poetic Sentiment than one who is merely filled with the general quality known as Ideality.

In the 1842 Longfellow review and later in more detail in his essay "The Poetic Principle," Poe named this basic human desire the quest for "supernal BEAUTY" and insisted that such a desire was not to be satisfied by any existing combination of forms in human experience. Furthermore, he suggested that although it was the task of the poet to try to satisfy this desire by combining existent forms of beauty or by combining combinations already created by previous poets, he insisted that achieving that perfect unity that would arouse the sense of ultimate Supernal Beauty was not humanly possible.

---

[3]For a complete discussion of Poe's development as a literary critic, see Robert D. Jacobs, *Poe: Journalist and Critic* (Baton Rouge: Louisiana University Press, 1969); Margaret Alterton, *Origins of Poe's Critical Theory* (Ames: University of Iowa Press, 1925); and Edd Winfield Parks, *Edgar Allen Poe as Literary Critic* (Athens: University of Georgia Press, 1964). For studies of specific sources of Poe's theories, see Floyd Stoval, "Poe's debt to Coleridge," *University of Texas Studies in English* (1930): 70–82; and Albert J. Lubell, "Poe and A. W. Schlegel," *Journal of English and Germanic Philology* 52 (1953): 1–12.

[4]Poe's reviews can be found in volumes 8–12 of *The Complete Works of Edgar Allan Poe,* ed. James A. Harrison (New York: Thomas Y. Crowell & Co., 1902).

The first time Poe refers to A. W. Schlegel's notion of the importance of "totality of interest" seems to be the 1836 Sigourney review. Poe argues that whereas in long works one may be pleased with particular passages, in short pieces the pleasure results from the perception of the oneness, the uniqueness, the overall unity of the piece — on the adaptation of all the constituent parts, which constitutes a totality of interest. In the same year, in a review of Dickens's *Watkins Tottle,* he uses the phrase "unity of effect" rather than "unity of interest" — a shift of emphasis from the source of the Poetic Sentiment in the artist to its arousal in the reader. As in the Sigourney review, Poe emphasized the importance of the overall design of the work as a means of achieving a sense of Supernal Beauty.

Poe uses the word "plot" in his 1842 Bulwer review as synonymous with what he means by the "unity" essential to arouse the Poetic Sentiment. He is careful here to distinguish between the usual notion of plot as merely those events that occur one after another and arouse suspense and his own definition of plot as an overall pattern, design, or unity. The 1842 review of Dickens's *Barnaby Rudge* presents the case for plot being synonymous with overall design even more emphatically. Poe makes a distinction here between story (the events as they might have happened) and plot (the events as the reader receives them) that is similar to the discrimination made by the Russian formalists in the 1920s.[5] Again, Poe emphasizes that by "plot" he means pattern and design, not simply the temporal progression of events. Only pattern can make the separate elements of the work meaningful, not mere realistic cause-and-effect. Moreover, Poe insists that only when the reader has an awareness of the "end" of the work, that is, the overall pattern, will seemingly trivial elements become relevant and therefore meaningful.

Related to the concept of unity, and important for understanding Poe's theory of how short fiction embodies theme, is his distinction between the way "meaning" is communicated by the techniques of allegory and the way meaning is communicated by the techniques of poetry. In the 1839 review of *Undine,* Poe refers to another concept he borrowed from Schlegel, the notion of a "mystic undercurrent" in the literary work, and suggests, without explaining why or how, that it is preferable to the way allegory is meaningful. Given Poe's theory of unity, one might suggest that Poe objected to allegory because it is built on a preestablished set of external ideas to which the various elements of the work refer; the notion of a mystic undercurrent is more like an atmosphere, a self-contained aesthetic realm of reality, created by the unity of the work. Poe objects to allegory more fully in the 1847 Hawthorne review, where he argues that the allegorist endangers both unity and verisimilitude in the work. Because allegory is so dependent on the structure of the external

---

[5]For discussion of this distinction, see *Russian Formalist Criticism,* ed. Lee T. Lemon and Marion J. Reis (Lincoln, Nebr.: Bison Books, 1965).

ideas it is meant to communicate, unity must be sacrificed and verisimilitude must be violated to preserve the integrity of those ideas. As Poe says, "if allegory ever establishes a fact, it is by dint of overturning a fiction."

There is little doubt that Poe was, if nothing else, a thoroughgoing formalist, always more interested in the work's pattern, structure, conventions, and techniques than its reference to the external world or its social or psychological theme. The meaning of the work for Poe *was* its technique, so much so that in many of his stories he thematizes aesthetic and literary theory issues, making the creation and explication of unity the central thematic "truth" of the work. Although Poe's formalism and his emphasis on the work's effect on the reader once alienated him from critics, recent structuralist and poststructuralist interest in form has made Poe's theories more acceptable. R. W. Foust has argued that Poe was America's first New Critic and that "Philosophy of Composition" can be read as a "proto-structuralist" analysis of the art work "conceived of as an objective aggregate of literary 'functions.'"[6] Three recent books on Poe have focused on the "life of writing," "the world of words," and the "fables of the mind" embodied in Poe's fiction.[7] Deconstructionist critics in particular have taken a new interest in Poe; in addition to the studies of "The Purloined Letter" by Jacques Lacan, Jacques Derrida, and Barbara Johnson, discussions by John T. Irwin, Joseph N. Riddel, and John Carlos Rowe have probed the ways that Poe's texts focus on their own means of signification.[8] Critics who once complained that "The Philosophy of Composition" was cold-blooded in its manipulation of the reader toward a preexistent effect are beginning to realize that for Poe the overall design was not a preestablished intention, totally in the mind of the writer before the work's composition, but rather that the pattern of the work was achieved in the actual working out of the intentions. The form of the work is the end of the work, not prior to it.[9]

---

[6]R. W. Foust, "Aesthetician of Simultaneity: E. A. Poe and Modern Literary Theory," *South Atlantic Quarterly* 46 (1981): 24.

[7]See J. Gerald Kennedy, *Poe, Death, and the Life of Writing* (New Haven: Yale University Press, 1987); Michael J. S. Williams, *A World of Words: Language and Displacement in the Fiction of Edgar Allan Poe* (Durham, N.C.: Duke University Press, 1988); and Joan Dayan, *Fables of Mind: An Inquiry into Poe's Fiction* (New York: Oxford University Press, 1987).

[8]The best source for discussion of the Lacan/Derrida controversy is *The Purloined Poe: Lacan, Derrida, and Psychoanalytic Reading,* ed. John P. Muller and William J. Richardson (Baltimore: Johns Hopkins University Press, 1988). See also John T. Irwin, *American Hieroglyphics* (New Haven: Yale University Press, 1980); Joseph N. Riddel, "'The Crypt' of Edgar Poe," *Boundry* 2 (1979): 117–44; and John Carlos Rowe, *Through the Custom-House: Nineteenth-Century American Fiction and Modern Theory* (Baltimore: Johns Hopkins University Press, 1982).

[9]For a detailed discussion of this issue in "The Philosophy of Composition," see Michael Black, "Why It Is So and Not Otherwise," *New Literary History* 6 (1975): 477–89.

Since no theory of the short prose tale had been developed when Poe was writing, he borrowed theoretical ideas from those genres that did possess a critical history, such as drama and poetry, and applied them to the gothic tale form that was popular during his time. The following generic elements are the most important ones Poe made use of: (1) the conventionalized and ritualized structure of the drama; (2) the metaphoric and self-contained unity of the lyric poem; (3) the technique of verisimilitude of the eighteenth-century novel; (4) the point of view and unifying tone of the eighteenth-century essay; and (5) the spiritual undercurrent and projective technique of the old romance and the gothic story. When you add to these the notion of prose assuming the spatial form of painting, which Poe suggested in the 1842 Hawthorne review, you have the basis for a new generic form. Poe's notion of short fiction as a picture is particularly important, as Robert Jacobs reminds us, for to see narrative as a painting is to see it as a design in space rather than a movement in time. Although the consequent implication of considering characters as static groupings in a composition means a loss of dramatic effect, this loss is compensated by a gain in emphasis on overall pattern, which is equivalent to thematic design.[10]

The 1842 Hawthorne review is the central document for understanding Poe's contribution to the theory of the short story, for it derives from his earlier discussions of the relationship between aesthetic unity and the concept of plot and looks forward to the ultimate implications of pattern and design presented in *Eureka*. The logic of the argument in the Hawthorne review is quite clear: what is most important in the literary work is unity; however, unity can only be achieved in a work that the reader can hold in the mind all at once. After the poem, traditionally the highest form of high literary art, Poe says that the short tale has the most potential for being unified in the way the poem is. The effect of the tale is synonymous with its overall pattern or design, which is also synonymous with its theme or idea. Form and meaning emerge from the unity of the motifs of the story.

Poe carries his concern with unity of effect even further in "The Philosophy of Composition," for here he asserts the importance of considering the work backward, that is, beginning with its end. Obviously, the possibility of beginning with the end is what distinguishes fiction from reality, what transforms reality into narrative discourse. A narrative, by its very nature, cannot be told until the events that it takes as its subject matter have already occurred. Therefore the "end" of the events, both in terms of their actual termination and in terms of the purpose to which the narrator binds them, is the beginning of the discourse. It is hardly necessary to say that the only narrative that the reader ever gets is that which is already discourse, already ended as an event, so there is nothing left for it but to move toward its end

---

[10]Robert D. Jacobs, *Poe: Journalist and Critic* (Baton Rouge: Louisiana State University Press, 1969), 163.

in an aesthetic, eventless way, that is, via tone, metaphor, and all the other purely artificial conventions of fictional discourse. Consequently, it is inevitable that events in the narrative will be motivated or determined by demands of the discourse, demands that do not necessarily have anything to do with psychological or phenomenological motivation of the narrated events in the real world.[11]

The full extent to which the concept of unity dominated Poe's work can be seen in *Eureka,* in which he attempted to create a cosmic theory based on his aesthetic principles. Reasoning backward from the fact that the basic desire for Supernal Beauty could only be partially fulfilled by the unity of poetry, Poe argued that the only One capable of achieving absolute unity was God; it therefore followed that the universe itself was a great poem, that is, a fully developed plan or plot (these are convertible terms for Poe) of God. Poe's presentation of *Eureka* as a poem is an inevitable implication of his theory that truth can only be tested by its coherence, not by its correspondence to anything external. Poe's theory is thus a paradigm in the sense that Thomas S. Kuhn uses that term in *The Structure of Scientific Revolutions.*[12] Its claim to truth lies in its explanatory power, its unity, and thus its intellectual beauty. To claim that the plots of God are perfect and that the universe is a plot of God is to make the artist who strives after the perfect plot one who attempts to fulfill the ultimate human desire: the creation of a freestanding unity dependent on nothing outside of itself. For Poe, the mind longs for symmetry and consistency; what is true is that which is consistent, unified. Thus, a perfect consistency is an absolute truth. This becomes Poe's central theme and the primary technical justification for his fiction.   [1991]

---

[11]For further discussion of these issues, see Peter Brooks, *Reading for the Plot* (New York: Alfred A. Knopf, 1984); and Jonathan Culler, *The Pursuit of Signs* (Ithaca, N.Y.: Cornell University Press, 1981).

[12]Thomas S. Kuhn, *The Structure of Scientific Revolutions,* 2d ed. (Chicago: University of Chicago Press, 1970).

HERMAN MELVILLE

*H*erman Melville *wrote an eloquent essay on Nathaniel Hawthorne's volume of short stories,* Mosses from an Old Manse, *for the New York periodical* Literary World *in August 1850. Unlike Edgar Allan Poe in his review of Hawthorne's short fiction, Melville did not use the opportunity to theorize about the form of the short story. Instead, he conveyed his enthusiasm for Hawthorne's tragic vision, what Melville saw as the "great power of blackness" in Hawthorne's writing that derived "its force from its appeals to that Calvinistic sense of Innate Depravity and Original Sin." This was the aspect* *of Hawthorne's work that seemed most congenial to Melville's own genius while he continued work that summer on his novel-in-progress,* Moby-Dick.

From *"Hawthorne and His Mosses"*

. . . It is curious how a man may travel along a country road, and yet miss the grandest or sweetest of prospects by reason of an intervening hedge, so like all other hedges, as in no way to hint of the wide landscape beyond. So has it been with me concerning the enchanting landscape in the soul of this Hawthorne, this most excellent Man of Mosses. His *Old Manse* has been written now four years, but I never read it till a day or two since. I had seen it in the bookstores—heard of it often—even had it rec-ommended to me by a tasteful friend, as a rare, quiet book, perhaps too deserving of popularity to be popular. But there are so many books called "excellent," and so much unpopular merit, that amid the thick stir of other things, the hint of my tasteful friend was disregarded, and for four years the *Mosses on the Old Manse* never refreshed me with their perennial green. It may be, however, that all this while the book, likewise, was only improving in flavor and body. At any rate, it so chanced that this long pro-crastination eventuated in a happy result. At breakfast the other day, a mountain girl, a cousin of mine, who for the last two weeks has every morning helped me to strawberries and raspberries, which, like the roses and pearls in the fairy tale, seemed to fall into the saucer from those straw-berry beds, her cheeks—this delightful creature, this charming Cherry says to me—"I see you spend your mornings in the haymow; and yester-day I found there Dwight's *Travels in New England.* Now I have some-thing far better than that, something more congenial to our summer on these hills. Take these raspberries, and then I will give you some moss." "Moss!" said I. "Yes, and you must take it to the barn with you, and good-by to Dwight."

With that she left me, and soon returned with a volume, verdantly bound, and garnished with a curious frontispiece in green; nothing less than a fragment of real moss, cunningly pressed to a fly-leaf. "Why, this," said I, spilling my raspberries, "this is the *Mosses from an Old Manse.*" "Yes," said Cousin Cherry, "Yes, it is that flowery Hawthorne." "Hawthorne and Mosses," said I, "no more it is morning: it is July in the country: and I am off for the barn."

Stretched on that new-mown clover, the hillside breeze blowing over me through the wide barn door, and soothed by the hum of the bees in the meadows around, how magically stole over me this Mossy Man! and how amply, how bountifully, did he redeem that delicious promise to his guests in the Old Manse, of whom it is written: "Others could give them pleasure, or amusement, or instruction—these could be picked up anywhere; but it was for me to give them rest—rest, in a life of trouble! What better could be done for those weary and world-worn spirits? . . . what better could be done for anybody who came within our magic circle than to throw the spell of a tranquil spirit over him?" So all that day, half buried in the new clover, I watched this Hawthorne's "Assyrian dawn, and Paphian sunset and moonrise from the summit of our eastern hill."

The soft ravishments of the man spun me round about in a web of dreams, and when the book was closed, when the spell was over, this wizard "dismissed me with but misty reminiscences, as if I had been dreaming of him."

What a wild moonlight of contemplative humor bathes that Old Manse!—the rich and rare distilment of a spicy and slowly-oozing heart. No rollicking rudeness, no gross fun fed on fat dinners, and bred in the lees of wine—but a humor so spiritually gentle, so high, so deep, and yet so richly relishable, that it were hardly inappropriate in an angel. It is the very religion of mirth; for nothing so human but it may be advanced to that. The orchard of the Old Manse seems the visible type of the fine mind that has described it—those twisted and contorted old trees, "they stretch out their crooked branches, and take such hold of the imagination that we remember them as humorists and odd-fellows." And then, as surrounded by these grotesque forms, and hushed in the noonday repose of this Hawthorne's spell, how aptly might the still fall of his ruddy thoughts into your soul be symbolized by: "In the stillest afternoon, if I listened, the thump of a great apple was audible, falling without a breath of wind, from the mere necessity of perfect ripeness." For no less ripe than ruddy are the apples of the thoughts and fancies in this sweet Man of Mosses. . . .

But it is the least part of genius that attracts admiration. Where Hawthorne is known, he seems to be deemed a pleasant writer, with a pleasant style,—a sequestered, harmless man, from whom any deep and weighty thing would hardly be anticipated—a man who means no meanings. But there is no man in whom humor and love, like mountain peaks, soar to such a rapt height as to receive the irradiations of the upper skies; there is no man in whom humor and love are developed in that high form called genius; no such man can exist without also possessing, as the indispensable complement of these, a great, deep intellect, which drops down into the universe like a plummet. Or, love and humor are only the eyes through which such an intellect views this world. The great beauty in such a mind is but the product of its strength. . . .

Now, it is that blackness in Hawthorne, of which I have spoken, that so fixes and fascinates me. It may be, nevertheless, that it is too largely developed in him. Perhaps he does not give us a ray of light for every shade of his dark. But however this may be, this blackness it is that furnishes the infinite obscure of his background—that background against which Shakespeare plays his grandest conceits, the things that have made for Shakespeare his loftiest but most circumscribed renown, as the profoundest of thinkers. For by philosophers Shakespeare is not adored, as the great man of tragedy and comedy: "Off with his head; so much for Buckingham!" This sort of rant, interlined by another hand, brings down the house—those mistaken souls, who dream of Shakespeare as a mere man of Richard the Third humps and Macbeth daggers. But it is those deep, far-away things in him; those occasional flashings-forth of the intuitive Truth in him; those short, quick probings at the very axis of reality,—these are the things that make Shakespeare, Shakespeare. Through the mouths of the dark characters of Hamlet, Timon, Lear, and Iago, he craftily says, or sometimes insinuates the things which we feel to be so terrifically true that it were all but madness for any good man, in his own proper character, to utter, or even hint of them. Tormented into desperation, Lear, the frantic king, tears off the mask, and speaks the same madness of vital truth. But, as I before said, it is the least part of genius that attracts admiration. And so, much of the blind, unbridled admiration that has been heaped upon Shakespeare has been lavished upon the least part of him. . . .

Some may start to read of Shakespeare and Hawthorne on the same page. They may say that if an illustration were needed, a lesser light might have sufficed to elucidate this Hawthorne, this small man of yesterday. But I am not willingly one of those who, as touching Shakespeare at least, exemplify the maxim of Rochefoucauld, that "we exalt the reputation of some, in order to depress that of others"—who, to teach all noble-souled aspirants that there is no hope for them, pronounce Shakespeare absolutely unapproachable. But Shakespeare has been approached. There are minds that have gone as far as Shakespeare into the universe. And hardly a mortal man, who, at some time or other, has not felt as great thoughts in him as any you will find in Hamlet. We must not inferentially malign mankind for the sake of any one man, whoever he may be. This is too cheap a purchase of contentment for conscious mediocrity to make. Besides, this absolute and unconditional adoration of Shakespeare has grown to be a part of our Anglo-Saxon superstitions. The Thirty-Nine Articles are now forty. Intolerance has come to exist in this matter. You must believe in Shakespeare's unapproachability, or quit the country. But what sort of a belief is this for an American, a man who is bound to carry republican progressiveness into Literature as well as into Life? Believe me, my friends, that men not very much inferior to Shakespeare are this day being born on the banks of the Ohio. And the day will come when you shall say, Who reads a book by an Englishman that is a modern? The great mistake seems to be, that even with those Americans who look forward to the coming of a great literary genius among us, they somehow fancy he will come in the costume of Queen Elizabeth's day; be a writer of dramas founded upon old English history or the tales of Boccaccio. Whereas, great geniuses are parts of the times, they themselves are the times, and possess a corresponding coloring. . . .

Now I do not say that Nathaniel of Salem is a greater man than William of Avon, or as great. But the difference between the two men is by no means immeasurable. Not a very great deal more, and Nathaniel were verily William.

This, too, I mean: that if Shakespeare has not been equaled, give the world time, and he is sure to be surpassed in one hemisphere or the other. Nor will it at all do to say that the world is getting gray and grizzled now, and has lost that fresh charm which she wore of old, and by virtue of which the great poets of past times made themselves what we esteem them to be. Not so. The world is as young today as when it was created; and this Vermont morning dew is as wet to my feet as Eden's dew to Adam's. Nor has nature been all over ransacked by our progenitors, so that no new charms and mysteries remain for this latter generation to find. Far from it. The trillionth part has not yet been said; and all that has been said but multiplies the avenues to what remains to be said. It is not so much paucity as super-abundance of material that seems to incapacitate modern authors.

Let America, then, prize and cherish her writers; yea, let her glorify them. They are not so many in number as to exhaust her goodwill. And while she has good kith and kin of her own to take to her bosom, let her not lavish her embraces upon the household of an alien. . . .

And now, my countrymen, as an excellent author of your own flesh and blood—an unimitating, and, perhaps, in his way, an inimitable man—whom better can I commend to you, in the first place, than Nathaniel Hawthorne? He is one of the new, and far better generation of your writers. The smell of young beeches and hemlocks is upon him; your own broad prairies are in his soul; and if you travel away inland into his deep and noble nature, you will hear the far roar of his Niagara. Give not over to future generations the glad duty of acknowledging him for what he is. Take that joy to yourself, in your own generation; and so shall he feel those grateful impulses on him, that may possibly prompt him to the full flower of some still greater achievement in your eyes. And by confessing him you thereby confess others; you brace the whole brotherhood. For genius, all over the world, stands hand in hand, and one shock of recognition runs the whole circle round. . . .   [1850]

J. HILLIS MILLER

J. Hillis Miller analyzed the effect of what he called "Bartleby's celebrated immobility" in the critical study Versions of Pygmalion *(1990). Miller was intent on examining "strange and unaccountable" versions of the Pygmalion myth in literature; each story he discussed "contains a character who does something like falling in love with a statue." In Miller's view, a story like "Bartleby, the Scrivener" is an occasion for "the act of personification essential to all storytelling and story-reading."*

A Deconstructive Reading of
Melville's "Bartleby, the Scrivener"

After the failure of all these strategies for getting rid of Bartleby, the narrator tries another. In part through charity but in part through the notion that it is his fate to have Bartleby permanently in his chambers, he decides to try to live with Bartleby, to take him as a permanent fixture in his office. The narrator looks into two quite different books that deny man free will in determining his life, "Edwards on the Will" and "Priestly on Necessity." For Jonathan Edwards man does not have free will because everything he does is predestined by God. For Joseph Priestly, on the other hand, man is bound within the chains of a universal material necessity. Everything happens through physical causality, and therefore everything happens as it must happen, as it has been certain through all time to happen. In either case Bartleby's presence in the narrator's rooms is something predestined:

> Gradually I slid into the persuasion that these troubles of mine touching the scrivener, had been all predestined from eternity, and Bartleby was billeted upon me for some mysterious purpose of an all-wise Providence, which it was not for a mere mortal like me to fathom. Yes, Bartleby, stay there behind your screen, thought I; I shall persecute you no more; you are harmless and noiseless as any of these old chairs; in short, I never feel so private as when I know you are here. At last I see it, I feel it; I penetrate to the predestinated purpose of my life. I am content. Others may have loftier parts to enact; but my mission in this world, Bartleby, is to furnish you with office-room for such period as you may see fit to remain.

This strategy fails too, when the narrator's clients and associates let him know that Bartleby's presence in his offices is scandalizing his professional reputation. It is then that the narrator, who is nothing if not logical, conceives his strangest way of dealing with Bartleby. Since Bartleby will not budge, he himself will leave. The immobility of Bartleby turns the narrator into a nomad: "No more then. Since he will not quit me, I must quit him. I will change my offices; I will move elsewhere."

When the new tenants and the landlord of his old premises come to charge the narrator with responsibility for the nuisance Bartleby is causing, "haunting the building generally, sitting upon the banisters of the stairs by day, and sleeping in the entry by night," the narrator tries first a new strategy of saying he is in no way related to Bartleby or responsible for him. But it is no use: "I was the last person known to have anything to do with him, and they held me to the terrible account."

The narrator then meets Bartleby once more face to face. He offers to set him up in a respectable position, as a clerk in a dry-goods store, a bartender, a bill collector, or a companion for young gentlemen traveling to

Europe. To all these ludicrous suggestions Bartleby replies that he is not particular, but he would prefer to remain "stationary." The narrator then, and finally, offers to take Bartleby home with him, like a stray cat, and give him refuge there. This meets with the same reply. The narrator flees the building and becomes truly a vagrant, wandering for days here and there in his rockaway.

The narrator's life and work seem to have been permanently broken by the irruption of Bartleby. It is not he but his old landlord who deals effectively with the situation. He has Bartleby "removed to the Tombs as a vagrant." This is just what the more intellectually consequent narrator has not been able to bring himself to do, not just because Bartleby is not, strictly speaking, a vagrant and not just because doing such violence to Bartleby would disobey the law of charity, but because he cannot respond with violence to a resistance that has been purely passive and has thereby "disarmed" or "unmanned" any decisive action: "Turn the man out by an actual thrusting I could not; to drive him away by calling him hard names would not do; calling in the police was an unpleasant idea. . . . You will not thrust him, the poor, pale, passive mortal, — you will not thrust such a helpless creature out of your door? you will not dishonor yourself by such cruelty? No, I will not, I cannot do that."

Even after the police have been called in and society has placed Bartleby where he belongs, the narrator continues to be haunted by a sense of unfulfilled responsibility. He visits him in the Tombs, the prison so called because it was in the Egyptian Revival style of architecture, but also no doubt in response to a deeper sense of kinship between incarceration and death: "The Egyptian character of the masonry weighed upon me with its gloom. But a soft imprisoned turf grew under foot. The heart of the eternal pyramids, it seemed, wherein, by some strange magic, through the clefts, grass-seed, dropped by birds, had sprung." Bartleby is appropriately placed in the Tombs since, if the prison courtyard where Bartleby dies is green life in the midst of death, Bartleby has been death in the midst of life. In the Tombs the narrator makes his last unsuccessful attempt to deal with Bartleby in a rational manner, to reincorporate him into ordinary life. He "narrates" to the prison authorities, as he says, "all I knew" about Bartleby, telling them Bartleby does not really belong there but must stay "till something less harsh might be done — though indeed I hardly knew what." He yields at last to the accounting for Bartleby that had been used by Ginger Nut: "I think, sir, he's a little *luny*." The narrator now tells the "grub-man" in the prison, Mr. Cutlets, "I think he is a little deranged." One powerful means society has for dealing with someone who does not fit any ordinary social category is to declare him insane.

Mr. Cutlets has his own curious and by no means insignificant way of placing Bartleby. He thinks Bartleby must be a forger. "Deranged? deranged is it? Well now, upon my word, I thought that friend of yourn was a gentleman forger; they are always pale and genteel-like, them forgers. I can't help pity 'em—can't help it, sir. Did you know Monroe Edwards?" To which the narrator answers, "No, I was never socially acquainted with any forgers." In a way Mr. Cutlets has got Bartleby right, since forgery involves the exact copying of someone else's handwriting in order to make a false document that functions performatively as if it were genuine. Bartleby is a species of forger in reverse. He copies documents all right, but he does this in such a way as to deprive them of their power to make anything happen. On the other hand, when the narrator has copied documents checked, corrected, and made functional, he is himself performing an act of forgery. He may not be socially acquainted with any forgers, but he is in a manner of speaking one himself.

The arrangement he makes with Mr. Cutlets to feed Bartleby in prison is the narrator's last attempt to reincorporate Bartleby into society. There is much emphasis on eating in the story, on what the narrator's different employees eat and drink and on how little Bartleby eats, apparently nothing at all in prison: "'I prefer not to dine to-day,' said Bartleby, turning away. 'It would disagree with me; I am unused to dinners.' So saying he slowly moved to the other side of the inclosure, and took up a position fronting the dead-wall." Eating is one of the basic ways to share our common humanity. This Bartleby refuses, or rather he says he would prefer not to share in the ritual of eating. To refuse that is in the end deadly. Bartleby's death makes him what he has been all along, a bit of death in the midst of life.

It is entirely appropriate that the narrator's account of Bartleby should end with Bartleby's death, not because any biography should end with the death of the biographee but because in death Bartleby becomes what he has always already been. As I have said, his "I would prefer not to" is strangely oriented toward the future. It opens the future, but a future of perpetual not-yet. It can only come as death, and death is that which can never be present. There, at the end, the narrator finds the corpse of Bartleby, "strangely huddled at the base of the wall, his knees drawn up, and lying on his side, his head touching the cold stones." In an earlier version, the "Bartleby" fragment in the Melville family papers in the Gansevoort-Lansing Collection at the New York Public Library, Bartleby is found by the narrator lying in a white-washed room with his head against a tombstone: "It was clean, well-lighted and scrupulously white washed. The head-stone was standing up against the wall, and stretched on a blanket at its base, his head touching the cold marble and his feet upon the threshold lay the wasted form of Bartleby."

The corpse of Bartleby is not the presence of Bartleby. It is his eternal absence. In death he becomes what he has always been, a cadaver who "lives without dining," as the narrator says to the grub-man. Bartleby returns at death, in the final version of the story, to a fetal position. He is the incursion into life of that unattainable realm somewhere before birth and after death. But the word "realm" is misleading. What Bartleby brings is not a realm in the sense of place we might go. It is the otherness that all along haunts or inhabits life from the inside. This otherness can by no method, such as the long series of techniques the narrator tries, be accounted for, narrated, rationalized, or in any other way reassimilated into ordinary life, though it is a permanent part of that ordinary life. Bartleby is the alien that may neither be thrust out the door nor domesticated, brought into the family, given citizenship papers. Bartleby is the invasion of death into life, but not death as something from outside life. He is death as the other side of life or the cohabitant with life. "Death," nevertheless, is not the proper name for this ghostly companion of life, as if it were an allegorical meaning identified at last. Nor is "Death" its generic or common name. "Death" is a catachresis for what can never be named properly.

The narrator's last method of attempting to deal with Bartleby is his narration, going all the way from "I am a rather elderly man" to "Ah Bartleby! Ah humanity!" This narration is explicitly said to be written down and addressed to a "reader." It repeats for a more indeterminate reader, that is, for whoever happens to read it, the quasi-legal deposition he has made before the proper officer of "the Tombs, or to speak more properly, the Halls of Justice." If the narrator can encompass Bartleby with words, if he can do justice to him, he may simultaneously have accounted for him, naturalized him after all, and freed himself from his unfulfilled obligation. He will have made an adequate response to the demand Bartleby has made on him. The narrator, that is, may have justified himself while doing justice to Bartleby.

This is impossible because Bartleby cannot be identified. His story cannot be told. But the reader at the end knows better just why this is so, since we have watched the narrator try one by one a whole series of strategies for accounting for someone and has seen them one by one fail. This failure leaves Bartleby still imperturbably bringing everything to a halt or indefinitely postponing everything with his "I would prefer not to." The narrator's account is not so much an account as an apology for his failure to give an adequate account.

The narrator's writing is also an attempt at a reading, a failed attempt to read Bartleby. In this sense it is the first in a long line of attempts to read Bartleby the scrivener, though the narrator's successors do this by trying to read the text written by Melville, "Bartleby, the Scrivener." Just as Bartleby by his immovable presence in the narrator's office has demanded to be read and accounted for by him, so Melville's strange story demands to be read and accounted for. Nor have readers failed to respond to the demand. A large secondary literature has grown up around "Bartleby," remarkable for its multiplicity and diversity. All claim in one way or another to have identified Bartleby and to have accounted for him, to have done him justice. They tend to exemplify that function of policing or putting things in their place which is entrusted by our society to literary studies as one realm among many of the academic forms of accounting or accounting for. In the case of the essays on "Bartleby" this accounting often takes one or the other of two main forms, as Warminski has observed. These forms could be put under the aegis of the two-pronged last paragraph of the story—"Ah Bartleby! Ah humanity!"—or they might be said to fly in the face either of Bartleby's "But I am not particular" or of the manifest failure of the narrator's attempt to draw close to Bartleby by way of "the bond of a common humanity." Many of the essays try to explain Bartleby either by making him an example of some universal type, for example "existential man," or by finding some particular original or explanatory context for him, for example one of Melville's acquaintances who worked in a law office, or some aspect of nineteenth-century capitalism in America. But Bartleby is neither general nor particular: he is neutral. As such, he disables reading by any of these strategies, any attempt to put "Bartleby, the Scrivener" in its place by answering the question, "In mercy's name, who is he?"

No doubt my own reading also claims to have identified Bartleby, in this case by defining him as the neutral in-between that haunts all thinking and living by dialectical opposition. All readings of the story, including my own, are more ways to call in the police. They are ways of trying to put Bartleby in his place, to convey him where we want to put him, to make sense of him, even if it is an accounting that defines him as the nonsense that inhabits all sense-making. All readings attempt in one way or another to fulfill what the narrator has tried and failed to do: to tell Bartleby's story in a way that will allow us to assimilate him and the story into the vast archives of rationalization that make up the secondary literature of our profession. We are institutionalized to do that work of policing for our society. None of these techniques of assimilation works any better than any of the narrator's methods, and we remain haunted by Bartleby, but haunted also by "Bartleby, the Scrivener: A Story of Wall-Street." I claim, however, that my accounting succeeds where the others fail by showing (though that is not quite the right word) why it is that "accounting for" in any of its usual senses cannot work, either for the story or for the character the story poses.   [1990]

MARY RUSSELL MITFORD

Mary Russell Mitford edited a three-volume collection titled Stories of American Life; by American Writers, *published in London in 1830. In her preface she explains that, in her view, the short story is the ideal form of literature for showing English readers "the Americans as they are."*

Stories of American Life

There are few things that give a completer picture of the habits of living, and the ways of thinking of a foreign country, than its lighter literature; which, composed with a view to domestic circulation, often displays unconsciously the nicest shades of national manners, and the broadest contrasts of national character.

In this branch of knowledge the Americans have hitherto had greatly the advantage of us; for whilst they pay us the compliment (and it is a compliment) of reprinting our popular productions almost as soon as they appear, our acquaintance with their lighter works has hitherto been confined to the whimsical pages of Salmagundi, the powerful though morbid rhapsodies of Brockden Brown, the moral tales of Miss Sedgwick, and the splendid novels of Mr. Cooper. With Mr. Washington Irving, indeed, we are sufficiently familiar; but, in spite of a few inimitable sketches of New York in its Dutch estate, his writings are essentially European, and must be content to take their station amongst the Spectators and Tatlers of the mother country.

To remedy this deficiency in our own literature, by presenting to the English public some specimens of the shorter American Stories, is the intention of the following work. The selection has been made partly from detached tales, but principally from a great mass of Annuals, Magazines, and other periodicals, embracing many of the most popular productions of the most popular living writers of the western world. Amongst these I am chiefly indebted to Messrs. Verplank, Paulding, Hall, Neal, Barker, Willis, and Stone, and though last, far from least, to Miss Sedgwick: some of the pieces are altogether anonymous, and of some the signature is evidently fictitious. The scenes described, and the personages introduced in these volumes, are as various as the authors, extending in geographical space from Canada to Mexico, and including almost every degree of civilization, from the wild Indian and the almost equally wild hunter of the forests and prairies, to the cultivated inhabitant of the city and the plain; from Otter-Bag and Pete Featherton, down to the fine lady in the Country Cousin, and Monsieur de Viellecour, most courtly of refugees.

In fixing on the different pieces, my principal aim has been to keep the book as national and characteristic as possible. Many a clever essay have I rejected, because it might have been written on this side of the Atlantic; and many a graceful tale has been thrown aside for no graver fault, than that, with an assortment of new names, it might have belonged to France, or Switzerland, or Italy, or to any land in Christendom, where love is spoken and tears are shed; whilst I have grasped at the broadest caricature, so that it contained indications of local manners; and clutched the wildest sketch, so that it gave a bold outline of local scenery. I wanted to show the Americans as they are; or rather, to make them show themselves, certain that the more graphic was the portraiture, the more favourable would be the impression.

It is not for me to say how far I have succeeded. Editors are generally accused of partiality; and I am not about to disclaim as a fault, that which I consider as an indispensable requisite. An Editor ought to be partial. I can only hope that the courteous reader, always gracious to merit of any sort, (especially when attended by novelty,) may like the collection with its acknowledged inequalities as well as I do. For my own part, I shall think my humble office most amply rewarded, if the attempt to make American manners better known in England, should tend, in the slightest degree, to promote kindly feelings between two nations, who, descended from a common ancestry, possessing the same rich and noble language, and alike distinguished by a love of public freedom and domestic virtue, ought, above all the people of the earth, to be to each other, in a social as well as a political sense, brethren and friends.   [1830]

FLANNERY O'CONNOR

*F*lannery O'Connor presented the analysis "Some Aspects of the Grotesque in Southern Fiction" as one of her lectures on the practice of writing. Throughout the essay she refers to novels, but as her editors Sally and Robert Fitzgerald understood, she felt that "her principal calling was to write stories." The piece is included in O'Connor's book of occasional prose, Mystery and Manners (1961).

Some Aspects of the Grotesque in Southern Fiction

I think that if there is any value in hearing writers talk, it will be in hearing what they can witness to and not what they can theorize about. My own approach to literary problems is very like the one Dr. Johnson's blind housekeeper used when she poured tea—she put her finger inside the cup.

These are not times when writers in this country can very well speak for one another. In the twenties there were those at Vanderbilt University who felt enough kinship with each other's ideas to issue a pamphlet called, *I'll Take My Stand,* and in the thirties there were writers whose social consciousness set them all going in more or less the same direction; but today there are no good writers, bound even loosely together, who would be so bold as to say that they speak for a generation or for each other. Today each writer speaks for himself, even though he may not be sure that his work is important enough to justify his doing so.

I think that every writer, when he speaks of his own approach to fiction, hopes to show that, in some crucial and deep sense, he is a realist; and for some of us, for whom the ordinary aspects of daily life prove to be of no great fictional interest, this is very difficult. I have found that if one's young hero can't be identified with the average American boy, or even with the average American delinquent, then his perpetrator will have a good deal of explaining to do.

The first necessity confronting him will be to say what he is not doing; for even if there are no genuine schools in American letters today, there is always some critic who has just invented one and who is ready to put you into it. If you are a Southern writer, that label, and all the misconceptions that go with it, is pasted on you at once, and you are left to get it off as best you can. I have found that no matter for what purpose peculiar to your special dramatic needs you use the Southern scene, you are still thought by the general reader to be writing about the South and are judged by the fidelity your fiction has to typical Southern life.

I am always having it pointed out to me that life in Georgia is not at all the way I picture it, that escaped criminals do not roam the roads exterminating families, nor Bible salesmen prowl about looking for girls with wooden legs.

The social sciences have cast a dreary blight on the public approach to fiction. When I first began to write, my own particular *bête noire* was that mythical entity, The School of Southern Degeneracy. Every time I heard about The School of Southern Degeneracy, I felt like Br'er Rabbit stuck on the Tar-baby. There was a time when the average reader read a novel simply for the moral he could get out of it, and however naïve that may have been, it was a good deal less naïve than some of the more limited objectives he now has. Today novels are considered to be entirely concerned with the social or economic or psychological forces that they will by necessity exhibit, or with those details of daily life that are for the good novelist only means to some deeper end.

Hawthorne knew his own problems and perhaps anticipated ours when he said he did not write novels, he wrote romances. Today many readers and critics have set up for the novel a kind of orthodoxy. They demand a realism of fact which may, in the end, limit rather than broaden the novel's scope. They associate the only legitimate material for long fiction with the movement of social forces, with the typical, with fidelity to the way things look and happen in normal life. Along with this usually goes a wholesale treatment of those aspects of existence that the Victorian novelist could not directly deal with. It has only been within the last five or six decades that writers have won this supposed emancipation. This was a license that opened up many possibilities for fiction, but it is always a bad day for culture when any liberty of this kind is assumed to be general.

The writer has no rights at all except those he forges for himself inside his own work. We have become so flooded with sorry fiction based on unearned liberties, or on the notion that fiction must represent the typical, that in the public mind the deeper kinds of realism are less and less understandable.

The writer who writes within what might be called the modern romance tradition may not be writing novels which in all respects partake of a novelistic orthodoxy; but as long as these works have vitality, as long as they present something that is alive, however eccentric its life may seem to the general reader, then they have to be dealt with; and they have to be dealt with on their own terms.

When we look at a good deal of serious modern fiction, and particularly Southern fiction, we find this quality about it that is generally described, in a pejorative sense, as grotesque. Of course, I have found that anything that comes out of the South is going to be called grotesque by the Northern reader, unless it is grotesque, in which case it is going to be called realistic. But for this occasion, we may leave such misapplications aside and consider the kind of fiction that may be called grotesque with good reason, because of a directed intention that way on the part of the author.

In these grotesque works, we find that the writer has made alive some experience which we are not accustomed to observe every day, or which the ordinary man may never experience in his ordinary life. We find that connections which we would expect in the customary kind of realism have been ignored, that there are strange skips and gaps which anyone trying to describe manners and customs would certainly not have left. Yet the characters have an inner coherence, if not always a coherence to their social framework. Their fictional qualities lean away from typical social patterns, toward mystery and the unexpected. It is this kind of realism that I want to consider.

All novelists are fundamentally seekers and describers of the real, but the realism of each novelist will depend on his view of the ultimate reaches of reality. Since the eighteenth century, the popular spirit of each succeeding age has tended more and more to the view that the ills and mysteries of life will eventually fall before the scientific advances of man, a belief that is still going strong even though this is the first generation to face total extinction because of these advances. If the novelist is in tune with this spirit, if he believes that actions are predetermined by psychic make-up or the economic situation or some other determinable factor, then he will be concerned above all with an accurate reproduction of the things that most immediately concern man, with the natural forces that he feels control his destiny. Such a writer may produce a great tragic naturalism, for by his responsibility to the things he sees, he may transcend the limitations of his narrow vision.

On the other hand, if the writer believes that our life is and will remain essentially mysterious, if he looks upon us as beings existing in a created order to whose laws we freely respond, then what he sees on the surface will be of interest to him only as he can go through it into an experience of mystery itself. His kind of fiction will always be pushing its own limits outward toward the limits of mystery, because for this kind of writer, the meaning of a story does not begin except at a depth where adequate motivation and adequate psychology and the various determinations have been exhausted. Such a writer will be interested in what we don't understand rather than in what we do. He will be interested in possibility rather than in probability. He will be interested in characters who are forced out to meet evil and grace and who act on a trust beyond themselves—whether they know very clearly what it is they act upon or not. To the modern mind, this kind of character, and his creator, are typical Don Quixotes, tilting at what is not there.

I would not like to suggest that this kind of writer, because his interest is predominantly in mystery, is able in any sense to slight the concrete. Fiction begins where human knowledge begins—with the senses—and every fiction writer is bound by this fundamental aspect of his medium. I do believe, however, that the kind of writer I am describing will use the concrete in a more drastic way. His way will much more obviously be the way of distortion.

Henry James said that Conrad in his fiction did things in the way that took the most doing. I think the writer of grotesque fiction does them in the way that takes the least, because in his work distances are so great. He's looking for one image that will connect or combine or embody two points; one is a point in the concrete, and the other is a point not visible to the naked eye, but believed in by him firmly, just as real to him, really, as the one that everybody sees.

It's not necessary to point out that the look of this fiction is going to be wild, that it is almost of necessity going to be violent and comic, because of the discrepancies that it seeks to combine.

Even though the writer who produces grotesque fiction may not consider his characters any more freakish than ordinary fallen man usually is, his audience is going to; and it is going to ask him—or more often, tell him—why he has chosen to bring such maimed souls alive. Thomas Mann has said that the grotesque is the true anti-bourgeois style, but I believe that in this country, the general reader has managed to connect the grotesque with the sentimental, for whenever he speaks of it favorably, he seems to associate it with the writer's compassion.

It's considered an absolute necessity these days for writers to have compassion. Compassion is a word that sounds good in anybody's mouth and which no book jacket can do without. It is a quality which no one can put his finger on in any exact critical sense, so it is always safe for anybody to use. Usually I think what is meant by it is that the writer excuses all human weakness because human weakness is human. The kind of hazy compassion demanded of the writer now makes it difficult for him to be anti-anything. Certainly when the grotesque is used in a legitimate way, the intellectual and moral judgments implicit in it will have the ascendency over feeling.

In nineteenth-century American writing, there was a good deal of grotesque literature which came from the frontier and was supposed to be funny; but our present grotesque characters, comic though they may be, are at least not primarily so. They seem to carry an invisible burden; their fanaticism is a reproach, not merely an eccentricity. I believe that they come about from the prophetic vision peculiar to any novelist whose concerns I have been describing. In the novelist's case, prophecy is a matter of seeing near things with their extensions of meaning and thus of seeing far things close up. The prophet is a realist of distances, and it is this kind of realism that you find in the best modern instances of the grotesque.

Whenever I'm asked why Southern writers particularly have a penchant for writing about freaks, I say it is because we are still able to recognize one. To be able to recognize a freak, you have to have some conception of the whole man, and in the South the general conception of man is still, in the main, theological. That is a large statement, and it is dangerous to make it, for almost anything you say about Southern belief can be denied in the next breath with equal propriety. But approaching the subject from the standpoint of the writer, I think it is safe to say that while the South is hardly Christ-centered, it is most certainly Christ-haunted. The Southerner, who isn't convinced of it, is very much afraid that he may have been formed in the image and likeness of God. Ghosts can be very fierce and instructive. They cast strange shadows, particularly in our literature. In any case, it is when the freak can be sensed as a figure for our essential displacement that he attains some depth in literature.

There is another reason in the Southern situation that makes for a tendency toward the grotesque and this is the prevalence of good Southern writers. I think the writer is initially set going by literature more than by life. When there are many writers all employing the same idiom, all looking out on more or less the same social scene, the individual writer will have to be more than ever careful that he isn't just doing badly what has already been done to completion. The presence alone of Faulkner in our midst makes a great difference in what the writer can and cannot permit himself to do. Nobody wants his mule and wagon stalled on the same track the Dixie Limited is roaring down.

The Southern writer is forced from all sides to make his gaze extend beyond the surface, beyond mere problems, until it touches that realm which is the concern of prophets and poets. When Hawthorne said that he wrote romances, he was attempting, in effect, to keep for fiction some of its freedom from social determinisms, and to steer it in the direction of poetry. I think this tradition of the dark and divisive romance-novel has combined with the comic-grotesque tradition, and with the lessons all writers have learned from the naturalists, to preserve our Southern literature for at least a little while from becoming the kind of thing Mr. Van Wyck Brooks desired when he said he hoped that our next literary phase would restore that central literature which combines the great subject matter of the middlebrow writers with the technical expertness bequeathed by the new critics and which would thereby restore literature as a mirror and guide for society.

For the kind of writer I have been describing, a literature which mirrors society would be no fit guide for it, and one which did manage, by sheer art, to do both these things would have to have recourse to more violent means than middlebrow subject matter and mere technical expertness.

We are not living in times when the realist of distances is understood or well thought of, even though he may be in the dominant tradition of American letters. Whenever the public is heard from, it is heard demanding a literature which is balanced and which will somehow heal the ravages of our times. In the name of social order, liberal thought, and sometimes even Christianity, the novelist is asked to be the handmaid of his age.

I have come to think of this handmaid as being very like the Negro porter who set Henry James' dressing case down in a puddle when James was leaving the hotel in Charleston. James was then obliged to sit in the crowded carriage with the satchel on his knees. All through the South the poor man was ignobly served, and he afterwards wrote that our domestic servants were the last people in the world who should be employed in the way they were, for they were by nature unfitted for it. The case is the same with the novelist. When he is given the function of domestic, he is going to set the public's luggage down in puddle after puddle.

The novelist must be characterized not by his function but by his vision, and we must remember that his vision has to be transmitted and that the limitations and blind spots of his audience will very definitely affect the way he is able to show what he sees. This is another thing which in these times increases the tendency toward the grotesque in fiction.

Those writers who speak for and with their age are able to do so with a great deal more ease and grace than those who speak counter to prevailing attitudes. I once received a letter from an old lady in California who informed me that when the tired reader comes home at night, he wishes to read something that will lift up his heart. And it seems her heart had not been lifted up by anything of mine she had read. I think that if her heart had been in the right place, it would have been lifted up.

You may say that the serious writer doesn't have to bother about the tired reader, but he does, because they are all tired. One old lady who wants her heart lifted up wouldn't be so bad, but you multiply her two hundred and fifty thousand times and what you get is a book club. I used to think it should be possible to write for some supposed elite, for the people who attend universities and sometimes know how to read, but I have since found that though you may publish your stories in *Botteghe Oscure,* if they are any good at all, you are eventually going to get a letter from some old lady in California, or some inmate of the Federal Penitentiary or the state insane asylum or the local poorhouse, telling you where you have failed to meet his needs.

And his need, of course, is to be lifted up. There is something in us, as storytellers and as listeners to stories, that demands the redemptive act, that demands that what falls at least be offered the chance to be restored. The reader of today looks for this motion, and rightly so, but what he has forgotten is the cost of it. His sense of evil is diluted or lacking altogether, and so he has forgotten the price of restoration. When he reads a novel, he wants either his senses tormented or his spirits raised. He wants to be transported, instantly, either to mock damnation or a mock innocence.

I am often told that the model of balance for the novelist should be Dante, who divided his territory up pretty evenly between hell, purgatory, and paradise. There can be no objection to this, but also there can be no reason to assume that the result of doing it in these times will give us the balanced picture that it gave in Dante's. Dante lived in the thirteenth century, when that balance was achieved in the faith of his age. We live now in an age which doubts both fact and value, which is swept this way and that by momentary convictions. Instead of reflecting a balance from the world around him, the novelist now has to achieve one from a felt balance inside himself.

There is no literary orthodoxy that can be prescribed as settled for the fiction writer, not even that of Henry James, who balanced the elements of traditional realism and romance so admirably within each of his novels. But this much can be said. The great novels we get in the future are not going to be those that the public thinks it wants, or those that critics demand. They are going to be the kind of novels that interest the novelist. And the novels that interest the novelist are those that have not already been written. They are those that put the greatest demands on him, that require him to operate at the maximum of his intelligence and his talents, and to be true to the particularities of his own vocation. The direction of many of us will be more toward poetry than toward the traditional novel.

The problem for such a novelist will be to know how far he can distort without destroying, and in order not to destroy, he will have to descend far enough into himself to reach those underground springs that give life to his work. This descent into himself will, at the same time, be a descent into his region. It will be a descent through the darkness of the familiar into a world where, like the blind man cured in the gospels, he sees men as if they were trees, but walking. This is the beginning of vision, and I feel it is a vision which we in the South must at least try to understand if we want to participate in the continuance of a vital Southern literature. I hate to think that in twenty years Southern writers too may be writing about men in gray-flannel suits and may have lost their ability to see that these gentlemen are even greater freaks than what we are writing about now. I hate to think of the day when the Southern writer will satisfy the tired reader.

[1961]

FRANK O'CONNOR

Frank O'Connor attempted a pioneering history of the short story in The Lonely Voice *(1963), a book often cited by later writers on the subject. In this excerpt from his introduction, he explains why he believes in "the superiority of the American short story over all others."*

From *The Lonely Voice*

Always in the short story there is this sense of outlawed figures wandering about the fringes of society, superimposed sometimes on symbolic figures whom they caricature and echo — Christ, Socrates, Moses. It is not for nothing that there are famous short stories called "Lady Macbeth of the Mtsensk District" and "A Lear of the Steppes" and — in reverse — one called "An Akoulina of the Irish Midlands." As a result there is in the short story at its most characteristic something we do not often find in the novel — an intense awareness of human loneliness. Indeed, it might be truer to say that while we often read a familiar novel again for companionship, we approach the short story in a very different mood. It is more akin to the mood of Pascal's saying: *Le silence éternel de ces espaces infinis m'effraie.*[1]

I have admitted that I do not profess to understand the idea fully: it is too vast for a writer with no critical or historical training to explore by his own inner light, but there are too many indications of its general truth for me to ignore it altogether. When I first dealt with it I had merely noticed the peculiar geographical distribution of the novel and the short story. For some reason Czarist Russia and modern America seemed to be able to produce both great novels and great short stories, while England, which might be called without exaggeration the homeland of the novel, showed up badly when it came to the short story. On the other hand my own country [Ireland], which had failed to produce a single novelist, had produced four or five storytellers who seemed to me to be first-rate.

I traced these differences very tentatively, but — on the whole, as I now think, correctly — to a difference in the national attitude toward society. In America as in Czarist Russia one might describe the intellectual's attitude to society as "It may work," in England as "It must work," and in Ireland as "It can't work." A young American of our own time or a young Russian of Turgenev's might look forward with a certain amount of cynicism to a measure of success and influence; nothing but bad luck could prevent a young Englishman's achieving it, even today; while a young

---

[1]The eternal silence of those infinite spaces terrifies me.

Irishman can still expect nothing but incomprehension, ridicule, and injustice. Which is exactly what the author of *Dubliners* got.

The reader will have noticed that I left out France, of which I know little, and Germany, which does not seem to have distinguished itself in fiction. But since those days I have seen fresh evidence accumulating that there was some truth in the distinctions I made. I have seen the Irish crowded out by Indian storytellers, and there are plenty of indications that they in their turn, having become respectable, are being outwritten by West Indians like Samuel Selvon.

Clearly, the novel and the short story, though they derive from the same sources, derive in a quite different way, and are distinct literary forms; and the difference is not so much formal (though, as we shall see, there are plenty of formal differences) as ideological. I am not, of course, suggesting that for the future the short story can be written only by Eskimos and American Indians: without going so far afield, we have plenty of submerged population groups. I am suggesting strongly that we can see in it an attitude of mind that is attracted by submerged population groups, whatever these may be at any given time — tramps, artists, lonely idealists, dreamers, and spoiled priests. The novel can still adhere to the classical concept of civilized society, of man as an animal who lives in a community, as in Jane Austen and Trollope it obviously does; but the short story remains by its very nature remote from the community — romantic, individualistic, and intransigent.

But formally as well the short story differs from the novel. At its crudest you can express the difference merely by saying that the short story is short. It is not necessarily true, but as a generalization it will do well enough. If the novelist takes a character of any interest and sets him up in opposition to society, and then, as a result of the conflict between them, allows his character either to master society or to be mastered by it, he has done all that can reasonably be expected of him. In this the element of Time is his greatest asset; the chronological development of character or incident is essential form as we see it in life, and the novelist flouts it at his own peril.

For the short-story writer there is no such thing as essential form. Because his frame of reference can never be the totality of a human life, he must be forever selecting the point at which he can approach it, and each selection he makes contains the possibility of a new form as well as the possibility of a complete fiasco. I have illustrated this element of choice by reference to a poem of Browning's. Almost any one of his great dramatic lyrics is a novel in itself but caught in a single moment of peculiar significance — Lippo Lippi arrested as he slinks back to his monastery in the early morning, Andrea Del Sarto as he resigns himself to the part of a complaisant lover, the Bishop dying in St. Praxed's. But since a whole lifetime must be crowded into a few minutes, those minutes must be carefully chosen indeed and lit by an unearthly glow, one that enables us to distinguish present, past, and future as though they were all contemporaneous. Instead of a novel of five hundred pages about the Duke of Ferrara, his first and second wives and the peculiar death of the first, we get fifty-odd lines in which the Duke, negotiating a second marriage, describes his first, and the very opening lines make our blood run cold:

> That's my last Duchess painted on the wall,
> Looking as if she were alive.

This is not the essential form that life gives us; it is organic form, something that springs from a single detail and embraces past, present, and future. In some book on Parnell there is a horrible story about the death of Parnell's child by Kitty O'Shea, his mistress, when he wandered frantically about the house like a ghost, while Willie O'Shea, the complaisant husband, gracefully received the condolences of visitors. When you read that, it should be unnecessary to read the whole sordid story of Parnell's romance and its tragic ending. The tragedy is there, if only one had a Browning or a Turgenev to write it. In the standard composition that the individual life presents, the storyteller must always be looking for new compositions that enable him to suggest the totality of the old one.

Accordingly, the storyteller differs from the novelist in this: he must be much more of a writer, much more of an artist—perhaps I should add, considering the examples I have chosen, more of a dramatist. For that, too, I suspect, has something to do with it. One savage story of J. D. Salinger's, "Pretty Mouth and Green My Eyes," echoes that scene in Parnell's life in a startling way. A deceived husband, whose wife is out late, rings up his best friend, without suspecting that the wife is in the best friend's bed. The best friend consoles him in a rough-and-ready way, and finally the deceived husband, a decent man who is ashamed of his own outburst, rings again to say that the wife has come home, though she is still in bed with her lover.

Now, a man can be a very great novelist as I believe Trollope was, and yet be a very inferior writer. I am not sure but that I prefer the novelist to be an inferior dramatist; I am not sure that a novel could stand the impact of a scene such as that I have quoted from Parnell's life, or J. D. Salinger's story. But I cannot think of a great storyteller who was also an inferior writer, unless perhaps Sherwood Anderson, nor of any at all who did not have the sense of theater.

This is anything but the recommendation that it may seem, because it is only too easy for a short-story writer to become a little too much of an artist. Hemingway, for instance, has so studied the artful approach to the significant moment that we sometimes end up with too much significance and too little information. I have tried to illustrate this from "Hills Like White Elephants." If one thinks of this as a novel one sees it as the love story of a man and a woman which begins to break down when the man, afraid of responsibility, persuades the woman to agree to an abortion which she believes to be wrong. The development is easy enough to work out in terms of the novel. He is an American, she perhaps an Englishwoman. Possibly he has responsibilities already—a wife and children elsewhere, for instance. She may have had some sort of moral upbringing, and perhaps in contemplating the birth of the child she is influenced by the expectation that her family and friends will stand by her in her ordeal.

Hemingway, like Browning in "My Last Duchess," chooses one brief episode from this long and involved story, and shows us the lovers at a wayside station on the Continent, between one train and the next, as it were, symbolically divorced from their normal surroundings and friends. In this setting they make a decision which has already begun to affect their past life and will certainly affect their future. We know that the man is American, but that is all we are told about him. We can guess the woman is not American, and that is all we are told about her. The light is focused fiercely on that one single decision about the abortion. It is the abortion, the whole abortion, and nothing but the abortion. We, too, are compelled to make ourselves judges of the decision, but on an abstract level. Clearly, if we knew that the man had responsibilities elsewhere, we should be a little more sympathetic to him. If, on the other hand, we knew that he had no other responsibilities, we should be even less sympathetic to him than we are. On the other hand, we should understand the woman better if we knew whether she didn't want the abortion because she thought it wrong or because she thought it might loosen her control of the man. The light is admirably focused but it is too blinding; we cannot see into the shadows as we do in "My Last Duchess."

> She had
> A heart—how shall I say?—too soon made glad,
> Too easily impressed; she liked whate'er
> She looked on, and her looks went everywhere.

And so I should say Hemingway's story is brilliant but thin. Our moral judgment has been stimulated, but our moral imagination has not been stirred, as it is stirred in "The Lady With the Toy Dog" in which we are given all the information at the disposal of the author which would enable us to make up our minds about the behavior of his pair of lovers. The comparative artlessness of the novel does permit the author to give unrestricted range to his feelings occasionally—to *sing;* and even minor novelists often sing loud and clear for several chapters at a time, but in the short story, for all its lyrical resources, the singing note is frequently absent.

That is the significance of the difference between the *conte* and the *nouvelle* which one sees even in Turgenev, the first of the great storytellers I have studied. Essentially the difference depends upon precisely how much information the writer feels he must give the reader to enable the moral imagination to function. Hemingway does not give the reader enough. When that wise mother Mme. Maupassant complained that her son, Guy, started his stories too soon and without sufficient preparation, she was making the same sort of complaint.

But the *conte* as Maupassant and even the early Chekhov sometimes wrote it is too rudimentary a form for a writer to go very far wrong in; it is rarely more than an anecdote, a *nouvelle* stripped of most of its detail. On the other hand, the form of the *conte* illustrated in "My Last Duchess" and "Hills Like White Elephants" is exceedingly complicated, and dozens of storytellers have gone astray in its mazes. There are three necessary elements in a story—exposition, development, and drama. Exposition we may illustrate as "John Fortescue was a solicitor in the little town of X"; development as "One day Mrs. Fortescue told him she was about to leave him for another man"; and drama as "You will do nothing of the kind," he said.

In the dramatized *conte* the storyteller has to combine exposition and development, and sometimes the drama shows a pronounced tendency to collapse under the mere weight of the intruded exposition—"As a solicitor I can tell you you will do nothing of the kind," John Fortescue said. The extraordinary brilliance of "Hills Like White Elephants" comes from the skill with which Hemingway has excluded unnecessary exposition; its weakness, as I have suggested, from the fact that much of the exposition is not unnecessary at all. Turgenev probably invented the dramatized *conte*, but if he did, he soon realized its dangers because in his later stories, even brief ones like "Old Portraits," he fell back on the *nouvelle*.

The ideal, of course, is to give the reader precisely enough information, and in this again the short story differs from the novel, because no convention of length ever seems to affect the novelist's power to tell us all we need to know. No such convention of length seems to apply to the short story at all. Maupassant often began too soon because he had to finish within two thousand words, and O'Flaherty sometimes leaves us with the impression that his stories have either gone on too long or not long enough. Neither Babel's stories nor Chekhov's leave us with that impression. Babel can sometimes finish a story in less than a thousand words, Chekhov can draw one out to eighty times the length.

One can put this crudely by saying that the form of the novel is given by the length; in the short story the length is given by the form. There is simply no criterion of the length of a short story other than that provided by the material itself, and either padding to bring it up to a conventional length or cutting to bring it down to a conventional length is liable to injure it. I am afraid that the modern short story is being seriously affected by editorial ideas of what its length should be. (Like most storytellers, I have been told that "nobody reads anything longer than three thousand words.") All I can say from reading Turgenev, Chekhov, Katherine Anne Porter, and others is that the very term "short story" is a misnomer. A great story is not necessarily short at all, and the conception of the short story as a miniature art is inherently false. Basically, the difference between the short story and the novel is not one of length. It is a difference between pure and applied storytelling, and in case someone has still failed to get the point, I am not trying to decry applied storytelling. Pure storytelling is more artistic, that is all, and in storytelling I am not sure how much art is preferable to nature. . . .

If I knew as much about American literature as I do about Irish literature, I feel I should probably be able to put my finger on Sherwood Anderson's *Winesburg, Ohio,* and say, "This is to America what *The Untilled Field* is to Ireland." The date itself—1919—is as significant as the date 1903 on the title page of Moore's book. Participation in the First World War had made Americans conscious for the first time since the Civil War that they were isolated, unique, and complacent; and the dissatisfaction it roused in them turned them into a generation of displaced persons, at home neither in America nor on the Continent. The year 1919 and Sherwood Anderson signaled the beginnings of a new self-consciousness; by 1920 Scott Fitzgerald was describing the return of the troops and the fresh complications this was creating, and within a couple of years Hemingway and Faulkner were sketching out the new literature.

When I said that I could think of no great storyteller who was not a great writer, I excluded Anderson, who did not really begin to write till he was in his forties. But few writers have had so clear a vision of what the short story could do. With absolute certainty he marked out his own submerged population—the lonely dreamers of the Middle West. Their loneliness is deeper and more tragic than that of George Moore's priests or Joyce's clerks, perhaps because, like Anderson himself, they come of pioneering stock, confident, competent men and women who do not understand what it means to be beaten almost from birth. There is an interesting comparison to be drawn between Joyce's "Eveline" and Anderson's "Adventure." Both deal with sensitive women who for one reason or another have been left on the shelf. Eveline is waiting to go with the man she loves to Buenos Aires, but when the boat is on the point of departure she leaves him and runs home, beaten before she starts at all. Alice Hindman, who has waited hopelessly for the return of a man she loves, strips herself and runs out into the street one rainy night to offer herself to the first man she meets, but he turns out to be old and deaf and says nothing but "What? What say?" So Alice returns to the house, goes to bed, and "turning her face to the wall, began trying to face bravely the fact that many people must live and die alone, even in Winesburg." It is a terrible moment for the American when his clear-sighted optimism gives place to an equally clear-sighted despondency. Anderson's characters understand their own hopeless position so well that I sometimes find myself wondering whether they are not really examples of that passive suffering which Yeats maintained was no material for art.

Those two terrible words, "alone" and "lonely," ring out in almost every story in *Winesburg, Ohio,* and with them the word "hands"—hands reaching out for a human contact that is not there. Yet contact itself is the principal danger, for to marry is to submit to the standards of the submerged population, and for the married there is no hope but to pass on the dream of escape to their children. The danger is the theme of the beautiful story, "The Untold Lie," and of a later, inferior story, "The Contract." The hope transmitted to the children is the theme of Anderson's finest story, "Death." In this, George Willard's grandfather, distrusting his son-in-law, leaves his daughter eight hundred dollars to be "a great open door" to her when the time comes for her to escape. Elizabeth, defeated in her turn, has saved it to be "a great open door" to her son, George, and hidden it a week after her marriage in a wall at the foot of her bed, where at the end of the story it still lies, plastered up and forgotten.

It is from this remarkable little book that the modern American short story develops, and the Americans have handled the short story so wonderfully that one can say that it is a national art form. I have given one reason for the superiority of the American short story over all others that I know, but of course, there are several reasons, and one is that America is largely populated by submerged population groups. That peculiar American sweetness toward the stranger — which exists side by side with American brutality toward everyone — is the sweetness of people whose own ancestors have been astray in an unfamiliar society and understand that a familiar society is the exception rather than the rule; that strangeness of behavior which is the very lifeblood of the short story is often an atavistic breaking out from some peculiar way of life, faraway and long ago. [1963]

GRACE PALEY

Grace Paley talked with Ann Charters about her experiences as a short story writer during lunch in her Greenwich Village apartment on a snowy day in February 1986. On the wall above the kitchen table hung an oil painting, a still life of vegetables painted by her father after his retirement from medicine. Paley mentions her father's interest in art in her story "A Conversation with My Father."

A Conversation with Ann Charters

Charters: Some literary critics think that short stories are more closely related to poetry than to the novel. Would you agree?

Paley: I would say that stories are closer to poetry than they are to the novel because first they are shorter, and second they are more concentrated, more economical, and that kind of economy, the pulling together of all the information and making leaps across the information, is really close to poetry. By leaps I mean thought leaps and feeling leaps. Also, when short stories are working right, you pay more attention to language than most novelists do.

Charters: Poe said unity was an essential factor of short stories. Do you have any ideas about this in your own work?

Paley: I suppose there has to be some kind of unity, but that's true in a novel too. It seems to me that unity is form. Form is really the vessel in which the story or poem or novel exists. The reason I don't have an answer for you is that there's really no telling — sometimes I like to start a story with one thing and end it with another. I don't know where the unity is in that case. I see the word *unity* meaning that something has to be whole, even if it ends in an open way.

Charters: You mean, as you wrote in "A Conversation with My Father," that "everyone, real or invented, deserves the open destiny of life."

Paley: Yes.

Charters: You started writing poetry before short stories, and the language of your fiction is often as compressed and metaphorical as the language of poetry. Can you describe the process of how you learned to write?

Paley: Let me put it this way: I went to school to poetry — that was where I learned how to write. People learn to write by doing various things. I suppose I also wrote a lot of letters, since it was the time of the Second World War. But apart from that I wrote poems, that's what I wrote. I thought about language a lot. That was important to me. That was my teacher. My fiction teacher was poetry.

Charters: What poets did you read when you were learning how to write?

Paley: I just read all the poets. If there was an anthology of poets, I read every single one. I knew all the Victorians. I read the Imagists. At a certain point I fell in love with the Englishmen who came to America — Christopher Isherwood, Stephen Spender, and W. H. Auden. I thought Auden was the greatest. And I loved the poetry of Dylan Thomas. Yeats meant a lot to me. I paid attention to all of them and listened to all of them. Some of them must have gotten into my ear. That's not up to me to say. That's for the reader to say. The reader of my stories will tell me, "This is whom you're influenced by," but I can't say that. I feel I was influenced by everybody.

Charters: Why did you stop writing poetry and start writing stories? What did the form of the short story offer you that the poem didn't?

Paley: First of all, I began to think of certain subject matter, women's lives specifically, and what was happening around me. I was in my thirties, which I guess is the time people start to notice these things, women's and men's lives and what their relationship is. I knew lots of women with small kids, and I was developing very close relationships with a variety of women. All sorts of things began to worry me, and I began to think about them a lot. I couldn't deal with any of this subject matter in poetry; I just didn't know how. I didn't have the technique. Other people can, but I didn't want to write poems saying "I feel this" and "I feel that." That was the last thing I wanted to do.

I can give you a definition that can be proven wrong in many ways, but for me it was that in writing poetry I wanted to talk to the world, I wanted to address the world, so to speak. But writing stories, I wanted to get the world to explain itself to me, to speak to me. And for me that was the essential difference between writing poetry and stories, and it still is, in many ways. So I had to get that world to talk to me. I had to reach out to it, a very different thing than writing poems. I had to reach out to the world and get it to tell me what it was all about, because I didn't understand it. I just didn't understand. Also, I'd always been very interested in people and told funny stories, and I didn't have any room for doing that in poems, again because of my own self. My poems were too literary, that's the real reason.

Charters: What do you mean, you had to get the world to tell you what it was all about?

Paley: In the first story I ever wrote, "The Contest," I did exactly what I just told you—I got this guy to talk. That's what I did. I had a certain guy in mind. In fact, I stuck pretty close to my notion of what he was, and the story was about a contest he had told me about. The second story I wrote was about Aunt Rose in "Goodbye and Good Luck." That began with my husband's aunt visiting us, and saying exactly the sentence I used to start the story: "I was popular in certain circles." But the rest has nothing to do with her life at all. She looked at us, this aunt of his, and she felt we didn't appreciate her, so she looked at us and she said to us, "Listen," she said. "I was popular in certain circles." That statement really began that particular story. That story was about lots of older women I knew who didn't get married, and I was thinking about them. These are two examples of how I began, how I got to my own voice by hearing and using all these other voices.

Charters: I suppose "A Conversation with My Father" isn't typical of your work, because the story you make up for him isn't what he wants, the old-fashioned Chekhov or Maupassant story, and it's not really one of your "voice" stories either, is it?

Paley: No. I'm just trying to oblige him.

Charters: So that may be one of the jokes of the story?

Paley: It could be, but I never thought of it that way. I think it's a good story. People have found it useful in literature classes, which I think is funny, but nice.

Charters: Did you make up the plot of "A Conversation with My Father," or did it actually happen when you were visiting him before he died?

Paley: My father was eighty-six years old and in bed. I spent a lot of time with him. He was an artist, and he painted pictures after he retired from being a doctor. I visited him at least once a week, and we were very close. We would have discussions. I never wrote a story for him about this neighbor, but he did say to me once, "Why can't you write a regular story, for God's sake?" something like that. So that particular story is both about literature and about that particular discussion, but it's also about generational differences, about different ways of looking at life. What my father thought could be done in the world was due to his own history. What I thought could be done in the world was different, not because I was a more open person, because he was also a very open person, but because I lived in a particularly open time, the late 1960s. The story I wrote for him was about all these druggies. It was made up, but it was certainly true. I could point out people on my block whose kids became junkies. Many of them have recovered from being junkies and are in good shape now.

Charters: Did you know any mothers in Greenwich Village who became junkies to keep their kids company?

Paley: Sure. It was a very open neighborhood then, with lots of freedom. But my father was born into a very different time. He was born in Czarist Russia and came over to America when he was twenty and worked hard and studied medicine and had a profession.

Charters: When you were growing up did you read the writers your father admired—Maupassant and Chekhov?

Paley: Actually, he had never mentioned Maupassant to me before. He did mention him in that conversation. He did read a lot, he loved Chekhov. And when he came to this country, he taught himself English by reading Dickens.

Charters: So the idea for the story came to you when he mentioned Maupassant?

Paley: Well, not really. He had just read my story "Faith in a Tree," and there are a lot of voices coming from all over in that story. And so he asked me, "What is this? All those voices? Voices from who knows where?" He wasn't actually that heavy. But when I wrote about our conversation it became a fiction, and it's different from what really happened.

Charters: It must have been fun for you to make up the two versions of the story about your neighbor in "A Conversation with My Father."

Paley: I enjoyed writing that story. Some stories you don't enjoy, because they're very hard. I didn't write it right off, but I enjoyed it.

Charters: How many days did it take you to write?

Paley: There's no such thing as days with me when I write a story. More like months. I write it and I write slow, and then I rewrite, and then I put it away, and then I take it out again. It's tedious in some respects. But that's the way it works.

Charters: When do you decide it's finished?

Paley: When I've gone over it and I can't think of another thing to change.

Charters: I was looking over your book *Enormous Changes at the Last Minute,* which is where "A Conversation with My Father" appears, and I noticed you've placed it between two very dark stories, "The Little Girl," about a runaway in the Village who commits suicide after she's raped, and "The Immigrant Story," about the starvation of the young children in a Jewish family in Poland before the mother emigrates to America. I assume you did this for a reason. When you put a collection of short fiction together, how do you order the stories?

Paley: I always have something in mind. I like to put one or two at the beginning that will be readable immediately, and then I just work it out. I like to mix the long and the short, and the serious and the funny ones. But I did put those two dark stories around "A Conversation with My Father" to show him I could look tragedy in the face. Remember he asks me at the end of the story, "When will you look it in the face?"

Charters: Was that one of the things he actually said to you when you visited him?

Paley: Well, he did tend to say that I wouldn't look things in the face. That things were hard, and I wasn't looking at it. I didn't see certain problems with my kids when they were small, and he was in some degree right. In "The Immigrant Story" a man tells me, "You have a rotten rosy temperament." But then she says, "Rosiness is not a worse windowpane than gloomy gray when viewing the world." They're both just prisms to look through.

Charters: Is that what you still believe?

Paley: Well, I do believe it, but I also believe that things are bad.

Charters: A theme that some students find when reading "A Conversation with My Father" is that one of the things you don't want to look in the face that your father is trying to prepare you for is his own death. Were you conscious of that when you wrote the story?

Paley: No.

Charters: Can you see that theme in it now?

Paley: No. But maybe you're right. As I said, that's not up to me to say. Maybe the reader of a particular story knows better than the writer what it means. But I know I wasn't thinking about that when I wrote it. I wasn't thinking of his death at all. I was thinking of him being sick and trying not to get him excited. [1986]

DOROTHY PARKER

Dorothy Parker discussed the phenomenon of the American short story as it flourished on the pages of popular magazines in an article for The New Yorker *on December 17, 1927. She came away from her immersion in the world of short fiction with a great respect for Edward O'Brien's stamina and judgment as he performed the task of editing* The Best American Short Stories *each year.*

The Short Story,
through a Couple of the Ages

There was a time, when I still had my strength, that I read nearly all the stories in the more popular magazines. I did not have to do it; I did it for fun, for I had yet to discover that there were other and more absorbing diversions that had the advantage of being no strain on the eyes. But even in those days of my vigor, nearly all the stories was the best that I could do. I could never go the full course. From the time I learned to read—which, I am pretty thoroughly convinced, was when I made my first big mistake—I was always unable to do anything whatever with stories that began in any of these following manners:

(1) "Ho, Felipe, my horse, and *pronto!*" cried *El Sol*. He turned to the quivering girl, and his mocking bow was so low that his *sombrero* swept the flags of the *patio*. "*Adiós,* then, *señorita,* until *mañana!*" And with a flash of white teeth across the lean young swarthiness of his face, he bounded to the back of his horse and was off, swift as a homing *paloma*.

(2) Everybody in Our Village loved to go by Granny Wilkins' cottage. Maybe it was the lilacs that twinkled a cheery greeting in the dooryard, or maybe it was the brass knocker that twinkled on the white-painted door, or maybe—and I suspect this was the real reason—it was Granny herself, with her crisp white cap, and her wise brown eyes, twinkling away in her dear little old winter apple of a face.

(3) The train chugged off down the long stretch of track, leaving the little new school-mistress standing alone on the rickety boards that composed the platform of Medicine Bend station. She looked very small indeed, standing there, and really ridiculously young. "I just won't cry!" she said fiercely, swallowing hard. "I won't! Daddy—Daddy would be disappointed in me if I cried. Oh, Daddy—Daddy, I miss you so!"

(4) The country club was a-hum, for the final match of the Fourth of July Golf Tournament was in full swing. Many a curious eye lingered on Janet DeLancey, rocking lazily, surrounded as usual by a circle of white-flanneled adorers, for the porch was a-whisper with the rumor that the winner of the match would also be the winner of the hitherto untouched heart of the blond and devastating Janet.

(5) I dunno ez I ought to be settin' here, talkin', when there's the vittles to git fer the men-folks. But, Laws, 'tain't often a body hez a chanct ter talk, up this-a-way. I wuz tellin' yuh 'bout li'l Mezzie Meigs, ol' Skinflint Meigs's da'ter. She wuz a right peart 'un, Mezzie wuz, and purty!

(6) "For God's sake, don't do it, Kid!" whispered Annie the Wop, twining her slim arms about the Kid's bull-like neck. "Yer promised me yer'd go straight, after the last time. The bulls'll get yer, Kid; they'll send yer up, sure. Aw, Kid, put away yer gat, and let's beat it away somewhere in God's nice, clean country, where yer can raise chickens, like yer always dreamed of doin'."

But, with these half-dozen exceptions, I read all the other short stories that separated the Ivory Soap advertisements from the pages devoted to Campbell's Soups. I read about bored and pampered wives who were right on the verge of eloping with slender-fingered, quizzical-eyed artists, but did not. I read of young suburban couples, caught up in the fast set about them, driven to separation by their false, nervous life, and restored to each other by the opportune illness of their baby. I read tales proving that Polack servant-girls have their feelings, too. I read of young men who collected blue jade, and solved mysterious murders, on the side. I read stories of transplanted Russians, of backstage life, of shop-girls' evening hours, of unwanted grandmothers, of heroic collies, of experiments in child-training, of golden-hearted cow-punchers with slow drawls, of the comicalities of adolescent love, of Cape Cod fisherfolk, of Creole belles and beaux, of Greenwich Village, of Michigan Boulevard, of the hard-drinking and easy-kissing younger generation, of baseball players, side-show artists, and professional mediums. I read, in short, more damn tripe than you ever saw in your life.

And then I found that I was sluggish upon awakening in the morning, spots appeared before my eyes, and my friends shunned me. I also found that I was reading the same stories over and over, month after month. So I stopped, like that. It is only an old wives' tale that you have to taper off.

Recently, though, I took the thing up again. There were rumors about that the American short story had taken a decided turn for the better. Crazed with hope, I got all the more popular and less expensive magazines that I could carry on my shoulders, and sat down for a regular old read. And a regular old read is just what it turned out to be. There they all were—the golden-hearted cow-punchers, the suburban couples, the baseball players, the Creole belles—even dear old Granny Wilkins was twinkling away, in one of them. There were the same old plots, the same old characters, the same old phrases—dear Heaven, even the same old illustrations. So that is why I shot myself.

It is true that in the magazines with quieter covers, with smaller circulations, and with higher purchasing prices, there are good short stories. Their scholarly editors have extended a courteous welcome to the newer writers. And the newer writers are good; they write with feeling and honesty and courage, and they write well. They do not prostitute their talents for money; they do not add words because they are to be paid by the word; scarcely, indeed, do they violate their amateur standing. But here, just as one did in the old days, does one get the feeling of reading the same stories over and over, month after month. There are no golden-hearted cow-punchers, but there are the inevitable Midwestern farm families; the laughing Creole belles have given place to the raw tragedies of the Bayou; but the formulae are as rigorous. You must write your story as starkly as it was written just before you did it; if you can outstark the previous author, you are one up. Sedulous agony has become as monotonous as sedulous sunshine. Save for those occasions when you come upon a Hemingway or an Anderson or a Lardner in your reading, the other stories that meet your eye might all have come from the same pen.

I do not see how Mr. Edward O'Brien stands the strain. Season after season, as inescapable as Christmas, he turns out his collection of what he considers to be the best short stories of their year. To do this, and he does it conscientiously, he must read and rate every short story in every American magazine of fiction. Me, I should liefer adopt the career of a blood donor.

The Best Short Stories of 1927 is distinguished by the inclusion in it of Ernest Hemingway's superb "The Killers." This is enough to make any book of stories a notable one. There is also Sherwood Anderson's "Another Wife," which seems to me one of his best. But in the other stories I can find only disappointment. They seem to me wholly conventional, in this recent conventionality of anguish. There is no excitement to them; they have all the dogged quiet of too-careful writing. Separate, each one might possibly—oh, possibly—grip you. Grouped together, they string out as flat as Kansas.

Their compiler shows himself, in this volume, to be more than ever the unsung hero. In the back of the book, where he lists all the short stories of the year, and grades them, unasked, without a star, with one star, with two stars, or with three stars, according to his notion of their merits, you may gain some idea of what the man has been through. I give you some of the titles of the stories that he has wrestled with:

"Vomen is Easily Veak-Minded"; "Ma Bentley's Christmas Dinner"; "Archibald in Arcady" (there is always one of those, every year); "Fred and Circuses"; "Willie Painter Stays on the Level"; "Sylvia Treads among the Goulds"; "Betty Use Your Bean"; "Daddy's Nondetachable Cuffs"; "Ann 'n' Andy"; "Freed 'Em and Weep" (I bet that was a little love); "Jerry Gums the Game"; "Blue Eyes in Trouble"; "Grandflapper" (you can practically write that one for yourself); "She Loops to Conquer"; "Yes, Sir, He's My Maybe"; and "Dot and Will Find Out What It Means to Be Rich," which last sets me wondering into the night just what were the titles that the author threw out as being less adroit.

They say Mr. O'Brien makes ample money, on his sales of these stories written by others, and I hope it is true. But no matter how much it is, he deserves more.   [1927]

EDGAR ALLAN POE

Edgar Allan Poe was one of the earliest writers to discuss the aesthetic qualities of the short story as a distinct prose narrative form. In his day literary criticism was still a new field in America, lacking a terminology and developed concepts. His two long reviews praising the tales of Nathaniel Hawthorne were published in Graham's Magazine *in 1842 and* Godey's Lady's Book *in 1847; they are pioneering examples of the analytic literary essay. The following is the 1842 review, in which Poe amplifies his theory of the short story and his views on the nature of originality in literature.*

Review of Hawthorne's *Twice-Told Tales*

We said a few hurried words about Mr. Hawthorne in our last number, with the design of speaking more fully in the present. We are still, however, pressed for room, and must necessarily discuss his volumes more briefly and more at random than their high merits deserve.

The book professes to be a collection of *tales,* yet is, in two respects, misnamed. These pieces are now in their third republication, and, of course, are thrice-told. Moreover, they are by no means *all* tales, either in the ordinary or in the legitimate understanding of the term. Many of them are pure essays; for example, "Sights from a Steeple," "Sunday at Home," "Little Annie's Ramble," "A Rill from the Town Pump," "The Toll-Gatherer's Day," "The Haunted Mind," "The Sister Years," "Snow-Flakes," "Night Sketches," and "Foot-Prints on the Sea-Shore." We mention these matters chiefly on account of their discrepancy with that marked precision and finish by which the body of the work is distinguished.

Of the essays just named, we must be content to speak in brief. They are each and all beautiful, without being characterised by the polish and adaptation so visible in the tales proper. A painter would at once note their leading or predominant feature, and style it *repose.* There is no attempt at effect. All is quiet, thoughtful, subdued. Yet this repose may exist simultaneously with high originality of thought; and Mr. Hawthorne has demonstrated the fact. At every turn we meet with novel combinations; yet these combinations never surpass the limits of the quiet. We are soothed as we read; and withal is a calm astonishment that ideas so apparently obvious have never occurred or been presented to us before. Herein our author differs materially from Lamb or Hunt or Hazlitt—who, with vivid originality of manner and expression, have less of the true novelty of thought than is generally supposed, and whose originality, at best, has an uneasy and meretricious quaintness, replete with startling effects unfounded in nature, and inducing trains of reflection which lead to no satisfactory result. The Essays of Hawthorne have much of the character of Irving, with more of originality, and less of finish; while, compared with the Spectator, they have a vast superiority at all points. The Spectator, Mr. Irving, and Mr. Hawthorne have in common that tranquil and subdued manner which we have chosen to denominate *repose;* but, in the case of the two former, this repose is attained rather by the absence of novel combination, or of originality, than otherwise, and consists chiefly in the calm, quiet, unostentatious expression of common-place thoughts, in an unambitious, unadulterated Saxon. In them, by strong effort, we are made to conceive the absence of all. In the essays before us the absence of effort is too obvious to be mistaken, and a strong under current of *suggestion* runs continuously beneath the upper stream of the tranquil thesis. In short, these effusions of Mr. Hawthorne are the product of a truly imaginative intellect, restrained, and in some measure repressed, by fastidiousness of taste, by constitutional melancholy and by indolence.

But it is of his tales that we desire principally to speak. The tale proper, in our opinion, affords unquestionably the fairest field for the exercise of the loftiest talent, which can be afforded by the wide domains of mere prose. Were we bidden to say how the highest genius could be most advantageously employed for the best display of its own powers, we should answer, without hesitation—in the composition of a rhymed poem, not to exceed in length what might be perused in an hour. Within this limit alone can the highest order of true poetry exist. We need only here say, upon this topic, that, in almost all classes of composition, the unity of effect or impression is a point of the greatest importance. It is clear, moreover, that this unity cannot be thoroughly preserved in productions whose perusal cannot be completed at one sitting. We may continue the reading of a prose composition, from the very nature of prose itself, much longer than we can persevere, to any good purpose, in the perusal of a poem. This latter, if truly fulfilling the demands of the poetic sentiment, induces an exaltation of the soul which cannot be long sustained. All high excitements are necessarily transient. Thus a long poem is a paradox. And, without unity of impression, the deepest effects cannot be brought about. Epics were the offspring of an imperfect sense of Art, and their reign is no more. A poem *too* brief may produce a vivid, but never an intense or enduring impression. Without a certain continuity of effort—without a certain duration or repetition of purpose—the soul is never deeply moved. There must be the dropping of the water upon the rock. De Beranger has wrought brilliant things—pungent and spirit-stirring—but, like all immassive bodies, they lack *momentum,* and thus fail to satisfy the Poetic Sentiment. They sparkle and excite, but, from want of continuity, fail deeply to impress. Extreme brevity will degenerate into epigrammatism; but the sin of extreme length is even more unpardonable. *In medio tutissimus ibis.*[1]

Were we called upon, however, to designate that class of composition which, next to such a poem as we have suggested, should best fulfil the demands of high genius—should offer it the most advantageous field of exertion—we should unhesitatingly speak of the prose tale, as Mr. Hawthorne has here exemplified it. We allude to the short prose narrative, requiring from a half-hour to one or two hours in its perusal. The ordinary

---

[1]For you the safest course is the middle one.

novel is objectionable, from its length, for reasons already stated in substance. As it cannot be read at one sitting, it deprives itself, of course, of the immense force derivable from *totality*. Worldly interests intervening during the pauses of perusal, modify, annul, or counteract, in a greater or less degree, the impressions of the book. But simple cessation in reading, would, of itself, be sufficient to destroy the true unity. In the brief tale, however, the author is enabled to carry out the fullness of his intention, be it what it may. During the hour of perusal the soul of the reader is at the writer's control. There are no external or extrinsic influences—resulting from weariness or interruption.

A skilful literary artist has constructed a tale. If wise, he has not fashioned his thoughts to accommodate his incidents; but having conceived, with deliberate care, a certain unique or single *effect* to be wrought out, he then invents such incidents—he then combines such events as may best aid him in establishing this preconceived effect. If his very initial sentence tend not to the outbringing of this effect, then he has failed in his first step. In the whole composition there should be no word written, of which the tendency, direct or indirect, is not to the one preestablished design. And by such means, with such care and skill, a picture is at length painted which leaves in the mind of him who contemplates it with a kindred art, a sense of the fullest satisfaction. The idea of the tale has been presented unblemished, because undisturbed; and this is an end unattainable by the novel. Undue brevity is just as exceptionable here as in the poem; but undue length is yet more to be avoided.

We have said that the tale has a point of superiority even over the poem. In fact, while the *rhythm* of this latter is an essential aid in the development of the poet's highest idea—idea of the Beautiful—the artificialities of this rhythm are an inseparable bar to the development of all points of thought or expression which have their basis in *Truth*. But Truth is often, and in very great degree, the aim of the tale. Some of the finest tales are tales of ratiocination. Thus the field of this species of composition, if not in so elevated a region on the mountain of Mind, is a table-land of far vaster extent than the domain of the mere poem. Its products are never so rich, but infinitely more numerous, and more appreciable by the mass of mankind. The writer of the prose tale, in short, may bring to his theme a vast variety of modes or inflections of thought and expression—(the ratiocinative, for example, the sarcastic, or the humorous) which are not only antagonistical to the nature of the poem, but absolutely forbidden by one of its most peculiar and indispensable adjuncts; we allude, of course, to rhythm. It may be added here, *par parenthèse*, that the author who aims at the purely beautiful in a prose tale is laboring at great disadvantage. For Beauty can be better treated in a poem. Not so with terror, or passion, or horror, or a multitude of such other points. And here it will be seen how full of prejudice are the usual animadversions against those *tales of effect*, many fine examples of which were found in the earlier numbers of Blackwood. The impressions produced were wrought in a legitimate sphere of action, and constituted a legitimate although sometimes an exaggerated interest. They were relished by every man of genius; although there were found many men of genius who condemned them without just ground. The true critic will but demand that the design intended be accomplished, to the fullest extent, by the means most advantageously applicable.

We have very few American tales of real merit—we may say, indeed, none, with the exception of "The Tales of a Traveller" of Washington Irving, and these "Twice-Told Tales" of Mr. Hawthorne. Some of the pieces of Mr. John Neal abound in vigor and originality; but in general, his compositions of this class are excessively diffuse, extravagant, and indicative of an imperfect sentiment of Art. Articles at random are, now and then, met with in our periodicals which might be advantageously compared with the best effusions of the British Magazines; but, upon the whole, we are far behind our progenitors in this department of literature.

Of Mr. Hawthorne's Tales we would say, emphatically, that they belong to the highest region of Art—an Art subservient to genius of a very lofty order. We had supposed, with good reason for so supposing, that he had been thrust into his present position by one of the impudent *cliques* which beset our literature, and whose pretensions it is our full purpose to expose at the earliest opportunity; but we have been most agreeably mistaken. We know of few compositions which the critic can more honestly commend than these "Twice-Told Tales." As Americans, we feel proud of the book.

Mr. Hawthorne's distinctive trait is invention, creation, imagination, originality—a trait which, in the literature of fiction, is positively worth all the rest. But the nature of originality, so far as regards its manifestation in letters, is but imperfectly understood. The inventive or original mind as frequently displays itself in novelty of *tone* as in novelty of matter. Mr. Hawthorne is original at *all* points.

It would be a matter of some difficulty to designate the best of these tales; we repeat that, without exception, they are beautiful. "Wakefield" is remarkable for the skill with which an old idea—a well-known incident— is worked up or discussed. A man of whims conceives the purpose of quitting his wife and residing *incognito,* for twenty years, in her immediate neighborhood. Something of this kind actually happened in London. The force of Mr. Hawthorne's tale lies in the analysis of the motives which must or might have impelled the husband to such folly, in the first instance, with the possible causes of his perseverance. Upon this thesis a sketch of singular power has been constructed.

"The Wedding Knell" is full of the boldest imagination—an imagination fully controlled by taste. The most captious critic could find no flaw in this production.

"The Minister's Black Veil" is a masterly composition of which the sole defect is that to the rabble its exquisite skill will be *caviare*. The *obvious* meaning of this article will be found to smother its insinuated one. The *moral* put into the mouth of the dying minister will be supposed to convey the *true* import of the narrative; and that a crime of dark dye (having refer-ence to the "young lady"), has been committed, is a point which only minds congenial with that of the author will perceive.

"Mr. Higginbotham's Catastrophe" is vividly original and managed most dexterously.

"Dr. Heidegger's Experiment" is exceedingly well imagined, and exe-cuted with surpassing ability. The artist breathes in every line of it.

"The White Old Maid" is objectionable, even more than the "Minis-ter's Black Veil," on the score of its mysticism. Even with the thoughtful and analytic, there will be much trouble in penetrating its entire import.

"The Hollow of the Three Hills" we would quote in full, had we space; — not as evincing higher talent than any of the other pieces, but as affording an excellent example of the author's peculiar ability. The subject is commonplace. A witch subjects the Distant and the Past to the view of a mourner. It has been the fashion to describe, in such cases, a mirror in which the images of the absent appear; or a cloud of smoke is made to arise, and thence the figures are gradually unfolded. Mr. Hawthorne has wonderfully heightened his effect by making the ear, in place of the eye, the medium by which the fantasy is conveyed. The head of the mourner is enveloped in the cloak of the witch, and within its magic folds there arise sounds which have an all-sufficient intelligence. Throughout this article also, the artist is conspicuous — not more in positive than in negative mer-its. Not only is all done that should be done, but (what perhaps is an end with more difficulty attained) there is nothing done which should not be. Every word *tells*, and there is not a word that does *not* tell. . . .

In the way of objection we have scarcely a word to say of these tales. There is, perhaps, a somewhat too general or prevalent *tone* — a tone of melancholy and mysticism. The subjects are insufficiently varied. There is not so much of *versatility* evinced as we might well be warranted in expect-ing from the high powers of Mr. Hawthorne. But beyond these trivial exceptions we have really none to make. The style is purity itself. Force abounds. High imagination gleams from every page. Mr. Hawthorne is a man of the truest genius. We only regret that the limits of our Magazine will not permit us to pay him that full tribute of commendation, which, under other circumstances, we should be so eager to pay.   [1842]

EARL ROVIT

Earl Rovit, a professor at the City College of New York, explores the connec-tion between the writing and the marketing of American short stories in his essay about James Thurber and The New Yorker. *Rovit's essay originally appeared in volume two of* The American Short Story, *edited by Calvin Skaggs (1980).*

On James Thurber and The New Yorker

Whenever the range of achievement in the American short story is discussed, one factor should receive more attention than it has — namely, the audience. For in a cultural interaction that is not always recognized, the American short story has developed its supple strengths partly as a result of its sensitivity to the demands of successive audiences. More directly than the other literary genres, the short story has been maintained by its authors' ability to apprehend and isolate a specific interest-group or audience — frequently before that audience was itself aware of its own existence.

We sometimes overlook the fact that the market for the short story in America is quite different from the market for poetry or the novel. In the case of those other genres, the writer can assume a relatively static, homogeneous, and very slowly changing readership to which he can address his work. But the economics of short-story publishing dictate a very different situation. Short stories are ephemeral; they are read quickly in disposable magazines. They rarely enjoy the luxury of being available on bookshelves until their moment has arrived; equally rarely is it possible to resavor their subtleties unless they are gathered up into collections. Consequently, short stories must be designed to work immediately and forcibly on the casual attention of a reader who happens to be leafing through the pages of a magazine — because he has nothing better to do or because he chooses not to be doing what he ought to be doing.

The writing and marketing of short stories, in other words, is very much a bread-and-butter proposition in which the writer strives to adapt his talents to the taste of a few easily distinguishable distributors (magazines) to which the prospective reader can come to shop, as it were, with reasonable expectations regarding what he will find there. And just as we would expect the contents of *Playboy* to differ from those of *National Geographic,* so famous American magazines like *The Dial, Atlantic Monthly, Vanity Fair, Smart Set, Saturday Evening Post,* and *Esquire* have flourished because they were able to consolidate their interests into a consistent style or tone that was identifiable and attractive to their respective customers.

Accordingly, except when we are dealing with the truly superior or original masters of our fiction like Hawthorne, James, Faulkner, or Hemingway, it is useful to consider some of our short-story writers almost as though they were functions of the magazines with which they were associated. Or, to turn the proposition around, an examination of the audience created and defined by a specific magazine can throw as much light on the work of a writer associated with that magazine as an exploration of his biography or an extended critical analysis of his career. If we can distinguish an audience similar in socioeconomic and ideological characteristics — one whose prejudices, fears, hopes, and composite self-image fall into a discernible pattern — then we already know a good deal about a writer whose career is inseparable from the magazine which is the repository and authority of that audience's taste. Specifically, James Thurber's relationship to *The New Yorker* offers a close-to-pure example of such symbiosis. And in this respect Thurber can stand as more or less representative of a group of writers and artists of the 1930s—E. B. White, S. J. Perelman, John O'Hara, Wolcott Gibbs, Ogden Nash, Dorothy Parker, Robert Benchley, Otto Soglow, Peter Arno—who, under the Mad Hatter orchestration of Harold Ross, were to establish the foundations for a kind of aesthetic style later to be exploited more profoundly by J. D. Salinger, John Cheever, Saul Steinberg, and John Updike.

The New Yorker was founded by Ross in 1925, some three years after the inaugural issues of *Reader's Digest* and *Time,* the two other powerhouses in the trinity of post–World War One American journalism. It is, of course, no accident that these one-man publishing ventures sprang into life at the same time that the advertising and public-relations businesses, radio, and the movies were taking their first steps toward forming what we now regard as the interlocked communications grid that controls our culture.

Thurber—quite typical of his peers in this respect—was born in Columbus, Ohio, in 1894, attended Ohio State University, and worked as a code clerk in Washington and Paris during the Great War. (He had lost the sight of his left eye in a childhood accident and was ineligible for active service.) Returning to America, he served a stint as a newspaperman, went back to Paris to fail at writing a novel, and finally joined *The New Yorker* in 1927 as a step up from his job as a reporter for the New York *Evening Post.* First as managing editor, later as regular author of "Talk of the Town," Thurber found in Ross and his *New Yorker* associates the perfect carnival environment for his antic sense of humor. And although he officially left his staff position in 1935 to free-lance, give shows of his drawings, and dabble in Broadway and Hollywood productions, it is primarily as a *New Yorker* writer-cartoonist that he should be identified.

Like his contemporaries, then, he was born in a rural and village-oriented America which Emerson and Lincoln would have found familiar. But he lived to see the bucolic stability of his youth dramatically changed as automobiles, telephones, radio, movies, airplanes, and television squeezed space and time to the dimensions of a fever blister, inevitably making accelerated mutability the central fact of modern consciousness. *The New Yorker*—even to the flaunting of its name and its famous motto ("It's not for the lady from Dubuque")—is one of the main chronicles as well as one of the more effective agents of this radical alteration of the American physical and mental landscape. One can hardly imagine the magazine, for example, except in terms of high-speed modern printing presses, a rapid transcontinental system of distribution to assure weekly delivery, and a gradual clustering of the most prestigious corporate images on its advertising accounts.

From its beginnings *The New Yorker* was peddling sophistication, and its natural audience came from the white, educated, mobile middle class— eager to clamber up the ladder of professionalism, trying to adapt to the frenetic pace of a changed America, and more than willing to learn the proper taste in furs, bourbon, automobiles, art, politics, and syntax. The weekly columns on theater, books, art exhibitions, sports, shopping, and New York City gossip; the smorgasbord mixture of fiction, profiles, causeries, poetry, reviews, and wisecracks blended with the glossy paper and the images of elegant advertising to mitigate anything too serious, too individualistic, too intellectual, too radical, or too vulgar. Wit, parody, and satire were central to the magazine's tone—as were poignancy and nostalgia if treated with a light enough touch. Thurber, White, and company had just the right balance of intelligent daring and restraint to execute charming performances under the cartoon rubric of Eustace Tilley. A more jagged artistic personality like Sinclair Lewis would have been decidedly out of place.

In a manner parallel to that by which *Time* sought out its audience of middle-class junior executives on the rise and *Reader's Digest* discovered a massive lower-middle-class audience avid for a twentieth-century version of *Poor Richard's Almanac,* the equally conservative *New Yorker* learned to transfer the "college humor" of the American campuses of the 1920s and the increasing consciousness of "fashion" to a readership of national breadth. Its editorial stance was irreverent without being caustic or fundamentally critical; it was judiciously hopeful in a pragmatic way, "liberal" and humanistic in its tolerances and aspirations, and, especially in the thirties and forties, before it had become an institution in its own right, generally playful and suspicious of solemnity. As *Time* prided itself on the accuracy of its research departments, *The New Yorker's* self-appointed role was that of the defender of grammar, syntax, and style—a kind of avuncular *Académie Française* for the benighted products of American mass education. Such essentially narrow concerns, of course, precluded attention to the more hazardous experiments in style or the more harrowing visions of human nature in the literature of the period. Faulkner, for example, was pretty much ignored in *The New Yorker* during the 1930s except for some notoriously condescending reviews by Clifton Fadiman; and at a time when leftist journals like *Partisan Review* were introducing Kafka and offering a genuine critique of capitalism to their readers, *The New Yorker* seems to have been fairly impervious to these new European currents beginning to seep into American intellectual life. By the time of World War Two, in other words, *The New Yorker* had become the unlikely replacement for the old *Atlantic Monthly* or *Harper's* of the late nineteenth century as the bastion or country club of a new genteel tradition. It sported a lighter and more delicate touch on morality, to be sure; it was somewhat more receptive to previously excluded minority groups; and it couched its authority in a far less ponderous style. But it was just as vitally concerned—in both the best and worst senses—with a zeal to define "manners" and suburban propriety.

Within these considerable limitations, Thurber's contributions to *The New Yorker* were exemplary. Never particularly interested in plot or serious character analysis, Thurber was a natural master of the *vignette*—which, after all, is a kind of verbal equivalent to the cartoon or illustration. In this mode—both written and drawn—he specialized in capturing the sudden comic flash of humiliation or triumph in the deliberately stereotyped lives of the new class which post–World War One prosperity and modern technology had spawned. His invention—the Thurberesque "little man," his trademark caricature of the suburban office-worker—was a *persona* which he both lovingly identified with and coldly despised. (He was himself a tall man and apparently not easily intimidated by any of the things that plague his typical protagonists.) Thurber's "little man" is characteristically surrounded by large threatening women, large—although usually quiescent—animals, and a large hostile machined environment. He tends to be permanently engaged in an unsuccessful balancing act as he tries ineptly to retain his remembered standards of a more stable life-style while he is being beset by a stepped-up work/play cycle geared to the commuter train, the interoffice memo, and the cocktail party. Wry, detached, whimsical—at their best, very funny—these stylized confrontations make a topsy-turvy assault against traditional notions of American heroism. At their very best they project a rather heroic "antihero" who—against all odds—emerges victorious from the fray.

The idea of heroism, in American culture, has often seemed contradictory. On the one hand the historical challenge of settling a vast continent and undertaking a precarious social experiment required of Americans an idealistic sense of mission; a willingness to undergo misfortune, deprivation, and frustration; and a consequent glorification of fortitude, courage, and readiness to take risks. On the other hand the theory of democratic egalitarianism resists the concept of heroes or superior men. If all men are created equal, then all ought to be appreciated equally; or, if we do accept heroes, the hero should come from the common stock—should be the Lincolnesque common man who is sometimes capable of doing uncommon things. In practice, denied a visible class of nobility which they could admire, Americans have been quick to elevate all sorts of candidates into heroic celebration—even at times into semideification. Ultimately we have demanded of our heroes (Emerson called them "representative men") a kind of impossible stature and range of achievement—one which requires both at base and pinnacle a *moral* superiority above and beyond mere success in a limited endeavor or pursuit of excellence. Our renowned generals and statesmen must also be paragons of virtue; our inventors, millionaires; and our popular artists, domestic saints of the most immaculate bearing.

Resolutely elitist in its role as arbiter of the new taste, *The New Yorker* was predictably antiheroic in its posture and prepared to be amused by the fanatic enthusiasm surrounding celebrities. Thurber's artistic willingness to deflate pretensions and to argue a satirical brief for the beleaguered "little man" dovetailed perfectly with *The New Yorker*'s editorial predilection. In *The Male Animal* (1940), a very successful play which he wrote with his old college chum, Elliot Nugent, a decidedly ineffectual college professor surprises everyone, including himself, by making a stalwart defense of academic freedom. In "The Catbird Seat" a characteristically woeful and seemingly helpless Thurber underdog outwits and dooms his formidable female oppressor. Walter Mitty, of course—undoubtedly Thurber's best-known "little man"—escapes the deadening torpor of hen-pecked domesticity by recourse to a series of delightful fantasies in which he can be in daydream the indomitable hero which reality makes decisively impossible. In these jaundiced responses to the heroic mode in American culture, Thurber is able to channel his malice (of which he appears to have had rather more than the normal portion) into the creation of small Chaplinesque triumphs—situations in which ineptitude gains a whimsical elegance and Thurber's "losers" can win our sympathy with only the barest modicum of our condescension. . . .

Even though Thurber began to lose the sight of his good eye in 1940 and suffered a series of futile operations for cataract and trachoma, he remained active in his writing up to his death in 1961. A minor talent when measured on the cold scales of universal greatness, producer of no single masterpiece even in a minor key, Thurber still deserves to be remembered and read for two reasons. First, his powerful shaping influence on *The New Yorker* style cannot be denied; and that style, in turn, has had immeasurable influence on the style and attitudes of at least two generations of American readers. Second, Thurber could do that rarest of things with an enviable degree of consistency: He could write sentences which make a reader smile and sometimes laugh.   [1980]

WILLIAM SAROYAN

William Saroyan wrote his preface to his first collection of short fiction, The Daring Young Man on the Flying Trapeze, *in 1934. In it he mentions the popular writer Ring Lardner (a close friend of F. Scott Fitzgerald), who had written a humorous analysis of how to write short stories. (See Lardner's "How to Write Short Stories," page 1385.)*

Writing Stories

In this early preface, when I have no idea how many copies of the book are going to be sold, the only thing I can do is talk about how I came to write these stories.

Years ago when I was getting a thorough grammar-school education in my home town I found out that stories were something very odd that some sort of men had been turning out (for some odd reason) for hundreds of years, and that there were rules governing the writing of stories.

I immediately began to study all the classic rules, including Ring Lardner's, and in the end I discovered that the rules were wrong.

The trouble was, they had been leaving me out, and as far as I could tell I was the most important element in the matter, so I made some new rules.

I wrote rule Number One when I was eleven and had just been sent home from the fourth grade for having talked out of turn and meant it.

Do not pay any attention to the rules other people make, I wrote. They make them for their own protection, and to hell with them. (I was pretty sore that day.)

Several months later I discovered rule Number Two, which caused a sensation. At any rate, it was a sensation with me. This rule was: Forget Edgar Allan Poe and O. Henry and write the kind of stories you feel like writing. Forget everybody who ever wrote anything.

Since that time I have added four other rules and I have found this number to be enough. Sometimes I do not have to bother about rules at all, and I just sit down and write. Now and then I stand and write.

My third rule was: Learn to typewrite, so you can turn out stories as fast as Zane Grey.[1]

It is one of my best rules.

But rules without a system are, as every good writer will tell you, utterly inadequate. You can leave out "utterly" and the sentence will mean the same thing, but it is always nicer to throw in an "utterly" whenever possible. All successful writers believe that one word by itself hasn't enough meaning and that it is best to emphasize the meaning of one word with the help of another. Some writers will go so far as to help an innocent word with as many as four and five other words, and at times they will kill an innocent word by charity and it will take years and years for some ignorant writer who doesn't know adjectives at all to resurrect the word that was killed by kindness.

Anyway, these stories are the result of a method of composition.

I call it the Festival or Fascist method of composition, and it works this way:

Someone who isn't a writer begins to want to be a writer and he keeps on wanting to be one for ten years, and by that time he has convinced all his relatives and friends and even himself that he *is* a writer, but he hasn't written a thing and he is no longer a boy, so he is getting worried. All he needs now is a system. Some authorities claim there are as many as fifteen systems, but actually there are only two: (1) you can decide to write like Anatole France or Alexandre Dumas or somebody else, or (2) you can decide to forget that you are a writer at all and you can decide to sit down

---

[1]A prolific American author of Western stories published in pulp magazines.

at your typewriter and put words on paper, one at a time, in the best fashion you know how—which brings me to the matter of style.

The matter of style is one that always excites controversy, but to me it is as simple as A B C, if not simpler.

A writer can have, ultimately, one of two styles: he can write in a manner that implies that death is inevitable, or he can write in a manner that implies that death is *not* inevitable. Every style ever employed by a writer has been influenced by one or another of these attitudes toward death.

If you write as if you believe that ultimately you and everyone else alive will be dead, there is a chance that you will write in a pretty earnest style. Otherwise you are apt to be either pompous or soft. On the other hand, in order not to be a fool, you must believe that as much as death is inevitable life is inevitable. That is, the earth is inevitable, and people and other living things on it are inevitable, but that no man can remain on the earth very long. You do not have to be melodramatically tragic about this. As a matter of fact, you can be as amusing as you like about it. It is really one of the basically humorous things, and it has all sorts of possibilities for laughter. If you will remember that living people are as good as dead, you will be able to perceive much that is very funny in their conduct that you perhaps might never have thought of perceiving if you did not believe that they were as good as dead.

The most solid advice, though, for a writer is this, I think: Try to learn to breathe deeply, really to taste food when you eat, and when you sleep, really to sleep. Try as much as possible to be wholly alive, with all your might, and when you laugh, laugh like hell, and when you get angry, get good and angry. Try to be alive. You will be dead soon enough.   [1934]

CHARLES SCRIBNER III

Charles Scribner III wrote a foreword to a volume of The Short Stories of F. Scott Fitzgerald *(1995). Fitzgerald's short fiction and novels had originally been accepted by Scribner's great-grandfather, who started the firm of Charles Scribner's Sons. Scribner's went on to publish all of Fitzgerald and Hemingway's work, as well as the writing of many other important American authors.*

On F. Scott Fitzgerald's Stories

"My whole theory of writing I can sum up in one sentence. An author ought to write for the youth of his own generation, the critics of the next, and the schoolmasters of ever afterward." So proclaimed the young Scott Fitzgerald in the first flush of success at the appearance of *This Side of*

Paradise in 1920. How magnificently—if, sad to say, posthumously—he fulfilled that ideal. His all too brief literary career—a dozen years of commercial and critical success followed by distractions and disappointments—ended in 1940 when he suffered a fatal heart attack at the age of forty-four. He was hard at work on the Hollywood novel he hoped would restore his literary fortunes, *The Last Tycoon*. At the time of his death his books were not, as was later supposed, out of print with his publisher. The truth is sadder: they were all in stock at our warehouse and listed in the catalogue, but there were no orders.

Now, a half century later, more copies of F. Scott Fitzgerald's books are ordered each year than were sold cumulatively throughout his entire lifetime. His novels and short stories are taught in virtually every high school and college across the country. This new, comprehensive collection of Fitzgerald's best short fiction is being published some seventy years—a biblical lifespan—after the author's first novel was accepted by my great-grandfather in 1919. I am struck by the realization that three generations (and namesakes) later I was the first of our family to have been introduced to Fitzgerald's work in the *classroom*. My grandfather, Fitzgerald's friend and publisher for the latter half of his career, died on the eve of the author's reappraisal and subsequent revival that gained momentum through the Fifties and has continued in full force down to the present time. It was my father who was to preside over Fitzgerald's literary apotheosis, a publishing phenomenon perhaps unprecedented in modern American letters. Through him I had the good fortune to meet and work with the author's talented and generous daughter, Scottie, and her collaborator and advisor, Matthew J. Bruccoli, whose prolific scholarship and infectious enthusiasm have long fanned the flames of Fitzgerald studies.

The day I met Professor Bruccoli fifteen years ago I asked what had prompted him to devote the lion's share of his scholarship to Fitzgerald. He told me exactly how it happened. One Sunday afternoon in 1949 Bruccoli, then a high school student, was driving with his family along the Merritt Parkway from Connecticut to New York City when he heard a dramatization of "The Diamond as Big as the Ritz" on the car radio. He later went to a library to find the story; the librarian had never heard of Scott Fitzgerald. But finally he managed to locate a copy—"and I never stopped reading Fitzgerald."

There is something magical about F. Scott Fitzgerald. Much has been written—and dramatized—about the Jazz Age personas and syncopated lives of Scott and Zelda. But the real magic lies embedded in his prose and it is perhaps nowhere more pervasive than in the amazing range and versatility of his short stories: the best sparkle with greater luster than ever in this new collection that displays them afresh in their proper literary and biographical settings. Each tale partakes of its creator's poetic imagination, his dramatic vision, his painstaking (if virtuosic and seemingly effortless) craftsmanship. Each bears Fitzgerald's distinctive hallmark, the indelible stamp of grace.

Fitzgerald once claimed to his agent Harold Ober that "good stories write themselves—bad ones have to be written." Yet a decade later he confessed that "there is no use of me trying to rush things." Even during his most prolific stages, he noted, "I could not turn out more than 8–9 top-price stories a year." The secret of success was not to be found in original themes. In his own view there were but "two basic stories of all times—*Cinderella* and *Jack the Giant Killer*—the charm of women and the courage of men." Nor should we look to the "booze and inspiration" school of thought, as he dubbed it: "You do not," he argued, "produce a short story for the *Saturday Evening Post* on a bottle." (Fitzgerald did, however, admit to writing his first novel with the aid of a liquid "stimulant"—Coca-Cola!) Some clues to his creative craftsmanship may be gleaned from his instructive if sometimes professorial letters to his daughter: "Stories are best written in either one jump or three, according to length. The three-jump story should be done on three successive days, then a day or so for revise and off she goes. This of course is the ideal. . . ." Still, he cautioned her, "nobody ever became a writer just by wanting to be one. If you have anything to say, anything you feel nobody has ever said before, you have got to feel it so desperately that you will find some way to say it that nobody has ever found before, so that the thing you have to say and the way of saying it blend as one matter—as indissolubly as if they were conceived together."

In the last year of his life Fitzgerald pondered in a poignant letter to his wife, Zelda, then hospitalized in an asylum, the loss of his former success in the genre: "It's odd that my old talent for the short story vanished. It was partly that times changed, editors changed, but part of it was tied up somehow with you and me—the happy ending. Of course every third story had some other ending, but essentially I got my public with stories of young love. I must have had a powerful imagination to project it so far and so often into the past." The key to Fitzgerald's enduring and elusive enchantment lies, I believe, in the power of his romantic imagination to transfigure his characters and settings—and indeed the very shape and sound of his prose. I shall never forget that evening train ride from Princeton to Philadelphia on which I first read "The Diamond as Big as the Ritz": a commute was converted into a fantastic voyage. And I can still see Anson Hunter, "The Rich Boy," whose self-conscious superiority will forever, in my eyes, embellish the gilded lobby of New York's Plaza Hotel. Fitzgerald's stories transform their external geography as thoroughly as the realm within. The ultimate effect, once the initial reverberations of imagery and language have subsided, transcends the bounds of fiction.   [1995]

FLOYD STOVALL

Floyd Stovall, an eminent professor and critic of American literature, ana-lyzed Henry James's "The Jolly Corner" in an essay prepared for Nineteenth-Century Fiction *in June 1957.*

Henry James's "The Jolly Corner"

There is in Spencer Brydon a double consciousness, but I cannot agree that it is explained as the selfish and selfless aspects of Brydon's soul. The ghost, or alter ego, is indeed himself as he might have been if he had remained in New York. Brydon does not see it and has only a vague idea of it; hence he mistakenly supposes the apparition of the entrance hall is the same ghost and it has come from behind the closed door and gone down before him. The ghost prefers the back rooms of the fourth floor because they are most remote from actuality. The apparition, on the contrary, is him-self as he actually is; it very properly seems to come from without through the vestibule doors and is seen by the dim light of breaking day. Brydon is puzzled by the apparition because he expects it to be his alter ego and therefore recognizable, yet the face is so horrible that he rejects it with loathing. For thirty-three years he has been false to his true self without realizing it. It is this false self that is revealed to him, as symbolized by the removal of the covering hands, though he does not yet recognize it as his.

Brydon is evidently confused by the working of his double conscious-ness: the consciousness of his actual self—which is the false self, the mask that he has worn during his European years—and the consciousness of his ghostly self—which is the self that might have been, the self that has been evoked by the strong sense of the past that he feels while in the house. The consciousness of the actual self belongs to the world outside, whereas the consciousness of the self that might have been is inseparable from the old house and is particularly strong in the back rooms of the fourth floor far-thest removed from the street. The combat that occurs within Brydon as he starts to mount the stairs on that last night of the story is the struggle between these two consciousnesses. He has an impulse to flee, which is the consequence of his fear of being lost to actuality and pulled into the ghostly world of his alter ego, but he conquers it for the moment. The rea-son James does not describe how Brydon gets to the fourth floor is that he wishes us to have the impression that the consciousness of actuality, the false self, remains below and the consciousness of himself as he might have been, the ghostly self, remains at the top. In the interval, the time during which he mounts the stairs, he is in effect without an operative conscious-ness, since the consciousness of his true self—so long buried under the consciousness of the actual self—has not yet been released. So it seems; yet the consciousness of actuality is never wholly lost, and even the consciousness of his true self, so long buried, has already begun to revive although Brydon does not yet realize what is happening to him. The crisis for him comes when he stands so long, unconscious of time, before the door of the innermost room, and finally abandons forever his pursuit of his alter ego and begs it not to trouble him further.

During the hours of this strange experience, Brydon's consciousness of his true self is struggling to emerge and has so far succeeded that when at last he does go downstairs the consciousness of actuality seems to rise before him in the apparition as something monstrous. This apparition is not a ghost in the sense that the alter ego on the fourth floor is a ghost. The false self, which he now sees in the apparition, has actually existed, whereas the self that might have been obviously has not except in his imagination. That the apparition belongs to the world without the house is symbolized by the fact that it is seen against the background of the open vestibule doors. The ghost, it will be remembered, remained unseen behind the door of the innermost room of the top floor, and there is no evidence that it comes out at all, though Brydon at first supposes that the apparition and the ghost are the same because he simply cannot otherwise account for what he sees, being still incompletely aware of his false self as false. The closed door above, which is not really closed, and the open doors below, which are not really open, are a part of his hallucination, but for the reader they are important symbolic keys to James's meaning.

Brydon does not recognize himself in the apparition with its evening dress, its double eyeglass, its two missing fingers, and its hideous face because it is the confused projection of his double consciousness. The symbols of both consciousnesses appear in the figure and contradict one another. The evening dress could belong to either, but the double eyeglass suggests to him that the apparition is himself as he would have become if he had remained in America. He actually uses a single eyeglass, but Americans prefer the double eyeglass. On the other hand, the missing fingers identify the apparition as himself as he actually is, his physical self. He has been an adventurer, a big-game hunter. If he had remained in New York he probably would not have lost the fingers. Brydon himself is not fully aware, as the reader is, of the workings of his double consciousness and quite naturally supposes the apparition to be the ghost that he had hoped would remain behind the closed door upstairs. When he sees the face, however, he cannot admit that his could ever have been so horrible. Neither is he ready to admit that it is himself as he actually is, in spite of the missing fingers. Yet when he rejects it, it becomes aggressive. This aggressiveness suggests that Brydon does recognize, after a moment, that the face is his own; that he continues to try to deny it to himself, but is no longer wholly self-deceived by such denial.

Alice Staverton understands him better than he understands himself.

She has seen the face of the apparition in a dream at the very moment it appeared to Brydon, and she had also seen it twice before in dreams, recognizing it at once as his false self. Their mutual love (though he has not until then acknowledged it) has produced for them a common psychic experience; indeed it is the power of Alice's love, which is wholly unselfish, that has determined the character of Brydon's strange adventure. It is she who saves him from the ghostly past and later releases his buried self. It is worthwhile to quote James's description of Brydon's feelings after he regains consciousness:

> It had brought him to knowledge, to knowledge — yes, this was the beauty of his state; which came to resemble more and more that of a man who has gone to sleep on some news of a great inheritance, and then, after dreaming it away, after profaning it with matters strange to it, has waked up again to serenity of certitude and has only to lie and watch it grow.

He still does not know how he has come to possess knowledge — the knowledge both of his true self and of his false — but he is at peace. He tells Alice that he must have died and she brought him to life again. Alice says, as I have mentioned already, that he has come to himself. She must mean, or James must mean, that Brydon has passed through an experience somewhat like religious conversion that is symbolized by death and resurrection. He has been blind all these years — as the double eyeglass symbolically suggests — to the truth about himself and the love she has been waiting to give him when he should realize his need of it.

When Alice Staverton tells Brydon that he "came to himself" her words have a double meaning. To Brydon they mean simply that he has recovered consciousness. To the reader they are intended to mean that Alice understands that Brydon has seen himself as he has lived during his European years. The double eyeglass, Alice says, is for his "poor ruined sight," clearly symbolic of Brydon's blindness to the true state of things. There are then three "selves" in the story: the real self that is released by Alice's love, the self that she has believed in throughout; the false self that for thirty-three years has overlaid Brydon's true self and caused him to refuse to acknowledge his love for Alice; and the self that might have been had he never left New York, which is the ghost of the back rooms on the fourth floor of the house on the jolly corner.   [1957]

RUTH SUCKOW

Ruth Suckow, a popular author of short stories, was invited to give her view of this literary genre in an article for the Saturday Review of Literature *of November 19, 1927.*

The Short Story

First of all — there is no such thing.

Why add to that statement? Especially when the title of this article at once suggests the most tiresome, hackneyed subject in the whole range of American literature! Because, while there is no fact, there is a great myth, a huge bug-a-boo, an enormous assumption; and this assumption has become one of the fundamental doctrines of American fiction. Contemporary writing is full of heresies against It. It no longer rules the young talent of this country. It never did rule the best talent, of course — no airtight doctrine ever does. But it still dominates the greater part of the magazines, the schools, and the reading public, and in spite of vigorous heresies, I am not at all sure that it is losing its hold. I ought to say that it dominates the market. Perhaps I ought to have said that first.

I am not going to add to my preliminary statement, however, by knocking down one dogma and setting up another, as is the usual method in the discussion of any form of art. "I know that you believe that The Short Story is not this but that," has often been said to me. I believe nothing of the kind. Because I myself write short stories of a certain type does not in the least mean to me that that is the way in which all short stories must be written — it means simply that I have found it the way best suited to my own intention. I admit a preference but not a theory. It seems unprofitable to me to attack one type of short story for the benefit of another. It is definition and formulæ themselves that I deny: the generalization of the specific. The definition formulated by Mr. Edgar Allan Poe defined *a* short story very well — the special kind of short story, of course, which he himself was bent upon writing. The trouble came when it was utilized to define *the* short story. As soon as any *a* is inflated into a *the* it becomes a menace to art. The doctrine of The Short Story has had, does have, a blighting influence upon the production of short stories in America.

In tracing the origin of this great myth, when it is admitted to be a myth, it is customary to blame Poe, or O. Henry, or Guy de Maupassant, or the schools, or the popular magazines. . . .

The rigidity of the definition is usually charged to the commercialization of popular magazines. That may explain its persistence, but not, I think, its origin. Many of the magazines themselves have been by-products of the definition. They owe their existence to The Short Story, and they have shown themselves very properly grateful. Commercialization does not explain even the persistence of the definition in the schools, outside of those "courses in The Short Story" that deal in marketable patterns with price-tags attached. It grew out of an aspiration and was held as an ideal. But, like most American ideals, it has been found a very profitable means of making money, preserving prosperity, and keeping the young people in line. The sardonic note seldom lacking in American humor is added by the fact that it was formulated by the chief literary rebel of his day. Its present conception is very remote from that original conception, as is the way with ideals and dogma. Other prophets and practitioners have added their bits. But it was Poe, struggling for precision, originality, and the perfection of accomplishment in the chaos of early American literature, who gave those very formalists and esthetic toadies who were his enemies the means of limiting the one vigorous native expression of American life in fiction and making all succeeding originality a cultural, artistic, and commercial sin.

It was the chaos, the unevenness, the diversity of American life that made short stories such a natural artistic expression in the first place. Roving, unsettled, restless, unassimilated, here and gone again—a chaos so huge, a life so varied and so multitudinous that its meaning could be caught only in fragments, perceived only by will-o'-the-wisp gleams, preserved only in tiny pieces of perfection. It was the first eager, hasty way of snatching little treasures of art from the great abundance of unused, uncomprehended material. Short stories were a way of making America intelligible to itself.

Within this chaos, two factions were and are forever struggling, both for an ideal which they call by the same name, each with an opposing conviction of the means of attainment. The ideal is called American culture, American art. Both struggle for standards. But one faction seeks to bring in these standards from the outside, the other to develop them from within. One is colonial-minded, and the other national-minded. One is very timid, and the other recklessly brave. Short stories are about the only form of literature in America which did not have their origin in England—as a form, that is, not a variation. There was, therefore, no external, ready-made standard to be applied to them. Poe, an originator even though a classicist, in the very fierceness of his originality was impelled to state his own standard as well as to write his own stories. He did so partly because nobody but himself believed in it. In this manner, Poe, the original artist, became the originator of the barren negation of original art that goes under the heading of The Short Story.

Poor hounded, discredited, thoroughly unrespectable Poe! I think that even his monstrous craving for power would have been daunted by the spectacle of the awful success of his own struggle. He gave American art a standard indeed. With tragic eagerness, the formalists who hate all that he stood for, flocked to it, upheld it, and declared it to be hereafter the law. Poe, being an artist, had a shop interest in method. What he wrote outside his own poems and his own stories was nearly all shop talk. His definition, therefore, was largely on the side of method, which, of course, was what formalists wanted. It enabled them to say, not: A short story *is* so and so; but, The Short Story *does* so and so. They knew, from the sacred book of English literature, what was poetry and what was prose, what constituted style, what was an epic and a lyric and a drama. But they did not know just what a short story was. Short stories, for many years, were only a sort of off-shoot from the main branch of English fiction, spare-time stuff in fact, with little dignity. Our cultured gentlemen had heard of tales, but not exactly of short stories. I doubt if they would have permitted an American to make a definition of a tale. Because of their own fundamental uncertainty in the field of art, they grasped at superficial certainties which they called "technique." Here was a form of American art, and the rules came with it! Now we could go on repeating and repeating forever and forever, at the same time being original and not derivative, because we were using an original form of American art. It was another bonanza.

In fact, the avidity with which American literary men rushed to The Short Story, and the childlike trust with which they have clung, always make me think of another piece of art very popular in America. It is a chromo, and it is called "The Rock of Ages." A very pure maiden in robes of white is clinging to a perfectly inexplicable and unreasonable cross in the midst of a raging sea, and in the completeness of her faith her brow is untroubled, her eyes are closed to the stormy waters. "Simply to the cross I cling."

So The Short Story, useful primarily as an esthetic method of dealing with diversity, multiplicity, and newness, soon became the chief tool in the standardization of American literature. For standardization itself grows out of the consciousness of variety. It is a hasty gloss applied deceptively to the surface of unevenness. The Short Story was the one form of American literature actually accepted by our schools on its own merit, but it never would have been accepted without definition. The definition also accounts largely for its commercial success. It is a known commodity. It is sure fire.

Because this is our one little lonely definition in the field of art, we Americans have cherished it with jealous tenacity. We have looked at interesting importations, but we have been able to discredit them at once, saying in the simplest manner: They are not Short Stories. In this way, we have pretty well kept the disturbing Chekhov out of our schools. For our professors all know Art even when they do not know what they like. They are unable to enjoy a short story without first definitely ascertaining that it is The Short Story. There are various ways in which this can be done. One is by scholarly analysis of technique to make certain that plot, climax, and an ending are all there. But this is a slow, plodding, patient way. Professors are willing to go through with it, but editors really do not have the time for it. So writers, for their benefit, tack on an introduction. Such a reassuring start as: "This is going to be a story," will put nearly any troubled editor at ease;

especially if the writer is careful to continue for a few lines: "The story of Stephen Harbison, of Harbison and—The Woman." Who, then, can doubt what is to follow?

All editors are not so sure as all professors that they know Art. Some of them even scorn to know it. But they know craftsmanship. That is a little different from technique—not quite so highfalutin. Craftsmanship consists in using the technical equipment of beginning, ending, plot, and climax in a slick manner to slap the simple elements of hackneyed fiction into a semblance of The Short Story. College courses in The Short Story teach technique; but correspondence courses teach only craftsmanship. That is really all that is needed to tell the folks how he and she got together this time.

So all our great wealth of raw material, year after year, goes into the big machines called courses, is rolled out, stamped flat, the pattern whacked down upon it, and turned into the market. The machine can be pretty well guaranteed to transform any idea into a commodity. It can also be guaranteed to change freshness into staleness, flavor into insipidity, truth of intention into semi-truth, native finish into gloss—a short story into The Short Story.

No, not all of our material. A great deal of it stays outside the definition. Still more of it begins outside and then, by means of a beginning or an ending or the distortion called plot, is brought within the fold. Otherwise, it gets slim pickings, and this in spite of the number of magazines publishing fiction in America. When a short story, fresh in treatment, unconventional in subject matter, far above the average in excellence was lately published in a magazine long established and devoted to culture, it was the occasion of a whole literary column of triumph in a New York newspaper and of a sort of manifesto, of apologia, on the part of the magazine editor. In the face of all the new and vigorous magazines that have lately been founded on a basis other than the blatantly commercial, I believe that the pickings are getting slimmer. For the place of fiction in our "better grade" magazine is shrinking. They have all become really serious!—all turned to the larger issues of controversy and instruction so relished by Americans, and away again from the piddling little arts. Soon the short stories in our more serious magazines will be reduced to the rank of fillers. An art does not stand loss of dignity much better than it stands being crammed into a pattern. Even now, our young American writers are driven to expedients. They get out thin little magazines each devoted to a single cult. They publish volumes of their own. They go abroad and renounce America. Or they submit to the tricks, saying that art must be democratic or that Shakespeare used a formula or that the purpose of fiction is amusement, and help to keep up the farce. If America continues to be the land of The Short Story, it will ultimately lose its short stories.

Yet I believe that this dogma held as an artistic creed is more blighting, futile, and deadly than when held as a commercial creed. Certainly it is more hide-bound. Trade, after all, has an eye to the market, and when the market changes, it is willing to change its commodities. Its creed is a utility, not a religion. The Short Story in America! An abstraction blindly erected in the very face of American short stories themselves—the stories of Stephen Crane, Sarah Orne Jewett, Willa Cather, Theodore Dreiser, Ring Lardner, all enjoyed, yet with fear and trembling, because of what they may do to The Short Story! The whole creed is founded upon another pathetic fallacy. Upon several fallacies, in fact. The fallacy that art and science can be united at the very point where essentially they differ. And beyond these, the colossal assumption that any form of art, or all art, is moving toward a millennium which will be brought by a savior in the form of a master, a method, or a movement. All discussions of art on the basis of "the" are thoroughly unprofitable. "The lyric." "The novel of the future." "The new poetry." "The Great Tradition." I never meet any of these "the's" without wanting to say "Boo!" to its pretentions. Of him that sets forth its dogma I feel that I must inquire gently, "And who are you, my little man?" As a speculation, they are endurable. They may be interesting when accepted with salt. But as soon as I come to—"the novel of the future will deal only with"—I throw away the article. The novel of the future will deal with whatever it pleases in any manner that comes to hand.

"The Short Story" is the worst of the lot. In its pathetic foolishness it offers a master key to beauty. It presupposes that form is an iron mould and not a living organism; that beauty is a rule and not an effect. If that effect is poignant, deep, and lasting, then the right means have been used, no matter what they may be—even plot, climax, and an ending! If it is not so, who cares about the means, anyway? . . . Short stories?—A running commentary upon life; fireflies in the dark; questions and answers; fragments, or small and finished bits of beauty; whatever, in fact, their author has the power to make of them. . . . But The Short Story?—A fundamental stupidity.   [1927]

MARK TWAIN

Mark Twain wrote "How to Tell a Story" in 1895 as a humorous essay about humorous stories. In the process he gracefully credited earlier authors who had influenced him, such as Charles Farrar Browne and Bill Nye, once immensely popular but now mostly unread.

How to Tell a Story

I do not claim that I can tell a story as it ought to be told. I only claim to know how a story ought to be told, for I have been almost daily in the company of the most expert story-tellers for many years.

There are several kinds of stories, but only one difficult kind—the humorous. I will talk mainly about that one. The humorous story is American, the comic story is English, the witty story is French. The humorous story depends for its effect upon the *manner* of the telling; the comic story and the witty story upon the *matter.*

The humorous story may be spun out to great length, and may wander around as much as it pleases, and arrive nowhere in particular; but the comic and witty stories must be brief and end with a point. The humorous story bubbles gently along, the others burst.

The humorous story is strictly a work of art — high and delicate art — and only an artist can tell it; but no art is necessary in telling the comic and the witty story; anybody can do it. The art of telling a humorous story — understand, I mean by word of mouth, not print — was created in America, and has remained at home.

The humorous story is told gravely; the teller does his best to conceal the fact that he even dimly suspects that there is anything funny about it; but the teller of the comic story tells you beforehand that it is one of the funniest things he has ever heard, then tells it with eager delight, and is the first person to laugh when he gets through. And sometimes, if he has had good success, he is so glad and happy that he will repeat the "nub" of it and glance around from face to face, collecting applause, and then repeat it again. It is a pathetic thing to see.

Very often, of course, the rambling and disjointed humorous story finishes with a nub, point, snapper, or whatever you like to call it. Then the listener must be alert, for in many cases the teller will divert attention from that nub by dropping it in a carefully casual and indifferent way, with the pretence that he does not know it is a nub.

Artemus Ward[1] used that trick a good deal: then when the belated audience presently caught the joke he would look up with innocent surprise, as if wondering what they had found to laugh at. Dan Setchell used it before him, Nye and Riley and others use it today.[2]

But the teller of the comic story does not slur the nub; he shouts it at you — every time. And when he prints it, in England, France, Germany, and Italy, he italicizes it, puts some whooping exclamation-points after it, and sometimes explains it in a parenthesis. All of which is very depressing, and makes one want to renounce joking and lead a better life.

---

[1] Pen name for Charles Farrar Browne (1834–1867), a famous humorist, journalist, and lecturer. Soon after meeting Twain in 1863, Ward helped him to publish "The Celebrated Jumping Frog of Calaveras County."

[2] Dan Setchell was a popular comedian and contemporary of Twain. Edgar Wilson "Bill" Nye (1850–1896) was a popular humorist, journalist, and lecturer. James Whitcomb Riley (1849–1916), "poet of the common people," was known for his poems in the Hoosier dialect of Indiana and for creating "Little Orphant Annie." Nye and Riley, with their combination of satire and sentiment, made a successful duo on the lecture circuit.

Let me set down an instance of the comic method, using an anecdote which has been popular all over the world for twelve or fifteen hundred years. The teller tells it in this way:

The Wounded Soldier

In the course of a certain battle a soldier whose leg had been shot off appealed to another soldier who was hurrying by to carry him to the rear, informing him at the same time of the loss which he had sustained; whereupon the generous son of Mars, shouldering the unfortunate, proceeded to carry out his desire. The bullets and cannon-balls were flying in all directions, and presently one of the latter took the wounded man's head off—without, however, his deliverer being aware of it. In no long time he was hailed by an officer, who said:

"Where are you going with that carcass?"

"To the rear, sir—he's lost his leg!"

"His leg, forsooth?" responded the astonished officer; "you mean his head, you booby."

Whereupon the soldier dispossessed himself of his burden, and stood looking down upon it in great perplexity. At length he said:

"It is true, sir, just as you have said." Then after a pause he added, *"But he* TOLD *me* IT WAS HIS LEG! ! ! ! !"

Here the narrator bursts into explosion after explosion of thunderous horse-laughter, repeating that nub from time to time through his gaspings and shriekings and suffocatings.

It takes only a minute and a half to tell that in its comic-story form; and isn't worth the telling, after all. Put into the humorous-story form it takes ten minutes, and is about the funniest thing I have ever listened to—as James Whitcomb Riley tells it.

He tells it in the character of a dull-witted old farmer who has just heard it for the first time, thinks it is unspeakably funny, and is trying to repeat it to a neighbor. But he can't remember it; so he gets all mixed up and wanders helplessly round and round, putting in tedious details that don't belong in the tale and only retard it; taking them out conscientiously and putting in others that are just as useless; making minor mistakes now and then and stopping to correct them and explain how he came to make them; remembering things which he forgot to put in in their proper place and going back to put them in there; stopping his narrative a good while in order to try to recall the name of the soldier that was hurt, and finally remembering that the soldier's name was not mentioned, and remarking placidly that the name is of no real importance, anyway—better, of course, if one knew it, but not essential, after all—and so on, and so on, and so on.

The teller is innocent and happy and pleased with himself, and has to stop every little while to hold himself in and keep from laughing outright; and does hold in, but his body quakes in a jelly-like way with interior chuckles; and at the end of the ten minutes the audience have laughed until they are exhausted, and the tears are running down their faces.

The simplicity and innocence and sincerity and unconsciousness of the old farmer are perfectly simulated, and the result is a performance which is thoroughly charming and delicious. This is art—and fine and beautiful, and only a master can compass it; but a machine could tell the other story.

To string incongruities and absurdities together in a wandering and sometimes purposeless way, and seem innocently unaware that they are absurdities, is the basis of the American art, if my position is correct. Another feature is the slurring of the point. A third is the dropping of a studied remark apparently without knowing it, as if one were thinking aloud. The fourth and last is the pause.

Artemus Ward dealt in numbers three and four a good deal. He would begin to tell with great animation something which he seemed to think was wonderful; then lose confidence, and after an apparently absent-minded pause add an incongruous remark in a soliloquizing way; and that was the remark intended to explode the mine—and it did.

For instance, he would say eagerly, excitedly, "I once knew a man in New Zealand who hadn't a tooth in his head"—here his animation would die out; a silent, reflective pause would follow, then he would say dreamily, and as if to himself, "and yet that man could beat a drum better than any man I ever saw."

The pause is an exceedingly important feature in any kind of story, and a frequently recurring feature, too. It is a dainty thing, and delicate, and also uncertain and treacherous; for it must be exactly the right length—no more and no less—or it fails of its purpose and makes trouble. If the pause is too short the impressive point is passed, and the audience have had time to divine that a surprise is intended—and then you can't surprise them, of course.

On the platform I used to tell a negro ghost story that had a pause in front of the snapper on the end, and that pause was the most important thing in the whole story. If I got it the right length precisely, I could spring the finishing ejaculation with effect enough to make some impressible girl deliver a startled little yelp and jump out of her seat—and that was what I was after. This story was called "The Golden Arm," and was told in this fashion. You can practise with it yourself—and mind you look out for the pause and get it right.

THE GOLDEN ARM

Once 'pon a time dey wuz a monsus mean man, en he live 'way out in de prairie all 'lone by hisself, 'cep'n he had a wife. En bimeby she died, en he tuck en toted her way out dah in de prairie en buried her. Well, she had a golden arm—all solid gold, fum de shoulder down. He wuz pow'ful mean—pow'ful; en dat night he couldn't sleep, caze he want dat golden arm so bad.

When it come midnight he couldn't stan' it no mo'; so he git up, he did, en tuck his lantern en shoved out thoo de storm en dug her up en got de golden arm; en he bent his head down 'gin de win', en plowed en plowed en plowed thoo de snow. Den all on a sudden he stop (make a considerable pause here, and look startled, and take a listening attitude) en say: "My *lan'*, what's dat!"

En he listen—en listen—en de win' say (set your teeth together and imitate the wailing and wheezing singsong of the wind), "Bzzz-z-zzz"—en den, way back yonder whah de grave is, he hear a *voice!*—he hear a voice all mix' up in de win'—can't hardly tell 'em 'part—"Bzzz-zzz-w-h-o—g-o-t—m-y—g-o-l-d-e-n arm?—zzz—zzz—W-h-o g-o-t m-y g-o-l-d-e-n *arm*?" (You must begin to shiver violently now.)

En he begin to shiver en shake, en say, "Oh, my! *Oh*, my lan'!" en de win' blow de lantern out, en de snow en sleet blow in his face en mos' choke him, en he start a-plowin' knee-deep towards home mos' dead, he so sk'yerd—en pooty soon he hear de voice agin, en (pause) it 'us comin' *after* him! "Bzzz—zzz—zzz—W-h-o—g-o-t—m-y—g-o-l-d-e-n—*arm*?"

When he git to de pasture he hear it agin—closter now, en a-*comin'!*—a-comin' back dah in de dark en de storm—(repeat the wind and the voice). When he git to de house he rush up-stairs en jump in de bed en kiver up, head and years, en lay dah shiverin' en shakin'—en den way out dah he hear it *again!*—en a-*comin'!* En bimeby he hear (pause—awed, listening attitude)—pat—pat—pat—*hit's a-comin' up-stairs!* Den he hear de latch, en he *know* it's in the room!

Den pooty soon he know it's a-*stannin' by de bed!* (Pause.) Den—he know it's a-*bendin' down over him*—en he cain't skasely git his breath! Den—den—he seem to feel someth'n *c-o-l-d*, right down 'most agin his head! (Pause.)

Den de voice say, *right at his year*—"W-h-o—g-o-t—m-y—g-o-l-d-e-n *arm*?" (You must wail it out very plaintively and accusingly; then you stare steadily and impressively into the face of the farthest-gone auditor—a girl, preferably—and let that awe-inspiring pause begin to build itself in the deep hush. When it has reached exactly the right length, jump suddenly at that girl and yell, "*You've* got it!"

If you've got the *pause* right, she'll fetch a dear little yelp and spring right out of her shoes. But you *must* get the pause right; and you will find it the most troublesome and aggravating and uncertain thing you ever undertook.)   [1895]

JOHN UPDIKE

John Updike offered his views on the importance of Sherwood Anderson's Winesburg, Ohio *in an essay for* Harper's Magazine *in March 1984.*

Twisted Apples: On *Winesburg, Ohio*

Sherwood Anderson's *Winesburg, Ohio* is one of those books so well known by title that we imagine we know what is inside it: a sketch of the population, seen more or less in cross section, of a small Midwestern town. It is this as much as Edvard Munch's paintings are portraits of the Norwegian middle class around the turn of the century. The important thing, for Anderson and Munch, is not the costumes and the furniture or even the bodies but the howl they conceal — the psychic pressure and warp underneath the social scene. Matter-of-fact though it sounds, *Winesburg, Ohio* is feverish, phantasmal, dreamlike. Anderson had accurately called this collection of loosely linked short stories *The Book of the Grotesque;* his publisher, B. W. Huebsch, suggested the more appealing title. The book was published in 1919, when Anderson was forty-three; it made his fame and remains his masterpiece.

"The Book of the Grotesque" is the name also of the opening story, which Anderson wrote first and which serves as a prologue. A writer, "an old man with a white mustache . . . who was past sixty," has a dream in which "all the men and women the writer had ever known had become grotesques."

> The grotesques were not all horrible. Some were amusing, some almost beautiful, and one, a woman all drawn out of shape, hurt the old man by her grotesqueness. When she passed he made a noise like a small dog whimpering.

Another writer, an "I" who is presumably Sherwood Anderson, breaks in and explains the old writer's theory of grotesqueness:

> . . . in the beginning when the world was young there were a great many thoughts but no such thing as a truth. Man made the truths himself and each truth was a composite of a great many vague thoughts. . . . It was the truths that made the people grotesques. The old man had quite an elaborate theory concerning the matter. It was his notion that the moment one of the people took one of the truths to himself, called it his truth, and tried to live his life by it, he became a grotesque and the truth he embraced became a falsehood.

Having so strangely doubled authorial personae, Anderson then offers twenty-one tales, one of them in four parts, all "concerning," as the table

1464

of contents specifies, one or another citizen of Winesburg; whether they come from the old writer's book of grotesques or some different set to which the younger author had access is as unclear as their fit within the cranky and fey anthropological-metaphysical framework set forth with such ungainly solemnity.

"Hands," the first tale, "concerning Wing Biddlebaum," introduces not only its hero, a pathetic, shy old man on the edge of town whose hyperactive little white hands had once strayed to the bodies of too many schoolboys in the Pennsylvania town where he had been a teacher, but also George Willard, the eighteen-year-old son of the local hotelkeeper and a reporter for the *Winesburg Eagle*. He seems a young representative of the author. There is also a "poet," suddenly invoked in flighty passages like:

> Let us look briefly into the story of the hands. Perhaps our talking of them will arouse the poet who will tell the hidden wonder story of the influence for which the hands were but fluttering pennants of promise.

A cloud of authorial effort, then, attends the citizens of Winesburg, each of whom walks otherwise isolated toward some inexpressible denouement of private revelation. Inexpressiveness, indeed, is what is above all expressed: the characters, often, talk only to George Willard, and then only once; their attempts to talk with one another tend to culminate in a comedy of tongue-tied silence.

Anderson himself took a long time to express what was in *Winesburg, Ohio*. Raised in the small Ohio town of Clyde, he worked successfully as a Chicago advertising man and an Elyria, Ohio, paint manufacturer, and acquired a wife and three children, but remained restless and, somehow, overwrought. In late 1912, in the kind of spasmodic sleepwalking gesture of protest that overtakes several of the pent-up and unfulfilled souls of Winesburg, he walked away from his paint factory. He was found four days later in Cleveland, suffering from exhaustion and aphasia, and, more gradually than his self-dramatizing memoirs admit, he shifted his life to Chicago and to the literary movement that included Dreiser, Sandburg, Ben Hecht, and Floyd Dell. Already Anderson had produced several long novels, but he later wrote, "They were not really mine." The first Winesburg stories, composed in 1915 as he lived alone in a rooming house in Chicago, were a breakthrough for him, prompted by his reading, earlier that year, of Edgar Lee Masters's *Spoon River Anthology* and Gertrude Stein's *Three Lives*. Masters's poetic inventory of a small Midwestern community stands in clear paternal relation to Anderson's rendering of his memories of Clyde; but perhaps Stein's elevation of humble lives into a curious dignity, along with her remarkably relaxed and idiomatic style, was the more nurturing influence in releasing Anderson into material that he *did* feel was really his and that gave him for the first time, as he later related, the conviction that he was "a real writer."

Both godparents of *Winesburg, Ohio* had a firmness and realism that was not part of Anderson's genius. Masters was a practicing lawyer, and his free-verse epitaphs state each case in almost legal prose; many have the form of arraignments, and a number of criminal incidents are fleshed out as each ghost gives its crisp testimony. Stein, before her confident and impudent mind went slack in its verbal enjoyments, showed an enlivening appetite for the particulars of how things are said and thought, a calm lack of either condescension or squeamishness in her social view, and a superb feel for the nuances of relationships, primarily but not only among women. For Anderson, society scarcely exists in its legal and affective bonds, and dialogue is generally the painful imposition of one monologue upon another. At the climax of the unconsummated love affair between George Willard and Helen White that is one of *Winesburg*'s continuous threads, the two sit together in the deserted fairground grandstand and hold hands:

> In that high place in the darkness the two oddly sensitive human atoms held each other tightly and waited. In the mind of each was the same thought. "I have come to this lonely place and here is this other," was the substance of the thing felt.

They embrace, but then mutual embarrassment overtakes them and like children they race and tumble on the way down to town and part, having "for a moment taken hold of the thing that makes the mature life of men and women in the modern world possible."

The vagueness of "the thing" is chronic, and only the stumbling, shrugging, willful style that Anderson made of Stein's serene run-on tropes affords him half a purchase on his unutterable subject, the "thing" troubling the heart of his characters. Dr. Reefy, who attends and in a sense loves George Willard's dying mother, compulsively writes thoughts on bits of paper. He then crumples them into little balls—"paper pills"—and shoves them into his pocket only to eventually throw them away. "One by one the mind of Dr. Reefy had made the thoughts. Out of many of them he formed a truth that arose gigantic in his mind. The truth clouded the world. It became terrible and then faded away and the little thoughts began again." What the gigantic thought was, we are not told.

Another questing medical man, Dr. Parcival, relates long tales that at times seem to George Willard "a pack of lies" and at others to contain "the very essence of truth." As Thornton Wilder's *Our Town* reminded us, small-town people think a lot about the universe (as opposed to city people, who think about one another). The agonizing philosophical search is inherited from religion; in the four-part story "Godliness," the author, speaking as a print-saturated modern man, says of the world fifty years before: "Men labored too hard and were too tired to read. In them was no desire for words printed upon paper. As they worked in the fields, vague, half-formed thoughts took possession of them. They believed in God and in God's power to control their lives. . . . The figure of God was big in the hearts of men." The rural landscape of the Midwest becomes easily confused in the minds of its pious denizens with that of the Bible, where God manifested himself with signs and spoken words. Jesse Bentley's attempt to emulate Abraham's offered sacrifice of Isaac so terrifies his grandson David that the boy flees the Winesburg region forever. Anderson writes about religious obsession with cold sympathy, as something that truly enters into lives and twists them. To this spiritual hunger sex adds its own; the Reverend Curtis Hartman breaks a small hole in the stained-glass window of his bell-tower study in order to spy on a woman in a house across the street as she lies on her bed and smokes and reads. "He did not want to kiss the shoulders and the throat of Kate Swift and had not allowed his mind to dwell on such thoughts. He did not know what he wanted. 'I am God's child and he must save me from myself,' he cried." One evening he sees her come naked into her room and weep and then pray; with his fist he smashes the window so all of it, with its broken bit of a peephole, will have to be repaired.

There are more naked women in *Winesburg* than one might think. "Adventure" shows Alice Hindman, a twenty-seven-year-old spinster jilted by a lover a decade before, so agitated by "her desire to have something beautiful come into her rather narrow life" that she runs naked into the rain one night and actually accosts a man—a befuddled old deaf man who goes on his way. In the following story, "Respectability," a fanatic and repulsive misogynist, Wash Williams, recalls to George Willard how, many years before, his mother-in-law, hoping to reconcile him with his unfaithful young wife, presented her naked to him in her (Dayton, Ohio) parlor. George Willard, his chaste relation to Helen White aside, suffers no lack of sexual invitation in Winesburg's alleys and surrounding fields. Sherwood Anderson's women are as full of "vague hungers and secret unnamable desires" as his men. The sexual quest and the philosophical quest blend: of George Willard's mother, the most tenderly drawn woman of all, the author says, "Always there was something she sought blindly, passionately, some hidden wonder in life. . . . In all the babble of words that fell from the lips of the men with whom she adventured she was trying to find what would be for her the true word." *Winesburg, Ohio* is dedicated to the memory of Anderson's own mother, "whose keen observations on the life about her first awoke in me the hunger to see beneath the surface of lives."

The author's hunger to see and express is entwined with the common hunger for love and reassurance and gives the book its awkward power and its limiting strangeness. The many characters of *Winesburg,* rather than standing forth as individuals, seem, with their repeating tics and uniform loneliness, aspects of one enveloping personality, an eccentric bundle of stalled impulses and frozen grievances. There is nowhere a citizen who, like Thomas Rhodes of Spoon River, exults in his material triumphs and impenitent rascality, nor any humbler type, like "real black, tall, well built, stupid, childlike, good looking" Rose Johnson of Stein's fictional Bridgepoint, who is happily at home in her skin. Do the Winesburgs of America lack such earthly successes; does the provincial orchard hold only, in Anderson's vivid phrase, "twisted apples"? No, and yet Yes, must be the answer; for the uncanny truth of Anderson's sad and surreal picture must awaken recognition within anyone who, like this reviewer, was born in a small town before highways and development filled all the fields and television imposed upon every home a degraded sophistication. The Protestant villages of America, going back to Hawthorne's Salem, leave a spectral impression in literature: vague longing and monotonous, inbred satisfactions are their essence; there is something perilous and maddening in the accommodations such communities extend to human aspiration and appetite. As neighbors watch, and murmur, lives visibly wrap themselves around a missed opportunity, a thwarted passion. The longing may be simply the longing to get out. The healthy, rounded apples, Anderson tells us, are "put in barrels and shipped to the cities where they will be eaten in apartments that are filled with books, magazines, furniture, and people." George Willard gets out in the end, and as soon as Winesburg falls away from the train windows "his life there had become but a background on which to paint the dreams of his manhood."

The small town is generally seen, by the adult writer arrived at his city, as the site of youthful paralysis and dreaming. Certainly Anderson, as Malcolm Cowley has pointed out,[1] wrote in a dreaming way, scrambling the time and logic of events as he hastened toward his epiphanies of helpless awakening, when the citizens of Winesburg break their tongue-tied trance and become momentarily alive to one another. Gertrude Stein's style, so revolutionary and liberating, has the haughtiness and humor of the *faux-naïve;* there is much genuine naïveté in Anderson, which in even his masterwork flirts with absurdity and which elsewhere weakens his work decisively. *Winesburg, Ohio* describes the human condition only insofar as unfulfillment and restlessness—a nagging sense that real life is elsewhere—are intrinsically part of it. Yet the wide-eyed eagerness with which Anderson pursued the mystery of the meager lives of Winesburg opened Michigan to Hemingway, and Mississippi to Faulkner; a way had been shown to a new directness and a freedom from contrivance. Though *Winesburg* accumulates external facts—streets, stores, town personalities—as it gropes along, its burden is a spiritual essence, a certain tart sweet taste to life as it passes in America's lonely lamplit homes. A nagging beauty lives amid this tame desolation; Anderson's parade of yearning wraiths constitutes in sum a democratic plea for the failed, the neglected, and the stuck. "On the trees are only a few gnarled apples that the pickers have rejected. . . . One nibbles at them and they are delicious. Into a little round place at the side of the apple has been gathered all of its sweetness." Describing a horse-and-buggy world bygone even in 1919, *Winesburg, Ohio* imparts this penetrating taste—the wine hidden in its title—as freshly today as yesterday.   [1984]

---

[1]See Cowley's introduction to *Winesburg, Ohio* (New York: Penguin, 1992) 4.

ALICE WALKER

Alice Walker wrote about Zora Neale Hurston in her collection In Search of Our Mothers' Gardens: Womanist Prose *(1983). There she also looked at Flannery O'Connor, Langston Hughes, Jean Toomer, and other writers from what she called her "womanist" perspective as a radical black woman. To clarify the meaning of her term, Walker added that "womanist is to feminist as purple is to lavender."*

Zora Neale Hurston: A Cautionary Tale and a Partisan View

During the early and middle years of her career Zora was a cultural revolutionary simply because she was always herself. Her work, so vigorous among the rather pallid productions of many of her contemporaries, comes from the essence of black folk life. During her later life she became frightened of the life she had always dared bravely before. Her work too became reactionary, static, shockingly misguided and timid. (This is especially true of her last novel, *Seraphs on the Sewannee,* which is not even about black people, which is no crime, but *is* about white people for whom it is impossible to care, which is.)

A series of misfortunes battered Zora's spirit and her health. And she was broke.

Being broke made all the difference.

Without money of one's own in a capitalist society, there is no such thing as independence. This is one of the clearest lessons of Zora's life, and why I consider the telling of her life "a cautionary tale." We must learn from it what we can.

Without money, an illness, even a simple one, can undermine the will. Without money, getting into a hospital is problematic and getting out without money to pay for the treatment is nearly impossible. Without money, one becomes dependent on other people, who are likely to be—even in their kindness—erratic in their support and despotic in their expectations of return. Zora was forced to rely, like Tennessee Williams's Blanche, "on the kindness of strangers." Can anything be more dangerous, if the strangers are forever in control? Zora, who worked so hard, was never able to make a living from her work.

She did not complain about not having money. She was not the type. (Several months ago I received a long letter from one of Zora's nieces, a bright ten-year-old, who explained to me that her aunt was so proud that the only way the family could guess she was ill or without funds was by realizing they had no idea where she was. Therefore, none of the family attended either Zora's sickbed or her funeral.) Those of us who have had "grants and fellowships from 'white folks' " know this aid is extended in precisely the way welfare is extended in Mississippi. One is asked, *curtly,* more often than not: How much do you need *just to survive?* Then one is—if fortunate—given a third of that. What is amazing is that Zora, who became an orphan at nine, a runaway at fourteen, a maid and manicurist (because of necessity and not from love of the work) before she was twenty—with one dress—managed to become Zora Neale Hurston, author and anthropologist, at all.

For me, the most unfortunate thing Zora ever wrote is her autobiography. After the first several chapters, it rings false. One begins to hear the voice of someone whose life required the assistance of too many transitory "friends." A Taoist proverb states that *to act sincerely with the insincere is dangerous.* (A mistake blacks as a group have tended to make in America.) And so we have Zora sincerely offering gratitude and kind words to people one knows she could not have respected. But this unctuousness, so out of character for Zora, is also a result of dependency, a sign of her powerlessness, her inability to pay back her debts with anything but words. They must have been bitter ones for her. In her dependency, it should be remembered, Zora was not alone—because it is quite true that America does not support or honor us as human beings, let alone as blacks, women, and artists. We have taken help where it was offered because we are committed to what we do and to the survival of our work. Zora was committed to the survival of her people's cultural heritage as well.

In my mind, Zora Neale Hurston, Billie Holiday, and Bessie Smith form a sort of unholy trinity. Zora *belongs* in the tradition of black women singers, rather than among "the literati," at least to me. There were the extreme highs and lows of her life, her undaunted pursuit of adventure, passionate emotional and sexual experience, and her love of freedom. Like Billie and Bessie she followed her own road, believed in her own gods, pursued her own dreams, and refused to separate herself from "common" people. It would have been nice if the three of them had had one another to turn to, in times of need. I close my eyes and imagine them: Bessie would be in charge of all the money; Zora would keep Billie's masochistic tendencies in check and prevent her from singing embarrassing anything-for-a-man songs, thereby preventing Billie's heroin addiction. In return, Billie could be, along with Bessie, the family that Zora felt she never had.

We are a people. A people do not throw their geniuses away. And if they are thrown away, it is our duty *as artists and as witnesses for the future* to collect them again for the sake of our children, and, if necessary, bone by bone.   [1979]

EUDORA WELTY

Eudora Welty commented on William Faulkner's "Spotted Horses" as one southern writer to another in The Eye of the Story *(1977). She developed her analysis as a way of illustrating her ideas on the importance of setting or "place" in short fiction. Her insistence on the humorous aspects of the story was based on her intimate knowledge of the landscape of "Faulkner country" as a fellow Mississippian.*

The Sense of Place in Faulkner's "Spotted Horses"

In humor place becomes its most revealing and at the same time is itself the most revealed. This is because humor, it seems to me, of all forms of fiction, entirely accepts place for what it is.

"Spotted Horses," by William Faulkner, is a good case in point. At the same time that this is just about Mr. Faulkner's funniest story, it is the most thorough and faithful picture of a Mississippi crossroads hamlet that you could ever hope to see. True in spirit, it is also true to everyday fact. Faulkner's art, which often lets him shoot the moon, tells him when to be literal too. In all its specification of detail, both mundane and poetic, in its complete adherence to social fact (which nobody knows better than Faulkner, surely, in writing today), by its unerring aim of observation as true as the sights of a gun would give, but Faulkner has no malice, only compassion; and even and also in the joy of those elements of harlequinade-fantasy that the spotted horses of the title bring in—in all that shining fidelity to place lies the heart and secret of this tale's comic glory.

Faulkner is, of course, the triumphant example in America today of the mastery of place in fiction. Yoknapatawpha County, so supremely and exclusively and majestically and totally itself, is an everywhere, but only because Faulkner's first concern is for what comes first—Yoknapatawpha, his own created world. I am not sure, as a Mississippian myself, how widely it is realized and appreciated that these works of such marvelous imaginative power can also stand as works of the carefulest and purest representation. Heightened, of course: their specialty is they are twice as true as life, and that is why it takes a genius to write them. "Spotted Horses" may not have happened yet; if it had, some others might have tried to make a story of it; but "Spotted Horses" could happen tomorrow—that is one of its glories. It could happen today or tomorrow at any little crossroads hamlet in Mississippi; the whole combination of irresistibility is there. We have the Snopses ready, the Mrs. Littlejohns ready, nice Ratliff and the Judge ready and sighing, the clowns, sober and merry, settled for the evening retro-spection of it in the cool dusk of the porch; and the Henry Armstids armed with their obsessions, the little periwinkle-eyed boys armed with their indestructibility; the beautiful, overweening spring, too, the moonlight on the pear trees from which the mockingbird's song keeps returning; and the little store and the fat boy to steal and steal away at its candy. There are undoubtedly spotted horses too, in the offing—somewhere in Texas this minute, straining toward the day. After Faulkner has told it, it is easy for one and all to look back and see it.

Faulkner, simply, knew it already; it is a different kind of knowledge from Flaubert's, and proof could not add much to it. He was born knowing, or rather learning, or rather prophesying, all that and more; and having it all together at one time available while he writes is one of the marks of his mind. If there *is* any more in Mississippi than is engaged and dilated upon, and made twice as real as it used to be and applies now to the world, in the one story "Spotted Horses," then we would almost rather not know it—but I don't bet a piece of store candy that there is. In Faulkner's humor, even more measurably than in his tragedy, it is all there.

It may be going too far to say that the exactness and concreteness and solidity of the real world achieved in a story correspond to the intensity of feeling in the author's mind and to the very turn of his heart; but there lies the secret of our confidence in him.

Making reality real is art's responsibility. It is a practical assignment, then, a self-assignment: to achieve, by a cultivated sensitivity for observing life, a capacity for receiving its impressions, a lonely, unremitting, unaided, unaidable vision, and transferring this vision without distortion to it onto the pages, . . . where, if the reader is so persuaded, it will turn into the reader's illusion. How bent on this peculiar joy we are, reader and writer, willingly to practice, willingly to undergo, this alchemy for it!

What is there, then, about place that is transferable to the pages of a [story]? The best things—the explicit things: physical texture. And as place has functioned between the writer and his material, so it functions between the writer and reader. Location is the ground conductor of all the currents of emotion and belief and moral conviction that charge out from the story in its course. These charges need the warm hard earth underfoot, the light and lift of air, the stir and play of mood, the softening bath of atmos-phere that gives the likeness-to-life that life needs. Through the story's trans-lation and ordering of life, the unconvincing raw material becomes the very heart's familiar. Life *is* strange. Stories hardly make it more so; with all they are able to tell and surmise, they make it more believably, more inevitably so.

I think the sense of place is as essential to good and honest writing as a logical mind; surely they are somewhere related. It is by knowing where you stand that you grow able to judge where you are. Place absorbs our earliest notice and attention, it bestows on us our original awareness; and our critical powers spring up from the study of it and the growth of experi-ence inside it. It perseveres in bringing us back to earth when we fly too

high. It never really stops informing us, for it is forever astir, alive, changing, reflecting, like the mind of man itself. One place comprehended can
make us understand other places better. Sense of place gives equilibrium;
extended, it is sense of direction too. Carried off we might be in spirit, and
should be, when we are reading or writing something good; but it is the
sense of place going with us still that is the ball of golden thread to carry us
there and back and in every sense of the word to bring us home.

What can place *not* give? Theme. It can present theme, show it to the
last detail — but place is forever illustrative: it is a picture of what man has
done and imagined, it is his visible past, result. Human life is fiction's only
theme.   [1977]

EDITH WHARTON

*E*dith Wharton included "Telling a Short Story" in her book The Writing of
Fiction *(1925), from which this excerpt is taken. Her disciplined attempt to
state a theory of narrative form was modeled on the example of her mentor,
Henry James. She took as the epigraph of her book a quotation from the early
English poet Thomas Traherne: "Order the beauty even of Beauty is." Concerned with defining the difference between the short story and longer forms of
prose narrative, Wharton was herself an accomplished writer of both.*

Every Subject Must Contain within Itself Its Own Dimensions

It is sometimes said that a "good subject" for a short story should
always be capable of being expanded into a novel.

The principle may be defendable in special cases; but it is certainly a
misleading one on which to build any general theory. Every "subject" (in
the novelist's sense of the term) must necessarily contain within itself its own
dimensions; and one of the fiction-writer's essential gifts is that of discerning
whether the subject which presents itself to him, asking for incarnation, is
suited to the proportions of a short story or of a novel. If it appears to be
adapted to both the chances are that it is inadequate to either.

It would be as great a mistake, however, to try to base a hard-and-fast
theory on the denial of the rule as on its assertion. Instances of short stories
made out of subjects that could have been expanded into a novel, and that
are yet typical short stories and not mere stunted novels, will occur to everyone. General rules in art are useful chiefly as a lamp in a mine, or a handrail
down a black stairway; they are necessary for the sake of the guidance they

give, but it is a mistake, once they are formulated, to be too much in awe of them.

There are at least two reasons why a subject should find expression in novel-form rather than as a tale; but neither is based on the number of what may be conveniently called incidents, or external happenings, which the narrative contains. There are novels of action which might be condensed into short stories without the loss of their distinguishing qualities. The marks of the subject requiring a longer development are, first, the gradual unfolding of the inner life of its characters, and secondly the need of producing in the reader's mind the sense of the lapse of time. Outward events of the most varied and exciting nature may without loss of probability be crowded into a few hours, but moral dramas usually have their roots deep in the soul, their rise far back in time; and the suddenest-seeming clash in which they culminate should be led up to step by step if it is to explain and justify itself.

There are cases, indeed, when the short story may make use of the moral drama at its culmination. If the incident dealt with be one which a single retrospective flash sufficiently lights up, it is qualified for use as a short story; but if the subject be so complex, and its successive phases so interesting, as to justify elaboration, the lapse of time must necessarily be suggested, and the novel-form becomes appropriate.

The effect of compactness and instantaneity sought in the short story is attained mainly by the observance of two "unities"—the old traditional one of time, and that other, more modern and complex, which requires that any rapidly enacted episode shall be seen through only one pair of eyes. . . .

One thing more is needful for the ultimate effect of probability; and that is, never to let the character who serves as reflector record anything not naturally within his register. It should be the story-teller's first care to choose this reflecting mind deliberately, as one would choose a building-site, or decide upon the orientation of one's house, and when this is done, to live inside the mind chosen, trying to feel, see and react exactly as the latter would, no more, no less, and, above all, no otherwise. Only thus can the writer avoid attributing incongruities of thought and metaphor to his chosen interpreter.   [1925]

WILLIAM CARLOS WILLIAMS

William Carlos Williams wrote "A Beginning on the Short Story" as a series of notes in 1949. As an experimental writer, he felt that the principal feature of the story is that it is short, "and so must pack in what it has to say, unless it be snipped off a large piece as prose-for-quality writing which might be justifiable." Williams also investigated using the story as "a practice sheet for the novel one might discover in it." Basically he considered it "a good medium for nailing down a single conviction. Emotionally." Williams felt that you can't study the work of a writer in order to "learn" to write a story. All you can learn is what the other writer did.

Notes on
"A Beginning on the Short Story"

The short story isn't a snippet from the newspaper. It isn't realism. It is, as in all forms of art, taking the materials of every day (or otherwise) and using them to raise the consciousness of our lives to higher levels by the use of the art: to get something said.

As in the poem, it must be stressed that the short story uses the same materials as rewrite, the same dregs—the same in fact as Shakespeare and Greek tragedy: the elevation of spirit that occurs when a consciousness of form, art in short, is imposed upon materials debased by dispirited and crassly cynical handling. What the newspaper uses on the lowest (sentimental) level, the short story had best elevate to the level of other interests.

This should make apparent that a mere "thrilling" account of an occurrence from daily life, a transcription of a fact, is not of itself and for that reason a short story. You get the fact, it interests you for whatever reason; of the fact you *make*, using words, a story. A thing. A piece of writing, as in the case of de Maup't, A Piece of String.[1] . . .

In other words when you begin to write a short story you should really know what you're writing about—because, if you write skilfully enough, sooner or later someone is going to find it out and judge you as a man for it.

Oh, but am I making a mistake? Perhaps all you want is to write a story and not be judged a liar because you lie. I'm really afraid I'm in the wrong bin. I'm taking the art of the short story seriously.

What will it do?

For instance—what was my problem or urge or opportunity for realization of my insights in 1932?

What was going on? A depression. Cheatery.

How did I resolve it? Why did I choose the short story and how much must it have been modified from stereotype to be serviceable to me?

I do not mean to imply that the choice was a conscious one altogether. I mean, looking back upon it, what were the elements involved in my coming upon the short story as a means?—that is during The Depression?

Answer: The character of the evidence: to accommodate itself to the heterogeneous character of the people, the elements involved, the situation

---

[1]A reference to Maupassant's story "The String."

in hand. In other words, the materials and the temporal situation dictated the terms.

I lived among these people. I knew them and saw the essential qualities, (not stereotype) the courage, the humor (an accident), the deformity, the basic tragedy of their lives—and the *importance* of it. You can't write about something unimportant to yourself. I was involved.

That wasn't all. I saw how they were maligned by their institutions of church and state—and "betters." I saw how all that was acceptable to the ear about them maligned them. I saw how stereotype falsified them.

Nobody was writing about them, anywhere, as they ought to be written about. There was no chance of writing anything acceptable, certainly not saleable, about them.

It was my duty to raise the level of consciousness, not to say discussion, of them to a higher level, a higher plane. Really to tell.

Why the short story? Not for a sales article but as I had conceived them. The briefness of their chronicles, its brokenness and heterogeneity—isolation, color. A novel was unthinkable.

And so to the very style of the stories themselves.

This wasn't the "acceptable," the unshocking stuff, the slippery, in the sense that it can be slipped into them while they are semiconscious of a Saturday evening. Not acceptable to a mag and didn't get into them. But one [that] was made for them by a guy who was broke. . . .

We speak of a man's "mettle"—it might better be metal. It is as with other metals, when it is heated it melts. It is when the metal is fluid the imagination can be said to become active; it is the melting, the rendering fluid of the imagination that describes the mind as entering upon creative work.

It must be melted to recreate itself, fluid, unfettered by anything. Maybe shock treatment may some day be part of the curriculum.

The characteristic of being melted is, for the object, to have lost the form it was in. It can be played with, made into a new form as we desire.

With the short story as with any sort of creation, I am trying to say, the imagination (that is the mind in a fluid state, is a melted state) has to be given play.

Now, we know by knowledge of the physiology of the brain that it acts only when it has been supplied oxygen in abundance. So it glows and sweats when it is active—as with anything else.

What is the origin of that heat? Something has stirred us, some perception linked with emotion. We are angry, we are committed to something in our lives, as with the poem. It doesn't matter what it has been— anything. We heat up, grow incandescent. This incentive is usually secret, it is guided by our fears perhaps. But we are heated and (if we can get quiet enough, as in jail, or running away—finally) we melt and the imagination is set to flow into its new mold.

The short story, since flights of the imagination, rocketlike, will be short, though they may penetrate far if we let them go—UP! I should say that the short story consists of one single flight of the imagination, complete: up and down.

What shall the story be written *about*. That's the final step. Obviously not, if it is serious, the mere sentimental characters. . . .

What then? Something that interests the writer seriously, as a writer (not necessarily a man, for in that case the interest would be moral and perhaps best NOT represented as a short story). He writes about the way his interests, as a writer, strike upon the materials, of some event, graphically presented.

The result is life, not morals. It is THE LIFE which comes alive in the telling. It is the life under specified conditions—so that it is relived in the telling—as it strikes off flashes from the materials. The material is the metal against which a flint of action makes sparks.

Thus anything can be used without fear of sentimentality. The THING we are writing, directing all our wit, our intelligence to discover and set down—is revealed as it hits against whatever may be in its path. That's the modern understanding—and I guess it's pretty hard to comprehend, whatever it may be for each man who writes. What good are you? Prove it. Or what do you see, young as you are? Do you think a prostitute is "bad" because she's a prostitute? And yet how shall you show her "good" except by speaking of her in the conditions of her prostitution. By using that material, graphically, specifically you must learn to tell all you want to tell—whatever YOU want to say. That is the art.   [1949]

SELECTED ANNOTATED BIBLIOGRAPHY
The American Short Story and Its Cultural Background

Abbott, Dorothy, and Susan Koppelman, eds. *The Signet Classic Book of Southern Short Stories.* New York: Penguin, 1991. *Thirty-three stories from 1829 to 1973, illustrating "the new shape of southern literature that has emerged when the riches of scholarship in African American literature and women's studies are joined to the white patriarchal tradition."*

Allen, Walter. *The Short Story in English.* Oxford: Clarendon, 1981. *A comprehensive study of the literary genre in England and the United States.*

"American Magazine-Literature of the Last Century." *The Atlantic Monthly* Apr. 1860: 429–38. *Summary of the early history of British and American magazines, concluding that periodical literature shows us "the transactions of the time in the light in which they were regarded by the parties engaged in them."*

Ammons, Elizabeth. *Conflicting Stories: American Women Writers at the Turn into the Twentieth Century.* New York: Oxford, 1991. *A revisionist history arguing that many so-called minor women writers were important participants in the American literary tradition, including Frances E. W. Harper, Charlotte Perkins Gilman, Sarah Orne Jewett, Alice Dunbar-Nelson, Kate Chopin, Gertrude Stein, Mary Austin, Sui Sin Far, Willa Cather, Edith Wharton, and Anzia Yezierska.*

Ammons, Elizabeth, and Valerie Rohy, eds. *American Local Color Writing, 1880–1920.* New York: Penguin, 1998. *Anthology of stories organized by region, with an introduction (pp. vii–xxviii) proposing that "regionalism offers, as a genre, a powerful literary allegory of what is now called multiculturalism."*

Aycock, Wendell M., ed. *The Teller and the Tale: Aspects of the Short Story.* Lubbock: Texas Tech, 1982. *A collection of essays discussing various aspects of short fiction, including its oral roots and realism versus antirealism.*

Barth, John. *The Friday Book.* New York: Putnam's, 1984. *A collection of nonfiction including "The Literature of Exhaustion," "The Future of Literature and the Literature of the Future," and "Some Reasons Why I Tell the Stories I Tell the Way I Tell Them Rather Than Some Other Sort of Stories Some Other Way."*

———. *Further Fridays: Essays, Lectures, and Other Nonfiction 1984–94.* Boston: Little, 1995. *Includes "It's a Short Story," "A Few Words about Minimalism," "Once Upon a Time: Storytelling Explained," and other choice reflections.*

Bates, H. E. *The Modern Short Story: A Critical Survey.* Boston: The Writer, 1941, 1972. *Three chapters on American writers, but primarily a historical survey of the European short story.*

Baxter, Charles. *Burning Down the House.* St. Paul: Graywolf, 1997. *Nine essays on various aspects of fiction, in which Baxter discusses the pathetic fallacy and the objective correlative, and analyzes stories by Donald Barthelme, Grace Paley, James Alan McPherson, Anton Chekhov, James Joyce, and others.*

Baym, Nina. *The Shape of Hawthorne's Career.* Ithaca: Cornell UP, 1976. *Analysis of Nathaniel Hawthorne's short fiction in the larger context of his career as an early American fiction writer.*

———. *Women's Fiction: A Guide to Novels by and about Women in America, 1820–1870.* Ithaca: Cornell UP, 1978. *Discussion of best-selling fiction by early American women writers that provides a context for the writing of women short story authors.*

Bierce, Ambrose. "The Short Story." *The Collected Works of Ambrose Bierce.* 1911. New York: Gordian, 1966. x, 234–48. *Early critical essay by this important author.*

Birkerts, Sven. *American Energies.* New York: Morrow, 1992. *Reviews and essays on contemporary American fiction, including "The School of Lish" (pp. 155–67), discussing editor Gordon Lish's influence on the prose style of Raymond Carver, Amy Hempel, Mary Robison, and others.*

Bone, Robert. *Down Home: A History of Afro-American Short Fiction from Its Beginnings to the End of the Harlem Renaissance.* New York: Capricorn, 1975. *Discusses African American folktales, the Brer Rabbit tales, and individual writers such as Paul Dunbar, Charles W. Chesnutt, Jean Toomer, Langston Hughes, and Arna Bontemps.*

Burnett, Whit, and Hallie Burnett. *Story Jubilee.* New York: Doubleday, 1965. *Anthology of fifty stories, with an introductory history of Story magazine (pp. ix–xiv).*

Canby, Henry S. *The Short Story in English.* 1909. New York: Holt, 1932. *Early analysis of the short story, arguing that Edgar Allan Poe is the most innovative storyteller in English since Chaucer.*

Coultrap-McQuin, Susan. *Doing Literary Business: American Women Writers in the Nineteenth Century.* Chapel Hill: U of North Carolina, 1990. *Discussion of the ambiguous cultural context for early women writers, and the ideals and economics of the literary marketplace as reflected in the careers of five best-selling novelists, including Harriet Beecher Stowe.*

Curnutt, Kirk. *Wise Economies: Brevity and Storytelling in American Short Stories.* Moscow: U of Idaho, 1997. *Analysis of the framing device in stories by Washington Irving, Nathaniel Hawthorne, and Herman Melville, and the "Cross-Gendered Text" in Rebecca Harding Davis's "Life in the Iron-Mills, or The Korl Woman."*

Current-Garcia, Eugene. *The American Short Story before 1850.* Boston: Twayne, 1985. *Comprehensive description of early types of short fiction in periodicals before 1820. Later chapters on Washington Irving, Nathaniel Hawthorne, Edgar Allan Poe, and William Gilmore Simms conclude with the discussion "Shifting*

Trends Toward Realism in Fiction." This entire volume is notable for being the work of a scholar specializing in early-nineteenth-century American short fiction.

Current-Garcia, Eugene, and Walton R. Patrick. *What Is the Short Story?* Glenview: Scott, 1961. *Case study in the development of the literary form through the presentation of twenty-seven critical statements from Edgar Allan Poe to W. Somerset Maugham, plus an anthology of thirty short stories.*

Davidson, Cathy N. *Revolution and the Word: The Rise of the Novel in America.* New York: Oxford UP, 1986. *Discussion of the early-nineteenth-century periodicals and publishers helping to establish the market for fiction in the United States.*

Douglass, Ann. *The Feminization of American Culture.* New York: Knopf, 1977. *Description of the polarization of literature in nineteenth-century America that prompted Nathaniel Hawthorne's comment about "the damned mob of scribbling women."*

Eichenbaum, Boris M. "O. Henry and the Theory of the Short Story." trans. I. R. Titunik. *Readings in Russian Poetics: Formalist and Structuralist Views.* Ed. L. Matejka and K. Pomorska. Cambridge: MIT, 1971. *Theoretical analysis of O. Henry's contribution to the short story.*

Fagin, N. Bryllion. *America through the Short Story.* Boston: Little, 1936. *Anthology arranged according to eight topics: "The Indian," "The Negro," "Other Minority Peoples," "Religion," "War," "Women," "Labor and Capital," and "Social Classes."*

Fetterley, Judith. *The Resisting Reader: A Feminist Approach to American Fiction.* Bloomington: Indiana UP, 1978. *Pioneering feminist work in which Fetterley develops her theory of "the immasculating imagination" in classic American literature. The chapters "Palpable Designs," "Growing Up Male in America," "Women Beware Science," and "A Rose" deal respectively with Washington Irving's "Rip Van Winkle," Sherwood Anderson's "I Want to Know Why," Nathaniel Hawthorne's "The Birthmark," and William Faulkner's "A Rose for Emily."*

Fetterley, Judith, and Marjorie Pryse, eds. *American Women Regionalists 1850–1910.* New York: Norton, 1992. *Generous sampling of the work of Harriet Beecher Stowe, Alice Carey, Rose Terry Cooke, Sarah Orne Jewett, Mary Noialles Murfree, Mary Wilkins Freeman, Kate Chopin, Alice Dunbar-Nelson, Sui Sin Far, Mary Austin, and Willa Cather, among others, with an introduction (pp. xi–xx) placing the writers in their context.*

Foley, Martha. *The Story of Story Magazine.* New York: Norton, 1980. *Covers the early years of the magazine, 1931–41, when Foley and coeditor Whit Burnett published hundreds of unknown short story writers.*

————, ed. *200 Years of Great American Short Stories.* Boston: Houghton, 1975. *Fifty-four stories from 1774 to 1974, including what Foley considers the first American short story, "A Pretty Story," along with an introduction by Foley (pp. 1–23) discussing her choices.*

Friedman, Norman. "What Makes a Short Story Short?" *Modern Fiction Studies* 4 (1958): 103–17. [Included in Charles E. May's *The New Short Story Theories.*] *Friedman uses literary theory to answer his question through an analysis of the conflict typically presented in short story narrative.*

Fusco, Richard. *Maupassant and the American Short Story*. University Park: Pennsylvania State UP, 1994. *The influence of the French author's use of the short story form on Ambrose Bierce, O. Henry, and Henry James at the turn of the century.*

Gardner, John. *On Writers and Writing*. Reading: Addison-Wesley, 1994. *Chapters on Herman Melville's "Bartleby, the Scrivener" and the stories of John Cheever.*

Geismar, Maxwell. "The American Short Story Today." *Studies on the Left* 4 (1964): 21–27. *Attack on popular writers J. D. Salinger, Philip Roth, Bernard Malamud, and John Updike for refusing to acknowledge contemporary social problems in their short fiction.*

Gelfant, Blanche H. *Women Writing in America*. Hanover: UP of New England, 1984. *Contains chapters on Grace Paley's and Ann Beattie's stories as documenting "The End of the Sixties."*

Gerlach, John. *Toward the End: Closure and Structure in the American Short Story*. Tuscaloosa: U of Alabama P, 1985. *Discusses the ending of individual stories in terms of the concept of closure.*

Griswold, Rufus Wilmot. *The Prose Writers of America*. Philadelphia: Parry, 1846. *Surveys "the intellectual history, condition, and prospects of the country" through selections by individual writers, including Washington Irving, James Hall, Catharine Maria Sedgwick, Lydia Maria Child, Ralph Waldo Emerson, James Fenimore Cooper, Caroline Kirkland, Nathaniel Hawthorne, William Gilmore Simms, Edgar Allan Poe, and others.*

Hanson, Clare, ed. *Re-reading the Short Story*. New York: St. Martin's, 1989. *Essays by various contributors include discussion of stories by Ernest Hemingway, F. Scott Fitzgerald, and Sylvia Plath as well as English and Irish writers.*

Hart, James D. *The Popular Book: A History of America's Literary Taste*. Berkeley: U of California P, 1963. *Well-written, scholarly history of publishing trends in the United States.*

Harte, Bret. "The Rise of the 'Short Story.'" *Cornhill Magazine* 7 (1899): 1–8. *Argues that the local-color story is the first "true" American story because Washington Irving took earlier German models for his short fiction.*

Kelley, M. *Private Woman, Public Stage: Literary Domesticity in Nineteenth-Century America*. New York: Oxford UP, 1984. *Description of the experiences of twelve best-selling nineteenth-century women writers as they became public figures, economic providers, and creators of culture.*

Kimbel, Bobby Ellen, ed. *American Short Story Writers, 1910–1945*. Detroit: Gale, 1989 (1st ser.), 1991 (2nd ser.). Vol. 86, 1st ser., and Vol. 102, 2nd ser., of the *Dictionary of Literary Biography*. *First series contains entries on twenty-five writers; second series includes thirty-seven writers. Each entry consists of a bibliography, a biographical and critical essay, and references.*

Kimbel, Bobby Ellen, and William E. Grant, eds. *American Short Story Writers before 1880*. Detroit: Gale, 1988. Vol. 74 of the *Dictionary of Literary Biography*. *Various contributors discuss thirty-six short story writers.*

———. *American Short Story Writers, 1880–1910*. Detroit: Gale, 1989. Vol. 78 of the *Dictionary of Literary Biography*. *Entries on thirty-one short story writers.*

Kiser, Michael, and Helene Barker. "Interview with Charles Baxter." *Sycamore Review* 4 (Winter 1992): 1–15. *Charles Baxter talks candidly about his early years writing poetry, his work habits, and the role of place in his character-driven fiction.*

Knopf, Marcy. *The Sleeper Wakes.* New Brunswick: Rutgers UP, 1993. *Harlem Renaissance stories by women, introduced with an essay by Nellie Y. McKay.*

Kroeber, Karl. *Artistry in Native American Myths.* Lincoln: U of Nebraska P, 1998. *Extensive commentary on a collection of Native American myths that analyzes their skillful verbal construction and emotional power.*

Levy, Andrew. *The Culture and Commerce of the American Short Story.* New York: Cambridge UP, 1993. *Proposes that America "built the short story as an image of itself, and continues to use the genre as a locale where political ideals can be rehearsed, debated, and turned into literary forms."*

Lohafer, Susan. *Coming to Terms with the Short Story.* Baton Rouge: Louisiana State UP, 1983. *Extended inquiry into the nature of the form, analyzing how a story offers a reading experience different from that offered by other narrative forms because the story is most directly dependent on the individual sentence.*

Lohafer, Susan, and J. E. Clarey, eds. *Short Story Theory at a Crossroads.* Baton Rouge: Louisiana State UP, 1989. *Fifteen essays giving an overview of contemporary short story theory and the evolution of the short story in relation to cultural contexts.*

Lundén, Rolf. *The United Stories of America: Studies in the Short Story Composite.* Amsterdam: Rodopi, 1999. *Narratological and general study of American twentieth-century short story composites/cycles.*

Marler, R. F. "From Tale to Short Story: The Emergence of a New Genre in the 1850s." *American Literature* 46 (1974–75): 153–69. *Historical analysis of the development of the early short story.*

Martindale, Colin, and Anne E. Martindale. "Historical Evolution of Content and Style in Nineteenth- and Twentieth-Century American Short Stories." *Poetics* 17 (1988): 333–55. *Traces the evolution of the genre as it reflects the constant demand for novelty by its readers.*

Matthews, Brander. *The Philosophy of the Short-Story.* New York: Longmans, 1901. *Elaboration of an 1884 article in which Matthews discusses the literary genre he named the "short-story."*

May, Charles E., ed. *The New Short Story Theories.* Athens: Ohio UP, 1994. *Comprehensive collection of essays by popular commentators, academic critics, and short story writers that provide significant theoretical directions for a reevaluation of the form.*

McClave, H., ed. *Women Writers of the Short Story.* Englewood Cliffs: Prentice, 1980. *Collection of critical essays on Sarah Orne Jewett by Warner Berthoff, on Edith Wharton by R. W. B. Lewis, on Willa Cather by Katherine Anne Porter and Lionel Trilling, on Katherine Anne Porter by Robert Penn Warren, on Eudora Welty by Robert Penn Warren, and on Flannery O'Connor by Robert Fitzgerald and Joyce Carol Oates, among others.*

Meanor, Patrick, ed. *American Short Story Writers Since World War II.* Detroit: Gale, 1993. Vol. 130 of the *Dictionary of Literary Biography. Contains essays on forty writers by various contributors.*

Mott, Frank Luther. *A History of American Magazines 1865–1905.* Cambridge: Harvard UP, 1938. *Comprehensive account of the role of periodicals in late-nineteenth-century America.*

Nagel, James, and Tom Quirk, eds. *The Portable American Realism Reader.* New York: Penguin, 1997. *Forty-seven stories published between 1865 and 1918, with a substantial introductory essay on the historical and literary context of the "Age of Realism."*

Nekola, Charlotte, and Paula Rabinowitz, eds. *Writing Red.* New York: Feminist, 1987. *Includes twelve stories illustrating radical "women's short fiction of the 1930s."*

Oates, Joyce Carol. *New Heaven, New Earth: The Visionary Experience in Literature.* New York: Vanguard, 1974. *Contains the essay "The Visionary Art of Flannery O'Connor" (pp. 37–68).*

———, ed. *The Oxford Book of American Short Stories.* New York: Oxford UP, 1992. *Fifty-six stories, both classic and little-known, introduced by a long essay (pp. 3–16).*

O'Brien, Edward J. *The Advance of the American Short Story.* Rev. ed. New York: Dodd, 1931. *Critical survey proposing that almost every American short story is "the product of one or more of four heresies": the heresy of types, the heresy of local color, the heresy of plot, and the heresy of the surprise ending.*

O'Connor, Flannery. *Mystery and Manners,* Ed. Sally and Robert Fitzgerald. New York: Farrar, 1969. *Critical essays on regional writing, the nature and aims of fiction, and the writer and religion.*

O'Connor, Frank. *The Lonely Voice: A Study of the Short Story.* Cleveland: World, 1963. *Pioneering book-length study of the unique qualities of the genre, with discussions of many important writers including Ivan Turgenev, Anton Chekhov, Guy de Maupassant, Rudyard Kipling, James Joyce, Katherine Mansfield, Ernest Hemingway, and Katherine Anne Porter.*

Our Famous Women. Hartford: Worthington, 1884. *Biographical essays on Harriet Beecher Stowe by Catherine E. Beecher, Rose Terry Cooke by Harriet Beecher Stowe and Harriet Prescott Spofford, Harriet Prescott Spofford by Rose Terry Cooke, Elizabeth Stuart Phelps by M. A. Livermore, Elizabeth Cady Stanton by Susan B. Anthony; and many more.*

Pattee, Fred Lewis. *The Development of the American Short Story.* New York: Harper, 1923. *Most comprehensive early history of the genre from Washington Irving and "The Arrival of the Annuals" to "O. Henry and the Handbooks."*

Paulin, Roger. *The Brief Compass: The Nineteenth-Century German Novelle.* Oxford: Clarendon, 1985. *Analysis of the development of nineteenth-century German short fiction and the influence of folklore and the oral tradition.*

Pauly, T. H. "The Literary Sketch in Nineteenth-Century America." *Texas Studies in Literature and Language* 17 (1975): 489–503. *Discussion of the earliest forms of short fiction in the United States.*

Ramsey, Jarold, ed. *Coyote Was Going There: Indian Literature of the Oregon Country.* Seattle: U of Washington P, 1977. *Representative Native American myths, legends, and stories from the oral tradition in Oregon, including the Shasta*

Indian tale "The Theft of Fire," collected from earlier anthropological and linguistic journals and monographs by a conscientious scholar who has "tried to keep emendations, rewordings, reorderings, and elisions to a minimum."

Reid, Ian. *The Short Story*. London: Methuen, 1977. *Brief survey defining the genre, analyzing its essential qualities, and describing its "tributary forms," such as the sketch, yarn, parable, and fable.*

Renza, Louis A. *"A White Heron" and the Question of a Minor Literature*. Madison: U of Wisconsin P, 1984. *Analysis of a Sarah Orne Jewett story as the basis for a theoretical interpretation of "minor" literature as a tool of literary resistance.*

Rhode, Robert D. *Setting in the American Short Story of Local Color: 1865–1900*. The Hague: Mouton, 1975. *Analysis of setting as background and ornament, as close relation to character, and as setting personified.*

Ross, Danforth. *The American Short Story*. Minneapolis: U of Minnesota P, 1961. *Brief pamphlet surveying the American short story from Washington Irving to the Beat writers, whose stories "tend to zigzag madly, reaching for moments of ecstasy, achieving them, and then plunging off in a new direction."*

Sedgwick, Ellery. *A History of the Atlantic Monthly 1857–1909*. Boston: U of Massachusetts P, 1994. *Focuses on the magazine's first seven editors: James Russell Lowell (1857–61), James T. Fields (1861–71), William Dean Howells (1871–81), Thomas Bailey Aldrich (1881–90), H. E. Scudder (1890–98), W. H. Page (1898–99), and Bliss Perry (1899–1909).*

Showalter, Elaine, ed. *Scribbling Women: Short Stories by 19th Century American Women*. New Brunswick: Rutgers UP, 1996. *Fourteen authors represented by one or more stories; a long introduction and a chronology of the authors' lives and times are included.*

———. *Sister's Choice: Tradition and Change in American Women's Writing*. Oxford: Clarendon, 1991. *Contains the chapters "American Female Gothic," discussing Charlotte Perkins Gilman and Joyce Carol Oates, and "Common Threads," analyzing stories by Susan Glaspell, Lydia Maria Child, Kate Chopin, Bobbie Ann Mason, and Alice Walker, among others.*

Stevick, Phillip. *Alternative Pleasures: Postrealist Fiction and the Tradition*. Urbana: U of Illinois P, 1981. *Discussion of short fiction by John Barth, Donald Barthelme, Richard Brautigan, William Gass, Robert Coover, and others.*

———, ed. *The American Short Story: 1900–1945*. Boston: Twayne, 1984. *Excellent overview of the period by Stevick, followed by essays by Ellen Kimbel on "The American Short Story: 1900–1920"; Thomas A. Gullason on "The 'Lesser' Renaissance: The American Short Story in the 1920s"; James G. Watson on "The American Short Story: 1930–1945"; and Mary Rohrberger on "The Question of Regionalism: Limitation and Transcendence."*

Tallack, Douglas. *The Nineteenth-Century American Short Story: Language, Form, and Ideology*. London: Routledge, 1993. *Deconstructivist approach to stories by Nathaniel Hawthorne, Edgar Allan Poe, Herman Melville, Charlotte Perkins Gilman, and Henry James.*

Tilton, Robert S. *Pocahontas: The Evolution of an American Narrative*. Cambridge: Cambridge UP, 1994. *Analyzes why this half-historic, half-legendary narrative has engaged the imaginations of Americans from the earliest days of the colonies to the present.*

Tompkins, Jane. *Sensational Designs: The Cultural Work of American Fiction.* New York: Oxford UP, 1985. *Discussion of how noncanonical texts by popular nineteenth-century authors can be read by considering the worldview they sprang from and helped to shape.*

Updike, John, and Katrina Kenison, eds. *The Best American Short Stories of the Century.* Boston: Houghton, 1999. *Fifty-five stories selected from the eighty-four volumes of* Best American Short Stories *since the series was launched by Edward J. O'Brien in 1915. Kenison's foreword sketches the history of the annual anthology; Updike's introduction explains his selection process: "I tried not to select stories because they illustrated a theme or portion of the national experience, but because they struck me as lively, beautiful, believable, and, in the human news they brought, important."*

Voss, Arthur. *The American Short Story: A Critical Survey.* Norman: U of Oklahoma P, 1973. *Survey of major writers and trends from Edgar Allan Poe to Katherine Anne Porter, with a final chapter on "The Short Story Since 1940."*

Watson, Noelle, ed. *Reference Guide to Short Fiction.* Detroit: St. James, 1993. *Large reference work with entries on many significant American writers, including short biographies, lists of each author's published work, and critical essays.*

Weaver, Gordon. *The American Short Story, 1945–1980.* Boston: Twayne, 1983. *Contains Weaver's introduction as well as essays by Jeffrey Walker on "Post–World War II Manners and Mores, 1945–1956"; E. P. Walkiewicz on "Toward Diversity of Form, 1957–1968"; and James C. Robison on "Experiment and Tradition, 1969–1980."*

Welty, Eudora. *The Eye of the Story.* New York: Random, 1978. *Essays on Katherine Anne Porter, Willa Cather, Anton Chekhov, and Isak Dinesen as well as seven essays on the art of writing and reading fiction.*

West, Ray B. *The Short Story in America: 1900–1955.* Chicago: Regnery, 1952. *Distinguishes two main divisions in the development of the American story: the "naturalistic" story based on social awareness (e.g., Theodore Dreiser, Sherwood Anderson, John Steinbeck), and the "traditional" story (e.g., F. Scott Fitzgerald, Katherine Anne Porter, Caroline Gordon).*

Wright, Austin. *The American Short Story in the Twenties.* Chicago: U of Chicago P, 1961. *Tribute to the artistry of Sherwood Anderson, F. Scott Fitzgerald, Ernest Hemingway, William Faulkner, and Katherine Anne Porter in the various ways that they perfected the short story genre.*

APPENDIX:
Chronological List of Stories
with Their Original Date and
Place of Publication

All dates refer to the original publication of a given story to the best of our knowledge. When two works are listed, the first is usually a periodical or anthology and the second is the author's own collection.

WASHINGTON IRVING, Rip Van Winkle (1819, *The Sketch Book*)

WILLIAM AUSTIN, Peter Rugg, the Missing Man (1824–27, *New England Galaxy*)

JAMES HALL, The Indian Hater (1830, *Western Souvenir*)

CATHARINE MARIA SEDGWICK, Cacoethes Scribendi (1830, *Atlantic Souvenir;* 1835, *Tales and Sketches by Miss Sedgwick*)

AUGUSTUS BALDWIN LONGSTREET, The Dance (1833, *Milledgeville Southern Recorder;* 1835, *Georgia Scenes*)

NATHANIEL HAWTHORNE, The Minister's Black Veil (1836, *The Token;* 1837, *Twice-Told Tales*)

EDGAR ALLAN POE, The Fall of the House of Usher (1839, *Gentlemen's Magazine;* 1840, *Tales of the Grotesque and Arabesque*)

THOMAS BANGS THORPE, The Big Bear of Arkansas (1841, *Spirit of the Times*)

LYDIA MARIA CHILD, Slavery's Pleasant Homes (1843, *The Liberty Bell;* 1997, *A Lydia Maria Child Reader*)

CAROLINE KIRKLAND, The Land-Fever (1845, *Western Clearings*)

WILLIAM GILMORE SIMMS, The Arm-Chair of Tustenuggee (1845, *The Wigwam and the Cabin*)

HARRIET BEECHER STOWE, The Two Altars; or, Two Pictures in One (1851, *New-York Evangelist;* 1852, *Liberty Tract*)

ELIZABETH STUART PHELPS, The Angel over the Right Shoulder (1852, *The Angel over the Right Shoulder* [Christmas pamphlet])

HERMAN MELVILLE, Bartleby, the Scrivener (1853, *Putnam's Magazine;* 1856, *Piazza Tales*)

FRANCES E. W. HARPER, The Two Offers (1859, *Anglo-African Magazine*)

HARRIET PRESCOTT SPOFFORD, Circumstance (1860, *The Atlantic Monthly;* 1863, *The Amber Gods and Other Stories*)

REBECCA HARDING DAVIS, Life in the Iron Mills, or The Korl Woman (1861, *The Atlantic Monthly;* 1972, *Life in the Iron Mills, or The Korl Woman*)

MARK TWAIN (SAMUEL LANGHORNE CLEMENS), The Celebrated Jumping Frog of Calaveras County (1865, *New York Saturday Press;* 1867, *The Celebrated Jumping Frog of Calaveras County and Other Sketches*)

BRET HARTE, The Luck of Roaring Camp (1868, *The Overland Monthly;* 1870, *The Luck of Roaring Camp, and Other Sketches*)

GEORGE WASHINGTON CABLE, Belles Demoiselles Plantation (1874, *Scribner's Monthly;* 1879, *Old Creole Days*)

CONSTANCE FENIMORE WOOLSON, Rodman the Keeper (1877, *The Atlantic Monthly;* 1880, *Rodman the Keeper: Southern Sketches*)

AMBROSE BIERCE, One of the Missing (1886, *The Wave;* 1891, *Tales of Soldiers and Civilians*)

HAMLIN GARLAND, The Return of a Private (1890, *The Arena;* 1891, *Main-Travelled Roads*)

MARY WILKINS FREEMAN, The Revolt of "Mother" (1890, *Harper's Magazine;* 1891, *A New England Nun and Other Stories*)

ROSE TERRY COOKE, How Celia Changed Her Mind (1891, *Huckleberries Gathered from New England Hills*)

CHARLOTTE PERKINS GILMAN, The Yellow Wallpaper (1892, *New England Magazine;* 1920, *The Great Modern American Stories*)

SARAH ORNE JEWETT, The Queen's Twin (1895, *The Atlantic Monthly;* 1899, *The Queen's Twin and Other Stories*)

MADELENE YALE WYNNE, The Little Room (1895, *Harper's Magazine;* 1920, *The Great Modern American Stories*)

KATE CHOPIN, Athénaïse (1896, *The Atlantic Monthly;* 1897, *A Night in Acadie*)

CHARLES W. CHESNUTT, The Wife of His Youth (1898, *The Atlantic Monthly;* 1899, *The Wife of His Youth and Other Stories of the Color Line*)

STEPHEN CRANE, The Bride Comes to Yellow Sky (1898, *McClure's Magazine;* 1898, *The Open Boat and Other Tales of Adventure*)

ALICE DUNBAR-NELSON, Tony's Wife (1899, *The Goodness of St. Rocque, and Other Stories*)

ZITKALA-SÄ (GERTRUDE SIMMONS BONNIN), The Trial Path (1901, *Harper's Magazine;* 1901, *Old Indian Legends, Retold by Zitkala-Sä*)

O. HENRY (WILLIAM SYDNEY PORTER), The Duplicity of Hargraves (1902, *Junior Munsey*)

WILLA CATHER, A Wagner Matinée (1904, *Everybody's Magazine;* 1905, *The Troll Gardens*)

EDITH WHARTON, The Other Two (1904, *Collier's Weekly;* 1904, *The Descent of Man*)

JACK LONDON, All Gold Canyon (1905, *Century Magazine;* 1906, *Moon-Face and Other Stories*)

MARY AUSTIN, The Walking Woman (1907, *The Atlantic Monthly;* 1909, *Lost Borders*)

HENRY JAMES, The Jolly Corner (1908, *English Review;* 1909, *The Novels and Tales of Henry James,* vol. XVII)

SUI SIN FAR (EDITH MAUD EATON), "Its Wavering Image" (1912, *Mrs. Spring Fragrance*)

SHERWOOD ANDERSON, Hands (1916, *Masses;* 1919, *Winesburg, Ohio*)

THEODORE DREISER, The Lost Phœbe (1916, *Century Magazine;* 1918, *Free and Other Stories*)

SUSAN GLASPELL, A Jury of Her Peers (1917, *Everyweek;* 1927, *A Jury of Her Peers*)

ANZIA YEZIERSKA, My Own People (1920, *Hungry Hearts*)

F. SCOTT FITZGERALD, Winter Dreams (1922, *Metropolitan Magazine;* 1926, *All the Sad Young Men*)

RING LARDNER, The Golden Honeymoon (1922, *Cosmopolitan;* 1929, *Round Up*)

GERTRUDE STEIN, Miss Furr and Miss Skeene (1922, *Geography and Plays*)

JEAN TOOMER, Blood-Burning Moon (1923, *Prairie;* 1923, *Cane*)

ERNEST HEMINGWAY, Soldier's Home (1925, *Contact Collection of Contemporary Writers;* 1925, *In Our Time*)

KATHERINE ANNE PORTER, He (1927, *New Masses;* 1930, *Flowering Judas and Other Stories*)

DOROTHY PARKER, You Were Perfectly Fine (1929, *The New Yorker;* 1930, *Lament for the Living*)

WILLIAM FAULKNER, Spotted Horses (1930, *Scribner's Magazine;* 1931, *These 13*)

ARNA BONTEMPS, A Summer Tragedy (1932, *Opportunity;* 1973, *The Old South*)

ZORA NEALE HURSTON, The Gilded Six-Bits (1933, *Story;* 1934, *The Story in America*)

LANGSTON HUGHES, Red-Headed Baby (1934, *The Ways of White Folks*)

WILLIAM SAROYAN, Seventy Thousand Assyrians (1934, *Story;* 1934, *The Daring Young Man on the Flying Trapeze*)

WILLIAM CARLOS WILLIAMS, The Use of Force (1934, *Blast;* 1938, *Life along the Passaic River*)

JOHN STEINBECK, The Snake (1935, *Monterey Beacon;* 1938, *The Long Valley*)

DELMORE SCHWARTZ, In Dreams Begin Responsibilities (1937, *Partisan Review;* 1938, *In Dreams Begin Responsibilities*)

JACK CONROY, He Is Thousands (1939, *New Masses*)

RICHARD WRIGHT, The Man Who Was Almost a Man (1940, *Harper's Bazaar;* 1961, *Eight Men*)

PEARL S. BUCK, His Own Country (1941, *Today and Forever*)

WALTER VAN TILBURG CLARK, The Portable Phonograph (1941, *Yale Review;* 1950, *The Watchful Gods and Other Stories*)

MARY MCCARTHY, The Man in the Brooks Brothers Shirt (1941, *Partisan Review;* 1942, *The Company She Keeps*)

CARSON MCCULLERS, A Tree. A Rock. A Cloud (1942, *Harper's Bazaar;* 1951, *The Ballad of the Sad Café*)

JAMES THURBER, The Catbird Seat (1942, *The New Yorker;* 1945, *The Thurber Carnival*)

RALPH ELLISON, Flying Home (1944, *Cross Section;* 1996, *Flying Home and Other Stories*)

GWENDOLYN BROOKS, We're the only colored people here (1945, *Portfolio;* 1953, *Maud Martha*)

KAY BOYLE, Winter Night (1946, *The New Yorker;* 1980, *Fifty Stories*)

JOHN CHEEVER, The Enormous Radio (1947, *The New Yorker;* 1953, *The Enormous Radio and Other Stories*)

CAROLINE GORDON, The Petrified Woman (1947, *Mademoiselle;* 1963, *Old Red and Other Stories*)

SHIRLEY JACKSON, The Lottery (1948, *The New Yorker;* 1949, *The Lottery; or, The Adventures of James Harris*)

TILLIE OLSEN, I Stand Here Ironing (1956, *Pacific Spectator;* 1961, *Tell Me a Riddle*)

JAMES BALDWIN, Sonny's Blues (1957, *Partisan Review;* 1965, *Going to Meet the Man*)

PHILIP ROTH, The Conversion of the Jews (1959, *Paris Review;* 1959, *Goodbye, Columbus and Five Short Stories*)

PETER TAYLOR, Promise of Rain (1959, *Happy Families Are All Alike*)

FLANNERY O'CONNOR, Everything That Rises Must Converge (1961, *New World Writing;* 1965, *Everything That Rises Must Converge*)

JOHN O'HARA, The Sharks (1961, *Assembly*)

KURT VONNEGUT JR., Harrison Bergeron (1961, *Fantasy and Science Fiction Magazine;* 1968, *Welcome to the Monkey House*)

EUDORA WELTY, Where Is the Voice Coming From? (1963, *The New Yorker;* 1980, *The Collected Stories of Eudora Welty*)

WILLIAM GASS, In the Heart of the Heart of the Country (1967, *New American Review;* 1968, *In the Heart of the Heart of the Country*)

JOHN BARTH, Title (1968, *Yale Review;* 1968, *Lost in the Funhouse*)

DONALD BARTHELME, The Police Band (1968, *The New Yorker;* 1968, *Unspeakable Practices, Unnatural Acts*)

JOYCE CAROL OATES, How I Contemplated the World from the Detroit House of Correction and Began My Life Over Again (1969, *TriQuarterly;* 1970, *The Wheels of Love and Other Stories*)

RICHARD BRAUTIGAN, 1/3, 1/3, 1/3 (1971, *Revenge of the Lawn: Stories, 1962–1970*)

GRACE PALEY, A Conversation with My Father (1971, *New American Review;* 1974, *Enormous Changes at the Last Minute*)

RAYMOND CARVER, Are These Actual Miles? (originally titled "What Is It?") (1972, *Esquire;* 1976, *Will You Please Be Quiet, Please?;* 1988, *Where I'm Calling From: New and Selected Stories*)

ALICE WALKER, Everyday Use (1973, *Harper's Magazine;* 1973, *In Love and Trouble*)

LESLIE MARMON SILKO, Yellow Woman (1974, *The Man to Send Rain Clouds;* 1981, *Storyteller*)

JOHN UPDIKE, Separating (1975, *The New Yorker;* 1979, *Too Far to Go*)

BOBBIE ANN MASON, Big Bertha Stories (1980, *The New Yorker;* 1989, *Love Life*)

AMY HEMPEL, In the Cemetery Where Al Jolson Is Buried (1985, *TriQuarterly;* 1985, *Reasons to Live*)

BHARATI MUKHERJEE, The Tenant (1986, *Literary Review;* 1988, *The Middleman and Other Stories*)

TIM O'BRIEN, The Things They Carried (1986, *Esquire;* 1990, *The Things They Carried*)

HELENA MARÍA VIRAMONTES, Miss Clairol (1988, *Chicana Creativity and Criticism: Charting New Frontiers in American Literature*)

ANN BEATTIE, Second Question (1991, *The New Yorker;* 1998, *Park City*)

URSULA K. LE GUIN, Texts (1991, *American Short Fiction;* 1991, *Searoad: Chronicles of Klatsand*)

JOHN EDGAR WIDEMAN, newborn thrown in trash and dies (1992, *Stories of John Edgar Wideman*)

SHERMAN ALEXIE, The Only Traffic Signal on the Reservation Doesn't Flash Red Anymore (1993, *The Lone Ranger and Tonto Fistfight in Heaven*)

MARY GAITSKILL, Tiny, Smiling Daddy (1993, *The Threepenny Review;* 1997, *Because They Wanted To*)

LORRIE MOORE, Four Calling Birds, Three French Hens (1993, *New York Times;* 1998, *Birds of America*)

GINA BERRIAULT, Who Is It Can Tell Me Who I Am? (1995, *Ploughshares;* 1996, *Women in Their Beds*)

EDWIDGE DANTICAT, New York Day Woman (1995, *Krik? Krak!*)

CHARLES BAXTER, Saul and Patsy Are in Labor (1997, *American Short Fiction;* 1997, *Believers*)

LAN SAMANTHA CHANG, Water Names (1998, *Hunger*)

ANNIE PROULX, The Bunchgrass Edge of the World (1998, *The New Yorker*) ·

Acknowledgments (continued from p. iv)

Sherwood Anderson. "Form, Not Plot, in the Short Story" from *A Story Teller's Story*. Copyright 1924 by B. W. Huebsch, Inc., renewed 1952 by Eleanor Copenhaver Anderson. Reprinted with the permission of Harold Ober Associates, Incorporated.

Mary Austin. "Regionalism in American Fiction" from Reuben J. Ellis (ed.), *Beyond Borders: Selected Essays of Mary Austin*. Originally published in *English Journal* (1932). Copyright 1932 by the National Council of Teachers of English. Reprinted with the permission of the publishers.

James Baldwin. "Sonny's Blues" from *Going to Meet the Man* (New York: Vintage Books, 1965). Originally published in *The Partisan Review*. Copyright © 1957 and renewed 1985 by James Baldwin. Reprinted with the permission of The James Baldwin Estate. "Autobiographical Notes" from *Notes of a Native Son*. Copyright © 1955 and renewed 1983 by James Baldwin. Reprinted with the permission of Beacon Press, Boston.

John Barth. "Title" from *Lost in the Funhouse*. Originally published in *Yale Review*. Copyright © 1968 by John Barth. Reprinted with the permission of Doubleday, a division of Random House, Inc. "It's a Short Story" from *Further Fridays: Essays, Lectures and Other Nonfiction, 1984-1994*. Originally published in *Mississippi Review*. Copyright © 1995 by John Barth. Reprinted with the permission of Little, Brown and Company.

Donald Barthelme. "The Police Band" from *Unspeakable Practices, Unnatural Acts* (New York: Farrar, Straus & Giroux, 1968). Originally published in *The New Yorker*. Copyright © 1965 by Donald Barthelme. Reprinted with the permission of The Wylie Agency, Inc.

H. E. Bates, "Hemingway's Short Stories" from *The Modern Short Story* (Nashville: Thomas Nelson & Sons, 1942). Reprinted by permission.

Charles Baxter. "Saul and Patsy Are in Labor" from *Believers*. Copyright © 1997 by Charles Baxter. Reprinted with the permission of Pantheon Books, a division of Random House, Inc.

Ann Beattie. "Second Question" from *Park City*. Copyright © 1998 by Ann Beattie. Reprinted with the permission of Alfred A. Knopf, Inc. "Where Characters Come From" from *The Mississippi Review* 1, no. 1 (April 1995). Copyright © 1995 by the Mississippi Review. Reprinted with the permission of the publishers.

Gina Berriault. "Who Is It Can Tell Me Who I Am?" from *Women in Their Beds* (Washington, D.C.: Counterpoint, 1996). Originally published in *Ploughshares* 21, no. 4. Copyright © 1996 by Gina Berriault. Reprinted with the permission of the author.

Arna Bontemps. "A Summer Tragedy" from *Opportunity*. Copyright 1932 by Arna Bontemps. "On Jean Toomer and *Cane*" from Herbert Hill (ed.), *Anger and Beyond: The Negro Writer in the U.S.* Copyright © 1966 by Harper & Row. Both reprinted with the permission of Harold Ober Associates Incorporated.

Kay Boyle. "Winter Night" from *Fifty Stories* (Garden City: Doubleday, 1980). Originally published in *The New Yorker*. Copyright 1946 by Kay Boyle. Reprinted with the permission of the Watkins/Loomis Agency, Inc.

Richard Brautigan. "⅓, ⅓, ⅓" from *Revenge of the Lawn*. Copyright © 1971 by Richard Brautigan. Reprinted with the permission of Houghton Mifflin Company. All rights reserved.

Gwendolyn Brooks. "We're the only colored people here" from *Maud Martha*. Originally published in *Portfolio*. Copyright 1953 by Harper & Row. Reprinted with the permission of the author.

Pearl S. Buck, "His Own Country" from *Today and Forever*. Copyright 1934, 1935, 1936, 1937, 1938, 1939, 1940, 1941 by Pearl S. Buck. Reprinted with the permission of HarperCollins Publishers, Inc.

Raymond Carver. "Are These Actual Miles?" from *Where I'm Calling From: New and Selected Stories*. Originally published in *Esquire* as "What Is It?" Copyright © 1988 by Raymond Carver. Reprinted with the permission of Grove/Atlantic. "Creative Writing 101" from the Foreword to John Gardner, *On Being a Novelist*. Copyright © 1983 by Raymond Carver. Reprinted with the permission of HarperCollins Publishers, Inc.

Willa Cather. "Miss Jewett" from *Not Under Forty*. Copyright 1925 by Willa Cather. Reprinted with the permission of Alfred A. Knopf, Inc.

Lan Samantha Chang. "Water Names" from *Hunger*. Copyright © 1998 by Lan Samantha Chang. Reprinted with the permission of W. W. Norton & Company, Inc.

John Cheever. "The Enormous Radio" from *The Enormous Radio and Other Stories*. Copyright 1947 by John Cheever. Reprinted with the permission of Alfred A. Knopf, Inc.

Walter Van Tilburg Clark. "The Portable Phonograph" from *The Watchful Gods and Other Stories* (New York: Random House, 1950). Copyright 1950 by Walter Van Tilburg Clark. Reprinted with the permission of International Creative Management.

Robert Coles. "Tillie Olsen: The Iron and the Riddle" from *That Red Wheelbarrow: Selected Literary Essays*. Copyright © 1988 by the University of Iowa Press. Reprinted with the permission of the publisher.

Jack Conroy. "He Is Thousands" from *The New Masses*. Copyright 1939 by Jack Conroy. Reprinted with the permission of the Estate of Jack Conroy.

Edwidge Danticat. "New York Day Woman" from *Krik? Krak!* Copyright © 1995 by Edwidge Danticat. Reprinted with the permission of Soho Press.

Ralph Ellison. "Flying Home" from *Flying Home and Other Stories.* Originally published in *Cross Section* (1944). Copyright 1944 by Ralph Ellison. Reprinted with the permission of Random House, Inc.

William Faulkner. "Spotted Horses" from *Uncollected Stories of William Faulkner.* Copyright 1931 and renewed © 1959 by William Faulkner. Copyright 1940 and renewed © 1968 by Estelle Faulkner and Jill Faulkner Summers. Reprinted with the permission of Random House, Inc.

Richard Ford, "Crazy for Stories" from *The New York Times Book Review* (August 9, 1992). Copyright © 1992 by Richard Ford. Reprinted with the permission of International Creative Management.

Mary Gaitskill. "Tiny, Smiling Daddy" from *Because They Wanted To.* Copyright © 1997 by Mary Gaitskill. Reprinted with the permission of Simon & Schuster.

William Gass. Excerpt from Preface and "In the Heart of the Heart of the Country" from *In the Heart of the Heart of the Country* (New York: Harper & Row, 1968). Copyright © 1968 by William Gass. Reprinted with the permission of International Creative Management.

Sandra M. Gilbert and Susan Gubar. "A Feminist Reading of Gilman's 'The Yellow Wallpaper'" from *The Madwoman in the Attic: The Woman Writer and the Nineteenth-Century Literary Imagination.* Copyright © 1979 by Yale University. Reprinted with the permission of Yale University Press.

Charlotte Perkins Gilman. "Undergoing the Cure for Nervous Prostration" from *The Living of Charlotte Perkins Gilman.* Copyright 1935 Katherine Beecher Stetson Chamberlin. Copyright © renewed 1963 by Radcliffe College. Reprinted with the permission of Radcliffe College c/o The Palmer & Dodge Agency, Boston.

Caroline Gordon. "The Petrified Woman" from *The Collected Stories of Caroline Gordon.* Copyright © 1981 by Caroline Gordon. Reprinted with the permission of Farrar, Straus & Giroux, Inc.

Ernest Hemingway. "Soldier's Home" from *In Our Time.* Copyright 1925 by Charles Scribner's Sons and renewed 1953 by Ernest Hemingway. Reprinted with the permission of Scribner, a division of Simon & Schuster.

Amy Hempel. "In the Cemetery Where Al Jolson Is Buried" from *Reasons to Live* (New York: Alfred A. Knopf, 1985). Originally published in *TriQuarterly* (1985). Copyright © 1985 by Amy Hempel. Reprinted with the permission of the Darhansoff & Verrill Literary Agency.

Langston Hughes. "Red-Headed Baby" from *The Ways of White Folks.* Copyright 1934 and renewed © 1962 by Langston Hughes. Reprinted with the permission of Alfred A. Knopf, Inc.

Zora Neale Hurston. "The Gilded Six-Bits" from *The Complete Stories of Zora Neale Hurston.* Compilation copyright © 1995 by Vivian Bowden, Lois J. Hurston Gaston, Clifford Hurston, Lucy Ann Hurston, Winifred Hurston Clark, Zora Mack Goins, Edgar Hurston, Sr., and Barbara Hurston Lewis. Reprinted with the permission of HarperCollins Publishers, Inc. "What White Publishers Won't Print" from *I Love Myself When I Am Laughing . . . And Then Again, When I Am Looking Mean and Impressive: A Zora Neale Hurston Reader.* Copyright © 1950 by Zora Neale Hurston. Reprinted with the permission of The Estate of Zora Neale Hurston.

Shirley Jackson. "The Lottery" from *The Lottery and Other Stories.* Copyright 1948, 1949 by Shirley Jackson, renewed © 1976, 1977 by Laurence Hyman, Barry Hyman, Mrs. Sarah Webster and Mrs. Joanne Schnurer. Reprinted with the permission of Farrar, Straus & Giroux, Inc. "The Morning of June 28, 1948, and 'The Lottery'" [editor's title; originally titled "Biography of a Story"] from *Come Along with Me.* Copyright 1948, 1952, © 1960 by Shirley Jackson. Reprinted with the permission of Viking Penguin, a division of Penguin Putnam, Inc.

Ring Lardner. "How to Write Short Stories" from *How to Write Short Stories.* Copyright 1924 by Charles Scribner's Sons, renewed 1952 by Ellis A. Lardner. Reprinted with the permission of Scribner, a division of Simon & Schuster.

Ursula Le Guin. "Texts" from *Searoad: Chronicles of Klatsand.* Copyright © 1990 by Ursula Le Guin/ PEN Syndicated Fiction Project. First appeared in *American Short Fiction* as part of the PEN Syndicated Fiction Project. Reprinted with the permission of author and the author's agent, Virginia Kidd Agency, Inc.

Susan Lohafer. Excerpt from the Introduction to Part I from Jo Ellyn Clarey and Susan Lohafer, *Short Story Theory at a Crossroads.* Copyright © 1989 by Louisiana State University Press. Reprinted with the permission of the publishers.

Bobbie Ann Mason. "Big Bertha Stories" from *Love Life* (New York: Harper & Row, 1989). Copyright © 1989 by Bobbie Ann Mason. "On Tim O'Brien's 'The Things They Carried'" from Ron Hansen and Jim Shepard (eds.), *You've Got to Read This: Contemporary American Writers Introduce Stories That Held Them in Awe* (New York: HarperCollins, 1994). Copyright © 1994 by Bobbie Ann Mason. Both reprinted with the permission of International Creative Management, Inc.

Charles E. May. "Edgar Allan Poe—Critical Context" from *Edgar Allan Poe: A Study in Short Fiction.* Copyright © 1991 by G. K. Hall & Company. Reprinted with the permission of the publishers.

Mary McCarthy. "The Man in the Brooks Brothers Shirt" from *Partisan Review* (Summer 1941). Reprinted in *The Company She Keeps*. Copyright 1942 and renewed © 1969 by Mary McCarthy. Reprinted with the permission of Harcourt Brace and Company.

Carson McCullers. "A Tree. A Rock. A Cloud" from *The Ballad of the Sad Café*. Copyright 1936, 1941, 1942, 1950, © 1955 by Carson McCullers, renewed © 1979 by Floria V. Lasky. Reprinted with the permission of Houghton Mifflin Company. All rights reserved.

J. Hillis Miller. "A Deconstructive Reading of Melville's 'Bartleby, the Scrivener' " [editor's title; originally titled "Who Is He? Melville's 'Bartleby the Scrivener' "] from *Versions of Pygmalion*. Copyright © 1990 by the President and Fellows of Harvard College. Reprinted with the permission of Harvard University Press.

Lorrie Moore. "Four Calling Birds, Three French Hens" from *Birds of America*. Copyright © 1998 by Lorrie Moore. Reprinted with the permission of Alfred A. Knopf, Inc.

Bharati Mukherjee. "The Tenant" from *The Middleman and Other Stories*. Copyright © 1988 by Bharati Mukherjee. Reprinted with the permission of Grove/Atlantic, Inc. and Penguin Books Canada Limited.

Joyce Carol Oates. "How I Contemplated the World from the Detroit House of Correction and Began My Life Over Again" from *The Wheel of Love and Other Stories*. Copyright © 1970 by Joyce Carol Oates. Reprinted with the permission of John Hawkins Associates, Inc.

Tim O'Brien. "The Things They Carried" from *Esquire* (August 1986). Reprinted in *The Things They Carried*. Copyright © 1986 by Tim O'Brien. Reprinted with the permission of Houghton Mifflin Company. All rights reserved.

Flannery O'Connor. "Everything That Rises Must Converge" from *Everything That Rises Must Converge*. Copyright © 1964, 1965 by The Estate of Mary Flannery O'Connor. "Some Aspects of the Grotesque in Southern Fiction" from *Mystery and Manners*. Copyright © 1969 by The Estate of Mary Flannery O'Connor. Both reprinted with the permission of Farrar, Straus & Giroux, Inc.

Frank O'Connor. Excerpt from *The Lonely Voice: A Study of the Short Story* (Cleveland: World Publishing Company, 1963). Copyright © 1963 by Frank O'Connor. Reprinted with the permission of The Estate of Frank O'Connor c/o Joan Daves Agency.

John O'Hara. "The Sharks" from *Assembly*. Copyright © 1961 by John O'Hara. Reprinted with the permission of Random House, Inc.

Tillie Olsen. "I Stand Here Ironing" from *Tell Me a Riddle*. Copyright © 1956, 1957, 1960, 1961 by Tillie Olsen. Reprinted with the permission of Delacourt Press/Seymour Laurence, a division of Random House, Inc.

Grace Paley. "A Conversation with My Father" from *Enormous Changes at the Last Minute*. Copyright © 1971, 1974 by Grace Paley. Reprinted with the permission of Farrar, Straus & Giroux, Inc.

Dorothy Parker. "You Were Perfectly Fine" from *The Portable Dorothy Parker*. Copyright 1928, © 1956 by Dorothy Parker. Reprinted with the permission of Viking Penguin, a division of Penguin Putnam, Inc. "The Short Story, Through a Couple of the Ages" from *The New Yorker* (December 17, 1927). Copyright 1927 by Dorothy Parker. Reprinted with the permission of the National Association for the Advancement of Colored People. All rights reserved.

Katherine Anne Porter. "He" from *The Flowering Judas and Other Stories*. Copyright 1930 and renewed © 1958 by Katherine Anne Porter. Reprinted with the permission of Harcourt Brace and Company.

E. Annie Proulx. "The Bunchgrass Edge of the World" from *The New Yorker* (November 30, 1998). Copyright © 1998 by E. Annie Proulx. Reprinted with the permission of the Darhansoff & Verrill Literary Agency.

Philip Roth. "The Conversion of the Jews" from *Goodbye, Columbus and 5 Short Stories*. Copyright © 1959 and renewed 1987 by Philip Roth. Reprinted with the permission of Houghton Mifflin Company. All rights reserved.

Earl Rovit. "On James Thurber and *The New Yorker*" from Calvin Shaggs (ed.), *The American Short Story, Volume 2* (New York: Dell, 1980). Copyright © 1980 by Learning in Focus, Inc. Reprinted with the permission of the author.

William Saroyan. "Writing Stories" from the Preface and "Seventy Thousand Assyrians" from *The Daring Young Man on the Flying Trapeze*. Copyright 1934, 1941 by The Modern Library, Inc. Reprinted with the permission of International Creative Management.

Delmore Schwartz. "In Dreams Begin Responsibilities" from *In Dreams Begin Responsibilities*. Copyright © 1961 by Delmore Schwartz. Reprinted with the permission of New Directions Publishing Corporation.

Charles Scribner III. "On F. Scott Fitzgerald's Stories" from *The Short Stories of F. Scott Fitzgerald*. Copyright © 1989 by Charles Scribner's Sons. Reprinted with the permission of Scribner, a division of Simon & Schuster.

Leslie Marmon Silko. "Yellow Woman" from *Storyteller*. Copyright © 1974 by Leslie Marmon Silko. Reprinted with permission of The Wylie Agency, Inc.

John Steinbeck. "The Snake" from *The Long Valley*. Copyright 1938 and renewed © 1966 by John Steinbeck. Reprinted with the permission of Viking Penguin, a division of Penguin Putnam, Inc.

Floyd Stovall. "On James's 'The Jolly Corner'" from *Nineteenth Century Fiction*, 12, no. 4 (March 1966). Copyright © 1966 by the Regents of the University of California. Reprinted with the permission of the University of California Press.

Ruth Suckow. "The Short Story" from *Saturday Review of Literature* (November 19, 1927). Copyright 1927 by Ruth Suckow. Reprinted with the permission of Barbara Camamo, Executor, Ruth Suckow Estate.

Peter Taylor. "Promise of Rain" from *Happy Families Are All Alike*. Copyright © 1959 by Peter Taylor. Reprinted with the permission of Doubleday, a division of Random House, Inc.

James Thurber. "The Catbird Seat" from *The Thurber Carnival* (New York: Harper & Row, 1945 and 1975). Originally published in *The New Yorker* (1942). Copyright 1942 by James Thurber. Reprinted with the permission of The Barbara Hogenson Agency, Inc.

Jean Toomer. "Blood-Burning Moon" from *Cane*. Copyright 1923 by Boni & Liveright; renewed 1951 by Jean Toomer. Reprinted with the permission of Liveright Publishing Corporation.

John Updike. "Separating" from *Too Far to Go*. Copyright © 1979 by John Updike. Reprinted with the permission of Alfred A. Knopf, Inc. "Twisted Apples: On *Winesburg, Ohio*" from *Harper's*, 268 (March 1984). Copyright © 1984 by *Harper's Magazine*. Reprinted by permission.

Helena María Viramontes. "Miss Clairol" from Maria Herrera Sobek and Helena María Viramontes (eds.), *Chicana Creativity and Criticism: Charting New Frontiers in American Literature, Second Edition*. Copyright © 1988 by Helena María Viramontes and Maria Herrera Sobek. Copyright © 1996 by The University of New Mexico Press. Reprinted with the permission of the publishers.

Kurt Vonnegut Jr. "Harrison Bergeron" from *Welcome to the Monkey House*. Copyright © 1961 by Kurt Vonnegut Jr. Reprinted with the permission of Delacourt Press/Seymour Lawrence, a division of Random House, Inc.

Alice Walker. "Everyday Use" from *In Love and Trouble*. Copyright © 1973 by Alice Walker. Reprinted with the permission of Harcourt Brace and Company. "Zora Neale Hurston: A Cautionary Tale and a Partisan View" from *In Search of Our Mothers' Gardens: Womanist Prose*. Copyright © 1983 by the Board of Trustees of the University of Illinois. Reprinted with the permission of the University of Illinois Press.

Eudora Welty. "Where Is the Voice Coming From?" from *The Collected Stories of Eudora Welty* (New York: Harcourt Brace, 1980). Originally published in *The New Yorker* (June 11, 1963). Copyright © 1963 by Eudora Welty. Reprinted with the permission of Russell & Volkening, Inc. "The Sense of Place in Faulkner's 'Spotted Horses'" from *The Eye of the Story: Selected Essays and Reviews*. Copyright © 1974 by Eudora Welty. Reprinted with the permission of Random House, Inc.

Edith Wharton. "Every Subject Must Contain Within Itself Its Own Dimensions" from *The Writing of Fiction*. Copyright 1925 by Charles Scribner's Sons, renewed 1953 by William R. Tyler. Reprinted with the permission of Scribner, a division of Simon & Schuster.

John Edgar Wideman. "newborn thrown in trash and dies" from *All Stories Are True*. Copyright © 1992 by John Edgar Wideman. Reprinted with the permission of Pantheon Books, a division of Random House, Inc.

William Carlos Williams. "The Use of Force" from *Life Along the Passaic River*. Copyright 1934 by William Carlos Williams. "Notes on 'A Beginning on the Short Story'" from *Selected Essays*. Copyright 1954 by William Carlos Williams. Both reprinted with the permission of New Directions Publishing Corporation.

Richard Wright. "The Man Who Was Almost a Man" from *Eight Men*. Copyright 1940, © 1961 by Richard Wright, renewed © 1989 by Ellen Wright. Reprinted with the permission of HarperCollins Publishers, Inc.

Anzia Yezierska. "My Own People" from *Hungry Hearts and Other Stories*. Copyright 1920 by A. Yezierska, renewed 1948 by Anzia Yezierska. Copyright © 1985 by Louise Levitas Henriksen. Reprinted with the permission of Persea Books, Inc.

ALPHABETICAL LISTING OF WRITERS

(Continued from the inside front cover)